OXFORD
UNIVERSITY PRESS

Great Clarendon Street, Oxford OX2 6DP

Oxford University Press is a department of the University of Oxford.
It furthers the University's objective of excellence in research, scholarship,
and education by publishing worldwide in

Oxford NewYork

Auckland Bangkok Buenos Aires Cape Town Chennai
Dar es Salaam Delhi Hong Kong Istanbul Karachi Kolkata
Kuala Lumpur Madrid Melbourne Mexico City Mumbai Nairobi
São Paulo Shanghai Singapore Taipei Tokyo Toronto

Oxford is a registered trade mark of Oxford University Press
in the UK and in certain other countries

British Library cataloguing in Publication Data available

ISBN 0-19-910729-7 (Hardback)

10 9 8 7 6 5 4 3 2 1

ISBN 0-19-910918-4 (Export paperback edition)

10 9 8 7 6 5 4 3 2

Typeset in Arial and OUP Swift

Printed in Great Britain by Clays Ltd, St Ives, plc

Do you have a query about words, their origin, meaning, use, spelling,
pronunciation, or any other aspect of the English language? Visit our
website at www.askoxford.com where you will be able to find answers
to your language queries.

Contents

Preface

The *Oxford Student's Dictionary* is a new dictionary specially written for use in schools. It has many extra features and a layout that is clear and easy to use.

The most distinctive feature of the dictionary is the special vocabulary of curriculum subjects. This includes many items not always found in dictionaries for adults: for example *bioreactor, gene transfer, homozygote, plasmid,* and *synapse*, all of which occur in science syllabuses. Many new words in more general use have also been included: notably, the language of information technology (*bulletin board, dot-com, e-commerce, virtual reality, WAP,* and others).

The information on word origins (etymologies) extends to every root word, and gives historical background as well as dealing with the development of word forms: for example, the colourful stories behind words such as *deadline, halibut,* and *trivial*.

The notes on usage have been written in line with current thinking on correctness in language and cover a broad range of issues to do with standards and sensitivities. Guidance needs to be clear and definite without being pedantic, and to explain the reasons for a particular difficulty as well as helping to resolve it. A large number of these notes deal with words that are often confused, for example the pairs *adverse* and *averse* and the trio *their, there,* and *they're*.

Students will also welcome the inclusion of sections giving synonyms. These have been chosen with great care and have only been included when they provide genuine and useful alternatives to words, especially to words that are overused (such as *get* and *nice*), or do not convey the full meaning intended, or are ambiguous, or are too informal in tone.

In compiling this dictionary we have made extensive use of the British National Corpus, a database of 100 million words of printed, written, and spoken British English collected by a consortium of publishers and academic institutions. This invaluable research tool has enabled linguists and lexicographers to gain deeper insights than is possible from their intuitions alone into the ways in which ordinary English words are used. It has led to a reappraisal of the core of English such as has not been possible since the compilation of the great *Oxford English Dictionary* at the end of the nineteenth century.

The editors and publishers would like to thank the many people who have helped them to write the dictionary: in particular, the schools that afforded access to their classrooms to find out how students use dictionaries and what problems they encounter, and the specialist advisers who provided substantial help in compiling and treating the curriculum vocabulary.

REA

AD

Dictionary features

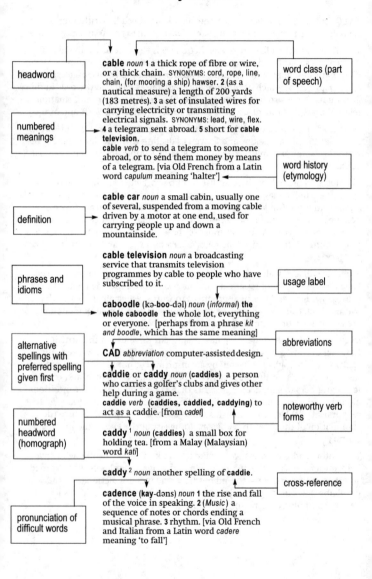

headword

cable *noun* **1** a thick rope of fibre or wire, or a thick chain. SYNONYMS: cord, rope, line, chain, (for mooring a ship) hawser. **2** (as a nautical measure) a length of 200 yards (183 metres). **3** a set of insulated wires for carrying electricity or transmitting electrical signals. SYNONYMS: lead, wire, flex.

numbered meanings

4 a telegram sent abroad. **5** short for **cable television**.
cable *verb* to send a telegram to someone abroad, or to send them money by means of a telegram. [via Old French from a Latin word *capulum* meaning 'halter']

word class (part of speech)

word history (etymology)

definition

cable car *noun* a small cabin, usually one of several, suspended from a moving cable driven by a motor at one end, used for carrying people up and down a mountainside.

phrases and idioms

cable television *noun* a broadcasting service that transmits television programmes by cable to people who have subscribed to it.

usage label

caboodle (kə-boo-dəl) *noun* (*informal*) **the whole caboodle** the whole lot, everything or everyone. [perhaps from a phrase *kit and boodle*, which has the same meaning]

alternative spellings with preferred spelling given first

CAD *abbreviation* computer-assisted design.

abbreviations

caddie or **caddy** *noun* (**caddies**) a person who carries a golfer's clubs and gives other help during a game.
caddie *verb* (**caddies, caddied, caddying**) to act as a caddie. [from *cadet*]

noteworthy verb forms

numbered headword (homograph)

caddy ¹ *noun* (**caddies**) a small box for holding tea. [from a Malay (Malaysian) word *kati*]

caddy ² *noun* another spelling of **caddie**.

cross-reference

cadence (kay-dəns) *noun* **1** the rise and fall of the voice in speaking. **2** (*Music*) a sequence of notes or chords ending a musical phrase. **3** rhythm. [via Old French and Italian from a Latin word *cadere* meaning 'to fall']

pronunciation of difficult words

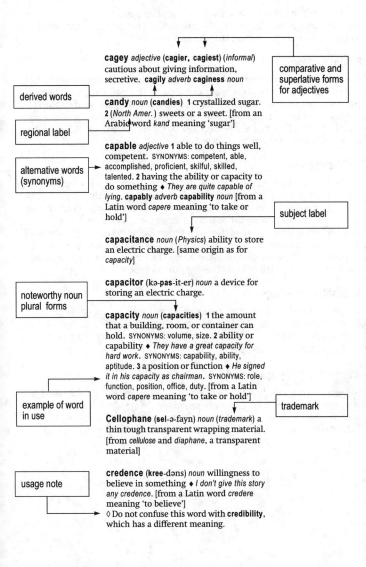

comparative and superlative forms for adjectives

cagey *adjective* (**cagier, cagiest**) (*informal*) cautious about giving information, secretive. **cagily** *adverb* **caginess** *noun*

derived words

regional label

candy *noun* (**candies**) **1** crystallized sugar. **2** (*North Amer.*) sweets or a sweet. [from an Arabic word *kand* meaning 'sugar']

alternative words (synonyms)

capable *adjective* **1** able to do things well, competent. SYNONYMS: competent, able, accomplished, proficient, skilful, skilled, talented. **2** having the ability or capacity to do something ♦ *They are quite capable of lying.* **capably** *adverb* **capability** *noun* [from a Latin word *capere* meaning 'to take or hold']

subject label

capacitance *noun* (*Physics*) ability to store an electric charge. [same origin as for *capacity*]

noteworthy noun plural forms

capacitor (kə-**pas**-it-er) *noun* a device for storing an electric charge.

capacity *noun* (**capacities**) **1** the amount that a building, room, or container can hold. SYNONYMS: volume, size. **2** ability or capability ♦ *They have a great capacity for hard work.* SYNONYMS: capability, ability, aptitude. **3** a position or function ♦ *He signed it in his capacity as chairman.* SYNONYMS: role, function, position, office, duty. [from a Latin word *capere* meaning 'to take or hold']

example of word in use

trademark

Cellophane (**sel**-ə-fayn) *noun* (*trademark*) a thin tough transparent wrapping material. [from *cellulose* and *diaphane*, a transparent material]

usage note

credence (**kree**-dəns) *noun* willingness to believe in something ♦ *I don't give this story any credence.* [from a Latin word *credere* meaning 'to believe']
◊ Do not confuse this word with **credibility**, which has a different meaning.

How to use the dictionary

You will see a diagram of the dictionary layout on pages vi-vii. This shows the main features of the entries, and the guidelines below will give you extra help with the types of information that the entries provide.

Finding a word

At the top of each page you will see a pair of words separated by an upright line. These tell you where the range of words on that particular page begins and ends. The word to the left of the upright line is the first word on the page and the word to the right is the last word on that page. So if you are looking for *able* you will find it on the second page of the dictionary, which contains all the words from *aberration* to *Aboriginal*.

The headword

Each dictionary entry has a headword in large bold type. This is followed by an explanation of how to pronounce the word when this is likely to cause difficulty (a list of letters used to show vowels and consonants is given on page ix) and by the word class (part of speech): noun, verb, adjective, adverb, pronoun, preposition, conjunction, or interjection. Different words that have the same spelling (such as *bat* the implement and *bat* the animal) are called homographs. These are distinguished by small numbers after the headword: see the two words spelt *caddy* in the diagram on page vi.

Alternative spellings

Some English words have more than one correct spelling: for example, *judgement* can also be spelt *judgment* (with only one *e*). In these cases the preferred form is given first and the variant is given after the word 'or':

judgement or **judgment** *noun*

Word class (part of speech)

The word class (part of speech), which shows the grammatical role a word has in a sentence, comes next. The names used are the standard ones: *noun, verb, adjective, adverb, pronoun, preposition, conjunction,* and *interjection*. You will find further information about these terms at their own entries in the dictionary.

Pronunciation

Guidance on pronunciation is given for words that cause difficulty.

The characters used to explain how words are pronounced are the ordinary letters of the English alphabet, with the addition of the inverted e character (called schwa) which represents the sound as in gard**en** and penc**il**.

Letters are used as follows:

vowels

a	as in	cat		i	as in	pin
ah	as in	calm		iy	as in	fine
air	as in	hair				
ar	as in	bar		o	as in	top
aw	as in	law		oh	as in	most
ay	as in	say		oi	as in	join
e	as in	bed		oo	as in	soon
ə	as in	garden, pencil,		oor	as in	poor
		rhythm		or	as in	corn
ee	as in	meet		ow	as in	cow
eer	as in	beer		u	as in	cup
er	as in	her		uu	as in	book
ew	as in	few				
ewr	as in	pure				

consonants

b	as in	bat		p	as in	pen
ch	as in	chip		r	as in	red
d	as in	day		s	as in	seat
f	as in	fat				
g	as in	get		sh	as in	shop
h	as in	hat		t	as in	top
j	as in	jam		th	as in	thin
k	as in	king		*th*	as in	this
l	as in	leg		v	as in	van
m	as in	man		w	as in	well
n	as in	not		y	as in	yes
ng	as in	sing, singer		z	as in	zebra
ngg	as in	finger		*zh*	as in	measure
nk	as in	think				

Letters are sometimes doubled (e.g. -ss-) to make the pronunciation clearer. The syllable that receives the main emphasis (called *stress*) in ordinary speech is shown in bold type. For example, the word **edifice** is pronounced (**ed**-i-fis) with the stress on the first syllable **ed-** .

Inflections

Some words change their endings to fit the grammar of the sentence (e.g.
changed, going, boxes). These special endings are called inflections. The
following inflections are given after the word class (part of speech) when they
cause difficulty:

Plurals of nouns:

facility *noun* (**facilities**)

Forms of verbs:

equal *verb* (**equalled, equalling**)

hear *verb* (past tense and past participle **heard**)

Comparatives and superlatives of adjective and adverbs:

mouldy *adjective* (**mouldier, mouldiest**)

Usage labels

Labels, which are printed in *italics*, give you information about when and
where a word is mainly used.

Some words are suitable for all occasions. Others are mainly used in particular
contexts: words labelled 'informal' are normally restricted to everyday
conversation, and words labelled 'formal' are normally found in print, for
example in reports or textbooks.

This aspect of the use of words is called 'register'.

The following labels are used to indicate register:

informal	normally used in conversation and informal writing, e.g. **barmy, cool** (= good or fashionable), **naff, oddball, OK, past it, tip-off**
formal	normally used in print and formal speaking, e.g. **ameliorate, beatific, behest, edifice, perambulate, regardful**
old use	no longer used by most speakers, but still sometimes found, e.g. **affray, betwixt, contumely, fisticuffs, perchance, raiment, smite, thither**
historical	still in use as a term but referring to people or things that existed or occurred in the past, e.g. **buccaneer, fealty, halberd, liege, ostler, parlourmaid**
humorous	normally used for a witty or amusing effect, e.g. **purloin, to have been in the wars**
derogatory	used in a disapproving way, or intended to offend or belittle, e.g. **popery, rabble**
offensive	likely to cause offence, whether intended or not, e.g. **halfcaste**
literary	normally found in literature, e.g. **aright, bard, espy, foe, perfidious, steed, yesteryear**

poetic	normally found in poetry, e.g. **argosy, bestrew, firmament, hark, lea**
dialect	used in a particular area but not part of the standard language, e.g. **aye**, **poll** (= head), **varmint**, **yon**

Regional labels

Words and meanings that are restricted to certain parts of the English-speaking world (and are not dialect words) are labelled to show this, e.g. *North Amer.* = mainly used in North America, *Austral.* = mainly used in Australia.

Subject labels

The following labels are used to indicate subjects that certain words and meanings belong to. For example, **cuticle** is used in Botany and Zoology.

Archaeology	Electronics	Mathematics
Architecture	Finance	Medicine
Art	Geography	Meteorology
Biochemistry	Geology	Music
Biology	Geometry	Philosophy
Botany	Grammar	Physics
Chemistry	Greek and Roman	Psychology
Computing	Mythology	Statistics
Ecology	Heraldry	Zoology
Electricity	Law	

Words that are used in technical contexts more generally are marked *technical*.

Meanings

The meanings of words are given next. If there is more than one meaning, the meanings are numbered.

If the meaning has a special application or typical context, this is given at the beginning of the definition, for example at **advanced**, meaning 4:

(said about ideas) new and not yet generally accepted.

Examples

An example of a word or meaning is given after the definition when it helps to make the meaning clearer, for example at the entry for **advent**:

the arrival of an important idea or development, or of an important person ◆ *the advent of the personal computer.*

Synonyms

Synonyms are words that are close in meaning to a particular word. For example, *benefit* is a synonym of *advantage*. You will find a list of synonyms when there are useful alternatives to the word you are looking up. Synonyms need to be used with care, as the meaning is rarely exactly the same and in many cases the grammar and usage of alternative words are different. For example, *danger* works as a synonym for *risk* in many of its meanings but you can only use *risk* in the expression *to take* (or *run*) *a risk*.

The synonyms are listed in order of usefulness, those closest in meaning to the headword coming first. Synonyms are not given separately when these would simply repeat the definition (for example, **possess**, **own**, and **hold** in the first meaning of **have**).

If a synonym is more formal or less formal in use than the headword, this is shown. For example, **convene** is given as a synonym of **assemble** and is marked 'more formal' (because **convene** would not be used in as wide a range of contexts as **assemble**) and **pluck** is given as an 'informal' synonym for **bravery**.

Phrases

At the end of some entries there are lists of phrases and idioms, also known as 'fixed expressions', i.e. items that can only be explained as a set of words, such as *off the peg* (at **peg**) and *at full pelt* (at **pelt**).

Derived words

Words that are formed from the headword are given at the end of entries when these can easily be understood from the meaning of the headword, for example **simplification** is a routine noun derived from the verb **simplify**, and **sincerely** is an adverb formed routinely from the adjective **sincere**. If there is any special non-routine feature of meaning or usage, derived words are given as headwords in their own right (for example, **equally**).

Word histories

The history and source (called the etymology) are given for root words, but not for all the words that are associated with them. For example, the word **east** is explained as being 'from Old English', and this applies also to the related words **easterly**, **eastern**, and so on, which either come from Old English as well or are derivatives of **east**.

Usage notes

Notes on points of usage are given for words that cause difficulty. Many of these are to do with words that are confused with one another (for example, **credence** and **credibility**: see the sample on p.vii)

Cross-references

A reference to another entry in the dictionary is shown in bold type:

muckle *noun* another word for **mickle**.

Trademarks

Words which the publishers have reason to believe are trademarks are marked *trademark*. Their inclusion does not imply any judgement about their legal status.

Abbreviations

There are a few special abbreviations used for this dictionary. General abbreviations, such as e.g. and i.e., are given in the main dictionary.

Austral.	Australia
North Amer.	North America
NZ	New Zealand

Aa

A 1 the first letter of the English alphabet. **2** (*Music*) the sixth note of the diatonic scale of C major. **A1** (*informal*) in perfect condition; first-rate.

A *abbreviation* ampere(s).

Å *abbreviation* ångström(s).

a *abbreviation* (*Physics*) the symbol for acceleration.

a *adjective* (called the *indefinite article*) **1** one person or thing but not any particular one ♦ *I need a knife*. **2** per ♦ *twice a day*. [from an Old English word meaning 'one']

a-[1] *prefix* (changing to **an-** before a vowel sound) not or without (as in *asymmetrical, anarchy*). [from Greek *a-* meaning 'not']

a-[2] *prefix* **1** on or towards (as in *ashore, aside*). **2** in the process of doing something (as in *go a-hunting*). [from an Old English word meaning 'on']

aardvark (ahd-vark) *noun* an African animal with a large heavy body like a pig, which feeds on termites. [from Afrikaans words *aarde* meaning 'earth' and *vark* meaning 'pig']

ab- *prefix* (changing to **abs-** before *c* and *t*) away; from (as in *abduct, abnormal, abstract*). [from the Latin word *ab* meaning 'away']

aback *adverb* **to be taken aback** to be upset or disconcerted by something that happens. [from Old English words related to *on* and *back*]

abacus (ab-ə-kəs) *noun* (**abacuses**) a frame with beads that slide along rods, used for counting. [via Latin from a Greek word *abax, abak-* meaning 'drawing board']

abandon *verb* **1** to leave a person or place without intending to return to them. SYNONYMS: desert, forsake (a person); leave (a person) stranded; leave, quit, forsake (a place). **2** to stop working on something ♦ *We decided to abandon the attempt.* **to abandon ship** to escape from a ship that is about to sink.
abandon *noun* a careless or reckless freedom of manner ♦ *They acted with carefree abandon.* **abandoned** *adjective* **abandonment** *noun* **to abandon oneself** to yield completely to an emotion or impulse ♦ *He abandoned himself completely*

to despair. [from an Old French word *bandon* meaning 'control']

abase *verb* to humiliate or degrade someone. **abasement** *noun* [from an Old French word *baissier* meaning 'to lower']

abashed *adjective* embarrassed or ashamed. [from an Old French word *esbair* meaning 'to astonish completely']

abate *verb* to become less; to die down ♦ *At last the storm abated.* **abatement** *noun* [from an Old French word *abatre* meaning 'to fell']

abattoir (ab-ə-twar) *noun* a slaughterhouse. [French, from *abattre* meaning 'to knock down or destroy']

abbess (ab-ess) *noun* a woman who is the head of an abbey of nuns.

abbey *noun* (**abbeys**) **1** a building occupied by monks or nuns living as a community, or the community itself. **2** a church or house that was once an abbey. [from an Old French word *abbeie* related to *abbot*]

abbot *noun* a man who is the head of an abbey of monks. [via Latin and Greek from an Aramaic word *abba* meaning 'father']

abbreviate *verb* to shorten a word or title. [from a Latin word *brevis* meaning 'short']

abbreviation *noun* a shortened form of a word or title ♦ *BBC is an abbreviation of British Broadcasting Corporation.*

ABC[1] *noun* **1** the alphabet. **2** the basic facts that you learn about a subject ♦ *the ABC of music.*

ABC[2] *abbreviation* Australian Broadcasting Corporation.

abdicate *verb* to give up a high office, especially the throne. **abdication** *noun* [from a Latin word *abdicare* meaning 'to renounce']

abdomen (ab-dəm-ən) *noun* **1** the part of the body below the chest and diaphragm, containing most of the digestive organs. **2** the hindmost section of the body of an insect, spider, or crustacean. **abdominal** (əb-dom-in-əl) *adjective* **abdominally** *adverb* [from Latin]

abduct *verb* to carry off a person illegally by force. SYNONYM: kidnap. **abduction** *noun* **abductor** *noun* [from a Latin word *abducere, abduct-* meaning 'to lead away']

aberrant (ab-e-rənt) *adjective* deviating from the normal type or accepted standard.

aberration (ab-er-ay-shən) *noun* 1 a deviation from what is normal. 2 a mental or moral lapse. 3 a distortion, e.g. of an image produced through an imperfect lens. [from a Latin word *aberrare* meaning 'to stray']

abet *verb* (**abetted, abetting**) to encourage or assist someone to commit an offence. **abetter** or **abettor** *noun* **abetment** *noun* [from an Old French word *abeter* meaning 'to urge']

abeyance (ə-bay-əns) *noun* in **abeyance** (said about a right, rule, problem, etc.) not in force or in use for a time. [from Old French]

abhor (əb-hor) *verb* (**abhorred, abhorring**) to detest something. [from a Latin word *abhorrere* meaning 'to shrink in fear']

abhorrent (əb-hor-rənt) *adjective* horrible or disgusting. **abhorrence** *noun*

abide *verb* 1 to bear or endure ♦ *I can't abide wasps.* 2 (*old use*) to remain or dwell in a place. **to abide by** to act in accordance with a rule or decision. [from an Old English word meaning 'to wait']

abiding *adjective* long-lasting, permanent.

ability *noun* (**abilities**) 1 the capacity or power to do something. 2 cleverness or talent. SYNONYMS: talent, skill, aptitude. [same origin as for *able*]

abiotic (ay-biy-ot-ik) *adjective* not having life, not derived from a living organism. [from *a-*[1] and a Greek word *bios* meaning 'life']

abject (ab-jekt) *adjective* 1 wretched and degrading ♦ *They lived for years in abject poverty.* 2 having no pride, undignified ♦ *He gave her an abject apology.* **abjectly** *adverb* [from *ab-* and a Latin word *-jectum* meaning 'thrown']

abjure (əb-joor) *verb* (*formal*) to renounce or repudiate something. **abjuration** *noun* [from a Latin word *abjurare* meaning 'to take an oath']

ablative (ab-lə-tiv) *noun* in some languages, the grammatical case of a noun, pronoun, or adjective that indicates the agent, instrument, or location of an action.

ablaze *adjective* burning fiercely.

able *adjective* 1 having the ability to do something. 2 having a lot of ability, very competent. SYNONYMS: skilful, skilled, capable, talented, accomplished, competent, proficient, gifted. **ably** *adverb* [from a Latin word *habilis* meaning 'handy']

-able *suffix* forming adjectives meaning 'that can be done' (as in *readable*). [from a Latin suffix *-abilis*]

able-bodied *adjective* physically fit and strong.

ablution (ə-bloo-shən) *noun* a ceremonial washing of the hands or vessels etc. **ablutions** *plural noun* (*informal or humorous*) washing of the body. [from a Latin word *abluere* meaning 'to wash away']

abnegate (ab-ni-gayt) *verb* (*formal*) to renounce or reject something valuable or desired. **abnegation** *noun* [from a Latin word *abnegare* meaning 'to renounce']

abnormal *adjective* different from what is normal. SYNONYMS: unusual, exceptional, odd, peculiar, strange, funny. **abnormally** *adverb* **abnormality** *noun* [from *ab-* and *normal*]

aboard *adverb* & *preposition* on or into a ship or aircraft or train. [from *a-*[2] and *board*]

abode *noun* (*old use*) a place where someone lives, a home. [from *abide*]

abolish *verb* to put an end to a practice or institution. SYNONYMS: get rid of, do away with, eliminate, end. **abolition** (abə-lish-ən) *noun* [from a Latin word *abolire* meaning 'to destroy']

abolitionist *noun* a person who favours abolishing capital punishment or (formerly) slavery.

A-bomb *noun* an atomic bomb.

abominable *adjective* 1 horrible or loathsome. 2 (*informal*) very bad or unpleasant. **abominably** *adverb* [same origin as for *abominate*]

Abominable Snowman *noun* a large animal like a bear, said to exist in the Himalayas; a yeti.

abominate *verb* to detest or loathe something. [from a Latin word *abominari* meaning 'to regard as a bad omen']

abomination *noun* 1 a feeling of loathing something. 2 something you detest or loathe.

aboriginal *adjective* (said about a people or about plants) living or growing in a land from the earliest times or from before the arrival of colonists.
aboriginal *noun* an aboriginal inhabitant.
Aboriginal *noun* an aboriginal inhabitant of Australia. [same origin as for *aborigine*]

aborigine (ab-er-ij-in-ee) *noun* (**aborigines**) an aboriginal inhabitant of a country. **Aborigine** *noun* (**Aborigines**) an aboriginal inhabitant of Australia. [from the Latin phrase *ab origine* meaning 'from the beginning']

abort (ə-bort) *verb* 1 to carry out the abortion of a fetus; (said about a fetus) to undergo abortion. 2 to end a scheme or activity because of a fault or failure; (said about an activity) to be ended in this way. [from a Latin word *aboriri* meaning 'to miscarry']

abortion *noun* 1 the expulsion of a fetus from the womb before it is able to survive. 2 (*informal*) a misshapen creature or thing.

abortionist *noun* a person who performs abortions, especially illegally.

abortive *adjective* unsuccessful, not producing the right result. **abortively** *adverb*

ABO system *noun* a system of classifying blood by four basic types, A, AB, B, and O.

abound *verb* 1 to be plentiful ♦ *Ferns abound on the hillside.* 2 to have in large quantities ♦ *The river abounds in fish.* [from a Latin word *abundare* meaning 'to overflow']

about *preposition* 1 approximately, roughly ♦ *about £100.* 2 in connection with, on the subject of ♦ *What is the film about?* 3 all around ♦ *round about the town.* **about** *adverb* 1 somewhere near, not far away ♦ *The children are somewhere about.* 2 in various places or directions ♦ *lying about* ♦ *running about.* 3 on the move, active ♦ *She will soon be about again.* **to be about to** to be on the point of doing something. [from a-² and an Old English word *butan* meaning 'outside']

about-face or **about-turn** *noun* 1 a turning movement to face the opposite direction. 2 a complete change of opinion or policy.

above *adverb* 1 at or to a higher point ♦ *See the stars above.* 2 earlier in a book or article ♦ *The picture is shown above.* **above** *preposition* 1 higher than ♦ *There is a sign above the door.* 2 more than ♦ *Don't pay above £20.* **above all** *adverb* especially, most importantly. [from Old English]

above-board *adjective* honest, done honestly or openly. [from card-players cheating by changing their cards under the 'board' or table]

abracadabra (abrə-kə-dab-rə) *noun* a formula supposed to be magical and used by conjurors when performing tricks. [a fanciful word derived from Greek]

abrade (ə-brayd) *verb* to scrape or wear something away by rubbing or eroding it. [from a Latin word *abradare* meaning 'to rub away']

abrasion (ə-bray-zhən) *noun* 1 a place or spot that has been worn by rubbing. 2 the action of rubbing something.

abrasive (ə-bray-siv) *adjective* 1 (said about a substance) suitable for polishing surfaces by rubbing or grinding them. 2 (said about a person) having a harsh or rough manner. **abrasive** *noun* a substance used to polish surfaces by rubbing.

abreast *adverb* side by side and facing the same way. **to keep abreast of** to be up to date with information or news about something.

abridge *verb* to shorten a story or text by using fewer words. **abridgement** *noun* [from Old French *abregier* meaning 'to shorten']

abroad *adverb* 1 in or to a foreign country. 2 over a large area ♦ *They scattered the seeds abroad.* 3 (*old use*) walking about out of doors ♦ *At that time of night no one was abroad.* [from a-² and *broad*]

abrogate (ab-rə-gayt) *verb* to cancel or repeal a law or agreement. **abrogation** *noun* [from a Latin word *abrogare* meaning 'to repeal']

abrupt *adjective* 1 sudden ♦ *The car came to an abrupt stop.* 2 speaking very curtly and almost rudely. SYNONYMS: blunt, sharp, gruff, curt, rude, unfriendly, short. 3 curt. 4 (said about a slope) very steep. **abruptly** *adverb* **abruptness** *noun* [from *ab-* and a Latin word *ruptum* meaning 'broken']

abscess (ab-sis) *noun* a swollen area that has formed in the body, containing pus. [from a Latin word *abscessus*, from *abscedere* meaning 'to go away']

abscissa (ab-sis-ə) *noun* (**abscissae**) a coordinate measured parallel to a horizontal axis; the x-axis of a graph. [a Latin word, from *abscindere* meaning 'to cut off']

abscond (əb-skond) *verb* to leave or escape secretly and without permission, especially after doing something wrong.

absconder noun [from a Latin word *abscondere* meaning 'to hide']

abseil (ab-sayl) verb to descend a rock-face using a doubled rope that is fixed at a higher point. [from German words *ab-* meaning 'down' and *Seil* meaning 'rope']

absence noun 1 the state of being away. 2 a lack or non-existence ♦ *in the absence of proof.*

absent [1] (ab-sənt) adjective 1 not present. SYNONYMS: away, missing, off. 2 non-existent. 3 having your mind on other things. **absently** adverb

absent [2] (əb-sent) verb to absent yourself to be absent or stay away. [from a Latin word *absens, absent-*, inflections of *abesse* meaning 'to be away']

absentee noun a person who is not present, especially when they are not at work or school.

absenteeism noun being often away from work or school.

absent-minded adjective having your mind on other things, forgetful.

absolute adjective 1 complete ♦ *The holiday was absolute bliss.* SYNONYMS: utter, complete, total, sheer. 2 without any limits ♦ *The dictators enjoyed absolute power.* SYNONYMS: total, complete, unlimited, unrestricted, unqualified. 3 independent, not relative ♦ *There is no absolute standard for beauty.* 4 (informal) utter, out-and-out ♦ *It was an absolute miracle we weren't injured.* [same origin as for *absolve*]

absolutely adverb 1 completely, utterly ♦ *It was absolutely beautiful.* 2 without restrictions, unconditionally. 3 (informal) used to agree with something a person has said.

absolute majority noun a majority of votes or seats in a parliament over all rivals combined.

absolute pitch noun 1 (Music) the ability to recognize or reproduce the pitch of a note exactly. 2 a fixed standard of pitch defined by the rate of vibration.

absolute temperature noun temperature measured in kelvins from absolute zero.

absolute zero noun the lowest temperature that is theoretically possible (−273.15°C).

absolution (absə-loo-shən) noun a priest's formal declaration that a person's sins are forgiven.

absolutism noun the principle of having a rule etc. that must apply in all cases.

absolve verb 1 to clear a person of blame or guilt. SYNONYMS: pardon, acquit, exonerate, clear. 2 to give a person absolution. 3 to free a person from an obligation. [from a Latin word *absolvere* meaning 'to set free']

absorb verb 1 to soak up liquid or other substances. SYNONYMS: soak up, assimilate. 2 to learn and remember information. SYNONYMS: assimilate, digest, take in. 3 to reduce the effect of something unwelcome ♦ *The buffers absorbed the impact.* SYNONYMS: cushion, lessen, soften. **absorbable** adjective **absorber** noun **absorption** noun [from *ab-* and a Latin word *sorbēre* meaning 'to suck in']

absorbent adjective able to absorb liquid or moisture. **absorbency** noun

absorbing adjective holding your interest, engrossing. SYNONYMS: engrossing, fascinating, captivating.

absorptive adjective able to absorb liquids or other substances.

abstain verb 1 to make yourself not do something you would like to, especially drinking alcohol. 2 to decide not to use your vote in an election. **abstainer** noun **abstention** noun [from *abs-* and a Latin word *tenēre* meaning 'to hold']

abstemious (əb-steem-iəs) adjective not eating or drinking much, or not having a lot of pleasure. **abstemiously** adverb **abstemiousness** noun [from *ab-* and a Latin word *temetum* meaning 'alcoholic drink']

abstention noun abstaining, especially a decision not to vote in an election. [same origin as for *abstain*]

abstinence (ab-stin-əns) noun abstaining, especially going without food or alcohol. **abstinent** adjective [same origin as for *abstain*]

abstract [1] (ab-strakt) adjective 1 not having any physical existence ♦ *Truth is an abstract quality.* 2 theoretical rather than practical. 3 (said about a painting or sculpture) using designs that show the creator's ideas and feelings without attempting to show a real person or thing. **abstract** noun 1 an abstract quality or idea. 2 a summary of a long book or article. 3 an abstract painting or sculpture. **abstractly** adverb **abstractness** noun [from *ab-* and a Latin word *tractum* meaning 'pulled']

abstract[2] (əb-**strakt**) *verb* **1** to take something out, to separate or remove something. **2** to make a written summary of a story or text. **abstractor** *noun*

abstracted *adjective* having your mind on other things, not paying attention.

abstraction *noun* **1** abstracting or removing something. **2** an abstract idea.

abstract noun *noun* a noun for a quality or state, or something that is not physical, for example *happiness* or *danger*.

abstruse (əb-**strooss**) *adjective* hard to understand, obscure or complicated. **abstruseness** *noun* [from a Latin word *abstrusus* meaning 'hidden']

absurd *adjective* having little sense, ridiculous or foolish. SYNONYMS: ridiculous, foolish, silly, laughable, ludicrous, preposterous, nonsensical. **absurdly** *adverb* [from a Latin word *absurdus* meaning 'out of tune']

absurdity *noun* (**absurdities**) **1** being absurd. **2** an absurd idea or suggestion.

ABTA *abbreviation* Association of British Travel Agents.

abundance *noun* a large amount of something, more than enough. [same origin as for *abound*]

abundant *adjective* **1** plentiful, being more than enough. SYNONYMS: plentiful, ample, copious, generous. **2** having plenty of something, rich ♦ *The land is abundant in minerals.* **abundantly** *adverb*

abuse[1] (ə-**bewss**) *noun* **1** a misuse of something, for example a machine or a drug. **2** treating someone cruelly, causing them pain or suffering. **3** an unjust or corrupt practice. **4** offensive or insulting language. [from *ab-* and *use*]

abuse[2] (ə-**bewz**) *verb* **1** to make a bad or wrong use of power or authority. **2** to treat someone cruelly. SYNONYMS: maltreat, hurt. **3** to attack someone in words, to insult someone. SYNONYMS: insult, swear at, curse, be rude to.

abusive (ə-**bew**-siv) *adjective* offensive or insulting, criticizing someone harshly or angrily. SYNONYMS: offensive, insulting, defamatory, rude. **abusively** *adverb*

abut (ə-**but**) *verb* (**abutted, abutting**) to have a common boundary; to touch at one side ♦ *Their land abuts ours* ♦ *Their land abuts on ours.* **abutment** *noun* [from an Old French word *abouter*]

abysmal (ə-**biz**-məl) *adjective* **1** (*informal*) extremely bad ♦ *Their taste is abysmal.* **2** very deep ♦ *He shows abysmal ignorance.* **abysmally** *adverb* [from *abyss*]

abyss (ə-**biss**) *noun* **1** a very deep hole or chasm. **2** disaster seen as likely to happen. [from Greek *abussos* meaning 'bottomless']

AC or **a.c.** *abbreviation* alternating current.

acacia (ə-**kay**-shə) *noun* a tree that grows in warm climates, having small yellow or white flowers. [via Latin from a Greek word *akakia*]

academic (akə-**dem**-ik) *adjective* **1** to do with a school, college, or university. **2** scholarly as opposed to technical or practical ♦ *academic subjects.* **3** having theoretical interest only, with no practical application. **academic** *noun* a scholar or academic person. **academically** *adverb* [from *academy*]

academician (ə-kad-ə-**mish**-ən) *noun* a member of an Academy.

academy *noun* (**academies**) **1** a school, especially for specialized training. **2** in Scotland, a secondary school. **Academy** *noun* a society of scholars or artists. [from *Akademeia*, the name of the garden where the Greek philosopher Plato taught his pupils in the 4th century BC]

acanthus *noun* a Mediterranean plant with bold spikes of flowers and large spiny leaves. [via Latin from Greek *akanthos*]

ACAS (**ay**-kass) *abbreviation* Advisory, Conciliation, and Arbitration Service.

accede (ək-**seed**) *verb* to take office, to become king or queen. **to accede to** to agree to a suggestion or idea. [from *ad-* and a Latin word *cedere* meaning 'to go']

accelerate *verb* **1** (said about a vehicle or its driver) to move steadily faster. **2** (said about an event) to happen earlier or more quickly. **3** to cause something to happen more quickly. **acceleration** *noun* [from *ad-* and a Latin word *celer* meaning 'swift']

accelerator *noun* **1** a device for increasing the speed of a vehicle, or the pedal for operating it. **2** (*Physics*) an apparatus for causing charged particles to move at high speeds.

accelerometer *noun* (*Physics*) an instrument for measuring acceleration or vibrations.

accent[1] (**ak**-sənt) *noun* 1 a particular way of pronouncing words, associated with a country, area, or social class. 2 the emphasis put on a syllable or word when pronouncing it. 3 a mark indicating an emphasis or the quality of a vowel sound. 4 the importance given to something ♦ *The accent is on quality.* [from *ad-* and a Latin word *cantus* meaning 'song']

accent[2] (ək-**sent**) *verb* 1 to pronounce a word with an accent. 2 to emphasize something.

accentuate (ək-**sen**-tew-ayt) *verb* to emphasize something or make it important. **accentuation** *noun* [same origin as for *accent*]

accept *verb* 1 to take something offered to you; to say yes to an offer or invitation. 2 to undertake a responsibility. 3 to treat someone as welcome ♦ *They were never really accepted by their neighbours.* 4 to be willing to agree to a suggestion or idea ♦ *I accept that I may have been wrong* ♦ *We do not accept your conclusions.* SYNONYMS: admit, acknowledge, agree, concede. **acceptance** *noun* **acceptor** *noun* [from *ad-* and a Latin word *capere* meaning 'to take']
◊ Do not confuse this word with *except*.

acceptable *adjective* 1 worth accepting, welcome. 2 tolerable or adequate ♦ *The quality was barely acceptable.* SYNONYMS: tolerable, adequate, satisfactory, passable. **acceptably** *adjective*

acceptor *noun* (*Physics*) an atom or molecule able to receive an extra electron or proton etc.

access (**ak**-sess) *noun* 1 a means of approaching or entering a place, a way in. 2 the right or opportunity of reaching or using something ♦ *Students need access to books.* 3 an attack of emotion ♦ *a sudden access of rage.*
access *verb* to retrieve information stored in a computer. [same origin as for *accede*]

accessible *adjective* 1 able to be reached or used easily. 2 (said about a person) friendly and easy to talk to. **accessibly** *adverb* **accessibility** *noun*

accession (ək-**sesh**-ən) *noun* 1 reaching a rank or position, especially that of king or queen ♦ *the Queen's accession to the throne.* 2 an addition to a library or other collection.

accessory (ək-**sess**-er-i) *noun* (**accessories**) 1 an extra or decorative thing that is added to something to make it more useful or attractive. 2 (*Law*) a person who helps someone to commit a crime, without taking part in it. [from a Latin word *accessorius* meaning 'added']

accidence (**ak**-si-dəns) *noun* the part of grammar that deals with the way words are inflected.

accident *noun* 1 an unexpected or unwelcome event, especially one causing injury or damage. SYNONYMS: misfortune, mishap. 2 chance or fortune ♦ *We met by accident.* SYNONYMS: chance, luck, coincidence. [from *ad-* and a Latin word *cadens* meaning 'falling']

accidental *adjective* happening or done by accident. SYNONYMS: unintentional, unplanned, fortuitous, coincidental.
accidental *noun* (*Music*) a sign attached to a single note, showing a temporary departure from the key signature. **accidentally** *adverb*

acclaim (ə-**klaym**) *verb* to welcome someone with shouts of approval, to applaud someone enthusiastically.
acclaim *noun* applause or praise. **acclamation** (aklə-**may**-shən) *noun* [from *ad-* and a Latin word *clamare* meaning 'to shout']

acclimatize *verb* to become used to a new climate or new conditions. **acclimatization** *noun* [from *ad-* and a French word *climat* meaning 'climate']

accolade (**ak**-ə-layd) *noun* 1 a special honour conferred as praise or approval. 2 a ceremonial touch of the shoulder with a sword, given when conferring a knighthood. [from *ad-* and a Latin word *collum* meaning 'neck' (because the king used to embrace a man round the neck when he was bestowing a knighthood on him)]

accommodate *verb* 1 to provide lodging or a room for someone. 2 to provide what someone wants or needs ♦ *The bank will accommodate you with a loan.* [from a Latin word *accommodare* meaning 'to make suitable for']

accommodating *adjective* willing to do what someone else wants.

accommodation *noun* 1 a room or building in which someone can live. SYNONYMS: housing, lodgings, shelter, quarters. 2 the process of adapting to what someone else needs.

accompaniment *noun* 1 (*Music*) an instrumental part which supports a solo

instrument or voice or a choir.
2 something that goes with something else.

accompanist *noun* a person who plays a musical accompaniment.

accompany *verb* (**accompanies, accompanied, accompanying**) 1 to go to a place with someone. 2 to be present with someone. 3 to provide a thing in addition to something. 4 (*Music*) to play an accompaniment to a singer or soloist. [from an Old French word *accompagner*, from *compaignon* meaning 'companion']

accomplice (ə-kum-plis) *noun* a person who helps someone to commit a crime. [via Old French from a Latin word *complex* meaning 'allied']

accomplish (ə-kum-plish) *verb* to succeed in doing something, to complete or achieve something. SYNONYMS: achieve, fulfil, complete, perform, manage. [from *ad-* and a Latin word *complere* meaning 'to complete']

accomplished *adjective* skilled, having many accomplishments. SYNONYMS: skilled, talented, gifted, expert, skilful, able.

accomplishment *noun* 1 something that a person can do well. 2 something that has been accomplished.

accord *noun* consent or agreement.
accord *verb* 1 to be in harmony or consistent with something. 2 (*formal*) to give or grant something to someone ♦ *We were accorded a rare privilege.* **of your own accord** without being asked or compelled. [via Old French from a Latin word *cor, cord-* meaning 'heart']

accordance *noun* agreement or conformity.

according *adverb* **according to** 1 as stated by a person or book ♦ *According to the encyclopedia light bulbs give out more heat than light.* 2 in a manner corresponding to or in proportion to ♦ *The eggs are classed according to size.*

accordingly *adverb* 1 according to what is known or said ♦ *They told us what to do and we acted accordingly.* 2 therefore, as a result.

accordion *noun* a musical instrument played by squeezing and stretching a set of bellows, and making the melody on keys or buttons. **accordionist** *noun* [via German from an Italian word *accordare* meaning 'to tune an instrument']

accost (ə-kost) *verb* to approach and speak to someone in a bold or challenging way. [from *ad-* and a Latin word *costa* meaning 'rib']

account *noun* 1 a description or report of something that happened. SYNONYMS: description, report, record, narrative, story. 2 an arrangement with a bank or firm to hold a customer's money or provide goods or services on credit. 3 a statement of money paid or owed for goods or services, or a bill stating the amount owed. 4 importance or value ♦ *Money is of no account to him.*
account *verb* to regard or consider someone in a special way ♦ *A person is accounted innocent until proved guilty.* **to account for** 1 to give or be an explanation of something. 2 to describe how you have used something, e.g. money. **to give a good account of oneself** to perform well. **on account** to be paid for fully at a later date. **on account of** because of something, for a stated reason. **on no account** under no circumstances, never. **to take into account** to make allowances for something. [from *ad-* and an Old French word *counte* meaning 'story' or 'sum']

accountable *adjective* 1 expected to give an explanation for what you have done, responsible. 2 able to be explained or understood. **accountability** *noun*

accountancy *noun* the profession of an accountant.

accountant *noun* a person who keeps or inspects business accounts as a profession.

accounting *noun* the business of keeping or inspecting accounts, accountancy.

accoutrements (ə-koo-trə-mənts) *plural noun* a soldier's equipment other than weapons and uniform. [a French word, from *cousture* meaning 'sewing']

accredited (ə-kred-itid) *adjective* 1 officially recognized or appointed to a position ♦ *our accredited representative in New York.* 2 generally accepted or believed. 3 certified as being of a prescribed quality. [from *ad-* and *credit*]

accretion (ə-kree-shən) *noun* 1 a growth or increase resulting from gradual additions. 2 the growing of separate things into one. [from *ad-* and a Latin word *crescere* meaning 'to grow']

accrue (ə-kroo) *verb* (**accrues, accrued,**

accruing) (said about a sum of money or a benefit) to be received at regular intervals, to accumulate ♦ *Interest on investments accrues annually.* **accrual** *noun* [same origin as for *accretion*]

accumulate *verb* **1** to acquire an increasing quantity of something. **2** to increase in quantity or amount. **accumulation** *noun* **accumulative** *adjective* [from *ad-* and a Latin word *cumulus* meaning 'heap']

accumulator *noun* **1** a large rechargeable electric battery. **2** a series of bets, with the winnings from each bet placed on the next.

accurate *adjective* **1** true or conforming to a standard. **2** precise or correct in all its details. SYNONYMS: correct, exact, precise. **accurately** *adverb* **accuracy** *noun* [from *ad-* and a Latin word *cura* meaning 'care']

accursed (ə-ker-sid) *adjective* **1** under a curse. **2** (*informal*) detestable, hateful. [from *ad-* and *curse*]

accusation *noun* **1** a charge that a person has committed a crime or wrongdoing. **2** accusing or being accused.

accusative (ə-kew-zə-tiv) *noun* (*Grammar*) the case used for the object of a verb etc., e.g. *him* in *We saw him.* [same origin as for *accuse*]

accuse *verb* to make a statement putting the blame for a crime or wrongdoing etc. on a named person. **the accused** the person accused in a court of law. **accuser** *noun* **accusingly** *adverb* [from *ad-* and a Latin word *causa* meaning 'cause']

accustom *verb* to make someone become used to something. **to be accustomed to** to be used to something. [from *ad-* and *custom*]

accustomed *adjective* usual, customary ♦ *He sat in his accustomed seat.*

ace *noun* **1** a playing card with one spot, usually having the highest value in its suit. **2** a person who is very good at something ♦ *an ace pilot.* **3** (in tennis) a service that is so good that the other player cannot return it. **ace** *adjective* (*informal*) extremely good, excellent. **within an ace of** very near to ♦ *They were within an ace of winning the game.* [from a Latin word *as* meaning 'unit']

acerbic (ə-serb-ik) *noun* having a sharp manner of speaking. **acerbity** *noun* [from a Latin word *acerbus* meaning 'sour-tasting']

acetate (ass-it-ayt) *noun* **1** a compound derived from acetic acid. **2** a fabric made from cellulose acetate.

acetic acid *noun* the acid that gives vinegar its special taste and smell. [from a Latin word *acetum* meaning 'vinegar']

acetone (ass-i-tohn) *noun* a colourless liquid used as a solvent.

acetylene (ə-set-i-leen) *noun* a gas that burns with a bright flame, used in cutting and welding metal.

ache *verb* **1** to suffer a dull continuous physical or mental pain. **2** to yearn. **ache** *noun* a dull continuous pain. **achy** *adjective* [an Old English word]

achieve *verb* to gain or reach something by an effort, to accomplish something. SYNONYMS: accomplish, fulfil, complete, perform, manage. **achievable** *adjective* **achievement** *noun* [from an Old French phrase *a chief* meaning 'to a head']

Achilles' heel (ə-kil-eez) *noun* a weak or vulnerable point. [named after the Greek mythical hero Achilles, who was dipped by his mother into the River Styx to make his body invulnerable, except for the heel by which she held him]

Achilles' tendon *noun* the tendon connecting the heel with the calf muscles.

acid *noun* **1** any of a class of substances containing hydrogen that can be replaced by a metal to form a salt. **2** a sour substance. **3** (*informal*) the drug LSD. **acid** *adjective* **1** sour or sharp-tasting. **2** looking or sounding bitter ♦ *He made some acid remarks.* **acidly** *adverb* [from a Latin word *acere* meaning 'to be sour']

acidic (ə-sid-ik) *adjective* of or like an acid.

acidify (ə-sid-i-fiy) *verb* (**acidifies, acidified, acidifying**) to make something acid, or to become acid.

acidity (ə-sid-iti) *noun* a state of being acid.

acid rain *noun* rain made acid by contamination, especially by waste gases from power-stations, factories, etc.

acid salt *noun* (*Chemistry*) a salt formed by incomplete replacement of the hydrogen of an acid.

acid test *noun* a conclusive test to see whether something is right or genuine. [so called because acid is applied to a metal to test whether it is gold or not]

ackee *noun* a West African tree or the fruit that grows on it. [from a West African word]

acknowledge *verb* **1** to admit that something is true or genuine. SYNONYMS: admit, accept, agree, concede. **2** to confirm that you have received something, or to express thanks for receiving it. **3** to show that you have noticed or recognized someone. **acknowledgement** *noun* [from an Old English word *oncnawan* meaning 'to confess', and an old meaning of *knowledge*]

acme (ak-mi) *noun* the highest point or achievement, the peak of perfection. [from a Greek word *akmē* meaning 'highest point']

acne (ak-ni) *noun* inflammation of the oil-glands of the skin, producing red pimples. [from a misreading in an old manuscript of the Greek word *akmē* (see *acme*) which meant 'highest point of eruption on the face']

acolyte (ak-ǝ-liyt) *noun* **1** a person who assists a priest in certain religious services. **2** an attendant. [via Latin from a Greek word *akolouthos* meaning 'follower']

aconite *noun* a perennial plant of the buttercup family, with a poisonous root. [from a Greek word *akoniton*]

acorn *noun* the fruit of the oak tree, with a base like a cup. [from an Old English word]

acoustic (ǝ-koo-stik) *adjective* **1** to do with sound or the sense of hearing; to do with acoustics. **2** (said about a musical instrument) amplifying the sound by natural means, such as a sound box; not electrically amplified.
acoustics *plural noun* the properties of sound; the qualities of a hall etc. that make it good or bad for carrying sound. **acoustically** *adverb* [from a Greek word *akouein* meaning 'to hear']

acquaint *verb* to make someone aware of something or familiar with it ♦ *You had better acquaint us with the facts.* **to be acquainted with** to know someone slightly. [via Old French from *ad-* and a Latin word *cognoscere* meaning 'to get to know']

acquaintance *noun* **1** being acquainted. **2** a person you know slightly.

acquiesce (akwi-ess) *verb* to agree willingly. **to acquiesce in** to accept something as an arrangement. [from *ad-* and a Latin word *quiescere* meaning 'to rest']

acquiescent (akwi-ess-ǝnt) *adjective* willing to agree to something. **acquiescence** *noun*

acquire *verb* to get possession of something. **acquirement** *noun* [from *ad-* and a Latin word *quaerere* meaning 'to seek']

acquired immune deficiency syndrome *noun* see **Aids**.

acquired taste *noun* something that you gradually get to like over time.

acquisition (akwi-zish-ǝn) *noun* **1** something you have acquired recently. **2** the process of acquiring something.

acquisitive (ǝ-kwiz-itiv) *adjective* wanting to have a lot of new things. **acquisitively** *adverb* **acquisitiveness** *noun*

acquit *verb* (**acquitted, acquitting**) in a court of law, to declare a person not guilty of the crime they were charged with. **to acquit oneself** to conduct oneself or perform in a certain way ♦ *She acquitted herself well in the test.* [from *ad-* and a late Latin word *quitare* meaning 'to set free']

acquittal (ǝ-kwi-tǝl) *noun* **1** the act of acquitting someone of a crime. **2** a verdict acquitting a person.

acre (ay-ker) *noun* a measure of land, equal to 4840 sq. yds. [from an Old English word *aecer* meaning 'field']

acreage (ay-ker-ij) *noun* the total number of acres in an area of land.

acrid (ak-rid) *adjective* **1** having a bitter smell or taste. **2** having a sharp temper or manner. **acridity** (ǝ-krid-iti) *noun* [from a Latin word *acer* meaning 'sharp', 'pungent']

acrimony (ak-ri-mǝni) *noun* bitterness of manner or words. **acrimonious** (akri-moh-niǝs) *adjective* **acrimoniously** *adverb* [same origin as for *acrid*]

acrobat *noun* someone who performs acrobatics. [from a Greek word *akrobatos* meaning 'walking on tiptoe']

acrobatics *plural noun* spectacular gymnastic exercises and movements. **acrobatic** *adjective* **acrobatically** *adverb*

acronym (ak-rǝ-nim) *noun* a word formed from the initial letters of other words and pronounced as a word in its own right, e.g. *Aids*, *Nato*. [from Greek words *akros* meaning 'top' and *onuma* meaning 'name']

acropolis (a-krop-ə-lis) *noun* the citadel or upper fortified part of an ancient Greek city, especially (**Acropolis**) Athens. [from a Greek word *acropolis* meaning 'summit of the city']

across *preposition & adverb* **1** from one side of a thing to the other. **2** to or on the other side of. **3** so as to be understood or accepted ♦ *He got his points across to the audience.* **4** so as to form a cross or intersect ♦ *They were laid across each other.* **across the board** applying to all members or groups. [from an Old French phrase *à croix* meaning 'crosswise']

acrostic (ə-**kros**-tik) *noun* a word puzzle or poem in which the first or last letters of each line form a word or phrase. [from Greek words *akron* meaning 'end' and *stikhos* meaning 'line of verse']

acrylic (ə-**kril**-ik) *adjective* of a synthetic material made from an organic acid. **acrylic** *noun* an acrylic fibre, plastic, or resin. [from *acrolein*, the substance from which acrylic is made. It is related to *acrid*]

act *noun* **1** something someone does. SYNONYMS: action, deed, feat, exploit. **2** the process of doing something ♦ *The thieves were caught in the act.* **3** a pose or pretence ♦ *His show of concern was just an act.* **4** each of a series of short performances in a programme ♦ *The next act will be the clowns.* **5** each of the main divisions of a play. **6** a decree or law made by a parliament. **act** *verb* **1** to behave or perform actions in a certain way ♦ *You have acted wisely.* SYNONYMS: behave, carry on, conduct yourself. **2** to function or do what is required ♦ *Will you act as referee?* ♦ *The brakes were slow to act.* **3** to have an effect on something ♦ *Acid acts on metal.* **4** to perform a part in a play ♦ *Stephen was chosen to act Hamlet.* SYNONYMS: perform, take part, play a part, appear. **5** to portray by actions as though taking part in a play ♦ *act the fool.* [from a Latin word *actus* meaning 'something done'. It is related to *action*]

acting *adjective* serving for a time as a substitute or replacement ♦ *the acting manager.*

action *noun* **1** the process of doing something to achieve a purpose. **2** the exertion of energy or influence ♦ *the action of acid on metal.* **3** a thing that

someone has done ♦ *Their prompt action prevented an accident.* SYNONYMS: act, deed, step. **4** a series of events in a story or play ♦ *The action is set in China.* **5** the mechanism or movements by which a machine or device works. **6** a lawsuit. **7** fighting in a war ♦ *Her brother was killed in action.* **out of action** not working or taking part. [from a Latin word *agere* meaning 'to do'. It is related to *act*]

actionable *adjective* giving good reason to take legal action.

action replay *noun* a playback of a piece of action in the broadcast of a sports event, often in slow motion.

activate *verb* to make something active. **activation** *noun* **activator** *noun*

active *adjective* **1** moving about, characterized by energetic action. SYNONYMS: lively, energetic, vigorous. **2** taking part in many activities. SYNONYM: busy. **3** (said about a machine) working or in operation. **4** (said about a volcano) erupting occasionally. **5** having an effect ♦ *the active ingredients.* **6** radioactive. **7** (*Grammar*) denoting the form of a verb used when the subject of the sentence is the person or thing that performs the action, e.g. *saw* in *We saw him* and *stops* in *When the train stops.* **active** *noun* (*Grammar*) the active form of a verb. **actively** *adverb*

activist *noun* someone who is very active and energetic, especially in politics. **activism** *noun*

activity *noun* (**activities**) **1** a situation in which things are happening or being done. **2** busy or energetic action. **3** that people do for exercise or interest ♦ *plenty of outdoor activities.*

actor *noun* someone who performs in a stage play or a film.

actress *noun* a female actor.

actual *adjective* existing in fact, real. SYNONYMS: real, true, genuine, authentic. **actually** *adverb* [from a Latin word *actualis* meaning 'active' or 'practical']

actuality (ak-tew-**al**-iti) *noun* what is real or happening.

actuary (**ak**-tew-er-i) *noun* (**actuaries**) an expert in statistics who calculates insurance risks and premiums. **actuarial** (ak-tew-**air**-iəl) *adjective* [from a Latin word *actuarius* meaning 'bookkeeper']

actuate *verb* **1** to start or activate a

movement or process. **2** to be a motive for a person's actions. **actuator** *noun* [same origin as for *act* and *action*]

acuity (ə-kew-iti) *noun* sharpness or acuteness. [same origin as for *acute*]

acumen (ak-yoo-men) *noun* shrewdness or sharpness of mind. [a Latin word meaning 'point']

acupressure (ak-yoo-presh-er) *noun* a system of applying pressure with the hands to certain points of the body, as a form of complementary medicine.

acupuncture (ak-yoo-punk-cher) *noun* a form of alternative medicine in which the tissues of the body are pricked with fine needles at special points thought to correspond to lines of energy.
acupuncturist *noun* [from the Latin word *acu* meaning 'with a needle' and *puncture*]

acute *adjective* **1** shrewd and perceptive, having a sharp mind. **2** sharp or severe in its effect ♦ *She felt an acute pain in her arm* ♦ *There was an acute shortage of food.* SYNONYMS: sharp (pain), intense, severe. **3** (said about an illness) coming sharply or quickly to a crisis ♦ *acute appendicitis.*
acutely *adverb* **acuteness** *noun* [from a Latin word *acus* meaning 'needle']

acute accent *noun* a mark put over a vowel in some languages, for example é in *café.*

acute angle *noun* an angle of less than 90°.

AD *abbreviation* (in dates) denoting the Christian era, placed after a date to indicate the number of years after the traditional date of the birth of Christ. [short for Latin *anno domini* meaning 'in the year of Our Lord']

ad- *prefix* (changing to **ac-, af-, ag-, al-, an-, ap-, ar-, as-, at-** before certain consonants) to; towards (as in *adapt, admit*). [from Latin *ad* meaning 'to']

adagio (ə-dahj-yoh) *adverb* (*Music*) to be played in slow time.
adagio *noun* (**adagios**) a movement to be played in this way. [an Italian word meaning 'at ease']

adamant (ad-ə-mənt) *adjective* refusing to change your mind, determined. [from a Greek word *adamas, adamant-* meaning 'untameable']

Adam's apple *noun* the projection of cartilage at the front of the neck, especially in men. [named after Adam, the first man in the Bible]

adapt *verb* **1** to make something suitable for a new use or situation. SYNONYMS: alter, adjust, convert, modify, transform. **2** to become used to a new situation. SYNONYMS: adjust, get used (to), acclimatize.
adaptation *noun* [from *ad-* and a Latin word *aptus* meaning 'fitted']

adaptable *adjective* **1** able to be adapted. **2** (said of a person) able to change to new circumstances or needs. **adaptability** *noun*

adaptor *noun* **1** a device used to connect different pieces of equipment. **2** a device allowing several electrical plugs to be put in one socket.

add *verb* **1** to join one thing to another to make it larger in size or quantity. **2** (also **add up**) to put numbers or amounts together to reach a total. SYNONYMS: total, reckon, count. **3** to reach a total. SYNONYMS: amount (to), come (to), total. **4** to make an extra remark ♦ *She added that it was time to leave anyway.* [from a Latin word *addere* meaning 'to add']

addenda *plural noun* extra text added at the end of a book or pamphlet. [a Latin word meaning 'things to be added']

adder *noun* a small poisonous snake, a viper. [from Old English. It was originally called *a nadder*, which became *an adder*]

addict (ad-ikt) *noun* a person who is addicted to something, especially to drugs. [from a Latin word *addictus* meaning 'given over'. It was used about a person who was given as a servant to someone he owed money to]

addicted (ə-dik-tid) *adjective* **1** doing or using something as a habit or compulsively. **2** enjoying an activity as a hobby or interest. **addiction** *noun*

addictive (ə-dik-tiv) *adjective* causing addiction.

addition *noun* **1** the process of adding or being added. **2** something added to something else. **in addition** as an extra thing, as well. [same origin as for *add*]

additional *adjective* added, extra. **additionally** *adverb*

additive (ad-it-iv) *noun* a substance added in small amounts to something, especially to colour or flavour food or to preserve it.

addle *verb* **1** (said about an egg) to become rotten and produce no chick. **2** to muddle or confuse ♦ *The din has addled my brains.* [from an Old English word *adela* meaning 'liquid filth']

address *noun* 1 the details of where a person lives or an organization is situated, as put on a letter or package for posting them. 2 a formal speech delivered to an audience. 3 (*Computing*) the part of a computer instruction that specifies the location of a piece of stored information.

address *verb* 1 to write the details of a person's or organization's address on an envelope or package. 2 to make a formal speech to an audience. 3 to direct a remark or statement to someone ♦ *At this point Jennifer addressed her brother.* 4 to use a particular style in speaking or writing to an important person ♦ *Do you know how to address an archbishop?* 5 (in golf) to take aim at the ball. **forms of address** words (such as *Mr, Sir, Your Majesty*) used in addressing a person. [via Old French from *ad-* and a Latin word *directus* meaning 'direct']

addressee (ad-ress-ee) *noun* a person to whom a letter or package is addressed.

adduce (ə-dewss) *verb* to mention or state something as an example or proof. **adducible** *adjective* [from *ad-* and a Latin word *ducere* meaning 'to lead']

adenoids (ad-in-oidz) *plural noun* a piece of spongy tissue between the back of the nose and the throat. **adenoidal** *adjective* [from a Greek word *aden* meaning 'gland']

adept (ad-ept) *adjective* very able or skilful. **adept** *noun* a skilful person. [from a Latin word *adept-*, an inflection of *adipisci* meaning 'to achieve']

adequate *adjective* 1 sufficient or satisfactory. 2 good enough but not outstanding. SYNONYMS: tolerable, acceptable, satisfactory, passable. **adequately** *adverb* **adequacy** *noun* [from *ad-* and a Latin word *aequus* meaning 'equal']

ADH *abbreviation* (*Biochemistry*) antidiuretic hormone, a hormone that decreases the flow of urine and increases blood pressure.

adhere (əd-heer) *verb* 1 to stick fast to a surface. 2 to continue to believe in something or to follow a course ♦ *We decided to adhere to our plan.* [from *ad-* and a Latin word *haerere* meaning 'to stick']

adherent *noun* someone who supports a political party or religious doctrine. **adherence** *noun*

adhesion (əd-hee-zhən) *noun* the state of sticking fast. [same origin as for *adhere*]

adhesive *adjective* causing things to adhere, sticky. **adhesive** *noun* an adhesive substance. **adhesiveness** *noun* [same origin as for *adhere*]

ad hoc *adjective & adverb* done or meant for a special purpose ♦ *They set up an ad hoc committee.* [a Latin phrase meaning 'for this']

adieu (ə-dew) *interjection & noun* (**adieus**) goodbye. [a French word, from the phrase *à Dieu* meaning 'to God']

Adi Granth (ah-di grunt) *noun* the sacred writings of Sikhism. [from an ancient Sanskrit name meaning 'first book']

ad infinitum (in-fin-iy-təm) *adverb* without limit, for ever. [a Latin phrase meaning 'to infinity']

adipose (ad-i-pohs) *adjective* of animal fat, fatty. **adiposity** (ad-i-**poss**-iti) *noun* [from a Latin word *adiposus* meaning 'fatty']

adjacent *adjective* lying near or adjoining something else. [from *ad-* and a Latin word *jacens* meaning 'lying']

adjective (aj-ik-tiv) *noun* a word added to a noun to describe it or change its meaning, e.g. *old, tall, Swedish, my, this*. **adjectival** (aj-ik-tiy-vəl) *adjective* **adjectivally** *noun* [from a Latin word *adicere* meaning 'to add']

adjoin *verb* to be next or nearest to something. [from *ad-* and a Latin word *jungere* meaning 'to join']

adjourn (ə-jern) *verb* 1 to break off a meeting for a time. 2 to stop doing something and go somewhere else. **adjournment** *noun* [from an Old French phrase *a jorn* meaning 'to (another) day']

adjudge *verb* to decide or award something formally ♦ *He was adjudged to be guilty.* [same origin as for *adjudicate*]

adjudicate (ə-joo-dik-ayt) *verb* 1 to act as judge in a court, tribunal, or competition. 2 to judge and pronounce a decision on a matter. **adjudication** *noun* **adjudicator** *noun* [from *ad-* and a Latin word *judicare* meaning 'to judge']

adjunct (ad-junkt) *noun* 1 something added or attached but subordinate. 2 (*Grammar*) a word, phrase, or clause used to modify a part of a sentence. [from *ad-* and a Latin word *junctum* meaning 'joined']

adjure (ə-joor) *verb* (*formal*) to command or urge someone to do something.

adjuration *noun* [from *ad-* and a Latin word *jurare* meaning 'to take an oath']

adjust *verb* **1** to arrange something or put it into the right position. **2** to alter a machine or device by a small amount to make it right for use ♦ *The steering needs adjusting.* SYNONYMS: alter, modify, correct, put right. **3** (said about a person) to be able to adapt to new circumstances. **4** (*Law*) to assess loss or damage in settlement of an insurance claim. **adjustable** *adjective* **adjuster** *noun* **adjustment** *noun* [from *ad-* and a Latin word *juxta* meaning 'near']

adjutant (aj-oo-tənt) *noun* an army officer who assists a superior officer with administrative work. [from *ad-* and a Latin word *juvare* meaning 'to help']

ad lib *adverb* as you want, without restraint.
ad-lib *adjective* said or done impromptu.
ad-lib *verb* (**ad-libbed, ad-libbing**) (*informal*) to speak impromptu, to improvise remarks or actions. [from the Latin phrase *ad libitum* meaning 'according to pleasure']

admin (ad-min) *noun* (*informal*) administration.

administer *verb* **1** to manage business affairs, to be an administrator. **2** to provide something or hand it out formally ♦ *They administered much comfort to the victims.* **3** to listen officially to someone taking an oath. [from *ad-* and a Latin word *ministrare* meaning 'to serve']

administrate *verb* to act as an administrator.

administration *noun* **1** the organization and running of public or business affairs. **2** the government, or the people who run an organization.

administrative *adjective* relating to or involving administration.

administrator *noun* **1** a person who organizes and runs a business or other organization. **2** a person appointed to administer an estate.

admirable *adjective* deserving to be admired, excellent. SYNONYMS: excellent, fine, wonderful, marvellous, praiseworthy, laudable, commendable, creditable.
admirably *adverb* [same origin as for *admire*]

admiral *noun* a naval officer of high rank, usually a commander of a fleet or squadron. [from an Arabic word *amir* meaning 'commander']

admire *verb* **1** to regard someone or something with pleasure or satisfaction, to think highly of them. SYNONYMS: praise, approve, approve of, marvel at, wonder at. **2** to look at something with enjoyment ♦ *to admire the view.* SYNONYMS: enjoy, appreciate.
admiration *noun* **admirer** *noun* [from *ad-* and a Latin word *mirari* meaning 'to wonder at']

admissible *adjective* valid or allowed to be included ♦ *admissible evidence.*
admissibility *noun* [same origin as for *admit*]

admission *noun* **1** the act of admitting someone to a place. **2** a charge made to admit someone. **3** a statement admitting something, a confession.

admit *verb* (**admitted, admitting**) **1** to allow someone to enter a place. **2** to accept someone into a hospital as a patient or into a school or college as a student. **3** to accept something as true or valid ♦ *The judge agreed to admit the new evidence.* SYNONYMS: accept, acknowledge, agree. **4** to state something reluctantly ♦ *We have to admit that we were wrong.* SYNONYM: concede. [from *ad-* and a Latin word *mittere* meaning 'to send']

admittance *noun* permission to enter a place.

admittedly *adverb* as you have to admit ♦ *It is admittedly rather late but I'd still like some tea.*

admixture *noun* something added as an ingredient. [*ad-* and *mixture*]

admonish (əd-mon-ish) *verb* **1** to advise or urge someone seriously to do something. **2** to reprimand someone gently but firmly. **admonition** (admən-ish-ən) *noun* **admonitory** (əd-mon-it-er-i) *adjective* [from *ad-* and a Latin word *monere* meaning 'to advise']

ad nauseam (naw-si-am) *adverb* to a sickening extent. [a Latin phrase meaning 'to sickness']

ado (ə-doo) *noun* fuss or excitement. [originally in *much ado* meaning 'much to do']

adobe (ə-doh-bi) *noun* sun-dried clay brick. [from Arabic words meaning 'the bricks']

adolescent (ad-ə-less-ənt) *adjective* at a time of life between childhood and adulthood.
adolescent *noun* an adolescent person.
adolescence *noun* [from *ad-* and a Latin word *alescere* meaning 'to grow up']

adopt *verb* 1 to take another person's child into your own family as the legal guardian. 2 to follow a decision or course of action. SYNONYMS: choose, follow. 3 to choose a person to be a candidate in an election. SYNONYMS: choose, select. 4 to take a position or attitude: ♦ *He adopted a standing position.* 5 (said about a local authority) to accept responsibility for maintenance of a road or piece of land. **adoption** *noun* [from *ad-* and a Latin word *optare* meaning 'to choose']

adoptive *adjective* (said about a child or parent) related by adoption.

adorable *adjective* 1 very lovable. 2 (*informal*) delightful. **adorably** *adverb*

adore *verb* 1 to love someone deeply. SYNONYMS: love, idolize, dote on, revere. 2 to worship a divine being. 3 (*informal*) to like something or someone very much. **adoration** *noun* **adorer** *noun* [from *ad-* and a Latin word *orare* meaning 'to pray']

adorn *verb* 1 to decorate something with ornaments. SYNONYMS: decorate, embellish. 2 to be an ornament to something. **adornment** *noun* [from *ad-* and a Latin word *ornare* meaning 'to decorate']

ADP *abbreviation* 1 adenosine diphosphate (compare **ATP**). 2 automatic data processing.

adrenal gland (ə-**dree**-nəl) *noun* each of two glands above the kidneys, which secrete adrenalin directly into the bloodstream. [from *ad-* and a Latin word *renes* meaning 'kidneys']

adrenalin (ə-**dren**-ə-lin) *noun* a hormone secreted by the adrenal glands or made synthetically, which increases rates of blood circulation and stimulates the nervous system.

adrift *adverb & adjective* 1 (said about a boat) drifting out of control. 2 (*informal*) loose or unfastened. [from *a-²* and *drift*]

adroit (ə-**droit**) *adjective* skilful or ingenious. **adroitly** *adverb* **adroitness** *noun* [from the French phrase *à droit* meaning 'according to right']

ADSL *abbreviation* (*Computing*) asymmetric digital subscriber line, a system of connection to the Internet.

adsorb *verb* (said about a solid) to hold particles of a gas or liquid as a thin film on its surface. **adsorption** *noun* [from *ad-* and *absorb*]

adulation (ad-yoo-**lay**-shən) *noun* too much flattery. **adulatory** (**ad**-yoo-layt-er-i) *adjective* [from a Latin word *adulari*, *adulat-* meaning 'to praise lavishly']

adult (**ad**-ult) *adjective* (said about a person) grown to full size or strength, mature. **adult** *noun* an adult person. **adulthood** *noun* [from a Latin word *adultus* meaning 'grown up']

adulterant *noun* an added substance that adulterates another substance.

adulterate *verb* to make a substance impure or poorer in quality by adding another substance. **adulteration** *noun* [from a Latin word *adulterare* meaning 'to corrupt']

adulterer *noun* a person who commits adultery. **adulteress** *feminine noun*

adultery *noun* the act of a married person having voluntary sexual intercourse with someone who is not their husband or wife. **adulterous** *adjective* [same origin as for *adulterate*]

advance *verb* 1 to move forward or make progress. SYNONYMS: proceed, approach, come near. 2 to make something go forward. 3 to bring forward or suggest something ♦ *We advanced a few ideas.* SYNONYMS: offer, present, suggest, propose. 4 to make an event happen at an earlier date. 5 to lend someone money or pay it before the date when it is due ♦ *advance her a month's salary.* 6 to help the progress of something ♦ *advance someone's interests.* **advance** *noun* 1 a forward movement. 2 an improvement or development. 3 an increase in price or amount. 4 a loan or payment made before the money is needed.
advance *adjective* 1 going ahead of others ♦ *an advance party.* 2 arranged or provided in advance ♦ *advance bookings.*
advances *plural noun* attempts to establish amorous relations or a business agreement. **in advance** ahead in place or time. [via Old French from a Latin word *abante* meaning 'in front']

advanced *adjective* 1 far on in life ♦ *He had reached an advanced age.* 2 having made good progress. 3 (said about a subject or studies) more complex and learned after the elementary stages. 4 (said about ideas) new and not yet generally accepted.

advanced gas-cooled reactor *noun* a nuclear reactor using uranium oxide as the fuel and carbon dioxide as the coolant.

Advanced Level noun in England, Wales, and Northern Ireland, a GCE examination at the higher of the two main levels.

advancement noun 1 an improvement or development; progress. 2 the promotion of a person in rank or position. 3 the process of promoting a plan or cause.

advantage noun 1 a condition or circumstance that helps you or is useful to you ♦ For Molly, being tall was quite an advantage. SYNONYMS: benefit, help, asset, bonus, convenience. 2 a benefit or profit ♦ There is no advantage in being the first to arrive. SYNONYMS: benefit, profit, gain. 3 (in tennis) the next point won after deuce. **to take advantage of** to make use of something or to exploit someone. [same origin as for advance]

advantageous (ad-van-**tay**-jəs) adjective giving an advantage, useful, or beneficial. SYNONYMS: useful, beneficial, helpful, favourable, worthwhile. **advantageously** adverb

advent noun the arrival of an important idea or development, or of an important person ♦ the advent of the personal computer. **Advent** noun 1 in Christian belief, the coming of Christ. 2 the season leading up to Christmas Day, when Christians celebrate the coming of Christ. [from ad- and a Latin word ventum meaning 'arrived']

Adventist noun a member of a religious sect believing that a second coming of Christ will happen in the near future.

adventitious (ad-ven-**tish**-əs) adjective 1 accidental, casual. 2 (said about the roots of a plant) occurring in an unusual place. **adventitiously** adverb

adventure noun 1 an exciting or dangerous experience. SYNONYMS: exploit, deed, feat, escapade, excitement. 2 willingness to take risks ♦ a spirit of adventure. **adventurous** adjective **adventurously** adverb [same origin as for advent]

adventurer noun 1 a person who enjoys adventures. 2 a person who makes money by risky or unscrupulous methods.

adverb noun a word that you use with a verb, adjective, or other adverb and tells how, when, or where something happened, e.g. gently, fully, soon. **adverbial** adjective **adverbially** adverb [from ad- and a Latin word verbum meaning 'word']

adversary (**ad**-ver-ser-i) noun (**adversaries**) an opponent or enemy. [same origin as for adverse]

adverse (**ad**-vers) adjective 1 critical or unfavourable ♦ an adverse report. 2 causing harm or misfortune ♦ The drug has no adverse effects. **adversely** adverb [from a Latin word adversus meaning 'opposite'] ◊ Do not confuse this word with averse.

adversity (əd-**vers**-iti) noun (**adversities**) difficulty or misfortune.

advert noun (informal) an advertisement.

advertise verb 1 to praise your own goods or services publicly in order to encourage people to buy or use them. SYNONYMS: promote, publicize. 2 to make something generally or publicly known. SYNONYMS: announce, make known, make public. 3 to give information about someone you need for a job ♦ The firm is advertising for a secretary. **advertiser** noun [via Old French from a Latin word advertere meaning 'to turn towards']

advertisement noun 1 a public notice or announcement advertising something. 2 the process of advertising.

advice noun 1 an opinion you give someone about what they should do or how they should behave. SYNONYMS: guidance, help, tip, suggestion. 2 a piece of information. [from ad- and a Latin word videre meaning 'to see'. The original meaning was 'opinion']

advisable adjective worth following as a course of action, sensible. **advisability** noun

advise verb 1 to give advice to someone. SYNONYMS: guide, help, counsel. 2 to recommend as a course of action ♦ What did the doctor advise? SYNONYMS: recommend, suggest, urge, advocate. 3 to give someone information about something ♦ They will advise us when to go in. SYNONYMS: inform, tell, notify. **adviser** noun [same origin as for advice]

advisory adjective giving advice or having the power to advise people ♦ an advisory council.

advocacy (**ad**-vək-əsi) noun 1 the advocating of an idea or policy. 2 the function of an advocate.

advocate [1] (ad-və-kayt) *verb* to recommend or be in favour of something ♦ *I advocate action.* [from *ad-* and a Latin word *vocare* meaning 'to call']

advocate [2] (ad-və-kət) *noun* **1** a person who favours or promotes a particular policy ♦ *She is an advocate of women's rights.* **2** a person, especially a lawyer in a lawcourt, who argues on behalf of another person.

adze *noun* an axe with a curved blade at right angles to the handle, used for trimming large pieces of wood. [from an Old English word *adesa*]

adzuki *noun* a small dark red bean, or the plant on which it grows. [from a Japanese word *azuki*]

aegis (ee-jis) *noun* protection or sponsorship ♦ *under the aegis of the Law Society.* [from a Greek word *aigis* denoting the magical shield of the god Zeus]

aeolian harp (ee-oh-li-ən) *noun* a stringed instrument giving musical sounds when exposed to wind. [from the name of Aeolus, god of the winds in Greek mythology]

aeon (ee-ən) *noun* a very long period of time. [from a Greek word *aion* meaning 'age']

aerate (air-ayt) *verb* to expose a substance to the chemical action of air ♦ *You can aerate the soil by digging a fork into it.* **aeration** *noun*

aerated *adjective* (said about a liquid) made fizzy or sparkling by having carbon dioxide added under pressure. [same origin as for *aero-*]

aerial (air-iəl) *noun* a metal rod or wire that receives or transmits radio or television signals.
aerial *adjective* **1** of or like air. **2** built or existing in the air or overhead ♦ *an aerial railway.* **3** done by or from aircraft ♦ *aerial bombardment.* **4** (said about a bird) spending a lot of its time in the air. [same origin as for *aero-*]

aero- *prefix* to do with air or aircraft (as in *aeronautics*). [from a Greek word *aer* meaning 'air']

aerobatics *plural noun* spectacular feats of flying aircraft, especially as an entertainment for spectators on the ground. **aerobatic** *adjective* [from *aero-* and *acrobatics*]

aerobic (air-oh-bik) *adjective* **1** using oxygen from the air. **2** (said about

exercises) designed to strengthen the heart and lungs.

aerobics *plural noun* aerobic exercises. [from *aero-* and a Greek word *bios* meaning 'life']

aerodrome *noun* a small airport or airfield. [from *aero-* and a Greek word *dromos* meaning 'running track']

aerodynamics *plural noun* **1** the movement of solid bodies (e.g. aircraft or bullets) through air. **2** the scientific study of this movement. **aerodynamic** *adjective* [from *aero-* and *dynamic*]
◊ In meaning **2** *aerodynamics* is usually treated as a singular noun.

aerofoil *noun* an aircraft wing, fin, or tailplane, shaped to produce good aerodynamics.

aeronautics *noun* the scientific study of the flight of aircraft. **aeronautic** *adjective* **aeronautical** *adjective* [from *aero-* and *nautical*]

aeroplane *noun* a flying vehicle which is heavier than the air it displaces and has one or more engines and fixed wings. [from *aero-* and *plane*]

aerosol *noun* **1** a container holding a liquid under pressure, with a device for releasing it as a fine spray. [from *aero-* and *solution*]

aerospace *noun* **1** the scientific study of aviation and space flight.

aesthete (ees-theet) *noun* a person who understands and loves great art and beauty.

aesthetic (iss-thet-ik) *adjective* **1** to do with beauty or the love of beauty. **2** artistic or tasteful. **aesthetically** *adverb*
aesthetics *plural noun* the study or principles of beauty, especially in art. [from a Greek word *aisthesthai* meaning 'to perceive']

aetiology (ee-ti-ol-əji) *noun* the scientific study of causes or reasons. **aetiological** *adjective* **aetiologically** *adverb* [from a Greek word *aitia* meaning 'a cause']

afar *adverb* far off, far away. [from *a-* [2] and *far*]

affable *adjective* good-natured and friendly. **affably** *adverb* **affability** *noun* [from *ad-* and a Latin word *fari* meaning 'to speak']

affair *noun* **1** a thing that has been done or has to be done, a matter or concern ♦ *How you do the work is your affair.* SYNONYMS: concern, business. **2** a thing or event that you want to comment on ♦ *The rest of the game was a dull affair.* **3** a temporary sexual relationship between two people who are not married to each other.

affairs *plural noun* the business that a person or organization has to deal with ♦ *I need a few days to put my affairs in order.* [from a French phrase *à faire* meaning 'to do']

affect *verb* **1** to have an effect on something or someone or make a difference to them ♦ *The weather may affect tomorrow's plans.* SYNONYMS: influence, alter, change, modify, have an effect on. **2** to make someone feel sad or sympathetic ♦ *The news of her death affected us deeply.* SYNONYMS: move, touch, upset, trouble. **3** to pretend to have a feeling or attitude ♦ *He decided to affect ignorance.* SYNONYMS: feign, pretend, simulate. [from *ad-* and a Latin word *facere* meaning 'to do']
◊ Do not confuse *affect* (which is a verb only) and *effect* (which is a noun and a verb).

affectation *noun* unnatural behaviour that is intended to impress other people.

affected *adjective* (said about behaviour) unnatural or pretended and meant to impress other people.

affection *noun* **1** a feeling of love or strong liking. **2** a disease.

affectionate *adjective* showing affection, loving. SYNONYMS: loving, caring, devoted, fond, tender. **affectionately** *adverb*

affidavit (af-i-**day**-vit) *noun* a written statement sworn on oath to be true and used as legal evidence. [a Latin word meaning 'he or she has stated on oath']

affiliate (ə-**fil**-i-ayt) *verb* to connect a person or organization to a larger organization as a member or branch ♦ *The club is affiliated to a national society.* **affiliation** *noun* [from Latin *ad-* and a Latin word *filius* meaning 'son'. The original meaning was 'to adopt someone as your son']

affinity (ə-**fin**-iti) *noun* (**affinities**) **1** a strong natural liking or attraction. **2** a relationship (especially by marriage) other than blood relationship. **3** a similarity, a close resemblance or connection. **4** the tendency of some substances to combine with others. [from *ad-* and a Latin word *finis* meaning 'boundary']

affirm *verb* **1** to assert something or state it as a fact. **2** (*Law*) to make an affirmation

instead of an oath. [from *ad-* and a Latin word *firmus* meaning 'firm']

affirmation (af-er-may-shən) *noun* **1** stating something as a fact. **2** a solemn declaration that a person makes in a lawcourt instead of an oath when they have no religion or do not want to use the name of God.

affirmative (ə-**ferm**-ətiv) *adjective* affirming or agreeing, giving the answer 'yes' ♦ *an affirmative reply.*
affirmative *noun* an affirmative word or statement. **in the affirmative** giving the answer 'yes'. **affirmatively** *adverb*

affix [2] (ə-**fiks**) *verb* **1** to stick or attach something to something else. **2** to add something in writing. [from *ad-* and a Latin word *fixare* meaning 'to fix']

affix [2] (**af**-iks) *noun* (*Grammar*) a prefix or suffix.

afflict *verb* to cause someone physical or mental pain or discomfort ♦ *He has been afflicted with rheumatism for years.* SYNONYMS: trouble, distress, burden, torment, plague. [from *ad-* and a Latin word *flictum* meaning 'struck']

affliction *noun* **1** pain or suffering. **2** something that causes this.

affluent (**af**-loo-ənt) *adjective* (usually said about groups of people) rich or wealthy. **affluently** *adverb* **affluence** *noun* [from a Latin word *affluens* meaning 'overflowing', from *ad-* and *fluens* meaning 'flowing']

afford *verb* **1** to have enough money or time for something. **2** to be able to do something without a risk ♦ *You can't afford to be critical.* **3** (*formal*) to provide something ♦ *The trees afforded some protection against the rain.* SYNONYMS: provide, offer, give. **affordable** *adjective* [from Old English]

afforest *verb* to plant an area with trees to make a forest. **afforestation** *noun*

affray (ə-**fray**) *noun* (*old use*) a breach of the peace by fighting or rioting in public. [from an Old French word *esfreer* meaning 'to riot']

affront (ə-**frunt**) *verb* to insult deliberately, to offend or embarrass.
affront *noun* a deliberate insult or show of disrespect. [from a Latin phrase *ad frontem* meaning 'to the face']

Afghan (**af**-gan) *noun* **1** a person born in Afghanistan or descended from people born there. 2 the language spoken in Afghanistan, Pashto.

Afghan *adjective* to do with or coming from Afghanistan.

aficionado (ə-fis-yon-ah-doh) *noun* (**aficionados**) someone who is very keen on a particular sport or pastime. [a Spanish word, in English originally used about bullfighting]

afield *adverb* at or to a large distance, far away from home. [from *a-²* and *field*]

aflame *adverb & adjective* in flames, burning. [from *a-²* and *flame*]

afloat *adverb & adjective* 1 floating, especially on the sea. 2 out of danger or difficulty. [from *a-²* and *float*]

afoot *adverb & adjective* happening or in progress ♦ *There's a scheme afoot to improve the roads.* [from *a-²* and *foot*. It originally meant 'on foot']

aforementioned or **aforesaid** *adjective* (*formal*) mentioned or said previously. [from *afore* meaning 'before' and *said* or *mentioned*]

aforethought *adjective* (*Law*) planned in advance, intended ♦ *with malice aforethought*.

afraid *adjective* feeling fear; alarmed or frightened. SYNONYMS: frightened, scared, alarmed, anxious, fearful, apprehensive, terrified. **I'm afraid** (*informal*) I regret to say ♦ *I'm afraid they've broken a window.* [from an Old English inflection of the verb *affray* meaning 'to attack', 'to frighten']

afresh *adverb* anew, beginning again. [from *a-²* and *fresh*]

African *adjective* to do with or coming from Africa.
African *noun* a person born in Africa or descended from people born there, especially a black person.

Afrikaans (af-ri-kahns) *noun* a language developed from Dutch and used in South Africa. [from a Dutch word meaning 'African']

Afrikaner (af-ri-kah-ner) *noun* a White person in South Africa whose first language is Afrikaans. [from a Dutch word meaning 'an African']

Afro (af-roh) *adjective* (said about a hairstyle) long and bushy, as naturally grown by some black people.

Afro- *combining form* African.

Afro-Caribbean *noun* a person of African descent living in or coming from the Caribbean area.
Afro-Caribbean *adjective* to do with Afro-Caribbeans.

aft *adverb* in or towards the stern of a ship or the tail of an aircraft. [a shortening of an Old English word *abaft*, related to *after*]

after *preposition* 1 at a later time ♦ *I won't arrive until after eight.* 2 behind in place or order ♦ *The police cars followed on after the procession.* 3 in spite of something ♦ *After all our help they still left without a word.* 4 as a result of something ♦ *After what she said, I can hardly like her.* 5 in pursuit or search of someone ♦ *I'd better run after him.* 6 about or concerning someone ♦ *Daphne was asking after you.* 7 in imitation of someone or in honour of them ♦ *They named their daughter Sibyl after her grandmother.*
after *adverb* 1 behind ♦ *Jill came tumbling after.* 2 later ♦ *They met again twenty years after.*
after *conjunction* at or in a time later than ♦ *They arrived after we had left.*
afters *plural noun* (*informal*) a course following the main course at a meal. [from an Old English word *aefter*]

afterbirth *noun* the placenta and fetal membrane discharged from the womb after childbirth.

afterburner *noun* an extra burner in the exhaust stream of a jet engine, to give it greater thrust.

aftercare *noun* 1 extra care or treatment of a patient who has left hospital. 2 extra support given to someone who has just left prison.

after-effect *noun* an effect that happens or arises after whatever caused it has stopped or gone away.

afterglow *noun* light still glowing in the sky after sunset.

afterlife *noun* (in some beliefs) a life that follows after death.

aftermath *noun* events or circumstances that come after something bad or unpleasant ♦ *Disease was the aftermath of war.*

afternoon *noun* the time from midday to early evening.

aftershave *noun* a soothing lotion for use on the skin after shaving.

afterthought *noun* something thought of or added later.

afterward adverb (North Amer.) afterwards.

afterwards adverb at a later time.

Ag abbreviation (Chemistry) the symbol for silver.

again adverb 1 another time, once more ♦ We decided to try again. 2 as before, in an original place or condition ♦ The doctor says you'll soon be well again. 3 what is more, besides ♦ Then again, she could have asked if she wanted help. 4 on the other hand ♦ I might, and again I might not. [from an Old English word ongean meaning 'in the opposite direction', 'back to the beginning']

against preposition 1 touching or hitting something ♦ Lean your bicycle against the wall. 2 in opposition to something ♦ We are against fox-hunting. 3 in contrast to something ♦ The picture looked beautiful against a dark background. 4 in preparation for ♦ You'll need a warm coat to protect you against the cold. [from again]

agape (ə-gayp) adjective gaping, open-mouthed. [from a-² and gape]

agar (ay-gah) noun a substance made from seaweed and used to thicken foods. [from a Malay word]

agate (ag-ət) noun a very hard stone with patches or concentric bands of colour. [from a Greek word akhatēs]

age noun 1 the length of time a person has lived or a thing has existed. 2 the later part of life, a person's old age. 3 a period of history, with special characteristics or events ♦ the Elizabethan Age ♦ the atomic age. SYNONYMS: period, time, era, epoch. 4 (informal) a very long time ♦ It took ages. **age** verb (**aged, ageing**) 1 to grow old and show signs of age. 2 (said about wine, cheese, etc.) to become mature. 3 to make someone seem old. **of age** having reached the age at which you have an adult's legal rights and obligations. [via Old French from a Latin word aevum meaning 'age', 'era']

aged adjective 1 (ayjd) having the age of ♦ a girl aged 10. 2 (ay-jid) very old ♦ He still lived at home with his aged mother. SYNONYMS: old, elderly.

age group noun all the people of the same age.

ageism noun discrimination against people because of their age.

ageless adjective never ageing or seeming to be old.

agency noun (**agencies**) 1 a business or place of business that provides a special service or does special work ♦ a travel agency ♦ The Child Support Agency. 2 the action that is done to achieve something ♦ Flowers are fertilized by the agency of bees. [same origin as for agent]

agenda (ə-jen-də) noun (**agendas**) a list of items of business to be dealt with at a meeting. [a Latin word meaning 'things to be done'] ◊ Although it is originally a Latin plural, agenda is normally used with a singular verb ♦ The agenda is rather long.

agent noun 1 someone who organizes the business side of the work of a writer, actor, etc., such as drawing up contracts. 2 someone who acts on behalf of another person or organization ♦ The Company has an agent in Paris. 3 something that produces an effect or change ♦ Soda is the active agent. [from a Latin word agens meaning 'doing things']

agent provocateur (azh-ahn prə-vok-ə-ter) (**agents provocateurs**) a person employed to prove that suspects are guilty by encouraging them to do something illegal. [a French phrase meaning 'provocative agent']

age of consent noun the age at which a person may legally agree to have sexual intercourse.

age-old adjective very old, having existed for a long time.

agglomerate¹ (ə-glom-er-ayt) verb to collect things or become collected into a mass. **agglomeration** noun [from ad- and a Latin word glomus meaning 'mass']

agglomerate² (ə-glom-er-ət) noun a collection or mass of things.

agglutinate (ə-gloo-tin-ayt) verb to stick or fuse together. **agglutination** noun **agglutinative** adjective [from ad- and a Latin word glutinare meaning 'to glue']

agglutinin (ə-gloo-tin-in) noun an antibody or other substance that causes bacteria or red blood cells to agglutinate.

aggrandize (ə-gran-diyz) verb to increase the power, wealth, or importance of a person or organization. **aggrandizement** noun [from ad- and a Latin word grandis meaning 'large']

aggravate verb 1 to make something worse or more serious. SYNONYMS: worsen, intensify, exacerbate. 2 (informal) to annoy or irritate someone. **aggravation** *noun* [from *ad-* and a Latin word *gravare* meaning 'to load heavily']

aggregate [1] (ag-ri-gət) *noun* **1** a mass or amount made by combining several parts. **2** a mixture of hard substances, such as sand, gravel, broken stone, mixed with cement to make concrete.
aggregate *adjective* combined or total ♦ *the aggregate amount.* [from *ad-* and a Latin word *gregatum* meaning 'herded together']

aggregate [2] (ag-ri-gayt) *verb* **1** to collect something or form into an aggregate, to unite. **2** (*informal*) to amount to a total. **aggregation** *noun*

aggression *noun* **1** the act of attacking someone without being provoked. **2** a hostile action, hostile behaviour. [from *ad-* and a Latin word *gressum* meaning 'gone' from *gradi* 'to go']

aggressive *adjective* **1** tending to make unprovoked attacks, showing aggression. SYNONYMS: hostile, belligerent, antagonistic, militant, warlike. **2** assertive or forceful ♦ *an aggressive salesman.* **aggressively** *adverb* **aggressiveness** *noun*

aggressor *noun* a person or country that attacks first or begins hostilities.

aggrieved (ə-greevd) *adjective* upset or resentful because of unfair treatment. [same origin as for *aggravate*]

aggro *noun* (*informal*) aggressive behaviour or trouble. [a shortening of *aggravation*]

aghast (ə-gahst) *adjective* filled with shock or dismay. [from an Old English word *gaesten* meaning 'to frighten']

agile *adjective* able to move about quickly and nimbly. SYNONYMS: nimble, graceful, sure-footed, lithe, sprightly. **agilely** *adverb* **agility** (ə-jil-iti) *noun* [from a Latin word *agilis* from *agere* meaning 'to do']

agitate *verb* **1** to stir up public interest or concern about something. **2** to shake or move something briskly. **3** to disturb someone or cause them anxiety. **agitation** *noun* **agitator** *noun* [from a Latin word *agitare* meaning 'to shake']

agitated *adjective* nervously anxious or worried. SYNONYMS: anxious, nervous, flustered, worried, restless, ruffled.

aglow *adjective* glowing brightly. [from *a-*[2] and *glow*]

AGM *abbreviation* annual general meeting.

agnostic (ag-**nos**-tik) *noun* a person who believes that we can know nothing about the existence of God. **agnosticism** *noun* [from *a-*[1] and a Greek word *gnōstikos* meaning 'knowing']

ago *adverb* in the past, before now ♦ *It happened ten days ago.* [from an old word *agone* meaning 'gone by']

agog (ə-**gog**) *adjective* eager or expectant.

agonize *noun* to worry a lot about something.

agonizing *adjective* causing great pain or worry. **agonizingly** *adverb*

agony *noun* (**agonies**) great physical or mental pain or suffering. SYNONYMS: pain, suffering, torment, torture, (mental) anguish, distress. [from a Greek word *agōn* meaning 'struggle']

agoraphobia (ag-er-ə-**foh**-biə) *noun* an abnormal fear of being in public places or open spaces. **agoraphobic** *noun* & *adjective* [from a Greek word *agora* meaning 'marketplace' and *phobia*]

AGR *abbreviation* advanced gas-cooled reactor.

agrarian (ə-**grair**-iən) *adjective* to do with agriculture and the cultivation of land. [from a Latin word *ager* meaning 'field']

agree *verb* (**agrees, agreed, agreeing**) **1** to have the same opinion as someone else ♦ *I'm afraid I don't agree with you.* SYNONYMS: concur, be of the same mind. **2** to say that you are willing to do something ♦ *The boy agreed to come and help.* SYNONYMS: consent, undertake, promise, be willing, assent. **3** (said about one person) to authorize or approve something ♦ *The Bank Manager has agreed an overdraft.* SYNONYMS: authorize, approve, allow. **4** (said about two or more people) to come to a decision about something ♦ *Can we agree a time to meet?* **5** to get on well together. **6** to be consistent with something else ♦ *Your story agrees with his.* SYNONYMS: correspond, accord. **7** (said about food) to be good for you or not harm you ♦ *I'm afraid curry doesn't agree with me.* **8** (*Grammar*) to have the right number, gender, case, or person in a phrase or sentence ♦ *the pronoun 'she' agrees with the noun 'woman'* ♦ *'he' agrees with 'man'.* [via Old French from Latin words *ad* meaning 'to' and *gratus* meaning 'pleasing']

agreeable *adjective* **1** pleasant or enjoyable ♦ *We had an agreeable time.* **2** willing to agree to something ♦ *I'll go if you are agreeable.* **agreeably** *adverb*

agreement *noun* 1 agreeing with someone. 2 having the same opinion or feeling. 3 an arrangement, such as a treaty or contract, agreed between people, organizations, or countries. SYNONYMS: settlement, contract, treaty (between states), deal, understanding.

agriculture *noun* the process of cultivating land on a large scale and rearing livestock. **agricultural** *adjective* **agriculturally** *adverb* [from Latin *agri* meaning 'of a field' and *culture*]

agrochemical *noun* a chemical used in agriculture.

agronomy (ǝ-gron-ǝmi) *noun* the scientific study of soil management and crop production. [from Greek *agros* meaning 'field' and *-nomia* meaning 'management']

aground *adverb & adjective* on or touching the bottom in shallow water ♦ *The ship has run aground.* [from *a-*² and *ground*]

ague (ay-gew) *noun* malaria or another illness involving a fit of shivering. [via Old French from a Latin word *acuta (febris)* meaning 'acute (fever)']

AH *abbreviation* (in dates) of the Muslim era. [short for Latin *anno Hegirae* meaning 'in the year of the Hegira']

ah *interjection* an exclamation of surprise, pity, admiration, etc.

ahead *adverb* 1 further forward in space or time. 2 having made more progress. **ahead of** before in time or space ♦ *We have a difficult task ahead of us.* [from *a-*² and *head*]

ahimsa (ǝ-him-sǝ) *noun* (in Hinduism, Buddhism, Jainism) the doctrine of non-violence or non-killing. [a Sanskrit word meaning 'without violence']

ahoy *interjection* a cry used by seamen to call attention.

AI *abbreviation* 1 artificial insemination. 2 artificial intelligence.

AID *abbreviation* artificial insemination by donor.

aid *verb* to help someone or support an activity. SYNONYMS: help, assist, support, facilitate (an activity). **aid** *noun* 1 help. SYNONYMS: help, assistance, support, cooperation. 2 something that helps you ♦ *a hearing aid.* 3 food, money, etc., sent to a country to help it. [from an Old French word *aide*]

aide *noun* an assistant. [a French word]

Aids *noun* a condition caused by the HIV virus, which breaks down a person's natural defences against illness. [from the initials of 'acquired immune deficiency syndrome']

AIH *abbreviation* artificial insemination by husband.

aikido *noun* a Japanese form of self-defence. [a Japanese word meaning 'way of adapting the spirit']

ail *verb* (old use) to make someone feel ill or uneasy. [from an Old English word]

aileron (ail-er-ǝn) *noun* a hinged flap on the rear side of an aeroplane wing, used to control balance. [from a French word *aile* meaning 'wing']

ailing *adjective* sick or unwell.

ailment *noun* a slight illness.

aim *verb* 1 to point or send a weapon towards its target; to direct (a blow, missile, remark, etc.) towards a specified object or goal. SYNONYMS: point, direct. 2 to attempt or try ♦ *aim to please.* SYNONYMS: try, attempt, intend, seek. **aim** *noun* 1 the act of aiming a weapon ♦ *The marksman took aim and fired.* 2 a purpose or intention ♦ *What are your aims in life?* [via Old French *amer* from Latin *aestimare* meaning 'to estimate']

aimless *adjective* without any purpose. **aimlessly** *adverb* **aimlessness** *noun*

ain't *verb* (informal) 1 am not, is not, or are not. 2 has not or have not.
◊ This word is common in dialect and informal speech, but is non-standard in ordinary use.

air *noun* 1 the mixture of gases (mainly oxygen and nitrogen) surrounding the earth. 2 the open space above the surface of the earth, especially as the space in which aircraft fly. 3 the earth's atmosphere, especially as a medium for transmitting radio waves. 4 a light wind or breeze. 5 an impression you get about a place ♦ *The house had an air of mystery.* 6 a tune or melody. **air** *verb* 1 to express an opinion publicly. 2 to broadcast a radio or television programme. 3 to expose a place to the air, especially to ventilate a room in order to make it cooler or fresher. 4 to put clothes or laundry in a warm place to finish drying. **by air** in or by aircraft. **in the air** evident or noticeable. **on the air**

broadcast or broadcasting by radio or television. **put on airs** to behave in an affectedly grand or pompous manner. [via Old French and Latin from a Greek word *aer* meaning 'air']

air bag *noun* a safety device in a vehicle, which inflates to protect occupants in an impact.

airbase *noun* a base for military aircraft.

airborne *adjective* **1** carried in the air or by aircraft. **2** (said about an aircraft) in flight after taking off.

air brake *noun* **1** a brake worked by compressed air. **2** a hinged flap on the wing of an aircraft, raised to reduce its speed.

airbrush *noun* a device for spraying paint by means of compressed air.
airbrush *verb* to paint over a surface with an airbrush.

air-conditioned *adjective* equipped with air conditioning.

air conditioning *noun* a system for controlling the humidity and temperature of the air in a room or building.

aircraft *noun* (**aircraft**) an aeroplane, helicopter, or other flying machine.

aircraft carrier *noun* a ship that carries and acts as a base for aeroplanes.

aircraftman or **aircraftwoman** *noun* the lowest rank in the RAF.

air cushion *noun* a layer of air under pressure that supports a hovercraft.

Airedale *noun* a large black-and-tan dog with a rough coat.

airfield *noun* an area of open level ground on which aircraft land and take off and are maintained.

airflow *noun* a flow of air past a vehicle or aircraft.

air force *noun* the branch of a country's armed forces that uses aircraft as the main means of fighting and defence.

airgun *noun* a gun which fires lead pellets by means of compressed air.

air hostess *noun* a female flight attendant in a passenger aircraft.

airless *adjective* **1** stuffy. **2** calm and still, with no wind. **airlessness** *noun*

air letter *noun* a sheet of light paper that is folded and sent as a letter by airmail.

airlift *noun* large-scale transport of troops or supplies by aircraft, especially in an emergency.
airlift *verb* to transport troops or supplies in this way.

airline *noun* an organization that provides a regular service of air transport for the public.

air line *noun* a pipe for supplying air.

airliner *noun* a large passenger aircraft.

airlock *noun* **1** a stoppage of the flow in a pump or pipe, caused by an air bubble. **2** a compartment with controlled pressure and a set of airtight doors at each end, allowing movement between areas having different pressures.

airmail *noun* a system of sending overseas mail by air transport.
airmail *verb* to send mail by airmail.

airman *noun* (**airmen**) a male aviator or member of an air force.

air pocket *noun* an area of low pressure that causes aircraft flying through it to lose height suddenly.

airport *noun* an area with hangars and runways for aircraft to land and take off, and passenger terminals and other buildings.

air quality *noun* the quality of the air in the immediate environment, and how free it is from pollution.

air raid *noun* an attack by aircraft dropping bombs on targets on the ground.

airscrew *noun* the propeller of an aircraft.

airship *noun* a power-driven aircraft containing helium or another gas that is lighter than air.

airsick *adjective* made sick or nauseous by the motion of an aircraft. **airsickness** *noun*

airspace *noun* the air above a country and subject to its control.

air speed *noun* the speed of an aircraft in relation to the air it is moving through.

airstream *noun* a current of air, especially over a flying aircraft.

airstrip *noun* a strip of ground for aircraft to land and take off.

airtight *adjective* not allowing air to enter or escape.

airtime *noun* the time during which a radio or television programme is being broadcast.

air traffic control *noun* an organization of people and equipment that monitors and controls the movement of aircraft in its area.

airway *noun* **1** a regular route used by aircraft. **2** the passage by which air goes into the lungs, or a tube to supply air to the lungs in an emergency.

airwoman *noun* (**airwomen**) a female aviator or member of an air force.

airworthy *adjective* (said about an aircraft) fit and safe to fly. **airworthiness** *noun*

airy *adjective* (**airier, airiest**) **1** (said about a building or room) having plenty of space and fresh air. **2** light as air, delicate. **3** careless and light-hearted ♦ *an airy manner.* **airily** *adverb* **airiness** *noun*

airy-fairy *adjective* (*informal*) vague or fanciful.

aisle (*rhymes with* mile) *noun* **1** a passage between rows of pews in a church, seats in a theatre or cinema, or shelves in a supermarket. **2** a side part of a church. [from a Latin word *ala* meaning 'wing']

ajar *adverb & adjective* (said about a door or window) slightly open. [from *a-²* and an old word *char* meaning 'a turn']

akimbo (a-kim-boh) *adverb* with the hands on the hips and the elbows pointed outwards. [from an Old Norse word]

akin *adjective* related or similar ♦ *I had a feeling akin to jealousy.* [from *a* meaning 'of' and *kin*]

alabaster (al-ə-bah-ster) *noun* a form of gypsum that is white and translucent, often carved into ornaments.

à la carte (ah lah kart) *adjective* (said about a restaurant meal) ordered as separate items from a menu. [a French phrase meaning 'from the menu']

alacrity (ə-lak-riti) *noun* eager willingness to do or take something ♦ *She accepted the offer with alacrity.* [from a Latin word *alacer* meaning 'brisk']

à la mode (ah lah mohd) *adjective* fashionable or up to date. [a French phrase meaning 'in the fashion']

alarm *noun* **1** sudden fear caused by expectation of danger. SYNONYMS: fright, fear, panic, anxiety, disquiet, consternation, trepidation. **2** a warning sound or signal, or a device that makes this. **3** an alarm clock.
alarm *verb* to frighten someone suddenly. SYNONYMS: frighten, startle, scare, panic, terrify. [from the Italian phrase *all'arme!* meaning 'to arms!', used as a rallying cry]

alarm clock *noun* a clock with a device that can be set to ring or bleep at a certain time.

alarmist *noun* someone who raises unnecessary or excessive alarm.

alas *interjection* an exclamation of pity or sorrow. [via Old French *a las* from a Latin word *lassus* meaning 'weary']

alb *noun* a white robe reaching to the feet, worn by some Christian clergy at church ceremonies. [from a Latin word *albus* meaning 'white']

albatross *noun* a large seabird with long narrow wings, related to the petrel. [via Spanish and Portuguese *alcatraz* from an Arabic word meaning 'the diver'. The English spelling is influenced by the Latin word *albus* meaning 'white'.]

albeit (awl-**bee**-it) *conjunction* (*literary*) although. [from the phrase *all be it*]

albino (al-**bee**-noh) *noun* (**albinos**) a person or animal with no colouring pigment in the skin and hair (which are white) and the eyes (which are normally pink). [from Latin *albus* meaning 'white']

album *noun* **1** a blank book for keeping a collection of autographs, photographs, postage stamps, etc. **2** a CD or LP with recordings of several items. [from a Latin word *album* denoting a white piece of stone for writing on]

albumen (al-bew-min) *noun* the white of an egg. [from Latin *albus* meaning 'white']

albumin (al-bew-min) *noun* a protein found in egg white, milk, and blood.

alchemy (al-kəmi) *noun* a form of chemistry in the Middle Ages, concerned mainly with attempts to turn ordinary metals into gold. **alchemist** *noun* [from an Arabic word *al-kimiya* meaning 'the art of changing metals']

alcohol *noun* **1** a colourless liquid made by fermenting sugar or starch and used as the intoxicant in wine, beer, and spirits. **2** a drink containing this. **3** a chemical compound of this type. [from an Arabic word *al-kuhl*]

alcoholic *adjective* containing alcohol or relating to the drinking of alcohol.

alcoholic *noun* a person suffering from alcoholism.

alcoholism *noun* an illness caused by continual heavy drinking of alcohol.

alcopop *noun* (*informal*) a bottled soft drink containing alcohol.

alcove *noun* 1 a recess in the wall of a room. 2 a recess forming an extension of a room etc. [from an Arabic word *al-kubba* meaning 'the arch']

aldehyde (al-di-hiyd) *noun* 1 a fluid with a suffocating smell, obtained from alcohol. 2 a compound with the same structure. [shortened from the Latin phrase *alcohol dehydrogenatum* meaning 'alcohol with hydrogen removed']

al dente *adjective & adverb* (said about food, especially pasta or vegetables) cooked so that it is still firm when bitten. [from an Italian phrase *al dente* meaning 'to the tooth']

alder (awl-der) *noun* a tree of the birch family with toothed leaves, bearing catkins and usually growing in marshy places and near rivers. [from an Old English word *aler*]

alderman (awl-der-mən) *noun* (**aldermen**) a co-opted member of an English county or borough council, next in dignity to the mayor. [from an Old English word *aldor* meaning 'older' and *man*]

ale *noun* beer other than lager or stout. [from an Old English word *alu*]

aleatory (ay-li-ə-ter-i) *adjective* (*formal*) depending on random choice. [from a Latin word *alea* meaning 'dice']

alert *adjective* watchful and ready to act. SYNONYMS: vigilant, watchful, sharp, observant, attentive, wary, quick, keen.
alert *noun* 1 a state of watchfulness or readiness. 2 a warning of danger.
alert *verb* to warn someone of danger. **on the alert** watchful and ready to act.
alertly *adverb* **alertness** *noun* [from the Italian phrase *all'erta!* meaning 'to the watchtower', used as a rallying cry]

aleurone *noun* (*Botany*) protein stored as granules in the cells of plant seeds. [from a Greek word *aleuron* meaning 'flour']

A level *noun* Advanced level in GCE.

alfalfa (al-fal-fə) *noun* a plant with leaves like clover and blue flowers, grown in SW Asia. [from the Arabic word *al-fasfasa* meaning 'a green fodder']

alfresco (al-**fres**-koh) *adjective & adverb* in the open air. [from the Italian phrase *al fresco* 'in the open air']

alga (al-gə) *noun* (**algae** (al-jee)) a water plant with no true stems or leaves. [from a Latin word *alga* meaning 'seaweed']

algebra (al-jib-rə) *noun* the branch of mathematics in which letters and symbols are used to represent quantities in formulae and equations. **algebraic** (alji-**bray**-ik) *adjective* **algebraically** *adverb* [from an Arabic word *al-jabr* meaning 'putting together broken parts']

Algol *noun* a high-level computer language using algebra. [from *algorithmic* and *language*]

algorithm (al-ger-ithəm) *noun* a process or set of rules for solving a problem, especially by a computer.

alias (ay-li-əs) *noun* (**aliases**) a false or assumed name.
alias *adverb* also known as ♦ *Norma Jean Baker, alias Marilyn Monroe.* [from a Latin word meaning 'at another time']

alibi (al-i-biy) *noun* (**alibis**) 1 a claim or piece of evidence that an accused person was not at the scene of a crime when it was committed. 2 (*informal*) an excuse or an answer to an accusation.

alien (ay-li-ən) *noun* 1 a person from another country, a foreigner. SYNONYMS: foreigner, stranger, outsider. 2 a being from another world.
alien *adjective* 1 not your own, foreign or unfamiliar ♦ *It took a while to get used to the alien customs of the place.* SYNONYMS: strange, foreign, unfamiliar. 2 not a part of something ♦ *Cruelty is alien to her character.* [from a Latin word *alius* meaning 'other']

alienate (ay-li-ən-ayt) *verb* to make someone become unfriendly or not willing to help you. **alienation** *noun* [same origin as for *alien*]

alight¹ *adjective* on fire, lit up. [from *a-*² and *light*¹]

alight² *verb* (*formal*) 1 to get down from a vehicle, especially a bus or train. 2 to rest or settle on something ♦ *A bird had alighted on a branch.* [from *a-*² and *light*²]

align (ə-liyn) *verb* 1 to arrange a number of things in their right positions in relation to each other. 2 to join a person or group as an ally ♦ *They decided to align themselves with the Tories.* **alignment** *noun* [from a French phrase *à ligne* meaning 'into line']

alike *adjective & adverb* like one another, in the same way. SYNONYMS: similar, identical. [from an Old English word]

alimentary canal (ali-**ment**-er-i) *noun* the long passage through which food passes from the mouth to the anus as it is digested and absorbed by the body. [from a Latin word *alimentum* meaning 'food']

alimony (**al**-i-mǝni) *noun* (*North Amer.*) an allowance that a person has to pay to a spouse after a separation or divorce. [from a Latin word *alimonia* meaning 'nourishment']
◊ In Britain this is called *maintenance*.

aliquot (**al**-i-kwot) *noun* **1** (*Chemistry*) a portion of a substance, especially a sample used for chemical analysis. **2** (*Mathematics*) a number that can be divided into a larger number without producing a fraction in the quotient. [a Latin word meaning 'some, so many']

alive *adjective* **1** living, not dead. SYNONYMS: living, live. **2** aware of something and able to deal with it ♦ *She seems alive to all the possible dangers.* **3** active or lively. SYNONYMS: active, lively, energetic, vigorous, sprightly. **4** full of living or moving things ♦ *The forest was alive with wildlife.* SYNONYMS: vibrant, active. [from an Old English phrase *on life* meaning 'in life']

alkali (**al**-kǝ-liy) *noun* (**alkalis**) a substance such as caustic soda, potash, or ammonia, which neutralizes acids and is neutralized by them, turns litmus blue, and forms caustic or corrosive solutions in water. **alkaline** (**al**-kǝ-liyn) *adjective* **alkalinity** (alkǝ-**lin**-iti) *noun* [from an Arabic word *al-kily* meaning 'the ashes']

alkaloid (**al**-kǝ-loid) *noun* a substance that contains nitrogen, is derived from plants, and is often used in medicine, for example morphine and quinine.

alkane *noun* a saturated hydrocarbon, e.g. methane, ethane, and propane.

alkene *noun* an unsaturated hydrocarbon containing a double bond, e.g. ethylene and propene.

alkyl (**al**-kilor **al**-kiyl) *adjective* denoting a hydrocarbon radical that is derived from an alkane by removing a hydrogen atom.

alkyne (**al**-kiyn) *noun* an unsaturated hydrocarbon containing a triple bond, e.g. acetylene.

all *adjective* the whole amount or number of something ♦ *all day* ♦ *all people.*

all *noun* **1** all people ♦ *All were agreed that we should wait.* **2** everything ♦ *All is lost.*
all *adverb* **1** completely ♦ *She was dressed all in white.* **2** (in scores) on both sides ♦ *A late goal made it three all.* **all but** very little short of ♦ *It is all but impossible to do.* **all for something** (*informal*) very much in favour of it. **all in** (*informal*) completely exhausted. **all in all** on the whole, for the most part. **all out** using all your strength or effort. **all set** (*informal*) ready to start. **all there** (*informal*) mentally alert, sane ♦ *I'm not sure he's quite all there.* **on all fours** crawling on hands and knees. [from an Old English word]

Allah (**al**-ǝ) the Muslim name for God. [from an Arabic word meaning 'the god']

allay (ǝ-**lay**) *verb* (**allayed, allaying**) to calm or reduce someone's fear or suspicion. [from an Old English word *alecgan* meaning 'to lay down']

all-clear *noun* a signal that a danger is over.

allegation (ali-**gay**-shǝn) *noun* an accusation made without any proof to support it.

allege (ǝ-**lej**) *verb* to say something without being able to prove that it is true. [from an Old French word *esligier*]

alleged *adjective* said to be, without any proof ♦ *The alleged culprit was a doctor.* **allegedly** *adverb*

allegiance (ǝ-**lee**-jǝns) *noun* loyalty or support someone gives to a government, sovereign, or cause. [from an Old French word related to *liege*]

allegory (**al**-ig-er-i) *noun* (**allegories**) a story, poem, or play in which the characters and events are made to represent a deeper underlying meaning. **allegorical** (alig-**o**-ri-kǝl) *noun* **allegorically** *adverb* [from a Greek word meaning 'other speaking']

allegro (ǝ-**leg**-roh) *adverb* (*Music*) fast and lively.
allegro *noun* (**allegros**) a movement to be played in this way. [an Italian word meaning 'happy']

alleluia *interjection & noun* an exclamation of praise to God. [from a Hebrew word]

Allen key *noun* (*trademark*) a kind of spanner for fitting a special type of screw with a six-sided socket in its head. [from the name of the American manufacturer]

allergic (ǝ-**ler**-jik) *adjective* **1** having an allergy ♦ *She is allergic to onions.* **2** caused by an allergy ♦ *She has had an allergic reaction.*

allergy (al-er-ji) *noun* (**allergies**) a condition producing an unfavourable reaction to certain foods, pollens, or other substances. [from a Greek word *allos* meaning 'other']

alleviate (ə-lee-vi-ayt) *verb* to lessen something unpleasant or make it less severe ♦ *The pills will alleviate the pain.* SYNONYMS: reduce, lessen, relieve, ease, moderate. **alleviation** *noun* [from *ad-* and a Latin word *levis* meaning 'light']

alley *noun* (**alleys**) 1 a narrow passage or street between houses or other buildings. 2 a path bordered by hedges or shrubbery. 3 a long channel along which balls are rolled in bowling and skittles. [from a French word *aller* meaning 'to go']

alliance *noun* a union or association formed by people, countries, or organizations who want to support each other. [same origin as for *ally*]

allied see *ally*[2].
allied *adjective* of the same kind, related.

alligator *noun* a reptile of the crocodile family, found especially in the rivers of tropical America and China. [from the Spanish words *el lagarto* meaning 'the lizard']

alliteration (ə-lit-er-ay-shən) *noun* the occurrence of the same letter or sound at the beginning of a group of words for special effect, e.g. *sing a song of sixpence.* **alliterative** (ə-lit-er-ətiv) *adjective* [from *ad-* and a Latin word *littera* meaning 'letter']

allocate (al-ə-kayt) *verb* to give resources or duties to various people or groups, to allot things. **allocable** *adjective* **allocation** *noun* **allocator** *noun* [from *ad-* and a Latin word *locus* meaning 'a place']

allot (ə-lot) *verb* (**allotted, allotting**) to give resources or duties as a share to various people or groups. [from an Old French word *aloter* meaning 'to distribute by lot']

allotment *noun* 1 a small area of public land let out to people for growing vegetables or flowers. 2 the process of allotting things, or a share allotted.

allotrope (al-ə-trohp) *noun* one of the physical forms in which an element can exist, for example charcoal, diamond, and graphite are allotropes of carbon. [from Greek words *allos* meaning 'other' and *tropos* meaning 'manner']

allotropy (ə-lot-rə-pi) *noun* the existence of a chemical element in different forms with different physical or chemical properties. **allotropic** (al-ə-trop-ik) *adjective*

allow *verb* 1 to let someone do something, to give someone permission or authority. SYNONYMS: permit, let, authorize. 2 to give someone something as their amount or share. SYNONYMS: allocate, assign, provide, grant. 3 to take account of something in making calculations ♦ *You should allow 10% for inflation.* 4 to agree that something is true or acceptable ♦ *They did allow that we might be right.* SYNONYMS: admit, concede, agree. 5 to authorize something ♦ *The tax inspector allowed their claim for expenses.* SYNONYMS: agree, authorize, approve. **allowable** *adjective* [via Old French from a Latin word *allaudare* meaning 'to praise']

allowance *noun* 1 allowing. 2 an amount or sum allowed to someone, especially a sum of money paid regularly to them. **to make allowances for something** to be lenient towards someone for a reason ♦ *We have to make allowances for his inexperience.*

alloy[1] (al-oi) *noun* 1 a metal made by mixing other metals or by mixing a metal and another substance. 2 an inferior metal mixed with one of greater value. [from an Old French word, related to *ally*]

alloy[2] (ə-loi) *verb* (**alloyed, alloying**) 1 to mix metals to form an alloy. 2 to weaken or spoil something by adding something that reduces its value.

all right *adjective* 1 feeling healthy or well. SYNONYMS: well, fine, healthy, fit, OK. 2 satisfactory or in good condition. SYNONYMS: satisfactory, acceptable, OK. 3 allowed ♦ *Is it all right to park here?* **all right** *adverb* fairly well, reasonably ♦ *It seemed to work all right.*

all-round *adjective* having many abilities or uses.

all-rounder *noun* someone who has a wide range of talents or abilities.

allspice *noun* 1 a spice made from the dried and ground berries of the pimento, a West Indian tree. 2 this berry.

all-time *adjective* not improved on up to now ♦ *an all-time long-jump record.*

allude (ə-lewd) *verb* to refer to something indirectly, without actually naming it. [from Latin words *ad* meaning 'towards' and *ludere* meaning 'to play']
◊ Do not confuse this word with *elude*.

allure (əl-**yoor**) *noun* attractiveness or appeal. **allurement** *noun* [from an Old French word *aleurier* meaning 'to attract', related to *lure*]

alluring *adjective* attractive or appealing.

allusion *noun* a reference made to something without actually naming it. [same origin as for *allude*]

allusive (ə-**loo**-siv) *adjective* containing allusions or indirect references to something. **allusively** *adverb*

alluvium (ə-**loo**-viəm) *noun* a deposit of soil and sand left by rivers or floods and usually very fertile. **alluvial** *adjective* [from a Latin word meaning 'washed against']

ally[1] (**al**-iy) *noun* (**allies**) a person, organization, or country that has agreed to help and support another. **the Allies** the nations opposed to Germany in each of the two World Wars. [via Old French from a Latin word *alligare* meaning 'to bind']

ally[2] (ə-**liy**) *verb* (**allies, allied, allying**) to become an ally, or make someone an ally.

alma mater (al- mə mah- tə) *noun* the school or university that a person attended. [a Latin phrase meaning 'generous mother']

almanac (**awl**-mən-ak) *noun* **1** an annual publication containing a calendar with important dates, astronomical data, and other information. **2** an annually published handbook for a sport or other activity. [from a Greek word *almenikhiaka*] ◊ Some publications use the older spelling *almanack* in their titles, e.g. *Whitaker's Almanack.*

almighty *adjective* **1** all-powerful. **2** (*informal*) very great ♦ *Then there was an almighty crash.* **the Almighty** a name for God.

almond (**ah**-mənd) *noun* **1** the nut-like kernel of the fruit of a tree related to the peach. **2** this tree. [via Old French from a Greek word *amugdalē*]

almond paste *noun* an edible paste like marzipan, made from ground almonds.

almost *adverb* very close to; nearly. SYNONYMS: nearly, practically. [from Old English words meaning 'for the most part']

alms (ahmz) *noun* (*old use*) gifts of money and food given to the poor. [from Old English, from a Greek word *eleos* meaning 'mercy']

almshouse *noun* a house founded by charity for poor elderly people.

aloe *noun* a tropical plant with thick sharp-pointed leaves and bitter juice. **aloes** *noun* this juice. [from an Old English word *alewe*]

aloft *adverb* high up, up in or into the air. [from an Old Norse phrase *a lopt* meaning 'in the air']

alone *adjective* not with others, on your own. SYNONYMS: single-handed, unaccompanied, by yourself. **alone** *adverb* only, exclusively ♦ *You alone can help me.* [from *all one*]

along *adverb* **1** forward or onward ♦ *Push it along.* **2** accompanying somebody, in addition ♦ *I've brought my brother along.* **along** *preposition* following or close to the length of something ♦ *We went for a walk along the river.* **all along** all the time, from the beginning ♦ *I knew the answer all along.* [from an Old English word *andlang*]

alongside *adverb* close to the side of something. **alongside** *preposition* beside.

aloof *adjective* unfriendly and keeping a distance from people. SYNONYMS: unfriendly, reticent, haughty, distant, cool, withdrawn. **aloofly** *adverb* **aloofness** *noun* [from *a-*[2] and *luff*, a ship's term meaning 'close to the wind' and so 'away from the shore']

aloud *adverb* in a voice loud enough to be heard. [from *a-*[2] and *loud*]

alp *noun* a high mountain. **the Alps** *plural noun* a high range of mountains in Switzerland and neighbouring countries. [from the Greek name *Alpeis*]

alpaca (al- **apak**- ə) *noun* a long- haired animal of South America, related to the llama. [from an American Indian word *allpaca*]

alpha (**al**-fə) *noun* the first letter of the Greek alphabet, equivalent to Roman *A, a.*

alphabet *noun* the set of letters used in writing a language, especially when arranged in a fixed order. [from *alpha* and *beta*, the first two letters of the Greek alphabet]

alphabetical *adjective* **1** following the order

of the letters of the alphabet. **2** to do with the alphabet. **alphabetically** adverb

alpha decay noun (Physics) radioactive decay that causes the emission of alpha particles.

alphanumeric (al-fə-new-merrik) adjective using or containing letters of the alphabet and numerals.

alpha particles plural noun helium nuclei emitted by radioactive substances.

alpine adjective to do with or growing on high mountains.
Alpine adjective to do with the Alps.
alpine noun a plant that grows in mountain regions or is grown in rock gardens. [from alp]

already adverb **1** before this time ♦ They had already gone. **2** as early as this ♦ Is she back already?

alright adverb another spelling of **all right**.
◊ Some people regard this spelling as incorrect.

Alsatian (al-**say**-shən) noun a large strong brown or black dog with smooth hair (also called German shepherd dog).

also adverb in addition, besides. [from an Old English word]

also-ran noun someone who is not among the winners or leaders in an activity. [originally a horse or dog that was not among the first three to finish in a race]

altar noun **1** the table on which bread and wine are consecrated in the Communion service. **2** any structure on which offerings are made to a god. [via Old English from a Latin word altus meaning 'high']

altarpiece noun a painting or other work of art placed above and behind an altar.

alter verb **1** to make something different; to change something in character or position. SYNONYMS: change, adjust, adapt, modify, transform. **2** to become changed or different. SYNONYMS: change, adapt.
alteration noun [from a Latin word alter meaning 'other']

altercation (ol-ter-**kay**-shən) noun a noisy argument or quarrel. [from a Latin word altercari meaning 'to wrangle']

alternate [1] (ol-ter-nət) adjective happening or following one after the other in turns ♦ We have to buy milk on alternate days.
alternately adverb
◊ See the note at **alternative**.

alternate [2] (ol-ter-nayt) verb **1** to occur or do something one after the other in turn. **2** to change repeatedly between two conditions. **alternation** noun

alternate angles plural noun two angles formed on opposite sides and at opposite ends of a line that cuts through two other lines.

alternating current noun an electric current that reverses its direction many times a second at regular intervals.

alternative (ol-ter-nə-tiv) adjective available instead of something else.
alternative noun one of two or more possibilities. **alternatively** adverb
◊ Do not confuse alternative with alternate. If there are alternative colours there is a choice of several colours, whereas alternate colours means that there is first one colour then another.

alternative energy noun energy using fuels that do not harm the environment.

alternative medicine noun unconventional forms of medical treatment, such as homoeopathy and hypnosis.

alternative technology noun technology using resources and methods that cause the least possible damage to the environment.

alternator (ol-ter-nay-ter) noun a dynamo that produces an alternating current.

although conjunction though. [from all and though]

altimeter (al-ti-meet-er) noun an instrument used in an aircraft to show its height. [from the Latin word altus meaning 'high' and meter]

altitude noun **1** the height of an object above sea level or ground level. **2** the distance of a star or other heavenly object above the horizon, measured as an angle. **3** (Geometry) the height of a triangle as measured by a line drawn from a vertex at right angles to the opposite side. [from Latin altus meaning 'high']

alto (al-toh) noun (altos) **1** the highest adult male singing voice. **2** the lowest female singing voice, a contralto. **3** a musical instrument having the second or third highest pitch in its family ♦ an alto saxophone. [from the Italian phrase alto canto meaning 'high song']

altocumulus (al-tə-kew-mew-ləs) noun

(**altocumuli** (al-tə-kew-mew-liy)) clouds resembling cumulus but higher in the sky. [from a Latin word *altus* meaning 'high' and *cumulus*]

altogether *adverb* **1** entirely, totally. SYNONYMS: completely, entirely, absolutely, quite, totally, utterly, wholly. **2** on the whole. SYNONYMS: on the whole, by and large.
◊ Do not confuse this word with *all together*. If you say *thirty people altogether* you mean a total of thirty people, whereas if you say *thirty people all together* you mean thirty people in one place.

altostratus (al-tə-strah-təs or al-tə-stray-təs) *noun* clouds in a continuous layer at medium altitude. [from a Latin word *altus* meaning 'high' and *stratus*]

altruism (al-troo-izm) *noun* concern for other people rather than yourself. **altruist** *noun* an unselfish person. **altruistic** *adjective* **altruistically** *adverb* [from an Italian word *altrui* meaning 'somebody else']

alum (al-əm) *noun* a white mineral salt used in medicine and dyeing. [from a Latin word *alumen*]

alumina (ə-loo-min-ə) *noun* an oxide of aluminium, e.g. corundum.

aluminium *noun* a strong lightweight silvery metal that is free of corrosion, a chemical element (symbol Al).

aluminize (ə-lew-mi-niyz) *verb* to coat a surface with aluminium.

aluminum *noun* an American spelling of aluminium.

alumnus *noun* (**alumni**) a former pupil or student of a school or university. [a Latin word meaning 'nursling', from *alere* meaning 'to nourish']

alveolus (al-vee-ə-ləs) *noun* (**alveoli** (al-vee-ə-liy)) **1** a small cavity such as a socket for a tooth or a cell in a honeycomb. **2** any of the tiny air-filled sacs in the lungs from which oxygen passes into the blood and through which carbon dioxide is removed from it. [a Latin word meaning 'small cavity']

always *adverb* **1** at all times, on all occasions. **2** whatever the circumstances ♦ *You can always sleep on the floor.* **3** constantly, repeatedly ♦ *He is always complaining.* SYNONYMS: constantly, continuously, repeatedly, all the time, unceasingly. [from the phrase *all ways*]

alyssum (al-iss-əm) *noun* a plant with small usually yellow or white flowers. [from a Greek word *alusson*]

Alzheimer's disease *noun* a brain disease of middle age or old age, causing mental deterioration and senility. [named after the German scientist Alois Alzheimer (1864–1915)]

AM *abbreviation* (in radio broadcasting) amplitude modulation.

am a form of *be*, used with *I*.

a.m. *abbreviation* before noon. [short for Latin *ante meridiem*]

amalgam *noun* **1** an alloy of mercury and another metal, as used for dental fillings. **2** a soft pliable mixture. [from Greek *malagma* meaning 'something that soothes or softens']

amalgamate *verb* to mix or combine ingredients. **amalgamation** *noun*

amaryllis (amə-ril-iss) *noun* a lily-like plant growing from a bulb. [from the Greek name *Amaryllis*, used for a country girl in pastoral poetry]

amass (ə-mass) *verb* to heap things up, to collect things ♦ *Over the years the family amassed a large fortune.* [from *a-²* and *mass*]

amateur (am-ə-ter) *noun* a person who does something, especially a sport or one of the performing arts, without pay rather than as a profession. [from Latin *amator* meaning 'lover']

amateurish (am-ə-ter-ish) *adjective* showing the limited ability of an amateur, clumsy or inept. **amateurishly** *adverb* **amateurishness** *noun*

amatory (am-ə-ter-i) *adjective* showing sexual love. [same origin as for *amateur*]

amaze *verb* to surprise someone greatly. SYNONYMS: astonish, astound, surprise, stagger, dumbfound, flabbergast. **amazement** *noun* [from an Old English word *amasian*]

amazing *adjective* surprising or highly remarkable. SYNONYMS: astonishing, astounding, staggering, remarkable, surprising, extraordinary, incredible.

Amazon (Greek Mythology) a woman of a race of female warriors.
amazon *noun* a tall and strong or athletic woman. **amazonian** (am-ə-zoh-niən) *adjective* [from a Greek word *Amazon*, which the ancient Greeks thought meant 'lacking a breast' (from *mazos* meaning 'breast'), from the legend that the

Amazons cut off one breast to make it easier to hold a bow]

ambassador noun 1 a diplomat sent by one country as its representative or on a special mission to another. 2 someone who actively promotes a cause ♦ *an ambassador for peace.*

amber noun 1 a hard clear yellowish resin used for making ornaments. 2 a yellow traffic light shown as a cautionary signal between red for 'stop' and green for 'go'. **amber** adjective made of amber or having the colour of amber.

ambergris (am-ber-grees) noun a wax-like substance from the intestines of the sperm whale, found floating in tropical seas and used in making perfumes.

ambidextrous (ambi-**deks**-trəs) adjective able to use the right and left hands equally well. [from Latin words *ambo* meaning 'both' and *dexter* meaning 'right-handed']

ambience (am-bi-əns) noun 1 the character a place has from its immediate surroundings. 2 the quality given to a sound recording by the acoustic in which it is made. **ambient** adjective [via French from a Latin word *ambire* meaning 'to go round']

ambiguous (am-**big**-yoo-əs) adjective 1 having more than one possible meaning. 2 doubtful or uncertain. **ambiguously** adverb **ambiguity** (ambig-**yoo**-iti) noun [from a Latin word *ambigere* meaning 'to waver' or 'to go around']

ambit noun the scope, extent, or limit of something.

ambition noun 1 a strong desire to achieve success. 2 something successful you want to achieve. SYNONYMS: goal, aim, intention, wish, objective, hope, aspiration. [from a Latin word *ambire* meaning 'to go round', with reference to going round to get votes in an election]

ambitious (am-**bish**-əs) adjective 1 (said about a person) having a lot of ambition. SYNONYMS: determined, keen, enterprising, enthusiastic. 2 (said about a plan or idea) difficult or demanding. **ambitiously** adverb

ambivalent (am-**biv**-ələnt) adjective with mixed feelings or conflicting ideas about something or someone. **ambivalently** adverb **ambivalence** noun [from Latin words *ambo* meaning 'both' and *valens* meaning 'strong']

amble verb to walk at a slow gentle pace. **amble** noun a slow gentle pace. **ambler** noun [from a Latin word *ambulare* meaning 'to walk']

ambrosia (am-**broh**-ziə) noun 1 (*Greek and Roman Mythology*) the food of the gods, which made them immortal. 2 something very pleasant to taste or smell. **ambrosial** adjective [a Greek word, from *ambrotos* meaning 'immortal']

ambulance noun a vehicle equipped to carry sick or injured people to and from hospital. [from a French phrase *hôpital ambulant* meaning 'mobile field hospital', from a Latin word *ambulare* meaning 'to walk']

ambulatory (am-**bew**-lə-ter-i) adjective 1 relating to or made for walking. 2 (said of a person or animal) able to walk. [same origin as for *amble*]

ambuscade (am-bəs-**kayd**) noun an ambush. [from a French word *embuscade*, from the same origin as *ambush*]

ambush noun a surprise attack by troops or bandits from a hidden position on an approaching enemy or victim. **ambush** verb to lie in wait for someone, to attack someone from an ambush. SYNONYMS: to attack, to jump out on, to pounce on, to swoop on, to intercept. [from an Old French word *embusche*, from a Latin word *boscus* meaning 'wood' (because ambushes were often made from the cover of woods)]

ameliorate (ə-**mee**-li-er-ayt) verb (*formal*) to make something better or to become better. **amelioration** noun [from *ad-* and a Latin word *melior* meaning 'better']

amen (ah-men or ay-men) interjection (said at the end of a prayer) so be it. [from a Hebrew word meaning 'truth, certainty']

amenable (ə-**meen**-əbəl) adjective willing to respond to advice or guidance ♦ *He was not amenable to persuasion.* **amenably** adverb **amenability** noun [from a French word *amener* meaning 'to lead']

amend verb to correct an error in something or to make minor alterations in it ♦ *We will have to amend the contract in two places.* SYNONYMS: change, alter, adjust, modify. **to make amends** to compensate or make up for something. **amendment** noun

amenity (ə-meen-iti) *noun* (**amenities**) **1** a useful or pleasant feature that a place has. **2** pleasantness of a place or circumstance. [from a Latin word *amoenus* meaning 'pleasant']

American *adjective* to do with or coming from the continent of America, or the USA.
American *noun* **1** a person born in America or descended from people born there. **2** a citizen of the USA.

American football *noun* a form of football played in the USA using an oval ball on a field marked out with a grid.

American Indian *noun* a member of one of the groups of original inhabitants of the continent of America, other than the Inuit.

Americanism *noun* a word or phrase mainly used or originally used in American English.

Amerindian *noun* an American Indian.

amethyst (am-i-thist) *noun* a precious stone formed from purple or violet quartz. [from the Greek word *amethustos* meaning 'not drunken' (because the stone was thought to prevent drunkenness if it was put in a drink)]

Amharic (am-ha-rik) *noun* the official language of Ethiopia. [from the name *Amhara*, a region of central Ethiopia]

amiable (aym-i-əbəl) *adjective* friendly and good-tempered. SYNONYMS: friendly, kind, affable, amicable, genial, agreeable, pleasant, nice. **amiability** *noun* **amiably** *adverb* [same origin as for *amicable*]

amicable (am-ik-əbəl) *adjective* pleasant and friendly. **amicability** *noun* **amicably** *adverb* [from a Latin word *amicus* meaning 'friend']

amid or **amidst** *preposition* in the middle of, during ♦ *The team arrived amid loud cheers.* [from *a-*[2] and *mid*]

amide (a-miyd) *noun* a compound in which an acid radical or metal atom replaces a hydrogen atom of ammonia. [from *ammonia*]

amidships *adverb* in the middle of a ship.

amine *noun* (*Chemistry*) an organic compound derived from ammonia by replacement of one or more hydrogen atoms by organic radicals. [from *ammonia*]

amino acid (ə-mee-noh) *noun* an organic acid found in proteins. [from *ammonia* (because the amino acids contain the same group of acids as ammonia)]

amir (ə-meer) *noun* another spelling of *emir*.

amiss *adjective* wrong or out of order. **amiss** *adverb* wrongly or faultily. **to take something amiss** to be offended by a remark or comment.

amity *noun* friendship, friendly relations. [from an Old French word *amitié*]

ammeter (am-it-er) *noun* an instrument that measures electric current in amperes.

ammo *noun* (*informal*) ammunition.

ammonia *noun* **1** a colourless gas with a strong smell. **2** a solution of this in water, used as a cleaning fluid. [from a Latin word]

ammonite (am-ə-niyt) *noun* the fossil of an extinct mollusc with a flat spiral shell. [from a medieval Latin phrase *cornu Ammonis* meaning 'horn of Ammon' (because the fossil looked like a ram's horn which was the symbol of the god Jupiter Ammon)]

ammunition *noun* **1** a supply of bullets and shells for use in guns and other weapons. **2** useful or persuasive facts and reasoning used in an argument. [from French *la munition*, wrongly understood as *l'ammunition*]

amnesia (am-nee-ziə) *noun* complete or partial loss of memory. **amnesiac** *adjective* & *noun* [from a Greek word meaning 'forgetfulness']

amnesty (am-nis-ti) *noun* (**amnesties**) an official pardon for people who have committed a crime, especially those convicted of political offences. [from a Greek word meaning 'forgetfulness' (because the offences are legally 'forgotten')]

amniocentesis (amni-ə-sen-tee-sis) *noun* the inserting of a hollow needle into the womb of a pregnant woman and withdrawing a sample of amniotic fluid, to test for abnormalities in the fetus. [from *amnion* and a Greek word *kentēsis* meaning 'pricking']

amnion (am-ni-ən) *noun* (**amnia**) the innermost membrane enclosing a fetus in the womb. [from a Greek word meaning 'caul']

amniotic fluid noun the fluid surrounding a fetus in the womb.

amoeba (ə-mee-bə) noun (**amoebae** (ə-mee-bee) (**amoebas**) a microscopic organism consisting of a single cell which changes shape constantly.

amok adverb **to run amok** to behave wildly, to cause damage or confusion. [from a Malay word meaning 'fighting mad']

among or **amongst** preposition **1** in or surrounded by ♦ Poppies were growing amongst the corn. **2** in the number of ♦ This is reckoned among her best works. **3** within the limits of, between ♦ We only have £5 amongst us ♦ They began to quarrel among themselves. [from an Old English word ongemang meaning 'in a crowd']

amoral (ay-mo-rəl) adjective having or showing no moral standards, not concerned with morality. [from a-¹ meaning 'not' and moral]

amorous (am-er-əs) adjective feeling or showing sexual love. SYNONYMS: passionate, loving, amatory. **amorously** adverb **amorousness** noun [from a Latin word amor meaning 'love']

amorphous (ə-mor-fəs) adjective not having any definite shape or form. [from a-¹ meaning 'not' and a Greek word morphē meaning 'form']

amount noun **1** the total of something in number or size. **2** a quantity ♦ Add a small amount of salt. SYNONYMS: quantity, volume. **amount** verb **to amount to 1** to add up to a total. **2** to be equivalent to something ♦ Their behaviour amounts to fraud. [from Latin ad montem meaning 'to the mountain','upwards']

amp noun **1** short for **ampere**. **2** (informal) short for **amplifier**.

ampere (am-pair) noun a unit for measuring electric current (symbol A). **amperage** noun [named after the French physicist A. M. Ampère (1775–1836)]

ampersand noun the sign & (= and). [based on the phrase and per se and meaning '& by itself is and', which pupils used to chant as an aid to learning the sign]

amphetamine (am-fet-ə-min) noun a drug used as a stimulant or to relieve congestion. [a shortening of its chemical name a(lpha)m(ethyl) phe(ne)t(hyl)amine]

amphibian (am-fib-iən) noun **1** an animal able to live both on land and in water, such as a frog, toad, newt, and salamander. **2** a vehicle that can move on both land and water. [from Greek words amphi meaning 'around' and bios meaning 'life']

amphibious (am-fib-iəs) adjective **1** able to live or operate both on land and in water. **2** (said about a military operation) involving both sea and land forces.

amphibole (am-fi-bohl) noun any of a group of minerals including hornblende. [from a Latin word amphibolus meaning 'ambiguous' (because the minerals have different structures)]

amphitheatre noun an oval or circular Roman theatre without a roof and with tiers of seats surrounding a central arena, used mainly for sports and gladiator contests. [from a Greek word amphi meaning 'around' and theatre]

amphoteric (am-fə-te-rik) adjective (Chemistry) (said about a substance) able to react as an acid or as a base. [from a Greek word amphoteros, from amphō meaning 'both']

ample adjective **1** plentiful, quite enough ♦ They have ample supplies. **2** (said about a person) large or stout. **amply** adverb [from a Latin word amplus meaning 'large, abundant']

amplifier noun an electronic device that increases the loudness of sounds or the power of audio or radio signals.

amplify verb (**amplifies**, **amplified**, **amplifying**) **1** to increase the strength of a sound. **2** to explain something more clearly or add details to it. **amplification** noun [from a Latin word amplificare meaning 'to make more ample']

amplitude noun **1** (Physics) the maximum extent of vibration, the largest amount by which an alternating current or electromagnetic wave can vary from its average. **2** breadth, largeness, or abundance. [same origin as for ample]

amplitude modulation noun the variation of the amplitude of a radio wave, without altering the frequency.

ampoule (am-pool) (Medicine) a small sealed glass container holding a liquid ready for injecting. [from a Latin word ampulla meaning 'flask']

amputate verb to cut off a part of the body by surgical operation. **amputation** noun [from a Latin word amputare]

amuck adverb another spelling of **amok**.

amulet (am-yoo-lit) *noun* a small ornament or piece of jewellery worn as a charm against evil or danger. [from a Latin word *amuletum*]

amuse *verb* 1 to cause someone to laugh or smile. SYNONYMS: delight, cheer, cheer up. 2 to entertain someone. SYNONYMS: entertain, divert, interest, absorb. [from a French word *amuser* meaning 'distract']

amusement *noun* 1 the process of amusing someone or of being amused. 2 something that amuses or entertains people.

amusement arcade *noun* an indoor area with slot machines and electronic games.

amusing *adjective* making people laugh or smile, entertaining. SYNONYMS: funny, witty, humorous, comical, hilarious. **amusingly** *adverb*

amylase (am-i-layz) *noun* (*Biochemistry*) an enzyme found in saliva, which converts starch into sugar as part of digestion (also called *diastase*). [from a Latin word *amylum* meaning 'starch']

an *adjective* the form of *a* used before vowel sounds ♦ *an egg* ♦ *an hour* (but *a unicorn*).

Anabaptist *noun* a member of a Protestant religious group, prominent in the 16th century, which held that baptism should be given only to consenting adults.

anabolic steroid (an-ə-bol-ik) *noun* a steroid hormone used to build up muscle tissue and sometimes (illegally) to improve athletic performance.

anabolism (ə-nab-əl-izm) *noun* (*Biochemistry*) a process in living organisms in which complex molecules are formed from simpler ones using energy. **anabolic** *adjective* [from a Greek word *anabolē* meaning 'going up, ascent']

anachronism (ən-ak-rən-izm) *noun* 1 the placing of something, especially in fiction and drama, in a historical period to which it does not belong. 2 something put in the wrong time. 3 a person, idea, or institution that is regarded as out of date. **anachronistic** (ə-nak-rən-**ist**-ik) *adjective* [from *ana-* and a Greek word *khronos* meaning 'time']

anaconda (anə-**kon**-də) *noun* a large snake related to the boa, native to parts of South America. [from a Sinhalese word *henakandaya*]

anaemia (ə-nee-miə) *noun* (*Medicine*) a lack of red corpuscles, or of their haemoglobin in blood. [from Greek words *an-* meaning 'without' and *haima* meaning 'blood']

anaemic (ə-nee-mik) *adjective* 1 suffering from anaemia. 2 pale or weak in colour. 3 lacking vigour or positive characteristics.

anaerobic (an-air-oh-bik) *adjective* not needing or using oxygen from the air ♦ *anaerobic bacteria*. **anaerobically** *adverb*

anaerobic respiration *noun* (*Biology*) the release of energy from food substances such as glucose without needing the presence of oxygen.

anaesthesia (anis-theez-iə) *noun* loss of physical sensation induced by use of anaesthetics. [from Greek words *an* meaning 'without' and *aisthēsis* meaning 'sensation']

anaesthetic (anis-thet-ik) *noun* a substance that produces loss of sensation and of ability to feel pain. **anaesthetic** *adjective* causing a loss of physical sensation.

anaesthetist (ən-ees-thət-ist) *noun* a medical specialist who administers anaesthetics.

anaesthetize (ən-ees-thətiyz) *verb* to administer an anaesthetic to a patient. **anaesthetization** *noun*

anagram (an-ə-gram) *noun* a word or phrase formed from the rearranged letters of another word or phrase (e.g. *carthorse* is an anagram of *orchestra*). [from Greek words *ana* meaning 'back' and *gramma* meaning 'letter']

anal *adjective* to do with or in the region of the anus.

analgesia (an-əl-jeez-iə) *noun* loss of ability to feel pain while still conscious. [from Greek words *an-* meaning 'without' and *algein* meaning 'to feel pain']

analgesic (an-əl-jee-sik) *adjective* relieving pain. **analgesic** *noun* a drug that relieves pain.

analogous (ə-nal-əgəs) *adjective* similar in certain respects. **analogously** *adverb* [from a Greek word *analogos* meaning 'proportionate']

analogue (an-ə-log) *noun* something that is analogous to something else. **analogue** *adjective* (said about a clock, watch, or other instrument) showing the time or information by using hands or a pointer. (Compare **digital**.)

analogue computer *noun* a computer that handles and calculates data measured in physical quantities such as length and volume, rather than digitally.

analogue signal *noun* a signal in which voltage or some other physical measure represents the value transmitted.

analogy (ə-nal-ə-ji) *noun* (**analogies**) partial likeness between two things which are compared ♦ *the analogy between the human brain and a computer.* [same origin as for *analogous*]

analyse *verb* 1 to examine a substance or its structure by separating it into its parts. 2 to study and interpret something ♦ *They tried to analyse the causes of their failure.* 3 to psychoanalyse someone. **analysable** *adjective* [from Greek words *ana* meaning 'up' and *lusis* meaning 'loosening']

analysis *noun* (**analyses** (ə-nal-i-seez)) 1 the process of analysing. 2 a statement of the result of analysing something. 3 psychoanalysis.

analyst (an-ə-list) *noun* 1 a scientist who analyses chemical substances. 2 a psychoanalyst.

analytical or **analytic** (anə-lit-ik-əl) *adjective* to do with analysis or using analysis. **analytically** *adverb*

anaphora (ə-naf-er-ə) *noun* the use of a short word (e.g. a pronoun such as *it* or a verb such as *do*) to refer back to a word or phrase used earlier, as in *When I tell you to leave you must do it.* [from Greek words *ana* meaning 'back' and *pherein* meaning 'to bear']

anarchism *noun* a belief that government should be abolished and society be based on voluntary cooperation.

anarchist (an-er-kist) *noun* a person who believes in anarchy as a political principle. **anarchistic** (an-er-kist-ik) *adjective*

anarchy (an-er-ki) *noun* 1 disorder or lawlessness caused by a lack of government or control. 2 a political system based on lack of government. **anarchic** (ən-ar-kik) *adjective* **anarchical** *adjective* [from Greek words *an-* meaning 'without' and *archē* meaning 'rule']

anathema (ən-ath-imə) *noun* 1 something you detest ♦ *Blood sports are anathema to them.* 2 a formal curse of the Church,

excommunicating someone or condemning something as evil. [from a Greek word *anathema* meaning 'something dedicated' and later 'something devoted to evil']

anatomy *noun* 1 the branch of medicine concerned with the study of the structure of the body, especially by cutting up specimens. 2 the bodily structure of an animal or plant. **anatomical** (anə-tom-ikəl) *adjective* **anatomically** *adverb* [from Greek words *ana-* meaning 'up' and *tomē* meaning 'cutting']

ANC *abbreviation* African National Congress.

ancestor *noun* any of the people from whom someone is descended, especially one more remote than grandparents. SYNONYMS: forebear, forefather. **ancestral** *adjective* [via Old French from a Latin word *antecedere* meaning 'to go before']

ancestry *noun* a line of ancestors.

anchor *noun* 1 a heavy metal object, usually with a shank and curved pieces (called *flukes*) at one end at right angles to the shank, used to moor a ship to the sea bottom or a balloon etc. to the ground. 2 something that gives stability or security. **anchor** *verb* 1 to make a ship or balloon etc. secure with an anchor. 2 (said about a ship) to be moored by an anchor. 3 to fix something firmly. [from a Greek word *ankura*]

anchorage *noun* a place where ships can be moored safely.

anchovy (an-chəvi) *noun* (**anchovies**) a small fish of the herring family, having a strong flavour. [from a Spanish or Portuguese word *anchova*]

ancient *adjective* 1 belonging to times in the distant past. SYNONYMS: old, early, prehistoric, primitive, archaic, primeval, primordial. 2 having lived or existed for a long time. SYNONYMS: old, aged, elderly, venerable. **the ancients** the people who lived in ancient times, especially ancient Greeks and Romans. [from an Old French word *ancien*, based on a Latin word *ante* meaning 'before']

ancient history *noun* the history of the period before the end of the Western Roman Empire in AD 476.

ancillary (an-**sil**-er-i) *adjective* providing extra support to a main activity or organization ♦ *ancillary services*. [from a Latin word *ancilla* meaning 'servant']

and *conjunction* a word used to link words, phrases, and parts of sentences ♦ *fish and chips* ♦ *Go away and don't come back* ♦ *It gets better and better* ♦ *Do that and I'll never speak to you again*.

andante (an-**dan**-ti) *adverb* (*Music*) at a moderately slow tempo.
andante *noun* a movement to be played in this way. [an Italian word meaning 'walking']

andiron (**and**-iy-ern) *noun* a metal support, usually one of two, for burning wood in a fireplace. [from an Old French word *andier*]

androgynous (an-**droj**-i-nəs) *adjective* partly male and partly female. [from Greek words *andros* meaning 'of a man' and *gunē* meaning 'woman']

android *noun* (in science fiction) a robot having the appearance of a human. [from a Greek word *anēr, andros* meaning 'man']

anecdote (an-**ik**-doht) *noun* a short entertaining story about a real person or event. [from a Greek word *anekdota* meaning 'things that have not been published']

anemometer (anim-**om**-it-er) *noun* an instrument for measuring the force of the wind. [from the Greek word *anemos* meaning 'wind' and *meter*]

anemone (ə-**nem**-əni) *noun* a plant related to the buttercup, with white, red, or purple flowers and divided leaves. [a Greek word meaning 'wind-flower' (perhaps because the flowers only open when the wind blows)]

aneroid barometer (**an**-er-oid) *noun* a barometer that measures air pressure by the effect the air has on the elastic lid of a box containing a vacuum. [from *a-*[1] meaning 'without' and the Greek word *neros* meaning 'water']

aneurysm (**an**- yoor- izm) *noun* (*Medicine*) a localized swelling of the wall of an artery. [from a Greek word *aneurisma*]

anew *adverb* again, or in a different way. [from an Old English word *of* meaning 'from' and *new*]

angel *noun* 1 in some beliefs, an attendant or messenger of God that is usually pictured as a being in human form with wings and dressed in long white robes. 2 an extremely beautiful or kind person. [from a Greek word *angelos* meaning 'messenger']

angel fish *noun* a fish with a flat upright body and large fins like wings.

angelic *adjective* 1 of or like an angel. 2 extremely beautiful or kind. **angelically** *adverb*

angelica (an-**jel**-ikə) *noun* a fragrant plant with stalks that are candied and used in cookery. [from the Latin name *herba angelica* meaning 'angelic herb' (because people believed it was effective against poisoning and disease)]

angelus (an-**jil**-əs) *noun* 1 in the Roman Catholic Church, a prayer to the Virgin Mary commemorating the Incarnation, said at morning, noon, and sunset. 2 a bell rung as a signal for this prayer. [from the opening words of the prayer in Latin, *Angelus Domini* meaning 'the angel of the Lord']

anger *noun* a strong feeling of displeasure or hostility. SYNONYMS: fury, rage, temper, wrath.
anger *verb* to make someone angry. SYNONYMS: enrage, annoy, infuriate, irritate, exasperate.

angina or **angina pectoris** (an-**jiy**-nə **pek**-ter-iss) *noun* a diseased condition of the heart, causing a sharp pain in the chest after strong physical exertion. [a Latin phrase meaning 'spasm of the chest']

angiosperm (**an**-ji-ə-sperm) *noun* a flowering plant belonging to a group that has seeds enclosed in an ovary. [from Greek words *angeion* meaning 'vessel' and *sperma* meaning 'seed']

Angle *noun* a member of a North German tribe that founded English kingdoms in the 5th century and finally gave their name to England and the English. [from the Latin name *Anglus* meaning 'inhabitant of Angul', a place in northern Germany from which some of the Angles came]

angle[1] *noun* 1 the space between two lines or surfaces that meet. 2 a point of view ♦ *The story is told from the victim's angle*.
angle *verb* 1 to move or place something in a slanting position. 2 to present news or information from a particular point of

view. [from a Latin word *angulus* meaning 'corner']

angle [2] *verb* **1** to fish with a hook and bait. **2** to try to get something you want by hinting ♦ *He was clearly angling for an invitation to the party.* **angler** *noun* [from an Old English word *angul* (a noun)]

Anglican *adjective* to do with the Church of England or a Church in communion with it.
Anglican *noun* a member of the Anglican Church. **Anglicanism** *noun* [same origin as for *Angle*]

anglicize (ang-li-siyz) *verb* to make something English in form or character.

Anglo- *prefix* English or British (and) ♦ *an Anglo-French agreement.* [same origin as for *Angle*]

Anglo-Catholic *adjective* of the section of the Church of England that has the strongest connection with the doctrine and forms of worship of the Roman Catholic Church.
Anglo-Catholic *noun* a member of this section of the Church.

Anglo-Indian *adjective* **1** to do with England and India. **2** (said about a person) of British descent but having lived for a long time in India. **3** of mixed British and Indian parentage.
Anglo-Indian *noun* an Anglo-Indian person.

Anglophile (an- gloh- fiyl) *noun* a person who is fond of England or Britain.

Anglo-Saxon *noun* **1** an English person of the period between the 5th century and the Norman Conquest in the 11th century. **2** the English language of this period, also called *Old English*. **3** a person of English descent.
Anglo-Saxon *adjective* to do with the Anglo-Saxons or their language.

angora *noun* **1** a long-haired variety of cat, goat, or rabbit. **2** a yarn or fabric made from the hair of angora goats or rabbits. [named after *Angora* (now called Ankara) in Turkey]

angry *adjective* (**angrier, angriest**) **1** feeling or showing anger. SYNONYMS: cross, furious, enraged, infuriated, irate, livid, annoyed, irritated, incensed, wrathful. **2** (said about a wound or sore place) red and inflamed. **angrily** *adverb* [same origin as for *anger*]

angst *noun* a feeling of anxious guilt or remorse. [a German word meaning 'fear']

ångström (ang-strəm) *noun* a unit of length for measuring wavelengths. [named after the Swedish physicist A. J. Ångström (1814–74)]

anguish *noun* severe mental or physical suffering. SYNONYMS: distress, suffering, torment, misery, agony, pain, torture. [same origin as for *anxious*]

anguished *adjective* feeling anguish.

angular *adjective* **1** having angles or sharp corners. **2** (said about a person) having a lean build with prominent bones. **3** measured by an angle. **angularity** (ang-yoo-la-riti) *noun*

angular momentum *noun* the momentum acquired by a body rotating around an axis.

aniline (an-ileen) *noun* an oily liquid found in coal tar and used in the manufacture of dyes and plastics. [from *anil* meaning 'indigo', from which aniline was originally obtained]

animadvert (anim-ad-**vert**) *verb* (*formal*) to criticize or censure something fiercely. **animadversion** *noun*

animal *noun* **1** a living organism that can feel, respond to stimuli, and move of its own accord. **2** a living organism of this kind other than a human being. **3** a four-footed animal as distinct from a bird, fish, reptile, or insect. **4** a cruel or uncivilized person.
animal *adjective* to do with or relating to animal life. [from a Latin word *animalis* meaning 'having breath']

animal liberation *noun* the freeing of animals from exploitation by humans.

animate [1] (an-im-ət) *adjective* living, having life. [from a Latin word *anima* meaning 'life, soul']

animate [2] (an-im-ayt) *verb* **1** to make something active or lively ♦ *A few anecdotes animated the discussion.* **2** to motivate someone ♦ *She was animated mainly by a feeling of loyalty.* **3** to produce as an animated cartoon. **animator** *noun*

animated *adjective* **1** lively, full of activity ♦ *an animated argument.* SYNONYMS: lively, excited, spirited, vigorous, energetic, vivacious. **2** (said about a cartoon or other film) giving an illusion of movement by using the technique of animation.

animation *noun* **1** the state of being animated or lively. **2** the technique of giving a film the illusion of movement by photographing a series of drawings that show successive positions.

animism *noun* the belief that natural things such as rocks, rivers, and winds, as well as living beings, have a living soul. **animistic** *adjective*

animosity (anim-**os**-iti) *noun* a feeling of strong hostility towards someone. [It originally meant 'courage', from a Latin word *animus* meaning 'spirit']

animus (an-imǝs) *noun* strong hostility shown in speech or action.

anion (an-iy-ǝn) *noun* (*Chemistry*) an ion with a negative charge. (Compare **cation**.) **anionic** (an-iy-**on**-ik) *adjective* [from *ana-* meaning 'up' and *ion*]

aniseed *noun* the seed of the plant called anise, having a sweet smell and used for flavouring and in herbal medicine. [from a Greek word *anison*, meaning 'anise']

ankle *noun* 1 the joint connecting the foot with the leg. 2 the narrow part of the leg between the ankle and the calf.

anklet *noun* an ornamental chain or band worn around the ankle.

annals (an-ǝlz) *plural noun* a history of events year by year, a set of historical records. [from a Latin word *annales* meaning 'yearly books']

anneal (ǝ-**neel**) *verb* to toughen glass or metal by heating it and then cooling it slowly. [from an Old English word meaning 'to set on fire']

annelid (an-il-id) *noun* a worm having a segmented body, for example an earthworm.

annex (ǝn-**eks**) *verb* 1 to add or join something to a larger thing. 2 to take possession of territory belonging to another country. **annexation** *noun* [from *ad-* and a Latin word *nexum* meaning 'tied']

annexe (an-eks) *noun* a building attached to a larger building or associated with it in some way.

annihilate (ǝ-**niy**-hil-ayt) *verb* to destroy something completely. SYNONYMS: destroy, exterminate, eliminate, obliterate, eradicate, wipe out. **annihilation** *noun* **annihilator** *noun* [from *ad-* and a Latin word *nihil* meaning 'nothing']

anniversary *noun* (**anniversaries**) 1 the date on which an important event took place

in a previous year. 2 a celebration of this. [from Latin words *annus* meaning 'year' and *versum* meaning 'turned']

Anno Domini (an-oh **dom**-in-iy) in the year of Our Lord (usually shortened to AD and put before a date, as in AD 1066). [a Latin phrase]

annotate (an-oh-tayt) *verb* to add notes giving a comment or explanation to a text, piece of writing, or diagram. **annotation** *noun* [from a Latin word *annotare* meaning 'to mark']

announce *verb* 1 to make a formal statement about an event, plan, or intention. SYNONYMS: declare, give out, proclaim, publish, report, broadcast. 2 to make known the arrival of a guest at a formal social occasion. **announcement** *noun* [from *ad-* and a Latin word *nuntius* meaning 'messenger']

announcer *noun* a person who announces items on radio or television.

annoy *verb* 1 to make someone slightly angry. SYNONYMS: irritate, bother, displease, exasperate, anger, upset, vex, trouble, aggravate. 2 to be troublesome to someone or harass them. SYNONYMS: pester, harass, bother. **annoyance** *noun* [from a Latin phrase *in odio* meaning 'hateful']

annual *adjective* 1 happening once every year. 2 calculated or reckoned by the year ♦ *Our annual income has increased.* 3 (said about a plant) lasting only one year or season.
annual *noun* 1 a plant that lives for one year or one season. 2 a book or periodical belonging to a series published once a year. **annually** *adverb* [from a Latin word *annus* meaning 'year']

annualized *adjective* (said about rates of interest or other financial figures) calculated on an annual basis from figures relating to a shorter period.

annuity (ǝ-**new**-iti) *noun* (**annuities**) a fixed annual allowance, usually provided by a form of investment. [same origin as for *annual*]

annul (ǝ-**nul**) *verb* (**annulled, annulling**) to make a contract or agreement invalid or void. [from *ad-* and the Latin word *nullus* meaning 'none']

annular (an-yoo-ler) *adjective* having the form of a ring. [same origin as for *annulus*]

annulus (an-yoo-ləs) *noun* (**annuli**) the ring-shaped space between two concentric circles. [a Latin word]

Annunciation *noun* 1 in Christian belief, the announcement by the angel Gabriel to the Virgin Mary that she was to be the mother of Christ. 2 the festival commemorating this on 25 March (also called *Lady Day*). [same origin as for *announce*]

anode (an-ohd) *noun* a positively charged electrode, by which electric current enters a device. (Compare **cathode**.) [from Greek words *ana* meaning 'up' and *hodos* meaning 'way']

anodize (an-ə-diyz) *verb* to coat metal with a protective layer by means of electrolysis. [same origin as for *anode*]

anodyne (an-ə-diyn) *noun* a drug that relieves pain.
anodyne *adjective* 1 relieving pain. 2 feebly dull or unexciting. [from a Greek word *anodunos* meaning 'painless']

anoint *verb* to rub a person with ointment or oil, especially as part of a religious ceremony. [via Old French from a Latin word *ungere*]

anomaly (ə-nom-əli) *noun* (**anomalies**) something that deviates from what is normal or expected ♦ *the many anomalies in our tax system*. **anomalous** *adjective* [from a-[1] meaning 'not' and a Greek word *homalos* meaning 'even']

anon (ə-non) *adverb* (*old use*) soon or presently ♦ *I will say more of this anon.* [from an Old English phrase *on ane* meaning 'in one, at once']

anon. *abbreviation* anonymous (with reference to an author).

anonymity (an-ən-im-iti) *noun* being anonymous.

anonymous (ə-non-im-əs) *adjective* 1 having a name that is not known ♦ *The gift came from an anonymous donor.* 2 written or given by a person whose name is not known ♦ *We have received an anonymous letter.* **anonymously** *adverb* [from a-[1] meaning 'not' and the Greek word *onuma* meaning 'name']

anorak (an-er-ak) *noun* 1 a waterproof jacket with a hood attached, worn as a protection against rain, wind, and cold. 2 (*informal*) a person who has solitary interests and is awkward on social occasions. [from a Greenland Eskimo word *anoraq*]

anorexia (an-er-eks-iə) *noun* a lack of appetite for food, especially in the meaning of *anorexia nervosa*. [from a-[1] meaning 'not' and a Greek word *orexis* meaning 'appetite']

anorexia nervosa *noun* a psychological condition involving an obsession with reducing weight by not eating.

anorexic or **anorectic** *adjective* relating to or suffering from anorexia.
anorexic or **anorectic** *noun* a person suffering from anorexia.

another *adjective* 1 additional, one more ♦ *Have another biscuit.* 2 different ♦ *If this one doesn't work I'll give you another.*
another *pronoun* another person or thing.

answer *noun* 1 something said, written, or done to deal with a question, accusation, or situation. SYNONYMS: reply, reponse, reaction. 2 something needed to resolve a problem or difficulty. SYNONYMS: solution, explanation, remedy.
answer *verb* 1 to make an answer to someone. SYNONYMS: reply (to), respond (to). 2 to be suitable or enough for something ♦ *This will answer the purpose.* SYNONYMS: satisfy, suit, meet, fill, fulfil. **to answer back** to answer a rebuke cheekily. **to answer for** to take responsibility for something ♦ *I will answer for his honesty* ♦ *They must answer for their crimes.* [from an Old English word]

answerable *adjective* 1 able to be answered. 2 having to account for something ♦ *You will be answerable to me for any mistakes.*

answering machine *noun* a machine that answers telephone calls by playing a recorded message and recording the caller's reply.

ant *noun* a small insect of which there are many species mostly without wings, which live in highly organized groups. [from an Old English word]

antacid (ant-**ass**-id) *noun* a substance that prevents or corrects acidity.

antagonism (an-**tag**-ən-izm) *noun* active opposition or hostility. SYNONYMS: opposition, hostility, antipathy, animosity, friction. [from *anti-* and a Greek word *agōn* meaning 'struggle']

antagonist (an-**tag**-ən-ist) *noun* 1 a person who is hostile to someone or something, an opponent. 2 (*Biochemistry*) either of a pair of organisms, drugs, or substances that counteract each other's effect.

antagonistic (an-tag-ən-**ist**-ik) *adjective* showing or feeling antagonism, hostile. **antagonistically** *adverb*

antagonistic muscle *noun* (*Anatomy*) a muscle whose action counteracts that of another muscle, for example relaxing while the other contracts.

antagonize *verb* to make someone feel hostile towards you.

Antarctic *noun* 1 the regions round the South Pole. 2 the Antarctic Ocean, the sea surrounding Antarctica.
Antarctic *adjective* relating to these regions. [from a Greek word *antarktikos* meaning 'opposite the north']

Antarctic Circle *noun* an imaginary line round the Antarctic regions at a latitude of 66° 30′ S.

ante (**an**-ti) *noun* a stake put up by a poker player before drawing new cards.

ante- *prefix* before (as in *ante-room*). [from a Latin word *ante* meaning 'before']

anteater *noun* an animal with a long nose and a sticky tongue, which feeds on ants and termites.

antecedent (ant-i-**seed**ənt) *noun*
1 something that happened before something else ♦ *We discussed the Great War and its antecedents.* 2 (*Grammar*) a noun or clause or sentence to which a following pronoun refers (in *the book which I have*, 'book' is the antecedent of 'which').
antecedent *adjective* previous.
antecedents *plural noun* a person's ancestors and social background. [from *ante-* and a Latin word *cedere* meaning 'to go']

antechamber *noun* a small room leading to a larger one, an ante-room.

antedate *verb* to put an earlier date on a document than the date on which it was issued.

antediluvian (anti-di-**loo**-viən) *adjective* 1 of the time before Noah's Flood as recounted in the Bible. 2 (*informal*) completely out of date. [from *ante-* and a Latin word *diluvium* meaning 'deluge']

antelope *noun* a fast-running animal like a deer, found especially in Africa, for example a chamois or gazelle. [from a late Greek word *antholops* (originally the name of a mythical creature)]

antenatal *adjective* before birth or during a pregnancy ♦ *an antenatal clinic.*

antenna *noun* 1 (**antennae** (an-**ten**-ee)) each of a pair of thin flexible extensions on the heads of insects and some other invertebrate animals, used as feelers. 2 (**antennas**) an aerial. [from a Latin word *antemna*]

antepenultimate (anti-pin-**ult**-imət) *adjective* last but two in a series.

anterior *adjective* coming before something in position or time. [from a Latin word meaning 'further forward']

ante-room *noun* a small room leading to a larger one, an antechamber.

anthem *noun* 1 a short musical composition for singing in religious services. 2 short for *national anthem*. 3 a rousing song sung by a large group of people, such as supporters of a sport. [from an Old English word]

anther *noun* the part of a flower's stamen that contains pollen. [from a Greek word *anthos* meaning 'flower']

anthill *noun* a mound built by ants over their nest.

anthology (an-**thol**-əji) *noun* (**anthologies**) a collection of poems or other pieces of literature. [from Greek words *anthos* meaning 'flower' and *-logia* meaning 'collection']

anthracite *noun* a hard form of coal that burns with little flame or smoke. [same origin as for *anthrax*]

anthrax *noun* a disease of sheep and cattle that can be transmitted to people. [from a Greek word *anthrax* meaning 'coal' or 'carbuncle']

anthropoid (**an**-thrəp-oid) *adjective* like a human being in form, especially with reference to the higher primates, including monkeys and apes.
anthropoid *noun* an anthropoid ape such as a gorilla or chimpanzee. [same origin as for *anthropology*]

anthropologist *noun* someone who studies anthropology.

anthropology (anthrə-**pol**-əji) *noun* the study of humankind, especially of human societies and cultures. **anthropological** (an-thrəp-ə-**loj**-ikəl) *adjective* **anthropologically** *adverb* [from a Greek word *anthrōpos* meaning 'human being']

anthropomorphic (an-thrəp-ə-**mor**-fik) *adjective* attributing human forms or characteristics to a god, animal, or object. **anthropomorphism** *noun* [from Greek words *anthrōpos* meaning 'human being' and *morphē* meaning 'form']

anthropomorphous (an-thrəp-ə-**mor**-fəs) *adjective* having a human form or nature.

anti *preposition* opposed to, against.

anti- *prefix* (changing to **ant-** before a vowel) **1** against or opposed to ♦ *anti-abortion.* **2** preventing or counteracting ♦ *antiperspirant.* [from a Greek word *anti* meaning 'against']

anti-aircraft *adjective* (said about a gun or missile) used against enemy aircraft.

antibiotic (anti-biy-**ot**-ik) *noun* a medicine that destroys bacteria or prevents their growth. **antibiotic** *adjective* acting in this way. [from *anti-* and a Greek word *bios* meaning 'life']

antibody (**an**-ti-bodi) *noun* (**antibodies**) a protein formed in the blood as a defence against certain substances which it then attacks and destroys.

anticipate *verb* **1** to take action in advance about something you are aware of ♦ *A good teacher learns to anticipate what students will ask.* SYNONYMS: foresee, predict. **2** to make use of something before the proper time. **3** to take action before someone else has had a chance to do so ♦ *The police were able to anticipate the thieves' movements.* SYNONYMS: forestall, prevent. **4** to expect ♦ *The result was much better than we anticipated.* SYNONYMS: expect, predict. **anticipation** *noun* [from Latin words *ante* meaning 'before' and *capere* meaning 'to take'] ◊ Some people regard meaning **4** as incorrect. It is better to avoid it and use *expect* instead.

anticipatory (an-tiss-i-**payt**-er-i) *adjective* showing anticipation.

anticlimax *noun* a disappointing ending to a series of events that seemed to be leading to a climax.

anticline *noun* a land formation in which strata are folded so that they slope down on opposite sides of a ridge. **anticlinal** *adjective* [from *anti-* and a Greek word *klinein* meaning 'to lean']

anticlockwise *adverb & adjective* moving in a curve in the opposite direction to the hands of a clock.

antics *plural noun* foolish or amusing behaviour. [from *antic* meaning 'strange' or 'grotesque', from an Italian word *antico* meaning 'ancient' or 'antique']

anticyclone *noun* a weather system in which atmospheric pressure is high, usually producing fine settled weather.

antidepressant (an- ti- di- **pres**- ənt) *noun* a drug used to reduce the symptoms of depression.

antidote (**an**-ti-doht) *noun* **1** a medicine that counteracts the effects of a poison or a disease. **2** anything that counteracts unpleasant effects. [from *anti-* and a Greek word *dotos* meaning 'given']

antifreeze *noun* a liquid added to water, especially in the radiator of a motor vehicle, to lower its freezing point and make it less likely to freeze.

antigen (**an**-ti-jən) *noun* a substance (e.g. a toxin) that the body recognizes as alien and that causes the body to produce antibodies. [from *anti-* and a Greek word *-genēs* meaning 'born']

anti-hero *noun* a central character in a story or drama who lacks the normal characteristics of a hero.

antihistamine (anti-**hist**-ə-min) *noun* a drug or other substance that counteracts the effects of histamine, used in treating allergies.

antilogarithm *noun* the number to which a given logarithm belongs.

antimacassar (anti-mə-**kas**-er) *noun* a small piece of cloth put over the backs or arms of chairs etc. to protect them from grease and dirt. [it was originally a protection against the Macassar oil that was used on hair]

antimony (**an**-ti-məni) *noun* a brittle silvery metal used in alloys, a chemical element (symbol Sb). [from a Latin word *antimonium*]

antiparticle *noun* an elementary particle having the same mass as a given particle but an opposite electric charge or magnetic effect.

antipasto (an-ti-**pah**-stoh) *noun* (**antipasti**) an Italian hors d'œuvre. [from Italian words *anti-* meaning 'before' and *pasto* meaning 'food']

antipathy (an-**tip**-ə-thi) *noun* a strong feeling of dislike for someone or something. SYNONYMS: opposition, hostility, antagonism, animosity, friction. [from *anti-* and a Greek word *pathos* meaning 'feeling']

antiperspirant (anti-**per**-spi-rənt) *noun* a substance that prevents or reduces perspiration.

antipodes (an-**tip**-ə-deez) *plural noun* places on opposite sides of the earth.
Antipodes Australia and New Zealand, as regarded by people in the northern hemisphere. **antipodean** (antip-ə-dee-ən) *adjective* [from a Greek word meaning 'having the feet opposite' (*podes* = feet)]

antiquarian *adjective* to do with the study of antiques or antiquities.
antiquarian *noun* an antiquary. [same origin as for *antique*]

antiquary (an-tik-wer-i) *noun* (**antiquaries**) a person who studies or collects antiques or antiquities.

antiquated (an-ti-kway-tid) *adjective* old-fashioned or out of date. SYNONYMS: old-fashioned, out of date, outdated, obsolete.

antique (an-**teek**) *adjective* 1 belonging to the distant past. 2 made in the style of past times.
antique *noun* an object, especially a piece of furniture or a decorative object, that has value because of its age. [from a Latin word *antiquus* meaning 'ancient']

antiquity (an-**tik**-witi) *noun* ancient times, especially the classical civilizations before the Middle Ages. **antiquities** *plural noun* objects dating from ancient times.

antirrhinum (anti-**riy**-nəm) *noun* a garden plant of a genus that includes the snapdragon.

anti-Semitic (anti-sim-**it**-ik) *adjective* hostile to or prejudiced against Jews. **anti-Semitism** (anti-**sem**-it-izm) *noun*

antiseptic *adjective* 1 preventing the growth of micro-organisms that cause disease. 2 completely clean and free from germs.
antiseptic *noun* an antiseptic substance. **antiseptically** *adverb* [from *anti-* and *septic*]

antisocial *adjective* 1 opposed to normal social institutions and conventions.
2 inconsiderate towards other people.
3 not sociable, keeping away from the company of others. **antisocially** *adverb*

antistatic *adjective* preventing the build-up of static electricity or reducing its effects.

antithesis (an-**tith**-i-sis) *noun* (**antitheses**)
1 someone or something that is the direct opposite of something or someone else.
2 in literature, the expression of a contrast of ideas. **antithetic** (anti-**thet**-ik) *adjective* **antithetical** *adjective* **antithetically** *adverb* [from *anti-* and a Greek word *thesis* meaning 'placing']

antitoxin *noun* an antibody that neutralizes a toxin and prevents it from having a harmful effect. **antitoxic** *adjective*

antitrade winds *plural noun* steady winds that blow in the opposite direction to a trade wind and at a different altitude.

antler *noun* a branched horn, one of a pair on a stag or other deer. **antlered** *adjective*

antonym (**ant**-ən-im) *noun* a word that is opposite in meaning to another word. [from *anti-* and a Greek word *onuma* meaning 'name']

anus (**ay**-nəs) *noun* the opening at the lower end of the alimentary canal, through which solid waste matter is passed out of the body. [from a Latin word *anus* meaning 'ring']

anvil *noun* a large block of iron on which a blacksmith hammers metal into shape. [from Old English words *an* meaning 'on' and *filt-* meaning 'beat']

anxiety *noun* (**anxieties**) 1 a feeling of being anxious. 2 something that causes this feeling.

anxious *adjective* 1 troubled and worried. SYNONYMS: nervous, worried, apprehensive, concerned, uneasy, fearful, jittery. 2 causing worry ♦ *A few anxious moments followed.*
3 eager ♦ *They are always anxious to please.* SYNONYMS: eager, keen. **anxiously** *adverb* [from a Latin word *anxius*, from *angere* meaning 'to choke']

any *adjective* 1 used to refer to one or some of a thing, or a number of things (usually more than two) when it is not important which are meant ♦ *Have you any bread?* ♦ *I don't have any books with me.* 2 every, whichever one you choose ♦ *Any fool knows that.* 3 in a significant amount ♦ *They did not stay any length of time.*
any *pronoun* any person, thing, or amount ♦ *I can't see any of them* ♦ *We haven't any left.*
any *adverb* at all, to some extent ♦ *Is that any better?* [from an Old English word]

anybody *noun pronoun* 1 any person. 2 a person of importance ♦ *Is she anybody?*

anyhow *adverb* **1** anyway. **2** in a careless or disorderly way ♦ *They just did the work anyhow.*

any more *adverb* any further, from now or then on ♦ *She didn't love him any more.*

anyone *noun & pronoun* anybody.

anything *noun & pronoun* a thing, no matter which ♦ *Anything will do* ♦ *I didn't see anything.* **anything but** far from being ♦ *It's anything but cheap.*

anyway *adverb* in any case.

anywhere *adverb* in or to any place. **anywhere** *pronoun* any place.

Anzac *noun* **1** a soldier in the Australian and New Zealand Army Corps (1914–18). **2** a person from Australia or New Zealand. [from the initial letters of the name of the Corps]

AOB *abbreviation* any other business.

aorta (ay-or-tə) *noun* the main artery of the body, through which blood is pumped into the circulatory system. **aortic** *adjective* [from a Greek word *aortē*, from *aeirein* meaning 'to raise']

apace *adverb* (*literary*) swiftly ♦ *Work continued apace.*

apart *adverb* **1** separately or by themselves ♦ *The children lived apart for many years.* **2** to or at a distance ♦ *Keep the tables apart.* **3** into pieces ♦ *I'll have to take it apart.* **apart from** excluding, other than. [from a French phrase *à part* meaning 'to the side']

apartheid (ə-part-hayt) *noun* the political policy that used to be followed in South Africa, of keeping Europeans and non-Europeans apart. [an Afrikaans word meaning 'being apart']

apartment *noun* a set of rooms, a flat.

apathy (ap-ə-thi) *noun* a feeling of not caring or not being interested. **apathetic** (apə-**thet**-ik) *adjective* **apathetically** *adverb* [from a-² and a Greek word *pathos* meaning 'feeling']

apatosaurus (ə-pa-tə-**sor**-əs) *noun* a large dinosaur with a long neck and tail, which fed on plants. [from Greek words *apatē* meaning 'deceit' (because its bones deceptively resembled other dinosaurs) and *sauros* meaning 'lizard']
◊ Another name often used for this dinosaur is **brontosaurus.**

ape *noun* any of the four primates (gorilla, chimpanzee, orang-utan, gibbon) most closely related to man.
ape *verb* to imitate or mimic someone.

apeman *noun* (**apemen**) an extinct being believed to have features of both apes and humans.

aperient (ə-peer-iənt) *adjective* (*Medicine*) used to relieve constipation, laxative. **aperient** *noun* a laxative medicine. [from a Latin word *aperiens* meaning 'opening']

aperitif (ə-pe-ri-teef) *noun* an alcoholic drink taken before a meal as an appetizer. [a French word, from a Latin word *aperire* meaning 'to open']

aperture *noun* an opening, especially one that admits light into a camera. [from a Latin word *aperire* meaning 'to open']

Apex *noun* a system of reduced fares for air or rail travel when booked in advance. [from *Advance Purchase Excursion*]

apex (ay-peks) *noun* (**apexes**) the tip or highest point of something, especially when it forms a point. [from a Latin word *apex* meaning 'peak' or 'tip']

aphasia (a- fay- ziə) *noun* (*Medicine*) the inability to understand or utter speech, as a result of brain damage. [from a Greek word *aphatos* meaning 'speechless']

aphid (ay-fid) *noun* a small bug, such as a greenfly or blackfly, that feeds off the sap of plants. [same origin as for *aphis*]

aphis (ay-fiss) *noun* (**aphides** (ay-fid-eez)) an aphid. [probably from a Greek word *koris*, which was misread as *aphis*]

aphorism (af-er-izm) *noun* a short saying that states a truth, a maxim. [from a Greek word *aphorismos* meaning 'definition']

aphrodisiac (afrə-diz-iak) *noun* a food or drink that arouses sexual desire.

apiary (ay-pi-er-i) *noun* (**apiaries**) a place with a number of hives where bees are kept. [from a Latin word *apis* meaning 'bee']

apiece *adverb* for or by each one of a group ♦ *They cost a pound apiece.*

aplomb (ə-plom) *noun* confident self-assurance. [from a French phrase *à plomb* meaning 'straight as a plumb line']

apocalypse (ə-pok-ə-lips) *noun* an event of great destruction or disaster.
Apocalypse *noun* the last book in the New Testament (also called the *Revelation of St John the Divine*), which includes a prophecy about the end of the world. [from a Greek word *apokaluptein* meaning 'to reveal']

apocalyptic (ə-pok-ə-**lip**-tik) *adjective* involving great disaster, catastrophic. **apocalyptically** *adverb*

Apocrypha (ə-**pok**-rif-ə) *noun* the books of the Old Testament that were not accepted by Jews as part of the Hebrew Scriptures and are omitted from some versions of the Bible. [from a Latin phrase *apocrypha scripta* meaning 'hidden writings']

apocryphal (ə-**pok**-rif-əl) *adjective* untrue or invented ♦ *He gave an apocryphal account of his travels.* **apocryphally** *adverb* [same origin as for *Apocrypha*]

apogee (**ap**-ə-jee) *noun* 1 the point in the orbit of the moon or a satellite when it is furthest from the earth. (Compare **perigee**.) 2 a climax. [from Greek words *apo* meaning 'away from' and *gē* meaning 'earth']

apolitical (ay-pə-**lit**-ikəl) *adjective* not political, not interested in politics.

apologetic *adjective* wanting to apologize for something; expressing regret. SYNONYMS: contrite, repentant, remorseful, regretful. **apologetically** *adverb*

apologetics *plural noun* a set of arguments that justify a doctrine, especially Christianity.

apologist *noun* a person who defends a doctrine by presenting an argument.

apologize *verb* to express regret for a wrongdoing or offence.

apology *noun* (**apologies**) 1 a statement of regret for having done wrong or caused offence. 2 an explanation or defence of beliefs. 3 a poor example of something ♦ *this feeble apology for a meal.* [from a Greek word *apologia* meaning 'a speech in your own defence']

apolune *noun* the point at which a spacecraft orbiting the moon is furthest from it. [from a Greek word *apo* meaning 'away from' and a Latin word *luna* meaning 'moon']

apophthegm (**ap**-əth-em) *noun* a short pithy saying or maxim. [from a Greek word meaning 'something spoken out']

apoplectic (apə-**plek**-tik) *adjective* 1 affected or overcome by apoplexy. 2 (*informal*) furious with rage. **apoplectically** *adverb*

apoplexy (**ap**-ə-plek-si) *noun* sudden inability to feel and move, caused by blockage or rupture of an artery in the brain. [from a Greek word *apoplexia* meaning 'a stroke']

apostate (ə-**poss**-tayt) *noun* a person who renounces a religious belief or political principle. **apostasy** (ə-**poss**-tə-si) *noun* [from a Greek word *apostatēs* meaning 'deserter']

apostatize (ə-**poss**-tə-tiyz) *verb* to renounce a belief or principle.

Apostle *noun* each of Christ's twelve disciples.
apostle *noun* a teacher or supporter of a new idea or cause. [from a Greek word *apostellein* meaning 'send out']

apostolic (apə-**stol**-ik) *adjective* 1 to do with the Apostles or their teaching. 2 to do with the pope as successor to St Peter.

apostolic succession *noun* the continuous transmission of spiritual authority from the Apostles through successive popes and other bishops.

apostrophe (ə-**pos**-trə-fi) *noun* 1 a punctuation mark (') used to show that letters or numbers have been omitted (as in *didn't* = did not; *'05* = 2005) or showing the possessive case (as in *Rachel's book*, *their parents' house*). 2 a part of a speech or a poem addressed to an absent person or an abstract idea. [from Greek words *apo* meaning 'away from' and *strophē* meaning 'turning']

apostrophize (ə-**pos**-trə-fiyz) *verb* to address an absent person or abstract thing in a speech or poem.

apothecary (ə-**poth**-ik-eri) *noun* (**apothecaries**) (*old use*) a person who prepared medicines. [from a Latin word *apothecarius*]

apotheosis (ə-**poth**-ee-**oh**-sis) *noun* 1 making a person divine, deification. 2 the highest point of perfection something reaches. [from Greek words *apo* meaning 'away from' and *theos* meaning 'god']

appal (ə-**pawl**) *verb* (**appalled, appalling**) to make someone feel horrified, to shock someone deeply. SYNONYMS: horrify, disgust, shock, outrage, dismay, alarm. [from an Old French word *apalir* meaning 'to become pale']

appalling *adjective* (*informal*) very bad or unpleasant. SYNONYMS: horrible, deplorable, shocking, revolting, awful, dreadful, horrifying.

apparatus *noun* 1 the equipment needed for doing something, especially the instruments, devices, and containers used in scientific experiments. 2 a complex piece of organization ♦ *the apparatus of government.* [from a Latin word *apparare* meaning 'to prepare or get ready']

apparel *noun* (*formal*) clothing. [from an Old French word *apareillier* meaning 'to make ready or fit']

apparent (ə-**pa**-rənt) *adjective* 1 clearly seen or understood. SYNONYMS: clear, evident, perceptible, obvious. 2 seeming to be true or real ♦ *She spoke with apparent feeling.* SYNONYMS: outward, seeming, ostensible. **apparently** *adverb* [same origin as for *appear*]

apparition (apə-**rish**-ən) 1 something remarkable or unexpected that appears suddenly. 2 a ghost. [same origin as for *appear*]

appeal *verb* (**appealed, appealing**) 1 to make a serious or formal request ♦ *The police appealed for calm.* SYNONYMS: ask (for), request. 2 to go or speak to someone with authority for an opinion. 3 in cricket, to call on the umpire to declare a batsman 'out'. 4 (*Law*) to take a case to a higher court for review of the decision of a lower court. 5 **appeal to** to be attractive or pleasing to someone ♦ *Air travel doesn't appeal to me.* SYNONYMS: attract, allure, interest, tempt.
appeal *noun* 1 the act of appealing, especially a formal request for donations to a cause. 2 attraction or pleasantness. 3 (*Law*) the process of appealing to a higher court. [from a Latin word *appellare* meaning 'to address']

appear *verb* 1 to become visible. 2 to start to exist or be used. 3 to give a certain impression ♦ *You appear to have forgotten.* SYNONYM: seem. 4 to give a public performance, especially on stage ♦ *Olivier appeared as Hamlet.* 5 to act as counsel in a lawcourt ♦ *I appear for the defendant.* 6 to be published ♦ *Her new novel will appear next month.* [from a Latin word *apparere* meaning 'to come in sight']

appearance *noun* 1 the act of appearing. 2 an outward sign, what something appears to be ♦ *He has an appearance of interest.* SYNONYMS: look, show, impression.

appease *verb* to make someone feel calm or quiet by giving them what they want. SYNONYMS: calm, pacify, mollify, soothe, assuage. **appeasement** *noun* [from a French phrase *à paix* meaning 'to peace']

appellant (ə-**pel**-ənt) *noun* a person who appeals against the ruling of a lawcourt. [same origin as for *appeal*]

appellation (ap-əl-**ay**-shən) *noun* (*formal*) a name or title.

append *verb* (*formal*) 1 to attach something. 2 to add something at the end of a text or document. [from *ad-* and the Latin word *pendere* meaning 'to hang']

appendage (ə-**pen**-dij) *noun* a thing attached to something larger or more important.

appendectomy (ap-en-**dek**-tə-mi) *noun* a surgical operation to remove the appendix. [from *appendix* and a Greek word *ektomē* meaning 'cutting out']

appendicitis *noun* inflammation of the appendix.

appendix *noun* 1 (**appendices**) a part at the end of a book or document, giving extra information. 2 (**appendixes**) a small tube of tissue closed at one end, attached to the lower end of the intestine. [same origin as *append*]

appertain (ap-er-**tayn**) *verb* to relate to something or be appropriate to it. [same origin as for *pertain*]

appetite *noun* 1 a physical desire, especially for food. SYNONYMS: desire, longing, hunger, craving. 2 a desire or liking ♦ *They have an appetite for power.* SYNONYMS: desire, longing, taste, relish. [from *ad-* and a Latin word *petere* meaning 'to seek']

appetizer *noun* a small amount of food or drink taken before a meal to stimulate the appetite.

appetizing *adjective* stimulating the appetite ♦ *an appetizing smell.* **appetizingly** *adverb*

applaud *verb* 1 to show approval of something or someone by clapping the hands. SYNONYMS: cheer, clap, acclaim. 2 to praise something ♦ *We all applaud your decision.* SYNONYMS: praise, commend, admire, approve of. [from *ad-* and a Latin word *plaudere* meaning 'to clap hands']

applause *noun* clapping by people to show approval.

apple *noun* 1 a round fruit of a tree related to the rose, with green or red skin and a firm juicy flesh. 2 the tree that bears this. [from an Old English word]

applet *noun* (*Computing*) a simple application program that is designed to perform a single task. [from *application* and *-let* as in *booklet*]

appliance *noun* a device or instrument. [same origin as for *apply*]

applicable (ap-lik-ə-bəl) *adjective* able to be applied, relevant, or appropriate. **applicability** (əplik-ə-**bil**-iti) *noun*

applicant (ap-lik-ənt) *noun* a person who applies for a job.

application *noun* **1** a formal request for something ♦ *His application has been refused.* **2** the action of putting something on a surface ♦ *The ointment is for external application only.* **3** putting something into effect or to practical use. **4** the ability to concentrate on a task. **5** a computer program or piece of software designed for a particular purpose.

applicator *noun* a device for putting a substance on a surface.

applied *adjective* (said about a subject of study) used for a practical purpose ♦ *applied mathematics.*

appliqué (ə-**plee**-kay) *noun* needlework in which pieces of material are sewn to a fabric background.
appliqué *verb* (**appliqués, appliquéd, appliquéing**) to decorate something with appliqué. [a French word meaning 'put on']

apply *verb* (**applies, applied, applying**) **1** to put one thing into contact with another; to spread something on a surface. **2** to bring into use or action ♦ *The United Nations voted to apply economic sanctions.* **3** (**apply to**) to be relevant to someone ♦ *The rules apply to everyone.* SYNONYMS: concern, affect, relate (to). **4** to make a formal request ♦ *I am applying for a job.* **to apply yourself** to concentrate on a task and work hard.

appoint *verb* **1** to choose a person for a job or special purpose. SYNONYMS: choose, select, name, nominate. **2** to decide or arrange something officially ♦ *We must appoint a time for the next meeting.* SYNONYMS: choose, decide, decide on, arrange, settle, fix. [from an Old French phrase *à point* meaning 'to a point']

appointment *noun* **1** an arrangement to meet at a particular time and place. **2** a job or position, or the act of appointing someone to it.

apportion (ə-**por**-shən) *verb* to share something out. **apportionment** *noun* [same origin as for *portion*]

apposite (**ap**-ə-zit) *adjective* (said about a remark) very apt or appropriate. **appositely** *adverb* [from a Latin word *apponere* meaning 'to apply']

apposition (apə-**zish**-ən) *noun* (*Grammar*) a relationship in which a word or phrase is placed with another, and both have the same grammatical role and refer to the same thing. For example, in the sentence *I met my friend Hannah*, *my friend* and *Hannah* are in apposition. [same origin as for *apposite*]

appraise *verb* to estimate the value or quality of something. **appraisal** *noun* [from an Old French word related to *price*]

appreciable (ə-**pree**-shə-bəl) *adjective* enough to be noticed or felt, considerable ♦ *an appreciable difference.* **appreciably** *adverb*

appreciate *verb* **1** to value something highly, to be grateful for something. **2** to enjoy something intelligently ♦ *It is good to perform for people who appreciate good singing.* SYNONYMS: enjoy, like, admire, value, approve of. **3** to understand ♦ *We appreciate their reluctance to give details.* **4** to increase in value ♦ *The value of the house has appreciated over the years.* **appreciation** *noun* [from *ad-* and a Latin word *pretium* mean 'price']

appreciative (ə-**pree**-shə-tiv) *adjective* feeling or showing pleasure or gratitude. **appreciatively** *adverb*

apprehend (apri-**hend**) *verb* **1** to seize or arrest someone who is doing wrong. **2** to understand something. **3** to expect something with fear or anxiety. [from *ad-* and a Latin word *prehendere* meaning 'to grasp']

apprehension (apri-**hen**-shən) *noun* **1** a feeling of fear about a danger or difficulty. **2** understanding. **3** the act of arresting someone.

apprehensive (apri-**hen**-siv) *adjective* anxious or fearful about a danger or difficulty. SYNONYMS: anxious, fearful, nervous, worried, concerned, uneasy, jittery. **apprehensively** *adverb* **apprehensiveness** *noun*

apprentice *noun* someone who is learning a craft from an employer.

apprentice *verb* to bind someone legally as an apprentice. **apprenticeship** *noun* [from a French word *apprendre* meaning 'to learn']

apprise (ə-**priyz**) *verb* (*formal*) to inform someone of something. [from a French word *apprendre* meaning 'to learn' or 'to teach']

approach *verb* 1 to come near or nearer to a place or time. 2 to set about doing a task ♦ *We must approach the problem in a practical way.* 3 to go to someone with a request or offer. 4 to be similar to something ♦ *Her generosity approaches extravagance.* **approach** *noun* 1 the action of approaching. 2 a way of reaching a place. 3 a method of doing or tackling something ♦ *We must try a more subtle approach.* 4 an effort to establish an agreement or friendly relations. [from an Old French word *approcher*]

approachable *adjective* (said about a person) friendly and easy to talk to. **approachability** *noun*

approbation (apra-**bay**-shən) *noun* approval. [same origin as for *approve*]

appropriate [1] (ə-**proh**-pri-ət) *adjective* suitable or proper. SYNONYMS: suitable, proper, fitting, apt, right. **appropriately** *adverb* **appropriateness** *noun* [from a Latin word *appropriare* meaning 'to make one's own']

appropriate [2] (ə-**proh**-pri-ayt) *verb* 1 to take and use something without permission as your own. 2 to set money aside for a special purpose. **appropriation** *noun* **appropriator** *noun*

approval *noun* feeling, showing, or saying that you approve of something. **on approval** (said about goods) taken by a customer with the right to return them if they are not satisfactory.

approve *verb* 1 (often **approve of**) to say or feel that something is good or suitable. 2 to agree formally to something ♦ *The committee has approved the expenditure.* SYNONYMS: authorize, allow, accept, agree to. [from a Latin word *approbare*]

approximate [1] (ə-**prok**-sim-ət) *adjective* nearly but not completely exact or correct.

approximate [2] (ə-**prok**-sim-ayt) *verb* 1 to be almost the same as something ♦ *His remarks approximated to an apology.* 2 to make something approximately the same. **approximation** *noun* [from *ad-* and a Latin word *proximus* meaning 'very near']

approximately *adverb* roughly, more or less. SYNONYMS: roughly, about, nearly, more or less.

APR *abbreviation* annual or annualized percentage rate, with reference to the rate of interest on a credit arrangement.

apricot *noun* 1 a juicy fruit containing a stone, related to the plum and peach. 2 the tree on which this grows. 3 the orange-pink colour of an apricot. [from Spanish and Portuguese, ultimately from an Arabic word]

April *noun* the fourth month of the year. [from the Latin name *Aprilis*]

April Fool's Day *noun* 1 April, by tradition a day for playing practical jokes on people.

apron *noun* 1 a garment you wear over the front part of the body to protect your clothes. 2 an extra part next to a larger one, for example a part of a theatre stage reaching in front of the curtain. 3 an area on an airfield used for loading and manoeuvring aircraft. [originally *napron*, from a French word *nappe* meaning 'tablecloth'. The *n* was lost when *a napron* was understood to be *an apron*.]

apropos (apra-**poh**) *adverb* appropriately, to the point. **apropos** *adjective* suitable or relevant to what someone is saying or doing. **apropos of** concerning or with reference to. [from a French phrase *à propos* meaning 'to the purpose']

apse *noun* a recess in a church, usually with an arched or domed roof. [from a Greek word *apsis* meaning 'arch' or 'vault']

apt *adjective* 1 suitable or appropriate ♦ *an apt quotation.* SYNONYMS: suitable, appropriate, fitting. 2 having a certain tendency, likely ♦ *They are apt to be careless.* SYNONYMS: liable, inclined, prone, likely. 3 quick at learning. **aptly** *adverb* **aptness** *noun* [from a Latin word *aptus* meaning 'fitted']

aptitude *noun* a natural ability or skill. [from an Old French word related to *apt*]

aqualung *noun* a portable breathing apparatus used by divers and consisting of cylinders of compressed air connected to a mask with a mouthpiece. [from a Latin word *aqua* meaning 'water' and *lung*]

aquamarine (akwa-ma-**reen**) *noun* 1 a bluish-green variety of beryl. 2 a bluish-green colour. [from Latin words *aqua marina* meaning 'seawater']

aquaplane *noun* a board for riding on water pulled by a speedboat.
aquaplane *verb* 1 to ride on an aquaplane. 2 (said about a road vehicle) to slide out of control on the wet surface of a road.

aquarium (ə-kwair-iəm) *noun* (**aquariums**) 1 a glass tank for keeping living fish and other water animals and plants. 2 a building containing a collection of fish in tanks. [a Latin word meaning 'of water']

Aquarius (ə-kwair-iəs) 1 a group of stars (the Water-carrier), seen as representing a figure of a man pouring water from a jug. 2 the sign of the zodiac which the sun enters about 21 January. **Aquarian** *adjective* & *noun* [same origin as for *aquarium*]

aquatic (ə-kwat-ik) *adjective* 1 growing in water or living in or near water ♦ *aquatic plants*. 2 taking place in or on water ♦ *aquatic sports*. [from a Latin word *aqua* meaning 'water']

aquatint *noun* an etching made on copper by using nitric acid. [from Italian words *acqua tinta* meaning 'coloured water']

aqueduct (ak-wi-dukt) *noun* an artificial water channel, especially a bridge carrying water across a valley or low ground. [from Latin words *aqua* meaning 'water' and *ducere* meaning 'to lead']

aqueous (ay-kwi-əs) *adjective* 1 like water, or containing water. 2 produced by water.

aqueous humour *noun* a transparent substance between the lens of the eye and the cornea.

aquifer (ak-wi-fer) *noun* a layer of rock that can hold or transmit water. [from Latin words *aqua* meaning 'water' and *ferre* meaning 'to bring']

aquilegia (akwi-lee-jə) *noun* a plant with showy flowers. [probably from a Latin word *aquilegus* meaning 'water-collecting']

aquiline (ak-wi-liyn) *adjective* (said about a person's nose) hooked like an eagle's beak. [from a Latin word *aquila* meaning 'eagle']

Arab *noun* 1 a member of a Semitic people living in parts of the Middle East and North Africa. 2 a horse of a breed originating in Arabia.
Arab *adjective* to do with the Arabs.

arabesque (a-rə-besk) *noun* 1 an elaborate design with intertwined leaves, branches, and scrolls. 2 (in ballet) a posture in which the dancer is poised on one leg with the torso extended forwards and the other leg stretched backwards horizontally.

Arabian *adjective* to do with Arabia, or living in Arabia.

Arabic *adjective* to do with the Arabs or their language.
Arabic *noun* the language of the Arabs.

Arabic numeral *noun* any of the numerals 0, 1, 2, 3, 4, 5, 6, 7, 8, and 9 (see also **roman numeral**).

arable (a-rə-bəl) *adjective* (said about land) suitable for growing crops.
arable *noun* arable land. [from a Latin word *arare* meaning 'to plough']

arachnid (ə-rak-nid) *noun* a member of the class of animals including spiders, scorpions, and mites. [from the Greek word *arachnē* meaning 'spider']

Aramaic (a-rə-may-ik) *noun* a Semitic language spoken in Syria and Palestine in New Testament times.

arbiter (ar-bit-er) *noun* 1 a person who has a strong influence over public opinion ♦ *the arbiters of fashion*. 2 a person given the power to settle a dispute, an arbitrator. [from a Latin word meaning 'judge' or 'supreme ruler']

arbitrary (ar-bit-rer-i) *adjective* 1 based on random choice or impulse ♦ *an arbitrary selection*. 2 unrestrained or autocratic ♦ *arbitrary powers*. **arbitrarily** *adverb* **arbitrariness** *noun* [same origin as for *arbiter*]

arbitrate *verb* to act as an arbitrator.

arbitration *noun* settlement of a dispute by an arbitrator.

arbitrator *noun* an independent person or group of people chosen to settle a dispute. [from a Latin word *arbitrari* meaning 'to judge']

arboreal (ar-bor-iəl) *adjective* to do with trees, or living in trees. [from a Latin word *arbor* meaning 'tree']

arboretum (ar-bor-ee-təm) *noun* (**arboreta**) a botanical garden where trees are grown for study and display. [same origin as for *arboreal*]

arbour (ar-ber) *noun* a shady alcove in a garden, formed with climbing plants growing over a framework. [same origin as for *arboreal*]

arc noun 1 a curve forming part of the circumference of a circle or other figure. 2 a luminous electric current passing across a gap between two terminals.
arc verb (**arced, arcing**) 1 to form an arc or curve. 2 to form an electrical arc. [from a Latin word *arcus* meaning 'a curve' or 'a bow']

arcade noun 1 a covered passage or walk with shops on one or both sides. 2 a series of arches along a wall. [from a French or Italian word, from a Latin word *arcus* meaning 'curve' (because early arcades had curved roofs)]

arcane (ar-**kayn**) adjective mysterious or secret. [from a Latin word *arcere* meaning 'to shut up', from *arca* meaning 'chest, box']

arch [1] noun 1 a curved structure built across an opening and supporting the weight above it. 2 a curve shaped like an arch. 3 the curved underside of the foot.
arch verb to form an arch, or to make something form an arch. [same origin as for *arc*]

arch [2] adjective self-consciously playful or mischievous ♦ *an arch smile.* **archly** adverb **archness** noun [same origin as for *arch-*]

arch- prefix 1 chief (as in *archbishop*). 2 extreme (as in *arch-enemy*). [from a Greek word *arkhos* meaning 'a chief']

archaeologist noun someone who studies archaeology.

archaeology (ar-ki-ol-ǝji) noun the study of ancient civilizations by digging for their physical remains and examining them. **archaeological** adjective [from a Greek word *arkhaios* meaning 'old' and *-logy*]

archaic (ar-**kay**-ik) adjective 1 belonging to ancient times. 2 old or old-fashioned. [from a Greek word *arkhē* meaning 'beginning']

archaism (ar-kay-izm) noun a word or expression that is now old or old-fashioned.

archangel noun an angel of high rank.

archbishop noun the chief bishop of a region.

archbishopric noun the office or region (called a *diocese*) of an archbishop.

archdeacon noun a senior priest, ranking next below a bishop. **archdeaconry** noun

archduke noun a chief duke, especially formerly as the title of a son of an Austrian emperor.

arch-enemy noun (**arch-enemies**) a chief or major enemy.

archer noun a person who shoots with bow and arrows. [from a Latin word *arcus* meaning 'a bow' or 'a curve']

archery noun the sport of shooting with bows and arrows.

archetype (ar-ki-tiyp) noun 1 an original model from which others are copied. 2 a typical example of something. **archetypal** adjective [from *arch-* and *type*]

Archimedean screw (arki-mee-diǝn) noun a device for raising water, consisting of a spiral screw rotating in a tube. [named after Archimedes, 3rd century BC Greek mathematician and inventor]

archipelago (arki-**pel**-ǝ-goh) noun (**archipelagos**) a large group of islands, or a sea containing such a group. [from *arch-* and a Greek word *pelagos* meaning 'sea']

architect noun 1 someone who designs buildings and supervises their construction. 2 someone who is responsible for a plan or strategy ♦ *the architect of victory.* [from *arch-* and a Greek word *tektōn* meaning 'builder']

architecture noun 1 the art or science of designing and constructing buildings. 2 the design or style of a building or buildings. **architectural** adjective **architecturally** adverb

architrave (ar-ki-trayv) noun 1 a horizontal beam resting along the top of a row of columns. 2 the surround of a doorway or window.

archive (ar-kiyv) noun a collection of the records or historical documents of an institution or community. [from a Greek word *arkheia* meaning 'public records']

archivist (ar-kiv-ist) noun a person qualified to organize and manage an archive.

archway noun a passageway under an arch.

arc lamp or **arc light** noun an artificial light using an electric arc.

Arctic noun 1 the regions round the North Pole. 2 the Arctic Ocean, the ocean surrounding the North Pole.
Arctic adjective relating to these regions.

arctic *adjective* (*informal*) extremely cold. [from a Greek word *arktos* meaning 'a bear' and 'pole star']

Arctic Circle *noun* an imaginary line round the Arctic regions at a latitude of 66° 30′ N.

arc welding *noun* welding by means of the heat produced by an electric arc.

ardent (**ar**-dənt) *adjective* very enthusiastic, full of ardour. SYNONYMS: enthusiastic, eager, passionate, keen, fervent, zealous. **ardently** *adverb* [from a Latin word *ardens* meaning 'burning']

ardour (**ar**-der) *noun* great enthusiasm or feeling.

arduous (**ar**-dew-əs) *adjective* very difficult and needing much effort. SYNONYMS: difficult, demanding, hard, onerous, laborious. **arduously** *adverb* [from a Latin word *arduus* meaning 'steep']

are [1] a form of **be**, used with plural nouns and with *we*, *you*, and *they*.

are [2] (ar) *noun* a former unit of area equal to 100 square metres. [same origin as for *area*]

area *noun* **1** the extent or measurement of a surface ♦ *The plane was flying over an area of desert.* SYNONYMS: expanse, stretch. **2** a region or district. SYNONYMS: region, district, locality, neighbourhood. **3** a space set aside for a purpose ♦ *a picnic area.* **4** the scope or range of an activity. **5** a sunken enclosure in front of the basement of a house. [from a Latin word *area* meaning 'a piece of ground']

areg plural of **erg** [2].

arena (ə-**ree**-nə) *noun* the level area in the centre of a sports stadium or amphitheatre. [from a Latin word *arena* meaning 'sand' (because ancient arenas were covered in sand)]

aren't (*informal*) **1** are not. **2** (*informal*) am not (only in questions ♦ *Aren't I coming too?*).

arête (a-**rayt**) *noun* a sharp ridge on a mountain. [a French word]

argon *noun* a chemical element (symbol Ar), an inert gas used in electric lamps. [from a Greek word *argos* meaning 'idle']

argosy (**ar**-gəsi) *noun* (*poetic*) a large merchant ship. [from an Italian word *Ragusea* meaning 'ship from Ragusa' (= Dubrovnik in Croatia)]

arguable *adjective* **1** able to be stated as a possibility. **2** open to doubt or discussion. **arguably** *adverb*

argue *verb* **1** to express disagreement; to exchange opposite views, especially with anger. SYNONYMS: quarrel, disagree, fight, wrangle, bicker, squabble. **2** to give reasons for or against something, to discuss an issue. [from a Latin word *arguere* meaning 'to make clear, to prove']

argument *noun* **1** a discussion involving disagreement, a quarrel. SYNONYMS: disagreement, dispute, quarrel, altercation, row, clash. **2** a reason or set of reasons in support of something. SYNONYMS: grounds, justification, evidence, proof, reason. **3** (*Mathematics*) an independent variable determining the value of a function.

argumentation *noun* systematic reasoning in support of something.

argumentative (arg-yoo-**ment**-ətiv) *adjective* arguing a lot. **argumentatively** *adverb*

aria (ah-riə) *noun* a song for one voice in an opera or oratorio. [an Italian word, related to *air*]

arid (ə-rid) *adjective* **1** (said about a region) dry and parched. SYNONYMS: barren, parched, dry, lifeless. **2** dull and uninteresting ♦ *an arid discussion.* **aridly** *adverb* **aridness** *noun* **aridity** (ə-**rid**-iti) *noun*

Aries (**air**-eez) **1** a group of stars (the Ram), seen as representing a figure of a ram. **2** the sign of the zodiac which the sun enters about 20 March. **Arian** (**air**-iən) *adjective & noun*

aright *adjective* (*literary*) rightly.

arise *verb* (**arose**, **arisen**) **1** to happen or come into existence ♦ *Some confusion arose about what happened next.* SYNONYMS: occur, emerge, ensue, develop, result. **2** (*old use*) to get up or stand up ♦ *Arise, Sir Francis.*

aristocracy (a-ri-**stok**-rəsi) *noun* (**aristocracies**) **1** the upper classes of people in a society, consisting of people of noble birth with inherited titles. **2** a form of government in which these people have power. [from a Greek word *aristos* meaning 'best' and *-cracy*]

aristocrat (a-**ris**-tə-krat) *noun* a member of the aristocracy, a noble.

aristocratic (a-ris-tə-**krat**-ik) *adjective* **1** to do with the aristocracy. **2** noble in style. **aristocratically** *adverb*

arithmetic [1] (ə-**rith**-mə-tik) *noun* **1** the part of mathematics concerned with numbers. **2** using numbers to count and calculate ♦ *His arithmetic is not very good.*

arithmetic [2] (a-rith-met-ik) or **arithmetical**
adjective to do with arithmetic or using
arithmetic. **arithmetically** adverb [from a
Greek word arithmos meaning 'number']

arithmetic mean noun see **mean** [3].

arithmetic progression noun a series of
numbers that increase or decrease by the
same amount each time, for example 1, 3,
5, 7, 9.

ark noun 1 the boat built by Noah at the
time of the Flood, according to the Bible.
2 a model of Noah's boat. [from a Latin
word arca meaning 'box']

Ark of the Covenant noun a wooden chest
in which the ancient writings of Jewish
Law were kept.

arm [1] noun 1 each of the two upper limbs of
the human body from the shoulder to the
hand. 2 a sleeve of a piece of clothing.
3 something shaped like an arm or
projecting from the main part of
something ♦ an arm of the sea. 4 each of
the raised parts of a chair, supporting the
arms of the person sitting in it. [an Old
English word]

arm [2] verb 1 to supply people with weapons.
2 to fit weapons to a vehicle or piece of
equipment. 3 to make a bomb ready to
explode.
arm noun each of the kinds of troops that
make up an army ♦ the Fleet Air Arm.
[from a Latin word arma meaning
'weapons']

armada (ar-**mah**-də) noun a fleet of
warships. **the Armada** or **the Spanish
Armada** the armada sent from Spain to
invade England in 1588. [a Spanish word
meaning 'navy', related to arm [2]]

armadillo (ar-mə-**dil**-oh) noun (**armadillos**) a
small burrowing animal of South America
with large claws and a body covered in
bony plates. [a Spanish word meaning
'little armed man']

Armageddon noun (ar-mə-**ged**-ən) 1 (in the
Bible) the scene of the final conflict
between good and evil at the end of the
world. 2 a decisive or catastrophic
conflict. [from Hebrew words meaning
'hill of Megiddo' (a place in ancient
Palestine)]

armament noun 1 the weapons and
equipment used by an army. 2 the
process of equipping armed forces for
war. [from a Latin word armamentum,
related to arm [2]]

armature (ar-mə-choor) noun 1 the rotating
coil of a dynamo or electric motor. 2 a
bar placed across the poles of a magnet to
preserve its power or transmit force to
support a load. 3 a framework round
which a clay or plaster sculpture is
modelled. [from a Latin word armatura
meaning 'armour', related to arm [2]]

armband noun 1 a band worn round the
upper part of an arm or sleeve. 2 an
inflatable plastic band worn round each
arm as a support in swimming.

armchair noun 1 a chair with arms or raised
sides. 2 (used with a noun) taking an
interest in an activity without any
practical experience of it ♦ an armchair
traveller.

armed forces or **armed services** plural
noun a country's army, navy, and air force.

armful noun (**armfuls**) as much as you can
hold in your arms.

armistice noun an agreement during a war
or battle to stop fighting for a time.
SYNONYMS: ceasefire, truce. [from Latin
words arma meaning 'weapons' and sistere
meaning 'to stop']

armlet noun an armband or bracelet.

armorial adjective to do with heraldry or
coats of arms. [from armory meaning
'heraldry', from an Old French word,
related to arm [2]]

armour noun 1 a metal covering formerly
worn to protect the body in fighting. 2 a
set of tough metal plates covering a
warship or military vehicle to protect it
from attack. 3 armoured fighting vehicles
collectively. [same origin as for arm [2]]

armoured adjective protected with armour
♦ an armoured car.

armoury (ar-mer-i) noun (**armouries**) 1 a
place where weapons and ammunition
are stored. 2 a supply of military weapons.

armpit noun a hollow under the arm below
the shoulder.

arms plural noun 1 weapons. 2 an emblem or
heraldic device. **up in arms** protesting
very strongly about something. [same
origin as for arm [2]]

arms control noun international
agreement to restrict the production of
military weapons.

arms race noun competition between
nations in developing and making more
powerful military weapons.

army noun (**armies**) **1** an organized military force equipped for fighting on land. **2** something compared to an army in being large or hostile ♦ an army of locusts. **3** a large group of people organized for a particular purpose ♦ an army of helpers. [via an Old French word armée from a Latin word armata meaning 'armed']

aroma (ə-roh-mə) noun a pleasant or special smell. **aromatic** (a-rə-mat-ik) adjective

aromatherapy noun the use of aromatic plant extracts and natural oils for medicinal and cosmetic purposes.

arose past tense of **arise**.

around adverb & preposition **1** all round, on every side, in every direction. **2** close at hand ♦ She's somewhere around. **3** about, approximately ♦ I'll be there around eight o'clock. [from a-² and round]

arouse verb **1** to waken from sleep. SYNONYMS: rouse, waken, awaken. **2** to stir up feelings. SYNONYMS: evoke, stir up, excite, stimulate, incite, provoke. [from rouse]

arpeggio (ar-pej-i-oh) noun (**arpeggios**) (Music) the notes of a chord played in succession instead of together. [from an Italian word arpa meaning 'harp' (because it is played this way on the strings of a harp)]

arrange verb **1** to put things into the right order or position. SYNONYMS: sort, order, put in order, classify, group. **2** to form plans or settle the details of something. SYNONYMS: plan, organize, fix. **3** to adapt a piece of music for voices or instruments other than those for which it was originally written, or to adapt a story or drama for broadcasting. **arrangement** noun **arranger** noun [from an Old French word, related to range]

arrangement noun **1** the process of arranging something. **2** something that has been arranged or organized ♦ It is too late to change the arrangements now. **3** the way in which something has been arranged.

arrant (a-rənt) adjective downright, out-and-out ♦ What arrant nonsense! [originally another form of the word errant meaning 'roving, wandering', as in arrant thief]

arras (a-rəs) noun a richly decorated tapestry or wall-hanging. [named after Arras, a town in France]

array verb **1** to arrange something in order

♦ The army was arrayed along the river. **2** to dress or clothe ♦ She was arrayed in her finest ball gown.

array noun **1** an impressive display of things ♦ There was a fine array of tools on the garage wall. SYNONYMS: display, show, collection, exhibition. **2** (Mathematics) an arrangement of figures or symbols in a grid or matrix. **3** (Computing) an arrangement of data in a computer. [from ad- and an old form of ready]

arrears plural noun money that is owed and should have been paid earlier. **in arrears** behind with a payment ♦ They are still in arrears with their rent ♦ The rent is in arrears. [from ad- and a Latin word retro meaning 'backwards', related to rear]

arrest verb **1** to seize someone suspected of having committed a crime and hold them by legal authority. SYNONYMS: seize, detain, apprehend, hold, take prisoner, take into custody, catch. **2** to stop or check a process or movement.

arrest noun **1** the act of arresting someone. **2** a stoppage. [from an Old French word, related to rest]

arrival noun **1** the act of arriving. **2** a person or thing that has arrived.

arrive verb **1** to reach a place you are going towards ♦ Some of the guests arrived early. SYNONYMS: appear, come; (informal) turn up, show up. **2** (said about an important moment) to come at last ♦ The day of the party arrived. **3** (said about a person) to be recognized as having achieved success in the world. **to arrive at** to come to a decision after discussion ♦ The two sides finally arrived at an agreement. [from an Old French word ariver meaning 'to reach the shore', from a Latin word ripa meaning 'shore']

arrogant (a-rə-gant) adjective proud and overbearing, thinking yourself to be superior. SYNONYMS: haughty, proud, conceited, boastful, bumptious, disdainful, self-important, vain; (informal) snooty. **arrogantly** adverb **arrogance** noun [from a Latin word arrogare meaning 'to claim' or 'to demand']

arrogate (a-rə-gayt) verb to claim or seize something for yourself without having the right to do so. **arrogation** noun [same origin as for arrogant]

arrow noun **1** a straight thin pointed stick for shooting from a bow. **2** a symbol of the outline of an arrow, used to show direction or position on a chart. [an Old English word, from Old Norse]

arrowhead *noun* the pointed end of an arrow.

arrowroot *noun* an edible starch prepared from the root of an American plant.

arsenal *noun* a store of weapons and ammunition. [from an Arabic word *dar-sinaa* meaning 'workshop']

arsenic (ar-sən-ik) *noun* **1** a brittle steel-grey chemical element (symbol As). **2** a highly poisonous white compound made from this. **arsenical** (ar-**sen**-ikəl) *adjective* [via Greek *arsenikon* from a Persian word *zar* meaning 'gold'. It was originally the name of arsenic sulphide, which is yellow]

arson *noun* the criminal act of deliberately setting fire to a house or other property. [from a Latin word *ardere* meaning 'to burn']

arsonist *noun* a person who is guilty of arson.

art [1] *noun* **1** the use of creative skill and imagination to produce something beautiful. **2** works such as paintings or sculptures produced by this skill. **3** any practical skill or ability ♦ *the art of sailing.* **4** cunning or artfulness.
arts *plural noun* subjects such as languages, literature, and history, dealing with human activity and creativity, as opposed to the sciences in which exact measurements and calculations are used.
the arts creative activity including painting, sculpture, music, literature, and dance. [from a Latin word *ars, artis*]

art [2] (*old use*) the present tense of **be**, used with *thou.*

art deco (**dek**-oh) *noun* a style of decorative art and architecture in the 1920s and 1930s, with strong colours and geometric patterns.

artefact (**ar**-ti-fakt) *noun* an object made by a human, especially a simple prehistoric tool or weapon. [from Latin words *arte factum* meaning 'made by art']

arterial (ar-**teer**-iəl) *adjective* of an artery.

arterial road *noun* an important main road.

arteriole *noun* a small artery.

arteriosclerosis (ar-teer-i-oh-skleer-**oh**-sis)
noun a condition in which the walls of arteries become harder and thicker so that blood circulation is hindered. [from *artery* and a Greek word *sklērōsis* meaning 'hardening']

artery *noun* (**arteries**) **1** any of the tubes carrying blood away from the heart to all parts of the body. **2** an important route in a traffic system. [from a Greek word *artēria*]

artesian well (ar-**tee**-zhən) *noun* a well sunk vertically into a place where water will rise to the earth's surface by natural pressure. [named after *Artois*, a region in France]

artful *adjective* crafty, cunningly clever.
SYNONYMS: crafty, clever, cunning, knowing, astute, sly, shrewd, wily. **artfully** *adverb* **artfulness** *noun*

arthritis (arth-**riy**-tiss) *noun* a disease causing pain and stiffness in the joints. **arthritic** (arth-**rit**-ik) *adjective & noun* [from a Greek word *arthron* meaning 'joint']

arthropod (**arth**-rə-pod) *noun* an animal of the group that includes insects, spiders, and crustaceans, having divided bodies and limbs with joints. [from a Greek word *arthron* meaning 'joint' and *pous, podos* meaning 'foot']

Arthurian (ar-**thewr**-iən) *adjective* to do with King Arthur, legendary king of the Britons in the 5th or 6th century and leader of the Knights of the Round Table at his court at Camelot.

artichoke *noun* a plant with a large flower consisting of thick scales like leaves, used as a vegetable. [via Italian and Spanish from an Arabic word]

article *noun* **1** a particular or separate object ♦ *Articles of clothing lay on the floor.* SYNONYMS: item, piece. **2** a short self-contained piece of writing in a newspaper or magazine. SYNONYMS: item, piece, essay. **3** a separate clause or item in a contract or agreement. **4** (*Grammar*) a word, such as *a* or *the*, used before a noun to show what it refers to: see **definite article, indefinite article.**
article *verb* to bind an apprentice by the terms of an apprenticeship. [from a Latin word *articulus* meaning 'small connecting part', from *artus* meaning 'joint']

articulate [1] (ar-**tik**-yoo-lət) *adjective* **1** (said about a person) able to express ideas clearly, good with words. **2** (said about

language) spoken clearly, well expressed.
articulately *adverb* [same origin as for *article*]

articulate [2] (ar-**tik**-yoo-layt) *verb* **1** to say something clearly and distinctly ♦ *Articulate each word with care.* **2** to form a joint ♦ *This bone articulates with the next.* **articulation** *noun*

articulated *adjective* (said about a vehicle, especially a large one) having sections connected by flexible joints.

artifice (ar-ti-fiss) *noun* a clever trick that is meant to mislead someone. [same origin as for *artificial*]

artificer (ar-tif-i-ser) *noun* a skilled craftsman or mechanic.

artificial *adjective* **1** made or done by human skill or effort as a copy of something natural. SYNONYMS: man-made, false, unnatural, bogus, faked, synthetic, unreal. **2** contrived or pretentious. SYNONYMS: insincere, pretentious, contrived, sham; (*informal*) phoney. **artificiality** (arti-fishi-al-iti) *noun* **artificially** *adverb* [from Latin words *ars* meaning 'art' and *facere* meaning 'make']

artificial insemination *noun* the injection of semen into the womb artificially so that conception can take place without sexual intercourse.

artificial intelligence *noun* the performance by computers of tasks normally needing human intelligence.

artificial respiration *noun* a process of stimulating natural breathing by forcing air into and out of the lungs, especially after injury.

artificial selection *noun* (*Biology*) the selective breeding of plants or animals in order to perpetuate certain desirable characteristics in the species.

artillery *noun* **1** large guns used in fighting on land. **2** the part of an army that uses large guns. **artillerist** *noun* [from an Old French word *atillier* meaning 'to equip' or 'to arm']

artisan (ar-ti-**zan**) *noun* a skilled worker or craftsman who makes things. [from an Italian word, related to *art*]

artist *noun* **1** a person who paints or produces other works of art. **2** a person who does something with great skill. **3** a professional entertainer.

artiste (ar-**teest**) *noun* a singer, dancer, or other professional entertainer. [a French word, related to *art*]

artistic *adjective* **1** showing the skill of an artist. SYNONYMS: creative, imaginative, attractive, tasteful, beautiful. **2** to do with art or artists. **artistically** *adverb*

artistry *noun* the skill of an artist.

artless *adjective* not artful, simple and natural. **artlessly** *adverb* **artlessness** *noun*

art nouveau (ar noo-**voh**) *noun* a style of art and architecture developed in the late 19th century, using ornamental and flowing designs. [a French phrase meaning 'new art']

arts and crafts *plural noun* decorative art and design used for practical purposes.

artwork *noun* pictures and other visual material included in a book or other publication.

arty *adjective* (**artier, artiest**) (*informal*) interested in the arts or in artistic design, especially in a showy or exaggerated way. **artiness** *noun*

arum (**air**-əm) *noun* a plant with arrow-shaped leaves and flowers consisting of a single petal-like part round a central spike. [via Latin from a Greek word *aron*]

arum lily *noun* a cultivated white arum.

Aryan (**air**-iən) *noun* **1** a member of a people who settled in northern India in the second millennium BC and spoke an Indo-European language. **2** (in Nazi Germany) a person of Caucasian and not Jewish descent.
Aryan *adjective* to do with the Aryans or their language. [from a Sanskrit word *arya* meaning 'noble']

as *adverb* **1** equally, in the same way ♦ *This one is just as good.*
as *preposition* in the function or role of ♦ *She was dressed up as an angel.*
as *conjunction* **1** at the same time that, when or while ♦ *We reached the platform as the train was leaving.* **2** because ♦ *As it's late we'd better go home now.* **3** in the way in which ♦ *Just leave it as it is.*
as *relative pronoun* that, who, or which ♦ *I had the same problem as you did.* **as for** with regard to ♦ *As for cabbage, I'd rather not have any.* **as if** or **as though** as it would be if ♦ *She said it as if she meant it.* **as it is** as things are, in the actual circumstances. **as it were** as if it was actually so ♦ *He*

became, as it were, a man without a country. **as well** in addition, too ♦ *I'm coming as well.* **as well as** in addition to. **as yet** until now, up to this time. [from an Old English word]

asbestos (ass-**best**-oss) *noun* a soft fibrous mineral substance that is made into fireproof material and used for heat insulation. [from a Greek word *asbestos* meaning 'unquenchable']

asbestosis (ass-best-**oh**-sis) *noun* a lung disease caused by inhaling asbestos particles.

ascend *verb* to go up or come up. SYNONYMS: climb, go up, come up, mount, scale. **to ascend the throne** to become king or queen. [from a Latin word *ascendere* meaning 'to climb up']

ascendancy (ǝ-**sen**-dǝn-si) *noun* the state of having great influence or being in control.

ascendant *adjective* ascending or rising. **in the ascendant** having greater control or influence.

ascension (ǝ-**sen**-shǝn) *noun* an ascent or going up.
Ascension in Christian belief, the ascent of Christ into heaven as witnessed by the Apostles and recorded in the New Testament.

ascent *noun* **1** ascending or going up. **2** a way up, an upward slope or path.

ascertain (ass-er-**tayn**) *verb* to find something out by asking or making enquiries. **ascertainable** *adjective* [from an Old French word *acertener*, from Latin *certus* meaning 'certain']

ascetic (ǝ-**set**-ik) *adjective* not allowing yourself any pleasures or physical comforts.
ascetic *noun* a person who leads a simple life without ordinary pleasures, often for religious reasons. **ascetically** *adverb* **asceticism** (ǝ-**set**-i-sizm) *noun* [from a Greek word *askētēs* meaning 'hermit']

ASCII (**as**- ki) *abbreviation* (*Computing*) American Standard Code for Information Interchange.

ascorbic acid (ǝ-**skor**-bik) *noun* vitamin C, found in citrus fruits and vegetables. [from a- and a Latin word *scorbutus* meaning 'scurvy']

ascribe (ǝ-**skryb**) *verb* to regard something as belonging to something else or caused by it ♦ *She ascribes her success to hard work.*

ascribable *adjective* **ascription** (ǝ-**skrip**-shǝn) *noun* [from ad- and a Latin word *scribere* meaning 'to write']

aseptic (ay-**sep**-tik) *adjective* clean and free from bacteria that cause things to become septic. **aseptically** *adverb* [from a-[1] and *septic*]

asexual (ay-**seks**-yoo-ǝl) *adjective* not having a sex or sex organs. **asexually** *adverb* [from a-[1] and *sexual*]

ash [1] *noun* the powder that is left after something has been burned. **the Ashes** a cricket trophy which England and Australia compete to win. **ashy** *adjective*

ash [2] **1** a tree with a silver-grey bark and leaves divided into several parts. **2** the hard pale wood of this tree. [from an Old English word]

ashamed *adjective* feeling great shame or guilt. SYNONYMS: sorry, remorseful, abashed, repentant, distressed, embarrassed, upset, mortified.

ashen *adjective* (said about a person's face) pale like ashes.

Ashkenazi (ash-ki-**nah**-zi) *noun* (**Ashkenazim**) a Jew of northern and eastern Europe (compare **Sephardi**). [named after *Ashkenaz*, a grandson of Noah in the Bible]

ashlar *noun* stonework for building, made of large square-cut stones. [via Old French from a Latin word *axilla* meaning 'little plank']

ashore *adverb* to or on the shore.

ashram *noun* a religious place in India where people go to learn and be restful, or a place modelled on this. [from a Sanskrit word *ashrama* meaning 'hermitage']

ashtray *noun* a small dish for putting tobacco ash into while smoking.

Asian (**ay**-shǝn) *adjective* to do with Asia, the continent extending from Europe to the Pacific Ocean.
Asian *noun* a person from Asia.

Asiatic (ay-si-**at**-ik) *adjective* situated in Asia, or coming from Asia.
◊ Use *Asian* when referring to people.

aside *adverb* **1** to or on one side ♦ *Please step aside.* **2** away, in reserve ♦ *I'm putting money aside for a holiday.*
aside *noun* (especially in acting) words spoken so that only certain people will hear them. **aside from** apart from.

asinine (**ass**-i-niyn) *adjective* very silly or foolish. **asininity** (ass-i-**nin**-iti) *noun* [same origin as for *ass*]

ask *verb* 1 to say something to get an answer, to address a question to someone. SYNONYMS: enquire (about something), find out (about something), question (someone). 2 to try to get something from someone ♦ *He has a favour to ask you* ♦ *We're asking £50 for it.* SYNONYMS: request, demand, seek, beg, implore. 3 to invite someone ♦ *I'm not going to ask him to the party.* **to ask for** to ask to be given something or to see someone. **to ask for it** or **to ask for trouble** to behave in a way that will cause trouble. [from an Old English word]

askance (ə-**skanss**) *adverb* **to look askance at** to regard someone or something with distrust or disapproval. [origin unknown]

askew *adverb* & *adjective* slightly crooked, not straight or level. [from *a-*[2] and *skew*]

asleep *adverb* & *adjective* 1 in or into a state of sleep. 2 (said about a limb) numbed ♦ *My foot is asleep.*

AS level *noun* Advanced Subsidiary level, an examination in England and Wales intermediate between GCSE and A level.

asp *noun* a small poisonous snake. [from a Greek word *aspis*]

asparagus (ə-**spa**-rə-gəs) *noun* a plant with tender shoots that are cooked and eaten as a vegetable. [from a Greek word *asparagos*]

aspect *noun* 1 one part or feature of a situation or event ♦ *The violence was the worst aspect of the crime.* SYNONYMS: part, feature, element, side, facet. 2 the look or appearance that a person or thing has ♦ *The forest had a sinister aspect.* SYNONYMS: look, face, appearance, manner. 3 the direction a thing faces, or a side facing this way ♦ *The house has a southern aspect.* SYNONYMS: outlook, prospect, view. [from *ad-* and a Latin word *specere* meaning 'to look']

aspen *noun* a tree related to the poplar, with leaves that tremble. [from an Old English word]

asperity (ə-**spe**-riti) *noun* a harsh or severe manner or tone. [from a Latin word *asper* meaning 'rough']

aspersions (ə-**sper**-shənz) *plural noun* **to cast aspersions** to attack someone's reputation or honesty. [from *asperse* meaning 'to spatter (with water or mud)', from *ad-* and a Latin word *spergere* meaning 'to sprinkle']

asphalt (**ass**-falt) *noun* a black sticky substance like coal tar, used to make surfaces for roads.
asphalt *verb* to cover a surface with asphalt. [from a Greek word *asphalton*]

asphyxia (ə-**sfiks**-iə) *noun* suffocation caused by lack of air in the lungs. [from a Greek word meaning 'stopping of the pulse', from *sphuxis* meaning 'pulse']

asphyxiate (ə-**sfiks**-i-ayt) *verb* to suffocate someone or be suffocated. **asphyxiation** *noun*

aspic *noun* a clear savoury jelly used for coating meat, eggs, etc. [from a French word, related to *asp*. The colours of the jelly were compared to a snake]

aspidistra *noun* a house plant with broad tapering leaves. [from a Greek word *aspis* meaning 'shield']

aspirant (**ass**-pər-ənt) *noun* a person who has an ambition about something.

aspirate[1] (**ass**-per-ət) *noun* the sound of 'h'.

aspirate[2] (**ass**-per-ayt) *verb* to pronounce a sound with an h.

aspiration (ass-per-**ay**-shən) *noun* 1 a strong hope or ambition. 2 the action of aspirating a sound. 3 the drawing of breath.

aspire *verb* to have a strong hope or ambition about something ♦ *He aspires to become president* ♦ *She aspires to the presidency.* [from *ad-* and a Latin word *spirare* meaning 'to breathe']

aspirin *noun* (**aspirins** or **aspirin**) a medicinal drug used to relieve pain and reduce fever, or a tablet of this. [from the German name]

ass *noun* 1 an animal of the horse family, smaller than a horse and with longer ears. 2 (*informal*) a foolish person. [from a Latin word *asinus* meaning 'donkey']

assail (ə-**sayl**) *verb* 1 to attack someone violently. 2 to begin a task with determination. [from a Latin word *assilire* = leap upon]

assailant *noun* an attacker.

assassin *noun* a person who assassinates someone. [from an Arabic word meaning 'hashish-takers', a name given to a group of Muslims at the time of the Crusades, who were believed to take hashish before murdering Christian leaders]

assassinate *verb* to kill an important person by violent means, usually from political or religious motives. **assassination** *noun*

assault *noun* 1 a violent attack. SYNONYMS: attack, onslaught. 2 (*Law*) an act that threatens another person, whether or not the person is harmed.
assault *verb* to make an assault on someone. SYNONYMS: attack, beat, beat up, set on, mug. [same origin as for *assail*]

assay (ə-**say**) *noun* a test of metal or ore (especially of gold or silver used for coin or bullion) for quality.
assay *verb* to make an assay of something. [from French *essai* = trial]

assegai (**ass**-ig-iy) *noun* a light spear with an iron tip, used by South African peoples. [from an Arabic word *al-zagayah* meaning 'the spear']

assemblage *noun* 1 the process of assembling. 2 a collection of things or a group of people that have been brought together.

assemble *verb* 1 to bring people or things together into a group. SYNONYMS: gather, get together, bring together, collect; (*more formal*) convene. 2 to come together into a group. SYNONYMS: gather, come together, collect, group, meet; (*more formal*) convene, congregate. 3 to fit or put parts together to make something. SYNONYMS: construct, erect, make, build, fit together, put together. [from an Old French word *asembler*]

assembler *noun* (*Computing*) a program that translates instructions from a low-level language into a form that can be understood and executed by a computer.

assembly *noun* (**assemblies**) 1 the process of assembling. 2 a group of people who have come together for a purpose.

assembly language *noun* (*Computing*) a low-level computer language for translation by an assembler.

assembly line *noun* in a factory, a sequence of workers and machines that assemble a product in successive stages.

assent *verb* to consent or express agreement.
assent *noun* formal consent or approval. [from *ad-* and a Latin word *sentire* meaning 'to think' or 'to feel']

assert *verb* 1 to state something firmly ♦ *They asserted their innocence* ♦ *They asserted that they were innocent.* SYNONYMS: state, claim, contend, declare, argue, insist, maintain, proclaim. 2 to make other people recognize a claim or right ♦ *The country began to assert its independence.* SYNONYMS: declare, profess, enforce. **to assert yourself** to behave in a confident or forceful way; to insist on your rights. [from *ad-* and a Latin word *serere* meaning 'to join']

assertion *noun* 1 a forcefully made statement that something is a fact. 2 the process of asserting.

assertive *adjective* acting forcefully and with confidence. **assertively** *adverb* **assertiveness** *noun*

assess *verb* 1 to decide the value or quality of something. SYNONYMS: estimate, calculate, work out, evaluate, determine, gauge, reckon. 2 to set the amount of a tax or fine for a person or property. **assessment** *noun* [from a Latin word *assessor* meaning 'assistant judge']

asset (**ass**-et) *noun* 1 a piece of property that has money value and could be used or sold to pay debts. 2 a useful or valuable quality or skill. 3 a useful or helpful person. [from an Old French word *asez* meaning 'enough']

assiduous (ə-**sid**-yoo-əs) *adjective* hard-working and conscientious. **assiduously** *adverb* **assiduity** (ass-id-**yoo**-iti) *noun* [from a Latin word *assiduus*]

assign *verb* 1 to give or allot something to someone ♦ *Rooms were assigned to us on the first floor.* SYNONYMS: allocate, provide (for), give. 2 to appoint a person to perform a task ♦ *The police assigned a team of detectives to the case.* SYNONYMS: appoint, designate, choose. 3 to regard something as correct or suitable ♦ *We cannot assign an exact date to Stonehenge.* SYNONYMS: attribute, determine (for). **assignable** *adjective* [from *ad-* and a Latin word *signare* meaning 'to mark out']

assignation (ass-ig-**nay**-shən) *noun* an arrangement to meet, especially a secret one.

assignment noun 1 a task or piece of work that is assigned to someone, especially as part of a course of study. 2 the process of assigning.

assimilate verb 1 to absorb nourishment into the body. 2 to take in and understand information or ideas. 3 to absorb something into a system or organization. 4 to change a sound in a word so that it is close to another in the same word or the next word (as in ♦ cupboard, where p is assimilated to b). **assimilation** noun [from ad- and a Latin word similis meaning 'like']

assist verb to help someone. SYNONYMS: help, aid, support. **assistance** noun [from a Latin word assistere meaning 'to stand by']

assistant noun 1 a person who serves customers in a shop. 2 a person who assists in a task, a helper. **assistant** adjective ranking next below a senior person and helping them in their work ♦ an assistant manager.

associate [1] (ə-soh-si-ayt) verb 1 to spend a lot of time with certain people. 2 to have regular dealings with a group of people. 3 to connect things in the mind ♦ I always associate forests with Germany. [from ad- and a Latin word socius meaning 'ally']

associate [2] noun 1 a partner or colleague in business. 2 someone who has limited membership of an association or organization, and is not a full member. **associate** adjective 1 associated. 2 having limited membership of an organization.

association noun 1 a group of people organized for a special purpose. 2 being associated with other people; companionship. 3 a mental connection between ideas.

Association Football noun a form of football played with a round ball that may not be handled during play except by the goalkeeper.

associative (ə-soh-shə-tiv) adjective 1 involving association. 2 (Mathematics) (said about a mathematical operation) producing the same result regardless of the way the elements are grouped, e.g. (4 + 5) + 6 = 15, and 4 + (5 + 6) = 15.

assonance (ass-ən-əns) noun similarity of vowel sounds in words that do not completely rhyme, as in vermin and furnish. [from ad- and a Latin word sonus meaning 'sound']

assorted adjective including different sorts put together ♦ assorted chocolates. SYNONYMS: various, different, diverse, miscellaneous, mixed. [from an Old French word, related to sort]

assortment noun a collection made up of several sorts of things. SYNONYMS: collection, selection, mixture, variety.

assuage (ə-swayj) verb 1 to soothe an unpleasant feeling or make it less severe. 2 to satisfy a thirst or appetite. [from ad- and a Latin word suavis meaning 'pleasant']

assume verb 1 to accept without proof that something is true or sure to happen ♦ We assume that you will be coming tomorrow. SYNONYMS: suppose, presume, imagine, believe, guess, expect, gather. 2 to take on a duty or responsibility. SYNONYMS: undertake, take on. 3 to begin to show a particular facial expression ♦ Then she assumed a stern look. [from ad- and a Latin word sumere meaning 'to take']

assumption noun 1 assuming something. 2 something that is accepted without proof. **Assumption** in Roman Catholic belief, the reception of the Virgin Mary in bodily form into heaven, or the festival commemorating this on 15 August.

assurance noun 1 a formal declaration or promise that something is true or will happen. SYNONYMS: guarantee, pledge, promise. 2 a kind of life insurance. 3 confidence in yourself ♦ She acted with great assurance. ◊ Insurance companies use the term assurance for policies that pay a sum of money after a fixed number of years or on the death of the insured person; they use insurance for policies that pay money in the event of some misfortune such as fire, accident, or death within an agreed period. In popular usage the word insurance is used in both cases.

assure (ə-shoor) verb 1 to declare that something is true or will happen ♦ I assure you there is no danger. SYNONYMS: promise, guarantee, give your word to, tell. 2 to make something certain ♦ The medicine will assure a complete recovery. 3 to insure a life by means of a policy of assurance. **to assure yourself** to convince yourself about something ♦ He tried the door to assure himself that it was locked. [from ad- and a Latin word securus meaning 'secure']

assured (ə-**shoord**) *adjective* **1** certain or sure ♦ *Complete victory is assured.* **2** confident ♦ *She has an assured manner.* **3** payable under an assurance policy ♦ *The sum assured is £200,000.*

assuredly (ə-**shoor**-idli) *adverb* certainly.

aster *noun* a garden plant with flowers of various colours like daisies. [from a Greek word *astēr* meaning 'star']

asterisk *noun* a star-shaped symbol (*) used in writing or printing, especially to mark a footnote.
asterisk *verb* to mark writing or printing with an asterisk. [from a Greek word *asteriskos* meaning 'little star']

astern *adverb* **1** at or towards the back (or stern) of a ship or the tail of an aircraft. **2** (said of a ship's engine) backwards.

asteroid (**ass**-ter-oid) *noun* **1** any of several small planets revolving round the sun. **2** a starfish. [same origin as for *aster*]

asthma (**ass**-mə) *noun* a disease that is often caused by allergies and leads to coughing and difficulties in breathing. [from a Greek word *asthma*, from *azein* meaning 'to breathe hard']

asthmatic (ass-**mat**-ik) *adjective* to do with asthma, or suffering from asthma.
asthmatic *noun* someone suffering from asthma. **asthmatically** *adverb*

astigmatism (ə-**stig**-mə-tizm) *noun* a defect in an eye or lens, preventing proper focusing. **astigmatic** (ass-tig-**mat**-ik) *adjective* **astigmatically** *adverb* [from *a-*[1] meaning 'not' and a Greek word *stigma* meaning 'point']

astir *adverb* & *adjective* moving about excitedly. [from *a-*[2] and *stir*]

astonish *verb* to surprise someone very much. SYNONYMS: amaze, astound, surprise, stagger, shock, dumbfound, flabbergast. **astonishment** *noun* [from an Old French word *estoner*, from Latin words *ex-* meaning 'out of' and *tonare* meaning 'thunder']

astound *verb* to surprise someone so they feel shocked. SYNONYMS: astonish, amaze, surprise, stagger, shock, dumbfound, flabbergast. [same origin as for *astonish*]

astrakhan (astrə-**kan**) *noun* **1** the dark tightly-curled wool of lambs from Astrakhan in southern Russia. **2** a fabric imitating this wool.

astral (**ass**-trəl) *adjective* to do with the stars, or like stars. [from a Greek word *astron* meaning 'star']

astray *adverb* & *adjective* away from the right path or direction. **to go astray** (said about things) to be lost or mislaid. **to lead astray** to make someone do something wrong. [from an Old French word related to 'stray']

astride *adjective* having the legs wide apart, or on either side of something.
astride *preposition* with a leg on each side of ♦ *She sat astride a horse.*

astringent (ə-**strin**-jənt) *adjective* **1** causing skin or body tissue to contract. **2** harsh or severe.
astringent *noun* an astringent lotion, used as a cosmetic or to treat minor damage to the skin. **astringency** *noun* [from *ad-* and a Latin word *stringere* meaning 'to bind tightly']

astrolabe (**ass**-trə-layb) *noun* an instrument formerly used for measuring the altitudes of stars. [from a Greek word *astrolabos* meaning 'star-taking']

astrologer *noun* someone who studies astrology.

astrology (ə-**strol**-əji) *noun* the study of the movements of stars, and their supposed influence on human affairs and the natural world. **astrological** *adjective* **astrologically** *adverb* [from a Greek word *astron* meaning 'star' and *-logy*]

astronaut *noun* a person trained to travel in a spacecraft. [from Greek words *astron* meaning 'star' and *nautes* meaning 'sailor']

astronautics *noun* the study and technology of space travel.

astronomer *noun* someone who studies astronomy.

astronomical *adjective* **1** to do with astronomy. **2** huge, enormous ♦ *We won an astronomical sum of money.* **astronomically** *adverb*

astronomy (ə-**stron**-əmi) *noun* the study of the stars and planets and their movements. [from a Greek word *astron* meaning 'star' and *-nomia* meaning 'arrangement']

astute (ə-**stewt**) *adjective* able to judge people and situations well, shrewd. SYNONYMS: shrewd, canny, sharp, perceptive, acute, clever, quick. **astutely** *adverb*

astuteness *noun* [from a Latin word *astus* meaning 'cunning' (noun)]

asunder (ə-**sun**-der) *adverb* apart or into pieces ♦ *torn asunder*. [from an Old English word]

asylum *noun* 1 refuge and safety offered by one country to political refugees from another. 2 a place of refuge. 3 (*old use*) an institution for the care of mentally ill people. [from a Greek word *asulon* meaning 'refuge']

asymmetry (ay- **sim**- ət- ri) *noun* lack of symmetry. **asymmetric** *adjective* **asymmetrical** *adjective* **asymmetrically** *adverb*

asymptote (**as**-im-toht) *noun* a straight line that continuously approaches a curve but does not touch it. **asymptotic** (a-sim-**tot**-ik) *adjective* [from a Greek word *asumptōtos* meaning 'not falling together']

at *preposition* 1 expressing position ♦ *at the top of the hill*. 2 expressing time ♦ *Come at six o'clock*. 3 expressing a state or occupation ♦ *We felt at ease* ♦ *They are all at work*. 4 indicating a price, amount, or age ♦ *They are sold at £5 each* ♦ *She left school at 15*. 5 expressing a reason or cause ♦ *I was annoyed at losing*. 6 expressing direction towards something ♦ *He drove straight at us* ♦ *Aim at the target*. **at all** in any way, to any extent, of any kind ♦ *The machine is no use at all now*. **at once** immediately; at the same time. [from Old English *æt*]

atavistic (at-ə-**vis**-tik) *adjective* following or imitating something done by a remote ancestor. **atavism** (**at**-ə-vizm) *noun* [from a Latin word *atavus* meaning 'forefather']

ate past tense of **eat**.

atheist (**ayth**-ee-ist) *noun* a person who believes there is no God. **atheism** *noun* **atheistic** (ayth-ee-**ist**-ik) *adjective* [from *a*-[1] meaning 'not' and a Greek word *theos* meaning 'god']

athlete *noun* a person who takes part in athletic sports.

athlete's foot *noun* a form of ringworm affecting the skin between the toes.

athletic *adjective* 1 to do with athletics or athletes. 2 physically fit and strong and active. **athletically** *adverb* **athleticism** *noun*

athletics *plural noun* sports based on physical exercises such as running, jumping, etc. [from a Greek word *athlein* meaning 'to compete for a prize' (*athlon* = prize)]

athwart *adverb* & *preposition* across from side to side. [from *a*-[2] and *thwart*]

Atlantic *noun* the Atlantic Ocean, the ocean separating the Americas from Europe and Africa.
Atlantic *adjective* to do with the Atlantic Ocean.

atlas *noun* a book of maps. [named after the Titan Atlas, who was punished for his part in the Titans' revolt against Zeus by being made to support the heavens. Early atlases had a picture of Atlas at the front]

ATM *abbreviation* automated teller machine, a machine that provides cash and other banking services when a machine-readable card is inserted.

atman *noun* (in Hinduism) the human soul or individual self, the supreme principle of life in the universe, identified with Brahman. [a Sanskrit word meaning 'essence' or 'breath']

atmosphere *noun* 1 the mixture of gases surrounding the earth or other planet. 2 the air in a place. 3 the psychological environment that a person lives in, a feeling or tone conveyed by something ♦ *The room had an atmosphere of peace and calm*. 4 a unit of pressure, equal to the pressure of the atmosphere at sea level. **atmospheric** *adjective* [from a Greek word *atmos* meaning 'vapour' and *sphere*]

atmospheric pressure *noun* the pressure of the earth's atmosphere at a particular point.

atmospherics *plural noun* electrical disturbances in the atmosphere, causing crackling sounds or other interference in telecommunications.

atoll (**at**-ol) *noun* a ring-shaped coral reef around a lagoon. [from a Maldivian (the language of the Maldives) word *atolu*]

atom *noun* 1 the smallest particle of a chemical element. 2 this particle as a source of atomic energy. 3 an extremely small quantity or thing ♦ *There's not an atom of truth in it*. [from a Greek word *atomos* meaning 'indivisible']

atom bomb or **atomic bomb** *noun* a bomb in which the rapid release of atomic energy creates immense destructive power.

atomic adjective to do with an atom or atoms, or using the power of atoms.

atomic clock noun a device for recording time with extreme accuracy, regulated by the natural vibrations of an atom or molecule.

atomic energy noun energy obtained from nuclear fission.

atomic mass noun the mass of an atom measured in atomic mass units (each equal to one twelfth of the mass of an atom of carbon-12).

atomic number noun the number of protons in the nucleus of an atom, as a characteristic of a chemical element.

atomic theory noun the theory that all matter is made up of atoms.

atomic weight noun the ratio between the mass of one atom of an element or isotope and one-twelfth the weight of an atom of the isotope carbon-12.

atomize verb to reduce a substance to atoms or fine particles. **atomization** noun

atomizer noun a device for converting a liquid into a fine spray.

atonal (ay-toh-nəl) adjective (said about music) not written in a particular key and using all the notes of the chromatic scale. [from a-¹ and tonal]

atone verb to make amends, to make up for an error or deficiency. [from at one]

atonement noun the act of making amends.

ATP abbreviation 1 adenosine triphosphate, a substance in living cells that provides energy when it is converted into ADP. 2 automatic train protection.

atrium (ay-tri-əm) noun (**atria** or **atriums**) 1 the central court, with an open roof, of an ancient Roman house. 2 each of the two upper cavities in the heart that receive blood from the veins. [a Latin word]

atrocious (ə-troh-shəs) adjective 1 extremely wicked or cruel ♦ an atrocious act of vandalism. SYNONYMS: wicked, terrible, dreadful, brutal, savage. 2 (informal) very bad or unpleasant ♦ The weather has been atrocious. **atrociously** adverb [from a Latin word atrox meaning 'cruel']

atrocity (ə-tross-iti) noun (**atrocities**) 1 an

extremely wicked or cruel act. 2 (informal) something bad or revolting.

atrophy (at-rə-fi) noun (said about body tissue or an organ) the process of wasting away through undernourishment or lack of use.
atrophy verb (**atrophies, atrophied, atrophying**) to undergo this process, to waste away. [from a-¹ and a Greek word -trophia meaning 'nourishment']

atropine (at-rə-peen) noun a poisonous drug obtained from deadly nightshade. [from the Latin name for deadly nightshade, Atropa belladonna]

attach verb 1 to fix or join something to something else. SYNONYMS: fasten, fix, join, tie, connect, link, secure. 2 to appoint someone to a particular group or to do a particular job. 3 to associate a quality with something ♦ We attach little importance to the report's conclusions. 4 to be ascribed to something or associated with it ♦ No blame attaches to the company. **attachable** adjective [from an Old French word atachier meaning 'to fasten']

attaché (ə-tash-ay) noun a person who is attached to the staff of an ambassador with a special area of responsibility ♦ The cultural attaché at the British Embassy. [a French word meaning 'attached']

attaché case noun a small rectangular case for carrying documents etc.

attached adjective 1 fixed or fastened to something. 2 having a lot of affection or fondness for someone or something ♦ She is very attached to her vegetable garden.

attachment noun 1 the act of attaching or being attached. 2 something that is attached or forms an extra part of something. 3 affection or fondness.

attack verb 1 to act violently against someone, or to start a fight with them. SYNONYMS: assault, beat, beat up, set on, molest, mug. 2 to criticize someone strongly. 3 to have a harmful effect on something ♦ Rust attacks most metals. 4 to start on a task with energy.
attack noun 1 an act of attacking someone or something. SYNONYMS: assault, ambush, onslaught. 2 a piece of strong or hostile criticism. 3 a sudden onset of an illness ♦ an attack of jaundice. SYNONYMS: onset, fit, bout. **attacker** noun [via French from an Italian word attaccare meaning 'to join battle']

attain verb to succeed in doing or getting something. [from ad- and a Latin word tangere meaning 'to touch']

attainable adjective able to be attained or reached.

attainment noun 1 attaining. 2 something someone attains, a personal achievement.

attainment target noun the level a student should reach during a year's work.

attar (at-er) noun a fragrant oil made from flowers ♦ attar of roses. [from an Arabic word meaning 'perfume']

attempt verb to make an effort to achieve something ♦ I was attempting to finish my letters. SYNONYMS: try, endeavour, strive, seek.
attempt noun 1 an effort to achieve something. 2 an attack or an effort to overcome something. [from ad- and a Latin word temptare meaning 'to try']

attend verb 1 to be present at a place, especially on a regular basis ♦ Children attend school from the age of 5. 2 (attend to) to give care and thought to something ♦ I will attend to the matter immediately. SYNONYMS: deal with, take care of, handle. 3 to take care of someone or look after them ♦ Which doctor is attending you? 4 to accompany someone as an attendant. [from ad- and a Latin word tendere meaning 'to stretch']

attendance noun 1 the act of attending or being present. 2 the number of people present ♦ an attendance of 5,000.

attendant noun 1 someone who provides a service to the public. 2 someone who is present at an occasion.
attendant adjective happening at the same time or as a result.

attention noun 1 the act of applying the mind to something, mental concentration. 2 awareness ♦ Try not to attract attention. 3 consideration or care ♦ She will get every attention. 4 (attentions) things you do for someone out of kindness or romantic interest. 5 a position of readiness taken by a soldier, with the feet together and arms stretched downwards ♦ to stand to attention.

attention deficit disorder noun a disorder especially in children, involving hyperactivity, loss of concentration, and learning difficulty.

attentive adjective 1 paying close attention, watchful. SYNONYMS: alert, paying attention, watchful, vigilant, observant, awake. 2 showing a lot of consideration or courtesy to another person. **attentively** adverb **attentiveness** noun

attenuate (ə-ten-yoo-ayt) verb 1 to make something slender or thin. 2 to make something weaker or reduce its force or value. **attenuation** noun [from a Latin word attenuare meaning 'to make something slender']

attest (ə-test) verb 1 to provide clear proof of something. 2 to declare that something is true or genuine. **attestation** (at-ess-tay-shən) noun [from ad- and a Latin word testari meaning 'be a witness']

attic noun a room or space below the roof of a building. [originally the name of an ancient style of architecture, named after Attica, the part of Greece in which Athens was situated]

attire noun (formal) clothes.
attire verb (formal) **to be attired** to be dressed in clothes of a particular kind ♦ The old man was attired in a tweed jacket. [from an Old French word atirer meaning 'to equip']

attitude noun 1 a position of the body or its parts. 2 a way of thinking or behaving, especially one you have for quite a long time. SYNONYMS: opinion, feeling, view, viewpoint, outlook, standpoint. [via French from an Italian word attitudine meaning 'fitness' or 'posture']

attorney (ə-ter-ni) noun (**attorneys**) 1 a person, usually a lawyer, who is appointed to act on behalf of someone else in business or legal matters. 2 (North Amer.) a lawyer who is qualified to act for clients in a lawcourt. **power of attorney** the legal authority to act on behalf of someone else. [from an Old French word atorne]

Attorney-General noun (**Attorneys-General**) the chief legal officer in some countries, appointed by the government.

attract verb 1 to make someone interested or pleased ♦ They were attracted by the colourful stalls in the market. SYNONYMS: allure, entice, fascinate, charm. 2 to bring people in by offering something interesting ♦ The game attracted a large crowd. 3 to draw something by means of a physical force (the opposite of repel) ♦ Magnets attract metals. [from ad- and a Latin word tractum meaning 'pulled']

attraction noun 1 the process of attracting, or the ability to attract. 2 something that attracts people by arousing their interest or pleasure.

attractive adjective having a pleasing appearance or effect. SYNONYMS: appealing, pleasant, agreeable, charming, beautiful (person). **attractively** adverb **attractiveness** noun

attribute[1] (ə-trib-yoot) verb to say that something was made or done by a certain person or group of people ♦ The painting is attributed to Rembrandt. **attributable** adjective **attribution** (at-rib-yoo-shən) noun

attribute[2] (at-rib-yoot) noun 1 a quality that is characteristic of a person or thing ♦ Kindness is one of his attributes. 2 an object that is regularly associated with a person or thing ♦ A pair of scales is an attribute of Justice. [from ad- and a Latin word tribuere meaning 'to allot']

attributive (ə-trib-yoo-tiv) adjective (Grammar) (said about an adjective or noun) placed before the word it describes and expressing an attribute, e.g. 'old' in the old dog. (Compare **predicative**.) **attributively** adverb

attrition (ə-trish-ən) noun 1 wearing something away by rubbing. 2 a process of wearing down someone's strength or stamina by constant attack or pressure ♦ a war of attrition. [from a Latin word atterere meaning 'to rub']

atypical (ay-tip-ikəl) adjective not typical; not conforming to a type. [from a-[1] and typical]

aubergine (oh-ber-zheen) noun 1 the purple fruit of a tropical plant, used as a vegetable. 2 the colour of an aubergine. [via French from an Arabic word al-badinjan]

aubrietia or **aubretia** (aw-bree-shə) noun an evergreen rock plant having thick foliage and purple, pink, or white flowers. [named after the French botanist Claude Aubriet (1665–1742)]

auburn (aw-bern) noun a reddish-brown colour.
auburn adjective having this colour.

AUC abbreviation denoting a date reckoned from the foundation of Rome, traditionally in 753 BC. [an abbreviation of a Latin phrase ab urbe condita, meaning 'from the founding of the city']

auction noun a public sale in which items are sold to the highest bidder.
auction verb to sell goods by auction. [from a Latin word auctum meaning 'increased']

auctioneer noun a person who is in charge of an auction.

audacious (aw-day-shəs) adjective bold or daring. SYNONYMS: bold, daring, intrepid, brave, courageous. **audaciously** adverb **audacity** (aw-dass-iti) noun [from a Latin word audax meaning 'bold']

audible adjective loud enough to be heard. **audibly** adverb **audibility** noun [from a Latin word audire meaning 'to hear']

audience noun 1 the people who have come to hear or watch something, especially a public performance in a theatre or cinema. 2 the people watching a television programme. 3 people who can hear what is being said. 4 the people for whom a book or speech is intended. 5 a formal interview with a distinguished person. [same origin as for audible]

audio noun 1 the reproduction of sound by electronic means.

audio frequency noun a frequency comparable to that of ordinary sound (about 20 Hz to 20 kHz).

audio tape noun magnetic tape for recording sound.

audio-visual adjective (said of teaching aids) involving both sight and sound, especially video.

audit noun an official scrutiny of financial accounts to see that they are in order.
audit verb (audited, auditing) to examine a set of accounts. [from a Latin word audire meaning 'to hear' (because audits were originally done orally)]

audition noun a practical demonstration given by an actor, musician, or other performer to test whether they are suitable for a particular role or job.
audition verb 1 to test someone with an audition. 2 to be tested in an audition. [same origin as for audible]

auditor noun a person who audits financial accounts.

auditorium (awdit-or-iəm) noun (auditoriums) the part of a theatre or hall in which an audience sits.

auditory (aw-dit-er-i) adjective to do with with hearing.

au fait (oh **fay**) *adjective* knowing a subject well. [a French phrase meaning 'to the fact']

auger (**awg**-er) *noun* a tool like a large corkscrew, for boring holes in wood. [originally *nauger*, from an Old English word *nafogar*. The *n* was lost when *a nauger* was understood to be *an auger*]

aught (awt) *noun* (*old use*) anything ♦ *for aught I know*. [from an Old English word]

augment (awg-**ment**) *verb* to add to something or to increase it. **augmentation** *noun* [from a Latin word *augere* meaning 'to increase']

augmented *adjective* (*Music*) said about an interval that is one semitone greater than the corresponding major or perfect interval.

augur (**awg**-er) *verb* to foretell a result or outcome ♦ *This augurs well for the future*. SYNONYMS: bode, portend, presage.
augur *noun* a religious official in ancient Rome who interpreted omens as signs of divine approval or disapproval of a proposed action. [from a Latin word *augur*]

August *noun* the eighth month of the year. [named after Augustus Caesar, the first Roman emperor]

august (aw-**gust**) *adjective* deserving honour or respect. [from a Latin word *augustus* meaning 'majestic']

Augustan (aw-**gus**-tən) *adjective* **1** to do with the reign of Augustus, the first Roman emperor, especially as an important period of Latin literature. **2** denoting the classical style of English literature in the 18th century.

auk *noun* a diving seabird with short narrow wings. [from an Old Norse word *alka*]

auld lang syne *noun* (*Scottish*) days of long ago. [from Scottish words meaning 'old long since']

aunt *noun* **1** the sister of your father or mother, or your uncle's wife. **2** (*informal*) a child's unrelated woman friend. [via Old French from a Latin word *amita*]

auntie *noun* (*informal*) an aunt.

au pair (oh **pair**) *noun* a young person from abroad, usually a woman, who helps with housework and the care of children in exchange for board and lodging. [a French phrase meaning 'on equal terms']

aura (**or**-ə) *noun* the atmosphere associated with a person or place ♦ *an aura of happiness*. [from a Greek word meaning 'breeze']

aural (**or**-əl) *adjective* to do with the ear or hearing. **aurally** *adverb* [from a Latin word *auris* meaning 'ear']
◊ Do not confuse this word with **oral**, which has a different meaning.

aureole (aw-ri-**oh**-l) or **aureola** (aw-ri-**oh**-lə) *noun* **1** a halo round the head of a figure in a painting, to indicate holiness. **2** a corona round the sun or moon. [from the Latin phrase *aureola corona* meaning 'Latin crown']

au revoir (oh rə-**vwar**) *interjection* goodbye for the moment. [a French phrase meaning 'to the seeing again']

auricle (**or**-i-kəl) *noun* **1** the part of the ear that is outside the head. **2** an atrium of the heart. [from a Latin word *auricula* meaning 'little ear']

aurora (aw-**ror**-ə) *noun* bands of coloured light appearing in the sky at night and probably caused by electrical radiation from the north and south magnetic poles. [from a Latin word *aurora* meaning 'dawn']

aurora australis *noun* the southern lights, an aurora in the southern hemisphere. [from a Latin word *australis* meaning 'southern']

aurora borealis (bor-i-**ay**-lis) *noun* the northern lights, an aurora in the northern hemisphere. [from a Latin word *borealis* meaning 'northern']

auspices (**aw**-spis-iz) *plural noun* patronage or protection ♦ *under the auspices of the Red Cross*. [from a Latin word *auspicium* meaning 'omen']

auspicious (aw-**spish**-əs) *adjective* showing signs that indicate success. SYNONYMS: favourable, propitious. **auspiciously** *adverb*

austere (aw-**steer**) *adjective* **1** severe in manner or appearance. **2** simple and lacking any comforts. **austerely** *adverb* [from a Greek word *austēros* meaning 'severe']

austerity (aw-**ste**-riti) *noun* a time or condition of hardship.

Australopithecus (oss-trə-lə-**pith**-i-kəs) *noun* an extinct form of primitive human being from the Lower Pleistocene era. **Australopithecine** *adjective & noun* [from a Latin word *australis* meaning 'southern' and a Greek word *pithēkos* meaning 'ape']

authentic *adjective* genuine, known to be true ♦ *an authentic signature.* **authentically** *adverb* **authenticity** *noun* [from a Greek word *authentikos* meaning 'genuine']

authenticate *verb* to prove that something is genuine. **authentication** *noun* **authenticator** *noun*

author *noun* 1 the writer of a book, article, or report. 2 someone who develops a plan or policy. **authoress** *noun* **authorship** *noun* [from a Latin word *auctor* meaning 'originator']

authoritarian (awth-o-ri-**tair**-iən) *adjective* demanding strict obedience to authority and limiting personal freedom. **authoritarianism** *noun*

authoritative (awth-**o**-ri-tə-tiv) *adjective* having a lot of authority, reliable. **authoritatively** *adverb*

authority *noun* (**authorities**) 1 the power or right to give orders and make people obey. 2 the power to take action ♦ *The police have the authority to close down the premises.* 3 a person or group having power or authority. 4 a person or book that can provide reliable information. [same origin as for *author*]

authorize *verb* 1 to give someone the authority to do something ♦ *We authorize you to conclude the deal on our behalf.* 2 to give permission for something ♦ *Has someone authorized this payment?* **authorization** *noun*

Authorized Version *noun* the English translation of the Bible made in 1611 by order of King James I.

autism (**aw**-tizm) *noun* a form of mental illness in which a person withdraws into a private world of fantasy and is unable to communicate with others. **autistic** (aw-**tiss**-tik) *adjective* [from a Greek word *autos* meaning 'self' and *-ism*]

auto- *prefix* (changing to **aut-** before a vowel) 1 yourself, your own (as in *autobiography*). 2 by yourself or itself, automatic (as in *automobile*). [from a Greek word *autos* meaning 'self']

autobahn (**aw**-tə-bahn) *noun* a German, Austrian, or Swiss motorway. [a German word, from *Auto* meaning 'car' and *Bahn* meaning 'road']

autobiography *noun* (**autobiographies**) the story of a person's life written by that person. **autobiographical** *adjective*

autocracy (aw-**tok**-rə-si) *noun* government by one person with total power. [from *auto-* and a Greek word *kratos* meaning 'power']

autocrat (**aw**-tə-krat) *noun* 1 a person who rules with total power. 2 a dictatorial person. **autocratic** (aw-tə-**krat**-ik) *adjective* **autocratically** *adverb*

autocross *noun* the sport of motor racing over rough country and unmade roads.

Autocue *noun* (*trademark*) a device which displays a text for a television presenter to read on air.

auto-da-fé (aw-toh-da-**fay**) *noun* the judgement and execution of heretics in special ceremonies during the Spanish Inquisition of the 16th century. [a Portuguese word meaning 'act of the faith']

autofocus *noun* a device in a camera that sets the correct focus automatically.

autogiro (aw-tə-**jiy**-roh) *noun* (**autogiros**) an aircraft like a helicopter but with wings that are not powered and rotate in the slipstream. [from a Spanish word, from *auto-* meaning 'self' and *giro* meaning 'circular movement']

autograph *noun* 1 a person's signature, especially the signature of a famous person. 2 a literary or musical manuscript written in the author's or composer's own handwriting. 3 a document signed by its author.
autograph *verb* to write a signature on something, especially a book or document. [from *auto-* and *-graph*]

automated *adjective* controlled or operated by automation ♦ *The process is fully automated.*

automatic *adjective* 1 (said about a machine or device) working by itself without direct human control. 2 (said about a gun) firing repeatedly until pressure on the trigger is released. 3 done without thought or from habit.
automatic *noun* 1 an automatic machine or device. 2 a motor vehicle with an automatic gearbox. **automatically** *adverb* [from a Greek word *automatos* meaning 'self-operating']

automatic pilot *noun* a device in an aircraft to keep it on its course.

automation *noun* the use of automatic equipment in factories and other processes.

automaton (aw-**tom**-ə-tən) *noun* **1** a mechanical device made in imitation of a human being, a robot. **2** someone who acts mechanically or without thinking. [same origin as for *automatic*]

automobile (aw-təm-ə-beel) *noun* (*North Amer.*) a motor car. [from *auto-* and *mobile*]

automotive (aw-təm-**oh**-tiv) *adjective* to do with motor vehicles.

autonomy (aw-**tonn**-ə-mi) *noun* **1** independence or self-government. **2** the freedom to act as you want to. **autonomous** *adjective* [from *auto-* and a Greek word *nomos* meaning 'law']

autopilot *noun* an automatic pilot in an aircraft.

autopsy (**aw**-top-si) *noun* (**autopsies**) a post-mortem examination of a body to find out the cause of death. [from a Greek word *autopsia* meaning 'seeing with your own eyes']

autostrada (aw-tə-**strah**-də) *noun* (**autostradas**) an Italian motorway. [an Italian word, from *auto* meaning 'motor car' and *strada* meaning 'road']

auto-suggestion *noun* the process of acting on your own subconscious thoughts and ideas.

autotrophic (aw-tə-**trof**-ik) *adjective* (said about bacteria) obtaining energy from light and able to assimilate carbon dioxide. [from *auto-* and a Greek word *trophē* meaning 'nourishment']

autumn *noun* the season between summer and winter. **autumnal** (aw-**tum**-nəl) *adjective* **autumnally** *adverb* [from a Latin word *autumnus*]

auxiliary (awg-**zil**-yer-i) *adjective* providing extra help or support. **auxiliary** *noun* a helper. **auxiliaries** *plural noun* foreign or allied troops used by a country in wartime. [from a Latin word *auxilium* meaning 'help']

auxiliary verb *noun* a verb such as *do*, *have*, and *will*, which is used to form parts of other verbs, for example *have* in *Have you finished?*

auxin (**awk**-sin) *noun* a hormone that stimulates the growth of plants. [from a Greek word *auxein* meaning 'to increase']

AV *abbreviation* Authorized Version (of the Bible).

avail *verb* to be of help or advantage ♦ *Nothing availed against the storm.* **to avail yourself of** to make use of something. **avail** *noun* **of** or **to no avail** having no use or benefit. [from a Latin word *valere* meaning 'to be strong']

available *adjective* ready to be obtained or used. SYNONYMS: obtainable, ready. **availability** *noun*

avalanche (**av**-ə-lahnsh) *noun* **1** a mass of snow or rock falling rapidly down a mountainside. **2** a large number of things coming at once ♦ *We've had an avalanche of letters.* [from a French word, from *avaler* meaning 'to descend']

avant-garde (av-ahn **gard**) *adjective* using a new style or approach, especially in art or literature. **avant-garde** *noun* an avant-garde group, or set of ideas. [a French word meaning 'vanguard']

avarice (**av**-er-iss) *noun* greed for wealth or gain. **avaricious** (av-er-**ish**-əs) *adjective* **avariciously** *adverb* [from a Latin word *avarus* meaning 'greedy']

avatar (**av**-ə-tar) *noun* (in Hinduism) the appearance on earth of a deity in human, animal, or superhuman form. [from a Sanskrit word *avatara* meaning 'descent']

Ave Maria (ah-vay mə-**ree**-ə) *noun* a prayer to the Virgin Mary in Catholic worship, a Hail Mary. [from the Latin words that open the prayer, meaning 'Hail, Mary']

avenge *verb* to take vengeance for a wrong that someone has done. **avenger** *noun* [from an Old French word *avengier*, related to *vindicate*]

avenue *noun* **1** a wide street or road, often one lined with trees. **2** a way of achieving something or making progress ♦ *There are other avenues to fame.* [from a French word *avenir* meaning 'to approach']

aver (ə-**ver**) *verb* (**averred**, **averring**) to state something definitely, to assert a fact. [from a Latin word *verus* meaning 'true']

average *noun* **1** a number obtained by adding several quantities together and dividing the total by the number of quantities. **2** the standard or level regarded as usual. **3** (*Law*) the allocation of responsibility for the costs arising from damage to a ship or its cargo. **average** *adjective* **1** found by making an average. **2** ordinary or usual ♦ *people of average intelligence*. SYNONYMS: ordinary, usual, normal, typical, standard, everyday,

commonplace. **3** not very good, mediocre.
average verb **1** to have as an average ♦ *The car averaged 40 miles to the gallon.* **2** to calculate the average of several quantities. [from an Arabic word meaning 'damage to a ship or cargo']

averse (ə-verss) adjective opposed to doing something ♦ *They seem averse to hard work.* [same origin as for *avert*]

aversion (ə-ver-shən) noun **1** a strong dislike. **2** something you dislike.

avert (ə-vert) verb **1** to turn something away ♦ *People averted their eyes.* SYNONYMS: deflect, turn away. **2** to prevent something bad or unwelcome ♦ *They managed to avert a disaster.* SYNONYMS: forestall, prevent, stave off, fend off, ward off. [from *ab-* meaning 'away' and a Latin word *vertere* meaning 'to turn']

Avesta (ə-vest-ə) noun the sacred writings of Zoroastrianism. [from a Persian word]

aviary (ay-vi-er-i) noun (**aviaries**) a large enclosure or building for keeping birds. [from a Latin word *avis* meaning 'bird']

aviation (ay-vi-ay-shən) noun the practice or business of flying aircraft. [from a Latin word *avis* meaning 'bird']

aviator (ay-vi-ay-ter) noun a pilot, especially in the early days of aviation.

avid (av-id) adjective eager or greedy. SYNONYMS: keen, eager, enthusiastic, fervent. **avidly** adverb **avidity** (ə-vid-iti) noun [from a Latin word *avere* meaning 'to long for']

avionics (ay-vi-on-iks) noun the use of electronic equipment in aviation.

avocado (av-ə-kah-doh) noun (**avocados**) a pear-shaped tropical fruit with a rough skin and thick smooth flesh. [via Spanish from a Nahuatl (Central American) word]

avocet (av-ə-set) noun a black and white wading bird with long legs and an upturned bill. [via French from an Italian word *avosetta*]

Avogadro's constant or **Avogadro's number** (av-ə-gad-rohz) noun (*Chemistry*) the number of atoms or molecules in one mole of a substance, equal to 6.023×10^{23}. [named after Amadeo Avogadro, 1776–1856, an Italian physicist famous for his work on gases]

avoid verb **1** to keep yourself away from something or someone dangerous or undesirable. SYNONYMS: evade, stay clear of, shun. **2** to refrain from doing something ♦ *Try to avoid making them angry.* SYNONYMS: refrain from, abstain from. **avoidable** adjective **avoidance** noun [from an Old French word *evuider* meaning 'to get rid of']

avoirdupois (av-er-dew-poiz) noun a system of weights based on the pound of 16 ounces or 7,000 grains. [from a French phrase *aveir de peis* meaning 'goods of weight']

avow verb (*formal*) to admit something or declare it openly. **avowal** noun **avowedly** (ə-vow-idli) adverb [via Old French from a Latin word *advocare* meaning 'to call in defence']

avuncular (ə-vunk-yoo-ler) adjective kind and friendly towards someone younger, like an uncle. [from a Latin word *avunculus* meaning 'uncle']

AWACS (ay-waks) abbreviation airborne warning and control system, a long-range radar system.

await verb **1** to wait for something ♦ *I await your reply.* **2** to be about to happen to someone ♦ *A surprise awaited us.* [from an Old French word, related to *wait*]

awake verb (**awoke, awoken**) **1** to wake up, to stop sleeping. **2** to become active. **3** to rouse someone from sleep.
awake adjective **1** not yet asleep, or no longer asleep. **2** alert or aware ♦ *The explorers were awake to the dangers around them.* [from an Old English word, related to *wake*]

awaken verb **1** to wake up, to stop sleeping. **2** to rouse someone from sleep. **3** to make someone experience a feeling ♦ *The sound awakened fears in all of them.* **awakening** noun

award verb to give someone an amount of money, a prize, or a penalty by an official decision.
award noun something given in this way, such as a sum of money or a prize. [from an Old French word]

aware adjective knowing or realizing something. SYNONYMS: conscious (of), sensitive (to). **awareness** noun [from an Old English word]

awash adjective washed over by water or waves. [from *a-²* and *wash*]

away adverb **1** to or at a distance, not at the usual place. **2** out of existence ♦ *The water had boiled away.* **3** constantly or continuously ♦ *We worked away at it.*

away *adjective* (said about a sports event) played at the opponent's ground ♦ *an away match*. [from an Old English word *aweg* meaning 'on one's way']

awe *noun* a mixed feeling of respect and fear or wonder. SYNONYMS: wonder, admiration, respect, reverence.
awe *verb* to fill someone with awe.

aweigh (ə-**way**) *adverb* (said about an anchor) hanging just clear of the sea bottom.

awesome *adjective* 1 inspiring awe.
2 (*informal*) very good.

awestricken or **awestruck** *adjective* filled with awe or wonder.

awful *adjective* 1 very bad or unpleasant ♦ *There has been an awful accident*. SYNONYMS: bad, severe, unpleasant, terrible, dreadful, horrible, nasty. 2 (*informal*) extreme, very great ♦ *This is an awful nuisance*. **awfully** *adverb* [from *awe* and *full*]

awhile *adverb* for a short time.

awkward *adjective* 1 difficult to do or deal with. SYNONYMS: troublesome, inconvenient, difficult. 2 (said about a person) clumsy, having little skill. SYNONYMS: clumsy, inept, ungainly, gawky. 3 inconvenient or unsuitable ♦ *They arrived at a very awkward time*. 4 slightly embarrassed ♦ *I feel awkward about it*. SYNONYMS: embarrassed, uncomfortable, disconcerted, self-conscious. **awkwardly** *adverb* **awkwardness** *noun* [from an Old Norse word *afugr* meaning 'turned the wrong way']

awl *noun* a small pointed tool for making holes in leather or wood. [from an Old English word]

awning *noun* a sheet of canvas or plastic stretched over a frame and fixed over a doorway or shop window as a protection against the sun or rain. [origin unknown]

awoke past tense of **awake**.

awoken past participle of **awake**.

AWOL (**ay**- wol) *abbreviation* absent without leave.

awry (ə-**riy**) *adverb* 1 twisted towards one side. 2 not as you intended, amiss ♦ *Our plans have gone awry*.
awry *adjective* crooked or wrong. [from *a-*[2] and *wry*]

axe *noun* 1 a large chopping tool with a heavy blade. 2 (*informal*) dismissal or redundancy ♦ *When the business closes, 30 staff will face the axe*.

axe *verb* to dismiss people or end a project suddenly. **to have an axe to grind** to have a personal interest in wanting to do something. [from an Old English word *aex*]

axial *adjective* forming an axis, or round an axis ♦ *axial rotation*. **axially** *adverb*

axil *noun* (*Botany*) the angle formed where a leaf joins a stem or branch. [from a Latin word *axilla* meaning 'armpit']

axillary (**aks**-il-er-i) *adjective* 1 in the armpit. 2 (*Botany*) growing from an axil. [same origin as for *axil*]

axiom (**aks**-i-əm) *noun* a truth or principle that is obviously true and that everyone accepts. [from a Greek word *axiōma*]

axiomatic (aks-i-əm-**at**-ik) *adjective* obviously true, self-evident.

axis *noun* (**axes**) 1 an imaginary line through the centre of an object, round which the object rotates. 2 a line about which a regular figure is symmetrically arranged. 3 a reference line for measuring coordinates. **the Axis** the alliance between Germany and Italy in the Second World War. [from a Latin word *axis* meaning 'axle']

axle *noun* a bar or rod on which a wheel or set of wheels turns. [from an Old Norse word]

ayatollah (iy-ə-**tol**-ə) *noun* a Shiite Muslim religious leader in Iran. [from an Arabic word *ayatu-llah* meaning 'sign from God']

aye[1] (iy) *adverb* (*old or dialect use*) yes.
aye *noun* a vote in favour of a proposal.
the ayes have it those voting in favour are in a majority.

aye[2] (ay) *adverb* (*old use*) always.

azalea (ə-**zay**-liə) *noun* a flowering shrub with brightly coloured flowers. [from a Greek word *azaleos* meaning 'dry' (because azaleas grow best in dry soil)]

azimuth (**az**-i-məth) *noun* 1 an arc of the sky from the zenith to the horizon. 2 the angle between this arc and the meridian. 3 the angle or direction of a compass bearing. [from an Arabic phrase *al samt* meaning 'the way']

Aztec *noun* 1 a member of an Indian people of Mexico before the Spanish conquest of the 16th century. 2 the language of this people.

Aztec *adjective* relating to the Aztecs or their language. [via Spanish from an Aztec word meaning 'person of Aztlan', their legendary home]

azure (**az**-yoor) *noun* a bright sky blue.
azure *adjective* having this colour. [via Old French from an Arabic word]

Bb

B 1 the second letter of the English alphabet. 2 (*Music*) the seventh note of the diatonic scale of C major. 3 (*Chemistry*) the symbol for boron.

BA *abbreviation* Bachelor of Arts.

baa *noun* the cry of a sheep or lamb. [an imitation of the sound]

babble *verb* 1 to talk quickly without making sense. 2 to make a continuous murmuring sound ♦ *a babbling brook.*
babble *noun* babbling talk or sound. [an imitation of the sound]

babe *noun* 1 (*poetic*) a baby. 2 (*informal*) an attractive young woman. [same origin as for *baby*]

babel (**bay**-bəl) *noun* a confused noise made by a lot of people talking at the same time. [from the Tower of *Babel* in the Old Testament, a high tower built in an attempt to reach heaven. God confused the languages of its builders so that they could not understand one another]

baboon *noun* a large African or Asian monkey with a long snout and large teeth. [from an Old French word *babuin*]

baby *noun* (**babies**) 1 a very young child or animal. 2 a timid or childish person. 3 (used before a noun) small of its kind ♦ *a baby helicopter.* 4 (*informal*) something that you have created and that means a lot to you ♦ *The drama group is really my baby.*
baby *verb* (**babies, babied, babying**) to treat someone like a baby, to pamper them. **to be left holding the baby** (*informal*) to be left with a responsibility that you do not want. **babyhood** *noun* [probably from the sounds a baby makes when it first tries to speak]

babyish *adjective* like a baby ♦ *Don't be so babyish!*

baby-sit *verb* (**baby-sat, baby-sitting**) to look after a child in its home while its parents are out.

baby-sitter *noun* a person who looks after a child in its home while its parents are out.

bachelor *noun* a man who has not married.
Bachelor *noun* a person who has taken a first degree at a university or college ♦ *Bachelor of Arts.* [from an Old French word *bacheler* meaning 'a young man aspiring to knighthood']

bacillus (bə-**sil**-əs) *noun* (**bacilli** (bə-**sil**-I)) a rod-like bacterium. [from a Latin word *baculus* meaning 'stick']

back¹ *noun* 1 the part or surface of something that is furthest from the front.
SYNONYMS: rear, end, stern (of a ship). 2 the rear surface of the human body from the shoulders to the buttocks. 3 the corresponding part of an animal's body.
SYNONYMS: hindquarters, rear, tail. 4 the part of a chair etc. that your back rests against when you sit down. 5 the part of a piece of clothing that covers the back. 6 a defending player near the goal in football, hockey, rugby, etc.
back *adjective* 1 situated at or near the back ♦ *the back teeth* ♦ *back streets.* 2 to do with your back ♦ *back pain.* 3 to do with a time in the past ♦ *back pay.*
back *adverb* 1 at or towards the back, away from the front or centre. 2 to the place you have come from ♦ *Go home back.* 3 in or to an earlier time or position ♦ *I'll be back at six* ♦ *Put the clocks back one hour.* 4 in return or in reply ♦ *Can you ring me back?* **the back of beyond** a very remote place. **back to front** with the back placed where the front should be. **behind someone's back** without a person knowing and in an unfair way. **to have your back to the wall** to be fighting for survival in a desperate situation. **on the back burner** not getting immediate attention. **to see the back of** (*informal*) to be rid of someone or something. **to turn your back on someone** to ignore someone or refuse to help them. [from an Old English word *baec*]

back² *verb* 1 to go or move backwards ♦ *I backed slowly out of the room.* 2 to make something move backwards ♦ *She backed the car into the garage.* 3 to give your support or help to someone. 4 to give financial support to something ♦ *He is backing the play.* 5 to put a bet on a horse, team, etc. ♦ *Did any of you back the winner?* 6 to cover the back of something ♦ *The rug* *is backed with canvas.* **7** (said about the wind) to change gradually in an anticlockwise direction. (Compare **veer**.) **to back down** to give up a claim, to withdraw your argument. **to back out** to refuse to do what you agreed to do. **to back someone up 1** to confirm something that someone else has said ♦ *I'm sure Emma will back me up.* **2** to give your support or help to someone. **to back something up** in computing, to make a spare copy of a file, disk, etc. to be stored in safety separately from the original ♦ *Make sure you back up your work at the end of each day.* **backer** *noun*

backache *noun* a pain in your back.

backbeat *noun* a strong accent on a beat of the bar that is not normally accented.

backbencher *noun* a Member of Parliament who does not hold an important position and is not entitled to sit on the front benches. (Compare **front-bencher**.)

backbiting *noun* saying unkind or nasty things about a person who is not present.

backblocks *plural noun* (*Austral.*) (*NZ*) land in the remote interior of a country.

backbone *noun* **1** the column of small bones down the centre of the back, the spine. **2** the people who give most support to an organization or institution ♦ *They are the backbone of the choral society.* **3** strength of character, courage.

backchat *noun* (*informal*) cheeky or rude remarks.

back-cross *noun* a cross between a hybrid plant or animal and of the same genetic type as one of its parents.

backdate *verb* to arrange for something such as a pay increase to be valid from some date in the past.

backdrop *noun* **1** a large painted cloth hung at the back of a stage set. **2** the setting or background for an event, story, etc.

backfire *verb* **1** (said about a car or its engine) to make a loud noise because of an explosion in the exhaust pipe. **2** (said about a plan or action) to go wrong and produce an undesired effect on the people who originated it.

backgammon *noun* a game played with draughts and dice on a double board marked with 24 triangular points. [from *back* (because sometimes pieces must go

back to the start) and an Old English word *gamen* meaning 'game']

background *noun* **1** the back part of a scene or picture, the setting for the main objects or people. **2** a person's family, upbringing, education, experience, etc. ♦ *She comes from a farming background.* **3** the circumstances and events surrounding and influencing something ♦ *Let me give you the background to this case.* **background** *adjective* (said about sounds, music, etc.) not very noticeable, used as an accompaniment to a play or film etc.

backhand *noun* a stroke in tennis etc. made with the back of the hand turned outwards. **backhand** *adjective*

backhanded *adjective* **1** made with the back of the hand turned outwards. **2** (said about a compliment or remark) ambiguous and suggesting some criticism behind the praise.

backhander *noun* **1** a backhanded stroke or blow. **2** (*informal*) a bribe.

backing *noun* **1** support for something ♦ *This campaign has the backing of the major political parties.* **2** a musical accompaniment to a pop singer. **3** material used to line the back of something.

backlash *noun* **1** a strong and hostile reaction by a lot of people to some event or development. **2** a recoil in machinery, excessive play between parts.

backless *adjective* **1** without a back. **2** (said about a dress) cut low at the back.

backlog *noun* an amount of work that should have been finished but is still waiting to be dealt with.

back number *noun* an old issue of a magazine or periodical.

backpack *noun* **1** a rucksack. **2** a package of equipment carried on the back.

backpacker *noun* a person who travels long distances with a backpack.

back-pedal *verb* (**back-pedalled**, **back-pedalling**) **1** to move the pedals of a bicycle backwards in order to brake. **2** to reverse your previous opinion or action, usually quickly.

back seat *noun* a seat at the back, especially in a car. **to take a back seat** to allow someone else to be in charge.

back-seat driver noun (informal) 1 a passenger in a car who keeps giving advice to the driver in an annoying way. 2 a person who has no responsibility but is eager to give orders to someone who has.

backside noun (informal) the buttocks.

backslide verb to slip back from good behaviour or habits into bad.

backspace verb to move a computer cursor one space back.
backspace noun the key on a computer keyboard used to move the cursor backwards.

backstage adverb behind the stage of a theatre, in the wings or dressing-rooms.
backstage adjective to do with this area in a theatre.

backstreet noun a small or minor street in a town.
backstreet adjective done secretly or illicitly.

backstroke noun a swimming stroke in which you lie on your back and lift your arms alternately back over your head.

backtrack verb 1 to go back the same way that you came. 2 to reverse your previous position or opinion.

back-up adjective kept in reserve in case it is needed.
back-up noun in computing, a spare copy of a file, disk, etc. made to be stored in safety separately from the original.

backward adjective 1 directed behind you or towards the back ♦ a backward glance. 2 having made less than normal progress. 3 diffident, lacking confidence ♦ She's not backward in expressing herself in class. 4 slow at learning or developing.
backward adverb backwards, away from the front. **backwardness** noun [from an old word abackward, from aback]
◊ The adverb backward is mainly used in American English. Backwards is the usual adverb in British English.

backwards adverb 1 away from the front, towards the back. 2 with the back facing forwards. 3 in reverse order ♦ Count backwards from 20. **to know something backwards** to know something very well indeed.

backwash noun a backward flow of water.

backwater noun 1 a stretch of stagnant water joining a stream. 2 a quiet place that has not been affected by progress or new ideas.

backwoods noun 1 remote uncleared forest, as in North America. 2 a remote or backward area. **backwoodsman** noun

backyard noun 1 a yard at the back of a house. 2 (North Amer.) a back garden.

bacon noun salted or smoked meat from the back or sides of a pig. **to save someone's bacon** (informal) to help someone escape death or injury. [via Old French from a Germanic word 'ham or flitch', related to back]

bactericide (bak-teer-i-siyd) noun a substance that kills bacteria. **bactericidal** adjective [from bacterium and a Latin word caedere meaning 'to kill']

bacteriology noun the scientific study of bacteria. **bacteriological** adjective **bacteriologist** noun [from bacterium and -logy]

bacterium (bak-teer-iəm) noun (bacteria) a microscopic organism. **bacterial** adjective [from a Greek word baktērion meaning 'little rod or cane']
◊ Note that it is a mistake to use the plural form bacteria as if it were the singular. It is incorrect to say 'a bacteria' or 'this bacteria'; correct usage is this bacterium or these bacteria.

bad adjective (**worse, worst**) 1 of poor quality or a low standard ♦ bad light ♦ The roads are bad round here. SYNONYMS: poor, awful, substandard, hopeless, (informal) lousy. 2 unpleasant or upsetting ♦ I have some bad news. 3 serious or severe ♦ a bad accident. SYNONYMS: dreadful, terrible, appalling. 4 wicked or evil. SYNONYMS: immoral, corrupt, villainous, sinful. 5 guilty or ashamed ♦ I feel bad about forgetting to invite you. 6 unhealthy or harmful ♦ Too much cholesterol is bad for you. 7 in ill health, diseased ♦ bad teeth ♦ How's your bad leg? 8 decayed or rotten ♦ This meat has gone bad. 9 (said about a debt) not able to be repaid.
bad adverb (North Amer.) (informal) badly ♦ Is he hurt bad? **not bad** (informal) quite good. **badness** noun [bad is probably from Old English; worse and worst are from an Old English word wyrsa, related to war]

bad blood noun ill feeling or enmity.

baddy noun (**baddies**) (informal) a villain in a film, book, etc.

bade past tense of **bid**².

bad form noun behaviour that offends against social conventions.

badge noun a piece of metal, cloth, plastic, etc. with a design on it, that you wear as a sign of who you are, what you belong to, or what you support. [origin unknown]

badger noun an animal of the weasel family that burrows in the ground and has a black and white head.
badger verb to keep asking someone to do something, to pester them. [perhaps from badge (because of the markings on a badger's head. The verb comes from the old sport of tormenting badgers)]

badinage (bad-in-ahzh) noun witty conversation. [from French badiner meaning 'to joke']

badlands plural noun a region of barren eroded land.

bad luck noun 1 misfortune. 2 an expression of real or mock sympathy at someone's misfortune.

badly adverb (**worse, worst**) 1 in an inferior, unsuitable, or defective way ♦ This book is badly written. 2 causing much injury, severely ♦ He was badly wounded. 3 (informal) very much ♦ I badly wanted to win the match.

badminton noun a game in which players use rackets to hit a light object called a shuttlecock across a high net. [named after Badminton in SW England, where the game was first played in about 1870]

bad-tempered adjective having or showing bad temper. SYNONYMS: short-tempered, irascible, irritable, testy, grumpy, crotchety.

baffle verb to puzzle or bewilder someone. SYNONYMS: perplex, mystify, fox, puzzle, bewilder, confound, stump.
baffle noun a screen placed in order to block or control the passage of sound, light, or fluid. **bafflement** noun [origin unknown, perhaps related to French words meaning 'to ridicule' or 'to deceive']

BAFTA (baf- tə) abbreviation British Academy of Film and Television Arts.

bag noun 1 a container made of flexible material with an opening at the top, used for holding or carrying things. 2 the contents of a bag, or the amount it contains. 3 the amount of game shot by a hunter.
bag verb (**bagged, bagging**) 1 to put something into a bag or bags. 2 to kill or catch a bird or animal ♦ They each bagged a pheasant. 3 (informal) to get something or stake a claim to it before anyone else can.

bags plural noun 1 folds of loose skin under the eyes. 2 (informal) plenty ♦ There's bags of room upstairs. **to be in the bag** (informal) to be as good as won or achieved. [from an Old Norse word]

bagatelle (bag-ə-tel) noun 1 a game in which you try to hit small balls into numbered holes on a board, with pins as obstructions. 2 something small and unimportant. [from an Italian word bagatella]

bagel (bay-gəl) noun a ring-shaped bread roll. [from a Yiddish word beygel]

bagful noun (**bagfuls**) as much as a bag will hold.

baggage noun all the suitcases and bags you take on a journey. [from either of the two Old French words bagage, from baguer meaning 'to tie up', or bagues meaning 'bundles']

baggy adjective (**baggier, baggiest**) (said about clothes) hanging in loose folds. **baggily** adverb **bagginess** noun

bagpipe or **bagpipes** noun a musical instrument with air stored in a bag and pressed out through pipes.

Baha'i (bah-hah-i) noun 1 a religion founded in Persia in the 19th century by Baha'ullah (1817–92) and his son, whose quest is for world peace and the unification of mankind. 2 a follower of this religion. **Baha'ism** noun [a Persian word, from an Arabic word baha' meaning 'splendour']

bail [1] noun 1 money that is paid or promised as a guarantee that a person accused of a crime will return to stand trial, if he or she is released temporarily. 2 permission for a person's release if this money is paid or promised.
bail verb to provide bail for a person. **to bail someone out** to give someone financial help in an emergency. **to jump bail** (informal) to fail to appear for trial after being released on bail. **out on bail** released after bail has been paid or promised. [from an Old French word bail meaning 'custody, jurisdiction']

bail [2] noun either of the two cross-pieces resting on top of the three stumps in cricket. [from an Old French word baile meaning 'palisade, enclosure']

bail[3] *verb* to scoop water out of a boat. [from a French word *baille* meaning 'bucket']

bailey *noun* (**baileys**) the outer wall of a castle, or a courtyard enclosed by this wall. [same origin as for *bail*[2]]

bailiff *noun* **1** a law officer who helps a sheriff by serving writs and performing arrests. **2** an official who takes people's property when they owe money. [from an Old French word *baillif*, related to *bail*[1]]

Bairam (biy-**rahm**) *noun* either of two annual Muslim festivals, **Lesser Bairam** (which follows Ramadan) in the tenth month and **Greater Bairam** in the twelfth month of the Islamic year. [a Turkish word]

bairn *noun* (*Scottish*) a child. [from an Old English word *bearn*]

Baisakhi (biy-**sa**-ki) *noun* a major Sikh festival, commemorating the formation of the Khalsa in 1699. [from Sanskrit]

bait *noun* **1** food that is placed on a hook or in a trap to help catch fish or animals. **2** something that is meant to tempt or entice someone.
bait *verb* **1** to place bait on or in something ♦ *You will need to bait the trap.* **2** to torment a person or animal by jeering at them. **to rise to the bait** to react to a provocation or temptation just as you were meant to. [from an Old Norse word *beita* meaning 'to hunt or chase']

baize *noun* thick green woollen cloth, used for covering snooker and card tables. [same origin as for *bay*[5] (because the cloth was originally reddish-brown)]

bake *verb* **1** to cook food by dry heat, usually in an oven. **2** to make something hard by heating it ♦ *The clay pots are now baked in a kiln.* **3** (*informal*) to become extremely hot ♦ *I'm baking in this heat!* [from an Old English word *bacan*]

baked beans *plural noun* cooked haricot beans, usually tinned and prepared with tomato sauce.

bakelite (**bay**-kə-liyt) *noun* a kind of plastic. [named after its Belgian-American inventor Leo H. Baekeland (1863–1944)]

baker *noun* a person who bakes and sells bread.

baker's dozen *noun* thirteen. [from the former custom of allowing the retailer to receive thirteen loaves for each twelve paid for]

bakery *noun* (**bakeries**) a place where bread is baked for sale.

baking *adjective* (*informal*) (said about weather etc.) extremely hot.

baking powder *noun* a mixture of powders used as a raising agent for cakes etc.

baking soda *noun* sodium bicarbonate, used in baking.

Balaclava (bal-ə-**klah**-və) *noun* a woollen hood covering the head and neck and part of the face. [named after *Balaclava*, a village in the Crimea (because these hoods were worn by soldiers fighting near there during the Crimean War)]

balalaika (bala- **liy**- kə) *noun* a Russian stringed instrument like a guitar, with a triangular body and usually three strings. [from a Russian word]

balance *noun* **1** a steady position, with the weight or amount evenly distributed. **2** your ability to keep steady and not fall over ♦ *She has learned how to keep her balance on a bicycle* ♦ *I nearly lost my balance.* **3** the amount of one thing in excess of another ♦ *The balance of the evidence suggests she is guilty.* **4** a device for weighing things, with two scales or pans hanging from a crossbar. **5** the difference between money paid into an account and money taken out of it. **6** the money that remains to be paid after something has been partly paid for.
balance *verb* **1** to keep steady and not fall over ♦ *Can you balance an egg on its end?* ♦ *a photo of a gymnast balancing on one hand.* **2** to consider something by comparing two things; to compare the value of one thing with another. **3** to be or put or keep something in a state of balance ♦ *a balanced diet.* **4** to compare the debits and credits of an account and make the entry needed to make these equal. **5** to have the debits and credits of an account equal ♦ *The cash account doesn't balance.* **in the balance** with the outcome still uncertain. **on balance** taking everything into consideration. [from a Latin word *bilanx* meaning 'having two scale-pans']

balance of payments *noun* the difference between the amount paid to foreign countries for imports and the amount received from them for exports in a certain period.

balance of power *noun* **1** a situation in which states of the world have roughly equal power. **2** the power held by a small group when the larger groups are of equal strength to each other.

balance sheet *noun* a written statement of assets and liabilities.

balcony (**bal**-kəni) *noun* (**balconies**) **1** a platform with a rail or parapet, sticking out from an outside wall of a building. **2** an upper floor of seats in a cinema or above the dress circle in a theatre. **balconied** *adjective* [from an Italian word *balcone*]

bald *adjective* **1** having little or no hair on the top of the head. **2** (said about animals) lacking the usual hair or feathers of the species. **3** (said about tyres) with the tread worn away. **4** bare, without details ♦ *a bald statement*. **baldly** *adverb* **baldness** *noun* [origin unknown, but probably from an Old English word meaning 'white patch']

balderdash *noun* nonsense. [origin unknown]

balding *adjective* becoming bald.

bale[1] *noun* a large bundle of hay, straw, paper, etc. tied up tightly.
bale *verb* to make something into a bale or bales. **baler** *noun* [probably from Dutch, related to *ball*]

bale[2] *verb* **to bale out** to make a parachute descent from an aircraft in an emergency. [a different spelling of *bail*[3]]

baleful *adjective* menacing or harmful ♦ *a baleful influence*. **balefully** *adverb* [from an Old English word *balu* meaning 'evil']

balk (bawlk) *verb* & *noun* another spelling of **baulk**.

ball[1] *noun* **1** a solid or hollow sphere, especially one used in games. **2** material that has been gathered or wound into a round mass ♦ *a ball of string*. **3** a single delivery of the ball by the bowler in cricket or by the pitcher in baseball.
ball *verb* to squeeze or wind something so that it forms into a ball. **the ball of the foot** the rounded part of the foot at the base of the big toe. **on the ball** (*informal*) alert or competent. **to start the ball rolling** to start a discussion or activity. [from Old Norse]

ball[2] *noun* a formal party where people dance. **to have a ball** (*informal*) to enjoy yourself greatly. [same origin as for *ballet*]

ballad *noun* **1** a song or poem that tells a story. **2** a slow romantic pop song. [from an Old French word *balade*]

ballade (ba-**lahd**) *noun* a poem with sets of three verses each ending with the same refrain line. [an earlier spelling of *ballad*]

ballast (**bal**-əst) *noun* **1** heavy material placed in a ship's hold to make it more stable. **2** gravel or coarse stone used to form the bed of a railway or road. [probably from a Scandinavian language]

ball bearing *noun* **1** a bearing using small steel balls. **2** one of these balls.

ballcock *noun* a device with a floating ball that controls the water level in a cistern. [from *ball*[1] and *cock* meaning 'tap']

ballerina (ba-ler-**ee**-nə) *noun* a female ballet dancer. [from an Italian word meaning 'female dancing teacher']

ballet (**bal**-ay) *noun* **1** a form of dancing and mime to music, usually telling a story. **2** a performance of this. [from an Old French word *baler* meaning 'to dance']

ballistic (bə-**lis**-tik) *adjective* to do with objects that are fired through the air (*projectiles*) such as bullets and missiles. **to go ballistic** (*informal*) to become extremely angry. **ballistics** *plural noun* the scientific study of objects that are fired through the air (*projectiles*) and of firearms. [from a Greek word *ballein* meaning 'to throw']

ballistic missile *noun* a missile that is initially powered and guided and then falls under gravity on its target.

balloon *noun* **1** a small inflatable rubber pouch with a neck, used as a child's toy or a decoration. **2** a large usually round bag inflated with hot air or light gases to make it rise in the air, often carrying a basket in which passengers may ride. **3** a balloon-shaped line enclosing the words or thoughts of a character in a comic strip or cartoon.
balloon *verb* **1** to swell like a balloon. **2** to kick or hit a ball or other object high in the air. **3** to travel by balloon. [from French or Italian, related to *ball*[1]]

balloonist *noun* a person who travels by balloon.

ballot *noun* **1** a secret method of voting, usually by making a mark on a piece of paper. **2** a piece of paper on which a vote is made. **3** the number of such votes recorded.
ballot *verb* (**balloted, balloting**) to invite and arrange for people to vote for

something by ballot ♦ *The union is to ballot its members on this issue.* [from an Italian word *ballotta* meaning 'little ball' (because originally this kind of voting was by dropping small coloured balls into a container)]

ballot box *noun* a sealed container for ballot papers.

ballot paper *noun* a paper used in voting by ballot, usually having the names of candidates etc. printed on it.

ballpark *noun* (*North Amer.*) a baseball ground. **in the right ballpark** (*informal*) approximately correct or accurate.

ballpoint pen *noun* a pen with a tiny ball as its writing point.

ballroom *noun* a large room where dances are held.

ballyhoo *noun* extravagant publicity or fuss. [an American word of unknown origin]

balm (bahm) *noun* **1** a sweet-scented ointment used to soothe or heal the skin. **2** something that soothes or heals you. [same origin as for *balsam*]

balmy (bah-mi) *adjective* (**balmier, balmiest**) **1** (said about the weather) pleasantly warm ♦ *a balmy breeze.* **2** sweet-scented, like balm.

baloney (bə-**loh**-ni) *noun* (*informal*) nonsense.

balsa or **balsa wood** (bawl-sə) *noun* very lightweight wood from a tropical American tree, often used for making models. [from a Spanish word *balsa* meaning 'little raft' (because balsa was used for building rafts and small boats)]

balsam (bawl-səm) *noun* **1** a sweet-smelling soothing oil produced by certain trees. **2** a kind of flowering plant. [via Latin from a Greek word *balsamon*]

balti (**bawl**-ti) *noun* a type of Pakistani curry, cooked in a bowl-shaped pan. [from an Urdu word *balti* meaning 'pail']

baluster (**bal**-əster) *noun* each of the short stone pillars in a balustrade. [same origin as for *balustrade*]

balustrade (bal-əs-**trayd**) *noun* a row of short posts or pillars supporting a rail or strip of stonework round a balcony or terrace. [from an Italian word *balustra* meaning 'pomegranate flower' (because the pillars of a balustrade were the same shape as the flower)]

bamboo (bam-**boo**) *noun* a giant tropical grass with hollow stems, used for making furniture. [from a Malay word *mambu*]

bamboozle *verb* (*informal*) to mystify or trick someone ♦ *This puzzle has completely bamboozled me.* [origin unknown]

ban *verb* (**banned, banning**) to forbid something officially ♦ *She is banned from driving for a year.* SYNONYMS: prevent, prohibit, outlaw, bar.
ban *noun* an order that bans something ♦ *a ban on exporting beef.* [from an Old English word *bannan* meaning 'to summon by a public proclamation']

banal (bə-**nahl**) *adjective* so familiar or obvious that it is uninteresting ♦ *a banal remark.* SYNONYMS: commonplace, hackneyed, trite. **banality** *noun* [from an Old French word *ban* meaning 'proclamation or summons' (which applied to everyone and was therefore 'commonplace')]

banana *noun* **1** a long curved fruit with a yellow or green skin and whitish flesh. **2** the tropical tree which bears this fruit. [via Spanish and Portuguese from Mande, a group of languages spoken in West Africa]

banana republic *noun* (*informal*) a small country dependent on a single export such as fruit and regarded as economically unstable.

band[1] *noun* **1** a narrow strip or loop of something ♦ *a rubber band* ♦ *a band of cloud.* **2** a range of values, wavelengths, etc. within a series.
band *verb* to put a band on or round something. [via an Old French word *bande*, of Germanic origin; related to *bind*]

band[2] *noun* **1** a small group of musicians who play pop, rock, or jazz music. **2** a group of musicians who play brass, wind, or percussion instruments. **3** an organized group of people doing something together ♦ *a band of pickpockets.*
band *verb* to join together in an organized group ♦ *We all banded together to buy her a present.* [from an Old French word *bande*, related to *banner*]

bandage *noun* a strip of material for binding up a wound.
bandage *verb* to bind up a wound with a bandage. [from French, related to *band*[1]]

bandanna (ban-**dan**-ə) *noun* a large coloured handkerchief or neckerchief. [probably via Portuguese from Hindi]

b. & b. *abbreviation* bed and breakfast.

bandeau (**ban**-doh) *noun* (**bandeaux** (**ban**-doh)) a strip of material worn round the head to hold the hair in place. [from French]

bandicoot (**ban**- di- koot) *noun* an insect- eating marsupial animal of Australia and New Guinea. [from a Telugu (South Indian) word *pandikokku* meaning 'pig- rat']

bandit *noun* a member of a gang of robbers who attack travellers. **banditry** *noun* [from an Italian word *bandito* meaning 'outlawed or banned']

bandmaster *noun* the conductor of a brass band.

bandolier (band-ə-**leer**) or **bandoleer** *noun* a shoulder belt with loops or pockets for ammunition. [from a French word *bandoulière*]

bandsaw *noun* a power saw consisting of a toothed steel belt running over wheels.

bandsman *noun* (**bandsmen**) a member of a musical band, especially a brass or military band.

bandstand *noun* a covered platform for a musical band to play outdoors, usually in a park.

bandwagon *noun* **to jump on the bandwagon** to seek to join something that has suddenly become successful or popular ◆ *Now everyone seems to be jumping on the Green bandwagon.*

bandwidth *noun* a range of frequencies used to transmit radio or television signals.

bandy[1] *verb* (**bandies, bandied, bandying**) to pass a name, story, etc. from one person to another ◆ *The story has been bandied about for weeks.* **to bandy words** to quarrel with someone. [probably from French]

bandy[2] *adjective* (**bandier, bandiest**) (said about legs) curving apart at the knees. **bandiness** *noun* [from an old word *bandy* meaning 'a kind of curved hockey stick']

bane *noun* a cause of trouble, worry, or annoyance ◆ *Traffic jams are the bane of my life!* [from an Old English word *bana*]

bang *noun* 1 a sudden loud noise like that of an explosion. 2 a sharp blow or knock ◆ *a nasty bang on the head.*
bang *verb* 1 to shut or hit something noisily ◆ *Don't bang the door!* 2 to hit something sharply against something else, especially by accident ◆ *I banged my head on the door frame.* 3 to make a sudden loud noise like an explosion.
bang *adverb* 1 (*informal*) exactly ◆ *We arrived bang on time* ◆ *The lake is bang in the middle of the park.* [an imitation of the sound]

banger *noun* 1 a firework that explodes noisily. 2 (*informal*) a sausage. 3 (*informal*) a noisy old car.

bangle *noun* a bracelet of rigid material. [from a Hindi word *bangli* meaning 'glass bracelet']

banish *verb* 1 to send someone away from a country as a punishment. SYNONYMS: exile, expel, deport. 2 to dismiss something from your mind ◆ *You must banish all thoughts of failure.* **banishment** *noun* [via an Old French word *banir*, of Germanic origin; related to *ban*]

banister *noun* the uprights and handrail at the side of a staircase. [a different spelling of *baluster*, related to *balustrade*]

banjo (**ban**-joh) *noun* (**banjos**) a stringed instrument rather like a guitar with a round body. [originally a black American word]

bank[1] *noun* 1 a financial organization that looks after people's money, pays money out on a customer's order, makes loans, etc. 2 a place for storing a reserve supply of something ◆ *a blood bank.* 3 the store of money used in some board games.
bank *verb* 1 to put money into a bank. 2 to have a bank account ◆ *Where do you bank?* **to bank on** to base your hopes on something ◆ *We are banking on your support.* [from an Italian word *banca* meaning 'bench', referring to a money dealer's table]

bank[2] *noun* 1 the land at the side of a river or canal. 2 a raised mass of earth, sand, etc. 3 a long mass of cloud, snow, or some other soft substance. 4 a set of lights, switches, etc. arranged in a line.
bank *verb* 1 to build or form a bank. 2 to tilt sideways while making a turn ◆ *The plane banked as it prepared to land.* 3 to cover a fire with coal so that it keeps burning slowly. [from an Old Norse word *bakki*]

banker *noun* 1 a person who runs a bank. 2 the player who is in charge of the store of money in a board game.

bank holiday *noun* a day on which banks are officially closed, usually kept as a public holiday.

banking *noun* the business of running a bank.

banknote *noun* a piece of paper money issued by a bank.

bankrupt *adjective* declared by a lawcourt to be unable to pay your debts. The estate of a person who has been declared bankrupt can be sold off for the benefit of the people who are owed money.
bankrupt *noun* someone who has been declared bankrupt.
bankrupt *verb* to make someone bankrupt.
bankruptcy *noun* [from *bank*¹ and a Latin word *ruptum* meaning 'broken']

banner *noun* 1 a strip of cloth with an emblem or slogan on it, hung up or carried on a crossbar or between two poles in a procession etc. 2 a flag. [from an Old French word *baniere*]

banns *plural noun* a public announcement in a Christian church of a forthcoming marriage between two named people. [from *ban* meaning 'proclamation']

banquet *noun* an elaborate formal meal for a lot of people.
banquet *verb* (**banqueted, banqueting**) to give or take part in a banquet. [from an Old French word *banquet* meaning 'little bench']

banshee (**ban**-shee) *noun* in Irish legend, a female spirit whose wail was believed to foretell a death in a house. [from the Irish words *bean sídhe* meaning 'woman of the fairies']

bantam *noun* a kind of small chicken. [named after the district of *Bantam* in Java]

bantamweight *noun* in boxing, a weight (54 kg) between featherweight and flyweight.

banter *noun* good-humoured teasing.
banter *verb* to joke in a good-humoured way. [origin unknown]

Bantu (ban-**too**) *noun* (**Bantu** or **Bantus**) 1 a member of a group of central and southern African peoples. 2 the group of languages spoken by these peoples, including Swahili, Xhosa, and Zulu. [a Bantu word meaning 'people']

banyan (ban-yən) *noun* an Indian fig tree with spreading branches from which roots grow downwards to the ground and form new trunks. [from the Hindi word *baniya*, from the Sanskrit word *vanija* meaning 'merchant' (because merchants used to meet in a pagoda under this tree)]

baobab (**bay**-oh-bab) *noun* an African tree with a massive trunk and large edible pulpy fruit. [probably from an African language]

bap *noun* a soft flat bread roll. [origin unknown]

baptism *noun* the Christian ceremony in which a person is sprinkled with or immersed in water to symbolize purification and admission to the Christian Church. **baptismal** *adjective*

Baptist *noun* a member of a Protestant Christian Church believing that baptism should be by immersion and performed at an age when the person is old enough to affirm his or her own faith before witnesses.

baptistery (**bap**-tist-eri) *noun* (**baptisteries**) 1 the part of a church used for baptism. 2 a tank used in a Baptist chapel for baptism by immersion.

baptize *verb* to perform baptism on someone. [from a Greek word *baptizein* meaning 'to dip']

bar¹ *noun* 1 a long piece of something hard, especially metal ♦ *the bars of a cage.* 2 a block of something ♦ *a bar of soap* ♦ *a chocolate bar.* 3 a narrow strip or band ♦ *bars of colour.* 4 a barrier or obstacle ♦ *a bar to promotion.* 5 one of the small equal units into which a piece of music is divided, shown on a score by vertical lines across the stave ♦ *three beats to the bar.* 6 a room or counter where alcoholic drinks are served. 7 a place where drinks and snacks are served across a counter ♦ *a coffee bar.* 8 a small shop or stall selling a single type of commodity or service. 9 (**the Bar**) barristers thought of collectively, or the profession of being a barrister. 10 a sandbank. 11 a strip of silver given as an additional award of the same honour ♦ *DSO and bar.*
bar *verb* (**barred, barring**) 1 to fasten something with a bar or bars ♦ *The door was barred.* 2 to forbid someone doing something or going somewhere ♦ *He was barred from the club for a month.* 3 to block or obstruct something ♦ *Two large men barred the way.*
bar *preposition* except for ♦ *It's all over bar the shouting.* **bar none** without exception. **behind bars** in prison. **to be called to the Bar** to become a barrister. [from French]

bar[2] *noun* a unit of pressure used in meteorology, equivalent to 100,000 newtons per square metre. [from a Greek word *baros* meaning 'weight']

barb *noun* 1 the backward-pointing part of an arrow, fish hook, etc. that is designed to make it difficult to pull out. 2 a deliberately hurtful remark. 3 a small pointed projecting part or filament. [from a Latin word *barba* meaning 'beard']

barbarian *noun* 1 in ancient times, a member of a people not belonging to the Greek, Roman, or Christian civilizations. 2 an uncivilized or brutal person. [from a Greek word *barbaros* meaning 'babbling, not speaking Greek']

barbaric (bar-ba-rik) *adjective* extremely cruel or brutal. **barbarically** *adverb*

barbarism (bar-bə-rizm) *noun* 1 an uncivilized condition or practice. 2 extreme cruelty or brutality.

barbarity (bar-ba-riti) *noun* (**barbarities**) savage cruelty, or a savagely cruel act.

barbarous (bar-ber-əs) *adjective* uncivilized or cruel. **barbarously** *adverb*

barbecue (bar-bi-kew) *noun* (**barbecues, barbecued, barbecuing**) 1 a metal frame for grilling food over a charcoal fire outdoors. 2 an outdoor party at which food is cooked in this way. **barbecue** *verb* to cook food on a barbecue. [via Spanish from an Arawak (South American) word *barbacoa* meaning 'a wooden frame on posts']

barbed *adjective* 1 having a barb or barbs. 2 deliberately hurtful ♦ *a barbed comment*.

barbed wire *noun* wire with short sharp spikes at intervals, used to make fences.

barber *noun* a men's hairdresser. [from a Latin word *barba* meaning 'beard']

barbershop *noun* a kind of unaccompanied close harmony singing, usually for four male voices.

barbican *noun* an outer defence of a castle or city, especially a double tower over a gate or bridge. [from an Old French word *barbacane*]

barbiturate (bar-**bit**-yoor-ət) *noun* a kind of sedative drug.

barcarole (bar-kə-**rol** or -**rohl**) *noun* 1 a song traditionally sung by Venetian gondoliers. 2 a piece of music with a steady lilting rhythm. [from an Italian word *barca* meaning 'boat']

bar chart *noun* a graph on which quantities are represented by bars of equal width but varying height.

bar code *noun* a pattern of black stripes printed on goods, library books, etc. containing information that can be read by a computer.

bard *noun* (*literary*) a poet. **the Bard of Avon** Shakespeare. **bardic** *adjective* [a Celtic word]

bare *adjective* 1 not covered by clothes ♦ *She walked home in her bare feet*. SYNONYMS: naked, unclothed. 2 without the usual or natural covering ♦ *bare floorboards* ♦ *The trees were bare*. 3 plain, without details ♦ *the bare facts*. 4 empty of stores ♦ *The cupboard was bare*. 5 only just enough ♦ *a bare majority* ♦ *the bare necessities of life*.
bare *verb* to uncover or reveal something ♦ *The dog bared its teeth in a snarl*. **with your bare hands** without using tools or weapons. **bareness** *noun* [from an Old English word *bær*]

bareback *adjective* & *adverb* on a horse without a saddle.

barefaced *adjective* shameless or undisguised ♦ *That's a barefaced lie*.

barefoot *adjective* & *adverb* wearing nothing on the feet.

bareheaded *adjective* not wearing a hat.

barely *adverb* 1 scarcely, only just ♦ *I barely know him*. 2 plainly or scantily ♦ *The room was barely furnished*.

bargain *noun* 1 an agreement between two or more people about what each one will do for the other. 2 something that you buy cheaply.
bargain *verb* to discuss the terms of an agreement. **bargain for** or **on** to be prepared for or expect something ♦ *I didn't bargain on his arriving so early* ♦ *He got more than he bargained for*. **into the bargain** in addition to other things ♦ *She's a good actress, and a fine musician into the bargain*. [from an Old French word *bargaigner* meaning 'to trade']

barge *noun* a large flat-bottomed boat used for carrying goods on canals or rivers.
barge *verb* to push or knock against someone roughly or clumsily. **barge in** to intrude or interrupt rudely. [from a Latin word *barca* meaning 'boat']

barite (**bair**-ryt) *noun* barium sulphate.

baritone noun **1** a male singing voice between tenor and bass. **2** a singer with such a voice. [from a Greek word *barus* meaning 'heavy' and *tone*]

barium (bair-iəm) noun **1** a chemical element (symbol Ba), a soft silvery-white metal. **2** a chemical substance (a mixture of barium sulphate and water) which is opaque to X-rays. It is swallowed or injected into the digestive tract when this is to be X-rayed. [from a Greek word *barus* meaning 'heavy']

bark [1] noun the sharp harsh sound made by a dog, fox, or seal.
bark verb **1** (said about a dog, fox, or seal) to give a bark. **2** to speak in a sharp commanding voice ♦ *The sergeant barked out his orders.* [from an Old English word *beorc*, an imitation of the sound]

bark [2] noun the outer layer of a tree's trunk and branches.
bark verb **1** to peel bark from a tree. **2** to scrape the skin off part of your body accidentally ♦ *I barked my shin on the gate.* [from Old Norse]

barley noun a kind of cereal plant, used to make malt. [from Old English]

barley sugar noun a sweet made of boiled sugar, often shaped into twisted sticks.

barley water noun a drink made from pearl barley.

barmaid noun a woman who serves behind a bar, especially in a pub.

barman noun (**barmen**) a man who serves behind a bar, especially in a pub.

bar mitzvah (mits-və) noun the ceremony at which a Jewish boy who has reached the age of 13 takes on the responsibilities of an adult under Jewish law. [a Hebrew word meaning 'son of the commandment']

barmy adjective (**barmier, barmiest**) (*informal*) crazy or foolish. [from the word *barm* meaning 'yeast or froth']

barn noun a large farm building used for storing grain, hay, etc. or for housing livestock. [from the Old English words *bere ern* meaning 'barley house']

barnacle noun a kind of shellfish that attaches itself to underwater surfaces, such as rocks and the bottoms of ships. [from Latin]

barnacle goose noun an Arctic goose with a white face and black neck that visits Britain in winter.

barn dance noun **1** an informal gathering for country dancing. **2** a kind of country dance.

barn owl noun an owl with a heart-shaped face, often breeding and roosting in farm buildings.

barnyard noun a yard beside a barn.

barograph (ba-rə-grahf) noun a barometer that produces a graph showing the atmospheric pressure. [from a Greek word *baros* meaning 'weight' and *graph*]

barometer (bə-rom-it-er) noun **1** an instrument that measures atmospheric pressure, used for forecasting the weather. **2** something that indicates change ♦ *The housing market is a barometer of the economy.* **barometric** (barə-met-rik) adjective [from a Greek word *baros* meaning 'weight' and *meter*]

baron noun **1** a member of the lowest rank of the British nobility. **2** in the Middle Ages, a person who held lands or property from the king. **3** a powerful owner of an industry or business ♦ *a press baron.* [from a Latin word *baro* meaning 'man or warrior']

baroness noun a female baron or a baron's wife.

baronet noun a British nobleman ranking below a baron but above a knight, having the title 'Sir'. **baronetcy** noun [same origin as for *baron*]

baronial (bə-roh-niəl) adjective to do with or suitable for a baron ♦ *a grand baronial hall.*

barony noun (**baronies**) the rank or lands of a baron.

baroque (bə-rok) adjective to do with an ornate style of European architecture, art, and music of the 17th and 18th centuries. **baroque** noun the baroque style or period. [from French]

barrack verb to jeer at someone while they are performing or speaking.

barracks noun a large building or group of buildings for soldiers to live in. [from a Spanish word *barraca* meaning 'soldier's tent']

barracuda (ba-rə-koo-də) noun a large tropical sea fish with a slender body and large jaws and teeth. [from Spanish]

barrage (ba-rahzh) noun **1** an artificial barrier across a river, used especially to prevent flooding. **2** heavy continuous gunfire. **3** a large number of questions or complaints all coming at the same time. [from a French word *barre* meaning 'a bar']

barrage balloon *noun* a large balloon anchored to the ground, acting as an obstacle to enemy aircraft.

barre *noun* a horizontal bar that ballet dancers use to steady themselves while exercising. [a French word]

barrel *noun* **1** a large round container with flat ends, used for liquids. **2** a metal tube of a gun, through which the shot is fired. **3** a measure of mineral oil equal to about 159 litres (35 gallons or 42 US gallons). **barrel** *verb* (**barrelled, barrelling**) to put something into barrels. **over a barrel** in a helpless position. [from a Latin word *barriculus* meaning 'a small cask']

barrel organ *noun* a small pipe organ played by turning a handle, which rotates a cylinder studded with pegs that open the pipes to produce a tune. Barrel organs used to be played in the street.

barren *adjective* **1** (said about land) not fertile enough to produce crops. **2** (said about a plant or tree) not producing fruit or seeds. **3** (said about a woman or female animal) not able to bear young. **barrenness** *noun* [from an Old French word *barhaine*]

barricade *noun* a barrier, especially one that is put up hastily across a door or street. **barricade** *verb* to block a door or street with a barricade. [French, from a Spanish word *barrica* meaning 'barrel' (because barrels were sometimes used to build barricades)]

barrier *noun* **1** a fence or wall that prevents people or animals getting past. **2** an obstacle that prevents people communicating, making progress, or understanding something ♦ *At first the language barrier made it difficult for us to get to know one another.* [from an Old French word *barriere*]

barrier reef *noun* a coral reef close to the shore but separated from it by a channel of deep water.

barring *preposition* except for; if not for ♦ *We should arrive on time, barring accidents.*

barrister (ba-ris-ter) *noun* a lawyer entitled to represent clients in the higher courts. [originally one who was allowed to pass the *bar*, a partition separating qualified lawyers from students]

barrow[1] *noun* **1** a wheelbarrow. **2** a two-wheeled cart pulled or pushed by hand, especially one used by someone selling goods in the street. [from an Old English word *bearwe* meaning 'carrier']

barrow[2] *noun* a mound of earth built over a prehistoric grave. [from an Old English word *beorg* meaning 'hill']

bartender *noun* a barman or barmaid.

barter *verb* to trade by exchanging goods or services for other goods or services, not for money. **barter** *noun* trading by exchanging goods and services, not by buying and selling. [from an Old French word *barater*] ◊ This word does not mean 'to bargain'.

baryon (ba-ri-on) *noun* a heavy elementary particle, such as a nucleon. [from a Greek word *barus* meaning 'heavy']

barysphere (ba-ri-sfeer) *noun* the dense interior of the earth, including the mantle and the core. [from a Greek word *barus* meaning 'heavy' and *sphere*]

basal (bay-səl) *adjective* forming or belonging to the base or the lowest level of something.

basal metabolic rate *noun* the rate at which the body uses energy while at rest to maintain vital functions such as breathing and keeping warm.

basalt (ba-sawlt) *noun* a kind of dark rock of volcanic origin. **basaltic** (bə-sawl-tik) *adjective* [from a Greek word *basanos* meaning 'touchstone']

base[1] *noun* **1** the lowest part of something, the part on which it stands or is supported. SYNONYMS: foot, bottom, stand, support. **2** a starting point. SYNONYMS: foundation, basis. **3** the main place where someone works or stays. **4** a place from which an expedition, military operation, etc. is directed and where its supplies are stored. **5** a substance which can combine with an acid to form a salt. **6** the number on which a system of counting and calculation is based. 10 is the base of the decimal system and 2 is the base of the binary system. **7** a substance into which other things are mixed ♦ *Some paints have an oil base.* **8** a cream or liquid applied to the skin as a foundation for make-up. **9** each of the four corners that must be reached by a runner in baseball.

base verb **1** to use one thing as the foundation for something else ♦ *The film is based on a true incident.* SYNONYMS: found, ground, establish. **2** to put someone somewhere as the main place where they work or stay ♦ *Where are you based now?* [from a Latin word *basis* meaning 'base, pedestal']

base [2] adjective **1** dishonourable or despicable ♦ *base motives.* **2** not made of precious metal ♦ *base coins.* **basely** adverb **baseness** noun [from a French word *bas* meaning 'low']

baseball noun a team game in which runs are scored by hitting a ball and running round a series of four bases, played mainly in the USA and Canada.

base jump noun a parachute jump from a fixed point such as the top of a high building.

baseless adjective without foundation in fact ♦ *baseless rumours.*

baseline noun **1** a line used as a base or starting point. **2** the line at each end of a tennis court.

basement noun the lowest storey of a building, below ground level. [probably via Dutch from Italian, related to *base* [1]]

base metal noun a common metal that is not considered precious, such as copper, tin, or zinc.

base rate noun the rate of interest that a bank uses as a basis for fixing the rates it charges to borrowers or pays to investors.

bash verb (informal) **1** to strike someone or something violently ♦ *We bashed into the back of another car.* **2** to criticize someone severely.
bash noun **1** a violent blow or knock. **2** a party. **to have a bash** (informal) to have a try. [an imitation of the sound]

bashful adjective shy and easily embarrassed. SYNONYMS: shy, demure, diffident, timid. **bashfully** adverb **bashfulness** noun [same origin as for *abashed*]

Basic noun an easy-to-learn computer language that was formerly used widely on microcomputers. [from the initials of Beginners' All-purpose Symbolic Instruction Code]

basic adjective **1** forming a base or starting point ♦ *basic principles.* SYNONYMS:

fundamental, essential, rudimentary, elementary, key, main, chief. **2** being the minimum that is needed or offered, with no extras ♦ *basic rates of pay* ♦ *The food was okay, but a bit basic.*

basics plural noun the essential facts or principles of a subject or skill. [from *base* [1]]

basically adverb at the simplest or most fundamental level.

basil noun a sweet-smelling herb. [from an Old French word *basile*]

basilica (bə-zil-ikə) noun a large oblong church with two rows of columns and an apse at one end. [a Latin word meaning 'royal palace']

basilisk (baz-il-isk) noun **1** a mythical reptile said to be able to kill people just by looking at them. **2** a small tropical American lizard. [from a Greek word *basilikos* meaning 'a kind of snake']

basin noun **1** a large bowl for holding liquids or soft substances or for mixing food. **2** a washbasin. **3** the area from which water drains into a river ♦ *the Amazon basin.* **4** a sheltered area of water for mooring boats ♦ *a yacht basin.* **basinful** noun (**basinfuls**) [from an Old French word *bacin*]

basis noun (**bases**) **1** a foundation or support for an idea, belief, etc. SYNONYMS: foundation, principle, ground, core. **2** the way that something is arranged or organized ♦ *You will be paid on a weekly basis.* [from a Greek word *basis* meaning 'step, stepping']

bask verb **1** to sit or lie comfortably warming yourself in the sun. **2** to enjoy someone's approval. [perhaps related to an Old Norse word *batha* meaning 'to bathe']

basket noun **1** a container for holding or carrying things, made of strips of flexible material or wire woven together. **2** the hoop through which players try to throw the ball in basketball, or a point scored in this way. **3** an assorted set of things ♦ *a basket of currencies.* [from an Old French word *basket*]

basketball noun **1** a game in which goals are scored by throwing a ball through high nets at each end of the court. **2** the ball used in this game.

basketry noun the craft of making baskets.

basketwork noun **1** material woven in the

style of a basket. **2** the art of making this.

basmati noun (baz-**mahh**-ti) a kind of long-grain Indian rice. [from a Hindi word meaning 'fragrant']

Basque (bahsk) noun **1** a member of a people living in the western Pyrenees. **2** their language. [from a Latin word *Vasco*]

bas-relief (**bas**-ri-leef) noun a style of sculpture or carving in which a design projects slightly from a flat surface; low relief. [from a French word *bas* meaning 'low']

bass [1] (bayss) noun **1** the lowest male singing voice, or a singer with such a voice. **2** the lowest-pitched member of a group of similar musical instruments. **3** a bass guitar or double bass.
bass adjective of the lowest pitch in music. **bassist** noun [from *base*[2] meaning 'low']

bass [2] (bas) noun (**bass**) an edible fish of the perch family. [from Old English]

basset hound (**bas**-it) noun a dog with short legs and long drooping ears, used for hunting hares etc. [from a French word *bas* meaning 'low']

bassoon (bə-**soon**) noun a woodwind instrument with a deep tone. **bassoonist** noun [from an Italian word *basso* meaning 'low']

bastard noun **1** (old use) an illegitimate child. **2** (informal) an unpleasant or difficult person or thing.
bastard adjective (old use) **1** of illegitimate birth. **2** no longer in its pure or original form. **bastardy** noun [from Old French]

baste [1] (bayst) verb to moisten meat with fat or juices during cooking. [origin unknown]

baste [2] (bayst) verb (in needlework) to tack material with long loose stitches. [from an Old French word *bastir* meaning 'to sew lightly']

bastinado (bas-tin-**ay**-doh) noun punishment or torture by caning someone on the soles of their feet. [from a Spanish word *bastón* meaning 'stick, cudgel']

bastion (**bas**-ti-ən) noun **1** a projecting part of a fortification. **2** something that protects a belief or way of life ♦ *a bastion of democracy.* [from an Italian word *bastire* meaning 'to build']

bat [1] noun **1** a shaped piece of wood used to hit the ball in games such as cricket and baseball. **2** a turn at batting ♦ *Have you had a bat yet?*
bat verb (**batted, batting**) **1** (in cricket) to have a turn at hitting the ball with a bat. **2** to hit something with a bat or as if with a bat. **off your own bat** without prompting or help from another person. [from an Old English word *batt* meaning 'club, stick']

bat [2] noun a flying nocturnal mammal with membranous wings. [from a Scandinavian language]

bat [3] verb (**batted, batting**) to flutter♦ *She batted her eyelashes at him.* **to not bat an eyelid** to not show any surprise or concern. [from an old word *bate* meaning 'flutter']

batch noun **1** a number of people or things dealt with or produced at one time. **2** (*Computing*) a group of records processed as a single unit.
batch verb **1** to arrange things in sets or groups. **2** (*Computing*) to group items for processing as a batch. [originally a number of loaves baked at the same time, related to *bake*]

bated (**bay**-tid) adjective **with bated breath** anxiously; hardly daring to speak. [from *abate*]

bath noun **1** a large container for water, in which you sit to wash your whole body. **2** washing the whole of your body while sitting in water ♦ *I need a bath.* **3** water for this ♦ *My bath is getting cold.* **4** a liquid in which something is immersed, or its container ♦ *an eye bath* ♦ *an acid bath.*
bath verb to wash someone or yourself in a bath.
baths plural noun **1** a public swimming pool. **2** a building with rooms where baths may be taken. [from an Old English word, related to *bathe*]

bathe verb **1** to take a swim ♦ *We bathed in the sea every day.* **2** to wash something gently in liquid to clean or soothe it ♦ *You should immediately bathe your eyes in water.* **3** to make something bright all over ♦ *The fields were bathed in sunlight.*
bathe noun a swim. **bather** noun [from an Old English word, related to *bath*]

batholith (ba-**thə**-lith) noun a huge mass of igneous rock extending from near the earth's surface to an unknown depth, e.g. Dartmoor. [from *bathos* and a Greek word *lithos* meaning 'stone']

bathos (bay-thoss) *noun* a sudden change in mood from something important or serious to something trivial or ridiculous. [a Greek word meaning 'depth']

bathroom *noun* 1 a room containing a bath. 2 (*North Amer.*) a toilet.

bathysphere (ba-thi-sfeer) *noun* a spherical diving-vessel for deep-sea observation, lowered by cable from a ship. [from *bathos* and *sphere*]

batik (bat-ik or ba-teek) *noun* a method of printing coloured designs on textiles by waxing the parts that are not to be dyed, originating in Java. [from Javanese]

batman *noun* (**batmen**) a soldier acting as an officer's personal servant. [from an Old French word *bat* meaning 'packsaddle']

baton (bat-ən) *noun* 1 a thin stick used by the conductor of an orchestra or choir for beating time and giving instructions. 2 a short stick passed from runner to runner in a relay race. 3 a police officer's truncheon. [from French]

baton round *noun* a rubber or plastic bullet, used by police dealing with riots.

batsman *noun* (**batsmen**) a player who is batting in cricket.

battalion *noun* an army unit made up of several companies and forming part of a regiment. [from an Italian word *battaglia* meaning 'battle']

batten [1] *noun* a strip of wood or metal that fastens or holds something in place. **batten** *verb* to fasten something down securely by fixing battens across it. **to batten down the hatches** to prepare for a difficult time ahead. [from an Old French word *batre* meaning 'to beat']

batten [2] *verb* **to batten on someone** to thrive or prosper at the expense of someone else. [from Old Norse]

batter [1] *verb* 1 to hit someone or something hard and often ♦ *Our ship was being battered by the waves.* 2 to subject someone to repeated violence ♦ *battered wives.* **batter** *noun* a beaten mixture of flour, eggs, and milk, used for making pancakes or for coating food before frying it. [from a Latin word *battuere* meaning 'to beat']

batter [2] *noun* a player who is batting in baseball.

battering ram *noun* 1 a heavy object rammed against a door to break it down. 2 a heavy iron-headed beam formerly used in war to break down walls or gates.

battery *noun* (**batteries**) 1 a device consisting of one or more electric cells, used for storing and supplying electricity. 2 a set of similar or connected units of equipment. 3 a series of cages in which poultry or animals are kept close together ♦ *battery farming.* 4 a group of heavy guns on land or on a warship. 5 (*Law*) the crime of inflicting unlawful blows or a menacing touch on another person ♦ *assault and battery.* [same origin as for *batter* [1]]

battle *noun* 1 a fight between organized armed forces. 2 a difficult contest or struggle ♦ *a battle of wits.* **battle** *verb* to fight or struggle with someone or to achieve something. [same origin as for *batter* [1]]

battleaxe *noun* 1 a heavy axe used as a weapon in ancient times. 2 (*informal*) a formidable aggressive woman.

battle cry *noun* a cry or slogan used in a battle or contest.

battledore *noun* a small racket used with a shuttlecock in the volleying game **battledore and shuttlecock.** [perhaps from a Provençal word *batedor* meaning 'beater']

battledress *noun* the everyday uniform worn by soldiers.

battlefield or **battleground** *noun* a piece of ground on which a battle is or was fought.

battlements *plural noun* a wall built along the top of a castle wall (*parapet*) with gaps at intervals, originally for firing from. [from an Old French word *bataillier* meaning 'to fortify with movable defence turrets']

battleship *noun* a heavily armed warship.

batty *adjective* (**battier, battiest**) (*informal*) crazy. **battiness** *noun* [from *bat* [2]]

bauble *noun* 1 a bright, showy but cheap ornament. 2 a decorative ball hung on a Christmas tree. [from an Old French word *baubel* meaning 'toy']

baud (bawd) *noun* a unit for measuring transmission speed in electronic signals, corresponding to one signal per second. [named after a French engineer J. M. E. Baudot]

baulk (bawlk) *verb* 1 to hesitate to do something difficult ♦ *She baulked at the idea of confronting him.* 2 (said about a horse) to stop and refuse to go on ♦ *The horse baulked at the fence.* **3** to prevent someone from doing or getting something.

baulk *noun* **1** the area of a billiard table within which the cue balls are placed at the start of a game. **2** a roughly squared timber beam. [from Old Norse]

bauxite (bawk-siyt) *noun* the clay-like substance from which aluminium is obtained. [from *Les Baux*, a place in France, where it was first found]

bawdy *adjective* (**bawdier, bawdiest**) referring to sex in a humorous way. **bawdily** *adverb* **bawdiness** *noun* [from an old word *bawd* meaning 'a brothel-keeper']

bawl *verb* **1** to shout at someone. **2** to cry noisily. [an imitation of the sound]

bay [1] *noun* a place where the coastline curves inwards. [from an Old French word *baie*]

bay [2] *noun* **1** an area or compartment used for a particular purpose ♦ *a parking bay.* **2** a window area that sticks outwards from a wall. [from a Latin word *batare* meaning 'to gape']

bay [3] *verb* (said about a dog) to make a deep drawn-out cry, especially in pursuit of a hunted animal. **bay** *noun* the sound of baying. **at bay** trapped or cornered but defiantly facing attackers. **to hold** or **keep something at bay** to prevent something from reaching you or causing harm ♦ *Somehow they managed to keep poverty at bay.* [from an Old French word *abaiier* meaning 'to bark']

bay [4] *noun* a kind of laurel with deep-green leaves that are dried and used for seasoning. [originally denoting the laurel berry, from a Latin word *baca* meaning 'berry']

bay [5] *adjective* reddish-brown. **bay** *noun* a bay horse. [from a Latin word *badius*]

bayonet (bay-ŏn-it) *noun* a long blade that can be fixed to the muzzle of a rifle and used in hand-to-hand fighting. **bayonet** *verb* (**bayoneted, bayoneting**) to stab someone with a bayonet. [named after *Bayonne* in France, where it was first used]

bay window *noun* a window that sticks out from the outside wall of a house. [from *bay*[2]]

bazaar *noun* **1** a market place in a Middle-Eastern country. **2** a sale of goods to raise money for charity. [from a Persian word *bazar* meaning 'market']

bazooka (bŏ-**zoo**-kŏ) *noun* a portable weapon for firing anti-tank rockets. [from an earlier meaning 'a musical instrument rather like a trombone']

BBC *abbreviation* British Broadcasting Corporation.

BC *abbreviation* **1** (in dates) before Christ. **2** British Columbia.

BCE *abbreviation* (in dates) before the Common Era.

BCG *abbreviation* Bacillus Calmette-Guérin, an anti-tuberculosis vaccine.

be *verb* (**am, are, is, was, were, been**) **1** to exist or occupy a position ♦ *The shop is on the corner.* **2** to take place ♦ *The wedding is tomorrow.* **3** to have a certain nature, quality, or condition ♦ *This is a very scary film.* **4** to become ♦ *He wants to be a pilot.* **be** *auxiliary verb* used to form parts of other verbs ♦ *She is studying electronics* ♦ *They were all killed.* **to have been** to have come or gone as a visitor ♦ *Have you been to Madrid?* **the be-all and end-all** the aspect of something that is of greater importance than anything else. [from an Old English word]

be- *prefix* used to form verbs (as in *befriend*, *belittle*) or to strengthen their meaning (as in *begrudge*).

beach *noun* the part of the shore at the edge of the sea, covered with sand or pebbles. **beach** *verb* **1** to bring something on to a beach from out of the water. **2** (said about a whale) to become stranded on a beach. [probably from an Old English word]

beachcomber (**beech**-koh-mer) *noun* a person who searches beaches for articles of value. **beachcombing** *noun*

beachhead *noun* a fortified position established on a beach by an invading army.

beacon *noun* **1** a fire lit on the top of a hill as a signal. **2** a light used as a signal or warning. **3** a radio transmitter signalling the position of a ship, aircraft, etc. [from an Old English word, related to *beckon*]

bead *noun* **1** a small shaped piece of glass, stone, plastic, etc. pierced for threading with others on a string or wire, or for sewing on to fabric. **2** a drop of liquid on a

surface ♦ *beads of sweat.* **3** a small knob forming the front sight of a gun.
beads *plural noun* a necklace or rosary of beads. **to draw a bead on something** to take aim at something with a gun. [from an Old English word *gebed* meaning 'prayer' (because people kept count of the prayers they said by moving the beads on a rosary)]

beaded *adjective* **1** decorated with beads. **2** forming or covered with beads of moisture ♦ *His forehead was beaded with sweat.*

beading *noun* **1** a decoration of beads. **2** a moulding or carving like a series of beads. **3** a strip of material with one side rounded, used as a trimming on edges of wood.

beady *adjective* (**beadier, beadiest**) (said about eyes) small and bright. **beadily** *adverb*

beagle *noun* a small short-legged hound, sometimes used for hunting hares. **beagling** *noun* hunting hares with beagles. [from Old French, related to *bay*[3]]

beak *noun* **1** the hard horny part of a bird's mouth. **2** a part of something that resembles a bird's beak, such as the projecting part at the prow of an ancient warship. **3** (*informal*) a magistrate. **beaked** *adjective* [from a Latin word *beccus*, of Celtic origin]

beaker *noun* **1** a tall plastic cup, often without a handle. **2** a small open glass vessel with straight sides and a lip for pouring liquids, used in laboratories. [from an Old Norse word *bikarr* meaning 'cup']

beam *noun* **1** a long thick piece of squared timber or other solid material, supported at both ends and carrying the weight of part of a building or other structure. **2** a ray or shaft of light or other radiation. **3** a happy smile. **4** a narrow length of wood used for balancing exercises in gymnastics. **5** a ship's breadth at its widest part. **6** the crossbar of a balance, from which the scales hang.
beam *verb* **1** to send out a beam of light or other radiation. **2** to transmit a radio signal or broadcast. **3** to smile happily. [from an Old English word]

bean *noun* **1** a kidney-shaped seed growing in long pods on certain plants. The seeds, and sometimes the pods, can be eaten as a vegetable. **2** a plant bearing beans. **3** a similar seed of coffee, cocoa, and certain other plants. **full of beans** (*informal*) lively, in high spirits. [from an Old English word]

beanbag *noun* **1** a small bag filled with dried beans and used for throwing or carrying in games. **2** a large cushion filled with plastic granules and used as a seat.

beanpole *noun* (*informal*) a tall thin person.

bean sprout *noun* a sprout of a bean seed that can be eaten either cooked or raw.

beanstalk *noun* the stem of a bean plant.

bear[1] *noun* **1** a large heavy mammal with thick fur. **2** a rough ill-mannered person. [from an Old English word *bera*]

bear[2] *verb* (**bore, borne**) **1** to carry or support something ♦ *They arrived bearing gifts* ♦ *She knew her ankle wouldn't bear her weight.* **2** to have or show a certain mark, characteristic, or feature ♦ *He still bears the scar* ♦ *The robbery bore all the marks of an inside job.* **3** to manage to tolerate something ♦ *He could hardly bear the pain* ♦ *I can't bear his brother.* SYNONYMS: tolerate, stand, endure, put up with, abide. **4** to be fit for something ♦ *His language doesn't bear repeating.* **5** to give birth to a child ♦ *She had borne him two sons.* **6** (said about land, trees, or plants) to produce flowers, fruit, etc. **7** to turn in a particular direction ♦ *Bear right when the road forks.* **to bear down on** to move rapidly or purposefully towards. **to bear someone a grudge** to feel resentment towards them. **to bear something in mind** to remember it and take it into account. **to bear on** to be relevant to ♦ *This matter bears directly on public health.* **to bear out** to confirm it ♦ *I can bear out what she said.* **to bear up** to remain cheerful even though you are having problems. **to bear with** to tolerate patiently ♦ *Please bear with me for a moment.* **to bear witness to** to provide evidence of the truth of something. **to bear yourself** to behave in a particular way ♦ *She bore herself bravely.* [from an Old English word *beran*]

bearable *adjective* able to be endured. **bearably** *adverb*

beard *noun* **1** hair growing on a man's chin and cheeks. **2** a similar hairy or bristly growth of hair on an animal or plant. **beard** *verb* to confront or challenge someone boldly. **bearded** *adjective* [from an Old English word; the verb originally meant 'to grab someone's beard']

bearer noun 1 a person who carries or bears something. 2 the person who presents a cheque at a bank.

bearing noun 1 a person's way of standing, walking, or behaving ♦ *his soldierly bearing.* 2 relevance to a situation ♦ *These events have no bearing on the case.* 3 a compass direction or position. 4 a device for reducing friction in a part of a machine where another part comes in contact with it. **to get your bearings** to work out where you are by recognizing landmarks etc. [from *bear*²]

bear market noun (on the Stock Exchange) a situation where share prices are falling rapidly.

bearskin noun a tall black fur headdress worn by some soldiers on ceremonial occasions.

beast noun 1 any large four-footed animal. 2 a cruel or vicious person. [from a Latin word *bestia*]

beastly adjective (**beastlier, beastliest**) (*informal*) unkind or unpleasant.

beast of prey noun an animal that kills other animals for food.

beat verb (**beat, beaten**) 1 to hit a person or animal repeatedly to hurt or punish them, especially using a stick. SYNONYMS: thrash, flog, batter, (*informal*) wallop. 2 to hit something repeatedly to make a noise, or to be hit like this ♦ *The rain was beating against the roof* ♦ *We heard the drums beating.* SYNONYMS: pound, hammer, buffet. 3 to defeat someone or do better than them ♦ *They beat us in the final.* SYNONYMS: overcome, conquer, vanquish, trounce, rout, (*informal*) lick. 4 to shape or flatten something by hitting it with a hammer. 5 to stir cooking ingredients vigorously to a frothy or smooth consistency ♦ *Now beat the eggs.* 6 (said about the heart) to expand and contract with a regular rhythm. 7 (said about a bird or insect) to move its wings up and down. 8 to sail towards the direction from which the wind is blowing, by tacking in alternate directions.
beat noun 1 a regular repeated stroke, or a sound of this ♦ *the beat of your heart.* 2 recurring emphasis marking rhythm in music or poetry. 3 the strongly marked rhythm of pop music. 4 the regular route of a police officer, or the area covered by this. **to beat about the bush** to discuss a subject without coming to the point. **to beat down** (said about the sun) to shine

with great heat. **to beat someone down** to force them to reduce the price they are asking. **to beat a retreat** to go away defeated. **to beat it** (*informal*) to go away. **to beat someone off** to drive someone off by fighting. **to beat time** to mark or follow the rhythm of music by waving a stick or by tapping. **to beat someone to it** to get there first. **to beat someone up** to assault someone violently and severely injure them. **it beats me** it is too difficult for me to understand or answer. **off the beaten track** away from the popular places. [from an Old English word]

beater noun a device for beating things.

beatific (bee-ə-tif-ik) adjective (*formal*) showing great happiness ♦ *a beatific smile.* **beatifically** adverb [same origin as for *beatify*]

beatification noun in the Roman Catholic Church, the Pope's official statement that a dead person has been beatified.

beatify (bee-at-i-fiy) verb (**beatifies, beatified, beatifying**) in the Roman Catholic Church, to honour a person who has died by declaring that he or she is among the Blessed, the first step towards declaring that person a saint. [from a Latin word *beatus* meaning 'blessed']

beatitude (bee-at-i-tewd) noun blessedness. [same origin as for *beatify*]

beatnik noun a young person associated with the beat generation of the 1950s and 1960s. [from *beat* and the Yiddish suffix *-nik*, perhaps influenced by the Russian word *Sputnik*, name for space satellites of that time]

Beaufort scale (boh-fert) noun a scale and description of wind velocity ranging from 0 (calm) to 12 (hurricane). [named after its inventor Sir F. Beaufort, English admiral (1774–1857)]

beautician (bew-tish-ən) noun a person whose job is to give people beauty treatments.

beautiful adjective 1 attractive to look at ♦ *a beautiful girl.* SYNONYMS: good-looking, pretty, lovely, gorgeous, stunning, exquisite, glamorous. 2 giving pleasure to the senses or the mind ♦ *beautiful music.* 3 of a high standard ♦ *a beautiful shot.* SYNONYMS: fine, superb, delightful, glorious. **beautifully** adverb

beautify verb (**beautifies, beautified, beautifying**) to make someone or something beautiful. **beautification** noun

beauty noun (**beauties**) 1 a combination of qualities that give pleasure to the sight or other senses or to the mind. 2 a beautiful woman. 3 a fine specimen or example. 4 an attractive feature or advantage of something ♦ *That's the beauty of the scheme – it doesn't cost you a penny.* [from an Old French word *beauté*]

beauty parlour or **beauty salon** noun an establishment for giving hairdressing, make-up, and other cosmetic treatments to the face and body.

beauty spot noun 1 a place with beautiful scenery. 2 a small natural or artificial mark on the face, said to heighten a person's beauty.

beaver noun 1 an animal with soft fur, a broad tail, and strong teeth that lives both on land and in water. Beavers gnaw through trees which they use to build dams across streams so they can make their homes in deep pools. 2 the soft brown fur of this animal.
Beaver noun a member of a junior branch of the Scout Association.
beaver verb (*informal*) to work hard ♦ *He's beavering away on the computer.* [from an Old English word]

bebop noun a kind of jazz music that originated in the 1940s. [an imitation of the typical rhythm of the music]

becalmed (bi-kahmd) adjective (said about a sailing ship) unable to move because there is no wind.

became past tense of **become**.

because conjunction for the reason that ♦ *I failed because I didn't do enough work.*
because of by reason of ♦ *He missed most of the season because of injury.* [from *by* and *cause*]

beck noun (*old use*) a gesture. **at someone's beck and call** always ready and waiting to obey his or her orders. [from *beckon*]

beckon verb (**beckoned, beckoning**) to make a gesture to someone asking them to come to you. [from an Old English word, related to *beacon*]

become verb (**became, become**) 1 to come or grow to be, to begin to be ♦ *She became a doctor.* ♦ *It became dark.* 2 to suit or look well on someone ♦ *That hairstyle becomes you.* **become of** happen to. ♦ *So what became of him?* [from an Old English word *becuman* meaning 'to happen, come to a place']

becoming adjective giving a pleasing appearance or effect, suitable.
becomingly adverb

becquerel (bek-er-əl) noun the SI unit of radioactivity. [named after A. H. Becquerel (1852–1908), French physicist]

bed noun 1 a piece of furniture that you sleep or rest on, especially one with a mattress and coverings. 2 an area of ground in a garden or park where flowers and plants are grown. 3 a flat base on which something rests, a foundation. 4 the bottom of the sea or a river. 5 a layer of rock, soil, etc. ♦ *a bed of clay.*
bed verb (**bedded, bedding**) 1 to provide someone with a place to sleep, or to go to bed ♦ *I found somewhere to bed down for the night.* 2 to plant seeds, plants, etc. in a garden bed ♦ *He was bedding out seedlings.* 3 to place or fix something in a foundation ♦ *The bricks are bedded in concrete.* [from an Old English word]

bedaub verb to smear something all over with something sticky.

bedbug noun a bug infesting beds.

bedclothes plural noun coverings for a bed, such as sheets and blankets.

bedding noun mattresses and bedclothes.

bedding plane noun (*Geology*) a surface that separates two layers or strata of rock.

bedevil verb (**bedevilled, bedevilling**) to constantly trouble someone or something ♦ *The project has been bedevilled with problems.*

bedfellow noun a person or thing that is closely connected with another, often in an unexpected way ♦ *Charity and rock music are no longer such strange bedfellows.*

bedlam (bed-ləm) noun a scene of uproar ♦ *Upstairs it was bedlam.* [from 'Bedlam', the popular name of the Hospital of St Mary of Bethlehem, a London mental institution in the 14th century]

Bedouin (bed-oo-in) noun (**Bedouin**) a member of an Arab people living in tents in the desert. [from an Arabic word *badawi* meaning 'desert dweller']

bedpan noun a pan used instead of a toilet by a person confined to bed.

bedpost noun one of the upright supports of a bedstead.

bedraggled (bi-**drag**-əld) *adjective* very untidy or messy, especially because of being soaked. [from *be-* and an old word *draggle* meaning 'to make dirty']

bedridden *noun* too ill or weak to get out of bed.

bedrock *noun* **1** solid rock beneath loose soil. **2** the fundamental facts or principles on which an idea or belief is based.

bedroom *noun* a room for sleeping in.

bedside *noun* the space beside a bed.

bedsitter or **bedsitting-room** *noun* a rented room used for both living and sleeping in.

bedsore *noun* a sore caused by pressure, developed by lying in bed for a long time.

bedspread *noun* a decorative covering spread over a bed during the day.

bedstead *noun* a framework supporting the springs and mattress of a bed. [originally the place where a bed stood; from *bed* and *stead* meaning 'place']

bee *noun* a four-winged stinging insect that produces wax and honey after gathering nectar from flowers. **to have a bee in your bonnet** to have a particular idea that occupies your thoughts continually. [from an Old English word]

beech *noun* **1** a kind of tree with smooth bark and glossy leaves. **2** the wood of this tree. [from an Old English word]

beechmast *noun* beech nuts.

beef *noun* **1** meat from an ox, bull, or cow. **2** (*informal*) muscular strength. **3** (*informal*) a grumble or complaint.
beef *verb* (*informal*) to grumble or complain. [from an Old French word *boef*]

beefburger *noun* a flat round cake of minced beef, served fried or grilled.

beefeater *noun* a guard at the Tower of London, wearing Tudor dress as uniform. [originally a scornful word for a fat, lazy servant]

beefsteak *noun* a slice of beef for grilling or frying.

beefy *adjective* (**beefier, beefiest**) having a solid muscular body. **beefiness** *noun*

beehive *noun* a box or other container in which bees are kept.

beeline *noun* **to make a beeline for somewhere** to go there quickly and directly. [so called because a bee was believed to fly in a straight line back to its hive]

been past participle of **be**.

beep *noun* a short high-pitched sound made by electronic equipment or a car horn.
beep *verb* to produce this sound. **beeper** *noun* [an imitation of the sound]

beer *noun* an alcoholic drink made from malt and flavoured with hops. **beery** *adjective* [from an Old English word]

beeswax *noun* a yellowish substance produced by bees, used for polishing wood.

beet *noun* (**beet** or **beets**) a plant with a fleshy root used as a vegetable or for making sugar. [from an Old English word]

beetle[1] *noun* an insect with hard wing covers. [from an Old English word, related to *bite*]

beetle[2] *noun* a heavy-headed tool for crushing or ramming things. [from an Old English word]

beetle-browed *adjective* with eyebrows that stick out.

beetroot *noun* the dark red root of a type of beet, used as a vegetable.

befall (bi-**fawl**) *verb* (**befell, befallen**) (*formal*) to happen to someone ♦ *A terrible fate was to befall her.* [from *be-* and an old word *fall* meaning 'to happen']

befit (bi-**fit**) *verb* (**befitted, befitting**) to be right and suitable for someone. **befitting** *adjective*

before *adverb, preposition, & conjunction* **1** at an earlier time; earlier than ♦ *Have you been here before?* ♦ *I was here before you.* **2** ahead of ♦ *You can go before me.* **3** in front of, in the presence of ♦ *He had to appear before the magistrate.* **4** rather than, in preference to ♦ *Death before dishonour!* [from an Old English word]

beforehand *adverb* in advance, in readiness. [from *before* and *hand*, with the idea of your hand doing something before someone else's does]

befriend *verb* to make friends with someone.

befuddled *adjective* muddled or confused.

beg *verb* (**begged, begging**) **1** to ask for money or food as charity. **2** to ask for something earnestly or humbly.

SYNONYMS: plead, beseech, implore, entreat.
3 to ask for something formally ♦ *I beg to differ.* **4** (said about a dog) to sit up expectantly, as it has been trained, with its front paws off the ground. **to beg the question** to argue in an illogical way by assuming the truth of the argument that you are trying to prove. **to go begging** to be available because other people do not want it. **I beg your pardon 1** I apologize. **2** I did not hear what you said. [probably from an Old English word]

began past tense of **begin**.

beget (bi-**get**) verb (**begot, begotten, begetting**) (old use) **1** to be the father of someone. **2** to give rise to something ♦ *War begets misery and ruin.* [from an Old English word]

beggar noun **1** a person who lives by begging for food or money. **2** (informal) a person ♦ *You lucky beggar!*
beggar verb to reduce someone to poverty. **to beggar belief** or **description** to be too extraordinary to be believed or described ♦ *The scenery simply beggars description.*

beggarly adjective (said about a sum of money) meagre and not at all generous.

beggary noun a state of extreme poverty.

begin verb (**began, begun, beginning**) **1** to do the earliest or first part of an activity. SYNONYMS: start, commence, launch into;(informal) get cracking. **2** to come into or bring something into existence. SYNONYMS: initiate, found, introduce, launch, originate. **3** to be the first to do something ♦ *Who would like to begin?* **4** to start speaking. **5** to have something as its first element or starting point ♦ *The word begins with the letter B.* [from an Old English word]

beginner noun a person who has just started to learn a subject or skill ♦ *an Italian class for beginners.*

beginning noun **1** the first part of something. **2** the starting point or origin of something.

begone (bi-**gon**) interjection (old use) go away at once ♦ *Begone dull care!* [from be- and gone]

begonia (bi-**goh**-niə) noun a garden plant with brightly coloured leaves and flowers. [named after Michel Bégon, a Frenchman who encouraged the study of plants]

begot or **begotten** past participle of **beget**.

begrudge verb to resent the fact that someone has something ♦ *I hope you don't begrudge me my success.*

beguile (bi-**giyl**) verb **1** to enchant or amuse someone. **2** to trick someone into doing something. **beguiling** adjective [from be- and guile]

begun past participle of **begin**.

behalf noun **on behalf of** for the benefit of someone else or as their representative ♦ *a lawyer speaking on behalf of his client.* [from an old phrase bi halve him meaning 'on his side']
◊ Do not use on behalf of when you mean on the part of. For example, do not say This was a serious mistake on behalf of the government when you mean a mistake made by the government.

behave verb **1** to act in a particular way ♦ *He has been behaving strangely all week.* **2** to show good manners ♦ *The children must learn to behave* ♦ *I wish you would behave yourself.* [from be- and have]

behaviour noun the way in which someone behaves. **behavioural** adjective

behead verb to cut a person's head off, especially as a form of execution. [from an Old English word]

beheld past tense and past participle of **behold**.

behest noun (formal) a command or request. **at a person's behest** done because they have asked or commanded you to do it ♦ *We attended the funeral at the behest of the family.* [from an Old English word]

behind preposition **1** at or to the back of, on the further side of ♦ *She had been hiding behind the curtain.* **2** responsible for or causing ♦ *What's behind all this trouble?* **3** supporting ♦ *We are all behind you.* **4** having made less progress than ♦ *Some countries are behind others in development.* **5** later than ♦ *We are a month behind schedule.*
behind adverb **1** remaining after others have gone ♦ *Would you stay behind for a few minutes?* **2** at a place you have left ♦ *Don't leave your coat behind.* **3** not making good progress; late ♦ *I'm behind with my rent.*
behind noun (informal) a person's bottom. **behind the scenes** hidden from public view or knowledge. **behind the times** having out-of-date ideas or practices. [from an Old English word]

behindhand adverb & adjective late or slow in doing something. [from behind and hand, on the pattern of beforehand]

behold verb (past tense and past participle **beheld**) (old use) to see or observe.
beholder noun [from an Old English word]

beholden adjective **to be beholden to someone** to be indebted to someone for something they have done. [same origin as for behold]

behove verb (formal) to be a person's duty or responsibility ♦ It behoves you to show loyalty to your comrades. [from an Old English word]

beige (bayzh) noun a very light brown colour.
beige adjective of this colour. [a French word]

being noun 1 existence ♦ When did the European Union come into being? 2 the essence or nature of a person or thing. 3 a living creature ♦ alien beings.

bejewelled adjective decorated with jewels.

belabour verb 1 to attack someone with blows or words. 2 to discuss a subject in too much detail.

belated (bi-lay-tid) adjective coming very late or too late. **belatedly** adverb

belay verb to fasten a rope by winding it round a peg or rock.
belay noun 1 the securing of a rope in this way. 2 a peg or rock used for belaying. [from a Dutch word]

belch verb 1 to send out wind from the stomach noisily through the mouth. 2 to send out a large amount of smoke or flames ♦ The front of the car was belching smoke.
belch noun an act or sound of belching. [from an Old English word]

beleaguered (bi-leeg-erd) adjective 1 experiencing a lot of difficulties or criticism ♦ the country's beleaguered government. 2 under siege. [from a Dutch word belegeren meaning 'to camp round']

belfry noun (**belfries**) a tower or part of a tower in which bells hang. [from an Old French word]

belie verb (**belies, belied, belying**) 1 to give a false idea of something ♦ The quality of her writing belies her youth. 2 to show that something is untrue ♦ His actions seem to belie these fine words. [from an Old English word]

belief noun (**beliefs**) 1 the feeling that something exists or is true. 2 trust or confidence ♦ I have belief in you. 3 something that a person believes. SYNONYMS: doctrine, ideology, tenet, creed. 4 acceptance of the teachings of a religion. SYNONYMS: faith, conviction. [from an Old English word]

believable adjective able to be believed.

believe verb 1 to accept that something is true or that someone is telling the truth. 2 to think or suppose ♦ I do believe it's raining. 3 to have religious faith. **to believe in** 1 to have faith in the existence of something ♦ Do you believe in ghosts? 2 to feel sure that something or someone is good or can be relied on. **believer** noun [from an Old English word]

belittle verb to suggest that something is unimportant or of little value ♦ I don't want to belittle their achievement. **belittlement** noun

bell noun 1 a cup-shaped metal instrument that makes a ringing sound when it is struck by the clapper hanging inside it. 2 a device making a ringing or buzzing sound to attract attention. 3 the sound of a bell, especially when used as a signal. 4 a bell-shaped object. **to ring a bell** to sound familiar. [from an Old English word]

belladonna noun 1 deadly nightshade. 2 a medicinal drug prepared from this. [from the Italian words bella donna meaning 'fair lady']

bell-bottomed adjective (said about trousers) widening from knee to ankle.

belle (bel) noun a beautiful girl or woman ♦ the belle of the ball. [a French word]

bellicose (bel-i-kohs) adjective aggressive and eager to fight. **bellicosity** (bel-i-**koss**-iti) noun [from a Latin word bellum meaning 'war']

belligerent (bi-lij-er-ənt) adjective 1 hostile and aggressive ♦ a belligerent reply. 2 taking part in a war ♦ the belligerent nations. **belligerently** adverb **belligerence** noun [from Latin words bellum meaning 'war' and gerens meaning 'waging']

bellow noun 1 the loud deep sound made by a bull. 2 a loud deep shout.
bellow verb to utter a bellow. [origin unknown]

bellows plural noun 1 a device that consists of an air bag that can be squeezed with two handles, used for blowing air into a fire. **2** a device or part that can be expanded or flattened in a series of folds. [from an Old English word]

belly *noun* (**bellies**) **1** a person's stomach or abdomen. **2** the underside of an animal's body. **3** a bulging or rounded part of something.
belly *verb* (**bellies, bellied, bellying**) to swell out, or to make something swell out. [from an Old English word *belig* meaning 'bag']

bellyache *verb* to complain tediously or noisily.

belly button *noun* (*informal*) a person's navel.

belly dance *noun* a style of dance originating in the Middle East, performed by a woman who moves her belly and hips in a circling motion. **belly dancer** *noun* **belly dancing** *noun*

bellyflop *noun* a dive into water in which you land flat on your front.

bellyful *noun* **to have a bellyful** (*informal*) to have more than enough of something ♦ *I've had a bellyful of your nagging.*

belong *verb* **1** to be the property of someone ♦ *The house belongs to me now.* **2** to rightly go with something else or be part of it ♦ *That lid belongs to this jar.* **3** to be a member of something ♦ *I belong to the local chess club.* **4** to fit in ♦ *I don't really belong here.* **5** to have a proper or usual place ♦ *The pans belong in the top cupboard.* [from *be-* and an old word *long* meaning 'owing to, because of']

belongings *plural noun* a person's possessions.

beloved *adjective* (bi-**luvd** or bi-**luv**-id) dearly loved ♦ *my beloved wife* ♦ *She was beloved by all.*
beloved *noun* (bi-**luv**-id) a much loved person.

below *adverb* **1** at or to a lower position. **2** mentioned further down ♦ *See chapter 6 below.*
below *preposition* **1** lower in position, amount, or rank, etc. than; under ♦ *It was ten degrees below zero.* [from *be-* and *low*[1]]

belt *noun* **1** a strip of cloth or leather etc. worn round the waist. **2** a continuous moving strap passing over pulleys and so driving machinery ♦ *a fan belt.* **3** a long narrow region or strip ♦ *A belt of rain will*

move eastwards ♦ *the asteroid belt.* **4** (*informal*) a heavy blow.
belt *verb* **1** to fasten something with a belt. **2** (*informal*) to hit or beat someone. **3** (*informal*) to rush along. **below the belt** unfair. **to belt up** (*informal*) **1** to wear a seat belt. **2** to be quiet. **under your belt** (*informal*) successfully obtained or achieved. [via Old English from Latin]

belvedere (**bel**-vi-deer) *noun* a summer house or gallery built to command a good view. [from an Italian word meaning 'fair sight']

bemused (bi-**mewzd**) *adjective* puzzled or confused. [from *be-* and *muse*, in the sense 'wonder']

bench *noun* **1** a long seat of wood or stone. **2** a long table for working at in a workshop or laboratory. **3** the place where judges and magistrates sit. **4** the judges or magistrates hearing a case. [from an Old English word *benc*, related to *bank*[2]]

benchmark *noun* **1** a standard or point of reference against which things can be compared or assessed. **2** a surveyor's mark indicating a point in a line of levels.

bend *verb* (past tense and past participle **bent**) **1** to make something curved or angular and no longer straight. SYNONYMS: twist, arch, bow, curl, warp, refract (light). **2** to move the top part of your body downwards, to stoop ♦ *She bent to pick it up.* **3** to turn in a new direction ♦ *The river bends ahead.*
bend *noun* a place where something bends, a curve or turn.
bends *plural noun* sickness due to too rapid decompression, e.g. after diving. [from an Old English word]

bender *noun* (*informal*) a drinking bout.

beneath *adverb* & *preposition* **1** below or underneath. **2** not worthy of ♦ *Cheating is beneath you.* [from an Old English word]

benediction (ben-i-**dik**-shən) *noun* a spoken blessing. **benedictory** *adjective* [from Latin words *bene* meaning 'well' and *dicere* meaning 'to say']

benefactor *noun* a person who gives money or other help. **benefactress** *feminine noun* [from Latin words *bene* meaning 'well' and *factor* meaning 'doer']

benefice (**ben**-i-fiss) *noun* the position of being in charge of a parish or parishes, for which a member of the clergy is paid. [same origin as for *beneficial*]

beneficial *adjective* having a good effect. SYNONYMS: advantageous, helpful, favourable, profitable. **beneficially** *adverb* [from a Latin word *beneficium* meaning 'favour' or 'support']

beneficiary (ben-i-fish-er-i) *noun* (**beneficiaries**) **1** a person who receives a benefit from something. **2** a person who is left a legacy under someone's will. [same origin as for *beneficial*]

benefit *noun* **1** an advantage that something brings. SYNONYMS: advantage, help, gain, asset. **2** a payment to which a person is entitled from an insurance policy or government funds. **3** a performance or game held in order to raise money for a particular player or for charity ♦ *a benefit match*.
benefit *verb* (**benefited, benefiting**) to receive or to bring an advantage. **benefit of clergy** the privilege (to which clergymen were formerly entitled) of being tried before a church court, not a secular one, or of being exempt from the sentence imposed. **the benefit of the doubt** the assumption that a person is innocent (or right) rather than guilty (or wrong) when nothing can be fully proved either way. [from Latin words *bene* meaning 'well' and *facere* meaning 'to do']

benevolent *adjective* **1** wishing to do good to others; kindly and helpful. **2** formed for charitable purposes ♦ *a benevolent fund*. **benevolently** *adverb* **benevolence** *noun* [from Latin words *bene* meaning 'well' and *volens* meaning 'wishing']

benighted *adjective* intellectually or morally ignorant.

benign (bi-niyn) *adjective* **1** kindly. **2** mild or favourable ♦ *a benign climate*. **3** (said about a tumour) not malignant. **benignly** *adverb* [from a Latin word *benignus* meaning 'kind-hearted']

bent *adjective* **1** curved or crooked. **2** (*informal*) dishonest or corrupt.
bent *noun* a natural talent or skill ♦ *She has a bent for photography*. **bent on** determined to do or have something ♦ *He was bent on mischief*.

bentwood *noun* wood that has been artificially bent into a permanent curve, used for making furniture.

benzene (**ben**-zeen) *noun* a colourless liquid obtained from petroleum and coal tar, used as a solvent, as fuel, and in the manufacture of plastics. [via French from an Arabic word *lubanjawi* meaning 'incense from Sumatra']

benzene ring *noun* a hexagonal ring of carbon atoms characteristic of the structure of benzene and most aromatic organic compounds.

benzine (**ben**-zeen) *noun* a colourless liquid mixture of hydrocarbons obtained from petroleum and used as a solvent in dry cleaning. [same origin as for *benzene*]

bequeath (bi-kwee*th*) *verb* to leave something to a person, especially in a will. [from *be-* and an Old English word *cwethan* meaning 'to say']

bequest (bi-**kwest**) *noun* something left to a person, especially in a will. [from *be-* and an Old English word *cwiss* meaning 'saying, a statement']

berate (bi-**rayt**) *verb* to scold someone angrily. [from *be-* and an old word *rate* meaning 'scold']

bereaved *adjective* (*formal*) having recently suffered the death of a close relative. **bereavement** *noun* [from *be-* and an old word *reave* meaning 'to take forcibly']

bereft *adjective* deprived of something ♦ *They were bereft of hope*. [old past participle of *bereave*]

beret (**be**-ray) *noun* a round flat cap with no peak. [a French word]

bergamot (**ber**-gǝ-mot) *noun* a fragrant herb. [named after Bergamo in northern Italy]

beriberi (be-ri-be-ri) *noun* a disease affecting the nervous system, caused by lack of vitamin B. [from a Sinhalese word]

berry *noun* (**berries**) **1** a small round juicy fruit without a stone. **2** (in botanical use) a fruit with seeds enclosed in a pulp, such as a banana or tomato. **3** an egg in the roe of fish or lobster. [from an Old English word]

berserk (ber-**zerk**) *adjective* frenzied. **to go berserk** to go into an uncontrollable and destructive rage. [from an Icelandic word *berserkr* meaning 'wild warrior' (*ber-* meaning 'bear', *serkr* meaning 'coat')]

berth *noun* **1** a place for a ship to tie up at a wharf or dock. **2** a bunk or sleeping place on a ship or train.
berth *verb* to moor at a berth. **to give someone or something a wide berth** to stay well away from them. [from *bear*²]

beryl *noun* a transparent usually green precious stone. [from French]

beryllium (bə-ril-iəm) *noun* a very light hard greyish-white metallic element (symbol Be), used in alloys where lightness and a high melting-point are important.

beseech *verb* (past tense and past participle **beseeched** or **besought**) to ask someone earnestly for something; to implore. [from be- and seek]

beset *verb* (**beset, besetting**) to surround or attack someone from all sides ♦ *We are beset with problems.* [from an Old English word]

beside *preposition* 1 by the side of, close to. 2 compared with ♦ *His work looks poor beside yours.* **to be beside yourself** to be very excited or upset. [from the Old English words be siden meaning 'by the side']

besides *preposition* in addition to, other than ♦ *He has no income besides his pension.* **besides** *adverb* also, in addition ♦ *And besides, it's the wrong colour.* [same origin as for beside]

besiege *verb* 1 to surround a place in order to capture it. 2 to crowd round someone with requests or questions ♦ *Fans besieged the singer after the concert.* **besieger** *noun* [from an Old French word]

besom (bee-zəm) *noun* a broom made by tying a bundle of twigs to a long handle. [from an Old English word]

besotted (bi-sot-id) *adjective* foolishly infatuated. [from be- and sot meaning 'make stupid']

besought past tense and past participle of **beseech**.

bespeak *verb* (**bespoke, bespoken, bespeaking**) 1 to be evidence of something. 2 to order or reserve goods in advance. [from an Old English word bisprecan meaning 'speak out']

bespoke past tense of **bespeak**.
bespoke *adjective* 1 (said about clothes or other goods) made to order ♦ *a bespoke suit.* 2 (said about a computer program) written or adapted for a specific user.

Bessemer process (bes-i-mer) *noun* a process formerly much used for converting pig iron into a material suitable for steel-making, devised by Sir Henry Bessemer (1813–98). Compressed air is forced through the iron in order to remove carbon, silicon, and other impurities.

best *adjective* of the most excellent kind; most satisfactory.
best *adverb* 1 in the best manner, to the greatest degree ♦ *I like this one best.* 2 most usefully or wisely ♦ *We had best go.*
best *noun* 1 that which is best ♦ *The best is yet to come.* 2 victory in a contest, especially by winning the majority of games etc. ♦ *Let's make it the best of three.*
best *verb* (*informal*) to defeat or outwit someone. [from an Old English word]

bestial (best-iəl) *adjective* like a beast, especially by being cruel or disgusting.
bestiality (best-i-al-iti) *noun* [from a Latin word bestia meaning 'beast']

bestir *verb* (**bestirred, bestirring**) to **bestir yourself** to rouse or exert yourself.

best man *noun* the bridegroom's chief attendant at a wedding.

bestow *verb* to present something to someone as a gift. **bestowal** *noun* [from be- and stow]

bestrew *verb* (*poetic*) to scatter or to lie scattered over something. **bestrewn** *adjective* [from an Old English word]

bestride *verb* (**bestrode, bestridden**) to sit or stand astride over something.

best-seller *noun* a book that sells in large numbers.

bet *noun* 1 an agreement that you will pay money if you are wrong in forecasting the result of a race, game, etc. and receive money if you are right. 2 the money that you agree to pay in this way. 3 (*informal*) a person or thing thought to be likely to be successful ♦ *She's a good bet to win the title.* 4 (*informal*) a prediction or opinion ♦ *My bet is that he won't come.*
bet *verb* (**bet** or **betted, betting**) 1 to make a bet ♦ *I bet you £10 they lose.* 2 (*informal*) to predict, to think most likely ♦ *I bet it rains tomorrow.* **you bet** (*informal*) definitely.
your best bet your best course of action ♦ *Your best bet is to call tomorrow.* [origin unknown]

beta (bee-tə) *noun* 1 the second letter of the Greek alphabet, equivalent to Roman B, b. 2 a second-class mark given for a piece of work.

beta blocker *noun* a drug used to prevent increased heart activity.

beta decay *noun* (*Physics*) radioactive decay in which an electron is emitted.

betake verb (**betook, betaken**) (poetic) to betake yourself to go.

beta particle or **beta ray** noun a fast-moving electron emitted by radioactive substances (originally regarded as rays).

betel (bee-təl) noun an Asian climbing plant, the leaves of which are chewed in eastern countries with the **betel nut** (the areca nut) as a mild stimulant. [via Portuguese from a Malayalam word]

bête noire (bayt nwar) (**bêtes noires** (bayt nwar)) a thing or person that you particularly dislike. [a French phrase meaning 'black beast']

betide verb (old use) to happen. **woe betide you** trouble will come to you. [from be- and an old word tide meaning 'to happen']

betoken verb to be a sign of something. [from an Old English word]

betook past tense of **betake**.

betray verb 1 to hand someone over to an enemy or give information to your country's enemy ♦ During the war he betrayed his country. 2 to be disloyal to someone ♦ She felt betrayed. 3 to reveal something unintentionally ♦ His shaking hand betrayed his nervousness. **betrayal** noun **betrayer** noun [from be- and a Latin word tradere meaning 'to hand over']

betroth (bi-trohth) verb (formal) to be **betrothed** to be engaged to be married. **betrothal** noun [from be- and troth]

better [1] adjective 1 more excellent, satisfactory, or desirable ♦ It would be better to start again. 2 partly or fully recovered from an illness ♦ Are you feeling better? **better** adverb 1 in a better manner, to a greater degree ♦ I like this one better. 2 more usefully or wisely ♦ We had better go.
better noun that which is better.
better verb to improve on or do better than something ♦ See if you can better that score.
betters plural noun people who are of higher status than yourself. **to better yourself** to get a better social position or status. [from an Old English word]

better [2] noun a person who bets.

betterment noun becoming better.

betting shop noun a bookmaker's office.

between preposition & adverb 1 in the space separating two or more points, lines, or objects. 2 connecting two or more people, places, or things ♦ the great love between them ♦ The train runs between London and Glasgow. 3 more than one amount or level and less than another. 4 in the period separating two points in time ♦ We'll arrive between 6.00 and 6.30. 5 separating ♦ the difference between right and wrong. 6 shared by ♦ Divide the money between you. 7 taking one and rejecting the other ♦ It is difficult to choose between them. [from an Old English word]
◊ The preposition between should be followed by the object form of the pronoun (me, her, him, them, or us). The expression 'between you and I' is incorrect; say between you and me.

betwixt preposition & adverb (old use) between. [from an Old English word]

bevel (bev-əl) noun 1 a sloping edge or surface. 2 a tool for making such slopes. **bevel** verb (**bevelled, bevelling**) to give a sloping edge to something. [from an Old French word]

beverage (bev-er-ij) noun any drink. [from an Old French word]

bevy (bev-i) noun (**bevies**) a large group ♦ a bevy of beauties. [origin unknown]

bewail verb to express great sorrow about something ♦ refugees bewailing their fate.

beware verb to be on your guard ♦ Beware of pickpockets. [from be- and ware meaning 'wary']

bewilder verb to puzzle or confuse someone completely. **bewilderment** noun [from be- and an old word wilder meaning 'to lose your way']

bewitch verb 1 to put someone under a magic spell. 2 to delight someone very much. [from be- and witch meaning 'put under a spell']

beyond adverb & preposition 1 at or to the further side of; further on ♦ They live beyond those hills. 2 outside the scope or limits of ♦ His bike is beyond repair ♦ This is beyond a joke. **to be beyond you** to be too difficult for you to do or to understand. [from an Old English word]

Bhagavadgita (bah-gə-vahd-**gee**-tə) noun the 'Song of the Lord' (i.e. Krishna), the most famous religious text of Hinduism. [a Sanskrit word]

bhangra noun a style of music that combines traditional Punjabi music with Western rock music. [from a Punjabi word]

bi- *prefix* **1** two (as in *bicycle*). **2** twice (as in *biannual*). [from a Latin word *bis* meaning 'twice']

biannual *adjective* appearing or happening twice a year. **biannually** *adverb*
◊ Do not confuse this word with *biennial*.

bias *noun* (**biases**) **1** an opinion or feeling that strongly favours one side in preference to another. **2** a distortion in statistical information because of a factor or influence that has not been taken account of. **3** the tendency of a ball in the game of bowls to swerve because of the way it is weighted. **4** a diagonal line across the threads of a piece of fabric. **5** a steady voltage, applied to an electronic device, that can be adjusted to change the way the device operates.
bias *verb* (**biased, biasing**) to give a bias to something, to influence something unfairly. **on the bias** cut with the threads running diagonally across the up-and-down lines of the dress etc. [from an Old French word]

biased *adjective* inclined to favour one side rather than another. SYNONYMS: partial, partisan, prejudiced, one-sided.

bib *noun* **1** a cloth or plastic covering put under a young child's chin to protect the front of its clothes while eating. **2** the front part of an apron, above the waist. [probably from a Latin word *bibere* meaning 'to drink']

Bible *noun* the sacred book of the Jews (the Old Testament) and of the Christians (the Old and New Testament).
bible *noun* **1** a copy of either of these. **2** a book regarded as authoritative ♦ *This should be every gardener's bible.* [from a Greek word *biblia* meaning 'books' (originally rolls of papyrus from Byblos, a port now in Lebanon)]

biblical *adjective* in or to do with the Bible.

bibliography (bibli-og-rəfi) *noun* (**bibliographies**) **1** a list of books or articles about a particular subject or by a particular author. **2** the study of the history of books and their production.
bibliographer *noun* **bibliographical** *adjective* [from a Greek word *biblion* meaning 'book' and *-graphy*]

bicameral (biy-kam-er-əl) *adjective* (said about a parliament) having two legislative chambers. [from *bi-* and a Latin word *camera* meaning 'chamber']

bicarbonate *noun* a carbonate containing a double proportion of carbon dioxide. [from *bi-* and *carbonate*]

bicentenary (biy-sen-teen-er-i) *noun* (**bicentenaries**) a 200th anniversary. [from *bi-* and *centenary*]

bicentennial (biy-sen-ten-iəl) *adjective* to do with a bicentenary.
bicentennial *noun* a bicentenary.

biceps (biy-seps) *noun* the large muscle at the front of the upper arm, which bends the elbow. [a Latin word meaning 'two-headed' (because its end is attached at two points)]

bicker *verb* to quarrel constantly over unimportant things. [origin unknown]

biconcave (biy-kon-kayv) *adjective* (said about a lens) having both its surfaces concave.

biconvex (biy-kon-veks) *adjective* (said about a lens) having both its surfaces convex.

bicuspid (biy-kusp-id) *adjective* having two cusps or points.
bicuspid *noun* a bicuspid tooth. [from *bi-* and a Latin word *cuspis* meaning 'sharp point']

bicycle *noun* a two-wheeled vehicle driven by pedals.
bicycle *verb* to ride on a bicycle. [from *bi-* and a Greek word *kuklos* meaning 'circle, wheel']

bicyclist *noun* a person who rides a bicycle.

bid[1] *noun* **1** an offer of an amount you are willing to pay for something, especially at an auction. **2** a statement of the number of tricks a player proposes to win in a card game. **3** an effort to obtain something ♦ *an unsuccessful bid for the title.*
bid *verb* (**bid, bidding**) to make a bid.
bidder *noun* [from an Old English word *beodan* meaning 'to offer or command']

bid[2] *verb* (**bid** or, **bade** (bad), **bid, bidding**) **1** to say something as a greeting or farewell ♦ *I bid you all good night.* **2** to command someone to do something ♦ *Do as you are bid.* [from an Old English word *biddan* meaning 'to ask']

biddable *adjective* meekly willing to obey.

bidding *noun* a command. **to do a person's bidding** to do what he or she tells you to do.

bide *verb* (*old use*) to wait. **to bide your time** to wait for a good opportunity to do something. [from an Old English word]

bidet (bee-day) noun a low oval washbasin that you can sit astride for washing the lower part of your body. [from a French word bidet meaning 'a pony']

biennial (biy-en-iəl) adjective 1 lasting or living for two years. 2 happening once every two years.
biennial noun a plant that lives for two years, flowering and dying in the second. **biennially** adverb [from bi- and a Latin word annus meaning 'year']
◊ Do not confuse this word with biannual.

bier noun a movable stand on which a coffin or a dead body is placed before burial. [from an Old English word]

biff verb (informal) to hit someone or something.
biff noun a blow. [an imitation of the sound]

bifocals (biy-foh-kəlz) plural noun spectacles with lenses made in two sections, an upper part for looking at distant objects and a lower part for reading.

big adjective (bigger, biggest) 1 large in size, amount, or intensity. SYNONYMS: high, tall, considerable, substantial, extensive, sizeable, spacious (room). 2 more grown up, elder ♦ my big sister. 3 important ♦ the big match. 4 boastful or pretentious ♦ big talk. 5 (informal) generous ♦ That's big of you. [origin unknown]

bigamist noun a person guilty of bigamy.

bigamy (big-a-mee) noun the crime of marrying a person when you are already married to someone else. **bigamous** adjective **bigamously** adverb [from bi- and a Greek word gamos meaning 'marriage']

big bang noun the theory that the universe originated when a fireball of radiation expanded suddenly and then cooled.

Big Brother noun a person or organization that exercises close supervision and control of people's lives. [named after the tyrannical leader in George Orwell's novel Nineteen Eighty-four (1949)]

big dipper noun a roller coaster.

big end noun the larger end of the connecting rod that encircles the crankshaft in a piston engine.

big game noun the larger animals hunted for sport.

big-head noun (informal) a conceited person. **big-headed** adjective

big-hearted adjective very kind, generous.

bight (biyt) noun 1 a long inward curve in a coastline ♦ the Great Australian Bight. 2 a loop of rope. [from an Old English word]

bigot (big-ət) noun a person who holds an opinion or belief obstinately and is intolerant of other people's opinions. **bigoted** adjective narrow-minded and intolerant. **bigotry** noun being a bigot or bigoted. [origin unknown]

big toe noun the first and largest toe.

big top noun the main tent at a circus.

bigwig noun (informal) an important person. [from the large wigs worn by distinguished men in the past]

bijou (bee-zhoo) adjective small and elegant ♦ a bijou flat. [a French word meaning 'jewel']

bike noun (informal) a bicycle or motorcycle. **bike** verb (informal) to ride a bicycle or motorcycle. **biker** noun [abbreviation of bicycle]

bikini noun a woman's two-piece swimsuit. [named after Bikini, an atoll in the West Pacific where an atomic bomb was tested in 1946, at about the time the bikini was first worn. Both were supposed to have had an 'explosive' effect]

bilateral (biy-lat-erəl) adjective 1 having or to do with two sides. 2 between two people or groups ♦ a bilateral agreement. **bilaterally** adverb [from bi- and lateral]

bilateral symmetry noun symmetry in which the left and right sides are mirror images of each other.

bilberry noun (bilberries) the small round dark-blue fruit of a shrub growing on heaths. [probably from Old Norse]

bile noun 1 a bitter yellowish liquid produced by the liver and stored in the gall bladder, helping the digestion of fats. 2 anger or bad temper. [from a Latin word bilis]

bilge noun the dirty water that collects at the bottom part of a ship called the **bilges**. [a different spelling of bulge]

bilingual (biy-ling-gwəl) adjective 1 able to speak two languages. 2 written in two languages. [from bi- and a Latin word lingua meaning 'language']

bilious (bil-yəs) adjective 1 feeling sick. 2 of a sickly yellowish colour or shade ♦ a bilious green. 3 spiteful or bad-tempered. **biliousness** noun [from bile]

bilk *verb* to avoid paying your debts to someone; to defraud someone. [origin unknown]

bill [1] *noun* 1 a written statement of charges for goods or services supplied. 2 the draft of a proposed law to be discussed by parliament. 3 (*North Amer.*) a banknote ♦ *a ten-dollar bill.* 4 a programme of entertainment at a theatre, cinema, etc. ♦ *Who's on the bill?* 5 a poster or notice. **bill** *verb* 1 to send a bill to someone. 2 to announce or advertise something ♦ *This has been billed as the match of the century.* **to fit** or **fill the bill** to be suitable for what is needed. [same origin as for *bull* [2]]

bill [2] *noun* a bird's beak. **bill** *verb* (said about doves) to stroke each other with their bills. [from an Old English word]

billabong *noun* (*Austral.*) a river branch that forms a backwater or a stagnant pool. [from an Aboriginal word]

billboard *noun* a hoarding for advertisements.

billet *noun* 1 a temporary lodging for soldiers, especially in a private house. **billet** *verb* (**billeted, billeting**) to house soldiers in a billet. [originally denoting an order to house troops, from a Latin word *bulla* meaning 'seal, sealed letter']

billhook *noun* a long-handled tool with a curved blade for lopping trees.

billiards *noun* a game played with cues and three balls on a cloth-covered table. [from a French word *billard* meaning 'cue']

billion *noun* 1 a thousand million. 2 (*old use*) a million million. **billionth** *adjective noun* [from *bi-* and *million*]
◊ Most people now use *billion* to mean 'a thousand million'. In the past, though, this meaning was the one used in American English, while in British English the word was used for 'a million million'. Notice that you say ♦ *three billion* and ♦ *a few billion*, not *billions*.

billionaire *noun* a person who possesses at least a billion pounds or dollars.

bill of exchange *noun* a written order to pay a specified sum of money on a particular date to a named person or to the bearer.

bill of fare *noun* a menu.

billow *noun* 1 a large rolling mass of cloud, smoke, or steam. 2 (*old use*) a huge wave. **billow** *verb* 1 to fill with air and swell outwards ♦ *His cloak billowed out behind him.* 2 to flow upwards and outwards ♦ *Smoke billowed forth.* [from an Old Norse word]

billy or **billycan** *noun* (**billies**) a tin can or enamelled container with a lid, used by campers etc. as a kettle or cooking pot. [from an Australian Aboriginal word *billa* meaning 'water']

billy goat *noun* a male goat. [from the name *Billy*]

biltong *noun* (in southern Africa) strips of lean meat salted and dried in the sun. [an Afrikaans word]

bimbo *noun* (**bimbos**) an attractive but unintelligent young woman. [an Italian word meaning 'little child']

bimetallic strip (biy-mə-tal-ik) *noun* a device used in thermostats, made of two bands of metals which expand at different rates when heated, so that the whole strip bends.

bimonthly *adjective* 1 happening every two months. 2 happening twice a month.

bin *noun* 1 a container for rubbish or litter. 2 a large container used for storing grain, flour, wine, etc. **bin** *verb* (**binned, binning**) to throw something away by putting it in a bin. [via Old English from a Celtic word]

binary (biy-ner-i) *adjective* 1 involving sets of two; consisting of two parts. 2 (*Mathematics*) using two as a base. **binary** *noun* (**binaries**) a binary star. [from a Latin word *bini* meaning 'two together']

binary code *noun* (*Computing*) a coding system using the two digits 0 and 1.

binary digit *noun* one of the two digits 0 and 1 used in the binary system.

binary number *noun* a number expressed in the binary system.

binary star *noun* two stars that revolve round each other.

binary system or **binary notation** *noun* a system of numbers using only the two digits 0 and 1, used in computing.

bind *verb* (past tense and past participle **bound**) 1 to tie or fasten something tightly. 2 to fasten a strip of material round something ♦ *Help me bind up the wound.* 3 to tie someone up. 4 to hold things together; to unite them ♦ *We are bound by ties of friendship.* 5 to fasten the pages of a book into a cover. 6 to stick ingredients together in a solid mass ♦ *Now*

bind the mixture with egg yolk. **7** to cover the edge of a piece of material in order to strengthen it or as a decoration. **8** to make someone agree to do something or place them under an obligation.
bind noun (informal) **1** a difficult or annoying situation. **2** a situation in which you cannot act freely. **to bind someone over** to put them under a legal obligation to keep the peace. [from an Old English word]

binder noun **1** a cover for holding magazines or loose papers together. **2** a bookbinder. **3** a machine that binds harvested corn into sheaves or straw into bales.

bindery noun (**binderies**) a workshop where books are bound.

binding noun **1** the covering, glue, etc. that hold the pages of a book together.
2 fabric used for binding the edges of a piece of material.
binding adjective (said about a promise or agreement) that must be carried out or obeyed ♦ The agreement is binding on both parties.

bindweed noun a twining plant with trumpet-shaped flowers.

bine noun the flexible stem of a climbing plant, especially of the hop plant. [a different spelling of bind]

binge (binj) noun (informal) a time spent eating or drinking too much.
binge verb to spend time eating to excess. [origin unknown]

bingo noun a gambling game with cards on which numbered squares are crossed out as the numbers are called out at random. [origin unknown]

binnacle (bin-ə-kəl) noun a non-magnetic stand for a ship's compass.

binocular (bin-ok-yoo-ler) adjective for or using both eyes ♦ binocular vision. [from Latin words bini meaning 'two together' and oculus meaning 'eye']

binoculars plural noun an instrument with lenses for both eyes, making distant objects seem nearer.

binomial (biy-noh-mi-əl) noun an algebraic expression consisting of two terms linked by a plus or minus sign. [from bi- and a Greek word nomos meaning 'part']

binomial theorem noun a formula for finding any power of a binomial without doing the series of multiplications.

bio- prefix life (as in biology). [from a Greek word bios meaning 'life']

biochemistry noun the study of the chemical composition and processes of living organisms. **biochemical** adjective **biochemist** noun

biochip noun a device that works like a microchip, with components made from biological molecules or structures.

biodegradable (biy-oh-di-gray-də-bəl) adjective able to be broken down by bacteria in the environment ♦ All our packaging is biodegradable. **biodegradability** noun **biodegradation** noun

biodiversity noun the variety of plant and animal life in an area.

bioengineering noun the application of engineering techniques to biological processes.

biofeedback noun electronic monitoring of a bodily function that is normally automatic, as a means of learning to control the function oneself.

biographer noun a person who writes a biography.

biography noun (**biographies**) the story of a person's life written by someone else.
biographical adjective [from bio- and -graphy]

biological adjective **1** to do with biology. **2** (said about a parent) related to a child by blood. **3** (said about a detergent) containing enzymes. **biologically** adverb

biological clock noun an innate mechanism that an organism has for controlling regular functions.

biological warfare noun the deliberate use of organisms to spread disease among an enemy.

biology noun the scientific study of the life and structure of living things. **biologist** noun [from bio- and -logy]

biomass (biy-oh-mas) noun the total quantity or weight of living things in a particular area.

bionic (biy-on-ik) adjective **1** to do with bionics. **2** having artificial body parts, especially (in science fiction) when these give a person superhuman powers. [from bio- and electronic]

bionics noun the study of mechanical systems that function like parts of living beings.

biophysics noun the science of the application of physics to the study of living organisms. **biophysical** adjective **biophysicist** noun

biopic (biy-oh-pik) noun (informal) a film about a person's life. [from biography and picture]

biopsy (biy-op-si) noun (**biopsies**) an examination of tissue cut from a living body, to find out the cause or extent of a disease. [from bio- and autopsy]

bioreactor noun (Biology) an apparatus in which a biological reaction or process is carried out, especially on an industrial scale. [from bio- and reactor]

biorhythm (biy-ə-rithm) noun any of the recurring cycles of physical, emotional, and intellectual activity said to occur in people's lives.

bioscope (biy-ə-skohp) noun (in southern Africa) a cinema.

biosynthesis noun the production of complex molecules in living organisms.

biotechnology noun the use of living micro-organisms and biological processes in industrial and commercial production.

biotic (biy-ot-ik) adjective to do with life or living things.

bipartisan (biy-parti-zan) adjective to do with or involving two political or other parties.

bipartite (biy-par-tiyt) adjective 1 involving or made by two groups ♦ a bipartite agreement. 2 having two parts. [from bi- and a Latin word partitum meaning 'divided, parted']

biped (biy-ped) noun a two-footed animal. [from bi- and a Latin word pedes meaning 'feet']

biplane (biy-playn) noun a type of aircraft with two sets of wings, one above the other. [from bi- and plane]

birch noun 1 a deciduous tree with smooth bark and slender branches. 2 the wood of this tree. 3 a bundle of birch twigs used in the past for flogging people.
birch verb to beat someone with a bundle of birch twigs. [from an Old English word]

bird noun 1 a feathered animal with two wings and two legs. 2 (informal) a young woman. [from an Old English word]

birdie noun 1 (informal) a little bird. 2 (in golf) a score of one stroke under par for a hole.

bird of paradise noun a New Guinea bird with brightly coloured plumage.

bird of prey noun a bird, such as an eagle or hawk, that kills animals for food.

birdseed noun special seed used as food for caged birds.

bird's-eye view noun a general view from above.

biretta (bir-et-ə) noun a square cap worn by Roman Catholic clergymen. [from an Italian word berretta]

biriani (bi-ri-ah-ni) noun an Indian dish made with rice and meat, fish, or vegetables. [an Urdu word]

Biro noun (trademark) a ballpoint pen. [named after its Hungarian inventor L. Biró (1900–85)]

birth noun 1 the process by which a baby or young animal comes out from its mother's body. 2 the beginning of something ♦ the birth of rock and roll. 3 a person's ancestry or parentage ♦ He is of noble birth. **to give birth** to bear a baby or young. [from an Old Norse word]

birth certificate noun an official document giving the date and place of a person's birth.

birth control noun using contraception and other ways of avoiding conceiving a baby.

birthday noun the anniversary of the day of your birth. **in your birthday suit** completely naked.

birthmark noun a coloured mark that has been on a person's skin since birth.

birth mother noun a person's natural mother, as distinct from an adoptive mother.

birthplace noun the house or district where you were born.

birth rate noun the number of children born in one year for every 1,000 people.

birthright noun a right or privilege to which a person is entitled through being born into a particular family or country.

biscuit (bis-kit) noun 1 a small flat kind of cake that has been baked until it is crisp. 2 (North Amer.) a soft cake like a scone. 3 a light brown colour. [from Latin words bis meaning 'twice' and coctus meaning 'cooked' (because originally they were baked and then dried out in a cool oven to make them keep longer)]

bisect (biy-**sekt**) *verb* to divide something into two equal parts. **bisection** *noun* **bisector** *noun* [from *bi-* and a Latin word *sectum* meaning 'cut']

bisexual (biy-**seks**-yoo-əl) *adjective* 1 sexually attracted to both men and women. 2 having both male and female sexual organs in one individual. **bisexual** *noun* a person who is sexually attracted to both men and women.

bishop *noun* 1 a high-ranking member of the Christian clergy with authority over the work of the church in a city or district (called *diocese*). 2 a chess piece shaped like a bishop's mitre. [via Old English from a Latin word *episcopus*]

bishopric *noun* the office or diocese of a bishop.

bismuth (**biz**-məth) *noun* 1 a chemical element (symbol Bi), a greyish-white metal used in alloys. 2 a compound of this used in medicines. [via modern Latin from German]

bison (**biy**-sən) *noun* (**bison**) a shaggy-haired wild ox of Europe and North America. [from a Latin word]

bistable (biy-**stay**-bəl) *adjective* (said about an electronic circuit or device) having two stable states which can be used to represent 0 and 1.

bistro (**bee**-stroh) *noun* (**bistros**) a small restaurant. [a French word]

bit[1] *noun* 1 a small piece or quantity ♦ *a bit of cheese.* SYNONYMS: piece, fragment, morsel, scrap, speck, crumb (of bread). 2 a fair amount ♦ *He took a bit of persuading.* [from an Old English word *bita* meaning 'bite, mouthful'; related to *bite*]

bit[2] *noun* 1 a metal bar forming the mouthpiece of a horse's bridle. 2 the part of a drill used for boring. 3 the part of a tool that cuts or grips when twisted. **to get the bit between your teeth** to begin to tackle a task in a determined way. [from an Old English word *bite* meaning 'biting, a bite']

bit[3] *noun* (*Computing*) the smallest unit of information, expressed as 0 or 1. [from *bi*nary dig*it*]

bit[4] past tense of **bite**.

bitch *noun* 1 a female dog, fox, wolf, or otter. 2 (*informal*) a spiteful woman. **bitchiness** *noun* **bitchy** *adjective* [from an Old English word *bicce*]

bite *verb* (**bit, bitten**) 1 to cut or take

something with the teeth. 2 to be in the habit of biting people ♦ *Does your dog bite?* 3 (said about an insect or snake) to pierce the skin with its sting or fangs. 4 (said about fish) to accept bait. 5 to grip or take hold on a surface ♦ *Tyres don't bite so well on a wet road.* 6 to have an unpleasant effect ♦ *The education cuts were beginning to bite.*
bite *noun* 1 an act of biting, or a mouthful cut off by biting ♦ *He took a bite of the pie.* 2 a wound or mark made by biting ♦ *She was covered in insect bites.* 3 a quick snack ♦ *Have we got time for a bite to eat?* 4 an attempt by a fish to take the bait. 5 the way the teeth close in biting. **biter** *noun* [from an Old English word *bitan*, related to *bit*[1]]

biting *adjective* 1 (said about the wind) intensely cold. 2 (said about remarks) sharp and critical.

bit part *noun* a small part in a play or film.

bitten past participle of **bite**.

bitter *adjective* 1 having a sharp unpleasant taste, like quinine or aspirin. SYNONYMS: sour, sharp, acid, acrid. 2 showing or feeling angry hurt or resentment ♦ *He still feels bitter about the way he was treated.* SYNONYMS: embittered, resentful, sour, acrimonious. 3 causing sorrow ♦ *a bitter disappointment.* SYNONYMS: heartbreaking, painful, galling. 4 very cold ♦ *a bitter wind.*
bitter *noun* beer that is strongly flavoured with hops and has a bitter taste. **bitterly** *adverb* **bitterness** *noun* [from an Old English word *biter*, related to *bite*]

bittern *noun* a marsh bird related to the heron, known for the male's deep booming call. [from an Old French word]

bittersweet *adjective* 1 sweet but with a bitter aftertaste. 2 pleasant but with a mixture of something sad or unpleasant.

bitty *adjective* (**bittier, bittiest**) made up of unrelated bits.

bitumen (**bit**-yoo-mən) *noun* a black sticky substance obtained from petroleum, used for covering roads etc. **bituminous** (bit-**yoo**-min-əs) *adjective* [from a Latin word]

bivalve (**biy**-valv) *noun* a shellfish, such as an oyster or mussel, that has a shell with two hinged parts.

bivouac (**biv**-oo-ak) *noun* a temporary camp without tents or other cover.
bivouac *verb* (**bivouacs, bivouacked,**

bivouacking) to camp in a bivouac. [from a French word]

biweekly *adjective* 1 happening every two weeks. 2 happening twice a week.

bizarre (biz-**ar**) *adjective* strikingly odd in appearance or effect. [from an Italian word *bizarro* meaning 'angry']

blab *verb* (**blabbed, blabbing**) to let out a secret. [an imitation of the sound]

black *adjective* 1 of the very darkest colour, like coal or soot. SYNONYMS: dark, jet-black, pitch-black, ebony, sable, inky. 2 having a dark skin. 3 to do with dark-skinned people or with their culture. 4 (said about coffee or tea) without milk. 5 very dirty. 6 not hopeful ♦ The outlook is black. 7 involving tragedy or disaster ♦ This has been a black day in our history. 8 (said about humour) presenting a tragic theme or situation in comic terms. 9 hostile or disapproving ♦ He gave me a black look. **black** *noun* 1 a black colour. 2 black clothes ♦ She was dressed in black. 3 a person with a dark skin, especially a person with African or Australian Aboriginal ancestry. 4 the black ball in snooker. 5 the player using the black pieces in chess. **black** *verb* 1 to make something black. 2 to polish something with blacking. 3 to refuse to handle goods as a form of industrial action. **to black out** to lose consciousness. **to black something out** to cover windows etc. so that no light can penetrate. **in black and white** recorded in writing or print. **in the black** not owing any money, in credit. **blackly** *adverb* **blackness** *noun* [from an Old English word]

blackball *verb* to prevent a person from being elected as a member of a club by voting against him or her at a secret ballot. [from the practice of voting against someone by placing a black ball in a ballot box]

blackberry *noun* (**blackberries**) 1 the bramble. 2 its small sweet dark berry. **blackberrying** *noun* picking blackberries.

blackbird *noun* a European songbird, the male of which is black.

blackboard *noun* a dark board for writing on with chalk.

black box *noun* (*informal*) an aircraft's flight recorder.

blackcock *noun* a male black grouse.

black economy *noun* an unofficial system of employing and paying people without paying income tax and National Insurance contributions.

blacken *verb* (**blackened, blackening**) 1 to make something black, or to become black. 2 to damage a person's reputation ♦ His enemies tried to blacken his name.

black eye *noun* an eye with the skin round it darkened by a bruise.

blackfly *noun* (**blackflies**) a kind of insect infesting plants.

blackguard (**blag**-erd) *noun* (*old use*) a man who behaves in a wicked or dishonourable way. **blackguardly** *adverb* [originally the black guard denoting the servants who did the dirty jobs]

blackhead *noun* a small black spot blocking a pore in the skin.

black hole *noun* a region in outer space with a gravitational field so intense that no matter or radiation can escape from it.

black ice *noun* hard thin transparent ice on roads.

blacking *noun* black polish for shoes.

blacklead *noun* graphite.

blackleg *noun* a person who continues to work while their fellow workers are on strike. **blackleg** *verb* (**blacklegged, blacklegging**) to act as a blackleg. [originally a disease affecting sheep]

blacklist *noun* a list of people who are disapproved of. **blacklist** *verb* to put someone on a blacklist.

black magic *noun* magic involving the summoning of evil spirits.

blackmail *verb* to demand payment or action from a person by threatening to do something, especially to reveal a secret which will damage their reputation. **blackmail** *noun* the crime of demanding payment or using threats in this way. **blackmailer** *noun* [from black and mail[2]; literally meaning 'black armour or protection']

black mark *noun* a record of the fact that someone has done something to earn disapproval or criticism.

black market *noun* the illegal buying and selling of goods or currencies.

black marketeer *noun* someone who trades in the black market.

blackout *noun* 1 a period of darkness when no light must be shown; the extinguishing of all lights. 2 a temporary loss of consciousness. 3 prevention of the release of information ♦ *a total news blackout.*

black pudding *noun* a large dark sausage containing blood, suet, etc.

black sheep *noun* a member of a family or other group who is seen as a disgrace to it.

blacksmith *noun* a person who makes and repairs iron things, especially someone who makes and fits horseshoes. [so called because of the dark colour of iron]

black spot *noun* a dangerous place.

blackthorn *noun* a thorny shrub bearing white flowers and sloes.

black tie *noun* a man's black bow tie worn with a dinner jacket.

black widow *noun* a poisonous spider found in tropical and subtropical regions. The female of a North American species devours its mate.

bladder *noun* 1 the bag-like part of the body in which urine collects. 2 the inflatable bag inside a football. [from an Old English word]

bladderwrack *noun* a seaweed with air-filled swellings among its fronds.

blade *noun* 1 the flat cutting edge of a knife, sword, chisel, etc. 2 the flat wide part of an oar, spade, propeller, etc. 3 a flat narrow leaf ♦ *blades of grass.* 4 a broad flattish bone ♦ *the shoulder blade.* [from an Old English word]

blame *verb* 1 to hold someone responsible for causing what is wrong ♦ *Police are blaming him for the accident.* SYNONYMS: accuse, charge. 2 to find fault with someone ♦ *I don't blame you for feeling angry.* SYNONYMS: criticize, condemn, denounce, reproach.
blame *noun* responsibility for what is wrong. [from an Old French word]

blameless *adjective* deserving no blame, innocent.

blanch *verb* 1 to make or become white or pale ♦ *He blanched with fear.* 2 to immerse fruit or vegetables briefly in boiling water. [from a French word *blanc* meaning 'white']

blancmange (bla-**monj**) *noun* a flavoured jelly-like pudding made with milk. [from French words *blanc* meaning 'white' and *manger* meaning 'to eat']

bland *adjective* 1 lacking flavour ♦ *bland foods.* 2 polite but dull ♦ *a bland reply.*
blandly *adverb* **blandness** *noun* [from a Latin word *blandus* meaning 'soothing']

blandishments *plural noun* flattering or coaxing words. [same origin as for *bland*]

blank *adjective* 1 not written, printed, or recorded on or decorated ♦ *Just leave a blank space* ♦ *a blank cheque* ♦ *a blank wall.* 2 showing no expression ♦ *a blank look.* SYNONYMS: expressionless, vacant, impassive, inscrutable. 3 empty ♦ *a blank cartridge.* 4 empty of thoughts ♦ *My mind's gone blank.*
blank *noun* 1 an empty space ♦ *In this puzzle you have to fill in the blanks* ♦ *His mind was a total blank.* 2 a blank cartridge.
blank *verb* **to blank something out** 1 to cross something out or obscure it. 2 to deliberately try to forget something. **to draw a blank** to fail to find what you are looking for. **to look blank** to appear puzzled. **blankly** *adverb* **blankness** *noun* [from a French word *blanc* meaning 'white']

blanket *noun* 1 a thick covering made of woollen or other fabric. 2 a thick soft mass of something that completely covers a place ♦ *a blanket of snow.*
blanket *adjective* covering all cases or instances ♦ *a blanket ban on tobacco advertising.*
blanket *verb* (**blanketed, blanketing**) to cover something completely with a thick layer. [originally denoting woollen cloth which had not been dyed; from a French word *blanc* meaning 'white']

blank verse *noun* verse written without rhyme, usually in lines of ten syllables.

blare *verb* to make a loud harsh sound like that of a horn or trumpet.
blare *noun* a loud harsh sound. [an imitation of the sound]

blarney *noun* smooth talk that flatters and deceives people. [named after Blarney Castle in Ireland where there is a stone said to give anyone who kisses it the ability to talk persuasively]

blasé (blah-**zay**) *adjective* bored or unimpressed by things because you have already experienced or seen them so often. [a French word]

blaspheme verb to talk or write irreverently about God or sacred things. **blasphemer** noun [from a Greek word *blasphēmos* meaning 'evil-speaking']

blasphemy (blas-fəmi) noun (**blasphemies**) contemptuous or irreverent talk about God and sacred things. **blasphemous** adjective **blasphemously** adverb

blast noun 1 a sudden strong rush of wind or air. 2 a wave of air from an explosion. 3 a single loud note from a trumpet, whistle, car horn, etc. **blast** verb 1 to blow something up with explosives. 2 to kick or hit a ball hard. 3 to cause a plant to wither or shrivel. **at full blast** at maximum power. **to blast off** to launch by the firing of rockets. [from an Old English word, related to *blow*¹]

blast furnace noun a furnace for smelting ore, with compressed hot air driven in.

blast-off noun the launching of a rocket or spacecraft.

blatant (blay-tənt) adjective very obvious and unashamed ♦ *a blatant lie.* **blatantly** adverb [from an Old word meaning 'noisy']

blaze¹ noun 1 a large hot fire. 2 a bright display of light or colour ♦ *The garden was a blaze of colour.* 3 an impressive show of something ♦ *The film opened in a blaze of publicity.* **blaze** verb 1 to burn or shine strongly and brightly. 2 to have an outburst of intense feeling or anger ♦ *He was blazing with anger.* [from an Old English word]

blaze² noun 1 a white mark on an animal's face. 2 a mark chipped in the bark of a tree to mark a route. **blaze** verb to mark a tree or route with blazes. **to blaze a trail** to be the first to do something and show the way for others to follow. [origin unknown]

blazer noun a type of jacket, often in the colours or bearing the badge of a school, club, or team. [from *blaze*¹ (because originally blazers were made in very bright colours and were thought of as shining or 'blazing')]

blazon (blay-zən) noun (old use) a heraldic shield or coat of arms. [from an Old French word *blason* meaning 'shield']

bleach verb to make something turn white by sunlight or chemicals. **bleach** noun a chemical used to bleach things and kill germs. [from an Old English word, related to *bleak*]

bleak adjective 1 cold and bare ♦ *a bleak landscape.* **SYNONYMS:** desolate, barren. 2 not at all hopeful ♦ *The future looks bleak.* **SYNONYMS:** hopeless, grim, dismal, depressing. **bleakly** adverb **bleakness** noun [from an Old English word, related to *bleach*]

bleary adjective (said about eyes) watery and not seeing clearly. **blearily** adverb **bleariness** noun [origin unknown]

bleat verb 1 to make the cry of a sheep, goat, or calf. 2 to speak or complain in a weak or foolish way ♦ *What are they bleating about now?* **bleat** noun a bleating sound. [an imitation of the sound]

bleed verb (past tense and past participle **bled**) 1 to lose blood. 2 to come out in water ♦ *Some dyes bleed.* 3 to draw blood from someone. 4 to take money away from someone ♦ *Local gangsters were bleeding him dry.* [from an Old English word, related to *blood*]

bleep verb to make the high-pitched sound of an electronic device. **bleep** noun a bleeping sound. [an imitation of the sound]

bleeper noun a small electronic device that bleeps when the wearer is contacted.

blemish noun a flaw that prevents something from being perfect; a mark that spoils the appearance of something. **blemish** verb to spoil something with a blemish ♦ *These allegations have blemished his reputation.* [from an Old French word *blemir* meaning 'to make pale, injure']

blench verb to flinch. [from an Old English word]

blend verb 1 to mix things together, or to become a mixture ♦ *Blend the eggs and milk together.* 2 to combine well with something ♦ *Their voices blend well.* 3 to join together so that nothing stands out from the rest ♦ *The sea and the sky seemed to blend into each other.* **blend** noun a mixture of different sorts ♦ *a blend of tea.* [probably from a Scandinavian word]

blender noun a machine for mixing food or turning it into liquid.

bless verb 1 (said about a priest) to ask for a person or thing to receive God's favour and protection, e.g. by making the sign of the cross over them. 2 to praise God or call God holy. **to be blessed with** to be fortunate in having something ♦ *She is* *blessed with good health.* [from an Old English word]

blessed (bles-id) *adjective* 1 holy or sacred, favoured by God ♦ *the Blessed Virgin.* 2 bringing happiness or relief ♦ *a few moments of blessed calm.* **blessedness** *noun*

blessing *noun* 1 a prayer that blesses a person or thing; being blessed. 2 a short prayer of thanks to God before or after a meal. 3 something that you are grateful for ♦ *It's a blessing no one was hurt.* **a blessing in disguise** something unwelcome at the time but which later turns out to have good results.

blew past tense of **blow**[1].

blight *noun* 1 a disease that withers plants, especially one caused by a fungus. 2 a thing that spoils or damages something ♦ *Poverty is a blight on their community.* 3 an unsightly area or landscape.
blight *verb* 1 to affect something with blight. 2 to spoil or damage something ♦ *Scandal has blighted his career.* [origin unknown]

blighter *noun* (*informal*) a person or thing, especially an annoying one.

blind *adjective* 1 without the ability to see. 2 without thought or understanding ♦ *blind obedience* ♦ *She was in a blind rage.* 3 (said about a corner or bend) impossible to see round. 4 (said about a tube, passage, or road) closed at one end. 5 (said about a plant) failing to produce a flower.
blind *adverb* without being able to see clearly.
blind *verb* 1 to make someone blind. 2 to dazzle someone with bright light. 3 to prevent you from realizing something ♦ *Her loyalty blinded her to his faults.*
blind *noun* 1 a screen, especially on a roller, for a window. 2 something used to hide your real intentions. **to blind someone with science** to confuse someone with a display of knowledge they do not understand. **to turn a blind eye** to pretend not to notice something. **blindly** *adverb* **blindness** *noun* [from an Old English word]

blind alley *noun* 1 an alley that is closed at one end. 2 a course of action that leads nowhere.

blind date *noun* a date between people who have not met before.

blindfold *noun* a strip of cloth tied round someone's eyes so that they cannot see.

blindfold *verb* to cover someone's eyes with a blindfold.
blindfold *adverb* with a blindfold covering the eyes. [from an Old English word *blindfeld* meaning 'struck blind', from *blind* and *fell*[2]]

blinding *adjective* (said about light) so bright that it hurts your eyes ♦ *a blinding flash.*

blindingly *adverb* **blindingly obvious** overwhelmingly obvious.

blind man's buff *noun* a game in which a blindfolded player tries to catch others who push him or her about. [from an old word *buff* meaning 'a blow']

blind spot *noun* 1 a point on the eye that is insensitive to light. 2 an area cut off from a motorist's vision. 3 a subject that you do not understand or know much about ♦ *I've got a blind spot about modern art.*

blink *verb* 1 to open and shut your eyes rapidly. 2 to shine unsteadily ♦ *a blinking light.*
blink *noun* 1 an act of blinking. 2 a quick gleam of light. **on the blink** (*informal*) not working properly. [from *blench*, influenced by a Dutch word *blinken* meaning 'shine']

blinker *verb* (**blinkered, blinkering**) 1 to put blinkers on a horse. 2 to make someone have a narrow or limited outlook.
blinkers *plural noun* leather pieces fixed on a bridle to prevent a horse from seeing sideways. [originally denoting a person who was half-blind; from *blink*]

blip *noun* 1 a very short high-pitched sound made by an electronic device. 2 a spot of light on a radar screen.
blip *verb* (**blipped, blipping**) to make a blip. [an imitation of the sound]

bliss *adjective* perfect happiness. **blissful** *adjective* **blissfully** *adverb* [from an Old English word, related to *blithe*]

blister *noun* 1 a bubble-like swelling on the skin, filled with watery liquid. 2 a raised swelling, e.g. on a painted surface.
blister *verb* (**blistered, blistering**) to cause a blister on the skin, or to be affected with blisters. [perhaps from an Old French word *blestre* meaning 'swelling, pimple']

blistering *adjective* 1 (said about heat) intense. 2 (said about criticism) very severe.

blithe (bliyth) *adjective* casual and carefree.

blithely adverb [from an Old English word, related to *bliss*]

blithering adjective (*informal*) complete, absolute ♦ *a blithering idiot.*

blitz noun 1 a sudden violent attack, especially from aircraft. 2 a burst of busy activity.
blitz verb to attack or damage a place in a blitz. [short for a German word *Blitzkrieg*, from *Blitz* meaning 'lightning' and *Krieg* meaning 'war']

blizzard noun a severe snowstorm. [origin unknown]

bloated adjective 1 swollen with fat, gas, or liquid. 2 puffed up with pride or excessive wealth. [from an Old Norse word *blautr* meaning 'soft']

bloater noun a salted smoked herring. [same origin as for *bloated*]

blob noun 1 a drop of thick liquid. 2 a round mass or spot. [so called because *blob* sounds squelchy, like liquid]

bloc noun a group of parties or countries who have formed an alliance. [a French word meaning 'block']

block noun 1 a solid piece of wood, stone, or other hard substance. SYNONYMS: chunk, hunk, lump, slab, bar. 2 a large building divided into separate flats or offices. 3 a group of buildings with streets on all sides ♦ *I went for a walk round the block.* 4 a large piece of wood on which condemned people were beheaded in the past. 5 the main part of a petrol engine, consisting of the cylinders. 6 a pad of paper for drawing or writing on. 7 an obstacle or obstruction ♦ *I've got a mental block about her name.* 8 a starting block in a race.
block verb 1 to obstruct something so that nothing can get through ♦ *The pipe is blocked* ♦ *A fallen tree was blocking the road.* SYNONYMS: clog, bung up, jam, obstruct. 2 to prevent something happening ♦ *The opposition will try to block the new proposals.* SYNONYMS: obstruct, impede, hinder, thwart. 3 (in cricket) to stop a bowled ball with the bat. **to block something in** to shade something roughly. [originally denoting a log or tree stump; via French from a Dutch word *blok*]

blockade noun the act of sealing off a place in order to prevent people and goods from going in or out.
blockade verb to set up a blockade of a place. [from *block*]

blockage noun something that blocks a pipe, tube, tunnel, etc.

block and tackle noun a system of pulleys and ropes used for lifting things.

blockbuster noun (*informal*) a film or book that is extremely successful.

block capitals plural noun plain capital letters.

block diagram noun a diagram showing the general arrangement of parts in an apparatus.

blockhead noun (*informal*) a stupid person.

block vote noun a voting system in which each voter has influence according to the number of people he or she represents.

bloke noun (*informal*) a man. [from Shelta (an ancient language used by Irish and Welsh gypsies)]

blonde or **blond** adjective 1 (said about hair) fair. 2 fair-haired.
blonde noun a woman with blonde hair. [from a medieval Latin word *blondus* meaning 'yellow']

blood noun 1 the red oxygen-bearing liquid circulating in the bodies of animals. 2 violence involving bloodshed. 3 family backgound, descent or parentage ♦ *Do you have any Irish blood?* 4 temper or passion.
blood verb 1 to initiate someone in a new activity. 2 to give a first taste of blood to a hound. **bad blood** hatred between people. **in cold blood** deliberately and cruelly. [from an Old English word, related to *bleed*]

blood bank noun a place where supplies of blood and plasma for transfusions are stored.

bloodbath noun a massacre.

blood count noun the number of corpuscles in a specified amount of blood.

blood-curdling adjective horrifying.

blood group noun any of the classes or types of human blood.

bloodhound noun a large dog with a very keen sense of smell, formerly used in tracking.

bloodless adjective 1 looking pale, drained of blood. 2 without violence or killing ♦ *a bloodless coup.* 3 without vitality, feeble.

blood money noun money paid as compensation to the family of someone who has been killed.

blood orange noun an orange with red-streaked pulp.

blood poisoning noun the condition that results when the bloodstream is infected with harmful micro-organisms that have entered the body, especially through a cut or wound.

blood pressure noun the pressure of blood within the arteries and veins.

bloodshed noun the killing or wounding of people.

bloodshot adjective (said about the eyes) streaked with red, usually because of tiredness.

blood sport noun a sport involving wounding or killing animals.

bloodstain noun a stain made by blood. **bloodstained** adjective

bloodstock noun thoroughbred horses.

bloodstream noun the blood circulating in the body.

bloodsucker noun an animal or insect that sucks blood.

blood sugar noun the proportion of glucose in the blood.

bloodthirsty adjective eager to use or watch violence.

blood vessel noun a vein, artery, or capillary tube carrying blood.

bloody adjective (bloodier, bloodiest) 1 covered in blood. 2 involving much killing and wounding ◆ a bloody battle. 3 (informal) used as a mild swear word. **bloody** verb (bloodies, bloodied, bloodying) to stain something with blood. **bloodily** adverb **bloodiness** noun

bloody-minded adjective deliberately awkward and unhelpful.

bloom noun 1 a flower. 2 a state of youthful beauty or health. 3 the fine powder on fresh ripe grapes etc. **bloom** verb 1 to bear flowers, to be in bloom. 2 to be in full beauty or health. **in bloom** in flower ◆ The apple trees are now in bloom. [from an Old Norse word]

bloomer noun a long rounded loaf with slashes along the top. [origin unknown]

bloomers plural noun (informal) women's loose-fitting knee-length knickers. [named after an American social reformer Mrs A. Bloomer (1818–94), who wore loose-fitting trousers]

blossom noun a flower or mass of flowers on a tree. **blossom** verb 1 to produce blossom. 2 to develop and flourish ◆ She has blossomed into a fine singer. **in blossom** producing blossom. [from an Old English word]

blot noun 1 a spot of ink. 2 a thing that spoils something ◆ a blot on his reputation. **blot** verb (blotted, blotting) 1 to make a blot or blots on something. 2 to dry something with blotting paper, to soak up. **to blot your copybook** to spoil your good record. **to blot something out** 1 to obscure something ◆ During a total eclipse the moon completely blots out the sun. 2 to make a deliberate effort to forget a painful memory or thought. [probably from a Scandinavian language]

blotch noun a large irregular mark or patch. **blotch** verb to mark something with blotches. **blotchy** adjective [related to blot]

blotting paper noun absorbent paper for drying ink when you are writing.

blouse noun 1 a woman's piece of clothing like a shirt. 2 a waist-length coat forming part of a military uniform. [from a French word]

blouson (bloo-zon) noun a short loose-fitting jacket. [a French word, related to blouse]

blow[1] verb (blew, blown) 1 to move or flow as a current of air does ◆ The wind was blowing hard ◆ It was blowing a gale. 2 to move something by sending out a current of air ◆ A gust of wind blew his wig off. 3 to be moved or carried by air or the wind ◆ The door blew open ◆ His hat blew off. 4 to send out a current of air from your mouth, or to make or sound something by doing this ◆ The kids were blowing bubbles ◆ The referee blew the whistle. 5 to shape molten glass by blowing into it. 6 to melt with too strong an electric current ◆ A fuse must have blown ◆ You must have blown the fuse. 7 to break something with explosives ◆ The thieves blew the safe. 8 (informal) to make a mess of something ◆ You've completely blown it! 9 (informal) to reveal something ◆ The spy's cover was blown. 10 (informal) to spend money recklessly ◆ He blew the lot on the horses. **blow** noun 1 an act of blowing. 2 exposure to fresh air. **to blow in** (informal) to arrive casually or unexpectedly. **to blow someone's mind** (informal) to impress someone very powerfully. **to blow your**

nose to clear your nose by breathing out through it. **to blow over** to die down without serious consequences ♦ *All this fuss will blow over in a few weeks.* **to blow your own trumpet** to praise yourself. **to blow your top** (*informal*) to show great anger. **to blow up 1** to explode. **2** to destroy something with an explosion. **3** to inflate or enlarge something ♦ *I'll blow up some balloons* ♦ *Would you like this photo blown up?* **4** to exaggerate. **5** to lose your temper. **6** to become a crisis ♦ *This problem has blown up recently.* [from an Old English word]

blow[2] *noun* **1** a hard knock or hit with the hand or a weapon. **2** a sudden shock or disappointment. [origin unknown]

blow-by-blow *adjective* telling all the details of an event in the order in which they occurred.

blow-dry *verb* (**blow-dries, blow-dried, blow-drying**) to use a hand-held dryer to style washed hair while drying it.

blower *noun* **1** a device that creates a current of air. **2** (*informal*) a telephone.

blowfly *noun* (**blowflies**) a fly that lays its eggs on meat.

blowhole *noun* the nostril of a whale or dolphin on the top of its head.

blowlamp *noun* a blowtorch.

blown past participle of **blow**[1].

blowout *noun* **1** a burst tyre. **2** a melted fuse. **3** a rapid uncontrolled upward rush of oil or gas from a well.

blowpipe *noun* **1** a tube for sending out darts or pellets by blowing. **2** a tube through which air or gas is blown.

blowsy (**blow-zi**) *adjective* (said about a woman) red-faced and coarse-looking. [from an old word *blowze* meaning 'beggar's female companion']

blowtorch *noun* a portable burner producing a very hot flame that can be directed on a selected spot.

blow-up *noun* an enlargement of a photograph.

blowy *adjective* (**blowier, blowiest**) windy.

blub *verb* (**blubbed, blubbing**) to weep noisily. [abbreviation of *blubber*]

blubber *noun* whale fat.
blubber *verb* to weep noisily. [originally denoting sea foam; probably related to *bubble*]

bludgeon (**bluj-ən**) *noun* a short stick with a thickened end, used as a weapon.
bludgeon *verb* **1** to beat someone with a heavy stick or other object. **2** to bully someone into doing something. [origin unknown]

blue *adjective* (**bluer, bluest**) **1** of the colour of a cloudless sky. **2** unhappy or depressed. **3** indecent or obscene ♦ *blue films.*
blue *noun* **1** blue colour. **2** blue clothes ♦ *She was dressed all in blue.* **3** (**the blue**) the sky or sea. **4** a person who has represented Oxford or Cambridge University in a sport.
blue *verb* (**blues, blued, blueing**) to make something blue, or to become blue. **once in a blue moon** very rarely. **out of the blue** unexpectedly. **blueness** *noun* [from an Old French word *bleu*, of Germanic origin]

bluebell *noun* a plant with blue bell-shaped flowers.

blueberry *noun* (**blueberries**) **1** a shrub with edible blue berries. **2** the fruit of this shrub.

blue blood *noun* aristocratic descent.
blue-blooded *adjective*

bluebottle *noun* a large fly with a bluish body. [origin unknown]

blue cheese *noun* cheese with veins of blue mould.

blue-chip *adjective* (said about companies or their shares) fairly reliable as an investment though less secure than gilt-edged. [from the high-valued blue chips in gambling games]

blue-collar *adjective* (said about a worker) involved in manual work, especially in industry.

Blue Peter *noun* a blue flag with a white square, hoisted by a ship about to leave port.

blueprint *noun* **1** a design plan or technical drawing. **2** a detailed plan or scheme. [so called because copies of plans used to be made on blue paper]

blues *noun* **1** a slow sad jazz song or tune, of black American folk origin. **2** (**the blues**) feelings of sadness or depression. [from *blue devils*, spiteful demons believed to cause depression]

blue tit *noun* a small bird with bright blue wings, tail, and top of head.

blue whale *noun* a bluish-grey rorqual, the largest living animal.

bluff[1] *verb* to try to deceive someone into believing that you are in a stronger position than you really are or that you are able to do something.
bluff *noun* an attempt to bluff someone, a threat that you make but do not intend to carry out. [from a Dutch word *bluffen* meaning 'to boast']

bluff[2] *adjective* frank and direct, but in a good-natured way.
bluff *noun* a headland or cliff with a broad steep front. **bluffness** *noun* [originally a sailor's word to describe a blunt ship's bow]

bluish *adjective* having a blue tinge.

blunder *noun* a mistake made especially through ignorance or carelessness.
blunder *verb* 1 to make a blunder. 2 to move clumsily and uncertainly ♦ *I could hear him blundering about upstairs.* **blunderer** *noun* [probably from a Scandinavian language]

blunderbuss *noun* an old type of hand-held gun that fired many balls at one shot. [from a Dutch word *donderbus* meaning 'thunder gun']

blunt *adjective* 1 with no sharp edge or point, not sharp. 2 speaking or expressed in plain terms ♦ *a blunt refusal*. SYNONYMS: direct, straightforward, forthright, curt, abrupt, brusque.
blunt *verb* to make something blunt, or to become blunt. **bluntly** *adverb* **bluntness** *noun* [probably from a Scandinavian language]

blur *noun* something that you cannot see, hear, or remember clearly ♦ *Without his glasses on, everything was a blur*.
blur *verb* (**blurred, blurring**) to make something less clear or distinct, or to become less clear or distinct. [origin unknown]

blurb *noun* a description of something praising it, e.g. on the back of a book. [first used by the American writer G. Burgess]

blurred *adjective* 1 not clear in outline, out of focus ♦ *a blurred photograph*. SYNONYMS: fuzzy, hazy. 2 difficult to distinguish ♦ *The boundary between right and wrong had become blurred*.

blurt *verb* to say something abruptly or tactlessly ♦ *He blurted it out before he had time to think*. [origin unknown]

blush *verb* to become red in the face because you are ashamed or embarrassed.

blush *noun* a reddening of the face. [from an Old English word *blyscan*]

blusher *noun* a cosmetic used to add red colour to the cheeks.

bluster *verb* 1 to talk aggressively, especially with empty threats. 2 (said about the wind or rain) to blow strongly in gusts.
bluster *noun* blustering talk. **blustery** *adjective* [an imitation of the sound]

BMA *abbreviation* British Medical Association.

BMX *noun* 1 organized bicycle racing on a dirt track. 2 a kind of strongly made bicycle suitable for this. [short for 'bicycle motocross']

boa or **boa constrictor** (boh-ə) *noun* a large non-poisonous South American snake that squeezes its prey in order to suffocate it. [from Latin]

boar *noun* 1 a wild pig. 2 an uncastrated domestic male pig. [from an Old English word]

board *noun* 1 a long thin flat piece of sawn timber. 2 a flat piece of wood or stiff material for a special purpose ♦ *a chopping board* ♦ *a chess board* ♦ *a diving board*. 3 a committee, the group of people who make the decisions in an organization. 4 daily meals obtained in return for payment or work ♦ *board and lodging*.
board *verb* 1 to get on or into a ship, aircraft, etc. 2 to receive meals and accommodation for payment. **to go by the board** to be ignored or rejected. **on board** on or in a ship, aircraft, etc. **to take something on board** to accept a new idea or situation and consider or act upon it. [from an Old English word *bord*]

boarder *noun* 1 a resident pupil at a boarding school. 2 a lodger who receives meals.

board game *noun* a game in which you move pieces around a board.

boarding house *noun* a private house where people obtain meals and lodging for payment.

boarding school *noun* a school where pupils live during the term.

boardroom *noun* a room where the meetings of the board of a company are held.

boardsailing *noun* another word for **windsurfing**.

boast *verb* 1 to speak with great pride about yourself in order to impress people. SYNONYMS: brag, crow, (*informal*) blow your own trumpet, swank. 2 to have something to be proud of ♦ *The town boasts a fine park.* **boast** *noun* 1 a boastful statement. 2 something you are proud of. **boaster** *noun* [origin unknown]

boastful *adjective* boasting frequently. **boastfully** *adverb* **boastfulness** *noun*

boat *noun* 1 a small vessel for travelling on water, propelled by paddle, oars, sails, or an engine. 2 a ship. **in the same boat** in the same predicament as others. **to rock the boat** to cause trouble. [from an Old English word]

boater *noun* a hard flat straw hat. [originally worn by men when rowing boats]

boathouse *noun* a shed at the water's edge for housing boats.

boatman *noun* (**boatmen**) a man who rows or sails boats or who rents out boats.

boat people *plural noun* refugees leaving a country by sea.

boatswain (boh-sən) *noun* a ship's officer in charge of rigging, boats, anchors, etc. [from *boat* and *swain* in the sense 'servant']

bob¹ *verb* (**bobbed, bobbing**) 1 to make a jerky movement, to move quickly up and down. 2 to cut hair short so that it hangs loosely and evenly all round the head. **bob** *noun* 1 a quick short movement up and down. 2 the style of bobbed hair. [origin unknown]

bob² *noun* (**bob**) (*informal*) a shilling, 5p. [origin unknown]

bobbin *noun* a small spool holding thread or wire in a machine. [from a French word]

bobble *noun* a small ball made of strands of wool, e.g. on a woolly hat. [origin unknown]

bobby *noun* (**bobbies**) (*informal*) a police officer. [named after Sir Robert Peel (1788–1850), founder of the Metropolitan Police Force]

bobsleigh (bob-slay) or **bobsled** *nouns* a sledge with two sets of runners and mechanical steering, used for racing down an ice-covered run. **bobsleighing** *noun* [origin unknown]

bode *verb* to be a sign or omen of what is to come ♦ *It doesn't bode well for their future.* [from an Old English word *bodian*]

bodice (bod-iss) *noun* 1 the upper part of a woman's dress, down to the waist. 2 a woman's piece of underclothing like a vest. [from *body*]

bodily *adjective* to do with the human body or physical nature. **bodily** *adverb* by taking hold of someone's body ♦ *She was dragged bodily off the stage.*

bodkin *noun* a blunt thick needle with a large eye. [origin unknown]

body *noun* (**bodies**) 1 the structure of bones, flesh, etc., of a human being or animal, living or dead. 2 the main part of the body apart from the head and limbs. 3 a corpse or carcass. 4 the main or central part of something ♦ *a car body* ♦ *the body of a concert hall.* 5 a group or quantity of people, things, or matter, regarded as a unit ♦ *the school's governing body.* 6 a distinct piece of matter, or an object in space. 7 a thick texture or full flavour ♦ *This wine has no body.* 8 another word for **bodysuit**. [from an Old English word]

body blow *noun* 1 a heavy punch. 2 a severe setback.

bodybuilding *noun* strengthening and enlarging your muscles by exercise such as weightlifting. **bodybuilder** *noun*

bodyguard *noun* a personal guard employed to protect an important person.

body language *noun* movements by which you communicate your feelings or moods.

body piercing *noun* the piercing of parts of the body for decoration.

body shop *noun* a garage that deals with repairs to the bodywork of vehicles.

bodysuit *noun* a tight-fitting piece of clothing worn by women on the upper part of the body.

bodywork *noun* the outer shell of a motor vehicle.

Boer (boh-er) *noun* 1 an Afrikaner. 2 (*old use*) an early Dutch inhabitant of South Africa. **Boer** *adjective* to do with the Boers. [from a Dutch word meaning 'farmer']

boffin *noun* (*informal*) a person involved in scientific or technical research. [origin unknown]

bog *noun* an area of ground that is permanently wet and spongy. **to be bogged down** to be stuck and unable to make progress. **boggy** *adjective* [from a Scottish Gaelic word *bogach* meaning 'soft']

bogey [1] *noun* (**bogeys**) (in golf) a score of one stroke over par at a hole. [same origin as for *bogey* [2]]

bogey [2] *noun* (**bogeys**) **1** an evil spirit. **2** something that frightens people. [perhaps from *Bogey*, denoting the Devil]

bogeyman *noun* (**bogeymen**) an imaginary man feared by children, especially in the dark.

boggle *verb* (*informal*) to be amazed or puzzled ♦ *The mind boggles at the idea.* [from a dialect word *bogle* meaning 'bogey']

bogie (boh-gi) *noun* an undercarriage fitted below a railway vehicle, pivoted at the end for going round curves. [origin unknown]

bogus *adjective* not genuine or true. [an American word; origin unknown]

Bohemian *adjective* not conventional in your way of living.
Bohemian *noun* a person who does not live in a socially conventional way. [from a French word *bohémien* meaning 'gypsy' (because gypsies were thought to come from Bohemia, a region of what is now the Czech Republic)]

boil [1] *verb* **1** (said about a liquid) to bubble up and change into vapour through being heated. **2** to heat a liquid or its container so that the liquid boils. **3** to cook or wash something in boiling water, to be heated or cooked in this way. **4** to be seething with anger. **5** (*informal*) to be very hot ♦ *I'm boiling!*
boil *noun* boiling point ♦ *Bring the milk to the boil.* **to boil down 1** to reduce or be reduced in quantity by boiling. **2** to express or be expressed in fewer words ♦ *It boils down to a question of money.* **to boil over** to overflow when boiling. **off the boil** having just stopped boiling. **on the boil** boiling. [from a Latin word *bulla* meaning 'a bubble']

boil [2] *noun* an inflamed swelling under the skin, filled with pus. [from an Old English word]

boiler *noun* **1** a container in which water is heated or clothes are boiled. **2** a water tank in which a hot-water supply is stored. **3** (*informal*) a chicken not tender enough to roast but suitable for boiling.

boiler suit *noun* a single piece of clothing combining overalls and shirt, worn for rough work.

boiling point *noun* **1** the temperature at which a liquid boils. **2** a state of great anger or excitement.

boisterous *adjective* **1** noisy and lively ♦ *boisterous children.* **2** wild and stormy ♦ *boisterous weather.* **boisterously** *adverb* [origin unknown]

bold *adjective* **1** confident and courageous. SYNONYMS: brave, daring, adventurous, intrepid, valiant. **2** (said about colours, designs, etc.) strong and vivid. SYNONYMS: striking, eye-catching. **3** without feelings of shame, impudent. SYNONYMS: cheeky, forward, brash, brazen. **4** printed in thick black type. **boldly** *adverb* **boldness** *noun* [from an Old English word *bald*]

boldface *noun* a type face with thick strokes.

bole *noun* the trunk of a tree. [from an Old Norse word *bolr*]

bolero *noun* (**boleros**) **1** (bə-**lair**-oh) a Spanish dance, or the music for this. **2** (**bol**-er-oh) a woman's short jacket with no front fastening. [from Spanish]

boll (bohl) *noun* the round seed vessel of plants such as cotton or flax. [originally denoting a bubble, from an early Dutch word *bolle* meaning 'rounded object']

bollard (bol-erd) *noun* **1** a short post for keeping traffic off a road or part of a road. **2** a short thick post on a quayside or ship to which a ship's rope may be tied. [probably the same origin as for *bole*]

boll weevil *noun* a destructive insect infesting the cotton plant.

bolshie *adjective* (*informal*) rebellious or uncooperative. **bolshiness** *noun* [from the *Bolsheviks*, the extremist faction of the Russian socialist party which was renamed the (Russian) Communist Party in 1918]

bolster *noun* a long pillow for placing across a bed under other pillows.
bolster *verb* to add extra strength or support to something ♦ *Winning the prize has really bolstered his confidence.* [from an Old English word]

bolt [1] *noun* **1** a sliding bar for fastening a door or window. **2** a strong metal pin that screws into a nut, used for fastening

things together. **3** the sliding bar that opens and closes the breech of a rifle. **4** an arrow shot from a crossbow. **5** a shaft of lightning.
bolt *verb* **1** to fasten something with a bolt or bolts ♦ *We bolted all the windows.* **2** to escape or run away. **3** (said about plants) to run to seed. **4** to gulp down food quickly. **a bolt from the blue** a complete surprise. **bolt upright** sitting or standing with your back straight. [from an Old English word]

bolt hole *noun* a place where someone can escape or hide.

bolus (boh-ləs) *noun* (**boluses**) **1** a quantity of food, chewed and mixed with saliva, as it is swallowed. **2** a large pill used in veterinary medicine. [from a Greek word *bolus* meaning 'clod']

bomb *noun* **1** a container filled with explosive or incendiary material to be set off by impact or by a timing device. **2** (**the bomb**) nuclear weapons. **3** (*informal*) a large sum of money ♦ *He must be making a bomb these days.*
bomb *verb* **1** to attack a place with bombs. **2** (*informal*) to fail badly. **to go like a bomb** (*informal*) to be very successful. [from a Greek word *bombos* meaning 'loud humming']

bombard *verb* **1** to attack a place with many missiles, especially from big guns. **2** to attack someone with constant questions or criticism. **3** to send a stream of high-speed particles against something. **bombardment** *noun* [same origin as for *bomb*]

bombardier *noun* a non-commissioned officer in the artillery. [same origin as for *bomb*]

bombast (bom-bast) *noun* pompous words or speech. [originally denoting cotton wool used for padding; later used to mean 'padded' language, with long or unnecessary words]

bombastic (bom-**bas**-tik) *adjective* using pompous words.

bomber *noun* **1** an aircraft that carries and drops bombs. **2** a person who plants bombs.

bomber jacket *noun* a waist-length jacket gathered into a band at the waist and cuffs.

bombshell *noun* something that comes as a great shock or disappointment.

bona fide (boh-nə fiy-di) genuine or real ♦ *bona fide customers.* [Latin words meaning 'with good faith']

bonanza (bə-**nan**-zə) *noun* a source of sudden great wealth or luck. [originally an American word referring to success when mining; from a Spanish word meaning 'good weather, prosperity']

bonbon *noun* a sweet. [from a French word *bon* meaning 'good']

bond *noun* **1** a close friendship or connection between two or more people ♦ *We hope to strengthen the bonds between our two countries.* SYNONYMS: link, tie, relationship, affinity. **2** (**bonds**) ropes or chains used to tie up a prisoner. **3** the strong force of attraction that holds atoms together in a molecule. **4** a document issued by a government or public company acknowledging that money has been lent to it and will be repaid, usually with interest. **5** a binding agreement, or a document containing this ♦ *My word is my bond.*
bond *verb* **1** to become closely linked or connected. **2** to establish a close relationship with someone ♦ *He has bonded well with his girlfriend's children.* [a different spelling of *band*¹]

bondage *noun* slavery or captivity.

bonded *adjective* (said about goods) stored in a bonded warehouse.

bone *noun* **1** one of the hard whitish parts that make up the skeleton of an animal's body. **2** the substance from which these parts are made.
bone *verb* to remove the bones from fish or meat. **to have a bone to pick with someone** to have a reason to be annoyed with someone. **to make no bones about** to not hesitate to do or speak about something unpleasant. [from an Old English word]

bone china *noun* fine china made of clay mixed with bone ash.

bone dry *adjective* extremely dry.

bonehead *noun* (*informal*) a stupid person.

bone idle *adjective* very lazy.

bonemeal *noun* crushed powdered bones used as a fertilizer.

boneshaker *noun* (*informal*) a vehicle that jolts.

bonfire *noun* a large fire built in the open air to destroy rubbish or as a celebration. [originally *bone fire*, denoting a fire to dispose of people's or animals' bones]

bongo *noun* (**bongos**) each of a pair of small drums held between the knees and played with the fingers. [from a Latin American Spanish word]

bonhomie (bon-*ə*mi) *noun* a good-natured friendly manner. [from French]

bonk *verb* (*informal*) 1 to hit someone. 2 to have sexual intercourse with someone. **bonk** *noun* a hit or thud. [an imitation of the sound]

bonkers *adjective* (*informal*) crazy. [origin unknown]

bonnet *noun* 1 a woman's or child's hat with strings that tie under the chin. 2 a Scottish cap like a beret. 3 a hinged cover over a car engine. [from a Latin word *abonnis* meaning 'a hat']

bonny *adjective* (**bonnier, bonniest**) 1 healthy-looking. 2 (*Scottish*) (*N. England*) good-looking. [from a French word *bon* meaning 'good']

bonsai (bon-siy) *noun* 1 a tree or shrub grown in miniature form in a pot by artificially restricting its growth. 2 the art of growing trees and shrubs like this. [from Japanese]

bonus *noun* (**bonuses**) 1 an extra payment in addition to a person's normal wages. 2 an extra benefit. [from a Latin word *bonus* meaning 'good']

bon voyage (bon voi-yahzh) *interjection* an expression of good wishes to someone starting a journey. [French words meaning 'good journey']

bony *adjective* (**bonier, boniest**) 1 having large or prominent bones, having bones with little flesh on them. 2 like or containing bones. **boniness** *noun*

bonze (bonz) *noun* a Buddhist priest in Japan or China. [from a Japanese word meaning 'priest']

boo *interjection* 1 a sound made to show disapproval or contempt. 2 an exclamation used to startle someone. **boo** *verb* to show disapproval by shouting 'boo'. [an imitation of the lowing of oxen]

boob¹ *noun* (*informal*) 1 an embarrassing mistake. 2 (*North Amer.*) a foolish person. **boob** *verb* to make an embarrassing mistake. [from a Spanish word]

boob² *noun* a woman's breast. [a shortening of a dialect word *booby*]

booby *noun* (**boobies**) a foolish person. [from a Spanish word]

booby prize *noun* a prize given as a joke to the competitor who comes last.

booby trap *noun* a hidden bomb placed so that it will explode when some apparently harmless object is touched or moved.

booby-trap *verb* (**booby-trapped, booby-trapping**) to place a booby trap in or on something.

boogie-woogie *noun* a style of playing blues on the piano, marked by a strong fast beat. [origin unknown]

book *noun* 1 a set of sheets of paper, usually with printing or writing on them, fastened together at one edge and enclosed in a cover. 2 each of the main divisions of a written work ♦ *the Books of the Bible.* 3 a number of cheques, stamps, tickets, matches, etc. fastened together in the shape of a book. 4 a libretto. 5 (**books**) a set of records or accounts.
book *verb* 1 to reserve a seat on a train, room in a hotel, etc.; to buy tickets in advance. 2 to enter a person in a police record ♦ *The police booked him for speeding.* 3 (said about a referee) to make a note of the name of a player who has committed a foul. **to book in** to register your arrival at a hotel. **to be booked up** to have all places, rooms, etc. reserved. **in someone's good** or **bad books** in favour (or not in favour) with them. **to throw the book at** to punish someone as severely as possible. **bookable** *adjective* [from an Old English word]

bookbinding *noun* binding books professionally. **bookbinder** *noun*

bookcase *noun* a piece of furniture with shelves for books.

book club *noun* a society for members who can buy books at a reduced price.

bookends *plural noun* a pair of supports for keeping a row of books upright.

bookie *noun* (*informal*) a bookmaker.

booking office *noun* an office where tickets are sold.

bookish *adjective* fond of reading.

bookkeeping *noun* keeping records of the money that is spent and received by a business. **bookkeeper** *noun*

booklet noun a small thin book with paper covers.

bookmaker noun a person whose business is taking bets. [so called because the bets used to be written down in a notebook]

bookmark noun 1 something placed between the pages of a book to mark a place. 2 (Computing) a record of the address of a file, Internet page, etc. so that you can find it again quickly.

bookseller noun a person whose business is selling books.

bookshop noun a shop selling books.

bookstall noun a stall or kiosk at which books and newspapers are sold.

bookworm noun 1 (informal) a person who enjoys reading. 2 a grub that eats holes in books.

Boolean adjective to do with a system of algebraic notation in expressing logical reasoning by means of the binary digits 0 (false) and 1 (true), especially in computing and electronics. [named after G. Boole (1815–64), the English mathematician who developed this system]

boom [1] verb 1 to make a hollow deep resonant sound. 2 to be growing and prospering ♦ *The economy is booming.* **boom** noun 1 a deep hollow sound. 2 a period of increased growth or prosperity. [an imitation of the sound]

boom [2] noun 1 a long pole used to keep the bottom of a sail stretched. 2 a floating barrier or a heavy chain across a river or a harbour entrance. 3 a long pole carrying a microphone or film camera. [from a Dutch word meaning 'beam, tree']

boomerang noun a curved wooden missile, especially one that can be thrown so that it returns to the thrower if it fails to hit anything, originally used by Australian Aborigines. [from an Australian Aboriginal word]

boon noun something very useful or practical. [from an Old Norse word *bón* meaning 'prayer']

boon companion noun a close friend. [from a French word *bon* meaning 'good']

boor noun a rough and bad-mannered person. **boorish** adjective **boorishly** adverb **boorishness** noun [same origin as for *Boer*]

boost verb to help something to increase in strength or value ♦ *Winning last night really* boosted the team's morale. SYNONYMS: lift, raise, encourage, bolster, build up, buoy up. **boost** noun 1 an increase in something ♦ *a boost in sales.* 2 help or encouragement ♦ *That gave my confidence a boost.* [origin unknown]

booster noun 1 a dose of a vaccine that increases or renews the effect of an earlier one. 2 the first stage of a rocket or spacecraft, used to give initial acceleration.

boot noun 1 a shoe that covers the foot and ankle or lower leg. 2 a compartment for luggage in a car. 3 (informal) a hard kick. **boot** verb 1 to kick something hard. 2 to start a computer and prepare it for use. **to get the boot** (informal) to be dismissed from your job. **to give someone the boot** (informal) to dismiss them from their job. [via Old Norse from an Old French word]

boot camp noun a prison for young offenders, run on military lines.

bootee noun a baby's knitted or crocheted boot.

booth noun 1 a small temporary shelter at a market or fair. 2 an enclosed compartment for a public telephone, for voting at elections, etc. [from an Old Norse word *buth*]

bootleg verb (**bootlegged, bootlegging**) 1 to smuggle alcohol. 2 to make and sell something illegally. **bootleg** adjective sold or distributed illegally ♦ *a bootleg recording.* **bootlegger** noun [from the smugglers' practice of hiding bottles in their boots]

booty noun valuable goods taken away by soldiers after a battle. [from an Old German word *buite* meaning 'exchange, sharing out']

booze noun (informal) alcoholic drink. **booze** verb (informal) to drink large quantities of alcohol. **boozer** noun **boozy** adjective [from an Old Dutch word *busen* meaning 'to drink too much alcohol']

bop verb (**bopped, bopping**) (informal) to dance to pop music. **bop** noun (informal) a dance to pop music. [an abbreviation of *bebop*]

boracic adjective containing boric acid.

borax noun a soluble white powder that is a compound of boron, used in making glass, enamels, and detergents. [via Latin and Arabic from Pahlavi, an old form of Persian]

border noun 1 the line dividing two countries or other areas. 2 something placed round an edge to strengthen or decorate it. 3 a strip of ground round a garden or a part of it.
border verb 1 to form a border around or along something. 2 (said about a country or area) to be next to another. **border on** to come close to something ♦ It borders on the absurd. [from an Old French word]

borderline noun the line that marks a boundary, especially between two countries.
borderline adjective only just belonging to a particular group or category ♦ You're a borderline pass.

bore¹ verb to make a hole or well with a drill or other tool.
bore noun the width of the inside of a gun barrel or engine cylinder. [from an Old English word]

bore² verb to make a person feel uninterested by being dull or tedious.
bore noun a dull and uninteresting person or thing. **boredom** noun [origin unknown]

bore³ noun a tidal wave with a steep front that moves up an estuary ♦ the Severn bore. [from an Old Norse word bara meaning 'wave']

bore⁴ past tense of **bear**².

bored adjective weary and uninterested because something is so dull.
◊ You can say that you are bored with something or bored by something. It is not acceptable in standard English to say bored of.

boric (bor-ik) adjective to do with boron.

boric acid noun a substance derived from boron, used as a mild antiseptic.

boring adjective dull and uninteresting. SYNONYMS: tedious, monotonous, dreary, humdrum.

born adjective 1 having a certain order, status, or place of birth ♦ first-born ♦ well-born ♦ French-born. 2 having a certain natural quality or ability ♦ a born leader.
born past participle of **bear** in some meanings (see the usage note at **borne**).
to be born to be brought forth by birth.
born of existing as a result of something ♦ Their courage was born of despair. [from an Old English word]

born-again adjective 1 denoting a person who has been converted to Christianity. 2 showing the enthusiasm of someone who has recently been converted to a cause ♦ a born-again vegetarian.

borne past participle of **bear**².
◊ The word borne is used as part of the verb to bear when it comes before by or after have, has, or had, e.g. children (who were) borne by Eve, She had borne him a son. The word born is used in a son was born.

boron (bor-on) noun a chemical element (symbol B) that is very resistant to high temperatures, used in metalwork and in nuclear reactors.

borough (bu-rə) noun 1 a town or part of a city that has its own council. 2 an administrative area of Greater London or of New York City. [from an Old English word burg meaning 'fortress or fortified town']

borrow verb 1 to get something to use for a time, with the intention of giving it back afterwards. 2 to obtain money as a loan. 3 to copy something ♦ We should borrow their methods. **to be living on borrowed time** to be living beyond an illness or crisis which could have ended your life.
borrower noun [from an Old English word borgian]
◊ Do not confuse borrow with lend, which means 'to give something for a time or as a loan'.

borscht (borsht) noun a Russian soup made with beetroot. [from a Russian word borshch]

borstal noun a type of prison to which young offenders were formerly sent. [named after the village of Borstal in southern England, where the first of these was established]

borzoi (bor-zoi) noun a large hound with a narrow head and silky coat. [from a Russian word borzyi meaning 'swift']

bosh noun (informal) nonsense. [from a Turkish word meaning 'empty, worthless']

bosom (buu-zəm) noun 1 a woman's breast or chest. 2 the centre of care or emotion ♦ He returned to the bosom of his family.
bosom adjective (said about a friend) very close. [from an Old English word]

boson (boh-zon) noun a subatomic particle, such as a photon. [named after the Indian scientist S. N. Bose (1894–1974)]

boss[1] noun (informal) a person who controls or gives orders to workers.
boss verb **to boss someone around** or **about** to order someone about. [from a Dutch word *baas* meaning 'master']

boss[2] noun a round raised knob or stud. [from an Old French word]

boss-eyed adjective (informal) cross-eyed. [from a dialect word *boss* meaning 'miss, bungle']

bossy adjective (**bossier, bossiest**) (informal) fond of ordering people about. **bossily** adverb **bossiness** noun

bosun (boh-sŏn) noun another word for **boatswain**.

botanical (bŏ-tan-ik-ăl) adjective to do with botany.

botanical garden noun a garden where plants and trees are grown for scientific study.

botanist noun an expert in botany.

botany noun the scientific study of plants. [from a Greek word *botane* meaning 'a plant']

botch verb (informal) to spoil something by poor or clumsy work ♦ *a botched job*.
botch noun a piece of work that has been badly done ♦ *He made a botch of the tiling.* [origin unknown]

both adjective & pronoun the two, not only the one ♦ *Are both films good?* ♦ *Both are old.*
both adverb **both ... and ...** not only ... but also ... ♦ *The house is both small and ugly.* [from an Old Norse word]

bother verb 1 to cause someone trouble, worry, or annoyance ♦ *Does the noise bother you?* SYNONYMS: worry, concern, disturb, upset, trouble, annoy, irritate. 2 to take the trouble to do something, to feel concern ♦ *You really shouldn't have bothered* ♦ *Don't bother to reply.*
bother interjection an exclamation of annoyance.
bother noun 1 trouble or worry. 2 a person or thing causing this. [from an Irish word *bodhraim* meaning 'to deafen' or 'to annoy']

bothersome adjective causing bother, troublesome.

bottle noun 1 a narrow-necked glass or plastic container for storing liquid. 2 a baby's feeding bottle. 3 a hot-water bottle. 4 (informal) courage ♦ *She's got bottle, I'll say that for her.*
bottle verb 1 to store liquid in bottles. 2 to preserve something in glass jars ♦ *bottled fruit.* **to bottle something up** to keep your feelings to yourself. **to hit the bottle** (informal) to start to drink alcohol heavily. [same origin as for *butt*[1]]

bottle bank noun a place where used glass bottles are deposited for recycling.

bottleneck noun 1 a narrow stretch of road where traffic cannot flow freely. 2 something that obstructs progress.

bottom noun 1 the lowest part of something, the lowest place. SYNONYMS: foot, base, floor, underside. 2 the part furthest away ♦ *the bottom of the garden.* 3 a person's buttocks. 4 the ground under a stretch of water. 5 a ship's keel or hull.
bottom adjective lowest in position, rank, or degree ♦ *the bottom shelf.*
bottom verb to reach or touch bottom. **to be at the bottom of** to be the underlying cause or origin of. **to get to the bottom of** to find out the cause or origin of. [from an Old English word *botm*]

bottomless adjective without a bottom, extremely deep.

bottom line noun 1 the final total of an account or balance sheet after profit and loss etc. have been calculated. 2 the basic and most important requirement.

botulism (bot-yoo-lizm) noun a kind of food poisoning caused by a bacterium growing on foods that have not been sterilized properly. [from a Latin word *botulus* meaning 'sausage']

boudoir (boo-dwar) noun a woman's private room. [French word meaning 'place to sulk in']

bougainvillea (boo-gŏn-vil-iŏ) noun a tropical shrub with red or purple bracts. [named after the French explorer L. A. de Bougainville (1729–1811)]

bough (bow) noun a large branch coming from the trunk of a tree. [from an Old English word]

bought past tense and past participle of **buy**.

bouillon (boo-yawn) noun clear soup, broth. [French, from *bouiller* meaning 'to boil']

boulder (bohl-der) noun a large rock. [from a Scandinavian word]

boulevard (boo-lŏ-vard) noun a wide street, often with trees on each side. [a French word, related to *bulwark*]

bounce verb 1 to spring back after hitting a hard surface. SYNONYMS: rebound, ricochet, recoil. 2 to make something do this ♦ *A boy was bouncing a ball against the wall.* 3 to jump suddenly, to move up and down repeatedly. SYNONYMS: leap, spring, bound, bob. 4 (*informal*) (said about a cheque) to be sent back by the bank because there is not enough money in the account. 5 (*informal*) to coerce someone into doing something. **bounce** noun 1 an act of bouncing a ball etc. 2 a strongly self-confident manner. [origin unknown]

bouncer noun 1 a person employed to stand at the door of a club etc. and stop unwanted people coming in or make troublemakers leave. 2 (in cricket) a bowled ball that bounces up near the batsman's head.

bouncing adjective (said about a baby) big and healthy.

bouncy adjective (**bouncier, bounciest**) 1 confident and lively. 2 suitable for bouncing on.

bouncy castle noun a large inflatable model castle on which children can play.

bound[1] verb 1 to move or run with large leaps. SYNONYMS: skip, hop, spring, leap, vault. **bound** noun a large leap. [from an Old French word *bondir*]

bound[2] past tense and past participle of **bind**. **bound** adjective obstructed or hindered by something ♦ *The airport was fog-bound.* **bound to** certain to ♦ *He is bound to fail.*

bound[3] verb 1 to form the boundary of something ♦ *Their land is bounded by the river.* 2 to limit or restrict something. **bounds** plural noun limits ♦ *This was beyond the bounds of possibility.* **out of bounds** outside the areas where you are allowed to go. [from an Old French word *bonde*]

bound[4] adjective going or heading towards ♦ *We are bound for Spain* ♦ *northbound traffic.* [from an Old Norse word]

boundary noun (**boundaries**) 1 a line that marks a limit. SYNONYMS: edge, limit, border, frontier, perimeter, margin, interface. 2 (in cricket) a hit that crosses the boundary, scoring four or six runs. [from *bound*[3]]

boundless adjective without limits.

bountiful adjective 1 plentiful or abundant ♦ *a bountiful harvest.* 2 giving generously.

bounty noun (**bounties**) 1 a reward paid for capturing or killing someone. 2 (*literary*) a generous gift or supply ♦ *the bounty of nature.* [from a Latin word *bonitas* meaning 'goodness']

bouquet (boo-**kay**) noun 1 a bunch of flowers. 2 the scent of wine. [a French word meaning 'group of trees']

bouquet garni (gar-**ni**) noun (**bouquets garnis**) a bunch of herbs used for flavouring. [French words meaning 'garnished bouquet']

bourbon (**ber**-bən) noun 1 an American whisky made mainly from maize. 2 a kind of chocolate-flavoured biscuit. [the whisky is named after Bourbon County, Kentucky, where it was first made]

bourgeois (boor-*zh*wah) adjective to do with the middle class, especially in having conventional ideas and tastes. [a French word, originally from a Latin word *burgus* meaning 'castle']

bourgeoisie (boor-*zh*wah-zi) noun the middle class in a society.

bout noun 1 a boxing or wrestling contest. 2 a period of exercise or work or illness ♦ *a bout of flu.* [probably from an Old German word]

boutique (boo-**teek**) noun a small shop selling fashionable clothes. [a French word]

bovine (**boh**-viyn) adjective 1 to do with or like cattle. 2 dull and stupid. [from a Latin word *bovis* meaning 'of an ox']

bow[1] (boh) noun 1 a knot made with two loops and two loose ends. 2 a piece of wood curved by a tight string joining its ends, used as a weapon for shooting arrows. 3 a rod with horsehair stretched between its ends, used for playing the violin etc. [from an Old English word *boga*]

bow[2] (bow) verb 1 to bend your body forwards to show respect or as a greeting. 2 to bend downwards under a weight. 3 to submit or give in ♦ *We must bow to the inevitable.* **bow** noun a bending of the head or body in greeting, respect, agreement, etc. **to bow out** to retire from a job or position. [from an Old English word *bugan*]

bow[3] (bow) noun the front end of a ship. [from an Old German or Dutch word]

bowdlerize (**bowd**-ler-riyz) verb to remove words or scenes from a play, novel, etc.

that are thought to be indecent or offensive. [named after T. Bowdler (1754–1825) who in 1818 produced a censored version of Shakespeare's plays]

bowel *noun* the intestine.
bowels *plural noun* the deepest inner parts of something. [from a Latin word *botellus* meaning 'little sausage']

bower *noun* a shady place under trees. [from an Old English word, related to *build*]

bowie knife (boh-i) *noun* a long hunting-knife with a double-edged point. [named after an American soldier J. Bowie (1796–1836)]

bowl [1] *noun* 1 a rounded usually deep container for food or liquid. 2 the hollow rounded part of a spoon, tobacco pipe, etc. 3 a stadium for sporting or musical events ♦ *the Hollywood Bowl*. [from an Old English word *bolla*]

bowl [2] *noun* 1 a ball used in the game of bowls. 2 a ball in tenpin bowling or skittles. 3 a period of bowling in cricket ♦ *Have you had a bowl yet?*
bowls *noun* a game played by rolling heavy balls that are weighted so that they roll in a curve.
bowl *verb* 1 to send a ball etc. rolling along the ground. 2 (in cricket) to send a ball to be played by a batsman; to get a batsman out by knocking down a wicket with the ball. 3 to go along quickly and smoothly ♦ *The cart was bowling along the road.* **to bowl someone over** 1 to knock someone down. 2 to overwhelm someone with surprise or emotion. [from an Old French word *boule*]

bow-legged *adjective* having legs that curve outwards at the knees.

bowler [1] *noun* 1 a person who bowls in cricket. 2 a person who plays at bowls.

bowler [2] or **bowler hat** *noun* a man's stiff felt hat with a rounded top. [named after a 19th-century hat-maker called Bowler]

bowline (boh-lin) *noun* a simple knot for forming a non-slipping loop at the end of a rope.

bowling *noun* 1 the game of knocking down skittles with a heavy ball. 2 the game of bowls.

bowsprit (boh-sprit) *noun* a long pole projecting from the stem of a ship, to which ropes from the front mast and sails are fastened. [from an early German word]

bow tie *noun* a man's necktie tied into a bow.

bow window *noun* a curved bay window.

box [1] *noun* 1 a container with a flat base and usually a lid. 2 a rectangular space to be filled in on a form, computer screen, etc. 3 a compartment in a theatre where several people can sit together, or one for the jury or witnesses in a law court ♦ *the witness box*. 4 a small hut or shelter ♦ *a sentry box*. 5 a facility at a newspaper office for receiving replies to an advertisement. 6 (**the box**) (*informal*) television.
box *verb* to put something into a box. **to box someone in** to surround someone so that they cannot move away. [from a Greek word *puxos* meaning 'box tree']

box [2] *verb* to fight with the fists as a sport.
box *noun* a slap on the side of someone's head. **to box a person's ears** to slap them. [origin unknown]

box [3] *noun* 1 a small evergreen tree, often used for hedges. 2 the hard wood of this tree. [from a Greek word *puxos*]

boxer *noun* 1 a person who boxes as a sport. 2 a dog resembling a bulldog.

boxer shorts *plural noun* men's underpants that look like shorts.

boxing *noun* the sport of fighting with the fists.

Boxing Day *noun* a public holiday on the first weekday after Christmas Day. [from the old custom of giving presents (Christmas boxes) to tradespeople on this day]

box junction *noun* a road junction marked with a grid, which vehicles may only enter if the exit is clear.

box number *noun* a number used to identify a box in a newspaper office or post office to which letters to an advertiser may be sent.

box office *noun* a place at a theatre, cinema, etc. where tickets are sold. [so called because boxes could be reserved there]

boxroom *noun* a very small room.

boy *noun* a male child or youth. **boyhood** *noun* [origin unknown]

boycott (boy-kot) *verb* to refuse to use, buy, or have anything to do with something ♦ *Customers have been boycotting these products.*

boycott *noun* an act of boycotting something ♦ *an Olympic boycott*. [from the name of Captain Boycott (1832–97), a harsh landlord in Ireland whose tenants refused to deal with him]

boyfriend *noun* a person's usual male companion in a romantic relationship.

boyish *adjective* like a boy. **boyishly** *adverb* **boyishness** *noun*

Boyle's law *noun* the scientific law stating that the volume of a fixed quantity of gas at constant temperature is inversely proportional to its pressure. [named after the English scientist Robert Boyle (1627–91)]

BP *abbreviation* (*Geology*) before the present (era).

bra *noun* a piece of underwear worn by women to support their breasts. [a shortening of **brassière**]

brace *noun* **1** a device that clamps things together or holds them in place. **2** a wire device fitted in the mouth to straighten the teeth. **3** (**brace**) a pair of birds or animals killed in hunting ♦ *a brace of pheasants*.
braces *plural noun* straps used to hold trousers up, fastened to the waistband and passing over the shoulders.
brace *verb* to support or give firmness to something. **to brace yourself** to prepare yourself for something unpleasant. [from a Latin word *brachia* meaning 'arms']

bracelet *noun* an ornamental band or chain worn on the arm. [same origin as for **brace**]

brachiopod (brak-i-ə-pod) *noun* any of a group of small sea creatures with an upper and lower shell and brachia fringed with hair-like organs (called *cilia*) that by their movement send water bearing microscopic food to the mouth. [from *brachium* and a Greek word *podos* meaning 'of a foot']

bracing *adverb* making you feel refreshed and healthy ♦ *the bracing sea breeze*.

bracken *noun* a large fern that grows on waste land, or a mass of such ferns. [from an Old Norse word]

bracket *noun* **1** any of the marks used in pairs for enclosing words or figures, e.g. (), []. **2** a support attached to a wall or other upright surface. **3** a group or range between certain limits ♦ *a high income bracket*.
bracket *verb* (**bracketed, bracketing**) **1** to enclose or join something by brackets. **2** to put a number of people or things together in a group because they are similar. [from a Latin word *bracae* meaning 'breeches']

brackish *adjective* (said about water) slightly salty. [from a German or Dutch word *brac* meaning 'salt water']

bract *noun* a leaf-like part of a plant, often highly coloured, e.g. in bougainvillea and poinsettia. [from a Latin word *bractea* meaning 'thin plate of metal']

bradawl *noun* a small tool for boring holes. [from an Old Norse word *broddr* meaning 'spike' and *awl*]

brae (bray) *noun* (*Scottish*) a hillside. [from an Old Norse word]

brag *verb* (**bragged, bragging**) to boast. SYNONYMS: boast, crow, show off, (*informal*) blow your own trumpet, swank.
brag *noun* a card game. [origin unknown]

braggart *noun* a person who brags.

Brahman or **Brahmin** (brah-mən) *noun* a member of the highest Hindu class, originally priests. **Brahmanism** *noun* [from a Sanskrit word *brahman* meaning 'priest']

braid *noun* **1** a plait of hair. **2** a strip of cloth with a woven decorative pattern, used as a trimming.
braid *verb* **1** to plait hair. **2** to trim something with braid. [from an Old English word *bregdan* meaning 'to make a sudden movement']

Braille (brayl) *noun* a system of representing letters etc. by patterns of raised dots which blind people can read by touch. [named after its inventor Louis Braille (1809–52)]

brain *noun* **1** the organ that is the centre of the nervous system in animals, a mass of soft grey matter in the skull. **2** a person's mind or intelligence ♦ *Use your brain!* ♦ *She's got both beauty and brains.*
brain *verb* (*informal*) to hit someone hard on the head. **to have something on the brain** to be obsessed with something. **the brains behind something** the person who supplies all the ideas or who originates a plan. [from an Old English word]

brainchild *noun* a person's invention or plan.

brain drain *noun* the loss from a country of clever and skilled people by emigration.

brainless *adjective* unintelligent or stupid.

brainpower *noun* mental ability or intelligence.

brainstorm *noun* 1 a moment of mental confusion. 2 a spontaneous group discussion organized to try to think of new ideas.
brainstorm *verb* to try to think of new ideas by having a spontaneous group discussion.

brainwash *verb* to use mental pressure to force someone to reject old beliefs and accept new ones.

brainwave *noun* 1 an electrical impulse in the brain. 2 a sudden clever idea.

brainy *adjective* (**brainier, brainiest**) (*informal*) intelligent. **braininess** *noun*

braise *verb* to cook food slowly with very little liquid in a closed container. [from a French word *braise* meaning 'burning coals']

brake *noun* 1 a device for slowing down or stopping a moving vehicle. 2 the pedal or lever that operates this device.
brake *verb* to slow down a moving vehicle by using a brake. [origin unknown]

brake drum *noun* a cylinder attached to a wheel, on which the brake shoe presses.

brake horsepower *noun* the power of an engine measured by the force needed to brake it.

brake shoe *noun* a long curved block acting on a wheel to brake it.

bramble *noun* a rough shrub with long prickly shoots, a blackberry bush. [from an Old English word; related to *broom*]

bran *noun* ground-up inner husks of grain, sifted out from flour. [from an Old French word]

branch *noun* 1 an arm-like part of a tree. 2 a part of a river, road, or railway that leads off from the main part. 3 a local shop or office etc. belonging to a larger organization. 4 a subdivision of a family or a group of languages or a subject.
branch *verb* 1 (said about a road, river, etc.) to divide into branches. SYNONYMS: fork, divide, split. 2 (said about a tree or plant) to send out branches. **to branch off** to leave a main route and take a minor one. **to**

branch out to start something new. [from a Latin word *branca* meaning 'a paw']

brand *noun* 1 a particular make of goods. 2 a company's trademark or label. 3 a characteristic kind of something ♦ *his strange brand of humour*. 4 a mark of identification made on livestock with a hot iron. 5 a piece of burning wood.
brand *verb* 1 to mark livestock with a hot iron to identify them. 2 to sell goods under a particular trademark. 3 to give a bad name to someone ♦ *He has been branded a liar*. [from an Old English word *brand* meaning 'burning']

brandish *verb* to wave something about. [via Old French from Germanic, related to *brand*]

brand name *noun* a name given to a product or range of products.

brand new *adjective* completely new. [from *brand* and *new*, with the idea 'straight from the fire']

brandy *noun* (**brandies**) a strong alcoholic spirit distilled from wine or from fermented fruit juice. [from a Dutch word *brandewijn* meaning 'burnt (distilled) wine']

brandy snap *noun* a thin crisp curled wafer of gingerbread.

brash *adjective* rudely or aggressively self-assertive. **brashly** *adverb* **brashness** *noun* [origin unknown]

brass *noun* 1 a yellow alloy of copper and zinc. 2 a brass ornament. 3 the brass wind instruments of an orchestra. 4 a brass memorial tablet in a church. 5 (*informal*) money. 6 (*informal*) high-ranking officers or officials ♦ *the top brass*.
brass *adjective* made of brass. **to get down to brass tacks** to start to consider the basic facts or practical details. [from an Old English word]

brass band *noun* a band playing brass and percussion instruments only.

brasserie (bras-er-i) *noun* an inexpensive restaurant, especially one serving French food. [a French word meaning 'brewery']

brassière (bras-i-air) *noun* a woman's bra. [a French word meaning 'child's vest']

brassy *adjective* (**brassier, brassiest**) 1 like brass in appearance or sound. 2 loud and vulgar. **brassiness** *noun*

brat *noun* (*informal*) a badly behaved child. [origin unknown]

bravado (brə-**vah**-doh) *noun* a display of boldness intended to impress people. [from a Spanish word *bravata*]

brave *adjective* having or showing courage. SYNONYMS: courageous, fearless, bold, daring, valiant, intrepid, plucky.
brave *verb* to face and endure something unpleasant or dangerous with courage ♦ *Are you ready to brave the elements?*
brave *noun* (*old use*) a Native American warrior. **bravely** *adverb* [from a Latin word *barbarus* meaning 'barbarous']

bravery *noun* courage. SYNONYMS: courage, valour, daring, (*informal*) guts, pluck, bottle.

bravo *interjection* & *noun* (**bravos**) a cry of 'well done!'. [an Italian word]

bravura (brə-**voor**-ə) *noun* great skill and brilliance. [an Italian word]

brawl *noun* a noisy quarrel or fight.
brawl *verb* to take part in a brawl. [origin unknown]

brawn *noun* 1 physical strength, in contrast to intelligence. 2 meat from a pig's or calf's head boiled, chopped, and pressed in a mould. [via Old French from Germanic]

brawny *adjective* (**brawnier**, **brawniest**) strong and muscular.

bray *verb* to make the loud harsh cry of a donkey.
bray *noun* a braying sound. [from an Old French word *braire* meaning 'to cry']

braze *verb* to join metal parts together with an alloy of brass and zinc. [from a French word *braser* meaning 'to solder']

brazen (**bray**-zən) *adjective* 1 bold and shameless. 2 made of brass or like brass.
brazen *verb* to brazen it out to behave, after doing wrong, as if you have nothing to be ashamed of. [from an Old English word meaning 'made of brass']

brazier (**bray**-zi-er) *noun* a basket-like stand for holding burning coals. [from a French word *braise* meaning 'coals, embers']

breach *noun* 1 the breaking or neglect of a rule, agreement, etc. ♦ *a breach of contract.* 2 a gap in a wall or barrier, especially one made by an attacking army.
breach *verb* 1 to make a gap in a wall or barrier. 2 to break a rule, agreement, etc. ♦ *The company has breached the code of conduct.* SYNONYMS: contravene, infringe, transgress, violate. **to step into the breach** to give help in a crisis, especially by

replacing someone. [via Old French from Germanic, related to *break*]

bread *noun* 1 a food made of flour, water, and yeast mixed together and baked. 2 (*informal*) money. [from an Old English word]

breadboard *noun* 1 a board for cutting bread on. 2 a board for making an experimental model of an electric circuit.

breadcrumb *noun* a small fragment of bread.

breaded *adjective* coated with breadcrumbs.

breadfruit *noun* the fruit of a tropical tree, with white pulp like new bread.

breadline *noun* on the breadline having barely enough means to live on.

breadth *noun* 1 the distance or measurement from side to side. 2 a wide range ♦ *She brings a breadth of experience to the job.* [from an Old English word]

breadwinner *noun* the member of a family who earns the money to support the others.

break *verb* (**broke**, **broken**) 1 to fall into pieces, or to cause something to do this, especially as a result of a blow or pressure ♦ *My sister broke her leg skiing.* SYNONYMS: shatter, fracture, snap, crack, smash, splinter. 2 to stop working properly, or to damage something so that it no longer works properly. SYNONYMS: damage, wreck, (*informal*) bust. 3 to fail to keep a promise, rule, or law. SYNONYMS: disobey, contravene, infringe, transgress, violate, flout. 4 to end or interrupt something ♦ *She finally broke her silence* ♦ *Let's break for coffee.* 5 to reveal news to someone, to become publicly known ♦ *When will you break the news to them?* ♦ *The story broke this morning.* 6 to make a rush or dash ♦ *The player broke clear with only the goalkeeper to beat.* 7 to surpass ♦ *He hopes to break the world record.* 8 to emerge or appear suddenly ♦ *Dawn had broken.* 9 to change suddenly ♦ *The weather broke.* 10 to find the solution to a code. 11 to destroy a person's spirit ♦ *The scandal broke him.* 12 to make the first stroke in a game of snooker, pool, etc. 13 (said about a voice) to change its even tone, either with emotion or (in the case of a boy's voice) by becoming suddenly deeper at puberty. 14 (said about waves) to fall in foam. 15 (said about a ball) to change direction after touching the ground. 16 (said about boxers) to come out of a clinch.

break noun 1 an instance of breaking, or the place where something is broken. 2 a sudden rush or dash. 3 a gap in something. 4 a short period during which you rest or do something different. SYNONYMS: rest, pause, interval, hiatus, respite, breathing space. 5 a short holiday. 6 a number of points scored continuously in snooker or billiards. 7 (in tennis) the winning of a game against your opponent's serve. 8 (informal) a piece of luck or an opportunity ♦ a lucky break. **to break down** 1 to stop working properly because of mechanical failure. 2 to end or collapse because of disagreements or problems ♦ The negotiations have broken down. 3 to start crying. 4 to act upon something chemically and reduce it to its constituent parts. **to break even** to make gains and losses that balance exactly. **to break in** 1 to force your way into a building. 2 to interrupt. 3 to accustom a horse to being ridden. **to break into** to suddenly start doing something ♦ He broke into a run. **break of day** (literary) dawn. **break off** 1 to bring something to an end ♦ The union announced it was breaking off negotiations. 2 to suddenly stop speaking. **break out** 1 to begin suddenly ♦ A fight broke out between rival supporters. 2 to force your way out. 3 to develop something unpleasant such as a rash ♦ The whole family have broken out in spots. **to break up** 1 to begin holidays when school closes at the end of term. 2 to bring or come to an end ♦ The party broke up about midnight. 3 to end your relationship with someone ♦ My brother and his girlfriend have broken up. **to break with** 1 to do something in a way different from the customary way ♦ He broke with tradition and asked his sister to be his best man. 2 to end your friendship with someone. **breakable** adjective [from an Old English word]

breakage noun something broken ♦ Breakages must be paid for.

breakaway noun becoming separate from a larger group. **breakaway** adjective separated from a large group.

break-dancing noun an energetic style of street dancing.

breakdown noun 1 mechanical failure, especially of a car ♦ We had a breakdown on the motorway. 2 failure or collapse ♦ the breakdown of law and order. 3 a period of

mental illness caused by anxiety or depression. 4 an analysis of accounts or statistics.

breaker noun a large wave that breaks on the coast or over a reef.

breakfast noun the first meal of the day. **breakfast** verb to eat breakfast. [from break and fast²]

break-in noun a forcible entry, especially by a thief.

breakneck adjective (said about speed) dangerously fast.

breakthrough noun a major advance in knowledge.

breakup noun the disintegration or dispersal of something.

breakwater noun a wall built out into the sea to protect a harbour or coast against heavy waves.

bream noun (bream) a yellowish freshwater fish with an arched back. [via Old French from Germanic]

breast (brest) noun 1 either of the two fleshy parts on the upper front of a woman's body that produce milk to feed a baby. 2 the upper front part of the human body or of a piece of clothing covering this. 3 the corresponding part in animals, especially a joint of poultry cut from here.
breast verb to face and move forwards against something ♦ We swam out, breasting the waves. [from an Old English word]

breastbone noun the flat vertical bone in the chest or breast, joined to the ribs.

breastfeed verb (past tense and past participle **breastfed**) to feed a baby with milk from the mother's breast. **breastfed** adjective

breastplate noun a piece of armour covering the chest.

breaststroke noun a swimming stroke performed on your front, with sweeping movements of the arms.

breath (breth) noun 1 air drawn into the lungs and sent out again. 2 breathing in ♦ Take six deep breaths. 3 a gentle blowing ♦ a breath of wind. 4 a hint or slight rumour ♦ There was not a breath of scandal. **in the same breath** immediately after saying something else. **out of breath** gasping for air after violent exercise. **to take your breath away** to surprise or delight you greatly. **under your breath** in a very quiet voice. [from an Old English word]

breathalyse *verb* to test someone with a breathalyser.

breathalyser *noun* a device used by police for measuring the amount of alcohol in a person's breath. [from *breath* and *analyse*]

breathe (breeth) *verb* 1 to draw air into the lungs and send it out again. 2 (said about plants) to respire. 3 (said about wine) to be exposed to fresh air. 4 to speak or utter ♦ *Don't breathe a word of this.* [from *breath*]

breather *noun* (*informal*) a pause for rest ♦ *Let's take a breather.*

breathing space *noun* a pause to recover from effort and decide what to do next.

breathless *adjective* 1 out of breath, panting. 2 holding your breath with excitement. **breathlessly** *adverb* **breathlessness** *noun*

breathtaking *adjective* very exciting, spectacular.

breathy (breth-i) *adjective* (**breathier**, **breathiest**) with a noticeable sound of breathing.

bred past tense and past participle of **breed**.

breech *noun* the back part of a gun barrel, where the bullets are put in. [from an Old English word *brec* meaning 'hindquarters']

breech birth *noun* a birth in which the baby's buttocks or feet appear first.

breeches (brich-iz) *plural noun* trousers reaching to just below the knees, worn for riding or as part of ceremonial dress. [same origin as for *breech*]

breed *verb* (past tense and past participle **bred**) 1 (said about animals) to produce offspring. SYNONYMS: reproduce, procreate, multiply. 2 to keep animals for the purpose of producing young. 3 to train someone or to bring them up. 4 to give rise to something ♦ *Familiarity breeds contempt.* SYNONYMS: create, foster, generate, induce. **breed** *noun* a variety of animals within a species, especially one that has been deliberately developed. SYNONYMS: variety, type, pedigree, strain. [from an Old English word, related to *brood*]

breeder *noun* 1 a person who breeds animals. 2 a nuclear reactor that produces more fissile material than it uses in operating.

breeding *noun* good manners resulting from training or background.

breeze *noun* a gentle wind.
breeze *verb* (*informal*) to move in a casual or lively manner ♦ *They breezed in halfway through the meal.* [probably from a Spanish word]

breeze block *noun* a lightweight building block made of sand, cinders, and cement. [same origin as for *brazier*]

breezy *adjective* (**breezier**, **breeziest**) 1 pleasantly windy. 2 (said about a person or their manner) relaxed and informal. **breezily** *adverb* **breeziness** *noun*

Bren gun *noun* a lightweight machine gun. [from *Br*no in Czechoslovakia and *En*field in England, the two places where Bren guns were made]

brent goose *noun* a small wild goose with a mainly black head and neck.

brethren *plural noun* (*old use*) brothers. [the old plural of *brother*]
◊ This word is used mainly in religious contexts, for example to mean 'fellow Christians'.

Breton (bret-ən) *adjective* to do with Brittany or its people or language.
Breton *noun* 1 a native of Brittany. 2 the Celtic language of Brittany. [from an Old French word meaning 'Briton']

breve (breev) *noun* 1 a note in music, equal to two semibreves. 2 a mark placed over a short or unstressed vowel (˘). [same origin as for *brief*]

breviary (breev-i-er-i) *noun* (**breviaries**) a book of prayers to be said daily by Roman Catholic priests. [from a Latin word *breviarium* meaning 'summary, abridgement']

brevity (brev-iti) *noun* shortness or briefness ♦ *the brevity of their visit.* [same origin as for *brief*]

brew *verb* 1 to make beer by boiling and fermentation. 2 to make tea or coffee by mixing it with hot water. 3 (said about tea or coffee) to be prepared in this way ♦ *The tea is brewing.* 4 to begin to develop ♦ *Trouble is brewing.*
brew *noun* 1 a kind of beer. 2 a drink of tea. [from an Old English word]

brewer *noun* a person whose trade is brewing beer.

brewery *noun* (**breweries**) a place where beer is brewed.

briar[1] noun a thorny bush, especially the wild rose. [from an Old English word]

briar[2] noun 1 a shrub with a hard woody root used for making tobacco pipes. 2 a pipe made of this. [from a French word *bruyère* meaning 'heath, heather']

bribe noun something, especially money, offered to someone to influence them to act in favour of the giver.
bribe verb to persuade someone to do something by offering them a bribe.
bribable adjective **bribery** noun [from an Old French word *briber* meaning 'to beg']

bric-a-brac (brik-ə-brak) noun odd items of furniture, ornaments, etc., of no great value. [from an old French expression *à bric et à brac* meaning 'at random']

brick noun 1 a block of baked or dried clay or other substance used to build walls. 2 bricks considered as a building material ♦ *Our garden shed is built of brick.* 3 (*informal*) a kind-hearted person.
brick verb to block something with bricks ♦ *We bricked up the fireplace.* [from an Old German or Dutch word]

brickbat noun 1 a piece of brick used as a missile. 2 a critical or uncomplimentary remark.

bricklayer noun a person whose job is building with bricks.

brick red noun a deep brownish red.

brickwork noun a structure made of bricks.

bridal adjective to do with a bride or wedding.

bride noun a woman on her wedding day, or a newly married woman. [from an Old English word *bryd*]

bridegroom noun a man on his wedding day, or a newly married man. [from an Old English word *brydguma* meaning 'bride's man']

bridesmaid noun a woman or girl attending the bride at a wedding.

bridge[1] noun 1 a structure providing a way across something or carrying a road or railway etc. across. 2 the raised platform on a ship from which the captain and officers direct its course. 3 the bony upper part of the nose.
bridge verb to make or form a bridge over something. [from an Old English word *brycg*]

bridge[2] noun a card game rather like whist. [origin unknown]

bridgehead noun a fortified area established in enemy territory, especially on the far side of a river.

bridging loan noun a loan given for the period between two transactions, e.g. between buying and selling houses.

bridle noun the part of a horse's harness that fits over its head.
bridle verb 1 to put a bridle on a horse. 2 to bring something under control. 3 to show you are offended by something. [from an Old English word; related to *braid*]

bridleway or **bridle path** noun a path suitable for horses but not for vehicles.

brief[1] adjective 1 lasting only for a short time ♦ *a brief visit.* SYNONYMS: short, quick, fleeting, momentary. 2 concise, using few words ♦ *a brief summary* ♦ *I'll be brief.* SYNONYMS: succint, pithy, crisp, abbreviated, compressed. 3 short in length ♦ *a brief skirt.*
briefs plural noun very short knickers or underpants. **in brief** in a few words.
briefly adverb **briefness** noun [from a Latin word *brevis* meaning 'short']

brief[2] noun 1 a summary of the facts of a case, drawn up for a barrister. 2 a case given to a barrister. 3 a set of instructions given to someone before they start a piece of work.
brief verb 1 to give someone all the instructions and information they need before starting a piece of work. 2 to give a brief to a barrister. **to hold no brief for** not to be obliged to support someone. [from a Latin word *breve* meaning 'note, dispatch']

briefcase noun a flat case for carrying documents.

briefing noun a meeting for giving someone instructions or information.

brier noun another spelling of **briar**.

brig noun a square-rigged sailing ship with two masts. [abbreviation of *brigantine*]

brigade noun 1 an army unit forming part of a division. 2 a group of people organized for a particular purpose ♦ *the fire brigade.* 3 (*informal*) a group of people with something in common ♦ *the anti-smoking brigade.* [from an Italian word *brigata* meaning 'a troop']

brigadier noun an army officer of the rank above colonel.

brigand (brig-ənd) *noun* a member of a band of robbers. [from an Italian word *brigante* meaning 'foot soldier']

bright *adjective* 1 giving out much light, or filled with light ♦ *a bright room.* SYNONYMS: light (room), shining, gleaming, dazzling, sparkling, glittering, brilliant, luminous. 2 (said about colours) vivid and bold. 3 quick-witted and clever. 4 cheerful ♦ *a bright smile.*
bright *adverb* brightly. **to look on the bright side** to be optimistic in spite of difficulties. **brightly** *adverb* **brightness** *noun* [from an Old English word]

brighten *verb* to make something brighter, or to become brighter.

brill[1] *noun* a flatfish like a turbot. [origin unknown]

brill[2] *adjective* (*informal*) brilliant, very good.

brilliant *adjective* 1 very bright or sparkling. SYNONYMS: dazzling, glittering, gleaming. 2 very clever or talented. 3 excellent, marvellous.
brilliant *noun* a cut diamond with many facets. **brilliance** *noun* **brilliancy** *noun* **brilliantly** *adverb* [from an Italian word *brillare* meaning 'to shine']

brim *noun* 1 the edge of a cup, bowl, or other container ♦ *The bucket was filled to the brim.* 2 the bottom part of a hat that sticks out.
brim *verb* (**brimmed, brimming**) to fill something to the brim, or to be full to the brim ♦ *Her eyes brimmed with tears.* **to brim over** to overflow. [origin unknown]

brimful *adjective* full to the brim.

brimstone *noun* (*old use*) sulphur. [from an Old English word *brynstan* meaning 'burning stone']

brindled (brin-dəld) *adjective* brown with streaks of other colour ♦ *a brindled cow.* [probably from a Scandinavian word]

brine *noun* salt water. [from an Old English word]

bring *verb* (past tense and past participle **brought**) 1 to cause a person or thing to come, especially by carrying or leading them. 2 to result in or cause something ♦ *War brought famine.* SYNONYMS: create, produce, generate, engender, induce, occasion. 3 to cause something to arrive at a particular state ♦ *Now bring it to the boil* ♦ *I managed to bring them to their senses.* 4 to put forward charges etc. in a law court

♦ *They brought an action for libel.* **to bring something about** to cause something to happen. **to bring the house down** to get loud applause or laughter from an audience. **to bring in** 1 to introduce something ♦ *The government brought in tough new anti-terrorist laws.* 2 to produce a sum of money as income or profit ♦ *How much did the sponsored walk bring in?* 3 to pronounce a particular verdict in court. **to bring something off** to succeed in doing it. **to bring something out** 1 to show a feature clearly ♦ *That sweater brings out the colour of your eyes.* 2 to publish a new book or launch a new product. **to bring yourself to do something** to force yourself to do something unpleasant. **to bring someone up** 1 to look after children while they are growing up. **to bring something up** 1 to mention a subject so it can be discussed. 2 to vomit. **to bring up the rear** to come last in a line. [from an Old English word *bringan*]

brink *noun* 1 the edge of a steep place or of a stretch of water. 2 the point beyond which something will happen ♦ *We were on the brink of war.* [from an Old Norse word *brekka* meaning 'hill, slope']

brinkmanship *noun* the pursuit of a dangerous policy to the brink of war, catastrophe, etc. before stopping.

briny *adjective* (**brinier, briniest**) salty.
briny *noun* (*informal*) the sea.

brioche (bree-osh) *noun* a small sweetened bread roll, circular in shape. [a French word]

briquette (brik-et) *noun* a block of compressed coal dust, used as fuel. [a French word meaning 'little brick']

brisk *adjective* 1 active, moving quickly ♦ *a brisk walk.* 2 (said about a person's manner) dealing with people quickly and in a businesslike way, perhaps slightly rudely. **briskly** *adverb* **briskness** *noun* [same origin as for *brusque*]

brisket (brisk-it) *noun* a joint of beef cut from the breast. [perhaps from an Old Norse word]

brisling (briz-ling) *noun* a small herring or sprat, processed like sardines. [a Norwegian word meaning 'sprat']

bristle (briss-əl) *noun* 1 a short stiff hair. 2 any of the stiff pieces of hair, wire, or plastic in a brush.
bristle *verb* 1 (said about an animal's hair or fur) to stand upright as a sign of anger

or fear. **2** to show indignation or irritation. **to bristle with** to have a lot of something ♦ *The kitchen bristled with gadgets.* [from an Old English word *byrst*]

bristly *adjective* full of bristles.

Britannic *adjective* (*old use*) to do with Britain ♦ *Her Britannic Majesty.*

Briton *noun* **1** a person born or living in Britain, especially an inhabitant of southern Britain before the Roman conquest.

brittle *adjective* hard but easy to break or snap. [from an Old English word]

broach *verb* **1** to raise a subject for discussion. **2** to make a hole in something and draw out liquid. [from an Old French word]

broad *adjective* **1** large across, wide. **2** measuring from side to side ♦ *50 ft. broad.* **3** large in scope ♦ *She has broad tastes in music.* SYNONYMS: wide-ranging, comprehensive, eclectic, catholic. **4** in general terms, not detailed ♦ *We were in broad agreement.* SYNONYMS: general, rough, non-specific. **5** clear and unmistakable ♦ *a broad hint.* **6** (said about a regional accent) very noticeable and strong. **7** rather coarse ♦ *broad humour.* **broad daylight** full daylight, the daytime. [from an Old English word]

broad bean *noun* an edible bean with large flat seeds.

broadcast *verb* (**broadcast, broadcast,** or **broadcasted**) **1** to send out a programme on television or radio. **2** to make a piece of news generally known. **3** to sow seed by scattering, not in drills.
broadcast *noun* a programme sent out on television or radio.
broadcast *adverb* scattered freely.
broadcaster *noun* [originally meaning 'to scatter widely', from *broad* and *cast*]

broaden *verb* to make something broad, or to become broad.

broadly *adverb* **1** in a broad way. **2** in a general way ♦ *Broadly speaking, I agree with you.*

broad-minded *adjective* having tolerant views, not easily shocked. SYNONYMS: tolerant, open-minded, liberal, enlightened, unshockable.

broadsheet *noun* a newspaper with a large format, thought of as more serious than the tabloids.

broadside *noun* **1** (*historical*) the firing of all guns on one side of a ship. **2** a strong attack in words. [originally denoting the side of a ship above the waterline]

broadsword *noun* a sword with a broad blade, used for cutting rather than thrusting.

brocade (brə-kayd) *noun* a rich fabric woven with raised patterns. **brocaded** *adjective* [from an Italian word *brocco* meaning 'twisted thread']

broccoli (brok-əli) *noun* a kind of cauliflower with greenish flowerheads. [an Italian word meaning 'cabbage heads']

brochure (broh-shə) *noun* a booklet or pamphlet containing information. [from a French word meaning 'stitching' (because originally the pages were roughly stitched together)]

brogue[1] (brohg) *noun* a strong shoe with ornamental perforated bands. [via Scottish Gaelic and Irish from an Old Norse word]

brogue[2] *noun* a dialectal accent, especially Irish. [origin unknown]

broil *verb* **1** to cook meat over direct heat. **2** to become very hot, especially from sunshine. [from a French word *brûler* meaning 'to burn']

broiler *noun* a young chicken suitable or specially reared for broiling or roasting.

broke past tense of **break**.
broke *adjective* (*informal*) having run out of money. SYNONYMS: penniless, insolvent, bankrupt, (*informal*) hard up, skint.

broken past participle of **break**.
broken *adjective* (said about a language) spoken imperfectly by a foreigner ♦ *broken English.* **brokenly** *adverb*

broken-hearted *adjective* overwhelmed by grief or disappointment.

broken home *noun* a family in which the parents are divorced or separated.

broker *noun* **1** a person who buys and sells things on behalf of others.
broker *verb* to arrange or negotiate a deal or plan. [originally denoting a retailer or pedlar]

brolly *noun* (**brollies**) (*informal*) an umbrella.

bromide (broh-myd) *noun* a compound of bromine, used in medicine to calm the nerves.

bromine (broh-meen) *noun* a dark red liquid chemical element (symbol Br), compounds of which are used in medicine and photography. [from a Greek word *brōmos* meaning 'a stink']

bronchial (bronk-iəl) *adjective* to do with the branched tubes (called *bronchi*) into which the windpipe divides before entering the lungs.

bronchiole *noun* (*Anatomy*) any of the tiny branches into which a bronchus divides.

bronchitis (brong-**kiy**-tiss) *noun* inflammation of the mucous membrane inside the bronchial tubes, which makes you cough a lot.

bronchus (brong-kəs) *noun* (**bronchi**, (brong-kiy)) either of the two main tubes into which the windpipe divides, leading to the lungs. [from a Greek word *bronkhos* meaning 'windpipe']

bronco (brong-koh) *noun* (**broncos**) a wild or half-tamed horse of western North America. [from a Spanish word meaning 'rough, rude']

brontosaurus (bront-ə-**sor**-əs) *noun* (**brontosauruses**) another name for **apatosaurus**. [from Greek words *brontē* meaning 'thunder' and *sauros* meaning 'lizard']

bronze *noun* 1 a brown alloy of copper and tin. 2 something made of bronze. 3 a bronze medal, awarded as third prize. 4 a yellowish-brown colour.
bronze *adjective* 1 made of bronze. 2 yellowish-brown.
bronze *verb* to make someone suntanned. [probably from a Persian word *birinj* meaning 'brass']

Bronze Age *noun* the period when weapons and tools were made of bronze.

brooch (brohch) *noun* an ornamental hinged pin fastened with a clasp. [a different spelling of *broach*]

brood *noun* the young birds or other animals that were hatched or born together.
brood *verb* 1 to keep thinking deeply or resentfully about something ♦ *I've been brooding over what you said last night.* 2 to sit on eggs to hatch them. [from an Old English word]

broody *adjective* (**broodier, broodiest**) 1 (said about a hen) wanting to sit on eggs. 2 (*informal*) (said about a woman) longing to have children. 3 thoughtful and depressed.

brook[1] *noun* a small stream. [from an Old English word *broc*]

brook[2] *verb* (*formal*) to tolerate something ♦ *He would brook no argument.* [from an Old English word *brucan*]

broom *noun* 1 a long-handled brush for sweeping floors. 2 a shrub with yellow or white flowers. [from an Old English word *brom* meaning 'the plant broom', from which brushes used to be made]

broomstick *noun* a broom handle.

Bros (bross) *abbreviation* Brothers.

broth *noun* a kind of thin soup. [from an Old English word]

brothel (broth-əl) *noun* a house where women work as prostitutes. [from an Old English word *breothan* meaning 'to become worse']

brother *noun* 1 a son of the same parents as another person. 2 a man who is a fellow member of a trade union, Christian Church, or other association. 3 a member of a religious order of men. **brotherly** *adjective* [from an Old English word *brothor*]

brotherhood *noun* 1 the relationship of brothers. 2 friendliness and companionship between men, or between people in general. 3 a society or association of men, or its members.

brother-in-law *noun* (**brothers-in-law**) the brother of a married person's husband or wife, or the husband of a person's sister.

brought past tense and past participle of **bring**.

brougham (broo-əm) *noun* (*historical*) 1 a four-wheeled closed carriage drawn by one horse or electrically driven. 2 a former type of motor car with the driver's seat open. [named after Lord Brougham (1778–1868)]

brow *noun* 1 a person's forehead. 2 an eyebrow. 3 the top of a hill. [from an Old English word]

browbeat *verb* (**browbeat, browbeaten**) to intimidate someone, especially with words.

brown *adjective* 1 of a colour between orange and black, like the colour of dark wood. 2 dark-skinned or suntanned. 3 (said about bread) brown in colour, especially through being made with wholemeal flour.
brown *noun* 1 brown colour. 2 brown clothes.

brown verb to make something brown, or to become brown. **to be browned off** (informal) to be fed up or annoyed. [from an Old English word]

brown coal noun a kind of coal, brownish in colour, in which the original plant or wood structures can usually be seen.

Brownian motion noun the irregular movements of microscopic particles (e.g. of smoke or pollen) in a liquid or gas, caused by molecules of the liquid or gas striking against them. [named after R. Brown, Scottish botanist]

brownie noun 1 a small square of chocolate cake. 2 a friendly elf.
Brownie noun a member of a junior branch of the Guides, for girls between about 7 and 10.

brownie point noun (informal) recognition that you have done something helpful.

browning noun a substance for colouring gravy.

brown sugar noun sugar that is only partly refined.

browse verb 1 to look through a book, or examine items for sale, in a casual leisurely way ♦ I'm just browsing, thank you. 2 (Computing) to search files on a network. 3 (said about animals) to feed on leaves or grass. [from an Old French word brost meaning 'young shoot']

browser noun (Computing) a program with a graphical user interface for displaying HTML files, used to search the World Wide Web.

brucellosis (broo-sel-oh-sis) noun a disease caused by bacteria, affecting cattle and some other farm animals. [from Brucella, the bacterium responsible, named after the Scottish physician David Bruce (1855–1931)]

bruise (brooz) noun 1 an injury caused by a blow or by pressure that makes a dark mark on the skin without breaking it. 2 a similar area of damage on a fruit or vegetable.
bruise verb 1 to cause a bruise or bruises to appear on a person's skin. 2 to be susceptible to bruises ♦ I bruise easily. [from an Old English word brysan meaning 'crush or injure']

bruit (broot) verb (old use) to spread a report or rumour. [from an Old French word bruit meaning 'noise']

brunch noun (informal) a late-morning meal combining breakfast and lunch. [from breakfast and lunch]

brunette (broo-net) noun a woman with dark brown hair. [from a French word brun meaning 'brown']

brunt noun the chief impact of something bad ♦ They bore the brunt of the attack. [origin unknown]

brush noun 1 an implement with bristles of hair, wire, or nylon set in a solid base, used for cleaning, smoothing, or painting things. 2 an act of brushing ♦ Give your hair a good brush. 3 a brief unpleasant encounter ♦ We had a brush with a group of hooligans. 4 a fox's bushy tail. 5 a brush-like piece of carbon or metal for making a good electrical connection. 6 each of a pair of thin sticks with long wire bristles for striking a drum or cymbal.
brush verb 1 to clean something or make something tidy with a brush ♦ I'll just brush my teeth. 2 to touch something lightly in passing ♦ Her hand brushed my cheek. **to brush something aside** to reject something casually or curtly. **to brush someone off** to reject someone in an abrupt way. **to brush something up** to improve your knowledge of a subject ♦ You need to brush up your Spanish before you go to Madrid. [from an Old French word broisse]

brush-off noun a curt rejection.

brushwood noun 1 undergrowth. 2 cut or broken twigs.

brushwork noun the style of the strokes made with a painter's brush.

brusque (bruusk) adjective abrupt and offhand in manner. **brusquely** adverb **brusqueness** noun [from an Italian word brusco meaning 'sour']

Brussels sprout noun one of the edible buds growing thickly on the stem of a kind of cabbage. [named after Brussels, the capital of Belgium]

brutal adjective cruel and violent ♦ a brutal attack. SYNONYMS: savage, vicious, barbaric, sadistic, ruthless, callous, merciless. **brutality** noun **brutally** adverb [same origin as for brute]

brutalize verb 1 to make someone brutal. 2 to treat someone brutally. **brutalization** noun

brute noun 1 a brutal person. 2 (informal) an unpleasant or difficult person or thing. 3 an animal in contrast to a human being. **brute** adjective merely physical ♦ We had to use brute force to get the door open. **brutish** adjective [from a Latin word brutus meaning 'stupid']

bryony (briy-əni) noun a climbing hedgerow plant with black or white berries. [from an Old English word]

bryophyte (briy-ə-fiyt) noun any of the group of plants that consists of mosses and liverworts. [from the Greek words bruon meaning 'moss' and phuta meaning 'plants']

BSc abbreviation Bachelor of Science.

BSE abbreviation bovine spongiform encephalopathy, a fatal disease of cattle that affects the nervous system and causes staggering. It is believed to be related to Creutzfeldt-Jakob disease in humans.

BSI abbreviation British Standards Institution.

BST abbreviation British Summer Time.

BT abbreviation British Telecom.

Bt abbreviation Baronet ♦ Sir John Davis, Bt.

bubble noun 1 a thin ball of liquid enclosing air or gas. 2 a small ball of air in a liquid or in a solidified liquid, such as glass. 3 a transparent domed cover. **bubble** verb 1 to send up or rise in bubbles. 2 to make the sound of bubbles rising in liquid ♦ The soup was bubbling away in the kitchen. 3 to show great liveliness or excitement ♦ She was bubbling with anticipation. [related to burble]

bubble and squeak noun cooked cabbage and potato that is chopped, mixed, and fried.

bubble chamber noun (Physics) a device containing superheated liquid in which the paths of charged particles, X-rays, and gamma rays can be observed by the trail of bubbles which they produce.

bubblegum noun chewing gum that can be blown into large bubbles.

bubble wrap noun plastic packaging in the form of sheets which contain lots of small air cushions, used to protect whatever it is wrapped around.

bubbly adjective (**bubblier, bubbliest**) 1 full of bubbles. 2 cheerful and lively. **bubbly** noun (informal) champagne or sparkling wine.

bubonic plague (bew-bon-ik) noun a contagious disease, transmitted by rat fleas, producing inflamed swellings (called buboes) in the groin or armpit. [from a Latin word bubo meaning 'a swelling']

buccaneer noun (historical) 1 a pirate. 2 an unscrupulous adventurer. **buccaneering** adjective [originally denoting European hunters in the Caribbean, from a French word boucanier]

buck¹ noun a male deer, hare, or rabbit. **buck** verb 1 (said about a horse) to jump with its back arched and kick out its back legs. 2 (informal) to resist or oppose something ♦ While other radio stations are losing listeners, we are bucking the trend. **to buck up** (informal) 1 to hurry up. 2 to become more cheerful. [from an Old English word]

buck² noun (North Amer.) (Austral.) (informal) a dollar. [origin unknown]

buck³ noun **to pass the buck** (informal) to shift the responsibility or blame for something to someone else. [from buck, a word used in poker meaning 'an article placed as a reminder before the person whose turn it is to deal']

bucket noun 1 a round open container with a handle, used for holding or carrying liquids or substances that are in small pieces. 2 the amount of liquid in a bucket ♦ You'll need three buckets to fill the bath. **buckets** plural noun (informal) large quantities of rain or tears ♦ I cried buckets at the end of the film. **bucket** verb (**bucketed, bucketing**) (informal) 1 (said about a vehicle) to move along quickly and jerkily. 2 to pour down heavily ♦ Rain was bucketing down. **bucketful** noun (**bucketfuls**) [from an Anglo-French word buquet meaning 'tub, pail']

bucket seat noun a seat with a rounded back, for one person.

bucket shop noun (informal) a travel agency that provides cheap air tickets.

buckle noun a device usually with a hinged tongue, through which a belt or strap is threaded to secure it. **buckle** verb 1 to fasten something with a buckle ♦ He buckled on his sword. 2 to bend and give way under pressure or intense heat ♦ My legs buckled and I fell to the floor ♦ The front wheel buckled in the accident. SYNONYMS: crumple, collapse, cave in, contort, warp. **to buckle down to** to start working at something with determination. [from a Latin word *buccula* meaning 'cheek strap of a helmet'; the second verb sense is from a French word *boucler* meaning 'bulge']

buckler *noun* a small round shield with a handle. [from an Old French word]

buckram (buk-rəm) *noun* stiffened cloth, especially that used for binding books. [from an Old French word]

buckshee *adjective* (*informal*) free of charge. [alteration of *baksheesh* meaning 'a small sum of money given as a tip or bribe']

buckshot *noun* coarse lead shot.

bucolic (bew-kol-ik) *adjective* to do with country life. [from a Greek word *boukolos* meaning 'herdsman']

bud *noun* 1 a small knob that will develop into a branch, flower, or cluster of leaves. 2 a flower or leaf before it opens. 3 an outgrowth that forms on the body of certain organisms (e.g. polyps) and develops into a new individual.
bud *verb* (**budded, budding**) to produce buds. **in bud** forming buds. [origin unknown]

Buddha (buud-ə) *noun* 1 the title (often treated as a name) of the Indian philosopher Gautama (5th century BC), and of a series of teachers of Buddhism. 2 a statue or carving representing Gautama Buddha. [from a Sanskrit word *buddha* meaning 'enlightened one']

Buddhism (buud-izm) *noun* an Asian religion based on the teachings of the Buddha. **Buddhist** *adjective & noun*

budding *adjective* beginning to develop ♦ *a budding poet.* [from *bud*]

buddleia (bud-liə) *noun* a shrub or tree with fragrant lilac or yellow flowers. [named in honour of the English botanist Adam Buddle (1660–1715)]

buddy *noun* (**buddies**) (*informal*) a friend. [probably from *brother*]

budge *verb* 1 to move or make something move slightly ♦ *The window wouldn't budge.* SYNONYMS: shift, stir. 2 to alter a position or opinion, or to make someone do this ♦ *She refused to budge on the matter* ♦ *We couldn't budge him.* SYNONYMS: sway, shift, persuade. [from a French word *bouger* meaning 'to stir']

budgerigar (buj-er-i-gar) *noun* a kind of Australian parakeet, often kept as a pet. [from Australian Aboriginal words *budgeri* meaning 'good' and *gar* meaning 'cockatoo']

budget *noun* 1 an estimate or plan of income and expenditure in a given period. 2 the amount of money set aside for a particular purpose ♦ *I have a budget of £30 for their present.* 3 (**the Budget**) a regular statement made by the Chancellor of the Exchequer about plans for government spending and raising revenue.
budget *verb* (**budgeted, budgeting**) to allow for an expense in a budget ♦ *I didn't budget for staying in a hotel.*
budget *adjective* inexpensive ♦ *budget fares.* **budgetary** *adjective* [from a French word *bouge* meaning 'leather bag'; the Chancellor was formerly said to 'open his budget']

budget account *noun* an account with a shop, bank, etc. into which a customer makes regular payments in order to cover bills.

budgie *noun* (*informal*) a budgerigar.

buff [1] *noun* 1 strong velvety dull-yellow leather. 2 the colour of this.
buff *adjective* dull yellow.
buff *verb* to polish something with soft material. **in the buff** naked. [from *buff leather* meaning 'leather of buffalo hide']

buff [2] *noun* (*informal*) a person who is interested in and knows a lot about a particular subject ♦ *a film buff.* [from *buff* [1], originally describing people who went to watch fires, from the buff-coloured uniforms once worn by New York volunteer firemen]

buffalo *noun* (**buffaloes** or **buffalo**) 1 a kind of domesticated ox found in Asia; a rather similar wild ox found in Africa. 2 an American bison. [from a Portuguese word]

buffer *noun* 1 one of a pair of plates on springs on the front and rear of a railway vehicle or at the end of a track, designed to reduce the effect of any impact. 2 something that reduces the effect of an impact or forms a barrier between two opposing sides. 3 (*Computing*) a temporary store in a system, used when editing text or transferring data. 4 (*informal*) an elderly or strange person ♦ *Who's the old buffer over there?*

buffer verb to lessen the impact of something. [from an old word buff meaning 'a blow', as in blind man's buff; related to buffet²]

buffer state noun a small country between two powerful ones, thought to reduce the chance of war between these.

buffet¹ (buu-fay) noun 1 a meal where guests serve themselves ♦ a buffet lunch. 2 a room or counter selling light meals or snacks ♦ the station buffet. [from a French word meaning 'stool']

buffet² (buff-it) verb (buffeted, buffeting) to hit or knock something ♦ Our aircraft was buffeted by strong winds. [from an Old French word buffe meaning 'a blow']

buffet car (buu-fay) noun a railway carriage serving light meals.

buffoon (buf-oon) noun a person who acts like a fool. **buffoonery** noun [from a medieval Latin word buffo meaning 'clown']

bug noun 1 an insect, especially one that infests dirty houses and beds. 2 (informal) a harmful micro-organism, or an illness caused by one ♦ a stomach bug. 3 (informal) an error in a computer program or system that prevents it working properly. 4 (informal) an enthusiasm for something ♦ They've caught the skiing bug. 5 (informal) a very small hidden microphone installed secretly.
bug verb (bugged, bugging) (informal) 1 to fit a room with a hidden microphone secretly so that conversations etc. can be overheard from a distance. 2 to annoy someone ♦ What's bugging you? [origin unknown]

bugbear noun something you fear or dislike. [from an old word bug meaning 'bogey']

bug-eyed adjective having bulging eyes.

buggy noun (buggies) 1 a small sturdy motor vehicle with an open top ♦ a beach buggy. 2 a light collapsible pushchair. 3 (old use) a light horse-drawn carriage. [origin unknown]

bugle noun a brass instrument like a small trumpet, used for sounding military signals. [originally bugle horn, denoting the horn of an ox used to give signals, via Old French from a Latin word buculus meaning 'ox']

bugler noun a person who sounds a bugle.

build verb (past tense and past participle built) 1 to construct something by putting parts or material together. SYNONYMS: construct, assemble, fabricate, erect, put up. 2 to develop something gradually ♦ We first need to build trust. 3 to accumulate or increase ♦ Traffic has been building all morning.
build noun the shape of a person's body ♦ He is of slender build. **to build on** to base new developments on something ♦ Let's try and build on what you've already learnt. [from an Old English word byldan]

builder noun someone whose trade is building houses etc.

building noun 1 a structure with a roof and walls. 2 the constructing of houses and other structures ♦ the building trade.

building society noun a financial organization that accepts deposits and lends out money for mortgages to people wishing to buy or build a house etc.

build-up noun 1 a gradual increase in something ♦ the build-up of nuclear weapons. 2 a favourable description in advance of a person's appearance, or a period of preparation before an event.

built past tense and past participle of build.
built adjective having a specified build ♦ a heavily built man.

built-in adjective forming an integral part of a structure ♦ a built-in wardrobe.

built-up adjective (said about a place) filled in with buildings ♦ a built-up area.

bulb noun 1 a thick rounded mass of scale-like leaves from which a stem grows up and roots grow down. 2 a plant grown from this, such as a daffodil. 3 a bulb-shaped object ♦ the bulb of a thermometer. 4 a glass globe that produces electric light. [from a Greek word bolbos meaning 'onion']

bulbous (bul-bəs) adjective 1 shaped like a bulb. 2 (said about a plant) growing from a bulb.

bulgar wheat noun a cereal food made from whole wheat that has been partially boiled and then dried. [from a Turkish word bulgur meaning 'bruised grain']

bulge noun a rounded swelling. SYNONYMS: bump, lump, protuberance.
bulge verb to swell outwards. [from a Latin word bulga meaning 'bag']

bulimia or **bulimia nervosa** (bew-lim-iə) noun a psychological condition causing someone to alternately overeat and fast, often making themselves vomit after eating. [from a Greek word meaning 'hunger of an ox']

bulk noun 1 the size of something, especially when it is large. 2 the greater part, the majority ♦ *The bulk of the population agree with this view.* 3 a large shape, body, or person ♦ *He raised his bulk from the armchair.*
bulk verb to increase the size or thickness of something ♦ *Use thicker paper to bulk it out.* **in bulk** in large quantities. [from an Old English word]

bulkhead noun a partition between separate compartments in a ship, aircraft, or vehicle. [from an Old Norse word *balkr* meaning 'partition' and *head*]

bulky adjective (**bulkier, bulkiest**) taking up a lot of space, awkwardly large.

bull [1] noun 1 an uncastrated male of any animal of the ox family. 2 the male of the whale, elephant, and other large animals. 3 the bullseye of a target. [from an Old Norse word *boli*]

bull [2] noun an official edict issued by the pope. [from a Latin word *bulla* meaning 'seal, sealed letter']

bulldog noun a powerful dog with short thick neck. [so called because it was used for attacking tethered bulls in the sport of 'bull-baiting']

bulldoze verb 1 to clear an area with a bulldozer. 2 (*informal*) to force someone to do something ♦ *He bulldozed them into accepting it.*

bulldozer noun a powerful tractor with a broad steel sheet mounted in front, used for shifting earth or clearing ground. [originally American; origin unknown]

bullet noun a small round or conical missile shot from a rifle or revolver. [from a French word *boulet* meaning 'little ball']

bulletin noun 1 a short official statement giving news. 2 a regular newsletter or report. [via French from Italian, related to *bull* [2]]

bulletin board noun (*Computing*) an information storage system that people can access via a network.

bulletproof adjective able to keep out bullets.

bullfighting noun the sport of baiting and killing bulls for public entertainment, as in Spain. **bullfight** noun **bullfighter** noun

bullfinch noun a songbird with a strong beak and a pinkish breast.

bullfrog noun a large American frog with a bellowing cry.

bullion noun bars of gold or silver, before coining or manufacture. [from an Old French word *bouillon* meaning 'a mint']

bull market noun (on the Stock Exchange) a situation where share prices are rising rapidly.

bull-nosed adjective with a rounded front end.

bullock noun a young castrated bull. [from an Old English word *bulloc* meaning 'young bull']

bullring noun an arena for bullfights.

bullseye noun 1 the centre of a target. 2 a large hard round peppermint sweet.

bull terrier noun a dog originally produced by crossing a bulldog and a terrier.

bully [1] noun (**bullies**) a person who tries to hurt or frighten people who are weaker.
bully verb (**bullies, bullied, bullying**) to use strength or power to hurt or frighten a weaker person. SYNONYMS: threaten, intimidate, coerce, domineer, tyrannize. **bully for you!** (*informal*) bravo! [probably from a Dutch word]

bully [2] verb (**bullies, bullied, bullying**) (in hockey) to start play by having two opposing players tap the ground and each other's sticks alternately three times before going for the ball.
bully noun (**bullies**) the start of a hockey game. [origin unknown]

bulrush noun a kind of tall rush with a thick velvety head. [probably from *bull* [1], suggesting something large]

bulwark (**buul-werk**) noun 1 a wall of earth built as a defence. 2 something that acts as a protection or defence.
bulwarks plural noun a ship's side above the level of the deck. [from German or Dutch]

bum [1] noun (*informal*) the buttocks. [origin unknown]

bum [2] noun (*North Amer.*) (*informal*) a tramp or lazy person.

bumble verb 1 to move or act in a clumsy way. 2 to ramble when speaking. [related to *boom* [1]]

bumblebee noun a large bee with a loud hum.

bump *verb* 1 to knock against something with a jolt ♦ *Our cars bumped into each other* ♦ *I bumped my head on the ceiling.* SYNONYMS: knock, hit, bang, strike, thump, collide. 2 to move along with a jolting movement ♦ *We bumped along the road.*
bump *noun* 1 a bumping sound, knock, or movement. SYNONYMS: bang, knock, thump, thud, crash, collision. 2 a swelling or lump on a surface. SYNONYMS: swelling, lump, bulge, hump, protuberance, protrusion. **to bump into** to meet someone by chance. **to bump someone off** (*informal*) to kill someone. **to bump something up** (*informal*) to increase something ♦ *They soon bumped up the price.* [an imitation of the sound]

bumper *noun* 1 a horizontal bar attached to the front or back of a motor vehicle to lessen the effect of a collision. 2 (in cricket) a ball that bounces high. **bumper** *adjective* unusually large or plentiful ♦ *a bumper crop.*

bumpkin *noun* a country person with awkward manners. [from a Dutch word]

bumptious (**bump-shəs**) *noun* annoyingly loud and conceited. **bumptiously** *adverb* **bumptiousness** *noun* [from bump, made up as a joke on the pattern of *fractious*]

bumpy *adjective* (**bumpier, bumpiest**) full of bumps; causing jolts ♦ *a bumpy ride.* **bumpiness** *noun*

bun *noun* 1 a small cake or bread roll. 2 hair twisted into a round bunch at the back of the head. [origin unknown]

bunch *noun* 1 a cluster ♦ *a bunch of grapes.* 2 a number of small similar things held or fastened together ♦ *a bunch of keys.* 3 (*informal*) a group of people. **bunch** *verb* to come or bring things together into a bunch. [origin unknown]

bundle *noun* 1 a number of things loosely fastened or wrapped together. 2 a set of sticks or rods tied together. 3 (*informal*) a large amount of money. **bundle** *verb* 1 to make a number of things into a bundle. 2 to put something away hastily and untidily ♦ *She bundled the letters into a drawer.* 3 to push someone hurriedly or carelessly ♦ *We bundled him into a taxi.* **to be bundled up** to be dressed in many warm clothes. [probably from Old German or Old Dutch]

bung *noun* a stopper for closing a hole in a barrel or jar. **bung** *verb* 1 to close something with a bung. 2 (*informal*) to throw or toss

something carelessly ♦ *Bung it over here.* **bunged up** blocked. [from an Old Dutch word]

bungalow *noun* a house with only one storey. [from a Hindi word *bangla* meaning 'of Bengal']

bungee jumping (**bun-jee**) *noun* the sport of jumping from a height with a long piece of elastic (called a *bungee*) tied to your legs to stop you from hitting the ground. [origin unknown]

bungle *verb* to make a mess of doing something. **bungle** *noun* a mistake or failure. **bungler** *noun* [origin unknown]

bunion *noun* a swelling at the side of the joint where the big toe joins the foot. [origin unknown]

bunk [1] *noun* a bed built like a shelf, e.g. on a ship. [origin unknown]

bunk [2] *verb* (*informal*) to leave school or work when you should be there. **to do a bunk** (*informal*) to depart hurriedly. [origin unknown]

bunk [3] *noun* (*informal, old use*) nonsense. [abbreviation of *bunkum*]

bunk beds *plural noun* a pair of single beds mounted one above the other as a unit.

bunker *noun* 1 a container for storing fuel. 2 a sandy hollow forming an obstacle on a golf course. 3 a reinforced underground shelter for use in wartime. [origin unknown]

bunkum *noun* (*old use*) nonsense. [from Buncombe County in North Carolina, mentioned in a nonsense speech by its Congressman]

bunny *noun* (**bunnies**) (*informal*) a child's name for a rabbit. [from a dialect word *bun* meaning 'rabbit']

Bunsen burner *noun* a small gas burner used in laboratories. [named after the German chemist R. Bunsen (1811–99), who invented it]

bunting [1] *noun* a bird related to the finches. [origin unknown]

bunting [2] *noun* flags and streamers for decorating streets and buildings. [origin unknown]

buoy (**boi**) *noun* an anchored floating object marking a navigable channel or showing the position of submerged rocks etc. **buoy** *verb* 1 to keep something afloat. 2 to mark something with a buoy or buoys. **to buoy someone up** to encourage someone or cheer them up ♦ *They were now buoyed up with new hope.* [from an Old Dutch word]

buoyant (boy-ənt) *adjective* 1 able to float. 2 cheerful and optimistic ♦ *He was in a buoyant mood.* **buoyancy** *noun* **buoyantly** *adverb* [from French or Spanish; related to *buoy*]

bur *noun* another spelling of **burr** (the seed case).

burble *verb* 1 to make a gentle murmuring sound. 2 to speak in a confused way and at length. [an imitation of the sound]

burden *noun* 1 a heavy load that has to be carried. 2 something difficult that you have to bear ♦ *the heavy burden of taxation.* SYNONYMS: affliction, handicap, obligation, onus, millstone. 3 the main theme of a speech, book, etc.
burden *verb* 1 to load someone heavily ♦ *She staggered in, burdened with shopping.* 2 to cause someone worry or hardship ♦ *I'm sorry to burden you with my troubles.* SYNONYMS: bother, trouble, encumber, (*informal*) saddle, lumber. [from an Old English word *byrthen*]

burdensome *adjective* troublesome.

bureau (bewr-oh) *noun* (**bureaux**) 1 a writing desk with drawers and a hinged flap for use as a writing surface. 2 an office or department ♦ *a travel bureau* ♦ *an information bureau.* [a French word meaning 'desk']

bureaucracy (bewr-ok-rəsi) *noun* (**bureaucracies**) 1 the use of too many rules and forms by officials, especially in government departments. SYNONYMS: red tape, paperwork, administration, officialdom. 2 government by state officials, not by elected representatives. [from *bureau* and *-cracy*]

bureaucrat (bewr-ə-krat) *noun* 1 an official who works in a government department. 2 someone who applies the rules of a department without exercising much judgement.

bureaucratic (bewr-ə-**krat**-ik) *adjective* 1 to do with bureaucracy. 2 to do with or like bureaucrats.

burette (bewr-et) *noun* a graduated glass tube with a tap, used for measuring small quantities of liquid. [a French word]

burgeon (ber-jən) *verb* to begin to grow rapidly ♦ *the country's burgeoning tourist industry.* [from an Old French word *bourgeonner* meaning 'to put out buds']

burger *noun* a hamburger or similar type of food. [short for *hamburger*, from Hamburg, a city in Germany; the first syllable was dropped because people thought it referred to ham]

burgess (ber-jis) *noun* (*old use*) 1 a citizen of a town or borough. 2 an MP for a borough or university. [from an Old French word *burgeis*, related to *borough*]

burgh (bu-rə) *noun* a borough in Scotland. [the Scots form of *borough*]

burglar *noun* a person who enters a building illegally, especially in order to steal. **burglary** *noun* [from a French word]

burgle *verb* to break into a building and steal things ♦ *We've been burgled!.* [from *burglar*]

burgundy *noun* (**burgundies**) 1 a rich red or white wine from Burgundy in France, or a similar wine from elsewhere. 2 a dark purplish red.

burial *noun* the burying of a dead body.

burka or **burkha** *noun* a loose piece of clothing covering the whole body including the head, worn in public by some Muslim women. [from an Arabic word]

burlesque (ber-lesk) *noun* a mocking imitation. [via French from an Italian word *burla* meaning 'ridicule, joke']

burly *adjective* (**burlier, burliest**) having a strong human body. **burliness** *noun* [from an Old English word]

burn[1] *verb* (past tense and past participle **burned** or **burnt**) 1 to be on fire, to blaze or glow. SYNONYMS: blaze, flame, smoulder, flicker, smoke. 2 to damage, hurt, or destroy something by fire, heat, or the action of acid ♦ *You should burn that letter* ♦ *I burnt my hand on the oven door.* 3 to use something as fuel ♦ *The stove burns wood.* 4 to char or scorch food you are cooking ♦ *Sorry, I've burnt the chops.* 5 to feel very hot ♦ *My face was burning.* 6 (said about the skin) to become red and painful from too much sunlight. 7 to feel great emotion ♦ *He was burning with desire.*
burn *noun* 1 a mark or sore made by burning. 2 the firing of a spacecraft's rockets. **to burn your boats** or **bridges** to do something deliberately that makes retreat impossible. **to burn the midnight oil** to work late into the night. **to have money to burn** to have so much that you do not

need to take care of it. [from an Old English word *birnan* meaning 'to be on fire']

◊ The form *burnt* (not *burned*) is always used when an adjective is required, e.g. in *burnt wood*. As parts of the verb, either *burned* or *burnt* may be used, e.g. *the wood had burned* or *had burnt completely*.

burn [2] *noun* (*Scottish*) a brook. [from an Old English word *burna*]

burner *noun* the part of a lamp or cooker that produces and shapes the flame.

burning *adjective* 1 intense ♦ *a burning ambition*. 2 hotly discussed, vital ♦ *a burning question*.

burnish *verb* to polish something by rubbing. [from an Old French word *burnir*]

burnous (ber-**noos**) *noun* a long loose hooded cloak worn by Arabs. [from an Arabic word *burnus*]

burnt past tense and past participle of **burn** [1].
burnt *adjective* of a deep shade ♦ *burnt sienna* ♦ *burnt umber*.

burp *noun* (*informal*) a belch.
burp *verb* (*informal*) 1 to belch. 2 to make a baby bring up wind from the stomach after feeding. [an imitation of the sound]

burr *noun* 1 a whirring sound. 2 the strong pronunciation of the letter 'r', as in some regional accents. 3 a prickly seed case or flower head that clings to hair or clothing. 4 a small drill.
burr *verb* to make a whirring sound. [a different spelling of *bur*]

burrow *noun* a hole or tunnel dug by a rabbit, fox, etc. as a dwelling.
burrow *verb* 1 to make a burrow. 2 to dig into or through something solid. 3 to push your way through or into something, to search deeply ♦ *She burrowed in her handbag*. [a different spelling of *borough*]

bursar (ber-ser) *noun* 1 a person who manages the finances and other business of a school or college. 2 (*Scottish*) a student who holds a bursary. [from a Latin word *bursa* meaning 'a bag']

bursary (ber-ser-i) *noun* (**bursaries**) a grant given to a student.

burst *verb* (past tense and past participle **burst**) 1 to break suddenly and violently apart, or to make something do this ♦ *One of my tyres has burst*. SYNONYMS: split, rupture, tear, pop (a balloon). 2 to be very full ♦ *My wardrobe is bursting with clothes*. 3 to enter loudly or suddenly ♦ *Three men burst into the room*. 4 to let out a strong and noisy expression of feeling ♦ *We all burst out laughing*.
burst *noun* 1 a bursting, a split. 2 a brief outbreak of something violent or noisy ♦ *a burst of gunfire*. 3 a period of continuous effort. **to be bursting to do something** to be very eager to do it ♦ *The kids are bursting to tell you the news*. **to burst into flame** to catch fire. **to burst into something** to suddenly start doing something ♦ *She burst into song* ♦ *The boy burst into tears*. [from an Old English word *berstan*]

burton *noun* **to go for a burton** (*informal*) to be lost or destroyed or killed. [perhaps referring to Burton ale, from Burton-upon-Trent]

bury *verb* (**buries, buried, burying**) 1 to place a dead body in the earth, a tomb, or the sea. 2 to put something in a hole in the ground and cover it up. 3 to cover something up ♦ *She buried her face in her hands*. **to bury the hatchet** to agree to stop quarrelling and become friendly. **to bury yourself in something** to involve yourself deeply in something ♦ *He buried himself in this work*. [from an Old English word *byrgan*]

bus *noun* (**buses**) 1 a large vehicle carrying passengers on a fixed route. 2 (*Computing*) a set of conductors in a system, to which pieces of equipment can be connected in parallel.
bus *verb* (**bussed, bussing**) 1 to travel or transport someone by bus. 2 to take children to a distant school by bus in order to counteract racial segregation. [short for *omnibus*]

busby (buz-bi) *noun* (**busbies**) a tall fur cap worn by some regiments on ceremonial occasions. [origin unknown]

bush [1] *noun* 1 a shrub. 2 wild uncultivated land, especially in Africa and Australia. [from an Old French or Old Norse word]

bush [2] *noun* 1 a metal lining for a round hole in which something fits or revolves. 2 a sleeve that protects an electric cable. [from an Old French word]

bushed *adjective* (*informal*) exhausted.

bushel *noun* a measure for grain and fruit equal to 8 gallons (36.4 litres). **to hide your light under a bushel** to conceal your abilities. [from an Old French word]

bushman *noun* (**bushmen**) a dweller or traveller in the Australian bush.

Bushman noun (**Bushmen**) a member of an aboriginal people of southern Africa, especially of the Kalahari Desert.

bush telegraph noun a way in which news or gossip is passed on unofficially.

bushy adjective (**bushier, bushiest**) 1 growing thickly ♦ bushy eyebrows. 2 covered with bushes. **bushiness** noun

business (**biz-nis**) noun 1 a person's regular trade or profession. 2 buying and selling things, trade ♦ We always do a lot of business at Christmas. 3 a shop or firm ♦ a grocery business. SYNONYMS: company, firm, establishment, practice, concern, enterprise. 4 a thing you are concerned about or need to deal with ♦ I have urgent business to see to. 5 a matter or affair ♦ I'm sick of the whole business. [from an Old English word bisignis meaning 'busyness']

businesslike adjective efficient and practical.

businessman or **businesswoman** noun (**businessmen** or **businesswomen**) a person working in commerce, especially at a senior level.

business studies plural noun the study of economics and management.

busker noun an entertainer who performs in the street for money. **busking** noun [from an old word busk meaning 'to be a pedlar']

busman noun (**busmen**) the driver of a bus.

busman's holiday noun leisure time spent doing the same thing that you do at work.

bus station noun an area where a number of buses stop.

bus stop noun a regular stopping place on a bus route.

bust[1] noun 1 a sculpture of a person's head, shoulders, and chest. 2 a woman's breasts. 3 the measurement round a woman's body at the bosom. [from a Latin word bustum meaning 'tomb']

bust[2] verb (past tense and past participle **busted** or **bust**) (informal) 1 to break or burst something ♦ Who's bust my radio? 2 to arrest someone. **bust** noun (informal) 1 a period of economic difficulty or depression. 2 a police raid. **bust** adjective (informal) 1 damaged or broken. 2 bankrupt. **to bust up** (informal) (said about a couple) to separate. **to go bust** (informal) to become bankrupt. [a different spelling of burst]

bustard noun a large swift-running bird. [from an Old French word]

bustier (**bus-ti-ay**) noun a tight-fitting top without straps, worn by women. [a French word]

bustle[1] verb 1 to hurry in a busy or excited way. 2 (said about a place) to be full of activity ♦ a bustling market town. **bustle** noun hurried or excited activity. [from an Old Norse word]

bustle[2] noun padding used to puff out the top of a woman's skirt at the back. [origin unknown]

bust-up noun (informal) a serious quarrel.

busy adjective (**busier, busiest**) 1 working or occupied, having much to do ♦ Look, I'm a bit busy at the moment. SYNONYMS: occupied, involved, engaged, employed, (informal) hard at it, on the go, up to your eyes. 2 full of activity ♦ a busy day ♦ It was busy in town today. 3 (said about a telephone line) engaged. 4 (said about a picture or design) too full of detail. **busy** verb (**busies, busied, busying**) to keep someone busy ♦ He busied himself in the kitchen. **busily** adverb **busyness** noun [from an Old English word bisig]

busybody noun (**busybodies**) a person who meddles or interferes.

but conjunction however, nevertheless ♦ I wanted to go, but I couldn't. **but** preposition except, other than ♦ There's no one here but me. **but** adverb only, no more than ♦ We can but try. **but** noun an objection ♦ You're coming, and no buts. **but for** except for ♦ I'd have drowned but for you. [from an Old English word]

butane (**bew-tayn**) noun a flammable gas produced from petroleum, used in liquid form as a fuel.

butch adjective (informal) masculine in appearance or behaviour. [perhaps an abbreviation of butcher]

butcher noun 1 a person who cuts up and sells meat in a shop. 2 a brutal or murderous person. **butcher** verb 1 to slaughter or cut up an animal for meat. 2 to kill someone needlessly or brutally. [from an Old French word]

butchery noun 1 a butcher's trade. 2 needless or brutal killing.

butene noun (*Chemistry*) a gaseous alkene, obtained from petroleum and used in manufacturing other organic compounds.

butler noun the chief manservant of a household. [from an Old French word *bouteillier* meaning 'bottler']

butt¹ noun a large cask or barrel. [from a Latin word *buttis* meaning 'cask']

butt² noun 1 the thicker end of a tool or weapon. 2 a short remnant, a stub ♦ *a cigar butt*. [from a Dutch word *bot* meaning 'stumpy']

butt³ noun 1 a person or thing that is a target for ridicule or teasing ♦ *She was sick of being the butt of their jokes.* 2 the mound of earth behind the targets on a shooting range.
butts plural noun a shooting range. [from an Old French word *but* meaning 'goal']

butt⁴ verb 1 (said about a ram or goat) to hit something with the head or horns. 2 to meet or place something edge to edge ♦ *The shop butted up against the row of houses* ♦ *The strips should be butted against each other, not overlapping.*
butt noun 1 a rough push with the head. 2 a butted join. **to butt in** to interrupt or meddle. [from a French word *buter* meaning 'to hit']

butte (bewt) noun (*North Amer.*) an isolated hill with steep sides and a flat top. [a French word meaning 'mound']

butter noun 1 a fatty food substance made from cream by churning. 2 a similar substance made from other materials ♦ *peanut butter.*
butter verb to spread, cook, or serve something with butter. **to butter someone up** (*informal*) to flatter them. **buttery** adjective [from an Old English word *butere*]

buttercup noun a wild plant with bright yellow cup-shaped flowers.

butterfingers noun (*informal*) a person who often drops things or fails to hold a catch.

butterfly noun (**butterflies**) 1 an insect with four often brightly coloured wings and knobbed feelers. 2 a swimming stroke in which both arms are lifted forwards at the same time. **to have butterflies in the stomach** (*informal*) to have a fluttering feeling in your stomach because you feel nervous.

buttermilk noun the liquid left after butter has been churned from milk.

butterscotch noun a kind of hard toffee.

buttock noun either of the two fleshy rounded parts at the lower or rear end of the back of the human or an animal body. [from an Old English word *buttoc*]

button noun 1 a knob or disc sewn on a piece of clothing as a fastener or ornament. 2 a knob pressed to operate a piece of electrical or electronic equipment.
button verb (**buttoned, buttoning**) to fasten a piece of clothing with a button or buttons. [from an Old French word]

buttonhole noun 1 a slit through which a button is passed to fasten clothing. 2 a flower worn in the buttonhole of a coat lapel.
buttonhole verb (*informal*) to come up to someone and talk to them for a long time.

buttress noun 1 a support built against a wall. 2 a thing that supports or reinforces something.
buttress verb 1 to support something with buttresses. 2 to support or strengthen something. [same origin as for *butt*⁴]

butty noun (**butties**) (*informal*) a sandwich.

buxom adjective (said about a woman) plump and having large breasts. [originally meaning 'compliant', from an Old English word *bugan* meaning 'to bend']

buy verb (past tense and past participle **bought**) 1 to obtain something in exchange for money ♦ *I'll buy you lunch.*
SYNONYMS: purchase, acquire, procure. 2 to get something by great effort or sacrifice ♦ *This victory was dearly bought.* 3 (*informal*) to believe or accept the truth of something ♦ *No one would buy that excuse.*
buy noun (*informal*) something that is bought ♦ *That suit was a good buy.* **to have bought it** (*informal*) to be killed. **to buy someone out** to own something completely by paying another person to give up their share. **to buy time** to delay something so that you have more time to improve your position. [from an Old English word *bycgan*]

buyer noun 1 a person who buys something. 2 an agent choosing and buying stock for a large shop.

buyer's market noun a state of affairs when goods are plentiful and prices are low.

buzz noun 1 a vibrating humming sound. 2 (*informal*) a telephone call. 3 (*informal*) a

thrill. **4** (*informal*) a rumour.
buzz *verb* **1** to make or be filled with a humming sound ♦ *My ears are buzzing.* **2** to signal with a buzzer ♦ *Buzz when you know the answer.* **3** to go about quickly and busily. **4** to threaten an aircraft by flying close to it. **to buzz off** (*informal*) to go away. [an imitation of the sound]

buzzard *noun* a kind of hawk. [from a Latin word *buteo* meaning 'falcon']

buzzer *noun* a device that produces a buzzing note as a signal.

buzzword *noun* (*informal*) a piece of fashionable jargon.

by *preposition* **1** near to, beside ♦ *She stood by the door.* **2** going past ♦ *We drove by your house today.* **3** through the agency or means of ♦ *I persuaded him by flattery.* **4** (said about numbers or measurements) taking it together with ♦ *Multiply six by four* ♦ *It measures ten metres by eight.* **5** not later than ♦ *Can you finish this by Friday?* **6** according to ♦ *You shouldn't judge by appearances* ♦ *They pay by the hour.* **7** to the extent of ♦ *He missed it by inches.* **8** during ♦ *They came by night.*
by *adverb* so as to go past ♦ *The soldiers marched by.*
by and by before long. **by and large** on the whole, considering everything. **by the way** incidentally. [from an Old English word]

bye *noun* **1** (in cricket) a run scored when the ball goes past the batsman without being touched. **2** the status of having no opponent for one round in a tournament and so going on to the next round as if you had won. **3** (in golf) a hole or holes remaining unplayed when a match is ended. [from *by-* meaning 'at the side, extra']

bye-bye *interjection* (*informal*) goodbye.

by-election *noun* an election to replace an MP who has died or resigned. [from *by-* meaning 'extra' (an 'extra' election between general elections)]

byeline *noun* the goal line of a football pitch.

bygone *adjective* belonging to the past. **let bygones be bygones** forgive and forget past offences.

by-law *noun* a law that applies only to a particular town or district. [from an Old Norse word *bjarlagu* meaning 'town law']

byline *noun* a line in a newspaper etc. naming the writer of an article.

bypass *noun* **1** a road taking traffic round a city or congested area. **2** a secondary channel allowing something to flow when the main route is blocked. **3** an operation to make an alternative passage to help the circulation of the blood ♦ *a heart bypass.*
bypass *verb* **1** to avoid a place by means of a bypass. **2** to omit or ignore procedures, regulations, etc. in order to act quickly.

by-product *noun* a substance produced during the making of something else. [from *by-* meaning 'at the side, besides']

byre *noun* a cowshed. [from an Old English word]

byroad *noun* a minor road.

bystander *noun* a person standing near but taking no part when something happens.

byte *noun* a fixed number of bits (binary digits) in a computer, often representing a single character. [an invented word, based on *bit* and *bite*]

byway *noun* a minor road or path.

byword *noun* **1** a person or thing spoken of as a notable example ♦ *The firm became a byword for mismanagement.* **2** a word or phrase that sums up a person's principles ♦ *Punctuality is my byword.* [from an Old English word *biwyrde* meaning 'proverb']

Byzantine (bi-**zan**-tiyn) *adjective* **1** to do with Byzantium or the Eastern Roman Empire. **2** extremely complicated and detailed. **3** devious or underhand. [from Byzantium, the city later called Constantinople and now Istanbul]

Cc

C **1** the third letter of the English alphabet. **2** (*Music*) the first note of the diatonic scale of C major. **3** the Roman numeral for 100. [meaning 3 is short for a Latin word *centum* meaning 'hundred']

C *abbreviation* **1** Celsius or centigrade. **2** (*Chemistry*) the symbol for carbon.

© *symbol* copyright.

c. *abbreviation* **1** cent or cents. **2** century. **3** (used before a date) about ♦ *c.1776*. [meaning 3 is short for a Latin word *circa* meaning 'about']

cab *noun* **1** a taxi. **2** a compartment for the driver of a train, bus, lorry, or crane. [short for *cabriolet*, a light carriage drawn by a horse]

cabal (kə-**bal**) *noun* a group of people involved in a plot. [from a French word *cabale*]

cabaret (kab-ə-ray) *noun* an entertainment provided for customers in a restaurant or nightclub. [from a French word meaning 'tavern']

cabbage *noun* a vegetable with green or purple leaves usually forming a round head. [from a French word *caboche* meaning 'head']

cabbage moth *noun* a brown moth whose caterpillars feed on cabbage leaves and other plants.

cabbage white *noun* a butterfly whose caterpillars feed on cabbage leaves.

cabby or **cabbie** *noun* (**cabbies**) (*informal*) a taxi driver.

caber (**kay**-ber) *noun* a roughly-trimmed tree trunk used in the Scottish Highland sport of tossing the caber. [from a Gaelic word *cabar* meaning 'pole']

cabin *noun* **1** a small wooden house or shelter. SYNONYMS: hut, chalet, shelter, shack, lodge. **2** a compartment in a ship or spacecraft. **3** the part of an aircraft in which passengers sit. **4** a driver's cab. [from an Old French word *cabane*]

cabinet *noun* **1** a cupboard or container with drawers or shelves for storage. **2** a cupboard or container for a television set, hi-fi, or other electronic equipment. **Cabinet** the group of ministers who are chosen by the Prime Minister and meet regularly to discuss government policy. [from *cabin*]

cable *noun* **1** a thick rope of fibre or wire, or a thick chain. SYNONYMS: cord, rope, line, chain, (for mooring a ship) hawser. **2** (as a nautical measure) a length of 200 yards (183 metres). **3** a set of insulated wires for carrying electricity or transmitting electrical signals. SYNONYMS: lead, wire, flex. **4** a telegram sent abroad. **5** short for **cable television**.

cable *verb* to send a telegram to someone abroad, or to send them money by means of a telegram. [via Old French from a Latin word *capulum* meaning 'halter']

cable car *noun* a small cabin, usually one of several, suspended from a moving cable driven by a motor at one end, used for carrying people up and down a mountainside.

cable television *noun* a broadcasting service that transmits television programmes by cable to people who have subscribed to it.

caboodle (kə-**boo**-dəl) *noun* (*informal*) **the whole caboodle** the whole lot, everything or everyone. [perhaps from a phrase *kit and boodle*, which has the same meaning]

cacao (kə-**kay**-oh) *noun* (**cacaos**) **1** a tropical tree producing a seed from which cocoa and chocolate are made. **2** the seed of this tree. [via Spanish from a Nahuatl (Central American) word *cacaua*]

cache (kash) *noun* **1** a hidden store of things, especially valuable things. **2** (*Computing*) an extra store of memory allowing high-speed access to data. **cache** *verb* to store something in a cache. [from a French word *cacher* meaning 'to hide']

cachet (**kash**-ay) *noun* **1** distinction or prestige. **2** a distinguishing mark or seal. **3** a flat capsule containing a medicine that is unpleasant to taste. [a French word, from *cacher* meaning 'to press']

cackle *noun* **1** the loud clucking noise a hen makes after laying. **2** noisy laughter or talk. **cackle** *verb* **1** to give a cackle. **2** to talk or laugh noisily. [from a German or Dutch word *kake* meaning 'jaw']

cacophony (kə-**kof**-əni) *noun* (**cacophonies**) a harsh unpleasant mixture of sounds. **cacophonous** *adjective* [from Greek words *kakos* meaning 'bad', and *phōnē* meaning 'sound']

cactus *noun* (**cacti** (**kak**-tiy)) a fleshy plant, usually with prickles and no leaves, from a hot dry climate. [from a Greek word *kaktos*]

CAD *abbreviation* computer-assisted design.

cad *noun* (*old use*) a person who behaves in a dishonourable way. **caddish** *adjective* [short for *caddie* or *cadet*]

cadaverous (kə-**dav**-er-əs) *adjective* gaunt and pale, like a corpse. [from a Latin word *cadaver* meaning 'corpse']

caddie or **caddy** *noun* (**caddies**) a person who carries a golfer's clubs and gives other help during a game.
caddie *verb* (**caddies, caddied, caddying**) to act as a caddie. [from *cadet*]

caddis fly *noun* a four-winged insect living near water. [origin unknown]

caddis worm *noun* the larva of a caddis fly.

caddy [1] *noun* (**caddies**) a small box for holding tea. [from a Malay (Malaysian) word *kati*]

caddy [2] *noun* another spelling of **caddie**.

cadence (**kay**-dəns) *noun* **1** the rise and fall of the voice in speaking. **2** (*Music*) a sequence of notes or chords ending a musical phrase. **3** rhythm. [via Old French and Italian from a Latin word *cadere* meaning 'to fall']

cadenza (kə-**den**-zə) *noun* an elaborate passage for a solo instrument or voice, inserted in a movement usually near the end. [same origin as for *cadence*]

cadet (kə-**det**) *noun* a young person being trained for the armed forces or the police. [from a French word meaning 'younger son']

cadge *verb* (*informal*) to get something you are not really entitled to, by asking repeatedly for it. SYNONYMS: scrounge, beg. **cadger** *noun* [from dialect words]

cadmium (**kad**-miəm) *noun* a metal that looks like tin, a chemical element (symbol Cd). [a Latin word]

cadre (**kah**-der) *noun* a small group of trained people who can form the core of a military or political unit. [via French and Italian from a Latin word *quadrus* meaning 'square']

caecilian (si-**sil**-iən) *noun* (*Zoology*) a member of a group of amphibians, mainly tropical and worm-like, with no limbs and poorly developed eyes. [from a Latin word *caecilia* meaning 'slow worm']

caecum (**see**-kəm) *noun* (**caeca**) a tubular pouch forming the first part of the large intestine. [from a Latin word *caecus* meaning 'blind']

Caesarean or **Caesarian section** (siz-**air**-iən) *noun* a surgical operation for delivering a baby by cutting through the wall of the mother's abdomen and into the womb. [from the name of the Roman general and statesman Julius Caesar (100–44 BC), who was said to have been born in this way]

caesium (**see**-zi-əm) *noun* a soft silver-white metallic element (symbol Cs). [from a Latin word *caesius* meaning 'greyish blue']

caesura (siz-**yoor**-ə) *noun* a short pause in a line of verse. [from a Latin word *caedere* meaning 'to cut']

café (**kaf**-ay) *noun* a small restaurant that sells drinks and light meals. SYNONYMS: cafeteria, coffee shop, coffee bar, snack bar. [a French word meaning 'coffee']

cafeteria (kaf-i-**teer**-iə) *noun* a café where customers serve themselves from a counter. [an American Spanish word meaning 'café']

caffeine (**kaf**-een) *noun* a stimulant substance found in tea and coffee. [from a French word *caféine*, from *café*]

caftan *noun* another spelling of **kaftan**.

cage *noun* **1** a container having a frame of wires or bars for keeping birds or animals. **2** an open framework forming the moving part of a lift.
cage *verb* to put or keep birds or animals in a cage. [via French from a Latin word *cavea*]

cagey *adjective* (**cagier, cagiest**) (*informal*) cautious about giving information, secretive. **cagily** *adverb* **caginess** *noun*

cagoule (kə-**gool**) *noun* a light waterproof jacket with a hood. [from a French word meaning 'cowl']

caiman *noun* (**caimans**) a kind of alligator found in South America. [via Spanish and Portuguese from a Carib word *acayuman*]

cairn *noun* a pile of loose stones set up as a landmark or monument. [from a Gaelic word *carn*]

caisson (**kay**-sən) *noun* a watertight box or chamber inside which construction work can be carried out underwater. [from a French word meaning 'large chest']

cajole (kə-**johl**) *verb* to coax or flatter someone into doing something. SYNONYMS: coax, entice, persuade, inveigle. **cajolery** *noun* [from a French word *cajoler*]

cake *noun* **1** a baked sweet food made from a mixture of flour, fats, sugar, eggs, etc. **2** a savoury food baked or fried in a round flat shape ♦ *fish cakes*. **3** a shaped or hardened mass of something ♦ *a cake of soap.*

cake *verb* **1** to harden a mixture into a compact mass. **2** to encrust something with a hardened mass. [from a Scandinavian language]

CAL *abbreviation* computer-assisted learning.

calamine *noun* a pink powder, chiefly zinc carbonate or oxide, used in skin lotions. [from a Latin word *calamina*]

calamity *noun* (**calamities**) a disaster. SYNONYMS: disaster, catastrophe, misfortune, tragedy, cataclysm. **calamitous** *adjective* [via Old French from a Latin word *calamitas*]

calcareous (kal-**kair**-iəs) *adjective* containing calcium carbonate.

calcify (**kal**-si-fiy) *verb* (**calcifies, calcified, calcifying**) to harden something by a deposit of calcium salts. **calcification** *noun*

calcium *noun* a greyish-white chemical element (symbol Ca), present in bones and teeth and forming the basis of lime. [from a Latin word *calcis* meaning 'of lime']

calculable *adjective* able to be calculated.

calculate *verb* **1** to get an answer by using mathematics, to count figures or values. SYNONYMS: work out, add up, compute, estimate, reckon, gauge, assess. **2** to plan something deliberately; to intend to do something. **3** (*North Amer.*) (*informal*) to suppose or believe something. **calculation** *noun* [from a Latin word *calculus* meaning 'small pebble' (as used on an abacus)]

calculated *adjective* (said about an action) done with knowledge of the consequences.

calculating *adjective* (said about a person) shrewd or scheming.

calculation *noun* **1** a process of getting an answer by using mathematics. **2** an assessment of the risks and benefits involved in a course of action.

calculator *noun* a small electronic device with a keyboard and display, used to make calculations.

calculus (**kal**-kew-ləs) *noun* **1** a branch of mathematics that deals with problems involving rates of variation. **2** (**calculi** (**kal**-kew-liy)) (*Medicine*) a stone formed in the body. [same origin as for *calculate*]

caldera (kahl-**dair**-ə) *noun* a large bowl-shaped depression formed where part of a volcano has collapsed. [via Spanish from a Latin word *caldaria* meaning 'boiling pot']

Caledonian (kali-**doh**-niən) *adjective* to do with Scotland. [from *Caledonia*, the Latin for northern Britain]

calendar *noun* **1** a chart or set of pages showing the days, weeks, and months of a particular year. **2** a device that displays the date. **3** a list of dates or events relating to a special activity ♦ *the Racing Calendar.* **4** the system by which time is divided into fixed periods ♦ *the Gregorian calendar.* [from a Latin word *kalendae* denoting the first day of the month]

calender *noun* a machine with rollers for pressing cloth or paper to glaze or smooth it.
calender *verb* to press cloth or paper in a calender. [from a French word *calendre*]

calends *plural noun* the first day of the month in the ancient Roman calendar. [same origin as for *calendar*]

calf[1] *noun* (**calves**) **1** a young cow or bull, or the young of the elephant, seal, whale, and certain other animals. **2** calfskin. [from an Old English word]

calf[2] *noun* (**calves**) the fleshy part at the back of the leg below the knee. [from an Old Norse word *kalfi*]

calfskin *noun* leather made from the skin of a calf.

calibrate (**kal**-i-brayt) *verb* **1** to mark a gauge or instrument with a scale of measurements. **2** to measure the calibre of a gun barrel. **calibration** *noun* **calibrator** *noun*

calibre (**kal**-i-ber) *noun* **1** the diameter of the inside of a gun barrel, or of a bullet or shell fired from it. **2** ability or importance ♦ *We need a person of your calibre.* [via French and Italian from an Arabic word *kalib* meaning 'mould']

calico *noun* a kind of plain white cotton cloth. [from *Calicut*, the name of a town in India]

caliph (**kal**-if or **kay**-lif) *noun* (*historical*) a Muslim civil and religious leader, regarded as a successor to Muhammad. **caliphate** *noun* [from Arabic *khalifa* meaning 'successor of Muhammad']

call *noun* **1** a shout or cry made to attract someone's attention. SYNONYMS: shout, cry,

yell. **2** a short visit. **3** a summons or invitation. SYNONYMS: invitation, summons, command. **4** an act of telephoning, or a conversation on the telephone. **5** the particular cry a bird makes. **6** a demand or claim ♦ *There's little call for this style of clothes now* ♦ *She has many calls on her time.* **7** a need or occasion ♦ *There's no call for you to be angry.* SYNONYMS: need, occasion, cause, reason, justification. **8** a shout made by an official in a game to show that a rule has been broken or that the ball has gone out of play.
call *verb* **1** to shout or speak loudly in order to attract someone's attention. SYNONYMS: shout, cry out, speak out, yell, (loudly) bawl, bellow. **2** to pay a short visit to someone ♦ *I'll call on them this afternoon* ♦ *Will you call at the library for my book on your way home?* SYNONYMS: visit, drop in (at, on). **3** to give someone a name, or use their name when addressing them ♦ *Why did you call your cat Albert?* ♦ *Please call me by my first name.* SYNONYMS: name, (old-fashioned) dub. **4** to describe someone or something in a certain way ♦ *I would certainly call her a friend* ♦ *I don't call that working.* **5** to summon someone or ask them to come to you ♦ *We'd better call the doctor.* **6** to telephone someone. SYNONYMS: ring, phone, telephone. **7** (said about a bird) to make its cry. **to call someone's bluff** to challenge someone to carry out a threat. **to call something off** to cancel or postpone an event or arrangement ♦ *The game has been called off.* SYNONYMS: cancel, postpone, put off, abandon, scrap. **to call the tune** to be in control of events. **to call to mind** to remember. **to call someone up 1** to telephone someone. **2** to summon someone for military service. **on call** available to be called out on duty. **caller** *noun* [from an Old Norse word]

callback *noun* a telephone call made to someone in reply to a call made by them.

call girl *noun* a female prostitute who accepts appointments by telephone.

calligraphy (kə-**lig**-rəfi) *noun* the art of elegant or decorative handwriting. **calligrapher** *noun* [from a Greek word *kalos* meaning 'beautiful' and *-graphy*]

calling *noun* an occupation, a profession or trade.

calliper (**kal**-i-per) *noun* a support for a weak or injured leg.
callipers *plural noun* compasses for measuring the width of tubes or round objects. [a different spelling of *calibre*]

callisthenics *plural noun* gymnastic exercises designed to improve fitness and good body movement. [from Greek words *kallos* meaning 'beauty' and *sthenos* meaning 'strength']

callous (**kal**-əs) *adjective* **1** unfeeling or cruel. SYNONYMS: cruel, brutal, unfeeling, heartless, pitiless, ruthless, hard-hearted. **2** (*Medicine*) having calluses. **callously** *adverb* **callousness** *noun* [from a Latin word *callosus* meaning 'hard-skinned']

callow *adjective* immature and inexperienced. **callowly** *adverb* **callowness** *noun* [from Old English]

call sign or **call signal** *noun* a tune or message transmitted by a radio station to identify itself or a particular broadcaster.

callus (**kal**-əs) *noun* (**calluses**) (*Medicine*) an area of thick hardened skin or tissue. [from a Latin word *callus* meaning 'hardened skin']

calm *adjective* **1** (said about a person) not excited or agitated. SYNONYMS: relaxed, untroubled, composed, cool, controlled, sedate, serene, tranquil. **2** quiet and still, not windy. SYNONYMS: quiet, still, peaceful, windless.
calm *noun* **1** a state or period of being calm. **2** a lack of strong winds or of rough sea.
calm *verb* (also **calm down**) to make someone or something calm, or to become calm. SYNONYMS: (with an object) soothe, pacify, comfort; (with or without an object) quieten, settle. **calmly** *adverb* **calmness** *noun* [from a Greek word *kauma* meaning 'heat of the day' (when people rested)]

Calor gas *noun* (*trademark*) liquefied butane stored under pressure in containers and used instead of mains gas or in camping.

calorie *noun* **1** a unit for measuring a quantity of heat, equal to the energy needed to raise the temperature of 1 gram of water by 1° Celsius (4.1868 joules). **2** a unit for measuring the energy produced by food. **caloric** *adjective* [from a Latin word *calor* meaning 'heat']

calorific *adjective* relating to the amount of energy produced by food or fuel.

calorimeter (kal-ə-**rim**-it-er) *noun* a device used to measure the amount of heat produced in a chemical process.

calumny (kal-əm-ni) *noun* (**calumnies**) the act of making an untrue statement that harms someone's reputation, a slander. [from a Latin word *calumnia*]

calve *verb* to give birth to a calf.

Calvinism *noun* the teachings of the French Protestant religious reformer John Calvin (1509–64), and his followers. **Calvinist** *noun* **Calvinistic** *adjective*

calx *noun* (**calces** (kal-seez)) a powdery substance that is formed when a metal or mineral is burned. [from a Latin word *calx* meaning 'lime']

calypso (ka-**lips**-oh) *noun* (**calypsos**) a West Indian song with a variable rhythm and with lyrics improvised on a topical theme. [origin unknown]

calyx (kay-liks) *noun* (**calyces**) a ring of leaves (called *sepals*) that surrounds an unopened flower bud. [from a Greek word *kalux* meaning 'case of a bud']

CAM *abbreviation* computer-assisted manufacturing.

cam *noun* a projecting part on a rotating wheel or shaft, which makes another part move up and down or back and forth. [from a Dutch word *kamrad* meaning 'cogwheel']

camaraderie (kamə-**rah**-der-i) *noun* trust and friendship between people. [a French word, from *camarade* meaning 'comrade']

camber *noun* a slight arched shape or upward curve given to a surface, especially of a road. **cambered** *adjective* [from a Latin word *camurus* meaning 'curved inwards']

cambium *noun* (*Botany*) a layer of tissue in the stems and roots of woody plants that increases their thickness by new tissue produced by division of its cells. [a Latin word meaning 'an exchange']

Cambrian *adjective* **1** Welsh. **2** (*Geology*) relating to the first period of the Palaeozoic era (about 570 to 510 million years ago). **Cambrian** *noun* this period. [from *Cambria*, the Latin name for Wales]

cambric *noun* a thin linen or cotton cloth. [from *Cambrai*, a town in France where it was first made]

camcorder *noun* a combined video camera and sound recorder. [from *camera* and *recorder*]

came *verb* past tense of **come**.

camel *noun* **1** a large animal with a long neck and either one or two humps on its back, used in desert countries for riding and for carrying goods. **2** the fawn colour of a camel. [from a Greek word *kamēlos*]

camellia (ka-**mel**-iə) *noun* an evergreen flowering shrub from China and Japan, related to the tea plant. [named after the 17th-century botanist Joseph Kamel (in Latin form *Camelius*)]

cameo (kam-i-oh) *noun* (**cameos**) **1** a small piece of hard stone carved with a raised design in a contrasting colour. **2** a short but vivid description in a novel, or a short part in a play or film, usually meant for a distinguished actor to perform. [from an Old French word]

camera *noun* a device for taking photographs, films, or television pictures. **in camera** (said about the hearing of evidence or lawsuits) in the judge's private room; in private, in secret. [a Latin word meaning 'a room or chamber']

cameraman *noun* (**cameramen**) a person whose job is to operate a film camera or television camera.

camera obscura *noun* **1** a small round building or room darkened inside and designed to admit rays of light which cast an image of the landscape on a surface inside the room. **2** a box with a hole or lens at one end, which projects an image of an outside object on to a screen inside the box.

camisole (kam-i-sohl) *noun* a woman's loose-fitting piece of underwear for the top of the body. [from a Latin word *camisa* meaning 'shirt' or 'nightgown']

camomile (kam-ə-miyl) *noun* another spelling of **chamomile**.

camouflage (kam-ə-flahzh) *noun* **1** an animal's natural colouring which enables it to blend in with its surroundings. **2** a way of disguising or hiding objects, especially military equipment, by colouring or covering them so that they look like part of their surroundings. **camouflage** *verb* to disguise objects in this way. [from a French word *camoufler* meaning 'to disguise']

camp[1] *noun* **1** a place where people live temporarily in tents, huts, or caravans. **2** a group of buildings for people on holiday to live in. **3** a place where soldiers are lodged or trained. **4** a group of people sharing the same ideas or plans.

camp verb 1 to make a camp. 2 to live in a camp, especially while on holiday.
camper noun [from a Latin word *campus* meaning 'field']

camp[2] adjective (*informal*) 1 (said about a man) rather effeminate. 2 exaggerated in style, especially for humorous effect. [origin unknown]

campaign noun 1 a series of battles or military operations with the same purpose, usually in one area. 2 an organized series of activities to achieve a purpose ♦ *an advertising campaign*.
SYNONYMS: effort, drive, crusade.
campaign verb to take part in a campaign.
campaigner noun [from a Latin word *campania* meaning 'a piece of open ground']

campanology (kamp-ən-ol-əji) noun the study of the making and use of bells.
campanologist noun [from a Latin word *campana* meaning 'bell']

campanula (kəm-pan-yoo-lə) noun a plant with bell-shaped blue, purple, or white flowers. [a Latin word meaning 'little bell']

camp bed noun a folding bed used in camping.

camphor noun a strong-smelling white substance used in medicine and mothballs and in making plastics.
camphorated adjective [via Old French and Arabic from a Sanskrit word]

campion noun a wild plant with pink or white flowers. [origin unknown]

campsite noun a camping site, especially one equipped for holidaymakers.

campus noun (**campuses**) the grounds and buildings of a university or college. [a Latin word meaning 'field']

camshaft noun a shaft carrying a series of cams, especially for operating the valves in an internal-combustion engine.

can[1] auxiliary verb past tense **could** 1 to have the ability or power to do something ♦ *Can you play the piano?* 2 to be allowed to do something ♦ *You can go if you promise to be back before dark.* [from an Old English word *cunnan* meaning 'know']
◊ Some people insist on using *may* for meaning 2 (♦ *You may go if you promise to be back before dark*), but *can* is common in this meaning in ordinary speech and there is nothing wrong with it.

can[2] noun 1 a sealed tin in which food or drink is preserved. 2 a metal or plastic container for liquids. **to carry the can** (*informal*) to bear the responsibility or blame for something.
can verb (**canned, canning**) to preserve food or drink in a sealed can. **canner** noun [from an Old English word *canne* meaning 'a container for liquids']

canal noun 1 an artificial river cut through land for boats to pass along or to irrigate an area of land. 2 a tube through which food or air passes in a plant or animal body ♦ *the alimentary canal.* [same origin as *channel*]

canapé (kan-əpi) noun a small piece of bread or pastry with a savoury topping, served with drinks. [a French word]

canary (kə-nair-i) noun (**canaries**) a small yellow songbird, often kept as a cage bird. [named after the Canary Islands off the NW coast of Africa, its original home]

canasta (kə-nas-tə) noun a card game played with two packs of 32 cards. [a Spanish word meaning 'basket']

cancan noun a lively stage dance with high kicking, originating in 19th-century music halls in Paris and performed by women in long skirts and petticoats. [from French, a child's word for *canard* meaning 'duck']

cancel verb (**cancelled, cancelling**) 1 to say that something already decided on will not after all take place ♦ *Tomorrow's match has been cancelled.* SYNONYMS: call off, postpone, put off, abandon, scrap. 2 to say that something is no longer valid, to revoke something ♦ *Her permit has been cancelled.* SYNONYMS: revoke, rescind, invalidate, annul, nullify. 3 to mark a stamp or ticket so that it can no longer be used. 4 to order a thing to be discontinued. 5 to neutralize the effect of something. 6 to cross out something written down. 7 (*Mathematics*) to divide the numerator and denominator of a fraction by the same factor, or to remove a common factor from two sides of an equation. **to cancel out** (said about two things) to neutralize the effect of each other. SYNONYMS: offset, counterbalance, neutralize. **cancellation** noun [from a Latin word *cancellare* meaning 'to cross out']

Cancer noun 1 a group of stars (the Crab), seen as representing a figure of a crab. 2 the sign of the zodiac which the sun enters about 21 June. **tropic of Cancer** see **tropic. Cancerian** (kan-seer-iən) adjective & noun

cancer noun 1 a tumour, especially a malignant one. 2 a disease in which malignant growths form in the body. 3 something bad or harmful that spreads rapidly ♦ *Racism is a cancer in our society.* **cancerous** adjective [from a Latin word *cancer* meaning 'crab']

candelabrum (kandi-**lahb**-rəm) noun (**candelabra**) a large branched candlestick or holder for lights. [from a Latin word *candela* meaning 'candle']

candid adjective open and truthful, not hiding one's thoughts. SYNONYMS: frank, open, truthful, honest, straightforward, blunt, ingenuous. **candidly** adverb **candidness** noun [from a Latin word *candidus* meaning 'white']

candidate noun 1 a person who is applying for a job or is trying to get elected to a public office such as MP. 2 a person who is taking an examination. **candidacy** (**kan**-did-ə-si) noun **candidature** (**kan**-did-ə-cher) noun [from a Latin word *candidus* meaning 'white' (because candidates for office in Roman times wore white togas)]

candied adjective coated with sugar, or preserved in sugar. [from *candy*]

candied peel noun pieces of peel of citrus fruits candied for use in cooking.

candle noun a stick of wax with a wick through it, which gives out light when it burns. [from an Old English word *candel*]

candlelight noun the light given out by a candle or candles.

Candlemas noun a Christian feast held on 2 February, commemorating the Purification of the Virgin Mary, when candles are blessed. [from an Old English word, related to *candle* and *mass*[2]]

candlestick noun a holder for one or more candles.

candlewick noun 1 a thick cotton fabric with a raised tufted pattern. 2 the yarn used to make this.

candour (**kan**-der) noun being open and honest in what you say, frankness. [same origin as for *candid*]

candy noun (**candies**) 1 crystallized sugar. 2 (*North Amer.*) sweets or a sweet. [from an Arabic word *kand* meaning 'sugar']

candyfloss noun a fluffy pink or white mass of spun sugar eaten on a stick.

candy-striped adjective having alternate stripes of white and pink (or sometimes another colour).

cane noun 1 the hollow jointed stem of tall reeds and grasses, especially bamboo or rattan. 2 the material of these plants used for making furniture and basketwork. 3 a piece of cane used as a walking stick or as a means of punishment. 4 a stem of raspberry plant. **cane** verb 1 to punish someone by beating them with a cane. 2 to weave cane into a piece of furniture. [from a Greek word *kanna*]

cane sugar noun sugar obtained from the juice of sugar cane.

canine (**kay**-nyin) adjective to do with dogs. **canine** noun 1 a dog. 2 a strong pointed tooth next to the front teeth (called *incisors*). [from a Latin word *canis* meaning dog]

canister noun 1 a metal box or other container. 2 a cylinder filled with shot or tear-gas, which bursts and releases its contents when fired from a gun or thrown. [from a Greek word *kanastron* meaning 'wicker basket' (the original meaning of the English word)]

canker noun 1 a fungus disease that rots the wood of plants and trees. 2 a disease that causes ulcers or sore places in animals. 3 a bad or corrupting influence. [same origin as for *cancer*]

cannabis (**kan**-ə-bis) noun 1 a mixture made from the leaves and flowers of a hemp plant and used for smoking or chewing as an intoxicant drug. 2 the plant from which the leaves are taken. [from *Cannabis*, the Latin name of the hemp plant]

canned adjective 1 (said about food) sealed in a can to preserve it. 2 (said about music) recorded for later reproduction.

cannelloni (kan-ə-**loh**-ni) plural noun pasta rolls stuffed with meat and seasoning. [an Italian word meaning 'large tubes']

cannery noun (**canneries**) a factory where food is put into cans.

cannibal noun 1 a person who eats human flesh. 2 an animal that eats animals of its own kind. **cannibalism** noun **cannibalistic** adjective [from the Spanish name *Canibales*, given to the original inhabitants of the Caribbean, who the Spanish thought ate people]

cannibalize verb to take a vehicle or machine to pieces to provide spare parts for other vehicles or machines. **cannibalization** noun

cannon noun 1 (**cannon**) an old type of large heavy gun that fired solid metal balls. 2 an automatic gun used in a military aircraft for firing shells. 3 a shot in billiards in which a ball hits two other balls in succession.
cannon verb (**cannoned, cannoning**) 1 to collide heavily with something. 2 to make a cannon at billiards.
◊ Do not confuse this word with *canon*.

cannonade noun continuous heavy gunfire.

cannonball noun a solid metal ball fired from a cannon.

cannon fodder noun soldiers regarded merely as material to be used up in a war.

cannot verb can not.

canny adjective (**cannier, canniest**) shrewd and clever, especially in business dealings. **cannily** adverb **canniness** noun [from *can*[1] in its old meaning 'to know']

canoe noun a light narrow boat with pointed ends, moved forwards with paddles.
canoe verb (**canoes, canoed, canoeing**) to paddle or travel in a canoe. **canoeist** noun [via Spanish from a Carib (Caribbean language) word *canaoua*]

canon noun 1 a general rule or principle. 2 a set of writings by a particular author that are regarded as genuine; the books of the Bible regarded as genuine. 3 a member of the clergy who is on the staff of a cathedral. 4 the central unchanging part of the Roman Catholic mass, including the words of consecration. 5 (*Music*) a passage or piece of music in which a theme is taken up by two or more parts that overlap. [from a Greek word *kanon* meaning 'rule']
◊ Do not confuse this word with *cannon*.

canonical (kə-non-ik-əl) adjective 1 ordered by the law of the Church. 2 included in the canon of the Bible. 3 standard, accepted.
canonicals plural noun the official dress worn by the clergy. **canonically** adverb

canonize verb in the Roman Catholic Church, to declare a dead person officially to be a saint. **canonization** noun

canon law noun the law of the Church.

canopied adjective having a canopy.

canopy noun (**canopies**) 1 a hanging cover forming a shelter above a throne, bed, person, etc. 2 any similar covering, or anything compared to a canopy, such as the high branches and foliage of a forest. 3 the part of a parachute that opens out like an umbrella. [from a Greek word *kōnōpeion* meaning 'bed with mosquito curtains', from *kōnops* meaning 'mosquito']

cant[1] noun 1 insincere talk. 2 the language or jargon associated with a particular group of people ♦ *thieves' cant*. [from a Latin word *cantare* meaning 'to sing']

cant[2] verb to slope or tilt.
cant noun a tilted or sloping position. [from a Dutch word *cant* meaning 'edge']

can't verb (*informal*) cannot.

Cantab. abbreviation of Cambridge University. [from *Cantabrigia*, the Latin name for Cambridge]

cantaloupe (kan-tə-loop) noun a small round melon with orange-coloured flesh. [from the name *Cantaluppi*, a place near Rome where it was first grown in Europe]

cantankerous (kan-tank-er-əs) adjective bad-tempered and quarrelsome.
SYNONYMS: bad-tempered, peevish, grumpy, quarrelsome, irritable, fractious, crotchety.
cantankerously adverb **cantankerousness** noun [origin unknown]

cantata (kan-tah-tə) noun (*Music*) a composition for singers, with a theme or narrative like an oratorio but shorter. [from an Italian word *cantare* meaning 'to sing']

canteen noun 1 a restaurant for the employees of a factory, office, etc. 2 a case or box containing a set of cutlery. 3 a small flask of water, carried by soldiers or campers. [via French from an Italian word *cantina* meaning 'cellar']

canter noun a horse's slow gentle gallop.
canter verb to ride at a canter, to gallop gently. [short for *Canterbury gallop*, the gentle pace at which pilgrims were said to travel to Canterbury in the Middle Ages]

canticle (kan-ti-kəl) noun a song or chant with words taken from the Bible, for example the Magnificat. [from a Latin word *canticulum*, meaning 'little song']

cantilever (kan-ti-lee-ver) noun a beam or girder fixed at one end only and supporting a bridge, balcony, or similar structure. [origin unknown]

canto *noun* (**cantos**) each of the sections into which some long poems are divided. [an Italian word meaning 'song']

canton *noun* a division or district of a country, especially Switzerland. [from an Old French word meaning 'corner']

Cantonese *adjective* to do with or coming from the city of Canton in China. **Cantonese** *noun* **1** (**Cantonese**) a person born or living in Canton. **2** a Chinese language spoken in southern China and Hong Kong.

cantor *noun* **1** in Christian worship, a singer in a religious service who sings solo verses to which the choir or congregation responds. **2** in Jewish worship, the leader of the prayers in a synagogue. [from a Latin word *canere* meaning 'to sing']

canvas *noun* **1** a strong coarse cloth used for making tents and sails etc. and by artists for oil paintings. **2** a piece of canvas as a surface for an oil painting. [from a Latin word *cannabis* meaning 'hemp', from whose fibres cloth was made]

canvass *verb* **1** to visit people to ask for their votes, opinions, etc. **2** to suggest a plan.
canvass *noun* an act of canvassing. **canvasser** *noun* [in an earlier meaning 'to toss in a canvas sheet', from *canvas*]

canyon (kan-yən) *noun* a deep valley gorge, usually with a river flowing through it. [from a Spanish word *cañón* meaning 'tube']

CAP *abbreviation* Common Agricultural Policy (of the European Union).

cap *noun* **1** a soft covering for the head, without a brim but usually with a peak. **2** a particular covering for the head worn for special reasons ♦ *a nurse's cap* ♦ *a shower cap.* **3** a cover or top like a cap. **4** a small amount of explosive in a paper or metal covering, a percussion cap.
cap *verb* (**capped, capping**) **1** to put a cap on something, to cover the top or end of something. **2** to award a sports cap to someone chosen to be in a team. **3** to reply to someone's story, joke, etc. with a better one ♦ *Can you cap that?* **4** to set a limit to the amount of something, especially the money available for

spending. [from a Latin word *cappa*, from *caput* meaning 'head']

capable *adjective* **1** able to do things well, competent. SYNONYMS: competent, able, accomplished, proficient, skilful, skilled, talented. **2** having the ability or capacity to do something ♦ *They are quite capable of lying.* **capably** *adverb* **capability** *noun* [from a Latin word *capere* meaning 'to take or hold']

capacious (kə-pay-shəs) *adjective* having a lot of space, able to hold a lot. SYNONYMS: spacious, roomy, sizeable, commodious. **capaciously** *adverb* **capaciousness** *noun* [same origin as for *capacity*]

capacitance *noun* (*Physics*) ability to store an electric charge. [same origin as for *capacity*]

capacitor (kə-pas-it-er) *noun* a device for storing an electric charge.

capacity *noun* (**capacities**) **1** the amount that a building, room, or container can hold. SYNONYMS: volume, size. **2** ability or capability ♦ *They have a great capacity for hard work.* SYNONYMS: capability, ability, aptitude. **3** a position or function ♦ *He signed it in his capacity as chairman.* SYNONYMS: role, function, position, office, duty. [from a Latin word *capere* meaning 'to take or hold']

cape¹ *noun* **1** a short cloak, usually without sleeves. **2** the top part of a longer coat or cloak, covering the shoulders. [from a Latin word *cappa* meaning 'hood']

cape² *noun* a large piece of high land that extends into the sea, a promontory. **the Cape** the Cape of Good Hope, a promontory at the southern end of Africa.

caper¹ *verb* to jump or run about playfully. SYNONYMS: frolic, gambol, bound, cavort, leap, skip.
caper *noun* **1** capering. **2** (*informal*) an activity or adventure. [from a Latin word *caper* meaning 'goat']

caper² *noun* **1** a bud from a shrub like a bramble, pickled and used in sauces. **2** the shrub from which these buds are taken. [from a Greek word *kapparis*]

capillary (kə-pil-er-i) *noun* (**capillaries**) any of the very fine branching blood vessels that connect veins and arteries. **capillary** *adjective* to do with a capillary; located in a narrow tube. [from a Latin word *capillus* meaning 'hair']

capital *adjective* **1** (said about a crime) involving the death penalty ◆ *Treason is still a capital offence.* **2** (said about a letter) having the form and size used to begin a name or a sentence ◆ *Andrew and Athens both begin with a capital A.* **3** principal or most important ◆ *a capital city.* **4** (*informal, old use*) very good, excellent ◆ *What a capital idea!*

capital *noun* **1** the most important city of a country or region, usually the centre of government. **2** a capital letter. **3** (*Architecture*) the top part of a column or pillar, usually broader and shaped and decorated in a distinct style. **4** money or property that is used to start a business or invested to earn interest. **to make capital out of** to use a situation to your own advantage. [from a Latin word *caput* meaning 'head']

capital gain *noun* a profit made from the sale of investments or property.

capitalism (kap-it-əl-izm) *noun* an economic system in which trade and industry are controlled by private owners for profit, and not by the state.

capitalist (kap-it-ə-list) *noun* **1** someone who has a lot of wealth invested, a rich person. **2** someone who supports or favours capitalism.
capitalist *adjective* relating to or favouring capitalism. **capitalistic** *adjective*

capitalize (kap-it-ə-lyz) *verb* **1** to write or print words in capital letters. **2** to convert something into capital (= money or property), to provide a business or enterprise with capital. **to capitalize on** to use an opportunity to your advantage. **capitalization** *noun*

capital sum *noun* a lump sum of money, especially an amount paid to a person from an insurance policy.

capitation *noun* a payment or fee calculated from the number of people involved, e.g. a grant paid to a school based on the number of pupils.

Capitol *noun* **1** the building in Washington DC in which the Congress of the USA meets. **2** the temple of Jupiter in ancient Rome. [same origin as for *capital*]

capitulate *verb* to give in to a demand, to surrender. SYNONYMS: surrender, give in, submit, succumb, yield. **capitulation** *noun* [from a Latin word *capitulare* meaning 'to arrange under headings', from *caput* meaning 'head']

cappuccino (kah-poo-chee-noh) *noun*

(**cappuccinos**) milky coffee made frothy with steam under pressure. [an Italian word for a Capuchin monk (because the colour of the coffee is like that of the monk's habit)]

caprice (kə-**prees**) *noun* **1** a whim or impulse, a sudden change of mood or behaviour. **2** (*Music*) a piece of music played in a lively fanciful style. [via French from an Italian word *capriccio*]

capricious (kə-**prish**-əs) *adjective* changing your mind often, impulsive. SYNONYMS: impulsive, changeable, erratic, unpredictable, temperamental. **capriciously** *adverb* **capriciousness** *noun*

Capricorn *noun* **1** a group of stars (the Goat), seen as representing a figure of a goat. **2** the sign of the zodiac which the sun enters about 21 December. **tropic of Capricorn** see **tropic**. **Capricornian** *adjective & noun* [from Latin words *caper* meaning 'goat' and *cornu* meaning 'horn']

capsicum (kap-si-kəm) *noun* **1** a hot-tasting seed from a tropical plant. **2** the plant from which these seeds are taken. [from a Latin word *capsa* meaning 'box' or 'chest']

capsize *verb* to overturn ◆ *A wave capsized the boat* ◆ *The boat capsized.* SYNONYMS: overturn, keel over, turn over, tip over, turn turtle. [origin unknown]

capstan (kap-stən) *noun* **1** a thick post that can be turned to pull in a rope or cable that winds round it, for example to raise a ship's anchor. **2** a small wheel that guides the tape in a tape recorder. **3** a revolving device for holding tools in a lathe, so that they can be used in turn. [from a Latin word *capere* meaning 'to seize']

capsule *noun* **1** a small soluble case containing a dose of medicine for swallowing. **2** a plant's seed-case that splits open when ripe. **3** a compartment of a spacecraft that can be separated from the main part. [from a Latin word *capsula* meaning 'little case', related to *case*]

captain *noun* **1** a person who has authority over a sports team or other group of people. **2** the person commanding a ship. **3** the pilot of a civil aircraft. **4** an army officer ranking below a major and above a lieutenant. **5** a naval officer ranking below a commodore and above a commander.
captain *verb* to act as the captain of a sports team or other group of people.
captaincy *noun* [same origin as for *capital*]

caption (kap-shən) *noun* 1 a short title or heading in a newspaper or magazine. 2 a group of words printed next to a picture to describe or explain it. 3 words shown on a cinema or television screen. [from a Latin word *captio* meaning 'a warrant', from *capere* meaning 'to take']

captious (kap-shəs) *adjective* (formal) fond of pointing out small mistakes or faults. **captiously** *adverb* **captiousness** *noun* [same origin as for *captive*]

captivate *verb* to charm someone or capture their fancy. SYNONYMS: charm, delight, enchant, entrance, enthral, bewitch. **captivation** *noun* [same origin as for *captive*]

captive *noun* a person or animal that has been captured. SYNONYMS: (person) prisoner, convict, hostage, detainee.
captive *adjective* 1 taken or kept as a prisoner. SYNONYMS: captured, imprisoned, jailed, locked up, confined. 2 unable to escape or choose an alternative ♦ *a captive audience*. [from a Latin word *capere* meaning 'to take']

captivity *noun* the state of being held captive.

captor *noun* someone who has captured a person or animal.

capture *verb* 1 to take hold of a person or animal and keep them by force. SYNONYMS: catch, seize, arrest, apprehend, take into custody, take prisoner. 2 to take a place by force or trickery ♦ *The castle was captured after a long siege*. SYNONYMS: take, win, seize, overrun. 3 (Computing) to put data in a form that can be stored in a computer. 4 in board games, to remove another player's piece when you have made a move that allows this.
capture *noun* 1 the act of capturing someone or something. 2 a person or thing that has been captured. [from a Latin word *capere* meaning 'to take']

car *noun* 1 a vehicle with a motor that can carry a small number of people, a motor car. 2 a railway carriage of a particular type ♦ *a dining car*. 3 the passenger compartment of an airship, balloon, cable railway, or lift. [from a Latin word *carrus* meaning 'wagon']

carafe (kə-raf) *noun* a glass bottle for serving wine or water at a meal. [via French and Italian from an Arabic word *gharrafa* meaning 'to draw water']

caramel *noun* 1 a kind of toffee tasting like burnt sugar. 2 burnt sugar used for colouring and flavouring food. [via French from a Spanish word *caramelo*]

caramelize *verb* to turn something into caramel, or to be turned into caramel. **caramelization** *noun*

carapace (ka-rə-payss) *noun* the shell on the back of a tortoise or a crab or other crustacean. [via French from a Spanish word *carapacho*]

carat (ka-rət) *noun* 1 a unit of weight for precious stones, equal to 200 milligrams. 2 a measure of the purity of gold, up to 24 carats for pure gold.

caravan *noun* 1 an enclosed carriage equipped for living in, able to be towed by a motor vehicle or a horse. 2 a group of people travelling together across desert country. **caravanning** *noun* [via French from a Persian word *karwan*]

caraway *noun* a plant with spicy seeds that are used for flavouring food. [from a Greek word *karon* meaning 'cumin']

carbide (kar-biyd) *noun* a compound of carbon with a metal or other element.

carbine (kar-biyn) *noun* a short light rifle. [from a French word *carabine*]

carbohydrate *noun* an organic compound, such as the sugars, starches, and cellulose, which contain carbon, oxygen, and hydrogen, and can be broken down to release energy in the body. [from *carbon* and *hydrate*]

carbolic *noun* a kind of disinfectant made from carbon.

carbon *noun* 1 a chemical element (symbol C) that is present in all living matter and occurs in its pure form as diamond and graphite. 2 a rod of carbon in an arc lamp. 3 carbon paper, or a copy made with it. [from a Latin word *carbo* meaning 'coal']

carbonate *noun* a compound that releases carbon dioxide when mixed with acid.

carbonated *adjective* (said about a drink) mixed with carbon dioxide to make it gassy or fizzy. **carbonation** *noun*

carbon copy *noun* 1 a copy of a letter or document made with carbon paper. 2 an exact copy of a thing or person ♦ *She is a carbon copy of her mother*.

carbon dating *noun* a method of finding the age of organic objects by measuring the decay of radiocarbon in them.

carbon dioxide noun a colourless gas that is formed by the burning of carbon or breathed out by animals in respiration.

carbon fibre noun a material consisting of carbon filaments, used as a strengthening material and in protective clothing.

carbon 14 noun a radioisotope used in carbon dating.

carbonic acid noun a weak acid formed from carbon dioxide and water.

carboniferous (kar-bən-if-er-əs) adjective producing coal.
Carboniferous adjective (Geology) of the period in the Palaeozoic era when many coal deposits were created.
Carboniferous noun this period. [from carbon and a Latin word ferre meaning 'to bear']

carbonize verb 1 to convert a substance that contains carbon into carbon alone, for example by heating or burning it. 2 to coat something with carbon.
carbonization noun

carbon monoxide noun a poisonous gas formed when carbon burns incompletely, e.g. in the exhaust of a motor vehicle.

carbon paper noun thin paper with a coloured coating, put between sheets of paper to make copies of what is written or typed on the top sheet.

carbon tax noun a tax on petrol and other fossil fuels.

carbon tetrachloride noun a colourless liquid used as a solvent in dry-cleaning etc.

carbon 12 noun a stable isotope of carbon, used as a standard in calculating atomic mass.

carbonyl (car-bən-il) noun (Chemistry) a chemical group present in aldehydes, ketones, and many other organic compounds, consisting of a carbon atom joined to an oxygen atom by a double bond.

car boot sale noun an outdoor sale at which people sell things they no longer want from the boots of their cars.

carborundum (kar-ber-un-dəm) noun a hard compound of carbon and silicon used for polishing and grinding things. [from carbon and corundum]

carboxyl (car-boks-il) noun (Chemistry) a chemical group present in organic acids.

carboxylic acid noun (Chemistry) an organic acid containing a carboxyl group, e.g. acetic acid.

carboy (kar-boi) noun a large round bottle surrounded by a protecting framework, used for holding or transporting dangerous liquids. [from a Persian word karaba meaning 'glass flagon']

carbuncle noun 1 a severe abscess in the skin. 2 a bright red round gem. [from a Latin word carbunculus meaning 'small piece of coal']

carburettor noun a device for mixing fuel and air in an internal-combustion engine. [from an old word carburet meaning 'to mix with carbon']

carcass noun 1 the dead body of an animal, especially one prepared for cutting up as meat. 2 the remains of a cooked bird after the meat has been eaten. 3 the framework of a building or ship. [from an Old French word charcois]

carcinogen (kar-sin-ə-jin) noun a substance that produces cancer. [from carcinoma and a Greek word -genēs meaning 'born']

carcinogenic (kar-sin-ə-jen-ik) adjective producing cancer.

carcinoma (kar-sin-oh-mə) noun (**carcinomas** or **carcinomata**) a cancerous growth in the body. [from a Greek word karkinos meaning 'crab']

card [1] noun 1 thick stiff paper or thin cardboard. 2 a small piece of this for writing or printing on, especially to send messages or greetings or to record information. 3 a small flat rectangular piece of plastic with machine-readable information on it, e.g. a bank card or credit card. 4 a playing card. 5 a card used for recording scores in games. 6 a programme of events at a race meeting. 7 (Computing) a circuit board with extra facilities. 8 (informal, old use) an odd or amusing person.
cards plural noun a game using playing cards. **to be on the cards** (informal) to be likely or possible. **to get your cards** (informal) to be dismissed from a job. **to put your cards on the table** to be honest and open about your intentions. [from a Latin word charta meaning 'papyrus leaf' or 'paper']

card [2] verb to clean or comb wool.
card noun a wire brush or toothed instrument for doing this. [from Old French words]

cardboard *noun* a type of thin board made of layers of paper or wood fibre.

card game *noun* a game using playing cards.

cardiac (kar-di-ak) *adjective* to do with the heart. [from a Greek word *kardia* meaning 'heart']

cardigan *noun* a woollen jumper fastened with buttons at the front. [named after the Earl of Cardigan, a commander in the Crimean War (19th century), whose troops were the first to wear cardigans]

cardinal *noun* 1 a senior dignitary of the Roman Catholic Church and a member of the Sacred College that elects the pope. 2 a deep scarlet colour like that of a cardinal's habit.
cardinal *adjective* chief or most important, fundamental. [from a Latin word *cardo* meaning 'hinge']

cardinal number *noun* a number that denotes an amount or quantity (*one*, *five*, *twenty*, etc.), as distinct from the ordinal numbers (*first*, *fifth*, *twentieth*, etc.)

cardinal point *noun* each of the four main points of the compass, North, East, South, and West.

card index *noun* an index in which each item is entered on a separate card.

cardiogram (kar-di-ə-gram) *noun* a record of the heart's movements, made by a cardiograph. [from a Greek word *kardia* meaning 'heart' and *-gram*]

cardiograph (kar-di-ə-grahf) *noun* an instrument that records the heart's movements.

cardiology (kar-di-ol-ə-ji) *noun* (*Medicine*) the study and treatment of diseases and abnormalities of the heart. **cardiological** *adjective* **cardiologist** *noun* [from a Greek word *kardia* meaning 'heart' and *-logy*]

card sharp *noun* a person who makes a living by cheating at card games.

care *noun* 1 serious attention and thought ♦ *The trip was planned with care.* SYNONYMS: attention, consideration, diligence, concentration. 2 caution to avoid damage or loss ♦ *Handle with care.* SYNONYMS: caution, vigilance. 3 the protection or supervision of a person ♦ *We left the child in her sister's care.* SYNONYMS: charge, protection, safe-keeping, custody. 4 worry or anxiety ♦ *freedom from care.* SYNONYMS: worry, anxiety, trouble, concern.
care *verb* 1 to feel concerned or interested in something ♦ *I care very much about the environment.* SYNONYMS: mind, bother, concern yourself, worry. 2 to feel affection or liking ♦ *His actions show that he cares.* 3 to be willing to do something ♦ *Would you care to come with us?* **to care for** 1 to look after someone. SYNONYMS: look after, mind, tend, take care of, watch over. 2 to like someone or something. **care of** to the address of someone who will deliver or forward post ♦ *Write to him care of his bank.* **in care** taken into the care of a local authority. **to take care** to be cautious. **to take care of** 1 to take charge of someone or look after them. 2 to deal with something. [from an Old English word *caru* meaning 'sorrow']

careen (kə-reen) *verb* 1 (said about a ship) to tilt or lean to one side. 2 to swerve. [via French and Italian from a Latin word *carina* meaning 'keel']

career *noun* 1 an occupation or way of making a living that a person follows, especially one with opportunities for promotion ♦ *She is taking up accountancy as a career.* SYNONYMS: job, occupation, profession. 2 (used before a noun) ambitious or keen to do well in a profession ♦ *a career politician.*
career *verb* to rush wildly or recklessly. SYNONYMS: rush, dash, hurtle, fly, speed. [from a Latin word, related to *car*]

careerist *noun* a person who is keen to do well in a career.

carefree *adjective* cheerful because you are free from anxiety or responsibility. SYNONYMS: happy, cheerful, cheery.

careful *adjective* 1 avoiding damage or danger, cautious ♦ *Be careful on the wet floors.* SYNONYMS: wary, watchful, alert. 2 giving serious thought and attention to something ♦ *He is a careful driver.* SYNONYMS: attentive, vigilant, observant. 3 done with care ♦ *She does careful work.* SYNONYMS: thorough, meticulous, methodical, conscientious. **carefully** *adverb* **carefulness** *noun*

careless *adjective* not giving enough care or attention to something. SYNONYMS: thoughtless, negligent, slapdash, inattentive. **carelessly** *adverb* **carelessness** *noun*

carer *noun* a person who looks after a sick, elderly, or disabled person at home.

caress (kə-ress) *noun* a loving touch or stroke.

caress *verb* to touch or stroke someone lovingly. SYNONYMS: stroke, fondle, cuddle, pet. [from a Latin word *carus* meaning 'dear']

caret (**ka-rit**) *noun* a mark (∧) put in a piece of writing or printing to show that something should be added. [a Latin word meaning 'it is lacking']

caretaker *noun* **1** a person employed to look after a house or building. **2** used before a noun to mean a person or group of people who hold office temporarily until a successor is appointed ♦ *a caretaker president.*

careworn *adjective* tired or unwell because of prolonged worry.

cargo *noun* (**cargoes**) goods carried on a ship or aircraft. [a Spanish word, from a Latin word *carcare* meaning 'to load']

Carib (**ka-rib**) *noun* **1** a member of a people living in the northern coastal regions of South America. **2** the language spoken by them. [from a Spanish word *caribe*]

Caribbean or **Caribbean Sea** (**ka-ri-bee-ən**) *noun* the part of the Atlantic Ocean off Central America and including the West Indies and other islands. **Caribbean** *adjective* relating to this region.

caribou (**ka-ri-boo**) *noun* (**caribou**) a North American reindeer. [from a Native American word meaning 'snow-shoveller' (because the caribou scrapes away the snow to feed on the grass underneath)]

caricature (**ka-rik-ə-choor**) *noun* a picture or description of a person or thing that exaggerates their well-known characteristics for comic effect. **caricature** *verb* to make a caricature of someone or something. **caricaturist** *noun* [from an Italian word *caricare* meaning 'to exaggerate']

caries (**kair-eez**) *noun* (**caries**) decay in the teeth or bones. [a Latin word]

carillon (**kə-ril-yən**) *noun* **1** a set of bells sounded either from a keyboard or mechanically. **2** a tune played on bells. [from an Old French word *quarregnon* meaning 'peal of four bells']

carmine (**kar-min**) *adjective* & *noun* deep red. [via French from an Arabic word *kirmiz*, related to *crimson*]

carnage (**kar-nij**) *noun* the killing of many people. [same origin as for *carnal*]

carnal (**kar-nəl**) *adjective* to do with the body's physical, especially sexual, needs.

carnally *adverb* [from a Latin word *carnis* meaning 'of flesh']

carnation *noun* a garden flower with dark green leaves and showy pink, white, or red flowers. [from an Arabic word, influenced by a French word *carnation* meaning 'flesh colour']

carnelian (**kar-nee-li-ən**) *noun* a dull red or reddish white semi-precious stone. [from Old French *corneline*, related to *carnal*]

carnival *noun* a festival, usually with a procession in fancy dress. [from a Latin word *carnis* meaning 'of flesh' (because a carnival was originally a celebration before Lent began, when people gave up meat until Easter), and Italian *levare* meaning 'to put away']

carnivore (**kar-niv-or**) *noun* an animal that feeds on the flesh of other animals. [from a Latin word *carnis* meaning 'of flesh' and *vorare* meaning 'to devour']

carnivorous (**kar-niv-er-əs**) *adjective* (said about an animal) feeding on the flesh of other animals.

carob *noun* the pod of an Arabian tree, producing a powder which is used as a substitute for chocolate. [from an Arabic word]

carol *noun* a joyful song, especially a Christmas hymn. **carol** *verb* (**carolled, carolling**) **1** to sing carols. **2** to sing joyfully. [from an Old French word]

Carolingian *adjective* relating to the Frankish dynasty founded by Charlemagne. **Carolingian** *noun* a member of this dynasty. [from Latin *Carolus* 'Charles']

carotene (**ka-rə-teen**) *noun* an orange or red substance in plants, a source of vitamin A. [from a Latin word *carota* meaning 'carrot']

carotid artery (**kə-rot-id**) *noun* either of the two great arteries, one on each side of the neck, that carry blood to the head. [from a Greek word *karōtis* meaning 'drowsiness' (because pressing on these arteries was thought to make people feel faint)]

carouse (**kə-rowz**) *verb* to have drinks and enjoy yourself with other people. **carousal** *noun* [from a German phrase *gar aus trinken* meaning 'to drink to the bottom of the glass']

carousel (**ka-roo-sel**) *noun* **1** a merry-go-round at a fair. **2** a conveyor belt or system that goes round in a circle, e.g. at an airport for passengers to collect their luggage. [via French from an Italian word *carosello*]

carp¹ *noun* (**carp**) an edible freshwater fish that lives in lakes and ponds. [from a Latin word *carpa*]

carp² *verb* to keep complaining or finding fault. [from a Latin word *carpere* meaning 'to slander']

carpal (**kar-pəl**) *adjective* to do with the wrist joint (called *carpus*).
carpal *noun* any of the bones in the wrist.

car park *noun* an area or building for parking cars.

carpel (**kar-pəl**) *noun* the pistil of a flower, in which the seeds develop. [from a Greek word *karpos* meaning 'fruit']

carpenter *noun* a person who makes or repairs wooden objects and structures. [from a Latin phrase *carpentarius artifex* meaning 'carriage-maker', from *carpentum* meaning 'wagon']

carpentry *noun* the work of a carpenter.

carpet *noun* **1** a thick soft covering for a floor, usually made from a woven material. **2** a thick layer of something on the ground ♦ *The path was covered in a carpet of leaves.*
carpet *verb* (**carpeted, carpeting**) **1** to cover a floor with a carpet. **2** (*informal*) to reprimand someone. **on the carpet** (*informal*) being reprimanded by someone in authority.

carpeting *noun* material for making carpets.

car phone *noun* a mobile telephone for use in a car.

carport *noun* an open-sided shelter for a car, built on to the side of a house.

carriage *noun* **1** a four-wheeled passenger vehicle pulled by horses. **2** a passenger vehicle forming part of a railway train. **3** the transporting of goods from place to place, or the cost of this ♦ *The price is £50 plus carriage.* **4** a support with wheels for moving a large gun or other heavy object. **5** a moving part for carrying or holding other parts in a machine, e.g. the roller of a typewriter. **6** the posture of the body when walking. [same origin as for *carry*]

carriage clock *noun* a small portable clock in a rectangular case with a handle on top.

carriage return *noun* **1** a key or lever on a typewriter for returning the roller to its left position for the start of a new line of typing. **2** a key on a computer keyboard that puts the cursor in a position at the left of the screen and performs other operations.

carriageway *noun* the part of the road on which vehicles travel.

carrier *noun* **1** a person or thing that carries something. **2** a business that transports goods or people for payment. **3** a person or animal that transmits a disease to others without being affected by it.

carrier bag *noun* a paper or plastic bag with handles, for carrying shopping.

carrier pigeon *noun* a homing pigeon trained to carry messages tied to its leg or neck.

carrion (**ka-ri-ən**) *noun* the decaying flesh of dead animals. [from a Latin word *caro* meaning 'flesh']

carrion crow *noun* a black crow that lives on carrion and small animals.

carrot *noun* **1** a tapering orange-coloured root eaten as a vegetable. **2** the plant from which this root comes. **3** something used to entice someone to do something, as distinct from the 'stick' or punishment.
carroty *adjective* [via French from a Greek word *karōton*]

carry *verb* (**carries, carried, carrying**) **1** to take something or someone from one place to another. SYNONYMS: take, bring, transport, convey, bear. **2** to have something with you constantly ♦ *The police now carry guns.* **3** to conduct or transmit ♦ *The cables carry a powerful electric current.* **4** to support the weight of something. SYNONYMS: support, hold (up), bear. **5** to involve or entail a consequence ♦ *The crime carries a life sentence.* **6** to hold or develop an idea or feeling ♦ *Don't carry the joke too far.* **7** to take an amount into the next column when adding figures. **8** to approve a proposed measure by a winning vote ♦ *The motion was carried by a large majority.* **9** (said about a newspaper or broadcasting station) to publish or broadcast something ♦ *The Sunday papers all carried the story.* **10** to hold and move the body in a certain way ♦ *She carried herself with dignity.* **11** to be transmitted clearly ♦ *The sound carried far across the valley.* **to carry off 1** to take something or someone by force. SYNONYMS: seize, bear off (a thing), kidnap, abduct (a person). **2** to cause the

death of someone ♦ *The plague carried off half the population.* SYNONYMS: kill, wipe out.
3 to win a prize. **4** to deal with a situation successfully. **to carry on 1** to continue doing something. SYNONYMS: continue, go on, keep on, persevere. **2** to take part in a conversation. **3** to manage or conduct a business or activity. **4** (*informal*) to behave excitedly. **to carry out** to achieve something or put it into practice. SYNONYMS: do, perform, implement, effect, complete, achieve, accomplish. **to carry weight** to be influential or important. **to get carried away** to become over-excited about something. [from an Old French word *carier*, related to *car*]

carrycot *noun* a portable cot for a baby.

carsick *adjective* feeling sick or queasy from the motion of a car. **carsickness** *noun*

cart *noun* an open vehicle used for carrying loads, pulled by a horse or by hand.
cart *verb* **1** to carry something in a cart, to transport a load. **2** (*informal*) to carry something heavy or tiring ♦ *We've carted these stones right across the field.* **to put the cart before the horse** to reverse the logical or usual order of things. [from an Old Norse word *cart*]

carte blanche (kart blahnsh) *noun* freedom or authority to act as you think best. [a French phrase meaning 'blank paper']

cartel (kar-**tel**) *noun* an agreement between business firms of the same kind to control the market and keep prices high. [from a German word *Kartell*, related to *card*]

Cartesian (kar-**tee**-ziǝn) *adjective* relating to the 17th-century French philosopher Descartes or his theories. [from *Cartesius*, the Latin form of the name Descartes]

Cartesian coordinates *plural noun* (*Mathematics*) coordinates measured from straight axes that intersect.

carthorse *noun* a strong horse used for pulling heavy loads.

cartilage *noun* tough white flexible tissue attached to a bone. **cartilaginous** (karti-**laj**-inǝs) *adjective* [from a Latin word *cartilago*]

cartography (kar-**tog**-rǝfi) *noun* the science of planning and drawing maps. **cartographer** *noun* **cartographic** (karto-**graf**-ik) *adjective* [from a French word *carte* meaning 'map' and *-graphy*]

carton *noun* a light cardboard or plastic container. [via French from an Italian word *cartone* meaning 'card']

cartoon *noun* **1** an amusing drawing, especially one in a newspaper intended as a comment on a topical subject. **2** a sequence of drawings that tell a story. **3** an animated film. **4** a full-size drawing made by an artist as a preliminary sketch for a painting, mural, or other work of art.
cartoon *verb* to show someone or something in a cartoon. [same origin as for *carton*; the earliest meaning is the 'full-size drawing' made on card]

cartoonist *noun* someone who draws cartoons.

cartouche (kar-**toosh**) *noun* **1** (*Architecture*) an ornament or feature in the shape of a scroll. **2** (*Archaeology*) an oval emblem containing the name in hieroglyphs of an ancient Egyptian king. [from a French word, related to *card*]

cartridge *noun* **1** a tube or case containing explosive for a bullet or shell. **2** a sealed case holding a length of film or recording tape, or an amount of ink, ready for insertion into a machine or pen, etc. **3** a device that holds the stylus of a record player. [same origin as for *cartouche*]

cartridge paper *noun* thick strong paper for drawing.

cartwheel *noun* **1** the wheel of a cart. **2** a handstand in which the body turns with the arms and legs spread like spokes of a wheel, balancing on each hand in turn.

cartwright *noun* someone who makes carts.

carve *verb* **1** to cut into solid material to make a design, inscription, etc. **2** to cut cooked meat into slices. **to carve up** to divide something into parts or shares. **carver** *noun* [from an Old English word *ceorfan*]

carving *noun* a carved object or design.

caryatid (ka-ri-**at**-id) *noun* a sculpture of a female figure used as a supporting pillar in a building. [from a Greek word *karuatis*, meaning 'a priestess of Artemis at Caryae' (a place in Asia Minor, modern Turkey)]

Casanova (kas-ǝ-**noh**-vǝ) *noun* a man with a reputation for having many love affairs. [named after an 18th-century Italian adventurer Jacopo Casanova]

cascade (kas-**kayd**) *noun* 1 a small waterfall or series of waterfalls. 2 a mass of something falling or hanging. 3 in a business organization, a system for passing information from managers in stages to other employees.
cascade *verb* to fall like a cascade. [from an Italian word *cascare* meaning 'to fall']

case [1] *noun* 1 an instance or example of something existing or occurring. SYNONYMS: instance, example, occurrence. 2 a condition of disease or injury, or a person suffering from this ♦ *two cases of measles.* 3 something being investigated by the police or other authorities ♦ *a murder case.* 4 a legal action in a court of law. SYNONYMS: lawsuit, suit, action. 5 a set of facts or arguments used to support something. 6 (*Grammar*) the form of a noun or pronoun that shows how it is related to other words. For example in *Tony's car, Tony's* is in the possessive case, and in *We saw him, him* is in the objective case. **in any case** whatever the facts are; whatever may happen. **in case** because something might happen ♦ *Take your umbrella in case.* **in case of** if something should occur ♦ *In case of fire leave by the staircase.* [from a Latin word *casus* meaning 'a fall' or 'an occasion']

case [2] *noun* 1 a container or protective covering. SYNONYMS: container, receptacle, box, chest, trunk, carton. 2 a piece of luggage. SYNONYMS: suitcase, bag, trunk.
case *verb* 1 to enclose something in a case. 2 (*informal*) to check over a place before carrying out a robbery. [from a Latin word *capsa* meaning 'box']

casein (**kay**-seen) *noun* the main protein found in milk and used to make cheese. [from a Latin word *caseus* meaning 'cheese']

casement *noun* a window that opens on hinges at the side, like a door. [same origin as for *case*[2]]

casework *noun* social work that involves dealing directly with people who have problems. **caseworker** *noun*

cash *noun* 1 money in the form of notes and coins. 2 immediate payment for things bought, as opposed to credit. 3 (*informal*) money or wealth ♦ *We're short of cash at the moment.*
cash *verb* to give or get cash for something ♦ *May I cash a cheque here?* **to cash in on** (*informal*) to gain a profit or advantage from something. **cashable**

adjective [via French from a Latin word *capsa* meaning 'box'; the English word originally meant a box for holding money]

cash card *noun* a plastic card used to withdraw cash from a cash dispenser.

cash desk *noun* a desk for making payments in a shop or restaurant.

cash dispenser *noun* a machine from which customers of a bank can withdraw cash by using a cash card.

cashew (**kash**-oo) *noun* 1 the small kidney-shaped edible nut of a tropical tree. 2 the tree from which these nuts come. [via Portuguese from a Tupi (South American) word]

cashflow *noun* the movement of money out of and into a business as goods are bought and sold, which affects its ability to make cash payments.

cashier [1] *noun* a person employed to receive and pay out money in a bank or to receive payments in a shop or business. [from a French word *caissier*, related to *cash*]

cashier [2] *verb* to dismiss someone in disgrace from the armed forces. [from a French word *casser* meaning 'to dismiss']

cashmere *noun* 1 a very fine soft wool, especially that from the Kashmir goat. 2 a fabric made from this. [an old spelling of *Kashmir* in Asia]

cash on delivery *noun* payment to be made when goods are delivered, not at the time they are bought.

cash register *noun* a machine in a shop that holds cash received and records the amount of each sale.

casing *noun* 1 a protective case or covering. 2 the frame round a door or window.

casino *noun* (**casinos**) a public building or room for gambling games. [an Italian word meaning 'little house']

cask *noun* a large barrel for holding liquid, especially alcoholic drinks. [via French from a Spanish word *casco* meaning 'helmet']

casket *noun* a small usually ornamental box for holding valuables etc. [origin unknown, but perhaps related to *case*[2]]

Caspian *noun* the Caspian Sea, a land-locked sea between SE Europe and Asia.

Cassandra (kə-**san**-drə) *noun* a person who predicts disaster. [named after a prophetess in Greek legend who foretold evil events but was doomed never to be believed]

cassata (kə-**sah**-tə) *noun* an ice cream containing fruit and nuts. [an Italian word]

cassava (kə-**sah**-və) *noun* a tropical plant with starchy roots used for food. [from a Taino (South American) word]

casserole *noun* **1** a covered dish for cooking food slowly in an oven. **2** food cooked in a casserole.
casserole *verb* to cook food in a casserole. [via French from a Greek word *kuathon* meaning 'little cup']

cassette (kə-**set**) *noun* a small sealed case containing a length of film or magnetic tape. [a French word meaning 'little case']

cassette player *noun* a device for playing audio cassettes.

cassock *noun* a long garment worn by Christian clergy and members of church choirs. [via French from an Italian word *casacca* meaning 'riding coat']

cassowary (kas-ə-**wer**-i) *noun* (**cassowaries**) a large bird that is unable to fly, found mainly in New Guinea. [from a Malay (Malaysian) word *kasuari*]

cast *verb* (past tense and past participle **cast**) **1** to throw something hard in a particular direction ♦ *The fishermen cast a net into the sea.* SYNONYMS: throw, fling, toss, hurl, pitch, heave; (*informal*) chuck, sling. **2** to shed or discard something. SYNONYMS: shed, discard, get rid of. **3** to make a shadow fall. **4** to direct your eye or your mind towards something ♦ *You'd better cast your eye over this letter* ♦ *Cast your thoughts back to what happened yesterday.* **5** to record or register a vote. **6** to make an object by pouring metal or plaster into a mould and leaving it to harden. **7** to choose the actors for a play or film.
cast *noun* **1** an act of casting or throwing something. **2** an object made by putting soft material into a mould to harden. **3** the actors taking part in a play or film. **4** a tinge of colour. **cast of mind** the way a person thinks. **to cast about for** to search or look for something. **to cast down** to make someone depressed or unhappy. **to cast off 1** to set a boat or ship free from its moorings. **2** to take the stitches off a knitting needle. **to cast on** to loop the stitches on to a knitting needle. [from an Old Norse word *kasta* meaning 'to throw']

castanets (kast-ə-**nets**) *plural noun* a pair of shell-shaped pieces of wood, ivory, or plastic, held in the hands and struck together with the fingers as an accompaniment to a Spanish dance. [from a Spanish word *castañetas* meaning 'little chestnuts']

castaway *noun* a person who has been shipwrecked and washed up in a deserted place.

caste (kahst) *noun* in India, each of the hereditary social groups into which Hindus are born. [from a Spanish word *casta* meaning 'descent from ancestors']

castellated (kas-təl-**ayt**-id) *adjective* (said about a wall or building) having turrets or battlements like a castle. [same origin as for *castle*]

caster *noun* another spelling of **castor**.

caster sugar *noun* fine white sugar.

castigate (**kas**-ti-gayt) *verb* to criticize someone harshly. **castigation** *noun* **castigator** *noun* [from a Latin word *castigare* meaning 'to punish']

casting vote *noun* a vote that decides which side will win when the votes on each side are equal.

cast iron a hard alloy of iron made by casting in a mould.
cast-iron *adjective* **1** made of cast iron. **2** very strong or effective ♦ *a cast-iron excuse.*

castle *noun* **1** a large fortified building or group of buildings. **2** a piece in chess, also called a rook.
castle *verb* in chess, to move the king two squares towards a rook and the rook to the square the king has crossed. [from a Latin word *castellum* meaning 'fort']

cast-offs *plural noun* clothes that someone no longer uses.

castor *noun* **1** a small container for sugar or salt, with holes in the top for sprinkling. **2** a small swivelled wheel fixed to each leg of a piece of furniture so that it can be moved easily. [from *cast*]

castor oil *noun* oil from the seeds of a tropical plant, used as a purgative and as a lubricant.

castor sugar *noun* another spelling of **caster sugar**.

castrate (kas-**trayt**) *verb* to remove the testicles of a male animal, to geld an animal. **castration** *noun*

casual *adjective* 1 happening by chance ♦ *a casual meeting*. SYNONYMS: chance, unforeseen, fortuitous, unplanned. 2 made or done lightly and without much care or thought ♦ *a casual remark*. SYNONYMS: flippant, offhand, nonchalant, light, light-hearted. 3 informal or meant for informal occasions ♦ *casual clothes*. SYNONYMS: informal, everyday. 4 available for a short time, not permanent ♦ *He found some casual work*.
casuals *plural noun* clothes or shoes for everyday use. **casually** *adverb* **casualness** *noun* [from a Latin word *casualis*, from *casus* meaning 'a fall', related to *case*[1]]

casualty *noun* (**casualties**) 1 a person who has been killed or injured in war or in an accident. SYNONYMS: victim, fatality. 2 a thing that has been lost or destroyed. 3 the casualty department of a hospital. [same origin as for *casual*; the original meaning was 'a chance occurrence']

casualty department *noun* the department of a hospital that deals with emergency patients.

casuistry (**kaz**-yoo-istri) *noun* clever reasoning that is false. **casuistic** *adjective* [same origin as for *case*[1]]

cat *noun* 1 a small furry domesticated animal often kept as a pet. 2 a wild animal of the same family as a domestic cat, e.g. a lion, tiger, or leopard. 3 (*informal*) a spiteful or malicious woman. 4 short for **cat-o'-nine-tails**. **to let the cat out of the bag** to give away a secret. [from an Old English word *catt*]

catabolism (kə-**tab**-ə-lizm) *noun* the breaking down of complex substances in the body to form simpler ones. **catabolic** (kat-ə-**bol**-ik) *adjective* [from a Greek word *katabolē* meaning 'descent']

cataclysm (**kat**-ə-klizm) *noun* a violent upheaval or disaster. **cataclysmic** (katə-**kliz**-mik) *adjective* [from Greek words *kata* meaning 'down' and *kluzein* meaning 'to wash']

catacombs (**kat**-ə-koomz) *plural noun* a series of underground galleries with recesses on each side for tombs. [from a Latin word *catacumbas*, the name of an ancient underground cemetery in Rome]

catafalque (**kat**-ə-falk) *noun* a decorated platform for the coffin of a distinguished person during the funeral or while it is lying in state. [via French from an Italian word *catafalco*]

Catalan *adjective* to do with or coming from Catalonia in NE Spain.
Catalan *noun* 1 a person born in Catalonia or descended from people born there. 2 the Romance language of Catalonia, closely related to Provençal and the Spanish of Castille. [from French and Spanish words]

catalepsy (**kat**-ə-lepsi) *noun* a medical condition in which the body becomes rigid and loses consciousness. **cataleptic** (katə-**lep**-tik) *adjective* [from Greek words *kata* meaning 'down' and *lēpsis* meaning 'seizure']

catalogue *noun* a list of items arranged in a systematic order.
catalogue *verb* (**catalogues, catalogued, cataloguing**) to list items in a catalogue. **cataloguer** *noun* [from a Greek word *katalogos* meaning 'a list']

catalyse (**kat**-ə-liyz) *verb* to produce or accelerate a chemical reaction by catalysis.

catalysis (kə-**tal**-i-sis) *noun* (**catalyses**) the process of producing or accelerating a chemical reaction. [from Greek words *kata* meaning 'down' and *lusis* meaning 'loosening']

catalyst (**kat**-ə-list) *noun* 1 a substance that produces or accelerates a chemical reaction while remaining unchanged itself. 2 a person or thing that brings about a change.

catalytic (kat-ə-**lit**-ik) *adjective* to do with or using catalysis.

catalytic converter *noun* a device in the exhaust system of a motor vehicle, with a catalyst that converts polluting gases into harmless products.

catamaran (kat-ə-mə-ran) *noun* a boat with twin hulls parallel to each other. [from a Tamil word *kattumaram* meaning 'tied wood']

catapult *noun* 1 a device with elastic for shooting small stones. 2 an ancient military weapon for hurling stones. 3 a device for launching a glider, or for launching an aircraft from the deck of a carrier.
catapult *verb* 1 to hurl a stone or other object from a catapult; to fling something

with force. **2** to rush violently. [from Greek words *kata* meaning 'down' and *pellein* meaning 'to throw']

cataract noun **1** a large waterfall or rush of water. **2** a cloudy area that forms on the lens of the eye and obscures sight. [from a Greek word *kataraktēs* meaning 'down-rushing']

catarrh (kə-tar) noun an inflammation of the nose and throat that causes a discharge of watery mucus. **catarrhal** adjective [from a Greek word *katarrhein* meaning 'to flow down']

catastrophe (kə-tas-trəfi) noun a sudden event that causes great damage or harm. SYNONYMS: disaster, calamity, misfortune, tragedy, cataclysm. **catastrophic** (katə-**strof**-ik) adjective **catastrophically** adverb [from a Greek word *katastrophē* meaning 'overturning']

catatonic (katə-ton-ik) adjective having abnormal bodily movement because of a disturbed mental state. [from Greek words *kata* meaning 'down' and *tonos* meaning 'tone' or 'tension']

cat burglar noun a burglar who enters a building by climbing to an upper storey.

catcall noun a shrill whistle or shout of disapproval.
catcall verb to make a catcall.

catch verb (past tense and past participle **caught**) **1** to grasp something moving and hold it. SYNONYMS: grab, seize, grasp, snatch, grip, clutch, take hold of. **2** to arrest or capture (someone). SYNONYMS: seize, capture, arrest, apprehend, take prisoner. **3** to come unexpectedly on someone or take them by surprise ♦ *The boys were caught leaving school early.* **4** to hear and understand something ♦ *I'm afraid I didn't catch what you said.* SYNONYMS: hear, grasp, understand, make out, comprehend. **5** in cricket, to get a batsman out by catching the ball before it hits the ground. **6** to capture an animal in a net or snare or after a chase. **7** to be in time to get on a train, bus, or other form of public transport. **8** to reach or overtake someone moving ahead of you. SYNONYMS: overtake, draw level with, reach. **9** to become infected with an illness ♦ *I was out in the rain and caught a cold.* SYNONYMS: get, develop, contract, come down with. **10** (informal) to manage to see a film or television programme or hear a radio broadcast ♦ *Did you catch yesterday's episode of the spy story?* **11** to become or make something

become trapped or entangled ♦ *I caught my dress in the lift doors.* **12** to hit someone lightly or unexpectedly ♦ *A twig caught him on the nose.* **13** to begin to burn.

catch noun **1** the act of catching something ♦ *That was a good catch.* **2** something caught or worth catching. SYNONYMS: haul, yield, find, acquisition. **3** someone thought to be worth having as a spouse or partner. **4** a difficulty or disadvantage that is hidden or not obvious. SYNONYMS: snag, drawback, disadvantage. **5** a device for fastening something such as a door or window. **6** (*Music*) a round for singing by three or more voices. **to catch someone's eye** to make someone notice you. **to catch hold of** to seize something or someone in the hands. **to catch it** (*informal*) to be scolded or punished. **to catch on** (*informal*) **7** to become fashionable or popular. **8** to understand what is meant. **to catch out** to discover someone in a mistake. **to catch sight of** to notice something or someone suddenly or briefly. **to catch up 1** to reach someone who is moving ahead of you. **2** to finish a task or piece of work that is overdue. [from a French word *cachier*, related to *chase*]

catcher noun **1** someone who catches something. **2** in baseball, a fielder who stands behind the batter.

catching adjective (said about an illness) infectious.

catchment area noun **1** the area from which a hospital takes patients or a school takes pupils. **2** the area from which rainfall drains into a river or reservoir.

catchphrase noun a sentence or phrase that people use often.

catch-22 noun (*informal*) a dilemma from which a person cannot escape, because the condition needed to escape cannot be fulfilled. [from the title of a novel by Joseph Heller (1961), set in the Second World War, in which the hero tries to avoid flying any more missions by going crazy, but is told that anyone who wants to get out of combat duty is not really crazy]

catchweight adjective & noun a category of weight in sports, in which there is no restriction.

catchword noun a memorable word or phrase that people often use; a slogan.

catchy *adjective* (**catchier, catchiest**) (said about a tune) pleasant and easy to remember.

catechism (kat-i-kizm) *noun* **1** a summary of the principles of a religion in the form of questions and answers, used for teaching. **2** a series of questions. [from a Greek word *katēkhizein* meaning 'to teach orally']

catechize (kat-i-kiyz) *verb* to teach someone by a series of questions and answers.

categorical (kat-ig-o-ri-kəl) *adjective* absolute or unconditional ♦ *She gave a categorical refusal.* SYNONYMS: absolute, definite, express, explicit, unconditional, direct. **categorically** *adverb*

categorize (kat-ig-eriyz) *verb* to put something in a particular category, to classify something. **categorization** *noun*

category (kat-ig-eri) *noun* (**categories**) a class of things having the same features or characteristics. SYNONYMS: class, type, set, group, grade, sort, kind. [from a Greek word *katēgoria* meaning 'statement' or 'accusation']

catenary (kə-teen-eri) *noun* (**catenaries**) a curve formed by a chain that hangs from points at each end, or the chain itself. [from a Latin word *catena* meaning 'chain']

cater (kay-ter) *verb* **1** to provide food or entertainment at a social occasion ♦ *We have to cater for 100 people.* **2** to provide what is needed ♦ *We cannot cater for all tastes.* **to cater to** to satisfy or pander to a demand or need. [from an Old French word *acateor* meaning 'a person who buys things']

caterer *noun* a person or business that provides food for social events.

caterpillar *noun* the larva of a butterfly or moth.
Caterpillar or **Caterpillar track** *noun* (*trademark*) a steel band passing round the wheels of a tractor or tank for travel over rough ground. [from an Old French word *chatepelose* meaning 'hairy cat']

caterwaul *verb* to make a shrill wailing sound. [from *cat* and a word *waul*, imitating the sound of a cat]

catfish *noun* (**catfishes** or **catfish**) a large freshwater or sea fish with feelers like whiskers round the mouth.

catgut *noun* a fine strong cord made from the dried intestines of animals (usually sheep or horses, but not cats), used for the strings of musical instruments and for sewing up surgical incisions.

catharsis (kə-thar-sis) *noun* the process of relieving strong feelings or tension through drama or art etc. **cathartic** *adjective*

cathedral *noun* the principal church of an area, often containing the bishop's throne. [from a Greek word *kathedra* meaning 'seat']

Catherine wheel *noun* a firework in the form of a coil that spins round. [named after St Catherine of Alexandria, who was tortured in the 4th century on a spiked wheel]

catheter (kath-it-er) *noun* a flexible tube that can be inserted into a body cavity to drain off fluid, especially into the bladder to extract urine. [from a Greek word *kathienai* meaning 'to send down']

cathode (kath-ohd) *noun* a negatively charged electrode, by which electric current leaves a device. (Compare **anode**.) [from *cata-* meaning 'down' and a Greek word *hodos* meaning 'way']

cathode-ray tube *noun* a vacuum tube used to produce images in a television set or computer screen, in which beams of electrons are directed against a fluorescent screen.

Catholic *adjective* **1** short for **Roman Catholic**. **2** relating to all Churches or all Christians.
Catholic *noun* a Roman Catholic.
Catholicism (kə-thol-i-sizm) *noun*

catholic *adjective* universal, including most things ♦ *She has catholic tastes in reading.* **catholicity** (kath-ə-liss-iti) *noun* [from a Greek word *katholikos* meaning 'universal']

cation (kat-iy-ən) *noun* (*Chemistry*) an ion with a positive charge. (Compare **anion**.) **cationic** (kat-iy-on-ik) *adjective* [from *cata-* meaning 'down' and *ion*]

catkin *noun* a spike of small soft flowers hanging from the willow and hazel and other trees. [from a Dutch word *katteken* meaning 'kitten']

catnap *noun* a short sleep during the day. **catnap** *verb* (**catnapped, catnapping**) to have a catnap.

catnip noun another word for catmint. [from *cat* and a dialect word *nep*, from a Latin word *nepeta* meaning 'catmint']

cat-o'-nine-tails noun a whip with nine knotted lashes, formerly used for flogging.

Catseye noun (trademark) each of a line of reflector studs marking the centre or edge of a road.

cat's cradle noun a child's game of making patterns with a loop of string held between the fingers of both hands.

cat's paw noun a person who is used by someone else to do something unpleasant or dangerous. [from the fable of the monkey who used the paw of his friend the cat to rake hot chestnuts out of the fire]

cattery noun (**catteries**) a place where cats are bred or boarded.

cattle plural noun large animals with horns and cloven hoofs, kept by farmers for their milk or meat. [from a French word *catel*, ultimately from a Latin word *caput* meaning 'head']

cattle grid noun a grid covering a ditch allowing vehicles to pass but not animals.

catty adjective (**cattier, cattiest**) spiteful, speaking spitefully. **cattily** adverb **cattiness** noun

catwalk noun 1 a raised narrow pathway. 2 a long platform that models walk along at a fashion show.

Caucasian (kaw-**kay**-zien) adjective 1 relating to the Caucasus, a mountainous region in SE Europe. 2 relating to the light-skinned race of humankind. **Caucasian** noun a Caucasian person.

caucus (**kaw**-kəs) noun 1 a small group within a political party or other organization, with its own concerns and plans. 2 a meeting of party leaders to decide policy or choose candidates. [from a Native American word meaning 'adviser']

caudal (**kaw**-dəl) adjective 1 of or like a tail. 2 at or near the tail of an animal. [from a Latin word *cauda* meaning 'tail']

caudate adjective having a tail.

caught verb past tense and past participle of **catch**.

caul (kawl) noun a membrane enclosing a fetus in the womb. [from an Old French word *cale* meaning 'head covering']

cauldron noun a large deep pot for boiling things in. [from a Latin word *caldarium* meaning 'hot bath']

cauliflower noun a cabbage with a large white flower head. [from a French phrase *chou fleuri* meaning 'flowered cabbage']

caulk (kawk) verb to make a boat or container watertight by filling its seams or joints with waterproof material, or by driving the edges of plating together. [from a Latin word *calcare* meaning 'to tread']

causal adjective relating to or forming a cause. **causally** adverb

causality (kaw-**zal**-iti) noun the relationship between cause and effect.

causation noun 1 the act of causing something. 2 the relationship between cause and effect.

causative (**kaw**-zə-tiv) adjective 1 acting as a cause. 2 (Grammar) expressing a cause.

cause noun 1 a person or thing that makes something happen or produces an effect. SYNONYMS: origin, basis, root, source, (person) instigator, originator. 2 a reason ♦ *There is no cause to worry.* SYNONYMS: reason, grounds, occasion, justification. 3 a purpose or aim for which people do work; a movement or charity. 4 a lawsuit or case. **cause** verb to be the cause of something or make it happen. SYNONYMS: effect, produce, bring about, result in, give rise to, lead to. [from a Latin word *causa*]

cause célèbre (kohz say-**lebr**) noun (**causes célèbres**) a controversial issue that causes great public interest. [a French phrase meaning 'famous case']

causeway noun a raised road or track across low or wet ground. [from an old word *causey* meaning 'embankment', and *way*]

caustic adjective 1 able to burn or corrode organic tissue by chemical action. 2 severely sarcastic. **caustic** noun a caustic substance. **caustically** adverb **causticity** (kaws-**tiss**-iti) noun [from a Greek word *kaustikos* meaning 'capable of burning']

cauterize verb to burn the surface of flesh to destroy infection or stop bleeding. **cauterization** noun [from a Greek word *kauterion* meaning 'branding iron']

caution noun 1 care taken to avoid danger or difficulty; attention to safety. SYNONYMS: heed, care, vigilance,

circumspection. **2** a warning ♦ *She let him off with a caution.*
caution *verb* to give someone a warning. [from a Latin word *cavere* meaning 'to take heed']

cautionary *adjective* serving as a warning.

cautious *adjective* showing caution, careful. SYNONYMS: careful, wary, chary, guarded, circumspect, prudent. **cautiously** *adverb* **cautiousness** *noun*

cavalcade (kav-əl-kayd) *noun* a procession of people on horseback or in vehicles. [from an Italian word *cavalcare* meaning 'to ride']

Cavalier *noun* a supporter of Charles I in the English Civil War of 1642–9.
cavalier *adjective* offhand or unconcerned ♦ *He showed a cavalier attitude to punctuality.* [from a French word *chevalier* meaning 'knight', from a Latin word *caballus* meaning 'horse']

cavalry *noun* soldiers who fight on horseback or in armoured vehicles. [from a Latin word *caballus* meaning 'horse']

cave *noun* a natural hollow underground or in the side of a hill or cliff.
cave *verb* **to cave in 1** to fall inwards or collapse. **2** to give way in an argument. [from a Latin word *cavus* meaning 'hollow']

caveat (kav-i-at) *noun* a warning, especially about a snag or exception. [a Latin word meaning 'let someone beware']

caveman *noun* (**cavemen**) a person of prehistoric times who lived in caves.

cavern *noun* a large cave or chamber in a cave. [from an Old French word *caverne*, related to *cave*]

cavernous *adjective* large and dark, like a cavern.

caviar (kav-i-ar) *noun* the pickled roe of sturgeon or other large fish, eaten as a delicacy. [from a French word *caviar*, probably from a late Greek word *khaviari*]

cavil *verb* (**cavilled, cavilling**) to raise trivial objections to something.
cavil *noun* a trivial objection. [from a Latin word *cavilla* meaning 'mockery']

caving *noun* exploring caves as a sport.

cavitation *noun* (*Physics*) the making of cavities in a structure or bubbles in a liquid.

cavity *noun* (**cavities**) a hollow or hole in a solid body. [same origin as for *cave*]

cavity wall *noun* a wall made of two thicknesses of bricks or blocks with a cavity between.

cavort (kə-vort) *verb* to caper about excitedly. [originally in American English, origin unknown]

caw *noun* the harsh cry of a rook, raven, or crow.
caw *verb* to make this sound. [an imitation of the sound]

cayenne (kay-en) *noun* a hot red powdered pepper. [from a Tupi (South American) word, later associated with *Cayenne*, capital of French Guiana in South America]

cayman *noun* another spelling of **caiman**.

CB *abbreviation* Citizens' Band (radio).

CBE *abbreviation* Commander of the Order of the British Empire.

CBI *abbreviation* Confederation of British Industry.

cc *abbreviation* **1** cubic centimetre(s). **2** carbon copy (put on a letter to show that it has also been sent to someone else).

CCTV *abbreviation* closed-circuit television.

CD *abbreviation* compact disc.

CDI *abbreviation* compact disc interactive.

CD-ROM *noun* a compact disc storing data as a read-only device for use in a computer. [abbreviation of *compact disc read-only memory*]

CDT *abbreviation* craft, design, and technology.

CE *abbreviation* Common Era.

cease *verb* to bring something to an end, or come to an end; to stop. SYNONYMS: stop, finish, break off, discontinue, end, terminate. **cease** *noun* **without cease** without stopping. [from an Old French word *cesser*, from a Latin word *cedere* meaning 'to yield']

ceasefire *noun* a signal to stop firing guns in war, a truce.

ceaseless *adjective* not ceasing, continuing constantly. **ceaselessly** *adverb*

cedar (see-der) *noun* an evergreen tree with hard sweet-smelling wood. [from a Greek word *kedros*]

cedarwood *noun* the wood of a cedar tree.

cede (seed) *verb* to give up rights to territory or possession of it. [from a Latin word *cedere* meaning 'to yield']

cedilla (si-**dil**-ə) *noun* a mark written under *c* in some languages to show that it is pronounced as *s*, as in ◆ *façade*. [a Spanish word meaning 'a little *z*']

Ceefax *noun* (*trademark*) a teletext information service produced by the BBC.

ceilidh (**kay**-li) *noun* a social gathering with traditional Scottish or Irish music and dancing. [from an Old Irish word *céile* meaning 'companion']

ceiling *noun* 1 the flat surface of the top of a room. 2 an upper limit or level to prices, wages, etc. 3 the maximum altitude at which a particular aircraft can fly. [perhaps from a Latin word *celare* meaning 'to hide']

celandine (**sel**-ən-diyn) *noun* a small wild plant with yellow flowers. [from a Greek word *khelidōn* meaning 'swallow' (because the plant flowered when the first swallows arrived for the summer)]

celebrate *verb* 1 to mark the importance of a day or event by doing something enjoyable or special. 2 to perform a religious ceremony. **celebration** *noun* [from a Latin word *celebrare*]

celebrated *adjective* famous, well known.

celebrity (si-**leb**-riti) *noun* (**celebrities**) 1 a famous person. 2 fame, being famous.

celeriac (si-**le**-ri-ak) *noun* a kind of celery with a swollen root like a turnip.

celerity (si-**le**-riti) *noun* (*literary*) speed, swiftness. [from a Latin word *celer* meaning 'swift']

celery *noun* a garden plant with crisp white or green stems used in salads or as a vegetable. [from a Greek word *selinon* meaning 'parsley']

celestial *adjective* 1 to do with the sky; in the sky ◆ *celestial bodies*. 2 to do with heaven, divine. [from a Latin word *caelum* meaning 'heaven']

celibate (**sel**-ib-ət) *adjective* remaining unmarried or not having sexual intercourse, especially for religious reasons. **celibacy** (**sel**-ib-əsi) *noun* [from a Latin word *caelebs* meaning 'unmarried']

cell *noun* 1 a small room in which a prisoner is locked up. 2 a small room for a monk in a monastery. 3 a microscopic unit of living matter. 4 a compartment of a honeycomb. 5 a device for producing electric current by chemical action. 6 a small group of people forming the core of

an organization, especially a political one. [from a Latin word *cella* meaning 'storeroom']

cellar *noun* 1 a room below ground level used for storage. 2 a stock of wine stored in a cellar. [same origin as for *cell*]

cellist (**chel**-ist) *noun* a person who plays the cello.

cello (**chel**-oh) *noun* (**cellos**) a musical instrument like a large violin, played upright by a seated player who holds it between the knees. [from an Italian word *violoncello* (also used in English; same origin as for *violin*)]

Cellophane (**sel**-ə-fayn) *noun* (*trademark*) a thin tough transparent wrapping material. [from *cellulose* and *diaphane*, a transparent material]

cellular (**sel**-yoo-ler) *adjective* 1 to do with cells, composed of cells. 2 (said about a fabric) woven with an open mesh that traps air and provides insulation ◆ *cellular blankets*. 3 (said about a telephone system) using short-range radio stations to transmit data.

cellulite (**sel**-yoo-liyt) *noun* a lumpy form of fat on the hips, thighs, and buttocks, producing puckering of the skin. [from a French word *cellule* meaning 'small cell']

celluloid (**sel**-yoo-loid) *noun* a kind of plastic made from nitrocellulose and camphor, formerly used for making cinema film.

cellulose (**sel**-yoo-lohz) *noun* 1 an organic substance forming the main part of plant tissues and textile fibres derived from these tissues. 2 a paint or lacquer made from this.

Celsius (**sel**-si-əs) *adjective* relating to or using a temperature scale in which water freezes at 0° and boils at 100°. [named after A. Celsius, a Swedish astronomer (1701–44) who devised the scale]

Celt (kelt) *noun* 1 a member of a group of ancient European peoples living in Britain and much of mainland Europe before the Roman period. 2 someone who lives in a region in which a Celtic language is spoken. [via Latin from a Greek word *Keltoi*]

Celtic (**kelt**-ik) *adjective* to do with the Celts or the languages spoken by them. **Celtic** *noun* a group of languages spoken by Celtic peoples, including Irish, Scottish

Gaelic, Welsh, Breton, Manx, and Cornish. [from a Latin word *Celticus*]

Celtic cross *noun* a Christian cross with a circle round the centre.

cement *noun* **1** a grey mixture of lime and clay that sets like stone when mixed with water and is used for building. **2** a glue that hardens when it sets.
cement *verb* **1** to put cement on something, to join something with cement. **2** to join things firmly together. [via French from a Latin word *caementum* meaning 'quarry stone']

cemetery *noun* (**cemeteries**) a large piece of ground where dead people are buried. [from a Greek word *koimētērion* meaning 'dormitory']

cenotaph (sen-ə-tahf) *noun* a monument like a tomb to honour people, especially soldiers, who are buried somewhere else. [from Greek words *kenos* meaning 'empty' and *taphos* meaning 'tomb']

Cenozoic *adjective* (*Geology*) relating to the era following the Mesozoic era, from about 65 million years ago to the present. [from Greek words *kainos* meaning 'new' and *zōion* meaning 'animal']

censer (sen-ser) *noun* a container in which incense is burnt in religious ceremonies, attached to a set of chains and swung to release a sweet-smelling smoke. [same origin as for *incense*]

censor (sen-ser) *noun* an official who examines films, books, letters, and other written material and removes or bans anything regarded as harmful.
censor *verb* to examine a film or other material and remove or ban harmful material. **censorship** *noun* [a Latin word for a magistrate with power to ban unsuitable people from ceremonies]
◊ Do not confuse this word with *censure*.

censorious (sen-sor-iəs) *adjective* severely critical. **censoriously** *adverb* **censoriousness** *noun*

censure (sen-sher) *noun* strong criticism or disapproval of something. SYNONYMS: criticism, disapproval, condemnation, stricture.
censure *verb* to blame or rebuke someone. SYNONYMS: rebuke, admonish, berate, castigate, reproach. [same origin as for *census*]
◊ Do not confuse this word with *censor*.

census (sen-səs) *noun* **1** an official count or survey of the population of a country or area. **2** an official survey of other things,

e.g. the amount of traffic. [from a Latin word *censere* meaning 'to estimate']

cent *noun* a unit or coin worth one hundredth of a dollar or of certain other metric units of currency. [from a Latin word *centum* meaning 'a hundred']

centaur (sen-tor) *noun* a creature in Greek mythology with the upper body, head, and arms of a man and the lower body of a horse. [from a Greek word *kentauros*]

centenarian (sen-tin-air-iən) *noun* a person who is a hundred years old or more.

centenary (sen-teen-eri) *noun* (**centenaries**) a hundredth anniversary. [from a Latin word *centenarius* meaning 'containing a hundred']

centennial (sen-ten-iəl) *adjective* to do with a centenary.
centennial *noun* (*North Amer.*) a centenary.

center *noun* & *verb* an American spelling of **centre**.

centi- *prefix* one hundredth. [from a Latin word *centum* meaning 'a hundred']

centigrade (sent-i-grayd) *adjective* relating to or using a temperature scale divided into 100 degrees, 0° being the freezing point of water and 100° the boiling point of water. [from *centi-* and a Latin word *gradus* meaning 'step']

centigram *noun* one hundredth of a gram.

centilitre *noun* one hundredth of a litre.

centimetre *noun* one hundredth of a metre (about 0.4 inch).

centipede *noun* a small crawling creature with a long thin body and many legs. [from *centi-* and a Latin word *pedes* meaning 'feet']

central *adjective* **1** at the centre of something or forming the centre. **2** chief or most important ♦ *Emma is the central character in the novel.* SYNONYMS: chief, principal, main, primary, leading. **centrally** *adverb* **centrality** (sen-tral-iti) *noun*

central heating *noun* a system of heating a building by heating water or air in one place and circulating it round the building through a system of pipes.

centralism *noun* a policy of concentrating power or authority in one place. **centralist** *noun*

centralize *verb* to concentrate power or control in one central authority. **centralization** *noun*

central nervous system *noun* the brain and spinal cord, which together control the activities of the body.

central processor or **central processing unit** *noun* the part of a computer that controls the activities of other units and performs the actions specified in a program.

central reservation *noun* the strip of land between the two carriageways of a motorway or major road.

centre *noun* 1 the middle point or part of something. SYNONYMS: middle, heart, kernel, nucleus, core. 2 a place from which an activity or process is controlled. 3 a place or group of buildings devoted to certain activities or facilities ♦ *a shopping centre*. 4 a political party or group holding moderate opinions between two extremes. 5 a player in the middle of the field in some games.
centre *adjective* to do with or at the centre of something.
centre *verb* (**centres, centred, centring**) 1 to place something in or at the centre. 2 to concentrate something or be concentrated at one point. 3 to kick or hit the ball from the wing towards the centre in some games. [via Latin from a Greek word *kentron* meaning 'sharp point']

centre back or **centre half** *noun* the middle player in the half-back line in some games.

centre forward *noun* the player in the middle of the forward line in football or hockey.

centre of gravity *noun* the point in a body about which its mass is evenly balanced.

centric *adjective* in or at the centre of something, central.

centricity (sen-**tris**-iti) *noun* being central or a centre.

centrifugal (sen-**tri**-few-gəl or sen-tri-**few**-gəl) *adjective* moving away from a centre or axis. **centrifugally** *adverb* [from a Latin word *centrum* meaning 'centre' and *fugere* meaning 'to flee']

centrifugal force *noun* a force that appears to act on a body that is travelling round a centre and make it fly outwards away from its circular path.

centrifuge (**sen**-tri-fewj) *noun* a machine that uses centrifugal force to separate substances, e.g. milk and cream.

centrifuge *verb* to subject something to the action of a centrifuge.

centripetal (sen-**trip**-itəl or sen-tri-**pee**-təl) *adjective* moving towards a centre or axis. [from a Latin word *centrum* meaning 'centre' and *petere* meaning 'to seek']

centurion (sen-**tewr**-iən) *noun* an officer in the ancient Roman army, originally one commanding a hundred foot soldiers. [same origin as for *century*]

century *noun* (**centuries**) 1 a period of a hundred years, especially when reckoned from the traditional date of the birth of Christ and ending in 99 or 00. 2 a hundred runs made by a batsman in one innings at cricket. 3 a unit of a hundred men in the ancient Roman army. [from a Latin word *centum* meaning 'a hundred']

cephalic (si-**fal**-ik) *adjective* to do with the head. [from a Greek word *kephalē* meaning 'head']

cephalopod (**sef**-ə-ə-pod) *noun* a mollusc (such as an octopus or squid) that has a distinct head with a ring of tentacles round the mouth. [from Greek words *kephalē* meaning 'head' and *podos* meaning 'of a foot']

ceramic (si-**ram**-ik) *adjective* made of pottery or to do with pottery. **ceramics** *plural noun* pottery, or the making of pottery. [from a Greek word *keramos* meaning 'pottery']

cereal *noun* 1 a grass that produces a grain used for food, such as wheat, rye, oats, or rice. 2 the grain produced by this grass. 3 a breakfast food made from this grain. [named after *Ceres*, Roman goddess of the corn]
◊ Do not confuse this word with *serial*.

cerebellum (se-ri-**bel**-əm) *noun* a small part of the brain located in the back of the skull and controlling the movement of muscles. [a Latin word meaning 'little brain']

cerebral (**se**-ri-brəl) *adjective* 1 to do with the brain. 2 intellectual.

cerebral palsy *noun* a form of paralysis with muscle spasms and sudden movements of the body, caused by brain damage at birth or before birth.

cerebrum (**se**-ri-brəm) *noun* the main part of the brain, located in the front of the skull. [a Latin word meaning 'brain']

ceremonial *adjective* to do with a ceremony or used in ceremonies, formal.

ceremonial *noun* 1 a ceremony or set of rites. 2 the formalities or behaviour that is suited to an occasion. **ceremonially** *adverb*

ceremonious *adjective* full of ceremony, elaborately performed. **ceremoniously** *adverb*

ceremony *noun* (**ceremonies**) 1 the formal actions carried out at a public event or at a religious act of worship. 2 formal politeness. [from a Latin word *caerimonia* meaning 'religious worship']

cerise (sər-**eez**) *noun & adjective* light clear red. [a French word meaning 'cherry']

certain *adjective* 1 feeling sure or convinced about something. SYNONYMS: sure, convinced, positive, assured, definite. 2 known without any doubt. SYNONYMS: definite, indisputable. 3 that can be relied on to happen or be true. 4 that is bound to happen ♦ *A rise in prices now seems certain*. SYNONYMS: inevitable, inescapable, unavoidable, sure. 5 specific but not named or stated for various reasons. 6 able to be recognized without being obvious or important ♦ *The house has a certain charm.* 7 not known to the hearer or reader ♦ *A certain John Smith then arrived.* **for certain** without doubt, as a certainty. **to make certain** to ensure, to make sure. [from a Latin word *certus* meaning 'sure']

certainly *adverb* 1 without doubt. 2 used to agree with something a person has said.

certainty *noun* (**certainties**) 1 the state of being certain. 2 something that is bound to happen or to be successful.

certifiable *adjective* 1 able to be certified. 2 needing to be certified as insane. **certifiably** *adverb*

certificate *noun* an official written or printed statement giving information about a fact or event, or about someone's achievement. **certificated** *adjective*

certify *verb* (**certifies, certified, certifying**) to declare something formally; to show something on a certificate or other document. **certification** *noun* [from a Latin word *certificare* meaning 'to make something certain']

certitude (**ser**-ti-tewd) *noun* a feeling of certainty.

cerulean (si-**roo**-li-ən) *adjective* (*literary*) sky blue.

cervical (ser-**viy**-kəl or **ser**-vik-əl) *adjective* 1 to do with the cervix of the womb ♦ *cervical cancer.* 2 to do with the neck ♦ *cervical vertebrae.*

cervical smear *noun* a specimen of cellular material taken from the cervix and examined under a microscope for early signs of cancer.

cervix (**ser**-viks) *noun* (**cervices**) 1 the passage forming the entrance to the womb. 2 a technical term for the neck. [a Latin word meaning 'neck']

cessation (sess-**ay**-shən) *noun* a ceasing or stopping. [from a Latin word *cessare* meaning 'to cease']

cession (**sesh**-ən) *noun* ceding or giving up a right or possession. [same origin as for *cede*]

cesspit or **cesspool** *noun* a covered pit where liquid waste or sewage is stored temporarily. [origin unknown]

cf. *abbreviation* compare. [short for the Latin word *confer*]

CFC *abbreviation* chlorofluorocarbon, a compound of carbon, hydrogen, and fluorine, formerly used in aerosols and refrigerants and now known to be harmful to the ozone layer.

CFE *abbreviation* College of Further Education.

chador (**chah**-dor) *noun* a cloak worn by Muslim women in some countries, consisting of a large piece of cloth that is wrapped round the head and upper body leaving only the face exposed. [from a Persian word *chadar* meaning 'veil']

chafe (chayf) *verb* 1 to make a part of the body sore from rubbing, or to become sore. 2 to warm a part of the body by rubbing. 3 to become irritated or impatient. [from a French word *chauffer* meaning 'to make warm']

chaff *noun* 1 husks of grain separated from the seed by threshing or winnowing. 2 hay or straw cut up as food for cattle. **chaff** *verb* to joke or tease someone in a good-humoured way. [from an Old English word]

chaffinch *noun* a common European finch. [from *chaff*, so called because it searched the chaff for seeds]

chafing-dish (**chay**-fing-dish) *noun* a pan with a heater under it for cooking food or keeping it warm at the table.

chagrin (**shag**-rin) *noun* a feeling of embarrassed annoyance or disappointment at a failure. **chagrined** *adjective* [a French word]

chain *noun* 1 a series of connected metal links, used for pulling or supporting weights or for restraining things or in jewellery. 2 a connected series or sequence of things ♦ *a mountain chain ♦ a chain of events.* SYNONYMS: series, sequence, succession, string. 3 a number of shops, hotels, or other businesses owned by the same company. 4 a unit of length for measuring land equal to 66 feet, or a jointed metal rod for measuring this. **chain** *verb* to secure or restrain something with a chain or chains. [via Old French from a Latin word *catena*, related to *catenary*]

chain letter *noun* a letter that the recipient is asked to copy and send to other people, who then do the same.

chain mail *noun* armour made of metal rings linked together.

chain reaction *noun* 1 a chemical or other change forming products that themselves cause more changes. 2 a series of events each of which causes or influences the next.

chainsaw *noun* a powered saw with teeth set on a continuous rotating chain.

chain-smoke *verb* to smoke continuously, often by lighting a new cigarette from the stub of the previous one. **chain-smoker** *noun*

chain stitch *noun* a looped stitch that looks like a chain, used in crochet or embroidery.

chain store *noun* one of a number of similar shops owned by the same firm.

chair *noun* 1 a movable seat with a back, for one person. 2 the person in charge at a meeting, a chairperson. 3 a university professorship. **chair** *verb* 1 to be in charge of a meeting. 2 to carry someone sitting in a chair held on the shoulders of a group, as a triumph or celebration. [from an Old French word, from a Greek word *kathedra*, related to *cathedral*]

chairlift *noun* a series of chairs hung from a moving cable, for carrying people up and down the side of a mountain.

chairman or **chairwoman** *noun* (**chairmen** or **chairwomen**) 1 a person in charge of a meeting or a committee. 2 a person who takes charge of a board of directors in a business. **chairmanship** *noun*
◊ The word *chairman* can be used about a man or a woman, but *chairperson* is now common to refer to a person of either gender.

chairperson *noun* a person in charge of a meeting, a chairman or chairwoman.

chaise longue (shayz **lawng**) *noun* a chair with a backrest at one end and a long seat for resting the legs. [a French phrase meaning 'long chair']

chalet (**shal**-ay) *noun* 1 a wooden house with eaves that overhang, found especially in the Swiss Alps. 2 a small villa. 3 a small cabin or hut in a holiday camp. [a Swiss French word, from an Old French word *chasel* meaning 'farmstead']

chalice (**chal**-iss) *noun* a large goblet for holding wine, especially one from which consecrated wine is drunk at the Christian Eucharist. [from a Latin word *calix* meaning 'cup']

chalk *noun* 1 a soft white limestone. 2 a white or coloured piece of a similar substance (calcium sulphate) used for drawing or writing. **chalk** *verb* to write or draw something with chalk, to mark or rub something with chalk. **by a long chalk** by far, by a long way. **chalky** *adjective* [from an Old English word *cealc*, from a Latin word *calx*]

challenge *noun* 1 a call to someone to take part in a contest or to show their ability or strength. 2 a task or undertaking that is new and exciting but also difficult or demanding. 3 a call to someone to respond, especially a sentry's call for someone approaching to identify themselves. 4 a formal objection, especially to the inclusion of a person in a jury. **challenge** *verb* 1 to issue a challenge to someone. 2 to raise a formal objection to a decision or proposal. 3 to question the truth or rightness of something. **challenger** *noun* [from an Old French word]

challenged *adjective* suffering from a handicap or disability ♦ *physically challenged.*

challenging *adjective* testing your ability, exciting or stimulating.

chamber *noun* 1 (*old use*) a room or bedroom. 2 a large room used for the meetings of a parliament or for other public events. 3 the group or body of people using a chamber. 4 a compartment in the body of an animal or plant, or in a machine. [same origin as for *camera*]

chamberlain (chaym-ber-lin) *noun* an official who manages the household of a sovereign or member of the nobility. [from an Old French word]

chambermaid *noun* a woman who cleans bedrooms in a hotel.

chamber music *noun* music written for a small number of players.

chamber pot *noun* a bowl kept in a bedroom for use as a toilet.

chameleon (kə-mee-li-ən) *noun* a small lizard that can change its colour to match its surroundings, as camouflage. [from a Greek word *khamaileōn* meaning 'ground lion']

chamfer (cham-fer) *verb* (**chamfered, chamfering**) to cut away a sharp edge or corner to make a rounded edge.
chamfer *noun* an edge or corner that has been chamfered. [from a French word *chaimfrain*]

chamois *noun* (**chamois**) 1 (sham-wah) a small mountain antelope of Europe and Asia. 2 (sham-i) a piece of soft yellow leather made from the skin of sheep, goats, or deer and used for washing and polishing. [a French word]

chamomile (kam-ə-miyl) *noun* a plant with sweet-smelling flowers like daisies, which are dried and used as a tonic. [from a Greek word *khamaimēlon* meaning 'earth apple' (because the flowers seemed to smell of earth)]

champ¹ *verb* 1 to munch food noisily. 2 to show impatience. [an imitation of the sound]

champ² *noun* (*informal*) a champion.

champagne *noun* a sparkling white wine from Champagne in France.

champion *noun* 1 a person or thing that has defeated all the others in a sport or competition. 2 a person who speaks or acts in support of another person or a cause.
champion *adjective* (*informal*) splendid, excellent.
champion *verb* to be active in supporting a person or cause. **championship** *noun* [from an Old French word]

chance *noun* 1 the way things happen without being planned or intended, luck, or fate. SYNONYMS: luck, fate, destiny, fortune. 2 a possibility or likelihood. SYNONYMS: possibility, likelihood, prospect. 3 an opportunity ♦ *Now is our chance to escape.* 4 (used before a noun) coming or happening without being planned ♦ *a chance meeting.*
chance *verb* 1 to happen without plan or intention. 2 (*informal*) to risk something ♦ *Let's chance it.* **by chance** as it happens or happened, without being planned. **to chance on** to come upon something or someone without planning to. [from an Old French word *cheance*]

chancel (chahn-səl) *noun* the part of a church near the altar, used by the clergy and choir. [from an Old French word, from a Latin word *cancelli* meaning 'crossbars']

chancellery (chahn-səl-er-i) *noun* (**chancelleries**) 1 the office or residence of a chancellor. 2 an office attached to an embassy or consulate.

chancellor *noun* 1 a senior state or legal official of various kinds. 2 the head of government in some European countries, for example Germany and Austria. 3 the honorary head of a university.
chancellorship *noun* [from a Latin word *cancellarius* meaning 'secretary']

Chancellor of the Exchequer *noun* the chief finance minister of the British government.

Chancery (chahn-ser-i) *noun* the Lord Chancellor's court, a division of the High Court of Justice.

chancy *adjective* (**chancier, chanciest**) (*informal*) risky or uncertain.

chandelier (shan-də-leer) *noun* a large ornamental fixture hanging from a ceiling, with supports for several lights. [from a French word *chandelle* meaning 'candle']

chandler *noun* someone who deals in ropes, canvas, and other supplies for ships. [same origin as for *chandelier*]

change *verb* 1 to make something different, or to become different. SYNONYMS: (with an object) alter, modify, adjust, adapt, amend; (with or without an object) vary. 2 to pass from one form or phase into another. 3 to take or use one thing instead of another. SYNONYMS: exchange, swop, substitute, replace, switch. 4 to put on fresh clothes or coverings ♦ *I'd better change before I go out.* 5 to put a clean nappy on a baby. 6 to go from one to another ♦ *We have to change trains at Crewe.* 7 to give smaller units of money, or money in another currency, for an amount of money ♦ *Can you change £20?*

change *noun* 1 the process of changing or becoming different. SYNONYMS: difference, alteration, variation, adjustment, modification. 2 a substitution of one thing for another; variety. 3 a fresh occupation or surroundings ♦ *I feel in need of a change.* 4 coins and notes in small units. 5 an amount of money given back to the payer as the balance when the price is less than the amount offered in payment. **to change hands** to pass to another owner. **to change over** to change from one system or situation to another. [from an Old French word]

changeable *adjective* 1 able to be changed. 2 changing frequently, unpredictable ♦ *changeable weather.* SYNONYMS: variable, unreliable, inconsistent, unpredictable, unsettled, erratic, unstable.

changeling (**chaynj**-ling) *noun* a child who is believed to have been substituted secretly for another, especially by fairies in stories.

change of heart *noun* a change in attitude or feelings about something.

changeover *noun* a change from one system or situation to another.

change-ringing *noun* ringing a peal of bells in a series of different sequences.

channel *noun* 1 a passage along which a liquid can flow, a sunken course or line along which something can move. 2 a stretch of water wider than a strait, connecting two seas. 3 the bed of a stream of water below normal ground level. 4 the part of a waterway in which ships can travel, deeper than the parts on each side. 5 any course by which news or information etc. may travel. 6 a band of frequencies used by a particular broadcasting station. 7 an electrical circuit for transmitting a signal. **the Channel** *noun* the English Channel, between Britain and mainland Europe. **channel** *verb* (**channelled, channelling**) 1 to direct something through the right channel or route. 2 to make a channel in something. [from a Latin word *canalis* meaning 'canal']

chant *noun* 1 a tune to which words with an irregular rhythm are fitted by singing several syllables or words to the same note, especially in church music. 2 a rhythmic call or shout by a crowd. 3 a monotonous or repetitive song.

chant *verb* 1 to sing a chant. 2 to call or shout repeatedly or monotonously. **chanter** *noun* [from a Latin word *cantare* meaning 'to sing']

chantry *noun* (**chantries**) a chapel founded for priests to sing masses for the soul of its founder. [from an Old French word *chanterie*, related to *chant*]

Chanukkah *noun* another spelling of **Hanukkah.**

chaos (**kay**-oss) *noun* great confusion or disorder. SYNONYMS: confusion, turmoil, havoc, mayhem, pandemonium, bedlam. [from a Greek word meaning 'bottomless pit']

chaos theory *noun* the branch of science concerned with the possible widespread effects on complex systems of very small changes within them.

chaotic (kay-ot-ik) *adjective* in great confusion, completely disorganized. SYNONYMS: confused, muddled, disorderly, disorganized, jumbled, topsy-turvy. **chaotically** *adverb*

chap [1] *noun* (*informal*) a man or boy. [short for *chapman*, an old word for a pedlar]

chap [2] *verb* (**chapped, chapping**) (said about the skin) to crack and become sore, especially in cold weather. [origin unknown]

chaparral (chap-er-al) *noun* an area of dense tangled shrubs and thorny bushes, especially in the southwestern USA and Mexico. [from a Spanish word *chaparra* meaning 'evergreen oak']

chapatti (cha-pah-ti) *noun* (**chapattis**) a flat cake of unleavened bread, used in Indian cookery. [a Hindi word, from *chapana* meaning 'to flatten or roll out']

chapel *noun* 1 a small building or room used for Christian worship. 2 a service in a chapel ♦ *They were on their way to chapel.* 3 a room or area with a separate altar within a larger church or cathedral. [from an Old French word *chapele*, from a Latin word *cappa* meaning 'cape' (because the first chapel was a place where the cloak of St Martin was preserved)]

chaperone (**shap**-er-ohn) *noun* an older woman in charge of a girl or young unmarried woman on social occasions. **chaperone** *verb* to act as chaperone to a girl or young woman. [from a French word *chaperon* meaning 'hood']

chaplain (**chap**-lin) *noun* a member of the clergy attached to a private chapel, institution, or military unit. [from an Old French word *chapelain*, related to *chapel*]

chaps *plural noun* long leather leggings worn over ordinary trousers by cowboys. [shortened from a Spanish word *chaparejos*]

chapter *noun* 1 a main division of a book, often numbered. 2 a distinct period of a person's life. 3 the canons of a cathedral or members of a monastic order. [from a Latin word *capitulum* meaning 'little head']

chapter house *noun* the building used for meetings of a cathedral chapter.

char[1] *noun* (*informal*) a charwoman.
char *verb* (**charred, charring**) to work as a charwoman.

char[2] *verb* (**charred, charring**) to make something black, or to become black, by burning. [from *charcoal*]

char[3] *noun* (*informal*) tea. [from a Chinese word *cha*]

charabanc (**sha**-rə-bang) *noun* an early form of bus with bench seats. [from a French word *char-à-banc* meaning 'carriage with benches']

character *noun* 1 all the distinct qualities that a person or thing has. SYNONYMS: nature, personality, disposition, manner, make-up, temperament. 2 a person's good reputation. 3 strength and purpose in a person's nature. SYNONYMS: integrity, honesty, honour, decency, morality. 4 an interesting or amusing person. 5 a person in a novel, play, or film. 6 a description of a person's qualities, a testimonial. 7 a letter, sign, or mark used in a system of writing or printing or appearing on a computer screen. 8 a physical characteristic of a plant or animal. **in character** in line with a person's usual behaviour. **out of character** not in line with a person's usual behaviour. [from a Greek word *kharaktēr* meaning 'a stamping tool']

characteristic *adjective* showing the character or nature of a person or thing, typical ♦ *She showed her characteristic good humour.* SYNONYMS: typical, distinguishing, distinctive.
characteristic *noun* 1 a quality or feature that forms part of the character of a person or thing. 2 (*Mathematics*) the part of the logarithm before the decimal point (contrasted with *mantissa*).

characteristically *adverb*

characterize *verb* 1 to be a characteristic of a person or thing. 2 to describe the character of a person or thing.
characterization *noun*

characterless *adjective* not having any distinct character.

charade (shə-**rahd**) *noun* 1 a scene acted out in a game of *charades* as a clue to a word that the players have to guess. 2 an absurd pretence that is meant to impress someone. [a French word]

charcoal *noun* a black substance used in drawing, and made by burning wood slowly in an oven with little air. [origin unknown, but probably related to *coal*]

charge *noun* 1 the price a seller asks for goods or services. SYNONYMS: price, cost, (for a service) fee. 2 an accusation that someone has done wrong or has committed a crime. SYNONYMS: accusation, allegation. 3 a rush forward, especially to attack. SYNONYMS: attack, assault. 4 the amount of explosive needed to fire a gun or make an explosion. 5 the amount of material that a device can hold at one time. 6 the electricity contained in a substance, or the electrical property (positive or negative) of a particle of matter. 7 energy stored chemically for conversion into electricity. 8 a task or duty, especially the care or custody of a person or thing. 9 a person or thing entrusted to someone's care. 10 formal instructions about a person's duty or responsibility.
charge *verb* 1 to ask a certain amount as a price for something. 2 to record an amount as a debt ♦ *Please charge it to my account.* 3 to accuse someone formally of having done wrong or committed a crime. SYNONYMS: accuse, prosecute. 4 to rush forward in attack. SYNONYMS: attack, assault, rush. 5 to load or fill a device with whatever it holds. 6 to give an electric charge to something, to store energy in a device. 7 to entrust someone with a task or duty. **in charge** in control or command. **to take charge** to take control. [via Old French from a Latin word *carcare* meaning 'to load']

chargeable *adjective* able or likely to be charged ♦ *A fee is chargeable for missed appointments.*

charge card *noun* a type of credit card in which the amount owed must be paid in full when an account is issued.

chargé d'affaires (shar-zhay da-**fair**) *noun* (**chargés d'affaires**) **1** an ambassador's deputy. **2** a state's representative in a small country. [a French phrase meaning 'in charge of affairs']

charger *noun* **1** a cavalry horse. **2** a device for charging a battery.

chariot *noun* a two-wheeled carriage drawn by horses, used in ancient warfare and racing. [from Old French, related to *car*]

charioteer *noun* the driver of a chariot.

charisma (kə-**riz**-mə) *noun* the ability a person has to inspire devotion and enthusiasm. [a Greek word meaning 'divine favour']

charismatic (ka-riz-**mat**-ik) *adjective* **1** having great personal charm and influence. **2** (said about religious groups or worship) emphasizing gifts and abilities conferred by God, e.g. the gift of prophecy.

charitable *adjective* **1** generous in giving help to people who need it. **2** to do with charity ♦ *charitable institutions.* **3** wanting to think well of people or what they do. **charitably** *adverb*

charity *noun* (**charities**) **1** loving kindness towards others. SYNONYMS: generosity, kindness, humanity, compassion. **2** thinking well about people or what they do. **3** help given freely to people in need. **4** an organization or fund set up to help people who are poor or have suffered disaster or hardship. [from a Latin word *caritas* meaning 'love']

charlady *noun* (**charladies**) a charwoman.

charlatan (**shar**-lə-tən) *noun* a person who falsely claims to have special knowledge or ability. [from an Italian word *ciarlatano* meaning 'babbler']

charm *noun* **1** the power a person has of arousing love or admiration. **2** an object or set of words that is believed to have magic power or bring good luck. **3** a small ornament worn on a chain or bracelet. **4** (*Physics*) a property that some elementary particles have, especially quarks.
charm *verb* **1** to give pleasure or delight to people. SYNONYMS: delight, enthral, attract, fascinate. **2** to influence someone by personal charm. SYNONYMS: bewitch, captivate, entrance, enchant, captivate. **3** to control something as if by magic.
charmer *noun* [via French from a Latin word *carmen* meaning 'song' or 'spell']

charming *adjective* **1** very pleasing, delightful. **2** (said about a person) friendly and likeable. SYNONYMS: delightful, lovely, appealing, attractive, captivating, enchanting.

charnel house (**char**-nəl) *noun* a place in which the bodies or bones of the dead are kept. [same origin as for *carnal*]

chart *noun* **1** a map designed for people sailing ships or flying aircraft. **2** an outline map for showing special information ♦ *a weather chart.* **3** a diagram, list, or table giving information in an orderly form.
the charts *plural noun* a published list of the best-selling pop records.
chart *verb* **1** to make a map of an area. **2** to put information into a chart. [from a Latin word *charta* meaning 'card']

charter *noun* **1** an official document giving certain rights to a person or organization. **2** the chartering of an aircraft, ship, or vehicle.
charter *verb* **1** to grant a charter to someone, or to found an organization by means of a charter. **2** to hire an aircraft, ship, or vehicle for a particular journey.
charterer *noun* [from Old French, related to *card*]

chartered *adjective* qualified as a member of a professional association which has a royal charter ♦ *a chartered accountant.*

charter flight *noun* a flight by an aircraft that has been chartered for that journey, as distinct from an airline's scheduled flights.

Chartism *noun* a movement for political and social reform in Britain (1837–48), with principles set out in a manifesto called *The People's Charter.* **Chartist** *noun*

chartreuse (shar-**trerz**) *noun* **1** a fragrant green or yellow liqueur made from brandy and herbs. **2** a pale green colour. **3** a dish of fruit set in jelly. [named after *La Grande Chartreuse*, a Carthusian monastery near Grenoble in France, where the liqueur was first made]

charwoman *noun* (**charwomen**) a woman employed as a cleaner in a house or office. [from an Old English word *cerr* meaning 'task']

chary (**chair**-i) *adjective* (**charier, chariest**) cautious or wary, especially about giving or taking something. [from an Old English word]

chase *verb* **1** to go quickly after a person or thing in order to capture them or catch them up, or to drive them away. **2** to hurry ◆ *We spent the morning chasing round the shops.* **3** (*informal*) to try to get or achieve something.

chase *noun* **1** an act of chasing, a pursuit. **2** hunting animals for sport. **3** a steeplechase. **4** (usually in place names) a piece of unenclosed parkland, originally used for hunting. **chaser** *noun* [via Old French from a Latin word *captare* meaning 'to capture']

chasm (kaz-əm) *noun* **1** a deep opening in the ground. **2** a wide difference in people's opinions or feelings. [from a Greek word *khasma* meaning 'wide hollow']

chassis (sha-see) *noun* (**chassis** (sha-seez)) **1** the base frame of a vehicle, on which other parts are mounted. **2** the framework of a piece of computer or audio equipment. [from a French word *châssis* meaning 'frame']

chaste (chayst) *adjective* **1** not having sexual intercourse at all, or only with the person you are married to. **2** simple in style, without decoration. **chastely** *adverb* [from a Latin word *castus* meaning 'pure']

chasten (chay-sən) *verb* to make someone realize they have done something wrong. [from a Latin word *castigare* meaning 'to castigate']

chastise (chas-tyz) *verb* to punish or reprimand someone severely. **chastisement** *noun* [same origin as for *chasten*]

chastity (chas-ti-ti) *noun* being chaste, especially by not having sexual intercourse.

chastity belt *noun* (*historical*) a belt that a woman was made to wear to prevent her from having sexual intercourse while her husband was away.

chasuble (chaz-yoo-bəl) *noun* a loose outer vestment worn over other vestments by a priest when celebrating Mass. [from a Latin word *casula* meaning 'little house' and then 'hooded cloak']

chat *noun* an informal or casual conversation.

chat *verb* (**chatted, chatting**) to talk in a friendly or informal way. **to chat someone up** to talk informally to someone, especially with romantic or sexual intentions. [a short form of *chatter*]

chateau (shat-oh) *noun* (**chateaux** (shat-ohz)) a castle or large country house in France. [from a French word *château*]

chatline *noun* a telephone service allowing several callers to have a conversation.

chat room *noun* an area on the Internet or other network in which users can exchange information in real time.

chat show *noun* a television or radio programme in which celebrities are invited to talk informally.

chattel *noun* a personal possession that can be moved about, as distinct from a house or land. [from an Old French word *chatel*, related to *cattle*]

chatter *verb* **1** to talk quickly and continuously about trivial things. **2** to make sounds like this, as some birds and animals do. **3** (said about the teeth) to make a repeated clicking or rattling sound. **chatter** *noun* **1** continuous trivial talk. **2** a series of short high-pitched sounds. **chatterer** *noun* [an imitation of the sound]

chatterbox *noun* (*informal*) a talkative person.

chatty *adjective* (**chattier, chattiest**) **1** fond of chatting. **2** (said about a conversation, letter, etc.) friendly and lively. **chattily** *adverb* **chattiness** *noun*

chauffeur (shoh-fer) *noun* a person employed to drive a car. **chauffeur** *verb* to drive someone about in a car. [a French word meaning 'stoker']

chauvinism (shoh-vin-izm) *noun* **1** an exaggerated belief that your own country is superior to others. **2** excessive loyalty to a group, especially to your own sex. **chauvinist** *noun* **chauvinistic** *adjective* [named after Nicolas Chauvin, a French soldier under Napoleon, known for his extreme patriotism]

cheap *adjective* **1** low in price, not expensive. **2** charging low prices ◆ *We are looking for a cheap hotel.* **3** poor in quality, of low value. **4** unfair or in bad taste ◆ *a cheap remark.* **cheap** *adverb* cheaply ◆ *We got it cheap.* **cheaply** *adverb* **cheapness** *noun* [from an Old English word *ceap* meaning 'bargain']

cheapen *verb* to make something cheap, or to become cheap.

cheat *verb* **1** to act dishonestly or unfairly in order to gain an advantage. SYNONYMS: trick, deceive, defraud, swindle; (*informal*) rip off, take in. **2** to break the rules in a game or examination in order to be successful. **3** to trick or deceive someone; to deprive someone of something by deceit ♦ *They were cheated out of all their money.*

cheat *noun* **1** a person who cheats, an unfair player. **2** an act of cheating, a piece of deception. [a shortening of an earlier word *escheat* meaning (in law) 'the passing of property to the state', from Old French]

check¹ *verb* **1** to make sure that something is correct or in good condition. SYNONYMS: verify, confirm, test, investigate. **2** to stop someone or something or make them go slower. SYNONYMS: curb, stop, slow down, hold back, hinder, impede. **3** to make a sudden stop. **4** (in chess) to make a move that threatens the opponent's king.
check *noun* **1** an act of checking that something is correct or in good condition. **2** a stopping or slowing; a pause or restraint. **3** (*North Amer.*) a bill in a restaurant. **4** (in chess) a situation in which a piece is threatening the opposing king. **in check** in chess, a position in which the king is threatened by an opposing piece. **to check in** to register on arrival at a hotel or an airport. **to check out** to settle a hotel bill when leaving. **to check up on** to make sure something or someone is all right. **checker** *noun* [from saying 'check 'in chess when the opposing king is threatened, from the Persian word *shah* meaning 'king']

check² *noun* a pattern of squares or crossing lines. **checked** *adjective* having a check pattern. [from *chequered*]

checkmate *noun* **1** a position in chess in which the king is in check and cannot escape. **2** a complete defeat.
checkmate *verb* **1** (in chess) to put the opposing king into checkmate. **2** to defeat someone finally. [from a Persian phrase *shah mat* meaning 'the king is dead']

checkout *noun* a place where customers pay for goods in a supermarket.

checkpoint *noun* a place at a frontier between countries where documents are checked.

check-up *noun* a routine medical or dental examination.

cheek *noun* **1** the side of the face below the eye. **2** rude or disrespectful talk or behaviour.

cheek *verb* to address someone in a cheeky manner. **cheek by jowl** close together, in close association. [from an Old English word]

cheeky *adjective* (**cheekier, cheekiest**) rather rude or disrespectful, without being unpleasant. SYNONYMS: rude, impolite, impertinent, insolent, impudent. **cheekily** *adverb* **cheekiness** *noun*

cheep *verb* to make the weak shrill cry of a young bird.
cheep *noun* this cry. [an imitation of the sound]

cheer *noun* **1** a shout of encouragement or applause. **2** cheerfulness ♦ *full of good cheer.*
cheer *verb* **1** to utter a cheer; to encourage or applaud with cheers. SYNONYMS: applaud, clap, shout. **2** to comfort or gladden someone. SYNONYMS: comfort, gladden, hearten, encourage. **to cheer up** to become more cheerful, or to make someone more cheerful. [originally in the meaning 'a person's expression', from an Old French word *chiere* meaning 'face']

cheerful *adjective* **1** looking or sounding happy. SYNONYMS: happy, jolly, lively, friendly, cheery, joyful. **2** bright and pleasant ♦ *cheerful colours.* **cheerfully** *adverb* **cheerfulness** *noun*

cheerio *interjection* (*informal*) goodbye.

cheerless *adjective* gloomy or dreary.

cheery *adjective* (**cheerier, cheeriest**) cheerful and happy. **cheerily** *adverb*

cheese *noun* **1** a solid or soft food made from curds of milk. **2** a thick stiff jam ♦ *damson cheese.* **cheesy** *adjective* [from an Old English word *cese*]

cheeseburger *noun* a hamburger with cheese in or on it.

cheesecake *noun* a tart with a filling of cream and soft cheese.

cheesecloth *noun* a thin loosely-woven cotton fabric.

cheese-paring *adjective* mean with money, stingy.

cheese straw *noun* a thin strip of pastry flavoured with cheese, eaten as a snack.

cheetah (**chee-tə**) *noun* a large spotted cat that can run extremely fast. [from a Hindi word *cita*]

chef (shef) *noun* a professional cook, especially the chief cook in a restaurant or hotel. [a French word meaning 'chief']

chemical *adjective* to do with chemistry, or produced by chemistry.
chemical *noun* a substance obtained by or used in chemistry. **chemically** *adverb* [from a Latin word *alchimia* meaning 'alchemy']

chemical engineering *noun* engineering concerned with processes that involve chemical change and with the equipment needed for these.

chemical warfare *noun* warfare using poison gas and other chemicals.

chemise (shəm-**eez**) *noun* **1** a loose-fitting piece of underwear formerly worn by women, hanging straight from the shoulders. **2** a dress of this shape. [from a Latin word *camisia* meaning 'shirt']

chemist *noun* **1** a person or firm that makes or sells medicinal drugs. **2** an expert in chemistry. [from a Latin word *alchimista* meaning 'alchemist']

chemistry *noun* **1** the study of substances and the ways in which they react with one another. **2** chemical structure, properties, and reactions. **3** the way in which two people react to each other emotionally and psychologically.

chemotherapy (keem-ə-**the**-rə-pi) *noun* the treatment of disease, especially cancer, by medicinal drugs and other chemical substances. [from *chemistry* and *therapy*]

chenille (shən-**eel**) *noun* a fabric with a long velvety pile, used for carpets and as trimmings for furniture. [a French word meaning 'hairy caterpillar']

cheque *noun* an order to a bank to pay out money from an account, written on a specially printed form. [a different spelling of *check*[1]]

cheque book *noun* a book of printed cheques.

cheque card *noun* a card guaranteeing payment of a bank customer's cheques.

chequered *adjective* **1** marked with a pattern of squares. **2** having alternating periods of success and failure ♦ *a chequered career*.

chequers (**chek**-erz) *noun* a pattern of squares of alternate colours. [from a Latin word *scaccarium* meaning 'chessboard']

cherish *verb* **1** to look after a person or thing lovingly. **2** to be fond of someone or something. **3** to have a deep feeling about something ♦ *We cherish hopes of their return*. [from a French word *cher* meaning 'dear']

cheroot (shə-**root**) *noun* a cigar with both ends open. [via French from a Tamil word meaning 'roll of tobacco']

cherry *noun* (**cherries**) **1** a small soft round fruit, usually bright or dark red, with a stone. **2** the tree from which this comes. **3** a deep red colour. [from an Old French word *cherise*, ultimately from a Greek word *kerasos*]

cherry-pick *verb* to pick out the best items from those available and reject the rest.

cherub (**cher**-əb) *noun* **1** (**cherubim** or **cherubs**) a winged angel, often represented in art as a chubby baby with wings. **2** a beautiful or angelic child. [from a Hebrew word]

cherubic (chə-**roo**-bik) *adjective* like a cherub, with a plump innocent face.

chervil *noun* a herb used for flavouring. [via Old English from a Greek word *khairephullon*]

Ches. *abbreviation* Cheshire.

chess *noun* a game for two players having 16 pieces each, played on a chequered board of 64 squares. [same origin as for *check*[1]]

chessboard *noun* a chequered board used for playing chess.

chest *noun* **1** a large strong box for storing or transporting things. **2** the front part of the body between the neck and the waist, containing the heart and lungs. **get something off your chest** (*informal*) to say something you have been wanting to say or have been anxious about. [from an Old English word]

chesterfield *noun* a sofa with a padded seat, back, and ends and curved outwards at the top. [named after an Earl of Chesterfield in the 19th century]

chestnut *noun* **1** a shiny hard brown nut that grows in a prickly green case. **2** the large tree from which this comes. **3** a deep reddish-brown colour. **4** a horse of reddish-brown or yellowish-brown colour. **5** (often **old chestnut**) an old joke or story. [from an Old English word *chesten*, from a Greek word *kastanea*]

chest of drawers *noun* a piece of furniture with drawers for storing clothes etc.

chevalier (shev-ə-**leer**) *noun* a member of certain orders of knighthood. [an Old French word, from a Latin word *caballarius* meaning 'horseman']

chevron (shev-rən) *noun* a bent line or stripe, especially one worn on the sleeve to show rank. [via Old French from a Latin word *caper* meaning 'goat']

chew *verb* to bite or grind food between the teeth to make it easier to swallow.
chew *noun* **1** the act of chewing. **2** something suitable for chewing. [from an Old English word]

chewing gum *noun* a sweetened and flavoured gum for chewing.

chewy *adjective* (**chewier, chewiest**) tough and needing to be chewed a lot.

chiaroscuro (ki-ar-ə-skoor-oh) *noun* the treatment of light and shade in drawing and painting. [from Italian words *chiaro* meaning 'clear' and *oscuro* meaning 'dark']

chic (sheek) *adjective* stylish and elegant.
chic *noun* stylishness and elegance. [a French word]

chicane (shi-kayn) *noun* an artificial barrier or obstacle on a motor-racing track. [same origin as for *chicanery*]

chicanery (shi-kayn-er-i) *noun* trickery used to get something you want. [from a French word *chicaner* meaning 'to quibble']

chick *noun* **1** a young bird, especially one that has just hatched. **2** (*informal*) a young woman. [a shortening of *chicken*]

chicken *noun* **1** a domestic fowl, especially a young one kept for its eggs or meat. **2** the flesh of a domestic fowl used as food. **3** (*informal*) a coward.
chicken *adjective* (*informal*) afraid to do something, cowardly.
chicken *verb* **chicken out** (*informal*) to be too afraid to take part in something. [from an Old English word]

chicken feed *noun* (*informal*) a small or trivial amount of something, especially money.

chickenpox *noun* an infectious disease that produces itchy red spots on the skin. [so called because the disease is mild compared to smallpox]

chickweed *noun* a weed with small white flowers.

chicory *noun* a blue-flowered plant grown for its leaves, which are used in salads, and for its root, which is roasted and ground and used with or instead of coffee. [from a Greek word *kikhorion*]

chide *verb* (past tense, **chided**, or **chid**; past participle, **chided**) (*old use*) to scold someone. [from an Old English word]

chief *noun* **1** a leader or ruler of a people. **2** a person with the highest authority.
chief *adjective* **1** highest in rank or authority. **2** most important ♦ *the chief reason.* SYNONYMS: main, principal, central, paramount, key, major. [from an Old French word *chief* or *chef*]

chief constable *noun* the head of the police force of an area.

chiefly *adverb* mainly, mostly.

chief of staff *noun* the most senior staff officer.

chieftain (cheef-tən) *noun* the leader of a people or of a group of people.

chiffon (shif-on) *noun* a very thin almost transparent fabric, usually of silk or nylon. [a French word, originally meaning 'trimmings on a woman's dress']

chignon (sheen-yawn) *noun* a knot or roll of long hair on the back of a woman's head. [a French word, originally meaning 'nape of the neck']

chihuahua (chi-wah-wə) *noun* a very small smooth-haired dog from a breed originating in Mexico. [named after *Chihuahua*, a city and state in Mexico]

chilblain *noun* a painful swelling on the hand or foot, caused by poor circulation and exposure to cold. [from *chill* and *blain* meaning 'a sore']

child *noun* (**children**) **1** a young human being before he or she has fully developed; a boy or girl. **2** a son or daughter of any age. [from an Old English word *cild*]

childbirth *noun* the process of giving birth to a child.

childhood *noun* the time or state of being a child.

childish *adjective* **1** like a child, unsuitable for a grown person. **2** (said about an adult) silly and immature. SYNONYMS: immature, silly, babyish, infantile, juvenile. **childishly** *adverb* **childishness** *noun*

childless *adjective* having no children.

childlike *adjective* (said about an adult) having the good qualities of a child, simple and innocent.

childminder *noun* someone who looks after children in their own home for payment.

children plural of **child**.

child's play *noun* something that is very easy or straightforward to do.

chill *noun* 1 an unpleasant feeling of coldness. 2 a mild illness with feverish shivering.
chill *adjective* unpleasantly cold.
chill *verb* 1 to keep food or drink at a low temperature. 2 to make someone feel cold. **to chill out** (*informal*) to relax. [from an Old English word, related to *cold*]

chill factor *noun* the perceived effect on the temperature caused by a cold wind.

chilli *noun* (**chillies**) a dried hot-tasting pod of red pepper used in sauces or as a seasoning. [via Spanish from a Nahuatl (Central American) word]

chilli con carne (kar-ni) *noun* a stew of minced beef and beans flavoured with chillies. [from a Spanish phrase *chile con carne* meaning 'chilli pepper with meat']

chilly *adjective* (**chillier, chilliest**) 1 slightly or unpleasantly cold. SYNONYMS: cold, cool, crisp, fresh, frosty, wintry. (*informal*) nippy. 2 (said about a person or manner) aloof and unfriendly. **chilliness** *noun*

chime *noun* a series of notes sounded by a set of bells or tuned metal bars or tubes.
chimes *plural noun* a set of bells or metal bars or tubes that make musical sounds.
chime *verb* 1 (said about bells) to ring. 2 (said about a clock) to show the hour by chiming. [origin unknown, but probably related to *cymbal*]

chimera (ki-meer-ə) *noun* a creature in Greek mythology with the head of a lion, the body of a goat, and the tail of a serpent. [from a Greek word *khimaira* meaning 'she-goat']

chimney *noun* (**chimneys**) a tall pipe or structure that carries smoke or gases away from a fire. [via French from a Greek word *kaminos* meaning 'oven']

chimney pot *noun* a short piece of pipe fitted to the top of a chimney.

chimney stack *noun* the part of a chimney above the roof, often with a number of chimneys together.

chimney sweep *noun* a person who cleans out soot from inside chimneys.

chimp *noun* (*informal*) a chimpanzee.

chimpanzee *noun* an African ape, smaller than a gorilla. [via French from an African language]

chin *noun* the front part of the lower jaw. [from an Old English word *cin*]

china *noun* 1 fine earthenware porcelain. 2 objects made from this ♦ *household china*. [from a Persian word *chini* meaning 'from China']

chinchilla (chin-chil-ə) *noun* 1 a small South American animal with grey fur and a long bushy tail. 2 the soft grey fur of a chinchilla. 3 a cat or rabbit of a breed with grey fur. [via Spanish from a South American language]

chine *noun* 1 an animal's backbone, or a joint of meat containing part of this. 2 a mountain ridge.
chine *verb* to cut a joint of meat along the backbone. [from an Old French word *eschine*, related to *shin*]

Chinese *adjective* to do with or coming from China.
Chinese *noun* 1 (**Chinese**) a person born in China or descended from people born there. 2 the language of China.

chink[1] *noun* a narrow opening or slit ♦ *The light came in through a chink in the curtains.* [from an Old English word]

chink[2] *verb* to make a sound like glasses or coins being struck together.
chink *noun* this sound. [an imitation of the sound]

chintz *noun* a shiny cotton cloth with a printed pattern, used for making curtains and furnishings. [from a Hindi word *chint* meaning 'stain'; in English the word was originally *chints*, a plural form]

chip *noun* 1 a thin piece cut or broken off something hard. 2 a part of an object where a thin piece has been broken off. 3 a fried oblong strip of potato. 4 (*Amer.*) a potato crisp. 5 a counter used to represent money in gambling games. 6 short for **microchip**.
chip *verb* (**chipped, chipping**) 1 to cut or break something at its surface or edge. 2 to cut potatoes into chips. **a chip off the old block** (*informal*) a child who is very like his or her father. **to chip in** (*informal*) to interrupt a conversation with a remark. 2 (*informal*) to give money to a collection. **to have a chip on your shoulder** to feel bitter or resentful about something. [from an Old English word *forcippian* meaning 'to cut off']

chipboard noun thin board made of wood chips pressed together with resin.

chipmunk noun a small North American animal like a squirrel, with light and dark stripes down its body. [from a Native American language]

chipolata (chipə-lah-tə) noun a small thin sausage. [from an Italian word *cipollata* meaning 'dish of onions', from *cipolla* meaning 'onion']

chippings plural noun small pieces of wood, stone, or other material.

chiropody (ki-rop-ədi) noun medical treatment of the feet. **chiropodist** noun [from a Greek word *kheir* meaning 'hand' and *podos* meaning 'foot' (because chiropody originally involved the hands as well as the feet)]

chiropractic (kiy-rə-prak-tik) noun a form of complementary medicine in which disorders are treated by manipulation of the joints, especially those of the spine, instead of by medicinal drugs or surgery. **chiropractor** noun [from a Greek word *kheir* meaning 'hand' and *prattein* meaning 'to do']

chirp verb to make the short sharp note of a small bird or a grasshopper.
chirp noun this sound. [an imitation of the sound]

chirpy adjective (**chirpier, chirpiest**) lively and cheerful.

chirrup verb (**chirruped, chirruping**) to make a series of chirps.
chirrup noun a series of chirps.

chisel noun a tool with a long blade ending in a bevelled edge, used with a hammer to shape wood, stone, or metal.
chisel verb (**chiselled, chiselling**) to cut or shape something with a chisel. **chiseller** noun [from an Old French word, from a Latin word *caedere* meaning 'to cut']

chit[1] noun an impudent young woman ♦ *a chit of a girl*. [originally a young animal, perhaps from a dialect word *chit* meaning 'sprout']

chit[2] noun a short written note, especially one recording an amount of money spent. [from a Hindi word *citthi* meaning 'note']

chit-chat noun chat or gossip.

chitty noun (**chitties**) (*informal*) same as **chit**[2].

chivalry (shiv-əl-ri) noun courtesy and considerate behaviour, especially towards people who are weaker. **chivalrous**

adjective [originally 'like a perfect knight' (same origin as for *cavalier*)]

chive noun a small herb with leaves tasting like onion. [via Old French from a Latin word *cepa* meaning 'onion']

chivvy verb (**chivvies, chivvied, chivvying**) (*informal*) to keep urging someone to hurry; to harass someone. [probably from *Chevy Chase*, the scene of a skirmish on the Scottish border, which was the subject of an old ballad]

chloral (klor-əl) noun a white crystalline compound used as a sedative or anaesthetic. [from *chlorine* and *alcohol*]

chloride (klor-ryd) noun a compound of chlorine and one other element ♦ *sodium chloride.*

chlorinate (klor-in-ayt) verb to treat or sterilize something with chlorine. **chlorination** noun

chlorine (klor-een) noun a chemical element (symbol Cl), a poisonous gas used in sterilizing water and in industry. [from a Greek word *khlōros* meaning 'green']

chlorofluorocarbon noun see CFC.

chloroform (klo-rə-form) noun a liquid that gives off vapour which causes unconsciousness when breathed in. [from a Greek word *khlōros* meaning 'green' and *formic acid*]

chlorophyll (klo-rə-fil) noun the substance that makes plants green. [from a Greek word *khlōros* meaning 'green' and *phullon* meaning 'leaf']

chloroplast (klo-rə-plast) noun a structure in a plant cell which contains chlorophyll and uses this in photosynthesis. [from a Greek word *khlōros* meaning 'green' and *plastos* meaning 'formed']

chock noun a block or wedge used to prevent something from moving, especially an aeroplane.
chock verb to secure something with a chock or chocks. [from an Old French word]

chock-a-block adjective (*informal*) crammed or crowded together.

chock-full adjective (*informal*) crammed full.

chocolate noun 1 a solid food or powder made from roasted cacao seeds. 2 a drink made by mixing milk or water with chocolate powder. 3 a sweet made of chocolate or covered with chocolate. 4 a dark-brown colour. [via French and Spanish from a Nahuatl (Central American) word *chocolatl*]

choice noun **1** the act of choosing. **2** the right to choose ♦ *Do we have a choice?* **3** a range of things from which to choose ♦ *There is a good choice of meals every day.* **4** a person or thing that has been chosen ♦ *This is my choice.*
choice adjective (said about food) of very high quality. [from Old French, related to *choose*]

choir (kwiy-ər) noun **1** an organized group of singers, especially in a church. **2** the part of the church where these singers sit. [from a Latin word *chorus*]

choirboy or **choirgirl** noun a boy or girl who sings in a church choir.

choke verb **1** to stop someone breathing properly by squeezing or blocking their windpipe. **2** to be unable to breathe properly. **3** to make someone unable to speak from emotion. **4** to clog or smother ♦ *The garden has become choked with weeds.*
choke noun a device controlling the flow of air into a petrol engine. [from an Old English word]

choker noun a close-fitting necklace.

cholera (kol-er-ə) noun an infectious disease that causes severe vomiting and diarrhoea and is often fatal. [from a Greek word *kholē* meaning 'bile']

choleric (kol-er-ik) adjective bad-tempered or irritable.

cholesterol (kəl-**est**-er-ol) noun a fatty substance in body tissue that can harden the arteries. [from Greek words *kholē* meaning 'bile' and *stereos* meaning 'stiff']

choose verb (**chose, chosen**) to take or decide on something or someone from a larger number that is available.
SYNONYMS: pick, adopt, decide on, select, settle on; name; appoint (a person), elect (a person), nominate (a person). **chooser** noun [from an Old English word]

choosy adjective (informal) (**choosier, choosiest**) taking a long time to choose, hard to please.

chop[1] verb (**chopped, chopping**) **1** to cut something with one or more blows with an axe or knife. **2** to hit something or someone with a short downward stroke or blow.
chop noun **1** a heavy cutting stroke with an axe or knife. **2** a chopping blow. **3** a

small thick slice of meat, usually including a rib. [origin unknown]

chop[2] verb (**chopped, chopping**) to chop and change (informal) to keep changing your mind or the way you behave. [from an earlier meaning 'to exchange']

chopper noun **1** a chopping tool or short axe. **2** (informal) a helicopter.

choppy adjective (**choppier, choppiest**) (said about the sea) slightly rough with a lot of short broken waves. **choppiness** noun

chops plural noun the jaws of an animal.

chopsticks plural noun a pair of small thin sticks used to lift Chinese and Japanese food to the mouth. [from a Pidgin English word *chop* meaning 'quick']

chop suey (chop **soo**-i) noun a Chinese dish of small meat pieces fried with vegetables and served with rice. [from a Chinese phrase *tsaap sui* meaning 'mixed bits']

choral (kor-əl) adjective written for a choir or chorus, or sung or spoken by them. **chorally** adverb [same origin as for *chorus*]

chorale (kor-ahl) noun a piece of music for a choir, using the words of a hymn.

chord[1] (kord) noun a group of three or more musical notes sounded together in harmony. [from *accord*]
◊ Do not confuse this word with **cord**, which has a different meaning.

chord[2] (kord) noun a straight line joining two points on a curve. [a different spelling of *cord*]

chore (chor) noun a tedious or routine task. [a different spelling of *char*]

chorea noun a nervous disorder involving involuntary jerky movements. [from a Greek word *khoreia* meaning 'dancing in unison']

choreography (ko-ri-**og**-rəfi) noun an arrangement of the sequence of steps in ballets or stage dances. **choreographer** noun **choreographic** adjective [from a Greek word *khoreia* meaning 'a dance', and *-graphy*]

chorister (ko-ris-ter) noun a member of a choir. [from an Old French word, related to *choir*]

choroid (kor-oid) noun a membrane in the eye between the retina and the iris.

chortle verb to laugh in a gleeful way.

chortle *noun* a chortling sound. [a mixture of *chuckle* and *snort*; invented by Lewis Carroll]

chorus (kor-əs) *noun* 1 a part of a poem or song that is repeated after each of the main parts. 2 a group of singers. 3 a piece of music written for a group of singers. 4 something said by a lot of people at once ♦ *There was a chorus of approval for the idea.* **chorus** *verb* (**choruses, chorused, chorusing**) to sing or speak together. **in chorus** speaking or singing together. [from a Greek word *khoros*]

chose past tense of **choose**.

chosen past participle of **choose**.

chough (chuf) *noun* a crow with a red or yellow bill that turns downward. [origin unknown]

choux pastry (shoo) very light pastry made with eggs. [from a French word *chou* (plural *choux*) meaning 'cabbage' (because of its shape)]

chow *noun* a long-haired Chinese dog. [from Pidgin English *chow chow*]

chowder *noun* a thick soup of fish or clams with vegetables. [perhaps from a French word *chaudière* meaning 'stew pot']

chow mein (mayn) *noun* a Chinese dish of fried noodles with shredded meat and vegetables. [from a Chinese phrase *chao mian* meaning 'fried noodles']

chrism (kri-zəm) *noun* consecrated oil used for anointing in some Christian Churches. [from a Greek word *khrisma* meaning 'anointing']

christen (kri-sən) *verb* 1 to admit someone to a Christian Church by baptism. 2 to give a name to someone or something. [from an Old English word *cristnian* meaning 'to make someone a Christian']

Christendom (kris-ən-dəm) *noun* Christians all over the world.

christening *noun* the ceremony of baptizing someone.

Christian *noun* a person who believes in Christianity or has been baptized in a Christian Church.
Christian *adjective* to do with Christians or their beliefs.

Christian era *noun* the period from the traditional date of Christ's birth.

Christianity *noun* the religion based on the teachings of Jesus Christ.

Christian name *noun* a name given at a christening, a person's given name.

Christian Science *noun* a religious system claiming that health and healing can be achieved through faith and prayer. **Christian Scientist** *noun*

Christmas *noun* (**Christmases**) 1 a Christian festival held on 25 December, commemorating Christ's birth. 2 the period just before and after this. [from *Christ* and *Mass*]

Christmas box *noun* a present given at Christmas to tradespeople.

Christmas cake *noun* a rich fruitcake covered in marzipan and icing, eaten at Christmas.

Christmas Day *noun* 25 December.

Christmas Eve *noun* the day before Christmas, 24 December.

Christmas pudding *noun* a rich dark pudding containing dried fruit, eaten at Christmas.

Christmas tree *noun* an evergreen or artificial tree decorated with lights and baubles at Christmas.

Christmassy *adjective* looking festive, like Christmas.

chromatic (krə-mat-ik) *adjective* to do with colour. [from a Greek word *khrōma* meaning 'colour']

chromatic scale *noun* (*Music*) a scale that goes up or down in semitones.

chromatin (kroh-mə-tin) *noun* (*Biology*) chromosome material in the nucleus of a cell that can be stained easily, so that it is clearly visible under a microscope.

chromatography (kroh-mə-tog-rə-fi) *noun* (*Chemistry*) separation of a mixture into the substances that make it up by passing it over material which absorbs the substances at different rates so that they appear as layers, often of different colours. **chromatographic** *adjective*

chrome (krohm) *noun* 1 chromium. 2 a yellow colouring matter obtained from a compound of chromium. [from a Greek word *khrōma* meaning 'colour' (because its compounds have brilliant colours)]

chromium (kroh-mi-əm) *noun* a hard shiny metal used in making stainless steel and for coating other metals, a chemical element (symbol Cr). [from *chrome*]

chromosome (kroh-mə-sohm) *noun* a tiny thread-like part of an animal or plant cell, carrying genes. [from Greek words *khrōma* meaning 'colour' and *sōma* meaning 'body']

chronic *adjective* 1 (said about a disease) affecting a person for a long time. 2 (said about a person) having had an illness or a habit for a long time ♦ *a chronic invalid.* **chronically** *adverb* [from a Greek word *khronikos* meaning 'of time']

chronicle (kron-ikəl) *noun* a record of important events in the order in which they happened.
chronicle *verb* to record events in a chronicle. **chronicler** *noun* [same origin as for *chronic*]

chronological (kron-ə-loj-ikəl) *adjective* arranged in the order in which things occurred. **chronologically** *adverb*

chronology (krən-ol-əji) *noun* (**chronologies**) 1 the study of the records of past events to decide when they occurred. 2 the arrangement of events in the order in which they occurred. [from a Greek word *khronos* meaning 'time', and *-logy*]

chronometer (krən-om-it-er) *noun* a device for measuring time exactly. [from a Greek word *khronos* meaning 'time', and *meter*]

chrysalis (kris-ə-lis) *noun* (**chrysalises**) an insect at a stage when it forms a sheath inside which it changes from a grub to an adult insect, especially a butterfly or moth. [from a Greek word *khrusos* meaning 'gold' (the colour of its covering)]

chrysanthemum *noun* a garden plant with bright flowers, blooming in autumn. [from Greek words *khrusos* meaning 'gold' and *anthemon* meaning 'flower']

chub *noun* (**chub**) a river fish with a thick body. [origin unknown]

chubby *adjective* (**chubbier, chubbiest**) round and plump. SYNONYMS: plump, podgy, dumpy, tubby. **chubbiness** *noun* [from *chub*]

chuck [1] *verb* 1 (*informal*) to throw something carelessly or casually. 2 to touch someone playfully under the chin. **chuck** *noun* a playful touch. **to chuck something in** (*informal*) to stop an activity suddenly. **to chuck someone out** (*informal*) to expel or get rid of someone. **to chuck something out** (*informal*) to throw

something away. [probably from a French word *chuquer* meaning 'to knock or bump']

chuck [2] *noun* 1 the part of a lathe that grips the drill, or the part of a drill that holds the bit. 2 a cut of beef from the neck to the ribs. [a different spelling of *chock*]

chuckle *noun* a quiet or suppressed laugh. **chuckle** *verb* to laugh quietly. [from an old word *chuck* meaning 'to cluck']

chuddar *noun* another spelling of **chador**.

chuffed *adjective* (*informal*) pleased.

chug *verb* (**chugged, chugging**) to make a repeated muffled explosive sound, like an engine running slowly. **chug** *noun* a sound of this kind. [an imitation of the sound]

chukka *noun* a period of play in polo. [from a Hindi word *cakkar*, from a Sanskrit word meaning 'circle' or 'wheel']

chum *noun* (*informal, old use*) a close friend. [short for *chamber fellow* meaning 'a person who shares a room']

chump *noun* (*informal*) a foolish person. [a mixture of *chunk* and *lump*]

chump chop *noun* a chop from the thick end of a loin of mutton.

chunk *noun* 1 a thick solid piece of something. 2 a large amount. [a different spelling of *chuck*[2]]

chunky *adjective* (**chunkier, chunkiest**) 1 short and thick. 2 in chunks, or containing chunks.

church *noun* 1 a building used for public worship by Christians. 2 a religious service in a church ♦ *I will see you after church.*
Church *noun* a Christian organization having its own doctrines and forms of worship. [from a Greek word *kuriakon* meaning 'belonging to the Lord']

churchman or **churchwoman** *noun* (**churchmen** or **churchwomen**) a member of the Christian clergy.

Church of England *noun* the English branch of the Western Christian Church, rejecting the pope's supremacy and having the monarch at its head.

Church of Scotland *noun* the national (Presbyterian) Church of Scotland.

churchwarden *noun* a representative of a parish who helps with the business of the church.

churchyard *noun* the ground round a church, often used as a graveyard.

churlish *adjective* ill-mannered and unfriendly, surly. **churlishly** *adverb* **churlishness** *noun* [from an old word *churl* meaning 'an impolite person' (originally, 'a peasant')]

churn *noun* 1 a large can in which milk is carried from a farm. 2 a machine in which milk is beaten to make butter.
churn *verb* 1 to make butter from milk in a churn. 2 to stir or swirl something vigorously. **to churn something out** to produce something in large numbers. **to churn something up** to break up the surface of something. [from an Old English word]

chute (shoot) *noun* 1 a steep channel for people or things to slide down. 2 (*informal*) a parachute. [from a French word meaning 'a fall']

chutney *noun* (**chutneys**) a strong-flavoured mixture of fruit, peppers, vinegar, and spices, eaten with meat or cheese. [from a Hindi word *catni*]

CIA *abbreviation* (in the USA) Central Intelligence Agency.

cicada (sik-**ah**-də) *noun* an insect like a grasshopper, which makes a shrill chirping sound. [from a Latin word *cicada*]

CID *abbreviation* (in Britain) Criminal Investigation Department.

cider *noun* an alcoholic drink made from apples. [via Old French and Latin from a Hebrew word *shekar* meaning 'strong drink']

cigar *noun* a roll of tobacco leaves for smoking. [from a Spanish word *cigarro*]

cigarette *noun* a roll of shredded tobacco in thin paper for smoking. [a French word meaning 'little cigar']

ciliary muscle (sil-eer-i) *noun* (*Anatomy*) a muscle controlling the shape of the lens of the eye.

cilium (sil-i-əm) *noun* (**cilia**) 1 each of the minute hairs fringing a leaf, an insect's wing, etc. 2 a hair-like vibrating organ on animal or vegetable tissue. **ciliary** *adjective* [a Latin word meaning 'eyelash']

cinch (sinch) *noun* (*informal*) something that is easy to do or certain to happen. [from a Spanish word *cincha* meaning 'girth']

cinder *noun* a small piece of partly burnt coal or wood. [from an Old English word *sinder* meaning 'slag']

cine-camera (sin-i) *noun* a camera used for taking moving pictures. [same origin as for *cinema*]

cinema *noun* 1 a theatre where films are shown. 2 making films as an art-form or an industry. **cinematic** *adjective* [from a Greek word *kinēma* meaning 'movement']

cinematographic (sini-matə-graf-ik) *adjective* used for taking or projecting cinema films.

cinematography (sini-mə-tog-rəfi) *noun* the art of making motion-picture films. [from *cinema* and *-graphy*]

cinnabar (sin-ə-bar) *noun* 1 a bright red mineral consisting of mercury sulphide. 2 a moth with black and red wings. [from a Latin word *cinnabaris*]

cinnamon (sin-a-mən) *noun* a yellowish-brown spice made from the inner bark of a south-east Asian tree. [from a Greek word *kinnamōmon*]

cipher (siy-fer) *noun* 1 the symbol 0, representing nought or zero. 2 a set of letters or symbols used as a code. 3 a person or thing of no importance. [from an Arabic word *sifr* meaning 'nought']

circa (ser-kə) *preposition* (used with dates) about, approximately ♦ *circa 1050*. [a Latin word meaning 'about']

circadian (ser-kay-diən) *adjective* occurring about once in a day. [from *circa* and a Latin word *dies* meaning 'day']

circle *noun* 1 a perfectly round flat figure or shape. 2 the line enclosing it, every point on which is the same distance from the centre. 3 something shaped like a circle, a ring. 4 a series of curved rows of seats above the lowest level in a theatre or cinema. 5 a number of people associated by similar interests ♦ *artistic circles*.
circle *verb* 1 to move in a circle. 2 to form a circle round something. [from a Latin word *circulus* meaning 'small ring']

circlet (ser-klit) *noun* a circular band worn as an ornament on the head.

circuit (ser-kit) *noun* 1 a line, route, or distance that goes in a circle round a place. 2 a track for motor racing. 3 a path for an electric current, or an apparatus through which an electric current passes. 4 a regular journey made by a judge round a particular district to hold courts. 5 a group of Methodist Churches in a district. **6** a series of sporting events ♦ *the American golf circuit.* **7** a chain of theatres or cinemas. [from Latin words *circum* meaning 'round' and *itum* meaning 'gone']

circuit-breaker *noun* a safety device for stopping an electric current in a circuit.

circuitous (ser-kew-it-əs) *adjective* (said about a route) longer than the usual way, indirect. **circuitously** *adverb*

circuitry (ser-kit-ri) *noun* electrical circuits, or the equipment forming them.

circular *adjective* **1** shaped like a circle, round. **2** moving round a circle, ending at the point at which it began ♦ *a circular tour.* **3** (in logic and reasoning) using the conclusion it is trying to prove as evidence in the reasoning process. **4** (said about a letter or advertisement) addressed or sent to a large number of people.
circular *noun* a circular letter or advertisement. **circularity** (ser-kew-la-riti) *noun*

circularize *verb* to send letters or leaflets to a large number of people.

circulate *verb* **1** to go round continuously ♦ *Blood circulates in the body.* **2** to pass from place to place. **3** to mix with people at a party and talk to them. **4** to give or send something to a large number of people ♦ *We will circulate your letter.*

circulation *noun* **1** movement that goes round something, the act of circulating. **2** the movement of blood round the body, pumped by the heart. **3** the number of copies of a newspaper or magazine that are sold or distributed.

circulatory (ser-kew-layt-er-i) *adjective* to do with the circulation of blood.

circum- *prefix* around (as in *circumference*). [from a Latin word *circum* meaning 'around']

circumcise *verb* **1** to cut off the foreskin of a man or boy, as a ritual among Jews and Muslims or for medical reasons. **2** to cut off the clitoris and sometimes the labia of a girl or young woman as a ritual in some societies. **circumcision** *noun* [from *circum*- and a Latin word *caedere* meaning 'to cut']

circumference (ser-kum-fer-əns) *noun* **1** the line round a circle. **2** the distance round something. [from *circum*- and a Latin word *ferens* meaning 'carrying']

circumflex accent (ser-kəm-fleks) *noun* a mark put over a vowel in some languages, e.g. *e* in *fête*.

circumlocution (ser-kəm-lə-kew-shən) *noun* **1** a roundabout expression, using many words where a few would do, e.g. *at this moment in time* instead of *now*. **2** evasive talk.

circumnavigate *verb* to sail completely round something. **circumnavigation** *noun*

circumscribe *verb* **1** to draw a line round something. **2** to limit or restrict an activity. **circumscription** *noun* [from *circum*- and a Latin word *scribere* meaning 'to write']

circumspect (ser-kəm-spekt) *adjective* cautious and watchful, wary. **circumspection** *noun* [from *circum*- and a Latin word *specere* meaning 'to look']

circumstance *noun* a condition or fact that is connected with an event, person, or action or influences it.
circumstances *plural noun* the conditions of a person's life, and how much money they have. [from *circum*- and a Latin word *stans* meaning 'standing']

circumstantial (ser-kəm-stan-shəl) *adjective* **1** (said about evidence) consisting of facts that strongly suggest something but do not directly prove it. **2** giving full details. **circumstantially** *adverb*

circumvent (ser-kəm-vent) *verb* to find a way round a difficulty ♦ *In the end we managed to circumvent the rules.* **circumvention** *noun* [from *circum*- and a Latin word *ventum* meaning 'to come']

circus *noun* **1** a travelling show usually performed in a tent, with clowns, acrobats, and sometimes trained animals. **2** (*informal*) a scene of lively or noisy activity. **3** (in place names) an open space in a town, where several streets meet ♦ *Piccadilly Circus.* **4** (in ancient Rome) a round or oval arena used for chariot races and other sports. [a Latin word meaning 'ring']

cirque (serk) *noun* (*Geology*) a bowl-shaped hollow with steep sides on a mountain. [a French word, related to *circus*]

cirrhosis (si-roh-sis) *noun* a chronic disease in which the liver hardens. [from a Greek word *kirrhos* meaning 'tawny' (the colour the liver often becomes)]

cirrus (si-rus) *noun* (**cirri**) cloud made up of light wispy streaks. [a Latin word meaning 'a curl']

CIS Commonwealth of Independent States, a group of countries most of which were republics of the former USSR.

cissy *noun* another spelling of **sissy**.

cistern (sis-tern) *noun* a tank or other container for storing water, especially as part of a flushing toilet. [from a Latin word *cisterna*]

citadel (sit-ə-dəl) *noun* 1 a fortress protecting or overlooking a city. 2 a meeting hall of the Salvation Army. [from an Italian word *cittadella*]

cite *verb* 1 to quote or mention an author or piece of writing as an example or in support of an argument. 2 to praise someone for their courage in an official military dispatch. **citation** *noun* [from a Latin word *citare* meaning 'to call']

citizen *noun* 1 a person who has full rights in a country or commonwealth by birth or by naturalization. 2 a person who lives in a particular city or town. **citizenry** *noun* **citizenship** *noun* [same origin as for *city*]

Citizens' Band *noun* a range of special radio frequencies which people can use to speak to one another over short distances.

citric acid (sit-rik) *noun* the sharp-tasting acid in the juice of lemons, limes, etc. [same origin as for *citrus*]

citrus (sit-rəs) *noun* any of a group of related trees including lemon, orange, and grapefruit. [a Latin word]

citrus fruit *noun* the fruit of a citrus tree.

city *noun* (**cities**) a large and important town, usually with special rights given by charter and usually containing a cathedral. [from a Latin word *civitas* meaning 'city']

cityscape *noun* a city landscape.

City Technology College *noun* (in Britain) a secondary school in a city, specializing in technology and science.

civet (siv-it) *noun* 1 a cat-like wild animal of central Africa. 2 a strong musky substance obtained from its glands, used in making perfumes. [via French from an Arabic word *zabad*]

civic (siv-ik) *adjective* to do with or belonging to a city or town, or to do with the citizens of a town.

civics *plural noun* the study of the rights and duties of citizens. [from a Latin word *civis* meaning 'citizen']

civic centre *noun* an area containing municipal offices and other public buildings.

civil *adjective* 1 polite and helpful. 2 to do with or belonging to citizens. 3 to do with civilians and not the armed forces or the Church ♦ *civil aviation* ♦ *a civil marriage*. 4 involving civil law and not criminal law ♦ *a civil dispute*. **civilly** *adverb* [from a Latin word *civilis*, related to *civic*]

civil defence *noun* the protection and organization of civilians in wartime or after a natural disaster.

civil disobedience *noun* a form of peaceful protest in which people refuse to obey certain laws or to pay taxes.

civil engineer *noun* an engineer who designs and builds roads, bridges, canals, and other public works. **civil engineering** *noun*

civilian *noun* an ordinary citizen, a person who is not serving in the armed forces.

civility *noun* (**civilities**) politeness, or an act of politeness.

civilization *noun* 1 the process of becoming civilized or making people civilized. 2 a stage in the development of human society, especially at an advanced stage ♦ *ancient civilizations*. 3 civilized conditions or social activity ♦ *far from civilization*.

civilize *verb* 1 to bring a primitive society to a more advanced stage of development. 2 to improve the behaviour of a person.

civilized *adjective* having good tastes and manners.

civil law *noun* law dealing with the private rights of citizens, not with criminal acts.

civil liberties *plural noun* a person's rights to freedom of speech and action subject to the laws that protect the community.

Civil List *noun* an allowance of money made by Parliament each year for the royal family's household expenses.

civil rights *plural noun* the rights of a citizen.

civil servant *noun* someone who works in the civil service.

civil service *noun* people employed by the government to run the state's affairs, other than the police and the armed forces.

civil war *noun* war between groups of citizens of the same country.

civvies (**siv-iz**) *plural noun* (*informal*) civilian clothes, as distinct from official uniform.

CJD *abbreviation* Creutzfeldt–Jakob disease.

cl *abbreviation* centilitre(s).

clack *verb* to make a short sharp sound like plates being struck together.
clack *noun* a sound of clacking. [an imitation of the sound]

clad *adjective* 1 clothed ♦ *He arrived clad in a heavy business suit.* 2 covered in cladding. [an old past tense of *clothe*]

cladding *noun* a metal or other material covering the surface of something to protect it.

cladistics *noun* (*Biology*) the study of the relationship of groups of living things by analysing their common features and their development from a common ancestor. [from a Greek word *klados* meaning 'a branch']

claim *verb* 1 to state that something is true or has happened, without being able to prove it. SYNONYMS: declare, assert, maintain, contend, profess, insist. 2 to request something as a right or debt. SYNONYMS: request, ask for, demand. 3 to cause people to die ♦ *The earthquake claimed over a thousand lives.*
claim *noun* 1 a statement claiming that something is true, an assertion. 2 a request for something as a right. 3 the right to something ♦ *A widow has a claim on her dead husband's estate.* 4 something that a person claims, especially land. [same origin as for *clamour*]

claimant *noun* a person who makes a claim, especially in law.

clairvoyant (klair-**voy**-ənt) *noun* a person who claims to have the power of knowing about future events or about things that are out of sight. **clairvoyance** *noun* [from French words *clair* meaning 'clear' and *voyant* meaning 'seeing']

clam *noun* a large shellfish with a hinged shell.
clam *verb* (**clammed, clamming**) **clam up** (*informal*) to refuse to talk. [from an Old English word *clam* meaning 'something that grips tightly', related to *clamp*]

clamber *verb* to climb slowly and with difficulty. [from *clamb*, an old past tense of *climb*]

clammy *adjective* (**clammier, clammiest**) unpleasantly damp and sticky. **clammily** *adverb* **clamminess** *noun* [from an Old English word *clæman* meaning 'to smear or make sticky']

clamorous *adjective* making a loud clamour or noise.

clamour *noun* 1 a loud confused noise, especially of shouting. 2 a loud protest or demand.
clamour *verb* to make a loud protest or demand. [from a Latin word *clamare* meaning 'to call out']

clamp *noun* a device for holding things tightly.
clamp *verb* to grip or fix something with a clamp. **to clamp down on** to become stricter about something or put a stop to it. [from an early Dutch or German word, related to *clam*]

clan *noun* 1 a group of related families, especially in the Scottish Highlands. 2 a large family forming a close group. [from a Gaelic word *clann* meaning 'offspring' or 'family']

clandestine (klan-**dest**-in) *adjective* done secretly, kept secret. **clandestinely** *adverb* [from a Latin word *clandestinus*, from *clam* meaning 'secretly']

clang *verb* to make a loud ringing sound.
clang *noun* a clanging sound. [an imitation of the sound]

clanger *noun* (*informal*) a bad or obvious mistake.

clangour (**klang**-er) *noun* a continuous clanging noise.

clank *verb* to make a dull metallic sound like pieces of metal banging together.
clank *noun* a clanking sound. [an imitation of the sound]

clannish *adjective* (said about a group of people) tending to cling together like a clan and exclude others.

clansman *noun* (**clansmen**) a male member of a clan.

clap *verb* (**clapped, clapping**) 1 to strike the palms of the hands together repeatedly, especially as applause. SYNONYMS: applaud, cheer. 2 (said about a bird) to flap its wings audibly. 3 to slap someone in a friendly way. 4 to impose a penalty abruptly on someone ♦ *The magistrate clapped a heavy* *fine on him for speeding.*

clap *noun* 1 the sudden sharp noise of thunder. 2 the sound of a person clapping; applause. 3 a friendly slap ♦ *Jem gave him a clap on the shoulder.* **to clap someone in jail** (*informal*) to put someone in prison. [from an Old English word *clappan* meaning 'to throb' or 'to beat']

clapped out *adjective* (*informal*) worn out, exhausted.

clapper *noun* the part of a bell (called the *tongue* or *striker*) that hits the side of the bell to make a sound.

claptrap *noun* nonsense. [from *clap* (because it originally meant 'something said to win applause')]

claret (kla-rət) *noun* a dry red wine from Bordeaux in France. [from the French phrase *vin claret* meaning 'clear wine', from a Latin word *clarus* meaning 'clear']

clarify *verb* (**clarifies, clarified, clarifying**) 1 to make something clear or easier to understand, or to become easier to understand. 2 to remove impurities from fats, especially by heating. **clarification** *noun* [from a Latin word *clarus* meaning 'clear']

clarinet (kla-rin-et) *noun* a woodwind musical instrument with finger-holes and keys. [from a French word *clarine* meaning 'a kind of bell']

clarinettist *noun* a person who plays the clarinet.

clarion (kla-ri-ən) *noun* an old type of trumpet. [same origin as for *clarify*]

clarity *noun* being clear to see or understand. [same origin as for *clarify*]

clash *verb* 1 (said about two groups of people) to come together and attack or fight one another. 2 to disagree or quarrel. 3 to strike cymbals together to make a loud harsh sound. 4 to happen inconveniently at the same time as something else ♦ *Tomorrow's party clashes with my birthday.* 5 (said about colours) to look unpleasant together. **clash** *noun* 1 a sound of clashing. 2 a disagreement or quarrel. 3 a clashing of colours. [an imitation of the sound]

clasp *noun* 1 a device for fastening things, with parts that lock together. 2 a grasp or handshake. **clasp** *verb* 1 to fasten something or join it with a clasp. 2 to grasp something or someone; to hold or embrace them closely. [origin unknown]

class *noun* 1 a set of children or students taught together, or a session when they are taught. 2 a group or set of similar people, animals, or things. SYNONYMS: category, type, set, group, grade, sort, kind. 3 people of a particular social or economic level ♦ *the middle class.* 4 a level of service or quality ♦ *first class* ♦ *tourist class.* 5 distinction or high quality ♦ *a tennis player with class.* **class** *verb* to place something in a class or category, to classify things. [from a Latin word *classis* meaning 'a social division']

classic *adjective* 1 generally recognized as important or outstanding ♦ *a classic novel.* 2 noticeably typical ♦ *the classic symptoms of cholera.* 3 simple and elegant in style ♦ *classic clothes.* **classic** *noun* 1 a book or work of art of outstanding value or importance. **classics** *plural noun* the study of ancient Greek and Roman literature and history. [from a Latin word *classicus* meaning 'of the highest class']

classical *adjective* 1 to do with ancient Greek and Roman art, literature, and culture. 2 simple and harmonious in style. 3 serious or conventional in form or style ♦ *classical music.* **classically** *adverb*

classicism *noun* following the ancient Greek and Roman principles of art and literature.

classicist *noun* someone who studies ancient Greek and Roman literature and history.

classification *noun* 1 the process of classifying things. 2 a category in which something is put. [via French from a Latin word *classis* meaning 'category']

classified *adjective* 1 (said about advertisements) arranged according to subject matter. 2 (said about information) officially secret and available only to specified people.

classify *verb* (**classifies, classified, classifying**) to arrange things systematically in classes or groups, or to put a single thing into a particular class. **classifiable** *adjective* [from *classification*]

classless *adjective* not divided into social classes.

classroom *noun* a room where a class of pupils or students is taught.

classy *adjective* (**classier, classiest**) (*informal*) stylish or superior. **classily** *adverb* **classiness** *noun*

clastic *adjective* (*Geology*) (said about rocks) formed from broken pieces of older rocks. [from a Greek word *klastos* meaning 'broken in pieces']

clatter *verb* to make a sound like hard objects rattling together.
clatter *noun* a clattering noise. [an imitation of the sound]

clause *noun* 1 a single part in a treaty, law, or contract. 2 (*Grammar*) a part of a sentence, with its own verb. There are two clauses in the sentence *We met the person who is going to be our leader.* [from a Latin word *claudere* meaning 'to shut or close']

claustrophobia (klaw-strə-foh-biə) *noun* abnormal fear of being in an enclosed space. **claustrophobic** *adjective* [from a Latin word *claustrum* meaning 'enclosed space' and *phobia*]

clavichord (klav-i-kord) *noun* a rectangular keyboard instrument with a very soft tone. [from Latin words *clavis* meaning 'key' and *chorda* meaning 'string']

clavicle (klav-ikəl) *noun* a technical term for the collarbone. [from a Latin word *clavicula* meaning 'little key' (because the bone has this shape)]

clavier (klav-i-er) *noun* a musical instrument played from a keyboard. [from a Latin word *clavis* meaning 'key']

claw *noun* 1 a sharp or pointed nail on an animal's or bird's foot. 2 the pincers of a lobster or other shellfish. 3 a device like a claw, used for grappling and holding things.
claw *verb* to grasp, pull, or scratch something with a claw or with the hands. [from an Old English word]

clay *noun* stiff sticky earth that becomes hard when baked, used for making bricks and pottery. **clayey** *adjective* [from an Old English word]

claymore *noun* a two-edged broadsword once used in Scotland. [from Gaelic words meaning 'great sword']

clay pigeon *noun* a disc of baked clay or other breakable material thrown up as a target for shooting.

-cle *suffix* forming nouns that were once diminutives (as in *article*). [from a Latin ending *-culus*]

clean *adjective* 1 without any dirt or impurities, not soiled. SYNONYMS: pure, washed, scrubbed, spotless. 2 fresh, not yet used. 3 morally pure, not indecent. 4 honourable and keeping to the rules ♦ *a clean fight.* 5 without projections or roughness, smooth and even. 6 (said about a catch in a game) done skilfully without any fumbling. 7 (said about a nuclear weapon) producing relatively little fallout. 8 (said about a driving licence) not having any endorsements.
clean *adverb* completely or entirely ♦ *I clean forgot their wedding anniversary.*
clean *verb* to make something clean. SYNONYMS: cleanse, wash.
clean *noun* an act of cleaning ♦ *I'll give the table a clean.* **to make a clean breast of** to own up about something. **cleanly** *adverb* **cleanness** *noun* [from an Old English word]

clean-cut *adjective* (usually said about a person's features) having a sharp outline.

cleaner *noun* 1 a person who cleans the rooms of a house or office. 2 something used for cleaning things.
cleaners *noun* a shop where clothes and fabrics are dry-cleaned.

cleanliness (klen-li-nəs) *noun* being clean, having clean habits.

cleanse (klenz) *verb* to make something thoroughly clean. **cleanser** *noun* something used for cleansing. [from an Old English word, related to *clean*]

clean-shaven *adjective* (said about a man) with the face and chin fully shaved.

clear *adjective* 1 transparent, not muddy or cloudy ♦ *clear glass* ♦ *clear water.* SYNONYMS: transparent, translucent, see-through, clean, colourless, pure. 2 easy to see or hear or understand. SYNONYMS: lucid, plain, simple, coherent, understandable, comprehensible, intelligible. 3 free from obstructions or from anything unwanted ♦ *At this time of the morning the streets are clear of traffic.* SYNONYMS: free, unobstructed. 4 not feeling guilt or regret ♦ *I have a clear conscience.* 5 evident or obvious ♦ *It was a clear case of cheating.* SYNONYMS: obvious, plain, definite, apparent, evident, palpable. 6 not having any doubt, not confused ♦ *Are you clear about what you have to do?* SYNONYMS: sure, certain, confident. 7 complete, without deductions ♦ *You have to give three clear days' notice* ♦ *We made a clear £1000.* 8 not touching something ♦ *One wheel was clear of the ground.*

clear *adverb* **1** clearly or distinctly ♦ *We can hear you loud and clear.* **2** completely ♦ *They got clear away.* **3** apart, not in contact ♦ *Stand clear of the doors!*

clear *verb* **1** to make something clear, or to become clear. **2** to get past or over an obstacle without touching it. **3** to get approval or authorization for something ♦ *We'll have to clear the goods through customs.* **4** to pass a cheque through a clearing house. **5** to make an amount of money as a net gain or profit. **to clear your throat** to free your throat of phlegm or huskiness by a slight cough. **to clear up** (said about the weather) to become fine or bright after rain or a storm. **to clear something up 1** to tidy something or remove a mess. **2** to explain or solve something ♦ *Can you clear up the mystery?* **in the clear** free of suspicion or difficulty. **clearly** *adverb* **clearness** *noun* [from a Latin word *clarus*]

clearance *noun* **1** the act of clearing something. **2** permission or authorization. **3** the space left clear when one object moves past another.

clear-cut *adjective* easy to see or understand, very distinct.

clearing *noun* an open space in a forest.

clearing bank *noun* a bank which is a member of a clearing house.

clearing house *noun* **1** an office at which banks exchange cheques and settle the balances. **2** an agency that collects and distributes information.

clearway *noun* (in Britain) a main road other than a motorway on which vehicles must not stop on the carriageway.

cleat *noun* **1** a short piece of wood or metal with projecting ends for fastening a rope. **2** one of several small studs on the sole of a boot or shoe, to make it grip better. **3** a wedge on a spar or tool to prevent it slipping. [from an old Germanic word, related to *clot*]

cleavage *noun* **1** the hollow between a woman's breasts. **2** a split or division made by cleaving.

cleave [1] *verb* (past tense, **clove**, **cleaved**, or **cleft**; past participle, **cloven**, **cleaved**, or **cleft**) **1** to split something or divide it by chopping, or to become split. **2** to make a way through something ♦ *We saw a bird cleave the clear water.* [from an Old English word *cleofan*]

cleave [2] *verb* (past tense and past participle **cleaved**) (*old use*) to cling to something. [from an Old English word *clifian*]

cleaver *noun* a tool with a large broad blade, for chopping meat.

clef *noun* (*Music*) a symbol on a stave, showing the pitch of the notes (e.g. treble or bass). [a French word meaning 'key']

cleft past tense and past participle of **cleave** [1].
cleft *adjective* split or partly divided.
cleft *noun* a split in something. **in a cleft stick** in an awkward situation.

cleft palate *noun* a defect in the roof of the mouth where two sides of the palate failed to join before birth.

clematis (**klem-ə-tiss** or **klim-ay-tiss**) *noun* a climbing plant with white, pink, or purple flowers. [from a Greek word *klēma* meaning 'vine branch']

clemency (**klem-ən-si**) *noun* gentleness or mildness, mercy. [from a Latin word *clementia*]

clement *adjective* (often said about the weather) mild and pleasant.

clementine (**klem-ən-tiyn**) *noun* a deep-coloured citrus fruit like a small orange. [from a French word *clémentine*, from the male name *Clément*]

clench *verb* **1** to close the teeth or fingers tightly. **2** to grasp something tightly. **3** to fasten a nail or rivet by hammering the point sideways after it is driven through. **clench** *noun* a clenching action, or a clenched state. [from an Old English word]

clerestory (**kleer-stor-i**) *noun* (**clerestories**) the upper part of the main body of a large church, with a row of windows admitting light to the nave. [from *clear storey*]

clergy *noun* (**clergies**) the people who have been ordained as priests or ministers of the Christian Church. [same origin as for *clerical*]

clergyman *noun* (**clergymen**) a man who is a member of the Christian clergy.

cleric (**kle-rik**) *noun* a member of the clergy.

clerical *adjective* **1** to do with the routine office work done by clerks. **2** to do with the clergy. [from a Greek word *klērikos* meaning 'belonging to the Christian clergy']

clerk (**klark**) *noun* **1** a person who keeps records or accounts in an office. **2** an official who keeps the records of a court or council etc. [same origin as for *clerical*; *clerk* originally meant a Christian minister]

clever *adjective* 1 quick at learning and understanding. SYNONYMS: bright, smart, intelligent, capable, able; (*informal*) brainy. 2 showing intelligent thought or skill ♦ *It's a clever idea.* SYNONYMS: shrewd, ingenious, cunning. **cleverly** *adverb* **cleverness** *noun* [origin unknown]

cliché (klee-shay) *noun* a phrase or idea that is used so often that it has little meaning. [a French word meaning 'stereotyped']

click *noun* a short sharp sound like two plastic objects coming abruptly into contact.
click *verb* 1 to make a click, or cause something to make a click. 2 to fasten something with a click. 3 (*Computing*) to press a button on a mouse in order to perform a task. 4 (*informal*) to become friendly, to get on well together. 5 (*informal*) to become understood. **clicky** *adjective* [an imitation of the sound]

client *noun* 1 a person who uses the services of a lawyer or architect or other professional or organization. 2 a customer of a shop or bank. 3 (*Computing*) a computer or workstation that gets information from a server in a network. [from a Latin word *cliens* meaning 'a person who listens']

clientele (klee-on-tel) *noun* the clients of a person or business, or the customers of a shop. [from a French word, related to *client*]

cliff *noun* a steep rock face, especially on a coast. [from an Old English word *clif*]

cliffhanger *noun* a tense and exciting ending to an episode of a story, leaving the audience anxious to know what happens next.

climacteric (kliy-mak-ter-ik) *noun* the period of a person's life when their physical powers begin to decline. [same origin as for *climax*]

climactic (kliy-mak-tik) *adjective* exciting, forming a climax.

climate *noun* 1 the regular weather conditions of an area. 2 an area with certain weather conditions ♦ *We enjoyed living in a warm climate.* 3 a general attitude or feeling ♦ *a climate of hostility.* **climatic** (kliy-mat-ik) *adjective* [via French from a Greek word *klima* meaning 'zone or region']

climax *noun* 1 the event or point in a series of events that reaches the greatest interest or excitement. 2 (in ecology) the point at which a community of plants has reached its fully developed form and reproduces itself without further change. **climax** *verb* to reach a climax, or bring something to a climax. [from a Greek word *klimax* meaning 'ladder']

climb *verb* 1 to go up or over something with an effort. 2 to move upwards or go higher. 3 (said about a plant) to grow up a wall or other support ♦ *a climbing rose.* **climb** *noun* climbing or going upwards. **to climb down** 1 to go down something with an effort. 2 to change your mind about something important and admit that you have been wrong. [from an Old English word]

climbdown *noun* (*informal*) an admission that you have been wrong about something important.

climber *noun* 1 a person who climbs, a mountaineer. 2 a climbing plant.

clime *noun* (*literary*) a region thought of in terms of its climate ♦ *We are off to sunnier climes.*

clinch *verb* 1 to settle something definitely ♦ *Their new offer clinched the deal.* 2 to fasten something securely. 3 to fight or grapple at close quarters. **clinch** *noun* 1 a fight at close quarters. 2 an embrace. [different spelling of *clench*]

cling *verb* (past tense and past participle **clung**) 1 to hold on tightly to something. 2 to become attached to something, to stick to something. 3 to be emotionally dependent on someone ♦ *She was a young child and continued to cling to her mother.* 4 to continue to believe in or hope for something ♦ *People often cling to their childhood ambitions.* [from an Old English word *clingan* meaning 'to stick together']

cling film *noun* a thin clinging plastic film used as a wrapping or covering for food.

clinic *noun* 1 a place where patients can get specialized medical treatment or advice. 2 a session at which a hospital doctor sees patients. [from a Greek phrase *klinikē tekhnē* meaning 'bedside art']

clinical *adjective* 1 relating to the treatment of patients ♦ *clinical medicine.* 2 used for treating patients ♦ *a clinical thermometer.* 3 based on observed signs and symptoms ♦ *clinical death.* 4 (said about a place) looking bare and hygienic. 5 (said about a person or behaviour) unemotional, cool and detached. **clinically** adverb

clink[1] verb to make a thin sharp sound like glasses striking together.
clink noun a clinking sound. [an imitation of the sound]

clink[2] noun (informal) prison ♦ in clink. [originally the name of a prison in Southwark, London]

clinker noun rough stony material left after coal has burnt, or a piece of this. [from a Dutch word klinken meaning 'to clink']

clip[1] noun 1 a fastener for holding things together, usually worked by a spring. 2 a piece of jewellery fastened by a clip. 3 a holder containing cartridges for an automatic weapon.
clip verb (**clipped, clipping**) to fix or fasten something with a clip. [from an Old English word clyppan meaning 'to hold']

clip[2] verb (**clipped, clipping**) 1 to cut or trim something with scissors or shears. 2 to punch a small piece from a ticket to show that it has been used. 3 (informal) to hit someone sharply.
clip noun 1 a short piece shown from a cinema or television film. 2 the act or process of clipping something, or a piece clipped off. 3 the wool cut from a sheep or flock at one shearing. 4 (informal) a sharp blow. 5 a fast pace ♦ The car was moving at quite a clip. [from an Old Norse word klippa]

clipboard noun a portable board with a spring clip at the top for holding papers.

clipper noun an old type of fast sailing ship.

clippers plural noun an instrument for clipping hair.

clipping noun a piece clipped from something, especially from a newspaper.

clique (kleek) noun a small group of people who support each other and keep others out. **cliquey** adjective **cliquish** adjective [a French word, from an Old French word cliquer meaning 'to make a noise']

clitoris (klit-er-iss) noun a small sensitive piece of flesh near the opening of a woman's vagina. **clitoral** adjective [from a Greek word kleitoris]

cloaca (kloh-ay-ka) noun (Zoology) the opening for excreting at the end of the intestinal canal in birds, reptiles, and some other animals. [a Latin word meaning 'sewer']

cloak noun 1 a sleeveless piece of outdoor clothing that hangs loosely from the

shoulders. 2 something that hides or covers ♦ the cloak of secrecy ♦ under the cloak of darkness.
cloak verb to cover or conceal something. [from an Old French word cloke, another form of cloche meaning 'bell']

cloak-and-dagger adjective (said about a story or series of events) involving secrecy and intrigue.

cloakroom noun 1 a room in a public building where outdoor clothes and bags may be left for a time. 2 a toilet in a house or public building.

clobber[1] noun (informal) clothing and personal belongings. [origin unknown]

clobber[2] verb (informal) 1 to hit someone hard or repeatedly. 2 to defeat someone heavily. 3 to criticize or punish someone severely. [origin unknown]

cloche (klosh or klohsh) noun 1 a small glass or plastic cover for outdoor plants. 2 a close-fitting bell-shaped hat worn by women. [a French word meaning 'bell']

clock noun 1 a device that measures the time and shows it with a dial and hands, or through a digital display. 2 any measuring device with a dial or digital display, such as a speedometer. 3 the downy seed head of a dandelion.
clock verb 1 to achieve or record a particular time, distance, or speed. 2 (informal) to hit someone. **to clock in** or **out** to register the time you arrive at work or leave work. **to clock something up** to reach a certain speed ♦ He clocked up 10 seconds for the 100 metres. **round the clock** all day and night. [from a Latin word clocca meaning 'bell']

clockwise adverb & adjective moving in a curve in the same direction as the hands of a clock. [from clock and -wise[2]]

clockwork noun a mechanism with a spring and toothed wheels, like that of a clock. **like clockwork** precisely and easily.

clod noun a lump of earth or clay. [a different spelling of clot]

clog noun a shoe with a heavy wooden sole. **clog** verb (**clogged, clogging**) to make something blocked, or to become blocked. [origin unknown]

cloister noun 1 a covered walk along the side of a church or other building, round a courtyard. 2 a monastery or convent. [from a Latin word claustrum meaning 'enclosed place']

cloistered *adjective* secluded or shut up.

clone *noun* an animal or plant made from the cells of another animal or plant and therefore exactly like it.
clone *verb* to produce a plant or animal as a clone of another. [from a Greek word *klōn* meaning 'twig' or 'cutting from a plant']

close[1] (klohs) *adjective* 1 only a short distance apart in space or time. SYNONYM: near. 2 belonging to the immediate family ♦ *a close relative of my father.* 3 fond or affectionate ♦ *They became close friends.* SYNONYMS: fond, devoted, firm, affectionate, intimate, loving. 4 detailed or concentrated ♦ *Pay close attention.* SYNONYMS: careful, thorough, detailed, intent. 5 strong or noticeable ♦ *There is a close resemblance between the two girls.* SYNONYMS: strong, clear, noticeable. 6 in which the competitors are nearly equal ♦ *It proved a close match.*
7 dense or compact ♦ *The carpet has a close texture.* 8 (said about information) closely guarded ♦ *The code was a close secret.*
9 (said about a person) stingy or mean. SYNONYMS: stingy, mean, niggardly, miserly, parsimonious. 10 (said about the weather) stuffy or humid. SYNONYMS: stuffy, muggy, humid, airless, oppressive, stifling.
close *adverb* at a point not far away ♦ *My cousin lives close by.*
close *noun* 1 a street that is closed at one end, a cul-de-sac. 2 the grounds round a cathedral or abbey. **at close quarters** very close together. **a close shave** a narrow escape from danger or difficulty. **closely** *adverb* **closeness** *noun* [via French from a Latin word *claudere* meaning 'to shut']

close[2] (klohz) *verb* 1 to move something so as to cover or block an opening, to shut something. 2 to move or be moved into this position ♦ *The door closed with a bang.* 3 to finish business at the end of a day, or for a longer period, at a shop or office ♦ *The shops close early on Wednesdays.* 4 to end something, or come to an end. 5 to bring two parts of something together ♦ *She closed the book and put out the light.* 6 to make an electric circuit continuous. 7 to come within fighting or striking distance.
close *noun* a conclusion or end. SYNONYMS: end, conclusion, finish, completion. **to close in** to surround someone or something gradually, especially to trap them or shut them in. [from a Latin word *clausus* meaning 'closed']

closed-circuit television *noun* a system of transmitting video signals to a small number of monitors, used especially for security surveillance.

closed shop *noun* a system in which all employees of a business must belong to an agreed trade union.

closet *noun* (*Amer.*) a cupboard or small storeroom.
closet *verb* (**closeted, closeting**) to shut yourself away in a private room. [from an Old French word, related to *close*[1]]

close-up (klohs-up) *noun* a photograph or piece of film taken at close range, with a lot of detail.

closure (kloh-zher) *noun* 1 the act of closing something, or the state of being closed. 2 a parliamentary procedure for ending a debate and taking a vote.

clot *noun* 1 a small mass of blood or other liquid that has become solid. 2 (*informal*) a foolish person.
clot *verb* (**clotted, clotting**) to form clots.

cloth *noun* 1 woven material or felt. 2 a piece of material used for a special purpose, such as a dishcloth or tablecloth. **the cloth** the clergy. [from an Old English word]

clothe *verb* (past tense and past participle **clothed** or **clad**) to put clothes on someone, or to provide them with clothes.

clothes *plural noun* things worn to cover the body and limbs. [from *cloth*]

clothier (kloh-thi-er) *noun* a person who makes or sells men's clothes.

clothing *noun* clothes collectively.

clotted cream *noun* cream that has been thickened by slowly heating and cooling milk, causing the cream to form lumps.

cloud *noun* 1 a mass of condensed water vapour floating in the sky. 2 a mass of smoke or dust in the air. 3 a mass of things moving in the air ♦ *a cloud of insects.* 4 a state of gloom or suspicion.
cloud *verb* 1 to cover or darken with clouds or gloom or trouble. 2 to become overcast or indistinct or gloomy. **to cloud over** to become cloudy. **under a cloud** under suspicion, in disgrace. **cloudless** *adjective* [from an Old English word]

cloudburst *noun* a sudden heavy rainstorm.

cloud chamber *noun* (*Physics*) a device containing vapour in a state that allows the paths of charged particles, X-rays, and gamma rays to be observed by the trail of tiny drops of condensed vapour which they produce.

cloudy *adjective* (**cloudier, cloudiest**) 1 full of clouds, or covered with clouds. SYNONYMS: overcast, dull, grey, gloomy. 2 not transparent ♦ *The glass held a cloudy liquid.* SYNONYMS: murky, milky, misty, opaque. **cloudiness** *noun*

clout *noun* (*informal*) 1 a heavy blow. 2 power or influence. 3 (*old use*) a piece of clothing ♦ *Cast ne'er a clout till May be out.* **clout** *verb* (*informal*) to hit someone hard. [from an Old English word]

clove[1] *noun* the dried bud of a tropical tree, used as a spice. [from Old French]

clove[2] *noun* each of the small bulbs in a compound bulb ♦ *a clove of garlic.* [from Old English]

clove[3] past tense of **cleave**[1].

clove hitch a knot used to secure a rope round a spar or pole. [from **clove**[3] (because the rope seems to be divided as parallel lines at the back of the knot)]

cloven past participle of **cleave**[1].

cloven hoof *noun* a divided hoof, like those of cattle or sheep.

clover *noun* a small plant, usually with three leaves on each stalk. [from an Old English word]

clown *noun* 1 a performer who performs comical tricks and actions, especially in a circus. 2 a person who does silly things. **clown** *verb* to do silly things to amuse other people. **clownish** *adjective* [origin unknown]

cloy *verb* to sicken or disgust with too much sweetness or pleasure. [from an old word *accloy* meaning 'to choke']

cloying *adjective* sickeningly sweet.

cloze test *noun* an exercise in which a person has to fill in gaps left in a piece of writing, to test their understanding of it. [short for *closure*]

club *noun* 1 a heavy stick with one end thicker than the other, used as a weapon. 2 (in golf) an implement for hitting the ball, consisting of a slender shaft with a heavy shaped head. 3 a playing card of the suit (called *clubs*) marked with black clover leaves. 4 a group of people who meet to enjoy a particular interest or activity, or the building where they meet. 5 an organization offering certain benefits to its subscribers ♦ *a book club.* **club** *verb* (**clubbed, clubbing**) 1 to hit someone with a club. 2 to join with other people in doing something, especially paying money ♦ *We clubbed together to buy a boat.* 3 to visit night clubs ♦ *to go clubbing.* [from an Old Norse word *klubba*]

clubbable *adjective* sociable and friendly, and therefore likely to be a good member of a social club.

club foot *noun* a foot that is deformed so that the sole cannot be put flat on the ground.

clubhouse *noun* the building used by a club.

cluck *verb* to make the throaty cry of a hen. **cluck** *noun* a clucking sound. [an imitation of the sound]

clue *noun* 1 a fact or idea that helps to solve a problem or mystery. 2 a word or phrase that gives a hint about what to put in a crossword puzzle. [originally a ball of thread (also spelt *clew*) used to escape from a labyrinth by unwinding it on the way in and rewinding it on the way out]

clued-up *adjective* (*informal*) well informed about something.

clueless *adjective* (*informal*) not knowing or understanding anything.

clump *noun* 1 a cluster or mass of things. 2 a clumping sound. **clump** *verb* 1 to form a cluster or mass. 2 to walk with a heavy tread. [related to *club*]

clumsy *adjective* (**clumsier, clumsiest**) 1 heavy and ungraceful in movement; likely to drop things or knock them over. SYNONYMS: awkward, ungainly, careless, fumbling, accident-prone. 2 large and difficult to handle or use. 3 done without much tact or skill ♦ *a clumsy apology.* **clumsily** *adverb* **clumsiness** *noun* [probably from a Scandinavian language]

clung past tense and past participle of cling.

clunk *verb* to make a dull sound like thick metal objects hitting each other. **clunk** *noun* this sound. [an imitation of the sound]

cluster *noun* a small close group of things.

cluster verb to bring things together, or come together, in a cluster. [from an Old English word clyster, perhaps related to clot]

cluster bomb noun a bomb that sprays metal pellets when it explodes.

clutch[1] verb to grasp something tightly. **clutch** noun 1 a tight grasp. 2 a device for connecting and disconnecting the engine and gears of a motor vehicle, especially when changing gear. **to clutch at** to try to get hold of something. [from an Old English word]

clutch[2] noun 1 a set of eggs that have been fertilized and laid at the same time. 2 a brood of chicks. [from an Old Norse word klekja meaning 'to hatch']

clutter noun 1 things lying about untidily. 2 a crowded untidy state. **clutter** verb to fill a place with clutter, or make it untidy. [from a dialect word clotter meaning 'to clot']

cm abbreviation centimetre(s).

Co. abbreviation 1 Company ♦ Briggs & Co. 2 County ♦ Co. Durham.

c/o abbreviation care of (used in addresses).

co- prefix together with, jointly ♦ co-author ♦ co-driver ♦ coexistence. [same origin as for com-]

coach noun 1 a well equipped single-decker bus used for long journeys. 2 a railway carriage. 3 a large four-wheeled carriage drawn by horses. 4 an instructor in sports. 5 a teacher giving private specialized tuition. **coach** verb to train or teach someone. [from a Hungarian phrase kocsi szekér meaning 'cart from Kocs', a town in Hungary]

coachwork noun the bodywork of a road or railway vehicle.

coagulate (koh-**ag**-yoo-layt) verb to change from liquid to semi-solid, to clot. **coagulation** noun [from a Latin word coagulare meaning 'to curdle']

coal noun 1 a hard black mineral used for burning to supply heat. 2 a piece of this, especially one that is burning. [from an Old English word col]

coalesce (koh-ə-**less**) verb to combine and form one whole thing. **coalescence** noun [from a Latin word coalescere meaning 'to grow together']

coalface noun the exposed surface of coal in a mine.

coalfield noun an area where there is coal underground.

coalition (koh-ə-**lish**-ən) noun 1 a temporary alliance, especially between political parties forming a joint government. [same origin as for coalesce]

coalmine noun a mine where coal is dug.

coalminer noun someone who mines coal.

coal tar noun a thick black liquid produced when gas is made from coal.

coarse adjective 1 composed of large particles. 2 rough or loose in texture. SYNONYMS: rough, thick, hard, scratchy, hairy, harsh. 3 (said about a person) rough or crude in manner or behaviour, not refined. SYNONYMS: crude, rough, rude, uncouth, vulgar. 4 inferior or common. **coarsely** adverb **coarseness** noun [origin unknown]

coarsen verb to make something coarse, or to become coarse.

coast noun the seashore and the land close to it. **coast** verb 1 to sail along a coast. 2 to move easily without using power. [from a Latin word costa meaning 'rib']

coastal adjective to do with the coast, or near the coast.

coastguard noun an official who keeps watch on the coast to assist ships in danger and prevent smuggling.

coastline noun the shape or outline of a coast.

coat noun 1 a piece of clothing with sleeves, worn outdoors over other clothes. 2 the hair or fur covering an animal's body. 3 a covering layer, especially of paint. **coat** verb 1 to cover something with a layer. 2 to form a covering to something. [from an Old French word cote]

coating noun a thin covering layer.

coat of arms noun a design on a shield, used as an emblem by a family, city, or institution.

coax verb 1 to persuade someone gently or gradually. SYNONYMS: entice, persuade, cajole, inveigle. 2 to achieve something in this way ♦ We managed to coax a brief smile out of him. [from an old word cokes meaning 'simpleton']

coaxial (koh-**aks**-iəl) adjective 1 having an

axis in common. **2** (said about a cable) having two conductors arranged so that one is inside the other with a layer of insulating material between. [from *co-* and *axis*]

cob *noun* **1** the central part of an ear of maize, on which the corn grows. **2** a male swan. **3** a sturdy horse for riding. **4** a loaf of bread with a rounded top. **5** a large kind of hazelnut. [origin unknown]

cobalt (koh-bollt) *noun* **1** a hard silvery-white metal used in many alloys and with radioactive forms used in medicine and industry, a chemical element (symbol Co). **2** colouring-matter made from this; its deep-blue colour. [from a German word *Kobalt* meaning 'demon' (because cobalt was believed to be harmful to the silver ore it was found with)]

cobalt blue *noun* a deep blue pigment made from cobalt, or this colour.

cobber *noun* (*Austral.*) (*NZ*) (*informal*) a friend or mate. [possibly related to an English dialect word *cob* meaning 'take a liking to']

cobble [1] or **cobblestone** *noun* a small rounded stone used for paving roads. **cobble** *verb* to pave a surface with cobblestones. **cobbled** *adjective* [from *cob*, in the meaning 'round']

cobble [2] *verb* to put together or mend something roughly. [from *cobbler*]

cobbler *noun* someone who mends shoes. [origin unknown]

COBOL (koh-bol) *noun* a computer programming language designed for use in business. [from the initials of *Common Business Oriented Language*]

cobra (koh-brə or kob-rə) *noun* (**cobras**) a poisonous Indian or African snake that can rise up at the front to attack or challenge an enemy. [from Portuguese words *cobra de capello* meaning 'snake with hood']

cobweb *noun* a spider's web, especially an old one covered in dust. **cobwebby** *adjective* [from an old word *coppe* meaning 'spider', and *web*]

coca (koh-kə) *noun* a tropical American shrub with leaves that are chewed as a stimulant and are the source of cocaine. [via Spanish from South American words]

cocaine (kə-kayn) *noun* an addictive drug made from coca, used in medicine as a local anaesthetic or illegally as a stimulant.

coccyx (kok-siks) *noun* a small triangular bone at the base of the spine. [from a Greek word *kokkux* meaning 'cuckoo' (because the bone looks like a cuckoo's beak)]

cochineal (koch-in-eel) *noun* a bright red dye used for colouring food, made from the crushed dried bodies of certain insects. [via French and Spanish from a Latin word *coccinus* meaning 'scarlet']

cochlea (kok-liə) *noun* the spiral cavity of the inner ear. [a Latin word meaning 'snail shell']

cock *noun* **1** a male bird, especially a domestic fowl. **2** a lever in the firing mechanism of a gun, which is raised ready to be released by the trigger. **3** a tap or spout for controlling the flow of a liquid.
cock *verb* to raise the cock of a gun ready for firing. **at half cock** not fully ready or prepared. [from an Old English word *cocc*]

cockade (kok-ayd) *noun* a rosette or knot of ribbon worn on a hat as a badge. [from a French word *coquard* meaning 'saucy']

cock-a-hoop *adjective* extremely pleased about something.

cock-and-bull story *noun* a silly or unlikely story that is hard to believe.

cockatoo *noun* (**cockatoos**) a crested parrot.

cockchafer (kok-chay-fer) *noun* a large flying beetle which destroys plants. [from *cock* (meaning 'large') and *chafer*, a kind of beetle]

cockcrow *noun* dawn, when cocks begin to crow.

cocked hat *noun* a triangular hat worn with some uniforms.

cockerel *noun* a young domestic cock. [a diminutive form of *cock*]

cocker spaniel *noun* a small spaniel with a silky golden-brown coat. [so called because it was once used to hunt woodcock]

cock-eyed *adjective* (*informal*) **1** crooked or slanting, not straight. **2** (said about an idea or plan) absurd or impractical. [from *cock* meaning 'to turn']

cockle *noun* **1** an edible shellfish. **2** a small shallow boat. **to warm the cockles of your heart** to make you feel pleased or contented. [from an Old French word *coquille* meaning 'shell']

cockney *noun* (**cockneys**) **1** a native of the East End of London. **2** the dialect or accent of this area. [origin unknown; an earlier meaning was 'a pampered child' and then 'a town-dweller' (regarded as puny by country-dwellers)]

cockpit *noun* **1** the compartment of an aircraft for the pilot and crew. **2** the driver's compartment in a racing car. [originally a pit in which cockfights were held]

cockroach *noun* an insect like a beetle with long legs and antennae, some kinds of which can be scavenging pests in houses. [from a Spanish word *cucaracha*]

cocksure *adjective* arrogantly confident or positive. [from an old use of *cock* as a substitute for *God* in oaths]

cocktail *noun* **1** an alcoholic drink made of a spirit mixed with other spirits or fruit juice. **2** a small dish of shellfish or fruit, served as an appetizer ♦ *prawn cocktail*. **3** a mixture of dangerous or unpleasant substances. [from an earlier meaning 'a horse with a docked tail' (because the tail stood up like a cock's tail)]

cocky *adjective* (**cockier, cockiest**) slightly over-confident or arrogant. **cockily** *adverb* **cockiness** *noun* [from the meaning 'proud as a cock']

cocoa *noun* **1** a powder made from crushed cacao seeds. **2** a drink made from this powder. [another spelling of *cacao*]

coconut *noun* **1** the large nut of the coco palm, with a hard shell containing a sweet milky juice. **2** the flaky white lining of this nut, used in sweets and cookery. [from a Spanish word *coco* meaning 'grinning face' (because the base of the nut looks like a monkey's face)]

coconut shy *noun* a fairground amusement in which balls are thrown to knock coconuts off stands.

cocoon (kə-koon) *noun* **1** the silky covering round a chrysalis. **2** a protective wrapping.
cocoon *verb* to protect something by wrapping it completely. [from a French word *cocon*]

COD *abbreviation* cash on delivery.

cod *noun* (**cod**) a large sea fish used for food. [origin unknown]

coda (koh-də) *noun* (*Music*) an extra passage played to finish a piece, after the main part. [an Italian word, from a Latin word *cauda* meaning 'tail']

coddle *verb* **1** to be too protective towards someone. **2** to cook eggs in water just below boiling point. [origin unknown]

code *noun* **1** a pre-arranged word or phrase representing a message, for secrecy. **2** a system of words, letters, or symbols used to represent others, either for secrecy or for transmitting by machine as in Morse code. **3** a set of rules or laws ♦ *the Highway Code*. **4** a set of numbers that represents an area in telephoning ♦ *Do you know the code for Southampton?* **5** (*Computing*) a set of programming instructions.
code *verb* to put something into code. [from a Latin word *codex* meaning 'book']

codeine (koh-deen) *noun* a white medicine made from morphine, used to relieve pain or induce sleep. [from a Greek word *kōdeia* meaning 'poppy head']

codger *noun* (*informal*) an elderly man. [perhaps related to *cadge*]

codicil (koh-di-sil) *noun* an extra clause added to a will. [from a Latin word *codicillus* meaning 'small book']

codify (koh-di-fiy) *verb* (**codifies, codified, codifying**) to organize laws or rules into a code. **codification** *noun* **codifier** *noun*

cod liver oil *noun* oil from cod livers, rich in vitamins A and D.

codomain *noun* (*Mathematics*) a set that contains all the possible values of a given function.

codpiece *noun* a pouch or flap to cover the genitals on men's breeches in the 15th and 16th centuries. [from an old word *cod* meaning 'scrotum']

codswallop *noun* (*informal*) nonsense. [origin uncertain, but associated with Hiram Codd, who invented a bottle for fizzy drinks (*wallop*) in the 19th century]

coeducation *noun* education of pupils of both sexes together. **coeducational** *adjective*

coefficient (koh-i-fish-ənt) *noun* (*Mathematics*) a number by which another number is multiplied, a factor. [from *co-* and *efficient* (because the numbers work together)]

coelacanth (seel-ə-kanth) *noun* a kind of large bony sea fish that was known from fossils and was thought to be extinct until a live one was found in 1938. [from Greek words *koilos* meaning 'hollow' and *akantha* meaning 'spine' (because its fins have hollow spines)]

coelenterate (si-**len**-ter-ət) *noun* a member of the group of aquatic animals including jellyfish, corals, and sea anemones, which have a simple tube-shaped or cup-shaped body and a digestive system with a single opening ringed with tentacles. [from Greek words *koilos* meaning 'hollow' and *enteron* meaning 'intestine']

coenzyme *noun* an organic compound with which an enzyme needs to combine to become active.

coequal *adjective* equal to one another.

coerce (koh-**erss**) *verb* to compel someone by threats or force. **coercion** (koh-**er**-shən) *noun* [from a Latin word *coercere* meaning 'to restrain']

coercive (koh-**er**-siv) *adjective* using coercion.

coeval (koh-**ee**-vəl) *adjective* having the same age or date of origin. [from *co-* and a Latin word *aevum* meaning 'age']

coexist *verb* to exist at the same time. **coexistence** *noun* **coexistent** *adjective*

coextensive *adjective* extending over the same area or time.

C. of E. *abbreviation* Church of England.

coffee *noun* 1 a hot drink made from the roasted and ground bean-like seeds of a tropical shrub. 2 the seeds of this shrub. 3 a light-brown colour. [from an Arabic word *kahwa*]

coffee bar or **coffee shop** *noun* a place serving coffee and light refreshments.

coffee table *noun* a small low table, normally used in a living room.

coffee-table book *noun* a large book with a large number of pictures, intended for browsing in.

coffer *noun* a large strong box for holding money and valuables. **coffers** *plural noun* the funds or financial resources of an organization. [from a Latin word *cophinus* meaning 'basket' or 'hamper']

cofferdam *noun* a watertight enclosure put round an area of water and pumped dry to allow building work or repairs to a ship to be done underwater.

coffin *noun* a long box in which a dead body is buried or cremated. [same origin as for *coffer*]

cog *noun* 1 each of a series of teeth on the edge of a wheel, fitting into and pushing those on another wheel. 2 a wheel with a series of cogs round it. [probably from a Scandinavian language]

cogent (koh-jənt) *adjective* logical and convincing ♦ *a cogent argument.* **cogently** *adverb* **cogency** *noun* [from a Latin word *cogere* meaning 'to compel']

cogitate (koj-i-tayt) *verb* to think deeply about something. **cogitation** *noun* [from a Latin word *cogitare* meaning 'to think']

cognac (kon-yak) *noun* French brandy, especially that made in Cognac in western France.

cognate (kog-nayt) *adjective* having the same source or origin.
cognate *noun* 1 a relative. 2 a word that has the same origin as another ♦ *Die and death are cognates.* [from *co-* and a Latin word *natus* meaning 'born']

cognition (kog-ni-shən) *noun* the faculty of knowing or perceiving things. [from a Latin word *cognoscere* meaning 'to know']

cognitive (kog-ni-tiv) *adjective* to do with cognition or knowing.

cognizant (kog-ni-zənt) *adjective* (*formal*) aware of something or having knowledge about it. **cognizance** *noun* [same origin as for *cognition*]

cohabit *verb* (**cohabited, cohabiting**) to live together and have a sexual relationship without being married. **cohabitation** *noun*

cohere (koh-**heer**) *verb* 1 to stick together or form a united mass. 2 (said about an argument or theory) to be logical or consistent. [from *co-* and a Latin word *haerere* meaning 'to stick']

coherent (koh-**heer**-ənt) *adjective* 1 (said about an argument) making sense. 2 (said about a person) able to speak sensibly and clearly. 3 (*Physics*) (said about waves) having a constant phase relationship. **coherently** *adverb* **coherence** *noun*

cohesion (koh-**hee**-zhən) *noun* a tendency to cohere or stick together. **cohesive** *adjective*

cohort *noun* 1 a division of the ancient Roman army, one-tenth of a legion. [from a Latin word *cohors*]

coiffure (kwahf-**yoor**) *noun* a hairstyle. [a French word, from coiffer meaning 'to arrange the hair']

coil *noun* 1 a length of something wound into a series of joined rings. 2 a length of wire wound in a spiral to conduct electric current. 3 a contraceptive device having the shape of a coil, for insertion into the womb.
coil *verb* to wind something into a coil. [same origin as for *collect*]

coin *noun* 1 a small round stamped piece of metal used for money. 2 money in the form of coins.
coin *verb* 1 to make coins by stamping metal. 2 (*informal*) to make a large amount of money as profit. 3 to invent a word or phrase. [from a French word *coin* meaning 'wedge' or 'die', from a Latin word *cuneus* meaning 'wedge']

coinage *noun* 1 coins collectively, or the system of coins in use. 2 making coins. 3 a new word or phrase.

coincide (koh-in-**siyd**) *verb* 1 to happen at the same time as something else ♦ *His holidays don't coincide with hers.* 2 to be in the same place or area. 3 to agree or be the same ♦ *We found that our tastes coincided.* [from co- and a Latin word *incidere* meaning 'to fall on']

coincidence (koh-**in**-si-dənss) *noun* 1 the fact or process of happening at the same time or being in the same place. 2 a remarkable occurrence of similar or corresponding events at the same time by chance.

coincident (koh-**in**-si-dənt) *adjective* happening at the same time or being in the same place.

coincidental (koh-in-si-**den**-təl) *adjective* happening at the same time by chance.
coincidentally *adverb*

coition (koh-**ish**-ən) or **coitus** (**koh**-it-əs) *noun* a technical word for sexual intercourse. [from a Latin word *coire* meaning 'to go together']

coke[1] *noun* the solid fuel left after gas and tar have been extracted from coal.

coke[2] *noun* (*informal*) cocaine.

col *noun* 1 a depression in a range of mountains. 2 (*Meteorology*) a region of low pressure between two anticyclones. [a French word meaning 'neck']

colander (**kul**-ən-der) *noun* a bowl-shaped container with holes for straining water from vegetables or other food after cooking. [from a Latin word *colare* meaning 'to strain']

cold *adjective* 1 having or at a low temperature, especially when compared with the human body. SYNONYMS: chilly, freezing, bitter, biting, wintry, raw, perishing, cool, frosty, icy; (*informal*) nippy. 2 not heated, having cooled after being heated or cooked ♦ *cold meat*. 3 (*informal*) unconscious ♦ *The blow knocked him cold.* 4 unfriendly or unwelcoming ♦ *We got a cold reception.* SYNONYMS: unfriendly, unkind, unfeeling, distant, aloof, indifferent. 5 (said about colours) suggesting coldness. 6 (said about the scent in hunting) faint because no longer fresh. 7 (in children's games) far from finding or guessing what is sought.
cold *noun* 1 lack of heat or warmth; a low temperature. 2 an infectious illness that can cause catarrh, a sore throat, and sneezing. **to get cold feet** to have doubts about doing something bold or ambitious. **to give someone the cold shoulder** to be deliberately unfriendly. **in cold blood** deliberately and ruthlessly. **coldish** *adjective* **coldly** *adverb* **coldness** *noun* [from an Old English word]

cold-blooded *adjective* 1 having a body temperature that changes with the temperature of surroundings, as fish have. 2 unfeeling, deliberately ruthless ♦ *a cold-blooded killer.*

cold-calling *noun* advertising goods or services by telephoning people from a list or telephone book.

cold chisel *noun* a strong steel chisel.

cold comfort *noun* poor consolation for something you have suffered.

cold cream *noun* ointment for cleansing and softening the skin.

cold war *noun* a state of hostility between nations without actual fighting.

coleopterous (kol-i-**op**-ter-əs) *adjective* of the group of animals (Coleoptera) consisting of beetles and weevils, insects with front wings serving as sheaths for the rear wings. [from Greek words *koleon* meaning 'sheath' and *pteron* meaning 'wing']

coleslaw *noun* a salad of finely shredded raw cabbage mixed with mayonnaise.

colic *noun* severe pain in the abdomen, caused by wind or an obstruction.

colicky adjective [from a Latin word colicus meaning 'to do with the colon']

collaborate verb 1 to work together on a piece of work. 2 to help your country's enemy. **collaboration** noun **collaborator** noun [from com- and a Latin word laborare meaning 'to work']

collage (kol-ahzh) noun a piece of art made by fixing bits of paper, cloth, string, etc. to a surface. [a French word meaning 'gluing']

collagen (kol-ə-jin) noun a protein substance found in bone and tissue. [from a Greek word kolla meaning 'glue']

collapse verb 1 to fall down or give way suddenly. 2 to lose strength or force suddenly ♦ Enemy resistance collapsed ♦ The pound collapsed against the dollar. 3 (said about a person) to fall down because of illness or physical breakdown. 4 to fold into a smaller size.
collapse noun 1 the collapsing of something. 2 a sudden breakdown or failure. [from com- and a Latin word lapsum meaning 'slipped']

collapsible adjective made so as to fold into a smaller size ♦ a collapsible chair.

collar noun 1 a band of material, turned over or upright, round the neck of a shirt, jacket, dress, or coat. 2 a band put round the neck of an animal. 3 a band, ring, or pipe holding part of a machine. 4 a cut of bacon from near the head.
collar verb (collared, collaring) (informal) to seize or catch someone. [from a Latin word collum meaning 'neck']

collarbone noun the bone joining the breastbone and shoulder blade, the clavicle.

collate (kə-layt) verb 1 to collect and arrange something systematically, especially information. 2 to compare things in detail. **collation** noun **collator** noun [from a Latin word collat-, an inflection of conferre meaning 'to compare']

collateral (kə-lat-er-əl) adjective 1 additional but less important ♦ collateral evidence. 2 side by side, parallel. 3 descended from the same ancestor but by a different line ♦ a collateral branch of the family.
collateral noun money or property that is pledged as security for repayment of a loan. [from com- and a Latin word lateralis meaning 'of a side']

collateral damage noun accidental damage to civilian areas in a war.

colleague noun a person you work with, especially in a business or profession. [from a Latin word collega meaning 'partner in office']

collect[1] (kə-lekt) verb 1 to bring people or things together from several places. SYNONYMS: gather, pile up (things), sweep (things), accumulate (things), assemble, bring together. 2 to come together. SYNONYMS: gather, assemble, converge, come together. 3 to get money or other contributions from a number of people. 4 to look for and acquire examples of particular things as a hobby or for study ♦ I've started collecting stamps. 5 to fetch or go and get something ♦ Will you collect my cleaning on your way home? SYNONYMS: fetch, bring, get, pick up. 6 to gather one's thoughts into systematic order or control. [from com- and a Latin word meaning 'to assemble' or 'to choose']

collect[2] (kol-ekt) noun a short prayer in some Christian Churches. [from a Latin word collecta meaning 'gathering']

collected adjective (said about a person) calm and self-controlled. **collectedly** adverb

collection noun 1 the process of collecting. 2 things collected systematically. 3 a number of things that have come together or been placed together. 4 money collected for a charity or at a church service.

collective adjective to do with a group taken as a whole ♦ Our collective response to the idea.
collective noun a collective enterprise. **collectively** adverb

collective bargaining noun negotiation about pay and working conditions by an organized group of employees.

collective noun noun (Grammar) a noun that is singular in form but denotes a group of individuals, e.g. army, cattle, government, herd.

collective ownership noun ownership of land or property by the community for everyone's benefit.

collector noun a person who collects things.

college noun 1 a place of education providing courses in higher or specialized forms of education for adults. 2 an independent part of a university with its own teachers and students. **3** (in names) a school ♦ *Eton College*. **4** an organized body of professional people ♦ *the Royal College of Surgeons*. [from a Latin word *collegium* meaning 'partnership']

collegiate (kə-**lee**-ji-ət) *adjective* to do with a college or college student, or belonging to a college.

collide *verb* **1** (said about a moving object) to strike violently against something. **2** (said about interests or opinions) to conflict. [from a Latin word *collidere* meaning 'to clash together']

collie *noun* a dog with a long pointed nose and shaggy hair. [origin unknown]

collier *noun* **1** a coalminer. **2** a ship that carries coal as its cargo.

colliery *noun* (**collieries**) a coalmine and its buildings. [from *coal*]

collinear (ko-lin-i-ə) *adjective* (Geometry) lying in the same straight line. [from *com-* and *linear*]

collision *noun* the act of colliding.

collocate *verb* **1** to bring things together to compare them. **collocation** *noun* **collocator** *noun* [from *com-* and *locate*]

collocation *noun* (Grammar) the words that are most often used in association with a particular word.

colloid *noun* **1** a gluey substance, especially a non-crystalline substance with very large molecules and a gluey texture, having special properties. **2** a substance consisting of many very fine particles suspended in a gas, liquid, or solid. **colloidal** *adjective* [from a Greek word *kolla* meaning 'glue']

colloquial (kə-**loh**-kwee-əl) *adjective* (said about a word or piece of language) suitable for ordinary conversation but not for formal speech or writing. **colloquially** *adverb* [from *com-* and a Latin word *loqui* meaning 'to speak']

colloquialism *noun* a colloquial word or phrase.

colloquy (kol-ə-kwi) *noun* (**colloquies**) a formal conference or conversation.

collusion (kə-**loo**-zhən) *noun* a secret agreement between two or more people who are trying to deceive or cheat someone. **collusive** *adjective* [from *com-* and a Latin word *ludere* meaning 'to play']

collywobbles *plural noun* (informal) **1** a

stomach pain. **2** a feeling of nervous anxiety.

cologne (kə-**lohn**) *noun* eau de cologne or other lightly scented liquid used on the skin.

colon [1] (**koh**-lən) *noun* the main part of the large intestine. **colonic** *adjective* [from a Greek word *kolon*]

colon [2] (**koh**-lən) *noun* **1** the punctuation mark (:), used to introduce a list or summary of what has gone before, or an elaboration or explanation. **2** the same mark used in mathematics, especially in statements of proportion (as in $1:3 = 2:6$). [from a Greek word *kōlon*]

colonel (**ker**-nəl) *noun* an army officer commanding a regiment, ranking next below a brigadier. [via French from an Italian word *colonello* meaning 'column of soldiers']

colonial *adjective* to do with a colony or colonies. **colonial** *noun* someone who lives in a colony.

colonialism *noun* the policy of acquiring or maintaining colonies.

colonist *noun* one of the first settlers in a colony.

colonization *noun* **1** the process of founding colonies. **2** the establishment of particular animals or plants in an area.

colonize *verb* to establish a colony in a place.

colonnade (kol-ən-**ayd**) *noun* a row of columns. [a French word, related to *column*]

colony *noun* (**colonies**) **1** an area of land in one country that people from another country settle in and control. **2** the people who live in a colony. **3** a group of people sharing the same background or interest ♦ *a nudist colony* ♦ *the artists' colony*. **4** a group of animals or plants of the same kind living close together. [from a Latin word *colonia* meaning 'farm' or 'settlement']

Colorado beetle (kolə-**rah**-doh) *noun* a black and yellow beetle that is very destructive to the potato plant. [named after *Colorado*, a state of the central USA]

coloration *noun* the process of colouring.

colossal *adjective* **1** very large, enormous. SYNONYMS: huge, enormous, gigantic, immense, massive. **colossally** adverb [from colossus]

colossus (kə-**los**-əs) noun (**colossi** (kə-**los**-I)) 1 a huge statue, much larger than lifesize. 2 a person of great importance and influence. [from the bronze statue of Apollo at Rhodes, the Colossus of Rhodes]

colostomy noun (**colostomies**) a surgical operation in which the colon is shortened and diverted to an opening formed in the abdominal wall.

colostrum (kə-**lost**-rəm) noun the clear fluid, rich in antibodies, that appears in the breasts of mammals before milk is produced. [a Latin word]

colour noun 1 the property an object has of producing a particular sensation on the eye by the way it reflects rays of light of different wavelengths. 2 a particular effect produced in this way ♦ Which colour did you choose for the bedroom? 3 the use of all colours, not only black and white, in photography or television. 4 the redness of a person's complexion. 5 the pigmentation of the skin, especially as an indication of racial origin. 6 a pigment, paint, or dye. 7 the flag of a ship or regiment.
colour verb 1 to put colour on something; to paint, stain, or dye something. 2 to change colour. 3 (said about a person) to blush. 4 to give a special character or bias to something ♦ His political opinions colour his writings. **colours** plural noun an award given to regular or leading members of a sports team. [from a Latin word color]

colourant noun a dye or pigment used to colour things.

colour-blind adjective unable to see the difference between certain colours.

coloured adjective 1 having colour. 2 wholly or partly of non-white descent. **Coloured** adjective (in South Africa) of mixed white and non-white descent. **coloured** noun a coloured person. **Coloured** noun (in South Africa) a person of mixed White and non-White descent.

colour-fast adjective not liable to lose its colour when washed.

colourful adjective 1 full of colour. 2 lively or exciting, with plenty of detail ♦ We heard a colourful account of their journey. **colourfully** adverb

colouring noun 1 the way in which something is coloured. 2 a substance used to colour things.

colourless adjective without colour.

colt noun a young male horse. [origin unknown]

columbine noun a garden flower with purple-blue flowers and slender pointed projections on its petals. [from a Latin word columba meaning 'dove' (because the flower was thought to resemble a cluster of doves)]

column noun 1 a round pillar. 2 something long or tall and narrow ♦ a column of smoke. 3 a section of printing or text down a page, especially in a newspaper or reference book. 4 a regular feature in a newspaper, devoted to a special subject ♦ Who writes the gardening column? 5 a long narrow formation of troops or vehicles. **columnar** (kə-**lum**-ner) adjective [from a Latin word columna]

columnist (**kol**-əm-ist) noun a journalist who regularly writes a column for a newspaper or magazine.

com- prefix (changing to **col-** before l, **cor-** before r, **con-** before many other consonants) with; together (as in ♦ combine, ♦ connect). [from a Latin word cum meaning 'with']

coma (**koh**-mə) noun a state of deep unconsciousness. [from a Greek word meaning 'deep sleep']

comatose (**koh**-mə-tohs) adjective 1 in a coma. 2 very tired or inactive.

comb noun 1 a strip of plastic or wood or other hard material with teeth, used for tidying the hair or holding it in place. 2 something shaped or used like this, e.g. to separate strands of wool or cotton. 3 the fleshy crest of a fowl. 4 a honeycomb.
comb verb 1 to tidy hair with a comb. 2 to search a place thoroughly. [from an Old English word]

combat noun a fight or contest.
combat verb (**combated, combating**) to take action to reduce the effects of something ♦ to combat the effects of alcohol. [from com- and a Latin word batuere meaning 'to fight']

combatant (**kom**-bə-tənt) noun a person or state that is actively fighting in a war. **combatant** adjective actively engaged in fighting.

combative (**kom**-bə-tiv) adjective eager to fight, aggressive.

combe (koom) *noun* a short valley on the side of a hill or running up from the coast.

combination *noun* **1** the process of combining things, or of being combined. **2** a number of people or things that are combined. **3** a sequence of numbers or letters used in opening a combination lock. **combinations** *plural noun* (*old use*) a one-piece item of clothing covering the body and legs.

combination lock *noun* a lock that is opened by turning a set of dials into the correct series of positions, shown by numbers or letters.

combine¹ (kəm-biyn) *verb* **1** to join things to form a set, group, or mixture. SYNONYMS: unite, pool, join, merge, amalgamate, add together, put together. **2** to come together; to unite or merge. [from *com-* and a Latin word *bini* meaning 'two together']

combine² (kom-biyn) *noun* a group of people or firms acting together in business. [from *com-* and a Latin word *bini* meaning 'pair']

combine harvester *noun* a machine that reaps and threshes grain in one operation.

combustible (kəm-bust-ibəl) *adjective* able to catch fire and burn, suitable for burning.
combustible *noun* something that will burn. **combustibility** *noun* [from a Latin word *comburere* meaning 'to burn up']

combustion (kəm-bus-chən) *noun* the process of burning, a chemical process (accompanied by heat) in which substances combine with oxygen in air.

come *verb* (**came, come**) **1** to move or be brought towards the speaker or to a place or point the speaker has in mind. **2** to arrive, to be happening ♦ *When spring comes we can have a holiday.* **3** to reach a result ♦ *Have you come to a decision yet?* **4** to take or occupy a specified position ♦ *The picture comes on the next page.* **5** to be available ♦ *The paint comes in a wide range of colours.* **6** to happen ♦ *How did you come to lose it?* **7** to occur as a result ♦ *That's what comes of being careless.* **8** to have as a home or origin ♦ *Where did that car come from?* **to come about** to happen. SYNONYMS: happen, occur, take place, befall. **to come across** to find or meet something or someone unexpectedly. SYNONYMS: encounter, find, run into, happen on, come upon. **to come**

along to make good progress ♦ *The painting is coming along nicely.* **to come by** to obtain something, often by chance. SYNONYMS: obtain, acquire, get, procure, secure. **to come clean** (*informal*) to own up. **to come down** to fall or collapse. **to come in 1** to have a useful role or function ♦ *A tool like this will come in useful.* **2** to finish a race or competition in a certain position ♦ *In the end we came in third.* **to come in for** to receive a share of something. **to come into** to inherit money or property. **to come of age** to become an adult. **to come off** to be successful, to take place. SYNONYMS: succeed, be successful, happen, take place. **to come on** to make progress, to be successful. **to come out 1** to become known. **2** to be published. **3** to say what you think about something ♦ *They came out in favour of the idea.* **to come out with** to say or admit something. **to come over 1** to affect someone ♦ *I don't know what came over me.* **2** (*informal*) to be affected with a feeling ♦ *She suddenly came over all faint.* **to come round 1** to make a brief visit. **2** to become conscious again after fainting. SYNONYMS: revive, wake up, awake, come to. **3** to agree in the end with what someone else has said. **to come to 1** to amount to or be equivalent to something. **2** to become conscious again. SYNONYMS: revive, wake up, awake, come round. **to come to pass** to happen. **to come up** to occur or need attention ♦ *A problem has just come up.* SYNONYMS: arise, occur; (*informal*) crop up. **to come upon** to find something or meet someone unexpectedly. SYNONYMS: encounter, find, run into, happen on, come across. **to come up to** to equal or match ♦ *The results did not come up to our expectations.* **to come up with** to contribute or find something that is needed ♦ *It was Fiona who came up with the answer.* SYNONYMS: submit, offer, present, propose. [from an Old English word]

comeback *noun* a return to former fame or success.

comedian *noun* **1** someone who entertains people by making them laugh. **2** a writer of comic plays.

comedienne (kə-mee-di-en) *noun* a female comedian.

comedown *noun* **1** a loss of importance or status. **2** a disappointment or anticlimax.

comedy *noun* (**comedies**) **1** entertainment that is meant to make people laugh. **2** humour. **3** a play or film that makes people laugh or has a light subject. [from Greek words *kōmos* meaning 'merry-making' and *ōidē* meaning 'song']

comely (kum-li) *adjective* (**comelier, comeliest**) handsome or good-looking. **comeliness** *noun* [from an old word *becomely* meaning 'suitable']

comestibles (kəm-**est**-i-bəlz) *plural noun* (*formal*) things to eat. [from a Latin word *comedere* meaning 'to eat up']

comet (kom-it) *noun* an object that moves round the sun, usually with a star-like centre and a tail pointing away from the sun. [from a Greek word *komētēs* meaning 'long-haired']

comeuppance *noun* (*informal*) a punishment or rebuke that someone deserves.

comfort *noun* 1 a state of ease and contentment. 2 relief of suffering or grief. 3 a person or thing that gives comfort. **comfort** *verb* to give comfort to someone. SYNONYMS: console, cheer up, reassure, calm, soothe, sympathize with. **comforter** *noun* [from a Latin word *comfortare* meaning 'to strengthen']

comfortable *adjective* 1 feeling at ease or in a state of comfort. 2 giving ease and contentment. 3 not close or restricted ♦ *won by a comfortable margin.* **comfortably** *adverb*

comfrey (kum-fri) *noun* (**comfreys**) a tall plant with large rough leaves and purple or white flowers, growing in ditches. [from a French word *cumfrie*, from a Latin word *confervere* meaning 'to heal' (because the plant was used in medicine)]

comfy *adjective* (**comfier, comfiest**) (*informal*) comfortable.

comic *adjective* 1 meant to make people laugh, amusing. 2 to do with comedy ♦ *a comic actor.*
comic *noun* 1 a comedian. 2 a children's paper containing comic strips. **comical** *adjective* **comically** *adverb* [from a Greek word *kōmikos*, related to *comedy*]

coming *adjective* approaching, next ♦ *this coming Wednesday.*
coming *noun* arriving ♦ *comings and goings.*

comma *noun* the punctuation mark (,), used to mark a slight pause or break between parts of a sentence, or separating words or figures in a list. [from a Greek word *komma* meaning 'clause']

command *noun* 1 a statement, based on authority, that some action must be performed. SYNONYMS: order, instruction. 2 the right to control others, authority. 3 knowledge or ability to use something ♦ *a good command of languages.* 4 a body of troops or staff. 5 an instruction to a computer to perform a function.
command *verb* 1 to give a command or order to someone. SYNONYMS: order, tell, instruct, require. 2 to have authority over someone. 3 to have something at your disposal ♦ *The firm commands international resources.* 4 to deserve and get something ♦ *They command our respect.* 5 to look down over or dominate someone. [from *com-* and a Latin word *mandare* meaning 'to impose a duty']

commandant (kom-ən-**dant**) *noun* a military officer in charge of a fortress or other military establishment.

commandeer *verb* 1 to take or seize something for military use. 2 to take something for your own use.

commander *noun* 1 the person in command of a group of people. 2 a naval officer ranking next below a captain. 3 a senior police officer.

commander-in-chief *noun* (**commanders-in-chief**) the overall commander.

commandment *noun* a divine command, especially one of the ten laws given by God to Moses.

commando *noun* (**commandos**) a member of a military unit specially trained for making raids and assaults. [from a Portuguese word, related to *command*]

commemorate *verb* 1 to keep a past event or person in the memory by means of a celebration or ceremony. 2 to be a memorial to a past event or person ♦ *A plaque commemorates the victory.* **commemoration** *noun* **commemorative** *adjective* [from *com-* and a Latin word *memor* meaning 'memory']

commence *verb* (*formal*) to begin. **commencement** *noun* [from *com-* and a Latin word *initiare* meaning 'to initiate']

commend *verb* 1 to praise a person or their actions. 2 to recommend someone. 3 to entrust something ♦ *We commend him to your care.* **commendation** *noun* [same origin as for *command*]

commendable *adjective* deserving praise. **commendably** *adverb*

commensal (kə-**men**-səl) *adjective* (*Biology*) (said about an organism) living in or with another plant or animal and obtaining food from it without harming it. **commensalism** *noun* [from *com-* and a Latin word *mensa* meaning 'table']

commensurable (kə-**men**-sher-əbəl) *adjective* able to be measured by the same standard.

commensurate (kə-**men**-sher-ət) *adjective* **1** of the same size or extent. **2** proportionate. [from *com-* and a Latin word *mensum* meaning 'measured']

comment *noun* an opinion given about an event or to explain something. **comment** *verb* to make a comment or comments. [from a Latin word *commentum* meaning 'interpretation']

commentary *noun* (**commentaries**) **1** a series of comments, especially describing a sports event while it is happening. **2** a book of explanatory comments on a text.

commentate *verb* to act as commentator.

commentator *noun* a person who gives a radio or television commentary.

commerce (**kom**-erss) *noun* trade and the services that assist trading, such as banking and insurance. [from *com-* and a Latin word *merx* meaning 'merchandise']

commercial *adjective* **1** to do with trade or commerce. **2** (said about television or radio) paid for by firms or organizations whose advertisements are included. **3** intended to produce profits. **commercial** *noun* an advertisement on radio or television. **commercially** *adverb* **commercialism** *noun*

commercialized *adjective* organized or altered to make a profit ♦ *Christmas has become very commercialized.* **commercialization** *noun*

commiserate (kə-**miz**-er-ayt) *verb* to express pity, to sympathize. **commiseration** *noun* [from *com-* and a Latin word *miserari* meaning 'to pity']

commissar (**kom**-i-sar) *noun* (*historical*) a communist official in the former Soviet Union. [from a Russian word, related to *commission*]

commissariat (kom-i-**sair**-iət) *noun* a military department supplying food and equipment.

commission *noun* **1** a task formally given to someone ♦ *a commission to paint a portrait.* **2** a body of people who are given a task. **3** an appointment to be an officer in the armed forces. **4** the act of committing something ♦ *the commission of a crime.* **5** a payment made to an agent for selling goods or services. **commission** *verb* to give a commission to someone or for a task to be done. **in commission** (said about military equipment) ready for service. **out of commission** not in working order. [from a Latin word *committere* meaning 'to entrust']

commissionaire (kə-mish-ən-**air**) *noun* a uniformed attendant at the entrance to a hotel, theatre, or other large building. [a French word, from a Latin word *commissarius* meaning 'person in charge']

commissioner *noun* **1** a person appointed to do a job or task by commission. **2** a member of a commission. **3** a government official in charge of a district abroad.

commissioner for oaths *noun* a solicitor authorized to hear oaths sworn by a person making an affidavit.

commit *verb* (**committed, committing**) **1** to do or perform something ♦ *to commit a crime.* **2** to entrust someone or something for safe keeping or treatment. **3** to send a person for trial in a lawcourt. **4** to agree to use time, money, or other resources for a particular purpose ♦ *The company has committed half its profits this year to providing new office accommodation.* **to commit to memory** to memorize something. **to commit yourself** to give a definite undertaking or opinion. [from *com-* and a Latin word *mittere* meaning 'to put' or 'to send']

commitment *noun* **1** the state of being involved in an obligation. **2** something you have agreed to do, an obligation.

committal *noun* **1** the process of committing a person to prison or other place of confinement. **2** the act of giving a body for burial or cremation.

committed *adjective* dedicated or pledged to support a belief or cause ♦ *a committed Christian.*

committee *noun* a group of people appointed to deal with special business or to manage the business of a club or other organization.

commode (kə-**mohd**) *noun* **1** a chair or

covered box with a chamber pot fitted in it. **2** an ornamental chest of drawers. [a French word meaning 'convenient']

commodious (kə-moh-di-əs) *adjective* spacious and comfortable. [same origin as for *commodity*]

commodity *noun* (**commodities**) something useful or valuable, a product or article of trade. [from a Latin word *commodus* meaning 'convenient']

commodore (kom-ə-dor) *noun* **1** a naval officer ranking above a captain and below a rear admiral. **2** the commander of a squadron or other division of a fleet. [via Dutch from a French word *commandeur* meaning 'commander']

common *adjective* **1** occurring frequently, usual or ordinary ♦ *Street crime is becoming more common.* SYNONYMS: usual, frequent, commonplace, familiar, normal. **2** to do with most people or with the whole community. **3** belonging to or shared by two or more people or things. **4** without special distinction, ordinary ♦ *the common sparrow.* **5** having no taste or refinement, vulgar.
common *noun* an area of land that everyone can use.
commons *plural noun* **1** (*historical*) the common people regarded as a political force. **2** short for **House of Commons. in common** shared by two or more people or things. **commonly** *adverb* **commonness** *noun* [from a Latin word *communis* meaning 'common']

common denominator *noun*
1 (*Mathematics*) a number that is a multiple of each of the denominators of two or more fractions. **2** a feature shared by members of a group.

commoner *noun* one of the common people, not a member of the nobility.

Common Era *noun* the Christian era.

common factor *noun* a factor which is common to two or more numbers. The common factors of 8 and 12 are 1, 2, and 4.

common ground *noun* views or opinions shared by all the people involved.

common law *noun* unwritten law based on custom and on former court decisions.

common-law husband or **common-law wife** *noun* a husband or wife recognized by common law without an official marriage.

Common Market *noun* a former name for the European Union.

common multiple *noun* a number which is a multiple of each of two or more numbers. 15 and 30 are common multiples of 3 and 5.

common or garden *adjective* (*informal*) of the ordinary or usual type.

commonplace *adjective* ordinary or usual.
commonplace *noun* something commonplace ♦ *Air travel is now a commonplace.*

common room *noun* a room in a school or college, used for social purposes by pupils, students, or teachers.

common sense *noun* ordinary good sense and judgement in practical matters.

common time *noun* (*Music*) a rhythmic pattern of two or four beats (especially four crotchets) in the bar.

commonwealth *noun* **1** an independent state or community, especially a democratic republic. **2** a federal association of states ♦ *the Commonwealth of Australia.*

Commonwealth *noun* **1** an association of the UK and its dependencies together with independent states that were formerly part of the British Empire. **2** the republican government of Britain established by Cromwell between the execution of Charles I in 1649 and the Restoration of Charles II in 1660. [from *common* and *wealth* in an old sense meaning 'welfare']

commotion *noun* uproar or disturbance. SYNONYMS: uproar, disturbance, tumult, rumpus. [from *com-* and a Latin word *motio* meaning 'movement' or 'motion']

communal (kom-yoo-nəl) *adjective* shared between the members of a group or community ♦ *a communal kitchen.*
communally *adverb* [same origin as for *common*]

commune [1] (kom-yoon) *noun* **1** a group of people living together and sharing certain possessions and domestic responsibilities. **2** a district of local government in France and some other European countries. [from a Latin word *communis* meaning 'common']

commune [2] (kə-mewn) *verb* to share intimate thoughts or feelings.

communicable *adjective* able to be communicated.

communicant *noun* a person who receives Holy Communion.

communicate *verb* 1 to give or share information ♦ *We will communicate the news to our friends.* 2 to transfer or transmit ♦ *There is a danger of communicating the disease to others.* 3 to exchange news or have social dealings. 4 to be connected ♦ *The passage communicates with the hall and stairs.* [from a Latin word *communicare* meaning 'to tell' or 'to share']

communication *noun* 1 the process of communicating. 2 something that communicates information from one person to another, such as a letter or message. 3 a means of communicating between places, such as a road, railway, telegraph line, or radio system.

communication cord *noun* a cord or chain in a train, which a passenger may pull to stop the train in an emergency.

communicative (kǝ-mew-nik-ǝtiv) *adjective* willing to talk and give information.

communion *noun* 1 religious fellowship, sharing beliefs or ideas. 2 social dealings between people. 3 a body of Christians belonging to the same denomination ♦ *the Anglican communion.*
Communion or **Holy Communion** *noun* the Christian sacrament in which bread and wine are consecrated and given to worshippers. [same origin as for *commune*[1]]

communiqué (kǝ-mew-ni-kay) *noun* an official message or announcement, especially one given to the press. [a French word meaning 'communicated']

communism *noun* a political and social system in which property is owned by the community and each member works for the common benefit.
Communism *noun* a political doctrine or movement based on Marxist principles, including state control of the means of production, and implemented in the former Soviet Union, China, and elsewhere. [from a French word *commun* meaning 'common']

communist *noun* a supporter of communism. **communistic** *adjective*

community *noun* (**communities**) 1 the people living in one place or country and considered as a whole. 2 a group with similar interests or origins ♦ *the farming community.* 3 the state of having interests in common. [same origin as for *commune*]

community service *noun* unpaid work for the community that an offender has to do instead of serving a prison sentence.

commutable *adjective* exchangeable, able to be exchanged for money.

commutative (kǝ-mew-tǝ-tiv) *adjective* (*Mathematics*) describing an operation that produces the same result regardless of the order in which the quantities are taken, e.g. $3 + 4 = 7$, $4 + 3 = 7$.

commutator *noun* a device for reversing the direction of flow of an electrical current.

commute *verb* 1 to travel regularly for some distance to and from work in a city. 2 to exchange one thing for another. 3 to change a punishment into something less severe. **commutation** *noun* [from *com-* and a Latin word *mutare* meaning 'to change']

commuter *noun* a person who commutes to and from work.

compact[1] (kom-pakt) *noun* 1 an agreement or contract. 2 a small flat container for face powder. [from *com-* and *pact*[1]]

compact[2] (kǝm-pakt) *adjective* 1 closely or neatly packed together. 2 concise or brief. **compact** *verb* to make something compact; to join or press things firmly together or into a small space. **compactly** *adverb* **compactness** *noun* [from a Latin word *compactum* meaning 'put together']

compact disc *noun* a small plastic disc on which music or computer data is stored and can be read by a laser beam.

companion *noun* 1 a person you spend time with or travel with. 2 the title given to a member of certain official orders ♦ *Companion of Honour.* 3 a person employed to live with and support someone who is old or unwell. 4 each of two things that match or go together. [from *com-* and a Latin word *panis* meaning 'bread'; the original meaning was 'a person who eats bread with another']

companionable *adjective* friendly or sociable. **companionably** *adverb*

companionship *noun* the friendly feeling of being with other people.

company *noun* (**companies**) 1 being with other people, companionship. SYNONYMS: friendship, society, companionship, fellowship. 2 a number of people who have come together for a social occasion. 3 the people you spend a lot of time with ♦ *He has got into bad company.* **4** a business organization or firm. **5** a ship's officers and crew. **6** a subdivision of an infantry battalion. [same origin as for *companion*]

comparable (kom-per-əbəl) *adjective* able to be compared with something else, similar. **comparably** *adverb* **comparability** *noun*

comparative *adjective* **1** involving a comparison with something else ♦ *a comparative study of the output of two firms.* **2** judged or estimated by comparing it with something else ♦ *They were living in comparative comfort.* **3** (*Grammar*) describing a form of an adjective or adverb that means 'more', such as *bigger, quicker, worse.*
comparative *noun* a comparative form of an adjective or adverb. **comparatively** *adverb*

compare *verb* **1** to judge how two or more things or people are similar and different. **to compare someone** or **something to** to say that one thing or person is like another. **to compare someone** or **something with 1** to consider things or people in detail to judge their similarities and differences. **2** to be worthy of comparison ♦ *Her new book does not compare with her earlier ones.* [from a Latin word *comparare* meaning 'to match with each other']
◊ Notice that you say *compare to* when you are showing that two or more people or things are similar (as in *She compared me to her cousin Helen*) and you say *compare with* when you make a more detailed judgement about how they are the same or different (as in *We have to compare this year's profits with last year's*).

comparison *noun* the act of comparing things or people.

compartment *noun* **1** one of the spaces into which a structure or other object is divided, a separate room or enclosed space. **2** a division of a railway carriage, separated by partitions. **compartmental** *adjective* [from *com-* and a Latin word *partiri* meaning 'to share']

compartmentalize (kom-part-ment-ə-liyz) *verb* to divide something into categories or compartments.

compass *noun* **1** a device that shows direction, with a needle pointing to the magnetic north. **2** the range or scope of something ♦ *The question of blame does not come within the compass of our inquiry.*

compasses *plural noun* an instrument for drawing circles, with two arms joined at one end. [via Old French from Latin words *com-* meaning 'together' and *passus* meaning 'a step or pace']

compassion *noun* a feeling of pity that makes you want to help or show mercy. **compassionate** *adjective* **compassionately** *adverb* [from *com-* and a Latin word *passum* meaning 'suffered']

compatible (kəm-pat-ibəl) *adjective* **1** able to exist or be used together ♦ *The printer is not compatible with all types of computer.* **2** (said about people) able to live together harmoniously. **compatibly** *adverb* **compatibility** *noun* [from a Latin word *compati* meaning 'to suffer together']

compatriot (kəm-pat-ri-ət) *noun* a person from the same country as another. [from *com-* and *patriot*]

compel *verb* (**compelled, compelling**) to use force or influence to make someone do something; to allow someone no choice of action. SYNONYMS: force, oblige, drive, make. [from *com-* and a Latin word *pellere* meaning 'to drive']

compelling *adjective* bringing attention or admiration.

compendious (kəm-pen-di-əs) *adjective* giving a lot of information in a concise form. [same origin as for *compendium*]

compendium (kəm-pen-di-əm) *noun* (**compendiums** or **compendia**) **1** a concise and comprehensive summary of information about a subject. **2** a collection of board games in one box. [a Latin word meaning 'a saving']

compensate *verb* **1** to give someone money or something else, to make up for a loss or injury. **2** to serve as a counterbalance ♦ *Our recent victory compensates for earlier defeats.* **compensation** *noun* [from a Latin word *compensare* meaning 'to weigh one thing against another']

compensatory (kom-pən-say-ter-i) *adjective* serving or helping to compensate for something.

compère (kom-pair) *noun* a person who introduces the performers in a variety show or broadcast.
compère *verb* to act as compère to a show etc. [a French word meaning 'godfather']

compete *verb* **1** to take part in a competition or other contest. **2** to try to

be more successful than your rivals.
SYNONYMS: contend, vie, strive. [from *com-* and a Latin word *petere* meaning 'to aim at']

competent (kom-pit-ənt) *adjective* 1 having the ability or authority to do a particular job or task. 2 adequate or satisfactory ♦ *He has a competent knowledge of Russian.* **competence** noun **competently** *adverb* [same origin as for *compete*]

competition *noun* 1 a game, race, or other contest in which people try to win. 2 the process of competing ♦ *There is strong competition in the book trade.* 3 people who are competing with you ♦ *We have strong foreign competition.*

competitive *adjective* 1 involving competition ♦ *competitive sports.* 2 as good as or better than others of the same kind ♦ *competitive prices.* **competitively** *adverb* **competitiveness** *noun*

competitor *noun* 1 someone who takes part in a competition. 2 a rival in business.

compile *verb* 1 to collect and arrange information into a list or book. 2 to make up a book of information in this way. 3 (*Computing*) (said about a computer program) to translate instructions from a high-level language into a form which can be understood by the computer. **compilation** (kom-pil-ay-shən) *noun* **compiler** *noun* [from an Old French word *compiler*]

complacent (kəm-play-sənt) *adjective* smug or self-satisfied. **complacency** *noun* **complacently** *adverb* [from *com-* and a Latin word *placens* meaning 'pleasing'] ◊ Do not confuse this word with **complaisant**, which has a different meaning.

complain *verb* to say that you are unhappy about something or that something is wrong. SYNONYMS: protest, grumble, object, protest, find fault, grouse, moan. **to complain of** to say that you are suffering from a pain or a symptom of illness. [via Old French from a Latin word *complangere* meaning 'to be very sorry about']

complaint *noun* 1 a statement complaining about something. 2 a cause of dissatisfaction ♦ *They produced a long list of complaints.* 3 a minor illness.

complaisant (kəm-play-zənt) *adjective* willing to do what pleases other people. **complaisance** *noun* [from a French word *complaire* meaning 'to acquiesce']

◊ Do not confuse this word with **complacent**, which has a different meaning.

complement (kom-pli-mənt) *noun* 1 something that makes a thing complete. 2 the number or quantity that fills something ♦ *The aircraft had its full complement of passengers.* 3 (*Grammar*) a word or words used after verbs such as *be*, *become*, and *make*, which completes what is said about the subject or object of the verb, e.g. *happy* in the sentence *We are happy* and *king of England* in the sentence *They made him king of England.* 4 (*Geometry*) the amount by which an angle is less than 90°.
complement *verb* to make something complete; to form a complement to something ♦ *The hat complements the outfit.* [same origin as for *complete*]
◊ Do not confuse this word with **compliment**, which has a different meaning.

complementary *adjective* 1 completing something or forming a complement. 2 (*Geometry*) (said about angles) adding up to 90°. 3 (said about colours) having the appearance of white light when mixed. ◊ Do not confuse this word with **complimentary**, which has a different meaning.

complementary medicine *noun* medical methods that are not officially recognized but are used as an alternative to conventional methods, e.g. acupuncture and homoeopathy.

complete *adjective* 1 having all its parts, not lacking anything. SYNONYMS: finished, entire, intact, whole. 2 finished ♦ *The work is now complete.* 3 thorough, in every way ♦ *The man is a complete stranger.*
complete *verb* 1 to add what is lacking to something to make it complete. 2 to finish a task or piece of work. SYNONYMS: finish, get done, conclude, end, accomplish, achieve. 3 to give the information asked for in a document ♦ *Please complete the questionnaire and return it in the envelope provided.* **completely** *adverb* **completeness** *noun* [from a Latin word *completum* meaning 'filled up']

completion (kəm-plee-shən) *noun* 1 the process of completing something. 2 something that completes a process, especially the selling of a house.

complex (kom-pleks) *adjective* 1 made up of several parts. 2 complicated. SYNONYMS:

complicated, intricate, involved.

complex noun 1 a set of buildings made up of related parts ♦ a sports complex. 2 a connected group of feelings or ideas that influence a person's behaviour or mental attitude ♦ an inferiority complex. **complexity** (kəm-pleks-iti) noun [from a Latin word complexum meaning 'embraced' or 'plaited']

complexion noun 1 the colour, texture, and appearance of the skin of the face. 2 the way things seem ♦ That puts a different complexion on the matter. [from an Old French word, related to complex]

complex number noun (Mathematics) a number containing real and imaginary numbers.

compliant (kəm-ply-ənt) adjective 1 (said about a person) willing to comply or obey. 2 meeting a standard or requirement. **compliance** noun

complicate verb to make something complex or complicated. [from com- and a Latin word plicare meaning 'to fold']

complicated adjective 1 made up of many parts. 2 difficult to understand or do. SYNONYMS: complex, intricate, involved.

complication noun 1 the process of complicating things. 2 a complex or confused condition or state. 3 something that complicates a situation or process or adds difficulties. 4 an illness or condition that arises during the course of another and makes it worse.

complicity (kəm-plis-iti) noun being involved in a crime or wrongdoing. [same origin as for complicate]

compliment noun something you say or do to show that you approve of a person or thing.
compliment verb to pay a compliment to someone, to congratulate someone.
compliments plural noun formal greetings conveyed in a message. [via French and Italian from a Latin word complementum meaning 'completion' or 'fulfilment']
◊ Do not confuse this word with **complement**, which has a different meaning.

complimentary adjective 1 expressing a compliment. 2 given free of charge ♦ complimentary tickets.
◊ Do not confuse this word with **complementary**, which has a different meaning.

compline (kom-plin) noun the last service of the day in some Christian Churches. [from an Old French word complie, related to complete]

comply (kəm-ply) verb (**complies, complied, complying**) to do what you are asked or ordered to do. **comply with** to obey ♦ You must comply with the rules. [from an Italian word complire, related to complete]

component (kəm-poh-nənt) noun each of the parts of which a machine or other thing is made.
component adjective forming a component of something. [from a Latin word componere meaning 'to put together']

compose verb 1 to form or make up a whole ♦ The class is composed of 20 students. 2 to write or create a work of art, especially music or poetry. 3 to arrange things into good order. **to compose yourself** to become calm. [same origin as for component]

composed adjective calm, having your feelings under control. **composedly** (kəm-pohz-id-li) adverb

composer noun a person who writes music.

composite (kom-pə-zit) adjective 1 made up of a number of different parts or styles. 2 (said about a plant, such as a daisy or dandelion) having a flower head of individual flowers forming one bloom. 3 (Mathematics) (said about a number) able to be divided exactly by one or more whole numbers as well as by itself and 1. [same origin as for compose]

composition noun 1 the process of putting things together into a whole. 2 something composed or written, especially a piece of music or writing. 3 the parts that make up something ♦ the composition of the soil. 4 the arrangement of the parts of a picture. 5 a compound artificial substance.

compositor noun a person who sets up type for printing.

compos mentis adjective in your right mind, sane. [a Latin phrase meaning 'having control of the mind']

compost noun 1 decayed leaves, grass, and other organic matter used as a fertilizer. 2 a mixture of soil and other ingredients for growing seedlings, cuttings, etc.
compost verb to treat something with compost; to make things into compost. [same origin as for compose]

composure *noun* the state of having a calm mind or manner.

compound [1] (kom-pownd) *adjective* made up of several parts or ingredients. **compound** *noun* a compound thing or substance. [from a Latin word *componere* meaning 'to put together']

compound [2] (kəm-**pownd**) *verb* 1 to put things together to form a whole, to combine things. 2 to make something that is already bad worse.

compound [3] (kom-pownd) *noun* a fenced area, often containing buildings. [via Portuguese and Dutch from a Malay (Malaysian) word *kampong*]

compound fraction *noun* a number that is made up of a whole number and a fraction, e.g. $\frac{53}{2}$.

compound fracture *noun* a fracture in which the damaged bone has pierced the skin.

compound interest *noun* interest that is paid on the original capital and on the interest that has already been added to it.

compound time *noun* (*Music*) a rhythm in which each beat is divided into three smaller units.

comprehend *verb* 1 to grasp something mentally, to understand something. 2 to include something. **comprehension** *noun* [from *com-* and a Latin word *prehendere* meaning 'to take or seize']

comprehensible *adjective* able to be understood. **comprehensibility** *noun* **comprehensibly** *adverb*

comprehensive *adjective* 1 including all or most of something ♦ *The new textbooks seem to be comprehensive.* 2 including all or many kinds of people or things. **comprehensive** *noun* a comprehensive school. **comprehensively** *adverb* **comprehensiveness** *noun*

comprehensive school *noun* a secondary school providing an education for children of all abilities in an area.

compress [1] (kəm-**press**) *verb* to press things together or into a smaller space. **compression** *noun* **compressor** *noun* [from *com-* and a Latin word *pressare* meaning 'to press']

compress [2] (kom-press) *noun* a soft pad or cloth pressed on the body to stop bleeding or to relieve inflammation.

compressible *adjective* able to be compressed.

compressor *noun* a machine for compressing air or other gases.

comprise (kəm-**priyz**) *verb* 1 to include or consist of several things ♦ *The pentathlon comprises five events.* 2 to form or make up a whole ♦ *These three rooms comprise the apartment.* [from a French word *comprendre*, related to *comprehend*]
◊ In meaning 2 it is better to use *compose* or *constitute*. It is incorrect to use *comprise* with *of*, as in *The group was comprised of twenty students*; instead you should say *The group was composed of twenty students.*

compromise (kom-prə-miyz) *noun* 1 settling a disagreement by each side accepting less than it originally demanded. 2 a settlement made in this way. 3 something that is halfway between opposite opinions or courses of action. **compromise** *verb* 1 to settle a dispute by a compromise. 2 to expose someone to danger or suspicion by indiscreet or unwise behaviour. [from *com-* and a Latin word *promittere* meaning 'to promise']

comptroller *noun* a controller (used in the title of some financial officers). [another spelling of *controller*, influenced by the French word *compte* meaning 'calculation']

compulsion *noun* 1 a strong and uncontrollable desire to do something. 2 the process of compelling someone to do something.

compulsive *adjective* 1 acting from a compulsion ♦ *a compulsive gambler.* 2 extremely exciting or interesting. **compulsively** *adverb*
◊ Do not confuse this word with **compulsory**, which has a different meaning.

compulsory *adjective* that must be done, required by a rule or law. **compulsorily** *adverb*
◊ Do not confuse this word with **compulsive**, which has a different meaning.

compunction *noun* a feeling of slight guilt or regret. [from *com-* and a Latin word *punctum* meaning 'pricked (by conscience)']

compute *verb* to calculate or reckon an amount mathematically. **computable** *adjective* **computation** *noun* [from *com-* and a Latin word *putare* meaning 'to reckon']

computer noun an electronic machine for making calculations, storing and analysing information put into it, or controlling machinery automatically.

computer-assisted adjective using computers to control or support a process ♦ computer-assisted learning.

computer graphics plural noun data displayed or printed out as graphics by a computer.

computerize verb 1 to process or store information by means of a computer. 2 to convert a process or set of machinery so that it can make use of or be controlled by a computer. **computerization** noun

computer science noun the study of the principles and use of computers.

comrade noun 1 a companion who shares your activities or is a fellow member of an organization. 2 a fellow socialist or communist. **comradeship** noun [from a Spanish word camarada meaning 'room-mate']

con [1] verb (**conned, conning**) (informal) to persuade or swindle someone after winning their confidence.
con noun (informal) a confidence trick. [a short form of confidence trick]

con [2] see pro and con.

concatenate (kən-kat-in-ayt) verb to link things together in a chain or series. **concatenation** noun [from com- and a Latin word catena meaning 'chain']

concave adjective curved like the inside surface of a ball. **concavity** (kən-kav-iti) noun [from com- and a Latin word cavus meaning 'hollow']

conceal verb to keep something secret or hidden. **concealment** noun [from com- and a Latin word celare meaning 'to hide']

concede (kən-seed) verb 1 to admit that something is true. 2 to grant or allow something ♦ The farmer conceded us the right to cross his land. 3 to admit defeat in a contest. [from com- and a Latin word cedere meaning 'to cede']

conceit noun too much pride in yourself. [from conceive, in an earlier meaning 'idea' or 'opinion']

conceited adjective being too proud of yourself. SYNONYMS: arrogant, boastful, self-important, bumptious, immodest, proud, self-satisfied; (informal) cocky. **conceitedly** adverb

conceivable adjective able to be imagined or believed. **conceivably** adverb

conceive verb 1 to become pregnant. 2 to form an idea or plan etc. in the mind, to imagine or think of something. [from a Latin word concipere meaning 'to take in' or 'to contain']

concentrate verb 1 to give all your thought or attention or effort to something. 2 to bring people or things together or to come together to one place. 3 to make a liquid less dilute.
concentrate noun a concentrated form of a substance, especially of food. [from com- and centre]

concentration noun 1 the process of concentrating. 2 the ability to concentrate on something. 3 the mass or amount of a substance contained in a specified amount of a solvent or in a mixture.

concentration camp noun a place where political prisoners are kept together.

concentric (kən-sen-trik) adjective having the same centre ♦ concentric circles. [from a Latin word, related to centre]

concept (kon-sept) noun an idea or general notion ♦ the concept of liberty. [same origin as for conceive]

conception noun 1 the process of conceiving a child. 2 the process of thinking up a plan or idea, or the idea itself. 3 the way in which you think of something.

concern verb 1 to be about something, or to have something as its subject ♦ The story concerns a family in wartime. 2 to be of importance to someone, or to affect someone ♦ What I am saying concerns everyone. SYNONYMS: affect, interest, involve, be important to, matter to. 3 to worry someone ♦ It concerned them that their son had not contacted them for several weeks. SYNONYMS: worry, bother, trouble, upset, distress.
concern noun 1 something of interest or importance, a responsibility ♦ That is not our concern. SYNONYMS: business, affair, matter. 2 a worry or anxiety. 3 a business or firm ♦ a printing concern. [from com- and a Latin word cernere meaning 'to sift']

concerned adjective 1 worried or anxious about something. 2 involved or interested in something.

concerning preposition about, to do with.

concert noun a musical entertainment given in public. **in concert** 1 acting together. 2 giving a concert. [from an Italian word concertare meaning 'to harmonize']

concerted (kən-**sert**-id) adjective 1 done in cooperation with others ♦ We made a concerted effort to finish on time. 2 (said about music) arranged in parts, of equal importance, for voices or instruments.

concertina noun a portable musical instrument with bellows, played by squeezing while pressing small keys or studs at each end.
concertina verb (**concertinas, concertinaed, concertining**) to fold or collapse like the bellows of a concertina. [from concert]

concerto (kən-**cher**-toh) noun (**concertos** or **concerti**) a piece of music for one or more solo instruments and an orchestra. [an Italian word, related to concert]

concession noun 1 something that you agree to concede to someone, especially in response to a demand or complaint. 2 a reduction in price for a certain category of person. 3 a right given by the owners of land to use it for a special purpose ♦ an oil concession. 4 a commercial operation set up in the premises of a larger one, such as a hairdresser in a department store. **concessionary** adjective [same origin as for concede]

conch (kongk or konch) noun the spiral shell of a kind of shellfish, sometimes used as a horn. [from a Latin word concha meaning 'shellfish']

conciliate verb 1 to make someone less angry or hostile by being friendly or pleasant to them. 2 to reconcile people who disagree. **conciliation** noun **conciliator** noun **conciliatory** (kən-**sil**-i-ətri) adjective [from a Latin word, related to council]

concise (kən-**syss**) adjective brief, giving much information in few words. **concisely** adverb [from com- and a Latin word caedere meaning 'to cut']

conclave (kon-**klayv**) noun a private meeting, especially of cardinals to elect a pope. [from com- and a Latin word clavis meaning 'key']

conclude verb 1 to bring something to an end, or to come to an end. SYNONYMS: end, close, finish, complete, round off, stop. 2 to arrange or settle something finally ♦ The two countries then concluded a treaty. 3 to

arrive at a belief or opinion by reasoning ♦ The inquiry concluded that the crash was caused by human error. SYNONYMS: decide, infer, deduce, judge. [from com- and a Latin word claudere meaning 'to shut']

conclusion noun 1 an end or ending. 2 a belief or opinion based on reasoning. 3 the arrangement or settling of something ♦ conclusion of the treaty.

conclusive adjective putting an end to all doubt or uncertainty, convincing. **conclusively** adverb

concoct (kən-**kokt**) verb 1 to make something by putting various ingredients together. 2 to invent something to say ♦ We'll have to concoct an excuse. **concoction** noun [from com- and a Latin word coctum meaning 'cooked']

concomitant (kən-**kom**-i-tənt) adjective naturally accompanying something or associated with it.
concomitant noun an accompanying thing. **concomitance** noun [from com- and a Latin word comitis meaning 'of a companion']

concord noun friendly agreement or harmony. **concordant** (kən-**kor**-dənt) adjective [from com- and a Latin word cor meaning 'heart']

concordance (kən-**kor**-dənss) noun an index of the words used in a book or in an author's works.

concordat noun an agreement made, especially between the Church and the government of a state. [from a Latin word concordatum meaning 'something agreed on']

concourse (kon-**korss**) noun 1 a crowd or gathering. 2 an open area through which people pass, e.g. at an airport. [same origin as for concur]

concrete [1] (kon-**kreet**) noun a mixture of cement with sand and gravel, used in building.
concrete adjective 1 existing in a physical form, able to be touched and felt. 2 definite or positive ♦ The police need concrete evidence. [from a Latin word concrescere meaning 'to grow together']

concrete [2] (kon-**kreet**) verb to cover a surface or area with concrete.

concrete jungle noun an unpleasant urban area with a concentration of unattractive modern buildings.

concretion (kən-**kree**-shən) noun a hard solid mass.

concubine (konk-yoo-biyn) *noun* in societies that practise polygamy, a woman who lives with a man but has a lower role than his wife. **concubinage** (kən-**kew**-bin-ij) *noun* [from *com*- and a Latin word *cubare* meaning 'to lie']

concur (kən-**ker**) *verb* (**concurred, concurring**) **1** to agree. **2** to happen together, to coincide. **concurrence** *noun* [from *com*- and a Latin word *currere* meaning 'to run']

concurrent (kən-**ku**-rənt) *adjective* existing or happening at the same time. **concurrently** *adverb*

concuss (kən-**kus**) *verb* to affect someone with concussion.

concussion (kən-**kush**-ən) *noun* injury to the brain caused by a hard blow. [from a Latin word *concussum* meaning 'shaken violently']

condemn *verb* **1** to express strong disapproval of someone or something. SYNONYMS: denounce, decry, censure, revile. **2** to pronounce someone guilty of a crime, to convict someone. **3** to sentence a criminal to a punishment ♦ *The murderer was condemned to death.* **4** to destine someone to an unhappy fate ♦ *After the war they were condemned to a life of poverty.* **5** to declare a building unfit for use. **condemnation** (kon-dem-**nay**-shən) *noun* [from *com*- and a Latin word *damnare* meaning 'to condemn']

condense *verb* **1** to make a liquid denser or more concentrated. **2** to change a substance from gas or vapour into liquid, or to be changed in this way ♦ *Steam was condensing on the windows.* **3** to express a thought or idea in fewer words. **condensation** (kon-den-**say**-shən) *noun* [from a Latin word *condensus* meaning 'thick or dense']

condensed milk *noun* milk that has been thickened by evaporation and sweetened.

condenser *noun* **1** a system of lenses for directing light. **2** a device for storing an electric charge.

condescend *verb* **1** to behave in a way that shows you feel superior. **2** to agree to do something even though you think it is beneath your diginity ♦ *In the end they condescended to come with us.* **condescension** *noun* [from a Latin word *condescendere* meaning 'to lower yourself']

condign (kən-**diyn**) *adjective* (*formal*) (said about a punishment) severe and well-deserved. [from *com*- and a Latin word *dignus* meaning 'worthy']

condiment (**kon**-di-mənt) *noun* a seasoning for food, such as salt or pepper.

condition *noun* **1** the state in which a person or thing is with regard to appearance, fitness, or working order ♦ *My bicycle is not in good condition.* **2** a state of physical fitness or fitness for use ♦ *I'm trying to get into condition.* **3** an illness or medical problem ♦ *a heart condition.* **4** something required as part of an agreement.

conditions *plural noun* the situation or surroundings that affect something ♦ *They wanted to improve their working conditions.*

condition *verb* **1** to bring something into the right condition needed for use. **2** to make someone physically fit. **3** to have a strong effect or influence on someone or something. **4** to train or accustom someone. **on condition that** only if; on the understanding that a certain thing will be done. [from a Latin word *condicere* meaning 'to agree on']

conditional *adjective* containing a condition or requirement ♦ *a conditional agreement.*

conditional *noun* (*Grammar*) a word or clause, or a form of a verb, that expresses a condition. **conditionally** *adverb*

conditioned reflex or **conditioned response** *noun* a reaction produced by training, not a natural reaction.

conditioner *noun* a substance put on something to improve its condition, such as a liquid for the hair.

condole (kən-**dohl**) *verb* to express sympathy. **condolence** *noun* [from *com*- and a Latin word *dolere* meaning 'to grieve']

condom (**kon**-dəm) *noun* a rubber sheath worn on the penis during sexual intercourse as a contraceptive or to prevent infection. [origin unknown]

condone (kən-**dohn**) *verb* to forgive or overlook a wrongdoing ♦ *We should not condone violence.* **condonation** (kon-dən-**ay**-shən) *noun* [from a Latin word *condonare* meaning 'to refrain from punishing']

condor *noun* a large vulture of South America. [via Spanish from a South American language]

conducive (kən-**dew**-siv) *adjective* helping to cause or produce something ♦ *We need an atmosphere that is conducive to work.* [same origin as for *conduct*]

conduct [1] (kən-**dukt**) *verb* 1 to lead or guide someone. 2 to direct the performance of an orchestra or choir. 3 to manage or direct an undertaking or business operation. 4 to have the property of allowing heat, light, sound, or electricity to pass along or through itself. **to conduct oneself** to behave in a specified way ♦ *We tried to conduct ourselves with dignity.* [from *com-* and a Latin word *ducere* meaning 'to lead']

conduct [2] (**kon**-dukt) *noun* 1 a person's behaviour. SYNONYMS: behaviour, manners. 2 the directing or managing of affairs.

conductance *noun* the degree to which a specified body conducts electricity.

conduction *noun* the transmission of heat or electricity.

conductive *adjective* able to conduct heat or electricity. **conductivity** *noun*

conductor *noun* 1 a person who directs the performance of an orchestra or choir. 2 an official who collects the fares on a bus. 3 a substance that conducts heat or electricity.

conduit (**kon**-dit or **kon**-dwit) *noun* 1 a pipe or channel for carrying liquids. 2 a tube or trough protecting insulated electric wires. [from a French word, related to *conduct*]

cone *noun* 1 an object with a round flat base, tapering to a point at the other end. 2 something shaped like this. 3 the dry fruit of certain evergreen trees, having woody scales arranged in a cone-like shape. 4 (*Anatomy*) a cone-shaped structure in the retina of the eye, sensitive to bright and coloured light (see also **rod**). [from a Greek word *kōnos*]

coney *noun* (**coneys**) rabbit fur used in making clothes. [from an Old French word *conin*]

confection *noun* 1 a dish or delicacy made from various sweet ingredients. 2 something made of various things put together. [from a Latin word *conficere* meaning 'to put together']

confectioner *noun* someone who makes or sells sweets and chocolates.

confectionery *noun* sweets and chocolates and other sweet things.

confederacy *noun* a union of states, a confederation.

confederate *adjective* allied, joined by an agreement or treaty.
confederate *noun* 1 a member of a confederacy. 2 an ally or accomplice. [from *com-* and a Latin word *foederatum* meaning 'allied']

confederated *adjective* united by an agreement or treaty.

Confederate States *plural noun* the 11 southern States which seceded from the United States in 1860–1 and formed a confederacy of their own, causing the American Civil War.

confederation *noun* 1 the process of joining in an alliance. 2 a group of people, organizations, or states joined together by an agreement or treaty.

confer *verb* (**conferred, conferring**) 1 to grant or bestow something. 2 to hold a discussion before deciding something. **conferrable** *adjective* [from *com-* and a Latin word *ferre* meaning 'to bring']

conference *noun* 1 a meeting for holding a discussion or a series of discussions. 2 a linking of telephones or computers so that several people can hold a discussion.

conferment (kən-**fer**-mənt) *noun* the granting or bestowing of something.

confess *verb* 1 to state openly that you have done wrong or have a weakness; to admit something. SYNONYMS: admit, acknowledge, own up. 2 to say something cautiously or reluctantly ♦ *I must confess that I am surprised.* 3 to declare your sins formally to a priest. [from a Latin word *confiteri* meaning 'to acknowledge']

confession *noun* 1 the act of confessing something. 2 something you confess, a statement of your wrongdoing. 3 a statement of your religious beliefs or principles.

confessional *noun* an enclosed compartment in a church, in which a priest hears confessions.

confessor *noun* 1 a priest who hears confessions and gives spiritual guidance. 2 a person who keeps to a religious faith in the face of danger ♦ *King Edward the Confessor.*

confetti noun small pieces of coloured paper thrown over the bride and bridegroom at a wedding. [an Italian word meaning 'sweets' (because sweets were once thrown at Italian weddings)]

confidant (kon-fid-**ant**) noun a person you confide in.
confidante noun a woman you confide in.

confide verb 1 to tell something to someone confidentially ♦ *Gemma decided to confide in her sister.* 2 to entrust something to someone. [from *com-* and a Latin word *fidere* meaning 'to trust']

confidence noun 1 firm trust ♦ *I have a lot of confidence in you.* 2 a feeling of certainty or self-assurance about what you can do ♦ *Does he have the confidence to do the task?* 3 something told confidentially ♦ *May I tell you a confidence?* **in confidence** as a secret. **to take someone into your confidence** to trust them with a secret. [same origin as for *confide*]

confidence trick noun swindling someone after persuading them to trust you.

confident adjective feeling confidence, bold and self-assured. SYNONYMS: optimistic, positive, certain, sure, hopeful. **confidently** adverb

confidential adjective 1 meant to be kept secret, said or written in confidence. 2 entrusted with private information ♦ *a confidential secretary.* **confidentiality** noun **confidentially** adverb

configuration noun 1 a method of arrangement of the parts of a machine or system. 2 a shape or outline.

confine (kən-**fyn**) verb 1 to keep or restrict someone or something within certain limits. 2 to keep someone shut up. **confines** (kon-**fiynz**) plural noun the limits or boundaries of an area. [from *com-* and a Latin word *finis* meaning 'limit' or 'end']

confined adjective (said about a space or area) narrow or restricted.

confinement noun 1 the state of being confined or shut up. 2 the time when a woman is giving birth to a baby.

confirm verb 1 to show that something is true or correct. SYNONYMS: prove, show, establish, demonstrate, verify. 2 to establish a feeling or idea more firmly ♦ *The incident confirmed his fear of dogs.* 3 to make something definite ♦ *Please write to confirm your reservation.* 4 to administer the Christian rite of confirmation to

someone. [from *com-* and a Latin word *firmare* meaning 'to strengthen']

confirmation noun 1 the act of confirming something. 2 something that confirms a thing. 3 a Christian rite admitting a baptized person as a full member of the Church. 4 a ceremony confirming a person in the Jewish faith.

confirmatory (kən-**ferm**-ə-ter-i) adjective serving to confirm something ♦ *We found confirmatory evidence.*

confiscate (kon-fis-kayt) verb to take or seize something with authority, especially as a punishment. **confiscation** noun [from a Latin word *confiscare* meaning 'to put away in a chest', from *fiscus* meaning 'chest']

conflagration (kon-flə-**gray**-shən) noun a large and destructive fire. [from *com-* and a Latin word *flagrare* meaning 'to blaze']

conflict[1] (**kon**-flikt) noun 1 a fight or struggle. 2 a disagreement between people having different ideas or beliefs. [from *com-* and a Latin word *flictum* meaning 'struck']

conflict[2] (kən-**flikt**) verb 1 to fight or struggle. 2 to have a disagreement. SYNONYMS: disagree, clash, differ.

confluence (kon-**floo**-əns) noun the place where two rivers unite. [from *com-* and a Latin word *fluens* meaning 'flowing']

conform verb 1 to keep to accepted rules or customs ♦ *They find it hard to conform.* 2 to be consistent or similar in type. **to conform to** to act or be in accordance with something. [from a Latin word *conformare* meaning 'to shape evenly']

conformation noun the structure or form of a thing.

conformist (kən-**form**-ist) noun a person who conforms to accepted rules or standards. **conformism** noun

conformity noun conforming to accepted rules or standards.

confound verb 1 to surprise or confuse someone. 2 to prove someone to be wrong. 3 to defeat a plan or hope. **to be confounded with** to be mixed up or confused with someone or something else. [from a Latin word *confundere* meaning 'to mix up']

confront (kən-**frunt**) verb 1 to face and challenge an opponent or enemy. 2 to be present as something you have to deal with ♦ *There are many problems confronting*

us. 3 to face up to a problem and deal with it ♦ *There are too many problems to confront all at once.* SYNONYMS: tackle, deal with, face up to. 4 to bring opponents face to face ♦ *They confronted him with his accusers.*
confrontation (kon-frun-**tay**-shən) *noun* [from *com-* and a Latin word *frons* meaning 'face']

Confucianism (kən-**few**-shən-izm) *noun* the moral and religious system founded by the Chinese philosopher Confucius (551–479 BC).

confuse *verb* 1 to make someone bewildered or muddled. SYNONYMS: bewilder, muddle, baffle, fluster, perplex. 2 to mistake one person or thing for another. 3 to make something unclear. **confusable** *adjective* **confusion** *noun* [from a Latin word *confundere* meaning 'mix up']

confused *adjective* 1 (said about a person) bewildered or muddled. 2 difficult to understand.

confute (kən-**fewt**) *verb* (*informal*) to prove a person or argument to be wrong. **confutation** (kon-few-**tay**-shən) *noun* [from *com-* and a Latin word *futare* meaning 'to refute']

conga *noun* 1 a Latin American dance in which people form a long winding line, one behind the other. 2 a tall narrow drum beaten with the hands. [a Spanish word, the feminine form of *congo* meaning 'Congolese']

congeal (kən-**jeel**) *verb* (said about a liquid) to become jelly-like, especially when it cools after being hot. [from a Latin word *congelare* meaning 'to freeze']

congenial (kən-**jeen**-iəl) *adjective* 1 pleasant through being similar to you or suiting your tastes ♦ *a congenial companion.* 2 suited or agreeable to you ♦ *a congenial climate.* [from *com-* and *genial*]

congenital (kən-**jen**-itəl) *adjective* existing in a person from birth ♦ *a congenital deformity.* **congenitally** *adverb* [from *com-* and a Latin word *genitus* meaning 'born']

conger (**kong**-ger) *noun* a large sea eel. [via Old French from a Greek word *gongros*]

congested *adjective* 1 too full or crowded. 2 (said about an organ or tissue of the body) abnormally full of blood. [from a Latin word *congestum* meaning 'heaped up']

congestion (kən-**jes**-chən) *noun* a congested or crowded condition.

conglomerate [1] (kən-**glom**-er-ət) *adjective* gathered into a mass.
conglomerate *noun* 1 a number of things gathered together to form a whole while keeping their individual identities. 2 a commercial group formed by merging several different firms. [from *com-* and a Latin word *glomus* meaning 'mass']

conglomerate [2] (kən-**glom**-er-ayt) *verb* to gather things into a mass, or to form a mass. **conglomeration** *noun*

congratulate *verb* to tell someone that you are pleased about their achievement or success. [from *com-* and a Latin word *gratulari* meaning 'to show joy']

congratulation *noun* the act of congratulating someone, or the words used for this.

congratulatory (kən-**grat**-yoo-lə-ter-i) *adjective* expressing congratulations.

congregate *verb* to come together, to form a crowd. [from *com-* and a Latin word *grex* meaning 'flock']

congregation *noun* a group of people who have come together to take part in religious worship. **congregational** *adjective*

Congregationalism *noun* a form of church organization in which each local church is independent. **Congregational** *adjective* **Congregationalist** *noun*

congress *noun* a formal meeting of representatives for a discussion or series of discussions.
Congress *noun* the law-making body of a country, especially of the USA. **congressional** *adjective* [from *com-* and a Latin word *gressus* meaning 'going']

congruent (kong-**groo**-ənt) *adjective* 1 suitable or consistent. 2 (*Geometry*) (said about two or more figures) having the same shape and size. **congruence** *noun* [from *com-* and a Latin word *ruere* meaning 'to fall' or 'to rush']

conic (**kon**-ik) *adjective* to do with a cone, or having the shape of a cone.

conical *adjective* cone-shaped. **conically** *adverb*

conic section *noun* a geometric figure formed by the intersection of a cone and a plane, such as a circle, ellipse, or parabola.

conifer (**kon**-i-fer or **koh**-ni-fer) *noun* a tree that bears cones. [from *cone* and a Latin word *ferens* meaning 'bearing']

coniferous (kə-nif-er-əs) *adjective* (said about a tree) bearing cones.

conjectural *adjective* based on conjecture.

conjecture *verb* to form a conclusion based on incomplete information, to guess.
conjecture *noun* a conclusion formed by conjecturing, a guess. [from a Latin word *conicere* meaning 'to put together in thought']

conjugal (kon-jəg-əl) *adjective* to do with marriage or the relationship between a husband and wife. [from *com-* and a Latin word *jugum* meaning 'yoke']

conjugate (kon-jəg-ayt) *verb* 1 (*Grammar*) to give the different forms of a verb, e.g. *get*, *gets*, *got*. 2 to unite or become fused. [same origin as for *conjugal*]

conjugation *noun* 1 (*Grammar*) a set of the inflected forms of a verb. 2 (*Biology*) the fusion of gametes in reproduction.

conjunction *noun* 1 (*Grammar*) a word that joins words or phrases or sentences, such as *and*, *but*, *or*. 2 a combination or union ♦ *The four countries acted in conjunction.* 3 the happening of things at the same time. [from a Latin word *conjunctum* meaning 'yoked together']

conjunctivitis *noun* inflammation of the membrane (called *conjunctiva*) forming the surface of the eyeball and the inside of the eyelid. [from a Latin phrase *membrana conjunctiva* meaning 'joined membrane']

conjure (kun-jer) *verb* 1 to perform tricks which appear to be magical, especially by movements of the hands. 2 to summon a spirit to appear. 3 to produce something as if from nothing ♦ *Meg managed to conjure up a meal.* **to conjure something up** to produce an image or memory in the mind ♦ *Mention of the desert conjures up visions of sand and sun.* [from a Latin word *conjurare* meaning 'to band together with an oath']

conjuror *noun* a person who performs conjuring tricks.

conk *noun* (*informal*) the nose. **to conk out** (*informal*) 1 to break down or fail. 2 to fall asleep from exhaustion. [perhaps another spelling of *conch*]

conker *noun* (*informal*) the hard shiny brown nut of the horse chestnut tree.
conkers *plural noun* a children's game in which each player has a conker on a string and hits another player's conker to try to break it. [from a dialect word meaning 'snail shell']

con man *noun* (*informal*) a man who swindles people by means of confidence tricks. [from *con*[1]]

connect *verb* 1 to join one thing to another, or to be joined. SYNONYMS: join, attach, fasten, fix, link. 2 (said about a train, bus, etc.) to arrive at a time that allows passengers to continue their journey on another train or bus etc. 3 to put someone into communication with another person by telephone. 4 to think of things or people as being associated with each other. [from *com-* and a Latin word *nectere* meaning 'to bind']

connection *noun* 1 the process of connecting or being connected. 2 a place or point where things connect; a connecting part. 3 a train, bus, etc. that leaves shortly after another arrives, so that passengers can change from one to the other. 4 a link or relationship ♦ *Most people accept that there is a connection between smoking and lung cancer.* 5 people you have contact with, either personally or in business.

connective *adjective* connecting or linking things.
connective *noun* (*Grammar*) a word that joins words or phrases or sentences, a conjunction.

connector *noun* a thing that connects others.

conning tower *noun* a raised structure on a submarine, containing the periscope.

connive (kə-niyv) *verb* to connive at to take no notice of wrongdoing, and so appear to approve of it. **connivance** *noun* [from a Latin word *connivere* meaning 'to shut the eyes']

connoisseur (kon-ə-ser) *noun* a person with a lot of experience and appreciation of something ♦ *a connoisseur of wine.* [a French word meaning 'someone who knows']

connote (kə-noht) *verb* (said about a word) to imply or suggest something in addition to the main meaning. (Compare **denote**.)
connotation *noun*

connubial (kə-new-biəl) *adjective* (*literary*) to do with marriage or the relationship between a husband and wife. [from *com-* and a Latin word *nubere* meaning 'to marry']

conoid (koh-noid) *adjective* shaped like a cone.
conoid *noun* an object shaped like a cone.

conquer *verb* **1** to defeat or overcome an opponent or enemy in war. SYNONYMS: defeat, beat, crush, subdue, overcome, overpower; (*formal*) vanquish. **2** to overcome something with an effort ♦ *I must learn to conquer my fear of heights.* SYNONYMS: overcome, control, master. **conqueror** *noun* [from a Latin word *conquirere* meaning 'to gain or win']

conquest *noun* **1** the act of conquering. **2** something won by conquering, especially territory.

conquistador (kon-**kwist**-ə-dor) *noun* a conqueror, especially one of the Spanish soldiers and adventurers who conquered Mexico and Peru in the 16th century. [a Spanish word meaning 'conqueror']

consanguineous (kon-sang-**win**-i-əs) *adjective* (*formal*) descended from the same ancestor. **consanguinity** *noun* [from *com*- and a Latin word *sanguis* meaning 'blood']

conscience *noun* a person's sense of what is right and wrong in what they do. **on your conscience** causing you to feel guilty or remorseful. [from *com*- and a Latin word *conscientia* meaning 'knowledge']

conscience-stricken *adjective* feeling deep remorse about a wrong you have done.

conscientious (kon-shi-**en**-shəs) *adjective* showing care and attention. SYNONYMS: diligent, hard-working, painstaking, careful, meticulous, thorough. **conscientiously** *adverb* **conscientiousness** *noun*

conscientious objector *noun* someone who refuses to serve in the armed forces because they believe it is morally wrong. [same origin as for *conscience*]

conscious *adjective* **1** awake and aware of your surroundings. **2** aware of something ♦ *We are conscious of the need for a quick answer.* **3** intentional ♦ *She spoke with conscious firmness.* **consciously** *adverb* **consciousness** *noun* [from a Latin word *conscius* meaning 'knowing']

conscript¹ (kən-**skript**) *verb* (said about a state or government) to make someone join the armed forces. **conscription** *noun* [from *com*- and a Latin word *scriptus* meaning 'written in a list']

conscript² (**kon**-skript) *noun* someone who has been made to join the armed forces.

consecrate *verb* **1** to make or declare something sacred. **2** to dedicate a place to the service or worship of God. **consecration** *noun* [from *com*- and a Latin word *sacer* meaning 'sacred']

consecutive (kən-**sek**-yoo-tiv) *adjective* following one after the other. **consecutively** *adverb* [from a Latin word *consecutum* meaning 'following']

consensus (kən-**sen**-səs) *noun* general agreement; the opinion of most people. [same origin as for *consent*]

consent *verb* to say that you are willing to do or allow what someone wishes. SYNONYMS: agree, acquiesce, concur, accede. **consent** *noun* agreement to what someone wishes, permission. [from *com*- and a Latin word *sentire* meaning 'to feel']

consequence *noun* **1** something that happens as a result of some event or action. **2** importance ♦ *a person of consequence.* **in consequence** as a result. **to take the consequences** to accept the results of your choice or action. [from a Latin word *consequi* meaning 'to follow closely']

consequent *adjective* happening as a result.

consequential (kon-si-**kwen**-shəl) *adjective* **1** happening as a result. **2** important. **consequentially** *adverb*

consequently *adverb* as a result, therefore.

conservancy *noun* (**conservancies**) **1** a group of people having the authority to control a port or river etc. ♦ *the Thames Conservancy.* **2** official conservation of natural resources.

conservation *noun* **1** the process of conserving or being conserved. **2** preservation, especially of the natural environment.

conservationist *noun* someone who supports conservation.

conservatism *noun* conservative principles, especially in politics.

conservative *adjective* **1** liking established ways and opposed to change. **2** moderate, avoiding extremes ♦ *a conservative estimate.*
Conservative *adjective* to do with the Conservative Party.
conservative *noun* a conservative person.
Conservative *noun* someone who supports the Conservative Party, a political party that favours private enterprise and freedom from state control.

conservatively adverb [same origin as for conserve]

conservatory noun (**conservatories**) a room with a glass roof and large windows, built against an outside wall of a house with a connecting door from the house.

conserve¹ (kən-**serv**) verb to keep something valuable or useful from being harmed or changed. [from com- and a Latin word servare meaning 'to keep safe']

conserve² (kən-**serv** or kon-**serv**) noun jam made from fresh fruit and sugar.

consider verb 1 to think carefully about something, especially in order to make a decision about it. SYNONYMS: think about, reflect on, contemplate. 2 to make allowances for something ♦ Please consider people's feelings. 3 to think a person or thing to be something ♦ Consider yourself lucky. [from a Latin word considerare meaning 'to examine']

considerable adjective fairly great in amount or extent etc. ♦ Their victory was a considerable achievement. **considerably** adverb

considerate adjective taking care not to inconvenience or hurt other people. SYNONYMS: kind, thoughtful, generous, friendly, helpful, obliging, polite. **considerately** adverb

consideration noun 1 careful thought or attention. 2 being considerate, kindness. 3 a fact that must be kept in mind ♦ Time is now an important consideration. 4 a payment given as a reward ♦ I will do it for a small consideration. **to take something into consideration** to allow for something when you are making a decision. **under consideration** being considered.

considering preposition taking something into consideration ♦ It's very warm, considering the time of year.

consign verb 1 to hand something over or deliver it formally. 2 to entrust something to someone's care. [from a Latin word consignare meaning 'to mark with a seal']

consignment noun a batch of goods sent to someone.

consist verb **to consist of** to be made up of ♦ The house consists of 3 floors. SYNONYMS: comprise, include, contain, be composed of, incorporate. **to consist in** to have something as a basis or essential feature

♦ Our happiness consists in hoping. [from a Latin word consistere meaning 'to stand firm or still']

consistency noun (**consistencies**) 1 the thickness or firmness of a liquid or soft mixture. 2 the state of being consistent.

consistent adjective 1 keeping to a regular pattern or style, not changing. 2 agreeing about content, giving the same account ♦ The second witness's account was consistent with the first. **consistently** adverb

consolation noun comfort for someone who has suffered a loss or disappointment.

consolation prize noun a prize given to a competitor who has just missed winning one of the main prizes.

console¹ (kən-**sohl**) verb to comfort someone who has suffered a loss or disappointment. SYNONYMS: comfort, cheer up, reassure, calm, soothe, sympathize with. **consolable** adjective [from com- and a Latin word solari meaning 'to comfort']

console² (**kon**-sohl) noun 1 a panel or unit containing a set of controls for electrical or other equipment. 2 a cabinet for a radio or television. 3 a frame containing the keyboards and stops of an organ. [a French word, related to consolidate]

consolidate verb 1 to make something secure and strong ♦ The team consolidated their lead with a second goal. 2 to combine two or more funds of money, organizations, etc. into one. **consolidation** noun [from com- + solid]

consommé (kən-**som**-ay) noun a clear meat soup. [a French word, related to consummate]

consonant noun 1 a letter of the alphabet that is not a vowel, in English b, c, d, f, g, h, j, k, l, m, n, p, q, r, s, t, v, w, x, y (as in yoke), z. 2 the speech sound represented by any of these letters. **consonant** adjective consistent or harmonious. [from com- and a Latin word sonans meaning 'sounding']

consort¹ (**kon**-sort) noun 1 a husband or wife, especially of a monarch. 2 a ship sailing in company with another. 3 a small group of musicians, especially one playing early music. [from a Latin word consors meaning 'sharer']

consort² (kən-**sort**) verb to keep regular company with someone ♦ He was often seen consorting with criminals.

consortium (kən-**sort**-iəm) noun (**consortia**) a combination of countries, companies, or other groups acting together. [same origin as for consort]

conspicuous adjective 1 easily seen, noticeable. 2 attracting attention. **conspicuously** adverb **conspicuousness** noun [from a Latin word conspicere meaning 'to look at attentively']

conspiracy noun (**conspiracies**) 1 a plot formed by planning secretly with others.

conspirator noun a person who conspires. **conspiratorial** adjective **conspiratorially** adverb

conspire verb 1 to plan secretly with others, especially to do something illegal. 2 (said about events or circumstances) to seem to be acting together with unfortunate results ◆ Events conspired to bring about their downfall. [from com- and a Latin word spirare meaning 'to breathe']

constable noun a police officer of the lowest rank. [from a Latin name comes stabuli meaning 'officer in charge of the stable']

constabulary (kən-**stab**-yoo-ler-i) noun (**constabularies**) a police force.

constancy noun the quality of being constant or loyal.

constant adjective 1 happening or continuing all the time, or happening repeatedly. SYNONYMS: continuous, endless, ceaseless, incessant, persistent; (repeatedly) continual. 2 unchanging, faithful ◆ He always remained constant to his principles. **constant** noun 1 something that is constant and does not vary.
2 (Mathematics) a number that expresses a physical property or relationship and remains the same in all circumstances or for the same substance in the same conditions. **constantly** adverb [from com- and a Latin word stans meaning 'standing']

constellation noun a group of stars forming a pattern. [from com- and a Latin word stella meaning 'star']

consternation noun great surprise causing anxiety or dismay. [from a Latin word consternare meaning 'to terrify']

constipated verb unable to empty the bowels easily or regularly. [from a Latin word constipare meaning 'to cram']

constipation noun difficulty in emptying the bowels.

constituency noun (**constituencies**) 1 a district that is represented by a Member of Parliament elected by its voters. 2 the body of voters in this district. [same origin as for constituent]

constituent adjective forming part of a whole.
constituent noun 1 one of the parts that forms a whole thing. 2 a member of a constituency. [from com- and a Latin word constituere meaning 'to set up']

constitute verb 1 to make up or form a whole ◆ 12 months constitute a year. 2 to establish or be something ◆ This does not constitute a precedent. [from com- and a Latin word statuere meaning 'to set up']

constitution noun 1 a set of rules and principles which state how a country is to be organized and governed. 2 the general condition and health of a person's body ◆ She has a strong constitution.

constitutional adjective 1 to do with a country's constitution ◆ constitutional reform. 2 permitted by a country's constitution. 3 to do with a person's physical or mental constitution ◆ a constitutional weakness. **constitutionally** adverb

constrain verb to force someone to act in a certain way; to compel someone. [from a Latin word constringere meaning 'to bind tightly together', related to constrict]

constraint noun 1 the act of constraining or being constrained; compulsion. 2 a restriction or limitation on what you can do. 3 a strained manner caused by holding back your real feelings.

constrict verb to tighten something by making it narrower; to squeeze something. **constriction** noun **constrictor** noun [from com- and a Latin word strictum meaning 'bound']

construct verb to make something by putting its parts together; to build something. SYNONYMS: build, erect, assemble, put up, make. **constructor** noun [from com- and a Latin word structum meaning 'built']

construction noun 1 the process of constructing or being constructed. 2 something constructed; a building. 3 two or more words put together to form a phrase, clause, or sentence. 4 an explanation or interpretation ◆ They have put a bad construction on our refusal. **constructional** adjective

constructive *adjective* offering helpful suggestions. **constructively** *adverb*

construe (kən-**stroo**) *verb* (**construes, construed, construing**) to interpret or explain what someone has said. [same origin as for *construct*]

consul *noun* 1 an official appointed by a state to live in a foreign city to support the state's interests and provide assistance to the state's citizens living there. 2 either of the two chief magistrates in ancient Rome. **consular** (**kons**-yoo-ler) *adjective* [a Latin word, related to *consult*]

consulate *noun* the office or building where a consul works.

consult *verb* 1 to seek information or advice from someone. 2 to confer with someone. **consultation** *noun* [from a Latin word *consulere* meaning 'to take advice or counsel']

consulting room *noun* a room in which a doctor sees patients.

consultant *noun* 1 a person who is qualified to give expert professional advice. 2 a senior hospital doctor or surgeon.

consultative (kən-**sult**-ə-tiv) *adjective* for consultation ♦ *a consultative committee.*

consume *verb* 1 to use something up ♦ *Much time was consumed in waiting.* 2 to eat or drink something. 3 to destroy something completely ♦ *Fire has consumed the buildings.* **consumable** *adjective* [from *com-* and a Latin word *sumere* meaning 'to take up']

consumer *noun* someone who buys goods or pays for services. (Compare **producer**.)

consumer goods *plural noun* goods that are bought and used by individual consumers.

consumerism *noun* 1 the protection of consumers' interests. 2 high consumption of goods and services.

consuming *adjective* overwhelming or dominating ♦ *He was driven by a consuming ambition.*

consummate [1] (kon-sə-**mayt**) *verb* 1 to make something complete or perfect. 2 to complete a marriage by having sexual intercourse. **consummation** *noun* [from *com-* and a Latin word *summus* meaning 'highest']

consummate [2] (kən-**sum**-ət) *adjective* highly skilled ♦ *a consummate artist.*

consumption *noun* 1 the process of consuming or destroying something. 2 the amount of something consumed. 3 (*old use*) tuberculosis of the lungs.

consumptive *adjective* (*old use*) suffering from tuberculosis of the lungs.

contact (**kon**-takt) *noun* 1 the act of touching or coming together. 2 the state of being in touch, communication. 3 a connection for an electric current. 4 someone who has recently been near a person with a contagious disease and who may carry the infection. 5 someone you can communicate with when you need information or help.
contact *verb* to get in touch with someone. [from *com-* and a Latin word *tactum* meaning 'touched']

contact lens *noun* a thin plastic lens worn directly on the surface of the eye to correct faulty vision.

contagion (kən-**tay**-jən) *noun* the spreading of disease from one person to another by close contact.

contagious (kən-**tay**-jəs) *adjective* (said about a disease) able to be spread by close contact with a person having it. (Compare **infectious**.) [from *com-* and a Latin word *tangere* meaning 'to touch']

contain *verb* 1 to have inside it ♦ *The atlas contains 100 maps* ♦ *The letter contained an invitation.* SYNONYMS: include, comprise. 2 to consist of something and amount or be equal to it ♦ *A kilometre contains 1,000 metres.* 3 to restrain something ♦ *We found it hard to contain our laughter.* SYNONYMS: restrain, control, check. 4 to keep something within limits ♦ *The enemy troops were contained in the valley.* [from *com-* and a Latin word *tenere* meaning 'to hold']

container *noun* 1 a box or bottle designed to contain something. 2 a large box-like receptacle of a standard design for transporting goods long distances by road, rail, sea, or air.

containerize *verb* to transport goods in containers. **containerization** *noun*

containment *noun* the practice of keeping a hostile country or influence within its present limits.

contaminate *verb* to make a thing dirty or impure; to pollute something. **contaminant** *noun* **contamination** *noun*

contaminator noun [from a Latin word contamen meaning 'contact' or 'pollution']

contemplate (kon-təm-playt) verb 1 to gaze at something or someone thoughtfully. 2 to consider something ♦ I contemplated going out. 3 to intend something or have it in mind as a possibility ♦ We are contemplating a trip to New York. 4 to meditate. **contemplation** noun [from a Latin word contemplari meaning 'to observe or survey']

contemplative (kən-tem-plə-tiv) adjective 1 fond of contemplating things, thoughtful. 2 devoted to religious contemplation.

contemporaneous adjective existing or happening at the same time.

contemporary (kən-tem-per-er-i) adjective 1 living in or belonging to the same period. 2 modern or up to date ♦ contemporary designs.
contemporary noun (**contemporaries**) a person living at the same time as someone else or who is about the same age ♦ Jan and Sarah were contemporaries at college. [from com- and a Latin word tempus meaning 'time']

contempt noun a feeling of despising a person or thing intensely. SYNONYMS: disgust, loathing, scorn. [from com- and a Latin word temnere meaning 'to despise']

contemptible adjective deserving contempt. **contemptibly** adverb **contemptibility** noun

contemptuous adjective feeling or showing contempt ♦ She gave me a contemptuous look. **contemptuously** adverb **contemptuousness** noun

contend verb 1 to struggle in a fight or battle, or against difficulties. 2 to argue or assert something ♦ The defendant contends that he is innocent. **contender** noun [from com- and a Latin word tendere meaning 'to strive']

content[1] (kən-tent) adjective happy, satisfied with what one has.
content noun being contented, satisfaction.
content verb to make someone feel content or satisfied. **to your heart's content** as much as you want. [from a Latin word contentum meaning 'restrained']

content[2] (kon-tent) noun or **contents** plural noun what something contains. [from a Latin word contenta meaning 'things contained']

contented adjective happy with what you have, satisfied. **contentedly** adverb

contention noun 1 the act of quarrelling or arguing. 2 an assertion made in arguing. [same origin as for contend]

contentious (kən-ten-shəs) adjective 1 likely to cause disagreement or argument. 2 (said about a person) fond of argument, quarrelsome. **contentiously** adverb

contentment noun a state of feeling happy or contented.

contest[1] (kon-test) noun 1 a competition, a test in which rivals try to obtain something or do best. 2 a struggle for superiority or victory. SYNONYMS: struggle, conflict, fight. [from a Latin word contestari meaning 'to call on someone to witness something']

contest[2] (kən-test) verb 1 to compete in something ♦ to contest an election. 2 to dispute or challenge a decision or ruling.

contestant noun someone who takes part in a contest, a competitor.

context noun 1 the words that come before and after a particular word or phrase and help to clarify its meaning. 2 the circumstances or background in which something happens. **out of context** without the surrounding words and therefore unclear or misleading. [from com- and a Latin word textum meaning 'woven']

contiguous (kən-tig-yoo-əs) adjective touching or adjoining ♦ The two countries are contiguous. **contiguity** (kon-tig-yoo-iti) noun [from a Latin word contiguus meaning 'touching']

continent[1] noun any of the earth's main land masses, Europe, Asia, Africa, North and South America, Australia, and Antarctica. **the Continent** the mainland of Europe as distinct from the British Isles. [from a Latin phrase terra continens meaning 'continuous land']

continent[2] adjective able to control the bladder and bowels. **continence** noun [same origin as for contain]

continental adjective 1 forming a continent, or to do with a continent. 2 (also **Continental**) to do with the mainland of Europe.
continental or **Continental** noun someone who lives in the mainland of Europe.

continental breakfast noun a light breakfast of coffee and bread rolls with butter and jam.

continental drift noun the slow drift of the continents to their present position, on a softer zone lying very deep within the earth.

continental shelf noun an area of seabed bordering a continent, where the sea is more shallow.

contingency (kən-**tin**-jən-si) noun (**contingencies**) something that may happen but cannot be known for certain. [from a Latin word *contingere* meaning 'to touch' or 'to happen to']

contingency plan noun a plan providing for an event that might happen.

contingent (kən-**tin**-jənt) adjective 1 depending on something that may or may not happen ♦ *His future is contingent on success in his exams.* 2 likely to occur but not certain ♦ *other contingent events.* **contingent** noun a group forming part of a larger group, especially a body of troops or police.

continual adjective continuing or happening constantly or frequently, with breaks between ♦ *We had continual interruptions during the meeting.* SYNONYMS: constant, repeated, incessant, recurrent. **continually** adverb
◊ See the usage note at **continuous**.

continuance noun (formal) the state of continuing.

continuation noun 1 the process of continuing, or of starting again after stopping or pausing. 2 a thing that continues something else ♦ *The continuation of the story will appear in next week's magazine.*

continue verb (**continues, continued, continuing**) 1 to keep doing an action, to do something without stopping ♦ *They continued to quarrel all evening* ♦ *We have to continue the campaign.* SYNONYMS: carry on, keep up, maintain, persist in, persevere with. 2 to remain in a certain place or condition ♦ *She will continue as manager.* 3 to go further ♦ *The road continues beyond the village.* 4 to begin again after stopping ♦ *Play will continue this afternoon.* SYNONYMS: resume, proceed. [same origin as for *contain*]

continuity (kon-tin-**yoo**-iti) noun 1 the state of being continuous. 2 the uninterrupted existence of something or succession of events. 3 the process of maintaining

continuous action with consistent details in a film or broadcast.

continuous adjective 1 continuing or happening without a break ♦ *There is a continuous hum of traffic from the bypass.* SYNONYMS: constant, endless, persistent, perpetual. 2 (*Mathematics*) (said about a set) such that any value that lies between any two elements of the set is also a member of that set. **continuously** adverb
◊ *Continuous* means 'going on all the time, without interruption', whereas *continual* means 'happening many times with breaks in between'. A noise is *continuous* when it goes on without a break and is *continual* when it stops and starts again over a period of time.

continuous assessment noun a system of regular assessment of a student's work throughout a course of study, with the evaluation contributing to the overall result.

continuum (kən-**tin**-yoo-əm) noun (**continua**) something that extends or changes gradually and continuously. [a Latin word, related to *continue*]

contort (kən-**tort**) verb to force or twist something out of its usual shape. **contortion** (kən-**tor**-shən) noun [from *com-* and a Latin word *tortum* meaning 'twisted']

contortionist (kon-tor-shən-ist) noun a performer who can twist their body into strange and unusual positions.

contour (**kon**-toor) noun 1 a line on a map joining the points that are the same height above sea level. 2 an outline. [from an Italian word *contornare* meaning 'to draw in outline']

contra- prefix against. [from a Latin word *contra* meaning 'against']

contraband noun goods that have been smuggled or imported illegally. [from *contra-* and an Italian word *bando* meaning 'a ban']

contraception (kon-trə-**sep**-shən) noun preventing pregnancy; birth control. [from *contra-* and *conception*]

contraceptive (kon-trə-**sep**-tiv) adjective preventing conception. **contraceptive** noun a device or drug that prevents conception.

contract [1] (**kon**-trakt) noun 1 a formal agreement to do something, made between people, organizations, or countries. 2 a document stating the terms of an agreement.

contract[2] (kən-**trakt**) *verb* 1 to make something smaller, or to become smaller. 2 to undertake something by the terms of a contract ♦ *The company has contracted to supply parts to the factory.* 3 to catch an illness. **contract in** to choose to take part in a scheme. **contract out** to choose not to take part in a scheme. [from *com-* and a Latin word *tractum* meaning 'pulled']

contractable *adjective* (said about a disease) able to be caught.

contractile *adjective* (*Biology*) able to contract or to produce contraction. **contractility** *noun*

contraction *noun* 1 the act of contracting. 2 a shortened form of a word, such as *can't* for *cannot*.

contractor *noun* a person or organization that makes a contract, especially for building work.

contractual (kən-**trakt**-yoo-əl) *adjective* to do with or stated in a contract. **contractually** *adverb*

contradict *verb* 1 to state that something said is untrue or that someone is wrong. 2 to state the opposite of something already said ♦ *These opinions contradict previous ones.* **contradictory** *adjective* [from *contra-* and a Latin word *dicere* meaning 'to say']

contradiction *noun* a statement that contradicts something already said. **a contradiction in terms** a statement that contradicts itself.

contradistinction *noun* a distinction made by contrasting two things or ideas.

contraflow *noun* a temporary arrangement of traffic in which vehicles from one carriageway use one of the lanes of the opposite carriageway.

contralto (kən-**tral**-toh) *noun* (**contraltos**) the lowest female singing voice, or a singer with this voice. [an Italian word, from *contra-* and *alto*]

contraption *noun* a strange or ingenious gadget or machine. [origin unknown; perhaps related to *contrive*]

contrapuntal *adjective* (*Music*) to do with counterpoint, or written in counterpoint. [from an Italian word *contrapunto*]

contrariwise (kən-**trair**-i-wiyz) *adverb* on the other hand, in the opposite way.

contrary[1] (kon-trə-ri) *adjective* 1 having an opposite nature or effect, opposed ♦ *They came, contrary to expectation.* 2 opposite in direction ♦ *a contrary wind.*

contrary *noun* the opposite.

contrary *adverb* against or in opposition ♦ *They were acting contrary to instructions.* **on the contrary** an assertion that the opposite is true. [from Latin *contra* meaning 'against']

contrary[2] (kon-**trair**-i) *adjective* (said about a person) doing the opposite of what is usual or advisable; obstinate or wilful. **contrariness** *noun*

contrast[1] (kon-**trahst**) *noun* 1 a difference clearly seen when things are compared or seen together. 2 something showing a clear difference. 3 the degree of difference between tones or colours. [from *contra-* and a Latin word *stare* meaning 'to stand']

contrast[2] (kon-**trahst**) *verb* 1 to compare or oppose two things to show their differences. 2 to show a clear difference when compared.

contravene (kon-trə-**veen**) *verb* to act against a rule or law ♦ *Parking in the High Street contravenes the traffic regulations.* **contravention** (kontrə-**ven**-shən) *noun* [from *contra-* and a Latin word *venire* meaning 'to come']

contretemps (kon-trə-tahn) *noun* a trivial disagreement or dispute. [a French word meaning 'out of time (in music)']

contribute (kən-**trib**-yoot) *verb* 1 to give money or help jointly with others. 2 to write an article for a newspaper, magazine, or book. 3 to help to bring something about ♦ *Drink contributed to his ruin.* **contribution** *noun* **contributor** *noun* [from *com-* and a Latin word *tribuere* meaning 'to bestow']

contributory (kən-**trib**-yoo-ter-i) *adjective* 1 contributing to a result. 2 involving contributions to a fund ♦ *a contributory pension scheme.*

contrite (kon-triyt) *adjective* feeling guilty or sorry for what you have done. **contritely** *adverb* **contrition** (kən-**trish**-ən) *noun* [from a Latin word *contritus* meaning 'ground down']

contrivance (kən-**triy**-vəns) *noun* 1 an ingenious device. 2 the process of contriving something. 3 a plan or scheme.

contrive verb to plan something cleverly or effectively; to find a way of doing or making something. **contriver** noun [from an Old French word *controver* meaning 'to invent']

control noun 1 the power to make people do things or to make things happen. SYNONYMS: power, authority, command, direction, jurisdiction. 2 a means of restraining or regulating something, especially a device for operating a machine. 3 restraint or self-restraint ♦ *He needed all his control to avoid losing his temper.* 4 something or someone used as a standard of comparison for checking the results of an experiment or survey. 5 a place from which an operation is directed or where something is checked or verified.
control verb (**controlled, controlling**) 1 to have the power to make people do things or to make things happen. SYNONYMS: direct, manage, regulate, supervise, oversee, monitor. 2 to operate a machine or direct an activity. 3 to restrain someone or something. SYNONYMS: restrain, check, contain. **in control** having control of something. **out of control** no longer able to be controlled. **under control** able to be controlled, in proper order. **controllable** adjective **controller** noun [from a French word *contreroller* meaning 'to keep a copy of a roll of accounts', from *contra-* and a Latin word *rotulus* meaning 'a roll']

control key noun a key on a computer keyboard which changes the function of another key when both are pressed together.

control tower noun a tall building from which air traffic is controlled at an airport.

control unit noun that part of a computer which controls the operation of the other units.

controversial (kontrə-**ver**-shəl) adjective likely to cause controversy.

controversy (kon-trə-**ver**-si or kən-**trov**-er-si) noun (**controversies**) a long argument or disagreement. [from *contra-* and a Latin word *versum* meaning 'turned']

controvert (kon-trə-**vert**) verb (formal) to contradict or deny the truth of something. [same origin as for *controversy*]

controvertible adjective able to be denied or disproved.

contumely (kon-**tewm**-li) noun (old use) insulting language or behaviour. [from a Latin word *contumelia*]

contusion (kən-**tew**-zhən) noun a technical term for a bruise. [from *com-* and a Latin word *tundere* meaning 'to beat']

conundrum (kə-**nun**-drəm) noun (**conundrums**) a difficult question or riddle. [origin unknown]

conurbation (kon-er-**bay**-shən) noun a large urban area where towns have spread into each other. [from *com-* and a Latin word *urbs* meaning 'city']

convalesce verb to regain health after illness. **convalescence** noun **convalescent** adjective [from *com-* and a Latin word *valescere* meaning 'to grow strong']

convection noun the transmission of heat within a liquid or gas by circulation of the heated parts. **convective** adjective [from *com-* and a Latin word *vectum* meaning 'carried']

convector noun a heater that circulates warm air by convection.

convene verb to summon or assemble people for a meeting. **convener** noun [from *com-* and a Latin word *venire* meaning 'to come']

convenience noun 1 the quality of being convenient; freedom from trouble or difficulty. 2 something that is convenient or easy to use. 3 a public toilet. **at your convenience** whenever you find it convenient, as it suits you.

convenience food noun a food sold in a form that needs little preparation by the user.

convenient adjective 1 suiting a person's plans or intentions ♦ *Would it be convenient to call tomorrow?* 2 easy to use or deal with, not causing any difficulty. 3 easy to find or reach ♦ *The house is convenient for the station and shops.* **conveniently** adverb [from a Latin word *convenire* meaning 'to suit']

convent noun 1 a place where nuns live and work. 2 a school run by nuns from a convent. [from a Latin word *conventus* meaning 'assembly', related to *convene*]

convention noun 1 an accepted way of doing things. 2 a formal assembly. 3 a formal agreement between countries ♦ *the Geneva Convention.*

conventional adjective 1 done or doing things in the accepted way; traditional. SYNONYMS: traditional, established, orthodox, customary, standard. **2** (said about weapons) not nuclear. **conventionality** *noun* **conventionally** *adverb*

converge *verb* to come to or towards the same point from different directions. **convergence** *noun* **convergent** *adjective* [from *com-* and a Latin word *vergere* meaning 'to turn']

conversant (kən-ver-sənt) *adjective* (*formal*) familiar with something ♦ *I am not conversant with the rules of this game*. [from *converse*[1]]

conversation *noun* informal talk between people. **conversational** *adjective* **conversationally** *adverb*

conversationalist *noun* a person who is good at conversation.

converse[1] (kən-verss) *verb* to talk informally with someone. [from a Latin word *conversari* meaning 'to keep company']

converse[2] (kon-verss) *adjective* opposite or contrary. **converse** *noun* an idea or statement that is the opposite of another. **conversely** *adverb* [same origin as for *convert*]

convert[1] (kən-vert) *verb* **1** to change from one form, character, or use to another. **2** to be made in such a way that its use can be changed ♦ *The sofa converts into a bed*. **3** to cause or influence someone to change their attitude or beliefs. **4** (in rugby football) to gain extra points after a try by kicking the ball over the bar. **conversion** *noun* **converter** *noun* [from *com-* and a Latin word *vertere* meaning 'to turn']

convert[2] (kon-vert) *noun* someone who has changed their beliefs, especially in religion.

convertible *adjective* designed so that its use can be changed. **convertible** *noun* a car with a roof that can be folded down or removed.

convex (kon-veks) *adjective* curved like the outside surface of a ball. **convexity** (kon-veks-iti) *noun* **convexly** *adverb* [from a Latin word *convexus* meaning 'arched']

convey *verb* (**conveyed, conveying**) **1** to transport or transmit something or somebody. SYNONYMS: transport, transmit, carry, take, deliver. **2** to communicate something as an idea or meaning. **conveyable** *adjective* [from an Old French word *conveier*, from *com-* and a Latin word *via* meaning 'way']

conveyance *noun* **1** the process of conveying something or someone. **2** a means of transporting people, a vehicle. **3** the transfer of the legal ownership of land or property, or a document bringing this about.

conveyancing *noun* the business of transferring the legal ownership of land or property from one person to another.

conveyor *noun* someone or something that conveys things or people.

conveyor belt *noun* a continuous moving belt for moving objects from one place to another in a factory or other large building.

convict[1] (kən-vikt) *verb* to prove or declare that a certain person is guilty of a crime.

convict[2] (kon-vikt) *noun* a convicted person who is in prison. [from *com-* and a Latin word *victum* meaning 'conquered']

conviction *noun* **1** the process of convicting a person of a crime. **2** the process of being convinced of something. **3** a firm opinion or belief.

convince *verb* to make someone feel certain that something is true. [from *com-* and a Latin word *vincere* meaning 'to conquer']

convivial (kən-viv-iəl) *adjective* sociable and lively. **conviviality** (kən-vivi-al-iti) *noun* **convivially** *adverb* [from a Latin word *convivium* meaning 'feast']

convocation *noun* **1** the process of calling people together for a meeting. **2** an assembly called together. [from *com-* and a Latin word *vocare* meaning 'to call']

convoke *verb* (*formal*) to call people together for a meeting.

convoluted (kon-və-loo-tid) *adjective* **1** coiled or twisted. **2** complicated or involved. [from *com-* and a Latin word *volutum* meaning 'rolled']

convolution (kon-və-loo-shən) *noun* **1** a coil or twist. **2** a complexity or difficulty.

convolvulus *noun* a twisting plant with trumpet-shaped flowers.

convoy (kon-voi) *noun* a group of ships or vehicles travelling together under the protection of an armed escort. **convoy** *verb* (said about a warship or armed troops) to escort and protect a group of ships or vehicles.

convulse verb to make someone have sudden or violent movements, especially with laughter. [from com- and a Latin word vulsum meaning 'pulled']

convulsion noun 1 a sudden or violent movement of the body. 2 a violent upheaval.

convulsive adjective producing upheaval or convulsions. **convulsively** adverb

cony noun another spelling of **coney**.

coo verb (**cooes, cooed, cooing**) to make the soft murmuring sound of a dove.
coo noun a cooing sound.
coo interjection (informal) an exclamation of surprise. [an imitation of the sound]

cook verb 1 to prepare food for eating by heating it. 2 to undergo this preparation ♦ Our meal is just cooking. 3 (informal) to alter accounts or other information falsely ♦ They were accused of cooking the books.
cook noun a person who cooks food, especially as a job. **to cook something up** (informal) to concoct or invent something ♦ We tried to cook up an excuse. [from an Old English word coc]

cookbook noun a cookery book.

cooker noun 1 an appliance consisting of an oven, hob, and grill, for cooking food. 2 an apple suitable for cooking rather than eating raw.

cookery noun the practice and skill of cooking food.

cookery book noun a book of recipes.

cookie noun 1 (Amer.) a sweet biscuit. 2 (Scottish) a plain bun. 3 (Computing) a set of data that an Internet server sends to a browser on a user's computer so that the server can identify the computer when the user accesses the server again. [from a Dutch word koekje meaning 'little cake']

cool adjective 1 fairly cold, not hot or warm. 2 (said about colours) suggesting coolness. 3 (said about a person) calm and confident ♦ He seemed quite cool about the whole thing. 4 not enthusiastic or friendly ♦ We got a cool reception. 5 (informal) good or fashionable. 6 full, complete ♦ It cost me a cool thousand.
cool noun 1 coolness; cool air or a cool place ♦ in the cool of the evening. 2 (informal) calmness or composure ♦ Try to keep your cool.

cool verb to make something cool, or to become cool. **coolly** adverb **coolness** noun [from an Old English word col]

coolant noun a liquid used for cooling an engine or machinery.

cooling curves plural noun (Physics) curves representing how a metal cools under constant conditions, plotting temperature against time.

cooling tower noun a tower for cooling water in an industrial process so that it can be used again.

coomb noun another spelling of **combe**.

coop noun a cage for poultry.
coop verb to **coop up** to confine people or animals or shut them in.

cooper noun a person who makes and repairs barrels and tubs. [from a German word Kupe meaning 'tub']

cooperate verb to work helpfully with another person or with other people. **cooperation** noun **cooperator** noun [from a Latin word cooperari meaning 'to work together']

cooperative adjective 1 willing to work helpfully with another person. 2 providing cooperation. 3 (said about a business or farm) owned and run jointly by its members with the profits shared between them.
cooperative noun a business or farm organized on cooperative principles. **cooperatively** adverb

co-opt verb to invite someone to become a member of a committee or other group of people, the invitation being issued by the other members. **co-option** noun **co-optive** adjective [from co- and a Latin word optare meaning 'to choose']

coordinate[1] (koh-**ord**-in-ət) noun each of a set of numbers or letters used to fix the position of a point on a graph or map. **coordinate** adjective equal in importance. **coordinately** adverb [from co- and a Latin word ordinare meaning 'to arrange']

coordinate[2] (koh-**ord**-in-ayt) verb to organize people or things to work properly together. **coordination** noun **coordinator** noun

coot noun a waterbird with a horny white patch on its forehead. [origin unknown]

cop verb (**copped, copping**) (informal) to catch or arrest someone.
cop noun (informal) 1 a police officer. 2 an arrest or capture ♦ It's a fair cop. **to cop it**

to get into trouble or be punished. **to cop out** to back out of an agreement or responsibility. [from a dialect word *cap* meaning 'to capture']

cope[1] *verb* to manage or deal with something successfully. [from a French word *cop* meaning 'a blow']

cope[2] *noun* a long loose cloak worn by clergy in certain ceremonies. [same origin as for *cape*[1]]

copier *noun* a machine for copying letters and documents, a photocopier.

co-pilot *noun* a second pilot in an aircraft.

coping (koh-ping) *noun* the top row of stones or bricks in a wall, usually slanted so that rainwater can run off it. [from *cope*[2]]

copious *adjective* in large amounts, plentiful. **copiously** *adverb* [from a Latin word *copia* meaning 'plenty']

coplanar *adjective* (*Geometry*) lying in the same plane.

cop-out *noun* (*informal*) the act of avoiding a commitment or responsibility.

copper[1] *noun* **1** a reddish-brown metal used to make pipes, wire, coins, etc.; a chemical element (symbol Cu). **2** a coin made of copper or a copper alloy. **3** a reddish-brown colour.
copper *adjective* **1** made of copper. **2** reddish-brown. [from a Latin word *cuprum* meaning 'Cyprus metal' (because the Romans got most of their copper from Cyprus)]

copper[2] *noun* (*informal*) a police officer. [from *cop*[1]]

copperplate *noun* neat clear handwriting. [so called because the books giving examples of this kind of writing for learners to copy were printed from copper plates]

coppice *noun* a group of trees and undergrowth. [from a Latin word *colpus* meaning 'a blow' (because the trees were periodically cut back and allowed to grow again)]

copra *noun* dried coconut kernels. [via Portuguese and Spanish from Malayalam (a language spoken in southern India)]

copse *noun* a small group of trees. [a different spelling of *coppice*]

Coptic *adjective* **1** to do with the Copts, an Egyptian people of the period from the mid 4th century BC onwards. **2** to do with the native Christian Church in Egypt.
Coptic *noun* the language of the Copts, now used only in the Coptic Church in Egypt. [via French and Latin from a Coptic word *Gyptios*, related to *Egyptian*]

copula *noun* (*Grammar*) a connecting word, especially a part of the verb *to be* connecting the predicate of a sentence with the subject. [a Latin word meaning 'connection']

copulate (kop-yoo-layt) *verb* to have sexual intercourse. **copulation** *noun* [from a Latin word *copulare* meaning 'to join together']

copy *noun* (**copies**) **1** a thing made to look like another. SYNONYMS: replica, reproduction, imitation, duplicate, facsimile, forgery, fake. **2** something written or printed out again from its original form. **3** one of a number of specimens of the same book, newspaper, or magazine. **4** material for printing.
copy *verb* (**copies, copied, copying**) **1** to make a copy of something. **2** to try to do the same as someone, to imitate someone. [from a Latin word *copia* meaning 'plenty']

copybook *noun* a book containing models of handwriting for learners to copy.

copycat *noun* (*informal*) a person who slavishly copies someone else.

copyright *noun* the exclusive legal right owned by a person or organization to print or publish a book or article, to reproduce a picture or film, or to perform or record a piece of music.
copyright *adjective* (said about a book, piece of music, etc.) protected by copyright.

coquettish (kə-ket-ish) *adjective* (said about a woman) often flirting. [from a French word *coquette* meaning 'wanton']

coracle (ko-rə-kəl) *noun* a small wickerwork boat covered with watertight material. [from a Welsh word *corwgl*]

coral *noun* **1** a hard red, pink, or white substance formed from the skeletons of tiny sea creatures massed together. **2** a reddish-pink colour.
coral *adjective* reddish-pink. **coralline** *adjective* [from a Greek word *korallion*]

cor anglais (kor ahn-glay) (**cors anglais**) an alto woodwind instrument of the oboe family, having a bulbous part at the lower end. [a French phrase, meaning 'English horn']

corbel (kor-bəl) *noun* a piece of stone or timber that sticks out from a wall to support something. **corbelled** *adjective* [from an Old French word, from a Latin word *corvus* meaning 'raven' (because early corbels had the shape of a raven's beak)]

cord *noun* 1 a long thin flexible strip of twisted strands, or a piece of this. 2 a structure like a cord in the body ♦ *the spinal cord*. 3 corduroy material. 4 a measure of cut wood (usually 128 cubic feet or 3.6 cubic metres).
cords *plural noun* corduroy trousers. [from an Old French word *corde*, from a Latin word *chorda*]
◊ Do not confuse this word with **chord**, which has a different meaning.

cordial *noun* a fruit-flavoured drink.
cordial *adjective* warm and friendly ♦ *They sent cordial greetings*. **cordially** *adverb* **cordiality** (kor-di-al-iti) *noun* [from a Latin word *cordis* meaning 'of the heart' (because a cordial was originally a drink given to stimulate the heart)]

cordite (kor-diyt) *noun* a smokeless explosive used in bullets and shells. [from *cord* (because it looks like cord)]

cordless *adjective* (said about a telephone or piece of electrical equipment) not connected by a flex to a central unit or mains supply.

cordon *noun* 1 a line of soldiers, police, or vehicles placed round an area to guard it or control the movement of people into and out of it. 2 a fruit tree trimmed so that it grows as a single stem against a wall or along wires.
cordon *verb* to enclose an area with a cordon. [from an Italian word *cordone*, related to *cord*]

cordon bleu (kor-dawn bler) *adjective* of the highest class in cookery. [a French phrase, meaning 'blue ribbon']

corduroy *noun* cotton cloth with velvety ridges. [from *cord* and *duroy* meaning 'a kind of woollen material']

core *noun* 1 the hard central part of an apple, pear, or other fruit, containing the seeds. 2 the central or most important part of something. 3 (*Computing*) a unit in the structure of a computer memory storing one bit of data. 4 the part of a nuclear reactor that contains the fissile material. 5 a piece of soft iron along the middle of an electromagnet or induction coil.

core *verb* to remove the core from a fruit.
to the core thoroughly, completely.
corer *noun* [origin unknown]

co-respondent (koh-ri-spon-dənt) *noun* a person who is named as having allegedly committed adultery with a person (in law called the *respondent*) being divorced.

corgi *noun* (**corgis**) a small dog of a Welsh breed with short legs and upright ears. [from Welsh words *cor* meaning 'dwarf' and *ci* meaning 'dog']

coriander (ko-ri-and-er) *noun* an aromatic plant with leaves and seeds used for flavouring. [from a Greek word *koriannon*]

Corinthian (kə-rinth-iən) *adjective* 1 to do with Corinth, a city of ancient Greece. 2 denoting a style of architecture, the most ornate of the five classical orders of architecture.

cork *noun* 1 a light tough substance made from the bark of a south European oak. 2 a bottle stopper made of cork or a similar material. 3 a piece of this substance used as a float.
cork *verb* to close or seal a bottle with a cork. [via Dutch and Spanish from a Latin word *quercus* meaning 'oak']

corkscrew *noun* 1 a tool with a spiral thread, for removing corks from bottles. 2 a spiral.

corm *noun* a rounded underground base of a stem, like a bulb and from which buds sprout. [from a Greek word *kormos*]

cormorant *noun* a large black seabird. [from a Latin phrase *corvus marinus* meaning 'sea raven']

corn¹ *noun* 1 the seed of wheat and similar plants. 2 a plant, such as wheat, grown for its grain. 3 (*Amer.*) maize. [from an Old English word]

corn² *noun* a small area of hardened skin on the foot. [from a Latin word *cornu* meaning 'horn']

corn dolly *noun* a model of a human figure, made from twisted straw.

cornea (korn-iə) *noun* the transparent layer over the front of the eyeball. **corneal** *adjective* [same origin as for *corn*²]

corned *adjective* preserved with salt ♦ *corned beef*. [from *corn*¹ (because the corns (= grains) of coarse salt that were used)]

cornelian *noun* another spelling of **carnelian**.

corner noun 1 the angle or area where two lines or sides or walls meet or where two streets join. 2 a difficult position, or one with no escape. 3 a hidden or remote place. 4 a free hit or kick from the corner of the field in hockey or football. 5 a situation in which one person or organization dominates the supply of a certain product or service, and can control its price.

corner verb 1 to drive a person or animal into a corner; to force someone into a position from which there is no escape. 2 to obtain all or most of something for yourself; to establish a monopoly of a product or service. 3 to move round a corner ♦ *The car was cornering much too fast.* [from a Latin word *cornu* meaning 'horn' or 'tip']

cornerstone noun 1 a stone built into the corner at the base of a building. 2 a vital or important feature on which an idea or activity is based.

cornet noun 1 a brass musical instrument like a trumpet but shorter and wider. 2 a cone-shaped wafer for holding ice cream. [from a French word *cornette* meaning 'small horn', from a Latin word *cornu* meaning 'horn']

cornfield noun a field in which corn grows.

cornflakes plural noun a breakfast cereal of toasted flakes made from maize flour.

cornflour noun flour made from maize or rice, used to thicken sauces.

cornflower noun a plant with blue flowers that grows wild in cornfields and is cultivated as a garden plant.

cornice (korn-iss) noun a band of ornamental moulding round the wall of a room just below the ceiling or at the top of a building. [via French and Italian from a Latin word *cornix* meaning 'crow']

Cornish adjective to do with Cornwall or its people or language.
Cornish noun the ancient language of Cornwall.

Cornish pasty noun a small pie containing a mixture of meat and potato or other vegetables.

cornucopia (kor-new-koh-piə) noun 1 a horn-shaped container overflowing with fruit and flowers, used as a symbol of plenty. 2 a plentiful supply of good things. [from Latin words *cornu* meaning 'horn' and *copiae* meaning 'of plenty']

corny adjective (**cornier, corniest**) (*informal*) repeated so often that people are tired of it ♦ *a corny joke.* **corniness** noun [from *corn*[1]]

corolla (kə-rol-ə) noun (**corollas**) (*Botany*) the part of a flower consisting of petals forming a bunch (called a *whorl*) around the stem. [a Latin word meaning 'small crown']

corollary (kə-rol-er-i) noun (**corollaries**) 1 a fact or proposition that follows as a logical consequence or result from something that has been proved. 2 a direct result or consequence. [from a Latin word *corollarium* meaning (in later Latin) 'deduction', related to *corolla*]

corona (kə-roh-nə) noun (**coronas**) 1 a circle or glow of light round something, especially round the sun or a star. 2 (*Botany*) the trumpet-shaped central part of a daffodil or narcissus. [a Latin word meaning 'crown']

coronary (ko-rən-er-i) adjective to do with the arteries supplying blood to the heart. **coronary** noun (**coronaries**) 1 a coronary artery. 2 short for **coronary thrombosis**. [from *corona* (because the coronary arteries surround the heart like a crown)]

coronary thrombosis noun a blockage of a coronary artery by a clot of blood.

coronation noun the ceremony of crowning a king or queen. [same origin as for *corona*]

coroner (ko-rən-er) noun a public official who holds an inquiry into the cause of a death thought to be from unnatural causes. [via French from a Latin title *custos placitorum coronae* meaning 'guardian of the Crown's pleas']

coronet noun 1 a small crown. 2 an ornamental band of gold or jewels for the head. [from an Old French word, related to *corona*]

corporal[1] adjective to do with the body. **corporality** noun [from a Latin word *corporis* meaning 'of the body']

corporal[2] noun a non-commissioned soldier ranking below a sergeant and above a private.

corporal punishment noun punishment on the body, such as spanking or caning.

corporate (kor-per-ət) adjective 1 shared by members of a group ♦ *corporate responsibility.* 2 united in one group ♦ *a* *corporate body.* [from a Latin word *corporare* meaning 'to unite in one body']

corporation *noun* 1 a group of people or group of companies legally authorized to act as one entity, especially in business. 2 a group of people elected to govern a town or borough.

corporation tax *noun* a tax on the profits of a business company.

corps (kor) *noun* (**corps** (korz)) 1 a military force or army unit. 2 a body of people working in the same activity ♦ *the diplomatic corps.* [a French word, from a Latin word *corpus* meaning 'body']

corpse *noun* a dead body, especially of a human. [from a Latin word *corpus* meaning 'body']

corpulent (kor-pew-lənt) *adjective* having a bulky body or fat. **corpulence** *noun* [same origin as for *corpse*]

corpus *noun* (**corpora** or **corpuses**) a large collection of writings or written texts. [a Latin word meaning 'body']

corpuscle (kor-pus-əl) *noun* (*Biology*) one of the red or white cells in the blood. [from a Latin word *corpusculum* meaning 'little body']

corral (kə-rahl) *noun* (*Amer.*) an enclosure for horses or cattle.
corral *verb* (**corralled, corralling**) (*Amer.*) to put animals into a corral. [from Spanish and Portuguese words]

correct *adjective* 1 true or accurate; not having any mistakes. SYNONYMS: right, accurate, exact, precise, true. 2 proper, done or said in the approved way.
correct *verb* 1 to make something correct by altering or adjusting it. SYNONYMS: rectify, remedy, put right, amend. 2 to mark the errors in a piece of work. 3 to point out the faults in a person, or to punish them. **correctly** *adverb* **correctness** *noun* **correctable** *adjective* [from *com-* and a Latin word *rectus* meaning 'straight']

correction *noun* 1 the process of correcting something or of being corrected. 2 an alteration made to something to make it correct.

corrective *adjective* meant to correct something bad or harmful.
corrective *noun* a measure that corrects something bad or harmful.

correlate (ko-rəl-ayt) *verb* 1 to compare or connect things systematically. 2 to have a systematic connection. **correlation** *noun* [from *com-* and *relate*]

correlative (kə-rel-ə-tiv) *adjective* 1 corresponding, having a systematic connection. 2 (*Grammar*) (said about words) regularly used together, such as *either* and *or*.

correspond *verb* 1 to match or be in agreement ♦ *Your story corresponds with what I've been told.* 2 to be similar or equivalent to something else ♦ *They have an official that corresponds to our mayor.* 3 to write letters to one other ♦ *Sarah and her cousin corresponded for many years.* [from *com-* and *respond*]

correspondence *noun* 1 agreement or similarity. 2 the process of writing letters to one another, or the letters themselves.

correspondence course *noun* a course of study in which the tutors and students correspond by post.

correspondent *noun* 1 a person who writes letters to someone else. 2 a person who works for a newspaper or radio station to gather news or write reports for them.

corresponding angles *plural noun* the equal angles that are formed on the same side of a straight line when parallel lines cut it.

corridor *noun* a long narrow passage from which doors open into rooms. [via French from an Italian word *corridoio* meaning 'running place']

corrigendum (ko-ri-gen-dəm) *noun* (**corrigenda**) an error in a book, for which a correction is printed. [a Latin word meaning 'thing to be corrected']

corroborate (kə-rob-er-ayt) *verb* to help to confirm a statement or theory. **corroboration** *noun* **corroborative** (kə-rob-er-ətiv) *adjective* [from *com-* and a Latin word *roborare* meaning 'to strengthen']

corrode *verb* to destroy a substance gradually by chemical action ♦ *Rust corrodes metal.* **corrosion** *noun* **corrosive** *adjective* **corrodable** *adjective* [from *com-* and a Latin word *rodere* meaning 'to gnaw']

corrugated *adjective* shaped into alternating ridges and grooves ♦ *corrugated iron.* **corrugation** *noun* [from *com-* and a Latin word *ruga* meaning 'wrinkle']

corrupt *adjective* 1 willing to act dishonestly or accept bribes. SYNONYMS:

dishonest, crooked, unscrupulous. **2** immoral or wicked. **3** (said about a text or computer data) unreliable because of errors.
corrupt verb **1** to make someone corrupt or dishonest. **2** to introduce errors into a text or computer data. **corruptible** adjective **corruption** noun [from com- and a Latin word ruptum meaning 'broken']

corsair (kor-sair) noun (old use) **1** a pirate ship. **2** a pirate. [from a French word, from a Latin word cursus meaning 'a raid']

corset noun a close-fitting piece of underwear worn to shape or support the body. [via French from a Latin word corpus meaning 'body']

cortège (kor-tayzh) noun a funeral procession. [a French word]

cortex noun (**cortices** (kor-ti-seez)) **1** an outer layer of tissue on an organ such as a kidney or a plant stem. **2** the outer grey matter of the brain. **cortical** adjective [a Latin word meaning 'bark of a tree']

cortisone (kor-tiz-ohn) noun a hormone produced by the adrenal glands or made synthetically, used against inflammation and allergy. [from parts of its chemical name]

coruscate (ko-rəs-kayt) verb (formal) to sparkle. [from a Latin word coruscare meaning 'to glitter']

corvette (kor-vet) noun a small fast warship designed for escorting merchant ships. [a French word, from a Dutch word korf meaning 'a kind of ship']

cos [1] (koss) noun a kind of lettuce with long crisp leaves. [from Kos, a Greek island where it was first grown]

cos [2] (koz or koss) abbreviation (Mathematics) cosine.

'cos (koz) adverb & conjunction (informal) because.

cosec (koh-sek) abbreviation (Mathematics) cosecant.

cosecant (koh-see-kənt) noun (Mathematics) the secant of the complement of a given angle.

cosh noun a heavy weapon used for hitting people.
cosh verb to hit someone with a cosh. [origin unknown]

cosine (koh-siyn) noun (Mathematics) (in a right-angled triangle) the ratio of the length of a side adjacent to one of the acute angles to the length of the hypotenuse.

cosmetic noun a substance such as a cream or liquid used on the skin to make it look more attractive.
cosmetic adjective used to improve the appearance ♦ cosmetic surgery. [from a Greek word kosmein meaning 'to arrange' or 'to decorate']

cosmic adjective **1** to do with the universe. **2** coming from outer space ♦ cosmic radiation. [from cosmos]

cosmonaut noun a Russian astronaut. [from cosmos and astronaut]

cosmopolitan adjective **1** to do with or coming from many parts of the world ♦ a cosmopolitan population. **2** including people from many parts of the world ♦ a cosmopolitan city. **3** interested in all parts of the world and not just your own country ♦ a cosmopolitan outlook.
cosmopolitan noun a cosmopolitan person. [from cosmos and a Greek word politēs meaning 'citizen']

cosmos (koz-moss) noun the universe. [from a Greek word kosmos meaning 'the world']

Cossack (koss-ak) noun a member of a people of southern Russia and neighbouring regions, famous as horsemen. [from a Turkish word meaning 'nomad']

cosset (koss-it) verb (**cosseted, cosseting**) to pamper someone. [from a French word]

cost noun **1** an amount you charge or have to pay for something. SYNONYMS: outlay, expense, charge. **2** the effort or loss needed to achieve something ♦ They shut the factory at a cost of 500 jobs.
cost verb (past tense and past participle **cost**) **1** to have a certain amount as its price or charge. **2** to need a certain effort or loss to achieve something. **3** to estimate the cost of something.
costs plural noun the expenses involved in a law case. **at all costs** no matter what the risk or loss might be. [from a French word, from a Latin word constare meaning 'to stand at a price']
◊ In meaning **3** the past tense and past participle is costed.

co-star noun a stage or cinema star appearing with another or others of equal importance.
co-star verb (**co-starred, co-starring**) **1** to

appear as a co-star. **2** (said about a film etc.) to have a performer as a co-star.

cost-effective *adjective* effective or beneficial enough to justify its cost.

costermonger (kost-er-mung-ger) *noun* a person who sells fruit and other things from a barrow in the street. [from old words *costard* meaning 'large apple' and *monger* meaning 'trader']

costly *adjective* (**costlier, costliest**) costing a lot, expensive. **costliness** *noun*

cost of living *noun* the general level of prices.

costume *noun* a set or style of clothes belonging to a particular place or time, or worn for a particular activity. [via French from an Italian word *costume* meaning 'habit' or 'fashion', related to *custom*]

costume drama *noun* a television or cinema drama set in a historical period.

costume jewellery *noun* jewellery made of inexpensive materials.

cosy *adjective* (**cosier, cosiest**) warm and comfortable.
cosy *noun* (**cosies**) a cover put over a teapot or boiled egg to keep it hot. **cosily** *adverb* **cosiness** *noun* [origin unknown]

cot[1] *noun* a small bed having high sides with bars, for a baby or young child. [from a Hindi word *khat* meaning 'bedstead']

cot[2] *abbreviation* (Mathematics) cotangent.

cotangent (koh-tan-jənt) *noun* (Mathematics) the tangent of the complement of a given angle.

cot death *noun* an unexplained death of a baby while sleeping.

coterie (koh-ter-i) *noun* a small group of people having the same interests or tastes. [a French word]

cottage *noun* a small simple house, especially in the country. [from a French word *cotage*]

cottage cheese *noun* soft white cheese made from curds without pressing.

cottage industry *noun* a light industry or business that can be carried on in a person's home.

cottage pie *noun* a dish of minced meat with a layer of browned mashed potato.

cotter pin *noun* **1** a bolt or wedge for securing parts of machinery etc. **2** a split pin that is passed through a hole and opened out on the other side. [origin unknown]

cotton *noun* **1** a soft white substance covering the seeds of a tropical plant, or the plant itself. **2** a thread made from this substance. **3** a cloth made from cotton thread.
cotton *verb* **to cotton on** (*informal*) to begin to understand something. [via French from an Arabic word *kutn*]

cotton wool *noun* soft fluffy wadding of a kind originally made from cotton.

cotyledon (kot-i-lee-dən) *noun* the first leaf growing from a seed. [from a Greek word *kotulēdōn* meaning 'cup-shaped cavity']

couch *noun* **1** a long soft seat like a sofa but with the back extending along half its length and only one raised end. **2** a sofa or settee. **3** a bed-like platform on which a doctor's patient can lie to be examined.
couch *verb* to express something in words of a certain kind ♦ *The request was couched in polite terms.* [from a French word *coucher* meaning 'to lay down flat']

couchant (cow-chənt) *adjective* (Heraldry) (said about an animal) lying with the body resting on the legs and the head raised. [a French word meaning 'lying down']

couchette (koo-shet) *noun* a compartment in a train, in which the seats can be converted to form beds for sleeping at night. [a French word meaning 'little couch']

cougar (koog-er) *noun* (Amer.) a puma. [via French from Guarani (a South American language)]

cough *verb* to send out air from the lungs with a sudden sharp sound.
cough *noun* **1** an act or sound of coughing. **2** an illness that makes you cough a lot. [an imitation of the sound]

could *auxiliary verb* **1** the past tense of **can**[2]. **2** to feel that you want to do something ♦ *I could laugh for joy.*

couldn't *verb* (*informal*) could not.

coulomb (koo-lom) *noun* a unit of electric charge. [named after a French engineer Charles-Augustin de Coulomb (1736–1806)]

council *noun* a group of people chosen or elected to organize or discuss something,

especially those elected to run the affairs of a town or county. [from a Latin word *concilium* meaning 'assembly']
◊ Do not confuse this word with **counsel**, which has a different meaning.

council house *noun* a house owned by a local council and let out to tenants.

councillor *noun* a member of a town or county council.
◊ Do not confuse this word with **counsellor**, which has a different meaning.

council tax *noun* a local tax introduced in Britain in 1993, based on the values of properties.

counsel *noun* 1 advice or suggestions ♦ *to give counsel.* 2 a barrister or group of barristers representing someone in a lawsuit.
counsel *verb* (**counselled, counselling**) 1 to advise or recommend something. 2 to give professional guidance to a person about personal or social problems. [from a Latin word *consulere* meaning 'to consult']
◊ Do not confuse this word with **council**, which has a different meaning.

counsellor *noun* an adviser.
◊ Do not confuse this word with **councillor**, which has a different meaning.

count [1] *verb* 1 to find the total of something by using numbers. SYNONYMS: calculate, add up, compute, total, reckon. 2 to say numbers in the right order. 3 to include something in a total ♦ *There were six of us, counting the dog.* 4 to be important ♦ *It's what you do that counts.* 5 to be a factor ♦ *I'm afraid his mistake will count against him.* 6 to regard or consider something in a certain way ♦ *I should count it an honour to be invited.*
count *noun* 1 the process of counting, a calculation. 2 a number reached by counting, a total. 3 any of the points being considered, e.g. in accusing someone of crimes ♦ *He was found guilty on all counts.* **to count down** to count numbers backwards to zero before a precisely timed event, e.g. when launching a space rocket. **to count on** to rely on something or someone. SYNONYMS: rely on, depend on, trust; (*informal*) bank on.
to keep count to know how many there have been. **to lose count** to forget how many there have been. **out for the count** defeated in a boxing match by being knocked to the floor and failing to get up within ten seconds. **countable** *adjective* [via French from a Latin word *computare*, related to *compute*]

count [2] *noun* a foreign nobleman.

countdown *noun* the process of counting numbers backwards to zero before a precisely timed event, e.g. when launching a space rocket.

countenance *noun* 1 a person's face, or the expression on it. 2 (*formal*) an appearance of approval ♦ *Their support lends countenance to the plan.*
countenance *verb* to allow something as acceptable or possible. [from a French word *contenance* meaning 'behaviour' or 'bearing']

counter [1] *noun* 1 a flat surface over which customers are served in a shop, bank, etc. 2 a small round playing piece used in some board games. 3 a token representing a coin. 4 a device for counting things. **under the counter** sold or obtained in an illegal or underhand way. [same origin as for *count*[1]]

counter [2] *adverb* opposite or contrary ♦ *This is counter to what we want.*
counter *adjective* opposed.
counter *verb* 1 to oppose or contradict someone or something. 2 to return an opponent's attack by hitting back. [via French from a Latin word *contra* meaning 'against']

counter- *prefix* 1 against or opposing; done in return (as in ♦ *counter-attack*). 2 corresponding (as in ♦ *countersign*). [same origin as for *counter*[2]]

counteract *verb* to take action against something and reduce or prevent its effects. **counteraction** *noun*

counter-attack *noun* an attack to oppose or return an enemy's attack.
counter-attack *verb* to make a counter-attack on an enemy.

counterbalance *noun* a weight or influence that balances another.
counterbalance *verb* to act as a counterbalance to something.

counterblast *noun* a strongly worded reply.

counterclockwise *adjective* & *adverb* (North Amer.) anticlockwise.

counter-espionage (es-pi-ən-ahzh) *noun* action taken to uncover and counteract spying by an enemy.

counterfeit (cownt-er-feet) *adjective* fake.

counterfeit *noun* a fake.
counterfeit *verb* to fake something, especially money. [from a French word *contrefait* meaning 'made in opposition']

counterfoil *noun* a section of a cheque or receipt that is torn off and kept by the sender as a record. [from *counter-* and *foil*[1] in its old meaning 'sheet of paper']

counter-intelligence *noun* counter-espionage.

countermand *verb* to cancel a command or order already given.
countermand *noun* a command or order cancelling an earlier one. [from *counter-* and a Latin word *mandare* meaning 'to command']

countermeasure *noun* an action taken to counteract a threat or danger.

counter-offensive *noun* a large-scale counter-attack.

counterpane *noun* a bedspread. [via French from a Latin phrase *culcitra puncta* meaning 'quilted mattress']

counterpart *noun* a person or thing that corresponds to another ♦ *Their President is the counterpart of our Prime Minister.*

counterpoint *noun* (*Music*) 1 a method of combining melodies in harmony according to fixed rules. 2 a melody added as an accompaniment to another. [from a French word *contrepoint*, from a Latin phrase *cantus contrapunctus* meaning 'song written opposite (to the original melody)']

counterpoise *noun* a counterbalance.
counterpoise *verb* to counterbalance something.

counterproductive *adjective* having the opposite of the effect that is wanted.

Counter-Reformation *noun* the reform of the Church of Rome in the 16th and 17th centuries, following on the Protestant Reformation.

countersign *verb* to add another signature to a document to give it authority.
countersignature *noun*

countersink *verb* (past tense and past participle **countersunk**) 1 to widen the top of a hole drilled for a screw so that the head of the screw is level with the surface. 2 to put a screw into a hole in this way.

countertenor *noun* a male singing voice higher than tenor, or a singer with this voice.

counterweight *noun* a counterbalancing weight or influence.

countess *noun* 1 the wife or widow of a count or earl. 2 a woman holding the rank of count or earl.

countless *adjective* too many to count.

countrified *adjective* like the country or country life.

country *noun* (**countries**) 1 a nation or state, or the land it occupies. 2 land away from a town, with fields and woods and few buildings. 3 an area of land with certain features ♦ *hill country.* [via French from a Latin phrase *contrata terra* meaning 'land lying opposite']

country-and-western *noun* a form of popular music based on American rural or cowboy songs sung to a guitar.

country dance *noun* a traditional English dance, often with couples face to face in long lines.

countryman or **countrywoman** *noun* (**countrymen** or **countrywomen**) 1 a man or woman living in the country, not in a town. 2 a man or woman from the same country as another person, a compatriot.

countryside *noun* country areas.

county *noun* (**counties**) 1 each of the main areas that a country is divided into for local government. 2 (*North Amer.*) a division of a state for administrative purposes. 3 the families of high social level long established in a county. [originally 'the land of a count' (*count*[2])]

county court *noun* a local court where civil cases are heard.

coup (koo) *noun* (**coups** (kooz)) 1 short for **coup d'état**. 2 a sudden and unexpectedly successful action. [a French word meaning 'a blow']

coup de grâce (koo də grahs) *noun* (**coups de grâce**) a stroke or blow that puts an end to something. [a French phrase, meaning 'mercy blow']

coup d'état (koo day-tah) *noun* (**coups d'état**) the sudden overthrow of a government by force or by unconstitutional means. [a French phrase, meaning 'blow of state']

coupé (koo-pay) *noun* a two-door car with a fixed roof and sloping back. [from a French phrase *carrosse coupé* meaning 'cut carriage']

couple *noun* 1 two people or things considered together, a pair. 2 a man and woman who are married to each other or romantically associated. **3** a pair of partners in a dance.

couple verb **1** to fasten or link things together; to join things with a coupling. **2** to have sexual intercourse. [via French from a Latin word *copula*]

couplet (kup-lit) noun two successive lines of rhyming verse in the same metre. [from a French word, related to *couple*]

coupling noun a device for connecting railway vehicles or parts of machinery.

coupon noun a small printed piece of paper that gives you the right to receive something or that can be used as an application form or an entry form for a competition. [a French word meaning 'a piece cut off']

courage noun the ability to face danger, difficulty, or pain even when you are afraid; bravery. SYNONYMS: daring, bravery, nerve, audacity, spirit; (*informal*) pluck, guts. [from a Latin word *cor* meaning 'heart']

courageous (kə-ray-jəs) adjective having or showing courage, brave. SYNONYMS: brave, bold, daring, fearless, valiant, intrepid; (*informal*) plucky. **courageously** adverb

courgette (koor-zhet) noun a kind of small vegetable marrow. [a French word meaning 'a small gourd']

courier (koor-i-er) noun **1** a messenger carrying news or important papers. **2** a person employed to guide and help a group of tourists. [from a Latin word *currere* meaning 'to run']

course noun **1** the route or direction taken or intended ◆ *Follow the course of the river* ◆ *The aircraft was off course.* **2** a movement forward or onward in space or time ◆ *in the ordinary course of events.* **3** a series of events or actions that can achieve something ◆ *Your best course is to start again.* **4** each part of a meal. **5** a series of lessons or talks in a particular subject. **6** a series of medical treatments or medicines given for a particular ailment or illness. **7** a stretch of land or water over which a race takes place. **8** a continuous layer of brick or stone in a wall.
course verb (said about something liquid) to move or flow freely ◆ *Tears coursed down his cheeks.* **in course of** in the process of ◆ *The building is in course of construction.* **of course** without a doubt, as was expected. [from a Latin word *cursus* meaning 'running']

coursework noun work done during a course of study and counting towards the final mark.

coursing noun the sport of hunting hares with dogs, using sight rather than scent.

court noun **1** the household and staff of a king or queen. **2** a yard surrounded by houses and opening off a street. **3** a courtyard. **4** an enclosed area for games, such as squash or tennis. **5** a lawcourt, or the judges in a lawcourt.
court verb **1** to try to win the favour or support of someone. **2** (*old use*) to try to win the love of someone, especially in order to marry them. **3** (said about animals) to try to attract a mate. **4** to behave as though trying to bring about something harmful ◆ *The climbers were courting danger.* [from an Old French word *cort*, from a Latin word *cohors* meaning 'yard' or 'retinue']

court card noun a playing card that is a king, queen, or jack.

courteous (ker-ti-əs) adjective polite and helpful. SYNONYMS: civil, polite, considerate, well-mannered, respectful. **courteously** adverb [from an Old French word *corteis*, related to *court*]

courtesan (kor-ti-zan) noun (*old use*) a prostitute having wealthy or upper-class clients. [via French from an obsolete Italian word *cortigiana* meaning 'female courtier']

courtesy (ker-ti-si) noun (**courtesies**) courteous behaviour. SYNONYMS: politeness, civility, good manners. **by courtesy of** by the permission or favour of.

courtier (kor-ti-er) noun (*old use*) one of a king's or queen's companions at court.

courtly (kort-li) adjective (**courtlier, courtliest**) dignified and polite. **courtliness** noun

court martial noun (**courts martial**) **1** a court for trying offences against military law. **2** a trial in this court.
court-martial verb (**court-martialled, court-martialling**) to try someone by a court martial.

courtship noun **1** a period of courting, especially for marriage. **2** the mating ritual of some birds and animals.

courtyard noun a space enclosed by walls or buildings.

cousin (kuz-ən) noun a son or daughter of your uncle or aunt. **cousinly** adverb

◊ A son or daughter of your uncle or aunt is also called a *first cousin*. A son or daughter of your parent's first cousin is called a *second cousin*, and a son or daughter of your first cousin is called a *first cousin once removed*.

couture (koo-tewr) *noun* the design and making of high-quality fashionable clothes. [a French word meaning 'sewing']

couturier (koo-tewr-i-ay) *noun* someone who designs and makes high-quality fashionable clothes.

covalent *adjective* (said about a chemical bond) formed by the sharing of one or more pairs of electrons between atoms. **covalency** *noun*

cove *noun* 1 a small bay or inlet on a coast. 2 a curved moulding where a ceiling and wall meet. [from an Old English word *cofa* meaning 'a hollow']

coven (kuv-ən) *noun* a gathering of witches. [same origin as for *convene*]

covenant (kuv-ən-ənt) *noun* a formal agreement or contract.
covenant *verb* to agree to something by covenant. **covenanter** *noun* [from an Old French word *covenir* meaning 'to agree', related to *convene*]

cover *verb* 1 to place one thing over or in front of another in order to protect or conceal it. 2 to spread something over a surface ♦ *Cover the wall with new paint.* 3 to lie or extend over a certain area ♦ *The grounds cover six acres.* 4 to travel over a distance ♦ *The marching soldiers covered thirty miles a day.* 5 to guard or protect a place by dominating the approach to it. 6 to have a target within a gun's range; to aim a gun at a target. 7 to protect someone or something by providing insurance or a guarantee ♦ *The policy covers you against fire or theft.* 8 to be enough money to pay for something ♦ *£20 should cover the fare.* 9 to include or deal with a subject ♦ *The book covers many aspects of modern art.* SYNONYMS: include, deal with, incorporate, encompass.
cover *noun* 1 a thing that covers something, such as a lid, wrapper, or envelope. 2 the binding of a book. 3 a place or area that gives shelter or protection ♦ *There was no cover from the sun's heat.* 4 a military force that gives protection ♦ *The ground troops needed air cover.* 5 a screen or pretence ♦ *They acted under cover of friendship.* 6 insurance

against a risk such as loss or damage. 7 a place laid at a table in a restaurant. **to cover for someone** to do someone's job for a time while they are unable to do it. **to cover something up** to conceal something, especially an awkward fact or piece of information. [from an Old French word *covrir*, from *co-* and a Latin word *operire* meaning 'to cover']

coverage *noun* 1 the area or amount covered by something. 2 the reporting of news in a newspaper or broadcast.

covert (kuv-ert or koh-vert) *adjective* concealed or done secretly ♦ *There were many covert glances across the table.*
covert *noun* (kuv-ert) 1 an area of thick bushes and undergrowth in which animals hide. 2 a bird's feather covering the base of another. **covertly** *adverb* [an Old French word meaning 'covered']

cover-up *noun* an attempt to conceal information about something, especially a crime or mistake.

covet (kuv-it) *verb* (**coveted, coveting**) to want very much to have something belonging to someone else. [from an Old French word, related to *cupidity*]

covetous (kuv-it-əs) *adjective* wanting something that belongs to someone else. **covetously** *adverb* **covetousness** *noun*

cow [1] *noun* 1 the fully-grown female of cattle or of some other large animals, such as an elephant, whale, or seal. [from an Old English word]

cow [2] *verb* to subdue someone by frightening or bullying them. [from an Old Norse word]

coward *noun* a person who has no courage and shows fear in a shameful way. [via French from a Latin word *cauda* meaning 'tail', perhaps referring to a frightened animal having its tail between its legs]

cowardice *noun* cowardly feelings or actions.

cowardly *adjective* lacking courage, showing cowardice. SYNONYMS: faint-hearted, timid, craven, spineless.

cowboy *noun* 1 a man in charge of grazing cattle on a ranch in the western USA. 2 (*informal*) a person who uses unscrupulous methods in trade or business.

cower *verb* to crouch or shrink back in fear. [from a German word *kuren* meaning 'to lie in wait']

cowhide noun the skin of a cow, or leather made from this.

cowl noun 1 a monk's hood or hooded robe. 2 a hood-shaped covering for a chimney or ventilation shaft. [from an Old English word]

cowling noun a removable cover over an engine.

cowrie noun a mollusc found in tropical seas, with a smooth, glossy, often brightly-coloured shell. [from a Hindi word *kauri*]

cowslip noun a wild plant with fragrant yellow spring flowers. [from an Old English word meaning 'cow slime']

cox noun a person who steers a boat with oars, a coxswain.
cox verb to act as cox of a racing boat.

coxswain (kok-swayn or kok-sən) noun 1 a person who steers a boat with oars. 2 a sailor with special duties. [from an old word *cock* meaning 'small boat' and *swain*]

coy adjective pretending to be shy or modest; bashful. **coyly** adverb **coyness** noun [from an Old French word *coi*, related to *quiet*]

coyote (koi-oh-ti) noun (**coyotes** or **coyote**) a wild dog like a wolf, found in North America. [via Mexican Spanish from a Nahuatl (Central American) word *coyotl*]

coypu (koi-poo) noun (**coypus**) a beaver-like water animal, originally from South America. [from an Araucanian (South American) word]

CPS abbreviation (in Britain) Crown Prosecution Service.

CPU abbreviation (*Computing*) central processing unit.

crab noun 1 a shellfish with ten legs, the first pair being a set of pincers. 2 the flesh of a crab used for food. **catch a crab** (in rowing) to get an oar jammed under the water by a faulty stroke. [from an Old English word *crabba*]

crab apple noun a kind of small sour apple. [perhaps from a Scottish and northern word *scrab*; it has nothing to do with *crab*]

crabbed adjective 1 bad-tempered. 2 (said about writing) difficult to read or decipher.

crack noun 1 a narrow line or opening on the surface of something where it is broken but has not come completely apart. SYNONYMS: chink, cleft, fissure. 2 a sudden sharp or explosive noise. 3 a sharp blow or knock ♦ *a crack on the head.* SYNONYMS: blow, knock, smack, rap.
4 (*informal*) a joke or wisecrack. 5 a narrow gap or chink ♦ *There was a crack in the curtains, and the light came through.* 6 a strong drug made from cocaine.

crack adjective first-class, excellent ♦ *a crack shot.*

crack verb 1 to break without coming completely apart. SYNONYMS: split, fracture. 2 to make a sudden sharp or explosive sound. 3 to break with a sharp sound. 4 (*informal*) to break into a safe. 5 (*informal*) to find the solution to a code or problem. 6 (said about a voice) to become suddenly harsh, especially with emotion. 7 (said about a person or group of people) to collapse under strain, to stop resisting. 8 (*Chemistry*) to break down heavy oils in order to produce lighter ones. **at the crack of dawn** at daybreak. **to crack down on** (*informal*) to take severe measures against something illegal or forbidden. **to crack a joke** (*informal*) to tell a joke. **to crack up** (*informal*) to have a physical or mental breakdown. **to get cracking** (*informal*) to start working or doing something with energy. [from an Old English word *cracian* meaning 'to make an explosive noise']

crackdown noun a series of severe measures taken against something illegal or forbidden.

cracked wheat noun grains of wheat crushed into small pieces.

cracker noun 1 a small paper toy that makes a bang and releases a small novelty when the ends are pulled. 2 a firework that explodes with a sharp crack. 3 a thin dry biscuit.

crackers adjective (*informal*) crazy.

cracking adjective (*informal*) 1 very good. 2 fast and exciting ♦ *They drove at a cracking pace.*

crackle verb to make a series of slight cracking sounds, or cause something to do this.
crackle noun a series of crackling sounds. [from *crack*]

crackling noun the crisp fatty skin on roast pork.

cracknel noun a brittle sweet made from melted sugar. [from an Old French word *craquelin*]

crackpot *adjective* (*informal*) crazy or impractical.
crackpot *noun* a person with crazy or impractical ideas.

-cracy *suffix* forming nouns meaning 'ruling' or 'government' (as in *democracy*). [from a Greek word *-kratia* meaning 'rule']

cradle *noun* 1 a small bed or cot for a baby, especially one mounted on rockers. 2 a supporting framework or structure. 3 a place where something begins ♦ *the cradle of civilization*.
cradle *verb* to hold or support something gently. [from an Old English word *cradol*]

craft *noun* 1 a job or occupation that needs skill. 2 a skill or technique. 3 cunning or deceit. 4 (**craft**) a ship or boat; an aircraft or spacecraft. [from an Old English word]

craftsman or **craftswoman** *noun* (**craftsmen** or **craftswomen**) a man or woman who is skilled in a craft.
craftsmanship *noun*

crafty *adjective* (**craftier**, **craftiest**)
1 cunning or deceitful. SYNONYMS: cunning, artful, deceitful, clever, foxy, wily. 2 ingenious ♦ *a crafty idea*. **craftily** *adverb*
craftiness *noun*

crag *noun* a steep or rugged rock face or cliff. [from a Celtic word]

craggy *adjective* (**craggier**, **craggiest**) 1 (said about a cliff or rock face) steep or uneven. 2 (said about a man's face) rugged and rough-looking in an attractive way. **cragginess** *noun*

cram *verb* (**crammed**, **cramming**) 1 to force too many things or people into something so that it is very full. SYNONYMS: jam, stuff, pack, crowd, squeeze. 2 to study intensively just before an examination. [from an Old English word *crammian*]

crammer *noun* a college or school that prepares students intensively for a particular examination.

cramp *noun* 1 a sudden painful tightening of a muscle. 2 a metal bar with bent ends for holding masonry together. 3 a clamp.
cramp *verb* 1 to hinder someone's freedom or growth. 2 to suffer from cramp. 3 to fasten something with a cramp. **to cramp someone's style** (*informal*) to prevent someone from acting freely or naturally. [via Old French from a Germanic word]

cramped *adjective* 1 too narrow or crowded, without enough room to move. 2 (said about handwriting) small and with letters close together.

crampon (**kram-pon**) *noun* an iron plate with spikes, worn on boots for walking or climbing on ice. [from an earlier meaning 'grappling hook', from an Old French word]

cranberry *noun* (**cranberries**) 1 a small sour red berry, used for making jelly and sauce. 2 the shrub that produces this berry. [from a German word *Kranbeere*]

crane *noun* 1 a machine for lifting and moving heavy objects, usually by suspending them from a jib by ropes or chains. 2 a large wading bird with long legs, neck, and bill.
crane *verb* to stretch out your neck in order to see something. [from an Old English word]

crane fly *noun* (**crane flies**) a flying insect with very long thin legs.

cranium (**kray-ni-ǝm**) *noun* (**craniums** or **crania**) the skull, especially the part enclosing the brain. [from a Greek word *kranion* meaning 'skull']

crank [1] *noun* an L-shaped part used for converting to-and-fro motion into circular motion.
crank *verb* to move something by means of a crank. **to crank something up 1** to start an engine by turning a crank. 2 (*informal*) to increase the intensity of something ♦ *The DJ decided to crank up the volume.* [from an Old English word *cranc*]

crank [2] *noun* a person with very strange or fanatical ideas. [from *cranky*]

crankshaft *noun* a shaft turned by a crank.

cranky *adjective* (**crankier**, **crankiest**) (*informal*) 1 (said about a person) odd or obsessive. 2 (*North Amer.*) bad-tempered.
crankiness *noun* [originally with the meaning 'sickly', perhaps from a Dutch or German word]

cranny *noun* (**crannies**) a small narrow space or opening. **crannied** *adjective* [from an Old French word *crane* meaning 'notched']

crash *noun* 1 the sudden violent noise of something breaking or banging together ♦ *The tree fell to the ground with a loud crash.* 2 an accident in which a car, train, aircraft, etc. violently collides with something. 3 the sudden failure of a business, economy, etc. ♦ *a stock market crash*.

crash *verb* **1** to collide violently with something. SYNONYMS: smash, knock, bang, bump. **2** (said about an aircraft) to fall from the sky and hit the ground or the sea. **3** to make a crash, or to move or go with a crash ♦ *The whole pile of tins crashed to the floor*. **4** (*Computing*) (said about a computer system) to stop working suddenly. **5** (said about a company's shares) to fall suddenly in value, leading to financial ruin. **6** (*informal*) to enter a party without permission, to gatecrash it ♦ *We decided to crash the party*.
crash *adjective* involving intense effort to achieve something rapidly ♦ *a crash course in Japanese*. **to crash out** (*informal*) to fall asleep. [an imitation of the sound]

crash barrier *noun* a protective fence erected where there is danger of vehicles leaving a road.

crash dive *noun* a sudden dive by an aircraft or submarine in an emergency. **crash-dive** *verb* to dive in this way.

crash helmet *noun* a padded helmet worn to protect the head in case of a crash.

crash landing *noun* an emergency landing of an aircraft, especially causing damage to it. **crash-land** *verb*

crass *adjective* stupidly insensitive or tactless. **crassly** *adverb* **crassness** *noun* [from a Latin word *crassus* meaning 'solid, thick']

crate *noun* **1** a packing case made of strips of wood. **2** a divided container for carrying bottles.
crate *verb* to pack something into a crate. [origin unknown]

crater *noun* **1** a bowl-shaped cavity or hollow caused by an explosion or impact. **2** the mouth of a volcano. [from a Greek word *kratēr* meaning 'mixing-bowl']

cravat (krə-**vat**) *noun* a short wide scarf worn by men round the neck and tucked into an open-necked shirt. [from a French word *Cravate* meaning 'Croatian' (because Croatian soldiers wore linen cravats)]

crave *verb* **1** to have a strong desire for something. **2** (*old use*) to beg for something ♦ *We crave your pardon*. [from an Old English word *crafian*]

craven *adjective* cowardly. **cravenly** *adverb* [from an Old French word *cravanté* meaning 'defeated']

craving *noun* a strong desire, a longing ♦ *I have a craving for chocolate*.

crawl *verb* **1** to move forward on your hands and knees. **2** to move with the body close to the ground or other surface ♦ *A snake was crawling towards him*. **3** to move slowly or with difficulty ♦ *The train crawled into the station*. **4** (*informal*) to seek favour from someone by behaving in a servile way. **5** (said about the skin) to feel as if it is covered with crawling things.
crawl *noun* **1** a crawling movement. **2** a very slow pace ♦ *The line of cars had slowed to a crawl*. **3** a swimming stroke with an overarm movement of each arm alternately. **to be crawling with** to be unpleasantly full of something ♦ *The place was crawling with reporters*. **crawler** *noun* [origin unknown]

crayfish *noun* (**crayfish**) a freshwater shellfish like a very small lobster. [from an Old French word *crevice*]

crayon *noun* a stick or pencil of coloured wax or chalk, used for drawing.
crayon *verb* to draw or colour something with crayons. [from a French word *craie* meaning 'chalk']

craze *noun* **1** a widespread but short-lived enthusiasm for something ♦ *a craze for yo-yos*. **2** the object of this. [probably from a Scandinavian language]

crazed *adjective* driven insane ♦ *a crazed killer*.

crazy *adjective* (**crazier, craziest**) **1** insane. **2** very foolish, not sensible ♦ *Who's crazy idea was this?* **3** very enthusiastic about something ♦ *He's crazy about books*. **crazily** *adverb* **craziness** *noun* [from *craze*]

crazy paving *noun* paving made up of oddly-shaped pieces of stone fitted together.

creak *noun* a harsh squeak like that of a stiff door hinge.
creak *verb* to make a sound like this ♦ *The door creaked open*. **creaky** *adjective* [an imitation of the sound]

cream *noun* **1** the fatty part of milk. **2** a yellowish-white colour. **3** a soft cream-like substance, especially one used as a cosmetic or for medical purposes ♦ *face cream*. **4** a food containing or like cream ♦ *chocolate cream*. **5** the very best part of something ♦ *the cream of British society*.
cream *adjective* yellowish-white.
cream *verb* **1** to make something creamy;

to beat ingredients into a smooth soft paste ♦ *Now cream the butter* ♦ *creamed potatoes.* 2 to rub a cosmetic cream into the skin. **to cream something off** to remove the best part of something. [from an Old French word *cresme*]

cream cheese *noun* a soft rich cheese made from unskimmed milk and cream.

cream cracker *noun* a dry unsweetened biscuit, often eaten with cheese.

creamery *noun* (**creameries**) a factory that produces butter and cheese.

cream of tartar *noun* a compound of potassium used in cookery.

creamy *adjective* (**creamier, creamiest**) 1 rich in cream. 2 like cream. **creaminess** *noun*

crease *noun* 1 a line made on cloth or paper by folding, crushing, or pressing it. 2 a wrinkle or furrow on the skin. 3 (in cricket) a line on the pitch marking the limit of the bowler's or batsman's position.
crease *verb* 1 to make a crease or creases in something. 2 to develop creases ♦ *This linen jacket creases easily.* **to crease up** (*informal*) to burst out laughing, or make someone do this. [a different spelling of *crest*]

create *verb* 1 to bring something into existence ♦ *God is said to have created the world in six days.* SYNONYMS: form, build, found, establish, generate, originate, concoct. 2 to produce something as a result of what you do ♦ *He was anxious to create a good impression* ♦ *I'll create a diversion.* 3 to give a new rank or position to someone ♦ *He was created Earl of Wessex.* 4 (*informal*) to make a fuss, to grumble. [from a Latin word *creare* meaning 'to produce']

creation *noun* 1 the act or process of creating something. 2 something which has been made or invented. **the Creation** the creating of the universe, especially when thought of as the work of God.

creative *adjective* 1 showing imagination and originality ♦ *her creative use of language.* 2 good at making things. **creatively** *adverb* **creativity** *noun*

creator *noun* someone who creates something. **the Creator** God.

creature *noun* 1 a living being, especially an animal. 2 a person ♦ *Who is this poor creature?* [from a Latin word *creatura* meaning 'a created being']

crèche (kresh) *noun* a place where babies and young children are looked after while their parents are at work. [a French word]

credence (**kree-dəns**) *noun* willingness to believe in something ♦ *I don't give this story any credence.* [from a Latin word *credere* meaning 'to believe']
◊ Do not confuse this word with **credibility**, which has a different meaning.

credentials (kri-**den**-shəlz) *plural noun* 1 a person's qualifications and past achievements that make them suitable for something ♦ *Her credentials for the job are impeccable.* 2 documents that prove a person's identity or qualifications ♦ *May I see your credentials?* [same origin as *credit*]

credibility *noun* 1 the quality of being believable or convincing ♦ *The defendant's story lacks credibility.* 2 acceptability among young or fashionable people.
◊ Do not confuse this word with **credence**, which has a different meaning.

credible *adjective* able to be believed, convincing ♦ *I find it scarcely credible that she could have stolen the money.* **credibly** *adverb* [same origin as *credit*]
◊ Do not confuse this word with **creditable**, which has a different meaning.

credit *noun* 1 an arrangement trusting a person to pay at a later date for goods or services supplied. 2 the amount of money you are allowed to owe or the length of time you are allowed to pay under this arrangement ♦ *We can offer you six months' credit.* 3 the amount of money in a person's bank account or entered in a financial account as paid in. 4 praise or acknowledgement given for some achievement or good quality ♦ *How come I did all the work and you got all the credit?* ♦ *I must give you credit for persistence.* 5 a source of pride ♦ *Your children are a credit to you.* 6 a grade above a pass in an examination. 7 (*Amer.*) the acknowledgement that a student has completed a course which counts towards a degree or diploma.
credits *plural noun* a list of the people who have helped to produce a film, television programme, or record.
credit *verb* (**credited, crediting**) 1 to say that someone has done or achieved something ♦ *Columbus is usually credited with the discovery of America.* 2 to enter an amount as a credit in a financial account. 3 to believe something that seems unlikely ♦ *You would hardly credit it, but she's been voted Best Singer of the Year.* **to be in**

credit to have money in an account. **to do someone credit** to be worthy of praise or admiration. **on credit** with an arrangement to pay later ♦ *They bought the computer on credit.* **to someone's credit** in their praise or defence ♦ *To his credit, he refused to go.* [from a Latin word *credere* meaning 'to believe, trust']

creditable *adjective* deserving praise ♦ *a creditable effort.* **creditably** *adverb*
◊ Do not confuse this word with **credible**, which has a different meaning.

credit card noun a plastic card authorizing a person to buy things on credit.

creditor noun a person or company to whom money is owed.

credo (**kree-doh**) noun (**credos**) a statement of a person's beliefs or principles. [a Latin word meaning 'I believe']

credulous (**kred-yoo-ləs**) *adjective* too ready to believe things. **credulity** (**krid-yoo-liti**) noun **credulously** *adverb* [from a Latin word *credulus* meaning 'trusting']

creed noun 1 a person's religion ♦ *No one should be discriminated against on the basis of their colour or creed.* 2 a formal summary of Christian beliefs. 3 a statement of a person's beliefs or principles. [from *credo*]

creek noun 1 a narrow inlet of water, especially on the coast. 2 (*North Amer.*) (*Austral.*) a stream or minor tributary of a river. **up the creek** (*informal*) 1 in difficulties. 2 stupid or misguided. [from an Old Norse word *kriki* meaning 'nook']

creel noun a fisherman's wicker basket for carrying fish. [origin unknown]

creep *verb* (past tense and past participle **crept**) 1 to move quietly or stealthily ♦ *She crept across the landing.* SYNONYMS: steal, slip, sneak, tiptoe. 2 to move along with the body close to the ground. SYNONYMS: crawl, slither, worm. 3 to move or progress very slowly ♦ *The tide was creeping up the beach.* SYNONYMS: edge, inch. 4 (said about a plant) to grow along the ground or other surface.
creep noun (*informal*) someone you dislike, especially because they are always flattering people to try to become popular. **to creep in** to begin to appear ♦ *Too many mistakes are creeping into your work.* **to give you the creeps** (*informal*) to produce a feeling of revulsion or fear ♦ *This place gives me the creeps.* **to make your flesh creep** (*informal*) to make you

feel disgusted or afraid. [from an Old English word]

creeper noun 1 a plant that grows along the ground or up a wall etc. 2 a person or thing that creeps.

creepy *adjective* (**creepier, creepiest**) frightening and sinister. SYNONYMS: spine-chilling, eerie, (*informal*) spooky, scary. **creepily** *adverb* **creepiness** noun

creepy-crawly noun (**creepy-crawlies**) (*informal*) a crawling insect, spider, or worm.

cremate *verb* to burn a dead person's body to ashes. **cremation** noun [from a Latin word *cremare* meaning 'to burn']

crematorium (**krem-ə-tor-iəm**) noun (**crematoria**) a place where the bodies of dead people are cremated.

crème de menthe (**krem də mahnt**) noun a green liqueur flavoured with peppermint. [French words meaning 'cream of mint']

crème fraiche (**krem fresh**) noun a type of thick sour cream. [French words meaning 'fresh cream']

crenellated (**kren-əl-ay-tid**) *adjective* having battlements. **crenellation** (**kren-əl-ay-shən**) noun [from an Old French word]

Creole (**kree-ohl**) noun 1 a descendant of European settlers in the West Indies or Central or South America; a white descendant of French settlers in the southern USA. 2 a person of mixed European and African descent, especially one living in the West Indies. 3 a language formed from the contact of a European language (especially English, French, or Portuguese) with a local language (especially an African one). **Creole** *adjective* to do with a Creole or Creoles. [via French and Spanish, probably from a Portuguese word *crioulo* meaning 'black person born in Brazil']

creosote (**kree-ə-soht**) noun 1 a thick brown oily liquid obtained from coal tar, used to prevent wood from rotting. 2 a colourless liquid obtained from wood tar, used as an antiseptic. **creosote** *verb* to treat a fence etc. with creosote. [via German from Greek words *kreas* meaning 'flesh' and *sōtēr* meaning 'saviour' (because of its use as an antiseptic)]

crêpe (**krayp**) noun 1 a thin fabric with a wrinkled surface. 2 rubber with a wrinkled texture, used for the soles of shoes. **3** a thin pancake. [from an Old French word *crespe* meaning 'curled']

crêpe paper *noun* thin paper with a wrinkled surface.

crept past tense and past participle of **creep**.

crepuscular (kri-pus-kew-ler) *adjective* (*formal*) to do with twilight; appearing or active at dusk or dawn, not at night or in full daylight. [from a Latin word *crepusculum* meaning 'twilight']

crescendo (kri-shen-doh) *noun* (**crescendos**) a gradual increase in loudness. [an Italian word meaning 'increasing']
◊ People often use this word as if it meant the same as *climax*. You should use *crescendo* when you are talking about something becoming louder and louder, and *climax* when you are talking about the loudest point that is reached at the end.

crescent *noun* **1** a narrow curved shape tapering to a point at each end, such as the waxing moon. **2** a curved street or terrace of houses. [originally denoting the new moon; from a Latin word *crescens* meaning 'growing']

cress *noun* any of various plants with hot-tasting leaves used in salads. [from an Old English word]

crest *noun* **1** a tuft of feathers, fur, or skin on the top of a bird's or animal's head. **2** a plume of feathers on a helmet. **3** the highest part of a hill or wave. SYNONYMS: crown, peak, brow, summit. **4** the highest point in one cycle of an electromagnetic or sound wave. **5** a design above the shield on a coat of arms, or used separately on a seal or notepaper ♦ *their family crest*. [from a Latin word *crista* meaning 'tuft, plume']

crested *adjective* (said about a bird or animal) having or bearing a crest.

crestfallen *adjective* downcast or disappointed. [originally referring to an animal with a fallen or drooping crest]

Cretaceous (kri-tay-shəs) *adjective* to do with the geological period in the Mesozoic era when chalk was deposited. **Cretaceous** *noun* this period. [from a Latin word *creta* meaning 'chalk']

cretin (kret-in) *noun* **1** a stupid person. **2** (*old use*) a person who is deformed and mentally undeveloped through lack of thyroid hormone. **cretinism** *noun* **cretinous**

adjective [via French from a Latin word *Christianus* meaning 'Christian', as a reminder that handicapped people were Christian souls, and should be cared for]

Creutzfeldt–Jakob disease (kroyts-felt-**yak**-ob) *noun* a fatal degenerative disease affecting nerve cells in the brain, a form of which (called *new variant*) is thought to be linked to BSE. [named after the German neurologists H. G. Creutzfeldt (1885–1964) and A. Jakob (1884–1931)]

crevasse (kri-vass) *noun* a deep open crack, especially in the ice of a glacier. [same origin as *crevice*]

crevice (krev-iss) *noun* a narrow opening or crack, especially in a rock or wall. [from an Old French word *crever* meaning 'to burst, split']

crew [1] *noun* **1** the group of people working in a ship, boat, or aircraft. **2** all these people except the officers. **3** a group of people working together ♦ *the camera crew*.
crew *verb* **1** to act as a member of a crew for a ship, boat, or aircraft. **2** to provide a ship, boat, or aircraft with a crew. [from an Old French word *creue* meaning 'increase']

crew [2] past tense of **crow** [2].

crew cut *noun* a very short haircut for men and boys.

crew neck *noun* a closely fitting round neckline of a knitted garment.

crib *noun* **1** a baby's cot. **2** a wooden framework from which animals can pull out fodder. **3** a model representing the Nativity of Jesus Christ. **4** something copied from another person's work. **5** (*informal*) a literal translation of something written in a foreign language, for use by students. **6** short for **cribbage**. **7** the cards discarded by the players and given to the dealer in the game of cribbage.
crib *verb* (**cribbed, cribbing**) (*informal*) to copy someone else's work. [from an Old English word]

cribbage *noun* a card game in which the dealer scores also from cards in the crib (see **crib** sense 7). [origin unknown]

crick *noun* a painful stiffness in the neck or back.
crick *verb* to cause a crick in your neck or back, especially by twisting it. [origin unknown]

cricket [1] *noun* a game played on a large grass field with a ball, bats, and wickets, between two sides of 11 players. [origin unknown]

cricket [2] *noun* a brown grasshopper-like insect that makes a shrill chirping sound. [from an Old French word *criquer* meaning 'to crackle', imitating the sound it makes]

cricketer *noun* a cricket player.

crime *noun* 1 a serious offence, especially one that breaks the law. SYNONYMS: misdemeanour, misdeed, felony. 2 such offences in general ♦ *the detection of crime.* 3 (*informal*) a pity or shame ♦ *It would be a crime to waste these tickets now.* [from a Latin word *crimen* meaning 'offence']

criminal *noun* a person who has committed a crime.
criminal *adjective* 1 involving crime ♦ *a criminal offence.* 2 to do with crime and its punishment ♦ *criminal law.* 3 (*informal*) shameful or shocking.

criminologist *noun* an expert in criminology.

criminology *noun* the scientific study of crime. [from a Latin word *crimen* meaning 'offence' and *-logy*]

crimp *verb* 1 to press material into small folds or ridges. 2 to make waves in hair with a hot iron. [from an Old English word]

crimson *noun* a deep red colour ♦ *He went crimson with embarrassment.* [from an Arabic word *kirmiz* meaning 'an insect which was used to make crimson dye']

cringe *verb* 1 to shrink back or crouch down in fear. 2 to feel extremely embarrassed or ashamed ♦ *My mother's rudeness made me cringe.* [from an Old English word *crincan* meaning 'to yield, fall in battle']

crinkle *verb* to make something wrinkled, or to become wrinkled.
crinkle *noun* a wrinkle or crease. **crinkly** *adjective* [same origin as for *cringe*]

crinoline (**krin-ə-lin**) *noun* a light framework formerly worn to make a long skirt stand out, or a skirt shaped by this. [from a French word, formed from the Latin words *crinis* meaning 'hair' and *linum* meaning 'thread']

cripple *noun* (*old use*) a person who is permanently lame through disability or injury.
cripple *verb* 1 to make someone lame. 2 to

weaken or damage something seriously ♦ *The project was crippled by lack of money.* [from an Old English word]

crisis *noun* (**crises** (**kriy-seez**)) a time of danger or great difficulty ♦ *a political crisis.* [from a Greek word *krisis* meaning 'decision']

crisp *adjective* 1 firm but brittle, breaking with a snap ♦ *crisp pastry.* 2 (said about paper) slightly stiff and crackling ♦ *a crisp £10 note.* 3 pleasantly cold and bracing ♦ *a crisp winter morning.* 4 brisk and decisive ♦ *She has a crisp manner.*
crisp *noun* a thin fried slice of potato, sold in packets and eaten as a snack.
crisp *verb* to make something crisp, or to become crisp. **crisply** *adverb* **crispness** *noun* [from a Latin word *crispus* meaning 'curled']

crispy *adjective* (**crispier, crispiest**) (said about food) pleasantly firm and crunchy ♦ *crispy bacon.*

criss-cross *noun* a pattern of crossing lines.
criss-cross *adjective* with crossing lines.
criss-cross *verb* 1 to move around a place by repeatedly going back and forth. 2 to form a criss-cross pattern. [from *Christ-cross*, the cross on which Christ died]

criterion (**kriy-teer-iən**) *noun* (**criteria**) a standard or principle by which something is judged. [a Greek word *kritērion* meaning 'means of judging']
◊ Note that the singular form is *criterion* and the plural form is *criteria*. It is incorrect to use the word *criteria* as if it were a singular, as in *a criteria* or *this criteria* or *these criterias.*

critic *noun* 1 a person who finds fault with something ♦ *His critics say he is too arrogant.* 2 a person who expresses judgements about books, art, music, etc. ♦ *a theatre critic.* [from a Greek word *kritēs* meaning 'judge']

critical *adjective* 1 looking for or pointing out faults ♦ *I'm sorry to be so critical.* SYNONYMS: derogatory, disparaging, censorious; (*informal*) nit-picking. 2 expressing judgements about books, art, music, etc. 3 at a point of crisis, very serious ♦ *The patient's condition is critical.* 4 having an important part to play in the success or failure of something ♦ *This is a critical moment in his career.* 5 (said about a nuclear reactor) maintaining a self-sustaining chain reaction. **critically** *adverb*

critical path noun the sequence in which a complex set of operations should be carried out in order to complete the work as quickly and efficiently as possible.

criticism noun 1 finding fault ♦ *She doesn't handle criticism well.* 2 a remark pointing out a fault ♦ *Could I make a criticism?* 3 expressing judgements about books, art, music, etc. ♦ *literary criticism.*

criticize verb 1 to say that a person or thing has faults. SYNONYMS: censure, condemn, attack, (*informal*) knock, pan. 2 to examine a book, piece of music, etc. and express judgements about it ♦ *We were asked to criticize a poem by Blake.*

critique (kri-*teek*) noun a critical essay or analysis. [from a French word, based on the Greek words *kritikē tekhnē* meaning 'critical art']

croak verb to make a deep hoarse cry or sound like that of a frog.
croak noun a croaking sound. [an imitation of the sound]

Croat (*kroh*-at) noun 1 a person born in Croatia in SE Europe, or descended from people born there. 2 the language of Croatia, close to Serbian but written in the Roman alphabet.
Croat adjective to do with or coming from Croatia.

crochet (*kroh*-shay) noun a kind of needlework in which a hooked needle is used to loop thread into a pattern of connected stitches.
crochet verb (**crocheted, crocheting**) to make something in this way. [a French word meaning 'little hook']

crock [1] noun 1 an earthenware pot or jar. 2 a broken piece of this. [from an Old English word *croc*]

crock [2] noun (*informal*) 1 someone who suffers from bad health or injury, especially an old person. 2 an old and worn-out vehicle. [origin unknown]

crockery noun household china. [from an old word *crocker* meaning 'potter']

crocodile noun 1 a large tropical reptile with a thick skin, long tail, and huge jaws. 2 its skin, used especially to make bags and shoes. 3 a long line of schoolchildren walking in pairs. [from a Greek word *krokodilos* meaning 'worm of the stones']

crocodile tears plural noun sorrow that is not sincere. [so called from the belief that crocodiles wept while devouring or luring their prey]

crocus noun (*kroh*-kəs) (**crocuses** or **croci** (*kroh*-ki)) a small plant growing from a corm in early spring, with yellow, purple, or white flowers. [from a Greek word *krokos*]

croft noun a small rented farm in Scotland.
croft verb to farm a croft. [from an Old English word]

crofter noun the tenant of a croft.

croissant (krwass-*ahn*) noun a crescent-shaped roll made of flaky pastry. [a French word meaning 'crescent']

cromlech (*krom*-lek) noun a prehistoric tomb consisting of a large flat stone laid on upright ones; a dolmen. [from the Welsh words *crom* meaning 'bent' and *llech* meaning 'flat stone']

crone noun an ugly old woman. [from an Old French word *carogne* meaning 'carrion']

crony noun (**cronies**) (*informal*) someone's close friend or supporter, especially when you do not approve of them. [from a Greek word *khronios* meaning 'long-lasting']

crook noun 1 (*informal*) a person who is dishonest or a criminal. 2 a shepherd's hooked stick or staff. 3 a bend in something ♦ *She carried the kitten in the crook of her arm.*
crook verb to bend your finger or arm ♦ *He crooked his finger to beckon us over.*
crook adjective (*Austral.*) (*NZ*) (*informal*) unwell, not working properly, or unsatisfactory. [from an Old Norse word]

crooked adjective 1 not straight or level ♦ *The picture is slightly crooked.* SYNONYMS: askew, lopsided, off-centre. 2 bent or twisted ♦ *a crooked road.* SYNONYMS: twisted, winding. 3 dishonest, not straightforward. SYNONYMS: corrupt, (*informal*) bent, shady.
crookedly adverb **crookedness** noun

croon verb to sing softly and gently.
crooner noun [an imitation of the sound]

crop noun 1 plants that are grown for food or other use, especially cereals. 2 the harvest from such plants ♦ *We had a good crop of barley this season.* 3 a group or quantity appearing or produced at one time ♦ *Who do you most admire among the current crop of players?* 4 a very short haircut. **5** the bag-like part of a bird's throat where food is broken up for digestion before passing into the stomach. **6** the handle of a whip, or a whip with a loop instead of a lash.

crop *verb* (**cropped, cropping**) **1** to cut something or bite it off ♦ *Sheep were cropping the grass.* **2** to cut hair very short. **3** to trim off the edges of a photograph. **4** (said about land or a plant) to produce a crop. **to crop up** to happen or appear unexpectedly ♦ *I'll have to go, something's cropped up.* [from an Old English word]

cropper *noun* **to come a cropper** (*informal*) **1** to fall heavily. **2** to fail badly. [origin unknown]

croquet (kroh-kay) *noun* a game played on a lawn with wooden balls that you drive through hoops with mallets. [perhaps a dialect form of a French word *crochet* meaning 'hook']

croquette (krə-ket) *noun* a ball or roll of potato, meat, or fish, fried in breadcrumbs. [from a French word *croquer* meaning 'to crunch']

crosier *noun* another spelling of **crozier**.

cross *noun* **1** a mark made by drawing one line across another, × or +. **2** an upright post with another piece of wood across it, used in ancient times for crucifixion. **3** (**the Cross**) the cross on which Christ was crucified, used as a symbol of Christianity. **4** a cross-shaped medal, emblem, or monument ♦ *the Victoria Cross.* **5** an annoying or distressing thing that someone has to bear. **6** an animal or plant produced by cross-breeding. SYNONYMS: hybrid, cross-breed, mongrel (dog). **7** a mixture of two different things. SYNONYMS: combination, blend, amalgam. **8** (in football) a pass of the ball across the field from the side towards the centre.

cross *verb* **1** to go across or to the other side of something. SYNONYMS: traverse, span. **2** to intersect ♦ *The roads cross near a little bridge.* **3** to pass a person or vehicle going in a different direction ♦ *The two planes crossed only a few metres apart.* **4** to place one thing across another in the shape of a cross ♦ *She crossed her arms* ♦ *Cross your fingers for luck.* **5** to draw a line across something or mark something with a cross. **6** (in football) to pass the ball across the field from the side towards the centre. **7** to frustrate or oppose someone ♦ *Don't cross me.* **8** to cross-breed animals or cross-fertilize plants.

cross *adjective* annoyed or bad-tempered. SYNONYMS: irritable, tetchy, testy, crotchety; (*informal*) grumpy. **to be at cross purposes** (said about two people) to have a misunderstanding because they do not realize they are talking about different things. **to cross a cheque** to mark it with two parallel lines so that it must be paid into a bank. **to cross something off** to remove something from a list by drawing a line through it ♦ *You can cross my name off the guest list.* **to cross your mind** to come briefly into your mind. **to cross something out** to draw a line through something to show that it is wrong or no longer wanted ♦ *He crossed out the word 'nice'.* **to cross swords** to have an argument or dispute with someone. **to cross yourself** to make the Christian sign of the cross as a sign of religious awe or to call upon God for protection. **to keep your fingers crossed** to hope that nothing unfortunate will happen, placing one finger over another to bring good luck. **crossly** *adverb* **crossness** *noun* [via Old Norse and Old Irish from a Latin word *crux*]

cross- *prefix* **1** across, crossing something (as in *cross-channel, crossbar*). **2** from two different kinds (as in *cross-breed*).

crossbar *noun* a horizontal bar between two uprights.

crossbow *noun* a powerful bow with a mechanism for pulling and releasing the string. [so called because the bow is mounted across the stock]

cross-breed *verb* (past tense and past participle **cross-bred**) to produce an animal by mating an animal with one of a different kind.

cross-breed *noun* an animal produced in this way.

cross-country *adjective & adverb* **1** across fields or open country ♦ *cross-country running.* **2** not keeping to main roads or to a direct road.

cross-examine *verb* to question a witness closely in a court of law in order to test answers given to previous questions. **cross-examination** *noun*

cross-eyed *adjective* having one or both eyes turned towards the nose.

cross-fertilize *verb* to fertilize a plant using pollen from another plant of the same species. **cross-fertilization** *noun*

crossfire *noun* gunfire from two or more points so that the lines of fire cross.

cross-grained *adjective* 1 (said about wood) with the grain running across the regular grain. 2 bad-tempered.

cross-hatching *noun* shading on a drawing done with sets of parallel lines that intersect.

crossing *noun* 1 a place where people can safely cross a street ♦ *a pedestrian crossing*. 2 a place where roads or railway lines cross. 3 a journey across water ♦ *We had a smooth crossing*.

cross-legged *adjective & adverb* with the ankles crossed and knees bent outwards.

crossover *noun* work in the arts that involves a new or different style from the performer's usual one, especially in music.

crosspatch *noun* (*informal*) a bad-tempered person.

crosspiece *noun* a bar or beam that goes across something.

cross-pollinate *verb* to pollinate a flower or plant with pollen from another.
cross-pollination *noun*

cross reference *noun* a note telling the reader to look at another part of a book, index, etc. for further information.

crossroads *noun* a place where two or more roads cross one another.

cross section *noun* 1 a diagram showing the internal structure of something as though it has been cut through. 2 a representative sample ♦ *We interviewed a cross section of the local community*.

cross stitch *noun* a stitch formed by two crossing stitches.

crosstalk *noun* 1 unwanted transfer of signals between communication channels. 2 witty dialogue or conversation.

crossways *adverb & adjective* in the form of a cross, with one thing crossing another.

crosswind *noun* a wind blowing across the direction of travel.

crosswise *adverb & adjective* in the form of a cross, with one thing crossing another.

crossword *noun* a puzzle in which intersecting words have to be worked out from clues and then written into the blank squares in a diagram.

crotch *noun* 1 the part of the body or of a piece of clothing between the tops of the legs. 2 a place where things fork. [a different spelling of *crutch*]

crotchet (kroch-it) *noun* (*Music*) a note lasting half as long as a minim. [from a French word *crochet* meaning 'small hook']

crotchety *adjective* bad-tempered. [from an old use of *crotchet* meaning 'whim']

crouch *verb* to lower your body with your legs bent and close to your chest. SYNONYMS: hunch, squat, stoop, huddle.
crouch *noun* a crouching position. [perhaps from an Old French word *crochir* meaning 'to be bent']

croup (kroop) *noun* a children's disease in which inflammation of the windpipe causes a hard cough and difficulty in breathing. [an imitation of the sound]

croupier (kroop-i-er) *noun* a person who rakes in the money at a gambling table and pays out winnings. [from a French word]

croûton (kroo-tawn) *noun* a small piece of fried or toasted bread served with soup. [a French word, related to *crust*]

crow[1] *noun* a large black bird of a family that includes the jackdaw, raven, and rook. [from an Old English word]

crow[2] *verb* (past tense and past participle **crowed** or **crew**) 1 (said about a cock) to make a loud shrill cry. 2 to boast about something or express great triumph ♦ *He's still crowing about winning the quiz*.
crow *noun* a crowing cry or sound. [an imitation of the sound]

crowbar *noun* a heavy iron bar with a flattened end, used as a lever. [so called because the end is shaped like a crow's beak]

crowd *noun* 1 a large number of people gathered together. SYNONYMS: multitude, throng, assembly, mob, horde. 2 the spectators at a sporting event.
crowd *verb* 1 to gather together in a crowd ♦ *People crowded round to listen to her*. SYNONYMS: mass, congregate, throng. 2 to fill a space almost completely so that there is little room to move ♦ *Shoppers crowded the streets*. [from an Old English word]

crowded *adjective* (said about a place) full of people. SYNONYMS: congested, teeming, packed.

crown *noun* **1** an ornamental headdress worn by a king or queen as a symbol of authority. **2 (the Crown)** the monarchy or sovereign ♦ *This land belongs to the Crown.* **3** a wreath worn on the head, especially as a symbol of victory. **4** in sport, the achievement of being world champion, winning a major competition, etc. ♦ *Bailey took the 100m crown in a thrilling race.* **5** the top part of something such as the head or a hat. **6** the highest part of something arched or curved ♦ *the crown of the road.* **7** the part of a tooth above the gum, or an artificial covering for this. **8** an old British coin with a value of five shillings (25p).

crown *verb* **1** to place a crown on someone as a symbol of royal power or victory. **2** to declare someone to be the best at a sport ♦ *He was crowned world champion.* **3** to form, cover, or decorate the top part of something. **4** to reward something or end it successfully ♦ *Our efforts were crowned with success.* **5** to put an artificial top on a tooth. **6** (*informal*) to hit someone on the head. [from a Latin word *corona* meaning 'garland or crown']

crown jewels *plural noun* the sovereign's crown, sceptre, orb, etc. used at coronations and other state occasions.

Crown Prince or **Crown Princess** *noun* the heir to the throne.

crow's feet *plural noun* wrinkles in the skin at the side of the eyes.

crow's-nest *noun* a platform high on the mast of a ship for a lookout to watch from.

crozier (kroh-zi-er) *noun* a hooked staff carried by a bishop as a symbol of office. [from an Old French word *croisier* meaning 'cross-bearer']

crucial (kroo-shəl) *adjective* **1** of the greatest importance in deciding what will happen ♦ *The next few days will be crucial* ♦ *a crucial decision.* SYNONYMS: decisive, critical, vital. **2** (*informal*) excellent. **crucially** *adverb* [from a Latin word *crucis* meaning 'of a cross']

crucible (kroo-si-bəl) *noun* a pot in which metals are melted. [from a Latin word *crucibulum* meaning 'night lamp']

cruciferous (kroo-sif-er-əs) *adjective* (*Botany*) to do with the family of plants bearing flowers with four equal petals arranged in a cross. [from Latin words *crucis* meaning 'of the cross' and *ferre* meaning 'to carry']

crucifix *noun* a model of a cross with a figure of Christ on it. [a Latin word meaning 'fixed to a cross']

crucifixion *noun* crucifying someone, or being crucified. **the Crucifixion** that of Christ.

cruciform (kroo-si-form) *adjective* cross-shaped. [from a Latin word *cruz* meaning 'cross']

crucify *verb* (**crucifies, crucified, crucifying**) **1** to put a person to death by nailing or binding their hands and feet to a cross. **2** to torment someone, or criticize or punish them severely.

crude *adjective* **1** in a natural state, not refined ♦ *crude oil.* **2** not well finished or worked out, rough ♦ *a crude carving* ♦ *a crude attempt.* SYNONYMS: simple, basic, rudimentary, primitive. **3** vulgar or indecent ♦ *a crude gesture.* SYNONYMS: coarse, smutty, rude, ribald, dirty. **crude** *noun* crude oil. **crudely** *adverb* **crudity** *noun* [from a Latin word *crudus* meaning 'raw, rough']

cruel *adjective* (**crueller, cruellest**) **1** deliberately causing suffering or pain to other people or animals ♦ *cruel remarks.* SYNONYMS: brutal, callous, heartless, barbaric, inhumane, sadistic. **2** causing pain or suffering ♦ *this cruel war.* **cruelly** *adverb* **cruelty** *noun* [from an Old French word, related to *crude*]

cruelty-free *adjective* (said about cosmetics) produced by methods that do not involve cruelty to animals.

cruet *noun* a stand holding small containers for salt, pepper, mustard, etc. for use at the table. [from an Old French word *crue* meaning 'pot']

cruise *verb* **1** to sail about from place to place for pleasure. **2** (said about a vehicle or aircraft) to travel at a constant moderate speed. **3** to achieve something with ease ♦ *Chelsea cruised to a 3-0 victory.* **cruise** *noun* a voyage on a ship taken as a holiday. [from a Dutch word *kruisen* meaning 'to cross']

cruise missile *noun* a missile that is able to fly at low altitude and is guided to its target by an on-board computer.

cruiser noun 1 a fast warship. 2 a yacht or motor boat for cruising.

crumb noun 1 a small fragment of bread, cake, or other food. 2 a small amount of something ♦ *a crumb of comfort.* 3 the soft inner part of bread.
crumb verb to cover food with breadcrumbs. **crumby** adjective [from an Old English word *cruma*]

crumble verb 1 to break or fall apart into small pieces. 2 to break food into small pieces ♦ *Crumble a stock cube into the liquid.*
crumble noun a pudding made with fruit cooked with a crumbly topping ♦ *apple crumble.* [from an Old English word, related to *crumb*]

crumbly adjective (**crumblier, crumbliest**) easily broken into small pieces.

crumpet noun a soft flat cake made from a yeast mixture, eaten toasted with butter. [origin unknown]

crumple verb to crush something or become crushed into creases. [from an Old English word *crump* meaning 'crooked']

crunch verb 1 to crush something noisily with the teeth. SYNONYMS: munch, champ, grind. 2 to walk over snow, gravel, etc. with a sound of crushing; to make a sound like this.
crunch noun 1 a crunching sound. 2 (**the crunch**) (*informal*) a decisive event or turning point. [an imitation of the sound]

Crusade (kroo-**sayd**) noun any of the military expeditions made by European Christians in the Middle Ages to recover the Holy Land from the Muslims.
crusade noun a campaign against something believed to be bad ♦ *her crusade against TV violence.*
crusade verb to take part in a crusade.
crusader noun [from a Latin word *crux* meaning 'cross']

crush verb 1 to press or squeeze something so that it becomes broken, injured, or wrinkled. SYNONYMS: squash, mangle. 2 to pound something into small fragments. SYNONYMS: pulverize, pulp. 3 to defeat or subdue someone completely ♦ *The rebellion was swiftly crushed* ♦ *I felt crushed by his reply.*
crush noun 1 a crowd of people pressed closely together. 2 a drink made from the juice of crushed fruit. 3 (*informal*) an infatuation that lasts only a short time. [from an Old French word *cruissir* meaning 'to gnash or crack']

crushable adjective able to be crushed easily.

crust noun 1 the hard outer layer of something, especially bread. 2 the rocky outer layer of the earth. [from a Latin word *crusta* meaning 'rind, shell']

crustacean (krus-**tay-shǝn**) noun an animal that has a hard shell, e.g. a crab, lobster, or shrimp. [same origin as for *crust*]

crusty adjective (**crustier, crustiest**) 1 having a crisp crust. 2 having a harsh or irritable manner. **crustily** adverb **crustiness** noun

crutch noun 1 a support for helping a lame person to walk, usually fitting under the armpit. 2 something used to support or reassure a person. 3 the crotch of the body or of a piece of clothing. [from an Old English word *crycc*]

crux noun (**cruces** (**kroo-**seez)) the vital part of a problem ♦ *This is the crux of the matter.* [a Latin word meaning 'a cross']

cry verb (**cries, cried, crying**) 1 to shed tears. SYNONYMS: weep, sob, blubber, snivel, whimper. 2 to shout or scream loudly ♦ *He cried out for help.* 3 (said about an animal) to utter its cry.
cry noun (**cries**) 1 a loud shout or scream. 2 the call of a bird or animal. 3 a spell of weeping ♦ *Go on, have a good cry.* 4 an urgent appeal or demand. **to cry off** to go back on a promise or fail to keep to an arrangement. **to cry out for** to clearly need something very much ♦ *The team is crying out for a decent striker.* **in full cry** calling out in hot pursuit. [from an Old French word *crier*]

crybaby noun (**crybabies**) a person who weeps easily without good cause.

cryogenics (kriy-ǝ-**jen-iks**) noun the scientific study of very low temperatures and their effects. [from Greek words *kruos* meaning 'frost' and -*genēs* meaning 'born']

crypt (kript) noun a room or vault below the floor of a church, used as a chapel or burial place. [same origin as for *cryptic*]

cryptic (**krip-**tik) adjective hiding its meaning in a puzzling way ♦ *a cryptic remark.* **cryptically** adverb [from a Greek word *kruptos* meaning 'hidden']

cryptogram (**krip-**tǝ-gram) noun something written in code. [from a Greek word *kruptos* meaning 'hidden' and -*gram*]

cryptography (krip-**tog**-rə-fi) *noun* the art of writing in codes or ciphers or of deciphering these. **cryptographer** *noun* [from a Greek word *kruptos* meaning 'hidden' and *-graphy*]

cryptosporidium (krip-toh-spor-**rid**-iəm) *noun* a single-celled parasite found in the intestines of some animals, often causing disease. [from a Greek word *kruptos* meaning 'hidden' and a Latin word *sporidium* meaning 'small spore']

crystal *noun* **1** a clear transparent colourless mineral, such as quartz. **2** a piece of this. **3** very clear glass of high quality. **4** each of the tiny symmetrical pieces into which certain substances solidify ♦ *ice crystals*.
crystal *adjective* as clear as crystal ♦ *the crystal waters of the Aegean Sea*. [from a Greek word *krustallos* meaning 'ice']

crystal ball *noun* a globe of glass used by fortune tellers for crystal-gazing.

crystal-gazing *noun* looking into a crystal ball in an attempt to see future events pictured there.

crystalline (krist-əliyn) *adjective* **1** having the structure and form of a crystal. **2** transparent, very clear.

crystallize *verb* **1** to form crystals. **2** (said about ideas or plans) to become clear and definite in form. **crystallization** *noun*

crystallized fruit *noun* fruit preserved in and coated with sugar.

CTC *abbreviation* City Technology College.

Cu *abbreviation* (*Chemistry*) the symbol for copper.

cu. *abbreviation* cubic.

cub *noun* a young animal, especially a fox, bear, or lion.
Cub or **Cub Scout** *noun* a member of the junior branch of the Scout Association.
cub *verb* (**cubbed, cubbing**) **1** to give birth to cubs. **2** to hunt fox cubs. [origin unknown]

cubbyhole *noun* a very small room or snug space. [from an old word *cub* meaning 'coop, hutch']

cube *noun* **1** a solid body with six equal square faces. **2** a block shaped like this ♦ *an ice cube*. **3** (*Mathematics*) the product of a number multiplied by itself twice ♦ *The cube of 3 is 27*.
cube *verb* **1** to cut food into small cubes. **2** to multiply a number by itself twice. [from a Greek word *kubos*]

cube root *noun* the number that produces a given number when it is cubed ♦ *The cube root of 27 is 3*.

cubic *adjective* **1** cube-shaped. **2** to do with three dimensions. **cubic metre, foot, etc.** the volume of a cube with sides one metre, foot, etc. long, used as a unit of measurement for volume.

cubicle *noun* a small enclosed space, screened off for privacy ♦ *a toilet cubicle*. [originally denoting a bedroom; from a Latin word *cubare* meaning 'to lie down']

cubism (kew-bizm) *noun* a style of painting in which objects are represented as geometrical shapes. **cubist** *noun*

cubit (kew-bit) *noun* an ancient measure of length, approximately equal to the length of the arm from elbow to fingertips. [from a Latin word *cubitum* meaning 'elbow']

cuboid (kew-boid) *adjective* cube-shaped. **cuboid** *noun* a solid body with six rectangular faces.

cuckold (kuk-əld) *noun* a man whose wife has committed adultery during their marriage. [from an Old French word *cucu* meaning 'cuckoo']

cuckoo *noun* a bird with a call that is like its name, which lays its eggs in the nests of other birds. [an imitation of its call]

cuckoo clock *noun* a clock that strikes the hour with a sound like a cuckoo's call.

cucumber *noun* **1** a long green-skinned fleshy fruit eaten raw or pickled. **2** the plant producing this. [from a Latin word *cucumis*]

cud *noun* half-digested food that a cow, sheep, etc. brings back from the stomach into the mouth and chews again. [from an Old English word]

cuddle *verb* to hold someone closely and lovingly in your arms.
cuddle *noun* an affectionate hug. [origin unknown]

cuddly *adjective* (**cuddlier, cuddliest**) soft and pleasant to cuddle ♦ *a cuddly toy*.

cudgel (kuj-əl) *noun* a short thick stick used as a weapon.
cudgel *verb* (**cudgelled, cudgelling**) to beat someone with a cudgel. **to cudgel your brains** to think hard about a problem. **to take up the cudgels for someone** to defend someone vigorously. [from an Old English word *cycgel*]

cue[1] *noun* something said or done which acts as a signal for something else to be done, e.g. for an actor to speak in a play.
cue *verb* (**cues, cued, cueing**) to give a cue to someone. **on cue** at the correct moment. [origin unknown]

cue[2] *noun* a long stick for striking the ball in snooker, billiards, and similar games. [from *queue*]

cuff[1] *noun* the end part of a sleeve that fits round the wrist.
cuffs *plural noun* (*informal*) handcuffs. **off the cuff** without rehearsal or preparation. [origin unknown]

cuff[2] *verb* to strike someone with an open hand.
cuff *noun* a slap. [origin unknown]

cufflink *noun* each of a pair of fasteners for shirt cuffs, used instead of buttons.

cuirass (kwi-**ras**) *noun* 1 a piece of armour consisting of a breastplate and a similar plate protecting the back. 2 (*Medicine*) a device for artificial respiration. [from an Old French word *cuirace*]

cuisine (kwi-**zeen**) *noun* a style of cooking ♦ *Italian cuisine*. [a French word meaning 'kitchen']

cul-de-sac (**kul**-də-sak) *noun* (**culs-de-sac**) a street or passage that is closed at one end. [a French phrase meaning 'bottom of a sack']

culinary (**kul**-in-er-i) *adjective* to do with cooking or the kitchen ♦ *culinary herbs*. [from a Latin word *culinarius* meaning 'to do with the kitchen']

cull *verb* 1 to select or gather things from a wide variety of sources ♦ *I've culled lines from several poems*. 2 to pick out and kill surplus wild animals from a herd.
cull *noun* a selective killing of wild animals, done to reduce the population ♦ *a seal cull*. [from a Latin word *colligere* meaning 'to collect']

culminate *verb* to reach its highest or final point ♦ *His career culminated in the award of the Nobel Prize for Literature*. **culmination** *noun* [from a Latin word *culmen* meaning 'summit']

culottes (kew-**lot**) *plural noun* women's knee-length trousers styled to look like a skirt. [a French word meaning 'knee breeches']

culpable (**kul**-pə-bəl) *adjective* deserving blame. **culpably** *adverb* **culpability** *noun* [from a Latin word *culpare* meaning 'to blame']

culprit *noun* the person who has done something wrong ♦ *Police are still looking for the culprits*. [from Old French words *culpable* meaning 'guilty' and *prit* meaning 'ready']

cult *noun* 1 a religious sect, especially one that is thought to control its members too much. 2 religious worship of a person or object, involving special rituals. 3 a film, TV programme, rock group, etc. that is popular only with a small group of people. [from a Latin word *cultus* meaning 'worship']

cultivar *noun* a variety of plant produced by cultivation. [from *cultivate* and *variety*]

cultivate *verb* 1 to prepare and use land for growing crops. 2 to produce crops by tending them. 3 to spend time trying to develop something ♦ *I've been cultivating a knowledge of art history*. **cultivation** *noun* [same origin as for *culture*]

cultivated *adjective* well-educated and well-mannered.

cultivator *noun* 1 a device for breaking up ground for cultivation. 2 a person who cultivates something.

cultural *adjective* to do with culture. **culturally** *adverb*

culture *noun* 1 the appreciation and understanding of literature, art, music, etc. 2 the customs, traditions, and civilization of a particular society or group of people ♦ *West Indian culture*. 3 (*Biology*) a quantity of bacteria or cells grown for study. 4 the cultivating of plants.
culture *verb* to grow bacteria or cells for study. [from a Latin word *colere* meaning 'to cultivate, look after, worship']

cultured *adjective* educated to appreciate literature, art, music, etc.

cultured pearl *noun* a pearl formed by an oyster when a speck of grit etc. is inserted into its shell.

culvert (**kul**-vert) *noun* a drain that crosses under a road or railway. [origin unknown]

cum *preposition* combined with ♦ *a bedroom-cum-study*. [a Latin word meaning 'with']

cumbersome (kum-ber-səm) *adjective* heavy and awkward to carry or use. [from *encumber* and *-some*]

cumin (kum-in) *noun* a plant with fragrant seeds that are used for flavouring, especially in curry powder. [from a Greek word *kuminon*]

cummerbund *noun* a sash worn round the waist. [from an Urdu word]

cumulative (kew-mew-lə-tiv) *adjective* increasing in amount by one addition after another. **cumulatively** *adverb* [from a Latin word *cumulus* meaning 'heap']

cumulonimbus (kew-mew-loh-**nim**-bəs) *noun* a tall dense mass of cloud present during thunderstorms. [from *cumulus* and a Latin word *nimbus* meaning 'cloud']

cumulus *noun* (**cumuli**) a form of cloud consisting of rounded masses heaped on a horizontal base. [a Latin word meaning 'a heap']

cuneiform (**kew**-ni-form) *adjective* written in or to do with the wedge-shaped strokes used in the inscriptions of ancient Assyria, Persia, etc.
cuneiform *noun* cuneiform writing. [from a Latin word *cuneus* meaning 'a wedge']

cunning *adjective* **1** skilled at deceiving people. SYNONYMS: crafty, devious, sly, wily. **2** cleverly designed or planned ♦ *a cunning device.*
cunning *noun* **1** skill in deceiving people. SYNONYMS: craftiness, guile, trickery, duplicity. **2** skill or ingenuity. [from an Old Norse word *kunnandi* meaning 'knowledge']

cup *noun* **1** a small container for drinking from, usually bowl-shaped and with a handle, used with a saucer. **2** the amount a cup contains, used as a measure in cookery. **3** something shaped like a cup. **4** a goblet-shaped vessel awarded as a prize. **5** a sports competition in which the winners receive a cup. **6** either of the two cup-shaped parts of a bra.
cup *verb* (**cupped, cupping**) **1** to form something into the shape of a cup ♦ *He cupped his hands under the waterfall.* **2** to hold something as if in a cup ♦ *She leant forward with her chin cupped in her hands.* **cupful** *noun* (**cupfuls**) [from a Latin word *cupa* meaning 'tub']

cupboard (**kub**-əd) *noun* a piece of furniture or recess with a door, used for storing things. [originally denoting a sideboard; from *cup* and *board*]

cupboard love *noun* a display of affection put on in the hope of obtaining a reward.

Cup Final *noun* the final match in a sports competition in which the winners receive a cup.

cupidity (kew-**pid**-iti) *noun* greed for money or possessions. [from a Latin word *cupido* meaning 'a desire']

cupola (**kew**-pə-lə) *noun* a small dome on a roof. [an Italian word]

cupro-nickel *noun* an alloy of copper and nickel, used to make silver-coloured coins.

cur *noun* a scruffy or bad-tempered dog. [from an Old Norse word *kurr* meaning 'grumbling']

curable *adjective* able to be cured.

curacy *noun* (**curacies**) the position of a curate.

curare (kewr-**ar**-i) *noun* a bitter substance obtained from certain South American plants, used by some Indian peoples there to poison their arrows. [from a Caribbean word]

curate *noun* a member of the clergy who assists a vicar or parish priest. [same origin as for *cure*]

curative (**kewr**-ə-tiv) *adjective* helping to cure illness.

curator (kewr-**ay**-ter) *noun* a person in charge of a museum or other collection. [same origin as for *cure*]

curb *noun* **1** something that restrains ♦ *The government has put a curb on spending.* **2** a chain or strap passing under a horse's lower jaw, used to restrain it.
curb *verb* to restrain something ♦ *Try to curb your impatience.* [from a Latin word *curvare* meaning 'to curve']
◊ Do not confuse this word with **kerb**, which has a different meaning.

curd *noun* (often **curds**) the thick soft substance formed when milk turns sour. [origin unknown]

curdle *verb* to separate into curds, or to make something do this. **to make your blood curdle** to fill you with horror. [from an old use of *curd* meaning 'to congeal']

cure *verb* **1** to bring someone back to health ♦ *Doctors are confident they can cure her.* **2** to get rid of a disease or illness ♦ *This condition cannot easily be cured.* SYNONYMS: remedy, relieve, alleviate. **3** to stop

something bad ♦ *measures to cure inflation*. SYNONYMS: correct, solve, rectify, (*informal*) fix.
4 to preserve meat, fruit, tobacco, or skins by salting, drying, or smoking ♦ *Fish can be cured in smoke*.

cure *noun* **1** a substance or treatment that cures a disease or illness, a remedy.
2 being cured of a disease or illness ♦ *We cannot guarantee a cure*. [from a Latin word *curare* meaning 'to take care of something']

curfew *noun* a signal or time after which people must remain indoors until the next day. [from an Old French word *cuevrefeu* meaning 'cover fire', from an old law saying that all fires should be covered or put out by a certain time each evening]

Curia *noun* the papal court, the government department of the Vatican. [from a Latin word]

curie *noun* **1** a unit of radioactivity. **2** a quantity of radioactive substance that has this amount of radioactivity. [named after the French physicists Pierre Curie (1859–1906) and Marie Curie (1867–1934)]

curio *noun* (**curios**) an object that is interesting because it is rare or unusual. [short for *curiosity*]

curiosity *noun* (**curiosities**) **1** a strong desire to find out and know things.
2 something that is of interest because it is rare or unusual.

curious *adjective* **1** eager to learn or know something. SYNONYMS: inquisitive, inquiring; (*informal*) nosey. **2** strange or unusual ♦ *Then a curious thing happened*. **curiously** *adverb* [from a Latin word *curiosus* meaning 'careful']

curl *verb* **1** to form a curved or spiral shape, or to make something do this ♦ *The snake curled itself round a branch*. SYNONYMS: coil, wind, entwine. **2** to move in a curve or spiral ♦ *Smoke curled upwards*.
curl *noun* **1** a piece of hair that curves round ♦ *His hair is a mass of red curls*.
2 something in a curved or spiral shape ♦ *a curl of smoke*. **3** a curling movement. [from an Old Dutch word *krul*]

curler *noun* a plastic tube which a piece of hair is wrapped round to curl it.

curlew (**kerl-yoo**) *noun* a wading bird with a long slender down-curved bill. [from an Old French word *courlieu*]

curlicue (**kerl-i-kew**) *noun* a decorative curl, especially in handwriting. [from *curly* and an old use of the word *cue* meaning 'pigtail']

curling *noun* a game played with large flat round stones which are sent along ice. [from *curl* (because the stones are made to 'curl round' opponents' stones to get to the target)]

curly *adjective* (**curlier, curliest**) full of curls ♦ *curly hair*. **curliness** *noun*

curmudgeon (**ker-muj-ən**) *noun* a bad-tempered person. [origin unknown]

currant *noun* **1** the dried fruit of a small seedless grape, used in cookery. **2** a small round red, white, or black berry; the shrub that produces it. [from an Old French phrase *raisins de Courauntz* meaning 'grapes from Corinth', a city in Greece]
◊ Do not confuse this word with **current**, which has a different meaning.

currency *noun* (**currencies**) **1** the money in use in a particular country. **2** the state of being in common or general use ♦ *The rumour soon gained currency*. [from *current*]

current *adjective* **1** belonging to the present time, happening now ♦ *See the current issue of the magazine*. **2** in general circulation or use ♦ *This term is no longer current*.
current *noun* **1** water or air flowing or moving in a certain direction. **2** the flow of electricity through something or along a wire or cable. [from a Latin word *currens* meaning 'running']
◊ Do not confuse this word with **currant**, which has a different meaning.

current account *noun* an account with a bank or building society from which money may be drawn without previous notice being given.

current affairs *plural noun* political events in the news at the present time.

currently *adverb* at the present time.

curricle *noun* an old type of light open two-wheeled carriage drawn by two horses side by side. [same origin as for *curriculum*]

curriculum (**kə-rik-yoo-ləm**) *noun* (**curricula**) a course of study in a school or university. [a Latin word meaning 'running, course']

curriculum vitae (**vee-tiy**) *noun* (**curricula vitae**) a brief account of someone's education, qualifications, previous jobs, etc., which they send when applying for a job. [a Latin phrase meaning 'course of life']

curried *adjective* (said about food) flavoured with hot-tasting spices.

curry [1] *noun* (**curries**) a dish of meat, vegetables, etc. cooked in a sauce made with hot-tasting spices. [from a Tamil word *kari* meaning 'sauce']

curry [2] *verb* (**curries, curried, currying**) **to curry favour** to try to win favour by flattering someone. [from an Old French word *correier* meaning 'to make ready']

curry powder *noun* a mixture of ground-up spices, used for making curry.

curse *noun* 1 a prayer or appeal to a supernatural power for someone to be harmed. 2 the harm resulting from this. 3 something very unpleasant or harmful ♦ *the curse of poverty.* 4 a swear word. 5 (**the curse**) (*old use*) menstruation.
curse *verb* 1 to put a curse on someone. 2 to use swear words. **to be cursed with something** to suffer from it ♦ *My grandmother is cursed with arthritis.* [origin unknown]

cursed (ker-sid) *adjective* (*old use*) hateful or annoying.

cursive *adjective* (said about writing) done with joined letters.
cursive *noun* cursive writing. [from a Latin word *currere* meaning 'to run']

cursor *noun* an indicator, usually a flashing light or line, on a computer screen, showing the position where the next piece of text you type in will appear. [a Latin word meaning 'runner']

cursory (ker-ser-i) *adjective* hasty and not thorough ♦ *a cursory inspection.* **cursorily** *adverb* [from a Latin word *cursorius* meaning 'of a runner']

curt *adjective* noticeably or rudely brief ♦ *a curt reply.* **curtly** *adverb* **curtness** *noun* [from a Latin word *curtus* meaning 'cut short']

curtail *verb* to cut something short, to reduce something ♦ *I had to curtail my visit to Scotland.* **curtailment** *noun* [from an old word *curtal* meaning 'horse with a docked tail'; related to *curt*]

curtain *noun* 1 a piece of cloth hung up as a screen, especially at a window. 2 the large cloth screen hung at the front of a stage. 3 the fall of a stage curtain at the end of an act or scene.
curtain *verb* to provide or shut something off with a curtain or curtains. [from an Old French word *cortine*]

curtain call *noun* applause calling for an actor, singer, etc. to take a bow after a performance.

curtsy *noun* (**curtsies**) a movement of respect made by a woman or girl, putting one foot behind the other and bending the knees.
curtsy *verb* (**curtsies, curtsied, curtsying**) to make a curtsy. [a different spelling of *courtesy*]

curvaceous (ker-vay-shəs) *adjective* (said about a woman) having an attractively curved figure.

curvature (ker-və-cher) *noun* the state of being curved; the curved shape that something has ♦ *the curvature of the earth.*

curve *noun* 1 a line or surface of which no part is straight or flat. 2 a line on a graph showing how one quantity varies in relation to another.
curve *verb* 1 to have a curved shape or move in a curve ♦ *The road curves to the left.* 2 to bend something so that it forms a curve. **curvy** *adjective* [from a Latin word *curvare* meaning 'to bend']

cushion *noun* 1 a bag of cloth filled with soft or springy material, used to make a seat more comfortable. 2 anything soft or springy that supports something or protects against jarring ♦ *A hovercraft travels on a cushion of air.* 3 the elastic border round a billiard table, from which the balls rebound.
cushion *verb* 1 to lessen the effect of an impact or blow ♦ *Luckily a pile of boxes cushioned his fall.* 2 to protect something from the effects of something harmful. [from an Old French word *cuissin*]

cushy *adjective* (**cushier, cushiest**) (*informal*) easy and pleasant ♦ *a cushy job.* [from a Hindi word *khush* meaning 'pleasant']

cusp *noun* 1 a pointed end where two curves meet, e.g. the tips of a crescent moon. 2 (in astrology) the time when one sign of the zodiac ends and the next begins. 3 the point at which one state ends and another begins. [from a Latin word *cuspis* meaning 'point']

cuss *verb* (*informal*) to swear or curse.
cuss *noun* (*informal*) 1 a swear word or curse. 2 a difficult person ♦ *an awkward cuss.* [a different spelling of *curse*]

cussed (kus-id) *adjective* (*informal*) awkward and stubborn. **cussedness** *noun*

custard *noun* 1 a sweet yellow sauce made with milk and flavoured cornflour. 2 a pudding made with beaten eggs and milk. [from an Old French word *crouste*, related to *crust*]

custodian (kus-toh-diən) *noun* a guardian or keeper, especially of a public building.

custody *noun* 1 the right or duty of taking care of something, guardianship ♦ *in safe custody*. 2 the legal responsibility to look after a child, given to one of the parents following a divorce ♦ *Custody was awarded to the mother.* 3 imprisonment. **to take someone into custody** to arrest them. **custodial** *adjective* [from a Latin word *custos* meaning 'guardian']

custom *noun* 1 an activity, ceremony, etc. that is traditional and part of the way of life of a particular society ♦ *Our customs can seem strange to foreigners* ♦ *an old Chinese custom.* 2 something that you usually do ♦ *It was his custom to take a walk every morning.* SYNONYMS: habit, practice. 3 the regular business from customers ♦ *We've lost a lot of custom since the hypermarket opened.*

customs *plural noun* taxes (called *duties*) charged by the government on goods imported from other countries.
Customs *plural noun* 1 the government department dealing with taxes on goods imported from other countries. 2 the area at a port or airport where Customs officials examine goods and baggage brought into a country. [from a Latin word *consuescere* meaning 'to become accustomed'. *Customs* are the taxes customarily charged]

customary *adjective* according to custom, usual. **customarily** *adverb*

custom-built *adjective* made according to a customer's order.

customer *noun* 1 a person who buys goods or services from a shop or business. 2 a person you have to deal with ♦ *He's a tough customer.* [originally a person who customarily used the same shop etc]

customize *verb* to modify something to suit the person using it ♦ *a customized car.*

cut *verb* (past tense and past participle **cut, cutting**) 1 to divide, shorten, or remove something with a knife, scissors, or other sharp instrument ♦ *I'll cut some bread.* SYNONYMS: slice (bread), carve (meat). 2 to

wound or puncture something ♦ *She cut her finger on a piece of glass.* 3 to be able to cut or to be cut easily ♦ *The cake cut beautifully* ♦ *The knife doesn't cut.* 4 to reduce something or remove part of it ♦ *The government has promised to cut taxes* ♦ *The producer cut two scenes from the play.* SYNONYMS: reduce, lower (taxes, prices, etc.), remove, edit (scenes). 5 to cross or intersect something ♦ *The line cuts the circle at two points.* 6 to go by a shorter route ♦ *They reached the gate by cutting across the grass.* 7 to switch off an engine or machine, or a source of power. 8 to lift and turn up part of a pack of cards, often to decide which player will deal. 9 in computing and word-processing, to delete part of a file or document, either completely or in order to insert it at another point. 10 in a film, to move to another shot or scene ♦ *The camera cut to a view of the mountains.* 11 to offend someone, or to ignore someone you know. 12 to miss an event or commitment deliberately ♦ *She cut all her classes that morning.* 13 in cricket and other games, to hit the ball with a chopping movement.

cut *noun* 1 an act of cutting. 2 a division or wound made by cutting. 3 a reduction or stoppage ♦ *There will be cuts in the local bus service* ♦ *Did you have a power cut?* 4 the removal of part of a play, film, piece of music, or other work. 5 (*informal*) a share of money or profits. SYNONYMS: share, quota, slice. 6 a piece of meat cut from the carcass of an animal. 7 the style in which clothes have been made. 8 a stroke with a sword, whip, or cane. 9 a hurtful or insulting remark. 10 (in cricket and other games) a stroke made by cutting the ball. **cut and dried** already decided, and difficult to change. **to cut and paste** (in computing and word-processing) to delete part of a file or document and insert it at another point. **to cut something back** 1 to reduce something. 2 to remove parts of something that is growing. **to cut both ways** 1 to support both sides of an argument. 2 to have advantages and disadvantages. **to cut corners** to do a piece of work hurriedly or cheaply and less well. **to cut something down** 1 to reduce something or use less of it. 2 to remove or destroy something that is growing. **to cut someone down to size** to make someone realize that they are not as important as they may think. **to cut in** 1 to interrupt a conversation. 2 in driving a vehicle, to return too soon to your own side of the road after overtaking another vehicle. **to cut no ice** (*informal*) to have little effect or importance. **to cut someone off 1** to disconnect someone's telephone. **2** to isolate someone or make it impossible for them to return ♦ *The swimmers were cut off by the tide.* **3** to prevent someone from speaking. **to cut something off 1** to remove a part of something by cutting it from the main part. **2** to discontinue something that is normally available to someone ♦ *The gas has been cut off.* **to be cut off** to have no contact with your friends or the people you work with. **to cut your losses** to abandon an unsuccessful scheme before you have lost too much money or time in it. **to cut something out 1** to remove something by cutting. **2** to make something by cutting it from something larger ♦ *The children cut out shapes from the paper.* **3** to exclude someone from an activity. **4** (said about an engine) to stop working. **to be cut out for something** to have the necessary skills or qualifications to do something. **to cut a tooth** to have a tooth that is starting to grow through the gum. **to cut something up** to divide something into small pieces by cutting. [from an Old English word]

cutaneous (kyoo-**tay**-niəs) *adjective* to do with the skin. [same origin as for *cuticle*]

cutaway *adjective* (said about a diagram or plan) having some parts left out to show the interior construction or workings.

cutback *noun* a reduction or saving ♦ *There have been cutbacks in library services.*

cute *adjective* **1** attractive in a pretty or quaint way ♦ *What a cute little dog.* **2** clever or ingenious. **cutely** *adverb* **cuteness** *noun* [a shorter form of *acute*]

cut glass *noun* glass with designs cut into it after it has been blown and has hardened.

cuticle (**kyoo**-ti-kəl) *noun* **1** (*technical*) the dead skin at the lower part of a fingernail or toenail. **2** (*Botany, Zoology*) the outer layer of an organism, especially a waxy protective layer covering the outer layer (called *epidermis*) of a plant or animal. [from a Latin word *cutis* meaning 'skin']

cutlass (**kut**-ləs) *noun* a short sword with a slightly curved blade, like those once used by sailors. [from a French word *coutelas*, from Latin; related to *cutlery*]

cutlery (**kut**-lə-ri) *noun* knives, forks, and spoons used for eating at a meal. [from a French word *coutellerie*, from Latin]

cutlet (**cut**-lit) *noun* a piece of meat, especially a chop taken from the neck of a sheep or lamb, or a small slice of veal. [via French from a Latin word *costa* meaning 'rib']

cut-off *noun* the point at which something is cut off or is no longer valid or permitted ♦ *The cut-off date for renewing your subscription is 30 September.*

cut-out *noun* **1** a shape or figure that has been cut out of something ♦ *a cardboard cut-out.* **2** a device that cuts off a supply or stops a machine working, usually for safety reasons.

cut-price *adjective* for sale at a reduced price ♦ *cut-price holiday deals.*

cutter *noun* **1** someone or something that cuts, especially a tailor who takes measurements and cuts the cloth for making clothes. **2** a small fast sailing ship. **3** a small boat carried by a larger ship.

cut-throat *noun* (*old use*) a murderer who kills victims by cutting their throats. **cut-throat** *adjective* intense or ruthless ♦ *The business faces cut-throat competition.*

cut-throat razor *noun* a razor with a long blade that can be folded into a handle.

cutting *noun* **1** a piece cut out of a newspaper and kept. **2** a piece cut from a plant for replanting or to produce a new shoot. **3** a channel cut through a piece of high ground for a road or railway to pass through.
cutting *adjective* (said about something said or written) hurtful or insulting ♦ *He made some cutting remarks.* **cuttingly** *adverb*

cuttlebone (**kut**-əl-bohn) *noun* the internal skeleton of the cuttlefish, crushed into a powder and used to make a polish or for feeding cage-birds.

cuttlefish (**kut**-əl-fish) *noun* (**cuttlefish** or **cuttlefishes**) a sea creature with ten arms, which sends out an inky liquid when attacked. [*cuttle* is an Old English word from a word *cod* meaning 'bag', which refers to the bag of ink it carries]

CV *abbreviation* curriculum vitae.

cwm (koom) *noun* a bowl-shaped hollow on a mountain in Wales; a cirque. [a Welsh word, related to *coomb*]

cyan (**siy**-ən) *noun* a greenish-blue colour. [from a Greek word *kuaneos* meaning 'dark blue']

cyanide (siy-ə-niyd) *noun* a highly poisonous chemical which is a salt or ester of hydrocyanic acid. [from a Greek word *kuanos* meaning 'dark blue mineral']

cybernetics (siy-ber-net-iks) *noun* the science of communication and control in machines (e.g. computers) and in animals (e.g. by the nervous system). **cybernetic** *adjective* [from a Greek word *kubernētēs* meaning 'steersman']

cyberspace (siy-ber-spays) *noun* the imagined world in which communication between computers and on the Internet is described as occurring.

cyclamate (siy-klə-mayt or sik-klə-mayt) *noun* an artificial sweetening substance.

cyclamen (sik-lə-mən) *noun* a plant with pink, purple, or white flowers with petals that turn back. [from a Greek word *kuklos* meaning 'circle' (because of its bulbous roots)]

cycle *noun* 1 a series of events that are regularly repeated in the same order ♦ *the cycle of the seasons.* 2 one complete occurrence of a continually recurring process such as electrical oscillation or alternation of electric current. 3 a complete set or series, e.g. of songs or poems. 4 short for **bicycle**.
cycle *verb* to ride a bicycle. [from a Greek word *kuklos* meaning 'circle']

cyclic (siy-klik) *adjective* 1 recurring in cycles or series. 2 forming a cycle. **cyclical** *adjective* **cyclically** *adverb*

cyclist *noun* a person who rides a cycle.

cyclo-cross *noun* cross-country racing on bicycles.

cycloid (siy-kloid) *noun* the curve traced by a point on a circle rolling along a straight line. [from a Greek word *kukloeidēs* meaning 'circular']

cyclone (siy-klohn) *noun* 1 a system of winds rotating round a calm central area; a depression. 2 a violent tropical storm. **cyclonic** (siy-klon-ik) *adjective* [from a Greek word *kuklōma* meaning 'wheel']

Cyclops (siy-klops) **(Cyclopses)** (*Greek Mythology*) a member of a race of one-eyed giants. [from a Greek word *Kuklōps* meaning 'round-eyed']

cyclotron (siy-klə-tron) *noun* an apparatus for accelerating charged particles by making them move spirally in a magnetic field.

cygnet (sig-nit) *noun* a young swan. [from a Latin word *cycnus* meaning 'swan']

cylinder *noun* 1 a solid or hollow object with straight sides and circular ends. 2 a machine part shaped like this, especially the chamber in which a piston moves in an engine. 3 a cylindrical container for gas in liquid form under pressure. **cylindrical** *adjective* [from a Greek word *kulindein* meaning 'to roll']

cymbal *noun* a percussion instrument consisting of a metal plate that is hit to make a ringing sound. [from a Greek word *kumbē* meaning 'cup']
◊ Do not confuse this word with **symbol**, which has a different meaning.

cynic (sin-ik) *noun* a person who believes that people's reasons for doing things are always selfish and dishonest, and shows this by sneering at them. **cynical** *adjective* **cynically** *adverb* [from a Greek word *kunikos* meaning 'surly']
◊ See the note at **sceptic**.

cynicism (sin-i-sizm) *noun* the attitude of a cynic.

cynosure (sin-əz-yoor) *noun* a person or thing that is the centre of attention. [originally denoting the constellation Ursa Minor, from a Greek word *kunosoura* meaning 'dog's tail', a name for Ursa Minor]

cypress *noun* a coniferous evergreen tree with dark feathery leaves. [from a Greek word *kuparissos*]

Cyrillic (si-ril-ik) *adjective* to do with the alphabet used by Slavic peoples of the Eastern Church, now used especially for Russian and Bulgarian.
Cyrillic *noun* the Cyrillic alphabet. [named after the 9th-century Greek missionary St Cyril, who is said to have introduced it]

cyst (sist) *noun* an abnormal swelling formed in or on the body, containing fluid or soft matter. [from a Greek word *kustis* meaning 'bladder']

cystic (sis-tik) *adjective* 1 to do with the bladder. 2 to do with cysts. [same origin as for *cyst*]

cystic fibrosis *noun* a hereditary disease which affects the glands, resulting in respiratory infections and the production of thick mucus.

cystitis (sis-tiy-tiss) *noun* inflammation of the bladder, causing painful urination.

cytology (siy-**tol**-əji) *noun* the scientific study of biological cells. **cytological** *adjective* [from a Greek word *kutos* meaning 'vessel' and *-logy*]

cytoplasm (**siy**-tə-plazm) *noun* (*Biology*) the content of a cell other than the nucleus. **cytoplasmic** *adjective*

czar (zar) *noun* another spelling of **tsar**.

Czech (chek) *adjective* to do with or coming from the Czech Republic or the former country of Czechoslovakia.
Czech *noun* 1 a person born in the Czech Republic or Czechoslovakia or descended from people born there. 2 the language of Czechoslovakia or the Czech Republic.

Dd

D 1 the fourth letter of the English alphabet. 2 (*Music*) the second note of the diatonic scale of C major. 3 the Roman numeral for 500.

d. *abbreviation* penny (before decimalization), pence. [short for the Latin word *denarius*]

dab [1] *noun* 1 a quick gentle touch, usually with something wet. 2 a small amount of a soft substance applied to a surface ♦ *a dab of paint*.
dab *verb* (**dabbed, dabbing**) 1 to touch something lightly or quickly. 2 to apply something to a surface with quick light strokes. [an imitation of the sound of dabbing something wet]

dab [2] *noun* a kind of flatfish. [origin unknown]

dabble *verb* 1 to move your hands or feet around gently in water. 2 (said about a duck or water bird) to move its bill around in shallow water while feeding.
to dabble in to study or work at something casually, not seriously ♦ *I dabble in astronomy*. **dabbler** *noun* [same origin as for *dab*[1]]

dabchick *noun* a small waterbird of the grebe family.

dab hand *noun* (*informal*) a person who is an expert at doing something. [origin unknown]

dace (dayss) *noun* (**dace**) a small freshwater fish related to the carp. [from an Old French word *dars*]

dacha (**dach**-ə) *noun* a Russian cottage or house in the country. [from a Russian word, originally meaning 'grant of land']

dachshund (**daks**-huund) *noun* a small dog with a long body and very short legs. [a German word meaning 'badger dog' (because dachshunds were originally used to dig badgers out of their setts)]

dactyl (**dak**-til) *noun* a metrical foot with one long or stressed syllable followed by two short or unstressed syllables, as in the word *corporal*. **dactylic** (dak-**til**-ik) *adjective* [from a Greek word *daktulos* meaning 'finger', from the idea that the three bones of the finger correspond to the three syllables]

dad *noun* (*informal*) father. [an imitation of the sounds a young child makes when it first tries to speak]

Dada (**dah**-dah) *noun* an international movement in art and literature in the early 20th century, which rejected the usual conventions and used startling and absurd effects. [a French word meaning 'hobby horse', the title of a review which appeared in Zurich in 1916]

daddy *noun* (**daddies**) (*informal*) father. [same origin as for *dad*]

daddy-long-legs *noun* (*informal*) a crane fly.

dado (**day**-doh) *noun* (**dados**) the lower part of the wall of a room or corridor when it is coloured or decorated differently from the upper part. [from an Italian word *dado* meaning 'dice or cube']

daffodil *noun* a yellow flower with a trumpet-shaped central part, growing from a bulb. [from *asphodel*, another plant with yellow flowers]

daft *adjective* (*informal*) silly or foolish. [an Old English word]

dagger *noun* a short pointed two-edged knife used as a weapon. **at daggers drawn** hostile and on the point of quarrelling. **to look daggers** to glare angrily. [from an Old French word]

daguerreotype (də-**ge**-rə-tiyp) *noun* an early kind of photograph taken on a silver-coated copper plate, giving an image of white on silver. [named after its French inventor, Louis Daguerre (1789–1851)]

dahlia (day-lia) *noun* a garden plant with large brightly-coloured flowers. [named after a Swedish botanist, Andreas Dahl (1751–87)]

Dáil (doil) *noun* (in full **Dáil Éireann** (doil air-ən)) the lower House of Parliament in the Republic of Ireland. [an Irish word meaning 'assembly']

daily *adjective* happening or produced every day or every weekday.
daily *adverb* once a day, every day.
daily *noun* (**dailies**) a daily newspaper.

dainty *adjective* (**daintier, daintiest**) **1** small, delicate, and pretty. **2** fastidious, especially about food. **daintily** *adverb* **daintiness** *noun* [via Old French from a Latin word *dignitas* meaning 'value, beauty']

dairy *noun* (**dairies**) **1** a room or building where milk, butter, etc. are processed. **2** a shop where dairies are sold.
dairy *adjective* **1** containing or made from milk. **2** to do with the production of milk ♦ *dairy farming*. [from an Old English word]

dairymaid *noun* (*old use*) a woman employed in a dairy.

dais (day-iss) *noun* a low platform, especially at one end of a room or hall. [from an Old French word *deis*]

daisy *noun* (**daisies**) a flower with many white petal-like rays surrounding a yellow centre. [from *day's eye* (because the daisy opens in daylight and closes at night)]

daisy wheel *noun* a printing head used in a kind of typewriter or computer printer, having characters arranged round the circumference of a segmented disc.

Dalai Lama (dal-iy lah-mə) *noun* the spiritual leader of Tibetan Buddhists. [from Tibetan words meaning 'ocean monk' (because he is thought of as 'the ocean of compassion')]

dale *noun* a valley, especially in north England. [from an Old English word]

dally *verb* (**dallies, dallied, dallying**) **1** to dawdle or waste time. **2** to show a casual interest in something. **3** to flirt. **dalliance** *noun* [from an Old French word *dalier* meaning 'to chat']

Dalmatian (dal-may-shən) *noun* a large white dog with dark spots. [from Dalmatia, a region of Croatia where the dog is thought to have originated]

dalton (dawl-tən) *noun* a unit used in expressing the molecular weight of proteins, equivalent to atomic mass unit. [named after the English chemist John Dalton (1766–1844)]

dam[1] *noun* **1** a barrier built across a river etc. to hold back water and control its flow or form a reservoir. **2** a barrier of branches in a stream made by a beaver to provide a deep pool and a lodge.
dam *verb* (**dammed, damming**) **1** to hold water back with a dam. **2** to obstruct a flow. [from an Old English word]

dam[2] *noun* the mother of a four-footed animal. [from *dame*]

damage *noun* something done or suffered that reduces the value or usefulness of a thing or spoils its appearance. SYNONYMS: harm, injury, destruction.
damages *plural noun* a sum of money paid as compensation for an injury or loss.
damage *verb* to cause damage to something. SYNONYMS: harm, break, spoil, destroy. [from a Latin word *damnum* meaning 'loss']

damask (dam-əsk) *noun* silk or linen material woven with a pattern that is visible on either side. [from *Damaske*, an early form of *Damascus*, the city in Syria where the fabric was first produced]

dame *noun* **1** (**Dame**) the title of a woman who has been awarded an order of knighthood (corresponding to the title of *Sir* for a knight). **2** a comic female character in pantomime, usually played by a man. **3** (*North Amer.*) (*informal*) a woman. [from a Latin word *domina* meaning 'lady']

damn *verb* **1** to condemn someone to eternal punishment in hell. **2** to condemn something as a failure. **3** to swear at someone or curse them.
damn *interjection* an exclamation of anger or annoyance. **I'll be damned** (*informal*) I am astonished. **I'm damned if I know** (*informal*) I certainly do not know. [from a Latin word *damnare* meaning 'to condemn']

damnable (dam-nə-bəl) *adjective* hateful or annoying. **damnably** *adverb*

damnation (dam-nay-shən) *noun* in some beliefs, being condemned to eternal punishment after death.

damned *adjective* hateful or annoying.

damp *adjective* slightly wet, not quite dry. SYNONYMS: moist, dank, humid, clammy.

damp noun moisture in the air, on a surface, or throughout something.
damp verb 1 to make something slightly wet. 2 to discourage or reduce the strength of something ♦ *The defeat damped their enthusiasm.* 3 to reduce the vibration of the strings of a musical instrument. **damply** adverb **dampness** noun [from a Germanic word]

damp course noun a layer of waterproof material built into a wall near the ground to prevent damp from rising.

dampen verb 1 to make something damp. 2 to reduce the strength of something.

damper noun 1 a felt pad that presses against a piano string to stop it vibrating. 2 a metal plate that can be moved to increase or decrease the flow of air into the fire in a stove or furnace. **to put a damper on something** to reduce people's enthusiasm or enjoyment. [from *damp*]

damsel (dam-zəl) noun (*old use*) a young unmarried woman. [from an Old French word *dameisele*]

damselfly noun (**damselflies**) an insect like a dragonfly but with wings that fold back along its body while it rests.

damson noun 1 a small dark purple plum. 2 the tree that bears this fruit. 3 dark purple. [from the Latin words *damascenum prunum* meaning 'plum from Damascus', a city in Syria]

dan noun 1 a degree of proficiency in judo or karate. 2 a person who reaches this. [from a Japanese word]

dance verb 1 to move with rhythmical steps or movements, usually to music. 2 to perform a particular dance ♦ *We learnt to dance the tango.* 3 to move in a quick or lively way.
dance noun 1 a piece of dancing. 2 a piece of music for dancing to. 3 a party or gathering where people dance. **dancer** noun [from an Old French word]

dandelion noun a wild plant with bright yellow flowers and jagged leaves. [from a French phrase *dent-de-lion* meaning 'tooth of a lion' (because the jagged edges of the leaves look like lion's teeth)]

dandle verb to move a baby or young child up and down on your knee. [origin unknown]

dandruff noun tiny white flakes of dead skin on the scalp and in the hair. [origin unknown]

dandy noun (**dandies**) a man who pays too much attention to the smartness of his appearance and clothes.
dandy adjective (**dandier, dandiest**) (*informal*) excellent. [origin unknown]

Dane noun 1 a person born in Denmark or descended from people born there. 2 a Scandinavian invader of England in the 9th–11th centuries. [from an Old English word]

Danegeld noun a land tax levied in Anglo-Saxon England, originally to bribe the invading Danes to go away. [from *Dane* and an Old Norse word *gjald* meaning 'payment']

Danelaw noun the north-eastern part of England that was settled or held by the Danes from the late 9th century until after the Norman Conquest.

danger noun 1 the possibility of suffering harm or death. SYNONYMS: peril, jeopardy, trouble. 2 something that is not safe or could harm you. 3 the possibility of something unpleasant happening ♦ *There's a danger they might be sold out.* SYNONYMS: risk, threat, chance, possibility. [from an Old French word *dangier* meaning 'power to harm']

dangerous adjective likely to kill or harm you. SYNONYMS: hazardous, perilous, risky, unsafe, toxic (substance). **dangerously** adverb

dangle verb 1 to hang or swing loosely. 2 to hold or carry something so that it swings loosely ♦ *She dangled her legs over the side of the boat.* **to keep someone dangling** to keep someone in an uncertain position. [from a Scandinavian word]

Danish adjective to do with or coming from Denmark.
Danish noun the Scandinavian language of Denmark.

Danish pastry noun a cake of sweet yeast pastry filled or topped with fruit or icing.

dank adjective unpleasantly damp, cold, and musty. [from a Scandinavian word]

dapper adjective dressed neatly and smartly ♦ *a dapper little man.* [from an Old German or Old Dutch word]

dapple verb to mark something with spots or patches of shade or a different colour. [probably from an Old Norse word *depill* meaning 'spot']

dapple grey adjective grey with darker markings.

dare verb 1 to be brave enough to do something ♦ *He didn't dare go* ♦ *I would never dare to argue with her.* 2 to challenge a person to do something risky.
dare noun a challenge to do something risky. **I dare say** it is very likely. [from an Old English word *durran*]

daredevil noun a person who enjoys doing dangerous things.

daren't verb dare not.

daring adjective 1 bold, taking risks boldly. SYNONYMS: bold, brave, adventurous, intrepid, fearless. 2 boldly dramatic or unconventional.
daring noun adventurous courage.
daringly adverb

dark adjective 1 with little or no light. SYNONYMS: black, dim, murky, gloomy, shadowy. 2 (said about a colour) of a deep shade closer to black than to white ♦ *dark grey* ♦ *a dark suit.* 3 (said about people) having a brown or black skin; having dark hair. 4 involving misery or suffering ♦ *the long dark years of the war.* 5 mysterious ♦ *a dark secret.* 6 remote and unexplored ♦ *in darkest Africa.* 7 evil or sinister ♦ *dark deeds.*
dark noun 1 absence of light. 2 a time of darkness, night or nightfall ♦ *Don't stay out after dark.* 3 a dark colour. **in the dark** having no information about something. **to keep something dark** to keep something secret. **darkly** adverb **darkness** noun [from an Old English word *deorc*]

Dark Ages plural noun the early part of the Middle Ages in Europe (about 500–1100), when learning and culture had declined.

darken verb 1 to make or become dark or darker. 2 to make or become angry or unhappy. **never to darken someone's door** to stay away from their home because you are unwelcome.

dark horse noun someone who might do surprisingly well, e.g. in a race or competition, because they have unexpected abilities.

darkroom noun a room kept dark for developing photographs.

darling noun someone who is loved very much.
darling adjective 1 dearly loved. 2 pretty or charming. [from an Old English word *deorling* meaning 'little dear']

darn verb to mend a hole by weaving threads across it.
darn noun a place mended by darning.

darning noun [from an Old English word *diernan* meaning 'to hide']

dart noun 1 a small metal-tipped object thrown in the game of darts. 2 a small pointed missile thrown or fired as a weapon. 3 a darting movement. 4 a tapering stitched tuck in a piece of clothing.
darts noun an indoor game in which darts are thrown at a dartboard.
dart verb 1 to move suddenly or rapidly. 2 to send something out rapidly ♦ *She darted an angry look at him.* [from an Old French word]

dartboard noun a circular board used as a target in the game of darts.

Darwinism noun the theory of the evolution of species by natural selection, put forward by the English naturalist Charles Darwin (1809–82).

dash verb 1 to run rapidly, to rush. 2 to knock or throw a thing with great force against something ♦ *He dashed the plate to the floor.* 3 to destroy or frustrate something ♦ *Our hopes were dashed.*
dash noun 1 a short rapid run, a rush ♦ *We made a dash for the door.* 2 a small amount of liquid or flavouring added ♦ *Add a dash of cream.* 3 the punctuation mark (—) used to mark a pause or to show that letters or words are missing. 4 a dashboard. 5 confidence and style ♦ *She plays with real dash.* 6 the longer of the two signals used in Morse code. **to dash something off** to write something hurriedly and without much effort ♦ *He dashed off a letter.* [origin unknown]

dashboard noun a panel with instruments and controls in front of the driver of a vehicle. [originally a board on the front of a carriage to keep out mud, which dashed against it]

dashing adjective attractive in a romantic, adventurous way.

dastardly adjective (old use) wicked and cruel. [originally meaning 'dull or stupid': from *dazed*]

DAT abbreviation digital audiotape.

data (**day**-ta) noun facts or information used as a basis for discussing or deciding something, or prepared for being processed by a computer etc. [from a Latin word, the plural of *datum*]
◊ Strictly speaking, this word is a plural noun (the singular is *datum*), so it should be used with a plural verb: *Here are the*

data. However, the word is widely used nowadays as if it were a singular noun and most people do not regard this as wrong: *Here is the data.*

databank *noun* a large store of computerized data.

database *noun* a structured store of computerized data.

datable *adjective* able to be dated to a particular time.

data capture *noun* the process of putting data into a form that is accessible by computer.

data processing *noun* the performance of operations on data, especially using a computer, to obtain or classify information.

data protection *noun* the process of ensuring that data stored in computers cannot be accessed except by people who are legally authorized to do so.

date¹ *noun* 1 the day of the month or year expressed by a number. 2 a day or year when something happened or will happen ♦ *We don't know the exact date of the battle.* 3 the period to which something belongs ♦ *What date are these ruins?* 4 (*informal*) an appointment to meet someone socially, especially at the start of what may become a romantic relationship. 5 (*informal*) a person you have a date with.
date *verb* 1 to mark something with a date ♦ *Is the letter dated?* 2 to give a date to something ♦ *Experts have been trying to date the fossil.* 3 to have existed from a particular date ♦ *The custom dates from Victorian times.* 4 to show signs of becoming out of date ♦ *Some fashions date quickly.* 5 (*informal*) to go on a date with someone. **out of date** see **out**. **to date** until now ♦ *Here are our sales figures to date.* **up to date** see **up**. [from a Latin word *data* meaning 'given or delivered (at a certain time)']

date² *noun* the small brown sweet edible fruit of the **date palm**, a palm-tree of North Africa and SW Asia. [from a Greek word *daktulos* meaning 'finger' (because of the finger-like shape of its leaves)]

dated *adjective* old-fashioned.

Date Line *noun* a line from north to south roughly along the meridian 180° from Greenwich, to the east of which the date is a day earlier than it is to the west.

dative *noun* (*Grammar*) the case of a word expressing the indirect object or a recipient, e.g. *me* in 'give me the book'. [same origin as for *datum*]

datum (**day**-təm) *noun* (**data**) (*formal*) 1 an item of information, a unit of data (see **data**). 2 the starting point from which something is measured or calculated. [a Latin word meaning 'something given']

datum line *noun* a set horizontal line from which measurements are taken.

daub *verb* 1 to coat or smear something roughly with a thick substance. 2 to paint or spread a thick substance on a surface in this way.
daub *noun* 1 a clumsily-painted picture. 2 a covering or smear of a thick substance. [from a Latin word *dealbare* meaning 'whitewash, plaster']

daughter *noun* 1 a female child in relation to her parents. 2 a female descendant ♦ *daughters of Eve.* [from an Old English word *dohtor*]

daughter-in-law *verb* (**daughters-in-law**) a son's wife.

daunt *verb* to make someone afraid or discouraged ♦ *She didn't seem daunted by the challenge ahead.* **daunting** *adjective* [from a Latin word *domitare* meaning 'to tame']

dauntless *adjective* brave and determined. **dauntlessly** *adverb*

dauphin (**daw**-fin) *noun* the title of the eldest son of the king of France in the days when France was ruled by a king. [from an Old French word]

Davy Jones's locker *noun* (*informal*) the bottom of the sea thought of as the grave of those who are drowned or buried at sea. [from *Davy Jones*, denoting the evil spirit of the sea]

Davy lamp *noun* a type of safety lamp for miners. [named after the English chemist Sir Humphry Davy (1778–1829), who invented it in 1816]

dawdle *verb* to walk slowly and idly, to take your time. **dawdler** *noun* [origin unknown]

dawn *noun* 1 the first light of the day just before sunrise. 2 the beginning of something ♦ *the dawn of civilization.*
dawn *verb* 1 to begin to grow light in the morning. 2 to begin to appear or become evident ♦ *The truth dawned on them.* **dawning** *noun* [from an Old English word]

day noun 1 the time during which the sun is above the horizon. 2 a period of 24 hours, especially from one midnight to the next, corresponding to one rotation of the earth on its axis. 3 the hours given to work ♦ She works an eight-hour day. 4 a period of time in the past or in a person's life ♦ in Queen Victoria's day ♦ I was a good player in my young days. **to call it a day** to decide to stop doing something. **day by day** each day, gradually and steadily. [from an Old English word]

daybreak noun the first light of day, dawn.

day centre noun a place where social and other facilities are provided for elderly or handicapped people during the day.

daydream noun pleasant thoughts of something you would like to happen, distracting your attention from the present.
daydream verb (past tense and past participle **daydreamed**) to have a daydream.

daylight noun 1 the natural light of day. 2 dawn. **to see daylight** to begin to understand something.

day return noun a ticket sold at a reduced rate for a return journey in one day.

day room noun a shared living room in a school, hospital, etc.

daytime noun the time of daylight.

daze verb to make someone feel stunned or bewildered.
daze noun a dazed state ♦ in a daze. [from an Old Norse word dasathr meaning 'weary']

dazzle verb 1 to make someone unable to see clearly because of too much bright light. 2 to amaze and impress or confuse someone by a splendid display.
dazzle noun blinding brightness. [from daze]

dB abbreviation decibel(s).

DBE abbreviation Dame Commander of the Order of the British Empire.

DC abbreviation direct current.

DCI abbreviation detective chief inspector.

D-Day noun 1 the day (6 June 1944) on which British and American forces invaded northern France in the Second World War. 2 the date on which an important operation is planned to begin. [from D for day and day]

DDT noun a white chlorinated hydrocarbon used as an insecticide but now banned in many countries.

de- prefix 1 removing (as in defrost). 2 down, away (as in descend). 3 completely (as in denude). [from a Latin word de meaning 'away from']

deacon noun 1 a member of the clergy ranking below a priest in Catholic, Anglican, and Orthodox Churches. 2 a lay person attending to church business in Nonconformist Churches. [from a Greek word diakonos meaning 'servant']

deaconess noun a woman with duties similar to those of a deacon.

dead adjective 1 no longer alive. 2 numb, without feeling ♦ My fingers have gone dead. 3 no longer used ♦ a dead language. 4 no longer active or functioning ♦ The microphone went dead. 5 not lively or interesting ♦ The town is dead on Sundays. 6 (said about a ball in games) out of play. 7 complete, abrupt, exact ♦ dead silence ♦ a dead stop ♦ dead centre.
dead adverb 1 completely, exactly ♦ dead drunk ♦ dead level. 2 (informal) very ♦ I'm dead sorry. **the dead of night** the quietest, darkest part of the night. **the dead of winter** the coldest part of winter. **dead to the world** (informal) fast asleep. **from the dead** from a state of death. [from an Old English word]

deaden verb to make pain or noise etc. weaker.

dead end noun the closed end of a road or passage, a blind alley.

dead-end job noun a job with no prospects of advancement.

dead heat noun the result of a race in which two or more competitors finish exactly level.

dead leg noun an injury caused by a numbing blow to a person's upper leg.

deadline noun the latest time or date by which something should be completed. [originally this meant the line round a military prison beyond which a prisoner could be shot]

deadlock noun a situation in which no progress can be made.
deadlock verb to reach a deadlock; to cause something to do this ♦ The negotiations are deadlocked. [from dead and lock]

deadly *adjective* (**deadlier, deadliest**)
1 likely to kill ♦ *a deadly poison.* SYNONYMS:
lethal, fatal, mortal. 2 extremely accurate or
effective ♦ *He has a deadly right foot.*
3 (*informal*) very boring.
deadly *adverb* 1 as if dead ♦ *deadly pale.*
2 extremely ♦ *I'm deadly serious.*
deadliness *noun*

deadly nightshade *noun* a plant with
poisonous black berries.

dead man's handle *noun* a safety lever on
a train etc. that shuts off the driving
power if it is released by the driver.

dead march *noun* a funeral march.

dead nettle *noun* a plant with nettle-like
leaves that does not sting.

deadpan *adjective & adverb* with an
expressionless face.

dead reckoning *noun* calculating a ship's
position by log and compass etc. when
observations are impossible.

dead shot *noun* an extremely accurate
marksman or markswoman.

dead weight *noun* a heavy inert weight.

deaf *adjective* 1 wholly or partly without
the sense of hearing. 2 refusing to listen
♦ *He was deaf to all advice.* **deafness** *noun*
[from an Old English word]

deaf aid *noun* a hearing aid.

deafen *verb* to make someone deaf or
unable to hear by a very loud noise.

deafening *adjective* extremely loud.

deaf mute *noun* a person who is deaf and
unable to speak.
◊ This term can cause offence and should
be avoided. Use *profoundly deaf* instead.

deal[1] *verb* (past tense and past participle
dealt) 1 to give out cards to players in a
card game. 2 to hand something out to
several people. 3 to do business, to trade
in something ♦ *He deals in scrap metal.* 4 to
give or inflict something ♦ *His father's
death dealt him a severe blow.*
deal *noun* 1 a business transaction or other
agreement ♦ *The deal fell through* ♦ *Okay,
it's a deal.* 2 treatment ♦ *Working mothers
don't get a fair deal.* 3 a player's turn to deal
at cards ♦ *Whose deal is it?* **a good** or **great
deal** a large amount. **to deal with** 1 to be
concerned with or to discuss a subject
♦ *This book deals with the history of cooking.*
2 to take action about something or cope
with something. 3 to do business with

someone. **dealer** *noun* [from an Old
English word *dælan* meaning 'to divide,
share out']

deal[2] *noun* sawn fir or pine timber. [from
an Old Dutch word *dele* meaning 'plank']

dealings *plural noun* a person's transactions
with another.

dean *noun* 1 a member of the clergy who is
head of a cathedral chapter. 2 a member
of the clergy with authority over a group
of parishes. 3 the head of a university,
college, or department. [from a Latin
word *decanus* meaning 'chief of a group of
ten']

deanery *noun* (**deaneries**) 1 the position of
dean. 2 a dean's official residence. 3 a
rural dean's area of office.

dear *adjective* 1 loved very much. 2 a polite
greeting in letters ♦ *Dear Sir.* 3 expensive.
SYNONYMS: expensive, costly, overpriced;
(*informal*) pricey.
dear *noun* a dear person.
dear *adverb* at a high cost ♦ *It cost us dear.*
dear *interjection* an exclamation of
surprise, sympathy, or distress. **dearness**
noun [from an Old English word]

dearly *adverb* 1 very much ♦ *I would dearly
love to come.* 2 at great cost.

dearth (derth) *noun* a scarcity or lack of
something. [from *dear* (because scarcity
made food etc. expensive)]

death *noun* 1 the process of dying, the end
of life. 2 the state of being dead. 3 the
ending or destruction of something ♦ *the
death of our hopes.* **at death's door** close to
death. **to be the death of someone** to cause
someone's death ♦ *Drink was the death of
him.* **to put someone to death** to kill or
execute them. **to death** extremely, to the
utmost limit ♦ *We were all bored to death.*
to the death until one or other is killed
♦ *a fight to the death.* [from an Old English
word]

deathbed *noun* the bed on which a person
dies or is dying.

death camp *noun* a prison camp, especially
for political prisoners or prisoners of war,
in which many die.

death certificate *noun* an official
statement of the date, place, and cause of
a person's death.

death duty *noun* tax levied on property
after the owner's death. It is now called
inheritance tax.

deathless *adjective* immortal.

deathly *adjective & adverb* like death ♦ *a deathly hush* ♦ *deathly pale*.

death penalty *noun* punishment for a crime by being put to death.

death rate *noun* the number of deaths in one year for every 1000 people.

death row *noun* a prison area housing prisoners sentenced to death.

death's head *noun* a picture of a skull as a symbol of death.

death toll *noun* the number of deaths resulting from a particular cause.

death trap *noun* a dangerous place or situation.

death warrant *noun* an order for the execution of a condemned person.

death-watch beetle *noun* a beetle whose larva bores holes in old wood and makes a ticking sound which was formerly believed to be a sign of an imminent death.

debacle (day-bahkl) *noun* an utter failure or disaster. [from a French word *débâcler* meaning 'to unbar']

debar *verb* (**debarred, debarring**) to forbid or ban someone from doing something ♦ *He was debarred from the contest.* [from *de-* and a French word *barrer* meaning 'to bar']

debark *verb* to leave a ship or aircraft. **debarkation** *noun* [from a French word]

debase *verb* 1 to reduce the quality or value of something. 2 to reduce the value of coins by using an alloy or inferior metal. **debasement** *noun* [from *de-* and *base*]

debatable *adjective* questionable, open to discussion or argument. **debatably** *adverb*

debate *noun* 1 a formal discussion. 2 an argument.
debate *verb* 1 to hold a debate about a subject. 2 to discuss or consider something. [from an Old French word]

debauch (di-bawch) *verb* to destroy a person's moral purity, to lead them into debauchery. **debauched** *adjective* [from a French word *débaucher* meaning 'to turn away from your duty']

debauchery (di-bawch-er-i) *noun* over-indulgence in sensual or immoral pleasures.

debenture (di-ben-cher) *noun* a certificate or bond acknowledging a debt on which fixed interest is being paid. [from a Latin word *debentur* meaning 'they are owed']

debilitate *verb* to make someone very weak and infirm ♦ *a debilitating illness.* [from a Latin word *debilis* meaning 'weak']

debility *noun* weakness of the body.

debit *noun* 1 an entry in an account of a sum owed. 2 the sum itself; the total of such sums.
debit *verb* (**debited, debiting**) to enter something as a debit in an account, to remove money from an account. [from a Latin word *debitum* meaning 'what is owed']

debit card *noun* a card that allows you to transfer money electronically from one bank account to another when making a purchase.

debonair (deb-ən-air) *adjective* having a carefree self-confident manner. [from a French phrase *de bon aire* meaning 'of good disposition']

debrief *verb* to question someone in order to obtain information about a mission just completed. **debriefing** *noun*

debris (deb-ree) *noun* scattered broken pieces or remains. [from a French word *débris* meaning 'broken down']

debt (det) *noun* something owed by one person to another. **to be in someone's debt** to owe gratitude to someone for a favour. **in debt** owing money. [same origin as for *debit*]

debtor (det-ər) *noun* a person who owes money to someone.

debug *verb* (**debugged, debugging**) 1 (*Computing*) to remove errors from a program or system. 2 to remove concealed listening devices from a room. 3 (*Amer.*) to remove insects from something.

debunk *verb* to show up a claim or theory, or a person's reputation, as exaggerated or false.

début (day-bew) *noun* the first public appearance of an actor or other performer. [from a French word *débuter* meaning 'to begin']

debutant (deb-yoo-tahn) *noun* a person making a debut.

debutante (deb-yoo-tahnt) *noun* a young upper-class woman making her first appearance in society.

Dec. *abbreviation* December.

deca- *prefix* ten (as in *decathlon*). [from a Greek word *deka* meaning 'ten']

decade (dek-ayd) *noun* a period of ten years. [from an Old French word]

decadent (dek-ə-dənt) *adjective* 1 falling to a lower standard of morality. 2 luxuriously self-indulgent. **decadence** *noun* [same origin as for *decay*]

decaffeinated (di-kaf-in-ayt-id) *adjective* (said about coffee or tea) with the caffeine removed.

decagon *noun* a geometric figure with ten sides. **decagonal** (di-kag-ən-əl) *adjective* [from *deca-* and a Greek word *gōnia* meaning 'angle']

decamp *verb* to go away suddenly or secretly. [from a French word *décamper*]

decant (di-kant) *verb* to pour liquid gently from one container into another, especially in order to separate the liquid from the sediment. [from a Latin word *decanthare*]

decanter (di-kant-er) *noun* a stoppered glass bottle into which wine or spirit may be decanted before serving. [from *decant*]

decapitate (di-kap-it-ayt) *verb* to cut someone's head off. **decapitation** *noun* [from *de-* and a Latin word *caput* meaning 'head']

decapod (dek-ə-pod) *noun* a crustacean with ten feet, e.g. a crab or lobster. [from *deca-* and a Greek word *podos* meaning 'of the foot']

decarbonize *verb* to remove the carbon deposit from an engine etc. **decarbonization** *noun*

decathlon (dik-ath-lən) *noun* an athletic contest in which each competitor takes part in ten events. [from *deca-* and a Greek word *athlon* meaning 'contest']

decay *verb* 1 to rot or cause something to rot. SYNONYMS: rot, decompose, perish, putrefy. 2 to lose quality or strength. 3 (said about a radioactive substance or particle) to undergo change to a different form by emitting radiation. **decay** *noun* 1 the state or process of decaying. 2 decayed matter or tissue. 3 radioactive change. [from *de-* and a Latin word *cadere* meaning 'to fall']

decease (di-seess) *noun* (*formal*) death. [from *de-* and a Latin word *cedere* meaning 'to go']

deceased *adjective* recently dead. **the deceased** the person who died recently.

deceit (di-seet) *noun* making a person believe something that is not true. SYNONYMS: deception, trickery, dishonesty, pretence, guile.

deceitful *adjective* deceiving people. SYNONYMS: dishonest, underhand, insincere. **deceitfully** *adverb* **deceitfulness** *noun*

deceive *verb* 1 to make someone believe something that is not true. SYNONYMS: fool, trick, mislead, dupe; (*informal*) con. 2 to give someone a mistaken impression ♦ *Don't be deceived by the cheap price of these CDs — they are of the highest quality.* **to deceive yourself** to persist in a mistaken belief. **deceiver** *noun* [from a Latin word *decipere* meaning 'to ensnare or cheat']

decelerate (dee-sel-er-ayt) *verb* to decrease your speed. **deceleration** *noun* [from *de-* and *accelerate*]

December *noun* the twelfth month of the year. [from a Latin word *decem* meaning 'ten' (because it was the tenth month of the ancient Roman calendar)]

decency *noun* decent behaviour.

decent *adjective* 1 conforming to the accepted standards of what is moral or proper, not immodest or obscene. 2 respectable and honest ♦ *ordinary decent people.* 3 quite good, satisfactory ♦ *She earns a decent salary.* 4 (*informal*) kind and generous ♦ *That's very decent of you.* **decently** *adverb* [from a Latin word *decere* meaning 'to be fit']

decentralize *verb* to divide and distribute powers etc. from a central authority to places or branches away from the centre. **decentralization** *noun*

deception *noun* 1 deceiving; being deceived. 2 something that deceives people.

deceptive *adjective* misleading; giving a false impression ♦ *Appearances can be deceptive.* **deceptively** *adverb*

deci-*prefix* one tenth part, as in *decigram*, *decilitre*. [same origin as for *decimal*]

decibel (dess-i-bəl) *noun* a unit for measuring the loudness of sound. [originally one tenth of the unit called a *bel*]

decide verb 1 to make up your mind; to come to a decision. SYNONYMS: resolve, determine, elect. 2 to settle a contest or argument by giving victory to one side ♦ A late goal decided the match. 3 to cause someone to reach a decision ♦ These letters of support decided me. [from a Latin word decidere meaning 'to determine']

decided adjective 1 noticeable, definite ♦ a decided improvement. 2 having clear and definite opinions; determined. **decidedly** adverb

decider noun a contest that settles the outcome of a series of contests.

deciduous (di-sid-yoo-əs) adjective (said about a tree) shedding its leaves annually. [from a Latin word decidere meaning 'to fall off']

decimal (dess-im-əl) adjective expressed or calculated in tens or tenths. **decimal** noun a decimal fraction. [from a Latin word decimus meaning 'tenth']

decimal currency noun a currency in which each unit is ten or one hundred times the value of the one next below it.

decimal fraction noun a fraction whose denominator is a power of 10, expressed in figures after a dot (called decimal point), e.g. $0.5 = \frac{5}{10}$, $0.52 = \frac{52}{100}$.

decimalize verb 1 to express a number as a decimal. 2 to change something, especially coinage, to a decimal system. **decimalization** noun

decimal place noun the position of a digit to the right of the decimal point in a decimal fraction.

decimal point noun the dot in a decimal fraction.

decimal system noun a system of weights and measures with each unit ten times that immediately below it.

decimate (dess-im-ayt) verb 1 to kill or destroy a large proportion of something ♦ The famine decimated the population. 2 to reduce the strength of something drastically. **decimation** noun [from a Latin word decimare meaning 'to kill every tenth man', from the practice of putting to death one in every ten of a body of soldiers guilty of mutiny in the ancient Roman army]
◊ Many people object to the looser and more general use in meaning 1.

decipher (di-siy-fer) verb 1 to make out the meaning of a coded message. 2 to succeed in understanding something that is unclear, especially something written badly. **decipherment** noun

decision noun 1 deciding, making a reasoned judgement about something. 2 what you have decided. SYNONYMS: conclusion, verdict, judgement, finding. 3 the ability to form clear opinions and act on them. [same origin as for decide]

decisive (di-siy-siv) adjective 1 settling something conclusively ♦ a decisive battle. 2 able to make decisions quickly. **decisively** adverb

deck noun 1 any of the horizontal floors in a ship. 2 a similar floor or platform, especially one of two or more ♦ the top deck of a bus. 3 a pack of playing cards. 4 the part of a piece of sound-reproduction equipment that contains a playing or recording mechanism for discs or tapes. **deck** verb to decorate something with bright and colourful decorations, to dress something up ♦ The front of the house was decked out with flags and balloons ♦ She was decked out in her finest clothes. **to hit the deck** (informal) to fall to the ground or floor. [from an Old Dutch word dec meaning 'a covering']

deckchair noun a portable folding chair with a wooden frame and a canvas seat. [so called because they were used on the decks of passenger ships]

declaim (di-klaym) verb to speak or say something impressively or dramatically. **declamation** (deklə-may-shən) noun **declamatory** adjective [from de- and a Latin word clamare meaning 'to shout']

declare verb 1 to say something clearly or firmly ♦ He declares that he is innocent. 2 to tell customs officials that you have goods on which you ought to pay duty ♦ Do you have anything to declare? 3 to announce something openly, formally, or explicitly. 4 (in cricket) to choose to close your side's innings before all the wickets have fallen. **to declare war** to announce that you are starting a war against someone. **declaration** noun **declarative** adjective **declaratory** adjective [from de- and a Latin word clarare meaning 'to make clear']

declension noun the variation of the form of a noun, adjective, or pronoun to give its grammatical case, number, and gender; the class by which a noun etc. is declined. [same origin as for decline]

declination (dek-lin-ay-shən) *noun* **1** the angle between the true north and the magnetic north. **2** (in astronomy) the angle between the direction of a star etc. and the celestial equator.

decline *verb* **1** to politely refuse ♦ *She reluctantly declined the offer.* **2** to become weaker or smaller ♦ *in her declining years.* **3** (said about the sun) to move downwards. **4** (*Grammar*) to give the forms of a noun, pronoun, or adjective that correspond to its cases, number, and gender.
decline *noun* a gradual decrease or loss of strength. **in decline** decreasing. [from *de-* and a Latin word *clinare* meaning 'to bend']

declivity (di-kliv-iti) *noun* (**declivities**) a downward slope. [from a Latin word *declivis* meaning 'sloping down']

decoction *noun* boiling down to extract an essence, or the extract itself. [from *de-* and a Latin word *coctum* meaning 'cooked']

decode *verb* **1** to put a coded message into plain language. **2** to translate coded characters in a computer.

decoder *noun* **1** a person or machine that decodes messages etc. **2** a device for analysing stereophonic signals and passing them to separate amplifier channels.

decommission *verb* to take a ship or piece of equipment out of service.

decompose *verb* **1** to decay, or to make something decay. **2** to separate a substance into its elements. **decomposition** *noun*

decompress *verb* **1** (*Computing*) to expand compressed data to the normal size. **2** to subject a diver to decompression.

decompression *noun* **1** reduction in air pressure. **2** the gradual and safe reduction of air pressure on a person who has been in compressed air.

decompression chamber *noun* an enclosed space where air pressure can be reduced, used to allow deep-sea divers to adjust to normal air pressure.

decompression sickness *noun* a condition of cramp, numbness, and paralysis that results when over-rapid decompression causes nitrogen bubbles to form in the tissues of the body.

decongestant (dee-kən-jest-ənt) *noun* a medicinal substance that relieves a blocked nose.

decontaminate *verb* to get rid of poisonous chemicals or radioactive material from a place, clothes, etc. **decontamination** *noun*

decontrol *verb* (**decontrolled, decontrolling**) to release a market or commodity from government control.

decor (day-kor) *noun* the style of furnishings and decoration used in a room. [a French word (compare *decorate*)]

decorate *verb* **1** to make something look more attractive or colourful by adding objects or details to it. **2** to put fresh paint or wallpaper on walls. **3** to give someone a medal or other award. [from a Latin word *decor* meaning 'beauty']

decoration *noun* **1** decorating. **2** something that decorates. **3** a medal or other award given and worn as an honour. **4** (**decorations**) streamers and other decorative objects put up at public celebrations.

decorative (dek-er-ətiv) *adjective* ornamental, pleasing to look at. **decoratively** *adverb*

decorator *noun* a person who decorates, especially someone whose job is to paint and paper the inside of houses.

decorous (dek-er-əs) *adjective* polite and dignified. **decorously** *adverb* [from a Latin word *decorus* meaning 'suitable, proper']

decorum (di-kor-əm) *noun* polite and dignified behaviour. [same origin as for *decorous*]

decoy [1] (dee-koi) *noun* a person or thing used to lure a person or animal into a trap or into danger. [from a Dutch word]

decoy [2] (di-koi) *verb* to lure a person or animal by means of a decoy.

decrease *verb* **1** to make something shorter, smaller, or fewer. SYNONYMS: reduce, lower, lessen, cut. **2** to become shorter, smaller, or fewer. SYNONYMS: fall, decline, dwindle, diminish, shrink.
decrease *noun* **1** decreasing. **2** the amount by which something decreases. [from *de-* and a Latin word *crescere* meaning 'to grow']

decree *noun* **1** an order given by a government or other authority that has the force of a law. **2** a judgement or decision of certain law courts.

decree verb (**decreed, decreeing**) to order something by decree. [from a Latin word *decretum* meaning 'what has been decided']

decree nisi (niy-siy) noun a provisional divorce order by a court of law, to be confirmed on a set date unless a reason is produced to prevent it. [from a Latin word *nisi* meaning 'unless']

decrepit (di-krep-it) adjective 1 old and weak. 2 worn out by long use. **decrepitude** noun [from a Latin word *decrepitus* meaning 'creaking']

decriminalize verb to stop treating something as a crime. **decriminalization** noun

decry (di-kriy) verb (**decries, decried, decrying**) to disparage something. [from a French word *décrier* meaning 'to cry down']

dedicate verb 1 to devote your time, energy, and loyalty to a special purpose ♦ *She has dedicated her life to animals.* 2 to devote a church or other building to a sacred purpose or use ♦ *This church is dedicated to St Peter.* 3 to address a book or piece of music etc. to a person as a compliment, putting his or her name at the beginning. **dedication** noun **dedicator** noun [from a Latin word *dedicare* meaning 'to devote or consecrate']

dedicated adjective 1 devoted to a task or purpose ♦ *a dedicated scientist.* 2 designed exclusively for a particular purpose ♦ *a dedicated high-speed rail link.*

deduce (di-dewss) verb to work something out by reasoning from observed facts. **deducible** adjective [from de- and a Latin word *ducere* meaning 'to lead']

deduct verb to take away an amount or quantity, to subtract something. **deductible** adjective [same origin as for *deduce*]

deduction noun 1 deducting; something that is deducted. 2 deducing; a conclusion reached by reasoning. 3 logical reasoning that something must be true because it is a particular case of a general law that is known to be true.

deductive adjective based on reasoning.

deed noun 1 something that someone has done, an act. 2 a legal document, especially one giving ownership or rights, bearing the giver's signature and seal. [from an Old English word]

deed poll noun (*Law*) a deed made by one party only, especially one that formally changes a person's name.

deem verb (*formal*) to consider or judge something ♦ *The concert was deemed a great success.* [from an Old English word]

deep adjective 1 going or situated far down or back or in ♦ *a deep well* ♦ *a deep cut* ♦ *deep cupboards.* 2 measured from top to bottom or front to back ♦ *a hole six feet deep.* 3 intense or strong ♦ *a deep sleep* ♦ *deep feelings.* 4 (said about colour) dark and intense ♦ *deep blue.* 5 low-pitched and resonant, not shrill ♦ *a deep voice.* 6 fully absorbed or overwhelmed ♦ *deep in thought.* 7 difficult to understand, obscure ♦ *That's too deep for me.* 8 (in cricket) distant from the batsman.
deep adverb deeply, far down or in.
deep noun (**the deep**) a deep place, especially the sea. **to go off the deep end** (*informal*) to give way to emotion or anger. **in deep water** (*informal*) in trouble or difficulty. **to be thrown in at the deep end** (*informal*) to face a difficult problem or situation with little experience. **deeply** adverb **deepness** noun [from an Old English word]

deepen verb to become or to make something become deep or deeper.

deep freeze noun a freezer.
deep-freeze verb (**deep-froze, deep-frozen**) to store or freeze something in a deep freeze.

deep-fry verb (**deep-fries, deep-fried, deep-frying**) to fry food in fat that covers it.

deep-seated adjective firmly established, not superficial ♦ *a deep-seated distrust.*

deep space noun the far distant regions beyond the earth's atmosphere or those beyond the solar system; outer space.

deer noun (**deer**) a fast-running graceful animal, the male of which usually has antlers. [from an Old English word *deor* meaning 'an animal']

deerskin noun leather made from a deer's skin.

deerstalker noun a soft cloth cap, originally worn for hunting, with one peak in front and another at the back.

deface verb to spoil or damage the surface of something, e.g. by scribbling on it. **defacement** noun [from an Old French word]

de facto (dee fak-toh) *adjective* existing in fact, whether by right or not ♦ *a de facto ruler*. [a Latin phrase meaning 'of fact']

defamatory (di-fam-ə-ter-i) *adjective* defaming.

defame (di-**faym**) *verb* to attack or damage a person's good reputation. **defamation** (def-ə-**may**-shən) *noun* [from *de-* and a Latin word *fama* meaning 'fame, reputation']

default *verb* to fail to do what you have agreed to do, especially to pay back a loan. **default** *noun* 1 failure to do something, especially to pay back a loan. 2 a pre-selected option adopted by a computer program when no alternative is specified. **by default** because of lack of opposition or positive action ♦ *The other team didn't arrive in time, so we won by default.* **in default** guilty of default. **defaulter** *noun* [from an Old French word *defaut*]

defeat *verb* 1 to win a victory over someone. SYNONYMS: beat, overcome, conquer, vanquish. 2 to baffle someone or be too difficult for them ♦ *The problem completely defeated me.* 3 to prevent something from being achieved ♦ *This defeats the object of the exercise.* **defeat** *noun* 1 defeating someone. 2 being defeated; a lost battle or contest. [from a Latin word *disfacere* meaning 'to undo, destroy']

defeatist *noun* a person who expects to fail or accepts failure too easily. **defeatist** *adjective* showing that you expect to fail. **defeatism** *noun*

defecate (def-ik-ayt) *verb* (*formal*) to get rid of waste matter from your body. **defecation** *noun* [from *de-* and *faeces*]

defect[1] (di-**fekt** or **dee**-fekt) *noun* a flaw or deficiency. SYNONYMS: flaw, fault, imperfection, weakness, bug (in computing). [from a Latin word *deficere* meaning 'to fail, leave, undo']

defect[2] (di-**fekt**) *verb* to abandon your country or cause in favour of another one. **defection** *noun* **defector** *noun*

defective *adjective* 1 imperfect or faulty. 2 lacking or deficient. **defectively** *adverb* **defectiveness** *noun*

defence *noun* 1 defending something from or resistance against attack. 2 something that defends or protects against attack. 3 a justification put forward in response to an accusation. 4 the defendant's case in a lawsuit. 5 the lawyers representing an accused person. 6 the players in a defending position in a game. **defensible** *adjective* **defensibly** *adverb*

defenceless *adjective* having no defence, unable to defend yourself.

defend *verb* 1 to protect something by warding off an attack. 2 to try to preserve or retain something ♦ *The champion is defending his title.* 3 to try to justify something ♦ *How can you defend such behaviour?* 4 to represent the defendant in a lawsuit. **defender** *noun* [from a Latin word *defendere*]

defendant *noun* a person accused of something or sued in a court of law. (Compare **plaintiff**.)

defensive *adjective* 1 used or done to defend or protect. 2 very anxious to challenge criticism ♦ *There's no need to be so defensive.* **on the defensive** ready to defend yourself against criticism. **defensively** *adverb*

defer[1] *verb* (**deferred, deferring**) to put something off to a later time, to postpone something. **deferment** *noun* [same origin as for *differ*]

defer[2] *verb* (**deferred, deferring**) **to defer to** to give way to a person's wishes, judgement, or authority ♦ *I defer to your superior knowledge.* [from a Latin word *deferre* meaning 'to grant']

deference (def-er-əns) *noun* polite respect; giving way to another person's wishes. **in deference to** out of respect for.

deferential (def-er-en-shəl) *adjective* showing deference. **deferentially** *adverb*

defiance *noun* open disobedience, bold resistance. [from an Old French word *defier* meaning 'to defy']

defiant *adjective* showing defiance, openly disobedient. **defiantly** *adverb*

deficiency (di-fish-ən-si) *noun* (**deficiencies**) 1 a lack or shortage. 2 a failing or defect.

deficiency disease *noun* a disease caused by lack of vitamins or other essential elements in the diet.

deficient (di-fish-ənt) *adjective* 1 not having enough of a quality or ingredient ♦ *This diet is deficient in vitamin B.* 2 insufficient or inadequate. [same origin as for *defect*]

deficit (def-i-sit) *noun* 1 the amount by which a total is smaller than what is required. 2 the amount by which spending is greater than income, or liabilities are greater than assets. [same origin as for *defect*]

defile[1] (di-fiyl) *verb* to make something dirty or impure, to pollute something. **defilement** *noun* [from an old word *defoul*]

defile[2] (di-fiyl) *noun* (also (**dee**-fiyl)) a narrow gorge or pass through which troops can pass only in file.
defile *verb* to march in file. [from a French word]

define *verb* 1 to give the meaning of a word or phrase. 2 to state or explain the scope of something ♦ *Customers' rights are defined by law.* 3 to show clearly the outline of something ♦ *a well-defined image.* 4 to mark out the boundary or limits of something. **definable** *adjective* [from *de-* and a Latin word *finis* meaning 'limit']

definite *adjective* 1 clear and unmistakable, not vague ♦ *I want a definite answer* ♦ *Let's fix a definite time.* 2 certain or settled ♦ *Is it definite that we are to move?* 3 having exact limits. [from a Latin word *definitus* meaning 'defined']

definite article *noun* the word 'the'.

definitely *adverb* without doubt.

definition *noun* 1 a statement of what a word or phrase means or what a thing is. 2 clearness of outline, especially of a photographic image ♦ *The faces lack definition.*

definitive (di-fin-itiv) *adjective* 1 finally fixing or settling something, decisive ♦ *a definitive answer.* 2 the most authoritative of its kind, not able to be bettered ♦ *the definitive history of French cinema.* [same origin as for *define*]

deflate *verb* 1 to let air or gas out of an inflated tyre, balloon, etc. 2 to make someone lose confidence or self-esteem. 3 to reduce or reverse inflation in a country's economy, e.g. by reducing the amount of money in circulation. [from *de-* and *inflate*]

deflation *noun* 1 deflating or being deflated. 2 reduction of the amount of money in circulation in an economy.

deflationary *adjective* causing deflation.

deflect *verb* to make something turn aside. **deflection** *noun* **deflector** *noun* [from *de-* and a Latin word *flectere* meaning 'to bend']

deflower *verb* (*old use*) to deprive a woman of her virginity.

defoliant (dee-**foh**-li-ənt) *noun* a chemical substance that destroys foliage.

defoliate (dee-**foh**-li-ayt) *verb* to remove leaves or foliage from trees or an area, especially by chemical means. **defoliation** *noun* [from *de-* and a Latin word *folium* meaning 'leaf']

deforest *verb* to clear away the trees from an area. **deforestation** *noun*

deform *verb* to spoil the form or appearance of something, to put it out of shape. **deformation** (dee-for-**may**-shən) *noun* [from *de-* and a Latin word *forma* meaning 'shape, form']

deformed *adjective* badly or abnormally shaped.

deformity *noun* (**deformities**) 1 the state of being deformed ♦ *spinal deformity.* 2 a deformed part of the body.

defraud *verb* to get money from someone by fraud. [from *de-* and a Latin word *fraudere* meaning 'to defraud']

defray *verb* to provide money to pay costs or expenses. **defrayal** *noun* [from *de-* and an Old French word *frais* meaning 'cost']

defrost *verb* 1 to thaw something out from frozen ♦ *The pie needs to be defrosted.* 2 to remove frost or ice from something ♦ *I've been defrosting the fridge.*

deft *adjective* skilful and quick, handling things neatly. **deftly** *adverb* **deftness** *noun* [from an Old English word]

defunct (di-**funkt**) *adjective* no longer existing or functioning. [from a Latin word *defunctus* meaning 'finished']

defuse *verb* 1 to remove the fuse from a bomb so that it cannot explode. 2 to make a situation less dangerous or tense.

defy *verb* (**defies, defied, defying**) 1 to resist something openly, to refuse to obey someone. 2 to challenge a person to try and do something that you believe cannot be done ♦ *I defy you to prove this.* 3 to offer difficulties that cannot easily be overcome ♦ *The door defied all attempts to open it.* [from *de-* and a Latin word *fidus* meaning 'faithful']

degauss (dee-**gowss**) *verb* to demagnetize something. [from *de-* and the name of the German physicist K. Gauss (1777–1855)]

degenerate[1] (di-**jen**-er-ayt) *verb* to become worse or lower in standard; to lose good qualities. **degeneration** *noun* [from a Latin word *degeneratus* meaning 'no longer of its kind']

degenerate[2] (di-**jen**-er-ət) *adjective* having become immoral or bad.
degenerate *noun* a morally degenerate person. **degeneracy** *noun*

degradable *adjective* able to be broken down by chemical or biological processes.

degrade *verb* 1 to humiliate or dishonour someone. 2 (*Chemistry*) to cause something to break down chemically or to decompose. 3 (*Physics*) to reduce energy to a less easily convertible form. **degradation** (deg-rə-**day**-shən) *noun* [from *de-* and a Latin word *gradus* meaning 'grade']

degrading *adjective* shaming or humiliating.

degree *noun* 1 a stage in intensity or amount ♦ *a high degree of skill.* 2 a unit for measuring temperature. 3 a unit for measuring angles or arcs, indicated by the symbol °, e.g. 45°. 4 a stage in a scale or series ♦ *third-degree burns.* 5 an academic rank awarded to a person who has successfully completed a course of study at a university or college or as an honour.
[from *de-* and a Latin word *gradus* meaning 'grade']

dehisce (di-**hiss**) *verb* (said especially about seed vessels) to gape or burst open when ripe. **dehiscence** *noun* **dehiscent** *adjective*
[from *de-* and a Latin word *hiscere* meaning 'to begin to gape']

dehumanize *verb* to take away human qualities from someone; to make something impersonal.

dehydrated *adjective* 1 (said about a person) having lost a large amount of water.
2 with all moisture removed. **dehydration** *noun* [from *de-* and a Greek word *hudros* meaning 'of water']

de-ice *verb* to remove ice from a windscreen or other surface. **de-icer** *noun*

deify (**dee**-i-fiy or **day**-i-fiy) *verb* (**deifies, deified, deifying**) to make a god of someone; to treat someone as a god.
deification *noun* [from a Latin word *deus* meaning 'god']

deign (dayn) *verb* to do something that you think is below your dignity ♦ *She did not deign to reply.* [from a Latin word *dignare* meaning 'to deem worthy']

deism (**day**-izm or **dee**-izm) *noun* belief in the existence of a god arising from reason. (Compare **theism**.) **deist** *noun*
[from a Latin word *deus* meaning 'god']

deity (**dee**-iti or **day**-iti) *noun* (**deities**) 1 a god or goddess ♦ *Roman deities.* 2 divine status or nature. [from a Latin word *deus* meaning 'god']

déjà vu (day-zha **vew**) *noun* the feeling that you have already experienced what is happening now. [a French phrase meaning 'already seen']

dejected *adjective* sad or depressed.
dejectedly *adverb* **dejection** *noun* [from *de-* and a Latin word *-jectum* meaning 'thrown']

delay *verb* 1 to make someone or something late, or to be late. SYNONYMS: detain, keep, hold up. 2 to put something off until later, to postpone something. 3 to wait or linger ♦ *Don't delay!* SYNONYMS: hesitate; (*informal*) hang about, drag your feet.
delay *noun* 1 delaying, being delayed.
2 the amount of time for which something is delayed ♦ *a two-hour delay.*
[from an Old French word *delayer*]

delectable *adjective* delightful or delicious.
delectably *adverb* [same origin as for *delight*]

delectation (dee-lek-**tay**-shən) *noun* (*formal*) pleasure or delight ♦ *an evening of song for your delectation.* [same origin as for *delight*]

delegate[1] (**del**-i-gət) *noun* a person who represents others and acts on their instructions.

delegate[2] (**del**-i-gayt) *verb* 1 to entrust a task, power, or responsibility to someone else ♦ *I'm going to delegate this job to one of my assistants.* 2 to appoint or send someone as a representative ♦ *James was delegated to meet the visitors.* [from a Latin word *delegare* meaning 'to entrust']

delegation (del-i-**gay**-shən) *noun* 1 a group of delegates. 2 delegating.

delete (di-**leet**) *verb* 1 to strike out something written or printed. 2 to remove a product from the catalogue of those available to be bought. **deletion** *noun* [from a Latin word *delere* meaning 'to blot out']

deleterious (del-i-**teer**-i-əs) *adjective* causing harm or damage. [from a Greek word *dēlētērios* meaning 'noxious' and *-ous*]

delft or **delftware** *noun* a kind of glazed earthenware, usually decorated in blue on a white background. [from Delft, a town in the Netherlands, where the pottery originated]

deliberate [1] (di-**lib**-er-ət) *adjective* **1** done on purpose, intentional. **2** slow and careful, unhurried ♦ *She entered the room with deliberate steps.* **deliberately** *adverb* [from *de-* and a Latin word *librare* meaning 'to weigh']

deliberate [2] (di-**lib**-er-ayt) *verb* to think over or discuss something carefully before reaching a decision.

deliberation *noun* **1** long and careful consideration or discussion. **2** careful slowness.

deliberative (di-**lib**-er-ətiv) *adjective* for the purpose of considering or discussing things ♦ *a deliberative assembly.*

delicacy *noun* (**delicacies**) **1** delicateness. **2** tact and sensitivity ♦ *Treat this matter with the utmost delicacy.* **3** a choice or expensive food.

delicate *adjective* **1** fine in texture, slender. **2** of exquisite quality or workmanship ♦ *delicate embroidery.* **3** (said about colour or flavour) pleasant and subtle. SYNONYMS: mild, faint, muted. **4** becoming ill easily. **5** fragile and easily damaged. **6** needing tact and careful handling ♦ *a delicate situation.* SYNONYMS: awkward, problematical; (*informal*) sticky. **7** skilful and sensitive ♦ *a player with a delicate touch.* **delicately** *adverb* **delicateness** *noun* [from a Latin word *delicatus* meaning 'delightful']

delicatessen (del-i-kə-**tess**-ən) *noun* a shop selling cooked meats, cheeses, salads, etc. [a German word meaning 'delicacies to eat']

delicious *adjective* tasting or smelling very pleasant. SYNONYMS: tasty, palatable, succulent, delectable, appetizing; (*informal*) mouth-watering, scrumptious, yummy. **deliciously** *adverb* [from a Latin word *deliciae* meaning 'delight, pleasure']

delight *verb* **1** to please someone greatly. SYNONYMS: thrill, gratify, gladden. **2** to take great pleasure in something ♦ *She delights in giving presents.* **delight** *noun* **1** great pleasure. **2** a cause of great pleasure. [from a Latin word *delectare* meaning 'to entice']

delightful *adjective* giving delight. **delightfully** *adverb*

delimit (dee-**lim**-it) *verb* (**delimited**, **delimiting**) to fix the limits or boundaries of something. **delimitation** *noun*

delineate (di-**lin**-i-ayt) *verb* to show something by drawing or describing it. **delineation** *noun* [from a Latin word *delineare* meaning 'to outline']

delinquent (di-**link**-wənt) *adjective* **1** guilty of committing minor crimes. **2** failing to perform a duty. **delinquent** *noun* a delinquent person, especially a young person who breaks the law. **delinquency** *noun* [from a Latin word *delinquere* meaning 'to offend']

deliquesce (del-i-**kwess**) *verb* **1** to become liquid, especially during decomposition. **2** (*Chemistry*) to dissolve in moisture absorbed from the air. **deliquescence** *noun* **deliquescent** *adjective* [from a Latin word *deliquescere* meaning 'to dissolve']

delirious (di-**li**-ri-əs) *adjective* **1** suffering from delirium. **2** wildly excited. **deliriously** *adverb* [same origin as for *delirium*]

delirium (di-**li**-ri-əm) *noun* **1** a state of mental confusion and agitation, especially during feverish illness. **2** wild excitement or emotion. [from a Latin word *delirium* meaning 'deranged']

deliver *verb* **1** to take letters, goods, etc. to the person they are addressed to or to the person who has bought them. **2** to give a speech or lecture. **3** to aim or launch a blow or an attack. **4** to rescue someone or set them free. **5** to provide something you have promised ♦ *We are waiting to see whether the government will deliver on its election pledges.* **6** to help with the birth of a baby. **7** to give birth to a child. **deliverer** *noun* [from *de-* and a Latin word *liberare* meaning 'to set free']

deliverance *noun* being rescued or set free.

delivery *noun* (**deliveries**) **1** delivering something, especially letters or goods ♦ *Your order is ready for delivery.* **2** a regular or scheduled distribution of letters or goods ♦ *We have two deliveries a day.* **3** the manner of delivering a speech ♦ *She has a rather clipped delivery.* **4** a ball bowled in cricket ♦ *the fastest delivery of the match.* **5** the process of giving birth.

dell *noun* a small wooded valley. [from an Old English word]

Delphic *adjective* of or like the ancient Greek oracle at Parnassus, which often gave obscure and enigmatic prophecies.

delphinium *noun* (**delphiniums**) a garden plant with tall spikes of blue flowers. [from a Greek word *delphinion*, related to *dolphin*]

delta *noun* **1** the fourth letter of the Greek alphabet, equivalent to Roman *D*, *d*. **2** a fourth-class mark in an examination. **3** a triangular area at the mouth of a river where it splits into two or more branches ♦ *the Nile Delta*. **deltaic** *adjective* [a Greek word]

delude (di-lood) *verb* to deceive or mislead someone. [from a Latin word *deludere* meaning 'to play unfairly']

deluge (del-yooj) *noun* **1** a great flood. **2** a heavy fall of rain. **3** anything coming in great numbers or a heavy rush ♦ *a deluge of questions*.
the Deluge the flood in Noah's time.
deluge *verb* **1** to come down on someone like a deluge ♦ *The company was deluged with complaints*. **2** to flood a place or region. [from an Old French word]

delusion *noun* **1** a false belief or impression. **2** a persistent false belief that is a symptom or form of madness.
delusional *adjective* **delusive** *adjective*

de luxe *adjective* of very high quality, luxurious. [a French phrase meaning 'of luxury']

delve *verb* **1** to reach inside a bag, drawer, etc. and search for something. **2** to search deeply for information ♦ *This programme delves into the history of gardening*. [from an Old English word *delfan* meaning 'to dig']

demagnetize *verb* to remove the magnetic properties from something.
demagnetization *noun*

demagogue (dem-ə-gog) *noun* a political leader who wins support by making emotional speeches rather than by reasoning. **demagogic** *adjective* [from Greek words *dēmos* meaning 'people' and *agōgos* meaning 'leading']

demand *noun* **1** a firm or forceful request. **2** a desire to have or buy something ♦ *an increase in demand for mobile phones*. **3** an urgent claim ♦ *There are many demands on my time*.
demand *verb* **1** to ask for something firmly or forcefully. **2** to need something ♦ *The work demands great skill*. **in demand** wanted or needed. **on demand** as soon as the demand is made ♦ *payable on demand*. [from *de-* and a Latin word *mandare* meaning 'to order']

demanding *adjective* **1** needing skill or effort ♦ *a demanding job*. **2** needing a lot of attention ♦ *a demanding child*.

demarcation (dee-mar-kay-shən) *noun* fixing the boundary or limits of something. [from a Spanish word *demarcación*]

demean *verb* to lower a person's dignity ♦ *I wouldn't demean myself to ask for it*. [from *de-* and *mean*²]

demeanour *noun* the way a person behaves. [from an Old French word *demener* meaning 'to lead']

demented *adjective* driven mad, crazy. [from *de-* and a Latin word *mentis* meaning 'of the mind']

dementia (di-men-shə) *noun* a serious mental disorder that is characterized by memory loss, personality changes, and impaired reasoning. [from a Latin word *demens* meaning 'out of your mind']

demerara (dem-er-air-ə) *noun* brown raw cane sugar. [named after Demerara in Guyana, South America]

demerit *noun* a fault or defect. [from an Old French word]

demersal (di-mer-səl) *adjective* (said about fish) living close to the bottom of the sea or of a lake. [from *de-* and a Latin word *mersum* meaning 'plunged']

demesne (di-meen) *noun* **1** a landed estate. **2** (*old use*) a domain. [from an Old French word *demeine* meaning 'belonging to a lord']

demi- *prefix* half (as in *demisemiquaver*). [from a French word]

demigod *noun* a partly divine being.

demilitarize *verb* to remove all military forces from an area ♦ *a demilitarized zone*. **demilitarization** *noun*

demise (di-myz) *noun* **1** the end or failure of something. **2** a person's death. [from an Old French word *desmettre* meaning 'to dismiss']

demisemiquaver *noun* (*Music*) a note lasting half as long as a semiquaver.

demist *verb* to clear misty condensation from a windscreen etc. **demister** *noun*

demo noun (**demos**) (*informal*) a demonstration.

demob verb (**demobbed, demobbing**) (*informal*) to demobilize troops.
demob noun (*informal*) demobilization.

demobilize verb to release soldiers etc. from military service. **demobilization** noun

democracy noun (**democracies**)
1 government of a country by representatives elected by the whole people. 2 a country governed in this way. [from a Greek word *dēmos* meaning 'the people' and *-cracy*]

democrat noun a person who supports democracy.
Democrat noun a member of the Democratic Party in the USA.

democratic adjective 1 of, like, or supporting democracy. 2 in accordance with the principle of equal rights for all ♦ a democratic decision.
Democratic adjective to do with the Democratic Party, one of the two main political parties in the USA.
democratically adverb

democratize (di-**mok**-rə-tiyz) verb to make a country etc. democratic.
democratization noun

demodulation noun the process of extracting a modulating radio signal from a modulated wave etc.

demography (di-**mog**-rəfi) noun the study of statistics of births, deaths, diseases, etc., as illustrating the conditions of life in communities. **demographic** adjective [from a Greek word *dēmos* meaning 'the people' and *-graphy*]

demolish verb 1 to pull or knock down a building. 2 to destroy something completely, especially a person's argument or theory etc. 3 (*informal*) to eat food up. **demolition** (dem-ə-**lish**-ən) noun [from *de-* and a Latin word *moliri* meaning 'to build']

demon (**dee**-mən) noun 1 a devil or evil spirit. 2 a forceful or skilful person ♦ a demon on the squash court. 3 a naughty, cruel, or destructive person ♦ She can be a little demon! **demonic** (di-**mon**-ik) adjective [from a Greek word *daimōn* meaning 'a spirit']

demoniac (di-**moh**-ni-ak) adjective 1 of or like a demon. 2 possessed by an evil spirit.

demonize verb to portray someone as wicked or threatening.

demonstrable (di-**mon**-strəb-əl) adjective able to be shown or proved.
demonstrably adverb

demonstrate verb 1 to show evidence of something, to prove it. SYNONYMS: exhibit, display, establish. 2 to show someone how to do something or how something works. 3 to take part in a public demonstration. **demonstrator** noun [from *de-* and a Latin word *monstrare* meaning 'to show']

demonstration noun 1 demonstrating; showing how to do or work something ♦ Let me give you a demonstration. 2 a show of feeling. 3 an organized gathering or march held to express the opinion of a group publicly.

demonstrative (di-**mon**-strə-tiv) adjective 1 showing or proving something. 2 expressing your feelings openly.
demonstratively adverb **demonstrativeness** noun

demonstrative pronoun noun (*Grammar*) a pronoun such as *this*, *that*, *these*, and *those*, that indicates the person or thing it refers to.

demoralize verb to weaken someone's confidence or morale. **demoralization** noun [from *de-* and *morale*]

demote (dee-**moht**) verb to give someone a less senior position. **demotion** noun [from *de-* and *promote*]

demur (di-**mer**) verb (**demurred, demurring**) to raise objections ♦ They demurred at working on Sundays.
demur noun an objection raised ♦ He accepted the decision without demur. [from a Latin word *demorari* meaning 'to delay']

demure (di-**mewr**) adjective shy and modest. **demurely** adverb **demureness** noun [origin unknown]

demystify verb (**demystifies, demystified, demystifying**) to make a subject easier to understand. **demystification** noun

den noun 1 a wild animal's lair. 2 a small room in which a person works or relaxes privately. 3 a place where people gather for some illegal activity ♦ an opium den. [from an Old English word *denn*]

denarius (di-**nair**-iəs) noun (**denarii**) an ancient Roman silver coin. [a Latin word meaning 'containing ten']

denary (**dee**-ner-i) adjective of ten, decimal.

denationalize verb to transfer an industry from public to private ownership. **denationalization** noun

denature verb (*Chemistry*) to make alcohol unfit for drinking by adding toxic or foul-tasting substances. **denaturation** noun

dendrite noun 1 any of the short usually branched outgrowths from a nerve cell, carrying signals into it. 2 a stone or mineral with a natural tree-like marking. 3 this marking. **dendritic** adjective [from a Greek word *dendron* meaning 'tree']

deniable adjective able to be denied.

denial noun 1 denying. 2 a statement that a thing is not true. 3 refusal of a request or wish.

denier (den-yer) noun a unit of weight for measuring the fineness of silk, rayon, or nylon thread. [from a French word]

denigrate (den-i-grayt) verb to blacken the reputation of someone or something. **denigration** noun [from de- and a Latin word *nigare* meaning 'to blacken']

denim noun a kind of strong, usually blue, cotton cloth used to make jeans etc. **denims** plural noun trousers made of denim. [from the French phrase *serge de Nîmes* meaning 'a fabric of Nîmes', a town in southern France]

denitrify (dee-nly-tri-fiy) verb (**denitrifies, denitrified, denitrifying**) to remove the nitrates or nitrites from soil or water. **denitrification** noun

denizen (den-i-zən) noun (*formal*) a person, animal, or plant living or often present in a particular place ♦ *Monkeys are denizens of the jungle.* [from an Old French word *deinz* meaning 'within']

denomination noun 1 a branch of a church or religion ♦ *Baptists and other Protestant denominations.* 2 a unit of money ♦ *coins of small denomination.* 3 (*formal*) a name or title. [from de- and a Latin word *nominare* meaning 'to name']

denominational adjective of a particular religious denomination.

denominator noun the number written below the line in a fraction, e.g. 4 in $\frac{3}{4}$, showing how many parts the whole is divided into. (Compare **numerator**.)

denote (di-**noht**) verb 1 to be the sign of something, to mean or indicate something ♦ *In road signs,* P *denotes a parking place.* 2 (said about a word) to have as its literal or basic meaning, without additional implications. (Compare **connote**.) **denotation** (dee-noh-**tay**-shən)

noun [from de- and a Latin word *notare* meaning 'to mark out']

dénouement (day-noo-mahn) noun the final part of a play or story in which the complications of the plot are cleared up. [a French word meaning 'unravelling']

denounce verb 1 to speak strongly against someone or something. 2 to give information against someone ♦ *They denounced him as a spy.* [from de- and a Latin word *nuntiare* meaning 'to announce']

dense adjective 1 thick, not easy to see through ♦ *dense fog.* 2 crowded or packed closely together ♦ *dense crowds.* 3 (*informal*) stupid. **densely** adverb **denseness** noun [from a Latin word *densus*]

density noun (**densities**) 1 a dense or concentrated condition ♦ *the density of the fog.* 2 the relation of mass to volume ♦ *The density of water is* $62\frac{1}{2}$ *pounds per cubic foot.*

dent noun a hollow in a surface where something has pressed or hit it. **dent** verb 1 to make a dent in something. 2 to have a bad effect on something ♦ *The experience has dented his confidence.* [a different spelling of *dint*]

dental adjective 1 to do with the teeth. 2 to do with dentistry ♦ *a dental practice.* [from a Latin word *dentis* meaning 'of a tooth']

dental surgeon noun a dentist.

dentifrice (dent-i-friss) noun a paste or powder for cleaning the teeth. [from Latin words *dentis* meaning 'of a tooth' and *fricare* meaning 'to rub']

dentine (den-teen) noun the hard dense tissue forming the main part of teeth. [from a Latin word *dent* meaning 'tooth']

dentist noun a person who is qualified to treat the diseases and conditions that affect the teeth and gums.

dentistry noun the work or profession of a dentist.

dentition noun the type and arrangement of teeth in a species or individual.

denture noun a set of artificial teeth. [a French word]

denude verb 1 to make something bare or naked, to strip the cover from something ♦ *The trees were denuded of their leaves.* 2 to take all of something away from a person ♦ *Creditors denuded him of every penny.* 3 (*Geology*) to expose a formation or layer of rock by removing what lies above it.

denudation (dee-new-**day**-shən) *noun*
[from *de-* and a Latin word *nudare* meaning
'to bare']

denunciation (di-nun-si-**ay**-shən) *noun* the
act of denouncing someone or something.
denunciatory *adjective*

deny *verb* (**denies, denied, denying**) 1 to say
that something is not true or does not
exist. SYNONYMS: reject, dispute, contradict,
gainsay. 2 to refuse to give or allow
something ♦ *She doesn't deny her children
anything.* **to deny yourself** to go without
pleasures. [from *de-* and a Latin word
negare meaning 'to say no']

deodorant (dee-oh-der-ənt) *noun* a
substance that removes or conceals
unwanted smells. [from *de-* and a Latin
word *odor* meaning 'a smell']

deodorize *verb* to remove unwanted smells.

deoxygenate *verb* to remove oxygen from
something.

deoxyribonucleic acid see **DNA**.

depart *verb* 1 to go away, to leave. 2 (said
about trains or buses) to start, to begin a
journey. 3 to stop following a particular
course ♦ *Today we will depart from our normal
procedure.* [from an Old French word
départir meaning 'to separate']

departed *adjective* **the departed** a dead
person or dead people.

department *noun* one of the sections into
which a business, shop, or organization is
divided ♦ *the hardware department.* [from a
French word *département* meaning
'division']

departmental (dee-part-**men**-təl) *adjective*
to do with a department. **departmentally**
adverb

department store *noun* a large shop in
which there are various departments
each dealing in a separate type of goods.

departure *noun* 1 departing, going away.
2 a new course of action or thought
♦ *Acting is a departure for me.*

depend *verb* **depend on** 1 to be controlled
or determined by something ♦ *It all
depends on the weather.* 2 to be unable to
do without something ♦ *She depends on my
help.* 3 to rely on someone or something
♦ *I'm depending on you to come.* SYNONYMS:
bank on, count on, rely on. [from *de-* and a
Latin word *pendere* meaning 'to hang']

dependable *adjective* able to be relied on.
dependably *adverb* **dependability** *noun*

dependant *noun* a person who depends on
someone else, especially financially ♦ *He
has four dependants.*
◊ In standard British English usage, the
spelling is *-ant* for the noun and *-ent* for
the adjective. In American English, *-ent* is
used for both.

dependence *noun* depending, being
dependent.

dependency *noun* (**dependencies**) a
country or province that is controlled by
another.

dependent *adjective* 1 depending or
conditional on something else ♦ *Promotion
is dependent on ability.* 2 unable to do
without something ♦ *He is dependent on
drugs.* 3 relying on someone or something
for financial support ♦ *She has three
dependent children.* 4 (*Grammar*) (said about
a clause, phrase, or word) in a subordinate
relation to a sentence or word.
◊ See the note at **dependant**.

depict *verb* 1 to show something in the
form of a picture. 2 to describe
something in words. **depiction** *noun* [from
de- and a Latin word *pictum* meaning
'painted']

depilatory (di-**pil**-ə-ter-i) *adjective* used to
remove unwanted hair.
depilatory *noun* (**depilatories**) a substance
that removes unwanted hair. [from *de-*
and a Latin word *pilus* meaning 'hair']

deplete (di-**pleet**) *verb* to reduce the supply
of something by using up large quantities
of it ♦ *Fish stocks are severely depleted.*
depletion *noun* [from *de-* and a Latin word
-pletum meaning 'filled']

depleted uranium *noun* uranium from
which most of the fissile isotope
uranium-235 has been removed.

deplorable *adjective* shockingly bad or
regrettable. **deplorably** *adverb*

deplore *verb* to feel or express strong
disapproval of something ♦ *We deplore
racism in any form.* [from *de-* and a Latin
word *plorare* meaning 'to weep']

deploy *verb* 1 to place troops or weapons in
position so that they are ready to be used
effectively. 2 to bring something into
effective action ♦ *He deployed his arguments
well.* **deployment** *noun* [from a French word
déployer]

deponent (di-**poh**-nənt) *adjective* (said
about certain verbs in Latin and Greek)

conjugated in the passive or middle voice but active in meaning. [from a Latin word *deponere* meaning 'to put down']

depopulate verb to reduce the population of a place. **depopulation** noun

deport verb to send an unwanted foreign person out of a country. **deportation** noun [from *de-* and a Latin word *portare* meaning 'to carry']

deportee noun a person who has been deported.

deportment noun a person's way of standing and walking. [from an Old French word]

depose verb to remove someone from power or office ♦ *The king was deposed in a military coup.* [from an Old French word *deposer* meaning 'to put down']

deposit noun 1 a sum of money paid into a bank or other account. 2 a sum of money paid as a guarantee or a first instalment. 3 a layer of solid matter deposited or accumulated naturally ♦ *New deposits of copper were found.*
deposit verb (**deposited, depositing**) 1 to put something down ♦ *She deposited the books on the desk.* 2 to store or entrust something for safe keeping, to pay money into a bank. 3 to pay money as a guarantee or first instalment. 4 to leave something as a layer or covering ♦ *Floods deposited mud on the land.* [from *de-* and a Latin word *positum* meaning 'placed']

deposit account noun a bank account that pays interest but from which money cannot be withdrawn without notice.

deposition noun 1 a written piece of evidence, given under oath. 2 the act of deposing someone from power or office. 3 (**the Deposition**) the taking down of Christ from the Cross, especially as a theme in art.

depositor noun a person who deposits money or property.

depository noun (**depositories**) a storehouse for furniture etc.

depot (dep-oh) noun 1 a place where things are stored, especially one used for military supplies. 2 a place where buses, trains, or other vehicles are kept and maintained. 3 (*North Amer.*) a railway or bus station. 4 the headquarters of a regiment. [same origin as for *deposit*]

deprave (di-prayv) verb to make someone morally corrupt. **depravation**

(dep-rǝ-**vay**-shǝn) noun [from *de-* and a Latin word *pravus* meaning 'perverse, wrong']

depraved adjective morally corrupt
♦ *depraved tastes.*

depravity (di-**prav**-iti) noun (**depravities**) moral corruption, wickedness.

deprecate (**dep**-ri-kayt) verb to feel and express disapproval of something. **deprecation** noun **deprecatory** (dep-ri-**kay**-ter-i) adjective [from a Latin word *deprecari* meaning 'to keep away misfortune by prayer']
◊ Do not confuse this word with **depreciate**, which has a different meaning.

depreciate (di-**pree**-shi-ayt) verb 1 to make or become lower in value over a period of time. 2 to disparage or belittle something. [from *de-* and a Latin word *pretium* meaning 'price']
◊ Do not confuse this word with **deprecate**, which has a different meaning.

depreciation noun a decline in value, especially the reduction in the value of a fixed asset charged as an expense when calculating profit and loss.

depreciatory (di-**pree**-shǝ-ter-i) adjective disparaging.

depredation (dep-ri-**day**-shǝn) noun the act of plundering or damaging something. [from *de-* and a Latin word *praedare* meaning 'to plunder']

depress verb 1 to make someone sad or dispirited. 2 to make something less active or lower the value of something ♦ *The stock market is depressed.* 3 to press something down ♦ *Now depress the lever.* **depressing** adjective **depressingly** adverb [from a Latin word *depressum* meaning 'pressed down']

depressant noun a substance that reduces the activity of the nervous system, a sedative.

depression noun 1 a state of great sadness or hopelessness, often with physical symptoms. 2 a long period when trade is very slack because no one can afford to buy things, with widespread unemployment. 3 (*Meteorology*) an area of low air pressure which may bring rain. 4 a sunken place or hollow on a surface. 5 pressing down.

depressive adjective involving or tending to cause depression.

depressive noun a person suffering from mental depression.

depressurize verb to cause the pressure inside an aircraft etc. to drop.

deprivation (dep-ri-vay-shən) noun 1 the lack of the basic benefits that most people have, such as a home and enough food. 2 the lack of something that you need ♦ sleep deprivation.

deprive verb to prevent someone from using or enjoying something ♦ The prisoner had been deprived of food. **deprival** noun [from de- and a Latin word privare meaning 'to rob']

deprived adjective 1 suffering from the effects of a poor or loveless home ♦ a deprived child. 2 with inadequate housing, employment, etc. ♦ a deprived area.

Dept. abbreviation Department.

depth noun 1 how deep something is, the distance from the top down, from the surface inwards, or from the front to the back. 2 being deep. 3 deep learning or thought or feeling ♦ The poem has great depth. 4 intensity of colour or darkness. 5 lowness of pitch in a voice or sound. 6 the deepest or most central part ♦ living in the depths of the country. **in depth** in great detail, thoroughly ♦ I have studied this subject in depth. **out of your depth** 1 in water that is too deep to stand in. 2 trying to do something that is too difficult for you. [from deep]

depth charge noun a bomb that will explode under water, for use against submarines etc.

deputation noun a group of people sent as representatives of others.

depute (di-pewt) verb 1 to appoint a person to do something on your behalf or as your representative ♦ We deputed John to take the message. 2 to delegate a task to someone ♦ We deputed the task to him. [from an Old French word deputer]

deputize verb to act as someone's deputy.

deputy noun (**deputies**) 1 a person appointed to act as substitute for another. 2 a member of a parliament in certain countries ♦ the Chamber of Deputies. [from a French word député meaning 'deputed']

derail verb to make a train leave the tracks. **derailment** noun

derailleur (di-ray-ler) noun a set of externally mounted bicycle gears in which the chain is moved from one gear wheel to another. [from a French word dérailler meaning 'to derail']

deranged adjective insane. **derangement** noun [from de- and a French word rang meaning 'rank']

Derby (dar-bi) noun 1 an annual flat race for three-year-old horses, run on Epsom Downs in Surrey. 2 a similar race or other important sporting contest.
derby noun (**derbies**) a sports match between two rival teams from the same area. [named after the 12th Earl of Derby, who founded the race in 1780]

deregulate verb to free something from regulations or controls. **deregulation** noun

derelict adjective abandoned and left to fall into ruin.
derelict noun 1 a person who is destitute. 2 an abandoned ship or other piece of property. [from de- meaning 'completely' and a Latin word relictum meaning 'left behind']

dereliction (derri-lik-shən) noun 1 neglect of duty. 2 abandoning or being abandoned.

derestrict verb to remove restrictions, especially speed limits, from something ♦ a derestricted road. **derestriction** noun

deride (di-ryd) verb to laugh at someone with contempt or scorn. [from de- and a Latin word ridere meaning 'to laugh']

derision (di-rizh-ən) noun scorn or ridicule. [same origin as for deride]

derisive (di-riy-siv) adjective scornful, showing derision ♦ derisive cheers. **derisively** adverb

derisory (di-riy-ser-i) adjective 1 so small that it is ridiculous ♦ a derisory pay offer. 2 scornful. [same origin as for deride]

derivation (derri-vay-shən) noun 1 deriving or obtaining something from a source. 2 the origin of a word from another language or from a simple word to which a prefix or suffix is added.

derivative (di-riv-ətiv) adjective derived from a source, not original ♦ Their music is rather derivative.
derivative noun 1 a thing that is derived from another. 2 (Mathematics) a quantity measuring the rate of change of another.

derive verb 1 to obtain something from a source ♦ He derived great satisfaction from his work. 2 to form or originate from something ♦ Some English words are derived *from Latin.* [from *de-* and a Latin word *rivus* meaning 'a stream']

derived function *noun* (*Mathematics*) a derivative of a function.

dermatitis (der-mə-**tiy**-tiss) *noun* inflammation of the skin. [from a Greek word *derma* meaning 'skin' and *-itis*]

dermatologist *noun* a specialist in dermatology.

dermatology (der-ma-**tol**-əji) *noun* the scientific study of the skin and its diseases. [from a Greek word *derma* meaning 'skin' and *-logy*]

dermis *noun* the layer of skin below the epidermis. [a Latin word, from a Greek word *derma* meaning 'skin']

derogatory (di-**rog**-ə-ter-i) *adjective* scornful or disparaging. [from a Latin word *derogare* meaning 'to make smaller']

derrick *noun* 1 a kind of crane with an arm pivoted to the base of a central post or to a floor. 2 a tall framework over an oil well, holding the drilling machinery. [this word originally meant 'a gallows', named after Derrick, a London hangman in about 1600]

derv *noun* diesel fuel for motor vehicles. [from the initials of *d*iesel-*e*ngined *r*oad *v*ehicle]

dervish *noun* a member of a Muslim religious order, vowed to live a life of poverty. [from a Persian word *darvish* meaning 'poor']

desalinate *verb* to remove the salt from seawater. **desalination** *noun*

descale *verb* to remove scale from a kettle or boiler etc.

descant *noun* a melody sung or played in accompaniment to the main melody. [from *dis-* and a Latin word *cantus* meaning 'song']

descend *verb* 1 to come or go down. 2 to slope or lead downwards. 3 to make a sudden attack or visit ♦ *I hope you don't mind us descending on you like this.* 4 to sink to immoral or unworthy behaviour ♦ *I never thought he would descend to violence.* 5 to be passed down by inheritance ♦ *The title descended to his son.* **to be descended from** to have someone as an ancestor; to come by birth from a certain person or family. [from an Old French word *descendre*]

descendant *noun* a person who is descended from another.

descent *noun* 1 descending. 2 a way by which you may descend. 3 a downward slope. 4 a person's family origin ♦ *She is of French descent.*

describe *verb* 1 to say what something is like ♦ *How would you describe your sister?* SYNONYMS: characterize, define, portray. 2 to give an account of something ♦ *Can you describe what happened?* SYNONYMS: recount, relate, outline, detail. 3 to draw the outline of something, to move in a certain pattern ♦ *The orbit of the Earth around the Sun describes an ellipse.* [from *de-* and a Latin word *scribere* meaning 'to write']

description *noun* 1 describing. 2 an account or picture in words. 3 a kind or class of thing ♦ *There's no food of any description.*

descriptive *adjective* 1 giving a description. 2 (said about grammatical rules etc.) describing or classifying what is actually done, not making judgements.

desecrate (**dess**-i-krayt) *verb* to treat a sacred thing with irreverence or disrespect. **desecration** *noun* **desecrator** *noun* [from *de-* and *consecrate*]

desegregate *verb* to end a policy of racial segregation. **desegregation** *noun*

deselect *verb* (said about a political party) to reject an existing MP as a candidate in a coming election. **deselection** *noun*

desert[1] (**dez**-ert) *noun* a large area of dry often sand-covered land. [from a Latin word *desertus* meaning 'abandoned']

desert[2] (di-**zert**) *verb* 1 to abandon a person or place without intending to return. 2 to leave service in the armed forces without permission. **deserter** *noun* **desertion** *noun* [same origin as for *desert*[1]]

deserted *adjective* empty or abandoned ♦ *a deserted house.*

desert island *noun* an uninhabited island.

deserts (di-**zerts**) *plural noun* what a person deserves ♦ *He got his deserts.* [from *deserve*]

deserve *verb* to be worthy of or entitled to something. [from a Latin word *deservire* meaning 'to serve someone well']

deservedly (di-**zerv**-idli) *adverb* according to what is deserved, justly.

deserving *adjective* worth rewarding or supporting ♦ *a deserving charity.*

desiccate verb (**dess**-i-kayt) to remove the moisture from something, especially to dry solid food in order to preserve it ♦ *desiccated coconut.* **desiccation** noun **desiccator** noun [from a Latin word *desiccare* meaning 'to make thoroughly dry']

design noun 1 a drawing that shows how something is to be made or built. 2 the art of making such drawings ♦ *She studied design.* 3 the way something is made or arranged ♦ *The design of the building is good.* 4 a combination of lines and shapes that form a decoration. 5 a mental plan or scheme.
design verb 1 to prepare a drawing or design showing how something is to be made. 2 to intend something for a specific purpose ♦ *The book is designed for students.* **by design** on purpose. **to have designs on** to plan to get hold of something. [from *de-* and a Latin word *signare* meaning 'to mark out']

designate [1] (**dez**-ig-nayt) verb 1 to give a name or title to something ♦ *It has been designated an area of outstanding natural beauty.* 2 to mark or point something out clearly, to specify something ♦ *The river was designated as the western boundary.* 3 to appoint someone to a position ♦ *He designated Smith as his successor.* [same origin as for *design*]

designate [2] (**dez**-ig-nət) adjective appointed to a job or office but not yet doing it ♦ *the bishop designate.* [same origin as for *design*]

designation (dez-ig-**nay**-shən) noun 1 designating. 2 an official name or title.

designer noun 1 someone who designs something, especially clothes. 2 (before a noun) exclusive or fashionable ♦ *designer drugs.*

desirable adjective 1 worth having or doing. 2 arousing sexual desire. **desirably** adverb **desirability** noun

desire noun 1 a feeling of wanting something very much. SYNONYMS: longing, craving, appetite, hunger, thirst, love, passion, yearning. 2 a request or wish ♦ *He expressed a desire to rest.* 3 something that you want very much ♦ *She has achieved her heart's desire.*
desire verb 1 to have a desire for something. 2 to want someone sexually. [from a Latin word *desiderare*]

desirous adjective having a desire or wish.

desist (di-**zist**) verb to stop doing something. [from a Latin word *desistere*]

desk noun 1 a piece of furniture with a flat top and often with drawers, used when writing or doing work. 2 a counter in a hotel, bank, airport, etc. ♦ *Ask at the information desk.* 3 the section of a news organization dealing with specified topics ♦ *the sports desk.* [from a late Latin word *desca*]

desktop publishing noun the production of high-quality printed matter using a computer and printer.

desolate (**dess**-ə-lət) adjective 1 uninhabited or barren ♦ *a desolate moor.* 2 forlorn and unhappy. [from a Latin word *desolare* meaning 'to abandon']

desolation noun 1 a desolate or barren condition. 2 grief or wretchedness.

despair noun complete loss or lack of hope.
despair verb to lose all hope ♦ *I despaired of ever seeing her again.* **to be the despair of** to be the cause of despair in someone. **despairing** adjective **despairingly** adverb [from *de-* and a Latin word *sperare* meaning 'to hope']

despatch noun & verb another spelling of **dispatch**.

desperate adjective 1 leaving little or no hope, extremely serious ♦ *a desperate situation.* 2 having a great need or desire for something ♦ *They are desperate to get tickets.* 3 reckless and ready to do anything. 4 done or used in a nearly hopeless situation. **desperately** adverb [same origin as for *despair*]

desperation noun 1 hopelessness. 2 being desperate; recklessness caused by despair.

despicable (di-**spik**-ə-bəl or **dess**-pik-ə-bəl) adjective deserving hatred and contempt. **despicably** adverb [from a late Latin word *despicari* meaning 'to look down on']

despise verb to regard someone as inferior or worthless, to feel disrespect for someone. [from *de-* and a Latin word *specere* meaning 'to look at']

despite preposition in spite of. [same origin as for *despise*]

despoil verb to plunder or rob a place. **despoliation** noun [from a Latin word *despoliare* meaning 'to rob or plunder']

despondent adjective in low spirits, dejected. **despondently** adverb **despondency** noun [from a Latin word *despondere* meaning 'to give up, resign']

despot (**dess**-pot) *noun* a tyrant, a ruler who has unrestricted power. [from a Greek word *despotēs* meaning 'master']

despotic (dis-**pot**-ik) *adjective* having unrestricted power. **despotically** *adverb*

despotism (**dess**-pət-izm) *noun* tyranny, government by a despot.

dessert (di-**zert**) *noun* the sweet course of a meal. [from a French word *desservir* meaning 'to clear the table']

dessertspoon *noun* a medium-sized spoon used for eating puddings etc. **dessertspoonful** *noun* (**dessertspoonfuls**)

destination *noun* the place to which a person or thing is going or being sent. [same origin as for *destiny*]

destine (**dess**-tin) *verb* **to be destined** to be chosen or set apart for a purpose, sometimes thought of as being determined in advance by fate ♦ *He was destined to become President.* [from a Latin word *destinare* meaning 'to fix, settle']

destiny *noun* (**destinies**) **1** fate considered as a power. **2** what will happen or has happened to a person or thing, thought of as determined in advance by fate. [from a Latin word *destinare* meaning 'to fix, settle']

destitute *adjective* **1** living in extreme poverty, without food, shelter, etc. **2** lacking in something ♦ *a landscape destitute of trees.* **destitution** *noun* [from a Latin word *destitutus* meaning 'left in the lurch']

destroy *verb* **1** to damage something so much that it is completely spoiled or made useless. SYNONYMS: wreck, demolish, annihilate. **2** to put an end to something ♦ *It destroyed our chances.* SYNONYMS: wreck, ruin, finish off. **3** to kill an animal by humane means ♦ *The dog had to be destroyed.* [from *de-* and a Latin word *struere* meaning 'to pile up']

destroyer *noun* **1** someone or something that destroys. **2** a small fast warship equipped with guns and torpedoes for protecting other ships.

destruction *noun* **1** destroying or being destroyed. **2** a cause of destruction or ruin ♦ *Greed was his destruction.*

destructive *adjective* causing destruction; frequently destroying things.

desultory (**dess**-əl-ter-i) *adjective* doing something in a half-hearted way, without enthusiasm or a definite plan. **desultorily**

adverb [from a Latin word *desultorius* meaning 'like an acrobat', someone who leaps about]

detach *verb* to release or remove one thing from something else or from a group. [from *de-* and *attach*]

detachable *adjective* able to be detached.

detached *adjective* **1** (said about a house) not joined to another. **2** free from emotion or bias; objective ♦ *Journalists need to remain detached.*

detachment *noun* **1** freedom from emotion or bias. **2** a group of soldiers, ships, etc. sent away from a larger group for a special duty. **3** detaching or being detached.

detail *noun* **1** a small individual item or feature. **2** the minor decoration in a building or picture etc. ♦ *Look at the detail in the carvings.* **3** a small detachment of soldiers or police officers given a special duty.
detail *verb* **1** to describe something fully, item by item. **2** to give soldiers etc. a special duty. **in detail** describing the individual parts or events etc. fully. [from *de-* and a French word *tailler* meaning 'to cut in pieces']

detailed *adjective* giving many details.

detain *verb* **1** to keep someone waiting or delay them. **2** to keep someone at a police station, prison, etc. [from *de-* and a Latin word *tenere* meaning 'to hold']

detainee (di-tayn-**ee**) *noun* a person who is held in custody, especially for political reasons.

detect *verb* **1** to discover the existence or presence of something. **2** to find a person doing something bad or secret. **detectable** *adjective* [from *de-* and a Latin word *tectum* meaning 'covered']

detection *noun* **1** detecting or being detected. **2** the work of a detective.

detective *noun* a person, especially a police officer, whose job is to investigate crimes.

detective story *noun* a story about crime and the detection of criminals.

detector *noun* a device for detecting the presence of something ♦ *a smoke detector.*

détente (day-**tahnt**) *noun* the easing of strained relations between countries. [a French word meaning 'relaxation']

detention *noun* **1** detaining or being detained. **2** being kept in school after hours as a punishment. **3** being kept in custody. [same origin as for *detain*]

detention centre *noun* an institution where young offenders are kept in detention for a short time.

deter *verb* (**deterred, deterring**) to discourage or prevent someone from doing something through fear or dislike of the consequences. [from *de-* and a Latin word *terrere* meaning 'to frighten']

detergent *noun* a substance used for cleaning or washing things, especially a synthetic substance other than soap. **detergent** *adjective* having a cleansing effect. [from *de-* and a Latin word *tergere* meaning 'to clean']

deteriorate (di-teer-ior-ayt) *verb* to become worse. **deterioration** *noun* [from a Latin word *deterior* meaning 'worse']

determinable *adjective* able to be settled or calculated ♦ *Its age is not determinable.*

determinant *noun* **1** a factor which determines the nature or outcome of something. **2** (*Mathematics*) the quantity obtained by adding the products of the elements of a square matrix according to a certain rule.
determinant *adjective* determining or deciding something.

determinate (di-ter-min-ət) *adjective* limited, of fixed and definite scope or nature.

determination *noun* **1** the firm intention to achieve what you have decided to achieve. **2** the process of deciding, determining, or calculating something.

determine *verb* **1** to find out or calculate something precisely ♦ *Can you determine the height of the mountain?* **2** to firmly decide to do something ♦ *He determined to confront her.* **3** to be the decisive factor or influence on something ♦ *Income determines your standard of living.* [from *de-* and a Latin word *terminare* meaning 'to set a limit']

determined *adjective* full of determination, with your mind firmly made up.
SYNONYMS: firm, resolute, adamant, resolved.
determinedly *adverb*

determinism *noun* the theory that human action is not free but is determined by external forces acting on the will.
determinist *noun* **deterministic** *adjective*

deterrent (di-te-rənt) *adjective* able or intended to deter people.

deterrent *noun* something that may deter people, such as a nuclear weapon that deters countries from attacking the one that has it. **deterrence** *noun*

detest *verb* to dislike something intensely, to loathe something. **detestation** *noun* [from a Latin word *detestari*]

detestable *adjective* intensely disliked, hateful. **detestably** *adverb*

dethrone *verb* to remove someone from a throne, to depose someone. **dethronement** *noun*

detonate (det-ən-ayt) *verb* to explode or cause something to explode. **detonation** *noun* [from *de-* meaning 'thoroughly' and a Latin word *tonare* meaning 'to thunder']

detonator *noun* a device for detonating an explosive.

detour (dee-toor) *noun* a roundabout route instead of the normal one ♦ *We had to make a detour.* [from a French word *détourner* meaning 'to turn away']

detoxify (dee-toks-i-fiy) *verb* (**detoxifies, detoxified, detoxifying**) to remove poison or harmful substances from something or someone. **detoxification** *noun* [from *de-* and a Latin word *toxicum* meaning 'poison']

detract *verb* **detract from** to take away a part or amount from something, to make something seem less valuable or impressive ♦ *It will not detract from our pleasure.* **detraction** *noun* [from *de-* and a Latin word *tractum* meaning 'pulled']

detractor *noun* a person who criticizes something unfavourably.

detriment (det-ri-mənt) *noun* harm or damage ♦ *She worked long hours, to the detriment of her health.* [from a Latin word *detrimentum* meaning 'worn away']

detrimental (det-ri-men-təl) *adjective* causing harm. **detrimentally** *adverb*

detritus (di-triy-təs) *noun* **1** loose pieces of gravel, silt, sand, etc. produced by erosion. **2** rubbish or debris. [from *de-* and a Latin word *tritum* meaning 'worn']

deuce[1] *noun* (in tennis) a score in which both sides have 40 points and must win two consecutive points to win. [from an Old French word *deus* meaning 'two']

deuce [2] *noun* (*old use*) used in exclamations of surprise or annoyance to mean 'devil'
♦ *What the deuce!* [from a Low German word *duus* meaning 'two', the worst throw at dice]

deus ex machina (day-əs eks mak-in-ə) *noun* an unexpected power or event that saves a seemingly impossible situation. [a Latin phrase meaning 'god from the machinery', with reference to the machinery by which, in ancient Greek theatre, gods were shown in the air]

deuterium (dew-teer-iəm) *noun* a stable isotope of hydrogen with a mass approximately twice that of the usual isotope. [from a Greek word *deuteros* meaning 'second']

deuteron (dew-ter-on) *noun* the nucleus of a deuterium atom.

Deutschmark (doich-mark) *noun* the unit of money in Germany. [from German words *deutsche Mark* meaning 'German mark']

deva (day-və) *noun* a member of a class of divine beings in the Vedic period, which in Indian mythology are benevolent and in Zoroastrianism are evil. (See also *asura*.) [a Sanskrit word meaning 'shining one']

devalue *verb* 1 to reduce the value of something. 2 to reduce the value of a country's currency in relation to other currencies or to gold. **devaluation** *noun*

devastate *verb* 1 to ruin or cause great destruction to something. 2 to overwhelm someone with shock or grief. **devastation** *noun* [from *de-* meaning 'thoroughly' and a Latin word *vastare* meaning 'to lay waste']

devastating *adjective* 1 causing great destruction. 2 causing great shock or grief ♦ *devastating news.*

develop *verb* (**developed, developing**) 1 to make or become larger or more advanced. SYNONYMS: grow, evolve, progress, flourish, advance, improve. 2 to bring or come gradually into existence ♦ *A storm developed.* 3 to begin to exhibit or suffer from something ♦ *They developed bad habits.* SYNONYMS: acquire, evolve, cultivate. 4 to use an area of land for building houses, shops, factories, etc. 5 to treat a photographic film or plate etc. with chemicals so that the picture becomes visible. [from a French word *développer*]

developer *noun* 1 a person or firm that develops land. 2 a substance used for developing photographic film etc.

developing country *noun* a poor agricultural country that is developing better economic and social conditions.

development *noun* 1 developing or being developed. 2 something that has developed, especially an event that changes a situation ♦ *the latest developments in the peace process.* 3 an area of land with new buildings on it.

deviant (dee-vi-ənt) *adjective* deviating from what is accepted as normal or usual. **deviant** *noun* a person who deviates from accepted standards in beliefs or behaviour.

deviate (dee-vi-ayt) *verb* to turn aside from a course or from what is usual or true. **deviator** *noun* [from *de-* and a Latin word *via* meaning 'way']

deviation *noun* 1 the action of deviating. 2 (*Statistics*) the amount by which a single measurement differs from a fixed value such as the mean.

device *noun* 1 a thing that is made or used for a particular purpose ♦ *a device for opening tins.* SYNONYMS: implement, instrument, tool, contraption, gadget, appliance. 2 a plan or scheme for achieving something. 3 a design used as a decoration or emblem. **to leave someone to their own devices** to leave them to do as they wish without help or advice. [same origin as for *devise*]

devil *noun* 1 (**the Devil**) in Jewish and Christian belief, the supreme spirit of evil and enemy of God. 2 an evil spirit. 3 a wicked or cruel person. 4 a clever or mischievous person ♦ *You cunning devil!* 5 something difficult or hard to manage. 6 (*informal*) a person ♦ *The lucky devil!* ♦ *You poor devil!.* **devilish** *adjective* [via Old English from Latin]

devilment *noun* mischief.

devilry *noun* wickedness or mischief.

devil's advocate *noun* a person who tests a theory by putting forward possible objections to it.

devious (dee-vi-əs) *adjective* 1 not straightforward, underhand. 2 (said about a route or journey) winding or roundabout. **deviously** *adverb* **deviousness** *noun* [same origin as for *deviate*]

devise (di-vyz) *verb* 1 to plan or invent something. 2 (*Law*) to leave real estate by will. [from an Old French word *deviser*]

devoid (di-**void**) *adjective* lacking or free from something ♦ *His work is devoid of merit.* [from *de-* and an Old French word *voider* meaning 'to make void']

devolution (dee-və-**loo**-shən) *noun* 1 handing over power from central government to local or regional government ♦ *Scottish devolution.* 2 the handing down of property to an heir. [same origin as for *devolve*]

devolve *verb* 1 to hand over power to a lower level, especially from central government to local or regional government. 2 to pass or be passed on to a deputy or successor ♦ *This work will devolve on the new manager.* [from a Latin word *devolvere* meaning 'to roll down']

devote *verb* to give something completely for a particular activity or purpose ♦ *He devoted all his time to sport.* [from *de-* and a Latin word *vovere* meaning 'to vow']

devoted *adjective* very loving or loyal. **devotedly** *adverb*

devotee (dev-ə-**tee**) *noun* a person who is devoted to something, an enthusiast.

devotion *noun* 1 great love, loyalty, or enthusiasm for someone or something. 2 religious worship. **devotions** *plural noun* prayers.

devotional *adjective* used in religious worship.

devour *verb* 1 to eat something hungrily or greedily. 2 to destroy something completely, to consume something ♦ *Fire devoured the forest.* 3 to take something in greedily with the eyes or ears ♦ *They devoured the story.* 4 to absorb the attention of someone ♦ *She was devoured by curiosity.* [from *de-* meaning 'completely' and a Latin word *vorare* meaning 'to swallow']

devout *adjective* 1 deeply religious. 2 earnest or sincere ♦ *a devout supporter.* **devoutly** *adverb* **devoutness** *noun* [same origin as for *devote*]

dew *noun* 1 small drops of moisture that condense on cool surfaces during the night from water vapour in the air. 2 moisture in small drops on a surface. [from an Old English word]

dewdrop *noun* a drop of dew.

dewlap *noun* a fold of loose skin that hangs from the throat of cattle and other animals.

dew point *noun* the temperature at which vapour condenses into dew.

dew pond *noun* an artificial shallow pond lined with clay etc., used to collect and store rainwater in areas where the supply from springs or surface drainage is inadequate.

dewy *adjective* (**dewier, dewiest**) wet with dew.

dewy-eyed *adjective* with eyes moist with tears because of sentimentality or nostalgia.

dexter *adjective* (*Heraldry*) of or on the right-hand side (the observer's left) of a coat of arms. [from a Latin word *dexter* meaning 'on the right-hand side']

dexterity (deks-**te**-riti) *noun* skill in using your hands or mind. [same origin as for *dexter*]

dexterous or **dextrous** (**deks**-trəs) *adjective* showing dexterity. **dexterously** *adverb*

dextrose (**deks**-trohs) *noun* the most common naturally occurring form of glucose.

DfEE *abbreviation* Department for Education and Employment.

dhal *noun* an Indian dish made from split pulses. [from a Hindi word]

dharma (**dar**-mə) *noun* in Indian religion, the eternal law of the Hindu cosmos, what is and what should be. [a Sanskrit word meaning 'decree']

dhobi *noun* (**dhobis**) (in the Indian subcontinent) a person who washes clothes for a living. [from a Hindi word]

dhoti (**doh**-ti) *noun* (**dhotis**) a loincloth worn by male Hindus. [from a Hindi word]

dhow (dow) *noun* a ship of the Arabian Sea, with a triangular sail on a slanting yard. [from an Arabic word]

DI *abbreviation* detective inspector.

di- *prefix* two or double (as in *dioxide*). [from a Greek word *dis* meaning 'twice']

dia- *prefix* through or across (as in *diagonal*). [from a Greek word *dia* meaning 'through']

diabetes (diy-ə-**bee**-teez) *noun* a disease in which sugar and starch are not properly absorbed by the body. [via Latin from a Greek word *diabētēs* meaning 'siphon']

diabetic (diy-ə-**bet**-ik) *adjective* to do with or having diabetes.

diabetic *noun* a person suffering from diabetes.

diabolical (diy-ə-**bol**-ikəl) *adjective* 1 like a devil, very cruel or wicked. 2 very clever or annoying ♦ *a diabolical puzzle.* **diabolically** *adverb* [from a Latin word *diabolus* meaning 'devil']

diadem (**diy**-a-dem) *noun* a jewelled crown or headband worn as a sign of sovereignty. [from a Greek word]

diaeresis (diy-**eer**-i-sis) *noun* (**diaereses**) a mark placed over a vowel to show that it is sounded separately, as in *naïve.* [from a Greek word *diairesis* meaning 'separation']

diagnose (**diy**-əg-nohz) *verb* to find out what disease a person has or what is wrong ♦ *Typhoid fever was diagnosed in six patients.*

diagnosis (diy-əg-**noh**-sis) *noun* (**diagnoses**) a statement of the nature of a disease or other condition made after observing its signs and symptoms. [from *dia-* and a Greek word *gignōskein* meaning 'to know']

diagnostic (diy-əg-**noss**-tik) *adjective* to do with or used in diagnosis ♦ *diagnostic procedures.*

diagonal (diy-**ag**-ən-əl) *adjective* slanting, crossing from corner to corner. **diagonal** *noun* a straight line joining two opposite corners. **diagonally** *adverb* [from *dia-* and a Greek word *gōnia* meaning 'angle']

diagram *noun* 1 an outline drawing that shows the parts of something or how it works. 2 a drawing explaining the course of a process or representing a series of quantities. [from *dia-* and *-gram*]

diagrammatic (diy-ə-grə-**mat**-ik) *adjective* in the form of a diagram. **diagrammatically** *adverb*

dial *noun* 1 a disc marked with a scale for measuring something and having a movable pointer that indicates the amount registered. 2 a disc on a radio or television set, turned to choose a wavelength or channel. 3 the face of a clock or watch. 4 a disc with finger-holes over a circle of numbers on an old type of telephone, turned in order to make a call. **dial** *verb* (**dialled, dialling**) to telephone a number by turning a telephone dial or pressing numbered buttons ♦ *He dialled the operator.* [from a Latin word *diale* meaning 'clock face', from *dies* meaning 'day']

dialect (**diy**-ə-lekt) *noun* the words and pronunciations that are used in a particular area and differ from what is regarded as standard in the language as a whole. [from a Greek word *dialektos* meaning 'way of speaking']

dialectic (diy-ə-**lek**-tik) *noun* (*Philosophy*) investigation of truths by systematic reasoning.

dialectical (diy-ə-**lek**-tik-əl) *adjective* to do with dialectic.

dialectical materialism *noun* the theory, put forward by Marx and Engels, that political and social conditions result from a conflict of social forces (the 'class struggle') produced by economic factors.

dialog box or **dialogue box** *noun* (*Computing*) a small area on a computer screen in which the user is prompted to choose commands or give information.

dialogue (**diy**-ə-log) *noun* 1 the words spoken by characters in a play, film, or story. 2 a conversation or discussion. [from a Greek word *dialogos*]

dialysis (diy-**al**-i-sis) *noun* (**dialyses**) purification of the blood by causing it to flow through a suitable membrane. [from *dia-* and a Greek word *lusis* meaning 'loosening']

diamanté (dee-ə-**mahn**-tay) *adjective* decorated with fragments of crystal or another sparkling substance. [a French word]

diameter (diy-**am**-it-er) *noun* 1 a line drawn straight across a circle or sphere and passing through its centre. 2 the length of this line. [from a Greek word *diametros* meaning 'measuring across']

diametrical (diy-ə-**met**-rik-əl) *adjective* 1 (said about opposites) complete or absolute ♦ *He is the diametrical opposite of my last boss.* 2 to do with or along a diameter. **diametrically** *adverb*

diamond *noun* 1 a very hard brilliant precious stone of pure crystallized carbon. 2 a figure or shape with four equal sides and with angles that are not right angles. 3 a playing card of the suit marked with red diamond shapes on it. **diamonds** *plural noun* in cards, the suit marked with red diamond shapes on it. **diamond** *adjective* made of or set with diamonds. [from a Greek word *adamas* meaning 'adamant', a very hard stone]

diamond jubilee noun the 60th anniversary of an event.

diamond wedding noun the 60th anniversary of a wedding.

diapason (diy-ə-**pay**-sən or -zən) noun (Music) 1 an organ stop sounding a main register of flue pipes. 2 a swelling burst of harmony. [via Latin from Greek words dia pasōn (khordōn) meaning 'through all (notes)']

diaper (diy-ə-per) noun (North Amer.) a baby's nappy. [from a Greek word diaspros meaning 'made of white cloth']

diaphanous (diy-**af**-ən-əs) adjective (said about fabric) light, delicate, and almost transparent. [from dia- and a Greek word phainein meaning 'to show']

diaphragm (diy-ə-fram) noun 1 the muscular layer inside the body that separates the chest from the abdomen and is used in breathing. 2 a dome-shaped contraceptive cap fitting over the neck of the womb. 3 a vibrating disc in a microphone or telephone receiver etc. 4 a device for varying the aperture of a camera lens. [from dia- and a Greek word phragma meaning 'fence']

diarist (**diy**-er-ist) noun someone who keeps a diary.

diarrhoea (diy-ə-**ree**-ə) noun a condition in which bowel movements are very frequent and watery. [from dia- and a Greek word rhoia meaning 'a flow']

diary noun (diaries) 1 a book for keeping a daily record of events. 2 a book for noting future appointments. [from a Latin word dies meaning 'day']

diaspora (diy-**ass**-per-ə) noun the dispersing of the Jews beyond Israel in the 8th to 6th centuries and later. [from a Greek word]

diastase (**diy**-ə-stayss) noun (Biochemistry) another word for amylase. [from a Greek word]

diastole (diy-**ass**-təli) noun the period between two contractions of the heart when the heart muscle relaxes and allows the chambers to fill with blood. (Compare systole.) **diastolic** (diy-ə-**stol**-ik) adjective [from a Greek word meaning 'separation']

diatom (**diy**-ə-tom) noun a one-celled microscopic alga found as plankton and forming fossil deposits. [from dia- and a Greek word tomē meaning 'cutting']

diatomic (diy-ə-**tom**-ik) adjective consisting of two atoms. [from di- and atom]

diatonic (diy-ə-**tonn**-ik) adjective (Music) using the notes of the major or minor scale only, not of the chromatic scale. [from a Greek word diatonikos meaning 'at intervals of one tone']

diatribe (**diy**-ə-tryb) noun a strong and bitter verbal attack. [from a French word]

diazepam (diy-**az**-ə-pam) noun a drug used as a tranquillizer and sedative.

dibble noun a hand tool used to make holes in the ground for seeds or young plants. [origin uncertain]

dice noun 1 (strictly the plural of die[2], but often used as a singular) (dice) a small cube marked on each side with a number of spots (1–6), used in games. 2 a game played with these.
dice verb to cut meat, vegetables, etc. into small cubes ♦ diced carrots. **to dice with death** to take dangerous risks. [plural of die[2]]

dicey adjective (dicier, diciest) (informal) risky or unreliable.

dichotomy (diy-**kot**-əmi) noun (dichotomies) a division into two entirely different parts or kinds ♦ a dichotomy between his public and private lives. [from Greek words dikho- meaning 'apart' and tomē meaning 'cutting']

dichromate (diy-**kroh**-mayt) noun a salt of an acid whose ions contain two chromium atoms.

dickens noun (informal) used in exclamation of surprise or annoyance ♦ What the dickens is going on? [a euphemism for 'devil', probably from a use of the surname Dickens]

dicotyledon (diy-kot-i-**lee**-dən) noun a flowering plant that has two cotyledons.

dictate verb 1 to say or read something aloud for someone else to type or write down. 2 to state or order something with the force of authority ♦ We are in a strong enough position to dictate terms. 3 to give orders in a bossy way ♦ I will not be dictated to. **dictation** noun [from a Latin word dictare meaning 'to keep saying']

dictates (dik-tayts) plural noun commands or principles that must be obeyed ♦ the dictates of conscience.

dictator noun 1 a ruler who has unlimited power, especially one who has taken control by force. 2 a person with supreme authority in any sphere. **3** a domineering person. **dictatorial** *adjective* **dictatorship** *noun*

diction (dik-shən) *noun* **1** a person's way of speaking or pronouncing words ♦ *clear diction*. **2** the choice of words used by a writer or poet. [from a Latin word *dictio* meaning 'saying, word']

dictionary *noun* (**dictionaries**) a book that lists and explains the words of a language or the words and topics of a particular subject, or that gives their equivalents in another language, usually in alphabetical order. [from a Latin word *dictio* meaning 'word']

dictum *noun* (**dicta** or **dictums**) **1** a formal expression of an opinion. **2** a saying or maxim. [from a Latin word meaning 'something said']

did past tense of **do**.

didactic (diy-dak-tik) *adjective* **1** meant to teach or give instruction. **2** having the manner of someone who is lecturing people. **didactically** *adverb* [from a Greek word *didaktikos* meaning 'teaching']

diddle *verb* (*informal*) to cheat or swindle someone. [origin unknown]

didn't *verb* (*informal*) did not.

die [1] *verb* (**dies, died, dying**) **1** to stop living or existing. SYNONYMS: expire, perish, pass away; (*informal*) kick the bucket, bite the dust. **2** to cease to function, to stop working ♦ *The engine sputtered and died.* **3** (said about a fire or flame) to go out. **4** to be forgotten ♦ *Her name will never die.* **5** to want to die or have something very much ♦ *We are all dying to see you* ♦ *I'm dying for a drink.* **to die away** to become fainter or weaker and then stop ♦ *The noise died away.* **to die down** to become less loud or less violent ♦ *The excitement died down.* **to die off** to die one by one. **to die out** to pass out of existence. [from an Old Norse word]

die [2] *noun* **1** a dice (see **dice**). **2** a device for stamping a design on coins or medals or for stamping, cutting, or moulding material into a particular shape. **the die is cast** a step has been taken and its consequences must follow. **as straight as a die 1** completely straight. **2** entirely open and honest.　[from an Old French word]

die-cast *adjective* made by pouring molten metal into a mould.

die-casting *noun* making metal objects by pouring molten metal into a mould.

diehard *noun* a person who stubbornly resists change. [from *die hard* meaning 'die painfully']

dielectric *adjective* that does not conduct electricity, insulating. **dielectric** *noun* an insulator.

diesel (dee-zəl) *noun* **1** an engine that works by burning oil in compressed air. **2** fuel for a diesel engine. [named after the German engineer Rudolf Diesel (1858–1913), who invented it]

diesel-electric *adjective* driven by electric current from a generator driven by a diesel engine.

die-stamping *noun* stamping with a die that leaves an embossed design.

diet [1] *noun* **1** the sort of foods that a person or animal usually eats ♦ *a healthy diet*. **2** a selection of food to which a person is restricted, especially for medical reasons or because they are trying to lose weight. **diet** *verb* (**dieted, dieting**) to keep to a diet, especially in order to control your weight. **dieter** *noun* [from a Greek word *diaita* meaning 'way of life']

diet [2] *noun* the parliament of certain countries, e.g. Japan. [from a Latin word *dieta* meaning 'day's business']

dietary (diy-it-er-i) *adjective* to do with or involving a diet.

dietetic (diy-i-tet-ik) *adjective* to do with diet and nutrition. **dietetics** *noun* the study of diet and nutrition.

dietitian (diy-i-tish-ən) *noun* an expert in dietetics.

differ *verb* **1** to be unlike something else ♦ *The two accounts differ in some important details*. **2** to disagree in opinion. [from *dis-* and a Latin word *ferre* meaning 'to carry']

difference *noun* **1** the state of being different or unlike. **2** the way in which things are different; the amount or degree of unlikeness ♦ *There's a big difference between borrowing and stealing.* **3** the remainder left after subtracting one number from another ♦ *The difference between 8 and 5 is 3.* **4** a disagreement in opinion, a quarrel.

different *adjective* **1** unlike, not the same ♦ *Your hair looks different* ♦ *Her attitude is different from the others*. **2** separate or

distinct ♦ *I called on three different occasions.*
3 unusual or novel ♦ *Try Finland for a holiday
that's a bit different.* **differently** *adverb*
◊ It is regarded as more acceptable to say
different from than *different to*, which is
common in less formal use. The phrase
different than is common in American
English, but should be avoided in
standard British English.

differential (dif-er-en-shəl) *adjective* **1** of,
showing, or depending on a difference.
2 (*Mathematics*) relating to infinitesimal
differences.
differential *noun* **1** an agreed difference in
wages between industries or between
different classes of workers in the same
industry. **2** a differential gear.

differential gear *noun* a system of gears
that allows a motor vehicle's driving
wheels to revolve at different speeds
when going round corners.

differentiate (dif-er-en-shi-ayt) *verb* **1** to
recognize differences between things, to
distinguish things ♦ *I don't differentiate
between them.* **2** to be a difference between
things, to make one thing different from
another ♦ *What are the features that
differentiate one breed from another?* **3** to
develop differences, to become different.
4 (*Mathematics*) to calculate the derivative
of a function. **differentiation** *noun*

difficult *adjective* **1** needing a lot of effort or
skill to do or understand. SYNONYMS: hard,
complicated; (*informal*) tricky, knotty. **2** full of
problems or hardships ♦ *These are difficult
times.* SYNONYMS: tough, arduous, taxing,
challenging, demanding. **3** not easy to please
or satisfy ♦ *a difficult employer.* [from *dis-*
and a Latin word *facilis* meaning 'easy']

difficulty *noun* (**difficulties**) **1** the state of
being difficult. **2** a difficult problem or
thing. SYNONYMS: problem, complication,
hurdle, obstacle, snag. **3** a difficult state of
affairs, trouble ♦ *They are in financial
difficulties.* SYNONYMS: adversity, plight,
predicament; (*informal*) jam, fix, spot, mess.

diffident (dif-i-dənt) *adjective* shy and
lacking self-confidence, hesitating to put
yourself or your ideas forward. **diffidently**
adverb **diffidence** *noun* [from *dis-* meaning
'not' and a Latin word *fidentia* meaning
'confidence']

diffract *verb* **1** to break up a beam of light
into a series of dark and light bands or the
coloured bands of the spectrum. **2** to
break up a beam of radiation or particles
into a series of high and low intensities.

diffraction *noun* [from *dis-* meaning 'apart'
and a Latin word *fractum* meaning
'broken']

diffuse [1] (di-**fewss**) *adjective* **1** spread
widely, not concentrated ♦ *diffuse light.*
2 wordy, not concise ♦ *a diffuse style.*
diffusely *adverb* **diffuseness** *noun* [from *dis-*
meaning 'apart' and a Latin word *fusum*
meaning 'poured']

diffuse [2] (di-**fewz**) *verb* **1** to spread or make
something spread over a wide area ♦ *The
Internet is being used to diffuse knowledge*
♦ *diffused sunlight.* **2** to mix liquids or gases
slowly, to become intermingled ♦ *Let the
milk diffuse in the water.* **diffuser** *noun*
diffusible *adjective* **diffusion** *noun*

dig *verb* (past tense and past participle **dug**;
digging) **1** to break up and move ground
with a tool or machine or claws etc.; to
make a hole or tunnel by doing this.
SYNONYMS: burrow, tunnel, excavate, hollow
out. **2** to obtain something from the
ground by digging ♦ *I spent the morning
digging potatoes.* **3** to excavate an
archaeological site. **4** to seek or discover
something by investigation ♦ *We dug up
some useful information.* **5** to poke or jab
something sharply ♦ *Its claws dug into my
hand.* **6** (old use, *informal*) to like or
appreciate something.
dig *noun* **1** a piece of digging. **2** an
archaeological excavation. **3** a thrust or
poke ♦ *a dig in the ribs.* **4** a cutting remark
♦ *That was a dig at me.*
digs *plural noun* lodgings. **to dig in**
(*informal*) to begin eating. **to dig your heels
in** to be obstinate, to refuse to give way.
[from an Old English word]

digest [1] (diy-**jest**) *verb* **1** to dissolve food in
the stomach and intestines so that the
body can absorb it. **2** to take information
into your mind and think it over ♦ *I need
time to digest this news.* **3** to summarize
information methodically. **digestible**
adjective [from a Latin word *digerere*
meaning 'to distribute' or 'to dissolve']

digest [2] (diy-**jest**) *noun* **1** a methodical
summary. **2** a periodical publication
giving excerpts and summaries of news,
writings, etc.

digestion *noun* **1** the process of digesting.
2 a person's ability to digest food ♦ *She has
a good digestion.*

digestive *adjective* **1** to do with or aiding
digestion. **2** having the function of
digesting food ♦ *the digestive system.*
digestive *noun* a digestive biscuit.

digestive biscuit noun a kind of wholemeal biscuit.

digger noun 1 someone who digs. 2 a mechanical excavator. 3 (Austral. & NZ) (informal) a friendly form of address for a man.

digit (dij-it) noun 1 any numeral from 0 to 9, especially when forming part of a number. 2 a finger or toe. [from a Latin word digitus meaning 'finger or toe']

digital (dij-it-əl) adjective 1 representing data as a series of binary digits ♦ a digital computer. 2 (said about a clock, watch, or other instrument) showing the time or information by displaying a row of figures. (Compare **analogue**.) 3 to do with or using fingers. **digitally** adverb

digital audiotape noun magnetic tape used to make digital recordings.

digitalin (dij-i-**tay**-lin) noun a drug containing the active ingredients of digitalis.

digitalis (dij-i-**tay**-lis) noun a drug prepared from dried foxglove leaves, used to stimulate the heart. [the genus name of the foxglove]

digital recording noun conversion of sound into electrical pulses that represent binary digits, for more reliable transmission.

digitize verb to convert analogue signals to digital ones for computer processing. **digitizer** noun

dignified adjective having or showing dignity.

dignify verb (dignifies, dignified, dignifying) 1 to give dignity to someone or something. 2 to make a thing sound more important than it is ♦ They dignified the school with the name of 'college'. [same origin as for dignity]

dignitary (**dig**-ni-ter-i) noun (dignitaries) a person holding a high rank or position. [same origin as for dignity]

dignity noun 1 a calm and serious manner or style, showing suitable formality or indicating that you deserve respect. SYNONYMS: decorum, propriety, gravitas. 2 the quality of being worthy of respect ♦ the dignity of labour. **beneath your dignity** not considered worthy enough for you to do. [from a Latin word dignus meaning 'worthy']

digraph (**diy**-grahf) noun a combination of two letters representing one sound (as in ph and ea). [from di- and -graph]

digress (diy-**gress**) verb to depart from the main subject. **digression** noun [from dis- meaning 'away' and a Latin word gressum meaning 'gone']

dike noun another spelling of **dyke**.

dilapidated adjective falling to pieces, in a state of disrepair. [from a Latin word dilapidare meaning 'to demolish, squander']

dilapidation noun a state of disrepair; bringing or being brought into this state.

dilatation (diy-lə-**tay**-shən) noun (Medicine) making a vessel or opening wider or larger, dilation.

dilate (diy-**layt**) verb 1 to make something wider or larger, or to become wider or larger ♦ dilated pupils. 2 to speak or write at length on a subject. **dilation** noun **dilator** noun [from dis- meaning 'apart' and a Latin word latus meaning 'wide']

dilatory (**dil**-ə-ter-i) adjective 1 slow in doing something, not prompt ♦ a dilatory response. 2 intended to cause delay. **dilatorily** adverb **dilatoriness** noun [from a Latin word dilator meaning 'someone who delays']

dilemma (dil-**em**-ə) noun 1 a situation in which a difficult choice has to be made between two or more alternatives. 2 (informal) a difficult situation or problem. [a Greek word meaning 'double proposal'] ◊ Strictly speaking, there should be some idea of choosing between two (or perhaps more) things. Some people dislike this word being used simply to mean a difficult situation or problem.

dilettante (dili-**tan**-ti) noun a person who dabbles in a subject for enjoyment and without serious study. [an Italian word meaning 'person loving the arts']

diligent (**dil**-i-jənt) adjective 1 hard-working, putting care and effort into what you do. 2 done with care and effort ♦ a diligent search. **diligently** adverb **diligence** noun [from a Latin word diligens meaning 'conscientious']

dill noun a yellow-flowered herb with spicy seeds used for flavouring pickles. [from an Old English word]

dilly-dally verb (dilly-dallies, dilly-dallied,

dilly-dallying) (*informal*) to dawdle, to waste time by not making up your mind. [from *dally*]

dilute (diy-**lewt**) *verb* 1 to make a liquid weaker or less concentrated by adding water or some other liquid. 2 to weaken or reduce the force or strength of something.
dilute *adjective* diluted ♦ *a dilute acid*.
dilution *noun* [from a Latin word *diluere* meaning 'to wash away']

dim *adjective* (**dimmer, dimmest**) 1 only faintly lit, not bright. 2 indistinct, not clearly seen, heard, or remembered. 3 not able to see clearly ♦ *eyes dim with tears*. 4 (*informal*) stupid.
dim *verb* (**dimmed, dimming**) to make something dim, or to become dim. **to take a dim view of something** (*informal*) to disapprove of something. **dimly** *adverb* **dimness** *noun* [from an Old English word]

dime *noun* (*North Amer.*) a ten-cent coin. [from an Old French word *disme*, denoting a tithe or tenth part]

dimension (diy-**men**-shən) *noun* 1 a measurement such as length, breadth, thickness, area, or volume ♦ *What are the dimensions of the room?* 2 size or extent ♦ *a structure of huge dimensions*. 3 an aspect or feature of something ♦ *His passing adds a new dimension to the team*. **dimensional** *adjective* [from a Latin word *dimensio* meaning 'measuring out']

diminish *verb* to make something smaller or less, or to become smaller or less. [same origin as for *diminutive*]

diminuendo (dim-in-yoo-**en**-doh) *adjective & adverb* (*Music*) gradually becoming quieter. [an Italian word]

diminution (dim-in-**yoo**-shən) *noun* 1 diminishing or being diminished. 2 a decrease.

diminutive (dim-**in**-yoo-tiv) *adjective* very small.
diminutive *noun* a word for a small specimen of something (e.g. *booklet, duckling*), or an affectionate form of a name etc. (e.g. *dearie, Johnnie*). [from a Latin word *diminuere* meaning 'to lessen']

dimmer *noun* a device for reducing the brightness of lights.

dimple *noun* a small hollow or dent, especially a natural one on the skin of the cheek or chin.
dimple *verb* 1 to produce dimples in

something. 2 to show dimples. [from an Old English word]

dim sum *noun* a Chinese dish of small steamed or fried savoury dumplings containing various fillings. [from Chinese words *tim* meaning 'dot' and *sam* meaning 'heart']

din *noun* a loud and annoying noise.
din *verb* (**dinned, dinning**) **to din something into** to force a person to learn something by continually repeating it. [from an Old English word]

dinar (dee-nar) *noun* the unit of currency in the states of Yugoslavia and certain countries of the Middle East and North Africa. [from an Arabic and Persian word]

dine *verb* 1 to eat dinner. 2 to give someone dinner ♦ *We were wined and dined*. [from an Old French word *disner*]

diner *noun* 1 a person who dines. 2 a dining car on a train. 3 (*North Amer.*) a small restaurant.

ding-dong *adjective & adverb* (*informal*) 1 with the sound of alternate chimes of a bell. 2 (said about a contest) fiercely fought, with each contestant having the better of it alternately.

dinghy (ding-gi) *noun* (**dinghies**) 1 a small open boat driven by oars or sails. 2 a small inflatable rubber boat. [from a Hindi word *dingi* meaning 'a small river boat']

dingo (**dingoes**) an Australian wild dog. [from an Australian Aboriginal word]

dingy (din-ji) *adjective* (**dingier, dingiest**) gloomy and drab, dirty-looking. **dingily** *adverb* **dinginess** *noun* [origin unknown]

dining room *noun* a room in which meals are eaten.

dinkum *adjective* (*Austral.*) (*NZ*) (*informal*) true or real. [origin unknown]

dinky *adjective* (*informal*) (**dinkier, dinkiest**) attractively small and neat. [from a Scots and north England dialect word *dink* meaning 'neat, trim']

dinner *noun* 1 the main meal of the day, either at midday or in the evening. 2 a formal evening meal in honour of a person or event. [same origin as for *dine*]

dinner jacket *noun* a man's short jacket for formal evening occasions, usually black and worn with a bow tie.

dinosaur (diy-nə-sor) *noun* 1 a prehistoric reptile of the Mesozoic era, often of enormous size. **2** a person or organization that has become out of date by failing to adapt to new circumstances. [from Greek words *deinos* meaning 'terrible' and *sauros* meaning 'lizard']

dint *noun* **by dint of** by means of ♦ *I got through the exam by dint of a good memory.* [from an Old English word *dynt*]

diocese (diy-ə-sis) *noun* a district under the care of a bishop in the Christian Church. **diocesan** (diy-**oss**-i-sən) *adjective* [from a Latin word *dioecesis* meaning 'governor's jurisdiction']

diode (diy-ohd) *noun* a semiconductor allowing the flow of current in one direction only and having two terminals. [from *di-* and *electrode*]

dioxide (diy-**ok**-siyd) *noun* an oxide with two atoms of oxygen to one of a metal or other element ♦ *carbon dioxide.* [from *di-* and *oxide*]

dip *verb* (**dipped, dipping**) **1** to put or lower something into liquid. SYNONYMS: immerse, submerge, plunge, duck, dunk. **2** to go under water and emerge quickly. **3** to go down ♦ *The sun dipped below the horizon.* **4** to lower something for a time, especially the beam of a vehicle's headlights. **5** to slope or extend downwards ♦ *The road dips after the bend.* **6** to become lower or smaller ♦ *Attendances have dipped this month.* **7** to put a hand, spoon, etc. into something in order to take something out. **8** to wash sheep in a vermin-killing liquid.
dip *noun* **1** dipping or being dipped. **2** a brief swim ♦ *He went for a dip in the sea.* **3** a downward slope. **4** a brief drop in an amount or level. **5** a creamy mixture into which pieces of food are dipped before eating. **6** a liquid into which something is dipped ♦ *sheep dip.* **to dip into 1** to read short passages here and there in a book ♦ *I've dipped into 'War and Peace'.* **2** to draw money from your financial resources and spend it ♦ *She had to dip into her savings.* [from an Old English word *dyppan*]

DipEd *abbreviation* Diploma in Education.

diphtheria (dif-**theer**-iə) *noun* an acute infectious disease that causes severe inflammation of a mucous membrane, especially in the throat. [from a Greek word *diphthera* meaning 'leather' (because a tough skin forms on the throat membrane)]

diphthong (dif-thong) *noun* a compound vowel sound produced by combining two simple ones in a single syllable, e.g. *oi* in *point*, *ou* in *loud*. [from *di-* and a Greek word *phthongos* meaning 'sound']

diplodocus (di-**plod**-əkəs) *noun* a large dinosaur with a long slender neck and tail, which fed on plants. [from Greek words *diplous* meaning 'double' and *dokos* meaning 'wooden beam']

diploid (dip-loid) *adjective* (said about a cell) having its chromosomes in pairs, with half of each pair coming from each parent. **diploidy** *noun* [from a Greek word *diplous* meaning 'double']

diploma *noun* a certificate awarded by a college etc. to a person who has successfully passed an examination or completed a course of study. [from a Greek word meaning 'folded paper']

diplomacy (dip-**loh**-mə-si) *noun* **1** the work or skill of making agreements with other countries. **2** skill in dealing with people and gently persuading them to agree to things; tact. [from a French word *diplomatie*]

diplomat (dip-lə-mat) *noun* **1** a person who represents their country officially abroad. **2** a tactful person. [from a Latin word *diploma* meaning 'an official letter' (given to travellers, saying who they were)]

diplomatic (diplə-**mat**-ik) *adjective* **1** to do with diplomats or diplomacy ♦ *the diplomatic service.* **2** tactful ♦ *a diplomatic reply.* **diplomatically** *adverb*

diplomatic immunity *noun* the right of foreign diplomats to be exempt from certain laws of the country they are working in.

dipole *noun* **1** an object with an opposite magnetization or electrical charge at two points or poles. **2** a molecule in which positive and negative charges are separated.

dipper *noun* **1** a kind of bird that dives for its food, especially the water ouzel. **2** a ladle or scoop. [from *dip*]

dipsomania (dip-sə-**may**-niə) *noun* an uncontrollable craving for alcohol. **dipsomaniac** *noun* [from a Greek word *dipsa* meaning 'thirst' and -*mania*]

dipstick *noun* a rod for measuring the depth of a liquid, especially oil in an engine.

dipterous (dip-ter-əs) *adjective* **1** (said about insects) having two wings. **2** (said about seeds) having two wing-like parts. [from *di-* and a Greek word *pteron* meaning 'wing']

diptych (dip-tik) *noun* a painting on two hinged wooden panels that can be closed like a book. [from the Greek word *diptukhos* meaning 'folded in two']

dire *adjective* **1** extremely serious or urgent ♦ *The refugees are in dire need.* **2** ominous, predicting trouble ♦ *dire warnings.* **3** (*informal*) of poor quality ♦ *a dire performance.* [from a Latin word *dirus* meaning 'fearful, threatening']

direct *adjective* **1** going from one place to another without changing direction or stopping ♦ *the direct route.* **2** with nothing or no one coming in between ♦ *Are you in direct contact with them?* ♦ *This is a direct result of all your hard work.* **3** going straight to the point, frank ♦ *a direct way of speaking.* SYNONYMS: frank, candid, forthright, blunt, straight, straightforward, plain. **4** exact, complete ♦ *the direct opposite.*
direct *adverb* by a direct route ♦ *We travelled to Rome direct.*
◊ Note that *directly* is not used with this meaning.
direct *verb* **1** to tell or show someone the way ♦ *Can you direct me to the station?* **2** to guide or aim something in a certain direction or to a target. **3** to supervise the acting, filming, etc. of a play, film, or opera. **4** to control or manage someone or something ♦ *There was no one to direct the workmen.* **5** to command or order something ♦ *The general directed his men to advance.* **directness** *noun* [from a Latin word *directum* meaning 'kept straight']

direct action *noun* the use of strikes, sabotage, or other active forms of protest to achieve your aims.

direct current *noun* an electric current flowing in one direction only.

direct debit *noun* an arrangement that you can set up with your bank, allowing bills to be paid directly from your account.

direction *noun* **1** the line along which something moves or faces ♦ *They are heading in the direction of London.* **2** directing or managing people.
directions *plural noun* instructions on how to use or do something or how to get somewhere.

directional *adjective* **1** to do with or indicating direction. **2** operating or sending radio signals in one direction only.

directive *noun* an official instruction or command.

directly *adverb* **1** in a direct line, in a direct manner. **2** without delay. **3** very soon.
◊ See also **direct** *adverb.*
directly *conjunction* (*informal*) as soon as ♦ *I went directly I knew.*

direct object *noun* (*Grammar*) the word that receives the action of a verb. In *She hit him*, *him* is the direct object. See **object**[1].

director *noun* **1** a person who supervises or manages things, especially a member of the board managing a business company on behalf of shareholders. **2** a person who directs a film or play. **directorial** *adjective* **directorship** *noun*

directorate *noun* **1** a part of a government department in charge of some activity. **2** a board of directors.

directory *noun* (**directories**) **1** a book containing a list of telephone subscribers, inhabitants of a district, members of a profession, business firms, etc. **2** (*Computing*) a file containing a group of other files. [from a Latin word *directorius* meaning 'guiding']

directrix *noun* (**directrices** (di-rek-tris-eez)) a fixed straight line used in drawing parabolas and certain other curves. [from a medieval Latin word meaning 'a female director']

direct speech *noun* words quoted in the form in which they were actually spoken (e.g. *Has he come?*), not altered by being reported (e.g. *She asked whether he had come*).

direct tax *noun* a tax, such as income tax, which is levied on the money that people earn rather than on the money that they spend.

dirge (derj) *noun* **1** a slow mournful song. **2** a lament for the dead. [from the first word of a song which used to be part of the Roman Catholic service for a dead person]

dirigible (di-rij-ibəl) *noun* a balloon or airship that can be steered in flight.
dirigible *adjective* capable of being guided. [from a Latin word *dirigere* meaning 'to direct']

dirk *noun* a kind of dagger, especially of a Scottish highlander. [origin unknown]

dirndl (dern-dəl) *noun* a full skirt gathered into a tight waistband. [from a German dialect word, a diminutive of *Dirne* meaning 'girl']

dirt *noun* **1** any unclean substance such as dust, soil, or mud. SYNONYMS: filth, grime; (*informal*) muck. **2** loose earth or soil. **3** unpleasant or unkind words or talk. [from an Old Norse word *drit* meaning 'excrement']

dirt track *noun* a course made of earth or rolled cinders, for flat racing or motorcycle racing.

dirty *adjective* (**dirtier, dirtiest**) **1** covered with an unclean substance, not clean ♦ *Your hands are dirty.* SYNONYMS: filthy, grimy, grubby, soiled, unclean; (*informal*) mucky. **2** making someone become dirty ♦ *a dirty job.* **3** unfair or dishonourable ♦ *a dirty trick* ♦ *a dirty fighter.* **4** indecent or obscene ♦ *dirty jokes.* SYNONYMS: smutty, crude, rude, coarse, vulgar. **5** (said about weather) rough and stormy. **6** (said about a nuclear weapon) producing a large amount of radioactive fallout.
dirty *verb* (**dirties, dirtied, dirtying**) to make something dirty. **dirtily** *adverb* **dirtiness** *noun*

dis- *prefix* (changing to **dif-** before *f*, **di-** before some consonants). **1** not; the reverse of (as in *dishonest*). **2** apart or separated (as in *disarm, disperse*). [from a Latin word meaning 'not; away']

disability *noun* (**disabilities**) **1** a physical or mental condition that limits a person's movements, senses, or activities. **2** a lack of something that prevents someone doing something.

disable *verb* **1** to limit a person's movements, senses, or activities. **2** to put something out of action. **disablement** *noun*

disabled *adjective* unable to use part of your body properly because of illness or injury.
◊ This term should be used instead of older words such as *crippled*, which can now cause offence.

disabuse (dis-ə-bewz) *verb* to free someone from a false idea ♦ *He was soon disabused of this notion.*

disaccharide (diy-sak-ə-riyd) *noun* any sugar whose molecule consists of two simple sugar molecules linked together.

disadvantage *noun* something that hinders or is unfavourable. SYNONYMS: drawback, hindrance, handicap, liability; (*informal*) minus.
disadvantage *verb* to put someone at a disadvantage.

disadvantaged *adjective* suffering from socially or economically unfavourable circumstances.

disadvantageous (dis-ad-vən-tay-jəs) *adjective* causing disadvantage.

disaffected *adjective* no longer willing to support someone or believe in something. **disaffection** *noun*

disagree *verb* (**disagrees, disagreed, disagreeing**) **1** to have or express a different opinion. **2** to fail to correspond or be consistent. **3** to quarrel. **to disagree with 1** to differ in opinion from someone. **2** (said about food or climate) to have a bad effect on someone ♦ *Rich food disagrees with me.* **disagreement** *noun* [from an Old French word *desagreer*]

disagreeable *adjective* **1** unpleasant. **2** unfriendly and bad-tempered. **disagreeably** *adverb* [from an Old French word *desagreable*]

disallow *verb* to refuse to allow or accept something as valid ♦ *The referee disallowed the goal.*

disappear *verb* **1** to stop being visible, to pass from sight. **2** to stop existing. SYNONYMS: vanish, fade, pass, evaporate, dissolve. **disappearance** *noun*

disappoint *verb* to fail to do what someone hoped for or desired or expected. **disappointment** *noun* [originally meaning 'to dismiss someone from an important position': from *dis-* and *appoint*]

disappointed *adjective* sad or dissatisfied because what you hoped for or expected has not happened.

disapprobation (dis-ap-rə-bay-shən) *noun* strong disapproval.

disapprove *verb* to have or express an unfavourable opinion of something. **disapproval** *noun*

disarm *verb* **1** to take away someone's weapons. **2** to reduce the size of the armed forces. **3** to remove the fuse from a bomb. **4** to make it difficult for a person to feel angry or hostile ♦ *We were completely disarmed by his honesty.* **disarming** *adjective* **disarmingly** *adverb* [from an Old French word *desarmer*]

disarmament *noun* reduction of a country's armed forces or weapons.

disarrange verb to make something disordered or untidy. **disarrangement** noun

disarray noun a state of disorder or untidiness. [from an Old French word]

disassemble verb to take something to pieces. **disassembly** noun

disassociate verb another word for **dissociate**.

disaster noun 1 an accident or natural event that causes great damage, injury, or loss of life. 2 a complete failure. SYNONYMS: catastrophe, fiasco, debacle; (informal) flop. [literally 'an unlucky star' from dis- and a Latin word astrum meaning 'star']

disaster area noun an area in which a major disaster, such as an earthquake, has recently occurred.

disastrous adjective 1 causing great damage. 2 resulting in complete failure. **disastrously** adverb

disavow verb to deny any knowledge of or responsibility for something. **disavowal** noun

disband verb (said about a group or organization) to break up, or cause it to break up ♦ We decided to disband the choir. [from an Old French word desbander]

disbelief noun refusal or unwillingness to believe something.

disbelieve verb to refuse or be unable to believe something. **disbeliever** noun

disburse verb to pay out money. **disbursal** noun **disbursement** noun [from dis- meaning 'apart' and a French word bourse meaning 'purse']

disc noun 1 a flat thin circular object. 2 something shaped or looking like this ♦ the sun's disc. 3 (**disk**) a computer storage device consisting of a rotatable disc on which data is stored either magnetically or optically ♦ a floppy disk ♦ a compact disk. 4 a layer of cartilage between vertebrae in the spine. 5 a CD or record. [from a Latin word discus meaning 'disc']

discard[1] (dis-**kard**) verb to get rid of something because it is no longer wanted or useful. SYNONYMS: dispose of, dump, jettison; (informal) ditch. [from an earlier meaning ' to throw out an unwanted playing card from a hand', from dis- and card]

discard[2] (dis-kard) noun something discarded.

disc brake noun a brake in which a flat plate presses against a plate at the centre of a wheel.

discern (di-**sern**) verb 1 to recognize or perceive something clearly ♦ Can you discern what her intentions are? 2 to be able to see or notice something, to make something out ♦ I could just discern a figure in the shadows. [from dis- meaning 'apart' and a Latin word cernere meaning 'to separate']

discernible (di-**sern**-ibəl) adjective able to be discerned.

discerning (di-**sern**-ing) adjective perceptive, showing good judgement.

discernment noun good judgement.

discharge (dis-**charj**) verb 1 to allow someone to leave ♦ My mother was discharged from hospital last week. 2 to dismiss someone from employment ♦ He was discharged from the army. 3 to send something out; to pour out ♦ The engine was discharging smoke. 4 to give out an electric charge, or to cause something to do this. 5 to carry out a duty or responsibility. 6 to fire a missile or gun. **discharge** (dis-**charj** or dis-charj) noun 1 discharging or being discharged. 2 something that has been discharged ♦ the discharge from the wound. 3 the release of an electric charge, especially with a spark. [from a Latin word discarricare meaning 'to unload']

disciple (di-**siy**-pəl) noun 1 a follower or pupil of a leader, teacher, or philosophy. 2 any of the original followers of Jesus Christ during his life. [from a Latin word discipulus meaning 'learner']

disciplinarian (dis-i-plin-**air**-iən) noun someone who believes in strict discipline.

disciplinary (**dis**-i-plin-er-i) adjective to do with or for discipline.

discipline (**dis**-i-plin) noun 1 training that produces obedience, self-control, or a particular skill. 2 controlled behaviour produced by such training. 3 a subject for study. **discipline** verb 1 to train someone to be obedient and self-controlled. 2 to punish someone ♦ Anyone who breaks the rules will be disciplined. [from a Latin word disciplina meaning 'training']

disc jockey *noun* a person who introduces and plays records on radio or at a disco.

disclaim *verb* to say that you do not have responsibility for or knowledge of something ♦ *They disclaim all responsibility for the accident.* [from an Old French word *desclamer*]

disclaimer *noun* a statement disclaiming something.

disclose *verb* to reveal something or make it known. **disclosure** *noun* [from an Old French word *desclore* meaning 'to open up']

disco *noun* (**discos**) (*informal*) a party or club where people dance to pop music. [from a French word *discothèque* meaning 'record library']

discolour *verb* 1 to spoil or change the colour of something. 2 to become changed in colour or stained. **discoloration** *noun* [from *dis-* meaning 'not' and a Latin word *colorare* meaning 'to colour']

discomfit (dis-kum-fit) *verb* (**discomfited, discomfiting**) to make someone feel uneasy or embarrassed. **discomfiture** (dis-**kum**-fi-cher) *noun* [from an Old French word *desconfit* meaning 'defeated']

discomfort *noun* 1 slight pain. 2 a feeling of uneasiness or embarrassment. [from an Old French word]

discompose *verb* to disturb or agitate someone. **discomposure** *noun*

disconcert (dis-kən-sert) *verb* to make a person feel uneasy. **disconcerting** *adjective* [from *dis-* meaning 'not' and a French word *concerter* meaning 'to make harmonious']

disconnect *verb* 1 to break a connection. 2 to put a piece of equipment out of action by detaching it from a power supply ♦ *The phone has been disconnected.* **disconnection** *noun*

disconnected *adjective* not joined together in a logical way ♦ *his disconnected ramblings.*

disconsolate (dis-kon-sə-lət) *adjective* unhappy at the loss of something. **disconsolately** *adverb* [from *dis-* meaning 'not' and a Latin word *consolatus* meaning 'consoled']

discontent *noun* lack of contentment or satisfaction. **discontentment** *noun*

discontented *adjective* not contented, feeling discontent.

discontinue *verb* to stop doing or providing something ♦ *The manufacturers have discontinued that line.* **discontinuance** *noun* [from *dis-* meaning 'not' and a Latin word *continuare* meaning 'to continue']

discontinuous *adjective* having gaps or intervals, not continuous. **discontinuity** (dis-kon-tin-**yoo**-iti) *noun*

discord (**dis**-kord) *noun* 1 disagreement or quarrelling. 2 (*Music*) a combination of notes producing a harsh or unpleasant sound. **discordance** *noun* **discordant** (dis-**kor**-dənt) *adjective* **discordantly** *adverb* [from *dis-* meaning 'not' and a Latin word *cordis* meaning 'of the heart']

discotheque (**dis**-kə-tek) *noun* a disco. [a French word meaning 'record library']

discount[1] (**dis**-kownt) *noun* an amount of money taken off the usual price or cost of something. **at a discount** below the usual price or cost. [from an Old French word]

discount[2] (dis-**kownt**) *verb* 1 to ignore or disregard a factor or possibility. 2 to reduce something in price. [from an Old French word]

discount store *noun* a shop selling goods regularly at less than the standard price.

discourage *verb* 1 to take away someone's enthusiasm or confidence. SYNONYMS: dishearten, deter, daunt, demoralize. 2 to try to persuade someone not to do something. 3 to show disapproval of something ♦ *Smoking is discouraged.* **discouragement** *noun* **discouraging** *adjective* [from an Old French word *descouragier*]

discourse[1] (**dis**-korss) *noun* a formal speech or piece of writing on a subject. [from a Latin word *discursus* meaning 'running to and fro']

discourse[2] (dis-**korss**) *verb* to speak or write at length about something.

discourteous (dis-**ker**-ti-əs) *adjective* lacking courtesy, rude. **discourteously** *adverb* **discourtesy** *noun*

discover *verb* 1 to find or become aware of something, especially by searching or other effort. SYNONYMS: come across, detect, track down, unearth; (*informal*) dig up, turn up. 2 to be the first person to find something ♦ *Herschel discovered the planet Uranus.* **discoverer** *noun* [from *dis-* meaning 'apart' and a Latin word *cooperire* meaning 'to cover']

discovery *noun* (**discoveries**) 1 discovering or being discovered. 2 something that is discovered.

discredit *verb* (**discredited, discrediting**) 1 to damage a person's reputation. 2 to cause an idea, piece of evidence, etc. to be disbelieved or doubted ♦ *This theory has since been discredited.*

discredit *noun* damage to a person's reputation ♦ *To her discredit, she never admitted her mistake.* [from *dis-* and *credit*]

discreditable *adjective* bringing discredit, shameful. **discreditably** *adverb*

discreet *adjective* 1 showing caution and good judgement in what you say or do; not giving away secrets ♦ *I'll make a few discreet inquiries.* 2 not showy or obtrusive. **discreetly** *adverb* [from a Latin word *discernere* meaning 'to be discerning'] ◊ Do not confuse this word with **discrete**, which has a different meaning.

discrepancy (dis-**krep**-ənsi) *noun* (**discrepancies**) lack of agreement between things which should be the same ♦ *There were several discrepancies between the witnesses' accounts.* [from a Latin word *discrepantia* meaning 'discord']

discrete (dis-**kreet**) *adjective* individually separate and distinct ♦ *a series of discrete scenes.* **discretely** *adverb* [from a Latin word *discretus* meaning 'separated'] ◊ Do not confuse this word with **discreet**, which has a different meaning.

discretion (dis-**kresh**-ən) *noun* 1 being discreet, keeping secrets ♦ *I hope I can rely on your discretion.* 2 freedom to decide for yourself ♦ *You can use your discretion.* [from *discreet*]

discretionary (dis-**kresh**-ən-er-i) *adjective* done or used at a person's discretion ♦ *a discretionary payment.*

discriminate *verb* 1 to notice and understand the differences between things. 2 to treat people differently or unfairly, usually because of their race, sex, age, or religion. **discrimination** *noun* **discriminatory** *adjective* [from a Latin word *discrimen* meaning 'separator']

discriminating *adjective* having or showing good taste or judgement.

discursive *adjective* wandering from one subject to another. [from a Latin word *discurrere* meaning 'to run away']

discus *noun* (**discuses**) a heavy thick-centred disc, thrown in athletic contests. [via Latin from a Greek word *diskos*]

discuss *verb* 1 to examine a subject in speech or writing. 2 to have a conversation in order to decide something. **discussion** *noun* [from a Latin word *discutere* meaning 'to dash to pieces']

disdain *noun* the feeling that someone or something is not worthy of your consideration or respect.

disdain *verb* 1 to regard something with disdain. 2 to refuse to do something because of disdain ♦ *She disdained to reply.* **disdainful** *adjective* **disdainfully** *adverb* [from *dis-* meaning 'not' and a Latin word *dignus* meaning 'worthy']

disease *noun* an unhealthy condition of the body or mind. [from *dis-* meaning 'not' and *ease*]

diseased *adjective* affected with disease.

disembark *verb* to get off a ship or aircraft. **disembarkation** *noun* [from a French word]

disembodied *adjective* 1 (said about the soul or spirit) separated or freed from the body. 2 (said about a voice) lacking any obvious source

disembowel *verb* (**disembowelled, disembowelling**) to take out the bowels or internal organs of a person or animal. [from *dis-* and *en-* and *bowel*]

disenchanted *adjective* no longer believing that something is worthwhile ♦ *She's become disenchanted with her job.* **disenchantment** *noun*

disenfranchise (dis-in-**fran**-chiyz) *verb* to take away someone's right to vote. **disenfranchisement** *noun*

disengage *verb* 1 to disconnect or detach something. 2 (said about an army etc.) to stop fighting and leave a battle area. **disengagement** *noun*

disentangle *verb* 1 to take the knots or tangles out of something. 2 to free something from difficulty or confusion, to extricate something. **disentanglement** *noun*

disestablish *verb* to deprive a national Church of its official connection with the State. **disestablishment** *noun*

disfavour *noun* dislike or disapproval.

disfigure verb to spoil the appearance of a person or thing. **disfigurement** noun [from dis- and a Latin word figura meaning 'a shape']

disgorge verb 1 to pour or send something out ♦ The pipe disgorged its contents. 2 to throw something out from the stomach or throat ♦ The whale swallowed Jonah and then disgorged him. [from dis- and a French word gorge meaning 'throat']

disgrace noun 1 shame, loss of approval or respect. SYNONYMS: dishonour, humiliation, discredit, ignominy. 2 something that is shameful or unacceptable ♦ The bus service is a disgrace.
disgrace verb to bring disgrace on someone. [from dis- and a Latin word gratia meaning 'grace']

disgraceful adjective shameful or unacceptable. **disgracefully** adverb

disgruntled adjective discontented or resentful. [from dis- meaning 'thoroughly' and gruntle meaning 'to grunt softly']

disguise verb 1 to make a person or thing look or seem different so that they cannot be recognized. 2 to conceal something ♦ She could not disguise her amazement. **disguise** noun 1 something worn or used for disguising your identity. 2 the state of being disguised ♦ in disguise. [from dis- and guise]

disgust noun a strong feeling of dislike or revulsion ♦ He turned away in disgust. SYNONYMS: loathing, repugnance, repulsion, antipathy, contempt, outrage.
disgust verb to cause disgust in someone. SYNONYMS: sicken, nauseate, repel; (informal) turn your stomach. **disgusted** adjective [from dis- meaning 'not' and a Latin word gustare meaning 'to taste']

disgusting adjective extremely unpleasant ♦ a disgusting habit. SYNONYMS: revolting, repulsive, repugnant, vile.

dish noun 1 a shallow flat-bottomed container for cooking or serving food. 2 a particular kind of food ♦ We specialize in vegetarian dishes. 3 a shallow concave object ♦ a soap dish. 4 a concave dish-shaped aerial used for receiving satellite communications and in radio astronomy. 5 (informal) an attractive person.
dish verb to dish something out to give out portions of something to people. to dish up or out to put food onto plates ready for serving. [from an Old English word disc]

disharmony noun lack of harmony. **disharmonious** adjective

dishcloth noun a cloth for washing dishes.

dishearten verb to cause someone to lose hope or confidence. **disheartening** adjective

dishevelled (dish-ev-əld) adjective ruffled and untidy ♦ his usual dishevelled appearance. **dishevelment** noun [from dis- meaning 'apart' and an Old French word chevel meaning 'hair']

dishonest adjective not honest. SYNONYMS: deceitful, insincere, untruthful, crooked, corrupt; (informal) shady, underhand. **dishonestly** adverb **dishonesty** noun [from an Old French word]

dishonour noun 1 loss of honour or respect, disgrace. 2 something that causes this. **dishonour** verb 1 to bring dishonour to someone, to disgrace someone. 2 to refuse to honour a cheque, agreement, etc. [from an Old French word]

dishonourable adjective not honourable, shameful. **dishonourably** adverb

dishwasher noun a machine for washing dishes automatically.

dishwater noun water in which dishes have been washed.

dishy adjective (dishier, dishiest) (informal) (said about a person) very attractive.

disillusion verb to get rid of someone's pleasant but mistaken beliefs. **disillusion** noun the state of being disillusioned. **disillusionment** noun

disincentive noun something that discourages an action or effort.

disinclination noun unwillingness to do something.

disincline verb to make a person feel reluctant or unwilling to do something.

disinfect verb to make something clean by destroying bacteria that may cause disease. **disinfection** noun [from a French word]

disinfectant noun a chemical liquid that destroys bacteria. [from a French word]

disinflation noun the process of reducing the rate of inflation without producing the disadvantages of deflation. **disinflationary** adjective

disinformation noun deliberately false information.

disingenuous (dis-in-**jen**-yoo-əs) *adjective* not frank or sincere, especially in pretending to know less about something than you really do. **disingenuously** *adverb*

disinherit *verb* to deprive a person of the right to inherit something, especially by making a will naming another person as your heir.

disintegrate *verb* **1** to break up into small parts or pieces. **2** to become weakened and come to an end ♦ *His marriage disintegrated under the strain.* **disintegration** *noun*

disinter (dis-in-**ter**) *verb* (**disinterred, disinterring**) to dig up something that has been buried. [from a French word]

disinterest *noun* **1** impartiality. **2** lack of interest.

disinterested *adjective* **1** not influenced by hope of gaining something yourself, impartial ♦ *She gave us some disinterested advice.* **2** not interested. **disinterestedly** *adverb*

◊ Although this word is commonly used to mean 'not interested', this sense is regarded by some people as unacceptable in standard English because it obscures a useful distinction between *disinterested* and *uninterested*.

disjointed *adjective* (said about talk or writing) not having parts logically fitting together and so difficult to understand. [from *dis-* and a Latin word *jungere* meaning 'to join']

disjunctive *adjective* (*Grammar*) (said about conjunctions such as *or* and *but*) introducing an alternative or contrast. [from *dis-* and a Latin word *junctum* meaning 'joined']

disk *noun* another spelling of **disc**, used in computing and in American English.

disk drive *noun* an apparatus that turns the disk on a computer while data is recorded or retrieved.

diskette *noun* a floppy disk.

dislike *noun* **1** a feeling of not liking someone or something. SYNONYMS: aversion, distaste, antipathy, hostility. **2** something that you do not like ♦ *She listed her likes and dislikes.* **dislike** *verb* to feel dislike for someone or something. [from *dis-* and *like*[1]]

dislocate *verb* **1** to move or force a bone from its proper position in a joint. **2** to put something out of order, to disrupt

something ♦ *Fog has dislocated the traffic.* **dislocation** *noun* [from *dis-* and a Latin word *locare* meaning 'to place']

dislodge *verb* to move or force something from its place. **dislodgement** *noun* [from a French word]

disloyal *adjective* not loyal. **disloyally** *adverb* **disloyalty** *noun* [from a French word]

dismal *adjective* **1** gloomy or dreary. **2** (*informal*) of poor quality, feeble ♦ *a dismal attempt at humour.* **dismally** *adverb* [from a Latin phrase *dies mali* meaning 'unlucky days']

dismantle *verb* to take something to pieces. [from *dis-* and an Old French word *manteler* meaning 'to fortify']

dismay *noun* a feeling of alarm and discouragement. SYNONYMS: consternation, dread, apprehension. **dismay** *verb* to fill someone with dismay. [from *dis-* and *may*[1]]

dismember *verb* **1** to tear or cut the limbs from a body. **2** to divide something into parts. **dismemberment** *noun* [from an Old French word *desmembrer*]

dismiss *verb* **1** to send someone away from your presence. **2** to tell someone that you will no longer employ them ♦ *She claims she was unfairly dismissed.* **3** to put something out of your thoughts because it is not worth thinking about. **4** to mention or discuss something only briefly. **5** to reject a legal case without further hearing ♦ *The court dismissed his appeal.* **6** (in cricket) to get a batsman or side out in cricket ♦ *He was dismissed for 6 runs.* **dismissal** *noun* [from *dis-* and a Latin word *missum* meaning 'sent']

dismissive *adjective* feeling or showing that something is not worth considering. **dismissively** *adverb*

dismount *verb* **1** to get off a horse or bicycle. **2** to remove something from its support.

disobedient *adjective* not obedient. SYNONYMS: insubordinate, rebellious, defiant, wilful. **disobedience** *noun* **disobediently** *adverb* [from an Old French word *desobedient*]

disobey *verb* to fail to obey someone, to refuse to follow rules or orders. [from an Old French word *desobeir*]

disobliging *adjective* refusing to help or cooperate with someone.

disorder noun 1 lack of order; untidiness or confusion. 2 a disturbance of public order, a riot. 3 disturbance of the normal working of the body or mind, an illness ♦ a nervous disorder.
disorder verb to throw something into disorder. **disordered** adjective

disorderly adjective 1 untidy or confused. 2 involving a disturbance of public order.

disorganized adjective 1 not properly planned or controlled. 2 (said about a person) not organized or efficient. **disorganization** noun

disorientate (dis-or-i-en-tayt) or **disorient** (dis-or-i-ənt) verb to confuse someone and make them lose their sense of direction. **disorientated** adjective **disorientation** noun **disoriented** adjective

disown verb to refuse to acknowledge that someone or something has any connection with you.

disparage (dis-pa-rij) verb to speak of someone or something in a slighting way, to belittle someone or something. **disparagingly** adverb **disparagement** noun [from dis- and an Old French word parage meaning 'equality in rank']

disparate (dis-per-ət) adjective different in kind. [from a Latin word disparare meaning 'separate']

disparity (dis-pa-riti) noun (**disparities**) difference or inequality. [from dis- and a Latin word paritas meaning 'equality']

dispassionate adjective free from emotion, calm and impartial. **dispassionately** adverb

dispatch verb 1 to send someone off to a destination or for a purpose ♦ Warships were dispatched to the region. 2 to complete or dispose of a task or problem quickly. 3 to kill a person or animal.
dispatch noun 1 dispatching or being dispatched. 2 an official message or report sent quickly, especially one concerning the latest situation in a war. 3 a news report sent in from abroad by a journalist. 4 promptness and efficiency ♦ He acted with dispatch. [from an Italian or Spanish word]

dispatch box noun 1 a container for carrying official documents. 2 (**Dispatch Box**) a box in the House of Commons where ministers stand to speak.

dispatch rider noun a messenger who travels by motorcycle.

dispel verb (**dispelled, dispelling**) to drive away doubts, fears, etc. ♦ We need to dispel these rumours of a takeover. [from dis- meaning 'apart' and a Latin word pellere meaning 'to drive']

dispensable adjective able to be done without, not essential.

dispensary noun (**dispensaries**) a place where medicines are dispensed ♦ the hospital dispensary.

dispensation noun 1 dispensing or distributing something ♦ the dispensation of justice. 2 exemption from a penalty, rule, or duty.

dispense verb 1 to distribute something to a number of people, to give something out ♦ a ruler who sought to dispense justice fairly. 2 (said about a machine) to supply a quantity of a product or money. 3 to prepare and give out medicines according to prescriptions. **to dispense with** to do without something; to make something unnecessary ♦ It's time we dispensed with such outdated ideas. [from dis- meaning 'separately' and a Latin word pensum meaning 'weighed']

dispenser noun 1 a person who dispenses medicines. 2 a device that supplies a quantity of something ♦ a soap dispenser.

dispersant noun a substance that disperses something.

disperse verb 1 to scatter something over a wide area. 2 (said about people) to leave and go in different directions, or to make them do this ♦ Police tried to disperse the crowd. **dispersal** noun [from a Latin word dispersum meaning 'scattered']

dispersion noun 1 the process of dispersing or being dispersed. 2 another word for **diaspora**. 3 (Physics) the separation of white light into colours or of any radiation according to wavelength.

dispirited adjective depressed and discouraged.

dispiriting adjective making you feel depressed and discouraged.

displace verb 1 to shift something from its usual place. 2 to take the place of a person or thing ♦ Weeds tend to displace other plants.

displaced person noun a person who is forced to leave his or her home country because of war, famine, etc.

displacement noun 1 displacing or being displaced. 2 the distance something is shifted. **3** the volume or weight of fluid displaced by something floating or immersed in it.

display verb **1** to show or arrange something so that it can be seen. **2** to reveal something ♦ *Don't display your ignorance.* SYNONYMS: show, demonstrate, exhibit, flaunt, expose, betray. **3** (said about birds and animals) to make a display. **display** noun **1** displaying or being displayed. **2** a collection of goods etc. displayed conspicuously. **3** an electronic device for visually presenting data. **4** a special pattern of behaviour used by birds and animals as a means of visual communication, especially when attracting a mate. [from *dis-* meaning 'separately' and a Latin word *plicare* meaning 'to fold']

displease verb to annoy or offend someone. [from an Old French word]

displeasure noun a feeling of annoyance or dissatisfaction.

disport verb to play about in a lively way ♦ *children disporting themselves on the beach.* [from *dis-* and a Latin word *portare* meaning 'to carry']

disposable adjective **1** designed to be thrown away after it has been used ♦ *a disposable razor.* **2** able to be disposed of. **3** available to be used as needed, at your disposal. **disposability** noun

disposable income noun the amount of income left after taxes have been deducted.

disposal noun getting rid of something. **at your disposal** available for you to use.

dispose verb **1** to make someone willing or ready to do something ♦ *Their friendliness disposed us to accept the invitation.* **2** to place or arrange something in position. **to be well disposed towards** to have kindly or favourable feelings towards someone or something. **to dispose of 1** to get rid of something. **2** to deal with something. [from *dis-* meaning 'away' and a French word *poser* meaning 'to place']

disposition noun **1** a person's natural qualities of mind and character ♦ *She has a cheerful disposition.* **2** a natural tendency or inclination. **3** setting in order, arrangement ♦ *the disposition of troops.*

dispossess verb to deprive a person of the possession of something. **dispossession** noun

disproportionate adjective out of proportion, relatively too large or too small. **disproportion** noun **disproportionately** adverb

disprove verb to prove that something is false or wrong. [from an Old French word]

disputable (dis-**pewt**-əbəl) adjective able to be disputed, questionable.

disputant (dis-**pew**-tənt) noun a person involved in a dispute.

disputation noun argument or debate.

dispute[1] (dis-**pewt**) verb **1** to argue or debate. **2** to quarrel. **3** to question whether something is true or valid ♦ *We dispute their claim.*

dispute[2] (dis-**pewt** or **dis**-pewt) noun **1** an argument or debate. **2** a quarrel. **3** a disagreement between management and employees that leads to industrial action. **in dispute** being argued about. [from *dis-* meaning 'apart' and a Latin word *putare* meaning 'to reckon']

disqualify verb (**disqualifies, disqualified, disqualifying**) **1** to bar someone from a competition because he or she has broken the rules or is not properly qualified to take part. **2** to make someone or something unsuitable or ineligible ♦ *Weak eyesight disqualifies him for military service.* **disqualification** noun

disquiet noun anxiety or uneasiness. **disquiet** verb to make someone anxious. **disquieting** adjective **disquietude** noun

disquisition (dis-kwi-**zish**-ən) noun a long elaborate spoken or written account of something. [from *dis-* and a Latin word *quaesitum* meaning 'sought']

disregard verb to pay no attention to something, to treat it as of no importance. **disregard** noun lack of attention to something, treating it as of no importance ♦ *She shows a complete disregard for her own safety.*

disrepair noun a poor condition caused by not doing repairs ♦ *The old cottage is in a state of disrepair.*

disreputable (dis-**rep**-yoo-təbəl) adjective not respectable in character or appearance. **disreputably** adverb

disrepute (dis-ri-**pewt**) noun the state of having a bad reputation or being discredited ♦ *He has been charged with bringing the game into disrepute.*

disrespect noun lack of respect, rudeness. **disrespectful** adjective **disrespectfully** adverb

disrobe verb 1 to take off official or ceremonial robes. 2 to undress.

disrupt verb to throw something into disorder, to interrupt the flow or continuity of something ♦ Floods disrupted traffic. **disruption** noun [from dis- meaning 'apart' and a Latin word ruptum meaning 'broken']

disruptive adjective causing disruption.

dissatisfaction noun lack of satisfaction or of contentment.

dissatisfied adjective not satisfied or pleased.

dissect (dis-**sekt**) verb 1 to cut something up in order to examine its internal structure. 2 to examine a theory etc. carefully in great detail. **dissection** noun **dissector** noun [from dis- meaning 'apart' and a Latin word sectum meaning 'cut']

dissemble verb to conceal your true feelings. [from a Latin word dissimulare meaning 'to disguise, conceal']

disseminate (dis-**sem**-in-ayt) verb to spread ideas etc. widely. **dissemination** noun [from dis- meaning 'apart' and a Latin word seminare meaning 'to sow (scatter seeds)']

dissension noun disagreement that gives rise to strife.

dissent verb to have or express a different opinion. **dissent** noun a difference in opinion. **dissenter** noun [from dis- meaning 'apart' and a Latin word sentire meaning 'to feel']

dissertation noun a long essay on an academic subject, especially one written as part of a university degree. [from a Latin word dissertare meaning 'to examine, discuss']

disservice noun a harmful action, especially one done when trying to help.

dissident (dis-i-dənt) noun someone who disagrees, especially someone who opposes the government. **dissident** adjective disagreeing. **dissidence** noun [from a Latin word dissidere meaning 'to sit by yourself']

dissimilar adjective not similar, unlike. **dissimilarity** noun

dissimulate verb to conceal your true feelings, to dissemble. **dissimulation** noun [same origin as for dissemble]

dissipate (dis-i-payt) verb 1 to disappear, or to make something disappear; to disperse ♦ The fog gradually dissipated. 2 to squander something or fritter it away. [from a Latin word dissipare meaning 'to scatter']

dissipated adjective indulging your vices, living an immoral life. **dissipation** noun

dissociate (dis-**soh**-si-ayt) verb to separate something in your thoughts ♦ It is difficult to dissociate the criminal from the crime. **to dissociate yourself from** to declare that you do not support or agree with something ♦ I wish to dissociate myself from these views. **dissociation** noun [from a Latin word dissociare meaning 'to separate']

dissoluble adjective able to be dissolved.

dissolute (dis-ə-loot) adjective having an immoral way of life. [from a Latin word dissolutus meaning 'loose']

dissolution noun 1 putting an end to a marriage or partnership. 2 formally ending a parliament or assembly. 3 the ending of the existence of monasteries in the reign of Henry VIII. [same origin as for dissolve]

dissolve verb 1 to mix something with a liquid so that it becomes part of the liquid; to become mixed in this way ♦ Wait for the tablet to dissolve. 2 to formally end an assembly or a parliament ♦ Parliament was dissolved and a general election was held. 3 to annul or put an end to a marriage or partnership. 4 to disappear gradually ♦ As she walked home, her anger dissolved. 5 to give way to emotion ♦ He dissolved into tears. [from dis- meaning 'separate' and a Latin word solvere meaning 'to loosen']

dissonant (dis-ən-ənt) adjective lacking harmony, discordant. **dissonance** noun [from dis- and a Latin word sonare meaning 'to sound']

dissuade verb to discourage someone from doing something; to persuade someone not to do something ♦ I tried to dissuade her from going. **dissuasion** noun **dissuasive** adjective [from dis- meaning 'apart' and a Latin word suadere meaning 'to advise']

distaff (dis-tahf) noun a cleft stick holding wool etc. for spinning into yarn. **on the distaff side** on the woman's side of the family. [from an Old English word]

distance noun 1 the length of space between one point and another. 2 a distant point or place ♦ *I could see a ship in the distance.* 3 being far away in space or time. **to distance yourself from** to show that you do not support or agree with something ♦ *I wish to distance myself from these views.*

distance learning noun a method of studying at home in which you take lessons by correspondence, watch lectures on television, etc.

distance runner noun an athlete who competes in long- or middle-distance races.

distant adjective 1 far away in space or time ♦ *the distant past.* 2 at a specified distance away ♦ *The town lay three miles distant.* 3 not friendly, aloof. SYNONYMS: remote, reserved, unapproachable; (*informal*) stand-offish. 4 not closely related ♦ *a distant cousin.* **distantly** adverb [from *dis-* meaning 'apart' and a Latin word *stans* meaning 'standing']

distaste noun dislike or aversion.

distasteful adjective unpleasant or offensive. **distastefully** adverb

distemper noun 1 a disease of dogs and certain other animals, causing coughing and weakness. 2 a kind of paint made from powdered pigment mixed with glue or size, used on walls.
distemper verb to paint a wall etc. with distemper. [from a Latin word *distemperare* meaning 'to soak']

distend verb to swell something or become swollen because of pressure from inside. **distension** noun [from *dis-* meaning 'apart' and a Latin word *tendere* meaning 'to stretch']

distil verb (**distilled, distilling**) 1 to purify a liquid by boiling it and condensing the vapour; to treat something by distillation. 2 to make spirits in this way. 3 to extract the essential meaning of something ♦ *Now you need to distil these ideas into a well-argued essay.* [from *dis-* meaning 'apart' and a Latin word *stillare* meaning 'to drip down']

distillate noun a product of distillation.

distillation noun 1 the process of turning a substance to vapour by heat, then cooling the vapour so that it condenses and collecting the resulting liquid, in order to purify it or separate its constituents or extract an essence. 2 something distilled.

distiller noun a person who makes alcoholic drinks such as whisky by distillation.

distillery noun (**distilleries**) a place where an alcoholic drink such as whisky is distilled.

distinct adjective 1 able to be perceived clearly by the senses ♦ *The distinct outline of a building* ♦ *a distinct improvement.* 2 clearly different or separate ♦ *There are three distinct possibilities.* **distinctly** adverb **distinctness** noun [from a Latin word *distinctus* meaning 'separated']
◊ See the note at **distinctive**.

distinction noun 1 a difference between things ♦ *What is the distinction between a hurricane and a cyclone?* 2 seeing or making a difference between things. 3 the quality of being excellent or distinguished ♦ *a person of distinction* ♦ *He has the distinction of being the youngest player to play for his country.* 4 the highest level of achievement in an examination. 5 a mark of honour.

distinctive adjective that distinguishes one thing from others ♦ *The school has a distinctive uniform.*
◊ Do not confuse this word with **distinct**. A *distinct* sign is one that can be seen clearly; a *distinctive* sign is one that is not found anywhere else.

distinguish verb 1 to see or point out a difference between two or more things ♦ *We must distinguish facts from rumours.* 2 to make one thing different from another, to be a characteristic mark or property of something ♦ *Speech distinguishes people from animals.* 3 to make something out by listening or looking ♦ *He cannot distinguish distant objects.* 4 to bring honour to yourself ♦ *She distinguished herself by her bravery.* **distinguishable** adjective [from a Latin word *distinguere* meaning 'to separate']

distinguished adjective 1 having a high reputation ♦ *a distinguished author.* 2 noble and dignified in appearance or behaviour.

distort verb 1 to pull or twist something out of its usual shape. 2 to give a false account or impression of something ♦ *This film deliberately distorts the truth.* 3 to change the quality of a sound that is being transmitted or amplified, often so that it sounds strange and unclear. **distortion** noun [from *dis-* meaning 'apart' and a Latin word *tortum* meaning 'twisted']

distract *verb* to take someone's attention away from something. SYNONYMS: deflect, divert, sidetrack. [from *dis-* meaning 'apart' and a Latin word *tractum* meaning 'pulled']

distracted *adjective* greatly upset by worry or distress.

distraction *noun* **1** something that distracts the attention and prevents concentration. **2** an amusement or entertainment. **3** great worry or distress ♦ *She had an air of distraction.* **to distraction** almost to a state of madness.

distraught (dis-trawt) *adjective* very worried and upset. [same origin as for *distract*]

distress *noun* **1** suffering caused by pain, worry, illness, or exhaustion. **2** the condition of being damaged or in danger and requiring help ♦ *a ship in distress*. **distress** *verb* **1** to cause distress to someone. SYNONYMS: upset; (*informal*) cut up. **2** to give artificial marks of wear to leather, furniture, etc. **distressing** *adjective* [from an Old French word]

distributary *noun* (**distributaries**) a branch of a river that does not return to it after leaving the main stream, e.g. in a delta.

distribute *verb* **1** to divide something and give a share to each of a number of people. **2** to hand something out ♦ *During the election he distributed leaflets.* **3** to place things at different points over an area. **to be distributed** to be spread over an area. **distribution** *noun* [from *dis-* meaning 'separate' and a Latin word *tributum* meaning 'given']

distributive *adjective* **1** to do with or concerned with distribution. **2** (*Mathematics*) (said about an operation applied to a sum of elements) producing the same result whether it is performed before or after the elements are added, e.g. $5(3 + 4) = (5 \times 3) + (5 \times 4) = 35$, $5(3 + 4) = 5 \times 7 = 35$.

distributor *noun* **1** someone who distributes things, especially an agent who supplies goods to retailers. **2** a device in an engine for passing electric current to each of the spark plugs in turn.

district *noun* part of a country, city, or county having a particular feature or regarded as a unit for a special purpose. [from a French word]

district attorney *noun* (in the USA) an official who acts as prosecutor for the state or federal government.

distrust *noun* lack of trust, suspicion. **distrust** *verb* to have little trust in someone or something. **distrustful** *adjective*

disturb *verb* **1** to spoil someone's peace, rest, or privacy. **2** to cause someone to worry. SYNONYMS: agitate, disconcert, unsettle, bother, fluster. **3** to cause something to move from a settled position. **disturbing** *adjective* [from *dis-* meaning 'thoroughly' and a Latin word *turbare* meaning 'to confuse, upset']

disturbance *noun* **1** disturbing or being disturbed. **2** an outbreak of social or political disorder.

disturbed *adjective* (said about a person) suffering from emotional or psychological problems.

disunion *noun* separation, lack of union.

disunited *adjective* lacking unity or agreement. **disunity** *noun*

disuse *noun* the state of being no longer used ♦ *The mine has fallen into disuse.*

disused *adjective* no longer used.

ditch *noun* a trench dug to hold water or carry it away, or to serve as a boundary. **ditch** *verb* **1** to bring an aircraft down in a forced landing on the sea. **2** (*informal*) to get rid of something. [from an Old English word]

dither *verb* to hesitate indecisively. **dither** *noun* a state of hesitation or agitation ♦ *in a dither*. [origin unknown]

ditto *noun* (used in lists to avoid repeating something) the same thing again. [from an Italian word *detto* meaning 'said']

ditto marks *plural noun* two small marks (resembling apostrophes) placed under an item in a list to indicate that it should be repeated.

ditty *noun* (**ditties**) a short simple song. [from an Old French word *dite* meaning 'composition']

diuretic (diy-yu-ret-ik) *adjective* causing an increase in the flow of urine. [from an Old French word]

diurnal (diy-ern-əl) *adjective* **1** of or during the day, not nocturnal. **2** occupying one day. [from a Latin word *diurnus* meaning 'of a day']

divalent (diy-vay-lənt) *adjective* having a valency of two.

Divali *noun* another spelling of Diwali.

divan (div-**an**) noun a low couch or bed without a raised back or ends. [a Persian word meaning 'cushioned bench']

dive verb 1 to plunge head first into water. 2 (said about an aircraft or bird) to plunge steeply downwards. SYNONYMS: plunge, plummet, swoop, nosedive. 3 (said about a submarine) to go to a deeper level in water. 4 to swim under water using breathing equipment. 5 to go down or out of sight suddenly; to rush headlong ♦ *We dived into a coffee shop.*
dive noun 1 an act of diving. 2 a sharp downward movement or fall. [from an Old English word]

dive-bomb verb to drop bombs from a diving aircraft.

diver noun 1 a person who dives under water as a sport or as part of their work. 2 a bird that dives for its food.

diverge (diy-**verj**) verb 1 to go in different directions from a common point or from each other; to become further apart ♦ *The path diverges here.* 2 to depart from something ♦ *This account diverges from the truth.* 3 to differ ♦ *Our views diverge on this matter.* **divergent** adjective **divergence** noun [from dis- meaning 'apart' and a Latin word vergere meaning 'to slope']

divers (diy-**verz**) adjective (old use) several or various. [from a Latin word diversus meaning 'diverted']

diverse (diy-**verss**) adjective of several different kinds. [a different spelling of divers]

diversify verb (diversifies, diversified, diversifying) 1 to introduce variety into something, to vary something. 2 (said about a company) to expand its range of products or services etc. **diversification** noun

diversion noun 1 diverting something from its course. 2 something intended to divert attention ♦ *You creep in while I create a diversion.* 3 an alternative route for traffic when a road is temporarily closed. 4 a leisure activity or entertainment. **diversionary** adjective

diversity (diy-**vers**-iti) noun variety.

divert verb 1 to make something change course or go by a different route ♦ *The stream has been diverted* ♦ *Police will divert traffic during the carnival.* 2 to distract someone's attention. 3 to entertain or amuse someone. [from dis- meaning 'apart' and a Latin word vertere meaning 'to turn']

diverting adjective entertaining or amusing.

divest (diy-**vest**) verb to take something away from someone, to deprive someone ♦ *They divested him of his power.* [from dis- and a Latin word vestire meaning 'to clothe']

divide verb 1 to separate something into parts, to split or break up ♦ *The river divides here into two* ♦ *Let me divide you into three groups.* 2 to form a boundary between two things or places ♦ *The Pyrenees divide France from Spain.* 3 to distribute something or share it out ♦ *Divide the prize money between you.* 4 to arrange things in separate groups, to classify. 5 to cause people to disagree ♦ *This controversy divided the party.* 6 (said about a legislative assembly) to separate into two groups to vote. 7 (Mathematics) to find how many times one number contains another ♦ *Divide 12 by 3.*
divide noun a dividing line ♦ *the divide between rich and poor.* **divided** adjective [from a Latin word dividere meaning 'to force apart, remove']

dividend noun 1 a share of profits paid to shareholders or winners in a football pool. 2 a benefit from an action ♦ *This policy will pay dividends in the future.* 3 (Mathematics) a number that is to be divided by another. [from a Latin word dividendum meaning 'something to be divided']

divider noun a screen or piece of furniture that divides a room into two parts.
dividers plural noun a pair of compasses for measuring distances.

divination (div-in-**ay**-shon) noun divining, foretelling future events or discovering hidden knowledge.

divine adjective 1 belonging to, coming from, or like God or a god. 2 (informal) excellent, very beautiful ♦ *this divine weather.*
divine verb 1 to discover something by guessing. 2 to discover or learn about future events by supernatural or magical means. **divinely** adverb **diviner** noun [from a Latin word divus meaning 'god']

diving bell noun an open-bottomed container supplied with air, in which a person can be lowered into deep water.

diving board noun a high board used for diving from.

diving suit noun a watertight suit, usually with a helmet, worn for working deep under water.

divinity noun (**divinities**) 1 being divine. 2 a god or goddess. 3 the study of religion.

divisible (di-viz-i-bəl) adjective able to be divided. **divisibility** noun

division noun 1 dividing or being divided. 2 the process of dividing one number by another. 3 one of the parts into which something is divided. 4 a major unit of an organization ♦ our export division. 5 a grouping of teams within a league. 6 a dividing line or partition. 7 (in Parliament) separation of members into two sections for counting votes. **divisional** adjective [from a Latin word dividere meaning 'to divide']

division of labour noun giving different parts of a task or process to different workers in order to improve efficiency.

division sign noun the sign ÷ (as in 12 ÷ 4) indicating that one number is to be divided by another.

divisive (di-viy-siv) adjective tending to cause disagreement among members of a group.

divisor (di-viy-zer) noun a number by which another is to be divided.

divorce noun the legal ending of a marriage.
divorce verb 1 to end a marriage by divorce. 2 to think of two things as being separate and not connected ♦ You can't divorce science from ethics. [from a French word divorce; related to divert]

divorcee (div-or-see) noun a divorced person.

divot (div-ət) noun a piece of turf cut out by a golf club in making a stroke. [origin unknown]

divulge (diy-vulj) verb to reveal information. [from dis- and a Latin word vulgare meaning 'to publish']

divvy noun (**divvies**) (informal) a dividend or share.
divvy verb (**divvies**, **divvied**, **divvying**) to share something out.

Diwali (di-wah-li) noun a Hindu religious festival at which lamps are lit, held in October or November. [from a Sanskrit word dipavali meaning 'row of lamps']

DIY abbreviation the activity of doing house repairs and decorations yourself. [an abbreviation of do it yourself]

dizzy adjective (**dizzier**, **dizziest**) 1 having the feeling that everything is spinning round; giddy. 2 causing giddiness ♦ dizzy heights. **dizzily** adverb **dizziness** noun [from an Old English word dysig meaning 'foolish']

dizzying adjective making you feel confused or amazed ♦ the dizzying rate of change.

DJ abbreviation 1 disc jockey. 2 dinner jacket.

DNA abbreviation deoxyribonucleic acid, a substance in chromosomes that stores genetic information.

do verb (**does**, **did**, **done**, **doing**) 1 to perform or carry out an action, to fulfil or complete work, a duty, etc. ♦ Have you done your homework? SYNONYMS: carry out, perform, accomplish, execute, finish. 2 to produce or make something ♦ She's done some lovely drawings. 3 to deal with or solve something ♦ I usually do the crossword. 4 to cover a distance in travelling ♦ We did 400 miles today. 5 (informal) to visit somewhere as a tourist ♦ We did Rome last year.
6 (informal) to undergo ♦ He did two years for fraud. 7 to act or proceed ♦ Do as you like. 8 to fare or get on ♦ How did you do in the exam? 9 to be suitable or acceptable, to serve a purpose ♦ It doesn't do to worry.
10 (informal) to swindle someone; to rob a place. 11 (informal) to regularly take a drug.

do auxiliary verb 1 used to indicate present or past tense ♦ What does he think? ♦ What did he think? 2 used for emphasis ♦ I do like chocolate. 3 used to avoid repetition of a verb you have just used ♦ We work as hard as they do.

do noun (**dos** or **do's**) (informal) a party or other social event. **to do away with** (informal) to get rid of something or kill someone. **to do for** (informal) to ruin or destroy something, to kill someone. **to do someone in** (informal) 1 to kill someone.
2 to tire someone out. **dos and don'ts** rules of behaviour. **to do something up** 1 to fasten, wrap, or arrange something.
2 (informal) to redecorate or renovate a room or building. **to do with** to need or want ♦ I could do with a cup of tea. **to do without** to manage without. [from an Old English word]

Dobermann pinscher noun a large German dog with a smooth coat and powerful jaws. [named after a German dog-breeder L. Dobermann, and a German word *Pinscher* meaning 'terrier']

docile (doh-siyl) adjective willing to obey or accept control. **docilely** adverb **docility** (də-sil-iti) noun [from a Latin word *docilis* meaning 'easily taught']

dock[1] noun an enclosed area of water in a port where ships are loaded, unloaded, or repaired.
dock verb 1 (said about a ship) to come into or bring it into a dock. 2 (said about a spacecraft) to join with a space station or another spacecraft in space. **docks** plural noun a dockyard. [from an Old German or Old Dutch word]

dock[2] noun an enclosure in a criminal court for a defendant on trial. [from a Flemish word *dok* meaning 'cage']

dock[3] noun a weed with broad leaves. [from an Old English word]

dock[4] verb 1 to take away part of someone's wages or a number of points from someone's score. 2 to cut short an animal's tail. [origin unknown]

docker noun a labourer who loads and unloads ships in a dockyard.

docket noun a document or label listing goods delivered or the contents of a package, or recording payment of duty etc. [origin unknown]

dockland noun the district near a dockyard.

dockyard noun an area with docks and equipment for building and repairing ships.

doctor noun 1 a person who is qualified to practise medicine. 2 a person who holds a doctorate (the highest university degree) ◆ *Doctor of Music.*
doctor verb 1 to tamper with or falsify something ◆ *Somebody has doctored the evidence.* 2 to castrate or spay an animal. [from a Latin word *doctor* meaning 'teacher']

doctoral (dok-ter-əl) adjective to do with a doctorate ◆ *a doctoral thesis.*

doctorate (dok-ter-ət) noun the highest degree at a university, entitling the holder to the title of 'doctor'.

doctrinaire (dok-trin-air) adjective applying theories or principles without taking account of practical considerations ◆ *doctrinaire socialism.*

doctrine (dok-trin) noun a set of principles and beliefs held by a religious or political or other group. **doctrinal** (dok-triy-nəl) adjective [same origin as for *doctor*]

docudrama (dok-yu-drah-mə) noun a dramatized television film based on real events.

document noun 1 a paper giving information or evidence about something. 2 (*Computing*) a file of text or graphics stored in a computer.
document verb 1 to provide written evidence to support or prove something. 2 to record something in detail.
documentation noun [from a Latin word *documentum* meaning 'lesson, official paper']

documentary (dok-yoo-ment-er-i) adjective 1 consisting of documents ◆ *documentary evidence.* 2 giving a factual filmed report of a subject or activity.
documentary noun (**documentaries**) a film giving information about real events. [same origin as for *document*]

dodder verb to walk unsteadily, especially because of old age. **dodderer** noun **doddery** adjective [origin unknown]

doddle noun (*informal*) a very easy task. [origin unknown]

dodecagon (doh-dek-ə-gən) noun a geometric figure with twelve sides. [from Greek words *dōdeka* meaning 'twelve' and *gōnia* meaning 'angle']

dodecahedron (doh-deka-hee-drən) noun (**dodecahedra** or **dodecahedrons**) a solid body with twelve faces. [from Greek words *dōdeka* meaning 'twelve' and *hedra* meaning 'base']

dodecaphonic (doh-dekə-fon-ik) adjective (said about music) using the twelve chromatic notes of the octave arranged in a chosen order, without a conventional key. [from Greek words *dōdeka* meaning 'twelve' and *phōnē* meaning 'sound']

dodge verb 1 to move quickly to one side; to avoid something by changing position or direction. 2 to evade something by cunning or trickery ◆ *He tried to dodge military service.*
dodge noun 1 a quick movement to avoid something. 2 (*informal*) a clever trick, an ingenious way of doing something.
dodger noun [origin unknown]

dodgem (doj-əm) *noun* a small electrically-powered car driven in an enclosure at a funfair, in which each driver tries to bump other cars and avoid being bumped by them. [from *dodge* and *'em* (them)]

dodgy *adjective* (**dodgier, dodgiest**) (*informal*) 1 not working properly. 2 dishonest. 3 risky or dangerous. [from *dodge* meaning 'a trick']

dodo (doh-doh) *noun* (**dodos** or **dodoes**) a large non-flying bird that used to live on the island of Mauritius but has been extinct since the 18th century. [from a Portuguese word *doudo* meaning 'fool' (because the bird had no fear of people)]

doe *noun* the female of the fallow deer, reindeer, hare, or rabbit. [from an Old English word]

doer *noun* a person who takes action rather than just thinking or talking about things.

doesn't (*informal*) *verb* does not.

doff *verb* to take something off ♦ *He doffed his hat.* [from *do off*; compare *don*[1]]

dog *noun* 1 a four-legged carnivorous animal, commonly kept as a pet or trained for use in hunting etc. 2 the male of this or of the wolf or fox. **dog** *verb* (**dogged, dogging**) to follow someone closely or persistently ♦ *Reporters dogged his footsteps.* **a dog in the manger** a person who prevents others from using something they do not need to use themselves. **a dog's life** a life of misery or harassment. **to go to the dogs** (*informal*) to reach a very poor standard. [from an Old English word]

dog collar *noun* 1 a collar for a dog. 2 (*informal*) a clerical collar.

doge (dohj) *noun* (*historical*) the chief magistrate of Venice or Genoa. [from a Latin word *dux* meaning 'leader']

dog-eared *adjective* (said about a book) having the corners of the pages turned down through constant use.

dogfight *noun* 1 a close fight between fighter aircraft. 2 a fierce struggle or fight.

dogfish *noun* (**dogfish**) a kind of small shark.

dogged (dog-id) *adjective* determined, not giving up easily. **doggedly** *adverb* **doggedness** *noun* [from *dog*]

doggerel (dog-er-əl) *noun* bad or comic verse. [origin unknown]

doggo *adverb* **to lie doggo** (*informal*) to lie motionless in order not to be noticed. [origin unknown]

doggy-paddle *noun* a simple swimming stroke with short quick movements of the arms and legs.

doghouse *noun* (*Amer.*) a dog's kennel. **in the doghouse** (*informal*) in disgrace.

dogma *noun* a belief or principle that a Church or other authority puts forward to be accepted as true without question. [from a Greek word *dogma* meaning 'opinion, decree']

dogmatic (dog-mat-ik) *adjective* firmly and arrogantly expressing personal opinions as if there is no question that they are true. **dogmatically** *adverb* **dogmatism** *noun* [from *dogma*]

dog rose *noun* a wild rose that grows in hedgerows.

dogsbody *noun* (**dogsbodies**) (*informal*) a person who is given boring, unimportant jobs to do.

dog-tired *adjective* tired out.

doh *noun* a name for the keynote of a scale in music, or the note C. [an Italian word]

doily *noun* (**doilies**) a small ornamental mat made of paper or lace, placed on a plate under cake etc. [named after a Mr *Doily* or *Doyley*, who sold household linen in the 17th century]

doing *noun* 1 performing a deed ♦ *It was my doing.* 2 effort ♦ *It will take some doing.*

Dolby *noun* (*trademark*) 1 a system for reducing background noise in tape recording. 2 a system of stereophonic sound used in cinemas. [named after the American engineer Ray M. Dolby (born 1933)]

doldrums *plural noun* 1 a period of inactivity. 2 the ocean regions near the equator where there is little or no wind. **in the doldrums** in low spirits. [origin unknown]

dole *verb* to distribute something ♦ *Can you dole out the pizza?*

dole noun (informal) money paid by the state to unemployed people ♦ He's been on the dole for six months. [from an Old English word]

doleful adjective mournful or sad. **dolefully** adverb [from an old word dole meaning 'grief']

doll noun a small model of a human figure, especially as a child's toy.
doll verb (**to doll yourself up**) (informal) to dress smartly. [an affectionate form of Dorothy]

dollar noun the unit of money in the USA and some other countries. [from a German word Thaler meaning 'a silver coin']

dollop noun (informal) a shapeless lump of something soft ♦ a dollop of cream. [perhaps from a Scandinavian word]

dolly noun (**dollies**) 1 (informal) a doll. 2 a movable platform for a film camera.

dolmen (dol-men) noun a prehistoric structure with a large flat stone laid on upright ones. [from a French word]

dolomite (dol-ə-miyt) noun a mineral or rock of calcium magnesium carbonate. [from a French word]

dolour (dol-er) noun (literary) sorrow or distress. **dolorous** adjective [from a Latin word dolor meaning 'pain']

dolphin noun a sea animal like a porpoise but larger and with a beak-like snout. [from a Greek word delphin]

dolt (dohlt) noun a stupid person. **doltish** adjective [perhaps related to dull]

domain (dəm-ayn) noun 1 an area under someone's control. 2 a field of knowledge or activity ♦ the domain of science. 3 (Computing) a distinct group of Internet addresses with the same suffix. 4 (Mathematics) the set of input values for a function. [from a French word domaine; related to dominion]

dome noun 1 a rounded roof with a circular base. 2 something shaped like this. [via French from an Italian word duomo meaning 'cathedral, dome']

domed adjective having a dome or shaped like a dome.

domestic adjective 1 to do with the home or household or family affairs. 2 to do with your own country, not foreign or international ♦ domestic air services. 3 (said about animals) kept by humans,

not wild.
domestic noun a household servant.
domestically adverb [from a Latin word domus meaning 'home']

domesticated adjective 1 (said about animals) trained to live with and be kept by humans. 2 (said about people) enjoying household work and home life.

domesticity (dom-es-**tiss**-iti) noun home or family life.

domicile (dom-i-siyl) noun (formal) the place where someone lives, residence.
domicile verb **to be domiciled** to have a particular country as your permanent home. [from a Latin word domus meaning 'home']

domiciliary (dom-i-sil-yer-i) adjective (formal) to do with a person's home.

dominant adjective 1 dominating. 2 (said about a species of plant or animal) most widespread in a particular area and influencing the type and abundance of other species. 3 (said about a gene or inherited characteristic) appearing in offspring even if a contrary gene or characteristic is also inherited.
dominant noun 1 a dominant species, characteristic, or gene. 2 (Music) the fifth note of a diatonic scale. **dominance** noun

dominate verb 1 to control someone or something by being stronger or more powerful than them. 2 to be the most influential or conspicuous person or thing. 3 (said about a high place) to tower over something ♦ The mountain dominates the whole valley. **domination** noun [from a Latin word dominus meaning 'master']

domineer verb to behave in a forceful or arrogant way, making others obey. **domineering** adjective [same origin as for dominate]

dominion noun 1 authority to rule others, control. 2 an area controlled by a ruler or government. [from a Latin word dominium meaning 'property']

domino noun (**dominoes**) each of the small oblong wooden or plastic pieces marked with up to 6 dots on each half, used in games.
dominoes noun a game played with these. [from a French word, denoting a hood worn by priests in winter]

domino effect noun the effect of a political or other event in one place seeming to cause similar events elsewhere, like a row of dominoes falling.

don [1] *verb* (**donned, donning**) to put on a piece of clothing. [from *do on*; compare *doff*]

don [2] *noun* a university teacher, especially a senior member of a college at Oxford or Cambridge.
Don *noun* a Spanish title put before a man's Christian name. [from a Latin word *dominus* meaning 'lord, master']

donate *verb* **1** to give money etc. for a good cause. **2** to give blood for transfusion or an organ for a transplant. [from a Latin word *donum* meaning 'gift']

donation *noun* **1** an act of donating. **2** a sum of money given to a charity.

done past participle of **do**.
done *adjective* **1** (*informal*) socially acceptable ♦ *the done thing*. **2** cooked thoroughly.
done *interjection* (in reply to an offer) I accept. **to be done for** (*informal*) to be in serious trouble. **done in** (*informal*) tired out. **done with** finished with, completed.

doner kebab (**don-er kə-bab**) *noun* layers of lamb or mutton cooked on a spit and sliced downwards, often served with pitta bread. [from a Turkish word *döner* meaning 'turning' and *kebab*]

donjon *noun* the great tower or keep of a castle. [an old spelling of *dungeon*]

donkey *noun* (**donkeys**) an animal of the horse family, with long ears and a braying call. **donkey's years** (*informal*) a very long time. [origin unknown]

Donna *noun* the title of an Italian, Spanish, or Portuguese lady.

donnish *adjective* like a college don, especially in being pedantic.

donor *noun* **1** someone who gives or donates something, especially to a charity. **2** someone who provides blood for transfusion or semen for insemination or tissue for transplantation. [from an Old French word *doneur*]

donor card *noun* a card someone carries giving their consent to the use of their organs for transplants in the event of their death.

don't *contraction* do not.

doodle *verb* to scribble or draw while thinking about something else.
doodle *noun* a drawing or marks made by doodling. [from an Old German word, denoting a foolish person]

doom *noun* a terrible fate that you cannot avoid, especially death or destruction ♦ *a sense of impending doom*.
doom *verb* to destine or condemn someone to a terrible fate. [from an Old English word]

doomed *adjective* bound to fail or suffer a bad fate.

doomsday *noun* the day of the Last Judgement, the end of the world. [from *doom* in an old sense meaning 'judgement']

door *noun* **1** a hinged, sliding, or revolving barrier used to open or close an entrance to a building, room, vehicle, or cupboard. **2** a doorway or entrance. [from an Old English word]

doorbell *noun* a bell inside a house, rung from outside by visitors as a signal.

doorkeeper *noun* a person on duty at the entrance to a building.

doorknob *noun* a knob for turning to release the latch of a door.

doorman *noun* (**doormen**) a man on duty at the entrance to a large building.

doormat *noun* **1** a mat placed at a door, for wiping dirt from shoes. **2** (*informal*) a person who meekly allows himself or herself to be bullied.

doorstep *noun* **1** a step leading up to the door of a house. **2** (*informal*) a thick slice of bread. **on your doorstep** very close.

doorstop *noun* a device for keeping a door open or preventing it from striking a wall when it opens.

door-to-door *adjective* (said about selling etc.) done at each house in turn.

doorway *noun* an opening into which a door fits.

dope *noun* (*informal*) **1** an illegal drug. **2** a drug given to an athlete, horse, or greyhound to affect performance. **3** a stupid person. **4** information.
dope *verb* **1** to give dope to an athlete, horse, or greyhound. **2** to take addictive drugs. **3** (*Electronics*) to add an impurity to a semiconductor to achieve a specific electrical property. [from a Dutch word *doop* meaning 'sauce']

dopey *adjective* (**dopier, dopiest**) (*informal*) **1** sleepy, acting as if drugged. **2** stupid. **dopiness** *noun*

doppelgänger (**dop-əl-geng-er**) *noun* **1** a ghost that looks exactly like a living person. **2** someone who looks exactly like someone else, a double. [a German word meaning 'double-goer']

Doppler effect or **Doppler shift** noun (*Physics*) an increase (or decrease) in the frequency of sound, light, or other waves as the source and observer move towards (or away) from each other. [named after the Austrian physicist J. C. Doppler (1803–53)]

Doric adjective (*Architecture*) denoting a classical order of architecture using sturdy columns and a plain style of decoration. [from a Greek word *Dōrikos*]

dormant adjective **1** temporarily inactive ♦ *a dormant volcano*. **2** sleeping, lying inactive as if in sleep. **3** (said about plants) alive but not actively growing. **dormancy** noun [from a French word meaning 'sleeping']

dormer window noun an upright window under a small gable built out from a sloping roof. [same origin as for *dormant*]

dormitory noun (**dormitories**) a room with a number of beds, especially in a school or institution. [from a Latin word *dormire* meaning 'to sleep']

dormitory town noun a town from which people travel to work elsewhere because there are few or no industries locally.

dormouse noun (**dormice**) a mouse-like rodent that hibernates in winter. [origin unknown]

dorsal adjective to do with or on the back of an animal or plant ♦ *a dorsal fin*. **dorsally** adverb [from a Latin word *dorsum* meaning 'the back']

DOS abbreviation (*Computing*) disk operating system.

dosage noun **1** the giving of medicine in doses. **2** the size of a dose.

dose noun **1** an amount of medicine taken at one time. **2** an amount of radiation received by a person or thing. **3** (*informal*) an amount of something, especially something that you do not want ♦ *a dose of punishment*. **dose** verb to give someone a dose of medicine. [from a Greek word *dosis* meaning 'something given']

doss verb (*informal*) to sleep, especially in a dosshouse. **dosser** noun [perhaps from a Latin word *dorsum* meaning 'back']

dosshouse noun (*informal*) a cheap lodging house for homeless people.

dossier (dos-i-er) noun a set of documents containing information about a person or event. [from a French word, denoting a bundle of papers with a label on the back]

dot noun **1** a small round mark or spot. **2** the shorter of the two signals used in Morse code. **dot** verb (**dotted**, **dotting**) **1** to mark something with a dot or dots. **2** to scatter things or be scattered here and there ♦ *Just dot a few cushions about* ♦ *The sea was dotted with ships*. **on the dot** exactly on time. **the year dot** (*informal*) a very long time ago. [from an Old English word *dott* meaning 'head of a boil']

dotage (doh-tij) noun the period of time in which someone is old and weak ♦ *He is in his dotage*. [from *dote*]

dotard (doh-terd) noun a person who is weak or senile.

dot-com noun a company that operates on the Internet. [from the suffix '.com' used in Internet addresses, signifying a commercial website]

dote verb **to dote on** to be very, perhaps foolishly, fond of someone. **doting** adjective [from an Old Dutch word *doten* meaning 'to be silly']

doth verb (old use) does.

dot matrix printer noun a printer in which each printed letter or number is made up of dots printed by the tips of small wires selected from a rectangular grid.

dotted line noun a line of dots showing where a signature should be written on a contract or other document.

dotty adjective (**dottier**, **dottiest**) (*informal*) slightly mad or eccentric. **to be dotty about** to be infatuated or obsessed with someone or something. **dottiness** noun [origin unknown]

double adjective **1** twice as much or twice as many ♦ *a double whisky*. **2** consisting of two things or parts that form a pair. **3** suitable for two people ♦ *a double bed*. **4** combining two things or qualities ♦ *The title has a double meaning*. **5** (said about flowers) having more than one circle of petals. **double** adverb twice the amount or quantity ♦ *It costs double what it cost last year*. **double** noun **1** a double quantity or thing. **2** a person or thing that looks exactly like another ♦ *You're the double of my cousin*. **3** (in darts) a hit between the two outer

circles of the board, scoring double.
doubles *plural noun* a game between two pairs of players.
double *verb* 1 to make something, or become, twice as much or as many. 2 to bend or fold something in two. 3 to turn sharply back from a course ♦ *The fox doubled back on its tracks.* **at the double** very fast, hurrying. **double as** to have another role or purpose as well as the main one. **doubly** *adverb* [from an Old French word]

double agent *noun* a spy who spies for two rival countries at the same time.

double-barrelled *adjective* 1 (said about a gun) having two barrels. 2 (said about a surname) having two parts joined by a hyphen.

double bass *noun* the largest and lowest-pitched instrument of the violin family. [from *double* and *bass*[1]]

double bluff *noun* an action or statement that is intended to appear as a bluff, but in fact is genuine.

double bond *noun* (*Chemistry*) a chemical bond in which two pairs of electrons are shared between two atoms.

double-breasted *adjective* (said about a jacket or coat) having two fronts that overlap to fasten across the body.

double-check *verb* to verify something twice or in two ways.

double chin *noun* a chin with a fold of loose flesh below it.

double cream *noun* thick cream with a high fat content.

double-cross *verb* to deceive or cheat someone who thinks you are working with them.
double-cross *noun* an act of double-crossing.

double-dealing *noun* deceit, especially in business.

double-decker *noun* a bus with two decks.

double Dutch *noun* talk that makes no sense at all.

double entendre (doobl ahn-**tahndr**) *noun* a word or phrase with two meanings, one of which is sexual or rude. [a French phrase, meaning 'double understanding']

double entry *noun* a system of bookkeeping in which each transaction is entered as a debit in one account and a credit in another.

double fault *noun* (in tennis) two consecutive faults in serving. **double-fault** *verb*

double figures *plural noun* any of the numbers from 10 to 99, as a total.

double glazing *noun* two layers of glass in a window, with an air space between.

double helix *noun* (*Chemistry*) the structure of the DNA molecule, consisting of two spiral chains coiled round the same axis.

double jeopardy *noun* (*Law*) a second prosecution of a person for an offence of which they have already been acquitted.

double-jointed *adjective* having very flexible joints that allow the fingers, arms, or legs to bend in unusual ways.

double-quick *adjective* & *adverb* (*informal*) very quick or quickly.

doublet (dub-lit) *noun* 1 a man's close-fitting jacket, with or without sleeves, worn in the 14th–17th centuries. 2 either of a pair of similar things. [from an Old French word meaning 'something folded']

double take *noun* a delayed reaction to something unexpected, coming immediately after your first reaction.

double time *noun* a rate of pay at twice the normal rate.

doubloon (dub-**loon**) *noun* a former Spanish gold coin. [from a French word *doublon*]

doubt *noun* 1 a feeling of uncertainty about something, an undecided state of mind. SYNONYMS: misgiving, qualm, reservation. 2 a feeling of disbelief.
doubt *verb* 1 to feel uncertain or undecided about something. 2 to hesitate to believe something. SYNONYMS: distrust, mistrust, question, suspect. **in doubt** 1 open to question. 2 feeling uncertain. **no doubt** certainly or probably. **doubter** *noun* [from a Latin word *dubitare* meaning 'to hesitate']

doubtful *adjective* 1 feeling doubt, unsure ♦ *He looked rather doubtful.* SYNONYMS: dubious, uncertain, sceptical. 2 making you feel doubt ♦ *It is doubtful that anyone will come.* 3 unreliable ♦ *a doubtful ally.* **doubtfully** *adverb*

doubting Thomas *noun* a person who refuses to believe something without proof.

doubtless *adverb* certainly, no doubt.

douche (doosh) *noun* 1 a jet of liquid applied to a part of the body to clean it or for medical purposes. 2 a device for producing such a jet.
douche *verb* to treat a part of the body with a douche; to use a douche. [from an Italian word *doccia* meaning 'a pipe']

dough (doh) *noun* 1 a thick mixture of flour and water, used for making bread, cake, or pastry. 2 (*informal*) money. **doughy** *adjective* [from an Old English word]

doughnut *noun* a small fried cake or ring of sweetened dough.

doughty (dow-ti) *adjective* (**doughtier, doughtiest**) (*old use*) brave and stout-hearted. [from an Old English word *dohtig*]

dour (door) *adjective* stern and gloomy-looking. **dourly** *adverb* **dourness** *noun* [from a Gaelic word *dur* meaning 'dull, obstinate']

douse (dows) *verb* 1 to put something into water, to throw water over something. 2 to extinguish a fire or light. [origin unknown]
◊ Do not confuse this word with **dowse**, which has a different meaning.

dove *noun* 1 a kind of bird that has short legs, a small head, and a thick body, makes a cooing sound, and resembles a pigeon. 2 a person who favours a policy of peace and negotiation. [from an Old Norse word]

dovecote *noun* a shelter for domesticated pigeons.

dovetail *noun* a wedge-shaped joint used to join two pieces of wood.
dovetail *verb* 1 to join pieces of wood with a dovetail. 2 to fit closely together, to combine neatly ♦ *My plans dovetailed with hers.* [so called because the wedge shape looks like a dove's tail]

dowager (dow-ə-jer) *noun* 1 a woman who holds a title or property after her husband has died ♦ *the dowager duchess.* 2 (*informal*) a dignified elderly woman. [from an Old French word *douage* meaning 'widow's share']

dowdy *adjective* (**dowdier, dowdiest**) 1 (said about clothes) unattractively dull, not stylish. 2 dressed in dowdy clothes.
dowdily *adverb* **dowdiness** *noun* [origin unknown]

dowel (dowl) *noun* a headless wooden or metal pin for holding two pieces of wood

or stone together by fitting into a corresponding hole in each.
dowel *verb* (**dowelled, dowelling**) to fasten something with a dowel. [probably from an Old German word]

dowelling *noun* round rods for cutting into dowels.

dower *noun* a widow's share of her husband's estate. [from an Old French word]

dower house *noun* a smaller house near a large one, forming part of a widow's dower.

Dow Jones index *noun* an index of figures indicating the relative price of shares on the New York Stock Exchange. [named after the American economists C. H. Dow (1851–1902) and E. D. Jones (1855–1920)]

down [1] *adverb* 1 into or towards a lower place; from an upright position to a horizontal one ♦ *It fell down.* 2 to or at a lower place; further south. 3 to or at a lower level or value; to a smaller size. 4 so as to be less active ♦ *Settle down!* 5 (said about a computer) out of action. 6 away from a central place or a university ♦ *She is down from headquarters.* 7 from an earlier to a later time ♦ *down to the present day.* 8 in writing ♦ *Take down these instructions.* 9 to the source or the place where something is ♦ *See if you can track it down.* 10 as a payment at the time of purchase ♦ *We will pay £50 down and the rest later.*
down *preposition* 1 downwards along or through or into, along, from top to bottom of ♦ *Pour it down the drain.* 2 at a lower part of ♦ *Oxford is further down the river.*
down *adjective* 1 directed downwards ♦ *a down draught.* 2 travelling away from a central place ♦ *a down train.*
down *verb* (*informal*) 1 to knock or bring something to the ground. 2 to swallow a drink.
down *noun* 1 a misfortune ♦ *ups and downs.* 2 (*informal*) a dislike, a grudge against someone ♦ *She has a real down on him.* **down in the mouth** looking unhappy. **to be down to** 1 to be attributable to something. 2 to be the responsibility of someone. [from an Old English word *adune*]

down [2] *noun* very fine soft furry feathers or short hairs. [from an Old Norse word]

down [3] or **downland** *noun* an area of open rolling land.

the Downs noun the chalk uplands of south England. [from an Old English word dun]

down and out adjective completely destitute.

down-and-out noun a destitute person.

down at heel adjective shabby.

downbeat noun (Music) an accented beat, for which the conductor's baton moves downwards.
downbeat adjective pessimistic or gloomy.

downcast adjective 1 looking downwards ♦ downcast eyes. 2 (said about a person) dejected.

downer noun (informal) 1 a depressant or tranquillizing drug. 2 something depressing.

downfall noun 1 a fall from prosperity or power. 2 something that causes this.

downgrade verb to reduce something to a lower grade or rank.

downhearted adjective in low spirits.

downhill adverb in a downward direction; further down a slope.
downhill adjective going or sloping downwards. **to go downhill** to deteriorate.

download verb (Computing) to transfer data from one system to another or to a disk.

downmarket adjective & adverb of or towards the cheaper end of the market.

down payment noun an initial payment made when buying something on credit.

downpipe noun a pipe for carrying rainwater from a roof to a drain.

downplay verb to make something seem less important than it really is.

downpour noun a heavy fall of rain.

downright adjective 1 thorough, complete ♦ a downright lie. 2 frank, straightforward.
downright adverb thoroughly ♦ He was downright rude.

downside noun the negative or disadvantageous aspect of something.

Down's syndrome noun an abnormal congenital condition that causes intellectual impairment and physical abnormalities such as short stature and a broad flattened skull. [named after the English physician J. L. H. Down (1828–96)]

downstage adjective & adverb at or towards the front of a theatre stage.

downstairs adverb down the stairs; to or on a lower floor.
downstairs adjective situated downstairs.

downstream adjective & adverb in the direction in which a stream or river flows.

down time noun the time when a computer system is out of action.

down-to-earth adjective sensible and practical.

downtrodden adjective oppressed or badly treated by people in power.

downturn noun a decline in something, especially economic activity.

down under adverb (informal) in Australia or New Zealand.

downward adjective moving, leading, or pointing towards a lower point or level ♦ a downward glance.
downwards or **downward** adverb towards a lower point or level ♦ The lawn slopes downwards towards the stream.

downwind adjective & adverb in the direction towards which the wind is blowing.

downy adjective (**downier, downiest**) like or covered with soft down.

dowry noun (**dowries**) property or money brought by a bride to her husband when she marries him. [from an Old French word dowarie; related to endow]

dowse verb to search for underground water or minerals by using a Y-shaped stick or rod. **dowser** noun [origin unknown]
◊ Do not confuse this word with **douse**, which has a different meaning.

doxology noun (**doxologies**) a formula of praise to God used in prayer. [from the Greek words doxa meaning 'glory' and logos meaning 'word']

doyen (doy-ən) or **doyenne** (doy-en) noun the most respected person in a particular field or profession. [a French word]
◊ The masculine form is **doyen** and the feminine form is **doyenne**.

doze verb to sleep lightly.
doze noun a short light sleep. **to doze off** to fall into a doze. [origin unknown]

dozen noun a group or set of twelve. [from an Old French word]
◊ Correct use is ten dozen, not ten dozens.

dozy adjective (**dozier, doziest**) 1 drowsy. 2 (informal) stupid or lazy.

Dr *abbreviation* Doctor.

drab *adjective* 1 dull or uninteresting ♦ *a drab life.* 2 of dull brownish colour.
drab *noun* a dull brownish colour. **drably** *adverb* **drabness** *noun* [from an Old French word]

drachma (drak-mə) *noun* (**drachmas** or **drachmae** (drak-mee)) the unit of money in Greece.

draconian (drə-koh-niən) *adjective* very harsh or severe ♦ *draconian laws.* [named after *Draco*, who is said to have established severe laws in ancient Athens in the 6th century BC]

draft *noun* 1 a rough preliminary written version ♦ *a draft of an essay.* 2 a written order for a bank to pay out money. 3 (*North Amer.*) conscription.
draft *verb* 1 to prepare a written draft of something ♦ *I've drafted the speech.* 2 to select someone for a special duty ♦ *He was drafted to the Paris branch.* 3 (*North Amer.*) to conscript someone. [a different spelling of *draught*]
◊ This is also the American spelling of **draught.**

drag *verb* (**dragged, dragging**) 1 to pull something along with effort or difficulty. SYNONYMS: haul, tug, tow, lug. 2 to take someone somewhere, especially against their will. 3 to trail or allow something to trail along the ground. 4 to move an image across a computer screen using a mouse. 5 to search the bottom of a river or lake with nets and hooks ♦ *The police dragged the river for a body.* 6 to continue slowly in a boring manner ♦ *The speeches dragged on.*
drag *noun* 1 (*informal*) something that is tedious or a nuisance. 2 women's clothes worn by men. **to drag your feet** to be deliberately slow or reluctant. **to drag something out** to prolong something unnecessarily. [from an Old Norse word *draga* meaning 'to draw']

dragon *noun* 1 a mythical monster resembling a reptile, usually with wings and able to breathe out fire. 2 a fierce person, especially a woman. [from a Greek word *drakōn* meaning 'serpent']

dragonfly *noun* (**dragonflies**) an insect with a long thin body and two pairs of transparent wings that spread out while it is resting.

dragoon *noun* a member of certain cavalry regiments, originally a mounted infantryman.

dragoon *verb* to force someone into doing something. [same origin as for *dragon*]

drag race *noun* a race between cars to see which can accelerate fastest from a standstill.

drain *noun* 1 a channel or pipe through which liquid or sewage is carried away. 2 something that takes away your strength or resources.
drain *verb* 1 to draw off liquid by means of channels or pipes etc. 2 to flow or trickle away. 3 to dry or become dried as liquid flows away. 4 (said about a river) to carry off the superfluous water from an area. 5 to gradually take away strength or resources. SYNONYMS: deplete, exhaust, consume, sap. 6 to drink the contents of a glass etc. [from an Old English word]

drainage *noun* 1 the process or means of draining ♦ *The land has poor drainage.* 2 a system of drains.

draining board *noun* a sloping surface beside a sink, on which washed dishes are put to drain.

drainpipe *noun* a pipe used for carrying rainwater or sewage from a building.

drake *noun* a male duck. [from a West Germanic word]

dram *noun* a small drink of spirits. [from an Old French word]

drama (drah-mə) *noun* 1 a play. 2 the art of writing and performing plays. 3 an exciting or emotional series of events. 4 dramatic quality ♦ *the drama of the situation.* [from a Greek word]

dramatic *adjective* 1 to do with drama. 2 exciting and impressive ♦ *a dramatic change.*
dramatics *plural noun* 1 the performance of plays. 2 exaggerated behaviour. **dramatically** *adverb*

dramatis personae (dram-a-tis per-sohn-iy) *plural noun* the characters in a play. [a Latin phrase meaning 'persons of the drama']

dramatist *noun* a person who writes plays.

dramatize *verb* 1 to make a story etc. into a play. 2 to make something seem more exciting. **dramatization** *noun*

drank past tense of **drink.**

drape *verb* 1 to arrange cloth or clothing loosely on or round something. 2 to cover something loosely with folds of cloth.

drapes plural noun (North Amer.) long curtains. [from a French word drap meaning 'cloth']

draper noun (old use) a retailer of cloth or clothing. [same origin as for drape]

drapery noun (draperies) cloth arranged in loose folds. [same origin as for drape]

drastic adjective having a strong or violent effect. **drastically** adverb [from a Greek word drastikos]

drat interjection used to express anger or annoyance. **dratted** adjective

draught (drahft) noun 1 a current of usually cold air indoors. 2 the depth of water needed to float a ship. 3 one continuous process of swallowing liquid; the amount swallowed.

draughts plural noun a game for two players using 24 round pieces, played on a chequered board of 64 squares. [from an Old Norse word]

draught animal noun an animal used for pulling heavy loads, such as a horse or ox.

draught beer noun beer drawn from a cask, not bottled or canned.

draughtboard noun a chequered board used for playing draughts, identical to a chessboard.

draughtsman noun (draughtsmen) 1 someone who makes detailed technical drawings or plans. 2 someone who is good at drawing. 3 a piece used in the game of draughts. **draughtsmanship** noun [draught is an old spelling of draft]

draughty adjective (draughtier, draughtiest) letting in sharp currents of air. **draughtiness** noun

draw verb (drew, drawn) 1 to produce a picture or diagram by making marks on a surface. 2 to pull something ♦ The horse drew a cart behind it ♦ She drew her bow. 3 to pull curtains shut or open. 4 to attract something ♦ The singer always draws large crowds ♦ Don't draw attention to yourself. 5 to take something in ♦ He hardly had time to draw breath. 6 to take something out ♦ People were drawing water from the well. 7 to obtain something in a raffle or lottery ♦ You've drawn the winning ticket. 8 to get information from someone ♦ He refused to be drawn about his plans. 9 to end a game or contest with the same score on both sides. 10 to move or come ♦ The boat drew nearer. 11 to reach a certain point in time ♦ The concert drew to a close. 12 to write out a cheque to be cashed. 13 (said about a fire or chimney) to allow air to flow freely so that a fire can burn. 14 to need a certain depth of water in which to float ♦ The ship draws 3 metres. 15 (said about tea) to infuse.

draw noun 1 a game or match that ends with the scores even. 2 a person or thing that draws custom or attention. 3 the drawing of lots, e.g. to decide the winner of a raffle or lottery. 4 the drawing out of a gun in order to shoot ♦ He was quick on the draw. **to draw a blank** to get no response or result. **to draw a conclusion** to form an opinion about something by thinking about the evidence. **to draw in** (said about the time of daylight) to become shorter ♦ The days are drawing in now. **to draw on** to use something as a resource ♦ You should draw on your imagination. **to draw someone out** to gently encourage a person to talk. **to draw something out** to make a discussion etc. last longer. **to draw the line at** to refuse to do or tolerate something. **to draw up** to come to a halt. **to draw something up** to prepare a contract or plan etc. in detail. **to draw yourself up** to stand or sit up with a straight back. [from an Old English word dragan]

drawback noun a disadvantage. [from draw back meaning 'to hesitate']

drawbridge noun a bridge over a moat, hinged at one end so that it can be raised or lowered.

drawee noun the person who has to pay the sum of money specified in a bill of exchange.

drawer noun 1 a sliding box-like compartment in a piece of furniture. 2 a person who draws something. 3 the person who writes out a cheque. **drawers** plural noun (old use) knickers or underpants.

drawing noun 1 a picture made with a pencil, ink, or crayon rather than paint. 2 the art or skill of doing these.

drawing board noun a flat board on which paper is stretched while a drawing is made. **to go back to the drawing board** to begin planning afresh.

drawing pin noun a flat-headed pin for fastening paper to a surface.

drawing room noun a room in a large private house in which guests can be received, a sitting room. [short for withdrawing room, a private room in a hotel etc., to which guests could withdraw]

drawl *verb* to speak lazily or with drawn-out vowel sounds.
drawl *noun* a drawling manner of speaking. [from an Old German or Old Dutch word *dralen* meaning 'to delay']

drawn past participle of **draw**.
drawn *adjective* looking strained from tiredness or worry.

drawstring *noun* a string that can be pulled to tighten or close an opening.

dray *noun* a strong low flat cart for heavy loads. [perhaps from an Old English word; related to *draw*]

dread *noun* great fear or apprehension.
dreads *plural noun* (*informal*) dreadlocks.
dread *verb* to feel worried or apprehensive about something.
dread *adjective* greatly feared. [from an Old English word]

dreadful *adjective* very bad or unpleasant ♦ *dreadful weather*. **dreadfully** *adverb*

dreadlocks *plural noun* hair worn in many ringlets or plaits, especially by Rastafarians.

dream *noun* 1 a series of pictures or events in a sleeping person's mind. 2 the state of mind in which someone is daydreaming or not fully aware of their surroundings ♦ *He goes around in a dream*. 3 an ambition or ideal. 4 (*informal*) a beautiful person or thing.
dream *verb* (past tense and past participle **dreamt** (dremt) or **dreamed** (dreemd)) 1 to have a dream or dreams while sleeping. 2 to have an ambition ♦ *He had always dreamt of being champion*. 3 to think of something as a possibility ♦ *I never dreamt it would happen* ♦ *I wouldn't dream of asking you to do it*. **to dream something up** to imagine or invent something. **like a dream** (*informal*) easily or effortlessly. **dreamer** *noun* **dreamless** *adjective* [from a Middle English word]

dreamy *adjective* (**dreamier, dreamiest**) 1 daydreaming. 2 like a dream. 3 (*informal*) wonderful. **dreamily** *adverb* **dreaminess** *noun*

dreary *adjective* (**drearier, dreariest**) dull, boring, or gloomy. **drearily** *adverb* **dreariness** *noun* [from an Old English word]

dredge [1] *noun* an apparatus for scooping things from the bottom of a river or the sea.
dredge *verb* to bring something up or clean something out with a dredge. **to**

dredge something up to mention a matter that someone would prefer to be forgotten about. [origin unknown]

dredge [2] *verb* to sprinkle food with sugar or flour. [from an old word *dredge* meaning 'sweetmeat']

dredger [1] *noun* a dredge, or a boat with a dredge.

dredger [2] *noun* a container with a perforated lid, used for sprinkling things.

dregs *plural noun* 1 the last drops of a liquid at the bottom of a glass, barrel, etc., together with any sediment. 2 the worst and most useless part ♦ *the dregs of society*. [from a Scandinavian word]

drench *verb* to make someone wet through ♦ *We got drenched in the rain*. [from an Old English word *drencan*; related to *drink*]

dress *noun* 1 a woman's or girl's piece of clothing with a bodice and skirt. 2 clothing, especially the visible part of it.
dress *verb* 1 to put on your clothes or put clothes on someone else. 2 to wear clothes in a particular way or of a particular type ♦ *She always dresses well* ♦ *The children are dressed in rags*. 3 to put on formal or evening clothes ♦ *They dress for dinner*. 4 to arrange a display in a window etc.; to decorate something. 5 to put a dressing on a wound. 6 to prepare poultry, crab, etc. for cooking or eating; to coat salad with dressing. **to dress up** to put on smart or formal clothes or fancy dress.
to dress something up to make something look or seem more interesting. [from a French word *dresser* meaning 'to prepare']

dressage (dress-ah*zh*) *noun* the training of a horse to perform various manoeuvres in order to show its obedience. [a French word meaning 'training']

dress circle *noun* the first level of seats above the ground floor in a theatre.

dresser [1] *noun* 1 someone who dresses in a particular way ♦ *a snappy dresser*. 2 someone who dresses a person or thing.

dresser [2] *noun* a kitchen sideboard with shelves above for displaying plates. [same origin as for *dress*]

dressing *noun* 1 a bandage, plaster, ointment, etc. for a wound. 2 a sauce of oil, vinegar, herbs, etc. for a salad.

dressing gown *noun* a loose robe worn when you are not fully dressed.

dressing room noun a room for dressing or changing your clothes.

dressing table noun a piece of bedroom furniture with a mirror and usually drawers, used while dressing or putting on make-up.

dressmaker noun a person who makes women's clothes. **dressmaking** noun

dress rehearsal noun the final rehearsal of a play in full costume.

dress shirt noun a man's shirt suitable for wearing with evening dress.

dressy adjective (**dressier, dressiest**) (said about clothes) elegant or elaborate, suitable for special occasions.

drew past tense of **draw**.

drey (dray) noun (**dreys**) a squirrel's nest. [origin unknown]

dribble verb 1 (said about a liquid) to flow or allow it to flow in drops. 2 to let saliva trickle out of your mouth. 3 to move the ball forward in football or hockey with slight touches of your feet or stick; to move the ball forward in basketball by continuous bouncing.
dribble noun 1 a thin stream of liquid. 2 an act of dribbling. [from drib, a different spelling of drip]

dribs and drabs plural noun small scattered amounts.

dried past tense and past participle of **dry**. **dried** adjective preserved by drying ♦ dried apricots.

drier noun a device for drying hair, laundry, etc.

drift verb 1 to be carried gently along by or as if by a current of water or air. 2 to walk along casually or aimlessly. 3 to move into a situation without meaning or planning to ♦ He drifted into teaching ♦ Over the years we drifted apart. 4 to be piled into drifts by wind ♦ The snow had drifted.
drift noun 1 a drifting movement from one place to another. 2 a mass of snow or sand piled up by wind. 3 deviation from a set course. 4 the general intention or meaning of what someone says ♦ I didn't understand it all, but I think I got the drift of it. 5 fragments of rock carried and deposited by wind, water, or a glacier. 6 (in South Africa) a ford. [from an Old Norse word drift meaning 'snowdrift']

drifter noun 1 a person who moves from place to place, without a fixed home or job. 2 a boat used for fishing with a drift net.

drift net noun a large net for catching herring etc., allowed to drift with the tide.

driftwood noun wood floating on the sea or washed ashore.

drill [1] noun 1 a pointed tool or a machine used for boring holes or sinking wells. 2 training in military exercises. 3 thorough training or instruction by practical exercises, usually with much repetition. 4 (informal) the correct or recognized procedure ♦ I expect you know the drill by now.
drill verb 1 to use a drill; to make a hole with a drill. 2 to teach someone to do something by making them do repeated exercises. [from an Old Dutch word drillen meaning 'to bore, turn in a circle']

drill [2] noun 1 a machine for making small furrows and sowing seed in them. 2 a small furrow for sowing seeds in.
drill verb to sow seed with a drill. [origin unknown]

drill [3] noun strong twilled linen or cotton cloth. [from a German word]

drily adverb in a dry way or manner.

drink verb (**drank, drunk**) 1 to swallow liquid. 2 (said about plants, the soil, etc.) to take in or absorb liquid. 3 to drink alcohol. 4 to express good wishes to someone or something by drinking, to toast someone ♦ Let's drink to your success.
drink noun 1 liquid for drinking. 2 a portion of liquid for drinking ♦ Would you like a drink of water? 3 an alcoholic drink. 4 (informal) the sea. **to drink something in** to watch or listen to something with delight or eagerness. **drinker** noun [from an Old English word]

drink-driving noun the crime of driving a vehicle with too much alcohol in the blood. **drink-driver** noun

drip verb (**dripped, dripping**) (said about liquid) to fall or let it fall in drops.
drip noun 1 a small drop of liquid ♦ a drip of paint. 2 the act or sound of liquid dripping. 3 a device that drips liquid, drugs, etc. into a patient's vein. 4 (informal) a weak or ineffectual person. [from an Old English word]

drip-dry verb (**drip-dries, drip-dried, drip-drying**) (said about a piece of clothing) to dry easily when hung up wet, without needing to be ironed.

drip-feed verb (past tense and past participle **drip-fed**) to feed someone with a drip.

dripping noun fat melted from roasted meat and allowed to set.
dripping adjective extremely wet. [from drip]

drive verb (**drove, driven**) 1 to operate a motor vehicle or train and direct its course. 2 to travel or carry someone in a car. 3 to urge or force someone to go in some direction by blows, threats, etc.
♦ Their bickering drove me into the kitchen.
4 to push, send, or carry something along. 5 to hit or kick a ball hard. 6 to force a nail etc. into something ♦ He drove the stake into the ground. 7 (said about steam or other power) to keep an engine or machine going. 8 to force or compel someone to do something ♦ Hunger drove them to steal. 9 to force someone into a state ♦ Her attitude was driving him mad.
drive noun 1 a trip or journey in a car. 2 a hard stroke made in cricket or golf etc. 3 the transmission of power to machinery or to the wheels of a vehicle ♦ front-wheel drive. 4 a psychological urge ♦ the sex drive. 5 determination and ambition. 6 an organized effort to achieve something ♦ a sales drive. 7 a social gathering to play whist etc., changing partners and tables. 8 (Computing) a disk drive. 9 a road or track leading to a house. **what someone is driving at** the point that someone is trying to make. [from an Old English word]

drive-in adjective (said about a cinema, restaurant, etc.) able to be used without getting out of your car.

drivel noun silly talk, nonsense.
drivel verb (**drivelled, drivelling**) to talk or write drivel. [from an Old English word dreflian meaning 'to dribble']

driven past participle of **drive**.

driver noun 1 a person or thing that drives something. 2 a golf club used for driving from a tee.

driveway noun a road or track leading to a house.

driving adjective 1 having a strong influence ♦ the driving force. 2 (said about rain) blown by the wind with great force.

drizzle noun very fine rain.
drizzle verb 1 to rain in very fine drops. 2 to trickle oil or some other liquid over

food in a thin stream. **drizzly** adjective [from an Old English word dreosan meaning 'to fall']

droll (drohl) adjective amusing in an odd way. **drolly** adverb [from a French word]

drollery (drohl-er-i) noun droll humour.

dromedary (drom-əd-er-i) noun (**dromedaries**) a camel with one hump, bred for riding on. [from a Greek word dromas meaning 'runner']

drone noun 1 a male bee which does not work in a colony but can fertilize a queen. 2 an idler. 3 a continuous deep humming sound. 4 the bass pipe of a bagpipe, or its continuous deep note.
drone verb 1 to make a deep humming sound. 2 to talk in a boring voice and for a long time ♦ What's he droning on about now? [from an Old English word]

drool verb 1 to water at the mouth, to dribble. 2 to show excessive admiration or desire for something. [from drivel]

droop verb to bend or hang downwards through tiredness or weakness.
droop noun an act of drooping. **droopy** adjective [from an Old Norse word]

drop verb (**dropped, dropping**) 1 to fall by force of gravity through not being held. 2 to allow something to fall ♦ Don't drop it! 3 to sink from exhaustion. 4 to put down a passenger or parcel etc. ♦ Drop me at the station. 5 to become or make something lower, weaker, or less ♦ The wind dropped. 6 to form a steep or vertical descent ♦ The cliff drops sharply to the sea. 7 to abandon or stop dealing with something ♦ The charges against him were dropped ♦ Just drop the subject! 8 to allow yourself to move to a position further back ♦ She dropped behind the others. 9 to mention or send something casually ♦ He dropped a few hints ♦ I'll drop it in the post to you. 10 to leave something out; to fail to pronounce or include something ♦ She's been dropped from the team ♦ Don't drop your h's. 11 (in rugby) to score by a drop kick. 12 (informal) to take a drug through your mouth.
drop noun 1 a small rounded or pear-shaped portion of liquid. 2 something shaped like this, e.g. a sweet or a hanging ornament ♦ a chocolate drop. 3 a very small quantity, especially of a drink ♦ There's just a drop left. 4 the act of dropping. 5 a fall or decrease ♦ a drop in prices. 6 a steep or vertical descent, the distance of this ♦ a drop of 20 feet. 7 the length of a hanging curtain.

drops *plural noun* liquid medicine to be measured by drops. **to drop by** or **drop in** to pay a casual visit. **to drop someone a line** to send someone an informal letter or note. **to drop off** to fall asleep. **to drop out** to stop taking part in something such as a race or course of study. [from an Old English word]

drop goal *noun* (in rugby) a goal scored by drop-kicking the ball over the crossbar.

drop kick *noun* **1** a kick made by dropping a football and kicking it as it falls to the ground. **2** a flying kick made while dropping to the ground. **drop-kick** *verb*

droplet *noun* a small drop of liquid.

drop-off *noun* a decline or decrease.

dropout *noun* someone who drops out from a course of study or from conventional society.

dropper *noun* a short glass tube with a rubber ball at one end, used for measuring out drops of liquid.

droppings *plural noun* the dung of animals or birds.

drop scone *noun* a small thick pancake made by dropping a spoonful of batter onto a hot pan or surface.

drop shot *noun* a tennis shot that drops abruptly over the net.

dropsy *noun* (*old use*) a disease in which watery fluid collects in the body. **dropsical** *adjective* [from an Old French word]

drosophila (dros-off-il-ə) *noun* a small fruit fly used in research on genetics. [from a Greek word *drosos* meaning 'dew' and *philos* meaning 'loving']

dross *noun* **1** rubbish. **2** scum on the surface of molten metal. [from an Old English word]

drought (drowt) *noun* a long period of dry weather. [from an Old English word]

drove past tense of **drive**.
drove *noun* **1** a herd or flock being driven or moving together. **2** a large number of people moving or doing something together ♦ *Tourists came in droves.* [from an Old English word; related to *drive*]

drover *noun* a person who herds cattle or sheep to market or pasture.

drown *verb* **1** to kill someone or be killed by suffocation under water. **2** to submerge or flood an area. **3** to make so much noise that another sound cannot be heard. [from an Old Norse word]

drowse *verb* to be half asleep. [from *drowsy*]

drowsy *adjective* (**drowsier, drowsiest**) sleepy ♦ *This drug may make you drowsy.* **drowsily** *adverb* **drowsiness** *noun* [from an Old English word; related to *dreary*]

drubbing *noun* (*informal*) a severe defeat ♦ *We gave them a real drubbing.* [from an Arabic word *daraba* meaning 'beat']

drudge *noun* a person who does hard, boring, or menial work. [origin unknown]

drudgery *noun* hard and boring work.

drug *noun* **1** a substance used in medicine. **2** a substance that acts on the nervous system, e.g. a narcotic or stimulant, especially one causing addiction.
drug *verb* (**drugged, drugging**) **1** to add a drug to food or drink. **2** to give a drug to someone, especially to make them unconscious. [from an Old French word *drogue*]

druggist *noun* (*North Amer.*) a pharmacist.

drugstore *noun* (*North Amer.*) a chemist's shop also selling many kinds of goods.

Druid (droo-id) *noun* a priest of an ancient Celtic religion in Britain and France. **Druidic** *adjective* **Druidism** *noun* [via Latin from a Celtic word]

drum *noun* **1** a percussion instrument consisting of a skin stretched tightly across a round frame. **2** the sound of a drum being struck, or a similar sound. **3** a cylindrical object or container ♦ *an oil drum.*
drum *verb* (**drummed, drumming**) **1** to play a drum or drums. **2** to make a drumming sound, especially by tapping continuously or rhythmically on something ♦ *She was drumming her fingers on the table.* **3** to drive a lesson, facts etc. into a person's mind by constant repetition. **to drum someone out** to dismiss someone in disgrace. **to drum something up** to obtain something through vigorous effort ♦ *We need to drum up more support.* [an imitation of the sound]

drumbeat *noun* a pattern of strokes on a drum.

drum brake *noun* a brake in which curved pads on a vehicle press against the inner cylindrical part of a wheel.

drumlin noun a long oval hill or ridge formed from material deposited by a glacier and shaped by its movement. [probably from a Scottish Gaelic and Irish word]

drum major noun a male leader of a marching band.

drum majorette noun a female leader or member of a marching band.

drummer noun a person who plays a drum or drums.

drumstick noun 1 a stick for beating a drum. 2 the lower part of a cooked fowl's leg.

drunk past participle of **drink**.
drunk adjective not able to control your behaviour through drinking too much alcohol.
drunk noun a person who is drunk or often drunk.
◊ See the note at **drunken**.

drunkard noun a person who is often drunk.

drunken adjective 1 drunk, or often drunk. 2 caused by drinking alcohol ♦ a drunken brawl. **drunkenly** adverb **drunkenness** noun
◊ This word is used before a noun (e.g. a drunken man), whereas drunk is usually used after a verb (e.g. he is drunk).

drupe noun (Botany) a fruit with juicy flesh round a stone with a kernel, e.g. a peach. [from a Greek word druppa meaning 'olive']

Druze or **Druse** noun a member of a political and religious sect of Islamic origin, concentrated in Lebanon and Syria. [via French from an Arabic word]

dry adjective (**drier, driest**) 1 containing no water or moisture ♦ Are the towels dry yet? 2 not producing water, oil, or milk ♦ a dry well. 3 without rain ♦ a dry spell. 4 eaten without butter etc. ♦ dry bread. 5 thirsty ♦ I'm feeling dry. 6 (said about wine) not sweet. 7 boring or dull ♦ a dry book. 8 (said about remarks or humour) said in a matter-of-fact or ironical way ♦ her dry wit. 9 not allowing the sale of alcohol ♦ a dry state.
dry verb (**dries, dried, drying**) 1 to make something dry, or to become dry. 2 to preserve food etc. by removing its moisture ♦ dried fruit. **to dry out** 1 to become completely dry. 2 (informal) to receive treatment to cure alcohol addiction. **to dry up** 1 to dry washed dishes. 2 to decrease and come to an end

♦ Our main source of income has dried up. 3 (informal) to stop talking. **drily** adverb **dryness** noun [from an Old English word]

dryad noun a wood nymph. [from a Greek word drus meaning 'tree']

dry-clean verb to clean clothes etc. by a solvent which evaporates very quickly, not by water. **dry-cleaning** noun

dry dock noun a dock that can be emptied of water, used for repairing ships.

dry-eyed adjective not crying.

dry ice noun solid carbon dioxide.

dry land noun land in contrast to the sea, a river, etc. ♦ I couldn't wait to reach dry land.

dry measure noun a measure of volume for dry goods, e.g. corn, sugar, or tea.

dry rot noun a fungus causing decay of wood that is not well ventilated.

dry run noun (informal) a rehearsal or practice.

drystone adjective (said about a stone wall) built without mortar.

dry valley noun a valley in which the stream or river that formed it has disappeared.

DTI abbreviation Department of Trade and Industry.

DTP abbreviation desktop publishing.

DTs abbreviation delirium tremens, a psychotic condition caused by chronic alcoholism.

dual adjective having two parts or aspects, double ♦ She has dual nationality. **duality** (dew-al-iti) noun [from a Latin word duo meaning 'two']

dual carriageway noun a road with a dividing strip between lanes of traffic in opposite directions.

dual-control adjective (said about a vehicle or aircraft) having two sets of controls, one of which is used by an instructor.

dub [1] verb (**dubbed, dubbing**) 1 to make a man a knight by touching him on the shoulder with a sword. 2 to give a person or thing a nickname or title. 3 to smear leather with grease. [from an Old French word adober meaning 'to equip with armour']

dub [2] verb (**dubbed, dubbing**) 1 to replace the original soundtrack of a film with one in a different language ♦ It is a Spanish film dubbed into English. 2 to add sound effects or music to a film or recording. **3** to add additional sounds to a recording.

dub noun **1** an instance of dubbing sound effects or music. **2** a style of popular music in which a recording of reggae music is remixed, with the main part of the tune removed and more bass and drum sounds added. [short for *double*]

dubbin noun thick grease used to soften leather and make it waterproof. [from an Old French word]

dubious (dew-bi-əs) adjective **1** doubtful or suspicious about something ♦ *I'm dubious about their motives.* **2** not to be relied on, questionable ♦ *a rather dubious character.* **dubiously** adverb [from a Latin word *dubium* meaning 'doubt']

ducal adjective to do with or like a duke.

ducat (duk-ət) noun a gold coin formerly used in most European countries. [from a Latin word]

duchess noun **1** a duke's wife or widow. **2** a woman whose rank is equal to that of a duke. [from a Latin word *ducissa*; related to *duke*]

duchy noun (**duchies**) the territory of a duke or duchess ♦ *the duchy of Cornwall.* [from an Old French word *duche*]

duck[1] noun **1** a swimming bird of various kinds. **2** the female of this. **3** the flesh of a duck as food. **4** (*informal*) dear. **5** (in cricket) a batsman's score of zero. **6** a ducking movement.
duck verb **1** to bend down quickly, especially to avoid being seen or hit. **2** to dip the head under water and emerge; to push a person under water ♦ *They ducked him in the pond.* **3** to avoid a task or duty ♦ *You shouldn't duck your responsibilities.* [from an Old English word *duce*]

duckbill noun a platypus.

duckboards plural noun boards forming a narrow path in a trench or over mud.

duckling noun a young duck.

duckweed noun a plant that grows on the surface of ponds etc.

duct noun **1** a tube or channel through which liquid, gas, air, cable, etc. can pass. **2** a vessel in the body through which fluid passes ♦ *tear ducts.*
duct verb to convey something through a duct. **ducting** noun [from a Latin word *ductum* meaning 'conveyed']

ductile adjective (said about metal) able to be drawn out into a thin wire. **ductility**

noun [from a Latin word *ducere* meaning 'to lead']

ductless adjective without a duct.

ductless glands noun glands that pour their secretions directly into the blood, not through a duct.

dud noun (*informal*) something that is useless or a fake or that fails to work properly.
dud adjective (*informal*) useless or defective. [origin unknown]

dude (dewd) noun (*North Amer.*) (*informal*) **1** a man ♦ *a cool dude.* **2** a dandy. [probably from a German dialect word *Dude* meaning 'fool']

dudgeon (duj-ən) noun deep resentment or indignation ♦ *He stormed out of the room in high dudgeon.* [origin unknown]

due adjective **1** expected; scheduled to do something or to arrive ♦ *When are they due?* ♦ *The train is due in ten minutes.*
2 owing; needing to be paid ♦ *Our thanks are due to him* ♦ *The rent was due on Monday.* **3** deserving something ♦ *You're due a bit of luck.* **4** that ought to be given to a person; proper or appropriate ♦ *with due respect.*
due adverb exactly or directly ♦ *We sailed due east.*
due noun something you deserve or have a right to ♦ *A fair hearing is my due.*
dues plural noun a fee ♦ *harbour dues.* **in due course** at the appropriate time. **due to as** a result of. **to give someone their due** to be fair to someone. [from a French word *dû* meaning 'what is owed']
◊ Traditionally, the correct use of *due to* is as in *His lateness was due to an accident.* Some people object to the use of *due to* without a preceding noun (e.g. 'lateness') to which it refers, and prefer to use *owing to* (as in *He was late owing to an accident*). However, such uses as *He was late due to an accident* are nowadays widely regarded as acceptable in standard English.

duel noun **1** a fight between two people, especially with swords or pistols. **2** a contest between two people or sides.
duel verb (**duelled, duelling**) to fight a duel. **duellist** noun [from an Italian word]

duet noun a piece of music for or performance by two players or singers. [from a Latin word *duo* meaning 'two']

duff adjective (*informal*) worthless or false. [origin unknown]

duffel *noun* heavy woollen cloth with a thick nap. [named after Duffel, a town in Belgium, where the cloth was first made]

duffel bag *noun* a cylindrical canvas bag closed by a drawstring.

duffel coat *noun* a hooded overcoat made of duffel, fastened with toggles.

duffer *noun* (*informal*) a person who is stupid or not good at doing something. [origin unknown]

dug¹ past tense and past participle of **dig**.

dug² *noun* an udder or teat of a female animal. [perhaps from an Old Norse word]

dugout *noun* **1** an underground shelter. **2** a shelter at the side of a sports field for a team's coaches and substitutes. **3** a canoe made by hollowing out a tree trunk.

duke *noun* **1** a nobleman of the highest hereditary rank. **2** the male ruler of a duchy or of certain small countries. [from a Latin word *dux* meaning 'leader']

dukedom *noun* the position or lands of a duke.

dulcet (**dul**-sit) *adjective* sweet-sounding. [from a Latin word *dulcis* meaning 'sweet']

dulcimer (**dul**-sim-er) *noun* a musical instrument with strings stretched over a sounding board or box, played by being struck with two hammers. [from an Old French word *doulcemer*]

dull *adjective* **1** not interesting or exciting, boring ♦ *a dull match*. **2** not bright or clear ♦ *a dull sky*. **3** slow in understanding, stupid. **4** not sharp; weak and indistinct ♦ *a dull ache* ♦ *a dull thud*.
dull *verb* to make something dull, or to become dull. **dully** *adverb* **dullness** *noun* [from an Old English word *dol* meaning 'stupid']

dullard *noun* a stupid person.

duly (**dew**-li) *adverb* **1** in the correct or suitable way. **2** as might be expected. [from **due**]

dumb *adjective* **1** without the ability to speak. **2** temporarily unable or unwilling to speak ♦ *We were struck dumb by this news*. **3** (*informal*) stupid.
dumb *verb* **to dumb something down** to reduce the intellectual content of something. **dumbly** *adverb* **dumbness** *noun* [from an Old English word]

dumb-bell *noun* a short bar with a weight at each end, lifted to exercise the muscles.

dumbfound *verb* to astonish someone, to strike someone dumb with surprise. [from **dumb** and **confound**]

dumbshow *noun* gestures without words.

dumbstruck *adjective* so shocked or surprised that you are unable to speak.

dumdum bullet *noun* a soft-nosed bullet that expands on impact. [named after Dum Dum in India, where it was first produced]

dummy *noun* (**dummies**) **1** a model of a human figure, especially one used to display clothes. **2** a rubber teat for a baby to suck. **3** an imitation or counterfeit article. **4** (in rugby or football) a pretended pass or kick. **5** in card games, a player whose cards are placed upwards on the table and played by his or her partner.
dummy *adjective* imitation.
dummy *verb* (**dummies, dummied, dummying**) to make a pretended pass or swerve. [from **dumb**]

dummy run *noun* a trial run, a practice.

dump *verb* **1** to deposit something as rubbish. **2** to get rid of something or someone that you do not want. **3** to put something down carelessly. **4** to market goods abroad at a lower price than is charged in the home market.
5 (*Computing*) to copy stored data to a different location.
dump *noun* **1** a rubbish heap; a place where rubbish may be left. **2** a temporary store ♦ *ammunition dump*. **3** (*informal*) a dull or unattractive place. [from a Scandinavian word]

dumpling *noun* a ball of dough cooked in a stew etc. or baked with fruit inside it. [same origin as for *dumpy*]

dumps *plural noun* (*informal*) **in the dumps** depressed or unhappy. [from an Old Dutch word *domp* meaning 'mist, dampness']

dumpy *adjective* (**dumpier, dumpiest**) short and fat. **dumpiness** *noun* [from an old word *dump* meaning 'dumpy person']

dun *adjective & noun* dull greyish-brown. [from an Old English word]

dunce *noun* a person who is slow at learning. [from John Duns Scotus, a Scottish philosopher in the Middle Ages, whose followers were said to be unable to understand new ideas]

dune (dewn) *noun* a mound of loose sand shaped by the wind. [via Old French from a Dutch word]

dung *noun* animal excrement. [from an Old English word]

dungarees *plural noun* trousers with a bib held up by straps over the shoulders, made of coarse cotton cloth. [from a Hindi word *dungri* denoting the cloth they were made of]

dung beetle *noun* a beetle whose larvae develop in dung.

dungeon (dun-jən) *noun* an underground prison cell, especially in a castle. [from an Old French word]

dunghill *noun* a heap of dung in a farmyard.

dunk *verb* 1 to dip a biscuit etc. into a drink before eating it. 2 to immerse someone or something in water. [from a German word]

duo (dew-oh) *noun* (**duos**) 1 a pair of performers ♦ *a comedy duo.* 2 a piece of music for two performers. [via Italian from a Latin word *duo* meaning 'two']

duodecimal (dew-ə-**dess**-iməl) *adjective* to do with a system of numerical notation that has twelve as a base. [from a Latin word *duodecim* meaning 'twelve']

duodenum (dew-ə-**deen**-əm) *noun* the part of the small intestine that is immediately below the stomach. **duodenal** *adjective* [from a Latin word *duodecim* meaning 'twelve' (because its length is about twelve times the breadth of a finger)]

duologue (dew-ə-log) *noun* a dialogue between two people. [from *duo* and a Greek word *logos* meaning 'word']

duopoly (dew-**op**-ə-li) *noun* (**duopolies**) a situation in which two suppliers dominate a market. [from *duo* and *monopoly*]

dupe *verb* to deceive or trick someone. **dupe** *noun* a person who is deceived or tricked. [from a French word]

duple (dew-pəl) *adjective* of or having two parts. [from a Latin word *duo* meaning 'two']

duple time *noun* (*Music*) time with two beats to the bar.

duplex (dew-pleks) *adjective* 1 having two parts. 2 (said about a flat) on two floors. [from Latin words *duo* meaning 'two' and *plicare* meaning 'to fold']

duplicate [1] (**dew**-plik-ət) *noun* 1 something that is exactly the same as something else. 2 an exact copy. **duplicate** *adjective* exactly like another thing; being a duplicate. **in duplicate** as two identical copies. [from a Latin word *duplex* meaning 'double']

duplicate [2] (**dew**-plik-ayt) *verb* 1 to make or be an exact copy of something. 2 to multiply something by two. 3 to repeat something, especially unnecessarily. **duplication** *noun* **duplicator** *noun*

duplicity (dew-**pliss**-iti) *noun* double-dealing, deceitfulness. **duplicitous** *adjective* [from a Latin word *duplex* meaning 'double']

durable *adjective* 1 hard-wearing, likely to last. 2 (said about goods) not for immediate consumption, able to be kept. **durability** *noun* **durably** *adverb* [from a Latin word *durare* meaning 'to endure']

duration *noun* the length of time that something lasts. [same origin as for *durable*]

duress (dewr-**ess**) *noun* the use of force or threats to make someone do something against their will. [from a Latin word *durus* meaning 'hard']

during *preposition* 1 throughout the course or duration of something ♦ *She slept during the film.* 2 at some point in the duration of something ♦ *He heard a scream during the night.* [from a Latin word *durans* meaning 'lasting, enduring']

dusk *noun* the darker stage of twilight. [from an Old English word]

dusky *adjective* (**duskier, duskiest**) darkish in colour. **duskiness** *noun*

dust *noun* 1 fine particles of earth or other solid material. 2 an act of dusting ♦ *These shelves need a dust.* **dust** *verb* 1 to wipe away dust from the surface of something. 2 to sprinkle something with dust or powder. [from an Old English word]

dustbin *noun* a bin for household rubbish.

dust bowl *noun* an area that has lost its vegetation because of drought or erosion.

duster *noun* a cloth for dusting things.

dust jacket *noun* a paper cover used to protect a book from dirt.

dustman *noun* (**dustmen**) a person employed to empty dustbins and take away household rubbish.

dustpan *noun* a pan into which dust is brushed from a floor.

dust sheet *noun* a sheet put over furniture to protect it from dust or while decorating.

dust-up *noun* (*informal*) a noisy argument, a fight.

dusty *adjective* (**dustier, dustiest**) **1** covered with or like dust. **2** uninteresting. **dustiness** *noun*

Dutch *adjective* to do with or coming from the Netherlands.
Dutch *noun* the language of the Netherlands.
the Dutch Dutch people. **to go Dutch** to share the cost of a meal equally. [from a Dutch word]

Dutch auction *noun* an auction in which the price asked is gradually reduced until a buyer is found.

Dutch barn *noun* a barn consisting of a roof supported on poles.

Dutch cap *noun* a contraceptive diaphragm.

Dutch courage *noun* courage obtained by drinking alcohol.

dutiable (dew-ti-ə-bəl) *adjective* (said about goods) needing customs or other duties to be paid.

dutiful *adjective* doing your duty, obedient. **dutifully** *adverb* [from *duty* and *-ful*]

duty *noun* (**duties**) **1** a moral or legal obligation. **2** a task that must be done, especially as part of someone's job. **3** a tax charged on certain goods or on imports. **on** or **off duty** actually doing (or not doing) what is your regular work. [same origin as for *due*]

duty-bound *adjective* obliged by duty.

duty-free *adjective* (said about goods) on which duty is not charged.

duvet (doo-vay) *noun* a thick soft quilt used instead of other bedclothes. [a French word meaning 'down' (soft feathers)]

DVD *abbreviation* digital videodisc, a compact disc that can record and play back sound and pictures.

dwarf *noun* (**dwarfs**) **1** a person, animal, or plant much below the usual size. **2** (in fairytales) a small human-like being, often with magic powers.
dwarf *adjective* of a kind that is very small in size.

dwarf *verb* **1** to make something seem small by contrast or distance ♦ *The ocean liner dwarfed the tugs that were towing it.* **2** to stunt the growth of something. [from an Old English word]

dwell *verb* (past tense and past participle **dwelt** or **dwelled**) (*formal*) to live somewhere. **to dwell on** to think, speak, or write about something for a long time. **dweller** *noun* [from an Old English word *dwellan* meaning 'to lead astray']

dwelling *noun* (*formal*) a house etc. where someone lives.

dwindle *verb* to become gradually less or smaller. [from an Old English word]

dye *noun* **1** a natural or synthetic substance used for changing the colour of cloth, hair, etc. **2** a colour produced by this.
dye *verb* (**dyes, dyed, dyeing**) to make something a particular colour with dye ♦ *She dyed her hair green.* **dyer** *noun* [from an Old English word]

dying present participle of **die**[1].

dyke *noun* **1** a long wall or embankment to hold back water and prevent flooding. **2** a ditch for draining water from land. [from an Old Norse word]

dynamic *adjective* **1** (said about force) producing motion (as opposed to *static*). **2** (said about a person) energetic, having force of character.
dynamics *noun* a branch of physics that deals with matter in motion. **dynamically** *adverb* [from a Greek word *dunamis* meaning 'power']

dynamite *noun* **1** a powerful explosive made of nitroglycerine. **2** something likely to cause violent or dangerous reactions ♦ *These latest revelations are dynamite.* **3** a very impressive person or thing.
dynamite *verb* to blow something up with dynamite. [same origin as for *dynamic*]

dynamo *noun* (**dynamos**) a machine for converting mechanical energy into electrical energy by rotating conducting coils in a magnetic field. [from a Greek word *dunamis* meaning 'power']

dynasty (din-ə-sti) *noun* (**dynasties**) a line of rulers or powerful people all from the same family. **dynastic** *adjective* [same origin as for *dynamic*]

dyne *noun* a unit of force. [from a Greek word *dunamis* meaning 'force, power']

dysentery (dis-ən-tri) *noun* a disease with inflammation of the intestines, causing severe diarrhoea. [from Greek words *dus-* meaning 'badly' and *entera* meaning 'bowels']

dysfunctional (dis-funk-shə-nəl) *adjective* not able to act or function normally. **dysfunction** *noun*

dyslexia (dis-leks-iə) *noun* abnormal difficulty in reading and spelling, caused by a brain condition. **dyslexic** *adjective & noun* [from Greek words *dus-* meaning 'badly' and *lexis* meaning 'speech']

dyspepsia (dis-pep-siə) *noun* indigestion. [from Greek words *dus-* meaning 'badly' and *peptikos* meaning 'able to digest']

dyspeptic *adjective* (dis-pep-tik) suffering from dyspepsia or the resulting irritability.

dystrophy (dis-trə-fi) *noun* a hereditary condition causing progressive weakening of the muscles ♦ *muscular dystrophy.* [from Greek words *dus-* meaning 'badly' and *-trophia* meaning 'nourishment']

Ee

E 1 the fifth letter of the English alphabet. **2** (*Music*) the third note of the diatonic scale of C major. **3** used with a number to indicate a product (especially a food additive) that conforms with the regulations of the EU.

E *abbreviation* east or eastern.

each *adjective* every one of two or more people or things ♦ *Each house has a garden* ♦ *Give a sheet of paper to each child.*
each *pronoun* each person or thing ♦ *Each of them has one* ♦ *Give them two each* ♦ *We see each other often.* [from an Old English word]

eager *adjective* wanting to have or do something very strongly, enthusiastic. SYNONYMS: keen, enthusiastic. **eagerly** *adverb* **eagerness** *noun* [via an Old French word *aigre* meaning 'keen' from a Latin word *acer* meaning 'sharp']

eagle *noun* **1** a large bird of prey. **2** (in golf) a score of two strokes under par or bogey

for a hole. [via Old French *aigle* from a Latin word *aquila*]

eagle eye *noun* a close watch. **eagle-eyed** *adjective*

eaglet *noun* a young eagle.

ear [1] *noun* **1** the organ of hearing and balance in humans and some animals, especially the external part of this. **2** the ability to hear and appreciate sounds ♦ *She has a good ear for music.* **3** willingness to listen; attention. **to be all ears** to listen closely. **to keep an ear to the ground** to be alert to opinions or information about events. [from an Old English word *eare*]

ear [2] *noun* the seed-bearing part of a cereal plant. [from an Old English word *ear*]

earache *noun* a pain in the eardrum.

eardrum *noun* a membrane inside the ear that vibrates when sounds strike it.

earl *noun* a British nobleman ranking below a marquis and above a viscount. [from an Old English word]

earldom *noun* the position or lands of an earl.

ear lobe *noun* the soft fleshy part at the lower end of the ear.

early *adjective & adverb* (**earlier, earliest**) **1** before the usual or expected time ♦ *We all arrived early for the film.* **2** near the beginning of a period of time ♦ *in the early years of this century.* **early on** at an early stage. **earliness** *noun* [from an Old English word, from *ere* and *-ly*]

early bird *noun* a person who gets up early in the morning or who arrives early.

earmark *noun* a distinguishing mark, originally one put on the ear of an animal. **earmark** *verb* **1** to set something aside for a particular purpose. **2** to put a distinguishing mark on an animal.

earn *verb* **1** to get or deserve something, especially money, as a reward for work or achievement. **2** (said about money lent or invested) to gain an amount as interest. [from an Old English word *earnian*]

earned income *noun* income you get from paid employment.

earnest *adjective* showing serious feeling or intentions. SYNONYMS: serious, conscientious, thoughtful, sincere. **in earnest 1** more seriously or with more determination ♦ *They now began to shovel the snow in earnest.* **2** sincere in intention.

earnestly adverb **earnestness** noun [from Old English words]

earnings plural noun money or income that you have earned.

earphone noun an electrical device worn on the ear to listen to radio or audio sounds.

earplug noun a piece of wax or cotton wool inserted in the ear to keep out noise or water.

earring noun a piece of jewellery worn on the ear, usually on the lobe.

earshot noun range of hearing ♦ *The dogs were now out of earshot.*

ear-splitting adjective unpleasantly loud.

earth noun 1 (also **Earth**) the planet that we live on, or the world we live in. 2 the surface of the planet, the ground or dry land ♦ *The rocket fell to earth in the desert.* 3 the substance of the surface of the earth; soil. 4 the underground home of a fox or badger. 5 connection to the ground in order to complete an electrical circuit. **earth** verb to connect an electrical circuit to earth. [from an Old English word *eorthe*]

earthen adjective 1 made of earth. 2 (said about a pot) made of baked clay.

earthenware noun pottery made of coarse baked clay.

earthly adjective 1 to do with the earth, or human life on it. 2 used to emphasize something ♦ *There is no earthly reason to be afraid.*

earthquake noun a violent shaking of the ground caused by a movement of part of the earth's crust.

earth sciences plural noun the branches of science to do with the composition of the earth and its atmosphere.

earthwork noun a large artificial bank of earth.

earthworm noun a burrowing worm that lives in the soil.

earthy adjective (**earthier, earthiest**) 1 like earth or soil. 2 crude or vulgar ♦ *He has an earthy sense of humour.* **earthiness** noun

earwig noun a small crawling insect with pincers at the end of its body. [so called because it was thought to crawl into people's ears]

ease noun 1 absence of trouble or difficulty ♦ *She climbed the tree with ease.* 2 freedom from anxiety or problems. SYNONYMS: leisure, comfort, contentment, relaxation, luxury, rest.
ease verb 1 to relieve someone from pain or anxiety. 2 to make something less difficult or severe. 3 to move something gently or gradually ♦ *The crane was slowly eased into position.* 4 to become less severe or troublesome. SYNONYMS: abate, lessen, decrease, be alleviated. **at ease** standing relaxed with the feet apart. **at one's ease** feeling relaxed and comfortable. [from an Old French word *aise*]

easel noun a wooden frame used to support a painting or a blackboard. [from a Dutch word *ezel* meaning 'donkey' (which carries a load)]

easily adverb 1 in an easy way, with ease. 2 by far ♦ *This was easily the best holiday we'd had.*

east noun 1 the point on the horizon where the sun rises, or the direction in which this point lies. 2 the part of a place or building that is towards the east. **east** adjective & adverb 1 towards or in the east. 2 (said about a wind) blowing from the east. **the East** the part of the world lying to the east of Europe, especially India, Japan, and China. [from an Old English word]

East End noun the eastern part of a city, especially of London.

Easter noun 1 a Christian festival celebrated on a Sunday in March or April, commemorating Christ's resurrection. 2 the period just before and after this. [named after *Eastre*, an Anglo-Saxon goddess whose feast was celebrated in spring]

Easter egg noun a chocolate artificial egg given as a gift at Easter.

easterly adjective 1 in or towards the east. 2 (said about a wind) blowing from the east.
easterly noun (**easterlies**) an easterly wind.

eastern adjective of or in the east.

easterner noun someone who lives in the east of a country or region.

easternmost adjective furthest east.

easting noun 1 a distance travelled or measured eastward, especially at sea. 2 an easterly direction.

eastward adjective & adverb in or towards the east.
eastwards adverb towards the east.

easy *adjective* (**easier, easiest**) **1** able to be done or understood without great effort or difficulty. SYNONYMS: simple, straightforward, elementary. **2** free from trouble or anxiety. SYNONYMS: leisurely, comfortable, carefree, untroubled, peaceful, restful. **3** (said about a person's manner) relaxed and pleasant, not awkward. **to take it easy** to rest or relax. **easiness** *noun* [from an Old French word *aisie*]

easy chair *noun* a large comfortable chair.

easygoing *adjective* pleasant and tolerant, not strict. SYNONYMS: tolerant, accommodating, good-tempered, amiable.

eat *verb* (**ate, eaten**) **1** to take food into the mouth and swallow it for nourishment; to chew and swallow the food. **2** to have a meal ♦ *When shall we eat?* **3** to destroy something gradually ♦ *Acids eat into metals* ♦ *Unexpected expenses ate up our savings.* **eats** *plural noun* (*informal*) food. **to eat your heart out** to suffer with longing, especially for something you cannot have. **to eat your words** to retract what you have said, especially in a humiliating way. [from an Old English word *etan*]

eatable *adjective* fit to be eaten. **eatables** *plural noun* food. ◊ Note that *eatable* describes food that is fit to be eaten, whereas *edible* describes something that can by its nature be eaten and is not harmful or poisonous.

eater *noun* **1** someone who is eating. **2** an eating apple.

eating apple *noun* an apple suitable for eating raw.

eau de cologne (oh-də-kə-lohn) *noun* a delicate perfume. [French words meaning 'water of Cologne' (in Germany, where it was first made)]

eaves *plural noun* the overhanging edge of a roof.

eavesdrop *verb* (**eavesdropped, eavesdropping**) to listen secretly to a private conversation. **eavesdropper** *noun* [from an early use of *eavesdrop* as a noun meaning 'the ground on which water drips from the eaves', as if you were standing there listening]

ebb *noun* **1** the movement of the tide when it is going out away from the land. **2** a low point or condition ♦ *Our courage was at a low ebb.* **ebb** *verb* **1** (said about a tide) to flow away from the land. **2** to weaken or become lower ♦ *Their strength was ebbing.* [from Old English words]

ebonite *noun* another term for vulcanite.

ebony *noun* the hard black wood of a tropical tree. **ebony** *adjective* black like ebony. [from a Greek word *ebenos* meaning 'ebony tree']

ebullient (i-bul-iənt) *adjective* cheerful, full of high spirits. **ebullience** *noun* **ebulliently** *adverb* [from *ex-* and a Latin word *bullire* meaning 'to boil']

eccentric *adjective* **1** slightly strange or unconventional in appearance or behaviour. SYNONYMS: unconventional, strange, odd, peculiar, weird. **2** (said about circles) not having the same centre. **3** (said about an orbit) not circular. **eccentric** *noun* **1** a person who is slightly strange or unconventional. **2** a disc or cam fitted off centre on a revolving shaft, in order to change rotary motion to motion backwards and forwards. **eccentrically** *adverb* **eccentricity** *noun* [from a Greek word *ekkentros* meaning 'away from the centre']

ecclesiastical (i-kleez-i-ast-ikəl) *adjective* to do with the Church or the clergy. [from a Greek word *ekklēsia* meaning 'church']

ecdysis (ek-dis-iss) *noun* the casting off of a reptile's shell or an insect's outer skin. [from a Greek word *ekdusis* meaning 'putting off']

ECG *abbreviation* electrocardiogram.

echelon (esh-ə-lən) *noun* **1** a level of rank or authority in an organization or profession ♦ *the upper echelons of the Civil Service.* **2** a formation of troops, vehicles, ships, or aircraft in a series of parallel rows, with each row extending further in one direction than the one in front. [from a French word *échelle* meaning 'ladder']

echidna (i-kid-nə) *noun* a spiny mammal of Australia and New Guinea, with a long snout. [from a Greek word *ekhidna* meaning 'viper']

echinoderm (i-kiy-nə-derm or ek-i-nə-derm) *noun* a sea animal of the group that includes starfishes and sea urchins. [from Greek words *ekhinos* meaning 'hedgehog' or 'sea urchin' and *derma* meaning 'skin']

echinoid (i-kiy-noid) *noun* a sea urchin. [from a Greek word *ekhinos* meaning 'hedgehog']

echo noun (**echoes**) 1 a repetition of a sound caused by the reflection of sound waves from a surface. 2 a reflected radio or radar beam. 3 something that closely imitates or resembles something else.
echo verb (**echoes, echoed, echoing**) 1 to repeat by an echo. 2 to repeat or imitate something or someone. [from a Greek word *ēkhē* meaning 'a sound']

echolocation noun location of objects by means of reflected sound.

echo sounder noun a sounding apparatus for measuring depth below the surface of the sea by recording the time taken for an echo to return to the listener. **echo sounding** noun

éclair (ay-klair) noun a finger-shaped cake of choux pastry with icing and a cream filling. [a French word meaning 'lightning']

eclampsia noun (*Medicine*) a condition in which a pregnant woman suffers convulsions, often leading to coma, caused by high blood pressure. [from a Greek word *eklampsis* meaning 'sudden development']

eclectic (i-klek-tik) adjective choosing or accepting ideas from a wide range of sources. **eclectically** adverb **eclecticism** noun [from a Greek word *eklegein* meaning 'to pick out']

eclipse noun 1 the blocking of light from or to one heavenly body by another, especially of the sun by the moon or of the moon by the earth. 2 a loss of power or reputation.
eclipse verb 1 to cause an eclipse of a heavenly body. 2 to make someone or something lose power or reputation. [from a Greek word *ekleipsis*, from *ekleipō* meaning 'to fail to appear']

ecliptic (i-klip-tik) noun a circle representing the sun's apparent path during the year, so called because an eclipse of the sun or moon can only occur when the moon crosses this circle.

eclogue (ek-log) noun a short pastoral poem. [from a Greek word *eklogē* meaning 'selection']

eco- prefix to do with ecology or the environment ♦ *eco-friendly*. [from *ecology*]

E. coli noun a bacterium found in the intestines of some animals, certain strains of which cause food poisoning. [from the name of the bacterium, *Escherichia coli*]

ecologist (ee-kol-ə-jist) noun someone who studies ecology.

ecology (ee-kol-əji) noun the study of living things in relation to each other and to their surroundings. **ecological** (ee-kə-loj-ikəl) adjective **ecologically** adverb [from a Greek word *oikos* meaning 'house' and -*logy*]

e-commerce noun commerce and business conducted electronically on the Internet. [a shortening of *electronic commerce*]

economic (ee-kə-nom-ik or ek-ə-nom-ik) adjective 1 to do with economics ♦ *the government's economic policies*. 2 providing enough profit on the money or effort that has been spent ♦ *The railway line was closed because it was not economic.*

economical (ee-kə-nom-ikəl) adjective careful in the use of resources; avoiding waste. SYNONYMS: thrifty, frugal, prudent, careful. **economically** adverb

economics noun the study of how money is used and how goods and services are provided and used.
economics plural noun the financial aspects of something ♦ *the economics of farming.*

economist (i-kon-əmist) noun an expert in economics.

economize verb to be economical, to use or spend less ♦ *We need to economize on fuel.*

economy noun (**economies**) 1 careful use of resources; being economical. 2 a saving ♦ *to make economies.* 3 the resources of a country or region and the way it uses these to produce wealth. **economy of scale** keeping the cost of single items low by producing or buying things in large quantities. [from a Greek word *oikos* meaning 'house' and -*nomia* meaning 'management']

ecosystem (ee-koh-sis-təm) noun a group of plants and animals that interact with each other and form an ecological unit.

ecotourism noun (*Geography*) tourism in natural environments, intended to support conservation efforts. [from *eco-* and *tourism*]

ecru (ay-kroo) noun a light fawn colour. [from a French word *écru* meaning 'unbleached']

ecstasy noun (**ecstasies**) a feeling of intense delight. SYNONYMS: bliss, rapture, elation, euphoria, joy, delight. **ecstatic**

adjective **ecstatically** *adverb* [from a Greek word *ekstasis* meaning 'standing outside yourself']

ECT *abbreviation* (*Medicine*) electroconvulsive therapy.

ectomorph (ekt-ə-mawf) *noun* a person with a light lean build. (Compare **endomorph**.) [from Greek words *ektos* meaning 'outside' and *morphē* meaning 'a form']

ectopic (ek-top-ik) *adjective* (*Medicine*) in an abnormal place or position, especially outside the womb in pregnancy. [from a Greek word *ektopos* meaning 'out of place']

ectoplasm (ek-tə-plazm) *noun* (*Biology*) the outer layer of the matter of an animal or vegetable cell. [from a Greek word *ektos* meaning 'outside' and *plasma*]

ecu (ay-kew) *abbreviation* a former term for **euro**. [short for *European currency unit*]

ecumenical (ee-kew-men-ikəl) *adjective* **1** to do with or including all the Christian Churches. **2** promoting worldwide Christian unity ♦ *the ecumenical movement*. [from a Greek word *oikoumenē* meaning 'the inhabited world']

eczema (ek-zim-ə) *noun* a skin disease causing rough itching patches. [a Greek word, from *ekzeō* meaning 'to boil over' or 'to break out']

edaphic (id-af-ik) *adjective* to do with, or produced by, the soil. [from a Greek word *edaphos* meaning 'floor']

Edda (ed-ə) *noun* either of two Icelandic collections of poetry compiled in the 13th century. [from the name of a character in a poem, or from an Old Norse word *othr* meaning 'poetry']

eddy *noun* (**eddies**) a patch of water swirling in circles like a small whirlpool. **eddy** *verb* (**eddies, eddied, eddying**) (said about water, air, or smoke) to move in swirling circles. [from Old English]

edelweiss (ay-dəl-viys) *noun* an alpine plant with dark green leaves and woolly white bracts round the flowers. [from German words *edel* meaning 'noble' and *weiss* meaning 'white']

Eden *noun* (also **the Garden of Eden**) the place where Adam and Eve lived, in the biblical account of the creation. **Eden** *noun* a place of great happiness and beauty. [from Hebrew and Sumerian words]

edge *noun* **1** the outside limit or boundary of an area or surface. SYNONYMS: border, boundary, limit, fringe, verge. **2** an area or strip next to a steep drop. SYNONYM: brink. **3** the sharpened side of a blade. **4** the sharpness of a blade or tool ♦ *The knife has lost its edge.* **5** the line where two surfaces meet at an angle. **edge** *verb* **1** to form the border of an area or surface. **2** to move gradually ♦ *As she spoke she was edging towards the door.* **to be on edge** to be tense and irritable. **to have the edge on someone** (*informal*) to have an advantage over someon. [from an Old English word *ecg*]

edgeways *adverb* with the edge forwards or outwards. **to get a word in edgeways** to manage to say something when someone else is talking a lot.

edging *noun* something placed round an edge to mark it or to strengthen or decorate it.

edgy *adjective* (**edgier, edgiest**) tense and irritable. **edginess** *noun*

edible *adjective* of a kind that can be eaten. **edibility** *noun* [from a Latin word *edere* meaning 'to eat']
◊ See the note at **eatable**.

edict (ee-dikt) *noun* an official order or command. [from *ex-* and a Latin word *dictum* meaning 'said']

edifice (ed-i-fis) *noun* (*formal*) a large or grand building. [from a Latin word *aedificium* meaning 'building']

edify (ed-i-fiy) *verb* (**edifies, edified, edifying**) to be an improving influence on a person's mind. **edification** *noun* [from a Latin word, related to *edifice*]

edit *verb* (**edited, editing**) **1** to act as editor of a newspaper or other publication. **2** to prepare written material for publication. **3** to reword writing for a special purpose. **4** to prepare a film or recording by choosing individual sections and putting them into a correct order. **5** to prepare data for processing by computer. [from *editor*]

edition *noun* **1** the form in which something is published ♦ *a paperback edition*. **2** all the copies of a book or newspaper issued at the same time ♦ *the first edition* ♦ *the early morning edition*. **3** a particular version or broadcast of a regular radio or televison programme.

editor *noun* **1** a person who is responsible for the content and writing of a newspaper or magazine or a section of one. **2** someone who edits written material for publication. **3** someone who edits cinema film or recording tape. **4** (*Computing*) a program that allows the user to edit text at a computer terminal. [from a Latin word *editor* meaning 'someone who produces something']

editorial *adjective* to do with editing or the work of an editor.
editorial *noun* a newspaper article giving an opinion on current affairs.

educate *verb* to train a person's mind and abilities; to provide education for someone. SYNONYMS: bring up, instruct, train. **educable** *adjective* **educator** *noun* [from a Latin word *educare* meaning 'to lead out', 'to train']

education *noun* the process of training a person's mind and abilities so that they can acquire knowledge and develop skills. **educational** *adjective* **educationally** *adverb*

educationist or **educationalist** *noun* someone who studies ways of educating people.

educative (ed-yoo-kə-tiv) *adjective* serving to educate people.

Edwardian (ed-wor-diən) *adjective* during or to do with the reign of King Edward VII (1901–10).
Edwardian *noun* a person living at this time.

EEG *abbreviation* electroencephalogram.

eel *noun* a long fish that looks like a snake. [from an Old English word]

eerie *adjective* (**eerier, eeriest**) mysterious and frightening. SYNONYMS: weird, mysterious, creepy, frightening, ghostly, scary, spooky. **eerily** *adverb* **eeriness** *noun* [from an Old English word]

efface *verb* to rub something out or obliterate it. **effacement** *noun* [from a French word *effacer*]

effect *noun* **1** a change that is produced by an action or cause, a result. **2** an impression produced on a spectator or hearer etc. ♦ *The news had a cheering effect on us.* SYNONYMS: influence, impact.
effect *verb* to accomplish something or bring it about ♦ *None of the doctors could effect a cure.* SYNONYMS: achieve, accomplish, bring about.
effects *plural noun* **1** property ♦ *personal effects.* **2** sounds and lighting etc. provided to accompany a broadcast or film. **to**

come into effect to become valid or operative ♦ *The law comes into effect next April.* **in effect** in fact, really ♦ *It is, in effect, a refusal.* **to take effect** to become operative, to start having an effect. **with effect from** coming into operation at a stated time. [from *ex-* and a Latin word *-fectum* meaning 'done']
◊ See the note at **affect**.

effective *adjective* **1** producing the effect that is wanted. **2** impressive or striking. **3** actual or existing. **4** in force, operative ♦ *The law is effective from 1 April.* **effectively** *adverb* **effectiveness** *noun*

effector *noun* (*Biology*) a muscle or other organ of the body that performs actions in response to a stimulus.

effectual *adjective* fulfilling its purpose; adequate to produce the effect that is wanted. **effectually** *adverb*

effeminate (i-fem-in-ət) *adjective* (said about a man) having qualities that are usually thought of as feminine. **effeminately** *adverb* **effeminacy** *noun* [from a Latin word *effeminatus* meaning 'made feminine']

effervesce (ef-er-vess) *verb* to give off small bubbles of gas, to fizz. **effervescent** *adjective* **effervescence** *noun* [from *ex-* and a Latin word *fervescere* meaning 'to come to the boil']

effete (ef-eet) *adjective* having lost vitality or effectiveness. **effeteness** *noun* [from a Latin word *effetus* meaning 'worn out from bearing young']

efficacious (ef-i-kay-shəs) *adjective* (*formal*) producing the result that is wanted. **efficacy** (ef-ik-əsi) *noun* [from a Latin word *efficere* meaning 'to succeed in doing something']

efficient (i-fish-ənt) *adjective* acting or working effectively, with little waste of effort. SYNONYMS: (said about a person) proficient, well-organized, competent, capable. **efficiently** *adverb* **efficiency** *noun* [from *ex-* and a Latin word *-ficiens* meaning 'doing']

effigy (ef-iji) *noun* (**effigies**) a sculpture or model of a person. [from a Latin word *effingere* meaning 'to form']

effloresce (ef-lor-ess) *verb* **1** (said about a substance) to turn to fine powder when exposed to air. **2** (said about salts) to come to the surface of brickwork and crystallize. **3** (said about a surface) to become covered with salt particles. **4** to reach a peak of development.

efflorescence *noun* **efflorescent** *adjective* [from *ex-* and a Latin word *florescere* meaning 'to begin to bloom']

effluence (ef-loo-əns) *noun* **1** something that flows out, such as light or electricity. **2** the process of flowing out. [from *ex-* and a Latin word *fluere* meaning 'to flow']

effluent (ef-loo-ənt) *noun* liquid sewage or other waste that flows into the sea or a river.

effort *noun* **1** the use of physical or mental energy to do something. **2** the energy used in this way. **3** something produced by using energy ♦ *The essay was a good effort.* [from *ex-* and a Latin word *fortis* meaning 'strong']

effortless *adjective* done without effort, or not needing any effort. **effortlessly** *adverb* **effortlessness** *noun*

effrontery (i-frunt-er-i) *noun* arrogant insolence. [from *ex-* and a Latin word *frons* meaning 'forehead']

effusion (i-few-zhən) *noun* **1** a pouring forth. **2** an unrestrained outpouring of thought or feeling. [from *ex-* and a Latin word *fusum* meaning 'poured']

effusive (i-few-siv) *adjective* making a great show of affection or enthusiasm. **effusively** *adverb* **effusiveness** *noun* [from *ex-* and a Latin word *fundere* meaning 'to pour']

e.g. *abbreviation* for example. [short for Latin *exempli gratia*]

egalitarian (i-gal-it-air-iən) *adjective* believing that all people are equal and deserve the same rights. **egalitarian** *noun* someone who holds this principle. **egalitarianism** *noun* [from a French word *égal* meaning 'equal']

egg [1] *noun* **1** a more or less round object produced by a female bird, fish, reptile, or insect, which can develop into a new individual if fertilized. **2** the hard-shelled egg of a hen or duck, used as food. **3** a reproductive cell produced by a female being or animal; an ovum. [from an Old Norse word]

egg [2] *verb* to urge someone to do something ♦ *He keeps egging us on.* [from an Old Norse word *eggja* meaning 'to sharpen' or 'to incite']

eggcup *noun* a small cup without a handle, for holding a boiled egg.

egghead *noun* (*informal*) an intellectual person.

eggplant *noun* (*North Amer.*) another word for **aubergine**.

eggshell *noun* the shell of an egg.
eggshell *adjective* **1** (said about china) very fragile. **2** (said about paint) having a slight sheen when it dries.

eglantine (eg-lən-tiyn) *noun* another word for **sweetbriar**.

ego (ee-goh *or* eg-oh) *noun* (**egos**) **1** a person's sense of importance or self-respect ♦ *The criticism has hurt their egos.* **2** (*Psychology*) the part of the mind that controls memory and personal identity. [a Latin word meaning 'I']

egocentric (eg-oh-sen-trik) *adjective* self-centred. **egocentricity** *noun*

egoism (eg-oh-izm) *noun* being self-centred.

egoist (eg-oh-ist) *noun* a self-centred person. **egoistic** *adjective* **egoistically** *adverb*

egotism (eg-oh-tizm) *noun* the practice of talking too much about yourself, conceit. **egotistic** *adjective* **egotistical** *adjective* **egotistically** *adverb*

egotist (eg-oh-tist) *noun* a conceited person.

ego trip *noun* (*informal*) something you do to increase your feeling of self-importance.

egregious (i-gree-jəs) *adjective* (*formal*) very bad or shocking ♦ *It was a piece of egregious folly.* [from a Latin word *egregius*, literally meaning 'standing out from the flock', from *ex-* and *grex* meaning 'flock']

egress (ee-gress) *noun* an exit or way out. [from *ex-* and a Latin word *gressus* meaning 'going']

egret (ee-grit) *noun* a kind of heron with white plumage and long tail feathers. [from an Old French word *aigrette*]

Egyptian *adjective* to do with or coming from Egypt in NE Africa.
Egyptian *noun* **1** a person born in Egypt or descended from people born there. **2** the language of ancient Egypt.

Egyptology *noun* the study of the language and antiquities of ancient Egypt. **Egyptologist** *noun*

eh (ay) *exclamation* (*informal*) expressing enquiry or surprise.

Eid (eed) *noun* a Muslim festival marking the end of the fast of Ramadan. [from an Arabic word meaning 'festival']

eiderdown *noun* a quilt stuffed with soft material. [originally the soft down of the *eider*, a kind of duck]

eight *adjective & noun* **1** the number 8, one more than seven. **2** an eight-oared rowing boat or its crew. [from an Old English word]

eighteen *adjective & noun* the number 18, one more than seventeen. **eighteenth** *adjective & noun*

eightfold *adjective & adverb* **1** eight times as much or as many. **2** consisting of eight parts.

eighth *adjective & noun* **1** next after seventh. **2** one of eight equal parts of a thing. **eighthly** *adverb*
◊ Note that there are two hs in *eighth*.

eighty *adjective & noun* (**eighties**) the number 80, equal to eight times ten.
eighties *plural noun* the numbers from 80 to 89, especially representing years of age or degrees of temperature. **eightieth** *adjective & noun*

eisteddfod (iy-**steth**-vod) *noun* an annual Welsh gathering of poets and musicians for competitions. [a Welsh word meaning 'session']

either (**iy**-*th*er or **ee**-ther) *adjective & pronoun* **1** one or the other of two ♦ *Either of you can do it.* **2** each of two ♦ *There are tall buildings on either side of the road.*
either *adverb & conjunction* **1** as one alternative, the other being expressed by *or* ♦ *He is either ill or drunk* ♦ *Either come in or go out.* **2** in the same way, what is more ♦ *I don't like it either.* [from an Old English word]

ejaculate (i-**jak**-yoo-layt) *verb* (*formal*) **1** to say something suddenly and sharply. **2** (said about a man or male animal) to eject semen from the penis at a sexual climax. **ejaculation** *noun* [from *ex-* and a Latin word *jacere* meaning 'to throw']

eject *verb* **1** to force or throw something out ♦ *The gun ejects spent cartridges.* **2** to expel someone or force them to leave. SYNONYMS: expel, drive out, banish. **3** (said about a pilot) to escape from an aircraft by using an ejector seat. **ejection** *noun* **ejector** *noun* [from *ex-* and a Latin word *-jectum* meaning 'thrown']

ejector seat *noun* an aircraft seat that in an emergency can eject the occupant, who then reaches the ground by parachute.

eke (eek) *verb* **to eke out** to make something last ♦ *They managed to eke out the meat with lots of vegetables.* **to eke out a living** to have just enough to live on. [from an Old English word]

elaborate [1] (i-**lab**-er-ət) *adjective* having many parts or details, complicated ♦ *The carpet has an elaborate pattern.* SYNONYMS: complicated, intricate, complex, involved. **elaborately** *adverb* [from *ex-* and a Latin word *laborare* meaning 'to work']

elaborate [2] (i-**lab**-er-ayt) *verb* to work something out or describe it in detail. **elaboration** *noun*

élan (ay-**lahn**) *noun* stylish or dashing vitality. [a French word]

eland (**ee**-lənd) *noun* a large African antelope with spirally twisted horns. [from a Dutch word meaning 'elk']

elapse *verb* (said about time) to pass. [from *ex-* and a Latin word *lapsum* meaning 'slipped']

elastic *adjective* **1** able to return to its original length or shape after being stretched or squeezed. **2** able to be used or understood flexibly ♦ *The rules are somewhat elastic.*
elastic *noun* cord or material that is woven with strands of rubber or plastic so that it can stretch and return to its original length or shape. **elastically** *adverb* **elasticity** (el-ass-**tiss**-iti) *noun* [from a Greek word *elastikos* meaning 'propelling', from *elaunein* meaning 'to drive']

elasticated *adjective* (said about material) made elastic by being interwoven with elastic thread.

elastomer (i-**last**-ə-mer) *noun* a natural or synthetic rubber or rubber-like plastic.

elate *verb* to make someone feel very happy or proud. **elated** *adjective* **elation** *noun* [from *ex-* and a Latin word *latum* meaning 'carried']

E-layer *noun* a layer of the ionosphere that reflects radio waves of medium frequency. [an arbitrary use of the letter *E*]

elbow *noun* **1** the joint between the forearm and upper arm. **2** the part of a sleeve covering this. **3** a sharp bend in a pipe.

elbow *verb* to poke or thrust someone with the elbow. [from an Old English word *elboga*]

elbow grease *noun* (*informal*) hard physical work.

elbow room *noun* plenty of room to work or move in.

elder[1] *adjective* older ♦ *Meet my elder sister.* **elder** *noun* 1 an older person ♦ *You must respect your elders.* 2 an official in certain Christian Churches. [an old form of *older*]

elder[2] *noun* a tree or shrub with white flowers and dark berries. [from an Old English word]

elderberry *noun* (**elderberries**) the berry of the elder, used to make wine and jam.

elderly *adjective* rather old, ageing.

elder statesman *noun* an experienced and influential politician or other public figure.

eldest *adjective* oldest or first-born ♦ *Peter is their eldest son.* [an old form of *oldest*]

eldorado (el-dor-**ah**-doh) *noun* (**eldorados**) a place of great wealth and riches. [from a Spanish phrase *El Dorado*, the name of a fabulously rich country or city formerly believed to exist in South America]

elect *verb* 1 to choose someone by a vote ♦ *The committee must elect a chairman.* SYNONYMS: choose, appoint. 2 to choose to do something ♦ *We elected to stay on for another week.* SYNONYMS: choose, decide. **elect** *adjective* chosen by a vote but not yet in office ♦ *the president elect.* [from *ex-* and a Latin word *lectum* meaning 'chosen']

election *noun* 1 the process of choosing someone or of being chosen, especially by a vote. 2 the process of electing MPs or other political representatives.

electioneer *verb* to take part in an election campaign. **electioneering** *noun*

elective *adjective* 1 having the power to elect someone ♦ *an elective assembly.* 2 chosen or filled by election ♦ *an elective office.*

elector *noun* someone who is eligible to vote in an election.

electoral *adjective* to do with elections or electors.

electorate *noun* all the people eligible to vote.

electric *adjective* 1 to do with or worked by electricity. 2 causing great or sudden excitement ♦ *The news had an electric effect.* [from a Greek word *ēlektron* meaning 'amber' (which is easily given a charge of static electricity)]

electrical *adjective* to do with or producing electricity ♦ *electrical engineering.* **electrically** *adverb*

electrical engineer *noun* an engineer who designs and builds electrical devices. **electrical engineering** *noun*

electric chair *noun* a chair in which criminals are executed by electrocution.

electric guitar *noun* a guitar with a built-in pickup which converts sound vibrations into electrical signals that are fed into an amplifier.

electrician (i-lek-**trish**-ən) *noun* a person whose job is to deal with electricity and electrical equipment.

electricity *noun* 1 a form of energy carried by certain particles of matter (electrons and protons). 2 a supply of electric current for lighting, heating, etc.

electric shock *noun* the sudden discharge of electricity through the body of a person or animal, stimulating the nerves and contracting the muscles.

electric storm *noun* a violent disturbance of the electrical condition of the atmosphere.

electrify *verb* (**electrifies, electrified, electrifying**) 1 to give an electric charge to something. 2 to supply a place, building, etc. with electric power, or to power a machine or device with electricity. 3 to startle or excite someone suddenly. **electrification** *noun*

electro- *prefix* to do with or using electricity.

electrocardiogram *noun* the pattern traced by an electrocardiograph.

electrocardiograph *noun* an instrument for detecting and recording the electric currents generated by heartbeats. **electrocardiography** *noun*

electroconvulsive therapy *noun* the treatment of mental illness by means of electric shocks that produce convulsions.

electrocute *verb* to kill or injure someone by an electric shock. **electrocution** *noun* [from *electro-* and *execute*]

electrode (i-lek-trohd) *noun* a solid conductor through which electricity enters or leaves a vacuum tube. [from *electro-* and a Greek word *hodos* meaning 'way']

electroencephalogram *noun* the pattern traced by an electroencephalograph.

electroencephalograph *noun* an instrument for detecting and recording the electric currents generated by activity of the brain. **electroencephalography** *noun*

electrolysis (i-lek-trol-ə-sis) *noun* 1 (*Chemistry*) chemical decomposition caused by an electric current. 2 the removal of blemishes, hair roots, etc. by means of an electric current. **electrolytic** (i-lek-trə-lit-ik) *adjective* [from *electro-* and a Greek word *lusis* meaning 'loosening']

electrolyte (i-lek-trə-liyt) *noun* a liquid or other solution that conducts an electric current, especially in an electric cell or battery. [from *electro-* and a Greek word *lutos* meaning 'released']

electromagnet *noun* a metal core that is magnetized by a coil carrying electric current and wound round it.

electromagnetic *adjective* having both electrical and magnetic properties. **electromagnetically** *adverb*

electromagnetic radiation *noun* emission of waves (called *electromagnetic waves*), including radio waves, heat and light rays, and X-rays, consisting of electric and magnetic fields that vary simultaneously.

electromagnetism *noun* magnetic forces produced by electricity.

electromotive *adjective* producing an electric current.

electromotive force *noun* a difference in potential that causes an electric current.

electron (i-lek-tron) *noun* (*Physics*) an elementary particle found in all atoms, which carries a charge of negative electricity and is the carrier of electric current in solids. [same origin as for *electric*]

electron beam *noun* (*Physics*) a stream of electrons, as emitted from a cathode.

electron gun *noun* (*Physics*) a device for producing a narrow beam of electrons from a heated cathode.

electronic (i-lek-tron-ik) *adjective* 1 making use of transistors and microchips and other components that control electric currents. 2 relating to or making use of electronics ♦ *electronic engineering.* 3 done by means of a computer network ♦ *electronic banking.* **electronically** *adverb*

electronic mail *noun* another term for **email**.

electronics *noun* the development and use of electronic devices in transistors, computers, etc. **electronics** *plural noun* electronic circuits.

electron microscope *noun* (*Physics*) a high-powered microscope that uses beams of electrons instead of rays of light.

electronvolt *noun* (*Physics*) a unit of energy, the amount of energy gained by an electron when accelerated through a potential difference of one volt.

electroplate *verb* to coat a metal object with a thin layer of silver etc. by electrolysis. **electroplate** *noun* objects plated in this way.

electroscope *noun* (*Physics*) an instrument for detecting and measuring electricity, especially to indicate the ionization of air by radioactivity.

electrostatic *adjective* to do with static electric charges.

electrostatic induction *noun* (*Physics*) the production of an electric charge in a conductor by the proximity of charges in another body.

electrostatics *noun* the study of static electricity.

electrotherapy *noun* the use of electricity to treat paralysis and other medical disorders.

elegant *adjective* graceful and dignified in appearance or style. SYNONYMS: handsome, graceful, noble, dignified, stately. **elegantly** *adverb* **elegance** *noun* [from a Latin word *elegans*]

elegiac (el-i-jiy-ək) *adjective* used for elegies; expressing sadness or sorrow. **elegiacs** *plural noun* elegiac verses.

elegy (el-i-ji) *noun* (**elegies**) a sorrowful or serious poem. [from a Greek word *elegos* meaning 'mournful']

element *noun* 1 each of the parts that make up the whole of something. SYNONYMS: component, constituent, part, ingredient. 2 a trace or aspect ♦ *There is an element of truth in their story.* 3 each of about 100 substances composed of atoms with the same atomic number. **4** each of the four substances (earth, water, air, and fire) that were regarded as the basic ingredients of matter in ancient and medieval philosophy. **5** a wire that becomes red and gives out heat in an electric heater or cooker. **6** (*Mathematics*) a member of a set.

elements *plural noun* **1** (**the elements**) the forces of the weather or atmosphere. **2** the basic or elementary principles of a subject ♦ *the elements of geometry*. **in your element** the situation or environment that suits you best. [from a Latin word *elementum* meaning 'particle']

elementary *adjective* to do with or dealing with the simplest facts of a subject; basic or easy. SYNONYMS: basic, fundamental, simple, easy. **elementarily** *adverb* **elementariness** *noun*

elementary particle *noun* each of the subatomic particles that are not known to be made up of simpler particles.

elephant *noun* a very large land animal with a trunk, large ears, and long curved ivory tusks. [from a Greek word *elephas* meaning 'ivory']

elephantine (el-i-**fan**-tiyn) *adjective* **1** to do with elephants, or like elephants. **2** clumsy and slow-moving.

elevate *verb* **1** to lift or raise something to a higher place or position. **2** to make a discussion, conversation, etc. more serious or intellectual. [from *ex-* and a Latin word *levare* meaning 'to lift']

elevation *noun* **1** the process of raising or lifting something. **2** the altitude of a place. **3** a low hill or a piece of rising ground. **4** the angle that the direction of something (e.g. a gun) makes with the horizontal. **5** a plan or drawing showing one side of a structure ♦ *The plan showed the north elevation of the house.*

elevator *noun* **1** something that lifts or raises things. **2** the movable part of a hinged flap on the tailplane of an aircraft, used to control its attitude. **3** (*North Amer.*) a lift in a building.

eleven *adjective & noun* **1** the number 11, one more than ten. **2** a team of eleven players in cricket, football, etc. [from an Old English word]

elevenfold *adjective & adverb* **1** eleven times as much or as many. **2** consisting of eleven parts.

elevenses *plural noun* (*informal*) a break for a snack or drink in the middle of the morning.

eleventh *adjective & noun* **1** next after tenth. **2** one of eleven equal parts of a thing. **at the eleventh hour** at the last possible moment; just in time.

elf *noun* (**elves**) in fairy tales, a small being with magic powers, usually shown with a large head and pointed ears. **elfish** *adjective* [from an Old English word]

elfin *adjective* small and delicate, like an elf.

elicit (i-**lis**-it) *verb* to draw out a response or information by argument or questioning. SYNONYMS: evoke, draw out, extract. [from a Latin word *elicere* meaning 'to draw out by trickery']

elide *verb* to omit part of a word by the process called elision. [same origin as for *elision*]

eligible (**el**-i-ji-bəl) *adjective* **1** qualified or suitable for a position or privilege. **2** (said about a person) regarded as suitable for marriage. **eligibility** *noun* [from a Latin word *eligere* meaning 'to choose']

eliminate (i-**lim**-in-ayt) *verb* **1** to get rid of something that is not wanted. **2** to exclude a competitor or team from the next stage of a competition when they are defeated. **elimination** *noun* **eliminator** *noun* [from *ex-* and a Latin word *limen* meaning 'entrance']

elision (i-**lizh**-ən) *noun* the omission of part of a word when speaking it (e.g. *I'm* for 'I am'). [from a Latin word *elidere* meaning 'to push out']

élite (ay-**leet**) *noun* a group of people who enjoy special privileges or are regarded as superior in some way. [from an Old French word *élit* meaning 'chosen']

élitist (ay-**leet**-ist) *noun* someone who likes to treat certain people as a superior élite. **élitism** *noun*

elixir (i-**liks**-er) *noun* a magical or medicinal liquid thought of as having special powers, such as changing metal to gold or making an old person young again. [from an Arabic word *aliksir*]

Elizabethan *adjective* during or to do with the reign of Queen Elizabeth I (1558–1603).
Elizabethan *noun* a person living at this time.

elk *noun* (**elk** or **elks**) a large deer of northern Europe and Asia. [from an Old English word]

ellipse (i-**lips**) *noun* a regular oval shape that can be divided into four identical quarters. [same origin as for *ellipsis*]

ellipsis (i-**lip**-sis) *noun* (**ellipses**) (*Grammar*) the omission of a word or words from speech and writing, usually leaving the meaning still clear (as in *Carl bought a large bottle and Shaun a small one*, which omits a second *bought* after *Shaun*). [from a Greek word *elleipsis* meaning 'fault' or 'omission']

elliptical (i-**lip**-ti-kəl) *adjective* 1 shaped like an ellipse. 2 (*Grammar*) containing an ellipsis, having omissions. **elliptically** *adverb*

elm *noun* 1 a tall deciduous tree with rough serrated leaves. 2 the wood of this tree. [from an Old English word]

elocution (el-ə-**kew**-shən) *noun* the art of speaking clearly and expressively. **elocutionist** *noun* [same origin as for *eloquent*]

elongated (ee-**long**-gayt-id) *adjective* made longer, prolonged. **elongation** *noun* [from *ex-* and a Latin word *longus* meaning 'long']

elope (i-**lohp**) *verb* (said about a couple) to run away secretly to get married. **elopement** *noun* [from an Old French word *aloper* meaning 'to run away']

eloquence (el-ə-**kwəns**) *noun* fluent and expressive speaking or writing. [from *ex-* and a Latin word *loqui* meaning 'to speak']

eloquent (el-ə-**kwənt**) *adjective* speaking fluently and expressively. **eloquently** *adverb*

else *adverb* 1 besides, other ♦ *I'll ask someone else.* 2 otherwise, if not ♦ *Run or else you'll be late.* [from an Old English word]

elsewhere *adverb* somewhere else.

ELT *abbreviation* English Language Teaching.

elucidate (i-**loo**-sid-ayt) *verb* to make something clear by explaining it. **elucidation** *noun* **elucidatory** *adjective* [same origin as for *lucid*]

elude (i-**lood**) *verb* 1 to avoid being caught by someone ♦ *He managed to elude all his pursuers.* SYNONYMS: avoid, evade, dodge, escape. 2 to escape a person's

understanding or memory ♦ *I'm afraid the answer eludes me.* **elusion** *noun* [from *ex-* and a Latin word *ludere* meaning 'to play']

elusive (i-**loo**-siv) *adjective* 1 difficult to find or achieve. 2 eluding a person's understanding or memory. **elusiveness** *noun*

elver *noun* a young eel. [from dialect words *eel-fare* meaning 'the movement of young eels up river']

elves plural of **elf**.

emaciated (i-**may**-si-ayt-id) *adjective* very thin from illness or starvation. **emaciation** *noun* [from *ex-* and a Latin word *macies* meaning 'leanness']

email *noun* a system of sending messages and data from one computer to another by means of a network. **email** *verb* to send a message or data by email. [a shortening of *electronic mail*]

emanate (em-ən-ayt) *verb* to come or originate from a particular source. **emanation** *noun* [from *ex-* and a Latin word *manare* meaning 'to flow']

emancipate (i-**man**-sip-ayt) *verb* to set someone free from slavery or some form of restraint. **emancipation** *noun* **emancipator** *noun* **emancipatory** *adjective* [from *ex-* and a Latin word *mancipium* meaning 'slave']

emasculated (i-**mas**-kew-layt-id) *adjective* made weaker or less effective. [the original meaning was 'castrated', from a Latin word *emasculare*]

embalm (im-**bahm**) *verb* to preserve a corpse from decay by using spices or chemicals. **embalmment** *noun* [from *en-* and *balm*]

embankment *noun* a long bank of earth or stone used to hold back water or to carry a road or railway. [from *en-* and *bank*²]

embargo (im-**bar**-goh) *noun* (**embargoes**) an official ban, especially on trade with a country. [from a Spanish word *embargar* meaning 'to restrain']

embark *verb* to go on board a ship or aircraft at the start of a journey, or to put something on board. **to embark on** to start to do something difficult or major. **embarkation** *noun* [from *en-* and a French word *barque* meaning 'sailing ship']

embarrass *verb* to make someone feel awkward or ashamed. SYNONYMS: discomfit, disconcert, discomfort, shame.

embarrassment noun [via French from a Spanish word *embarazar*]

embassy noun (**embassies**) **1** the building in which an ambassador's office is located. **2** a deputation sent to a foreign government. [from an Old French word, related to *ambassador*]

embattled adjective **1** prepared for battle or attack. **2** facing many difficulties or criticisms.

embed verb (**embedded, embedding**) to fix something firmly in a surrounding mass. [from en- and *bed*]

embellish (im-bel-ish) verb **1** to decorate something or add ornaments to it. SYNONYMS: decorate, adorn, beautify. **2** to improve a story by adding details that are entertaining but invented. SYNONYMS: embroider, elaborate. **embellishment** noun [from en- and a French word *bel* meaning 'beautiful']

embers plural noun small pieces of live coal or wood in a dying fire. [from an Old English word]

embezzle verb to take dishonestly for your own use money or property that has been placed in your care. **embezzlement** noun **embezzler** noun [from an Old French word *besiler* meaning 'to steal']

embittered adjective having bitter feelings about something.

emblazon (im-blay-zən) verb **1** to decorate something with bright or eye-catching designs or words. **2** to decorate something with a coat of arms. [from en- and an Old French word *blason* meaning 'shield']

emblem noun a symbol that represents something. [from a Latin word *emblema* meaning 'raised ornament']

emblematic (em-blim-at-ik) adjective serving as an emblem, symbolic.

embody verb (**embodies, embodied, embodying**) **1** to express principles or ideas in a visible or tangible form ♦ *The house embodies our idea of a modern home.* SYNONYMS: typify, represent, exemplify. **2** to incorporate or include something ♦ *Parts of the old agreement are embodied in the new one.* SYNONYMS: incorporate, include, encompass. **embodiment** noun

embolden verb to make someone bold, to encourage someone.

embolism (em-bəl-izm) noun (*Medicine*) obstruction of an artery or vein by a clot of blood or air bubble. [from a Greek word *embolismos*, from *emballein* meaning 'to insert']

emboss verb to decorate a flat surface with a raised design. **embossment** noun [from en- and an Old French word *boce* meaning 'boss' (a raised stud)]

embrace verb **1** to hold someone closely and lovingly in your arms. SYNONYMS: hug, hold, grasp, clasp. **2** to accept something eagerly ♦ *We will have to embrace the opportunity.* SYNONYMS: accept, adopt, espouse. **3** to adopt a cause or belief. **4** to include or contain something. **embrace** noun an act of embracing, a close hug. [from en- and a Latin word *brachium* meaning 'an arm']

embrasure (im-bray-zher) noun **1** an opening in a wall or parapet, widening towards the outside for shooting through. **2** an opening in an inside wall for a door or window, with widening sides to enlarge the area. [from a French word]

embrocation noun a liquid for rubbing on parts of the body to relieve aches or bruises. [from a Greek word *embrokhē* meaning 'lotion']

embroider verb **1** to decorate cloth with needlework. **2** to add interesting details to a story. SYNONYMS: elaborate, embellish. [from a French word *enbrouder*]

embroidery noun (**embroideries**) **1** the art or activity of embroidering. **2** embroidered cloth.

embroil verb to involve someone in an argument or quarrel. [from a French word *embrouiller* meaning 'to muddle']

embryo (em-bri-oh) noun (**embryos**) **1** a baby or young animal in the early stage of development in the womb, especially an unborn child in the first eight weeks after conception. **2** an unborn bird growing in an egg. **3** a rudimentary plant contained in a seed. **4** something in the early stages of its development. **in embryo** at an early stage before it has been developed. [from en- and a Greek word *bruein* meaning 'to grow']

embryonic (em-bri-on-ik) adjective at an early stage before it has been developed.

emend (i-mend) verb to alter something written in order to remove errors.

emendation (ee-men-**day**-shən) *noun* [from *ex-* and a Latin word *menda* meaning 'a fault']

emerald *noun* 1 a bright green precious stone. 2 the colour of an emerald. [from an Old French word *esmeraud* or *emeraud*, from Greek and Semitic words]

emerge (i-**merj**) *verb* 1 to come up or out into view. 2 (said about facts or ideas) to become known or obvious. SYNONYMS: come to light, transpire. **emergence** *noun* **emergent** *adjective* [from *ex-* and a Latin word *mergere* meaning 'to plunge']

emergency *noun* (**emergencies**) 1 a sudden and unexpected serious happening that needs urgent attention. 2 a medical condition needing immediate treatment. [from a late Latin word *emergentia*, related to *emerge*]

emery board *noun* a thin strip of card with a coarse gritty coating, used for filing fingernails. [from a Greek word *smuris* meaning 'polishing powder']

emery paper *noun* paper with a coarse gritty coating used for polishing hard surfaces.

emetic (i-**met**-ik) *noun* medicine used to cause vomiting. [from a Greek word *emein* meaning 'to vomit']

EMF *abbreviation* electromotive force.

emigrant *noun* someone who emigrates.

emigrate *verb* to leave your own country and go to settle in another. **emigration** *noun* [from *ex-* and *migrate*]

eminence (**em**-in-əns) *noun* 1 being famous or distinguished ♦ *a musician of great eminence*. 2 (*literary*) a piece of rising ground. 3 a title of a cardinal (in *Your Eminence* or *His Eminence*). [from a Latin word *eminentia*]

eminent (**em**-in-ənt) *adjective* 1 famous or distinguished. SYNONYMS: distinguished, famous, celebrated, illustrious. 2 outstanding or conspicuous ♦ *a person of eminent goodness*. **eminently** *adverb*

emir (em-**eer**) *noun* the title of a Muslim ruler. [from an Arabic word *amir* meaning 'ruler']

emirate (**em**-er-ət) *noun* the rank or territory of an emir.

emissary (**em**-iss-er-i) *noun* (**emissaries**) a person sent to conduct diplomatic negotiations. [from *ex-* and a Latin word *missum* meaning 'sent']

emission *noun* 1 the process of emitting something. 2 something that is emitted, especially fumes or radiation.

emit (i-**mit**) *verb* (**emitted, emitting**) 1 to send out light, heat, fumes, etc. SYNONYMS: discharge, give off, send out, exude. 2 to make a sudden or loud sound ♦ *When he saw her he emitted a cry of amazement.* **emitter** *noun* [from *ex-* and a Latin word *mittere* meaning 'to send']

emollient (i-**mol**-iənt) *adjective* softening or soothing the skin.
emollient *noun* an emollient substance.
[from *ex-* and a Latin word *mollis* meaning 'soft']

emolument (i-**mol**-yoo-mənt) *noun* (*formal*) a fee or payment for work, a salary. [from a Latin word *emolumentum* meaning 'payment for grinding', from *emolere* meaning 'to grind up']

emotion *noun* a strong mental feeling, such as anger, love, or hate. [from *ex-* and a Latin word *movere* meaning 'to move']

emotional *adjective* 1 to do with the emotions. 2 showing or arousing a lot of emotion ♦ *an emotional speech.* SYNONYMS: heartfelt, fervent, passionate, impassioned, ardent. **emotionally** *adverb* **emotionalism** *noun*

emotive (i-**moh**-tiv) *adjective* arousing emotion.

empathize (em-pə-thyz) *verb* to understand and share in someone else's feelings, to feel empathy.

empathy (**em**-pəthi) *noun* the ability to understand and share in someone else's feelings. **empathic** (em-pa-thik) *adjective* [from *en-* and a Greek word *pathos* meaning 'feeling']

emperor *noun* the ruler of an empire. [from a Latin word *imperator* meaning 'commander', related to *empire*]

emphasis (**em**-fə-sis) *noun* (**emphases**) 1 special importance given to something ♦ *The emphasis is on quality.* 2 strength of expression or feeling ♦ *She nodded her head with emphasis.* 3 the extra force used in speaking a particular syllable or word, or on a sound in music. [from *en-* and a Greek word *phanein* meaning 'to show']

emphasize (em-fə-siyz) *verb* to put emphasis on something. SYNONYMS: stress, underline, highlight, accentuate.

emphatic (im-**fat**-ik) *adjective* using or showing emphasis, expressing yourself with emphasis. **emphatically** *adverb*

emphysema (em- fi- **see**- mə) *noun* (*Medicine*) a condition in which excessive air is present in the body tissue, especially in the lungs, causing breathlessness. [from a Greek word *emphusan* meaning 'to puff up']

empire *noun* 1 a group of countries ruled by one person or government. 2 supreme power. 3 a large business organization controlled by one person or group. [from a Latin word *imperium* meaning 'command']

empirical (im-**pi**-ri-kəl) *adjective* (said about knowledge) based on observation or experiment, not on theory. **empirically** *adverb* [from a Greek word *empeiria* meaning 'experience']

emplacement *noun* a place or platform where a gun or set of guns is placed for firing.

employ *verb* 1 to give work to someone, to use the services of someone. SYNONYMS: engage, hire, take on. 2 to make use of something ♦ *How will you employ your spare time?* SYNONYMS: use, make us of, utilize, apply.
employ *noun* **in the employ of someone** (said about a person) employed by someone. **employable** *adjective* [from an Old French word *employer*]

employee (im-ploi-ee) *noun* a person who works for someone else in return for payment.

employer *noun* a person or organization that employs people.

employment *noun* 1 employing someone or something. 2 the state of being employed, having paid work. 3 work done as an occupation or to earn a living.

emporium (em-**por**-iəm) *noun* (**emporia** or **emporiums**) a large store selling a wide range of goods. [from a Greek word *emporos* meaning 'merchant']

empower *verb* to give someone the power or authority to do something.

empress *noun* 1 a woman ruler of an empire. 2 the wife or widow of an emperor. [from an Old French word *empresse*, related to *emperor*]

empty *adjective* (**emptier, emptiest**) 1 not containing anything. 2 not having a person or people in it ♦ *an empty chair*

♦ *empty streets.* SYNONYMS: (of a chair etc.) vacant, unoccupied; (of a place) deserted, uninhabited. 3 without real meaning or effectiveness ♦ *empty promises.* SYNONYMS: meaningless, hollow, useless, worthless.
empty *verb* (**empties, emptied, emptying**) 1 to make something empty, or to become empty. 2 to take out or transfer the contents of something ♦ *I'll empty the box on to the floor.* 3 (said about a river) to let its contents out into something ♦ *The river empties into a lake.*
empties *plural noun* bottles or other containers that no longer have any contents. **emptily** *adverb* **emptiness** *noun*

empty-handed *adjective* bringing or taking away nothing.

empty-headed *adjective* lacking sense or intelligence, foolish.

EMS *abbreviation* European Monetary System.

EMU *abbreviation* Economic and Monetary Union.

emu (ee-mew) *noun* (**emus**) a large Australian bird rather like an ostrich, with rough grey or brown feathers. [from a Portuguese word]

emulate (em-yoo-layt) *verb* to try to do as well as someone else; to imitate someone. **emulation** *noun* **emulator** *noun* [from a Latin word *aemulus* meaning 'a rival']

emulsify (i-mul-si-fiy) *verb* (**emulsifies, emulsified, emulsifying**) to convert something into an emulsion, or to be converted into an emulsion.

emulsion (i-mul-shən) *noun* 1 a creamy liquid with particles of oil or fat evenly distributed in it. 2 paint or medicine in this form. 3 a light-sensitive coating on photographic film, a mixture of silver compound in gelatine. [originally used of a milky liquid made by crushing almonds in water, from a Latin word *emulgere* meaning 'to milk out']

en- *prefix* (changing to **em-** before *b*, *m*, or *p*) in or into; on. [from a Latin word *in* or a Greek word *en*, both meaning 'in']

enable *verb* 1 to give someone the means or authority to do something. 2 to make something possible.

enact *verb* 1 to make a law by a formal process ♦ *Parliament will enact new laws controlling traffic in cities.* 2 to perform or act in a play.

enactment *noun* a law enacted.

enamel noun 1 a shiny substance with a surface like glass, used for coating metal or pottery. 2 paint that dries hard and glossy. 3 the hard outer covering of teeth.
enamel verb (**enamelled, enamelling**) to coat or decorate a surface with enamel. [from an Old French word]

enamoured (i-nam-erd) adjective very fond of someone or something. [from en- and a French word amour meaning 'love']

en bloc (ahn blok) adverb in a block, all at the same time. [a French phrase]

encamp verb to settle in a camp.

encampment noun a camp.

encapsulate verb 1 to enclose something in a capsule, or as if in a capsule. 2 to express an idea or set of ideas concisely. **encapsulation** noun [from en- and capsule]

encase verb to enclose something in a case.

encash verb to convert a cheque etc. into cash. **encashment** noun

encephalograph (en-sef-əloh-grahf) noun an instrument for recording the activity of the brain. **encephalography** noun [from a Greek word enkephalos meaning `brain']

enchant verb 1 to put someone under a magic spell. 2 to charm or delight someone. SYNONYMS: charm, delight, entrance, captivate, enthral, bewitch. **enchantment** noun **enchanter** noun **enchantress** noun [from an Old French word, related to chant]

encircle verb to surround someone or something. **encirclement** noun

enclave (en-klayv) noun a territory belonging to one country or state but lying entirely within the boundaries of another. [from an Old French word, from a Latin word clavis meaning 'key']

enclitic (en-klit-ik) adjective (said about a word) pronounced with hardly any emphasis, so that it forms part of the word before it.
enclitic noun a word of this kind. [from a Greek word enklinein meaning 'to lean on' (because it is thought of as leaning on the word before it)]

enclose verb 1 to put a wall or fence round something; to shut something in on all sides. SYNONYMS: confine, shut in, surround. 2 to put something into an envelope along with a letter or into a parcel along with the contents. [from an Old French word, related to include]

enclosed adjective (said about a religious community) living without any contact with the outside world.

enclosure noun 1 the process of enclosing or shutting in. 2 an enclosed area of ground. 3 something enclosed with a letter or the contents of a parcel.

encode verb 1 to put words into code. 2 (Computing) to put data into a coded form for processing by computer. **encoder** noun

encomium (en-koh-miəm) noun (**encomiums** or **encomia**) (formal) a speech or piece of writing expressing high praise. [from a Greek word enkōmion meaning 'eulogy']

encompass verb 1 to surround or encircle something. 2 to contain an idea or set of ideas. [from en- and compass in an old meaning 'circle']

encore (ong-kor) noun an extra item performed at a concert etc. after the main items have been performed and applauded.
encore verb to call for an extra item by applauding loudly. [a French word meaning 'again', used as a cry by audiences who want an encore]

encounter verb 1 to meet someone by chance or unexpectedly. SYNONYMS: come across, run into. 2 to find oneself faced with a challenge or difficulty. SYNONYMS: meet with, be faced with, experience.
encounter noun 1 a sudden or unexpected meeting with someone. 2 a confrontation or battle. [from en- and a Latin word contra meaning 'against']

encourage verb 1 to give hope or confidence to someone. SYNONYMS: hearten, reassure, inspire, embolden. 2 to urge someone to do something ♦ I encourage you all to try. 3 to stimulate or help develop an activity ♦ The new economic measures will encourage exports. **encouragement** noun [from a French word encourager, related to courage]

encroach verb 1 to intrude on someone's rights or property. 2 to extend beyond the original or proper limits ♦ The sea encroached gradually upon the land. **encroachment** noun [from en- and a French word crochier meaning 'to hook']

encrust verb 1 to cover something with a crust of hard material. 2 to decorate a surface with a layer of jewels or ornaments. **encrustation** noun [from a Latin word incrustare, related to crust]

encumber *verb* to hamper or be a burden to someone. [from *en-* and an Old French word *combre* meaning 'dam']

encumbrance *noun* a burden or difficulty.

encyclical (en-**sik**-lik-əl) *noun* a letter sent by the pope to the bishops of the Roman Catholic Church for wide circulation. [from a Greek word *enkuklios* meaning 'circular' or 'general']

encyclopedia *noun* a book or set of books giving information on many subjects, or on one subject in detail, usually arranged alphabetically. [from a Greek word *enkuklopaideia* meaning 'general education']

encyclopedic *adjective* having or providing information about many subjects or branches of one subject.

end *noun* 1 the last part or extreme point of something. SYNONYMS: limit, extremity, tip. 2 each half of a sports pitch or court, defended or occupied by one side or player. 3 the finish or conclusion of something, the final part. SYNONYMS: finish, close, conclusion, ending, completion, culmination. 4 destruction, downfall, or death. 5 a purpose or aim.
end *verb* 1 to bring something to an end, to finish something. SYNONYMS: conclude, finish, stop, terminate. 2 to come to an end. SYNONYMS: stop, finish, cease. 3 to reach a certain place or state, often by chance ♦ *We caught the wrong train and ended up in Preston.* **to keep your end up** (*informal*) to do what you can in spite of difficulties. **to make ends meet** to manage on a small income. **no end** (*informal*) very much ♦ *They liked it no end.* **no end of** (*informal*) a lot of ♦ *The storm caused no end of trouble.* **to put an end to something** to abolish or stop an activity, custom, etc. [from an Old English word]

endanger *verb* to cause danger to someone or something.

endangered species *noun* a species of animal or plant that is in danger of becoming extinct.

endear *verb* to cause someone to be loved ♦ *She endeared herself to us all.*

endearing *adjective* arousing love or affection.

endearment *noun* 1 a word or words that express love or affection. 2 liking or affection.

endeavour (in-**dev**-er) *verb* to attempt or try to do something.
endeavour *noun* an attempt. [from an old phrase *to put yourself in devoir* meaning 'to do your best' (from a French word *devoir* meaning 'duty')]

endemic (en-**dem**-ik) *adjective* (said about a disease) commonly found in a certain area or group of people. [from *en-* and a Greek word *dēmos* meaning 'people']

ending *noun* 1 the last part of something, especially a story or drama. 2 (*Grammar*) the part of a word that comes at the end, forming an inflection or suffix.

endive (**en**-div) *noun* 1 a plant with curly leaves, used as a salad. 2 (*North Amer.*) chicory. [from a Greek word *entubon*]

endless *adjective* 1 not ending or stopping ♦ *You need endless patience.* SYNONYMS: unlimited, unending, boundless, continuous, constant. 2 having the ends joined so that it forms a continuous strip for use in machinery etc. ♦ *an endless belt.*

endocrine (**end**-ə-kriyn or **end**-ə-krin) *adjective* (said about a gland) secreting its hormones or other products directly into the blood, not through a duct. [from Greek words *endon* meaning 'within' and *krinein* meaning 'to sift']

endogenous (end-**oj**-in-əs) *adjective* a technical term meaning originating from within. [from a Greek word *endon* meaning 'within' and *-genē* meaning 'of a certain kind']

endomorph (**end**-ə-mawf) *noun* a person with a soft rounded body and a large amount of fat tissue. (Compare **ectomorph**.) [from Greek words *endon* meaning 'within' and *morphē* meaning 'a form']

endorphin (en-**dor**-fin) *noun* any of a group of pain-killing hormones produced naturally within the brain and spinal cord. [from a Greek word *endon* meaning 'within' and *morphine*]

endorse *verb* 1 to sign or add a comment on a document. 2 to sign the back of a cheque in order to transfer the money to another person. 3 to make an official entry on a driving licence recording an offence committed by the holder. 4 to confirm a statement or approve of a course of action. SYNONYMS: approve, agree to, support, authorize. [from a Latin phrase *in dorsum* meaning 'on the back']

endorsement *noun* 1 approval of or

permission for a course of action. **2** a note added to a driving licence to record an offence committed by the holder.

endoscope *noun* an instrument for viewing internal parts of the body. [from Greek words *endon* meaning 'within' and *skopein* meaning 'to look']

endoskeleton *noun* (*Zoology*) an internal skeleton, such as vertebrates have. [from a Greek word *endon* meaning 'within' and *skeleton*]

endosperm *noun* (*Zoology*) the part of a seed that provides food material for a plant embryo. [from a Greek word *endon* meaning 'within' and *sperm*]

endothermic *adjective* (*Chemistry*) (said about a reaction) absorbing heat, not giving it off. (Compare **exothermic**.) [from Greek words *endon* meaning 'within' and *thermē* meaning 'heat']

endow *verb* **1** to provide a person or organization with a permanent income. **2** to provide someone with a power or quality. [from an Old French word, related to *dowry*]

endowment *noun* **1** the act of endowing something. **2** an endowed income. **3** a natural ability.

endowment insurance *noun* a form of life insurance in which a fixed sum is paid to the insured person on a specified date or to the person's estate if he or she dies before this date.

endowment mortgage *noun* a mortgage in which the capital is paid off after a fixed number of years by the proceeds of endowment insurance.

end product *noun* the product that is made by a manufacturing process.

endue *verb* (**endues, endued, enduing**) to provide someone with a talent or quality ♦ *Experience endues us with patience.* [from an Old French word *enduire*]

endurance *noun* the ability to withstand difficulty or pain for a long period.

endure *verb* **1** to experience or withstand difficulty or pain. SYNONYMS: withstand, suffer, bear, stand, undergo, put up with, submit to. **2** to tolerate something. **3** to remain in existence, to last. SYNONYMS: last, survive, persist, remain. **endurable** *adjective* [from *en-* and a Latin word *durus* meaning 'hard']

endways or **endwise** *adverb* **1** with its end foremost. **2** end to end.

enema (en-im-ə) *noun* (**enemas**) the medical process of inserting liquid into the rectum through the anus by means of a syringe. [from a Greek word *enienai* 'to put in']

enemy *noun* (**enemies**) **1** someone who is hostile towards another person and tries to harm them. **2** a country that is at war with another, or its armed forces. [from an Old French word *enemi*, from a Latin word *inimicus*]

energetic *adjective* showing or done with great energy. **energetically** *adverb*

energize (en-er-jiyz) *verb* **1** to give energy to someone or something. **2** to cause electricity to flow to a device.

energy *noun* (**energies**) **1** the capacity or strength to undertake activity. **2** the ability of matter or radiation to do work. **3** power obtained from fuel and other resources and used for light and heat, the operation of machinery etc. **energies** *plural noun* a person's physical powers used for a particular activity. [from *en-* and a Greek word *ergon* meaning 'work']

enervate (en-er-vayt) *verb* to cause someone to feel deprived of energy ♦ *an enervating climate.* [from a Latin word *enervare* meaning 'to weaken by removing the sinews']

enfeeble *verb* to weaken someone or make someone feeble.

enfold *verb* to surround or be wrapped round something.

enforce *verb* to compel someone to obey a rule or law. **enforceable** *adjective* **enforcement** *noun* [from an Old French word *enforcir*, from a Latin word *fortis* meaning 'strong']

enfranchise *verb* to give someone the right to vote in elections. **enfranchisement** *noun* [from *en-* and an Old French word *franc* meaning 'free']

engage *verb* **1** to arrange to employ someone ♦ *We need to engage a new secretary.* **2** to occupy the attention of someone ♦ *Douglas engaged her in conversation.* **3** to take part in an activity ♦ *She engaged in politics for many years.* **4** to begin a battle against an opponent ♦ *engaged the enemy troops.* **5** to promise or pledge to do something. **6** (said about a machine or engine part) to move into a position that allows it to operate or to connect with another part. [from an Old French word *engager*]

engaged *adjective* 1 having promised to marry someone. 2 busy or in use. 3 (said about a telephone line) already in use and therefore unavailable.

engagement *noun* 1 the process of engaging something. 2 a promise to marry someone. 3 an appointment made with another person. 4 a battle.

engaging *adjective* attractive or charming.

engender (in-**jen**-der) *verb* to cause something or give rise to it. [from an Old French word *engendrer*]

engine *noun* 1 a machine consisting of several parts working together to produce power or motion. 2 a vehicle that provides the power for a railway train; a locomotive. [from a Latin word *ingenium* meaning 'clever device', related to *ingenious*]

engineer *noun* 1 a person who is skilled in engineering. 2 a person who is in charge of machines or engines, e.g. on a ship. 3 someone who cleverly plans or organizes something.
engineer *verb* 1 to construct or control something as an engineer. 2 to make something happen by clever planning ♦ *He engineered a meeting between them.*

engineering *noun* the use of science and technology to build and use engines and other machines. (See also **civil engineering, electrical engineering, mechanical engineering.**)

English *adjective* to do with England or its people or language.
English *noun* the language of England, now used in several varieties throughout the world.
the English *plural noun* English people.
[from an Old English word]

Englishman or **Englishwoman** *noun* (**Englishmen** or **Englishwomen**) an English man or woman.

engrave *verb* 1 to cut or carve words or a design into a hard surface. 2 to fix an idea or memory deeply in the mind. **engraver** *noun* [from en- and an Old English word *grafan* meaning 'to carve']

engraving *noun* a print made from an engraved metal plate.

engross (in-**grohs**) *verb* to absorb all of someone's attention or efforts. SYNONYMS: absorb, preoccupy. [originally meaning 'to buy up all of something', from a French phrase *en gros* meaning 'wholesale']

engulf *verb* 1 to flow over something and cover or swamp it. 2 to overwhelm something.

enhance (in-**hahns**) *verb* to make something more attractive or of greater quality or value. **enhancement** *noun* [from an Old French word *enhaucer*]

enigma (in-**ig**-ma) *noun* (**enigmas**) something that is very puzzling or difficult to understand. [from a Greek word *ainigma* meaning 'riddle']

enigmatic (en-ig-**mat**-ik) *adjective* mysterious and puzzling. **enigmatically** *adverb*

enjoin *verb* to order or instruct someone to do something. [via Old French from a Latin word *injungere* meaning 'to impose']

enjoy *verb* 1 to get pleasure from something. SYNONYMS: appreciate, take pleasure in. 2 to have something as an advantage or benefit ♦ *She continues to enjoy good health.* ♦ **to enjoy yourself** to get pleasure from what you are doing. **enjoyment** *noun* [from en- and an Old French word *joir* meaning 'to rejoice']

enjoyable *adjective* giving enjoyment, pleasant. **enjoyably** *adverb*

enlarge *verb* 1 to make something larger, or to become larger. 2 to reproduce a photograph on a larger scale. 3 to talk or write about something in more detail.

enlargement *noun* 1 the process of enlarging something. 2 a larger copy made of a photograph.

enlarger *noun* an apparatus for making photographic enlargements.

enlighten *verb* to give more knowledge or understanding to someone. **enlightenment** *noun* [from en- and *lighten*[1]]

enlightened *adjective* tolerant and well-informed, free of prejudice.

enlist *verb* 1 to take someone into the armed forces, or to join the armed forces ♦ *He decided to enlist in the marines.* 2 to secure someone's help or support ♦ *They succeeded in enlisting our sympathy.* **enlistment** *noun*

enliven *verb* 1 to make someone more lively or cheerful. 2 to make something more interesting. **enlivenment** *noun*

en masse (ahn **mass**) *adverb* all together. [a French phrase, meaning 'in a mass']

enmesh *verb* to entangle something. [from *en-* and *mesh*]

enmity *noun* (**enmities**) a state of hostility between enemies. [from an Old French word, related to *enemy*]

ennoble *verb* 1 to make a person a noble. 2 to make someone or something more dignified. **ennoblement** *noun*

ennui (on-**wee**) *noun* a state of being weary from boredom. [a French word]

enormity (in-**orm**-iti) *noun* (**enormities**) 1 great wickedness ♦ *The country was shocked by the enormity of these crimes.* 2 a terrible crime or sin ♦ *It is difficult to comprehend such enormities.* 3 enormous size ♦ *They were quite daunted by the enormity of their task.* [same origin as for *enormous*] ◊ For the third meaning it is better to use *enormousness* or a different word such as *immensity* or *hugeness*.

enormous *adjective* huge, very large. SYNONYMS: huge, immense, massive, colossal, gigantic, vast. **enormously** *adverb* **enormousness** *noun* [from *ex-* and a Latin word *norma* meaning 'standard']

enough *adjective, noun,* & *adverb* as much or as many as necessary. SYNONYMS: sufficient, adequate, ample. [from an Old English word]

enquire *verb* to ask for information ♦ *He enquired if I was well.* [same origin as for *inquire*] ◊ The more usual spelling is *inquire* when the context is an official investigation.

enquiry *noun* (**enquiries**) 1 a question asking for information. 2 an investigation. [same origin as for *inquiry*] ◊ The more usual spelling is *inquiry* when referring to an official investigation.

enrage *verb* to make someone very angry.

enrapture *verb* to fill someone with intense delight.

enrich *verb* 1 to make someone rich or richer. 2 to improve the quality of something by adding things to it ♦ *The food has been enriched with vitamins.* **enrichment** *noun*

enriched uranium *noun* uranium containing an increased amount of the fissile isotope uranium-235.

enrol *verb* (**enrolled, enrolling**) 1 to become a member of a society or institution. 2 to admit someone as a member. **enrolment** *noun* [from *en-* and an Old French word *rolle* meaning 'roll']

en route (ahn **root**) *adverb* on the way from one place to another ♦ *We met them en route from Rome to London.* [a French phrase]

ensconce (in-**skons**) *verb* to settle someone securely or comfortably ♦ *He came in and ensconced himself in an armchair.* [from *en-* and an old word *sconce* meaning 'a shelter']

ensemble (on-**sombl**) *noun* 1 a collection of things regarded as a whole. 2 a group of musicians who perform together. 3 a matching outfit of clothes. [a French word]

enshrine *verb* 1 to place something precious in a special place or receptacle (such as a shrine). 2 to preserve an idea, memory, etc. with love or respect.

enshroud *verb* (*literary*) to cover something completely, as if in a shroud.

ensign (en-**syn**) *noun* a military or naval flag, especially one showing the nationality of a ship. [from an Old French word, related to *insignia*]

enslave *verb* to make a slave of someone. **enslavement** *noun*

ensnare *verb* to catch someone, as if in a snare.

ensue (ins-**yoo**) *verb* (**ensues, ensued, ensuing**) to happen afterwards or as a result ♦ *A violent quarrel ensued.*

en suite (on **sweet**) *adjective* & *adverb* (usually said about a bathroom) next to a bedroom, with a connecting door. [a French phrase meaning 'in sequence']

ensure *verb* to make something safe or certain ♦ *Good food will ensure good health.* ◊ Do not confuse this word with *insure*, which has a different meaning.

ENT *abbreviation* (*Medicine*) ear, nose, and throat.

entablature (in-**tab**-lə-cher) *noun* (*Architecture*) the section of a classical building above supporting columns, including the architrave, frieze, and cornice.

entail (in-**tayl**) *verb* 1 to involve something or make it necessary ♦ *These plans entail great expense.* SYNONYMS: involve, require, necessitate, mean. 2 (*Law*) to leave land or property to a succession of heirs with a stipulation that none of them can give it away or sell it.

entail noun (*Law*) the act of entailing land or property, or the land or property itself. [from en- and an Old French word *taillir* meaning 'to bequeath']

entangle verb 1 to make things become tangled. 2 to involve someone in something complicated. **entanglement** noun

entente (on-**tont**) noun a friendly understanding between countries. [a French word]

enter verb 1 to go in or come into a place. 2 to put a name or other details on a list or in a book. 3 to register someone as a competitor in a race or competition. 4 (said about an actor) to come on stage. 5 to become a member of an organization ♦ *When he was 18 he entered the Navy.* 6 to record something formally or present something for consideration ♦ *The accused entered a plea of not guilty.* **to enter into something** to begin to be involved in something. SYNONYMS: undertake, take on. [from a Latin word *intra* meaning 'within']

enteritis (en-ter-iy-tiss) noun (*Medicine*) a disease that involves inflammation of the intestines and diarrhoea. [from a Greek word *enteron* meaning 'intestine']

enterprise noun 1 a serious or difficult undertaking. 2 personal initiative or adventurousness ♦ *She showed a lot of enterprise.* 3 business activity ♦ *private enterprise.* [from en- and a Latin word *prehendere* meaning 'to take']

enterprising adjective showing initiative; adventurous.

entertain verb 1 to provide someone with amusement or enjoyment. 2 to treat someone to hospitality ♦ *After the meeting they entertained me to lunch.* 3 to have something in the mind ♦ *I think she is entertaining doubts.* 4 to consider something favourably ♦ *We refuse to entertain the idea.* [from an Old French word *entretenir*]

entertainer noun someone who entertains people, especially as a singer or comedian.

entertainment noun 1 the process of entertaining. 2 amusement. 3 something performed by an entertainer.

enthalpy (en-thəl-pi) noun (*Physics*) a thermodynamic quantity equivalent to the total heat content of a system. [from en- and a Greek word *thalpein* meaning 'to heat']

enthral (in-**thrawl**) verb (**enthralled, enthralling**) to fascinate someone or hold them spellbound. [from en- and an old word *thrall* meaning 'being in someone's power']

enthrone verb to place someone on a throne with ceremony. **enthronement** noun

enthuse (in-**thewz**) verb 1 to show interest and enthusiasm. 2 to fill someone with enthusiasm.

enthusiasm noun 1 a feeling of eager liking for something or interest in something. 2 something you are interested in ♦ *Skiing is one of my enthusiasms.* [from a Greek word *enthusiazein* meaning 'to be possessed by a god' (from *theos* meaning 'god')]

enthusiast noun someone who has a lot of enthusiasm for something ♦ *a sports enthusiast.*

enthusiastic adjective full of enthusiasm, eager. SYNONYMS: keen, eager. **enthusiastically** adverb

entice verb to attract or persuade someone by offering them something pleasant. SYNONYMS: coax, allure, lure, attract. **enticement** noun [from an Old French word *enticier*, from an older meaning 'to set on fire']

entire adjective whole or complete. **entirely** adverb [from an Old French word, related to *integer*]

entirety (in-**tiyr**-əti) noun the whole or total of something ♦ *He sold the family business in its entirety.*

entitle verb to give someone a right to do something ♦ *This ticket entitles you to free entrance to all the city's museums.* **entitlement** noun [from an Old French word, related to *title*]

entitled adjective having as a title ♦ *a poem entitled 'Spring'.*

entity (en-titi) noun (**entities**) something that exists as a distinct or separate thing. [from a French word *entité*]

entomb (in-**toom**) verb to place a body in a tomb. **entombment** noun

entomology (en-tə-**mol**-ə-ji) *noun* the study of insects. **entomological** (en-təm-ə-**loj**-ik-əl) *adjective* **entomologist** *noun* [from a Greek word *entomon* meaning 'insect' and *-logy*]

entourage (on-toor-**ah**zh) *noun* the people accompanying or attending an important person. [from a French word *entourer* meaning 'to surround']

entrails (en-traylz) *plural noun* the intestines of a person or animal. [via Old French from a Latin word *interanea* meaning 'internal things']

entrance[1] (en-trəns) *noun* **1** the act of entering. **2** a door or passage by which you enter a place. **3** the right to enter a public place, or the charge made for this. [from *enter*]

entrance[2] (in-trahns) *verb* to fill someone with intense delight. **entrancement** *noun* [from *en-* and *trance*]

entrant *noun* someone who enters for a competition or exam.

entrap *verb* (**entrapped, entrapping**) to catch someone or something, as if in a trap. **entrapment** *noun*

entreat *verb* to request someone earnestly or emotionally for something. **entreaty** *noun* [from an Old French word *entraitier*]

entrée (on-tray) *noun* **1** a dish served between the fish and meat courses of a formal dinner. **2** the right to enter a place. [a French word, originally referring to the first piece in a suite of music, related to *entry*]

entrench (in-**trench**) *verb* **1** to fix or establish a thought or idea firmly in the mind. **2** to establish a military force in a well-defended position. **entrenchment** *noun*

entrepreneur (on-trə-prən-**er**) *noun* a person who sets up a commercial undertaking, especially one involving commercial risk. **entrepreneurial** *adjective* [from a French word, related to *enterprise*]

entropy (en-trəp-i) *noun* (*Physics*) a measure of the disorder of molecules in substances that are mixed or in contact with each other, indicating the amount of energy that exists but is not available for use because it has become more evenly distributed instead of being concentrated. [from *en-* and a Greek word *tropē* meaning 'transformation']

entrust *verb* **1** to give something as a responsibility. **2** to place a person or thing in someone's care.

entry *noun* (**entries**) **1** the act of entering a place. **2** a place where you enter. **3** an alley between buildings. **4** an item entered in a list, diary, or reference book. **5** an entrant in a race or competition, or the total number of entrants.

entwine *verb* to twine one thing round another, to interweave things.

enumerate (i-**new**-mer-ayt) *verb* to count items, or to mention them one by one. **enumeration** *noun* **enumerator** *noun* [from *ex-* and a Latin word *numerare* meaning 'to number']

enunciate (i-**nun**-si-ayt) *verb* **1** to pronounce words. **2** to state something clearly. **enunciation** *noun* [from *ex-* and a Latin word *nuntiare* meaning 'to announce']

envelop (in-**vel**-əp) *verb* (**enveloped, enveloping**) to wrap something up or cover it completely. SYNONYMS: cover, enclose, enfold, wrap, sheathe. **envelopment** *noun* [from an Old French word *envoluper*, related to *develop*]

envelope (en-və-lohp) *noun* **1** a wrapper or covering, especially a folded cover for a letter. **2** the gas container of a balloon or airship.

enviable (en-vi-əbəl) *adjective* likely to arouse envy, desirable. **enviably** *adverb*

envious *adjective* full of envy. **enviously** *adverb*

environment *noun* **1** the surroundings in which people, animals, or plants live, and which affect their lives. **2** the natural world of the land, sea, and air. **environmental** (in-viyr-ən-**men**-təl) *adjective* [from an Old French word *environ* meaning 'surroundings']

environmentalist *noun* someone who wishes to protect or improve the environment.

environs (in-**viyr**-ənz) *plural noun* the surrounding districts, especially round a town ♦ *the environs of Manchester.* [same origin as for *environment*]

envisage (in-**viz**-ij) *verb* **1** to visualize or imagine something. **2** to consider something or think it possible ♦ *We envisage several changes in the new year.* [from *en-* and a French word *visage* meaning 'face']

envoy (en-voi) *noun* **1** an official

representative, especially one sent by one government to another. **2** a diplomatic minister ranking below an ambassador. [from a French word *envoyé* meaning 'sent']

envy *noun* **1** a feeling of discontent you have when someone else has something you want. **2** something that causes this feeling ♦ *Their new house is the envy of their friends.*

envy *verb* (**envies, envied, envying**) to have a feeling of envy towards someone or about something. [from Old French, related to *invidious*]

enzyme (en-ziym) *noun* **1** a protein formed in living cells, which assists chemical processes such as digestion. **2** a similar substance produced synthetically for use in chemical processes, household detergents, etc. [from a Greek word *enzumos* meaning 'leavened']

Eocene *adjective* (*Geology*) to do with the second epoch of the Tertiary period, about 56 to 35 million years ago, marked by the first appearance of horses, bats, and whales. [from Greek words *ēos* meaning 'dawn' and *kainos* meaning 'new']

epaulette (ep-ə-let) *noun* an ornamental flap attached to the shoulders of a uniform. [from a French word meaning 'little shoulder']

épée (ay-pay) *noun* a sharp-pointed sword used in duelling and (with the end blunted) in fencing. [a French word meaning 'sword']

ephemera (if-em-er-ə) *plural noun* things that are only useful or interesting for a short time. [from a Greek word *ephēmeros* meaning 'lasting a day']

ephemeral (if-em-er-əl) *adjective* lasting or useful only for a short time.

epi- *prefix* on; above; in addition. [from a Greek word *epi* meaning 'on']

epic *noun* **1** a long poem or story telling of heroic deeds or history. **2** a long book or film dealing with a similar subject. **epic** *adjective* to do with an epic or like an epic; on a grand scale. [from a Greek word *epos* meaning 'song']

epicentre *noun* the point at which an earthquake reaches the earth's surface. [from *epi-* and a Greek word *kentros* meaning 'centre']

epicure (ep-i-kewr) *noun* a person who enjoys good food, drink, literature, etc. **epicurism** *noun* [from the name of Epicurus, an ancient Greek philosopher (about 300 BC) who taught that pleasure was the highest good]

epicurean (ep-i-kewr-ee-ən) *adjective* fond of sensuous pleasure and luxury. **epicurean** *noun* an epicurean person. [same origin as for *epicure*]

epidemic *noun* an outbreak of a disease that spreads rapidly among the people of an area. [from *epi-* and a Greek word *dēmos* meaning 'people']

epidermis (epi-der-mis) *noun* the outer layer of the skin. [from *epi-* and a Greek word *derma* meaning 'skin']

epidural (epi-dewr-əl) *adjective* to do with or in the region (called the *dura mater*) of the nerves of the spinal cord. **epidural** *noun* an anaesthetic injection into this region, especially given during childbirth. [from *epi-* and *dura mater*]

epigeal (ep-i-jee-əl) *adjective* (*Botany*) growing or occurring above the ground. [from *epi-* and a Greek word *gē* meaning 'earth']

epiglottis (epi-glot-iss) *noun* a piece of cartilage at the root of the tongue, which descends to cover the windpipe during swallowing. [from *epi-* and a Greek word *glōtta* meaning 'tongue']

epigram *noun* a short witty saying or remark. **epigrammatic** *adjective* [from *epi-* and *-gram*]

epilepsy *noun* a disorder of the nervous system causing convulsions, sometimes with loss of consciousness. **epileptic** *adjective & noun* [from a Greek word *epilēpsia* meaning 'an attack' or 'a seizure']

epilogue (ep-i-log) *noun* a short section at the end of a book or play, added as a conclusion to or comment on what has gone before. [from *epi-* and a Greek word *logos* meaning 'speech']

Epiphany (i-pif-əni) *noun* a Christian festival celebrated on 6 January, commemorating the showing of Christ to the Magi. [from a Greek word *epiphainein* meaning 'to reveal clearly']

episcopal (ip-iss-kə-pəl) *adjective* **1** to do with a bishop or bishops. **2** (said about a Church) governed by bishops. [from a Greek word *episkopos* meaning 'bishop']

Episcopalian (ip-iss-kə-**pay**-li-ən) *adjective* to do with an episcopal Church, especially the Anglican Church in Scotland and the USA.
Episcopalian *noun* a member of an episcopal Church.

episcopate (ip-**iss**-kə-pət) *noun* the office of bishop.

episode *noun* 1 one incident or event in a sequence of happenings, either in real life or in fiction. SYNONYMS: incident, occurrence. 2 an instalment of a story or drama that is being serialized on radio or television. [from a Greek word *epeisodios* meaning 'coming in besides']

Epistle (ip-**iss**-əl) *noun* each of the books of the New Testament that are written in the form of letters to members of the Church.
epistle *noun* (*humorous*) a letter. [from a Greek word *epistolē*, from *epistellein* meaning 'to send out']

epitaph (ep-i-tahf) *noun* words inscribed on a tomb or in memory of a dead person. [from *epi-* and a Greek word *taphos* meaning 'tomb']

epithet (ep-i-thet) *noun* a word or phrase used to describe someone and often forming part of their name, e.g. 'the Great' in *Alfred the Great*. [from a Greek word *epithetos* meaning 'attributed']

epitome (ip-**it**-əmi) *noun* a person or thing that is a perfect example of a quality or type ♦ *She is the epitome of kindness.* [from a Greek word *epitomē* meaning 'shortening']

epitomize (ip-it-ə-myz) *verb* to be a perfect example of a quality or type.

epoch (ee-pok) *noun* 1 a period of history marked by certain events or circumstances. 2 (*Geology*) a division of a period. [from a Greek word *epokhē* meaning 'fixed point of time']

epoch-making *adjective* (said about an event) very significant or historic.

epoxy *noun* a plastic or adhesive made from synthetic organic compounds containing oxygen.

Epsom salts *plural noun* crystals of magnesium sulphate, used as a strong laxative. [named after Epsom in southern England, where a natural form of the salts was first found]

equable (ek-wə-bəl) *adjective* 1 (said about a person) calm and even-tempered. 2 (said about something natural, such as the climate) not changing much, constant.
equably *adverb* [from a Latin word, related to *equal*]

equal *adjective* 1 the same in size, amount, value, rank, etc. SYNONYMS: the same, identical, similar. 2 having the ability, strength, or courage needed ♦ *I'm not sure he's equal to the task.*
equal *noun* a person or thing that is equal to someone or something else.
equal *verb* (**equalled, equalling**) 1 to be equal to someone or something. 2 to match or rival another achievement ♦ *No one has yet equalled this score.* SYNONYMS: match, rival, compete with, compare with. [from a Latin word *aequus* meaning 'even' or 'level']

equality *noun* the state of being equal.

equalize *verb* 1 to make things equal, or to become equal. 2 (in games) to level the score by scoring a goal or point.
equalization *noun*

equalizer *noun* a goal or point that equalizes the score.

equally *adverb* 1 in equal amounts ♦ *The money was shared out equally.* 2 to the same extent or in the same way ♦ *The two problems are equally difficult.*

equanimity (ek-wə-**nim**-iti) *noun* a calm state of mind or temper. [from *equi-* and a Latin word *animus* meaning 'mind']

equate (i-kwayt) *verb* to consider someone or something as equal or equivalent to another.

equation (i-**kway**-zhən) *noun* 1 (*Mathematics*) a statement that two expressions (linked by the sign =) are equal. 2 (*Chemistry*) a formula indicating a chemical reaction by the use of symbols. 3 the process of making things equal.

equator (i-**kway**-ter) *noun* an imaginary line round the earth at an equal distance from the North and South Poles, dividing the earth into northern and southern hemispheres. [from a Latin phrase *circulus aequator diei et noctis* meaning 'circle equalizing day and night', related to *equal*]

equatorial (ek-wə-**tor**-iəl) *adjective* to do with the equator, or situated near the equator.

equerry (ek-**wer**-i) *noun* (**equerries**) a personal attendant of a member of the British royal family. [from an Old French word *esquierie* meaning 'company of squires', perhaps related to *equestrian*]

equestrian (i-**kwest**-riən) *adjective* **1** to do with horse riding. **2** (said about a portrait or statue) showing a figure on horseback. **equestrian** *noun* a person who is skilled at horse riding. [from a Latin word *equus* meaning 'horse']

equi- *prefix* equal; equally. [from a Latin word *aequus* meaning 'equal']

equidistant (ee-kwi-**dis**-tənt) *adjective* at an equal distance. [from *equi-* and *distant*]

equilateral (ee-kwi-**lat**-er-əl) *adjective* (said about a triangle or other figure) having all its sides equal. [from *equi-* and *lateral*]

equilibrium (ee-kwi-**lib**-riəm) *noun* (**equilibria**) **1** a state of balance between opposing forces or influences. **2** a balanced or calm state of mind. [from *equi-* and a Latin word *libra* meaning 'balance']

equine (**ek**-wiyn) *adjective* to do with horses, or like a horse. [from a Latin word *equus* meaning 'horse']

equinox (**ek**-win-oks) *noun* a time that occurs twice each year when day and night are of equal length (about 22 September and 20 March). **equinoctial** (ek-wi-**nok**-shəl) *adjective* [from *equi-* and a Latin word *nox* meaning 'night']

equip *verb* (**equipped, equipping**) to supply someone or something with what is needed. SYNONYMS: supply, fit out, prepare. [via French from an Old Norse word *skipa* meaning 'to man a ship']

equipment *noun* **1** the tools and other things needed for a particular job or undertaking. SYNONYMS: gear, kit, apparatus, tackle, materials. **2** the process of providing these items.

equitable (**ek**-wit-əbəl) *adjective* fair and just. **equitably** *adverb* [same origin as for *equity*]

equity (**ek**-wi-ti) *noun* fairness, impartiality. **equities** *plural noun* stocks and shares that do not yield a fixed rate of interest. [from a Latin word *aequitas*, related to *equal*]

equivalent *adjective* having the same value, importance, meaning, or status. **equivalent** *noun* an equivalent thing, amount, or word. **equivalence** *noun* [from *equi-* and a Latin word *valens* meaning 'worth']

equivocal (i-**kwiv**-əkəl) *adjective* deliberately vague and open to more than one interpretation, ambiguous. SYNONYMS: ambiguous, vague, misleading.

equivocally *adverb* [from *equi-* and a Latin word *vocare* meaning 'to call']

equivocate (i-**kwiv**-əkayt) *verb* to use ambiguous words to hide the truth. SYNONYMS: prevaricate, hedge. **equivocation** *noun* [same origin as for *equivocate*]

ER *abbreviation* Queen Elizabeth. [from *Elizabetha Regina*, the Latin form of the name]

era (**eer**-ə) *noun* **1** a distinct period of history. **2** (*Geology*) a major division of time, divided into periods.

eradicate (i-**rad**-ik-ayt) *verb* to get rid of something or remove all traces of it. **eradication** *noun* [from a Latin word *eradicare* meaning 'to root out' from *radix* meaning 'a root']

erase (i-**rayz**) *verb* **1** to rub out writing or other marks. SYNONYMS: rub out, efface, delete, obliterate, expunge. **2** to delete a recording from magnetic audio or video tape. [from *ex-* and a Latin word *rasum* meaning 'scraped']

eraser *noun* a piece of rubber or plastic used for rubbing out writing or other marks.

erasure (i-**ray**-zher) *noun* **1** the process of erasing something. **2** a mark or piece of writing that has been erased.

ere (air) *preposition & conjunction* (*old use*) before.

erect *adjective* **1** standing on end, upright, vertical. **2** (said about a part of the body, especially the penis) enlarged and rigid from sexual excitement. **erect** *verb* to build something or set it up. SYNONYMS: build, construct, put up, set up, raise, assemble. **erector** *noun* [from *erectus*, a form of *erigere* meaning 'to set up']

erectile (i-**rek**-tiyl) *adjective* (said about parts of the body) able to become enlarged and rigid.

erection *noun* **1** the process of erecting something. **2** something that has been erected, a building. **3** the swelling and hardening of the penis during sexual excitement.

erg *noun* (*Physics*) a unit of work or energy. [from a Greek word *ergon* meaning 'work']

ergo *adverb* therefore. [a Latin word]

ergonomics (ergə-**nom**-iks) *noun* the study of work and the most efficient ways of doing it. **ergonomic** *adjective*

ergonomically adverb [from Greek words ergon meaning 'work' and -nomia meaning 'management']

ERM abbreviation Exchange Rate Mechanism, a system for controlling the value of members' currencies in the European Monetary System of the EU.

ermine noun 1 an animal of the weasel family, with brown fur that turns white in winter. 2 the white fur of the ermine. [from an Old French word hermine, perhaps originally from the country name Armenia]

erode (i-rohd) verb to wear something away gradually, especially by rubbing or corroding. **erosion** (i-roh-zhən) noun **erosive** adjective [from ex- and a Latin word rodere meaning 'to gnaw']

erotic (i-rot-ik) adjective to do with sexual love, or arousing sexual desire. **erotically** adverb **eroticism** noun [from a Greek word erōs meaning 'sexual love']

err verb 1 to make a mistake, to be incorrect. 2 to do wrong. [from a Latin word errare meaning 'to wander']

errand noun a short journey to carry a message or to deliver or collect something, usually for someone else. [from an Old English word]

errant (e-rənt) adjective 1 (formal) misbehaving or doing wrong. 2 (literary) travelling in search of adventure ♦ a knight errant. [same origin as for err]

erratic (i-rat-ik) adjective irregular or uneven in movement or pattern. SYNONYMS: irregular, variable, changeable, unreliable. **erratically** adverb [same origin as for err]

erratum (e-rah-təm) noun (errata) an error in printing or writing. [a Latin word, related to err]

erroneous (i-roh-niəs) adjective incorrect or mistaken. **erroneously** adverb [same origin as for err]

error noun 1 a mistake. 2 the condition of being wrong in judgement or behaviour. 3 a technical term for the amount of inaccuracy in a calculation or a measuring device ♦ an error of 2 per cent. **in error** by mistake. [same origin as for err]

ersatz adjective substitute or imitation. [a German word meaning 'replacement']

Erse noun the Irish Gaelic language. [a form of the word Irish]

erstwhile adjective (formal) former. [from an Old English word, related to ere]

erudite (e-rew-diyt) adjective having great knowledge or learning. **erudition** (e-rew-dish-ən) noun [from a Latin word erudire meaning 'to instruct']

erupt verb 1 to break out suddenly and violently. 2 (said about a volcano) to shoot out lava. 3 to form spots or patches on the skin. **eruption** noun [from ex- and a Latin word ruptum meaning 'burst']

eruptive adjective erupting or liable to erupt.

erythrocyte (i-rith-rə-siyt) noun a red blood cell, which contains haemoglobin and carries oxygen through the body. [from Greek words eruthros meaning 'red' and kutos meaning 'vessel']

escalate (esk-ə-layt) verb to become greater, more serious, or more intense; to make something do this ♦ The street fighting soon escalated into a riot. **escalation** noun [same origin as for escalator]

escalator noun a staircase with an endless line of steps moving up or down. [via French from a Latin word scala meaning 'ladder']

escalope (esk-ə-lohp) noun a slice of boneless meat, especially veal. [same origin as for scallop]

escapade (esk-ə-payd) noun a reckless or mischievous adventure. [from a French word meaning 'an escape']

escape verb 1 to get yourself free from being confined or controlled. SYNONYMS: get free, get away, run away, break out. 2 to succeed in avoiding something dangerous or unpleasant ♦ The driver escaped injury by inches. SYNONYMS: avoid, evade, elude. 3 to be forgotten or unnoticed by someone ♦ Her name escapes me for the moment. 4 (said about a liquid or gas etc.) to get out of a container, to leak. SYNONYMS: leak, seep, ooze. 5 (said about words or sounds) to be uttered unintentionally.

escape noun 1 the act of escaping. 2 a means of escaping. 3 a leakage of liquid or gas. 4 a temporary distraction or relief from reality or worry. 5 short for **escape key**. **escaper** noun [via Old French from Latin words ex- meaning 'out' and cappa meaning 'cloak']

escapee (ess-kay-pee) noun someone who has escaped.

escape key noun (*Computing*) a key that cancels the present operation or instruction.

escapement noun a mechanism that controls the movement of a watch or clock etc. [from a French word, related to *escape*]

escapism noun escaping from the difficulties of life by thinking about or doing more pleasant things. **escapist** adjective & noun

escarpment noun a steep slope at the edge of a plateau or other high level ground. [via Old French from an Italian word *scarpa* meaning 'slope']

eschew (iss-**choo**) verb to avoid or abstain from a choice or action. [from an Old French word *eschiver*]

escort [1] (**ess**-kort) noun **1** one or more people, vehicles, or ships accompanying a person or thing to give protection or as an honour. **2** a person who accompanies a member of the opposite sex at a social occasion. [via French from an Italian word *scorgere* meaning 'to guide']

escort [2] (i-**skort**) verb to act as an escort to someone or something. SYNONYMS: accompany, attend.

escutcheon (i-**skuch**-ən) noun a shield or emblem bearing a coat of arms. [from a Latin word *scutum* meaning 'shield']

Eskimo noun (**Eskimos** or **Eskimo**) **1** a member of a people living near the Arctic coast of North America, Greenland, and Siberia. **2** the language of this people. [from an American Indian word meaning 'eaters of raw flesh']
◊ It is now more usual, and preferred by the people themselves, to use the name *Inuit* for those who live in northern Canada and Greenland, and *Yupik* for those who live in Alaska and Asia.

esoteric (ess-oh-**te**-rik) adjective intended only for people with special knowledge or interest. [from a Greek word *esōterikos*, comparative form of *esō* meaning 'within']

ESP abbreviation extrasensory perception.

espadrille (ess-pə-**dril**) noun a light canvas shoe with a sole of plaited fibre. [a French word, from a Latin word *spartum* meaning 'rope', related to *esparto*]

espalier (iss-**pal**-i-er) noun a fruit tree or ornamental shrub that is trained to grow against a wall or trellis. [via French from an Italian word *spalla* meaning 'shoulder', related to *spatula*]

especial adjective **1** special or outstanding ♦ *of especial interest*. **2** mainly suitable for one person or thing ♦ *for your especial benefit*. [same origin as for *special*]

especially adverb chiefly, more than in other cases.

Esperanto (ess-per-**an**-toh) noun an artificial language devised in 1887 as an international means of communication. [named after Dr Esperanto, assumed name of the Polish inventor of the language, based on the Latin word *sperare* meaning 'to hope']

espionage (ess-pi-ən-**ahzh**) noun spying or using spies to obtain secret information. [from a French word *espion* meaning 'a spy']

esplanade (ess-plən-**ayd**) noun a level area of ground where people may walk or ride for pleasure, especially beside the sea. [via French from a Latin word *explanatus* meaning 'levelled']

espouse (i-**spowz**) verb to adopt or support an idea or cause. **espousal** noun [from an earlier meaning 'to give someone in marriage', related to *spouse*]

espresso noun (**espressos**) strong black coffee made by forcing steam through ground coffee beans. [an Italian word meaning 'pressed out']

esprit de corps (ess-pree də **kor**) noun loyalty to the group you belong to. [a French phrase meaning 'spirit of the body']

espy verb (**espies**, **espied**, **espying**) (*literary*) to catch sight of someone or something. [from an Old French word]

Esq. abbreviation a courtesy title used in more formal correspondence, placed after a man's surname where no title is used before his name. [an abbreviation of *esquire*, originally a knight's attendant who carried his shield, from a Latin word *scutarius* meaning 'shield-bearer']

essay [1] (**ess**-ay) noun **1** a short piece of prose writing. **2** (*formal*) an attempt. [from a French word *essai* meaning 'trial']

essay [2] (ess-**ay**) verb (**essays**, **essayed**, **essaying**) (*formal*) to attempt to do something.

essayist noun a writer of essays.

essence noun 1 the nature or quality that makes a thing what it is. 2 a concentrated liquid taken from a plant or other substance, used for flavouring or as a perfume. [from a Latin word *esse* meaning 'to be']

essential adjective 1 that you have to do or have, indispensable. SYNONYMS: indispensable, necessary, crucial, vital, imperative. 2 making up a thing's nature or essence.
essentials plural noun things that you cannot do without. **essentially** adverb

essential oil noun a natural oil obtained from a plant.

establish verb 1 to set up a business or government on a permanent basis. SYNONYMS: set up, found, create, initiate, start. 2 to settle yourself or someone else in a place or position. 3 to cause people to accept a custom or belief etc. 4 to show something to be true ♦ *He succeeded in establishing his innocence.* SYNONYMS: prove, demonstrate, confirm, substantiate. [from a Latin word *stabilire* meaning 'to make firm', related to *stable*]

established adjective (said about a Church or religion) recognized as a country's official national Church or religion.

establishment noun 1 the process of establishing something. 2 an organized body, especially a household or staff of servants etc. 3 a business firm or other institution. **the Establishment** people who are established in positions of power and influence.

estate noun 1 a property consisting of a large house with extensive grounds. 2 an area of land with houses or factories built to a common plan and design. 3 all that a person owns at their death. 4 (old use) condition ♦ *the holy estate of matrimony*. [from Old French, related to *state*]

estate agent noun a person or organization that sells or lets houses and land.

estate car noun a car with a single compartment extended behind the passenger area and having a door at the back for loading goods.

esteem verb 1 to think highly of someone or something. 2 (formal) to consider or regard something in a certain way ♦ *I should esteem it an honour.*

esteem noun respect and admiration. [same origin as for *estimate*]

ester (**ess**-ter) noun (Chemistry) an organic compound formed when an acid and an alcohol interact in a certain way. [from German words *Essig* meaning 'vinegar' and *Äther* meaning 'ether']

estimable (**ess**-tim-əbəl) adjective worthy of respect or esteem.

estimate [1] (**ess**-tim-ət) noun 1 a judgement about the size or value of something. 2 a written or printed statement of what a piece of work is likely to cost. 3 a judgement of the character or qualities of a person or thing.

estimate [2] (**ess**-tim-ayt) verb 1 to calculate the size, value, or cost of something. SYNONYMS: work out, calculate, assess, evaluate, reckon. 2 to form an estimate of a person or thing. **estimation** noun [from a Latin word *aestimare* meaning 'to determine']

estranged adjective unfriendly after being friendly or loving. **estrangement** noun [from a Latin word *extraneare* meaning 'to treat someone as a stranger']

estuary (**ess**-tew-er-i) noun (**estuaries**) the mouth of a large river where it reaches the sea and the tide flows in and out. [from a Latin word *aestus* meaning 'tide']

et al. abbreviation and others. [short for a Latin phrase *et alii*]

etc. abbreviation and other similar things, and the rest. [short for *et cetera*, a Latin phrase meaning 'and the other things']

etch verb 1 to engrave a picture with acid on a metal plate, especially for printing. 2 to affect or impress someone deeply ♦ *The scene is etched on my mind.* **etcher** noun [from a Dutch word *etsen*]

etching noun a picture made from an etched metal plate.

eternal adjective 1 lasting or existing for ever. SYNONYMS: everlasting, unending, endless. 2 unchanging, not affected by time. 3 (informal) constant, too frequent ♦ *I'm tired of these eternal arguments.* **eternally** adverb [from a Latin word *aeternus*, from *aevum* meaning 'age']

eternity noun 1 time that goes on for ever. 2 (informal) a very long time.

ethane (**eth**-ayn or **ee**-thayn) noun (Chemistry) a carbon compound in the alkane series, found in natural gas. [from *ether*]

ethanoic acid (eth-ə-**noh**-ik) *noun* an acid that gives vinegar its special taste and smell.

ether (**ee**-ther) *noun* 1 a colourless liquid produced by the action of acids on alcohol, used as an anaesthetic and as a solvent. 2 (*literary*) the upper air beyond the clouds. [from a Greek word *aithēr*]

ethereal (i-**theer**-iəl) *adjective* 1 light and delicate. 2 to do with heaven, heavenly. **ethereally** *adverb*

ethic (**eth**-ik) *noun* a moral principle or set of principles. **ethics** *plural noun* the study of moral rights and principles. [from a Greek word *ēthos* meaning 'character']

ethical (**eth**-ikəl) *adjective* 1 to do with ethics. 2 morally right, honourable. **ethically** *adverb*

ethnic *adjective* 1 belonging to a group of people with a particular national or cultural identity. 2 (said about clothes etc.) resembling those of a non-Western people. **ethnically** *adverb* [from a Greek word *ethnos* meaning 'nation']

ethnic cleansing *noun* the mass expulsion or killing of one ethnic group by another in an area.

ethnology (eth-**nol**-əji) *noun* the study of the characteristics and conditions of peoples of the world. **ethnological** (eth-nə-**loj**-ikəl) *adjective* [from Greek words *ethnos* meaning 'nation' and *-logy*]

ethology (ee-**thol**-əji) *noun* the study of animal behaviour, or of human behaviour in its biological aspects. **ethologist** *noun* [from Greek words *ēthos* meaning 'character' and *-logy*]

ethos (**ee**-thoss) *noun* the characteristic spirit and beliefs of a society or organization. [a Greek word meaning 'character']

ethyl (**eth**-il) *noun* (*Chemistry*) a radical present in alcohol and ether.

ethylene (**eth**-i-leen) *noun* a carbon compound of the alkene series, used in the manufacture of polythene.

etiolated (**ee**-tiə-layt-id) *adjective* (said about a plant) pale and weak from lack of light. **etiolation** *noun* [from a French word]

etiquette (**et**-i-ket) *noun* the rules of correct behaviour in a society or profession. [from a French word]

Etruscan (i-**trus**-kən) *noun* 1 a native of ancient Etruria (modern Tuscany), a state of northwest Italy that was at its peak in the 6th century BC. 2 the language of the Etruscans. **Etruscan** *adjective* to do with Etruria or its people or language. [from the Latin name *Etruscus*]

étude (**ay**-tewd) *noun* (*Music*) a short musical composition, especially for piano. [a French word meaning 'study']

etymology (et-im-**ol**-əji) *noun* (**etymologies**) an account of the origin and development in meaning of a word. **etymological** (et-im-ə-**loj**-ikəl) *adjective* [from a Greek word *etumon* meaning 'original word' and *-logy*]

EU *abbreviation* European Union.

eu- (yoo) *prefix* well. [from a Greek word *eu* meaning 'well']

eucalyptus (yoo-kə-**lip**-təs) *noun* (**eucalyptuses**) 1 a kind of evergreen tree. 2 a strong-smelling oil obtained from its leaves. [from Greek words *eu* meaning 'well' and *kaluptos* meaning 'covered' (because the flower is covered by a cap before opening)]

Eucharist (**yoo**-kə-rist) *noun* the Christian sacrament in which bread and wine are consecrated and swallowed, commemorating the Last Supper of Christ and his disciples. **Eucharistic** *adjective* [from a Greek word *eukharistia* meaning 'thanksgiving']

eugenics (yoo-**jen**-iks) *noun* the science of developing a special human or animal population by controlled breeding. **eugenic** *adjective* **eugenically** *adverb* [from *eu-* and *gene*]

eulogize (**yoo**-lə-jiyz) *verb* to praise someone highly; to write a eulogy of someone. **eulogistic** *adjective*

eulogy (**yoo**-lə-ji) *noun* (**eulogies**) a speech or piece of writing in praise of a person or thing. [from *eu-* and a Greek word *-logia* meaning 'speaking']

eunuch (**yoo**-nək) *noun* a man who has been castrated. [from a Greek word *eunoukhos*]

euphemism (**yoo**-fim-izm) *noun* a mild or roundabout expression or phrase used instead of a more direct or frank one, e.g. *pass away* instead of *die*. **euphemistic** (yoo-fim-**ist**-ik) *adjective* **euphemistically** *adverb* [from *eu-* and a Greek word *phēmē* meaning 'speech']

euphonium (yoo-**foh**-niəm) *noun* a large brass wind instrument of the tuba family. [from *eu-* and a Greek word *phōnē* meaning 'sound']

euphony (**yoo**-fəni) *noun* pleasantness of sounds, especially made by words. **euphonious** (yoo-**foh**-niəs) *adjective* [same origin as for *euphonium*]

euphoria (yoo-**for**-iə) *noun* a feeling of general happiness. **euphoric** (yoo-**fo**-rik) *adjective* [from *eu-* and a Greek word *phoros* meaning 'bearing']

Eurasian (yoor-**ay**-zhən) *adjective* **1** of mixed European and Asian parentage. **2** to do with Europe and Asia. **Eurasian** *noun* a person of mixed European and Asian parentage. [from *European* and *Asian*]

eureka (yoor-**eek**-ə) *interjection* an exclamation of triumph at a great discovery. [from a Greek word *heurēka* meaning 'I have found it', said to have been uttered by the Greek mathematician Archimedes (3rd century BC) on discovering a way of determining the purity of gold]

eurhythmics (yoo- **rith**- miks) *noun* a system of rhythmical movements of the body done to music for therapeutic purposes. [from *eu-* and *rhythm*]

Euro- *prefix* Europe or European.

euro *noun* (**euros** or **euro**) the single currency introduced in the EU in 1999.

European *adjective* to do with or coming from Europe.
European *noun* a person born in Europe or descended from people born there.

europium *noun* a soft silvery-white metallic element. [from the name *Europe*]

Eurosceptic *noun* a person who is sceptical about the benefits of the European Union and is opposed to increasing its political role.

Eustachian tube (yoo-**stay**-shən) *noun* a narrow passage leading from the pharynx to the cavity of the middle ear, equalizing pressure on each side of the eardrum. [named after the 16th-century Italian anatomist Bartolomeo Eustachio]

euthanasia (yoo-thə-**nay**-ziə) *noun* the act of causing someone to die gently and without pain, especially when they are suffering from a painful incurable disease or in a permanent coma. [from *eu-* and a Greek word *thanatos* meaning 'death']

eutrophic (yoo-**troh**-fik or yoo-**trof**-ik) *adjective* (*Biology* and *Chemistry*) (said about a body of water) rich in nutrients and so supporting an abundant plant life. **eutrophication** *noun* [from *eu-* and a Greek word *trephein* meaning 'to nourish']

eV *abbreviation* electronvolt(s).

evacuate *verb* **1** to send people away from a place that has become dangerous. SYNONYMS: move out, clear, remove. **2** to make something empty of air, water, or other contents. **evacuation** *noun* [from *ex-* and a Latin word *vacuus* meaning 'empty']

evacuee *noun* a person who has been evacuated.

evade (i-**vayd**) *verb* to avoid a person or thing by cleverness or trickery. SYNONYMS: avoid, elude, dodge, escape. [from *ex-* and a Latin word *vadere* meaning 'to go']

evaluate *verb* to find out or state the value of something. **evaluation** *noun* [from a French word, related to *value*]

evangelical (ee-van-**jel**-ikəl) *adjective* **1** according to the teaching of the gospel or the Christian religion. **2** (in the Church of England) to do with a group that emphasizes the authority of the Bible and salvation through faith in the Atonement. **Evangelical** *noun* an evangelical Christian. **evangelicalism** *noun* [from a Greek word *euangelion* meaning 'good news', related to *angel*]

evangelism (i-**van**-jəl-izm) *noun* preaching or spreading of the gospel.

evangelist (i-**van**-jəl-ist) *noun* **1** each of the writers of the four Christian Gospels (Matthew, Mark, Luke, John). **2** a person who preaches the gospel. **evangelistic** *adjective*

evangelize *verb* to preach or spread the Christian gospel to people, to win people over to Christianity.

evaporate *verb* **1** to turn a liquid into vapour, or to be turned into vapour. **2** to cease to exist ♦ *Their hostility soon evaporated.* **evaporation** *noun* [from *ex-* meaning 'out' and a Latin word *vapor* meaning 'steam']

evaporated milk *noun* tinned sweetened milk that has been thickened by partial evaporation.

evasion (i-**vay**-zhən) noun 1 the act of evading someone or something. 2 an evasive answer or excuse.

evasive (i-**vay**-siv) adjective 1 evading an answer, not frank or straightforward. 2 seeking to avoid or prevent something ♦ to take evasive action. **evasively** adverb **evasiveness** noun

eve noun 1 the evening or day before an important festival ♦ Christmas Eve. 2 the time just before an important event ♦ on the eve of an election. 3 (old use) evening. [a short form of even[2]]

even[1] adjective 1 level and smooth, free from irregularities. SYNONYMS: level, flat, smooth. 2 not changing or varying, regular. SYNONYMS: regular, consistent. 3 (said about a person's temper) calm, not easily upset. SYNONYMS: calm, cool, placid. 4 equally balanced or matched ♦ The match was fairly even. 5 equal in number or amount ♦ At half time the scores were even. SYNONYMS: level, equal. 6 (said about a number) able to be divided exactly by two. 7 exact, not involving fractions ♦ an even dozen.
even adverb used to emphasize a word or statement ♦ She began to run even faster ♦ We couldn't even see it, let alone describe it. **even** verb to make something even, or to become even. **to be** or **get even with** to have revenge on someone. **evenly** adverb **evenness** noun [from an Old English word]

even[2] noun (poetic) evening.

even-handed adjective fair and impartial.

evening noun the part of the day between late afternoon and bedtime. [from an Old English word]

evening dress noun clothing worn at formal occasions in the evening.

evening star noun the planet Venus, seen shining brightly in the west after sunset.

even money noun (in betting) odds in which the amount to be won is the same as the stake.

evensong noun a service of evening prayers in the Church of England. [from even[2] and song]

event noun 1 something that happens, especially something important. SYNONYMS: happening, incident, occurrence, experience. 2 a race or competition that forms part of a sports contest. **at all events** or **in any event** in any case. [from ex- and a Latin word ventum meaning 'having come']

eventful adjective full of interesting or important happenings.

event horizon noun an imaginary boundary round a black hole, beyond which light and other radiation cannot escape.

eventide noun (old use) evening.

eventing noun a horse-riding competition that consists of several events including showjumping and dressage.

eventual adjective happening in the end or after a time ♦ his eventual success. **eventually** adverb [from a Latin word eventus meaning 'result' or 'event', modelled on actual]

eventuality (i-ven-tew-al-iti) noun (**eventualities**) something that may happen.

ever adverb 1 at all times, always ♦ We are ever hopeful. 2 at any time ♦ It was the best thing I ever did. 3 used for emphasis ♦ Why ever didn't you tell me? [from an Old English word]

evergreen adjective (said about a tree or shrub) having green leaves all the year round.
evergreen noun an evergreen tree or shrub.

everlasting adjective lasting for ever or for a long time. SYNONYMS: eternal, unending, endless. **everlastingly** adverb

evermore adverb (literary) for ever, always.

every adjective 1 each without any exception ♦ We enjoyed every minute. 2 each in a series of intervals ♦ The cleaners come every third day. 3 all that is possible ♦ They will be given every care. **every other** every second or alternate one ♦ The magazine is published every other Friday. **every so often** at intervals, occasionally. [from an Old English word]

everybody pronoun every person.

everyday adjective usual, ordinary ♦ everyday clothes.

everyone pronoun everybody.

everything pronoun 1 all things, all. 2 the most important thing ♦ Beauty is not everything.

everywhere adverb in every place.

evict (i-**vikt**) verb to use the law to make people leave the property they are living in. **eviction** noun [from a Latin word evictum meaning 'expelled']

evidence noun 1 a fact or piece of information that gives a reason for believing something. 2 statements made or objects produced in a lawcourt to prove or support a case.
evidence verb to be evidence of something. **to be in evidence** to be obvious or conspicuous. [from ex- and a Latin word videre meaning 'to see']

evident adjective obvious to the eye or mind. SYNONYMS: obvious, apparent, noticeable, clear, plain. **evidently** adverb

evidential (ev-i-den-shǝl) adjective (formal) based on or providing evidence.

evil adjective 1 morally bad, wicked. SYNONYMS: wicked, bad, vile, sinful, (said about a person) malevolent. 2 harmful or tending to do harm. 3 extremely unpleasant or troublesome ♦ an evil smell.
evil noun 1 extreme wickedness. 2 an evil thing. **evilly** adverb [from an Old English word]

evil-doer noun someone who does evil things.

evince (i-vins) verb (formal) to indicate a quality or feeling. [same origin as for evict]

eviscerate (i-vis-er-ayt) verb (formal) to take out the intestines of an animal or person. **evisceration** noun [from ex- and viscera]

evocative (i-vok-ǝtiv) adjective tending to bring back special memories or feelings. [same origin as for evoke]

evoke (i-vohk) verb 1 to bring back special memories or feelings ♦ The photographs evoked happy memories. SYNONYMS: arouse, awaken, excite, elicit. 2 to produce a particular response from someone. **evocation** (ev-ǝ-kay-shǝn) noun [from ex- and a Latin word vocare meaning 'to call']

evolution (ee-vǝ-loo-shǝn) noun 1 the process by which something evolves or changes. 2 the process by which living things develop from earlier forms. **evolutionary** adverb [same origin as for evolve]

evolve (i-volv) verb 1 to develop gradually, or develop something gradually ♦ We must try to evolve a plan. 2 (said about an organism) to develop by evolution. **evolvement** noun [from ex- and a Latin word volvere meaning 'to roll']

ewe noun a female sheep. [from an Old English word]

ewer (yoo-er) noun a large water jug with a wide mouth. [from a French word, from a Latin word aqua meaning 'water']

ex preposition (said about goods) as sold from a ship, factory, etc. ♦ ex-works. [from a Latin word ex meaning 'out of']

ex- prefix (changing to **ef-** before f, and to **e-** before many consonants). 1 out or away (as in ♦ extract). 2 thoroughly (as in ♦ exhilarate). 3 formerly (as in ♦ ex-president).

exacerbate (eks-ass-er-bayt) verb to make a pain, disease, or bad feeling worse. **exacerbation** noun [from ex- and a Latin word acerbus meaning 'harsh' or 'bitter']

exact adjective 1 correct in every detail. SYNONYMS: precise, correct, accurate. 2 clearly stated, giving all details ♦ Give me the exact instructions. 3 capable of being precise ♦ the exact sciences.
exact verb to insist on something and obtain it ♦ He exacted obedience from the recruits. **exactness** noun [from ex- and a Latin word actum meaning 'performed']

exacting adjective making great demands on your ability or stamina ♦ an exacting task.

exactitude noun exactness.

exactly adverb 1 in an exact manner; to an exact degree. 2 used to express agreement with what someone has said.

exaggerate verb to make something seem larger, better or worse, or more important than it really is. **exaggeration** noun [from a Latin word exaggerare meaning 'to heap up']

exalt (ig-zawlt) verb 1 to raise someone to a higher rank or level of power or dignity. 2 to praise someone or something highly. [from ex- and a Latin word altus meaning 'high']

exaltation noun 1 the process of exalting. 2 extreme happiness, delight.

exam noun a test or examination.

examination noun 1 the process of examining someone or something. 2 a formal test of a person's knowledge or ability by means of oral or written questions. 3 a formal questioning of a witness or an accused person in a lawcourt.

examine verb 1 to look at someone or something to check their condition or to get information about them. SYNONYMS: check, inspect, investigate, probe. 2 to test a person's knowledge or ability in an examination. **3** to question a witness or accused person in a lawcourt. **examiner** *noun* [from a Latin word *examinare* meaning 'to weigh accurately']

examinee *noun* a person being tested in an examination.

example *noun* **1** something that shows what others of the same kind are like or how they work. SYNONYMS: instance, case, illustration. **2** a person or thing that is good enough to imitate. **for example** by way of illustrating a general rule. **to make an example of** to punish someone as a warning to others. **to set an example** to behave in a way that is worthy of imitation. [from a Latin word *exemplum*]

exasperate *verb* to annoy someone very much. SYNONYMS: annoy, irritate, anger, aggravate. **exasperation** *noun* [from *ex-* and a Latin word *asper* meaning 'rough']

excavate *verb* **1** to make a hole or channel by digging; to dig out soil. **2** to reveal or extract something by digging. **3** to conduct an archaeological investigation by digging. **excavation** *noun* **excavator** *noun* [from *ex-* and a Latin word *cavus* meaning 'hollow']

exceed *verb* **1** to be greater or more numerous than something. SYNONYMS: beat, surpass, do better than, excel. **2** to go beyond the limit of what is normal or permitted ♦ *The police officer seems to have exceeded his authority.* [from *ex-* and a Latin word *cedere* meaning 'to go']

exceedingly *adverb* very, extremely.

excel *verb* (**excelled, excelling**) to be better at something than someone else or other people. **to excel yourself** to do better than you have ever done before. [from *ex-* and a Latin word *celsus* meaning 'lofty']

excellence *noun* very great quality or merit.

Excellency *noun* (**Excellencies**) the title of high officials such as ambassadors and governors.

excellent *adjective* extremely good. SYNONYMS: outstanding, superb, magnificent, splendid. **excellently** *adverb* [same origin as for *excel*]

except *preposition* not including, apart from ♦ *The guests have all arrived except three.*

except *verb* to exclude someone or something from a statement or calculation etc. [from *ex-* and a Latin word *-ceptum* meaning 'taken']

excepting *preposition* except.

exception *noun* **1** the process of excepting something or leaving something out. **2** a person or thing that is left out or does not follow the general rule. **to take exception to** to object to something. **the exception proves the rule** the existence of an exception shows that there is a rule. **with the exception of** except.

exceptionable *adjective* open to objection, causing disapproval.

exceptional *adjective* **1** forming an exception, very unusual. SYNONYMS: remarkable, outstanding, extraordinary, unusual, uncommon. **2** outstandingly good. **exceptionally** *adverb*

excerpt [1] (ek-serpt) *noun* an extract from a book, film, piece of music, etc. SYNONYMS: extract, passage, quotation. [from a Latin word *excerptum* meaning 'plucked out']

excerpt [2] (ek-serpt) *verb* to choose excerpts from something. **excerption** *noun*

excess *noun* **1** too much of something. SYNONYMS: surfeit, surplus. **2** the amount by which one number or quantity etc. is greater than another. **in excess of** more than. [same origin as for *exceed*]

excessive *adjective* more or greater than what is normal or necessary, too much or too great. SYNONYMS: inordinate, extreme. **excessively** *adverb*

exchange *verb* to give one thing and get another in its place. SYNONYMS: change, swap, trade, substitute, switch. **exchange** *noun* **1** the process of exchanging things. **2** the exchanging of money for its equivalent in another currency. **3** a place where things (especially stocks and shares) are bought and sold ♦ *a stock exchange.* **4** a place where telephone lines are connected to each other when calls are made. **exchangeable** *adjective* [from an Old French word, related to *change*]

exchange rate *noun* the value of one currency in relation to another.

exchequer *noun* a national treasury into which public money (such as taxes) is paid. [from a Latin word *scaccarium* meaning 'chessboard' (because the Norman kings kept their accounts by means of counters placed on a table covered with a chequered cloth)]

excise [1] (**ek**-siyz) noun a tax charged on certain goods and licences etc. [from a Dutch word *excijs* meaning 'tax']

excise [2] (ik-**siyz**) verb to remove something by cutting it out or away. **excision** (ik-**si**-zhən) noun [from *ex-* and a Latin word *caesum* meaning 'having been cut']

excitable adjective (said about a person) easily excited. **excitability** noun

excite verb 1 to rouse a person's feelings; to make someone eager about something. SYNONYMS: rouse, thrill, stir, stimulate. 2 to cause a feeling or reaction ♦ *The discovery excited great interest*. SYNONYMS: arouse, stir up, stimulate, cause. 3 to produce activity in a nerve or organ of the body etc. 4 to cause a substance to give out radiation. [from *ex-* and a Latin word *citare* meaning 'to rouse']

excited adjective showing excitement about something. SYNONYMS: thrilled, stimulated, eager, enthusiastic. **excitedly** adverb

excitement noun 1 a feeling of being excited or eager about something. 2 something that causes this feeling.

exciting adjective causing great interest or eagerness. **excitingly** adverb

exclaim verb to shout or cry out in eagerness or surprise. [from *ex-* and a Latin word *clamare* meaning 'to cry']

exclamation noun 1 the act of exclaiming. 2 a word or group of words that someone exclaims.

exclamation mark noun a punctuation mark (!) put at the end of an exclamation.

exclamatory (iks-**klam**-ə-ter-i) adjective having the form of an exclamation.

exclude verb 1 to keep someone or something out of a place, group, or privilege etc. SYNONYMS: ban, bar, shut out, keep out, prohibit. 2 to omit something or ignore it as irrelevant ♦ *We should not exclude this possibility*. SYNONYMS: omit, ignore, rule out. 3 to prevent something or make it impossible. **exclusion** noun [from *ex-* and a Latin word *claudere* meaning 'to shut']

exclusive adjective 1 not admitting or allowing other things, not true or valid if something else exists or is true ♦ *The two schemes are mutually exclusive*. 2 intended or available only for certain people, or

dealing only in expensive high-quality goods ♦ *an exclusive department store in Mayfair*. 3 (said about legal terms) excluding anything that is not specified. 4 (said about a newspaper article) not published anywhere else. 5 not shared by anyone else ♦ *The company has exclusive film rights to the book*. **exclusive of** excluding, not counting ♦ *There are twenty people coming exclusive of the family*. **exclusively** adverb **exclusiveness** noun **exclusivity** noun [same origin as for *exclude*]

excommunicate verb to deprive someone of membership of a Church. **excommunication** noun [from a Latin word *excommunicare* meaning 'to put out of the community']

excrement (**eks**-kri-mənt) noun waste matter excreted from the bowels, faeces.

excrescence (iks-**kress**-əns) noun 1 a growth or lump on an animal body or a plant. 2 an ugly addition or part. [from *ex-* and a Latin word *crescens* meaning 'growing']

excreta (iks-**kree**-tə) plural noun waste matter expelled from the body, faeces, and urine.

excrete (iks-**kreet**) verb to expel waste matter from the body. **excretion** noun **excretory** adjective [from *ex-* and a Latin word *cretum* meaning 'separated']

excruciating (iks-**kroo**-shi-ayting) adjective extremely painful, agonizing. [from *ex-* and a Latin word *cruciatum* meaning 'tortured']

exculpate (**eks**-kəl-payt) verb (formal) to clear a person from blame. **exculpation** noun [from *ex-* and a Latin word *culpa* meaning 'blame']

excursion noun a short journey made for pleasure. [from *ex-* and a Latin word *cursus* meaning 'course']

excursus (iks-**ker**-səs) noun (**excursuses**) a detailed digression in a book or text. [same origin as for *excursion*]

excusable adjective able to be excused. **excusably** adverb

excuse [1] (iks-**kewz**) verb 1 to overlook or pardon someone for an offence, especially a minor one. SYNONYMS: pardon, forgive, overlook. 2 to justify a fault or error ♦ *Nothing can excuse such rudeness*. SYNONYMS: justify, condone, vindicate. 3 to free someone from an obligation or duty ♦ *Steve was excused swimming because of his* *flu.* **to excuse oneself** to ask permission to leave a room or building. **excusable** *adjective* [from *ex-* and a Latin word *causa* meaning 'accusation']

excuse ² (iks-**kewss**) *noun* a reason given to explain a fault or offence.

ex-directory *adjective* (said about a telephone number or subscriber) not listed in a telephone directory, at the request of the subscriber.

execrable (eks-i-krə-bəl) *adjective* very bad or unpleasant. **execrably** *adverb* [from a Latin word *execrari* meaning 'to curse']

execrate (eks-i-krayt) *verb* to detest someone or something greatly. **execration** *noun* [same origin as for *execrable*]

execute *verb* 1 to put someone to death as a punishment. 2 to carry out an order or put a plan into effect. 3 to perform an action or manoeuvre ♦ *She executed a perfect somersault.* 4 to produce a work of art. 5 (*Law*) to make a will or other legal document valid, especially by signing it. [from *ex-* and a Latin word *sequi* meaning 'to follow']

execution *noun* 1 the carrying out or performance of something. 2 the executing of a condemned person.

executioner *noun* an official who executes a condemned person.

executive (ig-**zek**-yoo-tiv) *noun* 1 a senior person or group of people with authority to manage a business organization. 2 the branch of a government with responsibility for putting laws and decisions into effect.
executive *adjective* having the powers to put laws or decisions into effect.

executor (ig-**zek**-yoo-ter) *noun* (*Law*) a person appointed to carry out the terms of a person's will.

exemplary (ig-**zem**-pler-i) *adjective* 1 serving as an example to follow, very good ♦ *exemplary conduct.* 2 (said about a punishment) severe so as to serve as a warning to others.

exemplify (ig-**zem**-pli-fiy) *verb* (**exemplifies, exemplified, exemplifying**) to serve as an example of something. **exemplification** *noun*

exempt *adjective* free from an obligation or payment that is normally required.

exempt *verb* to make someone exempt from something. **exemption** *noun* [from *ex-* and a Latin word *emptum* meaning 'taken']

exercise *noun* 1 activity involving physical effort, done to improve your health. 2 an activity or task done to test or improve an ability. 3 the application or a right of process ♦ *the exercise of their authority.* SYNONYMS: use, application.
exercise *verb* 1 to make use of a power or right. 2 to take exercise, or train by means of exercises. 3 to perplex or worry someone. [from a Latin word *exercere* meaning 'to keep someone working']

exercise bike *noun* a stationary piece of exercise equipment like a bicycle.

exercise book *noun* a book with blank pages for writing in.

exert *verb* to make use of a quality or power ♦ *We needed to exert all our strength.* **to exert oneself** to make an effort. [from a Latin word *exsertum* meaning 'having been put forth']

exertion *noun* 1 the process of exerting. SYNONYMS: effort, toil, industry. 2 a great effort. SYNONYMS: effort, strain.

exeunt (**eks**-i-ənt) *verb* (as a stage direction) they leave the stage. [a Latin word meaning 'they go out']

ex gratia (eks **gray**-shə) *adverb & adjective* given as a concession, without any legal obligation ♦ *an ex gratia payment.* [a Latin phrase meaning 'from favour']

exhale *verb* to breathe out. **exhalation** *noun* [from *ex-* and a Latin word *halare* meaning 'to breathe']

exhaust *verb* 1 to make someone extremely tired. SYNONYMS: wear out, tire out, weary, drain. 2 to use up something completely. SYNONYMS: expend, use up, deplete, spend (usually time or money). 3 to find out or say all there is about a subject.
exhaust *noun* 1 the waste gases or steam from an engine. 2 the pipe or other device through which they are sent out.
exhaustible *adjective* [from *ex-* and a Latin word *haustum* meaning 'drained']

exhaustion (ig-**zaws**-chən) *noun* being exhausted; a complete loss of strength.

exhaustive *adjective* thorough, trying all the possibilities ♦ *The police made an exhaustive search.* **exhaustively** *adverb*

exhibit (ig-**zib**-it) *verb* to show or display something in public.

exhibit noun something on display in a museum or gallery. **exhibitor** noun [from a Latin word exhibitum meaning 'held out']

exhibition noun 1 a public display of works of art or other items in a museum or gallery. 2 the process of exhibiting something. 3 a display or show of feeling ♦ an exhibition of temper. **to make an exhibition of yourself** to behave foolishly in public.

exhibitionist noun someone who behaves in a way that is meant to attract attention. **exhibitionism** noun

exhilarate (ig-zil-er-ayt) verb to make someone very happy and excited. **exhilaration** noun [from ex- and a Latin word hilaris meaning 'cheerful', related to hilarious]

exhort (ig-zort) verb to urge someone earnestly. **exhortation** (eg-zor-tay-shon) noun [from ex- and a Latin word hortari meaning 'to encourage']

exhume (ig-zewm) verb to dig up a body that has been buried, especially to examine it. **exhumation** (eks-yoo-may-shon) noun [from ex- and a Latin word humare meaning 'to bury']

exigency (eks-i-jən-si) noun (**exigencies**) an urgent need or demand, an emergency. [same origin as for exact]

exigent (eks-i-jənt) adjective (formal) urgent or demanding. **exigently** adverb

exiguous (eg-zig-yoo-əs) adjective (formal) very small or scanty. **exiguousness** noun [from a Latin word exiguus meaning 'scanty']

exile noun 1 being sent away from your own country as a punishment. 2 an exiled person.
exile verb to send someone away from their own country. SYNONYMS: banish, expel, deport. [from a Latin word exilium meaning 'banishment']

exist verb 1 to be present as part of what is real ♦ Do ghosts exist? 2 to stay alive ♦ We c annot exist without food. SYNONYMS: survive, keep going, endure, subsist. 3 to occur or be found ♦ Various types of plant exist here. [from ex- and a Latin word sistere meaning 'to stand']

existence noun 1 the state of existing; occurrence or presence. 2 continuing to live ♦ the struggle for existence.

existent adjective existing or present.

existential (eg-zis-ten-shəl) adjective 1 to do with existence. 2 (Philosophy) to do with human experience as viewed by existentialism. **existentially** adverb

existentialism (eg-zis-ten-shəl-izm) noun (Philosophy) a theory emphasizing that an individual is responsible for his or her own actions and development. **existentialist** noun

exit noun 1 the way out of a room or building. 2 the act of going away or out of a room or building. 3 an actor's or performer's departure from the stage.
exit verb (**exited, exiting**) 1 to leave a room or building. 2 (as a stage direction) he or she leaves the stage. [a Latin word meaning 'he or she goes out']

exit poll noun a poll of people leaving a polling station after voting, to estimate the result.

exo- prefix outside, from outside (as in exoskeleton). [from a Greek word exō meaning 'outside']

exodus noun a departure of many people. **Exodus** the second book of the Old Testament, describing the exodus of the Jews from Egypt. [from a Greek word meaning 'a way out']

ex officio (eks ə-fish-i-oh) adverb & adjective because of a person's official position ♦ The director is a member of the committee ex officio. [a Latin phrase, meaning 'from office']

exonerate (ig-zon-er-ayt) verb to declare or prove that someone is not to blame for something. **exoneration** noun [from ex- and a Latin word oneris meaning 'of a burden']

exorbitant (ig-zorb-i-tənt) adjective (said about a price or demand) much too great, excessive. [from ex- and a Latin word orbita meaning 'orbit']

exorcize (eks-or-siyz) verb to drive out a supposed evil spirit from a person or place. **exorcism** noun **exorcist** noun [from ex- and a Greek word horkos meaning 'oath']

exoskeleton noun (Zoology) an external tough or bony covering on an animal, e.g. the shell of a lobster.

exosphere noun the outermost region of a planet's atmosphere.

exothermic adjective (Chemistry) (said about a reaction) giving off heat. (Compare endothermic.) [from exo- and a Greek word thermē meaning 'heat']

exotic (ig-**zot**-ik) *adjective* 1 from another part of the world. 2 strikingly colourful or unusual ♦ *exotic clothes.* **exotically** *adverb* [from a Greek word *exōtikos* meaning 'foreign']

expand *verb* 1 to make something larger, or to become larger. SYNONYMS: increase, extend, spread, build up. 2 to unfold something or spread it out. 3 (said about a person) to become more lively or talkative. **to expand on something** to describe something in more detail. **expandable** *adjective* **expander** *noun* [from *ex-* and a Latin word *pandere* meaning 'to spread']

expanse *noun* a wide area of open land, sea, or space. SYNONYMS: space, area, range, stretch, extent. [same origin as for *expand*]

expansion *noun* the process of expanding, an increase or extension.

expansionism *noun* the policy or practice of making a country or business expand. **expansionist** *noun* & *adjective*

expansive *adjective* 1 covering a wide area. 2 tending to expand. 3 (said about a person or manner) genial and communicating thoughts and feelings readily. **expansively** *adverb* **expansiveness** *noun*

expatiate (iks-**pay**-shi-ayt) *verb* to speak or write about a subject at length or in detail. **expatiation** *noun* **expatiatory** *adjective* [from *ex-* and a Latin word *spatium* meaning 'space']

expatriate [1] (eks-**pat**-ri-ət) *noun* a person living permanently abroad. **expatriate** *adjective* living abroad. [from *ex-* and a Latin word *patria* meaning 'native country']

expatriate [2] (eks-**pat**-ri-ayt) *verb* to settle abroad, or send someone to live abroad. **expatriation** *noun*

expect *verb* 1 to think or believe that something will happen. 2 to demand something or think it to be necessary ♦ *The shop expects prompt payment.* SYNONYMS: demand, require, count on, want. 3 to think, to suppose. [from *ex-* and a Latin word *spectare* meaning 'to look']

expectant *adjective* 1 expecting something to happen, hopeful. 2 (said about a woman) pregnant. **expectantly** *adverb* **expectancy** *noun*

expectation *noun* 1 a belief that something will happen. 2 something you expect to happen.

expectorant *noun* a medicine that causes a person to cough and spit out phlegm.

expectorate *verb* to cough and spit out phlegm from the throat or lungs. **expectoration** *noun* [from *ex-* and a Latin word *pectoris* meaning 'of the chest']

expedient (iks-**pee**-diənt) *adjective* 1 suitable or convenient. 2 useful or advantageous rather than right or just. **expedient** *noun* a convenient means of achieving something. **expediently** *adverb* **expediency** *noun* [same origin as for *expedite*]

expedite (**eks**-pi-diyt) *verb* to get something done quickly or efficiently. [from a Latin word *expedire* literally meaning 'to free someone's feet' (from *ped-* meaning 'foot')]

expedition *noun* 1 a journey or voyage made by a group of people for a special purpose. 2 the people or vehicles making such a journey. 3 (*formal*) speed or promptness. **expeditionary** *adjective* [from a French word, related to *expedite*]

expeditious (eks-pi-**dish**-əs) *adjective* quick and efficient. **expeditiously** *adverb*

expel *verb* (**expelled, expelling**) 1 to send or force something out ♦ *The fan expels stale air.* 2 to compel a person to leave a school or country etc. SYNONYMS: eject, throw out, banish, deport (from a country). [from *ex-* and a Latin word *pellere* meaning 'to drive']

expend *verb* to spend money or use time or care to get something done. [from *ex-* and a Latin word *pendere* meaning 'to pay']

expendable *adjective* 1 not worth keeping or preserving, suitable for sacrificing to gain an objective.

expenditure *noun* 1 the spending of money or other resources. 2 the amount spent.

expense *noun* 1 the cost of something. 2 something that you have to spend money on ♦ *The car has become a great expense.* **expenses** *plural noun* the amount spent in doing something. **at the expense of** with the loss of something or damage to it ♦ *He succeeded but at the expense of his health.* [same origin as for *expend*]

expensive *adjective* 1 costing a lot of money. 2 causing a lot of difficulty or trouble ♦ *an expensive mistake.* **expensively** *adverb* **expensiveness** *noun*

experience *noun* 1 actual practice in doing something or observation of facts or

events. **2** skill or knowledge gained over time. SYNONYMS: expertise, knowledge. **3** an event or activity that has an effect on you. SYNONYMS: event, episode, adventure, incident, happening.
experience verb **1** to have something happen to you. SYNONYMS: undergo, encounter; endure, suffer (something unpleasant). **2** to be affected by a feeling. [same origin as for *experiment*]

experienced adjective having a lot of knowledge or skill from much experience.

experiment noun a test or trial done to see how something works or to find out what happens.
experiment verb **1** to carry out an experiment. **2** to try out new things. **experimentation** noun [from a Latin word *experiri* meaning 'to test']

experimental adjective **1** based on untested ideas or processes and still to be completed. **2** to do with an experiment. **3** (said about ideas) new and innovative. **experimentally** adverb **experimentalism** noun

expert noun a person with great knowledge or skill in something. SYNONYMS: authority, specialist.
expert adjective having great knowledge or skill. SYNONYMS: skilled, qualified. **expertly** adverb [from a Latin word *expertus* meaning 'experienced']

expertise (eks-per-teez) noun expert knowledge or skill.

expert system noun (*Computing*) a program or set of programs designed to make the skills of experts available to others.

expiate (eks-pi-ayt) verb to make amends for something wrong you have done. **expiation** noun **expiatory** adjective [from a Latin word *expiare* meaning 'to appease with a sacrifice' (from *pius* meaning 'holy')]

expire verb **1** to stop being valid, to be no longer usable ♦ *Your ticket has expired.* SYNONYMS: run out, lapse. **2** a technical term meaning to breathe out air. **3** to breathe your last breath, to die. **expiration** (eks-per-ay-shən) noun [from *ex-* and a Latin word *spirare* meaning 'to breathe']

expiry noun the time when something expires or is no longer valid.

explain verb **1** to make something plain or clear, to show the meaning of something. SYNONYMS: describe, make clear, clarify; (*informal*) spell out. **2** to account for

something ♦ *That explains his absence.* [from *ex-* and a Latin word *planare* meaning 'to make level or plain']

explanation noun **1** the process of explaining something. **2** a statement or fact that explains something.

explanatory (iks-plan-ə-ter-i) adjective serving or intended to explain something.

expletive (iks-plee-tiv) noun an oath or swear word. [from a Latin word *explere* meaning 'to fill out']

explicable (eks-plik-əbəl) adjective able to be explained. [from a Latin word *explicare* meaning 'to unfold']

explicit (iks-pliss-it) adjective stating something openly and exactly. (Compare **implicit.**) **explicitly** adverb **explicitness** noun [from a Latin word *explicitus* meaning 'unfolded']

explode verb **1** to burst violently or suddenly release energy with a loud noise. SYNONYMS: blow up, detonate, go off. **2** (said about a person) to show sudden strong emotion, especially anger ♦ *When he heard about it he exploded with rage.* **3** (said about a population or a supply of goods etc.) to increase suddenly or rapidly. **4** to destroy an idea or theory by showing it to be false. [from an earlier meaning 'to drive a player off the stage by clapping and hissing', from *ex-* and a Latin word *plaudere* meaning 'to clap the hands']

exploded adjective (said about a diagram) showing the parts of a machine or mechanism in their correct positions but slightly separated from each other to make the structure clearer.

exploit[1] (eks-ploit) noun a bold or exciting deed. SYNONYMS: deed, feat, adventure. [via French from a Latin word *explicare* meaning 'to unfold']

exploit[2] (iks-ploit) verb **1** to develop a resource and get benefit from it. **2** to make unfair use of someone or something. **exploitation** noun

exploratory (iks-plo-rə-ter-i) adjective for the purpose of exploring.

explore verb **1** to travel into or through a country or region in order to learn about it. **2** to examine or investigate a subject or idea carefully ♦ *We will explore all the possibilities.* SYNONYMS: examine, investigate, analyse, inquire into, look into. **3** to examine

something by touch. **exploration** noun
[from a Latin word *explorare* meaning 'to
search out']

explorer noun a person who explores
unknown regions of the world.

explosion noun 1 the process or sound of
something exploding. 2 a sudden
outburst of anger, laughter, etc. 3 a
sudden great increase ♦ *a population
explosion.*

explosive adjective 1 able or likely to
explode. 2 likely to cause violent and
dangerous reactions ♦ *an explosive
situation.*
   explosive noun a substance that can
explode. **explosively** adverb

exponent (iks-poh-nǝnt) noun 1 someone
who favours a particular theory or policy.
2 (*Mathematics*) a raised number to the
right of another number (e.g. ^{3} in 2^3)
indicating how many times the first
number is to be multiplied by itself.
[from a Latin word, related to *expound*]

exponential (eks-pǝ-nen-shǝl) adjective
(*Mathematics*) indicated by an exponent.

export^1 (eks-port or eks-port) verb to send
goods to another country to be sold.
exportation noun **exporter** noun **exportable**
adjective [from *ex-* and a Latin word *portare*
meaning 'to carry']

export^2 (eks-port) noun 1 the process of
exporting goods. 2 something exported.

expose verb 1 to leave someone or
something uncovered or unprotected,
especially from the weather. 2 to subject
someone or something to a risk or
danger. 3 to allow light to reach
photographic film so as to take a picture.
4 to make something visible, to reveal
something. SYNONYMS: reveal, uncover,
show. 5 to reveal information about a
wrongdoing or the person who has
committed it. SYNONYMS: disclose, reveal,
make known. [from *ex-* and a Latin word
positum meaning 'having been put']

exposition noun 1 an explanatory account
of a plan or theory. 2 a large public
exhibition. 3 (*Music*) the part of a
movement in which themes are
presented.

expostulate (iks-**poss**-tew-layt) verb to
express strong disapproval or
disagreement about something.
expostulation noun [from a Latin word
expostulare meaning 'to demand']

exposure noun 1 the process of exposing
someone or something to air, cold, or
harm. 2 the process of exposing film to
the light so as to take a picture, or a piece
of film exposed in this way. 3 publicity.

expound verb to describe or explain
something in detail. [from a Latin word
exponere meaning 'to explain']

express^1 adjective 1 definitely and clearly
stated ♦ *These were her express instructions.*
2 going or sent quickly; designed for high
speed.
   express adverb at high speed, by an
express service.
   express noun a fast train stopping only at
a few stations.
   express verb to send something by
express service. **expressible** adjective
[from a Latin word *expressus* meaning
'pressed out']

express^2 verb 1 to put a thought or idea
into words; to make your feelings or ideas
known. SYNONYMS: describe, communicate,
utter, make known. 2 to represent
something by means of symbols, e.g. in
mathematics. 3 to press or squeeze
something out, especially liquid. **to
express yourself** to communicate your
thoughts or feelings.

expression noun 1 the process of
expressing thoughts or ideas. 2 a word or
phrase that expresses an idea. 3 a look on
someone's face that expresses their
feelings. SYNONYMS: face, appearance, look,
countenance. 4 speaking or playing music
in a way that shows feeling.
5 (*Mathematics*) a collection of symbols
expressing a quantity.

expressionism noun a style of painting,
drama, or music that tries to express the
artist's or writer's emotional feeling
rather than to represent what is in the
outside world. **expressionist** noun

expressionless adjective without any
expression, not revealing your thoughts
or feelings ♦ *an expressionless face.*

expressive adjective 1 expressing a lot of
feeling ♦ *an expressive voice.*
2 communicating a thought or feeling ♦ *a
tone expressive of contempt.* **expressively**
adverb **expressiveness** noun

expressly adverb 1 clearly and plainly
♦ *This was expressly forbidden.* 2 for a
particular purpose ♦ *The furniture was
designed expressly for children.*

expulsion noun the process of expelling someone or something. **expulsive** adjective

expunge (iks-punj) verb to wipe or rub something out, to delete something. [from ex- and a Latin word pungere meaning 'to prick']

expurgate (eks-per-gayt) verb to remove unsuitable or obscene material from a publication. **expurgation** noun **expurgator** noun [from a Latin word expurgare meaning 'to cleanse thoroughly']

exquisite (eks-kwiz-it) adjective 1 having great beauty and delicacy. SYNONYMS: beautiful, fine, delicate. 2 highly refined or sensitive ♦ exquisite taste. 3 acute or keenly felt ♦ the exquisite pain of love. **exquisitely** adverb [from ex- and a Latin word quaesitum meaning 'sought']

ex-serviceman or **ex-servicewoman** noun (**ex-servicemen** or **ex-servicewomen**) a man or woman who is a former member of the armed services.

extant (eks-tant) adjective still existing. [from a Latin word exstare meaning 'to exist' or 'to be apparent']

extemporary adjective spoken or done without preparation. [from extempore]

extempore (eks-tem-per-i) adverb & adjective spoken or done without preparation, impromptu. **extemporaneous** adjective [from a Latin phrase ex tempore meaning literally 'out of time']

extemporize (eks-tem-periyz) verb to speak or produce something extempore. **extemporization** noun

extend verb 1 to make something longer or larger. SYNONYMS: increase, expand, spread, build up. 2 to make something last longer. SYNONYMS: prolong, continue, lengthen. 3 to stretch out a hand or foot or limb etc. 4 to continue for a specified distance, to reach something ♦ The house has land that extends to the river. 5 to offer or grant something ♦ We extend a warm welcome to all our friends. **extendible** adjective **extensible** adjective [from ex- and a Latin word tendere meaning 'to stretch']

extended family noun a family including other relatives who live in the same household or nearby.

extension noun 1 the process of extending something. 2 extent or range. 3 something added on, especially an extra section added to a building. 4 an extra period for something to be done. 5 an individual telephone connected to a main telephone line or switchboard and having its own additional number.

extensive adjective 1 covering a large area ♦ extensive gardens. 2 large in scope, wide-ranging ♦ an extensive search. **extensively** adverb **extensiveness** noun

extensor noun (Anatomy) a muscle that extends or straightens out a part of the body.

extent noun 1 the space or length over which a thing extends. 2 the range or scope of something ♦ We need to find out the extent of the damage. SYNONYMS: size, level, range, scope. [from a Latin word extenta meaning 'extended']

extenuating (iks-ten-yoo-ayt-ing) adjective making an offence or error seem less great by providing a partial excuse ♦ There were extenuating circumstances. **extenuation** noun [from a Latin word extenuare meaning 'to reduce']

exterior adjective on the outside, or coming from the outside. **exterior** noun an exterior surface or part. [a Latin word meaning 'further out']

exterminate verb to kill or get rid of all the existing examples of something, to destroy something completely. **extermination** noun **exterminator** noun [from ex- and a Latin word terminus meaning 'boundary']

external adjective 1 on or belonging to or forming the outside or visible part of something. SYNONYMS: exterior, outside, outer. 2 on or for the outside of the body ♦ The lotion is for external use only. 3 coming or obtained from an independent or outside source ♦ external influences. 4 belonging to the world outside a person or people, not in the mind. **externally** adverb [from a Latin word exter meaning 'outside']

extinct adjective 1 (said about an animal or species) no longer alive or existing. 2 (said about a volcano) no longer active. [same origin as for extinguish]

extinction noun 1 making something extinct, or becoming extinct. 2 the process of extinguishing something.

extinguish verb 1 to put out a light, fire, or flame. 2 to end the existence of a hope or feeling etc. [from a Latin word extinguere meaning 'to quench']

extinguisher *noun* a portable device for sending out liquid chemicals or foam to extinguish a fire.

extirpate (eks-ter-payt) *verb* to search something out and destroy it completely. **extirpation** *noun* [from *ex-* and a Latin word *stirps* meaning 'a stem']

extol (iks-tohl) *verb* (**extolled, extolling**) to praise something or someone enthusiastically. [from *ex-* and a Latin word *tollere* meaning 'to raise']

extort *verb* to obtain something by force or threats. **extortion** *noun* **extortioner** *noun* [from *ex-* and a Latin word *tortum* meaning 'twisted']

extortionate (iks-tor-shən-ət) *adjective* charging or demanding far too much. **extortionately** *adverb* [from *extort*]

extra *adjective* additional, more than is usual or expected ♦ *Where did you find the extra money?*
extra *adverb* more than usually ♦ *The locks are extra strong.*
extra *noun* **1** an extra person or thing. **2** an item for which an extra charge is made. **3** a person taken on to form part of a crowd in a film or play. [a Latin word meaning 'outside']

extra- *prefix* outside or beyond (as in ♦ *extraterrestrial*).

extract [1] (iks-trakt) *verb* **1** to take something out or remove it, especially by force or effort. SYNONYMS: take out, remove, pull out. **2** to obtain money, information, etc. from someone who is reluctant to give it. **3** to obtain a substance or liquid by a special process. **4** to take or copy passages or quotations from a book, film, piece of music, etc. **extractor** *noun* [from *ex-* and a Latin word *tractum* meaning 'pulled']

extract [2] (eks-trakt) *noun* **1** a passage taken from a book, play, film, piece of music, etc. SYNONYMS: excerpt, passage, quotation. **2** a substance separated or obtained from another.

extraction *noun* **1** the process of extracting something. **2** descent or lineage ♦ *She is of Indian extraction.*

extradite (eks-trə-diyt) *verb* to hand over an accused person to the police of the country where the crime was committed. **extraditable** *adjective* **extradition** (eks-trə-dish-ən) *noun* [from *ex-* and a Latin word *traditum* meaning 'handed over']

extraneous (iks-tray-niəs) *adjective* **1** coming from outside. **2** not belonging to the matter or subject in hand. **extraneously** *adverb* [from a Latin word *extraneus*, related to *extra*]

extraordinary *adjective* **1** very unusual or remarkable. SYNONYMS: unusual, remarkable, exceptional, strange, amazing, astonishing. **2** (said about a meeting) specially called or arranged. **extraordinarily** *adverb* [from a Latin phrase *extra ordinem* meaning 'out of the ordinary']

extrapolate (iks-trap-ə-layt) *verb* to draw conclusions from available data about something unknown or beyond the range of the available data. **extrapolation** *noun* [from *extra-* and *interpolate*]

extrasensory perception *noun* the supposed ability to perceive things by means other than the known senses.

extraterrestrial *adjective* from beyond the earth or its atmosphere. **extraterrestrial** *noun* a fictional or supposed being from outer space.

extravagant *adjective* **1** spending or using much more than is necessary. **2** (said about prices) excessively high. **3** (said about ideas, behaviour, etc.) going beyond what is reasonable, not properly controlled. **extravagantly** *adverb* **extravagance** *noun* [from *extra-* and a Latin word *vagans* meaning 'wandering']

extravaganza (iks-trav-ə-gan-zə) *noun* a lavish or spectacular film or show. [from an Italian word *estravaganza*, related to *extravagance*]

extreme *adjective* **1** very great or intense ♦ *extreme cold.* SYNONYMS: intense, severe, acute, great. **2** furthest away, outermost ♦ *the extreme edge.* **3** going to great lengths in actions or opinions, not moderate ♦ *That is an extreme view.*
extreme *noun* **1** either end of something. **2** something extreme, either of two concepts or opinions that are as different from each other as they can be. **extremely** *adverb* [from a Latin word *extremus* meaning 'furthest outside']

extremist *noun* a person who holds extreme opinions, especially in politics. **extremism** *noun*

extremity (iks-trem-iti) *noun* (**extremities**) **1** an extreme point, the very end of something. **2** an extreme feeling or need or danger etc. **extremities** *plural noun* the hands and feet.

extricable (**eks**-trik-ə-bəl) *adjective* able to be extricated.

extricate (**eks**-trik-ayt) *verb* to free someone or something from a difficult position or state. **extrication** *noun* [from *ex-* and a Latin word *tricae* meaning 'entanglements']

extrovert (**eks**-trə-vert) *noun* a lively sociable person, or one more interested in external things than in internal thoughts. (Compare **introvert**.) **extroverted** *adjective* [from *extra-* and a Latin word *vertere* meaning 'to turn']

extrude *verb* 1 to thrust or squeeze something out. 2 to shape metal or plastic etc. by forcing it through a die. **extrusion** *noun* [from *ex-* and a Latin word *trudere* meaning 'to push']

extrusive *adjective* (*Geology*) (said about rock) produced by volcanic eruption. (Compare **intrusive**.)

exuberant (ig-**zew**-ber-ənt) *adjective* lively, full of high spirits. **exuberantly** *adverb* **exuberance** *noun* [from a Latin word *exuberare* meaning 'to grow thickly' (the English words can also have this meaning)]

exude (ig-**zewd**) *verb* 1 to give off moisture or a smell, or to ooze out in this way. 2 to display a feeling or quality openly ♦ *She exuded confidence.* **exudation** (eks-yoo-**day**-shən) *noun* [from *ex-* and a Latin word *sudare* meaning 'to sweat']

exult (ig-**zult**) *verb* to rejoice or feel triumphant. **exultation** *noun* [from a Latin word *exsilire* meaning 'to leap up']

exultant *adjective* rejoicing, exulting.

eye *noun* 1 the organ of seeing in humans and some animals. 2 the iris of the eye ♦ *She has lovely blue eyes.* 3 the power of seeing, observation ♦ *You'll need sharp eyes in this traffic.* 4 something compared to an eye, especially a leaf bud on a potato. 5 the hole in a needle through which the thread is passed.
eye *verb* (**eyes, eyed, eyeing**) to watch someone or something carefully. **to cast** or **run an eye over something** to read or study something quickly. **in the eyes of** in the opinion or judgement of someone. **to keep an eye on** 1 to watch someone or something carefully. 2 to take care of someone. **to keep an eye out** to watch out for someone or something. **to make eyes at** to look at someone with sexual interest. **to see eye to eye** to agree or

have the same opinion. **up to the eyes** deeply involved or occupied in something. **with an eye to** with the aim or intention of doing something. **with your eyes open** knowing all the circumstances full well. [from an Old English word]

eyeball *noun* the ball-shaped part of the eye inside the eyelids.

eyebrow *noun* the fringe of hair growing on the face above the eye.

eye-catching *adjective* striking or attractive.

eyeful *noun* (**eyefuls**) (*informal*) 1 a long close look ♦ *getting an eyeful.* 2 a striking or attractive person or thing.

eyeglass *noun* a single lens for a defective eye, a monocle.

eyelash *noun* each of the short hairs growing on the edge of the eyelids.

eyelet *noun* 1 a small hole through which a rope or cord is passed. 2 a metal ring strengthening this.

eyelid *noun* each of the two folds of skin that can close together to cover the eyeball.

eyeliner *noun* a cosmetic applied as a line round the eyes.

eye-opener *noun* (*informal*) something very surprising or revealing.

eyepiece *noun* the lens or lenses of a telescope or microscope that you put against the eye.

eyeshade *noun* a device to protect the eyes from strong light.

eyeshadow *noun* a cosmetic used to colour the skin round the eyes.

eyesight *noun* 1 the ability to see. 2 a range of vision ♦ *within eyesight.*

eyesore *noun* something that is ugly to look at.

eye tooth *noun* a canine tooth in the upper jaw, under the eye.

eyewash *noun* 1 a cleansing lotion for the eye. 2 (*informal*) nonsense.

eyewitness *noun* a person who saw a crime or other incident take place and can give information about it.

eyrie (**iy**-ri) *noun* the nest of an eagle or other bird of prey. [from a Latin word *area* meaning 'level piece of ground' and later 'nest of a bird of prey']

Ff

F 1 the sixth letter of the English alphabet. 2 (*Music*) the fourth note of the diatonic scale of C major. 3 (*Chemistry*) the symbol for fluorine.

F *abbreviation* Fahrenheit.

f *abbreviation* (*Music*) forte (loudly).

FA *abbreviation* Football Association.

Fabian (**fay**-bi-ən) *noun* a member or supporter of the Fabian Society, an English socialist society founded in 1884 with the aim of achieving social change through gradual reform. **Fabianism** *noun* [named after the Roman general Quintus Fabius Maximus (c.200 BC) who applied a strategy of caution and avoidance of pitched battle in the war against Hannibal]

fable *noun* 1 a short story, usually with animals as characters, intended to convey a moral. 2 these stories or legends collectively. [from a Latin word *fabula* meaning 'story']

fabled *adjective* 1 famous. 2 told of in fables, legendary.

fabric *noun* 1 material produced from woven or knitted textile fibres, cloth. 2 the basic structure or framework of something, especially the walls, floors, and roof of a building. [from a Latin word *fabrica* meaning 'something made']

fabricate *verb* 1 to construct or manufacture something. 2 to invent a story or excuse so as to deceive people. **fabrication** *noun* **fabricator** *noun* [from a Latin word *fabricare* meaning 'to make or forge']

fabulous *adjective* 1 told of in fables ♦ *a fabulous creature.* 2 incredibly great ♦ *fabulous wealth.* 3 (*informal*) wonderful, marvellous ♦ *We all had a fabulous time.* SYNONYMS: wonderful, marvellous, fantastic, amazing. **fabulously** *adverb* [same origin as for *fable*]

facade (fə-**sahd**) *noun* 1 the outer face of a building, especially the principal face. 2 an outward appearance, especially a deceptive one. [a French word, related to *face*]

face *noun* 1 the front part of the head from the forehead to the chin. 2 the expression on a person's face ♦ *She had a cheerful face.*

SYNONYMS: countenance, expression. 3 an aspect of something ♦ *the unacceptable face of capitalism.* 4 each of the surfaces of a three-dimensional object such as a cube. 5 the sloping or vertical side of a mountain or cliff. 6 the front of something, or the surface that is the one normally looked at or has a distinctive function ♦ *The playing cards were on the table face up.*

face *verb* 1 to have or turn the face in a specified direction. 2 to meet and deal with a difficulty or an opponent ♦ *She went in to face her accusers.* 3 to have the prospect of something unpleasant or difficult to deal with ♦ *The travellers faced further delays.* SYNONYMS: encounter, meet with. 4 to present itself to you ♦ *This is the problem that faces us.* SYNONYM: confront. 5 to cover a surface with a layer of different material. **to face the music** to face unpleasant consequences bravely. **to face up to** to face a difficulty resolutely. SYNONYMS: confront, accept, deal with. **in the face of** when confronted with, despite. **to lose face** to be humiliated or appear foolish. **to save face** to avoid humiliation. [from a Latin word *facies* meaning 'appearance']

facecloth *noun* 1 a small cloth for washing the face. 2 a smooth woollen cloth.

face flannel *noun* a small cloth for washing the face.

faceless *adjective* 1 not having an identity. 2 (said about an authority, organization, etc.) impersonal and inaccessible.

facelift *noun* 1 surgery done to improve the appearance of a person's face. 2 an alteration or renovation that improves the appearance of something, especially a building.

facet (**fas**-it) *noun* 1 each of the many sides of a cut stone or jewel. 2 one aspect of a situation or problem. [from a French word *facette* meaning 'small face']

facetious (fə-**see**-shəs) *adjective* trying to be amusing, especially at an unsuitable time. **facetiously** *adverb* **facetiousness** *noun* [from a Latin word *facetus* meaning 'witty']

face value *noun* the value printed or stamped on a coin, banknote, or postage stamp. **to take something at its face value** to assume that something is what it seems to be.

facia (**fay**-shə) *noun* another spelling of **fascia**.

facial (fay-shəl) *adjective* to do with or on the face.
facial *noun* a beauty treatment for the face.

facile (fa-siyl) *adjective* 1 done too easily, superficial ♦ *a facile solution.* 2 (said about a person) able to do something easily ♦ *a facile speaker.* [from a Latin word *facilis* meaning 'easy']

facilitate (fə-sil-i-tayt) *verb* to make something easy or easier to do.
facilitation *noun*

facility (fə-sil-iti) *noun* (**facilities**) 1 a building or piece of equipment used for a special purpose ♦ *sports facilities.* 2 ease or ability in doing something ♦ *She reads music with great facility.* 3 the quality of being easy, absence of difficulty.

facing *noun* 1 an outer layer covering a surface. 2 a layer of material covering part of a piece of clothing for contrast or to strengthen it.

facsimile (fak-sim-ili) *noun* (**facsimiles**) an exact copy of something written or printed. [from Latin words *fac* meaning 'make' and *simile* meaning 'a likeness']

fact *noun* 1 something that is known to have happened or to be true. SYNONYMS: reality, certainty. 2 a thing asserted to be true as a basis for reasoning. [from a Latin word *factum* meaning 'thing done']

faction (fak-shən) *noun* a small united group within a larger one, especially in politics. **factional** *adjective* **factionally** *adverb* [from a Latin word *factio*, from *facere* meaning 'to do']

factitious (fak-tish-əs) *adjective* made for a special purpose, contrived. [from a Latin word *facticius* meaning 'made by art']

factor *noun* 1 a circumstance or influence that helps to bring about a result ♦ *The weather was a decisive factor in the army's defeat.* SYNONYMS: aspect, circumstance, consideration. 2 (*Mathematics*) a number by which a larger number can be divided exactly ♦ *1, 2, 3, and 6 are factors of 6.* 3 a business agent, or (in Scotland) a land agent or steward. [from a Latin word *facere* meaning 'to do']

factorial *noun* (*Mathematics*) the product of a number and all the numbers below it, e.g. **factorial 4** (denoted by **4!**) is the product of $4 \times 3 \times 2 \times 1 = 24$.

factorize *verb* to find the factors of a number, to express a number in factors.

factorization *noun*

factor VIII *noun* a blood protein involved in clotting, a deficiency of which causes haemophilia.

factory *noun* (**factories**) a building or group of buildings in which goods are manufactured. [from a Latin word *facere* meaning 'to make or do']

factory farm *noun* a farm organized on industrial lines.

factotum (fak-toh-təm) *noun* (**factotums**) a servant or assistant who does all kinds of work. [from Latin words *fac* meaning 'do' and *totum* meaning 'everything']

facts of life *plural noun* information about sexual reproduction.

factual *adjective* based on facts or containing facts. SYNONYMS: actual, real, authentic. **factually** *adverb*

faculty (fak-əl-ti) *noun* (**faculties**) 1 any of the powers of the body or mind ♦ *the faculty of sight.* 2 a particular kind of ability ♦ *a faculty for learning languages.* 3 a department teaching a particular subject in a university or college ♦ *the faculty of music.* [from a Latin word *facultas*, related to *facile*]

fad *noun* 1 a temporary fashion or craze. 2 a person's particular like or dislike. **faddish** *adjective* [originally a dialect word]

faddy *adjective* (**faddier**, **faddiest**) having petty likes and dislikes, especially about food. **faddiness** *noun*

fade *verb* 1 to lose colour, freshness, or strength, or to make something or someone do this. SYNONYMS: grow pale, discolour, blanch; flag, droop, wilt. 2 (said about something seen or heard) to disappear gradually, to become indistinct. 3 to make the sound or picture in a cinema film or a television or radio recording decrease (*fade out*) or increase (*fade in*) gradually.
fade *noun* an act or sound of fading. [from an Old French word *fade* meaning 'dull' or 'feeble']

faeces (fee-seez) *plural noun* solid waste matter passed out of the body. **faecal** (fee-kəl) *adjective* [plural of a Latin word *faex* meaning 'dregs']

fag *noun* (*informal*) 1 a task that is tiring or unwelcome. 2 in British public schools, a junior pupil who has to run errands for a senior one. 3 a cigarette. **fagged out** tired out, exhausted. [origin unknown]

faggot noun 1 a bundle of sticks or twigs bound together. 2 a meatball made from chopped liver and baked. [via Old French and Italian from a Greek word *phakelos* meaning 'bundle']

Fahrenheit (fa-rən-hiyt) adjective relating to or using a temperature scale in which water freezes at 32° and boils at 212°. [named after G. D. Fahrenheit, a German physicist (1686–1736) who invented the mercury thermometer]

fail verb 1 to be unsuccessful in doing something or in trying to do it. SYNONYMS: misfire, go wrong, founder, fall through, come to grief. 2 to become weak or useless, to stop working ♦ *The brakes failed on a steep hill.* 3 to be or become insufficient; (said about crops) to produce a poor harvest. 4 to neglect or be unable to do something ♦ *They failed to warn us.* SYNONYMS: neglect, omit. 5 to disappoint the hopes of someone. 6 to become bankrupt. 7 to be unable to meet the standard needed in an examination. 8 to judge that a candidate has not passed an examination. **fail** noun a failure in an examination. **without fail** for certain, whatever happens. [from a Latin word *fallere* meaning 'to deceive']

failing noun a weakness or fault. **failing** preposition if a thing is not the case or does not happen ♦ *Failing that we will have to try something else.*

fail-safe adjective (said about equipment or machinery) returning to a safe state in the event of a failure or breakdown.

failure noun 1 the act of failing, a lack of success. 2 a situation in which power has failed, or a machine or a part of the body has stopped working ♦ *heart failure.* 3 a person or thing that has failed.

faint adjective 1 not clear to the senses, dim or indistinct. SYNONYMS: indistinct, dim, weak, unclear, hazy. 2 pale in colour. 3 weak or vague ♦ *There is a faint hope.* 4 timid or feeble. 5 (said about a person) weak and giddy, and about to lose consciousness. SYNONYMS: giddy, dizzy, unsteady, light-headed. **faint** verb to lose consciousness briefly when insufficient oxygen is supplied to the brain. SYNONYMS: pass out, black out, lose consciousness, collapse. **faint** noun an act or state of fainting. **faintly** adverb **faintness** noun [from an Old French word]

faint-hearted adjective timid or reserved.

fair [1] noun 1 right or just, in accordance with the rules ♦ *It was a fair decision to award a penalty.* SYNONYMS: just, proper, right, legitimate. 2 treating people equally and with justice. 3 (said about the hair or skin) light in colour; (said about a person) having fair hair. 4 (old use) beautiful. 5 (said about the weather) fine and dry. SYNONYMS: fine, clear, dry, bright. 6 moderate in quality or amount ♦ *A fair number of people had come.* **fair** adverb in a fair manner. **fair and square** 1 exactly or with accuracy. 2 honestly, straightforwardly. [from an Old English word *fæger*]

fair [2] noun 1 a gathering of shows and amusements for public entertainment. 2 a periodic gathering to sell goods. 3 an exhibition of commercial or industrial goods ♦ *the annual book fair.* [from a Latin word *feriae* meaning 'holiday']

fairground noun an open outdoor space where a fair is held.

fairing noun a structure added to the outside of a vehicle, ship, or aircraft to streamline it.

Fair Isle noun a traditional geometric design in coloured wools, of a kind originating in Fair Isle in the Shetlands.

fairly adverb 1 in a fair or just manner ♦ *She treated us fairly.* 2 moderately, somewhat ♦ *It seems fairly difficult.* 3 actually, really ♦ *He fairly jumped for joy.*

fair play noun equal opportunities and treatment for all.

fairway noun 1 a channel that shipping can use. 2 the part of a golf course between the tee and the green, where the grass is kept short.

fairy noun (**fairies**) an imaginary small being with magic powers. [from an old word *fay*, from Latin *fata* meaning 'the Fates', three goddesses who were believed to control people's lives]

fairy godmother noun a woman in fairy stories who brings unexpected good fortune to the hero or heroine.

fairyland noun 1 the world of fairies. 2 a very beautiful place.

fairy lights plural noun strings of small decorative coloured lights.

fairy story or **fairy tale** noun a story about imaginary or magical beings and places.

fait accompli (fayt ah-**kom**-pli) *noun* a thing that is already done and cannot be changed. [a French phrase meaning 'accomplished fact']

faith *noun* 1 strong trust or confidence in a person or thing. SYNONYMS: confidence, trust, belief. 2 belief in a religious doctrine, independent of proof or reasoning. 3 a system of religious beliefs ♦ *the Christian faith*. SYNONYMS: religion, belief. **in good faith** with honest intention. [from an Old French word, from a Latin word *fides*]

faithful *adjective* 1 loyal and trustworthy ♦ *faithful fans.* SYNONYMS: devoted, loyal, reliable, true, trustworthy. 2 sexually loyal to one partner. 3 true to the facts, accurate. SYNONYMS: accurate, true, exact. **the faithful** the believers in a particular faith, especially Islam. **Yours faithfully** see **yours. faithfully** *adverb* **faithfulness** *noun*

faith healing *noun* healing achieved by religious faith and prayer. **faith healer** *noun*

faithless *adjective* 1 not having a religious faith. 2 breaking promises, disloyal.

fake *noun* 1 something that looks genuine but is not, a forgery. SYNONYMS: forgery, counterfeit, imitation, sham. 2 a person who makes false claims in order to deceive others. SYNONYMS: cheat, fraud, impostor; (*informal*) phoney.
fake *adjective* false, not genuine.
fake *verb* 1 to make something that looks genuine, in order to deceive people. 2 to pretend something ♦ *He faked illness so as to stay at home.* **faker** *noun* [originally a slang word, of unknown origin]

fakir (**fay**-keer) *noun* a Muslim or Hindu religious beggar regarded as a holy man. [from an Arabic word meaning 'a poor man']

falafel (fə-**laf**-əl) *noun* a Middle Eastern dish of spiced mashed chickpeas made into balls and fried. [from an Arabic word meaning 'pepper']

falcon (**fawl**-kən) *noun* a kind of hawk often used in the sport of hunting other birds or game. [via Old French from a Latin word *falco*]

falconry *noun* the breeding and training of hawks.

fall *verb* (**fell, fallen**) 1 to come or go freely from a higher position to a lower one, usually by the force of weight, by losing balance, or by becoming detached. SYNONYMS: drop, plunge, tumble. 2 to hang down. 3 to slope downwards. 4 to become less in amount, number, or strength ♦ *House prices are falling at last.* SYNONYMS: come down, drop, decrease. 5 to happen or be noticed ♦ *An eerie silence fell on the crowd.* 6 to lose a position of power or authority. 7 (said about a person's face) to show disappointment by appearing to droop. 8 to die in battle. SYNONYMS: die, perish. 9 to be captured or overthrown ♦ *The city fell after a long siege.* 10 to pass into a specified state, to become something ♦ *We fell in love* ♦ *Then she fell asleep.* 11 to occur, to have as a date ♦ *Easter falls late this year.*
fall *noun* 1 the act of falling. 2 (*old use*) the act of giving way to temptation, especially by Adam and Eve in biblical accounts of the Creation. 3 the amount by which something falls or becomes less. SYNONYMS: decrease, decline. 4 (*North Amer.*) autumn, when leaves fall. **falls** *plural noun* a waterfall. **to fall back** to retreat. **to fall back on** to turn to someone or something for help in an emergency. **to fall down on** to fail in something. **to fall for** (*informal*) 1 to fall in love with someone. 2 to be tricked by a deception. **to fall foul of** to get into trouble or conflict with someone. **to fall in** 1 to collapse inwards. 2 to take your place in a military formation. **to fall in with** to agree to a proposal or suggestion. **to fall off** to decrease in size or number or quality. **to fall out** 1 to quarrel. SYNONYMS: quarrel, have a disagreement, clash, argue. 2 to happen. 3 to leave a military formation. **to fall through** (said about a plan) to fail, to come to nothing. [from an Old English word]

fallacious (fə-**lay**-shəs) *adjective* containing a fallacy, faulty. **fallaciously** *adverb* **fallaciousness** *noun*

fallacy (**fal**-əsi) *noun* (**fallacies**) 1 a false or mistaken belief. 2 faulty reasoning. [from a Latin word *fallere* meaning 'to deceive']

fallback *noun* an alternative plan adopted if all else fails.

fall guy *noun* (*informal*) an easy victim or scapegoat.

fallible (**fal**-ibəl) *adjective* liable to make mistakes. **fallibility** (fal-i-**bil**-iti) *noun* [same origin as for *fail*]

falling star *noun* a meteor.

Fallopian tubes (fə-loh-piən) *plural noun* the two tubes in female mammals carrying eggs from the ovaries to the uterus. [named after Gabriele Fallopio, a 16th-century Italian anatomist]

fallout *noun* particles of radioactive material carried in the air after a nuclear explosion.

fallow (fal-oh) *adjective* (said about land) ploughed but left without crops in order to restore its fertility. [from an Old English word *falu* meaning 'pale brown' (because of the colour of the bare earth)]

fallow deer *noun* a kind of small deer, which in the summer has a reddish-brown coat with white spots.

false *adjective* 1 incorrect or wrong. SYNONYMS: fictitious, incorrect, invalid, fabricated, made-up. 2 (said about a person) deceitful or unfaithful. SYNONYMS: unfaithful, disloyal, deceitful, dishonest, treacherous. 3 not genuine, artificial ♦ *false teeth.* **under false pretences** behaving in a way that is intended to deceive people. **falsely** *adverb* **falseness** *noun* [from a Latin word *falsum* meaning 'deceived']

falsehood *noun* 1 an untrue statement, a lie. 2 telling lies.

falsetto (fol-set-oh) *noun* (**falsettos**) a high-pitched voice above the natural range, especially when used by male singers. [an Italian word meaning 'little false one']

falsify *verb* (**falsifies, falsified, falsifying**) 1 to alter a document dishonestly. 2 to misrepresent facts. **falsification** *noun*

falsity *noun* (**falsities**) 1 falseness. 2 a falsehood or error.

falter *verb* 1 to move or function unsteadily. 2 to become weaker, to begin to give way ♦ *His courage began to falter.* 3 to speak or utter hesitatingly, to stammer. **falteringly** *adverb* [origin unknown]

fame *noun* 1 being known to many people, being famous. SYNONYMS: renown, glory, distinction, esteem. 2 a good reputation. [from a Latin word *fama* meaning 'report' or 'rumour']

famed *adjective* famous.

familiar *adjective* 1 well known, often seen or experienced ♦ *The old car was a familiar sight in the town.* SYNONYMS: well-known, common, everyday, normal, regular. 2 knowing something well ♦ *Are you familiar with this song?* 3 friendly and informal ♦ *She addressed him in familiar terms.* 4 too informal, over-friendly. **familiarly** *adverb* **familiarity** *noun* [same origin as for *family*]

familiarize *verb* to make someone well acquainted with a person or thing. **familiarization** *noun*

family *noun* (**families**) 1 parents and their children, sometimes including grandchildren and other relatives. 2 a person's children ♦ *They have a large family.* 3 all the descendants of a common ancestor; their line of descent. 4 a group of things that are alike in some way. 5 a group of related plants or animals ♦ *Lions belong to the cat family.* [from a Latin word *familia* meaning 'household']

family credit *noun* a regular payment made by the state to families with an income below a certain level.

family planning *noun* use of contraception to plan the size of a family, birth control.

family tree *noun* a diagram showing how people of successive generations in a family are related.

famine *noun* extreme scarcity of food in a region. [from a Latin word *fames* meaning 'hunger']

famished *adjectives* (*informal*) very hungry. [same origin as for *famine*]

famous *adjective* 1 known to many people. SYNONYMS: well-known, celebrated, prominent, distinguished, important. 2 (*informal*) splendid. **famously** *adverb* [same origin as for *fame*]

fan[1] *noun* a device or machine for creating a current of air in a room or building. **fan** *verb* (**fanned, fanning**) 1 to send a current of air on someone or something. 2 to stimulate flames with a current of air. 3 to spread from a central point ♦ *The troops fanned out to the left.* [from an Old English word *fann*, from a Latin word *vannus*]

fan[2] *noun* an enthusiastic admirer or supporter. [originally short for *fanatic*]

fanatic (fə-nat-ik) *noun* a person filled with excessive enthusiasm for something. **fanatical** *adjective* **fanatically** *adverb* **fanaticism** *noun*

fan belt *noun* a belt used to drive the fan that cools the radiator of a motor vehicle.

fancier *noun* a person with a special interest in a particular animal ♦ *a dog-fancier.*

fanciful *adjective* 1 highly imaginative and unrealistic. 2 existing only in the imagination. 3 (said about things) designed in a quaint or imaginative style. **fancifully** *adverb*

fan club *noun* an organized group of supporters or admirers.

fancy *noun* (**fancies**) 1 the power of imagining things, especially of an unreal or fantastic sort. 2 something imagined, an unfounded idea or belief. 3 a liking or desire for something.
fancy *adjective* (**fancier, fanciest**) 1 ornamental or elaborate. SYNONYMS: ornamental, decorated, elaborate.
fancy *verb* (**fancies, fancied, fancying**) 1 to imagine something ♦ *She fancied she saw a unicorn.* 2 to be inclined to believe or suppose something ♦ *I fancy he may be in love with Mary.* SYNONYMS: suppose, imagine. 3 (*informal*) to feel a wish or desire for something ♦ *Do you fancy a doughnut?* 4 (*informal*) to find someone sexually attractive. [originally a shortened spelling of *fantasy*]

fancy dress *noun* an unusual costume worn for a party, e.g. to make you look like a famous person or an animal.

fandango *noun* (**fandangoes** or **fandangos**) a lively Spanish dance for two people, or the music for this dance. [a Spanish word]

fanfare *noun* a short piece of loud music played on trumpets, especially as part of a ceremony. [from a French word]

fang *noun* 1 a long sharp tooth, especially of a dog or wolf. 2 a tooth a snake uses to inject its venom. [from an Old English word]

fanlight *noun* a small window, usually a half circle, above another window or a door. [so called because they often resemble the shape of an open fan]

fantasia (fan-**tay**-ziə) *noun* an imaginative piece of music or writing. [an Italian word related to *fantastic*]

fantasize (fan-tə-siyz) *verb* to imagine something strange or pleasant that you would like to happen. [from *fantasy*]

fantastic *adjective* 1 (*informal*) very remarkable, excellent. SYNONYMS: wonderful, marvellous, fabulous. 2 highly fanciful. 3 designed in an imaginative way. **fantastically** *adverb* [same origin as for *fantasy*]

fantasy *noun* (**fantasies**) 1 something imaginary or fantastic. 2 imagination used to produce fanciful ideas. 3 a fanciful design. 4 an imaginative piece of music or writing. [from a Greek word *phantazein* meaning 'to make visible']

FAQ *abbreviation* frequently asked question.

far *adverb* (**farther** or **further, farthest** or **furthest**) at or to a great distance ♦ *We shan't go far.*
far *adjective* distant or remote ♦ *They like to travel to far countries.* **a far cry from** very different from something. **by far** by a great amount. **far and away** by far. **far and wide** over a large area. [from an Old English word *feorr*]

farad (**fa**-rad) *noun* a unit of capacitance. [same origin as for *faraday*]

faraday (**fa**-rə-day) *noun* a unit of electrical charge. [named after the English physicist Michael Faraday (1791–1867)]

faraway *adjective* a long way away ♦ *faraway places.*

farce *noun* 1 a comedy in which the humour is exaggerated. 2 this kind of drama. 3 events that are absurd or useless. **farcical** (**far**-sik-əl) *adjective* **farcically** *adverb* [a French word meaning 'stuffing', the name given to a comic interlude between the acts of a play]

fare *noun* 1 the price charged for a passenger to travel. 2 a passenger who pays a fare, especially for a hired vehicle. 3 food and drink provided for people ♦ *There was only very simple fare.*
fare *verb* to have good or bad treatment, to progress ♦ *How did you fare?* [from an Old English word]

Far East *noun* China, Japan, and other countries of east and south-east Asia.

farewell *interjection* goodbye.
farewell *noun* an act of leaving or parting.

far-fetched *adjective* implausible, not very likely or convincing.

farinaceous (fa-rin-**ay**-shəs) *adjective* made of starch, like starch or a starchy substance. [from a Latin word *farina* meaning 'flour']

farm *noun* 1 an area of land and its buildings used for raising crops or rearing animals. 2 a farmhouse. 3 a stretch of water used for raising fish etc.

farm *verb* **1** to grow crops or rear farm animals. **2** to use land for this purpose. **3** to breed fish commercially. **to farm out** to give work to other people to do. [originally a payment of tax or rent, via French from a Latin word *firma* meaning 'fixed payment']

farmer *noun* a person who owns or manages a farm.

farmhand *noun* a worker on a farm.

farmhouse *noun* the main house on a farm, used by the farmer.

farmstead (**farm**-sted) *noun* a farm and its buildings.

farmyard *noun* the yard or area round farm buildings.

farrago (fə-**rah**-goh) *noun* (**farragos**) a confused muddle of things. [a Latin word meaning 'mixed fodder']

far-reaching *adjective* having important implications or consequences.

farrier (**fa**-ri-er) *noun* a smith who shoes horses. [from a Latin word *ferrum* meaning 'iron' or 'an iron horseshoe']

farrow (**fa**-roh) *noun* a litter of young pigs. **farrow** *verb* (said about a sow) to give birth to young pigs. [from an Old English word]

Farsi *noun* the modern form of the Persian language. [from an Arabic word, from the name *Fars* meaning 'Persia']

fart *verb* (*informal*) to let out wind from the anus.
fart *noun* the act or sound of wind let out of the anus. [from an Old English word]

farther *adverb & adjective* at or to a greater distance, more remote. [another spelling of *further*]
◊ *Farther* and *farthest* are only used when the meaning is of physical distance (e.g. *She lives farther from the school than I do*), but even then many people prefer to use *further* and *furthest*. When the meaning is 'more' or 'additional' (e.g. *We have further inquiries to make*), you have to use *further* and not *farther*. If you are not sure which to use, *further* or *furthest*, which are always correct.

farthest *adverb & adjective* at or to the greatest distance, most remote. [another spelling of *furthest*]
◊ See the note at **farther**.

farthing *noun* a former British coin worth one-quarter of a penny. [from an Old English word *feorthing* meaning 'one-fourth']

fasces (**fas**-eez) *plural noun* (in ancient Rome) a bundle of rods with a projecting axe blade, carried before certain officials as a symbol of authority. [plural of Latin *fascis* meaning 'bundle']

fascia (**fay**-shə) *noun* **1** a long flat board placed under the eaves of a building, or as a sign at the front of a shop. **2** the instrument panel of a motor vehicle, the dashboard. [a Latin word meaning 'band'or 'door frame']

fascinate *verb* to be very attractive or interesting to someone. SYNONYMS: enchant, captivate, charm, enthral.
fascination *noun* **fascinator** *noun* [from a Latin word *fascinare* meaning 'to cast a spell']

fascinating *adjective* having great attraction or interest. SYNONYMS: enchanting, captivating, charming, enthralling.

fascism (**fash**-izm) *noun* a system of extreme right-wing government based on authoritarian and nationalistic principles. **fascist** *noun* [from *fasces*, used as the emblem of the Italian Fascist party in the 1920s]

fashion *noun* **1** the popular style of dress or behaviour at a particular time. **2** a manner of doing something ♦ *We decided to continue in the same fashion*. SYNONYMS: manner, way, method, mode, style.
fashion *verb* to make something into a particular form or shape. **after a fashion** to some extent but not very satisfactorily. [from an Old French word *façon*, from a Latin word *facere* meaning 'to do']

fashionable *adjective* conforming to the current fashion, popular. **fashionably** *adverb*

fashion victim *noun* (*informal*) a slavish follower of popular fashions.

fast[1] *adjective* **1** moving or able to move at a high speed. SYNONYMS: quick, speedy, swift. **2** suitable for travel at high speed ♦ *a fast road*. **3** done or happening quickly ♦ *We need a fast response to our appeal*. SYNONYMS: quick, rapid, swift. **4** (said about a clock or watch) showing a time later than the correct time. **5** firmly fixed or attached. **6** (said about a person or activity) involved in or involving great or shocking excitement. **7** (said about colours or dyes)

not likely to fade or run. **8** (said about a film or lens) needing only a short exposure.
fast *adverb* **1** quickly. **2** firmly or tightly, securely ♦ *The window was stuck fast* ♦ *The children are fast asleep.* [from an Old English word *fæst*]

fast[2] *verb* to go without food or certain kinds of food, especially as a religious observance.
fast *noun* an act or time of fasting. [from an Old English word *fæstan*]

fast breeder reactor *noun* a nuclear reactor using high-speed neutrons to produce fissile material.

fasten *verb* **1** to fix something firmly in place, or tie or join things together. SYNONYMS: secure, fix. **2** to become fastened ♦ *The door fastens with a latch.* **to fasten on** to choose something and concentrate on it. [from an Old English word *fæstnian*]

fastener or **fastening** *noun* a device for fastening something.

fast food *noun* quickly-prepared food sold in a restaurant or snack bar for eating there or for taking away.

fast-forward *verb* to advance an audio or video tape at accelerated speed to reach a point further on in the recording.

fastidious (fas-tid-iəs) *adjective* **1** fussy and hard to please. **2** very careful about small details of dress or cleanliness. **fastidiously** *adverb* **fastidiousness** *noun* [from a Latin word *fastidium* meaning 'loathing']

fastness *noun* **1** a place protected by its natural surroundings. **2** the state of being fast or firm ♦ *colour fastness.*

fast track *noun* a quick route or method.

fat *noun* **1** a natural oily substance that is insoluble in water and is found in animal bodies and certain seeds. **2** oil or grease for use in cooking.
fat *adjective* (**fatter, fattest**) **1** containing much fat, covered with fat. SYNONYMS: plump, stout, tubby, podgy. **2** (said about a person) having a thick round body. **3** (said about an animal) made plump for slaughter. **4** thick ♦ *a fat book.* **a fat chance** (*informal*) no chance at all. **fatness** *noun* [from an Old English word *fætt*]

fatal *adjective* **1** causing or ending in death ♦ *a fatal wound.* SYNONYMS: lethal, deadly. **2** causing failure or disaster ♦ *a fatal mistake.* **fatally** *adverb* [from a Latin word *fatalis* meaning 'by fate']

fatalist *noun* a person who accepts whatever happens and regards it as inevitable. **fatalism** *noun* **fatalistic** *adjective*

fatality (fə-tal-iti) *noun* (**fatalities**) death caused by accident, war, or other disaster.

fate *noun* **1** an irresistible power that is thought to make things happen. **2** what has happened or will happen to a person. **Fates** *noun* (Greek Mythology) three goddesses who control people's lives and deaths. [from a Latin word *fatum* meaning 'what has been spoken']

fated *adjective* destined by fate, doomed.

fateful *adjective* bringing events that are important and usually unpleasant.

fathead *noun* (*informal*) a stupid person.

father *noun* **1** a male parent. **2** a male ancestor ♦ *land of our fathers.* **3** the founder or originator of something. **4** the **Father** (in Christian belief) God, the first person of the Trinity. **5** the title of certain priests, especially those belonging to religious orders.
father *verb* **1** to be the father of a child ♦ *He fathered six children.* **2** to be the founder or originator of an idea or plan. **fatherhood** *noun* [from an Old English word *fæder*]

Father Christmas *noun* an imaginary man traditionally having a long white beard and dressed in a red robe, said to bring presents for children at Christmas.

father figure *noun* an older man who is respected and trusted by others like a father.

father-in-law *noun* (**fathers-in-law**) the father of your wife or husband.

fatherland *noun* a person's native country.

fatherless *adjective* without a living or known father.

fatherly *adjective* like a father, especially in being protective and loving.

fathom *noun* a unit used to measure the depth of water, equal to 1.83 metres or 6 feet.
fathom *verb* **1** to understand something difficult. **2** to measure the depth of something. [from an Old English word *fæthm*]

fathomless *adjective* too deep to fathom.

fatigue *noun* **1** tiredness resulting from hard work or exercise. **2** weakness in metals, caused by constant stress. **3** (**fatigues**) the non-military duties of soldiers, such as cooking and cleaning. **fatigue** verb (**fatigues, fatigued, fatiguing**) to make someone very tired. [from a Latin word *fatigare* meaning 'to tire']

fatted adjective (said about an animal) fattened as food ♦ *the fatted calf.*

fatten verb to make something fat, or to become fat.

fatty adjective (**fattier, fattiest**) like fat or containing fat.

fatty acid noun an organic acid of the kind that occurs in natural oils.

fatuous (fat-yoo-əs) adjective pointless and silly. **fatuity** (fə-tew-iti) noun **fatuously** adverb **fatuousness** noun [from a Latin word *fatuus* meaning 'foolish']

fatwa noun a formal ruling on a point of Islamic law. [from an Arabic word]

faucet (faw-sit) noun 1 a tap for a barrel. 2 (North Amer.) a tap. [from an Old French word *fausset*]

fault noun 1 something that makes a person or thing imperfect, a flaw or weakness. SYNONYMS: defect, weakness, failing, imperfection, flaw. 2 a mistake or error. 3 an offence or wrongdoing. 4 the responsibility for something wrong ♦ *Whose fault is this?* 5 (Geology) a break in t he continuity of layers of rock, caused by movement of the earth's crust. 6 an incorrect serve in tennis and similar games. **fault** verb to find and comment on mistakes in someone or something. **at fault** responsible for a mistake or failure. **to find fault with** to find and comment on mistakes in someone or something. [from a Latin word *fallere* meaning 'to deceive']

faultless adjective not having any faults, perfect. **faultlessly** adverb **faultlessness** noun

faulty adjective (**faultier, faultiest**) having faults, imperfect.

faun (fawn) noun (Roman Mythology) an ancient rural god, shown as a man with a goat's legs, ears, horns, and tail. [from the name of the rural god Faunus (see *fauna*)]

fauna noun the animals of a particular area or period of time. (Compare **flora**.) [from the name of Fauna, an ancient Roman country goddess, sister of Faunus (see *faun*)]

faux pas (foh pah) noun (**faux pas** (foh pahz)) an embarrassing mistake or blunder. [a French expression, meaning 'false step']

favour noun 1 a kind act done specially to help someone. SYNONYMS: kindness, service, good deed, good turn. 2 approval or liking. 3 support or preference given to one person or group but not to another. SYNONYMS: partiality, favouritism, bias. **favour** verb 1 to regard or treat someone with approval or liking. SYNONYMS: approve of, like, prefer. 2 to be in favour of someone or something. 3 to give someone what they want ♦ *She favoured us with a song.* 4 (said about events or circumstances) to make something possible or easy. 5 (informal) to resemble a relative in facial features ♦ *The boy favours his father.* **to be in** or **out of favour** to have (or not have) a person's goodwill. **in favour of 1** in support of. 2 to the advantage of. [from a Latin word *favor*, from *favere* meaning 'to show kindness to']

favourable adjective 1 showing approval. 2 pleasing or satisfactory ♦ *I think we made a favourable impression.* 3 helpful or advantageous ♦ *favourable winds.* **favourably** adverb

favourite adjective liked or preferred above others. **favourite** noun 1 a favoured person or thing. 2 a competitor that is generally expected to win.

favouritism noun unfairly favouring one person or group and not another.

fawn[1] noun 1 a young deer in its first year. 2 light yellowish-brown. **fawn** adjective of a light yellowish brown colour. [from an Old French word *faon*, related to *fetus*]

fawn[2] verb 1 to get someone to like you by flattering or praising them too much. 2 (said about a dog or other animal) to show extreme affection for someone. [from an Old English word]

fax noun 1 an exact copy of a document transmitted electronically. 2 a machine used to transmit copies. **fax** verb to transmit a document by this process. [a short form of *facsimile*]

FBA abbreviation Fellow of the British Academy.

FBI abbreviation (in the USA) Federal Bureau of Investigation.

Fe *abbreviation* (*Chemistry*) the symbol for iron. [from a Latin word *ferrum* meaning 'iron']

fealty (**feel**-ti) *noun* (*historical*) loyalty or allegiance sworn by a feudal tenant or vassal to his lord ♦ *an oath of fealty*. [via Old French from a Latin word *fidelitas* (see *fidelity*)]

fear *noun* 1 an unpleasant feeling caused by the threat of danger or pain etc. 2 a danger or likelihood ♦ *There is no fear of that happening.*
fear *verb* 1 to feel fear; to be afraid of someone or something. **for fear of** because of the risk of. **without fear or favour** impartially. [from an Old English word *fær* meaning 'danger']

fearful *adjective* 1 feeling fear, afraid.
SYNONYMS: frightened, afraid, scared.
2 causing horror. 3 (*informal*) extremely bad. **fearfully** *adverb*

fearless *adjective* without fear. **fearlessly** *adverb* **fearlessness** *noun*

fearsome *adjective* frightening, alarming.

feasible (**fee**-zi-bəl) *adjective* 1 able to be done, possible ♦ *It will not be feasible to finish the work before tomorrow.* SYNONYMS: practicable, possible, realistic. 2 (*informal*) likely or probable ♦ *It is feasible that it will snow today.* **feasibility** (fee-zi-**bil**-iti) *noun* **feasibly** *adverb* [from an Old French word *faisible*, from *faire* meaning 'to make' or 'to do']
◊ The use of *feasible* to mean 'likely or probable' is not generally accepted in standard English.

feast *noun* 1 a large elaborate meal, especially to celebrate something. 2 an annual religious festival.
feast *verb* 1 to eat heartily. 2 to give a feast to people. **to feast one's eyes on** to gaze admiringly at. [from a Latin word *festus* meaning 'joyful']

feat *noun* a brave or remarkable action or achievement. [from an Old French word, related to *fact*]

feather *noun* any of the flat pieces that grow from a bird's skin and cover its body, consisting of a central shaft with a fringe of fine strands on each side.
feather *verb* 1 to cover or line something with feathers. 2 to turn an oar so that the blade passes through the air edgeways. 3 to make propeller blades rotate in such a way as to reduce the resistance of the air or water. [from an Old English word *fether*]

feather bed *noun* a mattress stuffed with feathers.

feather-brained *adjective* silly or absent-minded.

featherweight *noun* 1 in boxing, a weight (57 kg) between lightweight and bantamweight. 2 an unimportant person or thing.

feathery *adjective* 1 light and soft like feathers. 2 covered with feathers.

feature *noun* 1 a part of the face that helps to form its appearance (e.g. the mouth, nose, or eyes). 2 an important or noticeable quality that a thing has ♦ *The wooden ceiling is one of the interesting features of the old church.* SYNONYMS: detail, aspect. 3 a special newspaper or magazine article or radio or television programme dealing with a particular theme. 4 the main film in a cinema programme.
feature *verb* 1 to give special prominence to something. 2 to be a feature or important part of something. [from a Latin word *factura* meaning 'a creation']

featureless *adjective* not having any distinctive features.

February *noun* the second month of the year. [named after *februa*, the ancient Roman feast of purification held in this month]

feckless *adjective* feeble and incompetent, irresponsible. **fecklessly** *adverb* **fecklessness** *noun* [from a Scottish word *feck* meaning 'effect' and *-less*]

fecund (**feek**-ənd or **fek**-ənd) *adjective* highly fertile. **fecundity** (fi-**kund**-iti) *noun* [from a Latin word *fecundus*]

fed past tense and past participle of **feed**. **fed up** (*informal*) dejected or annoyed.

federal *adjective* 1 to do with a system of government in which several states are combined under a central authority but remain independent in internal affairs. 2 to do with the central government, as distinct from the separate parts, in such a system ♦ *federal laws.* **federally** *adverb* **federalism** *noun* [from a Latin word *foederis* meaning 'of a treaty']

federate *verb* to organize states on a federal basis, or to be organized in this way.

federation *noun* 1 the process of federating. 2 a federal group of states.

federative *adjective* federated or federal.

fee *noun* **1** a payment made to an official or a professional person for advice or services. **2** a payment made for a right or privilege, such as membership of a society, entrance for an examination, transfer of a footballer, etc. [from an Old French word *feu*, from a Latin word *feudum*]

feeble *adjective* **1** weak, lacking physical strength. SYNONYMS: poorly, sickly, weak, delicate, frail. **2** (said about a person) having a weak character, ineffective. **feebly** *adverb* **feebleness** *noun* [from Latin *flebilis* meaning 'wept over']

feeble-minded *adjective* foolish or stupid.

feed *verb* (past tense and past participle **fed**) **1** to give food to a person or animal. SYNONYMS: nourish, support, provide for. **2** to give something as food to animals ♦ *We feed oats to horses.* **3** (said about animals) to take food. **4** to serve as food for someone, to nourish someone. **5** to supply someone with material, water, power, etc. **6** (in ball games) to pass the ball to a player.
feed *noun* **1** a meal, especially for animals or babies. **2** food for animals. **3** a pipe or device for supplying material to a machine, or the supply of this material. [from an Old English word]

feedback *noun* **1** information about a product or service given to the supplier by its users, as a basis for improving it. **2** the return to its source of part of the output of an amplifier, microphone, or other device, especially so as to modify the output.

feeder *noun* **1** a person or animal that takes in food in a particular way ♦ *a greedy feeder.* **2** a container for feeding an animal or young child. **3** a hopper or feeding apparatus in a machine. **4** a road or rail route that links outlying areas with a central line or service.

feel *verb* (past tense and past participle **felt**) **1** to use touch to identify something or find out about it. SYNONYMS: touch, finger, caress. **2** to be physically or mentally aware of something ♦ *After a while she began to feel happier.* **3** to be affected by something ♦ *The old man felt the cold.* **4** to give a certain sensation or impression ♦ *The water feels warm.* **5** to have a vague conviction or impression of something. **6** to have something as an opinion, to consider something ♦ *We felt it was*

necessary to tell them. SYNONYMS: consider, think.

feel *noun* **1** the sense of touch. **2** an act of feeling. **3** the sensation produced by something touched ♦ *The curtains have a silky feel.* **to feel for someone** to sympathize with someone. **to feel like** (*informal*) to want something. [from an Old English word]

feeler *noun* **1** a long thin projection or organ on the bodies of certain animals, used to search for food or to test things by touch. **2** a cautious question or suggestion put forward to test people's reactions.

feel-good *adjective* (*informal*) making people feel happy or well off.

feeling *noun* **1** the ability to feel things ♦ *He had lost all feeling in his legs.* SYNONYMS: sensation, sensitivity. **2** mental awareness or emotion ♦ *a feeling of anger.* **3** an idea or belief not wholly based on reason ♦ *She had a feeling someone was watching her.* SYNONYMS: idea, impression, suspicion, inkling, intuition. **4** sensitivity, readiness to feel sympathy ♦ *They seemed to show no feeling for the sufferings of others.* **5** an opinion or attitude ♦ *The feeling of the meeting was against it.*
feelings *plural noun* **1** the emotional side of a person's nature, as distinct from the intellectual side. **2** emotional attitudes or responses ♦ *We have strong feelings on this matter* ♦ *You have hurt his feelings.*

feet plural of **foot**.

feign (fayn) *verb* to pretend to have a particular feeling or be in a particular state ♦ *When threatened, the animal feigns death.* [from a Latin word *fingere* meaning 'to form' or 'to plan']

feint[1] (faynt) *noun* a pretended attack or blow made to deceive an opponent.
feint *verb* to make a feint. [from a French word *feinte*, a form of the word *feindre* meaning 'to feign']

feint[2] (faynt) *adjective* (said about paper) ruled with faint lines as a guide for writing. [another spelling of *faint*]

feisty (fiy-sti) *adjective* (*informal*) (**feistier, feistiest**) (said about a person) lively and rather aggressive. [from an obsolete word *feist* meaning 'small dog']

feldspar *noun* a rock-forming mineral, an aluminium silicate combined with other metallic ions. [from a German word *Feldspat*, related to *field* and *spar*[2]]

felicitations (fi-liss-i-**tay**-shənz) *plural noun* (*formal*) congratulations. [same origin as for *felicity*]

felicitous (fi-**liss**-i-təs) *adjective* (said about words or remarks) well chosen, apt. **felicitously** *adverb* [same origin as for *felicity*]

felicity *noun* 1 great happiness. 2 a pleasing manner or style ♦ *He expressed himself with great felicity.* [from a Latin word *felicitas*, from *felix* meaning 'happy']

feline (**fee**-lyn) *adjective* to do with cats, cat-like.
feline *noun* an animal of the cat family. [from a Latin word *feles* meaning 'cat']

fell [1] past tense of **fall**.

fell [2] *verb* 1 to strike someone down with a hard blow. 2 to cut down a tree. [from an Old English word *fellan*]

fell [3] *noun* a stretch of hilly country or high moorland in the north of England. [from an Old Norse word *fjall* meaning 'hill']

fell [4] *adjective* (*poetic*) ruthless or cruel, destructive. **at one fell swoop** in a single action, all in one go. [from an Old French word *fel*, related to *felon*]

fellow *noun* 1 a man or boy. 2 a person who is associated with someone else, a comrade. 3 a thing of the same class or kind as another. 4 a member of a learned society, or of the governing body of certain colleges. [from an Old Norse word]

fellow feeling *noun* sympathy arising from a shared experience.

fellowship *noun* 1 friendly association with other people, companionship. 2 a society or group of friends. 3 the position of a college fellow.

felon (**fel**-ən) *noun* a person who has committed a felony. [from a Latin word *fellonis* meaning 'of an evil person']

felonious (fil-**oh**-ni-əs) *adjective* criminal.

felony (**fel**-əni) *noun* (**felonies**) (in the USA and formerly in Britain) a serious crime, especially one involving violence.

felspar *noun* another spelling of **feldspar**.

felt [1] past tense and past participle of **feel**.

felt [2] *noun* a thick fabric made of fibres of wool or fur etc. pressed together. **felt** *verb* to cover a surface with felt. [from an Old English word]

female *adjective* 1 to do with or belonging to the sex that can bear offspring or produce eggs. 2 (said about plants) able to produce fruit, having a pistil and no stamens. 3 to do with a woman or women. 4 (said about a fitting or machinery part) made hollow to receive a corresponding inserted part.
female *noun* a female person, animal, or plant. [from a Latin word *femina* meaning 'woman']

feminine *adjective* 1 to do with women or suitable for women. 2 having qualities traditionally associated with women. 3 (*Grammar*) (in some languages) belonging to the class that includes words referring to females or regarded as female.
feminine *noun* (*Grammar*) a feminine word or gender. **femininity** *noun* [from a Latin word *femina* meaning 'woman']

feminist *noun* someone who believes that women should have a status and rights equal to those of men. **feminism** *noun*

femur (**fee**-mer) *noun* (**femurs** or **femora**) the thigh bone. **femoral** *adjective* [a Latin word]

fen *noun* an area of low-lying marshy or flooded ground. [from an Old English word]

fence *noun* 1 a barrier made of wood or wire etc. put round a field or garden to mark a boundary or keep animals from straying. 2 a raised structure for a horse to jump over in showjumping or steeplechasing. 3 (*informal*) a person who deals in stolen goods.
fence *verb* 1 to surround an area with a fence. 2 to practise the sport of fencing. **fencer** *noun* [a shortened form of *defence*]

fencing *noun* 1 a set of fences, or a length of fence. 2 the sport of fighting with long narrow swords (called *foils*).

fend *verb* **to fend for yourself** to provide for and look after yourself. **to fend off** to defend yourself against an attack. [a shortened form of *defend*]

fender *noun* 1 a low frame round a fireplace to stop coals falling into the room. 2 a tyre or pad hung over the side of a ship to protect it when it is alongside a wharf or another ship.

feng shui (fung **shway**) *noun* (in Chinese thinking) a system of principles about the ways buildings and objects are laid out in relation to each other to achieve the best flow of energy. [from Chinese words meaning 'wind' and 'water']

fennel *noun* a fragrant herb with yellow flowers, used for flavouring. [from an Old English word, from a Latin word *faenum* meaning 'hay']

feral (feer-əl) *adjective* 1 (said about plants and animals) wild and untamed. 2 like a wild animal. [from a Latin word *fera* meaning 'wild animal']

ferment[1] (fer-ment) *verb* 1 to undergo a chemical change caused by the action of an organic substance such as yeast, especially when sugar is converted into alcohol to make wine or beer; to make something undergo this process. 2 to seethe with excitement or agitation. [from a Latin word *fermentum* meaning 'yeast']
◊ Do not confuse this word with **foment**, which has a different meaning.

ferment[2] (fer-ment) *noun* 1 a state of excitement or agitation. 2 the process of fermenting.

fermentation *noun* the process of fermenting.

fermium *noun* a radioactive chemical element (symbol Fm). [named after the Italian physicist Enrico Fermi (1901–54)]

fern *noun* a plant with feathery green leaves and no flowers. **ferny** *adjective* [from an Old English word *fearn*]

ferocious *adjective* fierce or savage. SYNONYMS: fierce, savage, wild, vicious, brutal, bloodthirsty. **ferociously** *adverb* **ferocity** (fi-ross-iti) *noun* [from a Latin word *ferox* meaning 'bold, fierce']

ferret *noun* a small animal of the weasel family kept for driving rabbits from burrows, killing rats, etc. **ferret** *verb* (**ferreted, ferreting**) 1 to search or rummage for something. 2 to hunt with ferrets. **to ferret out** to discover something by hard searching. [from a Latin word *fur* meaning 'thief']

ferrety *adjective* (said about a person's face) narrow and pointed like a ferret's.

ferric *adjective* made of or containing iron. [from a Latin word *ferrum* meaning 'iron']

Ferris wheel *noun* a large revolving wheel at a fairground, with cars round the edge for passengers to ride in. [named after its American inventor, George W. G. Ferris (1859–96)]

ferrite *noun* any of a class of iron oxides many of which have magnetic and insulating properties.

ferroconcrete *noun* reinforced concrete.

ferromagnetism *noun* the kind of magnetism found in substances such as iron, cobalt, nickel, and their alloys, with some ability to retain their magnetism after the magnetizing field is removed. **ferromagnetic** *adjective*

ferrous (fe-rəs) *adjective* containing iron ♦ *ferrous and non-ferrous metals.* [from a Latin word *ferrum* meaning 'iron']

ferrule (fe-rool) *noun* a metal ring or cap on the end of a stick, handle, or tube to strengthen it. [via Old French from a Latin word *viriae* meaning 'bracelets'. The form is probably influenced by the Latin word *ferrum* (see *ferrous*)]

ferry *noun* (**ferries**) a boat or ship used for transporting people or things across a short stretch of water. **ferry** *verb* (**ferries, ferried, ferrying**) to transport people or things across water or for a short distance, especially as a regular service. [from an Old Norse word]

ferryman *noun* (**ferrymen**) someone who operates a ferry.

fertile *adjective* 1 (said about soil) rich in the materials needed to produce good crops or vegetation. SYNONYMS: productive, fruitful, flourishing, lush. 2 (said about a person or animal) able to produce young or to conceive young; (said about a plant) able to produce fruit. 3 (said about seeds or eggs) able to develop into a new plant or animal, fertilized. 4 able to produce ideas, inventive ♦ *She has a fertile imagination.* SYNONYMS: inventive, vivid, prolific, resourceful. **fertility** *noun* [from a Latin word *fertilis*, from *ferre* meaning 'to bear']

fertilize *verb* 1 to make soil fertile or productive, especially by adding substances to it. 2 to introduce pollen into a plant or sperm into an egg or female animal so that it develops seed or young. **fertilization** *noun*

fertilizer *noun* a natural or artificial substance added to soil to make it more fertile.

fervent (fer-vənt) *adjective* showing warm or strong feeling. SYNONYMS: keen, enthusiastic, eager, avid, passionate, zealous. **fervency** *noun* **fervently** *adverb* [from a Latin word *fervens* meaning 'boiling']

fervid *adjective* extremely enthusiastic. **fervidly** *adverb* [same origin as for *fervent*]

fervour noun warm or strong feeling. [same origin as for *fervent*]

fester verb 1 (said about a wound or sore) to become septic and filled with pus. 2 (said about a difficulty or attitude) to cause a long period of resentment. [from an earlier meaning 'a festering sore']

festival noun 1 a day or time of celebration, especially for religious reasons. 2 an organized series of concerts, dramas, films, etc., especially one held annually in the same place ♦ *the Salzburg Festival*. [same origin as for *feast*]

festive adjective 1 to do with a festival. 2 suitable for a festival, joyful. SYNONYMS: joyful, joyous, cheerful, cheery.

festivity noun (**festivities**) a festive occasion or celebration.

festoon noun a chain of flowers or ribbons etc. hung as a decoration. **festoon** verb to decorate a room or place with hanging ornaments. [via French from an Italian word *festone* meaning 'festive ornament']

feta (fet-ə) noun a salty white Greek cheese made from the milk of goats or sheep. [from a modern Greek word *pheta*]

fetch verb 1 to go to get something or someone and bring them back. SYNONYMS: get, bring back, collect, pick up. 2 (said about goods) to sell for a price ♦ *Second-hand books don't fetch much these days*. **to fetch up** (informal) to arrive or end up at a place. [from an Old English word]

fetching adjective attractive. SYNONYMS: attractive, appealing, charming.

fête (fayt) noun an outdoor entertainment with stalls and sideshows, usually to raise money for a cause or charity. **fête** verb to honour a person with celebrations. [same origin as for *feast*]

fetid (fet-id or fee-tid) adjective smelling unpleasant. [from a Latin word *fetidus*]

fetish (fet-ish) noun 1 an object worshipped for its supposed magical powers. 2 something that a person has an obsession (especially a sexual obsession) about. [from a Portuguese word *feitiço* meaning 'a charm']

fetlock noun the part of a horse's leg above and behind the hoof. [from a Germanic language, related to *foot*]

fetter noun a chain or shackle put round a prisoner's ankle.

fetter verb 1 to put fetters on a prisoner. 2 to impede or restrict someone. [from an Old English word]

fettle noun **in fine fettle** in good health or condition. [from an Old English word]

fetus (fee-təs) noun (**fetuses**) a developing embryo, especially a human embryo more than eight weeks after conception. **fetal** adjective [a Latin word meaning 'offspring']

feud (fewd) noun a long-lasting quarrel or hostility between people, especially between two families. **feud** verb to carry on a feud. [via Old French from a Germanic language, related to *foe*]

feudal (few-dəl) adjective (in medieval Europe) relating to a system of holding land by which the tenant did work for the owner and owed him allegiance. **feudalism** noun **feudalistic** adjective [from a Latin word *feudum* (see *fee*)]

fever noun 1 an abnormally high body temperature, often with shivering, as a symptom of a disease. 2 a state of nervous excitement or agitation. [from a Latin word *febris*]

fevered adjective 1 affected with a fever. 2 highly excited.

feverish adjective 1 having a fever; caused or accompanied by a fever. 2 restless with excitement or agitation. SYNONYMS: hectic, frantic, excited. **feverishly** adverb **feverishness** noun

few adjective & noun not many. **a few** some, not none. **a good few** or **quite a few** (informal) a fairly large number. [from an Old English word] ◊ See the note at **less**.

fey (fay) adjective 1 having a strange other-worldly charm. 2 having clairvoyant powers. [from an Old English word]

fez noun (**fezzes**) a high flat-topped red hat with a tassel, worn by Muslim men in some countries. [named after Fez, a town in Morocco where fezzes were made]

ff abbreviation 1 (*Music*) fortissimo (very loudly). 2 the following pages (as in *134ff.*).

fiancé or **fiancée** (fee-ahn-say) nouns a man (**fiancé**) or woman (**fiancée**) to whom someone is engaged to be married. [a French word meaning 'betrothed']

fiasco (fi-**ass**-koh) *noun* (**fiascos**) a humiliating or ludicrous failure. [from an Italian phrase *far fiasco* meaning 'to make a bottle', and figuratively 'to fail in a performance']

fiat (**fiy**-at) *noun* an order or decree. [a Latin word meaning 'let it be done']

fib *noun* a trivial or unimportant lie. **fib** *verb* (**fibbed, fibbing**) to tell a fib. **fibber** *noun* [from *fable*]

Fibonacci series (fib-ən-ah-chi) *noun* a series of numbers (1, 1, 2, 3, 5, 8, 13, etc.) in which each number after the first two is the sum of the two preceding numbers. [named after the 13th-century Italian mathematician Leonardo Fibonacci, who discovered it]

fibre *noun* 1 a thin strand from which animal and vegetable tissue or a textile is made. 2 a substance made from fibres. 3 indigestible material in certain foods that stimulates the actions of the intestines. 4 strength of character ♦ *moral fibre*. [from a Latin word *fibra*]

fibreboard *noun* board made of compressed fibres.

fibreglass *noun* 1 textile fabric made from glass fibres. 2 plastic containing glass fibres.

fibre optics *noun* the use of thin flexible transparent fibres to transmit light signals, chiefly in telecommunications.

fibrin (**fiy**-brin) *noun* (*Biochemistry*) an insoluble protein formed as a mesh of fibres in the process of blood-clotting.

fibroid (**fiy**-broid) *adjective* consisting of fibres or fibrous tissue. **fibroid** *noun* (*Medicine*) a benign fibroid tumour in the womb.

fibrosis (fiy-**broh**-sis) *noun* (*Medicine*) the thickening and scarring of connective tissue, usually as a result of injury.

fibrous (**fiy**-brəs) *adjective* like fibres, or made of fibres.

fibula (fib-yoo-lə) *noun* (**fibulae** or **fibulas**) 1 (*Anatomy*) the bone on the outer side of the leg between the knee and the ankle, parallel to the tibia. 2 (*Archaeology*) a brooch or clasp. [a Latin word meaning 'brooch'. The bone is so called because with the tibia it forms the shape of a clasp]

fickle *adjective* constantly changing, not loyal or constant to one person or group.

SYNONYMS: unreliable, disloyal, unfaithful, changeable, inconstant. **fickleness** *noun* [from an Old English word]

fiction *noun* 1 prose writing, such as novels, that describes imaginary people and events. 2 something produced by the imagination. 3 a false idea or belief that is widely accepted because it is more convenient to do so. **fictional** *adjective* **fictionalize** *verb* **fictionally** *adverb* [from a Latin word *fictio* meaning 'pretending']

fictitious (fik-**tish**-əs) *adjective* imagined, not real or genuine. **fictitiously** *adverb*

fiddle *noun* 1 (*informal*) a violin. 2 (*informal*) a cheat or swindle. **fiddle** *verb* 1 to handle or fidget with something restlessly. 2 (*informal*) to cheat or swindle; to falsify accounts or records. 3 (*informal*) to play the fiddle. **fiddler** *noun* [from an Old English word]

fiddlesticks *interjection* (*informal*) nonsense.

fiddling *adjective* (*informal*) petty or trivial.

fiddly *adjective* (**fiddlier, fiddliest**) (*informal*) small and awkward to use or do.

fidelity (fid-**el**-iti) *noun* 1 faithfulness or loyalty. 2 accuracy or truthfulness. 3 the quality or precision with which sound is recorded and reproduced. [from a Latin word *fidelitas* meaning 'faithfulness']

fidget *verb* (**fidgeted, fidgeting**) 1 to make small restless movements because you are nervous or impatient. **fidget** *noun* a person who fidgets. [from a dialect word *fidge* meaning 'to twitch']

fidgety *adjective* fidgeting a lot, or inclined to fidget.

fie *interjection* (*old use*) an exclamation of disapproval.

field *noun* 1 a piece of open ground, especially one used for pasture or for growing crops. 2 an area of land rich in some natural product, such as gas or oil. 3 a battlefield ♦ *Thousands of dead lay on the field.* 4 a sports ground, or the playing area marked out on it. 5 (*Physics*) the region within which an electric, magnetic, or gravitational influence etc. can be felt. 6 the area that can be seen or observed ♦ *a field of vision.* 7 a branch of study or an area of activity or interest ♦ *an expert in the field of early music.* SYNONYMS: area, sphere, domain. 8 (*Computing*) one section of a record, representing a unit of information. 9 all the competitors in an outdoor contest or sport. 10 the scene or area of fieldwork ♦ *field archaeology.*

field *verb* **1** (in cricket and other ball games) to act as a fielder, to stop and return the ball. **2** to put a team into the field for a ball game. **3** to deal effectively with a series of questions. [from an Old English word *feld*]

field day *noun* **to have a field day** to have an opportunity for great activity or success, especially to someone else's disadvantage.

fielder or **fieldsman** *noun* (**fieldsmen**) a member of the side not batting in a ball game such as cricket.

field events *plural noun* athletic sports other than track races, such as jumping and throwing events.

field glasses *plural noun* binoculars for outdoor use.

Field Marshal an army officer of the highest rank.

field mouse *noun* a type of mouse found in open country.

field sports *plural noun* outdoor sports such as hunting, shooting, and fishing.

fieldwork *noun* practical work or research done in places outside libraries and laboratories, e.g. by surveyors and scientists, and by social workers who visit people in their homes. **fieldworker** *noun*

fiend (feend) *noun* **1** an evil spirit. **2** a very wicked or cruel person. **3** (*informal*) a devotee or addict ♦ *a fresh-air fiend.* [from an Old English word]

fiendish *adjective* **1** very wicked or cruel. **2** extremely difficult. **fiendishly** *adverb*

fierce *adjective* **1** angry and violent or cruel. SYNONYMS: ferocious, wild, savage, violent, brutal. **2** eager or intense ♦ *She showed a fierce loyalty to her friends.* SYNONYMS: intense, strong, eager, ardent. **3** unpleasantly strong or extreme ♦ *The heat is fierce in the middle of the day.* SYNONYMS: extreme, intense, strong. **fiercely** *adverb* **fierceness** *noun* [via Old French from a Latin word *ferus* meaning 'untamed']

fiery *adjective* (**fierier, fieriest**) **1** hot or flaming like fire. **2** looking like fire, bright red. **3** intense or passionate ♦ *He gave a fiery speech.* **4** easily made angry, quick-tempered. **fierily** *adverb* **fieriness** *noun*

fiesta (fee-est-ə) *noun* a religious festival in Spanish-speaking countries. [a Spanish word, related to *feast*]

FIFA *abbreviation* Fédération Internationale de Football Association, the international governing body for the sport.

fife *noun* a small shrill kind of flute used with a drum in military music. [from a German word *Pfeife* meaning 'pipe']

fifteen *adjective & noun* **1** the number 15. **2** a rugby team of fifteen players. **fifteenth** *adjective & noun* [from an Old English word]

fifth *adjective & noun* **1** next after fourth. **2** one of five equal parts of a thing. **3** (*Music*) an interval or chord spanning five alphabetical notes, e.g. C to G. **fifthly** *adverb*

fifth column *noun* an organized group working for the enemy within a country at war. **fifth columnist** *noun* [from the declaration by General Mola, who led four columns of troops towards Madrid in the Spanish Civil War, that he had a fifth column inside the city]

fifty *adjective & noun* (**fifties**) the number 50, equal to five times ten. **fifties** *plural noun* the numbers from 50 to 59, especially representing years of age or degrees of temperature. **fiftieth** *adjective & noun* [from an Old English word]

fifty-fifty *adjective & adverb* **1** shared or sharing equally between two people or groups. **2** evenly balanced ♦ *a fifty-fifty chance of success.*

fig *noun* **1** a soft fruit with a sweet dark flesh and many seeds. **2** the tree that produces this fruit. [from a Latin word *ficus*]

fig. *abbreviation* figure.

fight *verb* (past tense and past participle **fought**) **1** to take part in a struggle against a person or country in physical combat or in war. **2** to carry on a battle. **3** to struggle or strive hard to achieve something. **4** to strive to overcome or destroy something ♦ *They fought the fire for several hours.* **5** to make your way by fighting or effort ♦ *We had to fight our way out of the crowd.* **fight** *noun* **1** an act of fighting, a battle. SYNONYMS: battle, action, engagement. **2** a struggle or conflict. SYNONYMS: struggle, conflict, brawl, scrap, scuffle, clash. **3** a boxing match. [from an Old English word]

fighter *noun* **1** a person who is fighting. **2** a person who strives hard to achieve something. **3** a fast military aircraft designed for attacking other aircraft.

figment noun a thing that only exists in the imagination. [from a Latin word fingere meaning 'to contrive']

figurative (fig-yoor-ətiv) adjective (said about a word or expression) using or containing a figure of speech; metaphorical, not literal. **figuratively** adverb

figure noun 1 a written symbol that represents a number. SYNONYMS: number, numeral, digit, integer. 2 an amount or number ◆ There are a lot but it's hard to put a figure on it. 3 the external form or shape of something, especially of the human body ◆ Rose has a slim figure. SYNONYMS: form, shape, build, physique, outline. 4 a geometrical shape enclosed by lines or surfaces. 5 a representation of a person or animal in drawing, painting, sculpture, etc. 6 a decorative pattern; a pattern traced in dancing or skating. 7 a diagram or illustration in a book. 8 a person as seen or studied ◆ I could see a figure leaning against the door ◆ She is an important figure in twentieth-century history.
figure verb 1 to appear in something or form part of it ◆ He figures in all the books on the subject. 2 (North Amer.) to understand or consider something. 3 to picture something mentally, to imagine something. 4 to represent something or someone in a diagram or picture.
figures plural noun arithmetic, calculation by numbers ◆ I'm no good at figures. **to figure someone** or **something out** to understand someone or something. [from a Latin word figura meaning 'shape']

figurehead noun 1 a carved figure at the prow of a sailing ship. 2 a person who is at the head of a country or organization but has no real power.

figure of speech noun a word or phrase used for special effect and not meant literally (e.g. flood in We have had a flood of complaints).

figurine (fig-yoor-een) noun a small statue of a person, used as an ornament.

filament noun 1 a fine wire in an electric lamp, giving off light when heated by the current. 2 a thread-like fibre or strand. [from a Latin word filum meaning 'thread']

filch verb (informal) to steal something of small value. [origin unknown]

file¹ noun 1 a folder or box etc. for keeping papers in order. 2 (Computing) a collection of data stored under one name. 3 a line of people one behind the other.

file verb 1 to put something in a file. 2 to submit a document or form to be put on official record. 3 (said about a reporter) to send in a story or article. 4 to walk in a row one behind the other ◆ People were asked to file out slowly. [from a Latin word filum meaning 'thread' (because a string or wire was put through papers to hold them in order)]

file² noun a metal tool with a rough surface that is rubbed on surfaces to shape them or make them smooth.
file verb to shape or smooth a surface with a file. [from an Old English word]

filial (fil-iəl) adjective to do with a son or daughter ◆ to do your filial duty. [from Latin words filius meaning 'son' and filia meaning 'daughter']

filibuster noun an attempt to delay or prevent the passing of a law by making long speeches.
filibuster verb to delay legislation in this way. [from a Dutch word vrijbuiter meaning 'pirate']

filigree (fil-i-gree) noun ornamental lace-like work of twisted metal wire. **filigreed** adjective [from a Latin word filum meaning 'thread' and granum meaning 'grain']

filing cabinet noun a piece of office furniture with deep drawers for storing files.

filings plural noun tiny pieces of metal rubbed off by a file.

Filipino (fili-pee-noh) noun (**Filipinos**) a person born in the Philippine Islands in SE Asia, or descended from people born there. [from the Spanish name of the islands, Islas Filipinas]

fill verb 1 to make something full; to occupy the whole of something. 2 (said about a container, room, etc.) to become full. 3 to block up a hole or cavity. 4 to spread over or through an area ◆ Smoke began to fill the room. 5 to hold a position; to appoint a person to a vacant post. 6 to occupy a period of time.
fill noun 1 enough to fill something. 2 enough to satisfy a person's appetite or desire ◆ We ate our fill. **to fill in** to act as a substitute for someone. **to fill someone in** to give someone more detailed information. **to fill something in** 1 to add information needed to complete a form or document. 2 to complete a drawing by

shading or colouring inside an outline.
to fill out to become larger or plumper.
to fill something up to fill something completely. [from an Old English word]

filler *noun* something used to fill a cavity or to increase the bulk of something.

fillet *noun* 1 a piece of boneless meat or fish. 2 a strip of ribbon etc. worn round the head. 3 (*Architecture*) a narrow flat band between mouldings.
fillet *verb* (**filleted, filleting**) to remove the bones from fish or meat. [from a French word *filet* meaning 'thread', related to *file*[1]]

filling *noun* 1 material used to fill a hole or cavity, for example in a tooth.
2 something put in pastry to make a pie, or between layers of bread to make a sandwich.

filling station *noun* a place where petrol is sold to motorists from pumps.

fillip *noun* something that boosts or stimulates an activity. [related to *flip*]

filly *noun* (**fillies**) a young female horse. [from an Old Norse word *fylja*]

film *noun* 1 a motion picture shown in a cinema or on television. 2 a rolled strip or sheet coated with light-sensitive material and used for taking photographs or making a motion picture. 3 a thin coating or covering layer.
film *verb* 1 to record something on film; to make a film of a story etc. 2 to cover something, or become covered, with a thin coating or covering layer. [from an Old English word *filmen* meaning 'thin skin']

film star *noun* a well-known film actor or actress.

filmstrip *noun* a strip of transparencies for projection.

filmy *adjective* (**filmier, filmiest**) thin and almost transparent. **filminess** *noun*

filter *noun* 1 a device for holding back dirt or other unwanted material from a liquid or gas that is passed through it. 2 a screen for preventing light of certain wavelengths from passing through. 3 a device for suppressing electrical or sound waves of frequencies other than the ones required. 4 an arrangement for allowing traffic to pass in one direction while other traffic is stopped.
filter *verb* 1 to pass through a filter or put something through a filter; to remove impurities in this way. 2 to come or make

a way in or out gradually ♦ *News began to filter out* ♦ *People filtered into the hall.* 3 (said about traffic) to move forward in one direction while other traffic is stopped. [from *felt*[2], which was originally used for making filters]

filth *noun* 1 disgusting dirt. SYNONYMS: dirt, grime, muck. 2 obscene or offensive writing, pictures, or language. [from an Old English word]

filthy *adjective* (**filthier, filthiest**)
1 disgustingly dirty. SYNONYMS: dirty, grimy, mucky, foul. 2 (said about writing, pictures, or language) obscene or offensive. **filthily** *adverb* **filthiness** *noun*

filtrate *noun* liquid that has passed through a filter. **filtration** *noun*

fin *noun* 1 a thin flat part projecting from the body of a fish and used to guide it through the water. 2 a rubber flipper worn when swimming underwater. 3 a small projection on an aircraft or rocket, for helping its balance. [from an Old English word]

final *adjective* 1 coming at the end, last. 2 putting an end to doubt or discussion or argument.
final *noun* the last in a series of contests in sports or a competition.
finals *plural noun* examinations held at the end of a degree course. **finally** *adverb* [from a Latin word *finis* meaning 'end']

finale (fin-**ah**-li) *noun* the final section of a piece of music or an entertainment. [an Italian word, related to *final*]

finalist *noun* a competitor who takes part in a final.

finality (fiy-**nal**-iti) *noun* the state of being final, or ending doubt.

finalize *verb* 1 to put something into its final form. 2 to complete a deal or transaction. **finalization** *noun*

finance (fiy-**nanss**) *noun* 1 the management and use of money. 2 money used to support an undertaking.
finance *verb* to provide money for an undertaking.
finances *plural noun* the money resources and organization of a country, company, or person. [from an Old French word *finer* meaning 'to settle a debt']

finance company or **finance house** *noun* a company that is mainly concerned with lending money for credit transactions.

financial (fiy-nan-shǝl) *adjective* to do with finance. **financially** *adverb*

financial year *noun* a period of twelve months reckoned for accounting purposes, in Britain beginning on 6 April.

financier (fiy-nan-si-er) *noun* a person who is involved in managing the financial affairs of governments or business organizations.

finch *noun* any of a number of small birds most of which have a colourful plumage and short stubby bills. [from an Old English word]

find *verb* (past tense and past participle **found**) **1** to discover something or someone by looking for them or by chance. SYNONYMS: discover, come across, locate, uncover, unearth. **2** to become aware of something, to discover a fact by experience ♦ *He soon found that digging was hard work.* SYNONYMS: discover, realize, perceive. **3** to arrive at a state by a natural process ♦ *Water finds its own level.* SYNONYMS: establish, achieve. **4** to succeed in obtaining something ♦ *I haven't found time to do it yet.* **5** to decide and declare a verdict ♦ *The jury found him guilty.* **find** *noun* **1** the finding of something useful or pleasing. **2** a person or thing that proves to be useful. **to find favour** to be acceptable. **to find your feet 1** to become able to stand or walk. **2** to become established in an activity. **to find yourself** to discover natural powers or a vocation. **to find out 1** to get information about something. **2** to discover someone who has done wrong ♦ *They were afraid they might be found out.* [from an Old English word]

findings *plural noun* the conclusions reached from an inquiry, investigation, or experiment.

fine [1] *adjective* **1** of high quality, excellent. SYNONYMS: excellent, good, exceptional, outstanding, admirable. **2** (said about the weather) bright and clear. SYNONYMS: bright, sunny, clear, fair. **3** in good health, comfortable ♦ *I'm fine, thank you.* **4** slender or thin; consisting of small particles. **5** requiring very skilful workmanship. **6** difficult to distinguish ♦ *making fine distinctions.* SYNONYMS: subtle, precise, nice. **fine** *adverb* **1** finely. **2** (*informal*) very well ♦ *That will suit me fine.*

fine *verb* to become, or to make something become, finer, thinner, or less coarse. **finely** *adverb* **fineness** *noun* [same origin as for *finish*]

fine [2] *noun* a sum of money that has to be paid as a penalty. **fine** *verb* to punish someone with a fine. [from a Latin word *finis* meaning 'end' (because in the Middle Ages it meant the sum paid to settle a lawsuit)]

fine arts *plural noun* the arts that appeal to a sense of beauty, especially painting, sculpture, and architecture.

finery *noun* fine clothes or decorations.

finesse (fin-ess) *noun* tact and cleverness in doing something. [a French word meaning 'fineness']

fine-tooth comb *noun* a comb with narrow close-set teeth. **to go through something with a fine-tooth comb** to examine something in great detail.

fine-tune *verb* **1** to adjust something very precisely. **2** to make detailed adjustments to a plan in order to improve it.

finger *noun* **1** each of the four parts extending from each hand, or five including the thumb. **2** the part of a glove that fits over a finger. **3** an object having the shape of a finger. **finger** *verb* **1** to touch or feel something with the fingers. **2** to play a musical instrument with the fingers. [from an Old English word]

fingerboard *noun* a flat strip on the neck of a stringed instrument, against which the strings are pressed with the fingers to alter the pitch.

fingering *noun* a method of using the fingers in playing a musical instrument or in typing.

finger mark *noun* a mark left on a surface by a finger.

fingernail *noun* the nail on a finger.

fingerplate *noun* a plate fastened on a door to prevent finger marks.

fingerprint *noun* a mark made by the tiny ridges on a person's fingertip, especially as a means of identification.

fingertip *noun* the tip of a finger. **to have something at your fingertips** to be thoroughly familiar with a subject.

finial *noun* an ornament at the top of a gabled roof, canopy, etc. [from a Latin word *finis* meaning 'end']

finicky *adjective* 1 fussy about details, hard to please. 2 excessively detailed or elaborate.

finish *verb* 1 to bring something to an end, or to come to an end. SYNONYMS: end, conclude. 2 to reach the end of an undertaking. SYNONYMS: complete, accomplish. 3 to eat or drink all of something ♦ *Can you finish the pie?* 4 to complete the manufacture of something by giving it an attractive surface. **finish** *noun* 1 the last stage of something. SYNONYMS: end, conclusion, close. 2 the point at which a race ends. 3 the state of being finished or perfect. 4 the surface or coating on woodwork etc. **to finish something off** 1 to end something. 2 (*informal*) to kill someone. **to finish with** to have nothing more to do with someone or something. [from a Latin word *finis* meaning 'end']

finite (fy-nyt) *adjective* 1 limited, not infinite. 2 (*Mathematics*) (said about a set) having a finite number of elements. 3 (*Grammar*) (said about a verb) having a form that agrees with a subject in number and person, such as *was* and *takes*. [from a Latin word *finitum* meaning 'ended']

Finn *noun* a person born in Finland or descended from people born there.

Finnish *adjective* to do with or coming from Finland. **Finnish** *noun* the language of Finland.

fiord *noun* another spelling of **fjord**.

fir *noun* 1 an evergreen tree that produces cones and has needle-like leaves on its shoots. 2 the wood of this tree. [from an Old Norse word]

fire *noun* 1 the process of burning that produces light and heat. 2 burning that destroys property ♦ *They are insured against fire.* 3 something burning ♦ *They could see a fire in the distance.* SYNONYMS: blaze, inferno. 4 an amount of fuel burning in a grate or furnace; an electric or gas device that produces heat. 5 an angry or excited feeling, enthusiasm. 6 the firing of guns ♦ *Hold your fire.* **fire** *verb* 1 to shoot a gun; to send out a bullet or missile. SYNONYMS: shoot, discharge. 2 to deliver or utter a rapid succession of questions or statements. 3 (*informal*) to dismiss an employee from a job. SYNONYMS: dismiss, sack. 4 to set fire to something. 5 to catch fire; (said about an engine) to become ignited. 6 to supply a furnace etc. with fuel. 7 to bake pottery or bricks in a kiln. 8 to excite or stimulate someone ♦ *The idea fired them with enthusiasm.* **to fire away** (*informal*) to make a start on something. **on fire** burning. [from an Old English word]

fire alarm *noun* a device that gives off a loud sound to warn of fire.

firearm *noun* a small gun, such as a rifle, pistol, or revolver.

firebrand *noun* a person who stirs up trouble.

firebreak *noun* an obstacle to the spread of fire in a forest etc.

fire brigade *noun* an organized body of people trained to extinguish fires.

firecracker *noun* a loud explosive firework.

firedamp *noun* methane, making an explosive mixture with air in coalmines.

fire drill *noun* rehearsal of the procedure that needs to be followed in case of fire.

fire engine *noun* a large vehicle that carries firefighters and their equipment to the scene of a fire.

fire escape *noun* a special staircase or apparatus for escaping from a burning building.

firefighter *noun* a member of a fire brigade.

firefly *noun* a kind of beetle that gives off a phosphorescent light.

fire irons *plural noun* a set of equipment, including poker, tongs, and shovel, for tending a domestic fire.

firelight *noun* the light from a fire in a fireplace.

firelighter *noun* a piece of inflammable material to help start a fire in a grate.

fireman *noun* (**firemen**) 1 a male member of a fire brigade. 2 a person who tends a furnace.

fireplace *noun* 1 an open recess for a domestic fire, at the base of a chimney. 2 the structure built round this recess.

firepower *noun* the destructive capacity of guns and missiles.

fireproof *adjective* able to withstand fire or intense heat.

fire-raising *noun* setting fire to buildings, arson. **fire-raiser** *noun*

fireside *noun* the part of a room round a fireplace, regarded as the focus of a home.

fire station *noun* the headquarters of a fire brigade.

firestorm *noun* a fierce fire fanned by high winds and air currents.

fire trap *noun* a building without proper provision for escape in case of fire.

firewall *noun* **1** a wall or partition designed to check the spread of a fire. **2** (*Computing*) a part of a computer network that prevents unauthorized access.

firewood *noun* wood for use as fuel.

firework *noun* a device containing chemicals that burn or explode with spectacular effects, used at celebrations.

firing line *noun* **1** the front line of troops in a battle. **2** a situation in which you are vulnerable to criticism or blame.

firing squad *noun* a group of soldiers given the duty of shooting a condemned person.

firm [1] *adjective* **1** not giving way when pressed, hard or solid. SYNONYMS: hard, solid, rigid. **2** steady, not shaking or moving. SYNONYMS: steady, secure. **3** securely fixed. **4** definite, and unlikely to change ♦ *This is my firm belief.* SYNONYMS: definite, decided, unwavering.
firm *adverb* firmly ♦ *We must stand firm.*
firm *verb* to become firm or compact, or to make something firm; to fix something firmly. [from a Latin word *firmus*]

firm [2] *noun* a company or business organization. [from a Latin word *firmare* meaning 'to settle' (related to *firm* [1]), in the sense of confirming a legal contract by signing it, the signature being identified as the name of the business]

firmament *noun* (*poetic*) the sky with its clouds and stars. [from a Latin word *firmamentum*, related to *firm* [1]]

first *adjective* **1** coming before all others in time, order, or importance. **2** (*Music*) playing the leading part of two or more parts for the same instrument in a group ♦ *first violins.*
first *noun* **1** a person or thing that is first; the first day of a month. **2** the first time something is done or occurs. **3** first-class honours in a university degree. **4** first gear in a motor vehicle.
first *adverb* **1** before all others. **2** before something else happens or is done ♦ *I must finish this work first.* **3** for the first time ♦ *When did you first meet her?* **at first** at the

beginning. [from an Old English word]

first aid *noun* treatment given to an injured person before full medical treatment is available.

first-born *adjective* eldest of several brothers or sisters.

first class *noun* **1** a set of people or things grouped together as the best. **2** the best accommodation on a train, ship, or aircraft. **3** a category of mail that is to be delivered quickly.
first-class *adjective* **1** of the best quality. SYNONYMS: excellent, first-rate, superb. **2** using the best class of a service.

first cousin *noun* see **cousin**.

first-day cover *noun* an envelope with stamps postmarked on their day of issue.

first finger *noun* the index finger.

first-footing *noun* the practice of being the first person to cross someone's threshold in the New Year.

first gear *noun* the lowest gear in a motor vehicle.

first-hand *adjective & adverb* obtained directly from the original source.

first lady *noun* the wife of the US President.

firstly *adverb* first, as a first consideration.

first mate *noun* the officer who is second in command on a merchant ship.

first name *noun* someone's personal name, which comes before the family name.

first officer *noun* **1** the first mate on a merchant ship. **2** the officer who is second in command on an aircraft.

first person *noun* see **person**.

first-rate *adjective* of the best quality, excellent.

firth *noun* an estuary or narrow inlet of the sea in Scotland. [from an Old Norse word, related to *fjord*]

fiscal *adjective* to do with public finances. [from a Latin word *fiscus* meaning 'treasury']

fish *noun* (**fish** or **fishes**) **1** an animal with gills and fins, which lives and breathes wholly in water. **2** the flesh of a fish eaten as food.
fish *verb* **1** to try to catch fish. **2** to search or feel for something hidden. **3** to try to get something by hinting at it ♦ *He was obviously fishing for a compliment.* **to fish out** to pull something out of a place where it

is hidden or hard to find. [from an Old English word]

fishcake *noun* a small cake of shredded fish and mashed potato.

fisherman *noun* (**fishermen**) a person who catches fish for a living or for sport.

fishery *noun* (**fisheries**) 1 a part of the sea where fishing is carried on. 2 the business of catching fish.

fish finger *noun* a small oblong piece of fish in batter or breadcrumbs.

fishing *noun* the activity of catching fish for food or sport.

fishing rod *noun* a long rod with a line attached, used for fishing.

fishmonger *noun* a shopkeeper who sells fish.

fishnet *adjective* (said about a fabric) made in a kind of open mesh.

fishy *adjective* (**fishier, fishiest**) 1 smelling or tasting of fish. 2 (*informal*) causing doubt or suspicion. SYNONYMS: suspicious, doubtful. **fishiness** *noun*

fissile (fi-siyl) *adjective* 1 tending to split. 2 capable of undergoing nuclear fission. [same origin as for *fission*]

fission *noun* 1 the process of splitting the nucleus of an atom, in order to release energy. 2 the process of splitting or dividing biological cells as a method of reproduction. **fissionable** *adjective* [from a Latin word *fissum* meaning 'split']

fissure (fish-er) *noun* a narrow opening made when something splits or separates.

fist *noun* a tightly closed hand, with the fingers bent into the palm. [from an Old English word]

fisticuffs *noun* (*old use*) fighting with the fists. [from *fist* and *cuff* meaning 'to slap']

fistula (fiss-tew-lə) *noun* 1 (*Medicine*) an abnormal or surgically made passage in the body. 2 a natural pipe or spout in whales, insects, etc. **fistular** *adjective* [a Latin word meaning 'a flute']

fit¹ *adjective* (**fitter, fittest**) 1 suitable or well adapted for something, good enough ♦ *We had a meal fit for a king* ♦ *The old house was no longer in a fit state to live in.* SYNONYMS: suitable, appropriate, fitting, proper. 2 healthy or in good physical condition. SYNONYMS: healthy, strong, robust. 3 feeling in a suitable condition to do something.

fit *verb* (**fitted, fitting**) 1 to be the right shape and size for something. 2 to put clothing on a person and adjust it to the right shape and size. 3 to put something into place ♦ *We must fit a new catch on the window.* SYNONYMS: fix, install. 4 to make someone suitable or competent for an activity ♦ *Her training fitted her for the position.*
fit *noun* the way something fits ♦ *The coat is a good fit.* **to fit in** to get on well with a group of people; to be compatible or suitable. **to see** or **think fit** to decide or choose to do something, especially unwisely or without good reason. **fitly** *adverb* **fitness** *noun* [origin unknown]

fit² *noun* 1 a sudden attack of an illness, especially one causing convulsions or loss of consciousness. 2 a sudden attack of coughing. SYNONYMS: attack, spasm. 3 an outburst of strong feeling ♦ *a fit of rage.* 4 a short period of activity, an impulse ♦ *a fit of energy.* **in fits and starts** in short bursts of activity, not steadily or regularly. [from an Old English word]

fitful *adjective* happening in short periods, not regularly or steadily. **fitfully** *adverb*

fitment *noun* a piece of fixed furniture.

fitted *adjective* made to fit a particular space or cover something closely ♦ *a fitted carpet.*

fitter *noun* 1 a person who supervises the fitting of clothes. 2 a mechanic who fits together and adjusts the parts of machinery.

fitting *adjective* proper or suitable. SYNONYMS: suitable, appropriate, proper, right, apt.
fitting *noun* the process of having a piece of clothing fitted.
fittings *plural noun* the fixtures and fitments of a building.

five *adjective & noun* the number 5, one more than four. [from an Old English word]

fivefold *adjective & adverb* 1 five times as much or as many. 2 consisting of five parts.

fiver *noun* (*informal*) a five-pound note, or the sum of five pounds.

fives *noun* a game in which a ball is struck with gloved hands or a bat against the walls of a court. [the plural of *five* used as a singular noun]

fix verb 1 to fasten or place something firmly. SYNONYMS: fasten, attach, secure. 2 to make something permanent and unable to be changed. 3 to repair something or put it into working condition. SYNONYMS: repair, mend, put right. 4 to decide or specify an arrangement ♦ A date has been fixed for the trial. SYNONYMS: arrange, agree, settle. establish. 5 to put facts or ideas firmly in the mind or memory. 6 to direct your eyes or attention steadily. 7 (in photography) to make an image permanent by using a substance that prevents it from fading or changing colour. 8 (informal) to influence or affect the outcome of something fraudulently. SYNONYMS: rig, fiddle.
fix noun 1 (informal) an awkward situation ♦ Now we are in a fix. 2 (informal) a dose of a narcotic drug taken by an addict. 3 the position of a ship or aircraft determined by taking bearings. **to fix on** to choose or decide on something. **to fix something up** to arrange something. [from a Latin word fixus meaning 'fixed']

fixation noun 1 an abnormal emotional attachment to a person or thing. 2 an obsession or concentration on a single idea. **fixated** adjective

fixative noun 1 a substance for keeping things in position. 2 a substance for fixing colours, or for preventing perfumes from evaporating too quickly.

fixed assets plural noun the property and equipment owned by a company and used for carrying on its business activity.

fixedly (fiks-id-li) adverb with a fixed expression ♦ She stared at me fixedly.

fixer noun 1 a person or thing that fixes something. 2 a substance for fixing photographic images.

fixture noun 1 a piece of furniture or equipment that is fixed in position. 2 a person or thing that is firmly established and unlikely to leave. 3 a sporting event arranged for a particular date.

fizz verb to make a hissing sound, as when gas escapes in bubbles from a liquid. **fizz** noun 1 a hissing sound. 2 (informal) a fizzy drink. **fizzy** adjective **fizziness** noun [an imitation of the sound]

fizzle verb to make a slight fizzing sound. **to fizzle out** to end feebly or unsuccessfully. [from fizz]

fizzy adjective (**fizzier, fizziest**) (said about a drink) having a lot of small bubbles, effervescent.

fjord (fjord or fee-ord) noun a long narrow inlet of the sea between high cliffs, especially in Norway. [a Norwegian word]

flab noun (informal) soft loose flesh, fat. [from flabby]

flabbergasted adjective extremely surprised. [origin unknown]

flabby adjective (**flabbier, flabbiest**) fat and limp, not firm. **flabbily** adverb **flabbiness** noun [from an earlier form flappy, related to flap]

flaccid (flass-id or flak-sid) adjective soft and limp. **flaccidly** adverb **flaccidity** (flak-**sid**-iti) noun [from a Latin word flaccus meaning 'flabby']

flag ¹ noun 1 a piece of cloth with a distinctive pattern or design on it, raised on a pole as the emblem of a country or as a sign or signal. 2 a small piece of paper or plastic that looks like a flag.
flag verb (**flagged, flagging**) 1 to mark something out with flags. 2 to signal with a flag or with the arms ♦ A police officer flagged the vehicle down. 3 to hang down limply, to droop. 4 to lose vigour. SYNONYMS: tire, droop, weaken, fade, weary. [from an old word flag meaning 'drooping']

flag ² noun a flagstone.
flag verb (**flagged, flagging**) to pave an area with flagstones. [from an Old Norse word flaga meaning 'slab of stone']

flag ³ noun a plant with long flat leaves, especially an iris. [origin unknown]

flag day noun a day on which money is raised for charity and donors are given small paper flags to wear.

flagellate ¹ (flaj-əl-ayt) verb to whip someone, especially as a religious discipline. **flagellation** noun [from a Latin word flagellum meaning 'a whip']

flagellum (flə-jel-əm) noun (**flagella**) a long thin appendage on many bacteria and protozoans, which enables them to move. [a Latin word meaning 'little whip']

flageolet (flaj-ə-let) noun a small pipe blown like a recorder. [from an Old French word]

flag of convenience noun a flag of a country under which a ship is registered to evade taxation or regulations.

flagon noun a large container for holding or serving drinks. [from a Latin word flasco meaning 'flask']

flagpole or **flagstaff** noun a pole from which a flag is flown.

flagrant (flay-grənt) adjective (said about an offence or wrongdoing) very bad and noticeable. **flagrancy** noun **flagrantly** adverb [from a Latin word *flagrans* meaning 'blazing']

flagship noun 1 a ship that carries an admiral and flies the admiral's flag. 2 the best or most important part of an organization.

flagstone noun a flat slab of stone used for paving. [from *flag*² and *stone*]

flail noun an old-fashioned tool for threshing grain, consisting of a strong stick hinged on a long handle.
flail verb 1 to wave or swing about wildly. 2 to beat or flog someone. [same origin as for *flagellate*]

flair noun a natural ability or talent. [a French word meaning 'power to smell things']
◊ Do not confuse this word with **flare**, which has a different meaning.

flak noun 1 shells fired by anti-aircraft guns. 2 strong criticism. [a shortening of a German word *Fliegerabwehrkanone* meaning 'aircraft-defence cannon']

flake noun 1 a small light flat piece of snow. 2 a small thin piece of something.
flake verb 1 to come off in flakes. 2 to separate something into flakes. **flaky** adjective [origin unknown]

flambé (flahm-bay) adjective (said about food) covered with spirit and set alight briefly before eating. [a French word meaning 'singed']

flamboyant adjective 1 highly coloured or showy. 2 (said about a person) having a showy appearance or manner.
flamboyance noun **flamboyantly** adverb [a French word meaning 'blazing']

flame noun 1 a tongue-shaped portion of fire or burning gas. 2 a bright red colour. 3 an intense feeling or passion.
flame verb 1 to burn with flames, to send out flames. 2 to become bright red. [from a Latin word *flamma*]

flame-thrower noun a weapon that shoots out a jet of flame.

flamenco (flə-menk-oh) noun a lively Spanish style of song, guitar playing, and dance. [a Spanish word meaning 'Flemish' and 'like a gypsy']

flaming adjective very hot or bright.

flamingo (flə-ming-goh) noun (flamingoes) a wading bird with long thin legs, a long neck, and pinkish feathers. [from a Spanish word *flamengo*, related to *flamenco*]

flammable adjective easily set on fire. **flammability** noun [from a Latin word *flamma* meaning 'flame']
◊ See the note at **inflammable**.

flan noun a dish consisting of an open pastry case filled with a sweet or a savoury filling. [from an Old French word *flaon*]

flange (flanj) noun a projecting rim or edge. [perhaps from an Old French word *flanchir* meaning 'to bend']

flank noun 1 the side of a person's or animal's body between the ribs and the hip. 2 the side of a building or mountain. 3 the right or left side of a body of people, especially of an army.
flank verb to be positioned at the side of something. [from an Old French word *flanc*]

flannel noun 1 a soft loosely woven woollen or cotton fabric. 2 a soft cloth used for washing yourself. 3 (*informal*) bland meaningless talk used to get over a difficulty.
flannel verb (**flannelled, flannelling**) (*informal*) to talk blandly and meaninglessly.
flannels plural noun trousers made of flannel or similar fabric. [from a Welsh word *gwlanen* meaning 'woollen']

flannelette noun cotton fabric made to look and feel like flannel.

flap verb (**flapped, flapping**) 1 to sway loosely up and down or from side to side, to wave about. SYNONYMS: flutter, wave. 2 to give a light blow with something flat. 3 (*informal*) to fuss or panic about something.
flap noun 1 the action or sound of flapping. 2 a light blow with something flat. 3 a flat or broad piece that is hinged or fixed to something else at one side. 4 a hinged or sliding section of an aircraft wing, used to control lift. 5 (*informal*) a state of fuss or panic ♦ *in a flap*. [an imitation of the sound]

flapjack noun 1 a cake made from oats and syrup. 2 (*North Amer.*) a pancake. [from *flap* in the meaning 'to toss a pancake' and the name *Jack*]

flare verb 1 to blaze with a sudden bright flame. 2 to become suddenly angry or violent ◆ *Tempers flared.* **3** to become gradually wider ◆ *flared trousers.*

flare *noun* **1** a sudden outburst of flame or light. **2** a device producing a bright flame or light, especially as a signal or marker. **3** a gradually widening shape. **to flare up 1** to burst into flame. **2** to become suddenly angry. [origin unknown]
◊ Do not confuse this word with **flair**, which has a different meaning.

flash *verb* **1** to give out a brief or intermittent bright light. SYNONYMS: sparkle, glimmer, twinkle, shine, blaze. **2** to be suddenly visible or thought about ◆ *An idea flashed through my mind.* **3** to move rapidly ◆ *Several cars flashed past.* SYNONYMS: dash, speed, race, streak, speed. **4** to make something shine briefly. **5** to signal with a light or lights. **6** to send news or information by radio or telegraph.
flash *noun* **1** a sudden burst of bright flame or light. **2** a sudden occurrence or appearance of something ◆ *a flash of inspiration.* **3** a very short time ◆ *in a flash.* **4** a rush of water. **5** a brief news item on radio or television. **6** a camera attachment that makes a sudden bright light for taking photographs in poor natural light. **7** a bright patch of colour, especially as an emblem on a uniform.
flash *adjective* (*informal*) flashy. **a flash in the pan** something that makes a promising start and then fails. [origin unknown]
◊ A *flash in the pan* was originally an explosion of gunpowder in the 'pan' of an old gun which failed to fire the charge in the barrel.

flashback *noun* a scene in a story or film that is set at an earlier time than the main part of the story.

flashbulb *noun* a bulb used for flash photography.

flasher *noun* **1** a device that flashes a light intermittently. **2** someone who exposes their genitals in public.

flash flood *noun* a sudden local flood caused by heavy rainfall.

flashing *noun* a strip of metal used to seal a joint where a roof meets another surface.

flashlight *noun* an electric torch with a powerful beam.

flashpoint *noun* **1** a time or place at which anger or violence is about to break out. **2** the temperature at which vapour from oil etc. will ignite.

flashy *adjective* (**flashier, flashiest**) showy or gaudy. **flashily** *adverb* **flashiness** *noun*

flask *noun* **1** a bottle with a narrow neck. **2** a vacuum flask. [via Old English from a Latin word *flasca*]

flat *adjective* (**flatter, flattest**) **1** having a level surface, without curves or bumps. SYNONYMS: even, level, smooth. **2** level, not sloping. **3** spread out; lying at full length ◆ *Lie flat on the ground.* **4** having a broad level surface and little depth ◆ *a flat cap.* **5** (said about a tyre) having lost all or most of its air. **6** absolute or unqualified ◆ *We were given a flat refusal.* SYNONYMS: absolute, definite, unqualified, categorical. **7** dull or monotonous. SYNONYMS: dull, boring, monotonous. **8** (said about a drink) having lost its effervescence, no longer fizzy. **9** (said about a battery) unable to produce any more electric current. **10** (*Music*) below the correct pitch ◆ *Our singing was flat.*
flat *adverb* **1** so as to be flat ◆ *Lay it down flat.* **2** (*informal*) completely ◆ *I am flat broke.* **3** exactly ◆ *in ten seconds flat.* **4** (*Music*) below the correct pitch ◆ *He was singing flat.*
flat *noun* **1** a flat thing or part, level ground. **2** a set of rooms on one floor, used for living in. **3** (*Music*) a note that is a semitone lower than the natural note; the sign ♭ indicating this. **to fall flat** to fail to win approval or appreciation. **flat out** at top speed; using all your strength or resources. **flatly** *adverb* **flatness** *noun* [from an Old Norse word *flatr*]

flatbed *noun* (*Computing*) a scanner or other device that keeps the page flat during use.

flatfish *noun* a type of fish with a flattened body, which swims on its side.

flat-footed *adjective* having feet with arches that are lower than normal.

flat iron *noun* an old type of iron heated on a hotplate or fire.

flat race *noun* a horse race over level ground, with no fences to jump over.

flat rate *noun* a rate that is the same in all cases, not proportional.

flatten *verb* to make something flat, or to become flat.

flatter *verb* **1** to praise someone more than they deserve, especially to win their favour. **2** to please someone with an honour ◆ *We were flattered to receive an invitation.* **3** to make a person or thing seem more attractive than they really are ◆ *She* *thought the photograph flattered her.* **flatterer** *noun* [from an Old French word *flater* meaning 'to smooth down']

flattery *noun* **1** the act of flattering. **2** excessive or insincere compliments.

flattish *adjective* rather flat.

flatulent (flat-yoo-lnt) *adjective* affected by gas building up in the digestive tract. **flatulence** *noun* **flatulency** *noun* [from a Latin word *flatus* meaning 'blowing']

flatworm *noun* a kind of worm with a flattened body.

flaunt *verb* to display something in a showy or over-enthusiastic way ♦ *He liked to flaunt his expensive clothes and cars.* [origin unknown]
◊ Do not confuse this word with **flout**, which has a different meaning.

flautist (flaw-tist) *noun* a flute player. [from an Italian word *flauto* meaning 'flute']

flavour *noun* **1** a distinctive taste. SYNONYMS: taste, tang. **2** a special quality or characteristic ♦ *The story has a romantic flavour.*
flavour *verb* to give something a flavour, to season something. [from an Old French word *flaor*]

flavouring *noun* something used to give a flavour to food or drink.

flaw *noun* something that makes a person or thing imperfect. SYNONYMS: fault, defect, weakness, blemish, failing, imperfection.
flaw *verb* to spoil something with a flaw. [from an earlier meaning 'fragment or splinter', perhaps from an Old Norse word *flaga* meaning 'slab']

flawless *adjective* without a flaw, perfect. **flawlessly** *adverb* **flawlessness** *noun*

flax *noun* **1** a blue-flowered plant that produces fibres from which linen is made and seeds from which linseed oil is obtained. **2** textile fibre made from this plant. [from an Old English word *flæx*]

flaxen *adjective* **1** made of flax. **2** (*literary*) pale yellow-like flax fibres ♦ *flaxen hair.*

flay *verb* **1** to strip the skin from an animal. **2** to whip or beat someone. **3** to criticize someone fiercely. [from an Old English word *flēan*]

flea *noun* a small jumping insect that feeds on human and animal blood. **with a flea in someone's ear** (*informal*) with a sharp rebuke. [from an Old English word *flēa*]

flea market *noun* a street market selling second-hand goods.

fleck *noun* **1** a very small patch of colour. **2** a particle or speck. **flecked** *adjective* [origin unknown]

fled past tense and past participle of **flee**.

fledged *adjective* (said about young birds) having grown wing feathers and able to fly. [from an obsolete adjective *fledge* meaning 'ready to fly', from an Old English word]

fledgling *noun* a young bird that has grown wing feathers and is newly able to fly.

flee *verb* (**flees, fled, fleeing**) **1** to run or hurry away. SYNONYMS: run away, escape, rush, fly, dash. **2** to run away from a place ♦ *The criminals fled the country.* **3** to pass away swiftly, to vanish ♦ *All hope had fled.* [from an Old English word *fleon*]

fleece *noun* **1** the woolly hair of a sheep or similar animal. **2** a soft fabric, or a piece of clothing made from this.
fleece *verb* (*informal*) to swindle someone or deprive them of something by trickery. **fleecy** *adjective* [from an Old English word]

fleet[1] *noun* **1** the warships of a country, or a number of warships under one commander. **2** a number of ships, aircraft, or vehicles owned by a company or moving together. [from an Old English word *fleot* meaning 'ships']

fleet[2] *adjective* moving swiftly, nimble. **fleetly** *adverb* **fleetness** *noun* [from an Old Norse word]

fleeting *adjective* passing quickly, brief ♦ *We caught a fleeting glimpse of the Queen's car.*

Flemish *adjective* to do with Flanders in Belgium or its people or language.
Flemish *noun* the Flemish language.

flesh *noun* **1** the soft substance of a human or animal body, consisting of muscle and fat. **2** the body as opposed to the mind or soul. **3** the pulpy part of fruits and vegetables. **in the flesh** in person. [from an Old English word]

flesh wound *noun* a wound that does not reach a bone or vital organ.

fleshy *adjective* (**fleshier, fleshiest**) **1** having a lot of flesh, plump. **2** (said about plants or fruits) having a lot of pulp. **3** like flesh. **fleshiness** *noun*

fleur-de-lis (fler-də-lee) *noun* (**fleurs-de-lis**) a design of three petals joined together at their base, used in heraldry. [a French word meaning 'flower of lily']

flew past tense of **fly**².

flex ¹ *verb* to bend or stretch a limb or muscle. [from a Latin word *flexum* meaning 'bent']

flex ² *noun* a flexible insulated electric wire or cable. [a shortening of *flexible*]

flexible *adjective* 1 easy to bend or stretch. SYNONYMS: bendable, supple, pliable, pliant, elastic, springy. 2 adaptable, able to be changed to suit circumstances ♦ *Our plans are flexible.* **flexibility** *noun* **flexibly** *adverb*

flexion *noun* the bending or bent state of a joint or limb.

flexitime *noun* a system allowing workers to vary their working hours.

flexor *noun* (*Anatomy*) a muscle that bends a part of the body.

flick *noun* a quick light blow or movement. **flick** *verb* to hit or move something with a quick light blow. **to flick through** to turn over cards or pages quickly. [from a Middle English word]

flicker *verb* 1 to burn or shine unsteadily. 2 (said about a feeling such as hope) to occur briefly. 3 to move quickly to and fro.
flicker *noun* 1 a flickering light or movement or light. 2 a brief occurrence of a positive feeling. [from an Old English word]

flick knife *noun* a knife with a blade that springs out when a button is pressed.

flier *noun* another spelling of **flyer**.

flies *plural noun* (*informal*) a zip or set of buttons used to fasten the front of a pair of trousers. [plural of *fly*² *noun*]

flight *noun* 1 the process of flying; the movement of something through the air. 2 a journey in an aircraft. 3 a flock of birds or insects. 4 a number of aircraft regarded as a unit ♦ *the Queen's flight.* 5 the action of fleeing or escaping. 6 a series of stairs between two floors or levels. 7 a series of hurdles in a race. 8 a free exercise of the mind or thought ♦ *a flight of fancy.* 9 the feathers or fins on a dart or arrow. **to put to flight** to force someone to flee. **to take flight** to run away or escape. [from an Old English word *flyht*]

flight deck *noun* the cockpit of a large aircraft.

flightless *adjective* (said about birds, e.g. penguins) not able to fly.

flight lieutenant *noun* an RAF officer below squadron leader in rank.

flight path *noun* the plotted course of an aircraft.

flight recorder *noun* an electronic device in an aircraft, which records technical information about its flight and is used as evidence in case of an accident.

flighty *adjective* (**flightier, flightiest**) silly and frivolous.

flimsy *adjective* (**flimsier, flimsiest**) 1 light and thin; fragile or loose in structure. SYNONYMS: rickety, shaky, wobbly, fragile. 2 weak or unconvincing ♦ *a flimsy excuse.* **flimsily** *adverb* **flimsiness** *noun* [origin unknown]

flinch *verb* 1 to move or shrink back in fear, to wince. SYNONYMS: wince, recoil, shrink back, cringe, cower. 2 to shrink from a duty or obligation. [from an Old French word *flenchir* meaning 'to turn aside']

fling *verb* (past tense and past participle **flung**) 1 to throw something with great force. SYNONYMS: throw, hurl, toss, sling; (*informal*) chuck. 2 to send someone somewhere suddenly or forcefully ♦ *They have flung him into prison.* 3 to rush angrily or impulsively ♦ *She flung out of the room.* **fling** *noun* 1 a lively dance ♦ *the Highland fling.* 2 a short time of enjoyment ♦ *a final fling before the exams.* [origin unknown]

flint *noun* 1 a very hard kind of stone. 2 a piece of flint or hard metal used to produce sparks. [from an Old English word]

flintlock *noun* an old type of gun fired by a spark from a flint.

flinty *adjective* (**flintier, flintiest**) like flint, very hard.

flip ¹ *verb* (**flipped, flipping**) 1 to turn over or turn something over, with a quick movement. 2 to toss something in the air so that it turns over. 3 (*informal*) to lose your temper.
flip *noun* the action or movement of flipping.
flip *adjective* glib or flippant. [origin unknown]

flippant *adjective* not showing proper seriousness. **flippantly** *adverb* **flippancy** *noun* [from *flip*]

flipper *noun* 1 a limb that some sea animals such as seals, turtles, and penguins use for swimming. 2 a flat rubber attachment worn on the feet for underwater swimming.

flirt *verb* 1 to behave as though you are sexually attracted to someone. 2 to play or experiment in your mind with an idea ♦ *He flirted with the idea of moving abroad.* 3 to risk danger ♦ *to flirt with death.* **flirt** *noun* a person who flirts. **flirtation** *noun* **flirtatious** *adjective* [from an earlier meaning 'to give someone a sharp blow']

flit *verb* (**flitted, flitting**) 1 to fly or move lightly and quickly. 2 to run away secretly.
flit *noun* (*informal*) an act of running away secretly. [from an Old Norse word]

flitch *noun* 1 a side of bacon. 2 a slab of wood cut from a tree trunk. [from an Old English word *flicce*]

float *verb* 1 to stay or move on the surface of a liquid or in the air. 2 to make something do this. 3 to move lightly or gently. 4 (in ball games) to make the ball move gently in the air so that another player can reach it. 5 to allow a currency to have a variable rate of exchange. 6 to put forward an idea to test people's reactions to it. 7 to launch a business by getting financial support from the sale of shares.
float *noun* 1 a device that is designed to float on liquid. 2 a cork or other floating object used on a fishing line to show when the bait has been taken. 3 a floating device used as part of a valve to control the flow of water or other liquid. 4 a structure on an aircraft that allows it to float on water. 5 a small electric vehicle or cart, especially one used for delivering milk. 6 a vehicle with a platform for carrying a display in a parade or carnival. 7 a small amount of money kept for minor expenses or for giving change in a shop. [from an Old English word]

floating voter *noun* a person who has not decided how to vote, or who does not consistently support one political party.

flock [1] *noun* 1 a number of birds that are flying or resting together. 2 a number of sheep or goats that are kept together. 3 a large number of people together. 4 a number of people in someone's charge, especially a Christian congregation.

flock *verb* to gather together or move in a group. [from an Old English word *flocc*]

flock [2] *noun* 1 wool or cotton waste used for stuffing cushions or quilts. 2 a tuft of wool or cotton. [from a Latin word *floccus*]

floe *noun* a sheet of floating ice. [from a Norwegian word *flo* meaning 'layer']

flog *verb* (**flogged, flogging**) 1 to beat a person or animal with a stick or whip as a punishment. 2 (*informal*) to sell something. **flogging** *noun* [from a Latin word *flagellare* meaning 'to whip']

flood *noun* 1 a large amount of water over a place that is usually dry. 2 a great amount of something demanding or unwelcome ♦ *We have had a flood of requests.* SYNONYMS: spate, torrent, deluge, stream. 3 the movement of the tide when it is coming in towards the land.
flood *verb* 1 to cover or fill with a flood, to overflow. 2 (said about a river etc.) to become flooded. 3 to come in large amounts ♦ *The letters started to flood in.* SYNONYMS: pour, surge, gush. [from an Old English word *flod*]

floodgate *noun* a gate that can be opened or closed to control the flow of water, especially the lower gate of a lock.

floodlight *noun* a lamp that gives a broad bright beam to light up a stage, stadium, or large building.
floodlight *verb* (past tense and past participle **floodlit**) to light up a place with floodlights.

flood plain *noun* the flat area beside a river that becomes covered by water when the river floods.

flood tide *noun* an incoming tide.

floor *noun* 1 the surface of a room on which people stand and walk. 2 a storey of a building, all the rooms on the same level ♦ *Her office is on the third floor.* 3 the bottom of the sea or of a cave. 4 (in legislative assemblies) the part of the assembly hall where members sit.
floor *verb* 1 to put a floor into a building. 2 (*informal*) to baffle someone. 3 (*informal*) to knock someone down in a fight. **to have the floor** to have the right to speak next in a debate. [from an Old English word]

floorboard *noun* one of the boards forming the floor of a room.

flop *verb* (**flopped, flopping**) 1 to hang or sway heavily and loosely. 2 to fall or sit

down clumsily. SYNONYMS: slump, drop, collapse. 3 (*informal*) to be a failure.
flop *noun* 1 a flopping movement or sound. 2 (*informal*) a failure or disappointment. [a different spelling of *flap*]

floppy *adjective* (**floppier, floppiest**) hanging loosely, not firm or rigid. **floppily** *adverb* **floppiness** *noun*

floppy disk *noun* a flexible removable magnetic disk for storing data for use in a computer.

flora *noun* the plants of a particular area or period of time. (Compare **fauna**.) [from the name of Flora, the ancient Roman goddess of flowers, from a Latin word *flores* meaning 'flowers']

floral *adjective* made of flowers or to do with flowers. [from a Latin word *flores* meaning 'flowers']

Florentine (flo-rǝn-tiyn) *adjective* to do with Florence in northern Italy.

florescence (flor-**ess**-ǝns) *noun* the time or state of flowering or flourishing. [from a Latin word *florescere* meaning 'to begin to flower']

floret (**flor**-it) *noun* (*Botany*) 1 one of the small flowers that make up a composite flower such as a daisy. 2 one of the flowering stems that make up the head of a cauliflower. [same origin as for *floral*]

floribunda (flor-i-**bun**-dǝ) *noun* a rose or other plant that bears dense clusters of flowers. [from a Latin word *floribundus* meaning 'freely flowering']

florid (**flo**-rid) *adjective* 1 (said about a person's complexion) red and flushed. 2 elaborate and ornate. [same origin as for *floral*]

florin (**flo**-rin) *noun* 1 a former British coin worth two shillings. 2 a Dutch guilder. [from an Italian word *fiore* meaning 'flower' (because the name was originally given to an Italian coin which had a lily on one side)]

florist (**flo**-rist) *noun* a person who sells cut flowers. [same origin as for *floral*]

floss *noun* 1 a mass of silky fibres. 2 silky thread or fibres, used in embroidery. 3 a soft medicated thread pulled between the teeth to clean them. **flossy** *adjective* [from an Old French word *flosche* meaning 'nap of velvet']

flotation *noun* 1 the process of offering shares in a company on the stock market

in order to launch it or finance it. 2 the process of floating something.

flotilla (flǝ-**til**-ǝ) *noun* a small fleet of ships or boats. [a Spanish word meaning 'little fleet']

flotsam *noun* wreckage or cargo found floating after a shipwreck. **flotsam and jetsam** odds and ends. [from a French word *floter* meaning 'to float']

flounce [1] *verb* to go in an impatient or annoyed manner ♦ *She flounced out of the room.*
flounce *noun* a flouncing movement. [origin unknown]

flounce [2] *noun* a wide frill of material sewn to a skirt or dress. [from an Old French word *fronce*]

flounder [1] *verb* 1 to move clumsily and with difficulty, especially in mud or water. SYNONYMS: lurch, stagger, fumble, blunder. 2 to make mistakes or become confused when trying to do something. [perhaps a combination of *founder* and *blunder*]

flounder [2] *noun* a small flatfish used for food. [from an Old French word *flondre*]

flour *noun* a fine powder made from wheat or other grain, used in cooking.
flour *verb* to cover or sprinkle something with flour. **floury** *adjective* [an old spelling of *flower*]

flourish *verb* 1 to grow or develop strongly. 2 to prosper or be successful. SYNONYMS: prosper, thrive, succeed. 3 (said about a famous person) to be alive and working at a certain time. 4 to wave something about dramatically.
flourish *noun* 1 a dramatic sweeping gesture. 2 a flowing ornamental curve in writing or drawing. 3 a musical fanfare. [from a Latin word *florere* meaning 'to flower']

flout *verb* to disobey a rule or instruction openly or defiantly. [probably from a Dutch word *fluiten* meaning 'to whistle' or 'to hiss']
◊ Do not confuse this word with **flaunt**, which has a different meaning.

flow *verb* 1 to move continuously and freely in a stream. SYNONYMS: glide, stream, run. 2 to move steadily and continuously ♦ *It was important to keep the traffic flowing.* 3 to hang loosely ♦ *flowing hair.* 4 (said about water or other liquid) to gush out. 5 (said about the tide) to come in towards the land. 6 to come from a source, to be the result of something ♦ *Several*

consequences flowed from their actions.
7 (*technical*) (said about a solid substance) to change shape under stress without melting.
flow *noun* **1** a flowing movement or mass. **2** a steady continuous stream of something ♦ *the flow of traffic.* SYNONYMS: stream, movement. **3** the movement of the tide towards the land. [from an Old English word]

flow chart *noun* a diagram showing the successive stages of a process.

flower *noun* **1** the part of a plant from which the seed or fruit develops. **2** a blossom and its stem for use for decoration, usually in groups. **3** (*literary*) the best part of something ♦ *a man in the flower of his strength.*
flower *verb* **1** (said about a plant) to produce flowers. **2** to reach a peak of development. **in flower** (said about a plant) with its flowers fully developed. **flowered** *adjective* [from an Old French word *flour*, related to *flora*]

flowerpot *noun* an earthenware pot for growing a plant in.

flowery *adjective* **1** full of flowers. **2** (said about language) elaborate or rhetorical.

flown past participle of **fly**².

flu *noun* influenza or a similar infection.

fluctuate *verb* to vary irregularly, to rise and fall ♦ *Prices have been fluctuating.* **fluctuation** *noun* [from a Latin word *fluctus* meaning 'a wave']

flue *noun* **1** a duct in a chimney for smoke and gases to escape. **2** a channel for conveying heat.

fluent (floo-ənt) *adjective* **1** skilful at speaking clearly and without hesitating, especially in a foreign language. **2** (said about language) used with ease and clarity. **fluently** *adverb* **fluency** *noun* [from a Latin word *fluens* meaning 'flowing']

fluff *noun* **1** a light soft substance. **2** (*informal*) a mistake, especially in speaking.
fluff *verb* (*informal*) to bungle something. **to fluff up** to make something softer and rounder by patting it. [from a dialect word *flue* meaning 'down' or 'nap']

fluffy *adjective* (**fluffier, fluffiest**) having a soft mass of fur or fibres. SYNONYMS: woolly, fleecy, downy, soft, feathery. **fluffiness** *noun*

fluid *noun* a substance that is able to flow freely, a liquid or gas.

fluid *adjective* **1** able to flow freely, not solid or rigid. **2** (said about a situation) likely to change. **fluidity** (floo-**id**-iti) *noun* [from a Latin word *fluere* meaning 'to flow']

fluid ounce *noun* a unit of capacity equal to one-twentieth of a pint (0.028 litre), or to one-sixteenth of a US pint (0.03 litre).

fluke¹ *noun* an unexpected or unlikely stroke of good luck. [origin unknown]

fluke² *noun* **1** a flatworm found as a parasite in sheep's liver. **2** a broad triangular flat piece at the end of each arm of an anchor. **3** one of the lobes of a whale's tail. **4** a kind of flatfish, especially the flounder. [from an Old English word *floc*]

flummox *verb* (*informal*) to baffle someone. [origin unknown]

flung past tense and past participle of **fling**.

fluoresce (floo-er-**ess**) *verb* to become fluorescent.

fluorescent (floo-er-**ess**-ənt) *adjective* producing light from radiation ♦ *a fluorescent lamp.* **fluorescence** *noun* [from *fluorspar*, a fluorescent mineral]

fluoridate (floo-er-i-dayt) *verb* to add traces of fluoride to a water supply to reduce tooth decay. **fluoridation** *noun*

fluoride *noun* **1** a compound of fluorine and one other element ♦ *calcium fluoride.* **2** a substance added to the water supply or to toothpaste to reduce tooth decay.

fluorine (floo-er-een) *noun* a chemical element (symbol F), a pale yellow corrosive gas. [same origin as for *fluorescent*]

flurry *noun* (**flurries**) **1** a sudden short rush of wind, rain, or snow. **2** a short period of activity or excitement. **3** a number of things arriving together.
flurry *verb* (**flurries, flurried, flurrying**) to swirl about. [from an old word *flurr* meaning 'to throw about']

flush¹ *verb* **1** to become red in the face because of a rush of blood to the skin. SYNONYMS: blush, colour, go red, redden. **2** to cause the face to redden in this way. **3** to fill someone with pride ♦ *They appeared flushed with success.* **4** to cleanse something, especially a lavatory, with a fast flow of water. **5** (said about water) to rush out in a flood. **6** to drive a bird or animal out of its cover.
flush *noun* **1** a reddening of the face, a

blush. **2** a fast flow of water. **3** a feeling of excitement ♦ *in the first flush of victory.* **4** a fresh growth of leaves or vegetation. **5** (in card games) a hand of cards of the same suit. [an imitation of the sound of rushing water]

flush² *adjective* **1** level with the surrounding surface ♦ *The door was flush with the wall.* **2** (*informal*) having plenty of money. [from an earlier meaning 'perfect']

fluster *verb* to make someone feel nervous and confused.
fluster *noun* a flustered state. [from an earlier meaning 'to make slightly drunk', perhaps from a Scandinavian language]

flute *noun* **1** a wind instrument consisting of a tube with holes stopped by fingers or keys and held horizontally across the mouth. **2** (*Architecture*) an ornamental groove.
flute *verb* **1** to speak in melodious tones. **2** to make ornamental grooves in a surface. [from an Old French word *flahute*]

fluting *noun* a series of ornamental grooves.

flutter *verb* **1** to flap the wings rapidly in flying or trying to fly. **2** to wave or flap quickly and irregularly. **3** (said about the heart) to beat feebly and irregularly.
flutter *noun* **1** a fluttering movement or beat. **2** a state of nervous excitement. **3** (*informal*) a small bet ♦ *to have a flutter.* **4** (*Electronics*) rapid variation in the pitch or loudness of recorded sound. [from an Old English word]

fluvial (floo-vi-ǝl) *adjective* to do with rivers, or found in rivers. [from a Latin word *fluvius* meaning 'river']

flux *noun* **1** constant change ♦ *in a state of flux.* **2** the process of flowing. **3** (*Medicine*) an abnormal flow of blood from the body. **4** (*Physics*) the amount of radiation affecting an area in a given time. [from a Latin word *fluxus* meaning 'flowing']

fly¹ *noun* (**flies**) **1** a small flying insect with two wings. **2** a natural or artificial fly used as bait in fishing. **a fly in the ointment** a small annoyance that spoils the enjoyment of something. [from an Old English word *flycge*]

fly² *verb* (**flies, flew, flown, flying**) **1** to move through the air by means of wings as a bird does. SYNONYMS: glide, soar. **2** to travel through the air or through space. **3** to travel in an aircraft. **4** to direct or

control the flight of an aircraft; to transport people or cargo in an aircraft. **5** to raise a flag so that it waves; (said about a flag) to wave in the air. SYNONYMS: wave, flap, flutter. **6** to make a kite rise into the air. **7** to go or move quickly, to rush along. **8** (said about time) to pass quickly. **9** to be scattered violently ♦ *Sparks flew in all directions.* **10** to become suddenly angry ♦ *flew into a rage.* **11** to flee from a place ♦ *The traitors had to fly the country.*
fly *noun* (**flies**) **1** the front opening of a pair of trousers, closed with a zip or buttons. **2** a flap at the entrance of a tent. **3** (*historical*) a light carriage drawn by one horse. **to fly at** to attack someone violently, either physically or with words. **to fly in the face of** to disregard what is expected of you. **to fly off the handle** (*informal*) to lose your temper suddenly. **to send flying** to knock a person or thing aside. **with flying colours** with great distinction. [from an Old English word *fleogan*]

fly³ *adjective* (**flyer, flyest**) (*informal*) clever and knowing. [origin unknown]

flyblown *adjective* (said about meat) contaminated by contact with flies and flies' eggs.

flycatcher *noun* a bird that catches insects in the air.

flyer *noun* **1** a person or thing that flies. **2** (*informal*) an animal or vehicle that moves very fast. **3** a small poster advertising an event.

fly half *noun* (in rugby) a stand-off half.

flying buttress *noun* a buttress built on a separate structure, usually forming an arch with the wall it supports.

flying doctor *noun* a doctor who visits patients by air, especially in the Australian outback.

flying fish *noun* a tropical fish with wing-like fins, able to rise into the air and glide for some distance.

flying fox *noun* a large fruit bat with a face resembling a fox.

flying officer *noun* an RAF officer next in rank below flight lieutenant.

flying picket *noun* a person or group of people who travel to picket a place during an industrial dispute.

flying saucer *noun* in fiction, a saucer-shaped spaceship seen in the sky.

flying squad *noun* a team of police officers organized so that they can move rapidly from place to place.

flyleaf *noun* (**flyleaves**) a blank leaf at the beginning or end of a book.

flyover *noun* a bridge that carries one road or railway over another.

fly-past *noun* a ceremonial flight of aircraft past a person or place.

flysheet *noun* a cover over a tent for extra protection against bad weather.

flyweight *noun* (in boxing) a weight (51 kg) below bantamweight.

flywheel *noun* a heavy wheel revolving on a shaft to regulate machinery or build up a reserve of power.

FM *abbreviation* (in radio broadcasting) frequency modulation.

Fm *abbreviation* (*Chemistry*) the symbol for fermium.

foal *noun* a young horse or related animal. **foal** *verb* to give birth to a foal. **in foal** (said about a mare) pregnant. [from an Old English word]

foam *noun* **1** a mass of tiny bubbles formed on a liquid, froth. **2** a liquid containing many small bubbles. **3** a lightweight spongy form of rubber or plastic. **foam** *verb* to form or produce foam. **foamy** *adjective* [from an Old English word]

fob¹ *noun* **1** a chain for a pocket watch. **2** an ornament attached to a watch chain. **3** a tab on a key ring. [probably from a Germanic language]

fob² *verb* (**fobbed, fobbing**) **to fob off** to make someone accept something they don't really want. [probably from a German word]

focal *adjective* to do with a focus.

fo'c's'le (fohk-səl) *noun* another spelling of **forecastle**.

focus (foh-kəs) *noun* (**focuses** or **foci**, (foh-siy)) **1** the point at which rays appear to meet or from which they appear to spread out. **2** (*Geometry*) one of several fixed points used in drawing an ellipse, parabola, or other curve. **3** the point or distance from the eye or a lens at which an object is most clearly seen. **4** an adjustment on a lens for producing a clear image at different distances. **5** something that is an object of activity or attention.

focus *verb* (**focuses, focused, focusing**) **1** to adjust the focus of the eye or of a lens, camera, telescope, etc. **2** to concentrate or direct attention on something. [a Latin word meaning 'hearth', as the central point of a household]

focus group *noun* a group of people appointed to devise a strategy for marketing a new product, launching a political campaign, etc.

fodder *noun* food for horses and farm animals. [from an Old English word]

foe *noun* (*literary*) an enemy. [from an Old English word]

foetid (fee-tid) *adjective* another spelling of **fetid**.

foetus (fee-təs) *noun* another spelling of **fetus**.

fog *noun* **1** thick mist that is difficult to see through. **2** (in photography) cloudiness on a negative, obscuring the image. **3** a state of confusion or ignorance. **fog** *verb* (**fogged, fogging**) **1** to cover a surface with fog or condensed vapour, or to become covered in this way. **2** to cause cloudiness on a negative. **3** to bewilder or perplex someone. [origin unknown]

fogey *noun* (**fogeys**) a person with old-fashioned ideas ♦ *an old fogey*. [origin unknown]

foggy *adjective* (**foggier, foggiest**) **1** full of fog. **2** made opaque by condensed vapour, clouded. **3** obscure or vague ♦ *a foggy idea*. **fogginess** *noun*

foghorn *noun* a device that makes a deep booming sound as a warning to ships in fog.

foglamp *noun* a lamp for use in fog.

fogy *noun* (**fogies**) another spelling of **fogey**.

foible (foi-bəl) *noun* a minor peculiarity in a person's character. [from an Old French word, related to *feeble*]

foil¹ *noun* **1** metal hammered or rolled into a thin sheet ♦ *tin foil*. **2** a person or thing that makes another look better in contrast. [same origin as for *foliage*]

foil² *verb* to prevent someone or something from succeeding. SYNONYMS: thwart, frustrate, check, stop, prevent. [from an Old French word *fouler* meaning 'to trample']

foil[3] *noun* a long narrow sword with a button on the point, used in fencing. [origin unknown]

foist *verb* to make someone accept something inferior or unwelcome ♦ *They foisted the job on us.* [from an earlier meaning 'to use a loaded dice']

fold[1] *verb* 1 to bend or turn something so that one part lies on another. 2 to close or flatten something by pressing its parts together. 3 to become folded, or be able to be folded. 4 to embrace someone affectionately in the arms. 5 in cooking, to blend an ingredient by spooning one part over another. 6 (*informal*) (said about a business or undertaking) to collapse or fail.
fold *noun* 1 a line where something has been folded. 2 a folded part, a hollow between two thicknesses. 3 (*Geology*) a curvature of strata in the earth's crust. 4 a slight hollow among hills or mountains. **to fold your arms** to place your arms together and cross them across your chest. [from an Old English word *fealdan*]

fold[2] *noun* 1 an enclosure for sheep. 2 a community of people with the same beliefs or aims, especially the members of a Church. [from an Old English word *fald*]

folder *noun* 1 a folding cover for loose papers. 2 (*Computing*) a directory containing a set of files.

foliaceous (foh-li-**ay**-shəs) *adjective* of or like a leaf or leaves. [same origin as for *foliage*]

foliage (**foh**-li-ij) *noun* the leaves of a tree or plant. [from a Latin word *folium* meaning 'leaf']

foliate (**foh**-li-ət) *adjective* decorated with leaves or leaf-like designs.

foliated (**foh**-li-ayt-id) *adjective* (*Geology*) consisting of thin layers. **foliation** *noun*

folic acid (**foh**-lik) *noun* a vitamin of the B-group, found especially in green vegetables. [same origin as for *foliage*]

folio (**foh**-li-oh) *noun* (**folios**) 1 a large sheet of paper folded once to form two leaves (four pages) of a book. 2 a book made of these sheets. 3 the page number of a printed book. [same origin as for *foliage*]

folk *plural noun* 1 people in general. 2 the people of a certain country or place ♦ *country folk.*

folks *plural noun* a person's family or relatives. [from an Old English word *folc*]

folk dance *noun* a dance in the traditional style of a country.

folklore *noun* the traditional beliefs and tales of a community. **folklorist** *noun*

folk song *noun* a song in the traditional style of a country.

folksy *adjective* (**folksier, folksiest**) simple in style, especially in an affected or pretentious way.

follicle (**fol**-i-kəl) *noun* a small sac or cavity in the body, especially one containing the root of a hair. [from a Latin word *folliculus* meaning 'a little bellows']

follow *verb* 1 to go or come after someone or something. 2 to go after someone to watch them or check on them. SYNONYMS: go after, chase, pursue. 3 to go along a particular route ♦ *You follow the path all the way to the river.* 4 to succeed someone in a job or position ♦ *James I followed Elizabeth in 1603.* 5 to provide a sequel or continuation to something ♦ *The performers followed their act with a few jokes.* 6 to take someone or something as a guide or model ♦ *Try to follow your sister's example.* 7 to understand something or grasp its meaning ♦ *I didn't follow what he was saying.* 8 to take an interest in an activity, or to support a sports team etc. 9 to happen as a result of something. 10 to be necessarily true because of something else. **to follow on** (said about a side in cricket) to have to bat again immediately after the first innings. **to follow up** to do further work or take further action about something already started. [from an Old English word *folgian*]

follower *noun* 1 a person who supports or believes in a person or cause. 2 someone who follows.

following *noun* a body of believers or supporters ♦ *The local team has a large following.*
following *adjective* about to be mentioned ♦ *Answer the following questions.*
following *preposition* after or as a result of ♦ *Following the bomb attack, new security measures have been introduced.*

folly *noun* (**follies**) 1 foolishness, or a foolish act. 2 an ornamental building with no practical purpose, especially one in a park or large garden. [from a French word *folie* meaning 'madness']

foment (fə-**ment**) *verb* to arouse or stimulate trouble or discontent. **fomentation** *noun* [from a Latin word *fomentum* meaning 'poultice']
◊ Do not confuse this word with **ferment**, which has a different meaning.

fond *adjective* **1** loving or affectionate ♦ *We have fond memories of your visit.* SYNONYMS: loving, affectionate, tender. **2** (said about hopes) foolishly optimistic. **fond of** having a liking for someone or something. **fondly** *adverb* **fondness** *noun* [from an old word *fon* meaning 'a fool']

fondant *noun* a thick paste made with water and flavoured sugar, or a sweet made from this. [a French word meaning 'melting']

fondle *verb* to touch or stroke someone or something lovingly. SYNONYMS: caress, stroke. [from *fond*]

fondue (fon-**dew**) *noun* a dish of flavoured melted cheese. [a French word meaning 'melted']

font *noun* **1** a basin (often of carved stone) in a church, to hold water for baptism. **2** (in printing) a set of characters of a particular style of type. [from a Latin word *fontis* meaning 'of a fountain']

food *noun* any substance that an animal eats or drinks, or that a plant absorbs, to maintain its life and growth. [from an Old English word]

food chain *noun* a series of plants and animals each of which serves as food for the next.

food poisoning *noun* illness caused by bacteria or other toxins in food.

food processor *noun* an electrical device with blades for cutting or mixing food.

foodstuff *noun* something that can be used as food.

fool *noun* **1** a person who acts unwisely or lacks good sense and judgement. SYNONYMS: idiot, clot. **2** a jester or clown in the Middle Ages. **3** a creamy pudding made from fruit purée mixed with cream or custard.
fool *verb* **1** to behave in a joking way, to play about. **2** to trick or deceive someone. SYNONYMS: trick, deceive, take in. **to fool about** or **around** to behave in a joking way, to play about. [via Old French from a Latin word *follis* meaning 'bellows']

foolhardy *adjective* bold but rash or foolish; reckless. **foolhardiness** *noun* [from Old French words *fol* meaning 'fool' and *hardi* meaning 'bold']

foolish *adjective* without good sense or judgement, unwise. SYNONYMS: unwise, stupid, silly, senseless, crazy. **foolishly** *adverb* **foolishness** *noun*

foolproof *adjective* easy to understand or do.

foolscap *noun* a large size of paper. [said to be named after a watermark which showed a *fool's cap*, a jester's cap with bells]

fool's paradise *noun* a state of happiness maintained by ignoring realities.

foot *noun* (**feet**) **1** the lower part of the leg below the ankle, on which a person or animal stands and moves. **2** the lower end of a bed or table, opposite the head. **3** the part of a sock or stocking covering the foot. **4** a person's step or pace of movement ♦ *fleet of foot.* **5** the lowest supporting part of the leg of a table or other piece of furniture. **6** the part of a sewing machine that is lowered on to the material to hold it steady. **7** the lowest part of something that has height or length, especially the bottom of a hill, ladder, or page. **8** a measure of length, equal to 12 inches (30.48 cm). **9** a unit of rhythm in a line of poetry, usually containing a stressed syllable, e.g. each of the four divisions in ♦ *Jack/and Jill/went up/the hill.*
foot *verb* (*informal*) to meet the cost of something ♦ *In the end we had to foot the bill ourselves.* **by foot** or **on foot** walking rather than using a car or transport. **to have feet of clay** (said about something or someone usually honoured) to have a major weakness or failing. **to have one foot in the grave** to be very old or ill. **under foot** on the ground, in a position to be trodden on. **under your feet** in the way, in danger of being trodden on. [from an Old English word]

footage *noun* **1** an amount of cinema or television film. **2** a length of something measured in feet.

foot-and-mouth disease *noun* a contagious virus disease affecting cattle and sheep, causing ulcers on the hooves and around the mouth.

football *noun* **1** a ball game played by two teams who try to get the ball into their opponents' net. **2** a large inflated leather

or plastic ball used in this game.
footballer noun

football pools plural noun a form of gambling on the results of a number of football matches.

footbrake noun a brake in a motor vehicle, operated by the driver's foot.

footbridge noun a bridge for pedestrians.

footfall noun the sound of a footstep.

foothill noun one of the low hills near the bottom of a mountain or range of mountains.

foothold noun 1 a place wide enough to put a foot when climbing. 2 a secure position from which further progress can be made.

footing noun 1 a secure placing of the feet, a foothold ♦ He lost his footing and fell. 2 a status, conditions ♦ The talks were kept on a friendly footing.

footlights plural noun a row of lights along the front of a stage at floor level.

footling (foo-tling) adjective trivial.

footloose adjective independent, not having any responsibilities.

footman noun (footmen) a male servant who opens the door to visitors, serves at table, etc. [from an earlier meaning, a servant who accompanied his master on foot]

footmark noun a footprint.

footnote noun a note printed at the bottom of a page of a book.

footpath noun a path for pedestrians.

footplate noun a platform for the driver and crew of a railway locomotive.

footprint noun a mark left by a foot or shoe.

footslog verb (footslogged, footslogging) (informal) to walk hard over a long distance.

footsore adjective having feet that are sore from walking.

footstep noun a step taken in walking, or the sound of this. **to follow in someone's footsteps** to do what someone else did before.

footstool noun a stool for resting the feet on when sitting.

footwear noun shoes, boots, and other coverings for the feet.

footwork noun the manner of moving or using the feet in dancing or sport.

fop noun a man who is preoccupied with his own appearance. **foppery** noun **foppish** adjective [from an earlier meaning 'a fool']

for preposition 1 with regard to ♦ We're ready for anything. 2 as an objective or intention ♦ After lunch she went for a walk ♦ Are you still looking for a job? 3 in the direction of ♦ After that we set out for home. 4 intended to be given to ♦ a cage for the hamster. 5 in place of ♦ I need to change a five-pound note for pound coins. 6 so as to happen at a stated time ♦ I have an appointment for two o'clock. 7 because of, on account of ♦ The region is famous for its wine production. 8 to the extent or duration of ♦ The old man walked for several miles ♦ It will last for years. 9 as the price or penalty of ♦ She had been fined for speeding. 10 in defence or support of ♦ The solicitor was acting for three clients. **for** conjunction because ♦ They hesitated, for they were afraid. **to be for it** (informal) to be about to get into trouble or be punished. [from an Old English word]

for- prefix 1 away or off (as in forgive). 2 prohibiting (as in forbid). 3 neglecting or going without (as in forgo, forsake). [from an Old English word]

forage (for-ij) verb to go searching for something, especially food or fuel. **forage** noun 1 food for horses and cattle. 2 the act of foraging. **forager** noun [from an Old French word, related to fodder]

foramen (fŏ-ray-men) noun (foramina (fŏ-ram-i-nǎ)) (Anatomy) an opening or hole in a part of the body of an animal, especially in a bone. [a Latin word, from forare meaning 'to bore a hole']

foray (fo-ray) noun a sudden attack or raid. [from an Old French word, related to forage]

forbade past tense of forbid.

forbear verb (forbore, forborne) to refrain from doing something ♦ We forbore to mention it. [from an Old English word forberan]

forbearance noun patience or tolerance.

forbearing adjective & noun patient or tolerant.

forbid verb (forbade (for-bad), forbidden, forbidding) 1 to order someone not to do something ♦ I forbid you to go ♦ His mother forbade him from saying any more. 2 to refuse to allow something ♦ They can hardly forbid the marriage. SYNONYMS: prohibit, ban, bar, disallow. [from an Old English word]

forbidding *adjective* looking unfriendly or threatening.

forbore past tense of **forbear**.

forborne past participle of **forbear**.

force *noun* **1** physical strength or power. SYNONYMS: strength, power, energy, might, vigour. **2** (*Physics*) a measurable influence that causes movement of a body, or the intensity of this influence. **3** strong influence or coercion, especially when supported by the threat of physical action. **4** an organized body of soldiers, police, or workers. **5** effectiveness or validity ♦ *The new law has little force.* **force** *verb* **1** to use force in order to get or do something, or to make someone obey. SYNONYMS: compel, make, oblige, drive. **2** to break something open by using force ♦ *The intruder had forced the lock.* **3** to strain something to the utmost or too hard. **4** to impose or inflict something on someone. **5** to cause or produce something by effort ♦ *Despite her suffering she forced a smile.* **6** to cause plants to grow or bloom earlier than is normal. **to come into force** to become effective or legally valid. **to force someone's hand** to compel someone to take action. **to force the issue** to make it necessary to reach an immediate decision. **in force 1** legally valid. **2** in great strength or numbers. [from a Latin word *fortis* meaning 'strong']

forced landing *noun* an emergency landing of an aircraft.

forced march *noun* a fast march by troops over a long distance.

force-feed *verb* (past tense and past participle **force-fed**) to feed someone by force and against their will.

forceful *adjective* powerful and vigorous. **forcefully** *adverb* **forcefulness** *noun*

forcemeat *noun* finely chopped meat seasoned and used as stuffing. [from an obsolete word *force* meaning 'to stuff']

forceps (for-seps) *noun* (**forceps**) pincers or tongs used by dentists, surgeons, etc. [a Latin word meaning 'tongs']

forcible *adjective* done by force, forceful. **forcibly** *adverb*

ford *noun* a shallow place where a river can be crossed in a vehicle or on foot. **ford** *verb* to cross a river at a ford. **fordable** *adjective* [an Old English word]

fore *adjective* positioned at or towards the front.

fore *noun* the front or forward part of something.
fore *interjection* a cry warning a person in danger of being hit by a golf ball. [from an Old English word]

fore- *prefix* **1** before (as in ♦ *forecast*). **2** in front (as in ♦ *foreleg*).

fore and aft *adjective* (said about a ship's sails) set along the length of the boat (as opposed to *square-rigged*).

forearm [1] *noun* the arm from the elbow to the wrist or fingertips.

forearm [2] *verb* to arm or prepare someone in advance against a possible danger or attack.

forebears *plural noun* your ancestors. [from *fore-* and *beer* (from *be*) meaning 'someone who exists']

forebode *verb* (*literary*) to be an advance sign or token of trouble or difficulty. [from *fore-* and *bode*]

foreboding *noun* a feeling that trouble is coming.

forecast *verb* (past tense and past participle **forecast** or **forecasted**) to tell in advance what is likely to happen. SYNONYMS: predict, foretell, foresee. **forecast** *noun* a prediction about something likely to happen. [from *fore-* and *cast*]

forecastle (fohk-səl) *noun* the forward part of a ship below deck, where formerly the crew had their living quarters. [from *fore-* and *castle* (because originally this part was raised up like a castle to give command of the deck)]

foreclose *verb* (said about a bank or building society) to take possession of a property when the mortgage on it is not being repaid. **foreclosure** *noun* [from an earlier meaning 'to prevent from escaping']

forecourt *noun* an open area in front of a large building or petrol station.

forefathers *plural noun* your ancestors.

forefinger *noun* the finger next to the thumb.

forefoot *noun* (**forefeet**) an animal's front foot.

forefront *noun* the leading place or position ♦ *at the forefront of medical research.*

foregather *verb* (*formal*) to gather together, to assemble.

foregoing *adjective* preceding, previously mentioned.
◊ Note that this word is spelt *fore-* (with an e). Do not confuse it with **forgo**, which has a different meaning.

foregone conclusion *noun* a result that is predictable or bound to happen.

foreground *noun* 1 the part of a scene or picture that is nearest to an observer. 2 the most prominent position.

forehand *noun* a stroke in tennis and similar games played with the palm of the hand turned forwards. **forehanded** *adjective*

forehead (fo-rid or for-hed) *noun* the part of the face above the eyes.

foreign *adjective* 1 belonging to or coming from another country. 2 dealing with or involving other countries ♦ *foreign affairs.* 3 not belonging naturally to a place or to someone's character ♦ *Jealousy is foreign to her nature.* 4 coming from outside ♦ *a foreign body.* [from a Latin word *foris* meaning 'outside, abroad']

foreigner *noun* a person from another country.

Foreign Legion *noun* a part of the French army recruited from non-French people and originally established to fight France's colonial wars.

Foreign Secretary *noun* the British government minister in charge of the Foreign and Commonwealth Office, the department dealing with foreign affairs.

foreknowledge *noun* knowledge of something before it occurs.

foreland *noun* a cape or promontory.

foreleg *noun* an animal's front leg.

forelock *noun* a lock of hair growing just above the forehead.

foreman *noun* (**foremen**) 1 a worker who supervises a group of other workers. 2 a member of a jury who is in charge of its discussions and speaks on its behalf.

foremost *adjective* 1 most advanced in position or rank. 2 most important. **foremost** *adverb* in the front or most important position.

forename *noun* a person's first name.

forensic (fer-en-sik) *adjective* 1 to do with or used in lawcourts. 2 involving medical knowledge or science needed in legal matters or police investigations.

forensically *adverb* [from a Latin word *forum*, a place where courts of law were held]

forerunner *noun* a person or thing that comes before another and prepares the way.

foresee *verb* (**foresees, foresaw, foreseen, foreseeing**) to be aware of or realize something before it happens. SYNONYMS: predict, foretell, forecast.

foreseeable *adjective* able to be foreseen.

foreshadow *verb* to be a sign of something that is likely to happen.

foreshore *noun* the part of a shore between high-water and low-water marks, or between water and land that is cultivated or built on.

foreshorten *verb* 1 (in drawing) to represent an object with reduced depth or size, to give an effect of distance. 2 to shorten or reduce something in time or scale.

foresight *noun* 1 the ability to foresee and prepare for future needs. 2 the front sight of a gun.

foreskin *noun* the fold of skin covering the end of the penis.

forest *noun* trees and undergrowth covering a large area. **forested** *adjective* [from a Latin word *forestis* meaning 'outside']

forestall *verb* to prevent or foil a person or their plans by taking action first. [from an Old English word *foresteall* meaning 'to ambush']

forester *noun* a person who is in charge of a forest or expert in forestry.

forestry *noun* the science or practice of planting and managing forests.

foretaste *noun* an advance experience of something that is to come.

foretell *verb* (past tense and past participle **foretold**) to forecast or predict something.

forethought *noun* careful thought and planning for the future.

forever *adverb* 1 (also **for ever**) for all time, or for a long time. 2 continually or constantly ♦ *They are forever arguing.*

forewarn *verb* to warn someone about something so they can take action about it.

forewoman *noun* (**forewomen**) 1 a woman

who supervises a group of other workers. **2** a woman member of a jury who is in charge of its discussions and speaks on its behalf.

foreword noun a short introduction at the beginning of a book, often by a writer other than the author.

forfeit (for-fit) verb to have to pay something or give it up as a penalty. SYNONYMS: give up, concede, lose.
forfeit noun something that has to be paid or given up as a penalty.
forfeit adjective paid or given up as a penalty ♦ Their house and lands were forfeit to the king. **forfeiture** noun [from an Old French word forfaire meaning 'to transgress']

forgather verb another spelling of **foregather**.

forgave past tense of **forgive**.

forge¹ verb **to forge ahead** to move forward or make progress steadily. [probably a different spelling of force]

forge² noun **1** a workshop where metals are heated and shaped, especially a blacksmith's workshop. **2** a furnace or hearth for melting or refining metal.
forge verb **1** to shape metal by heating it in a fire and hammering it. **2** to make a copy or imitation of a document or banknote in order to use it fraudulently. **forger** noun [from an Old French word]

forgery noun (**forgeries**) **1** the act of forging a document or banknote. **2** a copy made by forging. SYNONYMS: fake, sham.

forget verb (**forgot, forgotten, forgetting**) **1** to fail to remember a fact, duty, commitment, etc. **2** to stop thinking about something. **to forget yourself** to behave thoughtlessly or badly. [from an Old English word]

forgetful adjective tending to forget things. **forgetfully** adverb **forgetfulness** noun

forget-me-not noun a plant with small blue flowers. [so called because in the Middle Ages the flower was worn by lovers]

forgive verb (**forgave, forgiven**) to stop feeling angry with someone for something they have done. SYNONYMS: pardon, absolve, excuse. **forgiveness** noun [from an Old English word]

forgiving adjective willing to forgive.

forgo verb (**forgoes, forwent, forgone,**

forgoing) to give something up or go without it. SYNONYMS: relinquish, give up, go without.
◊ See the note at **foregoing**.

forgot past tense of **forget**.

forgotten past participle of **forget**.

fork noun **1** a small device with prongs, used for lifting or holding food. **2** a large device with prongs, used for digging or lifting things. **3** something shaped like a fork. **4** a place where something separates into two or more parts ♦ a fork in the road. **fork** verb **1** to lift or dig something with a fork. **2** (said about an object or road) to form a fork by separating into two branches. **3** to follow one of the branches in a road or path ♦ Fork left. **to fork out** (informal) to have to pay out money. [from an Old English word forca]

forklift truck noun a truck with two metal bars pointing forward at the front, for lifting and moving heavy loads.

forlorn adjective left alone and unhappy. **forlornly** adverb [from for- and an old word lorn meaning 'lost']

form noun **1** the shape, appearance, or structure of something. SYNONYMS: outline, shape, figure, structure, appearance. **2** a person or animal as it can be seen or touched. **3** the way in which something exists ♦ Ice is a form of water. SYNONYMS: type, kind, sort, variety. **4** a document with blank spaces for writing in information. **5** a class in a school. **6** a customary or fixed method of doing something. **7** a set order of words in a prayer or ritual. **8** the condition of health and training of a person or animal, especially a competitor in a race or contest ♦ in good form. **9** a bench. **10** a wooden framework for holding concrete in shape while it is setting.
form verb **1** to shape or construct something. SYNONYMS: make, create, fashion, shape, mould. **2** to bring something into existence ♦ We formed a committee. **3** to be the material of something. SYNONYMS: make up, constitute. **4** to come into existence; to take shape or become solid ♦ It was so cold that icicles formed. SYNONYMS: develop, grow, appear, take shape. **5** to develop an idea or concept in the mind ♦ The boys formed a plan. **6** to arrange things in a certain way ♦ They formed the bricks into a large cube. [from a Latin word forma meaning 'a mould']

formal adjective **1** strictly following the

accepted rules or custom ♦ *formal dress*.
SYNONYMS: official, traditional. **2** following a
set structure or form ♦ *a formal education*.
SYNONYMS: regular, proper, standard.
3 outward or superficial ♦ *There was only a
formal resemblance*. **formally** *adverb* [from a
Latin word *formalis* meaning 'having a set
form']

formaldehyde (for-mal-di-hiyd) *noun*
(*Chemistry*) a colourless gas used in
solution as a preservative and
disinfectant. [from *formic* (acid) and
aldehyde]

formalin *noun* a solution of formaldehyde
in water.

formality (for-mal-iti) *noun* (**formalities**)
1 strict observance of rules and
conventions. **2** something done to obey a
law or custom.

formalize *verb* to make something formal
or official. **formalization** *noun*

format (for-mat) *noun* **1** the shape and size
of something, e.g. a book. **2** the way in
which something is organized or
presented. **3** (*Computing*) the way in which
data is organized for processing or storage
by a computer.
format *verb* (**formatted, formatting**)
(*Computing*) to organize data in the correct
format. [from a Latin word *formatus*
meaning 'formed or shaped']

formation *noun* **1** the process of forming
something. **2** something that has been
formed in a particular way ♦ *a rock
formation*. **3** a particular arrangement or
order of things ♦ *flying in formation*. [from
a Latin word *formare* meaning 'to mould']

formative (form-ətiv) *adjective* forming or
developing something.

former *adjective* belonging to an earlier
time ♦ *She is a former club president*. **the
former** the first of two people or things
mentioned. [from an Old English word,
related to *fore*]
◊ When you are referring to the first of
three or more people or things, use *the
first*, not *the former*.

formerly *adverb* at an earlier time.

Formica (for-miy-kə) *noun* (*trademark*) a
hard heat-resistant plastic used for
worktops and other surfaces. [origin
unknown]

formic acid *noun* (*Chemistry*) a colourless
acid contained in fluid emitted by ants.
[from a Latin word *formica* meaning 'ant']

formidable (for-mid-əbəl) *adjective*
1 difficult to do or overcome ♦ *a formidable
challenge*. **2** inspiring fear or awe ♦ *a
formidable woman*. **formidably** *adverb* [from
a Latin word *formido* meaning 'fear']

formless *adjective* not having any distinct
or regular form.

formula *noun* (**formulas** or **formulae**
(for-mew-lee) **1** a set of chemical symbols
showing what a substance is made of.
2 (*Mathematics*) a rule or statement
expressed in symbols or numbers. **3** a
fixed form of words, especially one used
on social or ceremonial occasions. **4** a list
of ingredients needed for making
something. **5** one of the groups by which
racing cars are classified, according to
their engine size. [a Latin word meaning
'little form']

formulate *verb* **1** to express an idea clearly
and exactly. **2** to express something in a
formula. **formulation** *noun* [from *formula*]

fornicate (for-ni-kayt) *verb* (*formal*) to have
sexual intercourse with someone you
are not married to. **fornication** *noun* [from
a Latin word *fornicis* meaning 'of a
brothel']

forsake *verb* (**forsook, forsaken**) (*literary*)
1 to give up or renounce something ♦ *They
were determined to forsake their former way of
life*. **2** to abandon someone ♦ *He forsook his
wife and children and travelled the world*.
SYNONYMS: abandon, desert, leave. [from an
Old English word]

forswear *verb* (**forswore, forsworn**) (*formal*)
to give up doing or using something, to
renounce something.

forsythia (for-siyth-iə) *noun* a shrub with
yellow flowers, blooming in spring.
[named after the botanist William
Forsyth (1737–1804), who is said to have
introduced the shrub into England from
China]

fort *noun* a fortified building or position.
[from a Latin word *fortis* meaning 'strong']

forte [1] (for-ti) *noun* a person's strong point.
[from French *fort* meaning 'strong']

forte [2] (for-ti) *adverb* (*Music*) to be played
loudly. [an Italian word meaning 'loud']

forth *adverb* (*old use, except in the idioms*)
1 out or into view ♦ *The travellers ventured
forth into the snow*. **2** onwards or forwards
♦ *from this day forth*. **and so forth** and so
on. **back and forth** to and fro. [from an
Old English word]

forthcoming *adjective* 1 about to happen or appear ◆ *forthcoming events.* 2 available when needed ◆ *The money was still not forthcoming.* 3 (said about a person) willing to talk or give information.

forthright *adjective* frank or outspoken.

forthwith *adverb* immediately.

fortieth see **forty**.

fortification *noun* 1 a wall or building constructed to make a place strong against attack. 2 the process of fortifying a place.

fortify *verb* (**fortifies, fortified, fortifying**) 1 to strengthen a place against attack by building strong walls and other defensive works. 2 to strengthen a person mentally or morally; to increase a person's vigour. 3 to increase the nutritional value of food by adding vitamins. 4 to strengthen wine with alcohol. [same origin as for *fort*]

fortissimo *adverb* (*Music*) to be played very loudly.

fortitude *noun* courage in bearing pain or trouble. [from a Latin word *fortis* meaning 'strong']

fortnight *noun* a period of two weeks. [from an old word meaning 'fourteen nights']

fortnightly *adverb & adjective* happening or appearing once a fortnight.

Fortran *noun* a high-level computer language used in scientific work. [from the first letters of *Formula Translation*]

fortress *noun* a fortified building or town. [from a French word *forteresse* meaning 'strong place']

fortuitous (for-tew-it-əs) *adjective* happening by chance, accidental. **fortuitously** *adverb* [from a Latin word *forte* meaning 'accidentally']
◊ Note that this word does not mean the same as *fortunate*.

fortunate *adjective* having or caused by good fortune. SYNONYMS: lucky, blessed. **fortunately** *adverb* [same origin as for *fortune*]

fortune *noun* 1 chance as a power affecting human affairs. 2 the events that chance brings to a person or undertaking. SYNONYMS: luck, chance, fate. 3 a person's destiny. 4 prosperity or success ◆ *He went abroad to seek his fortune.* 5 a very large amount of wealth ◆ *Her uncle had left her a fortune.* **to tell someone's fortune** to

predict what will happen to someone. [from a Latin word *fortuna* meaning 'luck']

fortune-teller *noun* a person who claims to predict future events in people's lives.

forty *adjective & noun* (**forties**) the number 40, equal to four times ten.
forties *plural noun* the numbers from 40 to 49, especially representing years of age or degrees of temperature. **fortieth** *adjective & noun* [from an Old English word]

forum *noun* 1 (**fora**) the public square in an ancient Roman city. 2 (**forums**) a meeting where a public discussion is held. [a Latin word meaning literally 'out of doors']

forward *adjective* 1 directed or moving towards the front; situated in the front. 2 having made more than normal progress. 3 too assertive or eager. SYNONYMS: bold, brazen, presumptuous, precocious. 4 ahead in time ◆ *forward buying.* **forward** *adverb* forwards or ahead; towards the future.
◊ The adverb *forward* is mainly used in American English. *Forwards* is the usual adverb in British English, but *forward* is used in the expressions *come forward, look forward to,* and *put forward.*
forward *noun* (in football or hockey) an attacking player in the front line of a team.
forward *verb* 1 to send on a letter or package to another address. 2 to send or dispatch (goods) to a customer. 3 to help someone to make progress. **forwardness** *noun* [from an Old English word]

forwards *adverb* 1 to or towards the front. 2 in the direction you are facing.

forwent past tense of **forgo**.

fossil *noun* the remains or traces of a prehistoric animal or plant embedded and preserved in rock. [from a Latin word *fossilis* meaning 'dug up']

fossil fuel *noun* a natural fuel such as coal or gas formed in the geological past.

fossilize *verb* to turn a plant or animal into a fossil, or to be turned into a fossil. **fossilization** *noun*

foster *verb* 1 to help a person to grow or develop. 2 to take care of and bring up a child who is not your own. [from an Old English word *foster* meaning 'food']

foster-child *noun* (**foster-children**) a child who is fostered. **foster-brother** *noun* **foster-daughter** *noun* **foster-sister** *noun* **foster-son** *noun*

foster home *noun* a family home in which a foster-child is brought up.

foster-parent *noun* a parent who fosters a child. **foster-father** *noun* **foster-mother** *noun*

fought past tense and past participle of **fight**.

foul *adjective* **1** having an offensive smell or taste, disgusting. SYNONYMS: disgusting, vile, repellent, obnoxious. **2** morally offensive, wicked. SYNONYMS: wicked, evil, vile. **3** (said about language) disgusting, obscene. **4** (said about the weather) wet and stormy. **5** contaminated or polluted with something. **6** colliding or entangled with something. **7** against the rules of a game, unfair ♦ *a foul stroke*.
foul *noun* an action that breaks the rules of a game.
foul *verb* **1** to make something foul, or to become foul. **2** to entangle or collide with something, to obstruct something. **3** to commit a foul against a player in a game or sport. **foully** *adverb* [from an Old English word]

foul-mouthed *adjective* using foul language.

foul play *noun* **1** unfair play in a game or sport. **2** a violent crime, especially murder.

found [1] past tense and past participle of **find**.

found [2] *verb* **1** to establish an organization or institution, or to provide money for starting one. SYNONYMS: establish, create, set up. **2** to base something ♦ *The story is founded on fact.* [from a Latin word *fundus* meaning 'bottom']

found [3] *verb* **1** to melt and mould metal. **2** to fuse materials for making glass. **3** to make an object in this way. [from a Latin word *fundere* meaning 'to melt' or 'to pour']

foundation *noun* **1** the solid base on which a building is built up, usually below ground level. **2** the underlying principle or idea on which something is based. **3** the founding of an organization or institution. **4** an organization or institution that has been established. **5** a fund of money established for a charitable purpose. **6** a cosmetic cream or powder applied to the skin as the first layer of make-up.

foundation stone *noun* a stone laid with a ceremony to celebrate the founding of a building.

founder [1] *noun* a person who founds an organization or institution.

founder [2] *verb* **1** to stumble or fall. **2** (said about a ship) to fill with water and sink. **3** to fail completely ♦ *Their plans foundered.* [same origin as for *found* [2]]

foundling *noun* a child that is found abandoned and whose parents are unknown.

foundry *noun* (**foundries**) a factory or workshop where metal or glass is made.

fount [1] *noun* **1** a source of something good or desirable. **2** (*poetic*) a spring or fountain.

fount [2] *noun* another spelling of **font** (in printing).

fountain *noun* **1** an ornamental structure in a pool or lake, in which a jet of water is made to spring into the air. **2** a structure providing a supply of drinking water in a public place. [via Old French *fontaine* from a Latin word *fons* meaning 'a spring']

fountain pen *noun* a pen that can be filled with a supply of ink.

four *adjective & noun* **1** the number 4, one more than three. **2** a four-oared boat or its crew. **on all fours** on hands and knees. [from an Old English word]

fourfold *adjective & adverb* **1** four times as much or as many. **2** consisting of four parts.

four-poster *noun* a bed with posts at each corner supporting a canopy.

foursome *noun* **1** a group of four people. **2** a golf match between two pairs, with partners playing the same ball.

four-square *adjective* solidly based, steady.

fourteen *adjective & noun* the number 14. **fourteenth** *adjective & noun* [from an Old English word]

fourth *adjective & noun* **1** next after third. **2** one of four equal parts of a thing. **3** a musical interval or chord spanning four alphabetical notes, e.g. C to F. **fourthly** *adverb*

fowl *noun* (**fowls** or **fowl**) a kind of bird kept to supply eggs and flesh for food. [from an Old English word]

fowling *noun* the sport of catching or shooting wildfowl. **fowler** *noun*

fox *noun* **1** a wild animal of the dog family with a pointed snout, reddish fur, and a bushy tail. **2** the fur of a fox. **3** a crafty person.

fox *verb* to deceive or confuse someone by cunning. **foxy** *adjective* [from an Old English word]

foxglove *noun* a tall plant with purple or white flowers like the fingers of a glove.

foxhound *noun* a kind of hound bred and trained to hunt foxes in packs.

fox terrier *noun* a kind of short-haired terrier.

foxtrot *noun* a ballroom dance with slow and quick steps, or the music for this dance.

foyer (foi-ay) *noun* the entrance hall of a large building, especially a theatre, cinema, or hotel. [a French word meaning 'hearth']

fracas (frak-ah) *noun* (**fracas** (frak-ahz)) a noisy quarrel or disturbance. [a French word]

fraction *noun* 1 a number that is not a whole number, e.g. $\frac{1}{2}$, 0.5. 2 a very small part or piece of something. [same origin as for *fracture*]

fractional *adjective* 1 expressed as a fraction. 2 very small ♦ *The difference is only fractional.* **fractionally** *adverb*

fractious (frak-shəs) *adjective* irritable or peevish. **fractiously** *adverb* **fractiousness** *noun* [from *fraction*]

fracture *noun* the breaking of something, especially of a bone.
fracture *verb* to break or make something break. [from a Latin word *fractum* meaning 'broken']

fragile *adjective* 1 easily damaged or broken. SYNONYMS: delicate, breakable. 2 (said about a person) having a weak constitution or health. **fragilely** *adverb* **fragility** (frə-jil-iti) *noun* [from a Latin word *frangere* meaning 'to break']

fragment[1] (frag-mənt) *noun* 1 a small piece broken off something. 2 a small part. [from a Latin word *fragmentum*, related to *fragile*]

fragment[3] (frag-ment) *verb* to break something into fragments, or to be broken into fragments. **fragmentation** *noun*

fragmentary (frag-mənt-er-i) *adjective* consisting of fragments.

fragrance *noun* 1 a sweet or pleasant smell. 2 something fragrant, a perfume. [from a Latin word *fragrare* meaning 'to smell sweet']

fragrant *adjective* having a sweet or pleasant smell.

frail *adjective* not strong, physically weak. SYNONYMS: weak, infirm, feeble, delicate. [from an Old French word *fraile*, related to *fragile*]

frailty *noun* (**frailties**) 1 the state of being frail, weakness. 2 a weakness in character or morals.

frame *noun* 1 a holder that fits round a picture or photograph. 2 a rigid structure built round a door, window, or other opening in a building. 3 a rigid structure supporting other parts of a building, vehicle, piece of furniture, etc. SYNONYMS: framework, shell, skeleton, structure. 4 a human or animal body in terms of its size ♦ *a small frame.* 5 a single exposure on a strip of cinema film. 6 a box-like structure for protecting plants from the cold. 7 a triangular structure for setting up the red balls in snooker; a round of play in snooker.
frame *verb* 1 to put or form a frame round something. 2 to express something in words ♦ *The question was framed awkwardly.* 3 (*informal*) to produce false evidence against an innocent person so that they appear guilty. **frame of mind** a person's mood or way of thinking at a particular time. [from an Old English word *framian* meaning 'to make the wooden parts of a building']

framework *noun* 1 the supporting structure of a building or other construction. 2 the structural basis of an organization or a plan.

franc *noun* the unit of money in France, Belgium, Switzerland, and other countries. [from the Latin title *Francorum rex* meaning 'King of the Franks', which was stamped on French gold coins in the Middle Ages]

franchise (fran-chiyz) *noun* 1 the right to vote in public elections, especially for MPs. 2 a licence or authorization to sell a firm's goods or services in a particular area.
franchise *verb* to grant a franchise to someone. [from an Old French word, related to *franc*]

Franco- *prefix* French (and) ♦ *a Franco-German treaty.*

Frank [1] *noun* a member of a Germanic people that conquered Gaul (modern France) in the 6th century. **Frankish** *adjective* [from an Old English word *Franca*, perhaps related to *franca* meaning 'javelin']

frank [1] *adjective* expressing your thoughts and feelings openly. SYNONYMS: direct, open, candid, sincere, honest, plain. **frankly** *adverb* **frankness** *noun* [via Old French from a medieval Latin word *francus* meaning 'free']

frank [2] *verb* to mark letters and packages automatically in a machine to show that postage has been paid. [from *frank* [1] in an earlier meaning 'free of obligation']

Frankenstein's monster (frank-in-stiynz) *noun* a creation that becomes terrifying to its creator. [the name of Baron Frankenstein, a character in Mary Shelley's novel *Frankenstein* (1818), who made a human monster which later destroyed him]

frankfurter *noun* a smoked sausage. [from the name of Frankfurt in Germany, where it was originally made]

frankincense *noun* a sweet-smelling gum resin burnt as incense. [from an Old French phrase *franc encens* meaning 'finest incense', related to *frank* [1]]

frantic *adjective* wildly excited or agitated. SYNONYMS: hectic, excited, wild, frenzied, furious. **frantically** *adverb* [from a Greek word *phrenetikos* meaning 'mad']

fraternal (frə-ter-nəl) *adjective* to do with a brother or brothers. **fraternally** *adverb* [from a Latin word *frater* meaning 'brother']

fraternity (frə-tern-iti) *noun* (**fraternities**) 1 brotherly feeling. 2 a religious brotherhood. 3 a group of people with common interests ♦ *the medical fraternity.*

fraternize (frat-er-niyz) *verb* to associate with other people in a friendly way. **fraternization** *noun* [same origin as for *fraternal*]

Frau (frow) *noun* (**Frauen** (frow-ən)) the title of a German-speaking married woman, equivalent to 'Mrs'.

fraud *noun* 1 criminal deception; a dishonest trick. 2 a person or thing that is not what they pretend to be, an impostor. [from a Latin word *fraudis* meaning 'of deceit']

fraudulent (fraw-dew-lənt) *adjective* involving or using fraud, deceitful or dishonest. SYNONYMS: deceitful, dishonest, underhand. **fraudulently** *adverb* **fraudulence** *noun*

fraught (frawt) *adjective* involving something unpleasant or unwelcome ♦ *an undertaking fraught with danger.* [from an older meaning 'loaded with freight']

Fräulein (froi-liyn) *noun* the title of a German-speaking unmarried woman, equivalent to 'Miss'.

fray [1] *noun* a fight or conflict ♦ *ready for the fray.* [same origin as for *affray*]

fray [2] *verb* 1 to make cloth or other material worn so that loose threads show. 2 to strain or upset a person's nerves or temper. 3 to become worn or frayed.

frazzle *noun* (*informal*) a completely exhausted state ♦ *worn to a frazzle.* **frazzled** *adjective* [perhaps from *fray* [1] and an obsolete word *fazle* meaning 'to tangle']

freak *noun* 1 a person or thing that is unusual or abnormal in form. 2 something very unusual or irregular ♦ *a freak storm.* 3 a person who is obsessed with a particular thing ♦ *a fitness freak.* [origin unknown]

freakish *adjective* like a freak.

freckle *noun* a light brown spot on the skin. **freckled** *adjective* **freckly** *adjective* [from an Old Norse word]

free *adjective* (**freer**, **freest**) 1 (said about a person) not in the power or control of someone else; able to do what you want and go where you want. 2 (said about a country or its inhabitants) not controlled by a foreign or despotic government; having private rights which are respected. 3 allowed to do something ♦ *You are free to leave.* 4 not fixed or held down, able to move without hindrance ♦ *Leave one end free.* 5 costing nothing, not requiring payment. SYNONYMS: complimentary, free of charge, gratis. 6 unrestricted, not controlled by rules ♦ *a free vote.* 7 open to anyone to join in ♦ *a free fight.* 8 not subject to or affected by something ♦ *free from blame* ♦ *The roads were free of ice.* 9 (said about a place or time) not occupied, not being used; (said about a person) not having any commitments or things to do. 10 given or giving readily ♦ *He is very free with his advice.* SYNONYMS: generous, lavish, unstinting.

free verb (**frees, freed, freeing**) 1 to make someone free. SYNONYMS: liberate, release, let go. 2 to relieve someone of something unwelcome ♦ *The court's verdict freed him from suspicion.* 3 to disengage or disentangle something. **free and easy** relaxed or informal. **a free hand** the right to act as you choose. **freely** adverb [from an Old English word]

Free Church noun a nonconformist Church.

freedom noun 1 the condition of being free, independence. SYNONYMS: independence, liberty. 2 being frank in what you say. 3 exemption or immunity from a duty. 4 unrestricted use of a facility ♦ *Students have the freedom of the library.*

freedom fighter noun someone who takes part in armed resistance to a government or regime.

free electron noun (*Physics*) an electron that is not bound in an atom or molecule.

free enterprise noun an economic system in which private businesses operate in competition with little or no state control.

free fall noun 1 the downward movement of a body towards earth under the force of gravity. 2 the movement of a spacecraft in space without thrust from the engines.

free flight noun the flight of a spacecraft or rocket without thrust from its engines.

free-for-all adjective a fight or discussion in which anyone present may join.

freehand adjective (said about a drawing) done without a ruler or other instrument.

freehold noun the holding of land or a house in absolute ownership. **freeholder** noun

free kick noun (in football) a kick allowed to be taken without interference from the other side, awarded for a foul or other infringement.

freelance adjective self-employed and available to do work for several companies.
freelance noun someone who works in this way.
freelance verb to work as a freelance. [from an earlier meaning 'mercenary solider', who carried a 'free lance']

freeman noun (**freemen**) 1 a free person, someone who is not a slave or serf. 2 a person who has been given the freedom of a city, as an honour.

Freemason noun a member of an international order set up to promote fellowship and mutual help, with elaborate secret ceremonies.
Freemasonry noun

free port noun 1 a port that is open to all traders. 2 a port that is free from duty on goods in transit.

free-range adjective (said about hens or their eggs) bred and kept in natural conditions.

freesia noun a small plant with fragrant colourful flowers, growing from a bulb. [named after the German physician H. T. Freese (1795–1876)]

free speech noun the right to express your opinions.

free-standing adjective not supported by a framework or other structure.

freestyle adjective (in sports) having few restrictions on the style or technique that may be used.

free trade noun trade left to its natural course, without restrictions on imports etc.

freewheel verb to ride a bicycle without pedalling; to act without effort.

free will noun the power to act free of the constraints of fate.

free world noun the non-Communist countries' name for themselves.

freeze verb (**froze, frozen**) 1 to change from a liquid to a solid as a result of extreme cold, or to make something change in this way. 2 to become full of ice or covered in ice. 3 to be so cold that water turns to ice ♦ *It was freezing last night.* 4 to preserve food by storing it at a very low temperature. 5 to become paralysed from fear or shock. 6 (said about a computer screen) to become locked because of a fault. 7 to prevent money or assets from being used for a period. 8 to hold prices or wages at a fixed level for a period.
freeze noun 1 a period of freezing or very cold weather. 2 the freezing of prices or wages. 3 to freeze up to obstruct something when ice forms over it. [from an Old English word]

freeze-dry verb (**freeze-dries, freeze-dried, freeze-drying**) to freeze food and then dry it by evaporating the ice in a vacuum.

freeze-frame *noun* a still picture taken from a film or video.

freezer *noun* a refrigerated cabinet or room for preserving and storing food at a very low temperature.

freezing point *noun* the temperature at which a liquid freezes.

freight (frayt) *noun* 1 the large-scale transport of goods by water, air, or land. 2 goods transported by freight, cargo. **freight** *verb* 1 to send or carry goods as cargo. 2 to load a ship with cargo. [from an early Dutch word *vrecht*]

freighter (frayt-er) *noun* a ship or aircraft mainly used for carrying freight.

French *adjective* to do with or coming from France.
French *noun* the language of France, also used in other countries. **the French** French people. **to take French leave** to go absent without permission. [from an Old English word, related to *Frank*]

French bean *noun* a kidney bean or haricot bean used as a vegetable.

French chalk *noun* finely powdered talc used as a dry lubricant and for marking cloth.

French dressing *noun* a salad dressing of seasoned oil and vinegar.

French fries *plural noun* (North Amer.) deep-fried potato chips.

French horn *noun* a brass wind instrument with valves and a long tube coiled in a circle and broadening into a wide opening.

French polish *noun* a shellac polish for producing a bright shine on wood.
french-polish *verb* to polish wood with shellac polish.

French window *noun* a long hinged window on an outside wall, also serving as a door to a garden or balcony.

frenzy *noun* (frenzies) wild excitement or agitation. **frenzied** *adjective* [from a Greek word *phrēn* meaning 'the mind']

frequency *noun* (frequencies) 1 being frequent, happening often. 2 the rate at which something happens. 3 the rate per second in the vibration of a sound, light, or radio wave; a band or group of similar radio frequencies.

frequency modulation *noun* the modulation of a wave by varying its frequency, used in broadcasting an audio signal by radio.

frequent [1] (free-kwənt) *adjective* happening or appearing often. SYNONYMS: constant, recurrent, continual. **frequently** *adverb* [from a Latin word *frequens* meaning 'crowded']

frequent [2] (fri-kwent) *verb* to be in a place often or go to it often.

fresco (fress-koh) *noun* (frescoes) a picture painted in watercolours on a wall or ceiling before the plaster is dry. [an Italian word meaning 'fresh']

fresh *adjective* 1 newly made, produced, or gathered, not stale. 2 new or different, not previously known or used. SYNONYMS: new, original, innovative. 3 (said about food) recently made, not preserved by being tinned, frozen, or salted. 4 not salty or bitter. 5 (said about the air or weather) cool, refreshing; (said about the wind) moderately strong. 6 bright and pure in colour, not dull or faded. 7 feeling vigorous or energetic. 8 impudent or presumptuous. **freshly** *adverb* **freshness** *noun* [from an Old English word]

freshen *verb* to make something fresh, or to become fresh.

fresher *noun* (informal) a first-year student at a college or university.

freshwater *adjective* living in fresh water, not sea water ♦ *freshwater fish*.

fret [1] *verb* (fretted, fretting) 1 to become anxious and unhappy, or to make someone do this. SYNONYMS: worry, fuss. 2 to wear something away by gnawing or rubbing it.
fret *noun* a state of worry and unhappiness. [from an Old English word]

fret [2] *noun* each of a series of raised bars or wires across the fingerboard of a guitar or other stringed instrument, against which the fingers stop the strings in playing. **fretted** *adjective* [origin unknown]

fretful *adjective* constantly worried or upset. **fretfully** *adverb* **fretfulness** *noun*

fretsaw *noun* a saw with a narrow blade stretched across a U-shaped frame, used for cutting patterns in thin wood. [from an Old French word *frete* meaning 'trellis']

fretwork *noun* carved ornamental work in wood, done with a fretsaw.

Freudian (froi- di- ən) *adjective* relating to the theories of the Austrian psychoanalyst Sigmund Freud (1856–

1939), especially in regard to human sexuality.

Freudian slip noun a slip made in speaking, regarded as revealing subconscious feelings or intentions.

friable (fry-ə-bəl) adjective easily crumbled. **friability** noun [from a Latin word friare meaning 'to crumble']

friar noun a member of certain Christian religious orders of men, especially the Franciscans, Augustinians, Dominicans, and Carmelites. [via Old French frere from a Latin word frater meaning 'brother']

friary noun (friaries) a building or community of friars.

fricassée (frik-ə-see) noun a dish of stewed or fried pieces of meat served in a thick sauce. [a French word]

friction noun 1 the resistance that one surface meets when it moves over another. 2 the action of one thing rubbing against another. 3 conflict or disagreement between people. **frictional** adjective [from a Latin word fricare meaning 'to rub']

Friday noun the day of the week following Thursday. [from an Old English word Frigedæg meaning 'day of Frigga']

fridge noun a refrigerator.

fried past and past participle of fry¹.

friend noun 1 a person you enjoy spending time with. SYNONYMS: acquaintance, companion; (informal) pal, chum, mate. 2 a helpful thing or quality ♦ Darkness was our friend. 3 someone who helps or supports a cultural organization such as a museum or concert hall.
Friend noun a member of the Society of Friends, a Quaker. **friendship** noun [from an Old English word]

friendless adjective without a friend.

friendly adjective (friendlier, friendliest) 1 behaving like a friend, kind and pleasant. SYNONYMS: kind, affectionate, amiable, pleasant, good-natured. 2 (said about a thing) favourable or helpful. **friendly** noun (friendlies) a sports match that is not part of a formal competition. **friendliness** noun

-friendly suffix 1 designed to be helpful to someone (as in user-friendly). 2 not harmful to something (as in environment-friendly).

friendly fire noun fire from one's own weapons in war, causing damage to one's own forces.

friendly society noun a mutual society providing sickness, insurance, and pension benefits to its members.

fries plural noun (North Amer.) another word for **French fries**.

Friesian (free-zhən) noun a large black-and-white dairy cow originally from Friesland in the Netherlands.

frieze noun a band of sculpture or decoration round the top of a wall or building. [from a Latin word frisium, from frigium opus meaning 'a work from Phrygia' (in Asia Minor, now Turkey)]

frigate (frig-ət) noun a small warship, smaller than a destroyer. [from an Italian word fregata]

fright noun 1 sudden great fear. SYNONYMS: fear, alarm, terror. 2 (informal) a person or thing that looks ridiculous. [from an Old English word]

frighten verb 1 to make someone afraid. SYNONYMS: scare, alarm, terrify. 2 to become afraid ♦ He doesn't frighten easily. 3 to force someone to do something from fear ♦ The man frightened them into admitting it. **to be frightened of** to be afraid of.

frightful adjective 1 very unpleasant or shocking ♦ It has caused a frightful scandal. SYNONYMS: terrible, awful, appalling, dreadful, shocking. 2 (informal) extreme, extremely bad ♦ The room was in a frightful mess. SYNONYMS: terrible, awful, dreadful. **frightfully** adverb

frigid (frij-id) adjective 1 intensely cold. 2 aloof and formal in manner. 3 (said about a woman) unable to be aroused sexually. **frigidly** adverb **frigidity** (fri-jid-iti) noun [from a Latin word frigidus meaning 'cold']

frill noun 1 a decorative gathered or pleated trimming attached at one edge to a dress, curtain, etc. 2 something extra that is pleasant but unnecessary ♦ We are looking for simple accommodation with no frills. **frilled** adjective **frilly** adjective [from a Flemish word frul]

fringe noun 1 a decorative edging with many threads or cords hanging down loosely. 2 something hanging over, such as part of a plant. 3 a straight line of hair hanging down over the forehead. 4 the edge of something. 5 not part of the main

activities ♦ *fringe theatre*.
fringe *verb* **1** to decorate something with a fringe. **2** to form a fringe to something. [from an Old French word *frenge*]

fringe benefits *plural noun* extra benefits provided for an employee in addition to wages or salary.

frippery *noun* (**fripperies**) showy unnecessary finery or ornaments. [from a French word *friperie*]

Frisian (friz-iən) *adjective* to do with Frisia (or Friesland) in the Netherlands, or its people or language.
Frisian *noun* the Germanic language spoken in northern parts of the Netherlands.

frisk *verb* **1** to play or skip about. **2** to run your hands over a person to search for something hidden on them. [from an Old French word *frisque* meaning 'lively']

frisky *adjective* (**friskier, friskiest**) lively or playful. SYNONYMS: playful, lively, sprightly, spirited. **friskiness** *noun*

frisson (free-sawn) *noun* a thrill of excitement or fear. [a French word meaning 'a shiver']

fritillary (fri-til-er-i) *noun* (**fritillaries**) **1** a plant with spotted bell-shaped flowers that hang over. **2** a butterfly with orange-brown and black wings.

fritter[1] *noun* a piece of sliced meat, fruit, or vegetable coated in batter and fried. [from a Latin word *frictum* meaning 'fried']

fritter[2] *verb* to waste time, money, or energy on unimportant things. SYNONYMS: squander, waste, misuse. [from an old word *fritters* meaning 'fragments']

frivolous *adjective* lacking a serious purpose, pleasure-loving. SYNONYMS: trivial, flippant, unimportant. **frivolously** *adverb* **frivolity** *noun*

frizz *verb* (said about hair) to form a mass of tight curls.
frizz *noun* a mass of curled hair. **frizzy** *adjective* **frizziness** *noun* [from a French word *friser*]

frizzle *verb* **1** to burn or cook food with a sizzling noise. **2** to burn or shrivel something by burning. [from *fry* and *sizzle*]

fro *adverb* **to and fro** see **to**.

frock *noun* a woman's or girl's dress. [from an Old French word *froc*]

frog *noun* **1** a small cold-blooded animal with long hind legs for leaping, living both in water and on land. **2** a horny pad growing on the sole of a horse's foot. **3** a fastener consisting of a button and an ornamentally looped cord. **a frog in your throat** (*informal*) a temporary inability to speak from hoarseness. [from an Old English word *frogga*]

frogman *noun* (**frogmen**) a swimmer equipped with a rubber suit, flippers, and breathing apparatus for swimming and working underwater.

frogmarch *verb* to force someone to move forward by holding their arms from behind and pushing them.

frolic *verb* (**frolicked, frolicking**) to play about in a lively cheerful way. SYNONYMS: cavort, gambol, caper, romp, skip.
frolic *noun* lively cheerful playing or entertainment. [from a Dutch word *vrolijk* meaning 'cheerful']

from *preposition* **1** indicating a starting point, either a place or a time ♦ *The group will travel from London* ♦ *Teas will be available from three o'clock.* **2** indicating a source or origin ♦ *I'll get a glass from the cupboard.* **3** indicating separation, release, or prevention ♦ *The men had escaped from prison* ♦ *Try to refrain from laughing.* **4** indicating difference or discrimination ♦ *I can't always tell red from green.* **5** indicating a cause or means ♦ *The children had died from starvation.* **6** indicating a material used to make something ♦ *Wine is made from grapes.* [from an Old English word]

frond *noun* a leaf-like part of a fern, palm tree, or other plant. [from a Latin word *frondis* meaning 'of a leaf']

front *noun* **1** the part or side of something that faces forward or is normally seen ♦ *A car was waiting at the front of the house.* **2** the most important side or surface of something. **3** the place where fighting is taking place in a war; the foremost line of an army. **4** a particular area of activity or concern ♦ *What is happening on the job front?* **5** an outward appearance or show; something serving as a cover for secret activities. **6** the leading edge of an advancing mass of cold or warm air. **7** a road or promenade by the sea at a seaside resort. **8** the part of a piece of clothing that covers the front of the body. **9** the part of a theatre where the audience sits, facing the stage. **10** (in names) an organized political group ♦ *the Patriotic Front.*

front *adjective* of the front; situated in front.

front *verb* 1 to face or have the front towards something ♦ *A hotel fronting the sea.* 2 to be the host of a television programme. **in front** at the front of something. **in front of** in the presence of someone. [from a Latin word *frontis* meaning 'of the forehead']

frontage *noun* 1 the front of a building. 2 the strip of land between the front of a large building and the road.

frontal *adjective* 1 of or at the front. 2 associated with a warm or cold weather front.

front bench *noun* the seats at the front on each side of the House of Commons, where members of the cabinet and shadow cabinet sit. **frontbencher** *noun*

frontier *noun* 1 the land border between two countries or regions. 2 the limit of achievement or understanding in a subject. [from an Old French word *frontiere*, from a Latin word *frontis* meaning 'of the front']

frontispiece (frunt-iss-peess) *noun* an illustration opposite the title page of a book. [from a Latin word *frontispicium* meaning 'facade']

front-runner *noun* the contestant who seems most likely to succeed in a race, competition, or election.

frost *noun* 1 a weather condition with the temperature below the freezing point of water. 2 a white powdery coating of frozen vapour produced in cold weather. 3 a chilling influence; great coolness of manner.
frost *verb* 1 to cover a surface with frost, or to become covered with frost. 2 to freeze. [from an Old English word, related to *freeze*]

frostbite *noun* injury to the tissue of the body caused by exposure to extreme cold. **frostbitten** *adjective*

frosted *adjective* (said about glass) made cloudy so that you cannot see clearly through it.

frosting *noun* sugar icing for cakes.

frosty *adjective* (**frostier, frostiest**) 1 cold with frost forming. SYNONYMS: freezing, icy, bitter. 2 aloof and unfriendly in manner. **frostily** *adverb* **frostiness** *noun*

froth *noun* a mass of tiny bubbles formed on a liquid, foam.

froth *verb* to make froth in a liquid, to form froth. **frothy** *adjective* [from an Old Norse word]

frown *verb* to wrinkle your brow because you are concentrating or worried, or disapprove of something.
frown *noun* a frowning movement or look. **to frown at** or **on** to disapprove of something. [from an Old French word *froigne*]

frowsty *adjective* (**frowstier, frowstiest**) fusty or stuffy. [from a dialect word]

frozen past participle of **freeze**.

FRS *abbreviation* Fellow of the Royal Society.

fructose (fruk-tohs) *noun* (*Chemistry*) sugar of the kind found in honey and fruit. [from a Latin word *fructus* meaning 'fruit']

frugal (froo-gəl) *adjective* 1 careful and economical with money. SYNONYMS: prudent, sparing, thrifty, careful, economical. 2 scanty or costing little ♦ *a frugal meal.* **frugally** *adverb* **frugality** *noun* [from a Latin word *frugalis*, related to *fruit*]

fruit *noun* 1 the juicy part of a plant that contains the seeds and can be used as food. 2 any plant product used as food ♦ *the fruits of the earth.* 3 the results or rewards of doing something.
fruit *verb* (said about a plant) to produce fruit. [from a Latin word *frui* meaning 'to enjoy']

fruiterer *noun* a shopkeeper who sells fruit.

fruitful *adjective* 1 producing a lot of fruit. SYNONYMS: fertile, productive. 2 producing good results ♦ *The talks are proving to be fruitful.* SYNONYMS: successful, profitable, useful. **fruitfully** *adverb* **fruitfulness** *noun*

fruition (froo-ish-ən) *noun* the achievement of what you intended or worked for.

fruitless *adjective* producing no useful results. SYNONYMS: unsuccessful, pointless, futile, useless. **fruitlessly** *adverb* **fruitlessness** *noun*

fruit machine *noun* a gambling machine worked by putting coins in a slot.

fruit salad *noun* a mixture of chopped fruit in juice or syrup.

fruity *adjective* (**fruitier, fruitiest**) 1 like fruit in smell or taste. 2 (said about a voice) deep and rich.

frump *noun* an unattractive woman who wears dowdy clothes. **frumpish** *adjective*

frumpy *adjective* [from an earlier meaning 'bad-tempered woman', probably from an old word *frumple* meaning 'wrinkle']

frustrate *verb* to prevent someone from doing what they want to do; to make someone's efforts useless. SYNONYMS: thwart, foil, check, stop, prevent. **frustration** *noun* [from a Latin word *frustra* meaning 'in vain']

fry [1] *verb* (**fries, fried, frying**) to cook food in hot fat, or (said about food) to be cooked in this way.
fry *noun* (**fries**) 1 a meal of fried food. [via Old French from a Latin word *frigere*]

fry [2] *plural noun* young or newly hatched fishes. [from an Old Norse word]

fryer *noun* a deep container for frying food.

frying pan or **frypan** *noun* a shallow pan used for frying food.

fry-up *noun* (*informal*) a meal of fried food.

ft. *abbreviation* foot or feet (as a measure).

FTP *abbreviation* (*Computing*) file transfer protocol, a procedure for transfering data over a network.

FTSE *abbreviation* a figure indicating the relative values of shares on the London Stock Exchange. [short for *Financial Times Stock Exchange*]

fuchsia (**few-shə**) *noun* an ornamental shrub with red, purple, or white drooping flowers. [named after the German botanist Leonhard Fuchs (1501–66)]

fuddled *adjective* in a confused state, especially from too much alcoholic drink. [origin unknown]

fuddy-duddy *noun* (**fuddy-duddies**) (*informal*) a person who is out of date or unable to accept new ideas. [from a dialect word]

fudge *noun* a soft sweet made of milk, sugar, and butter.
fudge *verb* to put something together in a makeshift or inadequate way. [probably from an old word *fadge* meaning 'to fit together']

fuel *noun* 1 material that is burnt or lit to produce heat or power. 2 something that causes or increases anger or other strong feelings.
fuel *verb* (**fuelled, fuelling**) to provide something with fuel. [from an Old French word, related to *focus*]

fug *noun* (*informal*) a stuffy atmosphere in a room. **fuggy** *adjective* [origin unknown]

fugitive (**few-ji-tiv**) *noun* a person who is running away from something.
fugitive *adjective* 1 running away or escaping. 2 quick to disappear, fleeting. [from a Latin word *fugere* meaning 'to flee']

fugue (**fewg**) *noun* (*Music*) a composition in which a theme is introduced by one part and taken up successively by others in complex patterns. [via French or Italian from a Latin word *fuga* meaning 'flight']

fulcrum (**ful-krəm**) *noun* (**fulcra** or **fulcums**) the point on which a lever turns. [a Latin word, from *fulcire* meaning 'to prop up']

fulfil *verb* (**fulfilled, fulfilling**) 1 to accomplish or carry out a task. SYNONYMS: achieve, accomplish, carry out. 2 to do what is required by a treaty or contract. SYNONYMS: comply with, satisfy. 3 to make a prophecy come true. **to fulfil yourself** or **be fulfilled** to develop and use your abilities. **fulfilment** *noun* [from an Old English word *fullfyllan* meaning 'to fill up' or 'to satisfy']

full *adjective* 1 holding or having as much or as many as possible, without any space for more. SYNONYMS: filled, packed, crowded. 2 having a large number or amount of something ♦ *a town full of visitors* ♦ *a girl full of vitality.* 3 preoccupied with something or unable to stop talking about it ♦ *They had just come back from their holiday and were full of it.* 4 having had enough to eat ♦ *By the end of the meal they were all feeling full.* 5 thorough or detailed ♦ *Please give the full story.* SYNONYMS: complete, thorough, detailed, comprehensive, exhaustive. 6 complete, reaching the usual or specified extent or limit etc. ♦ *flowers in full bloom* ♦ *We waited a full hour.* 7 (said about a person's figure) plump or rounded. 8 (said about clothes) fitting loosely, made with much material hanging in folds. 9 (said about the tone of a person's voice) deep and mellow. SYNONYMS: deep, mellow, rich.
full *adverb* 1 straight, directly ♦ *The ball hit him full in the face.* 2 very ♦ *We knew full well they weren't going to come.* **full of yourself** arrogant or conceited. **in full** with nothing left out; for the whole amount ♦ *We have paid in full.* **to the full** thoroughly, completely. [from an Old English word]

fullback *noun* a defensive player near the goal in football, hockey, and other ball games.

full-blooded *adjective* vigorous and hearty.

full-blown *adjective* fully developed, complete.

full board *noun* accommodation with all meals at a hotel or guest house.

fuller *noun* a person who cleans and thickens freshly woven cloth. [from a Latin word *fullo*]

fuller's earth *noun* a type of clay used by a fuller in cleaning cloth.

full face *adjective* with the whole face towards the viewer.

full-frontal *adjective* (said about a nude figure) fully exposed at the front.

full moon *noun* the phase of the moon in which its whole disc is lit.

fullness *noun* the state of being full. **in the fullness of time** at the proper time, eventually.

full-scale *adjective* 1 (said about a model) of the actual size. 2 complete, not reduced.

full stop *noun* the punctuation mark (.) used at the end of a sentence or in an abbreviation.

full time *noun* the end of a sports match. **full-time** *adjective* for the whole of the working day or week. **full-timer** *noun*

fully *adverb* 1 completely, entirely. 2 no less than ♦ *Fully ten thousand attended the rally.*

fully fledged *adjective* 1 (said about young birds) having grown wing feathers and able to fly. 2 fully trained or established.

fulmar *noun* a grey and white northern seabird. [from an Old Norse word *full* meaning 'stinking' (because it vomits when disturbed)]

fulminate (ful-min-ayt) *verb* to protest loudly and angrily. **fulmination** *noun* **fulminator** *noun* [from a Latin word *fulminis* meaning 'of lightning']

fulsome (fuul-sǒm) *adjective* praising something or thanking someone excessively and cloyingly.
◊ Note that *fulsome praise* does not mean 'generous praise' but 'excessive praise'.

fumble *verb* 1 to hold or handle something clumsily. 2 to grope about. [from German or Dutch words]

fume *noun* or **fumes** *plural noun* strong-smelling or dangerous smoke or gas.
fume *verb* 1 to give off fumes. 2 to be very angry. 3 to treat wood with chemical fumes in order to darken it. [from a Latin word *fumus* meaning 'smoke']

fumigate (few-mig-ayt) *verb* to disinfect something by using fumes. **fumigation** *noun*

fun *noun* 1 light-hearted amusement or enjoyment. SYNONYMS: amusement, enjoyment, entertainment. 2 something that provides this. **to make fun of** to ridicule a person or thing. SYNONYMS: ridicule, deride, jeer at, tease. [from an earlier meaning 'to cheat or hoax', of unknown origin]

function *noun* 1 the special activity or purpose that a person or thing is meant to perform. SYNONYMS: purpose, role. 2 an important social event or ceremony. 3 any of the basic operations done by a computer. 4 (*Mathematics*) a relation between several variables; a variable quantity whose value depends on the value of other variable quantities ♦ *X is a function of Y and Z.*
function *verb* to perform a function; to work properly. [from a Latin word *functum* meaning 'performed']

functional *adjective* 1 to do with a function or having a function. 2 working, able to be used ♦ *The computer network is not yet fully functional.* 3 designed to be practical and useful rather than attractive or luxurious. SYNONYMS: practical, serviceable, useful. **functionally** *adverb*

functionalism *noun* the principle that the design of a thing should be based on its practical use, especially in architecture and furnishing. **functionalist** *noun*

functionary *noun* (**functionaries**) an official.

fund *noun* 1 money collected or available for a particular purpose. 2 a stock or supply of something ♦ *a fund of good ideas.*
fund *verb* to provide someone or something with money.
funds *plural noun* the money a person or organization has, financial resources. SYNONYMS: money, resources, capital. [from a Latin word *fundus* meaning 'piece of landed property']

fundamental *adverb* 1 forming the basis or foundation of a subject, serving as a starting point. 2 very important, essential.
fundamentals *plural noun* basic facts or principles. **fundamentally** *adverb* [from a Latin word *fundamentum* meaning 'foundation']

fundamentalism *noun* strict observation of traditional beliefs in any religion, and a belief that a religion's holy writings should be understood and followed literally. **fundamentalist** *noun*

funeral *noun* the ceremony of burying or cremating a dead person. **your funeral** your concern or responsibility. [from a Latin word *funeris* meaning 'of a burial']

funeral director *noun* an undertaker.

funerary (**few**-ner-er-i) *adjective* to do with a funeral or burial.

funereal (few-**neer**-iəl) *adjective* suitable for a funeral; dismal or gloomy. **funereally** *adverb*

funfair *noun* a fair consisting of amusements and sideshows.

fungal *adjective* to do with a fungus.

fungicide (**fun**-ji-siyd) *noun* a substance that destroys fungus. **fungicidal** *adjective* [from *fungus* and a Latin word *caedere* meaning 'to kill']

fungoid (**fung**-goid) *adjective* like a fungus.

fungous (**fung**-əs) *adjective* like a fungus.

fungus *noun* (**fungi** (**fung**-giy)) a plant without leaves or flowers that grows on other plants or decayed material, including mushrooms, toadstools, and moulds. [a Latin word, related to *sponge*]

funicular (few-**nik**-yoo-ler) *adjective* (said about a cable railway) consisting of ascending and descending cars that counterbalance each other. [from a Latin word *funiculus* meaning 'a little rope']

funk[1] *noun* (*informal*) a state of fear or anxiety.
funk *verb* (*informal*) to avoid something from fear. [origin unknown]

funk[2] *noun* a style of popular music with a strong rhythm. [origin unknown]

funnel *noun* 1 a tube-shaped device that is wide at the top and narrow at the bottom, used for pouring liquid or powder into a small opening. 2 a metal chimney on a ship or steam engine.
funnel *verb* (**funnelled, funnelling**) to move or guide something through a funnel or a narrowing space. [from a Latin word *fundere* meaning 'to pour']

funny *adjective* (**funnier, funniest**) 1 causing amusement or laughter ♦ *a funny story*. SYNONYMS: amusing, humorous, witty, comic, entertaining. 2 strange or puzzling ♦ *a funny smell*. SYNONYMS: strange, odd, curious, peculiar, queer, unusual. 3 (*informal*) slightly unwell. **funnily** *adverb* [from *fun*]

funny bone *noun* part of the elbow over which a very sensitive nerve passes.

fun run *noun* (*informal*) a non-competitive sponsored run done for charity.

fur *noun* 1 short fine soft hair covering the bodies of some animals. 2 animal skin with the fur on it, used for making or trimming clothes; a fabric imitating this. 3 a coat made from real or imitation fur. 4 a coating formed on the tongue as a symptom of sickness or poor health. 5 a coating formed by hard water on the inside of a kettle or pipes.
fur *verb* (**furred, furring**) to cover a surface with fur, or to become covered with fur. [from an Old French word *forrer* meaning 'to line']

furbish *verb* to clean something or make it fresh and new. [from an Old French word *forbir*]

furcate (**fer**-kayt) *adjective* divided into branches or forks.
furcate *verb* to fork or divide. **furcation** *noun* [from a Latin word *furca* meaning 'a fork']

Furies *plural noun* (*Greek Mythology*) three avenging goddesses who punished wrongdoing.

furious *adjective* 1 very angry. SYNONYMS: angry, enraged, irate, livid. 2 violent or intense ♦ *They drove at a furious pace.* **furiously** *adverb* [from a Latin word *furiosus*, related to *fury*]

furl *verb* to roll up and fasten a sail, flag, or umbrella. [from a French word *ferler*]

furlong *noun* a measure of distance, equal to one-eighth of a mile or 220 yards. [from an Old English word *furlang* meaning 'a furrow long', denoting the length of a furrow in a common field]

furlough (**fer**-loh) *noun* leave of absence for a soldier to return home. [from a Dutch word *verlof*]

furnace *noun* 1 an enclosed chamber or structure for burning fuel, especially to heat water to a high temperature. 2 a very hot place. [from a Latin word *furnus* meaning 'oven']

furnish *verb* 1 to provide a room or building with furniture. 2 to provide or supply something. [from an Old French word *furnir*]

furnishings *plural noun* furniture, curtains, and other fittings in a room or building.

furniture *noun* 1 tables, chairs, and other movable articles needed in a room or building. 2 a set of accessories, especially the handles and lock fitted to a door.

furore (fewr-or-i) *noun* an outbreak of great anger or excitement. [from a Latin word *furor* meaning 'madness']

furrier (fu-ri-er) *noun* a person who buys and sells furs.

furrow *noun* 1 a long cut in the ground made by a plough or other implement. 2 a groove resembling this. 3 a deep wrinkle in the skin.
furrow *verb* to make furrows in a surface. [from an Old English word]

furry *adjective* (**furrier, furriest**) like fur, or covered with fur.

further *adverb & adjective* 1 more distant in space or time. 2 to a greater extent, more ♦ *We shall have to enquire further* ♦ *We have made further enquiries.*
further *verb* to help someone make progress ♦ *to further someone's interests.* [from an Old English word]
◊ See the note at **farther**.

furtherance *noun* development of a scheme or interest.

further education *noun* education for people above school age.

furthermore *adverb* also, moreover.

furthermost *adjective* most distant.

furthest *adjective* most distant.
furthest *adverb* to or at the greatest distance.
◊ See the note at **farther**.

furtive *adjective* stealthy, trying not to be seen. SYNONYMS: stealthy, secretive, shifty. **furtively** *adverb* **furtiveness** *noun* [from a Latin word *furtivus* meaning 'stolen']

fury *noun* (**furies**) 1 wild anger or rage. 2 extreme force or violence in nature, especially the weather ♦ *The storm's fury continued all night.*
Fury *noun* (*Greek Mythology*) each of the Furies (see **Furies**). [from a Latin word *furia* meaning 'rage' or 'an avenging spirit']

furze *noun* gorse. [from an Old English word *fyrs*]

fuse [1] *noun* a safety device in an electric circuit, consisting of a short piece of wire that is designed to melt and break the circuit if the current exceeds a safe level.

fuse *verb* 1 to blend or amalgamate materials, especially by melting. 2 to merge things together. 3 to fit an electric circuit or appliance with a fuse. 4 to stop functioning because a fuse has melted. [from a Latin word *fusum* meaning 'melted']

fuse [2] *noun* a length of material along which a flame moves to ignite an explosive or firework.
fuse *verb* to fit a fuse to an explosive device. [from a Latin word *fusus* meaning 'a spindle' (because originally the material was put into a tube)]

fuse box *noun* a box or panel containing the fuses of an electrical system.

fuselage (few-zəl-ahzh) *noun* the main body of an aeroplane. [a French word, from *fuseler* meaning 'to shape into a spindle']

fusible *adjective* able to be fused or melted. **fusibility** *noun*

fusillade (few-zi-layd) *noun* 1 a series of gunshots fired together or in quick succession. 2 an outburst of questions or criticism. [from a French word *fusil* meaning 'gun']

fusion (few-zhǒn) *noun* 1 the process of fusing or blending things into a whole. 2 the uniting of atomic nuclei to form a heavier nucleus, usually with a release of energy.

fuss *noun* 1 unnecessary excitement or concern. SYNONYMS: commotion, excitement, stir, bother. 2 an agitated protest or dispute.
fuss *verb* 1 to make a fuss about something. 2 to bother someone about something unimportant. **to make a fuss of** to treat someone with great attention or affection. [origin unknown]

fusspot *noun* (*informal*) a fussy person.

fussy *adjective* (**fussier, fussiest**) 1 fussing or inclined to fuss often. SYNONYMS: finicky, particular, fastidious. 2 choosing very carefully; hard to please. SYNONYMS: (*informal*) choosy, picky, faddy. 3 full of unnecessary details or decorations. **fussily** *adverb* **fussiness** *noun*

fusty *adjective* (**fustier, fustiest**) 1 (said about a room) smelling stale, damp, or stuffy. 2 (said about a person) having old-fashioned ideas. **fustiness** *noun* [from an Old French word]

futile (few-tiyl) *adjective* producing no useful result, useless. SYNONYMS: unsuccessful, pointless, useless, fruitless. **futility** (few-til-iti) *noun* [from a Latin word *futilis* meaning 'leaking']

futon (foo-tonn) *noun* 1 a light kind of Japanese mattress. 2 this mattress on a wooden frame, used as a couch or bed. [a Japanese word]

future *adjective* belonging or referring to the time that is still to come. **future** *noun* 1 future time or events. 2 (*Grammar*) the tense of a verb that expresses action or state in the future, expressed by using *shall*, *will*, or *be going to*. **in future** from now on, or from then on. [from a Latin word *futurus* meaning 'about to be']

future perfect *noun* the tense of a verb expressed in the form 'will have done'.

futuristic (few-tewr-ist-ik) *adjective* using the most modern technology or design, looking suitable for the future.

fuzz *noun* 1 something fluffy or frizzy. 2 (*informal*) the police. [from German or Dutch]

fuzzy *adjective* (**fuzzier, fuzziest**) 1 like fuzz; covered with fuzz. SYNONYMS: fluffy, woolly, downy. 2 frizzy. 3 blurred or unclear. SYNONYMS: blurred, unclear, hazy, indistinct. **fuzzily** *adverb* **fuzziness** *noun*

Gg

G 1 the seventh letter of the English alphabet. 2 (*Music*) the fifth note of the diatonic scale of C major.

g *abbreviation* 1 gram(s). 2 gravity; the acceleration due to this.

Ga *abbreviation* (*Chemistry*) the symbol for gallium.

gab *verb* (*informal*) (**gabbed, gabbing**) to chatter. **gab** *noun* chatter. **to have the gift of the gab** to be good at talking. [another spelling of *gob*]

gabble *verb* to talk so quickly that it is difficult to know what is being said.

gabble *noun* gabbled talk. **gabbler** *noun* [from an Old Dutch word *gabbelen*]

gaberdine (gab-er-deen) *noun* 1 a strong fabric woven in a twill pattern. 2 a raincoat made of this. [from an Old French word *gauvardine*, denoting a kind of cloak]

gable *noun* the triangular upper part of an outside wall, between two sloping roofs. [from an Old Norse word *gafl*]

gabled *adjective* having a gable or gables.

gad *verb* (**gadded, gadding**) **to gad about** or **around** (*informal*) to go about in search of pleasure. [from an old word *gadling* meaning 'wanderer, vagabond']

gadfly *noun* (**gadflies**) a fly that bites horses and cattle. [from *gad*]

gadget *noun* a small mechanical device or tool. **gadgetry** *noun* [originally a sailors' word; origin unknown]

Gael (gayl) *noun* a Gaelic-speaking person. [from a Scottish Gaelic word *Gaidheal*]

Gaelic (gay-lik or gal-ik) *noun* 1 the Celtic language of the Scots. 2 the Irish language. **Gaelic** *adjective* to do with Gaelic.

gaff [1] *noun* a stick with an iron hook for landing large fish caught with rod and line. **gaff** *verb* to seize a fish with a gaff. [from a French word *gaf* meaning 'hook']

gaff [2] *noun* **to blow the gaff** (*informal*) to reveal a plot or secret. [origin unknown]

gaffe *noun* an embarrassing blunder. [from a French word meaning 'boathook']

gaffer *noun* (*informal*) 1 a boss. 2 the chief electrician in a film or television production unit. [contraction of *godfather*]

gag [1] *noun* 1 something put into a person's mouth or tied across it to prevent them from speaking or crying out. 2 a device used by a dentist or surgeon for holding a patient's mouth open. 3 anything that prevents free speech. **gag** *verb* (**gagged, gagging**) 1 to put a gag on a person. 2 to prevent someone from speaking or writing freely ♦ We should not gag the press. 3 to retch or choke. [an imitation of the sound of retching]

gag [2] *noun* a joke or funny story, especially as part of a comedian's act. **gag** *verb* (**gagged, gagging**) to tell jokes. [origin unknown]

gaga (gah-gah) *adjective* (*informal*) senile or slightly mad. [from a French word]

gaggle *noun* **1** a flock of geese. **2** a disorderly group of people. [an imitation of the noise that a goose makes]

gaiety *noun* **1** cheerfulness, a happy and light-hearted manner. **2** fun or merrymaking. [from a French word *gaieté*; related to *gay*]
◊ See the note at **gay**.

gaily *adverb* **1** in a cheerful light-hearted manner. **2** in bright colours.

gain *verb* **1** to obtain something, especially something desirable. SYNONYMS: get, win, earn, acquire, procure. **2** to make a profit. **3** to increase the amount or rate of something, to build something up ♦ *He needs to gain some weight.* **4** to improve or increase ♦ *Salsa dancing is gaining in popularity.* **5** (said about a clock or watch) to become ahead of the correct time. **6** to reach a destination ♦ *At last we gained the shore.*
gain *noun* **1** an increase in wealth or possessions. **2** an improvement, an increase in amount or power. **to gain ground** to make progress. **to gain on** to come closer to someone or something you are chasing or racing. **to gain time** to improve your chances by arranging or accepting a delay. [via Old French from a Germanic word]

gainful *adjective* paid or profitable ♦ *gainful employment.* **gainfully** *adverb*

gainsay *verb* (past tense and past participle **gainsaid**) (*formal*) to deny or contradict something ♦ *There is no gainsaying it.* [from an old word *gain-* meaning 'against' and *say*]

gait *noun* **1** a person's manner of walking or running ♦ *a shuffling gait.* **2** any of the forward movements of a horse, such as trotting or cantering. [from a dialect word *gate* meaning 'going']

gaiter *noun* a covering of cloth or leather for the leg from knee to ankle, or for the ankle, or for part of a machine. [from a French word *guêtre*]

gala (gah-lə) *noun* **1** a festive entertainment or performance. **2** a sports meeting ♦ *a swimming gala.* [from an Old French word *gale* meaning 'rejoicing']

galactic (gə-lak-tik) *adjective* **1** to do with a galaxy or galaxies. **2** to do with the Galaxy or Milky Way.

galaxy (gal-ək-si) *noun* (**galaxies**) **1** any of the large independent systems of stars existing in space. **2** a large group of famous, important, or talented people. **3** (**the Galaxy**) the galaxy containing the solar system, the Milky Way. [originally referring to the Milky Way, from a Greek word *galaxias* meaning 'milky']

gale *noun* **1** very strong wind. **2** a noisy outburst, especially of laughter. [origin unknown]

gall [1] (gawl) *noun* **1** bold and impudent behaviour. **2** bitterness of feeling. **3** (*old use*) the contents of the gall bladder, bile. [from an Old English word *gealla*, denoting bile]

gall [2] (gawl) *noun* a sore spot on the skin of an animal caused by rubbing.
gall *verb* **1** to annoy or humiliate someone. **2** to rub the skin and make it sore. [from an Old English word *gealle* meaning 'sore on a horse']

gall [3] (gawl) *noun* an abnormal growth produced by an insect, fungus, or bacterium on a plant, especially on an oak tree. [from a Latin word *galla*]

gallant (gal-ənt, or in meaning 2 also gə-**lant**) *adjective* **1** brave or heroic ♦ *a gallant effort.* **2** (said about a man) chivalrous, courteous to women. **3** (*old use*) fine and stately ♦ *our gallant ship.*
gallantly *adverb* [originally meaning 'splendidly dressed'; from an Old French word *galant* meaning 'celebrating']

gallantry *noun* **1** bravery in battle. **2** polite attention or respect given by men to women.

gall bladder *noun* a pear-shaped organ attached to the liver, in which bile is stored.

galleon (gal-i-ən) *noun* a large Spanish sailing ship used in the 15th–17th centuries. [same origin as for *galley*]

gallery *noun* (**galleries**) **1** a room or building for showing works of art. **2** a balcony or platform projecting from the inner wall of a church or hall. **3** the highest balcony in a theatre. **4** the spectators at a golf tournament. **5** a long room or passage, especially one used for a special purpose ♦ *a shooting gallery.* **6** a raised covered platform or passage along the wall of a building. **to play to the gallery** to try to win favour by appealing to the taste of the general public. **galleried**

adjective [from an Italian word *galleria* meaning 'gallery, church porch', perhaps from *Galilee*. A church porch furthest from the altar was called a *galilee*, as Galilee was the province furthest from Jerusalem]

galley *noun* (**galleys**) **1** a long low medieval ship with sails and one or more banks of oars. **2** an ancient Greek or Roman warship propelled by oars. **3** the kitchen in a ship or aircraft. **4** a printer's proof in the form of long single-column strips. [from a Latin or Greek word *galea*]

Gallic (gal-ik) *adjective* **1** to do with France, typically French ♦ *a Gallic shrug.* **2** to do with ancient Gaul. [from a Latin word *Gallus* meaning 'a Gaul']

galling (gawl-ing) *adjective* annoying or humiliating. [from *gall*]

gallium *noun* a soft bluish-white metallic element (symbol Ga), used as a semiconductor in electronic components. [from a Latin word *Gallia* meaning 'France', so named by its French discoverer, the chemist Paul-Émile Lecoq de Boisbaudran]

gallivant *verb* (*informal*) to go from place to place in search of pleasure, to gad about. [origin unknown]

gallon *noun* a unit of volume for measuring liquids, equal to 8 pints (4.546 litres). [from an Old French word *galon*]

gallop *noun* **1** a horse's fastest pace, with all four feet off the ground together in each stride. **2** a ride on a horse at this pace. **gallop** *verb* (**galloped, galloping**) **1** to go or ride at a gallop. **2** to go very fast, to rush ♦ *The priest galloped through the service.* [from an Old French word *galop*; related to *wallop*]

gallows *noun* a framework with a suspended noose for hanging criminals. **the gallows** execution by hanging. [from an Old English word]

gallows humour *noun* grim and ironical humour.

gallstone *noun* a small hard mass that sometimes forms in the gall bladder.

Gallup poll *noun* (*trademark*) an estimate of public opinion, made by questioning a representative sample of people and used especially to forecast how people will vote in an election. [named after an American statistician G. H. Gallup (1901–84), who devised it]

galore *adverb* in great numbers or in a large amount ♦ *There will be bargains galore.* [from an Irish phrase *go leor* meaning 'to sufficiency']

galoshes *plural noun* waterproof rubber shoes worn over ordinary shoes. [from an Old French word]

galvanic (gal-van-ik) *adjective* **1** producing an electric current by chemical action ♦ *a galvanic cell.* **2** sudden and dramatic. [from the name of the Italian anatomist Luigi Galvani (1737–98), pioneer of research into the electrical properties of living things]

galvanize *verb* **1** to stimulate someone into sudden activity. **2** to coat iron with zinc to protect it from rust ♦ *galvanized iron.* **galvanization** *noun* [same origin as for *galvanic*]

galvanometer (gal-və-nom-it-er) *noun* an instrument for measuring small electric currents.

gambit *noun* **1** an action or remark intended to gain some advantage. **2** (in chess) an opening sequence of moves in which a player deliberately sacrifices a pawn or other piece in order to gain a favourable position. [from an Italian word *gambetto* meaning 'tripping up']

gamble *verb* **1** to play games of chance for money. **2** to bet a sum of money. SYNONYMS: stake, risk, wager. **3** to take a risk or chance ♦ *We gambled on its being a fine day.* **gamble** *noun* **1** an act of gambling, a bet. **2** a risky attempt or venture. **gambler** *noun* [from an Old English word *gamenian* meaning 'to play games']

gambol *verb* (**gambolled, gambolling**) to jump or skip about playfully. **gambol** *noun* a gambolling movement. [from a French word]

game [1] *noun* **1** a form of play or sport, especially one with rules. **2** a single section forming a scoring unit in games such as tennis. **3** a secret plan or a trick ♦ *So that's his little game!* **4** wild animals or birds hunted for sport or food. **5** their flesh as food ♦ *game pie.* **games** *plural noun* **1** a meeting for sporting contests ♦ *the Olympic Games.* **2** athletics or sports as a subject taught at school. **game** *adjective* eager and willing to do something new or difficult. **to give the game away** to reveal a secret or scheme.

gamely adverb **gameness** noun **gaming** noun [from an Old English word *gamen* meaning 'amusement, fun']

game[2] adjective lame ♦ *a game leg.* [origin unknown]

gamekeeper noun a person employed to protect and breed game.

gamelan (gam-ə-lan) noun a type of orchestra in Java and Bali, consisting mainly of bronze percussion instruments. [from a Javanese word]

game plan noun a strategy worked out in advance.

game show noun a television programme in which people compete to win prizes.

gamesmanship noun the art of winning contests by gaining a psychological advantage over your opponent.

gamete (gam-eet) noun a sexual cell which unites with another in reproduction, forming a *zygote*. **gametic** (gə-met-ik) adjective [from a Greek word *gamos* meaning 'marriage']

gamine (gam-een) noun a young woman with a mischievous, boyish appearance. [from a French word]

gaming noun playing games of chance for money.

gamma noun the third letter of the Greek alphabet, equivalent to Roman *G, g.* [via Latin from Greek]

gamma rays plural noun or **gamma radiation** noun X-rays of very short wavelength emitted by radioactive substances.

gammon noun 1 ham which has been cured like bacon. 2 the bottom piece of a flitch of bacon, including a hind leg. [from an Old French word *gambon*]

gammy adjective (informal) (said about a limb) unable to function properly because of a permanent injury ♦ *a gammy leg.* [a dialect form of *game*[2]]

gamut (gam-ət) noun 1 the whole range or scope of anything ♦ *He ran the whole gamut of emotion from joy to despair.* 2 the whole range of musical notes used in medieval or modern music. [related to *gamma*]

gander noun a male goose. [from an Old English word *gandra*]

gang noun 1 a band of people going about together or working together, especially for some criminal purpose. SYNONYMS: band, mob, ring. 2 a number of labourers working together ♦ *a roadmending gang.* **gang** verb to form a gang or group ♦ *They ganged together to complain.* **to gang up on** to join together against someone. [from an Old Norse word *gangr* meaning 'walking, going']

gangling adjective tall, thin, and awkward-looking. [from an Old English word]

ganglion noun (**ganglia** or **ganglions**) 1 a group of nerve cells from which nerve fibres radiate. 2 a cyst on a tendon sheath. **ganglionic** (gang-li-on-ik) adjective [from a Greek word *ganglion* meaning 'tumour on or near sinews or tendons']

gangplank noun a movable plank used as a bridge for walking into or out of a boat.

gangrene noun death and decay of body tissue, usually caused by blockage of the blood supply to that part. **gangrenous** (gang-rin-əs) adjective [from a Greek word *gangraina*]

gangster noun a member of a gang of violent criminals.

gangway noun 1 a gap left for people to pass between rows of seats. 2 a movable bridge that links a ship to the shore. 3 a passageway, especially on a ship. **gangway** interjection make way!

gannet (gan-it) noun a large seabird which catches fish by flying above the sea and then diving in. [from an Old English word *ganot*]

gantry noun (**gantries**) 1 a light bridge-like overhead framework for supporting equipment such as a crane, railway signals, etc. 2 a structure supporting a space rocket before it is launched. [from a Latin word *cantherius* meaning 'supporting frame']

gaol (jayl) noun another spelling of **jail**.

gaoler noun another spelling of **jailer**.

gap noun 1 a break or opening in something continuous such as a hedge or fence, or between hills. SYNONYMS: hole, breach, cleft. 2 a space ♦ *Mind the gap between the train and the platform.* 3 an interval. SYNONYMS: interlude, hiatus, lull, pause. 4 a wide difference in ideas or understanding. SYNONYMS: rift, gulf, divide. **gapped** adjective [from an Old Norse word meaning 'chasm']

gape verb 1 to stare with your mouth wide open, in surprise or wonder. 2 to be or

become wide open ♦ *a gaping chasm.*
gape noun **1** an open-mouthed stare. **2** a wide opening. [from an Old Norse word *gapa*; related to *gap*]

gap year noun a year taken off for other activities by a student, usually between school and university.

garage (ga-rahzh or ga-rij) noun **1** a building in which to keep a motor vehicle or vehicles. **2** a place which sells petrol or which repairs and services motor vehicles.
garage verb to put or keep a motor vehicle in a garage. [from a French word meaning 'a shelter']

garb noun clothing, especially of a distinctive kind ♦ *clerical garb.*
garb verb to dress someone in distinctive clothes. [via French from an Italian word *garbo* meaning 'elegance']

garbage noun rubbish, especially household rubbish. [origin unknown]

garble verb to distort or mix up a message or story so that it is difficult to understand ♦ *I received garbled instructions.* [from an Arabic word *garbala* meaning 'to sift, select' (because the real facts are 'sifted out')]

Garda noun the police force of the Republic of Ireland. [an Irish word meaning 'guard']

garden noun a piece of ground attached to a house, used for growing flowers, fruit, or vegetables.
gardens plural noun ornamental public grounds.
garden verb to tend a garden. **to lead someone up the garden path** to mislead someone deliberately. **gardening** noun [via Old French from a Germanic word]

garden centre noun an establishment where plants and gardening equipment are sold.

gardener noun a person who tends a garden, either as a job or as a hobby.

gardenia (gar-deen-iə) noun **1** a tree or shrub with large fragrant white or yellow flowers. **2** its flower. [named after the Scottish naturalist Alexander Garden (1730–91)]

garden party noun a party held on a lawn in a garden or park.

gargantuan (gar-gan-tew-ən) adjective gigantic. [from the name of Gargantua, a giant in a story by Rabelais]

gargle verb to wash or rinse the inside of your throat by breathing out through a liquid held at the back of your mouth.
gargle noun **1** an act of gargling. **2** a liquid used for this. [from a French word *gargouille* meaning 'throat']

gargoyle noun a grotesque carved face or figure, especially as a spout carrying water clear of a wall. [from a French word *gargouille* meaning 'throat' (because the water passes through the throat of the figure)]

garibaldi (ga-ri-bawl-di) noun (**garibaldis**) a thin biscuit containing a layer of currants. [named after the Italian patriot Giuseppe Garibaldi (1807–82)]

garish (gair-ish) adjective too bright or showy, gaudy. **garishly** adverb [origin unknown]

garland noun a wreath of flowers and leaves worn or hung as a decoration.
garland verb to put a garland or garlands on someone or something. [from an Old French word *garlande*]

garlic noun **1** a bulb that has a strong taste and smell, used as a flavouring. **2** the onion-like plant which produces this bulb. **garlicky** adjective [from an Old English word]

garment noun a piece of clothing. [from a French word *garnement* meaning 'equipment']

garner verb to gather or collect something ♦ *The film has garnered a host of awards.* [from a Latin word *granarium* meaning 'granary']

garnet noun a semi-precious stone of deep transparent red. [from an Old French word *grenat*]

garnish verb to decorate something, especially food for the table.
garnish noun something used to decorate food or give it extra flavour. **garnishing** noun [via Old French from a Germanic word]

garret noun a top-floor or attic room, especially one that is small and dismal. [from an Old French word *garite* meaning 'watchtower']

garrison noun **1** troops who stay in a town or fort to defend it ♦ *a garrison town.* **2** the building they live in.
garrison verb to provide a place with a garrison. [from an Old French word *garison* meaning 'defence']

garrotte (gə-rot) noun 1 a cord or wire used to strangle someone. 2 a method of capital punishment by strangulation with a metal collar, formerly used in Spain. 3 the apparatus used for this.
garrotte verb to kill someone with a garrotte. [from a Spanish word]

garrulous (ga-roo-ləs) adjective talkative. **garrulity** (gə-roo-liti) noun **garrulously** adverb **garrulousness** noun [from a Latin word garrire meaning 'to chatter']

garter noun a band worn round the leg to keep a stocking or sock up. [from an Old French word garet meaning 'bend of the knee']

gas noun (**gases**) 1 a substance with particles that can move freely, especially one that does not become liquid or solid at ordinary temperatures. Other gases are usually called 'vapours'. 2 any of the gases or mixtures of gases used for lighting, heating, or cooking ♦ a gas cooker. 3 poisonous gas used as a weapon in war. 4 nitrous oxide or another gas used as an anaesthetic. 5 (North Amer.) (informal) petrol.
gas verb (**gassed, gassing**) 1 to expose someone to gas, especially to kill them or make them unconscious. 2 (informal) to talk idly for a long time. **to be a gas** (informal) to be an entertaining or amusing person or thing. [an invented word suggested by the Greek word khaos]

gas chamber noun a room that can be filled with poisonous gas to kill people or animals.

gaseous (gas-ius or gay-siəs) adjective to do with or in the form of a gas.

gash noun a long deep cut or wound.
gash verb to make a gash in something. [from an Old French word garcer meaning 'to chap or crack']

gasket noun a flat sheet or ring of rubber or other soft material used for sealing a joint between two metal surfaces in an engine etc. [origin unknown]

gaslight noun light given by a jet of burning gas. **gaslit** adjective

gas mask noun a protective mask worn over the face to protect the wearer against poisonous gas.

gasoline noun (North Amer.) petrol. [from gas and a Latin word oleum meaning 'oil']

gasometer (gas-om-it-er) noun a large round tank in which gas is stored and from which it is distributed through pipes to users. [from a French word gazomètre meaning 'a container for measuring gas']

gasp verb 1 to breathe in sharply when you are shocked or surprised. 2 to struggle for breath with the mouth open ♦ We stood at the top of the hill, gasping for air. 3 to speak in a breathless way.
gasp noun a breath drawn in sharply. **to be gasping for** (informal) to be desperate to have something, especially a drink or a cigarette ♦ I'm gasping for a cup of tea. [from an Old Norse word geispa meaning 'to yawn']

gassy adjective (**gassier, gassiest**) full of gas, fizzy. **gassiness** noun

gastric adjective to do with the stomach. [from a Greek word gastēr meaning 'stomach']

gastric flu noun any stomach disorder involving sickness and diarrhoea.

gastritis (gas-triy-tiss) noun inflammation of the stomach.

gastro-enteritis (gas-troh-en-ter-iy-tiss) noun inflammation of the stomach and intestines.

gastronomy (gas-tron-əmi) noun the practice or art of eating and drinking well. **gastronomic** (gas-trə-nom-ik) adjective [from Greek words gastēr meaning 'stomach' and -nomia meaning 'management']

gastropod (gas-trə-pod) noun a mollusc that moves by means of a muscular 'foot' on its stomach, such as a snail or slug. [from Greek words gastēr meaning 'stomach' and podos meaning 'of the foot']

gasworks noun a place where gas for heating etc. is manufactured.

gate noun 1 a movable barrier, usually on hinges, used as a door in a wall or fence. 2 the opening it covers. 3 an exit from an airport building to an aircraft. 4 a barrier for controlling the flow of water in a dam or lock. 5 the total number of spectators who pay to attend a football match etc. 6 an arrangement of slots controlling the movement of a gear lever in a motor vehicle. 7 an electric circuit with an output that is activated only by a combination of input signals. [from an Old English word]

gateau (gat-oh) *noun* (**gateaus** or **gateaux**, (gat-ohz)) a large rich cake, usually containing cream or fruit. [from a French word *gâteau* meaning 'cake']

gatecrash *verb* to go to a private party without being invited. **gatecrasher** *noun*

gatehouse *noun* a house built at the side of or over a large gate.

gateway *noun* 1 an opening or structure containing a gate. 2 a way of entering or reaching something ♦ *the gateway to success.*

gather *verb* 1 to come together, to bring people or things together. SYNONYMS: meet, assemble, congregate, mass. 2 to collect something or obtain it gradually ♦ *We've been gathering information.* SYNONYMS: accumulate, assemble, amass. 3 to collect something as harvest ♦ *Gather the corn when it is ripe.* 4 to increase gradually ♦ *Downhill we gathered speed.* 5 to understand or conclude something ♦ *I gather your proposal was accepted.* 6 to summon something up ♦ *She hardly had time to gather her thoughts.* 7 to draw parts together in folds or wrinkles ♦ *His brow was gathered in thought.* 8 to pull cloth into folds by running a thread through it ♦ *a gathered skirt.* [from an Old English word *gaderian*]

gathering *noun* an assembly or meeting of people.

gauche (gohsh) *adjective* lacking in ease and grace of manner, socially awkward. [a French word meaning 'left-handed']

gaucho (gow-choh) *noun* (**gauchos**) a cowboy from the South American pampas. [from a Latin American Spanish word]

gaudy *adjective* (**gaudier**, **gaudiest**) showy or bright in a tasteless way. SYNONYMS: garish, flashy, lurid, loud. **gaudily** *adverb* **gaudiness** *noun* [from a Latin word *gaudere* meaning 'to rejoice']

gauge (gayj) *noun* 1 an instrument used for measuring, marked with regular divisions or units of measurement. 2 a standard measure of something, such as the thickness of sheet metal, the diameter of bullets, or the fineness of textiles. 3 the distance between the rails of a railway track. **gauge** *verb* 1 to measure something exactly. 2 to estimate or form a judgement of something. [from an Old French word]

gaunt *adjective* 1 lean and haggard. 2 (said about a place) grim or desolate-looking. **gauntness** *noun* [origin unknown]

gauntlet [1] *noun* 1 a heavy glove with a wide cuff covering the wrist. 2 a glove with metal plates worn by soldiers in the Middle Ages. **to throw down the gauntlet** to challenge someone to a contest or fight. [from a French word *gant* meaning 'glove']

gauntlet [2] *noun* **to run the gauntlet** to have to face criticism or hostility from a lot of people. [from a former military and naval punishment in which the victim was made to pass between two rows of men who struck him as he passed; from a Swedish word *gatlopp* meaning 'passage']

gauze (gawz) *noun* 1 thin transparent woven material of silk, cotton, etc. 2 fine wire mesh. **gauzy** *adjective* [from Gaza, a town in Palestine]

gave past tense of **give**.

gavel (gav-əl) *noun* a small hammer used by an auctioneer, judge, etc. to call for attention or order. [origin unknown]

gavotte (gə-vot) *noun* a lively French dance, popular in the 18th century. [from a French word *gavoto* meaning 'dance of the mountain people']

gawky *adjective* (**gawkier**, **gawkiest**) awkward and ungainly. **gawkiness** *noun* [perhaps from an old word *gaw* meaning 'to gaze']

gawp *verb* (*informal*) to stare in a rude or stupid way. [perhaps an alternative form of *gape*]

gay *adjective* 1 homosexual. 2 (*old use*) light-hearted and cheerful. 3 (*old use*) brightly coloured; dressed or decorated in bright colours. **gayness** *noun* [from an Old French word *gai*]
◊ Nowadays the most common meaning of *gay* is 'homosexual'. The older meanings of 'cheerful' and 'brightly coloured' are still sometimes used but are becoming less and less common in everyday use. *Gayness* is the noun from meaning 1 of *gay*. The noun that relates to the other two senses is *gaiety*.

gaze *verb* to look at something steadily and for a long time. **gaze** *noun* a long steady look. [origin unknown]

gazebo (gə-zee-boh) *noun* (**gazebos**) a small building in the garden of a house, giving a wide view of the surroundings. [perhaps from *gaze*]

gazelle *noun* a small graceful Asian or African antelope. [via Old French from an Arabic word]

gazette *noun* a journal or newspaper, especially the official one of an organization or institution. [from an Italian phrase *gazzetta de la novità* meaning 'a halfpenny worth of news'; a *gazetta* was a Venetian coin of small value]

gazetteer (gaz-it-eer) *noun* an index of place names, names of rivers and mountains, etc. [originally meaning 'journalist'; the first gazetteer was intended to help journalists]

gazump *verb* (*informal*) to make a higher offer for a house than someone whose offer has already been accepted, and so succeed in buying the house. [originally meaning 'to swindle', from a Yiddish word *gezumph* meaning 'to overcharge']

GB *abbreviation* 1 Great Britain. 2 gigabyte(s).

GCE *abbreviation* General Certificate of Education.

GCSE *abbreviation* General Certificate of Secondary Education.

GDP *abbreviation* gross domestic product.

gear *noun* 1 a set of toothed wheels working together to transmit motion from an engine to the driven parts, e.g. the road wheels of a motor vehicle. 2 a particular setting of these ♦ *in second gear.* 3 equipment or apparatus ♦ *camping gear* ♦ *the aircraft's landing gear.* SYNONYMS: tackle, kit, rig, stuff. 4 (*informal*) clothes ♦ *I've bought some new gear.*
gear *verb* 1 to change machinery to a different gear. 2 to fit something with gears. **to gear something to** to make something match or be suitable for something else ♦ *Our stores are geared to the young shopper.* **to gear something up** to prepare something ♦ *We are all geared up for your visit.* **in gear** with a gear engaged. **out of gear** with no gear engaged. [from an Old Norse word]

gearbox *nouns* a case enclosing a gear mechanism.

gearing *noun* a set or arrangement of gears.

gear lever or **gearstick** *noun* a lever used to engage or change gear in a motor vehicle.

gecko (gek-oh) *noun* (**geckos** or **geckoes**) a lizard of warm climates, able to climb walls by the adhesive pads on its toes. [from a Malay word]

gee *verb* (**gees, geed, geeing**) **to gee someone up** to encourage someone to work more quickly. **gee up!** a command to a horse to go faster. [origin unknown]

geese plural of **goose**.

geezer *noun* (*informal*) a man. [a dialect pronunciation of an old word *guiser* meaning 'mummer']

Geiger counter (giy-ger) *noun* an instrument for detecting and measuring radioactivity. [named after the German nuclear physicist Hans Geiger (1882–1945), who developed the first device of this kind]

geisha (gay-shə) *noun* a Japanese hostess trained to entertain men by dancing and singing. [a Japanese word meaning 'entertainer']

gel (jel) *noun* a jelly-like substance ♦ *hair gel.*
gel *verb* (**gelled, gelling**) 1 to set as a gel. 2 to smooth your hair with gel. [an abbreviation of *gelatin*]

gelatin (jel-ə-tin) or **gelatine** (jel-ə-teen) *noun* a clear tasteless substance made by boiling the bones, skins, and connective tissue of animals, used in foods, medicine, and photographic film. [same origin as for *jelly*]

gelatinize (jil-at-i-niyz) *verb* 1 to become or make something gelatinous. 2 to coat or treat something with gelatin. **gelatinization** *noun*

gelatinous (jil-at-in-əs) *adjective* having a jelly-like consistency.

geld *verb* to castrate or spay an animal. [from an Old Norse word *geldr* meaning 'barren']

gelding *noun* a castrated animal, especially a male horse.

gelignite (jel-ig-niyt) *noun* an explosive containing nitroglycerine, used especially for blasting rock. [from *gelatine* and a Latin word *lignis* meaning 'wood']

gem *noun* 1 a precious or semi-precious stone, especially when cut and polished. 2 something valued because of its excellence or beauty. [via Old English from a Latin word *gemma* meaning 'bud, jewel']

Gemini (jem-i-niy) 1 a group of stars (the Twins), seen as representing figures of the twins Castor and Pollux. 2 the sign of the zodiac which the sun enters about 21 May. **Geminian** *adjective & noun* [a Latin word meaning 'twins']

gemstone *noun* a precious or semi-precious stone, especially when cut, polished, and used in a piece of jewellery.

-gen *suffix* used in scientific language to form nouns meaning 'producing' or 'produced' (as in *oxygen*, *hydrogen*).

gen (jen) *noun* (*informal*) information. **gen** *verb* (**genned, genning**) **to gen up on** (*informal*) to learn or find out about something. [perhaps from *general information*]

gender *noun* 1 the class into which a noun or pronoun is placed in the grammar of some languages, e.g. masculine, feminine, or neuter. 2 a person's sex ♦ *Jobs should be open to all, regardless of race or gender.* [from a Latin word *genus* meaning 'a kind']

gene (jeen) *noun* a unit of heredity which is transferred from a parent to offspring and is held to determine some characteristic of the offspring, carried by a chromosome. [from a Greek word *-genēs* meaning 'born']

genealogy (jeen-i-al-ǝji) *noun* (**genealogies**) 1 an account or diagram showing how a person is descended from an ancestor, listing the intermediate people. 2 the study of family history and ancestors. **genealogical** (jeeni-ǝ-loj-ikǝl) *adjective* **genealogist** *noun* [from a Greek word *genea* meaning 'race of people' and *-logy*]

gene pool *noun* the stock of genes in an interbreeding population.

genera plural of **genus**.

general *adjective* 1 involving or affecting all or most people or things, not limited or particular ♦ *in general use.* SYNONYMS: widespread, universal, common, collective, shared. 2 involving various kinds, not specialized ♦ *a general education.* SYNONYMS: broad, comprehensive, wide-ranging, catholic. 3 involving only the main features, not detailed or specific ♦ *I've got the general idea.* SYNONYMS: broad, rough, loose, vague. 4 chief or head ♦ *the general manager.*

general *noun* 1 a commander of an army, or an army officer ranking below a Field Marshal. 2 a lieutenant general or major general. 3 the chief of the Jesuits, Salvation Army, or other religious order. **in general** as a general rule, usually. [from a Latin word *genus* meaning 'race, kind']

general anaesthetic *noun* an anaesthetic that affects the whole body and makes you lose consciousness.

general election *noun* an election of Members of Parliament for the whole country.

generalissimo *noun* (**generalissimos**) a commander of combined military, naval, and air forces, or of several armies. [an Italian word meaning 'having greatest authority']

generality (jen-er-al-iti) *noun* (**generalities**) 1 a general statement without precise details. 2 being general.

generalize *verb* 1 to make a statement that is true in most cases, to make a broad statement based on specific cases. 2 to bring something into general use. **generalization** *noun*

general knowledge *noun* knowledge of a wide variety of subjects.

generally *adverb* 1 usually, in most cases. 2 widely, for the most part ♦ *The plan was generally welcomed.* 3 in a general sense, without regard to details ♦ *I was speaking generally.*

general practitioner *noun* a doctor who treats cases of all kinds in a section of the community.

general strike *noun* a strike of workers in all or most industries.

generate *verb* to produce or create something. [from a Latin word *generatus* meaning 'fathered']

generation *noun* 1 all the people born about the same time and therefore of the same age ♦ *our parents' generation.* 2 the average period in which children grow up and have children of their own, usually thought of as about 30 years. 3 a single stage in a family ♦ *three generations of the Brown family.* 4 a set of models of a machine at one stage of development ♦ *a new generation of computers.* 5 generating or being generated. **generational** *adverb*

generation gap *noun* lack of understanding between people of different generations.

generator *noun* **1** an apparatus for producing gases, steam, etc. **2** a machine for converting mechanical energy into electricity.

generic (jin-e-rik) *adjective* **1** belonging to a whole class, group, or genus. **2** (said about goods) having no brand name. **generically** *adverb* [from a Latin word *genus* meaning 'stock, race']

generous *adjective* **1** giving or ready to give something freely, especially money. SYNONYMS: benevolent, charitable, unselfish, unstinting;*(formal)* bounteous. **2** given freely, plentiful ♦ *a generous gift* ♦ *a generous helping.* SYNONYMS: lavish, ample, copious, abundant. **3** kind and thoughtful in your treatment of other people. **generously** *adverb* **generosity** *noun* [from a Latin word *generosus* meaning 'noble']

genesis (jen-i-sis) *noun* the beginning or origin of something. [a Greek word meaning 'creation or origin']

gene therapy *noun* the treatment of genetic disorders by introducing normal genes into cells to replace defective ones.

genetic (ji-net-ik) *adjective* **1** to do with genes or heredity. **2** to do with genetics. **genetics** *noun* the scientific study of heredity. **genetically** *adverb* [from *genesis*]

genetically modified *adjective* (said about an organism) having genetic material that has been artificially altered to produce one or more different characteristics.

genetic code *noun* the system of storage of genetic information in chromosomes.

genetic engineering *noun* deliberate modification of hereditary characteristics by treatment to transfer certain genes.

genetic fingerprinting *noun* an analysis of body tissue or fluid to discover its DNA, used for identifying a person involved in a crime or for proving a family relationship.

geneticist (ji-net-i-sist) *noun* an expert in genetics.

gene transfer *noun* the introduction of genes from one species into another, e.g. by genetic engineering.

genial (jee-niəl) *adjective* **1** kindly, pleasant, and cheerful. **2** (*literary*) (said about the weather) pleasantly mild and warm ♦ *a genial climate.* **genially** *adverb* **geniality**

(jee-ni-al-iti) *noun* [from a Latin word *genialis* meaning 'productive']

genie (jee-ni) *noun* (in Arabian tales) a spirit with strange powers, especially one who can grant wishes. [from an Arabic word *jinni*]

genital (jen-i-təl) *adjective* to do with human or animal reproductive organs. **genitals** *plural noun* the external sexual organs of people and animals. [from an Old French word; related to *generate*]

genitalia (gen-i-tay-liə) *plural noun* (*formal*) the genitals.

genitive (jen-i-tiv) *noun* (*Grammar*) the case showing source or possession in certain languages, corresponding to the use of *of* or *from* in English. [from an Old French word]

genius *noun* (**geniuses**) **1** a person who has exceptional intelligence, creativity, or natural ability. **2** exceptional intelligence, creativity, or natural ability ♦ *He has a real genius for music.* [a Latin word meaning 'a spirit']

genocide (jen-ə-siyd) *noun* deliberate extermination of a race of people. [from a Greek word *genos* meaning 'a race' and a Latin word *caedere* meaning 'to kill']

genome (jeen-ohm) *noun* the complete set of an individual's chromosomes. [from *gene* and *chromosome*]

genre (zhahnr) *noun* a particular kind or style of art or literature, e.g. epic, romance, or western. [a French word meaning 'a kind']

gent *noun* (*informal*) a man, a gentleman. **the Gents**(*informal*) a men's public toilet.

genteel (jen-teel) *adjective* trying to seem polite and refined. **genteelly** *adverb* [from a French word *gentil* meaning 'well-born'; related to *gentle*]

gentian (jen-shən) *noun* an alpine plant usually with deep-blue bell-like flowers. [from a Latin word *gentiana*]

gentile (jen-tiyl) *noun* a person who is not Jewish. **gentile** *adjective* not Jewish. [from a Latin word *gens* meaning 'clan or race']

gentility (jen-til-iti) *noun* good manners and elegance. [same origin as for *gentle*]

gentle *adjective* **1** mild or kind, not rough. **2** moderate, not harsh or severe ♦ *a gentle breeze.* SYNONYMS: soft, delicate, faint, light.

gently adverb **gentleness** noun [from a Latin word gentilis meaning 'from a good family']

gentlefolk plural noun (old use) people of good family or social position.

gentleman noun (**gentlemen**) 1 a man of honourable and courteous behaviour. 2 a man of good social position. 3 (in polite use) a man. **gentlemanly** adjective

gentleman-at-arms noun a member of the monarch's bodyguard on ceremonial occasions.

gentleman's agreement noun an arrangement that is based on trust rather than being legally binding.

gentlewoman noun (**gentlewomen**) (old use) a woman of good family or social position, a lady.

gentrify verb (**gentrifies, gentrified, gentrifying**) to renovate or convert a house or area so that it conforms to middle-class taste. **gentrification** noun

gentry plural noun (old use) people of good social position, especially those next below the nobility in position. [from an Old French word genterie meaning 'nobility']

genuflect (jen-yoo-flekt) verb to briefly bend one knee to the ground, especially in worship. **genuflection** noun [from Latin words genu meaning 'knee' and flectere meaning 'to bend']

genuine adjective 1 really what it is said to be, authentic ♦ genuine pearls ♦ genuine pleasure. 2 (said about a person) sincere and honest. **genuinely** adverb **genuineness** noun [from a Latin word genu meaning 'knee' (because a father would take a baby onto his knee to show that he accepted it as his)]

genus (jee-nəs) noun (**genera** (jen-er-ə)) 1 a group of animals or plants with common characteristics, usually containing several species. 2 a kind or class. [a Latin word meaning 'family or race']

geo- prefix earth. [from a Greek word gē meaning 'earth']

geode (jee-ohd) noun 1 a small cavity lined with crystals. 2 a rock containing this. [from a Greek word geōdēs meaning 'earthy']

geodesy (jee-od-i-si) noun the scientific study of the earth's shape and size. **geodesic** (ji-o-dee-sik) adjective **geodetic**

(jee-ə-det-ik) adjective [from geo- and a Greek word -daisia meaning 'division']

geodesic dome or **geodetic dome** noun a dome built of short struts holding flat or triangular polygonal pieces, fitted together to form a rough hemisphere.

geographer noun an expert in geography.

geography noun 1 the scientific study of the earth's surface and its physical features, climate, products, and population. 2 the physical features and arrangement of a place. **geographic** adjective **geographical** adjective **geographically** adverb [from geo- and -graphy]

geologist noun an expert in geology.

geology (jee-ol-ə-ji) noun 1 the scientific study of the earth's crust and its strata. 2 the geological features of an area. **geological** adjective **geologically** adverb [from geo- and -logy]

geomagnetism (jee-oh-mag-nit-izm) noun the scientific study of the earth's magnetic properties. **geomagnetic** adjective

geometric adjective 1 to do with geometry. 2 (said about a design) using regular lines and shapes. **geometrical** adjective **geometrically** adverb

geometric mean noun the value obtained by multiplying two quantities together and finding the square root of their product, or by multiplying three quantities and finding the cube root, and so on.

geometric progression noun a series of numbers (such as 1, 3, 9, 27) in which each term is the product of a constant figure and the previous term.

geometry (jee-om-itri) noun the branch of mathematics dealing with the properties and relations of lines, angles, surfaces, and solids. [from geo- and a Greek word -metria meaning 'measurement']

geomorphology (jee-oh-mor-fol-ə-ji) noun the scientific study of the physical features of the earth's surface and their relation to its geological structures. [from geo- and a Greek word morphē meaning 'a form' and -logy]

geopolitics plural noun the politics of a country as influenced by its geographical features. **geopolitical** adjective

Geordie (jor-di) *noun* (*informal*) a person from Newcastle or Tyneside. [from the name *George*]

geostationary *adjective* (said about an artificial satellite) moving in an orbit at the same speed as the earth rotates so that it appears to be stationary above a fixed point on the surface.

geothermal (jee-oh-ther-məl) *adjective* to do with or using the heat produced in the earth's interior.

geotropism (jee-ə-**troh**-pizm) *noun* the way the growth of plants is affected by earth's gravity. **geotropic** (jee-ə-**trop**-ik) *adjective* [from *geo-* and a Greek word *tropē* meaning 'turning']

geranium *noun* a garden plant with red, pink, or white flowers. [from a Greek word *geranion*]

gerbil (jer-bil) *noun* a mouse-like desert rodent with long hind legs. [from a French word *gerbille*]

geriatric (je-ri-at-rik) *adjective* 1 to do with old people. 2 (*informal*) old or out of date. **geriatric** *noun* an old person, especially one receiving special care.
geriatrics *noun* the branch of medicine dealing with the diseases and care of old people. [from Greek words *geras* meaning 'old age' and *iatros* meaning 'doctor']

germ *noun* 1 a micro-organism, especially one causing disease. 2 a portion of a living organism capable of becoming a new organism; the embryo of a seed ♦ *wheat germ*. 3 an initial stage from which something may develop ♦ *the germ of an idea*. [from a Latin word *germen* meaning 'seed, sprout']

German *adjective* to do with Germany or its people or language.
German *noun* 1 a native of Germany. 2 the language of Germany.

germane (jer-mayn) *adjective* relevant to the subject you are discussing. [from a Latin word *germanus* meaning 'of the same parents']

Germanic (jer-man-ik) *adjective* having German characteristics.
Germanic *noun* 1 a group of languages spoken in northern Europe and Scandinavia. 2 an unrecorded language believed to be the ancestor of this group.

germanium (jer-may-nium) *noun* a brittle greyish-white semi-metallic element (symbol Ge). [from a Latin word *Germanus* meaning 'German']

German measles *noun* another term for **rubella**.

German shepherd dog *noun* another term for **Alsatian**.

germicide (jerm-i-syd) *noun* a substance that kills germs or micro-organisms. **germicidal** *adjective* [from *germ* and a Latin word *caedere* meaning 'to kill']

germinal *adjective* 1 to do with germs. 2 in the earliest stage of development. 3 producing new ideas. [same origin as for *germ*]

germinate *verb* 1 (said about a seed) to begin to develop and grow, to put forth shoots. 2 to cause a seed to do this. **germination** *noun* [same origin as for *germ*]

germ warfare *noun* the use of harmful micro-organisms as a military weapon.

gerontology (je-ron-**tol**-əji) *noun* the scientific study of the process of ageing and of old people's special problems. [from a Greek word *gerontos* meaning 'of an old man' and *-logy*]

gerrymander (je-ri-man-der) *verb* to arrange the boundaries of constituencies in order to give an unfair advantage to one party or class in an election. [named after Governor Gerry of Massachusetts, who rearranged boundaries for this purpose in 1812]

gerund (je-rənd) *noun* a form of a verb (in English ending in *-ing*) that functions as a noun, e.g. *scolding* in *what is the use of my scolding him?* **gerundial** (jə-run-di-əl) *adjective* [from a Latin word *gerundum* meaning 'doing']

gerundive (jə-run-div) *noun* a form of a Latin verb that functions as an adjective meaning 'that should or must be done'. [same origin as for *gerund*]

gesso (jes-oh) *noun* gypsum as used in painting or sculpture. [an Italian word]

Gestapo (ges-tah-poh) *noun* the German secret police of the Nazi regime. [from the German phrase *Geheime Staatspolizei* meaning 'secret state police']

gestation (jes-tay-shən) *noun* 1 the process of carrying or being carried in the womb between conception and birth. 2 the time this process takes. 3 the development of a plan or idea over time. **gestate** *verb* [from a Latin word *gestare* meaning 'to carry']

gesticulate (jes-tik-yoo-layt) *verb* to make expressive movements with your hands and arms. **gesticulation** *noun* [same origin as for *gesture*]

gesture (jes-cher) *noun* 1 a movement of any part of the body that expresses what a person feels. 2 something done to convey your intentions or attitude, especially your goodwill ♦ *It would be a nice gesture to send her some flowers.*
gesture *verb* to tell a person something by making a gesture ♦ *She gestured me to be quiet.* SYNONYMS: motion, signal, gesticulate. [from a Latin word *gestus* meaning 'action' or 'way of standing or moving']

get *verb* (past tense and past participle **got**; **getting**) 1 to come into possession of something, to obtain or receive something ♦ *What grade did you get?* SYNONYMS: acquire, gain, come by, procure, secure. 2 to become something ♦ *There's no need to get angry* ♦ *I got very wet.* 3 to bring or put someone or something into a certain condition ♦ *I need to get my hair cut* ♦ *You'll get us all into trouble.* 4 to fetch something ♦ *Get your coat.* 5 to travel by or catch a train, bus, taxi, etc. 6 to catch an illness or suffer a punishment ♦ *I got the flu over Christmas* ♦ *He got three years in jail.* 7 to catch and punish someone ♦ *I'll get him for that.* 8 (*informal*) to understand ♦ *I don't get that joke.* 9 to prepare a meal ♦ *I'll get supper.* 10 to move or go somewhere ♦ *Get off the grass.* 11 to reach a place ♦ *What time did you get here?* 12 to succeed in bringing something or persuading someone ♦ *I got a message to her* ♦ *How did you get her to agree?* **to get something across** to manage to communicate an idea clearly. **to get along** to be on friendly terms. **to get at 1** to reach somewhere. **2** (*informal*) to mean or imply something ♦ *What are you getting at?* **3** (*informal*) to keep criticizing someone subtly ♦ *She's always getting at the way I speak.* **4** (*informal*) to bribe or unfairly influence someone. **to get away** to escape. **to get away with** to do something and yet avoid blame or punishment. **to get back at** to take revenge on someone. **to get by** to manage to survive. **to get someone down** to make someone depressed. **to get down to** to begin working on something. **to get going** (*informal*) to begin moving or operating. **to get in** to arrive. **to get off 1** to begin a journey. **2** to escape with

little or no punishment, to be acquitted. **3** to go to sleep. **to get someone off** to obtain an acquittal for someone ♦ *A clever lawyer got him off.* **to get on 1** to make progress with something. **2** to be on friendly terms with someone. **to be getting on** (*informal*) to be advancing in age. **getting on for** (*informal*) nearly ♦ *It's getting on for midnight.* **to get your own back** (*informal*) to have your revenge. **to get out of** to avoid something. **to get over 1** to recover from an illness, shock, etc. **2** to overcome a difficulty. **to get something over** to manage to communicate an idea clearly. **to get something over with** to complete as soon as possible an unpleasant task that you have to do. **to get round 1** to influence someone in your favour, to coax someone. **2** to deal with a problem so that it does not stop you achieving something. **3** to evade a law or rule without actually breaking it. **to get round to** to find time to deal with something. **to get through 1** to finish something or use it up. **2** to endure a difficult experience. **3** to make contact with someone on the telephone. **to get through to** (*informal*) to make a person understand. **to get to** (*informal*) to annoy or upset someone. **to get up 1** to stand after sitting or kneeling etc. **2** to get out of your bed in the morning. **3** (said about the wind or sea) to become strong or rough. **to get someone up** to dress someone in an outfit or costume. **to get something up** to prepare or organize something. **to get up to** to become involved in mischief etc. **have got to** must. [from an Old Norse word *geta* meaning 'to obtain, beget']

getaway *noun* an escape, especially after committing a crime ♦ *They made their getaway in a stolen car.*

get-out *noun* a means of avoiding something.

get-together *noun* a social gathering.

get-up *noun* (*informal*) an outfit or costume, especially an elaborate or unusual one.

geyser *noun* 1 (gee-zer or giy-zer) a natural spring that shoots up a tall column of hot water and steam at intervals. 2 (gee-zer) a kind of water heater. [from the name of a hot spring in Iceland (*geysa* meaning 'to gush')]

ghastly *adjective* (**ghastlier**, **ghastliest**) 1 causing horror or fear ♦ *a ghastly accident.* 2 very unpleasant or bad ♦ *a*

ghastly mistake. **3** looking pale and ill.
ghastliness *noun* [from an old word *gast* meaning 'terrify'; related to *aghast* meaning 'horrified']

ghat (gaht) *noun* **1** (in India) a flight of steps leading down to a river, a landing-place. **2** (in India) a mountain pass. [a Hindi word]

ghee (gee) *noun* Indian clarified butter made from the milk of a buffalo or cow. [a Hindi word]

gherkin (ger-kin) *noun* a small cucumber used for pickling. [via Dutch from a Greek word *angourion* meaning 'cucumber']

ghetto (get-oh) *noun* (**ghettos** or **ghettoes**) an area of a city, often a slum area, occupied by a minority group (especially as a result of social or economic conditions). [from an Italian word *getto* meaning 'foundry' (the first ghetto was in Venice, on the site of a foundry)]

ghetto blaster *noun* (*informal*) a large portable stereo radio and cassette or CD player.

ghost *noun* **1** a person's spirit appearing after his or her death. SYNONYMS: apparition, spectre, phantom, wraith; (*informal*) spook. **2** a very slight trace of something ♦ *a ghost of a smile* ♦ *He hasn't a ghost of a chance.* **3** a faint duplicated image on a television or other screen.
ghost *verb* to write a book etc. as a ghostwriter. **to give up the ghost** to die or stop working. [from an Old English word *gast* meaning 'spirit']

ghosting *noun* the appearance of a shadowy second image on a television or VDU screen.

ghostly (**ghostlier, ghostliest**) *adjective* to do with or like a ghost. **ghostliness** *noun*

ghost town *noun* a town abandoned by all or most of the people who used to live there.

ghostwriter *noun* a person who writes a book, article, or speech for another person, who is the named author.
ghostwrite *verb*

ghoul (gool) *noun* **1** an evil spirit, especially one said to rob graves and devour the corpses in them. **2** a person who is interested in gruesome things such as death. [from an Arabic word *gul* denoting a demon that eats dead bodies]

ghoulish (gool-ish) *adjective* interested in gruesome things ♦ *a ghoulish fascination with murder cases.* **ghoulishly** *adverb*

GHQ *abbreviation* General Headquarters.

giant *noun* **1** in stories and myths, a being of human form but of very great height and size. **2** a person, animal, or plant that is much larger than the usual size. **3** a person of outstanding ability or influence ♦ *a literary giant.*
giant *adjective* of a kind that is very large in size. **giantess** *noun* [from a Greek word *gigas*]

giant-killer *noun* a person or team that surprisingly defeats a much more powerful opponent. **giant-killing** *noun*

gibber (jib-er) *verb* to talk very quickly without making sense, especially when shocked or terrified. [an imitation of the sound]

gibberish (jib-er-ish) *noun* unintelligible talk or sounds, nonsense. [perhaps from *gibber*]

gibbet (jib-it) *noun* **1** a gallows. **2** an upright post with an arm from which the body of an executed criminal was left hanging as a warning to others. [from an Old French word *gibet* meaning 'cudgel, gallows']

gibbon (jib-on) *noun* a small long-armed ape of SE Asia. [from a French word]

gibbous (jib-os) *adjective* **1** (said about the moon) having the bright part greater than a semicircle and less than a circle. **2** convex or sticking out. [from a Latin word *gibbus* meaning 'hump']

gibe (jiyb) *verb* to jeer.
gibe *noun* a jeering remark. [origin unknown]

giblets (jib-lits) *plural noun* the edible parts of the inside of a bird, such as the heart, liver, etc., that are taken out before it is cooked. [from an Old French word *gibelet* meaning 'game bird stew']

giddy *adjective* (**giddier, giddiest**) **1** having the feeling that everything is spinning round, dizzy. **2** causing this feeling ♦ *We looked down from this giddy height.* **3** frivolous and excited. **giddily** *adverb* **giddiness** *noun* [from an Old English word *gidig* meaning 'insane']

gift *noun* **1** something given without payment, a present. **2** a natural ability or talent ♦ *He has a gift for languages.* SYNONYMS: flair, aptitude, facility. **3** (*informal*) something that is very easy to do or cheap

to buy ♦ *Their first goal was an absolute gift.*
gift *verb* to give something as a gift. **to look a gift-horse in the mouth** to accept something ungratefully, examining it for faults. [from an Old Norse word *gipt*]

gifted *adjective* having great natural ability or talent.

gift wrap *noun* decorative paper used for wrapping presents.
gift-wrap *verb* (**gift-wrapped, gift-wrapping**) to wrap a present in decorative paper.

gig [1] *noun* (*informal*) a live performance by a musician, comedian, etc. [origin unknown]

gig [2] *noun* a light two-wheeled horse-drawn carriage. [from an old word *gig* meaning 'a flighty girl']

giga- *prefix* 1 denoting a factor of 10^9, one thousand million. 2 (*Computing*) denoting a factor of 2^{30}. [from a Greek word *gigas* meaning 'giant']

gigabyte (**gi-gə-biyt** or **ji-gə-biyt**) *noun* (*Computing*) a unit of information equal to one thousand million bytes, or (more precisely) 2^{30} bytes.

gigantic *adjective* extremely large.
gigantically *adverb* [from a Latin word *gigantis* meaning 'of a giant']

giggle *verb* to laugh in a silly or nervous way.
giggle *noun* 1 a silly or nervous laugh. 2 (*informal*) something amusing, a joke ♦ *We only did it for a giggle.* **giggly** *adjective* [an imitation of the sound]

gigolo (**jig-ə-loh**) or (**zhig-ə-loh**) *noun* (**gigolos**) a young man paid by an older woman to be her escort or lover.

gild *verb* to cover something with a thin layer of gold or gold paint. **to gild the lily** to spoil something already beautiful by trying to improve it. [from an Old English word *gyldan*]

gill (jil) *noun* a unit of liquid measure, equal to a quarter of a pint. [from an Old French word *gille* meaning 'measure or container for wine']

gills *plural noun* 1 the organ with which a fish breathes in water. 2 the vertical plates on the underside of a mushroom cap. **green about the gills** looking sickly. [from an Old Norse word]

gilt [1] *adjective* covered thinly with gold or gold paint.
gilt *noun* a thin covering of gold or gold paint.

gilts *plural noun* gilt-edged securities. [the old past tense of *gild*]

gilt [2] *noun* a young sow. [from an Old Norse word]

gilt-edged *noun* (said about stocks or securities) considered to be very safe as an investment.

gimbals (**jim-bəlz**) *plural noun* an arrangement of rings and pivots for keeping instruments horizontal in a moving ship or aircraft. [from an Old French word *gemel* meaning 'twin']

gimcrack (**jim-krak**) *adjective* showy, worthless, and flimsy ♦ *gimcrack ornaments.* [origin unknown]

gimlet *noun* a small tool with a screw-like tip for boring holes. [via Old French from a Germanic word]

gimlet-eyed *adjective* having piercing eyes.

gimmick *noun* a trick, device, or mannerism used to attract people's attention, or to make an entertainer etc. easily recognized and remembered.
gimmicky *adjective* [originally American; origin unknown]

gin [1] (jin) *noun* 1 a colourless alcoholic spirit flavoured with juniper berries. 2 gin rummy. [from the name of Geneva, a city in Switzerland]

gin [2] (jin) *noun* 1 a trap or snare for catching animals. 2 a machine for separating the fibres of the cotton plant from its seeds. 3 a kind of crane and windlass. [from an Old French word *engin* meaning 'engine']

ginger *noun* 1 the hot-tasting root of a tropical plant, or a flavouring made from this root, used especially in drinks and Eastern cooking. 2 this plant. 3 liveliness or energy. 4 a light reddish-yellow colour.
ginger *verb* to make something more lively ♦ *This will ginger things up!*
ginger *adjective* ginger-coloured. **gingery** *adjective* [via Old English, Latin, and Greek from Dravidian (an Indian language)]

ginger ale *noun* a ginger-flavoured fizzy drink.

ginger beer *noun* a slightly alcoholic ginger-flavoured drink.

gingerbread *noun* a ginger-flavoured cake or biscuit.

ginger group *noun* a group within a larger group or movement, urging stronger action on a particular issue.

gingerly *adverb* cautiously.

gingerly adjective cautious ♦ in a gingerly way. [perhaps from an Old French word gensor meaning 'delicate']

ginger nut noun a hard ginger-flavoured biscuit.

gingham (ging-əm) noun a cotton fabric often with a striped or checked pattern. [via Dutch from a Malay word genggang meaning 'striped']

gingivitis (jin-ji-viy-tiss) noun inflammation of the gums. [from a Latin word gingiva meaning 'gum']

gin rummy noun a form of the card game rummy for two players.

ginseng (jin-seng) noun 1 a plant found in eastern Asia and North America. 2 its root, used in medicine. [from a Chinese word]

gippy tummy (jip-i) noun (informal) diarrhoea affecting visitors to hot countries. [humorous alteration of Egyptian]

gipsy noun another spelling of **gypsy**.

giraffe noun a long-necked African mammal, the tallest living animal. [from an Arabic word zarafa]

gird verb (literary) to fasten or encircle something with a belt or band ♦ He girded on his sword. **to gird up your loins** to prepare yourself for an effort. [from an Old English word gyrdan]

girder noun a metal beam supporting part of a building or a bridge. [from an old use of gird meaning 'to brace or strengthen']

girdle noun 1 a belt or cord worn round the waist. 2 a woman's elastic corset covering from the waist to the thigh. 3 a connected ring of bones in the body ♦ the pelvic girdle.
girdle verb to surround something. [from an Old English word gyrdel]

girl noun 1 a female child. 2 a young woman. 3 a girlfriend. **girlhood** noun [origin unknown]

girlfriend noun a person's usual female companion in a romantic relationship.

girlish adjective like a girl. **girlishly** adverb **girlishness** noun

giro (jiy-roh) noun (giros) 1 a system, run by a bank or post office, by which one customer can make a payment to another by transferring credit from his or her own account to the other person's, instead of paying directly. 2 (informal) a cheque or payment by giro, especially a social security payment. [via German from an Italian word meaning 'circulation']
◊ Do not confuse this word with **gyro**, which has a different meaning.

girt adjective (poetic) girded. [old past tense of gird]

girth noun 1 the distance around the middle of something, especially a person's waist. 2 a band passing under a horse's body to hold the saddle in place. [from an Old Norse word]

gist (jist) noun the essential points or general sense of what someone says. [from an Old French word]

give verb (gave, given) 1 to let someone have something of yours, to provide someone with something. 2 to deliver a message. 3 to produce a sound ♦ He gave a sigh. SYNONYMS: utter, emit, let out. 4 to carry out an action ♦ She gave the door a kick. 5 to make someone experience or suffer something ♦ You gave me a fright. 6 to state or offer something ♦ Let me give my reasons. 7 to pledge something ♦ I've given my word. 8 to be the host at a party or meal. 9 to yield something as a product or result. 10 to be the source of something. 11 to allow a view of or access to a place ♦ The window gives on to the street. 12 (said about a referee, umpire, etc.) to deliver a judgement on whether a goal should be allowed, a player is out, etc. ♦ The referee didn't give the goal ♦ The umpire gave the batsman out. 13 to be flexible, to bend or collapse when pressed or pulled.
give noun springiness or elasticity. **give and take** willingness on both sides to make concessions. **to give someone away** 1 to betray someone or reveal who or where they are. 2 to hand over the bride to the groom at a wedding. **to give something away** to reveal a secret etc. unintentionally. **to give in** to admit that you are defeated. **to give something off** to produce and emit something ♦ Petrol gives off fumes. **give or take** (informal) adding or subtracting the amount mentioned in estimating something; more or less ♦ We should be there by midnight, give or take a few minutes. **to give out** 1 to become exhausted or used up. 2 to stop working ♦ The engine has given out at last. **to give something out** 1 to emit something ♦ The chimney was giving out smoke. 2 to distribute something ♦ Can you give the books out? **to give something over to** to devote a period of time to some activity

♦ *Afternoons are given over to sport.* **to give someone to understand** to tell someone something in an indirect or formal way ♦ *I was given to understand that there were no tickets left.* **to give up 1** to stop trying. **2** to admit that you are not able to do something. **to give something up 1** to stop doing something, especially a habit ♦ *She's given up smoking.* **2** to part with something you would prefer to keep. **to give way** see **way**. **giver** *noun* [from an Old English word *gefan*]

giveaway *noun* (*informal*) **1** something given without charge. **2** something that reveals a secret.

given past participle of **give**.
  given *adjective* **1** specified or stated ♦ *all the people in a given area.* **2** having a certain tendency ♦ *He is given to swearing.*
  given *preposition* taking into account
  ♦ *Given her ability, it's surprising she hasn't won more trophies.*

given name *noun* a person's first name, not their surname.

gizmo (giz-moh) *noun* (**gizmos**) (*informal*) a gadget, especially one that you do not know the name of. [origin unknown]

gizzard *noun* a bird's second stomach, in which food is ground up. [from an Old French word]

glacé (gla-say) *adjective* iced with sugar, preserved in sugar ♦ *glacé fruits.* [a French word meaning 'iced']

glacial (glay-shəl) *adjective* **1** icy. **2** to do with or from glaciers or other ice ♦ *glacial deposits.* **3** (said about a person) cold and unfriendly. **glacially** *adverb* [from a Latin word *glacialis* meaning 'icy']

glaciated (glas-i-ayt-id) *adjective* covered with glaciers, or affected by their action. **glaciation** *noun*

glacier (glas-i-er) *noun* a mass of ice moving very slowly. [same origin as for *glacial*]

glad *adjective* (**gladder**, **gladdest**) **1** pleased or happy. **2** making someone pleased or happy ♦ *We brought the glad news.* **to be glad of** to be grateful for or pleased with something. **gladly** *adverb* **gladness** *noun* [from an Old English word]

gladden *verb* to make a person glad.

glade *noun* an open space in a forest. [origin unknown]

gladiator (glad-i-ay-ter) *noun* a man trained to fight for public entertainment in ancient Rome. **gladiatorial** (gladi-ə-tor-iəl) *adjective* [from a Latin word *gladius* meaning 'sword']

gladiolus *noun* (**gladioli** (glad-i-oh-liy)) a garden plant with sword-shaped leaves and spikes of brightly coloured flowers. [same origin as for *gladiator*]

glamorize *verb* to make something seem glamorous or romantic.

glamorous *adjective* excitingly attractive. **glamorously** *adverb*

glamour *noun* **1** an attractive and exciting quality that something has, often because it involves famous and successful people ♦ *the glamour of Hollywood.* **2** physical attractiveness. [from an old use of *grammar* meaning 'magic']

glance *verb* **1** to look at something briefly. **2** to strike something at an angle and slide off it ♦ *a glancing blow* ♦ *The ball glanced off his bat.*
  glance *noun* a brief or hurried look. [probably from an Old French word *glacier* meaning 'to slip']

gland *noun* an organ of the body that separates substances from the blood that are to be used by the body or secreted from it. [from a Latin word *glandulae* meaning 'throat glands']

glandular (glan-dew-ler) *adjective* to do with or like a gland.

glandular fever *noun* a feverish illness in which the lymph glands are swollen.

glare *verb* **1** to shine with an unpleasantly strong or dazzling light. **2** to stare angrily or fiercely. SYNONYMS: glower, scowl; (*informal*) look daggers at.
  glare *noun* **1** a strong unpleasant light. **2** an angry or fierce stare. [from an Old German or Old Dutch word *glaren* meaning 'to gleam or glare']

glaring *adjective* **1** very obvious ♦ *a glaring error.* **2** bright and dazzling. **glaringly** *adverb*

glasnost (glaz-nost) *noun* the open reporting of news or giving of information, especially in the former Soviet Union. [from a Russian word meaning 'openness']

glass *noun* **1** a hard brittle substance, usually transparent, made by fusing sand with soda and lime. **2** a drinking container made of glass. **3** an object made of glass, such as a mirror or a covering for a watch face. **4** ornaments or other objects made of glass.

glasses *plural noun* a pair of lenses in a frame that rests on the nose and ears, used to correct or improve weak eyesight. **glass** *verb* to fit or enclose something with glass. [from an Old English word]

glass-blowing *noun* the craft of shaping semi-molten glass by blowing air into it through a tube. **glass-blower** *noun*

glass fibre *noun* a strong plastic or cloth reinforced with glass filaments.

glassful *noun* (**glassfuls**) the amount contained by a drinking glass.

glasshouse *noun* **1** a greenhouse. **2** (*informal*) a military prison.

glasspaper *noun* paper coated with powdered glass, used for smoothing wood etc.

glassy *adjective* (**glassier, glassiest**) **1** like glass, having a smooth surface. **2** with a dull expressionless stare ♦ *glassy-eyed*. **glassily** *adverb* **glassiness** *noun*

Glaswegian (glaz-wee-jən) *adjective* to do with or coming from Glasgow. **Glaswegian** *noun* a person born or living in Glasgow.

glaucoma (glaw-koh-mə) *noun* a condition caused by increased pressure of the fluid within the eyeball, causing gradual loss of sight. [from a Greek word *glaukōma*]

glaze *verb* **1** to fit a window or building with panes of glass. **2** to coat something with a glossy surface. **3** to become fixed or glassy ♦ *Her eyes glazed over with boredom*. **glaze** *noun* **1** a shiny surface or coating, especially on pottery, the substance used to form this. **2** a liquid such as milk or beaten egg, used to form a smooth shiny coating on food. [from *glass*]

glazier (glay-zi-er) *noun* a person whose job is to fit glass into windows and doors.

gleam *noun* **1** a beam or ray of soft light, especially one that comes and goes. **2** a small amount of some quality or emotion ♦ *a gleam of hope*. **gleam** *verb* to shine brightly, especially after cleaning or polishing. **gleaming** *adjective* [from an Old English word]

glean *verb* **1** to gather things, especially scraps of information, from various sources. **2** (*historical*) to pick up grain left by harvesters. **gleaner** *noun* [via Latin from a Celtic word]

gleanings *plural noun* things gleaned, especially scraps of information.

glebe (gleeb) *noun* a portion of land that formerly provided income for a rector or vicar. [from a Latin word *gleba* meaning 'a lump of earth']

glee *noun* **1** great delight. **2** a song with three or more male voice parts, often without accompaniment. [from an Old English word]

gleeful *adjective* full of glee, joyful. **gleefully** *adverb*

glen *noun* a narrow valley, especially in Scotland or Ireland. [from a Scottish Gaelic and Irish word *gleann*]

glib *adjective* ready with words but insincere or superficial. **glibly** *adverb* **glibness** *noun* [from an old word *glibbery* meaning 'slippery']

glide *verb* **1** to move along smoothly. SYNONYMS: slide, skim, skid, slip. **2** to fly in a glider or in an aeroplane without engine power. **3** (said about a bird) to fly without beating its wings. **glide** *noun* a gliding movement. [from an Old English word]

glider *noun* an aircraft without an engine that flies by floating on warm air currents called thermals.

glimmer *noun* **1** a faint, flickering light. **2** a faint sign or trace of something ♦ *a glimmer of hope*. **glimmer** *verb* to shine with a faint, flickering light. [probably from a Scandinavian word]

glimpse *noun* a brief view. **glimpse** *verb* to see something briefly. [probably from an Old English word; related to *glimmer*]

glint *noun* a very brief flash of light. **glint** *verb* to shine with brief flashes of light. [probably from a Scandinavian word]

glissade (glis-**ayd**) *verb* **1** to slide skilfully down a steep slope, especially in mountaineering. **2** to make a gliding step in dancing. **glissade** *noun* a glissading movement or step. [from a French word *glisser* meaning 'to slip, slide']

glisten *verb* to shine like something wet or polished. [from an Old English word *glisnian*]

glitch noun (informal) a sudden malfunction or setback. [origin unknown]

glitter verb to shine with tiny flashes of light, to sparkle.
glitter noun 1 tiny sparkling pieces used for decoration. 2 sparkling light. **glittery** adjective [from an Old Norse word glitra]

glitz noun (informal) extravagant display; show-business glamour. **glitzy** adjective [from glitter]

gloaming noun (literary) the evening twilight. [from an Old English word]

gloat verb to show how pleased you are about your success or someone else's misfortune, in a smug or mean way.
gloat noun an act of gloating. [origin unknown]

global adjective 1 to do with the whole world, worldwide. 2 involving all parts or aspects of something. 3 (Computing) applying to the whole of a file or program ♦ a global search. **globally** adverb [from globe]

global village noun the world regarded as a single community linked by telecommunications.

global warming noun the gradual increase in the temperature of the earth's atmosphere, caused by the greenhouse effect.

globe noun 1 an object shaped like a ball, especially one with the map of the earth on it. 2 the world ♦ She has travelled all over the globe. [from a Latin word globus]

globetrotter noun a person who travels all over the world.

globular (glob-yoo-ler) adjective shaped like a globe. [same origin as for globule]

globule (glob-yool) noun a small rounded drop. [from a Latin word globulus meaning 'small globe']

globulin (glob-yoo-lin) noun a kind of protein found in animal and plant tissue.

glockenspiel (glok-ən-speel) noun a musical instrument consisting of tuned steel bars fixed in a frame and struck with two small hammers. [a German word meaning 'bell play']

gloom noun 1 darkness or dimness. 2 a feeling of sadness and depression. [origin unknown]

gloomy adjective (gloomier, gloomiest) 1 dark, poorly lit. 2 depressed or sullen. 3 depressing or dismal. **gloomily** adverb

gloominess noun

glorified adjective pretending to be more impressive or special than it really is ♦ He still thinks a computer is just a glorified typewriter.

glorify verb (glorifies, glorified, glorifying) 1 to make something seem more splendid or admirable than it really is ♦ It is a film that glorifies war. 2 to praise someone highly. 3 to worship God. **glorification** noun [from glory]

glorious adjective 1 having or bringing glory. 2 splendid or magnificent ♦ a glorious view. SYNONYMS: marvellous, superb, spectacular, gorgeous, majestic. **gloriously** adverb

glory noun (glories) 1 fame and honour won by great deeds. 2 praise and worship offered to God. 3 beauty or magnificence ♦ the glory of a sunset. 4 a thing deserving praise and honour.
glory verb (glories, gloried, glorying) to rejoice or take pride in something ♦ We are all glorying in his success. [from a Latin word gloria]

gloss noun 1 the shine on a smooth surface. 2 an explanatory comment.
gloss verb to make something glossy. **to gloss something over** to mention a fault or mistake only briefly to make it seem less serious than it really is. [origin unknown]

glossary (glos-er-i) noun (glossaries) a list of technical or special words with their definitions. [from a Greek word glōssa meaning 'tongue, language']

gloss paint noun a paint with a glossy finish.

glossy adjective (glossier, glossiest) smooth and shiny.
glossy noun (glossies) (informal) a magazine printed on glossy paper, with many illustrations. **glossiness** noun

glottis noun the opening of the upper end of the windpipe between the vocal cords. **glottal** adjective [from a Greek word glōssa meaning 'tongue']

glove noun a covering for the hand, usually with separate parts for each finger and the thumb. [from an Old English word]

gloved adjective wearing a glove or gloves.

glove compartment noun a space in the dashboard of a motor vehicle, used for storing small items.

glove puppet *noun* a cloth puppet fitting over the hand so that the fingers can move it.

glow *verb* 1 to give out light and heat without flame. 2 to have a warm or flushed look or colour. 3 to express or feel great pleasure ♦ *She glowed with pride.* **glow** *noun* 1 brightness and warmth without flames. 2 a warm or cheerful feeling ♦ *We felt a glow of pride.* [from an Old English word]

glower (glow-ə) *verb* to scowl or stare angrily. [origin unknown]

glowing *adjective* very enthusiastic or favourable ♦ *a glowing report.*

glow-worm *noun* a kind of beetle that can give out a greenish light at its tail.

glucagon (gloo-kə-gon) *noun* (*Biochemistry*) a hormone produced in the pancreas which helps the breakdown of glycogen to glucose in the liver and so increases blood sugar. [from Greek words *glukus* meaning 'sweet' and *agōn* meaning 'leading' or 'bringing']

glucose (gloo-kohz) *noun* a form of sugar that is found in fruit juice and honey and is an important source of energy in living things. [same origin as for *glycerine*]

glue *noun* a sticky substance used for joining things.
glue *verb* (**glues, glued, gluing**) to fasten something with glue. **gluey** *adjective* [from an Old French word; related to *gluten*]

glum *adjective* (**glummer, glummest**) sad and gloomy. **glumly** *adverb* **glumness** *noun* [from a dialect word *glum* meaning 'to frown']

gluon *noun* (*Physics*) a hypothetical force binding quarks together. [from *glue*]

glut *noun* an excessive supply of something, a surfeit ♦ *a glut of apples.*
glut *verb* (**glutted, glutting**) to supply or fill something with much more than is needed ♦ *to glut the market.* [same origin as for *glutton*]

glutamate (gloo-tə-mayt) *noun* a substance used to bring out the flavour in food. [from *gluten*]

gluten (gloo-tən) *noun* a sticky protein substance that remains when starch is washed out of flour. [from a Latin word meaning 'glue']

glutinous (gloo-tin-əs) *adjective* glue-like or sticky. [same origin as for *gluten*]

glutton *noun* a person who eats far too much. **a glutton for punishment** a person who seems to enjoy doing something difficult or unpleasant. **gluttonous** *adjective* [from a Latin word *gluttire* meaning 'to swallow']

gluttony *noun* greed in eating.

glycogen (gliy-kə-jən) *noun* (*Biochemistry*) a polysaccharide found in the liver, the main form in which carbohydrate is stored in animals.

glycerine (glis-er-een) *noun* glycerol. [from a Greek word *glukus* meaning 'sweet']

glycerol (glis-er-ol) *noun* a thick sweet colourless liquid used in ointments and medicines and in the manufacture of explosives.

GM *abbreviation* genetically modified.

gm *abbreviation* gram(s).

GMT *abbreviation* Greenwich Mean Time.

gnarled (narld) *adjective* (said about a tree or a person's hands) knobbly and twisted. [from an Old German or Old Dutch word]

gnash *verb* 1 to grind your teeth together, especially in anger. 2 (said about teeth) to strike together. [perhaps from an Old Norse word *gnastan* meaning 'a gnashing of teeth']

gnat *noun* a small biting fly. [from an Old English word]

gnaw *verb* 1 to keep on biting at something so that it wears away. 2 to keep worrying or troubling someone ♦ *a gnawing doubt.* [from an Old English word *gnagan*]

gneiss (niyss) *noun* a kind of coarse-grained rock. [a German word]

gnome *noun* 1 a kind of dwarf in fairy tales and legends, living underground and guarding the treasures of the earth. 2 a garden ornament in the form of a bearded man with a pointed hat. [from a Latin word *gnomus*]

gnostic (nos-tik) *adjective* 1 to do with knowledge. 2 having special mystical knowledge. [from a Greek word *gnōstos* meaning 'known']

GNP *abbreviation* gross national product.

gnu (noo) *noun* a large African antelope that looks like an ox. [from a Khoisan (African) word]

GNVQ *abbreviation* General National Vocational Qualification.

go verb (**goes, went, gone**) **1** to move from one place to another ♦ *Where are you going?* **2** to leave ♦ *We must go at one o'clock.* **3** to pass into a certain condition, to become something ♦ *The milk has gone sour* ♦ *My mind went blank.* **4** to spend time doing something ♦ *Let's go shopping.* **5** to lead or stretch from one place to another ♦ *The road goes to York.* **6** to be in a certain state ♦ *They will just have to go hungry.* **7** to be working properly ♦ *The car won't go.* **8** (said about time) to pass. **9** to belong in some place or position ♦ *Plates go on the shelf.* **10** to match or look good with something else ♦ *Those shoes don't go with that suit.* **11** (said about a story, tune, etc.) to have a certain wording or content ♦ *I forget how the chorus goes.* **12** to make a specified sound ♦ *The gun went bang* ♦ *Has the bell gone yet?* **13** to turn out in a certain way ♦ *I hope the show goes well.* **14** to be sold ♦ *It's going cheap.* **15** (said about money or supplies) to be spent or used up. **16** to be given up or got rid of ♦ *Some luxuries will have to go.* **17** to disappear, fail, or die ♦ *My eyesight is going.* **18** to carry an action to a certain point ♦ *I'm not prepared to go any further with my offer.* **19** to be able to be put somewhere ♦ *Your clothes won't go into that suitcase.* **20** to be given or allotted to someone ♦ *His estate went to his nephew.* **21** to be allowable or acceptable ♦ *Anything goes.*
go noun (**goes**) **1** a turn or try ♦ *Can I have a go?* **2** energy or liveliness ♦ *She is full of go.* **3** busy activity ♦ *It's all go today.* **to go about** to tackle a job etc. ♦ *You've gone about it the wrong way.* **to go ahead** to proceed immediately. **to go along with** to accept or agree with something. **to go back on your word** to fail to keep a promise. **to go by** to be guided or directed by something. **to go down 1** to be received or accepted ♦ *The suggestion went down very well.* **2** to be recorded or remembered in a particular way ♦ *This will go down as a classic final.* **3** to catch an illness ♦ *She's gone down with the flu.* **4** (*informal*) to go to prison. **to go down with** to become ill with a disease. **to go far** to be successful in your career. **to go for 1** to like, prefer, or choose something. **2** (*informal*) to attack someone. **to go for it** (*informal*) to go all out for success. **go for it!** (*informal*) an encouragement to act vigorously. **to go in for 1** to enter a contest. **2** to enjoy doing something ♦ *I didn't know you went in for crosswords.* **to go into 1** to investigate something or describe it in detail. **2** (said about a whole number) to be able to be divided into another number, especially without a remainder. **to go it alone** to take action by yourself without assistance. **to go off 1** (said about a bomb or gun) to explode or fire. **2** (said about an alarm) to begin to sound. **3** to become stale. **4** to go to sleep. **5** to stop liking something ♦ *I've gone off tea lately.* **6** to lose quality ♦ *The programme has gone off recently.* **7** to proceed ♦ *The party went off well.* **to go on 1** to continue to do something. **2** to be taking place ♦ *There's an arts festival going on this week.* **3** to talk lengthily ♦ *He does go on a bit, doesn't he?* **4** to be spent on something ♦ *Most of my money goes on clothes.* **to be going on with** for the time being ♦ *That should be enough to be going on with.* **to go out 1** to stop burning or shining. **2** to go to social events. **3** to be broadcast ♦ *The programme goes out live.* **to go out with** to have someone as your regular romantic companion. **to go over** to examine or check something. **to go round** to be enough for everyone. **to go slow** to work at a deliberately slow pace as a form of industrial protest. **to go through 1** to experience a difficult or painful event or time. **2** to be approved or made official ♦ *We are waiting for our claim to go through.* **to go up** to explode or burn rapidly. **to go without** to put up with the lack of something. **to make a go of** to make a success of something. **on the go** very active or busy. **to go 1** remaining ♦ *just ten miles to go.* **2** (said about food or drink) to be eaten or drunk away from the restaurant or café where it has been bought. [from an Old English word]

goad noun **1** a pointed stick for prodding cattle to move onwards. **2** something that stimulates a person into action.
goad verb to stir someone into action, especially by being annoying ♦ *Don't let him goad you into retaliating.* [from an Old English word]

go-ahead noun (*informal*) permission to proceed.
go-ahead adjective (*informal*) willing to try new methods, enterprising.

goal noun **1** a structure or area into which the ball must be sent to score a point in football, hockey, etc. **2** a point scored in this way. **3** something that you are trying to reach or achieve. SYNONYMS: aim, purpose, end, objective, target, ambition. **in goal** in the position of a goalkeeper. [from an old word *gol* meaning 'boundary']

goal difference noun (in league football) the difference between the total of goals scored by a team and those scored against it in a series of matches.

goalie noun (informal) a goalkeeper.

goalkeeper noun a player who stands in the goal and tries to keep the ball out.

goal line noun the end line of a football or hockey pitch.

goalmouth noun the area just in front of a goal in soccer or hockey.

goalpost noun either of the pair of posts marking the limits of the goal.

goat noun 1 a hardy mammal with shaggy hair, horns, and (in the male) a beard, often kept for its milk and meat. 2 a related wild mammal ♦ mountain goat. **to get someone's goat** (informal) to irritate them. [from an Old English word]

goatee (goh-**tee**) noun a short pointed beard.

goatherd noun a person who looks after a herd of goats. [from goat and an old word herd meaning 'herdsman']

gob noun (informal) a person's mouth. [from a Scottish Gaelic word gob meaning 'beak, mouth']

gobble verb 1 to eat something quickly and greedily. SYNONYMS: bolt, guzzle, devour, gulp. 2 (said about a turkeycock) to make a throaty swallowing sound. [from an Old French word gober meaning 'to swallow']

gobbledegook noun (informal) the pompous and technical language that is often used by officials and is difficult to understand. [an imitation of the sound a turkeycock makes]

go-between noun a person who acts as a messenger or negotiator between others.

goblet noun 1 a drinking glass with a stem and a foot. 2 the container of liquid in a liquidizer. [from a French word gobelet meaning 'little cup']

goblin noun a mischievous ugly elf. [from an Old French word gobelin']

gobstopper noun a very large sweet for sucking.

god noun 1 a superhuman being regarded as having power over nature and human affairs ♦ Mars was the Roman god of war. 2 (**God**) the creator of the universe in Christian, Jewish, and Muslim belief; the supreme being. 3 a person or thing that is greatly admired or adored ♦ Money is his god. **the gods** (informal) the gallery of a theatre. **to play God** to behave as if you are all-powerful. [from an Old English word]

godchild noun (**godchildren**) a person in relation to his or her godparent.

god-daughter noun a female godchild.

goddess noun 1 a female god. 2 a woman who is adored for her beauty ♦ a Hollywood goddess.

godfather noun 1 a male godparent. 2 the mastermind behind an illegal organization.

godforsaken adjective (said about a place) wretched or dismal.

godhead noun divine nature. **the Godhead** God. [from god and an Old English word -had meaning '-hood']

godless adjective 1 not having belief in God. 2 wicked or profane. **godlessly** adverb **godlessness** noun

godlike adjective like God or a god.

godly adjective (**godlier, godliest**) sincerely religious. **godliness** noun

godmother noun a female godparent.

godparent noun a person who promises at a child's baptism to help to bring it up as a Christian.

godsend noun something very helpful that comes to you unexpectedly. [from an old phrase God's send meaning 'what God has sent']

godson noun a male godchild.

Godspeed interjection (old use) an expression of good wishes to a person starting a journey.

goer noun 1 a person who attends a place or event, especially regularly ♦ a cinema-goer ♦ a church-goer. 2 (informal) a person or thing that goes well.

gofer (goh-**fer**) noun (informal) a person who runs errands, a dogsbody. [from go for]

go-getter noun (informal) someone who is successful through being pushy or energetic. **go-getting** adjective

goggle verb to stare with wide open eyes. **goggles** plural noun large close-fitting spectacles for protecting your eyes from wind, water, dust, etc. [origin unknown]

goggle-box noun (informal) a television set.

goggle-eyed *adjective* with wide open eyes, especially through astonishment.

going present participle of **go**.
going *noun* 1 the state of the ground for walking or riding on ♦ *rough going*. 2 rate of progress ♦ *It was good going to get there by noon*.
going *adjective* 1 available or remaining ♦ *Is there any apple pie going?* 2 (said about a price etc.) current and fair ♦ *the going rate*. **to be going to do something** to be about to do it, to be likely to do it.

going concern *noun* a thriving business.

going-over *noun* (*informal*) 1 a thorough inspection or overhaul. 2 a thrashing.

goings-on *plural noun* surprising or suspicious behaviour or events.

goitre (goi-ter) *noun* a swelling in the neck caused by an enlarged thyroid gland. [from a French word]

go-kart *noun* a kind of miniature racing car.

gold *noun* 1 a yellow metal of very high value, a chemical element (symbol Au). 2 coins or other objects made of gold. 3 a deep yellow colour. 4 a gold medal, usually given as first prize. 5 something very good or precious.
gold *adjective* made of gold; coloured like gold. [from an Old English word]

gold dust *noun* 1 fine particles of gold. 2 something very valuable.

golden *adjective* 1 made of or coloured like gold. 2 precious or excellent ♦ *a golden memory* ♦ *a golden opportunity*.

golden age *noun* a time of great prosperity in the past.

golden boy or **golden girl** *noun* a popular or successful person.

golden eagle *noun* a large eagle with yellow-tipped head feathers.

golden handshake *noun* (*informal*) a payment given by a firm to one of its executives as compensation for being made redundant or forced to retire.

golden jubilee *noun* the 50th anniversary of an event.

golden mean *noun* neither too much nor too little.

golden retriever *noun* a retriever with a thick golden-coloured coat.

golden rule *noun* a basic principle which should always be followed.

golden syrup *noun* a kind of pale treacle.

golden wedding *noun* the 50th anniversary of a wedding.

goldfield *noun* an area where gold is found as a mineral.

goldfinch *noun* a songbird with a band of yellow across each wing.

goldfish *noun* (**goldfish**) a small reddish Chinese carp kept in a bowl or pond.

goldfish bowl *noun* 1 a round glass container for goldfish. 2 a place or situation with no privacy.

gold leaf *noun* gold that has been beaten into a very thin sheet.

gold mine *noun* 1 a place where gold is mined. 2 a source of great wealth ♦ *The shop was a little gold mine*.

gold-plated *adjective* coated with a thin layer of gold.

gold reserve *noun* gold held by a central bank to guarantee the value of a country's currency.

gold rush *noun* a rush of people to a newly discovered goldfield.

goldsmith *noun* a person who makes things in gold.

gold standard *noun* (*historical*) in the past, a system by which the value of money was based on that of gold.

golf *noun* a game played by hitting a small hard ball with clubs towards and into a series of holes on a special course and taking as few strokes as possible. **golfer** *noun* [origin unknown]

golf ball *noun* 1 a ball used in golf. 2 (**golfball**) a small ball-shaped device carrying the type in some electric typewriters.

golf club *noun* 1 a club used in golf. 2 an association for playing golf, or its premises.

golf course *noun* a course on which golf is played.

golly *interjection* (*informal*) an exclamation of surprise.

-gon *suffix* used to form nouns denoting figures with a certain number of angles and sides, as in *hexagon*. [from a Greek word *gōnia* meaning 'angle']

gonad (goh-nad) *noun* an animal organ, such as a testis or ovary, that produces gametes. [from a Greek word *gonē* meaning 'seed']

gondola (gon-dǝl-ǝ) *noun* 1 a boat with high pointed ends, used on the canals in Venice. 2 a cabin attached to a ski lift or hanging beneath a balloon or airship. [an Italian word]

gondolier (gond-ǝ-leer) *noun* a person who moves a gondola along by means of a pole.

gone past participle of **go**.
gone *adjective* departed or dead.
gone *preposition* past ♦ *It's gone six o'clock.*

goner *noun* (*informal*) a person or thing that is dead, ruined, or doomed.

gong *noun* 1 a round metal plate that makes an echoing sound when it is struck. 2 (*informal*) a medal or other award. [from a Malay word]

gonorrhoea (gon-ǝ-ree-ǝ) *noun* a venereal disease causing a thick discharge from the sexual organs. [from Greek words *gonos* meaning 'semen' and *rhoia* meaning 'a flow']

goo *noun* (*informal*) a sticky wet substance.

good *adjective* (**better, best**) 1 having the right or desirable properties, satisfactory ♦ *good food.* 2 appropriate or suitable ♦ *That would be a good thing to do.* 3 morally correct, virtuous. 4 strictly following the principles of a religion or cause ♦ *a good Catholic.* 5 kind ♦ *It was good of you to help us.* 6 (said about a child) well-behaved. 7 enjoyable or satisfying ♦ *We had a really good time.* 8 expressing good wishes on meeting ♦ *good morning.* 9 healthy, giving benefit ♦ *Exercise is good for you.* 10 skilled or talented ♦ *a good driver* ♦ *She's good at chess.* SYNONYMS: able, capable, accomplished, proficient, skilled. 11 thorough, considerable ♦ *Give it a good clean.* 12 at least, no less than ♦ *We've walked a good ten miles.* 13 used in exclamations ♦ *good God!*
good *noun* 1 benefit or advantage ♦ *It's for your own good.*
goods *plural noun* 1 movable possessions. 2 things that are bought and sold ♦ *leather goods.* 3 (used before a noun) freight ♦ *a goods train.* **as good as** very nearly, almost ♦ *The war was as good as over.* **to do someone good** to be beneficial, especially to their health. **for good** forever. **good for** beneficial to someone or something. **in good time** with no risk of being late. **up**

to no good doing something mischievous or criminal. [from an Old English word] ◊ In standard English, *good* cannot be used as an adverb. You can say *She's a good player* but not *She played good.* The adverb that goes with *good* is *well.*

goodbye *interjection* an expression used when you leave someone or at the end of a telephone call.
goodbye *noun* an instance of saying goodbye. [short for *God be with you*]

good-for-nothing *adjective* worthless.
good-for-nothing *noun* a worthless person.

Good Friday *noun* the Friday before Easter, when Christians commemorate the Crucifixion of Christ.

good-hearted *noun* kind and well-meaning.

good-looking *adjective* (said about a person) attractive.

goodness *noun* 1 the quality of being good. 2 the beneficial or nourishing part of food ♦ *The goodness is in the gravy.*
goodness *interjection* used instead of 'God' to express surprise, anger, relief, etc. ♦ *Goodness knows* ♦ *For goodness' sake!* ♦ *Thank goodness.* **to have the goodness to** to be kind enough to do something.

good-tempered *adjective* having or showing good temper.

goodwill *noun* 1 friendly or helpful feelings towards another person. 2 the established custom or reputation of a business, considered as an asset that can be sold.

goody *noun* (**goodies**) (*informal*) 1 a person of good character, especially one of the heroes in a story or film ♦ *the goodies and the baddies.* 2 something good or attractive, especially to eat ♦ *a plateful of goodies.*

goody-goody *adjective* smugly virtuous.
goody-goody *noun* (**goody-goodies**) a smugly virtuous person.

gooey *adjective* (*informal*) 1 wet and sticky. 2 sickly and sentimental.

goof *noun* (*informal*) 1 a mistake. 2 a stupid person.
goof *verb* (*informal*) to make a mistake, to blunder. [origin unknown]

goofy *adjective* (**goofier, goofiest**) (*informal*) 1 stupid or silly. 2 having front teeth that stick out or are crooked.

googly noun (**googlies**) (in cricket) a ball bowled so that it breaks in the opposite direction from the one the batsman expected. [origin unknown]

goon noun (informal) 1 a stupid person. 2 a hired thug, employed by a criminal to threaten or attack people. [perhaps from a dialect word gooney meaning 'booby']

goose noun (**geese**) 1 a large waterbird with a long neck and webbed feet, larger than a duck. 2 (informal) a foolish person. [from an Old English word]

gooseberry noun (**gooseberries**) 1 a small green fruit with a hairy skin. 2 the thorny shrub which bears this fruit. 3 an unwanted extra person, especially a third person with a pair of lovers who would prefer to be alone ♦ I don't want to play gooseberry. [probably from a French dialect word gozell]

gooseflesh noun or **goose pimples** plural noun skin that has turned rough with small bumps on it because of cold or fear. [so called because it looks like the skin of a plucked goose]

goose step noun a way of marching without bending the knees. **goose-step** verb

gopher noun 1 a burrowing American rodent with cheek pouches. 2 another spelling of **gofer**.

Gordian adjective **to cut the Gordian knot** to solve a difficult problem forcefully or by some unexpected means. [from the intricate knot tied by Gordius, king of ancient Phrygia. It was eventually cut, rather than untied, by Alexander the Great.]

gore[1] noun blood that has been shed, especially as a result of violence. [from an Old English word gor meaning 'dirt']

gore[2] verb (said about a bull or other animal) to pierce a person or animal with a horn or tusk. [origin unknown]

gorge noun a narrow steep-sided valley. **gorge** verb to eat a large amount greedily, to stuff yourself with food. **to make someone's gorge rise** to sicken or disgust them. [a French word meaning 'throat']

gorgeous adjective 1 strikingly beautiful. 2 (informal) very pleasant ♦ gorgeous weather. **gorgeously** adverb **gorgeousness** noun [from an Old French word gorgias meaning 'fine, elegant']

Gorgon noun (Greek Mythology) each of three sisters with hair made of snakes, who could turn anyone who looked at them to stone.
gorgon noun a terrifying or repulsive woman.

gorilla noun a large powerful ape of central Africa. [from a Greek word, probably from an African word denoting a wild or hairy person]
◊ Do not confuse this word with **guerrilla**, which can be pronounced in the same way.

gormless adjective (informal) stupid, lacking sense. [from a dialect word gaum meaning 'understanding']

gorse noun a wild evergreen shrub with yellow flowers and sharp thorns. [from an Old English word gors]

gory adjective (**gorier, goriest**) 1 involving bloodshed ♦ a gory battle. 2 covered with blood. **gorily** adverb **goriness** noun [from gore]

gosh interjection (informal) an exclamation of surprise. [used to avoid saying 'God']

goshawk (**goss**-hawk) noun a kind of large hawk with short wings. [from an Old English word]

gosling (**goz**-ling) noun a young goose. [from an Old Norse word]

go-slow noun a deliberately slow pace of work as a form of industrial protest.

gospel noun 1 the teachings of Jesus Christ as recorded in the first four books of the New Testament. 2 (**Gospel**) each of these books, describing the life and teachings of Jesus Christ. 3 something true or reliable ♦ You can take it as gospel. [from Old English words god spel meaning 'good news', translating a Latin word evangelium, related to evangelist]

gospel music noun a style of black American evangelical religious singing.

gossamer noun 1 a fine filmy piece of cobweb made by small spiders. 2 any flimsy delicate material. [from goose summer, a period of fine weather in the autumn (when geese were eaten), when gossamer is very common]

gossip noun 1 casual talk especially about other people's affairs. SYNONYMS: hearsay; (informal) tittle-tattle. 2 a person who is fond of gossiping.
gossip verb (**gossiped, gossiping**) to engage in or spread gossip. **gossipy**

adjective [from an Old English word *godsibb* meaning 'close friend' (literally 'god-brother or sister'), someone to gossip with]

gossip column *noun* a part of a newspaper giving gossip about well-known people. **gossip columnist** *noun*

got past tense and past participle of **get. to have got** to possess ♦ *Have you got a car?* **have got to do it** must do it.

Goth *noun* a member of a Germanic people that invaded the Roman Empire from the east in the 3rd–5th centuries. [from a Greek word *Gothoi*]

Gothic (**goth**-ik) *adjective* 1 to do with the Goths. 2 to do with the style of architecture common in western Europe in the 12th–16th centuries, with pointed arches and rich stone carving. **Gothic** *noun* 1 the Gothic style of architecture. 2 (in printing) the heavy black type formerly used for printing German.

gothic novel *noun* a kind of novel with sensational or horrifying events, popular in the 18th–19th centuries.

gotten an alternative form of **got**, used in the USA (♦ *He has gotten a job*) but not now used in standard English except in certain expressions such as ♦ *ill-gotten gains*.

gouache (goo-**ahsh**) *noun* 1 painting with opaque pigments ground in water and thickened with gum and honey. 2 these pigments. [from an Italian word *guazzo*]

gouge (gowj) *noun* a chisel with a concave blade, used for cutting grooves. **gouge** *verb* 1 to make a hole in a surface with a pointed object. 2 to scoop or force something out by pressing it. [from a Latin word *gubia* meaning 'a kind of chisel']

goulash (goo-**lash**) *noun* a stew of meat and vegetables, seasoned with paprika. [from a Hungarian word *gulyáshús* meaning 'herdsman's meat']

gourd (goord) *noun* 1 the hard-skinned fleshy fruit of a climbing plant. 2 this plant. 3 a bowl or container made from the dried hollowed-out rind of the gourd. [from an Old French word *gourde*]

gourmand (goor-mənd) *noun* a lover of food, a glutton. [origin unknown] ◊ This word is often applied to a person contemptuously, whereas *gourmet* is not.

gourmet (goor-**may**) *noun* a person who understands and appreciates good food and drink. [a French word meaning 'wine taster'] ◊ See the note under **gourmand**.

gout *noun* a disease that causes inflammation of the joints, especially the toes, knees, and fingers. **gouty** *adjective* [from an Old French or Latin word]

govern *verb* 1 to rule people with authority; to conduct the affairs of a country, state, organization, etc. 2 to influence, determine, or guide something ♦ *Everything she does is governed by her religious faith.* 3 to keep something under control ♦ *You need to govern your temper better.* 4 (*Grammar*) (said about a word) to require another word to be in a particular case. [from a Latin word *gubernare* meaning 'to steer or direct']

governance *noun* the act or manner of governing.

governess *noun* a woman employed to teach children in a private household.

government *noun* 1 the group of people who are in charge of the public affairs of a country. 2 the system or method of governing. **governmental** *adjective*

governor *noun* 1 a person who governs a province or colony. 2 the head of each state in the USA. 3 a member of the governing body of a school or other institution. 4 the person in charge of a prison. 5 (*informal*) a form of address to a man regarded as being of superior status. 6 a mechanism that automatically controls speed or the intake of gas or water etc. in a machine.

Governor General *noun* (**Governors General**) the representative of the Crown in a Commonwealth country that recognizes the British monarch as its head of the State.

gown *noun* 1 a loose flowing piece of clothing, especially a woman's long dress. 2 a piece of protective clothing worn by medical staff in a hospital. 3 a loose robe worn as official dress by judges, members of a university, etc. [from a Latin word *gunna* meaning 'a fur-lined robe']

gowned *adjective* wearing a gown.

GP *abbreviation* general practitioner.

GPS *abbreviation* Global Positioning System, a satellite navigational system.

Graafian follicle noun a very small sac in the ovary of a mammal, in which egg-cells (called *ova*) develop and mature. [named after the 17th-century Dutch anatomist R. de Graaf]

grab verb (**grabbed, grabbing**) 1 to take hold of something suddenly. SYNONYMS: clutch, grasp, snatch, seize. 2 to take advantage of something without hesitating ♦ *When the opportunity came, he grabbed it.* SYNONYMS: seize; (*informal*) jump at, snap up. 3 (*informal*) to make a favourable impression on someone ♦ *How does this idea grab you?*
grab noun 1 a sudden clutch or an attempt to seize something. 2 a mechanical device for gripping things or lifting them. **up for grabs** (*informal*) available for anyone to take. [from an Old German or Old Dutch word *grabben*]

grace noun 1 beauty and elegance of movement. 2 good manners or elegance of manner ♦ *At least he had the grace to apologize* ♦ *She lacks the social graces.* 3 a person's favour ♦ *I seem to have fallen from grace.* 4 a delay before something has to be completed or paid, allowed as a favour ♦ *Can you give me a week's grace?* 5 a short prayer of thanks said before or after a meal. 6 God's loving mercy towards mankind. 7 the title used in speaking of or to a duke, duchess, or archbishop ♦ *His Grace.*
grace verb 1 to bring honour to an event by agreeing to be present ♦ *I hope you will grace us with your presence.* 2 to make something more attractive. **to be in someone's good graces** to have their favour or approval. **with good grace** as if willingly, without complaining. [from a Latin word *gratus* meaning 'pleasing']

graceful adjective beautiful and elegant in movement or shape. **gracefully** adverb **gracefulness** noun

graceless adjective 1 inelegant or clumsy. 2 ungracious.

grace note noun (*Music*) an extra note that is not essential to the harmony but is added as an embellishment.

gracious adjective 1 kind, pleasant, and courteous. 2 showing the comfort and good taste made possible by wealth ♦ *gracious living.* 3 showing divine grace, merciful.
gracious interjection an exclamation of surprise ♦ *Good gracious!* **graciously**

adverb **graciousness** noun [same origin as for *grace*]

gradation (grə-**day**-shən) noun a process of gradual change, or a stage in such a process ♦ *the gradations of colour between blue and green.*

grade noun 1 a level of rank, quality, or value ♦ *a salary grade.* SYNONYMS: category, class, level, standard. 2 the mark given to a student for his or her standard of work. 3 a standard of musical skill at which someone has been tested ♦ *Piano Grade 5.* 4 a class of people or things of the same rank or quality etc. 5 a gradient or slope.
grade verb 1 to arrange people or things in grades ♦ *The eggs are next graded by size.* 2 to give a grade to a student. 3 to reduce the slope of a road. 4 to pass gradually from one level to another. **to make the grade** to reach the desired standard. [from a Latin word *gradus* meaning 'a step']

gradient (**gray**-di-ənt) noun 1 the steepness of a slope ♦ *The road has a gradient of 1 in 10.* 2 a sloping road or railway. [from *grade*]

gradual adjective 1 taking place or developing slowly and in stages ♦ *a gradual improvement.* 2 (said about a slope) not steep. **gradually** adverb [same origin as for *grade*]

graduate [1] (**grad**-yoo-ət) noun a person who holds a university or college degree. [same origin as for *grade*]

graduate [2] (**grad**-yoo-ayt) verb 1 to complete a university or college degree. 2 to progress to something more advanced ♦ *She has recently graduated from her tricycle to a bike.* 3 to mark something into regular divisions or units of measurement. **graduation** noun

Graeco-Roman (greek-oh-**roh**-mən) adjective to do with the ancient Greeks and Romans.

graffiti (grə-**fee**-ti) noun writing or drawings scribbled or sprayed on a wall or other public place. [an Italian word meaning 'scratchings']
◊ Strictly speaking, this word is a plural noun (the singular is *graffito*), so it should be used with a plural verb: *There are graffiti all over the wall.* However, the word is widely used nowadays as if it were a singular noun and most people do not regard this as wrong: *There is graffiti all over the wall.*

graft [1] noun 1 a shoot from one tree fixed

into a cut in another to form a new growth. **2** a piece of living tissue transplanted surgically to replace diseased or damaged tissue ♦ *a skin graft.* **3** an operation in which tissue is transplanted. **4** (*informal*) hard work.
graft *verb* **1** to put a graft in or on something. **2** to join one thing to another. **3** (*informal*) to work hard. [from a Greek word *grapheion* meaning 'pointed writing stick' (because of the pointed end of the shoot)]

graft² *noun* (*informal*) obtaining some advantage in business or politics by bribery or other unfair or dishonest means. [origin unknown]

Grail or **Holy Grail** *noun* the cup or the platter used by Christ at the Last Supper, sought in quests by knights in medieval legends. [from a Latin word *gradalis* meaning 'dish']

grain *noun* **1** a cereal plant such as wheat or rice, used as food. **2** a small hard seed of a cereal plant. **3** a small hard particle of a substance ♦ *a grain of sand.* **4** the smallest possible amount ♦ *There isn't a grain of truth in this story.* **5** the pattern of lines made by fibres in wood, paper, etc. or by layers in rock or coal etc.; the direction of threads in woven fabric. **6** a unit of weight, about 65 milligrams. **against the grain** against your natural inclinations or principles. [from a Latin word *granum*]

grainy *adjective* (**grainier, grainiest**) like grains in form, appearance, or texture. **graininess** *noun*

gram *noun* a metric unit of mass equal to one thousandth of a kilogram. [from a Latin word *gramma* meaning 'a small weight']

-gram *suffix* forming nouns meaning something written, drawn, or recorded (as in *diagram*). [from a Greek word *gramma* meaning 'thing written']

graminaceous (gram-in-ay-shǝs) *adjective* (*Botany*) of or like grass. [from a Latin word *gramen* meaning 'grass']

graminivorous (gram-in-iv-er-ǝs) *adjective* (said about an animal) feeding on grass. [from Latin words *graminis* meaning 'of grass' and *vorare* meaning 'to devour']

grammar *noun* **1** the study of words and of the rules for their formation and their relationships to each other in sentences. **2** the rules for using the words of a language correctly. **3** a book about these

rules. **4** speech or writing judged as good or bad according to these rules ♦ *His grammar is appalling.* [from a Greek word meaning 'the art of letters']

grammar school *noun* a secondary school for pupils of high academic ability.

grammatical *adjective* **1** in accordance with the rules of grammar. **2** to do with grammar. **grammatically** *adverb*

gramophone *noun* (*old use*) a record player, especially the kind that is not operated electrically. [altered from 'phonogram' (the name given to the first record player), from a Greek word *phōnē* meaning 'a sound' and *-gram*]

grampus *noun* (**grampuses**) a large dolphin-like sea animal that blows loudly and heavily. [from a Latin word *craspiscis* meaning 'fat fish']

gran *noun* (*informal*) grandmother.

granary *noun* (**granaries**) a storehouse for grain. [from a Latin word *granarium*]

grand *adjective* **1** large or impressive, splendid. SYNONYMS: imposing, majestic, magnificent, noble, stately, (*formal*) august. **2** of the highest rank, most important ♦ *the Grand Duke Alexis.* **3** haughty and pompous ♦ *She puts on a grand manner.* **4** (*informal*) very enjoyable or satisfactory ♦ *We had a grand time.*
grand *noun* **1** a grand piano. **2** (*informal*) a thousand pounds or dollars ♦ *five grand.*
grandly *adverb* **grandness** *noun* [from a Latin word *grandis* meaning 'fully-grown']

grandad *noun* (*informal*) **1** grandfather.

grandam *noun* (*old use*) a grandmother.

grandchild *noun* (**grandchildren**) the child of your son or daughter.

granddaughter *noun* the daughter of your son or daughter.

grandee (gran-dee) *noun* a person of high rank. [from a Spanish or Portuguese word *grande* meaning 'grand']

grandeur (grand-yer) *noun* impressive beauty or splendour. [from a French word]

grandfather *noun* the father of a person's father or mother.

grandfather clock *noun* a clock in a tall wooden case, worked by weights.

grandiose (gran-di-ohss) *adjective* **1** trying to seem impressive, pompous. **2** imposing, planned on a large scale.

grandiosity (grandi-**oss**-iti) noun [via French from an Italian word grandioso]

grandma noun (informal) grandmother.

grandmaster noun a chess player of the highest class.

grandmother noun the mother of a person's father or mother.

grand opera noun an opera in which everything is sung and there are no spoken parts.

grandpa noun (informal) grandfather.

grandparent noun a grandfather or grandmother.

grand piano noun a large full-toned piano with horizontal strings.

Grand Prix (grahn pree) noun any of several important international motor-racing contests. [a French phrase meaning 'great or chief prize']

grand slam noun 1 the winning of all the major competitions in the same year or season in tennis, golf, etc. 2 the winning of all 13 tricks in the game of bridge.

grandson noun the son of a person's son or daughter.

grandstand noun a building with a roof and rows of seats for spectators at a racecourse or sports ground.

grand total noun the final amount after everything is added up.

grange noun a country house with farm buildings that belong to it. [from an Old French word, related to grain]

granite (gran-it) noun a hard grey stone for building. [from an Italian word granito meaning 'granular' (because of the small particles you can see in the rock)]

granny noun (**grannies**) (informal) grandmother.

granny flat noun (informal) a flat in someone's house where an elderly relative can live independently but close to the family.

granny knot noun a reef knot with the threads crossed the wrong way and therefore likely to slip.

grant verb 1 to give or allow someone what he or she has asked for ♦ We have decided to grant your request. 2 to admit or agree that something is true ♦ I grant that your offer is generous. 3 to give a right or property to someone formally or legally.

grant noun a sum of money given by a government or public body for a particular purpose ♦ a research grant. **to take something for granted 1** to assume that something is true or sure to happen. **2** to be so used to having something that you no longer appreciate it. [from an Old French word granter meaning 'to consent to support']

granular (gran-yoo-ler) adjective like grains or granules. [from granule]

granulate (gran-yoo-layt) verb 1 to form something into grains or granules ♦ granulated sugar. 2 to make something rough and grainy on the surface. **granulation** noun

granule (gran-yool) noun a small grain. [from a Latin word granum meaning 'grain']

grape noun a green or purple berry growing in clusters on vines, used for making wine. [from an Old French word]

grapefruit noun (**grapefruit**) a large round yellow citrus fruit with an acid juicy pulp. [so called because they grow in clusters, like grapes]

grapevine noun 1 the kind of vine on which grapes grow. 2 a way by which news spreads unofficially, with people passing it on from one to another ♦ I heard it on the grapevine.

graph noun a diagram consisting of a line or lines showing the relationship between corresponding values of two quantities. **graph** verb to draw a graph of something. [from a Greek word -graphia meaning 'writing']

-graph suffix 1 forming nouns and verbs meaning something written or drawn etc. (as in photograph). 2 forming nouns meaning an instrument that records (as in seismograph). [same origin as for graph]

graphic (graf-ik) adjective 1 to do with drawing, lettering, or engraving ♦ the graphic arts ♦ a graphic artist. 2 giving a vivid description ♦ a graphic account of the fight.

graphics plural noun 1 the use of diagrams in calculation or in design. 2 diagrams, lettering, and drawings, especially pictures that are produced by a computer ♦ a computer game with superb graphics. [same origin as for graph]

graphical (graf-ik-əl) adjective 1 using diagrams or graphs. 2 to do with drawing, lettering, or engraving.

graphically adverb in a graphic or graphical way.

graphical user interface noun (Computing) the visual means by which a user communicates with a system, including windows and icons.

graphic design noun the art or skill of combining text and pictures in advertisements, magazines, or books.

graphic equalizer noun a device for varying the quality of an audio signal by controlling the strength of individual audio frequency bands independently of each other.

graphite noun a soft black form of carbon used in lead pencils, as a lubricant, and in nuclear reactors. [from a Greek word *graphein* meaning 'to write or draw' (because pencil lead is made of graphite)]

graphology (grǝ-fol-ǝji) noun the scientific study of handwriting, especially as a guide to the writer's character. **graphologist** noun [from *graph* and *-logy*]

graph paper noun paper ruled into small squares, used for drawing graphs.

-graphy suffix forming nouns which are the names of descriptive sciences (as in *geography*) or methods of writing, drawing, or recording (as in *photography*). [same origin as for *graph*]

grapnel noun 1 a grappling hook. 2 a small anchor with three or more flukes, used for boats and balloons. [via Old French from a Germanic word]

grapple verb 1 to struggle or wrestle at close quarters. 2 to struggle to deal with a problem etc. ♦ *I've been grappling with this essay all day*. [from an Old French word *grapil*; related to *grapnel*]

grappling hook or **grappling iron** noun a device with iron claws, attached to a rope and used for dragging or grasping.

grasp verb 1 to seize and hold something firmly, especially with your hands or arms. 2 to understand something ♦ *He couldn't grasp what we meant.* **grasp** noun 1 a firm hold or grip. 2 a person's ability to obtain or achieve something ♦ *The title is now within his grasp.* 3 a person's understanding of something ♦ *She has a thorough grasp of her subject.* [origin unknown]

grasping adjective greedy for money or possessions.

grass noun 1 any of a group of common wild low-growing plants with green blades and stalks that are eaten by animals. 2 any plant of the family that includes cereal plants, reeds, and bamboos. 3 ground covered with grass ♦ *Keep off the grass.* 4 (informal) cannabis. 5 (informal) a police informer. **grass** verb 1 to cover an area of ground with grass. 2 (informal) to inform the police of some criminal activity. **to put an animal out to grass** to put an animal out to graze. [from an Old English word]

grasshopper noun a jumping insect that makes a shrill chirping noise.

grassland noun a wide area covered in grass and with few trees.

grass roots noun the ordinary people who form the main part of the membership of a political party or other group.

grass snake noun a small harmless snake.

grass widow noun a wife whose husband is absent for some time.

grassy adjective (**grassier, grassiest**) like grass or covered with grass.

grate[1] noun 1 a metal frame that keeps fuel in a fireplace. 2 the recess of a fireplace. [from an Old French or Spanish word]

grate[2] verb 1 to shred food into small pieces by rubbing it against a jagged surface. 2 to make a harsh rasping sound. 3 to have an irritating effect. [via Old French from a Germanic word]

grateful adjective feeling or showing that you value or are thankful for something that has been done for you. SYNONYMS: appreciative, thankful, indebted, obliged, beholden. **gratefully** adverb [from a Latin word *gratus* meaning 'thankful, pleasing']

grater noun a device with a jagged surface for grating food.

gratify verb (**gratifies, gratified, gratifying**) 1 to give pleasure to someone. 2 to satisfy a feeling or desire ♦ *Please gratify our curiosity.* **gratification** noun **gratifying** adjective [from a Latin word *gratus* meaning 'pleasing']

grating[1] adjective 1 sounding harsh and unpleasant ♦ *a grating laugh*. 2 irritating. [from *grate*[2]]

grating[2] noun a screen of spaced metal or wooden bars placed across an opening. [from *grate*[1]]

gratis (**grah**-tiss) *adverb & adjective* free of charge. [a Latin word meaning 'out of kindness']

gratitude *noun* being grateful. [from a Latin word *gratus* meaning 'pleasing, thankful']

gratuitous (grə-**tew**-it-əs) *adjective* 1 given or done without good reason, uncalled for ♦ *a gratuitous insult.* 2 given or done without payment. **gratuitously** *adverb* [from a Latin word *gratuitus* meaning 'given freely, spontaneous']

gratuity (grə-**tew**-iti) *noun* (**gratuities**) (*formal*) money given to someone who has done you a service, a tip. [from a Latin word *gratuitas* meaning 'gift']

grave [1] *noun* 1 a hole dug in the ground to bury a corpse. 2 the place where a corpse is buried ♦ *She often visits her father's grave.* **the grave** death, being dead ♦ *He took his secret to the grave.* [from an Old English word *græf* meaning 'hole dug out']

grave [2] *adjective* 1 serious, causing great anxiety ♦ *grave news.* 2 solemn ♦ *a grave expression.* **gravely** *adverb* [from a Latin word *gravis* meaning 'heavy']

grave accent (grahv) *noun* a backward-sloping mark over a vowel, as in *à la carte*. [from a French word; related to *grave*[2]]

gravel *noun* small stones mixed with coarse sand, used to make roads and paths.
gravel *verb* (**gravelled, gravelling**) to cover something with gravel. [from an Old French word]

gravelly *adjective* 1 like gravel. 2 rough-sounding ♦ *a gravelly voice.*

gravestone *noun* a stone monument over a grave.

graveyard *noun* a burial ground beside a church.

gravitas *noun* dignity or solemnity of manner. [from a Latin word *gravis* meaning 'serious']

gravitate *verb* to move or be attracted towards something. [from a Latin word *gravitas* meaning 'weight']

gravitation *noun* 1 gravitating. 2 the force of gravity. **gravitational** *adjective*

gravity *noun* 1 the force that pulls all objects in the universe towards each other. 2 the force that attracts bodies towards the centre of the earth. 3 seriousness ♦ *the gravity of the situation.* 4 solemnity. [from a Latin word *gravitas* meaning 'weight']

gravy *noun* 1 the juices that come out of meat while it is cooking. 2 a sauce made from meat juices. 3 (*informal*) money or profit easily or unexpectedly earned. [from an Old French word]

gravy train *noun* (*informal*) a situation in which someone can easily make a lot of money.

grayling *noun* a silver-grey freshwater fish.

graze [1] *verb* 1 to feed on growing grass ♦ *cattle grazing in the fields.* 2 to put animals into a field to eat the grass. 3 (*informal*) to keep eating snacks rather than regular meals. [from an Old English word *græs* meaning 'grass']

graze [2] *verb* 1 to scrape the skin from a part of your body. 2 to touch something lightly in passing.
graze *noun* a raw place where the skin has been scraped. [perhaps from *graze*[1]]

grease *noun* 1 any thick semi-solid oily substance, especially one used as a lubricant. 2 melted animal fat.
grease *verb* to put grease on or in something. **to grease someone's palm** (*informal*) to bribe someone. **like greased lightning** (*informal*) very fast. [from a Latin word *crassus* meaning 'thick, fat']

greasepaint *noun* make-up used by actors.

greaseproof paper *noun* paper that grease cannot pass through, used in cooking.

greasy *adjective* (**greasier, greasiest**) 1 covered with grease. 2 containing or producing too much grease ♦ *greasy food* ♦ *greasy hair.* 3 slippery ♦ *The road was greasy after the storm.* 4 oily in manner. **greasily** *adverb* **greasiness** *noun*

great *adjective* 1 much above average in size, amount, or intensity. 2 larger than others of a similar kind ♦ *the great auk* ♦ *Great Malvern.* 3 of remarkable ability or character, important ♦ *one of the great painters.* SYNONYMS: celebrated, eminent, distinguished, prominent, renowned, noted. 4 doing something frequently or intensively or very well ♦ *She is a great reader.* 5 (*informal*) excellent ♦ *That's a great idea.* 6 used to describe a family relationship that is older or younger by one generation, as in *great-grandfather* or *great-niece.*

great *noun* an outstanding or distinguished person ♦ *He is one of the literary greats.* **greatness** *noun* [from an Old English word]

great ape *noun* a large ape of a family closely related to humans, including the gorilla and chimpanzees.

great circle *noun* a circle drawn on the surface of a sphere in such a way that its diameters pass through the centre of the sphere.

greatcoat *noun* a heavy overcoat.

Great Dane *noun* a large powerful smooth-haired dog.

greatly *adverb* very much.

Great War *noun* the First World War.

greave *noun* (*historical*) a piece of armour worn on the leg to protect the shin. [from an Old French word *greve* meaning 'shin, greave']

grebe (greeb) *noun* a diving bird. [from a French word]

Grecian (gree-shən) *adjective* to do with ancient Greece. [from a Latin word *Graecia* meaning 'Greece']

greed *noun* an excessive desire for food or wealth. SYNONYMS: (for food) gluttony, (for wealth) avarice. [from *greedy*]

greedy *adjective* (**greedier, greediest**) 1 wanting more food, wealth, or other things. SYNONYMS: (food) gluttonous, (wealth) avaricious, grasping. 2 very eager or keen for something ♦ *He is greedy for knowledge.* **greedily** *adverb* **greediness** *noun* [from an Old English word]

Greek *adjective* to do with Greece, its people, or their language. **Greek** *noun* 1 a member of the people living in ancient and modern Greece. 2 their language. **it's Greek to me** I cannot understand its meaning at all.

Greek Orthodox Church *noun* the Eastern Orthodox Church which uses the Byzantine rite in Greek, especially the national Church of Greece.

green *adjective* 1 of the colour between blue and yellow, the colour of growing grass. 2 covered with grass or with growing leaves. 3 unripe or unseasoned ♦ *This wood is still green and will not burn well.* 4 inexperienced or naive. 5 pale and sickly-looking. 6 concerned with protecting the natural environment. **green** *noun* 1 green colour. 2 a green

substance or material; green clothes. 3 a green light. 4 a piece of grassy land in the middle of a village. 5 a grassy area specially prepared for playing a game on, especially the area around a hole on a golf course ♦ *the 18th green* ♦ *a bowling green.* 6 (**Green**) (*informal*) a member of an environmentalist party or movement. **greens** *plural noun* green vegetables, such as cabbage and spinach. **greenness** *noun* **greeny** *adjective* [from an Old English word]

green belt *noun* an area of open land round a town, where the amount of building is restricted.

greenery *noun* green foliage or growing plants.

greenfield site *noun* a site for a new factory etc. which has not previously been built on.

greenfinch *noun* a finch with green and yellow feathers.

green fingers *noun* (*informal*) skill in making plants grow.

greenfly *noun* (**greenflies**) 1 a small green insect that sucks juices from plants. 2 these insects collectively.

greengage *noun* a round plum with a greenish skin.

greengrocer *noun* a shopkeeper selling vegetables and fruit.

greenhorn *noun* (*informal*) an inexperienced or naive person.

greenhouse *noun* a building with glass sides and roof, where plants are protected from cold weather.

greenhouse effect *noun* the process by which heat from the sun is trapped in the lower atmosphere, because visible radiation from the sun passes more easily than infrared radiation emitted from the earth's surface.

greenhouse gas *noun* any of the gases, especially carbon dioxide and methane, that are found in the earth's atmosphere and contribute to the greenhouse effect.

green light *noun* 1 a signal to proceed on a road. 2 permission to go ahead with a project.

Green Paper *noun* a government report of proposals which are being considered but are not yet accepted.

green pound *noun* the exchange rate for the pound according to which payments to agricultural producers are calculated in the EU.

green revolution *noun* greatly increased crop production in developing countries.

green room *noun* a room in a theatre or studio, used by actors when they are not performing.

greenstone *noun* 1 a kind of green rock. 2 a variety of jade found in New Zealand.

Greenwich Mean Time (gren-ich) *noun* the time on the line of longitude which passes through Greenwich in London, used as a basis for calculating time throughout the world.

greet *verb* 1 to speak in a welcoming way to someone who arrives or who you meet. 2 to receive something with a certain reaction ♦ *The news was greeted with dismay.* 3 (said about a sight or sound) to present itself to someone. [from an Old English word]

greeting *noun* 1 words or gestures used to greet a person. 2 expressions of goodwill ♦ *birthday greetings.*

gregarious (gri-gair-iəs) *adjective* 1 fond of company. 2 living in flocks or communities. **gregariously** *adverb* **gregariousness** *noun* [from a Latin word *gregis* meaning 'of a flock']

gremlin *noun* a mischievous spirit thought of as causing mishaps to machinery. [perhaps from *goblin*]

grenade *noun* a small bomb thrown by hand or fired from a rifle. [from an Old French phrase *pome grenate* meaning 'pomegranate' (because of the shape of the grenade)]

grew past tense of **grow**.

grey *adjective* 1 of the colour between black and white, coloured like ashes or lead. 2 (said about hair) turning grey with age. 3 (said about the weather) cloudy and dull, without sun. 4 dull, lacking individuality ♦ *an office full of grey men.* **grey** *noun* 1 grey colour. 2 a grey substance or material; grey clothes. 3 a grey horse. **grey** *verb* to become or make something grey. **greyish** *adjective* **greyness** *noun* [from an Old English word]

grey area *noun* an aspect of a subject that does not easily fit into any category and so is difficult to deal with.

grey-headed *adjective* with grey hair.

greyhound *noun* a slender smooth-haired dog noted for its swiftness, used in racing. [from an Old English word *grighund* meaning 'bitch-hound']

greylag *noun* a grey wild European goose. [origin unknown]

grey matter *noun* 1 the material of the brain and spinal cord. 2 (*informal*) intelligence.

grid *noun* 1 a network of squares printed on a map etc., numbered for reference. 2 a framework of spaced parallel bars. 3 an arrangement of electric-powered cables or gas-supply lines for distributing current or supplies over a large area. 4 a pattern of lines marking the starting places on a motor-racing track. [from *gridiron*]

griddle *noun* a round iron plate for cooking things on. [from an Old French word *gredil* meaning 'gridiron']

gridiron (grid-y-ern) *noun* 1 a framework of metal bars for cooking on. 2 a field on which American football is played, with parallel lines marking the area of play. [from *griddle*]

grid reference *noun* a set of numbers that allows you to describe the exact position of something on a map.

gridlock *noun* a traffic jam that affects a large number of intersecting streets. **gridlocked** *adjective*

grief *noun* 1 deep sorrow, especially at a person's death. SYNONYMS: anguish, desolation, heartache, mourning, woe. 2 something causing deep sorrow. **to come to grief** to meet with disaster, to fail. [same origin as for *grieve*]

grievance *noun* a real or imagined cause for complaint. [from an Old French word *grevance* meaning 'injury, hardship']

grieve *verb* 1 to feel deep sorrow, especially at a person's death. SYNONYMS: lament, mourn. 2 to make a person feel very sad ♦ *It grieves me to say this.* SYNONYMS: sadden, distress, pain, wound. [from an Old French word *grever* meaning 'to burden'; related to *grave*²]

grievous (gree-vəs) *adjective* (*formal*) extremely serious ♦ *a grievous error.* **grievously** *adverb*

grievous bodily harm *noun* (*Law*) serious physical injury to someone that is done deliberately.

griffin noun (Greek Mythology) a creature with an eagle's head and wings and a lion's body. [from an Old French word grifoun]

griffon noun 1 a dog like a terrier with coarse hair. 2 a kind of vulture. 3 another spelling of **griffin**. [a variant of griffin]

grill noun 1 a device on a cooker that radiates heat downwards. 2 a gridiron for cooking food on. 3 a dish of meat or other food cooked using a grill ♦ a mixed grill. 4 a restaurant that serves grilled food. 5 another spelling of **grille**.
grill verb 1 to cook food using a grill. 2 (informal) to question someone closely and severely ♦ The police grilled him for an hour. [same origin as for griddle]

grille noun a grating of bars or wires covering a window, piece of machinery, etc. [from a French word]

grilse noun a young salmon returning from the sea to fresh water to spawn for the first time. [origin unknown]

grim adjective (grimmer, grimmest) 1 stern or severe in appearance. 2 unattractive and depressing ♦ a grim place. 3 worrying, not hopeful ♦ The future looks grim ♦ a grim prospect. **like grim death** with great determination. **grimly** adverb **grimness** noun [from an Old English word]

grimace (grim-ayss) noun a twisted expression on the face showing pain or disgust, or intended to cause amusement. **grimace** verb to make a grimace. [from a Spanish word grima meaning 'fright']

grime noun dirt in a layer on a surface or on the skin. **griminess** noun **grimy** adjective [from an Old German or Old Dutch word]

grin verb (grinned, grinning) to smile broadly, showing your teeth.
grin noun a broad smile, showing your teeth. **to grin and bear it** to suffer pain or disappointment without complaining. [from an Old English word grennian meaning 'to bare the teeth in pain or anger']

grind verb (past tense and past participle **ground**) 1 to crush something or be crushed into grains or powder. SYNONYMS: pound, powder, pulverize, mill. 2 to sharpen or smooth something by rubbing it on a rough surface ♦ He was in the kitchen, grinding a knife. 3 to rub things harshly together ♦ She ground her teeth in fury. 4 to work a machine by turning a handle.
grind noun 1 the act of grinding. 2 hard

dull work ♦ the daily grind. **to grind to a halt** to stop completely, especially after moving more and more slowly ♦ The traffic finally ground to a halt. **grinder** noun [from an Old English word grindan]

grinding adjective oppressive and endless ♦ grinding poverty.

grindstone noun a thick revolving disc used for sharpening or grinding things. **to keep your nose to the grindstone** to work hard without rest.

grip verb (gripped, gripping) 1 to take a firm hold of something ♦ He gripped my hand ♦ These tyres don't grip very well. 2 to deeply affect someone ♦ She was gripped by fear. 3 to hold a person's attention ♦ The opening chapter really gripped me ♦ a gripping story.
grip noun 1 a firm grasp or hold. 2 the power of gripping ♦ These shoes don't have enough grip. 3 a way of holding something, especially a tennis racket, golf club, etc. 4 understanding ♦ He has a good grip of his subject. 5 control or influence ♦ The whole country is in the grip of lottery fever. 6 the part of a tool or machine etc. that grips things. 7 the part of a weapon or device designed to be held. 8 a travelling bag. 9 a hairgrip. **to come** or **get to grips with** to begin to deal with or understand something. **to get a grip on yourself** to regain your self-control. **to lose your grip** to become less competent than you used to be. [from an Old English word]

gripe verb 1 (informal) to grumble or complain. 2 to cause colic.
gripe noun (informal) a grumble or complaint. [from an Old English word]

gripe water noun (trademark) a medicine to relieve colic in babies.

grisly adjective (grislier, grisliest) causing horror or disgust ♦ a grisly death. [from an Old English word grislic meaning 'terrifying']

grist noun 1 corn that is ground to make flour. 2 malt crushed for brewing. **grist to the mill** experience or knowledge that you can make use of. [from an Old English word]

gristle noun tough flexible tissue of animal bodies, especially in meat. **gristly** adjective [from an Old English word]

grit noun 1 tiny pieces of stone or sand. 2 a kind of coarse sandstone, used for millstones. 3 courage and determination.

grit verb (**gritted, gritting**) to spread grit on an icy road or path. **to grit your teeth** 1 to clench your teeth. 2 to summon up your courage and determination when facing a difficult situation. [from an Old English word]

gritty adjective (**grittier, grittiest**) 1 full of or covered with grit. 2 showing courage and determination. **grittiness** noun

grizzle verb (informal) (said about a young child) to whimper or whine. **grizzle** noun a bout of grizzling. **grizzler** noun [origin unknown]

grizzled adjective streaked with grey hairs. [from an Old French word grisel meaning 'grey']

grizzly bear noun a large fierce brown bear with white-tipped fur, found in North America. [from grizzled]

groan verb 1 to make a long deep sound expressing pain, grief, or disapproval. 2 to make a creaking noise under a heavy load. **groan** noun a groaning sound. [from an Old English word]

groat noun an old English silver coin worth four old pence. [from an Old Dutch or Old German word]

groats plural noun crushed grain, especially oats. [from an Old English word grotan]

grocer noun a shopkeeper who sells food and other household goods. [originally meaning 'wholesaler'; from a Latin word grossus meaning 'gross' (because a wholesaler buys goods in the gross meaning 'in large quantities')]

grocery noun (**groceries**) a grocer's shop. **groceries** plural noun goods sold by a grocer.

grog noun 1 a drink of alcoholic spirits, usually rum, mixed with water, formerly given to sailors in the Royal Navy. 2 (informal) alcoholic drink. [from Old Grog, the nickname of Admiral Vernon, who ordered that sailors should be issued with grog instead of neat rum]

groggy adjective (**groggier, groggiest**) dizzy and unsteady, especially after being ill or drinking too much alcohol. **groggily** adverb **grogginess** noun [from an earlier meaning 'drunk'; from grog]

groin noun 1 the hollow between your thigh and the trunk of the body. 2 (informal) the area of the body where the genitals are situated. 3 (Architecture) the curved edge where two vaults meet in a roof. [origin unknown]

grommet noun 1 a protective eyelet placed in a hole that a rope or cable passes through. 2 a tube surgically placed in the eardrum to drain fluid from the middle ear. [origin unknown]

groom noun 1 a person whose job is to look after horses. 2 a bridegroom. 3 the title of certain officials of the royal household. **groom** verb 1 to clean and brush a horse or other animal. 2 to make something neat and tidy. 3 to prepare or train a person for a career or position ♦ She was being groomed for stardom. [origin unknown]

groove noun 1 a long narrow channel in the surface of a hard material. 2 a spiral cut on a gramophone record for the needle or stylus. 3 a way of living that has become a habit or routine. **groove** verb to make a groove or grooves in something. **grooved** adjective [from an Old Dutch word groeve meaning 'furrow or ditch']

grope verb to feel about with your hands for something you cannot see. [from an Old English word]

gross (grohss) adjective 1 unattractively large or bloated. 2 not refined, vulgar ♦ gross manners. 3 glaringly obvious, blatant ♦ gross negligence. 4 total, without anything being deducted ♦ gross income. (Compare **net**.) 5 (informal) repulsive, disgusting. **gross** noun (**gross**) twelve dozen, 144 ♦ ten gross. **gross** verb to total or earn an amount as total profit or income. **to gross someone out** (informal) to disgust someone. [from a Latin word grossus]

gross domestic product noun the total value of goods and services provided in a country in one year.

gross national product noun the gross domestic product plus the total of net income from abroad.

grotesque (groh-**tesk**) adjective 1 fantastically ugly or distorted. 2 so inappropriate that it is shocking or ridiculous ♦ The idea is simply grotesque. **grotesque** noun a comically distorted figure. **grotesquely** adverb **grotesqueness** noun [via French from an Italian phrase pittura grottesca meaning 'painting resembling that found in a grotto']

grotto (grot-oh) *noun* (**grottoes** or **grottos**) a small cave, especially an artificial and brightly decorated one in a garden. [from an Italian word *grotta*, related to *crypt*]

grotty *adjective* (**grottier**, **grottiest**) (*informal*) **1** unpleasant and of poor quality. **2** unwell. [from *grotesque*]

grouch *noun* (*informal*) **1** a bad-tempered person who is always grumbling. **2** a complaint or grumble.
grouch *verb* (*informal*) to complain or grumble. **grouchy** *adjective* [from an Old French word *grouchier* meaning 'to grumble, murmur']

ground[1] *noun* **1** the solid surface of the earth, especially contrasted with the air surrounding it. **2** earth or soil. **3** land of a certain kind ♦ *marshy ground*. **4** an area of land used for a certain purpose, especially a sports field ♦ *a football ground*. **5** the amount of a subject that is dealt with ♦ *The course covers a lot of ground*. **6** a position, point of view, or advantage ♦ *The party needs to make up some ground in the polls*. **7** a prepared surface to be worked upon in painting or embroidery.
grounds *plural noun* **1** an area of enclosed land belonging to a large house or an institution. **2** solid particles that sink to the bottom of a liquid ♦ *coffee grounds*. **3** reasons for doing or believing something ♦ *You have no grounds for complaint*. SYNONYMS: cause, base, basis, justification, foundation, argument.
ground *verb* **1** to prevent an aircraft or pilot from flying ♦ *All aircraft are grounded because of the fog*. **2** to give someone a good basic training in a subject. **3** to run a ship aground. **4** (*informal*) to keep a child indoors as a punishment. **to be grounded on** to be based on something ♦ *This theory is grounded on reliable evidence*. **to break new ground** to do something that has not been done before. **down to the ground** completely ♦ *This job suits me down to the ground*. **to gain ground** to make progress or become more popular or accepted. **to get off the ground** to make a successful start. **to lose ground** to lose your advantage. [from an Old English word *grund*]

ground[2] past tense and past participle of **grind**.

ground-breaking *adjective* innovative.

ground control *noun* the people and machinery that control and monitor an aircraft or spacecraft from the ground.

ground floor *noun* the floor of a building at ground level.

ground frost *noun* frost on the surface of the ground or in the top layer of soil.

ground glass *noun* glass made non-transparent by grinding.

grounding *noun* basic training or instruction in a subject ♦ *a good grounding in arithmetic*.

groundless *adjective* without basis, without good reason ♦ *Your fears are groundless*. **groundlessly** *adverb*

groundnut *noun* a peanut.

ground plan *noun* **1** a plan of a building at ground level. **2** the general outline of a scheme.

ground rent *noun* the rent paid for land that is leased for building.

ground rule *noun* a basic principle.

groundsel *noun* a plant of the daisy family with small starry flowers. [from an Old English word]

groundsheet *noun* a waterproof sheet for spreading on the ground, especially in a tent.

groundsman *noun* (**groundsmen**) a person employed to look after a sports ground.

groundswell *noun* **1** a build-up of opinion in a large section of the population. **2** heavy slow-moving waves caused by a distant or recent storm.

groundwork *noun* work that lays the basis for something.

group *noun* **1** a number of people or things gathered, placed, or classed together, or working together for some purpose. **2** a number of musicians who play together, especially a pop group. **3** a number of commercial companies under one owner. **4** (*Chemistry*) a combination of atoms that form a recognizable unit and are found in a number of compounds ♦ *an alkyl group*. **5** (*Mathematics*) a set, with an operation which combines any pair of its elements to yield a third, in which certain conditions are fulfilled.
group *verb* **1** to form or gather into a group or groups. **2** to place people or things in a group, or to organize them into groups. **grouping** *noun* [via French and Italian from a Germanic word]

group captain *noun* an officer in the RAF.

grouper (groo-per) *noun* a large fish of the sea bass family, used as food. [from a Portuguese word *garoupa*]

group practice *noun* a medical practice run by several doctors.

grouse [1] *noun* (**grouse**) a game bird with a plump body and feathered feet. [origin unknown]

grouse [2] *verb* (*informal*) to grumble or complain.
grouse *noun* (*informal*) a grumble or complaint. [origin unknown]

grout *noun* thin fluid mortar used to fill narrow cavities such as the gaps between stones or wall tiles.
grout *verb* to fill something in with grout. [perhaps from an Old English word meaning 'sediment, dregs']

grove *noun* a group of trees, a small wood. [from an Old English word]

grovel *verb* (**grovelled, grovelling**) 1 to lie or crawl on the ground in a show of humility or fear. 2 to act in an excessively humble way, e.g. by apologizing a lot. [from Old Norse words *a grufu* meaning 'face downwards']

grow *verb* (**grew, grown**) 1 (said about a living thing) to develop ♦ *Tadpoles grow into frogs.* 2 (said about a plant) to be capable of developing somewhere ♦ *Rice grows in warm climates.* 3 to increase in size, degree, or quantity; to become larger or greater. SYNONYMS: increase, develop, expand, spread, multiply, proliferate, thrive. 4 to become something gradually ♦ *It grew dark* ♦ *Over the years we grew apart.* 5 to arise or develop from something ♦ *The idea for this song grew out of a conversation I had a few weeks ago.* 6 to make or let something grow ♦ *He's growing a beard.* 7 to plant and look after flowers, crops, etc. ♦ *She grows roses.* SYNONYMS: cultivate, propagate. **to grow on** to become more acceptable or attractive to someone ♦ *It's a CD that grows on you.* **to grow out of** 1 (said about a growing child) to become too large to wear certain clothes. 2 to become too mature for something ♦ *He never really grew out of comics.* **to grow up** to become an adult. **growable** *adjective* [from an Old English word]

grower *noun* 1 a person who grows plants, fruit, or vegetables commercially. 2 a plant that grows in a certain way ♦ *a rapid grower.*

growl *verb* 1 (said especially about a dog) to make a low threatening sound. 2 to say something in a low grating voice.
growl *noun* a growling sound. **growler** *noun* [an imitation of the sound]

grown past participle of **grow**.
grown *adjective* 1 fully developed, adult ♦ *a grown man.* 2 covered with a growth ♦ *a wall grown over with ivy.*

grown-up *adjective* adult.
grown-up *noun* (*informal*) an adult.

growth *noun* 1 the process of growing or developing. 2 something that is growing or has grown ♦ *a thick growth of weeds.* 3 a tumour or other abnormal formation of tissue in the body.

growth industry *noun* an industry that is developing faster than most others.

growth ring *noun* any of the concentric rings visible in a cut tree trunk that are formed by the annual increase in the width of the tree.

groyne *noun* a structure of wood, stone, or concrete built out into the sea, preventing sand and pebbles from being washed away by the current. [from a dialect word *groin* meaning 'snout']

grub *noun* 1 the thick worm-like larva of an insect, especially a beetle. 2 (*informal*) food.
grub *verb* (**grubbed, grubbing**) 1 to dig around in the surface of the soil. 2 to search laboriously for something, to rummage. **to grub something up** to clear away roots by digging, or to dig something up by the roots. [origin unknown]

grubby *adjective* (**grubbier, grubbiest**) 1 dirty, unwashed. 2 sordid or disreputable. **grubbily** *adverb* **grubbiness** *noun*

grub screw *noun* a small headless screw.

grudge *noun* a feeling of resentment or ill will ♦ *She isn't the sort of person who bears a grudge.*
grudge *verb* 1 to resent having to give or allow something. 2 to resent that someone has achieved something and feel that they do not deserve it ♦ *I don't grudge him his success.* **grudging** *adjective* **grudgingly** *adverb* [from an Old French word *grouchier* meaning 'to grumble']

gruel (groo-əl) *noun* a thin porridge made by boiling oatmeal in milk or water, especially for invalids. [from an Old French word]

gruelling (groo-əl-ing) *adjective* extremely tiring or difficult. SYNONYMS: arduous, strenuous, demanding, punishing, taxing, hard, tough, exhausting. [from an old word *gruel* meaning 'to exhaust, punish']

gruesome (groo-səm) *adjective* filling you with horror or disgust ♦ *the gruesome details of the murder.* [from an old word *grue* meaning 'to shudder']

gruff *adjective* 1 (said about a voice) rough and low in pitch. 2 abrupt or surly in manner. **gruffly** *adverb* **gruffness** *noun* [from a Dutch word *grof* meaning 'coarse or rude']

grumble *verb* 1 to complain in a bad-tempered way. 2 to rumble ♦ *Thunder was grumbling in the distance.*
grumble *noun* a complaint, especially a bad-tempered one. **grumbler** *noun* [origin unknown]

grumpy *adjective* (**grumpier, grumpiest**) bad-tempered and sulky. SYNONYMS: cross, gruff, surly, testy, irascible, irritable. **grumpily** *adverb* **grumpiness** *noun* [an imitation of the muttering noises made by a grumpy person]

grunge *noun* 1 a style of rock music characterized by a harsh loud guitar sound. 2 a deliberately untidy-looking style of fashion. **grungy** *adjective* [perhaps a mixture of *grubby* and *dingy*]

grunt *verb* 1 (said about an animal, especially a pig) to make a short, low snorting sound. 2 (said about a person) to make a sound like this ♦ *When I asked if I could go in he just grunted.*
grunt *noun* a grunting sound. [from an Old English word *grunnettan*, an imitation of the sound]

gryphon (grif-ən) *noun* another spelling of **griffin**.

G-string *noun* a skimpy piece of underwear consisting of a narrow piece of cloth covering the genitals, attached to a band worn round the waist.

G-suit *noun* a close-fitting inflatable suit worn by fighter pilots and astronauts flying at high speed to prevent blood from draining away from the head and causing blackouts. [*G* meaning *gravity*]

GT *abbreviation* a high-performance car. [an abbreviation of the Italian words *gran turismo* meaning 'great touring']

guano (gwah-noh) *noun* 1 dung of seabirds, used as a fertilizer. 2 an artificial fertilizer, especially one made from fish. [from a Spanish word]

guarantee *noun* 1 a formal promise that a product will be repaired or replaced free if it develops a fault within a specified period ♦ *a watch with a five-year guarantee.* 2 a formal promise given by one person to another that he or she will be responsible for something to be done, or for a debt to be paid, by a third person. 3 something that makes it certain that something will happen ♦ *A good idea is no guarantee of success.* 4 a promise or assurance ♦ *She gave me a guarantee that it would not happen again.* SYNONYMS: pledge, undertaking. 5 something offered or accepted as security.
guarantee *verb* (**guaranteed, guaranteeing**) 1 to give or be a guarantee for something ♦ *If you are not satisfied, we guarantee to refund your money.* 2 to promise to pay another person's debts if he or she does not. 3 to promise something, to state something with certainty ♦ *I guarantee that you will enjoy the show.* 4 to make it certain that something will happen ♦ *Money does not guarantee happiness.* [from a Spanish word]

guarantor *noun* a person who gives a guarantee.

guard *verb* 1 to watch over and protect someone or something, to keep them safe. 2 to keep watch over someone, especially to prevent them from escaping. 3 to try to prevent something by taking precautions ♦ *We must guard against errors.* **guard** *noun* 1 a state of watchfulness or alertness for possible danger ♦ *Keep the prisoners under close guard.* 2 someone who guards a person or place. 3 a railway official in charge of a train. 4 a body of soldiers or others guarding a place or a person, serving as an escort, or forming a separate part of an army. 5 a device or part used to protect against injury ♦ *a fire guard.* 6 a defensive position taken by a person in boxing, fencing, cricket, etc. **Guards** *plural noun* the royal household troops of the British army. **off guard** or **off your guard** unprepared against attack or surprise. **on guard** or **on your guard** alert for possible danger or difficulty, vigilant. **to stand guard** to keep watch as a sentry. [via Old French from a Germanic word; related to *ward*]

guard cell *noun* (*Botany*) each of a pair of curved cells that surround a stoma.

guarded *adjective* cautious or discreet ♦ *a guarded reply.*

guardhouse *noun* a building used to accommodate a military guard or as a military prison.

guardian *noun* 1 someone who guards or protects. 2 a person who is legally responsible for a child whose parents have died. **guardianship** *noun* [via Old French from a Germanic word; related to *warden*]

guardian angel *noun* an angel thought of as watching over and protecting a person or place.

guardsman *noun* (**guardsmen**) 1 a soldier belonging to a body of guards. 2 a soldier of a regiment of Guards.

guava (**gwah**-və) *noun* 1 an edible orange-coloured fruit with pink juicy flesh. 2 the tropical American tree that bears this fruit. [from a Spanish word *guayaba*]

gudgeon[1] (**guj**-ən) *noun* a small freshwater fish used as bait. [from an Old French word]

gudgeon[2] (**guj**-ən) *noun* 1 a kind of pivot. 2 a socket for a boat's rudder. 3 a metal pin or rod. [from an Old French word]

gudgeon pin *noun* a pin holding a piston rod and a connecting rod together.

guernsey (**gern**-zi) *noun* (**guernseys**) a thick sweater made from oiled wool. [named after Guernsey, one of the Channel Islands]

guerrilla (gə-**ril**-ə) *noun* a member of a small unofficial army that fights a stronger official army by making surprise attacks. [from a Spanish word meaning 'little war']
◊ Do not confuse this word with **gorilla**, which can be pronounced in the same way.

guess *verb* 1 to form an opinion or make a statement or give an answer without enough information to be sure you are correct ♦ *I don't know the answer so I'll have to guess* ♦ *Guess who I saw today.* 2 to estimate or identify something correctly by guessing ♦ *It wasn't difficult to guess the reason.* 3 (*North Amer.*) (*informal*) to suppose or believe something ♦ *I guess we ought to be going.*
guess *noun* an opinion or answer arrived at by guessing ♦ *a good guess.* SYNONYMS: supposition, speculation, conjecture, hunch. **to**

keep someone guessing (*informal*) to keep them uncertain of your feelings or intentions. **guesser** *noun* [probably from an Old German or Old Dutch word]

guesstimate (**gess**-tim-ət) *noun* (*informal*) an estimate based on a mixture of guesswork and calculation. [from a mixture of *guess* and *estimate*]

guesswork *noun* the process or results of guessing.

guest *noun* 1 a person who is invited to visit another person's home or is being entertained to a meal. 2 a person staying at a hotel. 3 a person who takes part in another's show as a visiting performer ♦ *a guest artist.* [from an Old Norse word *gestr*]

guest house *noun* a private house that offers accommodation.

guff *noun* (*informal*) empty talk, nonsense. [originally meaning 'puff', an imitation of the sound]

guffaw *noun* a coarse noisy laugh.
guffaw *verb* to laugh noisily. [an imitation of the sound]

guidance *noun* 1 advice on how to overcome a difficulty or solve a problem. 2 controlling the course of something, especially a missile or rocket.

guide *noun* 1 a person who leads others or shows them the way. 2 a person employed to point out places of interest on a journey or visit. 3 something that influences your behaviour or decisions ♦ *My first impressions of people are usually a good guide.* 4 a book giving information about a place or subject ♦ *A Guide to Italy.* 5 a thing that marks a position, guides the eye, or steers moving parts.
Guide *noun* a member of a girls' organization corresponding to the Scout Association.
guide *verb* 1 to show someone the way or how to do something. 2 to direct the course of something. 3 to advise someone or influence their behaviour or decisions ♦ *I'll be guided by you.* [via Old French from a Germanic word; related to *wit*]

guidebook *noun* a book of information about a place for visitors or tourists.

guided missile *noun* a missile that is directed by remote control or by equipment inside it.

guide dog *noun* a dog trained to lead a blind person.

guidelines *plural noun* statements that give general advice about how something should be done.

Guider *noun* an adult leader in the Guides.

guild *noun* **1** a society of people with similar interests and aims. **2** any of the associations of craftsmen or merchants in the Middle Ages. [from an Old German or Old Dutch word *gilde*]

guilder (gild-er) *noun* the main unit of money in the Netherlands. [from a Dutch word]

guildhall *noun* **1** a hall built or used as a meeting place by a guild or corporation. **2** a town hall.

guile (giyl) *noun* cunning or craftiness. [via Old French from an Old Norse word]

guileful *adjective* full of guile.

guileless *adjective* without guile. **guilelessly** *adverb* **guilelessness** *noun*

guillemot (gil-i-mot) *noun* a kind of auk that nests on cliff ledges. [from a French word *Guillaume* meaning 'William']

guillotine (gil-ə-teen) *noun* **1** a machine with a heavy blade sliding down in grooves, used for beheading people. **2** a device with a long blade for cutting paper or metal. **3** the fixing of times for taking votes on a bill in parliament, in order to prevent it from being obstructed by an excessively long debate.
guillotine *verb* **1** to execute someone with a guillotine. **2** to cut something with a guillotine. [named after Dr Guillotin (1738–1814), who suggested its use in France in 1789]

guilt *noun* **1** the fact of having committed some offence or crime. SYNONYMS: blame, fault, culpability, liability. **2** a feeling that you are to blame for something or have failed to do something you should have done. SYNONYMS: regret, shame, remorse, contrition, penitence. [from an Old English word *gylt* meaning 'a crime or sin']

guiltless *adjective* without guilt, innocent.

guilty *adjective* (**guiltier, guiltiest**) **1** having done wrong ♦ *He was found guilty of murder.* **2** feeling or showing guilt ♦ *a guilty conscience.* SYNONYMS: ashamed, regretful, remorseful, contrite, sheepish, shamefaced, red-faced. **guiltily** *adverb* **guiltiness** *noun*

guinea (gin-ee) *noun* **1** a former British gold coin worth 21 shillings (£1.05). **2** the sum of money used in stating professional fees

or auction prices. [originally denoting a coin used by British traders in Africa; named after Guinea in West Africa]

guineafowl *noun* a domestic fowl of the pheasant family, with grey feathers spotted with white.

guinea pig *noun* **1** a small furry rodent without a tail, kept as a pet or a laboratory animal. **2** a person or thing used as the subject of an experiment. [from Guinea in West Africa, probably by mistake for Guiana, in South America, where the guinea pig comes from]

guise (giyz) *noun* an outward manner or appearance put on in order to conceal the truth, a pretence ♦ *They exploited him under the guise of friendship.* [via Old French from a Germanic word; related to *wise*]

guitar (gi-tar) *noun* a stringed musical instrument, played by plucking or strumming with the fingers or a plectrum. [from a Greek word *kithara* meaning 'a small harp']

guitarist *noun* a person who plays the guitar.

Gujarati (goo-jer-ah-ti) *noun* **1** a native or inhabitant of the Indian state of Gujarat. **2** a language descended from Sanskrit and spoken mainly in Gujarat.

gulch *noun* (North Amer.) a ravine in which a fast stream flows. [perhaps from a dialect word *gulch* meaning 'to swallow']

gulf *noun* **1** an area of sea, larger than a bay, that is partly surrounded by land. **2** a deep chasm or ravine. **3** a wide difference in opinions or outlook.
the Gulf *noun* the Persian Gulf. [from a Greek word *kolpos* meaning 'bosom, gulf']

gull *noun* a large seabird with long wings. [from a Celtic word]

gullet *noun* the passage by which food goes from the mouth to the stomach. [from an Old French word *gole* meaning 'throat']

gullible (gul-i-bəl) *adjective* easily deceived or tricked. **gullibility** (gul-i-bil-iti) *noun* [from an old word *gull* meaning 'to fool or deceive']

gully *noun* (**gullies**) **1** a narrow channel cut by water or made for carrying rainwater away from a building. **2** (in cricket) the fielding position between point and the slips; this position. [same origin as for *gullet*]

gulp *verb* **1** to swallow food or drink quickly or greedily. **2** to make a loud swallowing noise, especially because of fear.

gulp *noun* **1** the act of gulping. **2** a large mouthful of liquid drunk quickly. [an imitation of the sound]

gum[1] *noun* the firm flesh in which the teeth are rooted. [from Old English *goma*]

gum[2] *noun* **1** a sticky substance produced by some trees and shrubs. **2** a glue for sticking paper together, made from this. **3** chewing gum. **4** a hard transparent sweet made of gelatine or gum arabic ♦ *a fruit gum*. **5** a gum tree. **gum** *verb* (**gummed, gumming**) to smear or cover something with gum; to stick things together with gum. **to gum something up** (*informal*) to clog up a piece of machinery so it does not work properly. [from an Old French word *gomme*]

gum arabic *noun* a gum produced by some kinds of acacia and used as a glue and in incense.

gumboil *noun* a small abscess on the gum.

gumboot *noun* (*old use*) a long rubber boot, a wellington.

gumdrop *noun* a hard transparent sweet made of gelatine or gum arabic.

gummy *adjective* (**gummier, gummiest**) showing the gums, toothless ♦ *a gummy grin*. **gumminess** *noun*

gumption (**gump**-shən) *noun* (*informal*) common sense and initiative. [origin unknown]

gum tree *noun* a tree that produces gum, especially a eucalyptus. **up a gum tree** (*informal*) in great difficulties.

gun *noun* **1** a weapon that fires bullets or shells from a metal tube. **2** a starting pistol. **3** a device that forces a substance out of a tube ♦ *a grease gun*. **gun** *verb* (**gunned, gunning**) to shoot someone with a gun ♦ *He was gunned down in broad daylight*. **to be gunning for** to have someone as your target for attack or criticism. **to jump the gun** to act before the proper or agreed time. [probably from the Swedish girl's name Gunnhildr, from *gunnr* meaning 'war']

gunboat *noun* a small ship armed with heavy guns.

gun carriage *noun* a wheeled structure on which a gun is mounted for transport.

gun dog *noun* a dog trained to retrieve game that has been shot.

gunfire *noun* the repeated firing of guns.

gunge *noun* (*informal*) a sticky or messy mass of a substance. **gunge** *verb* (**gunged, gungeing**) (*informal*) to clog something with gunge ♦ *The pipe is completely gunged up*. [origin unknown]

gunman *noun* (**gunmen**) a man armed with a gun.

gunmetal *noun* a dull bluish-grey colour, like that of metal formerly used for guns.

gunner *noun* **1** a soldier in an artillery unit, the official term for a private in such a unit. **2** a member of an aircraft crew who operates a gun. **3** a naval warrant officer in the past who was in charge of a battery of guns.

gunnery *noun* the construction and firing of large guns.

gunpoint *noun* **at gunpoint** while being threatened by someone holding a gun.

gunpowder *noun* an explosive made from a powdered mixture of potassium nitrate, sulphur, and charcoal.

gunrunner *noun* a person who smuggles guns and ammunition into a country. **gunrunning** *noun*

gunship *noun* a heavily armed helicopter.

gunshot *noun* a shot fired from a gun.

gunsmith *noun* a person who makes and repairs small firearms.

gunwale (**gun**-əl) *noun* the upper edge of a small ship's or boat's side. [from *gun* and *wale* meaning 'a ridge' (because it was formerly used to support guns)]

guppy *noun* (**guppies**) a small West Indian freshwater fish. [named after the Trinidadian clergyman R. J. L. Guppy (1836–1916), who sent the first specimen to the British Museum]

gurdwara (gerd-**wah**-rə) *noun* a Sikh temple. [from Sanskrit words *guru* meaning 'teacher' and *dvara* meaning 'door']

gurgle *noun* a low bubbling sound. **gurgle** *verb* to make a low bubbling sound. [an imitation of the sound]

Gurkha (**ger**-kə) *noun* a member of a Hindu people in Nepal, forming regiments in the British army.

guru (goor-oo) *noun* (**gurus**) **1** a Hindu spiritual teacher or head of a religious sect. **2** an influential teacher, a mentor. [from a Sanskrit word meaning 'teacher']

gush *verb* **1** to flow or pour out quickly in great quantities. SYNONYMS: spurt, cascade, flood, stream, overflow. **2** to keep saying how much you admire or are pleased with something, especially in an exaggerated way.
gush *noun* **1** a sudden or great stream of liquid. **2** an outpouring of feeling, effusiveness. **gushing** *adjective* [an imitation of the sound]

gusset *noun* a piece of cloth inserted in a garment to strengthen or enlarge it. **gusseted** *adjective* [from an Old French word *gousset*]

gust *noun* **1** a sudden rush of wind. **2** a burst of rain or smoke or sound.
gust *verb* to blow in gusts. **gustily** *adverb* **gusty** *adjective* [from an Old Norse word *gustr*]

gusto *noun* great enjoyment or energy in doing something. [an Italian word, from a Latin word *gustus* meaning 'a taste']

gut *noun* **1** the lower part of the alimentary canal, the intestine. **2** the stomach or belly. **3** a thread made from the intestines of animals, used especially for violin and racket strings.
guts *plural noun* **1** the internal organs of the abdomen. **2** (*informal*) courage and determination. **3** the inside parts or essence of something ♦ *the guts of a problem.*
gut *verb* (**gutted, gutting**) **1** to remove the guts from a fish. **2** to destroy or remove the inside of a building ♦ *The factory was gutted by fire.* **to hate someone's guts** (*informal*) to hate them intensely. [from an Old English word]

gut feeling or **gut reaction** *noun* a feeling or reaction that you have instinctively.

gutless *adjective* (*informal*) lacking courage and determination.

gutsy *adjective* (**gutsier, gutsiest**) (*informal*) **1** showing courage and determination. **2** greedy.

gutta-percha *noun* a tough rubber-like substance made from the juice of various Malayan trees. [from the Malay words *getah* meaning 'gum' and *perca* meaning 'strips of cloth']

gutted *adjective* (*informal*) extremely disappointed or upset.

gutter *noun* **1** a shallow trough beneath the edge of a roof, or a channel at the side of a street, for carrying off rainwater. **2** a poverty-stricken or squalid environment or background.
gutter *verb* (said about a candle) to flicker and burn unsteadily so that melted wax flows freely down the sides. [from a Latin word *gutta* meaning 'a drop']

guttering *noun* the gutters of a building.

guttersnipe *noun* a poor child who plays in slum streets. [from *gutter* and *snipe*, which used to be used as an insult]

guttural (gut-er-əl) *adjective* throaty, harsh-sounding ♦ *a guttural voice.*
gutturally *adverb* [from a Latin word *guttur* meaning 'throat']

guy¹ *noun* **1** (*informal*) a man. **2** (*informal*) a person of either sex ♦ *Hi, guys.* **3** a figure in the form of a man dressed in old clothes, representing Guy Fawkes and burnt on 5 November in memory of the Gunpowder Plot.
guy *verb* to make fun of someone or something.

guy² *noun* a rope or line fixed to the ground to secure a tent. [probably from an Old German word]

guzzle *verb* to eat or drink something greedily. **guzzler** *noun* [from an Old French word *gosillier* meaning 'to chatter' or 'to vomit']

gym (jim) *noun* (*informal*) **1** a gymnasium. **2** gymnastics.

gymkhana (jim-kah-nə) *noun* an event in which people, especially children, take part in horse-riding competitions. [from an Urdu word]

gymnasium *noun* (**gymnasiums** or **gymnasia**) a hall or building equipped for physical training and gymnastics. [from a Greek word *gumnos* meaning 'naked' (because Greek men exercised naked)]

gymnast (jim-nast) *noun* a person who is trained in gymnastics.

gymnastic *adjective* to do with gymnastics.

gymnastics *plural noun* **1** physical exercises performed to develop the muscles or demonstrate agility and coordination. **2** other forms of physical or mental agility.

gymnosperm (jim-nə-sperm) *noun* (*Botany*) a member of the group of plants, mainly trees, that have seeds not enclosed in an ovary. [from a Greek word *gumnos* meaning 'naked' and *sperma* meaning 'seed']

gynaecologist (giy-ni-**kol**-ə-jist) *noun* a specialist in gynaecology.

gynaecology (giy-ni-**kol**-əji) *noun* the scientific study of the female reproductive system and its diseases. **gynaecological** *adjective* [from a Greek word *gunē* meaning 'woman' and -*logy*]

gypsophila (jip-**sof**-ilə) *noun* a garden plant with many small white flowers. [from Greek words *gupsos* meaning 'chalk, gypsum' and *philos* meaning 'loving']

gypsum (**jip**-səm) *noun* a chalk-like substance from which plaster of Paris is made, also used as a fertilizer. [from a Greek word *gupsos*]

gypsy *noun* (**gypsies**) a member of a travelling people of Europe, originally from India. Their language Romany is related to Hindi. [from *Egyptian* (because gypsies were originally thought to have come from Egypt)]

gyrate (jiy-**rayt**) *verb* to move round in circles or spirals. **gyration** (jiy-**ray**-shən) *noun* [from a Greek word *guros* meaning 'a ring or circle']

gyratory (jiy-**rayt**-er-i) *adjective* following a circular or spiral path. **gyratory** *noun* (**gyratories**) a traffic system that requires a circular flow of traffic.

gyrfalcon (**jer**-fawl-kən) *noun* a large falcon of northern countries. [from an Old French word *gerfaucon*]

gyro (**jiy**-roh) *noun* (**gyros**) (*informal*) a gyroscope or gyrocompass. ◊ Do not confuse this word with **giro**, which has a different meaning.

gyrocompass (**jiy**-rə-kum-pəs) *noun* a navigation compass using a gyroscope and therefore independent of the earth's rotation.

gyroscope (**jiy**-rə-skohp) *noun* a device consisting of a heavy wheel which, when spinning fast, keeps the direction of its axis unchanged, used in navigation instruments in ships, aircraft, missiles, etc. **gyroscopic** (jiy-rə-**skop**-ik) *adjective* [same origin as for *gyrate*]

Hh

H the eighth letter of the English alphabet.

H *abbreviation* **1** (said about a pencil lead) hard. **2** (*Physics*) henry. **3** (*Chemistry*) the symbol for hydrogen.

ha *interjection* an exclamation of triumph or surprise.

ha. *abbreviation* hectare(s).

habeas corpus (hay-bi-əs **kor**-pəs) *noun* an order requiring a person to be brought before a judge or into court, especially in order to investigate the right of the authorities to keep him or her imprisoned. [a Latin phrase meaning 'you must have the body']

haberdashery *noun* small articles, such as buttons, threads, and ribbons, used in sewing and dressmaking. **haberdasher** *noun* [origin unknown]

habit *noun* **1** something that you do often; a settled way of behaving ♦ *I got into the habit of walking home after work.* SYNONYMS: custom, practice, rule, routine. **2** something that is hard to give up ♦ *a smoking habit.* **3** the long dress worn by a monk or nun. [from a Latin word *habitus* meaning 'condition, appearance']

habitable *adjective* suitable for living in. [same origin as for *habitation*]

habitat (**hab**-i-tat) *noun* the natural environment of an animal or plant. [a Latin word meaning 'inhabits']

habitation *noun* **1** a place to live in. **2** inhabiting a place. [from a Latin word *habitare* meaning 'to inhabit']

habitual *adjective* **1** done constantly or as a habit. **2** regular or usual ♦ *She was sitting in her habitual place.* **3** doing something as a habit ♦ *a habitual smoker.* **habitually** *adverb* [same origin as for *habit*]

habituate *verb* to become or make someone accustomed to something. **habituation** *noun* [same origin as for *habit*]

hachures (ha-**shoorz**) *plural noun* parallel lines used on maps to indicate the degree of slope in hills. [from a French word]

hack¹ *verb* **1** to cut or chop something roughly. **2** to kick someone hard ♦ *He hacked at my shins.* **3** to break into a computer system. [from an Old English word *haccian* meaning 'to cut in pieces']

hack[2] noun **1** a person paid to do hard and uninteresting work, especially as a writer. **2** a horse for ordinary riding, or a horse that may be hired. [from Hackney in London (because many horses used to be kept on Hackney Marshes)]

hacker noun a person who breaks into a computer system.

hacking[1] adjective (said about a cough) dry and frequent.

hacking[2] noun riding on horseback at an ordinary pace, especially along roads.

hackles plural noun **1** the hairs along an animal's back, which rise when it is angry or alarmed. **2** the long feathers on the neck of a domestic cock and other birds. **to make someone's hackles rise** to make someone angry or indignant. [from an old word hatchel]

hackney carriage noun a taxi.

hackneyed (hak-nid) adjective (said about a phrase or idea) used so often that it is no longer interesting. SYNONYMS: banal, clichéd, overused, tired; (informal) corny. [same origin as for hack[2]: hack or hackney was used to mean a hired horse, one that everyone used]

hacksaw noun a saw for cutting metal, with a short blade in a frame.

had past tense and past participle of **have**.

haddock noun (**haddock**) a sea fish like cod but smaller, used for food. [from an Old French word hadoc]

Hades (hay-deez) noun **1** (Greek Mythology) the underworld, the place where the spirits of the dead go. **2** hell. [from a Greek word Haidēs, a name of Pluto, the god of the dead]

hadn't verb (informal) had not.

hadron noun (Physics) a subatomic particle, such as a baryon or meson, that can take part in the strong interaction. [from a Greek word hadros meaning 'bulky']

haematite (hee-mə-tiyt) noun ferric oxide in the form of reddish-black ore. [from a Greek word haima meaning 'blood']

haematology (hee-mə-tol-əji) noun the scientific study of blood and its diseases. [from a Greek word haima meaning 'blood' and -logy]

haemoglobin (heem-ə-gloh-bin) noun the red substance that carries oxygen in the blood. [from a Greek word haima meaning 'blood']

haemophilia (heem-ə-fil-iə) noun a disease, usually inherited, that causes a person to bleed severely from even a slight cut, because the blood does not clot quickly. **haemophilic** adjective [from Greek words haima meaning 'blood' and philia meaning 'loving']

haemophiliac (heem-ə-fil-iak) noun a person suffering from haemophilia.

haemorrhage (hem-er-ij) noun bleeding, especially inside a person's body. **haemorrhage** verb to bleed heavily. [from Greek words haima meaning 'blood' and rhēgnunai meaning 'to burst']

haemorrhoids (hem-er-oidz) plural noun varicose veins at or near the anus. [from Greek words haima meaning 'blood' and rhoia meaning 'a flow']

hafnium noun a hard-silver grey metallic element (symbol Hf). [from Hafnia, the Latin name for Copenhagen]

haft noun the handle of a knife, axe, or spear. [from an Old English word]

hag noun an ugly old woman. [from an Old English word]

haggard adjective looking ill or very tired. [from an Old French word hagard]

haggis noun a Scottish dish made from sheep's heart, lungs, and liver. [probably from an Old Norse word]

haggle verb to argue about price or terms when settling a bargain. [from an Old Norse word]

ha-ha noun a ditch strengthened by a wall, forming a boundary to a garden or park without interrupting the view. [from a French word, said to be from the cry of surprise on encountering such an obstacle]

haiku (hiy-koo) noun (**haiku** or **haikus**) a Japanese poem of 17 syllables, in three lines of five, seven, and five. [from the Japanese phrase haikai no ku meaning 'light or comic verse']

hail[1] noun **1** pellets of frozen rain falling in a shower. **2** something coming in great numbers ♦ a hail of blows. **hail** verb **1** to come down as hail ♦ It is hailing. **2** to come down or send something down like hail. [from an Old English word]

hail[2] verb **1** to call out to someone in order to attract their attention ♦ I tried to hail a taxi. **2** to acclaim someone or something ♦ His new novel has been hailed as a masterpiece.

hail interjection (old use) an exclamation of greeting. **to hail from** to come from ♦ She hails from Ireland. [from an Old Norse word heill]

hailstone noun a pellet of hail.

hailstorm noun a storm of hail.

hair noun 1 each of the fine thread-like strands that grow from the skin of people and animals or on certain plants. 2 a mass of these, especially on a person's head. **a hair's breadth** a very small margin ♦ We escaped by a hair's breadth. **to split hairs** to make distinctions of meaning that are too small to be of any real importance. **hairless** adjective [from an Old English word]

hairbrush noun a brush for smoothing your hair.

haircloth noun cloth woven from hair.

haircut noun 1 shortening the hair by cutting it. 2 the style in which someone's hair is cut.

hairdo noun (**hairdos**) (informal) the style of a woman's hair.

hairdresser noun a person whose job is to cut and arrange hair. **hairdressing** noun

hairdryer noun an electrical device for drying the hair with warm air.

hairgrip noun a strong springy clip for holding the hair in place.

hairline noun 1 the edge of a person's hair round the face. 2 a very thin line ♦ a hairline fracture.

hairpin noun a U-shaped pin for keeping the hair in place.

hairpin bend noun a sharp U-shaped bend in a road.

hair-raising adjective terrifying.

hair-splitting noun making distinctions of meaning that are too small to be of any real importance.

hairspring noun a fine spring regulating the balance wheel in a watch.

hairstyle noun a way in which someone's hair is cut or arranged.

hair trigger noun a trigger that causes a gun to fire at the very slightest pressure.

hairy adjective (**hairier, hairiest**) 1 having a lot of hair. 2 (informal) dangerous or risky. **hairiness** noun

haji (haj-i) noun a Muslim who has made the pilgrimage to Mecca.

hajj noun the pilgrimage to Mecca which all Muslims are expected to make at least once. [from an Arabic word]

hake noun (**hake**) a sea fish of the cod family. [from an Old English word haca meaning 'hook']

halal (hah-lahl) adjective to do with meat prepared according to Muslim law. **halal** noun meat prepared according to Muslim law. [from an Arabic word meaning 'lawful']

halberd noun (historical) a weapon that is a combined spear and battleaxe. [from a French word]

halcyon (hal-si-ən) adjective (said about a time in the past) happy and prosperous ♦ halcyon days. [named after a bird formerly believed to have the power of calming wind and waves while it nested on the sea]

hale adjective strong and healthy ♦ hale and hearty. [from an Old English word hal meaning 'whole']

half noun (**halves**) 1 each of two equal or corresponding parts into which a thing is divided. 2 either of the two equal periods into which a sports game or performance is divided. 3 a half-price ticket for a child on a bus or train. 4 (informal) half a pint of beer. 5 (informal) a halfback. **half** adjective amounting to a half ♦ a half share. **half** adverb 1 partly, not completely ♦ The meat is only half-cooked. 2 to a certain extent ♦ I half expected to find that nobody else had turned up. 3 (informal) half past ♦ half seven. **by half** excessively ♦ She is too clever by half. **to go halves** to share a thing equally. **to not do things by halves** to do things thoroughly or extravagantly. **not half** (informal) extremely ♦ Was he cross? Not half! [from an Old English word half]

half a dozen noun six.

half-and-half adjective being half of one thing and half of another.

halfback noun (in football and hockey) a player whose position is between the forwards and the fullbacks.

half-baked adjective not well planned or thought out.

half board noun provision of bed, breakfast, and one main meal at a hotel or guest house.

half-brother noun a brother you are related to by one parent but not by both parents.

half-caste noun (offensive) a person of mixed race.

half-hearted adjective not very enthusiastic. **half-heartedly** adverb

half holiday noun a day of which the afternoon is taken as a holiday.

half-hour noun 1 a period of thirty minutes. 2 a point of time 30 minutes after any hour o'clock. **half-hourly** adverb

half-life noun the time it takes for the radioactivity of a substance to fall to half its original value.

half mast noun a point about halfway up a mast, to which a flag is lowered as a mark of respect for a person who has died.

half measure noun a policy lacking thoroughness.

half nelson noun a hold in wrestling, with an arm under the opponent's arm and behind their back.

halfpenny (hayp-ni) noun (**halfpennies** for separate coins or **halfpence** for a sum of money) a former British coin worth half a penny.

half-sister noun a sister you are related to by one parent but not by both parents.

half-term noun a short holiday in the middle of a school term.

half-time noun the interval between the two halves of a game of football or hockey etc.

half-tone noun a black-and-white illustration in which light and dark shades are reproduced by means of small and large dots.

half-truth noun a statement conveying only part of the truth.

half-volley noun (in tennis and football) a return of the ball immediately after it bounces.

halfway adjective & adverb 1 at a point between and equally distant from two others. 2 to some extent ♦ halfway decent.

halfway house noun a compromise.

halfwit noun (informal) a stupid person.

half-witted adjective (informal) stupid.

halibut noun (**halibut**) a large flat fish used for food. [from holy and a dialect word butt meaning 'flatfish' (because it was eaten

on Christian holy days, when meat was forbidden)]

halide noun a chemical compound of a halogen with another element or radical.

halite noun common rock salt, the natural form in which sodium chloride is found. [from a Greek word hals meaning 'salt']

halitosis noun unpleasant-smelling breath. [from a Latin word halitus meaning 'breath']

hall noun 1 the room or space just inside the front entrance of a house. 2 a large room or a building for meetings, meals, concerts, etc. 3 a large country house. [from an Old English word]

hallelujah interjection & noun another spelling of **alleluia**.

halliard noun another spelling of **halyard**.

hallmark noun 1 an official mark made on gold, silver, and platinum to show its quality. 2 a characteristic by which something is easily recognized. [so called because the first such marks were made at the Goldsmiths' Hall in London]

hallmarked adjective marked with a hallmark.

hallo interjection & noun (**hallos**) another spelling of **hello**.

hallowed adjective honoured as being holy. [from an Old English word]

Hallowe'en noun 31 October, traditionally a time when ghosts and witches are believed to appear. [from All Hallow Even, the evening before the Christian festival honouring all the hallows, meaning 'saints']

hallucinate (ha-loo-sin-ayt) verb to experience hallucinations.

hallucination (hǝ-loo-sin-ay-shǝn) noun 1 the illusion of seeing or hearing something that is not actually present. 2 the thing seen or heard in this way. **hallucinatory** adjective [from a Latin word alucinari meaning 'to wander in your mind']

hallucinogen (hǝ-loo-sin-ǝ-jen) noun a drug that causes hallucinations. **hallucinogenic** adjective [from hallucinate and a Greek word -genēs meaning 'born']

halo noun (**haloes** or **halos**) 1 a circle of light shown round the head of a holy person in paintings etc. 2 a circle of diffused light round a luminous body such as the sun or moon. **haloed** *adjective* [from a Greek word *halos* meaning 'disc of the sun or moon']

halogen (hal-ə-jən) *noun* any of the five chemically related elements fluorine, chlorine, bromine, iodine, and astatine. [from a Greek word *halos* meaning 'of salt', and *-genēs* meaning 'born']

halon (hay-lon) *noun* (*Chemistry*) any of a number of compounds of carbon, bromine, and other halogens, used in fire extinguishers. [from *halogen*]

halt *noun* 1 a temporary stop, an interruption of progress ♦ *Work came to a halt.* 2 a minor stopping place on a railway line.
halt *verb* to stop or bring something to a stop. [from a German word *halten* meaning 'to hold']

halter *noun* 1 a rope or strap put round a horse's head so that it can be led or fastened to something. 2 a style of dress top held up by a strap passing round the back of the neck, leaving the back and shoulders bare. [from an Old English word]

halting *adjective* slow and hesitant. **haltingly** *adverb*

halve *verb* 1 to divide or share something equally between two. 2 to reduce something by half. 3 (in golf) to draw a hole or match with an opponent. 4 to fit crossing timbers together by cutting out half the thickness of each to make a *halving joint*. [from *half*]

halves plural of **half**.

halyard (hal-yerd) *noun* a rope used for raising or lowering a sail, yard, or flag on a ship. [from an old word *halier*]

ham[1] *noun* 1 meat from the upper part of a pig's leg, dried and salted or smoked. 2 the back of the thigh and buttock. [from an Old English word *ham* meaning 'the back of the knee']

ham[2] *noun* 1 (*informal*) an actor who overacts. 2 (*informal*) someone who operates a radio to send and receive messages as a hobby.
ham *verb* (**hammed, hamming**) (*informal*) (usually **to ham it up**) to overact or exaggerate your actions. [perhaps from the first syllable of *amateur*]

hamburger *noun* a flat round cake of minced beef served fried, often eaten in a bread roll. [short for *hamburger steak*; named after the city of Hamburg in Germany]

ham-fisted *adjective* (*informal*) clumsy.

hamlet *noun* a small village, usually one without a church. [via Old French from an Old German word]

hammer *noun* 1 a tool with a heavy metal head used for breaking things and driving in nails. 2 something shaped or used like this, e.g. part of the firing device in a gun, or the part of a piano mechanism that strikes the string. 3 an auctioneer's mallet. 4 a metal ball of about 7 kg, attached to a wire for throwing in an athletic contest.
hammer *verb* 1 to hit or beat something with a hammer. 2 to strike loudly. SYNONYMS: batter, pound, beat, knock. 3 to force someone to learn something by frequently repeating it ♦ *The rules of grammar were hammered into us at school.* 4 (*informal*) to defeat someone utterly. **hammer and tongs** with great energy and noise. **to hammer something out** to put great effort into working out the details of a plan or agreement. [from an Old English word *hamor*]

hammer and sickle *noun* the symbols of manual worker and peasant used as the emblem of the former USSR.

hammerhead *noun* a shark with a flattened hammer-shaped head.

hammock *noun* a hanging bed of canvas or rope network. [via Spanish from a Taino (South American) word]

hamper[1] *noun* 1 a large box-shaped basket with a lid, used for carrying food, cutlery, etc. on a picnic. 2 a hamper or box of food as a present. [from an Old French word *hanaper* meaning 'case for a goblet']

hamper[2] *verb* to prevent someone or something from moving or working freely. SYNONYMS: hinder, impede, frustrate, handicap, obstruct. [origin unknown]

hamster *noun* a small rat-like rodent with cheek pouches for carrying grain. [from a German word]

hamstring *noun* 1 any of the five tendons at the back of a person's knee. 2 the great tendon at the back of an animal's hock. **hamstring** *verb* (past tense and past participle **hamstrung**) 1 to cripple a person or animal by cutting the hamstrings. 2 to make it difficult for someone to achieve something ♦ *We were hamstrung by endless bureaucracy.* [from *ham* and *string*]

hand *noun* 1 the end part of the arm beyond the wrist. 2 a pointer on a clock or dial. 3 a manual worker in a factory or farm etc.; a member of a ship's crew ♦ *All hands on deck!* 4 the set of cards dealt to a player in a card game, or one round of a card game. 5 either the right or left side or direction ♦ *The queen sat at his right hand.* 6 each of two contrasted sides in an argument etc. ♦ *on the other hand.* 7 active help ♦ *Give him a hand with these boxes.* 8 control or care ♦ *I know my money is in safe hands* ♦ *They decided to take the law into their own hands.* 9 someone's influence or role in a situation or activity ♦ *Many people had a hand in it.* 10 a pledge of marriage ♦ *He asked for her hand.* 11 skill or style of workmanship ♦ *My mother has a light hand with pastry.* 12 a person's style of handwriting. 13 a unit of 4 inches (10.16 cm) used in measuring a horse's height. 14 (*informal*) a round of applause ♦ *Please give them all a big hand.*
hand *verb* 1 to give or pass something to someone ♦ *Hand it over.* 2 to help a person into a vehicle etc. **at hand** close by; about to happen. **at the hand** or **hands of** through the action of a particular person ♦ *At the end of the story, he dies at his brother's hands.* **by hand** 1 by a person and not a machine. 2 delivered by a messenger, not through the post. **to hand something down** to pass something from one generation to another. **hand in glove** working in close association with someone. **to hand something out** 1 to distribute something among a group of people. 2 to impose a penalty or misfortune on someone. **to hand someone or something over** to put a person or thing into the custody or control of another person. **hands down** (said about a victory won) easily and decisively. **to have your hands tied** to be unable to act freely. **in good hands** in the care or control of someone who can be trusted. **in hand** 1 being dealt with. 2 ready to be used if needed. **on hand** available. **out of hand** 1 out of control. 2 without taking time to think ♦ *They rejected the offer out of hand.* **to hand** within easy reach. [from an Old English word]

handbag *noun* a small bag for holding a purse and personal items.

handball *noun* 1 a game in which a ball is hit with the hand in a walled court. 2 (in

football) the foul of touching the ball with the hand or arm.

handbook *noun* a small book giving useful facts or instructions.

handbrake *noun* a brake operated by hand, used to hold a vehicle that has already stopped.

handcart *noun* a small cart pushed or drawn by hand.

handcuff *noun* each of a pair of linked metal rings for fastening a prisoner's wrists together.
handcuff *verb* to put handcuffs on a prisoner.

handful *noun* (**handfuls**) 1 as much as can be carried in one hand. 2 a small number of people or things. 3 (*informal*) a person who is difficult to control or deal with.

handgun *noun* a gun designed to be held in one hand.

handicap *noun* 1 anything that lessens your chance of success or makes progress difficult. SYNONYMS: disadvantage, impediment, drawback, hindrance, burden. 2 a physical or mental disability. 3 a disadvantage imposed on a superior competitor in golf or horse racing in order to make the chances more equal; a race or contest in which this is imposed. 4 the number of strokes by which a golfer normally exceeds par for the course.
handicap *verb* (**handicapped, handicapping**) 1 to impose a handicap on someone. 2 to put someone at a disadvantage.
handicapper *noun* [from *hand in cap*, from an old game in which forfeit money was deposited in a cap]

handicapped *adjective* suffering from a physical or mental disability.

handicraft *noun* artistic work done with the hands, e.g. woodwork, needlework, pottery, etc.

handily *adverb* in a handy way.

handiwork *noun* 1 something made by hand. 2 something done or made by a person ♦ *Is this mess your handiwork?* [from an Old English word *handgeweorc*]

handkerchief *noun* (**handkerchiefs** or **handkerchieves**) a small square of cloth, usually carried in a pocket, for wiping your nose. [from *hand* and *kerchief*]

handle *noun* 1 the part of a thing by which it is to be held, carried, or controlled. 2 a means of understanding or approaching something ♦ *I hope the following introduction*

will give you a handle on this complex issue.
handle *verb* **1** to touch, feel, or move something with your hands. **2** to be able to be driven or operated in a certain way ♦ *The car handles well.* **3** to manage or cope with something ♦ *Don't worry, I can handle it.* **4** to deal with someone or something ♦ *She knows how to handle people.* **5** to deal in goods. **6** to discuss or write about a subject. **to handle yourself** to conduct yourself in a certain way ♦ *I thought you handled yourself well during the interview.* [from an Old English word]

handlebar or **handlebars** *noun* the bar, with a handle at each end, that steers a bicycle or motorcycle.

handler *noun* **1** a person who handles things. **2** a police officer in charge of a trained dog.

handmade *adjective* made by hand rather than machine.

handmaid or **handmaiden** *noun* (*old use*) a female servant.

hand-me-down *noun* a piece of clothing that has been passed on from another person.

handout *noun* **1** money given to a needy person. **2** a sheet of information given out in a lesson or lecture.

hand-pick *verb* to choose people or things carefully.

handrail *noun* a narrow rail for people to hold on to as a support.

handset *noun* **1** the part of a telephone that you hold up to speak into and listen to. **2** a hand-held control device for a piece of electronic equipment.

hands-free *adjective* denoting a device that can be operated in a way that leaves the hands free once it has been activated.

handshake *noun* shaking hands with someone as a greeting or to show you agree to something.

handsome *adjective* **1** good-looking. **2** imposing and attractive ♦ *a handsome building.* **3** generous ♦ *a handsome present.* **4** (said about an amount) very large ♦ *a handsome profit.* **handsomely** *adverb* **handsomeness** *noun* [originally meaning 'easy to handle or use', from *hand* and *-some*]

hands-on *adjective* involving practical experience of using equipment ♦ *a hands-on computing course.*

handspring *noun* a somersault in which a person lands first on the hands and then on the feet.

handstand *noun* balancing on your hands with your feet in the air.

hand-to-hand *adjective* (said about fighting) at close quarters.

handwriting *noun* **1** writing done by hand with a pen or pencil. **2** a person's style of writing.

handwritten *adjective* written by hand.

handy *adjective* (**handier, handiest**) **1** convenient to handle or use. **2** conveniently placed for being reached or used. **3** good at using your hands. **to come in handy** to turn out to be useful. **handily** *adverb* **handiness** *noun*

handyman *noun* (**handymen**) a person who is good at or is employed to do household repairs and other odd jobs.

hang *verb* (past tense and past participle **hung** or (in meaning 5) **hanged**) **1** to support or be supported from above so that the lower end is free. **2** to attach a door or gate to hinges so that it swings freely to and fro, or to be attached in this way. **3** to stick wallpaper to a wall. **4** to decorate something with drapery or hanging ornaments ♦ *The tree was hung with lights.* **5** to execute or kill someone by hanging them from a rope that tightens round the neck, or to be executed in this way. **6** to droop or lean ♦ *People hung over the gate.* **7** to remain in the air ♦ *Smoke hung over the area.* SYNONYMS: hover, float, drift. **8** to remain as something unpleasant ♦ *The threat is still hanging over him.* **hang** *noun* the way something hangs. **to get the hang of** (*informal*) to learn how to do or use something. **to hang about** or **around** **1** to loiter or wait around. **2** to not go away. **to hang back** **1** to remain behind. **2** to show reluctance to act or move. **to hang fire** to delay in taking action. **to hang on** **1** to hold tightly. **2** (*informal*) to wait for a short time. **3** to depend on something ♦ *Much hangs on this decision.* **4** to pay close attention to something ♦ *They hung on his every word.* **to hang out** (*informal*) to spend time relaxing or enjoying yourself. **to hang up** to end a telephone conversation by replacing the receiver. [from an Old English word *hangian*]

hangar *noun* a large shed where aircraft are kept. [from a French word, originally meaning 'a shed']

hangdog *adjective* having a miserable or guilty expression.

hanger *noun* 1 a person who hangs things. 2 a loop or hook by which something is hung. 3 a shaped piece of wood, plastic, or metal for hanging clothes on ♦ *a coat hanger.*

hanger-on *noun* (**hangers-on**) a person who attaches himself or herself to another in the hope of personal gain.

hang-glider *noun* a device used for flying, consisting of a frame covered in fabric from which a person is suspended in a harness, controlling flight by their own movements. **hang-glide** *verb* **hang-gliding** *noun*

hanging *noun* a decorative piece of cloth hung on a wall.

hanging valley *noun* a valley that ends in a very steep descent to another valley, or to the sea.

hangman *noun* (**hangmen**) a man whose job is to hang people condemned to death.

hangnail *noun* torn skin at the root of a fingernail.

hang-out *noun* (*informal*) a place where you live or often visit.

hangover *noun* 1 a severe headache or other unpleasant after-effects from drinking too much alcohol. 2 something left from an earlier time.

hang-up *noun* (*informal*) an emotional problem or inhibition.

hank *noun* a coil or length of wool or thread. [from an Old Norse word]

hanker *verb* to feel a longing for something. [origin unknown]

hanky *noun* (**hankies**) (*informal*) a handkerchief.

hanky-panky *noun* (*informal*) 1 naughty behaviour, especially involving sexual activity. 2 dishonest dealing.

Hansard *noun* the official report of proceedings of the Houses of Parliament. [named after the English printer whose firm originally compiled it]

hansom or **hansom cab** *noun* (*historical*) a two-wheeled cab pulled by a horse, with space for two inside and the driver sitting behind. [named after the English architect Joseph Hansom (1803–82), who patented it]

Hanukkah (hah-nək-ə) *noun* an eight-day Jewish festival of lights, beginning in December, commemorating the rededication of the Temple at Jerusalem in 165 BC. [from a Hebrew word meaning 'consecration']

haphazard (hap-haz-erd) *adjective* done or chosen at random, not by planning. **haphazardly** *adverb* [from an old word *hap* meaning 'luck' and *hazard*]

hapless *adjective* unlucky. [from an old word *hap* meaning 'luck' and *-less* meaning 'without']

haploid (hap-loid) *adjective* 1 (said about a cell) having a single set of chromosomes not in pairs. 2 (said about an organism) having haploid cells. **haploid** *noun* a haploid cell or organism. [from a Greek word *haplous* meaning 'single']

ha'p'orth (hay-perth) *noun* 1 halfpenny-worth. 2 (*informal*) a very small amount ♦ *not a ha'p'orth of difference.*

happen *verb* 1 to take place or occur. SYNONYMS: arise, occur, take place, come about, transpire. 2 to do something by chance ♦ *I happened to see him.* 3 to be the fate or experience of someone or something ♦ *What happened to you?* **to happen on** to find someone or something by chance. [from an Old Norse word *happ* meaning 'luck']

happening *noun* something that happens, an event.

happy *adjective* (**happier, happiest**) 1 feeling or showing pleasure or contentment. SYNONYMS: glad, pleased, delighted, contented, blissful, joyful, cheerful, merry, elated, overjoyed, ecstatic. 2 fortunate ♦ *a happy coincidence.* 3 (said about words or behaviour) very suitable, pleasing ♦ *a happy turn of phrase.* **happily** *adverb* **happiness** *noun* [same origin as for *happen*]

happy-go-lucky *adjective* taking events cheerfully as they happen.

happy hour *noun* a period of the day when drinks are sold at reduced prices in a bar.

hara-kiri (ha-rə-ki-ri) *noun* suicide by disembowelment with a sword, formerly practised by Japanese army officers when in disgrace or under sentence of death. [from Japanese words *hara* meaning 'belly' and *kiri* meaning 'cutting']

harangue (hə-rang) *verb* to spend a long time criticizing someone aggressively.

harangue *noun* a forceful and aggressive speech. [from a late Latin word *harenga*]

harass (ha-rəs) *verb* to trouble and annoy someone continually. **harassment** (ha-rəs-mənt) *noun* [from an Old French word *harer* meaning 'to set a dog on someone']

◊ In American English, the main pronunciations are (hə-**ras**) and (hə-**ras**-mənt). Although also common in British English, these pronunciations are not fully accepted as standard British English.

harbinger (har-bin-jer) *noun* a person or thing whose presence is a sign of the approach of something. [from an Old French word]

harbour *noun* a place where ships can shelter or unload.
harbour *verb* 1 to keep a thought or feeling in your mind ◆ *I think she still harbours a grudge against them.* 2 to give shelter or refuge to someone ◆ *He was charged with harbouring a criminal.* [from an Old English word *herebeorg* meaning 'shelter']

hard *adjective* 1 firm, not yielding to pressure; not easily broken or cut. SYNONYMS: solid, firm, stiff, rigid. 2 difficult to do or understand or answer. SYNONYMS: difficult, complicated; (*informal*) tricky, knotty. 3 needing or using a lot of effort ◆ *a hard climb* ◆ *He's a hard worker.* SYNONYMS: tough, arduous, strenuous, gruelling, taxing. 4 causing unhappiness, difficult to bear. 5 strict, severe, and unsympathetic. 6 (said about people) tough and aggressive. 7 extreme and most radical ◆ *the hard left of the Labour party.* 8 (said about information) not able to be disputed ◆ *I'll give you some hard facts.* 9 (said about weather) severe, frosty ◆ *a hard winter.* 10 done with great force ◆ *a hard kick.* 11 (said about drinks) strongly alcoholic. 12 (said about drugs) strong and likely to cause addiction. 13 (said about water) containing mineral salts that prevent soap from lathering freely and cause a hard coating to form inside kettles, water tanks, etc. 14 (said about currency) not likely to drop suddenly in value. 15 (said about colours or sounds) harsh to the eye or ear. 16 (said about consonants) sounding sharp not soft. The letter 'g' is hard in 'gun' and soft in 'gin'.
hard *adverb* 1 with great effort or force, intensively ◆ *We worked hard* ◆ *It's raining hard.* 2 with difficulty ◆ *hard-earned money.* 3 so as to be hard ◆ *hard-baked.* **hard and**

fast fixed and not able to be altered to fit special cases ◆ *These are not hard and fast rules.* **hard at it** (*informal*) busily working. **hard by** close by. **hard going** difficult to enjoy or understand. **hard luck** used to express sympathy or commiserations. **hard of hearing** not able to hear well. **hardness** *noun* [from an Old English word]

hardback *noun* a book bound in stiff covers.

hardbitten *adjective* tough and cynical.

hardboard *noun* stiff board made of compressed wood pulp.

hard-boiled *adjective* 1 (said about eggs) boiled until the white and yolk have become solid. 2 (said about people) tough and cynical.

hard cash *noun* coins and banknotes, not a cheque or a promise to pay later.

hard copy *noun* a printed version on paper of computer data.

hard core *noun* 1 the most committed or active members of a group. 2 broken bricks and rubble used as a road foundation.

hard-core *adjective* (said about pornography) very explicit, obscene.

hard court *noun* a tennis court with a hard surface, not a grass one.

hard disk or **hard drive** *noun* a rigid disk fixed inside a computer, able to store large amounts of data.

harden *verb* to make something hard or harder, or to become hard. **to harden your heart** to become less sympathetic towards someone. **hardened** *adjective* **hardener** *noun*

hard-headed *adjective* tough and realistic, not sentimental.

hard-hearted *adjective* unfeeling or unsympathetic.

hard labour *noun* heavy manual work as a punishment.

hard line *noun* unyielding adherence to a firm policy. **hardliner** *noun*

hardly *adverb* 1 only just, scarcely. 2 only with difficulty.
◊ It is not acceptable in standard English to use 'not' with *hardly*, as in 'She can't hardly walk'.

hard-nosed *adjective* (*informal*) realistic and tough-minded.

hard-pressed *adjective* **1** closely pursued. **2** in difficulties.

hardship *noun* severe discomfort or lack of the necessaries of life ♦ *a life of hardship.* SYNONYMS: adversity, deprivation, suffering.

hard shoulder *noun* a strip of hardened land beside a motorway, for use by vehicles in an emergency.

hardstanding *noun* an area with a hard surface for a vehicle to stand on.

hard up *adjective* (*informal*) short of money.

hardware *noun* **1** heavy military equipment such as tanks and missiles. **2** the mechanical and electronic parts of a computer as opposed to the software. **3** tools and household implements etc. sold by a shop.

hard-wearing *adjective* able to stand a lot of wear.

hardwood *noun* the hard heavy wood obtained from deciduous trees, e.g. oak and teak.

hardy *adjective* (**hardier, hardiest**) **1** able to endure cold or difficult conditions. **2** (said about plants) able to grow in the open air all the year round. **hardiness** *noun* [from a French word *hardi* meaning 'bold or daring']

hare *noun* an animal like a rabbit but larger.
hare *verb* to run rapidly. [from an Old English word *hara*]

harebell *noun* a wild plant with blue bell-shaped flowers on a slender stalk.

hare-brained *adjective* wild and foolish, rash ♦ *a hare-brained scheme.*

Hare Krishna (hah-ri krish-nə) *noun* a Hindu religious cult founded in the USA in 1966.

harelip *noun* a birth defect consisting of a vertical slit in the upper lip.

harem (har-eem) *noun* **1** the women of a Muslim household, living in a separate part of the house. **2** their apartments. [from an Arabic word *harim* meaning 'forbidden']

haricot bean (ha-rik-oh) *noun* the white dried seed of a kind of bean. [from a French word]

hark *verb* (*poetic*) to listen. **to hark back** to return to an earlier subject. [probably from an Old English word; *hark back*

comes from a call telling hounds to retrace their steps to find a lost scent]

harlequin *adjective* in mixed colours. [named after Harlequin, a former pantomime character usually dressed in a diamond-patterned costume]

harlot *noun* (*old use*) a prostitute. **harlotry** *noun* [originally denoting a beggar or vagabond, from an Old French word]

harm *noun* damage or injury.
harm *verb* to damage or injure something or someone. SYNONYMS: hurt, damage, injure, impair, wound, spoil. **out of harm's way** in a safe place. [from an Old English word *hearm*]

harmful *adjective* causing harm. SYNONYMS: damaging, detrimental, injurious, unhealthy. **harmfully** *adverb*

harmless *adjective* **1** unlikely to cause harm. **2** inoffensive. **harmlessly** *adverb* **harmlessness** *noun*

harmonic *adjective* **1** to do with harmony in music. **2** (said about tones) produced by vibration of a string etc. in any of certain fractions (half, third, quarter, fifth, etc.) of its length. **3** harmonious.
harmonic *noun* a harmonic tone or overtone.

harmonica *noun* a small musical instrument played by passing it along the lips while blowing or sucking air; a mouth organ. [from a Latin word *harmonicus* meaning 'to do with melody']

harmonic progression *noun* (*Mathematics*) a series of quantities whose reciprocals are in arithmetical progression, such as $\frac{1}{3}, \frac{1}{5}, \frac{1}{7}, \frac{1}{9}$.

harmonious *adjective* **1** combining together in a pleasant and attractive way. **2** free from disagreement or ill feeling. **3** sweet-sounding, tuneful. **harmoniously** *adverb*

harmonium *noun* a musical instrument with a keyboard, in which notes are produced by air pumped through brass reeds. [same origin as for *harmony*]

harmonize *verb* **1** to make or be harmonious. **2** to combine together to form a pleasant or consistent whole. **3** to add notes to a melody to form chords. **harmonization** *noun*

harmony *noun* (**harmonies**) **1** the combination of musical notes to produce chords which sound pleasant together. **2** a sweet or melodious sound. **3** being friendly to each other and not quarrelling. [from a Latin word *harmonia* meaning 'agreement']

harness *noun* 1 the straps and fittings put round a horse's head and neck to control it and fasten it to the cart etc. that it pulls. 2 fastenings resembling this, e.g. for attaching a parachute to a person's body.
harness *verb* 1 to put a harness on a horse etc. 2 to control and make use of resources ♦ *Could we harness the power of the wind?* [via French from Old Norse words *herr* meaning 'army' and *nest* meaning 'provisions']

harp *noun* a musical instrument consisting of strings stretched on a roughly triangular frame, played by plucking with the fingers.
harp *verb* **to harp on** to keep on talking about something in a tiresome way ♦ *He is always harping on his misfortunes.* **harpist** *noun* [from an Old English word *hearpe*]

harpoon *noun* a spear-like missile with a rope attached, used for catching whales and other large sea creatures.
harpoon *verb* to spear something with a harpoon. [from a French word *harpe* meaning 'dog's claw']

harpsichord (harp-si-kord) *noun* a keyboard instrument with the strings sounded by a mechanism that plucks them. **harpsichordist** *noun* [from *harp* and a Latin word *chorda* meaning 'string']

harpy *noun* (**harpies**) (*Greek Mythology*) a creature with a woman's head and body and a bird's wings and claws. [from a Greek word *harpuiai* meaning 'snatchers']

harridan (ha-rid-ən) *noun* a strict or bad-tempered old woman. [perhaps from a French word *haridelle* meaning 'old horse']

harrier *noun* 1 a hound used for hunting hares. 2 a kind of falcon. [from *hare*]

harrow *noun* a heavy frame with metal spikes or discs which is dragged over ploughed land to break up or spread the soil.
harrow *verb* 1 to draw a harrow over land. 2 to distress someone greatly. [from an Old Norse word *herfi*]

harrowing *adjective* very upsetting or distressing ♦ *a harrowing film.*

harry *verb* (**harries, harried, harrying**) 1 to harass or worry someone. 2 to keep carrying out attacks on an enemy. [from an Old English word]

harsh *adjective* 1 rough and unpleasant, especially to the senses. 2 severe or cruel ♦ *harsh treatment.* SYNONYMS: tough, austere, severe, strict, draconian. **harshly** *adverb* **harshness** *noun* [from an Old German word *horsch* meaning 'rough or hairy']

hart *noun* an adult male deer. [from an Old English word *heorot*]

harvest *verb* 1 the time when farmers gather in the corn, fruit, or vegetables that they have grown. 2 the season's yield or crop.
harvest *verb* to gather in a crop. **harvester** *noun* [from an Old English word]

harvest festival *noun* a festival of thanksgiving for the harvest, held in church.

harvest moon *noun* the full moon nearest to the autumn equinox.

has *verb* a form of **have**, used with a singular noun and with *he, she,* or *it.*

has-been *noun* (**has-beens**) (*informal*) a person who is no longer as famous or successful as he or she used to be.

hash [1] *noun* 1 a dish of cooked meat cut into small pieces and reheated with potatoes. 2 a jumble or mess.
hash *verb* to make meat into a hash. **to make a hash of** (*informal*) to make a mess of something, to bungle something. [from a French word *hacher* meaning 'to cut up small']

hash [2] *noun* the symbol #. [probably from *hatch* [3]]

hashish *noun* cannabis. [from an Arabic word]

Hasid *noun* (**Hasidim**) a member of a devout mystical Jewish sect. **Hasidic** *adjective* [from a Hebrew word meaning 'pious']

hasn't *verb* (*informal*) has not.

hasp *noun* a hinged metal strip with a slit in it that fits over a metal loop through which a pin or padlock is then passed. [from an Old English word]

hassle *noun* (*informal*) 1 something that is troublesome and annoying. 2 harassment.
hassle *verb* (*informal*) to harass or pester someone. [origin unknown]

hassock *noun* a thick firm cushion for kneeling on in church. [origin unknown]

hast *verb* (*old use*) the present tense of **have**, used with **thou**.

haste *noun* urgency of movement or action, great hurry. **in haste** quickly, hurriedly ♦ *I am writing this in haste.* **to make haste** to be quick. [via Old French from a Germanic word]

hasten *verb* 1 to hurry. 2 to cause something to happen sooner than expected ♦ *This drug may have actually hastened her death.*

hasty *adjective* (**hastier, hastiest**) 1 hurried, acting too quickly. 2 said or made or done too quickly ♦ *a hasty decision.* **hastily** *adverb* **hastiness** *noun*

hat *noun* 1 a covering for the head, worn out of doors. 2 one of a person's positions or roles ♦ *I'm wearing my managerial hat today.* **to keep something under your hat** to keep it a secret. [from an Old English word]

hatch [1] *noun* 1 an opening in a wall between two rooms, especially one used for serving food. 2 a door in an aircraft, spacecraft, or submarine. 3 an opening in a ship's deck, or the cover for this. [from an Old English word]

hatch [2] *verb* 1 (said about a young bird, fish, or reptile) to emerge from its egg. 2 (said about an egg) to open and produce a young animal. 3 to cause eggs to produce young by incubating them. 4 to plan or devise something ♦ *They were hatching a plot.* **hatch** *noun* a newly hatched brood. [origin unknown]

hatch [3] *verb* to shade part of a drawing with close parallel lines. **hatching** *noun* [from an Old French word *hacher* meaning 'to inlay with strips of metal']

hatchback *noun* a car with a sloping back hinged at the top so that it can be opened.

hatchery *noun* (**hatcheries**) a place for hatching eggs, especially of fish ♦ *a trout hatchery.*

hatchet *noun* a light short-handled axe. [from an Old French word *hachette* meaning 'little axe']

hatchway *noun* a cover on a hatch in a ship's deck.

hate *noun* 1 extreme dislike. 2 (*informal*) a hated person or thing ♦ *Mobile phones are one of my pet hates.* **hate** *verb* 1 to feel hatred towards someone. 2 to dislike something greatly. SYNONYMS: detest, loathe, abhor, deplore, despise. 3 (*informal*) to be reluctant to do

something ♦ *I hate to interrupt you, but it's time to go.* **hater** *noun* [from an Old English word]

hateful *adjective* arousing hatred.

hath *verb* (*old use*) has.

hatred *noun* extreme dislike. SYNONYMS: antipathy, aversion, loathing, abhorrence. [from *hate*]

hatter *noun* a person who makes and sells hats.

hat-trick *noun* three successes in a row, especially (in cricket) the taking of three wickets by three successive balls and (in football) the scoring of three goals by one player. [originally referring to the club presentation of a new hat to a bowler taking three wickets]

haughty (haw-ti) *adjective* (**haughtier, haughtiest**) proud of yourself and looking down on other people. SYNONYMS: disdainful, supercilious, proud; (*informal*) snooty, hoity-toity, stuck-up. **haughtily** *adverb* **haughtiness** *noun* [from an Old French word *haut* meaning 'high']

haul *verb* 1 to pull or drag something with great effort. 2 to transport something in a truck or cart. 3 (said about a sailing ship) to turn course abruptly. **haul** *noun* 1 the amount of something gained as a result of effort ♦ *The robbers made a good haul.* 2 a number of fish caught at one time. 3 a distance to be travelled ♦ *It's only a short haul from here.* [via Old French from an Old Norse word]

haulage *noun* 1 the transport of goods. 2 a charge for this.

haulier (hawl-i-er) *noun* a person or firm who transports goods by road.

haunch *noun* 1 the fleshy part of the buttock and thigh. 2 the leg and loin of an animal as food. [via Old French from a Germanic word]

haunt *verb* 1 (said about ghosts) to appear often in a place. 2 to visit a place often. 3 to stay in your mind ♦ *The memory haunts me.* **haunt** *noun* a place often visited by the people named ♦ *The market is a favourite haunt of pickpockets.* [via Old French from a Germanic word]

haunted *adjective* 1 frequented by a ghost or ghosts ♦ *a haunted house.* 2 looking anxious or troubled ♦ *her haunted eyes.*

haunting *adjective* so beautiful and sad that it stays in your mind, poignant ♦ *a haunting melody.*

haute couture (oht koo-tewr) *noun* the designing and making of high-quality fashionable clothes by the leading fashion houses. [a French phrase meaning 'high dressmaking']

haute cuisine (oht kwee-zeen) *noun* high-quality cooking. [a French phrase meaning 'high cookery']

have *verb* (**has**; past tense and past participle **had**) 1 to possess, own, or hold something ♦ *We have two dogs* ♦ *He has many enemies.* 2 to contain something ♦ *This tin has biscuits in it* ♦ *The house has six rooms.* 3 to experience or undergo something ♦ *You've had quite a shock.* 4 to do or engage in something ♦ *Will you have a talk with him?* ♦ *We had a look round the town* ♦ *Let's have breakfast.* 5 to be obliged to do something ♦ *We have to go now.* 6 to put someone into a certain state ♦ *You had me worried.* 7 to allow or tolerate something ♦ *I won't have him bullied.* 8 to receive or accept something ♦ *We never have news of her now* ♦ *Will you have a banana?* 9 to cause something to be done for you by someone else ♦ *I'm having my hair cut.* 10 to give birth to a baby. 11 (*informal*) to cheat or deceive someone ♦ *We've been had!* 12 (*informal*) to have put someone at a disadvantage in an argument ♦ *Ah, you have me there.*
have *auxiliary verb* used to form the past tense of verbs ♦ *He has gone* ♦ *We had expected it.* **had better** ought to ♦ *We had better go now.* **to have had it** (*informal*) 1 to be beyond repair or near death ♦ *I think the car has had it.* 2 to have missed your chance. **to have it in for** (*informal*) to behave in a mean or hostile way towards someone. **to have it out** to settle a problem by discussing it openly and frankly. **to have someone on** (*informal*) to try to fool someone. **to have someone up** (*informal*) to bring a person before a court of justice. [from an Old English word *habban*]

haven *noun* a place of safety or refuge. [from an Old Norse word]

haven't *verb* (*informal*) have not.

haver (hay-ver) *verb* to hesitate. [origin unknown]

haversack *noun* a strong bag carried on your back or over your shoulder. [from an Old German word *Habersack* meaning 'oat bag', in which the German cavalry carried oats for their horses]

havoc (hav-ək) *noun* widespread destruction, great disorder. **to play havoc with** to disrupt something completely. [from an Old French word *havot*, an order to begin looting]

haw [1] *noun* a hawthorn berry. [from an Old English word *haga*]

haw [2] *verb* see **hum**.

hawk [1] *noun* 1 a bird of prey with very strong eyesight and rounded wings shorter than a falcon's. 2 a person who is in favour of an aggressive foreign policy. [from an Old English word *hafoc*]

hawk [2] *verb* to clear the throat of phlegm noisily. [an imitation of the sound]

hawk [3] *verb* to carry goods about and try to sell them. [from *hawker*]

hawker *noun* a person who travels about selling goods. [from a Dutch word]

hawser (haw-zer) *noun* a heavy rope or cable for mooring or towing a ship. [from an Old French word *haucier* meaning 'to hoist']

hawthorn *noun* a thorny tree or shrub with small dark red berries, called haws. [from an Old English word *hagathorn*]

hay *noun* grass that has been mown and dried for feeding to animals. **to make hay while the sun shines** to make good use of an opportunity while it lasts. [from an Old English word]

hay fever *noun* an allergy caused by pollen or dust, in which the nose, throat, and eyes become inflamed and irritated.

hayrick *noun* a haystack.

haystack *noun* a pile of hay firmly packed for storing, with a pointed or ridged top.

haywire *adjective* (*informal*) badly disorganized, out of control ♦ *In the film a robot goes haywire.* [so called because wire for tying up hay bales was often used for makeshift repairs]

hazard (haz-erd) *noun* 1 a danger or risk. 2 an obstacle, e.g. a pond or bunker, on a golf course.
hazard *verb* to risk something. **to hazard a guess** to venture to make a guess. [via French from a Persian or Turkish word *zar* meaning 'dice']

hazard lights *plural noun* flashing indicator lights on a vehicle, used especially to warn that the vehicle is stationary.

hazardous *adjective* risky or dangerous. **hazardously** *adverb*

haze *noun* 1 thin mist. 2 mental confusion or obscurity ♦ *He went to bed in an alcoholic haze.* [from *hazy*]

hazel *noun* 1 a shrub or small tree with small edible nuts. 2 a light brownish colour. [from an Old English word]

hazelnut *noun* the round brown nut of the hazel.

hazy *adjective* (**hazier, haziest**) 1 misty. 2 vague or indistinct ♦ *a hazy recollection.* 3 feeling confused or uncertain. **hazily** *adverb* **haziness** *noun* [origin unknown]

HB *abbreviation* hard black, a medium grade of pencil lead.

H-bomb *noun* a hydrogen bomb.

HE *abbreviation* His or Her Excellency.

He *abbreviation* (*Chemistry*) the symbol for helium.

he *pronoun* 1 the male person or animal mentioned. 2 a person, male or female ♦ *He who hesitates is lost.*
he *noun* a male animal ♦ *a he-goat.* [from an Old English word]

head *noun* 1 the part of the body containing the eyes, nose, mouth, and brain. 2 the top or upper end or front of something ♦ *at the head of the procession.* 3 the intellect, the imagination, the mind ♦ *Use your head!* 4 a mental ability, talent, or tolerance ♦ *She has a good head for heights.* 5 a person ♦ *It costs £12 a head.* 6 a number of animals ♦ *sixty head of dairy cattle.* 7 the person in charge of a group or organization. 8 a headteacher. 9 a thing like a head in form or position, e.g. the rounded end of a pin, the cutting or striking part of a tool etc., a rounded mass of leaves or petals etc. at the top of a stem, the flat surface of a drum or cask. 10 a body of water kept at a height (e.g. to work a watermill); a confined body of steam for exerting pressure. 11 the foam on top of a glass of beer. 12 (in place names) a promontory ♦ *Beachy Head.*
heads *noun* the side of a coin on which a head appears, turned upwards after the coin has been tossed.
head *adjective* chief or principal.
head *verb* 1 to be at the head or top of

something ♦ *United head the league table.* 2 to give a title or heading to something ♦ *The column is headed 'World's longest bridges'.* 3 (in football) to strike a ball with the head. 4 to move in a particular direction ♦ *We headed for the coast* ♦ *They are heading for disaster.* 5 to force someone to turn back or aside by getting in front of them ♦ *Let's see if we can head him off.* **to be on your own head** to be your responsibility and nobody else's. **to come to a head** (said about matters) to reach a crisis. **to get your head down** (*informal*) to concentrate on the work you have to do. **to give someone their head** to let them move or act freely. **to go to a person's head** 1 (said about alcohol) to make him or her slightly drunk. 2 (said about success) to make him or her conceited. **head over heels** 1 turning your body upside-down in a circular movement. 2 madly in love. **a head start** an advantage you are given or get at the beginning. **in your head** in your mind, not written down. **to keep your head** to remain calm in a crisis. **to lose your head** to lose your self-control or panic. **to make head or tail of** to be able to understand. **off your head** (*informal*) crazy. **off the top of your head** without much careful thought. **over your head** beyond your ability to understand. **to put heads together** to work together and share ideas. **to turn someone's head** to make them conceited. **headless** *adjective* [from an Old English word]

headache *noun* 1 a continuous pain in the head. 2 (*informal*) a worrying problem.

headband *noun* a band of cloth worn around the head, usually to keep the hair off the face.

headboard *noun* an upright panel along the head of a bed.

headcount *noun* a count of the number of people present.

headdress *noun* an ornamental covering or band worn on the head.

header *noun* (in football) a shot or pass made with the head.

headgear *noun* a hat, helmet, or headdress.

heading *noun* a word or words put at the top of a section of printing or writing as a title etc.

headlamp *noun* a headlight.

headland *noun* a narrow piece of high land that sticks out into the sea.

headlight noun 1 a powerful light at the front of a motor vehicle or railway engine. 2 the beam from this.

headline noun 1 a heading in a newspaper, especially the largest one at the top of the front page. 2 **(the headlines)** a summary of the main items of news.

headlong adverb & adjective 1 falling or plunging head first. 2 in a hasty and rash way.

headman noun **(headmen)** the chief or leader of a tribe.

headmaster noun a male headteacher.

headmistress noun a female headteacher.

head of state noun the chief public representative of a country, who may also be the head of government.

head-on adjective & adverb with the front parts colliding ♦ a head-on collision.

headphones plural noun a radio or telephone receiver held over the ears by a band fitting over the head.

headquarters noun the place from which an organization is controlled.
◊ You can use a singular or plural verb with this word: either ♦ The headquarters is in London or ♦ The headquarters are in London. You are more likely to use a singular verb when you are talking about a building, and a plural verb when you are talking about an organization or the people in it.

headroom noun the space between the top of a person's head and the ceiling.

headset noun a set of headphones with a microphone attached.

headship noun the position of head teacher in a school.

headstone noun a stone set up on a grave.

headstrong adjective determined to do as you want.

headteacher noun the person in charge of a school.

head-to-head adjective & adverb involving two sides confronting each other.

headwater noun the tributary stream that partly forms the source of a river.

headway noun forward movement or progress. **to make headway** to make progress.

head wind noun a wind blowing from directly in front.

headword noun a word forming a heading, especially to an entry in a dictionary.

heady adjective **(headier, headiest)** 1 (said about drinks) likely to make people drunk quickly. 2 making you feel very happy or excited ♦ the heady days of your youth. **headiness** noun

heal verb 1 to become or make part of the body healthy again ♦ The wound healed slowly. 2 to cure someone of a disease ♦ He went around healing the sick. 3 to put a situation right ♦ How can we heal the rift between them? **healer** noun [from an Old English word]

health noun 1 the condition of a person's body or mind ♦ His health is bad ♦ ill health. 2 the state of being well and free from illness ♦ She is bursting with health. SYNONYMS: fitness, vigour, well-being. [from an Old English word]

health centre noun an establishment where the practice of a group of doctors or several local medical services are based.

health farm noun an establishment where people seek improved health by dieting, exercise, etc.

health food noun food that contains only natural substances and is thought to be good for your health.

healthful adjective having or producing good health. **healthfully** adverb

health service noun a public service providing medical care.

health visitor noun a trained person visiting babies or sick or elderly people at their homes.

healthy adjective **(healthier, healthiest)** 1 having or showing good health. SYNONYMS: fit, well, hale and hearty. 2 producing good health ♦ a healthy diet. 3 normal, natural, and desirable ♦ She has a healthy respect for her opponent. 4 of a satisfactory size or amount ♦ a healthy profit. **healthily** adverb **healthiness** noun

heap noun a mound or pile, especially an untidy one. **heaps** plural noun (informal) a great amount, plenty ♦ We have heaps of room. **heap** verb 1 to put things in a pile. 2 to put large quantities on something ♦ She heaped the plate with food. [from an Old English word]

hear verb (past tense and past participle **heard**) 1 to take in sounds through the ears. **2** to listen to something ♦ *I heard them on the radio.* **3** to listen to and try a case in a lawcourt. **4** to receive news or information or a message or letter etc. ♦ *I hear that you have not been well* ♦ *Have you heard from Maria?* **to have heard of** to be aware of the existence of something ♦ *We have never heard of this firm.* **hear! hear!** used to show that you agree completely with something that has just been said in a speech. **to not hear of** to refuse to allow something ♦ *He wouldn't hear of my paying for it.* **hearer** noun [from an Old English word]

heard past tense and past participle of **hear**.

hearing noun **1** the ability to hear ♦ *My grandmother's hearing is poor.* **2** the distance within which you can hear something ♦ *He should not have said that in your hearing.* **3** an opportunity to state your case ♦ *She will be given a fair hearing.* **4** a trial of a case in a lawcourt, especially before a judge without a jury.

hearing aid noun a small sound-amplifier worn by a partially deaf person to improve their hearing.

hearsay noun information heard in a rumour or gossip.

hearsay evidence noun (*Law*) evidence given by a witness which is based on information they have received from other people rather than personal knowledge.

hearse (herss) noun a vehicle for carrying the coffin at a funeral. [from an Old French word]

heart noun **1** the hollow muscular organ that keeps blood circulating in the body by contracting rhythmically. **2** the part of the body where this is. **3** the centre of a person's emotions or affections or inmost thoughts ♦ *She knew it in her heart.* **4** the ability to feel emotion ♦ *He has no heart.* **5** courage or enthusiasm ♦ *They may lose heart as the work gets harder* ♦ *His heart isn't in it.* **6** the central, innermost, or most important part of something ♦ *the heart of the matter.* **7** the close compact head of a cabbage or lettuce. **8** a symmetrical figure conventionally representing a heart. **9** a playing card of the suit (called *hearts*) marked with red hearts. **at heart** basically. **to break someone's heart** to make someone very sad. **by heart** from memory. **a change of heart** a change of feeling towards something. **close** or **dear**

to your heart of deep interest and concern to you. **to have the heart to** to be hard-hearted enough to do something ♦ *I didn't have the heart to ask him.* **someone's heart is in the right place** he or she has kindly intentions. **my heart was in my mouth** I was violently alarmed. **to take something to heart** to be badly affected by criticism. **to your heart's content** as much as you wish. [from an Old English word *heorte*]

heartache noun deep sorrow or grief.

heart attack noun a sudden failure of the heart to work properly, which results in great pain or sometimes death.

heartbeat noun the pulsation of the heart.

heartbreak noun overwhelming unhappiness.

heartbreaking adjective causing overwhelming unhappiness.

heartbroken adjective suffering from overwhelming unhappiness.

heartburn noun a burning sensation in the lower part of the chest resulting from indigestion.

hearten verb to make a person feel cheerful or encouraged. **heartening** adjective

heart failure noun gradual failure of the heart to work properly, especially as a cause of death.

heartfelt adjective felt deeply and sincerely ♦ *my heartfelt thanks.*

hearth (harth) noun **1** the floor of a fireplace, or the area in front of it. **2** the fireside as a symbol of the home. **3** the bottom part of a furnace, where molten metal collects. [from an Old English word *heorth*]

heartily adverb **1** in a hearty manner. **2** very ♦ *I'm heartily sick of it.*

heartland noun the central or most important part of an area or country.

heartless adjective not feeling any pity or sympathy. **heartlessly** adverb **heartlessness** noun

heart-rending adjective very distressing.

heart-searching noun thinking hard about your own feelings and motives.

heart-throb noun (*informal*) a good-looking man who women are attracted to.

heart-to-heart adjective frank and personal ♦ *a heart-to-heart talk.*

heart-to-heart noun a frank and personal conversation.

heart-warming adjective making people feel happy and uplifted.

heartwood noun the dense inner part of a tree trunk, yielding the hardest wood.

hearty adjective (**heartier, heartiest**) 1 enthusiastic and sincere ♦ hearty congratulations. 2 strong and healthy ♦ hale and hearty. 3 (said about a meal or appetite) large. **heartily** adverb **heartiness** noun

heat noun 1 a form of energy produced by the movement of molecules. 2 the quality of being hot. 3 hot weather. 4 an intense feeling of anger or excitement ♦ I tried to take the heat out of the situation. 5 the most intense part or stage of something. 6 intense pressure or criticism ♦ The heat is on. 7 one of the preliminary rounds in a race or contest.
heat verb to make something hot or warm, or to become hot or warm. **in the heat of the moment** while angry or excited and without stopping to think. **on heat** (said about a female mammal) in a state of sexual excitement and ready for mating. [from an Old English word]

heated adjective (said about a person or discussion) angry ♦ a heated argument. **heatedly** adverb

heater noun a device for heating something, especially a room.

heath noun 1 an area of flat uncultivated land with low shrubs. 2 a small shrubby plant of the heather kind. [from an Old English word]

heathen (hee-thən) noun a person who is not a believer in any of the world's chief religions, especially someone who is neither Christian, Jewish, nor Muslim. **heathen** adjective to do with heathens. [from an Old English word]

heather noun an evergreen plant or shrub with small purple, pink, or white bell-shaped flowers, growing on uplands. [from an Old English word hadre]

heating noun equipment used to provide heat to a building.

heat-seeking adjective (said about a missile) guided to its target by infra-red radiation.

heat shield noun a device or coating on the outer covering of a spacecraft to protect it from the heat produced during re-entry into the earth's atmosphere.

heatstroke noun illness caused by too much exposure to heat or sun.

heat transfer noun (Physics) the transfer of heat energy by conduction, convection, or radiation.

heatwave noun a long period of very hot weather.

heave verb (past tense and past participle **heaved** or (in uses about ships) **hove**) 1 to lift or move something heavy with great effort. 2 (informal) to throw something ♦ One of the youths heaved a brick at him. 3 to rise and fall regularly like waves at sea. 4 to make an effort to vomit.
heave noun 1 the act of heaving. 2 (Geology) a sideways shift of strata at a fault in the earth's crust. **to heave a sigh** to utter a sigh. **to heave to** (said about a ship) to come to a stop without mooring or anchoring. **to heave into view** or **into sight** (said about a ship) to come into view. [from an Old English word hebban]

heaven noun 1 the place where God, angels, and good people after death are thought to live in some religions. 2 (informal) a state of great happiness or enjoyment. **heavens** plural noun the sky as seen from the earth, in which the sun, moon, and stars appear. **heavens** interjection an exclamation of surprise. [from an Old English word heofon]

heavenly adjective 1 to do with heaven, divine. 2 to do with the sky. 3 (informal) very pleasing.

heavenly body noun a planet, star, or other large mass in space.

heaven-sent adjective occurring at a fortunate time ♦ a heaven-sent opportunity.

Heaviside layer (hev-i-siyd) noun another name for E-layer. [named after the English physicist O. Heaviside (1850–1925), who discovered it]

heavy adjective (**heavier, heaviest**) 1 having great weight, difficult to lift or carry. SYNONYMS: hefty, weighty, leaden. 2 of more than average weight, amount, or force ♦ a heavy cold ♦ heavy rain ♦ He paid a heavy penalty. 3 (said about work) needing a lot of physical effort. 4 severe or intense ♦ a heavy sleeper. 5 dense ♦ a heavy mist. 6 (said about ground) clinging, difficult to travel over. 7 (said about food) stodgy and difficult to digest. 8 (said about the sky) gloomy and full of clouds. 9 clumsy or ungraceful in appearance, effect, or movement. **10** full of sadness or worry ♦ *with a heavy heart.* **11** important or serious ♦ *a heavy subject to talk about.* **12** strict or harsh. **to be heavy going** to be difficult or boring ♦ *I read that book, but it was heavy going.* **to make heavy weather of** to find something more difficult than it really is. **heavily** *adverb* **heaviness** *noun* [from an Old English word *hefig*]

heavy-duty *adjective* intended to withstand hard use.

heavy-handed *adjective* clumsy or insensitive.

heavy industry *noun* industry producing metal, large machines, etc.

heavy metal *noun* a type of loud rock music with a strong beat.

heavy water *noun* deuterium oxide, a substance with the same chemical properties as water but greater density.

heavyweight *noun* **1** a person of more than average weight. **2** the heaviest boxing weight. **3** a person of great influence or importance.
heavyweight *adjective* **1** of more than average weight. **2** having great influence or importance.

Hebrew *noun* **1** a member of an ancient Semitic people living in what is now Israel and Palestine. **2** the Semitic language of the Hebrews; a modern form of this used in Israel.
Hebrew *adjective* **1** to do with the Hebrews. **2** to do with Hebrew.

heck *interjection* used to express surprise or dismay or for emphasis. [an alteration of *hell*]

heckle *verb* to interrupt and harass a public speaker with awkward questions and abuse. **heckler** *noun* [originally, to use a *heckle* meaning 'a steel comb for hemp or flax']

hectare (hek-tar) *noun* a metric unit of area, equal to 10,000 square metres (2.471 acres). [from *hecto-* and a French word *are* meaning 'a hundred square metres']

hectic *adjective* full of frantic activity ♦ *a hectic day.* **hectically** *adverb* [from a Greek word *hektikos* meaning 'habitual']

hecto- *prefix* one hundred (as in *hectogram* = 100 grams). [from a Greek word *hekaton* meaning 'a hundred']

hector *verb* to talk to someone in a bullying way. **hectoring** *adjective* [from a gang of young bullies in London in the

17th century who named themselves after Hector, a Trojan hero in Greek legend]

he'd *verb* (*informal*) he had or he would.

hedge *noun* **1** a row of closely-planted bushes or shrubs forming a barrier or boundary. **2** a means of protecting yourself against possible loss ♦ *He bought diamonds as a hedge against inflation.*
hedge *verb* **1** to surround an area with a hedge or other barrier. **2** to avoid giving a direct answer or commitment. **3** to reduce the possible loss on an investment by making other speculations or transactions. **to hedge your bets** to avoid committing yourself when you are faced with a difficult choice. **hedger** *noun* [from an Old English word *hegg*]

hedgehog *noun* a small insect-eating animal with a pig-like snout and a back covered in stiff spines, able to roll itself up into a ball when attacked.

hedgerow *noun* a hedge of bushes etc. bordering a field.

hedonist (hee-dɔn-ist) *noun* someone who believes that pleasure is the main aim in life. **hedonism** *noun* **hedonistic** *adjective* [from a Greek word *hēdonē* meaning 'pleasure']

heebie-jeebies *plural noun* (*informal*) nervous anxiety or fear. [origin unknown]

heed *verb* to pay attention to someone or something. **to pay** or **take heed** to pay careful attention. [from an Old English word]

heedless *adjective* not taking care or paying attention. **heedlessly** *adverb* **heedlessness** *noun*

hee-haw *noun* a donkey's bray. [an imitation of the sound]

heel [1] *noun* **1** the rounded back part of the human foot. **2** the part of a sock or stocking covering this. **3** the part of a boot or shoe that supports a person's heel. **4** something like a heel in shape or position ♦ *the heel of a loaf.*
heel *verb* **1** to repair the heel of a shoe or boot. **2** (in rugby) to pass the ball with the heel. **at** or **on the heels of** following closely after. **to bring someone to heel** to bring someone under control. **to take to your heels** to run away. [from an Old English word *hela*]

heel [2] *verb* (said about a ship) to lean over to one side. [from an Old English word *hieldan*]

hefty *adjective* (**heftier, heftiest**) **1** (said about a person) big and strong. **2** (said about a thing) large, heavy, and powerful. **heftily** *adverb* **heftiness** *noun* [probably from a Scandinavian word; related to *heave*]

hegemony (hi-**jem**-ən-i or hi-**gem**-ən-i) *noun* leadership, especially by one country or group over others. [from a Greek word *hēgemōn* meaning 'leader']

Hegira (**hej**-i-rə) *noun* the flight of Muhammad from Mecca in AD 622, from which the Muslim era is reckoned. [from an Arabic word *hijra* meaning 'departure from a country']

heifer (**hef**-er) *noun* a young cow, especially one that has not given birth to a calf. [from an Old English word *heahfore*]

height *noun* **1** the measurement of someone or something from head to foot or from base to top. **2** the quality of being tall or high. **3** the distance of an object or position above ground level or sea level ◆ *What height are we flying at?* **4** a high place or area ◆ *I don't like heights.* **5** the highest point of something ◆ *at the height of the holiday season.* [from an Old English word]

heighten *verb* **1** to make something higher. **2** to become or make something more intense.

heinous (**hay**-nəs) *adjective* very wicked ◆ *a heinous crime.* [from an Old French word *hair* meaning 'to hate']

heir (air) *noun* a person who inherits property or rank from its former owner. [from a Latin word *heres*]

heir apparent *noun* (**heirs apparent**) **1** an heir whose claim cannot be set aside by the birth of a person with a stronger claim to inherit. **2** a person who is most likely to become the next leader etc.

heiress (**air**-ess) *noun* a female heir, especially to great wealth.

heirloom (**air**-loom) *noun* a valuable possession that has been handed down in a family for several generations. [from *heir* and an Old English word *geloma* meaning 'tool']

heir presumptive *noun* (**heirs presumptive**) an heir whose claim may be set aside by the birth of a person with a stronger claim to inherit.

held past tense and past participle of **hold** [1].

helical (**hel**-i-kəl) *adjective* like a helix.

helicopter *noun* a type of aircraft with horizontal revolving blades or rotors. [from *helix* and a Greek word *pteron* meaning 'wing']

heliotrope (**hee**-li-ə-trohp) *noun* **1** a plant with small sweet-smelling purple flowers. **2** a light purple colour. [from the Greek words *hēlios* meaning 'sun' and *tropē* meaning 'turning' (because the plant turns its flowers to the sun)]

helipad (**hel**-i-pad) *noun* a pad or landing ground for a helicopter.

heliport (**hel**-i-port) *noun* a place equipped for helicopters to take off and land.

helium (**hee**-li-əm) *noun* a chemical element (symbol He), a light colourless gas that does not burn, used in airships. [from a Greek word *hēlios* meaning 'sun']

helix (**hee**-liks) *noun* (**helices** (**hee**-li-seez)) a spiral, especially a three-dimensional one, either like a corkscrew or flat like a watch spring. [from a Greek word meaning 'coil']

hell *noun* **1** in some religions, a place where wicked people are thought to be punished after they die. **2** a place or state of great misery or suffering ◆ *The next few days were hell.* **hell** *interjection* an exclamation of anger. **to give someone hell** (*informal*) to tell someone off severely or make things unpleasant for them. **hell for leather** as fast as possible. **like hell** (*informal*) **1** very fast or hard ◆ *He tried like hell.* **2** used to show disagreement or scorn ◆ *'You don't mind staying behind, do you?' 'Like hell!'* [from an Old English word]

he'll *verb* (*informal*) he will.

hell-bent *adjective* determined to achieve something at all costs.

hellebore (**hel**-i-bor) *noun* a poisonous plant with white or greenish flowers. [from a Greek word *helleboros*]

Hellene (**hel**-een) *noun* a Greek. **Hellenic** *adjective* [from a Greek word *Hellēn* meaning 'a Greek']

Hellenistic *adjective* to do with the Greek language and culture of the 4th–1st centuries BC.

hellfire *noun* the fire of hell.

hellish *adjective* (*informal*) very difficult or unpleasant.

hello *interjection & noun* an exclamation used in greeting or to attract someone's attention or express surprise, or to answer a telephone call.

Hell's Angel *noun* a member of a gang of motorcyclists associated with rough and violent behaviour.

helm *noun* the tiller or wheel for steering a ship or boat. **at the helm** at the head of an organization etc., in control. [from an Old English word *helma*]

helmet *noun* a strong covering worn to protect the head. [from an Old French word]

helmsman *noun* (**helmsmen**) a person who steers a ship or boat.

helot (hel-ət) *noun* a serf in ancient Sparta. [from a Greek word]

help *verb* 1 to make it easier for someone to do something by doing some of the work or giving them what they need ♦ *Can you help with the washing-up?* 2 to make it easier for something to happen, to improve a situation ♦ *This will help ease the pain* ♦ *Shouting isn't going to help.* SYNONYMS: aid, assist, facilitate. 3 to prevent or avoid something ♦ *It can't be helped.*
help *noun* 1 the action of helping or being helped. SYNONYMS: aid, assistance, cooperation, backing, support. 2 a person or thing that helps ♦ *Thanks, you've been a great help.* 3 a person employed to help with housework. 4 (*Computing*) (used before a noun) giving assistance in the form of displayed instructions ♦ *a help menu.* **to help yourself to** 1 to serve yourself with food at a meal. 2 to take something without permission. **to help someone out** to give help, especially in a crisis. **helper** *noun* [from an Old English word *helpan*]

helpful *adjective* giving help, useful. **helpfully** *adverb* **helpfulness** *noun*

helping *noun* a portion of food given to one person at a meal.

helpless *adjective* 1 not able to manage without help, dependent on others. 2 incapable of action, or indicating this ♦ *Jack was helpless with laughter* ♦ *She gave him a helpless glance.* **helplessly** *adverb* **helplessness** *noun*

helpline *noun* a telephone service giving advice on problems.

helpmate *noun* a companion or partner who helps.

helter-skelter *adverb* in great haste.
helter-skelter *noun* a tower-shaped structure at a funfair, with a spiral track outside it which people slide down. [vaguely imitating the sound of many running feet]

hem *noun* the edge of a piece of cloth or clothing which has been turned under and sewn in place.
hem *verb* (**hemmed, hemming**) to turn and sew a hem on something. **to hem someone or something in** to surround and restrict the movement of someone or something ♦ *Enemy forces hemmed them in.* [from an Old English word]

he-man *noun* (*informal*) a strong masculine man.

hemisphere *noun* 1 a half of a sphere. 2 either of the halves into which the earth is divided either by the equator (the *Northern* and *Southern hemisphere*) or by a line passing through the poles (the *Eastern hemisphere*, including Europe, Asia, and Africa; the *Western hemisphere*, the Americas). [from a Greek word *hēmi-* meaning 'half' and *sphere*]

hemispherical (hem-iss-**fe**-ri-kəl) *adjective* shaped like a hemisphere.

hemline *noun* the lower edge of a skirt or dress.

hemlock *noun* 1 a poisonous plant of the parsley family with small white flowers. 2 the poison made from it. [from an Old English word *hymlice*]

hemp *noun* 1 the cannabis plant, from which coarse fibres are obtained for the manufacture of rope and cloth. 2 the drug cannabis. **hempen** *adjective* [from an Old English word]

hen *noun* a female bird, especially of the common domestic fowl. [from an Old English word *henn*]

hence *adverb* 1 from this time ♦ *five years hence.* 2 for this reason. 3 (*old use*) from here. [from an Old English word]

henceforth or **henceforward** *adverb* from this time on, in future.

henchman *noun* (**henchmen**) a trusted supporter or follower, especially one who uses violence. [origin unknown]

henge *noun* a prehistoric monument of wood or stone resembling the circle of stones at Stonehenge. [from *Stonehenge*]

henna *noun* **1** a reddish-brown dye used especially on the hair. **2** the tropical plant from which this is obtained.
henna *verb* (**hennaed, hennaing**) to dye hair etc. with henna. [from an Arabic word]

hen night or **hen party** *noun* (*informal*) a celebration for a woman who is about to get married, attended only by women.

henpecked *adjective* (said about a husband) nagged and ordered about by a domineering wife.

henry *noun* (**henries** or **henrys**) (*Physics*) a unit of inductance. [named after the American physicist J. Henry (1797–1878)]

hepatic (hip-at-ik) *adjective* to do with the liver. [from a Greek word *hēpatos* meaning 'of the liver']

hepatitis (hep-ə-tiy-tiss) *noun* inflammation of the liver. There are three forms, called **hepatitis A** (transmitted in food) and **hepatitis B** and **C** (both transmitted in infected blood).

hepta- *prefix* seven. [from a Greek word *hepta* meaning 'seven']

heptagon (hep-tə-gən) *noun* a geometric figure with seven sides. [from *hepta-* and a Greek word *gōnia* meaning 'angle']

heptathlon (hep-tath-lon) *noun* an athletic contest for women in which each competitor takes part in seven events.
heptathlete *noun* [from *hepta-* and a Greek word *athlon* meaning 'contest']

her *pronoun* **1** the form of *she* used as the object of a verb or after a preposition ♦ *We saw her.*
her *adjective* **1** of or belonging to her. **2** used in women's titles ♦ *Her Majesty.* [from an Old English word *hire*]

herald *noun* **1** an official in former times who made announcements and carried messages from a ruler. **2** a person or thing that indicates the approach of something ♦ *Spring is the herald of summer.* **3** an official employed to record people's pedigrees and grant coats of arms.

herald *verb* to show that something is approaching ♦ *Loud applause heralded the first runner to enter the stadium.* [from an Old French word *herault*]

heraldic (hi-ral-dik) *adjective* to do with heralds or heraldry.

heraldry *noun* the study of coats of arms and the right to bear them. [so called because a herald decided who could have a coat of arms and what should be on it]

herb *noun* **1** any plant whose leaves or seeds are used for flavouring or for making medicine. **2** (*Botany*) any soft-stemmed plant that dies down to the ground after flowering. **herby** *adjective* [from a Latin word *herba* meaning 'grass']

herbaceous (her-bay-shəs) *adjective* to do with or like herbs.

herbaceous border *noun* a garden border containing perennial flowering plants.

herbage *noun* grass and other field plants.

herbal *adjective* to do with herbs, or made from herbs.
herbal *noun* a book that describes herbs and their uses in medicine and cooking.

herbalist *noun* a dealer in medicinal herbs.

herbicide *noun* a substance that is poisonous to plants, used to destroy unwanted vegetation. [from Latin words *herba* meaning 'grass' and *caedere* meaning 'to kill']

herbivore (her-biv-or) *noun* an animal that feeds on plants. [from Latin words *herba* meaning 'grass' and *vorare* meaning 'to devour']

herbivorous (her-biv-er-əs) *adjective* feeding on plants.

herculean (her-kew-lee-ən) *adjective* needing great strength or effort ♦ *a herculean task.* [from the name of Hercules, a Greek hero famed for his prodigious strength]

herd *noun* **1** a large group of cattle or other animals feeding or staying together. **2** a mass of people, a mob.
herd *verb* **1** to move or gather in a large group ♦ *We all herded into the dining room.* **2** to look after a herd of animals. [from an Old English word *heord*]

herd instinct *noun* the instinct to think and behave like the majority of people do.

herdsman *noun* (**herdsmen**) a person who tends a herd of animals.

here adverb 1 in or at or to this place. 2 at this point in a process or a series of events.
here interjection used to attract someone's attention or as a reply in answer to a roll-call. **here and there** in various places. [from an Old English word]

hereabouts or **hereabout** adverb near this place.

hereafter adverb (formal) from now on or at some time in the future.
the hereafter noun life after death.

hereby adverb (formal) as a result of this, by this means.

hereditary (hi-**red**-it-er-i) adjective 1 inherited, able to be passed or received from one generation to another ♦ a hereditary disease. 2 holding a position by inheriting it ♦ a hereditary ruler. [from a Latin word]

heredity (hi-**red**-iti) noun inheritance of physical or mental characteristics from parents or ancestors. [from a Latin word heredis meaning 'to do with an heir']

herein adverb (formal) in this place, document, etc.

hereinafter adverb (formal) in a later part of this document.

hereof adverb (formal) of this document.

heresy (**herri**-si) noun (**heresies**) 1 a belief or opinion that disagrees with the accepted beliefs of the Christian Church, or with those on any subject. 2 the holding of such an opinion. [from a Greek word hairesis meaning 'choice']

heretic (**herri**-tik) noun a person who holds a heresy or is guilty of heresy. **heretical** (hi-**ret**-ikəl) adjective

herewith adverb (formal) with this letter ♦ A cheque is enclosed herewith.

heritable adjective able to be inherited.

heritage noun 1 the things that have been or may be inherited. 2 valued things such as historic buildings and traditions that have been passed down from previous generations. [from a Latin word hereditare meaning 'to inherit']

hermaphrodite (her-**maf**-rə-diyt) noun a person or animal that has both male and female sexual organs or other sexual characteristics. **hermaphroditic** (her-maf-rə-**dit**-ik) adjective [from a Greek word hermaphroditos, originally the name of the son of Hermes and Aphrodite who became joined in one body with a nymph]

hermetic adjective with an airtight closure ♦ a hermetic seal. **hermetically** adverb [from a Latin word]

hermit noun 1 a person who has withdrawn from human society and lives in solitude for religious reasons. 2 a person who lives alone away from other people. [from a Greek word erēmitēs meaning 'of the desert']

hermitage noun a hermit's home.

hermit crab noun a crab that uses a cast-off shell to protect its soft hinder parts.

hernia noun an abnormal condition in which a part or organ of the body pushes through a wall of the cavity (especially the abdomen) that normally contains it. [from a Latin word]

hero noun (**heroes**) 1 a man who is admired for his brave or noble deeds. 2 the chief male character in a story, play, or poem. [from a Greek word hērōs meaning 'a very strong or brave man, whom the gods love']

heroic adjective having the characteristics of a hero or heroine, very brave.
heroics plural noun over-dramatic talk or behaviour. **heroically** adverb

heroic couplet noun (in poetry) a pair of rhyming iambic pentameters.

heroin noun a powerful sedative drug prepared from morphine, used medically and by addicts. [from a German word]
◊ Do not confuse this word with **heroine**, which has a different meaning.

heroine noun 1 a woman who is admired for her brave or noble deeds. 2 the chief female character in a story, play, or poem. [a Greek word, the feminine of hērōs meaning 'hero']
◊ Do not confuse this word with **heroin**, which has a different meaning.

heroism noun heroic conduct or qualities.

heron noun a long-legged long-necked wading bird living in marshy places. [via Old French from a Germanic word]

hero worship noun excessive admiration for someone.
hero-worship verb (**hero-worshipped**, **hero-worshipping**) to admire someone excessively. **hero-worshipper** noun

herpes (her-peez) *noun* a virus disease causing blisters on the skin. [from a Greek word *herpēs* meaning 'shingles']

Herr (hair) *noun* (**Herren**) the title of a German man, equivalent to Mr.

herring *noun* a silvery North Atlantic fish much used for food. [from an Old English word]

herringbone *noun* a zigzag pattern or arrangement ♦ *herringbone tweed*. [so called because it looks like the spine and ribs of a herring]

herring gull *noun* a common gull with grey black-tipped wings.

hers *possessive pronoun* used to refer to a thing or things belonging to a female person or animal already mentioned ♦ *This bag must be hers* ♦ *Hers are best.* ◊ It is incorrect to write *her's*.

herself *pronoun* the form of *her* used in reflexive constructions (e.g. *She cut herself*) and for emphasis (e.g. *She herself told me* or *She told me herself*).

hertz *noun* (**hertz**) a unit of frequency of electromagnetic waves, equal to one cycle per second. [named after the German physicist H. R. Hertz (1857–94), a pioneer of radio communication]

he's *verb* (*informal*) he is or he has.

hesitant *adjective* slow to speak, act, or move because you feel uncertain or reluctant. SYNONYMS: diffident, tentative, indecisive, irresolute, wary. **hesitancy** *noun* **hesitantly** *adverb*

hesitate *verb* 1 to be slow to speak, act, or move because you feel uncertain or reluctant, to pause in doubt. SYNONYMS: delay, pause, waver, dither, vacillate; (*informal*) shilly-shally, be in two minds. 2 to be reluctant to do something ♦ *He wouldn't hesitate to break the rules if it suited him.* **hesitation** *noun* [from a Latin word *haesitare* meaning 'to get stuck']

hessian *noun* strong coarse cloth made of hemp or jute, used to make sacks and in upholstery. [named after Hesse in Germany, where it was made]

hetero- *prefix* other or different. [from a Greek word *heteros* meaning 'other']

heterodox (het-er-ə-doks) *adjective* not orthodox. **heterodoxy** *noun* [from *hetero-* and a Greek word *doxa* meaning 'opinion']

heterogeneous (het-er-ə-**jee**-niəs) *adjective* made up of people or things that are unlike each other. [from *hetero-* and a Greek word *genos* meaning 'a kind']

heterosexual *adjective* feeling sexually attracted to people of the opposite sex. **heterosexual** *noun* a heterosexual person. **heterosexuality** *noun*

heterotrophic (het-er-ə-trof-ik) *adjective* (*Biology*) (said about organisms) requiring carbon to sustain life. [from *hetero-* and a Greek word *trophos* meaning 'feeder']

heterozygote (het-er-ə-**ziy**-goht) *noun* (*Biochemistry*) an individual that has two different alleles for any one gene, being formed from gametes carrying different alleles. **heterozygous** *adjective* [from *hetero-* and *zygote*]

het up *adjective* (*informal*) angry and agitated ♦ *What is she so het up about?* [from a dialect word *het* meaning 'heated']

heuristic (hewr-**iss**-tik) *adjective* 1 helping someone to find out or discover something for themselves. 2 proceeding by trial and error. [from a Greek word *heuriskein* meaning 'to find']

hew *verb* (past participle, **hewn,** or **hewed**) 1 to chop or cut something with an axe or sword etc. 2 to cut a hard material into shape. **hewer** *noun* [from an Old English word]

hewn *adjective* made or shaped by hewing.

hex *noun* (*North Amer.*) a magic spell or a curse. [from a German word]

hexa- *prefix* six. [from a Greek word *hex* meaning 'six']

hexadecimal (heks-ə-**dess**-im-əl) *adjective* to do with or using a system of numerical notation that has 16 rather than 10 as a base. [from *hexa-* and *decimal*]

hexagon (heks-ə-gən) *noun* a geometric figure with six sides. **hexagonal** (heks-**ag**-ən-əl) *adjective* [from *hexa-* and a Greek word *gōnia* meaning 'angle']

hexagram *noun* a six-pointed star formed by two intersecting triangles. [from *hexa-* and *-gram*]

hexahedron (heks-ə-**hee**-drən) *noun* (**hexahedra** or **hexahedrons**) a solid body with six faces. **hexahedral** *adjective* [from *hexa-* and a Greek word *hedra* meaning 'base']

hexameter (heks-am-it-er) *noun* a line of verse consisting of six metrical feet. [from *hexa-* and a Greek word *metron* meaning 'measure']

hey *interjection* an exclamation used to attract attention or to express surprise or interest.

heyday *noun* the period when someone or something is at its most successful or popular ♦ *He was a superb player in his heyday.* [from an old word *heyday!*, an expression of joy or surprise]

Hf *abbreviation* (*Chemistry*) the symbol for hafnium.

HGV *abbreviation* heavy goods vehicle.

hi *interjection* used as a friendly greeting.

hiatus (hiy-ay-təs) *noun* (**hiatuses**) a pause or gap in a sequence or series. [a Latin word meaning 'gaping']

hibernate (hiy-ber-nayt) *verb* (said about an animal or plant) to spend the winter in a state like deep sleep. **hibernation** *noun* [from a Latin word *hibernus* meaning 'wintry']

Hibernian (hiy-ber-niən) *adjective* to do with Ireland. [from a Latin word *Hibernia* meaning 'Ireland']

hibiscus (hib-isk-əs) *noun* a cultivated shrub or tree with brightly coloured trumpet-shaped flowers. [from a Greek word *hibiskos* meaning 'marsh mallow']

hiccup or **hiccough** *noun* 1 a high gulping sound made when your breath is briefly interrupted. 2 a brief hitch or setback. **hiccup** *verb* (**hiccuped, hiccuping**) to make the sound of a hiccup. **hiccups** *plural noun* an attack of hiccuping. [an imitation of the sound]

hickory *noun* (**hickories**) 1 a North American tree related to the walnut. 2 the hard wood of this tree. [from a Native American word]

hid past tense of **hide**[2].

hidden past participle of **hide**[2].

hidden agenda *noun* a person's secret but real motive for doing something.

hide[1] *verb* (**hid, hidden**) 1 to put or keep something out of sight, to prevent something from being seen. SYNONYMS: conceal, secrete, stash, disguise, camouflage, mask, screen. 2 to keep something secret. 3 to conceal yourself ♦ *There was nowhere to hide.*

hide *noun* a camouflaged shelter used to observe wildlife at close quarters. [from an Old English word *hydan*]

hide[2] *noun* an animal's skin, especially when tanned or dressed. [from an Old English word *hyd*]

hide-and-seek *noun* a children's game in which one player looks for others who are hiding.

hideaway *noun* a hiding place, especially somewhere quiet away from people.

hidebound *adjective* narrow-minded, refusing to abandon old customs and prejudices. [originally referring to underfed cattle, with skin stretched tight over their bones, later of a tree whose bark was so tight it could not grow]

hideous *adjective* extremely ugly or unpleasant. **hideously** *adverb* **hideousness** *noun* [from an Old French word]

hideout *noun* a hiding place, especially one used by someone who has broken the law.

hidey-hole *noun* (*informal*) a hiding place.

hiding[1] *noun* being or remaining hidden ♦ *She went into hiding for a time.*

hiding[2] *noun* 1 a thrashing or beating. 2 (*informal*) a severe defeat. [from an old word *hide* meaning 'to beat the hide (skin)']

hierarchy (hiyr-ark-i) *noun* (**hierarchies**) 1 an organization or system that ranks people one above another according to the power or authority that they hold. 2 an arrangement according to relative importance. **hierarchical** (hiyr-**ark**-ikəl) *adjective* [from Greek words *hieros* meaning 'sacred' and *arkhein* meaning 'to rule']

hieroglyph (hiyr-ə-glif) *noun* 1 one of the pictures or symbols used in ancient Egypt and elsewhere to represent sounds, words, or ideas. 2 a written symbol with a secret or cryptic meaning.

hieroglyphic (hiyr-ə-glif-ik) *adjective* to do with or written in hieroglyphs. **hieroglyphics** *plural noun* writing consisting of hieroglyphs. [from a Greek word *hieros* meaning 'sacred' and *gluphē* meaning 'carving']

hi-fi *adjective* (**hi-fis**) (*informal*) high fidelity. **hi-fi** *noun* (*informal*) equipment for reproducing recorded sound with very little distortion.

higgledy-piggledy *adjective & adverb* completely mixed up, in great disorder. [a nonsense word based on *pig* (because of the way pigs huddle together)]

high *adjective* **1** reaching a long way upwards, extending above the normal or average level ♦ *high hills*. SYNONYMS: tall, lofty, towering. **2** situated far above the ground or above sea level ♦ *high clouds*. **3** measuring a specified distance from base to top ♦ *two metres high*. **4** ranking above others in importance or quality ♦ *High Admiral* ♦ *the higher animals*. **5** great in amount, value, or intensity ♦ *high temperatures* ♦ *high prices*. **6** (said about a period or movement) at its peak ♦ *high summer*. **7** noble or virtuous ♦ *high ideals*. **8** (said about a sound or voice) having rapid vibrations, not deep or low. SYNONYMS: high-pitched, shrill, piercing, sharp. **9** (said about meat) beginning to go bad. **10** (said about game) hung until slightly decomposed and ready to cook. **11** (*informal*) under the influence of drugs or alcohol. **high** *noun* **1** a high point, level, or figure ♦ *Exports reached a new high*. **2** an area of high barometric pressure. **3** (*informal*) a state of euphoria. **high** *adverb* **1** in, at, or to a high level or position ♦ *They flew high above us*. **2** in or to a high degree ♦ *Feelings were running high*. **high and dry** abandoned in a difficult situation ♦ *Our sponsors pulled out at the last moment, leaving us high and dry*. **high and low** everywhere ♦ *We hunted high and low for him*. **high and mighty** arrogant. **it is high time** it is past the time when something should have happened ♦ *It's high time we left*. [from an Old English word *heah*]

high altar *noun* the chief altar of a church.

highbrow *adjective* very intellectual, cultured. [from *highbrowed* meaning 'having a high forehead', thought to be a sign of intelligence]

high chair *noun* a small chair with long legs used by a baby or small child at mealtimes.

High Church *noun* the section of the Church of England that gives an important place to ritual and to the authority of bishops and priests.

high-class *adjective* of high quality.

high colour *noun* a flushed complexion.

high commission *noun* an embassy of one Commonwealth country in another.

high commissioner *noun* the head of a high commission.

High Court *noun* the supreme court dealing with civil law cases.

Higher *noun* the advanced level of the Scottish Certificate of Education.

higher animals *plural noun* mammals and other vertebrates, regarded as having relatively advanced characteristics.

higher education *noun* education above the level given in schools, especially to degree level.

higher plants *plural noun* vascular plants, regarded as having relatively advanced characteristics.

highest common factor *noun* the highest number that can be divided exactly into each of two or more numbers.

high explosive *noun* a powerful explosive with a violently shattering effect.

highfalutin *adjective* (*informal*) pompous or pretentious.

high fidelity *noun* reproduction of sound with little or no distortion.

high-flyer *noun* a person with the capacity to be very successful.

high frequency *noun* (in radio) a frequency of 3 to 30 megahertz.

high-handed *adjective* using authority in an arrogant way.

high jinks *plural noun* boisterous fun or mischief.

high jump *noun* an athletic competition in which competitors jump over a high horizontal bar. **for the high jump** about to be told off or punished.

highland *noun* (also **highlands**) mountainous country. **Highlands** *noun* the mountainous northern part of Scotland. **highlander** *noun*

high-level *adjective* **1** involving important or high-ranking people ♦ *high-level negotiations*. **2** (said about a computer language) designed for convenience in programming, often by resembling ordinary language.

high life or **high living** *noun* an extravagant or luxurious way of living.

highlight *noun* **1** the most interesting or outstanding feature of something ♦ *the highlight of the tour*. **2** a light or bright area in a painting etc. **3** a light-coloured streak in a person's hair.

highlight *verb* 1 to draw special attention to something. 2 to emphasize a section of text using a highlighter pen.

highlighter *noun* a felt-tip pen used to overlay transparent fluorescent colour on a section of text.

highly *adverb* 1 to a high degree, extremely ♦ *highly amusing.* 2 very favourably ♦ *We think highly of her.*

highly strung *adjective* nervous and easily upset.

high-minded *adjective* having strong moral principles.

Highness *noun* the title used in speaking of or to a prince or princess ♦ *His Highness* ♦ *Your Highness.*

high-pitched *adjective* (said about a voice or sound) high.

high priest *noun* the chief priest of a non-Christian religion.

high-profile *adjective* involving much publicity ♦ *a high-profile court case.*

high-rise *adjective* (said about a building) with many storeys.

high school *noun* a secondary school, often a grammar school.

high seas *plural noun* the open seas not under any country's jurisdiction.

high season *noun* the most popular time of year for a holiday, when prices are highest.

high-speed *adjective* operating at great speed.

high spirits *plural noun* cheerful and lively behaviour. **high-spirited** *adjective*

high street *noun* the main street of a town, with shops etc.

high table *noun* the table in the dining hall of a school or college where the high-ranking people sit.

hightail *verb* (*informal*) **to hightail it** to leave somewhere in a great hurry.

high tea *noun* an evening meal with tea and meat or other cooked food.

high-tech *adjective* using or involved in high technology.

high technology *noun* advanced technology, especially in electronics.

high-tensile *adjective* (said about metal) very strong under tension.

high tide *noun* the tide at its highest level.

high treason *noun* treason against your country or ruler.

high water *noun* high tide.

high-water mark *noun* the level reached by the sea at high tide, or by a river or lake when it floods.

highway *noun* 1 a public road. 2 a main route by land, sea, or air.

highwayman *noun* (**highwaymen**) (*historical*) a man, usually on horseback, who held up and robbed passing travellers.

high wire *noun* a high tightrope.

hijack *verb* to seize control of an aircraft, ship, or vehicle while it is in transit in order to steal its goods, take its passengers hostage, or force it to a new destination.
hijack *noun* a hijacking. **hijacker** *noun* [origin unknown]

hike *noun* 1 a long walk, especially a cross-country walk taken for pleasure. 2 (*informal*) a sharp increase in something ♦ *a price hike.*
hike *verb* 1 to go on a hike. 2 (*informal*) to increase a price sharply. **hiker** *noun* [origin unknown]

hilarious *adjective* extremely funny. SYNONYMS: hysterical, side-splitting, uproarious, rollicking. **hilariously** *adverb* **hilarity** (hi-la-riti) *noun* [from a Greek word *hilaros* meaning 'cheerful']

hill *noun* 1 a raised area of land, not as high as a mountain. 2 a slope in a road. 3 a heap or mound. **over the hill** (*informal*) old and past your best. [from an Old English word *hyll*]

hillbilly *noun* (**hillbillies**) (*informal*) a person from a remote rural area in a southern state of the US.

hillock *noun* a small hill or mound. [from *hill* and an Old English word *-oc* meaning 'small']

hillside *noun* the sloping side of a hill.

hilly *adjective* (**hillier, hilliest**) full of hills. **hilliness** *noun*

hilt *noun* the handle of a sword, dagger, or knife. **to the hilt** completely ♦ *I support you to the hilt.* [from an Old English word]

him *pronoun* the form of *he* used as the object of a verb or after a preposition. [from an Old English word]

himself *pronoun* the form of *him* used in reflexive constructions (e.g. *He cut himself*) and for emphasis (e.g. *He himself had said it, He told me himself*).

hind [1] *adjective* situated at the back ♦ *hind legs*. [probably from *behind*]

hind [2] *noun* a female deer. [from an Old English word]

hinder [1] (hin-der) *verb* to get in someone's way or make things difficult for them. SYNONYMS: hamper, impede, frustrate, handicap, obstruct, check. [from an Old English word *hindrian* meaning 'to damage']

hinder [2] (hiynd-er) *adjective* hind ♦ *the hinder part*. [perhaps from an Old English word *hinderweard* meaning 'backward']

Hindi (hin-di) *noun* one of the official languages of India. [from an Urdu word *Hind* meaning 'India']

hindmost *adjective* furthest back.

hindquarters *plural noun* an animal's hind legs and rear parts.

hindrance *noun* something that hinders.

hindsight *noun* looking back on an event with knowledge or understanding that you did not have at the time.

Hindu *noun* a person whose religion is Hinduism.
Hindu *adjective* to do with Hindus or Hinduism. [from an Urdu word]

Hinduism (hin-doo-izm) *noun* a major religion and philosophy of the Indian subcontinent, including belief in reincarnation and the worship of a large number of gods.

Hindustani (hin-də-stah-ni) *noun* 1 a group of languages and dialects spoken in NW India, especially Hindi and Urdu. 2 the dialect of Hindi spoken in Delhi, widely used throughout India.

hinge *noun* 1 a joint on which a lid, door, or gate etc. turns or swings. 2 a natural joint working in the same way. 3 a small piece of gummed paper for fixing stamps in an album.
hinge *verb* 1 to attach or be attached by a hinge or hinges. 2 to depend on something ♦ *Everything hinges on this meeting*. [from an old word *henge*, related to *hang*]

hinny *noun* (**hinnies**) an animal that is the offspring of a female donkey and a male horse. [from a Greek word *hinnos*]

hint *noun* 1 a slight indication, a suggestion made indirectly. SYNONYMS: clue, idea, inkling, pointer, intimation, insinuation. 2 a very small trace of something ♦ *white with a hint of pink*. SYNONYMS: dash, tinge, touch. 3 a small piece of practical information ♦ *household hints*.
hint *verb* to make a hint. SYNONYMS: suggest, indicate, imply, intimate, insinuate. **to hint at** to refer indirectly to something. [from an old word *hent* meaning 'grasp']

hinterland *noun* a district lying inland beyond a coast or port or other centre. [from German words *hinter* meaning 'behind' and *Land* meaning 'land']

hip [1] *noun* the bony part at the side of the body between the waist and the thigh. **hips** *plural noun* the measurement round the body here. **hipped** *adjective* [from an Old English word *hype*]

hip [2] *noun* the fruit of the wild rose. [from an Old English word *heope*]

hip [3] *adjective* (*informal*) aware of and understanding the latest trends. [origin unknown]

hip hop *noun* a style of popular music of American Black and Hispanic origin. [probably from *hip*[3]]

hippie *noun* another spelling of **hippy**.

hippo *noun* (**hippos**) (*informal*) a hippopotamus.

Hippocratic oath (hip-ə-krat-ik) *noun* an oath, formerly taken by people beginning medical practice, to observe the code of professional behaviour. [named after Hippocrates, a Greek physician of the 5th century BC]

hippodrome *noun* 1 (in names) a theatre or concert hall. 2 (in ancient Greece or Rome) a course for chariot or horse races. [from a Greek word *hippos* meaning 'horse' and *dromos* meaning 'running track']

hippopotamus *noun* (**hippopotamuses** or **hippopotami**) a large African river animal with massive jaws, short legs, and thick dark skin. [from Greek words *hippos* meaning 'horse' and *potamos* meaning 'river']

hippy *noun* (*informal*) (**hippies**) a young person who joins with others to live in an unconventional way, often based on ideas of peace and love. Hippies first appeared in the 1960s. [from *hip*[3]]

hire *verb* 1 to pay to use something

temporarily. SYNONYMS: rent, lease, charter.
2 to pay for someone's services. 3 to lend
something for payment ♦ He hires out
bicycles.
hire noun the act of hiring ♦ boats for hire.
hireable adjective **hirer** noun [from an Old
English word hyrian meaning 'to employ
for wages']

hireling noun a person hired to work for
someone, especially to do something
dishonest or illegal.

hire purchase noun buying something by
paying in regular instalments.

hirsute (herss-yoot) adjective (formal) hairy.
[from a Latin word hirsutus meaning
'rough or shaggy']

his adjective 1 of or belonging to him ♦ That
is his book. 2 used in men's titles ♦ His
Majesty.
his possessive pronoun the thing or things
belonging to him ♦ That book is his. [from
an Old English word]

Hispanic (hiss-pan-ik) adjective 1 to do with
Spain or other Spanish-speaking
countries. 2 to do with the
Spanish-speaking people of the USA.
[from a Latin word Hispania meaning
'Spain'] ·

hiss verb 1 to make a sound like that of
s ♦ The snakes were hissing. 2 to express
disapproval in this way.
hiss noun a hissing sound. [an imitation
of the sound]

histamine (hist-ə-min) noun a chemical
compound present in all body tissues,
causing some allergic reactions. [from
a Greek word histos meaning 'web,
tissue']

histogram (hist-ə-gram) noun a diagram
used in statistics, consisting of rectangles
whose sizes represent the values of a
variable quantity. [from a Greek word
histos meaning 'mast' and -gram]

histology (hist-ol-əji) noun the scientific
study of the structure of organic tissues.
histological adjective [from a Greek word
histos meaning 'web' and -logy]

historian noun a person who writes or
studies history.

historic adjective famous or important in
history; likely to be remembered ♦ a
historic town ♦ a historic meeting.
◊ Do not confuse this word with **historical**,
which has a different meaning.

historical adjective 1 that actually existed
or took place in the past ♦ The novel is
based on historical events ♦ a historical
character. 2 to do with history or based on
things that happened in the past
♦ historical research ♦ a historical novel.
historically adverb
◊ Do not confuse this word with **historic**,
which has a different meaning.

history noun (**histories**) 1 the study of past
events, especially of human affairs.
2 what happened in the past, either in
general or in connection with a particular
person or thing. 3 a continuous
methodical record of important past
events. 4 an interesting or eventful past
♦ The house has quite a history. **to make
history** to do something memorable or be
the first to do something. [from a Greek
word historia meaning 'finding out,
narrative']

histrionic (histri-on-ik) adjective dramatic
or theatrical in manner.
histrionics plural noun dramatic behaviour
intended to attract people's attention.
[from a Latin word histrio meaning 'actor']

hit verb (past tense and past participle **hit**;
hitting) 1 to aim a blow at someone or
something. SYNONYMS: strike, punch, thump,
slap; (informal) clout, belt, wallop. 2 to strike
a target ♦ The bridge was hit by a missile.
3 to come against something with force
♦ The car hit a tree. SYNONYMS: strike, knock,
bang, bump, clip; (informal) bash. 4 to have a
bad effect on someone; to cause someone
to suffer ♦ Famine has hit the poor countries.
5 to be realized by someone ♦ It suddenly
hit me what she was talking about. 6 to propel
a ball with a bat, racket, or club; to score
runs or points in this way. 7 to reach or
come to something ♦ I can't hit the high
notes ♦ We've hit a problem.
hit noun 1 a blow or stroke. 2 a shot that
hits its target. 3 a success, especially by
being popular ♦ You are certainly a hit with
my family. 4 a successful record, show, etc.
to hit back to retaliate. **to hit it off** to get
on well with a person. **to hit on** to
discover something suddenly or by
chance. **to hit out** to make a forceful
criticism of someone or something.
[from an Old Norse word hitta meaning 'to
come upon']

hit-and-miss adjective done or happening
at random.

hit-and-run adjective injuring someone in
an accident and driving off without
stopping ♦ a hit-and-run driver.

hitch verb 1 to raise or pull something with a slight jerk. 2 to fasten something or be fastened with a loop or hook. 3 to get a lift by hitch-hiking.
hitch noun 1 a slight difficulty that causes delay. 2 a type of knot or noose. **to get hitched** (informal) to marry. **hitcher** noun [origin unknown]

hitch-hike verb to travel by getting rides in passing vehicles. **hitch-hiker** noun

hi-tech adjective another spelling of **high-tech**.

hither adverb to or towards this place. **hither and thither** to and fro. [from an Old English word hider]

hitherto adverb until this time.

hit list noun (informal) a list of people to be killed for criminal reasons.

hit man noun (informal) a hired assassin.

Hittite noun a member of an ancient people who established an empire in Asia Minor and Syria in c.1700–1200 BC. [from a Hebrew word]

HIV abbreviation human immunodeficiency virus, a virus which causes Aids.

hive noun 1 a beehive. 2 the bees living in a beehive.
hive verb to gather bees in a hive. **to hive something off** to transfer work from a larger department or company to a smaller one. [from an Old English word hyf]

hives plural noun an itchy rash caused by an allergic reaction, especially nettlerash. [origin unknown]

HM abbreviation Her or His Majesty('s).

HMS abbreviation Her or His Majesty's Ship.

HMSO abbreviation Her or His Majesty's Stationery Office.

HNC abbreviation Higher National Certificate.

HND abbreviation Higher National Diploma.

Ho abbreviation (Chemistry) the symbol for holmium.

hoard noun a carefully saved store of money, food, or treasured objects.
SYNONYMS: store, stash, cache, stockpile.
hoard verb to save and store something away. **hoarder** noun [from an Old English word hord]
◊ Do not confuse this word with **horde**, which has a different meaning.

hoarding noun a fence of light boarding, often used for displaying advertisements. [from an Old French word]

hoar frost noun a white frost. [from an Old English word har meaning 'grey-haired' and frost]

hoarse adjective (said about a voice) sounding rough, as if from a dry throat.
SYNONYMS: husky, throaty, croaky, gruff.
hoarsely adverb **hoarseness** noun [from an Old English word has]

hoary adjective (hoarier, hoariest) 1 white or grey from age ♦ hoary hair. 2 with grey hair, aged. 3 (said about a joke etc.) old and corny. [from an Old English word]

hoax verb to deceive someone as a joke.
hoax noun a joking deception. **hoaxer** noun [probably from hocus-pocus]

hob noun 1 a flat heating surface on a cooker. 2 a flat metal shelf at the side of a fireplace, where a kettle or pan can be heated. [a different spelling of hub]

hobbit noun a member of an imaginary race of creatures, smaller than humans and with hairy feet, in stories by J. R. R. Tolkien. [invented by Tolkien in his book The Hobbit]

hobble verb 1 to walk awkwardly, especially because of pain. 2 to fasten together the legs of a horse in order to limit but not entirely prevent movement.
hobble noun 1 a hobbling walk. 2 a rope or strap used for hobbling a horse. [probably from an Old German word]

hobby noun (hobbies) something you do for pleasure in your spare time. [from hobby horse]

hobby horse noun 1 a stick with a horse's head, used as a toy. 2 a rocking horse. 3 a subject that a person is discussing whenever he or she gets the chance. [from hobby, a familiar form of the name Robin, often used for ponies, and horse]

hobgoblin noun a mischievous or evil spirit. [from hob, a familiar form of the name Robert or Robin, and goblin]

hobnail noun a heavy-headed nail used for the soles of boots. **hobnailed** adjective [from an old word hob meaning 'peg, pin' and nail]

hobnob verb (hobnobbed, hobnobbing) (informal) to spend time with someone socially ♦ I hear you've been hobnobbing with film stars. [from an old phrase to drink hob and nob meaning 'to drink to each other']

Hobson's choice *noun* a situation in which there is no alternative to the thing offered. [from the name of Thomas Hobson (1544–1631), who hired out horses and made customers take the one nearest the stable door]

hock[1] *noun* the middle joint of an animal's hind leg. [from an Old English word]

hock[2] *noun* a dry white wine from the German Rhineland. [from the German phrase *Hochheimer Wein* meaning 'wine from Hochheim']

hock[3] *verb* (*informal*) to pawn something. **hock** *noun* **in hock 1** that has been pawned. **2** in debt. [from a Dutch word *hok* meaning 'hutch, prison, debt']

hockey *noun* a game played on a field between two teams of players with curved sticks and a small hard ball. [origin unknown]

hocus-pocus *noun* meaningless talk used to trick or deceive people. [from an invented Latin phrase, used as a magic form of words by conjurors]

hod *noun* **1** a trough on a pole used by bricklayers for carrying mortar or bricks. **2** a coal scuttle. [from a dialect word *hot* meaning 'basket for carrying earth']

hoe *noun* a tool with a blade on a long handle, used for loosening soil or scraping up weeds.
hoe *verb* (**hoes, hoed, hoeing**) to dig up earth or plants with a hoe. [from an Old French word *houe*]

hog *noun* **1** a pig, especially a castrated male pig reared for meat. **2** (*informal*) a greedy person.
hog *verb* (**hogged, hogging**) (*informal*) to take more than your fair share of something; to hoard something selfishly.
to go the whole hog (*informal*) to do something completely or thoroughly. **hoggish** *adjective* [from an Old English word *hogg*]

hogback or **hog's back** *noun* a steep-sided hill ridge.

Hogmanay (hog-mə-nay) *noun* New Year's Eve in Scotland. [perhaps from an Old French word]

hogshead *noun* **1** a large cask. **2** a measure of liquid volume for various commodities, usually about 50 gallons.

hogwash *noun* (*informal*) nonsense or rubbish. [originally denoting kitchen swill for pigs]

hogweed *noun* any of several white-flowered weeds of the parsley family.

hoick *verb* (*informal*) to lift or pull something, especially with a jerk. [perhaps from *hike*]

hoi polloi (hoi pə-loi) *plural noun* the common people, the masses. [a Greek phrase meaning 'the many']

hoist *verb* **1** to lift or raise something with ropes and pulleys. **2** to haul something up ◆ *She hoisted herself up onto the wall.*
hoist *noun* an apparatus for hoisting things. [probably from a Dutch word]

hoity-toity *adjective* haughty. [origin unknown]

hold[1] *verb* (past tense and past participle **held**) **1** to take and keep something in your hands, arms, teeth, etc. SYNONYMS: take, seize, grasp, grip, clutch, clasp, cradle. **2** to keep something in a particular position or condition ◆ *Hold your head up.* **3** to keep someone and not allow them to leave, to detain them ◆ *The police are holding three men in connection with the robbery.* **4** to be able to contain a certain amount ◆ *The jug holds two pints.* **5** to have something that you have gained or achieved ◆ *He holds the record for the high jump* ◆ *She holds a law degree.* **6** to support or bear the weight of something ◆ *Will that branch hold your weight?* **7** to remain secure or unbroken under strain ◆ *I hope the shelf will hold with all these books on it.* **8** to remain in force or valid, to continue or last ◆ *My offer still holds* ◆ *How long will the fine weather hold?* **9** to have or occupy a job or position. **10** to defend a place successfully. **11** to manage to achieve a draw against an opponent. **12** to keep a person's attention by being interesting. **13** to stay on the phone and not ring off ◆ *Please hold while we will try to connect you* ◆ *Hold the line.* **14** to reserve something for someone ◆ *Can you hold the tickets for me?* **15** to arrange for something to take place ◆ *The meeting will be held in the village hall.* SYNONYMS: have, organize, convene, conduct, run. **16** to have in store ◆ *I don't know what the future holds.* **17** to believe or consider something ◆ *We will hold you responsible.*
hold *noun* **1** a grip on something. **2** something to hold on to for support; a handhold. **3** a means of exerting influence or control on a person. **to get hold of 1** to grasp something. **2** to obtain something. **3** (*informal*) to make contact with a person. **to hold something against** to allow

something to cause you to have a lower opinion of someone ♦ *It's all right, I don't hold it against you.* **to hold back** to hesitate. **to hold someone or something back** to prevent someone from doing something or something from happening ♦ *I couldn't hold back the tears.* **to hold forth** to speak at length. **to hold it** to wait or stop doing something. **to hold off** (said about bad weather) to not begin ♦ *I hope the rain will hold off.* **to hold something off 1** to resist an attack or challenge. **2** to postpone something. **to hold on 1** to wait or stop. **2** to keep going in difficult circumstances. **to hold out 1** to last ♦ *Our supplies will not hold out for much longer.* **2** to resist difficult circumstances. **to hold out for** to refuse to accept anything other than what you have asked for. **to hold out on** (*informal*) to conceal something from someone, or to refuse to give them something. **to hold something over 1** to postpone something. **2** to exert an influence on someone because you can threaten them with information you have. **to hold the fort** to cope on your own in an emergency. **to hold someone to** to insist that someone keeps a promise or agreement. **to hold your tongue** to remain silent or stop talking. **to hold true** to remain true. **to hold someone or something up 1** to hinder someone or something. **2** to rob someone by the use of threats or force. **3** to offer a person or thing as an example ♦ *He is sometimes held up as a model sportsman.* **to hold water** (said about a theory or argument) to be sound. **to hold with** (*informal*) to approve of something ♦ *We don't hold with bullying here.* **no holds barred** all methods are permitted. **on hold** waiting to be connected by telephone. **to take hold** to start to have an effect. **holder** *noun* [from an Old English word *haldan*]

hold [2] *noun* a storage space in the lower part of a ship or aircraft, where cargo is stored. [from an old word *holl*]

holdall *noun* a large bag with handles and a shoulder strap.

holding *noun* land held by lease.
holdings *plural noun* financial assets.

holding company *noun* a company formed to hold the shares of other companies which it then controls.

hold-up *noun* **1** a stoppage or delay. **2** a robbery by armed robbers.

hole *noun* **1** an empty space or opening in a solid body, mass, or surface. **2** an animal's burrow. **3** (*informal*) a small or unpleasant place. **4** (in golf) a hollow or cavity into which a ball must be sent.
hole *verb* **1** to make a hole or holes in something ♦ *The ship was holed.* **2** to hit a golf ball into a hole ♦ *Do you think he will hole it?* **to hole up** (*informal*) to hide yourself. [from an Old English word *hol*]

hole-and-corner *adjective* secret or underhand.

hole-in-one *noun* (**holes-in-one**) (in golf) a single shot of the ball from the tee into the hole.

holey *adverb* full of holes.

Holi (hoh-li) *noun* a Hindu spring festival celebrated in February or March. [via Hindi from a Sanskrit word *holi*]

holiday *noun* **1** (also **holidays**) a period of recreation, especially away from home. **2** a day of festivity or recreation, when no work is done.
holiday *verb* (**holidayed, holidaying**) to spend a holiday. [from *holy* and *day* (because holidays were originally religious festivals)]

holidaymaker *noun* a person on holiday.

holier-than-thou *adjective* self-righteous.

holiness *noun* being holy or sacred. **His Holiness** the title of the pope.

holistic (hol-ist-ik) *adjective* (said about medical treatment) treating the whole person, not just the symptoms. [from a Greek word *holos* meaning 'whole']

holler *verb* to shout loudly.
holler *noun* a loud shout.

hollow *adjective* **1** having a hole or empty space inside, not solid. **2** sunken or concave ♦ *hollow cheeks.* **3** (said about sound) echoing, as if from something hollow. **4** empty or worthless ♦ *a hollow victory.* **5** insincere or cynical ♦ *a hollow promise* ♦ *a hollow laugh.*
hollow *noun* **1** a hollow or sunken place. SYNONYMS: cavity, depression, indentation, dip, crater. **2** a small valley.
hollow *verb* to make something hollow, or to form something by doing this ♦ *Now hollow out the melon.* **hollowly** *adverb* [from an Old English word *holh* meaning 'cave']

holly *noun* an evergreen shrub with prickly dark green leaves and red berries. [from an Old English word *holegn*]

hollyhock *noun* a plant of the mallow family with large showy flowers on a tall stem. [from an Old English word]

holmium *noun* a soft silvery-white metallic element (symbol Ho). [from Holmia, the Latin name for Stockholm]

holm oak (hohm) *noun* an evergreen oak with dark green glossy leaves. [from a dialect word *hollin*]

holocaust (hol-ə-kawst) *noun* large-scale destruction, especially by fire or nuclear explosion ♦ *a nuclear holocaust.*
Holocaust the mass murder of Jews under the German Nazi regime in World War II. [from Greek words *holos* meaning 'whole' and *kaustos* meaning 'burnt']

Holocene (hol-ə-seen) *adjective* (*Geology*) to do with the second of the two epochs of the Quaternary period, lasting from about 10,000 years ago to the present day.
Holocene *noun* this epoch. [from Greek words *holos* meaning 'whole' and *kainos* meaning 'new']

hologram (hol-ə-gram) *noun* **1** a three-dimensional image formed by laser beams. **2** an image produced on photographic film in such a way that under suitable illumination a three-dimensional representation of an object is seen. **holographic** *adjective* **holography** *noun* [from a Greek word *holos* meaning 'whole' and -*gram*]

holster *noun* a leather case for a pistol or revolver, fixed to a belt or under the arm. [origin unknown]

holy *adjective* (**holier, holiest**) **1** to do with or belonging to God or religion ♦ *the Holy Bible.* **2** devoted to the service of God ♦ *a holy man.* SYNONYMS: devout, saintly, godly, pious. **3** consecrated or blessed ♦ *holy water.* [from an Old English word *halig*]

holy orders *plural noun* the status of being ordained as a member of the clergy.

Holy Week *noun* the week before Easter Sunday.

homage (hom-ij) *noun* **1** things said as a mark of respect ♦ *We paid homage to his achievements.* **2** a formal expression of loyalty to a ruler. [from an Old French word]

home *noun* **1** the place where you live, especially with your family. SYNONYMS: residence, abode, dwelling, domicile, habitation. **2** the place where you were born or where you have lived for a long time or where you feel you belong. **3** a house or flat. **4** an institution where those needing care may live ♦ *an old people's home.* **5** the natural environment of an animal or plant. **6** the finishing point in a race or in certain games.
home *adjective* **1** to do with or connected with your own home or country ♦ *home industries* ♦ *home produce.* **2** played on a team's own ground ♦ *a home match.*
home *adverb* **1** to or at home ♦ *Go home* ♦ *Is she home yet?* **2** into the intended or correct position ♦ *He drove the nail home.*
home *verb* **1** (said about a trained pigeon) to fly home. **2** to be guided to or make for a target ♦ *The missiles homed in on the airfield.* **at home 1** relaxed and at ease. **2** ready to receive visitors. **to bring something home to** to make someone realize something fully. **close to home** (said about a remark) so accurate that it makes you feel uncomfortable. **to come home to** to become fully realized by someone. **to drive something home** to stress a point forcefully. [from an Old English word]

homecoming *noun* arrival at home.

Home Counties *plural noun* the counties nearest to London.

home economics *noun* the study of cookery and household management.

home-grown *adjective* grown or produced in your own garden or country.

Home Guard *noun* the British volunteer force organized in 1940 against a possible German invasion.

home help *noun* a person employed to help with housework.

homeland *noun* **1** a person's native land. **2** any of the areas formerly reserved for the black population in South Africa and abolished in 1993.

homeless *adjective* having no home. **homelessness** *noun*

homely *adjective* (**homelier, homeliest**) **1** simple and informal, not pretentious ♦ *a homely meal.* **2** (*North Amer.*) (said about a person's appearance) plain, not beautiful. **homeliness** *noun*

home-made *adjective* made at home, not bought from a shop.

Home Office *noun* the British government department dealing with law and order, immigration, etc. in England and Wales.

homeopath noun (hohm-i-ǝ-path) a person who practises homeopathy.

homeopathy (hohm-i-**op**-ǝ-thi) noun the treatment of a disease by very small doses of natural susbstances that in a healthy person would produce symptoms like those of the disease itself. **homeopathic** (hohm-i-ǝ-**path**-ik) adjective [from Greek words homoios meaning 'alike' and pathos meaning 'suffering']

homeostasis (hoh-mi-ǝ-**stay**-sis) noun 1 (Biology) the tendency of the body to keep its own temperature, blood pressure, etc. at a constant level. 2 the tendency for plant and animal populations to remain constant in an area. [from Greek words homoios meaning 'alike' and stasis meaning 'standing']

homeotherm (hom-eer-therm) or **homoiotherm** (hom-oy-ǝ-therm) noun a warm-blooded animal. **homeothermic** adjective [from Greek words homoios meaning 'alike' and thermē meaning 'heat']

home page noun the introductory document of a website on the World Wide Web.

home rule noun government of a country by its own citizens.

home run noun (in baseball) a hit that allows the batter to make a complete circuit of the bases.

Home Secretary noun the government minister in charge of the Home Office.

homesick adjective upset because you are away from home. **homesickness** noun

homespun adjective 1 simple and unsophisticated ♦ homespun wisdom. 2 made of yarn spun at home.

homestead (hohm-sted) noun 1 a farmhouse or similar building with the land and buildings round it. 2 (North Amer.) an area of land formerly granted to a settler to be developed as a farm. [from home and an Old English word stede meaning 'a place']

home straight or **home stretch** noun the stretch of a racecourse between the last turn and the finishing line.

home truth noun an unpleasant truth about yourself that you are made to realize.

homeward adjective going or leading towards home.
homeward or **homewards** adverb towards home.

homework noun 1 school work that has to be done at home. 2 preparatory work that you need to do before discussing something, making a speech, etc.

homeworker noun a person who works from home.

homey adjective (**homier, homiest**) like a home, cosy.

homicide (hom-i-syd) noun 1 murder. 2 (old use) a murderer. **homicidal** adjective [from Latin words homo meaning 'person' and caedere meaning 'to kill']

homily noun (**homilies**) a sermon, a moralizing lecture. [from a Greek word homilia meaning 'sermon']

homing adjective 1 (said about a pigeon) trained to fly home from a great distance. 2 (said about a missile) having an inbuilt guidance system.

hominid (hom-in-id) noun (Zoology) a member of the family that includes humans and their fossil ancestors. **hominid** adjective belonging to this family. [from a Latin word homo meaning 'person']

homo- prefix the same (as in homosexual). [from a Greek word homos meaning 'same']

homogeneous (hom-ǝ-**jee**-niǝs) adjective formed of parts that are all of the same kind. **homogeneity** (hom-ǝ-jin-**ee**-iti) noun [from homo- and a Greek word genos meaning 'a kind']

homogenize (hǝ-**moj**-i-niyz) verb 1 to treat milk so that the particles of fat are broken down and cream does not separate. 2 to make something homogeneous. **homogenization** noun

homograph (hom-ǝ-graf) noun a word that is spelt like another but has a different meaning or origin, e.g. bat (a flying animal) and bat (for striking a ball). [from homo- and -graph]

homologous (hǝm-ol-ǝ-gǝs) adjective 1 having the same relation or relative position, corresponding. 2 (Biology) (said about chromosomes) pairing with each other in such a way that one member of each pair is carried by every gamete. **homology** noun [from homo- and a Greek word logos meaning 'proportion']

homonym (hom-ǝ-nim) noun a word with the same spelling or pronunciation as another but with a different meaning, e.g.

grate (meaning fireplace), grate (meaning to rub), great (meaning large). [from homo- and a Greek word onoma meaning 'name']

homophobia (hoh-mə-**foh**-bi-ə) noun strong dislike of homosexuals. **homophobic** adjective [from homo- and phobia]

homophone (hom-ə-fohn) noun a word with the same pronunciation as another, e.g. son, sun. [from homo- and a Greek word phōnē meaning 'sound']

homophonic (hom-ə-fon-ik) adjective (Music) with the accompanying parts moving in step with the melody.

Homo sapiens (hoh-moh sap-i-enz) noun human beings regarded as a species. [a Latin phrase meaning 'wise person']

homosexual (hoh-mə-**seks**-yoo-əl) adjective sexually attracted to people of the same sex as yourself.
homosexual noun a homosexual person.
homosexuality noun [from homo- and sexual]

homozygote (hom-ə-ziy-gooht) noun (Biochemistry) an individual that has two genes which are the same allele, being formed from gametes carrying the same allele. **homozygous** adjective [from homo- and zygote]

Hon. abbreviation 1 Honorary. 2 Honourable.

hone (hohn) verb 1 to sharpen something on a whetstone. 2 to spend time developing and improving an argument, skill, etc. [from an Old English word han meaning 'stone']

honest adjective 1 not likely to lie, cheat, or steal; able to be trusted ♦ an honest trader. SYNONYMS: trustworthy, honourable, upright, law-abiding. 2 truthful and sincere; free of deceit ♦ I haven't been completely honest with you ♦ Give me your honest opinion. SYNONYMS: sincere, truthful, genuine, open, candid. 3 earned by fair means ♦ He makes an honest living. 4 done with good intentions although misguided ♦ an honest mistake. [from a Latin word honestus meaning 'honourable']

honestly adverb 1 in an honest way. 2 really ♦ That's all I know, honestly.

honest-to-goodness adjective genuine and straightforward.

honesty noun 1 being honest. SYNONYMS: integrity, trustworthiness, probity, honour, truthfulness, veracity. 2 a plant with seeds that form in round translucent pods.

honey noun (**honeys**) 1 a sweet sticky yellowish substance made by bees from nectar. 2 a yellowish-brown colour. 3 (informal) something outstanding ♦ a honey of a house. 4 (informal) darling. [from an Old English word hunig]

honeybee noun the common bee that lives in a hive.

honeycomb noun 1 a bees' wax structure of six-sided cells for holding their honey and eggs. 2 a pattern or arrangement of six-sided sections.
honeycomb verb to fill something with holes or tunnels ♦ The rock was honeycombed with passages.

honeydew noun 1 a sweet sticky substance found on leaves and stems, secreted by aphids. 2 a variety of melon with pale skin and sweet green flesh.

honeymoon noun 1 a holiday spent together by a newly married couple. 2 an initial period of goodwill towards someone in a new job or position.
honeymoon verb to spend a honeymoon. [from honey and moon (because the first intensely passionate feelings gradually wane)]

honeysuckle noun a climbing shrub with fragrant yellow and pink flowers. [so called because people sucked the flowers for their sweet nectar]

honk verb 1 to sound the horn of a car. 2 to make the cry of a goose.
honk noun a honking sound. [an imitation of the sound]

honky-tonk noun (informal) ragtime music played on a piano, often with strings that give a tinny sound. [origin unknown]

honorarium (on-er-**air**-iəm) noun (**honorariums** or **honoraria**) a voluntary payment made for professional services where no fee is legally required. [from a Latin word]

honorary adjective 1 given as an honour ♦ an honorary degree. 2 (said about an office or its holder) unpaid ♦ the honorary treasurer. [from a Latin word honor meaning 'honour']

honour noun 1 great respect or public regard. SYNONYMS: repute, esteem, regard. 2 something given as a token of respect. SYNONYMS: accolade, kudos. 3 a title or decoration awarded by a monarch for service to the country. 4 a feeling of pleasure and pride from being shown respect ♦ It is a great honour to accept this position. 5 a person or thing that brings honour. 6 a clear sense of what is morally right and just ♦ *a man of honour.* **7** a title of respect given to certain judges or people of importance ♦ *your Honour.*

honour *verb* **1** to feel or show honour for a person. **2** to confer honour on someone ♦ *You honour us with your presence.* **3** to keep to the terms of an agreement or promise. **4** to acknowledge and pay a cheque etc. when it is due. **to do the honours** (*informal*) to perform a social duty for guests or visitors, especially serving food or drink. **in honour of** as an expression of respect for. [from a Latin word *honor*]

honourable *adjective* **1** having high moral principles, showing honour ♦ *She did the honourable thing and resigned.* **2** bringing or deserving honour ♦ *an honourable profession.*
Honourable *adjective* a courtesy title given to certain high officials, the children of certain peers, and used during debates by MPs to one another. **honourably** *adverb*

honours degree *noun* a university degree requiring a higher level of attainment than a pass degree.

hood *noun* **1** a covering for the head and neck, usually forming part of a coat or cloak. **2** a loose piece of clothing like a hood, forming part of academic dress. **3** something resembling a hood in shape or use, e.g. a folding roof over a car, a canopy over a machine etc. **4** (*North Amer.*) the bonnet of a car. [from an Old English word *hod*]

-hood *suffix* forms nouns denoting a condition or quality (as in *boyhood*).

hooded *adjective* **1** having or wearing a hood. **2** (said about animals) having a hood-like part.

hoodlum *noun* a hooligan or gangster. [origin unknown]

hoodwink *verb* to deceive or trick someone. [originally meaning 'to blindfold', from *hood* and *wink*]

hoof *noun* (**hoofs** or **hooves**) the horny part of the foot of a horse and other animals. **hoofed** *adjective* [from an Old English word *hof*]

hook *noun* **1** a bent or curved piece of metal etc. for catching hold of things or for hanging things on. **2** something shaped like this. **3** a curved cutting tool ♦ *a reaping hook.* **4** a hooked stroke in cricket or golf. **5** (in boxing) a short swinging blow with the elbow bent.

hook *verb* **1** to grasp or catch something with a hook; to fasten something with a hook or hooks. **2** to hit a ball in a curving path, in the direction of the follow-through. **3** (in rugby) to pass the ball backward with the foot. **to be hooked on** (*informal*) to be addicted to or captivated by something. **to hook something up** to connect something to electronic equipment. **off the hook** (*informal*) no longer in difficulty. [from an Old English word *hoc*]

hookah *noun* an oriental tobacco pipe with a long tube passing through a glass container of water that cools the smoke as it is drawn through. [from an Arabic word meaning 'casket' or ' jar']

hooked *adjective* **1** hook-shaped ♦ *a hooked nose.* **2** (said about a rug) made by looping yarn through canvas with a hook.

hooker *noun* (in rugby) a player in the front row of the scrum, who tries to get the ball by hooking it.

Hooke's law *noun* (*Physics*) a law stating that the strain in a solid is proportional to the applied stress, within the elastic limit of that solid. [named after the English scientist R. Hooke (1635–1703)]

hookey *noun* **to play hookey** (*North Amer.*) (*informal*) to play truant. [origin unknown]

hook-up *noun* a connection to a communications system or to mains electricity.

hookworm *noun* a worm, the male of which has hook-like spines, that can infest the intestines of people and animals.

hooligan *noun* a violent young troublemaker. **hooliganism** *noun* [from Hooligan, the surname of a fictional rowdy Irish family in a music-hall song]

hoop *noun* **1** a band of metal or wood etc. forming part of a framework. **2** a large ring used as a child's toy for bowling along the ground, or for circus performers to jump through. **3** a small metal arch used in croquet. **4** a horizontal band on a sports shirt.
hoop *verb* to bind or encircle something with hoops. [from an Old English word *hop*]

hoopla *noun* a game in which rings are thrown to encircle a prize.

hoopoe (hoo-poo) *noun* a bird with a fan-like crest, a long downcurved bill, and striped wings and tail. [from a Latin word *upupa*, imitating the bird's call]

hooray *interjection & noun* another spelling of **hurray**.

hoot *noun* 1 the cry of an owl. 2 the sound made by a horn, siren, etc. 3 a cry expressing scorn or disapproval. 4 an outburst of laughter. 5 (*informal*) an amusing person or thing ♦ *Your aunt really is a hoot.*
hoot *verb* 1 to make a hoot. 2 to sound a horn ♦ *The cars behind us started hooting.* 3 to receive someone or drive them away with scornful hoots ♦ *He was such a bad singer he was eventually hooted off the stage.* **to not care** or **give a hoot** (*informal*) to not care at all. [perhaps an imitation of the sound]

hooter *noun* 1 a siren or steam whistle used as a signal. 2 a vehicle's horn.

Hoover *noun* (*trademark*) a vacuum cleaner. **hoover** *verb* to clean a carpet with a vacuum cleaner.

hooves plural of **hoof**.

hop¹ *verb* (**hopped, hopping**) 1 (said about a person) to jump on one foot. 2 (said about an animal or bird) to jump with all its feet at once. 3 (*informal*) to jump over or on to something ♦ *We hopped on to the bus.* 4 (*informal*) to make a short quick trip. **hop** *noun* 1 a hopping movement. 2 a short journey, especially by plane. 3 an informal dance. **hop it** (*informal*) go away. **hopping mad** (*informal*) very angry. **on the hop** (*informal*) unprepared ♦ *You've caught me on the hop.* [from an Old English word *hoppian*]

hop² *noun* a climbing plant cultivated for its cones (called *hops*) which are used for giving a bitter flavour to beer. **hoppy** *adjective* [from an Old German or Old Dutch word]

hope *noun* 1 a feeling of expectation and desire; a desire for certain events to happen. 2 a person or thing that gives cause for hope. 3 what is hoped for. **hope** *verb* 1 to feel hope, to expect and desire something. 2 to intend if possible to do something. [from an Old English word *hopa*]

hopeful *adjective* 1 feeling hope. SYNONYMS: optimistic, confident. 2 causing hope, seeming likely to be favourable or successful. SYNONYMS: encouraging, heartening, promising, propitious. **hopefulness** *noun*

hopefully *adverb* 1 in a hopeful way ♦ *The dog looked up at him hopefully.* 2 it is to be hoped ♦ *Hopefully we shall be there by one o'clock.*
◊ The use in meaning 2 is regarded as incorrect by some people. However, it is very common, especially in conversation, and most people find it acceptable.

hopeless *adjective* 1 feeling no hope. 2 causing despair ♦ *a hopeless case.* 3 inadequate or incompetent ♦ *I am hopeless at tennis.* **hopelessly** *adverb* **hopelessness** *noun*

hoplite (hop-liyt) *noun* a heavily armed infantry soldier in ancient Greece. [from a Greek word *hoplon* meaning 'weapon']

hopper *noun* 1 a V-shaped container for grain, rock, etc. with an opening at the base through which its contents can be discharged into a machine etc. 2 a person or thing that hops, especially a hopping insect.

hopsack *noun* a kind of coarsely-woven fabric.

hopscotch *noun* a children's game of hopping and jumping over squares marked on the ground to retrieve a stone tossed into these.

horde *noun* a large group or crowd. [from a Polish word]
◊ Do not confuse this word with **hoard**, which has a different meaning.

horizon *noun* 1 the line at which the earth and the sky appear to meet. 2 the limit of a person's experience, knowledge, or interests. [from a Greek word *horizein* meaning 'to form a boundary']

horizontal *adjective* parallel to the horizon. **horizontally** *adverb*

hormone (hor-mohn) *noun* a substance produced within the body of an animal or plant, or made synthetically, and carried by the blood or sap to an organ which it stimulates. **hormonal** (hor-moh-nal) *adjective* [from a Greek word *hormōn* meaning 'setting in motion']

hormone replacement therapy *noun* a treatment using oestrogens to relieve the symptoms of the menopause.

horn *noun* 1 a hard pointed outgrowth on the heads of cattle, sheep, and other animals. 2 the hard smooth substance of which this consists. 3 a projection

resembling a horn. **4** any of various wind instruments with a trumpet-shaped end, originally made of horn, now usually of brass. **5** a device for sounding a warning signal.
horn verb (said about an animal) to gore a person or another animal with the horns. **to draw** or **pull in your horns** to become less ambitious or assertive. **on the horns of a dilemma** faced with a decision involving two equally unpleasant choices. **horned** adjective [from an Old English word]

hornbeam noun a tree with hard tough wood, often used in hedges. [so called because of the tree's hard wood]

hornbill noun a tropical bird with a horn-like projection on its large curved beak.

hornblende noun a black, green, or dark-brown mineral composed mainly of silicates of calcium, magnesium, and iron. [from a German word]

hornet noun a large kind of wasp inflicting a serious sting. **to stir up a hornets' nest** to cause an outbreak of angry feeling or controversy. [from an Old English word *hyrnet*]

horn of plenty noun another word for **cornucopia**.

hornpipe noun a lively dance usually for one person, traditionally performed by sailors.

horn-rimmed adjective (said about glasses) with frames made of a material like horn or tortoiseshell.

horny adjective (**hornier, horniest**) **1** of or like horn. **2** hard and rough ♦ *horny hands*. **3** (informal) sexually excited.

horoscope noun a forecast of a person's future based on the relative positions of the planets and stars at a particular time. [from Greek words *hōra* meaning 'hour (of birth)' and *skopos* meaning 'observer']

horrendous adjective extremely unpleasant. [from a Latin word *horrendus* meaning 'shuddering']

horrible adjective **1** causing horror ♦ *a horrible accident*. **2** (informal) very unpleasant. SYNONYMS: dreadful, nasty, ghastly, horrid, horrendous. **horribly** adverb [from a Latin word *horribilis*]

horrid adjective **1** causing horror. **2** (informal) very unpleasant. **horridly** adverb [from a Latin word *horrere* meaning 'to shudder']

horrific adjective causing horror. SYNONYMS: grisly, gruesome, shocking, appalling, sickening. **horrifically** adverb [same origin as for *horrid*]

horrify verb (**horrifies, horrified, horrifying**) to fill someone with horror, to shock someone. **horrified** adjective **horrifying** adjective [from a Latin word]

horror noun **1** a feeling of loathing, shock, or fear. **2** intense dislike or dismay. **3** (informal) a troublesome or mischievous person, especially a child. [same origin as for *horrid*]

horror film noun a film involving monsters and gruesome death, intended to frighten the audience.

hors-d'oeuvre (or-*dervr*) noun food served as an appetizer at the start of a meal. [a French phrase meaning 'outside the work']

horse noun **1** a four-legged animal with a flowing mane and tail, used for riding on or to carry loads or pull carts etc. **2** an adult male horse, as opposed to a mare or colt. **3** cavalry. **4** a frame on which something is supported, e.g. a clothes horse.
horse verb **to horse around** (informal) to fool about. **straight from the horse's mouth** (said about information) from a first-hand source. [from an Old English word *hors*]

horseback noun **on horseback** mounted on a horse.

horsebox noun a closed vehicle or trailer for transporting a horse.

horse brass noun a brass ornament worn by a horse.

horse chestnut noun **1** a large tree with conical clusters of white, pink, or red flowers. **2** the dark-brown nut of this tree, a conker.

horse-drawn adjective (said about a vehicle) pulled by a horse.

horsehair noun hair from a horse's mane or tail, used for padding furniture.

horse latitudes plural noun a belt of calm air and sea at the northern edge of the NE trade winds.

horseman noun (**horsemen**) a rider on horseback, especially a skilled one. **horsemanship** noun

horseplay noun rough boisterous play.

horsepower noun a unit for measuring the power of an engine (550 foot-pounds per second, about 750 watts).

horseradish noun a plant with a hot-tasting root used to make a sauce.

horseshoe noun 1 a U-shaped strip of metal nailed to a horse's hoof. 2 anything shaped like this ♦ *The seats were arranged in a horseshoe around the stage.*

horsewhip noun a whip for horses. **horsewhip** verb (**horsewhipped**, **horsewhipping**) to beat an animal or person with a horsewhip.

horsewoman noun (**horsewomen**) a woman rider on horseback, especially a skilled one.

horsey or **horsy** adjective (**horsier**, **horsiest**) 1 to do with or like a horse. 2 interested in horses and horse racing.

horticulture noun the art of garden cultivation. **horticultural** adjective [from a Latin word *hortus* meaning 'garden' and *culture*]

horticulturist noun an expert in horticulture.

hosanna interjection & noun a cry of praise or joy, especially expressing adoration to God and the Messiah. [from a Greek word]

hose noun 1 a flexible tube for taking water somewhere, used for watering plants and in firefighting. 2 (in shops) stockings, socks, and tights. 3 (old use) breeches ♦ *doublet and hose.*
hose verb to water or spray something with a hose ♦ *I'll just hose the car down.* [from an Old English word *hosa*]

hosepipe noun a hose.

hosier noun a dealer in stockings, socks, and tights.

hosiery noun (in shops) stockings, socks, and tights.

hospice (hos-pis) noun a home providing care for sick or terminally ill people. [from an earlier meaning 'lodge for travellers', from a French word]

hospitable (hos-pit-əbəl) adjective giving and liking to give hospitality. **hospitably** adverb [from an old French word *hospiter* meaning 'to receive a guest']

hospital noun an institution providing medical and surgical treatment and nursing care for people who are ill or injured. [from a Latin word *hospitium* meaning 'hospitality']

hospitality noun the friendly and generous reception and entertainment of guests or strangers. [from a Latin word *hospitalitas*]

hospitalize (hos-pit-ə-liyz) verb to send or admit a patient to a hospital. **hospitalization** noun

host [1] noun 1 a person who receives and entertains other people as guests. 2 the presenter of a television or radio programme. 3 (*Biology*) an organism on which another organism lives as a parasite.
host verb 1 to act as host at a meal, party, etc. 2 to present a television or radio programme. [same origin as for *hospital*]

host [2] noun a large number of people or things ♦ *a host of golden daffodils.* [same origin as for *hostile*]

host [3] noun the bread consecrated in the Eucharist. [from a Latin word *hostia* meaning 'sacrifice']

hostage noun a person seized or held as security until the holder's demands are met. **a hostage to fortune** something you say or do that might cause you trouble later. [from an Old French word]

hostel noun an establishment providing lodging and cheap food for young travellers, students, or other special groups ♦ *a youth hostel.* [same origin as for *hospital*]

hostelry noun (**hostelries**) (old use) an inn or pub. [from an Old French word]

hostess noun 1 a woman who receives and entertains other people as guests. 2 a stewardess on an aircraft or train.

hostile adjective 1 unfriendly ♦ *a hostile glance.* 2 opposed ♦ *They are hostile towards reform.* 3 belonging to a military enemy ♦ *hostile aircraft.* [from a Latin word *hostis* meaning 'an enemy']

hostility noun being hostile. **hostilities** plural noun acts of warfare.

hot adjective (**hotter**, **hottest**) 1 having great heat or a high temperature ♦ *a hot day* ♦ *a hot iron.* SYNONYMS: warm, baking, blistering, boiling, burning, roasting, scorching, sweltering. 2 having an uncomfortable feeling of heat ♦ *I'm too hot – let's go in.* 3 producing a burning sensation in the mouth. 4 passionate or excitable ♦ *a hot temper.* 5 currently popular, fashionable, or

interesting ♦ *They are a hot band at the moment.* **6** (said about the scent in hunting) fresh and strong. **7** (said about news) fresh. **8** (in children's games) very close to finding or guessing what is sought. **9** (*informal*) knowledgeable or skilful. **10** (*informal*) keen on or strict about something ♦ *He's hot on punctuality.* **11** (*informal*) good or promising ♦ *Things aren't looking too hot.* **12** (*informal*) radioactive. **13** (*informal*) (said about goods) recently stolen.
hot *verb* (**hotted, hotting**) (*informal*) **to hot up** (*informal*) to become more intense or exciting. **hotly** *adverb* **hotness** *noun* [from an Old English word *hat*]

hot air *noun* (*informal*) empty or boastful talk.

hotbed *noun* **1** a bed of earth heated by fermenting manure. **2** an environment favourable to the growth of something.

hot-blooded *adjective* excitable or passionate.

hotchpotch *noun* a confused mixture.

hot cross bun *noun* a bun marked with a cross, traditionally eaten hot on Good Friday.

hot dog *noun* a hot sausage served in a long soft roll of bread.

hotel *noun* a building where meals and rooms are provided for travellers and tourists. [from a French word *hôtel*]

hotelier (hoh-**tel**-i-er) *noun* a person who owns or manages a hotel. [from a French word]

hotfoot *adverb* in eager haste.
hotfoot *verb* **to hotfoot it** to hurry eagerly.

hothead *noun* an impetuous person.
hotheaded *adjective*

hothouse *noun* a heated building made of glass, for growing plants in a warm temperature.

hot key *noun* (*Computing*) a key that provides quick access to a function within a program.

hotline *noun* a direct telephone line set up for communication between heads of government or for some other special purpose.

hotplate *noun* a heated surface for cooking food or keeping it hot.

hotpot *noun* a stew containing meat and vegetables and covered with a layer of potato.

hot potato *noun* (*informal*) an issue or situation likely to cause trouble to the person handling it.

hot seat *noun* (*informal*) the position of someone who has difficult responsibilities or is being subjected to searching questions.

hot-tempered *adjective* easily becoming very angry.

hot-water bottle *noun* a rubber container that is filled with hot water and is used to warm a bed.

hound *noun* a dog used for hunting, especially a foxhound.
hound *verb* to harass or pursue someone ♦ *He was hounded out of society.* [from an Old English word *hund*]

hour *noun* **1** a twenty-fourth part of a day and night, 60 minutes. **2** a time of day, a point of time ♦ *Who is calling at this hour?* **3** a period set aside for a specified activity ♦ *the lunch hour.* **4** an important or special time ♦ *This was our finest hour* ♦ *Where were you in my hour of need?*
hours *plural noun* **1** a fixed period for daily work ♦ *Office hours are 9 a.m. to 5 p.m.* **2** the time according to the 24-hour clock ♦ *17.00 hours.* **on the hour** when the clock indicates an exact number of hours from midnight or midday ♦ *The bus leaves on the hour.* [from a Greek word *hōra* meaning 'season, hour']

hourglass *noun* a glass container with a very narrow part in the middle through which a quantity of fine sand trickles from the upper to the lower section, taking one hour.

houri (**hoor**-i) *noun* (**houris**) a young and beautiful woman of the Muslim paradise. [via French and Persian from an Arabic word]

hourly *adjective* **1** done or occurring every hour ♦ *an hourly bus service.* **2** reckoned hour by hour.
hourly *adverb* **1** every hour. **2** by the hour.

house[1] *noun* **1** a building made for people to live in. **2** a building used for a particular purpose ♦ *the opera house.* **3** a business firm ♦ *a publishing house.* **4** a building used by an assembly, the assembly itself ♦ *the Houses of Parliament.* **5** a family or dynasty ♦ *the House of Windsor.* **6** a group of pupils living in the same building at a boarding school. **7** each of the divisions of a school for sports competitions etc. **8** the audience of a theatre, or a performance in a theatre ♦ *a full house.* **9** a style of fast popular dance music produced electronically. **on the house** (said about drinks in a pub or bar) at the management's expense. [from an Old English word *hus*]

house [2] (howz) *verb* **1** to provide someone with accommodation or shelter. **2** to provide space for something. **3** to enclose or encase something.

house arrest *noun* being kept as a prisoner in your own house, not in prison.

houseboat *noun* a barge-like boat used as a dwelling.

housebound *adjective* unable to leave your house because of illness or old age.

housebreaking *noun* breaking into a building to commit a crime.
housebreaker *noun*

housefly *noun* (**houseflies**) a common fly found in houses.

houseful *noun* (**housefuls**) all that a house can hold.

household *noun* all the people who live together in the same house. [from *house* and an old sense of *hold* meaning 'possession']

householder *noun* a person who owns or rents a house.

household name *noun* a famous person or thing.

house-hunting *noun* the process of looking for a house to buy or rent.

house husband *noun* a man who lives with a partner and carries out the household duties traditionally done by a housewife.

housekeeper *noun* a person, typically a woman, employed to look after a household.

housekeeping *noun* **1** management of household affairs. **2** money set aside for this. **3** routine work such as record-keeping and administration.

housemaid *noun* a female servant in a house, especially one who cleans rooms.

houseman *noun* (**housemen**) a house officer.

house martin *noun* a bird of the swallow family that builds a mud nest on the walls of buildings.

housemaster or **housemistress** *nouns* a teacher in charge of a house at a boarding school.

House of Commons *noun* the assembly of elected representatives in the British Parliament.

house officer *noun* a recent medical graduate who is being trained in a hospital and acting as an assistant physician or surgeon.

House of Lords *noun* the upper assembly in the British Parliament, made up of peers and bishops.

house plant *noun* a plant for growing indoors.

house-proud *adjective* giving great attention to the care and appearance of your home.

house-sit *verb* to live in and look after a house while its owner is away.
house-sitter *noun*

house-to-house *adjective* calling at each house in turn.

house-trained *adjective* (said about animals) trained to be clean in the house.

house-warming *noun* a party to celebrate a move to a new home.

housewife *noun* (**housewives**) a married woman whose main occupation is looking after the household. **housewifely** *adjective* [from the old meaning of *wife* meaning 'woman' (as in *fishwife*), not 'married woman']

housework *noun* the regular work done in housekeeping, such as cleaning and cooking.

housing *noun* **1** houses and flats; accommodation. **2** a rigid casing enclosing a piece of machinery. **3** a shallow trench or groove cut in a piece of wood to allow another piece to be attached to it.

housing estate *noun* a set of houses planned and built together in one area.

hove past tense of **heave**.

hovel (hov-ǝl) *noun* a small shabby or squalid house. [origin unknown]

hover *verb* **1** (said about a bird or aircraft) to remain in one place in the air. **2** to wait about near someone or something. **3** to remain at or near a particular level. [from an old word *hove* meaning 'to hover' or 'to linger']

hovercraft noun (**hovercraft**) a vehicle that travels over land or water on a cushion of air thrust downwards from its engines.

hoverfly noun (**hoverflies**) a fly like a slim wasp that hovers with rapidly beating wings.

hoverport noun a port used by hovercraft.

how adverb 1 by what means, in what way. 2 to what extent or degree. 3 in what condition or health. **how do you do?** a formal greeting. **how many** what number. **how much** what amount or price. [from an Old English word *hu*]

however adverb 1 all the same, nevertheless ♦ *Later, however, she decided to go.* 2 in whatever way, to whatever extent ♦ *You will never catch him, however hard you try.*

howitzer noun a short gun for firing shells, with a steep angle of fire. [from a Dutch word]

howl verb 1 (said about an animal) to make a long loud wailing cry. 2 (said about a person) to weep loudly.
howl noun 1 a loud cry of amusement, pain, or scorn. 2 a similar noise made by a strong wind or in a loudspeaker. [an imitation of the sound]

howler noun (*informal*) a foolish mistake.

hoyden noun (*old use*) a girl who behaves boisterously. **hoydenish** adjective [probably from a Dutch word]

hp or **HP** abbreviation 1 high pressure. 2 hire purchase. 3 horsepower.

HQ abbreviation headquarters.

HRH abbreviation His or Her Royal Highness.

HRT abbreviation hormone replacement therapy.

HTML abbreviation (*Computing*) Hypertext Mark-up Language, a system of coding documents for the Internet.

HTTP abbreviation (*Computing*) Hypertext Transfer Protocol, a system for transferring documents over the Internet.

hub noun 1 the central part of a wheel, from which spokes radiate. 2 a central point of activity or interest ♦ *the financial hub of the city.* [origin unknown]

hubbub noun a loud confused noise of voices. [probably from an Irish word]

hubcap noun a round metal cover over the hub of a motor vehicle's wheel.

hubris (*hew-*bris) noun arrogant pride or presumption. **hubristic** adjective [from a Greek word *hubris*]

huckster noun 1 a person who sells small items from door to door. 2 (*North Amer.*) a person who uses aggressive methods to sell things. [probably from a German word]

huddle verb 1 to crowd together into a small space. 2 to curl your body into a small space.
huddle noun a number of people or things crowded together. **to go into a huddle** to gather together to hold a brief conference or receive instructions. [origin unknown]

hue[1] noun a colour or tint. SYNONYMS: shade, tone. [from an Old English word]

hue[2] noun **hue and cry** a public outcry of alarm or protest. [from an Old French word *huer* meaning 'to shout']

huff verb to blow out noisily.
huff noun a fit of annoyance ♦ *in a huff.* **to huff and puff** 1 to breathe heavily because you are exhausted. 2 to show your annoyance in an obvious way ♦ *After much huffing and puffing, he agreed to lend me the money.* [an imitation of the sound of blowing]

huffy adjective (**huffier, huffiest**) easily offended, in a huff.

hug verb (**hugged, hugging**) 1 to squeeze or hold someone or something tightly in your arms. SYNONYMS: embrace, cuddle, enfold. 2 to keep close to something ♦ *The ship hugged the shore.*
hug noun a tight embrace. **to hug yourself** to be very pleased with yourself. [from a Scandinavian word]

huge adjective extremely large, enormous. SYNONYMS: enormous, gigantic, colossal, giant, vast, immense, monumental, gargantuan. **hugeness** noun [from an Old French word *ahuge*]

hugely adverb very much ♦ *We are hugely grateful.*

Huguenot (*hew-*gǝ-noh) noun a member of the Calvinist French Protestants who were involved in almost continuous civil war with the Catholic majority during the 16th and 17th centuries. [from a French word]

hulk noun 1 the body or wreck of an old

ship. **2** a large clumsy person or thing. [from an Old English word *hulc* meaning 'fast ship']

hulking *adjective* (*informal*) bulky or clumsy.

hull *noun* **1** the framework of a ship or other vessel. **2** the outer covering of a fruit or seed, especially the pod of peas and beans. **3** the cluster of leaves on a strawberry or raspberry.
hull *verb* **1** to hit and pierce the hull of a ship. **2** to remove the hulls from strawberries or raspberries. [from an Old English word *hulu*]

hullabaloo *noun* a commotion or uproar. [origin unknown]

hullo *interjection & noun* another spelling of **hello.**

hum *verb* (**hummed, humming**) **1** to make a low steady continuous sound like that of a bee. **2** to sing a tune with your lips closed. **3** (*informal*) to be in a state of great activity ♦ *Things are really humming now.*
hum *noun* a low steady continuous sound.
hum *interjection* an exclamation of hesitation or disagreement. **to hum and haw** to hesitate, sometimes while uttering a slight sound. [an imitation of the sound]

human *adjective* **1** to do with or consisting of human beings ♦ *the human race.* **2** having the qualities that are characteristic of people as opposed to God, animals, or machines ♦ *human error.* **3** showing the better qualities of humankind, such as kindness, pity, etc.
human *noun* a human being. [from a Latin word *humanus*]

human being *noun* a man, woman, or child of the species *Homo sapiens.*

humane (hew-**mayn**) *adjective* **1** compassionate or merciful. **2** inflicting as little pain as possible, especially in killing animals. **humanely** *adverb* [an old spelling of *human*]

human geography *noun* geography that deals with how human activity affects or is influenced by the earth's surface.

human interest *noun* the aspect of a news story that appeals to personal emotions.

humanist (hew-**mǝnist**) *noun* a person who is concerned with people's needs and with finding rational ways to solve human problems, rather than using religious belief. **humanism** *noun* **humanistic** *adjective*

humanitarian (hew-man-i-**tair**-iǝn) *adjective* concerned with human welfare and the reduction of suffering.
humanitarian *noun* a humanitarian person. **humanitarianism** *noun*

humanity *noun* **1** the human race, people ♦ *crimes against humanity.* **2** being human, human nature. **3** being humane, compassion.
humanities *plural noun* arts subjects, such as literature, history, music, and philosophy, as opposed to the sciences.

humanize *verb* **1** to give a human character to something. **2** to make someone more humane. **humanization** *noun*

humankind *noun* human beings collectively.
◊ This is now often preferred to *mankind* because it is neutral as to gender.

humanly *adverb* **1** in a human way, from a human point of view. **2** by human means, with human limitations ♦ *as accurate as is humanly possible.*

humanoid *adjective* having a human form or human characteristics.
humanoid *noun* (in science fiction) a humanoid thing or being.

human rights *plural noun* rights that are believed to belong justifiably to any living person.

humble *adjective* (**humbler, humblest**) **1** having or showing a modest estimate of your own importance, not proud. SYNONYMS: modest, self-effacing, unassuming. **2** offered with such feelings ♦ *humble apologies* ♦ *in my humble opinion.* **3** of low rank or importance ♦ *He came from humble origins.* **4** not large, showy, or elaborate ♦ *a humble cottage.*
humble *verb* **1** to make someone feel humble, to lower the rank or self-importance of someone. **2** to defeat an opponent thought to be superior. **to eat humble pie** to make a humble apology. **humbly** *adverb* **humbleness** *noun* [from a Latin word *humilis* meaning 'lowly'. *Humble pie* is from *umble pie*, pie made with 'umbles', the edible offal of deer]

humbug *noun* **1** insincere or misleading talk or behaviour. **2** a hypocrite. **3** a kind of hard boiled sweet usually flavoured with peppermint. [origin unknown]

humdinger *noun* (*informal*) a remarkable or outstanding person or thing. [origin unknown]

humdrum *adjective* dull or monotonous ♦ *a humdrum existence.* [origin unknown]

humerus (hew-mer-əs) *noun* the bone in the upper arm, from shoulder to elbow. [from a Latin word meaning 'shoulder']

humid (hew-mid) *adjective* (said about the air or climate) warm and damp. SYNONYMS: muggy, clammy, steamy, sultry. [from a Latin word *humere* meaning 'to be moist']

humidifier (hew-mid-i-fiy-er) *noun* a device for keeping the air moist in a room or enclosed space.

humidify (hew-mid-i-fiy) *verb* (**humidifies, humidified, humidifying**) to increase the level of moisture in the air.

humidity (hew-mid-iti) *noun* (**humidities**) 1 the state of being humid. 2 the level of moisture in the air.

humiliate *verb* to make someone feel disgraced or ashamed. SYNONYMS: disgrace, shame, mortify, humble, abase, degrade. **humiliating** *adjective* **humiliation** *noun* [same origin as for *humble*]

humility *noun* a humble opinion of your own importance. [same origin as for *humble*]

hummingbird *noun* a small tropical bird that vibrates its wings rapidly, producing a humming sound.

hummock *noun* a hump in the ground. [origin unknown]

hummus (huu-məs) *noun* a dip made from ground chickpeas and sesame oil flavoured with lemon and garlic. [from an Arabic word]

humorist *noun* a writer or speaker who is noted for his or her humour.

humorous *adjective* 1 amusing. SYNONYMS: amusing, funny, droll, comic, comical, witty. 2 showing a sense of humour. **humorously** *adverb*

humour *noun* 1 the quality of being amusing. 2 the ability to enjoy comical things or situations ♦ *She has a good sense of humour.* 3 a mood or state of mind ♦ *He was in a good humour.* 4 (*old use*) each of the four bodily fluids (blood, phlegm, choler, and melancholy) formerly believed to determine a person's physical and mental qualities.
humour *verb* to keep a person contented by giving way to his or her wishes, even if they seem unreasonable. **humourless**

adjective [from a Latin word *humor* meaning 'moisture'; related to *humid*]

hump *noun* 1 a rounded lump or mound ♦ *a camel's hump.* 2 an abnormal outward curve at the top of a person's back. **hump** *verb* 1 (*informal*) to lift or carry something heavy with difficulty. 2 to form something into a hump. **to get the hump** (*informal*) to become annoyed or sulky. **humped** *adjective* [probably from an Old German word]

humpback *noun* a hunchback. **humpbacked** *adjective*

humpback bridge *noun* a small steeply-arched road bridge.

humph *interjection* used to express doubt or dissatisfaction.

humus (hew-məs) *noun* a rich dark organic material, formed by the decay of dead leaves and plants etc. and essential to the fertility of soil. [from a Latin word meaning 'soil']

Hun *noun* a member of an Asiatic people who invaded and ravaged Europe in the 4th–5th centuries. [from an Old English word]

hunch *verb* to bend the top of your body forward and raise your shoulders and back ♦ *She hunched her shoulders against the cold.*
hunch *noun* a feeling or guess based on intuition. [origin unknown]

hunchback *noun* 1 a back deformed by a hump. 2 (*offensive*) a person with a hump on his or her back. **hunchbacked** *adjective*

hunched *adjective* sitting or standing with your body bent forward and your shoulders raised ♦ *a hunched figure.*

hundred *adjective & noun* the number 100, equal to ten times ten ♦ *a few hundred.* **a hundred per cent** 1 entirely, completely. 2 (*informal*) completely fit and healthy ♦ *I'm not feeling a hundred per cent.* **hundredth** *adjective & noun* [from an Old English word]
◊ Notice that you say ♦ *three hundred* and ♦ *a few hundred*, not *hundreds.*

hundredfold *adjective & adverb* one hundred times as much or as many.

hundreds and thousands *plural noun* tiny coloured sweets used for decorating cakes and desserts.

hundredweight *noun* (**hundredweight**) a measure of weight equal to 112 lb (about 50.8 kg).

hung past tense and past participle of **hang**.

Hungarian adjective to do with or coming from Hungary.
Hungarian noun 1 a person born in Hungary or descended from people born there. 2 the language of Hungary.

hunger noun 1 need for food, the feeling you have when you have not eaten for some time. 2 a strong desire for something.
hunger verb to have a strong desire for something. [from an Old English word *hungor*]

hunger strike noun refusing to eat as a form of protest by a prisoner. **hunger striker** noun

hung jury noun a jury that is unable to agree on a verdict.

hung-over adjective suffering from a hangover.

hung parliament noun a parliament that has no political party with an overall majority.

hungry adjective (**hungrier, hungriest**)
1 feeling hunger. SYNONYMS: famished, ravenous, starving; (*informal*) peckish.
2 having a strong desire for something ♦ *hungry for power*. **hungrily** adverb [from an Old English word *hungrig*]

hunk noun 1 a large piece broken or cut off something ♦ *a hunk of bread*. 2 (*informal*) a muscular good-looking man. [probably from an old Dutch word]

hunt verb 1 to chase and kill wild animals for food or as a sport. 2 to pursue someone ♦ *Police are hunting three armed robbers*. 3 to search for something ♦ *I've been hunting for this pen everywhere*. 4 (said about an engine) to run too fast and too slow alternately.
hunt noun 1 hunting. 2 an association of people hunting with a pack of hounds, or the district where they hunt. **to hunt someone down** to pursue and capture someone. **hunting** noun [from an Old English word *huntian*]

hunted adjective looking alarmed or afraid, as if you were being hunted.

hunter noun 1 someone who hunts. 2 a horse used for hunting. 3 a watch with a hinged metal cover over the dial.

hunter's moon noun the first full moon after the harvest moon.

huntsman noun (**huntsmen**) 1 a person who hunts. 2 an official at a hunt in charge of

a pack of hounds.

hurdle noun 1 one of a series of upright frames to be jumped over by athletes in a race. 2 an obstacle or difficulty. 3 a portable rectangular frame with bars, used for a temporary fence.
hurdles plural noun a hurdle race ♦ *the 400 metre hurdles*.
hurdle verb 1 to run in a hurdle race. 2 to jump over an obstacle while running.
hurdler noun **hurdling** noun [from an Old English word *hyrdel* meaning 'temporary fence']

hurdy-gurdy noun (**hurdy-gurdies**) 1 a stringed musical instrument with a droning sound, played by turning a handle with the right hand and playing keys with the left. 2 (*informal*) a barrel organ. [probably an imitation of the instrument's sound]

hurl verb 1 to throw something with great force ♦ *She hurled the book across the room*. SYNONYMS: fling, cast, dash; (*informal*) chuck, sling. 2 to shout abuse or insults at someone ♦ *The crowd hurled insults at the prisoner*. [origin unknown]

hurling or **hurley** noun an Irish form of hockey played with broad sticks.

hurly-burly noun a rough bustle of activity. [from *hurl*]

hurray or **hurrah** interjection & noun an exclamation of joy or approval. [an alteration of an earlier word *huzza*, perhaps originally a sailors' cry when hauling]

hurricane (hurri-kən) noun 1 a storm with a violent wind, especially a tropical cyclone in the Caribbean. 2 a wind of 73 m.p.h. or more, force 12 on the Beaufort scale. [via Spanish and Portuguese from a Taino (South American) word meaning 'god of the storm']

hurricane lamp noun an oil lamp with the flame protected from violent wind.

hurried adjective done with great haste ♦ *a hurried meal*. **hurriedly** adverb

hurry verb (**hurries, hurried, hurrying**) 1 to move or do something with eager haste or too quickly. SYNONYMS: rush, hasten, dash, speed. 2 to try to make a person or thing move or proceed quickly ♦ *I'll have to hurry you for an answer*.
hurry noun 1 great haste. 2 a need for haste ♦ *What's the hurry?* **to hurry up** (*informal*) to make haste ♦ *Hurry up and get dressed*. **in a hurry** 1 hurrying or rushed. 2 (*informal*)

easily or willingly ♦ *You won't beat that in a hurry.* [an imitation of the sound]

hurt *verb* (past tense and past participle **hurt**) **1** to cause pain or injury to someone. **2** (said about a part of the body) to suffer pain ♦ *My leg hurts.* **3** to cause mental pain or distress to someone ♦ *I'm sorry if I hurt your feelings.* **4** to have a bad effect on something ♦ *A couple of late nights won't hurt.*
hurt *noun* physical or mental pain or injury.
hurt *adjective* upset and offended ♦ *a hurt look.* [from an Old French word *hurter*]

hurtful *adjective* causing mental pain or distress ♦ *a hurtful remark.* **hurtfully** *adverb*

hurtle *verb* to move at great or dangerous speed ♦ *The train hurtled along* ♦ *Roof tiles came hurtling down.* [from an old use of *hurt* meaning 'to knock or dash against something']

husband *noun* a man to whom a woman is married.
husband *verb* to use money, strength, etc. economically and try to save it ♦ *We must husband our resources.* [from an Old English word *husbonda* meaning 'master of a house]

husbandry *noun* **1** farming. **2** management of resources. [from an old use of *husband* meaning 'person who manages things']

hush *verb* to make something quiet or silent, or to become quiet or silent.
hush *noun* a silence. **to hush something up** to prevent something from becoming generally known. [an imitation of the soft hissing sound you make to get someone to be quiet]

hush-hush *adjective* (*informal*) highly secret or confidential.

husk *noun* the dry outer covering of certain seeds and fruits.
husk *verb* to remove the husk from something. [probably from an Old German word]

husky[1] *adjective* (**huskier, huskiest**) **1** (said about a person's voice) dry in the throat, hoarse. **2** big and strong, burly. **3** dry, like husks. **huskily** *adverb* **huskiness** *noun* [from *husk*]

husky[2] *noun* (**huskies**) a powerful dog used in the Arctic for pulling sledges. [from a Native American word *Huskemaw* meaning 'Eskimo']

Hussars (hǝ-**zarz**) *plural noun* any of several cavalry regiments. [from a Hungarian word]

hussy *noun* (**hussies**) (*old use*) an immoral or cheeky woman. [a short form of *housewife*]

hustings *noun* political speeches and campaigning just before an election. [originally a temporary platform from which candidates for parliament could address the electors, from an Old Norse word]

hustle *verb* **1** to push or shove someone roughly, to jostle someone. **2** to force someone to move hurriedly ♦ *The protestors were hustled away by the police.* **3** to make someone do something quickly and without time to consider things ♦ *I felt I had been hustled into making a hasty decision.* **4** (*informal*) to earn money by dishonest means or aggressive selling.
hustle *noun* busy movement and activity.
hustler *noun* [from a Dutch word *husselen* meaning 'to shake or toss']

hut *noun* a small roughly-made house or shelter ♦ *a beach hut.* [via French from an Old German word]

hutch *noun* a box or cage for keeping rabbits or other small pet animals. [from a Latin word]

hyacinth *noun* a plant with fragrant bell-shaped flowers, growing from a bulb. [from the name of Hyacinthus, a youth in Greek mythology from whose blood a flower grew when he was accidentally killed by Apollo]

hybrid *noun* **1** an animal or plant that is the offspring of two different species or varieties. **2** something made by combining two different elements.
hybrid *adjective* produced in this way, cross-bred. [from a Latin word *hybrida* meaning 'offspring of a tame sow and wild boar, child of a freeman and slave, etc.']

hydra *noun* a microscopic freshwater animal (called a *polyp*) with a tubular body and tentacles round the mouth. [named after the Hydra in Greek mythology, a water snake with many heads that grew again if cut off]

hydrangea (hiy-**drayn**-jǝ) *noun* a shrub with white, pink, or blue flowers growing in clusters. [from *hydro-* and a Greek word *angeion* meaning 'vessel', from the cup shape of its seed capsule]

hydrant *noun* a pipe from a water main, especially in a street, with a nozzle to which a hose can be attached for use in dealing with fires. [same origin as for *hydro-*]

hydrate *noun* a chemical compound of water with another compound or element.
hydrate *verb* to combine chemically with water; to cause a substance to absorb water. **hydration** *noun* [same origin as for *hydro-*]

hydraulic (hiy-**draw**-lik) *adjective* 1 (said about water, oil, etc.) conveyed through pipes or channels under pressure. 2 operated by the movement of water or other fluid ♦ *hydraulic brakes.* 3 to do with the science of hydraulics ♦ *a hydraulic engineer.* 4 hardening under water ♦ *hydraulic cement.*
hydraulics *noun* the science of transporting liquids through pipes and channels, especially as motive power. **hydraulically** *adverb* [from *hydro-* and a Greek word *aulos* meaning 'pipe']

hydro *noun* (**hydros**) (*informal*) 1 a hotel originally providing treatment by hydropathy. 2 a hydroelectric power plant.

hydro- *prefix* (changing to **hydr-** before a vowel) 1 water (as in *hydroelectric, hydraulic*). 2 (in chemical names) containing hydrogen (as in *hydrochloric*). [from a Greek word *hudōr* meaning 'water']

hydrocarbon *noun* any of a class of compounds of hydrogen and carbon which are found in petrol, coal, and natural gas.

hydrocephalus (hiy-droh-**sef**-ə-ləs) *noun* a condition, especially of children, in which fluid accumulates on the brain. [from *hydro-* and a Greek word *kephalē* meaning 'head']

hydrochloric acid (hiy-drə-**klor**-ik) *noun* a colourless corrosive acid containing hydrogen and chlorine.

hydrochloride *noun* a compound of an organic base with hydrochloric acid.

hydrocyanic acid *noun* a highly poisonous acid with an odour of bitter almonds; prussic acid.

hydrodynamics *noun* the scientific study of the force exerted by a moving liquid, especially water. **hydrodynamic** *adjective*

hydroelectric *adjective* using water power to produce electricity. **hydroelectricity** *noun*

hydrofoil *noun* 1 a boat equipped with a structure designed to raise the hull out of the water when the boat is in motion in order to increase its speed. 2 this structure. [from *hydro-*, based on *aerofoil*]

hydrogen *noun* a chemical element (symbol H), a colourless odourless tasteless gas. It is the lightest substance known and combines with oxygen to form water. [from *hydro-* and *-gen* meaning 'producing']

hydrogenate (hiy-**droj**-in-ayt) *verb* to charge a substance with hydrogen; to cause a substance to combine with hydrogen. **hydrogenation** *noun*

hydrogen bomb *noun* an immensely powerful bomb releasing energy by fusion of hydrogen nuclei.

hydrogenous (hiy-**droj**-in-əs) *adjective* to do with or containing hydrogen.

hydrography (hiy-**drog**-rəfi) *noun* the scientific study of seas, lakes, rivers, etc. **hydrographer** *noun* **hydrographic** *adjective* [from *hydro-* and *-graphy*]

hydrology (hiy-**drol**-əji) *noun* the scientific study of the properties of water, especially of its movement in relation to the land. **hydrological** *adjective* [from *hydro-* and *-logy*]

hydrolyse (hiy-drə-liyz) *verb* (*Chemistry*) to break down a compound by hydrolysis.

hydrolysis (hiy-**drol**-i-sis) *noun* (*Chemistry*) the chemical breakdown of a compound due to reaction with water. [from *hydro-* and a Greek word *lusis* meaning 'loosening']

hydrometer (hiy-**drom**-it-er) *noun* an instrument that measures the density of liquids.

hydropathy (hiy-**drop**-ə-thi) *noun* the treatment of illness through the use of water, either internally or externally.

hydrophilic (hiy-drə-**fil**-ik) *adjective* having a tendency to combine with water; able to be wetted by water. [from *hydro-* and a Greek word *philos* meaning 'loving']

hydrophobia (hiy-drə-**foh**-biə) *noun* 1 an abnormal fear of water, especially as a symptom of rabies. 2 rabies. **hydrophobic** *adjective* [from *hydro-* and *phobia*]

hydroplane *noun* a light fast motor boat designed to skim over the surface of water.

hydroponics (hiy-dra-**pon**-iks) *noun* the art of growing plants without soil in sand etc. containing water to which nutrients have been added. [from *hydro-* and a Greek word *ponos* meaning 'labour']

hydrosphere *noun* the waters of the earth's surface. [from *hydro-* and *sphere*]

hydrostatic *adjective* to do with the pressure and other characteristics of liquids at rest.
hydrostatics *noun* the scientific study of these characteristics. [from a Greek word]

hydrotherapy *noun* the use of water in the treatment of disease and abnormal physical conditions, especially exercises in a swimming pool.

hydrothermal *adjective* to do with hot water that occurs naturally underground. [from *hydro-* and a Greek word *thermē* meaning 'heat']

hydrotropism (hiy-dra-**trop**-izm) *noun* (*Botany*) the tendency of plant roots to turn towards moisture. **hydrotropic** *adjective* [from *hydro-* and a Greek word *tropē* meaning 'turning']

hydrous (**hiy**-dras) *adjective* (said about substances) containing water. [same origin as for *hydro-*]

hydroxide *noun* a compound of an element or radical with a hydroxyl.

hydroxyl (hiy-**droks**-il) *noun* a radical containing hydrogen and oxygen.

hyena *noun* a flesh-eating animal like a wolf, with a howl that sounds like wild laughter. [from a Greek word *huaina*]

hygiene (**hiy**-jeen) *noun* keeping things clean in order to remain healthy and prevent the spread of disease. [from a Greek word *hugieinē* meaning 'of health']

hygienic (hiy-**jeen**-ik) *adjective* **1** according to the principles of hygiene. **2** clean and not likely to cause disease. **hygienically** *adverb*

hygienist (hiy-**jeen**-ist) *noun* an expert in hygiene.

hygrometer (hiy-**grom**-it-er) *noun* an instrument that measures humidity. [from Greek words *hugros* meaning 'wet' and *metron* meaning 'measure']

hygroscopic (hiy-gra-**skop**-ik) *adjective* (said about a substance) tending to absorb moisture from the air.

hymen *noun* a membrane partly closing the external opening of the vagina of a girl or woman who is a virgin. [from a Greek word *humēn* meaning 'membrane']

hymenopterous (hiy-man-**op**-ter-as) *adjective* to do with the kind of insects that includes ants, bees, and wasps, having four membranous wings. [from Greek words *humēn* meaning 'membrane' and *pteron* meaning 'wing']

hymn *noun* a religious song, usually of praise to God. [from a Greek word *humnos* meaning 'ode or song in praise']

hymnal or **hymn book** *noun* a book of hymns.

hype *noun* (*informal*) extravagant or misleading publicity ♦ *Don't believe all the hype about this film.*
hype *verb* (*informal*) to promote a product with extravagant publicity. [origin unknown]

hyped up *adjective* (*informal*) overexcited or overstimulated.

hyper- *prefix* over or above; excessive. [from a Greek word *huper* meaning 'over']

hyperactive *adjective* (said about children) abnormally and excessively active. **hyperactivity** *noun*

hyperbola (hiy-**per**-bala) *noun* (*Mathematics*) the curve produced when a cone is cut by a plane that makes a larger angle with the base than the side of the cone does. **hyperbolic** (hiy-per-**bol**-ik) *adjective* [same origin as for *hyperbole*]

hyperbole (hiy-**per**-bali) *noun* a deliberately exaggerated statement that is not meant to be taken literally, e.g. *a stack of work a mile high.* **hyperbolical** (hiy-per-**bol**-ikal) *adjective* [from *hyper-* and a Greek word *bolē* meaning 'a throw']

hypercritical *adjective* excessively critical, especially of small faults. **hypercritically** *adverb*

hyperlink *noun* (*Computing*) a link from one document or part of a document to another, activated by selecting a highlighted word or image.

hypermarket *noun* a very large supermarket, usually situated outside a town. [from a French word]

hypersensitive *adjective* excessively sensitive.

hypersonic *adjective* 1 to do with speeds more than about five times that of sound. 2 to do with sound frequencies above about 1,000 megahertz. [from *hyper-* and *sonic*]

hyperspace *noun* (in science fiction) a space–time continuum in which it is possible to travel faster than light.

hypertension *noun* abnormally high blood pressure.

hypertext *noun* (*Computing*) a system of cross-referencing between linked sections of documents.

hypha *noun* (**hyphae** (**hiy-fee**)) any of the microscopic thread-like strands that form the main part of mould and similar fungi. [from a Greek word *huphē* meaning 'web']

hyphen *noun* the sign (-) used to link two words (e.g. *hot-tempered*) or to divide a word into parts, e.g. at the end of a line in print. [from a Greek word meaning 'together']

hyphenate *verb* to join words or divide a word with a hyphen. **hyphenated** *adjective* **hyphenation** *noun*

hypnosis (hip-**noh**-sis) *noun* 1 a sleep-like state produced in a person who is then very susceptible to suggestion and acts only if told to do so. 2 the producing of this state. [from a Greek word *hupnos* meaning 'sleep']

hypnotherapy *noun* the treatment of disease by hypnosis. **hypnotherapist** *noun*

hypnotic (hip-**not**-ik) *adjective* 1 to do with or producing hypnosis or a similar condition. 2 (said about a drug) producing sleep. 3 so fascinating that you are unable to turn your attention away ♦ *His voice had a hypnotic effect.*
hypnotic *noun* a drug that produces sleep. **hypnotically** *adverb*

hypnotism (**hip**-nə-tizm) *noun* the study or production of hypnosis.

hypnotist (**hip**-nə-tist) *noun* a person who produces hypnosis in another person.

hypnotize (**hip**-nə-tiyz) *verb* 1 to produce hypnosis in someone. 2 to fascinate someone, to hold their attention completely.

hypo- *prefix* below or under. [from a Greek word *hupo* meaning 'under']

hypocaust (**hiy**-pə-kawst) *noun* a system of under-floor heating by hot air, used in ancient Roman houses. [from *hypo-* and a Greek word *kaustos* meaning 'burnt']

hypochondria (hiy-pə-**kon**-driə) *noun* a mental condition in which a person constantly imagines that he or she is ill. [from a Greek word *hupokhondrios* meaning 'under the breastbone' (because the organs there were once thought to be the source of depression and anxiety)]

hypochondriac *noun* someone who suffers from hypochondria.

hypocrisy (hip-**ok**-risi) *noun* falsely pretending to be virtuous.

hypocrite (**hip**-ə-krit) *noun* a person who pretends to be more virtuous than he or she really is. **hypocritical** (hip-ə-**krit**-ikəl) *adjective* **hypocritically** *adverb* [from a Greek word meaning 'acting a part']

hypodermic *adjective* injected beneath the skin; used for such injections.
hypodermic *noun* a hypodermic syringe. **hypodermically** *adverb* [from *hypo-* and a Greek word *derma* meaning 'skin']

hypodermic syringe *noun* a syringe fitted with a hollow needle through which a liquid can be injected beneath the skin.

hypogeal (hiy-pə-**jee**-əl) *adjective* (*Botany*) growing or occurring under the ground. [from *hypo-* and a Greek word *gē* meaning 'earth']

hypotenuse (hiy-**pot**-i-newz) *noun* the longest side of a right-angled triangle, opposite the right angle. [from *hypo-* and a Greek word *teinein* meaning 'to stretch']

hypothalamus (hy-pə-**thal**-ə-məs) *noun* (**hypothalami** (hy-pə-**thal**-ə-my)) (*Anatomy*) the part of the brain which controls body temperature, appetite, and other involuntary functions. [from *hypo-* and *thalamus*, another part of the brain]

hypothermia *noun* the condition of having an abnormally low body temperature. [from *hypo-* and a Greek word *thermē* meaning 'heat']

hypothesis (hiy-**poth**-i-sis) *noun* (**hypotheses** (-seez)) a suggestion or possible explanation put forward to account for certain facts and used as a basis for further investigation by which it may be proved or disproved. [from *hypo-* and a Greek word *thesis* meaning 'placing']

hypothesize (hiy-**poth**-i-siyz) *verb* 1 to form a hypothesis. 2 to assume something as a hypothesis.

hypothetical (hiy-pə-thet-ik-əl) *adjective*
1 based on or serving as a hypothesis.
2 supposed but not necessarily true.
hypothetically *adverb*

hysterectomy (hiss-ter-ek-tə-mi) *noun*
(**hysterectomies**) the surgical removal of
the womb. [from Greek words *hustera*
meaning 'womb' and *-ectomy* meaning
'cutting out']

hysteria (hiss-teer-iə) *noun* wild
uncontrollable emotion, panic, or
excitement. [from a Greek word *hustera*
meaning 'womb' (once thought to be the
cause of hysterics)]

hysterical (hiss-te-ri-kəl) *adjective* 1 in a
state of hysteria ♦ *a crowd of hysterical fans.*
SYNONYMS: wild, frenzied, frantic,
uncontrollable. 2 (*informal*) extremely funny.
hysterically *adverb*

hysterics (hiss-te-riks) *plural noun* (*informal*)
1 a hysterical outburst. 2 uncontrollable
laughter ♦ *His speech had us all in hysterics.*

Hz *abbreviation* hertz.

Ii

I 1 the ninth letter of the English alphabet.
2 the Roman numeral for 1.

I *pronoun* used to refer to the person who is
speaking or writing. [from an Old English
word]

I *abbreviation* 1 (mostly used on maps)
island(s) or isle(s). 2 (*Chemistry*) the
symbol for iodine.

iambic (iy-am-bik) *adjective* of or using a
metrical foot (called an *iambus*) with one
short or unstressed syllable followed by
one long or stressed syllable.
iambics *plural noun* lines of verse in iambic
metre. [from a Greek word *iambos*, from
iaptein meaning 'to satirize' (because
iambic verse was first used in satirical
poetry)]

Iberian (iy-beer-iən) *adjective* to do with the
peninsula comprising Spain and Portugal.
[from the Latin name Iberia]

ibex (iy-beks) *noun* (**ibexes** or **ibex**) a wild
mountain goat with long curving horns.
[a Latin word]

ibid. *abbreviation* (in text references) in the
same book or passage already mentioned.
[short for Latin *ibidem* meaning 'in the
same place']

ibis (iy-bis) *noun* (**ibises**) a wading bird
with a long downward curved bill, a long
neck, and long legs. [from a Greek word]

-ible *suffix* forming adjectives meaning
'that can be done' (as in *legible*).

Ibo (ee-boh) *noun* another spelling of **Igbo**.

ICBM *abbreviation* intercontinental ballistic
missile.

ice *noun* 1 frozen water, a brittle
transparent solid. 2 an ice cream or water
ice.
ice *verb* 1 to become covered with ice
♦ *The pond has iced over.* 2 to make
something very cold ♦ *iced tea.* 3 to
decorate a cake with icing. [from an Old
English word]

ice age *noun* a period when much of the
earth's surface was covered with glaciers.

iceberg *noun* a huge mass of ice floating in
the sea with the greater part under water.
the tip of the iceberg a small discernible
part of a larger problem or difficulty that
lies concealed. [from a Dutch word
ijsberg, from *ijs* meaning 'ice' and *berg*
meaning 'hill']

icebox *noun* (*North Amer.*) a refrigerator, or
a compartment in a refrigerator for
making and keeping ice.

icecap *noun* a permanent covering of ice
and snow at the North and South Poles.

ice cream *noun* a sweet creamy frozen
food.

ice field *noun* a large expanse of floating
ice.

ice hockey *noun* a form of hockey played
on ice with a flat disc (called a *puck*)
instead of a ball.

Icelandic *adjective* to do with Iceland or its
people or language.
Icelandic *noun* the language of Iceland.

ice lolly *noun* a piece of flavoured water ice
on a stick.

ice rink *noun* a place made for skating on
ice.

ichthyology *noun* the study of fishes.
[from a Greek word *ikhthus* meaning 'fish']

ichthyosaurus (ik-thi-ə-sor-əs) *noun*
(**ichthyosauruses**) an extinct sea animal
resembling a dolphin, with a long head,

tapering body, four paddles, and a large tail. [from Greek words *ikhthus* meaning 'fish' and *sauros* meaning 'lizard']

-ician *suffix* forming nouns meaning 'a person skilled in something' (as in *musician*).

icicle *noun* a pointed hanging piece of ice, formed when dripping water freezes. [from an Old English word]

icing *noun* a sugary mixture used to decorate cakes and biscuits.

icing sugar *noun* powdered sugar used for making icing.

-icity *suffix* forming nouns from words ending in *-ic* (as in *publicity*).

icon (iy-kon) *noun* 1 a sacred painting, usually on wood, or mosaic of a holy person, especially in the Byzantine and other Eastern Churches. 2 (*Computing*) a small symbol or picture on a computer screen. 3 a famous person who is widely revered as an example or model. [from a Greek word *eikōn* meaning 'image']

iconoclast (iy-kon-ə-klast) *noun* a person who attacks cherished institutions or beliefs. **iconoclasm** *noun* **iconoclastic** *adjective* [from Greek words *eikōn* meaning 'image' and *klastos* meaning 'broken']

iconography (iy-kən-og-rə-fi) *noun* 1 the illustration of a subject by drawings or figures. 2 a study of the portraits of a person. [from a Greek word *eikōn* meaning 'image' and *-graphy*]

icosahedron (iy-koss-ə-hee-drən) *noun* a solid shape with twenty faces. [from Greek words *eikosi* meaning 'twenty' and *hedra* meaning 'base']

ICT *abbreviation* information and communication technology.

icy *adjective* (**icier**, **iciest**) 1 very cold ♦ *icy winds*. SYNONYMS: freezing, frosty, bitter, wintry, cold. 2 covered with ice ♦ *icy roads*. 3 hostile or unfriendly in manner ♦ *an icy voice*. SYNONYMS: aloof, chilly, cold, cool, unfriendly. **icily** *adverb* **iciness** *noun*

I'd *verb* (*informal*) 1 I had. 2 I would.

id *noun* (*Psychology*) a person's inherited psychological impulses considered as part of the unconscious.

idea *noun* 1 a plan or thought formed in the mind. SYNONYMS: concept, notion, plan, scheme. 2 a mental impression ♦ *I'll try to give you an idea of what is needed*. 3 an opinion or belief. 4 a vague belief or fancy, a feeling that something is likely ♦ *I had an idea this would happen*. SYNONYMS: feeling, notion, inkling, suspicion, hunch. [from a Greek word meaning 'form' or 'pattern']

ideal *adjective* 1 satisfying an idea of what is perfect or suitable ♦ *This is an ideal time for a meeting*. SYNONYMS: perfect, excellent. 2 existing only in an idea ♦ *in an ideal world*. **ideal** *noun* a person or thing or idea that is regarded as perfect or as a standard to follow. **ideally** *adverb* [from a Latin word *idealis*, related to *idea*]

ideal gas *noun* (*Chemistry*) an imaginary gas (used in calculations) whose behaviour conforms to the same simple law under all conditions.

idealist (iy-dee-əl-ist) *noun* a person who has high ideals and tries, often unrealistically, to achieve these. **idealism** *noun* **idealistic** *adjective*

idealize *verb* to regard or represent a person or thing as perfect, or as better than they are. **idealization** *noun*

identical *adjective* 1 one and the same ♦ *This is the identical place we visited last year*. SYNONYMS: same, very same, selfsame. 2 exactly alike ♦ *All the houses in the street looked identical*. 3 (said about twins) developed from a single fertilized ovum and therefore of the same sex and similar in appearance. **identically** *adverb* [same origin as for *identity*]

identify *verb* (**identifies, identified, identifying**) 1 to establish who or what a particular person or thing is, to recognize them as being a specified person or thing. 2 to associate someone closely in feeling or interest ♦ *The company identifies us with progress and efficiency*. 3 to think of yourself as sharing the characteristics or fortunes of another person ♦ *Anyone can identify with the hero of the play*. **identifiable** *adjective* **identification** *noun* [same origin as for *identity*]

Identikit *noun* (*trademark*) a picture of a person who is wanted by the police, assembled from features as described by witnesses.

identity *noun* (**identities**) 1 who or what a person or thing is. 2 the distinctive character of a person or thing. 3 the state of being identical, absolute sameness. [from a Latin word *idem* meaning 'same']

identity card noun a card that identifies the person who carries it for official purposes.

identity element noun (Mathematics) the element in a set which when combined with any other element leaves that element unchanged.

ideogram (id-i-ə-gram) noun a symbol that indicates the idea of a thing and not the sounds that form the name, e.g. numerals, Chinese characters, and symbols used in road signs. [from a Greek word idea meaning 'form' and -gram]

ideology (iy-dee-ol-əji) noun (**ideologies**) a set of ideas or beliefs that form the basis of an economic or political theory ♦ Marxist ideology. **ideological** adjective **ideologist** noun [from idea and -logy]

ides (iydz) plural noun (in the ancient Roman calendar) the 15th day of March, May, July, and October, and the 13th of other months.

idiocy noun (**idiocies**) 1 being an idiot or behaving stupidly. 2 a piece of stupid behaviour, a stupid action.

idiom (id-i-əm) noun 1 a phrase with a meaning that cannot be worked out from the individual words in it, e.g. ♦ in hot water and ♦ over the moon. 2 the use of words in a way that is natural in a language. 3 the language used by a particular group ♦ in the scientific idiom. 4 a characteristic style of expression in art or music. [from a Greek word idios meaning 'your own']

idiomatic (idi-ə-mat-ik) adjective 1 in accordance with the usage of a language. 2 full of idioms. **idiomatically** adverb

idiosyncrasy (idi-ə-sink-rəsi) noun (**idiosyncrasies**) a person's particular way of thinking or behaving. **idiosyncratic** (idi-ə-sin-krat-ik) adjective [from Greek words idios meaning 'your own', syn meaning 'with', and krasis meaning 'mixture']

idiot noun 1 (informal) a stupid or foolish person. 2 (old use) a person who is mentally deficient. [from a Greek word idiotēs meaning 'private citizen' or 'uneducated person']

idiotic adjective very stupid or foolish. SYNONYMS: stupid, foolish, ridiculous, absurd. **idiotically** adverb

idle adjective 1 (said about a person)

avoiding work, lazy. SYNONYMS: lazy, indolent. 2 (said about machinery) doing no work, not active or in use. SYNONYMS: inactive, unused, out of action. 3 (said about time) not spent in doing something. 4 worthless, having no purpose or basis ♦ idle gossip.

idle verb 1 to pass time without working, to be idle. 2 (said about an engine) to run slowly in a neutral gear. **idleness** noun **idler** noun **idly** adverb [from an Old English word]

idol noun 1 a statue or image of a god, used as an object of worship. 2 a famous person who is widely admired. [from a Greek word eidōlon meaning 'image']

idolatory (iy-dol-ə-tri) noun 1 the worship of idols. 2 great admiration or devotion. **idolater** noun **idolatrous** adjective [from idol and a Greek word latreia meaning 'worship']

idolize verb to show great admiration for or devotion to a person or thing. **idolization** noun

idyll (id-il) noun 1 a beautiful or peaceful scene or situation. 2 a short verse or prose description of a peaceful or romantic scene or incident, especially in country life. [from a Greek word eidullion meaning 'little picture']

idyllic (id-il-ik) adjective like an idyll, peaceful and happy. **idyllically** adverb

i.e. abbreviation that is, that is to say ♦ The person who wrote the play, i.e. Pinter. [short for the Latin phrase id est meaning 'that is']

if conjunction 1 on condition that, supposing that ♦ I'll do it if you pay me. 2 in the event that ♦ If you are tired we can rest. 3 supposing or granting that ♦ Even if she said it she didn't mean it. 4 even though ♦ We'll finish it, if it takes us all day. 5 whenever ♦ If they wanted anything, they got it. 6 whether ♦ See if the light works now. 7 used in exclamations of wish or surprise ♦ If only he would come! ♦ Well, if it isn't Simon!

if noun a condition or supposition ♦ There are too many ifs about it. [from an Old English word]

Igbo (ee-boh) noun (**Igbo** or **Igbos**) 1 a member of a black people of Nigeria. 2 their language.

igloo noun (**igloos**) a round Inuit house built of blocks of hard snow. [from an Inuit word meaning 'house']

igneous (ig-ni-əs) *adjective* (said about rocks) formed by the action of a volcano. [from a Latin word *igneus* meaning 'fiery']

ignite (ig-niyt) *verb* **1** to set fire to something. **2** to catch fire. [from a Latin word *ignis* meaning 'fire']

ignition (ig-nish-ən) *noun* **1** the process of igniting. **2** the process of producing a spark to ignite the fuel in an internal-combustion engine, or the device that does this.

ignoble *adjective* not noble in character, shameful or unworthy. **ignobly** *adverb*

ignominious (ignə-min-iəs) *adjective* bringing disgrace, humiliating. **ignominiously** *adverb* [from a Latin word *ignominia* meaning 'not a name']

ignominy (ig-nəm-ini) *noun* disgrace or humiliation.

ignoramus (ig-ner-ay-məs) *noun* (**ignoramuses**) an ignorant person. [a Latin word meaning 'we do not know']

ignorant *adjective* **1** not knowing about something or about many things. SYNONYMS: unaware, uninformed. **2** (*informal*) rude or impolite from not knowing how to behave. **ignorance** *noun* **ignorantly** *adverb* [same origin as for *ignore*]

ignore *verb* to take no notice of something or someone. SYNONYMS: disregard, overlook. [from a Latin word *ignorare* meaning 'not to know']

iguana (ig-wah-nə) *noun* a large tree-climbing tropical lizard. [via Spanish from a South American language]

iguanodon (ig-wah-nə-dən) *noun* a large plant-eating dinosaur with a broad stiff tail.

ileum (il-iəm) *noun* (**ilea**) the lowest part of the small intestine. [same origin as for *ilium*]

ilium (il-iəm) *noun* a broad bone forming the upper part of the pelvis. [from a Latin word *ilia* meaning 'entrails']

ilk *noun* **of that ilk** of that kind. [from an Old English word *ilca* meaning 'same']

I'll *verb* (*informal*) I shall or I will.

ill *adjective* **1** physically or mentally unwell, in bad health. SYNONYMS: sick, unwell, poorly; (*informal*) under the weather. **2** bad or harmful ♦ *There were no ill effects.* SYNONYMS: harmful, bad, unfavourable. **3** hostile or unkind ♦ *no ill feelings.* **ill** *adverb* **1** badly or wrongly ♦ *The child had*

been ill-treated. **2** imperfectly or scarcely ♦ *We can ill afford to do this.* **ill** *noun* harm or injury. **ill at ease** uncomfortable, embarrassed. [from an Old Norse word *illr* meaning 'evil']

ill-advised *adjective* unwise, not sensible.

ill-bred *adjective* having bad manners.

illegal *adjective* against the law. SYNONYMS: unlawful, forbidden, prohibited, illicit. **illegality** (ili-gal-iti) *noun* **illegally** *adverb*

illegible (i-lej-ibəl) *adjective* not clear enough to read. SYNONYMS: unreadable, indecipherable. **illegibly** *adverb* **illegibility** *noun*

illegitimate (ili-jit-im-ət) *adjective* **1** (said about a child) born of parents who are not married to each other. **2** not conforming to the law or to normal standards. **illegitimately** *adverb* **illegitimacy** *noun*

ill-fated *adjective* bound to fail, unlucky.

ill-gotten *adjective* obtained by unlawful means.

illicit (i-lis-it) *adjective* not allowed by the law or by custom. **illicitly** *adverb* [from *in-* meaning 'not' and a Latin word *licitus* meaning 'allowed']

illiterate (i-lit-er-ət) *adjective* **1** unable to read and write. **2** ignorant about a particular subject ♦ *He is politically illiterate.* **illiterate** *noun* a person who is unable to read or write. **illiterately** *adverb* **illiteracy** *noun*

ill-mannered *adjective* having bad manners.

ill-natured *adjective* bad-tempered or unkind.

illness *noun* **1** the state of being ill in body or mind. **2** a particular form of ill health. SYNONYMS: disease, sickness, infirmity, ailment, complaint.

illogical *adjective* not logical, having no sense. **illogically** *adverb* **illogicality** (i-loj-i-kal-iti) *noun*

ill-starred *adjective* unlucky.

ill-treat *verb* to treat someone or something badly or cruelly.

illuminate *verb* **1** to light something up or make it bright. **2** to throw light on a subject or make it understandable. **3** to decorate a place with lights. **4** to decorate a manuscript with coloured designs. **illumination** *noun* [from *in-* meaning 'in' and a Latin word *lumen* meaning 'light']

ill-use *verb* to ill-treat someone or something.

illusion (i-**loo**-zhən) *noun* 1 something unreal that a person supposes to exist. 2 a false idea or belief. [from a Latin word *illudere* meaning 'to mock']

illusionist *noun* a person who does tricks that deceive the eye, a conjuror.

illusory (i-**loo**-ser-i) *adjective* based on illusion, not real.

illustrate *verb* 1 to put drawings or pictures in a book, magazine, or newspaper. 2 to make something clear by giving examples or pictures etc. 3 to serve as an example of something. **illustrator** *noun* [from a Latin word *illustrare* meaning 'to add light or brilliance']

illustration *noun* 1 the process of illustrating something. 2 a drawing or picture in a book, magazine, or newspaper. 3 an example that is used to explain something.

illustrative (il-əs-trə-tiv) *adjective* serving as an illustration or example. **illustratively** *adverb*

illustrious (i-**lus**-triəs) *adjective* famous and distinguished. **illustriousness** *noun* [from a Latin word *illustris* meaning 'clear or bright']

ill will *noun* hostility, unkind feeling.

I'm *verb* (*informal*) I am.

image *noun* 1 something that represents the outward form of a person or thing, such as a statue or picture. 2 the appearance of something as seen in a mirror or through a lens. 3 a person or thing that is very much like another in appearance ♦ *She's the image of her mother.* 4 a mental picture of something. 5 the general impression or reputation of a person, organization, or product as seen by the public. 6 (*Mathematics*) a set formed by mapping. [from a Latin word *imago*]

imagery *noun* 1 the use of figurative or other special language to convey an idea to readers or hearers. 2 images; statues or carvings.

imaginable *adjective* able to be imagined or believed.

imaginary *adjective* existing only in the imagination, not real. SYNONYMS: unreal, fanciful, fictitious, invented.

imaginary number *noun* (*Mathematics*) a number which is expressed in relation to the hypothetical square root of minus one (represented by *i* or *j*).

imagination *noun* the power of imagining; the ability of the mind to imagine creatively or inventively.

imaginative *adjective* having or showing imagination. SYNONYMS: creative, inventive, original, ingenious. **imaginatively** *adverb*

imagine *verb* 1 to form a mental image of something, to picture something in the mind. SYNONYMS: picture, visualize, envisage, conceive. 2 to suppose or assume ♦ *Don't imagine you'll get away with this.* 3 to guess ♦ *I can't imagine what it will be like.* [same origin as for *image*]

imago (i-**may**-goh) *noun* (**imago** or **imagines** (i-**may**-jin-eez)) (*Zoology*) the fully developed stage of an insect. [same origin as for *image*]

imam (im-**ahm**) *noun* 1 the leader of prayers in a mosque. 2 the title of various Muslim religious leaders. [an Arabic word meaning 'leader']

imbalance *noun* a lack of balance or proportion.

imbecile (im-bi-**seel**) *noun* (*informal*) a stupid person. **imbecile** *adjective* (*informal*) stupid. **imbecility** (imbi-**sil**-iti) *noun* [from a Latin word *imbecillus* meaning 'not having a stick for support', from *baculum* meaning 'stick']

imbibe (im-**biyb**) *verb* (*formal*) 1 to drink, especially to drink an alcoholic drink. 2 to absorb ideas or information into the mind. [from *in-* meaning 'in' and a Latin word *bibere* meaning 'to drink']

imbroglio (im-**brohl**-yoh) *noun* (**imbroglios**) a confused situation, especially one involving a disagreement. [an Italian word, from *imbrogliare* meaning 'to confuse']

imbue (im-**bew**) *verb* (**imbues**, **imbued**, **imbuing**) to fill a person with a feeling or quality. [from a Latin word *imbuere* meaning 'to moisten']

IMF *abbreviation* International Monetary Fund.

imitate *verb* 1 to copy a person or their behaviour. 2 to mimic someone for amusement or entertainment. 3 to copy or be like something else. **imitable**

adjective **imitator** noun [from a Latin word *imitari* meaning 'to copy']

imitation noun **1** the process of imitating or copying a person or thing. **2** something produced by copying or imitating something. **3** the act of mimicking someone for entertainment ♦ *She does good imitations.*

imitative (im-it-ətiv) adjective imitating someone or something.

immaculate adjective **1** completely clean. **2** without any fault or blemish, free of mistakes. **immaculately** adverb **immaculacy** noun [from *in-* meaning 'not' and a Latin word *macula* meaning 'a spot or blemish']

immanent (im-ə-nənt) adjective **1** (said about a quality) existing within a person, inherent. **2** (said about God) permanently present in the universe. **immanence** noun [from a Latin word *immanere* meaning 'to remain within']
◊ Do not confuse this word with **imminent**, which has a different meaning.

immaterial adjective **1** of no importance or relevance ♦ *It is largely immaterial what you think.* **2** having no physical body ♦ *our immaterial souls.*

immature adjective not mature or developed, especially emotionally. SYNONYMS: childish, babyish, juvenile. **immaturity** noun

immeasurable adjective too large or too many to be measured. **immeasurably** adverb

immediate adjective **1** happening or done without any delay. **2** nearest, with nothing or no one between ♦ *our immediate neighbours.* **3** nearest in relationship ♦ *Their immediate family lived abroad.* **4** most urgent or pressing ♦ *Our immediate concern is to pay off the debt.* **immediacy** noun [from *in-* meaning 'in' and a Latin word *mediatus* meaning 'coming between']

immediately adverb at once, without any delay.
immediately conjunction as soon as ♦ *I came immediately you called.*

immemorial adjective going far back into the past ♦ *The town had immemorial rights to the land.* **from time immemorial** from the distant past. [from *in-* meaning 'not' and a Latin word *memoria* meaning 'memory']

immense adjective very large or great. SYNONYMS: huge, enormous, colossal, gigantic, massive. **immensity** noun [from *in-* meaning 'not' and a Latin word *mensum* meaning 'measured']

immensely adverb to a great extent, extremely.

immerse verb **1** to put something completely into a liquid. **2** to absorb or involve someone deeply in thought ♦ *She was immersed in her work.* [from *in-* meaning 'into' and a Latin word *mersum* meaning 'dipped']

immersion noun the process of immersing something in a liquid.

immersion heater noun an electric heating element that is fitted inside a hot-water tank so as to be immersed in the contents.

immigrant noun a person who comes into a foreign country to live there permanently.

immigrate verb to come into a foreign country to live there permanently. **immigration** noun [from *in-* meaning 'into' and *migrate*]

imminent adjective (of events) about to occur, likely to occur at any moment. **imminence** noun
◊ Do not confuse this word with **immanent**, which has a different meaning.

immiscible (i-mis-ibəl) adjective (said about liquids) not able to be mixed together.

immobile adjective not moving, or not able to move. **immobility** noun

immobilize verb to make something unable to move or work. **immobilization** noun

immoderate adjective excessive, lacking moderation. **immoderately** adverb

immodest adjective **1** not modest, indecent. **2** conceited. **immodestly** adverb **immodesty** noun

immolate (im-ə-layt) verb to sacrifice a person or animal by burning. **immolation** noun [from a Latin word *immolare* meaning 'to sprinkle with sacrificial meal', from *mola* meaning 'meal']

immoral adjective not conforming to the accepted standards of morality, morally wrong. SYNONYMS: bad, evil, wicked, wrong, sinful, depraved, unprincipled. **immorally** adverb **immorality** (im-er-al-iti) noun

immortal adjective **1** living for ever, not mortal. **2** famous for all time.

immortal *noun* an immortal being or person, especially an ancient deity. **immortality** *noun*

immortalize *verb* to make someone famous for all time.

immovable *adjective* 1 unable to be moved. 2 (said about a person) not willing to change an opinion or decision. 3 (said about property) consisting of land, houses, and other permanent things. **immovably** *adverb* **immovability** *noun*

immune *adjective* 1 resistant to a disease ♦ *She is not immune against infection* ♦ *He proved to be immune to the virus.* 2 safe from a danger or obligation ♦ *They are immune from prosecution.* [from a Latin word *immunis* meaning 'exempt']

immune system *noun* (*Medicine*) the body's means of resisting infection.

immunity *noun* (**immunities**) 1 (*Medicine*) the ability to resist infection. 2 special exemption from an obligation or penalty.

immunize *verb* (*Medicine*) to make someone immune to infection. **immunization** *noun*

immunodeficiency *noun* (*Medicine*) a reduced ability of the immune system to resist infection.

immunology (im-yoo-**nol**-əji) *noun* (*Medicine*) the branch of medicine concerned with resistance to infection. **immunological** *adjective*

immure (im-**yoor**) *verb* to imprison someone or shut them in. [from *in*-meaning 'into' and a Latin word *murus* meaning 'wall']

immutable (i-**mewt**-əbəl) *adjective* unchangeable. **immutably** *adverb* **immutability** *noun*

imp *noun* 1 a small devil. 2 a mischievous child.

impact[1] (**im**-pakt) *noun* 1 the action or force of one object coming into collision with another. 2 a significant effect or influence caused by something ♦ *the impact made by computers on our lives.* [from *in*- meaning 'in' and a Latin word *pactum* meaning 'driven']

impact[2] (im-**pakt**) *verb* 1 to collide or come into violent contact with something. 2 to have a significant effect on something.

impair *verb* to damage something or cause it to weaken ♦ *Smoking impairs your health.* **impairment** *noun* [from *in*- meaning 'in', and a Latin word *pejor* meaning 'worse']

impala (im-**pah**-lə) *noun* (**impala**) a small African antelope. [a Zulu word]

impale *verb* to fix or pierce something by passing a sharp-pointed object into it or through it. [from *in*- meaning 'in' and a Latin word *palus* meaning 'a stake']

impalpable (im-**palp**-əbəl) *adjective* 1 unable to be felt by touch. 2 not easily understood. **impalpably** *adverb* **impalpability** *noun*

impanel (im-**pan**-əl) *verb* (**impanelled, impanelling**) to list or select someone for service on a jury. [from *in*- meaning 'into' and *panel*]

impart *verb* 1 to give information. 2 to provide something with a quality ♦ *Lemon imparts a sharp flavour to drinks.* **impartation** *noun* [from a Latin word *impartire* meaning 'to give someone part of something']

impartial (im-**par**-shəl) *adjective* not favouring one person or side more than another. **impartiality** (im-par-shi-al-iti) *noun* **impartially** *adverb*

impassable *adjective* not able to be travelled along or over ♦ *The road is impassable because of flooding.* **impassably** *adverb* **impassability** *noun*

impasse (am-**pahss**) *noun* a situation in which no progress can be made; a deadlock. [a French word meaning 'impassable place']

impassioned (im-**pash**-ənd) *adjective* full of deep feeling ♦ *The aid workers made an impassioned appeal on behalf of the refugees.*

impassive *adjective* not feeling or showing any emotion. **impassively** *adverb* **impassiveness** *noun* **impassivity** *noun* [from *in*- meaning 'not' and *passive* in an old meaning 'suffering']

impasto *noun* (*Art*) a technique of laying on paint thickly to give a picture a textured quality. [from an Italian word *impastare*, from *in*- meaning 'on' and *pasta* meaning 'a paste']

impatient *adjective* 1 unable to wait patiently, restlessly eager ♦ *The boys are impatient to set off.* SYNONYMS: eager, anxious. 2 showing a lack of patience, irascible or intolerant. **impatiently** *adverb* **impatience** *noun*

impeach *verb* 1 to charge a person with a serious crime against the state; in the USA, to charge a person holding public office with misconduct. 2 to question a

practice or intention. **impeachment** noun
[from an Old French word empecher
meaning 'to impede']

impeccable adjective of the highest
standard, faultless. **impeccably** adverb
impeccability noun [from in- meaning 'not'
and a Latin word peccare meaning 'to sin']

impecunious (impi-kew-niəs) adjective
having little or no money. **impecuniosity**
noun [from in- meaning 'not' and a Latin
word pecunia meaning 'money']

impedance (im-pee-dəns) noun the total
resistance of an electric circuit to the flow
of alternating current. [from impede]

impede verb to hinder someone or
something. [from a Latin word impedire
meaning 'to shackle the feet', from in-
meaning 'in' and pedis meaning 'of a foot']

impediment noun 1 a hindrance or
obstruction. 2 a defect in a person's
speech, such as a lisp or stammer. [same
origin as for impede]

impel verb (impelled, impelling) 1 to urge or
drive someone to do something ♦ Curiosity
impelled her to investigate. 2 to send or drive
something forward, to propel something.
[from in- meaning 'towards' and a Latin
word pellere meaning 'to drive']

impending adjective soon to happen,
imminent. [from in- meaning 'in' and a
Latin word pendere meaning 'to hang']

impenetrable adjective 1 impossible to
enter or pass through. 2 impossible to
understand. **impenetrably** adverb
impenetrability noun

impenitent adjective not feeling sorrow or
regret for a wrongdoing. **impenitently**
adverb **impenitence** noun

imperative (im-pe-rə-tiv) adjective
1 expressing a command. 2 essential or
unavoidable ♦ Further economies are
imperative.
imperative noun 1 something essential or
unavoidable ♦ Speed is an imperative in this
operation. 2 (Grammar) a form of a verb
used in making commands (e.g. come in
come here!). [from a Latin word imperare
meaning 'to command']

imperceptible adjective so slight or gradual
that it is difficult to notice it.
imperceptibly adverb

imperfect adjective 1 not perfect;
incomplete. SYNONYMS: deficient, damaged,
defective, flawed. 2 (Grammar) (said about a
verb) in the tense used to denote past

action going on but not completed, as in
♦ She was laughing.
imperfect noun the imperfect tense.
imperfectly adverb

imperfection noun 1 the state of being
imperfect. 2 a fault or failing.

imperial adjective 1 to do with an empire or
its rulers. 2 majestic. 3 used to denote
non-metric weights and measures fixed
by law in the UK ♦ an imperial gallon.
imperially adverb [from a Latin word
imperium meaning 'supreme power']

imperialism noun the policy of extending a
country's influence by colonization or
military means. **imperialist** noun
imperialistic adjective

imperil verb (imperilled, imperilling) to
endanger someone or something.

imperious (im-peer-iəs) adjective
domineering or bossy. **imperiously** adverb
imperiousness noun [same origin as for
imperial]

impermanent adjective not permanent.
impermanence noun **impermanency** noun

impermeable (im-per-mi-əbəl) adjective not
allowing liquid to pass through.
impermeability noun

impersonal adjective 1 not influenced by
personal feeling, showing no emotion.
2 not referring to a particular person.
3 having no existence as a person,
♦ nature's impersonal forces. 4 (Grammar)
denoting a verb used with it to make
general statements such as it is raining or it
is hard to find one. **impersonality** noun
impersonally adverb

impersonate verb to pretend to be another
person, either for entertainment or
fraudulently. **impersonation** noun
impersonator noun

impertinent adjective 1 insolent, not
showing proper respect. 2 (formal) not
pertinent, irrelevant. **impertinence** noun
impertinently adverb

imperturbable (im-per-terb-əbəl) adjective
not easily excited, calm. **imperturbability**
noun **imperturbably** adverb

impervious (im-per-viəs) adjective 1 not
allowing water or heat etc. to pass
through ♦ impervious to water. 2 not
influenced by something or affected by it
♦ impervious to criticism. [from in- meaning
'not' and Latin words per meaning
'through' and via meaning 'way']

impetigo (imp-i-**tiy**-goh) *noun* a contagious skin disease causing spots that form yellowish crusts. [from a Latin word *impetere* meaning 'to attack']

impetuous (im-**pet**-yoo-əs) *adjective* **1** acting hastily without thinking. **2** moving quickly or violently ♦ *He made an impetuous dash for the exit.* **impetuously** *adverb* **impetuosity** *noun* [same origin as for *impetus*]

impetus (**im**-pit-əs) *noun* **1** the force or energy that makes a body move and keep moving. **2** a driving force ♦ *The ceasefire gave an impetus to peace talks.* [a Latin word meaning 'an attack']

impiety (im-**piy**-iti) *noun* (**impieties**) a lack of piety or reverence.

impinge *verb* **1** to influence something or have an important effect on it ♦ *The economic recession impinged on all aspects of our lives.* **2** to encroach on something. [from *in-* meaning 'in' and a Latin word *pangere* meaning 'to drive in']

impious (**imp**-iəs) *adjective* not reverent, wicked. **impiously** *adverb*

impish *adjective* like an imp, mischievous. **impishly** *adverb* **impishness** *noun*

implacable (im-**plak**-əbəl) *adjective* not able to be placated, relentless. **implacability** *adverb* **implacably** *adverb*

implant[1] (im-**plahnt**) *verb* **1** to plant or insert something. **2** to put an idea in the mind. **3** (*Medicine*) to insert tissue or other substance in a living thing. **implantation** *noun*

implant[2] (**im**-plahnt) *noun* something that has been implanted, especially an organ or piece of tissue inserted in the body.

implausible *adjective* not plausible or probable. **implausibility** *noun* **implausibly** *adverb*

implement[1] (**im**-pli-mənt) *noun* a tool or instrument for a special purpose. [from a Latin word *implere* meaning 'to fill up']

implement[2] (**im**-pli-ment) *verb* to put something into effect ♦ *We have already implemented the scheme.* **implementation** *noun*

implicate *verb* **1** to involve a person in a crime or act of wrongdoing, or to show that a particular person is involved. **2** to imply something as a meaning or consequence. [same origin as for *implicit*]

implication *noun* **1** the act of implicating

someone. **2** implying something, or something that is implied.

implicit (im-**pliss**-it) *adjective* **1** implied but not stated openly. (Compare **explicit**.) **2** absolute or unquestioning ♦ *She expects implicit obedience.* **implicitly** *adverb* [from a Latin word *implicitus* meaning 'folded in']

implode *verb* to burst or cause something to burst inwards. **implosion** *noun* [from *in-* meaning 'in', on the model of *explode*]

implore *verb* to beg someone to do something, to entreat someone. **imploring** *adjective* **imploringly** *adverb* [from *in-* meaning 'in' and a Latin word *plorare* meaning 'to weep']

imply *verb* (**implies**, **implied**, **implying**) **1** to suggest something without stating it directly. SYNONYMS: suggest, hint, indicate, intimate, make out. **2** to suggest or entail something as a consequence ♦ *A creation implies a creator.* [same origin as for *implicit*]

impolite *adjective* not polite. **impolitely** *adverb*

impolitic (im-**pol**-i-tik) *adjective* unwise, not advisable.

imponderable (im-**pon**-der-əbəl) *adjective* difficult or impossible to judge or estimate.
imponderable *noun* an imponderable factor, such as an emotion or subjective quality. [from *in-* meaning 'not' and a Latin word *pondus* meaning 'a weight']

import[1] (im-**port**) *verb* **1** to bring in goods from another country. **2** (*Computing*) to transfer data into a file or document. **importation** *noun* **importer** *noun* [from *in-* meaning 'into' and a Latin word *portare* meaning 'to carry']

import[2] (**im**-port) *noun* **1** something that has been imported from another country, or the process of importing goods. **2** a meaning implied by something. **3** importance ♦ *The message was of great import.*

important *adjective* **1** having or able to have a great effect. SYNONYMS: major, significant, fundamental. **2** having great authority or influence. SYNONYMS: prominent, distinguished, eminent, influential. **importantly** *adverb* **importance** *noun* [same origin as for *import*, in a meaning 'to have significance']

importunate (im-**por**-tew-nət) *adjective* making persistent or pressing requests.

importunity (im-per-*tewn*-iti) *noun* [from a Latin word *importunus* meaning 'inconvenient']

importune (im-per-*tewn*) *verb* to harass someone with persistent requests.

impose *verb* 1 to put a tax or obligation on someone or something ♦ *The government has imposed heavy duties on tobacco.* 2 to inflict a difficulty on someone ♦ *The expense of the trip imposed a great strain on their resources.* 3 to force something to be accepted ♦ *He was always imposing his ideas on the group.* **to impose on** to take unfair advantage of someone ♦ *We don't want to impose on your hospitality.* [from *in-* meaning 'on' and a Latin word *positum* meaning 'placed']

imposing *adjective* grand and impressive.

imposition *noun* 1 the act of imposing something. 2 a burden or obligation that has been imposed. 3 an unfair burden or inconvenience ♦ *I hope my visit won't be an imposition.*

impossible *adjective* 1 not possible, unable to be done or to exist. 2 difficult to deal with ♦ *an impossible person.* **impossibility** *noun* **impossibly** *adverb*

impostor *noun* a person who dishonestly pretends to be someone else. [same origin as for *impose*]

impotent (im-po-tənt) *adjective* 1 powerless, unable to take action. 2 (said about a man) unable to have an erection or to reach orgasm. **impotently** *adverb* **impotence** *noun*

impound *verb* 1 to seize someone's property and take it into legal custody, to confiscate something. 2 to shut up cattle in a pound. 3 (said about a dam) to collect or confine water in a natural or artificial lake. [from *in-* meaning 'into' and *pound*[2]]

impoverish *verb* 1 to make someone poor. 2 to make something poor in quality ♦ *impoverished soil.* **impoverishment** *noun* [from *in-* meaning 'into' and an Old French word *povre* meaning 'poor']

impracticable *adjective* not able to be done in practice. **impracticability** *noun* **impracticably** *adverb*

impractical *adjective* not practical, unwise. **impracticality** *noun*

imprecation (impri-*kay*-shən) *noun* (*formal*) a spoken curse. [from a Latin word *imprecari* meaning 'to invoke evil']

imprecise *adjective* not precise.

imprecisely *adverb* **imprecision** *noun*

impregnable (im-*preg*-nəbəl) *adjective* strong enough to be safe against attack ♦ *an impregnable fortress.* **impregnability** *noun* **impregnably** *adverb* [from *in-* meaning 'not' and an Old French word *prenable*, from a Latin word *prehendere* meaning 'to seize']

impregnate (im-*preg*-nayt) *verb* 1 to introduce sperm into a female animal or pollen into a plant to fertilize it. 2 to soak or saturate a substance ♦ *The cloth was impregnated with a cleaning liquid.* **impregnation** *noun* [from *in-* meaning 'into' and a Latin word *pregnare* meaning 'to be pregnant']

impresario (impri-*sar*-i-oh) *noun* (**impresarios**) a person who manages a theatre or music company and organizes productions. [an Italian word, from *impresa* meaning 'an undertaking']

impress[1] (im-*press*) *verb* 1 to make a person admire or respect someone or something. 2 to fix an idea firmly in the mind ♦ *We must impress on them the need for speed.* 3 to press a mark into something. [from *in-* meaning 'into' and an Old French word *presser* meaning 'to press']

impress[2] (im-*press*) *noun* a mark pressed into something.

impression *noun* 1 an effect produced on the mind. 2 a vague or unclear idea, belief, or memory. 3 an imitation of a person or sound, done for entertainment. 4 a mark pressed into a surface. 5 a printing of a book with few or no alterations to its contents. **to be under the impression** to think (that something is a fact).

impressionable *adjective* easily influenced or affected by someone else. **impressionably** *adverb* **impressionability** *noun*

impressionism *noun* 1 (*Art*) a style of painting in the late 19th century giving the general visual impression of a subject at a particular moment, especially by using the effects of light, rather than with accurate or elaborate detail. 2 a similar style in music or literature. **impressionist** *noun* **impressionistic** *adjective*

impressive *adjective* making a strong impression; bringing admiration and approval. SYNONYMS: striking, imposing, splendid. **impressively** *adverb*

imprint [1] (**im**-print) *noun* a mark made by pressing or stamping a surface. [from a Latin word *imprimere* meaning 'to press in']

imprint [2] (**im**-print) *verb* **1** to impress or stamp a mark on something. **2** to establish an idea firmly in the mind.

imprison *verb* to confine someone, especially in a prison. **imprisonment** *noun*

improbable *adjective* not likely to be true or to happen. **improbably** *adverb* **improbability** *noun*

impromptu (im-**promp**-tew) *adverb & adjective* without preparation or rehearsal.
impromptu *noun* (**impromptus**) a short improvised musical composition, usually for piano. [from a Latin phrase *in promptu* meaning 'in readiness']

improper *adjective* **1** unsuitable or wrong. **2** not conforming to the rules of social or lawful conduct. **3** indecent. SYNONYMS: indecent, crude, obscene, offensive. **improperly** *adverb*

improper fraction *noun* a fraction with a value greater than 1, with the numerator greater than the denominator, e.g $\frac{7}{3}$.

impropriety (im-prə-**priy**-iti) *noun* (**improprieties**) improper behaviour, or an improper act or remark.

improve *verb* to make something better, or to become better. **to improve on** to produce a thing that is better than something. **improvable** *adjective*

improvement *noun* **1** the process of improving something. **2** an addition or alteration that improves something or adds to its value.

improvident (im-**prov**-idənt) *adjective* not providing or planning for the future, wasting your resources. **improvidence** *noun* **improvidently** *adverb*

improvise (im-prə-**viyz**) *verb* **1** to compose or perform something without any preparation or rehearsal. **2** to make or provide something quickly with whatever is available ♦ *We had to improvise a bed from cushions and rugs.* **improvisation** *noun* **improviser** *noun* [from *in-* meaning 'in' and a Latin word *provisus* meaning 'provided for']

imprudent (im-**proo**-dənt) *adjective* unwise or rash. **imprudently** *adverb* **imprudence** *noun*

impudent (im-**pew**-dənt) *adjective* cheeky or disrespectful. **impudence** *noun* **impudently** *adverb* [from *in-* meaning 'in' and a Latin word *pudens* meaning 'ashamed']

impugn (im-**pewn**) *verb* to express doubts about the truth or honesty of a statement or attitude ♦ *We do not impugn their motives.* [from a Latin word *impugnare* meaning 'to attack']

impulse *noun* **1** a sudden desire to do something ♦ *I did it on impulse.* **2** a push or impetus. **3** (*Physics*) a force acting on a body for a short time ♦ *an electrical impulse.* [same origin as for *impel*]

impulsion *noun* **1** the force behind a process. **2** a strong desire to do something.

impulsive *adjective* acting or done on impulse, without much thought. **impulsively** *adverb* **impulsiveness** *noun*

impunity (im-**pewn**-iti) *noun* freedom from punishment or injury ♦ *Gangs were using violence with impunity.* [from *in-* meaning 'without' and a Latin word *poena* meaning 'penalty']

impure *adjective* **1** not pure, mixed with a foreign substance. SYNONYMS: contaminated, polluted, unclean, infected. **2** morally wrong, indecent.

impurity *noun* (**impurities**) **1** the state of being impure. **2** a foreign substance that makes another substance impure.

impute (im-**pewt**) *verb* to attribute or ascribe a fault to someone. **imputation** *noun* [from a Latin word *imputare* meaning 'to bring into consideration']

In *abbreviation* (*Chemistry*) the symbol for indium.

in *preposition* **1** expressing a position or state of being enclosed or surrounded by something ♦ *in the house* ♦ *in bed.* **2** expressing movement into an enclosed or surrounded position ♦ *Then we went in the garden.* **3** expressing a period of time that something takes ♦ *We did it in three hours.* **4** expressing an interval of time after which something will happen ♦ *The train will arrive in half an hour.* **5** expressing a state, condition, or arrangement ♦ *The curtain hung in folds* ♦ *She was dressed in red* ♦ *The serial is in four parts.* **6** expressing an activity or occupation ♦ *His father was in the army.* **7** expressing a method or means ♦ *He spoke in German* ♦ *I paid in cash.* **8** expressing identity ♦ *Kate found a true friend in Mary.* **9** expressing an influence

♦ *He rarely spoke in anger.*

in *adverb* **1** expressing position or movement that involves being enclosed or surrounded ♦ *I opened the door and Charlie came in.* **2** present at home or at some other regular place ♦ *Will the manager be in this afternoon?* **3** favourable or fashionable ♦ *My luck was in that day* ♦ *Long skirts are in again.* **4** (in cricket and baseball) batting ♦ *Which side is in?* **5** expressing arrival or receipt ♦ *The train is in already* ♦ *Get the harvest in.*

in *adjective* (*informal*) fashionable ♦ *It's the in thing to do.* **to be in for** to be about to experience something ♦ *She is in for a surprise.* **to be in on** to be aware of or involved in an activity or secret. **in all** in total. **the ins and outs** (*informal*) the details of an activity or process. **in so far as** to the extent that ♦ *He carried out orders only in so far as he did not openly disobey them.* [from an Old English word]

in. *abbreviation* inch(es).

in- *prefix* (changing to **il-** before *l*, **im-** before *b*, *m*, *p*, **ir-** before *r*) **1** not (as in *incorrect*, *indirect*). **2** in, into, towards, or on (as in *include*, *invade*).

inability *noun* being unable to do something.

in absentia (ab-**sent**-iə) *adverb* in his, her, or their absence. [a Latin phrase meaning 'in absence']

inaccessible *adjective* **1** (said about a place) not easy to find or reach. **2** (said about a person) not easy to approach or talk to. **inaccessibility** *noun* **inaccessibly** *adverb*

inaccurate *adjective* not accurate. **inaccuracy** *noun* **inaccurately** *adverb*

inaction *noun* lack of action when some action is expected; doing nothing.

inactive *adjective* not active or working. SYNONYMS: idle, dormant, immobile, inoperative. **inactively** *adverb* **inactivity** *noun*

inadequate *adjective* **1** not adequate, insufficient. **2** (said about a person) not sufficiently able to deal with a situation or to cope generally ♦ *I felt so inadequate.* **inadequately** *adverb* **inadequacy** *noun*

inadmissible *adjective* not allowable. **inadmissibly** *adverb* **inadmissibility** *noun*

inadvertent (in-əd-**ver**-tənt) *adjective* unintentional, not deliberate. **inadvertence** *noun* **inadvertency** *noun* **inadvertently** *adverb*

inadvisable *adjective* not advisable, unwise. **inadvisability** *noun* **inadvisably** *adverb*

inalienable (in-**ay**-li-ən-əbəl) *adjective* not able to be given away or taken away ♦ *an inalienable right.* **inalienability** *noun* **inalienably** *adverb*

inane *adjective* silly, having no sense. **inanely** *adverb* **inanity** (in-**an**-iti) *noun* [from a Latin word *inanis* meaning 'empty']

inanimate (in-**an**-im-ət) *adjective* **1** not having life in the way that animals and humans do. **2** showing no sign of life.

inapplicable (in-ap-**lik**-əbəl) *adjective* not applicable or relevant.

inappropriate (in-ə-**proh**-pri-ət) *adjective* not appropriate, unsuitable. SYNONYMS: unsuitable, inapt, out of place. **inappropriately** *adverb* **inappropriateness** *noun*

inarticulate (in-ar-**tik**-yoo-lət) *adjective* **1** unable to speak distinctly or to express ideas clearly. **2** not expressed in words ♦ *They heard an inarticulate cry from the landing.* **inarticulately** *adverb*

inartistic *adjective* showing no skill in art, not artistic. **inartistically** *adverb*

inasmuch as *conjunction* since, because.

inattention *noun* lack of attention, neglect.

inattentive *adjective* not attentive, not paying attention. **inattentively** *adverb* **inattentiveness** *noun*

inaudible (in-**aw**-dibəl) *adjective* unable to be heard, not audible. **inaudibility** *noun* **inaudibly** *adverb*

inaugural (in-**awg**-yoor-əl) *adjective* of or for an inauguration ♦ *an inaugural ceremony.*

inaugurate (in-**awg**-yoor-ayt) *verb* **1** to admit a person formally to office ♦ *Tomorrow they will inaugurate the new president.* **2** to begin or introduce an important project or undertaking. **inauguration** *noun* **inaugurator** *noun* [from a Latin word *inauguratus* meaning 'interpreted as omens']

inauspicious (in-aw-**spish**-əs) *adjective* not auspicious; unlikely to be successful. **inauspiciously** *adverb*

inborn *adjective* existing in a person or animal from birth, natural ♦ *an inborn ability.*

inbred *adjective* **1** produced by inbreeding. **2** inborn.

inbreeding noun breeding from closely related individuals.

in-built adjective built-in.

Inc. abbreviation (North Amer.) (in company names) Incorporated.

Inca noun (**Inca** or **Incas**) a member of a South American Indian people living in Peru and the central Andes before the Spanish conquest.

incalculable adjective too great to be calculated, enormous ♦ *The damage was incalculable.* **incalculably** adverb **incalculability** noun

incandescent (in-kan-dess-ənt) adjective **1** giving out light when heated, shining. **2** (informal) extremely angry. **incandescence** noun [from a Latin word *incandescere* meaning 'to become white']

incandescent lamp noun an electric lamp with a filament that glows white-hot as it gives off light.

incantation (in-kan-tay-shən) noun a set of words or sounds uttered as a magic spell or charm. **incantatory** adjective [from *in-* meaning 'in' and a Latin word *cantare* meaning 'to sing']

incapable adjective not able to do something ♦ *They seemed incapable of understanding the problem.* **incapability** noun **incapably** adverb

incapacitate (in-kə-pas-i-tayt) verb **1** to disable someone. **2** to make someone ineligible for something. **incapacitation** noun

incapacity noun **1** inability to do something or to manage your affairs. **2** lack of sufficient strength or power.

incarcerate (in-kar-ser-ayt) verb to imprison someone. **incarceration** noun [from *in-* meaning 'in' and a Latin word *carcer* meaning 'prison']

incarnate (in-kar-nət) adjective having a body or human form ♦ *a devil incarnate.* [from *in-* meaning 'in' and a Latin word *carnis* meaning 'of flesh']

incarnation (in-kar-nay-shən) noun the process of taking a human form. **the Incarnation** (in Christian teaching) God's taking a human form as Christ.

incautious (in-kaw-shəs) adjective not cautious, rash. **incautiously** adverb

incendiary (in-sen-di-er-i) adjective **1** (said about a bomb or other device) designed to cause widespread fires. **2** tending to stir up conflict.

incendiary noun (**incendiaries**) an incendiary bomb or other device. [same origin as for *incense*]

incense¹ (in-sens) noun a substance that produces a sweet-smelling smoke when it burns.
incense verb to perfume a place with incense or a perfume. [from a Latin word *incendere* meaning 'to set fire to']

incense² (in-sens) verb to make someone angry. [same origin as for *incense*¹]

incentive (in-sen-tiv) noun something that encourages a person to do something or to work harder. [from a Latin word *incentivum* meaning 'something that sets the tune']

inception (in-sep-shən) noun the beginning of an activity or institution. [from a Latin word *incipere* meaning 'to begin']

incessant (in-sess-ənt) adjective unceasing, continually repeated. SYNONYMS: constant, endless, continual, persistent. **incessantly** adverb [from *in-* meaning 'not' and a Latin word *cessare* meaning 'to cease']

incest (in-sest) noun sexual relations between people regarded as too closely related to marry each other. [from *in-* meaning 'not' and a Latin word *castus* meaning 'pure']

incestuous (in-sess-tew-əs) adjective involving or guilty of incest.

inch noun **1** a measure of length, equal to one twelfth of a foot (2.54 cm). **2** an amount of rainfall that would cover a surface to a depth of 1 inch. **3** a very small amount ♦ *They would not yield an inch.* **inch** verb to move slowly and gradually ♦ *The crows began to inch forward.* [from an Old English word]

incidence (in-si-dəns) noun **1** the rate at which something, especially crime or disease, occurs or affects people or things ♦ *the lower incidence of heart disease in Mediterranean countries.* **2** (Physics) the falling of something, e.g. a ray of light, on a surface. [from a Latin word *incidens* meaning 'happening']

incident noun **1** an event or happening, especially something short or relatively minor. **2** public disturbance or violence ♦ *The protest went off without incident.* **3** an event that attracts special attention. **incident** adjective **1** liable to happen as part of an activity ♦ *the dangers incident to mountaineering.* **2** (Physics) falling on a surface ♦ *incident light.*

incidental *adjective* **1** happening as a minor part of something else. SYNONYMS: secondary, unimportant, minor, trivial. **2** happening by chance.

incidental expenses *plural noun* minor expenses involved in an undertaking, such as train fares and meals.

incidental music *noun* music played as a background to the action of a film or play.

incidentally *adverb* **1** in an incidental way. **2** as an unconnected comment, by the way.

incinerate (in-sin-er-ayt) *verb* to destroy something, especially waste material, by burning it completely. **incineration** *noun* [from *in-* meaning 'in' and a Latin word *cineris* meaning 'of ashes']

incinerator (in-sin-er-ayt-er) *noun* a furnace or other device for burning waste material.

incipient (in-sip-iənt) *adjective* in its early stages, beginning ♦ *incipient decay.* [from a Latin word *incipere* meaning 'to begin']

incise (in-siyz) *verb* to cut or engrave something into a surface. [from *in-* meaning 'into' and a Latin word *caesum* meaning 'cut']

incision (in-si-zhən) *noun* **1** a cut, especially one made in a surgical operation.

incisive (in-siy-siv) *adjective* clear and sharp ♦ *incisive comments.* **incisively** *adverb* **incisiveness** *noun*

incisor (in-siy-zer) *noun* each of the sharp-edged front teeth in the upper and lower jaws.

incite (in-siyt) *verb* to urge someone on to action, to stir someone up. **incitement** *noun* [from *in-* meaning 'towards' and a Latin word *citare* meaning 'to rouse']

incivility *noun* (**incivilities**) rude or impolite remarks or behaviour.

inclement (in-klem-ənt) *adjective* (said about the weather) cold, wet, or stormy. **inclemency** *noun* [from *in-* meaning 'not' and a Latin word *clemens* meaning 'mild']

inclination *noun* **1** a natural tendency to act in a certain way. **2** a liking or preference. **3** a slope or slant; a leaning or bending movement.

incline [1] (in-kliyn) *verb* **1** to lean or slope. **2** to bend the head or body forward. **3** to cause someone to think a certain way ♦ *His behaviour inclines me to think he may be drunk.* **to be inclined** to have a certain

tendency or willingness ♦ *The window is inclined to rattle* ♦ *I'm inclined to agree with you.* [from a Latin word *inclinare* meaning 'to bend']

incline [2] (in-kliyn) *noun* a slope.

include *verb* **1** to have or treat something or someone as part of a whole. **2** to put something or someone into a certain category. **inclusion** *noun* [from a Latin word *includere* meaning 'to enclose']

inclusive *adjective* **1** including the limits mentioned and the part between ♦ *Read from pages 3 to 11 inclusive.* **2** including much or everything. **inclusively** *adverb*

incognito (in-kog-nee-toh or in-**kog**-nit-oh) *adjective & adverb* with your name or identity kept secret ♦ *The film star was travelling incognito.*
incognito *noun* (**incognitos**) an identity assumed by someone who is incognito. [an Italian word meaning 'unknown']

incoherent (in-koh-heer-ənt) *adjective* not speaking or reasoning in an intelligible way. **incoherently** *adverb* **incoherence** *noun*

incombustible *adjective* not able to be burnt by fire.

income *noun* money received regularly from doing work or from investments. SYNONYMS: pay, earnings, salary, wages. [from *in* and *come*]

income tax *noun* tax paid on a person's income.

incoming *adjective* **1** coming in ♦ *incoming phone calls.* **2** about to take over from someone else ♦ *the incoming chairman.*

incommensurate *adjective* not in proportion, out of keeping.

incommode (in-kə-mohd) *verb* (*formal*) to inconvenience someone. **incommodious** *adjective* [from *in-* meaning 'not' and a Latin word *commodus* meaning 'convenient']

incommunicable *adjective* unable to be communicated to other people.

incommunicado (in-kə-mew-ni-kah-doh) *adjective* not able or allowed to communicate with other people ♦ *The prisoner was held incommunicado.* [from a Spanish word *incomunicado* meaning 'deprived of communication']

incomparable (in-komp-er-əbəl) *adjective* without an equal, too good to be compared. **incomparably** *adverb* **incomparability** *noun*

incompatible (in-kəm-**pat**-ibəl) *adjective*
not able to exist or be used together.
incompatibly *adverb* **incompatibility** *noun*

incompetent (in-**kom**-pi-tənt) *adjective* not
able or skilled enough to do something.
SYNONYMS: ineffective, incapable, inept.
incompetently *adverb* **incompetence** *noun*

incomplete *adjective* not complete.
incompletely *adverb* **incompleteness** *noun*

incomprehensible (in-kom-pri-**hen**-sibəl)
adjective not able to be understood.
incomprehensibility *noun* **incomprehensibly**
adverb

incomprehension (in-kom-pri-**hen**-shən)
noun failure to understand.

inconceivable *adjective* **1** unable to be
imagined. **2** impossible to believe, most
unlikely. **inconceivably** *adverb*

inconclusive *adjective* (said about evidence
or an argument) not fully convincing, not
decisive. **inconclusively** *adverb*
inconclusiveness *noun*

incongruous (in-**kong**-groo-əs) *adjective*
not in keeping with its surroundings, out
of place. **incongruously** *adverb* **incongruity**
(in-kong-**groo**-iti) *noun* [from *in-* meaning
'not' and a Latin word *congruere* meaning
'to agree']

inconsequent (in-**kon**-si-kwənt) *adjective*
not following logically, irrelevant.
inconsequence *noun* **inconsequently** *adverb*

inconsequential (in-kon-si-**kwen**-shəl)
adjective not significant or important.
inconsequentially *adverb*

inconsiderable *adjective* not worth
considering, of small size or amount or
value.

inconsiderate *adjective* not considerate
towards other people. **inconsiderately**
adverb **inconsiderateness** *noun*

inconsistent *adjective* not consistent.
inconsistency *noun* **inconsistently** *adverb*

inconsolable (in-kən-**soh**-lə-bəl) *adjective*
too upset or distressed to be consoled.
inconsolably *adverb*

inconspicuous *adjective* not attracting
attention or clearly visible.
inconspicuously *adverb* **inconspicuousness**
noun

incontestable (in-kən-**test**-əbəl) *adjective*
not able to be disputed. **incontestably**
adverb

incontinent *adjective* unable to control the
bladder or bowels. **incontinence** *noun*

incontrovertible (in-kon-trə-**vert**-ibəl)
adjective unable to be denied,
indisputable. **incontrovertibility** *noun*
incontrovertibly *adverb* [from *in-* meaning
'not' and a Latin word *controversus*
meaning 'disputed']

inconvenience *noun* **1** the state of being
inconvenient or slightly troublesome.
2 something that is inconvenient or
slightly troublesome.
inconvenience *verb* to cause someone
slight trouble.

inconvenient *adjective* not convenient,
slightly troublesome. **inconveniently**
adverb

incorporate (in-**kor**-per-ayt) *verb* **1** to
include something as a part of a larger
thing ♦ *Your suggestions will be incorporated
in the plan.* **2** to form a company or
organization into a legal corporation.
incorporation *noun* [from *in-* meaning 'into'
and a Latin word *corpus* meaning 'body']

incorrect *adjective* not correct, wrong.
SYNONYMS: wrong, inaccurate, mistaken,
erroneous. **incorrectly** *adverb* **incorrectness**
noun

incorrigible (in-**ko**-ri-jibəl) *adjective* (said
about a person or behaviour) not able to
be reformed or improved ♦ *an incorrigible
liar.* **incorrigibility** *noun* **incorrigibly** *adverb*
[from *in-* meaning 'not' and a Latin word
corrigere meaning 'to correct']

incorruptible (in-kə-**rupt**-ibəl) *adjective*
1 not able to be corrupted, especially by
bribery. **2** not subject to decay or death.
incorruptibility *noun*

increase[1] (in-**kreess**) *verb* to make
something greater in size or amount, or
to become greater. SYNONYMS: extend,
lengthen, strengthen, raise (prices). [from *in-*
meaning 'in' and a Latin word *crescere*
meaning 'to grow']

increase[2] (in-**kreess**) *noun* **1** the process of
increasing. **2** an amount by which
something increases ♦ *an increase of 50%.*

increasingly *adverb* more and more.

incredible *adjective* **1** unbelievable. **2** hard
to believe, very surprising. **3** (*informal*)
very good. **incredibly** *adverb*
◊ Do not confuse this word with
incredulous, which has a different
meaning.

incredulous (in-kred-yoo-ləs) *adjective* not believing someone, showing disbelief. **incredulity** (in-kri-dew-liti) *noun* **incredulously** *adverb*
◊ Do not confuse this word with **incredible**, which has a different meaning.

increment (in-kri-mənt) *noun* an increase, an added amount, especially a regular increase in salary. **incremental** *adjective*

incriminate *verb* to show a person to have been involved in a crime. **incrimination** *noun* [from *in-* meaning 'into' and a Latin word *criminare* meaning 'to accuse of a crime']

incrustation *noun* 1 the process of forming a crust. 2 a crust or deposit that forms on a surface. [from *in-* meaning 'into' and a Latin word *crustare* meaning 'to form a crust']

incubate *verb* 1 to hatch eggs by keeping them warm. 2 to cause bacteria or a disease to develop. [from *in-* meaning 'on' and a Latin word *cubare* meaning 'to lie']

incubation *noun* the process of incubating.

incubation period *noun* the time it takes for symptoms of a disease to become apparent in an infected person.

incubator *noun* 1 a device for hatching eggs or developing bacteria by artificial warmth. 2 an apparatus in which a baby born prematurely can be kept at a controlled temperature and supplied with oxygen.

incubus (ink-yoo-bəs) *noun* (**incubuses**) an evil spirit that visits a sleeping person. [from a Latin word *incubo* meaning 'nightmare']

inculcate (in-kul-kayt) *verb* to influence someone with ideas by persistent instruction ◆ *They attempted to inculcate obedience in young children.* **inculcation** *noun* [from *in-* meaning 'on' and a Latin word *calcare* meaning 'to tread']

incumbency (in-kum-bən-si) *noun* (**incumbencies**) the position of an incumbent.

incumbent (in-kum-bənt) *adjective* forming an obligation or duty ◆ *It is incumbent on you to warn people of the danger.*
incumbent *noun* a person who holds a particular office. [from *in-* meaning 'on' and a Latin word *cumbens* meaning 'lying']

incur *verb* (**incurred, incurring**) to undergo something unwelcome as a result of your own actions ◆ *We incurred great expense on our journey.* [from *in-* meaning 'on' and a Latin word *currere* meaning 'to run']

incurable *adjective* unable to be cured. **incurable** *noun* a person with an incurable disease. **incurability** *noun* **incurably** *adverb*

incurious *adjective* feeling or showing no curiosity about something. **incuriously** *adverb*

incursion *noun* a sudden raid or brief invasion. [same origin as for *incur*]

indebted *adjective* owing money or gratitude to someone. **indebtedness** *noun*

indecent *adjective* offending against generally accepted standards of decency. SYNONYMS: improper, crude, obscene, offensive. **indecency** *noun* **indecently** *adverb*

indecent assault *noun* sexual assault not involving rape.

indecipherable *adjective* too difficult or untidy to be deciphered.

indecision *noun* inability to make up your mind, hesitation.

indecisive *adjective* not able to make decisions promptly. **indecisively** *adverb* **indecisiveness** *noun*

indecorous (in-dek-er-əs) *adjective* not in good taste, improper. **indecorously** *adverb*

indeed *adverb* 1 truly, really ◆ *It is indeed a remarkable story.* 2 used to make a meaning stronger ◆ *The house is very nice indeed.* 3 admittedly ◆ *It is, indeed, their first attempt.* 4 used to express surprise or disapproval ◆ *Does she indeed!* [from the phrase *in deed*, meaning 'in fact']

indefatigable (indi-fat-ig-əbəl) *adjective* not tiring easily, having a lot of stamina. **indefatigably** *adverb*

indefensible *adjective* not able to be defended or justified. **indefensibility** *noun* **indefensibly** *adverb*

indefinable (indi-fiy-nəbəl) *adjective* not able to be defined or described clearly. **indefinably** *adverb*

indefinite *adjective* not clearly defined or decided, vague.

indefinite article *noun* the word 'a' or 'an'.

indefinitely *adverb* 1 for an indefinite or unlimited time. 2 in an indefinite way.

indelible *adjective* 1 impossible to rub out or remove. 2 not able to be forgotten ◆ *The incident left an indelible impression on* *them.* **indelibly** *adverb* [from *in-* meaning 'not' and a Latin word *delere* meaning 'to destroy']

indelicate *adjective* **1** slightly indecent. **2** tactless. **indelicacy** *noun* **indelicately** *adverb*

indemnify (in-dem-ni-fiy) *verb* (**indemnifies, indemnified, indemnifying**) **1** to protect or insure someone against penalties incurred by their actions. **2** to compensate someone for harm or loss they have suffered. [same origin as for *indemnity*]

indemnity *noun* (**indemnities**) **1** protection or insurance against penalties incurred by your actions. **2** compensation for damage done. [from a Latin word *indemnis* meaning 'free from loss']

indent¹ (in-dent) *verb* **1** to make notches or recesses in something. **2** to start a line of print or writing further from the margin than the others. **3** to place an official order for goods or stores. **indentation** *noun* [from *in-* meaning 'in' and a Latin word *dens* meaning 'tooth' (because the indentations looked like teeth)]

indent² (in-dent) *noun* an official order for goods or stores.

indenture (in-den-cher) *noun* or **indentures** *plural noun* a written contract or agreement, especially one binding an apprentice to work for a particular employer.
indenture *verb* to bind an apprentice by means of indentures. [same origin as for *indent* (because each copy of the agreement had notches cut into it, so that the copies could be fitted together to show that they were genuine)]

independence *noun* **1** the state of being independent. **2** the time when a country is no longer politically dependent on another.

independent *adjective* **1** free from the control or authority of another person, country, or thing. SYNONYMS: free, autonomous, self-governing. **2** not depending on someone else for an income ♦ *He has independent means.* **3** separate, not connected with anything else. **4** (said about a person) wanting to avoid the influence of other people.
independent *noun* a politician who is not a member of any political party.
independently *adverb*

independent school *noun* a school that is not controlled by a local authority and does not receive a government grant.

in-depth *adjective* detailed and thorough.

indescribable *adjective* too unusual, extreme, or beautiful to be described. **indescribably** *adverb*

indestructible *adjective* not able to be destroyed. **indestructibility** *noun* **indestructibly** *adverb*

indeterminable *adjective* impossible to discover or decide. **indeterminably** *adverb* ◊ Do not confuse this word with **indeterminate**, which has a different meaning.

indeterminate *adjective* not fixed or decided exactly; vague. **indeterminately** *adverb* ◊ Do not confuse this word with **indeterminable**, which has a different meaning.

index *noun* (**indexes** or in technical uses **indices** (in-di-seez)) **1** an alphabetical list of names, titles, subjects, etc., especially one at the end of a book, showing where items occur in the text. **2** a number indicating how prices or wages have changed from a previous level ♦ *the retail price index.* **3** (*Mathematics*) a raised number (called an *exponent*) written to the right of another number to show how many times the main number is to be multiplied by itself.
index *verb* **1** to make an index to a book etc. **2** to enter an item in an index. **3** to link the level of prices or wages to a price index. **indexer** *noun* [a Latin word meaning 'pointer']

indexation *noun* the practice of making wages, pensions, etc. index-linked.

index finger *noun* the forefinger.

index-linked *adjective* (said about wages or prices) adjusted according to the level of a prices index.

Indian *adjective* to do with or coming from India in southern Asia.
Indian *noun* **1** a person born in India or descended from people born there. **2** a Native American.

Indian ink *noun* a deep black ink of a kind made originally in China and Japan.

Indian summer *noun* a period of dry sunny weather in late autumn; a period of tranquil enjoyment late in life.

India rubber noun a rubber for rubbing out pencil or ink marks.

indicate verb 1 to point something out or make it known. SYNONYMS: show, point out. 2 to be a sign of something or show its presence. SYNONYMS: signify, betoken, denote. 3 to show the need of a course of action ♦ Immediate hospital treatment is indicated. 4 to state something briefly ♦ He indicated that we should follow him. 5 (said of a driver) to use an indicator to show the intention of making a turn. **indication** noun [from in- meaning 'towards' and a Latin word dicatum meaning 'proclaimed']

indicative (in-dik-ətiv) adjective 1 giving an indication ♦ The damage is indicative of an accident. 2 (Grammar) (said about the form of a verb) used to make a statement, not a command or wish, e.g. He said or She is coming.
indicative noun the indicative form of a verb.

indicator noun 1 a thing that indicates or points to something. 2 a meter or gauge. 3 an information board at an airport or railway station. 4 a flashing light on a vehicle used to indicate a turn. 5 (Chemistry) a chemical compound (such as litmus) that changes colour in the presence of a particular substance or condition.

indict (in-diyt) verb to formally accuse someone of a serious crime. [from a Latin word indicere meaning 'to proclaim']

indictable (in-diyt-əbəl) adjective (said about an offence) making the person who commits it liable to be charged with a serious crime.

indictment (in-diyt-mənt) noun 1 a written statement of charges against an accused person. 2 a piece of information or evidence that shows something to be wrong or contemptible.

indie noun (informal) an independent film or record company.

indifferent adjective 1 not interested in something or not caring about it. SYNONYMS: unconcerned, uninterested, uncaring, apathetic. 2 not very good, fairly bad. **indifferently** adverb **indifference** noun

indigenous (in-dij-in-əs) adjective (said about plants, animals, or inhabitants) growing or originating in a particular country, native ♦ The koala bear is indigenous to Australia. [from a Latin word indigena meaning 'born in a country']

indigent (in-dij-ənt) adjective poor or needy. **indigence** noun [from a Latin word indigere meaning 'to lack']

indigestible (indi-jest-ibəl) adjective difficult or impossible to digest. **indigestibility** noun

indigestion (indi-jes-chən) noun pain or discomfort caused by difficulty in digesting food.

indignant adjective feeling or showing anger about something unjust. SYNONYMS: angry, annoyed, incensed, resentful. **indignantly** adverb [from a Latin word indignari meaning 'to regard as unworthy']

indignation noun anger at something unjust or wicked.

indignity noun (indignities) 1 the quality of causing shame or humiliation. 2 treatment that makes a person feel ashamed or humiliated.

indigo noun a deep-blue dye or colour. [via Portuguese from a Greek word indikon meaning 'Indian dye']

indirect adjective not direct. **indirectly** adverb

indirect object noun (Grammar) the word that receives the action of the verb but is not the primary or direct object. In 'she gave him a book', 'him' is the indirect object. (See object[1].)

indirect question noun a question contained in reported speech, as in She asked me if I felt well.

indirect speech noun another term for **reported speech**.

indirect tax noun a tax on money spent, not directly on income.

indiscipline noun lack of discipline, bad behaviour.

indiscreet adjective 1 revealing secrets or confidences too readily. 2 not cautious, unwise. **indiscreetly** adverb

indiscretion (in-dis-kresh-ən) noun 1 being indiscreet. 2 an indiscreet action or statement.

indiscriminate adjective showing no discrimination, not making a careful choice. **indiscriminately** adverb **indiscrimination** noun

indispensable adjective not able to be dispensed with, essential. **indispensability** noun **indispensably** adverb

indisposed *adjective* **1** slightly unwell. **2** unwilling to do something ♦ *They seem indisposed to help us.*

indisposition *noun* **1** a slight illness. **2** unwillingness.

indisputable (in-dis-pewt-əbəl) *adjective* not able to be challenged or denied. **indisputability** *noun* **indisputably** *adverb*

indissoluble (indi-sol-yoo-bəl) *adjective* not able to be dissolved or destroyed, firm and lasting. **indissolubly** *adverb*

indistinct *adjective* not distinct, unclear. **indistinctly** *adverb* **indistinctness** *noun*

indistinguishable *adjective* not able to be distinguished from something else. **indistinguishably** *adverb*

indium *noun* a soft silvery-white metallic element (symbol In) used in making semiconductors. [from *indigo* (because there are indigo lines in its spectrum)]

individual *adjective* **1** single or separate ♦ *Count each individual word.* **2** of or for one person ♦ *The gifts were wrapped in individual boxes.* **3** characteristic of one particular person or thing ♦ *She has a very individual style.* SYNONYMS: distinctive, characteristic, personal, particular.
individual *noun* **1** one person, plant, or animal considered separately. **2** (*informal*) a person ♦ *He is a most selfish individual.* **individually** *adverb* [from *in-* meaning 'not' and a Latin word *dividuus* meaning 'able to be divided']

individualist *noun* a person who is independent in thought or action. **individualism** *noun* **individualistic** *adjective*

individuality (indi-vid-yoo-al-iti) *noun* the special qualities or character that a person or thing has.

indivisible (indi-viz-ibəl) *adjective* not able to be divided. **indivisibility** *noun* **indivisibly** *adverb*

Indo- *prefix* Indian, Indian and (as in *Indo-Chinese*).

indoctrinate (in-dok-trin-ayt) *verb* to make someone believe particular ideas or doctrines by constantly instructing them. **indoctrination** *noun* [from *in-* meaning 'in' and *doctrine*]

Indo-European *adjective* to do with the family of languages spoken over most of Europe and Asia as far as north India. **Indo-European** *noun* **1** this family of languages. **2** a speaker of any of these languages.

indolent (in-dəl-ənt) *adjective* lazy. **indolence** *noun* **indolently** *adverb* [from *in-* meaning 'into' and a Latin word *dolere* meaning 'to suffer pain or trouble']

indomitable (in-dom-it-əbəl) *adjective* unwilling to yield to difficulty or opposition, unable to be overcome. **indomitability** *noun* **indomitably** *adverb* [from *in-* meaning 'not' and a Latin word *domitare* meaning 'to tame']

indoor *adjective* situated, used, or done inside a building ♦ *indoor games* ♦ *an indoor aerial.*

indoors *adverb* inside a building.

indubitable (in-dew-bit-əbəl) *adjective* not able to be doubted, certain. **indubitably** *adverb* [from *in-* meaning 'not' and a Latin word *dubium* meaning 'doubt']

induce (in-dewss) *verb* **1** to persuade someone to do something. **2** to produce or cause something. **3** to bring on labour in childbirth by artificial means. [from *in-* meaning 'in' and a Latin word *ducere* meaning 'to lead']

inducement *noun* **1** something that persuades someone to do something, an incentive.

induct *verb* to admit someone, especially a member of the clergy, formally into an office. [same origin as for *induce*]

inductance *noun* (*Physics*) the property of producing an electric current by induction.

induction *noun* **1** the process or ceremony of formally inducting someone into an office. **2** (*Philosophy*) logical reasoning that a general law exists because there are particular cases that seem to be examples of it. **3** (*Physics*) production of an electric or magnetic state in an object by bringing an electrified or magnetic object close to but not touching it. **4** (*Physics*) production of an electric current in a circuit by varying the magnetic field. **5** the drawing of a fuel mixture into the cylinders of an internal-combustion engine.

induction coil *noun* (*Physics*) a device like a transformer, for generating an intermittent high voltage from a low voltage.

inductive *adjective* **1** (*Philosophy*) of or using induction ♦ *inductive reasoning.* **2** (*Physics*) using or to do with electric or magnetic induction.

indulge verb 1 to allow someone to have whatever they want. 2 to gratify a wish. **to indulge in** to allow yourself something pleasant ♦ *He indulges in a warm bath before breakfast.* [from a Latin word *indulgere* meaning 'to give free rein to']

indulgence noun 1 enjoying yourself. 2 being indulgent towards someone else. 3 something enjoyable that you allow yourself.

indulgent adjective allowing someone to have whatever they want; kind and lenient. **indulgently** adverb

industrial adjective 1 to do with industry, or working or used in an industry ♦ *industrial machinery.* 2 having many highly developed industries ♦ *the industrial countries of the world.* **industrially** adverb

industrial action noun a strike or other action taken against an employer.

industrial estate noun an area of land developed as a site for industries.

industrialist noun a person who owns or manages an industrial business.

industrialized adjective (said about a country or area) having many industries. **industrialization** noun

industrial relations plural noun relations between workers and managers in industry.

Industrial Revolution noun the expansion of British industry by the use of machines in the late 18th and early 19th centuries.

industrious adjective hard-working. **industriously** adverb **industriousness** noun

industry noun (**industries**) 1 the manufacture or production of goods. 2 a particular branch of this, or any business activity ♦ *the motor industry* ♦ *the tourist industry.* 3 the quality of working hard. [from a Latin word *industria* meaning 'hard work']

inebriated (in-ee-bri-ayt-id) adjective drunk, intoxicated. **inebriation** noun [from *in-* meaning 'into' and a Latin word *ebrius* meaning 'drunk']

inedible adjective not suitable for eating.

ineducable (in-ed-yoo-kǝbǝl) adjective incapable of being educated.

ineffable (in-ef-ǝbǝl) adjective too great to be described ♦ *ineffable joy.* **ineffably** adverb [from *in-* meaning 'not' and a Latin word *effari* meaning 'to utter']

ineffective adjective 1 not effective. SYNONYMS: unsuccessful, useless, futile. 2 (said about a person) inefficient. **ineffectively** adverb

ineffectual adjective not producing the result that is wanted. **ineffectually** adverb

inefficacious adjective (said about a remedy etc.) not having the right effect.

inefficient adjective not making the best use of time and resources. **inefficiency** noun **inefficiently** adverb

inelastic adjective 1 (said about material) not elastic or able to be stretched. 2 (*Physics*) (said about a collision) involving a loss of total kinetic energy.

inelegant adjective not elegant, awkward. **inelegance** noun **inelegantly** adverb

ineligible adjective not eligible. **ineligibility** noun

ineluctable (in-i-luk-tǝbǝl) adjective not able to be resisted or avoided. [from *in-* meaning 'not' and a Latin word *eluctari* meaning 'to struggle out']

inept adjective lacking any skill, awkward or clumsy. **ineptitude** noun **ineptly** adverb [from *in-* meaning 'not' and a Latin word *aptus* meaning 'suitable']

inequality noun (**inequalities**) 1 lack of equality in size or status. 2 (*Mathematics*) a statement that two expressions are not equal.

inequitable (in-ek-wit-ǝbǝl) adjective unfair or unjust. **inequitably** adverb **inequity** noun

ineradicable (in-i-rad-ik-ǝbǝl) adjective not able to be eradicated or got rid of. **ineradicably** adverb

inert adjective 1 not having the power to move or act. 2 without active chemical or other properties, incapable of reacting ♦ *an inert gas.* 3 slow to move or take action. **inertly** adverb **inertness** noun [from a Latin word *iners* meaning 'idle']

inertia (in-er-shǝ) noun 1 slowness to take action. 2 (*Physics*) the property of matter by which it remains in a state of rest or uniform motion in a straight line unless an external force causes it to change. **inertial** adjective

inertia reel noun a type of reel that holds one end of a vehicle seat belt, so that the belt unwinds freely under normal conditions but locks on impact or rapid slowing.

inescapable adjective unavoidable.

inescapably adverb

inessential adjective not essential.
inessential noun an inessential thing.

inestimable (in-**est**-im-əbəl) adjective too great or precious to be estimated.
inestimably adverb

inevitable (in-**ev**-it-əbəl) adjective not able to be prevented, certain to happen.
SYNONYMS: unavoidable, inescapable, certain.
inevitability noun **inevitably** adverb [from in- meaning 'not' and a Latin word evitare meaning 'to avoid']

inexact adjective not exact. **inexactitude** noun **inexactly** adverb

inexcusable adjective not able to be excused or justified. **inexcusably** adverb

inexhaustible adjective not able to be used up, never ending.

inexorable (in-**eks**-er-əbəl) adjective 1 relentless. 2 not able to be persuaded by requests or entreaties. **inexorably** adverb [from in- meaning 'not' and a Latin word exorare meaning 'to plead']

inexpedient adjective not suitable or advisable. **inexpediency** noun

inexpensive adjective not expensive, offering good value for the price.
inexpensively adverb

inexperience noun lack of experience.
inexperienced adjective

inexpert adjective not expert, unskilful.
inexpertly adverb

inexplicable (in-**eks**-plik-əbəl or in-iks-**plik**-əbəl) adjective unable to be explained or accounted for. **inexplicably** adverb [from in- meaning 'not' and a Latin word explicare meaning 'to unfold']

inexpressible adjective not able to be expressed in words. **inexpressibly** adverb

inextricable (in-**eks**-trik-əbəl) adjective 1 unable to be extricated or separated. 2 unable to be disentangled or sorted out.
inextricably adverb

infallible (in-**fal**-ibəl) adjective 1 incapable of making a mistake or being wrong. 2 never failing, always effective ♦ an infallible remedy. SYNONYMS: dependable, reliable, foolproof, unfailing. **infallibility** (in-fali-**bil**-iti) noun **infallibly** adverb

infamous (**in**-fə-məs) adjective well known for some bad quality or action. **infamy** (**in**-fə-mi) noun

infancy noun 1 early childhood, babyhood. 2 an early stage of development.

infant noun a baby or young child. [from a Latin word infans meaning 'unable to speak']

infanta (in-**fant**-ə) noun (historical) the eldest daughter of the ruling king of Spain or Portugal. [a Spanish or Portuguese word, related to infant]

infanticide (in-**fant**-i-siyd) noun the act of killing an infant soon after its birth. [from infant and a Latin word caedere meaning 'to kill']

infantile (**in**-fən-tiyl) adjective 1 to do with infants or infancy. 2 very childish.

infantry noun soldiers who fight on foot. [from an Italian word infante meaning 'a youth']

infantryman noun (**infantrymen**) a soldier in an infantry regiment.

infatuated adjective having an intense but short-lived love for a person or thing.
infatuation noun [from in- meaning 'in' and a Latin word fatuus meaning 'foolish']

infect verb 1 to affect a person or organism with a disease or with bacteria that cause disease. 2 to cause someone to share a feeling ♦ Parents are infected by their children's humour. [from a Latin word infectum meaning 'tainted']

infection noun 1 the process of infecting or the state of being infected. 2 a disease that is spread by infecting people.

infectious adjective 1 (said about a disease) able to be spread by air or water. (Compare **contagious**.) 2 infecting someone with disease. 3 quickly spreading to others ♦ Her joy was infectious.

infer verb (**inferred, inferring**) to reach an opinion from what someone says or does, rather than from an explicit statement ♦ I infer from all your bags that you have been shopping. [from in- meaning 'into' and a Latin word ferre meaning 'to bring']
◊ Do not use **infer** to mean 'imply'. For example, you should say What are you implying?, and not What are you inferring?, to mean 'What are you suggesting?'

inference (**in**-fer-əns) noun 1 the process of inferring something. 2 something that you infer; a conclusion reached by reasoning. **inferential** (in-fer-**en**-shəl) adjective

inferior *adjective* less good or less important than someone or something else; lower in quality or ability.
inferior *noun* a person who is lower than someone else in rank or ability.
inferiority *noun* [from a Latin word meaning 'lower']

inferiority complex *noun* a feeling of being inferior or inadequate, sometimes leading to aggressive behaviour to compensate for it.

infernal *adjective* 1 to do with or like hell ♦ *the infernal regions.* 2 (*informal*) detestable or tiresome ♦ *an infernal nuisance.*
infernally *adverb* [from a Latin word *infernus* meaning 'below', used by Christians to mean 'hell']

inferno (in-**fer**-noh) *noun* (**infernos**) a raging fire; somewhere intensely hot; a place resembling hell. [an Italian word meaning 'hell', related to *infernal*]

infertile *adjective* 1 unable to produce young, not fertile. 2 (said about land) unable to bear crops or vegetation.
infertility *noun*

infest *verb* (said about pests or vermin) to be numerous and troublesome in a place.
infestation *noun* [from a Latin word *infestus* meaning 'hostile']

infidel (in-fid-ǝl) *noun* (used about people in the past) someone who did not believe in a religion. [from *in-* meaning 'not' and a Latin word *fidelis* meaning 'faithful']

infidelity *noun* (**infidelities**) unfaithfulness, or an unfaithful act.

infighting *noun* 1 hidden conflict within a group or organization. 2 boxing closer to an opponent than at arm's length.

infilling *noun* 1 placing of buildings to occupy gaps between existing buildings. 2 building material used to fill gaps and holes.

infiltrate (in-fil-trayt) *verb* 1 to enter a place or organization gradually and without being noticed, usually in order to harm or change it or to spy on it. 2 to pass fluid by filtration. **infiltration** *noun* **infiltrator** *noun* [from *in-* meaning 'into' and *filtrate*]

infinite (in-fin-it) *adjective* 1 having no limit, endless. SYNONYMS: endless, unlimited, limitless. 2 too great or too many to be measured or counted. SYNONYMS: countless, immeasurable. **infinitely** *adverb*

infinitesimal (in-fini-**tess**-imǝl) *adjective* extremely small. **infinitesimally** *adverb* [from a Latin word *infinitesimus*, related to *infinite*]

infinitive (in-**fin**-itiv) *noun* (*Grammar*) the basic form of a verb, not indicating a particular tense, number, or person, in English used with or without *to*, e.g. *stay* in *let them stay* or *allow them to stay.* [from *in-* meaning 'not' and a Latin word *finitivus* meaning 'definite']

infinitude *noun* 1 being infinite. 2 infinity.

infinity (in-**fin**-iti) *noun* 1 an infinite number or amount. 2 (*Mathematics*) a number greater than any countable number, having the symbol ∞.

infirm *adjective* physically weak, especially from old age or illness. [from *in-* meaning 'not' and a Latin word *firmus* meaning 'firm']

infirmary *noun* (**infirmaries**) 1 a hospital. 2 a place in a school or monastery etc. where sick people are cared for.

infirmity *noun* (**infirmities**) physical weakness, or a particular physical weakness.

inflame *verb* 1 to provoke someone to strong feelings or emotion, especially anger. 2 to cause a painful redness and swelling in a part of the body. [from *in-* meaning 'into' and a Latin word *flamma* meaning 'flame']

inflammable *adjective* able to be set on fire. ◊ This word means the same as *flammable*. If you want to say that something is not able to be set on fire, use *non-flammable*.

inflammation *noun* painful redness and swelling in a part of the body, especially as a reaction to injury or infection.

inflammatory (in-**flam**-ǝ-ter-i) *adjective* likely to cause anger or other strong feeling ♦ *an inflammatory speech on immigration.*

inflatable (in-**flayt**-ǝbǝl) *adjective* able to be inflated.

inflate *verb* 1 to fill something with air or gas so that it swells out. 2 to swell out from being filled with air or gas. 3 to puff someone up with pride etc. 4 to increase prices or wages more than is necessary or justified. 5 to cause inflation in a country's economy. [from *in-* meaning 'in' and a Latin word *flatum* meaning 'blown']

inflation *noun* 1 the process of inflating or being inflated. 2 a general increase of prices and fall in the purchasing value of money.

inflationary adjective causing inflation.

inflect verb 1 to change the pitch of the voice in speaking. 2 (Grammar) to change the ending or form of a word to show its tense (present, past, etc.), number (singular or plural), or grammatical relation to other words, e.g. sing changes to sang (past tense), singing (present participle), and sung (past participle), and child changes to children (plural). [from in- meaning 'in' and a Latin word flectere meaning 'to bend']

inflection noun an ending or form of a word used to inflect it, e.g. -ed and -ing.

inflexible adjective 1 not flexible, not able to be bent. 2 not able to be altered ♦ an inflexible rule. 3 refusing to change your mind or be persuaded. **inflexibility** noun **inflexibly** adverb

inflexion noun another spelling of inflection.

inflict verb to make a person suffer something painful or unpleasant. **infliction** noun [from in- meaning 'on' and a Latin word flictum meaning 'struck']

inflorescence (in-flor-ess-əns) noun 1 the process of flowering. 2 (Botany) the flower or flowers of a plant, or their arrangement on a stem. [from a Latin word inflorescere meaning 'to come into flower']

inflow noun 1 an inward flow ♦ the inflow of traffic. 2 an amount that flows in ♦ a large inflow of cash.

influence noun 1 the ability or power to affect the character or behaviour of someone or something. 2 a person or thing with this ability. 3 power arising from a person's position or authority. **influence** verb to have an influence on someone or something. SYNONYMS: affect, impress, have an effect on. [from in- meaning 'on' and a Latin word fluentia meaning 'flowing']

influential (in-floo-en-shəl) adjective having great influence. SYNONYMS: authoritative, important. **influentially** adverb

influenza noun a contagious virus disease causing fever, muscular pain, and catarrh. [an Italian word meaning literally 'influence']

influx noun an inflow, especially of people or things into a place. [from a Latin word influxus, related to influence]

inform verb to give information to someone. SYNONYMS: notify, advise, tell. **to inform on** to give information about someone to the police or other authorities. [from a Latin word informare meaning 'to form an idea about something']

informal adjective 1 not formal, unofficial ♦ an informal interview. 2 (said about clothes) suitable for casual or everyday wear. 3 (said about words or language) used in everyday speech.
◊ In this dictionary, words are described as informal when they are used in everyday speech rather than in more formal writing. **informality** (in-for-mal-iti) noun **informally** adverb

informant noun a person who gives information about someone else.

information noun 1 facts or knowledge learned or provided. 2 data put into a computer.

information science noun the study or use of processes for storing and retrieving information.

information superhighway noun the rapid availability of information, especially on the Internet.

information technology noun the study or use of computer systems for storing, retrieval, and sending information.

informative adjective giving useful information.

informed adjective having good or sufficient knowledge of something ♦ informed opinion.

informer noun a person who reveals information to the police etc. about secret or criminal activities.

infra- prefix below. [from a Latin word infra meaning 'below']

infraction (in-frak-shən) noun an infringement of a law or agreement. [from a Latin word infractio, related to infringe]

infra dig (informal) beneath your dignity. [from a Latin phrase infra dignitatem]

infra-red adjective (said about radiation) having a wavelength that is slightly longer than that of visible light-rays at the red end of the spectrum.

infrastructure *noun* the buildings, physical communications, and organization that form the basis of an enterprise.

infrequent *adjective* occasional, not frequent. SYNONYMS: rare, occasional, uncommon, unusual. **infrequency** *noun* **infrequently** *adverb*

infringe *verb* 1 to break a rule or agreement. 2 to encroach on a person's rights etc. **infringement** *noun* [from *in-* meaning 'into' and a Latin word *frangere* meaning 'to break']

infuriate *verb* to make someone very angry. **infuriating** *adjective* [from *in-* meaning 'into' and a Latin word *furia* meaning 'fury']

infuse *verb* 1 to inspire someone with a feeling ♦ *She infused them all with courage.* 2 to steep tea or herbs in a liquid to extract the flavour; (said about tea etc.) to undergo this process. **infuser** *noun* [from a Latin word *infusum* meaning 'poured in']

infusion *noun* 1 the process of infusing. 2 a liquid made by infusing.

ingenious *adjective* 1 clever at inventing things or devising methods. SYNONYMS: clever, imaginative, inventive. 2 cleverly made ♦ *an ingenious machine.* **ingeniously** *adverb* **ingenuity** (in-jin-yoo-iti) *noun* [from a Latin word *ingenium* meaning 'genius'] ◊ Do not confuse this word with **ingenuous**, which has a different meaning.

ingenuous (in-jen-yoo-əs) *adjective* without artfulness, innocent ♦ *an ingenuous manner.* **ingenuously** *adverb* **ingenuousness** *noun* ◊ Do not confuse this word with **ingenious**, which has a different meaning.

ingest (in-jest) *verb* to take food or drink into the body by swallowing it. **ingestion** *noun* [from a Latin word *ingestum* meaning 'brought in']

inglenook *noun* a space on each side of a recessed fireplace.

inglorious *adjective* 1 not worthy of honour. 2 not famous or well-known, obscure.

ingot (ing-gət) *noun* a rectangular block of cast metal, especially gold. [thought to be from *in-* meaning 'in' and an Old English word *geotan* meaning 'to pour' or 'to cast']

ingrained *adjective* 1 (said about habits or attitudes) firmly established. 2 (said about dirt) deeply embedded in a surface.

ingratiate (in-gray-shi-ayt) *verb* to ingratiate yourself to try to please or flatter someone. [from a Latin phrase *in gratiam* meaning 'into favour']

ingratitude *noun* lack of gratitude when it is due.

ingredient *noun* any of the parts or elements used in a mixture, especially one of the foods used in a recipe. [from a Latin word *ingrediens* meaning 'going in']

ingress *noun* the process of going into a place, or the right to go in. [from *in-* meaning 'in' and a Latin word *gressus* meaning 'going']

ingrowing *adjective* growing abnormally into the flesh ♦ *an ingrowing toenail.*

inhabit *verb* (**inhabited, inhabiting**) to live in a place as your home or environment. SYNONYMS: occupy, populate, live in. [from *in-* meaning 'in' and a Latin word *habitare* meaning 'to occupy']

inhabitable *adjective* suitable to be inhabited.

inhabitant *noun* a person who lives in a place.

inhalant (in-hay-lənt) *noun* a medicinal substance for inhaling.

inhale *verb* to breathe in; to draw air, smoke, gas, etc. into the lungs by breathing. **inhalation** (in-hə-lay-shən) *noun* [from *in-* meaning 'in' and a Latin word *halare* meaning 'to breathe']

inhaler *noun* a device used for relieving asthma and other disorders by inhaling a medicinal vapour.

inhere (in-heer) *verb* (*formal*) to be inherent.

inherent (in-heer-ənt) *adjective* existing in something as one of its natural or permanent characteristics or qualities. **inherence** *noun* **inherently** *adverb* [from *in-* meaning 'in' and a Latin word *haerere* meaning 'to stick']

inherit *verb* (**inherited, inheriting**) 1 to receive money, property, or a title by legal right when the previous owner or holder has died. 2 to receive something from a predecessor. 3 to receive a characteristic from your parents or ancestors. **inheritor** *noun* [from *in-* meaning 'in' and a Latin word *heres* meaning 'heir']

inheritance *noun* 1 the process of inheriting property. 2 money or property that is inherited.

inhibit verb (**inhibited, inhibiting**) 1 to restrain or prevent something ♦ *a substance that inhibits the growth of weeds.* SYNONYMS: restrain, prevent, impede. 2 to prevent or discourage someone from behaving naturally. SYNONYMS: restrain, deter, discourage, prevent. [from a Latin word *inhibere* meaning 'to restrain']

inhibition (in-hib-**ish**-ən) noun 1 the process of inhibiting. 2 a feeling of restraint that makes a person unwilling to act naturally.

inhospitable (in-**hoss**-pit-əbəl or in-hoss-**pit**-əbəl) adjective 1 not hospitable. 2 (said about a place or climate) providing no shelter or favourable conditions.

inhuman adjective cruel or brutal; without pity or kindness. SYNONYMS: cruel, brutal, barbaric, merciless, heartless, savage. **inhumanity** (in-hew-**man**-iti) noun

inhumane (in-hew-**mayn**) noun without pity for suffering; not humane. SYNONYMS: callous, merciless, pitiless, cruel.

inimical (in-**im**-ikəl) adjective hostile or harmful. **inimically** adverb [from *in-* meaning 'not' and a Latin word *amicus* meaning 'friend']

inimitable (in-**im**-it-əbəl) adjective impossible to imitate, unique. **inimitably** adverb

iniquitous (in-**ik**-wit-əs) adjective very unjust. [from *in-* meaning 'not' and *equity*]

iniquity (in-**ik**-witi) noun (**iniquities**) great injustice or wickedness. [from a Latin word *iniquitas* meaning 'inequality']

initial adjective belonging to the beginning of something ♦ *the initial stages of the project.*
initial noun the first letter of a word or name.
initial verb (**initialled, initialling**) to sign or mark a document with your initials. **initially** adverb [from a Latin word *initium* meaning 'the beginning']

initiate[1] (in-**ish**-i-ayt) verb 1 to make a process or activity begin. SYNONYMS: instigate, institute, undertake, embark on, begin, start. 2 to admit someone formally to a society or organization, often with a ceremony. 3 to give someone basic instruction or information about something that is new to them. **initiation** noun **initiator** noun **initiatory** adjective [same origin as for *initial*]

initiate[2] (in-**ish**-i-ət) noun a person who has been initiated.

initiative (in-**ish**-ə-tiv) noun 1 the first step in a process. 2 the power or right to begin something. 3 the ability or wish to do new things, enterprise ♦ *They show a great deal of initiative.* SYNONYMS: enterprise, resourcefulness, imagination. **on your own initiative** without being prompted by others. **to take the initiative** to be the first to take action.

inject verb 1 to put a medicine or drug into the body by means of a syringe. 2 to put liquid into something under pressure. 3 to introduce a new element or quality ♦ *We have tried to inject some energy into the project.* **injector** noun [from *in-* meaning 'in' and a Latin word *-jectum* meaning 'thrown']

injection noun 1 the process of injecting. 2 a liquid or other substance that is injected.

injudicious (in-joo-**dish**-əs) adjective showing a lack of good judgement, unwise. **injudiciously** adverb **injudiciousness** noun

injunction noun a command given with authority, especially an order from a lawcourt. [from a Latin word *injungere* meaning 'to impose']

injure verb 1 to harm or hurt someone. SYNONYMS: harm, hurt, damage. 2 to do wrong to someone. [from an earlier meaning 'to treat someone unfairly', from *in-* meaning 'not' and a Latin word *juris* meaning 'of right']

injurious (in-**joor**-iəs) adjective causing or likely to cause injury.

injury noun (**injuries**) 1 damage or harm. 2 a particular form of harm ♦ *a leg injury.* 3 a wrong or unjust act.

injustice noun 1 lack of justice. 2 an unjust action or treatment. **to do someone an injustice** to make an unfair judgement about someone.

ink noun a black or coloured liquid used in writing or printing.
ink verb to mark or cover something with ink. [from a Greek word *enkauston*, from *enkaiein* meaning 'to burn in']

inkling noun a hint, a slight knowledge or suspicion. SYNONYMS: suspicion, clue, hint, intimation. [from an old word *inkle* meaning 'to utter quietly']

inky adjective (**inkier, inkiest**) 1 covered or stained with ink. 2 black like ink ♦ *inky darkness.*

inlaid past tense and past participle of inlay¹.

inland adjective & adverb in or towards the interior of a country, away from the coast.

in-laws plural noun (informal) a person's relatives by marriage.

inlay ¹ (in-lay) verb (past tense and past participle **inlaid**) to set pieces of wood or metal into a surface to form a design.

inlay ² (in-lay) noun 1 an inlaid design or piece of material. 2 a dental filling shaped to fit the cavity in a tooth.

inlet noun 1 a strip of water reaching into the land from a sea or lake. 2 a passage or way in ♦ an air inlet.

inline skate noun a type of roller skate in which the wheels are set in a single line.

inmate noun a person living in an institution such as a hospital or prison.

in memoriam (mi-mor-i-am) preposition in memory of someone dead. [a Latin phrase meaning 'in memory']

inmost adjective furthest inward.

inn noun a hotel or public house, especially in the country. [from an Old English word]

innards plural noun (informal) 1 the internal organs of a person or animal, the entrails. 2 the inner working parts of a machine.

innate (in-ayt) adjective inborn, natural. **innately** adverb [from in- meaning 'in' and a Latin word natus meaning 'born']

inner adjective nearer to the inside or centre; interior, internal.

inner city noun the central area of a city, especially where there is overcrowding and poverty.

innermost adjective furthest in, closest to the centre.

inner tube noun a separate inflatable tube inside the casing of a pneumatic tyre.

innings noun (innings) (in cricket) a side's turn at batting or a particular player's turn.

innkeeper noun a person who runs an inn.

innocent adjective 1 not guilty of a particular crime or offence. SYNONYMS: blameless, guiltless. 2 free of wickedness or wrongdoing. SYNONYMS: blameless, guiltless, virtuous. 3 harmless, not intended to cause offence ♦ an innocent remark. SYNONYMS: harmless, inoffensive, innocuous. 4 foolishly trustful.

innocent noun a person, especially a child, who is free of wickedness or is foolishly trustful. **innocence** noun **innocently** adverb [from in- meaning 'not' and a Latin word nocens meaning 'doing harm']

innocuous (in-ok-yoo-əs) adjective harmless. **innocuously** adverb **innocuousness** noun [from in- meaning 'not' and a Latin word nocuus meaning 'harmful']

innovate verb to introduce a new process or way of doing things. **innovation** noun **innovator** noun **innovatory** adjective [from in- meaning 'in' and a Latin word novus meaning 'new']

innuendo (in-yoo-en-doh) noun (**innuendoes** or **innuendos**) an indirect reference to something rude or insulting. [a Latin word meaning 'by nodding or pointing']

innumerable adjective too many to be counted. SYNONYMS: countless, numberless. **innumerably** adverb [from in- meaning 'not' and a Latin word numerare meaning 'to count']

innumerate adjective having a poor basic knowledge of numbers and mathematics. **innumeracy** noun

inoculate verb to treat or inject a person or animal with a vaccine or serum as a protection against a disease. **inoculation** noun [from a Latin word inoculare meaning 'to implant']

inoffensive adjective not offensive, harmless.

inoperable (in-op-er-əbəl) adjective (said about a disease) not able to be cured by surgical operation.

inoperative adjective not functioning.

inopportune (in-op-er-tewn) adjective coming or happening at an unsuitable time. **inopportunely** adverb

inordinate (in-or-din-ət) adjective excessive. **inordinately** adverb

inorganic (in-or-gan-ik) adjective not made of living organisms, of mineral origin.

inpatient noun a patient who lives in hospital while receiving treatment.

input noun 1 what is put into something. 2 electrical or other energy supplied to a device or system. 3 (Computing) the data or programs put into a computer. **input** verb (past tense and past participle **input** or **inputted**; **inputting**) (Computing) to put data or programs into a computer.

inquest noun an official investigation to establish the facts about how a person died. [from an Old French word, related to inquire]

inquire verb to investigate something carefully or officially. **inquirer** noun [from in- meaning 'into' and a Latin word quaerere meaning 'to seek']
◊ See the note at enquire.

inquiry noun (**inquiries**) an investigation, especially an official one.
◊ See the note at enquiry.

inquisition (inkwi-**zish**-ən) noun a detailed questioning or investigation. **the Inquisition** a council of the Roman Catholic Church in the Middle Ages, especially the very severe one in Spain, set up to discover and punish heretics. [same origin as for inquire]

inquisitive adjective 1 curious or prying. 2 eagerly seeking knowledge. **inquisitively** adverb [same origin as for inquire]

inquisitor (in-**kwiz**-it-er) noun a person who questions another person harshly.

inquisitorial (in-kwiz-i-**tor**-iəl) adjective of or like an inquisitor, prying.

inroad noun a sudden attack made into a country. **make inroads on** or **into** to use up large quantities of stores or resources.

insalubrious (in-sə-**loo**-briəs) adjective (said about a place or climate) unhealthy.

insane adjective 1 not sane, mad. SYNONYMS: mad, crazy; (informal) barmy. 2 extremely foolish. SYNONYMS: foolish, senseless, silly, stupid, daft, crazy. **insanely** adverb **insanity** noun

insanitary adjective unclean and likely to be harmful to health.

insatiable (in-**say**-shə-bəl) adjective impossible to satisfy ♦ an insatiable appetite. **insatiability** noun **insatiably** adverb [from in- meaning 'not' and a Latin word satiare meaning 'to satiate or satisfy']

inscribe verb 1 to write or carve words or a design on a surface ♦ They inscribed their names on the stone. 2 (Geometry) to draw one geometrical figure inside another so that their boundaries touch but do not intersect. 3 to enter a name on a list or in a book. [from in- meaning 'on' and a Latin word scribere meaning 'to write']

inscription noun 1 words or names inscribed on a monument, coin, stone, etc. 2 the process of inscribing words or a design.

inscrutable (in-**skroot**-əbəl) adjective mysterious, impossible to understand or interpret. **inscrutability** noun **inscrutably** adverb [from in- meaning 'not' and a Latin word scrutari meaning 'to search']

insect noun a small animal with six legs, no backbone, and a body divided into three parts (head, thorax, and abdomen). [from a Latin word insectum meaning 'cut up']

insecticide noun a substance for killing insects. [from insect and a Latin word caedere meaning 'to kill']

insectivore (in-**sek**-ti-vor) noun an animal or plant that feeds on insects or other invertebrates. **insectivorous** (in-sek-**tiv**-er-əs) adjective [from insect and a Latin word vorare meaning 'to eat']

insecure adjective not secure or safe. SYNONYMS: unsafe, unsteady, precarious. **insecurely** adverb **insecurity** noun

inseminate (in-**sem**-in-ayt) verb to insert semen into the womb. **insemination** noun [from in- meaning 'in' and a Latin word seminare meaning 'to sow']

insensible adjective 1 unconscious or without feeling. 2 unaware of something ♦ They seemed insensible of the danger they were in. 3 too small or gradual to be noticed ♦ insensible changes. **insensibility** noun **insensibly** adverb

insensitive adjective showing little concern for other people's feelings, not sensitive. SYNONYMS: thoughtless, tactless, unfeeling, heartless. **insensitively** adverb **insensitivity** noun

insentient (in-**sen**-shənt) adjective incapable of feeling, not sentient.

inseparable adjective 1 unable to be separated. 2 liking to be constantly together ♦ The friends were inseparable. **inseparability** noun **inseparably** adverb

insert[1] (in-**sert**) verb to put something in, between, or among other things. **insertion** noun [from in- meaning 'in' and a Latin word serere meaning 'to plant']

insert[2] (in-**sert**) noun something inserted, especially a loose page or advertisement in a magazine.

in-service adjective undertaken by people in connection with their jobs while they are employed ♦ in-service training.

inset [1] (**in**-set) *verb* (past tense and past participle **inset** or **insetted; insetting**) to decorate something with something set into its surface ♦ *The crown is inset with jewels.*

inset [2] (**in**-set) *noun* 1 something set into a larger thing. 2 a small map printed within the frame of a larger one.

inshore *adverb & adjective* near or nearer to the shore.

inside *noun* 1 the inner side, surface, or part of something. SYNONYMS: interior, centre, core, middle. 2 (**insides**) (*informal*) the organs in the abdomen; the stomach and bowels.
inside *adjective* on or coming from the inside; in or nearest to the middle.
inside *adverb* 1 on or to the inside of something ♦ *Please come inside.* 2 (*informal*) in prison.
inside *preposition* on the inner side of, within ♦ *The rabbit is inside the box* ♦ *He arrived inside an hour.* **inside out** 1 with the inner surface turned to face the outside ♦ *She was wearing her jumper inside out.* 2 thoroughly ♦ *They know the subject inside out.*

insider *noun* a member of a group or organization, especially with access to private information.

insidious (in-**sid**-iəs) *adjective* causing harm gradually, without being noticed ♦ *an insidious influence.* **insidiously** *adverb* **insidiousness** *noun* [from a Latin word *insidiae* meaning 'an ambush']

insight *noun* 1 the ability to recognize and understand the truth about something. 2 knowledge obtained by this ability.

insignia (in-**sig**-niə) *plural noun* a badge or symbol that marks a military rank or a particular office or position. [a Latin word meaning 'signs', related to *sign*]

insignificant *adjective* having little or no importance or influence. SYNONYMS: unimportant, inconsequential, trivial, trifling. **insignificance** *noun* **insignificantly** *adverb*

insincere *adjective* not sincere. **insincerely** *adverb* **insincerity** *noun*

insinuate (in-**sin**-yoo-ayt) *verb* 1 to hint something unpleasant or offensive. 2 to introduce yourself gradually to a place ♦ *They insinuated themselves into the group.* **insinuation** *noun* [from *in-* meaning 'into' and a Latin word *sinuare* meaning 'to curve']

insipid (in-**sip**-id) *adjective* 1 lacking flavour. 2 not lively or interesting. **insipidity** (in-si-**pid**-iti) *noun* [from *in-* meaning 'not' and a Latin word *sapidus* meaning 'having flavour']

insist *verb* to say or ask for something firmly ♦ *We insist that you stay.* **to insist on** to demand something firmly ♦ *She insists on obedience.* [from a Latin word *insistere* meaning 'to stand firm']

insistent *adjective* 1 insisting, saying or demanding something firmly. 2 constant and demanding your attention ♦ *We could hear the insistent ring of a telephone.* **insistence** *noun* **insistently** *adverb*

in situ (**sit**-yoo) *adverb & adjective* in its original place. [a Latin phrase]

insobriety (in-sə-**briy**-iti) *noun* lack of sobriety, drunkenness.

insofar as *adverb* another spelling of **in so far as** (see in).

insole *noun* 1 the inner sole of a boot or shoe. 2 a loose piece of material put in the bottom of a shoe for warmth or to improve the fit.

insolent *adjective* behaving insultingly or arrogantly. SYNONYMS: impertinent, rude, disrespectful. **insolence** *noun* **insolently** *adverb* [from a Latin word *insolentia* meaning 'pride']

insoluble *adjective* 1 unable to be dissolved. 2 unable to be solved ♦ *an insoluble problem.* **insolubility** *noun* **insolubly** *adverb*

insolvent *adjective* unable to pay your debts. **insolvency** *noun*

insomnia *noun* habitual inability to sleep. [from *in-* meaning 'without' and a Latin word *somnus* meaning 'sleep']

insomniac *noun* a person who suffers from insomnia.

insomuch *adverb* 1 to such an extent. 2 inasmuch.

insouciant (in-**soo**-si-ənt or an-**soo**-si-ahn) *adjective* casual and unconcerned. **insouciance** *noun* [from *in-* meaning 'not' and a French word *souciant* meaning 'caring']

inspect *verb* 1 to examine something carefully and critically. SYNONYMS: examine, check, investigate. 2 to examine a place officially; to visit a place in order to make sure that regulations and standards are being followed. **inspection** *noun* [from *in-* meaning 'in' and a Latin word *specere* meaning 'to look']

inspector *noun* **1** an official who inspects places to ensure that regulations are being followed. **2** a police officer above sergeant and below superintendent.

inspiration *noun* **1** the process of inspiring someone. **2** an inspiring influence. **3** a sudden brilliant idea.

inspire *verb* **1** to fill someone with an urge to do something or with a strong feeling about something ♦ *She inspires confidence in everyone.* SYNONYMS: stimulate, arouse. **2** to inhale. [from *in-* meaning 'into' and a Latin word *spirare* meaning 'to breathe']

inspiriting *adjective* encouraging, filling people with enthusiasm.

instability *noun* lack of stability.

install *verb* **1** to put equipment or machinery in position and ready for use ♦ *They installed central heating in their house.* SYNONYMS: fit, put in, set up. **2** to place someone in office, especially with ceremonies. **3** to settle someone in a place ♦ *He was comfortably installed in an armchair.* [from *in-* meaning 'in' and a Latin word *stallum* meaning 'a place or position']

installation (in-stə-**lay**-shən) *noun* **1** the process of installing something. **2** equipment that is installed.

instalment *noun* each of the parts in which something is presented or paid for over a period of time.

instance *noun* a case or example of something.
instance *verb* to mention something as an instance or example. **in the first instance** to begin with, firstly. [from a Latin word *instantia* meaning 'presence' or 'urgency']

instant *adjective* **1** happening immediately ♦ *instant success.* SYNONYMS: immediate, instantaneous. **2** (said about food) designed to be prepared quickly and easily ♦ *instant coffee.*
instant *noun* **1** an exact point of time; the present moment ♦ *Come here this instant!* **2** a very short space of time, a moment. [from a Latin word *instans* meaning 'urgent']

instantaneous (in-stən-**tay**-niəs) *adjective* occurring or done instantly ♦ *Death was instantaneous.* **instantaneously** *adverb*

instantly *adverb* immediately.

instead *adverb* as an alternative or substitute for something else. [from *in-* meaning 'in' and *stead* meaning 'a place']

instep *noun* **1** the top of the foot between the toes and the ankle. **2** the part of a shoe that fits over or under this.

instigate *verb* **1** to urge or encourage someone to do something ♦ *He instigated them to make a formal complaint.* **2** to make something happen by using persuasion ♦ *We shall instigate an inquiry into the affair.* **instigation** *noun* **instigator** *noun* [from a Latin word *instigare* meaning 'to urge']

instil *verb* (**instilled, instilling**) to put ideas into someone's mind gradually. **instillation** *noun* **instilment** *noun* [from *in-* meaning 'in' and a Latin word *stilla* meaning 'a drop']

instinct *noun* **1** an inborn impulse or tendency to perform certain acts or behave in certain ways. **2** a natural ability ♦ *She has an instinct for saying the right thing.* [from a Latin word *instinctus* meaning 'impulse', related to *instigate*]

instinctive *adjective* involving or prompted by instinct. **instinctively** *adverb*

instinctual *adjective* to do with instinct, instinctive. **instinctually** *adverb*

institute *noun* a society or organization that promotes a particular scientific or educational activity.
institute *verb* **1** to establish or found an organization or practice. **2** to cause an inquiry to be started. [from *in-* meaning 'in' and a Latin word *statuere* meaning 'to set up']

institution *noun* **1** the process of instituting something. **2** an institute, especially one promoting a charitable or social activity. **3** a hospital or other organization that provides residential care for people with special medical needs. **4** an established custom or practice. **5** (*informal*) a person who has become a familiar figure in some activity.

institutional *adjective* to do with or like an institution.

institutionalize *verb* **1** to make something an institution or established practice. **2** to keep someone in a medical institution. **institutionalization** *noun*

instruct *verb* **1** to teach a person a subject or skill. SYNONYMS: teach, train, educate, coach, tutor. **2** to inform someone officially of something. **3** to tell someone what they must do. SYNONYMS: direct, order, tell, command. **4** to authorize a solicitor or counsel to act on your behalf. **instructor** *noun* [from a Latin word *instruere* meaning 'to teach']

instruction *noun* **1** a statement telling a person what they must do; an order. **2** the process of instructing someone. **3** knowledge or teaching that is given to someone. **4** (*Computing*) a code in a computer program that defines an operation and carries it out. **instructional** *adjective*

instructive *adjective* giving useful knowledge or information. **instructively** *adverb*

instrument *noun* **1** a tool or implement that is designed for delicate or scientific work. **2** a measuring device giving information about the operation of an engine or machine or used in navigation. **3** a device designed for producing musical sounds. **4** a person made use of or controlled by someone else. **5** a formal or legal document ♦ *an instrument of abdication.* [from a Latin word *instrumentum* meaning 'implement', related to *instruct*]

instrumental *adjective* **1** serving as a means of doing something ♦ *Her cousin was instrumental in finding her a job.* **2** (said about music) performed on musical instruments, without voices.

instrumentalist *noun* a musician who plays a musical instrument, as distinct from a singer.

instrumentation *noun* **1** the arrangement or composition of music for particular instruments. **2** the provision or use of mechanical or scientific instruments.

insubordinate *adjective* disobedient or rebellious. SYNONYMS: disobedient, rebellious, defiant, uncooperative. **insubordination** *noun*

insubstantial *adjective* **1** not existing in reality, imaginary. **2** lacking strength or force ♦ *The prosecution could only offer insubstantial evidence.*

insufferable *adjective* **1** unbearable ♦ *The weather was insufferable.* **2** unbearably conceited or arrogant. **insufferably** *adverb*

insufficient *adjective* not sufficient. **insufficiency** *noun* **insufficiently** *adverb*

insular (ins-yoo-ler) *adjective* **1** isolated from outside influences, narrow-minded ♦ *insular prejudices.* **2** like an island or forming an island. **insularity** (ins-yoo-la-riti) *noun* [from a Latin word *insula* meaning 'island']

insulate (ins-yoo-layt) *verb* **1** to cover or protect something to prevent heat, cold, electricity, etc. from passing in or out. **2** to isolate a person or place from external influences. **insulation** *noun* **insulator** *noun* [same origin as for *insular*]

insulin (ins-yoo-lin) *noun* a hormone produced in the pancreas, which controls the amount of glucose in the blood, and a lack of which causes diabetes. [from a Latin word *insula* meaning 'island' (because the cells in the pancreas that control the flow of glucose are called 'the islets of Langerhans')]

insult [1] (in-sult) *verb* to speak or act in a way that offends someone or makes them angry. SYNONYMS: offend, abuse, snub, be rude to. [from a Latin word *insultare* meaning 'to jump or trample on']

insult [2] (in-sult) *noun* an offensive or hurtful remark or action.

insuperable (in-soop-er-əbəl) *adjective* impossible to overcome ♦ *an insuperable difficulty.* [from *in-* meaning 'not' and a Latin word *superare* meaning 'to overcome']

insupportable *adjective* not able to be supported or justified; intolerable. **insupportably** *adverb*

insurance *noun* **1** an agreement that a company makes to provide compensation for loss, damage, or injury to a person or organization in return for a payment or series of payments (called a *premium*) made in advance. **2** the business of providing such contracts. **3** anything done as a safeguard against loss or failure. ◊ See the note at **assurance**.

insure *verb* to protect someone or something by a contract of insurance. **insurer** *noun* [same origin as for *ensure*] ◊ See the note at **ensure**.

insurgent (in-ser-jənt) *adjective* rebellious, rising in revolt. **insurgent** *noun* a rebel. **insurgence** *noun* [from *in-* meaning 'against' and a Latin word *surgere* meaning 'to rise']

insurmountable (in-ser-mownt-əbəl) *adjective* impossible to overcome, insuperable.

insurrection (in-ser-**ek**-shən) noun a rebellion. **insurrectionist** noun [same origin as for *insurgent*]

intact adjective undamaged, complete.
SYNONYMS: undamaged, unbroken, complete, whole. [from *in-* meaning 'not' and a Latin word *tactum* meaning 'touched']

intaglio (in-**tal**-yoh) noun (**intaglios**) 1 (*Art*) a kind of carving in which the design is engraved below the surface. 2 a gem carved in this way. [an Italian word, from *intagliare* meaning 'to carve']

intake noun 1 the process of taking something in. 2 the place where liquid or air is fed into something. 3 the number or quantity of people or things that are received or admitted ♦ *The school's annual intake of pupils is over 100.*

intangible (in-**tan**-jibəl) adjective not able to be touched, not material. **intangibly** adverb

integer (in-ti-jer) noun a whole number that is not a fraction, such as 0, 3, and 19. [a Latin word meaning 'whole']

integral (in-ti-grəl) adjective 1 forming an essential part, necessary to make something complete ♦ *The garage is an integral part of the building.* 2 complete, forming a whole ♦ *an integral design.* 3 (*Mathematics*) relating to or denoted by an integer.
integral noun (*Mathematics*) a quantity of which a given function is the derivative. **integrally** adverb [same origin as for *integer*]

integrate (in-ti-grayt) verb 1 to make parts into a whole, to combine parts. SYNONYMS: combine, merge, amalgamate, unite. 2 to join a community, or to bring a member into a community, on terms equal to the other members. 3 (*Mathematics*) to find the integral of a quantity. **integration** noun [from a Latin word *integrare* meaning 'to make whole']

integrated circuit noun an electronic circuit made from a small chip of material and replacing a conventional circuit of many components.

integrity (in-**teg**-riti) noun 1 being honest or incorruptible. SYNONYMS: honesty, sincerity, honour, principle. 2 wholeness. [from a Latin word *integritas* meaning 'wholeness' or 'purity']

integument (in-**teg**-yoo-mənt) noun a technical term for a tough outer skin. [from a Latin word *integere* meaning 'to cover over']

intellect (**in**-ti-lekt) noun power of the mind to reason and absorb knowledge, as distinct from feeling and instinct. [same origin as for *intelligent*]

intellectual (inti-**lek**-tew-əl) adjective 1 to do with the intellect. 2 needing to use the intellect ♦ *an intellectual activity.* 3 (said about a person) having a good intellect and a liking for knowledge.
intellectual noun an intellectual person. **intellectually** adverb

intelligence noun 1 the ability to absorb knowledge and to understand things. 2 information of military or political value. 3 the process of gathering this kind of information, or the people engaged in it.

intelligence quotient noun a number that shows how a person's reasoning ability compares with that of an average person, the average score being 100.

intelligent adjective 1 able to absorb knowledge and understand things. SYNONYMS: clever, bright, brainy, intellectual. 2 (said about a device in a computer system) containing a capacity to process information. **intelligently** adverb [from a Latin word *intelligere* meaning 'to understand']

intelligentsia (in-tel-i-**jent**-siə) noun intellectual people regarded as a class. [from Russian and Polish words, related to *intelligence*]

intelligible (in-**tel**-i-jibəl) adjective able to be understood. **intelligibility** noun **intelligibly** adverb

intemperate adjective 1 drinking too much alcohol. 2 lacking self-control ♦ *intemperate behaviour.* **intemperance** noun **intemperately** adverb

intend verb 1 to have something in mind as what you want to do or achieve. 2 to plan that something should be used or understood in a particular way. [from a Latin word *intendere* meaning 'to stretch' or 'to aim']

intense adjective 1 very strong or great ♦ *intense pain.* SYNONYMS: acute, sharp, extreme, strong. 2 (said about a person) feeling things strongly, highly emotional. **intensely** adverb **intensity** noun [from a Latin word *intensus* meaning 'stretched tight']

intensify verb (**intensifies, intensified, intensifying**) to become more intense, or to make something more intense. **intensification** noun

intensive *adjective* using a lot of effort over a short time, concentrated. **intensively** *adverb*

intensive care *noun* medical treatment of a dangerously ill patient, with constant supervision.

intent *noun* intention or purpose.
intent *adjective* **1** intending, having your mind fixed on a purpose ♦ *They are intent on finishing the building this week.* SYNONYMS: determined (to), eager (to), keen (to). **2** with the attention concentrated ♦ *an intent gaze.* **to all intents and purposes** practically, virtually. **intently** *adverb* **intentness** *noun* [same origin as for *intend*]

intention *noun* what a person intends to do or achieve, a purpose. SYNONYMS: aim, plan, objective, ambition, goal, purpose.

intentional *adjective* done on purpose, deliberate and not accidental. SYNONYMS: deliberate, intended. **intentionally** *adverb*

inter (in-ter) *verb* (**interred, interring**) to bury a dead body in the earth or in a tomb. [from *in-* meaning 'in' and a Latin word *terra* meaning 'earth']

inter- *prefix* between or among. [from a Latin word *inter* with the same meaning]

interact *verb* to have an effect on each other. **interaction** *noun*

interactive *adjective* **1** interacting. **2** (*Computing*) allowing information to be transferred immediately between a computer system and the user in both directions.

inter alia (ay-liə) *adverb* among other things. [a Latin phrase]

interbreed *verb* (past tense and past participle **interbred**) (said about animals of different species) to breed with each other; to cross-breed.

intercede (inter-seed) *verb* to intervene on behalf of another person or as a peacemaker. [from *inter-* and a Latin word *cedere* meaning 'to go']

intercept[1] (inter-sept) *verb* to stop or catch a person or thing while it is going from one place to another. **interception** *noun* **interceptor** *noun* [from *inter-* and a Latin word *captum* meaning 'seized']

intercept[2] (in-ter-sept) *noun* (*Mathematics*) the point at which a line intersects a coordinate axis.

intercession (inter-**sesh**-ən) *noun* interceding for someone. **intercessor** *noun*

interchange[1] (inter-**chaynj**) *verb* **1** to put each of two things into the other's place. **2** to give and receive one thing for another. **3** to alternate. **interchangeable** *adjective*

interchange[2] (in-ter-chaynj) *noun* **1** the process of interchanging. **2** a road junction on several levels, allowing traffic to move from one road to another without crossing other streams of traffic.

intercity *adjective* existing or travelling between cities.

intercom (in-ter-kom) *noun* a system of communication between parts of a building, operating like a telephone. [short for *intercommunication*]

interconnect *verb* to connect with each other. **interconnection** *noun*

intercontinental *adjective* relating to or travelling between two continents.

intercostal (int-ə-**kost**-əl) *adjective* (*Anatomy*) situated between the ribs ♦ *intercostal muscles.* [from *inter-* and a Latin word *costa* meaning 'rib']

intercourse *noun* **1** regular dealings or communication between people or countries. **2** short for **sexual intercourse**. [from a Latin word *intercursus* meaning 'running between']

interdependent *adjective* dependent on each other. **interdependence** *noun*

interdict[1] (in-ter-dikt) *noun* (*Law*) an order that forbids something, a prohibition. [from *inter-* and a Latin word *dictum* meaning 'said']

interdict[2] (inter-dikt) *verb* to prohibit or forbid something formally. **interdiction** *noun*

interdisciplinary *adjective* relating to or involving different branches of learning.

interest *noun* **1** a feeling of wanting to know about something or to become involved in it. **2** the quality of arousing this sort of feeling ♦ *The subject has no interest for me.* **3** a subject or activity that someone likes to follow ♦ *Music is one of her interests.* **4** an advantage or benefit ♦ *We need to protect our own interests.* **5** a legal right to a share in something, or a financial stake in a business. **6** money paid regularly in return for the use of money that has been lent.

interest *verb* 1 to arouse the interest of someone. SYNONYMS: attract, appeal to, intrigue, fascinate, absorb. 2 to lead someone to take an interest in something ♦ *He interested himself in welfare work.* [from a Latin word *interesse* meaning 'to be important']

interested *adjective* 1 feeling or showing interest or curiosity. 2 having a private interest in something ♦ *a meeting of all the interested parties.*

interesting *adjective* arousing interest. SYNONYMS: absorbing, exciting, appealing, engrossing, fascinating.

interface *noun* 1 a point or surface where two thing meet and interact. 2 (*Computing*) a piece of equipment enabling two items of hardware or software to exchange data or operate together, or enabling a user to access a system.
interface *verb* to connect with something by means of an interface.

interfacing *noun* a layer of material placed between two layers of fabric to give it extra support or firmness.

interfere *verb* 1 to take a part in other people's affairs without any right to do so ♦ *It's better not to interfere in their quarrel.* 2 to get in the way of something or make something difficult ♦ *The wind was interfering with the rescue operation.* SYNONYMS: (taking an object) hinder, impede, spoil. 3 (*Physics*) to produce interference. [from *inter-* and a Latin word *ferire* meaning 'to strike']

interference *noun* 1 the process of interfering. 2 disturbance to radio signals caused by atmospherics or unwanted signals. 3 (*Physics*) a combination of waves of the same wavelength from two or more sources, producing a new wave pattern.

interferon (inter-**feer**-on) *noun* (*Biochemistry*) a protein substance that prevents the development of a virus in living cells.

interglacial *adjective* (*Geology*) relating to a milder climate between glacial periods.

interim (in-ter-im) *noun* a period of time between two events ♦ *in the interim.*
interim *adjective* relating to a period of time when there is more to come, temporary ♦ *an interim report.* [a Latin word meaning 'meanwhile']

interior *adjective* nearer to the centre, inner.

interior *noun* 1 an inside part or region, the central or inland part of a country. 2 the inside of a building or room. [a Latin word meaning 'further in']

interior monologue *noun* a piece of writing that represents the thoughts of a character.

interject *verb* to add a remark when someone is speaking. [from *inter-* and a Latin word *jactum* meaning 'thrown']

interjection *noun* 1 the process of interrupting with a remark. 2 a remark made by interrupting. 3 an exclamation such as *oh!* or *good heavens!*

interlace *verb* to weave or lace things together.

interleaved *adjective* (said about a book) having blank leaves inserted between its normal pages.

interlock *verb* to fit into each other so that parts engage and work together.

interlocutor (inter-**lok**-yoo-ter) *noun* (*formal*) someone who takes part in a conversation. [from *inter-* and a Latin word *locutum* meaning 'spoken']

interloper *noun* someone who interferes in other people's affairs. [from *inter-* and *-loper* from an old word *landloper* meaning 'vagabond']

interlude *noun* 1 an interval or pause, especially between parts of a performance in a theatre etc. 2 something performed during an interval or between other events. 3 a temporary activity or diversion ♦ *a romantic interlude.* [from *inter-* and a Latin word *ludus* meaning 'game']

intermarry *verb* (intermarries, intermarried, intermarrying) 1 (said about peoples, families, etc.) to become connected by marriage. 2 to marry within your own family. **intermarriage** *noun*

intermediary (inter-**meed**-i-er-i) *noun* (intermediaries) someone who tries to settle a disagreement by negotiating with both sides; a mediator.
intermediary *adjective* intermediate in position or form. [from a Latin word *intermedius*]

intermediate *adjective* 1 coming between two things in time, place, or order. 2 having more than the basic knowledge of a subject but not yet advanced.

interment (in-ter-mənt) *noun* the burial of a dead person.

◊ Do not confuse this word with **internment**, which has a different meaning.

intermezzo (inter-**mets**-oh) *noun* (**intermezzi** or **intermezzos**) **1** a short musical composition played between parts of an opera or other musical work. **2** a light dramatic performance between the acts of a play. [an Italian word]

interminable (in-**ter**-min-əbəl) *adjective* seeming to be endless; long and boring. **interminably** *adverb* [from *in-* meaning 'not' and a Latin word *terminare* meaning 'to end']

intermingle *verb* to mix or mingle together, or to mix things together.

intermission *noun* **1** an interval during a play or film. **2** a pause in work or action. [same origin as for *intermittent*]

intermittent *adjective* happening at intervals, not continuous ♦ *periods of rain with intermittent sunshine*. **intermittently** *adverb* [from *inter-* and a Latin word *mittere* meaning 'to let go']

intermix *verb* to mix together, or to mix things together.

intermolecular *adjective* (*Biochemistry*) existing or occurring between molecules.

intern (in-**tern**) *verb* to confine someone as a prisoner, especially during a war. **intern** (in-**tern**) *noun* (*North Amer.*) a junior hospital doctor who has recently graduated, or a trainee doing work experience in other fields. [same origin as for *internal*]

internal *adjective* **1** of or on the inside of something. SYNONYMS: inside, inner, interior. **2** to do with the domestic affairs of a country. **3** used or applying within an organization. **4** to do with the mind or soul. **internally** *adverb* [from a Latin word *internus* meaning 'inward']

internal-combustion engine *noun* an engine that produces power by burning fuel inside the engine itself.

international *adjective* **1** to do with several countries or all countries. **2** agreed on by all or most countries ♦ *international law*. **international** *noun* **1** a sports contest between players representing different countries. **2** a player who has taken part in a contest of this kind. **internationally** *adverb*

International System of Units *noun* see SI.

internecine (inter-**nee**-siyn) *adjective* destructive to both sides in a war or other conflict. [from *inter-* and a Latin word *necare* meaning 'to kill']

internee (in-ter-**nee**) *noun* a person who has been interned.

Internet *noun* an international computer network that allows users throughout the world to communicate and exchange information with one another. [from *inter-* and *network*]

Internet café *noun* a place where the public can have access to the Internet for payment.

internment *noun* the process of interning, or the state of being interned. ◊ Do not confuse this word with **interment**, which has a different meaning.

interpersonal *adjective* to do with relations or communication between people.

interplanetary *adjective* travelling between planets.

interplay *noun* interaction between people or things.

Interpol *noun* a French-based organization that coordinates investigations made by the police forces of member countries into international crimes. [a shortening of *International Police*]

interpolate (in-**ter**-pəl-ayt) *verb* **1** to add a remark during a conversation. **2** to insert new material into a book, especially in order to mislead readers about its date. **3** (*Mathematics*) to estimate and insert a number or quantity between two others in a series. **interpolation** *noun* [from a Latin word *interpolare* meaning 'to alter']

interpose *verb* **1** to insert something between one thing and another. **2** to add a remark during a conversation. **3** to intervene. **interposition** *noun* [from *inter-* and a Latin word *positum* meaning 'put']

interpret (in-**ter**-prit) *verb* **1** to explain the meaning of something said or written, or of someone's actions. SYNONYMS: explain, clarify, elucidate. **2** to understand something in a specified way. **3** to translate the words of a speaker orally into a different language. **interpretation** *noun* [from a Latin word *interpretari* meaning 'to explain' or 'to translate']

interpreter *noun* a person who translates the words of a speaker orally into a different language.

interpretive *adjective* interpreting, explaining a meaning.

interregnum (inter-**reg**-nəm) *noun* (**interregnums** or **interregna**) 1 a period between the reign of one ruler and the next. 2 an interval or pause. [from *inter-* and a Latin word *regnum* meaning 'reign']

interrelated *adjective* related to each other. **interrelation** *noun*

interrogate (in-**te**-rə-gayt) *verb* 1 to question someone closely or formally. 2 to get information from a computer or database. **interrogation** *noun* **interrogator** *noun* [from *inter-* and a Latin word *rogare* meaning 'to ask']

interrogative (inter-**rog**-ətiv) *adjective* asking a question, or having the form of a question. **interrogatively** *adverb*

interrogative pronoun *noun* a pronoun such as *who*, *which*, and *what*, that asks a question.

interrogatory (inter-**rog**-ə-ter-i) *adjective* questioning.

interrupt *verb* 1 to break the continuity of a process, to prevent something continuing. 2 to break in on what someone is saying by inserting a remark. 3 to obstruct a view. **interruption** *noun* **interrupter** *noun* [from *inter-* and a Latin word *ruptum* meaning 'broken']

intersect *verb* 1 to divide something by passing or lying across it. 2 (said about lines or roads etc.) to cross each other. [from *inter-* and a Latin word *sectum* meaning 'cut']

intersection *noun* 1 the process of intersecting. 2 a place where lines or roads etc. cross each other. 3 (*Mathematics*) the elements common to two or more sets.

intersperse *verb* to insert things here and there in something different. [from *inter-* and a Latin word *sparsum* meaning 'scattered']

interstate *adjective* existing or carried on between States, especially of the USA.

interstellar *adjective* located or travelling between stars.

interstice (in-**ter**-stiss) *noun* a small intervening space. **interstitial** *adjective* [from a Latin word *interstitium*, from *intersistere* meaning 'to stand between']

intertwine *verb* to twist or twine several strands together.

interval *noun* 1 a time between two events or parts of an action. 2 a pause between two parts of a theatrical or musical performance. 3 a space between two objects or points. 4 (*Music*) the difference in pitch between two notes. **at intervals** with some time or distance between, not continuous. [from a Latin word *intervallum* meaning 'space between ramparts']

intervene (inter-**veen**) *verb* 1 to happen in the time between events ♦ *in the intervening years.* 2 to interrupt an action or process by happening ♦ *We should have finished our journey but a thunderstorm intervened.* 3 to join in a discussion or dispute in order to stop it or change its result. **intervention** (inter-**ven**-shən) *noun* [from *inter-* and a Latin word *venire* meaning 'to come']

interview *noun* a formal meeting or conversation with a person in order to obtain information about them. **interview** *verb* to hold an interview with someone. **interviewer** *noun* [from *inter-* and a French word *voir* meaning 'to see']

interviewee *noun* a person who is interviewed, especially as an applicant for a job.

interweave *verb* (**interwove, interwoven**) to weave strands into one another, or to become woven together.

intestate (in-**test**-ət) *adjective* (said about a person who has died) not having made a valid will. [from *in-* meaning 'not' and a Latin word *testatus* meaning 'witnessed']

intestine (in-**test**-in) *noun* the long tubular section of the passage in which food is digested (called the *alimentary canal*), from the stomach to the anus. **intestinal** *adjective* [from a Latin word *intestinus* meaning 'internal']

intifada (in-ti-**fah**-də) *noun* the Palestinian opposition to Israel's occupation of the West Bank and Gaza Strip. [from an Arabic word]

intimate [1] (in-**tim**-ət) *adjective* 1 having a close acquaintance or friendship with someone. SYNONYMS: friendly, familiar, close. 2 having a sexual relationship with someone. 3 private and personal ♦ *intimate thoughts.* 4 (said about knowledge) detailed and obtained from long experience or hard study. **intimate** *noun* an intimate friend. **intimacy** *noun* **intimately** *adverb* [from a Latin word *intimus* meaning 'close friend']

intimate ² (in-tim-ayt) *verb* to make something known, especially by hinting. **intimation** *noun*

intimidate (in-tim-i-dayt) *verb* to subdue or influence someone by frightening or threatening them. **intimidation** *noun* [from *in-* meaning 'in' and a Latin word *timidus* meaning 'timid']

into *preposition* 1 expressing movement or direction to a point within something ♦ *We went into the house* ♦ *The child fell into the river* ♦ *They talked far into the night.* 2 expressing change to a certain state or condition ♦ *You will get into trouble* ♦ *Soon she had grown into an adult* ♦ *His nephew went into politics.* 3 expressing active interest or involvement ♦ *She is into rock music.* 4 (*Mathematics*) expressing division ♦ *4 into 20 gives 5.*

intolerable *adjective* not able to be tolerated, unbearable. **intolerably** *adverb*

intolerant *adjective* not tolerant, unwilling to tolerate other ideas or beliefs. **intolerance** *noun* **intolerantly** *adverb*

intonation (in-tŏn-ay-shŏn) *noun* 1 the tone or pitch of the voice in speaking. 2 the action of intoning.

intone *verb* to say or recite words in a chanting voice, often on one note. [from *in-* meaning 'into' and a Latin word *tonus* meaning 'tone']

in toto *adverb* as a whole, completely. [a Latin phrase meaning 'in all']

intoxicant *noun* a drink or drug that makes you intoxicated.

intoxicated *adjective* (said about a person) drunk. **intoxication** *noun* [from *in-* meaning 'in' and a Latin word *toxicare* meaning 'to poison']

intra- *prefix* within. [from a Latin word *intra* meaning 'within']

intractable (in-trakt-ŏbŏl) *adjective* unmanageable, difficult to deal with or control ♦ *an intractable problem.* **intractability** *noun* [from *in-* meaning 'not' and a Latin word *tractare* meaning 'to handle']

intransigent (in-trans-i-jŏnt) *adjective* unwilling to change a decision or opinion, stubborn. **intransigence** *noun* [from *in-* meaning 'not' and a Latin word *transigere* meaning 'to come to an understanding']

intransitive (in-trans-itiv) *adjective* (*Grammar*) (said about a verb or a meaning of a verb) used without being followed by

a direct object, e.g. *play* in *The teams will play on Saturday* (but not in *The teams will play each other on Saturday*). **intransitively** *adverb*

intravenous (intrŏ-vee-nŏs) *adjective* (*Medicine*) directly into a vein ♦ *an intravenous injection.* **intravenously** *adverb* [from *intra-* and a Latin word *vena* meaning 'vein']

intrepid (in-trep-id) *adjective* fearless and brave. **intrepidity** (in-trip-id-iti) *noun* **intrepidly** *adverb* [from *in-* meaning 'not' and a Latin word *trepidus* meaning 'alarmed']

intricate *adjective* very complicated or detailed. SYNONYMS: complicated, complex, elaborate, involved. **intricacy** (in-trik-ŏsi) *noun* **intricately** *adverb* [from a Latin word *intricatum* meaning 'entangled']

intrigue (in-treeg) *verb* 1 to arouse a person's interest or curiosity ♦ *The subject intrigues me.* SYNONYMS: interest, fascinate, captivate. 2 to plot with someone in a devious way, especially to do harm. SYNONYMS: plot, scheme, conspire. **intrigue** (*also* in-treeg) *noun* devious or secret plotting; a secret plot. [from a Latin word *intricare* meaning 'to tangle', related to *intricate*]

intrinsic (in-trin-sik) *adjective* belonging naturally or essentially to a person or thing ♦ *The coin has little intrinsic value.* **intrinsically** *adverb* [from a Latin word *intrinsecus* meaning 'inward']

intro- *prefix* into or inwards. [from a Latin word *intro* meaning 'to the inside']

introduce *verb* 1 to bring an idea or practice into use. SYNONYMS: establish, initiate, bring in. 2 to make a person known by name to other people. SYNONYMS: present, make known. 3 to announce a speaker or broadcast programme to listeners or viewers. 4 to bring a bill before Parliament. 5 to cause a person to become acquainted with a subject. [from *intro-* and a Latin word *ducere* meaning 'to lead']

introduction *noun* 1 the process of introducing something. 2 the action of making a person known to other people. 3 a short explanatory section at the beginning of a book, speech, etc. 4 a book or course that teaches the basic aspects of a subject. 5 (*Music*) a short preliminary section leading to the main part of a composition.

introductory *adjective* serving as an introduction to a subject.

introspection *noun* the process of concentrating on your own thoughts and feelings.

introspective *adjective* concentrating on your own thoughts and feelings. [from *intro-* and a Latin word *specere* meaning 'to look']

introvert (in-trə-vert) *noun* a quiet reticent person, or one who is more concerned with inner thoughts and feelings than with external things. (Compare **extrovert**.) **introverted** *adjective* [from *intro-* and a Latin word *vertere* meaning 'to turn']

intrude *verb* to come or join in without being invited or wanted. SYNONYMS: interrupt, encroach, interfere, butt in. **intrusion** *noun* [from *in-* meaning 'in' and a Latin word *trudere* meaning 'to push']

intruder *noun* a person who intrudes, especially into a building to commit a crime.

intrusive *adjective* 1 intruding or getting in the way. 2 (*Geology*) (said about rock) forced into cracks or cavities in surrounding rocks by the pressure of molten matter below the earth's crust.

intuition (in-tew-ish-ən) *noun* the ability to know or understand something immediately without conscious reasoning or being taught. **intuitional** *adjective* [from a Latin word *intueri* meaning 'to contemplate']

intuitive (in-tew-itiv) *adjective* based on intuition, instinctive. **intuitively** *adverb*

Inuit (in-yoo-it) *noun* (**Inuit**) 1 a member of a people of northern Canada and parts of Greenland and Alaska. 2 the language of this people.

inundate (in-ən-dayt) *verb* 1 to flood an area or cover it with water. 2 to overwhelm someone with work or other matters to be dealt with ♦ *The television company was inundated with letters of complaint.* **inundation** *noun* [from *in-* meaning 'in' and a Latin word *unda* meaning 'a wave']

inure (in-yoor) *verb* to make someone used to something, especially something unpleasant ♦ *We've all become inured to their criticisms.* **inurement** *noun* [from an Old French phrase meaning 'in use']

in utero (in yoo-tə-roh) *adjective* & *adverb* in a woman's uterus (womb). [a Latin phrase]

invade *verb* 1 to attack and enter a country or region with armed forces in order to occupy it. SYNONYMS: occupy, overrun. 2 (said about a large number of people) to crowd into a place. 3 (said about a disease) to attack an organism or part of the body. 4 to intrude on someone ♦ *Our privacy is being invaded.* **invader** *noun* [from *in-* meaning 'into' and a Latin word *vadere* meaning 'to go']

invalid [1] (in-və-leed) *noun* a person who is ill or weakened by illness or injury. **invalid** *verb* 1 to take someone away from active military service because of ill health or injury ♦ *He was invalided home after the attack.* 2 to disable someone by injury or illness. [from *in-* meaning 'into' and a Latin word *validus* meaning 'strong or powerful']

invalid [2] (in-val-id) *adjective* not valid.

invalidate (in-val-i-dayt) *verb* to make an argument, proposition, or rule ineffective or not valid. **invalidation** *noun*

invalidity (in-və-lid-iti) *noun* 1 the state of being invalid. 2 the condition of being an invalid.

invaluable *adjective* extremely useful or valuable, having a value that is too great to be measured. **invaluably** *adverb*

invariable (in-vair-i-əbəl) *adjective* not variable, always the same.

invariably *adverb* without exception, always.

invasion *noun* the process of invading, especially of territory with an attacking army.

invasive (in-vay-siv) *adjective* invading or intruding.

invective (in-vek-tiv) *noun* strongly critical or abusive language. [from a Latin word *invehere* meaning 'to attack with words']

inveigh (in-vay) *verb* to speak or write with hostility or aggression ♦ *They inveighed against the company for the way they operated in the third world.* [same origin as for *invective*]

inveigle (in-vay-gəl) *verb* to entice someone into doing something ♦ *Their families had been inveigled into paying money.* [from an Old French word *aveugler* meaning 'to blind']

invent verb 1 to make or design something that did not exist before. SYNONYMS: devise, make up, contrive, create. 2 to make up a false story ♦ She was forced to invent an excuse. **inventor** noun [from a Latin word invenire meaning 'to discover']

invention noun 1 the process of inventing something. 2 something that has been invented.

inventive adjective skilled at inventing things, especially ideas.

inventory (in-vən-ter-i) noun (**inventories**) a detailed list of goods or furniture. **inventory** verb (**inventories**, **inventoried**, **inventorying**) to list items in an inventory.

inverse adjective reversed in position, direction, or order.
inverse noun 1 a thing that is the reverse or opposite of another. 2 (Mathematics) a reciprocal quantity. **inversely** adverb [same origin as invert]

inverse proportion noun a relation between two quantities in which one increases in the same proportion as the other decreases.

inversion noun 1 the process of inverting or reversing. 2 something that is inverted. 3 (Music) a form of a chord in which the root is not the lowest note.

invert verb 1 to turn something upside down. 2 to reverse the position or order of things. [from in- meaning 'in' and a Latin word vertere meaning 'to turn']

invertebrate (in-vert-ibrət) noun (Zoology) an animal without a backbone. **invertebrate** adjective not having a backbone.

inverted commas plural noun quotation marks ' ' or " ".

invest verb 1 to use money to make a profit, especially by buying stocks, shares, or property that earn dividends or interest. 2 to spend money, time, or effort on something useful or worthwhile. 3 to confer a rank, office, or power on a person. 4 to endow someone with a quality. 5 (old use) to lay siege to a fortified place. [from a Latin word investire meaning 'to clothe']

investigate verb 1 to make a careful study of something in order to discover the facts about it. 2 to make a search or systematic inquiry. **investigation** noun

investigator noun **investigatory** adjective [from a Latin word investigare meaning 'to trace out']

investigative adjective involving investigation or making inquiries, especially as distinct from merely reporting what is known ♦ investigative journalism.

investiture (in-vest-i-cher) noun the process or ceremony of investing a person with a rank, office, or honour.

investment noun 1 the process of investing money. 2 an amount of money invested. 3 something worthwhile in which money, time, or effort is invested.

investor noun a person who invests money.

inveterate (in-vet-er-ət) adjective firmly established, habitual ♦ an inveterate gambler. **inveterately** adverb [from a Latin word inveterare meaning 'to make old']

invidious (in-vid-iəs) adjective likely to cause resentment because of unfairness. **invidiously** adverb **invidiousness** noun [from a Latin word invidia meaning 'envy']

invigilate (in-vij-i-layt) verb to supervise candidates in an examination. **invigilation** noun **invigilator** noun [from in- meaning 'on' and a Latin word vigilare meaning 'to keep watch']

invigorate (in-vig-er-ayt) verb to fill someone with vigour, to give someone strength or courage. [from in- meaning 'into' and a Latin word vigor meaning 'vigour']

invincible (in-vin-si-bəl) adjective too powerful to be defeated. SYNONYMS: unbeatable, (said about a place) impregnable. **invincibly** adverb **invincibility** noun [from in- meaning 'not' and a Latin word vincere meaning 'to conquer']

inviolable (in-viy-əl-əbəl) adjective not to be violated or dishonoured. **inviolability** noun **inviolably** adverb

inviolate (in-viy-ə-lət) adjective not violated or harmed.

invisible adjective 1 not visible, unable to be seen. 2 (in economics) denoting earnings that a country receives or payments that it makes for services in which no physical imports and exports are involved, e.g. in insurance. **invisibility** noun **invisibly** adverb

invite [1] (in-viyt) verb 1 to ask someone in a friendly or formal way to come to your house or to a social event. 2 to ask

someone formally to do something ♦ *The company invites applications from suitably qualified candidates.* **3** to ask for comments or suggestions. **4** to act in a way that might bring a particular outcome or response ♦ *You are inviting disaster.*
invitation noun [from a Latin word *invitare*]

invite[2] (in-viyt) noun (*informal*) an invitation.

inviting adjective attracting you to do something pleasant and tempting.

in vitro adjective (said about a biological process) taking place in a test tube ♦ *in vitro fertilization.* [a Latin phrase meaning 'in glass']

invocation (invǝ-kay-shǝn) noun the act of invoking, especially calling on a deity in prayer.

invoice noun a list of goods sent or services performed, with prices and charges.
invoice verb **1** to make an invoice for goods or services. **2** to send an invoice to a person or company. [from a French word *envoyer* meaning 'to send']

invoke (in-vohk) verb **1** to call on a deity in prayer. **2** to appeal to an authority for support or protection ♦ *to invoke the law.* **3** to summon up a spirit with words or charms. **4** to call earnestly for vengeance etc. [from *in-* meaning 'in' and a Latin word *vocare* meaning 'to call']

involuntary adjective done without intention or conscious effort.
involuntarily adverb

involve verb **1** to have something as a part, to make something necessary as a condition or result ♦ *The job involves a lot of hard work.* SYNONYMS: require, entail. **2** to let someone share in an experience or undertaking ♦ *They want to involve us in their charity work.* SYNONYMS: include, concern. **3** to cause someone difficulties ♦ *The repairs will involve us in much expense.* **4** to show a person to be concerned in a crime or wrongdoing. **involvement** noun [from *in-* meaning 'in' and a Latin word *volvere* meaning 'to roll']

involved adjective **1** complicated. SYNONYMS: complicated, complex, elaborate, intricate. **2** concerned or sharing in something.

invulnerable (in-vul-ner-ǝbǝl) adjective impossible to harm, not vulnerable.
invulnerability noun

inward adjective **1** on the inside. **2** going or

facing towards the inside. **3** in the mind or spirit ♦ *inward happiness.*
inward adverb inwards.

inwardly adverb **1** on the inside. **2** in the mind or spirit.

inwards adverb **1** towards the inside. **2** in the mind or spirit.

iodine (iy-ǝ-deen) noun a chemical element (symbol I), a substance found in sea water and certain seaweeds, used in solution as an antiseptic. [from a Greek word *iōdēs* meaning 'violet-coloured' (because it gives off a violet-coloured vapour)]

ion (iy-ǝn) noun an electrically charged particle in certain substances. [from a Greek word *ion* meaning 'going']

Ionic (I-on-ik) adjective denoting a classical order of architecture using columns with a scroll-like decoration at the top.

ionic (iy-on-ik) adjective **1** using or containing ions. **2** (said about a chemical bond) linked by electrostatic attraction.

ionize (iy-ǝ-niyz) verb to convert an atom, molecule, or substance into ions, or to be converted into ions. **ionization** noun

ionosphere (iy-on-ǝ-sfeer) noun the region of the upper atmosphere above the mesosphere, with a high concentration of ions and able to reflect radio waves.

iota (iy-oh-tǝ) noun **1** the ninth letter of the Greek alphabet, equivalent to Roman I, i. **2** the smallest possible amount ♦ *It doesn't make an iota of difference.*

IOU noun a signed slip of paper acknowledging a debt. [an abbreviation of *I owe you*]

ipso facto (ip-soh fak-toh) adverb by that very fact or act, by the fact itself ♦ *The statement of the witness does not ipso facto prove the man's guilt.* [a Latin phrase]

IQ abbreviation intelligence quotient.

Ir abbreviation (*Chemistry*) the symbol for iridium.

IRA abbreviation Irish Republican Army.

irascible (i-ras-ibǝl) adjective irritable or bad-tempered. **irascibility** noun **irascibly** adverb [from a Latin word *irasci* meaning 'to become angry', from *ira* meaning 'anger']

irate (iy-rayt) adjective angry or enraged. **irately** adverb [from a Latin word *ira* meaning 'anger']

ire noun (literary) anger. [same origin as for *irate*]

iridescent (i-ri-**dess**-ənt) adjective showing bright colours that appear to change when looked at from different positions. **iridescence** noun [from a Greek word *iris* meaning 'rainbow']

iridium (i-**rid**-iəm) noun a metallic element (symbol Ir) resembling polished steel. [from a Greek word *iris* meaning 'rainbow' (because it forms compounds of different colours)]

iris noun 1 the coloured part of the eyeball, with a round opening (called the *pupil*) in the centre. 2 a plant with long pointed leaves and bright, often purple, flowers with large petals. 3 a diaphragm with a hole (called an *aperture*) that can be adjusted in size. [a Greek word meaning 'rainbow']

Irish adjective to do with or coming from Ireland.
Irish noun the Celtic language of Ireland.
the Irish Irish people.

Irish stew noun a stew made with mutton, potatoes, and onions.

irk verb to annoy someone, to be tiresome to someone. [from an Old Norse word *yrkja* meaning 'to work']

irksome adjective tiresome.

iron noun 1 a hard grey metal, a metallic element (symbol Fe), capable of being magnetized. 2 a device with a flat base that is heated for smoothing cloth or clothes. 3 a tool made of iron ◆ *a branding iron*. 4 a golf club with an iron or steel head. 5 a metal splint or support worn on the leg. 6 great strength or firmness ◆ *a will of iron*.
iron adjective 1 made of iron. 2 strong or unyielding ◆ *an iron constitution* ◆ *an iron will*.
iron verb to smooth cloth or clothes with an iron.
irons plural noun shackles, fetters. **to iron out** to sort out a difficulty or problem. **to have many irons in the fire** to have a large choice of things to use or do. [from an Old English word]

Iron Age noun a period of history that followed the Bronze Age, when weapons and tools were mostly made of iron.

Iron Curtain noun a notional barrier of secrecy and restriction between the Soviet bloc and the West between the end of the second World War and the collapse of communism in the late 1980s.

ironic (iy-**ron**-ik) or **ironical** (iy-**ron**-ikəl) adjective using irony, full of irony. **ironically** adverb

iron lung noun a rigid case fitting over a patient's body, used for giving a long period of artificial respiration by means of mechanical pumps.

ironmonger (iy-ern-mung-ger) noun a shopkeeper who sells tools and household implements.

ironmongery noun (**ironmongeries**) an ironmonger's shop or goods.

ironstone noun 1 rock containing hard iron ore. 2 a kind of hard white pottery.

ironwork noun articles made of iron, such as gratings or railings.

ironworks noun a place where iron is smelted or where heavy iron goods are made.

irony (iy-rən-i) noun (**ironies**) 1 the use of words that mean the opposite of what you really intend, done either for emphasis or for humour. For example, it is irony to say 'What a lovely day' when it is raining hard. 2 an oddly contradictory or perverse situation ◆ *The irony is that I had just told them to be careful when I tripped over myself.* [from a Greek word *eirōn* meaning 'someone who pretends not to know']

irradiate (i-ray-di-ayt) verb 1 to subject a substance to radiation. 2 to shine on something. **irradiation** noun

irrational (i-rash-ən-əl) adjective 1 not rational or logical ◆ *irrational fears* ◆ *irrational behaviour*. 2 not capable of reasoning. 3 (Mathematics) denoting numbers or a quantity that cannot be exactly expressed as a fraction, e.g. pi or the square root of 2. **irrationality** noun **irrationally** adverb

irreconcilable adjective not able to be reconciled. **irreconcilably** adverb

irrecoverable adjective unable to be recovered. **irrecoverably** adverb

irredeemable adjective not able to be saved or redeemed. **irredeemably** adverb

irreducible (i-ri-dew-sibəl) adjective not able to be reduced ◆ *an irreducible minimum.*

irrefutable (i-ref-yoo-təbəl) adjective not able to be refuted. **irrefutably** adverb

irregular adjective 1 not regular, uneven.

SYNONYMS: uneven, erratic. **2** contrary to the rules or to established custom. SYNONYMS: unusual, exceptional, peculiar, unorthodox, abnormal. **3** (said about troops) not in the regular armed forces. **irregularity** noun **irregularly** adverb

irrelevant (i-**rel**-i-vənt) adjective not relevant. **irrelevance** noun **irrelevantly** adverb

irreligious (i-ri-**lij**-əs) adjective not religious; irreverent.

irremediable (i-ri-**meed**-i-əbəl) adjective not able to be remedied or put right. **irremediably** adverb

irreparable (i-**rep**-er-əbəl) adjective not able to be repaired or made good ♦ The fire caused irreparable damage. **irreparably** adverb

irreplaceable adjective not able to be replaced if it is lost.

irrepressible (i-ri-**press**-ibəl) adjective not able to be repressed or restrained.

irreproachable adjective blameless, faultless.

irresistible adjective too strong or attractive to be resisted. **irresistibly** adverb

irresolute (i-**rez**-ə-loot) adjective feeling or showing uncertainty, hesitating. **irresolutely** adverb **irresolution** noun

irrespective adjective not taking something into account ♦ You can apply for a grant irrespective of your parents' income.

irresponsible adjective not behaving in a responsible way. **irresponsibly** adverb

irretrievable adjective not able to be retrieved. **irretrievably** adverb

irreverent adjective not reverent, not respectful. **irreverence** noun **irreverently** adverb

irreversible adjective not reversible, unable to be altered or revoked. **irreversibly** adverb

irrevocable (i-**rev**-ək-əbəl) adjective not able to be changed or revoked, final and unalterable. **irrevocably** adverb

irrigate verb **1** to supply land with water so that crops can grow. **2** (Medicine) to wash a wound with a constant flow of liquid. **irrigation** noun **irrigator** noun [from in- meaning 'into' and a Latin word rigare meaning 'to water']

irritable adjective **1** easily annoyed,

bad-tempered. SYNONYMS: bad-tempered, grumpy, touchy, irascible, peevish. **2** (Medicine) (said about an organ) abnormally sensitive. **irritability** noun **irritably** adverb

irritant noun something that causes irritation.

irritate verb **1** to annoy someone, to make someone angry or impatient. SYNONYMS: annoy, bother, aggravate, get on your nerves. **2** to cause itching. **irritation** noun [from a Latin word irritare, with the same meaning]

irrupt verb to go into a place forcibly or violently. **irruption** noun [from in- meaning 'into' and Latin ruptum meaning 'burst']

is see **be**.

ISA abbreviation individual savings account.

ischium (**isk**-iəm) noun the curved bone forming the base of each half of the pelvis. [from a Greek word ischion meaning 'hip joint']

ISBN abbreviation international standard book number.

ISDN abbreviation (Computing) integrated services digital network.

-ise suffix see **-ize**.

Islam (iz-**lahm**) noun **1** the Muslim religion, based on the teaching of Muhammad. **2** the Muslim world. **Islamic** (iz-**lam**-ik) adjective [from an Arabic word meaning 'submission to God']

island (**iy**-lənd) noun **1** a piece of land surrounded by water. **2** a thing that is compared to an island because it is detached or isolated, e.g. a paved or raised area in the middle of a road. [from an Old English word iegland, with the modern spelling influenced by isle (from Latin insula)]

islander (**iy**-lən-der) noun someone who lives on an island.

isle (iyl) noun (poetic and in place names) an island. [from a Latin word insula, with the same meaning]

islet (**iy**-lit) noun a small island.

isn't verb (informal) is not.

iso- prefix equal (as in isobar). [from a Greek word isos meaning 'equal']

isobar (**iy**-sə-bar) noun (Meteorology) a line on a map connecting points that have the same atmospheric pressure. **isobaric**

adjective [from *iso-* and a Greek word *baros* meaning 'weight']

isohyet (iy-so-hiy-it) *noun* (*Meteorology*) a line on a map connecting points that have the same amount of rainfall per year. [from *iso-* and a Greek word *huetos* meaning 'rain']

isolate *verb* 1 to place a person or thing apart or alone. SYNONYMS: separate, seclude, segregate, cut off. 2 to separate an infectious person from others. 3 to separate a substance from a mixture or compound. **isolation** *noun* [from an Italian word *isolato*, from a Latin word *insulatus* meaning 'made into an island']

isolationism *noun* the policy of not becoming involved in the politics of other countries. **isolationist** *noun*

isomer (iy-som-er) *noun* (*Chemistry*) each of two or more substances with molecules that have the same atoms in different arrangements. **isomeric** (iy-so-merrik) *adjective* **isomerism** (iy-som-er-izm) *noun* [from *iso-* and a Greek word *meros* meaning 'a part']

isometric (iy-so-met-rik) *adjective* 1 having equal size or dimensions. 2 (said about muscle action) developing tension without contraction of the muscle. 3 (said about a drawing or projection) representing a three-dimensional object without perspective, so that equal lengths along the three axes are drawn equal. 4 (*Geometry*) preserving shapes and sizes. [from *iso-* and a Greek word *metron* meaning 'measure']

isomorphic (iy-so-morf-ik) *adjective* having the same form or composition as another substance. **isomorphism** *noun* [from *iso-* and a Greek word *morphē* meaning 'form']

isosceles (iy-sos-i-leez) *adjective* (*Geometry*) (said about a triangle) having two sides that are equal. [from *iso-* and a Greek word *skelos* meaning 'leg']

isotherm (iy-so-therm) *noun* a line drawn on a map connecting points that have the same temperature. **isothermal** *adjective* [from *iso-* and a Greek word *thermē* meaning 'heat']

isotonic (iy-so-ton-ik) *adjective* (said about the action of muscles) taking place with normal contraction. [from *iso-* and a Greek word *tonos* meaning 'tone']

isotope (iy-so-tohp) *noun* a form of a chemical element that differs from other forms in atomic weight and nuclear properties but has the same chemical properties. **isotopic** (iy-so-top-ik) *adjective* [from *iso-* and a Greek word *topos* meaning 'place' (because the forms appear in the same place in the table of chemical elements)]

Israelite (iz-rə-liyt) *noun* a member of the ancient Hebrew nation. **Israelite** *adjective* to do with the ancient Hebrews.

issue *noun* 1 an important topic for thought or discussion. SYNONYMS: matter, concern, question, topic. 2 an outgoing or outflow. 3 the publication or release of things for use or for sale ♦ *The issue of passports is often delayed in the summer months.* 4 one set of publications in a series issued regularly ♦ *The May issue will be out at the end of April.* 5 offspring, children ♦ *Her grandfather had died without male issue.* **issue** *verb* (**issues, issued, issuing**) 1 to come or go or flow out. 2 to supply or distribute for use ♦ *The campers were issued with blankets.* 3 to put something out for sale, to publish something. 4 to send something out or make it known ♦ *The order to attack was issued at dawn.* **at issue** being considered or discussed. **to join** or **take issue** to start to discuss or argue about something. [from an Old French word, related to *exit*]

isthmus (iss-məs) *noun* (**isthmuses**) a narrow strip of land with sea on each side, connecting two larger pieces of land. [from a Greek word *isthmos*]

IT *abbreviation* information technology.

it *pronoun* 1 used to refer to a thing that has already been mentioned. 2 used to refer to a person being identified ♦ *Who is it?* ♦ *It's only me.* 3 used as the subject of a verb making a general statement about the weather (as in ♦ *It has been raining*) or about circumstances (as in ♦ *It is 50 miles to London*). 4 used as the subject or object of a verb, when a more specific reference follows ♦ *It is seldom that they fail* ♦ *I take it that you agree.* 5 exactly what is needed. 6 in children's games, the player who has to catch the others. [from an Old English word]
◊ See the note at **its**.

Italian *adjective* to do with or coming from Italy.
Italian *noun* 1 a person born in Italy or descended from people born there. 2 the language of Italy.

Italianate (i-**tal**-yən-ayt) *adjective* (said especially about art or architecture) Italian in style or appearance.

italic (i-**tal**-ik) *adjective* **1** printed with sloping letters *like this*. **2** (said about handwriting) compact and pointed like an early form of Italian handwriting.
italics *plural noun* sloping printed letters *like these*.

italicize (i-**tal**-i-siyz) *verb* to put printed words into italics.

ITC *abbreviation* Independent Television Commission.

itch *noun* **1** a tickling feeling in its skin that makes you want to scratch it. **2** (*informal*) a restless desire or longing to do something.
itch *verb* **1** to have or feel an itch. **2** (*informal*) to feel a restless desire or longing. [from an Old English word]

itchy *adjective* (**itchier, itchiest**) having or causing an itch. **to have itchy feet** (*informal*) to have an urge to travel or to live somewhere else. **itchiness** *noun*

item *noun* **1** a single thing in a list or number of things. SYNONYMS: article, object. **2** a single piece of news in a newspaper or bulletin. [from a Latin word *item* meaning 'in the same way, just so', used to introduce items in a list]

itemize *verb* to list or specify items.
itemization *noun*

iterate (it-er-ayt) *verb* **1** to say or do something repeatedly. **2** (*Mathematics*) to obtain a solution by repeating a process until a certain condition is satisfied.
iteration *noun* **iterative** *adjective* [from a Latin word *iterum* meaning 'again']

itinerant (iy-**tin**-er-ənt) *adjective* travelling from place to place ♦ *an itinerant preacher*. [same origin as for *itinerary*]

itinerary (iy-**tin**-er-er-i) *noun* (**itineraries**) a list of places to be visited on a journey; a route. [from a Latin word *itineris* meaning 'of a journey']

it'll (*informal*) *verb* it will.

its *possessive pronoun* of or belonging to it. ◊ Do not put an apostrophe in *its*, unless you mean 'it is' or 'it has' (see the next entry).

it's (*informal*) *verb* it is or it has ♦ *It's very hot* ♦ *It's broken all records.*
◊ Do not confuse this word, which has an apostrophe, with **its**, which has a different meaning (see the entry above).

itself *pronoun* **1** the reflexive form of *it*, used as the object of a verb or preposition when it is the same as the subject (normally a thing or an animal) ♦ *The cat was licking itself by the fire.* **2** used for emphasis ♦ *The town itself was hidden in fog.* **by itself** on its own, alone.

ITV *abbreviation* Independent Television.

IUD *abbreviation* intra-uterine device, a coil or loop placed inside the womb as a contraceptive.

IVF *abbreviation* in vitro fertilization.

ivory *noun* (**ivories**) **1** the hard creamy-white substance forming the tusks of elephants. **2** an object made of this. **3** a creamy-white colour.
ivory *adjective* creamy-white.

ivory tower *noun* a place or situation in which people live a privileged life away from the ordinary difficulties of the world.

ivy *noun* a climbing evergreen shrub with shiny five-pointed leaves.

-ize *suffix* forming verbs meaning 'to bring or come into a certain condition' (as in *civilize, privatize*), treat in a certain way (as in *pasteurize*), or have a certain feeling (as in *sympathize*). [from a Greek verb ending *-izein*]
◊ These verbs can also be spelt with the ending *-ise* (e.g. *privatise*). Some words ending in *-cise* and *-vise* have to be spelt with *-ise* (e.g. *exercise, supervise*).

Jj

J the tenth letter of the English alphabet.

J *abbreviation* joule(s).

jab *verb* (**jabbed, jabbing**) to poke something roughly with something pointed. SYNONYMS: prod, dig, stab.
jab *noun* **1** a sharp poke or blow, especially with something pointed. **2** (*informal*) a hypodermic injection. [originally a Scots word]

jabber *verb* to talk rapidly and unintelligibly ♦ *What are you jabbering on about?*

jabber *noun* jabbering talk. [an imitation of the sound]

jack *noun* **1** a portable device for lifting something heavy off the ground, especially one for raising the axle of a motor vehicle so that a wheel may be changed. **2** a playing card with a picture of a young man, ranking below a queen in card games. **3** a device using a single plug to connect an electrical circuit. **4** a star-shaped piece of metal or plastic used in tossing and catching games. **5** a small ship's flag flown at the bow of a ship to show its nationality. **6** the small white ball that players aim at in the game of bowls. **7** the male of various animals.
jacks *noun* a game played by tossing and catching jacks.
jack *verb* to lift something with a jack. **to jack it in** (*informal*) to give up or abandon an attempt. **jack of all trades** someone who can do many different kinds of work. **to jack something up** (*informal*) to increase something by a large amount. [from the name *Jack*, used for various sorts of tool, as though it was a person helping you]

jackal *noun* a wild animal of Africa and Asia, related to the dog, often hunting and scavenging in packs. [from a Persian word]

jackass *noun* **1** a male ass or donkey. **2** a stupid or foolish person. [from the name *Jack* and *ass*]

jackboot *noun* a large military boot reaching above the knee.

jackdaw *noun* a bird like a small crow with black and grey feathers, noted for its thieving habits. [from the name *Jack* and an old word *dawe* meaning 'jackdaw']

jacket *noun* **1** a short coat, usually reaching to the hips. **2** an outer covering round something, especially one round a boiler or water tank to keep the heat in. **3** a paper wrapper for a book. **4** the skin of a potato baked without being peeled. [from an Old French word *jaquet*]

jacket potato *noun* a baked potato served with the skin on.

Jack Frost *noun* a personification of frost.

jack-in-the-box *noun* a toy figure that springs out of a box when the lid is lifted.

jackknife *noun* (**jackknives**) **1** a large knife with a folding blade. **2** a dive in which the body is first bent double and then straightened.
jackknife *verb* **1** (said about an articulated vehicle) to bend into a V-shape in an uncontrolled skidding movement. **2** to move your body into a bent or doubled-up position.

jackpot *noun* a large cash prize or accumulated stake in a game or lottery. **to hit the jackpot** to have sudden great success or good fortune. [originally denoting a kitty which could be won only by playing a pair of jacks or cards of higher value: from *jack* and *pot*]

Jack Russell *noun* a small terrier with short legs. [named after the English clergyman Rev. John Russell (1795–1883), a breeder of terriers]

Jack tar *noun* (*informal, old use*) a sailor.

Jacobean (jak-ə-bee-ən) *adjective* from the reign of James I of England (1603–25). [from a Latin word *Jacobus* meaning 'James']

Jacobite (jak-ə-biyt) *noun* a supporter of the deposed James II of England after the revolution of 1688, or of the exiled Stuarts. [same origin as for *Jacobean*]

Jacuzzi (ja-koo-zi) *noun* (*trademark*) a large bath in which underwater jets of water massage the body.

jade *noun* **1** a hard green stone that is carved to make ornaments and jewellery. **2** a light bluish-green colour. [from a Spanish phrase *piedra de ijada* meaning 'colic stone' (because it was believed to cure diseases of the stomach)]

jaded *adjective* tired and no longer interested or enthusiastic. [from *jade*]

jagged (jag-id) *adjective* having an uneven edge or outline with sharp points. SYNONYMS: serrated, toothed, spiky. [from a Scots word *jag* meaning 'to stab']

jaguar *noun* a large flesh-eating animal of the cat family that has a yellowish-brown coat with black spots, found in tropical America. [via Portuguese from a Tupi (South American) word *yaguara*]

jail *noun* a prison.
jail *verb* to put someone into prison.
jailer or **gaoler** *noun* [from an Old French word *jaiole* meaning 'cage or prison']

jailbreak *noun* an escape from jail.

Jain (jayn) *noun* a follower of an Indian religion with doctrines like those of Buddhism.
Jain *adjective* to do with this religion.

Jainism noun **Jainist** noun [via Hindi from a Sanskrit word]

jalopy (jə-**lop**-i) noun (**jalopies**) (informal) a battered old car. [origin unknown]

jam¹ verb (**jammed, jamming**) **1** to squeeze or pack something tightly into a space ♦ Two hundred people were jammed into the hall. SYNONYMS: pack, cram, stuff, crush. **2** to make part of a machine become stuck so that the machine will not work; to become stuck in this way ♦ Something is jamming the printer. **3** to crowd or block a road or area with people or things. SYNONYMS: block, clog, obstruct; (informal) bung up. **4** to block a telephone line. **5** to push or apply something forcibly ♦ He jammed on the brakes. **6** to cause interference to a radio transmission so that it cannot be received clearly. **7** (informal) (said about musicians) to improvise together.
jam noun **1** a crowded mass making movement difficult ♦ a traffic jam. **2** a squeeze or crush. **3** (informal) a difficult situation ♦ I'm in a bit of a jam. SYNONYMS: predicament, quandary, plight; (informal) fix, hole, pickle. **4** (informal) an improvised performance by a group of musicians. [origin unknown]

jam² noun a sweet substance made by boiling fruit with sugar until it is thick.
jam verb (**jammed, jamming**) to make fruit into jam. [perhaps from jam¹]

jamb (jam) noun the vertical side post of a doorway or window frame. [from a French word jambe meaning 'leg']

jamboree (jam-ber-ee) noun a large party or celebration. [origin unknown]

jam-packed adjective (informal) extremely crowded or packed full.

jangle verb **1** to make or cause something to make a harsh ringing sound. **2** (said about your nerves) to be set on edge.
jangle noun a harsh ringing sound. [from an Old French word]

janissary (jan-i-ser-i) noun (**janissaries**) (historical) a Turkish soldier. [from Turkish words yeni meaning 'new' and çeri meaning 'troops']

janitor (jan-it-er) noun the caretaker of a building. **janitorial** (jan-i-**tor**-iəl) adjective [from a Latin word janua meaning 'door']

January noun the first month of the year. [named after Janus, a Roman god who was the guardian of doorways, gates, and beginnings, usually shown with two faces that look in opposite directions]

japan noun a kind of hard usually black varnish, especially a kind brought originally from Japan.
japan verb (**japanned, japanning**) to coat something with japan.

Japanese adjective to do with or coming from Japan.
Japanese noun **1** (**Japanese**) a person born in Japan or descended from people born there. **2** the language of Japan.

japonica (jə-**pon**-ikə) noun an ornamental variety of quince, with red flowers. [a Latin word meaning 'Japanese']

jar¹ noun **1** a cylindrical container made of glass or pottery. **2** this with its contents, or the amount it contains. [from an Arabic word jarra meaning 'pot']

jar² verb (**jarred, jarring**) **1** to make a harsh discordant sound. **2** to have a harsh or disagreeable effect on someone ♦ Her voice really jars on my nerves. **3** to cause an unpleasant jolt or vibration ♦ He jarred his neck in the fall. **4** to clash or conflict with something.
jar noun a sudden jolt or vibration. [an imitation of the sound]

jargon noun words or expressions used by a particular profession or group that are difficult for other people to understand ♦ scientists' jargon. [originally meaning 'twittering, chattering', from an Old French word jargoun]

jasmine noun a shrub with fragrant yellow or white flowers. [via French from an Arabic word]

jasper noun an opaque variety of quartz, usually red, yellow, or brown. [from an Old French word jaspe]

jaundice (**jawn**-dis) noun a condition in which the skin becomes abnormally yellow as a result of excessive bile in the bloodstream. [from a French word jaune meaning 'yellow']

jaundiced adjective **1** discoloured by jaundice. **2** filled with resentment or bitterness.

jaunt noun a short trip, especially one taken for pleasure. [origin unknown]

jaunty adjective (**jauntier, jauntiest**) **1** cheerful and self-confident in manner. **2** (said about clothes) stylish and cheerful.

jauntily adverb **jauntiness** noun [originally meaning stylish, elegant: from a French word gentil; related to gentle]

Java (jah-və) noun (Computing) a programming language that is compatible with different computer systems.

javelin (jav-ə-lin) noun a long light spear thrown in an athletics competition or as a weapon. [from an Old French word]

jaw noun 1 either of the two bones that form the framework of the mouth and in which the teeth are set. 2 the corresponding part of an insect or other invertebrate. 3 the lower part of the face ♦ He has a firm jaw.
jaws plural noun the gripping parts of a wrench or vice.
jaw verb (informal) to talk long and boringly; to gossip. [from an Old French word joe meaning 'cheek, jaw']

jawbone noun either of the bones of the jaw.

jay noun a bird of the crow family, especially a noisy chattering European bird with pinkish-brown plumage, a black tail, and a small blue patch on each wing. [from a French word]

jaywalking noun walking carelessly in a road, without looking out for traffic or signals. **jaywalker** noun [from an American meaning of jay meaning 'fool' and walk]

jazz noun a type of music with strong rhythm and much syncopation, often improvised. **to jazz something up** to make something more lively or interesting. [probably a black American meaning]

jazzy adjective (**jazzier, jazziest**) 1 of or like jazz. 2 bright and showy ♦ a jazzy sports car.

JCB noun a mechanical excavator with a shovel at the front and a digging arm at the rear. [from the name of the makers, J C Bamford]

jealous (jel-əs) adjective 1 feeling resentful or suspicious of a person who you feel is your rival or is better or luckier than yourself. SYNONYMS: envious, covetous, resentful. 2 careful in keeping something ♦ He is very jealous of his reputation. SYNONYMS: protective, possessive, vigilant.
jealously adverb **jealousy** noun [from an Old French word gelos]

jeans plural noun trousers made of denim or another strong cotton fabric. [from Genoa, a city in Italy, where such a cloth was once made]

Jeep noun (trademark) a small sturdy motor vehicle with four-wheel drive, especially one used in the army. [from G.P., short for 'general purpose']

jeer verb to laugh or shout at someone rudely and scornfully. SYNONYMS: taunt, deride, barrack, mock.
jeer noun a rude and mocking remark or shout. [origin unknown]

Jehovah (ji-hoh-və) noun the traditional English form of one of the Hebrew names for God, now often written as Yahweh. [from adding vowels to JHVH, the consonants of the Hebrew name of God]

Jehovah's Witness noun a member of a Christian sect preaching that the end of the world is near.

jejune (ji-joon) adjective 1 naive and simplistic. 2 dull and lacking imagination. [from a Latin word jejunus meaning 'fasting']

Jekyll and Hyde noun someone who alternately shows two sides of their personality, one good and one evil. [named after the hero of a story (by R. L. Stevenson) who could transform himself from the respectable Dr Jekyll into the evil Mr Hyde by means of a potion which he drank]

jell verb (informal) 1 to set as jelly. 2 to take a definite form or begin to work well ♦ Gradually our ideas began to jell. [from jelly]

jellied adjective set in jelly ♦ jellied eels.

jelly[1] noun (**jellies**) 1 a clear fruit-flavoured dessert set with gelatin. 2 a kind of jam made of strained fruit juice and sugar. 3 a savoury food made from meat stock and gelatin ♦ marrowbone jelly. 4 a substance of similar consistency ♦ petroleum jelly. [from a Latin word gelare meaning 'to freeze']

jelly[2] noun (informal) gelignite.

jellyfish noun (**jellyfish** or **jellyfishes**) a sea animal with a jelly-like body and stinging tentacles.

jemmy noun (**jemmies**) a short crowbar used by burglars to force doors, windows, and drawers.
jemmy verb (**jemmies, jemmied, jemmying**) to force open a door, window, or drawer with a jemmy. [from the name Jimmy; compare jack]

jenny noun (**jennies**) a female donkey. [from the name *Jenny*]

jeopardize (jep-er-diyz) verb to put someone in danger, to put something at risk.

jeopardy (jep-er-di) noun danger. [from an Old French word]

jerboa (jer-boh-ə) noun a small rat-like animal of the North African desert, with long hind legs used for leaping. [from an Arabic word]

Jeremiah (je-ri-miy-ah) noun a person who complains continually or foretells disaster. [from the name *Jeremiah*, a Hebrew prophet in the Old Testament]

jerk noun **1** a sudden sharp movement; an abrupt pull or push. **2** (*informal*) a stupid or insignificant person.
jerk verb to pull or move something with a jerk; to move with a jerk or in short uneven movements ♦ *The train jerked to a halt.* [origin unknown]

jerkin noun a sleeveless jacket. [origin unknown]

jerky adjective (**jerkier, jerkiest**) moving with abrupt starts and stops, not smoothly. **jerkily** adverb **jerkiness** noun

jerry-built adjective built badly and with poor materials. **jerry-builder** noun [origin unknown]

jerrycan noun a large flat-sided can for petrol or water.

jersey noun (**jerseys**) **1** a close-fitting woollen pullover with sleeves. **2** a shirt worn by a player in certain sports ♦ *a football jersey.* **3** a soft knitted fabric. **4** (**Jersey**) a breed of light-brown dairy cattle, originally from Jersey. [named after Jersey, one of the Channel Islands]

jest noun a joke.
jest verb to make jokes. **in jest** in fun, not seriously. [from an old word *gest* meaning 'a story']

jester noun a professional entertainer employed at a royal court in the Middle Ages.

Jesuit (jez-yoo-it) noun a member of the Society of Jesus, a Roman Catholic religious order. [from a Latin word *Jesuita* meaning 'follower of Jesus']

jet [1] noun **1** a stream of water, gas, flame, etc., shot out from a small opening. **2** a spout or opening from which a jet comes, a burner on a gas cooker. **3** a jet engine. **4** an aircraft powered by jet engines.
jet verb (**jetted, jetting**) **1** to spurt out in a jet. **2** to travel by jet aircraft. [from a French word *jeter* meaning 'to throw']

jet [2] noun **1** a hard black mineral that can be polished, used as a gem. **2** a deep glossy black colour ♦ *jet black hair.* [from an Old French word *jaiet*]

jet engine noun an engine using jet propulsion.

jet lag noun extreme tiredness that a person feels after a long flight between different time zones. **jet-lagged** adjective

jet-propelled adjective propelled by jet engines.

jet propulsion noun propulsion by engines that give forward thrust by sending out a high-speed jet of gases etc. at the back.

jetsam noun goods thrown overboard from a ship in distress and washed ashore. [from *jettison*]

jet set noun (*informal*) wealthy people who travel widely and frequently for pleasure.

jet ski noun (*trademark*) a small jet-propelled vehicle like a scooter, which skims across the surface of water.

jet stream noun **1** a strong wind blowing in a narrow range of altitudes in the upper atmosphere. **2** a flow of exhaust gases from a jet engine.

jettison verb **1** to throw goods overboard from a ship; to drop goods or fuel from an aircraft or spacecraft. **2** to get rid of something that is no longer wanted. [same origin as for *jet* [1]]

jetty noun (**jetties**) a landing stage or small pier. [from a French word *jetée* meaning 'thrown out (from the shore)']

Jew noun a person of Hebrew descent, or one whose religion is Judaism. [from a Hebrew word *yehudi* meaning 'belonging to the tribe of Judah']

jewel noun **1** a precious stone. **2** an ornament containing one or more precious stones. **3** a precious stone used as a bearing in a watch. **4** a person or thing that is highly valued. [from an Old French word]

jewelled adjective ornamented or set with jewels.

jeweller noun a person or company that makes or sells jewels or jewellery.

jewellery (joo-əl-ri or jool-er-i) *noun* ornaments that people wear made of jewels and precious metal.

Jewish *adjective* to do with Jews or Judaism.

Jewry *noun* the Jewish people.

Jew's harp *noun* a musical instrument consisting of a small U-shaped metal frame held in the teeth while a metal strip is twanged with a finger.

Jezebel (jez-ə-bəl) *noun* a shameless or immoral woman. [from Jezebel, the pagan wife of Ahab king of Israel in the Bible]

jib [1] *noun* 1 a triangular sail stretching forward from the mast. 2 the arm of a crane. **the cut of someone's jib** someone's manner or style. [origin unknown]

jib [2] *verb* (jibbed, jibbing) (said about a horse) to stop suddenly and refuse to go on. **to jib at** to be unwilling to do or accept something. [origin unknown]

jibba *noun* a long cloth coat worn by Muslim men in some countries. [from an Egyptian Arabic word]

jibe *verb & noun* another spelling of **gibe**.

jiffy or **jiff** *noun* (*informal*) a moment ♦ *I'll be with you in a jiffy.* [origin unknown]

jig *noun* 1 a lively jumping dance, or the music for this. 2 a device that holds a piece of work in place and guides the tools working on it. 3 a template. **jig** *verb* (jigged, jigging) to move or make something move up and down rapidly and jerkily. [origin unknown]

jiggered *adjective* (*informal*) exhausted or broken.

jiggery-pokery *noun* (*informal*) trickery, underhand dealing. [origin unknown]

jiggle *verb* to rock or jerk something lightly. [from *jig*]

jigsaw *noun* 1 a puzzle consisting of a picture printed on board or wood and cut into irregular pieces which have to be fitted together. 2 a mechanically operated saw with a small stiff blade that moves to and fro, used to cut curved lines.

jihad (ji-hahd) *noun* a holy war undertaken by Muslims. [an Arabic word]

jilt *verb* to abandon a boyfriend or girlfriend, especially after promising to marry him or her. [origin unknown]

jingle *verb* to make or cause something to make a metallic ringing or clinking sound like that of metal objects being shaken together ♦ *A set of keys jingled at her waist.* **jingle** *noun* 1 a jingling sound. 2 a short catchy slogan or tune, especially one used in advertising. [an imitation of the sound]

jingoism (jing-goh-izm) *noun* an aggressive attitude combining excessive patriotism and contempt for other countries. **jingoist** *noun* **jingoistic** *adjective* [from the saying *by jingo!*, used in a warlike popular song in the 19th century]

jinn *nouns* (jinn or jinns) 1 (in Arabian and Muslim mythology) any of the supernatural beings able to appear in human and animal form and to help or hinder human beings. 2 a genie. [from an Arabic word *jinni*; *jinn* is the plural in Arabic]

jinx *noun* a person or thing that is thought to bring bad luck. **jinx** *verb* to bring bad luck to someone. [probably a variation of *jynx* meaning 'wryneck', a bird used in witchcraft]

jitter *verb* (*informal*) to behave nervously. **the jitters** *plural noun* a feeling of extreme nervousness. **jitteriness** *noun* **jittery** *adjective* [origin unknown]

jive *noun* a style of lively dance performed to fast jazz music or rock and roll. **jive** *verb* to dance the jive. [origin unknown]

Jnr *abbreviation* Junior.

job *noun* 1 work that someone does regularly to earn a living ♦ *She's got a job at the hospital.* SYNONYMS: occupation, post, position, appointment, employment, trade, profession. 2 a piece of work to be done ♦ *Can you do a couple of jobs for me?* SYNONYMS: task, chore, errand, undertaking. 3 a responsibility or duty ♦ *It's your job to lock the gates.* 4 work done to improve or repair something ♦ *a nose job* ♦ *They've done a nice job on the car.* 5 (*Computing*) an operation or group of operations treated as a distinct unit. 6 (*informal*) a difficult task ♦ *You'll have a job to move it.* 7 (*informal*) a crime, especially a robbery. **a good job** (*informal*) a fortunate or satisfactory state of affairs ♦ *It's a good job you're here.* **just the job** (*informal*) exactly what is needed. [origin unknown]

jobber *noun* (*Finance*) a principal or wholesaler dealing on the Stock Exchange with brokers, not directly with the public.

jobbing *adjective* doing casual or occasional work for payment ♦ *a jobbing gardener.*

jobcentre *noun* a government office in a local area, providing information about available jobs and handling payment of benefits.

jobless *adjective* unemployed, out of work.

job lot *noun* a collection of miscellaneous articles bought together.

Job's comforter (johbz) *noun* someone who adds to the distress of the person they are supposed to be comforting. [from the story of Job, a Hebrew patriarch in the Bible]

job-share *verb* (said about two people) to jointly do a full-time job.
job-share *noun* an arrangement of this kind.

jockey *noun* (**jockeys**) a person who rides horses in horse races.
jockey *verb* (**jockeyed, jockeying**) to manoeuvre in order to gain an advantage ♦ *On the final bend the runners were jockeying for position.* [from a pet form of the name Jock]

jocose (jǝ-ohss) *adjective* (*formal*) humorous or playful. **jocosely** *adverb* [from a Latin word *jocus* meaning 'a joke']

jocular (jok-yoo-ler) *adjective* joking, avoiding seriousness. **jocularity** (jok-yoo-la-riti) *noun* **jocularly** *adverb* [from a Latin word *jocus* meaning 'a joke']

jocund (jok-ǝnd) *adjective* (*formal*) light-hearted or cheerful. [from a Latin word *jucundus* meaning 'pleasant or agreeable']

jodhpurs (jod-perz) *plural noun* trousers for horse riding, fitting closely below the knee and loose above it. [named after Jodhpur in India]

jog *verb* (**jogged, jogging**) 1 to run at a steady leisurely pace as a form of exercise. 2 (said about a horse) to move at a slow steady trot. 3 to give something a slight knock or push.
jog *noun* 1 a spell of jogging ♦ *He went out for his morning jog.* 2 a slow run or trot. 3 a slight knock or push. **to jog someone's memory** to help them to remember something. **jogger** *noun* [same origin as for *jagged*]

joggle *verb* to shake something slightly; to move by slight jerks.

joggle *noun* a joggling movement, a slight shake. [from *jog*]

jogtrot *noun* a slow steady trot.

joie de vivre (zhwah dǝ veevr) *noun* a feeling of great enjoyment of life. [a French phrase meaning 'joy of living']

join *verb* 1 to put things together, to link or connect things. SYNONYMS: attach, fix, combine, connect, link, unite, couple, marry. 2 to come together, to become united with something ♦ *The Cherwell joins the Thames at Oxford.* SYNONYMS: meet, converge, combine, link up. 3 to become a member or employee of a group or organization ♦ *He joined the company in 1998.* 4 to take part with others in doing something ♦ *We all joined in the chorus.* 5 to come into the company of other people ♦ *Will you join us for lunch?* 6 to become part of something or take your place in something ♦ *We joined the queue.*
join *noun* a place where two or more things are joined. **to join battle** (*formal*) to begin fighting. **to join forces** to combine efforts. **to join hands** to clasp each other's hands. **to join up** to become a member of the armed forces. [from a French word *joindre*]

joiner *noun* a person who makes doors, window frames, etc. and furniture out of wood.

joinery *noun* the work of a joiner.

joint *noun* 1 a place where two things are joined. 2 a structure in a body by which two bones are fitted together. 3 a place or device at which two parts of a structure are joined. 4 a large piece of meat cut ready for cooking ♦ *a joint of lamb.* 5 a crack or fissure in a mass of rock. 6 (*informal*) a cannabis cigarette.
joint *adjective* 1 shared, held, or done by two or more people together ♦ *a joint account.* 2 sharing in an achievement or activity ♦ *joint authors.*
joint *verb* 1 to connect things by a joint or joints. 2 to divide the body of an animal into joints ♦ *The book tells you how to joint a chicken.* 3 to fill up or point masonry or brickwork joints with mortar. **out of joint** 1 dislocated. 2 in disorder. [from a French word]

jointly *adverb* so as to be shared or done by two or more people together ♦ *You are jointly responsible for this accident.*

joint-stock company *noun* a business company with capital contributed and held jointly by a number of people.

joist noun any of the parallel beams, extending from wall to wall, on which floorboards or ceiling laths are fixed. [from an Old French word]

jojoba (hə-hoh-bə) noun an oil obtained from the seeds of a North American shrub, used in cosmetics. [from a Mexican Spanish word]

joke noun 1 something said or done to make people laugh. SYNONYMS: jest, quip, wisecrack, prank; (informal) gag. 2 a ridiculous person or thing.
joke verb 1 to make jokes. 2 to tease someone or not be serious ♦ It's all right, I'm only joking. **to be no joke** (informal) to be a serious or difficult matter. **to be beyond a joke** (informal) to be serious or worrying.
jokingly adverb [originally slang: probably from a Latin word jocus meaning 'jest, wordplay']

joker noun 1 a person who likes making jokes. 2 (informal) a foolish person. 3 an extra playing card with a jester on it, used as a wild card in certain card games.

jokey adjective joking, not serious.

jollification noun merrymaking or festivity.

jollity noun (jollities) cheerfulness and merriment.

jolly adverb (jollier, jolliest) full of high spirits, cheerful.
jolly adverb (informal) very ♦ jolly good. **jolly** verb (jollies, jollied, jollying) (informal) **to jolly someone along** or **up** to try to keep someone cheerful. [from an Old French word jolif, an earlier form of joli meaning 'pretty']

jolly boat noun a ship's boat, smaller than a cutter, built with overlapping planks.

Jolly Roger noun a black flag with a white skull and crossbones, traditionally associated with pirates.

jolt verb 1 to shake or dislodge something with a sudden sharp movement. 2 to move along jerkily, as on a rough road. 3 to give someone a shock.
jolt noun 1 a jolting movement or effect. 2 a surprise or shock. [origin unknown]

jonquil (jon-kwil) noun a kind of narcissus with clusters of fragrant flowers. [from a Spanish word]

josh verb (informal) to tease someone in a good-natured way. [origin unknown]

joss noun a Chinese idol. [from a Javanese word dejos]

joss house noun a Chinese temple.

joss stick noun a thin stick that burns to give off a smell of incense.

jostle verb to push or bump roughly against people, especially in a crowd. [from joust]

jot verb (jotted, jotting) to write something quickly ♦ Let me jot down your phone number.
jot noun a very small amount ♦ She doesn't care a jot about it. [from a Greek word iōta denoting the smallest letter of the Greek alphabet]

jotter noun a small notepad or notebook.

jottings plural noun brief notes.

joule (jool) noun an SI unit of work or energy, equal to the work done by a force of one newton to make an object move one metre. [named after the English physicist J. P. Joule (1818–89)]

journal (jer-nəl) noun 1 a newspaper or magazine dealing with a particular subject ♦ a physics journal. 2 a diary or logbook. 3 a daily record of business transactions. [from a Latin word meaning 'by day']

journalese (jer-nəl-eez) noun (informal) a style of language used in inferior newspaper writing, full of hackneyed or artificially elaborate phrases.

journalist (jer-nəl-ist) noun a person who writes for newspapers or magazines.
journalism noun **journalistic** adjective

journey noun (journeys) 1 going from one place to another. SYNONYMS: expedition, trip, jaunt, voyage (by sea), flight (by air). 2 the distance travelled or the time taken to travel somewhere ♦ The river is two days' journey from here.
journey verb (journeys, journeyed, journeying) to make a journey. [from a French word meaning 'a day's travel', from jour meaning 'day']

journeyman noun (journeymen) 1 a skilled workman who works for an employer. 2 a reliable but not outstanding worker.

joust (jowst) verb 1 to fight on horseback with lances. 2 to compete for superiority. **joust** noun a jousting contest. **jousting** noun [from an Old French word juster meaning 'to bring together']

Jove noun **by Jove!** an exclamation of surprise. [from Jove, the chief of the Roman gods, equivalent to Jupiter]

jovial (joh-vi-əl) *adjective* cheerful and good-humoured. **joviality** (joh-vi-**al**-iti) *noun* **jovially** *adverb* [from a Latin word *jovialis* meaning 'to do with Jupiter' (because people born under its influence were said to be cheerful)]

jowl *noun* **1** the lower part of a cheek, especially when it is drooping or fleshy. **2** an animal's dewlap. [from an Old English word *ceole*]

joy *noun* **1** a feeling of great pleasure or happiness. SYNONYMS: elation, bliss, rapture, delight. **2** a thing that causes joy. **no joy** (*informal*) no satisfaction or success. **joyless** *adjective* [from an Old French word *joie*]

joyful *adjective* full of joy ◆ *a joyful occasion.* **joyfully** *adverb* **joyfulness** *noun*

joyous *adjective* full of joy. **joyously** *adverb*

joypad *noun* a control device used for computer games, with buttons controlling an image on a screen.

joyride *noun* a fast ride in a stolen car for amusement. **joyrider** *noun* **joyriding** *noun*

joystick *noun* **1** the control lever of an aircraft. **2** a device for moving a cursor or image on a computer screen.

JP *abbreviation* Justice of the Peace.

Jr *abbreviation* Junior.

jubilant *adjective* happy and triumphant. [from a Latin word *jubilans* meaning 'shouting for joy']

jubilation *noun* a feeling of great happiness and triumph. [same origin as for *jubilant*]

jubilee *noun* **1** a special anniversary, especially one celebrating 25, 50, or 60 years. **2** a time of rejoicing. [from a Hebrew word *yobel* denoting a year when slaves were freed and property returned to its owners, held in ancient Israel every 50 years]
◊ A 25th anniversary is called a *silver jubilee*, a 50th anniversary is called a *golden jubilee*, and a 60th anniversary is called a *diamond jubilee*.

Judaic (joo-**day**-ik) *adjective* to do with or characteristic of Judaism or the ancient Jews.

Judaism (joo-day-izm) *noun* the religion of the Jewish people, with belief in one God and based on the teachings of the Old Testament and the Talmud. [same origin as for *Jew*]

Judas *noun* a person who betrays a friend. [from the name of *Judas* Iscariot who betrayed Christ]

judder *verb* to shake noisily or violently. **judder** *noun* a juddering movement or effect. [an imitation of the sound]

judge *noun* **1** a public officer appointed to hear and try cases in a law court. **2** a person appointed to decide who has won a contest. SYNONYMS: adjudicator, arbiter, referee, umpire. **3** a person who is able to give an authoritative opinion on something ◆ *She is a good judge of character.* **4** (in ancient Israel) any of the warrior leaders in the period between Joshua and the kings.
judge *verb* **1** to try a case in a law court. **2** to act as judge of a contest. **3** to form and give an opinion about something. **4** to estimate something ◆ *She judged the distance accurately.* [from a Latin word *judex* meaning 'judge', from *jus* meaning 'law' and *-dicus* meaning 'saying']

judgement or **judgment** *noun* **1** the ability to judge wisely, good sense ◆ *He lacks judgement.* SYNONYMS: common sense, acumen, discernment, wisdom. **2** an opinion or conclusion ◆ *It is in the judgement of most critics the film of the year.* SYNONYMS: opinion, estimation, assessment, valuation. **3** the decision of a judge or law court ◆ *The judgement was in his favour.* SYNONYMS: verdict, ruling, finding. **4** judging, or being judged.

judgemental (juj-**men**-təl) *adjective* **1** involving judgement. **2** inclined to make moral judgements ◆ *You shouldn't be so judgemental.* **judgementally** *adverb*

judicature (joo-dik-ə-choor) *noun* **1** the administration of justice. **2** a body of judges. [from a Latin word *judicare* meaning 'to judge']

judicial (joo-**dish**-əl) *adjective* **1** to do with law courts or the administration of justice ◆ *the British judicial system.* **2** to do with a judge or judgement. **judicially** *adverb* [from a Latin word *judicis* meaning 'of a judge']
◊ Do not confuse this word with **judicious**, which has a different meaning.

judiciary (joo-**dish**-er-i) *noun* (**judiciaries**) all the judges in a country.

judicious (joo-**dish**-əs) *adjective* judging wisely, showing good sense ◆ *a judicious choice.* **judiciously** *adverb* [same origin as for *judicial*]
◊ Do not confuse this word with **judicial**,

which has a different meaning.

judo *noun* a Japanese system of unarmed combat, derived from ju-jitsu. **judoist** *noun* [from Japanese words *ju* meaning 'gentle' and *do* meaning 'way']

judoka (joo-doh-kə) *noun* (**judoka**) a student of or expert in judo. [from *judo* and a Japanese word *ka* meaning 'person, profession']

jug *noun* 1 a container for holding and pouring liquids, with a handle and a shaped lip. 2 (*informal*) prison ♦ *He had to spend a night in the jug.*
jug *verb* (**jugged, jugging**) to stew or boil a hare or rabbit in a covered container.
jugful *noun* (**jugfuls**) [from a familiar form of Joan or Jenny]

juggernaut *noun* 1 a very large long-distance transport vehicle. 2 a large overwhelmingly powerful institution or other force. [via Hindi from a Sanskrit word *Jagannatha*, the name of an image of the Hindu god Krishna which was dragged in procession on a huge wheeled vehicle. Some devotees are said to have thrown themselves under its wheels]

juggle *verb* 1 to toss and catch a number of objects skilfully for entertainment, keeping one or more in the air at any time. 2 to cope with all the things you have to do by skilfully balancing the time you spend on each of them. 3 to rearrange facts or figures in order to achieve something or to deceive people. **juggler** *noun* [from an Old French word *jogler*]

jugular (jug-yoo-ler) *adjective* to do with the throat or neck. [from a Latin word *jugulum* meaning 'throat']

jugular vein *noun* either of the two great veins of the neck carrying blood from the head.

juice *noun* 1 the liquid from fruit or vegetables. 2 a drink made from this liquid. 3 liquid coming from meat or other food during cooking. 4 liquid secreted by an organ of the body ♦ *the digestive juices.* 5 (*informal*) electricity. 6 (*informal*) petrol. [from a Latin word *jus* meaning 'vegetable juice']

juicy *adjective* (**juicier, juiciest**) 1 full of juice. 2 (*informal*) interesting, especially because of its scandalous nature ♦ *juicy stories.* **juicily** *adverb* **juiciness** *noun*

ju-jitsu (joo-jit-soo) *noun* a Japanese method of self-defence using throws, punches,

etc., and seeking to use the opponent's strength and weight to his or her disadvantage. [from Japanese words *ju* meaning 'gentle' and *jutsu* meaning 'skill']

juju (joo-joo) *noun* 1 an object venerated in West Africa as a charm or fetish. 2 the magic attributed to this. [from a word of West African origin]

jujube *noun* a jelly-like sweet. [from a French word]

jukebox *noun* a machine that automatically plays a selected record when a coin is inserted. [probably from a West African word]

julienne (joo-li-en) *noun* a portion of food cut into thin strips. [from a French word]

July *noun* the seventh month of the year. [named after Julius Caesar, who was born in this month]

jumble *verb* to mix things up in a confused way.
jumble *noun* 1 a confused mixture of things, a muddle. SYNONYMS: clutter, tangle, muddle, hotchpotch. 2 articles collected for a jumble sale. [origin unknown]

jumble sale *noun* a sale of miscellaneous second-hand goods, usually to raise money for charity.

jumbo *noun* (**jumbos**) 1 something very large of its kind. 2 a jumbo jet.
jumbo *adjective* very large. [from the name of a very large elephant in London Zoo]

jumbo jet *noun* a very large airliner.

jump *verb* 1 to push yourself off the ground suddenly by bending and then extending the legs. SYNONYMS: leap, bound, bounce, spring, pounce. 2 to get into or out of a vehicle quickly ♦ *We jumped on the next train* ♦ *Jump in!* 3 to move somewhere suddenly and quickly ♦ *I jumped up to answer the door.* 4 to go over something by jumping ♦ *The horse jumped the fence.* SYNONYMS: clear, hurdle, vault. 5 to make a descent by parachute. 6 to pass over something to a point beyond it; to skip part of a book etc. in reading or studying. 7 to move suddenly in shock or excitement ♦ *You made me jump!* 8 to rise suddenly in amount or in price or value. 9 to pass abruptly from one subject or state to another ♦ *Your essay jumps from idea to idea too much.* 10 to pass through a red traffic light. 11 to pounce on someone, to attack someone without warning.
jump *noun* 1 a jumping movement. 2 a

startled movement. **3** a sudden rise in amount, price, or value. **4** an abrupt change to a different subject or state; a gap in a series of things. **5** a step taken or a move made by someone ♦ *He always seemed to be one jump ahead.* **6** an obstacle or distance to be jumped over. **7** a descent by parachute. **to jump at** to accept an opportunity eagerly. **to jump bail** to fail to come for trial when summoned after being released on bail. **to jump on someone** to start criticizing someone. **to jump ship** (said about a sailor) to desert a ship. **to jump the gun** to start something before you should. **to jump the queue** to obtain something without waiting for your proper turn. **to jump the rails** (said about a train) to leave the rails or track accidentally. **to jump to conclusions** to form an opinion too hastily. **to jump to it** (*informal*) to make an energetic start. [origin unknown]

jumped-up *adjective* (*informal*) thinking you are more important than you really are.

jumper¹ *noun* **1** a pullover or sweater. **2** the upper part of a sailor's uniform. [from a French word *jupe* meaning 'tunic']

jumper² *noun* **1** a person or animal that jumps ♦ *This horse is a good jumper.* **2** a short wire used to make or break an electrical circuit.

jumping-off place or **jumping-off point** *noun* a starting point.

jump jet *noun* a jet aircraft that can take off and land vertically.

jump lead *noun* a cable for conveying current from the battery of a motor vehicle to recharge the battery of another.

jump-off *noun* a deciding round in a showjumping competition.

jump-start *verb* to start a car with a flat battery by pushing it or by using jump leads.

jumpsuit *noun* a piece of clothing for the whole body, combining trousers and a top with sleeves. [so called because it first referred to a piece of clothing worn by parachutists]

jumpy *adjective* (**jumpier, jumpiest**) anxious or nervous.

junction *noun* **1** a point where two or more things join or meet. **2** a place where roads or railway lines meet. [from a Latin word *junctum* meaning 'joined']

juncture (**junk-cher**) *noun* **1** a particular point in time, especially an important one ♦ *The talks are at a critical juncture.* **2** a place where things join. [from a Latin word *junctura* meaning 'joint']

June *noun* the sixth month of the year. [named after the Roman goddess Juno]

jungle *noun* **1** an area of land with dense forest and tangled vegetation, especially in the tropics. **2** a wild tangled mass. **3** a scene of bewildering complexity or confusion, or of ruthless struggle ♦ *The city is a concrete jungle.* **jungly** *adjective* [from a Hindi word *jangal* meaning 'forest']

junior *adjective* **1** younger in age ♦ *Tom Brown junior.* **2** lower in rank or importance ♦ *a junior minister.* **3** for schoolchildren aged 7 to 11 ♦ *a junior school.*

junior *noun* **1** a person younger in age ♦ *He is six years her junior.* **2** a person employed to work in a junior capacity ♦ *the office junior.* **3** a child at a junior school. **4** (*North Amer.*) (*informal*) the son in a family. [a Latin word meaning 'younger']

juniper (**joo-nip-er**) *noun* an evergreen shrub with prickly leaves and dark purplish berries. [from a Latin word *juniperus*]

junk¹ *noun* (*informal*) rubbish or worthless stuff. [origin unknown]

junk² *noun* a kind of flat-bottomed ship with sails, used in the China Seas. [via Portuguese or French from a Malay word *jong*]

junket *noun* **1** a sweet food like custard, made of milk curdled with rennet and flavoured. **2** (*informal*) an extravagant trip or party, especially at public expense. **junket** *verb* (**junketed, junketing**) (*informal*) to have an extravagant trip or party. [from an Old French word *jonquette* meaning 'a rush basket ' (used to carry junket)]

junk food *noun* food that is not nutritious.

junkie *noun* (*informal*) a drug addict. [from a slang use of *junk* meaning 'heroin']

junk mail *noun* (*informal*) unwanted advertising material sent by post.

junk shop *noun* (*informal*) a shop selling miscellaneous second-hand goods or inexpensive antiques.

Junoesque (jew-noh-**esk**) *adjective* (said about a woman) tall and stately. [from the name of the Roman goddess Juno]

junta (**jun**-tə or **hun**-tə) *noun* a military or political group of people who combine to rule a country, especially after seizing power by force. [a Spanish word]

Jurassic (joor-**ass**-ik) *adjective* (Geology) to do with the second period of the Mesozoic era, a time when large reptiles were dominant and the first birds appeared. **Jurassic** *noun* this period. [from a French word]

jurisdiction (joor-iss-**dik**-shən) *noun* 1 authority to make legal decisions and judgements. 2 official power exercised within a particular sphere of activity. 3 the extent or territory over which legal or other power extends. [from Latin words *juris* meaning 'of the law' and *dictum* meaning 'said']

jurisprudence (joor-iss-**proo**-dəns) *noun* the study of law or of a particular part of law ♦ *medical jurisprudence.* **jurisprudential** *adjective* [from a Latin word *juris* meaning 'of law' and *prudentia* meaning 'knowledge']

jurist (**joor**-ist) *noun* a person who is skilled in the law. **juristic** *adjective* **juristical** *adjective* **juristically** *adverb*

juror (**joor**-er) *noun* a member of a jury.

jury *noun* (**juries**) 1 a group of people appointed to give a verdict on a case presented to them in a court of law. 2 a group of people appointed to judge a competition. [from a Latin word *jurare* meaning 'to take an oath']

jury-rigged *adjective* 1 (said about a ship) having makeshift rigging. 2 makeshift or improvised.

just *adjective* 1 giving proper consideration to the claims of everyone concerned. SYNONYMS: fair, equitable, even-handed. 2 deserved or appropriate ♦ *a just reward.* 3 well grounded in fact.
just *adverb* 1 exactly ♦ *It's just what I wanted.* 2 barely, by only a short distance or small amount ♦ *I just managed it* ♦ *just below the knee.* 3 at this moment or only a little time ago ♦ *She has just left.* 4 simply, only ♦ *We are just good friends.* 5 really, certainly ♦ *That idea is just ridiculous.* **just about** (*informal*) almost exactly or completely. **just in case** as a precaution. **just now** at this moment; a little time ago. **just so** 1 exactly arranged ♦ *She likes everything*

just so. 2 it is exactly as you say. **justly** *adverb* **justness** *noun* [from a Latin word *justus* meaning 'rightful']

justice *noun* 1 just treatment, fairness. 2 legal proceedings ♦ *a court of justice.* 3 a judge or magistrate; the title of a judge ♦ *Mr Justice Humphreys.* **to bring someone to justice** to arrest and try someone in court for a crime. **to do justice to** 1 to show something to full advantage. 2 to show due appreciation of something. **to do yourself justice** to perform as well as you can ♦ *I didn't do myself justice in the exam.* [same origin as for *just*]

Justice of the Peace *noun* a non-professional magistrate.

justiciary (jus-**tish**-er-i) *noun* (**justiciaries**) (*Scottish*) someone who administers justice. **Court of Justiciary** the supreme criminal court in Scotland.

justifiable *adjective* able to be justified. **justifiably** *adverb*

justify *verb* (**justifies, justified, justifying**) 1 to show or prove that something is fair, just, or reasonable. 2 to be a good reason for something ♦ *Increased production justifies an increase in wages.* 3 to adjust a line of type in printing so that the print forms a straight edge. **justification** *noun* [same origin as for *just*]

jut *verb* (**jutted, jutting**) to stick out ♦ *His chin juts out.* SYNONYMS: protrude, project, extend. [another spelling of *jet*]

Jute *noun* a member of a Low German people that invaded southern England in the 5th century and settled in Kent. [from an Old English word *Eotas*]

jute *noun* rough fibre from the bark of certain tropical plants, used for making sacks etc. [from a Bengali (a language spoken in Bangladesh and West Bengal) word]

juvenile (joo-və-niyl) *adjective* 1 youthful, childish. 2 to do with or for young people or animals.
juvenile *noun* 1 a young person or animal. 2 (*Law*) a person who is too young to be legally responsible for committing a crime. [from a Latin word *juvenis* meaning 'young person']

juvenile court *noun* a court for the trial of juveniles.

juvenile delinquent *noun* a juvenile who has repeatedly broken the law. **juvenile delinquency** *noun*

juxtapose (juks-tə-**pohz**) verb to put things side by side or close together.
juxtaposition noun [from a Latin word juxta meaning 'next' and positum meaning 'put']

Kk

K the eleventh letter of the English alphabet.

K abbreviation **1** kelvin(s). **2** kilobytes. **3** kilometres. **4** (informal) one thousand.

Kaaba (kah-ə-bə) noun a shrine at Mecca containing a sacred black stone. [from an Arabic word]

kabuki (kə-boo-ki) noun a form of classical Japanese theatre. [from Japanese words ka meaning 'song' and bu meaning 'dance' and ki meaning 'art']

Kaddish (kad-ish) noun a Jewish prayer sequence recited in the synagogue service and for the dead. [from an Aramaic word kaddis meaning 'holy']

kaftan (kaf-tən) noun **1** a long coat-like garment worn by men in the Middle East. **2** a woman's long loose dress. [from a Persian word]

kaiser (kiy-zer) noun (historical) the title of the German and Austrian emperors until 1918. [a German word meaning 'emperor', from the name of Julius Caesar]

kale noun a kind of cabbage with curly leaves that do not form a compact head. [from an Old English word]

kaleidoscope (kəl-iy-də-skohp) noun **1** a toy consisting of a tube containing mirrors and small brightly-coloured pieces of glass or paper which are reflected to form changing patterns as you turn the end of the tube. **2** a constantly changing pattern. **kaleidoscopic** (kəl-iy-də-**skop**-ik) adjective [from Greek words kalos meaning 'beautiful' and eidos meaning 'form' and skopein meaning 'to look at']

kame noun (Geology) a short irregular ridge of sand and gravel deposited by a stream running under a glacier. [a Scottish form of comb]

kameez (kə-meez) noun a long tunic worn by people from the Indian subcontinent. [from an Arabic word]

kamikaze (kam-i-kah-zi) noun **1** (in the Second World War) a Japanese aircraft loaded with explosives and suicidally crashed on an enemy target by its pilot. **kamikaze** adjective recklessly self-destructive. [from Japanese words kami meaning 'divinity' and kaze meaning 'wind']

kangaroo noun an Australian animal that jumps along on its strong hind legs, the female having a pouch on the front of the body in which young are carried. [from an Australian Aboriginal word]

kangaroo court noun an unofficial court formed by a group of people to settle disputes among themselves.

kangha (kang-gə) noun a comb worn in the hair by Sikhs. [a Punjabi word]

kaolin (kay-ə-lin) noun a fine white clay used in making porcelain and in medicine. [from a Chinese word gaoling, the name of a mountain where the clay is found]

kapok (kay-pok) noun a substance resembling cotton wool which grows around the seeds of a tropical tree, used for stuffing pillows and cushions. [from a Malay word kapoq]

kaput (kə-puut) adjective (informal) broken or useless; out of order. [from a German word kaputt]

kara noun a steel bracelet worn by Sikhs. [a Punjabi word]

karaoke (ka-rə-oh-ki or ka-ri-oh-ki) noun a form of entertainment in which people sing well-known songs over a pre-recorded backing track. [a Japanese word meaning 'empty orchestra']

karate (kə-rah-ti) noun a Japanese system of unarmed combat in which the hands and feet are used as weapons. [from Japanese words kara meaning 'empty' and te meaning 'hand']

karma noun (in Buddhism and Hinduism) the sum of a person's actions in successive existences, thought to decide their destiny. [a Sanskrit word meaning 'action' or 'fate']

karst noun (Geology) a limestone region with underground streams and many cavities. [from the name of Karst, a limestone region in Slovenia]

kart *noun* a kind of miniature racing car. **karting** *noun* [a short form of *go-kart*]

kasbah (kaz-bah) *noun* the citadel of an Arab city in North Africa, or the crowded area near this. [from an Arabic word *kasba* meaning 'citadel']

kauri (kowr-i) *noun* (kauris) a coniferous tree of New Zealand, which produces valuable wood and resin. [a Maori word]

kayak (kiy-ak) *noun* **1** an Inuit canoe with a sealskin covering that fits round the canoeist's waist. **2** a small covered canoe resembling this. **kayaking** *noun* [an Inuit word]

kazoo *noun* a simple musical instrument which produces a buzzing sound when you hum into it. [an imitation of the sound]

KB or **Kb** *abbreviation* kilobytes.

KBE *abbreviation* Knight Commander of the Order of the British Empire.

kc/s *abbreviation* kilocycles per second.

kea (kay-ə) *noun* an olive-green New Zealand mountain parrot, sometimes feeding on carrion. [a Maori word]

kebab (ki-bab) *noun* small pieces of meat, fish, or vegetables cooked on a skewer or spit. [from an Arabic word]

kedgeree (kej-er-ee) *noun* a cooked dish of smoked fish, rice, and hard-boiled eggs. [from a Hindi word *khichri*, denoting a dish of rice and split peas]

keel *noun* the timber or steel structure along the base of a ship, on which the ship's framework is built up. **to keel over 1** (said about a ship or ship) to turn over on its side. **2** to fall over or collapse. **on an even keel** steady. [from an Old Norse word]

keen[1] *adjective* **1** enthusiastic, very interested in or eager to do something ♦ *a keen swimmer* ♦ *I am keen to go.* SYNONYMS: eager, enthusiastic, committed, devoted, dedicated, avid, passionate, fervent, ardent, zealous. **2** sharp ♦ *a knife with a keen edge.* **3** quick and acute ♦ *keen wit.* SYNONYMS: acute, sharp, biting, acerbic, incisive. **4** (said about senses) perceiving things very distinctly ♦ *keen eyesight.* SYNONYMS: acute, clear, perceptive. **5** intense or strong ♦ *a keen rivalry.* **6** cold and biting ♦ *a keen wind.* **7** (said about prices) low because of competition. **keen on** very attracted to or fond of someone or something. **keenly**

adverb **keenness** *noun* [from an Old English word *cene* meaning 'wise, clever']

keen[2] *verb* to wail in grief for a dead person.
keen *noun* an Irish funeral song accompanied by wailing. [from an Irish word *caoinim* meaning 'I wail']

keep *verb* (past tense and past participle **kept**) **1** to stay or cause something to stay in a specified state, position, or condition ♦ *She kept quiet about it* ♦ *Keep still please* ♦ *I'll keep it hot for you.* **2** to have possession of something and not give or throw it away ♦ *You can keep the change* ♦ *She's kept the letter all these years.* SYNONYMS: retain, hold, save, conserve. **3** to continue doing something, to do something frequently or repeatedly ♦ *The strap keeps breaking.* **4** to continue in a specified direction ♦ *Keep straight on.* **5** to make someone late, to hold someone back from doing something ♦ *What kept you?* SYNONYMS: detain, delay, hold up. **6** to put or store something in its usual place ♦ *Where do you keep your mugs?* **7** to put something aside for a future time. **8** to respect and not break something ♦ *I always keep a promise.* **9** to celebrate a feast or ceremony. SYNONYMS: mark, observe. **10** to guard or protect someone or something ♦ *She kept them from harm.* **11** to provide someone with the necessities of life. **12** to own and look after an animal ♦ *They keep hens.* **13** to manage something ♦ *My grandparents keep a shop.* **14** to have a commodity regularly in stock or for sale. **15** to record something, to make entries in a diary or accounts etc. ♦ *Do you keep a diary?* **16** (said about food) to remain in good condition. **17** to be able to be put aside until later ♦ *The news will keep.*
keep *noun* **1** food, clothes, and the other essential things you need to live ♦ *She earns her keep.* **2** the central tower of a castle. **for keeps** (*informal*) permanently. **to keep a secret** to not tell it to others. **to keep something down 1** to keep something low in amount or number ♦ *This stuff keeps the weeds down.* **2** to eat and not vomit food. **to keep from** to avoid doing something. **to keep something from** to ensure that something remains a secret from someone. **to keep fit** to be and remain healthy. **to keep house** to look after a house or a household. **to keep something in** to restrain yourself from expressing a feeling. **to keep in with** to remain on good terms with someone. **to keep off** (said about bad weather) to fail to

happen ♦ *Let's hope the rain keeps off.* **to keep on 1** to continue to do something. **2** to speak about something repeatedly, to nag ♦ *Don't keep on about it.* **to keep your feet** to not fall. **to keep your hair on** (*informal*) to remain calm. **to keep your head above water** to keep out of debt. **to keep the peace** to obey the laws and refrain from causing trouble. **to keep to** to not move away from a path, road, or area. **to keep someone to** to make someone stick to a promise or agreement. **to keep to yourself** to avoid meeting people ♦ *He keeps himself to himself.* **to keep something to yourself** to keep a thing secret. **to keep up** to progress at the same pace as others. **to keep something up 1** to prevent something from sinking or getting low. **2** to continue to observe something ♦ *It's good to keep up old customs.* **3** to continue something ♦ *They kept up the attack all day.* **4** to maintain something in proper condition ♦ *the cost of keeping up a large house.* **to keep up with the Joneses** to try not to be outdone by your neighbours. [from an Old English word *cepan*]

keeper *noun* **1** a person who keeps or looks after something. **2** a goalkeeper or wicketkeeper. **3** a gamekeeper. **4** a person in charge of animals in a zoo.

keep-fit *noun* regular exercising done to improve your fitness and health.

keeping *noun* care or protection ♦ *I'll leave these keys in your safe keeping.* **in keeping with** suiting or appropriate for something ♦ *This modern furniture is not in keeping with such an old house.*

keepsake *noun* a gift to be kept in memory of the person who gave it.

keffiyeh (kef-ee-ay) *noun* a kerchief worn as a headdress by Bedouin Arab men. [an Arabic word]

keg *noun* a small barrel. [from an Old Norse word *kaggi*]

kelp *noun* a large brown seaweed. [origin unknown]

kelvin *noun* the SI base unit of thermodynamic temperature, equivalent to the degree Celsius. [named after the British physicist W. T. Kelvin (1824–1907), who invented the Kelvin scale]

Kelvin scale *noun* a scale of temperature with absolute zero as zero (−273.15°C).

ken *noun* the range of a person's knowledge ♦ *How the stock market works is beyond my ken.*
ken *verb* (*Scottish*) to know something or someone. [from an Old English word *cennan* meaning 'to make known']

kendo *noun* the Japanese art of fencing with two-handed bamboo swords. [from Japanese words *ken* meaning 'sword' and *do* meaning 'way']

kennel *noun* a small shelter for a dog. **kennels** *plural noun* an establishment where dogs are bred or where they can be looked after while their owners are away. **kennel** *verb* (**kennelled, kennelling**) to put a dog into a kennel or kennels. [from a Latin word *canis* meaning 'dog']

kept past tense and past participle of **keep**.

keratin (ke-rə-tin) *noun* a strong protein substance forming the basis of horns, claws, nails, feathers, and hair. [from a Greek word *keratos* meaning 'of horn']

kerb *noun* a stone edging to a pavement or raised path. **kerbstone** *noun* [a different spelling of *curb*]

kerchief *noun* **1** a square scarf worn on the head. **2** a handkerchief. [from Old French words *couvre* meaning 'cover' and *chief* meaning 'head']

kerfuffle *noun* (*informal*) fuss or commotion. [perhaps from a Scots word]

kernel *noun* **1** the softer part inside the shell of a nut, seed, or fruit stone. **2** the part of a grain or seed within the husk. **3** the central or most important part of something. [from an Old English word *cyrnel*]

kerosene (ke-rə-seen) *noun* a fuel oil distilled from petroleum; paraffin oil. [from a Greek word *keros* meaning 'wax']

kestrel *noun* a small falcon that hunts by hovering with rapidly beating wings. [probably from a French word]

ketch *noun* a small sailing boat with two masts. [probably from *catch*]

ketchup *noun* a thick sauce made from tomatoes and vinegar, used as a relish. [from a Chinese word *koechiap* meaning 'tomato juice']

ketone (kee-tohn) *noun* (*Chemistry*) any of a class of organic compounds to which acetone belongs. [from a German word *Aketon* meaning 'acetone']

kettle *noun* a container with a spout and handle, for boiling water in. **a different kettle of fish** something altogether different from what has just been mentioned. [from an Old English word *cetel*]

kettledrum *noun* a large bowl-shaped drum over which a piece of skin, parchment, or plastic is stretched.

kettle hole *noun* (*Geology*) a deep bowl-shaped depression in the ground formed where a large detached piece of glacier ice had become embedded in the boulder clay and then melted.

Kevlar *noun* (*trademark*) a synthetic fibre of high tensile strength used to reinforce rubber tyres etc.

key[1] *noun* 1 a small piece of metal shaped so that it will open or close a lock. 2 a similar instrument for turning something, e.g. for winding a clock or tightening a spring etc. 3 each of a set of small levers pressed by the fingers in playing a musical instrument or operating a computer etc. 4 a thing that helps you to achieve, understand, or solve something ♦ *a key to success* ♦ *the key to the mystery.* 5 a set of answers to problems or exercises. 6 a list of symbols used in a map or table. 7 a word or set of symbols for interpreting a code. 8 (*Music*) a system of related notes based on a particular note ♦ *the key of C major.* 9 the tone or pitch of someone's voice. 10 a piece of wood or metal inserted between others to hold them secure. 11 a device for making or breaking an electric circuit, e.g. to operate the ignition in a motor vehicle. 12 roughness of surface helping plaster or paint to stick to it. 13 the winged fruit of certain trees, e.g. sycamore.
key *adjective* very important or essential ♦ *a key figure in the affair.*
key *verb* (**keyed, keying**) 1 to enter data into a computer using a keyboard ♦ *Now key in your password.* 2 to link something closely with something else ♦ *The factory is keyed to the export trade.* 3 to roughen a surface so that plaster or paint will stick to it well. **to be keyed up** to be nervously tense or excited. [from an Old English word]

key[2] *noun* a reef or a low island, especially in the Caribbean. [from a Spanish word *cayo* meaning 'reef']

keyboard *noun* 1 the set of keys on a piano, computer, typewriter, etc. 2 an electronic musical instrument with keys arranged like a piano.
keyboard *verb* to key data into a computer system. **keyboarder** *noun*

keyhole *noun* the hole through which a key is put into a lock.

keyhole surgery *noun* surgery carried out through a very small incision, using fibre optics and special instruments.

keynote *noun* 1 (*Music*) the note on which a key is based ♦ *The keynote of C major is C.* 2 the main tone or theme of a speech or conference.

keypad *noun* a miniature keyboard or set of buttons used to operate a portable electronic device.

key ring *noun* a metal ring for holding keys together in a bunch.

Key Stage *noun* any of the four fixed stages into which the National Curriculum is divided.

keystone *noun* 1 the central wedge-shaped stone at the top of an arch, locking the others in position. 2 the central principle or part of a policy or system.

keystroke *noun* pressing down an individual key on a keyboard.

keyword *noun* 1 the key to a cipher or code. 2 a significant word or heading in an index or reference book.

kg *abbreviation* kilogram(s).

KGB *abbreviation* the former Soviet secret police. [from the Russian name *Komitet Gosudarstvennoi Bezopasnosti* meaning 'State Security Committee']

khaki (**kah-ki**) *noun* 1 cotton or wool fabric of a dull brownish-yellow colour, used for military uniforms. 2 a dull brownish-yellow colour. [from an Urdu word meaning 'dust-coloured']

khan (**kahn**) *noun* a title given to rulers and officials in central Asia. [from a Turkish word meaning 'lord' or 'prince']

Khedive (**ki-deev**) *noun* (*historical*) the title of the viceroy of Egypt under Turkish rule. [from a Persian word]

Khmer (**kmair**) *noun* 1 a native or inhabitant of the ancient kingdom of Khmer in SE Asia or of Cambodia. 2 the language of the Khmers, the official language of Cambodia.

kHz *abbreviation* kilohertz.

kibbutz (kib-**uuts**) *noun* (**kibbutzim**

(kib-uuts-**eem**)) a communal farming settlement in Israel. [from a Hebrew word *kibbus* meaning 'a gathering']

kibbutznik (kib-uuts-nik) *noun* a member of a kibbutz.

kiblah *noun* the direction of the Kaaba in Mecca, towards which Muslims turn in prayer. [an Arabic word]

kibosh (kie-bosh) *noun* **to put the kibosh on** (*informal*) to put an end to something. [origin unknown]

kick *verb* **1** to strike or move a person or thing with your foot. SYNONYMS: boot, punt. **2** to move your legs about vigorously. **3** to score by kicking the ball into goal. **4** (*informal*) to succeed in giving something up ♦ *She smoked a lot before she kicked the habit.* **5** (said about a gun) to recoil when fired.
kick *noun* **1** an act of kicking; a blow from being kicked. **2** (*informal*) a sharp stimulant effect ♦ *a drink with a real kick to it.* **3** (*informal*) a thrill, a pleasurable effect ♦ *He still gets a kick out of performing on stage* ♦ *They just did it for kicks.* **4** (*informal*) an interest or activity ♦ *He's on a health kick.* **5** the recoil of a gun when it is fired. **alive and kicking** (*informal*) fully active. **to kick around** or **about 1** to be unused or unwanted. **2** to go idly from place to place. **to kick someone around** or **about** to treat someone roughly or inconsiderately. **to kick something around** or **about** to discuss an idea casually. **to kick in** to come into effect. **a kick in the teeth** (*informal*) a serious setback or disappointment. **to kick off 1** to start a football game by kicking the ball. **2** (*informal*) to begin proceedings. **to kick your heels** to be kept waiting. **to kick someone out** (*informal*) to dismiss or get rid of someone forcibly. **to kick the bucket** (*informal*) to die. **to kick up a fuss** (*informal*) to create a fuss. **to kick yourself** to be annoyed with yourself. **kicker** *noun* [origin unknown]

kickback *noun* **1** a recoil. **2** (*informal*) a payment made to someone for help they have given, especially in doing something dishonest.

kick-boxing *noun* a form of martial art which combines boxing with elements of karate, especially kicking with bare feet. **kick-boxer** *noun*

kick-off *noun* the time a football match starts.

kick-start *verb* **1** to start the engine of a motorcycle by pushing down a lever with your foot. **2** to help something to get started or become active again ♦ *policies to kick-start the economy.*
kick-start *noun* an instance of kick-starting something.

kid *noun* **1** (*informal*) a child. **2** a young goat. **3** fine leather made from a young goat's skin.
kid *verb* (**kidded, kidding**) (*informal*) to deceive or lie to someone in fun. **to handle** or **treat someone with kid gloves** to deal with someone gently or carefully. [from an Old Norse word *kith*]

kidnap *verb* (**kidnapped, kidnapping**) to take someone away by force, usually in order to obtain a ransom. **kidnapper** *noun* [from *kid* and an old word *napper* meaning 'thief']

kidney *noun* (**kidneys**) **1** either of a pair of glandular organs that remove waste products from the blood and secrete urine. **2** the kidney of a sheep, ox, or pig eaten as food. [origin unknown]

kidney bean *noun* a dark red bean with a curved shape like a kidney.

kidney machine *noun* an apparatus that performs the functions of a kidney.

kilim (ki-leem) *noun* a Turkish or Middle Eastern rug or carpet woven without a pile. [from a Persian word]

kill *verb* **1** to cause the death of a person, animal, or plant. SYNONYMS: murder, slay, dispatch, put to death, assassinate (an important person), execute (a criminal), put down (an injured animal); (*informal*) bump off. **2** to destroy or put an end to something. **3** to pass time while waiting for something ♦ *We played cards to kill a few hours.* **4** (*informal*) to cause someone severe pain or mental suffering ♦ *My feet are killing me* ♦ *The suspense was killing us.* **5** (*informal*) to switch something off ♦ *Kill the engine.*
kill *noun* **1** the act of killing an animal ♦ *The lion has just made a kill.* **2** the animal or animals killed by a hunter or another animal. **to be in at the kill** to be present at the end of something. **to kill someone off** to bring about the death of a fictional character. **to kill something off** to destroy or get rid of something completely. **to kill two birds with one stone** to achieve two purposes with one action. **to kill yourself** to try too hard ♦ *Don't kill yourself to get here by 8.00.* **killer** *noun* [probably from an Old English word]

killer instinct *noun* a ruthless determination to win or succeed.

killer whale *noun* a large toothed whale with distinctive black-and-white markings.

killing *noun* an act causing death. **to make a killing** to make a lot of money.

killjoy *noun* a person who deliberately spoils or questions the enjoyment of others.

kiln *noun* an oven or furnace for hardening or drying things such as pottery, bricks, or hops, or for burning lime. [from a Latin word *culina* meaning 'kitchen']

kilo (kee-loh) *noun* (**kilos**) a kilogram.

kilo- *prefix* one thousand, as in *kilolitre*. [from a Greek word *khilioi* meaning 'thousand']

kilobyte *noun* (*Computing*) a unit of memory or data equal to 1,024 bytes.

kilocycle *noun* a kilohertz.

kilogram *noun* a unit of mass equal to 1,000 grams (2.205 lb).

kilohertz *noun* a unit of frequency of electromagnetic waves, equal to 1,000 cycles per second.

kilojoule *noun* 1,000 joules, especially as a measure of the energy value of foods.

kilolitre *noun* 1,000 litres.

kilometre (kil-ə-meet-er or kil-om-it-er) *noun* a unit of length equal to 1,000 metres (0.62 mile).
◊ The second pronunciation, influenced by words such as *speedometer*, is more common in North America but some people dislike it in British English.

kiloton or **kilotonne** (kil-ə-tun) *noun* a unit of explosive force equal to 1,000 tons of TNT.

kilovolt *noun* 1,000 volts.

kilowatt *noun* a unit of electrical power equal to 1,000 watts.

kilowatt-hour *noun* an amount of energy equal to one kilowatt operating for one hour.

kilt *noun* a knee-length skirt of pleated tartan wool, traditionally worn by men as part of Scottish Highland dress and also worn by women and girls. [probably from a word from a Scandinavian language]

kilted *adjective* wearing a kilt.

kilter *noun* **out of kilter** not balanced or in harmony. [origin unknown]

kimono (kim-oh-noh) *noun* (**kimonos**) 1 a long loose Japanese robe with wide sleeves, worn with a sash. 2 a dressing gown resembling this. [from Japanese words *ki* meaning 'wearing' and *mono* meaning 'thing']

kin *noun* a person's family and relatives. [from an Old English word *cynn*]

kind[1] *noun* 1 a class or type of similar people, animals, or things. SYNONYMS: sort, type, class, category, variety, breed, species, style, make. 2 character or nature ♦ *His criticisms varied in severity but not in kind.* **a kind of** something that belongs approximately to the class named. **in kind** 1 in the same way ♦ *She repaid his insults in kind.* 2 (describing payment) in goods or services, not in money. **kind of** (*informal*) slightly ♦ *I felt kind of sorry for him.* **of a kind** similar ♦ *They are three of a kind.* [from an Old English word *cynd* meaning 'nature'] ◊ In writing, correct usage is *this kind of thing* or *these kinds of things*, not 'these kind of things'.

kind[2] *adjective* 1 friendly, helpful, and considerate in your manner or conduct towards others. SYNONYMS: considerate, thoughtful, benevolent, kind-hearted. 2 not harmful ♦ *a washing-up liquid that's kind to hands.* **kindness** *noun* [from an Old English word *gecynd* meaning 'natural or proper']

kindergarten *noun* a school for very young children. [from German words *Kinder* meaning 'children' and *Garten* meaning 'garden']

kind-hearted *adjective* kind and sympathetic.

kindle *verb* 1 to set light to something, to start a fire burning. 2 to arouse or stimulate something ♦ *This news kindled our hopes.* [from an Old Norse word *kynda*]

kindling *noun* small pieces of dry wood used for lighting fires.

kindly *adjective* (**kindlier, kindliest**) kind in character, manner, or appearance ♦ *a kindly smile.*
kindly *adverb* 1 in a kind way. 2 please ♦ *Kindly shut the door.* **to look kindly on** to be sympathetic towards someone or something. **to not take kindly to** to not be pleased by something. **kindliness** *noun*

kindred (kin-drid) *noun* a person's family and relatives.
kindred *adjective* 1 related. 2 of a similar kind. [from *kin*]

kindred spirit *noun* a person whose tastes or attitudes are similar to your own.

kine *plural noun* (*old use*) cows, cattle.

kinesis (kiy-nee-sis) *noun* (*Biology*) movement of an organism in no particular direction in response to an external stimulus such as light (contrasted with *taxis*, directed movement in response to a stimulus). [from a Greek word *kinēsis* meaning 'movement']

kinetic (kin-et-ik or kiy-net-ik) *adjective* 1 to do with or produced by movement; characterized by movement ♦ *kinetic energy.* 2 (said about a work of art) depending for its effect on the movement of some of its parts, e.g. in air currents. **kinetics** *plural noun* 1 the study of the mechanisms and rates of chemical reactions or other processes. 2 another term for **dynamics**. [from a Greek word *kinētikos* meaning 'moving']

kinetic energy *noun* (*Physics*) energy which a body possesses by virtue of being in motion.

king *noun* 1 the male ruler of an independent country or state, especially one who inherits the position by right of birth. 2 a person or thing regarded as supreme in some way ♦ *The lion is the king of beasts.* 3 a large species of animal ♦ *king penguin.* 4 the most important chess piece, which has to be protected from checkmate. 5 a playing card with a picture of a king on it, ranking next below an ace. 6 a piece in draughts that has been crowned on reaching the opponent's end of the board. [from an Old English word *cyning*]

kingcup *noun* the marsh marigold.

kingdom *noun* 1 a country or state ruled by a king or queen. 2 a division of the natural world ♦ *the animal kingdom.* 3 an area of activity ♦ *the kingdom of the mind.* 4 the spiritual reign of God ♦ *thy Kingdom come.* **to kingdom come** (*informal*) into the next world ♦ *The bomb blew them all to kingdom come.* [from an Old English word *cyningdom*]

kingfisher *noun* a bird with bright bluish plumage, that dives to catch fish.

kingly *adjective* of, like, or suitable for a king.

kingpin *noun* 1 a vertical bolt used as a pivot. 2 an indispensable person or thing.

kingship *noun* being a king; a king's position or reign.

king-size or **king-sized** *adjective* extra large.

kink *noun* 1 a short twist or curve in a wire, rope, piece of hair, etc. 2 an unusual characteristic in a person's mind or personality.
kink *verb* to form or cause something to form a kink. [from an Old German word *kinke*]

kinky *adjective* (**kinkier, kinkiest**) 1 full of kinks. 2 (*informal*) involving unusual sexual behaviour.

kinsfolk *plural noun* (*formal*) a person's relatives.

kinship *noun* 1 a family relationship. 2 a close feeling between people who have similar attitudes or origins.

kinsman or **kinswoman** *noun* (**kinsmen** or **kinswomen**) (*formal*) one of a person's relatives.

kiosk (kee-osk) *noun* 1 a small hut or stall where newspapers, tickets, refreshments, etc. are sold. 2 a public telephone booth. [from a Persian word meaning 'pavilion']

kip *noun* (*informal*) a sleep.
kip *verb* (**kipped, kipping**) (*informal*) to sleep. [perhaps from a Danish word]

kipper *noun* a herring that has been split open, salted, and dried or smoked.
kipper *verb* to cure a herring in this way. [from an Old English word *cypera*]

kirk *noun* (*Scottish*) a church.
the Kirk *noun* the Church of Scotland. [from an Old Norse word *kirkja*]

Kirk session *noun* the lowest court in the Church of Scotland, composed of ministers and elders.

kirpan *noun* a Sikh sword. [a Punjabi word]

kirsch (keersh) *noun* a colourless brandy made from the juice of wild cherries. [from a German word *Kirsche* meaning 'cherry']

kismet (kiz-met) *noun* destiny, fate. [a Turkish word]

kiss *noun* touching someone with your lips as a sign of affection or as a greeting.
kiss *verb* 1 to give someone a kiss. 2 to touch something lightly. [from an Old English word *cyssan*]

kiss of death *noun* an apparently friendly act that in fact causes ruin.

kiss of life *noun* **1** mouth-to-mouth resuscitation. **2** something that rescues or revives an activity that seemed to be failing.

kissogram *noun* a greetings message delivered with a kiss.

Kiswahili (kis-wah-hee-li) *noun* the Swahili language.

kit *noun* **1** the equipment needed for a particular activity or situation ♦ *a first-aid kit*. **2** the clothing and personal equipment of a soldier, traveller, etc. **3** a set of parts sold ready to be fitted together ♦ *a bookcase in kit form*.
kit *verb* (**kitted, kitting**) to provide someone with the clothing or equipment they need ♦ *We were all kitted out for a day's skiing*. [from an Old Dutch word *kitte* meaning 'wooden vessel']

kitbag *noun* a long canvas bag for holding a soldier's kit.

kitchen *noun* a room in which meals are prepared. [from an Old English word *cycene*]

kitchenette *noun* a small room or part of a room used as a kitchen.

kitchen garden *noun* a garden for growing your own fruit and vegetables.

kitchen-sink *adjective* (said about drama) realistically dealing with drab or sordid subjects.

kite *noun* **1** a toy consisting of a light frame with thin material stretched over it, flown in a strong wind on the end of a long string. **2** a large bird of prey of the hawk family. **3** (*Geometry*) a shape like a diamond but with two short sides and two long sides. **to fly a kite** to try out an idea in order to gauge people's opinion. [from an Old English word]

Kitemark *noun* (*trademark*) an official kite-shaped mark put on goods approved by the British Standards Institution.

kith and kin *noun* friends and relatives. [from an Old English word *cyth* meaning 'what or who you know' and *kin*]

kitsch (kich) *noun* sentimentality and lack of good taste in art; art of this type. [a German word]

kitten *noun* **1** a young cat. **2** a young hare, rabbit, or ferret.
kitten *verb* to give birth to kittens. **to have kittens** (*informal*) to be very agitated or nervous. **kittenish** *adjective* [from an Old French word *chitoun* meaning 'small cat']

kitty [1] *noun* (**kitties**) **1** a fund of money for use by several people. **2** the pool of stakes to be played for in some card games. [origin unknown]

kitty [2] *noun* (**kitties**) a pet name for a cat.

kiwi (kee-wee) *noun* a New Zealand bird that does not fly, with a long bill, rudimentary wings, and no tail.
Kiwi *noun* (**Kiwis**) (*informal*) a New Zealander. [from a Maori word]

kiwi fruit *noun* a fruit with thin hairy skin, green flesh, and black seeds. [named after the kiwi (because the fruit was exported from New Zealand)]

kJ *abbreviation* kilojoule(s).

kl *abbreviation* kilolitre(s).

Klaxon *noun* (*trademark*) a powerful electric horn. [from the name of the manufacturers]

kleptomania (kleptə-may-niə) *noun* an uncontrollable urge to steal things.
kleptomaniac *noun & adjective* [from a Greek word *kleptēs* meaning 'thief' and *mania*]

km *abbreviation* kilometre(s).

knack *noun* **1** a skilful or effective way of doing something ♦ *There's a knack to putting up the sofa bed*. **2** a talent for doing something. [origin unknown]

knacker *noun* a person who buys and slaughters useless horses, selling the meat and hides. [origin unknown]

knackered *adjective* (*informal*) exhausted, worn out.

knap *verb* (**knapped, knapping**) to shape a stone by hitting it, in order to make a tool or a flat stone for building walls. [an imitation of the sound]

knapsack *noun* a bag with shoulder straps, carried on the back by soldiers, hikers, etc. [from a Dutch word]

knapweed *noun* a common weed like a thistle but without prickles. [from *knop* meaning 'knob' and *weed*]

knave *noun* **1** (*old use*) a dishonest man, a rogue. **2** the jack in playing cards. **knavery** *noun* **knavish** *adjective* [from an Old English word *cnafa* meaning 'a boy or male servant']

knead *verb* **1** to work dough or clay by pressing and stretching it with your hands. **2** to massage something with kneading movements. [from an Old English word *cnedan*]

knee *noun* 1 the joint between the thigh and the lower part of the leg. 2 a person's lap ♦ *Sit on my knee.* 3 something shaped like a bent knee.
knee *verb* (**knees, kneed, kneeing**) to strike someone with the knee. [from an Old English word]

knee breeches *plural noun* (*old use*) short trousers reaching to or just below the knee.

kneecap *noun* the small bone covering the front of the knee joint.
kneecap *verb* (**kneecapped, kneecapping**) to shoot someone in the knee or leg as a punishment.

knee-deep *adjective* 1 of or in sufficient depth to cover a person up to the knees. 2 deeply involved in something ♦ *knee-deep in work.*

knee-jerk *noun* an involuntary jerk of the leg when a tendon below the knee is struck.
knee-jerk *adjective* automatic and unthinking ♦ *a knee-jerk reaction.*

kneel *verb* (past tense and past participle **knelt**) to take or be in a position where the body is supported by the knees. [from an Old English word]

kneeler *noun* a cushion for kneeling on.

knell *noun* the sound of a bell rung solemnly after a death or at a funeral.
knell *verb* (said about a bell) to ring solemnly. [from an Old English word *cnyll*]

knelt past tense and past participle of **kneel**.

Knesset (knes-it) *noun* the parliament of the State of Israel. [a Hebrew word meaning 'gathering']

knew past tense of **know**.

knickerbockers *plural noun* loose-fitting breeches gathered in at the knee. [from D. Knickerbocker, the imaginary author of a book in which people were shown wearing knickerbockers]

knickers *plural noun* underpants worn by women and girls. [short for *knickerbockers*]

knick-knack *noun* a small ornament. [probably from an Old Dutch word]

knife *noun* (**knives**) 1 a cutting instrument or weapon consisting of a sharp blade with a handle. 2 the cutting blade of a machine.

knife *verb* to stab someone with a knife.
to have got the knife into someone (*informal*) to be persistently malicious or vindictive towards someone. **on a knife-edge** in a situation involving extreme tension or anxiety about the outcome. [from an Old English word *cnif*]

knife pleat *noun* a sharp narrow pleat on a skirt.

knight *noun* 1 a man who has been awarded a rank as an honour by the monarch and is entitled to use the title 'Sir'. 2 (*old use*) a man raised to an honourable military rank by a king etc. 3 a chess piece with the form of a horse's head.
knight *verb* to make someone a knight.
knightly *adverb* [from an Old English word *cniht* meaning 'young man']

knighthood *noun* the rank of knight.

knit *verb* (past tense and past participle **knitted** or **knit; knitting**) 1 to make something by looping together wool or other yarn, using long needles or a machine. 2 to make a plain stitch in knitting. 3 to unite or grow together ♦ *The broken bones had knit well.*
knit *noun* a piece of clothing made by knitting. **to knit your brow** to frown.
knitter *noun* [from an Old English word *cnyttan* meaning 'to tie in knots']
◊ The past tense of the verb in senses 1 and 2 is *knitted*. The past tense in sense 3 is usually *knit*.

knitting *noun* work in the process of being knitted.

knitting needle *noun* each of the long needles used for knitting by hand.

knitwear *noun* knitted garments.

knob *noun* 1 a round handle on a door or drawer. 2 a round button on a dial or machine. 3 a round lump on something. 4 a small round piece of something ♦ *a knob of butter.* **with knobs on** (*informal*) that and more. **knobby** *adjective* [from an Old German word *knobbe* meaning 'knot or knob']

knobbly *adjective* (**knobblier, knobbliest**) with many small lumps on it.

knock *verb* 1 to make a noise striking a surface with your hand or a hard object to attract attention ♦ *Someone's knocking on the door.* 2 to strike or bump into something with a sharp blow. 3 (said about an engine) to make a thumping or rattling noise while running. 4 to make something by knocking ♦ *The builders* knocked a hole in the wall. **5** to make something move or fall by hitting it ♦ *Can you knock a couple of nails in?* **6** (*informal*) to say critical or insulting things about something ♦ *People are always knocking this town.*

knock *noun* **1** an act or sound of knocking. **2** a sharp blow or collision. **3** a continual thumping or rattling noise made by an engine. **to knock about** (*informal*) to wander around casually. **to knock something down** (*informal*) to reduce the price of something. **to knock it off** (*informal*) to stop doing something. **to knock off** (*informal*) to stop work. **to knock something off** (*informal*) **1** to produce a piece of work quickly. **2** to deduct an amount from a price. **3** (*informal*) to steal something. **to be knocking on** (*informal*) to be getting old. **to knock someone out 1** to make someone unconscious. **2** to knock down a boxer for a count of ten. **3** to defeat someone in a knockout competition. **4** to greatly impress or astonish someone. **to knock something out** to produce work at a steady fast rate. **to knock spots off** (*informal*) to be easily superior to someone or something. **to knock up 1** to practise before starting a game of tennis etc. **2** (*informal*) to make someone pregnant. **to knock someone up** to wake someone by knocking at their door. **to knock something up 1** to make something hastily. **2** (in cricket) to score runs quickly. [from an Old English word *cnocian*]

knockabout *adjective* rough, boisterous ♦ *knockabout comedy.*

knock-down *adjective* (*informal*) (said about prices) very low.

knocker *noun* **1** a hinged metal flap for knocking against a door to summon a person. **2** (*informal*) a person who continually criticizes.

knock knees *plural noun* an abnormal inward curving of the legs at the knees. **knock-kneed** *adjective*

knock-on effect *noun* an indirect result of some action.

knockout *adjective* **1** (said about a competition) in which the loser in each successive round has to drop out. **2** that knocks a boxer out ♦ *a knockout punch.* **knockout** *noun* **1** a blow that knocks a boxer out. **2** a knockout competition. **3** (*informal*) an extremely attractive or outstanding person or thing.

knockout drops *plural noun* liquid added to a drink to cause unconsciousness when swallowed.

knock-up *noun* a practice or casual game at tennis etc.

knoll (nohl) *noun* a small round hill, a mound. [from an Old English word *cnoll*]

knot *noun* **1** a fastening made by intertwining one or more pieces of string or rope etc. and pulling the ends tight. **2** a tangle. **3** a hard mass in something, especially on a tree trunk where a branch joins it. **4** a round cross-grained spot in timber where a branch joined. **5** a cluster of people or things. **6** a unit of speed used by ships and aircraft, equal to one nautical mile (1,852 metres or 2,025 yards) per hour.
knot *verb* (**knotted, knotting**) **1** to tie or fasten something with a knot. **2** to become tangled up. **3** (said about a muscle) to become tense and hard. [from an Old English word *cnotta*]

knotgrass *noun* a common weed with nodes in its stems and small pale pink flowers.

knothole *noun* a hole in a piece of wood where a knot has fallen out.

knotty *adjective* (**knottier, knottiest**) **1** full of knots. **2** difficult or puzzling ♦ *a knotty problem.*

know *verb* (**knew, known**) **1** to have something in your mind or memory as a result of experience, learning, or information. **2** to be absolutely sure about something ♦ *I know I left it here!* **3** to recognize or have met a person; to be familiar with a place ♦ *I've known him for years* ♦ *How well do you know Glasgow?* **4** to understand and be able to use a subject, language, or skill ♦ *She knows how to please people.* **5** to recognize something with certainty ♦ *He knows a bargain when he sees one.* **in the know** (*informal*) having inside information. **knowable** *adjective* [from an Old English word]

know-all *noun* (*informal*) a person who behaves as if they know everything.

know-how *noun* practical knowledge or skill in a particular activity.

knowing *adjective* showing that you know or are aware of something ♦ *a knowing look.* **knowingly** *adverb*

knowledge *noun* **1** information and skills you have through experience or education. **2** awareness or familiarity gained by experience ♦ *I have no knowledge of that.* **3** all that is known ♦ *every branch of knowledge.* **to my knowledge** as far as I know. [from *know* and an Old English word *lac* meaning 'practice']

knowledgeable *adjective* well-informed. **knowledgeably** *adverb*

known past participle of **know**.

knuckle *noun* **1** a finger joint. **2** the knee joint of an animal, or the part joining the leg to the foot, especially as a joint of meat. **knuckle** *verb* to press or rub something with the knuckles. **to knuckle down** to begin to work earnestly. **to knuckle under** to yield or submit. **to rap someone over the knuckles** to tell someone off. [from an Old German word]

knuckleduster *noun* a metal guard worn over the knuckles in fighting to increase the injury done by a blow.

knurl (nerl) *noun* a small ridge or knob. [from an old word *knarre* meaning 'a rugged rock or stone']

knurled *adjective* having raised ridges or small knobs round the rim to provide grip.

KO *noun* (*informal*) a knockout in a boxing match. **KO** *verb* (**KO's, KO'd, KO'ing**) to knock someone out in a boxing match.

koala (koh-ah-lə) *noun* an Australian tree-climbing animal with thick grey fur and large ears, feeding on eucalyptus leaves. [from an Australian Aboriginal word]

kohl *noun* a black powder used as eye make-up, especially in eastern countries. [from an Arabic word *kuhl*]

kohlrabi (kohl-rah-bi) *noun* (**kohlrabies**) a cabbage with an edible turnip-shaped stem. [a German word]

kookaburra *noun* a very large Australian kingfisher that has a loud cackling call. [from an Australian Aboriginal word]

kop *noun* a high bank of terracing at a football ground. [an Afrikaans word, from a Dutch word meaning 'head']

koppie or **kopje** (kop-i) *noun* (in South Africa) a small hill. [an Afrikaans word]

Koran (kor-ahn) *noun* the sacred book of Islam believed by Muslims to be the word of God as dictated to Muhammad, written in Arabic. [from an Arabic word *kur'an* meaning 'reading']

korma *noun* a mild Indian meat or fish curry. [via Urdu from a Turkish word *kavurma*]

kosher (koh-sher) *adjective* **1** conforming to the requirements of Jewish law concerning the preparation of food. **2** (*informal*) genuine and legitimate. **kosher** *verb* to prepare food according to Jewish law. [from a Hebrew word *kasher* meaning 'proper']

kowtow *verb* to behave in an extremely submissive and respectful way towards a person. [the *kowtow* (Chinese *ketou*) was a former Chinese custom of kneeling and touching the ground with your forehead as a sign of worship or submission]

kph *abbreviation* kilometres per hour.

Kr *abbreviation* (*Chemistry*) the symbol for krypton.

kraal (krahl) *noun* (in South Africa) **1** a village of huts enclosed by a fence. **2** an enclosure for cattle or sheep. [an Afrikaans word]

kremlin *noun* a citadel within a Russian town. **the Kremlin** *noun* the citadel in Moscow, housing the Russian government. [from a Russian word *kreml* meaning 'citadel']

krill *noun* the mass of tiny crustaceans that forms the principal food of certain whales. [from a Norwegian word *kril* meaning 'tiny fish']

kris (krees or kris) *noun* a Malay or Indonesian dagger with a wavy blade. [from a Malay word *keris*]

krugerrand (kroog-er-ahnt) *noun* a South African gold coin bearing a portrait of President Kruger. [from the name P. Kruger, President of Transvaal 1883–99 and *rand*]

krypton (krip-ton) *noun* a chemical element (symbol Kr), a colourless odourless gas used in various types of lamps and bulbs. [from a Greek word *kruptos* meaning 'hidden']

Kshatriya (kshah-tri-ə) *noun* a member of the second of the four great Hindu classes, the warrior or baronial class. [from a Sanskrit word *kshatra* meaning 'rule']

kudos (kew-doss) *noun* honour and glory. [from a Greek word meaning 'praise']

kudu (koo-doo) *noun* (**kudu** or **kudus**) a large African antelope with white stripes and spiral horns. [from an Afrikaans word *koedoe*]

Kufic (kew-fik) *noun* an early form of the Arabic alphabet, found especially in inscriptions. [from the name of Kufa, a city in Iraq]

Ku Klux Klan *noun* a secret society in the USA that is hostile to and uses violence against black people, originally formed in the southern States after the Civil War. [perhaps from a Greek word *kuklos* meaning 'circle']

kukri (kuuk-ri) *noun* a heavy curved knife, broadening towards the point, used by Gurkhas as a weapon. [a Hindi word]

kulak (koo-lak) *noun* (*historical*) a peasant in Russia who was wealthy enough to own a farm. [a Russian word meaning 'fist']

kumkum (kuum-kuum) *noun* **1** a red powder used by Hindu women to make a small spot on the forehead. **2** this spot. [from a Sanskrit word meaning 'saffron']

kung fu (kuung foo) *noun* a Chinese form of unarmed combat, similar to karate. [from Chinese words *gong* meaning 'merit' and *fu* meaning 'master']

Kurd *noun* a member of a pastoral Islamic people of Kurdistan, a mountainous region of east Turkey, north Iraq, and NW Iran. **Kurdish** *adjective & noun*

kV *abbreviation* kilovolt(s).

kW *abbreviation* kilowatt(s).

kwashiorkor (kwo-shi-or-kor) *noun* a tropical disease of children, caused by protein deficiency. [the name given to the disease in Ghana]

kWh *abbreviation* kilowatt-hour(s).

kyle *noun* a narrow channel between an island and the mainland or another island in western Scotland. [from a Gaelic word *caol* meaning 'strait']

Ll

L 1 the twelfth letter of the English alphabet. **2** the Roman numeral for 50.

L *abbreviation* learner, especially a person learning to drive ♦ *L-driver.*

l *abbreviation* **1** length. **2** litre(s).

La *abbreviation* (*Chemistry*) the symbol for lanthanum.

laager (lah-ger) *noun* (in southern Africa) an encampment formed by tying wagons together in a circle. [an Afrikaans word]

lab *noun* (*informal*) a laboratory.

label *noun* **1** a slip of paper, cloth, etc. fixed on or beside something to show what it is or what it costs, or its owner or destination, etc. **2** a descriptive word or phrase classifying people or things.
label *verb* (**labelled, labelling**) **1** to attach a label to something. **2** to describe or classify something ♦ *He was labelled as a troublemaker.* [from an Old French word meaning 'ribbon']

labia (lay-bi-ə) *plural noun* the lips of the female genitals, consisting of the *labia majora*, the fleshy outer folds, and the *labia minora*, the inner folds. [a Latin word meaning 'lips']

labial (lay-bi-əl) *adjective* to do with the lips or the labia. [from a Latin word *labia* meaning 'lips']

labiate (lay-bi-ət) *adjective* (*Botany*) to do with the family of plants that have flowers with the corolla or the calyx divided into two parts resembling lips. [same origin as for *labial*]

laboratory (lə-bo-rə-ter-i) *noun* (**laboratories**) a room or building equipped for scientific experiments or research. [from a Latin word *laboratorium* meaning 'workplace']

laborious *adjective* **1** needing a lot of effort or perseverance ♦ *a laborious climb.* SYNONYMS: hard, tough, arduous, strenuous, gruelling. **2** explaining or discussing something at great length and with obvious effort ♦ *The book is written in laborious prose.* **laboriously** *adverb*

labour *noun* **1** work, especially hard physical work. SYNONYMS: exertion, toil, industry. **2** a difficult task. **3** the process of childbirth from the start of contractions of the womb to delivery. **4** workers, working people distinguished from management or considered as a political force.
Labour *noun* the Labour Party.
labour *verb* **1** to work hard. SYNONYMS: toil, slog, slave, strain. **2** to have to make a great effort. **3** (said about an engine) to work

noisily and with difficulty. **4** to explain or discuss something at great length or in excessive detail ♦ *I will not labour the point.*
to labour under to be misled by a mistaken belief. [from a Latin word *labor* meaning 'toil']

labour camp *noun* a prison camp with forced labour by prisoners.

Labour Day *noun* a public holiday held in honour of workers in some countries on 1 May or, in the USA, on the first Monday in September.

laboured *adjective* **1** showing signs of great effort. **2** not spontaneous or fluent.

labourer *noun* a person who does hard manual work, especially outdoors.

labour exchange *noun* a former term for jobcentre.

labour force *noun* the members of a population who are able to work.

labour-intensive *adjective* (said about an industry or activity) needing to have many people working or a large amount of work.

Labour Party *noun* a British political party, formed to represent the interests of working people and believing in social equality and socialism.

labour-saving *adjective* designed to reduce the amount of work or effort needed.

labrador *noun* a retriever dog with a smooth black or golden coat. [named after Labrador, a district in Canada, where it was bred]

labrum (lay-brəm) *noun* (labra) **1** the upper part of the mouth of an insect, crustacean, etc. **2** the outer edge of various kinds of shell. [a Latin word meaning 'lip']

laburnum *noun* an ornamental tree with hanging clusters of yellow flowers. [from a Latin word]

labyrinth (lab-er-inth) *noun* **1** a complicated network of paths or passages through which it is difficult to find your way. **2** a complex and confusing arrangement. **3** (*Anatomy*) the complex cavity of the inner ear. [from a Greek word *laburinthos*]

labyrinthine (lab-er-in-thiyn) *adjective* like a labyrinth, especially in being complicated or twisted.

lace *noun* **1** a delicate net-like material with decorative patterns of holes in it. **2** a cord or narrow leather strip threaded through holes or hooks to fasten a shoe or piece of clothing.
lace *verb* **1** to fasten something with a lace or laces. **2** to thread a lace through something. **3** to add alcohol to food or drink to flavour it or make it stronger. [from an Old French word]

lacerate (las-er-ayt) *verb* to injure flesh by cutting or tearing it. **laceration** *noun* [from a Latin word *lacer* meaning 'torn']

lachrymal (lak-rim-əl) *adjective* to do with tears, producing tears ♦ *lachrymal ducts.* [from a Latin word *lacrima* meaning 'a tear']

lachrymose (lak-rim-ohs) *adjective* (*formal*) tearful. [same origin as for *lachrymal*]

lack *noun* the state of being without or not having enough of something. SYNONYMS: absence, shortage, scarcity, deficiency, dearth, paucity.
lack *verb* to be without something ♦ *He lacks courage* ♦ *They lack for nothing.* [probably from an Old English word]

lackadaisical (lak-ə-day-zikəl) *adjective* **1** lacking energy or determination. **2** lazy and careless. [from *lack-a-day*, an old phrase expressing grief or surprise]

lackey *noun* (**lackeys**) **1** a footman or servant. **2** a person's servile follower. [from a French word *laquais*]

lacking *adjective* absent or deficient ♦ *Your essay is lacking in originality.*

lacklustre *adjective* **1** showing little energy or vitality. **2** not bright or shining, dull.

laconic (lə-kon-ik) *adjective* using very few words, terse ♦ *a laconic reply.* **laconically** *adverb* [from a Greek word *Lakōn* meaning 'a native of Laconia', an area in Greece (because the Laconians were famous for their terse speech)]

lacquer (lak-er) *noun* **1** a hard glossy varnish. **2** a chemical substance sprayed on hair to keep it in place.
lacquer *verb* to coat something with lacquer. [via French from a Portuguese word]

lacrosse (lə-kross) *noun* a game resembling hockey but with players using a stick with a net on it (called a *crosse*) to catch, carry, or throw the ball. [from a French word *la crosse* meaning 'the hooked stick']

lactate (lak-tayt) *verb* (said about a female mammal) to produce milk. **lactation** *noun* [from a Latin word *lac* meaning 'milk']

lacteal *adjective* to do with milk. [same origin as for *lactate*]

lactic *adjective* to do with or obtained from milk. [from a Latin word *lactis* meaning 'of milk']

lactic acid *noun* the acid found in sour milk and produced in the muscles during strenuous exercise.

lactose *noun* a sugar present in milk.

lacuna (lə-kew-nə) *noun* (**lacunae** (lə-kew-nee) or **lacunas**) a gap or missing section. [a Latin word meaning 'a pool']

lacy *adjective* (**lacier, laciest**) made of or like lace.

lad *noun* **1** (*informal*) a boy or young man. **2** (*informal*) a man who enjoys boisterous or rowdy behaviour ♦ *He's a bit of a lad.* [origin unknown]

ladder *noun* **1** a set of crossbars (called *rungs*) between two upright pieces of wood, metal, etc., used for climbing up or down something. **2** a vertical ladder-like flaw in a pair of stockings or tights caused by a stitch or stitches becoming undone through several rows. **3** a series of stages by which a person may advance in his or her career ♦ *the political ladder.*
ladder *verb* to cause a ladder in a pair of stockings or tights; to develop a ladder. [from an Old English word]

laddish *adjective* (*informal*) (said about young men) boisterous or rowdy. **laddishness** *noun*

laden *adjective* heavily loaded or weighed down. [from an Old English word *hladan* meaning 'to load a ship']

la-di-da *adjective* (*informal*) having an affected or pretentious manner or pronunciation. [an imitation of an affected manner of speech]

ladle *noun* a large deep spoon with a long handle, used for serving soup or sauce. **ladle** *verb* to serve out soup or sauce with a ladle. [from an Old English word]

lady *noun* (**ladies**) **1** (in polite or formal use) a woman. **2** a woman of good social position. **3** a well-mannered or kindly woman.
Lady *noun* a title used by peeresses, female relatives of peers, the wives and widows of knights, etc.
the Ladies *noun* a women's public toilet. [from an Old English word *hlaefdige* meaning 'a person who makes the bread' (compare *lord*)]

ladybird *noun* a small flying beetle, usually red with black spots.

Lady chapel *noun* a chapel within a large church, dedicated to the Virgin Mary.

Lady Day *noun* the Feast of the Annunciation, 25 March.

lady-in-waiting *noun* (**ladies-in-waiting**) a woman of good social position who attends a queen or princess.

ladylike *adjective* suitable for a lady, well-mannered and refined.

ladyship *noun* **Her** or **Your Ladyship** a title used in speaking about or to a woman of the rank of Lady.

lag [1] *verb* (**lagged, lagging**) to go too slowly, to fail to keep up with others. SYNONYMS: fall behind, dawdle, trail, straggle; (*informal*) bring up the rear.
lag *noun* a delay. **lagger** *noun* [origin unknown]

lag [2] *verb* (**lagged, lagging**) to wrap pipes, a boiler, etc. in a layer of insulating material to prevent loss of heat. **lagger** *noun* [probably from a word from a Scandinavian language]

lag [3] *noun* (*informal*) a convict ♦ *old lags.* [origin unknown]

lager (lah-ger) *noun* a kind of light beer. [from a German word *Lager* meaning 'a store']

lager lout *noun* (*informal*) a youth who behaves badly as a result of drinking too much.

laggard *noun* a person who lags behind. [from *lag*[1]]

lagging *noun* material used to lag pipes etc. [from *lag*[2]]

lagoon *noun* **1** a salt-water lake separated from the sea by a sandbank or coral reef etc. **2** a small freshwater lake near a larger lake or river. [from a Latin word *lacuna* meaning 'pool']

laid past tense and past participle of **lay**[1].

laid-back *adjective* (*informal*) relaxed and easy-going.

lain past participle of **lie**[2].

lair *noun* **1** a sheltered place where a wild animal lives. **2** a person's hiding place. [from an Old English word *leger* meaning 'resting place, bed']

laird *noun* (*Scottish*) a person who owns a large estate. [a Scots form of *lord*]

laissez-faire (lay-say-**fair**) *noun* a government's policy of not interfering. [a French phrase meaning 'to allow to do']

laity (**lay**-iti) *noun* lay people, not the clergy ♦ *the laity.* [from *lay²*]

lake¹ *noun* a large area of water entirely surrounded by land.
the Lakes *plural noun* the Lake District. [from a Latin word *lacus* meaning 'pool, lake']

lake² *noun* a kind of pigment, especially a reddish pigment once made from lac resin. [from the word *lac* denoting a type of resin, from a Hindi or Persian word]

Lake District *noun* a region of lakes and mountains in Cumbria.

lakh (lak) *noun* (in India) a hundred thousand ♦ *a lakh of rupees.* [via Hindi from a Sanskrit word]

lam *verb* (**lammed, lamming**) (*informal*) to hit someone hard and repeatedly, to thrash someone ♦ *She really lammed into him.* [perhaps from a word of Scandinavian origin]

lama (**lah**-mə) *noun* a Buddhist priest or monk in Tibet and Mongolia. [from a Tibetan word *blama* meaning 'superior']

lamaism (**lah**-mə-izm) *noun* Tibetan Buddhism.

lamasery (lə-**mah**-ser-i) *noun* (**lamaseries**) a monastery of lamas.

lamb *noun* 1 a young sheep. 2 meat from a lamb. 3 a gentle or endearing person ♦ *You poor lamb!*
lamb *verb* 1 (said about a ewe) to give birth to a lamb. 2 to tend lambing ewes.
lambing *noun* [from an Old English word]

lambaste (lam-**bayst**) or **lambast** (lam-**bast**) *verb* to criticize someone severely. [originally meaning 'to beat', from *lam* and an old use of *baste* meaning 'to thrash']

lambent *adjective* (*poetic*) (said about a flame or light) playing about a surface. [from a Latin word *lambens* meaning 'licking']

lambskin *noun* the skin of a lamb, either with its wool on or as leather.

lambswool *noun* soft fine wool used in making machine-knitted clothing.

lame *adjective* 1 unable to walk normally because of an injury or disability in a foot or leg. 2 (said about an excuse or explanation) weak or unconvincing.

SYNONYMS: feeble, poor, flimsy, thin.
lame *verb* to make a person or animal lame. **lamely** *adverb* **lameness** *noun* [from an Old English word *lama*]

lamé (**lah**-may) *noun* a fabric in which gold or silver thread is interwoven. [a French word]

lame duck *noun* a person or firm etc. that is in difficulties and unable to manage without help.

lament *noun* 1 a passionate expression of grief. 2 a song or poem expressing grief or regret.
lament *verb* 1 to mourn a person's death. 2 to feel or express regret about something. [from a Latin word *lamenta* meaning 'weeping']

lamentable (lam-ən-tə-bəl) *adjective* regrettable or deplorable. **lamentably** *adverb*

lamentation (lam-en-**tay**-shən) *noun* 1 lamenting. 2 a lament, an expression of grief.

lamented *adjective* mourned for ♦ *our late lamented friend.*

lamina (**lam**-in-ə) *noun* (**laminae**) (**lam**-i-nee) a technical term for a thin plate, scale, or layer of rock or tissue. [a Latin word meaning 'layer, plate']

laminate (**lam**-in-ət) *noun* a laminated material.

laminated *adjective* made of layers joined one upon the other ♦ *laminated plastic.* [from a Latin word *lamina* meaning 'layer']

lamp *noun* 1 a device for giving light, either by the use of electricity or gas or by burning oil or spirit. 2 a glass container enclosing a filament that is made to glow by electricity. 3 an electrical device producing radiation ♦ *an infra-red lamp.* [from a Greek word *lampas* meaning 'torch']

lampblack *noun* a black pigment made from soot.

lamplight *noun* the light given by a lamp.

lampoon (lam-**poon**) *noun* a piece of writing that attacks a person by ridiculing him or her.
lampoon *verb* to ridicule someone in a lampoon. [from a French word *lampon*]

lamppost *noun* a tall post supporting a street lamp.

lamprey noun (**lampreys**) a small eel-like water animal with a round mouth used as a sucker for attaching itself to things. [from an Old French word lampreie, probably from the Latin words lambere meaning 'to lick' and petra meaning 'stone']

lampshade noun a shade placed over a lamp to soften or screen its light.

LAN abbreviation (Computing) local area network.

Lancastrian adjective 1 to do with Lancashire. 2 to do with the House of Lancaster in the Wars of the Roses.
Lancastrian noun a Lancastrian person.

lance noun 1 a weapon consisting of a long wooden shaft with a pointed metal head, formerly used by mounted knights or cavalry. 2 a device resembling this, used for spearing fish etc.
lance verb 1 to prick or cut open a boil etc. with a surgical lancet. 2 to pierce someone or something with a lance. [from a Latin word lancea]

lance corporal noun a soldier ranking above a private and below a corporal. [origin unknown]

lancer noun a soldier of a cavalry regiment originally armed with lances.
lancers noun a kind of quadrille.

lancet (lahn-sit) noun 1 a pointed two-edged knife used by surgeons. 2 a tall narrow pointed arch or window. [from a French word lancette meaning 'small lance']

land noun 1 the solid part of the earth's surface, the part not covered by water. 2 an area of ground owned by someone or used for a particular purpose. 3 the ground or soil used for farming ♦ a lifetime spent working the land. 4 an expanse of country ♦ forest land. 5 a country, state, or region ♦ her native land. 6 property consisting of land.
land verb 1 to bring an aircraft or its passengers etc. down to the ground or other surface; to come down in this way. 2 to arrive or put people, goods, etc. on land from a ship. 3 to come to rest after a jump, fall, or throw ♦ One parachutist landed in a tree. 4 to succeed in getting or winning something ♦ She landed an excellent job. 5 to bring a fish out of the water. 6 to arrive or cause someone to arrive at a certain place, stage, or position ♦ They landed up in jail. 7 to strike someone with a blow ♦ He didn't land a single punch. 8 to present someone with something

difficult or unpleasant to deal with ♦ They landed me with the job of sorting it out. [from an Old English word]

landau (lan-daw) noun a kind of four-wheeled horse-drawn carriage. [named after Landau in Germany, where it was first made]

landed adjective 1 owning land ♦ landed gentry. 2 consisting of land ♦ landed estates.

landfall noun approach to land after a journey by sea or air.

landform noun a natural feature of the earth's surface.

landing noun 1 the process of coming to or bringing something to land or of alighting after a jump. 2 a place where people and goods can get on and off a boat. 3 a level area at the top of a flight of stairs or between such flights.

landing craft noun a boat specially designed for putting troops and military equipment ashore on a beach.

landing gear noun the wheeled structure which an aircraft uses when it lands on the ground.

landing stage noun a platform on which people and goods are taken on and off a boat.

landing strip noun an airstrip.

landlady noun (**landladies**) 1 a woman who lets out rooms etc. to tenants. 2 a woman who runs a public house.

landlocked adjective almost or entirely surrounded by land.

landlord noun 1 a person who lets land or a house or room etc. to tenants. 2 a person who runs a public house.

landlubber noun (informal) a person who is not accustomed to the sea or sailing. [from land and an old word lubber meaning 'an awkward, clumsy person']

landmark noun 1 a conspicuous and easily recognized object in or feature of a landscape. 2 an event that marks an important stage or development in the history of something.

land mass noun a continent or other large body of land.

landmine noun an explosive mine laid on or just under the surface of the ground.

landowner noun a person who owns land.

landscape noun 1 the scenery of a land area. 2 a picture of an area of countryside.

landscape *verb* to lay out a piece of land attractively, with natural features. [from a Dutch word *lantscap*]

landscape gardening *noun* laying out a garden or grounds, especially to imitate natural scenery. **landscape gardener** *noun*

landslide *noun* 1 a landslip. 2 an overwhelming majority of votes for one side in an election ♦ *The party won the General Election by a landslide.*

landslip *noun* a huge mass of soil and rocks sliding down a slope or mountain.

landward *adjective* facing towards the land. **landward** or **landwards** *adverb* towards the land.

lane *noun* 1 a narrow road or track, especially in the country. 2 (in names) a street ♦ *Drury Lane.* 3 a strip of road for a single line of traffic. 4 a strip of track or water for a runner, rower, or swimmer in a race. 5 a route prescribed for or regularly followed by ships or aircraft ♦ *shipping lanes.* [from an Old English word]

language *noun* 1 communication by the use of words. 2 a system of words used by a particular nation or people ♦ *the German language.* 3 any method of expressing or communicating meaning ♦ *body language* ♦ *the language of algebra.* 4 a system of symbols and rules used to write computer programs. 5 a particular style of wording. 6 the vocabulary of a particular group of people ♦ *medical language.* [from a Latin word *lingua* meaning 'tongue']

language laboratory *noun* a room equipped with audio equipment for learning a foreign language by repeated practice.

languid (lang-gwid) *adjective* 1 without energy or vitality. 2 weak or faint because of tiredness or illness. **languidly** *adverb* [same origin as for *languish*]

languish (lang-gwish) *verb* 1 to grow weak or feeble. 2 to be kept under miserable conditions, to be neglected ♦ *He had been languishing in prison for six months.* 3 (old use) to pine with love or grief. [from a Latin word *languere* meaning 'to be faint or weak']

languor (lang-ger) *noun* 1 a feeling of tiredness or laziness, lack of energy. 2 oppressive stillness of the air. **languorous** *adjective* [same origin as for *languish*]

laniard *noun* another spelling of **lanyard**.

lank *adjective* 1 (said about hair) long, straight, and limp. 2 tall and lean. [from an Old English word *hlanc* meaning 'thin']

lanky *adjective* (**lankier, lankiest**) ungracefully thin and tall. **lankiness** *noun*

lanolin (lan-ə-lin) *noun* fat extracted from sheep's wool and used as a base for ointments. [from Latin words *lana* meaning 'wool' and *oleum* meaning 'oil']

lantern *noun* a lamp with a transparent case for holding the light and shielding it against the wind. [from a Latin word *lanterna*; related to *lamp*]

lantern-jawed *adjective* having a long thin jaw and a chin that sticks out.

lanthanum (lan-thə-nəm) *noun* a silvery-white metallic element (symbol La). [from a Greek word *lanthanein* meaning 'to escape notice' (because it was not detected for a long time)]

lanyard *noun* 1 a short rope or line used on a ship to fasten something or secure it. 2 a cord worn round the neck or on the shoulder, to which a knife or whistle etc. may be attached. [from an Old French word *laniere*]

lap[1] *noun* the flat area formed by the upper part of the thighs when a person is sitting down. **to fall** or **drop into your lap** to be acquired by you without any effort. **in a person's lap** as his or her responsibility. **in the lap of the gods** open to chance, for fate to decide. **in the lap of luxury** in conditions of great comfort and wealth. [from an Old English word *laeppa* meaning 'fold, flap']

lap[2] *noun* 1 a single circuit of something, e.g. of a racetrack. 2 one section of a journey ♦ *the last lap.* 3 an overlapping part, or the amount of overlap. **lap** *verb* (**lapped, lapping**) 1 to overtake another competitor in a race to become one or more laps ahead. 2 to overlap something or fold it round. [from *lap*[1]]

lap[3] *verb* (**lapped, lapping**) 1 (said about an animal) to take up liquid by movements of the tongue. 2 (said about water) to wash against something with a gentle rippling sound ♦ *Waves lapped against the shore.* **to lap something up** to receive or watch something with great pleasure and appreciation. [from an Old English word *lapian*]

lapdog *noun* a small pampered pet dog.

lapel (lə-**pel**) *noun* each of the two flaps folded back against the front opening of a coat or jacket, below the collar. [from *lap*[1]]

lapidary (**lap**-id-er-i) *adjective* to do with the engraving, cutting, or polishing of stones. [from a Latin word *lapis* meaning 'a stone']

lapis lazuli (lap-iss **laz**-yoo-li) *noun* a bright blue semi-precious stone. [from a Latin word *lapis* meaning 'a stone' and a Persian word *lazward* meaning 'lapis lazuli']

Laplander *noun* a native or inhabitant of Lapland.

lap of honour *noun* a celebratory circuit of a sports field or racetrack by the winning person or team.

Lapp *noun* 1 a Laplander. 2 the language of Lapland. **Lappish** *adjective*

lapse *noun* 1 a slight error or failure, especially one caused by forgetfulness, weakness, or inattention ♦ *a lapse of memory.* 2 a decline to a lower state or standard. 3 a passing of time. 4 the loss of a privilege or legal right through disuse. **lapse** *verb* 1 to pass or slip gradually into a state or condition ♦ *He lapsed into unconsciousness.* 2 to fail to maintain your position or standard. 3 (said about rights and privileges) to be lost or no longer valid through not being used, claimed, or renewed ♦ *My insurance policy has lapsed.* SYNONYMS: expire, run out, terminate. 4 to no longer follow the rules and practices of a religion ♦ *a lapsed Catholic.* [from a Latin word *lapsum* meaning 'slipped']

laptop *noun* a portable computer for use while travelling.

lapwing *noun* a black and white bird with a crested head and a shrill cry. [from an Old English word *hleapewince*]

larceny (**lar**-sən-i) *noun* theft of personal property. **larcenous** *adjective* [from a Latin word *latro* meaning 'robber']

larch *noun* a cone-bearing deciduous tree of the pine family with bright green needles and tough wood. [via Old German from a Latin word *larix*]

lard *noun* a white greasy substance prepared from pig fat and used in cooking. **lard** *verb* 1 to place strips of fat or bacon in or on meat before cooking, in order to prevent it from becoming dry while roasting. 2 to insert contrasting material in a speech or piece of writing. **lardy**

adjective [from an Old French word meaning 'bacon']

larder *noun* a cupboard or small room for storing food. [originally denoting a store of meat, from a Latin word]

lardy cake *noun* a cake made with lard and containing currants.

large *adjective* 1 greater than normal in size or extent. SYNONYMS: big, sizeable, substantial, considerable, huge, immense. **at large** 1 free to roam about, not yet captured ♦ *Their killers are still at large.* 2 as a whole, in general ♦ *This is a problem for society at large.* **in large part** or **measure** to a great extent. **largeness** *noun* [from a Latin word *largus* meaning 'abundant' or 'generous']

large intestine *noun* the lower part of the intestine, including the caecum, colon, and rectum.

largely *adverb* to a great extent ♦ *His success was largely due to luck.*

large-scale *adjective* 1 extensive, involving large amounts ♦ *large-scale car production.* 2 drawn to a large scale so that many details can be shown ♦ *a large-scale map.*

largesse (lar-**jess**) *noun* 1 money or gifts given generously. 2 generosity. [from a French word, related to *large*]

largish *adjective* fairly large.

lariat (la-ri-ət) *noun* a lasso, a rope used to catch or tether a horse etc. [from Spanish words *la reata*, from *la* meaning 'the' and *reatar* meaning 'to tie again']

lark[1] *noun* 1 any of several small sandy-brown birds, especially the skylark. [from an Old English word]

lark[2] *noun* (*informal*) 1 a joke or piece of fun ♦ *We did it for a lark.* 2 an amusing incident. 3 a type of activity ♦ *I'm fed up with this queueing lark.* **lark** *verb* (*informal*) to have fun, especially playing mischief ♦ *We were just larking about.* **larky** *adjective* [origin unknown]

larkspur *noun* a plant with spur-shaped blue or pink flowers.

larrikin *noun* (*Austral.*) a lout or hooligan. [from an English dialect word]

larva *noun* (**larvae** (**lar**-vee)) an insect or other animal in the first stage of its life after coming out of the egg. **larval** *adjective* [from a Latin word meaning 'ghost, mask']

laryngitis (la-rin-jiy-tiss) *noun* inflammation of the larynx, causing hoarseness.

larynx (**la**-rinks) *noun* the part of the throat that contains the vocal cords. [from a Greek word *larunx*]

lasagne (lə-**san**-yeh) *noun* pasta in the form of sheets, usually cooked with minced meat and cheese sauce. [an Italian word]

lascivious (lə-**siv**-i-əs) *adjective* lustful. **lasciviously** *adverb* **lasciviousness** *noun* [from a Latin word *lascivia* meaning 'lustfully']

laser (**lay**-zer) *noun* a device that generates an intense and highly concentrated beam of light or other electromagnetic radiation. [from the initials of 'light amplification (by) stimulated emission (of) radiation']

laser printer *noun* a high-quality computer printer that uses a laser beam.

lash *verb* 1 to flick something violently in a whip-like movement ♦ *The crocodile lashed its tail.* 2 to strike a person or animal with a whip or stick. 3 to beat violently against something ♦ *Rain lashed against the panes.* 4 to fasten or secure something with a cord or rope ♦ *Lash the sticks together.* **lash** *noun* 1 a stroke with a whip or stick. 2 the flexible leather part of a whip. 3 an eyelash. **to lash out** 1 to attack someone with blows or words. 2 to spend money extravagantly. [origin unknown]

lashings *plural noun* (*informal*) a lot, plenty ♦ *lashings of cream.*

lass or **lassie** *noun* (*Scottish and N. England*) a girl or young woman. [from an Old Norse word *laskwa* meaning 'unmarried']

Lassa fever *noun* a serious disease of West Africa, caused by a virus. [named after the village of Lassa in Nigeria, where it was first reported]

lassitude *noun* physical or mental tiredness; lack of energy. [from a Latin word *lassus* meaning 'weary']

lasso (la-**soo**) *noun* (**lassoes**) a rope with a sliding noose at one end, used for catching cattle. **lasso** *verb* (**lassoes, lassoed, lassoing**) to catch an animal with a lasso. [from a Spanish word *lazo* meaning 'lace']

last[1] *adjective* 1 coming after all others in position or time, final. 2 latest, most recent ♦ *last night.* 3 only remaining ♦ *our last hope.* 4 least likely or suitable ♦ *She is the last person I'd have chosen.*
last *adv* 1 after all others, at the end ♦ *I'm afraid we came last.* 2 previously, most recently ♦ *A lot has happened since we last met.* 3 lastly ♦ *And last but not least this is Jake.*
last *noun* 1 the last person or thing. 2 the only remaining part ♦ *That's the last of the bread.* 3 the last mention or sight of something ♦ *We shall never hear the last of it.* **at last** or **at long last** finally, after much delay. **the last straw** a slight addition to your difficulties that finally makes them unbearable. **on your** or **its last legs** near death or the end of usefulness. **to the last** until the very end ♦ *He was brave to the last.* [from an Old English word *latost*]

last[2] *verb* 1 to continue for a period of time ♦ *The rain lasted all day.* SYNONYMS: continue, persist. 2 to be enough for your needs ♦ *The food will last us for three days.* 3 to keep fresh or in good health or condition ♦ *I don't think I'll be able to last long in this heat.* **to last out** to be strong enough or sufficient to last. [from an Old English word *læstan*]

last[3] *noun* a block of wood or metal shaped like a foot, used in making and repairing shoes. [from an Old English word *læste*]

last-ditch *adjective* being a desperate attempt to achieve something when everything else has failed.

lasting *adjective* able to last for a long time ♦ *a lasting peace.*

lastly *adverb* in the last place, finally.

last minute or **last moment** *adjective* the latest possible time before an event. **last-minute** *adjective*

last post *noun* a military bugle call sounded at sunset and played at military funerals and remembrance services.

Last Supper *noun* the meal eaten by Christ and his disciples on the night before the Crucifixion.

last word *noun* 1 a final or definitive statement on a subject. 2 the most modern or advanced example of something ♦ *the last word in mobile phones.*

latch *noun* 1 a small bar fastening a door or gate, lifted from its catch by a lever. 2 a spring lock that catches when the door is closed and can only be opened from the outside by a key. **latch** *verb* to fasten something or be fastened with a latch. **to latch on** to understand something. **to latch on to** (*informal*) to meet someone and follow them around all the time. **on the latch** fastened by a latch but not locked. [from an Old English word *læccan* meaning 'to grasp']

latchkey *noun* (**latchkeys**) the key of an outer door.

latchkey child *noun* a child left to look after himself or herself because neither parent is at home when he or she returns from school.

late *adjective & adverb* **1** after the usual or expected time ♦ *Sorry I'm late.* **2** far on in the day or night or a period of time or a series etc. ♦ *We arrived late in the afternoon* ♦ *in the late 1920s.* **3** of recent date or time ♦ *the latest news.* **4** no longer alive ♦ *the late president.* **at the latest** no later than a certain time. **of late** recently. **the latest** the most recent news. **lateness** *noun* [from an Old English word]

lately *adverb* recently, not long ago.

latent (lay-tǝnt) *adjective* existing but not yet active or developed or visible ♦ *her latent talent.* **latency** *noun* [from a Latin word *latens* meaning 'lying hidden']

latent heat *noun* (*Physics*) the heat needed to change a solid into liquid or vapour, or a liquid into a vapour, without a change in temperature.

later *adverb* at a time in the near future; afterwards.

lateral (lat-er-ǝl) *adjective* **1** to do with the side or sides. **2** sideways ♦ *lateral movement.* **laterally** *adverb* [from a Latin word *lateris* meaning 'of a side']

lateral line *noun* (*Zoology*) a line of pores opening into sensory organs along each side of a fish.

lateral thinking *noun* the solving of problems by thinking about them in an indirect and creative way.

latex (lay-teks) *noun* **1** a milky fluid produced by certain plants, e.g. the rubber tree. **2** a synthetic product resembling this, used to make paints and coatings. [a Latin word meaning 'liquid']

lath (lath) *noun* a narrow thin strip of wood, used in trellises or as a support for plaster etc. [from an Old English word *lætt*]

lathe (layth) *noun* a machine for holding and turning pieces of wood or metal against a tool that will cut them to shape. [perhaps from an Old Danish word *lad* meaning 'structure, frame']

lather *noun* **1** a frothy mass of bubbles produced by soap or detergent mixed with water. **2** frothy sweat, especially on horses. **3** (*informal*) a state of agitation.
lather *verb* **1** to form a lather. **2** to cover something with lather. **3** to cover or spread something with a substance. [from an Old English word]

Latin *noun* **1** the language of the ancient Romans. **2** a native or inhabitant of a country whose language developed from Latin, e.g. an Italian or Latin American.
Latin *adjective* **1** to do with or in Latin. **2** to do with the countries or peoples using languages developed from Latin, especially Italian, Spanish, and Portuguese. [from *Latium*, an ancient district of Italy including Rome]

Latin American *adjective* to do with the parts of Central and South America where Spanish or Portuguese is the main language.
Latin American *noun* a native or inhabitant of this region. [so called because these languages developed from Latin]

latitude *noun* **1** the distance of a place from the equator, measured in degrees. **2** freedom from restrictions on what people can do or believe.
latitudes *plural noun* regions with reference to their temperature and distance from the equator ♦ *northern latitudes* ♦ *low latitudes.* **latitudinal** *adjective* [from a Latin word *latitudo* meaning 'breadth']

latrine (lǝ-treen) *noun* a toilet in a camp or barracks. [from a French word; related to *lavatory*]

latter *adjective* **1** being the second of two people or things mentioned ♦ *He decided to take the latter course of action.* **2** nearer to the end than to the beginning ♦ *the latter half of the year.* **3** recent ♦ *in latter years.* **the latter** *noun* the second of two people or things just mentioned. [from an Old English word *lætra* meaning 'slower'] ◊ When you are referring to the last of three or more people or things, use *the last* or *the last-named*, not *the latter*.

latter-day *adjective* modern or recent ♦ *He is a latter-day Robin Hood.*

Latter-Day Saints *plural noun* the Mormons' name for themselves.

latterly *adverb* recently, nowadays.

lattice (lat-iss) *noun* 1 a framework of crossed strips or bars with spaces between, used as a screen or fence etc. 2 a structure or pattern resembling this. **latticework** *noun* [from an Old French word *lattis*]

lattice window *noun* a window made with small panes set in diagonally crossing strips of lead.

laud (lawd) *verb* (*formal*) to praise someone or something highly. [from a Latin word *laudare* meaning 'to praise']

laudable (law-də-bəl) *adjective* deserving praise ♦ *Their motives are laudable.* **laudably** *adverb* ◊ Do not confuse this word with **laudatory**, which has a different meaning.

laudanum (lawd-nəm) *noun* opium prepared for use as a sedative or painkiller. [from a Latin word]

laudatory (law-də-ter-i) *adjective* expressing praise ♦ *laudatory remarks.* ◊ Do not confuse this word with **laudable**, which has a different meaning.

laugh *verb* 1 to make the sounds and movements of the face and body that express lively amusement and sometimes also scorn. SYNONYMS: chuckle, chortle, snigger, giggle, titter, guffaw, roar. **laugh** *noun* 1 an act, sound, or manner of laughing. 2 (*informal*) an amusing incident or person. **to be laughing** (*informal*) to be in a fortunate or successful position. **to have the last laugh** to come off better in the end, to be finally proved to be right. **to laugh at** to make fun of someone or something. **to laugh something off** to dismiss something by treating it in a light-hearted way. **to laugh on the other side of your face** to change from amusement to dismay. **to laugh something out of court** to make fun of something so that no one gives it serious consideration. **no laughing matter** something serious that should not be joked about. [from an Old English word *hlaehhan*]

laughable *adjective* deserving to be laughed at, ridiculous.

laughing gas *noun* nitrous oxide, which can cause involuntary laughter in a person who inhales it.

laughing jackass *noun* (*Austral.*) the kookaburra.

laughing stock *noun* a person or thing that is the object of ridicule and scorn.

laughter *noun* the act or sound of laughing. [from an Old English word *hleahtor*]

launch [1] *verb* 1 to cause a boat or ship to move or slide from land into the water. 2 to send a rocket or missile upwards into space or into the air. 3 to send something on its course. 4 to bring a new product on to the market ♦ *The company has recently launched a new soft drink.* 5 to start something off ♦ *They launched an attack at dawn.* 6 to begin something with enthusiasm and energy ♦ *She launched into her speech.* **launch** *noun* 1 the process of launching a ship, rocket, etc. 2 the start of something. **to launch out** to start on an ambitious enterprise. [from an Old French word *launcher*]

launch [2] *noun* 1 a large motor boat. 2 (*historical*) a warship's largest boat. [from a Spanish word]

launch pad or **launching pad** *noun* a platform from which a rocket is launched.

launder *verb* 1 to wash and iron clothes and linen. 2 (*informal*) to transfer illegally obtained money in order to make its source seem legitimate. [same origin as for *laundry*]

launderette (lawn-der-et) *noun* an establishment fitted with washing machines that customers pay to use.

laundress *noun* a woman whose job is to launder clothes and linen.

laundry *noun* (**laundries**) 1 a batch of clothes and linen that needs to be washed or that has just been washed. 2 a place where clothes and linen are washed and ironed for customers. [from a Latin word *lavandaria* meaning 'things to be washed']

laureate (lorri-ət) *noun* 1 a person given an award for outstanding creative or intellectual achievement ♦ *a Nobel laureate.* 2 the Poet Laureate. **laureate** *adjective* wreathed with laurel as a mark of honour. **laureateship** *noun* [from *laurel* (because a laurel wreath was worn in ancient times as a sign of victory)]

laurel (lo-rəl) *noun* 1 an evergreen shrub with smooth glossy leaves. 2 (also **laurels**) a crown of of laurel leaves worn as an emblem of victory or mark of honour in classical times. **to look to your laurels** to beware of losing your position of superiority. **to rest on your laurels** to be so satisfied with what you have already achieved that you make no further effort. [from a Latin word *laurus*]

lava (lah-və) *noun* flowing molten rock that flows or erupts from a volcano, or the solid rock formed when this cools. [from a Latin word *lavare* meaning 'to wash']

lavatory *noun* (**lavatories**) 1 a toilet. 2 a room or compartment containing a toilet. [from a Latin word *lavatorium* meaning 'a place for washing']

lavender *noun* 1 a shrub with fragrant purple flowers that are dried and used to scent linen etc. 2 light purple. [from a Latin word *lavandula*]

lavender water *noun* a delicate perfume made from lavender.

lavish (lav-ish) *adjective* 1 giving or producing something in large quantities. 2 plentiful or luxurious ♦ *a lavish display.* **lavish** *verb* to give something in generous or plentiful quantities ♦ *Her latest novel has been lavished with praise.* **lavishly** *adverb* **lavishness** *noun* [from Old French *lavasse* meaning 'downpour of rain']

law *noun* 1 a rule or set of rules that everyone in a country or community must obey. 2 the use of these rules to provide a remedy against wrongs ♦ *law and order.* 3 the subject or study of these rules. 4 (*informal*) the police. 5 something that must be obeyed ♦ *His word was law.* 6 a rule of a sport or game ♦ *the laws of cricket.* 7 a factual statement of what always happens in certain circumstances, e.g. of regular natural occurrences ♦ *the laws of nature* ♦ *the law of gravity.* SYNONYMS: principle, theory, axiom. **to lay down the law** to tell someone what to do in a stern way or as if you are sure you are right. **to take the law into your own hands** to punish someone yourself, especially illegally, according to your own idea of justice. [via Old English from an Old Norse word *lag* meaning 'something laid down or fixed']

law-abiding *adjective* obeying the law.

lawbreaker *noun* a person who breaks the law.

law court *noun* a room or building in which legal cases are heard and judged.

lawful *adjective* allowed or accepted by the law. **lawfully** *adverb*

lawless *adjective* 1 (said about a place) where laws do not exist or are not applied. 2 not obeying the law ♦ *a lawless mob.* **lawlessly** *adverb* **lawlessness** *noun*

law lord *noun* a member of the House of Lords who is qualified to perform its legal work.

lawman *noun* (**lawmen**) (in the USA) a law-enforcement officer, especially a sheriff.

lawn [1] *noun* an area of mown grass in a garden or park. [from an Old French word *launde* meaning 'wooded district, heath']

lawn [2] *noun* fine linen or cotton material used for making clothes. [probably from *Laon*, a town in France where cloth was made]

lawnmower *noun* a machine with revolving blades for cutting the grass on a lawn.

lawn tennis *noun* see **tennis**.

lawsuit *noun* a dispute or claim that is brought to a law court to be settled.

lawyer (loi-er) *noun* a person who is trained in and qualified to practise law.

lax *adjective* slack, not strict or severe enough ♦ *Discipline was lax.* **laxity** *noun* **laxly** *adverb* [from a Latin word *laxus* meaning 'loose']

laxative (laks-ə-tiv) *noun* a drug or medicine that stimulates the bowels to empty.
laxative *adjective* having this effect. [from a Latin word *laxare* meaning 'to loosen']

lay [1] *verb* (past tense and past participle **laid**) 1 to put something down on a surface, especially in a horizontal position ♦ *He laid the letter on the table.* 2 to put something in a particular position or place ♦ *She laid a hand on his shoulder.* 3 to arrange things, especially for a meal ♦ *Can you lay the table?* 4 to place or assign something ♦ *He lays great emphasis on neatness* ♦ *She laid the blame on her brother.* 5 to formulate or prepare something ♦ *We laid our plans.* 6 to present something or put it forward for consideration ♦ *He laid his proposal before us.* 7 (said about a female bird, reptile, etc.) to produce an egg from inside its body. 8 to stake an amount of money in a wager or bet.
lay *noun* the way or position in which something is lying. **to lay claim to** to claim something as your right. **to lay**

something down 1 to establish something as a rule or instruction. **2** to store wine in a cellar. **3** to pay or wager money. **to lay a ghost** to cause a ghost to stop appearing. **to lay hands on** to find and take possession of something. **to lay hold of** to seize or grasp something. **to lay something in** to build up a stock of something you may need. **to lay into** (informal) **1** to thrash someone. **2** to reprimand someone harshly ♦ *His mother really laid into him.* **to lay it on the line** (informal) to speak frankly. **to lay someone low** (said about an illness) to affect someone severely. **to lay off** (informal) to stop doing something, especially annoying or causing trouble to someone. **to lay someone off** to stop employing someone for a while or permanently because of shortage of work. **to lay something on** to supply or provide something ♦ *We laid on a minibus to take people home after the party.* **to lay someone open to** to expose someone to the risk of something, especially criticism. **to lay someone out 1** to knock someone unconscious. **2** to prepare a person's body for burial. **to lay something out 1** to spread something out to its full extent. **2** to arrange or build something according to a plan. **3** to spend money for a purpose. **to lay someone to rest** to bury a person's body in a grave. **to lay someone up** to put someone out of action through illness or injury. **to lay something up** to store or save something. **to lay waste** to completely destroy the crops and buildings etc. of a district. [from an Old English word *lecgan*]

◊ Do not confuse *lay* ('to put down'; past tense is *laid*) with *lie* ('to recline'; past tense is *lay*). Correct uses are as follows: *Go and lie down. She and you lay down. Please lay it on the floor. They laid it on the floor.* Incorrect use is 'Go and lay down'.

lay[2] *adjective* **1** not ordained into the clergy ♦ *a lay preacher.* **2** not professionally qualified, especially in law or medicine. [from a Greek word *laos* meaning 'people']

lay[3] *noun* (old use) a poem meant to be sung, a ballad. [from an Old French word *lai*]

lay[4] past tense of **lie**[2].

layabout *noun* a person who lazily avoids doing any work.

lay-by *noun* (**lay-bys**) **1** an area at the side of a main road, where vehicles may stop

without obstructing the flow of traffic. **2** (Austral. and NZ) a system of reserving an article for later purchase, by payment of a deposit and instalments.

layer *noun* **1** a single thickness or coating of something, often one of several, laid over a surface. **2** a person or thing that lays something. **3** a shoot fastened down to take root while still attached to the parent plant.
layer *verb* **1** to arrange or cut something in layers. **2** to propagate a plant as a layer. [from *lay*[1]]

layer cake *noun* a cake consisting of layers with filling between.

layette *noun* the clothes and bedclothes prepared for a new-born baby. [from a French word]

lay figure *noun* a jointed wooden figure of the human body, used by artists. [from an old Dutch word *led* meaning 'joint']

layman or **layperson** *noun* (**laymen** or **laypeople**) **1** a person who does not have specialized knowledge or training, e.g. as a doctor or lawyer. **2** a person who is not ordained as a member of the clergy. [from *lay*[2] and *man*]

lay-off *noun* **1** a temporary or permanent discharge of a worker or workers. **2** a period during which someone cannot take part in a sport etc. because of injury or illness.

layout *noun* **1** the arrangement or plan of something ♦ *I like the layout of the gallery.* **2** the arrangement of text, illustrations, etc. on a page. **3** something displayed or set out ♦ *a model railway layout.*

lay reader *noun* (in the Anglican Church) a layperson licensed to conduct some religious services.

laywoman *noun* (**laywomen**) **1** a woman who is not ordained as a member of the clergy. **2** a woman who does not have specialized knowledge or training, e.g. as a doctor or lawyer. [from *lay*[2] and *woman*]

laze *verb* to spend time in a relaxed lazy manner.
laze *noun* a time spent lazing. [from *lazy*]

lazy *adjective* (**lazier, laziest**) **1** unwilling to work; doing little work. SYNONYMS: idle, indolent, slothful, work-shy, shiftless. **2** showing a lack of care or energy ♦ *a lazy yawn.* **lazily** *adverb* **laziness** *noun* [probably from an Old Dutch word]

lazybones *noun* (informal) a lazy person.

lb *abbreviation* pound(s) in weight. [short for a Latin word *libra*]

lbw *abbreviation* (in cricket) leg before wicket.

LCD *abbreviation* liquid crystal display.

LEA *abbreviation* Local Education Authority.

lea *noun* (poetic) an open area of grassy or arable land. [from an Old English word]

leach *verb* to make liquid, especially rainwater, percolate through soil or ore etc. in order to remove a soluble substance. [from an Old English word *leccan* meaning 'to water']

lead ¹ (leed) *verb* (past tense and past participle **led**) 1 to show someone the way by going in front or accompanying them. SYNONYMS: guide, conduct, escort, usher. 2 to make a person or animal go with you by pulling them along. 3 to be in first place or position in a race or contest, to be ahead ♦ *Rangers are leading by two goals to nil* ♦ *a country that leads the world in electronics.* 4 to be in charge of a group of people, to be the leader. SYNONYMS: head, preside over, direct, command, manage, captain. 5 to be a route or means of access ♦ *This path leads to the beach* ♦ *The door led into a passage.* 6 to have something as its result ♦ *This led to confusion.* 7 to be someone's reason or motive for something ♦ *What led you to become a journalist?* 8 to live or pass your life ♦ *He leads a dull life.* 9 (in boxing) to make your first punch in a series. 10 to play the first card in a round of a card game.
lead *noun* 1 a leading place or position, first place; the amount by which one competitor is in front ♦ *She took the lead on the final bend* ♦ *United now have a lead of 5 points.* 2 guidance or leadership given by being the first to do something ♦ *Britain should be taking a lead on this issue.* 3 a clue to be followed ♦ *The police have few leads.* 4 the chief part in a play or film, or the person who takes this part ♦ *He played the lead in 'Hamlet'.* 5 (used before a noun) playing the main part in a musical group ♦ *the lead singer.* 6 a strap or cord for leading a dog or other animal. 7 a wire carrying electric current from a source to a place of use. 8 the act or right of playing your card first in a round of a card game; the card played ♦ *Whose lead is it?* **to lead someone astray** to make someone think or do the wrong thing. **to lead someone on** to deceive someone into thinking that

you are attracted to them. **to lead someone up the garden path** (informal) to mislead someone. **to lead up to** to serve as an introduction to or preparation for something. [from an Old English word *lædan*]

lead ² (led) *noun* 1 a heavy metal of dull greyish colour, a chemical element (symbol Pb). 2 a thin stick of graphite forming the writing substance in a pencil. 3 a lump of lead suspended on a line to determine the depth of water.
leads *plural noun* strips of lead used to cover a roof. **to swing the lead** (informal) to pretend to be ill in order to avoid work. [from an Old English word *lead*]

leaded (led-id) *adjective* 1 covered or framed with lead; mixed with lead. 2 (said about petrol) containing a lead compound.

leaden (led-ən) *adjective* 1 heavy and slow. 2 lead-coloured, dark grey ♦ *leaden skies.* 3 (old use) made of lead.

leader *noun* 1 the person in charge of a group of people. 2 someone who is winning. 3 someone whose example is followed ♦ *a leader of fashion.* 4 the principal player in an orchestra. 5 a leading article in a newspaper.

leadership *noun* 1 being a leader. 2 ability to be a leader. 3 the leaders of a group.

lead-in *noun* an introduction to or the opening of something.

leading ¹ (leed-ing) *adjective* the most important or in first place.

leading ² (led-ing) *noun* the amount of blank space between lines of print.

leading aircraftman or **leading aircraftwoman** *noun* a member of the RAF ranking above aircraftman or aircraftwoman.

leading article *noun* an article in a newspaper giving the editorial opinion.

leading lady or **leading man** *noun* the actor taking the chief part in a play or film.

leading light *noun* a prominent or influential member of a group.

leading question *noun* a question that is worded so that it prompts a person to give the answer that is wanted.
◊ A *leading question* does not mean a 'challenging, searching, or embarrassing question'.

lead-up noun the sequence of events leading up to something.

leaf noun (**leaves**) **1** a flat, usually green, part of a plant growing from its stem or branch or directly from the root. **2** the state of having leaves out ♦ *The trees are now in leaf.* **3** a single thickness of the paper in a book. **4** a very thin sheet of metal ♦ *gold leaf.* **5** a hinged flap of a table, or an extra section that may be inserted to extend a table. **to leaf through** to turn over the pages of a book. **to take a leaf out of someone's book** to follow his or her example. **to turn over a new leaf** to make a fresh start and improve your behaviour. **leafless** adjective [from an Old English word]

leaflet noun **1** a printed sheet of paper giving information, especially one given out free. **2** a small leaf or leaf-like part of a plant.

leaf mould noun soil or compost consisting chiefly of decayed leaves.

leafy adjective (**leafier, leafiest**) covered in leaves; full of trees etc. ♦ *leafy suburbs.* **leafiness** noun

league [1] noun **1** a group of people or countries who combine formally for some common purpose. **2** a group of sports teams which compete against each other for a championship. **3** a class or level of quality or ability ♦ *As artists they are not remotely in the same league.*
league verb (**leagues, leagued, leaguing**) to join in a league or alliance. **in league with** working or plotting together. [from a Latin word *legare* meaning 'to bind']

league [2] noun an old measure of distance, about three miles. [from a Greek word]

league table noun **1** a table of competitors in a league ranked according to their performances. **2** a list in which things are ranked according to achievement or merit ♦ *school league tables.*

leak noun **1** a hole or crack through which liquid or gas may accidentally escape. **2** an escape of liquid or gas. **3** a similar escape of an electric charge, or the charge itself. **4** a deliberate disclosure of secret information.
leak verb **1** (said about liquid or gas) to escape accidentally through a hole or crack. **2** (said about a container) to let out liquid or gas in this way. **3** to deliberately reveal secret information ♦ *Someone leaked the report's findings to the press.* **to leak out** (said about a secret) to become

known despite efforts to keep it secret. [probably from an Old German or Dutch word]

leakage noun **1** leaking. **2** a thing or amount that has leaked out.

leaky adjective (**leakier, leakiest**) liable to leak.

lean [1] verb (past tense and past participle **leaned** or **leant**) **1** to bend your body towards or over something. **2** to be or put something in a sloping position. SYNONYMS: incline, slope, slant, tilt, tip, list. **3** to rest against or on something for support. **4** to rely or depend on someone for help.
lean noun a sloping position. **to lean on** (*informal*) to put pressure on someone to act in a certain way. **to lean to** or **towards** to tend to favour a particular point of view. [from an Old English word *hleonian*]
◊ The past tense is 'he *leaned* or he *leant* or he *had leant* against the wall'.

lean [2] adjective **1** (said about a person or animal) thin, without much flesh. **2** (said about meat) containing little or no fat. **3** efficient and with no wastage ♦ *a lean company.* **4** meagre or scanty ♦ *a lean harvest.*
lean noun the lean part of meat. **lean years** years of scarcity. **leanness** noun [from an Old English word *hlǽne*]

leaning noun a tendency or preference.

lean-to noun (**lean-tos**) a building with its roof resting against the side of a larger building.

leap verb (past tense and past participle **leaped** (leept or lept) or **leapt** (lept)) **1** to jump vigorously, to jump across something. SYNONYMS: jump, bound, spring, vault. **2** to move somewhere suddenly and quickly ♦ *He leapt out of his chair.* **3** to rise suddenly in amount or in price or value.
leap noun **1** a vigorous jump. **2** an abrupt change or increase. **a leap in the dark** a daring step you take without knowing what the consequences will be. **by** or **in leaps and bounds** with very rapid progress. **to leap at** to accept an opportunity eagerly. [from an Old English word]

leapfrog noun a game in which each player in turn jumps with legs apart over another who is bending down.
leapfrog verb (**leapfrogged, leapfrogging**) **1** to perform a jump of this kind. **2** to get ahead of someone who was in front of you.

leap year noun a year, occurring once every four years, with an extra day (29 February). [so called probably because the dates from March onwards 'leap' a day of the week. A date which would fall on a Monday in an ordinary year will be on Tuesday in a leap year]

learn verb (past tense and past participle **learned** (lernt or lernd) or **learnt** (lernt)) 1 to gain knowledge of or skill in something by study or experience or by being taught. 2 to memorize something ♦ I'll try to learn all your names. 3 to become aware of something by information or from observation. [from an Old English word leornian]
◊ It is not acceptable in standard English to use learn to mean 'to teach'.

learned (lern-id) adjective 1 having much knowledge acquired by study ♦ learned men. 2 to do with or for learned people ♦ a learned society. **learnedly** adverb

learner noun a person who is learning a subject or skill, especially to drive a car.

learning noun knowledge obtained by study.

learning curve noun the rate, often changing during its course, at which a person learns new information or abilities, regarded as a curve on a graph.

learning difficulties plural noun difficulties in learning, especially because of mental handicap.

lease noun a contract by which the owner of land or a building etc. allows another person to use it for a fixed period, usually in return for payment.
lease verb 1 to allow the use of a property by lease. 2 to obtain or take a property by lease. **a new lease of life** a chance to live more happily because of recovery from illness or anxiety, or to continue in use after repair. [from an Old French word lais]

leasehold noun the holding of land or a house or flat etc. by means of a lease. **leaseholder** noun

leash noun a dog's lead.
leash verb to put a leash on a dog. [from an Old French word lesse]

least adjective 1 smallest in amount or degree. 2 lowest in rank or importance.
least noun the least amount or degree ♦ The least you could do is apologize.
least adverb in the least degree. **at least** 1 not less than what is stated. 2 if

nothing else; anyway ♦ You could at least try. **not in the least** not at all ♦ I don't mind in the least. **to say the least** putting it mildly. [from an Old English word]

leather noun 1 material made from animal skins by tanning or a similar process. 2 a piece of leather for polishing with.
leathers plural noun leather clothes worn by a motorcyclist.
leather verb to cover something with leather. [from an Old English word lether]

leatherette (leth-er-et) noun imitation leather.

leatherjacket noun the tough-skinned larva of a type of crane fly.

leathery adjective as tough as leather.

leave [1] verb (past tense and past participle **left**) 1 to go away from a person or place ♦ What time did you leave the party? SYNONYMS: go, depart, disappear, set off, withdraw, retire. 2 to stop belonging to a group or organization; to stop working somewhere. 3 to cause or allow something to stay where it is or as it is ♦ Only a few crumbs were left ♦ You left the door open. 4 to go away without taking something ♦ I left my gloves on the bus. 5 to let someone deal with something without interfering or offering help ♦ We left him to get on with it ♦ I was left with the bill. 6 to refrain from eating or dealing with something ♦ She left the vegetables ♦ Let's leave the washing-up. 7 to entrust or commit something to another person ♦ Leave the shopping to me. 8 to have an amount as a remainder ♦ 11 from 43 leaves 32. 9 to give something as a legacy. 10 to deposit something to be collected or passed on ♦ You can leave your coat in the hall. ♦ Would you like to leave a message? 11 to abandon or desert someone or something ♦ His wife has left him ♦ A captain should never leave a sinking ship. **to leave someone or something alone** to allow a person or thing to remain undisturbed ♦ Leave the dog alone. **to leave off** to stop doing something. **to leave someone** or **something out** to fail to include someone or something. [from an Old English word]

leave [2] noun 1 time when you have official permission to be away from work ♦ three days' leave. 2 (formal) permission. **on leave** absent with official permission. **to take leave of your senses** to go mad. **to take your leave** (formal) to say goodbye and go away. [from an Old English word]

leaven (lev-ən) noun 1 a substance such as yeast that is added to dough to make it ferment and rise. 2 a quality or influence that lightens or enlivens something.
leaven verb 1 to add leaven to dough. 2 to modify something by an addition; to enliven it. [from a Latin word *levare* meaning 'to lighten or raise']

leave-taking noun an act of saying goodbye.

leavings plural noun things that have been left as worthless.

lecher noun a lecherous man.

lechery noun excessive sexual desire. **lecherous** adjective [via Old French from a Germanic word]

lectern noun a tall stand with a sloping top to hold a book or notes for someone to read from. [same origin as for *lecture*]

lecture noun 1 a speech or talk giving information about a subject to an audience or class. 2 a long serious speech, especially one giving a reprimand or warning.
lecture verb 1 to give a lecture or series of lectures. 2 to talk to someone seriously or reprovingly. **lecturer** noun [from a Latin word *lectum* meaning 'to read']

LED abbreviation light- emitting diode, a semiconductor that glows when a current passes through it.

led past tense and past participle of **lead**[1].

ledge noun a narrow horizontal projection, a narrow shelf ♦ *a mountain ledge* ♦ *a window ledge*. [origin unknown]

ledger noun a book of financial accounts. [from a Dutch word]

lee noun the sheltered side or part of something, away from the wind ♦ *under the lee of the hedge*. [from an Old English word]

leech noun 1 a small blood-sucking worm usually living in water. 2 a person who drains the resources of another. [from an Old English word]

leek noun a plant related to the onion but with broader leaves and a cylindrical white bulb, eaten as a vegetable. [from an Old English word]

leer verb to look at someone in a lustful or unpleasant way.
leer noun a leering look. **leering** adjective [origin unknown]

leery adjective (**leerier, leeriest**) (*informal*) wary, suspicious. [from *leer*]

lees plural noun the sediment of wine in the barrel. [from an Old French word]

leeward (lee-werd or loo-erd) adjective situated on the side turned away from the wind.
leeward noun the leeward side.

leeway noun 1 the amount of freedom to move or act that is available ♦ *These instructions give us plenty of leeway*. 2 a ship's sideways drift to leeward of its proper course. **to make up leeway** to make up lost time.

left[1] adjective 1 on or towards the side which is to the west when you are facing north. 2 to do with left-wing politics.
left adverb on or to the left side.
left noun 1 the left-hand side or direction. 2 a person's left fist, or a blow with this. 3 (often the Left) a political party or other group in favour of radical, reforming, or socialist views. [from an Old English word *lyft* meaning 'weak']

left[2] past tense and past participle of **leave**[1].

left-hand adjective of or towards the left side.

left-handed adjective 1 using the left hand usually. 2 operated by the left hand. 3 (said about a screw) to be tightened by turning anticlockwise. **left-handedness** noun

left-hander noun a left-handed person.

leftist noun a supporter of left-wing politics.
leftist adjective to do with the left wing in politics. **leftism** noun

left luggage noun luggage left temporarily at a railway station etc.

leftovers plural noun food not finished at a meal.
leftover adjective remaining after the rest has been used or finished.

left wing noun the radical, reforming, or socialist section of a political party or system. **left-wing** adjective **left-winger** noun

lefty or **leftie** noun (**lefties**) (*informal*) 1 a left-wing person. 2 a left-handed person.

leg noun 1 each of the limbs on which a person or animal stands or walks. 2 the leg of an animal or bird as food. 3 the part of a piece of clothing covering the leg. 4 each of the long thin supports beneath a chair or other piece of furniture. **5** any branch of a forked object. **6** a section of a journey. **7** each of a pair of matches between the same opponents in a round of a competition. **8** the side of a cricket field opposite the off side and behind the batsman. **to give someone a leg up** to help someone to climb up or over something. **to not have a leg to stand on** to have no facts or sound reasons to support your arguments or actions. **to leg it** (*informal*) to run away, to walk or run rapidly. **on your last legs** completely exhausted or worn out. [from an Old Norse word *leggr*]

legacy (leg-ə-si) *noun* (**legacies**) **1** something left to a person in a will. **2** something received from a predecessor or because of earlier events ♦ *a legacy of distrust.* [from a Latin word *legatus* meaning 'delegated or bequeathed']

legal *adjective* **1** in accordance with the law; authorized or required by law. **2** to do with or based on the law ♦ *my legal adviser.* **legally** *adverb* [from a Latin word *legis* meaning 'of a law']

legal aid *noun* payment from public funds towards the cost of legal advice or proceedings.

legality (lig-al-i-ti) *noun* (**legalities**) **1** the quality or state of being legal. **2** something you have to do by law.

legalize *verb* to make something legal. **legalization** *noun*

legate (leg-ət) *noun* an official representative, especially of the Pope. [from a Latin word *legare* meaning 'to depute or bequeath']

legatee (leg-ə-tee) *noun* a person who receives a legacy.

legation (lig-ay-shən) *noun* **1** a diplomatic minister and staff. **2** the official residence of a diplomat. [same origin as for *legate*]

legato (lig-ah-toh) *adverb* (*Music*) in a smooth flowing manner. [an Italian word]

leg before wicket *adjective & adverb* (said about a batsman in cricket) out because of illegally obstructing the ball with the leg or other part of the body when the ball would otherwise have hit the wicket.

legend (lej-ənd) *noun* **1** an old story, which may or may not be true, handed down from the past. **2** such stories collectively. **3** an extremely famous person ♦ *a screen*

legend. **4** an inscription, caption, or key. [from a Latin word *legenda* meaning 'things to be read']

legendary (lej-ən-der-i) *adjective* **1** to do with, based on, or described in legends. SYNONYMS: fabled, mythical. **2** famous, often talked about.

legerdemain (lej-er-də-mayn) *noun* **1** sleight of hand in conjuring tricks. **2** trickery. [a French word meaning 'light of hand']

leger line (lej-er) *noun* (*Music*) a short line added in a score for notes above or below the range of the stave. [another spelling of *ledger*]

leggings *plural noun* **1** a woman's tight-fitting stretchy piece of clothing covering the legs, hips, and bottom. **2** protective outer coverings for each leg from knee to ankle.

leggy *adjective* (**leggier**, **leggiest**) having noticeably long legs.

legible (lej-i-bəl) *adjective* (said about print or handwriting) clear enough to read. **legibility** *noun* **legibly** *adverb* [from a Latin word *legere* meaning 'to read']

legion (lee-jən) *noun* **1** a division of the ancient Roman army. **2** a national association of former servicemen and servicewomen ♦ *the British Legion.* **3** a vast number of people or things. **the Legion** *noun* the Foreign Legion. **legion** *adjective* great in number ♦ *Her fans are legion.* **legionary** *adjective* [from a Latin word *legere* meaning 'to choose or levy']

legionnaire (lee-jən-air) *noun* a member of a legion. [from a French word]

legionnaires' disease *noun* a serious form of bacterial pneumonia. [so-called because of an outbreak at a meeting of the American Legion of ex-servicemen in 1976]

legislate (lej-iss-layt) *verb* **1** to make or pass laws. **2** to bring something into effect by making laws. [from Latin words *legis* meaning 'of a law' and *latio* meaning 'proposing']

legislation (lej-iss-lay-shən) *noun* **1** legislating. **2** the laws themselves.

legislative (lej-iss-lə-tiv) *adjective* making laws ♦ *a legislative assembly.*

legislator (lej-iss-layt-er) *noun* a member of a legislative assembly.

legislature (lej-iss-lə-cher) *noun* a country's legislative assembly.

legitimate¹ (li-jit-i-mət) *adjective* 1 in accordance with the law or rules. 2 logical, justifiable ♦ *a legitimate reason for absence.* 3 (said about a child) born of parents who are married to each other. **legitimacy** *noun* **legitimately** *adverb* [from a Latin word *legitimare* meaning 'to make something lawful']

legitimate² (li-jit-i-mayt) *verb* to make something legitimate.

legitimize (li-jit-i-miyz) *verb* to make something legitimate.

legless *adjective* 1 without legs. 2 (*informal*) very drunk.

legroom *noun* space for someone sitting down to put their legs.

legume (leg-yoom) *noun* 1 a leguminous plant. 2 a fruit or pod of this, especially when edible. [from a Latin word *legere* meaning 'to pick']

leguminous (lig-yoo-min-əs) *adjective* (*Botany*) to do with the family of plants that bear their seeds in pods, e.g. peas and beans.

leg warmers *plural noun* a pair of very long socks without feet.

lei (lay) *noun* a Polynesian garland of flowers worn round the neck. [a Hawaiian word]

leisure (lezh-er) *noun* time that is free from work, time in which you can do what you like. **at leisure** 1 not occupied. 2 in an unhurried way. **at your leisure** when you have time. **leisured** *adjective* [from an Old French word *leisir*]

leisure centre *noun* a building or complex with recreational facilities of various kinds.

leisurely (lezh-er-li) *adjective & adverb* without hurry ♦ *a leisurely pace.* SYNONYMS: unhurried, relaxed, gentle, easy. **leisureliness** *noun*

leitmotif or **leitmotiv** (liyt-moh-teef) *noun* a theme associated with a particular person or idea etc. throughout a musical or literary composition. [a German word]

lemming *noun* a small mouse-like rodent of Arctic regions, one species of which migrates in large numbers and is said to continue running into the sea and drown. [from a Norwegian or Danish word]

lemon *noun* 1 an oval yellow citrus fruit

with a sour taste. 2 the tree that bears this fruit. 3 a pale yellow colour. 4 (*informal*) a useless or disappointing person or thing. **lemony** *adjective* [same origin as for *lime*]

lemonade *noun* a lemon-flavoured soft drink.

lemon curd or **lemon cheese** *noun* a thick creamy-textured jam made with lemons.

lemon sole *noun* a kind of plaice.

lemur (lee-mer) *noun* a monkey-like animal with a pointed snout and long tail, found only in Madagascar. [from a Latin word *lemures* meaning 'spirits of the dead', from their spectre-like faces]

lend *verb* (past tense and past participle **lent**) 1 to allow someone to use something of yours temporarily on the understanding that it will be returned. 2 to provide a sum of money under an agreement to pay it back later, often with interest. 3 to contribute or add a quality to something ♦ *She lent dignity to the occasion.* **to lend a hand** to help someone. **to lend an ear** to listen. **to lend itself to** to be suitable for something ♦ *This novel lends itself to TV dramatization.* **lender** *noun* [from an Old English word; related to *loan*]

length *noun* 1 how long something is; measurement or extent from end to end. 2 the quality of being long. 3 the amount of time occupied by something ♦ *the length of our holiday.* 4 the length of a horse or boat as a measure of the lead in a race. 5 the degree of thoroughness in taking a course of action ♦ *They went to great lengths to make us comfortable.* 6 a piece of cloth, rope, wire, etc. cut from a larger piece. **at length** 1 in detail, fully. 2 after a long time. [from an Old English word *lengthu*]

lengthen *verb* to make something longer, or to become longer ♦ *The days lengthen in the spring* ♦ *We'll need to lengthen the table.* SYNONYMS: draw out, extend, elongate, stretch, prolong.

lengthways *adverb* from end to end; along the longest part. **lengthwise** *adverb & adjective*

lengthy *adjective* (**lengthier, lengthiest**) very long. **lengthily** *adverb* **lengthiness** *noun*

lenient (lee-ni-ənt) *adjective* merciful, not severe. SYNONYMS: easygoing, indulgent, gentle, mild. **leniently** *adverb* **lenience** *noun* [from a Latin word *lenis* meaning 'gentle']

lens *noun* (**lenses**) 1 a piece of glass or other transparent substance with one or both sides curved, for use in optical instruments. 2 the transparent part of the eye, behind the pupil. 3 a contact lens. 4 a combination of lenses used in a camera. [from a Latin word *lens* meaning 'lentil' (because of its shape)]

Lent *noun* the period from Ash Wednesday to Easter Saturday, of which the 40 weekdays are observed as a time of fasting and penitence. **Lenten** *adjective* [from an Old English word *lencten* meaning 'the spring']

lent past tense and past participle of **lend**.

lentil *noun* 1 a kind of bean plant. 2 the edible seed of this plant ♦ *lentil soup*. [from an Old French word *lentille*; related to *lens*]

lento *adverb* (*Music*) slowly. [from an Italian word]

Leo (lee-oh) *noun* 1 a group of stars (the Lion), seen as representing a figure of a lion. 2 a sign of the zodiac which the sun enters about 21 July. [from a Latin word *leo* meaning 'lion']

leonine (lee-ə-niyn) *adjective* to do with or like a lion. [from a Latin word *leo* meaning 'lion']

leopard (lep-erd) *noun* a large mammal of the cat family (also called a **panther**), having a yellowish coat with dark spots, found in Africa and southern Asia. **leopardess** *noun* [from a Greek word *leopardos*]

leotard (lee-ə-tard) *noun* a close-fitting piece of clothing covering the body to the top of the thighs, worn for dance, exercise, and gymnastics. [named after the French trapeze artist, J. Léotard (1842–70), who designed it]

leper *noun* 1 a person with leprosy. 2 a person shunned by others ♦ *a social leper*. [same origin as for *leprosy*]

lepidopterous (lep-i-dop-ter-əs) *adjective* to do with the group of insects that includes moths and butterflies. [from Greek words *lepidos* meaning 'of a scale' and *pteron* meaning 'wing']

leprechaun (lep-rə-kawn) *noun* (in Irish folklore) an elf who looks like a little old man. [from an Irish word meaning 'a small body']

leprosy *noun* an infectious disease affecting the skin and nerves, resulting in mutilations and deformities. **leprous** *adjective* [from a Greek word *lepros* meaning 'scaly' (because white scales form on the skin)]

lepton *noun* (*Physics*) a type of subatomic particle, such as an electron or neutrino, that does not take part in the strong interaction. [from a Greek word *lepton* meaning 'small']

lesbian *noun* a homosexual woman. **lesbian** *adjective* to do with lesbians. **lesbianism** *noun* [named after the Greek island of Lesbos (because the ancient Greek poet Sappho, who wrote love poems to women, lived there)]

lesion (lee-zhən) *noun* a harmful change in the tissue of an organ of the body, caused by injury or disease. [from a Latin word *laesio* meaning 'injury']

less *adjective* 1 not as much, a smaller quantity of ♦ *Make less noise.* 2 smaller in amount or degree ♦ *It is less important.* **less** *adverb* to a smaller extent. **less** *noun* a smaller amount or quantity ♦ *He is paid less than he deserves.* **less** *preposition* minus, deducting ♦ *She earned £2000, less tax.* [from an Old English word]
◊ It is better not to use *less* when you are referring to a number of individual things, in which case use *fewer*: ♦ *If we use less batter we will make fewer pancakes.*

-less *suffix* forming adjectives meaning 'without' (as in *colourless*) or 'unable to be' (as in *countless*). [from an Old English word]

lessee (less-ee) *noun* a person who holds the lease of a property. [from an Old French word *lesse*]

lessen *verb* 1 to make something less. SYNONYMS: cut, reduce, decrease, ease, minimize, mitigate, assuage. 2 to become less. SYNONYMS: decrease, decline, diminish, dwindle, subside, abate, tail off.

lesser *adjective* not so great or important as the other ♦ *the lesser evil.*

lesson *noun* 1 an amount of teaching given at one time. 2 something to be learnt by a pupil or student. 3 an example or experience from which you should learn ♦ *Let this be a lesson to you!* 4 a passage from the Bible read aloud during a church service. [from an Old French word *leçon*; related to *lecture*]

lessor (less-or) *noun* a person who leases or lets a property to someone else.

lest *conjunction* (*formal*) **1** in order to prevent, to avoid the risk that ♦ *Lest we forget, let me remind you of her achievements.* **2** because of the possibility that ♦ *We were afraid lest we should be late.* [from an Old English word]

let[1] *verb* (past tense and past participle **let**; **letting**) **1** to allow someone or something to do something, to not prevent or forbid someone from doing something ♦ *Let me see* ♦ *You shouldn't let him speak to you like that.* **2** to cause something to happen ♦ *I'll let you know what happens.* **3** to allow or cause someone or something to come, go, or pass ♦ *Can you let the dog in?* ♦ *You need to let some of the air out of the tyre.* **4** used to express an intention, proposal, or instruction ♦ *Let's have a drink.* **5** used to express an assumption ♦ *Let AB equal CD.* **6** to allow someone to use a room or property in return for payment.
let *noun* the letting of a room or property ♦ *a long let.* **let alone** not to mention ♦ *We can't afford one, let alone three.* **to let** available for rent ♦ *Room to let.* **to let something alone** to refrain from interfering with or doing something. **to let someone** or **something be** to stop interfering with someone or something. **to let someone down 1** to fail to support or help someone. **2** to disappoint someone. **to let something down 1** to deflate a balloon or tyre. **2** to lengthen a piece of clothing by adjusting the hem. **to let fly** to attack someone, especially with words. **to let go** to loosen your hold of something. **to let someone go 1** to allow someone to go free. **2** to dismiss an employee. **to let yourself go 1** to behave in an uninhibited way. **2** to stop taking trouble about your appearance. **to let your hair down** to abandon usual restraint in your behaviour. **to let yourself in for** (*informal*) to involve yourself in something difficult or unpleasant. **to let something loose** to release something. **to let someone off 1** to give little or no punishment to someone. **2** to excuse someone from a task or duty. **to let something off** to fire a gun, make a bomb explode, or ignite a firework. **to let off steam** to do something that relieves your pent-up energy or feelings. **to let on** (*informal*) to reveal a secret. **to let something out 1** to make a sound or cry. **2** to make a piece of clothing looser by adjusting the seams. **3** to let rooms or

property to tenants. **to let up** (*informal*) **1** to become less intense. **2** to relax your efforts. [from an Old English word]

let[2] *noun* (in tennis etc.) an obstruction of the ball in certain ways, requiring the ball to be served again. **without let or hindrance** (*formal*) without any obstruction or stoppage. [from an Old English word *lettan* meaning 'to hinder']

let-down *noun* a disappointment.

lethal (lee-thəl) *adjective* deadly, causing or able to cause death. **lethally** *adverb* [from a Latin word *letum* meaning 'death']

lethargy (leth-er-ji) *noun* extreme lack of energy or vitality. **lethargic** (lith-ar-jik) *adjective* **lethargically** *adverb* [from a Greek word *lēthargos* meaning 'forgetful']

let-off *noun* (*informal*) a situation in which someone unexpectedly escapes or avoids something.

let-out *noun* (*informal*) a way of escaping an obligation.

let's *verb* (*informal*) let us.

letter *noun* **1** a symbol representing a sound used in speech. **2** a written message, usually sent by post.
letters *noun* literature ♦ *the world of letters.*
letter *verb* to inscribe or provide something with letters. **to the letter** paying strict attention to every detail. [from a Latin word *littera* meaning 'letter of the alphabet']

letter bomb *noun* an explosive device hidden in a package sent by post.

letter box *noun* **1** a slit in a door, with a movable flap, through which letters are delivered. **2** a postbox.

letterhead *noun* a printed heading on stationery, showing the sender's name and address.

lettering *noun* letters drawn or painted.

lettuce *noun* a garden plant with broad crisp leaves used in salads. [from a Latin word *lactuca*]

let-up *noun* (*informal*) a pause or reduction in the intensity of something.

leucocyte (lew-kə-siyt) *noun* a white cell which circulates in the blood and helps to counteract foreign substances and disease. [from Greek words *leukos* meaning 'white' and *kutos* meaning 'vessel']

leukaemia (lew-kee-miə) *noun* a disease in which the white corpuscles multiply uncontrollably in the body tissues and usually in the blood. [from Greek words *leukos* meaning 'white' and *haima* meaning 'blood']

Levant (li-vant) *noun* (*old use*) the countries and islands in the eastern part of the Mediterranean Sea. **Levantine** (lev-ən-tiyn) *adjective & noun* [from a French word meaning 'rising' (because the sun rises in the east)]

levee ² (lev-i) *noun* an embankment built up naturally along a river, or made artificially as a protection against floods. [from a French word]

level *noun* 1 an imaginary line or plane joining points of equal height. 2 a measured height or value etc., a position or stage on a scale ♦ *the level of alcohol in the blood.* 3 relative position in rank, class, or status ♦ *decisions at Cabinet level.* SYNONYMS: grade, rank, stage, status. 4 a more or less flat surface or area. 5 an instrument for testing a horizontal line. **level** *adjective* 1 having a flat horizontal surface. 2 (said about ground) flat, without hills or hollows. 3 at the same height as something else. 4 having the same relative position; not in front or behind. 5 calm and steady ♦ *a level voice.* **level** *verb* (**levelled, levelling**) 1 to make something level, or to become level. 2 to knock down buildings to the ground. 3 to aim a gun or missile. 4 to direct an accusation or criticism at a person. **to do your level best** to make all possible efforts. **on the level** (*informal*) honest or truthful. **leveller** *noun* **levelly** *adverb* [from a Latin word *libella* meaning 'a small balance']

level crossing *noun* a place where a railway and a road cross each other at the same level.

level-headed *adjective* (said about a person) sensible.

leveller *noun* 1 a person or thing that levels something. 2 a member of a group of radicals in the English civil War.

lever (lee-ver) *noun* 1 a bar or other device pivoted on a fixed point (called the *fulcrum*) in order to lift something or force something open. 2 a projecting handle used to operate or control a piece of machinery ♦ *a gear lever.* **lever** *verb* 1 to lift or move something by means of a lever. 2 to move yourself with an effort ♦ *She levered herself up onto the wall.* [from a Latin word *levare* meaning 'to raise']

leverage *noun* 1 the force you need when you use a lever. 2 the power to influence someone.

leveret (lev-er-it) *noun* a young hare. [from a French word *lièvre* meaning 'hare']

leviathan (li-viy-əth-ən) *noun* something of enormous size and power. [named after a sea monster in the Bible]

levitate *verb* to rise or cause something to rise and float in the air in defiance of gravity. **levitation** *noun* [same origin as for *levity*]

levity (lev-iti) *noun* a humorous attitude towards serious matters that should be treated with respect. [from a Latin word *levis* meaning 'lightweight']

levy *verb* (**levies, levied, levying**) to impose or collect a tax, fine, or other payment. **levy** *noun* (**levies**) 1 levying a tax, fine, etc. 2 an amount of money paid in tax. [same origin as for *lever*]

lewd *adjective* indecent or crude, treating sexual matters in a vulgar way. **lewdly** *adverb* **lewdness** *noun* [origin unknown]

lexical *adjective* 1 to do with the words of a language. 2 to do with a lexicon or dictionary. [from a Greek word *lexikos* meaning 'of words']

lexicography (leksi-kog-rəfi) *noun* the writing of dictionaries. **lexicographer** *noun* **lexicographical** *adjective* [from a Greek word *lexis* meaning 'word' and *-graphy*]

lexicon *noun* 1 the vocabulary of a person, field, etc. 2 a dictionary. [from a Greek word meaning 'book of words']

ley (lay) *noun* (**leys**) land that is temporarily sown with grass. [from an Old English word]

Leyden jar (lay-dən) *noun* a kind of electrical condenser consisting of a glass jar with layers of tin foil on the outside and inside. [named after Leyden (or Leiden), the city in the Netherlands where it was invented in 1745]

Li *abbreviation* (*Chemistry*) the symbol for lithium.

liability *noun* (**liabilities**) 1 being liable. 2 a debt or obligation. 3 a handicap or disadvantage ♦ *Our goalkeeper is proving a liability.*

liable (liy-əbəl) *adjective* **1** able or likely to do or suffer something ♦ *The cliff is liable to crumble* ♦ *She is liable to colds.* **2** held responsible by law; legally obliged to pay a tax or penalty etc. [probably from an Old French word *lier* meaning 'to bind']

liaise (lee-ayz) *verb* to act as a liaison or go-between. [from *liaison*]

liaison (lee-ay-zən) *noun* **1** communication and cooperation between people or groups. **2** a person who acts as a link or go-between. **3** a sexual relationship, especially a secretive one. [from a French word *lier* meaning 'to bind']

liar *noun* a person who tells lies. [from an Old English word]

lib *noun* (*informal*) liberation ♦ *women's lib.*

Lib Dem *noun* (*informal*) Liberal Democrat.

libel (liy-bəl) *noun* **1** an untrue written, printed, or broadcast statement that damages a person's reputation. **2** the act of publishing or broadcasting a libel ♦ *The newspaper was charged with libel.*
libel *verb* (**libelled**, **libelling**) to publish or broadcast a libel against someone. **libellous** *adjective* [from a Latin word *libellus* meaning 'little book']

liberal *adjective* **1** tolerant or open-minded. **2** (in politics) in favour of individual freedom and moderate political and social reform. **3** giving generously. **4** ample, given in large amounts. SYNONYMS: generous, abundant, copious, plentiful, lavish, unstinting. **5** not strict or literal ♦ *a liberal interpretation of the rules.* **6** (said about education) broadening the mind in a general way, not only training it in technical subjects.
Liberal *adjective* to do with the Liberal Democratic party.
liberal *noun* a person of liberal views.
Liberal *noun* a Liberal Democrat.
liberalism *noun* **liberality** (lib-er-al-iti) *noun*
liberally *adverb* [from a Latin word *liber* meaning 'free']

Liberal Democrat *noun* a member of the Liberal Democratic political party.

liberalize *verb* to make something less strict. **liberalization** *noun*

liberate *verb* to set someone free, especially from control by an authority that is considered to be oppressive.
liberation *noun* **liberator** *noun* [same origin as for *liberty*]

liberated *adjective* free from social conventions.

libertarian (lib-er-tair-iən) *noun* a person who believes in freedom of thought and action. [from *liberty*]

libertine (lib-er-teen) *noun* a person who lives an irresponsible and immoral life. [from a Latin word *libertinus* meaning 'freed man']

liberty *noun* (**liberties**) **1** freedom from imprisonment or oppression. **2** the right or power to do as you choose. **3** a right or privilege granted by authority. **4** (*informal*) a presumptuous remark or action. **at liberty 1** (said about a person) not imprisoned, free. **2** allowed or entitled to do something ♦ *You are at liberty to leave.* **to take liberties 1** to behave too familiarly towards a person. **2** to treat or interpret facts etc. too freely. **to take the liberty** to venture to do something without first asking permission. [from a Latin word *liber* meaning 'free']

libidinous (li-bid-in-əs) *adjective* having or showing excessive sexual desire, lustful.

libido (lib-ee-doh) *noun* (**libidos**) sexual desire. **libidinal** [a Latin word meaning 'lust']

Libra (leeb-rə) *noun* **1** a group of stars (the Scales or Balance), seen as representing a pair of scales. **2** a sign of the zodiac which the sun enters about 22 September. **Libran** *adjective* & *noun* [a Latin word]

librarian *noun* a person in charge of or assisting in a library. **librarianship** *noun* [from a Latin word *librarius* meaning 'relating to books']

library (liy-brə-ri) *noun* (**libraries**) **1** a building or room where books are kept for people to use or borrow. **2** a private collection of books. **3** a collection of videos, CDs, etc. for people to borrow or refer to. **4** a series of books issued in similar bindings as a set. [from a Latin word *libri* meaning 'books']

libretto (lib-ret-oh) *noun* (**librettos** or **libretti**) the words of an opera or other long musical work. **librettist** *noun* [an Italian word meaning 'little book']

lice plural of **louse**.

licence *noun* **1** an official permit to own or do something or to carry on a certain trade ♦ *a driving licence.* **2** permission. **3** freedom to disregard the usual rules or customs etc., or to behave without restraint. **4** a writer's or artist's exaggeration, or deliberate disregard of rules etc., to achieve a certain effect ♦ *poetic licence.* [from a Latin word *licere* meaning 'to be allowed']

license *verb* **1** to grant a licence to someone ♦ *We are licensed to sell alcohol.* **2** to authorize someone to do something. [from *licence*]

licensee *noun* a person who holds a licence, especially to sell alcoholic drinks.

licentiate (liy-**sen**-shi-ət) *noun* someone who holds a certificate showing that they are competent to practise a certain profession. [from a Latin word *licentia* meaning 'freedom']

licentious (liy-**sen**-shəs) *adjective* promiscuous and lacking principles in sexual matters. **licentiousness** *noun* [from a Latin word *licentiosus* meaning 'not restrained']

lichen (**liy**-kən or **lich**-ən) *noun* a dry-looking plant that grows on rocks, walls, and tree trunks, usually green or yellow or grey. [from a Greek word]

lick *verb* **1** to move the tongue over something in order to eat or clean it or make it wet. **2** (*said about waves or flames*) to move over something lightly and quickly like a tongue. **3** (*informal*) to defeat someone.
lick *noun* **1** an act of licking with the tongue. **2** (*informal*) a small amount or quick application of something ♦ *The walls could do with a lick of paint.* **3** (*informal*) a short phrase or solo in jazz or rock music. **at a lick** (*informal*) at a fast pace. **to lick something into shape** to make something presentable or efficient. **to lick your wounds** to spend some time trying to recover after a defeat. [from an Old English word *liccian*]

licking *noun* (*informal*) a defeat.

lid *noun* **1** a hinged or removable cover for the top of a container. **2** an eyelid. **lidded** *adjective* [from an Old English word *hlid*]

lido (**lee**-doh) *noun* (**lidos**) a public open-air swimming pool or bathing beach. [from the name of Lido, a bathing beach near Venice]

lie [1] *noun* **1** a statement that the person making it knows is untrue. SYNONYMS: falsehood, untruth; (*informal*) fib, whopper. **2** something that deceives ♦ *She has been living a lie.*

lie *verb* (**lies, lied, lying**) **1** to tell a lie or lies. **2** to give a false impression ♦ *The camera does not lie.* **to give the lie to** to show that something is untrue. [from an Old English word *leogan*]

lie [2] *verb* (**lay, lain, lying**) **1** to have or put your body in a flat or resting position horizontal to the ground ♦ *He lay on the grass* ♦ *The cat has lain here all night.* **2** (*said about a thing*) to rest on a surface ♦ *A book lay open on the table.* **3** to be buried somewhere ♦ *Here lies Anne Spencer.* **4** to be or remain in a particular state ♦ *These machines have lain idle for months* ♦ *Armed robbers had been lying in ambush.* **5** to be situated ♦ *The island lies to the north of here.* **6** to extend in front of you or behind you ♦ *A green valley lay before us* ♦ *Her whole life lies ahead of her.* **7** to exist or be found ♦ *The remedy lies in education and training.* **8** (*Law*) to be admissible or able to be upheld ♦ *Their appeal will not lie.*
lie *noun* the way or position in which something lies. **to let something lie** to take no action regarding something. **to lie behind** to be the real reason for something ♦ *What lies behind this announcement?* **to lie down** to have a brief rest on a bed or sofa. **to lie in** to stay in bed late in the morning. **to lie in state** (*said about a dead eminent person*) to be laid in a public place of honour before burial or cremation. **to lie low** to keep out of sight. **the lie of the land 1** the features of an area. **2** the way a situation is developing. **to take something lying down** to accept an insult etc. without protest. [from an Old English word *licgan*] ◊ See the note at **lay** [1].

lie detector *noun* an instrument that is designed to detect changes in a person's pulse rate, respiration, etc. brought on by the tension caused by telling lies.

lie-down *noun* a brief rest on a bed or sofa.

lief (leef) *adverb* **as lief** (*old use*) as gladly, as willingly ♦ *I would as lief stay as go.* [from an Old English word]

liege (leej) *noun* (*historical*) **1** (also **liege lord**) a person entitled to receive feudal service or allegiance. **2** a liegeman. [from an Old French word]

liegeman *noun* (**liegemen**) (*historical*) a person who was bound to give feudal service or allegiance to a nobleman.

lie-in *noun* staying in bed late in the morning.

lieu (lew) *noun* **in lieu** instead, in place ◆ *He accepted a cheque in lieu of cash.* [a French word meaning 'place']

lieutenant (lef-ten-ǝnt) *noun* **1** an army officer next below a captain. **2** a navy officer next below a lieutenant commander. **3** (used in the names of ranks) an officer ranking just below one specified ◆ *lieutenant colonel* ◆ *lieutenant commander.* **4** a deputy or chief assistant. [from French words *lieu* meaning 'place' and *tenant* meaning 'holding']

life *noun* (**lives**) **1** being alive, the ability to function and grow that distinguishes animals and plants from rocks and synthetic substances. **2** living things in general ◆ *plant life* ◆ *Is there life on Mars?* **3** the period between birth and death or between birth and the present time. **4** a living person ◆ *Many lives were lost in the earthquake.* **5** an aspect of someone's life or a type or manner of existence ◆ *in private life* ◆ *village life.* **6** a biography. **7** the length of time that something exists or continues to function ◆ *The battery has a life of two years.* **8** liveliness or energy ◆ *His music is full of life.* SYNONYMS: vitality, vivacity, zest, exuberance, verve, vigour. **9** human activities in general, especially the exciting or enjoyable aspects of human existence. **10** (*informal*) a life sentence. **11** (in certain games) each of a number of chances a player has before they are eliminated from the game. **12** a living form or model ◆ *The portrait is drawn from life.* **to come** or **bring something to life** to become or make something active, lively, or interesting. **for dear life** or **for your life** in order to escape death or as if to do this. **for the life of me** (*informal*) however hard I try ◆ *I can't for the life of me understand why he did it.* **not on your life** certainly not. **to see life** to gain a wide experience of the world. [from an Old English word]

life assurance *noun* another term for **life insurance.**

lifebelt *noun* a ring of buoyant or inflatable material used to support the body of a person who has fallen into the water.

lifeblood *noun* **1** (*poetic*) a person's or animal's blood, necessary to life. **2** an influence or force that gives strength and vitality to something.

lifeboat *noun* **1** a boat specially constructed for going to the help of people in danger at sea along a coast. **2** a small boat carried on a ship for use if the ship has to be abandoned at sea.

lifebuoy *noun* a device to keep a person afloat in the water.

life cycle *noun* the series of changes in the life of a living thing.

life expectancy *noun* the average length of time that a person of a specified age may be expected to live.

life form *noun* any living thing.

lifeguard *noun* a person whose job is to rescue swimmers who are in difficulty at a beach or swimming pool.

life imprisonment *noun* a long term of imprisonment, in theory (though rarely in practice) for the rest of the offender's life.

life insurance *noun* insurance that pays out a sum of money either on the death of the insured person or after a set period.

life jacket *noun* a sleeveless jacket of buoyant or inflatable material used to support a person's body in the water.

lifeless *adjective* **1** without life. **2** unconscious. **3** lacking vitality or excitement. **lifelessly** *adverb* **lifelessness** *noun*

lifelike *adjective* looking exactly like a real person or thing.

lifeline *noun* **1** a rope or line used in rescuing people, e.g. one attached to a lifebelt. **2** a diver's signalling line. **3** a vital means of communication or support on which someone relies.

lifelong *adjective* continuing for the whole of someone's life.

life peer or **life peeress** *noun* a peer or peeress whose title cannot be inherited. **life peerage** *noun*

life preserver *noun* a life jacket or lifebelt.

life raft *noun* an inflatable raft used in an emergency at sea.

lifesaver *noun* (*informal*) something that saves you from serious difficulty.

life sciences *plural noun* the sciences that deal with the study of living things, including biology, botany, zoology, and related subjects.

life sentence *noun* a punishment of life imprisonment.

life-size or **life-sized** *adjective* of the same size as the person or thing represented.

lifespan *noun* the length of a person's or animal's life.

lifestyle noun a person's way of life.

life support noun equipment and procedures that allow the body to continue functioning, e.g. when vital natural functions have failed or in an adverse environment such as space.

life-threatening adjective potentially fatal ♦ a life-threatening disease.

lifetime noun 1 the duration of a person's life or of a thing's existence. 2 (informal) a very long time.

lift verb 1 to raise something to a higher level or position. SYNONYMS: raise, elevate, hoist, jack up. 2 to pick something up and move it to a different position. 3 to dig something up. 4 to rise or go upwards. 5 (said about fog etc.) to disperse. 6 to remove or end something ♦ The ban has been lifted. 7 (informal) to steal or copy something.
lift noun 1 an apparatus for taking people or goods from one floor of a building to another. 2 a device for carrying people up or down a mountain ♦ a ski lift. 3 a free ride in someone else's car ♦ Can you give me a lift to the station? 4 lifting, or being lifted. 5 the upward pressure that air exerts on an aircraft in flight. 6 a feeling of increased confidence or cheerfulness ♦ Her words of encouragement gave me a real lift. **to lift a finger** to make the slightest effort to do something. **to lift off** (said about a rocket or spacecraft) to take off vertically. **to lift your eyes** to look up. [from an Old Norse word lypta]

lift-off noun the vertical take-off of a rocket or spacecraft.

ligament noun a short band of tough flexible tissue that holds bones together or keeps organs in place in the body. [from a Latin word ligare meaning 'to bind']

ligature (lig-ə-cher) noun 1 a thing used in tying something tightly, especially in surgical operations. 2 a tie in music. 3 joined printed letters such as œ.
ligature verb to tie something with a ligature. [from a Latin word ligare meaning 'to bind']

light [1] noun 1 the radiation that stimulates the sense of sight and makes things visible. 2 the presence, amount, or effect of this ♦ Have you got enough light to read in? ♦ The light is beautiful at this time of day. 3 something that provides light, especially an electric lamp ♦ Please leave the light on. 4 a flame or spark; something

used to produce this ♦ Do you have a light? 5 brightness; the bright parts of a picture etc. 6 enlightenment ♦ Light dawned in her eyes. 7 the way something appears to your mind ♦ I see the matter in a completely different light now. 8 a window or opening to let light in.
lights plural noun 1 traffic lights. 2 a person's mental ability, attitudes, or knowledge ♦ He did his best according to his lights.
light adjective 1 full of light, not in darkness. 2 pale ♦ light blue.
light verb (past tense, **lit**; past participle, **lit** or **lighted**) 1 to start something burning; to begin to burn. SYNONYMS: ignite, kindle. 2 to provide light for something ♦ A single spotlight lit the stage. 3 to guide someone with a light. 4 to brighten something. **to come to light** to become widely known or noticeable. **in the light of** taking something into consideration. **to light up** 1 to put lights on at dusk. 2 to become brightly lit. 3 to suddenly become animated with liveliness or happiness ♦ When she opened the box her whole face lit up. 4 to begin to smoke a pipe or cigarette. **to see the light** to realize or understand something. **to throw** or **shed** or **cast light on** to help to explain something. [from an Old English word leoht]
◊ The usual form for the past tense and past participle is lit: ♦ She lit a candle ♦ She had lit a candle. When the past participle is used as an adjective before a noun or pronoun, lighted is more usual: ♦ She came in with a lighted candle.

light [2] adjective 1 having little weight, easy to lift or carry. 2 of less than average weight, amount, or force ♦ light rain ♦ a light punishment. 3 (said about work) needing little physical effort. 4 not intense ♦ a light sleeper. 5 not dense ♦ light mist. 6 (said about food) small in quantity and easy to digest ♦ a light snack. 7 moving easily and quickly. 8 not serious or profound, intended as entertainment ♦ light music. 9 cheerful, free from worry ♦ I left with a light heart. **to make light of** to treat something as unimportant ♦ He made light of his injuries. **to travel light** to travel with very little luggage. **lightly** adverb **lightness** noun [from an Old English word liht]

light [3] verb (past tense and past participle **lit** or **lighted**) **to light on** or **upon** to come upon something by chance. [from an Old English word lihtan]

light bulb *noun* a glass bulb which provides light when an electric current is passed through it.

lighten[1] *verb* 1 to make something lighter, or to become lighter in weight. 2 to become or make something less serious or more cheerful. 3 to relieve someone or be relieved of care or worry.

lighten[2] *verb* to make something lighter, or to become lighter or brighter.

lighter[1] *noun* a device for lighting cigarettes.

lighter[2] *noun* a flat-bottomed boat used for transferring goods to and from ships in harbour. **lighterman** *noun* (**lightermen**)

light-fingered *adjective* apt to steal.

light-headed *adjective* dizzy and slightly faint.

light-hearted *adjective* 1 amusing and entertaining, not serious. 2 cheerful and free from worry.

lighthouse *noun* a tower or other structure containing a beacon light to warn or guide ships.

light industry *noun* an industry producing small or light articles.

lighting *noun* equipment for providing light to a room or building or street etc., or the light itself.

lighting-up time *noun* the time after which vehicles on a road must have their headlights on.

light meter *noun* an instrument measuring the intensity of light, used when taking photographs.

lightning *noun* a flash of bright light produced by natural electricity during a thunderstorm.
lightning *adverb* very quick ◆ *with lightning speed*. [from **lighten**[2]]

lightning conductor *noun* a metal rod or wire fixed on a building or other high place to divert lightning into the ground.

lightning strike *noun* a strike by workers begun without warning.

light pen *noun* a pen-like photoelectric device for communicating with a computer by movement, e.g. when passed over a bar code.

lights *plural noun* the lungs of sheep, pigs, etc., used as food for animals. [from **light**[2]]

lightweight *noun* 1 a boxing weight between welterweight and featherweight. 2 (*informal*) a person of little influence.
lightweight *adjective* 1 of thin material or build. 2 having little influence.

light year *noun* a unit of distance equivalent to the distance that light travels in one year, 9.4607×10^{12} km (nearly 6 million million miles).

ligneous (**lig**-ni-əs) *adjective* made of or like wood. [from a Latin word *lignum* meaning 'wood']

lignin (**lig**-nin) *noun* the material that stiffens the cell walls of woody tissue in plants. [same origin as for **ligneous**]

lignite (**lig**-nyt) *noun* a brown coal of woody texture. [same origin as for **ligneous**]

like[1] *preposition* 1 similar to or resembling ◆ *Those curtains are just like ours*. 2 used when asking for or giving a description of someone or something ◆ *What was the film like?* 3 in the manner of, to the same degree as ◆ *He swims like a fish*. 4 in a suitable state for ◆ *It looks like rain* ◆ *I feel like a cup of tea*. 5 such as ◆ *He's good at subjects like music and art*. 6 characteristic of ◆ *It was like him to do that*.
like *conjunction* (*informal*) 1 in the same way that, to the same degree as ◆ *You don't know her like I do*. 2 as if ◆ *She doesn't act like she belongs here*.
like *adjective* similar ◆ *We have like minds*.
like *noun* a similar person or thing ◆ *We shall not see his like again*. **and the like** and similar things. (**as**) **like as not** probably. **the likes of** a person such as. [from an Old Norse word *likr*]

like[2] *verb* 1 to think a person or thing is pleasant or satisfactory. SYNONYMS: enjoy, be fond of, be keen on, be partial to. 2 to wish for something ◆ *I would like to think it over*.
likes *plural noun* the things you like or prefer. [from an Old English word]

likeable *adjective* pleasant, easy to like.

likelihood *noun* being likely, probability.

likely *adjective* (**likelier, likeliest**)
1 probable, expected to happen or be true ◆ *He is likely to be late* ◆ *Rain is likely*.
2 seeming to be suitable or expected to be successful ◆ *the likeliest place*.
likely *adverb* probably ◆ *It is quite likely to rain*. **a likely story!** used to express disbelief. **not likely!** (*informal*) certainly not. **likeliness** *noun* [from **like**[1]]

◊ The use of *likely* as an adverb without *very*, *quite*, *most*, or *more* (e.g. in *The rain will likely die out*) is common in the USA but is not used in standard English.

like-minded *adjective* having similar tastes or opinions.

liken *verb* to point out the resemblance of one thing to another ♦ *He likened the heart to a pump.*

likeness *noun* 1 a similarity in appearance, a resemblance. 2 a copy, portrait, or picture.

likewise *adverb* 1 similarly. 2 moreover, also.

liking *noun* 1 what you like, your taste ♦ *Is it to your liking?* 2 a feeling that you like something ♦ *She has a liking for Italian food.*

lilac *noun* 1 a shrub with fragrant purple or white flowers. 2 pale purple.
lilac *adjective* of lilac colour. [from a Persian word *lilak* meaning 'bluish']

Lilliputian (lili-pew-shən) *adjective* very small.
Lilliputian *noun* a very small person or thing. [named after the inhabitants of Lilliput, a country in Swift's *Gulliver's Travels*, who were only six inches tall]

lilo (liy-loh) *noun* (**lilos**) an inflatable mattress used as a bed or for floating on water. [an alteration of *lie low*]

lilt *noun* 1 a pleasant gentle accent. 2 a light pleasant rhythm in a tune. [origin unknown]

lilting *adjective* having a light pleasant rhythm or accent.

lily *noun* (**lilies**) a garden plant growing from a bulb, with large white or reddish trumpet-shaped flowers. [from a Greek word *leirion*]

lily of the valley *noun* a spring flower with small fragrant white bell-shaped flowers.

lily pad *noun* a leaf of a water lily.

lily-white *adjective* 1 pure white. 2 completely innocent or pure.

limb *noun* 1 a leg, arm, or wing. 2 a large branch of a tree. 3 an arm of a cross. **out on a limb** 1 isolated. 2 in a position not supported by anyone else. [from an Old English word *lim*]

limber *adjective* flexible or supple. **to limber up** to exercise in preparation for an athletic activity. [origin unknown]

limbo [1] *noun* **in limbo** in an uncertain situation where you are waiting for something to happen or be decided ♦ *Lack*

of money has left our plans in limbo. [the name of a place formerly believed by Christians to be the abode of souls not admitted to heaven (e.g. because they were not baptized) but not condemned to punishment]

limbo [2] *noun* (**limbos**) a West Indian dance in which the dancer bends back and passes repeatedly under a horizontal bar which is gradually lowered. [from *limber*]

lime [1] *noun* quicklime, a white substance (calcium oxide) used in making cement and mortar and as a fertilizer.
lime *verb* to treat something with lime. [from an Old English word *lim*]

lime [2] *noun* 1 a green citrus fruit like a lemon but smaller and more acid. 2 a drink made from lime juice. 3 a bright light green colour. [from an Arabic word *lima* meaning 'citrus fruit']

lime [3] *noun* a tree with smooth heart-shaped leaves and fragrant yellow flowers, a linden. [from an Old English word *lind*]

limelight *noun* great publicity and attention. [named after the brilliant light, obtained by heating lime, formerly used to illuminate the stages of theatres]

limerick *noun* a type of humorous poem with five lines. [named after Limerick, a town in Ireland]

limestone *noun* a kind of hard rock composed mainly of calcium carbonate, used as building material and in cement.

Limey *noun* (**Limeys**) (*North Amer.*) (*Austral.*) (*informal*) a British person. [from *lime juice*, which was formerly issued to British sailors as a drink to prevent scurvy]

limit *noun* 1 the point, line, or level beyond which something does not continue.
SYNONYMS: boundary, frontier, bounds, edge, extent. 2 the greatest amount allowed ♦ *the speed limit.* ♦ *an age limit.* SYNONYMS: ceiling, threshold, maximum. 3 (*Mathematics*) a quantity which a function or the sum of a series can be made to approach as closely as desired.
limit *verb* (**limited, limiting**) 1 to keep something within certain limits.
SYNONYMS: restrict, curb, confine, circumscribe, ration, hold in check. 2 **to be a limit to something.** **to be the limit** (*informal*) to be more than you can tolerate ♦ *She really is the limit!* **off limits** out of bounds. **over the limit** (said about a driver) having more than the legally allowed level of alcohol

in the blood. **within limits** up to a point. [from a Latin word *limes* meaning 'boundary']

limitation *noun* 1 a restriction. 2 a lack of ability, a failing ♦ *He knows his limitations.*

limited *adjective* 1 kept within limits, not great ♦ *a limited choice* ♦ *limited experience.* 2 not great in ability ♦ *a limited player.*

limited company *noun* a business company whose shareholders are liable for its debts only to the extent of the amount of capital they invested.

limousine (lim-oo-zeen) *noun* a large luxurious car. [originally a hooded cape worn in Limousin, a district in France; the name was given to the cars because early ones had a canvas roof to shelter the driver]

limp[1] *verb* to walk or proceed with difficulty because of injury or damage. **limp** *noun* a limping walk. [origin unknown]

limp[2] *adjective* 1 not stiff or firm. 2 without strength or energy. **limply** *adverb* **limpness** *noun* [origin unknown]

limpet *noun* a small shellfish that attaches itself firmly to rocks. [via Old English from a Latin word *lampreda*]

limpid *adjective* (said about liquids) clear, transparent. **limpidity** *noun* [from a Latin word *limpidus*]

linchpin *noun* 1 a pin passed through the end of an axle to keep a wheel in position. 2 a person or thing that is vital to the success of an organization or plan etc. [from an Old English word *lynis* meaning 'linchpin' and *pin*]

linctus *noun* a soothing syrupy cough mixture. [from a Latin word *linctum* meaning 'licked']

linden *noun* a lime tree (see **lime**[3]). [from an Old English word *lind* meaning 'lime tree']

line[1] *noun* 1 a long narrow mark or band on a surface. 2 a wrinkle or crease in the skin. 3 (*Mathematics*) a straight or curved continuous extent of length without breadth. 4 an outline or edge of a shape. 5 a limit or boundary ♦ *the county line* ♦ *There's a thin line between genius and madness.* 6 a row or series of people or things. SYNONYMS: chain, column, file, queue. 7 a series of people coming one after the other or several generations of a family ♦ *a line of kings.* 8 each of a set of military

defences facing an enemy force. 9 a row of written or printed words. 10 the words of an actor's part ♦ *That's my favourite line in the film* ♦ *She is busy learning her lines.* 11 a brief letter ♦ *I wanted to drop you a line to say good luck.* 12 a direction, course, or track. 13 a railway track or route ♦ *the main line north.* 14 a series of ships, buses, or aircraft etc. regularly travelling between certain places, or a company running these. 15 a course or way of procedure, thought, or conduct ♦ *We've been thinking along quite different lines.* 16 a field of activity or type of business. 17 a range of goods. 18 something that a person is skilled at or interested in ♦ *Cooking is not really my line.* 19 a length of rope, string, wire, etc. used for a particular purpose ♦ *a washing line.* 20 the starting or finishing point in a race. 21 a wire or cable used to connect electricity or telephones. 22 a telephone connection.

line *verb* 1 to stand at intervals along something ♦ *Trees lined the pavement.* 2 to arrange things into a line or lines ♦ *Line them up.* 3 to mark something with lines ♦ *Use lined paper.* **to come** or **bring something into line** to conform or cause something to conform with others. **the end of the line** the point at which you can go no further. **to get a line on** (*informal*) to discover information about something. **in line** 1 forming a straight line. 2 under control. **in line for** likely to receive something ♦ *He is in line for promotion.* **in line with** in accordance with. **to line something up** to have something prepared ♦ *We have a great show lined up for you tonight.* **out of line** behaving in an unacceptable way. [from a Latin word *linea* meaning 'linen thread']

line[2] *verb* to cover the inside surface of something with a layer of different material. **to line your pockets** or **purse** to make a lot of money, especially by underhand or dishonest methods. [from *linen* (used for linings)]

lineage (lin-i-ij) *noun* ancestry, the line of descendants from an ancestor. [from an Old French word *lignage*]

lineal (lin-i-əl) *adjective* in a direct line of descent or ancestry. **lineally** *adverb* [same origin as for **line**[1]]

lineaments (lin-iə-mənts) *plural noun* (*literary*) the features of a face. [from a Latin word *lineare* meaning 'to make straight']

linear (lin-i-er) *adjective* **1** arranged in a line. **2** to do with a line or length. **3** (*Mathematics*) (said about an equation, function, etc.) in which only the first power of any variable occurs; able to be represented by a straight line on a graph. **linearity** *noun* [same origin as for *line*[1]]

line dancing *noun* a type of country and western dancing in which people dance in a line.

line drawing *noun* a drawing consisting only of lines.

linen *noun* **1** cloth made of flax. **2** sheets or clothes that were originally made of linen. [from a Latin word *linum* meaning 'flax']

linen basket *noun* a basket for clothes that need to be washed.

line of force *noun* (in a field of force) a line whose direction at any point is the direction of the magnetic field or electric field there.

line-out *noun* (in rugby) an arrangement of parallel lines of opposing forwards formed when the ball is thrown in.

liner[1] *noun* a large passenger ship. [from *line*[1]]

liner[2] *noun* a removable lining ♦ *nappy liners*.

linesman *noun* (**linesmen**) **1** an official in football or tennis etc. who decides whether or where a ball has crossed a line. **2** a person who repairs electrical or telephone wires.

line-up *noun* **1** a group of people or things assembled for a particular purpose. **2** an identity parade.

ling[1] *noun* a kind of heather. [from an Old Norse word *lyng*]

ling[2] *noun* a sea fish of northern Europe, usually eaten salted. [probably from an Old Dutch word]

-ling *suffix* forming nouns meaning 'having a certain quality' (as in *weakling*) or diminutives meaning 'little' (as in *duckling*). [from an Old English word]

linger *verb* **1** to stay for a long time, especially as if reluctant to leave. **2** to take a long time to disappear ♦ *The smell lingered in the kitchen for days* ♦ *a few lingering doubts*. **3** to spend a long time over something ♦ *We lingered over our meal.* **4** to remain alive although becoming weaker.

lingering *adjective* [from an Old English word; related to *long*[1]]

lingerie (lan-zher-ee) *noun* women's underwear and night clothes. [from a French word *linge* meaning 'linen']

lingo *noun* (**lingos** or **lingoes**) (*informal*) **1** a foreign language. **2** jargon ♦ *I don't understand all this legal lingo.* [via Portuguese from a Latin word *lingua* meaning 'tongue']

lingua franca (ling-gwə frank-ə) *noun* a language used as a common language between the people of an area where several languages are spoken. [from an Italian phrase meaning 'language of the Franks']

linguist (ling-gwist) *noun* **1** a person who knows foreign languages well. **2** a person who studies linguistics. [from a Latin word *lingua* meaning 'language']

linguistic (ling-gwist-ik) *adjective* to do with language or linguistics. **linguistics** *noun* the scientific study of language and its structure.

liniment *noun* a lotion for rubbing on parts of the body that ache; an embrocation. [from a Latin word *linire* meaning 'to smear']

lining *noun* **1** a layer of material used to cover the inside of something. **2** the tissue covering the inner surface of an organ of the body. [from *line*[2]]

link *noun* **1** one ring or loop of a chain. **2** a relationship or connection between people or things. SYNONYMS: connection, bond, association, affiliation; (*informal*) tie-up. **3** a means of communication or travel between people or places ♦ *a rail link.* **link** *verb* **1** to connect or join things together. SYNONYMS: connect, join, couple, amalgamate, associate, unite, yoke. **2** to be or become connected. [from an Old Norse word *hlekkr*]

linkage *noun* **1** linking or being linked. **2** a system of links.

linkman *noun* (**linkmen**) **1** a person who acts as a connection between others. **2** a person providing continuity in a radio or television programme.

links *noun* or *plural noun* a golf course, especially one near the sea. [from an Old English word *hlinc* meaning 'rising ground']

link-up *noun* a connection between two or more machines, systems, etc.

linnet (lin-it) *noun* a kind of finch. [from an Old French word *linette*, named because the bird feeds on linseed]

lino (liy-noh) *noun* (*informal*) linoleum.

linocut *noun* a print made from a design cut in relief on a layer of thick linoleum.

linoleum (lin-oh-liəm) *noun* a stiff shiny floor covering made by pressing a thick coating of powdered cork and linseed oil on to a canvas backing. [from Latin words *linum* meaning 'flax' and *oleum* meaning 'oil']

linseed *noun* the seeds of the flax plant. [from a Latin word *linum* meaning 'flax' and *seed*]

linseed cake *noun* linseed from which the oil has been pressed out, used as cattle food.

linseed oil *noun* oil extracted from linseed, used in paint and varnish.

lint *noun* **1** a soft material for dressing wounds, consisting of linen with one side scraped so that it is fluffy. **2** fluff. [probably from an Old French word *lin* meaning 'flax', from which lint was originally made]

lintel *noun* a horizontal piece of wood or stone etc. across the top of a door or window. [from an Old French word]

lion *noun* a large powerful flesh-eating animal of the cat family found in Africa and India. **the lion's share** the largest or best part of something that is divided. **lioness** *noun* [from a Greek word *leōn*]

lionize *verb* to treat someone as a celebrity.

lip *noun* **1** either of the two fleshy edges of the mouth opening; a similar edge. **2** the edge of a cup, crater, or other hollow container or opening. **3** a pointed part at the top of a jug etc. from which you pour things. **4** (*informal*) impudence. **to curl your lip** to sneer. **to pay lip service to** to say that you approve of something but do nothing to support it. **lipped** *adjective* [from an Old English word *lippa*]

lipase (lip-ayz) *noun* an enzyme able to break down fats. [from a Greek word *lipos* meaning 'fat']

lipid *noun* any of a group of compounds that are esters of fatty acids or fat-like substances and are found in living tissues.

liposuction *noun* a technique in cosmetic surgery for removing excess fat from under the skin by suction. [from a Greek word *lipos* meaning 'fat' and *suction*]

lip-read *verb* (past tense and past participle **lip-read** (lip-red)) to understand what a person is saying by watching the movements of their lips, not by hearing. **lip-reader** *noun*

lipsalve *noun* ointment for sore lips.

lipstick *noun* a cosmetic for colouring the lips in the form of a stick.

liquefy *verb* (**liquefies, liquefied, liquefying**) to make something liquid or become liquid. **liquefaction** *noun* [from a Latin word *liquefacere* meaning 'to make liquid']

liqueur (lik-yoor) *noun* a strong sweet alcoholic spirit with fragrant flavouring. [a French word meaning 'liquor']

liquid *noun* a substance like water or oil that flows freely but (unlike a gas) has a constant volume. **liquid** *adjective* **1** in the form of a liquid. **2** having the clearness of water. **3** (said about a sound) flowing clearly and pleasantly. **4** (said about assets) easily converted into cash. [from a Latin word *liquidus* meaning 'flowing']

liquidate *verb* **1** to close down a business and divide its assets between its creditors. **2** to convert assets into cash. **3** to pay off a debt. **4** (*informal*) to get rid of someone, especially by killing them. **liquidator** *noun* [from a Latin word *liquidare* meaning 'to make clear']

liquidation *noun* the process of liquidating a business. **to go into liquidation** (said about a business) to be closed down and its assets divided, especially in bankruptcy.

liquid crystal display *noun* a layer of liquid crystal which is made opaque when an electric current passes through, used as a visual display in electronic equipment.

liquidity (li-kwid-iti) *noun* **1** being liquid. **2** availability of liquid assets.

liquidize *verb* to make solid food into a liquid or pulp.

liquidizer *noun* a machine for liquidizing fruit and vegetables.

liquor (lik-er) *noun* **1** alcoholic drink, especially spirits. **2** liquid produced in cooking or in which food has been cooked. [from a Latin word]

liquorice (**lik**-er-iss) *noun* **1** a chewy black substance used in medicine and as a sweet. **2** the plant from whose root it is obtained. [from Greek words *glukus* meaning 'sweet' and *rhiza* meaning 'root']

lira (**leer**-ə) *noun* (**lire**) the unit of money in Italy and Turkey. [an Italian word, from a Latin word *libra* meaning 'pound']

lisle (liyl) *noun* a fine smooth cotton thread used for stockings. [from the name of Lille in France, where it was originally made]

lisp *noun* a speech defect in which *s* is pronounced like *th* in *thin* and *z* like *th* in *they*.
lisp *verb* to speak with a lisp. [from an Old English word *wlispian*]

lissom (**liss**-əm) *adjective* slim, supple, and graceful. [from *lithe*]

list[1] *noun* a number of names, items, figures, etc. written or printed one after another. SYNONYMS: inventory, catalogue, index, directory.
list *verb* **1** to make a list of people or things. SYNONYMS: itemize, enumerate, catalogue, index, record. **2** to enter a name etc. in a list. **to enter the lists** to make or accept a challenge. [from an Old English word *liste* meaning 'border']

list[2] *verb* (said about a ship) to lean over to one side.
list *noun* a listing position, a tilt. [origin unknown]

listed *adjective* (said about a building) protected from being demolished or altered because of its historical importance.

listen *verb* **1** to pay attention in order to hear something. **2** to make an effort to hear something. **3** to follow a piece of advice, suggestion, or request.
listen *noun* an act of listening ♦ *Have a listen to this.* **to listen in 1** to overhear a conversation, especially by telephone. **2** to listen to a radio broadcast. [from an Old English word *hlysnan* meaning 'to pay attention to']

listener *noun* **1** a person who listens ♦ *She is a good listener.* **2** a person listening to a radio broadcast.

listeria *noun* a bacterium active in certain foods which can cause disease in people and animals. [named after the English surgeon J. Lister (1827–1912)]

listeriosis *noun* a disease caused by infection by listeria.

listless *adjective* without energy or enthusiasm. **listlessly** *adverb* **listlessness** *noun* [from an old word *list* meaning 'desire' and *-less*]

lit past tense and past participle of **light**[1] and **light**[3].

litany *noun* (**litanies**) **1** a series of prayers and petitions to God, recited by a priest and with set responses by the congregation. **2** a long tedious list or recital ♦ *a litany of complaints.* [from a Greek word *litaneia* meaning 'prayer']

litchi *noun* (**litchis**) another spelling of **lychee**.

liter *noun* an American spelling of **litre**.

literacy (**lit**-er-əsi) *noun* the ability to read and write. [from *literate*]

literal *adjective* **1** meaning exactly what is said, not metaphorical or exaggerated. **2** keeping strictly to the words of the original ♦ *a literal translation.* SYNONYMS: word for word, verbatim, faithful. **3** (said about a person) tending to interpret things in a literal way, unimaginative. **literalness** *noun* [same origin as for *letter*]
◊ Do not confuse this word with **littoral**, which has a different meaning.

literally *adverb* really; exactly as stated ♦ *The old car was literally falling to pieces.*
◊ The word **literally** is often used to show that a familiar phrase or idiom should be understood in a real sense: ♦ *He literally jumped out of his seat.* It is also used informally in contexts where the literal meaning of what is said is absurd, and you need to be careful as this can sometimes disconcert or irritate people: ♦ *He literally jumped out of his skin.*

literary (**lit**-er-er-i) *adjective* **1** to do with literature. **2** knowing about or interested in literature. [same origin as for *letter*]

literate (**lit**-er-ət) *adjective* able to read and write.
literate *noun* a literate person. [same origin as for *letter*]

literature *noun* **1** written works such as novels, poetry, and plays, especially those considered to have been written well. **2** writings on a particular subject. **3** printed pamphlets, brochures, or leaflets etc. [same origin as for *letter*]

lithe *adjective* flexible and supple. [from an Old English word meaning 'gentle, meek']

lithium (lith-i-əm) noun a metallic element (symbol Li), with numerous commercial uses in alloys, lubricating greases, chemical reagents, etc. [from a Greek word lithos meaning 'stone']

litho (liyth-oh) noun (**lithos**) (informal) lithography, or a lithograph.

lithograph noun a print made by lithography. [from a Greek word lithos meaning 'stone' and -graph]

lithography (lith-og-rəfi) noun a process of printing from a smooth surface, e.g. a metal plate, treated so that ink will stick to the design to be printed and not to the rest of the surface. **lithographic** adjective

lithology (lith-ol-ə-ji) noun the scientific study of the nature and composition of stones and rocks. **lithological** adjective [from a Greek word lithos meaning 'stone' and -logy]

lithosphere (lith-ə-sfeer) noun (Geology) the solid crust of the earth, contrasted with the hydrosphere and the atmosphere. [from a Greek word lithos meaning 'stone' and sphere]

litigant (lit-i-gənt) noun a person who is involved in a lawsuit. [from a Latin word litigare meaning 'to start a lawsuit']

litigation (lit-i-gay-shən) noun a lawsuit; the process of going to law. [same origin as for litigant]

litigious (li-tij-əs) adjective tending to go to law to settle disputes. [same origin as for litigant]

litmus noun a blue substance that is turned red by acids and can be turned back to blue by alkalis. [from Old Norse words litr meaning 'dye' and mosi meaning 'moss' (because litmus is obtained from some kinds of moss)]

litmus paper noun paper stained with litmus, used to tell whether a solution is acid or alkaline.

litmus test noun 1 a test using litmus. 2 a conclusive test of the nature of something.

litre (lee-ter) noun a unit of capacity in the metric system (about 1¾ pints), used for measuring liquids. [a French word]

litter noun 1 rubbish or untidy things left lying about, especially in the street. 2 the young animals born to a mother at one time. 3 (also **cat litter**) absorbent material put down on a tray for a cat to urinate and defecate in indoors. 4 straw etc. put down as bedding for animals. 5 a kind of stretcher.
litter verb 1 to be scattered around a place making it untidy ♦ Paper cups and crisp packets littered the pavement. 2 to leave rubbish or objects lying around untidily ♦ Her room was littered with magazines. [from an Old French word litière meaning 'bed']

litterbug or **litter lout** noun (informal) a person who carelessly drops litter.

little adjective 1 small in size, amount, or degree. SYNONYMS: small, tiny, miniature, minute. 2 smaller than others of the same kind ♦ the little finger. 3 young or younger ♦ his little sister. 4 unimportant or trivial. SYNONYMS: inconsequential, slight, negligible, trifling.
little noun 1 only a small amount, some but not much. 2 a short time or distance.
little adverb 1 to a small extent only ♦ little-known authors. 2 not at all ♦ He little knew what really happened. **little by little** gradually. **to make little of** to dismiss something as not significant or important. **no little** considerable ♦ That was no little achievement. **not a little** very ♦ He was not a little annoyed. [from an Old English word lytel]

littoral adjective to do with or on the shore. **littoral** noun a region lying along the shore. [from a Latin word litoris meaning 'of the shore']
◊ Do not confuse this word with **literal**, which has a different meaning.

liturgy (lit-er-ji) noun (**liturgies**) a fixed form of public worship used in churches. **liturgical** (lit-ter-ji-kəl) adjective **liturgically** adverb [from a Greek word leitourgia meaning 'worship']

live¹ (liv) verb 1 to have life, to be or remain alive. 2 to have somewhere as your home ♦ She lives in Dublin. SYNONYMS: reside, dwell, abide, inhabit, occupy. 3 to pass your life in a certain way ♦ He lived as a hermit ♦ They lived a peaceful life in the country. 4 to get a livelihood from something ♦ They lived off her earnings ♦ Most people in the region live by farming. 5 to last or survive in someone's mind ♦ His name lives on. **to live something down** to succeed in making people forget a past mistake or embarrassment. **to live in** (said about an employee) to live on the premises. **to live on** 1 to use something as food ♦ They lived on fruit until they were rescued. 2 to depend on something for your living ♦ Do you have enough money to live on? **to live out** (said about an employee) to live off the premises. **to live it up** to enjoy yourself in a lively extravagant way, spending a lot of money. **to live up to** to live or behave in accordance with something ♦ *He did not live up to his principles.* **to live with** to accept or endure the effects of something. **to live with yourself** to be able to keep your self-respect ♦ *I couldn't live with myself if I let you down now.* [from an Old English word]

live [2] (liyv) *adjective* 1 alive. 2 (said about yogurt) containing living micro-organisms. 3 (said about a performance) actually taking place in front of an audience, not recorded. 4 (said about a broadcast) transmitted while it is actually happening or being performed, not recorded or edited. 5 actual or authentic ♦ *a real live princess.* 6 glowing or burning ♦ *live coals.* 7 (said about a shell or bomb) not yet exploded. 8 (said about a wire or cable) connected to a source of electric current. 9 of interest or importance at the present time ♦ *Pollution is a live issue.* SYNONYMS: topical, current, pressing, vital.
live *adverb* as or at a live performance ♦ *Have you seen them play live on stage?* [from *alive*]

liveable (liv-əbəl) *adjective* 1 worth living ♦ *She felt that life wasn't liveable.* 2 suitable for living in.

live action *noun* action in films involving real people or animals, as opposed to animation or computer-generated effects.

lived-in *adjective* 1 (said about a room or building) showing comforting signs of being used or occupied. 2 (*informal*) (said about a face) marked by life's experiences.

live-in *adjective* 1 living where you work ♦ *a live-in nanny.* 2 sharing a home ♦ *a live-in lover.*

livelihood (liyv-li-huud) *noun* a way of earning money or providing enough food to support yourself. [from Old English words *lif* meaning 'life' and *lad* meaning 'course or way']

livelong (liv-long) *adjective* (*poetic*) **the livelong day** the whole length of the day.

lively *adverb* (**livelier, liveliest**) full of life, energy, or activity. SYNONYMS: energetic, vivacious, exuberant, bubbly, frisky, spirited; (*informal*) perky. **to look lively** to move more quickly or energetically. **liveliness**

noun [from an Old English word meaning 'living']

liven *verb* to make something lively, or to become lively ♦ *I'll put some music on to liven things up* ♦ *The match livened up in the second half.*

liver *noun* 1 a large organ in the abdomen, that processes digested food, purifies the blood, and secretes bile. 2 an animal's liver, used as food. [from an Old English word *lifer*]

liveried *adjective* wearing a livery.

liverish *adjective* 1 suffering from a disorder of the liver. 2 irritable, bad-tempered.

Liverpudlian *adjective* to do with Liverpool, a city in NW England. **Liverpudlian** *noun* a native or inhabitant of Liverpool.

liverwort (liv-er-wert) *noun* any of a group of small creeping plants growing in damp places, of which some kinds have liver-shaped leaves and some resemble mosses. [from an Old English word, from *liver* and *wort*]

livery *noun* (**liveries**) 1 a distinctive uniform worn by a servant, an official, or a member of the London trade guilds (called *Livery Companies*). 2 the distinctive colour scheme used by a railway, bus company, etc. [originally meaning 'the giving of food or clothing': from a Latin word *liberare* meaning 'to set free or hand over']

livery stable *noun* a stable where horses are kept for their owner in return for a fee, or where horses may be hired.

lives plural of **life**.

livestock *noun* animals kept for use or profit, e.g. cattle, sheep, etc. on a farm.

live wire *noun* (*informal*) a forceful energetic person.

livid *adjective* 1 (*informal*) furiously angry. 2 of the colour of lead, bluish-grey ♦ *a livid bruise.* [from a Latin word *livere* meaning 'to be bluish']

living *adjective* 1 alive. 2 (said about a language) still spoken and used. 3 (said about rock) not detached from the earth. **living** *noun* 1 being alive. 2 a way of earning money or providing enough food to support yourself. 3 the way that a person lives ♦ *a good standard of living.* 4 a position held by a member of the clergy and providing them with an income or property. **the living image of** an exact copy or likeness of ♦ *She is the living image of her mother.* **within** or **in living memory** within the memory of people who are still alive.

living room *noun* a room for general use during the day.

living wage *noun* a wage on which it is possible to live.

lizard *noun* a reptile with a rough or scaly skin, four legs, and a long body and tail. [from a Latin word *lacertus*]

llama (lah-mə) *noun* a South American animal with woolly fur, related to the camel but with no hump. [via Spanish from Quechua, a South American language]

lm *abbreviation* lumen(s).

LMS *abbreviation* local management of schools.

lo *interjection* (*old use*) see. [from an Old English word]

load *noun* 1 something that is carried or transported. 2 the quantity that can be carried. 3 the weight carried by a wall or structure. 4 the amount of work to be done by a person or machine ♦ *a heavy teaching load.* 5 a burden of responsibility, worry, or grief ♦ *That's a load off my mind.* 6 (*informal*) a large amount ♦ *It's a load of nonsense.* 7 the amount of electric current supplied by a dynamo or generating station.
loads *plural noun* (*informal*) plenty ♦ *We've got loads of time.*
load *verb* 1 to put a load in or on something; to fill something with goods or cargo etc. ♦ *Help me load the dishwasher.* 2 (said about a ship or vehicle) to receive a load. 3 to make someone or something carry a lot of heavy things ♦ *A woman came out, loaded with parcels.* 4 to weight a thing with something heavy ♦ *loaded dice.* 5 to put ammunition into a gun or film into a camera ready for use. 6 to enter a program or data into a computer. **to get a load of** (*informal*) to pay attention to something. **loader** *noun* [from an Old English word]

loaded *adjective* 1 (said about a gun) containing bullets. 2 (*informal*) very rich.

loaded question *noun* a question that is worded so as to trap a person into saying something damaging.

load line *noun* another term for **Plimsoll line**.

load-shedding *noun* cutting off of supply of electric current from a power station when the demand is greater than the supply available.

loadstone *noun* another spelling of **lodestone**.

loaf¹ *noun* (**loaves**) a mass of bread shaped and baked in one piece. **to use your loaf** (*informal*) to use your common sense. [from an Old English word *hlaf*]

loaf² *verb* to spend time idly, to loiter or stand about. **loafer** *noun* [probably from a German word *Landläufer* meaning 'a tramp']

loam *noun* rich soil containing clay, sand, and decayed leaves etc. **loamy** *adjective* [from an Old English word]

loan *noun* 1 something lent, especially a sum of money. 2 lending, being lent ♦ *These books are on loan from the library.* **loan** *verb* to lend. [from an Old Norse word]
◊ Some people dislike the use of the verb except where it means to lend money, but it is now well established in standard English.

loath (lohth) *adjective* unwilling, reluctant ♦ *I was loath to go.* [from an Old English word *lath* meaning 'hostile']

loathe (loh*th*) *verb* to feel great hatred and disgust for something. [from an Old English word *lathian*; related to *loath*]

loathing *noun* a feeling of great hatred and disgust.

loathsome *adjective* making you feel great hatred and disgust, repulsive.

loaves *plural* of **loaf**¹.

lob *verb* (**lobbed, lobbing**) 1 to hit or kick a ball in a high arc in tennis, football, etc. 2 to throw something, especially in a high arc.
lob *noun* 1 a lobbed ball in tennis etc. 2 a slow underarm delivery in cricket. [probably from a Dutch word]

lobar (loh-ber) *adjective* (*Medicine*) to do with a lobe, especially of the lung ♦ *lobar pneumonia.*

lobby *noun* (**lobbies**) 1 a porch or entrance hall leading to other rooms. 2 (in the Houses of Parliament) a large hall where members of the public can meet MPs. 3 either of two corridors in the Houses of

Parliament to which MPs retire to vote
♦ *division lobby*. **4** a group of people
lobbying an MP etc. or seeking to
influence legislation ♦ *the anti-hunting
lobby*.

lobby *verb* (**lobbies, lobbied, lobbying**) to
try to persuade an MP or other person to
support your cause, by speaking to them
in person or writing letters. **lobbyist** *noun*
[same origin as for *lodge*]

lobe *noun* **1** a rounded flattish part or
projection, especially of an organ of the
body. **2** the lower soft part of the ear.
lobed *adjective* [from a Greek word *lobos*]

lobelia (lǝ-**bee**-liǝ) *noun* a low-growing
garden plant with blue, red, white, or
purple flowers, used especially for edging.
[named after the Flemish botanist M. de
Lobel (1538–1616)]

lobster *noun* **1** a large shellfish with eight
legs and two long claws that turns scarlet
after being boiled. **2** its flesh as food. [via
Old English from a Latin word *locusta*
meaning 'crustacean, locust']

lobster pot *noun* a basket for trapping
lobsters.

lobworm *noun* a large earthworm used as
fishing bait. [from an old sense of *lob*
meaning 'an object that hangs down']

local *adjective* **1** belonging to a particular
place or a small area ♦ *local politics*.
2 affecting a particular place or part, not
general ♦ *a local infection*.
local *noun* **1** someone who lives in a
particular district. **2** (*informal*) the pub
near to a person's home. **locally** *adverb*
[from a Latin word *locus* meaning 'place']

local anaesthetic *noun* an anaesthetic
affecting only the part of the body where
it is applied.

local authority *noun* the body of people
given responsibility for administration in
local government.

local colour *noun* details characteristic of
the place or time in which a story is set,
added to make it seem more real.

locale (lǝ-**kahl**) *noun* the scene or locality of
operations or events. [respelled from a
French word *local*]

local government *noun* the system of
administration of a town or county etc. by
the elected representatives of people who
live there.

locality (lǝ-**kal**-iti) *noun* (**localities**) **1** the
position or site of something. **2** a district

or neighbourhood. [same origin as for
local]

localize *verb* to restrict something to a
particular area ♦ *a localized infection*.

local time *noun* the time in a particular
place in the world, depending on which
time zone it is in.

locate *verb* to discover exactly where
something is ♦ *We need to locate the
electrical fault*. SYNONYMS: find, discover, track
down, detect, search out, unearth. **to be
located** to be situated in a particular
location ♦ *The cinema is located in the High
Street*. [from a Latin word *locare* meaning
'to place']

location *noun* **1** the place where something
is situated. SYNONYMS: whereabouts, site,
position, venue, locality, setting, spot. **2** the
actual place where a film or broadcast is
made. **3** finding a thing's location; being
found. **on location** filmed in a suitable
environment instead of in a film studio.

locative (lok-ǝ-tiv) *adjective* (*Grammar*) to do
with the grammatical case expressing
place or position.

loch (lok) *noun* (*Scottish*) **1** a lake. **2** (also **sea
loch**) an arm of the sea, especially when
narrow or partially landlocked. [from a
Scottish Gaelic word]

loci plural of **locus**.

lock[1] *noun* **1** a device for keeping a door,
lid, or container fastened, usually
needing a key to work it. **2** a section of a
canal or river where the water level
changes, fitted with gates and sluices so
that water can be let in or out to raise or
lower boats from one level to another.
3 the turning of a vehicle's front wheels
by use of the steering wheel. **4** (in
wrestling) a hold that keeps an
opponent's arm or leg from moving. **5** (in
rugby) a player in the second row of the
scrum.
lock *verb* **1** to fasten something or be able
to be fastened with a lock. **2** to shut
something into a place that is fastened by
a lock. **3** to store something away securely
or inaccessibly ♦ *His capital is locked up in
land*. **4** to make something fixed, or to
become fixed in one position ♦ *The wheels
have locked*. **5** to hold or engage someone
in something ♦ *She locked me in a warm
embrace* ♦ *Two gorillas were locked in combat*.
6 to go through a lock on a canal. **to lock
on to** to locate a target by radar etc. and
then track it. **to lock someone out** to shut
someone out by locking a door. **lock,**

stock, and barrel including everything. **to lock someone up** to put someone in prison. **lockable** *adjective* [from an Old English word *loc*]

lock² *noun* a portion of hair that hangs together.
locks *plural noun* a person's hair. [from an Old English word *locc*]

locker *noun* a small lockable cupboard or compartment, especially for an individual's use in a public place.

locket *noun* a small ornamental case holding a portrait or lock of hair etc., worn on a chain round the neck. [from an Old French word *locquet* meaning 'small latch or lock']

lockjaw *noun* a form of tetanus in which the jaws become rigidly closed.

lockout *noun* an employer's procedure of refusing to allow workers to enter their place of work until certain conditions are agreed to.

locksmith *noun* a person who makes and repairs locks.

lock-up *noun* 1 a temporary jail. 2 premises that can be locked up, especially a garage.

loco¹ *noun* (**locos**) (*informal*) a locomotive.

loco² *adjective* (*informal*) crazy. [a Spanish word meaning 'insane']

locomotion *noun* movement, the ability to move from place to place.

locomotive *noun* a railway engine used for pulling trains.
locomotive *adjective* to do with locomotion ♦ *locomotive power*. [from Latin words *locus* meaning 'place' and *motivus* meaning 'moving']

locum (*loh-kəm*) *noun* a deputy acting for a doctor or clergyman in his or her absence. [short for a Latin expression *locum tenens* meaning 'person holding the place']

locus (*loh-kəs*) *noun* (**loci** (*loh-siy* or *loh-kiy*)) 1 a technical term for the exact place of something. 2 (*Mathematics*) the line or curve etc. formed by all the points satisfying certain conditions. [a Latin word meaning 'place']

locust (*loh-kəst*) *noun* a kind of grasshopper that migrates in vast swarms and eats all the vegetation in an area. [from a Latin word *locusta* meaning 'locust, crustacean']

locution (*lə-kew-shən*) *noun* (*formal*) 1 a word, phrase, or idiom. 2 a person's style

of speech. [from a Latin word *locutum* meaning 'spoken']

lode *noun* a vein of metal ore. [from an Old English word *lad* meaning 'way']

lodestar *noun* a star used as a guide in navigation, especially the pole star. [from an old sense of *lode* meaning 'way' and *star*]

lodestone *noun* a piece of a magnetic oxide of iron, used as a magnet. [from an old sense of *lode* meaning 'way' (because it was used in compasses to guide travellers)]

lodge *noun* 1 a small house at the gates of a park or in the grounds of a large house, occupied by a gatekeeper or other employee. 2 a porter's room at the main entrance to a college or other large building. 3 a country house for use in certain seasons ♦ *a hunting lodge*. 4 a beaver's den. 5 the members or meeting place of a branch of a society such as the Freemasons.
lodge *noun* 1 to stay somewhere as a lodger. 2 to provide someone with somewhere to live temporarily. 3 to become or make something firmly fixed or embedded somewhere ♦ *The bullet lodged in his brain*. 4 to present something formally for attention ♦ *I wish to lodge a complaint*. [from an Old French word *loge* meaning 'hut'; related to *lobby*]

lodger *noun* a person who pays to live in another person's house.

lodging house *noun* a private house in which rooms can be rented.

lodgings *plural noun* a room or rooms, not in a hotel, rented for living in.

loess (*loh-iss*) *noun* a layer of fine light-coloured dust, found in large areas of Asia, Europe, and America and very fertile when irrigated, thought to have been deposited by winds during the Ice Age. [a German word]

loft *noun* 1 a space or room under the roof of a house. 2 a space under the roof of a stable or barn, used for storing hay etc. 3 a gallery or upper level in a church or hall ♦ *the organ loft*. 4 a backward slope in the face of a golf club. 5 a lofted stroke.
loft *verb* to send a ball in a high arc. [from an Old Norse word *lopt* meaning 'air, upper room']

lofty *adjective* (**loftier, loftiest**) 1 very tall, towering. 2 noble ♦ *a lofty ambition*. 3 haughty ♦ *a lofty manner*. **loftily** *adverb*

loftiness noun [from an old sense of *loft* meaning 'sky']

log [1] noun 1 a length of tree trunk that has fallen or been cut down. 2 a short piece of this, especially as firewood. 3 a detailed record of a ship's voyage or an aircraft's flight. 4 any detailed record ♦ *You need to keep a log of phone calls.* 5 a device for gauging a ship's speed.
log verb (**logged, logging**) 1 to enter facts in a logbook. 2 to achieve a certain speed, distance, or number of hours worked etc. ♦ *The pilot had logged 200 hours on jets.* 3 to cut down forest trees for timber. **to log in** or **on** to key in the necessary commands, passwords, etc. to become connected to a computer system. **to log out** or **off** to key in the necessary commands etc. to become disconnected from a computer system. **logger** noun **logging** noun [origin unknown]

log [2] noun a logarithm ♦ *log tables.*

loganberry noun (**loganberries**) a large dark-red cultivated fruit resembling a blackberry. [named after an American horticulturalist J. H. Logan (1841–1928), who first grew it]

logarithm (log-er-ith*əm*) noun a quantity representing the power to which a fixed number (called the *base*) must be raised to produce a given number. Logarithms can be used to work out problems by adding and subtracting numbers instead of multiplying and dividing. **logarithmic** adjective [from Greek words *logos* meaning 'reckoning' and *arithmos* meaning 'number']

logbook noun a book in which details of a voyage etc. or the registration details of a motor vehicle are recorded.

log cabin noun a hut built of logs.

loggerheads plural noun **at loggerheads** disagreeing or quarrelling. [from an old word *loggerhead* meaning 'a stupid person']

loggia (loj-*ə*) noun an open-sided gallery or arcade on the side of a building, especially one facing a garden. [an Italian word meaning 'lodge']

logic (loj-ik) noun 1 the science of reasoning. 2 a particular system or method of reasoning. 3 a chain of reasoning regarded as good or bad ♦ *I don't really understand your logic there.* 4 the ability to reason correctly. 5 the principles used in designing a computer

or electronic device; the circuits involved in this. **logician** noun [from a Greek word *logos* meaning 'word, reason']

logical (loj-ik*ə*l) adjective 1 to do with or according to logic, correctly reasoned. 2 in accordance with what seems reasonable or natural ♦ *That was the logical thing to do.* 3 capable of reasoning correctly. **logicality** (loj-i-kal-iti) noun **logically** adverb

-logical suffix forming adjectives from nouns ending in *-logy* (as in *biological*).

-logist suffix forming nouns meaning 'an expert in or student of something' (as in *biologist*). [same origin as for *-logy*]

logistics (l*ə*j-ist-iks) plural noun the organizing and coordinating of everything involved in a large complex operation. **logistic** adjective **logistical** adjective **logistically** adverb

logjam noun 1 a mass of logs blocking a river. 2 a deadlock. 3 a backlog.

logo (loh-goh or log-oh) noun (**logos**) a printed symbol or design used by an organization or business company as its emblem. [short for *logograph*, from a Greek word *logos* meaning 'word' and *-graph*]

-logy suffix forming nouns meaning 'a subject of study' (as in *biology*). [from a Greek word *-logia* meaning 'study']

loin noun 1 the side and back of the body between the ribs and the hip bone. 2 a joint of meat that includes the vertebrae of this part.
loins plural noun the region of the sexual organs. [from an Old French word *loigne*; related to *lumbar*]

loincloth noun a piece of cloth wrapped round the hips, worn by men in some hot countries as their only piece of clothing.

loiter verb to linger or stand around idly. **loiterer** noun [probably from an Old Dutch word]

loll verb 1 to stand, sit, or rest lazily; to lean lazily against something. 2 to hang loosely ♦ *The dog's tongue was lolling out.* [origin unknown]

lollipop noun 1 a large round usually flat boiled sweet on a small stick. 2 an ice lolly. [origin unknown]

lollipop lady or **lollipop man** noun (*informal*) an official using a circular sign on a stick to signal traffic to stop so that children can cross a road safely near a school.

lollop *verb* (**lolloped, lolloping**) (*informal*) to move about in clumsy bounds. [probably from *loll*]

lolly *noun* (**lollies**) (*informal*) 1 a lollipop. 2 (*Austral.*) a sweet. 3 (*informal*) money. [short for *lollipop*]

Londoner *noun* a native or inhabitant of London.

lone *adjective* solitary, without companions ♦ *a lone horseman*. [from *alone*]

lonely *adjective* (**lonelier, loneliest**) 1 sad because you are on your own or have no friends. 2 solitary, without companions. 3 (said about places) far from inhabited places, not often visited or used ♦ *a lonely road*. **loneliness** *noun* [from *lone*]

loner *noun* a person who prefers not to associate with others.

lonesome *adjective* lonely.

long[1] *adjective* 1 having great length, measuring a lot from one end to the other. 2 taking a lot of time ♦ *a long holiday*. SYNONYMS: lengthy, prolonged, protracted, drawn out, time-consuming, interminable. 3 having a certain length or duration ♦ *The river is twenty miles long*. 4 seeming to be longer than it really is ♦ *He was in prison ten long years*. 5 lasting, going far into the past or future ♦ *a long memory*. 6 (said about odds in betting) reflecting a low level of probability. 7 (said about vowel sounds) having a pronunciation that is considered to last longer than that of a corresponding 'short' vowel (e.g. *oo* is long in *moon* but short in *book*). **long** *adverb* 1 for a long time, by a long time ♦ *Have you been waiting long?* 2 at a distant time ♦ *They left long ago*. 3 throughout a period of time ♦ *all night long*. **as** or **so long as** provided that, on condition that. **to be long** to take a long time ♦ *Will you be long?* **to be long on** (*informal*) to have a lot of a certain quality ♦ *He's not long on tact*. **in the long run** or **term** in the end, over a long period. **the long and the short of it** all that need be said; the general effect or result. **long in the tooth** rather old. **longish** *adjective* [from an Old English word *lang*]

long[2] *verb* to feel a strong desire for something. SYNONYMS: crave, hanker after, pine, yearn, hunger, thirst, itch. [from an Old English word *langian* meaning 'to grow long']

longboat *noun* 1 the largest boat carried by a sailing ship. 2 a longship.

longbow *noun* a large bow drawn by hand and shooting a feathered arrow.

long-distance *adjective* travelling or operating between distant places.

long division *noun* the process of dividing one number by another with all the calculations written down.

longevity (lon-jev-iti) *noun* long life. [from Latin words *longus* meaning 'long' and *aevum* meaning 'age']

long face *noun* an unhappy or disappointed expression.

longhand *noun* ordinary writing, in contrast with shorthand or typing or printing.

longhorn *noun* an animal of a breed of cattle with long horns.

longing *noun* a strong desire or intense wish.

longitude (lonj-i-tewd) *noun* the distance east or west, measured in degrees, from the Greenwich meridian. [from a Latin word *longitudo* meaning 'length']

longitudinal (lonji-tew-din-ol) *adjective* 1 measured lengthways. 2 to do with longitude. **longitudinally** *adverb*

long johns *plural noun* (*informal*) underpants with legs down to the ankles.

long jump *noun* an athletic contest in which competitors jump as far as possible along the ground in one leap. **long jumper** *noun*

long-life *adjective* (said about perishable goods) remaining fresh or usable for a long time.

long-lived *adjective* having a long life.

long-playing *adjective* (said about a gramophone record) designed to rotate at $33\frac{1}{3}$ revolutions per minute, each side lasting about half an hour. **long-player** *noun*

long-range *adjective* 1 having a long range ♦ *a long-range missile*. 2 relating to a period far into the future ♦ *a long-range weather forecast*.

longship noun a long narrow warship, with oars and a sail, used by the Vikings.

longshore adjective found on or employed along the seashore. [from along shore]

longshore drift noun the movement of sand, shingle, etc., along a coast by the action of waves, tides, and currents.

longshoreman noun (**longshoremen**) (North Amer.) a docker.

long shot noun a guess or venture that is unlikely to be correct or successful.

long sight noun the ability to see clearly only what is at a distance.

long-sighted adjective having long sight.

long-standing adjective having existed for a long time ♦ a long-standing grievance.

long-suffering adjective putting up with things patiently.

long suit noun 1 (in bridge or whist) many playing cards of one suit in a hand. 2 something at which a person excels ♦ Modesty is not his long suit.

long-term adjective of or for a long period.

long ton see ton.

long wave noun a radio wave of a wavelength above one kilometre and a frequency less than 300 kilohertz.

longways or **longwise** adverb lengthways.

long-winded adjective talking or writing at tedious length.

loo noun (informal) a toilet. [origin unknown]

loofah (loo-fă) noun a rough sponge made from the dried pod of a kind of gourd. [from an Arabic word lufa]

look verb 1 to use your eyes, to turn your eyes in a particular direction. 2 to face in a certain direction. 3 to have a certain appearance, to seem to be something ♦ The fruit looks ripe ♦ These clothes make me look an idiot. 4 to try to find something ♦ I've been looking everywhere for those keys ♦ Keep looking. **look** noun 1 the act of looking, a gaze or glance. 2 an expression on someone's face. 3 a search or inspection ♦ I'll have a look for it. 4 appearance ♦ I don't like the look of this place ♦ He is blessed with good looks. **look** interjection used to call attention to what you are going to say. **to look after** 1 to protect or take care of someone. 2 to be in charge of something. **to look at** 1 to examine a matter ♦ She promised to look at my application. 2 to regard something in a certain way ♦ It all depends how you look at it. **to look down on** or **look down your nose at** to regard someone or something with contempt. **to look forward to** to be waiting, usually eagerly, for an expected thing or event. **look here!** an exclamation of protest. **to look in** to make a short visit. **to look into** to investigate something. **to look like** (informal) to be likely to be something ♦ It looks like rain. **to look on** to watch something without getting involved. **to look out** to be careful or vigilant. **to look something out** to search for something so that you can give it to someone ♦ I'll look out some books for you. **to look something over** to inspect something to see how good it is. **to look sharp** to be quick. **to look to** 1 to rely on someone to do something. 2 to hope to do something. **to look up** to improve ♦ Things are looking up. **to look something or someone up** 1 to search for a piece of information ♦ I looked up 'egregious' in the dictionary. 2 to go to visit someone ♦ Do look us up next time you're in England. **to look up to** to admire and respect someone. [from an Old English word]

lookalike noun a person or thing closely resembling another.

look-in noun (informal) a chance of participation or success.

looking glass noun a mirror.

lookout noun 1 a place from which you can keep watch. 2 a person whose job is to keep watch. 3 looking out or watching for something ♦ Be on the lookout for pickpockets. 4 (informal) a future prospect ♦ It's a poor lookout for us. 5 (informal) a person's own concern ♦ If he wastes his money, that's his lookout.

loom [1] noun an apparatus for weaving cloth. [from an Old English word geloma meaning 'tool']

loom [2] verb 1 to come into view suddenly; to appear close at hand or with threatening appearance ♦ An iceberg loomed up through the fog. 2 to seem about to happen. [probably from an Old Dutch word]

loony noun (**loonies**) (informal) a mad or silly person. **loony** adjective (**loonier, looniest**) (informal) mad or silly. [short for lunatic]

loop noun 1 the shape made by a curve that bends round and crosses itself. 2 a piece of thread, ribbon, wire, etc. in this shape, used as a fastening or handle. **3** any path or pattern roughly in this shape. **4** a series or process in which the end is connected to the beginning. **5** an endless strip of tape or film that continually repeats itself. **6** a complete circuit for an electrical current. **7** (*Computing*) a set of instructions that is carried out repeatedly until some specified condition is satisfied. **loop** *verb* **1** to form something into a loop or loops. **2** to follow a course that forms a loop or loops. **3** to fasten or join something with a loop or loops. **to loop the loop** (said about an aircraft) to fly in a vertical circle, turning upside down between climb and dive. [origin unknown]

loophole *noun* **1** a way of avoiding a law, rule, or contract, especially because of something missing, ambiguous, or not precise enough in its wording. **2** a narrow opening in the wall of a fort etc., for shooting arrows through. [from an old word *loop* meaning 'embrasure' and *hole*]

loop-the-loop *noun* a manoeuvre in which an aircraft flies in a vertical circle, turning upside down between climb and dive.

loose *adjective* **1** not firmly fixed in place ♦ *a loose tooth*. **2** not fastened or tied together; not packed in a box or packet. **3** not fitting tightly or closely ♦ *loose clothing* ♦ *a loose lid*. **4** not tied up or shut in. **5** (said about a ball in football etc.) not in any player's possession. **6** relaxed or slack, not tense or tight. **7** not strict or exact ♦ *a loose translation*. **8** careless and indiscreet ♦ *loose talk*. **9** not compact or dense, arranged at wide intervals ♦ *a loose weave*. **10** not organized strictly ♦ *a loose confederation*.
loose *adverb* loosely ♦ *loose-fitting*.
loose *verb* **1** to untie or release someone or something. **2** to loosen something. **at a loose end** with nothing to do. **to loose something off** to fire a gun or missile ♦ *He loosed off a round of ammunition.* **on the loose** escaped, free. **loosely** *adverb* **looseness** *noun* [from an Old Norse word *lauss*]

loose box *noun* a stall in which a horse can move about.

loose-leaf *adjective* with each sheet of paper separate and removable ♦ *a loose-leaf folder.*

loosen *verb* to make something looser, or to become loose or looser. SYNONYMS: relax, slacken, untie, unfasten, undo. **to loosen**

someone's tongue to make someone talk freely. **to loosen up 1** to relax. **2** to limber up.

loosestrife *noun* a kind of marsh plant. [from *loose* and *strife*]

loot *noun* **1** goods stolen by thieves or taken from an enemy in war. SYNONYMS: haul, spoils, booty, plunder; (*informal*) swag. **2** (*informal*) money.
loot *verb* **1** to steal from shops or houses left unprotected after a riot, battle, or other violent event. **2** to take something as loot. **looter** *noun* [a Hindi word]

lop *verb* (**lopped, lopping**) **1** to cut off branches or twigs. **2** to remove or cut something. [origin unknown]

lope *verb* to run with a long bounding stride.
lope *noun* a long bounding stride. [from an Old Norse word *hlaupa* meaning 'to leap']

lop-eared *adjective* having drooping ears. [from an old word *lop* meaning 'to droop']

lopsided *adjective* with one side lower or smaller than the other. [same origin as for *lop-eared*]

loquacious (lə-kway-shəs) *adjective* talkative. **loquaciously** *adverb* **loquacity** (lə-kwass-iti) *noun* [from a Latin word *loqui* meaning 'to speak']

lord *noun* **1** a master or ruler. **2** a male member of the nobility, especially one who is allowed to use the title 'Lord' in front of his name. **3** (in medieval times) a superior in a feudal system, especially the owner of a manor house.
Lord *noun* **1** the title or form of address to certain peers or high officials ♦ *the Lord Bishop of Oxford* ♦ *the Lord Chief Justice.* **2** a title for God or Christ.
the Lords *noun* the House of Lords. **to lord it over** to act in a superior or domineering way towards someone ♦ *At school Ruth always used to lord it over the rest of us.* [from an Old English word *hlaford* meaning 'a person who keeps the bread' (compare *lady*)]

Lord Chancellor *noun* the highest officer of the Crown, presiding over the House of Lords.

lordly *adjective* (**lordlier, lordliest**) **1** haughty, imperious. **2** suitable for a lord ♦ *a lordly mansion.*

Lord Mayor *noun* the title of the mayor of certain large cities.

lord of the manor *noun* (in the Middle Ages) the master from whom men held land and to whom they owed service.

lordship *noun* a title used in speaking to or about a man of the rank of 'Lord' ♦ *your lordship.*

Lord's Prayer *noun* the prayer taught by Christ to his disciples, beginning 'Our Father'.

lore *noun* a body of traditions and knowledge on a subject or possessed by a class of people ♦ *farming lore* ♦ *gypsy lore.* [from an Old English word]

lorgnette (lorn-yet) *noun* a pair of glasses held to the eyes on a long handle. [a French word, from *lorgner* meaning 'to squint']

lorry *noun* (**lorries**) a large heavy motor vehicle for carrying goods or troops. [origin unknown]

lose *verb* (past tense and past participle **lost**) 1 to become unable to find something ♦ *I've lost my keys.* 2 to be deprived of something ♦ *He lost a leg in a climbing accident.* 3 to no longer have or maintain something ♦ *She began to lose confidence* ♦ *Try not to lose your balance.* 4 to fail to keep something in sight or to follow a piece of reasoning mentally ♦ *We lost him in the crowd.* 5 to fail to obtain or catch something ♦ *They lost the contract.* 6 to get rid of something ♦ *He's trying to lose weight.* 7 to elude someone who is following you ♦ *We managed to lose our pursuers.* SYNONYMS: evade, elude, give the slip, shake off, throw off. 8 to be defeated in a contest or argument. 9 to waste time or an opportunity ♦ *You may have lost your chance.* SYNONYMS: waste, squander, fritter. 10 to earn less than you spend, to be worse off ♦ *We lost on the deal.* 11 (said about a clock or watch) to become slow ♦ *It loses two minutes a day.* **to lose ground** to be forced to retreat or give way. **to lose heart** to become discouraged. **to lose your heart** to fall in love. **to lose yourself in** to become deeply absorbed in something. **to lose your life** to be killed. **to lose your mind** (*informal*) to go insane. **to lose out** to be unsuccessful or suffer a disadvantage. **to lose your way** to not know where you are or which is the right path. **loser** *noun* [from an Old English word *losian* meaning 'to perish' or 'to destroy']

losing battle *noun* a struggle in which failure seems certain.

loss *noun* 1 losing something or someone. 2 a defeat in sport. 3 a disadvantage caused by losing something. 4 the suffering felt when a close relative or friend dies. 5 a person or thing lost. 6 money lost in a business transaction; the excess of spending over income. **to be at a loss** to be puzzled, to not know what to do or say. [from an Old English word *los* meaning 'destruction']

loss-leader *noun* a product sold at a loss to attract customers who will then buy other things.

lost past tense and past participle of **lose**.
lost *adjective* 1 not knowing where you are or not able to find your way ♦ *I think we're lost.* 2 missing, not able to be found ♦ *I want to report a lost wallet.* SYNONYMS: mislaid, misplaced, missing, astray. 3 strayed or separated from its owner ♦ *a lost dog.* 4 engrossed ♦ *She was lost in thought.* **to be lost on** to fail to be noticed or appreciated by someone ♦ *Our hints were lost on him.* **get lost!** (*informal*) go away!

lost cause *noun* an undertaking that can no longer be successful.

lot [1] *noun* 1 (*informal*) a large number or amount ♦ *She has a lot of friends* ♦ *There's lots of time.* SYNONYMS: plenty, abundance, profusion, wealth, plethora; (*informal*) loads, heaps, masses, stacks, tons. 2 much, a great deal ♦ *I'm feeling a lot better today.* 3 a number of people or things of the same kind ♦ *Come on, you lot!* **the lot** or **the whole lot** everything, all. [from *lot*[2]]

lot [2] *noun* 1 one of a set of objects used in choosing or deciding something by chance ♦ *We drew lots to see who would go first.* 2 this method of choosing or deciding ♦ *A leader was chosen by lot.* 3 a person's fate or condition in life. 4 an item or set of items put up for sale at an auction. 5 a piece of land, especially an area used for a particular purpose ♦ *a parking lot.* **a bad lot** a person of bad character. **to throw in your lot with** to decide to join and share the fortunes of someone. [from an Old English word *hlot* meaning 'share']

loth (lohth) another spelling of **loath**.

lotion *noun* a thick liquid for putting on the skin as a medicine or cosmetic. [from a Latin word *lotio* meaning 'washing']

lottery *noun* (**lotteries**) 1 a system of raising money by selling numbered tickets and giving prizes to the holders of numbers drawn at random. 2 something where the outcome depends on luck. [probably from a Dutch word]

lotto noun a game resembling bingo but with numbers drawn instead of called out. [an Italian word]

lotus (loh-təs) noun (**lotuses**) **1** a kind of tropical water lily. **2** (Greek Mythology) a legendary fruit represented as inducing a state of lazy and luxurious dreaminess and an unwillingness to leave. [from a Greek word lōtos]

lotus position noun a cross-legged position adopted for meditating.

louche (loosh) adjective appealingly dubious or disreputable. [a French word meaning 'squinting']

loud adjective **1** easily heard, producing much noise. SYNONYMS: noisy, deafening, ear-splitting, resounding, strident, rowdy (people). **2** strongly expressed ♦ loud protests. **3** (said about colours etc.) unpleasantly bright, gaudy.
loud adverb loudly. **out loud** aloud.
loudly adverb **loudness** noun [from an Old English word]

loudhailer noun a megaphone.

loudspeaker noun a device that converts electrical signals into audible sound, especially one used as part of a public address system.

lough (lok) noun (Irish) a lake or an arm of the sea. [from an Irish word loch]

lounge noun **1** a sitting room. **2** a public sitting room in a hotel or theatre. **3** a waiting room at an airport etc., with seats for waiting passengers ♦ the departure lounge.
lounge verb to sit or stand in a lazy and relaxed way. **lounger** noun [origin unknown]

lounge bar noun a more comfortable bar in a pub or hotel.

lounge suit noun a man's suit for ordinary day wear.

lour (low-ə) verb **1** (said about clouds or the sky) to look dark and threatening. **2** to frown or scowl. [origin unknown]

louse noun **1** (**lice**) a small insect that lives as a parasite on animals or plants. **2** (**louses**) (informal) a contemptible person. [from an Old English word]

lousy (low-zi) adjective (**lousier, lousiest**) **1** infested with lice. **2** (informal) very poor, bad, or ill.

lout noun a bad-mannered or aggressive man. **loutish** adjective [perhaps from an old word lout meaning 'to bow down']

louvre (loo-ver) noun each of a set of overlapping slats arranged to let air in but keep out light or rain. [from an Old French word lovier meaning 'skylight']

louvred (loo-verd) adjective fitted with louvres.

lovable adjective easy to love. **lovably** adverb

lovage (luv-ij) noun a herb with leaves that are used for flavouring soups and in salads. [from an Old French word]

love noun **1** an intense feeling of deep affection for a person. **2** sexual affection or passion. **3** strong liking for something ♦ a love of music. **4** affectionate greetings ♦ Send my love to your parents. **5** a person or thing that you love. **6** (informal) a friendly form of address. **7** (in tennis or squash etc.) no score, nil.
love verb **1** to feel love for someone. SYNONYMS: adore, cherish, dote on, worship. **2** to like something very much. **for love** for pleasure, not because you will be paid. **in love** feeling love for another person. **to make love** to have sexual intercourse. **not for love or money** (informal) not in any circumstances. [from an Old English word lufu]

love affair noun a romantic or sexual relationship between two people who are in love.

lovebird noun a kind of parakeet that seems to show great affection for its mate.

love child noun a child born to parents who are not married to each other.

love game noun a game in tennis or squash etc. in which the loser has not scored at all.

loveless adjective without love ♦ a loveless marriage.

love life noun the part of a person's life concerning relationships with lovers.

lovelorn adjective pining with love, especially when abandoned by a lover. [from love and an old word lorn meaning 'abandoned']

lovely adjective (**lovelier, loveliest**) **1** beautiful or attractive. **2** (informal) very pleasant or enjoyable ♦ We are having a lovely time. **loveliness** noun [from an Old English word luflic]

love match *noun* a marriage based on love.

lover *noun* 1 a person who someone is having a sexual or romantic relationship with but is not married to. 2 a person who likes or enjoys something ♦ *lovers of music* ♦ *an art lover*.

lovesick *adjective* longing for someone you love, especially someone who does not love you.

love song *noun* a song expressing love.

love story *noun* a novel or film etc. of which the main theme is romantic love.

loving *adjective* feeling or showing love or great care. **lovingly** *adverb*

low [1] *adjective* 1 not high or tall, not extending far upwards. 2 situated not far above the ground or above sea level ♦ *low clouds*. 3 ranking below others in importance or quality ♦ *Music seems to be given a low priority at the school*. SYNONYMS: inferior, minor, lowly, humble. 4 less than what is normal in amount, value, or intensity ♦ *low prices* ♦ *a low opinion*. 5 not noble, dishonest ♦ *low cunning*. 6 (said about a sound or voice) deep not shrill, having slow vibrations ♦ *low notes*. 7 not loud ♦ *She spoke in a low voice*. 8 lacking in energy, depressed.
low *noun* 1 a low point, level, or figure ♦ *Share prices reached a new low*. 2 an area of low barometric pressure.
low *adverb* 1 in, at, or to a low level or position ♦ *The plane was flying low*. 2 in or to a low degree. 3 in a low tone, at a low pitch. [from an Old Norse word]

low [2] *verb* to make the deep sound of cattle.
low *noun* a lowing sound. [from an Old English word]

lowbrow *adjective* (*informal*) not intellectual or cultured.

Low Church *noun* that section of the Church of England that gives only a low place to ritual and the authority of bishops and priests.

low-class *adjective* of low quality or social class.

Low Countries *plural noun* the Netherlands, Belgium, and Luxembourg.

low-down *noun* (*informal*) the true facts or relevant information.
low-down *adjective* (*informal*) mean and dishonourable.

lower [1] *adjective* 1 less high in place or position. 2 situated on less high land or to the south. 3 ranking below others. 4 (said

about a geological or archaeological period) earlier in its occurrence.
lower *adverb* in or to a lower position.
lower *verb* 1 to make something move downward; to let something down ♦ *The crew lowered the lifeboats*. 2 to make something lower, or to become lower ♦ *She lowered her voice*. 3 to reduce something in amount or quantity etc. SYNONYMS: cut, decrease, lessen; (*informal*) slash. **to lower your eyes** to direct your gaze downwards. **to lower yourself** to do something that is beneath your dignity.

lower [2] *verb* another spelling of **lour**.

lower animals *plural noun* invertebrate animals, regarded as having relatively primitive characteristics.

lower case *noun* small letters, not capitals.

Lower Chamber or **Lower House** *noun* the House of Commons as an assembly.

lower class *noun* the working class.

lower plants *plural noun* plants without vascular systems, regarded as having relatively primitive characteristics.

lowest common denominator *noun* 1 (*Mathematics*) the lowest common multiple of the denominators of several fractions. 2 the least desirable common feature of members of a group.

lowest common multiple *noun* (*Mathematics*) the lowest quantity that is a multiple of two or more given quantities.

low frequency *noun* (in radio) a frequency of 30 to 300 kilohertz.

low-key *adjective* restrained, not intense or emotional.

lowland *noun* (also **lowlands**) low-lying country.
Lowlands *noun* the part of Scotland lying south and east of the Highlands. **lowlander** *noun*

low-level *adjective* 1 involving people of low rank or little importance ♦ *low-level negotiations*. 2 (said about a computer language) close to machine code in form.

lowly *adjective* (**lowlier**, **lowliest**) of humble rank or condition. SYNONYMS: humble, modest, obscure. **lowliness** *noun*

low-lying *adjective* at a low height above sea level.

Low Mass *noun* (in the Catholic Church) a mass with no music and the minimum of ceremony.

low-pitched *adjective* (said about a voice or sound) low.

low-rise *adjective* (said about a building) with few storeys.

low season *noun* the least popular time of year for a holiday, when prices are lowest.

low spirits *plural noun* sadness and disappointment. **low-spirited** *adjective*

low tide *noun* the tide at its lowest level.

low water *noun* low tide.

low-water mark *noun* the level reached by the sea at low tide.

loyal *adjective* showing firm and constant support or allegiance to a person, cause, institution, etc. SYNONYMS: steadfast, faithful, true, constant, staunch, dedicated, dutiful, dependable. **loyally** *adverb* **loyalty** *noun* [from an Old French word]

loyalist *noun* a person who remains loyal, especially to the established government during a revolt.
Loyalist *noun* a person who is in favour of keeping Northern Ireland's link with Britain. **loyalism** *noun*

lozenge *noun* 1 a small flavoured tablet, especially one containing medicine, for dissolving in the mouth. 2 a diamond shape. [from an Old French word *losenge*]

LP *abbreviation* a long-playing record.

L-plate *noun* a sign bearing the letter 'L', fixed to a motor vehicle that is being driven by a learner driver.

LSD *noun* a powerful synthetic drug that produces hallucinations. [abbreviation of *lysergic acid diethylamide*]

Ltd *abbreviation* (after a company name) Limited.

lubricant (loo-brik-ənt) *noun* a substance such as oil or grease for lubricating an engine etc.

lubricate (loo-brik-ayt) *verb* to oil or grease machinery etc. so that it moves smoothly. **lubrication** *noun* **lubricator** *noun* [from a Latin word *lubricus* meaning 'slippery']

lucerne (loo-sern) *noun* another term for **alfalfa**. [from a French word]

lucid (loo-sid) *adjective* 1 clear and easy to understand. 2 showing an ability to think clearly. **lucidity** (loo-sid-iti) *noun* **lucidly** *adverb* [from a Latin word *lucidus* meaning 'bright']

luck *noun* 1 chance thought of as a force that brings either good or bad fortune ♦ *This is a game of luck rather than skill.* 2 good or bad fortune in your life ♦ *It is about time she had a change of luck.* 3 success or good fortune ♦ *This locket will bring you luck.* **in luck** having good fortune. **out of luck** not in luck. **to try your luck** to attempt something risky. [from an Old German word]

luckless *adjective* unlucky.

lucky *adjective* (**luckier, luckiest**) 1 bringing or resulting from good luck. SYNONYMS: fortunate, fortuitous, timely, opportune. 2 (said about a person) having good luck. **luckily** *adverb*

lucky dip *noun* a game in which small prizes are hidden in a container and taken out at random by people playing.

lucrative (loo-krə-tiv) *adjective* profitable, earning you a lot of money. **lucrativeness** *noun* [same origin as for *lucre*]

lucre (loo-ker) *noun* (*literary*) money or profit thought of as a motive for action. **filthy lucre** (*humorous*) money. [from a Latin word *lucrum* meaning 'profit']

Luddite (lud-diyt) *noun* 1 a member of the bands of English workers (1811–16) who destroyed newly introduced machinery which they thought would cause unemployment. 2 a person who opposes the introduction of new technology or methods. [probably named after Ned Lud, a participant in the destruction of machinery]

ludicrous (loo-dik-rəs) *adjective* ridiculous or laughable. **ludicrously** *adverb* [from a Latin word *ludere* meaning 'to play or have fun']

ludo *noun* a board game played with dice and counters. [from a Latin word meaning 'I play']

lug [1] *verb* (**lugged, lugging**) to drag or carry something heavy with great effort. [probably from a word from a Scandinavian language]

lug [2] *noun* 1 an ear-like part on an object, by which it may be carried or fixed in place. 2 (*informal*) an ear. [probably from a word from a Scandinavian language]

luge (loozh) *noun* a light toboggan ridden sitting or lying down. [a Swiss French word]

luggage *noun* suitcases and bags containing a person's belongings when travelling. [from lug[1]]

lugger *noun* a small ship with four-cornered sails. [from lugsail, from lug[2]]

lugubrious (lə-**goo**-briəs) *adjective* gloomy or mournful. **lugubriously** *adverb* [from a Latin word lugubris meaning 'mourning']

lugworm *noun* a large marine worm used as bait. [from its earlier name lug: origin unknown]

lukewarm *adjective* **1** only slightly warm. **2** not very enthusiastic ♦ *His latest book has got a lukewarm reception.* [from an old word luke meaning 'tepid' and warm]

lull *verb* **1** to soothe someone or send them to sleep. **2** to make someone feel safer or in a better position than they actually are ♦ *We were lulled into a false sense of security.* **3** to calm suspicions, fears, or doubts. **4** (said about a storm or noise) to lessen, to become quiet.
lull *noun* a temporary period of quiet or inactivity. [an imitation of the sounds you make to quieten a child]

lullaby *noun* (**lullabies**) a soothing song sung to send a young child to sleep. [from lull and bye as in bye-byes, a child's word for bed or sleep]

lumbago (lum-**bay**-goh) *noun* pain in the muscles of the lower back. [from a Latin word lumbus meaning 'loin']

lumbar *adjective* to do with the lower back area.

lumber *noun* **1** unwanted pieces of furniture stored away or taking up space. **2** (North Amer.) timber sawn into planks.
lumber *verb* **1** (informal) to leave someone with an unwanted or unpleasant task. **2** to move in a heavy clumsy way ♦ *I could hear him lumbering around upstairs.* [origin unknown]

lumberjack *noun* a person whose job is cutting down trees, cutting them into logs, or transporting them. [from lumber]

lumberjacket *noun* a thick jacket fastening up to the neck, usually with a bright check pattern.

lumber room *noun* a room for storing unwanted or bulky things.

lumen (loo-men) *noun* (*Physics*) the SI unit of flux of light. [from a Latin word meaning 'light']

luminescent (loo-min-**ess**-ənt) *adjective* giving out light without being hot. **luminescence** *noun* [from a Latin word lumen meaning 'light']

luminous (loo-min-əs) *adjective* giving out light, glowing in the dark. **luminosity** (loo-min-**oss**-iti) *noun*

lump[1] *noun* **1** a solid piece of something. SYNONYMS: chunk, hunk, block; (informal) dollop, wedge. **2** a swelling. **3** (informal) a heavy clumsy person.
lump *verb* to put or treat things together in a group because you think of them as alike in some way ♦ *For convenience I will lump these last few points together.* **a lump in the throat** a feeling of tightness in the throat caused by emotion. [origin unknown]

lump[2] *verb* **to lump it** (informal) to put up with something you dislike. [from an old word lump meaning 'to look sulky']

lumpish *adjective* heavy, clumsy, or stupid.

lump sum *noun* a single payment covering a number of items or paid all at once rather than in instalments.

lumpy *adjective* (**lumpier, lumpiest**) full of lumps or covered in lumps. **lumpiness** *noun*

lunacy *noun* (**lunacies**) **1** great foolishness. **2** insanity. [from lunatic]
◊ The meaning in sense 2 is no longer used in medical language and can be offensive.

lunar *adjective* to do with the moon. [from a Latin word luna meaning 'moon']

lunar month *noun* the interval between new moons (about $29\frac{1}{2}$ days); four weeks.

lunatic *noun* **1** someone who is extremely foolish or reckless. **2** an insane person. **lunatic** *adjective* **1** extremely foolish or reckless. **2** insane. [from a Latin word luna meaning 'moon' (because formerly people were thought to be affected by changes of the moon)]
◊ The meanings in sense 2 of the noun and adjective are no longer used in medical language and can be offensive.

lunatic asylum *noun* (*old use*) an institution for mentally ill people.

lunatic fringe *noun* a few eccentric or fanatical members of a political or other group.

lunch *noun* a meal eaten in the middle of the day.
lunch *verb* 1 to eat lunch. 2 to take someone out for lunch. [short for *luncheon*]

luncheon *noun* (*formal*) lunch. [origin unknown]

luncheon meat *noun* tinned meat loaf ready for serving, made from pork or ham.

lung *noun* either of the two breathing organs in the chest that draw in air when you breathe and bring it into contact with the blood. [from an Old English word *lungen*]

lunge *noun* 1 a sudden forward movement of the body towards something. 2 a sudden thrust with a sword. 3 a long rein on which a horse is held by its trainer while it is made to canter in a circle.
lunge *verb* (**lunged, lunging**) 1 to make a lunge. 2 to exercise a horse on a lunge. [from a French word *allonger* meaning 'to lengthen']

lupin *noun* a garden plant with tall tapering spikes of flowers, bearing seeds in pods. [from a Latin word *lupinus*]

lupine (loo-piyn) *adjective* to do with or like wolves. [from a Latin word *lupus* meaning 'wolf']

lurch[1] *noun* an unsteady swaying movement to one side.
lurch *verb* to lean suddenly to one side, to stagger. [originally a sailor's word: origin unknown]

lurch[2] *noun* **to leave someone in the lurch** to abandon someone so that they are left in an awkward situation without help. [from a French word *lourche*]

lurcher *noun* a dog that is a cross between a collie and a greyhound, originally used for hunting and by poachers. [from an old word *lurch*, another form of *lurk*]

lure *verb* to tempt someone to do something or to go somewhere.
SYNONYMS: entice, draw, seduce, inveigle, coax.
lure *noun* 1 something that tempts or entices a person or animal to do something. 2 the attractive qualities that something has ♦ *the lure of adventure.* 3 a bait or decoy for wild animals, or a device used to attract and recall a trained hawk. [from an Old French word *luere*]

lurid (lewr-id) *adjective* 1 in glaring colours. 2 sensationally and shockingly vivid ♦ *the lurid details of the murder.* **luridly** *adverb* **luridness** *noun* [from a Latin word *luridus* meaning 'pale and dismal']

lurk *verb* 1 to lie hidden while waiting to attack someone. 2 to wait where you cannot be seen. 3 to be present in a latent state ♦ *a lurking sympathy for the rebels.* [origin unknown]

luscious (lush-əs) *adjective* 1 having a delicious rich taste. 2 (said about a woman) sexually attractive. **lusciously** *adverb* **lusciousness** *noun* [perhaps from *delicious*]

lush *adjective* 1 growing thickly and strongly ♦ *lush vegetation.* 2 luxurious ♦ *lush furnishings.* 3 (said about music) beautifully rich ♦ *a lush orchestration.* **lushly** *adverb* **lushness** *noun* [origin unknown]

lust *noun* 1 strong sexual desire. 2 an intense desire for something ♦ *a lust for power.*
lust *verb* to have an intense desire for a person or thing ♦ *She lusted for adventure.* **lustful** *adjective* **lustfully** *adverb* [an Old English word meaning 'pleasure']

lustre (lus-ter) *noun* 1 the soft brightness of a smooth or shining surface. 2 glory or distinction ♦ *His presence added lustre to the assembly.* 3 a kind of metallic glaze on pottery and porcelain. **lustrous** (lus-trəs) *adjective* [from a Latin word *lustrare* meaning 'to illuminate']

lusty *adjective* (**lustier, lustiest**) strong and vigorous, full of vitality. **lustily** *adverb* **lustiness** *noun* [originally meaning 'lively and cheerful': same origin as for *lust*]

lute (loot) *noun* a stringed musical instrument with a pear-shaped body, played by plucking, popular in the 14th–17th centuries. [via French from an Arabic word]

lutenist or **lutist** *noun* a lute player.

lux noun the SI unit of illumination. [a Latin word meaning 'light']

luxuriant adjective 1 growing profusely. 2 (said about hair) thick and healthy. **luxuriance** noun [same origin as for luxury] ◊ Do not confuse this word with **luxurious**, which has a different meaning.

luxuriate verb to enjoy something as a luxury ♦ We've been luxuriating in the warm sunshine. [from a Latin word luxuriare meaning 'to grow in abundance']

luxurious adjective supplied with luxuries, very comfortable. SYNONYMS: sumptuous, opulent, lavish, grand, plush. **luxuriously** adverb **luxuriousness** noun [same origin as for luxury] ◊ Do not confuse this word with **luxuriant**, which has a different meaning.

luxury noun (**luxuries**) 1 something expensive that is enjoyable but not essential. 2 expensive and comfortable surroundings and food, dress, etc. ♦ a life of luxury. [from a Latin word luxus meaning 'plenty, excess']

-ly suffix 1 forming adjectives, as in friendly, heavenly, sickly. 2 forming adverbs from adjectives, as in boldly, sweetly, thoroughly. [from an Old English word]

lychee (liy-chi) noun 1 a small fruit with a sweet white scented pulp and a large stone in a thin brown shell. 2 the tree, originally from China, that bears this fruit. [from a Chinese word]

lychgate (lich-gayt) noun a churchyard gate with a roof over it. [from an Old English word lic meaning 'corpse' (because the coffin-bearers would shelter there until it was time to enter the church)]

Lycra noun (trademark) a kind of fabric containing elasticated threads, used especially for close-fitting sports clothing. [origin unknown]

lye noun a strongly alkaline solution for washing things. [from an Old English word]

lying present participle of lie[1] and lie[2].

lying-in-state noun the display of the corpse of an eminent person in a public place of honour before burial or cremation.

lymph (limf) noun a colourless fluid from tissues or organs of the body, containing white blood cells. **lymphatic** (lim-fat-ik) adjective [from a Latin word lympha meaning 'water']

lymphatic system noun a network of vessels through which lymph drains from the tissues into the blood.

lymph node or **lymph gland** noun a small mass of tissue in the lymphatic system where lymph is purified and lymphocytes are formed.

lymphocyte (limf-ə-siyt) noun a kind of white blood cell (called leucocyte) present in lymph nodes and in the spleen. [from lymph and a Greek word kutos meaning 'vessel']

lymphoma (lim-foh-mə) noun cancer of the lymph nodes.

lynch (linch) verb (said about a group of people) to execute someone without a proper trial, especially by hanging them. [named after an American judge, W. Lynch (1742–1820), who allowed this kind of punishment in about 1780]

lynx (links) noun a wild animal of the cat family with spotted fur, noted for its very sharp sight. [from a Greek word lunx]

lyre noun a musical instrument with strings fixed in a U-shaped frame, used especially in ancient Greece. [from a Greek word lura]

lyrebird noun an Australian bird, the male of which can spread its tail in the shape of a lyre.

lyric (li-rik) adjective to do with poetry that expresses the poet's emotions. **lyric** noun 1 (also **lyrics**) the words of a song. 2 a short poem that expresses emotions. [from lyre]

lyrical (li-ri-kəl) adjective 1 (said about writing, music, etc.) expressing the writer's emotions in an imaginative and beautiful way. 2 to do with the words of a popular song. 3 (informal) expressing yourself enthusiastically. **lyrically** adverb

lyricist (li-ri-sist) noun a writer of song lyrics.

lysin (liy-sin) noun (Biology) a substance that is able to cause disintegration of living cells or bacteria. [from a Greek word lusis meaning 'loosening']

Mm

M 1 the thirteenth letter of the English alphabet. **2** the Roman numeral for 1,000.

M *abbreviation* **1** mega-. **2** (in British road identifications) motorway ♦ *M25*.

M. *abbreviation* **1** Master. **2** Monsieur.

m *abbreviation* **1** metre(s). **2** mile(s). **3** million(s). **4** (*Physics*) the symbol for mass.

MA *abbreviation* Master of Arts.

ma *noun* (*informal*) mother.

ma'am (mam) *noun* madam (used in addressing the Queen or a royal lady).

mac *noun* (*informal*) a mackintosh.

macabre (mə-kahbr) *adjective* gruesome, strange, and horrible. [a French word, from the phrase *Dance Macabre* meaning 'dance of death']

macadam (mə-kad-əm) *noun* broken stone used in layers in road-making, each layer being rolled hard before the next is put down. **macadamed** *adjective* **macadamized** *adjective* [named after a Scottish engineer, J. McAdam (1756–1836), who first made roads of this kind]

macaroni *noun* a kind of pasta formed into narrow tubes. [from an Italian word *maccaroni*, from a Greek word *makaria* meaning 'food made from barley']

macaroon *noun* a small sweet cake or biscuit made with sugar, white of egg, and ground almonds or coconut. [from a French word *macaron*, related to *macaroni*]

macaw (mə-kaw) *noun* a brightly coloured parrot with a long tail, from Central and South America.

Maccabees (mak-ə-beez) *plural noun* **1** a family of Jewish patriots who led opposition to Syrian oppression from 168 BC. **2** four books of Jewish history, of which the first two are in the Apocrypha. **Maccabean** *adjective*

McCarthyism *noun* a policy of hunting out suspected Communists and removing them from public office, as pursued in the USA by Senator Joseph McCarthy from 1950 to 1954.

mace [1] *noun* a ceremonial staff carried or placed before an official, especially the one used in the House of Commons to symbolize the Speaker's authority. [from an Old French word]

mace [2] *noun* a spice made from the dried outer covering of nutmeg. [from a Latin word *macir*]

mach (mahk) *noun* **mach number** the ratio of the speed of a moving object to the speed of sound in the same medium. *Mach one* is the speed of sound, *mach two* is twice the speed of sound, and so on. [named after the Austrian physicist Ernst Mach (1838–1916)]

machete (mə-**chet**-i) *noun* a broad heavy knife used as a tool or weapon, originally in Central America and the West Indies. [a Spanish word, from *macho* meaning 'hammer']

Machiavellian (maki-ə-**vel**-iən) *adjective* cunning or deceitful in politics or business. [named after the Italian statesman Niccolo dei Machiavelli (1469–1527), whose work *The Prince* advised the use of unscrupulous methods in order to strengthen the State]

machinations (mash-in-**ay**-shənz) *plural noun* clever scheming or plotting. [from a Latin word *machinare* meaning 'to devise or plot', related to *machine*]

machine *noun* **1** an apparatus having several parts, each with a definite function, to perform a particular task. SYNONYMS: device, apparatus, appliance, contraption. **2** something operated by such apparatus, such as a bicycle or aircraft. **3** a complex or well-organized group of powerful people ♦ *the publicity machine*. **machine** *verb* to make something or work on something with a machine. [from a Greek word *mēkhanē* meaning 'device']

machine code or **machine language** *noun* a computer programming language that a computer can respond to directly without further translation.

machine gun *noun* an automatic gun that fires a rapid continuous series of bullets. **machine-gun** *verb* (**machine-gunned**, **machine-gunning**) to shoot at a person or thing with a machine gun.

machine-readable *adjective* (*Computing*) (said about data or text) in a form that a computer can respond to.

machinery *noun* **1** machines, or the parts of machines. **2** an organized system for doing something.

machinist noun a person who operates machine tools, or who makes machinery.

machismo (mə-**chiz**-moh) noun strong or aggressive male pride or exhibitionism. [same origin as for *macho*]

macho (**mach**-oh) adjective showing aggressive male pride. [a Spanish word meaning 'male']

mackerel noun (**mackerel**) a seafish used for food. [from an Old French word *maquerel*]

mackerel sky noun a sky marked by rows of small white fleecy clouds.

mackintosh noun 1 a waterproof raincoat. [named after the Scottish inventor of a waterproof material, C. Macintosh (1760–1843)]

macramé (mə-**krah**-mi) noun the art of making knotted thread or cord in decorative patterns as a trimming. [from a Turkish word *makrama* meaning 'towel' or 'tablecloth']

macrocosm (**mak**-rə-kozm) noun 1 the universe. 2 the whole of a complex organization or structure. (Compare *microcosm*.) [from the Greek words *makros* meaning 'large' and *kosmos* meaning 'world']

macromolecule noun (Chemistry) a molecule containing a very large number of atoms, such as a protein, nucleic acid, or synthetic polymer. **macromolecular** adjective

macroscopic (makrə-**skop**-ik) adjective 1 visible to the naked eye. 2 relating to large-scale organization or concepts. **macroscopically** adverb [from a Greek word *makros* meaning 'large' and *skopein* meaning 'to look at']

mad adjective (**madder, maddest**) 1 having something wrong with the mind, not sane. 2 extremely foolish or odd ♦ *It was a mad idea.* SYNONYMS: foolish, crazy, stupid, odd; (*informal*) barmy. 3 wildly enthusiastic ♦ *The girls are all mad about sport.* SYNONYMS: enthusiastic, wild; (*informal*) crazy. 4 (*informal*) very excited or annoyed. 5 frenzied ♦ *There was a mad scramble for the exits.* **like mad** (*informal*) with great energy or enthusiasm. **madly** adverb **madness** noun [from an Old English word]

madam noun 1 a word used in speaking politely to a woman ♦ *Can I help you madam?* 2 a conceited or presumptuous young woman ♦ *They all thought she was a bit of a madam.* [from a French phrase *ma dame* meaning 'my lady']

Madame (mə-**dahm**) noun (**Mesdames** (may-**dahm**)) the title of a French-speaking woman, equivalent to 'Mrs' or 'madam'.

madcap noun a wildly eccentric or impulsive person.

mad cow disease noun (*informal*) another term for **BSE**.

madden verb to make someone mad or angry; to irritate or annoy someone. SYNONYMS: anger, infuriate, irritate, annoy, exasperate, incense, enrage.

madder noun 1 a plant with yellowish flowers. 2 a red dye obtained from the root of this plant. [from an Old English word]

made past tense and past participle of **make**.

Mademoiselle (mad-mwə-**zel**) noun (**Mesdemoiselles** (mayd-mwə-zel)) the title of a French-speaking girl or unmarried woman, equivalent to 'Miss' or 'madam'.

madhouse noun (*informal*) 1 a scene of great confusion or uproar. 2 a former name for a mental home or mental hospital.

madman noun (**madmen**) a man who is mentally ill.

madonna noun a picture or statue of the Virgin Mary. [from an Italian phrase *ma donna* meaning 'my lady']

madras (mə-**dras**) noun a strong cotton fabric with a pattern of coloured stripes or checks. [named after the city of Madras in India]

madrigal (**mad**-ri-gəl) noun an old form of part song for several voices, often without instrumental accompaniment.

madwoman noun (**madwomen**) a woman who is mentally ill.

maelstrom (**mayl**-strəm) noun 1 a great whirlpool. 2 a state of great confusion. [from the Dutch words *malen* meaning 'whirl' and *stroom* meaning 'stream']

maestro (**miy**-stroh) noun (**maestros**) 1 a distinguished musician, especially a conductor. 2 a master of any art. [an Italian word meaning 'master']

Mafia (**ma**-fiə) noun an international criminal organization that originated in Sicily, having an elaborate code of behaviour and ruthless methods.

mafia *noun* any network of people who exert a hidden and sinister influence. [a Sicilian dialect word meaning 'bragging']

magazine *noun* 1 a paper-covered illustrated publication that is published regularly and contains articles, stories, or features by several writers. 2 a store for weapons and ammunition or for explosives. 3 a part of a gun that holds the cartridges. 4 a device that holds film for a camera or slides for a projector. [from an Arabic word *makhazin* meaning 'storehouses']

magenta (mə-jen-tə) *noun & adjective* bright purplish red. [named after Magenta, a town in north Italy, where Napoleon III of France won a battle in 1859, the year in which the dye was discovered]

maggot *noun* the larva of a bluebottle or other fly. **maggoty** *adjective* [perhaps from an Old Norse word]

Magi (may-jiy) *plural noun* the wise men from the East who brought offerings to the infant Jesus at Bethlehem (Matthew 2:1). [from a Persian word *magus* meaning 'priest' and later 'wizard']

magic *noun* 1 the art of supposedly influencing events or producing effects by a mysterious or supernatural power. SYNONYMS: sorcery, witchcraft, wizardry. 2 mysterious tricks performed for entertainment. 3 a mysterious and enchanting quality ♦ *the magic of a beautiful sunrise.*
magic *adjective* 1 to do with magic, or using magic ♦ *magic charms.* 2 (*informal*) very enjoyable or exciting.
magic *verb* (**magicked, magicking**) to make or produce something by magic or as if by magic. [same origin as for *Magi*]

magical *adjective* 1 to do with magic, or using magic. 2 wonderful to see or hear ♦ *The effect of the fireworks in the night sky was magical.* **magically** *adverb*

magic carpet *noun* a mythical carpet that is able to transport people through the air to distant places.

magic eye *noun* (*informal*) a photoelectric cell or other device used to detect the presence of people or things.

magician (mə-jish-ən) *noun* 1 a person who can do magic, a wizard. 2 a conjuror.

magic lantern *noun* (*historical*) a simple form of projector using glass slides.

magisterial (ma-jis-teer-iəl) *adjective* 1 to do with a magistrate. 2 having or showing authority, masterful. **magisterially** *adverb*

magistracy (maj-i-strə-si) *noun* (**magistracies**) 1 the office of magistrate. 2 magistrates collectively.

magistrate *noun* a legal official who hears and judges minor cases in a local law court. [from a Latin word *magister* meaning 'master']

magma *noun* hot fluid or semi-fluid material under the earth's crust, from which lava and other igneous rock is formed by cooling. [from a Greek word, from *massein* meaning 'to knead']

magnanimous (mag-nan-iməs) *adjective* generous and forgiving in behaviour, not petty-minded. **magnanimity** (mag-nə-nim-iti) *noun* **magnanimously** *adverb* [from the Latin words *magnus* meaning 'great' and *animus* meaning 'mind']

magnate (mag-nayt) *noun* a wealthy and influential person, especially in business. [from a Latin word *magnus* meaning 'great']

magnesia (mag-nee-zhə) *noun* a white powder that is a compound of magnesium, used in medicine. [from a Greek phrase *Magnēsia lithos* meaning 'stone of Magnesia', a place in Asia Minor (now Turkey)]

magnesium (mag-nee-ziəm) *noun* a chemical element (symbol Mg), a silvery-white metal that burns with an intensely bright flame.

magnet *noun* 1 a piece of iron or steel that can attract iron and that points north and south when suspended. 2 a person or thing that has a powerful attraction. [from a Greek phrase *magnēs lithos* meaning 'lodestone', related to *magnesia*]

magnetic *adverb* 1 having the properties of a magnet. 2 produced or acting by magnetism. 3 having the power to attract people ♦ *a magnetic personality.* **magnetically** *adverb*

magnetic field *noun* the area around a magnetic substance in which the force of magnetism acts.

magnetic needle *noun* a piece of magnetic steel that points north and south, used as an indicator on the dial of a compass.

magnetic north *noun* the direction in which a magnetic needle points, at a slight angle to true north.

magnetic pole *noun* each of two points, in the region of the geographical North and South Poles, indicated by the needle of a magnetic compass.

magnetic storm *noun* disturbance of the earth's magnetic field by charged particles from the sun.

magnetic tape *noun* a plastic strip coated with a magnetic substance for recording sound or pictures or storing computer data.

magnetism *noun* 1 the properties and effects of magnetic substances. 2 great personal charm and attraction.

magnetize *verb* 1 to give magnetic properties to a substance. 2 to attract things as a magnet does. 3 to exert charm or attraction on someone. **magnetization** *noun*

magneto (mag-nee-toh) *noun* (**magnetos**) a small electric generator using magnets.

magnification *noun* 1 the process of magnifying. 2 the amount by which a lens or microscope magnifies things.

magnificent *adjective* 1 grand or splendid in appearance. SYNONYMS: splendid, spectacular, grand, imposing, glorious, beautiful, gorgeous. 2 excellent in quality. SYNONYMS: superb, excellent, wonderful, marvellous. **magnificence** *noun* **magnificently** *adverb* [same origin as for *magnify*]

magnify *verb* (**magnifies**, **magnified**, **magnifying**) 1 to make an object appear larger than it really is, as a lens or microscope does. 2 to exaggerate something. **magnifier** *noun* [from Latin words *magnus* meaning 'great' and *facere* meaning 'to make']

magnifying glass *noun* a lens that magnifies things.

magnitude *noun* 1 largeness or size. 2 importance ♦ *We cannot overestimate the magnitude of the problem.* 3 the degree of brightness of a star. **of the first magnitude** very important. [from a Latin word *magnus* meaning 'great']

magnolia (mag-noh-liǝ) *noun* a tree with large waxy white or pale pink flowers.

magnum *noun* a wine bottle of about twice the standard size (about 1.5 litres). [a Latin word meaning 'large thing']

magpie *noun* 1 a large bird with a long tail, black and white feathers, and a loud cry. 2 someone who chatters constantly. 3 someone who collects things obsessively, as a magpie is supposed to do. [from *pie*, an old word for this bird, with *Mag* (short for Margaret) added at the beginning]

Magyar (mag-yar) *noun* 1 a member of a people living mainly in Hungary. 2 the language of this people, Hungarian. [from the Hungarian name]

maharaja (mah-hǝ-rah-jǝ) *noun* (historical) the title of certain Indian princes. [from a Hindi word meaning 'great rajah']

maharani (mah-hǝ-rah-ni) *noun* (historical) the title of a maharaja's wife or widow. [from a Hindi word meaning 'great rani']

Maharishi (mah-hǝ-rish-i) *noun* a Hindu wise man or leader. [from a Hindi word meaning 'great sage']

mahatma (mǝ-hat-mǝ) *noun* (in the Indian subcontinent) a title of respect for a distinguished person. [from a Sanskrit word meaning 'great soul']

Mahdi (mah-di) *noun* 1 a spiritual and temporal leader expected by Muslims to come and rule before the end of the world. 2 someone who claims this title, especially a leader in the Sudan (1843–85). [from an Arabic word *mahdiy* meaning 'he who is guided in the right way']

mah-jong *noun* a Chinese game for four people, played with pieces called tiles. [from a Chinese dialect word *ma-tsiang* meaning 'sparrows']

mahogany (mǝ-hog-ǝni) *noun* 1 a hard reddish-brown wood used to make furniture. 2 the tropical tree that produces this wood. 3 a rich reddish-brown colour. [origin unknown]

mahout (mǝ-howt) *noun* (in the Indian subcontinent) a person who rides and works with an elephant. [from a Hindi word *mahavat*]

maid *noun* 1 a female servant in a house. 2 (old use) a girl or young woman. [a short form of *maiden*]

maiden *noun* (old use) a girl or young unmarried woman.
maiden *adjective* 1 (said about a woman, especially an older one) unmarried ♦ *a maiden aunt.* 2 (said about a horse) that has not yet won a race. 3 first of its kind or in a series ♦ *a maiden speech* ♦ *a maiden*

voyage. **maidenhood** noun **maidenly** adjective [from an Old English word *mægden*]

maidenhair noun a fern with fine hair-like stalks and delicate foliage.

maidenhead noun (*old use*) virginity.

maiden name noun a woman's family name before she marries.

maiden over noun a cricket over in which no runs are scored.

maidservant noun (*old use*) a female servant.

mail [1] noun letters and packets sent by post. **mail** verb to send a letter or packet by post. [from an Old French word meaning 'bag']

mail [2] noun armour made of metal rings or plates ♦ *a suit of chain mail*. [from a Latin word *macula* meaning 'mesh']

mailbag noun 1 a large bag for carrying mail. 2 the letters received by an MP or public figure.

mailbox noun 1 a box into which mail is delivered. 2 (*Computing*) a computer file in which email messages are stored.

mailing list noun a list of addresses for sending mail to regularly, especially advertising material.

mail order noun a system of ordering goods by post.

maim verb to wound or injure someone so that part of the body is made useless. SYNONYMS: injure, disable, cripple, mutilate.

main adjective principal or most important; greatest in size or extent. SYNONYMS: principal, chief, foremost, primary, paramount. **main** noun 1 the main pipe or cable in a public system carrying water, gas, or (usually called **mains**) electricity. 2 (*old use*) the high seas. **in the main** for the most part, on the whole. [from an Old English word]

main clause noun (*Grammar*) a clause that can be a complete sentence in its own right.

mainframe noun (*Computing*) a large high-speed computer, as distinct from a PC.

mainland noun the main part of a country or continent, without the neighbouring islands.

mainly adverb for the most part, chiefly.

mainmast noun the tallest mast of a sailing ship.

mainspring noun 1 the principal spring of a watch or clock. 2 the chief force motivating or supporting the actions of a person or group.

mainstay noun 1 a strong cable that secures the mainmast of a sailing ship. 2 the chief support or main part.

mainstream noun the most widely held ideas or opinions about something. **mainstream** adjective belonging to a mainstream, widely held.

maintain verb 1 to cause a state or condition to continue, to keep something in existence. 2 to keep a building, vehicle, etc. in a good state of repair. SYNONYMS: keep up, preserve, take care of. 3 to support or provide for someone financially ♦ *They still have to maintain their son at college.* SYNONYMS: support, keep, provide for. 4 to state that something is true ♦ *She still maintained that she had never been to the place.* SYNONYMS: claim, assert, insist, declare, hold, profess. [from a Latin phrase *manu tenere* meaning 'to hold by the hand']

maintenance noun 1 the process of maintaining something. 2 the process of keeping buildings or equipment in repair. 3 provision of the means to support life. 4 money to be paid by a husband or wife to the other partner after a divorce.

maiolica (miy-ol-i-kə) noun a kind of fine earthenware originating in Renaissance Italy. [from the Italian name for Majorca]

maisonette (may-zən-et) noun 1 a small house. 2 part of a house, often on more than one floor, used as a separate dwelling. [from a French word *maisonnette* meaning 'little house']

maize noun 1 a tall cereal plant bearing grain on large cobs. 2 the grain of this plant. [via French and Spanish from a South American language]

majestic adjective stately and dignified, imposing. SYNONYMS: stately, imposing, dignified, grand, magnificent, splendid. **majestically** adverb

majesty noun (**majesties**) 1 impressive dignity or stateliness. 2 royal power. 3 **His** or **Her Majesty** the title of a king or queen or of a king's wife or widow. [from an Old French word, related to *major*]

majolica (mə-jol-i-kə) noun (*historical*) a kind of English earthenware made in imitation of Italian maiolica.

major adjective 1 greater, very important

♦ *The journey is quicker if you stick to the major roads.* **2** very important ♦ *There are three major reasons for doing this.* SYNONYMS: important, principal, chief, crucial, primary. **3** (*Music*) based on a scale which has a semitone next above the third and seventh notes and a whole tone elsewhere.

major *noun* **1** an army officer ranking below a lieutenant colonel and above a captain. **2** an officer in charge of a section of a band ♦ *drum major.*

major *verb* (*North Amer.*) to specialize in a certain subject at college or university. [from a Latin word meaning 'larger, greater']

major-domo (may-jer-doh-moh) *noun* (**major-domos**) the chief steward of a large household. [via Spanish and Italian from a Latin phrase *major domus* meaning 'highest official of the house']

major general *noun* an army officer ranking below a lieutenant general.

majority *noun* (**majorities**) **1** the greatest part of a group of people or things. **2** the number of votes by which a candidate or party in an election wins ♦ *She had a majority of over 5,000.* (Compare **minority**.) **3** the age at which a person gains full legal rights, usually 18 or 21 ♦ *He attained his majority.* [same origin as for *major*]

majority rule *noun* the principle that the largest group in a country should have most power.

majority verdict *noun* a jury's verdict that is not unanimous, with some (usually no more than two) members disagreeing.

make *verb* (past tense and past participle **made**) **1** to construct or create something, especially by putting parts together. SYNONYMS: produce, construct, create, build, assemble, manufacture; erect (a building). **2** to cause something to exist ♦ *They seem to be making difficulties.* SYNONYMS: cause, bring about, provoke. **3** to draw up a legal document or contract ♦ *She decided to make a will.* **4** to establish laws or rules. **5** to arrange the bedclothes tidily on a bed, ready for use. **6** to result in or amount to a total ♦ *Three and eight make eleven.* SYNONYMS: add up to, come to, amount to, total. **7** to cause someone to be in a certain state ♦ *The news made me happy.* **8** to succeed in arriving at a place or achieving a position ♦ *We only just made the shore by dark* ♦ *She has finally made the team.* SYNONYMS: get to, reach, achieve. **9** to

succeed in catching a train, bus, or other form of public transport ♦ *If you hurry you can make the last bus.* **10** to form or provide something ♦ *The letter makes pleasant reading.* **11** to gain or earn something ♦ *The company will make a profit this year.* **12** to reckon something ♦ *What do you make the time?* **13** to cause or compel someone to do something ♦ *I'd better make him stay.* SYNONYMS: compel, force, oblige, order, induce. **14** to perform an action ♦ *to make an attempt* ♦ *to make war.* **15** to ensure the success of something ♦ *A good wine can make a meal* ♦ *The news made my day.* **16** to act as if intending to do something ♦ *He suddenly made to go.*

make *noun* **1** the way a thing is made. **2** the manufacturer or place where a thing is made ♦ *What make is your car?* **to be made for** to be ideally suited to someone or something. **to have it made** (*informal*) to be sure of success. **to have the makings of** to have the essential qualities for a role or activity ♦ *She had all the makings of a good teacher.* **to make do** to manage with something that is not what you really want or need. **to make for 1** to be going towards a place or trying to reach it ♦ *They were making for home when the storm broke.* **2** to tend to cause something ♦ *It makes for domestic harmony.* **to make it** to achieve what you want, to be successful. **to make it up** to become reconciled after a quarrel. **to make it up to someone** to compensate someone for a loss. **to make love 1** to have sexual intercourse. **2** (*old use*) to try to win someone's love. **to make much** or **little of** to treat someone or something as important or unimportant. **to make off** to go away hastily. **to make off with** to carry something away, to steal something. **to make out 1** to manage to see, hear, or understand something. **2** to claim or pretend that something is true ♦ *They made out that they'd arrived early.* **to make room** to clear a space for something. **to make time** to find extra time to do something. **to make up 1** to build something or put the parts together. **2** to invent a story or excuse. **3** to compensate for something ♦ *This good news makes up for all our worries.* **4** to become reconciled after a quarrel. **5** to use cosmetics, to put on make-up. **to make up to** to try to win favour with someone. **on the make** (*informal*) wanting to make money. [from an Old English word *macian*]

make-believe *adjective* pretended, imagined.

make-believe noun pretending or imagining.
make believe verb to pretend or imagine something.

makeover noun a complete transformation of a person's appearance with cosmetics, hairstyling, etc.

maker noun someone who makes or produces something. **our Maker** God.

makeshift adjective improvised or used because there is nothing better ♦ We had to use an old box as a makeshift table.

make-up noun 1 cosmetics used on the face. 2 the way something is made up or built. 3 a person's character and temperament.

makeweight noun 1 something put on a scale to make up the full weight. 2 a person or thing added to make something complete.

mal- prefix bad; badly (as in ♦ malnourished). [from a Latin word male meaning 'badly']

malacca (mə-lak-ə) noun a brown cane made from the stem of a palm tree, used mainly for walking sticks and umbrella handles. [named after Malacca (or Melaka), a state of Malaysia]

malachite (mal-ə-kiyt) noun a bright green mineral that can be polished.

maladjusted adjective (said about a person) not able to cope with the normal demands of social life. **maladjustment** noun

maladministration noun (formal) bad or dishonest management of business or public affairs.

maladroit (mal-ə-droit) adjective inept or clumsy. **maladroitly** adverb **maladroitness** noun [from a French word]

malady (mal-ə-di) noun (maladies) a disease or ailment. [from a French word malade meaning 'ill']

Malagasy (malə-gas-i) noun (Malagasy or Malagasies) 1 a person born in Madagascar, an island country off the east coast of Africa, or descended from people born there. 2 the language of Madagascar. **Malagasy** adjective to do with or coming from Madagascar.

malaise (mal-ayz) noun a feeling of illness or discomfort. [from a French word meaning 'bad ease']

malapropism (mal-ə-prop-izm) noun a comical confusion of words, e.g. using hooligan instead of hurricane. [named after Mrs Malaprop in Sheridan's play The Rivals (1775), who made mistakes like this]

malaria (mə-lair-iə) noun a disease causing fever which recurs at intervals, transmitted by mosquitoes. **malarial** adjective [from an Italian phrase mala aria meaning 'bad air', which was once thought to cause the disease]

Malay (mə-lay) or **Malayan** noun 1 a member of a people living in Malaysia and Indonesia in SE Asia. 2 the language of the Malays.
Malay or **Malayan** adjective to do with or coming from Malaysia and Indonesia.

malcontent (mal-kən-tent) noun a discontented person who is likely to cause trouble.

male adjective 1 to do with or belonging to the sex that reproduces by fertilizing egg cells produced by the female. 2 (said about plants) having flowers that contain pollen-bearing organs and not seeds. 3 (said about a fitting or machinery part) designed to enter or fill a corresponding hollow part.
male noun a male person, animal, or plant. [from a Latin word mas, related to masculine]

male chauvinist noun a man who is excessively loyal to his own sex and is prejudiced against women.

malediction (mali-dik-shən) noun (formal) a curse. **maledictory** adjective [from mal- and diction]

malefactor (mal-i-fak-ter) noun a criminal or wrongdoer. **malefaction** (mal-i-fak-shən) noun [from mal- and a Latin word factor meaning 'doer']

malevolent (mə-lev-ə-lənt) adjective wishing harm to others. **malevolence** noun **malevolently** adverb [from mal- and a Latin word volens meaning 'wishing']

malformation noun an abnormal or faulty formation.

malformed adjective abnormally or faultily formed.

malfunction verb (said about equipment or machinery) to fail to work normally. **malfunction** noun a failure to work properly.

malice noun a vicious desire to harm other people. [from a Latin word *malus* meaning 'evil']

malicious (mə-**lish**-əs) adjective intending to harm other people. SYNONYMS: hurtful, vicious, spiteful, vindictive, malevolent. **maliciously** adverb

malign (mə-**liyn**) adjective 1 harmful ♦ *a malign influence.* 2 showing malice. **malign** verb to say unpleasant and untrue things about someone. **malignity** (mə-**lig**-niti) noun [from a Latin word *malignare* meaning 'to plot wickedly']

malignant (mə-**lig**-nənt) adjective 1 (said about a tumour) growing into areas of normal tissue and tending to regrow after it has been removed. 2 wanting to harm other people, malevolent. **malignancy** noun **malignantly** adverb

malinger (mə-**ling**-ger) verb to pretend to be ill or unwell in order to avoid work. **malingerer** noun [from an Old French word *malingre*]

mall (mal or mawl) noun 1 a sheltered walk or promenade. 2 a shopping area closed to traffic. [from the name of The Mall, a street in London]

mallard (**mal**-erd) noun (**mallard**) a wild duck, the male of which has a glossy green head. [from an Old French word, related to *male*]

malleable (**mal**-i-ə-bəl) adjective 1 able to be pressed or hammered into shape. 2 (said about a person) easy to influence, adaptable. **malleability** noun [from a Latin word *malleare* meaning 'to hammer']

mallet noun 1 a hammer with a large wooden head. 2 an implement with a long handle, used in croquet or polo for striking the ball. [from a Latin word *malleus* meaning 'a hammer']

mallow noun a plant with hairy stems and leaves and purple, pink, or white flowers. [from an Old English word, related to *mauve*]

malmsey (**mahm**-zi) noun a kind of strong sweet wine. [from the name of Monemvasia, a port in Greece]

malnutrition noun bad health from not having enough to eat or not enough of the right kind of food.

malodorous (mal-**oh**-der-əs) adjective stinking.

Malpighian layer (mal-**pig**-i-ən) noun (*Biology*) the layer of the epidermis that is next to the dermis and in which cell division takes place. [named after the Italian anatomist Marcello Malpighi (1628–94)]

malpractice noun wrong or negligent advice or treatment given by a professional person such as a doctor or lawyer.

malt noun 1 barley or other grain that has been allowed to sprout and then dried, used for brewing, distilling, or vinegar-making. 2 (*informal*) malt liquors. **malt** verb to make grain into malt. **malty** adjective [from an Old English word]

malted milk noun a drink made from dried milk and malt.

maltose noun (*Chemistry*) a sugar formed from starch by the action of saliva or malt.

maltreat verb to treat a person or animal badly or cruelly. **maltreatment** noun

malt whisky noun whisky made entirely from malted barley.

mama or **mamma** (mə-**mah**) noun (*old use*) mother.

mamba noun a poisonous black or green African snake. [from a Zulu word *imamba*]

mammal noun a member of the class of animals that give birth to live young which are fed from the mother's body. **mammalian** (mə-**may**-liən) adjective [from a Latin word *mamma* meaning 'breast']

mammary (**mam**-er-i) adjective to do with the breasts.

mammary gland noun a milk-secreting gland of female mammals.

mammogram noun an X-ray of the breasts, taken to locate and diagnose tumours.

Mammon noun wealth regarded as a bad influence. [via Greek from an Aramaic word *mamon* meaning 'riches', with reference to Christ's warning that 'you cannot serve both God and Mammon' in the New Testament (Matthew 6:24, Luke 16:13)]

mammoth noun a large extinct elephant with a hairy skin and curved tusks. **mammoth** adjective huge. [from a Russian word *mamot* (because the first examples were found in Siberia)]

man noun (**men**) 1 an adult male human being. SYNONYMS: gentleman, fellow; (*informal*) chap, bloke, guy. 2 a human

being, an individual person. SYNONYMS: person, human being, individual. **3** human beings in general. SYNONYMS: humankind, humanity, the human race, people. **4** a male member of a team, workforce, or army. **5** a playing piece used in a board game. **man** *verb* (**manned, manning**) to provide a place, piece of machinery, etc. with the people needed to run or work it. **the man in the street** a typical person, not an expert. **man to man** openly and frankly. **to a man** everyone without exception. [from an Old English word *mann*]
◊ It is better to avoid using *man* to mean 'human beings in general' because it can be regarded as sexist. Use any of the alternatives given above at sense 3:
♦ *Conservation measures taken for the good of humankind.*

manacle (man-ə-kəl) *noun* each of a pair of shackles for the hands.
manacle *verb* to tie someone's hands with manacles. [from a Latin word *manus* meaning 'hand']

manage *verb* **1** to have resources under your control. **2** to be in charge of a business or part of it, or a group of people. SYNONYMS: run, supervise, control, direct, lead, be in charge of, administer. **3** to succeed in doing or producing something in spite of difficulties ♦ *Can you manage without help?* SYNONYMS: cope, succeed; (*informal*) get along, get by. **4** to succeed in doing something unexpected or unwelcome ♦ *They've managed to lock themselves out.* [from a Latin word *manus* meaning 'hand']

manageable *adjective* able to be done or managed, feasible.

management *noun* **1** the process of managing a business or group of people. **2** the people who manage a business, managers.

manager *noun* **1** a person who is in charge of a business or group of people. **2** a person who directs the activity or performance of a sports team or entertainer. **managerial** (manə-jeer-iəl) *adjective*

manageress *noun* a woman manager, especially of a shop or hotel.

managing director *noun* a company director with the chief executive control or authority.

Mancunian (man-kew-niən) *adjective* to do with or coming from Manchester.

Mancunian *noun* a person born or living in Manchester.

mandala (man-də-lə) *noun* a symbolic pattern used in Hindu and Buddhist art and meditation. [a Sanskrit word meaning 'a disc']

mandarin (man-der-in) *noun* **1** an important or high-ranking official. **2** a kind of small flattened orange grown in China and North Africa.
Mandarin *noun* the standard literary and official form of Chinese. [via Portuguese from a Hindi word *mantri* meaning 'counsellor']

mandate *noun* authority given to someone to perform a task or carry out decisions.
mandate *verb* to give a person authority to perform a task. [from a Latin word *mandatum* meaning 'commanded']

mandatory (man-də-ter-i) *adjective* obligatory or compulsory. **mandatorily** *adverb*

mandible (man-dib-əl) *adjective* (*Anatomy and Zoology*) **1** a jaw, especially the lower one. (Compare **maxilla**.) **2** either of the parts of a bird's beak, or a similar part in insects. [from a Latin word *mandere* meaning 'to chew']

mandolin (man-dəl-in) *noun* a musical instrument of the lute family, played with a plectrum. [from an Italian word *mandolino*]

mandrake *noun* a poisonous plant with white or purple flowers and large yellow fruit. [from a Latin word *mandragora*, later associated with *man* and *drake* (in its old meaning 'dragon')]

mandrel *noun* **1** the shaft of a lathe, to which work is fixed while being turned. **2** a cylindrical rod round which metal or other material is forged or shaped. [origin unknown]

mane *noun* **1** the long hair on a horse's or lion's neck. **2** a person's long hair.

manful *adjective* brave or resolute. **manfully** *adverb*

manganese (mang-ə-neez) *noun* a hard and brittle grey metal that is a chemical element (symbol Mn). [via French from Italian, related to *magnesia*]

mange (maynj) *noun* a skin disease of dogs and other hairy animals, caused by a parasite. [via Old French from a Latin word *manducare* meaning 'to chew']

mangel-wurzel noun another word for mangold.

manger noun a long open trough in a stable for horses or cattle to eat from. [from a French word *manger* meaning 'to eat']

mangetout noun a kind of pea eaten together with the pod. [from French words meaning 'eat all']

mangle[1] noun a machine with rollers for drying and pressing wet laundry.
mangle verb to press laundry in a mangle. [from a Dutch word *mangel*]

mangle[2] verb to damage something badly by cutting or crushing it. SYNONYMS: crush, mutilate. [from a French word *mahangler*]

mango noun (**mangoes** or **mangos**) **1** a tropical fruit with a yellow flesh. **2** the tree that bears this fruit. [via Portuguese from an Indian language]

mangold noun a large beet used as food for cattle. [from a German word *Mangoldwurzel*, from *Mangold* meaning 'beet' and *Wurzel* meaning 'root']

mangrove noun a tropical tree or shrub which grows in muddy coastal swamps, having tangled roots that grow above the ground. [from a South American language]

mangy (mayn-ji) adjective (**mangier**, **mangiest**) **1** affected by mange. **2** squalid or shabby.

manhandle verb **1** to move something with difficulty by human effort alone. **2** to treat or push someone roughly.

manhole noun an opening, usually with a cover, through which a person can enter a sewer or a boiler etc. to inspect or repair it.

manhood noun **1** the state or time of being an adult man. **2** manly qualities or courage. **3** the men of a country.

manhunt noun an organized search for a person, especially a criminal.

mania (may-nia) noun **1** a mental illness marked by periods of excitement and over-activity. **2** an extreme enthusiasm for something. SYNONYMS: craze, fad, passion, obsession. [from a Greek word meaning 'madness']

maniac (may-ni-ak) noun **1** (old use) a person affected with mania. **2** a person who is behaving wildly or violently.

maniacal (mə-niy-ə-kəl) adjective like a mania or a maniac. **maniacally** adverb

manic (man-ik) adjective affected with mania.

manic depression noun a mental disorder with alternating bouts of excitement and depression. **manic-depressive** adjective & noun

manicure noun care and treatment of the hands and nails.
manicure verb to apply treatment to the hands and nails. **manicurist** noun [from Latin words *manus* meaning 'hand' and *cura* meaning 'care']

manifest adjective clear and obvious to see or understand.
manifest verb **1** to show a thing clearly
♦ *The crowd manifested its approval by cheering.* **2** (said about a ghost) to appear.
manifest noun a list of cargo or passengers carried by a ship or aircraft. **manifestly** adverb **manifestation** noun [from a Latin word *manifestare* meaning 'to make public']

manifesto noun (**manifestos**) a public statement of the policies and principles of a group or party. [an Italian word, related to *manifest*]

manifold adjective (formal or literary) of many kinds, very varied.
manifold noun in an engine or mechanism, a pipe or chamber with several openings that connect with other parts. [from *many* and *fold*[1]]

manikin noun **1** a very small person. **2** a model of the human body, with limbs that can be moved. [from a Dutch word *manneken*, related to *man*]

manila (mə-nil-ə) noun a brown paper used for wrapping and for envelopes. [from Manila, capital of the Philippines (because the paper was originally made from hemp from this area)]

manioc (man-i-ok) noun **1** cassava. **2** the flour made from cassava. [from a South American language]

manipulable adjective able to be manipulated.

manipulate verb **1** to handle or arrange something skilfully. **2** to control or influence someone cleverly. **3** to present or alter information so as to mislead people. SYNONYMS: falsify; (informal) doctor, fiddle, cook. **manipulation** noun **manipulator** noun [from a Latin word *manus* meaning 'hand']

mankind *noun* human beings in general, the human race. SYNONYMS: humankind, humanity, the human race, people.
◊ See the note at **man**.

manly *adjective* **1** having the qualities traditionally associated with men, such as strength and courage. SYNONYMS: brave, courageous, strong, virile. **2** suitable for a man. **manliness** *noun*

man-made *adjective* made by humans and not by nature.

manna *noun* **1** a substance miraculously supplied as food to the Israelites in the wilderness after the Exodus from Egypt, according to the account in the Bible (Exodus 16). **2** an unexpected or delightful benefit. [from a Hebrew word]

manned *adjective* (said about a spacecraft or other equipment) containing a human crew.

mannequin (man-i-kin) *noun* a dummy for displaying clothes in a shop window. [a French word, related to *manikin*]

manner *noun* **1** the way a thing is done or happens. SYNONYMS: way, fashion, style. **2** a person's way of behaving. SYNONYMS: disposition, demeanour, attitude, bearing. **3** a kind or sort ♦ *We saw all manner of things.* SYNONYMS: kind, sort, type, variety.
manners *plural noun* how a person behaves towards other people, polite behaviour. [from an Old French word, from a Latin word *manus* meaning 'hand']

mannered *adjective* **1** behaving in a certain way ♦ *well-mannered.* **2** (said about an artistic style) full of mannerisms.

mannerism *noun* **1** a person's distinctive habit or way of doing something. **2** (**Mannerism**) a style of European art in the 16th century, involving bright colours and contorted figures.

mannish *adjective* (said about a woman) having masculine characteristics, suitable for a man.

manoeuvre (mə-noo-ver) *noun* **1** a planned and controlled movement of a vehicle or a body of troops. **2** a skilful or crafty action or scheme.
manoeuvre *verb* (**manoeuvred, manoeuvring**)
1 to move a thing's position or course etc. carefully ♦ *She manoeuvred the car into the garage.* SYNONYMS: guide, negotiate, steer. **2** to perform military exercises. **3** to guide someone or something skilfully or craftily to get what you want ♦ *He*

gradually manoeuvred the conversation towards money.
manoeuvres *plural noun* large-scale exercises of troops or ships ♦ *on manoeuvres.* [via French from a Latin phrase *manu operari* meaning 'to work by hand']

man-of-war *noun* (**men-of-war**) (*historical*) an armed sailing ship.

manometer (mə-nom-it-er) *noun* an instrument for measuring the pressure on a column of fluid. [from Greek words *manos* meaning 'thin' and *metron* meaning 'measure']

manor *noun* **1** a large country house or the landed estate belonging to it. **2** a medieval estate in which a feudal lord had legal rights over the land and tenants. **3** (*informal*) an area of operation or influence. **manorial** (man-or-iəl) *adjective* [from a French word, related to *mansion*]

manpower *noun* the number of people working or available for work.

mansard (man-sard) *noun* a type of roof that has a steep lower part and a less steep upper part on all four sides of a building. [named after the French architect F. Mansard (1598–1666)]

manse *noun* a church minister's house, especially in Scotland. [same origin as for *mansion*]

manservant *noun* (**menservants**) a male servant.

mansion (man-shən) *noun* a large stately house. [from a Latin word *mansio* meaning 'a place to stay', 'a dwelling']

manslaughter *noun* the act of killing a person unlawfully but not intentionally.

mantel *noun* a structure of wood or marble above and around a fireplace. [a different spelling of *mantle*]

mantelpiece *noun* a shelf above a fireplace.

mantilla (man-til-ə) *noun* a lace veil worn by Spanish women over the hair and shoulders. [a Spanish word meaning 'little mantle']

mantis *noun* (also **praying mantis**) an insect like a grasshopper, with a triangular head and forelegs that it folds as if in prayer. [from a Greek word *mantis* meaning 'prophet']

mantissa noun (*Mathematics*) the part of a logarithm after the decimal point (contrasted with the *characteristic*). [from a Latin word meaning 'makeweight']

mantle noun 1 a loose sleeveless cloak. 2 a covering ♦ *a mantle of snow.* 3 a mesh cover fitted round the flame of a gas lamp, producing a strong light when heated. 4 (*Geology*) the region of very dense rock between the earth's crust and its core.
mantle verb (*literary*) to envelop or cover something. [from a Latin word *mantellum* meaning 'cloak']

mantra noun a word or sound chanted repeatedly as an aid to concentration in meditating, originally in Hinduism and Buddhism. [from a Sanskrit word meaning 'instrument of thought']

mantrap noun a trap for catching people, especially trespassers.

manual adjective 1 to do with the hands. 2 done or worked with the hands.
manual noun 1 a book giving information or instructions, a handbook. 2 an organ keyboard that is played with the hands, not with the feet. **manually** adverb [from a Latin word *manus* meaning 'hand']

manufacture verb 1 to make or produce goods on a large scale by machinery. 2 to invent something ♦ *I tried to manufacture an excuse.*
manufacture noun the process of manufacturing. **manufacturer** noun [from Latin words *manu* meaning 'by hand' and *facere* meaning 'to make']

manumission (man-yoo-**mish**-ən) noun (*formal*) the act of freeing a slave. [from Latin words *manu* meaning 'by hand', and *mittere* meaning 'to send']

manure noun animal dung used as a fertilizer.
manure verb to fertilize land with manure. [from an Old French word, related to *manoeuvre*]

manuscript (man-yoo-skript) noun 1 something written by hand, not printed. 2 a written or typed version of an author's work, before it is printed. [from Latin words *manu* meaning 'by hand' and *scriptum* meaning 'written']

Manx adjective to do with or coming from the Isle of Man.
Manx noun the Celtic language of the Manx people, now mainly confined to ceremonial use. [from an Old Norse word]

Manx cat noun a kind of domestic cat with no tail or only a short one.

many adjective (**more, most**) great in number, numerous. SYNONYMS: numerous, a lot of, countless; (*informal*) lots of, heaps of, umpteen.
many noun many people or things ♦ *Many have been found.* SYNONYMS: a great deal, a lot, plenty; (*informal*) lots, heaps, loads, masses. [from an Old English word]

Maoism (mow-izm) noun the communist principles of Mao Zedong (1893–1976) as formerly practised in China. **Maoist** noun & adjective

Maori (mow-ri) noun (**Maoris**) 1 a member of the aboriginal people of New Zealand. 2 the language of this people. [from the name in Maori]

map noun 1 a diagram of an area of land or of the earth's surface, showing the principal physical features. 2 a diagram of the sky or of another planet.
map verb (**mapped, mapping**) 1 to make a map of an area. 2 (*Mathematics*) to make each element of a set correspond to one of another set. **off the map** distant or remote. **to map out** to plan something in detail. [from a Latin phrase *mappa mundi* meaning 'sheet of the world']

maple noun a tree with broad leaves, grown for its wood or sugar. [from an Old English word]

mar verb (**marred, marring**) to damage or spoil something. SYNONYMS: spoil, damage, blemish, impair, disfigure. [from an Old English word]

marabou (ma-rə-boo) noun 1 a large African stork. 2 its down used as a trimming for clothing. [from an Arabic word *murabit* meaning 'holy man' (because the stork is regarded as holy by Muslims)]

maracas (mə-rak-əz) plural noun a pair of gourds or other club-like containers filled with beads or beans and shaken as a musical instrument. [via Portuguese from a South American language]

marathon noun 1 a long-distance running race, especially that of 26 miles 385 yards (42.195 km) in the modern Olympic Games. 2 any long race or test of endurance. [named after Marathon in Greece, where an invading Persian army was defeated in 490 BC. A man who fought at the battle is said to have run to Athens with news of the victory]

marauding (mə-**raw**-ding) *adjective* going about in search of plunder or prey. **marauder** *noun* [from a French word *maraud* meaning 'rogue']

marble *noun* 1 a kind of limestone polished and used in sculpture and building. 2 a piece of sculpture in marble ♦ *the Elgin Marbles.* 3 a small glass ball used in games. [from a Greek word *marmaros* meaning 'shining stone']

marbled *adjective* having a veined or mottled appearance.

marcasite (**mark**-ə-siyt) *noun* crystallized iron pyrites, or a piece of this used as an ornament. [from an Arabic word *markasita*]

March *noun* the third month of the year. [named after Mars, the Roman god of war]

march *verb* 1 to walk with regular steps. SYNONYMS: troop, stride, parade. 2 to walk purposefully ♦ *He marched up to the manager.* 3 to make someone march or walk ♦ *He marched them up the hill.* 4 to progress steadily ♦ *Time marches on.* 5 to take part in an organized procession as a form of protest.
march *noun* 1 marching; the distance covered in marching. 2 a piece of music for marching to. 3 progress ♦ *the march of events.* **on the march** marching, moving forward. **marcher** *noun* [from a French word *marcher* meaning 'to walk']

Marches *plural noun* border regions. [from an Old French word *marche*]

marchioness (mar-shən-ess) *noun* 1 the wife or widow of a marquess. 2 a woman holding the rank of marquess in her own right. [from a Latin word *marchionissa* meaning 'ruler of the border country']

mare *noun* a female horse or donkey. [from an Old English word *mere*]

mare's nest *noun* a discovery that is thought to be interesting but turns out to be false or worthless.

margarine (mar-jer-**een**) *noun* a substance used like butter, made from animal or vegetable fats. [via French from a Greek word *margaron* meaning 'pearl']

marge *noun* (*informal*) margarine.

margin *noun* 1 an edge or border. SYNONYMS: border, edge, verge. 2 a blank space between the edge of a page and the writing or pictures printed on it. 3 an amount over and above the necessary minimum ♦ *Keep your speed down to allow a* good safety margin. 4 (in commerce) the difference between the cost price and the selling price ♦ *large profit margins.* [from a Latin word *margo* meaning 'edge']

marginal *adjective* 1 written in a margin ♦ *marginal notes.* 2 of or at an edge. 3 very slight in amount ♦ *The difference is only marginal.* 4 (said about a parliamentary seat) having a very small majority in the previous election. **marginally** *adverb*

marguerite (marg-er-**eet**) *noun* a large daisy with a yellow centre and white petals. [from the French name for *Margaret*]

marigold *noun* a garden plant with golden or bright yellow flowers. [from the name *Mary* and *gold*]

marijuana (ma-ri-**hwah**-nə) *noun* a form of the drug cannabis, especially in the form of cigarettes. [an American Spanish word]

marimba (mə-**rim**-bə) *noun* a xylophone of Africa and Central America, or an orchestral instrument based on it. [from an African language]

marina (mə-**ree**-nə) *noun* a harbour for yachts and pleasure boats. [same origin as for *marine*]

marinade (ma-rin-**ayd**) *noun* a flavoured liquid in which meat or fish is soaked before being cooked.
marinade *verb* to soak meat or fish in a marinade. [via French from a Spanish word *marinada*]

marine (mə-**reen**) *adjective* 1 to do with the sea, or living in the sea ♦ *marine animals.* 2 to do with ships or shipping ♦ *marine insurance.* 3 for use at sea.
marine *noun* a member of a body of troops trained to serve on land or sea. [from a Latin word *mare* meaning 'sea']

mariner (ma-rin-er) *noun* (*formal or literary*) a sailor.

marionette (ma-ri-ə-net) *noun* a puppet worked by strings or wires. [from a French word meaning 'little Mary']

marital (ma-ritəl) *adjective* to do with marriage or the relations between husband and wife. **maritally** *adverb* [from a Latin word *maritus* meaning 'husband']

maritime (ma-ri-tiym) *adjective* 1 to do with the sea or ships. 2 living or found near the sea. [same origin as for *marine*]

marjoram (mar-jer-əm) *noun* a herb with a mild flavour, used in cooking. [from an Old French word *majorane*]

mark[1] *noun* **1** a small area on a surface that differs in appearance from the rest of the surface, especially a spot or stain that spoils it. SYNONYMS: stain, spot, blemish, smear, smudge, splodge. **2** a distinguishing feature or characteristic. **3** a sign or symbol of a quality or feeling ♦ *They all stood as a mark of respect.* **4** a lasting impression ♦ *Poverty had left its mark.* **5** a line or object serving to indicate a position. **6** a written or printed symbol ♦ *punctuation marks.* **7** a point awarded for the quality of a piece of work, or the total points awarded ♦ *She got high marks in her music exam* ♦ *She nearly got the highest mark.* **8** a target or standard to be aimed at. **9** used with a number to show the position of a product in a series ♦ *A Mark 10 Jaguar.*
mark *verb* **1** to make a mark on something. SYNONYMS: stain, blemish, scratch. **2** to distinguish or characterize something. **3** to assign points or a grade to a piece of work. SYNONYMS: correct, assess, evaluate, grade. **4** to notice or watch something carefully ♦ *Just you mark my words!* **5** (in ball games) to keep close to an opposing player so as to prevent them getting or passing the ball. **to make one's mark** to make a lasting impression or become famous. **to mark time 1** to march on the spot without moving forward. **2** to pass the time in routine activity while waiting to do something more useful. [from an Old English word *mearc*]

mark[2] *noun* the unit of money in Germany. [from an Old English word *marc*]

marked *adjective* clearly noticeable ♦ *a marked improvement.* **markedly** (mark-id-li) *adverb*

marker *noun* **1** something that serves to mark a position. **2** a pen with a broad felt tip. **3** a person who records the score in games.

market *noun* **1** a regular gathering of people to buy and sell goods or livestock. **2** a building or open space used for this. **3** a demand for a particular product or service ♦ *The new cereal found a ready market.* **4** a place or group of people where goods may be sold ♦ *foreign markets.* **5** the stock market.
market *verb* (**marketed, marketing**) to offer goods or services for sale. **on the market** offered for sale. [from a Latin word *merx* meaning 'merchandise']

marketable *adjective* able or fit to be sold.

market forces *plural noun* the working of supply and demand as an economic factor, without interference from government.

market garden *noun* a place where vegetables and fruit are grown for sale.

marketplace *noun* **1** an open space in a town, where a market is held. **2** the world of commercial buying and selling.

market research *noun* the study of what people want to buy and what type of products and services they prefer.

market town *noun* a town in which a market is held regularly.

market value *noun* the amount for which something can be sold.

marking *noun* **1** a mark that identifies something. **2** the colouring and pattern of marks on an animal's skin, feathers, or fur.

marksman *noun* (**marksmen**) a person who is skilled in shooting at a target. **marksmanship** *noun*

mark-up *noun* (in commerce) the amount a seller adds to the cost price of an article to determine its selling price.

marl *noun* a soil consisting of clay and lime, formerly used as a fertilizer. **marly** *adjective* [from an Old French word *marle*]

marlinspike *noun* a pointed tool used to separate strands of rope or wire. [from an old word *marl* meaning 'to fasten with a rope']

marmalade *noun* a kind of jam made from oranges or other citrus fruit. [via French from a Portuguese word *marmelo* meaning 'quince' (because quinces were once used to make marmalade)]

marmoset (mar-mə-zet) *noun* a small bushy-tailed monkey of tropical America. [from an Old French word]

marmot (mar-mət) *noun* a small burrowing animal of the squirrel family. [from a French word *marmotte*]

maroon[1] *noun* a dark brownish-red colour. **maroon** *adjective* of this colour. [from a French word *marron* meaning 'chestnut']

maroon[2] *verb* to abandon or isolate someone in a deserted place. SYNONYMS: abandon, desert, strand. [via French from a Spanish word *cimarrón* meaning 'runaway slave']

marque (mark) *noun* a make of car, as distinct from a specific model. [a French word meaning 'mark']

marquee (mar-**kee**) *noun* a large tent used for a party or exhibition. [from a French word, related to *marquis*]

marquess (mar-kwis) *noun* a British nobleman ranking between a duke and an earl. [same origin as for *marquis*]

marquetry (mar-kit-ri) *noun* inlaid work using small pieces of coloured wood or ivory. [from a French word *marqueterie*]

marquis (mar-kwis) *noun* a nobleman ranking between a duke and an earl. [from an Old French word]

marquise (mar-**keez**) *noun* 1 the wife or widow of a marquis. 2 a woman holding the rank of marquis in her own right.

marram (ma-rəm) *noun* a coarse grass that grows in sand by the shore. [from an Old Norse word *marr* meaning 'sea']

marriage *noun* 1 the state in which a man and a woman are formally united as husband and wife. 2 the act or ceremony of being married. [from an Old French word *mariage*]

marriageable *adjective* old enough or suitable to be married.

marron glacé (ma-ron gla-say) *noun* (**marrons glacés**) a chestnut preserved in sugar as a sweet. [a French phrase meaning 'iced chestnut']

marrow *noun* 1 a large gourd eaten as a vegetable. 2 the soft fatty substance inside bones. [from an Old English word]

marrowbone *noun* a bone containing edible marrow.

marrowfat *noun* a kind of large pea.

marry *verb* (**marries, married, marrying**) 1 to join two people in marriage. 2 to become a person's husband or wife. 3 to put things together as a pair. [from a Latin word *maritus* meaning 'husband']

marsh *noun* an area of wet low-lying ground. **marshy** *adjective* [from an Old English word]

marshal *noun* 1 an officer of the highest rank in the armed forces ♦ Air Marshal ♦ Field Marshal. 2 an official with responsibility for arranging public events or ceremonies. 3 an official accompanying a judge on circuit, with secretarial duties. 4 a federal law officer in the USA. 5 an official at a race.

marshal *verb* (**marshalled, marshalling**) 1 to arrange things in their proper order. 2 to make people assemble. 3 to usher people. [from an Old French word *mareschal* meaning 'commander']

marshland *noun* an area of marshy land.

marshmallow *noun* a soft spongy sweet, usually pink or white and made from sugar, egg white, and gelatine. [originally made from the root of the marsh mallow, a pink flower that grows in marshes]

marsupial (mar-**soo**-piəl) *noun* an animal such as the kangaroo or wallaby. The female has a pouch in which its young are carried until they are fully developed. [from a Greek word *marsupion* meaning 'pouch']

mart *noun* a market or place for trading. [from a Dutch word *marct* meaning 'market']

Martello tower *noun* each of a number of small circular forts erected along the coast of England during the Napoleonic Wars. [named after the tower at Cape Martello in Corsica, which the English found difficult to capture in 1794]

marten *noun* an animal like a weasel, with thick soft fur. [from an Old French phrase *peau martrine* meaning 'fur of the marten', from *martre*, the name for the animal]

martial (mar-shəl) *adjective* to do with war, or suitable for war. SYNONYMS: military, warlike. [from a Latin word *martialis*, meaning 'of Mars' (the Roman god of war)]

martial arts *plural noun* fighting sports such as judo and karate.

martial law *noun* government of a country by the armed forces in a time of crisis, during which ordinary law is suspended.

Martian (mar-shən) *adjective* to do with the planet Mars.
Martian *noun* (in fiction) an inhabitant of Mars.

martin *noun* a bird of the swallow family. [probably named after St Martin of Tours, who gave half his cloak to a beggar. The bird's markings look like a torn cloak.]

martinet (mar-tin-**et**) *noun* a person who enforces obedience strictly. [named after a French army officer Jean Martinet (died 1672), who imposed harsh discipline on his troops]

martyr *noun* 1 a person who is killed because of their religious beliefs. 2 a

person who puts up with great suffering in support of a cause or principle.
martyr verb to kill someone or make them suffer for their beliefs. **martyrdom** noun [from a Greek word martur meaning 'witness' and later 'martyr']

marvel noun a wonderful thing.
marvel verb (**marvelled, marvelling**) to be filled with wonder. [from an Old French word, from a Latin word mirabilis meaning 'wonderful']

marvellous adjective excellent, extremely good. SYNONYMS: excellent, outstanding, wonderful, remarkable, admirable, exceptional.
marvellously adverb

Marxism noun the political and economic theories of the German political philosopher and economist Karl Marx (1818–83), on which Communism is based. **Marxist** adjective & noun

marzipan (mar-zi-pan) noun a soft sweet food made of ground almonds, eggs, and sugar, often used as a covering on large cakes. [from an Italian word marzapane]

Masai (mah-siy or mə-siy) noun (**Masai**) 1 a member of a pastoral people living in Kenya and Tanzania. 2 the language of this people. [from the name in Masai]

masala (mə-sah-lə) noun a spice mixture used in Indian cookery. [from an Arabic word masalih meaning 'ingredients']

mascara noun a cosmetic for darkening the eyelashes. [from an Italian word meaning 'mask']

mascot noun a person or thing that is believed to bring good luck. [from a French word mascotte]

masculine adjective 1 to do with men or suitable for men. 2 having qualities traditionally associated with men. 3 (Grammar) (in some languages) belonging to the class that includes words referring to males or regarded as male.
masculine noun (Grammar) a masculine word or gender. **masculinity** noun [from a Latin word masculus meaning 'male']

maser (may-zer) noun a device for amplifying microwaves. [from the initial letters of microwave amplification by the stimulated emission of radiation]

mash verb to beat or crush something (especially food) into a soft mixture. SYNONYMS: pound, crush, grind.
mash noun 1 a soft mixture of cooked grain or bran, used as animal food. 2 (informal) mashed potatoes. [from an Old English word]

mask noun 1 a covering worn over the face to disguise or protect it. 2 a likeness of a person's face made in wax or clay. 3 a respirator worn over the face to filter air for breathing or to supply gas for inhaling.
mask verb 1 to cover the face with a mask. 2 to disguise or conceal something. SYNONYMS: hide, conceal, obscure, disguise, screen. [via French masque from an Italian word maschera]

masochist (mas-ə-kist) noun a person who gets sexual excitement from experiencing pain or humiliation. **masochism** noun **masochistic** adjective [named after the Austrian writer L. von Sacher-Masoch (1836–95), who wrote about masochism]

Mason noun a Freemason. **Masonic** (mə-sonn-ik) adjective **Masonry** noun

mason noun a person who builds or works with stone. [from an Old French word masson]

masonry noun the work of a mason, stonework.

masquerade (mas-ker-ayd) noun a false show or pretence.
masquerade verb to pretend to be what you are not ♦ He masqueraded as a doctor. [from a Spanish word máscara meaning 'mask']

mass noun 1 a coherent unit of matter with no specific shape. SYNONYMS: lump, chunk, hunk, dollop. 2 a large quantity or heap of something. SYNONYMS: heap, pile, mound, stack, load. 3 (Physics) the quantity of matter a body contains (in general usage called weight).
mass adjective involving a large number of people ♦ mass murder.
mass verb to gather into a mass, or assemble people or things into a mass.
the mass the majority. **the masses** the common people. [via French and Latin from a Greek word maza meaning 'barley cake']

Mass noun 1 (especially in the Roman Catholic Church) a celebration of the Eucharist. 2 the form of service used in this; a musical setting of certain parts of the text. [from an Old English word, from the Latin word missa]

massacre (mass-ə-ker) noun the killing of a large number of people.

massacre *verb* to slaughter people in large numbers. [from a French word]

massage (mas-ahzh) *noun* the rubbing and kneading of the body to lessen tension or pain.
massage *verb* to give someone a massage. [from a French word *masser*]

masseur (ma-ser) *noun* a person who provides massage professionally.

masseuse (ma-serz) *noun* a female masseur.

massif (ma-seef or ma-seef) *noun* a group of mountains forming a compact group. [a French word meaning 'massive']

massive *adjective* 1 large and heavy or solid. SYNONYMS: huge, immense, enormous, colossal, gigantic, mighty, vast. 2 unusually large or severe ♦ *a massive heart attack.* 3 substantial ♦ *a massive improvement.* **massively** *adverb* **massiveness** *noun* [from a French word, related to *mass*]

mass media *plural noun* the main media of news information, especially newspapers and broadcasting.

mass number *noun* (*Physics*) the total number of protons and neutrons in the nucleus of an atom.

mass-produce *verb* to manufacture products in large numbers by standardized processes. **mass production** *noun*

mast [1] *noun* 1 a long upright pole that supports a ship's sails. 2 a tall pole from which a flag is flown. 3 a tall steel structure holding the aerials of a radio or television transmitter. [from an Old English word]

mast [2] *noun* the fruit of beech, oak, chestnut, and other forest trees, used as food for pigs. [from an Old English word]

master *noun* 1 a man who has charge of people or things. 2 the male owner of a dog. 3 a male teacher. 4 a person with great skill, a great artist. 5 a chess player of proven ability at international level. 6 an original document, film, or recording from which copies can be made.
master *verb* 1 to overcome someone or something, to bring someone or something under control. SYNONYMS: control, subdue, subjugate, suppress. 2 to learn a subject or skill thoroughly. SYNONYMS: learn, grasp; (*informal*) get the hang of. [from a Latin word *magister* with the same meaning]

masterclass *noun* a class given to students by a distinguished musician.

masterful *adjective* 1 (said about a person) powerful or domineering. 2 very skilful.
masterfully *adverb*
◊ See the note at **masterly**.

master key *noun* a key that opens several locks, each of which has its own individual key.

masterly *adjective* worthy of a master, very skilful.
◊ Note that this word does not mean 'powerful or domineering'; use *masterful* for this meaning.

mastermind *noun* 1 a person with outstanding mental ability. 2 the person who is planning or directing a complex enterprise.
mastermind *verb* to plan and direct a complex enterprise.

Master of Arts *noun* (*Masters of Arts*) a person who has taken the degree higher than Bachelor of Arts.

master of ceremonies *noun* a person who introduces the speakers at a formal event, or the entertainers at a variety show.

Master of Science *noun* (*Masters of Science*) a person who has taken the degree higher than Bachelor of Science.

masterpiece *noun* an outstanding piece of work.

mastery *noun* 1 complete control over someone or something. 2 thorough knowledge or skill ♦ *his mastery of Arabic.*

masthead *noun* 1 the highest part of a ship's mast. 2 the title details of a newspaper at the top of the front page.

mastic *noun* 1 a gum or resin exuded from certain trees. 2 a filler or sealant used in building. [from a Greek word *mastikhē*]

masticate *verb* to chew food. **mastication** *noun* [from a Greek word *mastikhan* meaning 'to gnash the teeth']

mastiff *noun* a large strong dog with drooping ears. [from an Old French word *mastin*]

mastodon (mast-ə-don) *noun* a large extinct animal like an elephant. [from Greek words *mastos* meaning 'breast' and *odous* meaning 'tooth', referring to the rounded projections on its molar teeth]

mastoid *noun* part of a bone behind the ear. [from a Greek word *mastoeidēs* meaning 'breast-shaped']

masturbate *verb* to get sexual pleasure by stimulating the genitals with the hand. **masturbation** *noun* [from a Latin word *masturbari* with the same meaning]

mat *noun* 1 a piece of material used as a floor covering, a small carpet. 2 a small piece of material placed on a surface to prevent damage from an object placed on it. 3 a thick pad for landing on in gymnastics. 4 a small piece of material for resting a computer mouse on. **mat** *verb* (**matted, matting**) to become entangled or form a thick mass ♦ *matted hair.* [from an Old English word]

Matabele (mat-ə-bee-li) *noun* (**Matabele**) a member of a Bantu-speaking people of Zimbabwe.

matador (mat-ə-dor) *noun* a performer who challenges and kills the bull in a bullfight. [from a Spanish word *matar* meaning 'to kill']

match [1] *noun* a short thin piece of wood with a head made of material that bursts into flame when rubbed on a rough or specially prepared surface. [from an Old French word]

match [2] *noun* 1 a contest between people or teams in a game or sport. SYNONYMS: game, tie, contest. 2 a person or animal that is able to compete with another as an equal. 3 a person or thing exactly like or corresponding to another. 4 a marriage. 5 a person considered as a possible partner in marriage. **match** *verb* 1 to be the equal of someone else in quality or skill. SYNONYMS: equal, measure up to, compare with, live up to, rival; (*informal*) touch. 2 to place a competitor or team in a competition ♦ *Once again England and Scotland are matched against each other.* 3 to be like or harmonize with something else in colour or quality ♦ *His new hat matches his coat.* SYNONYMS: go with, suit. 4 to find something similar to another thing ♦ *I want to match this wool.* [from an Old English word]

matchboard *noun* a piece of board with a tongue cut along one edge which fits into a groove in the next piece.

matchbox *noun* a small box in which matches are sold.

matchless *adjective* having no equal, incomparable.

matchmaker *noun* a person who arranges marriages between other people. **matchmaking** *adjective & noun*

match point *noun* (in tennis and other sports) a point which will win a player the match.

matchstick *noun* the stem of a match.

matchwood *noun* wood that splinters easily, or that has been reduced to splinters.

mate [1] *noun* 1 (*informal*) a companion or friend. 2 each of a mated pair of birds or animals. 3 a fellow member or sharer of something ♦ *a team-mate* ♦ *a flat-mate.* 4 an officer on a merchant ship ranking next below the master. 5 an assistant or deputy in some trades ♦ *a plumber's mate.* **mate** *verb* 1 (said about birds or animals) to come together or bring two together in order to breed. 2 to put things together as a pair or because they correspond. [from a German word]

mate [2] *noun* a position in chess in which the king is in check and cannot escape, checkmate. **mate** *verb* (in chess) to put the opposing king into checkmate. [a shortening of *checkmate*]

mater (may-ter) *noun* (*old use*) mother. [a Latin word]

material *noun* 1 the substance or things from which something is or can be made. 2 cloth or fabric. 3 facts, information, or ideas that can be used in writing or composing something. 4 a person of a certain quality or suitability ♦ *He is a fine player but not international material.* **material** *adjective* 1 made of physical matter, as distinct from things of the mind or spirit. SYNONYMS: physical, real, tangible. 2 to do with bodily comfort ♦ *our material well-being.* 3 important or relevant ♦ *Your objection is not material to the issue we are discussing.* [from a Latin word *materia* meaning 'matter']

materialism *noun* 1 a tendency to regard material possessions as more important than spiritual or intellectual values. 2 (*Philosophy*) a belief that only the material world exists. **materialist** *noun* **materialistic** *adjective*

materialize *verb* 1 to appear or become visible ♦ *The ghost failed to materialize.* 2 to become a fact, to happen ♦ *The threatened strike did not materialize.* **materialization** *noun*

materially *adverb* significantly, considerably.

maternal (mə-ter-nəl) *adjective* 1 to do with a mother or with motherhood. 2 motherly. 3 related through your mother ♦ *my maternal uncle.* **maternally** *adverb* [from a Latin word *mater* meaning 'mother']

maternity (mə-ter-niti) *noun* 1 motherhood. 2 suitable for women in pregnancy or childbirth ♦ *maternity clothes.* [same origin as for *maternal*]

matey *adjective* (**matier, matiest**) (*informal*) sociable or friendly. **matily** *adverb* **matiness** *noun*

mathematician *noun* a person who is skilled in mathematics.

mathematics *noun* the science of numbers, measurements, and shapes. **mathematical** *adjective* **mathematically** *adverb* [from a Greek word *mathēma* meaning 'science']

maths *noun* (*informal*) mathematics.

matinée (mat-in-ay) *noun* an afternoon performance at a theatre or cinema. [a French word meaning 'morning' (as a period of activity), because performances used to be in the morning as well]

matins *noun* (in the Church of England) a service of morning prayer. [from a Latin word *matutinus* meaning 'in the morning']

matriarch (may-tri-ark) *noun* a woman who is the head of a family or tribe. **matriarchal** (may-tri-ark-əl) *adjective* [from a Latin word *mater* meaning 'mother' and a Greek word *arkhein* meaning 'to rule']

matriarchy (may-tri-ark-i) *noun* (**matriarchies**) 1 a social organization in which the mother is head of the family and descent is through the female line. 2 a system of government in which women have most of the authority.

matricide (may-tri-syd) *noun* 1 the act of killing one's mother. 2 a person who is guilty of this. **matricidal** *adjective* [from Latin words *mater* meaning 'mother' and *caedere* meaning 'to kill']

matriculate (mə-trik-yoo-layt) *verb* to be admitted as a member of a university. **matriculation** *noun* [from a Latin word *matricula* meaning 'register', related to *matrix*]

matrimony (mat-ri-məni) *noun* marriage. **matrimonial** (mat-ri-moh-niəl) *adjective* [from a Latin word *matrimonium*]

matrix (may-triks) *noun* (**matrices**) 1 a mould or framework in which something is made or allowed to develop. 2 (*Mathematics*) an array of quantities or expressions in rows and columns that is treated as a single quantity. 3 (*Computing*) an interconnected array of circuit elements that resembles a lattice or grid. [from a Latin word *matrix* meaning 'womb']

matron *noun* 1 a woman in charge of the domestic and medical arrangements at a boarding school. 2 a woman in charge of the nursing at a hospital or other institution, now officially called **senior nursing officer**. 3 a married woman, especially one who is dignified or elderly. [from a Latin word *matrona*, related to *maternal*]

matronly *adjective* like or suitable for a dignified married woman.

matron of honour *noun* a married woman attending the bride at a wedding.

matt *adjective* (said about a colour or surface) having a dull finish, not shiny. [from a French word *mat*]

matter *noun* 1 a substance or material that you can touch and see, as distinct from the mind and spirit. SYNONYMS: stuff, substance, material. 2 a particular substance or material ♦ *solid matter.* 3 material for thought or expression; the content of a book or speech as distinct from its form ♦ *subject matter.* 4 things of a specified kind ♦ *reading matter.* 5 something to be considered or thought about ♦ *a serious matter* ♦ *a matter for complaint.* SYNONYMS: topic, issue, concern, affair, question, business. 6 a quantity or amount ♦ *The ambulance arrived in a matter of minutes.* **matter** *verb* to be of importance ♦ *It doesn't matter.* **the matter** the thing that is causing a problem or difficulty ♦ *I can't think what the matter could be.* **for that matter** as well, as an important factor (in addition to another already mentioned). **as a matter of fact** in fact, indeed. **no matter** it is of no importance. [same origin as for *material*]

matter-of-fact *adjective* keeping to facts, not imaginative or emotional ♦ *She spoke about death in a very matter-of-fact way.*

matting *noun* rough material for covering floors.

mattock *noun* an agricultural tool with the blade set at right angles to the handle, used for loosening soil and digging out roots.

mattress *noun* a fabric covering filled with soft or springy material, used on or as a bed. [via French from an Arabic word *matrah* meaning 'carpet' or 'cushion']

maturation (mat-yoor-ay-shən) *noun* (*formal*) the process of maturing, ripening.

mature *adjective* **1** fully grown or developed. SYNONYMS: adult, fully-grown, developed. **2** having or showing fully developed mental powers, capable of reasoning and acting sensibly. **3** (said about wine) having reached a good stage of development. **4** (said about a bill) due for payment.
mature *verb* to become mature, or to make something mature. **maturely** *adverb*
maturity *noun* [from a Latin word *maturus* meaning 'ripe']

matzo *noun* (**matzos** or **matzoth**) a crisp biscuit of unleavened bread, eaten by Jews during Passover. [a Yiddish word]

maudlin *adjective* sentimental in a silly or tearful way. [from an old pronunciation of the name of Mary Magdalen (because pictures usually show her weeping)]

maul *verb* to injure a person or animal badly by treating them very roughly. [from an earlier meaning 'to knock down', from a Latin word *malleus* meaning 'hammer']

maunder *verb* to act or talk in a rambling way. [perhaps from an old word *maunder* meaning 'to beg']

Maundy money *noun* specially minted silver coins that the monarch gives to the poor in a ceremony on the Thursday before Easter (Maundy Thursday). [via Old French from a Latin word *mandatum* meaning 'commandment']

mausoleum (maw-sə-lee-əm) *noun* a large or magnificent tomb. [named after the tomb erected for King Mausolus of Caria in the 4th century BC at Halicarnassus in Asia Minor (modern Turkey)]

mauve (mohv) *noun* a pale purple colour. **mauve** *adjective* of this colour. [from a Latin word *malva* meaning 'mallow']

maverick (mav-er-ik) *noun* **1** a person who belongs to a group but often disagrees with its beliefs or acts independently. **2** (*North Amer.*) an unbranded calf or other young animal. [named after an American rancher, S. A. Maverick (1803–70), who did not brand his cattle]

maw *noun* the jaws or throat of an animal, especially one that eats large amounts of flesh. [from an Old English word]

mawkish *adjective* sentimental in a feeble or sickly way. [from an earlier meaning 'inclined to sickness', from an obsolete word *mawk* meaning 'maggot']

maxilla *noun* (**maxillae**) (*Anatomy and Zoology*) **1** the upper jaw or jawbone. (Compare **mandible**.) **2** a similar part in a bird or insect. [a Latin word meaning 'jaw']

maxim *noun* a short saying giving a general truth or rule of behaviour, e.g. 'Waste not, want not'. [from a Latin phrase *maxima propositio* meaning 'most important statement']

maximal *adjective* greatest or largest possible, being a maximum. **maximally** *adverb*

maximize *verb* **1** to make something as great or as large as possible. **2** to make the best use of something ♦ *The aim is to maximize our limited resources.* **maximization** *noun*

maximum *noun* (**maxima**) the greatest possible number or amount. **maximum** *adjective* greatest, greatest possible. [from a Latin word *maximus* meaning 'greatest']

May *noun* the fifth month of the year. [named after Maia, a Roman goddess]

may [1] *auxiliary verb* (see also **might** [2]) **1** expressing possibility ♦ *It may or may not be true.* **2** expressing permission ♦ *You may go if you like.* **3** expressing a wish ♦ *Long may she reign.* [from an Old English word] ◊ See the note at **can** [1].

may [2] *noun* hawthorn blossom.

Maya (miy-yə) *noun* (**Maya** or **Mayas**) **1** a member of an American Indian people of Mexico. **2** the language of this people. **Mayan** *adjective* [from the name in Maya]

maya (mah-yə) *noun* **1** (in Hinduism) the special power exercised by gods and demons. **2** (in Hindu and Buddhist philosophy) the power by which the universe exists and is visible; the material world, regarded as illusory. [from a Sanskrit word, from *ma* meaning 'to create']

maybe *adverb* perhaps, possibly.

May Day *noun* 1 May, celebrated in many countries as a spring festival with dancing or as an international day honouring workers.

Mayday *noun* an international radio signal of distress. [representing the pronunciation of French *m'aider* meaning 'help me']

mayfly *noun* (**mayflies**) an insect that lives for only a short time in the spring.

mayhem *noun* violent or damaging chaos or confusion. [from an Old French word, related to *maim*]

mayn't *verb* (*informal*) may not.

mayonnaise (may-ən-**ayz**) *noun* a creamy sauce made with egg yolks, oil, and vinegar, and eaten with salads. [a French word meaning 'from Mahon (on Minorca)', which the French had just captured when mayonnaise was first used]

mayor *noun* the head of the municipal corporation of a city or borough. **mayoral** (**mair**-əl) *adjective* [from an Old French word *maire*, related to *major*]

mayoress *noun* the wife of a mayor, or a woman holding the office of mayor.

maypole *noun* a tall pole for dancing round on May Day, with ribbons attached to the top.

maze *noun* 1 a confusing or disorganized amount of information. 2 a network of paths and hedges designed as a puzzle in which you try to find your way. [from *amaze*]

mazurka (mə-**zerk**-ə) *noun* a lively Polish dance in triple time, or the music for this. [from a Polish word *mazurka* meaning 'a woman from Mazovia' (a province of Poland)]

MBA *abbreviation* Master of Business Administration.

MBE *abbreviation* Member of the Order of the British Empire.

MC *abbreviation* 1 Master of Ceremonies. 2 Military Cross.

MCC *abbreviation* Marylebone Cricket Club, until 1969 the governing body that made the rules of cricket.

MD *abbreviation* Doctor of Medicine.

ME *abbreviation* myalgic encephalomyelitis, a medical condition of unknown cause with fever, fatigue, and muscular pain.

me *pronoun* the form of *I* used as the object of a verb or after a preposition. [from an Old English word]

mead *noun* an alcoholic drink made from fermented honey and water. [from an Old English word]

meadow *noun* a field of grass. [from an Old English word]

meadowsweet *noun* a plant with fragrant creamy-white flowers, often growing in damp meadows.

meagre (**meeg**-er) *adjective* scanty in amount, barely enough ♦ *a meagre diet.* SYNONYMS: scanty, sparse, inadequate. [from an Old French word *maigre*]

meal¹ *noun* 1 each of the regular occasions when food is eaten. 2 food eaten at this time. **to make a meal of** (*informal*) to carry out a task with unnecessary effort. [from an Old English word *mæl*]

meal² *noun* coarsely ground grain or pulse. **mealy** *adjective* [from an Old English word *melu*]

meal ticket *noun* a person or thing that provides you with a livelihood.

mealy-mouthed *adjective* reluctant or too timid to speak honestly and frankly.

mean¹ *verb* (past tense and past participle **meant**) 1 to have as your purpose or intention ♦ *They clearly mean to win.* SYNONYMS: intend, plan, aim, propose. 2 to design or intend something for a purpose ♦ *We mean the room to be an office.* 3 to intend to convey a significance or to refer to a thing ♦ *The sign means no entrance.* SYNONYMS: signify, indicate, convey, show. 4 (said about a word or expression) to have a significance as an equivalent in the same or another language ♦ *'Maybe' means 'perhaps'.* 5 to have something as a consequence or result ♦ *It means catching the early train* ♦ *This means war.* 6 to be of a specified importance to someone ♦ *The honour meant a lot to her.* **to mean business** (*informal*) to be ready to take action. **to mean it** to be serious about your intentions. [from an Old English word *mænan*]

mean² *adjective* 1 not generous, miserly. SYNONYMS: stingy, ungenerous, miserly, tight-fisted. 2 unkind or spiteful ♦ *It was mean to send them away.* SYNONYMS: unkind, unfriendly, nasty, spiteful, cruel. 3 poor in quality or appearance ♦ *a mean little house.* SYNONYMS: humble, lowly, inferior, shabby, scruffy, squalid. 4 vicious. **meanly** *adverb*

meanness noun [from an Old English word *mæne*]

mean [3] noun 1 a point or number midway between two extremes. 2 (also **arithmetic mean**) the average of two or more quantities. (See also **geometric mean**.) **mean** adjective midway between two points, average. **geometric mean** the value obtained by multiplying two quantities together and finding the square root of their product, or by multiplying three quantities and finding the cube root, and so on. **in the mean time** in the intervening period of time. [from an Old French word, related to *medial*]

meander (mee-an-der) verb 1 (said about a river or road) to take a winding course. 2 to wander about aimlessly. [named after the Maeander, a river in Turkey (now Menderes)]

meaning noun what you mean, or what something means.
meaning adjective full of meaning, expressive ♦ *She gave him a meaning look.*

meaningful adjective full of meaning, significant. **meaningfully** adverb

meaningless adjective having no meaning. **meaninglessly** adverb

means plural 1 a way of achieving something or producing a result ♦ *We will have to resort to other means.* 2 money or other wealth as a means of supporting someone ♦ *I think he must have private means.* SYNONYMS: money, funds, resources; (*informal*) wherewithal. **by all means** certainly. **by means of** using as a means or method ♦ *The load was moved by means of a crane.* **by no means** not nearly ♦ *It is by no means certain.* [from *mean*[3]]

means test noun an inquiry to see how much money or income a person has, in order to determine the level of state assistance they need.

meant past tense and past participle of **mean**[1].

meantime adverb (also **in the meantime**) meanwhile. [from *mean*[3] and *time*]

meanwhile adverb in the time between two events or while something else is happening. [from *mean*[3] and *while*]

measles noun an infectious disease producing small red spots on the skin. [probably from a German and Dutch word *masele* meaning 'pimple']

measly adjective (*informal*) miserably small or inadequate. [from earlier meanings 'affected by measles' and then 'blotchy', 'of poor quality']

measurable adjective able to be measured, or large enough to be measured.

measure verb 1 to find the size, amount, or extent of something by comparing it with a fixed unit or with an object of known size. SYNONYMS: calculate, assess, determine, gauge. 2 to be of a certain size ♦ *The room measures four metres by three.* 3 to estimate the value or quality of something by comparing it with a standard. SYNONYMS: assess, evaluate, estimate.
measure noun 1 action taken to achieve a purpose ♦ *The government will take measures to stop tax evasion.* 2 the size or quantity of something as found by measuring. 3 an extent or amount ♦ *They have had a measure of success.* 4 a unit or standard used in measuring ♦ *A kilometre is a measure of length.* 5 a device used in measuring. 6 the rhythm or metre of poetry or music. 7 a layer of rock or mineral. **made to measure** made to fit the measurements taken. **to measure out** to take or provide a measured quantity of something. **to measure up to** to reach the standard required by someone or something. [via Old French *mesure* from a Latin word *mensura*]

measured adjective 1 rhythmical or regular in movement ♦ *He walked with a measured tread.* 2 carefully considered ♦ *She spoke in measured language.*

measurement noun 1 the process of measuring something. 2 a size or amount found by measuring.

meat noun the flesh of an animal (especially a mammal) used as food. [from an Old English word *mete* meaning 'food']

meaty adjective (**meatier, meatiest**) 1 like meat. 2 full of meat, fleshy. 3 full of information or substance ♦ *a meaty book.*

Mecca noun a place that people with certain interests are eager to visit. [from the city of Mecca in Saudi Arabia, the chief place of pilgrimage for Muslims]

mechanic noun a person who maintains and repairs machinery.

mechanical adjective 1 to do with machines or machinery. 2 produced or worked by machinery. 3 done or doing things without much thought or effort. 4 to do with forces and motion. **mechanically** *adverb* [from a Greek word *mēkhanē* meaning 'machine']

mechanical engineer *noun* an engineer who designs and builds machines. **mechanical engineering** *noun*

mechanics *noun* 1 the scientific study of forces and motion. 2 the science of machinery.
mechanics *plural noun* the processes by which something is done or functions.

mechanism *noun* 1 the moving parts of a machine. 2 the way a machine works. 3 the process by which something is done ♦ *There is no mechanism for making complaints.*

mechanize (mek-ə-niyz) *verb* to equip a place or organization with machines. **mechanization** *noun*

medal *noun* a small flat piece of metal shaped like a coin, star, or cross and with an inscription or design, commemorating an event or given as an award for an achievement. [from a French word *médaille*, from a Latin word *medalia* for a coin worth half a denarius]

medallion (mid-al-yən) *noun* a large medal, usually worn round the neck as an ornament. [via French from an Italian word *medaglione*, related to *medal*]

medallist *noun* a competitor who wins a medal as a prize ♦ *a gold medallist.*

meddle *verb* 1 to interfere in people's affairs. SYNONYMS: interfere, pry, snoop, intrude. ♦ *Don't meddle with it.* SYNONYMS: tinker, interfere, play about. **meddler** *noun* [from an Old French word *medler*, related to *mix*]

meddlesome *adjective* often meddling or interfering.

Mede *noun* an inhabitant of the ancient kingdom of Media (now parts of Iraq, Iran, and Azerbaijan).

media (meed-iə) *plural noun* plural of **medium. the media** newspapers, radio, and television, which convey information to the public.
◊ This word is a plural noun and should have a plural verb, e.g. *The media have ignored this story.* It is incorrect to refer to one of them (e.g. television) as *a media* or *this media.*

mediaeval *adjective* another spelling of **medieval.**

medial (mee-di-əl) *adjective* situated in the middle. **medially** *adverb* [from a Latin word *medius* meaning 'middle']

median (mee-di-ən) *adjective* situated in or passing through the middle.
median *noun* 1 a middle point or line. 2 a medial number or point in a series.

mediate (mee-di-ayt) *verb* 1 to negotiate between the opposing sides in a dispute. SYNONYMS: negotiate, arbitrate, intercede. 2 to bring about a settlement by negotiation. **mediation** *noun* **mediator** *noun* [from a Latin word *medius* meaning 'middle']

medic *noun* (*informal*) a doctor or medical student.

medical *adjective* to do with medicine or the treatment of disease.
medical *noun* an examination to see how healthy and fit a person is. **medically** *adverb* [from a Latin word *medicus* meaning 'doctor']

medical practitioner *noun* a doctor or surgeon.

medicament (mid-ik-ə-mənt) *noun* (*formal*) a medicine, ointment, or other substance used in medical treatment. [same origin as for *medicated*]

medicated *adjective* treated or impregnated with a medicinal substance ♦ *medicated shampoo.*

medication *noun* 1 a medicine. 2 treatment using medicine.

medicinal (mid-iss-in-əl) *adjective* 1 to do with medicine. 2 having healing properties. **medicinally** *adverb*

medicine (med-sən) *noun* 1 a substance, usually swallowed, used to treat a disease or ailment. 2 the study and treatment of diseases and disorders of the body. **to give someone a dose of their own medicine** to give someone the same bad treatment that they have inflicted on others. [same origin as for *medical*]

medicine man *noun* (among some peoples) a shaman, a person who treats illness by calling on good and evil spirits.

medieval (med-i-ee-vəl) *adjective* belonging to or to do with the Middle Ages. [from a Latin word *medius* meaning 'middle' and *aevum* meaning 'age']

mediocre (meed-i-oh-ker) *adjective* only of medium quality, not very good.
SYNONYMS: indifferent, ordinary, second-rate, fair, commonplace, run-of-the-mill. **mediocrity**

(meed-i-**ok**-riti) *noun* [from a Latin word *mediocris* meaning 'of medium height']

meditate *verb* 1 to think deeply and quietly. 2 to plan something in the mind. SYNONYMS: consider, contemplate, ponder, cogitate. **meditation** *noun* [from a Latin word *meditari* meaning 'to contemplate']

meditative (med-it-ətiv) *adjective* meditating, or using meditation. **meditatively** *adverb*

Mediterranean *adjective* to do with the Mediterranean Sea, the sea which lies between Europe and Africa, or the countries round it. [from the Latin name *mare Mediterraneum* meaning 'sea in the middle of land' , from *media* meaning 'middle' and *terra* meaning 'land']

medium *noun* (**media** or **mediums**) 1 a middle quality or degree between two extremes. 2 a substance or surroundings in which something exists or moves or is transmitted ♦ *Air is the medium through which sound travels.* 3 a means for doing something ♦ *Television is a powerful medium for advertising.* 4 a liquid, such as oil or water, in which pigments are mixed for use in painting. 5 the material or form used by an artist or composer ♦ *Sculpture is his medium.* 6 (**mediums**) a person who claims to be able to communicate with the spirits of the dead.
medium *adjective* between two extremes or amounts; average, moderate ♦ *The suspect was described as being fair and of medium height.* SYNONYMS: average, middling, middle, normal, moderate, ordinary. [from a Latin word *medium* meaning 'middle thing']
◊ See also the entry for **media**.

medium wave *noun* a radio wave of a frequency between 300 kilohertz and 3 megahertz.

medlar *noun* 1 a fruit like a small brown apple that is not edible until it begins to decay. 2 the tree that bears this fruit. [from an Old French word *medle*]

medley *noun* (**medleys**) 1 an assortment of things. 2 a collection of musical items or songs played as a continuous piece. [from an Old French word *medlee*, related to *mix*]

medulla (mi-**dul**-ə) *noun* 1 (*Anatomy*) the central part of an organ or tissue, especially of a kidney or a hair. 2 (*Botany*) the soft internal tissue of plants. [a Latin word meaning 'pith' or 'marrow']

medulla oblongata (ob-long-**gah**-tə) *noun* (*Anatomy*) the lowest part of the brain, forming a continuation with the spinal cord in the skull.

meek *adjective* quiet and obedient. SYNONYMS: docile, obedient, compliant, quiet, unassuming, gentle, meek. **meekly** *adverb* **meekness** *noun* [from an Old Norse word *mjukr* meaning 'soft or gentle']

meerkat *noun* a small mongoose of southern Africa. [from Dutch words *meer* meaning 'sea' and *kat* meaning 'cat']

meerschaum (meer-shəm) *noun* a tobacco pipe with a bowl made from a white clay-like substance that darkens in use. [a German word meaning 'sea foam']

meet[1] *verb* (past tense and past participle **met**) 1 (said about one person) to come face to face with a person or people. SYNONYMS: encounter, come across, run into, see. 2 to make the acquaintance of a person for the first time ♦ *We met at a party.* 3 (said about several people) to come together, usually for a purpose. SYNONYMS: gather, assemble, come together, collect, congregate. 4 to come into contact, to touch. 5 (said about roads or paths) to join or cross each other. SYNONYMS: converge, merge, join, come together. 6 to come together as opponents ♦ *The teams will meet in the final next month.* 7 to go to a place to receive someone when they arrive ♦ *I will try to meet your train.* 8 to experience or receive something, usually unwelcome ♦ *They have met with difficulties* ♦ *He met his death.* 9 to satisfy or fulfil a demand or requirement; to pay a cost or debt.
meet *noun* a gathering of riders and hounds for a hunt. **to meet the eye** or **ear** to be visible or audible. [from an Old English word *metan*]

meet[2] *adjective* (*old use*) proper or suitable. [from an Old English word *gemæte*]

meeting *noun* 1 coming together. 2 a number of people who have come together for a discussion, contest, etc.

mega- (**meg**-ə)*prefix* 1 large or great (as in *megaphone*). 2 one million (as in *megavolts*, *megawatts*). [from a Greek word *megas* meaning 'great']

megadeath *noun* the death of one million people, as a unit in estimating the possible casualties in nuclear war.

megahertz *noun* a unit of frequency of electromagnetic waves, equal to one million hertz.

megalith (meg-ə-lith) *noun* (*Archaeology*) a huge stone forming the whole or part of a prehistoric monument. **megalithic** (megə-lith-ik) *adjective* [from *mega-* and a Greek word *lithos* meaning 'stone']

megalomania (meg-əl-ə-may-niə) *noun* **1** an exaggerated idea of your own importance. **2** an obsessive desire to do things on a grand scale. **megalomaniac** *noun* [from *mega-* and *mania*]

megalopolis (meg-ə-lop-ə-lis) *noun* a large heavily populated city. [from *mega-* and a Greek word *polis* meaning 'city']

megaphone *noun* a funnel-shaped device for amplifying the voice. [from *mega-* and a Greek word *phōnē* meaning 'voice']

megaton (meg-ə-tun) *noun* a unit of explosive power equal to that of one million tons of TNT.

megavolt *noun* a unit of electromotive force equal to one million volts.

megawatt *noun* a unit of electrical power equal to one million watts.

megohm *noun* a unit of electrical resistance equal to one million ohms.

meiosis (miy-oh-sis) *noun* **1** (*Biology*) a process of cell division in which daughter cells are formed, each containing half the number of chromosomes of the parent cell. (Compare **mitosis**.) **2** (*Grammar*) a figure of speech using understatement, as in *It's only a scratch* referring to a painful wound. [from a Greek word meaning 'lessening']

melamine (mel-ə-meen) *noun* a tough kind of plastic. [from *melam*, a chemical used to make melamine]

melancholia (mel-ən-koh-liə) *noun* mental depression. **melancholic** (mel-ən-kol-ik) *adjective*

melancholy (mel-ən-kəli) *noun* **1** depression or deep sadness. **2** an atmosphere of gloom.
melancholy *adjective* sad or gloomy. SYNONYMS: sad, unhappy, gloomy, downcast, dejected, depressed, despondent, miserable. [from Greek words *melas* meaning 'black' and *kholē* meaning 'bile']

Melanesian (mel-ə-nee-ziən) *adjective* to do with or coming from Melanesia, a group of islands in the SW Pacific.

Melanesian *noun* a person born in Melanesia, or descended from people born there. [from Greek words *melas* meaning 'black' and *nēsos* meaning 'island']

mélange (may-lahnzh) *noun* a mixture. [French]

melanin (mel-ən-in) *noun* a dark pigment found in skin and hair. [from Greek *melas* meaning 'black']

melanoma (melə-noh-mə) *noun* a form of skin cancer that develops in melanin-forming cells.

Melba toast *noun* thin crisp toast. [named after the Australian opera singer Dame Nellie Melba (1861–1931)]

mêlée (mel-ay) *noun* **1** a confused fight. **2** a muddle. [a French word meaning 'medley']

mellifluous (mel-if-loo-əs) *adjective* soft and pleasant to hear. [from Latin words *mel* meaning 'honey' and *fluere* meaning 'to flow']

mellow *adjective* **1** sweet and rich in flavour. SYNONYMS: ripe, sweet, mature. **2** (said about a sound or colour) soft and rich, free from harshness or sharp contrast. SYNONYMS: rich, ripe, soft, full. **3** (said about a person) made kindly and sympathetic by age or experience. SYNONYMS: genial, kind, amiable, good-natured, easygoing, tolerant.
mellow *verb* to make something or someone mellow, or to become mellow. **mellowly** *adverb* **mellowness** *noun* [perhaps related to *meal²*]

melodic (mil-od-ik) *adjective* **1** to do with melody. **2** pleasant-sounding.

melodious (mil-oh-diəs) *adjective* tuneful or pleasant-sounding. **melodiously** *adverb*

melodrama (mel-ə-drah-mə) *noun* **1** a play full of dramatic excitement and strong emotion. **2** plays of this kind. **3** language or behaviour resembling this. **melodramatic** (mel-ə-drə-mat-ik) *adjective* **melodramatically** *adverb* [from a Greek word *melos* meaning 'music' and *drama*]

melody *noun* (**melodies**) **1** sweet music or tunefulness. **2** a song or tune ♦ *old Irish melodies*. **3** the main part in a piece of harmonized music. [from Greek words *melos* meaning 'music' and *ōidē* meaning 'song']

melon noun a large sweet fruit with a yellow or green skin, a sweet flesh, and many pips. [from a Latin word melo]

melt verb 1 to become liquid, or to make something liquid, by heating. 2 (said about food) to be softened or dissolved easily ♦ It melts in the mouth. 3 to fade or disappear gradually ♦ The crowd slowly melted away. SYNONYMS: disappear, disperse, vanish, evaporate. 4 to make someone gentler through pity or love. SYNONYMS: soften, mellow. [from an Old English word]

meltdown noun 1 the overheating of the core of a nuclear reactor. 2 a disastrous collapse or failure.

melting point noun the temperature at which a solid melts.

melting pot noun a situation in which things change radically or need to be reconsidered ♦ The future of the industry is in the melting pot.

meltwater noun water formed from the melting of snow and ice, especially in a glacier.

member noun 1 a person or thing that belongs to a particular group or society. 2 a part of a complex structure. 3 (old use) a part of the body. [from a Latin word membrum meaning 'limb']

Member of Parliament noun a person elected to represent a constituency and take part in the proceedings of Parliament.

membership noun 1 being a member. 2 the total number of members.

membrane (mem-brayn) noun 1 a thin skin or similar covering. 2 (Zoology) a thin sheet-like covering, lining, or partition in an organism or cell. **membranous** (mem-brən-əs) adjective [from a Latin word membrum meaning 'limb']

meme noun (Biology) a characteristic that is passed on by non-genetic means, such as by imitation. [from a Greek word mimēma meaning 'something imitated']

memento (mim-ent-oh) noun (**mementos** or **mementoes**) a souvenir. [a Latin word meaning 'remember']

memo (mem-oh) noun (**memos**) (informal) a memorandum.

memoir (mem-wahr) noun a short personal biography written by the subject or someone who knew the subject. [from a French word mémoire meaning 'memory']

memorable (mem-er-əbəl) adjective 1 worth remembering ♦ a memorable experience. SYNONYMS: remarkable, outstanding, notable, impressive. 2 easy to remember ♦ a memorable tune. **memorability** noun **memorably** adverb

memorandum (mem-er-an-dəm) noun (**memoranda** or **memorandums**) 1 a note or record of events written as a reminder, for future use. 2 a note or message from one person to another in an organization. [a Latin word meaning 'thing to be remembered']

memorial noun 1 a structure or object put up in memory of a person or event. 2 an institution or custom established in memory of a person or event. **memorial** adjective serving as a memorial. [from a Latin word memoria meaning 'memory']

memorize verb to learn a thing so as to know it from memory.

memory noun (**memories**) 1 the ability to keep things in your mind and recall them at will. 2 something that you remember ♦ happy memories of childhood. 3 the length of time that people remember things ♦ within living memory. 4 the part of a computer in which data is stored for retrieval to operate programs. **in memory of** in honour of a person or thing remembered. [from a Latin word memor meaning 'remembering']

men plural of **man**.

menace noun 1 something that seems likely to bring harm or danger; a threat. 2 an annoying or troublesome person or thing. **menace** verb to threaten someone with harm or danger. SYNONYMS: threaten, intimidate, frighten, scare. **menacingly** adverb [from a Latin word minax meaning 'threatening']

ménage (may-nahzh) noun the members of a household. [a French word]

menagerie (min-aj-er-i) noun a collection of wild or strange animals kept in captivity for exhibition. [a French word, related to ménage]

mend verb 1 to repair something that is damaged or make it whole again. SYNONYMS: repair, fix. 2 to make something better, or to become better ♦ He said we should mend our manners. **mend** noun a repair or mended place in something. **on the mend** improving in health or condition. **mender** noun [from amend]

mendacious (men-**day**-shəs) adjective (formal) untruthful, telling lies. **mendaciously** adverb **mendacity** (men-**dass**-iti) noun [from a Latin word mendax meaning 'lying']

mendicant (men-**dik**-ənt) adjective begging, especially with reference to religious orders that were once dependent on alms. **mendicant** noun a beggar, or a member of a mendicant order of monks. [from a Latin word mendicans meaning 'begging']

menfolk plural noun men in general; the men of one's family.

menhir (men-**heer**) noun (Archaeology) a tall upright stone set up in prehistoric times. [from Breton words men meaning 'stone' and hir meaning 'long']

menial (meen-iəl) adjective lowly, not needing any skill ♦ menial tasks. **menial** noun a person who does menial tasks. **menially** adverb [from an Old French word]

meninges (min-**in**-jeez) plural noun (Anatomy) the membranes that enclose the brain and spinal cord. [from a Greek word mēninx]

meningitis (men-in-**jiy**-tiss) noun a disease caused by a virus, with inflammation of the meninges.

meniscus (min-**isk**-əs) noun (**menisci**) 1 (Physics) the curved upper surface of liquid in a tube, caused by surface tension. 2 a lens that is convex on one side and concave on the other. [from a Greek word mēniskos meaning 'crescent']

menopause (men-ə-pawz) noun the time of life (usually between 45 and 55) when a woman stops menstruating. **menopausal** adjective [from a Greek word mēnos meaning 'of a month' and pause]

menorah (mən-**or**-ə) noun 1 a candelabrum with seven branches, used in the Temple in ancient Jerusalem. 2 a candelabrum, usually with eight branches, used in modern synagogues and Jewish houses. [from a Hebrew word meaning 'candlestick']

menses plural noun blood and other matter discharged in menstruation. [a Latin word meaning 'months']

menstrual (men-stroo-əl) adjective to do with menstruating.

menstruate (men-stroo-ayt) verb to bleed from the womb about once a month, as girls and women do between puberty and middle age. **menstruation** noun [from a Latin word menstruus meaning 'monthly']

mensuration (men-sewr-**ay**-shən) noun 1 the process of measuring. 2 the mathematical rules for finding lengths, areas, and volumes. [from a Latin word mensura meaning 'a measure']

menswear noun (in shops) clothes for men.

mental adjective 1 to do with the mind, existing in or performed by the mind. 2 (informal) suffering from a disorder of the mind, mad. **mentally** adverb [from Latin mentis meaning 'of the mind']

mental age noun a person's mental ability expressed as the age at which an average person reaches this ability.

mental arithmetic noun calculations done in the head, without the aid of written figures.

mentality (men-**tal**-iti) noun (**mentalities**) a person's mental ability or attitude of mind.

menthol noun a solid white substance found in peppermint and other natural oils. [from a Latin word mentha meaning 'mint']

mentholated adjective impregnated with menthol.

mention verb to speak or write about a person or thing briefly; to refer to someone or something by name. SYNONYMS: refer to, speak about, allude to, comment on, touch on. **mention** noun an example of mentioning someone or something ♦ He didn't even get a mention. **not to mention** and as another important thing. [from a Latin word mentio (noun), related to mind]

mentor (men-tor) noun a trusted adviser. [from Mentor in Homer's Odyssey, who advised Odysseus' son Telemachus]

menu (men-yoo) noun (**menus**) 1 a list of dishes available in a restaurant. 2 (Computing) a list of options or commands displayed on a screen, from which the user makes a choice. [a French word meaning 'detailed list']

MEP abbreviation Member of the European Parliament.

mercantile (mer-kən-tiyl) adjective to do with trade or commerce. [from an Italian word mercante meaning 'merchant']

Mercator projection (mer-**kay**-ter) *noun* a system of map projection in which lines of latitude and longitude are straight lines with lines of latitude the same length as the equator. [named after Mercator, the name in Latin of the Flemish geographer Gerard Kremer (1512–94), who invented the system]

mercenary (mer-**sin**-er-i) *adjective* 1 working mainly for money or other gain. 2 (said about professional soldiers) hired to serve a foreign country. **mercenary** *noun* (**mercenaries**) a soldier hired to serve in a foreign country. **mercenariness** *noun* [from a Latin word *merces* meaning 'wages']

mercerized *adjective* (said about cotton fabric or thread) treated with a substance that gives it greater strength and a slight gloss. [named after a textile-maker John Mercer (1791–1866), who is said to have invented the process]

merchandise *noun* goods or commodities bought and sold, goods for sale. **merchandise** *verb* 1 to buy and sell goods. 2 to advertise an idea or person. [from a French word *marchand* meaning 'merchant']

merchant *noun* 1 a person involved in trade. 2 (*informal*) a person who is fond of an activity ♦ *a speed merchant*. [from a Latin word *mercari* meaning 'to trade']

merchantable *adjective* suitable for selling.

merchant bank *noun* a bank that gives loans and advice to businesses.

merchantman *noun* (**merchantmen**) a ship carrying merchandise.

merchant navy *noun* shipping used in commerce.

merciful *adjective* 1 showing mercy. SYNONYMS: kind, compassionate, humane, clement. 2 giving relief from pain or suffering ♦ *a merciful death*. **mercifully** *adverb*

merciless *adjective* showing no mercy, cruel. SYNONYMS: cruel, heartless, pitiless, ruthless, callous. **mercilessly** *adverb*

mercurial (mer-**kewr**-iəl) *adjective* 1 having sudden changes of mood. SYNONYMS: changeable, capricious, temperamental, unpredictable. 2 containing or involving mercury.

mercury *noun* a heavy silvery metal that is usually liquid, a chemical element (symbol Hg), used in some thermometers and barometers. **mercuric** (mer-**kewr**-ik) *adjective* **mercurous** *adjective* [named from the Roman god Mercury]

mercy *noun* (**mercies**) 1 kindness or compassion shown by not inflicting punishment or pain on an offender or enemy who is in your power. SYNONYMS: compassion, clemency, kindness. 2 something to be thankful for ♦ *It's a mercy no one was killed*. **at the mercy of** completely in the power of. [from an Old French word *merci* meaning 'pity' or 'thanks', related to *mercenary*]

mercy killing *noun* the killing of a person to release them from the suffering of an incurable disease.

mere¹ *adjective* nothing more than ♦ *He's a mere child*. **merely** *adverb* [from a Latin word *merus* meaning 'undiluted']

mere² *noun* (*poetic*) a lake.

merest *adjective* even very small or insignificant ♦ *The merest movement caused her pain*.

meretricious (merri-**trish**-əs) *adjective* showily attractive but cheap or false. [from a Latin word *meretrix* meaning 'prostitute']
◊ Do not confuse this word with **meritorious**, which has a different meaning.

merge *verb* 1 to unite or combine into a whole, or to make something do this ♦ *The two companies are going to merge* ♦ *The two companies will be merged*. SYNONYMS: amalgamate, combine, unite, join. 2 to pass slowly into something else, to blend or become blended. [from a Latin word *mergere* meaning 'to dip']

merger *noun* the combining of two business companies into one.

meridian (mer-**rid**-iən) *noun* a line on a map or globe passing from the North Pole to the South Pole and having a constant latitude. The meridian that passes through Greenwich in London is shown on maps as 0° longitude.

meringue (mer-**rang**) *noun* a crisp cake made from egg white and sugar. [a French word]

merino (mer-**ree**-noh) *noun* (**merinos**) 1 a kind of sheep with fine soft wool. 2 a kind of fine soft woollen material. [a Spanish word]

meristem (merri-stem) noun (*Botany*) plant tissue consisting of small cells that divide, producing new growth. [from a Greek word *meristos* meaning 'divisible']

merit noun 1 the quality of deserving praise, excellence. SYNONYMS: worth, value, quality, distinction, excellence. 2 a feature or quality that deserves praise ♦ *The book has the great merit of being short.*
merit verb (**merited, meriting**) to deserve something. SYNONYMS: deserve, earn, be entitled to. [from a Latin word *meritum* meaning 'deserved']

meritocracy (merri-tok-rəsi) noun (**meritocracies**) government by people of high ability. [from *merit* and *-cracy*]

meritorious (merri-tor-iəs) adjective having merit, deserving praise. SYNONYMS: praiseworthy, commendable, creditable. **meritoriously** adverb **meritoriousness** noun
◊ Do not confuse this word with **meretricious**, which has a different meaning.

merlin noun a kind of small falcon. [from an Old French word *esmerillon*]

mermaid noun a mythical sea creature having the body of a woman and the tail of a fish. **merman** noun [from *mere*[2] (in the meaning 'sea'), and *maid, man*]

merriment noun a lively time, fun or enjoyment.

merry adjective (**merrier, merriest**) 1 cheerful and lively, joyous. SYNONYMS: happy, cheerful, lively, bright, cheery, joyful, light-hearted, jolly. 2 (*informal*) slightly drunk. **to make merry** to have a lively time, to enjoy yourself. **merrily** adverb [from an Old English word *myrige* meaning 'pleasing' or 'delightful']

merry-go-round noun 1 a revolving machine with models of horses or cars for riding on for amusement. 2 a continuous series of occupations or events.

merrymaking noun a lively time, fun or enjoyment.

mescaline or **mescalin** (mesk-ə-leen or mesk-ə-lin) noun a drug that produces hallucinations, made from the dried disc-shaped tops of a Mexican cactus called mescal or peyote.

Mesdames plural of **Madame**.

Mesdemoiselles plural of **Mademoiselle**.

mesh noun 1 one of the spaces between threads in a net, sieve, or wire screen etc. 2 network fabric.
mesh verb (said about a toothed wheel etc.) to engage with one or more others. [probably from an Old English word]

mesmerism noun (*old use*) hypnosis.
mesmeric (mez-merrik) adjective [named after the Austrian physician F. A. Mesmer (1734–1815)]

mesmerize verb 1 (*old use*) to hypnotize someone. 2 to fascinate someone, to hold their attention completely. SYNONYMS: fascinate, enthrall, captivate.

Mesolithic (mess-ə-lith-ik) adjective (*Archaeology*) to do with or belonging to the period of time between the palaeolithic and the neolithic periods. [from Greek words *mesos* meaning 'middle' and *lithos* meaning 'stone']

meson (mee-zon) noun (*Physics*) a subatomic particle, between an electron and proton in mass, that binds nucleons together. [from a Greek word *mesos* meaning 'middle']

mesosphere (mess-ə-sfeer) noun the region of the earth's atmosphere above the stratosphere, between 50 and 80 km in altitude. [from a Greek word *mesos* meaning 'middle' and *sphere*]

Mesozoic (mess-ə-zoh-ik) adjective (*Geology*) belonging to the geological era lasting from about 248 to 65 million years ago. [from Greek words *mesos* meaning 'middle' and *zöion* meaning 'animal']

mess noun 1 a dirty or untidy condition, or an untidy collection of things. SYNONYMS: muddle, clutter, jumble, confusion, shambles, disarray. 2 a difficult or confused situation, trouble. SYNONYMS: difficulty, plight, predicament, quandary; (*informal*) pickle. 3 a portion of semi-solid food. 4 excrement left by a domestic animal. 5 a place where members of the armed forces have meals.
mess verb 1 to make something untidy or dirty. 2 (in the armed forces) to take meals with a group ♦ *The officers mess together.* **make a mess of** to bungle or mishandle something. **to mess about** or **around** to behave in a silly or playful way. **to mess up** to bungle or mishandle something. SYNONYMS: bungle, botch, mishandle, mismanage, spoil. **to mess with** to meddle or interfere with something. [from an Old French word *mes* meaning 'portion of food']

message noun 1 a spoken or written communication sent by one person to another. SYNONYMS: note, letter, communication. **2** the central theme or moral of a book, film, etc. **3** (*Scottish and Irish*) an errand. **to get the message** (*informal*) to understand what someone means. [via Old French from a Latin word *missus* meaning 'sent']

messenger *noun* someone who delivers a message.

messenger RNA *noun* a form of RNA (ribonucleic acid) in which genetic information is transferred from DNA to a ribosome.

Messiah (mi-siy-ə) *noun* **1** the expected deliverer and ruler of the Jewish people, whose coming was prophesied in the Old Testament. **2** Jesus Christ, regarded by Christians as the prophesied Messiah. **Messianic** *adjective* [from a Hebrew word meaning 'the anointed one']

Messieurs plural of **Monsieur**.

Messrs (mess-erz) *abbreviation* used as a plural of Mr to denote several people or a business name ♦ *Messrs Smith and Jones* ♦ *Messrs Brown & Co.*

messy *adjective* (**messier, messiest**) **1** untidy or dirty. SYNONYMS: untidy, dirty, disorderly, filthy; (*informal*) mucky. **2** causing a mess ♦ *a messy task.* **3** complicated and difficult to deal with. **messily** *adverb* **messiness** *noun*

met[1] past tense and past participle of **meet**[1].

Met *abbreviation* (*informal*) **1** the Meteorological Office. **2** The Metropolitan Police. **3** the Metropolitan Opera House in New York.

metabolism (mi-tab-əl-izm) *noun* the process by which food is built up into living material in a plant or animal, or used to supply it with energy. **metabolic** (met-ə-bol-ik) *adjective* [from a Greek word *metabolē* meaning 'a change']

metabolize (mi-tab-ə-liyz) *verb* to process food in metabolism.

metacarpus (met-ə-kar-pəs) *noun* the group of five bones of the hand between the wrist (called *carpus*) and the fingers. **metacarpal** *adjective*

metal *noun* a solid and usually hard mineral substance such as gold, silver, copper, iron, and uranium, or an alloy of any of these. **metal** *adjective* made of metal. **metal** *verb* (**metalled, metalling**) **1** to cover

or fit something with metal. **2** to make or mend a road with road metal. [from a Greek word *metallon*]

metallic (mi-tal-ik) *adjective* **1** of or like metal. **2** (said about a sound) like metal objects struck together, sharp and ringing. **metallically** *adverb*

metallurgy (mi-tal-er-ji) *noun* the study of the properties of metals and alloys. **metallurgical** (met-əl-er-jikəl) *adjective* **metallurgist** *noun* [from *metal* and a Greek word *-ourgia* meaning 'working']

metalwork *noun* **1** the art of making things from metal. **2** a shaped metal object.

metamorphic (met-ə-mor-fik) *adjective* (said about rock) that has had its structure or other properties changed by natural agencies such as heat and pressure, as in the transformation of limestone into marble. [from Greek words *meta-* meaning 'change' and *morphē* meaning 'form']

metamorphose (met-ə-mor-fohs) *verb* to change, or to change something, in form or character.

metamorphosis (met-ə-mor-fə-sis) *noun* (**metamorphoses**) a change of form or character. [same origin as for *metamorphic*]

metaphor (met-ə-fer) *noun* the use of a word or phrase in a special meaning that provides an image, as in *a blanket of fog* and *to take the rough with the smooth.* [from a Greek word *metapherein* meaning 'to transfer']

metaphorical (met-ə-fo-rikəl) *adjective* involving a metaphor, not literal. **metaphorically** *adverb*

metaphysics (met-ə-fiz-iks) *noun* **1** a branch of philosophy that deals with the nature of existence and of truth and knowledge. **2** (*informal*) abstract talk; mere theory. **metaphysical** (metə-fiz-ikəl) *adjective* [from a Latin word *metaphysica* meaning 'the things after the Physics', referring to a work of Aristotle that came after the work called Physics]

metatarsus (met-ə-tar-səs) *noun* the group of bones of the foot between the ankle (called *tarsus*) and the toes. **metatarsal** *adjective*

mete (meet) *verb* **to mete out** to give something that people deserve, usually something unpleasant such as punishment. [from an Old English word]

meteor (meet-i-er) *noun* a small body of matter from outer space that becomes luminous from compression of air as it enters the earth's atmosphere, and appears as a streak of light in the sky. [from a Greek word *meteōros* meaning 'high in the air']

meteoric (meet-i-o-rik) *adjective* 1 to do with meteors. 2 like a meteor in brilliance or sudden appearance ♦ *a meteoric career.*

meteorite (meet-i-er-riyt) *noun* a piece of rock or metal that has fallen to earth as a meteor.

meteoroid (meet-i-er-oid) *noun* a small body moving through space that would become a meteor if it entered the earth's atmosphere.

meteorological (meet-i-er-ə-loj-ik(ə)l) *adjective* to do with meteorology.

Meteorological Office *noun* a government department providing information and forecasts about the weather.

meteorology (meet-i-er-ol-ə-ji) *noun* the study of the conditions of the atmosphere, especially in order to forecast the weather. **meteorologist** *noun* [from a Greek word *meteōros* meaning 'high in the air' and *-logy*]

meter[1] *noun* a device that measures and indicates the quantity or rate of something, such as the amount of electricity used or the distance travelled. **meter** *verb* to measure the use of something by means of a meter. [from *mete*]
◊ Do not confuse this word with **metre**, which has a different meaning. See also **meter**[2].

meter[2] *noun* an American spelling of **metre**.

methane (mee-thayn) *noun* (*Chemistry*) an inflammable gas that is the main ingredient of natural gas. [from *methyl*, a chemical that methane contains]

methanol (meth-ən-ol) *noun* (*Chemistry*) an inflammable liquid hydrocarbon, used as a solvent.

methinks *verb* (*old use*) I think.

method *noun* 1 a procedure or way of doing something. SYNONYMS: way, procedure, means, manner, system, process, technique. 2 orderliness of thought or behaviour. [from a Greek word *methodos* meaning 'pursuit of knowledge']

methodical (mi-thod-ik(ə)l) *adjective* orderly or systematic. SYNONYMS: orderly, systematic, meticulous, painstaking. **methodically** *adverb*

Methodist *noun* a member of a Christian denomination originating in the 18th century and based on the teachings of John and Charles Wesley and their followers. **Methodism** *noun*

methodology (meth-ə-dol-ə-ji) *noun* (**methodologies**) a system or set of methods used in a particular activity.

methought *verb* (*old use*) I thought.

meths *noun* (*informal*) methylated spirit.

Methuselah (mi-thew-zə-lə) a very old person. [from the name of a Hebrew patriarch, the grandfather of Noah, who was said to have lived for 969 years]

methyl (meth-il) *noun* a chemical unit present in methane and in many organic compounds.

methyl alcohol *noun* methanol.

methylated spirit *noun* a form of alcohol used as a solvent and for heating, and made unpleasant for drinking by the addition of methyl and a violet dye.

meticulous (mi-tik-yoo-ləs) *adjective* very careful and precise. SYNONYMS: methodical, systematic, careful, precise, painstaking. **meticulously** *adverb* **meticulousness** *noun* [from a Latin word *meticulosus*, from *metus* meaning 'fear']

métier (met-yay) *noun* 1 a trade, profession, or field of activity. 2 what a person does best. [a French word]

metonymy (mi-ton-imi) *noun* a means of referring to an important or well-known person or institution by something it is closely associated with, such as the *Crown* for 'the Queen' or 'the King'. [from Greek words *meta-* meaning 'change' and *onuma* meaning 'name']

metre *noun* 1 a unit of length in the metric system (about 39.4 inches). 2 rhythm in poetry, or a particular form of it. [from a Greek word *metron* meaning 'measure']
◊ Do not confuse this word with **meter**, which has a different meaning.

metric *adjective* 1 of or using the metre or the metric system. 2 to do with metre in poetry. **metrically** *adverb*

metrical *adjective* to do with or composed in rhythmic metre, not prose ♦ *metrical psalms.*

metrication *noun* change to a metric system of measurement.

metric system *noun* a decimal system of weights and measures, using the metre, litre, and gram as units.

metric ton *noun* a unit of weight equal to 1,000 kilograms.

metro *noun* (*informal*) (**metros**) an underground railway in a city, especially Paris. [from a French word *métro*, a shortening of *métropolitain* meaning 'metropolitan (railway)']

metronome (met-rə-nohm) *noun* a device that makes a regular tick to indicate a tempo in music. [from a Greek word *metron* meaning 'measure' and *nomos* meaning 'law']

metropolis (mi-**trop**-əlis) *noun* the chief city of a country or region. [from a Greek word *mētēr* meaning 'mother' and *polis* meaning 'city']

metropolitan (metrə-**pol**-itən) *adjective* to do with or belonging to a metropolis.

Metropolitan Police *noun* the police force of London.

mettle *noun* a person's ability to deal with difficulties and challenges. **to be on your mettle** to be ready to show courage or ability. [a different spelling of *metal*]

mew *verb* to make the cry of a cat.
mew *noun* this cry. [an imitation of the sound]

mews *noun* a row of houses in a small street or square, converted from former stables. [first used of royal stables in London, built on the site of hawks' cages (called *mews*)]

Mexican *adjective* to do with or coming from Mexico in North America.
Mexican *noun* a person born in Mexico or descended from people born there.

Mexican wave *noun* a wave-like movement produced when successive sections of a seated crowd of spectators stand, raise their arms, and sit down again. [so called because it was first observed at World Cup football matches in Mexico City in 1986]

mezzanine (mets-ə-neen) *noun* an extra storey between the ground floor and first floor of a building, often in the form of a wide balcony. [from an Italian word *mezzano* meaning 'middle']

mezzo or **mezzo-soprano** (met-soh) *noun*

(**mezzos** or **mezzo-sopranos**) (*Music*) a voice between soprano and contralto, or a singer with this voice. [an Italian word meaning 'half']

mezzotint (met-soh-tint) *noun* a print made from an engraved copper or steel plate that has been roughened to give areas of shadow and smoothed to give areas of light. [from an Italian word *mezzotinto* meaning 'half tint']

Mg *abbreviation* (*Chemistry*) the symbol for magnesium.

MHz *abbreviation* megahertz.

miaow *verb* to make the cry of a cat.
miaow *noun* this cry. [an imitation of the sound]

miasma (mi-**az**-mə) *noun* unpleasant or unhealthy air. [from a Greek word meaning 'pollution']

mica (**miy**-kə) *noun* a mineral substance structured in layers, used to make electrical insulators. [a Latin word meaning 'crumb']

mice plural of **mouse**.

Michaelmas (**mik**-əl-məs) *noun* a Christian festival in honour of St Michael (29 September). [from Old English *Sanct Michaeles mæsse* meaning 'St Michael's Mass']

Michaelmas daisy *noun* an aster that flowers in autumn, with purple, dark-red, pink, or white flowers.

mickle *adjective* (*Scottish*) much, great.
mickle *noun* a large amount. [from an Old English word *micel* meaning 'great' or 'numerous']

micro- *prefix* **1** very small. **2** one-millionth of a unit (as in ♦ *microgram*). [from a Greek word *mikros* meaning 'small']

microbe *noun* a micro-organism, especially one that causes disease or is used for fermentation. [from *micro-* and a Greek word *bios* meaning 'life']

microbiology *noun* the study of micro-organisms. **microbiologist** *noun*

microchip *noun* a very small piece of silicon or similar material made to work like a complex wired electric circuit.

microclimate *noun* the climate of a very small area, such as part of a garden.

microcomputer *noun* a small computer with a microprocessor as its central processor.

microcosm (miy-krə-kozm) *noun* something regarded as resembling on a very small scale something much larger. (Compare **macrocosm**.) [from a Greek phrase *mikros kosmos* meaning 'little world']

microdot *noun* a photograph of a printed document reduced to the size of a dot.

microelectronics *noun* the design, manufacture, and use of microchips and microcircuits. **microelectronic** *adjective*

microfiche (miy-krə-feesh) *noun* a piece of film on which written or printed material is photographed in greatly reduced size. [from *micro-* and a French word *fiche* meaning 'slip of paper']

microfilm *noun* a length of film on which written or printed material is photographed in greatly reduced size. **microfilm** *verb* to make a microfilm of a document.

microhabitat *noun* (*Ecology*) the habitat of a very small area, differing from the areas round it.

microlight *noun* a very small aircraft for one person, like a hang-glider with a motor.

micrometer (miy-krom-it-er) *noun* an instrument for measuring small lengths or thicknesses.

micron (miy-kron) *noun* a unit of measurement equal to one-millionth of a metre.

micro-organism *noun* an organism that cannot be seen by the naked eye, e.g. a bacterium or virus.

microphone *noun* an instrument that picks up sound waves for amplifying, recording, or broadcasting. [from *micro-* and a Greek word *phōnē* meaning 'sound']

microprocessor *noun* an integrated circuit functioning as the processor of a computer.

microscope *noun* an instrument with lenses that magnify objects or details too small to be seen by the naked eye, [from *micro-* and a Greek word *skopein* meaning 'to look at']

microscopic *adjective* 1 to do with a microscope. 2 too small to be visible without the aid of a microscope. 3 (*informal*) extremely small. **microscopically** *adverb*

microscopy (miy-kros-kə-pi) *noun* the use of a microscope.

microsecond *noun* one-millionth of a second.

microsurgery *noun* intricate surgery done with miniature instruments and use of a microscope.

microswitch *noun* an electric switch that can be operated rapidly by a small movement.

microwave *noun* 1 an electromagnetic wave of length between about 30 cm and 1 mm. 2 a microwave oven.

microwave oven *noun* an oven that uses microwaves to heat or cook food quickly.

mid *adjective* 1 in the middle of ♦ *in mid-air.* 2 middle ♦ *He is in his mid thirties.* [from an Old English word]

midday *noun* the middle of the day, noon.

midden *noun* a heap of dung, a rubbish heap. [from a Scandinavian language]

middle *adjective* 1 at an equal distance from the extremes or outer limits of something. SYNONYMS: central, halfway, medial. 2 occurring halfway between the beginning and end of a process or period of time. 3 intermediate in rank or quality, moderate in size or importance ♦ *a person of middle height.*
middle *noun* 1 a middle point or position. 2 (*informal*) a person's waist ♦ *She grabbed him by his middle.* **in the middle of** during or halfway through a process or activity. [from an Old English word *middel*]

middle age *noun* the period between youth and old age. **middle-aged** *adjective*

Middle Ages *plural noun* the period of European history from about AD 1000 to 1400.

middlebrow *adjective* (*informal*) having or appealing to moderately intellectual tastes.

middle C *noun* (*Music*) the note C that occurs near the middle of the piano keyboard.

middle class *noun* the class of society between the upper and working classes, including business and professional people.

Middle East *noun* an area of SW Asia and northern Africa extending from the eastern Mediterranean to Iran and including Egypt and the Arabian Peninsula.

Middle English *noun* the form of English that developed after the Norman Conquest and lasted until about 1450.

middleman *noun* (**middlemen**) **1** a person who buys from producers of goods and sells to consumers; an intermediary. **2** a go-between or intermediary.

middle-of-the-road *adjective* favouring a moderate policy, avoiding extremes.

middle school *noun* a school for children aged from about 9 to 13 years.

middle-sized *adjective* of middle or average size.

middleweight *noun* a boxing weight between light heavyweight and welter-weight.

middling *adjective informal* moderate or average in size or quality. SYNONYMS: average, moderate, mediocre, run-of-the-mill. **middling** *adverb* fairly or moderately ♦ *The family is middling rich.*

midfield *noun* the central part of a football pitch away from the goals.

midge *noun* a small biting insect like a gnat. [from an Old English word *mycge*]

midget *noun* an extremely small person or thing.
midget *adjective* extremely small. [from *midge*]

midi system *noun* a compact hi-fi system consisting of stacking units. [from *mid*, on the pattern of *mini*]

midland *adjective* **1** to do with the middle part of a country. **2** to do with the Midlands.

Midlands *plural noun* the inland counties of central England.

midnight *noun* twelve o'clock at night, or the time near this.

Midrash *noun* an ancient Jewish commentary on part of the Hebrew scriptures. [from a Hebrew word meaning 'to expound']

midrib *noun* the central rib of a leaf, forming an extension of the stalk.

midriff *noun* the front part of the body or just above the waist. [from *mid* and an Old English word *hrif* meaning 'stomach']

midshipman *noun* (**midshipmen**) a rank in the navy between cadet and sub lieutenant.

midst *noun* **in the midst of** in the middle of

or surrounded by. **in our midst** among us. [from an old expression *in middes* meaning 'in the middle']

midsummer *noun* the middle part of summer, or the summer solstice.

Midsummer Day or **Midsummer's Day** *noun* 24 June.

midway *adverb* halfway.

midwife *noun* (**midwives**) a person trained to look after a woman who is giving birth. [from Old English words *mid* meaning 'with' and *wif* meaning 'woman']

midwifery (mid-wif-ri) *noun* the work of a midwife.

midwinter *noun* the middle of winter, or the winter solstice.

mien (meen) *noun* a person's manner or bearing. [probably from a French word *mine* meaning 'expression']

might [1] *noun* great strength or power. SYNONYMS: strength, power, force, energy. **with all your might** using all your strength and determination. [from an Old English word *miht*]

might [2] *auxiliary verb* **1** used as the past tense of **may** [1] ♦ *We told her she might go.* **2** used to express possibility ♦ *It might be true* ♦ *You might like to come with us.* **3** used to express annoyance ♦ *They might have told us!*

mightn't *verb* (*informal*) might not.

mighty *adjective* (**mightier, mightiest**) **1** very strong or powerful ♦ *He gave a mighty blow with his axe.* SYNONYMS: powerful, forceful, vigorous, tremendous. **2** (*informal*) very large or loud ♦ *There was a mighty crash from the kitchen.*
mighty *adverb* (*informal*) very ♦ *That was mighty good of them.* **mightily** *adverb* **mightiness** *noun*

migraine (mee-grayn) *noun* a severe kind of headache often affecting one side of the head. [via French from a Greek word *hēmikranion* meaning 'half skull']

migrant (miy-grənt) *noun* a person or animal that migrates or has migrated.
migrant *adjective* that migrates or has migrated.

migrate (miy-grayt) *verb* **1** to leave one place or country and settle in another. **2** (said about birds or animals) to go from one habitat to another according to the time of year. **migration** *noun* [from a Latin word *migrare* meaning 'to migrate']

migratory (miy-grə-ter-i) *adjective* involving migration; migrating.

mihrab (mee-rahb) *noun* a niche or slab in a mosque, showing the direction of Mecca for the congregation to face when praying. [from an Arabic word meaning 'place for prayer']

mikado (mi-kah-doh) *noun* (**mikados**) (*historical*) a title of the emperor of Japan. [a Japanese word meaning 'majestic gate', referring to an ancient place of audience]

mike *noun* (*informal*) a microphone.

milch cow *noun* 1 a cow that is kept for its milk rather than for beef. 2 a person or organization that is a source of ready money. [from an Old English word, related to *milk*]

mild *adjective* 1 moderate in intensity, not severe or harsh. SYNONYMS: gentle, soft, moderate. 2 (said about a person) gentle in manner. SYNONYMS: gentle, docile, affable, genial. 3 (said about food or drink) not strongly flavoured. 4 (said about weather) moderately warm and pleasant.
SYNONYMS: moderate, warm, pleasant, balmy. **mildly** *adverb* **mildness** *noun* [from an Old English word *milde*]

mildew *noun* a white coating formed by a minute fungus on things kept in damp conditions. **mildewed** *adjective* [from an Old English word meaning 'honeydew']

mile *noun* 1 a measure of length equal to 1,760 yards (about 1.609 kilometres). 2 (*informal*) a large distance or amount ♦ *It's miles too big.* [from a Latin word *mille* meaning 'a thousand (paces)']

mileage *noun* 1 a distance measured in miles. 2 the number of miles a vehicle travels on one gallon of fuel. 3 (*informal*) benefit or advantage ♦ *They got some mileage from having advance information about the deal.*

milepost *noun* a post marking the point one mile from the finish of a race.

milestone *noun* 1 a stone set beside a road to mark the distance between places. 2 an important event or stage in life or history.

milieu (meel-yer) *noun* (**milieux** (meel-yer)) environment or surroundings. [a French word, from *mi* meaning 'mid' and *lieu* meaning 'place']

militant *adjective* prepared to take strong or aggressive action in support of a cause. **militant** *noun* a militant person. **militancy**

noun [same origin as for *militate*]

militarism (mil-it-er-izm) *noun* belief in the use of military strength and methods. **militarist** *noun*

militaristic *adjective* favouring military methods, warlike.

militarize *verb* 1 to equip a country or people with military resources. 2 to give a place or organization a military character.

military *adjective* to do with soldiers or armed forces.
military *noun* (**the military**) the armed forces of a country. [from a Latin word *miles* meaning 'soldier']

militate (mil-i-tayt) *verb* to be a strong influence ♦ *Several factors militated against the success of our plan.* [from a Latin word *militare* meaning 'to be a soldier']
◊ Do not confuse this word with **mitigate**, which has a different meaning.

militia (mil-ish-ə) *noun* a military force, especially one raised from civilians. [same origin as for *military*]

milk *noun* 1 a white liquid that female mammals produce in their bodies as food for their young. 2 the milk of cows, used as food by human beings. 3 a milk-like liquid, e.g. that in a coconut.
milk *verb* 1 to draw milk from a cow or other animal. 2 to extract sap or juice from a tree etc. 3 to exploit a person or organization by illegally or unfairly taking money from them. [from an Old English word]

milk chocolate *noun* chocolate made with milk.

milk float *noun* a light low vehicle with open sides, used in delivering milk.

milkmaid *noun* a woman who milks cows or works in a dairy.

milkman *noun* (**milkmen**) a man who sells and delivers milk.

milkshake *noun* a cold drink made from milk whisked with ice cream and a flavouring.

milksop *noun* a timid or indecisive person.

milk tooth *noun* each of the first set of teeth that a child or young animal has, later replaced by adult teeth.

milkweed *noun* a wild plant with milky juice.

milky *adjective* (**milkier, milkiest**) 1 creamy or white like milk. 2 made with milk, or containing a lot of milk. **3** (said about a gem or liquid) cloudy, not clear. **milkiness** *noun*

Milky Way *noun* the broad band of stars formed by our galaxy.

mill *noun* **1** machinery for grinding corn to make flour, or a building containing this machinery. **2** a machine for grinding or crushing a solid substance into powder or pulp ♦ *a coffee mill.* **3** a factory or building for processing materials ♦ *a cotton mill* ♦ *a paper mill.*
mill *verb* **1** to grind or crush something in a mill. **2** to produce regular markings on the edge of a coin. **3** to cut or shape metal with a rotating tool. **to mill about** or **around** (said about people or animals) to move round in a confused crowd. **to put someone through the mill** to make someone undergo hard work or an unpleasant experience. [via Old English from a Latin word *molere* meaning 'to grind']

millennium (mil-en-iəm) *noun* (**millennia** or **millenniums**) **1** a period of 1,000 years. **2** (in Christian teaching) the thousand-year reign of Christ on earth prophesied in the Bible. **3** a period of great happiness and prosperity. [from Latin words *mille* meaning 'thousand' and *annus* meaning 'year']

millennium bug *noun* a fault in some older computer systems that prevented them from dealing with dates from 1 January 2000.

miller *noun* a person who owns or runs a grain mill.

millet *noun* **1** a cereal plant that produces a large crop of small seeds. **2** the seeds of this plant, used as food. [via French from a Latin word *milium*]

milli- *prefix* **1** one thousandth (as in *milligram*). **2** one thousand (as in *millipede*). [from a Latin word *mille* meaning 'thousand']

milliard *noun* one thousand million.

millibar *noun* (*Meteorology*) one thousandth of a bar as a unit of pressure.

milligram *noun* one thousandth of a gram.

millilitre *noun* one thousandth of a litre.

millimetre *noun* one thousandth of a metre (0.04 inch).

milliner *noun* a person who makes or sells women's hats. [from the meaning 'a person from Milan' in Italy, where

fashionable hats and accessories were made]

millinery *noun* **1** a milliner's work. **2** women's hats sold in a shop.

million *adjective* & *noun* **1** one thousand thousand (1,000,000). **2** (also **millions**) an enormous number. **millionth** *adjective* & *noun* [from a French word *million*, related to *milli-*]
◊ The plural is *million* when it follows a number (*three million*) or a few (*a few million*).

millionaire *noun* a person who owns a million pounds or dollars, or one who is extremely rich.

millipede (mil-i-peed) *noun* a small crawling creature like a centipede, with two pairs of legs on each segment of its body. [from Latin words *mille* meaning 'thousand' and *pedes* meaning 'feet']

millpond *noun* a pool formed by a mill dam, providing water for a water mill.

millstone *noun* **1** each of a pair of circular stones used for grinding corn between them. **2** a great burden of responsibility.

milometer (miy-lom-it-er) *noun* an instrument for measuring the number of miles travelled by a vehicle. [from *mile* and *meter*]

milt *noun* the sperm or roe of a male fish. [from an Old English word]

mime *noun* acting with movements of the body and without words.
mime *verb* to act with mime. [from a Greek word *mimos* meaning 'a mimic']

mimic *verb* (**mimicked, mimicking**) **1** to copy the appearance or ways of a person playfully or for entertainment. **2** to imitate someone or pretend to be someone. SYNONYMS: imitate, impersonate, copy, ape, parody.
mimic *noun* a person who mimics others, especially for entertainment. **mimicry** *noun* [same origin as for *mime*]

mimosa (mim-oh-zə) *noun* a tropical tree or shrub with clusters of small ball-shaped flowers. [from a Latin word]

minaret (min-er-et) *noun* a tall slender tower on or beside a mosque, with a balcony from which a muezzin calls Muslims to prayer. [from an Arabic word *manara* meaning 'lighthouse']

minatory (min-ə-ter-i) *adjective* (*formal*) threatening. [from a Latin word *minari* meaning 'to threaten']

mince verb 1 to cut food, especially meat, into small pieces in a machine with revolving blades. 2 to walk in an affected way with short quick steps and swinging hips.
mince noun minced meat. **to mince words** to criticize someone gently or discreetly.
mincer noun [from an Old French word *mincier*, related to *minute*²]

mincemeat noun a mixture of currants, raisins, apples, sugar, candied peel, spices, and suet, used in pies. **to make mincemeat of** (*informal*) to defeat someone completely. [from *mince* and *meat* in an old meaning 'food']

mince pie noun a small pie containing mincemeat.

mind noun 1 the ability to be aware of things and to think, remember, and reason. SYNONYMS: brain, intellect, reason, understanding. 2 a person's thoughts and attention ♦ *Try to keep your mind on the job.* 3 a way of thinking and feeling ♦ *What was his state of mind?*
mind verb 1 to take care of someone or something ♦ *Who is minding the children?* SYNONYMS: take care of, look after, supervise, watch, keep an eye on. 2 to be careful about something ♦ *Please mind the step.* SYNONYMS: heed, mark, take note of, watch out for. 3 to feel annoyed or discomforted by something ♦ *She doesn't seem to mind the cold* ♦ *Do you think they will mind if we stay?* SYNONYMS: object (to), resent, be annoyed (by), worry (about). 4 to concern yourself about something ♦ *Never mind the expense.* 5 to remember and take care ♦ *Mind you lock the door.* **to bear** or **keep in mind** to remember or consider something. **to be in two minds** to be unable to decide about something. **to be minded to** to intend or want to do something. **to change your mind** to have a different opinion about something. **to have something on your mind** to be worried or concerned about something. **to have a good mind** or **half a mind to** to feel tempted or inclined to do something. **in your right mind** sane. **to mind your Ps and Qs** to be careful to be polite. **out of your mind** insane. [from an Old English word *gemynd* meaning 'memory' or 'thought', related to a Latin word *mens* meaning 'mind']

minded adjective 1 having a mind of a certain kind ♦ *independent-minded.* 2 having certain interests ♦ *politically minded.*

minder noun informal a person who attends to or takes care of a person or thing.

mindful adjective taking thought or care about something ♦ *He is very mindful of his public image.*

mindless adjective without intelligence or thought. **mindlessly** adverb

mine ¹ possessive pronoun belonging to me. [from an Old English word]

mine ² noun 1 a place where metal, coal, or precious stones are dug out of the ground. 2 an abundant source of something ♦ *a mine of information.* 3 an explosive device placed in the ground or in water ready and detonated when anything passes over it.
mine verb 1 to dig coal or minerals from the ground. 2 to lay explosive mines in an area. [from an Old French word *mine*]

minefield noun 1 an area where explosive mines have been laid. 2 a subject or situation that has hidden dangers or problems.

miner noun a person who works in a mine.

mineral noun 1 an inorganic substance that occurs naturally in the ground. 2 an ore or other substance obtained by mining. 3 a cold fizzy non-alcoholic drink.
mineral adjective of or containing minerals. [from a Latin word *minera* meaning 'ore']

mineralogy (min-er-al-əji) noun the study of minerals. **mineralogical** adjective **mineralogist** noun [from *mineral* and *-logy*]

mineral water noun water that has dissolved mineral salts naturally present.

minestrone (mini-stroh-ni) noun an Italian soup containing vegetables and pasta. [an Italian word, from *ministrare* meaning 'to serve up a dish']

minesweeper noun a ship equipped for clearing away explosive mines laid in the sea.

Ming noun porcelain belonging to the time of the Ming dynasty in China (1368–1644).

mingle verb 1 to mix or blend, or to make things mix or blend. SYNONYMS: mix, blend, amalgamate. 2 to go about among people ♦ *The prime minister mingled with the crowd.* SYNONYMS: circulate, mix. [from an Old English word]

mingy adjective (**mingier**, **mingiest**) (*informal*) mean or stingy. [probably from *mean*² and *stingy*]

mini- *prefix* miniature. [short for *miniature*]

miniature (min-i-cher) *adjective* **1** very small. SYNONYMS: tiny, minute, diminutive. **2** imitating something on a small scale ♦ *a miniature railway*.
miniature *noun* **1** a small and detailed portrait. **2** a small-scale copy or model of something. **in miniature** on a very small scale. [from an Italian word *miniatura*, from a Latin word *miniare* meaning 'to mark with red', referring to the practice of marking words in manuscripts]

miniaturist *noun* a person who paints miniature portraits.

miniaturize *verb* to produce something in a small-scale version. **miniaturization** *noun*

minibus *noun* a small bus, seating about ten people.

minicab *noun* a car used as a taxi that must be booked in advance.

minidisc *noun* a disc like a small compact disc, capable of recording sound as well as playing it back.

minim *noun* **1** (*Music*) a note lasting half as long as a semibreve. **2** one sixtieth of a fluid drachm, about one drop of liquid. [same origin as for *minimum*]

minimal *adjective* very small, the least possible. **minimally** *adverb*

minimize *verb* **1** to reduce something to a minimum. **2** to estimate or represent something at less than its true value or importance ♦ *I have no wish to minimize the help they have given.*

minimum *noun* (**minima**) the lowest or the lowest possible number or amount. **minimum** *adjective* smallest, least possible. [from a Latin word *minimus* meaning 'smallest thing']

minion (min-yən) *noun* a subordinate assistant. [from a French word *mignon*]

miniskirt *noun* a short skirt ending at about the middle of the thighs.

minister *noun* **1** a member of the government who is in charge of a department or an area of policy ♦ *the Health Minister.* **2** a diplomatic representative, usually ranking below an ambassador. **3** a member of the clergy, especially in Presbyterian and Nonconformist Churches.
minister *verb* to attend to people's needs ♦ *The nurses ministered to the wounded.*
ministerial (min-iss-teer-iəl) *adjective* [a Latin word meaning 'servant']

ministry *noun* (**ministries**) **1** a government department headed by a minister ♦ *the Ministry of Defence.* **2** a period of government under one Prime Minister. **3** the work or office of the clergy.

mink *noun* **1** a small animal of the weasel family. **2** the highly valued fur of this animal, or a coat made from it. [from a Swedish word]

minnow (min-oh) *noun* a small freshwater fish of the carp family. [probably from Old English]

Minoan (min-oh-ən) *adjective* of the Bronze Age civilization of Crete (about 3000–1000 BC).
Minoan *noun* an inhabitant of Minoan Crete. [named after the legendary Cretan king Minos]

minor *adjective* **1** lesser or less important ♦ *The accident had only been a minor one.* SYNONYMS: small, trivial, insignificant, unimportant. **2** (*Music*) based on a scale which has a semitone next above the second note.
minor *noun* a person under the age of legal responsibility. [from a Latin word meaning 'smaller, lesser']

minority *noun* (**minorities**) **1** the smallest part of a group of people or things. (Compare **majority**.) **2** a small group that is different from others. **3** (in law) the state of being under the age of legal responsibility ♦ *during his minority.*

minor planet *noun* an asteroid.

Minotaur (miy-nə-tor) *noun* (*Greek mythology*) a creature who was half man and half bull, kept in the labyrinth on Crete by King Minos and killed by Theseus. [from *Minoan* and a Greek word *tauros* meaning 'bull']

minster *noun* a name given to certain large or important churches, often originally built as part of a monastery ♦ *York Minster.* [from an Old English word *mynster*]

minstrel *noun* a travelling singer and musician in the Middle Ages. [from an Old French word, related to *minister*]

mint¹ *noun* **1** a plant with fragrant leaves that are used for flavouring. **2** peppermint, or a sweet flavoured with peppermint. **minty** *adjective* [from a Latin word *mentha* meaning 'mint']

mint² *noun* **1** a place where a country's coins are made. **2** (*informal*) a huge amount of money.

mint *verb* 1 to make coins by stamping metal. 2 to invent or coin a word or expression. **in mint condition** in perfect condition as if newly made. [from a Latin word *moneta* meaning 'coins' or 'a mint']

minuet (min-yoo-et) *noun* a slow stately dance in triple time, or a piece of music suitable for this. [from a French word *menuet* meaning 'fine or delicate']

minus (miy-nəs) *preposition* 1 reduced by the subtraction of ♦ *seven minus three equals four (7 − 3 = 4).* 2 (*informal*) without, no longer having ♦ *They returned minus the dog.* **minus** *adjective* 1 (used before a number) less than zero ♦ *temperatures of minus 20 degrees.* 2 (used after a grade) slightly less ♦ *B minus.* **minus** *noun* 1 the sign −. 2 a disadvantage ♦ *There are pluses and minuses.* [a Latin word meaning 'less']

minuscule (min-əs-kewl) *adjective* extremely small.

minute[1] (min-it) *noun* 1 one sixtieth of an hour. 2 a very short time, a moment ♦ *It will only take a minute.* 3 an exact point of time ♦ *Come here this minute!* 4 one sixtieth of a degree (used in measuring angles). [from a Latin phrase *pars minuta prima* meaning 'first little part']

minute[2] (miy-newt) *adjective* 1 extremely small ♦ *a minute insect.* SYNONYMS: tiny, minuscule, microscopic, miniature, infinitesimal. 2 very detailed and precise ♦ *a minute examination.* SYNONYMS: detailed, precise, accurate, meticulous. **minutely** *adverb* [from a Latin word *minutus* meaning 'little']

minute[3] (min-it) *noun* an official memorandum. **minutes** *plural noun* a summary, serving as an official record, of points discussed at a meeting. **minute** *verb* to record a point in a set of minutes. [from a Latin phrase *minuta scriptura* meaning 'small writing']

minutiae (min-yoo-shi-ee) *plural noun* the small or precise details of something. [a Latin word meaning 'trifles']

minx *noun* a cheeky or mischievous girl. [origin unknown]

miracle *noun* 1 something wonderful and good that happens, especially something believed to have a supernatural or divine cause. 2 a remarkable example or specimen of something ♦ *a miracle of modern technology.* SYNONYMS: wonder, marvel. [from a Latin word *mirari* meaning 'to wonder']

miraculous *adjective* like a miracle, wonderful. SYNONYMS: marvellous, wonderful, remarkable, extraordinary, incredible, amazing. **miraculously** *adverb*

mirage (mi-rahzh) *noun* an optical illusion caused by atmospheric conditions, especially the appearance of a sheet of water in a desert or on a hot road. [a French word, from *se mirer* meaning 'to be reflected or mirrored']

mire *noun* 1 an area of swampy ground or bog. 2 mud or sticky dirt. **mire** *verb* 1 to plunge something in mud. 2 to involve someone or something in difficulties. 3 to cover or spatter something with mud. [from an Old Norse word]

mirror *noun* a piece of glass coated on the back with amalgam so that reflections can be seen in it. **mirror** *verb* to show a reflection of something. [from a Latin word *mirare* meaning 'to look at']

mirror image *noun* a reflection or copy in which the right and left sides of the original are reversed.

mirth *noun* merriment or laughter. **mirthful** *adjective* **mirthless** *adjective* [from an Old English word]

mis- *prefix* badly, wrongly. [from an Old English form *mis-*, related to *amiss*, or from a French form *mes-*, related to *minus*]

misadventure *noun* 1 a piece of bad luck. 2 (*Law*) death caused unintentionally by a deliberate act but with no crime involved. [from an Old French word *mesavenir* meaning 'to turn out badly']

misalliance *noun* an unsuitable alliance or marriage.

misanthrope (mis-ən-throhp) or **misanthropist** (mis-an-thrəp-ist) *nouns* a person who dislikes people.

misanthropy (mis-an-thrəpi) *noun* dislike of people in general. **misanthropic** (mis-an-throp-ik) *adjective* [from Greek words *misos* meaning 'hatred' and *anthrōpos* meaning 'human being']

misapprehend (mis-apri-hend) *verb* to misunderstand something. **misapprehension** *noun*

misappropriate (mis-ə-**proh**-pri-ayt) *verb* to take something dishonestly for your own use. **misappropriation** *noun*

misbegotten *adjective* 1 badly planned or designed. 2 contemptible.

misbehave *verb* to behave badly. **misbehaviour** *noun*

miscalculate *verb* to calculate something incorrectly. **miscalculation** *noun*

miscarriage (mis-**ka**-rij) *noun* 1 the spontaneous birth of a fetus before it has developed enough to survive outside the womb. 2 a mistake or failure to achieve the correct result ♦ *a miscarriage of justice*.

miscarry *verb* (**miscarries**, **miscarried**, **miscarrying**) 1 (said about a pregnant woman) to have a miscarriage. 2 (said about a scheme or intention) to go wrong, to fail. SYNONYMS: fail, founder, misfire, go wrong; (*informal*) come unstuck.

miscast *adjective* (said about an actor) cast in an unsuitable role.

miscellaneous (mis-ol-**ay**-niəs) *adjective* of various kinds, mixed ♦ *miscellaneous items* ♦ *a miscellaneous collection*. SYNONYMS: assorted, diverse, various, sundry, mixed. [from a Latin word *miscellus* meaning 'mixed']

miscellany (mi-**sel**-əni) *noun* (**miscellanies**) a collection of various items.

mischance *noun* misfortune, bad luck.

mischief *noun* 1 bad behaviour that causes trouble without being malicious. SYNONYMS: misbehaviour, misconduct, naughtiness. 2 harm or damage caused by bad behaviour ♦ *Their remarks did a lot of mischief*. **to make mischief** to cause discord or ill feeling. [from an Old French word *meschief*, from *meschever* meaning 'to come to an unfortunate end']

mischievous (mis-**chiv**-əs) *adjective* 1 (said about a person) behaving badly in a troublesome way. SYNONYMS: naughty, playful, troublesome. 2 (said about an action) causing trouble or harm. SYNONYMS: troublesome, harmful. **mischievously** *adverb*

miscible (mis-**ibəl**) *adjective* (said about liquids) able to be mixed. **miscibility** *noun* [from a Latin word *miscere* meaning 'to mix']

misconceive (mis-kən-**seev**) *verb* to misunderstand something, or to interpret something wrongly.

misconception (mis-kən-**sep**-shən) *noun* a mistaken idea.

misconduct (mis-**kon**-dukt) *noun* bad behaviour by someone in a responsible position.

misconstrue (mis-kən-**stroo**) *verb* (**misconstrues**, **misconstrued**, **misconstruing**) to understand or interpret something wrongly. **misconstruction** *noun*

miscount *verb* to count something wrongly. **miscount** *noun* an incorrect count.

miscreant (**mis**-kri-ənt) *noun* a wrongdoer or criminal. [from an earlier meaning 'disbeliever', from an Old French word *mescreire* meaning 'to disbelieve']

misdeed *noun* a wrong or illegal act.

misdemeanour (mis-dim-**een**-er) *noun* a minor misdeed or wrongdoing.

misdirect *verb* to direct someone wrongly. **misdirection** *noun*

miser *noun* a person who hoards money and spends as little as possible. **miserly** *adjective* **miserliness** *noun* [same origin as for *misery*]

miserable *adjective* 1 wretchedly unhappy or uncomfortable. SYNONYMS: sad, unhappy, dejected, depressed, despondent, wretched, melancholy, gloomy. 2 disagreeable or unpleasant ♦ *miserable weather*. 3 wretchedly poor or inadequate ♦ *a miserable attempt* ♦ *miserable housing*. **miserably** *adverb*

misericord (miz-e-ri-kord) *noun* a small ledge projecting from the underside of a hinged seat in a church choir stall, giving support to someone standing when the seat is turned up. [from a Latin word *misericordia* meaning 'compassion']

misery *noun* (**miseries**) 1 a feeling of great unhappiness or discomfort. SYNONYMS: sorrow, distress, unhappiness, anguish, despair, melancholy, sadness, hardship, grief. 2 something that causes unhappiness. 3 (*informal*) a person who is constantly unhappy or disagreeable. [from a Latin word *miser* meaning 'wretched']

misfire *verb* 1 (said about a gun) to fail to fire correctly. 2 (said about an engine) to fail to start or function correctly. 3 to fail to have the intended effect ♦ *The joke misfired*. **misfire** *noun* a failure of this kind.

misfit *noun* 1 a person who does not fit in well with other people or with their surroundings. **2** a piece of clothing that does not fit well.

misfortune *noun* **1** bad luck. SYNONYMS: adversity, bad luck. **2** an unfortunate event. SYNONYMS: mishap, calamity, disaster, mischance.

misgiving *noun* a feeling of doubt or slight fear or mistrust. [from an old word *misgive* meaning 'to give someone bad feelings about something']

misgovernment *noun* bad government.

misguided *adjective* showing bad judgement or reasoning. **misguidedly** *adverb*

mishandle *verb* to deal with something badly or inefficiently.

mishap (mis-hap) *noun* an unlucky accident. SYNONYMS: misfortune, calamity, disaster, mischance.

mishear *verb* (past tense and past participle **misheard**) to hear something incorrectly.

mishit *verb* (**mishit, mishitting**) to hit a ball faultily or badly.
mishit *noun* a faulty or bad hit.

mishmash *noun* a confused mixture.

Mishnah *noun* a collection of decisions on Jewish law and ritual that form the main text of the Talmud. [from a Hebrew word *mishnah* meaning '(teaching) by repetition']

misinform *verb* to give wrong information to someone.

misinterpret *verb* to interpret something wrongly. **misinterpretation** *noun*

misjudge *verb* **1** to form a wrong opinion of someone or something. **2** to estimate an amount or distance incorrectly. **misjudgement** *noun*

mislay *verb* (past tense and past participle **mislaid**) to lose something temporarily because you cannot remember where you put it.

mislead *verb* (past tense and past participle **misled**) to give someone a wrong impression about something. SYNONYMS: deceive, delude, fool, hoodwink, bluff, trick; (*informal*) kid, take in.

mismanage *verb* to manage affairs badly or wrongly. SYNONYMS: bungle, botch, mishandle, mess up, spoil. **mismanagement** *noun*

mismatch *verb* to match something unsuitably or incorrectly.

mismatch *noun* a bad match.

misnomer (mis-noh-mer) *noun* an unsuitable name or description for something. [from *mis-* and a Latin word *nomen* meaning 'name']

misogynist (mis-oj-in-ist) *noun* a person who hates women. **misogyny** *noun* [from Greek words *misos* meaning 'hatred' and *gunē* meaning 'woman']

misplace to put something in the wrong place. **misplacement** *noun*

misplaced *adjective* unsuitable or inappropriate ♦ *misplaced humour.*

misprint *noun* an error in printing.

mispronounce *verb* to pronounce a word incorrectly. **mispronunciation** *noun*

misquote *verb* to quote something or someone incorrectly. **misquotation** *noun*

misread *verb* (past tense and past participle **misread** (mis-red)) to read or interpret something incorrectly.

misrepresent *verb* to represent someone or something in a false or misleading way. **misrepresentation** *noun*

misrule *noun* bad government.

miss [1] *verb* **1** to fail to hit, reach, or catch something. **2** to fail to see, hear, or understand someone or something ♦ *I missed what you said* ♦ *Did you miss the signpost?* **3** to fail to catch a train, bus, etc., or to keep an appointment with someone. **4** to omit or lack something. **5** to notice the absence or loss of something. **6** to feel sorrow or regret because someone or something is not with you ♦ *Katie missed her family terribly.* SYNONYMS: yearn for, pine for, long for, want. **7** to avoid something ♦ *Go this way and you'll miss the traffic.* **8** (said about an engine) to misfire.
miss *noun* failure to hit or reach what is aimed at. **to give something a miss** (*informal*) to avoid something or leave it alone. **to miss out** to omit something. **to miss out on** to fail to get any benefit or enjoyment from something that others have enjoyed. **to miss the boat** (*informal*) to lose an opportunity. [from an Old English word *missan*]

miss [2] *noun* **1** a girl or unmarried woman. **2** (**Miss**) a title used to refer to a girl or unmarried woman ♦ *Miss Smith.* [short for *mistress*]

missal *noun* a book containing the prayers used in the Mass in the Roman Catholic Church. [from a Latin word *missalis* meaning 'to do with the mass' (see *Mass*)]

missel thrush *noun* another spelling of **mistle thrush**.

misshapen *adjective* distorted or badly shaped. SYNONYMS: distorted, contorted, malformed, twisted. [from *mis-* and *shapen*, an old past participle of the verb *shape*]

missile *noun* **1** a weapon that is guided remotely to its target. **2** an object that is thrown at a target. [from a Latin word *missum* meaning 'sent']

missing *adjective* **1** lost, not in the proper place ◆ *Two chairs are missing.* **2** absent, not available ◆ *He's always missing when we need him.* **3** absent from home and with whereabouts unknown ◆ *She's listed as a missing person.* **4** (said about a soldier) not present after a battle and not known to have been killed.

missing link *noun* a hypothetical type of animal supposed to have existed between the apes and the development of humans.

mission *noun* **1** an important task or assignment, especially one involving travel abroad. SYNONYMS: assignment, task, objective. **2** a group of people sent on a mission. **3** an organization for spreading a religious belief, or the place where it is based. **4** a military or scientific expedition. **5** what a person wants to do or thinks they must do ◆ *a mission in life.* [from a Latin word *missio* meaning 'a sending']

missionary *noun* (**missionaries**) a person who is sent to another country to spread a religious faith.

missis *noun* another spelling of **missus**.

missive *noun* a letter or written message. [same origin as for *missile*]

misspell *verb* (past tense and past participle **misspelt** or **misspelled**) to spell a word incorrectly.

misspend *verb* (past tense and past participle **misspent**) to spend time or money badly or unwisely.

missus *noun* (*informal*) **1** a person's wife ◆ *How's the missus?* **2** a form of address to a woman.

mist *noun* **1** a cloud of water vapour in tiny drops near the ground, limiting visibility less severely than fog does. **2** condensed water vapour clouding a window or other surface. **3** something resembling mist in its form or effect.

mist *verb* to become covered with mist ◆ *The windscreen has misted up* ◆ *My glasses misted over.* [from an Old English word]

mistakable *adjective* able to be mistaken for another person or thing.

mistake *noun* **1** something done incorrectly ◆ *I've made some mistakes in the accounts.* SYNONYMS: error, slip; (*informal*) gaffe, howler. **2** an incorrect idea or opinion ◆ *It would be a mistake to think they don't care.* SYNONYMS: misconception, error.

mistake *verb* (**mistook, mistaken**) **1** to be wrong about something ◆ *Don't mistake my meaning.* **2** to choose or identify a person or thing wrongly ◆ *She is often mistaken for her sister.*

mistaken *adjective* **1** having a wrong opinion ◆ *You are mistaken if you think that.* **2** badly judged or used ◆ *Their kindness seems to have been mistaken.* **mistakenly** *adverb*

mister *noun* (*informal*) a form of address to a man.

mistime *verb* to say or do something at an inappropriate time.

mistle thrush *noun* a large thrush with a spotted breast, which feeds on mistletoe berries.

mistletoe *noun* a plant with white berries that grows as a parasite on trees. [from an Old English word]

mistook past tense of **mistake**.

mistral (**mis-**trəl or mis-**trahl**) *noun* a strong cold north-west wind in southern France. [via French from a Latin phrase *magistralis ventus* meaning 'master wind']

mistreat *verb* to treat someone or something badly. **mistreatment** *noun*

mistress *noun* **1** a woman who has charge of people or things. **2** the female owner of a dog. **3** a female teacher. **4** a woman who is a married man's female lover but is not his wife. [from an Old French word *maistresse*, a feminine form of *maistre* meaning 'master']

mistrial *noun* a trial made invalid by an error in procedure.

mistrust *verb* to feel no trust in someone or something. SYNONYMS: disbelieve, distrust, suspect.

mistrust *noun* a lack of trust. SYNONYMS: distrust, doubt, suspicion. **mistrustful** *adjective* **mistrustfully** *adverb*

misty adjective (**mistier, mistiest**) 1 full of mist. 2 not clear or distinct. **mistily** adjective **mistiness** noun

misunderstand verb (past tense and past participle **misunderstood**) to understand someone or something incorrectly ♦ Please don't misunderstand me.

misuse[1] (mis-yooz) verb 1 to use something wrongly or incorrectly. 2 to treat a person or thing badly.

misuse[2] (mis-yooss) noun wrong or incorrect use of something.

mite noun 1 a tiny spider-like animal, many of which are parasites. 2 a small child or animal. 3 a very small amount ♦ He only offered a mite of comfort. [from an Old English word]

mitigate (mit-i-gayt) verb to make something less serious or severe. **mitigating circumstances** facts that explain or partly excuse a wrongdoing. **mitigation** noun [from a Latin word mitigare meaning 'to make mild']
◊ Do not confuse this word with **militate**, which has a different meaning.

mitochondrion (miy-toh-kon-dri-ɘn) noun (**mitochondria**) (Biology) a rod-shaped structure existing in large quantities in most living cells, in which important chemical reactions take place and energy is produced. [from Greek words mitos meaning 'thread' and khondrion meaning 'granule']

mitosis (miy-toh-sis) noun (Biology) a process of cell division in which daughter cells are formed, each containing the same number of chromosomes as the parent cell. (Compare **meiosis**.) [from a Greek word mitos meaning 'thread']

mitre (miy-ter) noun 1 a tall headdress worn by bishops and senior abbots, tapering to a point at the front and back. 2 a joint of two pieces of wood or cloth with their ends evenly tapered so that together they form a right angle. **mitre** verb (**mitred, mitring**) to join pieces of wood or cloth with a mitre. [from a Greek word mitra meaning 'turban']

mitt noun a mitten.

mitten noun a glove that leaves the fingers and tip of the thumb exposed or that has no partition between the fingers. [from a French word mitaine]

mix verb 1 to put different things together so that they form a whole and are no longer distinct. SYNONYMS: blend, combine, integrate. 2 to be capable of being mixed to form a whole ♦ Oil will not mix with water. 3 to combine things or put things together ♦ to mix business with pleasure. 4 (said about a person) to get on well with other people.
mix noun 1 a mixture of people or things. SYNONYMS: mixture, combination. 2 a mixture prepared for making something ♦ a cake mix ♦ a concrete mix. **to be mixed up in** to be involved in something, especially a wrongdoing. **to mix up** 1 to mix things thoroughly. SYNONYMS: blend, combine, mingle. 2 to confuse things in the mind. SYNONYMS: confuse, muddle. 3 to make a person feel confused. SYNONYMS: confuse, muddle, perplex. [from mixed]

mixed adjective 1 consisting of different kinds of things or people. SYNONYMS: assorted, miscellaneous, diverse, various, sundry. 2 involving people from different races or social classes. 3 for people of both sexes ♦ a mixed school. [from a Latin word mixtus meaning 'mingled']

mixed blessing noun something that has advantages and disadvantages.

mixed economy noun an economy in which some industries and businesses are run by the state, and others by private enterprise.

mixed farming noun farming of both crops and livestock.

mixed feelings plural noun a mixture of pleasure and regret about something.

mixed marriage noun a marriage between people of different races or religions.

mixed media plural noun the use of different media in art or entertainment.

mixed number noun a number made up of a whole number and a fraction.

mixed-up adjective (informal) suffering from emotional or psychological problems.

mixer noun 1 a machine or device for mixing or blending things ♦ a food mixer. 2 a person who gets on in a certain way with others ♦ He is a good mixer. 3 a soft drink for mixing with an alcoholic drink.

mixture noun 1 the process of mixing. 2 something made by mixing different things together. 3 a combination of different things. SYNONYMS: assortment, variety, collection, jumble.

mix-up noun (informal) a confusion or misunderstanding.

mizzen or **mizzenmast** *noun* the mast nearest to and behind the main mast of a ship. [from an Italian word *mezzano* meaning 'middle']

ml *abbreviation* millilitre(s).

mm *abbreviation* millimetre(s).

MMR *abbreviation* measles, mumps, and rubella (vaccination).

Mn *abbreviation* (*Chemistry*) the symbol for manganese.

mnemonic (nim-on-ik) *noun* a verse or saying that helps you to remember something. [from a Greek word *mnēmonikos* meaning 'for the memory']

MO *abbreviation* 1 Medical Officer. 2 money order.

Mo *abbreviation* (*Chemistry*) the symbol for molybdenum.

mo *noun* (*informal*) a moment ♦ *I'll be there in half a mo.*

moa *noun* a large extinct bird of New Zealand, resembling an emu. [from a Maori word]

moan *noun* 1 a long low sound of pain or suffering. 2 (*informal*) a grumble.
moan *verb* 1 to make a moan. 2 (said about the wind) to make a sound like a moan. 3 (*informal*) to complain or grumble. SYNONYMS: complain, grumble, grouse. [probably from Old English]

moat *noun* a deep wide ditch round a castle or large house, usually filled with water.
moated *adjective* [from an Old French word *mote* meaning 'mound']

mob *noun* 1 a large disorderly crowd of people. 2 (*informal*) a group of people.
mob *verb* (**mobbed, mobbing**) to crowd round a person or place. [from a Latin phrase *mobile vulgus* meaning 'excitable crowd']

mob cap *noun* a large round cap worn indoors by women in the 18th and early 19th centuries. [from an old word *mob* meaning 'slut' or 'prostitute']

mobile (moh-biyl) *adjective* 1 able to move or be moved easily and quickly. SYNONYMS: movable, portable. 2 installed in a vehicle so as to travel about ♦ *a mobile library.* 3 able to be carried about, not fixed ♦ *a mobile phone.* 4 (said about a person) able or willing to change jobs or move to a different area.
mobile *noun* 1 a decoration for hanging from a ceiling so that its parts move freely in currents of air. 2 a mobile phone.
mobility (moh-bil-iti) *noun* [from a Latin word *movere* meaning 'to move']

mobile home *noun* a large caravan that is permanently parked and used as a home.

mobile phone *noun* a portable telephone that uses a cellular radio system.

mobilize (moh-bi-liyz) *verb* 1 to organize troops for active service in war. 2 to bring people or resources together for a particular purpose. **mobilization** *noun*

mobster *noun* (*informal*) a gangster.

moccasin (mok-ə-sin) *noun* a soft leather shoe. [a Native American word]

mocha (moh-kə) *noun* a kind of coffee, or a flavouring made with this. [named after Mocha on the Red Sea, where the coffee first came from]

mock *verb* 1 to make fun of someone or something by imitating them. SYNONYMS: ape, parody, mimic, ridicule; (*informal*) send up. 2 to taunt or defy someone with scorn. SYNONYMS: taunt, ridicule, deride, make fun of, scoff at.
mock *adjective* imitation, not real ♦ *mock exams.* [from an Old French word *mocquer* meaning 'to deride']

mockery *noun* (**mockeries**) 1 ridicule or contempt. 2 a ridiculous imitation, a travesty.

mockingbird *noun* a long-tailed American bird that mimics the notes of other birds.

mock turtle soup *noun* soup made from calf's head or other meat, to resemble turtle soup.

mock-up *noun* a model of something, made to test or study it.

MOD *abbreviation* Ministry of Defence.

mod *noun* (*informal*) (in the 1960s) a young person belonging to a group noted for its smart style of clothes.
mod *adjective* (*informal*) modern or stylish.

modal (moh-dəl) *adjective* to do with mode or form rather than substance.

modal verb *noun* (*Grammar*) an auxiliary verb (e.g. *would*) that is used to indicate the mood of another verb.

mod cons *plural noun* (*informal*) modern conveniences, especially in houses and buildings.

mode *noun* 1 the way in which a thing is done. 2 (*Computing*) a way of operating a system. 3 (*Statistics*) the value that occurs

most frequently in a set of values.
4 (*Music*) each of a number of traditional scale systems. 5 the current fashion. [from a Latin word *modus* meaning 'measure']

model *noun* 1 a copy or reproduction of something, usually on a smaller scale. SYNONYMS: replica, reproduction. 2 a particular design or version of a product, especially a car ♦ *This year's models have improved steering.* SYNONYMS: design, version, type. 3 a person or thing that is an excellent example of some quality ♦ *She is a model of patience.* SYNONYMS: paragon, example, ideal, archetype. 4 a person or thing that is worth imitating ♦ *Take this essay as your model.* SYNONYMS: example, standard, prototype. 5 a person who poses for an artist. 6 a person who displays clothes in a shop or at a fashion show by wearing them. 7 a simplified description of a system or process, often in mathematical terms.
model *adjective* excellent of its kind, worth imitating ♦ *a model patient.*
model *verb* (**modelled, modelling**) 1 to make a model of something. 2 to use a material to make a model ♦ *The sculptor was modelling clay into a bust.* SYNONYMS: mould, form, shape, fashion. 3 to design or plan something using another thing as an example ♦ *The new system is modelled on the old one.* 4 to work as an artist's model or as a fashion model; to display clothes as a model. [from a French word *modelle*, from a Latin word *modulus*]

modem (moh-dəm) *noun* a device that links a computer system to a telephone line for transmitting data. [from *modulator* and *demodulator*]

moderate[1] (mod-er-ət) *adjective* 1 average or medium in amount or quality. SYNONYMS: fair, reasonable, average, middling, ordinary. 2 not extreme or excessive ♦ *a moderate climate.* 3 not extreme or unreasonable ♦ *moderate political views.*
moderate *noun* a person with moderate views, especially in politics. **moderately** *adverb* [from a Latin word *moderari* meaning 'to restrain']

moderate[2] (mod-er-ayt) *verb* to make something moderate or less intense, or to become moderate. SYNONYMS: (with object) temper, modify, soften, relieve, reduce; (without object) soften, moderate, abate.

moderation *noun* being moderate. **in moderation** in moderate amounts.

moderator *noun* 1 an arbitrator or mediator. 2 a Presbyterian minister presiding over a church court or assembly. 3 (*Physics*) a substance used in a nuclear reactor to slow down neutrons.

modern *adjective* 1 belonging to the present or recent times ♦ *modern history.* 2 in current fashion, using methods or materials that are new or recent. 3 (said about art or literature) new and experimental, not following traditional styles.
modern *noun* a person of modern times or with modern tastes or style. **modernity** (mə-dern-iti) *noun* [from a Latin word *modernus*]

modern dance *noun* an expressive style of dancing distinct from classical ballet.

modernism *noun* modern views or methods.

modernist *noun* someone who favours modern views or methods. **modernistic** *adjective*

modernize *verb* 1 to make something more modern. SYNONYMS: renovate, update. 2 to adapt to modern ideas or tastes. **modernization** *noun*

modest *adjective* 1 not vain or boastful, unassuming. SYNONYMS: unassuming, humble. 2 moderate in size or amount ♦ *The staff will get a modest pay rise next year.* SYNONYMS: moderate, small, reasonable, limited. 3 not showy or pretentious, ordinary. SYNONYMS: ordinary, unpretentious, simple, plain. 4 behaving or dressing decently or decorously. **modestly** *adverb* **modesty** *noun* [from a Latin word *modestus* meaning 'keeping the proper measure']

modicum (mod-i-kəm) *noun* a small amount. [from a Latin word *modicus* meaning 'moderate']

modify *verb* (**modifies, modified, modifying**) 1 to change something in small ways ♦ *Some clauses in the agreement have been modified.* SYNONYMS: adjust, alter, change, revise. 2 to make something less severe or harsh. SYNONYMS: moderate, temper, soften, relieve, reduce. 3 (*Grammar*) to qualify a word or phrase by describing it ♦ *Adjectives modify nouns.* **modification** *noun* [from a Latin word *modificare* meaning 'to limit']

modish (moh-dish) *adjective* fashionable. **modishly** *adverb* **modishness** *noun* [from *mode*]

modular adjective consisting of independent units or modules.

modulate verb 1 to adjust or regulate something. 2 to vary the tone or pitch of your voice. 3 (Music) to change from one key to another. 4 to alter the amplitude, frequency, or phase of a carrier wave so as to convey a particular signal. **modulation** noun [from a Latin word modulare, related to model]

module (mod-yool) noun 1 each of a set of standardized parts or units used to make something more complex. 2 a section of a course of study. 3 a self-contained unit attached to a spacecraft. [same origin as for modulate]

modulo arithmetic noun a form of arithmetic using a limited set of consecutive numbers beginning with 0, which can be set out in a circle for doing calculations. In modulo 12 arithmetic, the 12 numbers from 0 to 11 are used.

modus operandi (moh-dəs op-er-an-di) noun a particular way of doing something. [a Latin phrase meaning 'way of operating']

Mogul (moh-gəl) noun a member of a Muslim dynasty of Mongol origin in India in the 16th–19th centuries. [from the Persian word mugul meaning 'Mongol']

mogul (moh-gəl) noun (informal) an important or powerful person. [named after the Mogul dynasty]

mohair noun 1 the silky hair of the angora goat. 2 a yarn or fabric made from this. [from an Arabic word meaning 'special' or 'choice']

mohican noun a hairstyle in which the head is shaved except for a strip of hair along the top, which is worn upright and often brightly coloured. [from Mohican, the name of an American Indian people with whom this style was wrongly associated]

moire (mwah) noun a fabric that looks like watered silk. [a French word meaning 'mohair']

moist adjective slightly wet, damp. SYNONYMS: damp, wet, watery. **moistness** noun [from an Old French word]

moisten (moi-sən) verb to make something moist, or to become moist.

moisture noun water or other liquid in a substance or present in the air as vapour or condensed on a surface.

moisturize verb to make the skin less dry by using cosmetics. **moisturizer** noun

moksha noun (in Hinduism) release from the cycle of rebirth required by the law of karma. [from a Sanskrit word moksa]

molar [1] (moh-ler) noun any of the wide teeth at the back of the mouth used for grinding. [from a Latin word mola meaning 'millstone']

molar [2] (moh-ler) adjective (Chemistry) 1 to do with one mole of a substance. 2 (said about a solution) containing one mole of solute per litre of solvent.

molarity noun (molarities) (Chemistry) the concentration of a solution expressed as the number of moles of solute per litre of solvent.

molasses (mə-las-iz) noun dark syrup made from raw sugar. [from a Latin word mellaceus meaning 'like honey']

mole [1] noun 1 a small burrowing animal with dark velvety fur and very small eyes. 2 a spy working within an organization and passing information to another organization or country. [probably from a German and Dutch word mol]

mole [2] noun a small dark spot on the skin. [from an Old English word mal]

mole [3] noun a structure built out into the sea as a breakwater or causeway. [from a Latin word moles meaning 'mass']

mole [4] noun (Chemistry) a unit of amount of a substance equal to the quantity containing as many elementary units as there are atoms in 0.012 kg of carbon-12. [from a German word Mol, from Molekül meaning 'molecule']

molecule (mol-i-kewl) noun 1 the smallest unit, usually a group of atoms, into which a substance can be divided without changing its chemical qualities. 2 a small particle of something. **molecular** (mə-lek-yoo-ler) adjective [from a Latin word molecula meaning 'little mass']

molehill noun a small mound of earth thrown up by a burrowing mole. **to make a mountain out of a molehill** to exaggerate the seriousness of a problem.

molest (mə-lest) verb 1 to annoy or pester someone in a hostile way. SYNONYMS: harass, pester, annoy. 2 to assault or abuse someone sexually. **molestation** noun [from a Latin word molestus meaning 'troublesome']

mollify *verb* (**mollifies, mollified, mollifying**) to make someone less angry. SYNONYMS: calm, pacify, appease, soothe, assuage. [from a Latin word *mollis* meaning 'soft']

mollusc (mol-əsk) *noun* any of a group of animals including snails, slugs, and mussels, with soft bodies and (in some cases) external shells. [from a Latin word *molluscus* meaning 'soft thing']

mollycoddle *verb* to pamper someone.

Molotov cocktail *noun* a crude improvised incendiary bomb thrown by hand. [named after the Russian statesman V. M. Molotov (1890–1986), who organized their production during World War II]

molten (mohl-tən) *adjective* melted, made liquid by great heat. [an old past participle of *melt*]

molybdenum (mə-lib-din-əm) *noun* a metallic element (symbol Mo), used as a strengthening agent in steels and other alloys. [from a Greek word *molubdos* meaning 'lead']

moment *noun* **1** a very short period of time ♦ *It will only take a moment.* SYNONYMS: instant, second, minute. **2** a particular or suitable time ♦ *It was not the moment to mention the broken window.* SYNONYMS: time, occasion, opportunity. **3** (*formal*) importance ♦ *These are questions of great moment.* SYNONYMS: importance, significance, consequence. **at any moment** very soon. **at the moment** now. **for the moment** for now, for the time being. **in a moment** soon. **moment of truth** a time of test or crisis. [from a Latin word *movere* meaning 'to move'. The phrase *moment of truth* comes from a Spanish phrase used in bullfighting to refer to the sword thrust that kills the bull]

momentary (moh-mən-ter-i) *adjective* lasting only a moment. SYNONYMS: brief, fleeting, passing, transient, transitory. **momentarily** *adverb*

momentous (mə-ment-əs) *adjective* very important or significant. SYNONYMS: important, crucial, significant, serious, grave.

momentum (mə-ment-əm) *noun* impetus gained by movement ♦ *The boulder gathered momentum as it rolled down the hill.* [a Latin word meaning 'movement']

monarch (mon-erk) *noun* **1** a ruler with the title of king, queen, emperor, or empress. **2** a large orange and black butterfly. **monarchic** (mən-ark-ik) *adjective*

monarchical (mən-ark-ikəl) *adjective* [from Greek words *monos* meaning 'alone' and *arkhein* meaning 'to rule']

monarchist (mon-er-kist) *noun* a person who favours government by a monarch. **monarchism** *noun*

monarchy (mon-er-ki) *noun* (**monarchies**) **1** government by a monarch. **2** a country ruled by a monarch.

monastery (mon-ə-ster-i) *noun* (**monasteries**) a building occupied by monks living as a secluded community, or the community itself. [from a Greek word *monazein* meaning 'to live alone']

monastic (mən-ast-ik) *adjective* to do with monks or monasteries. **monastically** *adverb*

monasticism (mən-ast-i-sizm) *noun* the way of life practised by monks.

Monday *noun* the day of the week following Sunday. [from an Old English word *monandæg* meaning 'day of the moon']

monetarism (mun-it-er-izm) *noun* control of the supply of money as a means of stabilizing the economy of a country. **monetarist** *noun* & *adjective*

monetary (mun-it-er-i) *adjective* to do with money or currency.

money *noun* **1** coins and banknotes used as a medium of exchange for goods and services. SYNONYMS: cash, change, notes, coins, silver, funds. **2** wealth. **3** (**moneys** or **monies**) a sum of money. [from a Latin word *moneta*, related to *mint*[2]]

money box *noun* a closed box with a slit for dropping coins through.

moneyed *adjective* wealthy or affluent.

money-grubbing *adjective* (*informal*) too keen to make money; greedy.

moneylender *noun* a person who lends money to be repaid with interest.

money order *noun* a printed order for the payment of a sum of money, issued by a bank or Post Office.

money-spinner *noun* something that makes a lot of money.

Mongol (mong-gəl) *noun* a person born in Mongolia, a country north of China, or descended from people born there. **Mongol** *adjective* to do with or coming from Mongolia.

mongolism (mong-gəl-izm) *noun* Down's syndrome.
◊ This term is now considered to be offensive. Use *Down's syndrome* instead.

mongoose (mon-gooss) *noun* (**mongooses**) a small tropical animal like a stoat, which can attack and kill snakes. [from a southern Indian language]

mongrel (mung-grəl) *noun* 1 a dog of no identifiable type or breed, or of mixed breeds. [related to *mingle*]

monitor *noun* 1 a device used for observing or testing the operation of something. 2 a television screen used in a studio to check and control transmissions. 3 a screen that displays data and images produced by a computer. 4 a person who listens to and reports on foreign broadcasts. 5 a pupil who is given special duties in a school.
monitor *verb* to record or test or control the working of something. SYNONYMS: survey, supervise, observe, control. [from a Latin word *monere* meaning 'to warn']

monk *noun* a member of a community of men who live apart from the world under the rules of a religious order. [via Old English from a Greek word *monakhos* meaning 'single' or 'solitary']

monkey *noun* (**monkeys**) 1 an animal of a group closely related to humans, having long arms and hands with thumbs, and often a tail. 2 a mischievous person, especially a child. 3 (*informal*) a sum of £500.
monkey *verb* (**monkeys, monkeyed, monkeying**) to tamper with something ♦ *Please don't monkey with the switches.* [origin unknown]

monkey business *noun* (*informal*) 1 mischief. 2 underhand dealings.

monkey nut *noun* a peanut.

monkey puzzle *noun* an evergreen tree with stiff needle-like leaves and intertwining branches.

monkey wrench *noun* a large spanner with adjustable jaws.

monkshood *noun* a poisonous plant with blue hood-shaped flowers.

mono *adjective* monophonic.
mono *noun* (**monos**) monophonic sound or recording.

mono- *prefix* one, single. [from a Greek word *monos* meaning 'alone']

monochrome (mon-ə-krohm) *adjective* done in one colour or in black and white.

monochromatic (mon-ə-krə-mat-ik) *adjective* [from *mono-* and a Greek word *khrōma* meaning 'colour']

monocle (mon-ə-kəl) *noun* a lens worn over one eye and held in place by the muscles round the eye. [from *mono-* and a Latin word *oculus* meaning 'eye']

monocotyledon (monə-kot-i-lee-dən) *noun* (*Botany*) a flowering plant that has a single cotyledon. **monocotyledonous** *adjective*

monocular (mən-ok-yoo-ler) *adjective* with one eye, using or intended for use with one eye. [same origin as for *monocle*]

monogamy (mən-og-əmi) *noun* the practice of being married to only one person at a time. (Compare **polygamy**.) **monogamous** *adjective* [from *mono-* and a Greek word *gamos* meaning 'marriage']

monogram (mon-ə-gram) *noun* a design made up of a letter or letters, especially a person's initials. [from *mono-* and *-gram*] **monogrammed** *adjective*

monograph (mon-ə-grahf) *noun* a scholarly book or article on a single subject or topic. [from *mono-* and *-graph*]

monolith (mon-ə-lith) *noun* a large single upright block of stone. [from *mono-* and a Greek word *lithos* meaning 'stone']

monolithic (monə-lith-ik) *adjective* 1 formed from a single block of stone. 2 (said about an organization) large and difficult to change.

monologue (mon-ə-log) *noun* 1 a speech by one actor in a play. 2 a long tedious speech by one person in a group. [from *mono-* and a Greek word *logos* meaning 'word']

monomania (monə-may-niə) *noun* an obsession with one idea or interest. **monomaniac** *noun* [from *mono-* and *mania*]

monomer (mon-ə-mer) *noun* (*Chemistry*) 1 a molecule that can unite with other identical molecules to form a polymer. **monomeric** *adjective* [from *mono-* and a Greek word *meros* meaning 'a part']

monophonic (mon-ə-fon-ik) *adjective* (said about sound reproduction) using only one transmission channel. (Compare **stereophonic**.) [from *mono-* and a Greek word *phōnē* meaning 'sound']

monoplane *noun* a type of aeroplane with only one set of wings.

monopolist (mən-**op**-əlist) *noun* a person who has a monopoly. **monopolistic** *adjective*

monopolize *verb* to control or use something so that other people are excluded ♦ *My uncle always seems to monopolize the conversation.* **monopolization** *noun*

monopoly (mən-**op**-əli) *noun* (**monopolies**) 1 the exclusive right or opportunity to sell a commodity or service. 2 complete possession or control of something by one person or group. [from *mono-* and a Greek word *pōlein* meaning 'to sell']

monorail *noun* a railway in which the track consists of a single rail, usually built above ground level.

monosaccharide *noun* (*Chemistry*) a sugar that cannot be broken down by hydrolysis into simpler sugars.

monosodium glutamate (mo- noh- **soh**- di- əm **gloo**- tə- mayt) *noun* a compound made by the breakdown of vegetable protein and used to enhance flavour in food.

monosyllable (**mon**-ə-sil-əbəl) *noun* a word of only one syllable. **monosyllabic** (monə-sil-**ab**-ik) *adjective*

monotheism (**mon**-əth-ee-izm) *noun* the belief that there is only one God. **monotheist** *noun* **monotheistic** *adjective* [from *mono-* and a Greek word *theos* meaning 'god']

monotone (**mon**-ə-tohn) *noun* a level unchanging sound or tone of voice in speaking or singing.

monotonous (mən-**ot**-ən-əs) *adjective* 1 dull or tedious because it does not change much. SYNONYMS: dull, tedious, boring, dreary, repetitive, wearisome. 2 lacking in variation of tone or pitch. **monotonously** *adverb* [from *mono-* and a Greek word *tonos* meaning 'tone']

monotony (mən-**ot**-ən-i) *noun* a dull or tedious situation.

monovalent (mon-oh-vay-lənt) *adjective* (*Chemistry*) having a valency of one. [from *mono-* and *valency*]

monoxide (mə-**nok**-siyd) *noun* (*Chemistry*) an oxide with one atom of oxygen.

Monseigneur (mawn-sen-**yer**) *noun* a title or form of address for an eminent Frenchman, such as a prince or bishop. [a French word, from *mon* meaning 'my' and *seigneur* meaning 'lord']

Monsieur (məs-**yer**) *noun* (**Messieurs** (mes-**yer**)) the title of a Frenchman, equivalent to 'Mr' or 'sir'. [a French word, from *mon* meaning 'my' and *sieur* meaning 'lord']

Monsignor (mon-**seen**-yor) *noun* the title of certain Roman Catholic priests and officials. [an Italian word, modelled on *Monseigneur*]

monsoon *noun* 1 a strong seasonal wind that blows in the region of the Indian subcontinent and South Asia. 2 the rainy season accompanying the monsoon blowing from the south-west. [from an Arabic word *mausim* meaning 'fixed season']

monster *noun* 1 a large ugly or frightening creature. 2 a huge thing. 3 an animal or plant that is very abnormal in form. 4 an extremely cruel or wicked person. [from a Latin word *monstrum* meaning 'marvel']

monstrosity (mon-**stros**-iti) *noun* (**monstrosities**) a huge and ugly thing.

monstrous (**mon**-strəs) *adjective* 1 huge and ugly. 2 outrageously wrong or unjust. SYNONYMS: wicked, terrible, outrageous, atrocious, appalling. **monstrously** *adverb*

montage (mon-**tah**zh) *noun* 1 the process of making a composite work of art, music, or film by putting together separate pieces or pieces from other works. 2 a work produced in this way. [a French word, from *monter* meaning 'to mount']

month *noun* 1 any of the twelve named periods into which a year is divided. 2 a period between the same dates in successive months. [from an Old English word *monath*, related to *moon* (because time was measured by changes in the moon's appearance)]

monthly *adjective* happening or produced once a month.
monthly *adverb* once a month, every month.
monthly *noun* (**monthlies**) a monthly magazine.

monument *noun* 1 a statue or building intended to celebrate or commemorate an important person or event. 2 a building or site that is preserved because of its historical importance. [from a Latin word *monumentum*, from *monere* meaning 'to remind']

monumental *adjective* 1 belonging to or serving as a monument ♦ *monumental arches and gateways.* 2 extremely great or important ♦ *a monumental achievement.*

SYNONYMS: outstanding, remarkable, tremendous, wonderful.

moo verb (**moos, mooed, mooing**) to make the low deep sound of a cow.
moo noun (**moos**) a mooing sound. [an imitation of the sound]

mooch verb (informal) to loiter in a bored or listless manner. [from an earlier meaning 'to hoard', probably from a French word muscher meaning 'to hide' or 'to skulk']

mood noun 1 a temporary state of mind or spirits ♦ She seemed to be in a subdued mood. SYNONYMS: temper, humour, disposition, state of mind. 2 a fit of bad temper or depression ♦ He's in one of his moods. 3 the tone or atmosphere conveyed by a literary or artistic work. 4 (Grammar) a form of a verb that shows whether it is a statement, command, question, or wish. **in the mood** in a willing state of mind. [from an Old English word]

moody adjective (**moodier, moodiest**) 1 gloomy or sullen. SYNONYMS: sulky, sullen, morose, peevish, irritable. 2 having sudden changes of mood for no apparent reason. **moodily** adverb **moodiness** noun

moon noun 1 the natural satellite of the earth, visible from light reflected from the sun. 2 the moon when it is visible ♦ There's no moon tonight. 3 a natural satellite of another planet.
moon verb 1 to move or pass time in a dreamy or listless manner. 2 (informal) to expose your bottom as an insult or joke. [from an Old English word, related to month]

moonbeam noun a ray of moonlight.

moonless adjective without a moon.

moonlight noun light from the moon.
moonlight verb (past tense and past participle **moonlighted**) (informal) to have a second job, especially in the evening when your main job is during the day.

moonlit adjective lit by the moon.

moonshine noun 1 foolish talk or ideas. 2 (North Amer.) illicit liquor.

moonstone noun a pearly white semi-precious stone, especially of feldspar.

moonstruck adjective unable to act sensibly, especially when in love.

moony adjective (**moonier, mooniest**) dreamy or listless. **moonily** adverb

Moor noun a member of a Muslim people of north-west Africa. **Moorish** adjective [from a Greek word Mauros meaning 'inhabitant of Mauretania', an ancient region of north Africa]

moor[1] noun 1 a stretch of open uncultivated land with heather and other low shrubs. [from an Old English word]

moor[2] verb to secure a boat to the shore or to a fixed object by means of a cable. [probably from a German word]

moorhen noun a small waterbird. [from moor[1] in an old meaning 'fen']

mooring noun or **moorings** plural noun 1 a place where a boat is moored. 2 cables and ropes for mooring a boat.

moorland noun an area of moor.

moose noun (**moose**) a North American elk. [from a Native American language]

moot adjective debatable or undecided ♦ That's a moot point.
moot verb to raise a question for discussion. [from an Old English word mot meaning 'assembly or meeting']

mop noun 1 a bunch or pad of soft material fastened to the end of a long handle, used for cleaning floors. 2 a thick mass of hair.
mop verb (**mopped, mopping**) to clean or wipe a floor or other surface with a mop. **to mop up** 1 to wipe up with a mop. 2 to clear an area of remaining enemy troops after a victory. [origin unknown]

mope verb to be listless and in low spirits. SYNONYMS: sulk, brood. [probably from a Scandinavian language]

moped (moh-ped) noun a kind of small motorcycle that can be pedalled. [from motor and pedal]

moraine (mə-rayn) noun (Geology) a mass of rocks and debris carried down and deposited by a glacier. [via French from an Italian word morena]

moral adjective 1 to do with what is right and wrong in human behaviour ♦ moral philosophy. 2 good or virtuous. SYNONYMS: virtuous, honest, good, honourable. 3 following the accepted rules of behaviour. SYNONYMS: decent, righteous, proper. 4 based on a sense of what is right or just rather than on legal rights ♦ We had a moral obligation to help. 5 psychological or mental, not physical ♦ moral courage.
moral noun a lesson in right behaviour taught by an event or story.

morals *plural noun* standards of behaviour. **morally** *adverb* [from a Latin word *mores* meaning 'customs']

morale (mə-**rahl**) *noun* the spirits and confidence of a person or group at a particular time. [same origin as for *moral*]

moralist *noun* a person who expresses or teaches moral principles. **moralistic** *adjective*

morality (mə-**ral**-iti) *noun* (**moralities**) 1 moral principles or rules. 2 a particular system of morals ♦ *financial morality*. 3 conforming to moral principles; goodness or rightness.

moralize *verb* to talk or write about the principles of right and wrong in human behaviour.

moral majority *noun* the majority of people, regarded as supporting good standards of behaviour.

moral philosophy *noun* the branch of philosophy concerned with the right and wrongs of human behaviour.

moral support *noun* support that is psychological, giving a person confidence, rather than physical.

morass (mo-**rass**) *noun* 1 a marsh or bog. 2 a confused mass. [via Dutch from an Old French word *marais* meaning 'marsh']

moratorium (mo-rə-**tor**-iəm) *noun* (**moratoriums** or **moratoria**) 1 a temporary ban imposed on an activity. 2 legal authorization to debtors to delay payment. [from a Latin word *morari* meaning 'to delay']

morbid *adjective* 1 concerned with or interested in gloomy or unpleasant things. SYNONYMS: gloomy, glum, melancholy, gruesome. 2 (*Medicine*) caused by or indicating disease, unhealthy ♦ *a morbid growth*. **morbidity** (mor-**bid**-iti) *noun* **morbidly** *adverb* **morbidness** *noun* [from a Latin word *morbus* meaning 'disease']

mordant (**mor**-dənt) *adjective* (said about humour) sharp or critical. **mordant** *noun* a chemical substance used to fix dyes on fabric. [from a French word meaning 'biting']

more *adjective* greater in amount or degree. **more** *noun* a greater amount or number. **more** *adverb* 1 to a greater extent ♦ *more beautiful*. 2 again ♦ *once more*. **more or less** to a greater or less extent; approximately ♦ *We have more or less finished*. [from an Old English word]

morello (mə-**rel**-oh) *noun* (**morellos**) a dark cherry with a bitter taste. [an Italian word meaning 'blackish']

moreover *adverb* besides, in addition to what has already been said.

morganatic (mor-gən-**at**-ik) *adjective* (said about a marriage) concluded between people of different social rank, in which the spouse of lower rank, and the children of the marriage, have no claim to the other spouse's possessions or title. **morganatically** *adverb* [from a Latin phrase *matrimonium ad morganaticam* meaning 'marriage with a morning gift' (because a gift given by a husband on the morning after the marriage was all the wife was entitled to)]

morgue (morg) *noun* a mortuary. [a French word, originally the name of a Paris mortuary]

MORI *abbreviation* Market and Opinion Research Institute.

moribund (**mo**-ri-bund) *adjective* 1 in a dying state. 2 lacking energy or vigour. [from a Latin word *moribundus*, from *mori* meaning 'to die']

Mormon (**mor**-mən) *noun* a member of a religious organization, the Church of Jesus Christ of Latter-Day Saints, founded in the USA in 1830. [from *The Book of Mormon*, a collection of supposed revelations attributed to a prophet called Mormon]

morn *noun* (*poetic*) morning. [from an Old English word]

morning *noun* 1 the early part of the day, up to noon or lunchtime. 2 sunrise or dawn ♦ *when morning broke*. [from *morn*]

morning dress *noun* formal dress for a man consisting of a tailcoat, striped trousers, and a top hat.

morning star *noun* a planet, especially Venus, seen in the east before sunrise.

morocco *noun* a fine flexible leather originally made in Morocco from goatskins.

moron (**mor**-on) *noun* (*informal*) a very stupid person. **moronic** (mə-**ron**-ik) *adjective* [from a Greek word *mōros* meaning 'foolish']

morose (mə-**rohss**) *adjective* bad-tempered and gloomy. SYNONYMS: sullen, gloomy, moody, peevish, irritable, bad-tempered. **morosely** *adverb* **moroseness** *noun* [from a Latin word *morosus* meaning 'peevish']

morphia (mor-fiə) *noun* (old use) morphine.

morphine (mor-feen) *noun* a drug made from opium, used for relieving pain. [named after Morpheus, the Roman god of sleep]

morris dance *noun* a traditional English folk dance performed by dancers in costume with ribbons and bells. [originally *Moorish dance* (because it was thought to have come from the Moors)]

morrow *noun* (old use or poetic) the following day. [same origin as for *morn*]

Morse code *noun* a system of signalling, in which letters of the alphabet are represented by combinations of short and long sounds or flashes of light (dots and dashes). [named after its American inventor S. F. B. Morse (1791–1872)]

morsel *noun* a small piece of food. SYNONYMS: scrap, mouthful, bit, bite. [from a Latin word *morsus* meaning 'bite']

mortal *adjective* 1 not living for ever, bound to die ♦ *All humans are mortal.* 2 causing death, fatal ♦ *He suffered a mortal wound.* SYNONYMS: fatal, lethal, deadly; terminal (illness). 3 lasting until death ♦ *mortal enemies* ♦ *in mortal combat.* 4 (informal) intense ♦ *in mortal fear.* 5 (informal) without exception ♦ *They took every mortal thing.* 6 (in Christian teaching, said about a sin) serious enough to deprive the soul of divine grace.
mortal *noun* an ordinary human being, especially contrasted with a god or spirit.
mortally *adjective* [from a Latin word *mortis* meaning 'of death']

mortality (mor-tal-iti) *noun* 1 the state of being mortal and bound to die. 2 loss of life on a large scale.

mortar *noun* 1 a mixture of lime or cement with sand and water, for joining bricks or stones. 2 a hard bowl in which substances are pounded with a pestle. 3 a short cannon for firing shells at a high angle.
mortar *verb* 1 to join bricks with mortar. 2 to attack an enemy with shells fired from a mortar. [from an Old French word *mortier*]

mortar board *noun* an academic cap with a stiff square top. [so called because it looks like the board used by builders to hold mortar]

mortgage (mor-gij) *noun* a loan from a bank or building society to buy a house or other property, with the property as security for the loan.

mortgage *verb* to offer a property as security for a loan taken out to buy the property ♦ *The house is mortgaged with a building society.* [from an Old French word meaning literally 'dead pledge']

mortician (mor-tish-ən) *noun* (North Amer.) an undertaker. [same origin as for *mortal*]

mortify *verb* (**mortifies, mortified, mortifying**) 1 to humiliate someone or make them feel very ashamed. SYNONYMS: humiliate, shame, chasten. 2 to subdue physical desires by discipline or self-denial. 3 (said about flesh) to be affected by gangrene.
mortification *noun* [from an earlier meaning 'to kill or destroy', from a Latin word *mors* meaning 'death']

mortise (mor-tiss) *noun* a hole or slot made in a piece of wood so that a projecting part (called a *tenon*) on the end of another piece can be inserted in it to hold the two pieces together.
mortise *verb* to join pieces of wood with a mortise. [from an Old French word *mortaise*]

mortise lock *noun* a lock that is set into the framework of a door.

mortuary (mor-tew-er-i) *noun* (**mortuaries**) a place where dead bodies are kept until they are buried. [from a Latin word *mortuus* meaning 'dead']

Mosaic (mə-zay-ik) *adjective* to do with Moses, the Jewish patriarch of the Old Testament, or his teaching ♦ *Mosaic Law.*

mosaic (mə-zay-ik) *noun* a picture or design made by putting together small pieces of glass or stone of different colours. [via French from a Latin word *musivum* meaning 'decoration with small square stones']

Moslem (moz-ləm) *adjective* & *noun* another spelling of **Muslim**.

mosque (mosk) *noun* a building in which Muslims worship. [via French and Italian from an Arabic word *masgid*]

mosquito (mos-kee-toh) *noun* (**mosquitoes**) a kind of gnat, the female of which bites and sucks blood. [a Spanish word meaning 'little fly', from a Latin word *musca* meaning 'fly']

moss *noun* a small plant with no flowers, which forms a dense growth on moist surfaces or in bogs. **mossy** *adjective* [from an Old English word]

most *adjective* greatest in amount or degree.

most *noun* the greatest amount or number.

most *adverb* **1** to the greatest extent. **2** very ♦ *It is a most interesting story.* **at most** or **at the most** not more than, and no more ♦ *There were twenty people at the most.* **for the most part** in most cases, in most of its extent. **to make the most of something** to use something to the best advantage. [from an Old English word]

mostly *adverb* for the most part.

Most Reverend *adjective* a title given to an archbishop or Irish Roman Catholic bishop.

MOT *abbreviation* **1** (in Britain) a compulsory annual test of motor vehicles of more than a specified age. [an abbreviation of Ministry of Transport, the government department that introduced it]

mote *noun* a speck. [from an Old English word *mot*]

motel (moh-**tel**) *noun* a hotel built near a major road and providing accommodation for motorists and their cars. [from *motor* and *hotel*]

motet (moh-**tet**) *noun* a short piece of sacred choral music. [from an Old French word meaning 'little word']

moth *noun* an insect resembling a butterfly, which usually flies at night. **mothy** *adjective* [from an Old English word *moththe*]

mothball *noun* a small ball of naphthalene etc. placed in stored clothes to keep away moths. **in mothballs** stored out of use for a considerable time.

moth-eaten *adjective* **1** damaged by moth larvae. **2** old or shabby.

mother *noun* **1** a female parent. **2** a woman who is head of a female religious community ♦ *Mother Superior.* **mother** *verb* to look after someone in a motherly way. **motherhood** *noun* [from an Old English word *modor*]

motherboard *noun* (*Computing*) a board with a printed circuit used in a microcomputer.

mother country *noun* a country in relation to its colonies.

Mothering Sunday the fourth Sunday in Lent, when people give cards and gifts to their mothers.

mother-in-law *noun* (**mothers-in-law**) the mother of your wife or husband.

motherland *noun* a person's native country.

motherless *adjective* without a living or known mother.

motherly *adjective* like a mother, especially in being caring and protective. **motherliness** *noun*

mother-of-pearl *noun* a pearly substance lining the shells of oysters and mussels, and some other molluscs.

Mother's Day *noun* a day on which mothers are honoured, especially Mothering Sunday.

mother tongue *noun* the language a person speaks as their first or only language.

motif (moh-**teef**) *noun* **1** an image or feature forming a repeated part of a design. **2** a distinctive theme in a literary work or piece of music. **3** a decorative design sewn on a piece of clothing. [a French word]

motion *noun* **1** the action of moving or changing position. **2** a particular movement or gesture. SYNONYMS: movement, gesture, gesticulation, sign, signal. **3** a formal proposal put before a meeting for discussion. **4** an emptying of the bowels; excrement. **motion** *verb* to make a gesture directing someone to do something ♦ *She motioned him to sit beside her.* **to go through the motions** to do something in a routine or unthinking manner. **in motion** moving, not still. [from a Latin word *motio* meaning 'movement']

motionless *adjective* not moving.

motion picture *noun* a film shown in a cinema.

motivate *verb* **1** to give a motive or incentive to someone. SYNONYMS: induce, incite, influence, stimulate, prompt. **2** to arouse the interest of someone. **motivation** *noun*

motivated *adjective* having a definite and positive desire to do things.

motive *noun* what makes a person do something or act in a certain way. SYNONYMS: incentive, inducement, motivation, stimulus, reason. **motive** *adjective* producing movement or action ♦ *The engine provides motive power.* [from a Latin word *motivus* meaning 'moving']

motley *adjective* **1** varied in colour or appearance. **2** made up of various sorts ♦ *a motley group of people*.
motley *noun* (*old use*) a jester's costume of different colours. [origin unknown]

motocross *noun* a motorcycle race over rough ground.

motor *noun* **1** a machine that supplies motive power for a vehicle or machinery; an engine. **2** (*informal*) a motor car.
motor *adjective* giving or producing motion.
motor *verb* to travel in a motor car. [from a Latin word *motor* meaning 'mover']

motorbike *noun* a motorcycle.

motorcade *noun* a procession or parade of motor vehicles. [from *motor* and *cavalcade*]

motor car *noun* a car.

motorcycle *noun* a two-wheeled road vehicle with an engine. **motorcyclist** *noun*

motorist *noun* the driver of a car.

motorized *adjective* **1** equipped with a motor. **2** equipped with motor vehicles.

motor neuron *noun* a nerve cell carrying impulses from the brain or spinal cord to a muscle or gland.

motor neuron disease *noun* a disease of the motor neurons, causing severe weakening of the muscles.

motor vehicle *noun* a road vehicle with an engine.

motorway *noun* a road designed for fast motor traffic, with several lanes in each direction and restricted access.

motte *noun* (*Archaeology*) a mound forming the site of an ancient castle or camp. [a French word meaning 'mound']

mottled *adjective* marked with spots or patches of colour. SYNONYMS: speckled, spotted, spotty, blotchy. [probably from *motley*]

motto *noun* (**mottoes** or **mottos**) a short phrase or saying summarizing an ideal or principle and adopted as a guide for behaviour. SYNONYMS: saying, slogan, proverb, maxim. [an Italian word meaning 'word']

mould[1] *noun* **1** a hollow container of a particular shape, into which a soft or liquid substance is poured to set or cool into this shape. **2** a pudding made in a mould. **3** a distinctive style or character ♦ *a cricketer in the mould of Botham.*

mould *verb* **1** to make something in a particular shape. SYNONYMS: shape, form, fashion, model, cast, sculpt. **2** to influence or guide the development of something ♦ *The experience helped to mould his character.* SYNONYMS: shape, form, guide, influence, direct. [from a Latin word *modulus* meaning 'little measure']

mould[2] *noun* a fine furry growth of very small fungi that forms on things that are kept in moist warm conditions. [probably from a Scandinavian language]

mould[3] *noun* soft loose earth that is rich in organic matter ♦ *leaf mould.* [from an Old English word *molde*]

moulder *verb* to decay or rot slowly. [perhaps from *mould*[3]]

moulding *noun* (*Architecture*) an ornamental strip of plaster or wood used as a decoration.

mouldy *adjective* (**mouldier**, **mouldiest**) **1** covered with mould. **2** stale and smelling of mould. **3** (*informal*) dull or tedious. **mouldiness** *noun*

moult (mohlt) *verb* (said about an animal) to shed its skin, hair, or feathers to make way for a new growth.
moult *noun* the process of moulting. [via Old English from a Latin word *mutari* meaning 'to change']

mound *noun* **1** a built-up pile of earth or stones. SYNONYMS: heap, pile, mass. **2** a small hill. SYNONYMS: hill, hillock, knoll, rise, hump. [origin unknown]

mount[1] *noun* (*old use, or in place names*) a mountain or hill ♦ *Mount Everest.* [from a Latin word *mons* meaning 'mountain']

mount[2] *verb* **1** to go upwards, to rise to a higher level. SYNONYMS: rise, ascend, climb. **2** to get on to a horse or bicycle so as to ride it. **3** to increase in amount or intensity ♦ *The excitement was mounting.* SYNONYMS: grow, increase, intensify, escalate. **4** to fix something in position for use or display ♦ *You can mount your photographs in an album.* **5** to take action to achieve something ♦ *The enemy mounted a strong offensive.* SYNONYMS: stage, initiate, begin. **6** to place someone on guard ♦ *to mount sentries.*
mount *noun* **1** a horse for riding. **2** something on which a thing is mounted for support or display. [from an Old French word *munter*]

mountain *noun* **1** a mass of land that rises to a large height compared with the surrounding land. **2** a large heap or pile; a large amount ♦ *a mountain of work*. **3** a large surplus stock of a product ♦ *a butter mountain*. [from an Old French word *montaigne*, related to *mount*¹]

mountain ash *noun* a rowan tree.

mountain bike *noun* a bicycle with a strong lightweight frame, thick tyres, and multiple gears, suitable for riding on rough and hilly terrain.

mountaineer *noun* a person who climbs mountains. **mountaineering** *noun*

mountainous *adjective* **1** having many mountains ♦ *mountainous country*. **2** huge.

mountebank (**mownt-i-bank**) *noun* a swindler or charlatan. [from an earlier meaning 'a person who sold medicines in public places', from an Italian word *montambanco*, from the phrase *monta in banco!* meaning 'climb on the bench!', referring to the raised platform used for addressing the public]

mounted *adjective* serving on horseback ♦ *mounted police*.

Mountie *noun* (*informal*) a member of the Royal Canadian Mounted Police.

mourn *verb* **1** to feel or show deep sorrow for someone who has died. SYNONYMS: grieve, lament, (without an object) sorrow. **2** to regret something that has been lost. [from an Old English word *murnan*]

mourner *noun* a person who attends a funeral as a relative or friend of the dead.

mournful *adjective* feeling or showing sorrow or grief. SYNONYMS: sorrowful, forlorn, melancholy, despondent. **mournfully** *adverb* **mournfulness** *noun*

mourning *noun* **1** the process of showing sorrow for someone who has died. **2** black or dark clothes worn in mourning.

mouse *noun* (**mice**) **1** a small rodent with a long thin tail and a pointed nose. **2** a quiet or timid person. **3** (**mice** or **mouses**) (*Computing*) a small hand-held device which is dragged across a flat surface to control the position of a cursor on a VDU screen. [from an Old English word]

mousetrap *noun* a trap for catching mice.

mousing *noun* hunting mice, especially by a cat.

moussaka (**moo-sah-kə**) *noun* a Greek dish consisting of layers of minced meat and aubergine with a cheese sauce. [from a Turkish word *musakka*]

mousse (**mooss**) *noun* **1** a creamy light pudding of fruit or chocolate whipped with cream or egg white. **2** a savoury dish of meat or fish purée mixed with cream and shaped in a mould. **3** a frothy creamy substance used for styling the hair. [a French word meaning 'froth']

moustache (**məs-tahsh**) *noun* a strip of hair growing on a man's upper lip. [via French from an Italian word *mostaccio*]

mousy *adjective* (**mousier, mousiest**) **1** (said about hair) dull or light brown in colour. **2** (said about a person) quiet and timid.

mouth ¹ (mowth) *noun* **1** the opening in the face through which food is taken into the body and from which sounds are made. **2** the place where a river enters the sea. **3** the opening of something hollow or enclosed, such as a cave, horn, etc. **4** (*informal*) talkativeness or impudence. [from an Old English word]

mouth ² (mowth) *verb* **1** to form words with the lips, usually without saying them aloud. **2** to declaim words pompously or with exaggerated distinctness. **to mouth off** (*informal*) to talk in an opinionated or abusive way.

mouthful *noun* (**mouthfuls**) **1** a quantity of food or drink that fills the mouth. **2** a long or awkward word or phrase that is difficult to say.

mouth organ *noun* a small musical instrument played by passing it along the lips while blowing or sucking air; a harmonica.

mouthpiece *noun* **1** the part of a musical instrument or other device (such as a telephone) that is placed between or near the lips. **2** someone who speaks on behalf of another person or an organization.

mouthwash *noun* a liquid for cleansing the mouth or for gargling.

movable *adjective* able to be moved. **movables** *plural noun* property that can be moved, not buildings or land.

movable feast *noun* a religious feast day that changes from year to year, such as Easter.

move *verb* **1** to change in position or posture, or to make something do this. SYNONYMS: shift, budge, stir. **2** to go in a certain direction, or to make something do this. SYNONYMS: (without an object) go, travel. **3** to change your job or the place where you live. SYNONYM: relocate. **4** to

make progress ♦ *The work moves slowly.*
SYNONYMS: progress, advance, proceed. **5** to
provoke a strong feeling in someone,
especially sorrow or sympathy ♦ *They were
deeply moved by the story.* SYNONYMS: affect,
touch, stir. **6** to prompt or motivate
someone to do something ♦ *What moved
them to invite us?* SYNONYMS: prompt, make,
induce. **7** to propose an item for discussion
and decision at a meeting. SYNONYMS:
propose, submit, suggest. **8** to take prompt
action ♦ *We need to move quickly.* SYNONYMS:
act, take action. **9** to live or be active in a
particular group ♦ *She moves in the best
circles.* **10** to make a move in a board game.
11 to cause the bowels to empty.
move *noun* **1** the act or process of moving.
2 a player's turn to move a piece in a
board game. **3** an action done to achieve a
purpose ♦ *The union has made a move
towards settling the dispute.* **to get a move on**
(*informal*) to hurry. **to make a move 1** to
take action. **2** to leave. **to move in** to
take possession of a new house or other
property. **to move over** or **up** to change
position and make room for someone
else. **on the move** moving from one place
to another; making progress. **mover** *noun*
[from a Latin word *movere* meaning 'to
move']

movement *noun* **1** an act of moving. **2** the
moving parts in a mechanism, especially
a clock or watch. **3 a** a group of people
working together to advance a cause, or
the cause itself. **4** a trend or fashion ♦ *the
movement towards more flexible working hours.*
5 (*Music*) each of the principal divisions in
a long work.
movements *plural noun* a person's activity
during a period of time.

movie *noun* (*chiefly North Amer.*) a cinema
film. [short for *moving picture*]

moving *adjective* arousing strong
emotions, especially of sorrow or
sympathy ♦ *It was a very moving story.*
SYNONYMS: touching, poignant, emotional,
affecting.

moving staircase *noun* an escalator.

mow *verb* (past participle **mowed** or **mown**)
to cut down grass or a cereal crop with a
machine or a scythe. **to mow down** to kill
or destroy people at random or in great
numbers. [from an Old English word]

mower *noun* a machine for mowing.

mozzarella (mot-sə-**rel**-lə) *noun* a hard
white Italian cheese. [an Italian word,
from *mozzare* meaning 'to cut off']

MP *abbreviation* Member of Parliament.
◊ In the plural, *MPs* (meaning 'Members of
Parliament') does not need an
apostrophe. The possessive forms are
(singular) *an MP's salary*, (plural) *MPs'
salaries.*

m.p.g. *abbreviation* miles per gallon.

m.p.h. *abbreviation* miles per hour.

Mr *noun* (**Messrs**) **1** a title put before a
man's name ♦ *Mr Brown* ♦ *Mr John Brown.*
2 a title put before the name of an office
when addressing the holder ♦ *Mr
President.* [short for *mister*]

Mrs *noun* (**Mrs**) a title put before a married
woman's name ♦ *Mrs Jones* ♦ *Mrs Sheila
Jones.* [short for *mistress*]

MS *abbreviation* **1** (**MSS**) manuscript.
2 multiple sclerosis.

Ms (miz) *noun* a title put before a woman's
name regardless of her married or
unmarried status ♦ *Ms Green* ♦ *Ms Mary
Green.* [from *Mrs* and *Miss*]
◊ You put *Ms* before a woman's name if
she does not want to be called 'Miss' or
'Mrs', or if you do not know whether she
is married.

MS-DOS *abbreviation* (*Computing*) (*trademark*)
Microsoft disk operating system.

MSG *abbreviation* monosodium glutamate.

MSP *abbreviation* Member of the Scottish
Parliament.

Mt. *abbreviation* Mount.

much *adjective* existing in a large amount
♦ *much noise.*
much *noun* a large quantity.
much *adverb* **1** to a great extent ♦ *much to
my surprise.* **2** approximately ♦ *They are
much the same.* **much of a muchness**
(*informal*) hardly different, nearly the
same. [from an Old English word]

muck *noun* **1** farmyard manure. **2** dirt or
filth.
muck *verb* to make something dirty. **to
muck in** (*informal*) to contribute to tasks or
expenses. **to muck out** to remove muck or
dirt from a place ♦ *He is mucking out the
stables.* [probably from a Scandinavian
language]

muckle *noun* another word for **mickle**.

muckraking *noun* (*informal*) seeking for and
exposing scandal.

mucky *adjective* (**muckier, muckiest**) covered with muck, dirty.

mucous (mew-kəs) *adjective* of or like mucus, or covered with mucus.

mucous membrane *noun* a moist skin lining the nose, mouth, throat, and other hollow organs of the body.

mucus (mew-kəs) *noun* a moist sticky substance secreted by a mucous membrane and forming a protective covering inside hollow organs of the body. [from a Latin word]

mud *noun* 1 wet soft earth. 2 information that can cause harm or damage reputations. **your name is mud** (*informal*) you are unpopular or in disgrace. [probably from a German word]

muddle *verb* 1 to make something confused or disorganized. SYNONYMS: confuse, disorganize, jumble, mix up. 2 to confuse someone mentally. SYNONYMS: confuse, bewilder, puzzle, perplex. 3 to confuse or mistake one person or thing for another.
muddle *noun* a muddled state or condition, confusion or disorder. SYNONYMS: clutter, mess, jumble, disarray. **to muddle along** or **through** to cope as best you can. **muddler** *noun* [from an earlier meaning 'to wallow in mud', related to *mud*]

muddle-headed *adjective* liable to muddle things, mentally confused.

muddy *adjective* (**muddier, muddiest**) 1 like mud, or full of mud. 2 (said about a colour) dull, not clear or bright. **muddy** *verb* (**muddies, muddied, muddying**) to make something muddy or unclear. **muddiness** *noun*

mudflat *noun* a stretch of muddy land left uncovered at low tide.

mudguard *noun* a curved cover over the wheel of a bicycle, to protect the rider from mud thrown up.

mudlark *noun* 1 a person who scavenges for objects of value in mud beside a tidal river.

mud-slinging *noun* (*informal*) the spreading of accusations and insults about people.

muesli (mooz-li) *noun* a breakfast food of mixed cereals, dried fruit, and nuts. [from a Swiss German word]

muezzin (moo-ez-in) *noun* a Muslim crier who proclaims the hours of prayer from a minaret. [from an Arabic word *mu'addin* meaning 'calling to prayer']

muff [1] *noun* a short tube-shaped piece of warm material into which the hands are placed for warmth, one at each end. [from a Dutch word *mof*]

muff [2] *verb* (*informal*) to bungle something. [origin unknown]

muffin *noun* 1 a flat round bun, eaten toasted and buttered. 2 a small round sponge cake containing fruit or chocolate chips. [origin unknown]

muffle *verb* 1 to wrap or cover something to protect it or keep it warm. SYNONYMS: wrap, clothe, cover, swathe. 2 to wrap or pad a source of sound in order to deaden its sound. 3 to deaden or reduce a sound. SYNONYMS: stifle, soften, deaden, suppress. [from an Old French word *moufle* meaning 'thick glove']

muffler *noun* 1 a scarf worn round the neck for warmth. 2 a device for muffling sound.

mufti *noun* ordinary clothes worn by someone who usually wears a uniform. [from an Arabic word]

mug [1] *noun* 1 a large drinking vessel with a handle, used without a saucer. 2 (*informal*) a person's face or mouth. 3 (*informal*) a person who is easily deceived. **mug** *verb* (*informal*) (**mugged, mugging**) to rob someone with violence in a public place. **a mug's game** (*informal*) an activity that is likely to fail or bring discredit. **mugger** *noun* [probably from a Scandinavian language]

mug [2] *verb* (**mugged, mugging**) **to mug up** (*informal*) to learn a subject by studying hard. [origin unknown]

muggins *noun* (*informal*) a person, especially the person speaking or writing, who is easily deceived or victimized. [a use of the surname Muggins, perhaps with reference to *mug* [1]]

muggy *adjective* (**muggier, muggiest**) (said about the weather) oppressively damp and warm. SYNONYMS: humid, close, oppressive, sultry. **mugginess** *noun* [from a dialect word *mug* meaning 'mist' or 'drizzle']

mujahedin (muu-jah-hi-deen) *plural noun* a group of Islamic guerrilla fighters. [from an Arabic word meaning 'a person who fights a war']

mulberry *noun* (**mulberries**) **1** a purple or white fruit rather like a blackberry. **2** the tree that bears this fruit. **3** a dark purplish red colour. [from an Old English word]

mulch *noun* a mixture of leaves, grass, or compost spread on the ground to protect plants or to enrich the soil.
mulch *verb* to cover the ground with a mulch. [probably from a dialect word *mulch* meaning 'soft']

mulct *verb* (*formal*) to take money from someone, especially by a fine or taxation or by fraudulent means. [from a Latin word *mulcta* meaning 'a fine']

mule [1] *noun* **1** an animal that is the offspring of a mare and a donkey, used for carrying loads. **2** a stubborn person. [from an Old English word]

mule [2] *noun* a light shoe or slipper without a back. [from a French word meaning 'slipper']

muleteer (mew-li-teer) *noun* a person who drives mules.

mulish (mewl-ish) *adjective* stubborn, as a mule is supposed to be. **mulishly** *adverb* **mulishness** *noun*

mull [1] *verb* to heat wine or beer and add sugar and spices to it. [origin unknown]

mull [2] *verb* to mull over to think carefully about something. SYNONYMS: consider, think about, ponder on, reflect on. [perhaps related to *mill*]

mull [3] *noun* (in Scottish place names) a promontory ♦ *the Mull of Kintyre*. [from a Scottish Gaelic word *maol*]

mullah (mul-ə) *noun* a Muslim who has studied Islamic theology and sacred law. [from an Arabic word *mawla*]

mullet (mul-it) *noun* a kind of fish used for food. [via French from a Greek word *mullos*]

mulligatawny (mul-ig-ə-taw-ni) *noun* a spicy hot soup originally made in India. [from a Tamil word *milagutannir* meaning 'pepper water']

mullion (mul-iən) *noun* an upright bar between the panes of a tall window. [from an Old French word *moinel* meaning 'middle']

multi- *prefix* many (as in *multicultural*). [from a Latin word *multus* meaning 'many']

multicellular *adjective* (*Biology*) (said about an organism) consisting of many cells.

multicoloured *adjective* having many colours.

multicultural *adjective* made up of people of different races and cultures ♦ *a multicultural society*.

multifarious (multi-fair-iəs) *adjective* of many kinds, very varied. **multifariously** *adverb* [from a Latin word *multifarius*]

multilateral (multi-lat-er-əl) *adjective* (said about an agreement or treaty) made between three or more people, organizations, or countries. **multilaterally** *adverb* [from a Latin word *multilaterus* meaning 'many-sided']

multimedia *adjective* using more than one medium of communication ♦ *a multimedia show with pictures, lights, and music*.
multimedia *noun* (*Computing*) the use of audio and video material with links to computer data.

multimillionaire *noun* a person with a fortune of several million pounds or dollars.

multinational *adjective* (said about a business company) operating in several countries.
multinational *noun* a multinational company.

multiple *adjective* having several parts or elements.
multiple *noun* a number that contains another number (called a *factor*) an exact amount of times without a remainder ♦ *8 and 12 are multiples of 4*. [same origin as for *multiply*]

multiple sclerosis *noun* a chronic disease of the nervous system in which patches of tissue harden in the brain or spinal cord, causing partial or complete paralysis.

multiplex *adjective* having many parts or forms, or consisting of many elements.
multiplex *noun* a large cinema complex with many screens. [from *multi-* and a Latin word *-plex* meaning '-fold']

multiplicand *noun* a number that is to be multiplied by another number (called the *multiplier*).

multiplication *noun* **1** multiplying or being multiplied. **2** the process of multiplying one number by another.

multiplication sign *noun* the sign × (as in 2 × 3) indicating that one number is to be multiplied by another.

multiplication table *noun* a list showing the results when a number is multiplied by a series of numbers, usually 1 to 12.

multiplicity (multi-plis-iti) *noun* a great variety or large number.

multiplier *noun* **1** a number by which another number (called the *multiplicand*) is multiplied. **2** a device for increasing a small electric current so that it can be used or measured more easily.

multiply *verb* (**multiplies, multiplied, multiplying**) **1** (*Mathematics*) to take a number and obtain another number which contains the first number a specified number of times ♦ *Multiply 8 by 4 and get 32.* **2** to increase in number. SYNONYMS: increase, grow, proliferate. **3** to increase by breeding ♦ *Rabbits multiply rapidly.* [from a Latin word *multiplicare*, from *multus* meaning 'many']

multiracial (multi-**ray**-shǝl) *adjective* consisting of people of many different races.

multi-storey *adjective* (said about a building) having several storeys.

multitude *noun* a large number of things or people. [from a Latin word *multitudo*]

multitudinous (multi-**tewd**-in-ǝs) *adjective* very numerous.

mum [1] *noun* (*informal*) mother. [short for *mummy* [1]]

mum [2] *adjective* (*informal*) silent ♦ *Try to keep mum.* **mum's the word** say nothing about this. [an imitation of a sound made with closed lips]

mumble *verb* to speak indistinctly so you cannot easily be heard. SYNONYMS: mutter, murmur, whisper.
mumble *noun* indistinct speech. **mumbler** *noun* [from *mum* [2]]

mumbo-jumbo *noun* (*informal*) **1** meaningless talk or ritual. **2** obscure words or actions that are meant to mystify or confuse people. [from a name *Mumbo Jumbo* for a supposed African idol]

mummer *noun* an actor in a traditional mime. [from an Old French word *momer* meaning 'to act in a mime']

mummify *verb* (**mummifies, mummified, mummifying**) (especially in ancient Egypt) to preserve a corpse as a mummy by embalming it.

mummy [1] *noun* (*informal*) (**mummies**) mother. [from *mama*]

mummy [2] *noun* (**mummies**) (especially in ancient Egypt) a corpse treated with oils and wrapped in cloth to preserve it for burial. [from an Arabic word *mumiya* meaning 'an embalmed body']

mumps *noun* a virus disease that causes painful swellings in the neck. [from an old word *mump* meaning 'to pull a face' (because the glands in the face sometimes swell)]

munch *verb* to chew food steadily and vigorously. SYNONYMS: crunch, chew, chomp. [an imitation of the sound]

mundane (mun-**dayn**) *adjective* **1** dull or routine. SYNONYMS: routine, dull, everyday, commonplace, humdrum, run-of-the-mill, ordinary. **2** concerned with practical matters, not ideals. [from a Latin word *mundus* meaning 'world']

municipal (mew-**nis**-i-pǝl) *adjective* to do with a town or city or its local government.

municipality (mew-nis-i-**pal**-iti) *noun* (**municipalities**) a town or district that has local government. [from a Latin word *municipium* denoting a town whose citizens have the rights of Roman citizens]

munificent (mew-**nif**-i-sǝnt) *adjective* extremely generous. **munificence** *noun* **munificently** *adverb* [from a Latin word *munus* meaning 'gift']

munitions (mew-**nish**-ǝnz) *plural noun* military weapons, ammunition, and equipment. [from a Latin word *munitum* meaning 'fortified']

muntjac (munt-jak) *noun* a kind of small deer, originally from southern Asia and now also found in western Europe. [from a Sundanese (Indonesian) word *minchek*]

muon (**mew**-on) *noun* (*Physics*) an unstable meson with a mass around 200 times that of an electron. [a shortening of the earlier name *mu-meson*]

mural (**mewr**-ǝl) *noun* a wall painting.
mural *adjective* on or to do with a wall. [from a Latin word *murus* meaning 'wall']

murder *noun* **1** the intentional and unlawful killing of one person by another. **2** (*informal*) something very difficult or unpleasant.

murder *verb* 1 to kill a person unlawfully and intentionally. 2 (*informal*) to punish someone brutally. **murderer** *noun* [from an Old English word]

murderous *adjective* 1 involving murder; capable of or intent on murder. SYNONYMS: savage, vicious, brutal, homicidal. 2 (*informal*) very difficult or unpleasant.

murk *noun* darkness or poor visibility.

murky *adjective* (**murkier, murkiest**) 1 dark and gloomy. SYNONYMS: gloomy, dark, dim, shadowy. 2 (said about water) muddy or full of sediment. 3 scandalous or immoral in an obscure way ♦ *a family with a murky past.* **murkily** *adverb* **murkiness** *noun*

murmur *noun* 1 a low continuous background sound. 2 softly spoken words. 3 a subdued expression of feeling ♦ *There were murmurs of discontent.* 4 (*Medicine*) a low abnormal sound made by the heart as a symptom of disease or weakness and heard through a stethoscope.
murmur *verb* to make a murmur; to speak or utter something in a low voice. SYNONYMS: mutter, mumble, whisper. [from an Old French word *murmure*]

muscat (**musk-**ət) *noun* a kind of grape with a musky scent, used for making wine. [a French word, from a Provençal word *musc* meaning 'musk']

muscle *noun* 1 a band or bundle of fibrous tissue able to contract and relax and so produce movement in parts of the body. 2 physical power. 3 political power or strength ♦ *government committees with plenty of muscle.*
muscle *verb* **to muscle in** (*informal*) to force your way into someone else's affairs. [from a Latin word *musculus* meaning 'little mouse' (because some muscles are thought to resemble a mouse in form)]

muscular *adjective* 1 of or affecting the muscles. 2 having well-developed muscles. **muscularity** (mus-kew-la-riti) *noun*

muscular dystrophy (mus- kew- lə dis- trə- fi) *noun* a hereditary condition marked by a progressive weakening and wasting of the muscles.

Muse *noun* (*Greek and Roman Mythology*) each of nine goddesses who are sources of inspiration for learning and the arts.
muse *noun* a writer's or artist's source of inspiration, regarded as a woman. [from a Greek word *mousa*]

muse *verb* to ponder deeply about something. SYNONYMS: ponder, reflect, ruminate. [from an Old French word *muser* meaning 'to meditate']

museum *noun* a building in which objects of historical, cultural, or scientific interest are collected and exhibited. [from a Greek word *mouseion* meaning 'place of the Muses']

mush *noun* 1 soft pulp. 2 feeble sentimentality. **mushy** *adjective* [another spelling of *mash*]

mushroom *noun* 1 an edible fungus with a stem and domed cap. 2 a pale yellowish- brown colour.
mushroom *verb* 1 to grow or appear rapidly in large numbers ♦ *Estate agents mushroomed along the High Street.* 2 to rise and spread in the shape of a mushroom. [from an Old French word *mousseron*]

mushrooming *noun* gathering mushrooms.

music *noun* 1 the art of arranging the sounds of voices or instruments in a harmonious and pleasing sequence or combination. 2 the sounds or compositions produced in this way, or a set of written or printed symbols showing these sounds. **music to your ears** something pleasant to hear. [from a Greek phrase *mousikē tekhnē* meaning 'art of the Muses']

musical *adjective* 1 to do with music. 2 producing music ♦ *a musical instrument.* 3 (said about a person) fond of or skilled in music. 4 accompanied by music; set to music.
musical *noun* a play or film containing a large number of songs. **musically** *adverb*

musical box *noun* a box with a mechanical device that produces music when the lid is opened.

musical chairs *plural noun* a party game in which players walk round chairs, always one fewer than the number of players, while music is played. When the music stops at the end of each round, the player who fails to find a chair is eliminated.

music centre *noun* equipment combining a radio, record player or CD player, and tape recorder.

music hall *noun* 1 a form of variety entertainment popular in Britain from about 1850 to 1918. 2 a theatre where this took place.

musician noun a person who plays a musical instrument or is musically accomplished.

musk noun 1 a strong-smelling substance secreted by the male musk deer, used as an ingredient in perfumes. 2 a plant with a musky smell.

musket noun a gun with a long barrel, formerly used by infantry soldiers. [via French from an Italian word *moschetto* meaning 'crossbow bolt']

musketeer noun (*historical*) 1 a soldier armed with a musket. 2 in France, a soldier of the king's household troops in the 17th and 18th centuries.

muskrat a large North American water animal wih a musky smell, valued for its fur (called *musquash*).

musky adjective (**muskier, muskiest**) smelling like musk.

Muslim noun a person who follows the Islamic faith.
Muslim adjective to do with Muslims or their faith. [from an Arabic word meaning 'someone who submits to God']

muslin noun a thin cotton cloth. [named after the city of Mosul in Iraq, where it was first made]

musquash (**mus-kwosh**) noun the fur of the muskrat.

muss verb **muss up** (*North Amer.*) (*informal*) to make something untidy. [probably another spelling of *mess*]

mussel noun a black shellfish, a bivalve mollusc, some forms of which can be eaten. [from an Old English word]

must[1] auxiliary verb 1 used to express necessity or obligation ♦ *We must try to find them.* 2 used to express certainty or probability ♦ *The train must be late.* 3 used to express insistence ♦ *I must emphasize that I did everything possible.*
must noun (*informal*) a thing that should not be overlooked or missed ♦ *This job is a must.* [from an Old English word]

must[2] noun grape juice before or during fermentation. [from *musty*]

mustang noun a wild horse of Mexico and the south-west USA. [from Spanish words meaning 'wild cattle']

mustard noun 1 a hot-tasting yellow or brownish paste made from the seeds of certain plants and used to flavour food. 2 a plant with yellow flowers and black or

white sharp-tasting seeds in long pods, from which mustard paste is made. 3 a darkish-yellow colour.
mustard adjective darkish yellow. [from an Old French word]

mustard gas noun a kind of poison gas that burns the skin.

muster verb 1 to come together, or bring people or things together. 2 to summon something you need ♦ *to muster up your strength.*
muster noun an assembly or gathering of people or things. **to pass muster** to be up to the required standard. [from a Latin word *monstrare* meaning 'to show']

mustn't verb (*informal*) must not.

musty adjective (**mustier, mustiest**) 1 smelling or tasting mouldy or stale. SYNONYMS: mouldy, stale, damp. 2 antiquated or outdated. **mustily** adverb **mustiness** noun [probably from *moist*]

mutable (**mew-tə-bəl**) adjective able or likely to change. **mutability** noun [from a Latin word *mutare* meaning 'to change']

mutagen (**mew-tə-jən**) noun (*Biology*) a substance which causes genetic mutation. [from *mutation* and *-gen*]

mutant (**mew-tənt**) noun (*Biology*) a living thing that differs basically from its parents as a result of genetic change (called *mutation*).
mutant adjective differing in this way. [same origin as for *mutable*]

mutate (**mew-tayt**) verb to undergo mutation, or cause something to undergo mutation.

mutation noun 1 a change or alteration in form. 2 (*Biology*) a change in the structure of a gene which may be transmitted to later generations. 3 a mutant.

mute adjective 1 silent, not speaking. SYNONYMS: silent, speechless. 2 (*old use*) unable to speak or make sounds. 3 not expressed in words ♦ *He looked in mute adoration.* 4 (said about a letter) not pronounced ♦ *The k in 'knife' is mute.*
mute noun 1 (*old use*) a person who is unable to speak. 2 a device fitted to a musical instrument to deaden its sound.
mute verb 1 to deaden or muffle the sound of a musical instrument. 2 to make something quieter or less intense. **mutely** adverb **muteness** noun [from a Latin word *mutus* meaning 'silent']

mutilate *verb* to injure or damage something by breaking or cutting off part of it. SYNONYMS: damage, disfigure, deface, vandalize, maim, cripple. **mutilation** *noun* **mutilator** *noun* [from a Latin word *mutilus* meaning 'maimed']

mutineer (mew-tin-**eer**) *noun* a person who mutinies.

mutinous (mew-tin-əs) *adjective* rebellious, ready to mutiny. SYNONYMS: rebellious, insubordinate, insurgent. **mutinously** *adverb*

mutiny (mew-tin-i) *noun* (**mutinies**) an open rebellion against authority, especially by members of the armed forces against their officers. SYNONYMS: rebellion, revolt, rising, insurgence.
mutiny *verb* (**mutinies, mutinied, mutinying**) to engage in mutiny. SYNONYMS: rebel, revolt. [from a French word *mutin* meaning 'mutineer']

mutter *verb* 1 to speak or utter something in a low unclear voice. SYNONYMS: mumble, murmur, whisper. 2 to grumble quietly or in private.
mutter *noun* muttering; muttered words. [an imitation of the sound]

mutton *noun* the flesh of sheep eaten as food. [from a French word *moton*]

mutual (mew-tew-əl) *adjective* 1 (said about a feeling or action) felt or done by each of two or more people towards or to the other ♦ *mutual affection* ♦ *mutual assistance.* 2 (said about people) having the same relationship to each other ♦ *mutual enemies.* 3 shared by two or more people ♦ *a mutual friend.* 4 (said about a building society or fund) owned by its member and sharing its profits among them. **mutually** *adverb* [from a Latin word *mutuus*]

Muzak (mew-zak) *noun* (trademark) recorded light music played through speakers in public places. [an alteration of *music*]

muzzle *noun* 1 the projecting nose and mouth of dogs and some other animals. 2 the open end of a gun. 3 a cover put over an animal's head to prevent it from biting or feeding.
muzzle *verb* 1 to put a muzzle on an animal. 2 to prevent a person or organization from expressing opinions openly. [from an Old French word *musel*]

muzzy *adjective* (**muzzier, muzziest**) confused or blurred. **muzzily** *adverb* **muzziness** *noun* [origin unknown]

my *adjective* 1 belonging to me. 2 used in forms of address ♦ *my lord* ♦ *my dear.* 3 used to express surprise ♦ *my God!* [originally a form of *mine*[1] used before consonants]

mycelium (miy-**see**-li-əm) *noun* (**mycelia**) (*Botany*) a mass of fine white thread-like strands of a fungus that divide and reproduce. [from a Greek word *mukēs* meaning 'mushroom']

Mycenaean (miy-sin-**ee**-ən) *adjective* (*Archaeology*) to do with an ancient Bronze Age civilization of Greece, remains of which were found at Mycenae in the Peloponnese and elsewhere.
Mycenaean *noun* a Greek of the Mycenaean period.

mycology (miy-kol-əji) *noun* the study of fungi. **mycologist** *noun* [same origin as for *mycelium*]

myelin sheath (my-ə-lin) *noun* (*Anatomy and Zoology*) a fatty insulating layer around the fibres of some nerve cells in vertebrates. [from a Greek word *muelos* meaning 'marrow']

mynah (miy-nə) *noun* a southern Asian or Australasian bird of the starling family, some kinds of which can mimic human speech. [from a Hindi word *maina*]

myopia (miy-oh-piə) *noun* short-sightedness. [from Greek words *muein* 'to shut' and *ōps* meaning 'eye']

myopic (miy-op-ik) *adjective* short-sighted. **myopically** *noun*

myriad (mi-ri-əd) *noun* (*literary*) a vast number. [from a Greek word *murioi* meaning '10,000']

myriapod (mi-ri-ə-pod) *noun* (*Zoology*) a small crawling creature with many legs. [from *myriad* and a Greek word *podos* meaning 'of the foot']

myrrh[1] (mir) *noun* a fragrant gum resin used in perfumes, incense, and medicine. [via Old English from a Greek word *murra*]

myrrh[2] *noun* a fragrant herb with white flowers. [from a Greek word *murris*]

myrtle (mer-təl) *noun* an evergreen shrub with dark leaves and scented white flowers. [from a Greek word *murtos*]

myself *pronoun* used to refer to the person speaking when that person is also the subject of the sentence ♦ *I have hurt myself* ♦ *I myself think so.* [from Old English, related to *me* and *self*]

mysterious *adjective* full of mystery, puzzling. SYNONYMS: strange, puzzling, baffling, bewildering, mystifying, inexplicable, unknown. **mysteriously** *adverb*

mystery *noun* (**mysteries**) 1 something that cannot be explained or understood ♦ *The whereabouts of the cat remained a mystery.* SYNONYMS: puzzle, problem, enigma. 2 the quality of being unexplained or obscure ♦ *Its origins are wrapped in mystery.* 3 a religious truth that the human mind is incapable of understanding. 4 a story or play that deals with a puzzling crime. [from a Greek word *mustērion* meaning 'a secret thing' or 'a secret ceremony']

mystery play *noun* a kind of medieval religious drama.

mystic (mis-tik) *adjective* 1 having hidden or symbolic meaning, especially in religion ♦ *mystic ceremonies.* 2 inspiring a sense of mystery and awe.
mystic *noun* a person who seeks to obtain union with God by deep religious meditation. [from a Greek word *mustikos* meaning 'secret']

mystical (mis-tik-əl) *adjective* 1 to do with mystics or mysticism. 2 having spiritual meaning, value, or symbolism. **mystically** *adverb*

mysticism (mis-ti-sizm) *noun* 1 a spiritual quality. 2 the beliefs or practices of mystics.

mystify *verb* (**mystifies, mystified, mystifying**) to cause a person to feel puzzled. SYNONYMS: puzzle, perplex, baffle, bewilder. **mystification** *noun*

mystique (mis-**teek**) *noun* an air of mystery or mystical power. [a French word meaning 'mystic']

myth *noun* 1 a traditional story containing ideas or beliefs about ancient times or about supernatural beings. 2 these stories collectively ♦ *in myth and legend.* 3 an imaginary person or thing. 4 an idea that forms part of the beliefs of a group or class but is not founded on fact. [from a Greek word *muthos* meaning 'story']

mythical (mith-i-kəl) *adjective* 1 to do with myths, or existing in myths. 2 imaginary, found only in myths. SYNONYMS: legendary, fabulous, imaginary, mythological.

mythology (mith-ol-ə-ji) *noun* 1 a body of myths ♦ *Greek mythology.* 2 the study of myths. **mythological** *adjective* **mythologist** *noun* [from *myth* and *-logy*]

myxomatosis (miksə-mə-**toh**-sis) *noun* a fatal virus disease of rabbits. [from a Greek word *muxa* meaning 'mucus' (because the mucous membranes swell up)]

Nn

N the fourteenth letter of the English alphabet.

N *abbreviation* 1 north or northern. 2 (*Chemistry*) the symbol for nitrogen.

Naafi (naf-i) *noun* a canteen for servicemen, organized by the Navy, Army, and Air Force Institutes.

naan *noun* another spelling of **nan**².

nab *verb* (**nabbed, nabbing**) (*informal*) 1 to catch someone doing wrong. 2 to seize or grab something. [origin unknown]

nabob (nay-bob) *noun* (*historical*) 1 a Muslim official under the Mogul empire. 2 a wealthy person. [via Spanish and Portuguese from an Urdu word]

nacre (nay-ker) *noun* mother-of-pearl. **nacreous** (nay-kri-əs) *adjective* [from a French word]

nadir (nay-deer) *noun* 1 (in astronomy) the part of the sky that is directly below the observer. 2 the lowest or most unsuccessful point. [from an Arabic word *nazir* meaning 'opposite (to the zenith)']

naff *adjective* (*informal*) lacking taste; unfashionable. [origin unknown]

nag¹ *verb* (**nagged, nagging**) 1 to bother someone by constantly criticizing, complaining, or asking for things. SYNONYMS: criticize, pick on, find fault with; pester. 2 (said about pain or worry) to keep on hurting or bothering you. [origin unknown]

nag² *noun* (*informal*) a horse. [origin unknown]

naiad (niy-ad) *noun* (*Greek and Roman Mythology*) a water nymph. [from a Greek word *naias*, from *naein* meaning 'to flow']

nail *noun* 1 a hard covering on the upper surface of the tip of a finger or toe. 2 a claw or talon. 3 a small metal spike, often with a flattened head, driven into wood or other materials with a hammer to hold pieces together.

nail verb **1** to fasten wood or other materials with a nail or nails. **2** to catch or arrest someone in the act of doing wrong. **to hit the nail on the head** to state the truth exactly. **on the nail** (said about payment) made immediately. [from an Old English word *nægel*]

nail file noun a small file for smoothing and shaping the fingernails and toenails.

naive (niy-eev) adjective **1** showing a lack of experience or judgement, innocent and trusting. **2** (said about artists or their work) using a simple style that avoids sophisticated techniques. **naively** adverb **naivety** (niy-eev-ə-ti) noun [a French word, related to *native*]

naked adjective **1** without any clothes on, nude. SYNONYMS: nude, bare, undressed, unclothed. **2** without the usual coverings or protection ♦ *a naked sword*. SYNONYMS: uncovered, bare. **3** obvious or undisguised ♦ *the naked truth*. **naked eye** the eye unassisted by a telescope or microscope etc. **nakedly** adverb **nakedness** noun [from an Old English word *nacod*]

namaste (nah-ma-stay) noun a traditional Indian greeting with the hands held together as if in prayer. [via Hindi from a Sanskrit word *namas* meaning 'bowing']

namby-pamby adjective lacking character, feeble or sentimental. [a fanciful variation of the name *Ambrose*, from Ambrose Philips, an 18th-century English writer whose poetry was regarded in this way]

name noun **1** the word or words by which a person, animal, place, or thing is known. **2** a reputation ♦ *This place has got a bad name*. **3** a famous person ♦ *The film has some big names in it*. **name** verb **1** to give a name to a person, place, or thing ♦ *They named their cat Albert*. SYNONYMS: call; (humorous) dub. **2** to state the name of a person, place, or thing ♦ *Can you name the people in the photograph?* SYNONYMS: identify, recognize. **3** to appoint someone to a job or role ♦ *She was named captain for the next game*. SYNONYMS: appoint, choose. **4** to mention or specify a piece of information ♦ *Name your price*. **name and shame** to publicize the actions of a person or group that is considered to be doing wrong, especially in a newspaper article. **to call a person names** to speak abusively to or about someone. **to make a name for**

yourself to become well-known or famous. **to name the day** to fix a date for an event, especially a wedding. **nameable** adjective [from an Old English word *nama*]

nameless adjective **1** having no name or no known name. **2** not mentioned by name ♦ *There are others who shall be nameless*. **3** difficult or too bad to describe ♦ *Nameless misfortunes hit the village*.

namely adverb that is to say, specifically ♦ *My two best subjects, namely French and German*.

namesake noun a person or thing with the same name as another.

nan [1] noun (informal) a person's grandmother. [a shortening of *nanny*]

nan [2] noun a type of flat leavened Indian bread. [an Urdu and Persian word]

nankeen (nan-keen) noun a kind of yellow cotton cloth. [from the name of Nanking in China, where it was originally made]

nanny noun (nannies) **1** a person employed to look after a child in its own home. **2** (informal) a person's grandmother. **3** a nanny goat. [a familiar form of the name *Ann*]

nanny goat noun a female goat.

nanny state noun a government that is regarded as interfering too much in people's lives.

nano- prefix **1** one thousand millionth ♦ *nanosecond*. **2** extremely small. [from a Greek word *nanos* meaning 'dwarf']

nanotechnology noun chemical and biological engineering concerned with the manipulation of molecules.

nap [1] noun a short sleep, especially during the day. SYNONYMS: snooze, sleep, rest. **nap** verb (napped, napping) to have a nap. **to catch someone napping** to catch someone when they are unprepared. [from an Old English word]

nap [2] noun short raised fibres on the surface of cloth or leather. [from a German or Dutch word]

nap [3] noun a card game in which players have five cards and declare how many tricks they expect to take. [short for *napoleon*, the original name of the game]

napalm (nay-pahm) noun a sticky jelly-like petrol substance used in incendiary bombs. [from *naphtha* and *palmitic acid*, two chemicals from which napalm is made]

nape *noun* the back part of the neck. [origin unknown]

naphtha (naf-thə) *noun* (*Chemistry*) an inflammable oil obtained from coal or petroleum. [via Latin and Greek from an oriental word]

napkin *noun* 1 a piece of cloth or paper used at meals to protect your clothes or for wiping your lips or fingers. 2 a baby's nappy. [from a French word *nappe* meaning 'tablecloth']

nappy *noun* (**nappies**) a piece of towelling or other absorbent material put round a baby's bottom and legs to absorb or hold its urine and faeces. [a shortened form of *napkin*, formerly used in this meaning]

narcissism (nar-sis-izm) *noun* abnormal interest in or admiration for yourself. **narcissistic** (nar-sis-ist-ik) *adjective* [from Narcissus, the name of a beautiful youth in Greek mythology who fell in love with his own reflection in a pool]

narcissus (nar-sis-əs) *noun* (**narcissi**) a daffodil with white or pale outer petals and an orange or yellow centre. [from a Greek word *narkissos*, perhaps from *narkē* meaning 'numbness' (because of the narcotic effects of the flower)]

narcosis (nar-koh-sis) *noun* (*Medicine*) a state of sleep or drowsiness produced by drugs. [from a Greek word *narkē* meaning 'numbness']

narcotic (nar-kot-ik) *noun* 1 (*Medicine*) a drug that causes sleep or drowsiness, and relieves pain. 2 a drug or other substance, often illegal, that affects a person's mood and behaviour.
narcotic *adjective* causing sleep or drowsiness.

nark *noun* (*informal*) a police informer.
nark *verb* (*informal*) to annoy someone. [from a Romany word *nak* meaning 'nose']

narrate (nə-rayt) *verb* to tell a story or give an account of events in the order in which they happened. SYNONYMS: relate, recount, describe, tell. **narration** *noun* **narrator** *noun* [from a Latin word *narrare* meaning 'to relate']

narrative (na-rə-tiv) *noun* a spoken or written account of something.
narrative *adjective* in the form of a narrative.

narrow *adjective* 1 small in width compared to length. SYNONYMS: thin, slender, slim. 2 having or allowing little space ♦ *within narrow bounds*. 3 with little scope or variety, small ♦ *a narrow circle of friends*. 4 uncomfortably close, only just achieved ♦ *We had a narrow escape* ♦ *He won by a narrow majority*.
narrow *verb* to make something narrower, or to become narrower. **narrowly** *adverb* **narrowness** *noun* [from an Old English word *nearu*]

narrowboat *noun* a long narrow boat used on canals.

narrow-minded *adjective* not willing to consider other people's opinions, prejudiced. SYNONYMS: intolerant, prejudiced, bigoted.

narwhal (nar-wəl) *noun* a small Arctic whale, the male of which has a long tusk with a spiral groove. [from a Dutch word *narwal*, from an Old Norse word *nar* meaning 'corpse' (because the colour of the animal's skin resembled that of a corpse)]

NASA *abbreviation* (in the USA) National Aeronautics and Space Administration.

nasal (nay-zəl) *adjective* 1 to do with the nose. 2 (said about a voice or speech) sounding as if the breath comes out through the nose. **nasally** *adverb* [from a Latin word *nasus* meaning 'nose']

nasturtium (nə-ster-shəm) *noun* (**nasturtiums**) a garden plant with round flat leaves and bright orange, yellow, or red flowers. [from Latin words *nasus* meaning 'nose' and *torquere* meaning 'to twist' (because of its sharp smell)]

nasty *adjective* (**nastier, nastiest**) 1 very unpleasant or repulsive. SYNONYMS: bad, unpleasant, disgusting, repulsive, disagreeable. 2 unkind or spiteful. SYNONYMS: unkind, unpleasant, unfriendly, cruel, spiteful. 3 difficult to deal with ♦ *a nasty problem*. SYNONYMS: difficult, tricky. **nastily** *adverb* **nastiness** *noun* [origin unknown]

natal (nay-təl) *adjective* 1 to do with birth. 2 from or since birth. [from a Latin word *natus* meaning 'born']

nation *noun* a large community of people most of whom have the same ancestors, language, history, and customs, and who live in the same part of the world under one government. [from a Latin word *natio* meaning 'birth' or 'race']

national *adjective* to do with a nation, or belonging to a whole nation.
national *noun* a citizen or subject of a particular country. **nationally** *adverb*

national anthem *noun* the official song of a nation, played on important occasions.

national curriculum *noun* a curriculum of study that has to be taught in state schools.

national debt *noun* the total amount of money borrowed by a government.

national grid *noun* 1 a network of high-voltage electric power lines between major power stations. 2 a metric system of geographical coordinates used in maps of the British Isles.

National Health Service *noun* the public service in Britain that provides medical care.

National Insurance *noun* a system of compulsory payments made by employees and employers to provide state assistance for people who are ill, unemployed, or retired.

nationalism *noun* 1 patriotic feeling, principles, or efforts. 2 a movement favouring independence for a country that is controlled by another or forms part of another.

nationalist *noun* a supporter of nationalism. **nationalistic** *adjective*

nationality *noun* (**nationalities**) the condition of belonging to a particular nation.

nationalize *verb* to put an industry or business under state ownership or control. **nationalization** *noun*

national park *noun* an area of countryside which is protected by the state for the public to visit.

national service *noun* a period of compulsory service in the armed forces in peacetime.

nationwide *adjective & adverb* extending over the whole of a nation.

native *adjective* 1 belonging to a person or thing by nature; inborn or natural ♦ *a native ability.* 2 belonging to a person because of their place of birth ♦ *a native language;* (said about a person) belonging to a particular place by birth. 3 grown or originating in a specified place ♦ *a plant native to China.* 4 to do with the people born in a place.
native *noun* 1 a person who was born in a particular place ♦ *She is a native of Sweden.* 2 a local inhabitant of a place. 3 an animal or plant grown or originating in a

particular place. [from a Latin word *nativus* meaning 'born']

Native American *noun* one of the original inhabitants of North and South America and the Caribbean Islands.

nativity *noun* (**nativities**) the time when a person is born.
Nativity *noun* the birth of Jesus Christ.

nativity play *noun* a play based on the birth of Christ, performed at Christmas.

natter *verb* (*informal*) to chat informally.
natter *noun* (*informal*) a chat. [an imitation of the sound]

natterjack *noun* a small toad with a yellow stripe down its back. [from *natter* (probably because of its loud cry) and *jack*]

natty *adjective* (**nattier, nattiest**) (*informal*) neat and trim; dapper. **nattily** *adverb* [probably from *neat*]

natural *adjective* 1 produced or done by nature, not by people or machines. 2 in accordance with nature, normal ♦ *He died a natural death.* 3 (said about a person) having certain inborn qualities or abilities ♦ *She seemed to be a natural leader.* SYNONYM: instinctive. 4 not looking artificial; not affected in manner ♦ *Their behaviour was very natural.* 5 not surprising, to be expected ♦ *Anger was a natural reaction to the news.* SYNONYMS: normal, unsurprising, expected, typical. 6 (*Music*) neither sharp nor flat ♦ *B natural.*
natural *noun* 1 a person or thing that seems to be naturally suited for something. 2 (*Music*) a natural note; the sign ♮ indicating this. 3 a pale fawn colour. **naturally** *adverb* **naturalness** *noun*

natural childbirth *noun* a system of childbirth based on exercises and relaxation and avoiding medical intervention and use of drugs.

natural gas *noun* gas found naturally underground, not manufactured.

natural history *noun* the study of plants and animals.

naturalism *noun* (in art and literature) the theory or practice of drawing, painting, or describing things as they are in nature. **naturalistic** *adjective*

naturalist *noun* someone who studies natural history.

naturalize *verb* 1 to give a person of foreign birth the right of citizenship of a country. 2 to adopt a foreign word or custom, often

adapting it so that it fits local practice.
3 to cause a plant or animal to grow or live
naturally in a country where it is not
native. **naturalization** noun

natural selection noun a theory that
organisms that are best adapted to their
environment will survive while the less
well adapted ones will die out.

nature noun **1** the world with all its features
and living things, as distinct from things
made by humans. **2** the physical force
regarded as producing living things. **3** a
kind or sort of thing ♦ *They like things of this
nature.* **4** the qualities and characteristics
of a person or thing ♦ *She has a loving
nature.* [from a Latin word *natus* meaning
'born']

nature study noun the practical study of
plant and animal life.

nature trail noun a path through woods or
countryside, with signposts showing
interesting natural features.

naturist noun a nudist. **naturism** noun

naught noun (*old use*) nothing. **to come to
naught** to be unsuccessful, to fail.
[another spelling of *nought*]

naughty adjective (**naughtier, naughtiest**)
1 behaving badly, disobedient. SYNONYMS:
disobedient, mischievous, unruly. **2** mildly
shocking or indecent. **naughtily** adverb
naughtiness noun [from *naught*]

nausea (**naw-zi**ə) noun a feeling of sickness
or disgust. [from an earlier meaning
'seasickness', from a Greek word *naus*
meaning 'ship']

nauseate (**naw-zi-ayt**) verb to make
someone feel nausea.

nauseous (**naw-zi-ə**s) adjective **1** feeling
nausea. **2** causing a feeling of nausea.

nautical adjective to do with ships or
sailors. [from a Greek word *nautēs*
meaning 'sailor']

nautical mile noun a measure of distance
at sea, equal to 2,025 yards or 1.852
kilometres.

nautilus (**naw-til-ə**s) noun (**nautiluses**) a
mollusc with a spiral shell divided into
compartments. [from a Greek word
nautilos meaning 'sailor']

naval adjective to do with ships or sailors.
[from a Latin word *navis* meaning 'ship']

nave noun the main part of a church apart
from the chancel, aisles, and transepts.
[from a Latin word *navis* meaning 'ship'
(because the form of a church was
compared to that of a ship)]

navel (**nay-v**əl) noun **1** the small hollow in
the centre of the abdomen where the
umbilical cord was attached. **2** the central
point of a place. [from an Old English
word *nafela*]

navel orange noun a large seedless orange
with a navel-like formation at the top.

navigable (**nav-ig-ə**bəl) adjective **1** suitable
for ships to sail in ♦ *a navigable river.*
2 (said about a boat or ship) able to be
steered and sailed. **navigability** noun

navigate verb **1** to sail in or through a sea
or waterway. **2** to direct the course of a
ship, aircraft, or vehicle. SYNONYMS: steer,
direct; (ship or aircraft) pilot. **navigation** noun
navigator noun [from Latin words *navis*
meaning 'ship' and *agere* meaning 'to
drive']

navvy noun (**navvies**) a labourer digging a
road, railway, or canal. [short for *navigator*
meaning 'a person who constructs a
navigation (= canal)']

navy noun (**navies**) **1** a country's warships
and the crews trained to use them. **2** (also
navy blue) a dark blue colour like that of
naval uniform. [from a Latin word *navis*
meaning 'ship']

nawab (**nə-wahb**) noun (in India) **1** the title
of a Muslim nobleman or person of high
status. **2** the title of a governor or
nobleman at the time of the Mogul
empire. [from an Urdu word *nawwab* and
an Arabic word *nuwwab*]

nay adverb (*old use*) no. [from an Old Norse
word *nei*]

Nazi (**nah-tsi**) noun (**Nazis**) a member of the
National Socialist party in Germany
under Hitler, having Fascist beliefs.
Nazism noun [from the German
pronunciation of *Nationalsozialist*]

NB abbreviation take note of something.
[from a Latin phrase *nota bene* meaning
'note well']

NCO abbreviation non-commissioned
officer.

NE abbreviation north-east or north-eastern.

Ne abbreviation (*Chemistry*) the symbol for
neon.

Neanderthal (ni-an-der-təl) *noun* an extinct type of human who lived in Europe during the early Stone Age.

neap *noun* **neap tide** the tide when there is the least rise and fall of water, halfway between spring tides.

Neapolitan (nee-ə-pol-itan) *adjective* **1** to do with or coming from Naples in southern Italy. **2** (said about an ice cream) made in layers of different colours and flavours. [from Neapolis, the Latin name of Naples]

near *adverb* **1** at or to a short distance. SYNONYMS: close, nearby. **2** a short time away in the future. **3** nearly ♦ *This is correct as near as I can tell.*
near *preposition* not far away from ♦ *The house is near the station.*
near *adjective* **1** with only a short distance or interval between ♦ *in the near future.* **2** closely related. **3** with little margin ♦ *a near escape.* SYNONYMS: close, narrow.
near *verb* to come near to something ♦ *The ship neared the harbour.* **a near thing** something achieved or missed by only a narrow margin. **nearness** *noun* [from an Old Norse word]

nearby *adjective* near in position ♦ *a nearby house.*
near by *adverb* not far off ♦ *They live near by.*

Near East *noun* an area of SW Asia extending from the eastern Mediterranean to Iran and including the Middle East.

nearly *adverb* almost ♦ *We have nearly finished.* SYNONYMS: almost, practically. **not nearly** nothing like ♦ *That is not nearly enough.*

near miss *noun* **1** a situation in which a collision is only narrowly avoided. **2** a bomb or shot that narrowly misses its target.

nearside *noun* the side of a vehicle that is by the kerb.

near-sighted *adjective* short-sighted.

neat *adjective* **1** simple and clean and tidy. SYNONYMS: tidy, orderly. **2** done or doing things in a precise and skilful way. **3** undiluted ♦ *neat whisky.* **4** (*North Amer.*) excellent. **neatly** *adverb* **neatness** *noun* [from a Latin word *nitidus* meaning 'clean' or 'shining']

neaten *verb* to make something neat, or to become neat.

nebula (neb-yoo-lə) *noun* (**nebulae** (neb-yoo-lee)) a bright or dark patch in the sky caused by a distant galaxy or a cloud of dust or gas. **nebular** *adjective* [a Latin word meaning 'mist']

nebulous (neb-yoo-ləs) *adjective* indistinct or vague ♦ *nebulous ideas.* [same origin as for *nebula*]

necessarily *adverb* as a necessary result, inevitably.

necessary *adjective* **1** essential in order to achieve something. SYNONYMS: essential, indispensable, obligatory. **2** unavoidable, happening as an inevitable result ♦ *Suffering is the necessary consequence of their actions.* SYNONYMS: unavoidable, inevitable, inescapable.
necessaries *plural noun* food, warmth, and other basic needs of life. **the necessary** (*informal*) the money or action needed for a purpose. [from a Latin word *necessarius*, from *necesse* meaning 'to be needful']

necessitate (ni-sess-i-tayt) *verb* to make something necessary, to involve something as a condition or result.

necessitous (ni-sess-i-təs) *adjective* needy.

necessity (ni-sess-iti) *noun* (**necessities**) **1** the state or fact of being necessary ♦ *the necessity for complete discretion.* SYNONYMS: need, requirement. **2** something that is necessary. SYNONYMS: requirement, essential, prerequisite.

neck *noun* **1** the part of the body connecting the head to the rest of the body. **2** the part of a piece of clothing that covers the neck. **3** a narrow opening or connecting part of anything, especially of a bottle near its mouth. **4** the length of a horse's head and neck as a measure of its lead in a race. **to get it in the neck** (*informal*) to be severely reprimanded or punished. **neck and neck** running level in a race or contest. **to risk** or **save your neck** to risk or save your own life. **up to your neck in** (*informal*) deeply or busily involved in something. [from an Old English word]

neckerchief *noun* a square of cloth worn round the neck.

necklace *noun* an ornamental string of beads or precious stones worn round the neck.

neckline *noun* the edge of a woman's piece of clothing at or below the neck.

necromancy (nek-rǝ-man-si) *noun* 1 the supposed practice of communicating with the dead in order to predict future events. 2 witchcraft or sorcery. **necromancer** *noun* [from Greek words *nekros* meaning 'corpse' and *manteia* meaning 'divination']

necropolis (nek-rop-ǝ-lis) *noun* (*Archaeology*) a large ancient cemetery. [from Greek words *nekros* meaning 'corpse' and *polis* meaning 'city']

nectar *noun* 1 a sugary sweet fluid produced by plants and collected by bees for making honey. 2 (*Greek and Roman Mythology*) the drink of the gods. 3 a delicious drink. [from a Greek word *nektar*]

nectarine (nek-ter-in) *noun* a kind of peach with a thin smooth skin.

nectary (nek-ter-i) *noun* (**nectaries**) (*Botany*) the part of a plant or flower that produces nectar.

née (nay) *adjective* born (used in giving a married woman's maiden name ♦ *Mrs Jane Smith, née Jones*). [a French word meaning 'born']

need *verb* 1 to be without something you should have, to require something ♦ *We need two more chairs*. 2 to be under an obligation to do something ♦ *You do not need to answer*.

need *noun* 1 circumstances in which something is needed ♦ *There was no need for them to stay*. SYNONYMS: necessity, obligation, requirement. 2 a situation of great difficulty or misfortune ♦ *a friend in need*. SYNONYMS: distress, crisis, difficulty, trouble. 3 lack of the basic necessities of life, poverty. SYNONYMS: poverty, destitution, penury, indigence. 4 something you need or want ♦ *My needs are few*. **if need be** if necessary. **needs must** it is necessary or unavoidable. [from an Old English word]

needful *adjective* (*formal*) necessary.

needle *noun* 1 a small thin piece of metal with a point at one end and a hole for thread at the other, used in sewing. 2 a long thin piece of metal or plastic with one or both ends pointed, used in knitting. 3 something that is long, thin, and sharp ♦ *The ground was covered in pine needles*. 4 the pointer of a compass or gauge.
needle *verb* to annoy or provoke someone.

needlecord *noun* a fine corduroy fabric.

needlecraft *noun* skill in needlework.

needlepoint *noun* a kind of fine embroidery on canvas.

needless *adjective* not needed, unnecessary. **needlessly** *adverb*

needlewoman *noun* (**needlewomen**) a woman with a particular skill in sewing ♦ *a good needlewoman*.

needlework *noun* sewing or embroidery.

needn't *verb* (*informal*) need not.

needy *adjective* (**needier, neediest**) lacking things necessary for life, extremely poor. SYNONYMS: poor, deprived, destitute, impoverished. **neediness** *noun*

ne'er *adverb* (*poetic*) never.

ne'er-do-well *noun* a person who is lazy and irresponsible.

nefarious (ni-fair-iǝs) *adjective* wicked or criminal. **nefariously** *adverb* [from a Latin word *nefas* meaning 'wrong']

negate (ni-gayt) *verb* 1 to make something ineffective. 2 to disprove or deny something. **negation** *noun* [from a Latin word *negare* meaning 'to deny']

negative *adjective* 1 denying or disagreeing, giving the answer 'no'. 2 involving the absence of something sought or in question ♦ *Her pregnancy test was negative*. 3 (said about a quantity) less than zero, minus. 4 (*Electricity*) containing or producing the kind of electric charge carried by electrons. 5 (in photography, said about an image) having the light and shade or the colours of the original reversed.
negative *noun* 1 a negative word or statement. 2 a negative quality or quantity. 3 a negative photographic image, from which positive prints can be made.
◊ The opposite of *negative* in meaning 1 is *affirmative*, and in the other meanings is *positive*.
negative *verb* 1 to reject or veto something proposed. 2 to contradict a statement. 3 to neutralize an effect. **negatively** *adverb* [from a Latin word *negare* meaning 'to deny']

negative feedback *noun* feedback that tends to reduce the effect by which it is produced, as when an amplifier returns a part of its output back to the input, in order to reduce distortion.

negative pole *noun* the south-seeking pole of a magnet.

negative sign *noun* the sign –.

neglect verb 1 to fail to take proper care of someone or something. 2 to pay no attention or too little attention to something. SYNONYMS: disregard, ignore, overlook. 3 to omit or fail to do something ♦ They neglected to tell us their new address. SYNONYMS: omit, fail, forget.
neglect noun neglecting or being neglected, failure to do something.
neglectful adjective [from Latin words nec meaning 'not' and legere meaning 'to choose']

negligee (neg-li-zhay) noun a woman's light flimsy dressing gown. [from a French word négliger meaning 'to neglect']

negligence (neg-li-jəns) noun failure to take proper care or attention, carelessness. **negligent** adjective **negligently** adverb [same origin as for neglect]

negligible (neg-lij-ibəl) adjective so small or insignificant as to be not worth taking into account. **negligibly** adverb [from a French word négliger meaning 'to neglect']

negotiable (nig-oh-shə-bəl) adjective 1 able to be changed after being discussed ♦ The salary is negotiable. 2 (said about a cheque) able to be converted into cash or transferred to another person. [from negotiate]

negotiate (nig-oh-shi-ayt) verb 1 to discuss a matter with others in order to reach an agreement or arrangement about it. 2 to arrange an agreement after discussion ♦ The countries negotiated a peace treaty. SYNONYMS: agree on, work out, conclude, arrange. 3 to get or give money in exchange for a cheque or bonds. 4 to get over an obstacle or difficulty successfully. **negotiation** noun **negotiator** noun [from a Latin word negotium meaning 'business']

Negress noun a woman or girl of black African origin.
◊ See the note at **Negro**.

Negro noun (**Negroes**) a member of a dark-skinned people originating in Africa. [from a Latin word niger meaning 'black']
◊ Negro and Negress are usually considered to be old-fashioned and offensive. Black is the term that is generally prefered.

neigh (nay) verb (said about a horse) to make a long high-pitched cry.
neigh noun this cry. [from an Old English word, an imitation of the sound]

neighbour noun 1 a person who lives next to or near to another. 2 a person or thing situated near or next to another. [from an Old English word neahgebur meaning 'near dweller']

neighbourhood noun 1 the surrounding district or area. 2 a part of a town where people live ♦ We live in a quiet neighbourhood. SYNONYMS: district, area, locality, region, vicinity. **in the neighbourhood of** somewhere near, approximately.

neighbourhood watch noun a system of vigilance by the householders of an area to deter burglary and other local crime.

neighbouring adjective living or situated near by.

neighbourly adjective kind and friendly to the people living near you. SYNONYMS: considerate, helpful, kind, friendly. **neighbourliness** noun

neither (niy-ther or nee-ther) adjective & pronoun not either ♦ Neither road is the right one ♦ Neither of them likes it.
neither adverb & conjunction 1 not either ♦ We neither know nor care. 2 also not ♦ They don't know and neither do I. **neither here nor there** not important or relevant. **neither ... nor ...** not one or the other of two specified things. [from Old English words related to no and whether]
◊ Note that neither is followed by a singular verb (♦ Neither road is the right one, ♦ Neither of them likes it); but when one of its subjects is plural you use a plural verb: ♦ Neither he nor his children like it.

nelson noun a kind of hold in wrestling, with the arm placed under the opponent's arm and the hand round the back of the opponent's neck. [thought to be from the name Nelson]

nematode (nem-ə-tohd) noun (Zoology) a kind of slender worm. [from a Greek word nematos meaning 'of a thread']

nemesis (nem-i-sis) noun deserved punishment that comes to someone who hoped to escape it. [named after Nemesis, goddess of retribution in Greek mythology]

neo- prefix new, or a new form of something (as in neoclassical). [from a Greek word neos meaning 'new']

neoclassical adjective to do with a style of art, literature, or music that is based on a classical style. **neoclassicism** noun

neolithic (nee-ə-lith-ik) *adjective*
(*Archaeology*) to do with the later part of
the Stone Age. [from *neo-* and a Greek
word *lithos* meaning 'stone']

neologism (ni-ol-ə-jizm) *noun* a newly
coined word or expression. [from *neo-* and
a Greek word *logos* meaning 'word']

neon (nee-on) *noun* a chemical element
(symbol Ne), a kind of gas that glows
orange-red when electricity is passed
through it. [from a Greek word *neos*
meaning 'new']

nephew (nef-yoo) *noun* the son of your
brother or sister. [from a Latin word
nepos]

nephritis (ni-friy-tiss) *noun* (*Medicine*)
inflammation of the kidneys. [from a
Greek word *nephros* meaning 'kidney']

nepotism (nep-ə-tizm) *noun* showing
favouritism to relatives in appointing
them to jobs. [from a Latin word *nepos*
meaning 'nephew']

nerve *noun* 1 any of the fibres in the body
that carry impulses of sensation or
movement between the brain or spinal
cord and parts of the body. 2 courage or
calmness in the face of danger ♦ *It took a
lot of nerve to walk through the wood in the
dark.* SYNONYMS: courage, pluck, daring,
bravery; (*informal*) guts. 3 (*informal*)
impudence ♦ *They had the nerve to ask for
more money.*
nerve *verb* to give strength or courage to
someone.
nerves *plural noun* a state of being nervous
and easily upset. **to get on a person's
nerves** to be irritating to someone.
[from a Latin word *nervus* meaning
'sinew']

nerve centre *noun* 1 a cluster of neurons.
2 the place from which a system or
organization is controlled.

nerve gas *noun* a poison gas that affects
the nervous system.

nerveless *adjective* 1 lacking strength or
feeling. 2 not nervous, confident.

nerve-racking *adjective* causing great
stress or anxiety.

nervous *adjective* 1 easily agitated or
excited. SYNONYMS: anxious, uneasy,
apprehensive, worried, nervy, edgy, jumpy.
2 to do with the nerves or the nervous
system ♦ *a nervous disorder.* **nervously**
adverb **nervousness** *noun*

nervous breakdown *noun* a mental illness
resulting from severe depression and
anxiety.

nervous system *noun* the system that
sends electrical messages from one part
of the body to another, consisting of the
brain, spinal cord, and nerves.

nervy *adjective* (**nervier, nerviest**) easily
agitated or nervous. **nerviness** *noun*

-ness *suffix* forming nouns from adjectives
(as in *kindness, happiness*).

nest *noun* 1 a structure or place in which a
bird lays its eggs and feeds its young. 2 a
place where certain creatures live, such as
mice or wasps. 3 a snug place. 4 a set of
similar things that fit inside each other
♦ *a nest of tables.*
nest *verb* 1 to make or have a nest.
2 (*Computing*) to structure a set of
commands so that one operates within
another. [from an Old English word]

nest egg *noun* a sum of money saved up for
the future. [originally an egg left in the
nest to encourage a hen to lay more eggs]

nesting *noun* collecting wild birds' nests or
eggs.

nestle *verb* 1 to curl up comfortably. 2 (said
about a place) to lie in a sheltered
position. [from an Old English word
nestlian meaning 'to nest']

nestling *noun* a bird that is too young to
leave the nest.

net¹ *noun* 1 material of thread, cord, or
wire, etc. woven or joined in an open
mesh. 2 a piece of this used to cover or
protect something. 3 a structure with a
net used in various games, e.g. as a goal in
football or to divide a tennis court. 4 a
piece of net attached to the end of a rod,
used to catch fish.
net *verb* (**netted, netting**) 1 to make
something by forming threads into a net;
to make netting. 2 to cover something
with a net. 3 to hit a ball into a net in a
game. [from an Old English word]

net² *adjective* 1 (said about an amount or
value) after tax, expenses, etc. have been
deducted. 2 (said about a weight)
excluding the packing. 3 (said about an
effect or result) overall, excluding
incidental factors.
net *verb* (**netted, netting**) to earn or
acquire money as a net profit ♦ *They netted
over a million on the deal.* [from a French
word *net* meaning 'neat']

netball noun a team game in which players try to throw a ball into a net hanging from a ring on a high post.

nether (neth-er) adjective lower in position ♦ the nether regions. **nethermost** adjective [from an Old English word]

netting noun a piece of net fabric.

nettle noun a wild plant with leaves that sting and redden the skin when they are touched.
nettle verb to irritate or provoke someone.

nettle rash noun a rash of red patches on the skin, caused by an allergy.

network noun 1 an arrangement or pattern of intersecting lines or parts ♦ a railway network. 2 a chain of interconnected people or operations ♦ a spy network. 3 a group of radio or television stations which broadcast the same programmes. 4 (Computing) a set of computers which are linked to one another.

neural (new-rəl) adjective to do with a nerve or the nervous system. [from a Greek word neuron meaning 'nerve']

neuralgia (new-ral-jə) noun (Medicine) a sharp pain along the line of a nerve, especially in the head or face. **neuralgic** adjective [from Greek words neuron meaning 'nerve' and algos meaning 'pain']

neuritis (new-riy-tiss) noun (Medicine) inflammation of a nerve or nerves.

neurology (new-rol-əji) noun the study of nerve systems and their diseases. **neurological** adjective **neurologist** noun [from a Greek word neuron meaning 'nerve' and -logy]

neuron (new-ron) or **neurone** (new-rohn) noun a cell that is part of the nervous system and sends impulses to and from the brain. [from a Greek word meaning 'nerve']

neurosis (new-roh-sis) noun (neuroses) a mental disorder producing depression or abnormal behaviour, sometimes with physical symptoms but with no evidence of disease.

neurosurgery noun surgery performed on the nervous system.

neurotic (new-rot-ik) adjective 1 subject to abnormal anxieties or obsessive behaviour. 2 of or caused by a neurosis. **neurotically** adverb

neuter (new-ter) adjective 1 (Grammar) (said about a noun) belonging to a class that is neither masculine nor feminine. 2 (said about a plant) without male or female parts. 3 (said about an insect) sexually undeveloped, sterile.
neuter noun 1 a neuter word. 2 a neuter plant or insect. 3 a castrated animal.
neuter verb to remove an animal's sexual organs so that it cannot breathe. [from a Latin word meaning 'neither']

neutral adjective 1 not supporting either side in a war or dispute. SYNONYMS: impartial, unbiased. 2 having no positive or distinctive characteristics; not definitely one thing or the other. 3 (said about colours) not strong or positive; grey or fawn. 4 (Chemistry) neither acid nor alkaline, with a pH value of about 7.
neutral noun 1 a neutral person or country; or a person who is a subject of a neutral country. 2 a neutral colour. 3 a position of a set of gears in which the engine is disconnected from the driven parts. **neutrality** (new-tral-iti) noun **neutrally** adverb [from a Latin word neuter meaning 'neither']

neutralize verb 1 to make something ineffective by applying an opposite force or effect. 2 to make a substance chemically neutral. **neutralization** noun

neutrino (new-tree-noh) noun (neutrinos) an elementary particle with zero electric charge and a mass close to zero. [an Italian word, related to neutral]

neutron (new-tron) noun a particle with no electric charge, present in the nuclei of all atoms except those of ordinary hydrogen. [from neutral]

neutron bomb noun a nuclear bomb that kills people by intense radiation but does little damage to property.

never adverb 1 at no time, on no occasion. 2 not at all ♦ Never doubt it. 3 (informal) surely not ♦ You never left the key in the lock! **never** interjection (informal) surely not. [from an Old English word, from ne meaning 'not' and ever]

nevermore adverb at no future time.

never-never noun (informal) hire purchase ♦ We bought it on the never-never.

nevertheless adverb & conjunction in spite of this, although this is a fact.

new adjective 1 not existing before; recently made, invented, discovered, or experienced. SYNONYMS: fresh, recent, original, unused, brand new. 2 unfamiliar or unaccustomed ♦ The work was new to me ♦ I

was new to the work. **3** recently changed or renewed, different ♦ *His mother has got a new house.*
new *adverb* newly, recently ♦ *a new-born baby* ♦ *new-laid eggs.* **newness** *noun* [from an Old English word]

New Age *noun* a modern cultural movement that rejects many traditional Western values and promotes peace and interest in spiritual and environmental concerns.

newcomer *noun* a person who has recently arrived in a place.

newel (new-əl) *noun* **1** an upright post to which the handrail of a staircase is fixed at each end. **2** the central pillar of a spiral or winding stair. [from an Old French word *nouel* meaning 'knob']

newfangled *adjective* new and unfamiliar, used especially about something you do not like. [from *new* and an Old English word *fang* meaning 'to seize']

newish *adjective* fairly new.

newly *adverb* **1** recently. **2** again, afresh.

newly-wed *noun* someone who is recently married.

news *noun* **1** information about recent events, or a broadcast report of this. **2** new information ♦ *That's news to me.*

newsagent *noun* a shopkeeper who sells newspapers.

newsflash *noun* a single item of important news that is broadcast to interrupt normal programmes.

newsletter *noun* a short informal report giving information to members of an organization.

newspaper *noun* **1** a daily or weekly publication printed on large sheets of paper, containing news reports, articles and features, advertisements, etc. **2** the sheets of paper forming a newspaper ♦ *Wrap it in newspaper.*

newsprint *noun* the type of paper on which a newspaper is printed.

newsreel *noun* a short cinema film of news and current affairs.

news-stand *noun* a stand from which newspapers are sold.

newsworthy *adjective* important or interesting enough to be reported as news.

newsy *adjective* (*informal*) full of news.

newt *noun* a small animal like a lizard, which can live in water or on land.

New Testament *noun* the second part of the Christian Bible, including the four gospels recording the life and teaching of Jesus Christ and other writing of the early Church.

newton *noun* a unit for measuring force. [named after the English scientist Sir Isaac Newton (1642–1727)]

new town *noun* a town established as a new settlement in a rural or undeveloped area.

New World *noun* North and South America, as distinct from Europe, Asia, and Africa.

new year *noun* **1** the calendar year that is about to begin or has just begun. **2** 1 January and the days immediately following.

New Year's Day *noun* 1 January.

New Year's Eve *noun* 31 December.

next *adjective* **1** being nearest to something ♦ *The house is next to a playing field.* SYNONYMS: adjacent, close. **2** coming immediately after ♦ *It happened on the next day.* SYNONYMS: following, subsequent.
next *adverb* in the next place; on the next occasion ♦ *Shall I tell you what happened next?*
next *noun* the next person or thing. **next to** almost ♦ *It seemed next to impossible.*
the next world (in some religious beliefs) life after death. [from an Old English word]

next-best *adjective* second-best.

next door *adverb* in the next house or room.

next-door *adjective* situated next door ♦ *in the next-door house.*

next of kin *noun* a person's closest living relative.

nexus *noun* (**nexus** or **nexuses**) a connected group or series. [a Latin word, from *nectere* meaning 'to bind']

NHS *abbreviation* National Health Service.

Ni *abbreviation* (*Chemistry*) the symbol for nickel.

nib *noun* the metal tip of a pen. [from a German or Dutch word]

nibble *verb* **1** to take small quick or gentle bites of something. **2** to eat food in small amounts. **3** to show initial interest in an offer or proposal.

nibble noun 1 a small quick bite. 2 a small piece of food. [probably from a German or Dutch word]

nibs noun his nibs (informal) a humorous title used to refer to a self-important man. [origin unknown]

Nicam noun a digital system for producing high-quality stereo sound in television broadcasting. [a shortening of near instantaneously companded (= compressed and expanded) audio multiplex]

nice adjective 1 pleasant or satisfactory. SYNONYMS: pleasant, agreeable, enjoyable. 2 (said about a person) kind and considerate. SYNONYMS: kind, friendly, considerate, likeable, genial. 3 precise or subtle ♦ a nice distinction. **nicely** adverb **niceness** noun [from earlier meanings 'stupid' and later 'coy, reserved', from a Latin word nescius meaning 'ignorant']

nicety (niy-sit-i) noun (niceties) 1 precision or accuracy. 2 a small or precise distinction or detail. [from nice]

niche (nich or neesh) noun 1 a shallow recess, especially in a wall ♦ The vase stood in a niche. 2 a suitable job or position in life ♦ He has found his niche. 3 a specialized part of the market for selling goods or services. [via French from a Latin word nidus meaning 'nest']

nick noun 1 a small cut or notch. 2 the nick (informal) a police station or prison. **nick** verb 1 to make a nick in something. 2 (informal) to steal something. 3 (informal) to catch or arrest a criminal. in good nick (informal) in good condition. in the nick of time only just in time. [origin unknown]

nickel noun 1 a chemical element (symbol Ni), a hard silvery-white metal used in alloys. 2 (North Amer.) a five-cent piece. [from a German word Kupfernickel used of the copper-coloured ore from which nickel was produced]

nickel silver noun an alloy of nickel, zinc, and copper.

nickname noun a familiar or humorous name for a person. **nickname** verb to give a nickname to someone. [from an earlier form nekename, from an eke-name, from eke meaning 'additional' and name]

nicotine (nik-ə-teen) noun a poisonous oily liquid found in tobacco. [from the name of the French diplomat J. Nicot (1530–1600), who introduced tobacco into France in 1560]

nictitating membrane noun (Zoology) a membrane forming an inner eyelid of birds, reptiles, and some mammals. [from a Latin word nictare meaning 'to blink']

niece noun the daughter of your brother or sister.

nifty adjective (informal) (niftier, niftiest) particularly good or stylish. [origin unknown]

niggard noun a mean or stingy person. [from a Middle English word nig meaning 'a mean person']

niggardly (nig-erd-li) adjective mean or stingy. **niggardliness** noun

niggle verb to fuss over details or small faults. **niggling** adjective [probably from a Scandinavian language]

nigh (niy) adverb & preposition (old use) near. [from an Old English word]

night noun 1 the hours between sunset and sunrise, when it is dark. 2 the darkness of this time ♦ He opened the door and walked out into the night. 3 a particular night or evening ♦ Tonight is the first night of the play. [from an Old English word]

nightcap noun 1 (historical) a soft cap for wearing in bed. 2 an alcoholic or hot drink taken at bedtime.

nightclub noun a club that is open at night where people go to drink and dance.

nightdress noun a light loose dress worn by a woman or girl in bed.

nightfall noun the beginning of darkness at the end of the day.

nightgown noun a nightdress or nightshirt.

nightie noun (informal) a nightdress.

nightingale noun a small reddish-brown bird that sings sweetly, often at night. [from an Old English word nihtegala meaning 'night singer']

nightjar noun a bird with a harsh cry, which flies at night.

night light noun a lamp left on to provide a dim light at night.

nightly adjective 1 happening or done in the night. 2 happening or done every night. **nightly** adverb once a night, every night.

nightmare noun 1 a frightening or horrid dream. 2 an unpleasant or terrifying experience ♦ The journey was a nightmare.

nightmarish *adjective* [from *night* and an Old English word *mare* meaning 'evil spirit']

night safe *noun* a bank safe into which money and other items can be deposited when the bank is closed.

night school *noun* an educational institution providing evening classes.

nightshade *noun* any of several wild plants with poisonous berries.

nightshirt *noun* a long shirt worn by a man or boy in bed.

night-time *noun* the time between evening and morning.

nightwatchman *noun* (**nightwatchmen**) a person who guards a building at night.

nihilism (niy-il-izm) *noun* 1 the rejection of all religious and moral principles. 2 (*Philosophy*) the theory that nothing has real existence. **nihilist** *noun* **nihilistic** *adjective* [same origin as for *nil*]

nil *noun* nothing or nought. [from a Latin word *nihil* meaning 'nothing']

nimble *adjective* 1 able to move quickly, agile. SYNONYMS: agile, deft, skilful, fleet. 2 able to think quickly. **nimbleness** *noun* **nimbly** *adverb* [from an Old English word]

nincompoop *noun* a foolish person. [perhaps from the name Nicholas]

nine *adjective* & *noun* the number 9, one more than eight. **dressed up to the nines** dressed very smartly. [from an Old English word *nigon*]

ninefold *adjective* & *adverb* 1 nine times as much or as many. 2 consisting of nine parts.

ninepins *noun* the game of skittles played with nine pins.

nineteen *adjective* & *noun* the number 19, one more than eighteen. **talk nineteen to the dozen** to talk a great deal. **nineteenth** *adjective* & *noun*

ninety *adjective* & *noun* (**nineties**) the number 90, equal to nine times ten. **nineties** *plural noun* the numbers from 90 to 99, especially representing years of age or degrees of temperature. **ninetieth** *adjective* & *noun*

ninny *noun* (**ninnies**) (*informal*) a foolish person. [perhaps from *innocent*]

ninth *adjective* & *noun* 1 next after eighth. 2 one of nine equal parts of a thing. **ninthly** *adverb*

nip [1] *verb* (**nipped, nipping**) 1 to pinch or squeeze something sharply. 2 to remove something by pinching or squeezing. 3 (*informal*) to go quickly somewhere. 4 to bite something with the front teeth. 5 (said about the wind or cold) to cause pain or harm.
nip *noun* 1 a sharp pinch or bite. 2 sharp coldness ♦ *a nip in the air*. **to nip something in the bud** to suppress or destroy something at an early stage. [probably from a German or Dutch word]

nip [2] *noun* a small drink of spirits. [a shortening of an old word *nipperkin* meaning 'a small measure']

nipper *noun* 1 (*informal*) a young child. 2 the claw of a lobster or similar animal. **nippers** *plural noun* pincers or forceps for gripping things or cutting things off.

nipple *noun* 1 a small projecting part at the centre of a mammal's breasts, in females containing the outlets for secreting milk. 2 the teat of a feeding bottle. 3 a projection on a machine from which oil or other fluid is secreted. [origin unknown]

nippy *adjective* (*informal*) (**nippier, nippiest**) 1 nimble or quick. 2 sharply cold. **nippiness** *noun*

nirvana (ner-**vah**-nə) *noun* (in Buddhism and Hinduism) the state of perfect happiness achieved when the soul is freed from all suffering and absorbed into the supreme spirit. [from a Sanskrit word]

Nissen hut *noun* a tunnel-shaped hut of corrugated iron with a cement floor. [named after the British engineer Peter Nissen (1871–1930)]

nit *noun* (*informal*) 1 the egg or young form of a louse or other parasite, found in the hair. 2 a stupid or foolish person. [from an Old English word]

nit-picking *noun* (*informal*) petty criticism or fault-finding.

nitrate (niy-trayt) *noun* (*Chemistry*) 1 a salt of ester of nitric acid. 2 potassium or sodium nitrate used as a fertilizer.

nitric acid (niy-trik) *noun* (*Chemistry*) a colourless caustic highly corrosive acid.

nitrify (ny-tri-fy) *verb* (**nitrifies, nitrified, nitrifying**) (*Chemistry*) (said about bacteria) to oxidize ammonia or other nitrogen compounds in the soil, converting them into nitrates. **nitrification** *noun* [from a French word *nitrifier*]

nitrocellulose *noun* a flammable material made by treating cellulose with concentrated nitric acid, used to make explosives and celluloid.

nitrogen (niy-tro-jən) *noun* a chemical element (symbol N), a colourless odourless gas forming about four-fifths of the atmosphere. **nitrogenous** (niy-**troj**-in-əs) *adjective* [from *nitre*, a substance once thought to be a vital part of the atmosphere]

nitrogen cycle *noun* the series of processes by which nitrogen from the air is converted into compounds that are deposited in the soil, assimilated by plants, and eaten by animals, then returned to the atmosphere when these organic substances decay.

nitroglycerine (niy-trə-**gliss**-er-een) *noun* a powerful explosive made by adding glycerine to a mixture of nitric acid and sulphuric acid.

nitrous (niy-trəs) *adjective* made of or containing nitrogen.

nitrous oxide *noun* a colourless gas used as an anaesthetic.

nitty-gritty *noun* (*informal*) the basic facts or aspects of a matter.

nitwit *noun* (*informal*) a stupid or foolish person.

No. or **no.** *abbreviation* number. [from a Latin word *numero* meaning 'by number']

no *adjective* **1** not any ♦ *We have no money left.* **2** not a, quite the opposite of ♦ *It was no easy task.*
no *adverb* **1** used to deny or refuse something ♦ *Will you come? No.* **2** not at all ♦ *The result is no better than before.*
no *noun* (**noes**) a negative reply or decision, especially in voting. [from *none*]

no-ball *noun* (in cricket and rounders) a ball delivered in a way that is against the rules.

nobble *verb* (*informal*) **1** to tamper with a racehorse to prevent it from winning. **2** to thwart or influence a process by underhand means. **3** (*informal*) to accost someone. **4** (*informal*) to steal something. [probably from a dialect word *knobble* meaning 'to strike with the knuckles']

Nobel Prize (noh-**bel**) *noun* any of six international prizes awarded annually for outstanding achievements in physics, chemistry, physiology or medicine, literature, economics, and the promotion of peace. [named after the Swedish inventor of dynamite, Alfred Nobel (1833–96), who funded the prizes]

nobility (noh-**bil**-iti) *noun* **1** the quality of being noble. **2** people of aristocratic birth or rank, titled people.

noble *adjective* **1** belonging to the aristocracy by birth or rank. SYNONYMS: aristocratic, upper-class. **2** having fine qualities or character; free from pettiness or meanness. SYNONYMS: honourable, upright, worthy. **3** grand or impressive in appearance ♦ *a noble building.* SYNONYMS: stately, imposing, grand, majestic, elegant, impressive.
noble *noun* a person of noble birth or rank. **nobleness** *noun* **nobly** *adverb* [from a Latin word *nobilis* meaning 'high-born']

noble gas *noun* any of a group of gases that rarely or never combine with other elements to form compounds.

nobleman or **noblewoman** *noun* (**noblemen** or **noblewomen**) a person of noble birth or rank.

nobody *pronoun* no person.
nobody *noun* (**nobodies**) a person of no importance or authority ♦ *He's a nobody.*

nocturnal (nok-**ter**-nəl) *adjective* **1** happening at night. **2** active at night ♦ *nocturnal animals.* **nocturnally** *adverb* [from a Latin word *noctis* meaning 'of the night']

nocturne (nok-**tern**) *noun* a short romantic piece of music. [a French word, related to *nocturnal*]

nod *verb* (**nodded, nodding**) **1** to lower and raise the head quickly as a sign of agreement or casual greeting. **2** to let the head fall forward in drowsiness; to be drowsy. **3** (said about plumes or flowers etc.) to bend downwards and sway.
nod *noun* a nodding movement used to express agreement or as a casual greeting.
to nod off (*informal*) to fall asleep. [perhaps from a German word]

node *noun* **1** a swelling like a small knob. **2** (*Botany*) a point on the stem of a plant from which a leaf or bud grows. **3** (*Mathematics*) a point at which a curve crosses itself. **4** (*Physics*) a point of minimum disturbance in a standing wave system. [from a Latin word *nodus* meaning 'knot']

nodule (**nod**-yool) *noun* a small rounded lump or node. **nodular** *adjective*

noggin noun 1 (informal) the head. 2 a small measure of alcohol, usually a quarter of a pint. [from an earlier meaning 'a small mug']

no-go area noun an area that certain people or groups may not enter.

Noh noun a form of traditional Japanese drama. [from a Japanese word]

nohow adverb (informal) in no way.

noise noun 1 a sound, especially one that is loud or unpleasant. SYNONYMS: din, row, racket, rumpus. 2 (Electronics) disturbances or fluctuations which interfere with the sound or picture or data being processed. **noiseless** adjective [from a French word, related to nausea]

noisome (noi-səm) adjective (literary) smelling unpleasant; harmful. [from annoy and -some]

noisy adjective (**noisier, noisiest**) making a lot of noise. SYNONYMS: loud, rowdy, blaring, deafening. **noisily** adverb **noisiness** noun

nomad (noh-mad) noun 1 a member of a tribe that moves from place to place looking for pasture for its animals. 2 a wanderer. **nomadic** (nə-mad-ik) adjective **nomadism** noun [from a Greek word nomas meaning 'roaming']

no man's land noun 1 a piece of land that no one owns or is responsible for. 2 an area of territory between two opposing armies in war.

nom de plume (nom də ploom) noun a writer's pseudonym. [from French words meaning 'pen name', although the phrase is not used in French]

nomenclature (nə-men-klə-cher) noun a system of names, especially those used in a science such as botany or zoology. [from a Latin word nomenclatura, from nomen meaning 'name' and clatura meaning 'calling']

nominal (nom-in-əl) adjective 1 in name only ♦ The president is the nominal ruler, but real power lies with the generals. 2 (said about a sum of money) small but charged or paid as a token that payment is required ♦ a nominal fee. **nominally** adverb [from a Latin word nomen meaning 'name']

nominate (nom-in-ayt) verb 1 to propose someone as a candidate for an office or honour. SYNONYMS: appoint, designate, select, choose, name. 2 to appoint someone to a job. 3 to specify something formally.

nomination noun **nominator** noun [from a Latin word nominare meaning 'to name']

nominative (nom-in-ə-tiv) noun (Grammar) the case used for the subject of a verb etc., e.g. we in 'We saw him'. [same origin as for nominate]

nominee (nom-in-ee) noun a person who is nominated for an office or honour.

non- prefix not. [from a Latin word non meaning 'not']

nonagenarian (noh-nə-jin-**air**-iən) noun a person aged between 90 and 99. [from a Latin word nonageni meaning 'ninety each']

nonchalant (non-shə-lənt) adjective calm and relaxed, not feeling or showing anxiety or excitement. **nonchalance** noun **nonchalantly** adverb [from French words non meaning 'not' and chaloir meaning 'to be concerned']

non-combatant (non-com-bə-tənt) noun 1 a member of an army whose duties do not involve fighting, e.g. a doctor or chaplain. 2 a civilian during a war.

non-commissioned adjective not holding a commission ♦ non-commissioned officers.

non-committal (non-kə-mi-təl) adjective not committing yourself to a particular policy or decision; not revealing your thoughts or opinions.

non-conductor noun a substance that does not conduct heat or electricity.

nonconformist noun a person who does not conform to established principles. **Nonconformist** noun a member of a Protestant Church that does not conform to the teaching or practices of the Church of England or other established Churches.

non-contributory adjective not involving payment of contributions ♦ a non-contributory pension scheme.

non-cooperation noun failure or refusal to cooperate, especially as a protest.

nondescript (non-dis-kript) adjective having no distinctive characteristics and therefore difficult to describe or classify. SYNONYMS: ordinary, unexceptional, run-of-the-mill. **nondescript** noun a nondescript person or thing.

none pronoun 1 not any. 2 no one ♦ What the truth is, none can tell. ◊ Note that none can be followed by a singular or plural verb. A singular verb

emphasizes each individual (♦ *None of them has come yet*), whereas a plural verb emphasizes the group collectively (♦ *None of them want to go*).
none *adverb* by no amount, not at all ♦ *She is none the worse for her experience.* **none other** no other person. **none too** not very, not at all ♦ *He's feeling none too well.* [from an Old English word *nan*]

nonentity (non-en-titi) *noun* (**nonentities**) an unimportant person or thing. [from *non-* and *entity*]

nonetheless *adverb* in spite of that; nevertheless.

non-event *noun* an event that was meant to be important but proves to be disappointing.

non-existent *adjective* not existing or real.

non-ferrous *adjective* (said about a metal) not iron or steel.

non-fiction *noun* a class of literature that includes books in all subjects other than fiction.

non-flammable or **non-inflammable** *adjective* not easily catching fire.
◊ See the note at **inflammable**.

non-intervention *noun* the policy of not interfering in the disputes of other people.

nonpareil (non-pə-**rayl**) *noun* an unrivalled person or thing. [a French word meaning 'not equal']

nonplus (non-**plus**) *verb* (**nonplussed**, **nonplussing**) to surprise or perplex someone completely. [from a Latin phrase *non plus* meaning 'not further']

non-proliferation *noun* preventing the spread of something, especially nuclear weapons.

non-resident *adjective* 1 not living on the premises ♦ *a non-resident caretaker*. 2 (said about a job or course) not requiring residence at the place of work or study. **non-resident** *noun* a person not staying at a place, especially a hotel ♦ *The restaurant is open to non-residents.*

nonsense *noun* 1 words that do not make any sense. SYNONYM: gibberish. 2 absurd or foolish talk, ideas, or behaviour. SYNONYMS: rubbish, balderdash; (*informal*) rot, tripe. [from *non-* and *sense*]

nonsensical (non-**sens**-ikəl) *adjective* not making any sense, absurd or foolish.

SYNONYMS: absurd, senseless, foolish, ridiculous, ludicrous. **nonsensically** *adverb*

non sequitur (non **sek**-wit-er) *noun* a conclusion that does not follow from the evidence given. [a Latin phrase meaning 'it does not follow']

non-smoker *noun* a person who does not smoke.

non-starter *noun* 1 a horse which is entered for a race but does not run in it. 2 (*informal*) a person or an idea that has no chance of succeeding or is not worth considering.

non-stick *adjective* (said about a pan or surface) coated with a substance that food will not stick to during cooking.

non-stop *adjective* 1 (said about a passenger vehicle or journey) not stopping at places on the way. 2 not stopping or pausing ♦ *The room was full of non-stop chatter.* SYNONYMS: constant, ceaseless, endless, incessant. **non-stop** *adverb* without stopping or pausing ♦ *They chatted for hours non-stop.* SYNONYMS: constantly, ceaselessly, endlessly, incessantly.

non-U *adjective* (*informal*) (said about language or behaviour) not characteristic of the upper social classes.

non-union *adjective* not belonging to a trade union.

non-white *adjective* (said about a person) not white.

noodle *noun* (*informal*) 1 a foolish or silly person. 2 the head. [origin unknown]

noodles *plural noun* pasta made in narrow strips and used in soups or Chinese dishes. [from a German word *Nudel*]

nook *noun* a secluded corner or recess. [origin unknown]

noon *noun* twelve o'clock in the day, midday. [via Old English from a Latin phrase *nona hora* meaning 'ninth hour']

no one *noun* no person, nobody.

noose *noun* a loop of rope with a knot that tightens when pulled. [perhaps from a Latin word *nodus* meaning 'knot']

nor *conjunction* and not ♦ *She didn't say anything; nor did I* ♦ *They neither care nor understand.*

Nordic *adjective* (said about a person) belonging to a racial type that is tall and blond with blue eyes, found especially in Scandinavia. [from a French word *nord* meaning 'north']

norm *noun* 1 a standard or type considered to be typical or representative of a group. 2 a required or acceptable standard ♦ *the norms of good behaviour.*

normal *adjective* 1 conforming to what is standard or typical. SYNONYMS: usual, typical, accustomed, customary, conventional, regular. 2 (said about a person) free from mental or emotional disorders. 3 (*Geometry*) (said about a line) crossing a line or surface at right angles, perpendicular.
normal *noun* 1 the normal state or condition ♦ *His temperature is well above normal.* 2 (*Geometry*) a line at right angles to a line or surface. **normality** *noun* **normally** *adverb*

normalize *verb* to make something normal, or to become normal. **normalization** *noun*

Norman *noun* a member of the people of Normandy in northern France, who conquered England in 1066.
Norman *adjective* to do with the Normans or Normandy. [from an Old Norse word *northmathr* meaning 'man from the north' (because the Normans were partly descended from the Vikings of Scandinavia)]

normative (norm-ə-tiv) *adjective* relating to or establishing a norm or standard.

Norse *adjective* to do with ancient Norway or Scandinavia.
Norse *noun* the Norwegian language or the Scandinavian group of languages. [from a Dutch word *noord* meaning 'north']

Norseman *noun* (**Norsemen**) a Viking.

north *noun* 1 the point on the horizon that a compass needle normally indicates, or the direction in which this point lies, to the left of a person facing east. 2 the part of a place or building that is towards the north.
north *adjective & adverb* 1 towards or in the north. 2 (said about a wind) blowing from the north. [from an Old English word]

north country *noun* the northern part of England.

north-east *noun* the point or direction midway between north and east.
north-east *adjective* 1 situated in the north-east. 2 (said about a wind) blowing from the north-east.
north-east *adverb* in or towards the north-east. **north-easterly** *adjective & noun* **north-eastern** *adjective*

northeaster *noun* a north-east wind.

northerly *adjective* 1 in or towards the north. 2 (said about a wind) blowing from the north.
northerly *noun* (**northerlies**) a northerly wind.

northern *adjective* of or in the north.

northerner *noun* someone who lives in the north of a country or region.

Northern Lights *plural noun* the aurora borealis, which appears in the northern hemisphere.

northernmost *adjective* furthest north.

North Pole *noun* the northernmost point of the earth.

North Star *noun* the Pole Star.

northward *adjective & adverb* towards the north. **northwards** *adverb*

north-west *noun* the point or direction midway between north and west.
north-west *adjective* 1 situated in the north-west. 2 (said about a wind) blowing from the north-west.
north-west *adverb* in or towards the north-west. **north-westerly** *adjective & noun* **north-western** *adjective*

northwester *noun* a north-west wind.

Norwegian *adjective* to do with or coming from Norway.
Norwegian *noun* 1 a person born in Norway, or descended from people born there. 2 the language of Norway. [from *Norvegia*, the medieval Latin name for Norway]

Nos. or **nos.** *abbreviation* numbers.

nose *noun* 1 the organ above the mouth in humans and animals, used for breathing and smelling. 2 a sense of smell. 3 an ability or instinct for detecting things of a particular kind ♦ *She has a nose for scandal.* 4 the front end of a vehicle or aircraft. 5 the aroma of wine or other substance.
nose *verb* 1 to detect or search something by using your sense of smell. 2 to smell something. 3 to rub something with the nose; to push the nose against or into something. 4 to push your way cautiously ahead ♦ *The car nosed slowly through the crowd.* **to cut off your nose to spite your face**

to act spitefully although it causes you to suffer too. **to pay through the nose** to pay an unfairly high price. **to put someone's nose out of joint** to make someone envious because of another person's success or good fortune. **to rub a person's nose in it** to remind someone humiliatingly of an error. **to turn up one's nose at** to reject or ignore something contemptuously. **under a person's nose** where someone can or should see it clearly. **with your nose in the air** haughtily. [from an Old English word]

nosebag noun a bag containing fodder, for hanging on a horse's head.

nosebleed noun a spell of bleeding from the nose.

nosedive noun 1 a steep downward plunge by an aircraft. 2 a sudden drop or worsening.
nosedive verb 1 to plunge steeply downward. 2 to drop suddenly in amount or value ♦ *The Company's profits nosedived the following year.*

nosegay noun a small bunch of flowers. [from *nose* and an old word *gay* meaning 'an ornament']

nosh noun (*informal*) food.
nosh verb (*informal*) to eat something. [from a Yiddish word]

nostalgia (noss-tal-jə) noun a sentimental memory of or longing for things of the past. **nostalgic** adjective [from an earlier meaning 'homesickness', from Greek words *nostos* meaning 'return home' and *algos* meaning 'pain']

nostril noun each of the two openings in the nose through which air is admitted. [from an Old English word *nosthryl* meaning 'nose hole']

nostrum (noss-trəm) noun a quack or bogus remedy. [a Latin word meaning 'our thing']

nosy adjective (**nosier, nosiest**) inquisitive. SYNONYMS: inquisitive, prying, meddlesome. **nosily** adverb **nosiness** noun

nosy parker noun (*informal*) a nosy or inquisitive person.

not adverb expressing a negative or opposite. [from *nought*]

notable adjective worth noticing, remarkable or famous. SYNONYMS: (said about an achievement) remarkable, striking, memorable, noteworthy; (said about a person) famous, well-known, renowned.

notable noun a famous or eminent person. SYNONYMS: celebrity, dignitary.

notably adverb 1 remarkably. 2 in particular, especially.

notary (noh-ter-i) noun (**notaries**) a person officially authorized to witness the signing of documents and to perform other legal formalities. **notarial** adjective [from a Latin word *notarius* meaning 'secretary']

notate verb to write something in notation.

notation noun a system of signs or symbols representing numbers, quantities, or musical notes.

notch noun 1 a small cut or indentation in a surface or on the edge of something. 2 each of a row of holes into which the tongue of a buckle fits. 3 a point or level in a graded system or scale.
notch verb 1 to make a notch or notches in the surface or an edge of something. 2 to score something ♦ *The team notched up another win.* [from an Old French word *osche*]

note noun 1 a brief written record of information or thoughts, used as an aid to the memory. 2 a short or informal letter or message. SYNONYMS: message, letter; (*informal*) line. 3 a short comment on or explanation of a word or passage in a book or text. 4 a banknote ♦ *a £5 note.* 5 a single tone of definite pitch made by a voice or musical instrument, or by a machine or engine. 6 (*Music*) a written sign representing the pitch and duration of a sound. 7 any of the keys on a piano or other instrument with a keyboard. 8 a significant sound or indication of feeling ♦ *a note of optimism.* SYNONYMS: sound, tone. 9 eminence or distinction ♦ *a family of note.* 10 notice or attention ♦ *Take note of what they say.*
note verb 1 to notice or pay attention to something. 2 to write something down. [from a Latin word *nota* meaning 'a mark']

notebook noun a book with blank pages on which to write notes.

notecase noun a wallet for holding banknotes.

noted adjective famous or well-known.

notelet noun a small sheet of folded paper, often with a design on the front, used for short informal letters.

notepaper noun paper for writing letters.

noteworthy *adjective* worth noting, remarkable. SYNONYMS: remarkable, striking, memorable, notable.

nothing *noun* 1 no thing, not anything. 2 no amount, nought. 3 a person or thing of no importance.
nothing *adverb* not at all, in no way ♦ *It's nothing like as good.* **for nothing** without payment, free. [from an Old English phrase *nan thing* meaning 'no thing']

notice *noun* 1 a publicly displayed sheet of written or printed information or instructions. SYNONYMS: announcement, poster, placard. 2 attention or observation ♦ *It escaped my notice.* 3 information about something that is about to happen. 4 a formal announcement that you are about to end an agreement or leave a job at a specified time ♦ *You will need to give a month's notice.* SYNONYMS: warning, notification. 5 an account or review in a newspaper.
notice *verb* 1 to become aware of something or take notice of it. SYNONYMS: observe, discern, perceive, see, note. 2 to remark on something or speak of it. **at short notice** with little warning or time for preparation. **to take notice** to show signs of interest. [from a Latin word *notus* meaning 'known']

noticeable *adjective* easily seen or noticed. **noticeably** *adverb*

noticeboard *noun* a board for displaying notices.

notifiable *adjective* that must be reported officially ♦ *a notifiable disease.*

notify *verb* (**notifies, notified, notifying**) 1 to inform someone officially or formally. SYNONYMS: inform, advise, tell. 2 to report something or make it known. SYNONYMS: report, declare, make known, communicate. **notification** *noun*

notion *noun* 1 an idea or opinion, especially one that is vague or probably incorrect. SYNONYMS: idea, concept, conception, opinion. 2 an understanding or intention ♦ *He has no notion of how to behave.* [from a Latin word *notio* meaning 'getting to know']

notional (noh-shən-əl) *adjective* imaginary or hypothetical; assumed to be correct or valid ♦ *an estimate based on notional figures.* **notionally** *adverb*

notorious (noh-tor-iəs) *adjective* well-known for a bad quality or deed. SYNONYMS: infamous, disreputable. **notoriety**

(noh-ter-iy-iti) *noun* **notoriously** *adverb* [from a Latin word *notus* meaning 'known']

notwithstanding *preposition* in spite of. **notwithstanding** *adverb* nevertheless.

nougat (noo-gah) *noun* a chewy sweet made from nuts, sugar or honey, and egg white. [a French word]

nought (nawt) *noun* 1 the figure 0. 2 nothing. [from an Old English word *nowiht* meaning 'not anything']

noun *noun* a word or phrase used as the name of a person, place, or thing. [from a Latin word *nomen* meaning 'name']
◊ Nouns can be *common nouns*, which refer to a whole kind of people or things (e.g. *boy, dog, chair, pleasure*), or *proper nouns*, which refer to a particular person or thing (*Churchill, Thames, Paris*).

nourish (nu-rish) *verb* 1 to keep a person, animal, or plant alive and well by means of food. SYNONYMS: feed, sustain. 2 to foster or cherish a feeling. **nourishment** *noun* [from a Latin word *nutrire*]

nous (nows) *noun* (*informal*) common sense. [from a Greek word meaning 'the mind']

nouveau riche (noo-voh reesh) *noun* a person who has only recently become rich. [a French phrase meaning 'new rich']

nouvelle cuisine (noo-vel kwi-zeen) *noun* a style of cooking that avoids traditional rich sauces and emphasizes fresh ingredients and attractive presentation of the dishes. [a French phrase meaning 'new cookery']

nova (noh-və) *noun* (**novae** (noh-vee) or **novas**) a star that suddenly becomes much brighter for a short time. [a Latin word meaning 'new']

novel *noun* a fictional story that fills an entire book.
novel *adjective* of a new kind, original ♦ *It was a novel way of solving the problem.* SYNONYMS: new, original, different, unusual. [from a Latin word *novus* meaning 'new']

novelette *noun* a short novel.

novelist *noun* a person who writes novels.

novelty *noun* (**novelites**) 1 the quality of being new or original. SYNONYMS: newness, originality. 2 a novel thing or occurrence. 3 a small unusual object, suitable as a small gift. SYNONYMS: trinket, bauble. [same origin as for *novel*]

November noun the eleventh month of the year. [from a Latin word *novem* meaning 'nine' (because it was the ninth month of the ancient Roman calendar)]

novice (nov-iss) noun 1 a beginner or inexperienced person. SYNONYMS: beginner, learner. 2 a person who belongs to a religious order but has not yet taken final vows. [via French from a Latin word *novus* meaning 'new']

now adverb 1 at the present time, or at the time being spoken or written of. 2 immediately ♦ We have to leave now. 3 used in conversation to draw attention to something ♦ Now why didn't I think of that?
now conjunction as a result of or at the same time as ♦ Now that you have come, we'll start.
now noun the present time ♦ They ought to be here by now. **for now** until a later time ♦ Goodbye for now. **now and again** or **now and then** occasionally. [from an Old English word *nu*]

nowadays adverb at the present time, as contrasted with the past.

nowhere adverb not anywhere.
nowhere pronoun no place ♦ Nowhere is as beautiful as this.

nowt noun (N. England) nothing.

noxious (nok-shəs) adjective unpleasant and harmful. [from a Latin word *noxius* meaning 'harmful']

nozzle noun the spout at the end of a pipe, hose, or tube. [from a word meaning 'little nose']

NT abbreviation New Testament.

nth adjective (Mathematics) denoting an unspecified member of a series of numbers.

nuance (new-ahns) noun a slight difference or shade of meaning. [from a French word meaning 'shade']

nub noun 1 a small knob or lump. 2 the central point of a matter or problem. [from a dialect word *knub* meaning 'protuberance']

nubbly adjective full of small lumps.

nubile (new-biyl) adjective (said about a girl or woman) young but sexually mature and attractive. [from a Latin word *nubilis* meaning 'suitable for marriage']

nuclear adjective 1 to do with a nucleus or nuclei. 2 using energy that is released or absorbed during reactions taking place in the nuclei of atoms ♦ nuclear weapons ♦ nuclear power.

nuclear family noun a father, mother, and their child or children.

nuclear physics noun the branch of physics dealing with atomic nuclei and their reactions.

nuclear power noun 1 power generated by a nuclear reactor. 2 a country that has nuclear weapons.

nuclear reactor noun an apparatus that produces nuclear energy.

nucleate (new-kli-ayt) verb 1 to form a nucleus. 2 to form around a central area. **nucleated** adjective

nucleic acid (new-klee-ik) noun an acid of either of the two types (DNA and RNA) present in all living cells.

nucleon noun (Physics) a proton or neutron.

nucleotide noun (Biochemistry) an organic compound that forms the basic structural unit of a nucleic acid.

nucleus (new-kli-əs) noun (nuclei (new-kli-iy)) 1 the part in the centre of something, round which other things are grouped. 2 something that forms the basis of a developing thing ♦ The collection of books will form the nucleus of a new library. SYNONYMS: core, heart, centre, starting point, essence. 3 (Physics) the central positively charged portion of an atom. 4 (Biology) the central part of a seed or of a plant or animal cell. [a Latin word meaning 'kernel']

nude adjective not wearing any clothes. SYNONYMS: naked, bare, undressed, unclothed. **nude** noun a naked human figure as a subject in painting or photography. **in the nude** not wearing any clothes. **nudity** noun [from a Latin word *nudus* meaning 'bare']

nudge verb 1 to poke someone gently with the elbow, especially to get their attention discreetly. SYNONYMS: poke, prod, elbow. 2 to push something slightly or gradually.
nudge noun a light touch or push. [origin unknown]

nudist (newd-ist) noun a person who believes that going naked is enjoyable and good for the health. **nudism** noun

nugatory (new-gə-ter-i) adjective 1 trivial or

futile. **2** useless or invalid. [from a Latin word *nugari* meaning 'to trifle']

nugget (nug-it) *noun* **1** a rough lump of gold or platinum as found in the earth. **2** a small but valuable fact ♦ *The article contained several nuggets of new information.* [probably from a dialect word *nug* meaning 'lump']

nuisance *noun* a person or thing that causes annoyance or inconvenience. SYNONYMS: annoyance, pest, bother, irritation. [from a French word *nuire* meaning 'to hurt someone']

null *adjective* not having any legal force ♦ *The agreement is null and void.* **nullity** *noun* [from a Latin word *nullus* meaning 'none']

nullify *verb* (**nullifies, nullified, nullifying**) **1** to make something null and void. SYNONYMS: invalidate, revoke, annul. **2** to cancel or neutralize the effect of something. **nullification** *noun*

numb *adjective* temporarily unable to feel or move ♦ *numb with cold* ♦ *numb with shock.* **numb** *verb* to make someone or a part of the body numb. **numbly** *adverb* **numbness** *noun* [from an Old English word]

number *noun* **1** a symbol or word indicating a quantity or amount, a numeral or figure. SYNONYMS: numeral, figure, digit, integer. **2** a numeral or set of numerals assigned to a person or thing to identify it ♦ *a telephone number.* **3** a single issue of a magazine or newspaper. **4** a song or piece of music, especially as an item in a performance. **5** (*informal*) an article of clothing or other object regarded with favour or affection ♦ *She wore a little black number.* **6** a quantity or amount ♦ *We could see a number of new houses.* **7** (*Grammar*) the category in which a noun is singular or plural. **8** (**Numbers**) the fourth book of the Old Testament, telling of the wanderings of the Israelites in the desert. ◊ Note that *a number of*, meaning 'several', should be followed by a plural verb: ♦ *A number of problems remain.*
number *verb* **1** to count things. **2** to amount to a certain number ♦ *The crowd numbered 10,000.* SYNONYMS: amount to, total, add up to. **3** to assign a number to each in a series. **4** to include someone or something in a certain class or category ♦ *I number him among my dearest friends.* **without number** too many to count. [from an Old French word *nombre*, related to *numeral*]

numberless *adjective* too many to count.

number one *noun* (*informal*) yourself ♦ *You must take care of number one.*

number plate *noun* a plate on a motor vehicle, bearing its registration number.

numbskull *noun* (*informal*) a stupid person.

numerable *adjective* able to be counted.

numeral (new-mer-əl) *noun* a symbol that represents a certain number, a figure. SYNONYMS: figure, digit, integer, number. [from a Latin word *numerus* meaning 'number']

numerate (new-mer-ət) *adjective* having a good basic knowledge of numbers and mathematics. **numeracy** *noun* [from a Latin word *numerus* meaning 'number', on the model of *literate*]

numeration (new-mer-ay-shən) *noun* numbering. [from a Latin word *numerare* meaning 'to number']

numerator (new-mer-ayter) *noun* the number written above the line in a fraction, e.g. 3 in $\frac{3}{4}$, showing how many of the parts indicated by the denominator are to be taken. (Compare **denominator**.)

numerical (new-merri-kəl) *adjective* of a number or series of numbers ♦ *in numerical order.* **numerically** *adverb*

numerous (new-mer-əs) *adjective* many, consisting of many items. SYNONYMS: many, innumerable, countless, several. [from a Latin word *numerus* meaning 'number']

numinous (new-min-əs) *adjective* having a strong religious quality. [from a Latin word *numen* meaning 'a presiding deity']

numismatics (new-miz-mat-iks) *noun* the study of coins and medals. **numismatist** (new-miz-mə-tist) *noun* [from a Greek word *nomisma* meaning 'coin']

nun *noun* a member of a community of women who live apart from the world under the rules of a religious order. [via Old English *nonne* from a Church Latin word *nonna* with the same meaning]

nunnery (nunneries) a religious house for nuns.

nuptial (nup-shəl) *adjective* to do with marriage or a wedding. **nuptials** *plural noun* a wedding. [from a Latin word *nuptiae* meaning 'wedding']

nurse *noun* **1** a person trained to look after people who are ill or injured. **2** (*old use*) a woman employed to look after young children.
nurse *verb* **1** to work as a nurse. **2** to look

after people as a nurse. SYNONYMS: care for, look after, tend. **3** to feed a baby at the breast. SYNONYMS: feed, breastfeed. **4** to hold something carefully or protectively. **5** to give special care to something. [same origin as for *nourish*]

nursemaid *noun* a young woman employed to look after young children.

nursery *noun* (**nurseries**) **1** a room or place where young children are looked after or play. **2** a place where young plants are grown for sale.

nurseryman *noun* (**nurserymen**) a person who owns or works in a plant nursery.

nursery rhyme *noun* a simple traditional song or poem for children.

nursery school *noun* a school for children below normal school age.

nursing home *noun* a privately run hospital or home for invalids.

nurture (ner-cher) *verb* **1** to bring up a child. **2** to cherish an idea or hope. **nurture** *noun* upbringing and education. [from an Old French word *nourture* meaning 'nourishment']

nut *noun* **1** a fruit consisting of a hard shell round an edible kernel. **2** the hard kernel of this fruit. **3** (*informal*) the head. **4** (*informal*) a crazy or eccentric person. **5** a small piece of metal with a hole in its centre, for screwing on a bolt. **6** a small lump of a solid substance, e.g. coal or butter. **nuts and bolts** the basic practical details of a scheme or plan. [from an Old English word *hnutu*]

nutcrackers *plural noun* a pair of pincers for cracking nuts.

nuthatch *noun* a small climbing bird that feeds on nuts and insects.

nutmeg *noun* the hard seed of a tropical tree, grated as a spice in cooking. [from a Latin phrase *nux muscata* meaning 'spicy nut']

nutrient (new-tri-ənt) *noun* a substance that nourishes people. [from a Latin word *nutrire* meaning 'to nourish']

nutriment (new-trim-ənt) *noun* nourishing food.

nutrition (new-trish-ən) *noun* **1** nourishment. **2** the study of what nourishes people. **nutritional** *adjective* **nutritionally** *adverb*

nutritious (new-trish-əs) *adjective* containing nutrients, nourishing. SYNONYMS: nourishing, wholesome. **nutritiousness** *noun*

nutritive (new-tri-tiv) *adjective* **1** to do with nutrition. **2** nourishing.

nuts *adjective* (*informal*) crazy or eccentric.

nutshell *noun* the hard outer shell of a nut. **in a nutshell** stated or explained very briefly.

nutty *adjective* (**nuttier, nuttiest**) **1** full of nuts. **2** tasting like nuts. **3** (*informal*) crazy or eccentric. **nuttiness** *noun*

nuzzle *verb* to press or rub someone or something gently with the nose.

NW *abbreviation* north-west, north-western.

nylon *noun* **1** a strong light synthetic fibre or fabric. [invented on the model of *rayon* and *cotton*]

nymph (nimf) *noun* **1** (*Mythology*) a spirit in the form of a beautiful maiden, living in the sea or woods. **2** (*Zoology*) the immature form of the dragonfly or certain other insects. [from a Greek word *numphē* meaning 'bride']

NZ *abbreviation* New Zealand.

Oo

O 1 the fifteenth letter of the English alphabet. **2** the number zero, especially when spoken in a sequence of numbers.

O *abbreviation* (*Chemistry*) the symbol for oxygen.

oaf *noun* (**oafs**) a stupid badly-behaved or clumsy man. [from an Old Norse word]

oafish *adjective* like an oaf.

oak *noun* **1** a deciduous forest tree with irregularly-shaped leaves, bearing seeds called acorns. **2** the hard wood of this tree. [from an Old English word]

oak apple *noun* an abnormal growth or gall (see **gall**³) on an oak tree.

oaken *adjective* (*old use*) made of oak.

oakum *noun* loose fibre obtained by picking old rope to pieces, formerly used for caulking wooden ships. [from an Old English word]

OAP *abbreviation* old-age pensioner.

oar *noun* **1** a pole with a flat blade at one end, used to row or steer a boat through the water. **2** a rower ♦ *He was known to be a good oar.* **to put** or **stick your oar in** to give an opinion about something without being asked. [from an Old English word]

oarsman or **oarswoman** *noun* (**oarsmen** or **oarswomen**) a rower. **oarsmanship** *noun*

oasis (oh-ay-sis) *noun* (**oases** (oh-ay-seez)) a fertile spot in a desert, with a spring or well of water. [from a Greek word]

oast *noun* a kiln for drying hops. [from an Old English word]

oast house *noun* a building containing an oast.

oatcake *noun* a thin biscuit made of oatmeal.

oath *noun* **1** a solemn promise to do something or that something is true, sometimes appealing to God as witness. SYNONYMS: pledge, vow. **2** a swear word, especially one using the name of God or Jesus. SYNONYMS: curse, expletive, obscenity, profanity, blasphemy. **on** or **under oath** having sworn to tell the truth, especially in a court of law. [from an Old English word]

oatmeal *noun* **1** ground oats, used to make porridge etc. **2** a greyish-fawn colour.

oats *plural noun* **1** a hardy cereal plant grown in cool climates for food (*oats* for horses, *oatmeal* for people). **2** the grain of this plant. **to sow your wild oats** to lead a wild life while young, before settling down. [from an Old English word]

ob- *prefix* (changing to **oc-** before *c*, **of-** before *f*, **op-** before *p*) **1** to or towards (as in *observe*). **2** against (as in *opponent*). **3** in the way, blocking (as in *obstruct*). [from a Latin word *ob* meaning 'towards, against']

obbligato (obli-gah-toh) *noun* (**obbligatos** or **obbligati**) an important accompanying part in a musical composition. [an Italian word meaning 'obligatory']

obdurate *adjective* (**ob**-dewr-ət) *adjective* stubbornly refusing to change your mind. **obduracy** *noun* [from *ob-* and a Latin word *durare* meaning 'to harden']

OBE *abbreviation* Order of the British Empire.

obeah (oh-bee-ə) *noun* a kind of sorcery practised especially in the Caribbean. [from a West African word *bayi* meaning 'sorcery']

obedient *adjective* doing what you are told to do, willing to obey. SYNONYMS: compliant, acquiescent, biddable. **obedience** *noun* **obediently** *adverb* [same origin as for *obey*]

obeisance (ə-bay-səns) *noun* **1** an attitude of great respect or deference. **2** a deep bow or curtsy showing respect. **obeisant** *adjective* [from an Old French word *obeissant* meaning 'obeying']

obelisk (ob-əl-isk) *noun* a tall pillar set up as a monument or landmark. [from a Greek word *obeliskos* meaning 'small pillar']

obese (ə-beess) *adjective* very fat. **obesity** (ə-bee-siti) *noun* [from a Latin word *obesus* meaning 'having overeaten']

obey *verb* (**obeyed, obeying**) **1** to do what you are told to do; to be obedient. SYNONYMS: comply, conform, submit. **2** to behave in accordance with a scientific law or rule ♦ *Even pole vaulters must eventually obey the law of gravity.* SYNONYMS: comply with, follow, keep to, abide by. [from *ob-* and a Latin word *audire* meaning 'to listen or hear']

obi *noun* another spelling of **obeah**.

obituary (ə-bit-yoo-eri) *noun* (**obituaries**) a notice of a person's death, especially in a newspaper, often with a short account of his or her life and achievements. [from a Latin word *obitus* meaning 'death']

object[1] (ob-jikt) *noun* **1** something solid that can be seen or touched. **2** a person or thing to which some action or feeling is directed ♦ *She has become an object of pity.* **3** a purpose or intention. **4** (*Grammar*) a noun or its equivalent acted upon by a transitive verb or by a preposition ('him' is the object in *the dog bit him* and *against him*). **no object** not an obstacle or problem ♦ *Money is no object.* [from *ob-* meaning 'in the way' and a Latin word *-jectum* meaning 'thrown']

object[2] (əb-jekt) *verb* to say that you are not in favour of something or do not agree ♦ *Many residents objected to the plans for a new supermarket.* SYNONYMS: oppose, disapprove, protest, take exception to, dissent, mind, grumble; (*informal*) moan. **objector** *noun*

objection noun 1 a feeling of disapproval or opposition; a statement of this. 2 a reason for objecting; a drawback in a plan etc.

objectionable adjective causing objections or disapproval, unpleasant or nasty. **objectionably** adverb

objective (ǝb-**jek**-tiv) adjective 1 not influenced by personal feelings or opinions ♦ an objective account of the problem. 2 having real existence outside a person's mind, not subjective ♦ Dreams have no objective existence. 3 (Grammar) to do with the objective case.
objective noun what you are trying to achieve or reach. **objectively** adverb

objective case noun (Grammar) the form of a word used when it is the object of a verb or preposition.

object lesson noun a striking practical example of some principle.

objet d'art (ob-zhay **dar**) noun (**objets d'art** (ob-zhay **dar**)) a small artistic or decorative object. [a French phrase meaning 'object of art']

oblate (**ob**-layt) adjective (Geometry) (said about a spheroid) flattened at the poles. [from a Latin word oblatus]

oblation (ǝb-**lay**-shǝn) noun an offering to God or a god. [from a Latin word offerre meaning 'to offer']

obligation noun 1 what you must do in order to comply with an agreement or law etc., your duty. 2 being obliged to do something. **under an obligation** having a debt of gratitude to another person for some service or favour.

obligatory (ǝ-**blig**-ǝ-ter-i) adjective required by law, rule, or custom; compulsory, not optional.

oblige verb 1 to force or compel someone by law, agreement, custom, or necessity ♦ You are not obliged to answer our questions. 2 to help someone by performing a service or favour ♦ Can you oblige me with a loan? **to be obliged to someone** to feel gratitude to a person who has helped you. [from ob- meaning 'to' and a Latin word ligare meaning 'to bind']

obliging adjective willing to be helpful or do a favour. **obligingly** adverb

oblique (ǝ-**bleek**) adjective 1 slanting. 2 expressed indirectly, not going straight to the point ♦ an oblique reply. **obliquely** adverb [from a Latin word obliquus]

oblique angle noun an acute or obtuse angle.

obliterate (ǝ-**blit**-er-ayt) verb 1 to destroy something completely, leaving no traces. 2 to blot something out. **obliteration** noun [from a Latin word obliterare meaning 'to erase', from ob meaning 'over' and littera meaning 'letter']

oblivion (ǝ-**bliv**-iǝn) noun 1 the state of being unconscious or unaware of what is happening around you. 2 the state of being forgotten. [from a Latin word oblivisci meaning 'to forget']

oblivious (ǝ-**bliv**-iǝs) adjective completely unaware of what is happening around you ♦ She seemed oblivious to the danger ♦ I was oblivious of my surroundings. [same origin as for oblivion]

oblong noun a rectangular shape that is longer than it is wide.
oblong adjective having this shape. [from a Latin word oblongus meaning 'fairly long']

obnoxious (ǝb-**nok**-shǝs) adjective extremely unpleasant. **obnoxiously** adverb [from ob- and a Latin word noxa meaning 'harm']

oboe (**oh**-boh) noun a woodwind instrument of treble pitch. **oboist** noun [from French words haut meaning 'high' and bois meaning 'wood']

obscene (ǝb-**seen**) adjective indecent in a very offensive way. SYNONYMS: indecent, pornographic, coarse, dirty, filthy, vulgar, smutty; (informal) blue. **obscenely** adverb [from a Latin word obscaenus meaning 'ill-omened or abominable']

obscenity (ǝb-**sen**-iti) noun (**obscenities**) 1 being obscene. 2 an obscene action or expression ♦ Some members of the crowd shouted obscenities at him.

obscure adjective 1 hard to see properly, indistinct. 2 not easy to understand, not clearly expressed. 3 not known about, uncertain ♦ His reasons for resigning remain obscure. 4 not well known ♦ an obscure poet of the eighteenth century.
obscure verb 1 to keep something from being seen ♦ Clouds obscured the sun. 2 to make something unclear. **obscurely** adverb **obscurity** noun [from a Latin word obscurus meaning 'dark']

obsequies (**ob**-si-kwiz) plural noun funeral rites. [from a Latin word exsequiae meaning 'funeral rites']

obsequious (əb-**see**-kwi-əs) *adjective* showing too much respect or too willing to obey or serve someone; servile. **obsequiously** *adverb* **obsequiousness** *noun* [from *ob*- and a Latin word *sequi* meaning 'follow']

observance *noun* 1 the keeping of a law, rule, or custom etc. 2 the keeping or celebrating of a religious festival or of a holiday.

observant *adjective* quick at noticing things. **observantly** *adverb*

observation *noun* 1 watching something carefully ♦ *This will test your powers of observation.* 2 detailed examination ♦ *The patient is under observation.* 3 a comment or remark.

observatory (əb-**zerv**-ə-ter-i) *noun* (**observatories**) a room or building equipped with a telescope etc. for scientific observation of the stars or weather.

observe *verb* 1 to see and notice something; to watch something carefully. SYNONYMS: watch, view, scrutinize, study, monitor. 2 to pay attention to a rule or law. 3 to keep or celebrate a custom, religious festival, or holiday. 4 to make a remark. SYNONYMS: comment, remark, declare. **observable** *adjective* **observer** *noun* [from *ob*- meaning 'towards' and a Latin word *servare* meaning 'to watch']

obsess (əb-**sess**) *verb* to occupy a person's thoughts continually ♦ *My sister is obsessed with clothes.* [from a Latin word *obsessum* meaning 'haunted or besieged']

obsession (əb-**sesh**-ən) *noun* 1 obsessing or being obsessed. 2 a persistent idea that dominates a person's thoughts. SYNONYMS: preoccupation, fixation; (*informal*) thing, bee in your bonnet. **obsessional** *adjective*

obsessive *adjective* causing or showing obsession. **obsessively** *adverb*

obsidian (əb-**sid**-i-ən) *noun* a dark glassy kind of hardened lava or volcanic rock. [from a Latin word]

obsolescent (obsə-**less**-ənt) *adjective* becoming obsolete, going out of use or out of fashion ♦ *an obsolescent missile system.* **obsolescence** *noun*

obsolete (**ob**-sə-leet) *adjective* no longer used, out of date. [from a Latin word *obsoletus* meaning 'worn out']

obstacle *noun* something that stands in the way or hinders progress. SYNONYMS: hurdle, hindrance, impediment, obstruction, barrier, snag. [from *ob*- meaning 'in the way' and a Latin word *stare* meaning 'to stand']

obstacle race *noun* a race in which artificial or natural obstacles have to be passed.

obstetrician (ob-sti-**trish**-ən) *noun* a doctor or surgeon who specializes in obstetrics.

obstetrics (əb-**stet**-riks) *noun* the branch of medicine and surgery that deals with childbirth. **obstetric** *adjective* [from a Latin word *obstetrix* meaning 'midwife']

obstinate *adjective* 1 stubbornly refusing to change your mind, not easily persuaded. SYNONYMS: stubborn, obdurate, intransigent, inflexible, wilful, headstrong; (*informal*) pig-headed, bloody-minded. 2 not easily overcome ♦ *an obstinate problem.* **obstinacy** *noun* **obstinately** *adverb* [from a Latin word *obstinare* meaning 'to persist']

obstreperous (əb-**strep**-er-əs) *adjective* noisy and unruly. **obstreperously** *adverb* [from *ob*- and a Latin word *strepere* meaning 'to make a noise']

obstruct *verb* 1 to be or get in the way of something ♦ *A parked car was obstructing the entrance to their house.* 2 to prevent something from making progress ♦ *The Opposition have said they intend to obstruct the immigration bill.* [from *ob*- and a Latin word *structum* meaning 'built']

obstruction *noun* 1 obstructing or being obstructed. 2 a thing that obstructs.

obstructive *adjective* causing or intended to cause obstruction.

obtain *verb* 1 to get or come into possession of something. SYNONYMS: acquire, gain, secure, procure, come by. 2 (*formal*) to apply or be in use as a rule or custom ♦ *This custom still obtains in some districts.* **obtainable** *adjective* [from *ob*- meaning 'to' and a Latin word *tenere* meaning 'to hold']

obtrude (əb-**trood**) *verb* 1 to become obtrusive. 2 to force yourself or your opinions on someone. **obtrusion** *noun* [from *ob*- and a Latin word *trudere* meaning 'to push']

obtrusive (əb-**troo**-siv) *adjective* unpleasantly noticeable ♦ *Didn't you find the music obtrusive?* **obtrusively** *adverb* [same origin as for *obtrude*]

obtuse (əb-**tewss**) adjective 1 slow to understand something. 2 of blunt shape, not sharp or pointed. **obtusely** adverb **obtuseness** noun [from ob- meaning 'towards' and a Latin word tusum meaning 'blunted']

obtuse angle noun an angle of more than 90° but less than 180°.

obverse (ob-**verss**) noun the side of a coin or medal that bears the head or the principal design. [from ob- meaning 'towards' and a Latin word versum meaning 'turned']

obviate (ob-vi-ayt) verb to make something unnecessary ♦ The bypass obviates the need to drive through the town. [from a Latin word obviare meaning 'to prevent']

obvious adjective easy to see or recognize or to understand. SYNONYMS: apparent, evident, clear, straightforward, conspicuous, manifest, palpable, patent, blatant. **obviously** adverb [from a Latin phrase ob viam meaning 'in the way']

ocarina (oka-**ree**-nə) noun a small wind instrument with holes for the fingers, usually in the shape of a bird. [an Italian word, from oca meaning 'goose' (because of its shape)]

occasion noun 1 the time at which a particular event takes place. 2 a special event or celebration ♦ The wedding was a very happy occasion. 3 a suitable time for doing something, an opportunity. 4 (formal) a need, reason, or cause ♦ I have little occasion to visit them these days. **occasion** verb (formal) to cause something. **on occasion** from time to time. [from a Latin word occidere meaning 'to go down or set']

occasional adjective 1 happening from time to time but not regularly or frequently ♦ occasional showers. SYNONYMS: infrequent, rare, odd, intermittent, spasmodic, sporadic. 2 produced, used, or meant for a special event ♦ an occasional table. **occasionally** adverb

Occident (**oks**-i-dənt) noun (formal or poetic) the countries of the West, as opposed to the Orient. [from a Latin word meaning 'sunset']

occidental (oksi-**den**-təl) adjective western. **Occidental** noun a native or inhabitant of the West.

occiput (**ok**-si-pət) noun (Anatomy) the back of the head. **occipital** (ok-**sip**-i-təl) adjective [from ob- and a Latin word caput meaning 'head']

occlude verb to obstruct something or stop it up. **occlusion** noun [from a Latin word occludere meaning 'to shut up']

occluded front noun (Meteorology) the atmospheric condition that occurs when a cold front overtakes a mass of warm air, and warm air is driven upwards, producing a long period of steady rain.

occult (ə-**kult**) adjective to do with the supernatural or magic. **the occult** noun supernatural beliefs or events. [from a Latin word occultum meaning 'hidden']

occupant noun a person who occupies a place or position. **occupancy** noun

occupation noun 1 a person's job or profession. 2 something you do to keep yourself busy or pass the time. 3 capturing a country or region by military force.

occupational adjective to do with or caused by your occupation ♦ an occupational disease.

occupational hazard noun a risk accepted as a consequence of a certain job.

occupational therapy noun creative activities designed to help people recover from certain illnesses. **occupational therapist** noun

occupy verb (occupies, occupied, occupying) 1 to live or work in a place, to inhabit somewhere. 2 to take up or fill space or time ♦ Looking after the baby seems to occupy most of her time. 3 to keep someone busy ♦ She has plenty to occupy herself with in her retirement. 4 to capture a country or region and keep troops there. 5 to enter and stay in a building etc. as a form of protest. 6 to hold a position or job ♦ He occupies the post of finance director. **occupier** noun [from a Latin word occupare meaning 'to seize']

occur verb (occurred, occurring) 1 to happen or take place. 2 to be found to exist in some place or conditions ♦ These plants occur in marshy areas. SYNONYMS: appear, arise, exist; (informal) turn up, crop up. **to occur to** to come into a person's mind ♦ An idea has just occurred to me. [from a Latin word occurrere meaning 'to go to meet']

occurrence (ə-**ku**-rəns) noun 1 occurring. 2 an incident or event.

ocean noun the expanse of sea surrounding the continents of the earth, especially one of the very large named areas of sea ♦ *the Pacific Ocean*. [from Oceanus, the river that the ancient Greeks thought surrounded the world]

ocean-going *adjective* (said about ships) made for crossing the sea, not for coastal or river journeys.

oceanic (oh-shi-an-ik) *adjective* to do with the ocean.

oceanography (oh-shǝn-og-rǝfi) *noun* the scientific study of the sea. **oceanographer** *noun* [from *ocean* and *-graphy*]

ocelot (oss-il-ot) *noun* a leopard-like animal of Central and South America. [via French from a Nahuatl (Central American) word *ocelotl* meaning 'jaguar']

ochre (oh-ker) *noun* 1 a yellow, red, or brownish mineral consisting of clay and iron oxide, used as a pigment. 2 pale brownish yellow. [via French from a Greek word *okhros* meaning 'pale yellow']

o'clock *adverb* 1 used to specify the hour when telling the time ♦ *six o'clock*. 2 according to a method for indicating relative position by imagining a clock face with the observer at the centre, 'twelve o'clock' being directly ahead or above ♦ *Enemy aircraft are approaching at two o'clock*. [short for *of the clock*]

octa- *prefix* eight (as in *octagon*). [from a Greek word *oktō* meaning 'eight']

octagon (ok-tǝ-gǝn) *noun* a geometric figure with eight sides. [from *octa-* and a Greek word *gōnia* meaning 'angle']

octagonal (ok-tag-ǝn-ǝl) *adjective* having eight sides.

octahedron (okta-hee-drǝn) *noun* (**octahedra** (okta-hee-drǝ) or **octahedrons**) a solid geometric shape with eight faces. [from *octa-* and a Greek word *hedra* meaning 'base']

octane (ok-tayn) *noun* (*Chemistry*) a liquid hydrocarbon compound occurring in petrol. [from *octa-* (because it contains eight carbon atoms)]

octave (ok-tiv) *noun* 1 (*Music*) the series of eight notes filling the interval between one note and the next note of the same name above or below it. 2 (*Music*) a note that is six whole tones above or below a given note. 3 a group or stanza of eight lines of verse. [from a Latin word *octavus* meaning 'eighth']

octet (ok-tet) *noun* a group of eight musicians, or a musical composition for eight voices or instruments. [from *octo-*]

octo- *prefix* eight (as in *octopus*). [from a Greek word *oktō* meaning 'eight']

October *noun* the tenth month of the year. [from a Latin word *octo* meaning 'eight' (because it was the eighth month of the ancient Roman calendar)]

octogenarian (ok-toh-jin-air-iǝn) *noun* a person who is between 80 and 89 years old. [from a Latin word *octogeni* meaning '80 each']

octopus *noun* (**octopuses**) a sea creature with eight long tentacles and a soft body. [from *octo-* and a Greek word *pous* meaning 'foot']

ocular (ok-yoo-ler) *adjective* to do with the eyes or vision. [from a Latin word *oculus* meaning 'eye']

oculist (ok-yoo-list) *noun* a specialist in the treatment of diseases and defects of the eyes. [from a Latin word *oculus* meaning 'eye']

OD *abbreviation* overdose.

odd *adjective* 1 strange or unusual in appearance or nature ♦ *This is all very odd* ♦ *an odd sort of person*. SYNONYMS: peculiar, weird, curious, eccentric, extraordinary. 2 not at regular or fixed intervals, occasional ♦ *I do the crossword at odd moments.* 3 (said about a number) not even, not exactly divisible by two. 4 left over after the rest has been used ♦ *I made the bird table from odd bits of wood.* 5 being part of a pair or set when the other ones are missing ♦ *an odd glove* ♦ *several odd volumes of an encyclopedia* ♦ *You're wearing odd socks.* 6 in the region of, more than ♦ *They've been married forty-odd years.* **odd one out** a person or thing differing in some way from the others in a group or set. **oddly** *adverb* **oddness** *noun* [from an Old Norse word]

oddball *noun* (*informal*) a strange or eccentric person.

oddity *noun* (**oddities**) 1 strangeness. 2 a strange person or thing.

odd jobs *plural noun* casual pieces of work, especially household repairs.

oddment *noun* something left over from a larger piece or set.

odds *plural noun* 1 the chances that a certain thing will happen; this expressed as a ratio ♦ *The odds are 5 to 1 against throwing a six.* 2 the ratio between amounts staked by people taking part in a bet ♦ *The bookmakers are giving odds of 3 to 1.* **3** She balance of advantage or strength ♦ *She somehow won against all the odds.* **at odds with** in disagreement or conflict with someone. **it makes no odds** it makes no difference.

odds and ends *plural noun* miscellaneous items or pieces left over.

odds-on *adjective* with success more likely than failure; with betting odds in favour of its success ♦ *the odds-on favourite.*

ode *noun* a poem expressing noble feelings, often addressed to a person or thing or celebrating an event. [from a Greek word *ōidē* meaning 'song']

odious (oh-di-əs) *adjective* extremely unpleasant; detestable. **odiously** *adverb* **odiousness** *noun* [same origin as for *odium*]

odium (oh-di-əm) *noun* widespread hatred or disgust felt towards a person or actions. [a Latin word meaning 'hatred']

odometer (od-**om**-it-er) *noun* an instrument for measuring the distance travelled by a wheeled vehicle. [from a Greek word *hodos* meaning 'way' and *meter*]

odour (oh-der) *noun* a smell, especially an unpleasant one. **odorous** *adjective* **odourless** *adjective* [from a Latin word *odor* meaning 'smell']

odyssey (od-iss-i) *noun* (**odysseys**) a long adventurous journey. [named after the *Odyssey*, a Greek epic poem telling of the wanderings of Odysseus on his journey home from Troy]

oedema (i-dee-mə) *noun* an excess of watery fluid in the cavities or tissues of the body. [from a Greek word *oidein* meaning 'to swell']

Oedipus complex (ee-dip-əs) *noun* unconscious sexual feeling towards your parent of the opposite sex. [named after Oedipus who, in Greek mythology, unwittingly killed his father and married his mother]

o'er *preposition* & *adverb* (old use, poetic) over.

oesophagus (ee-sof-ə-gəs) *noun* (**oesophagi** (ee-**sof**-ə-jiy) or **oesophaguses**) the tube from the throat to the stomach, the gullet. [from a Greek word *oisophagos*]

oestrogen (ees-trə-jən) *noun* a hormone capable of developing and maintaining female bodily characteristics. [from a Greek word]

of *preposition* **1** belonging to; originating from or created by ♦ *a friend of mine* ♦ *the poems of Ted Hughes.* **2** concerning or showing ♦ *news of the disaster* ♦ *a map of France.* **3** composed or made from ♦ *a house built of brick* ♦ *a farm of 100 acres.* **4** with reference or regard to ♦ *I've never heard of it.* **5** for, involving, or directed towards ♦ *the love of your country.* **6** so as to bring separation or relief from ♦ *He has been cured of drug addiction.* [from an Old English word]

off *adverb* **1** away, at or to a distance ♦ *The bandits rode off* ♦ *My exams are six months off.* **2** out of position, not touching or attached, separate ♦ *Can you take the lid off?* **3** disconnected, not working, no longer obtainable, cancelled ♦ *Turn the gas off* ♦ *The match is off because of snow* ♦ *You had better take the day off.* **4** to the end, completely ♦ *Finish it off.* **5** as regards money or supplies ♦ *How are you off for cash?* **6** (in a theatre) behind or at the side of the stage ♦ *noises off.*
off *preposition* **1** not on; away or down from ♦ *She fell on a ladder.* **2** abstaining from, not attracted by something for the time being ♦ *Jack is off his food today.* **3** leading from, not far from ♦ *We live in a road off the High Street.* **4** deducted from ♦ *£10 off the price.* **5** at sea a short distance from ♦ *The ship sank off Cape Horn.*
off *adjective* **1** (said about food) no longer fresh. **2** not satisfactory. **3** (said about a part of a vehicle, horse, or road) on the right-hand side ♦ *the off-side front wheel.*
off *noun* **1** (in cricket) the side of the field towards which the batsman's feet are pointing. **2** (*informal*) the start of a race or journey ♦ *I think we're ready for the off now.* **off and on** from time to time. [from an Old English word]

offal *noun* the organs of an animal (e.g. heart, kidneys, liver) used as food. [originally meaning 'waste products': from *off* and *fall*]

offbeat *adjective* (*informal*) unconventional or unusual.

off chance *noun* a slight possibility.

off-colour *adjective* slightly unwell.

offcut *noun* a piece of wood, hardboard, etc. that is left behind after cutting a larger piece.

offence *noun* **1** breaking of the law, an illegal act. **2** a feeling of annoyance or resentment ♦ *I didn't think anyone would take offence.*

offend *verb* **1** to cause offence or displeasure to someone. **2** to do wrong or commit a crime ♦ *criminals who persistently offend*. **offended** *adjective* **offender** *noun* [from *ob-* and a Latin word *fendere* meaning 'to strike']

offensive *adjective* **1** causing offence ♦ *offensive remarks*. **2** disgusting or repulsive ♦ *an offensive smell*. **3** used in attacking ♦ *offensive weapons*. **offensive** *noun* a forceful attack or campaign. **to be on the offensive** to be ready to act aggressively. **offensively** *adverb* **offensiveness** *noun*

offer *verb* **1** to present something so that people can accept it if they want. SYNONYMS: proffer, tender, put forward. **2** to say you are willing to do something for someone else ♦ *Thanks for offering to help*. SYNONYMS: volunteer, come forward; (*informal*) show willing. **3** to state what you are willing to do, pay, or give. **4** to provide something, to give opportunity ♦ *The job offers prospects of promotion*. **offer** *noun* **1** an expression of willingness to give, do, or pay something. **2** an amount offered ♦ *offers above £500*. **3** a specially reduced price. **on offer 1** available. **2** for sale at a reduced price. [from *ob-* meaning 'to' and a Latin word *ferre* meaning 'to bring']

offering *noun* something that is offered.

offertory *noun* (**offertories**) **1** in the Christian Church, the offering of bread and wine for consecration at the Eucharist. **2** a collection of money made at a religious service. [same origin as for *offer*]

offhand *adjective* rather casual and without thought or consideration, often in a way that seems rude ♦ *an offhand manner*. **offhand** *adverb* without previous thought or preparation ♦ *Offhand I can't think of anyone who would be suitable*. **offhanded** *adjective* **offhandedly** *adverb*

office *noun* **1** a room or building used as a place of business, especially for clerical and similar work or for a special department ♦ *the enquiry office* ♦ *an office job*. **2** a government department ♦ *the Foreign and Commonwealth Office*. **3** an important position of authority or trust, the holding of an official position ♦ *He has announced that he seeks office as president* ♦ *She holds the office of Attorney-General*. **4** an authorized form of Christian worship ♦ *the Office for the Dead*. **5** a piece of

kindness or a service done for others ♦ *through the good offices of his friends*. **in** or **out of office** (describing a political party) in or out of power. [from a Latin word *officium* meaning 'a service or duty']

office block *noun* a large building designed to contain business offices.

office boy or **office girl** *noun* a young man or woman employed to do minor jobs in a business office.

officer *noun* **1** a person holding a position of authority or trust, an official ♦ *customs officers*. **2** a person who holds authority in any of the armed forces, especially with a commission. **3** a member of the police force.

office worker *noun* an employee in a business office.

official *adjective* **1** to do with an authority or public body or in an official capacity. **2** done or said by someone with authority; properly authorized ♦ *The news is official*. **official** *noun* a person holding a position of authority. **officially** *adverb* ◊ Do not confuse this word with **officious**, which has a different meaning.

officiate (ə-**fish**-i-ayt) *verb* to be in charge of a meeting, ceremony, etc. [from a Latin word *officiare* meaning 'to hold a service']

officious (ə-**fish**-əs) *adjective* too ready to give orders, bossy. **officiously** *adverb* [from a Latin word *officiosus* meaning 'ready to do your duty'] ◊ Do not confuse this word with **official**, which has a different meaning.

offing *noun* **in the offing** likely to happen soon.

off-key *adjective* & *adverb* (*Music*) out of tune.

off-licence *noun* a shop with a licence to sell alcoholic drinks to be drunk away from the shop.

off-limits *adjective* out of bounds.

off-line *adjective* not directly controlled by or connected to a computer.

offload *verb* **1** to unload goods. **2** to get rid of something.

off-peak *adjective* in or used at a time that is less popular or less busy ♦ *off-peak electricity*.

off-putting *adjective* unpleasant or disconcerting.

off season *noun* the time of year when business etc. is fairly slack.

offset *verb* (past tense and past participle **offset; offsetting**) to counterbalance or compensate for something.
offset *noun* **1** a side shoot on a plant. **2** a method of printing in which the ink is transferred to a rubber surface and from this to paper.

offshoot *noun* **1** a side shoot on a plant. **2** something that develops from something else.

offshore *adjective* **1** at sea some distance from the shore ♦ *an offshore island*. **2** (said about wind) blowing from the land towards the sea.

offside *adjective & adverb* (said about a player in football etc.) in a position where the rules do not allow him or her to play the ball.

offspring *noun* (**offspring**) **1** a person's child or children. **2** the young of an animal. [from an Old English word *ofspring*]

offstage *adjective & adverb* not on the stage, not visible to the audience.

off-white *noun* white with a grey or yellowish tinge. **off-white** *adjective*

Ofsted *abbreviation* Office for Standards in Education.

oft *adverb* (*old use*) often. [from an Old English word]

Oftel *abbreviation* Office of telecommunications.

often *adverb* **1** frequently, many times. **2** in many cases. [from *oft*]

ogee (oh-jee) *noun* (*Architecture*) an S-shaped curve or line. [from *ogive*]

ogive (oh-jiyv) *noun* (*Architecture*) **1** a pointed arch. **2** a diagonal groin or rib of a vault. [from a French word]

ogle (oh-gəl) *verb* to stare at someone you find attractive, especially in a lustful way. [probably from an Old Dutch word]

ogre *noun* **1** a man-eating giant in fairy tales and legends. **2** a terrifying person. **ogress** *noun* [from a French word]

oh *interjection* **1** an exclamation of surprise, delight, disappointment, etc. **2** used for emphasis ♦ *Oh yes I will!*

ohm (ohm) *noun* a unit of electrical resistance. [named after the German physicist G. S. Ohm (1787–1854), who studied electrical currents]

ohmmeter (ohm-meet-er) *noun* an instrument for measuring electrical resistance in ohms.

OHMS *abbreviation* On Her (or His) Majesty's Service.

OHP *abbreviation* overhead projector.

oil *noun* **1** a thick slippery liquid that will not dissolve in water. **2** a form of petroleum used as fuel or lubricant. **3** petroleum. **4** oil paint.
oil *verb* to put oil on something, especially to make it work smoothly. [from a Latin word *oleum* meaning 'olive oil']

oilcake *noun* cattle food made from linseed or similar seeds after the oil has been pressed out.

oilcan *noun* a can with a long nozzle through which oil flows, used for oiling machinery.

oilcloth *noun* strong fabric treated with oil to make it waterproof.

oilfield *noun* an area where oil is found in the ground or beneath the sea.

oil-fired *adjective* (said about a heating system or power station) using oil as fuel.

oil paint *noun* paint made by mixing powdered pigment in oil.

oil painting *noun* a picture painted in oil paints.

oil rig *noun* a structure with equipment for drilling for oil.

oilskin *noun* cloth made waterproof by treatment with oil.
oilskins *plural noun* waterproof clothing made of oilskin.

oily *adjective* (**oilier, oiliest**) **1** containing, covered, or soaked in oil. **2** like oil. **3** behaving in an insincerely polite and smooth way; trying to win favour by flattery. **oiliness** *noun*

oink *noun* the grunting sound that a pig makes.
oink *verb* to make this sound. [an imitation of the sound]

ointment *noun* a thick slippery paste rubbed on the skin to heal sore skin and cuts. [from an Old French word *oignement*]

OK *adverb & adjective* (*informal*) **1** all right, satisfactory. **2** allowed.

OK noun (informal) approval, agreement to a plan etc.
OK verb (**OK's**, **OK'ed**, **OK'ing**) (informal) to give your approval or agreement to something. [perhaps from the initials of oll (or orl) korrect, a humorous spelling of all correct, first used in the USA in 1839]

okapi (ə-kah-pi) noun (**okapis**) an animal of Central Africa, like a giraffe but with a shorter neck and a striped body. [a local word]

okay(informal) another spelling of **OK**.

okra (oh-krə or uk-rə) noun a tropical plant with seed pods that are used as a vegetable. [from a West African word]

old adjective 1 having lived or existed for a long time. SYNONYMS: aged, elderly (people). 2 made or built long ago: SYNONYMS: ancient, antiquated, antique, vintage. 3 known, used, or established for a long time ♦ They are old friends of mine. 4 shabby from age or wear. 5 of a particular age ♦ He is ten years old ♦ a ten-year-old. 6 not recent or modern ♦ in the old days. 7 former or original ♦ in its old place. 8 (informal) used to express affection, familiarity, etc. ♦ good old Winnie. **of old 1** in or belonging to the past. **2** since a long time ago ♦ We know him of old. **the old** old people. **the old days** a period in the past. **oldish** adjective **oldness** noun [from an Old English word ald]

old age noun the period of a person's life from about 65 or 70 onwards.

old-age pension noun a state pension paid to people above a certain age. **old-age pensioner** noun

old boy noun 1 a former male pupil of a school. 2 (informal) an elderly man. 3 an affectionate term of address for a man.

old country noun a person's native country.

olden adjective of former times ♦ the olden days.

Old English noun the English language from about 700 to 1150, also called Anglo-Saxon.

old-fashioned adjective having the styles, views, or tastes current a long time ago; no longer fashionable. SYNONYMS: out of date, outdated, outmoded, dated, antiquated, archaic; (informal) old hat.

old girl noun 1 a former female pupil of a

school. 2 (informal) an elderly woman. 3 an affectionate term of address for a woman.

old gold noun a dull gold colour.

old hand noun a person with a lot of experience.

oldie noun (informal) an old person or thing.

old maid noun a single woman thought of as too old to get married.

old man noun (informal) your father, husband, or male partner.

old master noun 1 a great painter of former times, especially the 13th–17th centuries in Europe. 2 a painting by such a painter.

Old Nick noun a name for the Devil.

Old Norse noun the language spoken by Vikings, the ancestor of modern Scandinavian languages.

Old Testament noun the first part of the Christian Bible, corresponding to the Hebrew Bible and telling of the history of the Jews and their beliefs.

old-time adjective belonging to former times.

old-timer noun (informal) 1 a person with long experience or who has served a long time. 2 (North Amer.) an old person.

old wives' tale noun a traditional belief for which there is little scientific evidence.

old woman noun 1 (informal) your mother, wife, or female partner. 2 a fussy or timid person.

Old World noun Europe, Asia, and Africa, as distinct from the Americas.

old year noun the year just ended or about to end.

oleaginous (oh-li-aj-in-əs) adjective 1 oily or greasy. 2 flattering or complimenting someone too much; obsequious. [from a Latin word oleum meaning 'oil']

oleander (oh-li-an-der) noun a poisonous evergreen shrub of Mediterranean regions, with red, white, or pink flowers. [origin unknown]

olfactory (ol-fak-ter-i) adjective to do with the sense of smell ♦ olfactory organs. [from a Latin word olfacere meaning 'to smell']

oligarch (ol-i-gark) noun a ruler in an oligarchy.

oligarchy (ol-i-gar-ki) noun (**oligarchies**) 1 government by a small group of people. 2 a small group of people who rule a country in this way. **3** a country governed in this way. [from Greek words *oligoi* meaning 'few' and *arkhein* meaning 'to rule']

oligopoly (ol-i-**gop**-ə-li) *noun* (**oligopolies**) a market in which there are only a few producers or sellers. [from Greek words *oligoi* meaning 'few' and *pōlein* meaning 'to sell']

olive *noun* **1** a small oval fruit with a hard stone and bitter flesh from which olive oil is obtained. **2** the evergreen tree that bears it. **3** a greyish-green colour like that of an unripe olive.
olive *adjective* **1** greyish-green like an unripe olive. **2** (said about the complexion) yellowish-brown. [from a Greek word *elaion* meaning 'oil']

olive branch *noun* something done or offered to show that you want to make peace. [from a story in the Bible, where the dove brings Noah an olive branch as a sign that God is no longer angry with mankind]

olive oil *noun* an oil obtained from olives, used in cookery and salad dressings.

-ology *suffix* see **-logy**.

Olympiad (ə-**limp**-i-ad) *noun* **1** a celebration of the modern Olympic Games. **2** a period of four years between celebrations of the Olympic Games, used by the ancient Greeks in dating events.

Olympian (ə-**limp**-i-ən) *adjective* **1** to do with Mount Olympus in Greece, traditional home of the Greek gods. **2** fit for or like a god; majestic, imposing, or aloof. **3** Olympic.
Olympian *noun* a competitor in the Olympic Games.

Olympic (ə-**limp**-ik) *adjective* to do with the Olympic Games.
Olympics *plural noun* the Olympic Games.

Olympic Games *plural noun* **1** an international sports festival held every four years in a different part of the world. **2** a festival of athletic and other contests held every four years at Olympia in Greece in ancient times.

om (in Buddhism and Hinduism etc.) a mystic syllable considered the most sacred mantra. [from a Sanskrit word]

omasum (ə-**may**-səm) *noun* (*Zoology*) the third stomach of a ruminant animal. [from a Latin word]

ombudsman (om-**buudz**-mən) *noun* (**ombudsmen**) an official appointed to investigate individuals' complaints against government organizations etc. [a Swedish word meaning 'legal representative']

omega (oh-**mig**-ə) *noun* the last letter of the Greek alphabet, equivalent to Roman *o*. [from a Greek phrase *ō mega* meaning 'great O']

omelette (**om**-lit) *noun* a dish made of beaten eggs cooked in a frying pan, often served folded round a savoury filling. [from a French word]

omen (**oh**-men) *noun* an event regarded as a sign of what is going to happen in the future. [from a Latin word]

ominous (**om**-in-əs) *adjective* making you think that something bad is going to happen ♦ *an ominous silence.* SYNONYMS: forbidding, sinister, menacing, portentous, threatening. **ominously** *adverb* [from *omen*]

omission *noun* **1** omitting or being omitted. **2** something that has been omitted or not done.

omit *verb* (**omitted, omitting**) **1** to leave or miss something out. **2** to fail to do something. [from *ob-* and a Latin word *mittere* meaning 'to let go']

omni- *prefix* all. [from a Latin word *omnis* meaning 'all']

omnibus *noun* **1** a book containing a number of books or stories previously published separately. **2** a single edition of two or more radio or television programmes previously broadcast separately. **3** (*old use*) a bus. [a Latin word meaning 'for everybody']

omnipotent (əm-**nip**-ə-tənt) *adjective* having unlimited power or very great power. **omnipotence** *noun* [from *omni-* and *potent*]

omnipresent *adjective* present everywhere.

omniscient (om-**niss**-iənt) *adjective* knowing everything. **omniscience** (om-**niss**-iəns) *noun* [from *omni-* and a Latin word *sciens* meaning 'knowing']

omnivore (**om**-niv-or) *noun* an omnivorous animal.

omnivorous (om-**niv**-er-əs) *adjective* **1** feeding on both plants and animal flesh. **2** reading or taking in whatever comes your way. [from *omni-* and a Latin word *vorare* meaning 'to devour']

on preposition 1 supported by, attached to, or covering something ♦ *We sat on the floor* ♦ *Have you got any money on you?* 2 close to, in the area or direction of ♦ *They live on the coast* ♦ *The army advanced on Paris.* 3 (said about time) exactly at, during ♦ *on the next day* ♦ *on my birthday.* 4 having something as a basis or reason ♦ *Two men were arrested on suspicion* ♦ *profits on sales.* 5 as a member of ♦ *She sits on the student-teacher committee.* 6 in a certain manner or state ♦ *The house was on fire* ♦ *Be on your best behaviour.* 7 about or concerning ♦ *a book on grammar.* 8 doing or taking part in something ♦ *We're going on holiday tomorrow.* 9 taking a drug or medicine ♦ *I've been on antibiotics for a week.* 10 paid for by ♦ *The drinks are on me.* 11 added to ♦ *5p on the price of petrol.*
on adverb 1 so as to be supported by, attached to, or covering something ♦ *Make sure you put the lid on tightly.* 2 being worn by someone ♦ *He had a straw hat on.* 3 further forward, towards something ♦ *Let's move on to another subject* ♦ *from that day on.* 4 with continued movement or action ♦ *She slept on all morning.* 5 in operation or activity; running or functioning ♦ *Someone left the light on all night.* 6 taking place or being performed or broadcast ♦ *Where is the film on?* 7 due to take place, not cancelled ♦ *Despite all the rain, the match is still on.* 8 (said about an employee) on duty.
on noun (in cricket) the part of the field opposite the off side and in front of the batsman. **to be on** to be acceptable or practical ♦ *This plan just isn't on.* **to be on about** (*informal*) to keep talking about something in a boring way ♦ *He's always on about his pigeons.* **to be** or **keep on at** (*informal*) to nag someone. **to be on to something** to have a good idea or realize the importance of something. **on and off** from time to time, not continually. **on and on** continually, at great length. **on high** in or to a high place. **on to** to a position on. See the note at **onto**. [from an Old English word]

once adverb 1 for one time or on one occasion only ♦ *They came only once.* 2 formerly ♦ *people who once lived here.* **once** conjunction as soon as ♦ *You can go once I have taken your names.* **once** noun one time or occurrence ♦ *Once is enough.* **at once** 1 immediately. 2 at the same time. **once and for all** finally, now and for the last time. **once in a while** from time to time, not often. **once more** or **again** one more time. **once upon a time** at some time in the past. [from *one*]

once-over noun (*informal*) a rapid inspection or search ♦ *I'd better give the tyres the once-over.*

oncology (on-**col**-ə-ji) noun (*Medicine*) the study and treatment of tumours.

oncoming adjective approaching, coming towards you ♦ *oncoming traffic.*

one adjective 1 single. 2 individual or united. **one** noun 1 the smallest whole number, 1. 2 a single thing or person. **one** pronoun 1 a person or thing previously mentioned ♦ *The town is full of restaurants but I've yet to find one I like.* 2 a person ♦ *loved ones.* 3 any person; the speaker or writer as representing people in general ♦ *One doesn't want to seem mean.* **one another** each other. **one by one** separately and in succession. **one day** at some unspecified time. **one or two** a few. [from an Old English word]

one-armed bandit noun (*informal*) a fruit machine operated by pulling down a long handle at the side.

one-man band noun 1 a street performer who plays several instruments at the same time. 2 a person who runs a business alone.

one-off adjective done or happening only once, not repeated.

onerous (**ohn**-er-əs) adjective difficult to bear or do; burdensome. [from a Latin word *onus* meaning 'burden']

oneself pronoun the form of the pronoun *one* used in reflexive constructions (e.g. *One must avoid cutting oneself*) and for emphasis (e.g. *One does it oneself*).

one-sided adjective 1 with one side or person in a contest, conversation etc. being much stronger or doing it more than the other ♦ *a one-sided match.* 2 showing only one point of view in an unfair way ♦ *This is a very one-sided account of what happened.*

one-time adjective former.

one-track mind noun (*informal*) a mind that can think of only one subject, especially sex.

one-upmanship noun the art of gaining a psychological advantage over someone else.

one-way adjective where traffic is allowed to travel in one direction only.

one-way ticket *noun* a single ticket, not a return.

ongoing *adjective* continuing, still in progress.

onion *noun* a vegetable with an edible rounded bulb that has a strong smell and flavour. **oniony** *adjective* [from an Old French word *oignon*]

online *adjective & adverb* connected to a computer, the Internet, etc.

onlooker *noun* a spectator.

only *adjective* **1** being the one specimen or all the specimens of a class, sole ♦ *my only wish.* **2** most or best worth considering ♦ *In my opinion athletics is the only sport.*
only *adverb* **1** no more than, without anything or anyone else ♦ *There are only three cakes left.* **2** no longer ago than ♦ *I saw her only yesterday.*
only *conjunction* except that, but then ♦ *He often makes promises, only he never keeps them.* **only just 1** by a very small degree or amount. **2** very recently. **only too** extremely ♦ *We'd be only too pleased to help.* [from an Old English word]

only child *noun* a child who has no brothers or sisters.

o.n.o. *abbreviation* or nearest offer.

onomatopoeia (on-ə-mat-ə-**pee**-ə) *noun* the formation of words that imitate or suggest what they stand for, e.g. *cuckoo, plop, sizzle.* **onomatopoeic** *adjective* [from a Greek word meaning 'word-making']

onrush *noun* a surging rush forward.

onset *noun* the beginning of something ♦ *the onset of winter.*

onshore *adjective* **1** situated or occurring on land. **2** (said about wind) blowing from the sea towards the land.

onside *adjective & adverb* not offside.

onslaught (on-**slawt**) *noun* a fierce attack. [from Old Dutch *aan* meaning 'on' and *slag* meaning 'a blow']

onto *preposition* to a position on.
◊ Note that *onto* cannot be used where *on* is an adverb, e.g. *We walked on to the river* (continued walking until we reached it). Compare this with *We walked onto the escalator.*

ontology (on-**tol**-əji) *noun* a branch of philosophy dealing with the nature of being. **ontological** *adjective* [from a Greek word *ontos* meaning 'of a being' and *-logy*]

onus (**oh**-nəs) *noun* a duty or responsibility ♦ *The onus is on the prosecution to prove he did it.* [a Latin word meaning 'burden']

onward *adverb & adjective* going or moving forward, further on. **onwards** *adverb*

onyx (**on**-iks) *noun* a stone like marble with different colours in layers. [from a Greek word *onux*]

oodles *noun* (*informal*) a great quantity. [origin unknown]

ooze *verb* **1** (said about liquid) to trickle or flow out slowly. SYNONYMS: seep, trickle. **2** to allow a liquid to trickle or flow out slowly ♦ *The wound oozed blood.* **3** to show a feeling strongly or freely ♦ *She oozes confidence on the tennis court.*
ooze *noun* mud at the bottom of a river or sea. [from an Old English word]

opacity (ə-**pas**-iti) *noun* being opaque.

opal *noun* a quartz-like stone with a rainbow sheen, often used as a gem. [via French or Latin from a Sanskrit word *upala* meaning 'precious stone']

opalescent (oh-pə-**less**-ənt) *adjective* having a rainbow sheen like an opal. **opalescence** *noun*

opaque (ə-**payk**) *adjective* **1** not able to be seen through; not transparent. **2** not clear, difficult to understand. [from a Latin word *opacus* meaning 'shady or dark']

op art *noun* a form of abstract art that gives an illusion of movement by using pattern and colour. [the word *op* is short for *optical*]

OPEC (**oh**-pek) *abbreviation* Organization of Petroleum Exporting Countries.

open *adjective* **1** not closed; not sealed or locked. **2** not covered or blocked up. **3** not limited or restricted ♦ *an open championship.* **4** letting in visitors or customers. **5** spread out, unfolded. **6** with wide empty spaces ♦ *open country* ♦ *open texture.* **7** honest and frank; not secret or secretive ♦ *with open hostility.* **8** not yet settled or decided ♦ *an open mind.* **9** available ♦ *Three courses are open to us.* **10** willing to receive ♦ *We are open to offers.* **11** vulnerable or susceptible ♦ *You will leave yourself open to attack.* **12** (said about a cheque) not crossed.
open *verb* **1** to make something open, or to become open or more open ♦ *Open your books on page 72.* **2** to begin or establish something, to make a start ♦ *Who would like to open the discussion?* ♦ *The play opens*

next month ♦ *Open fire!* **3** to give access to somewhere ♦ *The French windows open on to a beautiful garden.* **4** to declare something in a special ceremony to be open to the public.

open *noun* **1** (**the open**) open space or open air. **2** (**Open**) a championship or competition with no restriction on who can take part. **in the open air** not inside a house or building. **openness** *noun* [from an Old English word]

open-and-shut *adjective* (*informal*) perfectly straightforward ♦ *an open-and-shut case.*

opencast *adjective* (said about a mine or mining) with layers of earth removed from the surface and worked from above, not from underground shafts.

open day *noun* a day when the public may visit a place that is not normally open to them.

open-ended *adjective* with no fixed limit ♦ *an open-ended ticket.*

opener *noun* **1** a device for opening tins or bottles. **2** a person or thing that opens something. **for openers** (*informal*) to start with.

open-handed *adjective* generous in giving.

open-hearted *adjective* warm and kindly.

open-heart surgery *noun* surgery with the heart exposed and with blood circulating temporarily through a bypass.

open house *noun* a place where all visitors are welcome.

opening *noun* **1** a space or gap; a place where something opens. SYNONYMS: aperture, hole, gap, breach, break, mouth, orifice (in the body). **2** the beginning of something. **3** a ceremony at which something is declared open to the public. **4** an opportunity.

open letter *noun* a letter of comment or protest addressed to a person by name but printed in a newspaper.

openly *adverb* without secrecy; frankly or honestly.

open mind *noun* a mind that is willing to consider new ideas or is not yet decided. **open-minded** *adjective*

open-plan *adjective* (said about a room or building) having no or few dividing walls between areas ♦ *an open-plan office.*

open prison *noun* a prison with few physical restraints on the prisoners.

open question *noun* a matter on which no final verdict has yet been made or on which none is possible.

open sandwich *noun* a sandwich without a top slice of bread.

open secret *noun* a secret known to so many people that it is no longer a secret.

open-topped *adjective* (said about a vehicle) having no roof or a roof that can be removed ♦ *an open-topped bus.*

open verdict *noun* (*Law*) a verdict that does not specify whether a crime is involved in the case of a person's death.

openwork *noun* a pattern with spaces between threads or strips of metal, leather etc.

opera *noun* **1** a play in which the words are sung to a musical accompaniment. **2** dramatic works of this kind. **opera** *plural noun* the plural of **opus**. [from a Latin word meaning 'work']

operable *adjective* **1** able to be treated by a surgical operation. **2** able to be operated.

opera glasses *plural noun* small binoculars used at the opera or theatre.

opera house *noun* a theatre where operas are performed.

operate *verb* **1** to make a machine, process, etc. work or function ♦ *He operates the lift.* **2** to be in action; to produce an effect ♦ *The new tax operates to our advantage.* **3** to perform a surgical or other operation. [from a Latin word *operari* meaning 'to work']

operatic *adjective* to do with or like opera.

operating system *noun* the software that controls a computer's basic functions.

operating theatre *noun* a room for surgical operations.

operation *noun* **1** operating or being operated. **2** the way a thing works. **3** a piece of work, something to be done ♦ *begin operations.* **4** a business organization. **5** an act performed by a surgeon on part of the body to take away or repair a diseased, injured, or deformed part. **6** (*Mathematics*) a procedure in which one of the rules of addition, multiplication, differentiation, etc. is applied to a number or quantity. **7** strategic military activities in war or during manoeuvres. **in operation** working or in use ♦ *When does the new system come into operation?*

operational *adjective* 1 in or ready for use ♦ *Is the system operational yet?* 2 to do with the operation of an organization.

operative *adjective* 1 working or functioning. 2 (said about a word) having most significance in a phrase. 3 to do with surgical operations.
operative *noun* a worker, especially a skilled one.

operator *noun* 1 a person who operates a machine or equipment. 2 a person or company that runs a business etc. 3 a person who makes connections of lines at a telephone exchange. 4 (*Mathematics*) a symbol or function denoting an operation, e.g. +, ÷, ×.

operculum (ə-per-kew-ləm) *noun* (**opercula**) a movable flap or plate etc. covering a fish's gills or the opening of a mollusc's shell. [from a Latin word meaning 'lid, covering']

operetta *noun* a short or light opera. [from an Italian word meaning 'little opera']

ophthalmia *noun* (off-thal-miə) *noun* inflammation of the eye, especially conjunctivitis. [same origin as for *ophthalmic*]

ophthalmic (off-thal-mik) *adjective* to do with or for the eyes. [from a Greek word *ophthalmos* meaning 'eye']

ophthalmic optician *noun* a person who is qualified to examine a person's eyes and to prescribe glasses and contact lenses as well as to sell them.

ophthalmology (off-thal-mol-əji) *noun* the scientific study of the eye and its diseases. **ophthalmologist** *noun* [from *ophthalmic* and *-logy*]

opiate (oh-piət) *noun* 1 a sedative drug containing opium. 2 something that soothes the feelings or dulls activity.

opine (ə-piyn) *verb* (*formal*) to express an opinion. [same origin as for *opinion*]

opinion *noun* 1 what you think of something. SYNONYMS: assessment, estimation, evaluation, view, attitude, impression, feeling, idea. 2 a judgement or belief that is held firmly but without actual proof of its truth; a view held as probable. 3 a judgement or comments given by an expert who is consulted ♦ *a medical opinion*. [from a Latin word *opinari* meaning 'to believe']

opinionated *adjective* having strong opinions and holding them obstinately.

opinion poll *noun* an estimate of public opinion made by questioning a representative sample of people.

opium *noun* an addictive drug made from the juice of certain poppies, smoked or chewed as a narcotic, and occasionally used in medicine as a sedative. [from a Greek word *opion* meaning 'poppy juice']

opossum (ə-poss-əm) *noun* a small furry American or Australian marsupial that lives in trees. [from a word from a Native American language]

opponent *noun* a person or group opposing another in a contest or war. [from a Latin word *opponere* meaning 'to set against']

opportune (op-er-tewn) *adjective* 1 (said about a time) convenient or suitable for a purpose. 2 done or happening at a favourable time. **opportunely** *adverb* [from *ob-* and a Latin word *portus* meaning 'harbour', originally used of wind blowing a ship towards a harbour]

opportunist (op-er-tewn-ist) *noun* a person who is quick to take advantage of opportunities, often in an unprincipled way. **opportunism** *noun*

opportunistic *adjective* taking advantage of opportunities, often in an unprincipled way.

opportunity *noun* (**opportunities**) a suitable time or set of circumstances for doing something. SYNONYMS: chance, time, moment, opening, break. [same origin as for *opportune*]

opportunity cost *noun* (*Economics*) the price that must be paid for choosing one alternative rather than another, e.g. the loss of arable land to provide space for new housing.

opposable *adjective* (*Zoology*) (said of the thumb of a primate) capable of facing and touching the other parts of the hand, as in humans.

oppose *verb* 1 to argue or fight against someone or something. 2 to place something or be in opposition to something else. **to be opposed to** to be strongly against something. **as opposed to** in contrast with. [from a French word *opposer*, related to *opponent*]

opposite *adjective* 1 having a position on the other or further side, facing ♦ *on the opposite side of the road*. 2 moving away from or towards each other ♦ *The trains were travelling in opposite directions*. 3 as different as possible from ♦ *opposite characters* ♦ *the opposite end of the price range*.

opposite *noun* an opposite person or thing. SYNONYMS: antithesis, converse.

opposite *adverb* & *preposition* in an opposite place, position, or direction to a person or thing ♦ *I'll sit opposite* ♦ *They live opposite the school*. [from a Latin word *oppositus* meaning 'placed against']

opposite number *noun* a person holding a similar position to yourself in another group or organization.

opposite sex *noun* women in relation to men, or men in relation to women ♦ *As a young man he was nervous with the opposite sex*.

opposition *noun* 1 resistance, being hostile or in conflict or disagreement. 2 the people who oppose something; your competitors or rivals. 3 a contrast. **the Opposition** the chief parliamentary party opposing the one that is in power.

oppress *verb* 1 to govern or treat someone harshly, cruelly, or unjustly. 2 to weigh someone down with worry or unhappiness. **oppression** *noun* **oppressor** *noun* [from *ob-* meaning 'against' and *press*]

oppressive *adjective* 1 cruel or harsh ♦ *an oppressive regime*. 2 worrying and difficult to bear. 3 (said about weather) unpleasantly hot and humid. **oppressively** *adverb* **oppressiveness** *noun*

opprobrious (ə-proh-briəs) *adjective* (said about words etc.) showing scorn or reproach.

opprobrium (ə-proh-briəm) *noun* 1 harsh criticism or scorn. 2 great disgrace brought by shameful conduct. [from a Latin word meaning 'infamy']

opt *verb* to make a choice. **to opt out** 1 to choose not to take part in something. 2 (said about a school or hospital) to decide to be no longer controlled by the local authority. [from a Latin word *optare* meaning 'to wish for']

optative (op-tay-tiv) *adjective* (Grammar) to do with the form of a verb used in Greek in expressing a wish. [same origin as for *opt*]

optic *adjective* to do with the eye or the sense of sight.
optic *noun* a device for measuring out spirits from a bottle.

optics *noun* the scientific study of sight and the behaviour of light. [from a Greek word *optos* meaning 'seen']

optical *adjective* 1 to do with the sense of sight. 2 aiding sight ♦ *optical instruments*. **optically** *adverb* [from *optic*]

optical fibre *noun* thin glass fibre used in fibre optics.

optical illusion *noun* a mental misinterpretation of something you see, caused by its deceptive appearance.

optician (op-tish-ən) *noun* a person qualified to prescribe and dispense glasses and contact lenses, and to detect eye diseases (*an ophthalmic optician*), or to make and supply glasses and contact lenses (*a dispensing optician*). [from a French word, related to *optic*]

optimal *adjective* best or most favourable. [from a Latin word *optimus* meaning 'best']

optimism *noun* a tendency to take a hopeful view of things, or to expect that results will be good. **optimist** *noun* [from a Latin word *optimus* meaning 'best']

optimistic *adjective* showing optimism, hopeful. **optimistically** *adverb*

optimize *verb* to make something as effective or favourable as possible. **optimization** *noun*

optimum *adjective* best or most favourable. **optimum** *noun* the best or most favourable conditions or amount etc. [a Latin word meaning 'best thing']

option *noun* 1 a thing that is or may be chosen ♦ *None of the options is satisfactory*. 2 the behaviour of the options. 2 the freedom or right to choose ♦ *He had no option but to go*. 3 the right to buy or sell something at a certain price within a set time ♦ *We have 10 days' option on the house*. **to keep** or **leave your options open** to avoid committing yourself, so that you still have a choice. [same origin as for *opt*]

optional *adjective* available to be chosen but not compulsory. **optionally** *adverb*

opulent (op-yoo-lənt) *adjective* 1 wealthy or luxurious. 2 plentiful or abundant. **opulence** *noun* **opulently** *adverb* [from a Latin word *opes* meaning 'wealth']

opus (oh-pəs) *noun* (**opuses** or **opera**, (op-er-ə)) 1 a musical composition numbered as one of a composer's works ♦ *Beethoven opus 15*. 2 any artistic work. [a Latin word meaning 'work']

or *conjunction* **1** used to join choices or alternatives ◆ *Do you want rice or chips?* **2** used to introduce a synonym or explanation ◆ *hydrophobia or rabies.* [from *other*]

-or *suffix* forming nouns meaning 'a person or thing that does something' (as in *tailor, refrigerator*). [from a Latin or Old French word]

oracle *noun* **1** a place where the ancient Greeks consulted one of their gods for advice or a prophecy. **2** the reply given. **3** a person or thing thought of as able to give wise guidance. **oracular** (or-**ak**-yoo-ler) *adjective* [from a Latin word *orare* meaning 'to speak']

oracy (or-ǝ-si) *noun* the ability to express yourself well in speaking. [same origin as for *oral*, on the pattern of *literacy*]

oral (or-ǝl) *adjective* **1** spoken, not written ◆ *oral evidence.* **2** to do with the mouth; done or taken by the mouth.
oral *noun* a spoken examination or test.
orally *adverb* [from a Latin word *oris* meaning 'of the mouth']
◊ Do not confuse this word with **aural**, which has a different meaning.

oral history *noun* the collection and study of people's tape-recorded accounts of past events.

orange *noun* **1** a round juicy citrus fruit with reddish-yellow peel. **2** a drink made from orange juice. **3** a reddish-yellow colour.
orange *adjective* reddish yellow. [via French, Arabic, and Persian from a Sanskrit word]

orangeade *noun* a fizzy orange-flavoured soft drink.

Orangeman *noun* (**Orangemen**) a member of the Orange Order, a Protestant political society in Ireland, especially in Northern Ireland. [named after William of Orange (William III)]

orange stick *noun* a small thin stick, typically made of wood from an orange tree, for manicuring the nails.

orang-utan (or-ang-oo-tan) *noun* a large long-armed ape with long red hair, native to Borneo and Sumatra. [from Malay words *orang hutan* meaning 'man of the forest']

oration (ǝ-**ray**-shǝn) *noun* a long formal speech, especially one given on a ceremonial occasion. [from a Latin word *orare* meaning 'to speak']

orator *noun* a person who is good at making speeches in public.

oratorical (o-rǝt-o-ri-kǝl) *adjective* to do with or like oratory.

oratorio (o-rǝ-**tor**-i-oh) *noun* (**oratorios**) a musical composition for solo voices, chorus, and orchestra, usually with a religious theme. [from an Italian word, related to *oration*]

oratory[1] (o-rǝ-ter-i) *noun* **1** the art of public speaking. **2** eloquent speech. [from a Latin word *oratorius* meaning 'to do with an orator']

oratory[2] (o-rǝ-ter-i) *noun* (**oratories**) a small chapel or place for private worship. [from an Old French word]

orb *noun* **1** a sphere or globe. **2** an ornamental globe with a cross on top, held on ceremonial occasions by a monarch. [from a Latin word *orbis* meaning 'circle']

orbit *noun* **1** the curved path of a planet, satellite, or spacecraft etc. around a star or planet ◆ *The spacecraft was now in orbit around the moon.* **2** the range of someone's influence or control.
orbit *verb* (**orbited, orbiting**) to move in an orbit around a star or planet ◆ *The satellite has been orbiting the earth since 1986.*
orbiter *noun* [from a Latin word *orbis* meaning 'circle']

orbital (or-bitǝl) *adjective* **1** (said about a road) passing round the outside of a city. **2** to do with an orbit ◆ *orbital velocity.*
orbitally *adverb*

Orcadian (or-**kay**-diǝn) *adjective* to do with the Orkney Islands.

orchard *noun* a piece of land planted with fruit trees. [from an Old English word *ortgeard*, from a Latin word *hortus* meaning 'garden' and *yard*]

orchestra *noun* **1** a large group of people playing various musical instruments, including stringed and wind instruments. **2** (also **orchestra pit**) the part of a theatre where the orchestra plays, in front of the stalls and lower than the stage. **orchestral** (or-**kess**-trǝl) *adjective* [a Greek word denoting 'the space where the chorus danced during a play']

orchestrate (or-kis-trayt) verb 1 to compose or arrange music for performance by an orchestra. 2 to coordinate things deliberately ♦ *an orchestrated series of protests*. **orchestration** noun [from *orchestra*]

orchid (or-kid) noun 1 a plant of a family with showy often irregularly-shaped flowers. 2 its flower. [from a Latin word]

orchis (or-kis) noun an orchid, especially a wild one. [from a Greek word]

ordain verb 1 to make a person a member of the clergy in the Christian Church. 2 to declare or order something by law. 3 (said about God or fate) to decide something in advance ♦ *Providence ordained that they should meet*. [from an Old French word *ordeiner*; related to *order*]

ordeal (or-deel) noun a difficult or horrific experience that lasts a long time. [from an Old English word]

order noun 1 a state in which everything is in its proper place; tidiness. 2 the way in which things are arranged or placed in relation to one another ♦ *in alphabetical order* ♦ *Are these pages in the right order?* SYNONYMS: arrangement, organization, sequence, classification. 3 a state in which everything is in a normal or efficient state ♦ *The boiler is in good working order*. 4 a state of peace and obedience to the laws ♦ *Order was restored to the streets* ♦ *law and order*. 5 a system of rules or procedure. 6 a command, an instruction given with authority. SYNONYMS: command, instruction, directive, decree, edict. 7 a request for goods to be supplied or food to be served; the goods themselves. 8 a written instruction to pay money. 9 a kind, sort, or quality ♦ *She showed courage of the highest order*. 10 a rank or class in society ♦ *the lower orders*. 11 a group of monks or nuns who live by certain religious rules ♦ *the Franciscan Order*. 12 a company of people to which distinguished people are admitted as an honour or reward; the insignia worn by its members ♦ *the Order of the Garter*. 13 a style of ancient Greek or Roman architecture distinguished by the type of column used. 14 (*Biology*) a group of plants or animals classified as similar in many ways.
order verb 1 to issue a command to someone, to command that something shall be done. 2 to give an order for goods etc. to be supplied; to tell a waiter what food you want. 3 to put things in order, to arrange things methodically.

orders plural noun the status of being ordained as a member of the clergy ♦ *in holy orders*. **in order 1** in the correct condition to work or be used. **2** appropriate in the circumstances ♦ *I think congratulations are in order*. **in order to** or **that** with the intention that, for the purpose of. **on order** (describing goods) ordered but not yet received. **out of order 1** not working properly or at all. **2** (*informal*) not acceptable or wrong. **to order someone about** to keep on giving commands to someone. [from a Latin word *ordo* meaning 'a row, series, or arrangement']

ordered adjective arranged in order.

orderly adjective 1 well arranged, tidy. 2 methodical ♦ *an orderly mind*. SYNONYMS: organized, well-organized, systematic. 3 well-behaved and obedient ♦ *an orderly crowd*.
orderly noun (**orderlies**) 1 an attendant in a hospital. 2 a soldier whose job is to assist an officer or carry orders. **orderliness** noun

orderly room noun a room where business is conducted in a military barracks.

order of magnitude noun a classification by size, especially in powers of ten.

Order Paper noun a written or printed programme of the day's business for parliament.

ordinal number noun a number that denotes a position in a series (*first, fifth, twentieth*, etc.), as distinct from the cardinal numbers (*one, five, twenty*, etc.). [same origin as for *ordinary*]

ordinance noun an order or rule made by authority, a decree. [from a Latin word *ordinare* meaning 'to put in order']

ordinand (or-din-and) noun a candidate for ordination.

ordinary adjective usual or normal, not special. SYNONYMS: standard, typical, average, regular, conventional, everyday, commonplace, common; (*informal*) common or garden, run-of-the mill. **out of the ordinary** unusual. **ordinarily** adverb [from a Latin word *ordinis* meaning 'of a row or an order']

ordinary seaman noun a sailor in the Royal Navy ranking lower than an able seaman.

ordinary shares plural noun shares whose holders are entitled to dividends which vary in amount depending on the profits of the company. (Compare **preference shares**.)

ordinate (or-din-ət) noun (*Mathematics*) a coordinate on a graph measured usually vertically. [from a Latin phrase *linea ordinata applicata* meaning 'line applied parallel']

ordination noun ordaining or being ordained as a member of the clergy.

ordnance noun 1 weapons and other military equipment. 2 the government service dealing with military stores and equipment. [from an Old French word *ordenance* meaning 'ordinance']

Ordnance Survey noun an official survey organization that prepares accurate and detailed maps of the British Isles. [so called because the maps were originally made for the army]

ordure (or-dewr) noun dung or excrement. [from an Old French word *ord* meaning 'foul'; related to *horrid*]

ore noun solid rock or mineral, found in the earth's crust, from which metal or other useful or valuable substances can be extracted ♦ *iron ore*. [from an Old English word]

oregano (o-ri-gah-noh) noun the dried leaves of wild marjoram used as a herb in cooking. [via Spanish from a Greek word]

organ noun 1 a large musical instrument consisting of pipes that sound notes when air is forced through them, played by keys pressed with the fingers and pedals pressed with the feet. 2 a smaller instrument without pipes that produces similar sounds electronically. 3 a part of an animal or plant body with a particular function ♦ *digestive organs* ♦ *organs of speech*. 4 a newspaper or journal that puts forward the views of a particular group. [from a Greek word *organon* meaning 'tool']

organdie noun a kind of thin stiff cotton fabric, used for dresses. [from a French word]

organelle noun (*Biology*) a structure within a living cell. [from *organ*]

organic (or-gan-ik) adjective 1 to do with or formed from living things ♦ *organic matter*. 2 to do with or affecting an organ or organs of the body ♦ *organic diseases*. 3 (said about food etc.) produced without the use of artificial fertilizers or pesticides ♦ *organic farming*. 4 organized or arranged as a system of related parts ♦ *The business forms an organic whole*. 5 developing or growing naturally. **organically** adverb

organic chemistry noun chemistry of carbon compounds, which are present in all living matter and in substances derived from it.

organism noun a living being, an individual animal or plant. [from a French word *organisme*]

organist noun a person who plays the organ.

organization noun 1 an organized body of people, such as a business, charity, or government department. 2 the organizing of something. **organizational** adjective

organize verb 1 to make arrangements or preparations for something ♦ *He helped to organize a fund-raising concert*. 2 to form people into a group for a common purpose. 3 to arrange things in an orderly or systematic way. **organizer** noun [same origin as for *organ*]

organza (or-ganzə) noun thin stiff transparent dress fabric of silk or synthetic fibre. [probably from *Lorganza*, a US trademark]

orgasm (or-gazm) noun the climax of sexual excitement. **orgasmic** (or-gaz-mik) adjective [from a Greek word *orgasmos*]

orgy noun (**orgies**) 1 a wild party that involves a lot of drinking and sex. 2 an extravagant activity ♦ *an orgy of spending*. [from a Latin word *orgia* meaning 'secret rites', held in honour of Bacchus, the Greek and Roman god of wine]

oriel window (or-i-əl) noun a kind of projecting window in an upper storey. [from an Old French word *oriol* meaning 'gallery']

Orient (or-i-ənt) noun the countries of the East, especially east Asia. [from a Latin word meaning 'sunrise']

orient (or-i-ənt) verb 1 to place or determine the position of a thing with regard to the points of the compass ♦ *orient a map*. 2 to face or direct something towards a certain direction. **to orient yourself** 1 to get your bearings. 2 to become accustomed to a new situation.

oriental (or-i-en-təl) adjective to do with the countries east of the Mediterranean Sea, especially China and Japan.
Oriental noun (*often offensive*) a person of Far Eastern descent.

orientate (or-i-ən-tayt) *verb* to orient something or yourself. [originally meaning 'to turn to face the east': same origin as for *Orient*]

orientation (or-i-ən-**tay**-shən) *noun* 1 orienting or being oriented. 2 position relative to surroundings. 3 the direction of a person's attitude or interest, especially sexual or political.

orienteering (or-i-ən-**teer**-ing) *noun* the sport of finding your way on foot across rough country with a map and compass. [from a Swedish word *orientering* meaning 'orientating']

orifice (o-ri-fiss) *noun* an opening in the body. [from a Latin word *oris* meaning 'of the mouth']

origami (o-ri-**gah**-mi) *noun* the Japanese art of folding paper into attractive shapes and figures. [from Japanese words *ori* meaning 'fold' and *kami* meaning 'paper']

origin *noun* 1 the point, source, or cause from which a thing begins its existence. SYNONYMS: source, root, derivation. 2 a person's ancestry or social background ♦ *a man of humble origins*. SYNONYMS: background, stock, pedigree. 3 (*Mathematics*) the point on a graph where two or more axes meet. [from a Latin word *origo* meaning 'source']

original *adverb* 1 existing from the start, earliest. 2 being a thing from which a copy or translation has been made. 3 new in character or design, not copying something else. 4 thinking or acting for yourself, inventive, creative ♦ *an original mind*.
original *noun* 1 a document, painting, etc. which was the first one made and from which another is copied. 2 the language in which something was first written. **originality** *noun* **originally** *adverb* [same origin as for *origin*]

original sin *noun* (in Christianity) the condition of wickedness thought to be common to all human beings since Adam's sin.

originate *verb* 1 to cause something to begin, to create something. 2 to have its origin, to begin ♦ *This feud seems to have originated in a childhood rivalry.* **origination** *noun* **originator** *noun*

oriole (or-i-ohl) *noun* a kind of bird of which the male has black and yellow plumage. [from a Latin word *aureolus* meaning 'little golden thing']

ormolu (or-mə-loo) *noun* 1 a gold-coloured alloy of copper, zinc, and tin, used in decorating furniture and making ornaments. 2 articles made of or decorated with this. [from a French phrase *or moulu* meaning 'powdered gold']

ornament *noun* 1 an object displayed or worn as a decoration. 2 decoration ♦ *This candlestick is for use, not for ornament.*
ornament *verb* to decorate something with beautiful things. **ornamentation** *noun* [from a Latin word *ornare* meaning 'to adorn']

ornamental *adjective* serving as an ornament.

ornate (or-**nayt**) *adjective* 1 elaborately decorated. 2 (said about writing) using unusual words and complicated constructions. [from a Latin word *ornatum* meaning 'adorned']

ornithologist *noun* an expert in ornithology.

ornithology (orni-**thol**-əji) *noun* the scientific study of birds. **ornithological** *adjective* [from a Greek word *ornithos* meaning 'of a bird' and *-logy*]

orphan *noun* a child whose parents are dead.
orphan *verb* to make a child an orphan. [from a Greek word *orphanos* meaning 'bereaved']

orphanage *noun* a home for orphans.

Orphism (or-fizm) *noun* 1 an ancient Greek mystic religion associated with the legendary musician Orpheus. 2 an artistic movement in the early 20th century using the techniques of cubism but with a less austere style. **Orphic** *adjective*

orris or **orris root** (o-riss) *noun* the fragrant root of a kind of iris which is dried for use in perfumery and medicine. [from *iris*]

ortho- *prefix* right; straight; correct (as in *orthodontics*). [from a Greek word *orthos* meaning 'straight']

orthodontics (ortho-**don**-tiks) *noun* the treatment of irregularities in the teeth and jaws. **orthodontic** *adjective* [from *ortho-* and a Greek word *odontos* meaning 'of a tooth']

orthodontist noun a specialist in orthodontics.

orthodox adjective 1 holding beliefs that are traditional or generally accepted, especially in religion. 2 conventional or normal. **orthodoxy** noun [from ortho- and a Greek word doxa meaning 'opinion']

Orthodox Church noun the Christian Churches of eastern Europe, recognizing the Greek patriarch of Constantinople as their head.

Orthodox Judaism noun a major branch within Judaism which involves following traditional observances strictly.

orthographic projection noun (in engineering) a way of drawing a three-dimensional object without showing perspective.

orthography (or-thog-rə-fi) noun (orthographies) the spelling system of a language. **orthographic** adjective [from ortho- and -graphy]

orthopaedics (orthə-pee-diks) noun the branch of surgery dealing with the correction of deformities of bones or muscles. **orthopaedic** adjective [from ortho- and a Greek word paideia meaning 'rearing of children' (because the treatment was originally of children)]

orthoptics (or-thop-tiks) noun treatment of irregularities of the eye muscles. **orthoptic** adjective **orthoptist** noun [from ortho- and optic]

OS abbreviation 1 (Computing) operating system. 2 Ordnance Survey.

Oscar noun the name for a gold statuette awarded by the Academy of Motion Picture Arts and Sciences for excellence in the acting or directing of films.

oscillate (oss-i-layt) verb 1 to move to and fro like a pendulum. 2 to vary between extremes of opinion or emotion. 3 (said about an electric current) to reverse its direction with high frequency. **oscillation** noun **oscillator** noun [from a Latin word oscillare meaning 'to swing']

oscilloscope (ə-sil-ə-skohp) noun a device for showing oscillations as a display on the screen of a cathode ray tube.

osier (oh-zi-er) noun 1 a kind of willow with flexible twigs used in making baskets. 2 a twig from this. [from an Old French word]

-osis suffix 1 a diseased condition (as in tuberculosis). 2 an action or process (as in metamorphosis). [from a Latin or Greek word]

osmoregulation noun (Biology) regulation of the diffusion of fluids, especially in the body of a living organism. [from osmosis and regulation]

osmosis (oz-moh-sis) noun 1 diffusion of fluid through a porous partition into another more concentrated fluid. 2 the process of gradually or unconsciously acquiring knowledge or ideas. **osmotic** (oz-mot-ik) adjective [from a Greek word osmos meaning 'a push']

osprey (oss-pri) noun (ospreys) a large bird preying on fish in inland waters. [from an Old French word ospres]

ossicle noun (Anatomy and Zoology) a small bone or piece of bone-like substance in the skeleton of an animal. [from a Latin word ossiculum meaning 'little bone']

ossify verb (ossifies, ossified, ossifying) 1 to change into bone; to become hard like bone. 2 to stop developing. **ossification** noun [from a Latin word os meaning 'bone']

ostensible (oss-ten-sibəl) adjective apparently true, but actually concealing the true reason. **ostensibly** adverb [from a Latin word ostendere meaning 'to show']

ostensive (oss-ten-siv) adjective showing something directly. [same origin as for ostensible]

ostentation noun a showy display intended to impress people. **ostentatious** (oss-ten-tay-shəs) adjective **ostentatiously** adverb [same origin as for ostensible]

osteopath (oss-ti-əp-ath) noun a person who treats certain diseases and abnormalities by manipulating and massaging a patient's bones and muscles. [from Greek words osteon meaning 'bone' and -patheia meaning 'suffering']

osteoporosis (osti-oh-pə-roh-sis) noun a medical condition in which the bones become brittle and fragile, usually as a result of hormonal changes or vitamin deficiency. [from Greek words osteon meaning 'bone' and poros meaning 'passage' or 'pore']

osteopathy (osti-op-əthi) noun the treatment given by an osteopath. **osteopathic** (osti-əp-ath-ik) adjective

ostler (**oss**-ler) *noun* (*historical*) a person who looked after the horses of people staying at an inn. [from an Old French word *hostelier* meaning 'innkeeper']

ostracize (**oss**-trə-siyz) *verb* to exclude someone from a group or from society and completely ignore them. **ostracism** *noun* [from a Greek word *ostrakon* meaning 'piece of pottery' (because people voted that a person should be banished by writing his or her name on this)]

ostrich *noun* **1** a large long-legged African bird that can run very fast but cannot fly. It is said to bury its head in the sand when pursued, in the belief that it then cannot be seen. **2** a person who refuses to face an awkward truth. [from an Old French word *ostriche*]

OT *abbreviation* Old Testament.

other *adjective* **1** additional or remaining ♦ *one of my other friends* ♦ *She has no other income* ♦ *Try the other shoe.* **2** different, not the same ♦ *Can you phone some other time?* ♦ *We wouldn't want her to be other than she is.* **other** *noun* & *pronoun* the other person or thing ♦ *Where are the others?* **the other day** or **week** etc. a few days or weeks etc. ago. [from an Old English word]

otherwise *adverb* **1** if things happen differently; or else ♦ *Write it down, otherwise you'll forget.* **2** in a different way ♦ *We could not do otherwise.* **3** in other respects ♦ *There's a small mistake in the first line but your answer is otherwise correct.* **otherwise** *adjective* in a different state or situation ♦ *The truth is quite otherwise.* [from *other* and *-wise*]

otter *noun* a fish-eating animal with webbed feet, a flat tail, and thick brown fur, living near water. [from an Old English word *otr*]

Ottoman *adjective* to do with the Turkish dynasty founded by Osman or Othman (1259–1326), his branch of the Turks, or the empire ruled by his descendants (late 13th–early 20th century). **Ottoman** *noun* a Turk of the Ottoman period. [from an Arabic word]

ottoman *noun* **1** a long cushioned seat without back or arms. **2** a storage box with a padded top. [from *Ottoman* (because the ottoman originated in Turkey)]

oubliette (oo-bli-et) *noun* a secret dungeon to which entrance is through a trapdoor. [from a French word *oublier* meaning 'to forget']

ouch *interjection* an exclamation of sudden pain.

ought *auxiliary verb* expressing duty, rightness, advisability, or strong probability ♦ *We ought to feed them* ♦ *You ought to take more exercise* ♦ *At this speed, we ought to be there by noon.* [from an Old English word *ahte* meaning 'owed']

oughtn't *verb* (*informal*) ought not.

Ouija board (**wee**-jə) *noun* (*trademark*) a board marked with the alphabet, used in spiritualistic seances. [from a French word *oui* meaning 'yes' and a German word *ja* meaning 'yes']

ounce *noun* a unit of weight equal to one-sixteenth of a pound (about 28 grams). [from a Latin word]

our *adjective* to do with or belonging to us. [from an Old English word]

ours *possessive pronoun* belonging to us; the things belonging to us ♦ *These seats are ours.* ◊ It is incorrect to write *our's*.

ourselves *pronoun* the form of *we* and *us* used in reflexive constructions (e.g. *We blame ourselves*) and for emphasis (e.g. *We wrote it all ourselves*).

oust (owst) *verb* to drive a person out from office or a position or employment. [from an Old French word *ouster* meaning 'to take away']

out *adverb* **1** away from or not in a place or position; not in its normal or usual state. **2** outdoors. **3** not at home. **4** (said about the tide) falling or at its lowest level. **5** not in action or use; no longer in fashion. **6** (said about a light or fire etc.) no longer burning. **7** in error ♦ *The estimate was 10% out.* **8** no longer visible ♦ *I'll paint the sign out.* **9** not possible or not worth considering ♦ *Skating is out until the ice thickens.* **10** unconscious. **11** into the open; into existence or hearing or view etc., visible, revealed ♦ *The sun came out* ♦ *Our secret is out.* **12** (said about a flower) open, no longer in bud. **13** (said about the ball in tennis, squash, etc.) outside the playing area. **14** (in cricket) no longer batting. **15** to or at an end, completely ♦ *I'm tired out* ♦ *The CD is sold out.* **16** in finished form ♦ *Now print the whole thing out.* **17** without restraint; boldly or loudly ♦ *Speak out!* **18** (in radio conversations) transmission ends. **out** *preposition* (*informal*) out of. **out** *noun* a way of escape. **to be out to** to intend to do something ♦ *They are out to make trouble*. **out for** keen to have something ♦ *Now she is out for revenge*. **out of 1** from within or among. **2** so as to be without a supply of something. **3** beyond the range of ♦ *out of hearing*. **out of doors** in the open air. **out of the way 1** no longer an obstacle. **2** remote. **out of this world** incredibly good. [from an Old English word]

out- *prefix* **1** away from, out of (as in *outcast*). **2** external, separate (as in *outhouse*). **3** more than, so as to exceed (as in *outbid*, *outgrow*).

out and out *adjective* thorough, absolute ♦ *an out and out villain*.

outback *noun* the remote inland districts of Australia.

outbid *verb* (**outbid, outbidding**) to bid more for something than another person does.

outboard *adjective* (said about a motor) fitted to the outside of the stern of a boat.

outbreak *noun* a sudden or violent breaking out of war, disease, etc.

outbuilding *noun* a small building in the grounds of a main building.

outburst *noun* a sudden bursting out of anger, laughter, etc. SYNONYMS: fit, attack, eruption, surge, rush.

outcast *noun* a person who has been driven out of a group or rejected by society.

outclass *verb* to be far superior to someone.

outcome *noun* the result or effect of something that takes place.

outcrop *noun* part of an underlying layer of rock that sticks out on the surface of the ground. [*out* and *crop* meaning 'outcrop']

outcry *noun* (**outcries**) **1** a strong protest. **2** a loud cry.

outdated *adjective* out of date, obsolete.

outdistance *verb* to get far ahead of someone in a race etc.

outdo *verb* (**outdid, outdone**) to do better than another person.

outdoor *adjective* **1** done or used in the open air. **2** enjoying open-air activities ♦ *She's not an outdoor type*.

outdoors *adverb* in or into the open air. **outdoors** *noun* anywhere outside buildings or shelter.

outer *adjective* outside or external; further from the centre or from the inside. **outer** *noun* the division of a target furthest from the bullseye.

outermost *adjective* furthest from the centre, most distant.

outer space *noun* the universe beyond the earth's atmosphere.

outface *verb* to disconcert someone by your defiant or confident manner.

outfall *noun* an outlet where water falls or flows out.

outfield *noun* the outer part of a cricket or baseball field.

outfight *verb* (past tense and past participle **outfought**) to beat someone in a fight.

outfit *noun* **1** a set of clothes to be worn together. **2** a complete set of equipment needed for a particular purpose. **3** (*informal*) an organization, a group of people regarded as a unit.

outfitter *noun* a shop selling equipment or men's clothing.

outflank *verb* to move round the side of an enemy in order to outmanoeuvre them.

outflow *noun* **1** an outward flow. **2** an amount of water, money, etc. that flows out.

outgoing *adjective* **1** sociable and friendly. **2** going out; leaving an office or position ♦ *the outgoing chairman*. **outgoings** *plural noun* regular expenditure.

outgrow *verb* (**outgrew, outgrown**) **1** to grow out of clothes or habits. **2** to grow faster than another person or thing.

outgrowth *noun* **1** something that grows out of another thing. **2** a natural development or result.

outhouse *noun* a small building, such as a shed or barn, belonging to but separate from a house.

outing *noun* a short trip taken for pleasure.

outlandish *adjective* looking or sounding strange or unfamiliar. **outlandishness** *noun* [from an Old English word *utland* meaning 'a foreign land']

outlast *verb* to last longer than something else.

outlaw *noun* **1** a fugitive from the law. **2** (in the Middle Ages) a person who was punished by being placed outside the protection of the law. **outlaw** *verb* **1** to declare something to be illegal; to ban something. SYNONYMS: ban, forbid, prohibit, proscribe. **2** to make a person an outlaw. [from an Old English word]

outlay noun what is spent on something.

outlet noun **1** a way out for water or gas etc. **2** the mouth of a river. **3** a means of expressing your feelings or energies. **4** a place from which goods are sold or distributed.

outline noun **1** a line round the outside of something, showing its shape or boundary. **2** a statement or summary of the main features of something. **3** a symbol in shorthand.
outline verb **1** to make an outline of something. **2** to give a summary of something. **in outline** giving only an outline.

outlive verb to live longer than another person.

outlook noun **1** a person's mental attitude or way of looking at something. **2** a view you look out on ♦ *a pleasant outlook over the lake.* **3** future prospects ♦ *The outlook is bleak.*

outlying adjective situated far from the centre, remote ♦ *the outlying districts.*

outmanoeuvre verb to use skill and cunning to gain an advantage over someone.

outmoded (owt-**moh**-did) adjective old-fashioned.

outnumber verb to be more numerous than another group.

out of date adjective **1** old-fashioned. **2** no longer valid ♦ *This rail card is out of date* ♦ *an out-of-date passport.*

outpace verb to go faster than someone or something else.

outpatient noun a person who visits a hospital for treatment but does not stay there overnight.

outplay verb to play better than another player or team ♦ *We were completely outplayed in the first half.*

outport noun a port that serves a nearby major port, often being in a better position for receiving large ships ♦ *Avonmouth is an outport of Bristol.*

outpost noun **1** a small military camp at a distance from the main army. **2** a remote branch or settlement.

output noun **1** the amount produced. **2** the data produced by a computer.
output verb (past tense and past participle **output** or **outputted**; **outputting**) (said about a computer) to produce or supply data.

outrage noun **1** an act that shocks and angers people by being very wicked and cruel. **2** great anger or indignation.
outrage verb to shock and anger people greatly. [from an Old French word *outrer* meaning 'to go beyond, exaggerate', influenced by *rage*]

outrageous adjective **1** greatly exceeding what is moderate or reasonable, shocking. **2** very bold and unusual.
outrageously adverb

outrank verb to have a higher rank than someone else.

outré (oo-tray) adjective unusual and rather shocking. [a French word meaning 'exaggerated']

outrider noun a person riding on a motorcycle as an escort or guard.

outrigger noun **1** a beam, spar, or structure sticking out from the side of a ship for various purposes. **2** a strip of wood fixed parallel to a canoe by struts sticking out from it, to give stability. **3** a boat with either of these. [origin unknown]

outright adverb **1** completely, altogether. **2** not by degrees or instalments ♦ *We were able to buy the house outright.* **3** openly, frankly ♦ *I told him outright he was a fool.*
outright adjective thorough, complete ♦ *an outright fraud.*

outrun verb (**outran**, **outrun**, **outrunning**) **1** to run faster or further than another person or animal. **2** to exceed something.

outsell verb (past tense and past participle **outsold**) **1** to be sold in greater quantities than something else. **2** to sell more of something than someone else does.

outset noun the beginning of something ♦ *from the outset of his career.*

outshine verb (past tense and past participle **outshone**) **1** to shine more brightly than something else. **2** to be much better than something else.

outside noun **1** the outer side, surface, or part of something. **2** the outer appearance of someone or something ♦ *On the outside she seemed calm enough.*
outside adjective **1** on, near, or coming from the outside. **2** not connected with your work or studies ♦ *He never stops*

working and has few outside interests. **3** (said about a player in football, hockey, etc.) positioned nearest to the edge of the field ♦ *outside left.*

outside *adverb* on or at or to the outside; outdoors ♦ *Leave it outside* ♦ *It's cold outside.*

outside *preposition* **1** on the outer side of; at or to the outside of ♦ *Leave it outside the door.* **2** beyond the limits or scope of something ♦ *He has no interests outside his work.* **at the outside** at the most. **an outside chance** a remote possibility.

outside broadcast *noun* a broadcast made on location and not in a studio.

outsider *noun* **1** a person who does not belong to a certain group. **2** a horse or person thought to have no chance of winning a race or competition.

outsize *adjective* much larger than average.

outskirts *plural noun* the outer parts of a town or city.

outspoken *adjective* frank in giving your opinions.

outspread *adjective* spread out.

outstanding *adjective* **1** exceptionally good. **2** clearly noticeable. **3** not yet paid or dealt with ♦ *Some of his debts are still outstanding.* **outstandingly** *adverb*

outstay *verb* to stay longer than you are expected to.

outstretched *adjective* stretched out.

outstrip *verb* (**outstripped, outstripping**) **1** to run faster or further than someone else. **2** to surpass someone in achievement or success. [from *out-* and a Middle English word *strypen* meaning 'to move quickly']

out-take *noun* a scene cut from the final version of a film.

outvote *verb* to defeat someone by a majority of votes.

outward *adjective* **1** situated on the outside. **2** going out or away from a place. **3** to do with the external appearance of something rather than its true nature. **outward** *adverb* outwards. **outwardly** *adverb*

Outward Bound *noun* (*trademark*) an organization running adventure training and other outdoor activities for young people.

outwards *adverb* towards the outside.

outwash *noun* a deposit of silt, sand, and gravel washed out from a glacier by meltwater.

outweigh *verb* to be greater in weight, importance, or significance than something else.

outwit *verb* (**outwitted, outwitting**) to get the better of a person by your cleverness or craftiness.

outwork *noun* an outer part of a fortification.

outworn *adjective* worn out, damaged by wear.

ouzel (oo-zəl) *noun* **1** a small bird of the thrush family ♦ *ring ouzel.* **2** a kind of diving bird ♦ *water ouzel.* [from an Old English word]

ova plural of **ovum.**

oval *noun* a rounded symmetrical shape longer than it is broad. **oval** *adjective* having this shape. [from a Latin word *ovum* meaning 'egg']

ovary (oh-ver-i) *noun* (**ovaries**) **1** either of the two organs in which egg cells are produced in a woman's or female animal's body. **2** (*Botany*) part of the pistil in a plant, from which fruit is formed. **ovarian** (ə-vair-iən) *adjective* [same origin as for *oval*]

ovation (ə-vay-shən) *noun* enthusiastic applause. [from a Latin word *ovare* meaning 'to rejoice']

oven *noun* **1** an enclosed compartment in which things are cooked. **2** a small kiln or furnace. [from an Old English word *ofen*]

ovenproof *adjective* (said about dishes etc.) able to be used in an oven.

ovenware *noun* ovenproof dishes.

over *adverb* **1** with movement outwards and downwards from the top or edge or from an upright position ♦ *He fell over.* **2** with movement from one side to the other or so that a different side is showing ♦ *Turn it over.* **3** across a street or other space or distance ♦ *Let's cross over at the lights* ♦ *She is over here from America.* **4** so as to cover or touch a whole surface ♦ *The lake froze over.* **5** transferring or changing from one hand or one side or one owner etc. to another ♦ *Hand it over* ♦ *Do you believe he's gone over to the enemy?* **6** (in radio conversation) it is your turn to transmit. **7** remaining, more than is needed ♦ *There are a few bits of wood left*

over. **8** with repetition ♦ *ten times over.*
9 thoroughly, with detailed consideration
♦ *Think it over.* **10** at an end, finished ♦ *The battle is over.*
over *preposition* **1** in or to a position higher than. **2** across the top of something and covering it; on or to the other side of ♦ *a hat over his eyes* ♦ *We flew over the Alps.*
3 out and down from; down from the edge of ♦ *The car must have driven straight over the cliff.* **4** throughout the length or extent of, during ♦ *over the years* ♦ *You can stay over the weekend.* **5** so as to visit or examine all parts ♦ *Someone's coming to look over the house* ♦ *Let's go over the plan again.*
6 transmitted by ♦ *I heard it over the radio.*
7 during, while engaged with ♦ *We can talk over dinner.* **8** on the subject of ♦ *They are always quarrelling over money.* **9** more than ♦ *It's over a mile away.* **10** in superiority or preference to ♦ *their victory over United.*
over *noun* (in cricket) a series of six balls bowled in succession. **to be over something** to be no longer affected or upset by something. **over and above** in addition to. **over and over** repeated many times. [from an Old English word *ofer*]

over- *prefix* **1** over, above (as in *overturn, overlay*). **2** too much, excessively (as in *overanxious*).

overact *verb* to act your part in an exaggerated manner.

overactive *adjective* excessively active.

overall *noun* a type of coat worn over other clothes to protect them when working.
overalls *plural noun* a combined piece of clothing covering the body and legs, worn over other clothes to protect them.
overall *adjective* **1** including everything, total ♦ *the overall cost.* **2** taking everything into account.
overall *adverb* taken as a whole.

overarm *adjective & adverb* **1** (in cricket etc.) bowling or bowled with the hand brought forward and down from above shoulder level. **2** (in swimming) with the arm lifted out of the water and stretched forward beyond the head.

overawe *verb* to overcome or inhibit a person with awe.

overbalance *verb* to lose balance and fall over, or to cause a person or thing to do this.

overbear *verb* (**overbore, overborne**) to overcome someone by emotional pressure or physical force.

overbearing *adjective* domineering or overpowering.

overblown *adjective* **1** exaggerated or pretentious. **2** (said about a flower etc.) too fully open, past its prime.

overboard *adverb* from a ship into the water ♦ *She jumped overboard.* **to go overboard 1** to be very enthusiastic. **2** to go too far.

overbook *verb* to book more passengers or visitors for an aircraft flight or a hotel etc. than there is room for.

overburden *verb* to burden someone excessively.

overcast *adjective* (said about the sky or weather) covered with cloud.
overcast *verb* (past tense and past participle **overcast**) to stitch over an edge to prevent it from fraying.

overcharge *verb* **1** to charge too high a price. **2** to put too much electric charge into a battery.

overcoat *noun* a warm outdoor coat.

overcome *verb* (**overcame, overcome**) **1** to defeat someone. **2** to have a strong physical or emotional effect on someone and make them helpless ♦ *One of the firefighters was overcome by gas fumes* ♦ *She was overcome with grief.* **3** to find a way of dealing with a problem.

overcrowd *verb* to crowd too many people into a place or vehicle. **overcrowded** *adjective* **overcrowding** *noun*

overdo *verb* (**overdid, overdone**) **1** to do something too much or use too much of something. **2** to cook food too long. **to overdo it** or **things** to exhaust yourself, to work too hard.

overdose *noun* too large a dose of a drug.
overdose *verb* to take an overdose.

overdraft *noun* a debt in a bank account, caused by taking out more money than there is in the account.

overdraw *verb* (**overdrew, overdrawn**) to draw more money from a bank account than the amount you have in it. **to be overdrawn** to have taken more money from your bank account than you have in it.

overdrive *noun* a mechanism providing an extra gear above the normal top gear in a vehicle. **to go into overdrive** to become highly active.

overdue *adjective* **1** not paid or arrived etc. by the due or expected time. **2** (said about a library book) kept longer than allowed.

overeat *verb* (**overate**, **overeaten**) to eat too much.

overestimate *verb* to form too high an estimate of something.
overestimate *noun* an excessively high estimate.

overexpose *verb* to expose something for too long. **overexposure** *noun*

overfeed *verb* (past tense and past participle **overfed**) to feed a person or animal too much.

overfill *verb* to fill something too full or to overflowing.

overfish *verb* to catch so many fish from a certain area that next season's supply is reduced.

overflow *verb* **1** to flow over the edge, limits, or banks etc. **2** (said about a crowd) to spread beyond the limits of a room etc.
overflow *noun* **1** what overflows. **2** an outlet for excess liquid.

overfly *verb* (**overflew**, **overflown**) to fly over or beyond a place or territory.

overfull *adjective* too full.

overground *adverb* & *adjective* on or above the ground.

overgrown *adjective* **1** covered with weeds or unwanted plants. **2** grown too large.
overgrowth *noun*

overhang *verb* (past tense and past participle **overhung**) to jut out over something.
overhang *noun* an overhanging part.

overhaul *verb* **1** to examine something thoroughly and repair it if necessary. **2** to overtake someone or something.
overhaul *noun* an examination and repair of something.

overhead *adverb* & *adjective* **1** above the level of your head. **2** in the sky.
overheads *plural noun* the expenses involved in running a business (e.g. rent, heating, cleaning) that are not directly related to a particular product or department etc.

overhead projector *noun* a projector that gives an image of a transparency on a vertical screen by means of an overhead mirror.

overhear *verb* (past tense and past participle **overheard**) to hear something accidentally or without the speaker intending you to hear it.

overheat *verb* to make something too hot, or to become too hot or too intensive.

overjoyed *adjective* extremely happy.

overkill *noun* **1** a surplus of capacity for destruction above what is needed to defeat or destroy an enemy. **2** excessive use or treatment of something.

overland *adverb* & *adjective* by land, not by sea or air.

overlap *verb* (**overlapped**, **overlapping**) **1** to lie across something and partly cover it. **2** to partly coincide ♦ *Our holidays overlap.*
overlap *noun* overlapping; an overlapping part or amount. [from *over* and *lap*²]

overlay¹ *verb* (**overlaid**) **1** to cover something with a surface layer. **2** to lie on top of something.

overlay² *noun* a thing laid over another.

overleaf *adverb* on the other side of the page.

overlie *verb* (**overlay**, **overlain**, **overlying**) to lie on top of something.

overload *verb* to put too great a load on someone or something.
overload *noun* a load that is too great.

overlook *verb* **1** to fail to notice or consider something. **2** to deliberately ignore something, to allow an offence to go unpunished. SYNONYMS: disregard, excuse, pardon, gloss over; (*informal*) turn a blind eye to. **3** to have a view of a place from above.

overlord *noun* a supreme lord.

overly *adverb* excessively.

overman *verb* (**overmanned**, **overmanning**) to provide a ship, factory, department, etc. with too many people as workers or crew etc.

overmantel *noun* ornamental shelves etc. over a mantelpiece.

overmuch *adverb* too much.

overnight *adverb* for the length of a night or during a night.
overnight *adjective* for or during a night ♦ *an overnight stop in Rome.*

overpass *noun* a road that crosses another by means of a bridge.

overpay *verb* (past tense and past participle **overpaid**) to pay someone too much.

overplay verb to give too much importance to something. **to overplay your hand** to take unjustified risks by overestimating your strength.

overpower verb to defeat someone by greater strength or numbers.

overpowering adjective (said about heat or feelings) extremely intense.

overrate verb to have a higher opinion of something than it deserves.

overreach verb **to overreach yourself** to fail through being too ambitious.

overreact verb to respond more emotionally or strongly than is justified. **overreaction** noun

override verb (**overrode, overridden**) 1 to set aside an order by having superior authority. 2 to be more important than something else ♦ Safety overrides all other considerations. 3 to interrupt the operation of an automatic mechanism.
override noun a device on a machine for overriding an automatic mechanism.

overriding adjective more important than any other considerations.

overripe adjective too ripe.

overrule verb to reject or disallow a suggestion, decision, etc. by using your authority.

overrun verb (**overran, overrun, overrunning**) 1 to spread over and occupy a place in large numbers ♦ The place is overrun with mice. 2 to go on for longer than it should. [from an Old English word oferyrnan]

overseas adverb & adjective across or beyond the sea, abroad.

oversee verb (**oversaw, overseen**) to watch over or supervise people working. **overseer** noun

oversew verb (past participle, **oversewn** or **oversewed**) to sew together two edges so that each stitch lies over the edges.

overshadow verb 1 to tower above something and cast a shadow over it. 2 to cast a gloom over something. 3 to make a person or thing seem unimportant or unsuccessful in comparison.

overshoe noun a shoe worn over an ordinary one as a protection against wet etc.

overshoot verb (past tense and past participle **overshot**) to pass beyond a target or limit etc. ♦ The plane overshot the runway when landing.

oversight noun 1 a failure to notice or do something. 2 supervision.

oversimplify verb (**oversimplifies, oversimplified, oversimplifying**) to give a false impression of a problem or issue by stating it in terms that are too simple. **oversimplification** noun

oversized adjective of more than the usual size.

oversleep verb (past tense and past participle **overslept**) to sleep longer or later than you intended.

overspend verb (past tense and past participle **overspent**) to spend too much.

overspill noun 1 what spills over or overflows. 2 the surplus population of a town etc. who seek accommodation in other districts.

overstaff verb to provide an organization etc. with more than the necessary number of staff.

overstate verb to exaggerate something. **overstatement** noun

overstay verb to stay longer than the duration or limits of something. **to overstay your welcome** to stay so long that you are no longer welcome.

overstep verb (**overstepped, overstepping**) to go beyond a limit. **to overstep the mark** to go beyond what is acceptable.

overstrung adjective (said about a piano) with strings in sets crossing each other obliquely.

oversubscribed adjective 1 with applications for an issue of shares etc. in excess of the number offered. 2 (said about a course of study) having more applications than available places.

overt (oh-**vert**) adjective done or shown openly ♦ overt hostility. **overtly** adverb [from an Old French word meaning 'open']

overtake verb (**overtook, overtaken**) 1 to pass a person or vehicle by moving faster. 2 to catch up with someone. 3 to exceed a compared value or amount.

overtax verb 1 to tax someone too heavily. 2 to put too heavy a burden or strain on someone.

overthrow verb (**overthrew, overthrown**) to remove someone from power by force ♦ The rebel forces overthrew the government. SYNONYMS: depose, oust, bring down, topple.
overthrow noun 1 a downfall or defeat. 2 a fielder's throwing of a ball beyond an intended point.

overtime adverb in addition to normal working hours.
overtime noun 1 time spent working outside the normal hours. 2 payment for this.

overtone noun 1 an additional or subtle quality or implication ♦ There were overtones of malice in his comments. 2 (Music) any of the tones above the lowest in a harmonic series.

overtook past tense of **overtake**.

overture noun a piece of music written as an introduction to an opera or ballet etc.
overtures plural noun a friendly approach showing willingness to begin negotiations or start a relationship. [from an Old French word meaning 'opening']

overturn verb 1 to turn over or upside down, or to make something do this. 2 to reverse a legal decision.

overuse (oh-ver-yooz) verb to use something too much.
overuse (oh-ver-yoos) noun excessive use.

overview noun a general review or summary.

overweight adjective weighing more than is normal, required, or allowed.

overwhelm verb 1 to bury or drown something or someone beneath a huge mass. 2 to defeat someone completely, especially by force of numbers. 3 to have a strong emotional effect on someone ♦ I was overwhelmed by their generosity.
overwhelming adjective [from over and a Middle English word whelm meaning 'to turn upside down']

overwind verb (past tense and past participle **overwound**) to wind a watch etc. beyond the proper stopping point.

overwork verb 1 to work or make someone work too hard. 2 to use something too often or too much ♦ an overworked phrase.
overwork noun excessive work causing exhaustion.

overwrought (oh-ver-rawt) adjective in a state of nervous excitement or anxiety.

oviduct (oh-vi-dukt) noun (Anatomy, Zoology) a canal through which ova pass from the ovary, especially in egg-laying creatures. [from ovum and duct]

oviparous (oh-vip-er-os) adjective (Zoology) producing young from eggs that are laid by the parent and then hatched (in contrast to viviparous). [from ovum and a Latin word -parus meaning 'bearing']

ovipositor (oh-vi-poz-it-er) noun (Zoology) a pointed tube-shaped organ through which a female insect or fish deposits its eggs. [from ovum and a Latin word positum meaning 'placed']

ovoid (oh-void) adjective egg-shaped.
ovoid noun an ovoid shape or mass. [from ovum]

ovulate (ov-yoo-layt) verb to produce or discharge an ovum from an ovary.
ovulation noun [from a Latin word ovum meaning 'egg']

ovule (oh-vewl) noun 1 (Botany) a small part in a plant's ovary that develops into a seed when fertilized. 2 an unfertilized ovum. [from a Latin word ovum meaning 'egg']

ovum (oh-vəm) noun (ova) (Biology) a female egg cell capable of developing into a new individual when fertilized by male sperm. [a Latin word meaning 'egg']

owe verb 1 to have an obligation to pay or repay money etc. in return for what you have received. 2 to be under an obligation to show or offer something to someone ♦ I think I owe you an apology. 3 to have something because of the work or action of another person or cause ♦ We owe this discovery to Newton ♦ He owes his success to luck. 4 to feel gratitude etc. towards someone in return for a service. [from an Old English word]

owing adjective owed and not yet paid.
owing to because of or on account of. ◊ See the note at **due**.

owl noun a bird of prey with a large head, large eyes, and a hooked beak, usually flying at night. [from an Old English word]

owlet noun a small or young owl.

owlish adjective like an owl. **owlishly** adverb

own[1] adjective to do with or belonging to the person or thing specified. **to come into your own** to have the opportunity to show your qualities or abilities. **to get your own back** (informal) to have your revenge. **to hold your own** to succeed in holding your position against competition or attack. **of your own** belonging to yourself exclusively. **on your own** alone; independently. [from an Old English word]

own² verb 1 to have something as your property, to possess something. 2 (formal) to acknowledge or admit to something ♦ She owns to having said it. **to own up** to admit that you have done something wrong or embarrassing. **owner** noun [from an Old English word]

own goal noun a goal scored by a member of a team against his or her own side.

ox noun (**oxen**) 1 an animal of the kind kept as domestic cattle or related to these. 2 a fully grown bullock, used as a draught animal or as food. [from an Old English word oxa]

oxbow lake noun a curved lake formed from a horseshoe-shaped bend in a river, where the river cuts across the narrow end and leaves the curve of water isolated. [from oxbow meaning the U-shaped collar on the yoke of oxen]

Oxbridge noun the universities of Oxford and Cambridge.

oxen plural of **ox**.

oxidant noun an oxidizing agent.

oxidation noun (Chemistry) the process of combining or causing a substance to combine with oxygen.

oxide noun (Chemistry) a compound of oxygen and one other element.

oxidize verb 1 to combine or cause a substance to combine with oxygen. 2 to form or make something form a layer of metal oxide, as when something becomes rusty. **oxidization** noun

Oxon. abbreviation 1 Oxfordshire. 2 of Oxford University.

oxtail noun the tail of an ox, used in making soup.

oxyacetylene (oksi-ǝ-**set**-i-leen) adjective using a very hot flame produced by mixing oxygen and acetylene, especially in the cutting and welding of metals.

oxygen noun a chemical element (symbol O), a colourless odourless tasteless gas existing in air and combining with hydrogen to form water. [from a French word]

oxygenate verb to supply, treat, or mix something with oxygen. **oxygenation** noun

oxyhaemoglobin (oks-i-heem-ǝ-**gloh**-bin) noun a bright red compound of oxygen and haemoglobin present in oxygenated blood.

oxymoron (oksi-**mor**-ǝn) noun putting together words which seem to contradict one another, e.g. bitter-sweet, living death. [from a Greek word oxumōros meaning 'pointedly foolish', from oxus meaning 'sharp' and moros meaning 'foolish']

oxytocin (oksi-**toh**-sin) noun a hormone controlling contractions of the womb. [from a Greek word oxutokia meaning 'sudden delivery', from oxus meaning 'sharp' and tokos meaning 'childbirth']

oyez (oh-**yez**) interjection a cry uttered, usually three times, by a public crier or court officer to call for attention before an announcement. [from an Old French word meaning 'hear!']

oyster noun a kind of shellfish used as food, some types of which produce pearls inside their shells. [from an Old French word oistre]

oz. abbreviation ounce(s).

ozone (oh-zohn) noun 1 a form of oxygen with a sharp smell. 2 (informal) invigorating air at the seaside. [from a Greek word ozein meaning 'to smell']

ozone-friendly adjective not containing chemicals that can damage the ozone layer.

ozone layer noun a layer in the stratosphere where ozone is generated, serving to protect the earth from harmful ultraviolet rays from the sun.

Pp

P the sixteenth letter of the English alphabet.

P abbreviation 1 (on road signs) parking. 2 (Chemistry) the symbol for phosphorus.

p abbreviation 1 page. 2 penny or pence. 3 (Music) piano (softly).

PA *abbreviation* 1 personal assistant.
2 public address.

pa *noun* (*informal*) father. [short for *papa*]

pace [1] *noun* 1 a single step taken in walking or running. 2 the distance covered by this ♦ *We measured out twenty paces.* 3 speed of walking or running ♦ *a player with real pace.* 4 the rate of progress or change in some activity. 5 a manner of walking or running, especially of horses.
pace *verb* 1 to walk at a steady speed, especially up and down a room. 2 to measure a distance in paces ♦ *We paced out the length of a cricket pitch.* 3 to set the pace for a runner etc. **to keep pace with** to advance at the same speed as something else. **to pace yourself** to do something at a restrained rate. **to put someone through their paces** to test someone's abilities. **to set the pace** to set the speed, especially by leading. **to stand** or **stay the pace** to be able to keep up with others. **pacer** *noun* [from a Latin word *passus* meaning 'a stretch of the leg']

pace [2] (**pay-si** or **pah-chay**) *preposition* with due respect to a named person who disagrees. [a Latin word meaning 'in peace']

pacemaker *noun* 1 a competitor who sets the pace in a race. 2 an electrical device placed on the heart to stimulate contractions.

pachyderm (**pak-i-derm**) *noun* a large thick-skinned mammal, such as an elephant, rhinoceros, or hippopotamus.
pachydermatous *adjective* [from Greek words *pakhus* meaning 'thick' and *derma* meaning 'skin']

pacific (**pǝ-sif-ik**) *adjective* peaceful; making or loving peace.
Pacific *noun* the Pacific Ocean, the ocean separating the Americas from Asia and Australia.
Pacific *adjective* to do with the Pacific Ocean. **pacifically** *adverb* [from a Latin word *pacis* meaning 'of peace']

pacifist (**pas-i-fist**) *noun* a person who totally opposes war, believing that disputes should be settled by peaceful means. **pacifism** *noun* [from a French word *pacifier* meaning 'to pacify']

pacify (**pas-i-fiy**) *verb* (**pacifies, pacified, pacifying**) 1 to calm a person down.
SYNONYMS: soothe, appease, placate, mollify.
2 to bring peace to a country or warring sides. **pacification** *noun* [same origin as for *pacific*]

pack [1] *noun* 1 a set of things wrapped or tied together for carrying or selling ♦ *a pack of envelopes* ♦ *a family pack of biscuits* ♦ *an information pack.* 2 a set of 52 playing cards. 3 a bag carried on your back. 4 a number of people or things ♦ *a pack of lies.* 5 a group of wolves etc. that live and hunt together. 6 a group of hounds kept for hunting. 7 a group of Cub Scouts or Brownies. 8 a rugby football team's forwards.
pack *verb* 1 to put things into a suitcase, bag, box, etc. in order to move or store them ♦ *Have you packed yet?* 2 to put food or goods into a box, wrapper, etc. ready to be sold. 3 to be able to be folded up and packed ♦ *This table packs away neatly.* 4 to cram a large number of things into something ♦ *Each of these books is packed with useful information.* 5 to crowd into a place and fill it ♦ *By 7 o'clock the hall was packed out.* 6 to cover or protect a thing with something pressed tightly on, in, or round it. **to pack a gun** (*informal*) to carry a gun regularly. **to pack a punch** to hit someone hard or have a powerful effect. **to pack something in** (*informal*) to stop doing something. **to pack someone off** (*informal*) to send someone away. **to pack up** 1 to put your things together to get ready for leaving or stopping work.
2 (*informal*) (said about a machine) to break down. **to send someone packing** to dismiss them abruptly. **packer** *noun* [from an Old German or Dutch word]

pack [2] *verb* to fill a jury or committee with people whose decisions are likely to be in your favour. [probably related to *pact*]

package *noun* 1 something wrapped up, a parcel. 2 a box or other container in which goods are packed. 3 a number of separate items or proposals offered together as a whole. 4 (*Computing*) a set of programs designed for a particular purpose.
package *verb* 1 to put things together in a box or wrapping. 2 to present something in a particular way. [from *pack*]

package holiday or **package tour** *noun* a holiday with travel, accommodation, meals, etc. all included in the price.

packaging *noun* wrappings or containers for goods.

pack animal *noun* 1 an animal used to carry packs. 2 an animal that lives and hunts in a pack.

packet *noun* 1 a paper or cardboard

container. **2** (*informal*) a large sum of money ♦ *She must be earning a packet.* **3** (*old use*) a mail boat. [from *pack*]

packhorse *noun* a horse for carrying loads.

pack ice *noun* large crowded floating pieces of ice in the sea.

packing case *noun* a large strong box for packing goods in.

pact *noun* an agreement or treaty. [from a Latin word *pactum* meaning 'something agreed']

pad [1] *noun* **1** a thick piece of soft material used to protect against jarring, to add bulk, to hold or absorb fluid, etc. **2** a piece of soft material used to protect your leg and ankle in cricket and other games. **3** the soft fleshy part under an animal's foot or at the end of a finger or toe. **4** a set of sheets of blank paper fastened together at one edge. **5** a flat surface from which rockets and spacecraft are launched or where helicopters take off and land. **6** (*informal*) a person's home. **pad** *verb* (**padded, padding**) **1** to cover something with a pad or pads. **2** to stuff something. **3** to fill a book or speech etc. with unnecessary material in order to lengthen it. [probably from an Old Dutch word]

pad [2] *verb* (**padded, padding**) to walk with soft steady steps. [from a Dutch word *pad* meaning 'path']

padded cell *noun* a room with padded walls in a psychiatric hospital.

padding *noun* material used to pad things.

paddle [1] *noun* **1** a short oar with a broad blade. **2** something shaped like this. **3** one of the boards on a paddle wheel. **paddle** *verb* **1** to move a boat along by using a paddle or paddles. **2** (said about a bird or animal) to swim with short fast strokes. **to paddle your own canoe** to be independent. **paddler** *noun* [origin unknown]

paddle [2] *verb* to walk about with bare feet in shallow water. **paddle** *noun* a spell of paddling. [probably from an Old Dutch word]

paddle steamer or **paddle boat** *noun* a boat powered by steam and moved along by paddle wheels.

paddle wheel *noun* a large wheel with boards round its rim that drives a paddle steamer.

paddling pool *noun* a shallow pool for children to paddle in.

paddock *noun* **1** a small field where horses are kept. **2** an enclosure at a racecourse or track where horses or racing cars are brought together before a race. **3** (*Austral.*) (*NZ*) a field or plot of land. [from an old word *parrock*]

paddy [1] *noun* (**paddies**) **1** a field where rice is grown. **2** rice that is still growing or in the husk. [from a Malay word *padi* meaning 'rice']

paddy [2] *noun* (*informal*) a fit of temper. [pet form of *Patrick*]

padlock *noun* a detachable lock with a U-shaped bar or a chain etc. that fastens through the loop of a staple or ring. **padlock** *verb* to fasten something with a padlock. [origin unknown]

padre (pah-dray) *noun* (*informal*) a chaplain in the armed forces. [an Italian, Spanish, and Portuguese word meaning 'father']

paean (pee-ən) *noun* a song of praise or triumph. [from a Greek word *paian* meaning 'hymn']

paediatrician (peed-i-ə-trish-ən) *noun* a specialist in paediatrics.

paediatrics (peed-i-at-triks) *noun* the branch of medicine dealing with children and their diseases. **paediatric** *adjective* [from Greek words *paidos* meaning 'of a child' and *iatros* meaning 'doctor']

paedophile (pee-də-fiyl) *noun* a person who is sexually attracted to children. **paedophilia** *noun* [from Greek words *paidos* meaning 'of a child' and *philos* meaning 'loving']

paella (piy-el-ə) *noun* a Spanish dish of rice, chicken, seafood, etc. cooked and served in a large shallow pan. [via Catalan and Old French from a Latin word *patella* meaning 'pan']

pagan (pay-gən) *noun* a person whose religion is not one of the main world religions. **pagan** *adjective* not believing in one of the main world religions. **paganism** *noun* [same origin as for *peasant*]

page [1] *noun* **1** a piece of paper that is part of a book or newspaper etc. **2** one side of this, or what is written or printed on it. **page** *verb* (*Computing*) to move through text and display one screen of it at a time ♦ *Use this key to page down the text.* [from a Latin word *pagina* meaning 'page']

page [2] *noun* **1** a boy or man employed in a hotel or club to go on errands, open doors, etc. **2** a young boy attending a bride at a wedding. **3** (*historical*) a boy training to be a knight and acting as a servant to a knight.
page *verb* **1** to summon a person over a public address system or by calling their name. **2** to contact a person by means of a pager. [from a Greek word *paidion* meaning 'small boy']

pageant (paj-ənt) *noun* a public show consisting of a procession of people in elaborate costumes, or an outdoor performance of a historical play. [origin unknown]

pageantry *noun* elaborate ceremony.

pageboy *noun* a page in a hotel or attending a bride at a wedding.

pager *noun* a small radio device which bleeps or vibrates to tell you that someone wants to contact you or that it has received a short message.

paginate *verb* to number the pages of a book etc. **pagination** *noun*

pagoda (pə-goh-də) *noun* a Hindu temple shaped like a pyramid, or a Buddhist tower with several storeys, in India and countries of the Far East. [via Portuguese from a Persian word *butkada* meaning 'temple of idols']

paid past tense and past participle of **pay**.
paid *adjective* receiving payment or a salary ♦ *a paid assistant* ♦ *paid holidays*. **to put paid to** (*informal*) to put an end to someone's hopes, prospects, or activities.

paid-up *adjective* with all the necessary payments made.

pail *noun* a bucket. [from an Old English word]

pain *noun* **1** an unpleasant feeling caused by injury or illness. SYNONYMS: ache, discomfort, soreness, twinge, stab, sting, throb, pang. **2** mental suffering or distress. **3** (*informal*) an annoying or tedious person or thing.
pains *plural noun* careful effort, trouble taken ♦ *He's taken great pains with the work*. **pain** *verb* to cause suffering or distress to someone. **on** or **under pain of** with the threat of. [from a Latin word *poena* meaning 'punishment']

pained *adjective* distressed and annoyed ♦ *a pained look*.

painful *adjective* **1** (said about a part of the body) affected with pain. SYNONYMS: sore, tender, aching, splitting (head). **2** causing pain. SYNONYMS: agonizing, excruciating. **3** causing trouble or difficulty ♦ *a painful decision*. **painfully** *adverb* **painfulness** *noun*

painkiller *noun* a medicine or drug that relieves pain.

painless *adjective* **1** not causing pain. **2** involving little effort or stress. **painlessly** *adverb* **painlessness** *noun*

painstaking *adjective* very careful and thorough. **painstakingly** *adverb*

paint *noun* a substance spread over a surface in liquid form to colour it.
paints *plural noun* a collection of tubes or cakes of paint.
paint *verb* **1** to coat or decorate something with paint. **2** to make a picture with paints. **3** to apply a liquid to a surface using a brush. **4** to describe something vividly. **5** (*Computing*) to create a display or graphics using a special program. [from a Latin word *pingere* meaning 'to paint']

paintbox *noun* a box holding dry paints for use by an artist.

paintbrush *noun* a brush for applying paint.

painted lady *noun* an orange butterfly with black and white spots.

painter [1] *noun* a person who paints as an artist or as a decorator.

painter [2] *noun* a rope attached to the bow of a boat for tying it up. [from an Old French word *penteur* meaning 'rope']

painting *noun* a painted picture.

paintwork *noun* a painted surface in a building or on a vehicle.

pair *noun* **1** a set of two things used or thought of together. **2** something made of two joined corresponding parts ♦ *a pair of scissors*. **3** the other member of a matching pair ♦ *I can't find the pair to this glove*. **4** two people thought of together, especially a couple. **5** two mating animals. **6** two playing cards of the same rank. **7** either or both of two MPs of opposite parties who are absent from voting by mutual arrangement.
pair *verb* **1** to put two things together as a pair; to arrange things in groups of two. **2** (said about animals) to mate. **3** to partner a person with a member of the opposite sex. **4** to make a pair in Parliament. **to pair off** or **up** to form a

couple. [from a Latin word *paria* meaning 'equal things']

paisley noun a pattern of tapering petal-shaped figures with much detail. [named after Paisley in Scotland]

pal noun (*informal*) a friend.
pal verb (**palled, palling**) **to pal up** (*informal*) to become friends. [from a Romany word *pal* meaning 'brother']

palace noun 1 the official residence of a sovereign, president, archbishop, etc. 2 a large splendid house or other building. [from Palatium, the name of a hill on which the house of the emperor Augustus stood in ancient Rome]

palaeography (pal-i-og-rəfi) noun the study of ancient writing and documents.
palaeographer noun **palaeographic** adjective [from a Greek word *palaios* meaning 'old' and *-graphy*]

Palaeolithic (pal-i-ə-lith-ik) adjective (*Archaeology*) belonging to the early part of the Stone Age, up to the end of the glacial period.
Palaeolithic noun this period. [from Greek words *palaios* meaning 'old' and *lithos* meaning 'stone']

palaeontology (pal-i-on-tol-əji) noun the scientific study of fossil animals and plants. **palaeontologist** noun [from a Greek word *palaios* meaning 'old' and *ontology*]

Palaeozoic (pal-i-ə-zoh-ik) adjective (*Geology*) to do with the era between the Precambrian and Mesozoic, lasting from about 570 to 245 million years ago.
Palaeozoic noun this era. [from Greek words *palaios* meaning 'old' and *zōion* meaning 'animal']

palanquin (pal-ən-keen) noun a covered litter for one person, used in eastern countries. [via Portuguese from a Sanskrit word *palyanka* meaning 'bed, couch']

palatable (pal-ə-tə-bəl) adjective 1 pleasant to taste. 2 acceptable.

palate (pal-ət) noun 1 the roof of the mouth. 2 a person's sense of taste. **palatal** adjective [from a Latin word *palatum*]
◊ Do not confuse this word with **palette** or **pallet**, which have different meanings.

palatial (pə-lay-shəl) adjective like a palace, spacious and grand. **palatially** adverb [same origin as for *palace*]

palaver (pə-lah-ver) noun (*informal*) a fuss or time-consuming procedure ♦ *What a palaver!* [from a Portuguese word *palavra* meaning 'word']

pale [1] adjective 1 (said about colour or light) faint, not bright or vivid ♦ *the pale moonlight*. 2 (said about a person's face) having little colour, almost white.
SYNONYMS: anaemic, ashen, pallid, pasty; (*informal*) peaky, washed-out. 3 inferior ♦ *a pale imitation*.
pale verb 1 to turn pale. 2 to seem less important ♦ *Their other problems paled into insignificance in the light of this news.* **palely** adverb **paleness** noun [from a Latin word *pallidus* meaning 'pallid']

pale [2] noun 1 a wooden stake forming part of a fence. 2 a boundary. **beyond the pale** outside the bounds of acceptable behaviour. [from a Latin word *palus* meaning 'pointed stick set in the ground']

palette (pal-it) noun a thin board on which an artist mixes colours when painting. [from a French word meaning 'little shovel']
◊ Do not confuse this word with **palate** or **pallet**, which have different meanings.

palette knife noun 1 an artist's knife for mixing or spreading paint. 2 a knife with a long blunt round-ended flexible blade for spreading or smoothing soft substances in cookery etc.

palindrome (pal-in-drohm) noun a word or phrase that reads the same backwards as forwards, e.g. *radar* or *Madam, I'm Adam*. [from a Greek word *palindromos* meaning 'running back again']

paling noun 1 a fence made from wooden posts. 2 one of its posts. [from *pale*[2]]

palisade (pal-i-sayd) noun a fence of pointed stakes. [same origin as for *pale*[2]]

palisade layer noun (*Botany*) a layer of long cells that are parallel to each other and often at right angles to the surface of the structure (especially a leaf) of which they form part.

pall [1] (pawl) noun 1 a cloth spread over a coffin. 2 a dark cloud or covering of something ♦ *a pall of smoke*. [from a Latin word *pallium* meaning 'cloak']

pall [2] (pawl) verb to become less interesting or enjoyable ♦ *The summer holidays soon began to pall.* [from *appal*]

Palladian (pə-lay-diən) adjective to do with or in the neoclassical style of the 16th-century Italian architect Andrea Palladio (1508–80).

pall-bearer *noun* a person helping to carry the coffin at a funeral.

pallet [1] *noun* 1 a mattress stuffed with straw. 2 a simple or makeshift bed. [from an Old French word *paille* meaning 'straw']
◊ Do not confuse this word with **palate** or **palette**, which have different meanings.

pallet [2] *noun* a large tray or platform for carrying goods that are being lifted, stacked, or stored, especially one that can be raised by a forklift truck. [from a French word *palette* meaning 'little blade']
◊ Do not confuse this word with **palate** or **palette**, which have different meanings.

palliasse (pal-i-ass) *noun* a straw mattress. [from a French word *paillasse*]

palliate (pal-i-ayt) *verb* to make something less serious or less severe. **palliation** *noun* [same origin as for **pall**[1]]

palliative (pal-i-ətiv) *adjective* reducing the bad effects of something.
palliative *noun* something that does this.

pallid (pal-id) *adjective* pale, especially from illness. [from a Latin word *pallidus* meaning 'pale']

pallor (pal-er) *noun* paleness in a person's face, especially from illness. [from a Latin word *pallere* meaning 'to be pale']

pally *adjective* (**pallier, palliest**) (*informal*) friendly.

palm *noun* 1 the inner surface of the hand between the wrist and the fingers. 2 (also **palm tree**) a kind of tree growing in warm or tropical climates, with no branches and with large leaves growing in a mass at the top. 3 a palm leaf thought of as a symbol of victory ♦ *It was last year's winner who again carried off the palm.*
palm *verb* to pick up something secretly and hide it in the palm of your hand. **in the palm of your hand** under your control. **to palm something off** to deceive a person into accepting something. [from a Latin word *palma*]

palmate (pal-mayt) *adjective* (*Botany and Zoology*) shaped like a hand with the fingers spread out. [same origin as for *palm*]

palmist (pah-mist) *noun* a person who is skilled in palmistry.

palmistry (pahm-ist-ri) *noun* the supposed art of telling someone's future or

interpreting their character by examining the lines on the palm of their hand.

Palm Sunday *noun* the Sunday before Easter, when Christians commemorate Christ's triumphal entry into Jerusalem when the people spread palm leaves in his path.

palmtop *noun* a small light computer that can be held in one hand.

palmy (pahm-i) *adjective* (**palmier, palmiest**) 1 flourishing or prosperous ♦ *in their former palmy days.* 2 covered with palms.

palp *noun* (*Zoology*) an organ at or near the mouth of certain insects and crustaceans, used for feeling and tasting things. [same origin as for *palpable*]

palpable (pal-pə-bəl) *adjective* 1 easily perceived, obvious ♦ *a palpable sense of loss.* 2 able to be touched or felt.
palpability *noun* **palpably** *adverb* [from a Latin word *palpare* meaning 'to feel or touch']

palpate (pal-payt) *verb* to examine a part of the body by feeling with the hands, especially as part of a medical examination. **palpation** *noun* [same origin as for *palpable*]

palpitate (pal-pit-ayt) *verb* 1 (said about the heart) to beat rapidly. 2 (said about a person) to quiver with fear or excitement. **palpitation** *noun* [same origin as for *palpable*]

palsied (pawl-zid) *adjective* affected with palsy.

palsy (pawl-zi) *noun* (*old use*) paralysis, especially with involuntary tremors. [same origin as for *paralysis*]

paltry (pol-tri) *adjective* (**paltrier, paltriest**) very small and almost worthless ♦ *a paltry amount.* [origin unknown]

pampas (pam-pəs) *noun* vast grassy plains in South America. [via Spanish from a Quechua (South American) word *pampa* meaning 'plain']

pampas grass *noun* a kind of tall South American grass with feathery plumes.

pamper *verb* to treat someone very indulgently. SYNONYMS: indulge, spoil, coddle, cosset. [probably from an Old German or Old Dutch word]

pamphlet (pamf-lit) *noun* a leaflet or booklet containing information or arguments on a subject. [from *Pamphilet*, the name of a long 12th-century poem in Latin]

pan [1] *noun* **1** a metal container with a flat base, sometimes with a lid, used for cooking food in. **2** something shaped like this. **3** the bowl of a pair of scales. **4** the bowl of a toilet.
pan *verb* (**panned, panning**) **1** to wash gravel in a pan in search of gold. **2** (*informal*) to criticize something severely. **to pan out** (said about circumstances or events) to turn out in a particular way, especially successfully. [from an Old English word *panne*]

pan [2] *verb* (**panned, panning**) **1** to turn a camera horizontally to give a panoramic effect or follow a moving object. **2** (said about a camera) to turn in this way. [short for *panorama*]

pan- *prefix* **1** all (as in *panorama*). **2** to do with the whole of a continent or racial group etc. (as in *pan-African*). [from a Greek word *pan* meaning 'all']

panacea (pan-ə-see-ə) *noun* a remedy or solution for all kinds of diseases or troubles. [from *pan-* and a Greek word *akos* meaning 'remedy']

panache (pən-ash) *noun* a confident stylish manner. [originally denoting a plume of feathers on a helmet or headdress, via French and Italian from a Latin word *pinnaculum* meaning 'little feather']

panama (pan-ə-mah) *noun* a wide-brimmed hat made of fine straw-like material. [from Panama in Central America (because the hats were originally made from the leaves of a plant which grows there)]

pancake *noun* **1** a thin round cake of batter fried on both sides, sometimes rolled up with filling. **2** theatrical make-up in the form of a flat cake. [from *pan* [1] and *cake*]

Pancake Day *noun* Shrove Tuesday, on which pancakes are traditionally eaten.

panchromatic (pan-krə-mat-ik) *adjective* (said about black-and-white film) sensitive to all colours of the visible spectrum. [from *pan-* and a Greek word *khrōma* meaning 'colour']

pancreas (pank-ri-əs) *noun* a gland near the stomach producing a digestive secretion into the duodenum and insulin into the blood. **pancreatic** (pank-ri-at-ik) *adjective* [from *pan-* and a Greek word *kreas* meaning 'flesh']

panda *noun* **1** (also **giant panda**) a large rare bear-like black-and-white animal living in the mountains of south-west China. **2** (also **red panda**) a raccoon-like animal of the Himalayas. [from a Nepali word]

panda car *noun* (*informal*) a police patrol car, originally white with black stripes on the doors.

pandemic (pan-dem-ik) *adjective* (said about a disease) occurring over a whole country or the whole world. **pandemic** *noun* an outbreak of such a disease. [from *pan-* and a Greek word *dēmos* meaning 'people']

pandemonium (pandi-moh-niəm) *noun* uproar and complete confusion. [from Pandemonium, John Milton's name for the capital of hell in his poem *Paradise Lost*, from *pan-* and *demon*]

pander *verb* **to pander to** to indulge someone by giving them whatever they want or satisfying a weakness
♦ *Newspapers just pander to the public interest in scandal.* [from Pandare, a character in an old poem who acted as go-between for two lovers]

Pandora's box *noun* a process that once begun will generate many unmanageable problems. [from Pandora in Greek mythology, who opened a jar which let loose all kinds of misfortunes upon mankind]

p. & p. *abbreviation* postage and packing.

pane *noun* a single sheet of glass in a window or door. [from a Latin word *pannus* meaning 'piece of cloth']

panegyric (pan-i-ji-rik) *noun* a speech or piece of writing praising a person or thing. [from a Greek word *panēgurikos* meaning 'of public assembly']

panel *noun* **1** a long flat piece of wood, metal, etc. that forms a section of a wall, door, piece of furniture, vehicle, etc. **2** a strip of material set lengthwise in or on a garment. **3** a flat board with controls or instruments on it. **4** a rectangular section on a printed page, containing text or illustrations. **5** a group of people brought together to discuss or decide something, or to form a team in a quiz. **6** a list of jurors, or a jury.
panel *verb* (**panelled, panelling**) to cover or decorate something with panels. [from an Old French word, related to *pane*]

panel game *noun* a television or radio quiz played by a panel of people.

panelling noun 1 a series of panels in a wall. 2 wood used for making panels.

panellist noun a member of a panel.

pang noun a sudden sharp feeling of pain or a painful emotion ♦ *pangs of jealousy*. [from *prong*]

panic noun sudden uncontrollable fear or anxiety, especially when this affects a large group of people.
panic verb (**panicked, panicking**) to feel panic or to make someone feel panic. SYNONYMS: (*informal*) go to pieces, lose your head, flap. **panicky** adjective [from the name of Pan, an ancient Greek god thought to be able to cause sudden fear]

panic button noun a button to be pressed to summon help in an emergency.

panic stations plural noun (*informal*) a state of alarm or emergency.

panic-stricken adjective affected with panic.

panicle noun (*Botany*) a loose branching cluster of flowers. [from a Latin word *panus* meaning 'ear of millet']

panjandrum noun a pompous person who has or claims to have a lot of authority or influence. [from the name of a character in a nonsense poem by Samuel Foote, written in 1755]

pannier noun 1 a large basket, especially one of a pair carried on either side of a pack animal. 2 a bag or container carried similarly on a motorcycle or bicycle. [from a Latin word *panarium* meaning 'bread basket']

panoply (pan-ə-pli) noun a splendid display or collection of things. [from *pan-* and a Greek word *hopla* meaning 'weapons']

panorama noun 1 a view or picture of a wide area. 2 a view of a constantly changing scene or series of events. **panoramic** (pan-er-am-ik) adjective [from *pan-* and a Greek word *horama* meaning 'view']

pan pipes plural noun a musical instrument consisting of a row of short pipes fixed together side by side. [from the name of the Greek god Pan]

pansy noun (**pansies**) a small brightly coloured garden flower of the violet family, with velvety petals. [from a French word *pensée* meaning 'thought']

pant verb 1 to breathe with short quick breaths, usually after running or working hard. SYNONYMS: gasp, wheeze, puff; (*informal*) huff and puff. 2 to utter something breathlessly. 3 to be extremely eager to do or have something.
pant noun a short quick breath. [from an Old French word *pantaisier* meaning 'to be agitated, to gasp']

pantaloons plural noun 1 (*historical*) men's tight-fitting trousers, fastened below the calf or at the foot. 2 baggy trousers gathered at the ankle. [from Pantalone, a character in old Italian comedies who wore pantaloons]

pantechnicon (pan-tek-nik-ən) noun a large van for transporting furniture. [originally the name of a large art and craft gallery in London, which was later used for storing furniture: from *pan-* and a Greek word *tekhnē* meaning 'art']

pantheism (pan-thi-izm) noun the belief that God is everything and everything is God. **pantheist** noun **pantheistic** adjective [from *pan-* and a Greek word *theos* meaning 'god']

pantheon (pan-thi-ən) noun 1 all the gods of a people or religion collectively. 2 a temple dedicated to all the gods. 3 a collection of famous or important people ♦ *His place in the sporting pantheon is assured.* [from *pan-* and a Greek word *theos* meaning 'god']

panther noun a leopard, especially a black one. [from a Greek word]

panties plural noun (*informal*) short knickers. [from *pants*]

pantile (pan-tyl) noun a curved roof tile. [from *pan*[1] and *tile*]

panto noun (**pantos**) (*informal*) a pantomime.

pantomime noun 1 a type of theatrical entertainment, usually based on a fairy tale and produced around Christmas. 2 acting with movements of the body and without words to express a meaning or tell a story.
pantomime verb to use movements of the body and no words to express a meaning or tell a story. [from *pan-* and *mime* (because in its most ancient form an actor mimed the different parts)]

pantry noun (**pantries**) a small room for storing food; a larder. [from a Latin word *panis* meaning 'bread']

pants plural noun 1 (*North Amer.*) trousers. 2 underpants or knickers. [short for *pantaloons*]

pantyhose *plural noun* (*North Amer.*) women's thin nylon tights.

panzer (**panz**-er) *noun* a German armoured unit ♦ *panzer divisions*. [from a German word *Panzer* meaning 'coat of mail']

pap *noun* **1** soft or semi-liquid food suitable for babies or invalids. **2** worthless or trivial reading matter or entertainment. [probably via Old German from a Latin word *pappare* meaning 'to eat']

papa *noun* (*old use*) father. [from a Greek word *papas* meaning 'father']

papacy (**pay**-pə-si) *noun* (**papacies**) the office or authority of the pope. [from a Latin word *papa* meaning 'pope']

papal (**pay**-pəl) *adjective* to do with the pope or the papacy.

paparazzi (pap-ə-**rat**-si) *plural noun* photographers who chase famous people to get photographs of them. [from an Italian word]

papaw (pə-**paw**) *noun* another spelling of **pawpaw**.

papaya (pə-**py**-ə) *noun* **1** an oblong orange-coloured edible fruit. **2** the palm-like tropical American tree bearing this fruit. [from a Spanish and Portuguese word]

paper *noun* **1** a substance manufactured in thin sheets from wood fibre, rags, etc., used for writing or printing or drawing on or for wrapping things. **2** a newspaper. **3** wallpaper. **4** a set of examination questions ♦ *the biology paper*. **5** a document ♦ *Can I see your papers?* **6** an essay or dissertation, especially one read to an academic society.
paper *verb* to cover a wall or room with wallpaper. **on paper 1** in writing. **2** in theory, though not necessarily in practice ♦ *The scheme looked fine on paper*. **to paper over** to try to hide a difficulty instead of dealing with it. [from *papyrus*]

paperback *noun* a book bound in a flexible paper binding, not in a stiff cover.

paper boy or **paper girl** *noun* a boy or girl who delivers newspapers.

paper clip *noun* a piece of bent wire or plastic for holding a few sheets of paper together.

paperknife *noun* (**paperknives**) a blunt knife used for slitting open envelopes.

paper money *noun* money in the form of banknotes, not coins.

paper tiger *noun* a person or thing that has a threatening appearance but can do no harm.

paperweight *noun* a small heavy object placed on loose papers to keep them in place.

paperwork *noun* all the writing of reports, keeping of records, etc. that someone has to do as part of their job.

papier mâché (pap-yay ma-shay) *noun* moulded paper pulp used for making models, ornaments, etc. [a French phrase meaning 'chewed paper']

papilla (pə-**pil**-ə) *noun* (**papillae** (pə-**pil**-ee)) a small projection on a part of an animal or plant, e.g. one of those forming the surface of the tongue. **papillary** *adjective* [a Latin word meaning 'nipple']

papist (**pay**-pist) *noun* a derogatory term for a Roman Catholic. [from a French word]

papoose (pə-**pooss**) *noun* a bag for carrying a baby, worn on the back. [from an Algonquian (North American) word *papoos*]

paprika (**pap**-rik-ə or pə-**pree**-kə) *noun* a powdered spice made from red pepper. [a Hungarian word]

papyrus (pə-**py**-rəs) *noun* **1** a reed-like water plant with thick fibrous stems from which a kind of paper was made by the ancient Egyptians. **2** this paper. **3** (**papyri**) a manuscript written on this paper. [from a Greek word *papuros* meaning 'paper reed']

par *noun* **1** the usual or expected amount, condition, or degree ♦ *I was feeling well below par that morning*. **2** (in golf) the number of strokes that a good player should normally take for a particular hole or course. **3** the face value of stocks and shares etc., not their market value. **on a par with** equal to in amount or quality. **par for the course** what you would expect. [from a Latin word *par* meaning 'equal']

para *noun* (*informal*) **1** a parachutist or paratrooper. **2** a paragraph.

para- *prefix* **1** beside (as in *parallel*). **2** beyond (as in *paradox*). [from a Greek word *para* meaning 'beside or past']

parable *noun* a simple story told to illustrate a moral or spiritual truth, especially one of those told by Jesus Christ. [from a Greek word *parabolē* meaning 'comparison'; same origin as for *parabola*]

parabola (pə-**rab**-ə-lə) *noun* a curve like the path of an object thrown into the air and falling back to earth. [from *para-* and a Greek word *bolē* meaning 'a throw']

parabolic (pa-rə-**bol**-ik) *adjective* 1 to do with or like a parabola. 2 to do with or expressed in a parable.

paracetamol (pa-rə-**see**-tə-mol) *noun* a medicinal drug used to relieve pain and reduce fever. [an abbreviation of its chemical name]

parachute *noun* a rectangular or umbrella-shaped device used to slow the descent of a person or heavy object falling from a great height, especially from an aircraft.
parachute *verb* 1 to descend by parachute. 2 to drop supplies etc. by parachute.
parachutist *noun* [from French words *para* meaning 'protection against' and *chute* meaning 'a fall']

parade *noun* 1 a public procession celebrating a special day or event. 2 a formal assembly of troops for inspection or display. 3 an ostentatious display ♦ *He likes to make a parade of his virtues.* 4 a row of shops or a promenade.
parade *verb* 1 to march or walk in a parade. 2 to make a display of something ♦ *The quiz was an opportunity for her to parade her knowledge of pop history.* [from a Spanish or Italian word meaning 'display']

parade ground *noun* a place where troops gather for parade.

paradigm (**pa**-rə-diym) *noun* something serving as an example or model of how things should be done. [from *para-* and a Greek word *deiknunai* meaning 'to show']

paradise *noun* 1 heaven or a heavenly place. 2 (**Paradise**) the Garden of Eden. [from a Greek word *paradeisos* meaning 'a royal park']

paradox (**pa**-rə-doks) *noun* 1 a statement that seems to contradict itself or to conflict with common sense but which contains a truth (e.g. 'more haste, less speed'). 2 a person or thing that combines qualities that seem to contradict one another. **paradoxical** (pa-rə-**doks**-ik-əl) *adjective* **paradoxically** *adverb* [from *para-* and a Greek word *doxa* meaning 'opinion']

paraffin *noun* an oil obtained from petroleum or shale, used as a fuel and solvent. [via German from Latin words *parum* meaning 'hardly' and *affinis* meaning 'related' (because paraffin does not combine readily with other substances)]

paraffin wax *noun* paraffin in its solid form, used in candles, waterproofing, etc.

paragliding *noun* the sport of gliding through the air while being supported by a wide parachute after jumping from or being hauled to a height. **paraglider** *noun*

paragon (**pa**-rə-gən) *noun* a person or thing that seems to be a model of excellence or perfection. [from an Italian word *paragone* meaning 'touchstone']

paragraph *noun* one or more sentences on a single theme, forming a distinct section of a piece of writing and beginning on a new line, usually slightly in from the margin of the page.
paragraph *verb* to arrange a piece of writing in paragraphs. [from *para-* and *-graph*]

parakeet (**pa**-rə-keet) *noun* a kind of small parrot, often with a long tail. [from an Old French word *paroquet*]

parallax (**pa**-rə-laks) *noun* an apparent difference in the position or direction of an object when you look at it from different points. **parallactic** (pa-rə-**lak**-tik) *adjective* [from *para-* and a Greek word *allassein* meaning 'to change']

parallel *adjective* 1 (said about lines, planes, etc.) side by side and the same distance apart from each other at every point ♦ *The road runs parallel to the railway.* 2 occurring or existing at the same time or in a similar way; corresponding ♦ *When petrol prices rise there is a parallel rise in bus fares.*
parallel *noun* 1 something similar or corresponding ♦ *There are interesting parallels between the two cases.* 2 a comparison ♦ *You can draw a parallel between the two situations.* 3 an imaginary line on the earth's surface or a corresponding line on a map parallel to and passing through all points equidistant from the equator. 4 a line that is parallel to another.
parallel *verb* (**paralleled, paralleling**) 1 to run or lie parallel to something. 2 to be similar or corresponding to something.
in parallel 1 taking place at the same time and having some connection.
2 (describing electrical components or circuits) connected to common points at each end, so that the current is divided between them. **parallelism** *noun* [from *para-* and a Greek word *allēlos* meaning 'each other']

parallelogram (pa-rə-lel-ə-gram) noun a plane four-sided figure with its opposite sides parallel to each other. [from *parallel* and *-gram*]

paralyse verb 1 to affect a person or part of the body with paralysis, to make someone unable to act or move normally ♦ *She was paralysed with fear.* SYNONYMS: freeze, numb, deaden, immobilize, petrify. 2 to bring something to a standstill ♦ *The strike paralysed the country's transport system.* [from a French word *paralyser*]

paralysis noun 1 loss of the power of movement, caused by disease or an injury to nerves. 2 inability to move or act normally. [from Greek words *para* meaning 'on one side' and *lusis* meaning 'loosening']

paralytic (pa-rə-lit-ik) adjective 1 affected by paralysis. 2 (informal) very drunk. **paralytic** noun a person affected by paralysis.

paramecium (pa-rə-mee-si-əm) noun (Zoology) a very small single-celled animal that is roughly oval in shape and fringed with minute hairs (called *cilia*). [from a Greek word *paramēkēs* meaning 'oval']

paramedic noun a person who is trained to do medical work, especially emergency first aid, but is not a fully qualified doctor. **paramedical** adjective

parameter (pə-ram-it-er) noun 1 (Mathematics) a quantity that is constant in the case in question but varies in different cases. 2 a characteristic of a system that can be measured or quantified. 3 a limiting factor that defines the scope of something ♦ *We are working within the parameters of time and money.* [from *para-* meaning 'beside' and a Greek word *metron* meaning 'measure']
◊ Do not confuse this word with **perimeter**, which has a different meaning.

paramilitary adjective organized like a military force but not part of the armed services.
paramilitary noun (**paramilitaries**) a member of a paramilitary organization. [from *para-* and *military*]

paramount adjective more important than anything else ♦ *Secrecy is paramount.* [from an Old French word *paramont* meaning 'above']

paramour (pa-rə-moor) noun (old use) a lover, especially a married person's lover. [from a French phrase *par amour* meaning 'by love']

paranoia (pa-rə-noi-ə) noun 1 a mental disorder in which a person has delusions of being persecuted or of self-importance. 2 an unjustified suspicion and mistrust of others. **paranoiac** (pa-rə-noi-ak) adjective & noun [a Greek word meaning 'distraction']

paranoid (pa-rə-noid) adjective to do with, like, or suffering from paranoia. **paranoid** noun a person suffering from paranoia.

paranormal (pa-rə-nor-məl) adjective beyond what is normal and can be rationally explained; supernatural.

parapet (pa-rə-pit) noun a low protective wall along the edge of a balcony, roof, or bridge. [via French from an Italian word *parapetto* meaning 'chest-high wall']

paraphernalia (pa-rə-fer-nay-liə) noun numerous small pieces of equipment or other belongings. [from a Greek word denoting the personal articles that a woman could keep after her marriage, as opposed to her dowry which went to her husband (from Greek words *para* meaning 'beside' and *phernē* meaning 'dowry')]

paraphrase (pa-rə-frayz) verb to give the meaning of a passage by using different words.
paraphrase noun a rewording of a passage in this way. [from *para-* and *phrase*]

paraplegia (pa-rə-plee-jiə) noun paralysis of the legs and lower body. **paraplegic** adjective & noun [from *para-* and a Greek word *plēxis* meaning 'a stroke']

parapsychology (pa-rə-siy-kol-əji) noun the scientific study of mental phenomena, such as clairvoyance and telepathy, that seem to be outside normal mental abilities.

paraquat (pa-rə-kwot) noun (trademark) an extremely poisonous weedkiller. [from *para-* and *quaternary*]

parasite noun 1 an animal or plant that lives on or in another from which it draws its nourishment. 2 a person who lives off others and gives nothing in return. **parasitic** (pa-rə-sit-ik) adjective **parasitically** adverb [from a Greek word *parasitos* meaning 'guest at a meal']

parasol noun a light umbrella used to shade yourself from the sun. [from Italian words *para* meaning 'protection against' and *sole* meaning 'sun']

paratha (pə-**rah**-tə) noun a kind of Indian unleavened bread, fried in butter, ghee, etc. [from a Hindi word]

paratrooper noun a member of the paratroops.

paratroops plural noun troops trained to be dropped from aircraft by parachute. [from *parachute* and *troops*]

paratyphoid (pa-rə-**tiy**-foid) noun a fever resembling typhoid but milder. [from *para-* and *typhoid*]

parboil verb to boil food until it is partly cooked. [from Latin words *per-* meaning 'thoroughly' and *bullire* meaning 'to boil' (*per-* was later confused with *part*)]

parcel noun 1 a thing or things wrapped up for carrying or for sending by post. 2 a piece of land.
parcel verb (**parcelled, parcelling**) 1 to wrap something up as a parcel. 2 to divide something into portions ♦ *I've decided to parcel out the work between you.* [same origin as for *particle*]

parch verb to make something dry because of great heat. [origin unknown]

parched adjective very thirsty.

parchment noun 1 a heavy paper-like material made from animal skins. 2 a kind of paper resembling this. [from the city of Pergamum, now in Turkey, where parchment was made in ancient times]

pardon noun 1 forgiveness for a mistake or offence. 2 cancellation of the punishment for an offence ♦ *a free pardon.* SYNONYMS: reprieve, amnesty.
pardon verb 1 to forgive or excuse someone for something. 2 to cancel the punishment for an offence.
pardon interjection (also **I beg your pardon** or **pardon me**) used to mean 'I didn't hear or understand what you said' or 'I apologize'. [from an Old French word]

pardonable adjective able to be pardoned.
pardonably adverb

pare (pair) verb 1 to trim something by cutting away the edges. 2 to reduce something little by little ♦ *We had to pare down our expenses.* [from a Latin word *parare* meaning 'to prepare']

parent noun 1 a father or mother. 2 an animal or plant from which others are derived. 3 an ancestor. 4 an organization or company which owns or controls a number of subsidiaries.
parent verb to be a parent of a child etc.
parenthood noun [from a Latin word *parens* meaning 'producing offspring']

parentage (**pair**-ən-tij) noun who your parents are.

parental (pə-**ren**-təl) adjective to do with parents.

parenthesis (pə-**ren**-thi-sis) noun (**parentheses**) 1 an additional word, phrase, or sentence inserted in a passage which is grammatically complete without it, and usually marked off by brackets, dashes, or commas. 2 either of the pair of round brackets (like these) used to mark off words from the rest of a sentence. **in parenthesis 1** between brackets as a parenthesis. **2** as an aside or digression in a speech etc. [a Greek word meaning 'putting in besides']

parenthetic (pa-rən-**thet**-ik) adjective 1 to do with or as a parenthesis. 2 put in as an aside or digression. **parenthetical** adjective **parenthetically** adverb

par excellence (par-**eks**-el-ahns) adjective more than all others, to the highest degree. [a French phrase meaning 'by excellence']

pariah (pə-**riy**-ə) noun an outcast. [from a Tamil word]

parings (**pair**-ingz) plural noun pieces pared off from something.

parish noun 1 an area within a Christian diocese, having its own church and clergy ♦ *the parish church.* 2 (also **civil parish**) the smallest unit of local government in rural areas. 3 the people of a parish. [from a Greek word *paroikia* meaning 'neighbourhood' (from Greek words *para* meaning 'beside' and *oikein* meaning 'to dwell')]

parish council noun the administrative body in a civil parish.

parishioner (pə-**rish**-ən-er) noun an inhabitant of a parish.

parish register noun a book recording the christenings, marriages, and burials that have taken place at a parish church.

parity (**pa**-riti) noun 1 equality in status, pay, or value. 2 equivalence between one currency and another. [same origin as for *par*]

park noun **1** a large public garden or recreation ground for public use in a town. **2** an enclosed area of grassland or woodland attached to a country house. **3** a parking area for vehicles ♦ *a coach park*. **4** an area of land for a particular activity ♦ *a wildlife park* ♦ *a science park*.
park verb **1** to leave a vehicle somewhere for a time. **2** (*informal*) to leave something somewhere until you need it ♦ *You can park your bag by the door.* **to park yourself** (*informal*) to sit down. [from an Old French word *parc*]

parka noun **1** a windproof jacket with a hood, worn in cold weather. **2** a hooded jacket made of animal skin, worn by Inuits. [via an Eskimo language from a Russian word]

parking meter noun a coin-operated machine in which fees are inserted for parking a vehicle beside it in the street.

parking ticket noun a notice of a fine imposed for parking a vehicle illegally.

Parkinson's disease noun a disease of the nervous system that makes a person's arms and legs shake and the muscles become stiff. [named after the English surgeon J. Parkinson (1755–1824)]

parkland noun open grassland with scattered trees.

parky adjective (**parkier, parkiest**) (*informal*) chilly. [origin unknown]

parlance (par-ləns) noun a way of using words, phraseology ♦ *medical parlance* ♦ *a word in common parlance.* [same origin as for *parley*]

parley noun (**parleys**) a discussion between enemies or opponents to settle points in dispute.
parley verb (**parleyed, parleying**) to hold a parley. [from a French word *parler* meaning 'to speak']

parliament (par-lə-mənt) noun an assembly that makes the laws of a country. **Parliament** noun the parliament of the UK, consisting of the House of Commons and the House of Lords. [from an Old French word *parlement* meaning 'speaking']

parliamentarian (parlə-men-**tair**-iən) noun **1** a person who is skilled at debating in parliament and has a good knowledge of its procedures. **2** a supporter of Parliament in the English Civil War.

parliamentary (parlə-ment-eri) adjective to do with parliament.

parlour noun **1** (*old use*) a sitting room in a private house. **2** a place for milking cows. **3** a shop or business ♦ *an ice-cream parlour.* [originally denoting a room in a monastery where the monks were allowed to talk: from a French word *parler* meaning 'to speak']

parlour game noun an indoor game, especially a word game.

parlourmaid noun (*historical*) a maid employed to wait on a household at meals.

parlous (par-ləs) adjective (*old use*) precarious, hard to deal with ♦ *the parlous state of the economy.* [from *perilous*]

Parmesan (par-mi-zan) noun a kind of hard dry Italian cheese, usually grated before use. [from an Italian word *Parmigiano* meaning 'of Parma']

parochial (pə-roh-kiəl) adjective **1** to do with a church parish. **2** merely local; showing interest in your own area only ♦ *a narrow parochial attitude.* **parochialism** noun [from an Old French word]

parody (pa-rə-di) noun (**parodies**) **1** an amusing imitation of the style of a writer, composer, literary work, etc. **2** a poor or grotesque imitation of something ♦ *a parody of a smile.*
parody verb (**parodies, parodied, parodying**) to produce a parody of something. [from *para-* meaning 'beside' and a Greek word *ōidē* meaning 'song']

parole (pə-rohl) noun the release of a convicted person from a prison before the end of his or her sentence, on condition of good behaviour.
parole verb to release a prisoner on parole. [from a French word meaning 'word of honour']

paroxysm (pa-rək-sizm) noun a sudden attack or outburst of pain, rage, or laughter etc. [from a Greek word *paroxunein* meaning 'to annoy or exasperate']

parquet (par-kay) noun flooring of wooden blocks arranged in a pattern. [from a French word meaning 'little park']

parrot noun a tropical bird with a short hooked bill and often with brightly coloured plumage.
parrot verb (**parroted, parroting**) to repeat another person's words, especially without understanding what you are saying. [from a French word]

parry verb (**parries, parried, parrying**) 1 to turn aside an opponent's weapon or blow by using your own weapon etc. to block the thrust. 2 to avoid an awkward question skilfully.
parry noun (**parries**) an act of parrying. [from an Italian word *parare* meaning 'to defend']

parse (parz) verb to identify the grammatical form and function of words in a sentence. [from a Latin word *pars* meaning 'part (of speech)']

parsec (par-sek) noun (in astronomy) a unit of distance equal to about $3\frac{1}{4}$ light years. [from *parallax* and *second*]

Parsee (par-see) noun a person who believes in Zoroastrianism, especially one living in India. [from a Persian word]

parsimonious (par-si-moh-niəs) adjective stingy, very sparing in the use of resources. **parsimoniously** adverb **parsimony** (par-sim-əni) noun [from a Latin word *parcere* meaning 'to be sparing']

parsley noun a garden plant with crinkled green leaves used for seasoning and decorating food and in sauces. [via Old French from a Latin word]

parsnip noun 1 a large yellowish tapering root with a sweet flavour that is used as a vegetable. 2 the plant that produces this root. [from an Old French word *pasnaie*]

parson noun a member of the clergy, especially a rector or vicar. [from an Old French word *persone* meaning 'person']

parsonage noun a rectory or vicarage.

parson's nose noun (informal) the rump of a cooked fowl.

part noun 1 some but not all of a thing or number of things; anything that belongs to something bigger. SYNONYMS: portion, bit, constituent, component, element, unit, section, segment. 2 a division of a book or television serial etc., especially as much as is published or broadcast at one time ♦ Henry IV, Part II. 3 a component of a machine ♦ spare parts. 4 each of several equal portions of a whole ♦ Add three parts oil to one part vinegar. 5 a region ♦ What brings you to these parts? SYNONYMS: district, neighbourhood, quarter, vicinity. 6 an integral element ♦ We think of her as part of the family. 7 a distinct portion of a human or animal body or of a plant. 8 the character played by an actor or actress; the words spoken by this character. 9 the melody or other line of music assigned to a particular voice or instrument. 10 how much someone is involved in something ♦ She played a huge part in her daughter's success. 11 a side in an agreement or in a dispute.
part adverb in part, partly ♦ part comedy, part tragedy.
part verb 1 to separate or divide; to cause something to do this. 2 to separate the hair on either side of a parting with a comb. 3 (said about two people) to leave each other. **for my part** as far as I am concerned. **in part** partly. **a man of (many) parts** a man with many abilities. **on the part of** used to say who is responsible for something. **part and parcel of** an essential part of. **to part company** to go different ways after being together; to cease to be together. **to part with** to give something away or get rid of it. **to take something in good part** to not take offence at something. **to take part** to join in or be involved in an activity. [from a Latin word *pars*]

partake verb (**partook, partaken**) 1 to join in something. 2 to eat or drink something. **partaker** noun [from *part* and *take*]

part exchange noun a transaction in which you give something that you own as part of the payment for something more expensive you are buying.

parthenogenesis (par-thin-ə-jen-i-sis) noun (Biology) reproduction from gametes without fertilization. **parthenogenetic** (par-thin-oh-jin-et-ik) adjective [from a Greek word *parthenos* meaning 'virgin' and *genesis*]

Parthian shot (par-thi-ən) noun a sharp remark made on leaving, a parting shot. [named after the horsemen of Parthia (an ancient kingdom in what is now Iran), who were famous for turning to shoot their arrows at the enemy while retreating]

partial (par-shəl) adjective 1 in part but not complete or total ♦ a partial eclipse. 2 favouring one side more than the other; biased. **to be partial to** to have a strong liking for something. **partially** adverb [from an Old French word]

partiality (par-shi-al-iti) noun 1 bias, favouritism. 2 a strong liking.

participate (par-tiss-i-payt) verb to take part in something. **participant** noun **participation** noun [from Latin words *pars* meaning 'part' and *capere* meaning 'to take']

participle (par-tiss-ipəl) *noun* (*Grammar*) a word formed from a verb (e.g. *going*, *gone*; *burning*, *burnt*) and used with an auxiliary verb to form certain tenses (e.g. *It has gone*, *It is going*) or the passive (e.g. *We were guided to our seats*), or as an adjective (e.g. *a guided missile*, *a going concern*). The **past participle** (e.g. *burnt*, *frightened*, *wasted*) describes a completed action or past condition. The **present participle** (e.g. *burning*, *frightening*, *wasting*) describes a continuing action or condition.
participial (par-ti-**sip**-iəl) *adjective* [from a Latin word *particeps* meaning 'taking part']

particle *noun* 1 a very small portion of matter. 2 (*Physics*) a subatomic constituent of the physical world, e.g. an electron or proton. 3 (*Grammar*) a part of speech that does not inflect and has a grammatical function, e.g. *in*, *up*, *off*, or *over*. [from a Latin word meaning 'little part']

particle physics *noun* the branch of physics dealing with the properties and behaviour of subatomic particles.

particoloured *adjective* coloured partly in one colour and partly in another or others.

particular *adjective* 1 relating to one person or thing as distinct from others, individual ♦ *This particular stamp is very rare*. SYNONYMS: specific, individual, distinct, certain. 2 especially great ♦ *Take particular care when handling these substances.* 3 selecting carefully, insisting on certain standards ♦ *He is very particular about what he eats.*
particular *noun* a detail, a piece of information ♦ *Here are the particulars of the case.* **in particular** 1 particularly, especially ♦ *We liked this one in particular.* 2 special ♦ *We did nothing in particular.*
particularity (pə-tik-yoo-la-riti) *noun*
particularly *adverb* [same origin as for *particle*]

particularize *verb* (*formal*) to treat something individually or in detail.
particularization *noun*

parting *noun* 1 leaving or separation. 2 a line where hair is combed away in different directions.

parting shot *noun* a sharp remark made by a person on leaving.

partisan (parti-**zan**) *noun* 1 a strong supporter of a person, group, or cause. 2 a member of an armed group resisting the authorities in a conquered country.
partisan *adjective* strongly supporting a particular cause. **partisanship** *noun* [via French from an Italian word *partigiano*]

partition (par-**tish**-ən) *noun* 1 a thin wall that divides a room or space. 2 dividing something, especially a country, into separate parts. 3 a part formed in this way.
partition *verb* 1 to divide something into separate parts. 2 to divide a room or space by means of a partition. [from a Latin word *partitio* meaning 'division']

partly *adverb* to some extent but not completely or wholly.

partner *noun* 1 a person who shares in some activity with one or more other people, especially in a business firm where risks and profits are shared. 2 either of two people doing something as a pair, such as dancing together or playing tennis or cards etc. on the same side. 3 a person that someone is married to or is having a sexual relationship with. **partner** *verb* to be the partner of someone. **partnership** *noun* [from a Latin word *partiri* meaning 'to divide or share']

part of speech *noun* one of the classes into which words are divided in grammar, e.g. noun, adjective, pronoun, verb, adverb, preposition, conjunction, and interjection; a word class.

partook past tense of **partake**.

partridge *noun* (**partridge** or **partridges**) a game bird with brown feathers and a plump body. [from an Old French word *pertriz*]

part song *noun* a song with three or more voice parts, often without accompaniment.

part-time *adjective* & *adverb* for only part of the usual working day or week ♦ *a part-time job.*

part-timer *noun* a person employed in part-time work.

parturition (par-tewr-**ish**-ən) *noun* a technical term for giving birth; childbirth. [from a Latin word *parturire* meaning 'to be in labour']

party *noun* (**parties**) 1 a social gathering, usually of invited guests. 2 a political group organized on a national basis to put forward its policies and candidates for office. 3 a number of people travelling or

working together as a unit ♦ *a search party.*
4 a person or group forming one side in an
agreement or dispute. **5** (*informal*) a
person. **to be (a) party to** to be involved in
something. [from *part*]

party line *noun* **1** the set policy of a political
party. **2** a shared telephone line.

party wall *noun* a wall that is common to
two rooms or buildings which it divides.

Pascal (pas-kahl) *noun* a computer
language, used especially in training.
[named after the French mathematician,
physicist, and religious philosopher
Blaise Pascal (1623–62)]

pascal (pas-kəl) *noun* a unit of pressure,
equal to one newton per square metre.
[named after Blaise Pascal]

paschal (pas-kəl) *adjective* (*formal*) **1** to do
with the Jewish Passover. **2** to do with
Easter. [from a Latin word *pascha*
meaning 'feast of Passover']

pas de deux (pah der der) *noun* (**pas de deux**)
(in ballet) a dance for two people. [a
French phrase meaning 'step of two']

Pashto (push-toh) *noun* the language of the
Pathans, spoken in parts of Afghanistan
and Pakistan.

pass [1] *verb* **1** to go or move past something
or to the other side of something ♦ *An old
man passed me on the stairs.* **2** to go or move
in a certain direction ♦ *The road passes
through the centre of town.* **3** to move
something across, over, or past another
thing ♦ *Pass the cord through the ring.* **4** to
hand or transfer something to another
person ♦ *Could you pass me the butter?* **5** to
go from one person to another, to be
transferred ♦ *His title passed to his eldest
son.* **6** (in ball games) to kick or throw the
ball to another player of your own side.
7 to change from one state or condition to
another. **8** to go away ♦ *The pain soon
passed.* SYNONYMS: fade, disappear, vanish.
9 to happen, to be done or said ♦ *We heard
what passed between them.* **10** (said about
time) to go by. SYNONYMS: elapse, lapse.
11 to occupy time ♦ *I passed the time doing a
crossword.* **12** to be accepted or currently
known in a certain way ♦ *You could easily
pass for 18.* **13** to be tolerated, allowed, or
ignored ♦ *Let it pass.* **14** to be successful in
a test or examination; to be accepted as
satisfactory. **15** to judge the performance
or standard of someone or something to
be satisfactory. **16** to approve a law or
measure, especially by voting on it. **17** to
go beyond something. **18** to utter
remarks; to pronounce a judgement or

sentence ♦ *I don't like to pass criticism.* **19** to
discharge urine etc. from the body. **20** (in
a card game or a quiz) to let your turn go
by or choose not to answer.

pass *noun* **1** moving past or through
something. **2** a success in an examination.
3 a permit to go into or out of a place or
travel on a bus etc. **4** (in ball games)
kicking or throwing the ball to another
player of your own side. **5** a critical state
of affairs ♦ *Things have come to a pretty pass.*
to make a pass at (*informal*) to try to
attract someone sexually. **to pass away** to
die. **to pass someone by** to happen
without someone really noticing. **to pass
off** (said about an event) to take place in a
particular way ♦ *The meeting passed off
smoothly.* **to pass something off 1** to evade
or dismiss an awkward remark etc.
lightly. **2** to offer or sell something under
false pretences ♦ *He passed it off as his own
work.* **to pass out 1** to faint. **2** to complete
your military training. **to pass someone
over** to ignore the claims of a person to
promotion etc. **to pass something over** to
disregard something. **to pass something
up** to refuse to accept an opportunity. **to
pass water** to urinate. [from a Latin
word *passus* meaning 'pace']

pass [2] *noun* a gap in a mountain range,
allowing access to the other side.

passable *adjective* **1** satisfactory, fairly
good but not outstanding. **2** able to be
travelled along or over ♦ *The road is now
passable again.* **passably** *adverb*

passage *noun* **1** a way through something,
especially with walls on either side. **2** the
process of passing ♦ *the passage of time.*
3 a particular section of a piece of writing
or music. SYNONYMS: excerpt, extract,
quotation, piece. **4** a journey by sea or air.
5 the right to pass through somewhere;
the right of being carried as a passenger
by sea or air. [from an Old French word]

passageway *noun* a corridor or other
passage between buildings or rooms.

passbook *noun* a book recording a
customer's deposits and withdrawals
from a bank or building society account.

passé (pas-ay) *adjective* no longer
fashionable. [a French word meaning
'passed']

passenger *noun* **1** a person who travels in a
vehicle or ship or aircraft, other than the
driver, pilot, or members of the crew. **2** a
member of a team who does no effective
work. [same origin as for *passage*]

passer-by noun (**passers-by**) a person who happens to be going past something.

passim (pas-im) adverb at various places throughout a book or article etc. [a Latin word meaning 'everywhere']

passing adjective not lasting long, casual ♦ *a passing glance.*
passing noun the end of something, a death. **in passing** briefly and casually.

passing note noun (*Music*) a note that does not belong to the harmony but is put in to make a smooth transition.

passion noun 1 strong emotion. 2 an outburst of strong emotion, especially anger ♦ *He spoke with passion.* SYNONYMS: vehemence, intensity, force, fervour. 3 sexual love. SYNONYMS: ardour, desire, lust. 4 great enthusiasm for something, or the object of this ♦ *Chess is his passion.*
Passion noun 1 the suffering and death of Jesus Christ. 2 a musical setting of this. [from a Latin word *passio* meaning 'suffering']

passionate adjective 1 full of passion, showing or moved by strong emotion. 2 (said about emotion) intense.
passionately adverb

passion flower noun a climbing plant with flowers thought to resemble the crown of thorns and other things associated with the Passion of Christ.

passion fruit noun the edible fruit of some kinds of passion flower.

Passion Sunday noun the fifth Sunday in Lent.

passive adjective 1 acted upon by an external force; not active. 2 not resisting or opposing what happens or what others do. SYNONYMS: submissive, compliant, docile. 3 lacking initiative or forceful qualities. 4 (*Grammar*) denoting the form of a verb used when the subject of the sentence receives the action, e.g. *they were killed* as opposed to *he killed them.* 5 (*Chemistry*) (said about substances) inert, not active.
passive noun (*Grammar*) the passive form of a verb. **passively** adverb **passiveness** noun **passivity** (pa-siv-iti) noun [from a Latin word *passivus* meaning 'capable of suffering']

passive resistance noun non-violent resistance to authority by a refusal to cooperate.

passive smoking noun breathing in smoke from cigarettes etc. smoked by others, considered as a health risk.

pass key noun 1 a key to a door or gate. 2 a master key.

Passover noun a Jewish festival commemorating the liberation of the Jews from slavery in Egypt. [from *pass over* (because God spared the Jews from the fate which affected the Egyptians)]

passport noun 1 an official document issued by a government identifying the holder as one of its citizens and entitling him or her to travel abroad under its protection. 2 a thing that enables you to obtain something ♦ *Hard work alone is not a passport to success.* [from *pass*[1] and *port*[1]]

password noun 1 a secret word or phrase used to distinguish friends from enemies. 2 a word you need to key in to gain access to certain computer files.

past adjective 1 belonging or referring to the time before the present ♦ *in past centuries* ♦ *his past achievements.* 2 just gone by ♦ *the past twelve months.* 3 (*Grammar*) (said about a tense) denoting an action or state that went on before the time of speaking or writing (e.g. *he came, he had come*).
past noun 1 time that is gone by ♦ *I've been there in the past.* 2 past events ♦ *She looks back on the past with regret.* 3 a person's earlier life or career, especially when this is disreputable ♦ *a man with a past.* 4 (*Grammar*) the past tense.
past preposition 1 up to and beyond ♦ *She hurried past me.* 2 after, later than ♦ *It is past midnight* ♦ *ten past six.* 3 beyond the limits, power, range, or stage of something ♦ *What they did next is past belief* ♦ *He's past caring what happens to him.*
past adverb beyond in time or place, up to and further ♦ *I looked into the window as I walked past.* **to not put it past someone** (*informal*) to regard someone as capable of doing something wrong or rash. **past it** (*informal*) too old to be able to do something. [the old past participle of *pass*]

pasta (pas-tə) noun 1 an Italian food consisting of a dried paste made with flour and produced in various shapes (e.g. spaghetti, lasagne). 2 a cooked dish made with this. [an Italian word meaning 'paste']

paste noun 1 a moist fairly stiff mixture, especially of a powdery substance and a liquid. 2 an adhesive. 3 a creamy mass of ground meat or fish etc., for spreading on bread ♦ anchovy paste. 4 an edible doughy mixture ♦ almond paste. 5 a hard glass-like substance used to make imitation jewellery.
paste verb 1 to stick something onto a surface with paste. 2 to coat something with paste. 3 (Computing) to insert a section of text into a document.
4 (informal) to beat or thrash someone. [from a Greek word]

pasteboard noun thin board made of layers of paper or wood fibres pasted together.

pastel (pas-təl) noun 1 a chalk-like crayon. 2 a drawing made with this. 3 a light delicate shade of a colour. [from a Latin word pastellus meaning 'woad']

pastern (pas-tern) noun the part of a horse's foot between the fetlock and the hoof. [from an Old French word pasturon]

pasteurize (pahs-chŏriyz) verb to sterilize milk etc. partially by heating and then chilling it. **pasteurization** noun [named after the French chemist and bacteriologist Louis Pasteur (1822–95), who invented the process]

pastiche (pas-teesh) noun a piece of music or writing etc. in a style that imitates another work, artist, or period. [from a Latin word pasta meaning 'paste']

pastille (pas-təl) noun a small sweet or lozenge. [from a Latin word pastillus meaning 'lozenge']

pastime noun something you do regularly for enjoyment. SYNONYMS: hobby, pursuit, interest, recreation, diversion.

past master noun a person who is experienced in and skilled at a subject or activity.

pastor (pah-ster) noun a member of the Christian clergy in charge of a church or congregation. [a Latin word meaning 'shepherd']

pastoral (pah-ster-əl) adjective 1 to do with shepherds or country life ♦ a pastoral scene. 2 to do with the giving of spiritual guidance ♦ pastoral theology. 3 to do with a teacher's responsibility to look after the general well-being of students or pupils.

pastry noun (pastries) 1 a dough made of flour, fat, and water, used for covering pies or holding a filling. 2 a cake of sweet pastry with a cream, jam, or fruit filling. [from paste]

pasturage (pahs-cher-ij) noun 1 pasture land. 2 the right to graze animals on pasture land.

pasture noun 1 land covered mainly with grass, suitable for grazing cattle or sheep. 2 grass and other plants growing on such land.
pasture verb 1 to put animals to graze in a pasture. 2 (said about animals) to graze. [from a Latin word pastura meaning 'grazing']

pasty[1] (pas-ti) noun (pasties) pastry with a filling of meat and vegetables, baked without a dish. [from an Old French word pasté meaning 'paste or pastry']

pasty[2] (pay-sti) adjective (pastier, pastiest) 1 of or like paste. 2 unhealthily pale ♦ a pasty-faced boy.

pat verb (patted, patting) 1 to tap something gently with the open hand or with something flat. 2 to flatten or shape something by doing this.
pat noun 1 a patting movement or sound. 2 a small mass of butter or other soft substance.
pat adjective & adverb readily given or prepared in advance ♦ a pat answer ♦ He had his excuses off pat. **a pat on the back** praise or congratulations. [probably an imitation of the sound]

patch noun 1 a piece of material or metal etc. put over a hole or damaged place to mend it. 2 a shield worn over the eye, to protect it. 3 a piece of material containing a drug and worn on the skin so that the drug can be gradually absorbed ♦ a nicotine patch. 4 a large or irregular area on a surface, differing in colour or texture etc. from the rest. 5 a piece of ground, especially for growing vegetables ♦ a cabbage patch. 6 an area for which a person is responsible or where they do their job. 7 a small area or piece of something ♦ patches of fog. 8 a short period ♦ Their marriage was going through a bad patch.
patch verb 1 to sew a patch on something. 2 to piece things together. **not a patch on** (informal) not nearly as good as. **to patch something up** 1 to repair something roughly. 2 to settle a quarrel or dispute. [probably from an Old French word pieche meaning 'piece']

patch pocket *noun* a pocket made by sewing a piece of cloth on the surface of a piece of clothing.

patchwork *noun* 1 needlework in which assorted small pieces of cloth are joined edge to edge, often in a pattern. 2 anything made of assorted pieces or elements.

patchy *adjective* (**patchier, patchiest**) 1 existing in small isolated areas ♦ *patchy fog*. 2 uneven in quality. **patchily** *adverb* **patchiness** *noun*

pate (payt) *noun* (*old use*) the top of a person's head. [origin unknown]

pâté (pa-tay) *noun* a rich paste made of meat or fish. [a French word]

patella (pə-tel-ə) *noun* (*Anatomy*) the kneecap. [from a Latin word *patina* meaning 'shallow dish']

paten (pat-ən) *noun* a metal plate on which bread is placed during the Eucharist. [from a Greek word meaning 'a plate']

patent[1] (pat-ənt or pay-tənt) *noun* 1 the official right given to an inventor to make or sell his or her invention and to prevent other people from copying it. 2 an invention or process protected in this way.

patent[2] (pay-tənt) *adjective* 1 obvious, unconcealed ♦ *his patent dislike of the plan*. 2 protected by a patent ♦ *patent medicines*. **patent** *verb* to obtain a patent for an invention. **patently** *adverb* [originally, in *letters patent*, an open letter from a monarch or government recording a contract or granting a right: from a Latin word *patens* meaning 'lying open']

patentee (pay-tən-tee or pat-ən-tee) *noun* a person who holds a patent.

patent leather *noun* leather with a glossy varnished surface.

Patent Office *noun* the government office from which patents are issued.

pater (pay-ter) *noun* (*old use*) father. [a Latin word]

paternal (pə-ter-nəl) *adjective* 1 to do with a father or fatherhood. 2 fatherly. 3 related through your father ♦ *my paternal grandmother*. **paternally** *adverb* [from a Latin word *pater* meaning 'father']

paternalism (pə-ter-nəl-izm) *noun* the policy of treating people in a paternal way, providing for their needs but giving them no responsibility. **paternalistic** *adjective*

paternity (pə-tern-iti) *noun* 1 being the father of a particular child. 2 descent from a father. [from a Latin word *pater* meaning 'father']

paternoster (pat-er-nost-er) *noun* the Lord's Prayer, especially in Latin. [from Latin words *pater noster* meaning 'our father', the first words of the Lord's Prayer]

path *noun* 1 a way by which people or animals can walk, a track. 2 a line along which a person or thing moves. 3 a course of action. [from an Old English word]

Pathan (pə-tahn) *noun* a member of a people living in parts of Afghanistan and Pakistan. [from a Hindi word]

pathetic (pə-thet-ik) *adjective* 1 making you feel pity or sadness. 2 (*informal*) miserably inadequate or useless ♦ *a pathetic attempt*. **pathetically** *adverb* [same origin as for *pathos*]

pathetic fallacy *noun* giving human feelings to inanimate things or animals.

pathfinder *noun* a person who goes ahead and shows other people the way.

pathname *noun* (*Computing*) a description of where an item is to be found in a hierarchy of directories.

pathogen (path-ə-jən) *noun* (*Medicine*) a bacterium, virus, or other micro-organism that can cause disease. [from a Greek word *pathos* meaning 'suffering' and *-gen*]

pathological (pa-thə-loj-ikəl) *adjective* 1 to do with pathology. 2 to do with or caused by disease. 3 (*informal*) compulsive ♦ *a pathological liar*. **pathologically** *adverb*

pathologist (pə-thol-ə-jist) *noun* an expert in pathology.

pathology (pə-thol-əji) *noun* 1 the scientific study of diseases of the body. 2 abnormal changes in body tissue, caused by disease. [from a Greek word *pathos* meaning 'suffering, disease' and *-logy*]

pathos (pay-thoss) *noun* a quality of making people feel pity or sadness. [a Greek word meaning 'suffering']

pathway *noun* a path or track.

-pathy *suffix* forming nouns meaning 'feeling or suffering something' (as in *sympathy, telepathy*). [from a Greek word *patheia* meaning 'suffering, feeling']

patience *noun* 1 the ability to put up calmly with delay, inconvenience, or annoyance without becoming angry or upset. SYNONYMS: tolerance, endurance, forbearance, stoicism. 2 a card game for one player in which cards have to be brought into a particular arrangement. **to lose patience** to be unable to keep your temper.

patient *adjective* having or showing patience.
patient *noun* a person receiving or registered to receive medical treatment by a doctor or dentist etc. **patiently** *adverb* [from a Latin word *patiens* meaning 'suffering']

patina (pat-in-ə) *noun* 1 an attractive green film on the surface of old bronze. 2 a gloss on the surface of wooden furniture produced by age and polishing. [from a Latin word *patina* meaning 'shallow dish']

patio (pat-i-oh) *noun* (**patios**) 1 a paved area beside a house, used for outdoor meals or relaxation. 2 an inner courtyard, open to the sky, in a Spanish or Spanish-American house. [a Spanish word meaning 'courtyard']

patois (pat-wah) *noun* a dialect. [a French word meaning 'rough speech']

patriarch (pay-tri-ark) *noun* 1 the male head of a family or tribe. 2 a powerful old man. 3 one of the men in the Bible named as the ancestors of mankind or of the tribes of Israel. 4 a bishop of high rank in the Orthodox Christian Churches. **patriarchal** (pay-tri-**ar**-kəl) *adjective* [from Greek words *patria* meaning 'family' and *arkhein* meaning 'to rule']

patrician (pə-**trish**-ən) *noun* 1 an aristocrat or nobleman. 2 a member of the noble class in ancient Rome.
patrician *adjective* aristocratic. [from a Latin word *patricius* meaning 'having a noble father']

patricide (pat-ri-siyd) *noun* 1 the crime of killing your own father. 2 a person who kills their own father. [from a Latin word *pater* meaning 'father' and *caedere* meaning 'to kill']

patrimony (pat-rim-ə-ni) *noun* (**patrimonies**) 1 property inherited from your father or ancestors, a heritage. 2 a church's endowed income or property. [from a Latin word *patris* meaning 'of a father']

patriot (**pay**-tri-ət or **pat**-ri-ət) *noun* a person who loves their country and supports it loyally. [from a Greek word *patris* meaning 'fatherland']

patriotic (pat-ri-ot-ik) *adjective* loyally supporting your country. **patriotically** *adverb* **patriotism** (**pat**-riə-tizm) *noun*

patrol *verb* (**patrolled, patrolling**) to walk or travel regularly over an area in order to guard it and see that all is well.
patrol *noun* the people, ships, or aircraft whose job is to patrol an area. **on patrol** patrolling. [from a French word *patouiller* meaning 'to paddle in mud']

patrolman *noun* (**patrolmen**) (North Amer.) a patrolling police officer.

patron (**pay**-trən) *noun* 1 a person who supports a person or cause with money or encouragement. 2 a famous or important person who takes an honorary position in a charity. 3 a regular customer of a restaurant, hotel, shop, etc. 4 a patron saint. **patroness** *noun* [from a Latin word *patronus* meaning 'protector']

patronage (pat-rən-ij) *noun* 1 support given by a patron. 2 the power to appoint people to office. 3 patronizing behaviour. 4 regular custom.

patronize (pat-rə-niyz) *verb* 1 to talk to someone in a way that shows you think they are stupid or inferior to you. 2 to be a regular customer at a restaurant, shop, etc. 3 to act as a patron towards a person or organization.

patronizing *adjective* condescending. **patronizingly** *adverb*

patron saint *noun* a saint who is thought to give special protection to a person, place, or activity.

patronymic (pat-rə-nim-ik) *noun* a person's name that is taken from the name of the father or a male ancestor. [from Greek words *patros* meaning 'of a father' and *ōnoma* meaning 'name']

patter [1] *verb* 1 to make a series of light quick tapping sounds ♦ *Rain pattered on the window panes.* 2 to run with short quick steps.
patter *noun* a series of light quick tapping sounds. [from *pat*]

patter [2] *noun* the rapid continuous talk of a comedian, conjuror, salesperson, etc. [originally meaning 'to recite a prayer': from *patemoster*]

pattern noun 1 a repeated arrangement of lines, shapes, or colours; a decorative design. 2 the regular way in which something happens ♦ *James Bond films follow a set pattern* ♦ *behaviour patterns*. 3 a model, design, or instructions according to which something is to be made ♦ *a dress pattern*. 4 a sample of cloth or other material. 5 an excellent example or model.
pattern verb 1 to decorate something with a pattern. 2 to model something according to a pattern. [same origin as for *patron*]

patty noun (**patties**) 1 a small pie or pasty. 2 a small flat cake of minced meat etc. [from *pâté*]

paucity (paw-siti) noun (*formal*) smallness of supply or quantity. [from a Latin word *pauci* meaning 'few']

paunch noun a large stomach that sticks out. [from an Old French word]

pauper noun a very poor person. [from a Latin word meaning 'poor']

pause noun 1 a temporary stop in speaking or doing something. SYNONYMS: break, interlude, interval, interruption, lull, hiatus, respite. 2 a control that temporarily interrupts the playing of a CD, video tape, etc.
pause verb 1 to stop speaking or doing something for a short time. 2 to temporarily interrupt the playing of a CD, video tape, etc. **to give pause to** to cause someone to hesitate or think carefully. [from a Greek word *pausein* meaning 'to stop']

pavane (pə-van) noun a kind of stately dance, or the music for this. [via French from an Italian word]

pave verb to cover a road or path etc. with stones or concrete etc. to make a hard surface. **to pave the way** to prepare the way for changes etc. [from a Latin word *pavire* meaning 'to ram down']

pavement noun 1 a paved path for pedestrians at the side of a road. 2 (*Geology*) a horizontal area of bare rock with cracks or joints ♦ *a limestone pavement*.

pavilion noun 1 a building on a sports ground for use by players and spectators, especially at a cricket ground. 2 an ornamental building or shelter used for dances, concerts, exhibitions, etc. 3 a light building or other structure used as a shelter in a park or large garden. [from a French word *pavillon* meaning 'tent']

paving stone noun a slab of stone for paving.

pavlova (pav-loh-və) noun an open meringue case filled with cream and fruit. [named after the Russian ballerina Anna Pavlova (1885–1931)]

paw noun 1 the foot of an animal that has claws. 2 (*informal*) a person's hand.
paw verb 1 to feel or scrape something with a paw or hoof. 2 (*informal*) to touch something awkwardly or rudely with the hands. [from an Old French word *poue*]

pawl noun a bar or lever with a catch that fits into the notches of a ratchet. [origin unknown]

pawn [1] noun 1 the least valuable chess piece. 2 a person used by others for their own purposes. [from a Latin word *pedo* meaning 'foot soldier']

pawn [2] verb to leave something with a pawnbroker as security for money borrowed. **in pawn** the state of being pawned. [from an Old French word *pan* meaning 'pledge']

pawnbroker noun a shopkeeper who lends money at interest to people in return for objects that they leave as security.

pawnshop noun a pawnbroker's shop.

pawpaw noun 1 another word for *papaya*. 2 a North American tree with edible yellow fruit with sweet pulp. 3 the fruit of this tree. [from a Spanish and Portuguese word *papaya*]

pay verb (past tense and past participle , **paid**) 1 to give someone money in return for work, goods, or services. SYNONYMS: spend; (*informal*) fork out, cough up, stump up. 2 to give what is owed ♦ *I always pay my debts* ♦ *Have you paid the rent?* SYNONYMS: settle, clear, meet. 3 to be profitable or worthwhile ♦ *It pays to advertise*. 4 to suffer a penalty or misfortune. 5 to give or express something ♦ *Now pay attention* ♦ *We paid them a visit last week* ♦ *She was not used to people paying her compliments*. 6 to let out a rope by loosening it gradually.
pay noun money paid for work. **in the pay of** employed by. **to pay someone back** to take revenge on someone. **to pay for** to suffer or be punished because of a mistake etc. **to pay its way** to make enough profit to cover costs. **to pay off** (*informal*) to yield good results ♦ *The risk paid off*. **to pay someone off** to dismiss an

employee with a final payment. **to pay something off** to pay a debt in full. **to pay your way** to earn enough to cover your expenses. **to pay up** to pay the full amount you owe. **payer** noun [from a Latin word *pacare* meaning 'to appease']

payable adjective needing to be paid.

pay-as-you-earn noun a method of collecting income tax by deducting it at source from an employee's wages.

PAYE abbreviation pay-as-you-earn.

payee (pay-ee) noun a person to whom money is paid or is to be paid.

payload noun 1 the part of an aircraft's load from which revenue is derived, i.e. passengers or cargo. 2 an explosive warhead carried by an aircraft or missile.

paymaster noun 1 a person who pays someone else to do something and so controls them. 2 an official who pays troops or workers.

Paymaster General noun the minister at the head of the department of the Treasury through which payments are made.

payment noun 1 paying or being paid. 2 money given in return for work, goods, or services.

pay-off noun (informal) 1 a payment, especially one made as a bribe or on leaving a job. 2 the return on investment or on a bet. 3 a final outcome or climax, especially of a joke or story.

payola (pay-oh-lə) noun a bribe offered to promote a commercial product. [from *pay* and *-ola* in Victrola, an old make of gramophone (because it originally meant a bribe given to a disc jockey to play a record)]

payphone noun a public telephone operated by coins or a card.

payroll noun a list of a firm's employees receiving regular pay.

Pb abbreviation (Chemistry) the symbol for lead. [from the Latin word *plumbum* meaning 'lead']

PC abbreviation 1 personal computer. 2 police constable. 3 politically correct.

p.c. abbreviation 1 per cent. 2 postcard.

PDSA abbreviation People's Dispensary for Sick Animals.

PE abbreviation physical education.

pea noun 1 a small round green seed eaten as a vegetable. 2 the climbing plant bearing these seeds in pods. [via an old word *pease* meaning 'pea', from a Greek word *pison*]

peace noun 1 freedom from or the ending of war. 2 a treaty ending a war ♦ *After three years of conflict, the peace was signed.* 3 freedom from civil disorder ♦ *a breach of the peace.* 4 undisturbed quietness and calm ♦ *peace of mind.* SYNONYMS: serenity, tranquillity, stillness. 5 a state of harmony between people. **at peace** 1 free from anxiety or distress. 2 dead. **to keep the peace** to not disturb civil order, or stop others from doing so. **to make (your) peace** to become reconciled. [from a Latin word *pax* meaning 'peace']

peaceable adjective 1 not quarrelsome, wanting to be at peace with others. 2 peaceful, without strife. **peaceably** adverb

peaceful adjective 1 quiet and calm. SYNONYMS: serene, tranquil, still, placid, pacific, undisturbed. 2 not involving war or violence. **peacefully** adverb **peacefulness** noun

peacekeeping noun maintaining a truce, especially by an international military force. **peacekeeper** noun

peacemaker noun a person who brings about peace.

peace offering noun something offered to show that you are willing to make peace.

peacetime noun a period when a country is not at war.

peach noun 1 a round juicy fruit with downy yellowish or reddish skin and a large rough stone. 2 the tree that bears this fruit. 3 a yellowish-pink colour. 4 (informal) something that is greatly admired ♦ *a peach of a shot.* **peach** adjective yellowish-pink. **peachy** adjective [from an Old French word *pesche*]

peach Melba noun a dish of ice cream and peaches with raspberry syrup. [from the name of the Australian operatic soprano Dame Nellie Melba (1861–1931)]

peacock noun a male bird with a long brightly-coloured tail that it can spread upright like a fan. [via Old English from a Latin word *pavo*]

peacock blue noun a greenish-blue colour like that of the feathers on a peacock's neck.

pea green noun a bright green colour.

peahen noun the female of a peacock, which has drabber colours and a shorter tail than the male.

peak noun 1 a pointed top of a mountain. 2 a mountain with a pointed top. 3 any shape, edge, or part that tapers to form a point. 4 the part of a cap that sticks out in front. 5 a point on a curve or graph which is higher than those around it. 6 the point of highest value, achievement, or activity ♦ *Traffic reaches its peak between 8 and 9 a.m* ♦ *the peak of her career.* SYNONYMS: pinnacle, culmination, acme, zenith, apogee. **peak** verb to reach its highest point or value. **peak** adjective 1 maximum. 2 when use or demand is at its highest ♦ *peak viewing hours.* [origin unknown]

peaked adjective (said about a cap) having a peak.

peaky adjective (**peakier, peakiest**) looking pale from illness or fatigue. **peakiness** noun [from an old word *peak* meaning 'to decline in health and spirits']

peal noun 1 the loud ringing of a bell or set of bells. 2 a set of bells with different notes. 3 a loud burst of thunder or laughter. **peal** verb (said about bells) to ring loudly. [from *appeal*]

peanut noun 1 a plant bearing pods that ripen underground, containing two edible seeds. 2 this seed, eaten as a snack or used to make oil. **peanuts** noun (informal) a small or trivial amount of money ♦ *She still works for peanuts.*

peanut butter noun a paste of ground roasted peanuts.

pear noun 1 a rounded fleshy fruit that tapers towards the stalk. 2 the tree that bears this fruit. [via Old English from a Latin word *pirum*]

pearl noun 1 a round usually white mass of a shiny substance formed inside the shells of some oysters and valued as a gem ♦ *a string of pearls.* 2 an artificial imitation of this. 3 something resembling a pearl ♦ *pearls of dew.* 4 something valued because of its excellence or beauty ♦ *pearls of wisdom.* 5 a pale greyish-white colour. **pearl** adjective made of or set with pearl or mother-of-pearl. **to cast pearls before swine** to offer a good thing to someone who is not capable of appreciating it. [from an Old French word *perle*]

pearl barley noun barley grains ground small.

pearly adjective (**pearlier, pearliest**) like pearls. **pearliness** noun

Pearly Gates plural noun (informal) the gates of heaven.

pearly king or **pearly queen** noun a London costermonger or his wife wearing traditional clothes decorated with lots of pearl buttons.

peasant (pez-ənt) noun 1 a member of the class of farm labourers and small farmers, especially in a poor country. 2 (informal) an ignorant, rude, or uncultured person. [from a Latin word *paganus* meaning 'villager']

peasantry noun peasants.

pease pudding noun a dish of split peas boiled with onion and carrot and mashed to a pulp. [from an old word *pease* meaning 'pea']

pea-shooter noun a toy tube from which dried peas are shot by blowing.

peat noun vegetable matter decomposed by the action of water in bogs etc. and partly carbonized, used in gardening or cut in pieces as fuel. **peaty** adjective [from a Latin word *peta*, probably from a Celtic word]

pebble noun a small stone worn round and smooth by the action of water. **pebbly** adjective [from an Old English word]

pebble-dash noun mortar with pebbles in it, used as a coating for an outside wall. **pebble-dashed** adjective

pecan noun 1 a smooth pinkish-brown nut like a walnut. 2 a tree of the southern USA which produces these nuts. [from a French word]

peccadillo (pek-ə-dil-oh) noun (**peccadilloes** or **peccadillos**) a small and unimportant fault or offence. [from a Spanish word *pecadillo* meaning 'little sin']

peck[1] verb 1 to bite or strike something with the beak. 2 to kiss someone lightly on the cheek. **peck** noun 1 a quick bite or stroke made with the beak. 2 a light kiss on the cheek. **to peck at** to eat food daintily or without interest. [probably from an Old German word]

peck[2] noun a measure of capacity for dry goods, equivalent to 2 gallons (9.092 litres). [from an Old French word *pek*]

pecker *noun* to keep your pecker up (*informal*) to stay cheerful. [from *pecker* meaning 'beak']

pecking order *noun* a series of ranks of status or authority in which people dominate those below themselves and are dominated by those above, originally as observed among hens.

peckish *adjective* (*informal*) hungry. [from *peck*[1] and *-ish*]

pectin *noun* a jelly-like substance found in ripe fruits, used to make jams and jellies set. [from a Greek word *pektos* meaning 'fixed or set']

pectoral (pek-ter-əl) *adjective* 1 to do with, in, or on the chest or breast ♦ *pectoral muscles*. 2 worn on the chest or breast ♦ *a pectoral cross*.
pectoral *noun* a pectoral muscle or fin. [from a Latin word *pectoris* meaning 'of the breast']

peculate (pek-yoo-layt) *verb* (*formal*) to embezzle money. **peculation** *noun* **peculator** *noun* [same origin as for *peculiar*]

peculiar *adjective* 1 strange or odd.
SYNONYMS: curious, funny, odd, weird.
2 belonging exclusively to a particular person, place, or thing ♦ *customs peculiar to the 18th century*. SYNONYMS: distinctive, individual, characteristic. 3 (*formal*) particular or special ♦ *a point of peculiar interest*. [from a Latin word *peculium* meaning 'private property']

peculiarity *noun* (**peculiarities**) 1 an unusual or distinctive characteristic or habit. 2 being peculiar.

peculiarly *adverb* 1 in a peculiar way. 2 especially ♦ *peculiarly annoying*.

pecuniary (pi-kew-ni-er-i) *adjective* (*formal*) to do with money ♦ *pecuniary aid*. [from a Latin word *pecunia* meaning 'money' (from *pecu* meaning 'cattle' (because in early times wealth consisted of cattle and sheep)]

pedagogic (ped-ə-gog-ik or ped-ə-goj-ik) *adjective* to do with teaching. **pedagogical** *adjective* **pedagogically** *adverb* [from *pedagogue*]

pedagogue (ped-ə-gog) *noun* (*formal*) a teacher, especially one who teaches in a pedantic way. [from a Greek word *paidagōgos* denoting a slave who took a boy to school]

pedal *noun* a lever pressed by the foot to operate a bicycle, car, or other machine, or in certain musical instruments.
pedal *verb* (**pedalled, pedalling**) 1 to move or operate something by means of pedals; to ride a bicycle. 2 to work the pedals of something. [from a Latin word *pedis* meaning 'of a foot']

pedalo (ped-ə-loh) *noun* (**pedalos**) a small pleasure boat operated by pedals.

pedant (ped-ənt) *noun* a person who is too concerned with minor detail or with the strict observance of formal rules.
pedantic (pid-an-tik) *adjective* **pedantically** *adverb* **pedantry** (ped-ən-tri) *noun* [same origin as for *pedagogue*]

peddle *verb* 1 to go from house to house selling goods. 2 to sell illegal drugs. 3 to try to get people to accept an idea, way of life, etc. [from *pedlar*]

peddler *noun* someone who sells illegal drugs.
◊ See also **pedlar**, which is sometimes used in this meaning and also has other meanings.

pederast (peed-er-ast) *noun* a man who has sexual intercourse with a boy. **pederasty** *noun* [from a Greek word *paidos* meaning 'of a boy' and *erastēs* meaning 'lover']

pedestal *noun* 1 the raised base on which a column, pillar, or statue etc. stands. 2 each of the two supports of a kneehole desk. 3 the supporting column or base of a washbasin or toilet. **to put someone on a pedestal** to admire or respect someone greatly or uncritically. [from an Italian word *piede* meaning 'foot' and *stall*[1]]

pedestrian *noun* a person who is walking, especially in a street.
pedestrian *adjective* 1 to do with walking; to do with or for pedestrians. 2 dull and unimaginative. [from a Latin word *pedis* meaning 'of a foot']

pedestrian crossing *noun* a place where pedestrians can cross the road safely.

pedestrianize *verb* to make a street or area accessible only to pedestrians. **pedestrianization** *noun*

pedigree *noun* 1 the record of an animal's descent that shows pure breeding. 2 a line or list of a person's ancestors.
pedigree *adjective* (said about animals) having a recorded line of descent that shows pure breeding. [from an Old French phrase *pé du grue* meaning 'crane's

foot', from the shape made by the lines on a family tree]

pediment (ped-i-mənt) *noun* (*Architecture*) a wide triangular part decorating the top of the front of a building. [origin unknown]

pedlar *noun* **1** a person who goes from house to house selling small goods. **2** a person who sells illegal drugs. [from an old word *ped* meaning 'a hamper or basket', in which a pedlar carried goods] ◊ See also **peddler**, which is also sometimes used in meaning 2.

pedometer (pid-om-it-er) *noun* an instrument that calculates the distance a person walks by counting the number of steps taken. [from a Latin word *pedis* meaning 'of a foot' and *meter*]

peek *verb* to have a quick or sly look at something.
peek *noun* a quick or sly look. [origin unknown]

peel [1] *noun* the skin or rind of certain fruits and vegetables.
peel *verb* **1** to remove the peel from a fruit or vegetable. **2** to pull off an outer layer or covering. **3** (said of a surface) to lose its outer layer in small strips or pieces ♦ *The walls have begun to peel.* **to peel off** (said about an aircraft or vehicle) to veer away from the main group. **to peel something off** to take off a piece of clothing. **peeler** *noun* [from a Latin word *pilare* meaning 'to cut off the hair']

peel [2] *noun* a small square tower built as a fortification in the 16th century near the border between England and Scotland. [from an Old French word *pel* meaning 'stake, palisade']

peelings *plural noun* strips of skin peeled from potatoes etc.

peep [1] *verb* **1** to look quickly or surreptitiously through a narrow opening or from a hidden place. **2** to come briefly or partially into view ♦ *The moon peeped out from behind the clouds.*
peep *noun* a brief or surreptitious look. [origin unknown]

peep [2] *noun* **1** a weak high chirping sound like that made by young birds. **2** a brief high-pitched electronic sound.
peep *verb* to make a peep. [an imitation of the sound]

peephole *noun* a small hole to peep through.

peer [1] *verb* **1** to look at something closely or with difficulty. **2** to be just visible. [from *appear*]

peer [2] *noun* **1** a member of the nobility in Britain, including the ranks of duke, marquess, earl, viscount, and baron. **2** a person of the same age, status, or ability as someone else ♦ *She has no peer.* [from a Latin word *par* meaning 'equal']

peerage *noun* **1** peers as a group. **2** the rank of peer or peeress ♦ *He was raised to the peerage.* **3** a book containing a list of peers.

peeress *noun* **1** a female peer. **2** a peer's wife.

peer group *noun* a group of people of roughly the same age or status.

peerless *adjective* without an equal; better than the others.

peer pressure *noun* the pressure to do what others in your peer group do.

peeve *verb* (*informal*) to annoy or irritate someone.
peeve *noun* (*informal*) a cause of annoyance. [from *peevish*]

peevish *adjective* irritable. **peevishly** *adverb* **peevishness** *noun* [origin unknown]

peewit *noun* a lapwing. [an imitation of its call]

peg *noun* **1** a short pin or bolt for hanging things on, fastening things together, holding a tent rope taut, or marking a position. **2** a clothes peg. **3** a wooden pin for adjusting the strings of a violin etc. **4** a suitable pretext or occasion for the treatment of a wider matter ♦ *The priest used the incident as a peg on which to hang his sermon.* **5** (*informal*) a person's leg.
peg *verb* (**pegged, pegging**) **1** to fix or mark something by means of a peg or pegs. **2** to keep wages or prices at a fixed level. **off the peg** (describing clothes) ready-made. **to peg away** to work hard over a long period. **to peg out** (*informal*) to die. **to take someone down a peg (or two)** to reduce a person's pride, to humble him or her. [probably from an Old Dutch word]

pegboard *noun* a board with holes and pegs.

pejorative (pij-o-rə-tiv) *adjective* showing disapproval or contempt. **pejoratively** *adverb* [from a Latin word *pejor* meaning 'worse']

Pekinese or **Pekingese** *noun* (**Pekinese** or

Pekingese) a small dog with short legs, a flat face, and long silky hair. [from Peking, the old name of Beijing, the capital of China, where the breed came from]

pelagic (pil-**aj**-ik) *adjective* (said about fish) living near the surface of the open sea. [from a Greek word *pelagos* meaning 'sea']

pelargonium (pel-er-goh-niəm) *noun* a plant with showy flowers and fragrant leaves. The cultivated variety is usually called *geranium*. [from a Greek word *pelargos* meaning 'stork']

pelican *noun* a large waterbird of warm regions, with a pouch in its long bill for scooping up and storing fish. [from a Greek word *pelekan*]

pelican crossing *noun* a pedestrian crossing controlled by lights that signal traffic to stop. [from *pe(destrian) li(ght) con(trolled)*]

pelisse (pel-**eess**) *noun* (*historical*) **1** a woman's long cloak with armholes or sleeves. **2** a fur-lined cloak, especially as part of a hussar's uniform. [from a French word]

pellagra (pil-**ag**-rə) *noun* a deficiency disease causing cracking of the skin and mental disorders. [from an Italian word *pelle* meaning 'skin']

pellet *noun* **1** a small rounded closely-packed mass of a soft substance. **2** a small metal ball fired from an airgun etc. **3** a small mass of undigested food regurgitated by a bird of prey. [from a Latin word *pila* meaning 'ball']

pelleted *adjective* formed into pellets.

pell-mell *adverb & adjective* in a confused rush; headlong. [from an Old French phrase]

pellucid (pil-**oo**-sid) *adjective* very clear. [from a Latin word *perlucere* meaning 'to shine through']

pelmet (**pel**-mit) *noun* an ornamental strip of cloth or wood fitted across the top of a window, used to conceal a curtain rail. [probably from a French word *palmette* meaning 'little palm']

pelt¹ *verb* **1** to throw a lot of things at someone. SYNONYMS: bombard, shower. **2** (said about rain etc.) to fall heavily. **3** to run fast. **at full pelt** as fast as possible. [origin unknown]

pelt² *noun* an animal skin, especially with the fur or hair still on it. [from a Latin word *pellis* meaning 'skin or leather']

pelvis *noun* the basin-shaped framework of bones at the lower end of the body. **pelvic** *adjective* [from a Latin word *pelvis* meaning 'basin']

pemmican *noun* a food made from a paste of dried pounded meat. [from a North American Indian word]

pen¹ *noun* an instrument for writing with ink. **pen** *verb* (**penned, penning**) to write or compose something. [from a Latin word *penna* meaning 'feather' (because a pen was originally a sharpened quill)]

pen² *noun* a small fenced enclosure, especially for sheep, pigs, hens, etc. **pen** *verb* (**penned, penning**) **1** to shut animals in a pen. **2** to force someone to stay in a restricted space ♦ *Once the scandal broke, reporters kept him penned up at home.* [from an Old English word *penn*]

pen³ *noun* a female swan. [origin unknown]

penal (**pee**-nəl) *adjective* **1** to do with the punishment of criminals, especially in prisons. **2** punishable by law ♦ *a penal offence.* **3** extremely severe ♦ *penal taxation.* [same origin as for *penalty*]

penalize *verb* **1** to inflict a penalty on someone. **2** to place someone at a serious disadvantage. **penalization** *noun*

penalty *noun* (**penalties**) **1** a punishment for breaking a law, rule, or contract. **2** a disadvantage or hardship brought on as a result of some action or error ♦ *the penalties of fame* ♦ *She forgot to put on suncream and paid the penalty.* **3** a disadvantage imposed on a sports player or team for breaking a rule. **4** a penalty kick, or a goal scored for this. **under** or **on penalty of** under the threat of. [from a Latin word *poena* meaning 'pain, punishment']

penalty area or **penalty box** *noun* (in football) an area in front of the goal in which a foul by a defender involves the award of a penalty kick.

penalty kick *noun* **1** (in football) a free kick at goal awarded as a penalty. **2** (in rugby) a free kick.

penance (**pen**-əns) *noun* **1** a punishment that you willingly suffer to express your regret for something wrong that you have done. **2** (in the Roman Catholic and Orthodox Church) a sacrament including confession, absolution, and the performing of a penance imposed by the priest. [from a Latin word *poenitentia* meaning 'penitence']

pence a plural of **penny**.

penchant (pahn-shahn) *noun* a liking or inclination ♦ *He has a penchant for old films.* [a French word]

pencil *noun* **1** an instrument for drawing or writing, consisting of a thin stick of graphite or coloured chalk etc. enclosed in a cylinder of wood or fixed in a metal case. **2** something used or shaped like this.
pencil *verb* (**pencilled, pencilling**) to write, draw, or mark something with a pencil.
to pencil something in to enter a suggested date or estimate etc. provisionally. [from a Latin word *pencillium* meaning 'paintbrush']

pendant *noun* a piece of jewellery that hangs from a chain worn round the neck. [from a Latin word *pendens* meaning 'hanging']

pendent *adjective* hanging down. [same origin as for *pendant*]

pending *adjective* **1** waiting to be decided or settled. **2** about to happen ♦ *A decision on the new stadium is pending.*
pending *preposition* while waiting for, until ♦ *He was held in custody pending trial.* [same origin as for *pendant*]

pendulous (pen-dew-ləs) *adjective* hanging downwards. [from a Latin word *pendulus* meaning 'hanging down']

pendulum (pen-dew-ləm) *noun* **1** a weight hung from a cord so that it can swing to and fro. **2** a rod with a weighted end that regulates the movement of a clock. **3** something that regularly changes from one extreme to another ♦ *the pendulum of public opinion.* [from a Latin word *pendulum* meaning 'something hanging down']

penetrable (pen-i-trə-bəl) *adjective* able to be penetrated. **penetrability** *noun*

penetrate *verb* **1** to make a way into or through something. **2** to enter and permeate something ♦ *Damp has penetrated into the walls.* SYNONYMS: permeate, pervade, suffuse, seep into. **3** to see through something ♦ *Our eyes could not penetrate the darkness.* **4** to discover or understand something ♦ *It took us a few days to penetrate the mystery.* **5** to be

absorbed by the mind ♦ *My broad hints didn't seem to penetrate at all.* **6** (said about a man) to insert his penis in the vagina or anus of a sexual partner. **penetration** *noun* **penetrator** *noun* [from a Latin word *penitus* meaning 'inside']

penetrating *adjective* **1** having or showing great insight ♦ *a penetrating mind.* **2** (said about a voice or sound) clearly heard above or through other sounds.

penetrative (pen-i-trə-tiv) *adjective* able to penetrate, penetrating.

penfriend *noun* a friend who you write to without meeting.

penguin *noun* a black and white seabird of the Antarctic and nearby regions, with wings developed into flippers used for swimming. [origin unknown]

penicillin (pen-i-sil-in) *noun* an antibiotic obtained from mould fungi. [from the Latin name of the mould used]

peninsula (pən-ins-yoo-lə) *noun* a long narrow piece of land sticking out into the sea or a lake. **peninsular** *adjective* [from a Latin word *paene* meaning 'almost' and *insula* meaning 'island']

penis (pee-nis) *noun* the part of the body with which a male animal has sexual intercourse and, in mammals, urinates. [a Latin word meaning 'tail']

penitent *adjective* feeling or showing regret that you have done wrong.
penitent *noun* a penitent person.
penitence *noun* **penitently** *adverb* [from a Latin word *paenitere* meaning 'to make someone sorry']

penitential (pen-i-ten-shəl) *adjective* to do with penitence or penance.

penitentiary (pen-i-ten-sher-i) *noun* (**penitentiaries**) (*North Amer.*) a prison for people convicted of a serious crime.

penknife *noun* (**penknives**) a small folding knife. [originally used for sharpening quill pens]

pen name *noun* a name used by an author instead of his or her real name.

pennant (pen-ənt) *noun* **1** a long narrow triangular flag flown on a ship for identification or signalling. **2** any similar flag. [a mixture of *pendant* and *pennon*]

penne (pe-nay) *plural noun* pasta in the form of short wide tubes. [an Italian word meaning 'quills']

penniless *adjective* having no money, very poor.

pennon *noun* **1** a long narrow triangular or swallow-tailed flag. **2** a long pointed streamer on a ship. **3** any flag or banner. [via Old French from a Latin word *penna* meaning 'feather']

penn'orth *noun* (*informal*) pennyworth.

penny *noun* (**pennies** or **pence**) **1** a British bronze coin worth $\frac{1}{100}$ of £1. **2** a former British coin worth $\frac{1}{12}$ of a shilling. **3** (*North Amer.*) (*informal*) a cent. **4** a very small sum of money ♦ *It won't cost you a penny*. **to be two** or **ten a penny** to be very common and so of little value. **in for a penny, in for a pound** once involved in something, you might as well be fully involved and see it through to the end. **the penny dropped** understanding finally came. [from an Old English word *penig*] ◊ The plural form is *pennies* for a number of coins and *pence* for a sum of money.

penny black *noun* the first adhesive postage stamp (1840), printed in black.

penny-farthing *noun* an early type of bicycle with a very large front wheel and a small rear one.

penny-pinching *adjective* unwilling to spend money; miserly.
penny-pinching *noun* miserliness.

pennyworth *noun* the amount a penny will buy.

penology (pee-**nol**-əji) *noun* the scientific study of the punishment of crime and of prison management. [from a Latin word *poena* meaning 'punishment' and *-logy*]

pen-pusher *noun* (*informal*) a person who does clerical work.

pension [1] (pen-shən) *noun* an income consisting of regular payments made by a government or firm, or from an investment fund, to someone who is retired, widowed, or disabled.
pension *verb* to pay a pension to someone. **to pension someone off** to allow someone to retire or make them redundant with a pension. [from a Latin word *pensio* meaning 'payment']

pension [2] (pahn-si-awn or pen-shən) *noun* a small hotel or boarding house in France and other European countries. [a French word]

pensionable *adjective* **1** entitled to receive a pension. **2** (said about a job) entitling a person to receive a pension.

pensioner *noun* a person who receives a retirement or other pension.

pensive *adjective* deep in thought; thoughtful and gloomy. **pensively** *adverb* **pensiveness** *noun* [from a Latin word *pensare* meaning 'to consider']

penta- *prefix* five. [from a Greek word *pente* meaning 'five']

pentagon (pen-tə-gən) *noun* a geometric figure with five sides.
the Pentagon a five-sided building near Washington DC, the headquarters of the US Department of Defense. [from *penta-* and a Greek word *gōnia* meaning 'angle']

pentagonal (pen-**tag**-ən-əl) *adjective* having five sides.

pentagram (pen-tə-gram) *noun* a five-pointed star. [from *penta-* and *-gram*]

pentameter (pen-**tam**-it-er) *noun* a line of verse with five rhythmic beats. [from *penta-* and a Greek word *metron* meaning 'measure']

Pentateuch (pen-tə-tewk) *noun* the first five books of the Old Testament and Hebrew Scriptures. [from *penta-* and a Greek word *teukhos* meaning 'book']

pentathlon (pen-**tath**-lən) *noun* an athletic contest in which each competitor takes part in five events. **pentathlete** *noun* [from *penta-* and a Greek word *athlon* meaning 'contest']

pentatonic (pen-tə-**tonn**-ik) *adjective* (*Music*) to do with a scale consisting of five notes. [from *penta-* and *tonic*]

Pentecost (pen-ti-kost) *noun* **1** a Christian festival occurring on Whit Sunday and commemorating the descent of the Holy Spirit on the apostles. **2** the Jewish harvest festival of Shavuoth, fifty days after the second day of Passover. [from a Greek word *pentēkostē* meaning 'fiftieth day']

Pentecostal (pen-ti-**kos**-təl) *adjective* to do with any of the Christian groups characterized by an emphasis on the gifts of the Holy Spirit and a fundamental interpretation of the Bible.

penthouse *noun* a flat on the top floor of a tall building. [from a Latin word *appendicium* meaning 'something added on', later confused with a French word *pente* meaning 'slope' and with *house*]

pent-up *adjective* shut in; kept from being expressed ♦ *pent-up anger*. [from *pen* [2]]

penultimate (pən-ul-tim-ət) *adjective* last but one. [from a Latin word *paene* meaning 'almost' and *ultimate*]

penumbra (pin-um-brə) *noun* an outer area of shadow that is partly but not fully shaded, e.g. during a partial eclipse. **penumbral** *adjective* [from a Latin word *paene* meaning 'almost' and *umbra* meaning 'shade']

penurious (pin-yoor-iəs) *adjective* (*formal*) 1 in great poverty. 2 mean or stingy.

penury (pen-yoor-i) *noun* (*formal*) great poverty. [from a Latin word *penuria* meaning 'poverty']

peony (pee-əni) *noun* (**peonies**) a garden plant with large round red, pink, or white flowers. [named after Paion, physician of the Greek gods (because the plant was once used in medicines)]

people *plural noun* 1 human beings in general. 2 the men, women, and children belonging to a place or forming a group or social class; the mass of citizens in a country. SYNONYMS: population, populace, citizenry, public, community. 3 a person's parents or other relatives.
people *noun* a community, tribe, race, or nation ♦ *a warlike people* ♦ *the English-speaking peoples*.
people *verb* to fill a place with people, to populate a place. [from a Latin word *populus* meaning 'people']

PEP *abbreviation* personal equity plan, an investment scheme with certain tax advantages.
◊ PEPs were replaced by ISAs (Individual Savings Accounts) in 1999.

pep *noun* (*informal*) vigour or energy.
pep *verb* (**pepped, pepping**) (*informal*) **to pep someone or something up** to make someone or something more lively. [from *pepper*]

peplum *noun* a short frill of material sewn to the waist of a woman's jacket or dress. [from a Greek word *peplos* meaning 'outer robe or shawl']

pepper *noun* 1 a hot-tasting powder made from the dried berries of certain plants, used to season food. 2 a kind of capsicum grown as a vegetable ♦ *a green pepper*.
pepper *verb* 1 to sprinkle food with pepper. 2 to sprinkle or scatter things here and there. 3 to pelt someone or something with small objects. [from an Old English word *piper*]

peppercorn *noun* the dried black berry from which pepper is made.

peppercorn rent *noun* a very low rent, virtually nothing. [from the former practice of requiring the payment of a peppercorn as a nominal rent]

pepper mill *noun* a mill for grinding peppercorns by hand.

peppermint *noun* 1 a kind of mint grown for its strong fragrant oil, used in medicine and in sweets etc. 2 the oil obtained from this mint. 3 a sweet flavoured with this mint. [so called because of its sharp taste]

pepperoni *noun* beef and pork sausage seasoned with pepper. [from an Italian word *peperone* meaning 'chilli']

pepper pot *noun* a small container with a perforated lid for sprinkling pepper.

peppery *adjective* 1 like pepper, containing much pepper. 2 hot-tempered.

pep pill *noun* (*informal*) a pill containing a stimulant drug.

pepsin *noun* an enzyme contained in gastric juice, helping to digest food. [from a Greek word *pepsis* meaning 'digestion']

pep talk *noun* (*informal*) a talk given to someone to encourage them.

peptic *adjective* to do with digestion. [from a Greek word *peptikos* meaning 'able to digest']

peptic ulcer *noun* an ulcer in the stomach or duodenum.

peptide *noun* (*Biochemistry*) a compound consisting of a chain of amino acids, chemically linked. [from a German word]

per *preposition* 1 for each ♦ *The charge is £12 per person*. 2 in accordance with ♦ *I have signed and returned the contract, as per instructions*. 3 by means of ♦ *per post*. [from a Latin word meaning 'through']

per- *prefix* 1 through (as in *perforate*). 2 thoroughly (as in *perturb*). 3 away entirely; towards badness (as in *pervert*). [from a Latin word *per* meaning 'through']

perambulate (per-am-bew-layt) *verb* (*formal*) 1 to walk about. 2 to walk round an area in order to inspect it. **perambulation** *noun* [from *per-* and a Latin word *ambulare* meaning 'to walk']

perambulator *noun* (*formal*) a baby's pram.

per annum *adverb* for each year; yearly. [from *per* and a Latin word *annus* meaning 'year']

per capita (**kap-it-ə**) *adverb & adjective* for each person. [a Latin phrase meaning 'by heads']

perceive *verb* 1 to see, notice, or become aware of something ♦ *His friends had perceived a change in his behaviour.* SYNONYMS: discern, detect, distinguish, identify, recognize, observe, make out. 2 to regard or understand something in a particular way ♦ *I perceived the situation quite differently.* [from a Latin word *percipere* meaning 'to seize, understand']

per cent *adverb* in or for every hundred ♦ *three per cent* (3%). [from *per* and a Latin word *centum* meaning 'hundred']

percentage (**per-sen-tij**) *noun* 1 an amount or rate expressed as a proportion of 100. 2 a proportion or share of something.

perceptible *adjective* able to be seen or noticed. **perceptibility** *noun* **perceptibly** *adverb*

perception *noun* 1 the process of receiving information through the senses and making sense of it. 2 the ability to notice or understand something. [same origin as for *perceive*]

perceptive *adjective* quick to notice or understand things. SYNONYMS: astute, sharp, shrewd, percipient, penetrating, perspicacious. **perceptively** *adverb* **perceptiveness** *noun* **perceptivity** (**per-sep-tiv-iti**) *noun*

perceptual *adjective* to do with or involving perception.

perch¹ *noun* 1 a place where a bird sits or rests; a bar or rod provided for this purpose. 2 a high seat or place on which a person sits. **perch** *verb* 1 to rest on a perch. 2 to position something on the edge or at the very top of something. [from a Latin word *pertica* meaning 'pole']

perch² *noun* (**perch**) an edible freshwater fish with spiny fins. [from a Greek word *perkē*]

perchance *adverb* (old use) perhaps. [from an Old French phrase *par cheance* meaning 'by chance']

percipient (**per-sip-i-ənt**) *adjective* quick to notice or understand things; perceptive. **percipience** *noun* [same origin as for *perceive*]

percolate (**per-kəl-ayt**) *verb* 1 to filter or cause something to filter, especially through small holes. 2 to prepare coffee in a percolator. 3 to spread gradually through a group of people. **percolation** *noun* [from *per-* and a Latin word *colum* meaning 'strainer']

percolator *noun* a machine for making coffee, in which boiling water is made to circulate through ground coffee held in a perforated drum.

percussion (**per-kush-ən**) *noun* 1 the percussion instruments in an orchestra. 2 the striking of one object against another. **percussive** *adjective* [from a Latin word *percussum* meaning 'hit']

percussion cap *noun* a small metal or paper device containing explosive powder that explodes when it is struck, used as a detonator or in a toy pistol.

percussion instrument *noun* a musical instrument, such as a drum or cymbals, played by being struck or shaken.

perdition (**per-dish-ən**) *noun* (in Christian belief) eternal damnation. [from a Latin word *perditum* meaning 'destroyed']

peregrine (**pe-ri-grin**) *noun* a kind of falcon that can be trained to hunt and catch small animals and birds. [from a Latin word *peregrinus* meaning 'travelling' (because it migrates)]

peremptory (**per-emp-ter-i**) *adjective* giving an urgent command and expecting to be obeyed at once. **peremptorily** *adverb* **peremptoriness** *noun* [from a Latin word *peremptorius* meaning 'final, decisive']

perennial (**per-en-yəl**) *adjective* 1 lasting a long time; continually recurring ♦ *a perennial problem.* 2 (said about a plant) living for several years. **perennial** *noun* a perennial plant. **perennially** *adverb* [from *per-* and a Latin word *annus* meaning 'year']

perestroika (**pe-res-troi-kə**) *noun* restructuring a system, especially the political and economic system of the former Soviet Union. [a Russian word meaning 'restructuring']

perfect¹ (**per-fikt**) *adjective* 1 having all its essential qualities or characteristics ♦ *in perfect health.* 2 so good that it cannot be made any better ♦ *a perfect score.* SYNONYMS: faultless, flawless, ideal, immaculate. 3 exact or precise ♦ *a perfect circle.* 4 complete, total ♦ *It made perfect sense to me* ♦ *a perfect stranger.* 5 excellent

or satisfactory in every respect ♦ *It's been a perfect day.* **6** (*Grammar*) (said about a verb) in the tense used to denote a completed past action, as in ♦ *He has returned.*
perfect *noun* (*Grammar*) the perfect tense. [from a Latin word *perfectum* meaning 'completed']

perfect² (per-**fekt**) *verb* to make something perfect.

perfect interval *noun* (*Music*) a fourth or fifth interval in its usual form.

perfection *noun* **1** making or being perfect. **2** a person or thing thought of as perfect.

perfectionist *noun* a person who is only satisfied if something is perfect. **perfectionism** *noun*

perfectly *adverb* **1** in a perfect way. **2** completely, quite ♦ *perfectly satisfied.*

perfect number *noun* (*Mathematics*) a number equal to the sum of all its factors, e.g. $6 = 1 + 2 + 3$.

perfect pitch *noun* the ability to recognize the pitch of a note or produce any given note.

perfidious (per-**fid**-iəs) *adjective* (*literary*) treacherous or disloyal. **perfidiously** *adverb* **perfidy** (per-fid-i) *noun* [from *per-* meaning 'becoming bad' and a Latin word *fides* meaning 'faith']

perforate *verb* **1** to pierce something with a row or rows of tiny holes so that parts can be torn off easily. **2** to pierce something and make a hole in it. **perforation** *noun* [from *per-* and a Latin word *forare* meaning 'to bore through']

perforce *adverb* (*formal*) by force of circumstances, necessarily. [from an Old French phrase *par force* meaning 'by force']

perform *verb* **1** to do or carry out something ♦ *I'd like to perform a little experiment* ♦ *to perform a ceremony.* SYNONYMS: accomplish, complete, execute, conduct, discharge, effect. **2** to function or work ♦ *The car performs well at low speeds.* **3** to do something in front of an audience. **performer** *noun* [from an Old French word *parfourmer*]

performance *noun* **1** the process or manner of performing a task or function. **2** the performing of a play or other entertainment. **3** the way a person performs a song, piece of music, part in a play, etc. **4** (*informal*) a fuss ♦ *What a performance!*

performance art *noun* an art form that combines visual art with dramatic performance.

performing arts *plural noun* the arts that involve public performance, e.g. dance, drama, and music.

perfume *noun* **1** a fragrant liquid for giving a pleasant smell, especially to the body. **2** a pleasant smell.
perfume *verb* to give a pleasant smell to something; to apply perfume to something. [from *per-* and *fume*, originally used of smoke from burning substances]

perfumery (per-**fewm**-er-i) *noun* (**perfumeries**) **1** the process of producing and selling perfumes. **2** a shop that sells perfumes.

perfunctory (per-**funk**-ter-i) *adjective* done as a duty or routine but without much care or interest ♦ *a perfunctory glance.* **perfunctorily** *adverb* **perfunctoriness** *noun* [from a Latin word *perfunctorius* meaning 'careless']

pergola (per-**gə**lə) *noun* an arched structure forming a framework for climbing or trailing plants. [from an Italian word]

perhaps *adverb* it may be, possibly. [from *per* and an old word *hap* meaning 'luck']

peri- *prefix* around (as in *perimeter*). [from a Greek word *peri* meaning 'around']

pericardium *noun* (**pericardia**) (*Anatomy*) the membranous sac enclosing the heart. [from *peri-* and a Greek word *kardia* meaning 'heart']

pericarp (pe-ri-karp) *noun* (*Botany*) the seed casing of a fruit that develops from the wall of the ovary. [from *peri-* and a Greek word *karpos* meaning 'fruit']

periglacial *adjective* (*Geology*) to do with the area around a glacier.

peril *noun* serious danger. **at your peril** at your own risk. [from a Latin word *periculum* meaning 'danger']

perilous *adjective* full of risk, dangerous. **perilously** *adverb*

perimeter (per-im-it-er) *noun* **1** the outer edge or boundary of something ♦ *a perimeter fence.* **2** the distance round the edge. [from *peri-* and a Greek word *metron* meaning 'measure']
◊ Do not confuse this word with **parameter**, which has a different meaning.

period noun 1 a length of time. SYNONYMS: time, while, spell, stint, phase. 2 a time with particular characteristics ♦ the colonial period. SYNONYMS: age, era. 3 the time allocated for a lesson in school. 4 the time when a woman menstruates. 5 a full stop in punctuation.
period adjective (said about furniture, dress, drama, etc.) belonging to a past historical time. [from a Greek word periodos meaning 'course or cycle' (of events)]

periodic adjective occurring or appearing at intervals.

periodical adjective occurring or appearing at intervals.
periodical noun a magazine etc. published at regular intervals. **periodically** adverb

periodic table noun a table of the chemical elements arranged in order of their atomic numbers, in which chemically related elements tend to appear in the same column or row.

peripatetic (pe-ri-pə-**tet**-ik) adjective 1 going from place to place. 2 (said about a teacher) working in more than one school or college. [from peri- and a Greek word patein meaning 'to walk']

peripheral (per-if-er-əl) adjective 1 of minor but not central importance to something. 2 to do with or on the periphery.
peripheral noun (Computing) any device that can be attached to and used with a computer but is not an integral part of it.

periphery (per-if-er-i) noun (peripheries) 1 the boundary of a surface or area; the region immediately inside or beyond this. 2 the fringes of a subject, group, etc. [from a Greek word meaning 'circumference']

periphrasis (per-if-rə-sis) noun (periphrases) a roundabout way of saying something; a circumlocution. [from peri- and a Greek word phrasis meaning 'speech']

periscope noun a device with a tube and mirrors by which a person in a submerged submarine or behind a high obstacle can see things that are otherwise out of sight. [from peri- and a Greek word skopein meaning 'to look at']

perish verb 1 to die or be destroyed. 2 to rot or decay ♦ The rubber ring has perished. [from per- and a Latin word ire meaning 'to go']

perishable adjective likely to rot or go bad in a short time.
perishables plural noun perishable foods.

perished adjective (informal) feeling very cold.

perishing adjective (informal) freezing cold ♦ It's perishing outside!

peristalsis (pe-ri-stal-sis) noun the automatic muscular movements by which the digestive tract moves its contents along. **peristaltic** adjective [from a Greek word peristellein meaning 'to wrap around']

peritoneum (pe-ri-tə-nee-əm) noun the membrane lining the abdomen. [from a Greek word peritonos meaning 'stretched round']

peritonitis (pe-ri-tə-niy-tiss) noun inflammation of the peritoneum.

periwig noun a man's wig worn in the 17th and 18th centuries. [from an old word peruke]

periwinkle [1] noun an evergreen trailing plant with blue or white flowers. [from a Latin word pervinca]

periwinkle [2] noun a winkle. [origin unknown]

perjure (per-jer) verb to perjure yourself to commit perjury.

perjured adjective 1 involving perjury ♦ perjured evidence. 2 guilty of perjury.

perjury (per-jer-i) noun (perjuries) the deliberate giving of false evidence while on oath; the evidence itself. **perjurious** (per-joor-iəs) adjective [from a Latin word perjurare meaning 'to break an oath']

perk [1] verb to perk up to become or cause a person or thing to become more cheerful or lively. [from perch [1]]

perk [2] noun (informal) a benefit given to an employee in addition to normal pay, such as health insurance or the use of a company car. [short for perquisite]

perky adjective (perkier, perkiest) lively and cheerful. **perkily** adverb **perkiness** noun [from perk [1]]

perm [1] noun treatment of the hair with chemicals to give it long-lasting waves or curls.
perm verb to give a perm to someone's hair. [short for permanent wave]

perm [2] noun (informal) a permutation, especially a selection of matches in a football pool.
perm verb (informal) 1 to select a specified number of things from a larger number. 2 to change the order or arrangement of a

set of numbers or things. [short for *permutation*]

permafrost *noun* the permanently frozen subsoil in polar regions. [from *permanent* and *frost*]

permanent *adjective* lasting for always; meant to last indefinitely. SYNONYMS: everlasting, never-ending, perennial, constant, irreversible. **permanence** *noun* **permanency** *noun* **permanently** *adverb* [from *per-* and a Latin word *manens* meaning 'remaining']

permanent wave *noun* a perm (see **perm**[1]).

permanganate (per-mang-ən-ayt) *noun* (*Chemistry*) a salt of an acid containing manganese.

permeable (per-mi-əbəl) *adjective* allowing liquids or gases to pass through. **permeability** *noun* [same origin as for *permeate*]

permeate (per-mi-ayt) *verb* to pass or spread into every part of something. SYNONYMS: pervade, penetrate, percolate, suffuse, seep into. **permeation** *noun* [from *per-* and a Latin word *meare* meaning 'to pass']

Permian (per-mi-ən) *adjective* (*Geology*) to do with the final period of the Palaeozoic era.
Permian *noun* this period. [from Perm, the name of a Russian province with extensive deposits from this period]

permissible *adjective* permitted or allowable. **permissibly** *adverb*

permission *noun* the right to do something, given by someone in authority. SYNONYMS: approval, consent, authorization, leave, clearance, dispensation, licence; (*informal*) go-ahead. [same origin as for *permit*]

permissive *adjective* 1 allowing a lot of freedom in behaviour, especially in sexual matters ♦ *the permissive society.* 2 allowing something without making it obligatory ♦ *permissive legislation.* **permissively** *adverb* **permissiveness** *noun*

permit[1] (per-mit) *verb* (**permitted, permitting**) 1 to give someone permission or consent to do something. SYNONYMS: allow, let, agree to, consent to, authorize, license, tolerate. 2 to make something possible or give someone the opportunity to do something ♦ *We're having a barbecue tomorrow, weather permitting.* [from *per-* and a Latin word *mittere* meaning 'to send']

permit[2] (per-mit) *noun* an official document giving someone permission to do something or go somewhere.

permutate (per-mew-tayt) *verb* to change the order or arrangement of a set of things. [from *permutation*]

permutation (per-mew-tay-shən) *noun* 1 variation of the order or arrangement of a set of things. 2 any one of these arrangements ♦ *3, 1, 2 is a permutation of 1, 2, 3.* 3 a selection of specified items from a larger group, to be arranged in a number of combinations, e.g. in a football pool. [from *per-* and a Latin word *mutare* meaning 'to change']

pernicious (per-nish-əs) *adjective* having a harmful effect, especially in a subtle way. [from a Latin word *pernicies* meaning 'destruction']

pernickety *adjective* (*informal*) fussy about small details. [origin unknown]

peroration (pe-rer-ay-shən) *noun* the concluding part of a speech. [from *per-* and a Latin word *oratio* meaning 'speech, oration']

peroxide *noun* 1 hydrogen peroxide, used for bleaching hair. 2 (*Chemistry*) a compound containing two oxygen atoms bonded together in its molecule. **peroxide** *verb* to bleach hair with hydrogen peroxide. [from *per-* and *oxide*]

perpendicular *adjective* 1 at an angle of 90° to another line or surface. 2 at an angle of 90° to the horizontal; upright or vertical. 3 (said about a cliff etc.) having a vertical face.
Perpendicular *adjective* to do with the style of English Gothic architecture in the 14th–15th centuries, with vertical tracery in large windows.
perpendicular *noun* a perpendicular line or direction. **perpendicularity** *noun* **perpendicularly** *adverb* [from a Latin word *perpendiculum* meaning 'plumb line']

perpetrate (per-pit-rayt) *verb* to commit or be guilty of something wrong, such as a crime or error. **perpetration** *noun* **perpetrator** *noun* [from *per-* and a Latin word *patrare* meaning 'to make something happen']

perpetual *adjective* 1 never ending. 2 frequent, often repeated ♦ *I'm sick of this perpetual quarrelling.* **perpetually** *adverb* [from a Latin word *perpes* meaning 'uninterrupted']

perpetuate verb to cause something to last or continue ♦ *The statue will perpetuate his memory.* **perpetuation** noun

perpetuity (per-pi-**tew**-iti) noun the state or quality of lasting forever. **in perpetuity** forever.

perplex verb to bewilder or puzzle someone. **perplexed** adjective **perplexedly** (per-**pleks**-idli) adverb [from *per-* and a Latin word *plexum* meaning 'twisted together']

perplexity noun bewilderment.

perquisite (per-**kwiz**-it) noun (formal) a benefit or perk. [originally denoting property that you got yourself, as opposed to property left to you: from *per-* and a Latin word *quaerere* meaning 'to seek']

perry noun (**perries**) a drink like cider, made from the fermented juice of pears. [from an Old French word *pere*; related to *pear*]

per se (per say) adverb by or in itself ♦ *I don't object to violence in films per se, but there just seems to be too much of it these days.* [from a Latin phrase]

persecute verb 1 to be continually hostile and cruel to someone, especially because you disagree with their beliefs. 2 to keep harassing someone. **persecution** noun **persecutor** noun [from a Latin word *persecutum* meaning 'pursued']

persecution complex noun a strong but irrational feeling that you are being persecuted.

persevere verb to go on doing something even though it is difficult or tedious. SYNONYMS: keep going, carry on, keep at, persist; (informal) stick at, plug away. **perseverance** noun [from *per-* and a Latin word *severus* meaning 'strict']

Persian adjective to do with Persia, a country in the Middle East now called Iran, or its people or language. **Persian** noun 1 a native or inhabitant of Persia. 2 the language of Persia. 3 a cat with long silky fur.

persiflage (per-si-**flahzh**) noun (formal) banter. [from a French word *persifler* meaning 'to banter']

persist verb 1 to continue doing something firmly or obstinately in spite of opposition or failure ♦ *She persists in breaking the rules.* 2 to continue to exist ♦ *The custom persists in some countries* ♦ *Rain will persist throughout the night.*

SYNONYMS: last, go on, keep on, keep going. **persistence** noun **persistency** noun **persistent** adjective **persistently** adverb [from *per-* and a Latin word *sistere* meaning 'to stand']

person noun (**people** or **persons**) 1 an individual human being. 2 an individual's body ♦ *She had a microphone concealed on her person.* 3 (Grammar) any of the three classes of personal pronouns and verb forms. The **first person** (= *I, me, we, us*) refers to the person speaking. The **second person** (= *you*) refers to the person spoken to. The **third person** (= *he, him, she, her, it, they, them*) refers to the person spoken about. 4 (in Christian teaching) each of the three ways in which God is said to exist, i.e. the Father, the Son, and the Holy Spirit. **in person** physically present ♦ *You have to buy tickets for the match in person.* [from a Latin word *persona* meaning 'actor's mask, character in a play']
◊ The normal plural is *people*. Persons is used in more formal contexts, such as official document.

persona (per-**soh**-nə) noun (**personas** or **personae**) 1 a role or character taken by a writer or actor. 2 the aspect of a person's character that other people are aware of. [same origin as for *person*]

personable (**per**-sən-əbəl) adjective pleasant in appearance and manner.

personage (**per**-sən-ij) noun an important or distinguished person.

personal adjective 1 to do with or belonging to a particular person ♦ *The story is clearly written from personal experience.* 2 done, dealt with, or made in person ♦ *I will give it my personal attention* ♦ *several personal appearances.* 3 designed for use by one person ♦ *a personal stereo.* 4 to do with a person's private life ♦ *This is a personal matter.* 5 making remarks about a person's appearance, character, or private affairs, especially in an offensive way ♦ *There's no need to get personal.* 6 to do with a person's body ♦ *personal hygiene.*
◊ Do not confuse this word with **personnel**, which has a different meaning.

personal assistant noun a secretary or administrative assistant working for one particular person.

personal column noun the part of a newspaper that includes private messages or advertisements.

personal computer noun a microcomputer designed to be used by one person at a time.

personality noun (**personalities**) 1 a person's own distinctive character ♦ *She has a cheerful personality.* SYNONYMS: character, nature, temperament, disposition. 2 the qualities that make someone interesting or popular. 3 a celebrity ♦ *a TV personality.*

personalize verb 1 to make something personal, especially by marking it with your initials, name, etc. or by making it fit your individual requirements. 2 to cause an argument or discussion to become concerned with personalities rather than with general issues. 3 to personify something.

personally adverb 1 in person, not through someone else ♦ *The chairman showed us round personally.* 2 as a person, in a personal capacity ♦ *We don't know him personally.* 3 in a personal manner ♦ *Don't take it personally.* 4 as regards yourself ♦ *Personally, I like it.*

personal organizer noun 1 a loose-leaf notebook with separate sections including a diary and address book. 2 a hand-held computer used for the same purpose.

personal pronoun noun each of the pronouns (*I, me, we, us, you, he, him, she, her, it, they, them*) that indicate person, gender, number, and case.

personal stereo noun a small portable cassette, CD, or minidisc player with a set of headphones.

persona non grata (per-soh-nə non grah-tə) noun a person who is not welcome or acceptable. [from Latin words *persona* meaning 'character' and *non* meaning 'not' and *grata* meaning 'pleasing']

personify (per-**sonn**-i-fiy) verb (**personifies, personified, personifying**) 1 to represent an idea in human form or a thing as having human characteristics ♦ *Justice is personified as a blindfolded woman holding a pair of scales.* 2 to embody a quality in your life or behaviour ♦ *He was vanity personified.* **personification** noun

personnel (per-sən-el) noun 1 the body of people employed by a firm or other large organization. 2 the department in a firm etc. dealing with employees and their welfare. [a French word meaning 'personal']

◊ Do not confuse this word with **personal**, which has a different meaning.

perspective noun 1 the art of drawing solid objects on a flat surface so as to give the impression of depth and space and relative distance. 2 the apparent relationship between visible objects as to position, distance, etc. 3 a balanced understanding of the relative importance of things ♦ *Try to keep a sense of perspective.* 4 a particular way of thinking about something. 5 a view of a scene giving a strong sense of distance. **in perspective** 1 drawn according to the rules of perspective. 2 giving a well-balanced view of things. [from a Latin word *perspicere* meaning 'to look at closely']

Perspex noun (*trademark*) a tough transparent plastic material. [from a Latin word *perspectum* meaning 'looked through']

perspicacious (per-spi-**kay**-shəs) adjective having or showing great insight. **perspicaciously** adverb **perspicacity** (per-spi-**kas**-iti) noun [same origin as for *perspective*]

perspicuity (per-spi-**kew**-iti) noun clearness of statement or explanation.

perspicuous (per-**spik**-yoo-əs) adjective expressed or expressing things clearly. **perspicuously** adverb **perspicuousness** noun [from a Latin word *perspicuus* meaning 'transparent']

perspire verb to sweat. **perspiration** noun [from *per-* and a Latin word *spirare* meaning 'to breathe']

persuade verb 1 to make someone believe or agree to do something by reasoning with him or her. SYNONYMS: bring round, talk into, get, induce, coax, inveigle, prevail upon, win over. 2 to be a good reason for someone to do something. **persuadable** adjective **persuasible** adjective [from *per-* and a Latin word *suadere* meaning 'to advise or induce']

persuasion noun 1 persuading, or being persuaded. 2 persuasiveness. 3 belief, especially religious belief ♦ *people of the same persuasion.*

persuasive adjective 1 good at persuading someone to do or believe something. 2 providing sound reasoning or argument. **persuasively** adverb **persuasiveness** noun

pert adjective 1 lively or cheeky. 2 neat and jaunty. **pertly** adverb **pertness** noun [from an Old French word *apert*]

pertain (per-**tayn**) *verb* **1** to be relevant to or connected with something ♦ *evidence pertaining to the case.* **2** to belong to something as a part ♦ *the mansion and lands pertaining to it.* [from a Latin word *pertinere* meaning 'to belong']

pertinacious (per-tin-**ay**-shas) *adjective* (*formal*) stubbornly persistent and determined. **pertinaciously** *adverb* **pertinacity** (per-tin-**ass**-iti) *noun* [from *per-* and a Latin word *tenax* meaning 'holding fast, tenacious']

pertinent *adjective* relevant to what you are talking about. **pertinence** *noun* **pertinency** *noun* **pertinently** *adverb* [same origin as for *pertain*]

perturb *verb* to make someone anxious or uneasy. **perturbation** *noun* [from *per-* and a Latin word *turbare* meaning 'to disturb']

peruse (per-**ooz**) *verb* (*formal*) to read something carefully. **perusal** (per-**oo**-zal) *noun* [from *per-* and a Latin word *usitari* meaning 'to use often']

pervade *verb* to spread or be present throughout something. **pervasion** *noun* [from *per-* and a Latin word *vadere* meaning 'to go']

pervasive (per-**vay**-siv) *adjective* widespread. **pervasively** *adverb* **pervasiveness** *noun*

perverse (per-**verss**) *adjective* **1** deliberately or obstinately doing something different from what is reasonable or normal. **2** indicating or characterized by a tendency of this kind ♦ *He takes a perverse satisfaction in annoying me.* **perversely** *adverb* **perverseness** *noun* **perversity** *noun* [same origin as for *pervert*]

perversion *noun* **1** perverting, or being perverted. **2** a perverted form of something. **3** abnormal sexual behaviour.

pervert¹ (per-**vert**) *verb* **1** to turn something from its proper course or use ♦ *They were charged with perverting the course of justice.* **2** to cause someone to behave wickedly or abnormally.

pervert² (per-vert) *noun* a person whose sexual behaviour is thought to be abnormal or disgusting. [from *per-* and a Latin word *vertere* meaning 'to turn']

perverted *adjective* characterized by sexually abnormal behaviour.

pervious (per-vi-as) *adjective* allowing liquids to pass through, permeable. [from *per-* and a Latin word *via* meaning 'way']

Pesach (pay-sahk) *noun* the Passover festival. [a Hebrew word]

peseta (pa-**say**-ta) *noun* the unit of money in Spain. [a Spanish word]

pesky *adjective* (**peskier, peskiest**) (*informal*) annoying. [perhaps related to *pest*]

peso (pay-soh) *noun* (**pesos**) the unit of money in Chile and several Latin-American countries, and in the Philippines. [a Spanish word]

pessimism *noun* a tendency to take a gloomy view of things, or to expect that results will be bad. **pessimist** *noun* [from a Latin word *pessimus* meaning 'worst']

pessimistic *adjective* showing pessimism, gloomy. **pessimistically** *adverb*

pest *noun* **1** an insect or animal that is destructive to crops or to stored food etc. **2** a troublesome or annoying person or thing. [from a Latin word *pestis* meaning 'plague']

pester *verb* to keep annoying someone with frequent requests or questions. SYNONYMS: bother, badger, nag, harass, importune, besiege. [from a French word *empestrer* meaning 'to infect with plague']

pesticide *noun* a substance for killing harmful insects and other pests. [from *pest* and a Latin word *caedere* meaning 'to kill']

pestilence *noun* (*old use*) a deadly epidemic disease. [same origin as for *pest*]

pestilential (pest-i-**len**-shal) *adjective* troublesome or harmful. [same origin as for *pest*]

pestle *noun* a tool with a heavy rounded end for pounding substances in a mortar. [from a Latin word *pinsere* meaning 'to pound']

pet *noun* **1** an animal that is tamed and treated with affection, kept for companionship and pleasure. **2** a person treated as a favourite. **3** used as an affectionate form of address. **pet** *adjective* **1** kept or treated as a pet ♦ *a pet lamb.* **2** favourite or particular ♦ *Sport is his pet subject* ♦ *My pet hate is the sound of mobile phones.* **pet** *verb* (**petted, petting**) **1** to stroke or pat an animal. **2** to stroke or fondle someone sexually. **petting** *noun* [origin unknown]

petal *noun* each of the coloured outer parts of a flower head. [from a Greek word *petalos* meaning 'spread out, unfolded']

petard (pit-**ard**) *noun* (*historical*) a kind of small bomb. **to be hoist with** or **by your own petard** to be the victim of your own schemes against others. [from a French word *péter* meaning 'to break wind'. The phrase is from Shakespeare, *Hamlet* Act III, scene iv, 207]

peter *verb* **to peter out** to become gradually less and cease to exist. [origin unknown]

petiole (pet-i-ohl) *noun* (*Botany*) a slender stalk joining a leaf to a stem. [from a Latin word *petiolus* meaning 'little foot, stalk']

petit bourgeois (pe-ti boor-zhwah) *noun* a member of the lower middle class. **petit bourgeois** *adjective* characteristic of the lower middle class, especially in being conventional. [a French phrase meaning 'little citizen']

petite (pǝ-**teet**) *adjective* (said about a woman) of small dainty build. [a French word meaning 'small']

petite bourgeoisie (pe-ti boor-zhwah-**zee**) *noun* the lower middle class. [a French phrase meaning 'little townsfolk']

petition *noun* **1** a formal written request appealing to an authority for some action to be taken, especially one signed by a large number of people. **2** an earnest request. **3** a formal application made to a court of law for a writ or order etc. **petition** *verb* to make or address a petition to someone. **petitioner** *noun* [from a Latin word *petere* meaning 'to seek']

petits pois (pe-ti pwah) *plural noun* small peas. [a French phrase]

pet name *noun* a name used to express affection or familiarity.

petrel *noun* a kind of seabird that flies far from land, named after St. Peter, who tried to walk on the water (because the bird flies just over the waves with its legs dangling)]

Petri dish (pet- ri) *noun* a shallow round dish with a loose lid, used for growing micro- organisms. [named after the German bacteriologist Julius R. Petri (1852–1922)]

petrify *verb* (**petrifies, petrified, petrifying**) **1** to make someone so terrified that he or she cannot move. **2** to turn something into stone. **petrification** *noun* [from a Greek word *petra* meaning 'rock']

petrochemical *noun* a chemical substance obtained from petroleum or natural gas.

petrodollar *noun* a dollar earned by a country that exports petroleum oil.

petrol *noun* an inflammable liquid made from petroleum, used as fuel in engines. [same origin as for *petroleum*]

petroleum (pi-troh-liam) *noun* a mineral oil found underground, refined for use as fuel (e.g. petrol, paraffin) or in the manufacture of plastics, solvents, etc. [from a Greek word *petra* meaning 'rock' and a Latin word *oleum* meaning 'oil']

petroleum jelly *noun* a greasy translucent substance obtained from petroleum, used as a lubricant or ointment.

petrol station *noun* a place selling petrol for motor vehicles.

petticoat *noun* a woman's or girl's dress-length piece of underwear worn hanging from the shoulders or waist beneath a dress or skirt. [from *petty* meaning 'little' and *coat*]

pettifogging *adjective* paying too much attention to unimportant details. [from an old slang word *pettifogger* meaning 'a lawyer who dealt with trivial cases']

pettish *adjective* unreasonably impatient, petulant. **pettishly** *adverb* **pettishness** *noun*

petty *adjective* (**pettier, pettiest**) **1** unimportant or trivial ♦ *petty regulations*. **2** minor, on a small scale ♦ *petty crime*. **3** small-minded ♦ *petty spite*. **pettily** *adverb* **pettiness** *noun* [from a French word *petit* meaning 'small']

petty cash *noun* a small amount of money kept by an office for small payments.

petty officer *noun* an NCO in the navy.

petty sessions *noun* a meeting of magistrates for the summary trial of minor offences.

petulant (pet-yoo-lǝnt) *adjective* irritable or bad-tempered, especially in a childish way. **petulance** *noun* **petulantly** *adverb* [from an Old French word]

petunia *noun* a garden plant with funnel-shaped flowers in bright colours. [from *petun*, an old word for tobacco (because it is related to the tobacco plant)]

pew *noun* **1** a long bench with a back and sides, one of a number fixed in rows for the congregation in a church. **2** (*informal*) a seat ♦ *Take a pew.* [from an Old French word *puye* meaning 'balcony'; related to *podium*]

pewter *noun* **1** a grey alloy that used to be made of tin and lead and is nowadays made of tin, copper, and antimony. Pewter is used for making tankards and dishes etc. **2** articles made of this. [from an Old French word *peutre*]

pfennig *noun* a German coin worth $\frac{1}{100}$ of a mark. [a German word]

PG *abbreviation* (in film classification) parental guidance.

pH *noun* (*Chemistry*) a measure of the acidity or alkalinity of a solution. Pure water has a pH of 7, acids have a pH between 0 and 7, and alkalis have a pH between 7 and 14. [from the initial letter of a German word *Potenz* meaning 'power' and *H*, the symbol for hydrogen]

phaeton (fay-tən) *noun* an old type of open horse-drawn carriage with four wheels. [from a French word *phaéton*, named after Phaethon, son of the sun god Helios in Greek mythology, who was allowed to drive the solar chariot for a day with fatal results]

phagocyte (fag-ə-siyt) *noun* (*Biology*) a type of body cell, especially a white blood cell, that can absorb bacteria and other small particles. [from Greek words *phagein* meaning 'to eat' and *kutos* meaning 'vessel']

phalanx *noun* a number of people or soldiers forming a compact mass or banded together for a common purpose. [a Greek word]

phallic (fal-ik) *adjective* to do with or resembling an erect penis, often symbolizing male reproductive power. [from a Greek word *phallos* meaning 'penis']

phallus (fal- əs) *noun* a representation of an erect penis, especially as a symbol of fertility.

phantasm (fan-tazm) *noun* (*literary*) an illusion or apparition. **phantasmal** *adjective* [from a Greek word *phantasma* meaning 'vision or ghost']

phantasmagoria (fan-taz-mə-gor-iə) *noun* a shifting scene of real or imagined images, as if in a dream. [originally the name of a London exhibition of optical illusions]

phantom *noun* **1** a ghost or apparition. **2** something that does not really exist, a figment of the imagination. **phantom** *adjective* imaginary, not really existing. [from a Greek word *phantazein* meaning 'to make visible']

Pharaoh (fair-oh) *noun* the title of the king of ancient Egypt. [from an ancient Egyptian word *pr-'o* meaning 'great house']

Pharisee *noun* **1** a member of an ancient Jewish sect represented in the New Testament as making a show of sanctity and piety. **2** a hypocritical self-righteous person. **pharisaical** (fa-ri-**say**-ikəl) *adjective* [from an Aramaic word meaning 'separated ones']

pharmaceutical (farm-ə-**sewt**-ikəl) *adjective* to do with medicinal drugs or with pharmacy. [from a Greek word *pharmakeutēs* meaning 'pharmacist']

pharmaceutics (farm-ə-**sew**-tiks) *noun* the preparation and dispensing of medicinal drugs; pharmacy.

pharmacist (farm-ə-sist) *noun* a person who is trained to prepare and sell medicinal drugs.

pharmacology (farm-ə-**kol**-əji) *noun* the scientific study of medicinal drugs and their effects on the body. **pharmacological** *adjective* **pharmacologist** *noun* [from a Greek word *pharmakon* meaning 'drug' and -*logy*]

pharmacopoeia (farm-ə-kə-**pee**-ə) *noun* **1** a book containing a list of medicinal drugs with directions for their use. **2** a stock of medicinal drugs. [from a Greek word *pharmakopoiia* meaning 'art of preparing drugs']

pharmacy (farm-əsi) *noun* (**pharmacies**) **1** a place where medicinal drugs are prepared and sold. **2** the preparation and dispensing of medicinal drugs. [from a Greek word *pharmakon* meaning 'drug']

pharyngitis (fa-rin-**jiy**-tiss) *noun* (*Medicine*) inflammation of the pharynx.

pharynx (fa-rinks) *noun* (**pharynges**) the cavity at the back of the nose and throat. [from a Greek word *pharunx* meaning 'throat']

phase *noun* **1** a stage in a process of change or development. **2** any of the forms in which the moon or a planet appears as part or all of its disc is seen illuminated. **3** the stage that a regularly varying

quantity, e.g. an alternating electric current, has reached in relation to zero or another chosen value.
phase verb to carry something out in stages, not all at once ♦ *a phased withdrawal*. **to phase something in** or **out** to bring something gradually into or out of use. [from a French word *phase*, based on a Greek word *phasis* meaning 'appearance']

PhD abbreviation Doctor of Philosophy; a university degree awarded to someone who has done advanced research in their subject.

pheasant (fez-ənt) noun a long-tailed game bird with bright feathers. [from a Greek word]

phenobarbitone (feen-ə-bar-bit-ohn) noun a medicinal drug used to calm the nerves and induce sleep and in treating epilepsy.

phenol (fee-nol) noun (Chemistry) 1 a mildly acidic toxic white crystalline solid obtained from coal tar and used in chemical manufacture. 2 any of a group of mildly acidic organic compounds, many of which are used as antiseptics. [from a French word *phène* meaning 'benzene']

phenomenal adjective extraordinary or remarkable. **phenomenally** adverb

phenomenon (fin-om-inən) noun (**phenomena**) 1 a fact or occurrence that can be observed ♦ *Snow is a common phenomenon in winter.* 2 a remarkable or extraordinary person or thing. [from a Greek word *phainomenon* meaning 'visible thing']
◊ Note that *phenomena* is a plural noun. It is not correct to say *this phenomena* or *these phenomenas*.

phenotype (fee-nə-tiyp) noun (Biology) an individual's visible set of characteristics, determined by the genotype and the environment.

pheromone (ferrə-mohn) noun (Zoology) a substance secreted by an animal, that is detected by others of the same species and produces a response in them. [from a Greek word *pherein* meaning 'to convey' and *hormone*]

phew interjection (informal) an exclamation of relief, wonder, discomfort, etc. [an imitation of puffing]

phial (fiy-əl) noun a small glass bottle, especially for perfume or liquid medicine. [from a Greek word]

philander (fil-and-er) verb (said about a man) to have casual affairs with women. **philanderer** noun [from a Greek word *philandros* meaning 'fond of men', though later taken to mean 'a loving man']

philanthropic (fil-ən-throp-ik) adjective concerned with the welfare of your fellow human beings, especially by donating money to good causes. **philanthropically** adverb

philanthropist (fil-an-thrəp-ist) noun a philanthropic person.

philanthropy (fil-an-thrəp-i) noun concern for your fellow human beings, especially as shown by kind and generous acts that benefit large numbers of people. [from *philo-* and a Greek word *anthrōpos* meaning 'human being']

philately (fil-at-əl-i) noun stamp-collecting. **philatelic** (fil-ə-tel-ik) adjective **philatelist** noun [from *philo-* and a Greek word *ateleia* meaning 'not needing to pay' (because postage has been paid for by buying a stamp)]

philharmonic (fil-ar-mon-ik) adjective (in the names of orchestras) devoted to music. [from *philo-* and a French word *harmonique* meaning 'harmonic']

philistine (fil-i-stiyn) noun a person who dislikes culture and the arts. **philistine** adjective having or showing uncultured tastes. [from the Philistines in the Bible, a people in ancient Palestine who were enemies of the Israelites]

Phillips adjective (trademark) (said about a screw) with a cross-shaped slot in the head.

philo- prefix (changing to **phil-** before vowels and h) fond of; lover of (as in *philosophy*). [from a Greek word *philein* meaning 'to love']

philology (fil-ol-əji) noun the study of the structure and development of a language. **philological** adjective **philologist** noun [from *philo-* and a Greek word *logos* meaning 'word']

philosopher noun 1 someone who studies or is an expert in philosophy. 2 a person who speaks or behaves philosophically.

philosopher's stone noun a mythical substance sought in alchemy, which was supposed to turn any metal into gold or silver.

philosophical adjective 1 to do with philosophy. 2 calm in the face of

disappointment or misfortune.
philosophically adverb

philosophize verb to reason like a philosopher.

philosophy noun (**philosophies**) 1 the study by logical reasoning of the fundamental nature of knowledge, reality, and existence. 2 a system of ideas of a particular philosopher ♦ Kantian philosophy. 3 a system of principles for the conduct of life or behaviour. 4 advanced learning in general ♦ Doctor of Philosophy. 5 calm endurance of disappointment or misfortune. [from philo- and a Greek word sophia meaning 'wisdom']

philtre (fil-ter) noun a love potion. [from a Greek word philein meaning 'to love']

phlegm (flem) noun 1 thick mucus in the throat and bronchial passages, ejected by coughing. 2 calmness of temperament. [from a Greek word phlegma meaning 'inflammation', and denoting one of the four bodily humours, associated with calmness, in medieval science]

phlegmatic (fleg-mat-ik) adjective not easily excited or agitated. **phlegmatically** adverb [same origin as for phlegm]

phloem (floh-em) noun (Botany) the tissue in plant stems that carries the food materials made by photosynthesis to all parts of the plant. [from a Greek word phloos meaning 'bark']

phlox (floks) noun a plant with a cluster of reddish, purple, or white flowers at the end of each stem. [from a Greek word meaning 'flame']

phobia (foh-biə) noun an extreme or irrational fear or great dislike of something. **phobic** adjective [from a Greek word phobos meaning 'fear']

-phobia suffix forming nouns meaning 'fear or great dislike of something' (as in hydrophobia).

Phoenician (fin-ish-ən) noun a member of an ancient Semitic people of the eastern Mediterranean.
Phoenician adjective to do with the Phoenicians.

phoenix (fee-niks) noun a mythical bird of the Arabian desert, said to live for hundreds of years and then burn itself on a funeral pyre, rising from its ashes young again to live for another cycle. [from a Greek word]

phone noun a telephone.

phone verb to telephone someone. **on the phone** 1 using the telephone. 2 connected to a telephone system. [short for telephone]

phone book noun a telephone directory.

phonecard noun a plastic card that you can use instead of money to make calls from some public telephones.

phone-in noun a radio or television programme in which listeners or viewers telephone the studio and take part in a discussion.

phoneme (foh-neem) noun a unit of significant sound in a language (e.g. the sound of c in cat, which differs from the b in bat and distinguishes the two words). **phonemic** (foh-neem-ik) adjective [from a Greek word phōnēma meaning 'sound, speech']

phonetic (fə-net-ik) adjective 1 representing each speech sound by a particular symbol which is always used for that sound ♦ the phonetic alphabet. 2 (said about spelling) corresponding to pronunciation. 3 to do with phonetics.
phonetics noun the study of speech sounds. [from a Greek word phōnein meaning 'to speak']

phoney adjective (**phonier, phoniest**) (informal) not genuine. SYNONYMS: fake, bogus, sham, false.
phoney noun (**phonies**) (informal) a phoney person or thing. [origin unknown]

phonograph (fohn-ə-grahf) noun 1 (old use) an early form of gramophone. 2 (North Amer.) a record player. [from a Greek word phōnē meaning 'sound' and -graph]

phonology (fə-nol-oji) noun the study of the speech sounds in a language. [from a Greek word phōnē meaning 'sound' and -logy]

phosphate (foss-fayt) noun (Chemistry) a salt or ester of phosphoric acid; an artificial fertilizer composed of or containing this. [from a French word phosphore meaning 'phosphorus']

phosphor (foss-fer) noun a synthetic fluorescent or phosphorescent substance. [from phosphorus]

phosphoresce (foss-fer-ess) verb to be phosphorescent.

phosphorescent (foss-fer-ess-ənt) adjective glowing with a faint light without burning or perceptible heat.
phosphorescence noun [from phosphorus]

phosphoric (foss-**fo**-rik) *adjective* to do with or containing phosphorus.

phosphorus (foss-**fer**-əs) *noun* a chemical element (symbol P) existing in several forms, including a yellowish wax-like form that appears luminous in the dark and is highly inflammable. [from Greek words *phōs* meaning 'light' and *-phoros* meaning 'bringing']

photo *noun* (**photos**) a photograph.

photo- *prefix* **1** light (as in *photograph*). **2** photography (as in *photofit*). [from a Greek word *phōtos* meaning 'of light']

photocopier *noun* a machine for making photocopies.

photocopy *noun* (**photocopies**) a photographic copy of something produced by a process involving the action of light on a specially prepared surface.
photocopy *verb* (**photocopies, photocopied, photocopying**) to make a photocopy of something.

photoelectric *adjective* to do with or using the electrical effects of light.
photoelectricity *noun*

photoelectric cell *noun* an electronic device which emits an electric current when light falls on it, used e.g. to measure light for photography, in burglar alarms, or to cause a door to open when someone approaches it.

photoemission *noun* the emission of electrons from a surface as a result of light falling on it.

photo finish *noun* a very close finish of a race, where the winner can only be identified from a photograph of competitors crossing the line.

photofit *noun* a likeness of a person, especially someone the police are looking for, that is put together by assembling photographs of separate features.

photogenic (foh-tə-**jen**-ik) *adjective* coming out well in photographs. [from *photo-* and *-genic* meaning 'producing']

photograph *noun* a picture formed by means of the chemical action of light or other radiation on a sensitive surface.
photograph *verb* **1** to take a photograph of something. **2** to come out in a certain way when photographed ♦ *I don't photograph well.* [from *photo-* and *-graph*]

photographer *noun* a person who takes photographs.

photographic *adjective* to do with or used in or produced by photography.
photographically *adverb*

photographic memory *noun* an ability to remember what was seen in great detail.

photography *noun* the taking and processing of photographs.

photon (**foh**-tonn) *noun* (*Physics*) an indivisible unit of electromagnetic radiation. [from a Greek word *phōs* meaning 'light']

photo opportunity *noun* an occasion on which a star or celebrity poses for journalists to take photographs.

photosensitive *adjective* reacting to light.

photosynthesis (foh-toh-**sin**-thi-sis) *noun* the process by which green plants use sunlight to turn carbon dioxide (taken from the air) and water into complex substances, giving off oxygen. [from *photo-* and *synthesis*]

phototransistor *noun* a transistor that responds to light falling on it by generating and amplifying an electric current.

phototropic (foh-tə-**trop**-ik) *adjective* (*Biology*) (said about the movement or growth of a plant) responding to the direction from which light falls upon it.
phototropism (foh-tə-**troh**-pizm) *noun* [from *photo-* and a Greek word *tropē* meaning 'turning']

phrase *noun* **1** a group of words without a finite verb, forming a unit within a sentence or clause. **2** an expression someone uses, especially an idiom or a striking or clever way of saying something. **3** the way someone words something ♦ *a nice turn of phrase.* **4** (*Music*) a short distinct passage forming a unit in a melody.
phrase *verb* **1** to put something into words. **2** to divide music into phrases. [from a Greek word *phrazein* meaning 'to declare']

phrase book *noun* a book listing useful expressions and their equivalents in a foreign language, for use by travellers.

phraseology (fray-zi-**ol**-əji) *noun* (**phraseologies**) the words someone chooses to express things. [from *phrase* and *-logy*]

phylactery (fi-lak-ter-i) noun (**phylacteries**) a small leather box containing Hebrew texts, worn by Jewish men at weekday morning prayer. [from a Greek word *phulassein* meaning 'to protect']

phylum (fiy-ləm) noun (**phyla**) (*Zoology*) any of the larger groups into which plants and animals are divided, containing species with the same general form. [from a Greek word *phulon* meaning 'race']

physic (fiz-ik) noun (*old use*) medicinal drugs or medical treatment. [same origin as for *physics*]

physical adjective 1 to do with the body rather than the mind or feelings ♦ *physical fitness* ♦ *a physical examination.* 2 to do with things that you can touch or see, as opposed to moral, spiritual, or imaginary things ♦ *the physical world.* SYNONYMS: material, concrete, tangible. 3 to do with physics.
physical noun a physical examination.
physically adverb [same origin as for *physics*]

physical chemistry noun a branch of chemistry in which physics is used to study substances and their reactions.

physical education or **physical training** noun instruction in physical exercise and games done at school.

physical geography noun a branch of geography dealing with the natural features of the earth's surface, e.g. mountains, lakes, and rivers.

physician (fiz-ish-ən) noun a doctor, especially one who practises medicine as distinct from surgery. [from an Old French word *fisicien* meaning 'physicist']

physicist (fiz-i-sist) noun an expert in physics.

physics (fiz-iks) noun 1 the scientific study of the properties and interactions of matter and energy, e.g. heat, light, sound, movement. 2 the physical properties of something. [from a Greek word *phusikos* meaning 'natural']

physio noun (physios) (*informal*) physiotherapy or a physiotherapist.

physiognomy (fiz-i-on-əmi) noun (**physiognomies**) the features of a person's face. [from Greek words *phusis* meaning 'nature' and *gnomon* meaning 'indicator']

physiology (fiz-i-ol-əji) noun 1 the scientific study of the bodily functions of living organisms and their parts. 2 the way in which a living organism or bodily part functions. **physiological** (fizi-ə-loj-ikəl) adjective **physiologist** noun [from a Greek word *phusis* meaning 'nature' and *-logy*]

physiotherapy (fiz-i-oh-the-rə-pi) noun the treatment of a disease, injury, deformity, or weakness by massaging, exercises, heat, etc., not by drugs or surgery. **physiotherapist** noun [from a Greek word *phusis* meaning 'nature' and *therapy*]

physique (fiz-eek) noun a person's physical build and muscular development. [a French word meaning 'physical']

phytoplankton (fiy-tə-plank-tən) noun (*Biology*) plankton consisting of tiny plants. [from a Greek word *phuton* meaning 'plant' and *plankton*]

pi (pie) noun 1 a letter of the Greek alphabet (π), equivalent to Roman *P, p.* 2 this letter used as a symbol for the ratio of the circumference of a circle to its diameter (approximately 3.14159). [the numerical use comes from the initial letter of a Greek word *periphereia* meaning 'circumference']

pianissimo adverb (*Music*) very softly. [an Italian word]

pianist noun a person who plays the piano.

piano[1] (pee-an-oh) noun (**pianos**) a large keyboard musical instrument in which metal strings are struck by hammers operated by pressing the keys. [short for *pianoforte*]

piano[2] (pee-ah-noh) adverb (*Music*) softly. [an Italian word]

piano accordion noun an accordion in which the melody is played on a small piano-like keyboard.

pianoforte (pi-ah-noh-for-ti) noun (*formal*) a piano. [from Italian words *piano* meaning 'soft' and *forte* meaning 'loud' (because it can produce soft notes and loud notes)]

piastre (pee-ast-er) noun a small coin of various Middle Eastern countries. [from an Italian word *piastra* meaning 'plate']

piazza (pee-ats-ə) noun a public square in an Italian town. [an Italian word]

pica (piy-kə) noun 1 a unit of length for measuring printing type, about one sixth of an inch (4.2mm). 2 a size of typewriter type, with 10 characters per inch (about 3.9 per centimetre). [from a medieval Latin word *pica* meaning 'magpie', referring to a book of rules about religious festivals]

picador (pik-ǝ-dor) *noun* (in bullfighting) a person on horseback with a lance. [a Spanish word, from *picar* meaning 'to prick']

picaresque (pik-er-**esk**) *adjective* (said about a style of fiction) dealing with the adventures of a likeable rogue in a series of episodes. [via French from a Spanish word *picaro* meaning 'rogue']

piccalilli *noun* a pickle of chopped vegetables, mustard, and hot spices. [probably from *pickle* and *chilli*]

piccolo *noun* (**piccolos**) a small flute sounding an octave higher than the ordinary one. [an Italian word meaning 'small']

pick¹ *verb* 1 to choose or select something. SYNONYMS: choose, select, decide on, settle on, opt for, nominate, prefer. 2 to separate a flower or fruit from the plant bearing it. 3 to take hold of something and lift or move it ♦ *She bent down to pick up the milk bottle.* 4 to use a finger or pointed instrument in order to remove bits from something.
pick *noun* 1 choice ♦ *Take your pick.* 2 the best of a group ♦ *The last song on the CD is the pick of the bunch.* **to pick a fight** to provoke a quarrel or fight deliberately. **to pick a lock** to use a piece of wire or a pointed tool to open a lock without using a key. **to pick at** 1 to eat food in small bits or without appetite. 2 to keep pulling at something with your fingers. **to pick someone's brains** (*informal*) to get information from someone for your own use. **to pick holes in** to find fault with something. **to pick someone or something off** to select and shoot or destroy members of a group one by one, especially from a distance. **to pick on** to single someone out as a target for criticism or unkind treatment. **to pick something out** 1 to select something from among a number of things. 2 to distinguish something from surrounding objects or areas. 3 to recognize something. 4 to play a tune by searching for the right notes. **to pick something over** to examine something carefully, especially in order to select the best ones. **to pick someone's pocket** to steal from it. **to pick up** to get better or recover ♦ *The game picked up in the second half.* **to pick someone up** 1 to call for someone and take them with you, especially in a

vehicle. 2 (said about police etc.) to catch someone or find them and take them into custody. 3 (*informal*) to meet someone casually and become acquainted with them, especially in the hope of sexual relations. 4 to return to a point or remark made by someone in order to criticize it ♦ *I must pick you up on that last point.* **to pick something up** 1 to collect something that has been left somewhere. 2 to get, acquire, or learn something. 3 to catch an illness or infection. 4 to manage to hear or detect something. 5 to resume something. **to pick up speed** to accelerate. **to pick your way** to walk slowly and carefully. **picker** *noun* [origin unknown]

pick² *noun* 1 a pickaxe. 2 a plectrum. [another spelling of *pike*]

pickaxe *noun* a tool consisting of a curved iron bar with one or both ends pointed, mounted on a long handle, used for breaking up hard ground or rock. [from an Old French word *picois*, later confused with *axe*]

picket *noun* 1 a person or group of people standing outside their place of work and trying to persuade other people not to enter during a strike. 2 a pointed wooden stake set into the ground as part of a fence.
picket *verb* (**picketed, picketing**) to act as a picket during a strike. [from a French word *piquet* meaning 'pointed post']

pickings *plural noun* 1 scraps of food etc. remaining. 2 profits or gains, especially those made dishonestly or without any effort ♦ *There were rich pickings for thieves that day.*

pickle *noun* 1 a food consisting of vegetables or fruit preserved in vinegar or brine. 2 vinegar or brine used to preserve food. 3 (*informal*) a difficult situation.
pickle *verb* 1 to preserve food in vinegar or brine. 2 to clean the surface of a metal object by the use of an acid solution. [from an Old German or Old Dutch word]

pickled *adjective* (*informal*) drunk.

pick-me-up *noun* (*informal*) something that makes you feel more energetic or cheerful.

pickpocket *noun* a thief who steals from people's pockets or bags.

pickup *noun* 1 a small open truck or van. 2 the part of a record player that holds the stylus.

picky adjective (**pickier, pickiest**) (*informal*) fussy or choosy, especially excessively so. **pickiness** noun

picnic noun an informal meal eaten in the open air away from home.
picnic verb (**picnicked, picnicking**) to have a picnic. **to be no picnic** (*informal*) to be difficult or unpleasant. **picnicker** noun [from a French word *pique-nique*]

pico- (**pee-koh**) prefix one million millionth of a unit ♦ *picosecond*. [from a Spanish word *pico* meaning 'beak, little bit']

picric acid noun (*Chemistry*) a bitter yellow substance used in dyeing and in explosives. [from a Greek word *pikros* meaning 'bitter']

Pict noun a member of an ancient people of northern Britain. **Pictish** adjective [from a Latin word *Picti* meaning 'painted or tattooed people']

pictograph or **pictogram** noun 1 a pictorial symbol used as a form of writing. 2 a chart or graph using pictures to represent statistical information. **pictographic** adjective [from a Latin word *pictum* meaning 'painted' and *-graph*]

pictorial adjective with or using pictures. **pictorial** noun a newspaper or magazine in which pictures are the main feature. **pictorially** adverb [from a Latin word *pictor* meaning 'painter']

picture noun 1 a painting, drawing, or photograph. 2 a portrait. 3 an image on a television screen. 4 how something seems; the impression formed about something ♦ *A full picture of the incident is yet to emerge.* 5 a cinema film ♦ *Let's go to the pictures.* 6 a perfect example of something ♦ *She looked a picture of health.* **picture** verb 1 to represent something in a picture. 2 to describe something vividly. 3 to form a mental image of something ♦ *Can you picture the flat we used to live in?* SYNONYMS: imagine, visualize, envisage, envision, conceive. **to be** or **look a picture** 1 to look beautiful. 2 to look startled in an amusing way. **to get the picture** to understand or appreciate the situation. **in the picture** (*informal*) fully informed. [from a Latin word *pictum* meaning 'painted']

picture postcard noun a postcard with a picture on one side.

picturesque (**pik-cher-esk**) adjective 1 forming a striking and pleasant scene ♦ *a picturesque village.* 2 (said about words or a description) very expressive, vivid ♦ *picturesque language.* **picturesquely** adverb **picturesqueness** noun [via French from an Italian word]

picture window noun a large window made from a single sheet of glass, usually looking out on a view.

piddling adjective (*informal*) trivial, unimportant. [from *piddle* meaning 'to urinate']

pidgin (**pij-in**) noun a simplified form of English or another language, containing elements of the local language and used for communication between people speaking different languages ♦ *pidgin English.* [from the Chinese pronunciation of *business* (because it was used by traders)]

pie noun a baked dish of meat, fish, or fruit etc. enclosed in or covered with pastry. **pie in the sky** (*informal*) a prospect of future happiness that is very unlikely to happen. [perhaps from *magpie* (because the contents of a pie look like the bits and pieces a magpie collects in its nest)]

piebald adjective (said about a horse etc.) having irregular patches of white and black or other dark colour. (Compare **skewbald**.) [from *pie* meaning 'magpie' and *bald*]

piece noun 1 one of the distinct portions of which a thing is composed or into which it is divided or broken. 2 one of a set of things ♦ *a three-piece suite.* 3 an instance of something ♦ *a fine piece of work* ♦ *a crucial piece of evidence.* 4 a musical, literary, or artistic composition ♦ *a piece of music.* 5 a coin ♦ *a 50p piece.* 6 one of the set of objects used to make moves in a game on a board ♦ *a chess piece.* **piece** verb **to piece something together** 1 to discover what happened by putting together several different pieces of information. 2 to make something by joining or adding pieces together. **to give someone a piece of your mind** to reproach or scold someone giving your frank criticisms. **to go to pieces** (said about a person) to become so upset or nervous that you cannot do things properly. **in one piece** not harmed or damaged. **of a piece** of the same kind, consistent. **to say your piece** to give your opinion or make a prepared statement. [from an Old French word]

pièce de résistance (pee-ess də ray-zee-stahns) noun the most important or remarkable item. [a French phrase]

piecemeal adjective & adverb done or made a bit at a time. [from piece and an Old English word mael meaning 'a measure']

piecework noun work paid according to the quantity done, not by the time spent on it.

pie chart noun a type of graph in which a circle is divided into sectors to represent the way in which a quantity is divided up.

pied adjective having two or more different colours ♦ a pied wagtail. [from an earlier meaning 'black and white like a magpie']

pier (peer) noun 1 a long structure built out into the sea for people to walk on or as a landing stage for boats. 2 a pillar supporting an arch or bridge. 3 solid masonry between windows etc. [from a Latin word pera]

pierce verb 1 to make a hole in or through something with a sharp pointed object. SYNONYMS: perforate, puncture, penetrate, poke through, prick. 2 to force or cut a way through something ♦ A shrill voice pierced the air. [from an Old French word percer]

piercing adjective 1 (said about a voice or sound) very loud and shrill. 2 (said about cold or wind etc.) penetrating sharply.

piety (piy-iti) noun (pieties) 1 being very religious and devout; piousness. 2 a pious action or remark. [from a Latin word pietas meaning 'dutiful behaviour']

piffle noun (informal) nonsense, worthless talk. [originally a dialect word]

piffling adjective (informal) trivial, worthless.

pig noun 1 a domestic or wild animal with short legs, cloven hooves, and a broad blunt snout. 2 (informal) a greedy, dirty, or unpleasant person. 3 (informal) a difficult or unpleasant task. 4 an oblong mass of metal from a smelting furnace; pig iron. pig verb (pigged, pigging) to pig yourself or pig out (informal) to gorge yourself with food. [origin unknown]

pigeon [1] noun a plump bird of the dove family. [from an Old French word pijon meaning 'young bird']

pigeon [2] noun (informal) a person's responsibility or business ♦ That's not really my pigeon. [from a Chinese pronunciation of the word business]

pigeonhole noun 1 a small recess for a pigeon to nest in. 2 one of a set of small compartments in a desk, on a wall, etc., used for holding papers, letters, or messages.
pigeonhole verb to decide that a person belongs only to a particular category or group ♦ He doesn't want to be pigeonholed simply as a stand-up comedian.

pigeon-toed adjective having the toes or feet turned inwards.

piggery noun (piggeries) a place where pigs are bred or kept.

piggy adjective like a pig ♦ piggy eyes.

piggyback noun a ride on a person's shoulders and back.
piggyback adverb carried in this way. [from an earlier word pick-a-back]

piggy bank noun a money box made in the shape of a hollow pig.

pig-headed adjective obstinate or stubborn.

pig iron noun crude iron that has been processed in a smelting furnace, in the form of oblong blocks. [so called because the blocks of iron reminded people of pigs]

piglet noun a young pig.

pigment noun 1 a substance that colours skin or other tissue in animals and plants. 2 a substance that gives colour to paint, inks, dyes, etc.
pigment verb to colour skin or other tissue with natural pigment. pigmentation noun [from a Latin word pingere meaning 'to paint']

pigskin noun leather made from the skin of a pig.

pigsty noun (pigsties) 1 a pen for pigs. 2 a filthy room or house.

pigtail noun long hair worn hanging in a plait at the back of the head.

pike [1] noun (pike) a large voracious freshwater fish with a long narrow snout. [from pike[2] (because of the fish's pointed jaw)]

pike [2] noun 1 (historical) a long wooden shaft with a pointed metal head, used as a weapon. 2 a hill with a peaked top in the Lake District ♦ Scafell Pike. [from a French word piquer meaning 'to pierce']

pike [3] noun a position in diving or gymnastics with the legs straight and forming an angle with the body at the hips. [origin unknown]

pikelet *noun* a thin crumpet. [from a Welsh word]

pikestaff *noun* the wooden shaft of a pike. **plain as a pikestaff** quite plain or obvious. [from *packstaff*, a pedlar's smooth staff]

pilaf (pi-laf) or **pilau** (pi-low) *noun* an Indian or Middle Eastern dish of spiced rice with meat and vegetables. [from a Turkish word]

pilaster (pil-ast-er) *noun* a rectangular column, especially an ornamental one that sticks out from a wall. [via French and Italian from a Latin word *pila* meaning 'pillar']

pilchard *noun* a small sea fish related to the herring. [origin unknown]

pile[1] *noun* 1 a number of things lying on top of one another. SYNONYMS: heap, mound, stack, mass. 2 (*informal*) a large quantity ◆ *I've a pile of work to do.* SYNONYMS: load, stack, mountain. 3 (*informal*) a lot of money ◆ *He's making a pile now.* 4 a large imposing building.
pile *verb* 1 to put things into a pile. 2 to crowd somewhere ◆ *They all piled into one car.* **to pile it on** (*informal*) to exaggerate. **to pile up** to form a pile or a large quantity. [from a Latin word *pila* meaning 'pillar']

pile[2] *noun* a heavy beam of metal, concrete, or timber driven vertically into the ground as a foundation or support for a building or bridge. [from a Latin word *pilum* meaning 'spear']

pile[3] *noun* a raised surface on a carpet or fabric, consisting of many small upright threads. [from a Latin word *pilus* meaning 'hair']

piledriver *noun* 1 a machine for driving piles into the ground. 2 (*informal*) a powerful punch or blow.

piles *plural noun* haemorrhoids.

pile-up *noun* (*informal*) a road accident that involves a number of vehicles.

pilfer *verb* to steal small items or in small quantities. **pilferage** *noun* **pilferer** *noun* [from an Old French word *pelfrer* meaning 'to pillage']

pilgrim *noun* a person who travels to a sacred or revered place as an act of religious devotion. [same origin as for *peregrine*]

pilgrimage *noun* 1 a pilgrim's journey. 2 a journey made to a place as a mark of respect, e.g. to a person's birthplace.

pill *noun* a small ball or flat round piece of medicine for swallowing whole. **the pill** *noun* (*informal*) a contraceptive pill. **pill** *verb* (said about fabric) to form tiny balls of fluff on the surface. **a bitter pill** something unpleasant or painful that is necessary. [from a Latin word *pila* meaning 'ball']

pillage *verb* to carry off goods using violence, especially in a war. **pillage** *noun* the act of pillaging. **pillager** *noun* [from an Old French word *piller* meaning 'to plunder']

pillar *noun* 1 a tall vertical structure, usually made of stone, used as a support or ornament. 2 something resembling this in shape ◆ *a pillar of rock.* 3 a person who is one of the chief supporters of something ◆ *He is a pillar of the local community.* **from pillar to post** from one place or situation to another. [from a Latin word *pila* meaning 'pillar']

pillar box *noun* a large red cylindrical postbox standing in the street.

pillbox *noun* 1 a small round box for holding pills. 2 a hat shaped like this. 3 a small concrete shelter for a gun emplacement.

pillion *noun* a seat for a passenger behind the driver of a motorcycle. **to ride pillion** to ride on this as a passenger. [from a Scottish Gaelic word *pillean* meaning 'cushion']

pillory *noun* (**pillories**) a wooden framework with holes for a person's head and hands, into which offenders were formerly locked and exposed to public ridicule as a punishment.
pillory *verb* (**pillories, pilloried, pillorying**) 1 to put someone in a pillory as a punishment. 2 to ridicule, attack, or abuse publicly ◆ *Football managers get used to being pilloried in the newspapers.* [from an Old French word *pilori*]

pillow *noun* a cushion for a person's head to rest on, especially in bed. **pillow** *verb* to rest the head on something soft ◆ *She pillowed her head on her arms.* [from an Old English word *pyle*]

pillowcase or **pillowslip** *noun* a cloth cover for a pillow.

pilot *noun* 1 a person who operates the flying controls of an aircraft. 2 a person qualified to take charge of ships entering or leaving a harbour or travelling through a difficult stretch of water.

pilot *adjective* testing on a small scale how something will work before it is introduced ♦ *a pilot scheme.*

pilot *verb* (**piloted, piloting**) **1** to be the pilot of an aircraft or ship. **2** to guide or steer something. **3** to test a scheme etc. before introducing it more widely.
pilotless *adjective* [from a Greek word *pēdon* meaning 'oar or rudder']

pilotage *noun* piloting, or the charge for this.

pilot light *noun* **1** a small jet of gas kept alight and lighting a larger burner when this is turned on, especially on a boiler or gas cooker. **2** an electric indicator light.

pilot officer *noun* an officer of the lowest commissioned rank in the RAF.

pimento (pim-ent-oh) *noun* (**pimentos**) **1** another word for **allspice**. **2** another spelling of **pimiento**. [same origin as for *pimiento*]

pimiento (pim-yent-oh) *noun* (**pimientos**) a red sweet pepper. [via Spanish from a Latin word *pigmentum* meaning 'spice']

pimp *noun* a man who gets clients for prostitutes and lives off their earnings. [origin unknown]

pimpernel (pimp-er-nel) *noun* a wild plant with small scarlet, blue, or white flowers that close in cloudy or wet weather. [from an Old French word]

pimple *noun* a small hard inflamed spot on the skin. **pimply** *adjective* [via Old English from a Latin word]

PIN *abbreviation* personal identification number, a number allocated by a bank etc. to a customer, e.g. for use with a card for obtaining cash from an automatic device.

pin *noun* **1** a short thin piece of metal with a sharp point and a rounded head, used for fastening pieces of fabric or paper etc. together. **2** a drawing pin, safety pin, or hairpin. **3** a brooch or badge fastened to clothing with a pin. **4** a peg of wood or metal used for various purposes. **5** one of the parts of an electric plug that sticks out and fits into a socket. **6** a stick with a flag on it, placed in a hole on a golf course to mark its position. **7** a skittle in bowling.
pins *plural noun* (*informal*) legs ♦ *He's not as quick on his pins as he used to be.*
pin *verb* (**pinned, pinning**) **1** to fasten something with a pin or pins. **2** to fix blame or responsibility on someone

♦ *They pinned the blame for the mix-up on her.* **3** to hold someone firmly so that they are unable to move ♦ *He was pinned under the wreckage.* **to pin someone down 1** to force someone to make a definite arrangement or to state clearly their intentions. **2** to prevent an enemy from moving by firing at them. **to pin something down** to establish something clearly. **to pin your hopes on** to count on someone to succeed. [via Old English from a Latin word *pinna* meaning 'point, tip, edge']

pinafore *noun* an apron. [from *pin* and *afore* meaning 'in front' (because originally the bib of the apron was pinned to the front of the dress)]

pinafore dress *noun* a dress without collar or sleeves, worn over a blouse or jumper.

pinball *noun* a game played on a sloping board across which you shoot small metal balls so that they strike various targets in order to score points.

pinboard *noun* a board to which messages and pictures may be pinned.

pince-nez (panss-nay) *noun* (**pince-nez**) a pair of glasses with a spring that clips on the nose and no side pieces. [a French word meaning 'pinch-nose']

pincer *noun* a front claw of a lobster, crab, etc.
pincers *plural noun* a tool for gripping and pulling things, consisting of a pair of pivoted jaws with handles that are pressed together to close them. [from an Old French word *pincier* meaning 'to pinch']

pincer movement *noun* an attack in which forces converge from each side on an enemy.

pinch *verb* **1** to squeeze something tightly or painfully between two surfaces, especially between the finger and thumb. **2** to live in a frugal way. **3** (*informal*) to steal something. **4** (*informal*) to arrest someone.
pinch *noun* **1** a pinching movement. **2** the amount that can be held between the tips of the thumb and forefinger ♦ *a pinch of salt.* **at a pinch** if absolutely necessary. **to feel the pinch** to suffer from lack of money. [same origin as for *pincer*]

pinched *adjective* having a drawn appearance from feeling tense or cold.

pincushion *noun* a small pad into which pins are stuck to keep them ready for use.

pine[1] *noun* 1 an evergreen tree with needle-shaped leaves growing in clusters. 2 the soft wood of this tree. [from a Latin word *pinus*]

pine[2] *verb* 1 to feel an intense longing for someone or something ♦ *She pined for the mountains of her homeland.* 2 to suffer and become ill through grief or a broken heart. [from an Old English word]

pineapple *noun* 1 a large juicy tropical fruit with a tough prickly skin and yellow flesh. 2 the plant that bears this fruit. [from *pine*[1] and *apple* (because it looks like a pine cone)]

ping *verb* to make a short sharp ringing sound.
ping *noun* a pinging sound. **pinger** *noun* [an imitation of the sound]

ping-pong *noun* (*informal*) table tennis. [from the sound of the bats hitting the ball]

pinion[1] (pin-yən) *noun* a bird's wing, especially the outer part.
pinion *verb* 1 to hold or fasten someone's arms or legs in order to prevent them from moving. 2 to clip a bird's wings to prevent it from flying. [from a Latin word *pinna* meaning 'feather']

pinion[2] (pin-yən) *noun* a small cogwheel that fits into a larger one or into a rod (called a *rack*). [from a Latin word *pinus* meaning 'pine tree' (because the wheel's teeth reminded people of a pine cone)]

pink[1] *noun* 1 pale red. 2 a garden plant with fragrant white, pink, or variegated flowers.
pink *adjective* 1 of pale red colour. **in the pink** (*informal*) in good health. **pinkish** *adjective* **pinkness** *noun* [origin unknown]

pink[2] *verb* to cut a zigzag edge on cloth. [probably from an Old Dutch word]

pink[3] *verb* (said about an engine) to make slight explosive sounds when running imperfectly. [an imitation of the sound]

pinking shears *plural noun* dressmaker's scissors with serrated blades for cutting a zigzag edge.

pin money *noun* a small sum of money someone earns for spending on personal expenses. [originally denoting an allowance to a woman from her husband for dress and other personal expenses]

pinnacle *noun* 1 a pointed ornament on a roof. 2 a high pointed piece of rock. 3 the highest or most successful point ♦ *It was the pinnacle of her career.* [from an Old French word]

pinny *noun* (**pinnies**) (*informal*) a pinafore.

pinpoint *adjective* absolutely precise ♦ *with pinpoint accuracy.*
pinpoint *verb* to locate or identify something precisely.

pinprick *noun* 1 a prick caused by a pin. 2 a small annoyance.

pins and needles *noun* a tingling sensation in a limb.

pinstripe *noun* 1 one of the very narrow stripes that form a pattern on cloth. 2 cloth with parallel stripes of this kind. **pinstriped** *adjective*

pint *noun* 1 a measure for liquids, equal to one eighth of a gallon (in Britain 0.568 litres, in the USA 0.473 litres). 2 a pint of beer. [from an Old French word *pinte*]

pint-sized *adjective* (*informal*) very small.

pin-tuck *noun* a very narrow ornamental tuck.

pin-up *noun* 1 a picture of an attractive or famous person, for pinning on a wall. 2 a famous person thought of as sexually attractive.

pion (piy-on) *noun* a meson with a mass around 270 times that of an electron. [a shortening of the earlier name *pi-meson*]

pioneer (piy-ən-eer) *noun* 1 someone who is the first to explore or settle a new region. 2 someone who is the first to investigate a new subject or develop new methods.
pioneer *verb* to be the first person to develop new methods etc. **pioneering** *adjective* [from a French word *pionnier* meaning 'foot soldier', later denoting one of the troops who went ahead of the army to prepare roads etc.]

pious *adjective* 1 devoutly religious. SYNONYMS: devout, godly, saintly, holy. 2 ostentatiously virtuous. **piously** *adverb* **piousness** *noun* [from a Latin word *pius* meaning 'dutiful']

pip[1] *noun* a small hard seed of an apple, pear, orange, etc. [short for *pippin*]

pip[2] *noun* a short high-pitched sound, especially one used to give a time signal on the radio. [an imitation of the sound]

pip[3] *noun* 1 a star, indicating rank, on the shoulder of an army officer's uniform. 2 a spot on a domino, dice, or playing card. [origin unknown]

pip⁴ verb (**pipped, pipping**) (*informal*) to defeat someone by a small amount. **to pip someone at the post** to defeat someone at the last moment. [from *pip*¹ or *pip*³]

pipe noun 1 a tube through which something can flow. 2 a narrow tube with a bowl at one end in which tobacco burns for smoking. 3 a wind instrument consisting of a single tube. 4 each of the tubes by which sound is produced in an organ.
the pipes plural noun bagpipes.
pipe verb 1 to convey water etc. through pipes. 2 to transmit music or other sound by wire or cable. 3 to play music on a pipe or the bagpipes. 4 to signal a person's arrival or departure by playing a pipe or bagpipes ♦ *The royal party was piped on board.* 5 to say or sing something in a shrill voice. 6 to decorate a dress etc. with piping. 7 to force icing or cream through a nozzle to decorate a cake. **to pipe down** (*informal*) to be quiet. **to pipe up** to begin to say something. [from an Old English word]

pipe cleaner noun a piece of wire covered with fibre, used to clean a tobacco pipe.

pipe dream noun an impractical hope or scheme. [perhaps from dreams produced by smoking opium]

pipeline noun 1 a pipe for carrying oil, gas, water, etc. over long distances. 2 a channel of supply or information. **in the pipeline** in the process of being prepared or developed.

piper noun a person who plays a pipe or bagpipes.

pipette (pip-et) noun a slender glass tube, usually filled by suction, used in a laboratory for transferring or measuring small quantities of liquids. [a French word meaning 'little pipe']

piping noun 1 lengths of pipe. 2 a decorative line of icing or cream piped on a cake or dessert. 3 a long narrow pipe-like fold, often enclosing a cord, decorating edges or seams of clothing or upholstery. **piping hot** (describing water or food) very hot.

pipistrelle (pip-i-**strel**) noun a small insect-eating bat. [from a French word]

pipit noun a kind of small bird resembling a lark. [an imitation of its call]

pippin noun a kind of apple. [from an Old French word *pepin*]

pipsqueak noun (*informal*) a small or insignificant person.

piquant (pee-kənt) adjective 1 pleasantly sharp in its taste or smell. 2 pleasantly stimulating or exciting to the mind. **piquancy** noun **piquantly** adverb [same origin as for *pique*]

pique (peek) noun a feeling of hurt pride ♦ *She left in a fit of pique.*
pique verb (**piques, piqued, piquing**) 1 to hurt the pride or self-respect of someone. 2 to stimulate something ♦ *Their curiosity was piqued.* [from a French word *piquer* meaning 'to prick']

piqué (pee-kay) noun a firm fabric woven in a ribbed or raised pattern. [from a French word meaning 'backstitched']

piranha (pi-rahn-ə) noun a tropical South American freshwater fish that has sharp teeth and eats flesh. [via Portuguese from a Tupi (South American) word]

pirate noun 1 a person on a ship who attacks and robs other ships at sea. 2 someone who reproduces or uses another person's work without legal permission ♦ *pirate videos.* 3 someone who broadcasts illegally ♦ *a pirate radio station.*
pirate verb to reproduce or use another person's work without legal permission. **piracy** (piyr-əsi) noun **piratical** adjective [from a Greek word *peiraein* meaning 'to attack']

pirated adjective reproduced or used for profit without legal permission.

pirouette (pi-roo-et) noun a spinning movement of the body made while balanced on the point of the toe or the ball of the foot.
pirouette verb to perform a pirouette. [a French word meaning 'spinning top']

Pisces (piy-seez) noun 1 a group of stars (the Fishes), seen as representing a pair of fishes. 2 the sign of the zodiac which the sun enters about 20 February. **Piscean** adjective & noun [from a Latin word *piscis* meaning 'a fish']

pistachio (pis-**tash**-i-oh) noun (**pistachios**) a kind of nut with an edible green kernel. [from a Greek word *pistakion*]

piste (peest) noun a ski track of compacted snow. [a French word meaning 'racetrack']

pistil noun (Botany) the part of a flower that produces the seed, comprising the ovary, style, and stigma. [from a Latin word *pistillum* meaning 'pestle' (because of its shape)]

pistol noun a small gun held in one hand. [via French and German from a Czech word]

pistol grip noun a handle shaped and held like the butt of a pistol.

piston noun 1 a sliding disc or cylinder fitting closely inside a tube in which it moves up and down as part of an engine or pump. 2 the sliding valve in a trumpet or other brass wind instrument. [via French from an Italian word *pestone* meaning 'pestle']

pit noun 1 a large hole in the ground, especially one from which material is dug out ♦ *a chalk pit.* 2 a coal mine. 3 a depression or hollow in the skin or in any surface. 4 an area at the side of a track where racing cars are serviced and refuelled during a race. 5 a sunken area in a workshop floor, giving access to the underside of motor vehicles. 6 seats on the ground floor of a theatre behind the stalls.
pit verb (**pitted, pitting**) 1 to make holes or hollows in something ♦ *The runway was pitted with craters.* 2 to set someone in competition with someone else ♦ *He found himself pitted against the champion.* **the pits** (*informal*) the worst or most despicable person, place, or thing. **pitted** adjective [from a Latin word *puteus* meaning 'a well']

pit-a-pat noun a quick tapping sound.
pit-a-pat adverb with this sound. [an imitation of the sound]

pit bull terrier noun a small strong and fierce dog.

pitch ¹ noun 1 a piece of ground marked out for football, cricket, or another game. 2 the degree of highness or lowness of a musical note or a voice. 3 a level of intensity or strength ♦ *Excitement was at fever pitch.* 4 the steepness of a slope ♦ *the pitch of the roof.* 5 the act or process of pitching. 6 (in golf) a high shot on to the green. 7 a place at which a street performer or trader etc. is stationed. 8 persuasive talk, especially when selling something.
pitch verb 1 to throw or fling something. 2 to erect and fix a tent or camp. 3 to fall heavily ♦ *She pitched forward into the*

blackness. 4 (said about a ship or vehicle) to plunge forward and backward alternately. 5 to set a piece of music at a particular pitch. 6 to set or aim something at a particular degree or level ♦ *I hope I've pitched this talk at the right level.* 7 (in baseball) to throw the ball to the batter. 8 (in golf) to hit the ball on to the green with a high shot. 9 (said about a bowled ball in cricket) to strike the ground in a particular spot. **to make a pitch** to make a bid for something. **to pitch in** (*informal*) to join in an activity with enthusiasm. [origin unknown]

pitch ² noun a dark resinous tarry substance that sets hard, used for caulking seams of ships etc.
pitch verb to coat something with pitch. [from an Old English word *pic*]

pitch-black or **pitch-dark** adjective completely dark.

pitchblende noun a mineral ore (uranium oxide) from which radium is obtained. [from *pitch* ² and a German word *blenden* meaning 'to deceive' (because it looks like pitch)]

pitched battle noun a battle fought by troops in prepared positions, not a skirmish.

pitcher ¹ noun a large jug. [from an Old French word *pichier* meaning 'pot']

pitcher ² noun (in baseball) the player who delivers the ball to the batter.

pitchfork noun a long-handled fork with two prongs, used for lifting hay.
pitchfork verb 1 to lift something with a pitchfork. 2 to thrust a person forcibly into a position or office etc. [originally *pickfork*: from *pick* ¹]

pitch pine noun a kind of pine tree that yields a lot of resin.

piteous adjective making you feel pity.
piteously adverb [from an Old French word *piteus*; related to *piety*]

pitfall noun an unsuspected danger or difficulty.

pith noun 1 the spongy substance in the stems of certain plants or lining the rind of citrus fruits. 2 the essential part of something ♦ *the pith of the argument.* [from an Old English word *pitha*]

pithead noun the top of a mineshaft and the area around it.

pithy adjective (**pithier, pithiest**) 1 like pith; containing much pith. 2 brief and full of meaning ♦ *pithy comments*. **pithily** *adverb* **pithiness** *noun*

pitiable *adjective* making you feel pity; pitiful. **pitiably** *adverb*

pitiful *adjective* 1 making you feel pity. 2 miserably inadequate or useless ♦ *a pitiful attempt*. **pitifully** *adverb*

pitiless *adjective* showing no pity. **pitilessly** *adverb*

piton (pee-tonn) *noun* a spike or peg with a hole through which a rope can be passed, driven into a rock or crack as a support in rock climbing. [from a French word meaning 'eye bolt']

pitot or **pitot tube** (pee-toh) *noun* an open-ended tube bent at right angles, used in instruments that measure wind speed, the rate of flow of liquids, etc. [named after the French scientist H. Pitot (1695–1771)]

pit stop *noun* (in motor racing) a brief stop at a pit for servicing and refuelling.

pitta *noun* a kind of flat bread with a hollow inside, originally from Greece and the Middle East. [from a modern Greek word meaning 'cake or pie']

pittance *noun* a very small or inadequate amount of money. [originally meaning 'pious gift': same origin as for *pity* and *piety*]

pitter-patter *noun* a sound of quick light taps or steps. [from *patter*]

pituitary or **pituitary gland** (pit-yoo-it-eri) *noun* (**pituitaries**) a small ductless gland at the base of the brain, with important influence on growth and bodily functions. [from a Latin word *pituitarius* meaning 'secreting phlegm']

pity *noun* (**pities**) 1 the feeling of being sorry because someone is in pain or trouble. SYNONYMS: compassion, sympathy, mercy. 2 a cause for regret or disappointment ♦ *What a pity you can't come*.
pity *verb* (**pities, pitied, pitying**) to feel pity for someone. **to take pity on** to feel concern for someone in need or difficulty and therefore help them. **pitying** *adjective* **pityingly** *adverb* [same origin as for *piety*]

pivot *noun* 1 a central point or shaft etc. on which something turns or swings. 2 a person or thing that plays a central part in an activity or organization.
pivot *verb* (**pivoted, pivoting**) 1 to turn or

fix something on a pivot. 2 to depend on something. [from a French word]

pivotal *adjective* 1 to do with a pivot. 2 of crucial importance ♦ *a pivotal moment in the match*.

pixel (piks-əl) *noun* one of the tiny illuminated dots on a computer display screen from which the image is composed. [short for *picture element*]

pixie *noun* a small supernatural being in fairy tales, like a small human with pointed ears and a pointed hat. [origin unknown]

pizza (peets-ə) *noun* an Italian dish consisting of a layer of dough baked with a savoury topping. [an Italian word meaning 'pie']

pizzicato (pits-i-kah-toh) *adverb* (*Music*) plucking the strings of an instrument with the finger instead of using a bow. [an Italian word meaning 'pinched or twitched']

placard *noun* a poster or other notice for displaying, especially one carried at a demonstration.
placard *verb* to cover a wall with placards. [from an Old French word *plaquier* meaning 'to lay flat']

placate (plə-kayt) *verb* to make someone feel calmer and less angry. SYNONYMS: appease, mollify, pacify, soothe. **placatory** *adjective* [from a Latin word *placare* meaning 'to please or appease']

place *noun* 1 a particular part of space, especially where something belongs; an area or position. SYNONYMS: location, point, position, spot, region, area. 2 a particular town, district, or building ♦ *This is one of the places we want to visit*. SYNONYMS: district, locality, neighbourhood, quarter. 3 (*informal*) a person's home ♦ *They had a place in the country*. SYNONYMS: house, property; (*formal*) residence. 4 the part of a book a reader has reached ♦ *I've lost my place*. 5 a proper position for a thing, or a position in a series ♦ *Put each piece in its place*. 6 a space or seat or other accommodation for a person ♦ *Save me a place on the train*. 7 a person's rank or position. SYNONYMS: standing, status, position, rank. 8 a duty or responsibility associated with a person's rank or position ♦ *It is not my place to argue*. SYNONYMS: responsibility, duty, concern. 9 a vacancy or available position, e.g. at a university. 10 any of the first three (or sometimes four) positions at the end of a race. 11 the position of a figure after a decimal point ♦ *The figure is correct to 4 decimal places.*

place *verb* **1** to put something in a particular place or position ♦ *Place the vase on the table.* SYNONYMS: put, position, lay, rest, set, deposit; (*informal*) stick. **2** to identify someone or something in relation to circumstances or memory ♦ *I know her face but can't quite place her.* SYNONYMS: identify, recognize, remember. **3** to arrange for an instruction or request to be carried out ♦ *We have placed an order with a German company.* **to be placed** to be among the first three (or sometimes four) winners in a race. **in the first place** as the first point to be considered. **in place of** instead of. **out of place** in the wrong position or environment; unsuitable. [from a Greek word *plateia* meaning 'broad way']

placebo (plǝ-**see**-boh) *noun* (**placebos**) a harmless substance given as if it were medicine, to reassure a patient or as part of an experiment. [a Latin word meaning 'I shall please']

place kick *noun* (in football) a kick made with the ball first placed on the ground.

placement *noun* the action of placing something.

placenta (plǝ-**sent**-ǝ) *noun* an organ that develops in the womb during pregnancy and supplies the developing fetus with nourishment through the umbilical cord. **placental** *adjective* [from a Greek word *plakous* meaning 'flat cake' (because of its shape)]

place setting *noun* a set of dishes and cutlery for one person at table.

placid *adjective* calm and peaceful, not easily made anxious or upset. SYNONYMS: mild, calm, gentle, easy-going, peaceful. **placidity** (plǝ-**sid**-iti) *noun* **placidly** *adverb* [from a Latin word *placidus* meaning 'gentle']

placket *noun* an opening in a piece of clothing, covering a fastening or giving access to a pocket. [another spelling of *placard* in an old meaning 'a piece of clothing worn under a coat']

plagiarize (**play**-ji-ǝ-riyz) *verb* to take another person's ideas or writings and use them as your own. **plagiarism** *noun* **plagiarist** *noun* [from a Latin word *plagiarius* meaning 'kidnapper']

plague (playg) *noun* **1** a deadly contagious disease that spreads very quickly. **2** a large number of pests infesting a place or causing damage to it ♦ *a plague of greenfly.* **plague** *verb* (**plagues, plagued, plaguing**) to annoy or pester someone. [from a Latin word *plaga* meaning 'a stroke' or 'a wound']

plaice *noun* (**plaice**) a flat sea fish used for food. [from a Greek word *platus* meaning 'broad']

plaid (plad) *noun* **1** a piece of cloth with a chequered or tartan pattern. **2** a long piece of this worn over the shoulder as part of Highland dress. [from a Scottish Gaelic word]

plain *adjective* **1** easy to see or hear or understand. SYNONYMS: clear, obvious, apparent, evident, unmistakable. **2** simple, not elaborate or intricate ♦ *a plain design* ♦ *plain cooking.* SYNONYMS: simple, basic. **3** frank and straightforward ♦ *We could do with some plain speaking.* SYNONYMS: honest, blunt, candid, frank, straightforward. **4** ordinary in manner, without affectation. **5** not pretty or beautiful, ordinary looking. **plain** *adverb* plainly or simply ♦ *The idea is plain stupid.* **plain** *noun* **1** a large area of flat country. **2** an ordinary stitch in knitting, made by putting the needle through the front of the stitch from left to right. (Compare **purl**.) **plainly** *adverb* **plainness** *noun* [from a Latin word *planus* meaning 'flat'] ◊ Do not confuse this word with **plane**, which has a different meaning.

plain chocolate *noun* dark slightly bitter chocolate made without milk.

plain clothes *plural noun* civilian clothes worn instead of a uniform, especially by police officers.

plain flour *noun* flour that does not contain a raising agent.

plain sailing *noun* a course of action that is free from difficulties.

plainsong or **plainchant** *noun* medieval unaccompanied church music for voices singing in unison in free rhythm.

plain-spoken *adjective* frank and direct in what you say.

plaintiff *noun* the person that brings an action in a court of law. (Compare **defendant**.) [from a Latin word *planctus* meaning 'complaint']

plaintive *adjective* sounding sad. SYNONYMS: sad, sorrowful, doleful, melancholy.

plaintively *adverb* **plaintiveness** *noun* [from a French word *plaintif* meaning 'grieving' or 'complaining']

plait (plat) *verb* to weave or twist three or more strands of hair or rope to form one thick length.
plait *noun* a length of hair or rope that has been plaited. [from a Latin word *plicatum* meaning 'folded']

plan *noun* 1 a detailed scheme or method for doing something. SYNONYMS: scheme, idea, proposal, strategy. 2 a drawing showing the layout and parts of something, especially a building. SYNONYMS: design, diagram, drawing, chart. 3 a map of a town or district.
plan *verb* (**planned, planning**) 1 to make detailed arrangements for doing something ♦ *Have you planned your holiday?* SYNONYMS: organize, prepare, arrange, work out, think out. 2 to intend or propose to do something ♦ *We are planning to stay for longer this year.* SYNONYMS: propose, intend, aim. 3 to make a plan or design of something. SYNONYMS: design, map out. **planner** *noun* [from a French word *plan* meaning 'flat surface']

planar (play-ner) *adjective* (*Mathematics*) of or in the form of a plane.

plane¹ *noun* 1 a flat or level surface. 2 an imaginary flat surface in an object. 3 a level of thought or existence ♦ *on a spiritual plane.*
plane *adjective* lying in a plane, level ♦ *a plane figure.* SYNONYMS: flat, level. [from a Latin word *planum* meaning 'a flat surface']
◊ Do not confuse this word with **plain**, which has a different meaning.

plane² *noun* an aeroplane.

plane³ *noun* a tool with a blade projecting from the base, used for smoothing the surface of wood or metal by paring shavings from it.
plane *verb* to smooth or pare a surface with a plane. [from a Latin word *planare* meaning 'to make level']

plane⁴ *noun* a tall spreading tree with broad leaves. [from a Greek word *platus* meaning 'broad']

planet *noun* any of the bodies that move in an orbit round the sun. **planetary** *adjective* [from a Greek word *planētēs* meaning 'wanderer' (because it was not a 'fixed star')]

planetarium (plan-i-tair-iəm) *noun* a room with a domed ceiling on which images of stars and planets are projected.

plangent (plan-jənt) *adjective* (said about a sound) loud and resonant, with a mournful tone. **plangency** *noun* [from a Latin word *plangens* meaning 'lamenting']

plank *noun* 1 a long flat piece of wood used in building. 2 one of the basic principles of a political programme. [from a Latin word *planca* meaning 'board']

plankton *noun* microscopic organisms (plants and animals) that float in the sea or in fresh water. **planktonic** *adjective* [from a Greek word *planktos* meaning 'wandering']

planning permission *noun* formal permission from a local authority to erect or alter buildings or to develop land in other ways.

plant *noun* 1 a living organism, including trees, shrubs, grasses, ferns, and mosses, that absorbs water and other substances through its roots and lacks the power of movement that animals have. 2 a small plant, as distinguished from a tree or shrub. 3 a factory or its machinery and equipment. 4 (*informal*) something deliberately placed for other people to discover, especially to trick or incriminate someone. 5 (*informal*) a person put into a group to act as a spy or informer.
plant *verb* 1 to place a seed, bulb, or plant in the ground or in soil for growing. 2 to fix something firmly in position. 3 to station a person as a lookout or spy. 4 to put something in a place where other people will discover it, especially to trick or incriminate someone. [from a Latin word *planta* meaning 'a shoot']

Plantagenet (plan-taj-in-it) *noun* each of the kings of England of a dynasty lasting from Henry II to Richard III (1154–1485).

plantain¹ (plan-tin) *noun* a wild plant with broad flat leaves, bearing seeds that are used as food for cage birds. [from a Latin word *planta* meaning 'sole of the foot' (because of the shape of its leaves)]

plantain² (plan-tin) *noun* a tropical tree and fruit resembling the banana. [probably from a Spanish word *plantano* meaning 'plane tree']

plantation *noun* 1 a large area of land on which crops such as cotton, sugar, tobacco, or tea are grown. 2 an area where trees have been planted, especially for commercial uses. **3** (*historical*) a colony.

planter *noun* **1** a person who owns or manages a plantation, especially in a tropical country. **2** a machine for planting seeds or bulbs. **3** a container for decorative plants.

plaque (plak) *noun* **1** a flat piece of metal or porcelain fixed on a wall as an ornament or memorial. **2** a filmy substance that forms on teeth, where bacteria can live. [via French from a Dutch word *plak* meaning 'tablet']

plasma (plaz-mə) *noun* **1** the colourless liquid part of blood, which carries the corpuscles. **2** (*Physics*) a kind of gas containing positively and negatively charged particles in approximately equal numbers. [from a Greek word *plasma* meaning 'a mould or shape', from *plassein* meaning 'to shape']

plasmid *noun* (*Biology*) a genetic structure in a cell that can replicate independently of the chromosomes, especially a small circular DNA strand in a bacterium or protozoan. [from *plasma*]

plasmolysis (plaz-mol-i-sis) *noun* (*Botany*) contraction of the protoplasm of a plant cell as a result of loss of water, often causing the plant to die. [from *plasma* and a Greek word *lusis* meaning 'loosening']

plaster *noun* **1** a soft mixture of lime, sand, and water, used for covering walls and ceilings. **2** plaster of Paris, or a cast made of this to hold broken bones in place. **3** a piece of sticking plaster.
plaster *verb* **1** to cover a wall or ceiling with plaster or a similar substance. **2** to cover a surface with something thick. **plasterer** *noun* [via Old English from a Latin word *plastrum*]

plasterboard *noun* board made of paper sheets with a core of plaster between, used for lining walls and making partitions.

plaster of Paris *noun* white paste made from gypsum, used for making moulds or casts.

plastic *noun* a strong light synthetic substance that can be moulded into any permanent shape.
plastic *adjective* **1** made of plastic. **2** able to be shaped or moulded ♦ *Clay is a plastic substance.* **3** involving shaping or

moulding. **plasticity** (plas-**tiss**-iti) *noun* [from a Greek word *plastos* meaning 'moulded' or 'formed', from *plassein* meaning 'to shape']

plastic arts *plural noun* forms of visual art that make use of moulding or modelling.

plasticine *noun* (*trademark*) a soft modelling material used especially by children.

plasticize (plast-i-siyz) *verb* to make a substance mouldable. **plasticizer** *noun*

plastic surgery *noun* surgery done by transferring tissue to repair deformed or injured parts of the body. **plastic surgeon** *noun*

plate *noun* **1** an almost flat dish, usually circular in shape, from which food is eaten or served. **2** dishes and other domestic utensils made of gold, silver, or other metal. **3** a flat thin sheet of metal, glass, or other rigid material. **4** an illustration on special paper in a book. **5** plated metal, or objects made of this. **6** a silver or gold cup as a prize for a horse race, or the race itself. **7** a flat piece of metal on which something is engraved or bearing a name or other identification. **8** a thin flat structure or formation in a plant or animal body. **9** a piece of plastic material moulded to the shape of the gums or roof of the mouth for holding artificial teeth.
plate *verb* **1** to cover a surface with plates of metal. **2** to coat metal with a thin layer of silver, gold, or tin. **on a plate** (*informal*) involving little or no effort. [from a Latin word *platus* meaning 'broad or flat']

plateau (plat-oh) *noun* (*plateaux* (plat-oh)) **1** an area of high level ground. **2** a state or period of inactivity or no change, following a period of progress or change. [from a French word *plat* meaning 'flat']

plateful *noun* (*platefuls*) as much as a plate will hold.

plate glass *noun* thick glass of fine quality for windows and doors, of a kind originally cast in plates.

platelet *noun* a small colourless disc found in the blood and involved in clotting.

platform *noun* **1** a flat surface that is above the rest of the ground or floor, especially one from which a speaker addresses an audience. **2** a raised area along the side of the line at a railway station, where passengers wait for and get on and off trains. **3** a floor area at the entrance to a bus or tram. **4** the declared policy or

programme of a political party or group.
5 (*Computing*) a standard for the hardware
of a computer system. [from a French
word *plateforme* meaning 'a flat surface']

platinum *noun* a silver-white metal, a
chemical element (symbol Pt), that does
not tarnish. [from a Spanish word *plata*
meaning 'silver']

platinum blonde *noun* a woman with very
light blonde hair.

platitude (plat-i-tewd) *noun* a trite or
insincere remark that is commonly used.
platitudinous (plat-i-tewd-in-əs) *adjective* [a
French word, from *plat* meaning 'flat']

Platonic (plə-tonn-ik) *adjective* to do with
the Greek philosopher Plato (5th century
BC) or his teaching.
platonic *adjective* (said about love or
friendship) close and affectionate but not
sexual.

platoon *noun* a small group of soldiers, a
subdivision of a military company. [from
a French word *peloton* meaning 'little
ball']

platter *noun* **1** a large flat dish or plate. **2** a
selection of food served on a platter.
[from a French word *plater*, related to *plate*]

platypus (plat-i-pəs) *noun* (**platypuses**) an
Australian animal with a beak like a
duck's and a flat tail, that lays eggs but is
a mammal and suckles its young. [from
Greek words *platus* meaning 'broad' and
pous meaning 'foot']

plaudits (plaw-dits) *plural noun* applause or
strong approval. [from a Latin word
plaudere meaning 'to clap', related to
applaud]

plausible (plaw-zib-əl) *adjective* **1** (said
about a statement) seeming to be
reasonable or probable but perhaps
deceptive. SYNONYMS: convincing, believable,
credible. **2** (said about a person) persuasive
but perhaps not trustworthy. **plausibility**
noun **plausibly** *adverb* [from a Latin word
plausibilis meaning 'deserving applause']

play *verb* **1** to take part in a game or sport
or other activity for enjoyment ♦ *On
Saturdays we play hockey* ♦ *The children were
playing in the garden.* **2** to compete against a
player or team in a game ♦ *France play Italy
in the final.* **3** to occupy a specified position
in a game ♦ *Jones played in goal.* **4** to move
a piece or put a card on the table in a
game. **5** to perform a part in a drama or
film. **6** to perform a part in a process or
undertaking ♦ *She played an important role
in reaching an agreement.* **7** to perform
music on a musical instrument. **8** to
make a radio or other piece of equipment
produce sounds. **9** to move lightly or
quickly ♦ *A smile played on her lips.* **10** to
allow light or water to fall on something.
11 (said about a fountain or hosepipe) to
send out water. **12** (in fishing) to allow a
fish to exhaust itself on the line before
pulling it in.
play *noun* **1** games and other activities
done for enjoyment, especially by
children. SYNONYMS: recreation, amusement,
fun. **2** a dramatic work written for
performance on the stage or for
broadcasting. **3** activity or operation
♦ *Other factors come into play.* SYNONYMS:
operation, consideration. **4** free movement
♦ *The bolts should have a small amount of play.*
in or **out of play** (describing a ball in a
game) available or not available to be
played according to the rules. **to play
along** to pretend to cooperate. **to play at**
to do something in a trivial or half-
hearted way. **to play back** to play music
or sounds that have been recorded. **to
play ball** (*informal*) to cooperate. **to play by
ear 1** to perform music without having
seen a written score. **2** to do something
step by step by using instinct or reacting
to results. **to play something down** to
minimize the importance of something.
SYNONYMS: minimize, trivialize. **to play into
someone's hands** to do something that
unwittingly gives someone an advantage.
to play off to play an extra match to
decide a draw or tie. **to play someone off**
to make one person oppose another in
order to serve your own interests. **to play
on** to make use of a person's sympathy or
weakness. **to play the game** to behave
honourably. **to play up 1** (*informal*) (said
about a person) to cause trouble.
SYNONYMS: misbehave, fool about, make
trouble. **2** (said about a machine) to fail to
work properly. **to play up to** to humour
or flatter someone. **to play with fire** to
take foolish risks that could bring danger.
[from an Old English word]

playa (plah-yə) *noun* a piece of flat dried out
land at the bottom of a sunken area in a
desert. [a Spanish word meaning 'beach']

play-act *verb* **1** to act in a play. **2** to pretend
in a dramatic way.

playback *noun* the action of playing music
or other sounds that have been recorded.

playboy *noun* a wealthy man who spends
his time seeking pleasure.

player noun 1 a person who takes part in a game. SYNONYMS: competitor, contestant, participant. 2 a person who plays a musical instrument. SYNONYMS: performer, instrumentalist. 3 an actor. 4 a device for playing compact discs or cassettes.

playful adjective 1 fond of fun and amusement. SYNONYMS: lively, vivacious, high-spirited, frisky. 2 done in fun, not meant seriously. SYNONYMS: friendly, teasing, skittish. **playfully** adverb **playfulness** noun

playground noun a piece of ground for children to play on.

playgroup noun a group of young children who play together regularly under supervision.

playhouse noun 1 a theatre. 2 a toy house for children to play in.

playing card noun each of a set of oblong pieces of card (usually 52 divided into four suits) marked on one side with numbers and symbols to show their rank, used to play various games.

playing field noun a field used for outdoor games.

playmate noun a friend that a child plays with regularly.

play-off noun an extra match played to decide a draw or tie in previous matches.

playpen noun a portable enclosure for a young child to play in.

playroom noun a room for children to play in.

plaything noun 1 a toy. 2 a person exploited for amusement and not taken seriously.

playwright noun a person who writes plays, a dramatist. [from play and wright meaning 'maker']

plaza (plah-zə) noun 1 a public square or open space in a town. 2 (North Amer.) a shopping centre. [from a Spanish word meaning 'place']

PLC abbreviation Public Limited Company.

plea noun 1 an appeal or entreaty ♦ The villagers made a plea for help after the floods. SYNONYMS: appeal, request, petition, entreaty. 2 an excuse ♦ He stayed at home on the plea of a headache. 3 a formal statement of 'guilty' or 'not guilty' made in a law court by a person accused of a crime. [same origin as for please]

plead verb 1 to put forward a plea of 'guilty' or 'not guilty' in a law court. 2 to address a law court or put forward a case. 3 to make an appeal or entreaty. SYNONYMS: beg, appeal, implore, entreat, beseech. 4 to offer an excuse ♦ She stayed at home, pleading her work. **to plead with** to entreat. [from an earlier meaning 'to wrangle', related to please]

pleasant adjective 1 pleasing, giving pleasure or enjoyment. SYNONYMS: agreeable, enjoyable, satisfying, nice; (informal) lovely. 2 (said about a person) having a friendly manner. SYNONYMS: friendly, kind, genial, likeable, amiable, agreeable, nice. **pleasantly** adverb **pleasantness** noun

pleasantry noun (pleasantries) a humorous remark.

please verb 1 to give pleasure to someone or make them feel satisfied or glad. SYNONYMS: delight, gladden, gratify, content, satisfy. 2 to like or think suitable ♦ Do as you please.
please adverb used to make a polite request or order ♦ Please close the door. **if you please** used to express surprise or indignation ♦ Then, if you please, they left without payng! **to please yourself** to do as you choose. [from a Latin word placere meaning 'to satisfy']

pleased adjective feeling or showing pleasure or satisfaction. SYNONYMS: glad, happy, content, contented, satisfied.

pleasurable adjective causing pleasure, enjoyable. **pleasurably** adverb

pleasure noun 1 a feeling of satisfaction or enjoyment. SYNONYMS: contentment, satisfaction, enjoyment, joy, delight. 2 something that causes pleasure or enjoyment. SYNONYMS: delight, amusement, recreation. 3 choice or wish ♦ at your pleasure. 4 (used before a noun) used or done for enjoyment ♦ a pleasure boat. [from a French word plaisir meaning 'to please']

pleat noun a flat fold made by doubling cloth on itself.
pleat verb to make a pleat or pleats in cloth. [from plait]

plebeian (pli-bee-ən) adjective 1 belonging to the ordinary people as distinct from the upper classes. 2 lacking in refinement, uncultured.
plebeian noun a member of the ordinary people. [originally with reference to ancient Rome, from a Latin word plebs meaning 'the common people']

plebiscite (pleb-i-sit) *noun* a referendum. [from Latin words *plebs* meaning 'the common people' and *scitum* meaning 'a decree']

plebs *plural noun* (*informal*) the ordinary people.

plectrum *noun* (**plectrums** or **plectra**) a small piece of metal or bone or plastic for plucking the strings of a guitar or other stringed instrument. [from a Greek word *plēktron* meaning 'something to strike with']

pledge *noun* 1 a formal or solemn promise ♦ *They gave a pledge that they would return.* SYNONYMS: promise, assurance, guarantee, vow, oath, word. 2 a thing that is given as security for payment of a debt or fulfilment of a contract, and is liable to be forfeited in case of failure. 3 a token of something ♦ *He offered money as a pledge of his support.* SYNONYMS: token, guarantee. 4 (*old use*) a toast drunk to someone's health.
pledge *verb* 1 to deposit an article as a pledge. 2 to promise solemnly to do something. SYNONYMS: promise, swear, vow. [from an Old French word *plege*]

plenary (pleen-er-i) *adjective* attended by all members ♦ *a plenary session of the council.* [from a Latin word *plenus* meaning 'full']

plenipotentiary (plen-i-pə-ten-sher-i) *noun* (**plenipotentiaries**) a diplomat or representative who has full powers to take action or make decisions on behalf of a government.
plenipotentiary *adjective* having full powers. [from Latin words *plenus* meaning 'full' and *potentia* meaning 'power']

plenteous (plen-ti-əs) *adjective* (*literary*) plentiful. **plenteously** *adverb*

plentiful *adjective* producing or existing in large quantities, abundant. SYNONYMS: abundant, profuse, copious. **plentifully** *adverb*

plenty *noun* quite enough, as much as is needed or wanted.
plenty *adverb* (*informal*) quite or fully ♦ *It's plenty big enough.* [from a Latin word *plenus* meaning 'full']

plethora (pleth-er-ə) *noun* an excess or over-abundance. [from a Greek word *plēthein* meaning 'to be full']

pleura (ploor-ə) *noun* (**pleurae** (ploor-ii)) (*Medicine*) each of two membranes that line the chest and surround the lungs.
pleural *adjective* [from a Greek word meaning 'side of the body']

pleurisy (ploor-i-si) *noun* inflammation of the pleurae, causing pain in breathing.

pliable *adjective* 1 bending easily, flexible. SYNONYMS: flexible, bendable, supple, pliant, elastic, springy. 2 (said about a person) easily influenced or persuaded. **pliability** *noun* **pliably** *adverb* [from a French word *plier* meaning 'to bend']

pliant (pliy-ənt) *adjective* pliable. **pliancy** *noun* **pliantly** *adverb*

pliers *plural noun* pincers having jaws with flat surfaces, used for gripping small objects or bending wire. [from a French word *plier* meaning 'to bend']

plight [1] *noun* a dangerous or difficult situation for someone. SYNONYMS: difficulty, predicament, quandary. [from a French word *plit* meaning 'a fold']

plight [2] *verb* (*old use*) to pledge devotion or loyalty. [from an Old English word *plihtan* meaning 'to endanger']

plimsoll *noun* a canvas sports shoe with a rubber sole. [same origin as for *Plimsoll line* (because the thin sole resembled a Plimsoll line)]

Plimsoll line *noun* a mark on a ship's side showing how deeply it may legally go down in the water when loaded. [named after an English politician Samuel Plimsoll (1824–98) who in the 1870s protested against the practice of sending overloaded ships to sea, from which the owners made a profit from the insurance if they sank]

plinth *noun* a block or slab forming the base of a column or a support for a statue or vase. [from a Greek word *plinthos* meaning 'tile or brick']

PLO *abbreviation* Palestine Liberation Organization.

plod *verb* (**plodded, plodding**) 1 to walk slowly and heavily. SYNONYMS: trudge, tramp, stomp, clump. 2 to work at a slow but steady rate. SYNONYMS: slog, toil.
plod *noun* a slow heavy walk. **plodder** *noun* [origin unknown]

plonk [1] *verb* (*informal*) to put something down heavily or clumsily. [probably an imitation of the sound]

plonk [2] *noun* (*informal*) cheap inferior wine. [probably an alteration of the French word *blanc* in *vin blanc* meaning 'white wine']

plop verb (**plopped, plopping**) to make a sound like something dropping into water without a splash.
plop noun a plopping sound. [an imitation of the sound]

plot noun 1 a small measured piece of land ♦ a building plot. SYNONYMS: patch, allotment. 2 the story in a play, novel, or film. SYNONYMS: story, narrative. 3 a secret plan or conspiracy. SYNONYMS: conspiracy, intrigue.
plot verb (**plotted, plotting**) 1 to make a plan or map of a place. 2 to mark a point on a chart or diagram. 3 to plan something secretly. SYNONYMS: conspire, scheme, plan. **plotter** noun [origin unknown]

plough (plow) noun 1 a farming implement pulled by horses or a tractor for cutting furrows in the soil and turning it over, in preparation for planting seeds. 2 an implement that works like a plough ♦ a snow plough. 3 (**the Plough**) a group of seven stars in the constellation Ursa Major (Great Bear).
plough verb 1 to turn over the soil with a plough. 2 to go through something with great effort or difficulty ♦ He had to plough through a pile of work. 3 (said about a vehicle) to move in a fast and uncontrolled manner ♦ The train ploughed into the buffers. [from an Old English word ploh]

ploughman noun (**ploughmen**) (old use) a man who guides a plough.

ploughman's lunch noun a meal of bread and cheese with pickle and salad.

ploughshare noun the main cutting blade of a plough. [from plough and an Old English word scear meaning 'blade', related to shear]

plover (pluv-er) noun a kind of wading bird. [from a Latin word pluvia meaning 'rain']

ploy noun a cunning action or plan designed to gain an advantage. [originally Scots: origin unknown]

pluck verb 1 to take hold of something and quickly pull or remove it from its place. SYNONYMS: pick, pull, take. 2 to pull a flower from the ground or fruit from a tree or bush. 3 to strip a bird of its feathers. 4 to sound the string of a musical instrument by pulling it with the fingers or a plectrum and then releasing it.
pluck noun 1 courage or spirit. SYNONYMS: boldness, courage, spirit, nerve; (informal) guts. 2 an action of plucking, a pull. **to pluck up courage** to summon up courage

and overcome fear. [from an Old English word]

plucky adjective (**pluckier, pluckiest**) showing pluck; brave or spirited. **pluckily** adverb

plug noun 1 a piece of solid material fitting into a hole to stop or fill it. SYNONYMS: bung, stopper, cork. 2 a device with metal pins that fit into a socket to make an electrical connection; (informal) an electrical socket. 3 short for **spark plug**. 4 a piece of tobacco cut off a larger piece for chewing. 5 (informal) a piece of unofficial or spontaneous publicity promoting a commercial product.
plug verb (**plugged, plugging**) 1 to put a plug into a hole or cavity to stop or fill it. SYNONYMS: stop, stop up, block up. 2 (informal) to promote an event or commercial product by mentioning it favourably. SYNONYMS: publicize, promote, advertise. 3 (informal) to shoot or hit someone or something. **to plug away** (informal) to work steadily or persistently. **to plug something in** to connect a device to an electrical supply by putting its plug into a socket. [from a German and Dutch word plugge]

plum noun 1 a soft fleshy fruit with a flattish pointed stone. 2 the tree that bears this fruit. 3 a reddish-purple colour. 4 (usually used before a noun) the best of its kind ♦ a plum job. [via Old English from a Latin word prunum, related to prune¹]

plumage (ploo-mij) noun a bird's feathers. [same origin as for plume]

plumb¹ (plum) verb 1 to measure the depth of water. 2 to explore or experience something fully ♦ She plumbed the depths of misery.
plumb noun a piece of lead tied to the end of a cord, used for finding the depth of water or testing whether an upright surface is vertical.
plumb adverb 1 (informal) exactly ♦ It landed plumb in the middle. 2 (North Amer.) completely ♦ They must be plumb crazy. [from a Latin word plumbum meaning 'lead (the metal)']

plumb² (plum) verb to fit a room or building with a plumbing system. **to plumb something in** to install a washing machine or dishwasher so that it is connected directly to the water supply and drainage pipes.

plumber (plum-er) noun a person who fits and repairs plumbing.

plumbing (plum-ing) noun 1 the water pipes, water tanks, and drainage pipes in a building. 2 the work of a plumber. [from a Latin word *plumbum* meaning 'lead' (because the pipes used to be made of lead)]

plumb line noun a line with a plumb weight on the end of it.

plume (ploom) noun 1 a large feather or set of feathers used by a bird for display or worn as a decoration. 2 something like a feather in shape ♦ *a plume of smoke.* [from a Latin word *pluma* meaning 'feather']

plumed (ploomd) adjective decorated with large feathers.

plummet verb (**plummeted, plummeting**) 1 to fall or plunge suddenly and without control. SYNONYMS: plunge, pitch, nosedive. 2 to decrease rapidly in value ♦ *Share prices plummeted.*
plummet noun 1 a plumb or plumb line. 2 a sudden decrease or decline. [from an Old French word *plommet* meaning 'small lead for sounding', related to *plumb*[1]]

plummy adjective (**plummier, plummiest**) (*informal*) (said about a voice) affectedly full and rich in tone.

plump[1] adjective having a full rounded shape; slightly fat. SYNONYMS: stout, podgy, chubby, tubby, portly, rotund, dumpy, fat.
plump verb to make something full and rounded ♦ *to plump a cushion.* **plumpness** noun [from German and Dutch words]

plump[2] verb to drop or plunge abruptly ♦ *He plumped down in a chair.*
plump adverb with a sudden or heavy fall. **to plump for** to choose or decide on something or someone. [from a German word *plompen* meaning 'to plop']

plumule (ploom-yool) noun 1 (*Botany*) the rudimentary stem of an embryo plant. 2 a bird's down feather. [from a Latin word *plumula* meaning 'little feather']

plunder verb to rob a place or person by force, especially in a time of war or other disturbance. SYNONYMS: loot, raid, ransack, pillage, rifle.
plunder noun 1 the action of plundering. 2 property taken by plundering. SYNONYMS: booty, loot, spoils. **plunderer** noun [from a German word *plunder* meaning 'household goods']

plunge verb 1 to push or thrust a thing forcefully into something soft or liquid. 2 to fall or drop suddenly and without control. SYNONYMS: plummet, pitch, nosedive. 3 to jump or dive into water. 4 to embark suddenly or impetuously on a course of action. 5 to bring someone into a certain condition suddenly or impetuously ♦ *They plunged the world into war.*
plunge noun the action of plunging, a dive. **to take the plunge** (*informal*) to take a bold decisive step. [from an Old French word *plungier* meaning 'to thrust down', related to *plumb*[1]]

plunge pool noun a deep pool at the foot of a waterfall, formed from the action of the falling water.

plunger noun 1 the part of a mechanism that works with a plunging or thrusting movement. 2 a rubber cup on a handle used for clearing blocked pipes by alternate thrusting and suction.

pluperfect (ploo-per-fikt) adjective (*Grammar*) (said about the tense of a verb) used to denote an action completed before some past point of time, as in *We had arrived.* [from a Latin phrase *plus quam perfectum* meaning 'more than the perfect (tense)']

plural (ploor-ǝl) adjective 1 more than one. 2 (*Grammar*) (said about a form of a noun or verb) used when it refers to more than one person or thing ♦ *The plural form of 'child' is 'children'.*
plural noun a plural word or form. **plurality** noun [from a Latin word *pluris* meaning 'of more']

plus preposition 1 with the addition of ♦ *15 plus 6 equals 21.* 2 (*informal*) together with ♦ *The family arrived plus dog and parrot.*
plus adjective 1 denoting a grade slightly higher ♦ *B plus.* 2 denoting a number above zero ♦ *a temperature between minus ten and plus ten degrees.*
plus noun 1 the sign +. 2 an advantage. [a Latin word meaning 'more']

plush noun a thick velvety cloth used in furnishings.
plush adjective 1 made of plush. 2 luxurious. [from a Latin word *pilus* meaning 'hair']

plushy adjective (**plushier, plushiest**) luxurious. **plushiness** noun

plutocrat (ploo-tǝ-krat) noun a person who is powerful because of their wealth. **plutocratic** adjective [from Greek words *ploutos* meaning 'wealth' and *-kratia* meaning 'power']

plutonium (ploo-**toh**-niəm) *noun* a chemical element (symbol Pu), a radioactive substance used in nuclear weapons and reactors. [named after the planet Pluto]

ply¹ *noun* (**plies**) 1 a thickness or layer of wood or cloth etc. 2 a strand in yarn ♦ *4-ply wool.* 3 plywood. [from a French word *pli* meaning 'a fold']

ply² *verb* (**plies, plied, plying**) 1 to use or wield a tool or weapon. 2 to work steadily at something ♦ *Weavers plied their trade.* 3 to keep offering or supplying something ♦ *They plied her with food.* 4 to go regularly along a route ♦ *The boat plies between the two ports.* [from *apply*]

plywood *noun* strong thin board made of layers of wood glued and pressed together.

PM *abbreviation* Prime Minister.

p.m. *abbreviation* after noon. [short for Latin *post meridiem*]

PMS *abbreviation* premenstrual tension.

pneumatic (new-**mat**-ik) *adjective* filled with or worked by compressed air ♦ *a pneumatic drill.* **pneumatically** *adverb* [from a Greek word *pneuma* meaning 'wind']

pneumonia (new-**moh**-niə) *noun* a serious illness caused by inflammation of one or both lungs. [from a Greek word *pneumōn* meaning 'lung']

PO *abbreviation* 1 postal order. 2 Post Office.

poach¹ *verb* 1 to cook an egg removed from its shell in or over boiling water. 2 to cook fish or fruit by simmering it in a small amount of liquid. **poacher** *noun* [from an Old French word *pochier* meaning 'to enclose in a bag']

poach² *verb* 1 to steal game or fish from private land or water. 2 to take something unfairly from someone else ♦ *The company has been poaching staff from its rivals.* **poacher** *noun* [same origin as *poach*]

pock *noun* a pockmark. **pocked** *adjective* [from an Old English word *poc* meaning 'pustule']

pocket *noun* 1 a small bag-shaped part sewn into or on a piece of clothing, for holding small articles. 2 a person's supply of money ♦ *The cost is beyond my pocket.* 3 a pouch-like compartment in a suitcase or on a car door etc. 4 each of the pouches at the corners or sides of a billiard table, into which balls are driven. 5 an isolated group or area ♦ *The army met* small pockets of resistance.

pocket *adjective* small enough to carry in a pocket ♦ *a pocket calculator.*

pocket *verb* (**pocketed, pocketing**) 1 to put something into your pocket. 2 to take something for yourself, especially dishonestly. 3 (in billiards or snooker) to send a ball into a pocket. **in pocket** having money to spare. **out of pocket** having lost money in a transaction. [from an Old French word *pochet* meaning 'little pouch']

pocketbook *noun* 1 a notebook. 2 (*North Amer.*) a wallet or purse.

pocket borough *noun* (in the 19th century) a borough in which election of an MP was controlled by a private person or family.

pocketful *noun* (**pocketfuls**) the amount that a pocket will hold.

pocket knife *noun* a penknife.

pocket money *noun* 1 money regularly given to a child by its parents. 2 money for minor expenses.

pockmark *noun* a scar or mark left on the skin by a spot or pustule. **pockmarked** *adjective*

pod *noun* a long seed container of the kind found on a pea or bean plant.
pod *verb* (**podded, podding**) 1 (said about plants) to bear or form pods. 2 to remove peas or beans from their pods.

podgy *adjective* (**podgier, podgiest**) short and fat. SYNONYMS: plump, stout, chubby, tubby, portly, rotund, dumpy, fat. [origin unknown]

podium (**poh**-di-əm) *noun* (**podiums** or **podia**) a pedestal or platform. [from a Greek word *podion* meaning 'little foot']

podzol *noun* an infertile soil found in regions with a cold climate, in which minerals have been washed below the surface. [from Russian words *pod* meaning 'under' and *zola* meaning 'ashes']

poem *noun* a piece of writing in verse, usually arranged in short lines with a particular rhythm or set of rhythms, and expressing deep feeling or noble thought in an imaginative way. [from a Greek word *poiēma* meaning 'thing made']

poet *noun* someone who writes poems.

poetess *noun* a female poet.

poetic *adjective* to do with poetry, like poetry.

poetical *adjective* written in verse ♦ *poetical works*. **poetically** *adverb*

poetic justice *noun* suitable and well-deserved punishment or reward, as found in literature.

poetic licence *noun* departing from the normal rules and conventions of writing in order to create an artistic effect.

Poet Laureate *noun* an eminent poet appointed to write poems for important state occasions.

poetry *noun* writing in verse, poems collectively.

pogrom (pog-rəm) *noun* an organized massacre of an ethnic group of people, originally that of Jews in eastern Europe in the early 20th century. [from a Russian word meaning 'destruction']

poignant (poin-yənt) *adjective* arousing sympathy, deeply moving to the feelings. SYNONYMS: moving, emotional, touching, affecting. **poignancy** *noun* **poignantly** *adverb* [from a French word, literally meaning 'pricking']

poikilotherm (poi-kil-ə-therm) *noun* (*Zoology*) a cold-blooded animal. **poikilothermic** *adjective* [from Greek words *poikilos* meaning 'changeable' and *thermē* meaning 'heat']

poinsettia (poin-set-iə) *noun* a plant with large scarlet petal-like bracts. [named after an American diplomat and botanist Joel R. Poinsett (1779–1851)]

point *noun* 1 the tapered or sharp end of a tool, weapon, pencil, or other object. SYNONYMS: tip, end, prong. 2 a dot used as a punctuation mark; a decimal point. 3 a particular place or time, or a particular stage in a process ♦ *At this point in the game the home team was winning*. SYNONYMS: stage, juncture; (of time) moment; (of place) spot, place, location, position. 4 each of the directions marked on the compass, or a corresponding direction towards the horizon. 5 a unit of measurement, value, or scoring. 6 (*Geometry*) something that has position but not magnitude, such as the intersection of two lines. 7 a separate item or detail ♦ *The two sides differed on several points*. 8 a distinctive feature or characteristic ♦ *The plan has some good points*. 9 the thing that matters or is under discussion ♦ *I'll try to come to the point*. 10 the important feature of a story, joke, or remark. 11 aim or purpose ♦ *The point of the game is to get rid of all your cards*.

SYNONYMS: aim, object, intention. 12 advantage or value ♦ *There's no point waiting any longer*. SYNONYMS: advantage, sense, use, value. 13 (in cricket) the position of a fieldsman near the batsman on the off side. 14 an electrical socket ♦ *a power point*. 15 a place where two railway lines meet, with a pair of tapering rails which can be moved horizontally to allow a train to pass from one line to the other. 16 a narrow piece of land jutting out into the sea, a promontory.

point *verb* 1 to direct or aim something ♦ *The man was pointing a gun at her*. SYNONYMS: aim, direct, level. 2 to show where something is, especially by holding out a finger towards it ♦ *He pointed to the post office across the road*. 3 to be evidence of something ♦ *It all points to murder*. 4 to sharpen something. 5 to fill in the joints of brickwork or stonework with mortar or cement. **to make a point of** to make sure that you do something, or to do it with special care or attention. **on the point of** about to do something. **the point of no return** the point in a journey or undertaking at which you have to keep going to the end. **point of view** a way of thinking about something, an opinion. SYNONYMS: standpoint, viewpoint, perspective. **to point something out** to indicate something or draw attention to it. **to point something up** to emphasize something. SYNONYMS: emphasize, highlight, stress. **to the point** relevant; relevantly. [from a Latin word *punctum* meaning 'pricked']

point-blank *adjective* 1 (said about a shot) aimed or fired at very close range. 2 (said about a remark) direct or straightforward ♦ *We got a point-blank refusal*. **point-blank** *adverb* directly, in a point-blank manner ♦ *They refused point-blank*.

pointed *adjective* 1 tapering or sharpened to a point. 2 (said about a remark or look) clearly aimed at a particular person or thing, unambiguous. **pointedly** *adverb*

pointer *noun* 1 a stick, rod, or mark used to point at something. 2 a long thin piece of metal that points to figures or other marks on a dial or scale. 3 a hint or indication. 4 a dog that scents game and then stands rigidly with its muzzle pointing towards it.

pointillism (pwan-til-izm) *noun* (*Art*) a technique of neo-Impressionist painting in which the paint is applied in tiny spots of various colours which are blended by the viewer's eye. **pointillist** noun [from a French word *pointillisme*, from *pointiller* meaning 'to mark with dots']

pointless adjective **1** having no purpose or meaning. SYNONYMS: futile, useless, fruitless, senseless. **2** not having scored any points. **pointlessly** adverb

point-to-point noun a steeplechase for horses across country between certain landmarks.

poise verb **1** to balance something, or to be balanced. **2** to hold something suspended or supported.
poise noun **1** a dignified self-confident manner. **2** balance, the way something is poised. [from an earlier meaning 'weight', via French from a Latin word *pensum* meaning 'weight']

poised adjective (said about a person) dignified and self-confident.

poison noun **1** a substance that can harm or destroy a living thing. **2** a harmful influence. **3** (*Physics*) an impurity that retards nuclear fission by absorbing neutrons.
poison verb **1** to kill someone with poison. **2** to put poison on or in something living. **3** to corrupt someone or make them prejudiced ♦ *He poisoned their minds with his ideas.* **poisoner** noun [from a French word *poison* meaning 'magic potion', related to *potion*]

poisonous adjective **1** containing or having the effect of poison. **2** likely to corrupt people ♦ *a poisonous influence.*

poison pen letter noun an anonymous letter that is malicious or abusive.

poke [1] verb **1** to prod or jab something with the end of a finger or a long thin object. SYNONYMS: prod, jab, dig. **2** to thrust something forward, or to be thrust forward. SYNONYMS: stick, thrust. **3** to produce something by poking ♦ *She poked a hole in it with her finger.*
poke noun a poking movement, a thrust or nudge. **to poke about** or **around** to search casually for something. **to poke fun at** to ridicule someone or something. **to poke your nose into** (*informal*) to pry or intrude into someone else's affairs. [from a German or Dutch word]

poke [2] noun (*Scottish*) a small bag or pouch. **a pig in a poke** something you buy without seeing it or knowing much about it. [same origin as for *pocket*]

poker [1] noun a stiff metal rod for poking a fire.

poker [2] noun a card game in which players bet on the value of their cards, often using bluff. [perhaps from a German word *pochen* meaning 'to brag']

poky adjective (**pokier, pokiest**) small and cramped ♦ *The family live in one poky little room.* **pokiness** noun [from *poke*[1]]

polar adjective **1** to do with or near the North Pole or South Pole. **2** to do with one of the poles of a magnet. **3** directly opposite in character or tendency.

polar bear noun a white bear living in Arctic regions.

polar coordinates plural noun (*Geometry*) a pair of coordinates that use a distance and an angle to fix a position.

polarity (poh-la-riti) noun the property of possessing negative and positive poles.

polarize verb **1** (*Physics*) to restrict similar vibrations of (a light wave or other transverse wave) to a single direction or plane. **2** (*Physics*) to cause something to have polarity. **3** to separate into two extremes of opinion ♦ *The debate has become polarized.* **polarization** noun

Polaroid noun (*trademark*) **1** a material that polarizes the light passing through it, used in the lenses of sunglasses to protect the eyes from glare. **2** a type of camera that develops and prints a photograph rapidly when each exposure is made.

Pole noun a person born in Poland or descended from people born there.

pole [1] noun a long slender rounded piece of wood or metal, especially one used as a support.
pole verb to push a boat along by using a pole. [via Old English from a Latin word *palus* meaning 'stake']

pole [2] noun **1** either of the two points on the earth's surface which are at the ends of its axis of rotation, the North Pole or South Pole. **2** each of the two opposite points in a magnet which most strongly attract or repel magnetic bodies. **3** the positive or negative terminal of an electric cell or battery. **4** each of two opposed principles or ideas. **to be poles apart** to be widely different. [from a Greek word *polos* meaning 'axis']

poleaxe noun **1** a battleaxe. **2** a butcher's axe for slaughtering animals.
poleaxe verb **1** to strike someone down

with or as if with a poleaxe. **2** to shock someone greatly.

polecat noun **1** a small dark brown animal of the weasel family with an unpleasant smell. **2** (North Amer.) a skunk. [from an Old French word *pole* meaning 'chicken' and *cat*]

polemic (pəl-em-ik) noun a verbal attack on a belief or opinion.
polemic or **polemical** adjective
1 controversial. **2** argumentative. [from a Greek word *polemos* meaning 'war']

pole position noun the most favourable position on the starting grid in a motor race, in the front row and on the inside of the first bend. [from a use of *pole*¹ in horse racing to mean the starting position next to the inside boundary fence]

Pole Star noun a star above the North Pole.

pole vault noun an athletic event in which competitors vault over a high crossbar with the help of a long flexible pole held in the hands.
pole-vault verb to perform a pole vault.

police noun **1** a civil force responsible for keeping public order and detecting crime. **2** a force responsible for enforcing the regulations of an organization ♦ *military police*.
police verb to keep order in a place by means of a police force. [from an earlier meaning 'public order', same origin as for *political*]

policeman noun (**policemen**) a male police officer.

police officer noun a member of a police force.

police state noun a country (usually a totalitarian state) in which political police supervise and control citizens' activities.

police station noun the office of a local police force.

policewoman noun (**policewomen**) a female police officer.

policy¹ noun (**policies**) a course or general plan of action adopted by a government, party, or person. SYNONYMS: strategy, plan, approach. [same origin as for *political*]

policy² noun (**policies**) a contract of insurance. [via French from a Greek word *apodeixis* meaning 'evidence']

polio (poh-li-oh) noun short for **poliomyelitis**.

poliomyelitis (poh-li-oh-miy-ə-liy-tiss) noun an infectious disease caused by a virus, producing temporary or permanent paralysis. [from Greek words *polios* meaning 'grey' and *muelos* meaning 'marrow']

Polish adjective to do with or coming from Poland.
Polish noun the language of Poland.

polish verb **1** to make something smooth and shiny by rubbing, or to become smooth and shiny. **2** to improve or perfect a piece of work by correcting it or adding the finishing touches.
polish noun **1** smoothness and glossiness. SYNONYMS: gloss, shine, sheen, lustre, brightness, glossiness. **2** the process of polishing. **3** a substance for polishing a surface. **4** elegance or refinement of manner. SYNONYMS: elegance, refinement, sophistication. **to polish something off** to finish it quickly. **polisher** noun [from a Latin word *polire*]

polished adjective **1** elegant or refined ♦ *polished manners*. SYNONYMS: elegant, refined, suave, cultivated. **2** done with great ability and distinction ♦ *The singers gave a polished performance*. SYNONYMS: accomplished, masterly, distinguished.

politburo (pol-it-bewr-oh) noun (**politburos**) the chief policy-making committee of a communist country, especially of the former Soviet Union.

polite adjective **1** respectful and well-mannered towards other people. SYNONYMS: courteous, respectful, considerate, civil. **2** refined ♦ *polite society*. SYNONYMS: refined, civilized, elegant. **politely** adverb **politeness** noun [from a Latin word *politus* meaning 'polished']

politic adjective prudent and wise. [same origin as for *political*]

political adjective **1** to do with the government or public affairs of a country or region. **2** to do with status and power within an organization. **politically** adverb [from a Greek word *politeia* meaning 'government']

political asylum noun refuge and safety offered by one country to political refugees from another.

politically correct adjective using language and behaviour that avoid discrimination against or insensitivity towards certain groups of people, especially minorities. **political correctness** noun

political prisoner noun a person imprisoned for political beliefs or activities.

political science noun the study of political activity and principles.

politician noun a person who is professionally involved in politics, especially a holder of an elected political office.

politics noun 1 the activities and principles involved in governing a country or region. 2 political affairs or life. 3 activities aimed at enhancing power and status within an organization ♦ *office politics*.
politics plural noun political affairs or activities.

polka noun a lively dance of Bohemian origin. [from a Czech word *pulka* meaning 'half-step']

polka dot noun each of a number of round dots evenly spaced to form a pattern on fabric.

poll (pohl) noun 1 the process of voting at an election ♦ *to go to the polls*. 2 the number of votes cast in an election ♦ *a heavy poll*. 3 an opinion poll. 4 (*dialect*) the head.
poll verb 1 to vote at an election. 2 (said about a candidate) to receive a specified number of votes ♦ *The winner polled over 20,000 votes*. 3 to cut off the horns of an animal, especially a young cow. 4 to cut off the top of a tree or plant. [originally in the meaning 'the head' and later 'the number of people determined by counting heads', probably from a German or Dutch word]

pollard (pol-erd) noun a tree that is cut off at the top to produce a close head of young branches.
pollard verb to cut the top off a tree. [from *poll* meaning 'head']

pollen noun a fine powdery substance produced by the anthers of flowers, containing male cells for fertilizing other flowers. [from a Latin word meaning 'fine flour']

pollen count noun an index of the amount of pollen in the air, published as information for people who are allergic to pollen.

pollinate verb to fertilize a flower or plant with pollen. **pollination** noun **pollinator** noun

polling booth noun a booth or cubicle in which a vote is made.

polling station noun a place used for people to vote in an election.

poll tax noun a tax that every adult has to pay regardless of income.

pollutant noun a substance that causes pollution.

pollute verb 1 to make the air, water, etc. dirty or impure, especially by adding harmful or offensive substances. SYNONYMS: contaminate, poison. 2 to corrupt someone or someone's mind. **pollution** noun [from a Latin word *polluere*, with the same meaning]

polo noun a game like hockey, played by teams on horseback with long-handled mallets. [from a Tibetan word meaning 'ball']

polonaise (pol-ə-**nayz**) noun a stately dance of Polish origin, or the music for this. [from a French word *polonais* meaning 'Polish']

polo neck noun a high close-fitting collar turned over at the top.

polo shirt noun a casual shirt with short sleeves and a collar and buttons at the neck.

poltergeist (pol-ter-gyst) noun a ghost or spirit that supposedly causes a disturbance by throwing things about. [from German words *poltern* meaning 'to make a disturbance' and *Geist* meaning 'ghost']

poltroon (pol-troon) noun (*old use*) a coward. [probably from an Italian word *poltro* meaning 'sluggard']

poly (pol-i) noun (**polys**) (*informal*) short for polytechnic.

poly- prefix 1 many (as in *polymath*). 2 (in names of plastics) polymerized. [from a Greek word *polus* meaning 'much']

polyamide noun a natural or synthetic fibre such as silk or nylon, that is composed of polymers of the same amide group.

polyandry (pol-i-an-dri) noun the custom or practice of having more than one husband at a time. **polyandrous** adjective [from poly- and a Greek word *andros* meaning 'of a man']

polyanthus *noun* a cultivated primrose produced from hybridized primulas. [from *poly-* and a Greek word *anthos* meaning 'flower']

polychrome (pol-i-krohm) *adjective* painted, printed, or decorated in several colours. [from *poly-* and a Greek word *khrōma* meaning 'colour']

polyester *noun* a polymerized synthetic resin or fibre used to make clothing.

polygamy (pə-lig-əmi) *noun* the custom or practice of having more than one wife at a time. (Compare **monogamy**.) **polygamist** *noun* **polygamous** *adjective* [from *poly-* and a Greek word *gamos* meaning 'marriage']

polyglot (pol-i-glot) *adjective* 1 knowing or using several languages. 2 (said about a book) translated into several languages. **polyglot** *noun* a person who knows several languages. [from *poly-* and a Greek word *glōtta* meaning 'language']

polygon (pol-i-gən) *noun* (*Geometry*) a plane figure with many sides, usually at least five. **polygonal** (pə-lig-ən-əl) *adjective* [from *poly-* and a Greek word *gōnia* meaning 'corner']

polyhedron (poli-hee-drən) *noun* (*Geometry*) a solid figure with many faces, usually at least seven. **polyhedral** *adjective* [from *poly-* and a Greek word *hedra* meaning 'base']

polymer (pol-im-er) *noun* (*Chemistry*) a compound whose molecule is formed from a large number of simple molecules combined. **polymerize** *verb* [from *poly-* and a Greek word *meros* meaning 'part']

polyp (pol-ip) *noun* 1 (*Zoology*) a simple organism with a tube-shaped body, e.g. one of the organisms of which coral is made. 2 (*Medicine*) an abnormal growth projecting from a mucous membrane. [from a Latin word *polypus*]

polyphonic (pol-i-fon-ik) *adjective* (*Music*) (said about music, especially vocal music) written in counterpoint. [from *poly-* and a Greek word *phōnē* meaning 'sound']

polyploid *adjective* (*Biochemistry*) (said about a cell or nucleus) having more than two sets of chromosomes. [from *poly-*, made to look like *haploid* and *diploid*]

polypropylene or **polypropene** *noun* (*Chemistry*) any of a number of plastics or fibres that are polymers of propene.

polysaccharide *noun* (*Biochemistry*) a carbohydrate that can be broken down into two or more simple sugars.

polystyrene (poli-stiyr-een) *noun* a kind of plastic which is a polymer of styrene, used for insulation and in packaging.

polysyllabic (poli-sil-ab-ik) *adjective* (said about a word) having several syllables.

polytechnic (poli-tek-nik) *noun* an institution of higher education giving courses to degree level, especially in vocational subjects. From 1992, most British polytechnics were entitled to use the name 'university'. [from *poly-* and a Greek word *tekhnē* meaning 'art' or 'skill']

polytheism (pol-ith-ee-ism) *noun* the belief in or worship of more than one god. **polytheist** *noun* **polytheistic** *adjective* [from *poly-* and a Greek word *theos* meaning 'god']

polythene *noun* a kind of tough light plastic material used mainly in packaging. [from *polyethylene*, a polymer from which it is made]

polyunsaturated *adjective* (*Chemistry*) denoting a fat or oil that is not associated with the formation of cholesterol in the blood.

polyurethane (poli-yoor-i-thayn) *noun* a kind of synthetic resin or plastic.

polyvinyl (poli-viy-nil) *adjective* (said about a synthetic resin) made from polymerized vinyl.

polyvinyl acetate *noun* a soft plastic polymer used in paints and adhesives.

polyvinyl chloride *noun* a plastic used for insulation of electrical wiring etc. and as fabric for furnishings etc.

pomander (pəm-an-der) *noun* a ball or container of mixed sweet-smelling substances, used to perfume a room or cupboard.

pomegranate (pom-i-gran-it) *noun* 1 a tropical fruit with a tough rind and reddish pulp enclosing many seeds. 2 the tree that bears this fruit. [from a Latin word *pomum* meaning 'apple' and *granatum* meaning 'having many seeds']

Pomeranian (pom-er-ayn-iən) *noun* a small dog with a silky coat and a pointed nose. [from Pomerania, a region of central Europe]

pommel (pum-əl) *noun* 1 a part that projects upward at the front of a saddle. 2 a knob on the handle of a sword or dagger. **pommel** *verb* (**pommelled**, **pommelling**) another spelling of **pummel**. [from a Latin word *pomum* meaning 'apple']

Pommy noun (Austral. and NZ) (informal) (**Pommies**) a British person, especially a recent immigrant. [origin unknown]

pomp noun the splendour and ceremony that is associated with important state occasions. SYNONYMS: splendour, pageantry, grandeur, ceremony, magnificence, majesty. [from a Greek word *pompē* meaning 'procession']

pom-pom noun an automatic quick-firing gun of a kind formerly used to fire on aircraft from the deck of a ship. [an imitation of the sound it makes when it is fired]

pompom or **pompon** noun 1 a ball of coloured threads used as a decoration. 2 a dahlia or similar flower with small tightly clustered petals. [from a French word *pompon*]

pompous adjective affectedly solemn and self-important in manner. SYNONYMS: self-important, haughty; (informal) stuck-up. **pomposity** (pom-**poss**-iti) noun **pompously** adverb [from *pomp*]

poncho noun (**ponchos**) a short cloak of a kind originally worn in South America, consisting of a piece of cloth like a blanket with a slit in the centre for the head. [a South American Spanish word]

pond noun a small area of still water, especially in a town or village or on a common. [from *pound*^{2}]

ponder verb 1 to be deep in thought. 2 to think long and carefully about something. SYNONYMS: reflect, consider, deliberate. [from a Latin word *ponderare* meaning 'to weigh']

ponderous adjective 1 heavy and clumsy. SYNONYMS: cumbersome, clumsy, unwieldy. 2 dull and laborious in style. **ponderously** adverb [from a Latin word *ponderis* meaning 'of weight']

pondweed noun a submerged plant that grows in still water.

pong noun (informal) an unpleasant smell. **pong** verb (informal) to smell unpleasantly. [origin unknown]

pontiff noun 1 the Pope. 2 a bishop or chief priest. [from a Latin word *pontifex* meaning literally 'bridge builder', then 'chief priest']

pontifical (pon-**tif**-ikəl) adjective 1 to do with a pontiff, papal. 2 having a pompous air or manner. **pontifically** adverb

pontificate^1 (pon-**tif**-i-kayt) verb to express opinions in a pompous or self-important way. **pontificator** noun

pontificate^2 (pon-**tif**-i-kət) noun the office of pope or bishop.

pontoon^1 noun 1 each of a number of boats or hollow metal cylinders used to support a temporary bridge over a river. 2 a kind of flat-bottomed boat. [from a Latin word *pontis* meaning 'of a bridge']

pontoon^2 noun 1 a card game in which players try to get cards with a face value totalling 21. 2 a score of 21 from two cards in this game. [from a French word *vingt-et-un* meaning 'twenty-one']

pony noun (**ponies**) 1 a small horse. 2 (informal) a sum of £25. [from a French word *poulenet* meaning 'small foal']

ponytail noun long hair drawn back and tied at the crown of the head so that it hangs down.

pony-trekking noun travelling across country on ponies for pleasure.

poodle noun a dog with thick curly hair that is often clipped and partly shaved. [from a German word *Pudelhund* meaning 'water-dog']

pooh interjection (informal) 1 an exclamation of disgust at an unpleasant smell. 2 an exclamation of impatience or contempt.

pooh-pooh verb (informal) to dismiss an idea or suggestion scornfully.

pool^1 noun 1 a small area of still water, especially one that is naturally formed. 2 a puddle or shallow patch of water or other liquid lying on a surface. 3 a swimming pool. 4 a deep place in a river. [from an Old English word *pol*]

pool^2 noun 1 a common fund of money that several contributors pay into, providing financial support for something. 2 the total of players' stakes in gambling. 3 a shared supply of vehicles, personnel, or resources that can be drawn on when needed. 4 a game resembling billiards. **pool** verb to put money or other resources into a common fund or supply, for sharing. **the pools** short for **football pools**. [from a French word *poule* meaning 'stake' or 'kitty']

poop noun the raised deck at the stern of a ship. [from a Latin word *puppis* meaning 'stern']

poor adjective 1 having too little money or other resources to live a normal or comfortable life. SYNONYMS: needy, hard up, badly off, impoverished. **2** lacking in something ♦ *soil poor in minerals*. **3** of a low quality or standard ♦ *The work was poor*. SYNONYMS: inferior, inadequate, unsatisfactory, deficient. **4** lacking in spirit, despicable. **5** deserving pity or sympathy ♦ *The poor man could hardly speak*. **poorness** noun [via Old French from a Latin word *pauper* meaning 'poor']

poorly adverb in a poor way, badly.
poorly adjective unwell ♦ *She is feeling poorly*. SYNONYMS: unwell, sick, ill, indisposed.

pop[1] noun **1** a small sharp explosive sound. **2** a fizzy drink.
pop verb (**popped, popping**) **1** to make a pop, or to cause something to make a pop. **2** to put something quickly somewhere ♦ *I'll pop it in the microwave*. **3** to come or go quickly or suddenly or unexpectedly ♦ *He's just popped out for a newspaper*. [an imitation of the sound]

pop[2] noun (also **pop music**) popular music of a kind promoted commercially since the 1950s.
pop adjective to do with pop music. [short for *popular*]

popadom noun another spelling of **poppadom**.

pop art noun art that uses themes drawn from popular culture.

popcorn noun maize heated so that it bursts to form fluffy balls.

pope noun the Bishop of Rome as head of the Roman Catholic Church. [from a Greek word *papas* meaning 'father']

popery noun (derogatory) Roman Catholicism.

pop-eyed adjective (informal) having bulging eyes.

popgun noun a child's toy gun that shoots a cork or pellet with a popping sound.

popinjay noun (old use) a vain or conceited person. [via Old French and Spanish from an Arabic word *babbaga*]

popish adjective (derogatory) Roman Catholic.

poplar noun a kind of tall slender tree with leaves that quiver easily. [from an Old French word *poplier*]

poplin noun a plain woven fabric usually of cotton. [from an Old French word *papeline*]

poppadom (pop-ə-dəm) noun (in Indian cookery) a thin crisp biscuit made of lentil flour. [from a Tamil word]

popper noun (informal) a press stud.

poppet noun (informal) a small and lovable person, especially a child. [from a Latin word *puppa* meaning 'doll' or 'girl']

popping crease noun (in cricket) a line marking the limit of the batsman's position at the wicket.

poppy noun (**poppies**) a plant with showy flowers and milky juice. [from an Old English word *popig*]

poppycock noun (informal) nonsense. [from a Dutch dialect word *pappekak* meaning 'soft dung']

populace (pop-yoo-ləs) noun the general public. [via French from an Italian word *popolaccio* meaning 'common people']

popular adjective **1** liked or enjoyed by many people. **2** intended for the general public. **3** (said about a belief or attitude) held by many people ♦ *popular superstitions*. **popularity** noun **popularly** adverb [from a Latin word *populus* meaning 'people']

popular front noun a political party representing left-wing groups.

popularize verb **1** to make something popular or suitable for the general public. **2** to present a subject, especially a technical one in a way that can be understood by ordinary people. **popularization** noun

populate verb to supply a place with a population; to inhabit a place.

population noun all the inhabitants of a place, or the total number of these.

populous adjective having a large population.

porcelain (por-səl-in) noun the finest kind of china. [from a French word *porcelaine*]

porch noun a covered shelter outside the entrance of a building. [from a Latin word *porticus*, related to *portico*]

porcupine noun a small animal with a body and tail covered with protective spines. [from a Latin word *porcus* meaning 'pig' and *spine*]

pore[1] noun each of many tiny openings on the skin or other surface, through which moisture can pass. [from a Greek word *poros* meaning 'passage']

pore[2] *verb* **pore over** to study something closely and with great interest. [origin unknown]
◊ Do not confuse this word with **pour**, which has a different meaning.

pork *noun* meat from a pig. [from a Latin word *porcus* meaning 'pig']

porker *noun* a young pig raised for its meat.

porn *noun* (*informal*) short for **pornography**.

pornography *noun* pictures or descriptions that are intended to stimulate sexual excitement. **pornographic** *adjective* [from a Greek word *pornē* meaning 'prostitute' and *-graphy*]

porous (por-əs) *adjective* having pores, allowing liquid or air to pass through. **porosity** (por-**oss**-iti) *noun*

porphyry (por-fi-ri) *noun* a kind of rock containing crystals of minerals. [from a Greek word *porphura* meaning 'purple']

porpoise (por-pəs) *noun* a sea animal resembling a dolphin or small whale, with a blunt rounded snout. [from Latin words *porcus* meaning 'pig' and *piscis* meaning 'fish']

porridge *noun* a food of oatmeal or other cereal boiled in water or milk. [an alteration of the word *pottage*]

porringer *noun* (*historical*) a small bowl for holding porridge or soup.

port[1] *noun* 1 a town or city with a harbour where goods are imported or exported by ship, especially one with a customs office. 2 the left-hand side of a ship or aircraft when facing forward, the opposite to **starboard**.
port *verb* to turn a ship or its helm to the port side. [from a Latin word *portus* meaning 'harbour']

port[2] *noun* 1 an opening in the side of a ship for boarding or loading. 2 a porthole. 3 a socket in a computer or computer network into which a device can be plugged.
port *verb* (*Computing*) to transfer data from one system or device to another. [from a Latin word *porta* meaning 'gate']

port[3] *noun* a sweet fortified red wine of Portugal. [from the city of Oporto in Portugal]

portable *adjective* suitable or light enough to be carried ♦ *a portable television.*
portable *noun* a portable device.
portability *noun* [from a Latin word *portare* meaning 'to carry']

portal *noun* a doorway or gateway, especially a large imposing one. [from a Latin word *porta* meaning 'gate']

portcullis *noun* a strong heavy grating that can be lowered in grooves to block a gateway. [from a French phrase *porte coleice* meaning 'sliding door']

portend (por-tend) *verb* to be a sign that something important or calamitous will happen. SYNONYMS: bode, augur, presage. [from Latin words *pro-* meaning 'forwards' and *tendere* meaning 'to stretch']

portent (por-tent) *noun* a sign that something important or calamitous will happen. SYNONYMS: omen, presage, sign.

portentous (por-tent-əs) *adjective* indicating that something important or calamitous will happen. SYNONYMS: ominous, momentous, foreboding.

porter[1] *noun* a person employed to look after the entrance to a large building and help people coming in. [from a Latin word *porta* meaning 'gate']

porter[2] *noun* 1 a person employed to carry luggage or other goods. 2 a kind of dark beer. [from Latin *portare* meaning 'to carry']

portfolio *noun* (**portfolios**) 1 a case for holding loose documents or drawings. 2 a set of investments held by one investor. 3 the position of a Minister or Secretary of State. 4 a set of creative work intended to demonstrate a person's abilities. [from Italian words *portare* meaning 'to carry' and *foglio* meaning 'sheet of paper']

porthole *noun* a small window in the side of a ship or aircraft.

portico (port-i-koh) *noun* (**porticoes** or **porticos**) a structure consisting of a roof supported by columns, usually forming a porch to a building. [from a Latin word *porticus* meaning 'porch']

portion *noun* 1 a part or share of something. SYNONYMS: share, part, allocation, amount. 2 an amount of food given to one person. SYNONYMS: helping, serving.
portion *verb* to divide something into portions and share it out. [via French from a Latin phrase *pro portione* meaning 'in proportion']

Portland cement *noun* a kind of cement coloured like limestone (called *Portland stone*) from the Isle of Portland in Dorset.

portly adjective (**portlier, portliest**) large and rather fat. **portliness** noun [from an earlier meaning 'dignified', from an old word *port* meaning 'bearing' or 'deportment']

portmanteau (port-man-toh) noun (**portmanteaus** or **portmanteaux**) a large travelling bag made of stout material that opens into two equal parts. [from French words *porter* meaning 'to carry' and *manteau* meaning 'coat']

portmanteau word noun an invented word that combines the sounds and meanings of two other words, e.g. *brunch* for *breakfast* and *lunch*.

portrait noun 1 a picture of a person or animal. SYNONYMS: likeness, representation. 2 a description in words. SYNONYMS: description, profile, portrayal. **portraitist** noun

portray (por-tray) verb 1 to make a picture of a person or animal. 2 to describe someone or something in words or represent them in a play or film ♦ *The queen is portrayed as a lonely and pathetic character.* SYNONYMS: depict, represent, picture. **portrayal** noun [from an Old French word *portraire*, from *traire* meaning 'to draw']

Portuguese adjective to do with or coming from Portugal.
Portuguese noun 1 (**Portuguese**) a person born in Portugal or descended from people born there. 2 the language of Portugal, also spoken in Brazil.
◊ Note that there is a second letter *u* after the *g* in this word.

Portuguese man-of-war noun a sea animal with stinging tentacles.

pose verb 1 to take a position for being painted or photographed for a portrait, or to put someone in this position. 2 to take a particular attitude for effect. 3 to pretend to be someone ♦ *The man was posing as a police officer.* 4 to put forward or present something that needs attention ♦ *The increasing costs pose a major problem.*
pose noun 1 a position or attitude that a person takes for a portrait. SYNONYMS: position, attitude, stance, posture. 2 a way of behaving that someone adopts to give a particular impression. [via Old French from a Latin word *ponere* meaning 'to put']

poser noun 1 a puzzling question or problem. 2 a poseur.

poseur (poh-**zer**) noun a person who behaves in an affected way to impress others. [a French word, related to *pose*]

posh adjective (*informal*) 1 smart or luxurious ♦ *a posh restaurant.* SYNONYMS: smart, grand, elegant, fancy. 2 upper-class ♦ *a posh accent.* [the suggestion is often made that this word is derived from the initials of 'port out, starboard home', referring to the more comfortable side (out of the heat of the sun) for accommodation on ships that used to travel between England and India; but this is not correct]

posit (poz-it) verb (**posited, positing**) to propose something as a fact or a basis for argument. [same origin as for *position*]

position noun 1 the place occupied by a person or thing. SYNONYMS: location, point, place, spot. 2 the correct or usual place for something ♦ *The chair is out of position.* 3 an advantageous situation, especially in competition with others ♦ *The runners were manoeuvring for position.* 4 the way in which a person or thing is placed or arranged ♦ *She was in a sitting position* ♦ *Make a note of our chess positions.* 5 a situation or set of circumstances ♦ *They explained the position to us.* SYNONYMS: situation, circumstances. 6 a situation in relation to other people or things ♦ *I am in no position to argue with you.* 7 a policy or point of view ♦ *What is the Bank's position about loans?* SYNONYMS: policy, attitude, standpoint. 8 rank or status, high social standing ♦ *a family of position.* 9 a job or paid employment. SYNONYMS: job, post, appointment.
position verb to place something or someone in a certain position. SYNONYMS: put, place, lay, rest, set, deposit; (*informal*) stick. [from a Latin word *positus* meaning 'placed', from *ponere* meaning 'to put']

positive adjective 1 agreeing, giving the answer 'yes' ♦ *Their reply was a positive one.* 2 definite, leaving no room for doubt ♦ *There is positive proof of their guilt.* SYNONYMS: definite, absolute, firm, conclusive, unequivocal. 3 holding an opinion confidently ♦ *I am positive that was George.* SYNONYMS: sure, certain, confident, convinced. 4 constructive and helpful ♦ *She made some positive suggestions.* SYNONYMS: constructive, helpful, useful, productive. 5 involving the presence of something sought or in question ♦ *The result of her pregnancy test was positive.* 6 (said about a quantity) greater than zero. 7 (*Electricity*)

containing or producing the kind of electric charge opposite to that carried by electrons. **8** (said about a photographic image) having the light and shade or the colours of the original. **9** (*Grammar*) said about the basic or primary form of an adjective or adverb (e.g. *big*, *quickly*) as distinct from the comparative (*bigger*, *more quickly*) or superlative (*biggest*, *most quickly*).
positive *noun* **1** a positive quality or character. **2** a positive photographic image. **positively** *adverb* **positiveness** *noun* [from a Latin word *positivus* meaning 'placed' or 'settled']

positive pole *noun* the north-seeking pole of a magnet.

positive sign *noun* the sign +.

positron (poz-i-tron) *noun* (*Physics*) an elementary particle with the mass of an electron and an equal but positive charge. [from *positive* and *electron*]

posse (poss-i) *noun* (*historical*) a body of men summoned by a sheriff to enforce the law. [from a Latin phrase *posse comitatus* meaning 'force of the county']

possess *verb* **1** to have something as belonging to you, to own something. **2** to control or dominate the thoughts or actions of someone ♦ *What possessed you to do such a thing?* **possessor** *noun* [from a Latin word *possidere* meaning 'to occupy' or 'to hold']

possession *noun* **1** something you possess or own. SYNONYMS: (possessions) belongings, property, goods. **2** the state of possessing something or of being possessed. **3** (in some ball games) one side's control and use of the ball for a time. **to take possession of** to become the owner or possessor of something.

possessive *adjective* **1** wanting to keep what you possess for yourself and not to share it. **2** demanding someone's total attention and love. **3** (*Grammar*) denoting a form of a word that indicates possession, such as *hers* and *Jack's*. **possessively** *adverb* **possessiveness** *noun*

possessive pronoun *noun* a pronoun that indicates possession, such as *hers* and *theirs*.

possibility *noun* (**possibilities**) **1** something that is possible or might happen. **2** the fact or condition of being possible.

possible *adjective* able to exist or happen or to be done or used. SYNONYMS: (able to be done) feasible, practical.
possible *noun* a candidate who may be successful for a job or membership of a team. [from a Latin word *posse* meaning 'to be able']

possibly *adverb* **1** in terms of what is possible ♦ *I could not possibly do it.*
2 perhaps ♦ *They are possibly right about that.*

possum *noun* **1** an Australian animal with a pouch and a long tail. **2** (*North Amer.*) (*informal*) an opossum. **to play possum 1** to pretend to be unconscious or dead (as an opossum does when threatened). **2** to pretend not to know something is happening. [a shortening of *opossum*]

post[1] *noun* **1** a piece of wood, concrete, or metal etc. set upright in the ground to support something or to mark a position. SYNONYMS: pillar, column, pole, stake, upright. **2** the starting post or finishing post in a race ♦ *Several runners were left at the post.*
post *verb* to announce something by putting up a notice or placard about it. [from a Latin word *postis* with the same meaning]

post[2] *noun* **1** the place where a soldier is on watch, a place of duty ♦ *The sentries are at their posts.* **2** a place occupied by soldiers, especially a frontier fort; the soldiers there. **3** a place occupied for purposes of trade, especially in a region that is not yet fully settled, ♦ *trading posts.* **4** a position of paid employment, a job. SYNONYMS: job, position, appointment.
post *verb* **1** to place or station people somewhere ♦ *Sentries are posted at the gates.* **2** to appoint someone to a post or command ♦ *Her husband was posted to Washington.* [via French and Italian from a Latin word *positum* meaning 'placed']

post[3] *noun* **1** the collection and delivery of letters, parcels, etc. **2** the letters and parcels sent in this way. **3** a single collection or delivery of letters and parcels ♦ *Is there an afternoon post on Saturdays?*
post *verb* **1** to put a letter or parcel into a post office or postbox for delivery to an address. **2** to enter information in an official ledger. **to keep someone posted** to keep someone informed about something. [from a French word *poste*, related to *post*[2] (because originally mail was carried in relays by riders posted along the route)]

post- *prefix* after (as in *post-war*). [from a Latin word *post* meaning 'after']

postage *noun* the charge for sending something by post.

postage stamp *noun* a small adhesive stamp for sticking on things to be posted, showing the amount paid.

postal *adjective* **1** to do with the post. **2** by post ♦ *a postal vote.* **postally** *adverb*

postal order *noun* a money order bought from a post office for sending to a named recipient.

postbox *noun* a large container with a slot into which letters are put for posting.

postcard *noun* a card for sending a message by post without an envelope.

postcode *noun* a group of letters and figures included in a postal address to assist sorting.

post-date *verb* to put a date on a document or cheque etc. that is later than the actual one.

poster *noun* a large printed notice or picture put up to announce something or as decoration. [from *post*¹]

poste restante (pohst ress-tahnt) *noun* a department in a post office where letters are kept until called for. [a French phrase, meaning 'post remaining']

posterior *adjective* situated behind or at the back.
posterior *noun* the buttocks. [from a Latin word meaning 'further back']

posterity (poss-te-riti) *noun* future generations of people ♦ *We need to preserve these documents for posterity.* [from a Latin word *posterus* meaning 'following, future']

postern (poss-tern) *noun* a small entrance at the back or side of a fortress or other large building. [from an Old French word *posterne*, related to *posterity*]

postgraduate *adjective* to do with studies carried on after taking a first degree.
postgraduate *noun* a student engaged in these studies.

post-haste *adverb* with great speed or haste. [from *post*³ and *haste* (because post was the quickest means of communication)]

posthumous (poss-tew-məs) *adjective* coming or happening after a person's death ♦ *a posthumous award for bravery.*

posthumously *adverb* [from a Latin word *postumus* meaning 'last']

postilion *noun* a rider on a nearside horse pulling a coach or carriage, when there is no coachman. [via French from an Italian word *postiglione* meaning 'post boy']

postman *noun* (**postmen**) a person who delivers or collects letters and parcels.

postmark *noun* an official mark stamped on something sent by post, giving the place and date and cancelling the stamp.
postmark *verb* to mark a letter or parcel with a postmark.

postmaster or **postmistress** *noun* an official in charge of a post office.

post-mortem *noun* **1** an examination of a dead body to determine the cause of death. **2** a detailed discussion of something, especially a failure, after it is over. [a Latin word meaning 'after death']

post-natal *adjective* occurring in or to do with the period after childbirth. [from *post-* and a Latin word *natus* meaning 'born']

post office *noun* **1** a public department or corporation responsible for postal services. **2** a building in which postal business is conducted.

post office box *noun* a numbered place in a post office where letters are kept until called for.

postpone *verb* to arrange for an event to take place at a later time than originally planned ♦ *The match has been postponed until next week.* SYNONYMS: put off, delay, defer, (of a meeting) adjourn. **postponement** *noun* [from *post-* and a Latin word *ponere* meaning 'to place']

postscript *noun* a remark or paragraph added at the end of a letter, after the signature. [from *post-* and a Latin word *scriptum* meaning 'written']

postulant (poss-tew-lənt) *noun* someone who has applied to join a religious order. [same origin as for *postulate*¹]

postulate¹ (poss-tew-layt) *verb* to assume something to be true, especially as a basis for reasoning or argument. **postulation** *noun* [from a Latin word *postulare* meaning 'to claim']

postulate² (poss-tew-lət) *noun* something postulated.

posture (poss-cher) *noun* a particular position of the body, or the way in which a person stands, sits, or walks. SYNONYMS: attitude, pose, stance, position. [same origin as for *position*]

post-war *adjective* existing or occurring after a war.

posy *noun* (**posies**) a small bunch of flowers. [from a French word *poésie* meaning 'poetry']

pot [1] *noun* 1 a deep rounded container, especially one made of earthenware. 2 a flowerpot. 3 a receptacle for a child to urinate or defecate into. 4 (*informal*) a large amount of something ♦ *pots of money*.
pot *verb* (**potted, potting**) 1 to plant something in a pot. 2 (in billiards and snooker) to put a ball into a pocket. 3 to hit or kill something by shooting at it. 4 (*informal*) to put a child to sit on a pot.
to go to pot (*informal*) to deteriorate or become ruined. [from an Old English word *pott*]

pot [2] *noun* (*informal*) cannabis. [short for Mexican Spanish *potiguaya* meaning 'cannabis leaves']

potable (poh-tə-bəl) *adjective* (*formal*) drinkable. [from a Latin word *potare* meaning 'to drink']

potash *noun* a potassium compound, especially potassium carbonate. [from *pot* and *ash* [2] (because it was first obtained from vegetable ashes washed in a pot)]

potassium (pə-tas-iəm) *noun* a soft silvery-white metallic element (symbol K) that is essential for living things. [from *potash*]

potato *noun* (**potatoes**) 1 a plant with starchy tubers that are used as food. 2 one of these tubers. [from a South American word *batata* (because potatoes were first brought to Europe from South America)]

pot belly *noun* a fat rounded stomach.

potent (poh-tənt) *adjective* having a powerful effect ♦ *a potent drug*. SYNONYMS: powerful, strong, effective. **potency** *noun* [from a Latin word *potens* meaning 'able']

potentate (poh-tən-tayt) *noun* a monarch or ruler. [same origin as for *potent*]

potential (pə-ten-shəl) *adjective* capable of coming into being or of being developed or used ♦ *a potential source of energy*. SYNONYMS: likely, possible, future.
potential *noun* 1 an ability or resources available for development or use. SYNONYMS: capacity, promise. 2 (*Electricity*) the voltage between two points.
potentiality *noun* **potentially** *adverb* [from a Latin word *potentia* meaning 'power']

potentiometer (pə-ten-shi-om-it-er) *noun* (*Electricity*) an instrument for measuring or adjusting electrical potential.

pothole *noun* 1 a deep underground cave formed in rock by the action of water. 2 a hole in the surface of a road.
pothole *verb* to explore underground potholes. **potholer** *noun*

potion (poh-shən) *noun* a liquid for drinking as a medicine or drug. SYNONYMS: medicine, mixture, draught. [from a Latin word *potus* meaning 'having drunk something']

pot luck *noun* a chance taken with whatever happens to be available.

pot-pourri (poh-poor-ee) *noun* (**pot-pourris**) 1 a mixture of dried petals and spices put in a bowl to perfume a room. 2 a mixture of things, a medley. [a French word meaning 'rotten pot']

potsherd (pot-sherd) *noun* (*Archaeology*) a broken piece of earthenware.

pot shot *noun* a shot aimed casually at something.

pottage *noun* (*old use*) a soup or stew. [from an Old French word *potage* meaning 'what is put into a pot']

potted *adjective* 1 (said about a piece of writing) shortened or abridged from a longer version. 2 (said about food) preserved in a pot ♦ *potted shrimps*.

potter [1] *noun* a person who makes pottery.

potter [2] *verb* to work or move about in a leisurely relaxed way. **potterer** *noun* [from an old word *pote* meaning 'to push or poke']

pottery *noun* (**potteries**) 1 vessels and other objects made of baked clay. 2 the work of making pottery, or the place where it is made.

potting shed *noun* a shed used for potting plants and keeping garden tools.

potty [1] *adjective* (**pottier, pottiest**) (*informal*) 1 crazy or foolish ♦ *a potty idea*. 2 extremely keen on something ♦ *potty about football*. [origin unknown]

potty [2] *noun* (**potties**) (*informal*) a chamber pot for a child.

pouch *noun* a small bag, or something shaped like a bag.

pouch *verb* to put something into a pouch or pocket. [from a French word *poche* meaning 'bag or pocket']

pouffe (poof) *noun* a padded stool. [a French word]

poulterer *noun* someone who sells poultry and game.

poultice (pohl-tiss) *noun* a soft heated dressing applied to an inflamed or sore area of skin.
poultice *verb* to apply a poultice to the skin. [from a Latin word *pultes* meaning 'soft food' or 'pap']

poultry (pohl-tri) *noun* domestic fowls such as ducks, geese, chickens, and turkeys, kept for their eggs and meat. [from an Old French word *poulet* meaning 'pullet']

pounce *verb* to jump or swoop down quickly on something.
pounce *noun* a pouncing movement. **to pounce on** to notice a mistake or weakness and take quick advantage of it. [from an earlier meaning 'claw' or 'talon', perhaps related to *puncture*]

pound[1] *noun* 1 a measure of weight equal to 16 oz. avoirdupois (0.4536 kg) or 12 oz. troy (0.3732 kg). 2 the unit of currency of Britain and some other countries. [from an Old English word *pund*]

pound[2] *noun* 1 a place where stray dogs are taken and kept until claimed. 2 an enclosure for motor vehicles impounded by the police. [origin unknown]

pound[3] *verb* 1 to crush or beat something with heavy repeated strokes. SYNONYMS: grind, crush, beat, mash. 2 to walk or run with heavy steps ♦ *He pounded down the stairs.* 3 to beat or throb with a heavy rhythm. SYNONYMS: throb, pulsate. 4 (said about the heart) to beat heavily, to thump. **to pound out** to produce a document or piece of music using heavy strokes of a keyboard. [from an Old English word *punian*]

poundage *noun* a payment or charge of so much for each pound.

pound note *noun* a banknote having the value of £1.

pour *verb* 1 to flow or cause liquid to flow in a stream or shower. SYNONYMS: (without an object) flow, gush, run, stream, cascade. 2 to prepare and serve a drink. 3 to rain heavily. 4 to come or go in large amounts ♦ *Letters of complaint poured in.* **to pour something out** to express your feelings

openly and at length. **pourer** *noun* [origin unknown]

pout *verb* to push out your lips when you are annoyed or sulking.
pout *noun* a pouting expression. [probably from a Scandinavian language]

poverty *noun* 1 the state of being poor, a lack of money or resources. SYNONYMS: hardship, need, privation. 2 a scarcity or lack of something. SYNONYMS: scarcity, lack, paucity. 3 a renunciation of possessions, as part of a religious way of life. [via Old French from a Latin word *pauper* meaning 'poor']

poverty line *noun* the minimum income level needed to be sure of the basic necessities of life.

poverty trap *noun* a situation in which there is no advantage in an increased income because this would be offset by a loss of state benefits which a lower income brings.

POW *abbreviation* prisoner of war.

powder *noun* 1 a mass of fine dry particles produced by grinding or crushing a solid substance. 2 a medicine or cosmetic made as a powder. 3 gunpowder.
powder *verb* 1 to apply powder to something; to cover a surface with powder. 2 to reduce a substance to powder. **powdered** *adjective* [from a Latin word *pulveris* meaning 'of dust']

powder puff *noun* a soft pad for putting powder on the skin.

powder room *noun* a woman's toilet in a public building.

powdery *adjective* like powder.
powderiness *noun*

power *noun* 1 strength or energy. SYNONYMS: strength, energy, vigour, might, force. 2 the ability to do something ♦ *the power of speech.* SYNONYMS: ability, capacity, capability. 3 political control or authority ♦ *the party in power.* 4 legal right or authority ♦ *the power to levy taxes.* 5 an influential person, country, or organization. 6 (*Mathematics*) the product of a number multiplied by itself a given number of times ♦ *the third power of 2 = 2 × 2 × 2 = 8.* 7 mechanical or electrical energy as opposed to hand labour ♦ *power tools.* 8 an electricity supply ♦ *a power failure.* 9 (*Physics*) the rate of doing work, measured in watts or horsepower. 10 the magnifying capacity of a lens.
power *verb* 1 to equip a place with

mechanical or electrical power. **2** to travel with great speed or strength. [via Old French from a Latin word *posse* meaning 'to be able']

power cut *noun* a temporary failure of an electricity supply.

powerful *adjective* having great power, strength, or influence. SYNONYMS: strong, vigorous, forceful; influential. **powerfully** *adverb*

powerhouse *noun* a person with great energy and determination.

powerless *adjective* having no power to take action, wholly unable.

power shower *noun* a shower producing a high-pressure spray by means of an electric pump.

power station *noun* a building where electrical power is generated for distribution.

powwow *noun* (*informal*) a meeting for discussion.

pp *abbreviation* **1** pages (as in *pp. 25-6*). **2** (*Music*) pianissimo (very softly).

PPP *abbreviation* public–private partnership (in financing public services).

PPS *abbreviation* **1** Parliamentary Private Secretary. **2** post postscript, an additional postscript.

PR *abbreviation* **1** proportional representation. **2** public relations.

practicable *adjective* able to be done. **practicability** *noun*

practical *adjective* **1** involving activity as distinct from study or theory ♦ *She has had practical experience.* **2** likely to be useful ♦ *a clever invention but not very practical.* SYNONYMS: useful, usable, functional, sensible. **3** (said about a person) adept at making things and doing useful things. SYNONYMS: competent, capable. **4** virtual, very nearly so ♦ *He now has practical control of the business.* **practicality** (prakti-**kal**-iti) *noun* [from a Greek word *prattein* meaning 'to do']

practical joke *noun* a trick played on someone to make them appear foolish.

practically *adverb* **1** in a practical way. **2** virtually, almost ♦ *I have practically finished.*

practice *noun* **1** actual use of a plan or method as opposed to theory ♦ *It works well in practice.* SYNONYMS: reality, actuality. **2** a habitual action or custom ♦ *It is her practice to work until midnight.* SYNONYMS: custom, habit, routine. **3** repeated exercise to improve a skill ♦ *You need to do more piano practice.* **4** the business or professional work done by a doctor, lawyer, etc., or the building where this is done ♦ *There is a doctors' practice near the bank.* **out of practice** less skilful in something from lack of practice.
◊ Note that the noun is spelt **practice** and the verb is spelt **practise**.

practise *verb* **1** to do something repeatedly in order to become more skilful at it. **2** to do something actively or habitually ♦ *Practise what you preach.* **3** to follow the teaching and rules of a religion. **4** (said about a doctor or lawyer etc.) to be actively doing professional work. [same origin as for *practical*]
◊ See the note at **practice**.

practised *adjective* experienced or expert. SYNONYMS: experienced, accomplished, expert, adept, proficient.

practitioner (prak-**tish**-ən-er) *noun* a professional or practical worker, especially a doctor.

pragmatic (prag-**mat**-ik) *adjective* treating things in a practical way ♦ *Take a pragmatic approach to the problem.* SYNONYMS: practical, functional, realistic. **pragmatically** *adverb* [from a Greek word *pragmatikos* meaning 'businesslike']

pragmatism (**prag**-mə-tizm) *noun* treating things in a practical way. **pragmatist** *noun*

prairie *noun* a large area of flat grassland, especially in North America. [from a Latin word *pratum* meaning 'meadow']

praise *verb* **1** to express approval or admiration of someone or what they have done. SYNONYMS: applaud, acclaim, congratulate, commend, pay tribute to; (*formal*) extol. **2** to express honour or reverence for a deity.
praise *noun* words that praise someone or something. SYNONYMS: acclaim, commendation. [from a Latin word *pretium* meaning 'value']

praiseworthy *adjective* deserving praise.

praline (**prah**-leen) *noun* a sweet made by boiling nuts in sugar and grinding the mixture, used especially as a filling for chocolates. [named after the French soldier Marshal de Plessis-Praslin (1598–1675), whose cook invented it]

pram *noun* a four-wheeled carriage for a baby, pushed by a person walking. [short for *perambulator*]

prana (**prah-nə**) *noun* (in Hinduism) breath as the life-giving force. [from a Sanskrit word]

prance *verb* to move about in a lively or eager way. SYNONYMS: jump, bound, leap, dance, skip, frisk. [origin unknown]

prang *verb* (*informal*) to crash or damage a vehicle.
prang *noun* (*informal*) a crash or damage to a vehicle. [an imitation of the sound]

prank *noun* a practical joke or piece of mischief. SYNONYMS: trick, antic, practical joke. [probably from German or Dutch words]

prattle *verb* to chatter foolishly.
prattle *noun* foolish chatter. [from a German word *pratelen*]

prawn *noun* an edible shellfish like a large shrimp. [origin unknown]

pray *verb* 1 to say prayers. 2 to wish or hope earnestly for something.
pray *adverb* (*formal*) used to make a polite request ♦ *Pray continue.* [via Old French from a Latin word *precari* meaning 'to entreat']

prayer *noun* 1 a solemn request or thanksgiving to God or to another deity. 2 a set form of words used in this ♦ *the Lord's Prayer.* 3 a religious service ♦ *morning prayer.* 4 the act of praying. 5 an earnest wish or hope.

prayer book *noun* a book of set prayers.

prayer mat *noun* a small carpet on which Muslims kneel to pray.

prayer wheel *noun* (in Buddhism) a revolving cylindrical box inscribed with or containing prayers.

pre- *prefix* before or beforehand (as in *prehistoric*). [from a Latin word *prae* meaning 'before']

preach *verb* 1 to give a sermon or a religious or moral talk. 2 to urge people to adopt a certain practice or principle ♦ *They preached economy.* SYNONYMS: advocate, recommend. 3 to give moral advice ostentatiously or self-righteously ♦ *What right have they to preach to us?* SYNONYMS: moralize, pontificate. **preacher** *noun* [via Old French from a Latin word *praedicare* meaning 'to proclaim']

preamble (**pree-am-bəl**) *noun* a preliminary statement; the introductory part of a document or law etc. [from *pre-* and a Latin word *ambulare* meaning 'to go']

pre-arrange *verb* to arrange something in advance. **pre-arrangement** *noun*

precarious (**pri-kair-iəs**) *adjective* not very safe or secure. SYNONYMS: unsafe, insecure, dangerous, hazardous, perilous. **precariously** *adverb* [from a Latin word *precarius* meaning 'uncertain']

pre-cast *adjective* (said about concrete) cast in blocks before use.

precaution *noun* something done in advance to prevent trouble or danger. **precautionary** *adjective* [from *pre-* and a Latin word *cavere* meaning 'to take care']

precede (**pri-seed**) *verb* to come or go before someone or something else. [from *pre-* and a Latin word *cedere* meaning 'to go']
◊ Do not confuse this word with **proceed**, which has a different meaning.

precedence (**press-i-dənss**) *noun* the right of something to be put first, or of someone or something to go first, because they are more important or urgent. **to take precedence** to have priority.

precedent (**press-i-dənt**) *noun* a previous action or decision that is taken as an example to be followed in other cases of the same kind.

precentor (**pri-sent-er**) *noun* 1 a member of the clergy of a cathedral who is in general charge of music there. 2 a person who leads a congregation in singing or prayers. [from a Latin word *praecinere* meaning 'to sing before']

precept (**pree-sept**) *noun* a rule or principle about how people should act or behave. [from a Latin word *praecipere* meaning 'to warn' or 'to instruct']

preceptor (**pri-sept-er**) *noun* a teacher or instructor.

precinct (**pree-sinkt**) *noun* 1 an area round a place, especially round a cathedral or college. 2 an area in a town set aside for some purpose, especially one closed to traffic ♦ *a pedestrian precinct.* 3 (*North Amer.*) an administrative division of a county or city. [from a Latin word *praecingere* meaning 'to encircle']

precious *adjective* 1 having great value or worth. SYNONYMS: valuable, invaluable, priceless. 2 greatly loved by someone.

SYNONYMS: dear, beloved, loved. **3** affectedly refined or elegant. SYNONYMS: affected, pretentious. **4** (informal) (usually said with irony) considerable ♦ *A precious lot of good that did!* **precious little** (informal) not very much. **preciously** adverb **preciousness** noun [from a Latin word *pretium* meaning 'value']

precious metals plural noun gold, silver, and platinum.

precious stone noun a valuable and attractive piece of mineral used in jewellery.

precipice (press-i-piss) noun a very steep or vertical rock face or cliff. [from a Latin word *praeceps* meaning 'headlong']

precipitate[1] (pri-sip-i-tayt) verb **1** to throw something down headlong ♦ *The shove precipitated him through the window.* SYNONYMS: hurl, cast, fling, propel, throw. **2** to send something rapidly into a certain state or condition ♦ *The attack precipitated the country into war.* **3** to cause something to happen suddenly or without warning ♦ *The remarks precipitated an argument.* SYNONYMS: cause, bring about, result in. **4** (Chemistry) to cause a substance to be deposited in solid form from a solution in which it is present. **5** (Chemistry) to condense vapour into drops which fall as rain or dew etc. **precipitation** noun [same origin as for *precipice*]

precipitate[2] (pri-sip-i-tət) adjective **1** headlong or sudden ♦ *a precipitate fall in popularity.* SYNONYMS: abrupt, headlong. **2** (said about a person or action) hasty or rash. SYNONYMS: hasty, rash, foolhardy, reckless, impetuous. **precipitate** noun (Chemistry) a substance precipitated from a solution. **precipitately** adverb ◊ Do not confuse the adjective with **precipitous**, which has a different meaning.

precipitous (pri-sip-itəs) adjective like a precipice, steep. **precipitously** adverb ◊ Do not confuse this word with **precipitate**[2], which has a different meaning.

precis (pray-see) noun (**precis** (pray-seez)) a written or spoken summary of a text or speech. **precis** verb (**precised, precising**) to make a summary of a text or speech. [from a French word *précis* meaning 'precise']

precise adjective **1** exact, correctly and clearly stated. SYNONYMS: exact, correct, accurate. **2** (said about a person) taking care to be exact. SYNONYMS: careful, meticulous, conscientious. [from a Latin word *praecisus* meaning 'cut short']

precisely adverb **1** in a precise manner, exactly. **2** used to express agreement with what someone has said.

precision (pri-sizh-ən) noun **1** the quality of being precise, accuracy. **2** (used before a noun) designed for precise and accurate use ♦ *precision tools.*

preclude (pri-klood) verb to prevent something or exclude the possibility of its happening. [from a Latin word *praeclaudere* meaning 'to shut before']

precocious (pri-koh-shəs) adjective **1** (said about a child) having developed certain abilities at an earlier age than usual. **2** (said about abilities or knowledge) showing this kind of development. **precociously** adverb **precocity** (pri-koss-iti) noun [from a Latin word *praecox* meaning 'ripe very early']

preconceived adjective (said about an idea or opinion) formed before full knowledge or information is available.

preconception noun a preconceived idea.

precondition noun a condition that must be fulfilled before something else can happen or be done.

precursor (pri-ker-ser) noun a person or thing that comes before another of the same kind, a forerunner. [from a Latin word *praecurrere* meaning 'to run beforehand']

predation (pri-day-shən) noun (Zoology) the preying of one animal on others. **predate** verb [same origin as for *predator*]

predator (pred-ə-ter) noun **1** an animal that hunts or preys on others. **2** a person or organization that exploits or threatens others. [from a Latin word meaning 'plunderer']

predatory (pred-ə-ter-i) adjective **1** (said about an animal) hunting or preying on others. **2** plundering or exploiting others.

predecease (pree-di-seess) verb to die earlier than another person.

predecessor (pree-di-sess-er) noun **1** someone who held an office or position before the present holder. **2** a thing that has been followed or replaced by another. [from pre- and a Latin word *decessor* meaning 'person departed']

predestination noun the Christian doctrine that God has foreordained all that happens, and that some people are destined for salvation and others are not.

predestine verb to destine something beforehand, to determine an outcome in advance.

predetermine verb to determine an outcome in advance. **predetermination** noun

predicament (pri-dik-ə-mənt) noun a difficult or unpleasant situation. SYNONYMS: difficulty, plight, quandary. [same origin as for *predicate*]

predicate (pred-i-kət) noun (Grammar) the part of a sentence that says something about the subject, e.g. 'is short' in *Life is short.* [from a Latin word *praedicare* meaning 'to proclaim']

predicative (pri-dik-ətiv) adjective (Grammar) forming part of the predicate, e.g. 'old' in *The dog is old.* (Compare **attributive**.) **predicatively** adverb

predict verb to say what will happen in the future, to foretell something. SYNONYMS: foretell, foresee, forecast, prophesy. **prediction** noun **predictor** noun [from a Latin word *praedictum* meaning 'said beforehand']

predictable adjective 1 able to be predicted. 2 tediously or boringly behaving in the same way always. **predictability** noun **predictably** adverb

predilection (pree-di-lek-shən) noun a special liking or preference. [from a Latin word *praedilectum* meaning 'selected beforehand']

predispose verb 1 to influence someone in advance so that they are likely to take a particular attitude ♦ *We were predisposed to help them.* 2 to make someone liable to a disease.

predisposition noun a state of mind or body that makes a person liable to act or behave in a certain way or to be subject to certain diseases.

predominant adjective being the main force or element. SYNONYMS: dominant, prevailing, prevalent. **predominantly** adverb **predominance** noun

predominate verb 1 to be the largest or most important or powerful element. 2 to have or exert control.

pre-eminent adjective excelling all others, outstanding. **pre-eminence** noun **pre-eminently** adverb

pre-empt verb to take action to prevent an attack or other expected event from happening; to forestall something. **pre-emption** noun [from a Latin word *praeemptum* meaning 'bought in advance']

pre-emptive adjective serving to prevent or forestall something ♦ *a pre-emptive attack.*

preen verb (said about a bird) to smooth its feathers with its beak. **to preen yourself** 1 to make yourself look attractive. 2 to congratulate yourself ostentatiously. [perhaps from dialect words]

prefab noun (informal) a prefabricated building.

prefabricate verb to manufacture a building or piece of furniture in sections ready for assembly when they are delivered to a site. **prefabrication** noun

preface (pref-əs) noun 1 an introduction to a book, outlining its contents and aims. 2 a part of the Eucharist service in some Christian Churches. **preface** verb 1 to begin a speech with some introductory words ♦ *She prefaced her remarks with a round of thanks.* 2 to introduce or lead up to an event ♦ *The ceremony was prefaced by grand music.* [from a Latin word *praefatio* meaning 'something said beforehand']

prefatory (pref-ə-ter-i) adjective serving as a preface, introductory ♦ *prefatory remarks.*

prefect noun 1 a senior pupil in a school, given authority to help maintain discipline. 2 a regional official in France, Japan, and some other countries. 3 any of various senior officials in ancient Rome. [from a Latin word *praefectus* meaning 'overseer']

prefer verb (preferred, preferring) 1 to choose or like one person or thing as being better or more desirable than another. 2 (formal) to put forward an accusation for consideration by an authority ♦ *They have preferred charges of fraud against him.* 3 (old use) to promote someone. [from a Latin word *praeferre* meaning 'to carry before']

preferable (pref-er-əbəl) adjective more desirable or suitable. **preferably** adverb

preference (pref-er-əns) noun 1 a choice or greater liking for one person or thing over another. 2 a person or thing preferred. 3 a prior right to something. 4 favour shown to one person or country over another. **in preference to** as a person or thing preferred to another.

preference shares *plural noun* shares on which a dividend is paid before profits are distributed to holders of ordinary shares.

preferential (pref-er-en-shəl) *adjective* showing or based on a preference ♦ *preferential treatment*. **preferentially** *adverb*

preferment *noun* appointment or promotion to an office or job.

prefigure *verb* to be an early version of something.

prefix *noun* 1 a word or syllable placed in front of a word to add to or change its meaning (as in *dis*order, *non*-existent, *out*stretched, *un*happy). 2 a title placed before a name (e.g. *Dr*).
prefix *verb* to add something as a prefix or introduction. [from a Latin word *praefixum* meaning 'fixed in front']

pregnant *adjective* 1 (said about a woman or female animal) having a child or young animal developing in the womb. 2 full of meaning or significance ♦ *There was a pregnant silence*. **pregnancy** *noun* [from *pre-* and a Latin word *gnasci* meaning 'to be born']

prehensile (pri-hen-siyl) *adjective* (said about an animal's limb or tail) able to grasp things. [from a Latin word *prehendere* meaning 'to grasp']

prehistoric *adjective* 1 to do with the ancient period of time before written records of events were made. 2 (*informal*) old or out of date.

prehistory *noun* prehistoric times.

prejudge *verb* to form a judgement about a person or action before all the information is available.

prejudice *noun* 1 an unfavourable opinion or dislike formed on the basis of preconceived ideas and without regard to the actual facts or circumstances. SYNONYMS: bias, discrimination. 2 (*Law*) harm done to a person's rights.
prejudice *verb* 1 to cause a person to have a prejudice. SYNONYMS: bias, influence. 2 (*Law*) to cause harm to a person's rights. **without prejudice** (*Law*) (describing an offer made to settle a dispute) which must not be taken as an admission of liability or as affecting other rights. [from a Latin word *praejudicium* meaning 'judgement in advance']

prejudiced *adjective* having a prejudice. SYNONYMS: biased, partial, bigoted.

prejudicial (prej-oo-dish-əl) *adjective* harmful to a person's rights or claims.

prelate (prel-ət) *noun* (*formal*) a bishop or other clergyman of high rank. [from a Latin word *praelatus* meaning 'preferred']

preliminary *adjective* coming before an important action or event and preparing for it. SYNONYMS: introductory, preparatory. **preliminary** *noun* (**preliminaries**) a preliminary action or event. [from *pre-* and a Latin word *limen* meaning 'threshold']

prelude (prel-yood) *noun* 1 an action or event that precedes another and leads up to it. 2 the introductory part of a poem or other literary work. 3 (*Music*) an introductory movement preceding a fugue or forming the first piece of a suite, or a short piece of music of similar type. [from *pre-* and a Latin word *ludere* meaning 'to play']

premarital (pree-ma-ritəl) *adjective* to do with or happening in the time before marriage.

premature (prem-ə-tewr) *adjective* 1 occurring or done before the usual or proper time, too early. 2 (said about a baby) born three or more weeks before the full term of gestation. **prematurely** *adverb*

premeditated (pree-med-i-tayt-id) *adjective* (said about an action, especially a crime) planned beforehand. SYNONYMS: deliberate, calculated, conscious, intentional. **premeditation** *noun*

premenstrual (pree-men-stroo-əl) *adjective* to do with or experienced in the time immediately before menstruation.

premenstrual tension *noun* emotional tension and other symptoms experienced by some women just before menstruation.

premier (prem-i-er) *adjective* first in importance, order, or time. **premier** *noun* a prime minister or other head of government. **premiership** *noun* [a French word meaning 'first']

premiere (prem-yair) *noun* the first public performance or showing of a play or film. **premiere** *verb* to give a premiere of a play or film. [a French word (the feminine form of *premier*), meaning 'first']

premise (prem-iss) *noun* a statement used as a basis for reasoning. [from a Latin phrase *praemissa propositio* meaning 'proposition put in front']

premises (prem-i-siz) *plural noun* a house or other building with its grounds and outbuildings. SYNONYMS: property, establishment.

premiss (prem-iss) *noun* another spelling of **premise**.

premium (pree-mi-əm) *noun* 1 an amount or instalment paid for an insurance policy. 2 an extra charge or payment. 3 (used before a noun) superior or more expensive ♦ *a premium service.* **at a premium** 1 in demand but scarce. 2 above the nominal or usual price. **to put a premium on** to regard something as especially valuable or important. [from a Latin word *praemium* meaning 'reward']

Premium Bond *noun* a government security that pays no interest but is entered in a regular draw for cash prizes.

premolar (pree-moh-ler) *noun* a tooth in front of the molars, nearer the front of the mouth.

premonition (prem-ə-nish-ən) *noun* a strong feeling that a particular thing is going to happen, a presentiment. [from *pre-* and a Latin word *monere* meaning 'to warn']

preoccupation *noun* 1 the state of being preoccupied. 2 a thought or activity that preoccupies someone.

preoccupy *verb* (preoccupies, preoccupied, preoccupying) to occupy someone's thoughts completely, excluding other thoughts. SYNONYMS: engross, absorb. **preoccupied** *adjective*

preordain *verb* to decide or determine something beforehand.

prep *noun* (*informal*) school work or homework done outside lessons. [short for *preparation*]

pre-pack *verb* to pack goods ready for sale before distributing them.

preparation *noun* 1 the process of preparing something. 2 something done to make ready for an event or activity. 3 a substance or mixture prepared for use, especially a food or medicine.

preparatory (pri-pa-rə-ter-i) *adjective* preparing for an event or activity ♦ *preparatory training.*

preparatory school *noun* a school for pupils between the ages of seven and thirteen or (in the USA) for pupils preparing for college or university.

prepare *verb* 1 to get ready, or to make something ready. 2 to make food ready for cooking or eating. **to be prepared to** to be ready and willing to do something. [from *pre-* and a Latin word *parare* meaning 'to make ready']

preparedness (pri-pair-id-niss) *noun* a state of being prepared or ready.

prepay *verb* (past tense and past participle **prepaid**) to pay for something in advance, especially to pay the postage on a letter or parcel by fixing a stamp on it. **prepayment** *noun*

preponderant (pri-pond-er-ənt) *adjective* predominant in influence or importance. **preponderance** *noun* **preponderantly** *adverb* [from a Latin word *praeponderare* meaning 'to outweigh']

preponderate (pri-pond-er-ayt) *verb* to be greater than others in number or importance.

preposition *noun* (*Grammar*) a word used with a noun or pronoun to show place, position, time, or means, e.g. *at* home, *in* the hall, *on* Sunday, *by* train. **prepositional** *adjective* [from *pre-* and a Latin word *positum* meaning 'placed']

prepossessing *adjective* attractive, making a good impression ♦ *The front of the house is not very prepossessing.*

preposterous (pri-poss-ter-əs) *adjective* utterly absurd or ridiculous. SYNONYMS: absurd, ridiculous, ludicrous, nonsensical. **preposterously** *adverb* [from a Latin word *praeposterus* meaning 'back to front', from *prae* meaning 'before' and *posterus* meaning 'behind']

prep school *noun* a preparatory school.

Pre-Raphaelite (pree-raf-ə-liyt) *noun* a member of a group of 19th-century artists who aimed at producing work in the style of Italian artists before the time of Raphael.

prerequisite (pree-rek-wiz-it) *noun* something that is required as a condition or in preparation for something else ♦ *Knowledge of a foreign language is normally a prerequisite for working abroad.* SYNONYMS: condition, precondition.

prerogative (pri-**rog**-ətiv) *noun* a right or privilege that belongs to a particular person or group. [from a Latin word *praerogativa* meaning 'the people voting first']

presage [1] (**pres**-ij) *noun* an omen or portent. [from a Latin word *praesagium*, from *praesagire* meaning 'to forbode']

presage [2] (pri-**sayj**) *verb* to be an advance sign or warning of something about to happen.

presbyter (**prez**-bit-er) *noun* a priest or elder in certain Christian Churches. [from a Greek word *presbuteros* meaning 'elder']

Presbyterian (prezbi-**teer**-iən) *adjective* denoting a Christian Church governed by elders who are all of equal rank, especially the national Church of Scotland.
Presbyterian *noun* a member of a Presbyterian Church. **Presbyterianism** *noun*

presbytery (**prez**-bit-er-i) *noun* (**presbyteries**) 1 the house of a Roman Catholic parish priest. 2 a body of presbyters. 3 the eastern part of a church chancel.

pre-school *adjective* to do with the time before a child is old enough to attend school.

prescribe *verb* 1 to advise and authorize the use of a medicine, usually by providing a written prescription. 2 to recommend or lay down a procedure or rule to be followed. SYNONYMS: recommend, advise, suggest. [from a Latin word *praescribere* meaning 'to direct in writing'] ◊ Do not confuse this word with **proscribe**, which has a different meaning.

prescript (**pree**-skript) *noun* (formal or old use) a rule or command. [from a Latin word *prescriptum* meaning 'something directed in writing']

prescription *noun* 1 a doctor's written instruction for a medicine or treatment to be provided to a patient. 2 an authorization or recommendation.

prescriptive *adjective* 1 stating or laying down rules. 2 (said about a right or title) established by usage or custom.

presence *noun* 1 the state or fact of being present in a place ♦ *The bird seemed unaware of our presence.* 2 the impressive bearing or manner of a person ♦ *She has a fine presence.* 3 a person or thing that is or

seems to be present in a place ♦ *We could all feel a presence in the room.* **presence of mind** the ability to act quickly and sensibly in a difficult situation.

present [1] (**prez**-ənt) *adjective* 1 being in a particular place ♦ *Three people were present when the alarm went off.* 2 being dealt with or considered ♦ *in the present case.* 3 existing or occurring now ♦ *The estate then passed to the present Duke.* 4 (*Grammar*) (said about a tense) denoting an action or state that is going on at the time of speaking or writing, or occurs habitually. **present** *noun* 1 present time, the time now passing. 2 (*Grammar*) the present tense. **at present** now. **for the present** for now, temporarily. [from a Latin word *praesens* meaning 'being at hand']

present [2] (**prez**-ənt) *noun* something given or received as a gift.

present [3] (pri-**zent**) *verb* 1 to give something as a gift or award, to offer something for acceptance. SYNONYMS: award, give, hand over. 2 to introduce someone to another person or to others, or to an audience. 3 to put a performance or exhibition before the public. SYNONYMS: perform, put on. 4 to show or reveal ♦ *They presented a brave front to the world.* 5 to level or aim a weapon. **to present arms** to hold a rifle vertically in front of the body as a salute. **to present oneself** to attend for an examination or interview. **presenter** *noun*

presentable *adjective* fit to be presented to other people, of good appearance.

presentation *noun* 1 the process of presenting something. 2 something that is presented. 3 a talk in which information is presented to an audience.

present-day *adjective* to do with present times, modern.

presentiment (pri-**zent**-i-mənt) *noun* a feeling or foreboding about the future. [from *pre-* and an obsolete French word *sentiment* meaning 'feeling']

presently *adverb* 1 after a short time, soon. SYNONYMS: soon, shortly, in a while. 2 at the present time, now.

preservation *noun* the process of preserving something.

preservative *noun* a substance that preserves food, wood, or other perishable substances.
preservative *adjective* serving to preserve things.

preserve verb 1 to keep something safe or in an unchanged condition. SYNONYMS: maintain, conserve, safeguard. 2 to treat food to prevent it from decaying. 3 to keep someone safe from harm.
preserve noun 1 jam made with preserved fruit. 2 an area where game or fish are protected for private hunting or fishing. 3 an activity or interest that is regarded as belonging to a particular person or group.
preserver noun [from a Latin word praeservare meaning 'to keep in advance']

preset verb (past tense and past participle, **preset; presetting**) to set a function of a device to operate at a certain time or in a certain way.
preset noun a function that has been preset.

pre-shrunk adjective (said about a fabric or piece of clothing) shrunk before being used or sold, to prevent further shrinking in use.

preside verb to have the position of authority or control at a meeting, in a law court, etc. [from pre- and a Latin word sedere meaning 'to sit']

president noun 1 the elected head of a state that is a republic. 2 the head of a club, society, or other organization. **presidency** noun **presidential** (prez-i-den-shǝl) adjective [same origin as for preside]

presidium (pri-sid-iǝm) noun a standing executive committee in a communist state. [same origin as for preside]

press[1] verb 1 to apply weight or force steadily to something. SYNONYMS: push, push down, squeeze. 2 to make something by pressing. 3 to squeeze juice from fruit. 4 to flatten or smooth clothes by ironing them. SYNONYMS: iron, smooth. 5 to exert pressure on an enemy or opponent. 6 to urge or demand something insistently ♦ The union pressed for a 35-hour week. 7 to force someone to accept something ♦ They kept pressing sweets upon us. 8 to insist on ♦ We had better not press the point. 9 to throng closely. 10 to push your way.
press noun 1 a device or machine for pressing, flattening, or shaping something. 2 the process of pressing something ♦ Give your shirt a quick press. 3 crowding, a throng of people. 4 a printing press. 5 a printing or publishing firm. 6 newspapers and periodicals, or the people involved in producing them ♦ a press photographer. **to be pressed for** to have barely enough of ♦ We are a little

pressed for time. [from a Latin word pressum meaning 'squeezed']

press conference noun a meeting with journalists to make an announcement or answer questions.

press cutting noun a cutting from a newspaper.

press gang noun (historical) a group of men employed to force people to enlist in the army or navy.

pressing adjective 1 needing quick action, urgent ♦ a pressing need. 2 urging something strongly ♦ a pressing invitation.
pressing noun a thing made by pressing, especially a gramophone record.

press release noun an official statement or announcement made to journalists on a particular matter.

press stud noun a small fastener with two parts that engage when pressed together.

press-up noun an exercise in which a person lies face downwards and presses down on the hands so that the shoulders and trunk are raised.

pressure noun 1 the exertion of a continuous physical force on something. SYNONYMS: force, power, strength. 2 the force with which something presses. 3 the force exerted by the atmosphere ♦ Pressure is high in eastern areas. 4 a strong influence that persuades you to do something ♦ The government is under pressure to reduce taxes.
pressure verb to influence or persuade someone to take a certain action. [from a Latin word pressura, related to press]

pressure cooker noun an airtight pan in which things can be cooked quickly by steam under high pressure.

pressure group noun an organized group that tries to influence public policy by concerted action.

pressurize verb 1 to keep a closed compartment, e.g. an aircraft cabin, at a constant atmospheric pressure. 2 to influence or persuade someone to take a certain action. **pressurization** noun

pressurized-water reactor noun a nuclear reactor in which the coolant is water at high pressure.

prestige (press-teezh) noun respect and admiration for a person or organization resulting from a widespread high opinion of their achievements or quality. SYNONYMS: esteem, distinction, renown. [from an earlier meaning 'conjuring trick', from a Latin word *praestigium* meaning 'an illusion']

prestigious (press-**tij**-əs) *adjective* having or bringing prestige. SYNONYMS: distinguished, esteemed, acclaimed, renowned.

presto *adverb* (*Music*) quickly. [an Italian word meaning 'quick, quickly']

pre-stressed *adjective* (said about concrete) strengthened by means of stretched rods or wires inserted during manufacture.

presumably *adverb* as you may presume.

presume *verb* **1** to take something for granted, or suppose it to be true. SYNONYMS: suppose, assume, imagine, believe, guess, expect, gather. **2** to take the liberty of doing something, to venture ♦ *May I presume to advise you?* SYNONYMS: venture, dare. **3** to be presumptuous. **to presume on** to make use of something you are not entitled to ♦ *They have been presuming on her good nature.*

presumption *noun* **1** the act of presuming something to be true. **2** an idea that is presumed to be true. **3** presumptuous behaviour.

presumptive *adjective* **1** presumed when no further information is available. **2** (*Law*) giving grounds for a particular inference.

presumptuous (pri-**zump**-tew-əs) *adjective* behaving too boldly, or acting without authority. SYNONYMS: arrogant, bold, audacious, forward, impertinent, insolent. **presumptuously** *adverb* **presumptuousness** *noun*

presuppose *verb* **1** to assume something to be the case before having all the information. **2** to require something as a prior condition ♦ *Exceptions presuppose the existence of a rule.* **presupposition** *noun*

pre-tax *adjective* before tax has been deducted ♦ *the Company's pre-tax profits.*

pretence *noun* **1** the act of pretending. **2** a false or over-ambitious claim. **3** pretentious behaviour.

pretend *verb* **1** to act or talk in a way that falsely suggests something to be the case, either in play or so as to deceive other people. **2** to claim falsely that one has or is something. SYNONYMS: fake, feign. **3** to put forward a claim ♦ *The son of James II*

pretended to the British throne. **pretendedly** *adverb* [from a Latin word *praetendere* meaning 'to put forward or claim']

pretender *noun* a person who claims a throne or title.

pretension *noun* **1** a claim or aspiration, especially a false one. **2** pretentious behaviour.

pretentious (pri-**ten**-shəs) *adjective* trying to impress by claiming greater importance or merit than is actually the case. **pretentiously** *adverb* **pretentiousness** *noun*

preternatural (pree-ter-**nach**-er-əl) *adjective* outside what is normal or natural. **preternaturally** *adverb* [from a Latin word *praeter* meaning 'beyond' and *natural*]

pretext (**pree**-tekst) *noun* a reason put forward to conceal the true reason. SYNONYMS: excuse, pretence. [from a Latin word *praetextus* meaning 'an outward display']

prettify *verb* (**prettifies, prettified, prettifying**) to make something look superficially pretty or pleasing.

pretty *adjective* (**prettier, prettiest**) **1** attractive in a delicate way. SYNONYMS: attractive, lovely, appealing, charming. **2** (*informal*) (said with irony) unwelcome or unpleasant ♦ *That cost me a pretty penny.* **pretty** *adverb* fairly, moderately ♦ *The food was pretty good.* **pretty much** or **nearly** or **well** almost. **prettily** *adverb* **prettiness** *noun* [from an Old English word, with earlier meanings 'clever, skilful']

pretzel (**pret**-zəl) *noun* a crisp biscuit baked in the form of a stick or knot and flavoured with salt. [a German word]

prevail *verb* **1** to be victorious, to be more powerful or successful. SYNONYMS: succeed, triumph, win. **2** to be the most usual or most frequently occurring. SYNONYMS: predominate, be prevalent. **to prevail on** to persuade someone. SYNONYMS: persuade, convince, induce. [from *pre-* and a Latin word *valere* meaning 'to have power']

prevailing wind *noun* a wind that is blowing from the most usual direction.

prevalent (**prev**-ə-lənt) *adjective* most usual or most frequently occurring. SYNONYMS: dominant, prevailing, predominant. **prevalence** *noun* **prevalently** *adverb* [same origin as for *prevail*]

prevaricate (pri-va-ri-kayt) *verb* to speak evasively or misleadingly. SYNONYMS: equivocate, hedge. **prevarication** *noun* **prevaricator** *noun* [from a Latin word *praevaricari* meaning 'to walk crookedly']

prevent *verb* **1** to keep something from happening, or make it impossible. SYNONYMS: preclude, prohibit, stop, thwart. **2** to keep someone from doing something. SYNONYMS: stop, hinder, deter, thwart, discourage. **preventable** *adjective* **prevention** *noun* [from a Latin word *praeventum* meaning 'hindered']

preventative *adjective* preventive. **preventative** *noun* a preventive.

preventive *adjective* designed or serving to prevent something. **preventive** *noun* a thing that prevents something, especially a medicine.

preventive medicine *noun* medical treatment intended to prevent disease.

preview *noun* an advance showing or viewing of a film or play etc. before it is shown to the general public.

previous *adjective* **1** coming before in time or order. SYNONYMS: past, earlier, former, prior. **2** (*informal*) done or acting prematurely. **previously** *adverb* [from a Latin word *praevius* meaning 'going before']

pre-war *adjective* existing or occurring before a major war, especially before the World War of 1939–45.

prey (pray) *noun* **1** an animal that is hunted or killed by another animal for food. SYNONYMS: victim, quarry. **2** a person or thing that falls victim to an enemy or to fear, disease, etc. **prey** *verb* (**preys, preyed, preying**) to prey on **1** (said about an animal) to hunt and kill other animals for food. **2** to cause anxiety or worry to someone ♦ *The problem was preying on his mind.* [from a Latin word *praeda* meaning 'booty']

price *noun* **1** the amount of money for which something is bought or sold. SYNONYMS: cost, charge, expense. **2** something that must be given or done in order to achieve something ♦ *Loss of freedom is a high price to pay in defence of one's principles.* SYNONYMS: cost, sacrifice. **3** odds in betting ♦ *a starting price.* **price** *verb* to fix or estimate the price of something. **a price on someone's head** a reward offered for someone's capture or death. **at any price** no matter what the cost or sacrifice. [via Old French from a Latin word *pretium* meaning 'value' or 'reward']

priceless *adjective* **1** so valuable that its price cannot be determined. SYNONYMS: valuable, invaluable, precious. **2** (*informal*) very amusing or absurd.

price tag *noun* **1** a label on an item showing its price. **2** the cost of an undertaking or activity.

pricey *adjective* (**pricier, priciest**) (*informal*) expensive.

prick *verb* **1** to pierce something slightly or make a tiny hole in it. SYNONYMS: pierce, puncture. **2** to make someone feel anxious or guilty ♦ *My conscience has been pricking me.* **3** to feel a pricking sensation. SYNONYMS: prickle, sting, tingle. **4** to hurt someone with the tip of a pin or other sharp object. **5** to mark a pattern or design with pricks or dots. **prick** *noun* **1** an act of pricking. **2** a mark or puncture made by pricking. **to prick up your ears 1** (said about a dog) to raise its ears erect when on the alert. **2** (said about a person) to become suddenly attentive. **pricker** *noun* [from an Old English word *prician*]

prickle *noun* **1** a small thorn. **2** one of the hard pointed spines on a hedgehog, cactus, etc. **3** a pricking sensation. **prickle** *verb* to feel or cause someone to feel a sensation of pricking. SYNONYMS: prick, sting, tingle. [from an Old English word *price*] meaning 'an instrument for pricking', related to *prick*]

prickly *adjective* (**pricklier, prickliest**) **1** covered in prickles. SYNONYMS: spiky, thorny. **2** causing a prickling feeling. **3** (said about a person) irritable or touchy. SYNONYMS: irritable, touchy, testy, bad-tempered, peevish. **prickliness** *noun*

prickly pear *noun* **1** a kind of cactus with pear-shaped edible fruit. **2** the fruit of this cactus.

pride *noun* **1** a feeling of deep pleasure or satisfaction derived from your actions, qualities, or possessions etc. SYNONYMS: satisfaction, contentment. **2** a person or thing that causes you pride. **3** a proper sense of what is fitting for your position or character, self-respect. **4** an unduly high opinion of your qualities or merits. SYNONYMS: conceit, vanity, self-importance, arrogance. **5** a group of lions. **pride** *verb* to pride oneself on to be proud of an achievement or quality. **pride of**

place the most prominent or important position. [from an Old English word *pryde*, related to *proud*]

priest *noun* 1 an ordained member of the clergy in certain Christian Churches. 2 a person who performs rites in a non-Christian religion. **priesthood** *noun* [from an Old English word *preost*]

priestess *noun* a female priest of a non-Christian religion.

priestly *adjective* like a priest, or suitable for a priest.

prig *noun* a person who self-righteously displays or demands moral correctness. **priggery** *noun* **priggish** *adjective* **priggishness** *noun* [origin unknown]

prim *adjective* (**primmer, primmest**) stiffly formal and precise in manner or behaviour, disliking what is rough or improper. SYNONYMS: proper, precise, correct, strait-laced. **primly** *adverb* **primness** *noun* [from an Old French word *prin*, from a Latin word *primus* meaning 'first']

prima ballerina (pree-mə) *noun* the chief female dancer in a ballet. [an Italian phrase, meaning 'first ballerina']

primacy (priy-mə-si) *noun* pre-eminence.

prima donna (pree-mə don-ə) *noun* 1 the chief female singer in an opera. 2 a self-important and demanding person. [an Italian phrase, meaning 'first lady']

prima facie (priy-mə fay-shee) *adjective & adverb* at first sight, based on a first impression. [a Latin phrase, meaning 'at the first appearance']

primal (priy-məl) *adjective* primitive or primeval. [from a Latin word *primus* meaning 'first']

primary (priy-mə-ri) *adjective* 1 of the first importance, chief ♦ *Safety is our primary concern.* SYNONYMS: main, principal, chief, first, prime. 2 earliest in time or order, first in a series ♦ *the primary stage in a process.* **primary** *noun* (**primaries**) (in the USA) a first election to choose the candidates for a presidential election, or to appoint delegates to a party conference. **primarily** (priy-mer-ili) *adverb* [same origin as for *prime*[1]]

primary care *noun* health care provided by doctors and clinics in the community.

primary colour *noun* any of the colours from which all others can be made by mixing, (of paint) red, yellow, and blue, (of light) red, green, and violet.

primary education *noun* education for children between the ages of five and eleven.

primary school *noun* a school for children between the ages of five and eleven.

primate (priy-mət) *noun* 1 a chief bishop or archbishop. 2 (*Zoology*) a member of the highly developed order of animals that includes humans, apes, and monkeys. [from a Latin word *primas*, related to *prime*[1]]

prime[1] *adjective* 1 chief or most important ♦ *the prime cause.* SYNONYMS: main, principal, chief, first, primary. 2 excellent or first-rate ♦ *prime quality.* 3 (*Mathematics*) (said about a number) that can be divided only by itself or one, e.g. 2, 3, 5, and 7. **prime** *noun* the best or most fully developed part or stage of something ♦ *in the prime of life.* [from a Latin word *primus* meaning 'first']

prime[2] *verb* 1 to prepare something, especially a weapon or bomb, for use or action. 2 to cause liquid to flow into a pump to start it working. 3 to prepare a surface for painting by coating it with a substance that prevents the first coat of paint from being soaked in. 4 to prepare someone for an undertaking or situation by providing information or instructions. [from an earlier meaning 'to fill' or 'to load', related to *prime*[1]]

prime factor *noun* (*Mathematics*) a factor that is a prime number, e.g. the prime factors of 12 are 3, 2, and 2.

prime minister *noun* the chief minister in a government.

prime number *noun* a number that can be divided exactly only by itself and one (e.g. 2, 3, 5, 7, 11).

primer[1] (priy-mer) *noun* a substance used to prime a surface for painting.

primer[2] (priy-mer) *noun* an elementary textbook. [from a Latin phrase *primarius liber* meaning 'primary book']

primeval (priy-mee-vəl) *adjective* to do with the earliest time in history. **primevally** *adverb* [from Latin words *primus* meaning 'first' and *aevum* meaning 'age']

primitive *adjective* 1 at an early stage of history or civilization ♦ *primitive peoples.* SYNONYMS: early, ancient, prehistoric. 2 simple or crude, not developed or advanced ♦ *primitive tools.* SYNONYMS: simple, crude, basic, rudimentary. 3 (said about feelings or behaviour) emotional, not based on reason. **primitively** *adjective* [from a Latin word *primitivus* meaning 'first of its kind']

primogeniture (priy-mə-jen-i-cher) *noun* **1** the fact or status of being a first-born child. **2** the system by which an eldest son inherits all his parents' property. [from Latin words *primo* meaning 'first' and *genitus* meaning 'born']

primordial (priy-mor-di-əl) *adjective* to do with the earliest time in history, primeval. **primordially** *adverb*

primrose *noun* **1** a plant bearing pale yellow flowers in spring. **2** a pale yellow colour. [from a Latin phrase *prima rosa* meaning 'first rose']

primula *noun* a perennial plant of a kind that includes primroses and polyanthuses, having clusters of flowers in various colours. [from a Latin word *primulus* meaning 'first little one']

Primus (priy-məs) *noun* (*trademark*) a portable cooking stove that burns vaporized oil.

prince *noun* **1** a male member of a royal family, especially a son or grandson of the reigning queen or king. **2** a ruler of a small state. **3** a nobleman in certain European countries. [from a Latin word *princeps* meaning 'chieftain']

prince consort *noun* the husband of a reigning queen when he himself is a prince.

princeling *noun* a young or minor prince.

princely *adjective* **1** relating to or suitable for a prince. **2** splendid, generous.

princess *noun* **1** the wife of a prince. **2** a female member of a royal family; especially a daughter or granddaughter of the reigning queen or king. [from an Old French word *princesse*, related to *prince*]

princess royal *noun* a title that may be conferred on the eldest daughter of the British sovereign.

principal *adjective* chief or most important. SYNONYMS: main, chief, first, foremost, primary, prime.
principal *noun* **1** the most important or senior person in an organization. **2** the head of certain schools or colleges. **3** a person who takes a leading part in an activity or in a play or musical performance. **4** a person for whom

another person acts as a representative. **5** a capital sum as distinguished from the interest or income earned on it. [same origin as *prince*]
◊ Do not confuse this word with **principle**, which has a different meaning.

principal boy or **principal girl** *noun* a woman who plays the leading male or female part in a pantomime.

principality (prin-si-pal-iti) *noun* (**principalities**) a country ruled by a prince. [from a Latin word *principalis*, related to *principal*]

principally *adverb* for the most part, chiefly.

principle *noun* **1** a basic truth or general rule used as a basis of reasoning or behaviour. SYNONYMS: rule, precept, tenet, truth. **2** a personal code of moral conduct ♦ *a person of principle*. SYNONYMS: honour, integrity. **3** a scientific rule or natural law shown in the way a thing works or used as the basis for the construction of a machine etc. **in principle** in theory, as regards the main elements but not necessarily the details. **on principle** because of the principles of conduct someone believes in ♦ *We refused their offer on principle*. [from a Latin word *principium* meaning 'source']
◊ Do not confuse this word with **principal**, which has a different meaning.

print *verb* **1** to produce lettering on a book or newspaper etc. by transferring text or designs to paper by various mechanical or electronic processes. **2** to publish books or newspapers in this way. **3** to press a mark or design on a surface. SYNONYMS: press, imprint, stamp. **4** to impress or stamp a surface or fabric etc. with a mark or design. **5** to write letters clearly without joining them up. **6** (in photography) to produce a positive picture from a negative or transparency.
print *noun* **1** printed lettering or writing, the text of a book or newspaper etc. **2** a printed picture or design. **3** a piece of printed cotton fabric. **4** a mark made by something pressing on a surface. SYNONYMS: impression, imprint. **in print** available from a publisher, not out of print. **out of print** no longer available from a publisher. [from an Old French word *preinte* meaning 'pressed', from a Latin word *premere* meaning 'to press']

printed circuit *noun* an electronic circuit made with thin strips of a conducting material on an insulating board.

printer *noun* **1** a person whose job or business is the printing of books, newspapers, etc. **2** a machine for printing text or pictures.

printing press *noun* a machine for printing from raised type.

printout *noun* material produced in printed form from a computer or teleprinter.

prion (pree-on) *noun* a microscopic protein particle believed to be the cause of BSE and other brain diseases. [from the first letters of *protein* and *infectious*]

prior [1] *adjective* earlier or more important than something else ♦ *a prior engagement.* **prior** *adverb* **prior to** before ♦ *prior to our meeting.* [from a Latin word *prior* meaning 'former' or 'more important']

prior [2] *noun* a monk who is the head of a religious house or order, or who is next below an abbot in an abbey. [from an Old English word, a noun use of *prior*[1]]

prioress *noun* a nun who is the head of a religious house or order, or who is next below an abbess in an abbey.

priority *noun* (**priorities**) **1** the fact or state of being earlier or more important, the right to be first. **2** something that is considered more important than other items or considerations. [from *prior*[1]]

priory *noun* (**priories**) a community of monks governed by a prior, or of nuns governed by a prioress. [from a French word *priorie*, related to *prior*[2]]

prise *verb* to force something open or apart by leverage. [from an Old French word *prise* meaning 'taking hold']
◇ Do not confuse this word with **prize**, which has a different meaning.

prism *noun* **1** (*Geometry*) a solid geometric shape with ends that are similar, equal, and parallel. **2** a transparent object having this form and usually with triangular ends, which breaks up light into a spectrum. [from a Greek word *prisma* meaning 'sawn object']

prismatic (priz-mat-ik) *adjective* **1** of or having the form of a prism. **2** (said about colours) formed or distributed as if by a prism, like a rainbow. **prismatically** *adverb*

prison *noun* **1** a building used to confine criminals or people accused of crimes. **2** any place of custody or confinement. **3** imprisonment as a punishment ♦ *Prison works.* [from an Old French word *prisun*, from a Latin word *prehendere* meaning 'to seize']

prison camp *noun* a camp where prisoners of war or political prisoners are kept.

prisoner *noun* **1** a person kept in prison as a legal punishment for a crime. SYNONYM: convict. **2** a person who is being held in custody and on trial for a criminal offence. **3** a person who has been captured and confined. SYNONYMS: captive, hostage. **4** a person who is trapped by circumstances.

prisoner of war *noun* a person captured and imprisoned by the enemy in a war.

prissy *adjective* (**prissier, prissiest**) fussily respectable or prim. **prissily** *adverb* **prissiness** *noun* [probably a blend of *prim* and *sissy*]

pristine (pris-teen) *adjective* **1** in its original condition, unspoilt. **2** fresh as if new ♦ *a pristine layer of snow.* [from a Latin word *pristinus* meaning 'former']

privacy (priv-ǝsi) *noun* a state of being private and not disturbed by other people.

private *adjective* **1** of or belonging to a particular person or group, not public ♦ *private property.* **2** (said about thoughts, feelings, or statements) confidential, not to be shared with other people. SYNONYMS: personal, confidential, intimate. **3** not holding public office or having an official position ♦ *a private citizen.* **4** (said about a place) quiet and secluded. SYNONYMS: quiet, secluded, hidden. **5** (said about a service or industry) run as a commercial operation and not by the state. **6** to do with medical care for which patients pay fees, as distinct from the National Health Service. **private** *noun* a soldier of the lowest rank. **in private** without the presence of people who are not involved. **privately** *adverb* [from a Latin word *privatus* meaning 'withdrawn from public life', from *privus* meaning 'individual']

private enterprise *noun* business or industry run by private individuals or companies as distinct from the state.

private eye *noun* (*informal*) a private detective.

private life *noun* a person's personal relationships and interests, as distinct from their work or professional activity.

private means *plural noun* income obtained from investments, property, etc., as distinct from income earned from employment.

private member *noun* an MP who does not hold a government appointment.

private parts *plural noun* the genitals.

private practice *noun* medical practice that is not part of the National Health Service.

private school *noun* a school supported wholly by the payment of fees or endowments.

private sector *noun* businesses and industries run by private enterprise as distinct from the state.

private soldier *noun* an ordinary soldier who is not an officer.

privation (priy-vay-shən) *noun* the loss or lack of essentials, such as food and warmth. [from a Latin word *privatus* meaning 'deprived']

privatize (priv-ə-tiyz) *verb* to transfer a business or industry from state ownership to private enterprise. **privatization** *noun*

privet (priv-it) *noun* a bushy evergreen shrub with small leaves, used to make hedges. [origin unknown]

privilege *noun* a special right or advantage given to one person or group. SYNONYMS: right, advantage, prerogative. [from Latin words *privus* meaning 'an individual' and *legis* meaning 'of law']

privileged *adjective* having privileges or advantages over other people.

privy *adjective* (old use) hidden or secret. **privy** *noun* (privies) (old use) a lavatory. **to be privy to** to be sharing in the knowledge of something secret. **privily** *adverb* [same origin as for *private*]

Privy Council *noun* a body of distinguished people who advise the sovereign on matters of state.

privy counsellor *noun* a member of the Privy Council.

privy purse *noun* an allowance from public revenue for the sovereign's private expenses.

privy seal *noun* a seal put on state documents.

prize *noun* 1 an award given as a reward to a winner or to acknowledge an outstanding achievement. SYNONYMS: award, trophy. 2 something valuable that is worth striving for. 3 something that can be won in a lottery or other game of chance. 4 a ship or property captured at sea during a war. **prize** *adjective* winning or likely to win a prize; excellent of its kind. **prize** *verb* to value something highly. SYNONYMS: value, appreciate, treasure, cherish. [from *price*]

prizefighter *noun* a professional boxer.

pro [1] *noun* (pros) (*informal*) a professional.

pro [2] *adjective & preposition* for, in favour of. **pro** *noun* (pros) a reason for or in favour of something, an advantage. **pros and cons** reasons for and against something, advantages and disadvantages. [from a Latin word *pro* meaning 'for'; *con* is from a Latin word *contra* meaning 'against']

pro- *prefix* 1 favouring or supporting (as in *pro-choice*). 2 deputizing or substituted for (as in *pronoun*). 3 onwards or forwards (as in *proceed*). [from a Latin word *pro* meaning 'for' or 'in front of']

probability *noun* (probabilities) 1 the state of being probable. 2 something that is probable; the most probable event. 3 a ratio expressing the chances that a certain event will occur.

probable *adjective* likely to happen or be true. **probable** *noun* a person who is likely to be chosen or be successful. **probably** *adverb* [from a Latin word *probare* meaning 'to prove']

probate (proh-bayt) *noun* 1 the official process of proving that a will is valid. 2 a copy of a will with a certificate that it is valid, handed to executors. [from a Latin word *probatum* meaning 'tested, proved']

probation *noun* 1 the process of testing a person's character and abilities in a certain role. 2 a system whereby certain offenders are not sent to prison but have to complete a period of good behaviour under supervision. **probationary** *adjective* [same origin as for *prove*]

probationer *noun* 1 a person who is serving a period of probation in a job. 2 an offender who is on probation.

probe noun 1 a device for exploring an otherwise inaccessible place or object. 2 a blunt-ended surgical instrument for exploring a wound or part of the body. 3 an unmanned exploratory spacecraft. 4 a thorough investigation.
probe verb 1 to explore something with a probe. 2 to penetrate something with a sharp object. 3 to make a thorough investigation of something. SYNONYMS: investigate, examine, explore, inquire into. [from a Latin word probare meaning 'to test']

probity (**proh**-biti) noun honesty or integrity. [from a Latin word probus meaning 'good' or 'honest']

problem noun 1 something difficult to deal with or understand. 2 something that has to be done or answered. [from a Greek word problēma meaning 'an exercise']

problematic or **problematical** adjective difficult to deal with or understand. **problematically** adverb

proboscis (prə-**boss**-iss) noun (**probosces**) (prə-**boss**-eez) 1 a long flexible snout, such as an elephant's trunk. 2 an elongated mouthpart in certain insects, used for sucking things. [from Greek words pro meaning 'in front' and boskein meaning 'to feed']

procedure noun an established series of actions for doing something. SYNONYMS: process, method, system. **procedural** adjective [from a French word procédure, related to proceed]

proceed (prə-**seed**) verb 1 to go forward or onward. SYNONYMS: advance, progress. 2 to go on to do something ♦ She proceeded to tell us the latest news. SYNONYMS: go on, continue. 3 to carry on an activity ♦ We told the builders to proceed with the work. 4 (Law) to start a lawsuit against someone. 5 to originate with or be caused by something ♦ the evils that proceed from war. SYNONYMS: originate, issue, result, spring, stem. [from pro- and a Latin word cedere meaning 'to go']
◊ Do not confuse this word with **precede**, which has a different meaning.

proceedings plural noun 1 an event or series of activities that follows a set procedure. 2 a lawsuit ♦ His wife has started proceedings for divorce. 3 the activities and discussions that take place at a conference.

proceeds (**proh**-seedz) plural noun the money raised by a sale or activity.

process [1] (**proh**-sess) noun 1 a series of actions or operations involved in making or doing something. SYNONYMS: procedure, method, system. 2 a natural operation or series of changes ♦ the digestive process. 3 a course of events or time. 4 (Law) a summons or writ to appear in court. 5 (Biology) a natural projection on an organism.
process verb 1 to put something through a process or course of treatment. SYNONYMS: treat, deal with, prepare. 2 (Computing) to perform operations on data. [same origin as for proceed]

process [2] (prə-**sess**) verb to walk in procession. [from procession]

procession noun a line of people or vehicles moving steadily forward, especially in a ceremony. **processional** adjective

processor noun 1 a machine that processes things. 2 (Computing) a central processing unit.

proclaim verb 1 to announce something officially or publicly. SYNONYMS: announce, declare, give out, publish, report, broadcast. 2 to show something clearly ♦ He had an accent that proclaimed him a Glaswegian. **proclamation** noun [from a Latin word proclamare meaning 'to shout out']

proclivity (prə-**kliv**-iti) noun (**proclivities**) a tendency or inclination. [from a Latin word proclivis meaning 'inclined']

procrastinate (prə-**kras**-tin-ayt) verb to keep delaying or postponing action. SYNONYMS: delay, stall, dilly-dally. **procrastination** noun **procrastinator** noun [from pro- and a Latin word crastinus meaning 'of tomorrow']

procreate (**proh**-kri-ayt) verb to produce young by the natural process of reproduction. **procreation** noun **procreative** adjective [from a Latin word procreatus meaning 'brought forth']

Procrustean (prə-**krust**-iən) adjective making people or things conform even when they cannot naturally do so. [from Procrustes, a robber in Greek legend who fitted victims to his bed by stretching them or cutting parts off them]

procurator (prok-yoor-ayt-er) noun an agent or proxy. **procurator fiscal** (in Scotland) the public prosecutor and coroner of a district.

procure verb to obtain or acquire something, often by special effort.

procurable *adjective* **procurement** *noun* [from a Latin word *procurare* meaning 'to take care of']

prod *verb* (**prodded, prodding**) 1 to poke something or someone. SYNONYMS: poke, dig, jab. 2 to urge or stimulate someone into action. SYNONYMS: urge, stimulate, prompt, spur, stir.
prod *noun* 1 a poke. 2 a stimulus to action. 3 a pointed instrument for prodding things. [origin unknown]

prodigal *adjective* 1 wasteful or extravagant. 2 lavish.
prodigal *noun* a wastefully extravagant person. **prodigality** (prod-i-**gal**-iti) *noun* **prodigally** *adverb* [from a Latin word *prodigus* meaning 'generous']

prodigious (prə-**dij**-us) *adjective* remarkably large or impressive. **prodigiously** *adverb*

prodigy (**prod**-iji) *noun* (**prodigies**) 1 a person, especially a child or young person, with exceptional abilities or talents. 2 a marvellous or unusual thing. [from a Latin word *prodigium* meaning 'good omen']

produce[1] (prə-**dewss**) *verb* 1 to make or manufacture something ♦ *The factory produces washing machines.* SYNONYMS: make, manufacture, assemble. 2 to bring something forward for consideration or use. SYNONYMS: show, bring out, reveal, disclose, present. 3 to organize the performance of a play, making of a film, etc. 4 to cause something to exist or occur ♦ *The remarks produced a round of applause.* 5 (*Geometry*) to extend a straight line ♦ *Produce the base of the triangle.* [from *pro-* and a Latin word *ducere* meaning 'to lead']

produce[2] (**prod**-yewss) *noun* 1 things that have been produced, especially things grown or farmed for food.

producer *noun* 1 a person who produces goods or produce. (Compare **consumer**.) 2 a person who directs the performance of a play or controls the business of a film or broadcast programme.

product *noun* 1 something manufactured or produced by agriculture. 2 a substance produced during a natural process. 3 (*Mathematics*) the result obtained by multiplying two amounts together (e.g. 12 in 3 × 4 = 12). [from a Latin word *productum* meaning 'produced']

production *noun* 1 the process of producing things. 2 something produced, especially a play or film. 3 the amount produced ♦ *Production has increased this year.*

production line *noun* in a factory, a sequence of workers and machines that assemble a product in successive stages.

productive *adjective* 1 able to produce things in large quantities. 2 useful, producing good results ♦ *The two countries have had productive talks on arms control.* SYNONYMS: useful, helpful, constructive. **productively** *adverb* **productiveness** *noun*

productivity *noun* efficiency in industrial production.

profane (prə-**fayn**) *adjective* 1 secular and not religious. 2 irreverent or blasphemous.
profane *verb* to treat something with irreverence or lack of due respect. **profanely** *adverb* **profanity** (prə-**fan**-iti) *noun* [from a Latin word *profanus* meaning 'outside the temple']

profess *verb* 1 to claim that you have a quality or feeling ♦ *She professed ignorance.* 2 to affirm your faith in a religion. [from a Latin word *professus* meaning 'declared publicly']

professed *adjective* 1 openly acknowledged by the person concerned ♦ *a professed Christian.* 2 falsely claiming to be something ♦ *a professed friend.* 3 having taken the vows of a religious order ♦ *a professed nun.* **professedly** (prə-**fess**-idli) *adverb*

profession *noun* 1 an occupation that involves special knowledge and training, such as medicine and law. SYNONYMS: occupation, calling, vocation. 2 the people engaged in a profession. 3 a declaration or avowal ♦ *They made many professions of loyalty.* [from a Latin word *professio* meaning 'public declaration']

professional *adjective* 1 to do with or belonging to a profession. 2 having or showing the skill of a professional. SYNONYMS: competent, expert, skilful. 3 doing work or an activity for payment or as a livelihood and not as an amateur ♦ *a professional writer.*
professional *noun* 1 a person working or performing for payment. 2 someone who is highly skilled. **professionally** *adverb*

professionalism *noun* the qualities or skills expected of professional people.

professor *noun* a university teacher of the highest rank. **professorial** (prof-i-**sor**-iəl) *adjective* **professorship** *noun*

proffer (prof-er) *verb* to offer something. [from *pro-* and *offer*]

proficient (prə-**fish**-ənt) *adjective* doing something correctly and competently through training or practice, skilled. SYNONYMS: competent, able, capable, qualified, skilled. **proficiency** *noun* **proficiently** *adverb* [from a Latin word *proficiens* meaning 'making progress']

profile (proh-fiyl) *noun* 1 a side view of a person's face. 2 an outline. 3 a vertical cross section of a structure. 4 a short description of a person's character or career.
profile *verb* 1 to represent someone in profile. 2 to describe someone in a profile. [from an obsolete Italian word *profilare* meaning 'to draw in outline', from a Latin word *filum* meaning 'thread']

profit *noun* 1 an advantage or benefit obtained from doing something. SYNONYMS: advantage, benefit, gain. 2 the money gained in a business transaction, especially the excess of the amount earned from selling goods or services over the cost of producing them. SYNONYMS: gain, surplus.
profit *verb* (**profited, profiting**) 1 to bring an advantage to someone. SYNONYMS: benefit, serve, help. 2 to obtain an advantage or benefit ♦ *Criminals should not be allowed to profit from their crimes.* SYNONYMS: benefit, gain. [from a Latin word *profectus* meaning 'progress' or 'profit']

profitable *adjective* providing a profit or benefits. SYNONYMS: lucrative, beneficial. **profitability** *noun* **profitably** *adverb*

profiteer *noun* a person who makes large profits unfairly, especially in time of war or scarcity.

profiteering *noun* making large profits unfairly, being a profiteer.

profiterole (prə-fit-er-ohl) *noun* a small hollow ball of choux pastry filled with cream and covered in chocolate sauce. [from a French word meaning 'little profit']

profit-sharing *noun* a system by which the employees of a company share directly in its profits.

profligate (prof-lig-ət) *adjective* 1 recklessly wasteful or extravagant. 2 indulging too much in pleasure.
profligate *noun* a profligate person. **profligacy** *noun* [from a Latin word *profligare* meaning 'to ruin']

profound *adjective* 1 very deep or intense ♦ *We have made some profound changes.* 2 having or showing great knowledge or insight. SYNONYMS: deep, learned, scholarly, serious, wise. 3 needing deep study or thought. **profoundly** *adverb* **profundity** *noun* [from a Latin word *profundus* meaning 'deep']

profuse (prə-fewss) *adjective* lavish or plentiful ♦ *The guests made profuse apologies for being so late.* **profusely** *adverb* **profuseness** *noun* [from a Latin word *profusus* meaning 'poured out']

profusion (prə-few-zhən) *noun* an abundance or plentiful supply ♦ *a profusion of ideas.*

progenitor (prə-jen-it-er) *noun* an ancestor.

progeny (proj-ini) *noun* offspring or descendants. [from *pro-* and a Latin word *gignere* meaning 'to create' or 'to father']

progesterone (prə-jest-er-ohn) *noun* a hormone that stimulates the uterus to prepare for pregnancy.

prognosis (prog-noh-sis) *noun* (**prognoses**) a forecast or advance indication, especially about the way a disease will develop. [from Greek words *pro* meaning 'before' and *gnōsis* meaning 'knowing']

prognostic (prog-nost-ik) *adjective* making or giving a prediction about a course of events.

prognosticate (prog-nost-i-kayt) *verb* to predict or be an advance indication of something. **prognostication** *noun* **prognosticator** *noun*

program *noun* 1 (*North Amer.*) another spelling of **programme**. 2 (*Computing*) a series of coded instructions for a computer.
program *verb* (**programmed, programming**) (*Computing*) to input instructions in a computer by means of a program. **programmable** *adjective* **programmer** *noun*

programme *noun* 1 a planned series of events, especially of related activities having a particular objective. 2 a plan of what is going to happen or what is going to be done. 3 a sheet or booklet giving details of the items and performers at an event. 4 a radio or television broadcast. **programme** *verb* to plan events according to a programme. [from a Greek word *programma* meaning 'public notice']

progress¹ (**proh**-gress) *noun* **1** forward or onward movement towards a destination. **2** a development or improvement. SYNONYMS: development, improvement, advance. **in progress** taking place, in the course of occurring. [from a Latin word *progressus* meaning 'going forward']

progress² (prə-**gress**) *verb* **1** to move forward or onward. **2** to develop or improve, or to make something develop. SYNONYMS: develop, improve, advance.

progression *noun* **1** a gradual movement or advance towards a destination. **2** a gradual development or improvement.

progressive *adjective* **1** making continuous forward movement. **2** proceeding steadily or in regular degrees ♦ *a progressive reduction in pollution levels.* **3** in favour of political or social change or reform. **4** (said about a card game or dance) involving successive changes of partners. **5** (said about a disease) becoming gradually more severe. **6** (said about a tax) calculated on a scale with higher rates paid on higher levels of income. **progressive** *noun* someone who favours a progressive policy. **progressively** *adverb* **progressiveness** *noun*

prohibit *verb* (**prohibited, prohibiting**) to forbid something. SYNONYMS: forbid, ban, bar, disallow. **prohibition** *noun* **prohibitor** *noun* [from a Latin word *prohibere* meaning 'to keep in check']

prohibitive *adjective* **1** serving to prevent or prohibit something. **2** (said about a charge or price) unacceptably high. **prohibitively** *adverb*

project¹ (prə-**jekt**) *verb* **1** to extend outward ♦ *a projecting balcony.* SYNONYMS: protrude, stick out, jut out. **2** to cause something to move forward or outward. **3** to cause an image or shadow to fall on a surface. SYNONYMS: cast, throw. **4** to cause a sound to be heard further away. **5** to present or promote an idea ♦ *The advertisements were meant to project a strong brand image.* SYNONYMS: present, offer. **6** to imagine something or oneself in another situation or time. **7** to estimate or forecast future trends on the basis of the present situation. **8** to plan a scheme or course of action. **9** (*Geometry*) to represent a solid systematically on a plane surface, as maps of the earth are made. [from a Latin word *projectum* meaning 'something thrown forward']

project² (**proj**-ekt) *noun* **1** an undertaking aimed at achieving a particular objective; a plan or scheme. SYNONYMS: plan, scheme, undertaking. **2** an educational task of conducting research into a topic and writing up the results. SYNONYMS: assignment, topic.

projectile (prə-**jek**-tiyl) *noun* a missile that can be fired or thrown at a target.

projection *noun* **1** something that projects from a surface. **2** the process of projecting a sound or image. **3** the process of projecting thoughts and mental images. **4** something that is projected. **5** an estimate or forecast of future situations or trends based on a study of the present ones. **6** a representation of the surface of the earth on a plane surface.

projectionist *noun* a person who works a projector.

projector *noun* a device for projecting photographs or film on to a screen.

prolapse (**proh**-laps) *noun* a movement of an organ of the body, in which it slips forward or down out of its place. **prolapsed** (proh-**lapsd**) *adjective* [from *pro-* meaning 'forward' and a Latin word *lapsum* meaning 'fallen']

proletarian (proh-li-**tair**-iən) *adjective* of the proletariat. **proletarian** *noun* a member of the proletariat.

proletariat (proh-li-**tair**-iət) *noun* the working class, especially as contrasted with the bourgeoisie in Marxist thinking. [from a Latin word *proletarius* meaning 'a person who produces offspring', from *proles* meaning 'offspring'. In ancient Rome this was the name for the lowest class of citizens, who lacked wealth and served the state by producing children]

pro-life *adjective* opposed to abortion and euthanasia.

proliferate (prə-**lif**-er-ayt) *verb* **1** to produce new growth or offspring rapidly. **2** to increase rapidly in number. **proliferation** *noun* [from Latin words *proles* meaning 'offspring' and *ferre* meaning 'to bear']

prolific (prə-**lif**-ik) *adjective* **1** producing much fruit or many flowers or offspring. **2** producing many works ♦ *a prolific writer.* **prolifically** *adverb* [same origin as for *proliferate*]

prolix (**proh**-liks) *adjective* (said about speech or writing) tediously wordy or lengthy. **prolixity** (prə-**liks**-iti) *noun* [from a Latin word *prolixus* meaning 'poured forth']

prologue (**proh**-log) *noun* 1 an introduction to a poem or play etc. 2 an act or event that leads to another. [from Greek words *pro-* meaning 'before' and *logos* meaning 'speech']

prolong (prə-**long**) *verb* 1 to make something last longer. SYNONYMS: extend, lengthen, protract. 2 a technical term meaning to make something greater in length. SYNONYMS: lengthen, increase, extend. **prolongation** (proh-long-**gay**-shən) *noun*

prolonged *adjective* continuing for a long time, lengthy ♦ *prolonged periods of rain*.

prom *noun* (*informal*) 1 a promenade along a sea front. 2 a promenade concert. 3 (*North Amer.*) a formal dance at a high school or college.

promenade (prom-ən-**ahd**) *noun* 1 a paved public walk, especially along a sea front. 2 a leisurely walk in a public place. **promenade** *verb* to go for a promenade. [from a French word, from *se promener* meaning 'to walk']

promenade concert *noun* a concert at which all or part of the audience stands or walks about in an open area without seating.

promethium (prə- **mee**- thi- əm) *noun* a radioactive metal, a chemical element (symbol Pm). [named after Prometheus, a demigod in Greek mythology who stole fire from the gods and gave it to the human race]

prominent *adjective* 1 important or well-known ♦ *prominent politicians*. SYNONYMS: important, well-known, distinguished, famous, eminent. 2 conspicuous or noticeable ♦ *The house stood in a prominent position*. 3 projecting or jutting out ♦ *a low ceiling with prominent oak beams*. **prominence** *noun* **prominently** *adverb* [from a Latin word *prominere* meaning 'to jut out']

promiscuous (prə-**miss**-kew-əs) *adjective* 1 having casual sexual relations with many people. 2 indiscriminate. **promiscuity** (prom-iss-**kew**-iti) *noun* **promiscuously** *adverb*

promise *noun* 1 an assurance that you will do or not do a certain thing. SYNONYMS: assurance, pledge, undertaking, guarantee, vow. 2 an indication that something is likely to occur ♦ *the promise of thunderstorms*. 3 an indication of future success or excellence ♦ *The work shows promise*.
promise *verb* 1 to make a promise to someone, to declare that you will do or not do a certain thing. SYNONYMS: undertake, guarantee, pledge, vow. 2 to make something seem likely. [from a Latin word *promittere* meaning 'to put forth' or 'to promise']

Promised Land *noun* the land of Canaan, which in the Bible (Genesis 12:7) was promised by God to Abraham and his descendants.

promising *adjective* likely to succeed or produce good results. SYNONYMS: encouraging, hopeful. **promisingly** *adverb*

promissory (prom-iss-er-i) *adjective* conveying a promise.

promissory note *noun* a signed promise to pay a sum of money on a certain date.

promontory (prom-ən-ter-i) *noun* (**promontories**) a piece of high land jutting out into the sea or a lake. [from a Latin word *promontorium*]

promote *verb* 1 to give someone a higher rank or more senior office. 2 to help the progress of something, to support or encourage something ♦ *promoting friendship between nations*. SYNONYMS: support, encourage, foster, back, progress. 3 to publicize a product in order to sell it. **promoter** *noun* [from *pro-* and a Latin word *motum* meaning 'moved']

promotion *noun* 1 activity that supports or encourages something. 2 the process of promoting someone to a higher position. **promotional** *adjective*

prompt *adjective* 1 made or done without delay ♦ *We would like a prompt reply*. SYNONYMS: speedy, swift. 2 doing something in good time, punctual. **prompt** *adverb* in good time, punctually. **prompt** *verb* 1 to urge or encourage someone to do something. SYNONYMS: urge, encourage, spur, stir, induce. 2 to cause a certain feeling, thought, or action. 3 to help an actor or speaker by reminding them of words they have forgotten. **promptly** *adverb* **promptness** *noun* [from a Latin word *promptum* meaning 'produced']

prompter *noun* a person out of sight of the audience who prompts actors during the performance of a play.

promulgate (prom-əl-gayt) *verb* to make something known to the public, to proclaim something. **promulgation** *noun* **promulgator** *noun* [from a Latin word *promulgare*]

prone *adjective* 1 likely to do or suffer something ♦ *He is prone to sudden changes of mood* ♦ *Some of the players seemed injury-prone.* SYNONYMS: (prone to) apt to, likely to, inclined to, given to. 2 lying face downwards. **proneness** *noun* [from a Latin word *pronus* meaning 'leaning forward']

prong *noun* 1 each of the pointed parts of a fork. 2 each of the separate parts of an attack. **pronged** *adjective* [origin unknown]

pronoun (proh-nown) *noun* a word used in place of a noun, such as *I, me, us, this, which.* [from *pro-* meaning 'in place of' and *noun*]
◊ See the separate entries for different kinds of pronoun: **demonstrative pronoun, interrogative pronoun, personal pronoun, reflexive pronoun, relative pronoun.**

pronounce *verb* 1 to utter a speech sound in a particular way ♦ *'Two' and 'too' are pronounced the same.* 2 to declare something formally ♦ *I now pronounce you man and wife.* SYNONYMS: declare, proclaim. 3 to declare something as an opinion ♦ *The baby was immediately pronounced gorgeous.* [from *pro-* and a Latin word *nuntiare* meaning 'to announce']

pronounced *adjective* definite or noticeable ♦ *The man had a pronounced limp.*

pronouncement *noun* a declaration.

pronto *adverb* (*informal*) immediately. [a Spanish word, related to *prompt*]

pronunciation *noun* the way in which a word is pronounced.
◊ Note that this word should not be written or spoken as 'pronounciation'.

proof *noun* 1 a fact or piece of evidence that shows something to be true. SYNONYMS: authentication, validation, confirmation. 2 a demonstration that something is true or valid ♦ *The measures are a proof of their intention to help pensioners.* 3 a standard of strength for distilled alcoholic liquors ♦ *80% proof.* 4 a trial impression of the pages of a book or other printed work, produced so that corrections can be made before it is finally printed. 5 a trial print of a photograph.
proof *adjective* able to resist or withstand penetration or damage ♦ *a bulletproof jacket.*

proof *verb* 1 to make a proof of printed matter. 2 to make a fabric waterproof. [from an Old French word *proeve*, related to *prove*]

proof-read *verb* (past tense and past participle, **proof-read** (proof-red)) to read a proof of printed matter and mark corrections. **proof-reader** *noun*

prop[1] *noun* 1 a support, especially one made of a long piece of wood or metal, used to keep something from falling or sagging. SYNONYMS: support, upright, strut. 2 a person or thing you depend on for support or help.
prop *verb* (**propped, propping**) 1 to support something with or as if with a prop. 2 to lean something against an upright surface ♦ *Prop your bicycle against the wall.* SYNONYMS: lean, rest. **to prop someone up** to give someone help or support to prevent them failing. **to prop something up** to support something and prevent it falling. [from a Dutch word *proppe* meaning 'support (for vines)']

prop[2] *noun* a movable object or piece of furniture used on the set of a play or film. [short for *property*]

prop[3] *noun* (*informal*) an aircraft propeller.

propaganda *noun* biased or misleading publicity that is intended to promote a political point of view. [from the Latin name of a religious body *congregatio de propaganda fide* meaning 'congregation for propagating the faith']

propagandist *noun* a person who spreads propaganda.

propagate *verb* 1 to breed or reproduce animals or plants from a parent stock. 2 to spread information or ideas widely. 3 to transmit something ♦ *The vibrations are propagated through the rock.* **propagation** *noun* **propagator** *noun* [from a Latin word *propago* meaning 'young shoot']

propane (proh-payn) *noun* (*Chemistry*) a hydrocarbon found in petroleum and used as a fuel. [from *propionic acid* a fatty acid, from a Greek word *pīon* meaning 'fat']

propanol (proh-pə-nol) *noun* (*Chemistry*) a liquid alcohol used as a solvent.

propel *verb* (**propelled, propelling**) to drive or push something forward, to give an onward movement to something. SYNONYMS: drive, impel, thrust, push. [from *pro-* and a Latin word *pellere* meaning 'to drive']

propellant noun a substance that propels things, such as an explosive that fires a bullet or a fuel that drives a rocket.

propellent adjective able to propel something.

propeller noun a device consisting of a shaft with blades that spin round to propel a ship or aircraft.

propene (proh-peen) or **propylene** noun (Chemistry) an alkene obtained by cracking petroleum, a colourless gas used in the manufacture of many organic chemicals.

propensity (prə-pen-siti) noun (**propensities**) a tendency or inclination ♦ a propensity for violence. [from a Latin word propendere meaning 'to lean forward' or 'to hang down']

proper adjective 1 genuinely or fully what something is called ♦ It will be good to sleep in a proper bed again. 2 correct or suitable ♦ You need to make your application at the proper time ♦ What is the proper way to address a bishop? SYNONYMS: correct, suitable, appropriate, right. 3 according to social conventions, respectable ♦ Their behaviour did not seem quite proper. SYNONYMS: decent, respectable, seemly, becoming. **properly** adverb [from a Latin word proprius meaning 'your own']

proper fraction noun a fraction that is less than 1, with the numerator less than the denominator, e.g. $\frac{1}{3}$.

proper name or **proper noun** noun the name of an individual person or thing, e.g. Mary, London, Spain.

property noun (**properties**) 1 a thing or things that someone owns. SYNONYMS: possessions, belongings. 2 a building and the land belonging to it ♦ Their property borders on ours. 3 a quality or characteristic ♦ It has the property of becoming soft when heated. [same origin as for proper]

prophecy (prof-i-si) noun (**prophecies**) 1 the power of foreseeing the future. 2 a statement that predicts what will happen.

prophesy (prof-i-siy) verb (**prophesies, prophesied, prophesying**) to predict what will happen. SYNONYMS: predict, foretell, foresee, forecast. [from Greek pro meaning 'before' and phanai meaning 'to speak']

prophet noun 1 a person who predicts the future. 2 a religious teacher inspired by God. **the Prophet** a name used by Muslims for Muhammad. **prophetess** noun

prophetic or **prophetical** adjective 1 predicting the future. 2 to do with a prophet or prophecy. **prophetically** adverb

prophylactic (proh-fil-ak-tik) adjective tending to prevent a disease. **prophylactic** noun a prophylactic medicine or course of treatment. **prophylactically** adverb [from a Greek word prophulaxis meaning 'guarding']

propinquity (prə-pink-witi) noun (formal) nearness.

propitiate (prə-pish-i-ayt) verb to win the favour or forgiveness of someone, to placate someone. **propitiation** noun **propitiatory** (prə-pish-ə-ter-i) adjective [same origin as for propitious]

propitious (prə-pish-əs) adjective favourable, providing a suitable opportunity. SYNONYMS: favourable, auspicious. **propitiously** adverb [from a Latin word propitius meaning 'favourable']

proponent (prə-poh-nənt) noun a person who puts forward a theory or proposal. [from pro- and a Latin word ponere meaning 'to place']

proportion noun 1 a part or share of something considered in relation to the whole. SYNONYMS: part, share, portion. 2 the ratio of one thing to another ♦ the proportion of skilled workers to unskilled. SYNONYMS: ratio, balance. 3 the correct relation in size or amount between one thing and another or between parts of a thing. SYNONYMS: symmetry, balance. **proportion** verb to give the correct proportions to things, to make one thing proportionate to another. **proportions** plural noun size or dimensions ♦ a palace of vast proportions. [from pro- and a Latin word portio meaning 'portion' or 'share']

proportional adjective corresponding in size or amount to something. **proportionally** adverb

proportional representation noun an electoral system in which each party has a number of seats in proportion to the number of votes for its candidates.

proportionate adjective in proportion, corresponding ♦ Penalties are proportionate to the seriousness of the offence. **proportionately** adverb

proposal noun 1 the process of proposing something. 2 something proposed, a plan or suggestion. SYNONYMS: suggestion, plan, proposition, scheme. **3** an offer of marriage.

propose *verb* **1** to put forward an idea or plan for consideration. SYNONYMS: suggest, advance, submit, recommend. **2** to plan or intend to do something ♦ *We propose to wait here.* SYNONYMS: intend, aim, mean, plan. **3** to nominate someone as a candidate. **4** to make an offer of marriage. **proposer** *noun* [from *pro-* and a Latin word *positum* meaning 'put']

proposition *noun* **1** a statement or assertion. **2** a suggestion or proposal. **3** something to be considered or dealt with ♦ *The work was not an attractive proposition.* **4** (*informal*) an offer of sexual intercourse.
proposition *verb* (*informal*) to make an offer to someone, especially of sexual intercourse.

propound *verb* to put forward an idea or suggestions for consideration.
propounder *noun* [same origin as for *proponent*]

proprietary (prǝ-**priy**-ǝt-er-i) *adjective* **1** manufactured and sold by one firm as a registered trademark ♦ *proprietary medicines*. **2** to do with an owner or ownership. [same origin as for *property*]

proprietor (prǝ-**priy**-ǝt-er) *noun* the owner of a shop or business. [same origin as for *property*]

proprietorial (prǝ-priy-ǝ-**tor**-iǝl) *adjective* of or indicating ownership.

propriety (prǝ-**priy**-ǝti) *noun* **1** being proper or suitable. SYNONYMS: decency, decorum, courtesy. **2** correct behaviour or morals. [same origin as for *property*]

propulsion *noun* the process of propelling or driving something forward.

propylene (**prop**- i- leen) *noun* a gaseous hydrocarbon of the alkene series. [from *propane*]

pro rata (proh **rah**-tǝ) *adjective & adverb* in proportion. [a Latin phrase, meaning 'according to the rate']

prorogue (prǝ-**rohg**) *verb* (**prorogues, prorogued, proroguing**) to discontinue the meetings of a parliament or assembly without dissolving it. **prorogation** (proh-rǝ-**gay**-shǝn) *noun* [from a Latin word *prorogare* meaning 'to prolong']

prosaic (prǝ-**zay**-ik) *adjective* **1** in the style of prose writing. **2** unimaginative, plain and ordinary. SYNONYMS: unimaginative, dull,

plain, ordinary, commonplace, tedious, boring. **prosaically** *adverb*

proscenium (prǝ-**seen**-iǝm) *noun* (**prosceniums** or **proscenia**) the part of a theatre stage in front of the curtain. [from Greek words *pro* meaning 'before' and *skēnē* meaning 'stage']

proscribe *verb* **1** to forbid something by law. **2** to denounce or condemn a practice etc. **proscription** *noun* **proscriptive** *adjective* [from a Latin word *proscribere* meaning 'to outlaw']
◊ Do not confuse this word with **prescribe**, which has a different meaning.

prose *noun* ordinary written or spoken language that is not in verse. [from a Latin phrase *prosa oratio* meaning 'plain speech']

prosecute *verb* **1** to start legal proceedings against someone. **2** to continue an activity so as to complete it ♦ *The state prosecuted the war with determination.* **prosecutor** *noun* [from Latin *prosecutus* meaning 'pursued']

prosecution *noun* **1** the process of starting legal proceedings against someone. **2** the party prosecuting someone in a lawsuit.

proselyte (**pross**-i-liyt) *noun* a person who has been converted to a religion or opinion, especially to Judaism. [from a Greek word *prosēluthos* meaning 'stranger' or 'convert']

proselytize (**pross**-il-i-tiyz) *verb* to convert people to your own beliefs or opinions.

prosody (**pross**-ǝ-di) *noun* **1** the patterns of sound and rhythm used in poetry. **2** the study of these patterns. [from a Greek word *prosōidia* meaning 'song sung to music']

prospect[1] (**pross**-pekt) *noun* **1** a possibility or expectation of something ♦ *The prospects of success are quite good.* SYNONYMS: chance, possibility, likelihood, expectation. **2** a mental picture of a future event. **3** a chance of success or advancement ♦ *She has a job with good prospects.* **4** a person regarded as a potential customer or as likely to succeed. **5** a wide or extensive view. SYNONYMS: view, vista, panorama. [from a Latin word *prospicere* meaning 'to look forward']

prospect[2] (prǝ-**spekt**) *verb* to search for something, especially mineral deposits ♦ *prospecting for gold.* **prospector** *noun*

prospective (prə-**spek**-tiv) *adjective* expected to happen or exist ♦ *prospective customers.*

prospectus (prə-**spek**-təs) *noun* (**prospectuses**) a booklet describing and advertising a school, university, or business. [a Latin word meaning 'view or prospect']

prosper *verb* to be successful, especially financially. SYNONYMS: flourish, thrive, succeed. [from a Latin word *prosperare*]

prosperous *adjective* financially successful. SYNONYMS: wealthy, affluent, well-off, rich. **prosperity** *noun* **prosperously** *adverb*

prostate (**pross**-tayt) *noun* a gland round the neck of the bladder in males, which releases semen. **prostatic** (prə-**stat**-ik) *adjective* [from a Greek word *prostatēs* meaning 'one that stands before']

prostitute *noun* a person, usually a woman, who takes part in sexual activity for payment.
prostitute *verb* to put something worthwhile to an unworthy use ♦ *They were accused of prostituting their artistic abilities.* **prostitution** *noun* [from a Latin word *prostitutus* meaning 'for sale']

prostrate[1] (**pross**-trayt) *adjective* **1** lying on the ground face downwards. **2** overcome with emotion or exhaustion ♦ *prostrate with grief.* [from a Latin word *prostratum* meaning 'laid flat']

prostrate[2] (**pross**-trayt) *verb* **to prostrate yourself** to throw yourself flat on the ground as an act of reverence or submission. **prostration** *noun*

prosy (**proh**-zi) *adjective* (**prosier, prosiest**) (said about speech or writing) prosaic, dull or unimaginative. **prosily** *adverb* **prosiness** *noun*

protagonist (proh-**tag**-ən-ist) *noun* **1** the chief character, or one of the leading characters, in a drama or narrative. **2** an important figure in a real situation. **3** someone who supports a cause or idea. [from *proto-* and a Greek word *agōnistēs* meaning 'actor']

protean (**proh**-tiən or proh-**tee**-ən) *adjective* able to adapt or take many forms. [from Proteus, the name of an ancient Greek sea god who was able to change his shape whenever he wanted]

protease (**proh**-ti-ayz) *noun* (*Biology*) an enzyme that breaks down proteins.

protect *verb* to keep someone or something from harm or injury. SYNONYMS: safeguard, shelter, look after, defend. [from *pro-* and a Latin word *tectum* meaning 'covered']

protection *noun* **1** the process of protecting someone or something. **2** a person or thing that protects. **3** a form of extortion involving payment of money to criminals to avoid being attacked by them.

protectionism *noun* a policy of protecting domestic industries from foreign competition, e.g. by controlling imports. **protectionist** *noun*

protective *adjective* serving to protect something or someone. **protectively** *adverb*

protector *noun* a person or thing that protects something.

protectorate *noun* a country that is under the official protection and partial control of a stronger country.

protégé or **protégée** (**prot**-ezh-ay) *noun* someone who is being helped and supported by an older or more experienced person. [a French word meaning 'protected']
◊ The masculine form is *protégé* and the feminine form is *protégée.*

protein (**proh**-teen) *noun* (*Biology*) an organic compound containing nitrogen, which is found in plant and animal tissue and is an essential part of the food of animals.

pro tem *adverb* & *adjective* (*informal*) for the time being, temporarily. [short for Latin *pro tempore*]

protest[1] (**proh**-test) *noun* a statement or action showing disapproval of something. SYNONYMS: objection, complaint; (*informal*) gripe, grouse. **under protest** unwillingly and after making protests.

protest[2] (prə-**test**) *verb* **1** to express disapproval of something. SYNONYMS: object, complain; (*informal*) gripe, grouse. **2** to declare something firmly or solemnly ♦ *All the accused men protested their innocence.* **protester** *noun* [from *pro-* and a Latin word *testari* meaning 'to say on oath']

Protestant (**prot**-i-stənt) *noun* a member of any of the western Christian Churches that separated from the Roman Catholic Church at the Reformation.

Protestantism noun [so called because in the 16th century many people protested (= declared firmly) their opposition to the Catholic Church]

protestation (prot-i-**stay**-shən) noun a firm declaration about something ♦ *He was full of protestations of goodwill towards us.*

proto- prefix first or original (as in *prototype*). [from a Greek word *prōtos* meaning 'first' or 'earliest']

protocol (**proh**-tə-kol) noun 1 the correct or official procedure for dealing with certain situations, especially affairs of state or diplomacy. 2 the first or original draft of a diplomatic agreement, especially one containing the terms of a treaty, signed by those making it. [from a Greek word *prōtokollon* meaning 'first page']

proton (**proh**-ton) noun (*Physics*) a particle of matter with a positive electric charge. [from a Greek word *prōtos* meaning 'first' or 'earliest']

protoplasm (**proh**-tə-plazm) noun (*Biology*) the contents of a living cell, consisting of the cell membrane, nucleus, and cytoplasm. **protoplasmic** adjective [from *proto-* and *plasma*]

prototype (**proh**-tə-tiyp) noun a first or original example of something from which others are developed, especially a trial model of a vehicle or aircraft. [from *proto-* and *type*]

protozoon (proh-tə-**zoh**-ən) noun (**protozoa**) a microscopic animal such as an amoeba. **protozoan** adjective & noun [from *proto-* and a Greek word *zōion* meaning 'animal']

protract (prə-**trakt**) verb to prolong something or make it last longer. **protraction** noun [from *pro-* and a Latin word *tractum* meaning 'drawn out']

protractor noun an instrument for measuring angles, usually a flat semicircle marked with degrees round the curved edge.

protrude verb to stick out or project from a surface. SYNONYMS: project, stick out, jut out. **protrusion** noun **protrusive** adjective [from *pro-* and a Latin word *trudere* meaning 'to thrust']

protuberance noun a part that bulges out from a surface. [from *pro-* and a Latin word *tuber* meaning 'a swelling']

protuberant (prə-**tew**-ber-ənt) adjective bulging out from a surface.

proud adjective 1 feeling or showing pride or satisfaction in what you have done or in what someone else has done. SYNONYMS: satisfied, gratified, pleased. 2 causing a feeling of pride ♦ *This is a proud day for us.* 3 full of self-respect and independence ♦ *They were too proud to ask for help.* 4 having an unduly high opinion of yourself. SYNONYMS: vain, conceited, arrogant. 5 slightly projecting from a surface. **to do someone proud** (*informal*) to treat them with great attention or honour. **proudly** adverb [via Old English from an Old French word *prud* meaning 'brave']

prove verb 1 to show that something is true, to give or be a proof of something. SYNONYMS: establish, demonstrate, verify, show, confirm. 2 (*Law*) to establish the validity of a will. 3 to be seen or found to be something ♦ *The forecast proved to be correct.* 4 (said about dough) to rise from the action of yeast, before being baked. **to prove yourself** to show that you have the necessary character or abilities. **provable** adjective [from a Latin word *probare* meaning 'to test']

proven (**proh**-vən or **proo**-vən) adjective proved or established ♦ *a person of proven ability.* **not proven** (in Scottish law) a verdict that the evidence is insufficient to establish either guilt or innocence.

provenance (**prov**-in-əns) noun a place of origin. [from *pro-* and a Latin word *venire* meaning 'to come']

provender (**prov**-in-der) noun animal fodder. [from an Old French word *provendre* meaning 'to provide']

proverb noun a short well-known saying stating a general truth or piece of advice, such as *many hands make light work.* [from *pro-* and a Latin word *verbum* meaning 'word']

proverbial (prə-**verb**-iəl) adjective 1 of or like a proverb, or mentioned in a proverb or idiom ♦ *She was up in the morning like the proverbial early bird.* 2 well-known ♦ *His generosity is proverbial.* **proverbially** adverb

provide verb 1 to make something available for someone to use. SYNONYMS: equip, supply, furnish, offer. 2 to supply the necessities of life ♦ *She has to provide for a large family.* 3 to make suitable preparation or arrangements for something ♦ *Try to provide for emergencies.* **provider** noun [from a Latin word *providere* meaning 'to foresee']

provided *conjunction* on the condition that
♦ They can stay provided that they help.
◊ You can also say ♦ They can stay provided
they help.

providence *noun* 1 being provident. 2 care
and protection seen as being provided by
God or by nature. [same origin as for *provide*]

provident *adjective* taking care to be ready
for future needs or events, thrifty.

providential (prov-i-den-shəl) *adjective*
happening at a fortunate time,
opportune. **providentially** *adverb*

providing *conjunction* on the condition that
♦ They can stay providing that they help.
◊ You can also say ♦ They can stay providing
they help.

province *noun* 1 one of the principal
administrative divisions of a country or
empire. 2 (in a Christian Church) a district
consisting of a group of dioceses, under
the charge of an archbishop. 3 a person's
special area of knowledge or
responsibility ♦ I'm afraid chemistry is not my
province. **the provinces** the parts of a
country outside its capital city. [from a
Latin word *provincia* meaning 'charge' or
'province']

provincial (prə-vin-shəl) *adjective* 1 to do
with a province or provinces ♦ provincial
government. 2 to do with the parts of a
country outside the capital, especially
when regarded as culturally limited or
narrow-minded ♦ provincial attitudes.
provincial *noun* a person born or living in a
province or the provinces. **provincialism**
noun

provision *noun* 1 the act of providing
something. 2 preparation of resources for
future needs ♦ They made good provision for
their old age. 3 a statement or requirement
in a legal document ♦ the provisions of a will.
provision *verb* to supply someone with
provisions.
provisions *plural noun* supplies of food and
drink, especially for a journey. SYNONYMS:
food, supplies, rations. [from a Latin word
provisum meaning 'provided']

provisional *adjective* arranged or agreed
upon for the time being but possibly to be
altered later.
Provisional *noun* a member of the
Provisional wing of the IRA, taking its
name from the 'Provisional Government
of the Republic of Ireland' which was
declared in 1916. **provisionally** *adjective*

proviso (prə-viy-zoh) *noun* (**provisos**) a
condition that is insisted on in advance.

provisory (prə-viy-zeri) *adjective* subject to
a proviso, conditional.

provocation *noun* 1 the process of
provoking. 2 something said or done that
provokes anger or retaliation.

provocative (prə-vok-ətiv) *adjective*
1 arousing or likely to arouse anger or
other strong feeling. 2 intended to arouse
sexual desire or interest. **provocatively**
adverb

provoke *verb* 1 to make someone angry.
SYNONYMS: annoy, anger, upset, irritate,
enrage, incense. 2 to rouse or incite a
person to action. 3 to produce a reaction
or effect. [from *pro-* and a Latin word
vocare meaning 'to summon']

provost (prov-əst) *noun* 1 a Scottish official
with authority comparable to that of
mayor in England and Wales. 2 the head
of certain colleges. 3 the head of the
chapter in certain cathedrals. [from an
Old English word *profost* meaning 'head of
a chapter']

prow *noun* the pointed front part of a ship.
[from an Old French word *proue*]

prowess (prow-ess) *noun* great ability or
daring. [from an Old French word *prou*
meaning 'valiant']

prowl *verb* 1 to go about stealthily in search
of prey or plunder or to catch other
people unawares. SYNONYMS: lurk, creep,
slink. 2 to pace or wander restlessly.
prowl *noun* an act of prowling ♦ on the
prowl. **prowler** *noun* [origin unknown]

proximate (proks-im-ət) *adjective* closest or
nearest, next before or after. [from a
Latin word *proximus* meaning 'nearest']

proximity (proks-im-iti) *noun* being near in
space or time. **in the proximity of** near to.

proxy *noun* (**proxies**) 1 the authority to act
for another person. 2 a person authorized
to represent or act for another person. [a
shortening of an earlier word *procuracy*,
related to *procure*]

prude (prood) *noun* a person who is easily
shocked by matters relating to sex or
nudity. **prudery** *noun* [from a French word
prud'homme meaning 'good man and true']

prudent *adjective* acting with or showing
care and foresight, not rash or reckless.
SYNONYMS: careful, sensible, cautious,
sagacious. **prudence** *noun* **prudently** *adverb*
[from French, related to *provide*]

prudential (proo-**den**-shəl) *adjective* showing prudence. **prudentially** *adverb*

prudish (**proo**-dish) *adjective* like a prude, easily shocked. **prudishly** *adverb* **prudishness** *noun*

prune[1] *noun* a dried plum. [from a Greek word *prounon* meaning 'plum']

prune[2] *verb* 1 to trim a tree or shrub by cutting away dead or overgrown branches or shoots. 2 to shorten and improve a speech or book etc. by removing unnecessary parts. [from an Old French word *proignier*]

Prussian *adjective* to do with Prussia, a former country of north Europe. **Prussian** *noun* a person from Prussia.

Prussian blue *noun* a deep blue colour.

prussic acid *noun* a highly poisonous acid with an odour of bitter almonds; hydrocyanic acid.

pry[1] *verb* (**pries, pried, prying**) to look or enquire intrusively. SYNONYMS: snoop, interfere, meddle.

pry[2] *verb* (**pries, pried, prying**) (*North Amer.*) another word for **prise**.

PS *abbreviation* postscript.

psalm (sahm) *noun* a sacred song, especially one of those in the Book of Psalms in the Old Testament. **psalmist** *noun* [from a Greek word *psalmos* meaning 'song sung to the harp']

psalter (**sol**-ter) *noun* a copy of the Book of Psalms. [from a Greek word *psaltērion* meaning 'stringed instrument']

pseudo-*prefix* false. [from a Greek word *pseudēs* meaning 'false']

pseudonym (**syoo**-dən-im) *noun* a false name used by an author. [from *pseudo-* and a Greek word *onoma* meaning 'name']

PSV *abbreviation* public service vehicle.

psych (siyk) *verb* (*informal*) **be psyched up** to be emotionally prepared for something.

psyche (**siy**-ki) *noun* the human soul or mind. [from a Greek word *psukhē* meaning 'breath' or 'spirit']

psychedelic (siy-ki-**del**-ik) *adjective* 1 producing hallucinations. 2 having vivid or luminous colours. [from *psyche* and a Greek word *dēlos* meaning 'clear']

psychiatrist (siy-**kiy**-ə-trist) *noun* a doctor who treats people with mental illnesses.

psychiatry (siy-**kiy**-ə-tri) *noun* the study and treatment of mental illnesses. **psychiatric** (siy-ki-**at**-rik) *adjective* [from *psycho-* and a Greek word *iatreia* meaning 'healing']

psychic (**siy**-kik) *adjective* 1 to do with the mind or the soul. 2 to do with processes that seem to be outside normal physical laws, especially those involving extrasensory perception or clairvoyance. **psychical** *adjective* **psychically** *adverb*

psycho- *prefix* to do with the mind. [from *psyche*]

psychoanalyse *verb* to treat a person by psychoanalysis.

psychoanalysis *noun* a method of examining or treating mental illnesses by bringing certain memories that are in a person's unconscious mind into their consciousness, as a way of releasing repressed fears and inhibitions that may be influencing their behaviour and mental state. **psychoanalytic** *adjective* **psychoanalytical** *adjective*

psychoanalyst *noun* a specialist in psychoanalysis.

psychological *adjective* 1 to do with or affecting the mind and its working. 2 to do with psychology. **psychologically** *adverb*

psychologist *noun* a specialist or expert in psychology.

psychology *noun* 1 the study of the human mind and its workings, especially as these affect behaviour. 2 mental characteristics. [from *psycho-* and *-logy*]

psychopath (**siy**-kə-path) *noun* a person suffering from a severe mental disorder with aggressive or violent antisocial behaviour. **psychopathic** (siy-kə-**pa**-thik) *adjective*

psychosis (siy-**koh**-sis) *noun* (**psychoses**) a severe mental disorder involving a person's whole personality.

psychosomatic (siy-kə-sə-**mat**-ik) *adjective* 1 involving both the mind and the body. 2 (said about an illness) caused or made worse by psychological factors such as stress. **psychosomatically** *adverb* [from *psycho-* and a Greek word *sōmatos* meaning 'of the body']

psychotherapy (siy-kə-**the**-rəpi) *noun* treatment of mental illness by psychological methods. **psychotherapist** *noun*

psychotic (siy-**kot**-ik) *adjective* to do with or suffering from a psychosis.
psychotic *noun* a person suffering from a psychosis.

PT *abbreviation* physical training.

Pt *abbreviation* (*Chemistry*) the symbol for platinum.

pt. *abbreviation* pint.

PTA *abbreviation* parent–teacher association.

ptarmigan (**tar**-mig-ən) *noun* a bird of the grouse family with plumage that turns white in winter. [from a Scottish Gaelic word *tarmachan*, with the spelling influenced by Greek words beginning *pt*-]

pterodactyl (te-rə-**dak**-til) *noun* an extinct flying reptile with a long neck, thin head, and large wings. [from Greek words *pteron* meaning 'wing' and *daktulos* meaning 'finger' (because one of the 'fingers' on its frontleg was enlarged to support its wing)]

pterosaur (**te**-rə-sor) *noun* an extinct flying reptile, such as a pterodactyl. [from Greek words *pteros* meaning 'wing' and *sauros* meaning 'lizard']

PTO *abbreviation* please turn over.

ptomaine (**toh**- mayn) *noun* an amine compound of unpleasant taste and smell found in rotting flesh and vegetable matter, formerly thought to be the cause of food poisoning. [from a Greek word *ptōma* meaning 'corpse']

Pu *abbreviation* (*Chemistry*) the symbol for plutonium.

pub *noun* a building licensed to sell beer and other alcoholic drinks to the general public for drinking on the premises. [short for *public house*]

puberty (**pew**-ber-ti) *noun* the stage at which a young person becomes sexually mature and is capable of producing offspring. **pubertal** *adjective* [from a Latin word *puber* meaning 'adult']

pubic (**pew**-bik) *adjective* to do with the lower part of the abdomen at the front of the pelvis ♦ *pubic hair*. [from a Latin word *pubes* meaning 'groin' or 'genitals']

public *adjective* belonging to or known to people in general, not private. SYNONYMS: communal, common, shared, general.

public *noun* (**the public**) people in general or a particular group of people ♦ *the British public*. **in public** openly, not in private. [from a Latin word *publicus* meaning 'of the people']

public address system *noun* a system of amplifiers and loudspeakers used to make speech or music audible over a wide area.

publican *noun* 1 the keeper of a public house. 2 (in the Bible) a tax-collector.

publication *noun* 1 the process of publishing or being published. 2 something published, e.g. a book or newspaper.

public health *noun* protection of the public from infection and disease.

public house *noun* (*formal*) a pub.

publicity *noun* 1 public attention directed upon a person or thing. 2 the process of drawing public attention to a person or thing; the spoken, written, or other material by which this is done.

publicize *verb* to bring something to the attention of the public, to advertise something.

public limited company *noun* a business company whose shares may be bought and sold on the open market.

publicly *adverb* in public, openly.

public prosecutor *noun* a law officer conducting prosecutions on behalf of the state or in the public interest.

public relations *plural noun* the promotion of goodwill between an organization and the general public.

public school *noun* 1 a secondary school that charges fees. 2 (especially in North America) a school supported by public funds.

public sector *noun* all the businesses and industries that are owned or controlled by the state and not by private enterprise.

public spirit *noun* willingness to do things for the benefit of people in general. **public-spirited** *adjective*

publish *verb* 1 to issue copies of a book, newspaper, magazine, or piece of music to the public. SYNONYMS: issue, bring out, release. 2 to make something generally known. SYNONYMS: circulate, make known. 3 to announce something formally ♦ *They will publish the results of the competition next month*. SYNONYMS: announce, declare, release, disclose. [from a Latin word *publicare* meaning 'to make public']

publisher *noun* a person or firm that issues copies of a book, newspaper, magazine, or piece of music to the public.

puce (pewss) *noun* a brownish purple colour.
puce *adjective* of this colour. [from a French phrase *couleur puce* meaning 'the colour of a flea']

puck *noun* a hard rubber disc used in ice hockey. [origin unknown]

pucker *verb* to come together in small wrinkles or folds, or to cause something to do this.
pucker *noun* a wrinkle or fold.

puckish *adjective* impish or mischievous. [from Puck, the name of a sprite]

pud *noun* (*informal*) short for pudding.

pudding *noun* 1 a cooked sweet dish, or the sweet course of a meal. 2 a sweet or savoury cooked food made with a mixture of flour and other ingredients. 3 a kind of sausage ◆ *black pudding*. [from an Old French word *boudin* meaning 'black pudding', from a Latin word *botellus* meaning 'sausage']

puddle *noun* a shallow patch of liquid on a surface, especially of water on a road.
puddle *verb* 1 to stir molten iron so as to expel carbon and produce wrought iron. 2 to work something into a wet mixture.

pudenda (pew-den-də) *plural noun* a person's genitals, especially a woman's.
pudendal *adjective* [from a Latin word *pudere* meaning 'to be ashamed']

pudgy *adjective* (**pudgier, pudgiest**) (*informal*) podgy.

pueblo (pewb-loh) *noun* (**pueblos**) a Native American settlement in Mexico or the south-west USA. [a Spanish word meaning 'people']

puerile (pyoo-riyl) *adjective* immature or childish ◆ *asking puerile questions*. **puerility** (pyoo-**ril**-iti) *noun* [from a Latin word *puer* meaning 'boy']

puerperal fever (pew-er-per-əl) *noun* a fever caused by an infection of the womb after childbirth. [from Latin words *puer* meaning 'boy' and -*parus* meaning 'bearing']

puff *noun* 1 a short blowing of breath, wind, etc. SYNONYMS: gust, breath. 2 a small amount of smoke or vapour sent out by this. 3 a soft pad for putting powder on the skin. 4 a cake of light pastry filled with cream or a sweet filling. 5 (*informal*) a complimentary review or advertisement for a book or play etc.
puff *verb* 1 to breathe with short hard gasps. SYNONYMS: pant, gasp. 2 to blow smoke or dust in puffs. 3 to smoke a cigarette, cigar, or pipe. 4 to swell or become inflated, or to make something do this. 5 (*informal*) to advertise something with extravagant praise. [an imitation of the sound]

puff adder *noun* a large poisonous African viper that puffs out the upper part of its body when threatened.

puffball *noun* a fungus with a large round spore case that bursts open when ripe.

puffin *noun* a seabird with a large brightly coloured bill. [perhaps related to *puff*]

puff pastry *noun* very light flaky pastry.

puffy *adjective* (**puffier, puffiest**) swollen or puffed out. **puffiness** *noun*

pug *noun* a small dog like a bulldog, with a flat nose and a wrinkled face. [probably from a Dutch or German word]

pugilist (pew-jil-ist) *noun* (*old use*) a boxer. **pugilism** *noun* **pugilistic** *adjective* [from a Latin word *pugil* meaning 'boxer']

pugnacious (pug-nay-shəs) *adjective* eager or quick to fight, aggressive.
pugnaciously *adverb* **pugnacity** (pug-**nas**-iti) *noun* [from a Latin word *pugnare* meaning 'to fight']

pug-nosed *adjective* having a short flattish nose.

puissance (pwee-səns) *noun* (in showjumping) a test of a horse's ability to jump large obstacles. [via Old French from a Latin word *posse* meaning 'to be able']

puja (poo-jə) *noun* a Hindu act of worship, often involving an offering of flowers. [a Sanskrit word meaning 'worship']

puke *verb* (*informal*) to vomit. [origin unknown]

pukka (puk-ə) *adjective* (*informal*) 1 real or genuine. 2 excellent. [from a Hindi word *pakka* meaning 'cooked' or 'ripe']

pull *verb* 1 to exert force on something or someone so as to move them towards you or towards the source of the force. SYNONYMS: tug, jerk, wrench. 2 to grip something and apply force to it so that it moves along behind you. SYNONYMS: tow, drag, draw, haul. **3** to remove something by pulling it. **4** to propel a boat by pulling on its oars. **5** (in cricket) to strike the ball to the leg side; (in golf) to hit the ball to the left. **6** (said about a vehicle or engine) to exert a pulling or driving force. **7** to attract people ♦ *The new exhibition is pulling the crowds.*

pull noun **1** the act of pulling, or the force exerted by it. **2** a means of exerting influence. **3** a deep draught of a drink, or a draw at a cigarette, cigar, or pipe. **4** a prolonged effort in walking, climbing, etc. ♦ *We felt tired from our long pull up the hill.* **to pull a fast one** (*informal*) to act unfairly in order to gain an advantage. **to pull back** to retreat or withdraw, or to cause someone to do this. **to pull something down** to demolish a building. **to pull in 1** (said about a train) to enter and stop at a station. **2** (said about a vehicle) to move to the side of the road. **to pull someone in** (*informal*) to take someone into custody. **to pull something in** (*informal*) to earn money as wages or profit. **to pull someone's leg** to tease someone. **to pull something off** (*informal*) to succeed in achieving or winning something. SYNONYMS: achieve, accomplish, manage. **to pull out 1** to withdraw from an activity or commitment. **2** (said about a train) to move out of a station. **3** (said about a vehicle) to move away from the side of a road, or from behind another vehicle to overtake it. **to pull yourself together** to regain your self-control. **to pull your punches** to avoid using your full force. **to pull rank** to make unfair use of your senior position to get what you want. **to pull round** to recover from an illness. **to pull strings** to use your influence to get what you want. **to pull through** to recover from an illness or difficulty. SYNONYMS: recover, get better, improve, survive. **to pull together** to cooperate. **to pull up** (said about a vehicle) to stop abruptly. **to pull someone up** to scold or reprimand someone. **to pull your weight** to do your fair share of work. **to pull your finger out** (*informal*) to stop delaying and start to act. [from an Old English word *pullian* meaning 'to snatch']

pullet noun a young hen less than one year old. [from an Old French word *poulet*]

pulley noun (**pulleys**) a wheel with a grooved rim over which a rope, chain, or belt passes, used to lift heavy objects. [from an Old French word *polie*]

Pullman noun (**Pullmans**) a type of railway carriage providing passengers with a high level of comfort. [named after its American designer, George M. Pullman (1831–97)]

pull-out noun a middle part of a magazine, which can be pulled out to form a separate section.

pullover noun a knitted garment put on over the head and covering the top part of the body.

pulmonary (pul-mən-er-i) adjective to do with or affecting the lungs. [from a Latin word *pulmo* meaning 'lung']

pulp noun **1** a soft moist mass of material, especially of wood fibre as used for making paper. **2** the soft moist part of fruit. **3** the soft tissue inside a tooth. **4** (used before a noun) indicating cheap popular publications of a kind originally printed on rough paper made from wood pulp ♦ *pulp magazines.* **pulp** verb to become pulp, or to make something into pulp. [from a Latin word *pulpa*]

pulpit noun a raised enclosed platform for a preacher in a church or chapel. [from a Latin word *pulpitum* meaning 'a scaffold or platform']

pulpy adjective soft like pulp, or containing a lot of pulp. **pulpiness** noun

pulsar noun an object in space that gives out radio signals that pulsate in a rapid regular rhythm. [from *pulsating star*, modelled on *quasar*]

pulsate (pul-**sayt**) verb to expand and contract rhythmically; to vibrate or quiver. **pulsation** noun **pulsator** noun [from a Latin word *pulsare* meaning 'to throb']

pulse [1] noun **1** the rhythmical throbbing of the arteries as blood is propelled along them. **2** a steady throb. **3** a single beat or throb. **4** the central point of an activity ♦ *the financial pulse of the nation.* **pulse** verb to pulsate. [from a Latin word *pulsum* meaning 'driven' or ' beaten']

pulse [2] noun the edible seed of peas, beans, lentils, etc. [via Old French from a Latin word *puls* meaning 'porridge of meal']

pulverize verb **1** to become powder, or to crush something into powder. **2** (*informal*) to defeat someone thoroughly. **pulverization** noun [from a Latin word *pulveris* meaning 'of dust']

puma (pew-mə) *noun* a large brown American animal of the cat family. [via Spanish from a South American language]

pumice (pum-iss) *noun* a light porous kind of lava used for rubbing stains from the skin or as powder for polishing. [via Old French from a Latin word *pumex*]

pummel *verb* (**pummelled**, **pummelling**) to strike something or someone repeatedly with the fists. [a different spelling of *pommel*]

pump [1] *noun* a machine or device that forces liquid, air, or gas into or out of something, or along pipes.
pump *verb* 1 to move liquid, air, or gas with a pump. 2 (also **pump up**) to fill something with air, especially to inflate it. 3 to move something vigorously up and down like the handle of a pump. 4 (*informal*) to question someone persistently to get information. [origin unknown]

pump [2] *noun* 1 a plimsoll. 2 a light dancing shoe. [origin unknown]

pumpernickel *noun* (pum-pə-ni-kəl) German wholemeal rye bread. [a German word meaning 'bumpkin']

pumpkin *noun* 1 a large round fruit with a hard orange skin and flesh that is used as a vegetable. 2 the trailing plant that produces this fruit. [from a Greek word *pepōn* meaning 'a large melon']

pun *noun* a humorous use of a word to suggest another that sounds the same, as in 'Deciding where to bury him was a *grave* decision'.
pun *verb* (**punned**, **punning**) to make a pun. [origin unknown]

punch [1] *verb* to strike someone or something with the fist.
punch *noun* 1 a blow with the fist. 2 (*informal*) force or vigour ♦ *a speech with plenty of punch*. [same origin as for *puncture*]

punch [2] *noun* 1 a device for making holes in paper or metal. 2 a tool or machine for stamping a design on material.
punch *verb* to make a hole in something with a punch. [same origin as for *puncture*]

punch [3] *noun* a drink made of wine or spirits mixed with fruit juices, spices, etc. [from a Sanskrit word meaning 'five' (because it originally had five ingredients)]

punchbowl *noun* a deep bowl for making and serving punch.

punch-drunk *adjective* stupefied through being severely punched.

punchline *noun* words that give the climax of a joke or story.

punchy *adjective* (**punchier**, **punchiest**) forceful or effective.

punctilious (punk-til-iəs) *adjective* very careful about correct behaviour and detail. **punctiliously** *adverb* **punctiliousness** *noun* [from a Latin word *punctillum* meaning 'little point']

punctual *adjective* arriving or doing things at the correct time. SYNONYMS: prompt, on time. **punctuality** *noun* **punctually** *adverb* [from a Latin word *punctum* meaning 'point']

punctuate *verb* 1 to put punctuation marks in a piece of writing. 2 to put something in at intervals ♦ *His speech was punctuated with cheers*. [same origin as for *punctual*]

punctuation *noun* 1 the use of marks such as comma, full stop, and question mark to clarify the structure and meaning of a piece of writing. 2 the set of marks used in this.

puncture *noun* a small hole made by something sharp, especially one made accidentally in a tyre.
puncture *verb* 1 to make a puncture in something, or to receive a puncture. 2 to cause a mood or feeling to disappear suddenly ♦ *The criticism punctured his pride*. [from a Latin word *punctum* meaning 'pricked']

pundit *noun* a person who is an authority on a subject. [from a Sanskrit word *pandita* meaning 'learned']

pungent (pun-jənt) *adjective* 1 having a strong sharp taste or smell. 2 (said about remarks) sharp or caustic. **pungency** *noun* **pungently** *adverb* [from a Latin word *pungens* meaning 'pricking']

punish *verb* 1 to cause someone to suffer a penalty for doing wrong. SYNONYMS: discipline, penalize, chastise. 2 to inflict a punishment for a wrongdoing ♦ *Vandalism should be severely punished*. 3 to treat or test someone severely ♦ *The race was run at a punishing pace*. **punishable** *adjective* [from a Latin word *poena* meaning 'penalty']

punishment *noun* 1 the process of punishing someone. 2 the penalty that someone suffers for doing wrong. 3 (*informal*) rough treatment.

punitive (pew-nit-iv) *adjective* inflicting or intended as a punishment.

punk *noun* 1 (also **punk rock**) a loud aggressive form of rock music. 2 a person who enjoys this music.
punk *adjective* (North Amer.) (*informal*) worthless. [origin unknown]

punnet (pun-it) *noun* a small container for fruit or vegetables. [origin unknown]

punt[1] *noun* a flat-bottomed boat with square ends, usually moved along a river by pushing a pole against the bottom of the river while standing at one end of the punt.
punt *verb* 1 to move a punt forward with a pole in this way. 2 to travel in a punt. **punter** *noun* [from a Latin word *ponto*, related to *pontoon*[1]]

punt[2] *verb* to kick a ball after it has dropped from the hands and before it touches the ground.
punt *noun* a kick of this kind. **punter** *noun* [probably from a dialect word *punt* meaning 'to push forcibly']

punt[3] *verb* (*informal*) to bet or gamble. [from a French word *ponte*]

punter *noun* 1 (*informal*) a customer or client. 2 a person who bets, a gambler.

puny (pew-ni) *adjective* (**punier, puniest**) 1 small or undersized. 2 weak or feeble. [from an Old French word *puisne* meaning 'a younger person' or 'inferior', which is pronounced like *puny*]

pup *noun* 1 a young dog. 2 a young wolf, rat, seal, or other mammal.
pup *verb* (**pupped, pupping**) to give birth to a pup or pups. **sell someone a pup** (*informal*) to swindle a person by selling them something less valuable than is claimed. [short for *puppy*]

pupa (pew-pə) *noun* (**pupae** (pew-pee)) a chrysalis. **pupal** *adjective* [from a Latin word *pupa* meaning 'girl' or 'doll']

pupil *noun* 1 a person who is taught by a teacher, especially at a school. 2 an opening in the centre of the iris of the eye, through which light passes to the retina. [from a Latin word *pupilla* meaning 'little girl or doll'. The use in sense 2 refers to the tiny images of people and things that can be seen in the eye]

puppet *noun* 1 a kind of doll that can be made to move by pulling strings attached to it or by putting a hand inside it. 2 a person or group whose actions are controlled by someone else. **puppetry** *noun* [a different spelling of *poppet*]

puppy *noun* (**puppies**) a young dog. [from an Old French word *poupee* meaning 'doll' or 'toy', related to *pupil*]

puppy fat *noun* temporary fat on the body of a child or young adolescent.

purblind (per-bliynd) *adjective* 1 having defective vision, partially blind. 2 dim-witted. [from *pure* meaning 'utterly' and *blind*]

purchase *verb* to buy something.
purchase *noun* 1 the process of buying something. 2 something bought. 3 a firm hold to pull or raise something or prevent it from slipping. **purchaser** *noun* [from an Old French word *pourchacier* meaning 'to seek to obtain']

purdah (per-də) *noun* 1 the custom in certain Muslim and Hindu communities of keeping women from the sight of men or strangers by means of a curtain or of clothes that cover the entire body except for the eyes. 2 complete seclusion from company. [from a Persian or Urdu word *parda* meaning 'veil']

pure *adjective* 1 not mixed with any other substance, free from impurities.
SYNONYMS: clean, clear, undiluted. 2 mere, nothing but ♦ *What they said was pure nonsense*. SYNONYMS: sheer, utter, absolute, complete, total, perfect. 3 morally good, free from evil or sin. SYNONYMS: virtuous, chaste. 4 (said about a subject) dealing with the theory only and not with its practical applications ♦ *pure mathematics*. **pureness** *noun* [via Old French from a Latin word *purus*]

purée (pewr-ay) *noun* fruit or vegetables made into pulp.
purée *verb* (**purées, puréed, puréeing**) to make fruit or vegetables into a purée. [a French word meaning 'squeezed']

purely *adverb* 1 in a pure way. 2 entirely, only ♦ *We came purely out of interest*.

purgative (per-gə-tiv) *noun* a strong laxative. [same origin as for *purge*]

purgatory (per-gə-ter-i) *noun* 1 (in Roman Catholic belief) a place or condition in which souls undergo purification by temporary punishment before they can enter heaven. 2 a place or condition of suffering, especially of mental anguish. **purgatorial** (per-gə-tor-iəl) *adjective* [same origin as for *purge*]

purge (perj) verb 1 to rid a place or organization of people or things considered to be undesirable or harmful. 2 to remove something by a cleansing process. 3 to empty the bowels of a person by means of a laxative. 4 (Law) to atone for an offence, especially contempt of court.
purge noun an act of purging or ridding a place of undesirable people or things. [from a Latin word purgare meaning 'to make pure']

purify verb (purifies, purified, purifying) to make something pure or cleanse it of impurities. SYNONYMS: cleanse, refine. **purification** noun **purificatory** adjective **purifier** noun

purist (pewr-ist) noun someone who insists on correctness, especially in language. **purism** noun

Puritan noun an English Protestant of the 16th and 17th centuries who wanted simpler forms of church ceremony and strictly moral behaviour.
puritan noun a person who is extremely strict in morals and who regards some kinds of pleasure and enjoyment as sinful. **puritanical** adjective [from a Latin word puritas meaning 'purity']

purity noun a pure state, pureness.

purl [1] noun a knitting stitch that makes a ridge towards the person knitting. (Compare **plain**.)
purl verb to make this stitch. [origin uncertain]

purl [2] verb (literary) (said about a brook) to flow with a swirling motion and babbling sound. [probably from a Scandinavian language]

purlieus (perl-yooz) plural noun the outskirts of a place. [probably from an early French word puralee meaning 'a going round to fix the boundaries']

purloin (per-loin) verb (formal or humorous) to steal something. [from an early French word purloigner meaning 'to put away']

purple adjective 1 of a deep reddish blue colour. 2 (said about writing) very ornate and literary.
purple noun purple colour.
purple verb to become purple. **born in** or **into the purple** born into a reigning or aristocratic family. **purplish** adjective **purply** adjective [via Old English from a Latin word purpura, from a Greek word porphura meaning 'mollusc that gives a crimson dye']

purport [1] (per-port) noun the general meaning or intention of something said or written. [from pro- meaning 'forward' and a Latin word portare meaning 'to carry']

purport [2] (per-port) verb to pretend or be intended to seem, especially falsely ♦ The letter purports to come from you. **purportedly** adverb

purpose noun 1 something that you intend to do or achieve, an intended result ♦ This will serve our purpose. SYNONYMS: intention, aim. 2 wanting to get something done, determination ♦ They acted with a real sense of purpose.
purpose verb (formal) to intend something, to have something as a purpose. **on purpose** deliberately, not by chance. **to no purpose** with no result. [same origin as for propose]

purposeful adjective 1 having a particular purpose. 2 determined, resolute. **purposefully** adverb **purposefulness** noun

purposeless adjective without a purpose.

purposely adverb deliberately, on purpose.

purr verb 1 (said about a cat) to make a low murmuring sound expressing contentment. 2 (said about machinery etc.) to make a similar sound when working smoothly.
purr verb a purring sound. [an imitation of the sound]

purse noun 1 a small leather or plastic pouch for carrying money. 2 (North Amer.) a handbag. 3 an amount of money available for a purpose. 4 a sum of money given as a prize in a sporting competition.
purse verb to pucker the lips, especially in indignation. **to hold the purse strings** to have control of expenditure. [from a Latin word bursa meaning 'a bag']

purser noun an officer on a ship who is in charge of the accounts, especially the chief steward on a passenger ship.

pursuance noun (formal) the performance or carrying out of something ♦ in pursuance of my duties.

pursuant adverb (formal) **pursuant to** in accordance with.

pursue verb (pursues, pursued, pursuing) 1 to chase someone or something in order to catch or attack them. SYNONYMS: chase, go after, follow. 2 to be a constant trouble to

someone ♦ *They are pursued by misfortunes.*
SYNONYM: dog. **3** to continue or proceed along a course or route. **4** to be occupied in an activity ♦ *She would like to pursue a career as a journalist.* SYNONYM: follow.
pursuer *noun* [via early French from a Latin word *prosequi* meaning 'to prosecute']

pursuit *noun* **1** the act of pursuing someone or something. SYNONYMS: chase, hunt. **2** an activity to which you devote time.
SYNONYMS: interest, activity, hobby, pastime, occupation.

purvey (per-**vay**) *verb* to supply articles of food as a trader. **purveyor** *noun* [same origin as for *provide*]

pus *noun* thick yellowish matter produced in inflamed or infected tissue, e.g. in an abscess or boil. [from a Latin word]

push *verb* **1** to exert force on something or someone so as to move them away from you or away from the source of the force.
SYNONYMS: force, shove, thrust, press. **2** to grip something and apply force to it so that it moves along in front of you. **3** to move oneself forcibly into a position ♦ *Several people pushed to the front.*
SYNONYMS: move, surge, shove. **4** to extend something by an effort ♦ *The frontier was pushed further north.* **5** to make a vigorous effort in order to succeed or to surpass others. **6** to urge someone to do something ♦ *We must push you for prompt payment.* **7** (*informal*) to promote the sale or use of something. **8** (*informal*) to sell illegal drugs.
push *noun* **1** the act of pushing, or the force used in this. **2** a vigorous effort, especially a military attack made in order to advance. **3** determination or enterprise. **at a push** (*informal*) if necessary and only with difficulty. **to be pushing** (*informal*) to be close to a specified age ♦ *He is already pushing forty.*
to give or **get the push** (*informal*) to dismiss someone or be dismissed from a job. **to push someone around** to treat someone contemptuously and unfairly; to bully someone. **to push off** (*informal*) to go away. **to push one's luck** (*informal*) to take undue risks. **pusher** *noun* [from an Old French word *pousser*, related to *pulse*[1]]

pushchair *noun* a folding chair on wheels, for pushing a baby or young child along.

pushover *noun* (*informal*) something that is easily done; a person who is easily convinced or charmed etc.

pushy *adjective* (**pushier, pushiest**) too assertive or ambitious.

pusillanimous (pew-zi-**lan**-imǝs) *adjective* timid or cowardly. [from a Latin word *pusillus* meaning 'small' and *animus* meaning 'mind']

puss or **pussy** *noun* (*informal*) (**pussies**) a cat. [from a German or Dutch word]

pussyfoot *verb* **1** to move stealthily. **2** to act cautiously and avoid committing yourself.

pussy willow *noun* a willow with furry catkins.

pustule (**pus**-tewl) *noun* a small pimple or blister containing pus. **pustular** *adjective* [from a Latin word *pustula*, with the same meaning]

put *verb* (past tense and past participle, **put**; **putting**) **1** to move something to a specified place or position ♦ *Put the bag on the table.* SYNONYMS: place, set, lay, stand, leave; (*informal*) stick. **2** to cause something or someone to be in a certain state ♦ *Put the light on* ♦ *Try to put them at their ease.* **3** to express or state something in a certain way ♦ *I will put it as tactfully as I can.* SYNONYMS: express, state, explain, say. **4** to subject something to a process ♦ *Put it to the test.* **5** to estimate an amount ♦ *I put the cost at £1000.* **6** to impose or assign something ♦ *I put the blame on the visitors* ♦ *The government will put a higher tax on large incomes.* **7** to invest money, or stake money in a bet. **8** (said about a ship) to move in a specified direction ♦ *The ferry put into harbour.*
put *noun* a throw of the shot or weight. **to be hard put** to have difficulty in doing or providing something. **to put something across** to succeed in communicating an idea or making it seem acceptable. **to put something by** to save money for future use. **to put someone down 1** to snub someone or make them look foolish. **2** to enter someone's name in a list or register.
to put something down 1 to write something down or make a note of it. **2** to have an animal destroyed. **3** to suppress a revolt or rebellion. **4** to pay a specified sum as a deposit. **5** to identify the reason for something ♦ *I put his behaviour down to nervousness.* **to put something in** to submit a claim or proposal. **to put in for** to apply for a job or position. **to put someone off 1** to postpone or cancel an appointment with someone. **2** to make someone less enthusiastic

about something. SYNONYMS: dissuade, discourage, deter. **3** to distract someone. SYNONYMS: distract, disconcert, disturb; (informal) throw. **to put something off** to postpone an arrangement, meeting, etc. SYNONYMS: postpone, defer, delay. **to put something on 1** to stage a performance of a play. **2** to switch on a device ♦ I'll put the radio on. **3** to display a certain feeling or emotion. **to put your foot down** (informal) **4** to insist on something firmly. **5** to accelerate a motor vehicle. **to put your foot in it** (informal) to make an embarrassing mistake. **to put someone out** to annoy or inconvenience someone. SYNONYMS: annoy, inconvenience, discomfort. **to put something out** to extinguish a fire, light, etc. **to put something over** to succeed in communicating an idea or making it seem acceptable. **to put the shot** or **weight** to hurl a shot or weight as an athletic sport. **to put two and two together** to draw an obvious conclusion from the facts. **to put someone up** to provide someone with accommodation for a short period. SYNONYMS: accommodate, lodge. **to put something up 1** to construct or build something. SYNONYMS: construct, build, erect. **2** to raise the price of something. SYNONYMS: increase, raise. **3** to provide or contribute the necessary resources ♦ The company will put up the money. SYNONYMS: provide, contribute, supply, furnish. **4** to display a notice or sign. **5** to present an idea or proposal. **6** to attempt or offer something ♦ The enemy put up no resistance. **to put someone up to** (informal) to involve someone in an activity, especially an illicit or suspect one ♦ Who put him up to it? **to put up with** to endure or tolerate something unpleasant or unwelcome. SYNONYMS: endure, tolerate, bear, stand; (informal) stick. [from an Old English word]

putative (pew-tə-tiv) adjective supposed or considered to be ♦ his putative father. [from a Latin word putare meaning 'to think']

putrefy (pew-tri-fiy) verb (**putrefies, putrefied, putrefying**) to decay or make something decay. **putrefaction** (pew-tri-fak-shən) noun [from a Latin word puter meaning 'rotten']

putrescent (pew-tress-ənt) adjective decaying or rotting. **putrescence** noun

putrid (pew-trid) adjective **1** decomposed or rotting. **2** smelling bad. **3** (informal) very distasteful or unpleasant.

putsch (puuch) noun a violent attempt to overthrow a government. [a Swiss German word meaning 'thrust' or ' blow']

putt verb to strike a golf ball gently to make it roll along the ground. **putt** noun a stroke of this kind.

putter noun a golf club used in putting.

putting green noun (in golf) an area of smooth cut grass round a hole.

putty noun a soft paste that sets hard, used for fitting glass in a window frame. [from a French word potée, meaning 'potful']

put-up job noun (informal) something concocted to deceive people.

puzzle noun **1** a difficult question or problem. SYNONYMS: mystery, problem, enigma. **2** a game or toy that sets a problem to solve or a difficult task to complete. **puzzle** verb **1** to confuse someone or cause them uncertainty. SYNONYMS: baffle, perplex, confuse, bewilder, fox, stump. **2** to make hard thought necessary ♦ It is a puzzling problem. **to puzzle something out** to solve or understand a problem by patient thought or ingenuity. **puzzlement** noun [origin unknown]

puzzler noun a puzzling problem.

PVA abbreviation polyvinyl acetate.

PVC abbreviation polyvinyl chloride.

pygmy (pig-mi) noun (**pygmies**) **1** a person or thing of unusually small size. **2** a member of certain unusually short peoples of equatorial Africa and SE Asia. **pygmy** adjective very small.

pyjamas plural noun a suit of loose-fitting jacket and trousers for sleeping in. [from Persian and Urdu words pay jama meaning 'leg clothes']

pylon noun **1** a tall framework made of steel strips, used for carrying overhead electricity cables. **2** a structure marking a path for aircraft or other vehicles. [from a Greek word pulē meaning 'gateway']

PYO abbreviation pick-your-own (fruit and vegetables).

pyramid noun **1** a structure with a square base and sloping sides that meet at the top. **2** a stone structure shaped like this, especially an ancient Egyptian tomb. **pyramidal** (pi-ram-idəl) adjective [from a Greek word puramis]

pyre noun a pile of wood or other material for burning a corpse as part of a funeral ceremony. [from a Greek word *pur* meaning 'fire']

pyrethrum (piy-**ree**-thrəm) noun 1 a kind of chrysanthemum with brightly coloured flowers and finely divided leaves. 2 an insecticide made from the dried flowers of this plant. [from a Greek word *purethron* meaning 'feverfew']

Pyrex noun (*trademark*) a hard heat-resistant glass.

pyrites (piy-**riy**-teez) noun a shiny yellow mineral that is a sulphide of iron (**iron pyrites**) or copper and iron (**copper pyrites**). [from a Greek word *puritēs* meaning 'of fire']

pyromania (piyr-ə-**may**-niə) noun an obsessive desire to set things on fire.
pyromaniac noun [from a Greek word *pur* meaning 'fire' and *mania*]

pyrotechnic (piy-rə-**tek**-nik) adjective to do with fireworks.
pyrotechnics plural noun 1 a firework display. 2 the art of making or staging fireworks. 3 a spectacular performance or display. [from Greek words *pur* meaning 'fire' and *tekhnē* meaning 'art' or 'skill']

pyrrhic victory (pi-rik) noun a victory gained at so great a cost that it cannot be exploited. [named after King Pyrrhus of Epirus, who defeated a Roman army at Asculum in 279 BC but suffered heavy losses and was unable to follow up his advantage]

python noun a large snake that squeezes its prey so as to suffocate it. [named after Python, a huge serpent in Greek mythology, killed by Apollo]

Qq

Q the seventeenth letter of the English alphabet.

QC abbreviation Queen's Counsel.

QED abbreviation quod erat demonstrandum, put at the end of a formal proof to show that the proposition has been proved. [a Latin phrase meaning 'which was the thing that had to be proved']

qibla noun another spelling of **kiblah**.

qt. abbreviation quart(s).

qua (kway) conjunction formal in the capacity or character of ♦ *Although she is a solicitor, she was giving her advice qua friend.* [a Latin word meaning 'in which']

quack[1] verb to make the harsh cry of a duck.
quack noun this cry. [an imitation of the sound]

quack[2] noun a person who falsely claims to have medical skill or to have remedies for curing diseases. [from a Dutch word *quacken* meaning 'to boast']

quad (kwod) noun 1 a quadrangle. 2 a quadruplet.

quadrangle (**kwod**-rang-gəl) noun a rectangular court with buildings on each side. [from *quadri-* and *angle*[1]]

quadrant (**kwod**-rənt) noun 1 a quarter of a circle. 2 (*historical*) an instrument consisting of a quarter circle marked off in degrees, used for measuring angles. [from a Latin word *quadrans* meaning 'quarter']

quadratic equation (kwod-**rat**-ik) noun (*Mathematics*) an equation in which one or more of the unknown quantities or variables is raised to the power of two, but no higher. [from a Latin word *quadrare* meaning 'to square']

quadri- prefix four. [from a Latin word *quattuor* meaning 'four']

quadriceps (**kwod**-ri-seps) noun (**quadriceps**) (*Anatomy*) the large muscle at the front of the thigh which straightens the leg. [from a Latin word meaning 'four-headed' (because the end of the muscle is attached at four points)]

quadrilateral (kwod-ri-**lat**-er-əl) noun a flat figure with four sides.
quadrilateral adjective having four sides. [from *quadri-* and *lateral*]

quadrille (kwod-**ril**) noun a square dance for four couples, or the music for this. [via French from an Italian word *quadriglia* meaning 'a troop or company']

quadriplegia (kwod-ri-**plee**-jiə) noun paralysis of both arms and both legs.

quadriplegic *adjective & noun* [from *quadri-* and a Greek word *plēxis* meaning 'a stroke']

quadruped (kwod-ruu-ped) *noun* an animal with four feet. [from *quadri-* and a Latin word *pedis* meaning 'of a foot']

quadruple *adjective* **1** consisting of four parts, or involving four people or groups ♦ *a quadruple alliance.* **2** four times as much ♦ *The glass contained a quadruple measure of whisky.*
quadruple *verb* **1** to multiply something by four. **2** to increase fourfold ♦ *The cost of the new building had quadrupled in two years.*
quadruply *adverb* [from a Latin word *quadruplus*, related to *quadri-*]

quadruplet (kwod-ruu-plit) *noun* each of four children born at one birth.

quadruplicate (kwod-roo-plik-ət) *noun* each of four identical things or copies.

quaff (kwof) *verb* to drink something heartily. [origin unknown]

quagmire (kwag-miyr) *noun* a bog or marsh. [from an old word *quag* meaning 'marsh' and *mire*]

quail [1] *noun* (quail or quails) a game bird with a short tail, related to the partridge. [from an Old French word *quaille*]

quail [2] *verb* to show fear or apprehension. [origin unknown]

quaint *adjective* pleasingly or attractively odd or old-fashioned. SYNONYMS: charming, old-fashioned; (*informal*) cute. **quaintly** *adverb* **quaintness** *noun* [from an earlier meaning 'ingenious', from an Old French word *cointe*]

quake *verb* **1** to shake or tremble from unsteadiness. SYNONYMS: tremble, quiver. **2** to tremble with fear. SYNONYMS: tremble, shake, quaver, quiver, shudder, shiver.
quake *noun* **1** a quaking movement. **2** (*informal*) an earthquake. [from an Old English word *cwacian*]

Quaker *noun* a member of the Religious Society of Friends, a Christian movement founded by George Fox in the 17th century, which rejects formal acts of worship and emphasizes peaceful principles. **Quakerism** *noun* [originally an insult, probably based on a statement attributed to George Fox, that people should 'tremble at the name of the Lord']

qualification *noun* **1** the process of qualifying or being qualified. **2** something that qualifies a person to do something or to have a certain right ♦ *She wants to get a good teaching qualification.* **3** a statement that limits or restricts another statement ♦ *We welcome the report without any qualifications.* **qualificatory** *adjective*

qualify *verb* (qualifies, qualified, qualifying) **1** to give someone the right or competence to do something. SYNONYMS: entitle, make eligible. **2** to have the right or competence to do something; to have fulfilled the conditions for something. **3** to limit or restrict a statement or make it less general or extreme. **4** to describe someone or something in a certain way. **5** (*Grammar*) (said of a word or phrase) to describe or add meaning to another word, especially a noun. **qualifier** *noun* [via French from a Latin word *qualis* meaning 'of what kind']

qualitative (kwol-i-tə-tiv) *adjective* to do with the presence or quality of a substance and not its quantity ♦ *qualitative analysis.* (Compare **quantitative**.)

quality *noun* (qualities) **1** how good something is in relation to others of the same kind ♦ *The quality of English wine has improved in the last decade.* SYNONYMS: standard, level, grade, class. **2** general excellence ♦ *They are producing work of quality.* **3** a special characteristic or ability ♦ *The paper has a shiny quality.* SYNONYMS: look, property, condition. [same origin as for **qualify**]

qualm (kwahm) *noun* a doubt or misgiving about what you have done or might do. SYNONYMS: doubt, misgiving, compunction, scruple. [perhaps related to an Old English word *cwalm* meaning 'pain']

quandary (kwon-der-i) *noun* (quandaries) a state of uncertainty about what to do for the best. SYNONYMS: predicament, dilemma. [perhaps related to a Latin word *quando* meaning 'when']

quango *noun* (quangos) an administrative body with financial support from and senior appointments made by the government but acting independently. [from the initials of *quasi-autonomous non-governmental organization*]

quantify (kwon-ti-fiy) *verb* (quantifies, quantified, quantifying) to express something as a quantity. **quantifiable** *adjective* **quantification** *noun* [same origin as for *quantity*]

quantitative (kwon-ti-tə-tiv) *adjective* to do with quantity ♦ *quantitative analysis.* (Compare **qualitative**.)

quantity *noun* (**quantities**) **1** how much of something there is, or how many of a certain thing there are. SYNONYMS: amount, volume; number, total, sum. **2** a large number or amount. **3** the property of something that can be measured. **in quantity** in a large amount or number. [from a Latin word *quantus* meaning 'how much']

quantum (kwon-təm) *noun* (**quanta**) **1** (*Physics*) a minimum amount of a physical quantity (such as energy) which can exist in a given situation. **2** the amount required or allowed. [same origin as for *quantity*]

quantum leap or **quantum jump** *noun* a sudden great advance or increase.

quantum theory *noun* (*Physics*) a theory based on the assumption that energy exists in indivisible units.

quarantine (kwo-rən-teen) *noun* **1** isolation imposed on people or animals who may have been exposed to a disease which could spread to others. **2** the period or place of this isolation.
quarantine *verb* to put a person or animal into quarantine. [from an Italian word *quaranta* meaning 'forty' (because the original period of isolation was 40 days)]

quark *noun* (*Physics*) any of a group of hypothetical components of elementary particles. [an invented word, based on 'three quarks for Muster Mark' in James Joyce's *Finnegans Wake* (1939)]

quarrel *noun* **1** an angry argument or disagreement. SYNONYMS: argument, row, disagreement, altercation, fight, dispute; (*informal*) tiff, bust-up. **2** a cause for complaint against someone ♦ *We have no quarrel with them.*
quarrel *verb* (**quarrelled**, **quarrelling**) **1** to have a quarrel, to disagree angrily. SYNONYMS: argue, disagree, fight, squabble, bicker, fall out, wrangle. **2** to complain about something ♦ *We are not quarrelling with this decision.* [from a Latin word *querela* meaning 'complaint']

quarrelsome *adjective* likely to quarrel often with people. SYNONYMS: argumentative, irascible, contentious. **quarrelsomeness** *noun*

quarry [1] *noun* (**quarries**) **1** an animal being hunted. **2** a person or thing that is being sought or pursued. [from an Old French word *cuiree*, from a Latin word *cor* meaning 'heart' (because *quarry* originally meant the parts of the animal, including the heart, that were given to the hounds)]

quarry [2] *noun* (**quarries**) a pit or other open place from which stone or other materials are obtained.
quarry *verb* (**quarries**, **quarried**, **quarrying**) to dig stone etc. from a quarry. [via Old French from a Latin word *quadrum* meaning 'a square']

quart *noun* a unit of volume for measuring liquids, equal to 2 pints or a quarter of a gallon. [via Old French from a Latin phrase *quarta pars* meaning 'fourth part']

quarter *noun* **1** each of the four equal parts into which a thing is or can be divided. **2** (*North Amer.*) a quarter of a dollar, 25 cents. **3** a period of three months, one fourth of a year. **4** a fourth part of a lunar month. **5** a point of time 15 minutes before or after every hour. **6** a direction or point of the compass. **7** a district or division of a town ♦ *the artists' quarter.* SYNONYMS: district, area, neighbourhood, region. **8** a person or group, especially regarded as a possible source of help or information etc. ♦ *We got no sympathy at all from that quarter.* **9** mercy towards an enemy or opponent ♦ *The enemy gave no quarter.* SYNONYMS: mercy, clemency, compassion.
quarter *verb* **1** to divide something into quarters. **2** to put soldiers etc. into lodgings. SYNONYMS: accommodate, billet, lodge. **3** (*Heraldry*) to place a symbol in each of the divisions of a shield or coat of arms. **4** (said about an animal) to search the ground in every direction.
quarters *plural noun* lodgings or accommodation. [from a Latin word *quartus* meaning 'fourth']

quarter day *noun* each of four days reckoned as the start and end of some tenancies and as points at which certain payments become due.
◊ The quarter days in England are 25 March, 24 June, 29 September, and 25 December, and in Scotland are 2 February, 15 May, 1 August, and 11 November.

quarterdeck *noun* the part of the upper deck of a ship nearest the stern, usually reserved for the ship's officers.

quarter-final *noun* each of the matches or rounds preceding a semi-final, in which there are eight contestants or teams. **quarter-finalist** *noun*

quarterly *adjective* happening or produced once every three months.
quarterly *adverb* once every three months.

quarterly noun (**quarterlies**) a quarterly magazine.

quartermaster noun 1 (in the army) a regimental officer in charge of stores and allocating quarters. 2 a naval petty officer in charge of steering and signals.

quartet noun 1 a group of four musicians or singers. 2 a musical composition for four performers. 3 a set of four people or things. [via French and Italian from a Latin word *quartus* meaning 'fourth']

quartile (**kwor**-tiyl) noun 1 each of three points at which a range of statistical data is divided to make four groups of equal size. 2 each of these groups. [same origin as for *quarter*]

quarto noun (**quartos**) 1 a size of paper made by folding a sheet of standard size twice to form four leaves. 2 a book of this size.

quartz (kwortz) noun a hard mineral occurring in various forms. [from a German word *Quarz*]

quartz clock or **quartz watch** a clock or watch operated by electric vibrations of a quartz crystal.

quasar (**kway**-zar) noun a distant object with the appearance of a star, a source of intense electromagnetic radiation. [from *quasi-* and *stellar*]

quash verb 1 to reject something as invalid by legal authority ♦ *The appeal judges quashed the conviction.* SYNONYMS: overthrow, revoke, rescind, annul, reject. 2 to suppress something, such as a rebellion or hostile rumour. SYNONYMS: suppress, crush, quell, put down, subdue, overcome. [from a Latin word *cassus* meaning 'null and void']

quasi- (**kway**-ziy) prefix seeming to be something but not really so ♦ *a quasi-scientific explanation.* [from a Latin word *quasi* meaning 'as if']

quatercentenary (kwat-er-sen-**teen**-er-i) noun (**quatercentenaries**) a 400th anniversary. [from a Latin word *quater* meaning 'four times' and *centenary*]

quaternary adjective fourth in rank or order.
Quaternary adjective (*Geology*) to do with the most recent period of the Cenozoic era, extending from about 1.64 million years ago to the present. [from a Latin word *quater* meaning 'four times']

quatrain (**kwot**-rayn) noun a stanza of four lines. [from a French word *quatre* meaning 'four']

quatrefoil (**kat**-rə-foil) noun an ornamental design of four leaves or lobes, like a flower or clover leaf. [from Old French words *quatre* meaning 'four' and *foil* meaning 'leaf']

quattrocento (kwah-troh-**chen**-toh) noun the 15th century as a period of Italian art. [an Italian word meaning '400', shortened from *milquattrocento* meaning '1400']

quaver verb 1 to tremble or vibrate. SYNONYMS: tremble, shake, quake, quiver, shudder, shiver. 2 to speak in a trembling voice.
quaver noun 1 a quavering sound. 2 (*Music*) a note lasting half as long as a crotchet. [from an Old English word, related to *quake*]

quay (kee) noun a landing place where ships can be tied up for loading and unloading. [from an Old French word *kay*]

quayside noun a quay and the area around it.

queasy adjective (**queasier**, **queasiest**) 1 feeling slightly sick. 2 slightly nervous or anxious. **queasiness** noun [origin unknown]

queen noun 1 the female ruler of an independent country or state, especially one who inherits the position by right of birth. 2 the wife of a king. 3 a female person or thing regarded as supreme in some way. 4 a playing card with a picture of a queen on it, ranking next below a king. 5 the most powerful piece in chess, able to move in any direction. 6 a female bee, wasp, or ant that is capable of reproduction. 7 an adult female cat that has not been spayed. 8 (*informal*) a flamboyant male homosexual.
queen verb (in chess) to convert a pawn to a queen when it reaches the opponent's end of the board. **to queen it** (said about a woman) to behave in a domineering manner. [from an Old English word *cwēn*. The spelling changed in Middle English under the influence of French spellings.]

queenly adjective like a queen in appearance or manner. **queenliness** noun

queen mother noun the widow of a king who is the mother of a reigning king or queen.

Queen's Counsel noun a senior barrister.

queer *adjective* **1** strange or eccentric. SYNONYMS: odd, strange, peculiar, funny, curious, weird, unusual. **2** (*informal*, usually *derogatory*) homosexual. **3** (*informal*, *old use*) slightly ill or faint.
queer *verb* to spoil something. **to queer someone's pitch** to spoil their chances beforehand. **queerly** *adverb* **queerness** *noun* [origin unknown]

quell *verb* to suppress something, especially a rebellion, by force. SYNONYMS: suppress, crush, quash, put down, subdue, overcome. [from an Old English word *cwellan* meaning 'to kill']

quench *verb* **1** to satisfy your thirst by drinking. **2** to put out a fire or flame. **3** to cool hot metal rapidly. **4** to stifle a feeling. [from an Old English word *acwencan* meaning 'to put out or extinguish']

querulous (kwe-rew-ləs) *adjective* complaining in a peevish or petulant manner. **querulously** *adverb* [from a Latin word *queri* meaning 'to complain']

query *noun* (**queries**) a question, especially one that expresses a doubt or uncertainty. SYNONYMS: question, enquiry.
query *verb* (**queries, queried, querying**) to ask a question or express a doubt about something. SYNONYMS: question, ask about, dispute. [from a Latin word *quaere* meaning (as an instruction) 'ask!']

quest *noun* the act of seeking something, a search.

question *noun* **1** a sentence that asks for information or an answer. **2** something being discussed or for discussion; a problem requiring a solution. SYNONYMS: concern, matter, issue, point. **3** doubt or uncertainty ♦ *There is some question about whether he is fit.*
question *verb* **1** to ask questions of someone. SYNONYMS: interrogate, examine. **2** to express doubt about something ♦ *He seemed to be questioning her competence.* SYNONYMS: doubt, dispute, query. **a question of** what is required or involved ♦ *It is only a question of time.* **in question** under discussion or in dispute ♦ *The period in question extends from April to June* ♦ *Their honesty is not in question.* **no question of** no possibility of. **out of the question** not possible or practicable. **questioner** *noun* [from a Latin word *quaesitum* meaning 'sought for']

questionable *adjective* **1** open to doubt or suspicion. SYNONYMS: doubtful, dubious, uncertain, suspect. **2** not certainly advisable or honest. **questionably** *adverb*

question mark *noun* the punctuation mark (?) placed after a question.

questionnaire (kwes-chən-**air**) *noun* a list of questions seeking information from people for use in a survey or statistical study. [a French word, related to *question*]

question time *noun* a period in Parliament when MPs may question ministers.

queue *noun* **1** a line or series of people or vehicles waiting to move forward or for their turn for something. **2** (*Computing*) a list of items to be processed by a computer.
queue *verb* (**queues, queued, queuing**) to wait in a queue. [via French from a Latin word *cauda* meaning 'tail']

quibble *noun* a minor or petty objection or complaint.
quibble *verb* to make petty objections. **quibbler** *noun* [from an old word *quib* meaning 'a petty objection', thought to be from a Latin word *quibus* meaning 'for which?', often used in legal documents]

quiche (keesh) *noun* an open tart with a savoury filling. [a French word]

quick *adjective* **1** moving fast or taking only a short time to do something. **2** done in a short time. SYNONYMS: fast, rapid, swift, speedy. **3** (said about a person) able to think well, alert and intelligent. SYNONYMS: astute, able, intelligent, alert, perceptive. **4** (said about a person's temper) easily roused. **5** (*old use*) alive, living ♦ *the quick and the dead.*
quick *noun* (**the quick**) the sensitive flesh below the nails.
quick *adverb* quickly ♦ *quick-drying.* **to be cut to the quick** to be deeply offended or insulted. **quickly** *adverb* **quickness** *noun* [from an Old English word *cwic*]

quicken *verb* **1** to make something quicker, or to become quicker. SYNONYMS: speed up, accelerate, go faster. **2** to stimulate a feeling, or to become stimulated ♦ *Our interest began to quicken.* **3** (said about a fetus) to reach a stage when it makes movements in the womb that can be felt by the mother.

quickie *noun* (*informal*) something done or dealt with quickly, especially a drink or an act of sexual intercourse.

quicklime *noun* a white substance (calcium oxide) used in making cement and mortar and as a fertilizer.

quicksand *noun* an area of loose wet deep sand that sucks in anything resting or falling on top of it.

quicksilver *noun* liquid mercury.

quickstep *noun* a ballroom dance with quick steps, or the music for this dance.

quick-witted *adjective* quick at understanding a situation or responding to it.

quid [1] *noun* (**quid**) (*informal*) one pound sterling. [origin unknown]

quid [2] *noun* a lump of tobacco for chewing. [a different spelling of *cud*]

quid pro quo *noun* something given in return for something else. [a Latin phrase meaning 'something for something']

quiescent (kwi-**ess**-ənt) *adjective* quiet or inactive. **quiescence** *noun* [from a Latin word *quiescens* meaning 'becoming quiet']

quiet *adjective* **1** making little or no sound, not loud or noisy. SYNONYMS: silent, noiseless; (of a voice) low, soft, hushed. **2** with little or no movement. SYNONYMS: still, motionless, calm, tranquil. **3** free from disturbance or vigorous activity, peaceful. SYNONYMS: calm, tranquil, peaceful, untroubled. **4** silent ♦ *Please be quiet.* **5** discreet or restrained ♦ *We all had a quiet laugh about it.* **6** (said about colours or dress etc.) subdued, not bright.
quiet *noun* quietness.
quiet *verb* (**quieted, quieting**) to make someone or something quiet, or to become quiet. **on the quiet** discreetly or secretly. **quietly** *adverb* **quietness** *noun* [from a Latin word *quietus* meaning 'calm']

quieten *verb* to make someone or something quiet, or to become quiet.

quietude (**kwiy**-i-tewd) *noun* a state of quiet or calm.

quiff *noun* an upright tuft of hair above a man's forehead. [origin unknown]

quill *noun* **1** each of the large feathers on the wing or tail of a bird. **2** an old type of pen made from a bird's feather. **3** each of the spines on a porcupine or hedgehog. **4** the hollow stem of a feather, or a plectrum or other device made from this. [probably from an early German word *quiele*]

quilt *noun* a padded cover for a bed.

quilt *verb* to line material with padding and fix it with lines of stitching. [via Old French from a Latin word *culcita* meaning 'mattress' or 'cushion']

quin *noun* (*informal*) a quintuplet.

quince *noun* **1** a hard yellowish pear-shaped fruit used for making jam. **2** the tree bearing this fruit. [via Old French from a Latin phrase *malum cydonium* meaning 'apple of Cydonia' (= Chania, a place in Crete)]

quinine (kwin-**een**) *noun* a bitter-tasting medicinal drug used to treat malaria and as a tonic. [from a Spanish word *quina* meaning 'cinchona (a South American tree) bark']

quinsy (**kwin**-zi) *noun* inflammation of the throat, especially an abscess on one of the tonsils. [via Old French from a Greek word *kunankhē* meaning 'a disease of dogs', from *kun-* meaning 'dog']

quintessence (kwin-**tess**-əns) *noun* **1** a perfect example of a quality. **2** an essence of a substance. **3** the most essential or intrinsic part of something. [via French from a Latin phrase *quinta essentia* meaning 'fifth essence']

quintet *noun* **1** a group of five musicians or singers. **2** a musical composition for five performers. **3** a set of five people or things. [from a Latin word *quintus* meaning 'fifth']

quintuple *adjective* **1** consisting of five parts, or involving five people or groups ♦ *a quintuple alliance*. **2** five times as much. **quintuple** *verb* **1** to multiply something by five. **2** to increase fivefold. **quintuply** *adverb* [from a Latin word *quintuplus* from *quintus* meaning 'fifth']

quintuplet (kwin-**tew**-plit) *noun* each of five children born at one birth.

quip *noun* a witty remark.
quip *verb* (**quipped, quipping**) to make a quip. [origin unknown]

quire *noun* **1** a set of four sheets of paper folded to form eight leaves in a book or manuscript. **2** 25 (formerly 24) sheets of writing paper. [via Old French from a Latin word *quaterni* meaning 'set of four']

quirk *noun* **1** a peculiarity of a person's behaviour. SYNONYMS: peculiarity, eccentricity, oddity, idiosyncrasy, foible. **2** a strange occurrence or trick of fate. [origin unknown]

quisling (**kwiz**-ling) noun a traitor who collaborates with an invading enemy. [from the name of Vidkun Quisling (1887–1945), a pro-Nazi Norwegian leader in the Second World War]

quit verb (past tense and past participle **quitted** or **quit; quitting**) 1 to leave or go away from a place. SYNONYMS: leave, abandon. 2 (informal) to resign from a job. 3 (informal) to stop doing something ♦ He wants to quit smoking. SYNONYMS: stop, give up, discontinue.
quit adjective (**quit of**) rid of ♦ We are glad to be quit of them. [same origin as for quiet]

quite adverb 1 completely or utterly ♦ I haven't quite finished ♦ We are all quite exhausted. SYNONYMS: completely, entirely, totally, utterly. 2 fairly, somewhat ♦ The news was quite bad, though not as bad as we feared. SYNONYMS: rather, somewhat, fairly. 3 really or actually ♦ It's quite a change. 4 used as an expression of agreement. [from an obsolete adjective quite, another spelling of quit]
◊ You sometimes need to be careful about using quite, because it can have either the strong meaning 'completely or utterly' or the weaker meaning 'fairly, somewhat'. For example, if you say ♦ I am quite happy, this can mean 'I am completely happy' or only 'I am fairly happy'. In speech your tone of voice usually makes it clear which you mean. In writing, if people need to be sure which you mean, it is sometimes better to use one of the alternative words given above.

quits adjective on equal terms after a retaliation or repayment.

quitter noun (informal) a person who gives up too easily.

quiver¹ verb to shake or tremble with a slight rapid motion. SYNONYMS: tremble, shake, quake, quaver, shudder, shiver.
quiver noun a quivering movement or sound. [from an Old English word cwifer meaning 'nimble' or 'quick']

quiver² noun a case for holding arrows. [from an early French word quiveir]

qui vive (kee veev) noun **on the qui vive** on the alert, watchful. [a French phrase meaning '(long) live who?' used as a sentry's challenge]

quixotic (kwik-**sot**-ik) adjective chivalrous and unselfish, often to an extravagant or impractical extent. **quixotically** adverb [from the name of Don Quixote, the hero of a Spanish story by Cervantes]

quiz noun (**quizzes**) a series of questions testing general knowledge, especially as a form of entertainment.
quiz verb (**quizzed, quizzing**) to question someone. [origin unknown]

quizzical (**kwiz**-ikəl) adjective showing mild curiosity or amusement ♦ a quizzical look. **quizzically** adverb

quoit (koit) noun a ring of metal or rubber or rope thrown round an upright peg in the game called **quoits**. [probably from a French word]

quorate (**kwor**-ət) adjective (said about a meeting) having a quorum.

quorum (**kwor**-əm) noun (**quorums**) the minimum number of people that must be present at a meeting for its proceedings to be valid. [a Latin word meaning 'of which people']

quota noun (**quotas**) 1 a fixed share that must be done, given, or received. SYNONYMS: share, allocation, ration, allowance. 2 the maximum number of people or things that can be allowed or admitted, e.g. imported goods into a country. [from a Latin word quot meaning 'how many']

quotable adjective worth quoting.

quotation noun 1 a passage or group of words from a book or speech that is repeated by someone other than the original writer or speaker. 2 the process of quoting or being quoted. 3 a statement or estimate of a price.

quotation marks plural noun punctuation marks (either single '' or double "") put round words that are being quoted or have some special significance.
◊ These are also called inverted commas.

quote verb 1 to repeat words that were first used by someone else, e.g. in a book or speech. 2 to mention something in support of a statement ♦ Can you quote a recent example? SYNONYMS: cite, refer to. 3 to state the price of goods or services, to give a quotation or estimate.
quote noun a quotation. [from a Latin word quotare meaning 'to number']

quoth (kwohth) verb (old use) said. [from an obsolete word quethe meaning 'to say']

quotient (**kwoh**-shənt) noun (Mathematics) the result obtained when one amount is divided by another (e.g. 3 in $12 \div 4 = 3$). [from a Latin word quotiens meaning 'how many times']

q.v. *abbreviation* used to direct a reader to another part of a book or text for further information. [short for Latin *quod vide* meaning 'which see']

Rr

R the eighteenth letter of the English alphabet.

R *abbreviation* 1 Regina (Queen) ♦ *Elizabeth R.* 2 Rex (King) ♦ *George R.* 3 (in names) river. 4 (*Chemistry*) the symbol for electrical resistance.

r *abbreviation* radius.

RA *abbreviation* 1 Royal Academician. 2 Royal Academy. 3 Royal Artillery.

Ra *abbreviation* (*Chemistry*) the symbol for radium.

rabbi (rab-iy) *noun* (**rabbis**) a Jewish religious leader. [a Hebrew word meaning 'my master']

rabbinic (rǝ-bin-ik) or **rabbinical** (rǝ-bin-ikǝl) *adjective* to do with rabbis or Jewish teachings or law.

rabbit *noun* a burrowing animal with long ears and a short furry tail.
rabbit *verb* (**rabbited, rabbiting**) 1 to hunt rabbits. 2 (*informal*) to chatter or talk lengthily. **rabbity** *adjective* [perhaps from an Old French word]

rabble *noun* a disorderly crowd or mob.
the rabble *noun* (*informal, derogatory*) the common people. [probably from an Old German or Old Dutch word]

rabble-rouser *noun* a person who stirs up a crowd. **rabble-rousing** *adjective & noun*

rabid (rab-id) *adjective* 1 extreme or fanatical ♦ *a rabid socialist.* 2 suffering from rabies. **rabidity** (rǝ-bid-iti) *noun* **rabidly** *adverb* [from a Latin word *rabidus* meaning 'raving']

rabies (ray-beez or ray-biz) *noun* a dangerous contagious virus disease affecting dogs and other mammals, transmitted to humans usually by the bite of an infected animal. [from a Latin word *rabere* meaning 'to be mad']

raccoon *noun* a North American animal with a bushy striped tail, sharp snout, and greyish-brown fur. [from an Algonquan (North American) word *aroughcun*]

race [1] *noun* 1 a contest of speed in reaching a certain point or in doing something. 2 a situation in which people compete to be the first to achieve or get something ♦ *the arms race.* 3 a strong fast current of water ♦ *the tidal race.* 4 a channel for the balls in a ball bearing.
race *verb* 1 to take part in a race; to have a race with someone. 2 to prepare and enter an animal or vehicle for races ♦ *He races pigeons.* 3 to move or go quickly. 4 to operate or cause an engine etc. to operate at full speed. **a race against time** an effort to get something done before a certain time. **racer** *noun* **racing** *noun* [from an Old Norse word meaning 'current']

race [2] *noun* 1 each of the major divisions of humankind with certain inherited physical characteristics in common, e.g. colour of skin, type of hair, shape of eyes and nose. 2 racial origin ♦ *discrimination on grounds of race.* 3 a number of people related by common descent. 4 a group of people with a common feature ♦ *Librarians are a fairly quiet race.* 5 a genus, species, breed, or variety of animals or plants. **the human race** human beings collectively. [via French from an Italian word *razza*]

racecourse *noun* a ground or track where horse races are run.

racehorse *noun* a horse bred or kept for racing.

raceme (rǝ-seem) *noun* (*Botany*) a cluster of flowers evenly spaced along a central stem, with the ones at the base opening first, as in lupins, hyacinths, etc. [from a Latin word *racemus* meaning 'bunch of grapes']

race relations *plural noun* relations between members of different races within a country.

racetrack *noun* a track for horse or vehicle races.

racial (ray-shǝl) *adjective* to do with a particular race or based on race. **racially** *adverb*

racialism (ray-shǝl-izm) *noun* racism. **racialist** *noun & adjective*

racism (ray-sizm) *noun* 1 the belief that there are characteristics, abilities, or qualities specific to each race. 2 discrimination against or hostility towards people of other races. **racist** noun & adjective

rack[1] noun 1 a framework, usually with bars or pegs, for holding things or for hanging things on. 2 a shelf or framework of bars for holding light luggage in a train or bus etc. 3 a bar or rail with teeth or cogs into which those of a wheel or gear etc. fit. 4 an instrument of torture on which people were tied and stretched.
rack verb to inflict great physical or mental pain on someone ♦ *He was racked with guilt.* **to rack your brains** to think hard, especially when you are trying to remember something. **to rack something up** to accumulate or achieve something ♦ *She has racked up a succession of impressive victories this year.* [from an Old German or Old Dutch word]

rack[2] noun **to go to rack and ruin** to gradually become worse in condition due to neglect. [another spelling of *wreck*]

rack[3] noun a joint of meat including the front ribs ♦ *rack of lamb.* [origin unknown]

racket[1] noun a bat with strings stretched across a frame, used in tennis, badminton, and squash.
rackets noun a ball game for two or four people played with rackets in a four-walled court. [from an Arabic word *rahat* meaning 'palm of the hand']

racket[2] noun 1 a loud noise. SYNONYMS: din, clamour, cacophony, hubbub, commotion. 2 (*informal*) a business or other activity in which dishonest methods are used. 3 (*informal*) a person's line of business. **rackety** adjective [perhaps an imitation of the sound of clattering]

racketeer noun a person who runs or works in a racket or dishonest business. **racketeering** noun

rack railway noun a railway having a cogged rail with which a cogged wheel on the train engages for driving the train up a steep slope.

raconteur (rak-on-ter) noun a person who tells anecdotes well. [a French word]

racoon noun another spelling of **raccoon**.

racquet noun another spelling of **racket**[1].

racy adjective (**racier**, **raciest**) 1 slightly shocking or indecent. 2 lively or spirited. **racily** adverb **raciness** noun [originally meaning 'having a particular quality': from *race*[2]]

radar noun 1 a system for detecting the presence, position, or movement etc. of objects by sending out short radio waves which are reflected back off the object. 2 apparatus used for this. [from the initial letters of *radio detection and ranging*]

radar trap noun a system using radar to detect vehicles travelling faster than the speed limit.

raddled adjective worn out. [from *raddle* meaning 'red colouring for marking sheep']

radial (ray-di-əl) adjective 1 to do with rays or radii. 2 having spokes or lines radiating from a central point. 3 (also **radial-ply**) (said about a tyre) having fabric layers with cords lying radial to the hub of the wheel, not crossing each other.
radial noun 1 a radial tyre. 2 a radial part. **radially** adverb [same origin as for *radius*]

radial symmetry noun symmetry about a central axis.

radian (ray-di-ən) noun a unit of measurement of angles equal to about $57.3°$; the angle at the centre of a circle formed by the radii of an arc equal in length to the radius.

radiant adjective 1 shining or glowing brightly. 2 looking very happy and healthy. 3 transmitting heat by radiation. 4 (said about heat) transmitted in this way. **radiance** noun **radiancy** noun **radiantly** adverb [same origin as for *radiate*]

radiate verb 1 to send out light, heat, or other energy in the form of rays or waves; to be sent out in this way. 2 to give out a strong feeling or quality ♦ *She radiated confidence.* 3 to spread outwards from a central point like the spokes of a wheel; to cause something to do this. [from a Latin word *radius* meaning 'ray']

radiation noun 1 (*Physics*) the sending out of the rays and atomic particles characteristic of radioactive substances; these rays and particles. 2 the action or process of radiating.

radiation sickness noun illness caused by exposure to X-rays, gamma rays, or other radiation.

radiator noun 1 a device that radiates heat, especially a metal case through which steam or hot water circulates, or one heated electrically. 2 a device that cools the engine of a motor vehicle or an aircraft. [from *radiate*]

radical *adjective* **1** going to the root or foundation of something, fundamental. **2** drastic, thorough ♦ *radical changes.* **3** wanting to make great reforms; holding extremist views.
radical *noun* **1** a person who wants to make great reforms or holds extremist views. **2** (*Chemistry*) a group of atoms forming part of a compound and remaining unaltered during its ordinary chemical changes. **3** the root of a word. **4** (*Mathematics*) a quantity forming or expressed as the root of another.
radicalism *noun* **radically** *adverb* [from a Latin word *radicis* meaning 'of a root']

radicchio (ra-**dee**-ki-oh) *noun* a kind of chicory with dark red leaves. [an Italian word meaning 'chicory']

radicle *noun* (*Botany*) an embryo root, e.g. of a pea or bean. [from a Latin word meaning 'little root']

radio *noun* (**radios**) **1** the process of sending and receiving messages etc. by electromagnetic waves. **2** sound broadcasting; a sound-broadcasting station ♦ *She works in radio* ♦ *Radio Oxford.* **3** an apparatus for receiving radio programmes or for sending or receiving radio messages; a transmitter or receiver.
radio *adjective* **1** to do with or operated by radio. **2** broadcast on radio.
radio *verb* (**radioes**, **radioed**, **radioing**) to send a message or communicate with someone by radio. [from a Latin word *radius* meaning 'ray']

radio- *prefix* **1** to do with radio. **2** to do with rays or radiation.

radioactive *adjective* to do with or showing radioactivity.

radioactivity *noun* **1** the property of having atoms that break up spontaneously and send out radiation capable of penetrating opaque bodies and producing electrical and chemical effects. **2** radioactive particles.

radio astronomy *noun* the branch of astronomy concerned with radio signals emitted from objects in space.

radio beacon *noun* an instrument that sends out radio signals, which aircraft use to find their way.

radiocarbon *noun* a radioactive form of carbon that is present in organic materials and is used in carbon dating.

radio frequency *noun* a range of electromagnetic wave frequencies used in radio and television transmission.

radiographer (ray-di-og-rəfer) *noun* a person who is skilled in radiography.

radiography (ray-di-og-rəfi) *noun* the production of X-ray photographs. [from *radio-* and -*graphy*]

radiologist (ray-di-ol-əjist) *noun* a specialist in radiology.

radiology (ray-di-ol-əji) *noun* the scientific study of X-rays and similar radiation, especially in treating diseases. [from *radio-* and -*logy*]

radio telescope *noun* an instrument used to detect radio waves emitted from space, whether from natural celestial objects or from artificial satellites.

radiotherapy *noun* the treatment of cancer or other disease by X-rays or similar forms of radiation.

radish *noun* **1** a crisp hot-tasting red-skinned root that is eaten raw in salads. **2** the plant that produces this root. [from a Latin word *radix* meaning 'root']

radium *noun* a radioactive metallic element (symbol Ra), obtained from pitchblende, often used in radiotherapy. [from a Latin word *radius* meaning 'ray']

radius (ray-di-əs) *noun* (**radii** (ray-di-iy) or **radiuses**) **1** a straight line from the centre of a circle or sphere to its circumference. **2** the length of this line; the distance from a centre ♦ *They could be anywhere within a radius of 20 miles by now.* **3** (*Anatomy and Zoology*) the thicker of the two long bones in the forearm; the corresponding bone in animals. [from a Latin word *radius* meaning 'a spoke or ray']

radon *noun* a radioactive gas and chemical element (symbol Rn) formed by the decay of radium and used in radiotherapy. [from *radium*]

RAF *abbreviation* Royal Air Force.

raffia *noun* soft fibre from the leaves of a kind of palm tree, used for making mats, baskets, etc. [from a Malagasy (Madagascar) word]

raffish *adjective* slightly disreputable, but attractively so. **raffishness** *noun* [from *riff-raff*]

raffle *noun* a lottery with an object as the prize, especially as a method of raising money for a charity.

raffle verb to offer something as the prize in a raffle. [probably from a French word]

raft noun 1 a flat floating structure made of timber or other materials, used especially as a boat. 2 a small inflatable boat.
raft verb to travel or transport something on a raft. **rafting** noun [from an Old Norse word]

rafter noun any of the sloping beams forming the framework of a roof. [from an Old English word]

rag[1] noun 1 a piece of old cloth, especially one torn from a larger piece. 2 (informal) a newspaper of low quality.
rags plural noun old and torn clothes. [from ragged]

rag[2] noun a series of entertainments and activities held by students to collect money for charity.
rag verb (**ragged, ragging**) to tease or play jokes on someone. [origin unknown]

rag[3] noun a piece of ragtime music.

raga (rah-gə) noun 1 (in Indian music) a pattern of notes used as a basis for improvisation. 2 a piece of music using a particular raga. [a Sanskrit word meaning 'colour; musical tone']

ragamuffin noun a person in ragged dirty clothes. [from rag]

rag-and-bone man noun an itinerant dealer in old clothes and other second-hand articles.

ragbag noun 1 a bag in which scraps of fabric etc. are kept for future use. 2 a miscellaneous collection.

rage noun 1 violent anger that is difficult to control, or a fit of this. 2 a fit of violent anger associated with some activity ♦ road rage ♦ air rage.
rage verb 1 to show violent anger. SYNONYMS: boil, fume, seethe, storm, rave. 2 (said about a storm or battle etc.) to continue violently or with great force. **to be all the rage** to be temporarily very popular or fashionable. **raging** adjective [from an Old French word rage; related to rabies]

ragged (rag-id) adjective 1 torn or frayed. 2 dressed in torn clothes. 3 jagged. 4 uneven or irregular ♦ That crew's rowing is a bit ragged. **raggedly** adverb **raggedness** noun [from an Old Norse word roggvathr meaning 'tufted']

ragged robin noun a pink-flowered campion with ragged petals.

raglan adjective (said about a sleeve) continuing to the neck and joined to the body of the coat, jumper, etc. by sloping seams.
raglan noun an overcoat with raglan sleeves. [named after the British military commander Lord Raglan (1788–1855)]

ragout (ra-**goo**) noun a stew of meat and vegetables. [from a French word ragoûter meaning 'to revive the taste of']

ragtag adjective 1 consisting of an odd and varied mixture. 2 untidy. [from rag[1] and tag[1]]

ragtime noun a form of jazz music played especially on the piano. [perhaps from ragged time]

ragwort noun a wild plant with yellow flowers and ragged leaves.

raid noun 1 a sudden surprise attack. 2 a surprise visit by police to arrest suspected people or seize illegal goods.
raid verb 1 to make a raid on a place. 2 to sneak into a place in order to take something ♦ Who's been raiding the fridge? **raider** noun [from an Old English word]

rail[1] noun 1 a horizontal or sloping bar forming part of a fence or barrier or the top of banisters, or for hanging things on. 2 any of the lines of metal bars on which trains or trams run. 3 railways as a means of transport ♦ We sent the parcel by rail. 4 a horizontal piece in the frame of a panelled door or sash window.
rail verb to fit or protect something with a rail ♦ The painting has been railed off. **to go off the rails** (informal) to start behaving oddly or out of control. [from an Old French word reille meaning 'iron rod'; related to rule]

rail[2] verb to complain strongly about a person or thing ♦ He stood there railing at the failure of the judicial system. [via French from a Portuguese word]

rail[3] noun a kind of small wading bird. [from an Old French word]

railing noun a fence of rails supported on upright metal bars.

raillery noun good-humoured joking or teasing. [from a French word raillerie]

railman noun (**railmen**) a railwayman.

railroad noun (North Amer.) a railway.
railroad verb to rush or force someone into hasty action ♦ He felt he had been railroaded into accepting.

railway noun 1 a set of rails on which trains

run. 2 a system of transport using these; the organization and people required for its working.

railwayman noun (**railwaymen**) a railway employee.

raiment noun (old use) clothing. [from array]

rain noun 1 condensed moisture of the atmosphere falling in separate drops. 2 a large quantity of things coming down ♦ a rain of blows.
the rains plural noun the rainy season in tropical countries.
rain verb 1 to fall as rain ♦ It's been raining all day. SYNONYMS: pour, pelt, drizzle; (informal) bucket down. 2 to come down or send something down like rain ♦ It was just raining glass ♦ They rained blows on him.
to be rained off (said about an event) to be prevented by rain from taking place or finishing. **to take a rain check** (informal) to defer your acceptance of an offer until a later date. [from an Old English word regn]

rainbow noun an arch of all the colours of the spectrum formed in the sky when the sun's rays are reflected and refracted through rain or spray. [from an Old English word regnboga]

raincoat noun a waterproof or water-resistant coat.

raindrop noun a single drop of rain.

rainfall noun the total amount of rain falling within a given area in a given time.

rainforest noun a thick forest in tropical areas where there is heavy rainfall.

rain shadow noun a region in the lee of mountains where the rainfall is low because it is sheltered from the prevailing winds.

rainstorm noun a storm with heavy rain.

rainwater noun water that has fallen as rain.

rainy adjective (**rainier, rainiest**) having a lot of rainfall. **to save something for a rainy day** to save money for a time when you may need it.

raise verb 1 to move or lift something to a higher or upright position. SYNONYMS: lift, elevate, hoist, jack up. 2 to increase the amount, level, or strength of something ♦ We may need to raise prices. SYNONYMS: increase, put up, boost; (informal) up. 3 (Mathematics) to multiply a quantity to a particular power. 4 to collect, assemble, or manage to obtain something ♦ The duke

had no difficulty raising an army ♦ an auction to raise money for charity. 5 to bring up a child ♦ She had to raise her family alone. 6 to breed or grow animals or plants ♦ We used to raise sheep. 7 to give rise to something ♦ These revelations raised serious doubts in my mind ♦ Some of the jokes will raise a smile or two. SYNONYMS: arouse, provoke, stimulate, foster, build up. 8 to put something forward ♦ Does anyone have questions they would like to raise? SYNONYMS: pose, bring up, present, broach. 9 to wake someone from sleep or bring someone back from death. 10 to make something come or appear ♦ a spell for raising a ghost. 11 to make contact with someone by radio or telephone. 12 to bring a siege, blockade, or embargo to an end. 13 (in poker) to bet more than the previous player.
raise noun (North Amer.) an increase in salary. **to raise the alarm** to give a warning of imminent danger. **to raise your glass** to drink a toast to a person or thing. **to raise hell** (informal) 1 to make an uproar. 2 to complain noisily. **to raise your voice** to speak more loudly. [from an Old Norse word reisa]

raisin noun a partially dried grape. [from a French word meaning 'grape']

raising agent noun a substance, e.g. yeast or baking powder, that makes bread or cake etc. swell and become light in texture.

raison d'être (ray-zawn detr) noun (**raisons d'être**) the reason or purpose for a thing's existence. [a French phrase meaning 'reason for being']

Raj (rahj) noun the period of Indian history when the country was ruled by Britain. [a Hindi word meaning 'reign']

raja or **rajah** (rah-jə) noun (historical) an Indian king or prince. [a Hindi word]

rake [1] noun 1 a tool with prongs used for drawing together leaves, cut grass, etc. or for smoothing loose soil or gravel. 2 an implement resembling this, used e.g. by a croupier for drawing in money at a gambling table.
rake verb 1 to gather or smooth something with a rake. 2 to search through something ♦ He's been raking through all his old records. 3 to direct gunfire or your eyes along a line from end to end. **to rake it in** (informal) to make a lot of money. **to rake something up** to remind people of an old quarrel, scandal, or other incident that is

best forgotten. [from an Old English word]

rake [2] *noun* the angle at which something slopes, such as a stage or seating.
rake *verb* to set something at a sloping angle. [origin unknown]

rake [3] *noun* a man who lives an irresponsible and immoral life. [from an old word *rakehell*]

rake-off *noun* (*informal*) a commission or share of profits.

rakish *adjective* jaunty and dashing in appearance. **rakishly** *adverb* **rakishness** *noun* [from *rake* [3]]

rally *verb* (**rallies, rallied, rallying**) 1 to bring people together, or come together, for a united effort ◆ *She's been trying to rally support for the election campaign* ◆ *All his family rallied round.* 2 to reassemble for another effort after being scattered or defeated. 3 to summon up or revive something ◆ *It's time to rally our courage.* 4 to recover your strength after illness. 5 (said about share prices) to increase again after a fall.
rally *noun* (**rallies**) 1 a mass meeting of people to support a cause, protest about something, or share an interest. 2 a driving competition for cars or motorcycles over public roads or rough country. 3 (in tennis etc.) a series of strokes between players before a point is won. 4 a recovery of energy or spirits etc. [from a French word *rallier*]

rallying *adjective* calling people to action ◆ *a rallying cry.*

RAM *abbreviation* (*Computing*) random-access memory.

ram *noun* 1 an uncastrated male sheep. 2 a battering ram or similar device. 3 a striking or plunging device in various machines.
ram *verb* (**rammed, ramming**) 1 to force something into place by pressure. 2 to crash against or drive into something with great force. **rammer** *noun* [from an Old English word *ram*]

Ramadan (ram-ə-dan) *noun* the ninth month of the Muslim year, when Muslims fast between sunrise and sunset. [an Arabic word, from *ramida* meaning 'to be parched']

ramble *noun* a walk in the countryside taken for pleasure.
ramble *verb* 1 to take a ramble. 2 to talk or write in a confused or disorganized way, to wander from the subject. [origin unknown]

rambler *noun* 1 someone who goes for a ramble. 2 a climbing rose.

rambling *adjective* 1 (said about speech or writing) confused or disorganized, wandering from one subject to another. 2 (said about a plant) growing over walls and fences; climbing. 3 (said about a house, street, or village etc.) extending in various directions irregularly.

ramekin (ram-i-kin) *noun* 1 a small dish for baking and serving an individual portion of food. 2 something baked and served in this ◆ *cheese ramekins.* [from a French word *ramequin*]

ramification *noun* 1 one of the complicated consequences of something ◆ *This decision is bound to have widespread ramifications.* 2 an arrangement of branching parts. 3 a part of a complex structure or process. [from a Latin word *ramificare* meaning 'to branch out']

ramify *verb* (**ramifies, ramified, ramifying**) to form or cause something to form into branching parts. [same origin as for *ramification*]

ramin (rah-meen) *noun* a light-coloured hardwood from Malaysia. [from a Malay word]

ramjet *noun* a type of jet engine in which air is drawn in and compressed by motion through the air.

ramp *noun* 1 a slope joining two different levels of floor or road etc. 2 a movable set of steps put beside an aircraft so that people can enter or leave. 3 a ridge built across a road to control the speed of traffic. [from a French word *ramper* meaning 'to climb']

rampage [1] (ram-payj) *verb* to rush about wildly or destructively. SYNONYMS: run amok, run riot, go wild, go berserk. [origin unknown]

rampage [2] (ram-payj) *noun* **on the rampage** rushing about wildly or destructively.

rampant *adjective* 1 unrestrained, flourishing or spreading excessively ◆ *Disease was rampant in the poorer districts.* 2 (*Heraldry*) (said about an animal on a coat of arms) standing upright on one hind leg with the other legs raised ◆ *a lion rampant.* [same origin as for *ramp*]

rampart noun a defensive wall of a castle or walled city, having a broad top with a walkway. [from a French word *remparer* meaning 'to fortify']

ram raid noun a robbery in which a shop window is rammed with a vehicle and looted. **ram-raider** noun **ram-raiding** noun

ramrod noun an iron rod formerly used for ramming an explosive charge into muzzle-loading guns.

ramshackle adjective in a state of severe disrepair ♦ *a ramshackle hut*. SYNONYMS: dilapidated, rickety, run-down, tumbledown. [from an old word *ransackle* meaning 'to ransack']

ran past tense of **run**.

ranch noun a large farm in North America where cattle or other animals are bred. **ranch** verb to farm on a ranch. **rancher** noun [from a Spanish word *rancho* meaning 'group of people eating together']

rancid (ran-sid) adjective smelling or tasting unpleasant like stale fat. [from a Latin word *rancidus* meaning 'stinking']

rancour (rank-er) noun bitter feeling or ill will. **rancorous** adjective **rancorously** adverb [from an Old French word; related to *rancid*]

rand (rand or rant) noun 1 the unit of money in South Africa. 2 (*South African*) a ridge of high ground on either side of a river. [an Afrikaans word meaning 'edge']

R & B abbreviation rhythm and blues.

R & D abbreviation research and development.

random adjective done or made or taken etc. without any method or conscious decision ♦ *a random choice*. SYNONYMS: arbitrary, haphazard, chance. **at random** using no particular method or conscious decision ♦ *numbers chosen at random*. **randomly** adverb **randomness** noun [via Old French from a Germanic word]

random access noun (*Computing*) the process of retrieving or storing information in a computer without having to read through items stored previously.

randy adjective (**randier, randiest**) (*informal*) sexually aroused or excited; lustful. **randiness** noun [perhaps from an old word *rand* meaning 'to rant or rave']

rang past tense of **ring**[2].

range noun 1 the limits between which something varies ♦ *the age range 15 to 18* ♦ *What price range do you have in mind?* 2 a set of different things of the same type ♦ *a lovely range of colours* ♦ *a wide range of backgrounds*. 3 a set of products made by a company or available in a shop ♦ *our new range of summer clothing*. 4 the scope or extent of something ♦ *Such questions fall outside the range of this enquiry*. 5 the extent of pitch which a particular singing voice or musical instrument is capable of. 6 the distance over which you can see or hear, or to which a sound, signal, or missile can travel; the distance that a ship or aircraft etc. can travel without refuelling. 7 the distance to a thing being aimed at or looked at ♦ *at close range*. 8 a line or series of mountains or hills. 9 a large stretch of open land for grazing or hunting. 10 a place with targets for shooting practice ♦ *a firing range*. 11 a kitchen fireplace with ovens etc. for cooking in.
range verb 1 to vary between certain limits ♦ *Prices range from £20 to £50*. 2 to include a variety of different things ♦ *She's had numerous jobs, ranging from taxi driver to lifeguard*. 3 to cover a number of different subjects ♦ *Our discussion ranged over several key topics*. 4 to arrange things in a row or ranks or in a specified way ♦ *Decorative plates were ranged on the shelves*. 5 to wander or travel about a wide area. [from an Old French word *range* meaning 'row, rank']

rangefinder noun an instrument for calculating the distance of an object to be shot at or photographed.

ranger noun 1 a keeper of a park or forest. 2 a member of a body of mounted troops policing a thinly populated area. **Ranger** noun a senior Guide. [from *range*]

ranging pole noun a rod used in surveying for setting a straight line.

rangy (rayn-ji) adjective (said about a person) tall and thin.

rani (rah-nee) noun (*historical*) a Hindu queen. [a Hindi word]

rank[1] noun 1 a position or grade in a hierarchy ♦ *the rank of colonel* ♦ *ministers of Cabinet rank*. 2 high social position ♦ *people of rank*. 3 a line or row of people or things. 4 a place where taxis stand to wait for passengers.
the ranks plural noun 1 ordinary soldiers, not officers. 2 people belonging to a group or class ♦ *the ranks of the unemployed*.

rank verb 1 to give someone or something a rank. 2 to have a certain rank ◆ *He ranks among the great statesmen.* 3 to arrange things in a row or sequence. **to close ranks** to maintain solidarity. **to pull rank** to use your superior position or status to get what you want. [via Old French from a Germanic word]

rank [2] adjective 1 growing too thickly ◆ *rank vegetation.* 2 smelling very unpleasant. 3 unmistakably bad, out-and-out ◆ *rank injustice.* **rankly** adverb **rankness** noun [from an Old English word *ranc* meaning 'proud, rebellious, sturdy']

rank and file noun the ordinary people of an organization, not the leaders. [referring to the 'ranks' and 'files' into which privates and non-commissioned officers form on parade]

ranking noun a position in a hierarchy or scale.

rankle verb to cause lasting and bitter annoyance or resentment. [from an Old French word *rancle* meaning 'festering sore']

ransack verb 1 to rob a place, causing damage. 2 to search somewhere thoroughly or roughly. [from an Old Norse word *rannsaka*]

ransom noun money that has to be paid for a captive to be set free.
ransom verb 1 to free someone by paying a ransom. 2 to get a ransom for someone. **to hold someone to ransom** 1 to hold someone captive and demand payment for their release. 2 to demand concessions from someone by threatening some damaging action. [same origin as for *redeem*]

rant verb to speak or shout loudly and wildly.
rant noun a spell of ranting. [from a Dutch word *ranten* meaning 'to talk nonsense']

rap verb (**rapped, rapping**) 1 to strike something quickly and sharply. 2 to make a knocking or tapping sound. 3 to speak words rapidly and rhythmically to a backing of rock music. 4 (*informal*) to chat.
rap noun 1 a quick sharp knock or blow. 2 a knocking or tapping sound. 3 (*informal*) a criminal charge ◆ *a murder rap.* 4 words recited rapidly and rhythmically to a backing of rock music; a type of popular music in which this is done. 5 (*informal*) a reprimand. 6 (*informal*) a chat. **to rap something out** to say something suddenly or sharply. **to take**

the rap (*informal*) to be punished or blamed for something. **rapper** noun [an imitation of the sound]

rapacious (rə-**pay**-shəs) adjective greedy and grasping, especially for money. **rapaciously** adverb **rapacity** (rə-**pas**-iti) noun [from a Latin word *rapax* meaning 'grasping']

rape [1] noun 1 the act or crime of having sexual intercourse with a person without their consent, usually by using force. 2 spoiling or destroying a place ◆ *the rape of the countryside.*
rape verb 1 to commit rape on a person. 2 to spoil or destroy a place. [from a Latin word *rapere* meaning 'to take by force']

rape [2] noun a plant with bright yellow flowers, grown as food for sheep and for its seed from which oil is obtained. [from a Latin word *rapum* meaning 'turnip', to which it is related]

rapid adjective happening in a short time or at great speed. SYNONYMS: quick, fast, swift, brisk, speedy; (*informal*) nippy.
rapids plural noun a fast-flowing part of a river, caused by a steep downward slope in the river bed. **rapidity** (rə-**pid**-iti) noun **rapidly** adverb [from a Latin word *rapere* meaning 'to take by force']

rapier (**rayp**-i-er) noun a thin light sharp-pointed sword, used for thrusting. [from a French word *râpe* meaning 'grater' (because the perforated hilt looks like a grater)]

rapine (**ra**-piyn) noun (*literary*) plundering. [from an Old French word]

rapist (**ray**-pist) noun a person who commits rape.

rapport (rap-**or**) noun a harmonious and understanding relationship between people. [a French word]

rapscallion noun (*old use*) a rascal. [perhaps from *rascal*]

rapt adjective very intent and absorbed, enraptured. **raptly** adverb [from a Latin word *raptum* meaning 'seized']

rapture noun intense pleasure or joy. **in raptures** feeling or expressing rapture. **rapturous** adjective **rapturously** adverb [from an Old French word; related to *rapt*]

rare [1] adjective 1 not often found or happening. SYNONYMS: uncommon, unusual, scarce, infrequent; (*informal*) few and far between. 2 exceptionally good, remarkable ◆ *a player of rare skill.* **rarely** adverb **rareness** noun [from a Latin word *rarus*]

rare [2] *adjective* (said about meat) lightly cooked so that the inside is still red. [from an old word *rear* meaning 'half-cooked']

rarebit *noun* a dish of melted cheese on toast.

rare earth *noun* (*Chemistry*) any of a group of metallic elements with similar chemical properties.

rarefied (rair-i-fiyd) *adjective* **1** (said about air) of lower pressure than usual; thin. **2** very high in rank ♦ *These days he moves in rarefied social circles.* **3** (said about an idea etc.) remote from everyday life ♦ *the rarefied atmosphere of the university.* SYNONYMS: esoteric, abstruse. [from a Latin word *rarefacere* meaning 'to grow thin, become rare']

rare gas *noun* another term for **noble gas**.

raring (rair-ing) *adjective* (*informal*) very eager to do something ♦ *We're all raring to go.* [from *rare*, a dialect variation of *rear* [2]]

rarity (rair-iti) *noun* (**rarities**) **1** rareness. **2** something uncommon; a thing valued because it is rare.

rascal *noun* a mischievous or cheeky person. **rascally** *adjective* [from an Old French word *rascaille* meaning 'rabble']

rash [1] *noun* **1** an outbreak of spots or patches on a person's skin. **2** a number of unwelcome events happening in a short time ♦ *a rash of accidents.* [probably from an Old French word]

rash [2] *adjective* acting or done without careful consideration of the possible effects or risks. SYNONYMS: reckless, impetuous, foolhardy, impulsive, incautious. **rashly** *adverb* **rashness** *noun* [probably from an Old English word]

rasher *noun* a slice of bacon. [origin unknown]

rasp *noun* **1** a coarse file with raised sharp points on its surface. **2** a rough grating sound. **rasp** *verb* **1** to scrape or rub something roughly, especially with a rasp. **2** to make a rough grating sound ♦ *a rasping voice.* **3** to say something gratingly ♦ *He rasped out orders.* [via Old French from a Germanic word]

raspberry *noun* (**raspberries**) **1** an edible sweet red conical berry. **2** the bramble that bears this berry. **3** (*informal*) a rude sound made with the tongue and lips to express disapproval or contempt. [origin unknown]

Rasta *noun* (*informal*) a Rastafarian.

Rastafarian (ras-tə-fair-iən) *noun* a member of a religious group that originated in Jamaica. They regard blacks as a people chosen for salvation and revere Haile Selassie, the former emperor of Ethiopia, as God. **Rastafarian** *adjective* to do with Rastafarians. [from *Ras Tafari* (*ras* meaning 'chief'), the name by which Haile Selassie was known]

rat *noun* **1** a rodent resembling a mouse but larger. **2** (*informal*) a treacherous or despicable person. **rat** *verb* (**ratted, ratting**) to hunt or kill rats. **to rat on someone** (*informal*) to betray, desert, or inform on someone. **to rat on something** (*informal*) to break an agreement or promise. [from an Old English word]

ratafia (rat-ə-fee-ə) *noun* **1** a liqueur flavoured with almonds or fruit kernels. **2** a small biscuit flavoured with almonds. [from a French word]

ratatouille (rat-ə-too-i) *noun* a vegetable dish consisting of onions, courgettes, tomatoes, and peppers, stewed in oil. [a French dialect word]

ratchet (rach-it) *noun* **1** a series of notches on a bar or wheel in which a device (called a *pawl*) catches to allow movement in one direction only. **2** the bar or wheel bearing these. **ratchet** *verb* (**ratcheted, ratcheting**) to work something using a ratchet. **to ratchet something up** or **down** to make something increase or decrease to a higher or lower level or stage. [from a French word *rochet*]

rate *noun* **1** a measure obtained by expressing the quantity or amount of one thing with respect to another ♦ *Assume we are walking at a rate of four miles per hour* ♦ *a high pass rate.* **2** a fixed charge, cost, or value ♦ *Postal rates have gone up* ♦ *a rate of pay.* **3** speed of movement or change ♦ *He drove at a great rate* ♦ *Our rate of progress has been good.* SYNONYMS: speed, pace, tempo, velocity. **rates** *plural noun* a local tax assessed on the value of commercial land and buildings and formerly also levied on private property. **rate** *verb* **1** to estimate the worth or value of a person or thing; to give a value or rank to a person or thing ♦ *She is highly rated as a musician* ♦ *He is rated the third best player in the world.* SYNONYMS: evaluate, assess, appraise, gauge, judge, rank. **2** to regard someone or something in a certain way ♦ *We rate him among our closest friends.* **3** to rank or be regarded in a certain way ♦ *Today's game rates as one of the team's worst performances of the season.* **4** to deserve or be worthy of something ♦ *That joke didn't even rate a smile.* **5** (*informal*) to have a high opinion of someone or something. **6** to value property for the purpose of assessing rates. **at any rate** no matter what happens; at least. **at this** or **that rate** (*informal*) if things continue in this or that way. [from a Latin word *ratum* meaning 'reckoned']

rateable *adjective* liable to payment of rates.

rateable value *noun* the value at which a commercial property is assessed for rates.

ratepayer *noun* a person liable to pay rates.

rather *adverb* **1** slightly or somewhat ♦ *It's rather dark.* **2** preferably, sooner ♦ *I would rather have tea than coffee.* **3** more accurately ♦ *I crashed my car, or rather my mother's car.* **4** instead of; as opposed to ♦ *Why don't you help, rather than get in my way?* ♦ *He is lazy rather than incompetent.* **5** on the contrary ♦ *The concert wasn't the disaster I expected. Rather, it was quite a success.* **6** (*informal, old use*) yes indeed ♦ *'Do you like it? ' 'Rather!'* [from an Old English word *hrathor* meaning 'earlier, sooner']

ratify *verb* (**ratifies, ratified, ratifying**) to give formal consent to something or make something officially valid ♦ *The council voted to ratify the treaty.* **ratification** *noun* [from a Latin word *ratus* meaning 'fixed or established']

rating *noun* **1** a classification assigned to a person or thing based on quality, standard, etc. **2** the amount payable as local rates. **3** a sailor who is not an officer. **ratings** *plural noun* the estimated audience size of a particular television or radio programme. [from *rate*]

ratio (ray-shi-oh) *noun* (**ratios**) the relationship between two amounts expressed as the number of times one contains the other. [from a Latin word meaning 'reckoning']

ratiocinate (rat-i-**oss**-in-ayt) *verb* (*formal*) to reason using logic. **ratiocination** *noun* [from a Latin word *ratiocinari* meaning 'to deliberate or calculate']

ration *noun* a fixed quantity of something, especially food, allowed to one person. **rations** *plural noun* a fixed daily amount of food supplied to a soldier etc.
ration *verb* **1** to limit the supply of food etc. to a fixed ration. **2** to allow someone only a certain amount of something. [same origin as for *ratio*]

rational *adjective* **1** capable of reasoning or thinking sensibly. **2** based on reason or logic ♦ *a rational explanation.* **3** (*Mathematics*) denoting numbers or a quantity that can be exactly expressed as a fraction. **rationality** (rash-ən-**al**-iti) *noun* **rationally** *adverb* [same origin as for *ratio*]

rationale (rash-ən-**ahl**) *noun* a fundamental reason, the logical basis of something. [same origin as for *ratio*]

rationalism *noun* basing opinions and actions on reason rather than on religious belief or emotions. **rationalist** *noun*

rationalize *verb* **1** to try to justify something with a rational explanation ♦ *I think you are just rationalizing your fears.* **2** to make something logical and consistent ♦ *Attempts to rationalize English spelling have failed.* **3** to make a company or industry more efficient by getting rid of any staff, equipment, processes, etc. that are not needed. **rationalization** *noun*

rat race *noun* (*informal*) a fiercely competitive struggle to maintain your position in work or life.

rattle *verb* **1** to make or cause something to make a rapid series of short sharp hard sounds; to make such sounds by shaking something. **2** to move or travel with a rattling noise ♦ *Trains rattled past.* **3** (*informal*) to make someone feel nervous, flustered, or irritated.
rattle *noun* **1** a rattling sound. **2** a device or baby's toy for making a rattling sound. **3** a gurgling sound in the throat. **to rattle something off** to say or recite something rapidly ♦ *He rattled off a few prayers.* [an imitation of the sound]

rattlesnake *noun* a poisonous American snake with a rattling structure in its tail.

ratty *adjective* (**rattier, rattiest**) (*informal*) bad-tempered and irritable. **rattily** *adverb* **rattiness** *noun* [from *rat*]

raucous (raw-kəs) *adjective* loud and harsh-sounding. **raucously** *adverb* **raucousness** *noun* [from a Latin word *raucus* meaning 'hoarse']

raunchy *adjective* (**raunchier, raunchiest**) (*informal*) earthy and sexually explicit ♦ *a raunchy novel.* [origin unknown]

ravage *verb* to do great damage to something, to devastate something. **ravages** *plural noun* damaging effects ♦ *the ravages of war.* [same origin as for *ravine*]

rave *verb* 1 to talk wildly or incoherently. 2 to speak with great enthusiasm or admiration about something. **rave** *noun* (*informal*) 1 a very enthusiastic review. 2 a large party or event with dancing to loud fast electronic music. 3 a person or thing that is popular or inspires enthusiasm. [from an Old French word]

ravel *verb* (**ravelled, ravelling**) to untangle something or separate it into threads. **ravel** *noun* a tangle. [probably from a Dutch word *ravelen* meaning 'to fray out, tangle']

raven *noun* a large bird with glossy black feathers and a hoarse cry. **raven** *adjective* (said about hair etc.) glossy black. [from an Old English word]

ravening (rav-ən-ing) *adjective* hungrily seeking prey ♦ *a ravening beast.*

ravenous (rav-ən-əs) *adjective* very hungry. **ravenously** *adverb* [from a French word *raviner* meaning 'to rush, ravage']

rave-up *noun* (*informal*) a lively party.

ravine (rə-veen) *noun* a deep narrow gorge with steep sides. [from a French word meaning 'a rush of water' (because a ravine is cut by rushing water)]

raving *adjective & adverb* (*informal*) 1 completely mad. 2 complete, absolute ♦ *a raving beauty.* **ravings** *plural noun* wild or incoherent talk.

ravioli (rav-i-oh-li) *noun* an Italian dish consisting of small pasta cases containing meat. [an Italian word]

ravish *verb* (*old use*) 1 to rape someone. 2 to fill someone with delight, to enrapture someone. **ravishment** *noun* [from an Old French word *ravir*; related to *rape*[1]]

ravishing *adjective* very beautiful.

raw *adjective* 1 not cooked. 2 in its natural state, not processed or treated ♦ *raw hides.* 3 (said about data) not organized or analysed. 4 inexperienced, fresh to something ♦ *raw recruits.* 5 stripped of skin and with the underlying flesh exposed ♦ *a raw wound.* 6 (said about the nerves) very sensitive. 7 (said about an emotion or quality) strong and apparent. 8 (said about weather) damp and chilly ♦ *a raw morning.* 9 crude in artistic quality, lacking finish. 10 (said about an edge of cloth) not having a hem or selvedge. **in the raw** 1 in its true state, without a softening or refining influence ♦ *nature in the raw.* 2 (*informal*) naked. **a raw deal** unfair treatment. **rawness** *noun* [from an Old English word]

raw-boned *adjective* gaunt and bony.

rawhide *noun* untanned leather.

raw material *noun* the basic material from which a product is made.

ray[1] *noun* 1 a single line or narrow beam of light or other radiation. SYNONYMS: beam, shaft, streak. 2 a ray of something good ♦ *a ray of hope.* 3 each of a set of lines or parts extending from a centre. [from a Latin word *radius* meaning 'ray']

ray[2] *noun* any of several large sea fish with a flattened body and a long tail, related to the shark. [from a Latin word *raia*]

rayon *noun* a synthetic fibre or fabric made from cellulose. [a made-up word, probably based on a French word *rayon* meaning 'a ray of light' (because of its shiny surface)]

raze *verb* to destroy a building or town completely, to tear something down to the ground. [from a Latin word *rasum* meaning 'scraped']

razor *noun* an instrument with a sharp blade or cutters, used to shave hair from the face or body. [from *raze*]

razor blade *noun* a thin flat piece of metal with sharp edges used in a razor.

razor wire *noun* wire set with small sharp pieces of metal, used as fencing.

razzle *noun* **on the razzle** (*informal*) out celebrating or enjoying yourself. [from *razzle-dazzle*]

razzle-dazzle *noun* another term for **razzmatazz**. [from *dazzle*]

razzmatazz or **razzamatazz** *noun* (*informal*) showy publicity or display. [probably from *razzle-dazzle*]

RC *abbreviation* Roman Catholic.

Rd *abbreviation* (used in street names) Road.

RDS *abbreviation* radio data system.

RE *abbreviation* religious education.

re (ree) *preposition* in the matter of, about, concerning. [from a Latin word *res* meaning 'thing']

re- *prefix* 1 again (as in *redecorate, revisit*). 2 back again, with return to a previous state (as in *re-enter, reopen*). [a Latin word]

reach *verb* 1 to arrive at or go as far as a place or thing. 2 to stretch out your hand or arm in order to touch, grasp, or take something ♦ *He reached for his gun* ♦ *Can you reach the ceiling?* ♦ *Can you reach down that pan for me?* 3 to stretch out or extend to a place or point ♦ *The carpet does not quite reach to the door.* 4 to make contact with someone ♦ *You can reach me on this number.* 5 to achieve or attain something ♦ *The cheetah can reach a speed of 70 m.p.h* ♦ *The committee has yet to reach a conclusion.* 6 to sail with the wind blowing from the side.
reach *noun* 1 an act of reaching. 2 the distance a person or thing can reach. 3 a distance you can easily travel ♦ *We live within reach of the sea.* 4 the extent or range of a thing's effect or influence. 5 a continuous stretch of a river between two bends or of a canal between two locks.
reachable *adjective* [from an Old English word]

react *verb* 1 to act in response to something. 2 to undergo a chemical change. **to react against** to respond in a hostile or opposing way to something. [from re- and a Latin word *agere* meaning 'to act or do']

reactant *noun* (*Chemistry*) a substance that takes part in and undergoes change during a reaction.

reaction *noun* 1 what someone feels, does, etc. as a result of something that happens ♦ *My immediate reaction was one of shock.* 2 a response by the body to a drug or other substance ♦ *an allergic reaction.* 3 a chemical change produced by two or more substances acting upon each other. 4 (*Physics*) a force exerted by a body in response to another force applied to it, which is equal in strength and acts in the opposite direction. 5 a change from one condition to its opposite after a period of time, e.g. to depression after excitement. **reactions** *plural noun* a person's ability to respond physically and mentally to a stimulus.

reactionary *adjective* opposed to progress or reform.
reactionary *noun* (**reactionaries**) a person who holds reactionary views.

reactivate *verb* to restore something to a state of activity. **reactivation** *noun*

reactor *noun* or **nuclear reactor** an apparatus for the controlled production of nuclear energy.

read (reed) *verb* (past tense and past participle **read** (red)) 1 to be able to understand the meaning of something written or printed. 2 to speak written or printed words etc. aloud ♦ *She reads to the children every night* ♦ *Read me a story.* 3 to learn about something by reading ♦ *We read about the accident.* 4 to spend time reading books ♦ *Do you read much?* 5 to carry out a course of study ♦ *She is reading Chemistry at Oxford.* 6 to have a certain wording ♦ *The sign reads 'Keep Left'.* 7 (said about a computer) to copy, search, or transfer data; to enter or extract data in an electronic storage device. 8 (said about a measuring instrument) to indicate or register a value ♦ *The thermometer reads 20° Celsius.* 9 to interpret something, especially by looking at it ♦ *Do you know how to read a map?* 10 to inspect and record the value on a measuring instrument ♦ *I've come to read your gas meter.*
read *noun* 1 a time spent reading ♦ *I've been having a nice quiet read.* 2 a book thought of in terms of how readable it is ♦ *Her latest novel is an exciting read.* **to read between the lines** to discover a hidden or implicit meaning in something. **to read something into** to find implications in something ♦ *Don't read too much into it.* **to read someone's mind** or **thoughts** to tell what someone is thinking. **to read up on** to find out about a subject by reading. [from an Old English word]

readable *adjective* 1 pleasant and interesting to read. 2 legible. **readability** *noun*

readdress *verb* to change the address on a letter etc.

reader *noun* 1 a person who reads. 2 a book containing passages for practice in reading by students of a language ♦ *a Latin reader.* 3 a machine which produces an image on a screen from a microfiche or microfilm.

readership *noun* the readers of a newspaper or magazine; the number of these.

readily *adverb* 1 without reluctance, willingly. 2 without any difficulty.

readiness *noun* being ready.

reading *noun* 1 the ability or activity of reading. 2 the act of being read aloud ♦ *a reading of a will.* 3 books etc. intended to be read. 4 the way in which something is read or interpreted ♦ *What's your reading of the situation?* 5 a gathering of people at which something is read aloud ♦ *a poetry reading.* 6 the value that is indicated or registered by a measuring instrument. 7 a stage of debate in parliament that a bill must pass through before it can become law.

reading age *noun* a person's reading ability measured by comparing it with the average ability of children of a particular age.

reading room *noun* a room in a library, club, etc. set aside for people who want to read.

readjust *verb* 1 to adjust something again. 2 to adapt yourself to a new situation or environment. **readjustment** *noun*

read-only memory *noun* (*Computing*) a storage device whose contents can be copied, searched, or transferred but not changed by program instructions.

ready *adjective* (**readier, readiest**) 1 fully prepared to do something ♦ *Are you ready to go?* 2 completed and available to be used ♦ *The meal's ready.* 3 willing to do something ♦ *She's always ready to help a friend.* SYNONYMS: eager, keen, pleased, inclined, disposed. 4 about or likely to do something ♦ *The woman looked ready to collapse.* 5 quick or prompt ♦ *a ready wit.* 6 easily available ♦ *Keep your tickets ready to hand* ♦ *He found a ready market for his paintings.* SYNONYMS: handy, at hand, accessible.
ready *adverb* beforehand ♦ *This meat is ready cooked.*
readies *plural noun* (*informal*) available money; cash.
ready *verb* (**readies, readied, readying**) to make something ready. **at the ready** ready for immediate use or action. **to make ready** to prepare for something. [from an Old English word]

ready-made *adjective* 1 (said about clothes) made for selling in standard shapes and sizes, not to individual customers' orders. 2 (said about food) sold ready to be served, sometimes after being heated up. 3 (said about opinions or excuses etc.) of a standard type, not original.

ready money *noun* money in the form of cash that is immediately available.

ready reckoner *noun* a book of tables for working out calculations needed in business etc.

reagent (ree-ay-jənt) *noun* a substance used to produce a chemical reaction, especially to detect another substance. [from *re-* and *agent*]

real *adjective* 1 actually existing, not imaginary. 2 actual or true ♦ *That's not the real reason.* 3 genuine, not imitation ♦ *real pearls.* SYNONYMS: genuine, authentic, actual. 4 proper, worthy of the name ♦ *She's been a real friend to me.* 5 (said about food or drink) regarded as superior because it is produced by traditional methods ♦ *real ale.* 6 (said about income or value etc.) measured with regard to its purchasing power ♦ *in real terms.* 7 consisting of immovable property such as land or houses ♦ *real property* ♦ *real estate.*
real *adverb* (*North Amer.*) (*informal*) really, very. **for real** in earnest, seriously. [from a Latin word *res* meaning 'thing']

real estate *noun* (*North Amer.*) property consisting of land and buildings.

realign *verb* 1 to change something to a different or former position. 2 to change your position or attitude with regard to something. **realignment** *noun*

realism *noun* 1 accepting a situation as it really is; the attitude of a realist. 2 (in art and literature) representing things in a way that is accurate and true to life.

realist *noun* a person who faces facts and accepts a situation as it really is.

realistic *adjective* 1 representing things in a way that is accurate and true to life. SYNONYMS: lifelike, true-to-life, convincing, faithful. 2 facing facts, having a sensible and practical idea of what can be achieved or expected. 3 (said about wages or prices) high enough to pay the worker or seller adequately. **realistically** *adverb*

reality *noun* (**realities**) 1 all that is real; the state of things as they actually exist as distinct from imagination or fantasy ♦ *You must face reality* ♦ *He seems to have lost his grip on reality.* 2 something that exists or that is real ♦ *Her worst fears had* become a reality ♦ *the realities of the situation.* **3** the quality of being lifelike; resemblance to an original. **4** the state or quality of having existence.

realize *verb* **1** to be fully aware of something, to accept something as a fact ♦ *Almost at once he realized his mistake.* SYNONYMS: appreciate, recognize, see, understand; (*informal*) twig, cotton on, catch on. **2** to achieve something or make it happen ♦ *She realized her ambition to become an astronomer.* SYNONYMS: fulfil, effect, accomplish. **3** to convert a security or property into money by selling it. **4** to be sold for a particular amount or bring an amount in as profit. **realization** *noun* [from *real* and *-ize*]

really *adverb* **1** truly or in fact. **2** very, indeed ♦ *a really nice girl.* **3** an expression of interest, surprise, doubt, or protest.

realm (relm) *noun* **1** a kingdom ♦ *peers of the realm.* **2** a field of knowledge, activity, or interest ♦ *the realms of science.* [from an Old French word *reaume*; related to *regiment*]

real tennis *noun* see **tennis**.

real-time *adjective* (said about a computer system) able to receive continually changing data from outside sources, process these data rapidly, and supply results that can influence their sources ♦ *real-time processing.*

ream *noun* a quantity of paper (about 500 sheets) of the same size. **reams** *plural noun* a great quantity of written matter. [via French from an Arabic word *rizma* meaning 'bundle']

reap *verb* **1** to cut or gather a crop or harvest. **2** to receive something as the result of something done ♦ *reap a reward.* **reaper** *noun* [from an Old English word *ripan*]

reappear *verb* to appear again. **reappearance** *noun*

reappraise *verb* to think about or examine something again. **reappraisal** (ree-ə-**pray**-zəl) *noun* [from *re-* and *appraise*]

rear [1] *noun* the back part of something. **rear** *adjective* situated at the back. **to bring up the rear** to come last in a line or race. [from a Latin word *retro-* meaning 'back']

rear [2] *verb* **1** to bring up and educate children. **2** (said about an animal) to care for its young until fully grown. **3** to breed

and look after animals; to cultivate crops. **4** (said about a horse etc.) to raise itself upright on its hind legs. **5** to build or set up a monument etc. **6** (said about a structure) to extend to a great height. [from an Old English word]

rear admiral *noun* a rank of naval officer, above commodore.

rearguard *noun* a body of troops whose job is to protect the rear of the main force, especially when it is retreating. **to fight a rearguard action** to go on defending or resisting something even though it is likely you will lose. [from an Old French word *rereguarde*]

rear light or **rear lamp** *noun* a light on the back of a vehicle.

rearm *verb* to get or supply someone with a new supply of weapons. **rearmament** *noun*

rearmost *adjective* furthest back.

rearrange *verb* to arrange something in a different way or order. **rearrangement** *noun*

rearward *adjective* & *adverb* towards the back. **rearwards** *adverb*

reason *noun* **1** a cause, explanation, or justification of something. SYNONYMS: cause, motive, grounds, pretext, occasion. **2** the ability to think, understand, and draw conclusions. **3** a person's sanity ♦ *Later in the play Lear loses his reason.* **4** good sense or judgement; common sense ♦ *She won't listen to reason.* **reason** *verb* **1** to use your ability to think, understand, and draw conclusions. **2** to try to persuade someone by giving reasons ♦ *We tried reasoning with the protestors.* [from an Old French word *reisun*; related to *ratio*]
◊ The phrase *the reason is* should not be followed by *because* (which means the same thing). Correct usage is *We are unable to come; the reason is that we both have flu* (not 'the reason is because we both have flu').

reasonable *adjective* **1** fair and sensible ♦ *a reasonable person.* **2** in accordance with reason, not absurd ♦ *a reasonable argument.* SYNONYMS: plausible, sound, tenable. **3** not too expensive ♦ *reasonable prices.* **4** acceptable or fairly good ♦ *a reasonable standard of living.* **reasonableness** *noun* **reasonably** *adverb*

reassemble *verb* to assemble again; to put something back together.

reassure (ree-ə-**shoor**) *verb* to restore someone's confidence by removing fears and doubts. **reassurance** *noun*

rebate [1] (**ree**-bayt) *noun* a reduction in the amount to be paid, a partial refund. [from *re-* and a French word *abattre* meaning 'to abate']

rebate [2] *noun* a step-shaped channel cut along the edge of a piece of wood etc. to receive another piece or the glass of a window etc.
rebate *verb* **1** to cut a rebate in something. **2** to join or fix something with a rebate. [from an earlier spelling *rabbet*, from an Old French word *rabbat* meaning 'recess']

rebel [1] (**reb**-əl) *noun* a person who rebels, especially against the government or against accepted standards of behaviour.

rebel [2] (ri-**bel**) *verb* (**rebelled, rebelling**) **1** to resist an established government or ruler; to take up arms against it. **2** to resist authority, control, or convention. SYNONYMS: disobey, dissent, mutiny, revolt. [from *re-* and a Latin word *bellare* meaning 'to fight', originally referring to a defeated enemy who began to fight again]

rebellion *noun* open resistance to authority, especially organized armed resistance to an established government. SYNONYMS: uprising, rising, revolt, revolution, insurrection, mutiny.

rebellious *adjective* rebelling, not easily controlled ♦ *a rebellious child.* **rebelliously** *adverb* **rebelliousness** *noun*

rebirth *noun* a return to life or activity, a revival.

reboot *verb* to boot a computer system again.

rebound [1] (ri-**bownd**) *verb* **1** to bounce back after hitting something. **2** to have an unexpected adverse effect on the person doing something. [from *re-* and an Old French word *bondir* meaning 'to bounce up']

rebound [2] (**ree**-bownd) *noun* an act or instance of rebounding. **on the rebound** **1** (said about a hit or catch) made to a ball that is bouncing back. **2** while still upset after the ending of a romantic relationship.

rebuff *noun* an unkind or contemptuous refusal. SYNONYMS: snub, slight; (*informal*) brush-off.

rebuff *verb* to give someone a rebuff. [from *re-* and an Italian word *buffo* meaning 'a gust']

rebuild *verb* (past tense and past participle **rebuilt**) **1** to build something again after it has been destroyed. **2** to restore something ♦ *She needs to rebuild her confidence.*

rebuke *verb* to speak severely to someone who has done something wrong.
rebuke *noun* a sharp or severe criticism. [originally meaning 'to force back': from *re-* and an Old French word *buker* meaning 'to hit']

rebus (**ree**-bəs) *noun* (**rebuses**) a puzzle in which a name or word is represented by means of a picture or pictures suggesting its syllables. [from a Latin word *res* meaning 'thing']

rebut (ri-**but**) *verb* (**rebutted, rebutting**) to claim or prove that a criticism or accusation is not true. **rebuttal** *noun* [from *re-* and *butt* [4]]

recalcitrant (ri-**kal**-si-trənt) *adjective* disobedient, resisting authority or discipline. **recalcitrance** *noun* [from a Latin word *recalcitrare* meaning 'to kick back']

recall *verb* **1** to remember or cause someone to remember something. **2** to ask or order a person to return. **3** to ask for something to be returned.
recall *noun* **1** the ability to remember; remembering. **2** an order to return. [from *re-* and *call*]

recant (ri-**kant**) *verb* to state formally and publicly that you no longer hold an opinion or belief that you used to hold, rejecting it as wrong or heretical. **recantation** *noun* [from *re-* and a Latin word *cantare* meaning 'to sing']

recap (**ree**-kap) *verb* (**recapped, recapping**) (*informal*) to recapitulate.
recap *noun* (*informal*) a recapitulation.

recapitulate (ree-kə-**pit**-yoo-layt) *verb* to state again the main points of what has been said or discussed. **recapitulation** *noun* [from *re-* and a Latin word *capitulum* meaning 'chapter']

recapture *verb* **1** to capture a person or animal that has escaped or something that has been lost to an enemy. **2** to succeed in experiencing a former state, mood, or emotion again.
recapture *noun* recapturing.

recast verb (past tense and past participle **recast**) to cast something again, to put something into a different form.

recce (rek-i) noun (informal) a reconnaissance.

recede verb 1 to move back or further away ♦ The floods receded ♦ The shore receded as we sailed away. 2 (said about a man's hair) to stop growing at the temples and above the forehead. 3 to slope backwards ♦ a receding forehead. [from re- and a Latin word cedere meaning 'to go']

receipt (ri-seet) noun 1 a written statement that money has been paid or something has been received. 2 receiving, or being received ♦ on receipt of your letter.
receipts plural noun the total amount of money received over a period by an organization. [via Old French from a Latin word recepta meaning 'received']

receive verb 1 to get, accept, or take something offered, sent, or given. 2 to be awarded something ♦ She received the OBE in 1998. 3 to experience or be treated with something ♦ One man received injuries to his face and hands. SYNONYMS: meet with, sustain, undergo, suffer. 4 to react to something in a particular way ♦ How did he receive the news? 5 to pick up broadcast signals. 6 to support or take the weight of something. 7 to serve as a receptacle for something. 8 to allow someone to enter as a member or guest. 9 to greet someone on arrival. 10 to buy or accept stolen goods while knowing them to be stolen. [from re- meaning 'back again' and a Latin word capere meaning 'to take']

received pronunciation noun the standard form of British English pronunciation, based on educated speech in southern England.

receiver noun 1 a person or thing that receives something. 2 a radio or television set that receives broadcast signals and converts them into sound or a picture. 3 the part of a telephone that receives the incoming sound and is held to the ear. 4 (also **official receiver**) an official who takes charge of the financial affairs of a bankrupt business. 5 a person who buys or accepts stolen goods while knowing them to be stolen.

receivership noun the state of being managed by an official receiver.

recent adjective not long ago, happening or begun in a time shortly before the present. **recency** noun **recently** adverb [from a Latin word recens]

receptacle noun something for holding or containing what is put into it. [same origin as for receive]

reception noun 1 receiving, or being received. 2 the way a person or thing is received ♦ The speech got a cool reception. 3 a formal party or gathering held to welcome someone or celebrate an event ♦ a wedding reception. 4 a place in a hotel, office, etc. where visitors are greeted. 5 the first class in an infant school. 6 the quality with which broadcast signals are received ♦ Reception on our TV is poor. [same origin as for receive]

receptionist noun a person employed to greet and deal with visitors, clients, patients, etc.

reception room noun 1 a living room in a house or flat as distinct from a bedroom, kitchen, etc. 2 a room in a hotel suitable for receptions or other functions.

receptive adjective able or willing to receive knowledge, ideas, or suggestions etc. **receptiveness** noun **receptivity** noun

receptor noun an organ of the body that is able to respond to a stimulus, such as light or pressure, and transmit a signal through a sensory nerve.

recess (ri-sess or ree-sess) noun 1 a part or space set back from the line of a wall etc.; a small hollow place inside something. 2 a time when work or business is stopped for a while ♦ while parliament is in recess.
recesses plural noun secluded or secret places.
recess verb to set something back into a wall or surface. [same origin as for recede]

recession noun 1 a temporary decline in economic activity or prosperity. 2 receding from a point or level.

recessive adjective 1 tending to recede. 2 (said about inherited characteristics) remaining latent when a dominant characteristic is present.

recharge verb to charge a battery or gun etc. again. **rechargeable** adjective

recherché (rǝ-shair-shay) adjective rare, exotic, or obscure. [a French word meaning 'carefully sought out']

recidivist (ri-**sid**-i-vist) *noun* a person who constantly commits crimes and seems unable to be cured of criminal tendencies. **recidivism** *noun* [from *re-* and a Latin word *cadere* meaning 'to fall']

recipe *noun* 1 instructions for preparing or cooking a dish. 2 a course of action likely to lead to something ♦ *a recipe for disaster.* [a Latin word meaning 'take' (used at the beginning of a list of ingredients)]

recipient (ri-**sip**-iənt) *noun* a person who receives something.

reciprocal (ri-**sip**-rə-kəl) *adjective* 1 given or felt by each towards the other, mutual ♦ *reciprocal affection.* 2 given or done in return ♦ *a reciprocal favour.* 3 (*Grammar*) (said about a pronoun or verb) expressing mutual relationship or action. **reciprocal** *noun* (*Mathematics*) the quantity obtained by dividing the number 1 by a given quantity. The reciprocal of 5 is ⅕. **reciprocally** *adverb* [from a Latin word *reciprocus* meaning 'moving backwards and forwards']

reciprocate (ri-**sip**-rə-kayt) *verb* 1 to return a feeling, gesture, etc. to someone who gives it to you; to do the same thing in return ♦ *She did not reciprocate his love.* 2 (said about a machine part) to move backwards and forwards alternately. **reciprocation** *noun* [same origin as for *reciprocal*]

reciprocity (ress-i-**pross**-iti) *noun* 1 a reciprocal condition or action. 2 the giving of privileges in return for similar privileges.

recital *noun* 1 a musical performance given by a soloist or small group. 2 reciting. 3 a long account of a series of events.

recitation *noun* 1 reciting. 2 a thing recited.

recitative (ress-i-tə-**teev**) *noun* a narrative or conversational part of an opera or oratorio, sung in a rhythm imitating that of ordinary speech. [from an Italian word *recitativo* meaning 'something recited']

recite *verb* 1 to repeat a passage aloud from memory, especially before an audience. 2 to state facts in order. [from a Latin word *recitare* meaning 'to read aloud']

reckless *adjective* ignoring risk or danger. SYNONYMS: rash, daredevil, foolhardy, irresponsible, incautious. **recklessly** *adverb* **recklessness** *noun* [from an old word *reck* meaning 'heed' and *-less* meaning 'without']

reckon *verb* 1 to calculate or count up something ♦ *Let's just reckon up the cost.* 2 to regard something in a particular way ♦ *She is generally reckoned an expert on the subject.* 3 to include something in a total or as a member of a particular class. 4 (*informal*) to have something as your opinion ♦ *I reckon we shall win.* 5 to rely or base your plans on something ♦ *We reckoned on your support.* **to reckon with** to take something into account ♦ *We didn't reckon with the train strike when we planned the journey.* **to be reckoned with** that must not be underestimated ♦ *She is clearly a woman to be reckoned with.* [from an Old English word]

reckoning *noun* 1 an opinion or judgement. 2 the working out of consequences or punishment for your actions ♦ *a terrible reckoning.* **day of reckoning** the time when you must atone for your actions or be punished. **into** or **out of the reckoning** into or out of contention for selection, victory, etc.

reclaim *verb* 1 to take action in order to get something back. 2 to make flooded or waste land able to be used again, e.g. by draining or irrigating it. 3 to recycle something. **reclamation** (rek-lə-**may**-shən) *noun* [from *re-* and a Latin word *clamare* meaning 'to shout']

recline *verb* 1 to lean or lie back. 2 (said about a seat) to have a back which can move into a sloping position. [from *re-* and a Latin word *clinare* meaning 'to bend']

recluse (ri-**klooss**) *noun* a person who lives alone and avoids mixing with people. **reclusive** *adjective* **reclusiveness** *noun* [from *re-* meaning 'away' and a Latin word *clausum* meaning 'shut']

recognition *noun* recognizing, or being recognized ♦ *a presentation in recognition of his services.*

recognizance (ri-**kog**-ni-zəns) *noun* (*Law*) a pledge made to a court or magistrate that a person will observe some condition, e.g. to appear when summoned. [from an Old French word *reconnaistre* meaning 'to recognize']

recognize *verb* 1 to know who someone is or what something is because you have seen that person or thing before. SYNONYMS: know, identify, place, spot, discern. 2 (said about a computer etc.) to identify and respond correctly to a command, character, etc. 3 to realize or admit the

nature of something ♦ *She recognized the hopelessness of the situation.* SYNONYMS: accept, acknowledge, appreciate, understand, concede. **4** to acknowledge or accept something formally as genuine, valid, or lawful ♦ *France has recognized the island's new government.* **5** to show appreciation of ability or service etc. by giving an honour or reward. **6** (said about someone chairing a meeting or debate) to allow a particular person the right to speak next.
recognizable *adjective* **recognizably** *adverb* [from *re-* and a Latin word *cognoscere* meaning 'to know']

recoil *verb* **1** to draw yourself back in fear or disgust. **2** to have a feeling like this at the thought of something. **3** (said about a gun) to jerk backwards when it is fired. **4** (said about an action) to have an adverse effect on the person who did it ♦ *His scheme appears to have recoiled on him.*
recoil *noun* the act or sensation of recoiling. [from an Old French word *reculer* meaning 'to move back']

recollect *verb* to remember something.
recollection *noun* [from *re-* and a Latin word *colligere* meaning 'to collect']

recommence (ree-kə-menss) *verb* to begin or make something begin again.
recommencement *noun*

recommend *verb* **1** to praise someone or something as suitable for something. **2** to advise a course of action. **3** (said about qualities or conduct) to make something acceptable or desirable ♦ *This plan has much to recommend it.* **recommendation** *noun* [from *re-* and a Latin word *commendare* meaning 'to commend']

recompense (rek-əm-penss) *verb* **1** to repay or reward someone. **2** to compensate someone for a loss or injury.
recompense *noun* compensation or reward for something. [from *re-* and a Latin word *compensare* meaning 'to compensate']

reconcile (rek-ən-siyl) *verb* **1** to make people who have quarrelled become friendly again. **2** to get someone to accept an unwelcome fact or situation ♦ *It took him a while to reconcile himself to wearing glasses.* **3** to make facts or statements etc. compatible ♦ *I cannot reconcile what you say with what you do.* **reconcilable** *adjective*
reconciliation *noun* [from *re-* and a Latin word *conciliare* meaning 'to conciliate']

recondite (rek-ən-diyt) *adjective* (said about a subject) obscure. [from *re-* and a Latin word *conditum* meaning 'hidden']

recondition *verb* to overhaul and make any necessary repairs to something.

reconnaissance (ri-kon-i-səns) *noun* **1** an exploration or examination of an area in order to gather information about it, especially for military purposes. **2** a preliminary survey. [a French word meaning 'recognition']

reconnoitre (rek-ən-oi-ter) *verb* to make a reconnaissance of an area; to make a preliminary survey. [an Old French word meaning 'to recognize']

reconsider *verb* to consider something again and perhaps change your earlier decision. **reconsideration** *noun*

reconstitute *verb* **1** to form something again, especially in a different way. **2** to make dried food edible again by adding water. **reconstitution** *noun*

reconstruct *verb* **1** to construct or build something again. **2** to create or enact past events again, e.g. in investigating the circumstances of a crime. **reconstruction** *noun*

record[1] (rek-ord) *noun* **1** information kept in a permanent form, especially in writing. **2** (*Computing*) a number of related pieces of information dealt with as a unit. **3** a disc on which sound has been recorded; a piece of music recorded on a disc. **4** facts known about a person's past life, performance, or career ♦ *He has a superb record at Wimbledon.* **5** a criminal record. **6** the best performance or most remarkable event etc. of its kind that is known ♦ *She holds the world record for the 100 metres.*
record *adjective* best, highest, or most extreme recorded up to now ♦ *a record crop.* **for the record** so that the true facts are recorded or known. **off the record** stated unofficially or not for publication or broadcast. **on record** preserved in written records. **to put** or **set the record straight** to correct a mistaken belief. [from an Old French word *record* meaning 'remembrance']

record[2] (ri-kord) *verb* **1** to put something down in writing or other permanent form. SYNONYMS: log, note, enter, document, register, transcribe, take down. **2** to store sound or visual scenes, especially television pictures, on a disc or magnetic tape etc. so that they can be played or shown later. **3** (said about a measuring instrument) to show or register a figure.

record-breaking *adjective* surpassing all previous records. **record-breaker** *noun*

recorded delivery *noun* a postal delivery in which a signature is obtained from the recipient as proof of delivery.

recorder *noun* 1 a kind of flute held forward and downwards from the mouth as it is played. 2 a machine for recording sound, pictures, or data. 3 a person who keeps records. 4 a barrister appointed to serve as a part-time judge.

recording *noun* 1 a process by which audio or video signals are recorded for later reproduction. 2 the disc or tape etc. produced. 3 the recorded material.

recording angel *noun* an angel popularly supposed to register people's good and bad actions.

record player *noun* an apparatus for reproducing sound from discs on which it is recorded.

recount¹ (ri-kownt) *verb* to give an account of something ♦ *Breathlessly he recounted his adventures.* [from an Old French word *reconter* meaning 'to tell again']

recount² (ree-kownt) *verb* to count something again.
recount *noun* a second counting, especially of election votes to check the totals.

recoup (ri-koop) *verb* 1 to recover what you have lost or its equivalent ♦ *We expect to recoup our investment by the end of the year.* 2 to reimburse or compensate someone ♦ *They promised to recoup him for his losses.* [from a French word *recouper* meaning 'to cut back']

recourse (ri-korss) *noun* a source of help. **to have recourse to** to turn to a person or thing for help. [from an Old French word *recours*]

recover *verb* 1 to get something back again after losing it. SYNONYMS: retrieve, regain, restore. 2 to get well again after being ill or weak. SYNONYMS: get better, improve, recuperate, convalesce, rally. 3 to obtain something as compensation ♦ *We sought to recover damages from the company.* **to recover yourself** to regain calmness or your balance. **recoverable** *adjective* [from an Old French word *recoverer*; related to *recuperate*]

recovery *noun* (**recoveries**) 1 a return to a state of health or strength ♦ *Doctors expect him to make a speedy recovery.* 2 the act or

process of recovering something ♦ *a reward for the recovery of the jewels.*

recreate *verb* to create something again.

recreation (rek-ri-ay-shǝn) *noun* 1 the process of refreshing or entertaining yourself after work by some enjoyable activity. 2 a game or hobby etc. that is an enjoyable activity. **recreational** *adjective* [from *re-* and a Latin word *creatio* meaning 'creation']

recreation ground *noun* a piece of public land used for sports and games.

recriminate *verb* to make recriminations.

recrimination *noun* an accusation made against a person who has criticized or blamed you. [from *re-* and a Latin word *criminare* meaning 'to accuse']

recrudesce (rek-roo-dess) *verb* (*formal*) (said about a disease or sore or discontent) to break out again. **recrudescence** *noun* **recrudescent** *adjective* [from *re-* and a Latin word *crudescere* meaning 'to become raw']

recruit *noun* 1 a person who has just joined the armed forces and is not yet trained. 2 a new member or employee of a society, company, or other group.
recruit *verb* 1 to enlist someone in the armed forces. 2 to find new people to join a society, company, or other group. 3 to persuade someone to do or help with something. **recruitment** *noun* [from a French word *recroître* meaning 'to increase again']

rectal *adjective* to do with the rectum.

rectangle *noun* a four-sided geometric figure with four right angles, especially one with adjacent sides unequal in length. [from a Latin word *rectus* meaning 'straight or right' and *angle*]

rectangular *adjective* shaped like a rectangle.

rectifier *noun* a device that converts alternating current to direct current.

rectify *verb* (**rectifies, rectified, rectifying**) 1 to correct or put something right ♦ *We will rectify the error at once.* 2 to convert alternating current to direct current. **rectifiable** *adjective* **rectification** *noun* [from a Latin word *rectus* meaning 'right']

rectilinear (rek-ti-lin-i-er) *adjective* bounded by straight lines ♦ *a rectilinear figure.* [from a Latin word *rectus* meaning 'straight' and *linear*]

rectitude noun (formal) morally correct behaviour. [from a Latin word rectus meaning 'right']

recto noun (rectos) the right-hand page of an open book, or the front of a sheet of paper. [a Latin word meaning 'on the right'] (Compare verso.)

rector noun 1 a member of the clergy in charge of a parish; (in the Church of England) one formerly entitled to receive all the tithes of the parish. 2 the head of certain universities, colleges, schools, and religious institutions. 3 the students' elected representative on the governing body of a Scottish university. [a Latin word meaning 'ruler']

rectory noun (rectories) a rector's house.

rectum noun the last section of the large intestine, ending at the anus. [a Latin word meaning 'straight (intestine)']

recumbent adjective lying down, reclining. [from re- and a Latin word cumbens meaning 'lying']

recuperate (ri-koo-per-ayt) verb 1 to get better after an illness or exhaustion. 2 to recover losses. **recuperation** noun **recuperative** adjective [from a Latin word recuperare meaning 'to regain']

recur verb (recurred, recurring) 1 to happen again, to keep on happening. 2 (said about a thought) to come back to your mind. [from re- and a Latin word currere meaning 'to run']

recurrent (ri-ku-rənt) adjective happening often or repeatedly ♦ a recurrent problem. **recurrence** noun

recurring decimal noun a decimal fraction in a figure or group of figures that is repeated indefinitely, e.g. 0.666 ... .

recurve (ri-kerv) verb (Biology) to bend backwards or bend something backwards ♦ a flower with recurved petals.

recusant (rek-yoo-zənt) noun a person who refuses to submit to authority or to comply with a regulation. [from a Latin word recusare meaning 'to refuse']

recycle verb 1 to convert waste material into a form in which it can be reused. 2 to use something again. **recyclable** adjective

red adjective (redder, reddest) 1 of the colour of blood. 2 (said about hair or fur) of a reddish-brown colour. 3 (said about the face) flushed with embarrassment or anger. 4 (said about wine) made from dark

grapes and dark red in colour. 5 (informal) communist or socialist.
red noun 1 red colour. 2 a red substance or material; red clothes. 3 a red light. 4 (informal) a communist or socialist. **in the red** having spent more than is in your bank account, in debt. **to see red** (informal) to become very angry suddenly. **redly** adverb **redness** noun [from an Old English word]

red admiral noun a butterfly with dark wings with red bands and white spots.

red blood cell noun another term for **erythrocyte**.

red-blooded adjective (said about a man) vigorous or virile.

red-brick adjective (said about a British university) founded in the 19th century or later, as distinct from Oxford and Cambridge.

redcap noun (informal) a member of the military police.

red card noun a red card shown by the referee in a football match to a player being sent off the field.

red carpet noun 1 a long narrow red carpet for an important visitor to walk along. 2 privileged treatment given to an important visitor.

Red Crescent noun the equivalent of the Red Cross in Muslim countries.

Red Cross noun an international organization for the treatment of the sick and wounded in war and for helping those affected by large-scale natural disasters.

red deer noun a kind of large deer with a reddish-brown coat, found in Europe and Asia.

redden verb to make something red, or to become red.

reddish adjective rather red.

red dwarf noun a small faint cool star.

redecorate verb to decorate a room etc. freshly. **redecoration** noun

redeem verb 1 to make up for faults or deficiencies ♦ His one redeeming feature is his generosity. 2 to buy something back, to recover a thing in exchange for payment. 3 to clear a debt by paying it off ♦ to redeem a mortgage. 4 to exchange a coupon or token for goods or cash. 5 to save a person from damnation or from the consequences of sin. 6 (old use) to obtain the freedom of a person by payment. **to redeem yourself** to make up for performing or behaving poorly in the past. **redeemable** *adjective* [from *re-* and a Latin word *emere* meaning 'to buy']

redeemer *noun* someone who redeems someone or something.
the Redeemer Christ as the redeemer of mankind.

redemption *noun* redeeming, or being redeemed. **redemptive** *adjective*

red ensign *noun* the flag of the merchant navy.

redeploy *verb* to deploy something again or differently. **redeployment** *noun*

redevelop *verb* (**redeveloped, redeveloping**) to develop land etc. in a different way. **redeveloper** *noun* **redevelopment** *noun*

red giant *noun* a very large cool star.

red-handed *adjective* **to catch someone red-handed** to catch someone while they are actually committing a crime or doing something wrong.

redhead *noun* a person with reddish hair.

red herring *noun* a misleading clue; something that draws attention away from the main subject. [so called because a red smoked herring (kipper) drawn across a fox's path put hounds off the scent]

red-hot *adjective* **1** so hot that it glows red. **2** extremely exciting or popular. **3** very passionate.

red-hot poker *noun* a garden plant with spikes of red or yellow flowers.

redial *verb* (**redialled, redialling**) to dial a telephone number again.
redial *noun* the facility on a telephone by which a number just dialled can be redialled by pressing a single button.

rediffusion *noun* the relaying of broadcast programmes from a central receiver.

Red Indian *noun* an old-fashioned term for American Indian.

redirect *verb* to send or direct someone or something to a different place. **redirection** *noun*

rediscover *verb* to discover something again. **rediscovery** *noun*

redistribute *verb* to distribute something again or differently. **redistribution** *noun*

red lead *noun* red oxide of lead, used as a pigment.

red-letter day *noun* a special or memorable day. [from the practice of highlighting a festival in red on a calendar]

red light *noun* a red light that is a signal to stop on a road or railway.

red-light district *noun* an area in a city where there are many prostitutes, strip clubs, etc.

red meat *noun* meat, such as beef or lamb, that is red when raw.

redo (ree-doo) *verb* (**redoes, redid, redone**) **1** to do something again or differently. **2** to redecorate a room again.

redolent (red-ə-lənt) *adjective* **1** strongly suggesting or reminding you of something ♦ *a castle redolent of history and romance.* **2** (*literary*) smelling strongly ♦ *redolent of onions.* **redolence** *noun* [from *re-* and a Latin word *olens* meaning 'smelling']

redouble *verb* **1** to double something again. **2** to make something greater, or to become greater or more intense ♦ *We must redouble our efforts in the second half.*

redoubt (ri-dowt) *noun* a temporary fortification with no defences flanking it. [from a Latin word *reductum* meaning 'withdrawn']

redoubtable *adjective* formidable, especially as an opponent. [from a French word *redouter* meaning 'to fear']

redound *verb* (*formal*) to cause someone credit or honour ♦ *This will redound to our credit.* [from a Latin word *redundare* meaning 'to overflow']

redox (ree-doks) *noun* (*Chemistry*) a chemical reaction in which one substance is oxidized and another reduced.
redox *adjective* to do with or involving this reaction.

red pepper *noun* the ripe red fruit of a sweet pepper.

redress (ri-dress) *verb* to remedy or set something right ♦ *How can this injustice ever be redressed?*
redress *noun* compensation or amends for a wrong done ♦ *You should seek redress for this damage.* **to redress the balance** to make things equal again. [from an Old French word *redresser*]

redshank *noun* a kind of large sandpiper.

red shift *noun* a displacement of the spectrum to longer wavelengths in the light from a distant galaxy or other object moving away from the universe.

redstart noun a kind of songbird with a red tail.

red tape noun use of too many rules and forms in official business. [so called because bundles of official papers are tied up with red or pink tape]

reduce verb 1 to make something less. SYNONYMS: decrease, lessen, curtail, diminish, cut, condense, compress, trim. 2 to become less. SYNONYMS: dwindle, shrink, contract. 3 to boil a sauce or other liquid so that it becomes thicker and more concentrated. 4 to force someone into an undesirable state or condition ♦ *This news reduced her to despair* ♦ *He was reduced to borrowing from his parents.* 5 to change something into a simpler or more basic form ♦ *Reduce the fraction to its lowest terms* ♦ *The problem may be reduced to two main elements.* 6 (*Chemistry*) to cause a substance to combine with hydrogen or lose oxygen. 7 to make someone lower in rank or status. 8 to restore a dislocated bone to its proper position. **reducer** noun [from *re-* and a Latin word *ducere* meaning 'to bring']

reduced circumstances plural noun poverty after a period of prosperity.

reducible adjective able to be reduced.

reduction noun 1 reducing, or being reduced. 2 the amount by which something is reduced, especially in price.

redundant adjective 1 no longer needed or useful; superfluous. 2 (said about workers) no longer needed for any available job and therefore dismissed. 3 (said about part of a machine) being a duplicate in case another part fails. **redundancy** noun [same origin as for *redound*]

reduplicate verb to double a letter or syllable, e.g. *bye-bye, goody-goody.*

redwing noun a thrush with red flanks.

redwood noun 1 a very tall evergreen coniferous tree of California. 2 the reddish wood of this tree.

re-echo verb (**re-echoes, re-echoed, re-echoing**) to echo again or to go on echoing.

reed noun 1 a water or marsh plant with tall straight hollow stems. 2 the stem of this plant. 3 a thin strip that vibrates to produce the sound in certain wind instruments. [from an Old English word]

reedy adjective (**reedier, reediest**) 1 (said about a voice) having a thin high tone. 2 full of reeds. 3 (said about a person) tall and thin. **reediness** noun

reef¹ noun a ridge of rock, coral, or sand that reaches to or close to the surface of the sea. [via Old German or Old Dutch from an Old Norse word]

reef² noun each of several strips at the top or bottom of a sail that can be drawn in to reduce the area of sail exposed to the wind.
reef verb to shorten a sail by drawing in a reef or reefs. [via Dutch from an Old Norse word]

reefer noun (*informal*) a cannabis cigarette. [origin unknown]

reefer jacket noun a thick double-breasted jacket.

reef knot noun a symmetrical double knot that is very secure. [from *reef*²]

reek verb 1 to have a foul smell. 2 to strongly suggest something ♦ *The whole thing reeks of corruption.*
reek noun a foul smell. [from an Old English word meaning 'to give off smoke']

reel noun 1 a cylinder or similar device on which film, cotton, wire, etc. is wound. 2 a length of something wound on a reel. 3 a lively Scottish or Irish folk dance, or the music for this.
reel verb 1 to wind something on or off a reel. 2 to pull a thing in by using a reel. 3 to stagger or lurch. 4 to feel giddy or confused ♦ *I am still reeling from the shock.*
to reel something off to say something quickly and without effort. [from an Old English word]

re-elect verb to elect someone again. **re-election** noun

re-enter verb to enter something again.

re-entrant adjective (said about an angle) pointing inwards, reflex.

re-entry noun (**re-entries**) 1 re-entering something. 2 the return of a spacecraft or missile into the earth's atmosphere.

reeve noun (*historical*) the chief magistrate of a town or district. [from an Old English word]

re-examine verb to examine something again. **re-examination** noun

ref noun (*informal*) a referee.

refectory (ri-fek-teri) *noun* (**refectories**) the dining room of a college, monastery, or similar establishment. [from a Latin word *refectum* meaning 'refreshed']

refer *verb* (**referred, referring**) 1 to mention or speak about someone or something ♦ *I wasn't referring to you.* 2 to send or direct a person to some authority, specialist, or source of information. 3 to describe or denote something ♦ *Who does the phrase 'the Bard of Avon' refer to?* 4 to turn to a book, table, etc. for information ♦ *We referred to the list of rules.* **referable** (ri-fer-əbəl) *adjective* [from *re-* meaning 'back' and a Latin word *ferre* meaning 'to bring']

referee *noun* 1 an official who closely watches a game or match and makes sure that people keep to the rules. 2 a person to whom disputes are referred for decision. 3 a person willing to testify about the character or ability of someone applying for a job.
referee *verb* (**referees, refereed, refereeing**) to act as referee in a football match etc. [literally meaning 'someone who is referred to']

reference *noun* 1 the act of mentioning something ♦ *The report made no reference to recent events.* 2 a direction to a book, page, file, etc. where information can be found; the book or passage etc. to which the reader is directed. 3 a source of facts or information. 4 a letter from a previous employer testifying to someone's ability or reliability.
reference *verb* to provide a book or article with references. **in** or **with reference to** in connection with, about. **terms of reference** the scope or limits of an investigation.

reference book *noun* a book giving information for reference but not designed to be read straight through.

reference library *noun* a library containing books that can be consulted but not taken away.

referendum *noun* (**referendums** or **referenda**) the referring of a single political question to the people of a country etc. for direct decision by a general vote; a vote taken in this way. [a Latin word meaning 'referring']

referral (ri-fer-əl) *noun* referring someone or something, especially the directing of a patient by a GP to a specialist.

refill¹ (ree-fil) *verb* to fill something again.

refill² (ree-fil) *noun* a second or later filling, or a glass that is refilled ♦ *Would you like a refill?*

refine *verb* 1 to remove impurities or defects from something. 2 to improve something by making small changes to it. [from *re-* and an old word *fine* meaning 'to make pure']

refined *adjective* 1 purified or processed ♦ *refined oil.* 2 having good taste or good manners. SYNONYMS: cultured, cultivated, discerning, civilized, genteel, polished.

refinement *noun* 1 refining, or being refined. 2 elegance of behaviour or manners. 3 an improvement added to something.

refiner *noun* someone whose business is to refine crude oil, metal, or sugar etc.

refinery *noun* (**refineries**) a factory where crude substances are refined ♦ *an oil refinery.*

refit¹ (ree-fit) *verb* (**refitted, refitting**) to replace or repair the machinery, equipment, and fittings in a ship, building, etc. **refitment** *noun*

refit² (ree-fit) *noun* the refitting of a ship, building, etc.

reflate *verb* to cause reflation of a financial system.

reflation *noun* the process of restoring a financial system to its previous condition when deflation has been carried out too fast or too far. **reflationary** *adjective*

reflect *verb* 1 to throw back light, heat, or sound. 2 to be thrown back in this way. 3 (said about a mirror etc.) to show an image of something. 4 to be a sign of something or make it apparent ♦ *Her hard work was reflected in her exam results.* 5 to think deeply or carefully about something. SYNONYMS: ponder, deliberate, ruminate, contemplate. 6 to bring about a good or bad impression of something ♦ *This failure reflects badly upon the whole industry.* [from *re-* and a Latin word *flectere* meaning 'to bend']

reflection *noun* 1 reflecting, or being reflected. 2 reflected light or heat etc.; a reflected image. 3 something that brings discredit. 4 a serious thought or consideration; an idea or statement produced by this.

reflective *adjective* 1 reflecting ♦ *a reflective surface.* 2 thoughtful ♦ *in a reflective mood.*

reflector *noun* 1 a thing that reflects light,

heat, sound, etc. **2** a red disc or panel on the back of a vehicle, making it visible in the dark by reflecting the lights of vehicles behind it.

reflex (ree-fleks) *noun* an involuntary or instinctive movement in response to a stimulus.
reflex *adjective* **1** (said about an action) done as a reflex. **2** (said about an angle) more than 180°. [from *reflect*]

reflex camera *noun* a camera in which the image given by the lens is reflected by an angled mirror to the viewfinder.

reflexive *adjective* (Grammar) (said about a word or form) referring back to the subject of the verb, in which the action of the verb is performed on its subject, e.g. *he washed himself.*
reflexive *noun* a reflexive word or form.

reflexive pronoun *noun* any of the pronouns *myself, himself, itself, themselves,* etc., which refer back to the subject of the verb.

reflexology *noun* a system of massage used to treat illness and relieve tension, based on the theory that there are reflex points on the feet, hands, and head linked to every part of the body. **reflexologist** *noun*

refloat *verb* to set a stranded ship afloat again.

reforest *verb* to replant an area with trees. **reforestation** *noun*

reform *verb* **1** to make changes in something in order to improve it. **2** to give up a criminal or immoral lifestyle, or to make someone do this.
reform *noun* **1** reforming, or being reformed. **2** a change made in order to improve something. **reformed** *adjective* **reformer** *noun* [from *re-* and a Latin word *formare* meaning 'to form']

re-form *verb* to form or make something form again.

reformat *verb* (**reformatted, reformatting**) to give a new format to something, especially in computing.

reformation (ref-er-may-shǝn) *noun* the action or process of reforming.
the Reformation *noun* a religious movement in Europe in the 16th century intended to reform certain teachings and practices of the Roman Church, resulting in the establishment of the Reformed and Protestant Churches.

reformatory (ri-form-ǝ-ter-i) *noun*

(**reformatories**) (*North Amer.*) (*old use*) an institution where young offenders against the law are sent as an alternative to prison.

Reformed Church *noun* a Church that accepted the principles of the Reformation, especially a Calvinist Church.

reformist *adjective* supporting gradual reform rather than abolition or revolution.
reformist *noun* a supporter of this policy.

Reform Judaism *noun* a liberalized form of Judaism in which Jewish law is not strictly observed.

refract (ri-frakt) *verb* to bend a ray of light at the point where it enters water or glass etc. at an angle. **refraction** *noun* **refractive** *adjective* **refractor** *noun* [from *re-* and a Latin word *fractum* meaning 'broken']

refractory *adjective* (formal) **1** resisting control or discipline, stubborn ♦ *a refractory child.* **2** (said about a disease etc.) not yielding to treatment. **3** (said about a substance) resistant to heat; hard to fuse or melt. [from *re-* and a Latin word *frangere* meaning 'to break']

refrain[1] *verb* to keep yourself from doing something ♦ *Please refrain from talking.* [from a Latin word *refrenare* meaning 'to bridle']

refrain[2] **1** a repeated line or number of lines in a poem or song, usually at the end of each verse. **2** the music for a refrain. [from an Old French word]

refresh *verb* to give new strength or energy to a tired person etc. by food, drink, or rest. SYNONYMS: revive, revitalize, invigorate, fortify; (*informal*) perk up. **to refresh someone's memory** to stimulate someone's memory by going over previous information. **refresher** *noun* [from an Old French word *refreschier*]

refresher course *noun* a training course enabling a qualified person to keep up to date with recent developments in the subject.

refreshing *adjective* **1** restoring strength and energy ♦ *a refreshing sleep.* **2** welcome and interesting because it is new or different ♦ *refreshing honesty.*

refreshment *noun* the giving of fresh strength or energy.

refreshments *plural noun* drinks and snacks provided as a light meal, especially at an event.

refrigerant *noun* a substance used for cooling things or for keeping things cold.

refrigerate *verb* to make food or drink extremely cold, especially in order to preserve it and keep it fresh. **refrigeration** *noun* [from *re-* and a Latin word *frigus* meaning 'cold']

refrigerator *noun* a cabinet or room in which food is stored at a very low temperature.

refuel *verb* (**refuelled, refuelling**) to supply a ship or aircraft with more fuel.

refuge *noun* 1 a place or state of safety from pursuit, danger, or trouble. 2 a traffic island. **to take refuge** to go somewhere or do something so that you are protected ♦ *She decided to take refuge in silence.* [from *re-* and a Latin word *fugere* meaning 'to flee']

refugee *noun* a person who has had to leave their country and seek refuge elsewhere, e.g. because of war, persecution, or famine.

refund¹ (ri-**fund**) *verb* to pay back money received or expenses that a person has paid out. SYNONYMS: repay, reimburse. [from a Latin word *refundere* meaning 'to pour back']

refund² (**ree**-fund) *noun* money paid back.

refurbish *verb* to make something clean or bright again; to redecorate and repair something.

refusal *noun* refusing, or being refused. **first refusal** the right to accept or refuse something before the choice is offered to others ♦ *If I decide to sell it, I'll give you first refusal.*

refuse¹ (ri-**fewz**) *verb* 1 (said about a person) to say or show that you are unwilling to accept or give or do something ♦ *I refused to go* ♦ *Your request has been refused* ♦ *They refused me permission to go.* 2 (said about a thing) to show an unwillingness to do something ♦ *The car refused to start.* 3 (said about a horse) to be unwilling to jump a fence. [from an Old French word *refuser*]

refuse² (**ref**-yooss) *noun* what is rejected as worthless, waste material.

refute *verb* to prove that a statement, opinion, or theory is false or wrong. **refutable** *adjective* **refutation** (ref-yoo-**tay**-shən) *noun* [from a Latin word *refutare*

meaning 'to repel']
◊ This word is sometimes used to mean 'to deny' or 'to repudiate', but this meaning is not fully accepted as part of standard English and should be avoided.

regain *verb* 1 to get something back again after losing it. SYNONYMS: recover, retrieve, recapture, win back. 2 to reach a place again ♦ *Eventually we regained the shore.*

regal (**ree**-gəl) *adjective* like or fit for a king or queen, especially in being magnificent or dignified. **regality** (ri-**gal**-iti) *noun* **regally** *adverb* [from a Latin word *regis* meaning 'of a king']

regale (ri-**gayl**) *verb* 1 to entertain someone with conversation ♦ *She regaled us with stories of her life in the theatre.* 2 to feed someone well ♦ *They regaled themselves on caviare.* [from a French word *régaler*]

regalia (ri-**gay**-li-ə) *plural noun* 1 the emblems of royalty used at coronations ♦ *The regalia include crown, sceptre, and orb.* 2 distinctive clothing and ornaments worn at formal occasions as a sign of high office. [from a Latin word meaning 'royal privileges']

regard *verb* 1 to consider or think of something in a certain way ♦ *We regard the matter as serious.* 2 to look steadily at someone or something. **regard** *noun* 1 heed or consideration ♦ *You acted without regard to the safety of others.* 2 high opinion, respect ♦ *We have a great regard for her.* 3 a steady gaze. **regards** *plural noun* kindly greetings or wishes sent in a message ♦ *Give him my regards.* **as regards** concerning ♦ *He is innocent as regards the first charge.* **in this** or **that regard** in connection with the point just mentioned. **with** or **in** or **having regard to** as concerns, in respect of. [from *re-* and a French word *garder* meaning 'to guard']

regardful *adjective* (*formal*) mindful.

regarding *preposition* about or concerning ♦ *There are laws regarding picketing.*

regardless *adverb* paying no attention to something ♦ *Do it, regardless of the cost.*

regatta *noun* a series of boat or yacht races organized as a sporting event. [from an Italian word meaning 'a fight or contest']

regency *noun* (**regencies**) 1 being a regent. 2 a period when a country is ruled by a regent. 3 a group of people acting as regent.

the Regency the period 1811–20 in England, when George, Prince of Wales, acted as regent.

regenerate[1] (ri-**jen**-er-ayt) *verb* **1** to give new life or strength to something. **2** to reform someone spiritually or morally. **3** to grow new tissues or organs to replace damaged ones. **regeneration** *noun* [from a Latin word *regenerare* meaning 'to create again']

regenerate[2] (ri-**jen**-er-ət) *adjective* spiritually born again, reformed.

regent *noun* a person appointed to rule a country while the monarch is too young or unable to rule, or is absent.
regent *adjective* acting as regent ♦ *Prince Regent.* [from a Latin word *regens* meaning 'ruling']

reggae (**reg**-ay) *noun* a West Indian style of popular music with a strongly accented subsidiary beat. [origin unknown]

regicide (**rej**-i-siyd) *noun* **1** the killing of a king. **2** a person who does this. [from Latin words *regis* meaning 'of a king' and *caedere* meaning 'to kill']

regime (ray-**zheem**) *noun* a system of government or administration ♦ *a fascist regime.* [from a French word; related to *regiment*]

regiment *noun* **1** a permanent unit of an army, usually divided into companies or troops or battalions. **2** a large number of people or things.
regiment *verb* to organize people, work, data, etc. rigidly into groups or into a pattern. **regimentation** *noun* [from a Latin word *regimentum* meaning 'rule, governing']

regimental *adjective* to do with an army regiment.
regimentals *plural noun* the uniform of an army regiment.

Regina (ri-**jiy**-nə) *noun* a reigning queen; the Crown in lawsuits ♦ *Regina v. Adams.* [a Latin word meaning 'queen']

region *noun* **1** an area of a country or of the world ♦ *in tropical regions.* SYNONYMS: area, territory, locality, zone. **2** an administrative division of a city or country. **3** an area of the body ♦ *the abdominal region.* **in the region of** approximately ♦ *The cost will be in the region of £100.* **regional** *adjective* **regionally** *adverb* [from a Latin word *regio* meaning 'boundary']

register *noun* **1** an official list recording names or items etc., or a book containing this list ♦ *the electoral register.* **2** a record of attendance at school. **3** the range of a human voice or musical instrument. **4** a device for indicating or recording information automatically ♦ *a cash register.* **5** the kinds of words (e.g. informal, formal, literary) and the manner of speaking or writing that vary according to the situation and the relationship of the people involved. **6** (in printing) exact correspondence of position, especially of colours.
register *verb* **1** to put a name etc. on a register. **2** to put your name and address in a hotel register when you arrive. **3** to present something for consideration ♦ *I wish to register a complaint.* **4** (said about an instrument) to indicate or show something ♦ *The thermometer registered 100°.* **5** to make an impression on someone ♦ *His name did not register with me.* **6** to express an emotion on your face or by gesture ♦ *Her face registered disappointment.* **7** to notice or become aware of something. **8** to send a letter or parcel by registered post. [from a Latin word *regesta* meaning 'things recorded']

registered post *noun* a system of sending a letter or parcel by post with special precautions for its safety.

register office *noun* a place where civil marriages are performed and where records of births, marriages, and deaths are kept.

registrar (rej-i-**strar**) *noun* **1** an official with responsibility for keeping written records or registers. **2** the chief administrative officer in a university. **3** a judicial and administrative officer of the High Court. **4** a doctor undergoing hospital training to be a specialist. [same origin as for *register*]

registration *noun* **1** registering, or being registered. **2** (also **registration number**) a series of letters and figures identifying a motor vehicle.

registration plate *noun* another term for **number plate**.

registry *noun* (**registries**) **1** a place where written records or registers are kept. **2** registration.

registry office *noun* another term for **register office**.

regnant *adjective* reigning. [from a Latin word *regnare* meaning 'to reign']

regress [1] (ri-gress) *verb* to go back to an earlier or less advanced form, state, or way of behaving. **regression** *noun* [from re- and a Latin word *gressus* meaning 'gone']

regress [2] (ree-gress) *noun* regressing.

regressive *adjective* tending to regress.

regressive tax *noun* a tax that takes a proportionately greater amount from those on lower incomes.

regret *noun* 1 a feeling of sorrow, disappointment, or repentance. 2 a polite expression of sorrow or apology, especially when refusing an invitation ♦ My mother is unable to come to your wedding and sends her regrets.
regret *verb* (**regretted, regretting**) to feel regret about something ♦ He regrets what he has done ♦ We regret that we cannot offer you the job. **regretful** *adjective* **regretfully** *adverb* [from an Old French word *regreter* meaning 'to mourn for the dead']

regrettable *adjective* that is to be regretted ♦ a regrettable incident.

regrettably *adverb* it is regrettable that ♦ Regrettably I will not be able to meet you at the airport.

regroup *verb* to form people or things into fresh groups.

regular *adjective* 1 happening or repeated in a uniform manner, or constantly at a fixed time or interval ♦ Her pulse is regular ♦ Plant the seeds at regular intervals ♦ He has no regular income. 2 happening often and at fixed times ♦ Try to eat regular meals. 3 even or symmetrical ♦ regular teeth ♦ a regular pentagon. 4 usual or normal ♦ When is their regular bedtime? ♦ regular customers. 5 belonging to a country's permanent armed forces ♦ regular soldiers. 6 (Grammar) (said about a verb or noun etc.) having inflections that are of a normal type. 7 (informal) complete or absolute ♦ You're a regular Florence Nightingale, aren't you? 8 of medium size ♦ a regular coffee.
regular *noun* 1 a member of the permanent armed forces of a country. 2 a frequent customer or client. **regularity** *noun* **regularly** *adverb* [from a Latin word *regula* meaning 'a rule']

regularize *verb* 1 to make something regular. 2 to make something lawful or correct ♦ We need to regularize the situation. **regularization** *noun*

regulate *verb* 1 to control or direct something by means of rules and restrictions. 2 to adjust or control a machine or the amount or rate of something so that it works correctly or according to your requirements ♦ You can regulate the heat using the thermostat. **regulator** *noun* [same origin as for *regular*]

regulation *noun* 1 a rule, law, or restriction. 2 regulating, or being regulated. **regulation** *adjective* as required by regulations. [same origin as for *regular*]

regurgitate (ri-gerj-it-ayt) *verb* 1 to bring swallowed food up again to the mouth. 2 to repeat information without really thinking about or understanding it. **regurgitation** *noun* [from re- and a Latin word *gurgitare* meaning 'to swallow']

rehabilitate *verb* 1 to restore a person to health or normal life by training and treatment after a period of imprisonment, addiction, or illness. 2 to restore the reputation of a person or thing. 3 to restore a building etc. to a good condition or for a new purpose. **rehabilitation** *noun* [from re- and a Latin word *habilitare* meaning 'to enable']

rehash [1] (ree-hash) *verb* to use old ideas or material again with no great change or improvement. [from re- and *hash* [1]]

rehash [2] (ree-hash) *noun* something made of rehashed material.

rehearsal *noun* 1 a practice or trial performance. 2 rehearsing.

rehearse *verb* 1 to practise something before performing to an audience. 2 to train a person by doing this. 3 to recite a list of points, especially ones that have been made many times before ♦ You will be given an opportunity to rehearse your grievances. [from an Old French word *rehercier* meaning 'to repeat aloud']

reheat *verb* to heat something again.

rehouse (ree-howz) *verb* to provide someone with new accommodation.

Reich (ryk) *noun* the former German state, especially the **Third Reich**, the Nazi regime (1933–45). [a German word meaning 'empire']

reign (rayn) *noun* 1 the period during which a king or queen rules. 2 the period during which someone or something is dominant or in control ♦ a reign of terror. **reign** *verb* 1 to rule a country as king or queen. 2 to prevail or dominate ♦ Confusion reigned. [from a Latin word

regnum meaning 'royal authority']
◊ Do not confuse this word with **rein**, which has a different meaning.

reigning *adjective* currently holding a particular title ♦ *the reigning champion.*

reimburse *verb* to repay money that has been spent or lost ♦ *Your travelling expenses will be reimbursed.* **reimbursement** *noun* [from *re-* and an old word *imburse* meaning 'to pay']

rein *noun* **1** a long narrow strap fastened to the bit of a bridle and used to guide or check a horse being ridden or driven. **2** a similar device to restrain a young child. **reins** *plural noun* the power to control something ♦ *The company has prospered since she took over the reins.* **rein** *verb* to check or control a horse by pulling on its reins. **to give free rein to** to allow freedom to something ♦ *Give your imagination free rein.* **to keep a tight rein on** to strictly control something. **to rein something in** or **back** to restrain something. [same origin as *retain*]
◊ Do not confuse this word with **reign**, which has a different meaning.

reincarnate [1] (ree-in-kar-nayt) *verb* to cause someone to be born again in another body.

reincarnate [2] (ree-in-kar-nət) *adjective* born again in another body.

reincarnation *noun* **1** the belief that after death the soul is born again in another body. **2** a person or animal in whom a soul is believed to have been reborn.

reindeer *noun* (**reindeer** or **reindeers**) a kind of deer with large antlers, living in Arctic regions. [from an Old Norse word]

reinforce *verb* **1** to strengthen or support something by additional people or material. **2** to emphasize or increase something ♦ *These setbacks only served to reinforce my determination.* [from *re-* and an Old French word *enforcer* meaning 'to enforce']

reinforced concrete *noun* concrete with metal bars or wire embedded in it to increase its strength.

reinforcement *noun* **1** reinforcing, or being reinforced. **2** something that reinforces. **reinforcements** *plural noun* additional troops or ships etc. sent to strengthen armed forces.

reinstate *verb* to restore a person or thing to a previous position. **reinstatement** *noun* [from *re-* and *in-* and *state*]

reissue *verb* to make a book, record, etc. available for sale again. **reissue** *noun* something reissued.

reiterate (ree-it-er-ayt) *verb* to say something again or repeatedly. **reiteration** *noun* [from *re-* and a Latin word *iterare* meaning 'to repeat']

reject [1] (ri-jekt) *verb* **1** to refuse to accept, believe, or agree to something ♦ *The committee has rejected the latest proposals.* **2** to discard or not use something, especially because it is below standard. **3** (said about the body) to fail to accept tissue or an organ that has been transplanted ♦ *Her body may reject the new heart.* **4** to fail to give due affection to someone ♦ *The child was rejected by both his parents.* **rejection** *noun* [from *re-* meaning 'away' and a Latin word *-jectum* meaning 'thrown']

reject [2] (ree-jekt) *noun* a person or thing that is rejected, especially as being below standard.

rejig *verb* (**rejigged, rejigging**) **1** (*informal*) to rearrange something. **2** (*old use*) to re-equip a factory etc. for a new type of work.

rejoice *verb* to feel or show great joy. [from an Old French word *rejoir*]

rejoin [1] (ree-join) *verb* **1** to join something together again. **2** to return to something ♦ *What time did you rejoin the party?*

rejoin [2] (ri-join) *verb* to say something in reply; to retort. [from an Old French word]

rejoinder *noun* a sharp or witty reply. [from an Old French word]

rejuvenate (ri-joo-vən-ayt) *verb* to make a person seem young again. **rejuvenation** *noun* [from *re-* and a Latin word *juvenis* meaning 'young']

rekindle *verb* **1** to relight a fire. **2** to revive something that has been lost.

relapse *verb* **1** (said about a sick or injured person) to get worse after a period of improvement. **2** to return to a worse or less active state. **relapse** *noun* relapsing, especially after partial recovery from illness. [from *re-* and a Latin word *lapsum* meaning 'slipped']

relate verb 1 to tell a story or give an account of something. 2 to establish a link between one thing and another ♦ *I've been trying to relate these effects to a possible cause.* **to relate to 1** to concern or have a link with something ♦ *He notices only what relates to himself.* 2 to understand and get on well with someone ♦ *She relates to children extremely well.* [from a Latin word *referre* meaning 'to bring back']

related adjective 1 connected. 2 connected by birth or marriage.

relation noun 1 the way in which two or more people or things are connected or related to one another. 2 being connected by birth or marriage. 3 a relative. 4 telling a story or giving an account.
relations plural noun 1 dealings with others ♦ *the country's foreign relations.* 2 (*formal*) sexual intercourse ♦ *She had relations with him.* **in relation to** in connection with.

relationship noun 1 the way in which two or more people or things are connected or related to one another. SYNONYMS: connection, link, association, correlation, bond, tie. 2 the way in which two or more people or groups think of and behave towards each other. 3 an emotional or sexual association between two people.

relative adjective 1 considered in relation or proportion to something else ♦ *the relative merits of the two plans* ♦ *They lived in relative comfort.* 2 having a connection with something ♦ *Let's review the facts relative to the matter in hand.* 3 (*Grammar*) referring or attached to an earlier noun, clause, or sentence ♦ *relative pronoun,* e.g. *who* in *the man who came to dinner.*
relative noun 1 a person who is related to another by birth or marriage. 2 a species related to another by common origin. 3 (*Grammar*) a relative pronoun or adverb.
relatively adverb **relativeness** noun

relative atomic mass noun (*Chemistry*) atomic weight, the mass of one atom of an element relative to a standard mass.

relative density noun the ratio of the density of a substance to that of a standard substance (usually water for liquids and solids and air for gases).

relative molecular mass noun (*Chemistry*) the sum of the relative atomic masses of the atoms in a molecule.

relative pronoun noun any of the pronouns *who, whom, whose, which,* and *that,* which refer back to an earlier noun or phrase as in *the people who know us.*

relativism noun the idea that morality, truth, etc. are not absolute but may vary in different situations, cultures, and historical periods. **relativist** adjective & noun

relativity noun 1 the state or quality of being relative. 2 (*Physics*) a description of matter, energy, space, and time according to Einstein's theory of the universe, in which measurements are relative to the position or motion of the observer making them.

relaunch verb to launch something again or in a different form.
relaunch noun an instance of relaunching ♦ *a product relaunch.*

relax verb 1 to stop working and rest or enjoy yourself. 2 to become or cause someone to become less tense or anxious ♦ *Relax! Everything will be fine.* 3 to make a limb or muscle become less rigid. 4 to make a rule etc. less strict or severe ♦ *They have decided to relax the entry requirements slightly.* 5 to let something become less intense ♦ *We can't relax our vigilance for a second.* **relaxation** noun [from *re-* meaning 'back' and a Latin word *laxus* meaning 'loose']

relaxed adjective 1 calm and not anxious. 2 not insisting on rules being strictly followed ♦ *My parents had a relaxed attitude to discipline.* SYNONYMS: easygoing, lax; (*informal*) laid-back. 3 friendly and informal ♦ *The hotel has a relaxed atmosphere.*

relay [1] (ree-lay) noun 1 a fresh set of people or animals taking the place of others who have completed a spell of work ♦ *The firefighters operated in relays.* 2 a race between teams in which each person in turn covers a part of the total distance. 3 an electronic device that receives and passes on a signal, often strengthening it. 4 an electronic device activated by a current in one circuit to open or close another circuit. 5 a relayed message or transmission. [from an Old French word *relaier* meaning 'to leave behind']

relay [2] (ree-lay) verb (past tense and past participle **relayed**) to receive and pass on or retransmit a message or broadcast etc.

relay [3] verb (past tense and past participle **relaid**) to lay something again.

release verb 1 to set someone or something free. 2 to make a film, record, information, etc. available to the public. 3 to unfasten something or remove it from a fixed position ♦ *Now release the* *handbrake.* **4** to let a thing fall or fly or go out ♦ *One of the archers released an arrow.*

release *noun* **1** releasing, or being released. **2** something released. **3** information or a film or record etc. released to the public ♦ *a press release.* **4** a handle or catch etc. that unfastens a device or machine part. [from an Old French word *relesser*; related to *relax*]

relegate (rel-i-gayt) *verb* **1** to put or send someone or something to a less important position or rank. **2** to transfer a sports team to a lower division of a league. **relegation** *noun* [from *re-* meaning 'back' and a Latin word *legatum* meaning 'sent']

relent *verb* **1** to abandon your harsh intentions and become more lenient. **2** to become less intense. [from *re-* meaning 'back' and a Latin word *lentus* meaning 'flexible']

relentless *adjective* **1** (said about people) not relenting. SYNONYMS: implacable, inexorable, remorseless. **2** not becoming less severe ♦ *relentless pressure.* SYNONYMS: unremitting, unrelenting, unyielding, sustained. **relentlessly** *adverb* **relentlessness** *noun*

relevant (rel-i-vənt) *adjective* related to what is being discussed or dealt with. SYNONYMS: germane, applicable, pertinent, material, apropos. **relevance** *noun* [from a Latin word *relevare* meaning 'to raise up']

reliable *adjective* able to be relied on. **reliability** *noun* **reliably** *adverb*

reliance *noun* depending on something; trust or confidence felt about something ♦ *Don't place too much reliance on his promises.* **reliant** *adjective* [from *rely*]

relic (rel-ik) *noun* **1** something that has survived from an earlier time. **2** a surviving trace of an old custom, belief, or practice. **3** part of a holy person's body or belongings kept after their death as an object of reverence.
relics *plural noun* the remnants or residue of something. [same origin as *relinquish*]

relief *noun* **1** ease given by the ending or lessening of pain, anxiety, or difficulty. **2** a feeling or cause of relief ♦ *That's a relief, the film's not started yet.* **3** something that relaxes tension or breaks up monotony ♦ *a humorous scene serving as comic relief.* **4** help or assistance given to people in need ♦ *a relief fund for the earthquake victims.* **5** a person or group taking over another's turn of duty. **6** a bus etc. supplementing an ordinary service. **7** the raising of the

siege of a besieged town ♦ *the relief of Mafeking.* **8** a method of carving or moulding in which the design stands out from the surface. **9** a piece of carving etc. done in this way. **10** a similar effect achieved by the use of colour or shading. [via Old French from a Latin word *relevare* meaning 'to raise again, to alleviate']

relief map *noun* a map showing hills and valleys either by shading or by their being moulded in relief.

relief road *noun* a road taking traffic around, rather than through, a congested area.

relieve *verb* **1** to remove or lessen pain, anxiety, or difficulty. SYNONYMS: alleviate, ease, soothe, assuage. **2** to give help or assistance to someone in need. **3** to release a person from a duty or task by taking their place or providing a substitute. **4** to make something less monotonous or boring. **5** to take something from a person ♦ *A pickpocket had relieved him of his wallet.* **6** to raise the siege of a town. **to relieve yourself** to urinate or defecate. [from *re-* and a Latin word *levare* meaning 'to raise or lighten']

relieved *adjective* no longer feeling anxious.

religion *noun* **1** belief in the existence of a superhuman controlling power, especially of God or gods, usually expressed in worship. **2** a particular system of faith and worship ♦ *the Christian religion.* **3** an interest that someone is devoted to and that seems to take over their life ♦ *Football is his religion.* [from a Latin word *religio* meaning 'reverence']

religious *adjective* **1** to do with religion ♦ *a religious service.* **2** believing firmly in a religion and paying great attention to its practices. **3** to do with a monastic order. **4** very conscientious or scrupulous ♦ *with religious attention to detail.* **religious** *noun* (**religious**) a person bound by monastic vows. **religiously** *adverb*

relinquish *verb* **1** to give up a plan, belief, struggle, etc. **2** to surrender possession or control of something ♦ *She has relinquished control of the company.* **3** to release your hold of something ♦ *He finally had to relinquish the reins.* **relinquishment** *noun* [from *re-* meaning 'behind' and a Latin word *linquere* meaning 'to leave']

reliquary (rel-i-kwer-i) *noun* (**reliquaries**) a container for holy relics. [from a French word *reliquaire*]

relish *noun* 1 great enjoyment of food or other things. SYNONYMS: appetite, enthusiasm, zest, gusto. 2 anticipating something with pleasure. 3 a strong-tasting sauce or pickle eaten with plainer food to add flavour.
relish *verb* 1 to enjoy something greatly. 2 to look forward to something with pleasure ♦ *I don't relish the prospect of driving home in this weather.* [from an Old French word *reles* meaning 'remainder']

relive *verb* to remember an experience or feeling very vividly, as though it was happening again.

reload *verb* to load something again.

relocate (ree-lə-**kayt**) *verb* to move your home or business from one place to another. **relocation** *noun*

reluctant *adjective* unwilling and slow to do something. **reluctance** *noun* **reluctantly** *adverb* [from a Latin word meaning 'struggling against something']

rely *verb* (**relies, relied, relying**) to rely on or upon 1 to trust a person or thing to help or support you ♦ *You can rely on me not to tell anyone.* 2 to be dependent on something ♦ *Many people rely on this local bus service.* [from an Old French word *relier* meaning 'to bind together']

REM *abbreviation* rapid eye movement, referring to a type of sleep that occurs at intervals during the night and is characterized by dreaming with extensive bodily movement.

remain *verb* 1 to be in the same place or condition during further time, to continue to be ♦ *We remained in London for another two years* ♦ *You must remain alert.* 2 to be left over after other parts have been removed, used, or dealt with. [from *re-* meaning 'behind' and a Latin word *manere* meaning 'to stay']

remainder *noun* 1 the remaining people or things or part. 2 the number left after dividing one quantity into another. **remainder** *verb* to dispose of unsold copies of a book at a reduced price. [same origin as for *remain*]

remains *plural noun* 1 what remains after other parts or things have been removed, used, or destroyed. SYNONYMS: remnants, traces, vestiges, debris, dregs, leftovers (of a meal), offcuts (of wood etc.). 2 ancient buildings or other things that have survived when others are destroyed. 3 a person's body after death ♦ *his mortal remains.*

remake *verb* (past tense and past participle **remade**) to make something again or differently.
remake *noun* something remade, especially a film.

remand *verb* (*Law*) to send a person accused of a crime back into custody while further evidence is being gathered. **remand** *noun* remanding someone. **on remand** in custody or on bail while waiting for a trial. [from *re-* and a Latin word *mandare* meaning 'to entrust']

remand centre *noun* a place where people accused of a crime are sent temporarily while waiting for their trial.

remark *noun* a written or spoken comment, anything that is said. SYNONYMS: comment, observation, reflection. **remark** *verb* 1 to make a remark. SYNONYMS: mention, comment, observe, note, declare. 2 to notice something. [from a French word *remarquer* meaning 'to note again']

remarkable *adjective* extraordinary or striking ♦ *a remarkable achievement.* SYNONYMS: notable, noteworthy, significant, outstanding, exceptional, astonishing. **remarkably** *adverb* [from *remark*]

remarry *verb* (**remarries, remarried, remarrying**) to marry again. **remarriage** *noun*

rematch *noun* a second game or match between two teams or players.

remedial (ri-**meed**-iəl) *adjective* 1 helping to cure an illness or deficiency. 2 to do with the teaching of children with learning difficulties. [same origin as for *remedy*]

remedy *noun* (**remedies**) something that cures or relieves a disease etc. or that puts a matter right.
remedy *verb* (**remedies, remedied, remedying**) to be a remedy for something, to put something right. **remediable** (ri-**meed**-i-əbəl) *adjective* [from *re-* and a Latin word *mederi* meaning 'to heal']

remember *verb* 1 to bring something back into your mind. SYNONYMS: recall, recollect, reminisce. 2 to keep something in your mind ♦ *Remember to lock the door.* 3 to make a present to someone ♦ *My Uncle Paul remembered me in his will.* 4 to mention someone as sending greetings ♦ *Please remember me to your mother.* **to remember yourself** to recover your manners after a lapse. [from *re-* and a Latin word *memor* meaning 'mindful']

remembrance 1 remembering, or being remembered. **2** something that is remembered. **3** something kept or given as a reminder or in commemoration of someone.

Remembrance Sunday noun the Sunday nearest to 11 November, when those killed in the First and Second World Wars are commemorated.

remind verb to cause someone to remember or think of something ♦ *Remind me to phone Jack* ♦ *She reminds me of my history teacher.* [from *re-* and an old sense of *mind* meaning 'to put into someone's mind, to mention']

reminder noun **1** a thing that reminds someone of something. **2** a letter sent to remind someone to pay a bill.

reminisce (rem-in-iss) verb to think or talk about past events and experiences.

reminiscence (rem-in-iss-ens) noun **1** thinking or talking about past events and experiences. **2** a spoken or written account of what you remember ♦ *He wrote his reminiscences of his life as a diplomat.* **3** a thing that is reminiscent of something else. [from a Latin word *reminisci* meaning 'to remember']

reminiscent (rem-in-iss-ent) adjective **1** tending to remind you of something ♦ *His style is reminiscent of Picasso's.* **2** inclined to reminisce ♦ *in reminiscent mood.* **reminiscently** adverb

remiss (ri-miss) adjective negligent, careless about doing what you ought to do ♦ *You have been remiss in your duties* ♦ *That was remiss of me.* [same origin as for *remit*]

remission noun **1** the cancellation of a debt or penalty. **2** the shortening of a prison sentence, especially for good behaviour while in prison. **3** a temporary lessening of the intensity of an illness or pain. **4** (formal) forgiveness of sins.

remit [1] (ri-mit) verb (remitted, remitting) **1** to cancel a debt or refrain from inflicting a punishment. **2** to send money in payment to a person or place ♦ *Please remit the interest to my home address.* **3** to send a matter for decision to some authority. **4** (said about God) to forgive sins. [from *re-* meaning 'back' and a Latin word *mittere* meaning 'to send']

remit [2] (ree-mit) noun the task or area of activity officially given to a person or organization ♦ *Staff training is outside the remit of this committee.*

remittance noun **1** the sending of money to a person. **2** the money sent.

remix [1] (ree-miks) verb to produce a different version of a musical recording by changing the balance of the separate tracks.

remix [2] (ree-mix) noun a remixed recording.

remnant noun **1** a part or piece left over from something. **2** a small piece of cloth left when the rest of the roll has been used or sold. **3** a surviving trace of something. [from an Old French word *remenant*; related to *remain*]

remodel verb (remodelled, remodelling) **1** to model something again or differently. **2** to change the structure or form of something.

remonstrance (ri-mon-strens) noun a forceful protest.

remonstrate (rem-en-strayt) verb to make a forceful protest ♦ *We remonstrated with him about his behaviour.* [from *re-* meaning 'against' and a Latin word *monstrare* meaning 'to show']

remorse noun deep regret for your wrongdoing. SYNONYMS: regret, guilt, contrition, repentance, penitence, self-reproach, pangs of conscience. **remorseful** adjective **remorsefully** adverb [from *re-* meaning 'back' and a Latin word *morsum* meaning 'bitten']

remorseless adverb relentless. **remorselessly** adverb

remote adjective (remoter, remotest) **1** far away in place or time ♦ *the remote past.* **2** far from the main centres of population; isolated ♦ *a remote village.* **3** not close in relationship or connection ♦ *a remote ancestor.* **4** slight ♦ *a remote chance* ♦ *I haven't the remotest idea.* **5** aloof and unfriendly ♦ *I find him a rather remote individual.* **remotely** adverb **remoteness** noun [from a Latin word *remotum* meaning 'removed']

remote control noun **1** controlling something from a distance, usually by means of electricity or radio. **2** a device used to do this. **remote-controlled** adjective

remould [1] (ree-mohld) verb **1** to mould something again. **2** to put a new tread on a worn tyre.

remould [2] (ree-mohld) noun a worn tyre that has been given a new tread.

remount verb **1** to get on a horse, bicycle, etc. again. **2** to put a new frame or mount on a picture.

removable *adjective* able to be removed.

removal *noun* **1** removing, or being removed. **2** the transfer of furniture etc. when moving house.

remove *verb* **1** to take something off or away from where it was. **2** to get rid of something ♦ *This removes the last of my doubts.* SYNONYMS: eliminate, dispose of, dispense with, eradicate, obviate. **3** to take off clothing. **4** to dismiss someone from office.

remove *noun* **1** a stage or degree away from something ♦ *This is several removes from the truth.* **2** a class or form in some British schools. **remover** *noun* [from *re-* and a Latin word *movere* meaning 'to move']

removed *adjective* **1** separated or distant ♦ *a dialect not far removed from Cockney.* **2** (said about cousins) separated by a particular number of steps of descent ♦ *his first cousin once removed.*

remunerate (ri-mewn-er-ayt) *verb* to pay or reward a person for work done or services rendered. **remuneration** *noun* [from *re-* and a Latin word *muneris* meaning 'of a gift']

remunerative (ri-mewn-er-ətiv) *adjective* giving good remuneration, profitable.

Renaissance (rə-nay-sɒns) *noun* the revival of art and literature in Europe, influenced by classical forms, in the 14th–16th centuries.
renaissance *noun* a revival of something. [a French word meaning 'rebirth']

renal (ree-nəl) *adjective* to do with the kidneys. [from a Latin word *renes* meaning 'kidneys']

rename *verb* to give a new name to a person or thing.

rend *verb* (past tense and past participle **rent**) (*literary*) **1** to tear something apart with force. **2** to pierce the silence with a loud noise ♦ *Loud screams rent the air.* [from an Old English word *rendan*]

render *verb* **1** to cause a person or thing to become something ♦ *The shock rendered us all speechless.* **2** to give something, especially in return or exchange or as something due ♦ *a reward for services rendered.* **3** to present or send in an account for payment. **4** to represent or perform something ♦ *The artist has rendered her features with great delicacy.* **5** to translate something ♦ *Underneath, the inscription has been rendered into English.* **6** to melt down fat. **7** to cover stone or

brick with a first coat of plaster. [from a Latin word *reddere* meaning 'to give back']

rendezvous (ron-day-voo) *noun* (**rendezvous** (ron-day-vooz)) **1** a meeting with someone at an agreed time and place. **2** a place arranged for this.
rendezvous *verb* (**rendezvoused, rendezvousing**) to meet at an agreed time and place. [from a French phrase *rendez-vous* meaning 'present yourselves']

rendition (ren-dish-ən) *noun* the way a dramatic role or musical piece etc. is rendered or performed. [same origin as for *render*]

renegade (ren-i-gayd) *noun* **1** someone who deserts a group, cause, or faith etc. for another. **2** an outlaw. [from *re-* meaning 'back' and a Latin word *negare* meaning 'to deny']

renege (ri-nayg or ri-neeg) (to **renege on** to break your word or an agreement. [from *re-* meaning 'back' and a Latin word *negare* meaning 'to deny']

renew *verb* **1** to begin or make or give something again ♦ *It's time we renewed our acquaintance* ♦ *They renewed their requests for help.* **2** to arrange for something to be valid for a further period of time ♦ *I'd like to renew my passport.* **3** to give new strength to something ♦ *We ran out for the second half with renewed enthusiasm.* **4** to replace something with a fresh supply ♦ *The tyres need renewing.* **renewal** *noun*

renewable *adjective* able to be renewed.

renewable energy *noun* an energy source (such as power from the sun, wind, or waves) that can never be used up, or which can be renewed.

rennet (ren-it) *noun* a substance used to curdle milk in making cheese, originally obtained from the stomachs of calves. [probably from an Old English word]

rennin *noun* the enzyme in rennet that causes milk to curdle. [from *rennet*]

renounce *verb* **1** to give up a claim or right etc. formally ♦ *He decided to renounce his title.* **2** to reject or abandon a belief, way of life, etc. ♦ *This former terrorist has renounced violence completely.* **renouncement** *noun* [from *re-* meaning 'back' and a Latin word *nuntiare* meaning 'to announce']

renovate (ren-ə-vayt) *verb* to repair something and make it look new. **renovation** *noun* **renovator** *noun* [from *re-* and a Latin word *novus* meaning 'new']

renown *noun* fame. [from *re-* and a French word *nomer* meaning 'to name']

renowned *adjective* famous or celebrated.
SYNONYMS: eminent, noted, distinguished, prominent, well-known.

rent [1] *noun* **1** a regular payment made for the use of land or accommodation. **2** a sum paid to hire something.
rent *verb* **1** to pay rent for temporary use of something. **2** to allow something to be used in return for payment. **rentable** *adjective* [from an Old French word *rente*]

rent [2] past tense and past participle of **rend**.
rent *noun* a large tear in a piece of material. [from *rend*]

rental *noun* **1** the amount paid or received as rent. **2** renting something.

renumber *verb* to change the number or numbering of something.

renunciation (ri-nun-si-ay-shon) *noun* renouncing, giving something up.

reopen *verb* to open something or be opened again.

reorder *verb* **1** to order something again; to order further supplies of something. **2** to put something into a different sequence.

reorganize *verb* to change the way in which something is organized.
reorganization *noun*

rep [1] *noun* (*informal*) a business firm's travelling representative.

rep [2] *adjective* (*informal*) repertory ♦ *a rep theatre.*
rep *noun* a repertory theatre or company.

repaint *verb* to paint something again or differently.

repair [1] *verb* **1** to put something into good condition after damage or the effects of wear and tear. **2** to put something right ♦ *Attempts to repair their marriage failed.*
repair *noun* **1** the act or process of repairing something ♦ *The pier is currently under repair.* **2** a part that has been repaired ♦ *Look, the repair is hardly visible.*
in good repair in good condition; well maintained. **repairer** *noun* [from *re-* and a Latin word *parare* meaning 'to make ready']

repair [2] *verb* (*formal or humorous*) to go ♦ *The guests repaired to the dining room.* [same origin as for *repatriate*]

repairable *adjective* able to be repaired.

reparable (rep-er-ǝbǝl) *adjective* able to be repaired or put right.

reparation (rep-er-ay-shon) *noun* making amends; paying for damage or loss.
reparations *plural noun* compensation for war damage paid by the defeated nation. [same origin as for *repair*]

repartee (rep-ar-tee) *noun* witty replies and remarks. [from a French word *repartir* meaning 'to answer back']

repast (ri-pahst) *noun* (*formal*) a meal. [from *re-* and a Latin word *pascere* meaning 'to feed']

repatriate (ree-pat-ri-ayt) *verb* to send a person back to their own country.
repatriation *noun* [from *re-* and a Latin word *patria* meaning 'native country']

repay *verb* (past tense and past participle **repaid**) **1** to pay back money borrowed or owed. **2** to do or make or give something in return ♦ *How can we ever repay you for your kindness?* **3** to be worth having something done to it ♦ *This poem looks simple enough but repays a closer reading.*
repayable *adjective* **repayment** *noun*

repeal *verb* to cancel a law officially.
repeal *noun* the repealing of a law. [from *re-* and a French word *appeler* meaning 'to appeal']

repeat *verb* **1** to say or do something again. **2** to say aloud something you have heard or learnt by heart ♦ *Repeat the oath after me.* **3** to tell to another person something told to yourself. **4** (said about food) to produce a taste in your mouth some time after being eaten.
repeat *noun* **1** repeating. **2** something that is repeated ♦ *There are too many repeats on television* ♦ *a repeat prescription.* **to repeat itself** to recur in the same form ♦ *History has a way of repeating itself.* **to repeat yourself** to say or do the same thing more than once, especially in a boring way.
repeatable *adjective* **repeater** *noun* [from *re-* and a Latin word *petere* meaning 'to seek']

repeatedly *adverb* again and again.

repel *verb* (**repelled, repelling**) **1** to drive someone or something away ♦ *They fought bravely and repelled the attackers.* **2** to produce a feeling of disgust in someone.
SYNONYMS: disgust, revolt, sicken, nauseate, offend. **3** (*formal*) to refuse to accept something ♦ *She repelled all offers of help.* **4** (said about a substance) to not allow another substance to penetrate or mix

with it ♦ *The surface repels moisture.* **5** to push something away from itself by means of a physical force (the opposite of *attract*) ♦ *One north magnetic pole repels another.* [from *re-* and a Latin word *pellere* meaning 'to drive']

repellent *adjective* **1** causing disgust or distaste. **2** not able to be penetrated by a specified substance ♦ *The fabric is water-repellent.*
repellent *noun* a substance that repels something ♦ *insect repellents.* **repellence** *noun*

repent *verb* to feel regret about what you have done or failed to do. **repentance** *noun* **repentant** *adjective* [from an Old Fench word *repentir*]

repercussion (ree-per-**kush**-ən) *noun* **1** a consequence of an event or action. **2** (*old use*) the recoil of something after impact. **3** (*old use*) an echo. [from *re-* and a Latin word *percutere* meaning 'to strike']

repertoire (**rep**-er-twar) *noun* a stock of songs, plays, or acts etc. that a person or company knows and is able to perform. [from a French word *répertoire*; related to *repertory*]

repertory (**rep**-er-ter-i) *noun* (**repertories**) **1** theatrical performances of various plays for short periods, not for long runs. **2** a repertoire. [from a Latin word *repertorium* meaning 'a list or catalogue']

repertory company *noun* a theatrical company that gives performances of various plays for short periods.

repetition *noun* **1** repeating, or being repeated. **2** something repeated.

repetitious (rep-i-**tish**-əs) *adjective* repetitive.

repetitive (ri-**pet**-it-iv) *adjective* characterized by repetition. **repetitively** *adverb*

rephrase *verb* to express something in an alternative way.

repine (ri-**piyn**) *verb* (*literary*) to fret or be discontented. [from *re-* and *pine*[2]]

replace *verb* **1** to take the place of another person or thing. **2** to find or provide a substitute for something. **3** to put something back in its place. **replaceable** *adjective* **replacement** *noun*

replay[1] (**ree**-play) *noun* **1** a playback of a piece of action in the broadcast of a sports event, often in slow motion. **2** the playing of a match again.

replay[2] (ree-**play**) *verb* **1** to play a match again. **2** to play back a recording.

replenish *verb* **1** to fill something up again. **2** to add a new supply of something. **replenishment** *noun* [from *re-* and a Latin word *plenus* meaning 'full']

replete (ri-**pleet**) *adjective* **1** well stocked or supplied. **2** feeling full after eating. **repletion** *noun* [from *re-* and a Latin word -*pletum* meaning 'filled']

replica (**rep**-lik-ə) *noun* an exact copy or reproduction of something. [from an Italian word]

replicate *verb* **1** to make or be an exact copy of something. **2** to reproduce itself ♦ *a computer virus that replicates itself.* **3** to repeat a scientific experiment satisfactorily. [from *re-* and a Latin word *plicare* meaning 'to fold']

reply *verb* (**replies, replied, replying**) to say, write, or do something in answer or response.
reply *noun* (**replies**) **1** replying. **2** a spoken or written response. [from an Old French word *replier*]

report *verb* **1** to give an account of something you have seen, done, or studied. **2** to give information about something or make something known ♦ *Do you have much progress to report?* **3** to write or give an account of a news story for publication or broadcasting. **4** to make a formal complaint or accusation ♦ *I wish to report a break-in.* **5** to present yourself as having arrived or as ready to do something ♦ *Visitors are asked to report to reception.* **6** to be responsible to a certain person as your manager or supervisor.
report *noun* **1** a spoken or written account of something you have seen, done, or studied. **2** an account of a news story for publication or broadcasting. **3** a regular statement about a pupil's or employee's work and conduct. **4** a rumour or piece of gossip. **5** an explosive sound like that made by a gun. [from *re-* meaning 'back' and a Latin word *portare* meaning 'to carry']

reportage (rep-or-**tahzh**) *noun* the reporting of news by journalists; a typical style of doing this.

reportedly *adverb* according to reports.

reported speech *noun* a speaker's words as reported by another person and put into the tense of the reporting verb (such as *said* or *replied*), as in *She said I was not looking well.*

reporter noun a person whose job is to report news for publication or broadcasting.

repose [1] noun 1 rest or sleep. 2 a peaceful state or effect, tranquillity.
repose verb to rest or lie somewhere. [from *re-* and a Latin word *pausare* meaning 'to pause']

repose [2] verb to place your trust or confidence in a person or thing. [from *re-* and *pose*]

repository noun (**repositories**) 1 a place where things are stored. 2 a store or source of information or knowledge ♦ *My grandfather is a repository of family stories.* [from a Latin word *reponere* meaning 'to replace']

repossess verb to take back possession of property or goods on which payments have not been kept up. **repossession** noun

repoussé (ri-poo-say) adjective (said about metalwork) hammered into relief from the reverse side. [from *re-* and a French word *pousser* meaning 'to push']

reprehend (rep-ri-hend) verb to reprimand someone. [from *re-* and a Latin word *prehendere* meaning 'to grasp']

reprehensible (rep-ri-hen-sibəl) adjective extremely bad and deserving blame or rebuke. **reprehensibly** adverb [from a Latin word *reprehendere* meaning 'to blame, rebuke']

represent verb 1 to act or speak on someone's behalf ♦ *As an MP my duty is to represent my constituents.* 2 to constitute or amount to something ♦ *This announcement represents a U-turn by the government.* 3 to be an example or expression of something ♦ *The election results represent the views of the electorate.* 4 to symbolize or stand for something ♦ *In Roman numerals, C represents 100.* 5 to show a person, thing, or scene in a picture or play etc. SYNONYMS: depict, portray, picture, render. 6 to describe or declare someone or something to be something ♦ *He has been falsely representing himself as an expert.* 7 (*formal*) to state or point out something ♦ *We must represent to them the risks involved.* [from *re-* and a Latin word *praesentare* meaning 'to present']

representation noun 1 representing, or being represented. 2 a picture, model, or other depiction of something.

representations plural noun formal statements, complaints, or demands made to an authority.

representative adjective 1 typical of a group or class. 2 containing examples of a number of types ♦ *a representative selection.* 3 consisting of elected representatives; based on representation by these ♦ *representative government.*
representative noun 1 a person chosen or appointed to act or speak on behalf of others, or to take part in a legislative assembly on their behalf. 2 a firm's agent who travels to potential clients to sell its products. 3 a sample or specimen of something.

repress verb 1 to keep your feelings or desires under control. SYNONYMS: suppress, stifle; (*informal*) bottle up. 2 to subdue people by force. **repression** noun [from a Latin word *reprimere* meaning 'to press back']

repressed adjective suffering from repression of your feelings and desires.

repressive adjective harshly restricting people's freedom ♦ *a repressive regime.* **repressively** adverb

reprieve (ri-preev) noun 1 postponement or cancellation of a punishment, especially of the death sentence. 2 temporary relief from danger; postponement of trouble. **reprieve** verb to give a reprieve to someone. [from an Old French word *repris*]

reprimand (rep-ri-mahnd) noun an expression of disapproval, especially a formal or official one.
reprimand verb to give someone a reprimand. SYNONYMS: criticize, censure, rebuke, admonish, castigate, reproach, condemn, scold, upbraid; (*informal*) tell off, tick off. [from a French word *réprimande*; related to *repress*]

reprint [1] (ree-print) verb to print something again in the same or a new form.

reprint [2] (ree-print) noun 1 the reprinting of a book. 2 a copy of a book or photograph etc. that has been reprinted.

reprisal (ri-priy-zəl) noun an act of retaliation ♦ *It is feared the guerrillas will take reprisals.* [from an Old French word *reprisaille*]

reprise (ri-preez) noun a repeated passage of music or performance of something.

reprise *verb* to repeat a piece of music or a performance. [from a French word meaning 'taken up again']

reproach *verb* to express disapproval to a person for a fault or offence.
reproach *noun* an expression of disapproval or disappointment. **above** or **beyond reproach** deserving no blame or criticism; perfect. **reproachful** *adjective* **reproachfully** *adverb* [from an Old French word *reprochier*]

reprobate (rep-rə-bayt) *noun* an immoral or unprincipled person. [from a Latin word *reprobare* meaning 'to disapprove']

reproduce *verb* 1 to produce a copy of something. 2 to produce further members of the same species by natural means; to produce offspring. 3 to cause something to be seen or heard again or to happen again ♦ *Scientists are trying to reproduce these conditions in a laboratory.* 4 to come out in a particular way when copied ♦ *Some colours don't reproduce well.* **reproducible** *adjective*

reproduction *noun* 1 reproducing, or being reproduced. 2 a copy of something, especially a work of art. 3 the process of producing offspring.
reproduction *adjective* (said about furniture) made in imitation of an earlier style.

reproductive *adjective* to do with or belonging to reproduction ♦ *the reproductive system.*

reprographic (ree-prə-**graf**-ik) *adjective* to do with or involving the copying of printed material by photocopying etc. [from *reproduce* and *-graph*]

reproof *noun* an expression of condemnation for a fault or offence. [from an Old French word *reprover* meaning 'to reprove']

reprove *verb* to rebuke or reprimand someone. [from a Latin word *reprobare* meaning 'to disapprove']

reptile *noun* a member of the class of cold-blooded animals with a backbone and relatively short legs or no legs at all, e.g. snakes, lizards, crocodiles, tortoises.
reptilian (rep-**til**-iən) *adjective & noun* [from a Latin word *reptilis* meaning 'crawling']

republic *noun* a country in which the supreme power is held by the people and their elected representatives, and which

has an elected or nominated president rather than a monarch. [from Latin words *res publica* meaning 'public affairs']

republican *adjective* to do with, like, or in favour of a republic.
republican *noun* a person who is in favour of republican government.
Republican *noun* 1 a member or supporter of the **Republican Party**, one of the two main political parties in the USA. 2 a supporter of the union of Northern Ireland and Eire.

repudiate (ri-**pew**-di-ayt) *verb* 1 to refuse to deal with or be associated with someone or something. 2 to deny or reject something ♦ *I utterly repudiate the accusation.* **repudiation** *noun* **repudiator** *noun* [from a Latin word *repudiare* meaning 'to divorce']

repugnant (ri-**pug**-nənt) *adjective* distasteful or objectionable. **repugnance** *noun* [from *re-* meaning 'against' and a Latin word *pugnans* meaning 'fighting']

repulse *verb* 1 to drive back an attacking force. 2 to reject an offer or help etc. firmly. 3 to make someone feel strong distaste or disgust. [same origin as for *repel*]

repulsion *noun* 1 repelling, or being repelled. 2 a feeling of strong distaste or disgust.

repulsive *adjective* 1 disgusting. SYNONYMS: revolting, repugnant, repellent, vile, hideous, loathsome, obnoxious. 2 repelling things ♦ *a repulsive force.* **repulsively** *adverb* **repulsiveness** *noun*

reputable (**rep**-yoo-təbəl) *adjective* having a good reputation. **reputably** *adverb*

reputation *noun* 1 the opinion that is generally held about a person or thing. 2 public recognition for your abilities or achievements ♦ *He has built up quite a reputation for himself.* SYNONYMS: name, repute, renown, standing, prestige. [from a Latin word *reputare* meaning 'to consider']

repute (ri-**pewt**) *noun* reputation ♦ *I know him by repute* ♦ *designers of international repute.* [same origin as for *reputation*]

reputed (ri-**pewt**-id) *adjective* said or thought to have done or to be something ♦ *This is reputed to be the best hotel in the area.* **reputedly** *adverb*

request *noun* 1 asking or being asked for a thing or to do something. 2 a thing asked for ♦ *Do you have any requests?* ♦ *a record* request show.

request verb to make a request for something. **by** or **on request** in response to a request. [from an Old French word; related to *require*]

request stop noun a bus stop at which the bus stops only on a passenger's or intended passenger's request.

requiem (rek-wi-em) noun a special Mass for someone who has died; a musical setting for this. [a Latin word meaning 'rest']

require verb 1 to need or depend on something ♦ *Cars require regular servicing.* 2 to demand that someone does something; to oblige someone ♦ *These measures are required by law* ♦ *Civil Servants are required to sign the Official Secrets Act.* 3 to wish to have something ♦ *Will you require tea?* [from re- and a Latin word *quaerere* meaning 'to seek']

requirement noun a thing required; a need.

requisite (rek-wiz-it) adjective required by circumstances, necessary to success. **requisite** noun a thing needed for some purpose. [same origin as for *require*]

requisition noun an official order laying claim to the use of something, especially by the army; a formal written demand for something that is needed. **requisition** verb to take something over for official use. [same origin as for *require*]

requite (ri-kwiyt) verb (formal) 1 to make a return for a service or to a person. 2 to avenge a wrong or injury etc. **requital** noun [from re- and an old word *quite* meaning 'to quit']

reredos (reer-doss) noun (**reredos**) an ornamental screen covering the wall above the back of an altar. [from Old French words *arere* meaning 'behind' and *dos* meaning 'back']

re-route (ree-root) verb to send or carry something by a different route.

rerun verb (**reran**, **rerun**, **rerunning**) 1 to run a race again. 2 to broadcast a programme, film, etc. again. **rerun** noun 1 a race that is run again. 2 a repeat of a programme, film, etc.

resale noun sale to another person of something you have bought.

rescind (ri-sind) verb to repeal or cancel a law or rule etc. **rescission** noun [from re- and a Latin word *scindere* meaning 'to cut']

rescue verb to save a person or thing from danger, harm, etc.; to free someone from captivity. **rescue** noun rescuing, or being rescued. **rescuer** noun [from an Old French word *rescoure*]

research (ri-serch or ree-serch) noun careful study and investigation, especially in order to discover new facts or information. **research** verb to carry out research into something. **researcher** noun [from an Old French word *recerche* meaning 'careful search']

◊ The first pronunciation is the one traditionally used in British English. The US pronunciation, with the stress on the second syllable, is also now commonly used in British English and is perfectly acceptable.

resell verb (past tense and past participle **resold**) to sell what you have bought to another person.

resemble verb to look like or have features in common with another person or thing. **resemblance** noun [from re- and a Latin word *similis* meaning 'like']

resent (ri-zent) verb to feel bitter and indignant about something, to feel insulted by something said or done. **resentment** noun [from re- meaning 'against' and a Latin word *sentire* meaning 'to feel']

resentful adjective feeling bitter and indignant about something. **resentfully** adverb

reservation noun 1 reserving, or being reserved. 2 a reserved seat, table, room, etc. ♦ *our hotel reservations.* 3 an area of land set aside for the exclusive use of North American Indians or Australian Aboriginals. 4 a limit on how far you agree with or accept an idea etc. ♦ *We accept the plan in principle but have certain reservations* ♦ *I can recommend her for the job without reservation.* 5 a strip of land between the carriageways of a road.

reserve verb 1 to put something aside for a later occasion or for special use. 2 to order or set aside seats, tickets, accommodation, etc. for a particular person to use at a future date. 3 to retain or hold something ♦ *The company reserves the right to offer a substitute.* 4 to postpone something until you have had time to consider it properly ♦ *I will reserve judgement on his chances of winning the title.*

reserve noun 1 something kept back for future use; an extra amount or stock kept available for use when needed ♦ *dwindling oil reserves*. 2 (also **reserves**) forces outside the regular armed services and liable to be called out in an emergency. 3 an extra player chosen in case a substitute should be needed in a team. 4 an area of land set aside for some special purpose ♦ *a nature reserve*. 5 a limitation on your agreement or acceptance of an idea etc. 6 a tendency to avoid showing your feelings and to lack warmth towards other people. **in reserve** in a state of being unused but available. [from *re-* meaning 'back' and a Latin word *servare* meaning 'to keep']

reserved adjective (said about a person) restrained in your behaviour, unwilling to show your feelings.

reserve price noun the lowest price that will be accepted for something sold in an auction.

reservist noun a member of a country's reserve forces.

reservoir (rez-er-vwar) noun 1 a natural or artificial lake that is a source of water supply for a town etc. 2 a supply or collection of information etc. 3 a container for a supply of fuel or other liquid. [from a French word *réservoir*, related to *reserve*]

reshuffle verb 1 to rearrange the posts or responsibilities of a group of people, especially government ministers. 2 to shuffle cards again.
reshuffle noun reshuffling ♦ *a Cabinet reshuffle*.

reside verb 1 to have your permanent home in a certain place. 2 to be present in or belong to a person or thing ♦ *Supreme authority resides in the President*. [from *re-* and a Latin word *-sidere* meaning 'to sit']

residence noun 1 the place where a person lives. 2 a house, especially a large or impressive one ♦ *the ambassador's official residence* ♦ *desirable residence for sale*. 3 the fact of living in a place ♦ *When can I take up residence in college?* **in residence** (said about an artist, writer, etc.) working in a specified place for a period of time ♦ *The local museum has appointed a writer in residence*.

residency noun (**residencies**) 1 the fact of living in a place ♦ *She has been granted permanent residency*. 2 a band's or singer's regular appearance at a particular venue. 3 a residential post held by an artist or writer.

resident noun 1 a person living somewhere, not a visitor. 2 a person staying overnight at a hotel.
resident adjective residing, in residence. [from *re-* and a Latin word *-sidens* meaning 'sitting']

residential (rez-i-den-shəl) adjective 1 containing or suitable for private houses ♦ *a residential area*. 2 providing accommodation ♦ *a residential course*. 3 connected with or based on residence ♦ *residential qualifications for voters*.

residual (ri-zid-yoo-əl) adjective left over as a residue, remaining.
residual noun something left over as a residue. **residually** adverb

residuary (ri-zid-yoo-er-i) adjective 1 a technical term for residual. 2 (*Law*) to do with the residue of an estate.

residue (rez-i-dew) noun 1 the remainder, what is left over. 2 a substance that remains after a process such as combustion or evaporation. [from a Latin word *residuus* meaning 'remaining']

residuum (ri-zid-yoo-əm) noun (**residua**) a chemical residue, especially after combustion or evaporation. [same origin as for *residue*]

resign verb to give up your job or position. **to resign yourself to** to accept that something cannot be avoided and you must put up with it. [from a Latin word *resignare* meaning 'to unseal']

resignation noun 1 resigning. 2 a document stating that you wish to resign. 3 a resigned attitude or expression.

resigned adjective having or showing patient acceptance of something unwelcome that cannot be avoided. **to be resigned to** to resign yourself to something. **resignedly** (ri-ziyn-idli) adverb

resilient (ri-zil-iənt) adjective 1 able to spring back into shape after being bent or stretched. 2 (said about a person) able to recover quickly from difficult circumstances. **resilience** noun **resiliently** adverb [from a Latin word *resilire* meaning 'to jump back']

resin (rez-in) noun 1 a sticky substance that oozes from fir and pine trees and from many other plants. 2 a similar substance made synthetically, used in making plastics, paints, varnishes, etc. **resinous** adjective [from a Latin word *resina*]

resist verb 1 to use force in order to prevent something from happening or being successful ♦ *He was charged with resisting arrest.* 2 to oppose or refuse to accept something ♦ *I would definitely resist any plans to close the school down.* 3 to be undamaged or unaffected by something ♦ *pans that resist heat.* 4 to refrain from yielding to something although you are tempted by it ♦ *I find it difficult to resist chocolate.* ♦ *She can't resist interfering.* [from re- meaning 'against' and a Latin word sistere meaning 'to stand firmly']

resistance noun 1 resisting; the power to resist something. 2 an influence that hinders or stops something. 3 the ability of a substance to resist the passage of heat or electricity; the measure of this. 4 (also **Resistance**) a secret organization resisting the authorities, especially in a conquered or enemy-occupied country. **the line of least resistance** the easiest method or course.

resistant adjective offering resistance, capable of resisting ♦ *heat-resistant plastics.*

resistive adjective 1 a technical term for resistant. 2 (Physics) having electrical resistance.

resistivity (rez-iss-tiv-iti) noun (Physics) the power of a specified material to resist the passage of electric current.

resistor noun a device having resistance to the passage of electric current.

resit verb (past tense and past participle **resat**; **resitting**) to sit an examination again after a previous failure.
resit noun an examination that you sit again.

resolute (rez-ə-loot) adjective showing great determination. **resolutely** adverb **resoluteness** noun [same origin as for resolve]

resolution noun 1 the quality of being resolute, great determination. 2 a formal decision or statement of opinion agreed on by a committee or assembly. 3 a mental pledge, something you intend to do ♦ *New Year resolutions.* 4 the solving of a problem or question. 5 the process of separating something or being separated into constituent parts. 6 the degree to which a photographic or television image can reproduce fine detail.

resolve verb 1 to solve or settle a problem or doubts etc. 2 to decide something firmly. 3 (said about a committee or assembly) to pass a resolution. 4 (Music) to convert a discord into a pleasing chord. 5 to separate something into constituent parts.
resolve noun a firm decision or determination ♦ *She said she would give up smoking and she kept her resolve.* [from re- and a Latin word solvere meaning 'to loosen']

resolved adjective (said about a person) determined, resolute.

resolving power noun the ability of an optical instrument or type of film to distinguish between objects that are very close together or to reproduce fine detail.

resonant (rez-ən-ənt) adjective 1 (said about a sound, room, etc.) resounding or echoing. 2 suggesting or bringing to mind a feeling, memory, etc. **resonance** noun [from re- and a Latin word sonans meaning 'sounding']

resonate (rez-ən-ayt) verb to be resonant, to resound. **resonator** noun

resort (ri-zort) verb 1 to turn to and make use of a course of action to help you deal with a situation ♦ *You should never need to resort to violence.* 2 (formal) to go somewhere, especially on a regular basis.
resort noun 1 a place where people go for relaxation or holidays. 2 a course of action resorted to; resorting to something ♦ *I'm sure you can persuade him without resort to threats.* **as a last resort** when everything else has failed. [from re- and a French word sortir meaning 'to go out']

resound (ri-zownd) verb 1 (said about a voice or sound etc.) to fill a place with sound; to produce echoes. 2 (said about a place) to be filled with sound; to echo. [from re- and a Latin word sonare meaning 'to sound']

resounding adjective 1 loud and echoing. 2 (said about a success, victory, etc.) clear and emphatic ♦ *a resounding victory.* **resoundingly** adverb

resource noun 1 something that can be used to achieve a purpose. 2 a teaching aid.

resources plural noun 1 a source of wealth to a country ♦ *The country's natural resources include coal and oil.* 2 available assets, especially money ♦ *We pooled our resources.* 3 a person's qualities and abilities that help them in difficult circumstances.

resource *verb* to provide money or other resources for something. [from an Old French word *resourdre* meaning 'to rise again'; related to *resurgence*]

resourceful *adjective* clever at finding ways of dealing with difficulties. **resourcefully** *adverb* **resourcefulness** *noun*

respect *noun* 1 admiration felt towards a person or thing that has good qualities or achievements. 2 consideration or attention ♦ *You should show more respect for other people's feelings.* 3 a particular detail or aspect ♦ *In this respect he is like his sister.* **respects** *plural noun* polite greetings ♦ *I'd like to pay my respects to your mother.* **respect** *verb* 1 to feel or show respect for a person or thing. SYNONYMS: admire, revere, look up to. 2 to agree to abide by a rule, agreement, etc. **with respect to** or **in respect of** as regards; with reference to ♦ *This is true with respect to English but not to French.* **respecter** *noun* [from *re-* meaning 'back' and a Latin word *specere* meaning 'to look']

respectable *adjective* 1 honest and decent; of good social standing. 2 fairly good; adequate or acceptable ♦ *a respectable score.* **respectability** *noun* **respectably** *adverb*

respectful *adjective* showing respect. **respectfully** *adverb* **respectfulness** *noun*

respecting *preposition* concerning, with respect to.

respective *adjective* belonging separately to each one mentioned ♦ *We went off to our respective rooms* ♦ *All four brothers are successful in their respective fields.*

respectively *adverb* for each separately in the order mentioned.

respiration *noun* 1 breathing. 2 (*Biology*) a process in living organisms involving the production of energy, especially a plant's taking in of oxygen and release of carbon dioxide. [from a Latin word *respirare* meaning 'to breathe out']

respirator *noun* 1 a device worn over the nose and mouth to filter or purify the air before it is inhaled. 2 an apparatus for giving artificial respiration.

respiratory (**ress**-per-ayt-er-i or ri-**spyr**-ə-ter-i) *adjective* to do with or involving respiration.

respire *verb* 1 to breathe. 2 (*Biology*) (said about plants) to perform the process of respiration. [same origin as for *respiration*]

respite (**ress**-pyt) *noun* a short period of rest or relief from something difficult or unpleasant. [from an Old French word *respit*]

resplendent *adjective* impressively bright and colourful. **resplendently** *adverb* [from *re-* and a Latin word *splendens* meaning 'glittering']

respond *verb* 1 to speak or write in reply. 2 to act or behave in answer to or because of something ♦ *The British public have responded marvellously to our appeal.* 3 to show a favourable reaction to something ♦ *The disease did not respond to treatment* ♦ *She responds to kindness.* [from *re-* and a Latin word *spondere* meaning 'to promise']

respondent *noun* 1 the defendant in a lawsuit, especially in a divorce case. 2 someone who responds to a questionnaire or advertisement.

response *noun* 1 an answer ♦ *She made no response.* 2 a reaction to something ♦ *The appeal for help met with an enthusiastic response.* [same origin as for *respond*]

responsibility *noun* (**responsibilities**) 1 being responsible. 2 the opportunity to work independently and take your own decisions without being told what to do. 3 something for which a person is responsible.

responsible *adjective* 1 legally or morally obliged to take care of something or to carry out a duty, and having to take the blame if something goes wrong. 2 being the main cause of something ♦ *This faulty piece of equipment was responsible for many deaths.* 3 reporting to someone; having to account for your actions ♦ *You will be responsible to the president himself.* 4 involving important duties or decisions ♦ *a responsible position.* 5 reliable and trustworthy ♦ *a responsible person.* **responsibly** *adverb* [same origin as for *respond*]

responsive *adjective* responding well or quickly to something. **responsiveness** *noun*

respray *verb* to spray something with a new coat of paint. **respray** *noun* the act or process of respraying.

rest[1] *verb* 1 to be still, to stop moving or working, especially in order to relax or recover your strength. 2 to allow something to be inactive in order to recover or save strength or energy ♦ *Sit* down and rest your feet. **3** to place something or be placed somewhere for support ♦ *Rest the ladder against the wall.* **4** to depend or be based on something ♦ *The entire case rests on evidence of identification.* **5** (said about a look) to be directed in a particular direction ♦ *His gaze rested on his son.* **6** (said about a matter under discussion) to be left without further discussion or investigation ♦ *And there the matter rests.*

rest *noun* **1** a time of sleep or inactivity as a way of recovering your strength. **2** an interval of silence between notes in music; a sign indicating this. **3** an object used to hold or support something. **at rest 1** not moving. **2** free from trouble or anxiety. **to come to rest** to slow down and stop. **to rest with** to be someone's responsibility to deal with ♦ *It rests with you to suggest a date.* [from an Old English word *ræst* meaning 'bed']

rest ² *verb* to remain in a specified state ♦ *Rest assured, we will do everything we can.* **the rest** *noun* the remaining part of something; the others. [from a Latin word *restare* meaning 'to stay behind']

restaurant *noun* a place where people pay to sit and eat meals that are cooked there. [from a French word meaning 'restoring']

restaurateur (rest-ə-rə-tur) *noun* a person who owns and manages a restaurant. [a French word]

rested *adjective* refreshed by resting.

restful *adjective* giving rest or a feeling of rest ♦ *a restful holiday.* **restfully** *adverb* **restfulness** *noun*

restitution *noun* **1** restoring something to its proper owner or its original state. **2** compensation for injury or damage. [from re- and a Latin word *statutum* meaning 'established']

restive *adjective* restless or impatient because of delay, boredom, or restraint. **restively** *adverb* **restiveness** *noun* [originally describing a horse and meaning 'refusing to move', from an Old French word *restif*]

restless *adjective* **1** unable to keep still. SYNONYMS: restive, fidgety, jumpy, jittery, edgy. **2** without rest or sleep ♦ *a restless night.* **restlessly** *adverb* **restlessness** *noun*

restock *verb* to fill something with a new stock of something ♦ *We need to restock the freezer.*

restoration *noun* **1** restoring, or being restored. **2** a model or drawing representing the supposed original form of an extinct animal, ruined building, etc. **the Restoration** *noun* the re-establishment of the monarchy in Britain in 1660 when Charles II became king.

restorative (ri-sto-rə-tiv) *adjective* tending to restore health or strength. **restorative** *noun* a restorative food, drink, or medicine.

restore *verb* **1** to bring something back to its original state, e.g. by repairing or rebuilding it. **2** to bring someone back to good health or full strength. **3** to return something that was lost or stolen to its original owner. **4** to establish something again ♦ *The new head's priority was to restore discipline.* **restorer** *noun* [from a Latin word *restaurare* meaning 'to rebuild, restore']

restrain *verb* **1** to hold someone back, to stop them moving or doing something. **2** to keep something under control ♦ *You must try to restrain your anger.* SYNONYMS: check, curb, stifle, suppress, rein in. [from a Latin word *restringere* meaning 'to tie up firmly, to confine']

restrained *adjective* showing restraint.

restraint *noun* **1** restraining, or being restrained. **2** something that restrains, a limiting influence. **3** the ability to keep calm and control your emotions. **4** avoidance of exaggeration in literary or artistic work. [same origin as for *restrain*]

restrict *verb* to put a limit on something, to subject something to limitations. SYNONYMS: limit, confine, inhibit, restrain. **restriction** *noun* [from a Latin word *restrictus* meaning 'restrained']

restrictive *adjective* restricting.

restrictive practice *noun* an agreement between manufacturers that restricts competition, e.g. by limiting the price at which goods can be sold.

restructure *verb* to organize something differently.

result *noun* **1** what is produced by an activity or operation, an effect or consequence. SYNONYMS: outcome, repercussion, upshot. **2** a statement of the score or marks or the name of the winner in a sporting event, competition, or examination. **3** a satisfactory outcome, such as a victory. **4** an answer or formula etc. obtained by calculation. **result** *verb* **1** to happen as a result ♦ *All sorts of troubles resulted from the merger.* **2** to have a specified result ♦ *The match resulted in a draw.* **to get results** to achieve a significant and satisfactory result. [from a Latin word *resultare* meaning 'to result']

resultant *adjective* happening as a result ♦ *the resultant profit.*
resultant *noun* (*Mathematics*) a vector whose effect is equal to the combined effects of two or more given vectors.

resume *verb* 1 to begin again or continue after stopping for a while. 2 to get or take or occupy something again ♦ *You may now resume your seats.* **resumption** *noun* [from *re-* and a Latin word *sumere* meaning 'to take up']

résumé (rez-yoom-ay) *noun* a summary. [a French word meaning 'summed up']

resurgence (ri-**ser**-jəns) *noun* a rise or revival after a period of decline or inactivity ♦ *a resurgence of interest in Latin.* **resurgent** *adjective* [from *re-* and a Latin word *surgens* meaning 'rising']

resurrect *verb* to bring something back into use or existence ♦ *Perhaps it is time to resurrect this old custom.* [from *resurrection*]

resurrection *noun* 1 coming back to life after being dead. 2 the revival of something after disuse.
Resurrection *noun* in the Christian religion, the resurrection of Jesus Christ three days after his death. [same origin as for *resurgence*]

resuscitate (ri-**sus**-i-tayt) *verb* 1 to revive a person from unconsciousness or apparent death. 2 to revive a custom or institution etc. **resuscitation** *noun* [from *re-* and a Latin word *suscitare* meaning 'to revive']

retail *noun* the selling of goods to the general public.
retail *adverb* being sold in such a way.
retail *verb* 1 to sell something or be sold to the general public. 2 to recount or relate the details of something. **retailer** *noun* [from an Old French word *retaille* meaning 'a piece cut off']

retail price index *noun* an index of the variation in the prices of retail goods and other items.

retain *verb* 1 to keep something in your possession or use. 2 to continue to have something and not lose it ♦ *The fire had retained its heat.* 3 to keep something in your memory ♦ *She retained a clear impression of the building.* 4 to hold something in place. 5 to book the services

of a barrister. [from *re-* and a Latin word *tenere* meaning 'to hold']

retainer *noun* 1 a thing that holds something in place. 2 a sum of money regularly paid to someone so that they will work for you when needed. 3 a servant who has worked for a person or family for a long time.

retaining wall *noun* a wall that holds back a mass of earth or water on one side of it.

retake *verb* (**retook, retaken**) to take a test or examination again.
retake *noun* 1 a test or examination taken again. 2 a scene filmed again.

retaliate (ri-**tal**-i-ayt) *verb* to repay an injury or insult etc. with a similar one; to attack someone in return for a similar attack. **retaliation** *noun* **retaliatory** (ri-**tal**-yə-ter-i) *adjective* [from *re-* and a Latin word *talis* meaning 'the same kind']

retard (ri-**tard**) *verb* to slow down or delay the progress or development of something. **retardation** *noun* [from *re-* and a Latin word *tardus* meaning 'slow']

retarded *adjective* 1 slowed down or delayed. 2 (said about a person) mentally less developed than is usual for their age.

retch *verb* to strain your throat as if vomiting. [from an Old English word] ◊ Do not confuse this word with **wretch**, which has a different meaning.

retell *verb* (past tense and past participle **retold**) to tell a story etc. again.

retention *noun* retaining or keeping something. [same origin as for *retain*]

retentive *adjective* able to retain things ♦ *a retentive memory.* **retentiveness** *noun*

rethink *verb* (past tense and past participle **rethought**) to think about something again; to plan something again and differently.
rethink *noun* an instance of rethinking.

reticent (**ret**-i-sənt) *adjective* not revealing your thoughts and feelings readily. **reticence** *noun* **reticently** *adverb* [from a Latin word *reticere* meaning 'to keep silent']

reticulated (ri-**tik**-yoo-layt-id) *adjective* divided into a network or into small squares with intersecting lines. **reticulation** *noun* [same origin as for *reticulum*]

reticule (ret-i-kewl) *noun* (*historical*) a woman's drawstring handbag of woven or other material. [from a French word *réticule*]

reticulum (ri-tik-yoo-ləm) *noun* (**reticula**) (*Zoology*) a ruminant's second stomach. [a Latin word meaning 'a small net']

retina (ret-in-ə) *noun* (**retinas**) a layer of membrane at the back of the eyeball, sensitive to light. [from a Latin word *rete* meaning 'net']

retinol (ret-in-ol) *noun* either of two forms of vitamin A.

retinue (ret-in-yoo) *noun* a number of attendants accompanying an important person. [from an Old French word *retenue* meaning 'restrained, in someone's service']

retire *verb* 1 to give up your regular work because you are getting old. 2 (said about a sports player) to stop playing competitively. 3 to withdraw from a race, match, etc. because of injury. 4 to go to bed or to a private room. **retired** *adjective* **retirement** *noun* [from a French word *retirer* meaning 'to draw back']

retiring *adjective* shy, avoiding company.

retort[1] *verb* to make a sharp, witty, or angry reply. **retort** *noun* a sharp, witty, or angry reply. [from *re-* and a Latin word *tortum* meaning 'twisted']

retort[2] *noun* 1 a glass vessel with a long downward-bent neck, used in distilling liquids. 2 a container or furnace used in making gas or steel. [from a French word *retorte*]

retouch *verb* to improve or alter a picture or photograph by making minor alterations or removing flaws etc.

retrace *verb* 1 to go back over the route that you have just taken ♦ *We retraced our steps and returned to the ferry.* 2 to trace something back to the source or beginning. **retraceable** *adjective*

retract *verb* 1 to pull something or be pulled back or in ♦ *The snail retracts its horns.* 2 to withdraw a statement or accusation. 3 to go back on an agreement or promise. **retractable** *adjective* **retraction** *noun* **retractor** *noun* [from *re-* and a Latin word *tractum* meaning 'pulled']

retractile (ri-trak-tiyl) *adjective* (*Zoology*) (said about a part of the body) able to be retracted.

retrain *verb* to teach or learn new skills for a different job.

retread[1] (ree-tred) *verb* to put a fresh tread on a worn tyre by moulding rubber to a used foundation.

retread[2] (ree-tred) *noun* a retreaded tyre.

retreat *verb* 1 to go back after being defeated or to avoid danger or difficulty. 2 to go away to a quiet or secluded place. **retreat** *noun* 1 retreating; the military signal for this. 2 a quiet or secluded place. 3 a period of withdrawal from worldly activities for prayer and meditation. [same origin as for *retract*]

retrench *verb* 1 to reduce your costs or spending ♦ *The company has been forced to retrench.* 2 (*formal*) to reduce the amount of something ♦ *We will have to retrench our operations.* **retrenchment** *noun* [from a French word *retrencher*; related to *truncate*]

retrial *noun* a second or further trial.

retribution (ret-ri-bew-shən) *noun* a deserved punishment. [from *re-* and a Latin word *tributum* meaning 'assigned']

retributive (ri-trib-yoo-tiv) *adjective* happening or inflicted as retribution.

retrievable *adjective* able to be retrieved.

retrieval *noun* retrieving, or being retrieved.

retrieve *verb* 1 to bring or get something back. 2 to find or extract information stored in a computer. 3 (said about a dog) to find and bring back killed or wounded game. 4 to rescue or save something; to restore something to a flourishing state ♦ *His quick thinking retrieved the situation* ♦ *I have a plan that might retrieve our fortunes.* 5 to set right a loss or error. **retrieve** *noun* possibility of recovery ♦ *The match was now beyond retrieve.* [from an Old French word *retrover* meaning 'to find again']

retriever *noun* a dog that can be trained to retrieve game.

retro- *prefix* back; backwards (as in *retrograde*). [from a Latin word *retro* meaning 'backwards']

retroactive *adjective* taking effect from a date in the past. **retroactively** *adverb*

retrograde *adjective* 1 going backwards ♦ *retrograde motion.* 2 reverting to an earlier and less good condition. [from *retro-* and a Latin word *gradus* meaning 'a step']

retrogress (ret-rə-**gress**) *verb* to go back to an earlier and less good condition. **retrogression** *noun* **retrogressive** *adjective* [from *retro-* and *progress*]

retrorocket *noun* an auxiliary rocket fired in the opposite direction to the main rockets, used for slowing a spacecraft or missile.

retrospect *noun* a survey of past time or events. **in retrospect** when you look back on a past event or situation. [from *retro-* and *prospect*]

retrospection *noun* looking back into the past.

retrospective *adjective* 1 looking back on the past. 2 taking effect from a date in the past ♦ *The law could not be made retrospective.* **retrospectively** *adjective*

retroussé (rə-**troo**-say) *adjective* (said about a person's nose) turned up at the tip. [a French word meaning 'tucked up']

retry *verb* (**retries**, **retried**, **retrying**) to try a lawsuit or a defendant again.

return *verb* 1 to come or go back. 2 to bring, give, put, or send something back. 3 to say something in reply. 4 (in tennis etc.) to hit the ball back to an opponent. 5 to state or present something officially ♦ *The jury returned a verdict of not guilty.* 6 to elect someone as an MP ♦ *She was returned as MP for Finchley.*
return *noun* 1 coming or going back. 2 bringing, giving, putting, or sending back. 3 the proceeds or profits of a transaction ♦ *He is confident of receiving a good return on his investment.* 4 something that has been returned, such as an unwanted theatre ticket. 5 a return ticket. 6 a return match or game. 7 a formal report or statement, e.g. of a set of transactions ♦ *an income-tax return.* 8 (also **return key**) a key on a computer keyboard that you press to move the cursor from the end of one line to the start of the next. **returnable** *adjective* [from *re-* and a Latin word *tornare* meaning 'to turn']

returning officer *noun* an official who conducts an election in a parliamentary constituency and announces the result.

return match or **return game** *noun* a second match or game played between the same opponents.

return ticket *noun* a ticket for a journey to a place and back again.

reunify *verb* (**reunifies**, **reunified**, **reunifying**) to make a divided country into one again ♦ *How long has Germany been reunified?* **reunification** *noun*

reunion *noun* 1 reuniting, or being reunited. 2 a meeting of people who were formerly associated and have not seen each other for some time ♦ *a school reunion.*

reunite *verb* to come together or bring people together after a period of separation.

reusable *adjective* able to be reused.

reuse[1] (ree-**yooz**) *verb* to use something again.

reuse[2] (ree-**yooss**) *noun* using or being used again.

Rev. *abbreviation* Reverend ♦ *the Rev. John Smith.*

rev *noun* (*informal*) a revolution of an engine.
rev *verb* (**revved**, **revving**) to make an engine run quickly, especially when starting. [short for *revolution*]

revalue *verb* (**revalues**, **revalued**, **revaluing**) 1 to make a new valuation of something. 2 to give a new value, especially a higher one, to a currency in relation to other currencies. **revaluation** *noun*

revamp *verb* to improve the appearance of or give a new structure to something. **revamp** *noun* an improved version of something.

Revd *abbreviation* Reverend.

reveal *verb* 1 to make something known ♦ *The police have not yet revealed the victim's name.* SYNONYMS: disclose, divulge, unveil. 2 to uncover and allow something to be seen. SYNONYMS: expose, show, display, bare. [from a Latin word *revelare* meaning 'to unveil']

revealing *adjective* 1 giving interesting or significant information ♦ *a revealing slip of the tongue.* 2 (said about a piece of clothing) allowing a lot of someone's body to be seen.

reveille (ri-**val**-i) *noun* a military waking signal sounded on a bugle or drums. [from a French word *réveillez* meaning 'wake up!']

revel *verb* (**revelled, revelling**) 1 to take great delight in something ♦ *Some people revel in gossip.* 2 to enage in lively and noisy festivities.

revels plural noun lively and noisy festivities. **reveller** noun [from an Old French word *reveler* meaning 'to rise up'; related to *rebel*]

revelation noun 1 something revealed, especially something surprising. 2 the revealing or making known of something that was secret or hidden. [same origin as for *reveal*]

revelatory adjective revealing.

revelry noun (**revelries**) revelling or revels.

revenge noun 1 harming or punishing someone in return for what they have made you suffer. SYNONYMS: retribution, vengeance, retaliation, reprisal. 2 a desire to inflict such harm or punishment. **revenge** verb to get satisfaction by inflicting revenge; to avenge ♦ *I will be revenged!* **revengeful** adjective [from an Old French word *revencher*; related to *vindicate*]

revenue (rev-ən-yoo) noun 1 a company's income. 2 a country's annual income from taxes, duties, etc., used for paying public expenses. [from an Old French word meaning 'returned']

reverberate (ri-verb-er-ayt) verb 1 (said about a loud noise) to be repeated as an echo. 2 to have continuing serious effects. **reverberant** adjective **reverberation** noun **reverberative** adjective [from *re-* and a Latin word *verberare* meaning 'to lash']

revere (ri-veer) verb to feel deep respect or admiration for someone. [from *re-* and a Latin word *vereri* meaning 'to fear']

reverence noun 1 a feeling of deep respect. 2 a title given to a member of the clergy, especially a priest in Ireland ♦ *His Reverence*. **reverence** verb to feel or show reverence towards someone. [same origin as for *revere*]

Reverend adjective a title or form of address to members of the clergy ♦ *the Reverend Brian Smith*. **reverend** noun (*informal*) a member of the clergy. [from a Latin word *reverendus* meaning 'person to be revered'] ◊ The title *Very Reverend* is used for a dean, *Right Reverend* is used for a bishop, and *Most Reverend* is used for an archbishop or Irish Roman Catholic bishop.

Reverend Mother noun the title of the Mother Superior of a convent.

reverent adjective showing reverence.

reverential adjective **reverently** adverb [from a Latin word meaning 'revering']

reverie (rev-er-i) noun a daydream, a state of daydreaming. [from a French word]

revers (ri-veer) noun (**revers**, (ri-veerz)) a turned-back edge of a piece of clothing, especially at the lapel. [a French word meaning 'reverse']

reversal noun 1 a change to an opposite direction, position, or course of action. 2 a piece of bad luck.

reverse verb 1 to put or turn something the other way round or up, or inside out. 2 to move or make something move backwards or in an opposite direction ♦ *He reversed the car out of the drive.* 3 to make an engine or machine work in the opposite direction to normal. 4 to change something to the opposite of what it was ♦ *If elected, they have promised to reverse that policy.* 5 to cancel a decision, judgement, or decree. SYNONYMS: overturn, quash, countermand, annul, rescind. **reverse** adjective 1 facing or moving in the opposite direction. 2 opposite in character or order. **reverse** noun 1 the opposite or contrary of something. 2 a complete change of direction or action. 3 the reverse side or face of something. 4 a setback or defeat ♦ *They suffered several reverses.* 5 reverse gear. **in reverse** the opposite way round ♦ *The name was printed in reverse.* **to reverse the charges** to make the person receiving a telephone call pay for it, not the caller. **reversely** adverb [same origin as for *revert*]

reverse gear noun a gear that allows a vehicle to be driven backwards.

reversible adjective 1 able to be reversed. 2 (said about a piece of clothing) able to be worn with either side turned outwards.

reversion noun 1 reverting to a previous state, practice, or belief. 2 the legal right to possess something when its present holder relinquishes it; the returning of a right or property in this way. **reversionary** adjective ◊ Note that *reversion* does not mean the same as *reversal*.

revert verb 1 to return to a previous state, practice, or belief. 2 to return to a subject in talk or thought. 3 (*Law*) (said about property etc.) to return or pass to another owner by reversion. [from *re-* meaning 'back' and a Latin word *vertere* meaning 'to turn']

review noun **1** a re-examination or reconsideration of something ♦ *The salary scale is under review.* **2** a published report assessing the merits of a book, film, play, etc. **3** a general survey of past events or of a subject. **4** a ceremonial inspection of troops or a fleet etc.
review verb **1** to re-examine or reconsider something. **2** to write a review of a book, film, play, etc. **3** to inspect troops or a fleet etc. ceremonially. **reviewer** noun [from a French word *revoir* meaning 'to see again']
◊ Do not confuse this word with **revue**, which has a different meaning.

revile verb to criticize someone angrily in abusive language. **revilement** noun [from *re-* and an Old French word *vil* meaning 'vile']

revise verb **1** to go over work that you have already learnt in preparation for an examination. **2** to change or amend something ♦ *I have revised my opinion about her.* **3** to examine something again and correct any faults in it. **4** to prepare a new edition of a book. [from *re-* and a Latin word *visere* meaning 'to examine']

revision noun **1** revising, or being revised. **2** a revised edition, version, or form.

revisit verb (**revisited, revisiting**) to pay another visit to a place.

revitalize verb to put new strength or vitality into something. [from *re-* and *vital* and *-ize*]

revival noun **1** an improvement in the condition or strength of something. **2** something brought back into use, popularity, or fashion. **3** a reawakening of interest in religion, especially by means of evangelistic meetings.

revivalist noun a person who organizes or conducts meetings to promote a religious revival. **revivalism** noun

revive verb **1** to come or bring something back to life, consciousness, or strength. **2** to restore interest in or the popularity of something. **3** to restore or improve the position or condition of something. **reviver** noun [from *re-* and a Latin word *vivere* meaning 'to live']

revocable (rev-ə-kə-bəl) adjective able to be revoked.

revoke (ri-vohk) verb to withdraw or cancel a decree or licence etc. [from *re-* and a Latin word *vocare* meaning 'to call']

revolt verb **1** to take part in a rebellion. SYNONYMS: mutiny, rise up. **2** to be in a mood of protest or defiance. **3** to cause someone to feel strong disgust.
revolt noun **1** an attempt to end the authority of someone by rebelling. **2** a refusal to obey or conform. [same origin as for *revolve*]

revolting adjective causing disgust.

revolution noun **1** substitution of a new system of government, especially by force. **2** a complete or drastic change ♦ *a revolution in the treatment of burns.* **3** turning or moving around an axis; a single complete turn of a wheel, engine, etc. [same origin as for *revolve*]

revolutionary adjective **1** involving a great change ♦ *revolutionary new ideas.* **2** to do with political revolution.
revolutionary noun (**revolutionaries**) a person who begins or supports a political revolution.

revolutionize verb to alter a thing completely ♦ *The Internet is going to revolutionize our lives.*

revolve verb **1** to turn or cause something to turn round. SYNONYMS: rotate, spin, gyrate, swivel, twirl, whirl. **2** to move in a circular orbit. **3** to treat something as the most important point or element ♦ *His life revolves around his children.* [from *re-* and a Latin word *volvere* meaning 'to roll']

revolver noun a pistol with a revolving mechanism that makes it possible to fire it a number of times without reloading.

revolving door noun an entrance to a large building in which four partitions turn about a central axis.

revue noun an entertainment consisting of songs, sketches, etc., often about current events. [a French word meaning 'review']
◊ Do not confuse this word with **review**, which has a different meaning.

revulsion noun a feeling of strong disgust. [from *re-* and a Latin word *vulsus* meaning 'pulled']

reward noun **1** something given or received in return for what is done or for a service or merit. **2** a sum of money offered for the detection of a criminal or return of lost property etc.
reward verb to give a reward to someone. [originally meaning 'to consider, take notice'; related to *regard*]

rewarding *adjective* giving satisfaction and a feeling of achievement ♦ *a rewarding job.*

rewind *verb* (past tense and past participle **rewound**) to wind a film or tape back to or towards the beginning.
rewind *noun* a mechanism for rewinding a film or tape.

rewire *verb* to renew the electrical wiring of something.

reword *verb* to put something into different words.

rewrite *verb* (**rewrote, rewritten**) to write something again in a different form or style.

Rex *noun* a reigning king; the Crown in lawsuits ♦ *Rex v. Jones.* [a Latin word meaning 'king']

Rh *abbreviation* rhesus.

rhapsodize *verb* to talk or write about something in an extremely enthusiastic way.

rhapsody *noun* (**rhapsodies**) 1 an extremely enthusiastic and emotional written or spoken statement. 2 (*Music*) a romantic and emotional composition written in an irregular form. [from a Greek word *rhapsōidos* meaning 'someone who stitches songs together']

rheostat (ree-ə-stat) *noun* an instrument used to control the current in an electrical circuit by varying the amount of resistance in it. [from a Greek word *rheos* meaning 'a stream' and *statos* meaning 'stationary']

rhesus factor (ree-səs) *noun* a substance present in the blood of most people and some animals, causing a blood disorder in a new-born baby whose blood is **rhesus positive** (containing this substance) while its mother's blood is **rhesus negative** (not containing it). [from *rhesus monkey*, in which the substance was first observed]

rhesus monkey *noun* a small monkey common in northern India. [from a Latin word]

rhetoric (ret-er-ik) *noun* 1 the art of using words impressively, especially in public speaking. 2 language used for its impressive effect, but often lacking sincerity or meaningful content. [from a Greek word *rhētōr* meaning 'orator']

rhetorical (rit-o-ri-kəl) *adjective* 1 expressed in a way that is designed to be impressive. 2 to do with rhetoric. **rhetorically** *adverb*

rhetorical question *noun* a question asked for dramatic effect and not intended to get an answer, e.g. ♦ *Who cares?* (i.e. nobody cares).

rheumatic (roo-mat-ik) *adjective* to do with or affected with rheumatism. **rheumatics** *plural noun* (*informal*) rheumatism. **rheumatically** *adverb* **rheumaticky** *adjective* [same origin as for *rheumatism*]

rheumatic fever *noun* a serious form of rheumatism with fever, mainly affecting children.

rheumatism (room-ə-tizm) *noun* any of several diseases causing pain in the joints, muscles, or fibrous tissue, especially a form of arthritis. **rheumatoid** *adjective* [from a Greek word *rheuma* meaning 'stream', denoting a substance in the body which was once believed to cause rheumatism]

rhinestone *noun* an imitation diamond.

rhino *noun* (**rhino** or **rhinos**) (*informal*) a rhinoceros.

rhinoceros *noun* (**rhinoceros** or **rhinoceroses**) a large thick-skinned animal of Africa and south Asia, with a horn or two horns on its nose. [from Greek words *rhinos* meaning 'of the nose' and *keras* meaning 'horn']

rhizome (riy-zohm) *noun* (*Botany*) a root-like stem growing along or under the ground and sending out both roots and shoots. [from a Greek word *rhiza* meaning 'root']

rhododendron (roh-də-den-drən) *noun* an evergreen shrub with large clusters of trumpet-shaped flowers. [from Greek words *rhodon* meaning 'rose' and *dendron* meaning 'tree']

rhomboid (rom-boid) *adjective* shaped like a rhombus.
rhomboid *noun* a parallelogram with adjacent sides not equal.

rhombus (rom-bəs) *noun* a geometric figure shaped like the diamond on playing cards, a parallelogram with all sides equal. [from a Greek word *rhombos*]

rhubarb *noun* a garden plant with fleshy reddish leaf stalks that are used like fruit. [from a Latin word *rheubarbarum*]

rhyme *noun* 1 identity of sound between words or syllables or the endings of lines of verse (e.g. *line/mine/pine, visit/is it*). 2 a poem with rhymes. 3 a word that rhymes with another.

rhyme *verb* to form a rhyme; to have rhymes. **without rhyme or reason** with no sensible or logical reason. [from an Old French word; related to *rhythm* (originally used of a kind of rhythmic verse which usually rhymed)]

rhyme scheme *noun* the pattern of rhymes in a poem or verse.

rhyming slang *noun* a type of slang based on words or phrases that rhyme with the word in question, often with the rhyming part omitted, e.g. *butcher's (hook)* for *look*.

rhythm (rith-əm) *noun* **1** the pattern produced by emphasis and duration of notes in music or by long and short or stressed syllables in words. SYNONYMS: beat, tempo, time, metre. **2** a movement with a regular succession of strong and weak elements ♦ *the rhythm of the heart beating*. SYNONYMS: pulse, throb. **3** a constantly recurring sequence of events. **rhythmic** *adjective* **rhythmical** *adjective* **rhythmically** *adverb* [from a Greek word *rhuthmos*]

rhythm and blues *noun* a kind of popular music with elements of blues and jazz.

ria (ree-ə) *noun* (*Geography*) a long narrow inlet of the sea formed where part of a river valley has become submerged. [from a Spanish word *ria* meaning 'estuary']

rib *noun* **1** each of the curved bones round the chest. **2** a cut of meat from this part of an animal. **3** a curved structural part resembling a rib, e.g. a curved timber forming part of a ship's hull. **4** each of the hinged rods forming the framework of an umbrella. **5** a vein in a leaf or an insect's wing. **6** a raised pattern of lines in knitting.
rib *verb* (**ribbed, ribbing**) **1** to support a structure with ribs. **2** (*informal*) to tease someone. [from an Old English word]

ribald (rib-əld) *adjective* humorous in a cheerful but vulgar or disrespectful way. **ribaldry** *noun* [via Old French from a Germanic word]

riband (rib-ənd) *noun* (*old use*) a ribbon. [from an Old French word *riban*]

ribbed *adjective* **1** having a pattern of raised ridges. **2** (*Architecture*) strengthened with ribs.

ribbon *noun* **1** a narrow band of silk, nylon, etc. used for decoration or for tying something. **2** a ribbon of special colour or pattern worn to indicate the award of a medal or order etc. **3** a long narrow strip of material, e.g. an inked strip used in a typewriter or printer. [a different spelling of *riband*]

ribbon development *noun* the building of houses along a main road, extending outwards from a town or village.

ribcage *noun* the framework of ribs round the chest.

ribonucleic acid see RNA.

ribose (riy-bohz) *noun* a sugar which is a constituent of DNA and several vitamins and enzymes. [alteration of *arabinose*, the name of a related sugar]

ribosome (riy-bə-zohm) *noun* (*Biochemistry*) a minute particle of RNA (ribonucleic acid) involved in producing proteins from amino acids.

rice *noun* **1** a cereal plant grown in flooded fields in hot countries, producing seeds that are used as food. **2** the seeds of this plant used as food. [from a Greek word *oruza*]

ricepaper *noun* thin edible paper made from the pith of an oriental shrub, used for painting and in cookery.

rich *adjective* **1** having a lot of wealth. SYNONYMS: wealthy, affluent, prosperous, well-off; (*informal*) flush, well-heeled, loaded. **2** having a large supply of something ♦ *The country is rich in natural resources*. **3** splendid or elaborate, made of costly materials ♦ *rich furnishings*. **4** producing or produced abundantly ♦ *rich soil* ♦ *a rich harvest*. **5** (said about food) containing a large proportion of fat, butter, eggs, or spices etc. **6** (said about the mixture in an internal-combustion engine) containing a high proportion of fuel. **7** (said about colour, sound, or smell) pleasantly deep or strong. **8** varied or complex in an interesting way. **9** highly amusing or ridiculous. **richness** *noun* [from an Old English word]

riches *plural noun* a great quantity of money, property, or valuable possessions.

richly *adjective* **1** in a rich way. **2** fully or thoroughly ♦ *Her success is richly deserved*.

Richter scale (rik-ter) *noun* a scale for measuring the magnitude of earthquakes. [named after the American seismologist C. F. Richter (1900–85)]

rick[1] *noun* a built stack of hay, corn, or straw. [from an Old English word]

rick[2] *noun* a slight sprain or strain. **rick** *verb* to sprain or strain your neck or back slightly. [origin unknown]

rickets *noun* a children's disease caused by deficiency of vitamin D, resulting in softening and deformity of the bones. [origin unknown]

rickety *adjective* poorly made and likely to fall down ♦ *a rickety bridge*. **ricketiness** *noun* [from *rickets*]

rickrack *noun* a zigzag braid trimming. [origin unknown]

rickshaw *noun* a light two-wheeled hooded vehicle used in countries of the Far East, pulled by one or more people. [from a Japanese word *jin-riki-sha* meaning 'person-power-vehicle']

ricochet (rik-ə-shay) *verb* (**ricocheted** (rik-ə-shayd), **ricocheting** (rik-ə-shay-ing)) (said about a bullet etc.) to rebound off a surface ♦ *One of the bullets must have ricocheted off the wall.* **ricochet** *noun* a shot or hit that ricochets. [from a French word]

ricotta *noun* a kind of soft Italian cheese made from sheep's milk. [an Italian word]

rid *verb* (past tense and past participle **rid**; **ridding**) to free a person or place from something unpleasant or unwanted ♦ *First we had to rid the house of mice.* SYNONYMS: free, deliver, clear, purge. **to be rid of** to be freed of something ♦ *Frankly I was glad to be rid of him.* **to get rid of** to cause something to go away, to dispose of something. [from an Old Norse word *rythja*]

riddance *noun* getting rid of someone or something. **good riddance** used to express relief that you are free of a person or thing.

ridden past participle of **ride**. **ridden** *adjective* full of or dominated by something ♦ *rat-ridden cellars* ♦ *guilt-ridden*.

riddle[1] *noun* **1** a question or statement designed to test ingenuity or give amusement in finding its answer or meaning. SYNONYMS: puzzle, conundrum; (*informal*) brain-teaser, poser. **2** something puzzling or mysterious. [from an Old English word *rædels* meaning 'opinion, riddle']

riddle[2] *noun* a coarse sieve for gravel or cinders etc. **riddle** *verb* **1** to pass gravel or ashes through a riddle. **2** to pierce something with many holes ♦ *The car was riddled with bullets.* **3** to fill or permeate something thoroughly ♦ *Doctors found that she was riddled with cancer.* [from an Old English word *hriddel*]

ride *verb* (**rode**, **ridden**) **1** to sit on a horse, bicycle, or motorcycle and control it as it carries you along. **2** to travel in a car, bus, train, etc. **3** to be carried over or supported by something; to float or seem to float ♦ *The ship rode the waves* ♦ *The moon was riding high.* **4** to yield to a blow in order to reduce its impact. **ride** *noun* **1** a spell of riding. **2** a journey or lift in a vehicle ♦ *Come on, I'll give you a ride.* **3** a track for riding on, especially through woods. **4** a roundabout, roller coaster, etc. on which people ride at a fair or amusement park. **to let something ride** to take no further action over something. **to ride high** to be successful. **to ride on** to depend on ♦ *There's a lot of money riding on this decision.* **to ride something out** to come safely through something. **to ride up** (said about a piece of clothing) to work upwards when worn. **a rough** or **easy ride** a difficult or easy time. **to take someone for a ride** (*informal*) to deceive or swindle someone. [from an Old English word]

rider *noun* **1** a person who rides a horse, bicycle, or motorcycle. **2** an extra clause added to a document or statement; an expression of opinion added to a verdict.

riderless *adjective* without a rider.

ridge *noun* **1** a long narrow hilltop or mountain range. **2** a narrow raised strip, a line where two upward-sloping surfaces meet. **3** (*Meteorology*) an elongated region of high barometric pressure. [from an Old English word *hrycg* meaning 'spine, crest']

ridged *adjective* formed into ridges.

ridgeway *noun* a road or track along a ridge.

ridicule *noun* words or behaviour intended to make a person or thing appear ridiculous; mockery or derision. **ridicule** *verb* to make fun of a person or thing. SYNONYMS: mock, deride, taunt, jeer at, sneer at; (*informal*) send up, take the mickey out of. [from a Latin word *ridere* meaning 'to laugh']

ridiculous *adjective* **1** so silly or foolish that it makes people laugh or despise it. **2** not worth serious consideration, preposterous. **ridiculously** *adverb*

Riding *noun* one of the former administrative divisions of Yorkshire ♦ *West Riding*. [from an Old Norse word *thrithjungr* meaning 'third part']

rife *adjective* **1** happening frequently, widespread ♦ *Crime was rife in the city.* **2** full of something ♦ *The country was rife with rumours of war.* [probably from an Old Norse word]

riffle *verb* to flick through pages or papers quickly and casually. [perhaps from *ruffle*]

riff-raff *noun* disreputable or undesirable people. [from an Old French expression *rif et raf* meaning 'everybody or everything']

rifle[1] *noun* a gun with a long barrel cut with spiral grooves (called *rifling*) to make the bullet spin and so travel more accurately when fired.
rifle *verb* **1** to cut spiral grooves in a gun barrel. **2** to hit or kick a ball hard and straight. [from a French word *rifler* meaning 'to scratch']

rifle[2] *verb* to search and rob a place ♦ *They had rifled the safe.* [from an Old French word *rifler* meaning 'to plunder']

rift *noun* **1** a crack, split, or break in something. **2** a serious break in friendly relations between people or in the unity of a group. [from a Scandinavian word]

rift valley *noun* a steep-sided valley formed by subsidence of the earth's crust.

rig[1] *verb* (**rigged, rigging**) **1** to provide someone with clothes or equipment ♦ *Everyone was rigged out in waterproofs.* **2** to fit a ship with spars, ropes, sails, etc. **3** to set up a structure quickly or with makeshift materials ♦ *We've managed to rig up a shelter for the night.*
rig *noun* **1** the way a ship's masts and sails etc. are arranged. **2** equipment for a special purpose, e.g. for drilling an oil well ♦ *a test rig* ♦ *an oil rig.* **3** (*informal*) an outfit of clothes. [probably from a Scandinavian word]

rig[2] *verb* (**rigged, rigging**) to manage or control something fraudulently ♦ *There were protests that the election had been rigged.* [origin unknown]

rigging *noun* the ropes etc. used to support masts and to set or work the sails on a ship.

right *adjective* **1** on or towards the side which is to the east when you are facing north. **2** to do with right-wing politics. **3** proper, correct, or true ♦ *the right answer* ♦ *Is this paint the right colour?* **4** (said about conduct or actions etc.) morally good, in accordance with justice. SYNONYMS: honourable, ethical, just, principled. **5** in a good or normal condition ♦ *All's right with the world.* **6** (*informal*) real, properly so called ♦ *You've made a right old mess of things.*
right *adverb* **1** on or to the right side ♦ *Turn right here.* **2** correctly or appropriately ♦ *Did I do that right?* **3** straight ♦ *Go right on.* **4** (*informal*) immediately ♦ *I'll be right back.* **5** all the way, completely ♦ *We went right round the town centre.* **6** exactly ♦ *right in the middle.*
right *noun* **1** the right-hand side or direction. **2** what is morally right or just. **3** something that people are entitled to ♦ *People over 18 have the right to vote in elections.* **4** a person's right fist, or a blow with this. **5** (often **the Right**) the right wing of a political party or other group.
right *verb* **1** to restore something to a proper or correct or upright position ♦ *The crew managed to right the boat.* **2** to set something right, to make amends or take vengeance for something ♦ *This wrong must be righted.* **3** to correct something ♦ *The fault should right itself.*
right *interjection* all right, that is correct, I agree. **as of right** or **by right** because of having a legal or moral claim. **by rights** if things were fair or correct ♦ *By rights that prize should have been mine.* **in the right** having justice or truth on your side. **in your own right** as a result of your own claims, qualifications, or efforts. **to put someone right** to tell someone the true facts. **right away** immediately. [from an Old English word *riht*]

right angle *noun* an angle of 90°. **at right angles** placed at or turning through a right angle.

right-angled *adjective* having a right angle.

righteous *adjective* **1** doing what is morally right, making a show of this. **2** morally justifiable ♦ *full of righteous indignation.* **righteously** *adverb* **righteousness** *noun* [from an Old English word *rihtwis*]

rightful *adjective* in accordance with what is deserved, just, or proper ♦ *in her rightful place.* **rightfully** *adverb*

right-hand *adjective* of or towards the right side.

right-handed *adjective* 1 using the right hand usually. 2 operated by the right hand. 3 (said about a screw) to be tightened by turning clockwise. **right-handedness** *noun*

right-hander *noun* a right-handed person.

right-hand man *noun* a person's trusted, indispensable, or chief assistant.

Right Honourable *adjective* a title given to certain high officials such as Privy Counsellors and government ministers.

rightist *noun* a member of the right wing of a political party. **rightist** *adjective* to do with the right wing in politics. **rightism** *noun*

rightly *adverb* justly, correctly, properly, or justifiably ♦ *He was quite rightly disappointed with the team's efforts.*

right-minded *adjective* having ideas and opinions which are sensible and morally good.

rightness *noun* being just, correct, proper, or justifiable.

right of way *noun* 1 the right to pass over someone else's land, a path that is subject to such a right. 2 the right of one vehicle to pass or cross a junction etc. before another.

Right Reverend *adjective* a title given to a bishop.

right-thinking *adjective* right-minded.

right wing *noun* the section of a political party or system supporting more conservative or traditional policies. **right-wing** *adjective* **right-winger** *noun*

rigid *adjective* 1 not able to bend or be forced out of shape. SYNONYMS: stiff, firm, inflexible. 2 strict and inflexible ♦ *rigid rules.* **rigidity** (ri-jid-iti) *noun* **rigidly** *adverb* [from a Latin word *rigere* meaning 'to be stiff']

rigmarole (rig-mǝ-rohl) *noun* 1 a complicated formal procedure. 2 a long rambling statement. [from an old word *ragman* meaning 'a legal document']

rigor mortis (rig-ǝ mor-tiss) *noun* stiffening of the body after death. [a Latin phrase meaning 'stiffness of death']

rigorous (rig-er-ǝs) *adjective* 1 strictly accurate or detailed ♦ *a rigorous search.* 2 strict or severe ♦ *rigorous discipline.* 3 harsh or unpleasant ♦ *a rigorous climate.* **rigorously** *adverb*

rigour (rig-er) *noun* 1 severity or strictness. 2 strict precision ♦ *We must apply scientific rigour to this investigation.* 3 harshness of weather or conditions ♦ *the rigours of famine.* [from a Latin word *rigor* meaning 'stiffness']

rig-out *noun* (*informal*) an outfit of clothes.

rile *verb* (*informal*) to annoy or irritate someone. [probably from an Old French word]

rill *noun* a small stream. [probably from an Old Dutch word]

rim *noun* 1 the upper or outer edge of something more or less circular. 2 the outer edge of a wheel, on which a tyre is fitted. [from an Old English word *rima* meaning 'a border, coast']

rime *noun* frost. [from an Old English word]

rimed *adjective* (*literary*) coated with frost.

rimless *adjective* (said about glasses) made without frames.

rimmed *adjective* edged or bordered ♦ *red-rimmed eyes.*

rind *noun* a tough outer layer or skin on fruit, cheese, bacon, etc. [from an Old English word]

ring[1] *noun* 1 a small circular band, often made of precious metal, worn on the finger. 2 the outline of a circle. 3 something shaped like this, a circular band. 4 a flat circular device forming part of a gas or electric hob. 5 a circular or other enclosure for a circus, sports event, cattle show, etc. 6 a square area in which a boxing match or wrestling match takes place. 7 a group of people acting together, especially in some illegal activity ♦ *a drugs ring.*
ring *verb* 1 to put or draw a ring round something. 2 to surround or encircle something. 3 to put a ring on the leg of a bird to identify it. **to run rings round** to outwit someone easily. [from an Old English word *hring*]

ring[2] *verb* (**rang, rung**) 1 to make a loud clear resonant sound, like that of a bell when struck. SYNONYMS: chime, peal, toll, knell, tinkle, ping. 2 to make a bell to do this. 3 to sound a bell as a summons; to signal something by ringing ♦ *Church bells rang out the old year.* 4 to be filled with sound ♦ *The stadium rang with cheers.* 5 (said about ears) to be filled with a buzzing or humming sound. 6 to telephone someone ♦ *I'll ring you tomorrow.*

ring *noun* 1 the act of ringing a bell. 2 a ringing sound or tone. 3 a quality given by something you have heard ♦ *This story does have the ring of truth.* **to give someone a ring** (*informal*) to telephone someone. **to ring a bell** (*informal*) to arouse a vague memory, to sound faintly familiar. **to ring off** to end a telephone call by replacing the receiver. **to ring the changes** to vary things. **to ring down** or **up the curtain** 1 to lower or raise the curtain on a theatre stage. 2 to mark the beginning or end of something. **to ring true** to sound as though it is true. **to ring someone up** to make a telephone call to someone. **to ring something up** to record an amount on a cash register. [from an Old English word *hringan*]

ring finger *noun* the finger next to the little finger, especially of the left hand, on which a wedding ring is worn.

ringing *adjective* clear and forceful ♦ *a ringing endorsement.*

ringleader *noun* a person who leads others in doing something illegal or mischievous. [from *ring*¹]

ringlet *noun* a long spiral-shaped curl of hair.

ringmaster *noun* the person in charge of a circus performance.

ring road *noun* a bypass encircling a town.

ringside *noun* the area immediately beside a boxing ring.

ringworm *noun* a skin disease producing round scaly patches on the skin, caused by a fungus.

rink *noun* (also **ice rink**) a place made for skating on ice. [originally a Scots word, perhaps from an Old French word *renc* meaning 'rank']

rinse *verb* 1 to wash something in clean water to remove soap or dirt. 2 to wash something lightly with water. **rinse** *noun* 1 rinsing. 2 an antiseptic solution for cleaning the mouth. 3 a solution washed through hair to tint or condition it. [from an Old French word *rincer*]

riot *noun* 1 a wild and violent disturbance by a crowd of people. 2 a profuse display of something ♦ *a riot of colour.* 3 (*informal*) a very amusing thing or person. **riot** *verb* to take part in a riot. **to read the Riot Act** to give someone a severe reprimand or warning. **to run riot** 1 to behave in an unruly way. 2 to grow or spread in an uncontrolled way. **rioter** *noun* [from an Old French word *rioter* meaning 'to quarrel']

riot gear *noun* protective clothing, helmets, shields, etc. worn or carried by police or soldiers dealing with riots.

riotous *adjective* 1 disorderly or unruly. 2 boisterous or unrestrained ♦ *riotous laughter.* **riotously** *adverb*

RIP *abbreviation* (used on graves) rest in peace. [short for a Latin phrase *requiescat* (or *requiescant*) *in pace*]

rip *verb* (**ripped, ripping**) 1 to tear something apart roughly, to remove something by pulling it roughly. 2 to become torn. 3 to rush along. **rip** *noun* a rough tear or split. **to let rip** (*informal*) 1 to do something without restraint. 2 to express yourself vehemently. **to rip someone off** (*informal*) to cheat or defraud someone. **to rip something off** (*informal*) to steal or copy something, especially someone else's idea. **to rip something up** to tear something into small pieces. **ripper** *noun* [origin unknown]

ripcord *noun* a cord that is pulled to release a parachute from its pack.

ripe *adjective* 1 (said about fruit or grain) ready to be gathered and eaten. 2 fully matured ♦ *ripe cheese.* 3 ready, prepared or able to undergo something ♦ *The time is ripe for revolution.* **ripely** *adverb* **ripeness** *noun* [from an Old English word]

ripen *verb* to make something ripe or to become ripe.

rip-off *noun* (*informal*) 1 something that is greatly overpriced. 2 an inferior imitation.

riposte (ri-**posst**) *noun* 1 a quick clever reply. 2 a quick return thrust in fencing. **riposte** *verb* to deliver a riposte. [from an Italian word *risposta* meaning 'response']

ripple *noun* 1 a small wave or series of waves. 2 something resembling this in appearance or movement. 3 a gentle sound that rises and falls ♦ *a ripple of laughter.* **ripple** *verb* to form or cause ripples. [origin unknown]

rip-roaring *adjective* full of energy, wildly noisy.

ripsaw *noun* a saw for sawing wood along the grain.

rise *verb* (**rose**, **risen**) **1** to come or go upwards; to grow or extend upwards. **2** to get up from lying, sitting, or kneeling. **3** to get out of bed. **4** (said about a meeting or court) to finish sitting for business, to adjourn. **5** to increase in amount, number, or intensity ♦ *House prices are rising* ♦ *Her spirits rose.* SYNONYMS: climb, soar, mount, escalate, spiral. **6** to reach a higher position or status ♦ *He rose to the rank of colonel.* **7** to become upright or erect. **8** to come back to life ♦ *Christians believe that Jesus rose from the dead.* **9** to rebel ♦ *Eventually the people rose in revolt against the tyrant.* **10** (said about the sun etc.) to become visible above the horizon. **11** (said about a river) to begin its course ♦ *The Thames rises in the Cotswolds.* **12** (said about the wind) to begin to blow more strongly. **13** (said about bread or cake etc.) to swell by the action of yeast or other raising agent.
rise *noun* **1** rising, an upward movement. **2** an upward slope; a small hill. **3** an increase in salary or wages. **4** an increase in amount, number, or intensity. **5** an upward movement in rank or status. **to get** or **take a rise out of** (*informal*) to draw a person into a display of annoyance or into making a retort. **to give rise to** to cause something. **on the rise** increasing. **to rise to** to cope well with a challenging situation ♦ *I was pleased to see how well you rose to the occasion.* [from an Old English word]

riser *noun* **1** a person or thing that rises ♦ *an early riser.* **2** a vertical piece between treads of a staircase.

risible *adjective* so ridiculous that it provokes laughter. **risibility** *noun* **risibly** *adverb* [from a Latin word *ridere* meaning 'to laugh']

rising *noun* a revolt.
rising *adjective* nearing a particular age ♦ *rising five.*

rising damp *noun* moisture absorbed from the ground into a wall.

risk *noun* **1** a situation involving the chance of suffering injury or loss. **2** the possibility that something unpleasant will happen ♦ *There is a small risk of rain.* SYNONYMS: danger, threat, chance, possibility. **3** a person or thing insured or similarly representing a source of risk ♦ *Her insurers do not think she is a good risk* ♦ *a fire risk.* **risk** *verb* **1** to expose someone or something to the chance of injury or loss ♦ *She risked her life to save the children.* **2** to accept the risk of something unpleasant happening ♦ *He risks injury each time he climbs.* **at your own risk** taking responsibility for your own safety or possessions. **to run** or **take a risk** to act in a way that exposes you to danger. [via French from an Italian word *risco* meaning 'danger']

risky *adjective* (**riskier**, **riskiest**) involving risk. **riskily** *adverb* **riskiness** *noun*

risotto (ri-**zot**-oh) *noun* (**risottos**) an Italian dish of rice cooked with vegetables and meat or seafood. [an Italian word, from *riso* meaning 'rice']

risqué (**risk**-ay) *adjective* (said about a story etc.) slightly indecent. [a French word]

rissole *noun* a cake of minced meat coated with breadcrumbs and fried. [from a French word]

rite *noun* a religious or other solemn ceremony. [from a Latin word *ritus* meaning 'religious ceremony']

rite of passage *noun* a ceremony or event marking an important stage in someone's life.

ritual *noun* **1** the series of actions used in a religious or other ceremony; a particular form of this. **2** a procedure that is regularly followed.
ritual *adjective* to do with or done as a ritual. **ritualistic** *adjective* **ritually** *adverb* [from a Latin word *ritus* meaning 'rite']

rival *noun* **1** a person or thing competing with another. SYNONYMS: adversary, opponent, competitor, contender. **2** a person or thing that can equal another in quality. **rival** *adjective* being a rival or rivals. **rival** *verb* (**rivalled**, **rivalling**) to be comparable to something else, to seem or be as good as something else ♦ *scenery that cannot be rivalled anywhere in the world.* **rivalry** *noun* [from a Latin word *rivalis* meaning 'person using the same stream', from *rivus* meaning 'stream']

riven (**riv**-ən) *adjective* torn apart. [from an Old Norse word]

river *noun* **1** a large natural stream of water flowing in a channel. **2** a great flow of something ♦ *rivers of blood.* [from a Latin word *ripa* meaning 'bank']

riverside *noun* the land along a river bank.

rivet (**riv**-it) *noun* a short metal pin or bolt for holding two pieces of metal together, its headless end being beaten or pressed down to form a head when it is in place.

rivet verb (**riveted, riveting**) **1** to fasten something with rivets. **2** to fix something or hold it firmly ♦ *We stood riveted to the spot.* **3** to attract and hold someone's complete attention ♦ *The concert was riveting.* **riveter** noun [from an Old French word *river* meaning 'to fix or clinch']

riviera (rivi-air-ə) noun a coastal region with a subtropical climate and vegetation. **the Riviera** noun the region along the Mediterranean coast of SE France, Monaco, and NW Italy, famous for its natural beauty and containing many holiday resorts. [from an Italian word meaning 'seashore']

rivulet (riv-yoo-lit) noun a small stream. [from a Latin word *rivus* meaning 'stream']

RM abbreviation Royal Marines.

RMM abbreviation (*Chemistry*) relative molecular mass.

RN abbreviation Royal Navy.

Rn abbreviation (*Chemistry*) the symbol for radon.

RNA abbreviation (*Biochemistry*) ribonucleic acid, a type of substance similar to DNA that is involved in the synthesis of proteins.

roach noun (**roach**) a small freshwater fish related to the carp. [from an Old French word *roche*]

road noun **1** a level way with a hard surface made for traffic to travel on. **2** a way of achieving something ♦ *the road to success.* **on the road 1** on a long journey or series of journeys. **2** moving from place to place without a home.   [from an Old English word]

roadblock noun a barrier set up across a road by the police or army to stop and check vehicles.

road hog noun (*informal*) a reckless or inconsiderate driver.

roadholding noun the ability of a vehicle to remain stable and under control when cornering, especially when travelling fast.

road rage noun violent or aggressive behaviour by a driver towards other drivers.

road sense noun ability to behave safely on roads, especially in traffic.

roadshow noun a series of radio or television programmes broadcast live on location from different places.

road tax noun a tax on motor vehicles using public roads.

road test noun **1** a test of a vehicle by using it on the road. **2** a test of equipment carried out in working conditions.

road-test verb to give a car or piece of equipment a road test.

roadway noun the middle part of the road, used by traffic.

roadworks plural noun construction or repair of roads.

roadworthy adjective (said about a vehicle) fit to be used on the road. **roadworthiness** noun

roam verb to wander over a wide area. **roam** noun a wander. [origin unknown]

roan adjective (said about an animal) having a coat that is thickly sprinkled with white or grey hairs. **roan** noun a roan horse or other animal. [from an Old French word]

roar noun **1** a long deep loud sound, like that made by a lion. **2** loud laughter. **roar** verb **1** to give a roar. **2** to express something in this way, to laugh loudly ♦ *The crowd roared its approval.* **3** to travel quickly making a loud noise. **roarer** noun [from an Old English word]

roaring adjective (*informal*) unmistakable, emphatic ♦ *a roaring success.* **to do a roaring trade** (*informal*) to do very good business.

roast verb **1** to cook meat etc. in an oven or by exposing it to heat. **2** to undergo roasting. **3** to make something very hot, or to become very hot. **roast** adjective roasted ♦ *roast beef.* **roast** noun roast meat; a joint of meat for roasting. [via Old French from a Germanic word]

roaster noun a fowl etc. suitable for roasting.

roasting adjective (*informal*) very hot and dry. **roasting** noun (*informal*) a severe reprimand.

rob verb (**robbed, robbing**) **1** to steal from a person or place; to commit robbery. **2** to deprive someone of something they need or deserve ♦ *Our noisy neighbours robbed us of a good night's sleep again.* **to rob Peter to pay Paul** to pay one debt by borrowing what you need and so incurring another. **robber** noun [from an Old French word *robe* meaning 'booty']

robbery noun (**robberies**) 1 robbing a person or place. 2 overcharging or swindling someone.

robe noun a long loose piece of clothing, especially a ceremonial one or one worn as an indication of rank, office, or profession.
robe verb to dress someone or yourself in a robe. [via Old French from a Germanic word]

robin noun a small brown red-breasted European bird. [from an Old French word meaning 'Robert']

robot (roh-bot) noun 1 (in science fiction) a machine that resembles and can act like a person. 2 an automatic machine programmed to perform specific tasks. 3 a person who seems to work or act like a machine. 4 (in South Africa) a set of traffic lights. [from a Czech word *robota* meaning 'forced labour']

robotic (rə-bot-ik) adjective 1 to do with or using robots. 2 behaving in a mechanical or unemotional way.
robotics noun the study of the design, construction, and use of robots.

robust (rə-bust) adjective 1 strong and vigorous. 2 sturdily built. **robustly** adverb **robustness** noun [from a Latin word *robustus* meaning 'firm and hard']

roc noun a gigantic bird of Eastern legend. [from a Persian word]

rock [1] noun 1 the hard part of the earth's crust, under the soil. 2 a mass of this; a large stone or boulder. 3 a hard sugar sweet made in cylindrical sticks, usually flavoured with peppermint. **on the rocks** (informal) 1 (said about a drink) served neat with ice cubes. 2 experiencing difficulties and likely to fail. [from an Old French word *rocque*]

rock [2] verb 1 to move or be moved gently backwards and forwards or from side to side. 2 to shake something violently ♦ *The earthquake rocked the city.* 3 to disturb or shock someone greatly ♦ *The scandal rocked the financial world.*
rock noun 1 (also **rock music**) a kind of popular modern music usually with a strong beat. 2 rock and roll. 3 a rocking movement. **to rock the boat** (informal) to do something that upsets the plans or progress of your group. [from an Old English word *roccian*]

rock and roll noun a kind of popular dance music with a strong beat, originating in the 1950s.

rock-bottom adjective (informal) at the lowest possible level ♦ *rock-bottom prices.*
rock bottom noun the lowest possible level ♦ *She felt she had finally reached rock bottom.*

rock cake noun a small fruit cake with a flat base and a hard rough surface.

rock climbing noun the sport of climbing rock faces. **rock climber** noun

rocker noun 1 a fan or performer of rock music. 2 a member of a group of young people in the 1960s often associated with leather clothes and motorcycles. 3 a rocking chair. 4 each of the curved bars on which a rocking chair etc. is mounted. 5 a rocking device in a machine. **off your rocker** (informal) mad.

rockery noun (**rockeries**) a mound or bank in a garden, where plants are made to grow between large rocks.

rocket [1] noun 1 a firework or similar device that shoots high into the air when ignited and then explodes. 2 a structure that flies by sending out a backward jet of gases that are the products of combustion, used to send up a warhead or a spacecraft; a bomb or shell propelled by this. 3 (informal) a severe reprimand.
rocket verb (**rocketed, rocketing**) to move rapidly upwards or away ♦ *House prices are rocketing.* [from an Italian word *rocchetto* meaning 'small distaff' (because of its shape)]

rocket [2] noun a Mediterranean plant of the cabbage family, eaten in salads. [from a French word *roquette*]

rock face noun a bare vertical surface of natural rock.

rock garden noun a rockery, or a garden containing rockeries.

rocking chair noun a chair mounted on rockers or with springs so that it can be rocked by the person sitting on it.

rocking horse noun a wooden horse mounted on rockers or springs so that it can be rocked by a child sitting on it.

rock 'n' roll noun another spelling of **rock and roll.**

rock plant noun a plant that grows on or among rocks.

rock pool noun a pool of water among rocks on a shoreline.

rock salmon *noun* dogfish sold as food.

rock salt *noun* common salt (sodium chloride) as it is found naturally in the earth.

rock solid *adjective* completely firm or stable.

rocky[1] *adjective* (**rockier, rockiest**) 1 like or made of rock. 2 full of rocks.

rocky[2] *adjective* (**rockier, rockiest**) unsteady or unstable. **rockily** *adverb* **rockiness** *noun*

rococo (rə-**koh**-koh) *noun* an ornate style of decoration common in Europe in the 18th century.
rococo *adjective* to do with or in this style. [from a French word]

rod *noun* 1 a thin straight round stick or metal bar. 2 a fishing rod. 3 a stick used for caning or flogging people. 4 (*Anatomy*) a rod-shaped structure in the retina of the eye, not sensitive to coloured light (see also **cone**). [from an Old English word *rodd*]

rode past tense of **ride**.

rodent *noun* an animal, e.g. rat, mouse, or squirrel, with strong front teeth used for gnawing things. [from a Latin word *rodens* meaning 'gnawing']

rodeo (roh-**day**-oh) *noun* (**rodeos**) 1 a display of cowboys' skill in riding and handling horses, roping calves, etc. 2 an exhibition of motorcycle riding. 3 a round-up of cattle on a ranch, for branding and counting. [a Spanish word, from *rodear* meaning 'to go round']

roe[1] *noun* a mass of eggs in a female fish's ovary (**hard roe**); the ripe testes of a male fish (**soft roe**). [from an Old German or Old Dutch word]

roe[2] *noun* (**roe** or **roes**) a kind of small deer of Europe and Asia. [from an Old English word]

roebuck *noun* a male roe deer.

roentgen (**runt**-yən or **ront**-yən) *noun* a unit of ionizing radiation. [named after the German physicist and discoverer of X-rays W. C. Röntgen (1845–1923)]

roger *interjection* (in radio communication) your message has been received and understood. [from the name *Roger*]

rogue *noun* 1 a dishonest or unprincipled person. 2 a mischievous but likeable person. 3 a wild animal driven away from the herd or living apart from it ♦ *a rogue elephant*. 4 something that is defective or found in an unexpected place. **roguery** *noun* [origin unknown]

rogues' gallery *noun* (*informal*) a collection of photographs of criminals.

roguish *adjective* playful and mischievous ♦ *a roguish smile.* **roguishly** *adverb* **roguishness** *noun*

roister *verb* to enjoy yourself in a noisy or boisterous way. **roisterer** *noun* [from an Old French word *rustre* meaning 'ruffian']

role *noun* 1 an actor's part. 2 a person's or thing's purpose or function ♦ *the role of computers in education.* [from a French word *rôle* meaning 'roll', originally the roll of paper on which an actor's part was written]

role model *noun* a person looked to by others as an example of how to behave.

role playing *noun* an exercise in which people act out imaginary roles.

roll *verb* 1 to move or cause something to move along in contact with a surface, either on wheels or by turning over and over. 2 to turn on an axis or over and over; to cause something to revolve. 3 to turn something over and over on itself to form it into a cylindrical or spherical shape. 4 to rock or sway from side to side. 5 to flatten something by pushing a roller over it ♦ *Now roll out the pastry.* 6 to pass steadily ♦ *The years rolled by.* 7 to move forward or stretch out with undulations ♦ *The hills rolled down to the sea.* 8 to make a long continuous vibrating sound ♦ *Thunder rolled overhead.* 9 to pronounce an 'r' sound with a trill.
roll *noun* 1 a cylinder formed by turning flexible material over and over on itself. 2 something having this shape, an undulation ♦ *rolls of fat.* 3 a small individual portion of bread baked in a rounded shape; one of these split and containing a filling. 4 an official list or register of names. 5 a rolling movement. 6 a long steady vibrating sound ♦ *a drum roll.* **to be rolling in it** or **in money** (*informal*) to be very rich. **on a roll** (*informal*) experiencing a continuing spell of good luck or success. **to roll in** (*informal*) 1 to arrive in great numbers or quantities ♦ *Offers of help soon started to roll in.* 2 to arrive casually at a later time than expected. **rolled into one** combined in one person or thing. **to roll up** (*informal*) to arrive. **to roll up your sleeves** to prepare to fight or to work. **to strike**

someone off the roll to debar a solicitor from practising as a penalty for dishonesty etc. [from a Latin word *rotula* meaning 'little wheel']

roll-call *noun* the calling out of a list of names to check who is present.

rolled gold *noun* a thin coating of gold applied to another metal.

roller *noun* 1 a cylinder used for flattening or spreading things, or on which something is wound. 2 a small cylinder on which hair is rolled in order to produce curls. 3 a long swelling wave.

rollerball *noun* a ballpoint pen using a smaller ball and thinner ink so that it writes very smoothly.

Rollerblade *noun* (*trademark*) a boot like an ice-skating boot, with a line of wheels in place of the skate, for rolling smoothly on hard ground. **rollerblading** *noun*

roller blind *noun* a window blind fitted on a roller.

roller coaster *noun* a type of railway used for amusement at fairgrounds etc. with a series of alternate steep descents and ascents.

roller skate *noun* a boot or metal frame fitted under a shoe, with small wheels on it so that the wearer can roll smoothly over the ground. **roller skating** *noun*

roller towel *noun* a long towel with its ends joined so that it is continuous, hung over a roller.

rollicking *adjective* full of boisterous high spirits. [from *romp* and *frolic*]

rolling *adjective* 1 steady and continuous ♦ *a rolling programme of reforms.* 2 (said about land) stretching out in gentle undulations ♦ *rolling hills.*

rolling mill *noun* a machine or factory for rolling metal into sheets.

rolling pin *noun* a cylindrical device for rolling out dough.

rolling stock *noun* the railway engines, carriages, wagons, etc. used on a railway.

roll of honour *noun* a list of people whose achievements are honoured.

roll-on *adjective* (said about a deodorant or cosmetic) applied by means of a ball that rotates in the neck of a container.

roll-on roll-off *adjective* (said about a ferry etc.) that vehicles can be driven on to and off.

rollover *noun* (in a lottery) a jackpot prize which has not been won and is carried over to be added to the prize money for the following draw.

roll-top desk *noun* a writing desk with a flexible cover that slides in curved grooves.

roly-poly *noun* (**roly-polies**) a pudding consisting of suet pastry spread with jam, rolled up, and steamed or baked.
roly-poly *adjective* round and plump. [a nonsense word based on *roll*]

ROM *abbreviation* (*Computing*) read-only memory.

Roman *adjective* 1 to do with ancient or modern Rome. 2 to do with the ancient Roman republic or empire.
Roman *noun* an inhabitant of ancient or modern Rome.
roman *noun* plain upright type (not italic) used in printing.

Roman alphabet *noun* the alphabet in which most European languages are written.

Roman candle *noun* a tubular firework that sends out coloured sparks.

Roman Catholic *adjective* belonging to or to do with the Christian Church that acknowledges the Pope as its head.
Roman Catholic *noun* a member of this Church.

Roman Catholicism *noun* the faith of the Roman Catholic Church.

romance (rə-**manss**) *noun* 1 a feeling of excitement and wonder associated with love. 2 a love affair. 3 a love story. 4 a quality or feeling of mystery, excitement, and remoteness from everyday life ♦ *the romance of ocean cruises.* 5 a medieval story about the adventures of heroes.
romance *verb* to exaggerate or distort the truth in an imaginative way. [from an Old French word *romanz*]

Romance languages *plural noun* the group of European languages descended from Latin (French, Italian, Spanish, etc.).

Romanesque (roh-mən-**esk**) *adjective* to do with a style of architecture in Europe in about 900–1200, with massive vaulting and round arches.
Romanesque *noun* this style of architecture.

Romanian (roh-**may**-niən) *adjective* to do with or coming from Romania.
Romanian *noun* 1 a person born in

Romania, or descended from people born there. **2** the language of Romania.

Roman nose noun a nose with a high bridge.

Roman numeral noun any of the letters representing numbers in the Roman system: I = 1, V = 5, X = 10, L = 50, C = 100, D = 500, M = 1,000 (see also **arabic numeral**).

romantic adjective **1** to do with or characterized by romance. **2** enjoying or producing thoughts and feelings of love, especially sentimental or idealized love ♦ *a romantic dinner for two*. **3** dealing with sentimental love and adventure ♦ *romantic fiction*. **4** idealistic, not at all realistic or practical. SYNONYMS: idealistic, quixotic, starry-eyed. **5** (also **Romantic**) (said about music or literature) richly imaginative, not conforming to classical conventions. **romantic** noun a person with romantic beliefs or attitudes. **romantically** adverb [same origin as for *romance*]

romanticize verb to describe or think about something in an idealized or unrealistic way.

Romany (rom-ə-ni) noun (**Romanies**) **1** a gypsy. **2** the language of gypsies. **Romany** adjective to do with Romanies or their language. [from a Romany word *rom* meaning 'man']

romp verb to play about together in a rough and lively way, as children do. **romp** noun a spell of romping. **to romp home** or **in** to win a race or competition easily. [origin unknown]

rompers plural noun a piece of clothing for a baby or young child, covering the body and legs.

rondavel (ron-**dah**-vəl) noun (in southern Africa) a traditional round hut with a cone-shaped thatched roof. [from an Afrikaans word *rondawel*]

rondeau (ron-doh) noun (**rondeaux**) a short poem with only two rhymes throughout and the opening words used twice as a refrain. [from a French word *rond* meaning 'round']

rondo noun (**rondos**) a piece of music with a theme that recurs several times. [an Italian word, from a French word *rondeau* meaning 'circle']

rood noun **1** a crucifix, especially one raised on the middle of the rood screen. **2** (*historical*) a quarter of an acre. [from an Old English word]

rood screen noun a carved wooden or stone screen separating the nave from the chancel in a church.

roof noun (**roofs**) **1** a structure covering the top of a house or building. **2** the top of a car or tent etc. **3** the top inside surface of something ♦ *the roof of the mouth*. **roof** verb to cover something with a roof; to be the roof of something. **to go through the roof** (*informal*) (said about prices etc.) to become extremely high. **to have a roof over your head** to have somewhere to live. **to hit** or **go through the roof** (*informal*) to suddenly become very angry. [from an Old English word *hrof*]

roof garden noun a garden on the flat roof of a building.

roofing noun material used for a roof.

roof rack noun a framework for carrying luggage on the roof of a vehicle.

rook[1] noun a black crow that nests in colonies. **rook** verb (*informal*) to swindle or overcharge someone. [from an Old English word *hroc*]

rook[2] noun a chess piece with a top shaped like battlements. [from an Arabic word *rukk*]

rookery noun (**rookeries**) **1** a colony of rooks; a place where rooks nest. **2** a colony or breeding place of penguins or seals.

rookie noun (*informal*) a new recruit or novice. [origin unknown]

room noun **1** space that is or could be occupied by something ♦ *Do you have enough room?* ♦ *Make room for your sister.* **2** a part of a building enclosed by walls, floor, and ceiling. **3** the people present in a room ♦ *The whole room fell silent.* **4** opportunity or scope for something ♦ *There is definitely room for improvement.* **rooms** plural noun a set of rooms rented out to a person or family. [from an Old English word]

room-mate noun a person sharing a room with another.

roomful noun (**roomfuls**) the amount that a room will hold.

room service noun providing food and drink to hotel guests in their rooms.

room temperature noun a comfortable surrounding temperature, about 20°C.

roomy adjective (**roomier, roomiest**) having plenty of room to contain things.
SYNONYMS: spacious, sizeable, capacious, voluminous.

roost noun a place where birds settle to rest at night.
roost verb (said about birds) to settle for rest. [from an Old English word]

rooster noun (North Amer.) a male domestic fowl.

root [1] noun 1 the part of a plant that attaches it to the earth and absorbs water and nourishment from the soil. 2 a similar part attaching ivy etc. to its support, a rhizome. 3 a vegetable which grows as a root, such as a carrot or turnip ♦ root crops. 4 the part of a bodily organ or structure that is embedded in tissue ♦ the root of a tooth. 5 a source or basis ♦ The love of money is the root of all evil ♦ We need to get to the root of the matter. 6 (Mathematics) a number that when multiplied by itself one or more times produces a given number ♦ 3 is the square root of 9 ♦ 2 is the cube root of 8 ($2 \times 2 \times 2 = 8$).
roots plural noun a person's family origins, or their sense of belonging to a place where they or their family live or used to live ♦ Although I've lived in London for many years, my roots are in Manchester.
root verb 1 to take root, or to cause something to take root. 2 to cause someone to stand fixed and unmoving ♦ He was rooted to the spot by fear. 3 to establish something deeply and firmly ♦ The feeling is deeply rooted in our society. **at root** fundamentally. **root and branch** thorough and radical. **to root something out** or **up** to find and get rid of something. **to take root** 1 to send down roots. 2 (said about an idea etc.) to become established. [from an Old Norse word]

root [2] verb 1 (said about an animal) to turn up the ground with its snout in search of food. 2 to rummage; to find or extract something by doing this ♦ I've managed to root out some facts and figures. **to root for** (informal) to support someone enthusiastically. [from an Old English word]

rootless adjective 1 having no root or roots. 2 (said about a person) having no roots in a community.

root mean square noun (Mathematics) the square root of the arithmetic mean of the squares of a set of numbers.

rootstock noun a rhizome.

rope noun 1 a length of strong thick cord made of twisted strands of fibre. 2 a quantity of similar things strung together ♦ a rope of pearls.
rope verb 1 to fasten, catch, or secure something with rope. 2 to fence something off with rope. **on the ropes** in a desperate position. **to rope someone in** to persuade someone to take part in an activity. **the ropes** (informal) the procedure for doing things in an organization, activity, etc. ♦ I'll show you the ropes. [from an Old English word]

rope ladder noun a ladder made of two long ropes connected by short crosspieces.

ropy adjective (**ropier, ropiest**) 1 (said about a substance) forming long sticky threads. 2 (informal) poor in quality or health.
ropiness noun

Roquefort (rok-for) noun (trademark) a kind of soft blue cheese, made from ewes' milk. [from the name of a village in southern France]

rosary noun (**rosaries**) 1 a set series of prayers used in the Roman Catholic Church. 2 a string of beads for keeping count of these prayers or of prayers in some other religions. [from a Latin word rosarium meaning 'rose garden']

rose [1] noun 1 a prickly bush or shrub bearing ornamental usually fragrant flowers. 2 a flower from this bush or shrub. 3 the perforated sprinkling nozzle of a watering can, hosepipe, or shower. 4 a deep pink colour.
rose adjective deep pink. [via Old English from a Latin word rosa]

rose [2] past tense of **rise**.

rosé (roh-zay) noun a light pink wine. [a French word meaning 'pink']

roseate (roh-zi-ət) adjective deep pink, rosy.

rosebud noun the bud of a rose.

rose-coloured adjective 1 of a deep pink colour. 2 (also **rose-tinted**) involving an unduly cheerful or favourable view of things ♦ You tend to see things through rose-coloured spectacles.

rosemary (rohz-mer-i) *noun* an evergreen shrub with fragrant leaves used as a herb in cooking. [from Latin words *ros marinus* meaning 'dew of the sea']

rosette *noun* 1 a rose-shaped badge or decoration made of ribbon, awarded as a prize or worn by supporters of a team, political party, etc. 2 a rose-shaped carving. [from a French word meaning 'little rose']

rose water *noun* a fragrant liquid perfumed with roses.

rose window *noun* a circular window in a church, with a pattern of tracery.

rosewood *noun* any of several fragrant close-grained woods used for making furniture.

Rosh Hashana or **Rosh Hashanah** *noun* the Jewish New Year festival. [a Hebrew phrase meaning 'head of the year']

rosin (roz-in) *noun* a kind of resin. [same origin as for *resin*]

RoSPA *abbreviation* Royal Society for the Prevention of Accidents.

roster (ros-ter) *noun* a list showing people's turns to be on duty.
roster *verb* to place someone on a roster. [from a Dutch word *rooster* meaning 'list']

rostrum (ros-trəm) *noun* (rostra or rostrums) a raised platform for one person, especially for public speaking or conducting an orchestra. [from a Latin word meaning 'beak, prow of a warship' (because a rostrum in ancient Rome was decorated with the prows of captured enemy ships)]

rosy *adjective* (rosier, rosiest) 1 rose-coloured, deep pink ♦ *rosy cheeks.* 2 promising or hopeful ♦ *a rosy future.* **rosily** *adverb* **rosiness** *noun*

rot *verb* (rotted, rotting) 1 to decompose or decay by chemical action caused by bacteria or fungi; to make something do this. 2 to gradually become worse in condition through lack of use or activity ♦ *The two men were left to rot in jail.*
rot *noun* 1 rotting or decay. 2 a process of becoming worse in standard or condition ♦ *Isn't there anything we can do to stop the rot?* 3 (*informal*) nonsense or rubbish. [from an Old English word *rotian*]

rota (roh-tə) *noun* a list of duties to be done and the order in which people are to take their turn in doing them. [a Latin word meaning 'wheel']

Rotarian (roh-tair-iən) *noun* a member of Rotary, an international charitable association formed by business and professional people.

rotary *adjective* rotating; acting by rotating ♦ *a rotary drill.* [from a Latin word *rota* meaning 'wheel']

rotate *verb* 1 to go round like a wheel, to move in a circle around an axis; to make something do this. 2 to arrange or deal with something in a set sequence. 3 to take turns at doing something, to be used in turn ♦ *The crews rotate every three weeks.*
rotator *noun* [same origin as for *rota*]

rotation *noun* 1 the action of rotating. 2 the practice of growing a different crop each year on a plot of land in a regular order, to avoid exhausting the soil.

rotational *adjective* to do with or using rotation.

rotatory (roh-tə-ter-i) *adjective* rotating.

rotavator (roh-tə-vay-tə) *noun* (*trademark*) a machine with rotating blades for breaking up or tilling the soil. [from *rotary* and *cultivator*]

rote *noun* **by rote** by memory or routine without fully understanding the meaning ♦ *It is a poem I learnt by rote at school.* [origin unknown]

rotisserie (rə-tiss-er-i) *noun* a cooking device for roasting food on a revolving spit. [from a French word]

rotor *noun* 1 a rotating part of a machine. 2 a horizontally-rotating vane of a helicopter. [from *rotate*]

rotten *adjective* 1 suffering from decay; breaking easily or falling to pieces from age or use. 2 morally corrupt. 3 (*informal*) very bad or unpleasant ♦ *rotten weather.*
rotten *adverb* (*informal*) very much ♦ *Your grandparents spoil you rotten.* **rottenly** *adverb* **rottenness** *noun* [from an Old Norse word *rotinn*]

rotten borough *noun* (in the 19th century) a borough that was able to elect an MP although it had only a few voters.

rotter *noun* (*informal*) (*old use*) a mean or unkind person.

rottweiler (rot-viy-ler) *noun* a large black German dog. [a German word, from Rottweil, a town in Germany where the dog was bred]

rotund (rə-tund) *adjective* 1 (said about a person) plump. 2 rounded in shape.

rotundity noun [from a Latin word *rotundus* meaning 'round']

rotunda (rə-**tun**-də) noun a circular domed building or hall. [from an Italian word *rotonda* (*camera*) meaning 'round (chamber)']

rouble (**roo**-bəl) noun the unit of money in Russia and some other countries. [via French from a Russian word]

roué (**roo**-ay) noun a debauched elderly man. [a French word meaning 'broken on a wheel', referring to an instrument of torture thought to be deserved by such a person]

rouge (roozh) noun a reddish cosmetic for colouring the cheeks.
rouge verb to colour the cheeks with rouge. [a French word meaning 'red']

rough adjective 1 having an uneven or irregular surface; not level or smooth. 2 not gentle, restrained, or careful; violent ♦ *a rough push.* 3 (said about weather or the sea) wild and stormy. SYNONYMS: turbulent, tempestuous, choppy. 4 (said about a person) coarse or rude. 5 (informal) difficult and unpleasant ♦ *She's had a rough time recently.* 6 not finished in detail ♦ *a rough draft.* 7 approximate, not exact ♦ *a rough estimate.*
rough noun 1 a ruffian or hooligan. 2 (on a golf course) the area of longer grass around the fairway and the green. 3 a rough drawing or design etc.
rough verb to make something rough. **in the rough** in a natural or unfinished state. **to rough it** (informal) to do without ordinary comforts. **to rough someone up** (informal) to beat someone up. **to sleep rough** to sleep out of doors, not in a proper bed. **to take the rough with the smooth** to accept the difficult or unpleasant aspects of life as well as the good. **roughness** noun [from an Old English word]

roughage noun indigestible material in plants which are used as food (e.g. bran, green vegetables, and certain fruits), that stimulates the action of the intestines.

rough and ready adjective 1 crude or hastily put together, but effective or adequate. 2 not refined or sophisticated.

rough and tumble noun disorderly fighting or rough play.

roughcast noun plaster of lime, cement, and gravel, used for covering the outsides of buildings.

roughcast verb (past tense and past participle **roughcast**) to coat a building with this.

rough diamond noun 1 a diamond not yet cut. 2 a person of good nature but lacking manners or education.

roughen verb to make something or become rough.

rough grazing noun pasture in a natural state.

rough house noun (informal) a disturbance with violent behaviour or fighting.

rough justice noun treatment or punishment that is approximately fair although often not following the proper procedures.

roughly adverb 1 in a rough manner. 2 approximately.

roughneck noun 1 a worker on an oil rig. 2 (informal) a rough uncouth person.

roughshod adjective (old use) (said about a horse) having shoes with the nail heads left sticking out to prevent slipping. **to ride roughshod over** to treat someone inconsiderately or arrogantly.

roulette (roo-**let**) noun a gambling game in which players bet on where the ball on a revolving wheel will come to rest. [a French word meaning 'little wheel']

round adjective 1 having a curved shape or outline; shaped like a circle, ball, or cylinder. SYNONYMS: circular; (ball-shaped) spherical, globular. 2 (said about a number) expressed to the nearest whole number or the nearest ten, hundred, etc. 3 full or complete ♦ *a round dozen.*
round preposition 1 on all sides of; circling or enclosing. 2 at points on or near the circumference of ♦ *We sat round the table.* 3 in a curve or circle at an even distance from a central point ♦ *The earth moves round the sun.* 4 from place to place in, to all parts of ♦ *Let me show you round the house.* 5 on or to the further side of ♦ *the shop round the corner.*
round adverb 1 in a circle or curve; surrounding something ♦ *Go round to the back of the house* ♦ *Gather round, everyone.* 2 so as to face in a different direction ♦ *Turn your chair round.* 3 to all people present; in every direction ♦ *Hand the biscuits round.* 4 from place to place ♦ *We wandered round for a while.* 5 to a person's house or office etc. ♦ *I'll be round in an hour.*
round noun 1 a round object. 2 a series of visits made by a doctor, postman, etc.,

especially in a fixed order as part of their duties ♦ *a paper round* ♦ *a doctor on her rounds.* **3** a recurring course or series, or one event in a series ♦ *the daily round* ♦ *another round of negotiations.* **4** one stage in a competition or struggle; one section of a boxing match ♦ *He was knocked out in the first round.* **5** the playing of all the holes on a golf course once. **6** a single shot or volley of shots from a gun; ammunition for this. **7** a slice of bread; a sandwich made with two slices of bread. **8** a song for two or more voices in which each sings the same melody but starts at a different time. **9** a set of drinks bought for all the members of a group.

round *verb* **1** to make something round in shape, or to become round. **2** to make an amount into a round figure or number ♦ *Let's round the distance up to the nearest kilometre.* **3** to travel or go round something ♦ *The car rounded the bend.* **to come round** to become conscious again. **to do** or **go the rounds** (said about a story or piece of news) to be passed round among a lot of people. **in the round** **1** (said about a theatre) with seats on all sides of the stage. **2** fully and thoroughly ♦ *We need to look at this problem in the round.* **round about 1** near by. **2** approximately. **round and round** turning or going round several times. **to round something off 1** to complete something in a pleasant way ♦ *Let's round the evening off with a nightcap.* **2** to make the edges of something smooth. **to round on** to make a verbal attack on someone, especially unexpectedly. **round the clock** continuously throughout day and night. **to round something up** to gather animals, people, or things into one place. **roundish** *adjective* **roundness** *noun* [from an Old French word; related to *rotund*]

roundabout *noun* **1** a road junction with a circular structure round which traffic has to pass in the same direction. **2** a circular revolving ride in a playground or a merry-go-round at a funfair. **roundabout** *adjective* indirect, not using the shortest or most direct route or phrasing etc. ♦ *I heard the news in a roundabout way.*

rounded *adjective* **1** round or curved. **2** well developed, complete ♦ *a rounded character.*

round dance *noun* a dance in which dancers form one large circle.

roundel *noun* a circular identifying mark on an aircraft etc. [from an Old French word *rondel*]

rounder *noun* the unit of scoring in rounders.

rounders *noun* a team game played with bat and ball, in which players have to run round a circuit of bases.

Roundhead *noun* a supporter of the Parliamentary party in the English Civil War. [so called because they wore their hair cut short at a time when long hair was in fashion for men]

roundly *adverb* **1** thoroughly or severely ♦ *She was roundly scolded.* **2** in a circular or roughly circular shape.

round robin *noun* **1** a statement or petition signed by a number of people, often with signatures written in a circle to conceal who signed first. **2** a competition in which each player or team plays in turn against every other one.

round-shouldered *adjective* with the shoulders bent forward, so that the back is rounded.

roundsman *noun* (**roundsmen**) a trader's employee who delivers goods on a regular round.

round-table *adjective* involving people meeting on equal terms to discuss something ♦ *round-table talks.*

round-the-clock *adjective* lasting or happening all day and all night.

round trip *noun* a journey to a place and back to where you started.

round-up *noun* **1** a gathering together of people or things ♦ *a police round-up of suspects.* **2** a summary ♦ *a round-up of the news.*

roundworm *noun* a kind of worm that lives as a parasite in the intestines of animals and birds.

rouse *verb* **1** to cause someone to wake up. **2** (said about a person or animal) to wake up. **3** to cause someone to become active or excited. SYNONYMS: excite, stimulate, provoke, galvanize, incite, stir up. [probably from an Old French word]

rousing *adjective* loud or stirring ♦ *a rousing speech.*

roustabout *noun* a labourer, especially one on an oil rig. [from the word *roust* meaning 'to rouse']

rout *noun* utter defeat; a disorderly retreat of defeated troops.
rout *verb* to defeat an enemy completely and force them to retreat. [via Old French from a Latin word *rumpere* meaning 'to break']

route (root) *noun* the course or way taken to get from a starting point to a destination.
route *verb* (present participle **routeing** or **routing**) to send someone by a certain route. [from an Old French word *rute* meaning 'road']

router (row-ter) *noun* a tool for cutting grooves and shaping mouldings etc. in wood. [from the word *rout* meaning 'to cut a groove in']

routine (roo-teen) *noun* 1 a standard way of doing things; a series of acts performed regularly in the same way. 2 a set sequence in a performance, especially in a comedy act. 3 a sequence of instructions to a computer.
routine *adjective* 1 performed as part of a regular procedure ♦ *a routine inspection*. 2 in accordance with routine, not varying.
routinely *adverb* [from a French word; related to *route*]

route march *noun* a long training march for soldiers.

roux (roo) *noun* a mixture of heated fat and flour used as a basis for a sauce. [from French words *(beurre) roux* meaning 'browned (butter)']

rove *verb* to roam or wander. **rover** *noun* [probably from a Scandinavian word]

roving *adjective* travelling for your work, with no fixed base ♦ *our roving reporter*.

row[1] (roh) *noun* 1 a number of people or things in a line. SYNONYMS: line, column, file, rank, chain. 2 a line of seats across a theatre etc. **in a row** in succession. [from an Old English word *raw*]

row[2] (roh) *verb* 1 to make a boat move by using oars. 2 to carry someone or something in a boat that you row. 3 to take part in the sport of rowing.
row *noun* a spell of rowing. [from an Old English word *rowan*]

row[3] (row) *noun* (*informal*) 1 a noisy quarrel or argument. 2 a loud noise or uproar.
row *verb* (*informal*) to quarrel or argue noisily. [origin unknown]

rowan (roh-ən) *noun* a tree that bears hanging clusters of scarlet berries. [from a Scandinavian word]

rowdy *adjective* (**rowdier, rowdiest**) noisy and disorderly. SYNONYMS: boisterous, obstreperous, unruly.
rowdy *noun* (**rowdies**) a rowdy person.
rowdily *adverb* **rowdiness** *noun* **rowdyism** *noun* [originally North American; origin unknown]

rowing machine *noun* an exercise machine with oars and a sliding seat.

rowlock (rol-ək) *noun* a device on the side of a boat serving as a fulcrum for an oar and keeping it in place. [from an earlier word *oarlock*, with *row*[3] in place of *oar*]

royal *adjective* 1 to do with, suitable for, or worthy of a king or queen. SYNONYMS: regal, majestic, imperial. 2 to do with or belonging to the family of a king or queen. 3 splendid, of exceptional size or quality.
royal *noun* (*informal*) a member of the royal family. **royally** *adverb* [from an Old French word *roial*, related to *regal*]

royal blue *noun* a deep vivid blue.

royal icing *noun* hard icing for cakes, made with icing sugar and egg white.

royalist *noun* a person who favours the idea of a monarchy.
Royalist *noun* a supporter of the monarchy in the English Civil War.
royalist *adjective* giving support to the monarchy.

royalty *noun* (**royalties**) 1 a royal person or royal people ♦ *in the presence of royalty*. 2 being royal. 3 a payment made to an author or composer for each copy of a book sold or for each public performance of a work; a payment to a patentee for the use of the patent. 4 payment by a mining or oil company to the owner of the land used.

RP *abbreviation* received pronunciation.

rpm *abbreviation* revolutions per minute.

RSPB *abbreviation* Royal Society for the Protection of Birds.

RSPCA *abbreviation* Royal Society for the Prevention of Cruelty to Animals.

RSVP *abbreviation* (in an invitation) please reply. [short for a French phrase *répondez s'il vous plaît*]

Rt Hon. *abbreviation* Right Honourable.

Rt Revd or **Rt Rev.** *abbreviation* Right Reverend.

rub *verb* (**rubbed, rubbing**) **1** to press something against a surface and move it back and forth ♦ *He rubbed his eyes* ♦ *She rubbed some suncream on her arms.* **2** to polish or clean something by rubbing; to make something dry or smooth in this way ♦ *Rub your hair dry with a towel.* **3** to keep moving against a surface and make it sore or worn ♦ *The heel of my shoe is rubbing.* SYNONYMS: chafe, abrade. **4** to take an impression of a brass memorial tablet by rubbing wax, pencil, or chalk over paper laid upon it.
rub *noun* **1** the act or process of rubbing. **2** the chief difficulty or problem ♦ *There's the rub.* **to rub something down** to dry, smooth, or clean something by rubbing. **to rub it in** (*informal*) to emphasize or remind a person constantly of an unpleasant or embarrassing fact. **to rub off 1** to be removed by rubbing. **2** to be transferred through close contact ♦ *I hope some of your good luck rubs off on me.* **to rub something out** to remove pencil marks by using a rubber. **to rub shoulders with** to associate or come into contact with certain people. **to rub someone up the wrong way** to irritate a person by your actions. [origin unknown]

rubber [1] *noun* **1** a tough elastic substance made from the latex of certain tropical plants or synthetically, used for making tyres, balls, hoses, etc. **2** a piece of rubber used for rubbing out pencil or ink marks. [from *rub*]

rubber [2] *noun* **1** a contest consisting of a series of matches between the same sides in cricket, tennis, etc. **2** (in bridge) a match of three successive games. [origin unknown]

rubber bullet *noun* a bullet made of rubber, used especially in riot control.

rubberize *verb* to treat or coat something with rubber.

rubberneck *noun* (*informal*) someone who stares inquisitively.
rubberneck *verb* (*informal*) to stare inquisitively.

rubber plant *noun* a tall evergreen plant with tough shiny leaves, often grown as a house plant.

rubber stamp *noun* a device with lettering or a design on it, which is inked and used to mark paper etc.

rubber-stamp *verb* to give official approval to a decision without thinking properly about it.

rubber tree *noun* a tropical tree from which rubber is obtained.

rubbery *adjective* like rubber.

rubbing *noun* an impression made of a memorial brass or other relief design by placing paper over it and rubbing with pigment.

rubbish *noun* **1** waste material to be thrown away. SYNONYMS: refuse, litter, garbage, trash, waste, junk, detritus. **2** something that is worthless. **3** nonsense.
rubbish *verb* (*informal*) to criticize something severely or dismiss it as being worthless.
rubbish *adjective* (*informal*) very poor in quality. **rubbishy** *adjective* [from an Old French word *rubbous*]

rubble *noun* broken pieces of stone, brick, or concrete, especially those left after a building has been demolished. [perhaps from an Old French word]

rubella *noun* an infectious disease which causes a red rash, and which can damage a baby if the mother catches it early in pregnancy. [from a Latin word *rubellus* meaning 'reddish']

Rubicon (roo-bi-kən) *noun* **to cross the Rubicon** to take a decisive step that commits you to doing something. [The river Rubicon, in NE Italy, was the ancient boundary between Gaul and Italy; by crossing it into Italy Julius Caesar committed himself to war against the Roman Senate]

rubicund (roo-bik-ənd) *adjective* having a ruddy complexion. [same origin as for *ruby*]

rubric (roo-brik) *noun* words put as a heading or a note of explanation or instructions of how something must be done ♦ *Make sure you read the rubric at the top of the examination paper.* [from a Latin word *rubeus* meaning 'red' (because rubrics used to be written in red)]

ruby *noun* (**rubies**) **1** a red gem. **2** a deep red colour.
ruby *adjective* deep red. [from a Latin word *rubeus* meaning 'red']

ruby wedding *noun* the 40th anniversary of a wedding.

ruche (roosh) *noun* a frill or pleat of fabric. **ruched** *adjective* [from a French word]

ruck [1] *noun* **1** (in rugby) a loose scrum with the ball on the ground. **2** a tightly packed crowd of people. [probably from a Scandinavian word]

ruck [2] *verb* to form creases or wrinkles ♦ *Your dress has rucked up at the back.* **ruck** *noun* a crease or wrinkle. [from an Old Norse word *hrukka*]

rucksack *noun* a bag worn slung by straps from both shoulders and resting on the back, used by walkers and climbers. [from a German word *Rücken* meaning 'back' and *sack* [1]]

ructions *plural noun* (*informal*) angry protests or arguments; trouble. [origin unknown]

rudder *noun* a vertical piece of metal or wood hinged to the stern of a boat or rear of an aircraft and used for steering. [from an Old English word]

ruddy *adjective* (**ruddier, ruddiest**) **1** having a healthy reddish colour ♦ *a ruddy complexion.* **2** (*informal, old use*) bloody. **ruddily** *adverb* **ruddiness** *noun* [from an Old English word *rudig*]

rude *adjective* **1** impolite, bad-mannered. SYNONYMS: discourteous, uncivil, ill-mannered. **2** indecent or vulgar. SYNONYMS: coarse, crude, improper, saucy. **3** roughly made, not sophisticated ♦ *rude stone implements.* **4** vigorous or hearty ♦ *rude health.* **5** abrupt or startling ♦ *a rude awakening.* **rudely** *adverb* **rudeness** *noun* [from a Latin word *rudis* meaning 'raw, wild']

rudiment (roo-dim-ənt) *noun* (*Biology*) a part or organ that is incompletely developed. **rudiments** *plural noun* the basic or elementary principles of a subject ♦ *This book will teach you the rudiments of chemistry.* [same origin as for *rude*]

rudimentary (roodi-ment-er-i) *adjective* **1** involving or limited to basic principles; elementary. **2** not fully developed ♦ *Penguins have rudimentary wings.*

rue [1] *verb* (**rues, rued, ruing**) to regret something and wish it had not happened ♦ *You'll live to rue the day you betrayed your friends.* [from an Old English word]

rue [2] *noun* a shrub with bitter leaves used in herbal medicine. [via Old French and Latin from a Greek word]

rueful *adjective* showing or feeling good-humoured regret. **ruefully** *adverb*

ruff *noun* **1** a deep starched pleated frill worn around the neck in the 16th century. **2** a collar-like ring of feathers or fur round the neck of a bird or animal. **3** a bird of the sandpiper family. [a different spelling of *rough*]

ruffian *noun* a violent or lawless person. [via French and Italian from a Germanic word]

ruffle *verb* **1** to disturb the smoothness or evenness of something. **2** (said about a bird) to make its feathers stand up in anger or display. **3** to upset the calmness or even temper of someone. **4** to become ruffled. **ruffle** *noun* a gathered ornamental frill. **ruffled** *adjective* [origin unknown]

rug *noun* **1** a small carpet or thick mat for the floor. **2** a thick woollen blanket. [probably from a Scandinavian word]

rugby or **rugby football** *noun* a kind of football played with an oval ball which may be kicked or carried. [named after Rugby School in Warwickshire, where it was first played]

rugby league *noun* a form of rugby played in teams of 13 players.

rugby union *noun* a form of rugby played in teams of 15 players.

rugged *adjective* **1** having a rocky and uneven surface ♦ *a rugged landscape.* **2** (said about a man's face) having strong masculine features. **3** needing or showing toughness and determination. **ruggedly** *adverb* **ruggedness** *noun* [probably from a Scandinavian word]

rugger *noun* (*informal*) rugby.

ruin *noun* **1** severe damage or destruction. **2** complete loss of your fortune, resources, or prospects. **3** a building, or the remains of a building, that has fallen down or been badly damaged ♦ *The house was a ruin* ♦ *the ruins of Pompeii.* **4** a cause of ruin. **ruin** *verb* **1** to damage something so severely that it is useless; to bring something into a ruined condition. **2** to make someone bankrupt. **in ruins** in a state of utter failure ♦ *Her hopes for a gold medal are now in ruins.* **ruination** *noun* [from a Latin word *ruere* meaning 'to fall']

ruinous *adjective* **1** bringing or likely to bring ruin. **2** falling to pieces, in a state of disrepair ♦ *The house is in a ruinous condition.* **ruinously** *adverb*

rule noun 1 a statement of what can, must, or should be done in a certain set of circumstances or in playing a game. SYNONYMS: regulation, law, principle. 2 control or government ♦ *countries that were under French rule.* 3 the customary or normal state of things or course of action ♦ *Seaside holidays became the rule.* 4 a straight often jointed measuring device used by carpenters etc. 5 a thin printed line or dash.
rule verb 1 to have control or power over people or a country, to govern. 2 to have a powerful influence over something ♦ *Don't let your heart rule your head.* 3 to give a decision as judge or other authority ♦ *The chairman ruled that the question was out of order.* 4 to be the normal thing that happens, to prevail ♦ *a world in which anarchy rules.* 5 to draw a straight line using a ruler or other straight edge; to mark parallel lines on writing paper etc. **as a rule** usually, more often than not. **to rule something out** to exclude something as a possibility. **to rule the roost** to be the dominant person. [from a Latin word *regula* meaning 'a rule']

rule of thumb noun a rough practical method of procedure.

ruler noun 1 a person who governs. 2 a straight strip of wood or metal etc. used for measuring or for drawing straight lines.

ruling noun an authoritative decision or judgement.

rum¹ noun a strong alcoholic drink distilled from sugar-cane residues or molasses. [origin unknown]

rum² adjective (**rummer, rummest**) (*informal, old use*) strange or odd. [origin unknown]

rumba noun a lively ballroom dance of Cuban origin, or music for this. [from a Latin American Spanish word]

rumble verb 1 to make a deep heavy continuous sound like thunder. 2 to move with a sound like this. 3 (*informal*) to detect the true character of a person or thing, to see through a deception. **rumble** noun a rumbling sound. **to rumble on** (said about a dispute) to continue. [probably from an Old Dutch word *rommelen*]

rumble strip noun a series of raised strips on a road that warns drivers of the edge of the roadway, or tells them to slow down, by making vehicles vibrate.

rumbustious adjective (*informal*) boisterous or unruly. [probably from an old word *robustious* meaning 'boisterous or robust']

ruminant (roo-min-ənt) noun an animal that chews the cud, such as cattle, sheep, deer, etc.
ruminant adjective to do with ruminants. [from a Latin word *ruminari* meaning 'to chew over again']

ruminate (roo-min-ayt) verb 1 to chew the cud. 2 to think deeply about something. **rumination** noun **ruminative** adjective

rummage verb to search for something by turning things over or moving them about in an untidy way.
rummage noun a search of this kind. [from an Old French word *arrumage* meaning 'stowing of a cargo in a ship's hold']

rummage sale noun a jumble sale.

rummy noun a card game in which players try to form sets or sequences of cards. [origin unknown]

rumour noun a story or report that spreads to a lot of people by word of mouth but may not be true.
rumour verb **to be rumoured** to be spread as a rumour. [from a Latin word *rumor* meaning 'noise']

rump noun 1 the hind part of an animal's or bird's body. 2 a person's buttocks. 3 a cut of meat from an animal's hindquarters. [probably from a Scandinavian word]

rumple verb to make something look untidy or dishevelled. [from a Dutch word]

rump steak noun a piece of meat from the rump of a cow.

rumpus noun (*informal*) an uproar or an angry dispute. SYNONYMS: commotion, uproar, disturbance, tumult. [origin unknown]

run verb (**ran, run, running**) 1 to move with quick steps, never having both or all feet on the ground at the same time. 2 to go or travel smoothly or swiftly. 3 to pass over or through something, or to make something do this ♦ *She ran her fingers through her hair* ♦ *His eyes ran over the names on the list.* 4 to flow, to produce mucus or other liquid ♦ *Tears ran down his cheeks* ♦ *Her nose was running.* SYNONYMS: flow, pour, gush, stream, dribble, trickle. 5 to produce a flow of liquid ♦ *Run some water into it.* 6 to compete in a race or contest; to seek election ♦ *The senator announced that he was running for President.* 7 (said about dye, ink,

etc.) to spread when it is wet ♦ *Wash this separately in case the colours run.* **8** to work, function, or operate ♦ *Have you left the engine running?* **9** to continue or proceed ♦ *Everything's running according to plan.* **10** to extend in distance or time ♦ *A fence runs round the estate* ♦ *The play ran for six months.* **11** to manage or organize something ♦ *She runs a coffee shop* ♦ *Who is running the country?* **12** to show or broadcast a film, television programme, etc. **13** to publish a story in a newspaper or magazine, or to be published. **14** to make a regular journey on a particular route ♦ *The bus runs every hour.* **15** to travel or take someone in a vehicle ♦ *We'll run you to the station.* **16** to be current or valid ♦ *The lease runs for 20 years.* **17** to recur as a characteristic ♦ *Musical ability runs in the family.* **18** to pass or make something pass into a specified condition ♦ *Supplies are running low.* **19** to make something run, go, extend, or function; to cause a computer program to operate. **20** to own and use a vehicle etc. **21** (*informal*) to fail to stop at a red traffic light. **22** to smuggle goods. **23** (said about salmon) to go up river in large numbers from the sea. **24** (said about a boat) to be travelling with the wind blowing from astern.
run *noun* **1** an act or spell or course of running ♦ *I'm just going for a run.* **2** a journey, especially in a car. **3** a point scored in cricket or baseball. **4** a continuous stretch, sequence, or spell ♦ *He's had a run of bad luck.* **5** a sequence of playing cards of the same suit. **6** a general demand for goods ♦ *There has been a run on bread* ♦ *a run on the dollar.* **7** the average or usual type ♦ *She stands out from the general run of TV presenters.* **8** an enclosed area where domestic animals can run freely in the open ♦ *a chicken run.* **9** a track for some purpose ♦ *a ski run.* **10** permission to make unrestricted use of something ♦ *You can have the run of the house.* **11** a ladder in a pair of stockings or tights. **12** a large number of salmon going up river from the sea. **to be run off your feet** to be extremely busy. **to make a run for it** to try to escape by running away. **on the run** running away from pursuit or capture. **to run across** to happen to meet or find a person or thing. **to run after** to chase someone. **to run away 1** to leave a place quickly or secretly. **2** to try to avoid facing up to something. **to run away with 1** to win a prize or competition easily. **2** to escape someone's control ♦ *Your imagination is running away with you.* **3** to

elope with a person. **to run down 1** to stop working gradually because of loss of power. **2** to deteriorate gradually. **to run someone down 1** to knock someone down with a moving vehicle. **2** to criticize someone unkindly or unfairly. **to run something down 1** to reduce the numbers or supply of something. **2** to discover something after a search. **to run dry 1** (said about a well or river) to stop flowing or no longer have any water. **2** (said about a supply) to be completely used up. **to run for it** to try to escape by running away. **to run high** (said about feelings) to be very strong. **to run someone in** (*informal*) to arrest someone and take them into custody. **to run something in** (*informal*) to run a new engine gently. **to run into 1** to collide with someone or something. **2** to meet someone by chance. **3** to experience a problem or difficulty. **to run low** or **short** (said about a supply) to become depleted. **to run off** to run away or escape. **to run something off** to produce a copy of something on a machine. **to run on** to continue for longer than expected. **to run out 1** (said about time or a stock of something) to become used up. **2** (said about a person) to have used up your stock of something. **3** to be no longer valid ♦ *Your travel card has run out.* **4** to jut out. **to run someone out** (in cricket) to knock over the wicket of a running batsman. **to run over 1** to overflow. **2** to exceed a limit ♦ *The best man's speech ran over by about ten minutes.* **to run someone or something over** to knock down or crush someone or something with a vehicle. **to run risks** to take risks. **to run a temperature** to be suffering from a high temperature. **to run someone through** to stab someone and kill them. **to run through** or **over** to examine, repeat, or rehearse something quickly. **to run to 1** to be sufficient for something; to be able to afford something ♦ *I can't run to a holiday this year.* **2** to show a tendency towards something. **to run something up 1** to allow a bill or score to mount up. **2** to make something quickly, especially by sewing ♦ *My mother said she would run up some curtains.* **3** to raise a flag on a mast. **to run up against** to experience or meet a difficulty or problem. **the runs** (*informal*) diarrhoea. [from an Old English word *rinnan*]

runaway *noun* a person who has run away. **runaway** *adjective* **1** having run away or become out of control. **2** won easily ♦ *a runaway victory.*

rundown *noun* a brief analysis or summary.

run-down *adjective* 1 tired and in bad health, especially from working too hard. 2 in bad condition; dilapidated.

rune (roon) *noun* any of the letters in an alphabet used by early Germanic peoples. **runic** *adjective* [from an Old Norse word meaning 'magic sign']

rung¹ *noun* one of the crosspieces of a ladder. [from an Old English word *hrung*]

rung² past participle of **ring**².

run-in *noun* 1 the approach to an action or event. 2 (*informal*) a quarrel or argument.

runner *noun* 1 a person or animal that runs, especially in a race. 2 a messenger. 3 a creeping stem that grows away from the main stem and takes root. 4 a groove, rod, or roller for something to move on; each of the long strips on which a sledge slides. 5 a long narrow rug or strip of carpet. 6 (*informal*) an idea that has a chance of being accepted.

runner bean *noun* a kind of climbing bean with long green pods which are eaten.

runner-up *noun* a person or team finishing second in a contest.

running *adjective* 1 done while running ♦ *a running jump.* 2 following each other without interval ♦ *It rained for four days running.* 3 continuous ♦ *a running joke.* **in** or **out of the running** with a good chance, or no chance, of winning. **to make the running** to set the pace.

running commentary *noun* a verbal description of events, given as they happen.

running mate *noun* an election candidate for the lesser of two linked political posts, e.g. for the post of vice-president.

running repairs *plural noun* repairs carried out on machinery while it is in use.

running stitch *noun* a line of evenly spaced stitches made by a straight thread passing in and out of the material.

runny *adjective* (**runnier, runniest**) 1 liquid or watery ♦ *runny honey.* 2 (said about a person's nose) producing a flow of liquid.

run-off *noun* 1 (*Geography*) the draining away of rainfall from the surface of an area. 2 a further contest to decide a tie.

run-of-the-mill *adjective* ordinary, not special.

run-out *noun* (in cricket) the dismissal of a batsman by being run out.

runt *noun* an undersized animal, especially the smallest in a litter. [origin unknown]

run-through *noun* 1 a rehearsal. 2 a brief outline or summary.

run-up *noun* 1 the period leading to an event. 2 the running a person does before taking a jump, bowling a ball, etc.

runway *noun* a strip of hard ground along which aircraft take off and land.

rupee (roo-**pee**) *noun* the unit of money in India, Pakistan, and certain other countries. [via Hindi from a Sanskrit word]

rupture *verb* 1 to break or burst suddenly, or cause something to do this. 2 to disturb a friendship or other relationship. **rupture** *noun* 1 breaking; a breach. 2 an abdominal hernia. **to be ruptured** or **rupture yourself** to suffer an abdominal hernia. [from a Latin word *ruptum* meaning 'broken']

rural *adjective* to do with, in, or like the countryside rather than the town. SYNONYMS: pastoral, rustic, bucolic. [from a Latin word *ruris* meaning 'of the country']

ruse (rooz) *noun* a deception or trick. [from an Old French word *ruser* meaning 'to use trickery']

rush¹ *verb* 1 to go, come, or take something with great speed ♦ *We rushed here as soon as we heard the news* ♦ *The survivors were rushed to hospital.* 2 to do something with urgent, perhaps excessive, haste, or make someone do this ♦ *Don't rush me - I need to think about it.* 3 to flow strongly. 4 to dash towards a person or place in an attempt to attack or capture them or it. **rush** *noun* 1 rushing; an instance of this. 2 a period of great activity. 3 a sudden great demand for goods. **rushes** *plural noun* the first prints of a cinema film before it is cut and edited. **to rush something out** to produce and distribute something very quickly. [from an Old French word *ruser* meaning 'to drive back']

rush² *noun* a marsh plant with slender pithy stems used for making mats, chair seats, baskets, etc. [from an Old English word *risc*]

rush hour *noun* the time each day when traffic is busiest.

rusk noun a kind of dry biscuit, especially one used for feeding babies. [from a Spanish or Portuguese word *rosca* meaning 'coil or roll of bread']

russet adjective soft reddish brown.
russet noun 1 a reddish-brown colour. 2 an apple with a rough skin of this colour. [from a Latin word *russus* meaning 'red']

Russian adjective to do with or coming from Russia.
Russian noun 1 a person born in Russia or descended from people born there. 2 the language of Russia.

Russian roulette noun a dangerous game of chance in which a revolver is loaded with a single bullet and the people taking part spin the cylinder in turn and fire the gun at their head.

Russo- prefix Russian and
♦ *Russo-Japanese*.

rust noun 1 a reddish-brown or yellowish-brown coating of iron oxide that forms on iron or steel by the effect of moisture, and gradually corrodes it. 2 a reddish-brown colour. 3 a plant disease with rust-coloured spots; the fungus causing this.
rust verb 1 to be affected with rust. 2 to lose quality or efficiency by lack of use. **rustless** adjective [from an Old English word]

rustic adjective 1 having the qualities that country people or peasants are thought to have; simple and unsophisticated, or rough and unrefined. 2 to do with living in the country. 3 made of rough branches or timber ♦ *a rustic bridge*.
rustic noun a country person, a peasant. [same origin as for *rural*]

rusticate verb 1 to suspend a student from a university as a punishment. 2 to make masonry with sunken joints or a roughened surface. 3 (*old use*) to settle in the country and live a rural life. **rustication** noun [from *rustic*]

rustle verb 1 to make a soft crackling sound like that of paper being crumpled; to cause something to do this. 2 to steal horses or cattle.
rustle noun a rustling sound. **to rustle something up** (*informal*) to prepare or produce something quickly ♦ *I'll see if I can rustle up something to eat.* **rustler** noun [an imitation of the sound]

rustproof adjective not affected by corrosion by rust.

rustproof verb to make something rustproof.

rusty adjective (**rustier, rustiest**) 1 affected with rust. 2 rust-coloured. 3 weakened by lack of use or practice ♦ *My French is a bit rusty.* **rustiness** noun

rut[1] noun 1 a deep track made by the wheels of vehicles. 2 a course of life that has become dull but is hard to change ♦ *We are getting into a rut.* [probably related to *route*]

rut[2] noun a period of sexual excitement in male deer and other mammals during which they fight each other for females.
rut verb (**rutted, rutting**) to be affected with this. [from a Latin word *rugire* meaning 'to roar']

ruthless adjective having no pity or compassion. SYNONYMS: heartless, pitiless, merciless, brutal, vicious, callous. **ruthlessly** adverb **ruthlessness** noun [from an old word *ruth* meaning 'pity']

rutted adjective marked with ruts.

rye noun 1 a kind of cereal used for making flour or as food for cattle. 2 a kind of whisky made from rye. [from an Old English word *ryge*]

rye bread noun a dense chewy bread made with rye flour.

Ss

S the nineteenth letter of the English alphabet.

S abbreviation 1 Saint. 2 siemens. 3 south or southern. 4 (*Chemistry*) the symbol for sulphur.

SA abbreviation South Africa.

sabbath noun a weekly religious day of rest, observed on Saturday by Jews and on Sunday by Christians. [from a Hebrew word *shabat* meaning 'rest']

sabbatical (sə-bat-ik-əl) noun a period of paid leave granted to a university teacher for study or travel.
sabbatical adjective of or like the sabbath. [from a Greek word *sabbatikos* meaning 'of the sabbath'. The noun is so called because leave was traditionally granted

once every seven years, just as the sabbath is one in every seven days]

sable noun 1 a small weasel-like animal native to Japan and Siberia. 2 its dark brown fur.
sable adjective (poetic) black. [via Old French from a Latin word sabelum]

sabotage (sab-ə-tahzh) noun deliberate damage done to machinery or materials for political or military purposes.
sabotage verb 1 to commit sabotage on something. 2 to make something useless or impossible ♦ Their arrival sabotaged all my plans. [from a French word saboter meaning 'to kick with sabots (wooden shoes)']

saboteur (sab-ə-ter) noun a person who commits sabotage.

sabre (say-ber) noun 1 a heavy sword with a curved blade. 2 a light fencing sword with a tapering blade. [from a Hungarian word szablya]

sac noun a bag-shaped part in an animal or plant. [a French word, from a Latin word saccus meaning 'sack or bag']

saccharin (sak-er-in) noun a sweet substance used as a substitute for sugar. [from a Greek word sakkharon meaning 'sugar']

saccharine (sak-er-een) adjective unpleasantly sweet or sentimental ♦ a saccharine smile.

sachet (sash-ay) noun a small sealed packet or bag containing a small amount of something. [a French word meaning 'little sack']

sack [1] noun 1 a large bag of strong material for storing and carrying goods. 2 (**the sack**) (informal) dismissal from a job or position ♦ They gave him the sack.
sack verb 1 (informal) to dismiss someone from a job. SYNONYMS: dismiss, fire. 2 to put something into a sack or sacks. [via Old English from a Latin word saccus, with the same meaning]

sack [2] verb to plunder a captured town in a violent destructive way. SYNONYMS: plunder, loot, pillage, raid.
sack noun the act of sacking a place. [from a French phrase mettre à sac meaning 'to put in a sack']

sackbut noun an early form of trombone. [from a French word saquebute]

sackcloth noun a coarse fabric made from flax or hemp. **sackcloth and ashes** a symbol of regret and repentance (from the ancient custom of wearing sackcloth and sprinkling ashes on the head in penitence or mourning).

sackful noun (**sackfuls**) the amount that a sack will hold.

sacking noun material for making sacks.

sack race noun a children's race in which each competitor is tied in a sack up to the waist and moves forward by jumping.

sacral (say-krəl) adjective 1 (Anatomy) to do with the sacrum. 2 of or for sacred rites.

sacrament noun 1 an important Christian religious ceremony, such as baptism and the Eucharist. 2 the consecrated elements in the Eucharist, especially the bread.
sacramental adjective [same origin as for sacred]

sacred adjective 1 associated with or dedicated to God or a god, and so deserving to be worshipped or venerated. SYNONYMS: holy, blessed. 2 dedicated to some person or purpose ♦ sacred to the memory of those who fell in battle. 3 used in connection with religion, not secular ♦ sacred music. 4 sacrosanct. [from a Latin word sacer meaning 'holy']

sacred cow noun an idea or institution which its supporters will not allow to be criticized. [with reference to the Hindu respect for the cow as a sacred animal]

sacrifice noun 1 the slaughter of a victim or the presenting of a gift or doing of an act in order to win the favour of a god. 2 giving up something you value for the sake of something that is more important or more valuable. 3 something offered or given up.
sacrifice verb 1 to offer something or give something up as a sacrifice. SYNONYMS: give up, forgo, surrender. 2 to give up something in order to achieve something else ♦ Their description of the events sacrificed brevity to accuracy. **sacrificial** (sak-ri-**fish**-əl) adjective [from a Latin word sacrificium]

sacrilege (sak-ri-lij) noun disrespect or damage to something regarded as sacred.
sacrilegious (sak-ri-lij-əs) adjective [from Latin words sacer meaning 'sacred' and legere meaning 'to take away']

sacristan (sak-ri-stən) noun a person in charge of the sacred vessels and other contents of a church. [from a Latin word sacristanus]

sacristy (**sak**-rist-i) *noun* (**sacristies**) the place in a church where the priest prepares for a service and where the sacred vessels are kept. [via French from a Latin word *sacristia*]

sacrosanct (**sak**-roh-sankt) *adjective* sacred and respected and therefore not to be violated or damaged. [from Latin words *sacro* meaning 'by a sacred rite' and *sanctus* meaning 'holy']

sacrum (**say**-krəm) *noun* (*Anatomy*) a triangular bone that forms the back of the pelvis. [from a Latin phrase *os sacrum* meaning 'sacred bone' (because people believed the soul was located there)]

SAD *abbreviation* seasonal affective disorder.

sad *adjective* (**sadder, saddest**) 1 feeling sorrow, unhappy. SYNONYMS: unhappy, despondent, down-hearted, sorrowful, dejected, downcast, miserable, glum. 2 causing sorrow ♦ *There is a sad story in the newspaper about an abandoned baby.* SYNONYMS: distressing, touching, poignant, pathetic, pitiful. 3 regrettable ♦ *It is a sad fact that one in three marriages ends in divorce.* SYNONYMS: regrettable, deplorable, unfortunate. 4 (*informal*) inadequate or unfashionable. **sadly** *adverb* **sadness** *noun* [from an Old English word *sæd*]

sadden *verb* to make someone sad.

saddle *noun* 1 a seat placed on a horse or other animal. 2 the seat of bicycle. 3 a ridge of high land between two peaks. 4 a joint of meat consisting of the two loins. 5 a shaped support for a pipe or cable. **saddle** *verb* 1 to put a saddle on an animal. 2 to burden someone with a task or responsibility. **in the saddle** 1 on horseback. 2 in a position of responsibility or control. [from an Old English word *sadol*]

saddleback *noun* a black pig with a white stripe round its body.

saddlebag *noun* a bag fixed behind a saddle or as one of a pair slung over a horse.

saddler *noun* someone who makes or deals in saddles and other equipment for horses.

saddlery *noun* a saddler's goods or business.

saddle stitch *noun* a decorative stitch made with thick thread.

sadhu (**sah**-doo) *noun* (in India) a Hindu or Jain holy man or sage. [from a Sanskrit word meaning 'holy man']

sadism (**say**-dizm) *noun* sexual or general pleasure derived from inflicting or watching pain. **sadist** *noun* **sadistic** (sə-**dis**-tik) *adjective* **sadistically** *adverb* [from the name of the French novelist Marquis de Sade (1740–1814), who wrote descriptions of sadism]

sadomasochism (say-doh-**mas**-ə-kizm) *noun* a sexual tendency that combines sadism and masochism. **sadomasochist** *noun*

sae *abbreviation* stamped addressed envelope.

safari (sə-**far**-i) *noun* (**safaris**) an expedition to hunt or observe wild animals in their environment, especially in East Africa. [from an Arabic word *safara* meaning 'to travel']

safari jacket *noun* a belted lightweight jacket with patch pockets.

safari park *noun* a park where wild animals are kept in the open for observation by visitors driving through.

safe *adjective* 1 free or protected from risk or danger. SYNONYMS: secure, protected. 2 not causing or resulting in harm or injury. SYNONYMS: harmless, innocuous. 3 (said about a place) providing security or protection. SYNONYMS: secure, reliable. **safe** *noun* 1 a strong locked cupboard or cabinet for keeping valuables. 2 a cabinet for storing food. **to be on the safe side** to allow a margin of security against risks. **safely** *adverb* **safeness** *noun* [from a Latin word *salvus* meaning 'uninjured']

safe conduct *noun* the right to pass through an area without risk of arrest or harm, especially in time of war.

safe deposit *noun* a safe or strongroom in a bank or hotel.

safeguard *noun* a measure taken to prevent a danger or mishap. **safeguard** *verb* to protect something by means of a safeguard. SYNONYMS: protect, defend, look after.

safe period *noun* the time in a woman's menstrual cycle when sexual intercourse is least likely to result in conception.

safe sex *noun* sexual activity in which people take precautions, such as the use of condoms, to avoid the spread of diseases.

safety *noun* a state of being safe, freedom from risk or danger. SYNONYMS: security, protection.

safety catch *noun* a device that prevents a gun being fired or a machine being operated accidentally or dangerously.

safety lamp *noun* a miner's lamp with the flame protected so that it will not ignite firedamp.

safety net *noun* a net placed to catch an acrobat in case of a fall.

safety pin *noun* a U-shaped pin with a guard covering the point when it is closed.

safety razor *noun* a razor with a guard to prevent the blade from cutting the skin deeply.

safety valve *noun* **1** a valve that opens automatically to relieve excessive pressure. **2** a harmless way of releasing feelings of anger or excitement.

saffron *noun* an orange-coloured spice used for colouring and flavouring food, made from the stigmas of a kind of crocus. [from an Old French word *safran*]

sag *verb* (**sagged, sagging**) **1** to sink or curve down in the middle under weight or pressure. SYNONYMS: bend, bow, dip, slump. **2** to hang down loosely and unevenly.
sag *noun* an instance of sagging. [from a German word]

saga (**sah**-gə) *noun* a long story with many episodes. [from an Old Norse word]

sagacious (sə-**gay**-shəs) *adjective* showing wisdom in your judgement and behaviour. SYNONYMS: wise, prudent, judicious, shrewd. **sagaciously** *adverb* **sagacity** (sə-**gas**-iti) *noun* [from a Latin word *sagax* meaning 'wise']

sage[1] *noun* a herb with fragrant greyish green leaves used to flavour food and formerly in medicine. [from an Old French word *sauge*, from a Latin word *salvia* meaning 'healing plant']

sage[2] *noun* a wise and respected person. **sage** *adjective* wise. **sagely** *adverb* [via Old French from a Latin word *sapere* meaning 'to be wise']

Sagittarius (saj-i-**tair**-iəs) **1** a group of stars (the Archer), seen as representing a centaur carrying a bow and arrow. **2** the sign of the zodiac which the sun enters about 22 November. **Sagittarian** *adjective* & *noun* [from a Latin word *sagittarius* meaning 'archer']

sago *noun* a starchy food in the form of hard white grains obtained from a palm and used in puddings. [from a Malay word *sagu*]

sahib (**sah**-ib) *noun* (in India) a title or form of address for a man. [from an Arabic word meaning 'friend' or 'lord']

said past tense and past participle of **say**.

sail *noun* **1** a piece of canvas or other material spread on rigging to catch the wind and make a ship or boat move. **2** these sails collectively. **3** a journey by ship or boat, used especially in indications of distance ♦ *Portsmouth is four hours' sail from St Malo.* **4** an arm on a windmill for catching the wind.
sail *verb* **1** to travel on water in a ship or boat. **2** to start on a voyage ♦ *We sail at noon.* **3** to travel on or over water in a ship or boat ♦ *ancestors who sailed the seas.* **4** to control the navigation of a ship or boat. **5** to move swiftly and smoothly, or in a stately manner. [from an Old English word *segel*]

sailboard *noun* a board with a mast and a sail fitted to it, used in windsurfing.

sailcloth *noun* **1** canvas for sails. **2** a strong dress material like canvas.

sailing ship *noun* a ship driven by sails.

sailor *noun* **1** a member of a ship's crew, or of a country's navy, especially one below the rank of officer. **2** a traveller considered as prone or not prone to seasickness ♦ *a poor sailor.*

sailplane *noun* a glider designed for a long period of flight.

saint *noun* **1** in Christian belief, a holy person, especially one considered to have won a high place in heaven and to be worthy of veneration. **2** a title given to such a person ♦ *Saint Anne.* **3** (*informal*) an exceptionally virtuous or unselfish person. **sainthood** *noun* [from a Latin word *sanctus* meaning 'holy']

St Elmo's fire *noun* a luminous electrical discharge seen on a ship or aircraft during a storm. [from St Elmo, the patron saint of sailors]

saintly *adjective* (**saintlier, saintliest**) like a saint, very virtuous. **saintliness** *noun*

St Vitus's dance *noun* a children's disease in which the limbs twitch uncontrollably.

saithe (saith) *noun* a fish related to the cod. [from an Old Norse word *seithr*]

sake *noun* **for the sake of 1** in order to please or honour someone ♦ *They organized a holiday for their children's sake.* **2** in order to achieve or obtain something ♦ *For the sake of clarity, each question has a number.* [from an Old English word]

salaam (sə-lahm) *noun* a gesture of greeting in Arabic and Muslim countries, made by lowering the head and body and touching the forehead with the fingers. **salaam** *verb* to make a salaam. [from an Arabic word *salam* meaning 'peace']

salacious (sə-lay-shəs) *adjective* sexually indecent. **salaciously** *adverb* **salaciousness** *noun* [from a Latin word *salax*, from *salire* meaning 'to jump']

salad *noun* a dish consisting of raw vegetables and other cold ingredients. [from a French word *salade*, from a Latin word *sal* meaning 'salt']

salad days *plural noun* a time of youth and inexperience. [from Shakespeare, *Antony and Cleopatra* I.v.72]

salamander (sal-ə-mand-er) *noun* **1** a lizard-like amphibian animal related to the newts. **2** (in mythology) a lizard-like animal said to live in fire. [from a Greek word *salamandra*]

salami (sə-lah-mi) *noun* a strongly flavoured sausage, originally from Italy. [an Italian word, from a Latin word *sal* meaning 'salt']

salaried *adjective* receiving a salary.

salary *noun* (**salaries**) a fixed payment made by an employer at regular intervals (usually monthly) to an employee, calculated on an annual basis. [from a Latin word *salarium* meaning 'salt money', i.e. money given to Roman soldiers to buy salt]

sale *noun* **1** the process of selling or being sold. **2** a transaction in which something is sold. **3** the amount sold, or the profit from being sold ♦ *Sales were up last year.* **4** an event at which goods are sold, especially by public auction or for charity. **5** a time when goods are sold at a reduced price. **for** or **on sale** available to be bought. [via Old English from a Norse word *sala*]

saleable *adjective* fit to be sold, likely to be bought.

saleroom *noun* a room in which auctions are held.

salesman or **saleswoman** *noun* (**salesmen** or **saleswomen**) a person who sells goods commercially.

salesmanship *noun* skill in selling goods commercially.

salesperson *noun* (**salespersons** or **salespeople**) a salesman or saleswoman.

salient (say-li-ənt) *adjective* **1** most noticeable ♦ *the salient features of the plan.* **2** projecting or prominent. **salient** *noun* a projecting piece of land or part of a fortification. [from a Latin word *saliens* meaning 'leaping']

saline (say-liyn) *adjective* containing salt or salts. **salinity** (sə-lin-iti) *noun* [from a Latin word *sal* meaning 'salt']

saliva (sə-liy-və) *noun* a natural liquid secreted into the mouth by various glands, used to help chewing and swallowing. **salivary** *adjective*

salivate (sal-i-vayt) *verb* to produce saliva. **salivation** *noun*

sallow[1] *adjective* (said about the skin or complexion) slightly yellow. **sallowness** *noun* [from an Old English word *salo* meaning 'dusky']

sally *noun* (**sallies**) **1** a sudden rush forward. SYNONYMS: charge, foray, sortie, attack, assault. **2** a lively or witty remark. **sally** *verb* (**sallies, sallied, sallying**) **sally out** or **forth** to make a sally, to set forth. [same origin as for *salient*]

salmon (sam-ən) *noun* **1** (**salmon**) a large fish with light pink flesh, used for food. **2** a salmon pink colour.

salmonella (sal-mə-nel-lə) *noun* a bacterium that causes food poisoning. [from the name of an American veterinary surgeon D. E. Salmon (1850–1914)]

salon *noun* **1** a room or establishment where a hairdresser, beauty specialist, or couturier etc. receives clients. **2** a large elegant room used for receiving guests. [from a French word *salon* meaning 'room']

saloon *noun* **1** a public room for a specified purpose ♦ *billiard saloon.* **2** a public room on a ship. **3** (*North Amer.*) (*historical*) a place where alcoholic drinks may be bought and drunk. **4** a saloon car. [via French from an Italian word *salone* meaning 'large hall']

saloon bar noun a comfortable bar in a pub.

saloon car noun a passenger car with a closed body.

salsa noun 1 a hot spicy tomato sauce. 2 a type of Latin American dance music with jazz and rock elements, or a dance to this music. [a Spanish word meaning 'sauce']

salsify (sal-si-fi) noun a plant with a long fleshy root cooked as a vegetable. [from a French word salsifis]

salt noun 1 sodium chloride, a crystalline substance that gives seawater its taste and is used to flavour and preserve food. 2 a chemical compound of a metal and an acid. 3 (usually **old salt**) (informal) an experienced sailor.
salt adjective 1 impregnated with or preserved with salt. 2 tasting of salt.
salt verb 1 to season food with salt. 2 to preserve food in salt. 3 to put salt on a road surface to melt snow or ice. 4 (informal) to make a mine appear rich by fraudulently inserting precious metal into it before it is viewed.
salts plural noun a substance resembling salt in form, especially a laxative. **to salt something away** to put money aside for the future. **salt of the earth** people with a wholesome influence upon society. **to take something with a grain** or **pinch of salt** be cautious about believing a statement. **worth your salt** deserving your position or reputation. [from an Old English word sealt]

salt cellar noun a small dish or perforated pot holding salt for use at meals. [cellar from a French word salier meaning 'salt box']

salting noun a marsh that is covered by the sea when the tide rises.

saltire (sal-tiyr) noun (Heraldry) a diagonal cross dividing a shield into four compartments. [from an Old French word saultoir meaning 'stirrup cord']

salt marsh noun a marsh that is flooded by the sea at high tide.

salt pan noun a hollow by the sea where salt water evaporates and leaves a deposit of salt.

saltpetre (solt-peet-er) noun a salty white powder (potassium nitrate) used in making gunpowder. [from a Latin phrase sal petrae meaning 'salt of rock']

salty adjective (**saltier, saltiest**) containing or tasting of salt. **saltiness** noun

salubrious (sə-loo-bri-əs) adjective good for people's health. SYNONYMS: healthy, wholesome. **salubrity** noun [from a Latin word salubris, from salus meaning 'health']

saluki (sə-loo-ki) noun (**salukis**) a tall swift slender dog with a silky coat. [from an Arabic word saluki]

salutary (sal-yoo-ter-i) adjective (said about something unpleasant) having a beneficial effect. [from Latin salus meaning 'health']

salutation (sal-yoo-tay-shən) noun a statement or gesture of greeting or respect.

salute noun 1 a gesture of respect or recognition. 2 a formal movement to denote respect, especially the raising of the hand to the head by a soldier acknowledging a superior or in reply to this. 3 a firing of guns in a ceremony to show respect or as a celebration. 4 an expression of respect or admiration.
salute verb 1 to perform a formal military salute, or to greet someone with this. 2 to greet someone with a polite gesture. SYNONYMS: hail, greet, acknowledge. 3 to express respect or admiration for someone or something. SYNONYMS: acclaim, recognize, extol, pay tribute to. [from a Latin word salus meaning 'health']

salvage verb 1 to rescue a wrecked or damaged ship or its cargo at sea. 2 to rescue goods from a building destroyed by fire.
salvage noun 1 the rescue of property, especially of a ship or its cargo, or of the contents of a building destroyed by fire. 2 the goods or property saved. [from a Latin word salvare meaning 'to save']

salvation noun 1 (in some religious beliefs) the saving of the soul from sin and its consequences. 2 preservation from loss or calamity. 3 a source or means of being saved ♦ The loan was our salvation.

Salvation Army noun an international Christian organization founded on military lines to do charitable work and spread Christianity.

salve noun 1 a soothing ointment. 2 something that soothes a person's conscience or feelings.

salve verb to soothe a person's conscience or feelings. [from an Old English word *sealfe*]

salver noun a metal tray on which letters, cards, or refreshments are placed for handing to people on formal occasions. [from a French word *salve*, from a Spanish word *salva* meaning 'sampling of food', for which such a tray was originally used]

salvo noun (**salvos** or **salvoes**) **1** the firing of a number of guns together as a salute. **2** a volley of applause. [from an Italian word *salva* meaning 'salutation']

sal volatile (sal və-lat-ili) noun a flavoured solution of ammonium carbonate, used as smelling salts. [a Latin phrase, meaning 'volatile salt']

SAM abbreviation surface- to- air missile.

Samaritan noun someone who readily gives help to a person in need. [named after the parable of the Good Samaritan (= person from Samaria) in the Bible (Luke 10:33)]

same adjective **1** of one kind, not changed or changing or different ♦ We hear the same story every time. **2** identical, the very one ♦ Is that the same man you saw yesterday? **3** used to refer to something or someone previously mentioned.
same pronoun **1** (**the same**) the same person or thing ♦ I would do the same again. **2** (**the same**) in the same manner ♦ We still feel the same about it. **sameness** noun [from an Old Norse word *sami*]

samizdat (**sam**-iz-dat) noun a system of secret publication of literature banned by the state, especially in the former communist countries of eastern Europe. [from a Russian word meaning 'self-publishing house']

samosa (sə-**moh**-sə) noun a triangular fried pastry containing meat or a spiced vegetable filling. [from Persian and Urdu words]

samovar (**sam**-ə-var) noun a metal tea urn with an interior heating tube to keep water at boiling point, used in Russia and elsewhere. [from a Russian word meaning 'self-boiler']

sampan noun a small flat-bottomed boat used along coasts and rivers in China. [from a Chinese word *sanpan*, from *san* meaning 'three' and *pan* meaning 'boards']

samphire (**sam**-fiyr) noun a plant with fragrant fleshy leaves, growing near the sea. [from a French phrase *herbe de Saint Pierre* meaning 'St Peter's herb']

sample noun a small part or amount of something that shows what the whole is like. SYNONYMS: specimen, example.
sample verb to take a sample of something. SYNONYMS: try, test, experience. [from an Old French word *essample* meaning 'example']

sampler noun **1** a piece of embroidery worked in various stitches to show skill in needlework. **2** a typical sample or part of something. **3** a thing that takes samples.

samsara (sam-**sar**-ə) noun (in Hinduism and Buddhism) the cycle of life, death, and rebirth that the soul experiences. [from a Sanskrit word meaning 'a wandering through']

samurai (**sam**-oor-iy) noun (**samurai**) (historical) a member of a powerful military caste in feudal Japan. [from a Japanese word]

sanatorium noun (**sanatoriums** or **sanatoria**) a hospital for treating chronic diseases or convalescents. [from a Latin word *sanare* meaning 'to heal']

sanctify verb (**sanctifies, sanctified, sanctifying**) to make something or someone holy or sacred. **sanctification** noun [from a Latin word *sanctus* meaning 'holy']

sanctimonious (sank-ti-moh-niəs) adjective making a show of being righteous or pious. **sanctimoniously** adverb **sanctimoniousness** noun [from a Latin word *sanctimonia* meaning 'sanctity']

sanction noun **1** action taken by one country or several countries against a country or organization to force it to conform to a law or principle of behaviour that it is considered to have violated. **2** a threatened penalty for disobeying a law. **3** formal permission or approval for an action. SYNONYMS: agreement, approval, permission, consent, authorization.
sanction verb to give official permission for an action. SYNONYMS: authorize, approve, agree to, allow, permit, endorse. [from a Latin word *sancire* meaning 'to make holy']

sanctity noun being sacred, holiness.

sanctuary noun (**sanctuaries**) **1** a sacred place. **2** the holiest part of a temple. **3** the part of the chancel of a church containing the main altar. **4** an area where birds or wild animals are protected and encouraged to breed. **5** refuge, or a place of refuge ♦ *to seek sanctuary*. SYNONYMS: refuge, shelter, asylum. [from a Latin word *sanctus* meaning 'holy']

sanctum *noun* **1** a person's private room. **2** a holy place. [a Latin word meaning 'holy thing']

sand *noun* **1** a substance consisting of fine loose particles resulting from the wearing down of rock and covering the ground in deserts and on beaches, the seabed, and river beds. **2** (**sands**) an expanse of sand ♦ *a walk along the sands*. **3** a light brown colour like that of sand.
sand *verb* **1** to sprinkle or cover a surface with sand. **2** to smooth or polish a surface with sandpaper or another abrasive. [from an Old English word]

sandal *noun* a light shoe consisting of a sole with straps or thongs over the foot.
sandalled *adjective*

sandalwood *noun* a kind of scented wood from a tropical tree. [*sandal* via Latin from a Sanskrit word *candana*]

sandbag *noun* a bag filled with sand, used to build defences, e.g. to protect a wall or building against floods, and as ballast in a boat.
sandbag *verb* (**sandbagged, sandbagging**) to protect a place with sandbags.

sandbank *noun* a bank of sand under water, causing the water to be shallow at that point.

sandblast *verb* to clean a surface with a jet of sand under pressure.

sandcastle *noun* a model of a castle made in sand on the seashore.

sand dune *noun* loose sand formed into a mound by the wind.

sander *noun* a device for sanding surfaces.

sandpaper *noun* paper with a coating of sand or another abrasive, used for smoothing or polishing surfaces.
sandpaper *verb* to smooth or polish a surface with sandpaper.

sandpiper *noun* a bird with a long pointed bill and long legs, living in sandy coastal areas.

sandpit *noun* a shallow box or hollow partly filled with sand for children to play in.

sandstone *noun* rock formed of compressed sand.

sandstorm *noun* a storm of wind in the desert, carrying huge clouds of sand.

sandwich *noun* **1** a food consisting of two or more slices of bread with a filling such as meat, jam, cheese, etc. between them. **2** a cake made of two or more layers with jam or cream between them.
sandwich *verb* to insert something tightly between two other things. [said to have been invented by the Earl of Sandwich (1718–92) so that he could eat while gambling]

sandwich board *noun* a linked pair of boards bearing advertisements, hung over a person's shoulders.

sandwich course *noun* a training course with alternating periods of instruction and practical experience.

sandy *adjective* (**sandier, sandiest**) **1** like sand, or covered with sand. **2** (said about the hair) light yellowish brown.
sandiness *noun*

sane *adjective* **1** having a sound mind, not mad ♦ *It was an odd thing for a sane person to do*. SYNONYMS: rational, normal, reasonable, right-minded. **2** sensible and practical.
sanely *adverb* [from a Latin word *sanus* meaning 'healthy']

sang past tense of **sing**.

sangfroid (sahn-**frwah**) *noun* calmness at a time of danger or difficulty. [from a French word *sang-froid* meaning 'cold blood']

sangha (sang-gə) *noun* the Buddhist monastic order, including monks, nuns, and novices. [from a Sanskrit word *samgha* meaning 'community']

sanguinary (sang-gwin-er-i) *adjective* **1** full of bloodshed. **2** bloodthirsty. [from a Latin word *sanguis* meaning 'blood']

sanguine (sang-gwin) *adjective* hopeful or optimistic. [same origin as for *sanguinary* (because good blood was believed to be the cause of cheerfulness)]

sanitary (san-it-er-i) *noun* **1** to do with hygiene or health, hygienic. **2** to do with sanitation. [same origin as for *sane*]

sanitary towel *noun* an absorbent pad worn by a woman to absorb blood during menstruation.

sanitation *noun* arrangements for drainage and the disposal of sewage.

sanitize *verb* to make something hygienic.

sanity *noun* the state of being sane.

sank past tense of **sink**.

Sanskrit *noun* the ancient and sacred language of the Hindus in India, one of the oldest known Indo-European languages.

sans serif (san-**se**-rif) *noun* a style of typeface without small projections (called *serifs*) on the ends of letters.
sans serif *adjective* without serifs. [from a French word *sans* meaning 'without' and *serif*]

Santa Claus *noun* Father Christmas. [from the Dutch name *Sante Klaas* meaning 'St Nicholas']

sap[1] *noun* **1** the liquid that circulates in plants, carrying food to all parts. **2** strength or energy. **3** (*informal*) a foolish person.
sap *verb* (**sapped, sapping**) to take away a person's strength gradually. SYNONYMS: exhaust, drain, use up. [from an Old English word *sæp*]

sap[2] *noun* a trench or tunnel made in order to get closer to an enemy. [via French and Italian from an Arabic word *sarab* meaning 'underground passage']

sapele (sə-**pee**-li) *noun* a large West African tree, with a hard reddish brown wood like mahogany. [from the name of a port in Nigeria]

sapient (**say**-pi-ənt) *adjective* (*formal*) wise. [from a Latin word *sapiens* meaning 'wise']

sapling *noun* a young tree. [from *sap*[1]]

saponify (sə-**pon**-i-fiy) *verb* (**saponifies, saponified, saponifying**) (*Chemistry*) to make fat or oil into soap by combining with an alkali. **saponification** *noun* [from a Latin word *sapo* meaning 'soap']

sapper *noun* a soldier who lays or detects mines, especially a private in the Royal Engineers. [from *sap*[2]]

sapphire *noun* **1** a transparent blue precious stone. **2** a bright blue colour. **sapphire** *adjective* bright blue. [via French and Latin from a Greek word *sappheiros*]

saprophyte (**sap**-rə-fiyt) *noun* (*Biology*) a fungus or similar plant that lives on decaying matter. **saprophytic** (sap-rə-**fit**-ik) *adjective* [from Greek words *sapros* meaning 'putrid' and *phuton* meaning 'plant']

sapwood *noun* the soft outer layers of recently formed wood in a tree, between the heartwood and the bark.

saraband (**sa**-rə-band) *noun* a slow Spanish dance, or the music for it. [via French from a Spanish word *zarabanda*]

Saracen (**sa**-rə-sən) *noun* an Arab or Muslim of the time of the Crusades. [via French from a Greek word *Sarakēnos*]

sarcasm (**sar**-kazm) *noun* the use of wit and irony to mock or criticize someone. [from a Greek word *sarkazein* meaning 'to tear the flesh']

sarcastic (sar-**kas**-tik) *adjective* using or showing sarcasm. SYNONYMS: caustic, cutting, sardonic. **sarcastically** *adverb*

sarcoma (sar-**koh**-mə) *noun* (*Medicine*) a malignant tumour on connective tissue. [from a Greek word *sarkōma*, from *sarkoun* meaning 'to become fleshy']

sarcophagus (sar-**kof**-ə-gəs) *noun* (**sarcophagi**) an ancient stone coffin, often decorated with carvings. [from Greek words *sarkos* meaning 'of flesh' and *-phagos* meaning 'eating']

sardine *noun* a young pilchard or other small fish, tinned as food tightly packed in oil. [probably from the name Sardinia, an island in the Mediterranean Sea]

sardonic (sar-**don**-ik) *adjective* humorous in a grim or sarcastic way. **sardonically** *adverb* [from a Greek word *sardonios* meaning 'of Sardinia', also used to describe scornful laughter]

sargassum (sar-**gas**-əm) *noun* a kind of seaweed with air vessels like berries, usually floating in large masses. [from a Portuguese word *sargaço*]

sari (**sar**-i) *noun* (**saris**) a length of cloth worn draped round the body as a traditional item of dress by Indian women. [from a Hindi word]

sarong (sə-**rong**) *noun* a skirt-like piece of clothing worn by men and women in SE Asia, consisting of a strip of cloth worn tucked round the waist or under the armpits. [from a Malay word]

sarsen (**sar**-sən) *noun* a large sandstone boulder of the kind found in southern England. [probably another spelling of *Saracen*]

sartorial (sar-**tor**-iəl) *adjective* to do with tailoring or clothes ♦ *sartorial taste*. [from a Latin word *sartor* meaning 'tailor']

SAS *abbreviation* Special Air Service, a regiment of the British armed services trained in commando techniques.

sash [1] *noun* a long strip of cloth worn round the waist or over one shoulder and across the body for ornament or as part of a uniform. [from an Arabic word *shash* meaning 'turban']

sash [2] *noun* each of a pair of frames holding the glass panes of a window and sliding up and down in grooves. [from a French word *châssis* meaning 'frame']

sash cord *noun* a strong cord used for attaching a weight to each end of a sash so that it can be balanced at any height.

Sassenach (sas-ǝn-ak) *noun* (*Scottish and Irish*) (*derogatory*) an English person. [from a Gaelic word meaning 'Saxon']

SAT *abbreviation* standard assessment task.

sat past tense and past participle of **sit**.

Satan *noun* a name for the Devil. [via Old English and Latin from a Hebrew word *satan* meaning 'adversary']

satanic (sǝ-tan-ik) *adjective* to do with Satan or satanism.

satanism *noun* the worship of Satan, involving parodies of Christian symbols and worship. **satanist** *noun*

satchel *noun* a small bag with a strap, used especially for school books and hung over the shoulder or carried on the back. [from a Latin word *saccellus* meaning 'little sack']

sate *verb* to satisfy someone fully, to satiate someone. [from an Old English word *sadian* meaning 'to become sated or weary', related to *sad*]

sateen (sǝ-teen) *noun* a cotton fabric with a glossy surface resembling satin.

satellite *noun* 1 a spacecraft or other artificial body put in orbit round a planet to collect information or transmit communications signals. 2 a heavenly body revolving round a planet. 3 a small country that is dependent on a larger and more powerful neighbouring country. [from an earlier meaning 'follower', from a Latin word *satelles* meaning 'attendant']

satellite dish *noun* a bowl-shaped aerial for receiving broadcasting signals transmitted by satellite.

satellite television *noun* television broadcasting in which the signals are transmitted by means of a communications satellite.

satellite town *noun* a smaller town dependent on a larger one near it.

satiate (say-shi-ayt) *verb* to satisfy someone fully, to sate someone. **satiation** *noun* [from a Latin word *satis* meaning 'enough']

satin *noun* a silky material woven in such a way that it is glossy on one side only. **satin** *adjective* smooth like satin. **satiny** *adjective* [via Old French from an Arabic word *zaytuni* meaning 'of Tsinkiang', a town in China]

satinwood *noun* 1 the smooth hard wood of a tropical tree, used for making furniture. 2 a tree producing this wood.

satire *noun* 1 the use of ridicule, irony, or sarcasm to show up apparent weaknesses of people and institutions. 2 a novel, play, etc. that uses satire. **satirist** *noun* [from a Latin word *satira*]

satirical (sǝ-ti-ri-kǝl) *adjective* using or containing satire. **satirically** *adverb*

satirize (sat-i-ryz) *verb* to attack or criticize someone by using satire.

satisfaction *noun* 1 the state or feeling of being satisfied. 2 something that satisfies a desire or gratifies a feeling. 3 compensation for injury or loss ♦ *The victims are demanding satisfaction.*

satisfactory *adjective* satisfying expectations or needs, adequate. SYNONYMS: adequate, acceptable, sufficient. **satisfactorily** *adverb*

satisfy *verb* (**satisfies, satisfied, satisfying**) 1 to give someone what they want or demand, to make someone pleased or contented. SYNONYMS: content, please, placate. 2 to put an end to a demand or craving by giving what is required ♦ *to satisfy your hunger.* 3 to provide someone with sufficient evidence of something, to convince someone ♦ *The police are satisfied that the death was accidental.* SYNONYMS: convince, persuade. 4 to pay a creditor. **to be satisfied with** to regard something as adequate. [from Latin words *satis* meaning 'enough' and *facere* meaning 'to make']

satrap *noun* 1 a provincial governor in the ancient Persian empire. 2 a local ruler owing allegiance to a more powerful ruler. [via Old French and Latin from a Persian word]

satsuma (sat-**soo**-mə) *noun* a kind of tangerine with a loose skin, originally grown in Japan. [named after Satsuma, a former province of Japan]

saturate *verb* 1 to soak something with liquid, to make something thoroughly wet. SYNONYMS: soak, drench. 2 to cause a substance to combine with or absorb the greatest possible amount of another substance. 3 to cause something to absorb as much as possible until no more can be absorbed ♦ *The market for used cars is saturated.*

saturation *noun* the state of being saturated, maximum absorption.

saturation point *noun* the point at which no more can be absorbed.

Saturday *noun* the day of the week following Friday. [from an Old English word Sæternesdæg meaning 'day of Saturn']

saturnine (**sat**-er-niyn) *adjective* (said about a person) having a gloomy and forbidding appearance. [from a Latin word *saturninus* meaning 'of Saturn' (because people born under the influence of the planet Saturn were believed to be gloomy)]

satyr (**sat**-er) *noun* 1 (*Greek and Roman Mythology*) a woodland god with a man's body and a goat's ears, tail, and legs. 2 a man with strong sexual desires.

sauce *noun* 1 a thick liquid served with food to add flavour or richness. 2 (*informal*) cheek, impudence. [via Old French from a Latin word *salsus* meaning 'salted']

saucepan *noun* a round metal cooking pan with a long handle at the side, used for boiling things over heat.

saucer *noun* 1 a small shallow curved dish on which a cup is placed. 2 something having a similar shape.

saucy *adjective* (**saucier, sauciest**) (*informal*) 1 sexually suggestive. 2 cheeky or impudent. SYNONYMS: cheeky, impudent, disrespectful, insolent, rude. **saucily** *adverb* **sauciness** *noun*

sauerkraut (**sowr**-krowt) *noun* a German dish of chopped pickled cabbage. [a German word, from *sauer* meaning 'sour' and *Kraut* meaning 'cabbage']

sauna (**saw**-nə) *noun* a steam bath, or a building or room for this. [from a Finnish word]

saunter *verb* to walk in a slow relaxed manner. SYNONYMS: stroll, amble, wander, roam.
saunter *noun* a leisurely walk. [origin unknown]

saurian (**sor**-iən) *adjective* of or like a lizard.
saurian *noun* a large reptile, especially a dinosaur. [from a Greek word *sauros* meaning 'lizard']

sausage *noun* 1 a tube of minced seasoned meat enclosed in a skin and eaten grilled or fried. 2 a tube of cooked or preserved seasoned meat sold cold for eating in slices. [from an early French word *saussiche*, related to *sauce*]

sausage meat *noun* spiced minced meat for use in sausages.

sausage roll *noun* a piece of sausage meat cooked in a roll of pastry.

sauté (**soh**-tay) *adjective* fried quickly in a small amount of fat ♦ *sauté potatoes.*
sauté *verb* (**sautés, sautéd, sautéing**) to cook food in this way. [from a French word *sauter* meaning 'to jump']

savage *adjective* 1 wild and brutal ♦ *They were victims of a savage attack.* SYNONYMS: wild, fierce, vicious, brutal, cruel, ferocious. 2 fiercely hostile ♦ *The book came in for some savage criticism.* SYNONYMS: fierce, hostile. 3 (said about a people) primitive or uncivilized.
savage *noun* a member of a people regarded as primitive or uncivilized.
savage *verb* to attack someone fiercely, to maul someone. **savagely** *adverb*
savageness *noun* **savagery** *noun* [from a Latin word *silvaticus* meaning 'of the woods, wild']

savannah (sə-**van**-ə) *noun* a grassy plain in hot regions, with few or no trees. [via Spanish from a South American language]

savant (**sav**-ənt) *noun* a learned person. [a French word meaning 'knowing (person)']

save *verb* 1 to rescue someone or something or keep them from danger or harm. SYNONYMS: free, liberate, rescue, release, set free; protect, safeguard. 2 to keep something (especially money) so that it can be used later. SYNONYMS: keep, put by. 3 (in Christianity) to keep a soul from damnation. 4 to avoid wasting something ♦ *We must try to save fuel.* SYNONYM: preserve. 5 to make something unnecessary ♦ *Sending it by post will save you a journey.* 6 (in football or other sports) to prevent an opponent from scoring.

save noun the act of saving in football or other sports.

save preposition except ♦ in all cases save one. **to save your breath** to keep silent because it would be pointless to speak.

saver noun [via French from a Latin word salvus meaning 'safe']

saving noun a reduction or economy in money, time, or other resource.
saving adjective avoiding or preventing the need for something ♦ labour-saving devices.
saving preposition except.
savings plural noun money put aside for future use.

saving grace noun a good quality that redeems a person or thing whose other qualities are not good.

savings bank noun a bank that holds and pays interest on small deposits but does not offer other banking facilities.

savings certificate noun a document issued by the government guaranteeing a rate of interest on a deposit of savings.

saviour noun a person who rescues or delivers people from harm or danger. **the** or **our Saviour** (in Christianity) Christ as the saviour of mankind.

savoir faire (sav-wahr-**fair**) noun knowledge of how to behave in any social situation. [a French phrase, meaning 'knowing how to do']

savory noun a herb with a spicy smell and flavour, used in cooking. [probably from an Old English word]

savour verb 1 to enjoy the taste or smell of something. SYNONYMS: relish, appreciate, enjoy. 2 to have a certain taste or smell. 3 to suggest or show a trace of something ♦ The reply savoured of arrogance.
savour noun the taste or smell of something. [from a Latin word sapor meaning 'flavour']

savoury adjective 1 (said about food) salty or piquant rather than sweet. 2 having an appetizing taste or smell.
savoury noun (**savouries**) a savoury dish or snack. **savouriness** noun

savoy noun a hardy cabbage with dense wrinkled leaves. [named after Savoie, a region of SE France]

savvy noun (informal) common sense or good understanding.

savvy verb (**savvies, savvied, savvying**) (informal) to know or understand something. [from a Spanish phrase sabe usted meaning 'you know']

saw [1] noun a tool with a toothed edge for cutting wood etc. with a backwards and forwards movement.
saw verb (past tense **sawed**; past participle **sawn**) 1 to cut something with a saw. 2 to make a backwards and forwards movement as in sawing. [from an Old English word saga]

saw [2] past tense of **see** [1].

saw [3] noun a proverb or saying. [from an Old English word sagu meaning 'a saying']

sawdust noun powdery fragments of wood produced when sawing.

sawfish noun a large sea fish having a blade-like snout with jagged edges.

sawfly noun (**sawflies**) an insect that pierces plant tissues with a jagged organ in order to lay its eggs.

sawmill noun a factory with power-operated saws for cutting timber.

sawn past participle of **saw** [1].

sawn-off adjective (said about a gun) having a shortened barrel to make it easier to handle.

sawyer noun a person who saws timber.

sax noun (informal) a saxophone.

saxifrage (**saks**-i-frij) noun a rock plant with clusters of small white, yellow, or red flowers. [from Latin words saxum meaning 'rock' and frangere meaning 'to break']

Saxon noun 1 a member of a Germanic people who occupied parts of England in the 5th–6th centuries. 2 the language of this people.
Saxon adjective to do with the Saxons or their language.

saxophone noun a brass wind instrument with a reed in the mouthpiece and keys like those of a clarinet, used especially for jazz and dance music. [named after a Belgian instrument maker Adolphe Sax (1814–94), who invented it]

saxophonist (saks-**off**-ən-ist) noun a person who plays the saxophone.

say verb (past tense and past participle **said**) 1 to speak words to make a statement ♦ I said we ought to be leaving.

SYNONYMS: mention, state, remark, observe.
2 to express a fact, feeling, etc. ♦ *Colin tried to say what he really thought.* SYNONYMS: express, state, convey, explain, communicate. **3** to utter something ♦ *She was too angry to say his name.* SYNONYMS: utter, speak, mention. **4** (said about something written or printed) to have a specified wording ♦ *The notice said 'no parking'.* **5** to offer something as an argument or excuse ♦ *There's much to be said on both sides.* **6** to give something as an opinion or decision ♦ *It's hard to say which of them is better.* **7** to take a specified amount as being near enough ♦ *We'll allow, say, an hour for the meeting.*
say *noun* the power to decide something ♦ *He has no say in the matter.* SYNONYMS: voice, authority, influence. **to have your say** to give your opinion. **I'll say** (*informal*) an expression of approval or agreement. **I say** (*old use*) an expression of surprise or admiration, or used to call attention. [from an Old English word *secgan*]

saying *noun* a well-known phrase or proverb.

say-so *noun* (*informal*) **1** the power to decide something; a command. **2** a mere assertion offered without proof.

scab *noun* **1** a hard crust that forms over a wound or sore as it heals. **2** a skin disease or plant disease that causes rough scab-like patches. **3** (*informal*) a term of contempt for a person, especially a blackleg.
scab *verb* (**scabbed, scabbing**) to become covered by a scab. **scabby** *adjective* [from an Old Norse word *skabb*]

scabbard *noun* a sheath for the blade of a sword or dagger. [from an early French word *escalberc*]

scabies (**skay**-beez) *noun* a contagious skin disease causing severe itching. [from a Latin word *scabere* meaning 'to scratch']

scaffold *noun* **1** a wooden platform formerly used for public executions. **2** a structure of scaffolding.
scaffold *verb* to fit scaffolding to a building. [from an early French word, related to *catafalque*]

scaffolding *noun* **1** a temporary structure made of metal poles and planks to provide a platform or series of platforms for working on the outside of a building. **2** the poles and planks used to make this.

scalable *adjective* **1** able to be scaled or climbed. **2** able to be changed in scale.

scalar (**skay**-ler) *adjective* (*Mathematics and Physics*) having magnitude but not direction.
scalar *noun* a scalar quantity, such as speed. [same origin as for *scale³*]

scald *verb* **1** to injure someone with hot liquid or steam. **2** to heat milk to near boiling point.
scald *noun* a burn or other injury caused by scalding. [from a Latin word *excaldare* meaning 'to wash in hot water']

scale ¹ *noun* **1** each of the thin overlapping hard or horny plates protecting the skin of fishes and reptiles. **2** a dry flake of skin. **3** a flaky deposit inside a boiler or kettle etc., resulting from use of hard water. **4** a flaky deposit on the teeth.
scale *verb* **1** to remove scales or scale from something. **2** to come off in scales or flakes. [from an Old French word *escale* meaning 'flake']

scale ² *noun* each of the pans of a balance.
scales *plural noun* an instrument for weighing things. **to tip** or **turn the scales** to be the decisive factor in a situation. [from an Old Norse word *skál* meaning 'bowl']

scale ³ *noun* **1** a regular series of units, degrees, or qualities etc. for measuring or grading something. **2** (*Music*) an arrangement of notes ascending or descending by fixed intervals. **3** the ratio of the actual measurements of something and those of a drawing, map, or model of it. **4** the relative size or extent of something ♦ *bribery on a grand scale.*
scale *verb* **1** to climb something tall and precipitous, such as a cliff face. SYNONYMS: climb, ascend. **2** to represent something in measurements proportional to those of the original. **to scale up** or **down** to make something larger or smaller in proportion. **to scale** with measurements in proportion to those of the original. [from a Latin word *scala* meaning 'ladder']

scale model *noun* a model made to scale.

scalene (**skay**-leen) *adjective* (*Mathematics*) (said about a triangle) having unequal sides. [from a Greek word *skalēnos* meaning 'unequal']

scallop (**skol**-əp) *noun* **1** a shellfish with two hinged fan-shaped shells. **2** one shell of this, used as a dish for cooking and serving food. **3** each of a series of curves forming an ornamental edging.

scallop verb (**scalloped, scalloping**) to decorate something with ornamental scallops. **scalloping** noun [from an Old French word *escalope*]

scallywag noun (*informal*) a rascal.

scalp noun **1** the skin covering the top and back of the head. **2** (*historical*) the scalp with the hair cut away from an enemy's head as a trophy.
scalp verb to take the scalp of an enemy. [probably from a Scandinavian language]

scalpel (skal-pəl) noun a knife with a small sharp blade, used by a surgeon. [from a Latin word *scalprum* meaning 'chisel']

scaly adjective (**scalier, scaliest**) **1** covered in scales or scale (see **scale**[1]). **2** (*said about skin*) dry and flaky. **scaliness** noun

scamp noun (*informal*) a mischievous child. [same origin as for *scamper*]

scamper verb to run hastily; to run about playfully as a child does. SYNONYMS: scurry, scuttle, scoot, dash, hurry, rush.
scamper noun a scampering run. [from an earlier meaning 'to run away', probably from an early Dutch word *schampen* meaning 'to slip away']

scampi (skamp-i) plural noun large prawns. [an Italian word]

scan verb (**scanned, scanning**) **1** to glance at different parts of something quickly in order to check for something ♦ *He scanned the newspaper for a report of the incident.* SYNONYMS: look through, skim, peruse, study. **2** to sweep a radar or electronic beam over an area in search of something. **3** to resolve a picture into elements of light and shade for television transmission. **4** to analyse the metre of a line of verse. **5** (*said about verse*) to be correct in rhythm ♦ *This line doesn't scan.*
scan noun an act of scanning. [from a Latin word *scandere* meaning 'to climb']

scandal noun **1** an act that is regarded as morally wrong and causes widespread public disapproval. SYNONYMS: outrage, sensation. **2** gossip or disapproval about people's behaviour. [from a Greek word *skandalon* meaning 'stumbling block']

scandalize verb to shock someone by doing something considered to be shameful or disgraceful.

scandalmonger noun a person who invents or spreads scandal.

scandalous adjective causing scandal, shameful or disgraceful. SYNONYMS: shameful, disgraceful, shocking, outrageous. **scandalously** adverb

Scandinavian adjective to do with or coming from Scandinavia (Norway, Sweden, and Denmark, and sometimes also Finland, Iceland, and the Faroe Islands).
Scandinavian noun a person born in Scandinavia or descended from people born there.

scanner noun **1** (*Medicine*) a machine for examining the body by radiation, ultrasound, or other means, as an aid in diagnosis. **2** (*Computing*) a device for converting printed text and images into machine-readable data.

scansion (skan-shən) noun **1** the scanning of lines of verse. **2** the rhythm of a line of verse.

scant adjective barely enough or adequate ♦ *We were treated with scant courtesy.* [from an Old Norse word *skamt*]

scanty adjective (**scantier, scantiest**) **1** small in amount or extent. **2** barely enough. SYNONYMS: sparse, meagre, inadequate. **scantily** adverb **scantiness** noun

scapegoat noun a person who is made to take the blame or punishment for what others have done. [named after the goat which the ancient Jews allowed to escape into the desert after the high priest had symbolically laid the sins of the people on it]

scapula (skap-yoo-lə) noun (**scapulae** (skap-yoo-lee) or **scapulas** (skap-yoo-lee)) a technical term for the shoulder blade.

scar[1] noun **1** a mark left where an injury or sore has healed. **2** a mark left on a plant at the point where a leaf has fallen. **3** an ugly trace left by damage or building ♦ *The new road made a scar on the hillside.* **4** a lasting effect left by an unpleasant experience.
scar verb (**scarred, scarring**) to mark something with a scar, or to form a scar. SYNONYMS: disfigure, mark. [from a Greek word *eskhara* meaning 'scab']

scar[2] noun a steep mountainside or high cliff. [from an Old Norse word *sker* meaning 'low reef']

scarab (ska-rəb) noun an ancient Egyptian carving of a beetle, engraved with symbols on the flat side and used in ancient Egypt as a charm. [from a Greek word *skarabeios*]

scarce *adjective* not enough to supply a demand or need, rare. SYNONYMS: sparse, scanty, rare. **to make yourself scarce** (*informal*) to leave or keep out of the way. [from an early French word *escars*]

scarcely *adverb* **1** only just, almost not ♦ *She is scarcely 10 years old* ♦ *I scarcely know him.* **2** surely not ♦ *You can scarcely expect me to believe that.*

scarcity *noun* (**scarcities**) a state of being scarce, a shortage.

scare *verb* to frighten a person or animal, or to become frightened suddenly. SYNONYMS: frighten, alarm, startle, terrify. **scare** *noun* **1** a sudden fright. SYNONYMS: fright, shock. **2** a sudden widespread sense of alarm about something ♦ *a bomb scare.* [from an Old Norse word *skirra* meaning 'to frighten']

scarecrow *noun* an object made to resemble a human figure dressed in old clothes, set up in a field to scare birds away from crops.

scaremonger *noun* a person who raises unnecessary or excessive alarm. **scaremongering** *noun* [from *scare* and an old word *monger* meaning 'trader']

scarf [1] *noun* (**scarves**) **1** a length of material worn round the neck for warmth or decoration. **2** a square of material worn round the neck or tied over a woman's hair. [from a French word *escarpe*]

scarf [2] *noun* a joint made by thinning the ends of two pieces of timber or metal, so that they overlap without an increase of thickness. **scarf** *verb* to join timber or metal in this way. [probably from an Old Norse word]

scarify [1] (ska-ri-fiy or skair-i-fiy) *verb* (**scarifies, scarified, scarifying**) **1** to loosen the surface of soil etc. **2** to make light surgical cuts in the skin or tissue.

scarify [2] (skair-i-fiy) *verb* (**scarifies, scarified, scarifying**) (*informal*) to scare someone.

scarlatina (skar-lə-teen-ə) *noun* another term for **scarlet fever**.

scarlet *adjective* of a brilliant red colour. **scarlet** *noun* **1** scarlet colour. **2** scarlet clothes. [via French and Arabic from a Latin word *sigillatus* meaning 'decorated with small images']

scarlet fever *noun* an infectious fever caused by bacteria, producing a scarlet rash.

scarp *noun* a steep slope on a hillside.

scarper *verb* (*informal*) to run away. [from an Italian word *scappare* meaning 'to escape']

scary *adjective* (**scarier, scariest**) (*informal*) frightening, causing alarm. **scarily** *adverb*

scathing (**skay**-thing) *adjective* severely scornful or critical. [from an Old Norse word]

scatter *verb* **1** to throw or move something in different directions. SYNONYMS: throw, strew, spread. **2** to leave in different directions after being in a group. SYNONYMS: disperse, break up. **scatter** *noun* **1** an amount of something scattered about. **2** (*Statistics*) the degree to which measurements or readings differ within a sample. [a different spelling of *shatter*]

scatterbrain *noun* a person who is disorganized and absent-minded. **scatterbrained** *adjective*

scatter diagram *noun* (*Statistics*) a graph giving information about the relationship between the values of two variables by plotting them along two axes, causing a scattering or clustering of the resulting points.

scattered *adjective* situated at various points apart from each other ♦ *There were scattered huts down the hillside.*

scatty *adjective* (**scattier, scattiest**) (*informal*) scatterbrained, absent-minded. **scattily** *adverb* **scattiness** *noun*

scavenge *verb* **1** (said about an animal) to search for decaying flesh as food. **2** to search for useful objects or material among rubbish or discarded things. **scavenger** *noun* [from an early French word *escauver* meaning 'to inspect']

scenario (sin-ar-i-oh) *noun* (**scenarios**) **1** an outline of a story. **2** a detailed summary of the action of a play, with notes on scenery and special effects. **3** an imagined sequence of events. [an Italian word, related to *scene*]

scene *noun* **1** the place at which something happened ♦ *Police were at the scene of the crime.* SYNONYMS: location, setting, site, place. **2** a piece of continuous action in a play or film, or an incident thought of as resembling this. **3** a dramatic or public outburst of temper or emotion ♦ *Try not to make a scene.* SYNONYMS: fuss, disturbance, commotion. **4** pieces of scenery used on a stage. **5** a landscape or view as seen by a spectator. SYNONYMS: view, landscape, vista, prospect. **6** (*informal*) an area of activity ♦ *the drugs scene.* **to be on the scene** to be present. [from a Greek word *skēnē* meaning 'stage']

scenery *noun* **1** the natural features of a landscape regarded in terms of their visual effect. **2** painted background and other equipment used on a theatre stage to represent features in the scene of the action.

scenic (**seen**-ik) *adjective* having fine natural scenery ♦ *the scenic route along the coast.* **scenically** *adverb*

scent *noun* **1** a distinctive pleasant smell. **2** a sweet-smelling liquid made from essence of flowers or aromatic chemicals; perfume. **3** the trail left by an animal and perceptible to other animals, especially to hounds in pursuit. **4** an animal's sense of smell.
scent *verb* **1** to discover something by a sense of smell ♦ *The dog had scented a rat.* **2** to begin to suspect the presence or existence of something ♦ *She scented trouble.* **3** to put scent on something to make it fragrant. **scented** *adjective* [from a Latin word *sentire* meaning 'to perceive']

sceptic (**skep**-tik) *noun* a sceptical person, someone who doubts the truth of beliefs and claims. [from a Greek word *skeptikos* meaning 'thoughtful']
◊ Note the difference between *sceptic* and *cynic*. A sceptic tends by nature to doubt the things that people say, whereas a cynic doubts the integrity and worth of the people saying them.

sceptical (**skep**-tik-əl) *adjective* inclined to question or disbelieve things, not believing easily. SYNONYMS: doubtful, disbelieving, incredulous, distrustful. **sceptically** *adverb*

scepticism (**skep**-ti-sizm) *noun* a sceptical attitude of mind.

sceptre (**sep**-ter) *noun* a staff or rod carried by a king or queen as a symbol of their power. [via Old French from a Greek word *skēptron*]

schedule (**shed**-yool) *noun* a plan for carrying out work or completing a sequence of events, with times for the completion of each stage. SYNONYMS: timetable, programme, plan.

schedule *verb* **1** to include an item or event in a schedule. **2** to organize or arrange something for a certain time ♦ *We are scheduled to arrive at ten o'clock.* **on schedule** on time according to a schedule. [from a Latin word *schedula* meaning 'little piece of paper']

schematic (skee-**mat**-ik) *adjective* **1** having the form of a diagram or chart. **2** (said about thoughts or ideas) following a set scheme or formula, not varied or imaginative. **schematically** *adverb*

schematize (**skee**-mə-tyiz) *verb* to put something into a schematic form; to organize information in a regular order. **schematization** *noun*

scheme (skeem) *noun* **1** a systematic or detailed plan of action or work. SYNONYMS: plan, programme. **2** a secret or underhand plan, a plot. SYNONYMS: plot, conspiracy, intrigue. **3** a planned arrangement of something ♦ *a colour scheme.*
scheme *verb* to make plans, especially in a secret or underhand way. SYNONYMS: plot, conspire, intrigue. **schemer** *noun* [from a Greek word *skhēma* meaning 'form']

scherzo (skairts-oh) *noun* (**scherzos**) (*Music*) a lively piece of music, usually forming part of a longer work such as a symphony. [an Italian word meaning 'joke']

schism (sizm) *noun* the division of a group or organization, especially a religious body, into opposing sections because of an important difference in belief or opinion. **schismatic** *adjective* [from a Greek word *skhisma* meaning 'a split']

schizoid (**skitz**-oid) *adjective* resembling or suffering from schizophrenia.
schizoid *noun* a person suffering from schizophrenia.

schizophrenia (skitz-ə-**freen**-iə) *noun* a mental illness in which a person becomes unable to relate their thoughts and feelings to reality, often leading to a withdrawal into fantasy and delusion. [from Greek words *skhizein* meaning 'to split' and *phrēn* meaning 'mind']

schizophrenic (skitz-ə-**fren**-ik) *adjective* to do with or suffering from schizophrenia. **schizophrenic** *noun* a schizophrenic person.

schmaltz (shmawlts) *noun* (*informal*) cloying sentimentality, especially in music or literature. **schmaltzy** *adjective* [a German word meaning 'lard']

schnapps (shnaps) *noun* a strong alcoholic drink like gin. [a German word, from a Dutch word *snaps* meaning 'mouthful']

schnitzel (shnits-əl) *noun* a cutlet of veal or other pale meat, coated in breadcrumbs and fried. [a German word meaning 'slice']

scholar *noun* **1** a person with great knowledge of a particular subject, especially in the humanities. **2** a university student who holds a scholarship. **scholarly** *adjective* [from a Latin word *scholaris* meaning 'to do with a school']

scholarship *noun* **1** a grant of money to pay for a person's education, usually awarded on the basis of academic achievement. **2** the work of scholars, advanced academic work.

scholastic (skəl-**ast**-ik) *adjective* to do with schools or education, academic. **scholastically** *adverb*

school[1] *noun* **1** an institution for educating children. **2** an institution for teaching a particular subject or activity ♦ *a driving school*. **3** the pupils of a school. **4** the process of being educated in a school ♦ *He always hated school.* **5** the time during which teaching is done at a school ♦ *School ends at 4.30 p.m.* **6** a department of a university ♦ *the School of Medicine.* **7** experience as a way of teaching people about life ♦ *She learned her methods in a hard school.* **8** a group of people following the same teachings or principles.
school *verb* to train or educate someone. SYNONYMS: train, educate, teach, instruct. **of the old school** following traditional standards. **school of thought** a particular way of thinking about something. [from a Greek word *skholē* meaning 'leisure' or 'lecture place']

school[2] *noun* a large group of sea mammals or fish. [from an early German or Dutch word *schole* meaning 'a troop']

schoolchild *noun* (**schoolchildren**) a child at school. **schoolboy** *noun* **schoolgirl** *noun*

schooling *noun* education received at a school.

schoolmaster *noun* a male schoolteacher.

schoolmistress *noun* a female schoolteacher.

schoolteacher *noun* a teacher in a school.

schooner (skoo-ner) *noun* **1** a sailing ship with two or more masts. **2** a tall glass for serving sherry. [origin unknown]

sciatic (siy-**at**-ik) *adjective* **1** to do with the hip. **2** to do with a nerve (called the *sciatic nerve*), the largest nerve in the human body, which runs from the lower end of the spinal cord to the thigh.

sciatica (siy-**at**-ik-ə) *noun* a pain in the sciatic nerve, affecting the back, hip, and outer side of the leg.

science *noun* **1** a branch of knowledge concerned with the physical world, studied by means of observation and experiment, e.g. physics, chemistry, and biology. **2** any study involving experiment and observation of data, as distinct from creative or imaginative study. [from a Latin word *scientia* meaning 'knowledge']

science fiction *noun* stories about imaginary scientific discoveries or about space travel and life on other planets.

science park *noun* an area in which scientific and technological industries are located.

scientific *adjective* **1** to do with science or scientists. **2** using careful and systematic study and methods. **scientifically** *adverb*

scientist *noun* someone who studies or is an expert in one or more of the natural or physical sciences.

Scientology *noun* a religious system based on the seeking of self-knowledge and spiritual fulfilment through courses of study and training. **Scientologist** *noun*

sci-fi (**siy**-fiy) *noun* (*informal*) science fiction.

scimitar (**sim**-it-er) *noun* a short sword with a curved blade, originally used in oriental countries.

scintilla (sin-**til**-ə) *noun* a slight trace ♦ *There is not a scintilla of evidence.* [a Latin word meaning 'spark']

scintillate (**sin**-til-ayt) *verb* **1** to give off sparks or flashes of light. **2** to be lively and witty ♦ *The conversation was scintillating.* **scintillation** *noun* [from a Latin word *scintilla* meaning 'spark']

scion (**siy**-ən) *noun* a descendant of a noble family or one with a long lineage. [from an Old French word *cion* meaning 'a twig']

scissors *plural noun* a cutting instrument made of two blades with handles for the thumb and fingers of one hand, pivoted in the middle so that the cutting edges can be closed on what is being cut. [from a Latin word *scissum* meaning 'cut']

sclera (**skleer**-ə) noun (Anatomy) the white outer layer of the eyeball. [from a Greek word sklēros meaning 'hard']

sclerosis (skleer-**oh**-sis) noun (Medicine) an abnormal hardening of body tissue, especially of the arteries. **sclerotic** adjective [from a Greek word sklērōsis meaning 'hardening']

scoff[1] verb to speak with scorn or contempt about something. SYNONYMS: sneer, jeer; (with object) mock. **scoffer** noun [probably from a Scandinavian language]

scoff[2] verb (informal) to eat food quickly or greedily. [from a dialect word scaff meaning 'food']

scold verb to rebuke someone angrily. SYNONYMS: rebuke, reprimand, chide, upbraid, tell off; (informal) tick off. **scold** noun (old use) a woman who constantly nags or grumbles. [probably from an Old Norse word]

sconce noun an ornamental wall bracket for holding a candle or electric light. [from an Old French word esconce meaning 'lantern']

scone (skon or skohn) noun a soft flat unsweetened or slightly sweetened cake made from flour, fat, and milk, baked quickly and eaten buttered. [perhaps from a Dutch word schoonbroot meaning 'fine bread']

scoop noun 1 a tool like a spoon with a deep bowl, used for taking liquids or other substances out of a container. 2 a scooping movement. 3 (informal) an important piece of news published by one newspaper ahead of its rivals. **scoop** verb 1 to lift something out with a scoop. 2 to make a hollow with a scoop. 3 (informal) to be ahead of a rival newspaper with a news story. [from an early German word schope meaning 'bucket for a waterwheel']

scoot verb 1 to go away or leave somewhere hurriedly. 2 to propel a bicycle or scooter by sitting or standing on it and pushing one foot against the ground. [origin unknown]

scooter noun 1 a child's toy for riding on, with a footboard on wheels and a long handle for steering. 2 a kind of lightweight motorcycle with small wheels and a protective shield below the handlebars.

scope noun 1 the range or limit of an activity or task ♦ This topic is outside the scope of the inquiry. SYNONYMS: range, compass. 2 an opportunity or possibility for doing something ♦ She is looking for work that gives her scope for her abilities. [from a Greek word skopos meaning 'target']

scorch verb 1 to make something go brown by burning it slightly, or to become brown in this way. 2 (informal) to drive or ride at high speed. **scorch** noun a mark made by scorching. [origin unknown]

scorcher noun (informal) 1 a very hot day. 2 something remarkable.

scorching adjective (informal) extremely hot.

score noun 1 the number of points or goals achieved by each player or side in a game or competition. 2 a reason or motive ♦ He was rejected on the score of being too young. 3 (old use) a set of twenty. 4 a large amount or number ♦ I have written scores of letters. 5 a line or mark cut into a surface. 6 (Music) a written version of a composition showing the notes on sets of staves. 7 (historical) an informal record of money that someone owes, e.g. in a pub. ◊ The plural in meaning 3 is **score**: three score and ten= 70. **score** verb 1 to gain a point or goal in a game. 2 to keep a record of the score. 3 to be worth a certain number of points in a game ♦ A goal scores 3 points. 4 to achieve something ♦ She scored a great success with her first novel. 5 to have an advantage ♦ He scores by knowing the language well. 6 to cut a line or mark into a surface. SYNONYMS: scratch, mark. 7 (Music) to write out a composition as a musical score, or to arrange a piece of music for particular instruments. **on that score** for that reason, because of that ♦ You needn't worry on that score. **to score off** (informal) to defeat someone in an argument. **to score something out or through** to cancel words etc. by drawing a line through them. **scorer** noun [from an Old Norse word skor meaning 'a notch or tally' or 'twenty']

scoreboard noun a board where the score is displayed.

scoria noun dark rock formed from pieces of lava ejected by a volcano. [from a Greek word skōria meaning 'refuse']

scorn noun strong contempt openly expressed. SYNONYMS: contempt, derision, disdain. **scorn** verb 1 to show strong contempt for something or someone. SYNONYMS: disdain, deride, despise. **2** to reject or refuse something with scorn ♦ *He put his head over the parapet, scorning the use of a periscope.* SYNONYMS: spurn, reject. [from an Old French word *escarn*, from a Germanic language]

scornful *adjective* feeling or showing scorn. SYNONYMS: disdainful, contemptuous, derisive. **scornfully** *adverb* **scornfulness** *noun*

Scorpio *noun* a sign of the zodiac (the Scorpion) which the sun enters about 23 October. **Scorpian** *adjective* & *noun* [a Latin word meaning 'scorpion']

scorpion *noun* a small animal of the spider family with claws like a lobster and a long jointed tail that bends over and has a sting at the end.

Scot *noun* a native of Scotland.

Scotch *adjective* (*old use*) to do with Scotland or Scottish people.
Scotch *noun* **1** (*old use*) the form of English used in Scotland. **2** short for Scotch whisky.
◊ *Scottish* and *Scots* are the words now generally used. See the note at **Scottish**.

scotch *verb* to put an end to something ♦ *The rumour had to be scotched without delay.*

Scotch broth *noun* soup or stew containing pearl barley and vegetables.

Scotch egg *noun* a hard-boiled egg enclosed in sausage meat and breadcrumbs and fried.

Scotch whisky *noun* whisky distilled in Scotland, especially from malted barley.

scot-free *adjective* without being punished or harmed. [*scot* from an old word meaning 'tax']

Scots *adjective* Scottish.
Scots *noun* the form of English used in Scotland.

Scotsman or **Scotswoman** *noun* (**Scotsmen** or **Scotswomen**) a man or woman born in Scotland or descended from people born there.

Scottie *noun* (*informal*) a Scottish terrier.

Scottish *adjective* to do with or coming from Scotland.
◊ *Scottish* is the word most widely used to describe things connected with Scotland and its people: ♦ *Scottish education* ♦ *Scottish mountains. Scots* is mainly used to describe people: ♦ *a young Scots girl.*

Scotch is only used in established names for things, such as ♦ *Scotch egg* and ♦ *Scotch whisky.*

Scottish terrier *noun* a small terrier with rough hair and short legs.

scoundrel *noun* a dishonest or wicked person. SYNONYMS: blackguard, knave, villain, rascal. **scoundrelly** *adjective*

scour [1] *verb* **1** to cleanse or brighten something by rubbing it. SYNONYMS: rub, scrub. **2** to clear out a pipe or channel by the force of water flowing through it.
scour *noun* the action of scouring.
scourer *noun* [via Old French from a Latin word *excurare* meaning 'to clean thoroughly']

scour [2] *verb* to search an area thoroughly. SYNONYMS: search, comb. [origin unknown]

scourge (skerj) *noun* **1** (*historical*) a whip for flogging people. **2** a person or thing that causes great trouble or difficulty. SYNONYMS: misfortune, affliction, blight, curse, bane.
scourge *verb* **1** to whip someone with a scourge. **2** to cause someone great trouble or difficulty. [from an Old French word *escorge*, from Latin words *ex-* meaning 'thoroughly' and *corrigia* meaning 'thong' or 'whip']

Scouse (skowss) *noun* (*informal*) **1** (also **Scouser**) a person born or living in Liverpool. **2** the dialect of Liverpool.
Scouse *adjective* (*informal*) to do with or coming from Liverpool. [a shortening of *lobscouse* (a kind of stew formerly eaten by sailors)]

scout *noun* **1** a person sent out to collect information, e.g. about an enemy's movements or strength. **2** a ship or aircraft used for reconnaissance. **3** (**Scout**) a member of the Scout Association, an organization for boys.
scout *verb* **1** to act as scout. **2** to make a search. [via Old French from a Latin word *auscultare* meaning 'to listen']

scowl *noun* a severe or angry frown.
scowl *verb* to make a scowl. SYNONYMS: frown, glare, glower. [probably from a Scandinavian language]

scrabble *verb* **1** to grope or struggle to find or obtain something. **2** to make a scratching movement or sound with the hands or feet. [from a Dutch word *schrabben* meaning 'to scrape']

scrag *verb* (**scragged, scragging**) (*informal*) to seize or handle someone roughly. [from a dialect word *crag* meaning 'neck']

scrag-end *noun* the bony part of a neck of mutton.

scraggy *adjective* (**scraggier, scraggiest**) thin and bony.

scram *verb* (**scrammed, scramming**) (*informal*) to go away. [from *scramble*]

scramble *verb* 1 to move hurriedly and with difficulty over rough ground, often using the hands and feet. SYNONYMS: clamber, climb, crawl. 2 to struggle to do or obtain something ♦ *Everyone scrambled for the ball.* SYNONYMS: struggle, tussle, fight. 3 (said about an aircraft or the crew) to hurry and take off quickly, especially to attack an invading enemy. 4 to mix things together indiscriminately. SYNONYMS: jumble, muddle, mix up. 5 to cook eggs by mixing them and heating the mixture in a pan until it thickens. 6 to alter the frequency of a radio or telephone signal so that the information transmitted is unintelligible except to a person with a decoding device. **scramble** *noun* 1 a climb or walk over rough ground, using the hands and feet. 2 an eager struggle to do or obtain something. SYNONYMS: struggle, tussle, fight. 3 a motorcycle race over rough ground. **scrambler** *noun* [perhaps related to dialect words *scamble* meaning 'to stumble' and *cramble* meaning 'to crawl']

scrap [1] *noun* 1 a small piece of something, especially when it is left after the rest has been used. SYNONYMS: bit, piece, fragment. 2 rubbish or waste material, especially discarded metal suitable for reprocessing. SYNONYMS: junk, rubbish, waste. **scrap** *verb* (**scrapped, scrapping**) to discard something that is useless or unwanted ♦ *In the end we had to scrap the idea.* SYNONYMS: discard, abandon, reject. [from an Old Norse word *skrap*, related to *scrape*]

scrap [2] *noun* (*informal*) a fight or quarrel. **scrap** *verb* (**scrapped, scrapping**) (*informal*) to fight or quarrel. [probably from *scrape*]

scrapbook *noun* a book of blank pages for sticking in newspaper cuttings, drawings, etc.

scrape *verb* 1 to pass a hard or sharp object across a surface. 2 to make something clean, smooth, or level by doing this. 3 to remove something by doing this ♦ *You should scrape the mud off your shoes.* 4 to make something by scraping ♦ *to scrape a hole.* 5 to damage something by scraping. 6 to make the sound of scraping. 7 to pass along or through something with difficulty. 8 to obtain or accumulate something with difficulty or by careful saving ♦ *They managed to scrape a living* ♦ *We will scrape the money together somehow.* 9 to be very economical. **scrape** *noun* 1 a scraping movement or sound. 2 a mark or injury made by scraping. 3 an awkward situation resulting from mischief or foolishness. SYNONYMS: mess, fix, jam, difficulty. 4 a thinly applied layer of butter etc. on bread. **to scrape the barrel** or **the bottom of the barrel** (*informal*) to be forced to use your last and poorest resources when others are no longer available. **to scrape through** to get through a difficult situation or pass an examination by only a small margin. **scraper** *noun* [from an Old English word *scrapian*]

scrap heap *noun* a heap of waste or discarded material.

scrappy *adjective* (**scrappier, scrappiest**) made up of an odd or untidy assortment of things. **scrappily** *adverb* **scrappiness** *noun*

scrapyard *noun* a place where scrap is collected.

scratch *verb* 1 to make a shallow mark or wound on a surface with something sharp. 2 to form something (e.g. a design or letter) by scratching ♦ *The lovers scratched a pair of hearts on the tree.* 3 to scrape the skin with the fingernails to relieve itching. 4 to make a thin scraping sound. 5 to obtain something with difficulty ♦ *They managed to scratch a living.* 6 to cancel something by drawing a line through it ♦ *I'll scratch it out.* 7 to withdraw from a race or competition. **scratch** *noun* 1 a mark or wound made by scratching. 2 the action or a spell of scratching. 3 a line from which competitors start in a race when they receive no handicap. **scratch** *adjective* collected from whatever is available ♦ *a scratch team.* **to start from scratch** to begin at the very beginning or with nothing prepared. **up to scratch** up to the required standard. [origin unknown]

scratchy *adjective* (**scratchier, scratchiest**) 1 tending to cause itching. 2 (said about a pen) making a scratching sound when writing. **scratchily** *adverb* **scratchiness** *noun*

scrawl noun hurried or careless handwriting that is difficult to read. **scrawl** verb to write in a scrawl. [origin unknown]

scrawny adjective (**scrawnier, scrawniest**) thin and bony. **scrawniness** noun

scream verb 1 to make a long piercing cry of pain, fear, anger, or excitement. SYNONYMS: shriek, screech, yell, cry out. 2 to utter something in a screaming tone. 3 (said about the wind or a machine etc.) to make a loud piercing sound. 4 to laugh uncontrollably.
scream noun 1 a screaming cry or sound. SYNONYMS: shriek, screech, yell, cry. 2 (informal) an extremely amusing person or thing. [origin unknown]

scree noun a mass of loose stones on a mountainside. [from an Old Norse word skritha meaning 'landslip']

screech noun a harsh high-pitched scream or sound.
screech verb 1 to make a screech. 2 to utter something with a screech. [an imitation of the sound]

screech owl noun an owl that makes a screeching cry instead of a hoot.

screed noun 1 a long and tedious piece of writing. 2 a strip of plaster or other material placed on a surface as a guide to the correct thickness of plaster or concrete to be laid. 3 a finishing layer of mortar, cement, etc. spread over a floor or other surface. [from an earlier meaning 'fragment', related to shred]

screen noun 1 an upright partition used to divide an area or to conceal or protect something. SYNONYMS: partition, panel, divider; shield. 2 something providing protection ♦ under the screen of night. 3 a windscreen of a motor vehicle. 4 a blank surface on which pictures, cinema films, television transmissions, or computer data are projected or displayed. 5 a large sieve or riddle, especially one used for sorting grain or coal etc. into sizes.
screen verb 1 to shelter, conceal, or protect someone or something. SYNONYMS: shelter, protect, shield; conceal, disguise. 2 to protect someone from discovery or deserved blame by diverting suspicion away from them. 3 to show a film or television pictures on a screen. 4 to pass grain or coal etc. through a screen. 5 to examine or test people for the presence or absence of a disease. 6 to examine an applicant for a post or position of authority to ensure they are suitable. [from an Old French word escren, from a Germanic language]

screenplay noun the script of a film, with directions for the movement and behaviour of the actors.

screen printing noun a printing process like stencilling with ink or dye forced through a prepared sheet of fine fabric.

screen test noun a trial to see if a person is suitable for a part in a film.

screw noun 1 a metal pin with a spiral ridge (called a thread) round its length, used for holding things together by being twisted in, or secured by a nut. 2 a thing turned like a screw and used for tightening something or exerting pressure. 3 a propeller, especially of a ship or motor boat. 4 the act of turning a screw. 5 (informal) a prison officer.
screw verb 1 to fasten or tighten something with a screw. 2 to turn a screw. 3 to turn something with a twisting movement. 4 (informal) to swindle someone. 5 (informal) to have sexual intercourse with someone. **to have a screw loose** (informal) to be eccentric or slightly mad. **to put the screw** or **screws on** (informal) to intimidate or put pressure on someone. **to screw something up** 1 to crush a piece of paper or material into a tight mass. 2 to tense the muscles of the face or eyes. 3 to summon up courage. 4 (informal) to bungle or mismanage something. [from an Old French word escroue]

screwball noun (North Amer.) (informal) a crazy or eccentric person.

screw cap noun a cap that can be screwed on the opening of a container.

screwdriver noun a tool with a narrow end that fits into the slot on the head of a screw to turn it.

screw top noun a top that can be screwed on the opening of a container.

screwy adjective (**screwier, screwiest**) (informal) crazy or eccentric.

scribble verb 1 to write hurriedly or untidily. 2 to make meaningless marks. **scribble** noun something written or drawn hurriedly or untidily. **scribbler** noun [same origin as for scribe]

scribe noun 1 (historical) a person who made copies of writings before the development of printing. 2 a professional religious scholar in New Testament times. **3** (*informal*) a writer, especially a journalist. **scribal** *adjective* [from a Latin word *scribere* meaning 'to write']

scrim *noun* a coarse cotton fabric. [origin unknown]

scrimmage *noun* a confused struggle or fight. [from *skirmish*]

scrimp *verb* to skimp.

scrip *noun* an issue of additional shares to shareholders in a company in place of a dividend ♦ *a scrip issue*. [short for *subscription receipt*]

script *noun* **1** handwriting, especially as distinct from print. **2** the text of a play, film, or broadcast. **3** a candidate's written answers in an examination.
script *verb* to write a script for a film or broadcast. [from a Latin word *scriptum* meaning 'written']

scripture *noun* **1** the sacred writings of a religion. **2** the biblical writings of the Christians (the Old and New Testaments) or the Jews (the Old Testament).
scriptural *adjective* [same origin as for *script*]

scrofula (skrof-yoo-lǝ) *noun* a disease causing glandular swellings. **scrofulous** *adjective* [a Latin word, from *scrofa* meaning 'breeding sow' (because sows were said to be subject to the disease)]

scroll *noun* **1** a roll of paper or parchment for writing on. **2** an ornamental design resembling a partly unrolled scroll.
scroll *verb* (*Computing*) to move the display on a computer screen up or down in order to view different parts of it. [from an old word *scrow* meaning 'roll']

Scrooge *noun* a person who is mean with money. [named after Ebenezer Scrooge, a miserly character in Dickens's novel *A Christmas Carol*]

scrotum (skroh-tǝm) *noun* a pouch of skin that contains the testicles. **scrotal** *adjective* [a Latin word]

scrounge *verb* (*informal*) to get something you are not really entitled to, especially by stealth. SYNONYMS: cadge, beg.
scrounge *noun* (*informal*) an act of scrounging. **scrounger** *noun* [from a dialect word *scrunge* meaning 'to steal']

scrub[1] *verb* (**scrubbed, scrubbing**) **1** to rub a surface hard with something coarse or bristly, especially in order to clean it. SYNONYMS: rub, scour. **2** (*informal*) to cancel

or scrap an arrangement ♦ *We'll have to scrub all our plans now.*
scrub *noun* the action of scrubbing ♦ *I'll give it a scrub.* **to scrub up** (said about a surgeon) to clean the hands and arms thoroughly before performing an operation. [probably from a German word *schrobben*]

scrub[2] *noun* vegetation consisting of stunted trees or shrubs, or land covered with this. [from *shrub*]

scrubby *adjective* (**scrubbier, scrubbiest**) small and shabby. [from *scrub*[2]]

scruff *noun* the back of the neck as used to grasp, lift, or drag a person or animal. [from a dialect word *scuff*]

scruffy *adjective* (**scruffier, scruffiest**) shabby and untidy. SYNONYMS: shabby, untidy, dishevelled, dirty, scrappy, tatty. **scruffily** *adverb* **scruffiness** *noun* [a different spelling of *scurfy*]

scrum *noun* **1** (in rugby) a formation in which the forwards on each side push against each other and try to get possession of the ball when this is thrown on the ground between them. **2** a milling or disorderly crowd. [a shortening of *scrummage*]

scrum half *noun* (in rugby) a halfback who puts the ball into the scrum.

scrummage *noun* a scrum. [a different spelling of *scrimmage*]

scrumping *noun* (*informal*) stealing fruit from an orchard or garden. [from a dialect word *scrump* meaning 'withered apple']

scrumptious *adjective* (*informal*) **1** (said about food) delicious. **2** (said about a person) very attractive. [origin unknown]

scrumpy *noun* (*informal*) rough strong cider. [same origin as for *scrumping*]

scrunch *verb* **1** to make a loud crunching noise. **2** to crush or crumple something. [an imitation of the sound]

scruple *noun* a feeling of doubt or hesitation about doing or allowing something because you think it may be wrong. SYNONYMS: misgiving, doubt, compunction, qualm.
scruple *verb* to hesitate to do something you think may be wrong. [from a Latin word *scrupus* meaning 'rough pebble' and then 'anxiety']

scrupulous (skroo-pew-lǝs) *adjective* **1** very careful and conscientious. SYNONYMS:

careful, conscientious, meticulous, punctilious, painstaking. **2** very concerned not to do wrong. **scrupulously** *adverb* **scrupulousness** *noun*

scrutineer *noun* a person who scrutinizes something, especially voting in a ballot or election.

scrutinize *verb* to look at or examine something carefully. SYNONYMS: examine, look at, look over, study, inspect.

scrutiny *noun* (**scrutinies**) a careful look at or examination of something. [from a Latin word *scrutari* meaning 'to sort rubbish' and then 'to search']

SCSI *abbreviation* (*Computing*) small computer system interface.

scuba diving *noun* swimming underwater using a breathing apparatus strapped to the back. [from the initials of *self-contained underwater breathing apparatus*]

scud *verb* (**scudded, scudding**) to move quickly and lightly ♦ *Clouds scudded across the sky.* [origin unknown]

scuff *verb* **1** to scrape or drag your feet in walking. **2** to mark or damage a shoe or boot by doing this. **3** to scrape something with your foot. **scuff** *noun* a mark made by scuffing. [origin unknown]

scuffle *noun* a brief confused struggle or fight at close quarters. SYNONYMS: tussle, struggle, fight, brawl. **scuffle** *verb* to take part in a scuffle. [probably from a Scandinavian language, related to *shove* and *shuffle*]

scull *noun* **1** each of a pair of small oars used by a single rower. **2** an oar that rests on the stern of a boat, worked with a side-to-side movement. **scull** *verb* to row with sculls. [origin unknown]

scullery *noun* (**sculleries**) a small room where dishes etc. are washed up. [via Old French from a Latin word *scutella* meaning 'small dish']

scullion *noun* (*old use*) a servant who did menial tasks in a kitchen. [origin unknown, but perhaps related to *scullery*]

sculpt *verb* (*informal*) to make sculptures.

sculptor *noun* a person who makes sculptures.

sculpture *noun* **1** the art of making three-dimensional shapes and figures in wood, stone, or metal. **2** a work made in this way. **sculpture** *verb* to make a sculpture to represent a person or thing. **sculptural** *adjective* [from a Latin word *sculptura*, from *sculpere* meaning 'to carve']

scum *noun* **1** a layer of dirt or froth on the surface of a liquid. **2** (*informal*) a worthless or contemptible person or group of people. **scum** *verb* (**scummed, scumming**) **1** to remove the scum from something. **2** to form a scum. **scummy** *adjective* [from a German or Dutch word]

scupper *noun* an opening in a ship's side to let water drain from the deck. **scupper** *verb* **1** to sink a ship deliberately. **2** (*informal*) to wreck or thwart a plan or intention. [perhaps from an Old French word *escopir* meaning 'to spit']

scurf *noun* **1** flakes of dry skin, especially from the scalp. **2** a dry scaly matter forming on a surface. **scurfy** *adjective* [from an Old English word *sceorf*]

scurrilous (sku-ril-əs) *adjective* **1** abusive and insulting ♦ *scurrilous attacks in the newspapers.* SYNONYMS: abusive, defamatory, insulting, derogatory. **2** coarsely humorous. **scurrility** (sku-ril-iti) *noun* **scurrilously** *adverb* [from a Latin word *scurra* meaning 'buffoon']

scurry *verb* (**scurries, scurried, scurrying**) to run hurriedly with quick short steps. SYNONYMS: scamper, scuttle, scoot, dash, hurry, rush. **scurry** *noun* (**scurries**) **1** the act of scurrying, a rush. **2** a flurry of rain or snow. [a shortening of *hurry-scurry*, a fanciful formation on *hurry*]

scurvy *noun* a disease caused by lack of vitamin C in the diet. [a different spelling of *scurfy*]

scut *noun* the short tail of a rabbit, hare, or deer. [origin unknown]

scuttle [1] *noun* **1** a container for coal in a room of a house. **2** the part of a car body between the windscreen and the bonnet. [from a Latin word *scutella* meaning 'dish']

scuttle [2] *noun* a small opening with a lid on a ship's deck or side. **scuttle** *verb* to let water into a ship in order to sink it. [from a Spanish word *escotar* meaning 'to cut out']

scuttle [3] *verb* to scurry or hurry away. SYNONYMS: scamper, scurry, scoot, dash, hurry, rush.

scuttle *noun* the act or sound of someone scuttling. [from *scud*]

scythe (siyth) *noun* a tool with a long curved blade for cutting long grass or crops.
scythe *verb* to cut grass or crops with a scythe. [from an Old English word *sithe*]

SDLP *abbreviation* (in Northern Ireland) Social Democratic and Labour Party.

SE *abbreviation* south-east or south-eastern.

Se *abbreviation* (*Chemistry*) the symbol for selenium.

sea *noun* 1 the expanse of salt water that covers most of the earth's surface and surrounds the continents. 2 a particular named part of this ♦ *the Black Sea*. 3 a large inland lake ♦ *the Sea of Galilee*. 4 the waves of the sea, especially in relation to their movement or state ♦ *a heavy sea*. 5 a large expanse of something ♦ *a sea of faces*. **at sea** 1 in a ship on the sea. 2 confused, not knowing what to do. **by sea** carried or conveyed in a ship. **to get your sea legs** to become used to the motion of a ship at sea. **on the sea** 1 in a ship on the sea. 2 situated at a coast. [from an Old English word]

sea anchor *noun* a bag or other object dragged in the water to slow the drifting of a vessel.

sea anemone *noun* a tube-shaped sea animal with short tentacles round its mouth.

seabed *noun* the ground under the sea.

seabird *noun* a bird that frequents the sea or coastal areas.

seaboard *noun* the coastline or the region near it.

seafarer *noun* a person who travels or works in the sea.

seafaring *adjective & noun* working or travelling by sea, especially as an occupation.

sea fish *noun* a fish living in the sea, as distinct from a freshwater fish.

seafood *noun* fish or shellfish from the sea eaten as food.

seafront *noun* the part of a coastal town next to and facing the sea.

seagoing *adjective* 1 (said about a ship) suitable for travelling on the sea. 2 (said about a person) travelling by sea.

sea green *noun* a pale bluish green colour.

seagull *noun* a gull.

sea horse *noun* a small fish that swims in an upright position, with a head and neck like that of a horse.

seakale *noun* a plant with young shoots that are used as a vegetable.

seal ¹ *noun* a sea mammal that breeds on land, with thick fur or bristles and short limbs that serve as flippers. [from an Old English word *seolh*]

seal ² *noun* 1 a device or substance used to close an opening or joint and prevent air or liquid etc. from passing through it. 2 a gem or piece of metal with an engraved design that is pressed on wax or other soft material to leave an impression. 3 a piece of wax bearing this impression, attached to a document as a guarantee of its authenticity. 4 a confirmation or guarantee ♦ *They gave the report their seal of approval*. 5 a small decorative paper sticker resembling a postage stamp.
seal *verb* 1 to fasten or close something securely. 2 to attach a seal to something. 3 to stamp or certify a document as authentic by attaching a seal. 4 to close something with a seal. 5 to settle or decide something ♦ *His fate was sealed*. **to seal something off** to prevent access to an area. [via Old French from a Latin word *sigillum* meaning 'small picture']

sealant *noun* a substance used for coating a surface to make it watertight.

sea level *noun* the level corresponding to that of the surface of the sea halfway between high and low water.

sealing wax *noun* a substance that is soft when heated but hardens when cooled, used for sealing documents.

sea lion *noun* a kind of large seal that lives in the Pacific Ocean.

sealskin *noun* the skin or prepared fur of a seal used as a clothing material.

Sealyham (see-li-əm) *noun* a terrier that has short legs and wiry hair. [named after Sealyham in Wales, where the dog was first bred]

seam *noun* 1 a line where two pieces of fabric are joined together. 2 a line where two pieces of wood or other material meet each other. 3 a surface line such as a wrinkle or scar. 4 a layer of a mineral such as coal or gold in the ground.
seam *verb* 1 to join pieces of fabric by means of a seam. 2 to mark something

with a wrinkle or scar. [from an Old English word]

seaman noun (**seamen**) a sailor, especially one below the rank of officer in the navy.

seamanship noun skill in seafaring.

seamstress (sem-stris) noun a woman who sews, especially for a living.

seamy adjective (**seamier, seamiest**) disreputable or sordid. **the seamy side** the less presentable or less attractive aspect of something. [originally the 'wrong' side of a piece of sewing, where the rough edges of the seams show]

seance (say-ahns) noun a meeting at which people try to make contact with the dead. [from a French word séance meaning 'sitting']

seaplane noun an aeroplane with floats instead of wheels, designed to land on and take off from water.

seaport noun a town or city with a harbour on the coast.

seaquake noun an earthquake below the seabed, causing disturbance of the sea.

sear verb to burn or scorch something with a strong heat. [from an Old English word]

search verb 1 to look carefully and thoroughly in a place in order to find something. SYNONYMS: scour, comb, hunt. 2 to examine the clothes and body of a person to see if something is concealed there. 3 to examine something thoroughly ♦ Try to search your memory. **search** noun the action of searching. **searcher** noun [via Old French from a Latin word circare meaning 'to go round']

search engine noun (Computing) a program that searches for computer data, especially on the Internet.

searching adjective thorough or probing.

searchlight noun an outdoor electric light with a powerful beam that can be turned in any direction.

search party noun a group of people organized to search for a missing person or thing.

search warrant noun a legal warrant allowing the police or other officials to enter private premises.

searing adjective (said about a pain) felt as a sudden burning sensation.

sea salt noun salt obtained from sea water by evaporation.

seascape noun a picture or view of the sea.

sea serpent noun a fictional sea monster like a serpent.

seashell noun the shell of a mollusc living in salt water.

seashore noun land close to the sea.

seasick adjective sick or unwell from the motion of a ship. **seasickness** noun

season noun 1 each of the four main parts of the year (spring, summer, autumn, and winter) marked by particular characteristics of weather and daylight. 2 the time of year when a particular fruit, vegetable, etc. is plentiful, or when a particular activity takes place ♦ the football season. **season** verb 1 to give extra flavour to food by adding salt, pepper, or other sharp-tasting substances. 2 to dry and treat timber to make it fit for use. **in season** 1 (said about food) plentiful and in good condition. 2 (said about a female mammal) ready to mate. [via French from a Latin word satio meaning 'time for sowing seed']

seasonable adjective 1 suitable for a particular season ♦ Hot weather is seasonable in summer. 2 (old use) timely or opportune. **seasonably** adverb ◊ Do not confuse this word with **seasonal**, which has a different meaning.

seasonal adjective done in or associated with a particular season of the year ♦ the seasonal migration of birds ♦ Fruit-picking is seasonal work. ◊ Do not confuse this word with **seasonable**, which has a different meaning.

seasonal affective disorder noun depression associated with the onset of winter and thought to be caused by a lack of light.

seasoned adjective experienced and competent because of training and practice ♦ a seasoned soldier.

seasoning noun a substance used to season food.

season ticket noun a ticket that can be used repeatedly over a given period.

seat noun 1 a piece of furniture or other object made or used for sitting on. 2 the level part of a chair on which a sitter's body rests. 3 a place where someone can sit, especially a place for one person to sit in a theatre or vehicle. 4 a place as a member of a council or committee. **5** a parliamentary constituency as offering a right to sit in parliament ♦ *She won the seat at the last election.* **6** a part in a machine that supports another part. **7** the buttocks, or the part of a skirt or trousers covering them. **8** a place where something is based or located ♦ *a seat of learning.* SYNONYMS: centre, base, heart, cradle, focus. **9** a country estate belonging to an aristocratic family ♦ *the family seat in Scotland.* **10** a manner of sitting on a horse. **seat** *verb* **1** to give someone a place to sit ♦ *We've seated you at the end of the table.* **2** to provide sitting accommodation for a particular number of people ♦ *The hall seats 1,000.* **3** to put a piece of machinery into position. **to be seated** to sit down. [from an Old Norse word *sæti*]

seat belt *noun* a belt for securing a person to a seat in a motor vehicle or aircraft.

seated *adjective* sitting down.

sea urchin *noun* a sea animal with a round shell covered in sharp spikes.

sea wall *noun* a wall or embankment built to prevent the sea from encroaching on an area of land.

seaward *adjective & adverb* towards the sea. **seawards** *adverb*

seaweed *noun* a plant that grows in the sea or on rocks washed by the sea.

seaworthy *adjective* (said about a ship) in a fit condition for a sea voyage.

sebum (*see-bəm*) *noun* a natural oil produced by glands (called *sebacious glands*) in the skin to lubricate the skin and hair. [a Latin word meaning 'grease']

sec *abbreviation* (*Mathematics*) secant.

secant (*see-kənt*) *noun* **1** (*Mathematics*) the ratio of the length of the hypotenuse (in a right-angled triangle) to the length of the side adjacent to that angle. **2** (*Geometry*) a straight line that cuts a circle or curve at two or more points. [from a Latin word *secans* meaning 'cutting']

secateurs (*sek-ə-terz* or *sek-ə-terz*) *plural noun* clippers used with one hand for pruning plants. [from a Latin word *secare* meaning 'to cut']

secede (*si-seed*) *verb* to withdraw formally from membership of an organization. [from *se-* meaning 'aside' and a Latin word *cedere* meaning 'to go']

secession (*si-sesh-ən*) *noun* the action of seceding from membership of an organization.

seclude *verb* to keep someone away from other people. [from *se-* meaning 'aside' and a Latin word *claudere* meaning 'to shut']

secluded *adjective* (said about a place) sheltered from view, private. SYNONYMS: isolated, sheltered, private, remote.

seclusion (*si-kloo-zhən*) *noun* being secluded and private.

second[1] (*sek-ənd*) *adjective* **1** next after first. **2** another after the first ♦ *We deserve a second chance.* SYNONYMS: extra, further, additional. **3** inferior or less good ♦ *second quality.* **4** (*Music*) playing the subordinate part of two or more parts for the same instrument in a group ♦ *second violins.* **second** *noun* **1** a person or thing that is second. **2** the second day of a month. **3** second-class honours in a university degree. **4** an attendant of a person taking part in a boxing match or duel. **5** a sixtieth part of a minute of time or of a degree in measuring angles. **6** (*informal*) a short time ♦ *Can you wait a second?* SYNONYMS: moment, while, bit. **second** *adverb* **1** in second place or position. **second** *verb* **1** to assist someone. **2** to support a motion formally in a debate. **seconds** *plural noun* **1** goods of second-class quality, sold at a reduced price. **2** (*informal*) a second helping of food at a meal. **at second hand** obtained indirectly, not from the original source. **to have second thoughts** to have doubts or change your mind about a previous decision. **to get your second wind** to recover normal breathing after being out of breath. **seconder** *noun* [from a Latin word *secundus* meaning 'following' or 'second']

second[2] (*si-kond*) *verb* to transfer a person temporarily to another job or department. **secondment** *noun*

secondary *adjective* **1** coming after something that is primary. **2** of lesser importance or rank than the first. SYNONYMS: ancillary, subsidiary. **3** derived from what is primary or original ♦ *secondary sources.* **secondarily** *adverb*

secondary colour *noun* a colour made by mixing two primary colours.

secondary education *noun* education for children over the age of about eleven.

secondary picketing *noun* picketing of firms that are not directly involved in an industrial dispute in order to increase the effect of a strike.

secondary school *noun* a school for children over the age of about eleven.

second-best *adjective* of second or inferior quality. **to come off second-best** to come off worse in an argument or contest.

second class *noun* **1** a set of people or things grouped together as second-best. **2** the second-best accommodation on a train, ship, or aircraft. **3** a category of mail that is less urgent than first class. **second-class** *adjective* of second or inferior quality.

second cousin *noun* see **cousin**.

second fiddle *noun* a subsidiary or secondary role ♦ *He always had to play second fiddle to his older brother.*

second gear *noun* the second lowest gear in a motor vehicle.

second-hand *adjective* **1** (said about goods) bought after use by a previous owner. **2** obtained or experienced at second hand.

second in command *noun* the person next in rank to the commanding officer or chief official.

second lieutenant *noun* an army officer immediately below lieutenant.

secondly *adverb* second, as a second consideration.

second name *noun* a surname.

second nature *noun* a habit or characteristic that has become automatic ♦ *Secrecy is second nature to him.*

second officer *noun* the assistant mate on a merchant ship.

second person *noun* see **person**.

second-rate *adjective* of inferior or poor quality. SYNONYMS: inferior, poor, substandard.

second sight *noun* the supposed power to foresee future events.

second teeth *plural noun* the permanent teeth of adults, appearing after the milk teeth have fallen out.

secrecy *noun* a state of keeping things secret ♦ *We were pledged to secrecy.*

secret *adjective* **1** not known or seen by other people, or not meant to be known or seen by them. SYNONYMS: hidden, concealed; confidential, private, personal; (*informal*) hush-hush. **2** working or operating without other people knowing. SYNONYMS: hidden, clandestine, covert, surreptitious.
secret *noun* **1** a fact or piece of information that is kept or meant to be kept secret. **2** something no one fully understands ♦ *the secrets of nature.* **3** a method that is not known to everyone for achieving something ♦ *the secret of good health.* **in secret** without other people knowing.   **secretly** *adverb* [from a Latin word *secretum* meaning 'set apart']

secret agent *noun* a spy acting for a country.

secretarial (sek-ri-**tair**-iəl) *adjective* to do with the work a secretary does.

secretariat (sek-ri-**tair**-i-at) *noun* an administrative office or department of a government or international body.

secretary (**sek**-rə-tri) *noun* (**secretaries**) **1** a person employed in an office to help deal with correspondence and filing, answer the telephone, make business arrangements for people, and similar work. **2** an official of a society or organization in charge of the correspondence and keeping records. **3** the principal assistant of a government minister or ambassador. [from a Latin word *secretarius* meaning 'confidential officer']

secretary bird *noun* a long-legged African bird with a crest that looks like a quill pen placed behind a writer's ear.

Secretary General *noun* the chief administrator of a large organization.

Secretary of State *noun* **1** (in Britain) the head of a major government department. **2** (in the USA) a senior official responsible for foreign affairs.

secret ballot *noun* a ballot in which individual voters' choices are not made public.

secrete (si-**kreet**) *verb* **1** to put something in a hidden place. SYNONYMS: conceal, hide. **2** (said about an organ or cell) to produce a substance for use in the body (such as bile) or for excretion from the body (such as urine). SYNONYMS: discharge, exude. **secretor** *noun* **secretory** *adjective* [same origin as for *secret*]

secretion (si-**kree**-shən) *noun* **1** the process of secreting substances. **2** a substance secreted by an organ or cell of the body.

secretive (**seek**-rit-iv) *adjective* wanting to keep things secret and not make information known. SYNONYMS: uncommunicative, reticent, unforthcoming, furtive. **secretively** *adverb* **secretiveness** *noun*

secret police *noun* a police force operating in secret for political purposes.

secret service *noun* a government department responsible for conducting espionage.

secret society *noun* a society whose members are sworn to secrecy about its activities.

sect *noun* a group of people whose religious or other beliefs differ from those more generally accepted. [from a Latin word *secta* meaning 'following', from *sequi* meaning 'to follow']

sectarian (sek-**tair**-iən) *adjective* 1 to do with or belonging to a sect or sects. 2 putting the beliefs or interests of a sect before more general interests.

section *noun* 1 a distinct part or portion of something. SYNONYMS: part, portion, bit, segment. 2 a division of an organization. SYNONYMS: department, branch, division, sector. 3 a cross section. 4 (*Medicine*) the process of cutting or separating a part of the body by surgery.
section *verb* to divide something into sections. [from a Latin word *sectum* meaning 'having been cut']

sectional *adjective* 1 made in sections that can be separated and put back together ♦ *a sectional fishing rod*. 2 to do with one section of a group or community as distinct from others or from the whole. 3 to do with a section or sections.

sector *noun* 1 a division of an area of military operations. SYNONYMS: zone, region. 2 a distinct division of an activity ♦ *the private sector of industry*. 3 (*Geometry*) a section of a circular area between two lines drawn from its centre to its circumference. [from a Latin word *secare* meaning 'to cut']

secular (**sek**-yoo-ler) *adjective* 1 to do with worldly affairs rather than spiritual or religious ones. 2 not involving or belonging to religion ♦ *secular music*. **secularity** (sek-yoo-la-riti) *noun* [from a Latin word *saecularis* meaning 'worldly']

secure *adjective* 1 safe, especially against attack. SYNONYMS: safe, protected, defended, invulnerable. 2 well fixed or fitted, certain

not to slip or fall. SYNONYMS: firm, fixed, fastened, steady. 3 certain or reliable. SYNONYMS: certain, reliable, assured, sure.
secure *verb* 1 to make something secure. 2 to fasten something securely. SYNONYMS: fasten, lock. 3 to obtain something. SYNONYMS: obtain, acquire, procure. 4 to guarantee a loan by pledging something as security ♦ *The loan is secured on the house*. **securely** *adverb* [from a Latin word *securus* meaning 'free from worry', from *se-* meaning 'apart' and *cura* meaning 'care']

security *noun* (**securities**) 1 a state or feeling of being secure. SYNONYMS: safety, protection, assurance. 2 something that gives this feeling. 3 precautions taken to protect a country or organization from dangers such as espionage or theft. 4 a thing that serves as a guarantee or pledge for a loan. 5 a certificate showing ownership of financial stocks or shares.

sedan (si-**dan**) *noun* 1 (*North Amer.*) a saloon car. 2 a sedan chair. [origin unknown]

sedan chair *noun* an enclosed chair for one person, mounted on two poles and carried by two bearers, used in the 17th–18th centuries.

sedate¹ (si-**dayt**) *adjective* calm and dignified. SYNONYMS: calm, dignified, tranquil, composed, serene. **sedately** *adverb* **sedateness** *noun* [from a Latin word *sedatum* meaning 'made calm']

sedate² (si-**dayt**) *verb* to treat someone with sedatives. **sedation** *noun*

sedative (**sed**-ə-tiv) *noun* a medicine that makes a person calm or sends them to sleep.
sedative *adjective* having a calming or soothing effect. [same origin as for *sedate*]

sedentary (**sed**-ən-ter-i) *adjective* 1 involving a lot of sitting down and not much physical exercise ♦ *sedentary work*. 2 spending a lot of time sitting down ♦ *sedentary workers*. [from a Latin word *sedens* meaning 'sitting']

sedge *noun* a grass-like plant growing in marshes or near water. [from an Old English word *secg*]

sediment *noun* 1 fine particles of solid matter that float in a liquid or settle at the bottom of it. 2 (*Geology*) solid matter such as sand and gravel that is carried by water or wind and settles on the surface of land. [from a Latin word *sedere* meaning 'to sit']

sedimentary (sed-i-ment-er-i) *adjective* (Geology) formed from particles that have settled on a surface ♦ *sedimentary rocks.*

sedimentation *noun* (Geology) the process of depositing a sediment.

sedition (si-dish-ən) *noun* actions or speech that make people rebel against the authority of the state. **seditious** (si-dish-əs) *adjective* [from a Latin word *seditio*, from *se-* meaning 'aside' and *itio* meaning 'going']

seduce (si-dewss) *verb* 1 to persuade someone to do wrong by offering temptations ♦ *He was seduced into betraying his country.* 2 to persuade someone to have sexual intercourse. **seducer** *noun* [from a Latin word *seducere*, from *se-* meaning 'aside' and *ducere* meaning 'to lead']

seduction *noun* 1 the process of seducing someone or of being seduced. 2 something tempting or attractive ♦ *the seductions of city life.*

seductive *adjective* tending to seduce someone, temptingly attractive or alluring. SYNONYMS: alluring, captivating, enticing. **seductively** *adverb* **seductiveness** *noun*

sedulous (sed-yoo-ləs) *adjective* diligent and persevering. **sedulously** *adverb* **sedulousness** *noun* [from a Latin word *sedulus*]

see [1] *verb* (**saw, seen**) 1 to perceive something or someone with the eyes. SYNONYMS: observe, catch sight of, discern, perceive, spot. 2 to have or use the power of perceiving with the eyes. 3 to understand something with the mind, to understand something ♦ *Do you see what I mean* SYNONYMS: perceive, understand, comprehend, appreciate. 4 to have a certain opinion about something ♦ *This is the way I see it.* SYNONYMS: regard, consider. 5 to visualize or imagine something or someone in a certain way ♦ *I just can't see him as a singer.* SYNONYMS: imagine, visualize, picture. 6 to consider or think about something ♦ *We must see what we can do.* SYNONYMS: consider, reflect on, think about. 7 to find out about something ♦ *I'll go and see who is at the door.* SYNONYMS: find out; (formal) ascertain. 8 to watch an entertainment or be a spectator at an event ♦ *They went to see a film.* 9 to look at a specified place for information ♦ *For more information, see your local telephone directory.* SYNONYMS: consult, refer to, look in. 10 to meet or recognize someone ♦ *She said she had seen me in town.*

SYNONYMS: recognize, notice. 11 to experience or undergo something ♦ *He saw active service in the war.* 12 to visit someone briefly ♦ *I am going to see my aunt tomorrow.* 13 to consult or obtain an interview with someone ♦ *You should see a doctor about your cough.* 14 to escort or conduct someone ♦ *I'll see you to the door.* SYNONYMS: escort, accompany, conduct. 15 to make sure of something ♦ *See that the windows are shut.* SYNONYMS: ensure, make sure, make certain. **to see about** to attend to something. **to see the light** 1 to understand something after failing to do so. 2 to realize one's mistakes. **to see someone off** 1 to go to the station, airport, etc. with someone who is leaving. 2 to chase away an intruder. **to see red** to be suddenly angry. **to see things** to have hallucinations. **to see through** 1 to understand the true nature of something. 2 to remain undeceived by someone or something. **to see something through** to complete a task despite difficulties. **to see to** to attend to something. [from an Old English word *seon*]

see [2] *noun* the district of which a bishop or archbishop has charge ♦ *the see of Canterbury.* [from a Latin word *sedes* meaning 'seat']

seed *noun* (**seeds** or **seed**) 1 a fertilized part of a plant, capable of developing into a new plant. 2 a quantity of seeds for sowing. 3 (old use) a man's semen. 4 (old use) offspring or descendants ♦ *Abraham and his seed.* 5 something that can give rise to a feeling or tendency ♦ *The remarks sowed the seeds of hope in their minds.* 6 each of several players in a tournament who are identified as especially strong so as not to be matched against each other in early rounds. **seed** *verb* 1 to plant seeds in something. 2 to remove seeds from fruit. 3 to place particles in a cloud to cause condensation and produce rain. 4 to identify the strong players in a tournament and arrange for them not to be matched against each other in early rounds. **to go** or **run to seed** 1 to stop flowering as the seed develops. 2 to deteriorate in appearance or ability. [from an Old English word]

seedbed *noun* a bed of fine soil in which seeds are sown.

seed cake *noun* cake containing caraway seeds as flavouring.

seedless *adjective* not containing seeds.

seedling *noun* a very young plant growing from a seed.

seed potato *noun* a potato kept for seed.

seedy *adjective* (**seedier, seediest**) (*informal*) shabby and disreputable. SYNONYMS: shabby, squalid, disreputable, sleazy. **seedily** *adverb* **seediness** *noun*

seeing *conjunction* because, since ♦ *I'll have to do it, seeing you won't be here.* ◊ You can also say ♦ *seeing that you won't be here.*

seek *verb* (past tense and past participle **sought**) **1** to try to find something or someone. **2** to try to obtain or do something. SYNONYMS: aim, try, endeavour, strive. **to seek something** or **someone out** to look specially for them. [from an Old English word *secan*]

seem *verb* to give the appearance or impression of being something ♦ *She seems worried about her work.* SYNONYMS: appear, look, sound. [from an Old Norse word]

seeming *adjective* giving the impression of being something but not necessarily being this in fact.

seemly *adjective* proper or suitable, in accordance with accepted standards of good taste. **seemliness** *noun*

seen past participle of **see**[1].

seep *verb* (said about a liquid) to ooze slowly out or through something. SYNONYMS: ooze, trickle. [probably from an Old English word]

seepage (seep-ij) *noun* the process of seeping, or the amount that seeps out.

seer *noun* a prophet, a person who sees visions. [from *see*[1]]

seersucker *noun* a fabric woven with a puckered surface. [from a Persian phrase *shir o shakar* meaning 'milk and sugar' and then 'a striped garment']

see-saw *noun* **1** a long board balanced on a central support so that a person (especially a child) can sit on each end and make it go up and down by pushing the ground alternately with their feet. **2** an up-and-down change that is constantly repeated.
see-saw *verb* **1** to ride on a see-saw. **2** to change rapidly from one state to another and back again. SYNONYMS: fluctuate, vacillate, oscillate. [from an old rhyme which imitated the rhythm of a saw going

to and fro, later used by children on a see-saw]

seethe *verb* **1** to bubble or surge like water when it boils. **2** to be very angry or excited. [from an Old English word *seothan*]

see-through *adjective* (said about clothing) able to be seen through, translucent.

segment (seg-mənt) *noun* a part that is cut off or separates naturally from other parts ♦ *a segment of an orange.* **segmental** (seg-men-təl) *adjective* **segmented** (seg-men-tid) *adjective* [from a Latin word *segmentum*, from *secare* meaning 'to cut']

segmentation *noun* division into segments.

segregate (seg-ri-gayt) *verb* **1** to put something apart from the rest, to isolate something. **2** to separate people of different races, sex, religion, etc. **segregation** *noun* [from a Latin word *segregare*, from *se-* meaning 'apart' and *gregatum* meaning 'herded']

seigneur (sayn-yer) *noun* a feudal lord. **seigneurial** *adjective* [same origin as for *senior*]

seine (sayn) *noun* a large fishing net that hangs vertically in the water with floats at the top and weights at the bottom, the ends being drawn together to enclose the fish as it is pulled ashore. [from an Old English word *segne*]

seismic (siy-zmik) *adjective* **1** to do with earthquakes or other vibrations of the earth. **2** having an enormous importance or effect. **seismically** *adverb* [from a Greek word *seismos* meaning 'earthquake']

seismogram (siyz-mə-gram) *noun* a record produced by a seismograph.

seismograph (siy-zmə-grahf) *noun* an instrument that detects, records, and measures earthquakes. [from a Greek word *seismos* meaning 'earthquake' and *-graph*]

seismology (siyz-mol-ə-ji) *noun* the study and recording of earthquakes and other vibrations of the earth. **seismological** *adjective* **seismologist** *noun* [from a Greek word *seismos* meaning 'earthquake' and *-logy*]

seismometer (siyz-mom-it-er) *noun* a seismograph. [from a Greek word *seismos* meaning 'earthquake' and *meter*]

seize *verb* **1** to take hold of a person or thing suddenly or forcibly. SYNONYMS:

grab, grasp, snatch, clutch, take hold of. **2** to take possession of something by force or by legal authority ♦ *Customs officers seized the smuggled goods.* SYNONYMS: appropriate, confiscate, take possession of. **3** to affect someone suddenly and intensely ♦ *Panic seized us.* **4** to seize up. **to seize on** to make use of an opportunity eagerly. **to seize up** (said about machinery) to become stuck or jammed because of friction or undue heat. [from an Old French word *seizir*, from a Latin word *sacire* meaning 'to claim']

seizure (see-zher) *noun* **1** the process of seizing something. **2** a sudden fit or attack, such as a stroke or a heart attack.

seldom *adverb* rarely, not often. [from an Old English word *seldan*]

select *verb* to choose something or someone carefully as being the best or most suitable.
select *adjective* **1** carefully chosen ♦ *a select group of pupils.* **2** (said about a club, society, etc.) admitting only certain people as members, exclusive. **selector** *noun* [from a Latin word *selectus* meaning 'chosen', from *se-* meaning 'apart' and *legere* meaning 'to choose']

select committee *noun* a small committee of parliament appointed for a special purpose.

selection *noun* **1** the process of selecting, or of being selected. **2** a person or thing that has been selected. **3** a group selected from a larger group. **4** a range of things from which to make a choice. SYNONYMS: collection, assortment, range, variety.

selective *adjective* **1** chosen or choosing carefully. SYNONYMS: discerning, fastidious, choosy, fussy. **2** involving or allowing a choice. **selectively** *adverb* **selectivity** *noun*

selenium (si-leen-iəm) *noun* a chemical element (symbol Se) that is a semiconductor and has various applications in electronics. [from a Greek word *selēnē* meaning 'moon']

self *noun* (**selves**) **1** a person as an individual ♦ *one's own self.* **2** a person's special nature ♦ *She has fully recovered and is her old self again.* **3** a person's own interests or advantage ♦ *He always puts self first.* **4** myself, herself, himself, etc., especially as the person writing or signing a document ♦ *Make the cheque payable to self.* [from an Old English word]

self- *prefix* of or to or done by yourself or itself.

self-addressed *adjective* (said about an envelope for containing a reply) addressed to yourself.

self-assured *adjective* confident in yourself. **self-assurance** *noun*

self-catering *adjective* catering for yourself, instead of having meals provided.

self-centred *adjective* thinking chiefly of yourself or your own affairs, selfish. SYNONYMS: selfish, egocentric.

self-confessed *adjective* openly admitting oneself to be something ♦ *a self-confessed traitor.*

self-confident *adjective* confident of your own abilities. SYNONYMS: assured, sure of yourself. **self-confidence** *noun*

self-conscious *adjective* embarrassed or awkward in manner because you know that people are watching you. SYNONYMS: awkward, embarrassed, ill at ease, uncomfortable, bashful. **self-consciously** *adverb* **self-consciousness** *noun*

self-contained *adjective* **1** complete in itself. **2** (said about accommodation) having all the necessary facilities without having to share. **3** (said about a person) able to do without the company of others, reserved.

self-control *noun* ability to control your behaviour and emotions. **self-controlled** *adjective*

self-defeating *adjective* (said about a policy or course of action) frustrating the purpose for which it was intended.

self-defence *noun* defence of yourself or of your rights or reputation against attack.

self-denial *noun* deliberately going without the things you would like to have.

self-destruct *verb* (said about a device) to destroy itself automatically.

self-determination *noun* a country's right to rule itself and choose its own government.

self-drive *adjective* (said about a hired vehicle) to be driven by the hirer.

self-effacing *adjective* keeping yourself in the background. **self-effacement** *noun*

self-employed *adjective* working independently and not for an employer. **self-employment** *noun*

self-esteem *noun* confidence in your own worth and abilities.

self-evident *adjective* clear without needing to be explained or proved. SYNONYMS: patent, manifest, clear, plain, obvious.

self-explanatory *adjective* understandable without needing explanation.

self-governing *adjective* (said about a country) governing itself. **self-government** *noun*

self-help *noun* use of your own powers and abilities to achieve things, without depending on help from others.

self-important *adjective* having a high opinion of your own importance, pompous. SYNONYMS: pompous, arrogant, overbearing. **self-importance** *noun*

self-indulgent *adjective* indulging your own pleasures and comforts. **self-indulgence** *noun*

self-interest *noun* your own personal advantage.

selfish *adjective* concerned with your own wishes and needs and ignoring those of other people. SYNONYMS: self-centred, inconsiderate, thoughtless. **selfishly** *adverb* **selfishness** *noun*

selfless *adjective* thinking of other people, unselfish. **selflessly** *adverb* **selflessness** *noun*

self-loading *adjective* (said about a gun) reloading itself automatically after being fired.

self-made *adjective* rich or successful from your own efforts.

self-pity *noun* too much sorrow and pity for yourself and your own problems.

self-portrait *noun* a portrait or description by an artist or writer, with himself or herself as the subject.

self-possessed *adjective* calm and dignified. SYNONYMS: calm, dignified, collected. **self-possession** *noun*

self-preservation *noun* protection of yourself from harm or injury, especially as a basic instinct for survival.

self-raising *adjective* (said about flour) containing its own raising agent, without the need for baking powder.

self-regard *noun* regard for oneself.

self-reliant *adjective* relying on your own abilities and resources, independent.

self-reliance *noun*

self-respect *noun* proper regard for yourself and your own principles and standing.

self-righteous *adjective* smugly sure that you are thinking or behaving rightly. SYNONYMS: sanctimonious, smug, priggish.

self-sacrifice *noun* sacrifice of your own interests and needs so that other people can benefit. **self-sacrificing** *adjective*

selfsame *adjective* the very same ♦ *He died in the selfsame house where he was born.*

self-satisfied *adjective* ostentatiously pleased with yourself and your own achievements, conceited. **self-satisfaction** *noun*

self-seeking *adjective* selfishly seeking to promote your own interests and welfare.

self-service *adjective* (said about a restaurant, shop, etc.) at which customers help themselves and pay at a checkout.

self-sown *adjective* (said about a plant) grown from seed that has dropped naturally from a plant.

self-styled *adjective* using a name or description that you may not be entitled to ♦ *self-styled pundits telling people what to do.*

self-sufficient *adjective* able to produce or provide what you need without help from other people.

self-supporting *adjective* earning enough to support yourself without needing financial help.

self-taught *adjective* having taught yourself without receiving formal teaching.

self-willed *adjective* obstinately doing what you want, stubborn. SYNONYMS: obstinate, stubborn, determined, intransigent, wilful.

sell *verb* (past tense and past participle **sold**) 1 to transfer the ownership of goods, or to provide a service, in exchange for money. 2 to keep a stock of goods for sale, to be a dealer in a commodity ♦ *Do you sell umbrellas?* SYNONYMS: stock, deal in, market, handle. 3 to promote the sales of something ♦ *The author's name alone will sell many copies.* 4 (said about goods) to be bought ♦ *The book is selling well.* 5 to be on sale at a certain price ♦ *It sells for £3.99.* 6 to convince someone of the merits of something ♦ *We tried to sell him the idea of*

merging the two departments.
sell *noun* (*informal*) **1** an act of selling something, or the manner of selling something. **2** a deception or disappointment. **to sell someone down the river** (*informal*) to betray or defraud someone. **to sell something off** to dispose of something by selling it at a reduced price. **to sell out 1** to sell all the stock of a commodity. **2** to abandon your principles to gain an advantage. **to sell someone out** to betray someone for your own advantage. **to sell up** to sell a house or business and change location or line of work. [from an Old English word *sellan*]

seller *noun* **1** a person who sells something. **2** a thing that sells well or badly ♦ *The new models are proving to be good sellers.*

seller's market *noun* a state of affairs when goods are scarce and prices are high.

sell-off *noun* the selling of all assets, especially at a low price.

sell-out *noun* **1** the selling of all the tickets for an entertainment etc. **2** a great commercial success. **3** a betrayal.

Sellotape *noun* (*trademark*) a transparent adhesive tape.
sellotape *verb* to fix or seal something with this tape. [from *cellulose* and *tape*]

selvedge or **selvage** *noun* an edge of cloth woven so that it does not unravel. [from *self* and *edge*]

selves plural of **self**.

semantic (sim-**an**-tik) *adjective* to do with meaning in language.
semantics *noun* **1** the study of language concerned with meaning. **2** the meaning or connotation of a word or phrase. [from a Greek word *sēma* meaning 'sign']

semaphore (**sem**-ə-for) *noun* a system of signalling by holding the arms in positions that indicate letters of the alphabet.
semaphore *verb* to send a message by semaphore. [from Greek words *sēma* meaning 'sign' and *phoros* meaning 'carrying']

semblance (**sem**-bləns) *noun* **1** an outward appearance or show ♦ *She spoke with a semblance of friendship.* SYNONYMS: appearance, aspect, air, show, façade. **2** a resemblance or likeness to something.

semen (**see**-men) *noun* a white fluid containing sperm, produced by male animals. [a Latin word meaning 'seed']

semester (sim-**est**-er) *noun* a half-year term or course of study at a school or university, especially in America. [from a Latin word *semestris* meaning 'six-monthly']

semi *noun* (**semis**) (*informal*) a semi-detached house.

semi- *prefix* half or partly. [from a Latin word *semi* meaning 'half']

semibreve (**sem**-i-breev) *noun* (*Music*) the longest note in normal use, lasting twice as long as a minim and four times as long as a crotchet.

semicircle *noun* half of a circle.
semicircular *adjective*

semicolon (sem-i-**koh**-lən) *noun* the punctuation-mark (;), used to separate parts of a sentence where there is a more distinct break than that marked by a comma.

semiconductor *noun* a substance that can conduct electricity but not as well as most metals do. **semiconducting** *adjective*

semi-detached *adjective* (said about a house) joined to another house on one side by a common wall, but not joined on the other side.

semi-final *noun* each of the matches or rounds preceding a final, in which there are four contestants or teams.
semi-finalist *noun*

seminal (**sem**-in-əl) *adjective* **1** to do with seed or semen. **2** giving rise to new ideas or developments ♦ *seminal ideas.* [from a Latin word *semen* meaning 'seed']

seminar (**sem**-in-ar) *noun* a small class or meeting for advanced discussion and research. [from a German word, related to *seminary*]

seminary (**sem**-in-er-i) *noun* (**seminaries**) a training college for priests or rabbis.
seminarist *noun* [from a Latin word *seminarium* meaning 'seedbed']

semi-permeable *adjective* allowing small molecules to pass through but not large ones.

semi-precious *adjective* (said about a mineral or gem) considered to be less valuable than those called precious.

semiquaver *noun* (*Music*) a note lasting half as long as a quaver.

semi-skilled *adjective* having or requiring some training but not extensive training.

Semite (see-miyt) *noun* a member of the group of people speaking a Semitic language, including the Jews and Arabs and formerly the Phoenicians and Assyrians.

Semitic (sim-it-ik) *adjective* to do with the Semites or their languages.

semitone *noun* (*Music*) the smallest interval used in European music, half of a tone.

semolina *noun* hard round grains left when flour has been milled, used to make puddings and pasta. [from an Italian word *semola* meaning 'bran']

sempstress *noun* another spelling of **seamstress**.

senate (sen-ət) *noun* 1 the state council of the ancient Roman Republic and Roman Empire. 2 the upper house of the parliamentary assemblies of the USA, France, and certain other countries. 3 the governing body of a university or college. [from a Latin word *senatus* meaning 'council of elders']

senator (sen-ə-ter) *noun* a member of a senate. **senatorial** (sen-ə-tor-iəl) *adjective*

send *verb* (past tense and past participle **sent**) 1 to cause someone or something to go or be taken to a place. SYNONYMS: (people or things) dispatch, convey; (things) transmit, post. 2 to make someone or something move, especially violently ♦ *The blow sent him flying* ♦ *The illness sent his temperature up.* 3 to put a person or animal into a certain state ♦ *The buzzing sent him mad* ♦ *The lecture sent everyone to sleep.* **send away for** to order goods by post. **send someone down** 1 to expel a student from a university. 2 to send a convicted person to prison. **send for** 1 to order someone to come to you. SYNONYMS: summon, call, call for. 2 to order goods to be brought or delivered. **to send something up** (*informal*) to make fun of something by imitating it. **to send word** to send information. **sender** *noun* [from an Old English word *sendan*]

send-off *noun* a friendly demonstration at a person's departure.

send-up *noun* (*informal*) a humorous parody or imitation.

seneschal (sen-i-shəl) *noun* (*historical*) the steward of a medieval great house. [from a medieval Latin word *seniscalcus*, from

Germanic words meaning 'old' and 'servant']

senile (see-niyl) *adjective* suffering from the physical or mental weaknesses of old age. **senility** (sin-il-iti) *noun* [from a Latin word *senilis* meaning 'old']

senior *adjective* 1 older than someone else. 2 higher in rank or authority. 3 to do with children above a certain age ♦ *senior school.* **senior** *noun* 1 an older person ♦ *She is my senior.* 2 a senior person, especially a member of a senior school. **seniority** *noun* [a Latin word meaning 'older', from *senex* meaning 'old']

senior citizen *noun* an elderly person, especially a pensioner.

senna *noun* the dried pods or leaves of a tropical tree, used as a laxative. [via Latin from an Arabic word *sana*]

señor (sen-yor) *noun* (**señores**) the title of a Spanish-speaking man, equivalent to 'Mr' or 'sir'.

señora (sen-yor-ə) *noun* the title of a Spanish-speaking woman, equivalent to 'Mrs' or 'madam'.

señorita (sen-yor-eet-ə) *noun* the title of a Spanish-speaking girl or unmarried woman, equivalent to 'Miss' or 'madam'.

sensation *noun* 1 a physical feeling or awareness resulting from stimulation of a sense organ or of the mind. 2 the ability to feel this stimulation ♦ *loss of sensation in the fingers.* SYNONYMS: feeling, perception. 3 a condition of great public interest or excitement ♦ *The news caused a sensation.* [same origin as for *sense*]

sensational *adjective* 1 producing great public interest or excitement. SYNONYMS: shocking, startling. 2 (*informal*) wonderful, amazing. SYNONYMS: wonderful, amazing, marvellous, dazzling, remarkable. **sensationally** *adverb*

sensationalism *noun* the use of sensational subjects or language to produce public interest or excitement. **sensationalist** *noun* & *adjective*

sense *noun* 1 the ability to see, hear, touch, taste, or smell things. 2 ability to perceive or feel or be conscious of a thing ♦ *He has no sense of shame* ♦ *sense of humour.* 3 the power to make good decisions; a sound practical judgement ♦ *They had the sense to keep out of the way.* SYNONYMS: wisdom, intelligence, gumption, prudence; (*informal*)

nous. **4** the meaning, or one of the meanings, of a word, phrase, or passage ♦ *The word 'set' has many senses.*
sense *verb* **1** to perceive something with one of the senses. **2** to become aware of something ♦ *He sensed that he was unwelcome.* SYNONYMS: perceive, realize, become aware (of), suspect. **3** (said about a machine) to detect something. **to come to your senses 1** to regain consciousness. **2** to behave sensibly after being foolish. **to make sense 1** (said about words or language) to have a meaning you can understand. **2** (said about an idea or scheme) to be sensible and practicable. **to make sense of** to find a meaning in something. [from a Latin word *sensus* meaning 'faculty of feeling']

senseless *adjective* **1** not showing good sense, foolish. SYNONYMS: foolish, absurd, pointless, fatuous, stupid, ridiculous, ludicrous. **2** unconscious, having no sensation. **senselessness** *noun*

sense organ *noun* any of the organs, such as the eye or ear, by which the body's senses are stimulated.

sensibility *noun* (**sensibilities**) sensitiveness, delicacy of feeling. ◊ This word does not mean 'being sensible' or 'having good sense'.

sensible *adjective* **1** having or showing good sense. SYNONYMS: practical, intelligent, prudent. **2** (*formal*) aware ♦ *We are sensible of the fact that maths is not a popular subject generally.* **3** (said about clothing) practical rather than fashionable ♦ *sensible shoes.* **sensibly** *adverb*

sensitive *adjective* **1** affected by or responsive to a physical stimulus ♦ *Plants are sensitive to light.* **2** receiving impressions quickly and easily ♦ *She has sensitive fingers.* **3** easily hurt or damaged ♦ *sensitive skin.* SYNONYMS: tender, delicate. **4** alert and considerate about other people's feelings. **5** (said about a person) easily hurt or offended. SYNONYMS: touchy, highly-strung, emotional. **6** (said about a subject) requiring tactful treatment. SYNONYMS: awkward, delicate. **7** (said about an instrument etc.) readily responding to or recording slight changes of condition. **sensitively** *adverb* **sensitivity** *noun*

sensitize *verb* to make something sensitive or abnormally sensitive. **sensitization** *noun*

sensor *noun* a device that measures or reacts to a physical property.

sensory (**sen**-ser-i) *adjective* to do with the senses or sensation ♦ *sensory nerves.*

sensual (**sens**-yoo-əl) *adjective* **1** to do with the physical senses, especially as a source of pleasure. **2** liking physical or sexual pleasures, or suggesting these. **sensually** *adverb*
sensuality (sens-yoo-al-iti) *noun*
◊ See the note at **sensuous**.

sensuous (**sens**-yoo-əs) *adjective* affecting or giving pleasure to the senses, especially on account of beauty or delicacy. **sensuously** *adverb*
◊ This word does not have the implication of undesirable behaviour that *sensual* can have.

sent past tense and past participle of **send**.

sentence *noun* **1** a group of words, usually containing a verb, that expresses a complete thought and forms a statement, question, exclamation, or command. **2** the punishment given by a law court to a person convicted of a crime.
sentence *verb* to give a convicted person a sentence in a law court ♦ *The judge sentenced him to a year in prison.* [from a Latin word *sententia* meaning 'opinion']

sententious (sen-ten-shəs) *adjective* giving moral advice in an affected or self-satisfied way. **sententiously** *adverb* **sententiousness** *noun*

sentient (sen-shənt) *adjective* capable of perceiving and feeling things ♦ *sentient beings.* [from a Latin word *sentiens* meaning 'feeling']

sentiment *noun* **1** an opinion or mental attitude produced by your feeling about something. **2** emotion as opposed to reason, sentimentality. [from a Latin word *sentire* meaning 'to feel']

sentimental *adjective* **1** showing or affected by feelings of tenderness, sadness, or nostalgia. **2** having these feelings in an exaggerated or self-indulgent way. SYNONYMS: emotional, mawkish, maudlin; (*informal*) soppy. **to have sentimental value** to be of value because of personal or emotional associations rather than actual worth. **sentimentality** (senti-men-tal-iti) *noun* **sentimentally** *adverb*

sentinel *noun* a guard or sentry. [via French from an Italian word *sentinella*]

sentry *noun* (**sentries**) a soldier posted to keep watch and guard something. [origin unknown; perhaps related to *sentinel*]

sentry box *noun* a wooden structure providing shelter for a single standing sentry.

sepal (sep-əl) *noun* (*Botany*) each of the leaf-like parts forming the calyx of a flower. [via French from a Greek word *skepē* meaning 'covering']

separable (sep-er-əbəl) *adjective* able to be separated. **separability** *noun* **separably** *adverb*

separate¹ (sep-er-ət) *adjective* forming a unit by itself, not joined or united with others. SYNONYMS: detached, distinct, discrete. **separately** *adverb*

separate² (sep-er-ayt) *verb* 1 to divide something or make or keep it separate. SYNONYMS: detach, remove, set apart. 2 to be between two places ♦ *The Channel separates England from France.* 3 to become separate, to go different ways. SYNONYMS: (of paths, roads, etc.) diverge, branch, split; (of people) disperse. 4 to withdraw from a union. 5 to stop living together as a couple. SYNONYMS: part, split up. [from a Latin word *separare* meaning 'to divide', from *se-* meaning 'apart' and *parare* meaning 'to make ready']

separation *noun* 1 the process of separating, or of being separated. 2 a legal arrangement by which a couple live apart while remaining married.

separatism (sep-er-ə-tizm) *noun* a policy of separation from a larger unit, especially in order to achieve political independence. **separatist** *noun*

separator *noun* a machine that separates things (e.g. cream from milk).

Sephardi (si-far-di) *noun* (**Sephardim**) a Jew of Spanish or Portuguese descent, as distinct from an Ashkenazi. **Sephardic** *adjective* [from a Hebrew word *separad* used in the Old Testament to refer to a country thought to be Spain]

sepia (seep-iə) *noun* 1 a brown colouring matter originally made from the black fluid of the cuttlefish, used in inks and water colours. 2 a rich reddish-brown colour of a kind found in early photographic prints.
sepia *adjective* having this colour. [from a Greek word *sēpia* meaning 'cuttlefish']

sepoy (see-poi) *noun* (*historical*) a native Indian soldier serving under British or other European orders. [from an Urdu and Persian word *sipahi* meaning 'soldier']

sepsis *noun* (*Medicine*) a condition in which harmful bacteria are present in a wound. [from a Greek word *sēpsis*, from *sēpein* meaning 'to make rotten']

September *noun* the ninth month of the year. [from a Latin word *septem* meaning 'seven' (because it was the seventh month of the ancient Roman calendar)]

septet *noun* a group of seven musicians, or a musical composition for seven voices or instruments. [from a Latin word *septem* meaning 'seven']

septic *adjective* (*Medicine*) (said about a part of the body) infected with harmful bacteria that cause pus to form. [same origin as for *sepsis*]

septicaemia (septi-**seem**-iə) *noun* blood poisoning caused by bacteria. [from *septic* and a Greek word *haima* meaning 'blood']

septic tank *noun* a tank, usually underground, in which sewage is stored and decomposes by the action of bacteria until it is able to drain away.

septuagenarian (sep-tew-ə-jin-**air**-iən) *noun* a person who is between 70 and 79 years old. [from a Latin word *septuageni* meaning '70 each']

Septuagint (sep-tew-ə-jint) *noun* the Greek version of the Old Testament. [from a Latin word *septuaginta* meaning '70' (because of the tradition that 72 translators were involved in producing the Greek text)]

septum *noun* (**septa**) (*Anatomy*) a partition separating two cavities, such as the one in the nose between the nostrils. [from a Latin word *saeptum* meaning 'enclosed']

sepulchral (sip-ul-krəl) *adjective* 1 to do with or having the form of a tomb ♦ *a sepulchral monument.* 2 (said about a voice) sounding deep and hollow.

sepulchre (sep-əl-ker) *noun* a tomb. [from a Latin word *sepulcrum* meaning 'burial place', from *sepelire* meaning 'to bury']

sequel *noun* 1 a book or film etc. that continues the story of an earlier one. 2 something that happens after an earlier event or as a result of it. [via Old French from a Latin word *sequi* meaning 'to follow']

sequence *noun* 1 the following of one thing after another in a regular or continuous way. SYNONYMS: succession, course. 2 the order in which things occur. SYNONYMS: order, arrangement. 3 a series or

set of things that belong next to each other in a particular order. **4** a section dealing with one scene or topic in a film or broadcast.
sequence *verb* to arrange things in sequence. SYNONYMS: order, arrange. [from a Latin word *sequens* meaning 'following']

sequential (si-**kwen**-shəl) *adjective*
1 forming a sequence or regular order.
2 happening as a result. **sequentially** *adverb*

sequester (si-**kwest**-er) *verb* **1** to isolate or seclude someone or something. **2** to confiscate something. [via Old French from a Latin word *sequestrare* meaning 'to commit for safe keeping']

sequestrate (si-**kwes**-trayt) *verb* to confiscate something. SYNONYMS: confiscate, appropriate, seize. **sequestration** *noun* **sequestrator** *noun*

sequin (**see**-kwin) *noun* a small bright disc, one of several sewn on clothing for decoration. **sequinned** *adjective* [via French and Italian from an Arabic word *sikka* meaning 'a die for making coins']

sequoia (si-**kwoi**-ə) *noun* a coniferous tree of California, growing to a great height. [named after Sequoya, a Cherokee Indian]

seraglio (si-**rahl**-yoh) *noun* (**seraglios**) the women's apartments in a Muslim palace, a harem. [via Italian and Turkish from a Persian word *saray* meaning 'palace']

seraph *noun* (**seraphim** or **seraphs**) a member of the highest order of angels in ancient Christian belief. [from a Hebrew word]

seraphic (ser-**af**-ik) *adjective* like a seraph, angelic ♦ *a seraphic smile.* **seraphically** *adverb*

Serb *noun* a person born in Serbia, part of Yugoslavia, or descended from people born there.

Serbian *noun* **1** another word for **Serb**. **2** the language of Serbia, close to Croat but written in the Cyrillic alphabet. **Serbian** *adjective* to do with or coming from Serbia.

Serbo-Croat (ser-boh-**kroh**-at) *noun* the language spoken in Serbia, Croatia, and elsewhere in the former republics of Yugoslavia.

serenade *noun* a song or tune of a kind played by a man under his lover's window.

serenade *verb* to sing or play a serenade to someone. [via French from an Italian word *sereno* meaning 'serene']

serendipity (se-rən-**dip**-iti) *noun* the ability or habit of making pleasant or interesting discoveries by accident. **serendipitous** *adjective* [coined by the 18th-century writer Horace Walpole, from the title of a story *The Three Princes of Serendip* (who had this ability)]

serene *adjective* calm and peaceful. SYNONYMS: calm, peaceful, tranquil, placid. **serenely** *adverb* **serenity** (ser-**en**-iti) *noun* [from a Latin word *serenus*, with the same meaning]

serf *noun* in the Middle Ages, a farm labourer who worked for a landowner and was not allowed to leave the place where he worked. **serfdom** *noun* [same origin as for *servant*]

serge *noun* a strong woven fabric used for making clothes. [from an Old French word *sarge*, related to *silk*]

sergeant (**sar**-jənt) *noun* **1** a soldier ranking below a sergeant major and above a corporal. **2** a police officer ranking below an inspector. [via Old French from a Latin word *servire* meaning 'to serve']

sergeant major *noun* a warrant officer in the British army who assists the adjutant of a regiment or battalion.

serial *noun* a story or film etc. that is shown in separate instalments.
serial *adjective* to do with or forming a series. **serially** *adverb* [from *series*]

serialism *noun* (*Music*) a technique of composition using the twelve notes of the chromatic scale arranged in a fixed order.

serialize *verb* to produce a story or film etc. as a serial. **serialization** *noun*

serial number *noun* a number that identifies one item in a series of things.

series *noun* (**series**) **1** a number of similar things that are related to each other or come one after another. SYNONYMS: set, sequence, succession. **2** a number of separate television or radio programmes on the same theme. **3** a number of games or matches between the same competitors. **4** a set of stamps or coins etc. issued at one time or in one reign. **in series** (said about electrical components or circuits) arranged so that the current passes through each in turn. [from a Latin word meaning 'row or chain']

serif (**se**-rif) *noun* a slight projection finishing off the stroke of a printed letter (as in T contrasted with sans serif T).

serious *adjective* 1 solemn and thoughtful, not smiling. SYNONYMS: grave, earnest, thoughtful, solemn. 2 sincere and earnest, not casual or light-hearted ♦ *He made a serious attempt to improve.* 3 needing serious thought, important ♦ *This is a serious matter.* SYNONYMS: important, significant, weighty, urgent. 4 causing great concern, not slight ♦ *She had recovered from a serious illness.* SYNONYMS: critical, acute. **seriously** *adverb* **seriousness** *noun* [from a Latin word *serius*, with the same meaning]

serjeant-at-arms *noun* (**serjeants-at-arms**) an official of a parliament, responsible for security and maintaining order and having ceremonial duties.

sermon *noun* 1 a talk on a religious or moral subject, especially one given by a member of the clergy during a religious service. 2 a long or tedious talk admonishing or rebuking someone. [from a Latin word *sermo* meaning 'discourse or talk']

sermonize *verb* to give a long moralizing talk.

serpent *noun* 1 a large snake, especially in stories. 2 (*historical*) a brass musical instrument made with three U-shaped turns. [from a Latin word *serpens* meaning 'creeping']

serpentine *adjective* twisting and curving like a snake ♦ *a serpentine road.*

SERPS *abbreviation* state earnings-related pension scheme.

serrated (ser-**ay**-tid) *adjective* having a jagged or notched edge like the teeth of a saw. **serration** *noun* [from a Latin word *serratum* meaning 'sawn']

serried *adjective* (said about rows of people or things) arranged or standing close together. [originally a form of an old verb *serry* meaning 'to press close']

serum (**seer**-əm) *noun* (**sera** or **serums**) 1 a thin pale yellow fluid that remains from blood when the rest has clotted. 2 this fluid taken from an animal and used in inoculations to provide immunity. [a Latin word meaning 'whey']

servant *noun* 1 a person employed to work in a household or as a personal attendant. 2 a person working for a government. 3 an employee regarded as performing services for an employer ♦ *a faithful servant of the company.* [from a Latin word *servus* meaning 'slave']

serve *verb* 1 to perform duties or services for a person, organization, country, etc. 2 to be employed as a member of the armed forces ♦ *He served in the Navy for many years.* 3 to be suitable for something ♦ *This will serve our purpose very well.* SYNONYMS: suit, answer, fulfil, meet. 4 to provide a facility for people, a community, etc. ♦ *The area is served by a number of buses.* 5 to spend time in something, to undergo something ♦ *He had served a long prison sentence.* 6 to attend to customers in a shop. 7 to set out or present food or drink for people. 8 (said about an amount of food) to be enough for a specified number of people ♦ *The recipe serves six.* 9 (in tennis and other games) to hit the ball to your opponent to start play. 10 to assist the priest officiating in a religious service. 11 to deliver a legal writ etc. to the person named. 12 to treat someone in a certain way ♦ *She was most unjustly served.* **serve** *noun* a service in tennis etc. **it serves you right** it is what you deserve. **server** *noun* [same origin as for *servant*]

service *noun* 1 the status or process of working for a person or organization. 2 a period of employment with a particular employer ♦ *She retired after 30 years' service.* 3 a department of people employed by the state or by a public organization ♦ *the Secret Service.* 4 a system or arrangement that supplies people with their needs ♦ *a train service.* 5 a branch of the armed forces, the army, navy, or air force. 6 a religious ceremony following a prescribed form. 7 (*Law*) the process of serving a legal writ. 8 an act that helps or benefits someone ♦ *Doing the shopping for us was a great service.* SYNONYMS: help, support, benefit, favour. 9 the process of serving food or drink in a restaurant etc. ♦ *The service was slow that day.* 10 the process of attending to customers in a shop etc. 11 a regular process of maintaining and repairing a motor vehicle or piece of machinery. SYNONYMS: maintenance, overhaul. 12 a set of dishes, plates, etc. for serving a meal ♦ *a dinner service.* 13 (in tennis and other games) the act or manner of serving, or the game in which a particular player serves ♦ *He lost his service twice in the next set.*

service *verb* **1** to maintain or repair a motor vehicle or piece of machinery. SYNONYMS: maintain, overhaul. **2** to supply someone with a service or services. **3** to pay the interest on a debt. **4** (said about a male animal) to mate with a female animal. **to be in service** to be employed as a servant. **to be of service** to be of use, to be helpful. **to do someone a service** to do something to help them. [via Old French from a Latin word *servitium* meaning 'slavery']

serviceable *adjective* **1** serving its purpose well, practical. SYNONYMS: practical, functional, usable. **2** suitable for ordinary use or wear, hard-wearing. **serviceability** *noun* **serviceably** *adverb*

service area *noun* an area beside a main road or motorway where petrol and other services are available to motorists.

service charge *noun* **1** an amount added to a hotel or restaurant bill to cover service. **2** a charge made to tenants in addition to rent for maintaining the building they occupy.

service industry *noun* an industry that provides services (such as gas and electricity) rather than goods.

serviceman or **servicewoman** *noun* (**servicemen** or **servicewomen**) a man or woman serving in the armed services.

service station *noun* a place beside a road, where petrol and other services are available.

serviette *noun* a table napkin. [from an Old French word, from *servir* meaning 'to serve']

servile (ser-viyl) *adjective* **1** to do with slaves or slavery. **2** excessively submissive or willing to serve others. SYNONYMS: slavish, submissive, obsequious, deferential. **servilely** *adverb* **servility** (ser-vil-iti) *noun* [same origin as for *servant*]

serving *noun* a portion of food at a meal.

servitude *noun* the condition of having to work for others and having no freedom or independence.

servo or **servomechanism** *noun* (**servos** or **servomechanisms**) a mechanism that provides additional power in a mechanical process such as the braking or steering system of a motor vehicle. [same origin as for *serve*]

sesame (sess-ǎ-mi) *noun* **1** a plant of tropical Asia with seeds that are used as food or as a source of oil. **2** the seeds of this plant. **open sesame** a special way of gaining access to a place or thing that is usually inaccessible (from the words used in one of the Arabian Nights stories to cause a door to open). [via Greek from an Arabic word *simsim*]

session *noun* **1** a meeting or series of meetings for discussion ♦ *The Queen will open the new session of Parliament.* **2** a period spent in an activity ♦ *a recording session.* SYNONYMS: period, stint, spell. **3** the academic year in certain universities. **4** the governing body of a Presbyterian Church. **in session** assembled for business. [from a Latin word *sessio* meaning 'sitting']

set *verb* (past tense and past participle **set**; **setting**) **1** to put or place something in position ♦ *Set the vase on the table.* SYNONYMS: place, put, lay, stand, leave; (*informal*) stick. **2** to fix something in position. **3** to adjust a clock or other mechanism. **4** to arrange the things on a table ready for a meal. SYNONYMS: lay, arrange, prepare. **5** to represent a story or film etc. as happening in a certain place or at a certain time ♦ *The story is set in Russia at the time of the Revolution.* **6** to provide music for words ♦ *The composer also set several poems by Blake.* **7** to fix or decide on something ♦ *Have they set a date for the wedding?* SYNONYMS: fix, decide, settle, establish, name, determine, appoint. **8** to arrange and protect a broken bone so that it will heal. **9** to fix the hair while it is damp so that it will dry in the style wanted. **10** to place a jewel in a framework, or to decorate something with jewels ♦ *The bracelet is set with emeralds.* **11** to establish something ♦ *She has set a new record for the high jump.* **12** to offer or assign something as a task to be done ♦ *She set them an essay to write over the weekend.* **13** to put someone or something into a specified state ♦ *The soldiers set them free* ♦ *An explosion set the doors rattling.* **14** to become firm or hard, or to make something do this ♦ *Leave the jelly to set.* SYNONYMS: harden, solidify, thicken. **15** (said about the sun) to appear to move towards or below the horizon by the earth's movement. **16** (in certain dances) to face another dancer and make certain steps ♦ *Set to your partners.*

set *noun* **1** a number of people or things

that belong together or are used together.
2 (*Mathematics*) a collection of things having a common property. **3** a radio or television receiver. **4** (in tennis and other games) a group of games forming a unit or part of a match. **5** the way something sets or is set or placed or arranged ♦ *the set of his jaw.* **6** the process or style of setting hair. **7** the scenery used for a play or film, or the stage or location where this is being performed. **8** a paving block. **9** a slip or shoot for planting ♦ *onion sets.* **10** another spelling of **sett**.

set *adjective* **1** fixed or arranged in advance ♦ *a set time.* **2** (said about a substance) having become solid. **3** ready or prepared to do something. **4** (said about a statement etc.) having a fixed wording. **to be set against** to be opposed to something. **to be set on** to be determined about doing something. **to set about 1** to begin a task. SYNONYMS: begin, start, embark on, tackle. **2** to attack someone physically or verbally. **to set something** or **someone back** to halt or slow the progress of something or someone. SYNONYMS: halt, delay, retard. **to set eyes on** to see something or someone. **to set fire to** to cause something to burn. **to set forth** to start on a journey. SYNONYMS: leave, depart, set off, set out; (*informal*) get going. **to set in** to become established ♦ *Depression had set in.* **to set off** to start on a journey. SYNONYMS: leave, depart, set out, set forth; (*informal*) get going. **to set something off 1** to make it begin working or cause it to happen ♦ *to set off a chain reaction.* **2** to cause a bomb, firework, etc. to explode. **3** to improve the appearance of something by providing a contrast. **to set your hand to** to begin a task. **to set out 1** to start on a journey. SYNONYMS: leave, depart, set off, set forth; (*informal*) get going. **2** to intend to do something. **to set something out** to display something for people to see. **to set sail** to begin a voyage by sea. **to set to 1** to begin doing something with energy. **2** (*informal*) to begin fighting or arguing. **to set someone up 1** (*informal*) to lead someone on in order to cheat or incriminate them. **2** to establish someone in a role. **to set something up 1** to put something on view. **2** to arrange or organize something. **3** to start a business or undertaking. SYNONYMS: establish, institute, create. **4** to begin making a noise. [from an Old English word *settan*]

set-aside *noun* the policy of paying farmers to take land out of use because there is a surplus of produce.

setback *noun* something that stops or slows progress. SYNONYMS: snag, complication, difficulty, hold-up.

set book *noun* a book that has to be studied for an examination.

set piece *noun* **1** a formal or elaborate arrangement in art or literature. **2** an arrangement of fireworks on a framework.

set square *noun* an instrument in the shape of a right-angled triangle, used for drawing lines in a certain relation to each other.

sett *noun* a badger's burrow. [a different spelling of *set*]

settee *noun* a long soft seat with a back and arms, for two or more people; a sofa. [probably from *settle*]

setter *noun* **1** a long-haired dog that is trained to stand rigid when it scents game. **2** a person or thing that sets something.

set theory *noun* (*Mathematics*) the study of the properties and applications of sets.

setting *noun* **1** the way or place in which something is set. **2** music for the words of a song etc. **3** a set of cutlery or crockery for one person at a meal.

settle[1] *verb* **1** to arrange or deal with something, especially to end a disagreement or dispute. SYNONYMS: resolve, reconcile, sort out; (*informal*) patch up. **2** to agree or decide on something ♦ *We still have to settle where we are going for our holiday.* SYNONYMS: decide, agree on, fix, finalize. **3** to become calm and able to concentrate, especially after being restless, or to make someone do this ♦ *I'm finding it hard to settle to work.* **4** to relax in a comfortable position ♦ *Rose settled in a chair and closed her eyes.* SYNONYMS: relax, sit back, rest. **5** to establish someone or something more or less permanently, or to become established in this way. **6** to make your home in a place ♦ *The family settled in Canada at the end of the nineteenth century* ♦ *Colonists settled the coast.* **7** to come to rest in a certain position, or to become compact by doing this ♦ *The snow has settled on minor roads* ♦ *Let the earth settle after digging.* **8** to place something so that it stays in position. **9** to pay a debt or claim. **10** to bestow something legally on someone ♦ *He settled all his property on his wife.* **to settle down 1** to become settled after movement or restlessness. **2** to follow a steady lifestyle, especially by establishing a home or family. **to settle up** to pay the bill at a restaurant, hotel, etc. [from an Old English word *setlan*]

settle [2] *noun* a wooden seat for two or more people, with a high back and arms and often a box-like compartment under the seat. [from an Old English word *setl* meaning 'a place to sit']

settlement *noun* **1** the process of settling something. **2** a business or financial arrangement. **3** an amount or property settled legally on a person. **4** a place where people establish a community or colony.

settler *noun* a person who goes to live in a place, especially one that was previously uninhabited.

set-to *noun* (*informal*) a fight or argument.

set-up *noun* (*informal*) the structure of an organization.

seven *adjective & noun* the number 7, one more than six.

sevenfold *adjective & adverb* **1** seven times as much or as many. **2** consisting of seven parts.

seventeen *adjective & noun* the number 17, one more than sixteen. **seventeenth** *adjective & noun*

seventh *adjective & noun* **1** next after sixth. **2** one of seven equal parts of a thing. **in seventh heaven** delighted or overjoyed. **seventhly** *adverb*

Seventh-Day Adventist *noun* a member of a strict Protestant sect that observes the sabbath on Saturday and preaches the imminent second coming of Christ.

seventy *adjective & noun* (**seventies**) the number 70, equal to seven times ten. **seventies** *plural noun* the numbers from 70 to 79, especially representing years of age or degrees of temperature. **seventieth** *adjective & noun*

sever (sev-er) *verb* **1** to separate or divide something by cutting. **2** to end a connection or relationship. SYNONYMS: break off, end, terminate. [via French from a Latin word *separare*, related to *separate*]

several *adjective & noun* **1** more than two but not many. **2** separate or individual ♦ *They all went their several ways.* [same origin as for *sever*]

severally *adverb* separately.

severance (sev-er-əns) *noun* **1** the action of ending a connection or relationship. **2** the action of severing or cutting.

severance pay *noun* an amount of money paid to an employee when an employment contract is ended early.

severe (si-veer) *adjective* **1** strict or harsh. SYNONYMS: strict, harsh, stern, austere. **2** (said about something bad, unwelcome, or demanding) great or intense ♦ *Severe gales are expected* ♦ *The pace was severe.* SYNONYMS: intense, strong, fierce, acute. **3** plain and without decoration ♦ *a severe style of architecture.* SYNONYMS: plain, austere. **severely** *adverb* **severity** (si-ve-riti) *noun* [from a Latin word *severus*]

Seville orange *noun* a bitter orange used for making marmalade. [named after Seville in Spain]

sew (soh) *verb* (past participle, **sewn** or **sewed**) **1** to join or repair material by passing thread many times through it, using a needle or sewing machine. **2** to make or fasten something by sewing. **3** to work with a needle and thread or with a sewing machine. **sewer** *noun* [from an Old English word *siwan*]
◊ Do not confuse this word with **sow**, which has a different meaning.

sewage (soo-ij) *noun* waste water and excrement carried away from buildings in drains. [from *sewer*]

sewage farm *noun* a place where sewage is treated for use as manure.

sewage works *noun* a place where sewage is treated and purified so that it can be discharged into a river or sea.

sewer (soo-er) *noun* an underground pipe for carrying away sewage and drainage water. [via Old French from Latin words *ex aqua* meaning 'from water']

sewerage *noun* a system of sewers.

sewing machine *noun* a machine for sewing or stitching material.

sewn past participle of **sew**.

sex *noun* **1** each of the two main groups (**male** and **female**) into which human beings and other living things are placed according to their reproductive functions. **2** the attraction between members of the two sexes, sexual feelings or impulses. **3** sexual activity, especially sexual intercourse ♦ *to have sex with someone.*

sex *verb* to judge the sex of a living thing ♦ *to sex chickens.* **sexer** *noun* [from a Latin word *secus* meaning 'division']

sex act *noun* an act of sexual intercourse.

sexagenarian (seks-ə-jin-**air**-iən) *noun* a person who is between 60 and 69 years old. [from a Latin word *sexageni* meaning '60 each']

sex appeal *noun* sexual attractiveness.

sex chromosome *noun* a chromosome that contributes to determining which sex an organism is to be.

sexism *noun* discrimination against members of one sex, especially women. **sexist** *noun* & *adjective*

sexless *adjective* 1 lacking sexual desire or attractiveness. 2 neither male nor female. **sexlessly** *adverb*

sextant *noun* an instrument for finding your position by measuring the altitude of the sun and stars, used in navigating and surveying. [from a Latin word *sextus* meaning 'sixth' (because early sextants consisted of an arc of one-sixth of a circle)]

sextet *noun* a group of six musicians, or a musical composition for six voices or instruments. [from a Latin word *sextus* meaning 'sixth']

sexton *noun* a person who looks after a church and churchyard. [from an Old French word, related to *sacristan*]

sextuple (seks-**tew**-pəl) *adjective* 1 consisting of six parts, or involving six people or groups ♦ *a sextuple alliance.* 2 six times as much.

sextuplet (seks-**tew**-plit) *noun* each of six children born at one birth. [from a Latin word *sextus* meaning 'sixth']

sexual *adjective* 1 to do with sex or the sexes, or with the attraction between the sexes. 2 (said about reproduction) involving the fusion of male and female cells. **sexually** *adverb*

sexual harassment *noun* the process of annoying or upsetting someone, especially a woman, by touching her or making indecent remarks or suggestions.

sexual intercourse *noun* a sexual act between two people, in which a man puts his erect penis into a woman's vagina, leading to orgasm and ejaculation of semen.

sexuality (seks-yoo-al-iti) *noun* 1 the fact of

belonging to one of the sexes. 2 sexual characteristics or impulses, or the capacity for having these.

sexy *adjective* (**sexier, sexiest**) sexually attractive or stimulating. **sexiness** *noun*

SF *abbreviation* science fiction.

shabby *adjective* (**shabbier, shabbiest**) 1 worn and threadbare, not kept in good condition. SYNONYMS: worn, threadbare, dirty, scrappy, tatty. 2 (said about a person) poorly dressed. SYNONYMS: scruffy, untidy, dishevelled. 3 unfair or dishonourable ♦ *a shabby trick.* **shabbily** *adverb* **shabbiness** *noun* [from a dialect word *shab* meaning 'scab']

shack *noun* a roughly built hut or shed. **to shack up with** (*informal*) to live with someone, especially as their lover. [perhaps from a Mexican word *jacal* meaning 'wooden hut']

shackle *noun* each of a pair of iron rings joined by a chain, for fastening a prisoner's wrists or ankles. **shackle** *verb* 1 to put shackles on a person, especially a prisoner. 2 to restrict or limit someone ♦ *They felt shackled by tradition.* [from an Old English word *scacul* meaning 'fetter']

shade *noun* 1 slight darkness or coolness produced when something blocks rays of light or heat. 2 shelter from the light and heat of the sun, or a place providing this shelter. 3 the darker part of a picture. 4 a colour, or the degree or depth of a colour. 5 a slight difference ♦ *The word has many shades of meaning.* 6 a small amount ♦ *It's a shade warmer today.* 7 (*literary*) a ghost. 8 a screen or cover used to block or reduce light or heat. SYNONYMS: screen, blind, awning. 9 a lampshade. 10 (*North Amer.*) a window blind.
shade *verb* 1 to block the rays of a source of light or heat, or to protect something from these. SYNONYMS: screen, shield, protect, mask, cover. 2 to give shade to something, to make something dark. 3 to darken parts of a drawing or painting so as to give effects of light and shade or differences of colour. 4 to pass gradually from colour or variety to another ♦ *The blue here shades into green* ♦ *where socialism shaded into communism.* **shades of** a reminder of someone or something ♦ *shades of the 1960s.* [from an Old English word *scadu*]

shadow *noun* 1 a dark area or shape produced when an object comes between

a source of light and a surface. **2** partial darkness, shade. **3** someone who attends or accompanies a person closely. **4** a slight trace ♦ *no shadow of doubt*. **5** a shaded part of a picture. **6** a feeling of sadness or gloom ♦ *The news cast a shadow over the rest of the holiday*. **7** (used before a noun) a member of the Opposition in Parliament who has responsibility for a particular area of politics ♦ *the shadow chancellor*.
shadow *verb* **1** to cast a shadow over a surface. **2** to follow and watch someone secretly. SYNONYMS: follow, pursue, tail, stalk. **3** to accompany and observe a person doing their work, so as to learn about it. **shadower** *noun* [same origin as for *shade*]

shadow boxing *noun* boxing against an imaginary opponent as a form of training.

Shadow Cabinet *noun* members of the Opposition in Parliament who speak on matters for which Cabinet ministers hold responsibility.

shadowy *adjective* **1** like a shadow. **2** full of shadows.

shady *adjective* (**shadier, shadiest**) **1** giving shade ♦ *a shady tree*. **2** situated in the shade ♦ *a shady corner*. **3** (*informal*) disreputable, not completely honest ♦ *shady dealings*. SYNONYMS: disreputable, dishonest; (*informal*) dodgy. **shadily** *adverb* **shadiness** *noun*

shaft *noun* **1** a long narrow straight part of something ♦ *the shaft of an arrow*. **2** a spear or arrow or similar device, or its long slender stem. **3** a ray of light. SYNONYMS: ray, beam, gleam. **4** a forceful or provocative remark ♦ *shafts of wit*. **5** a large rotating rod transmitting power in a machine. **6** each of a pair of long bars between which a horse is harnessed to a vehicle. **7** a deep passage or opening giving access to a mine or giving an outlet for air or smoke. [from an Old English word]

shag *noun* **1** a rough mass of hair or fibre. **2** a carpet with a rough pile. **3** a strong coarse kind of tobacco. **4** a kind of cormorant with a long curly crest. [from an Old English word *sceacga* meaning 'rough matted hair']

shaggy *adjective* (**shaggier, shaggiest**) **1** having long rough hair or fibre. SYNONYMS: hairy, bushy, woolly. **2** thick and untidy ♦ *shaggy hair*. **shaggily** *adverb* **shagginess** *noun*

shaggy-dog story *noun* a long rambling story with a peculiar twist of humour at the end.

shah *noun* (*historical*) the title of the former ruler of Iran. [from a Persian word meaning 'king']

shake *verb* (**shook, shaken**) **1** to move quickly up and down or from side to side, or to make something do this. SYNONYMS: tremble, quiver, vibrate, agitate. **2** to dislodge something by shaking ♦ *She shook the rain off her umbrella*. **3** to shock or disturb someone, or to upset their calmness ♦ *The bad news shook him for a moment*. SYNONYMS: shock, trouble, disturb, disconcert, ruffle, unsettle. **4** to make something less firm. **5** (said about a voice) to tremble or sound weak or faltering. **6** to shake hands ♦ *Shall we shake on it?*
shake *noun* **1** an act of shaking, or a shaking movement. **2** (*informal*) a milk shake. **in two shakes** (*informal*) very quickly. **no great shakes** (*informal*) not very good. **to shake down** to become settled. **to shake hands** to clasp right hands in greeting or parting or as a token of agreement. **to shake someone up** to rouse someone from sluggishness or apathy. **to shake something up 1** to mix something by shaking it. **2** to make radical changes to an organization or procedure. [from an Old English word *sceacan*]

shakedown *noun* (*informal*) **1** a radical change or reorganization. **2** a test of a new product. **3** a temporary or makeshift bed.

shaker *noun* a container in which ingredients are mixed by being shaken. **Shaker** *noun* a member of an American Christian sect that lives a simple life (so named from the wild movements they make during worship).

shake-up *noun* (*informal*) a radical reorganization.

shaky *adjective* (**shakier, shakiest**) **1** shaking or unsteady. SYNONYMS: unsteady, wobbly, rickety, flimsy. **2** unsafe or unreliable. SYNONYMS: unsafe, unreliable, tenuous, weak. **shakily** *adverb* **shakiness** *noun*

shale *noun* a kind of stone that splits easily into fine layers, like slate. [probably from a German word *Schale*, related to an English dialect word *shale* meaning 'dish']

shall *auxiliary verb* **1** used with *I* and *we* to express the ordinary future tense in

statements and questions ♦ *I shall arrive tomorrow* ♦ *Shall I close the door?* **2** used with words other than *I* and *we* to express a promise or obligation ♦ *You shall have a party.* [from an Old English word *sceal*]
◊ Note that in meaning **1** *will* is used with words other than *I* and *we*: ♦ *They will arrive tomorrow* ♦ *Will you close the door? Will*, as well as *shall*, can be used with *I* and *we* in statements: ♦ *I will arrive tomorrow.*

shallot (shə-lot) *noun* a plant producing an onion-like bulb that is used in cookery. [from a French word *eschalotte*]

shallow *adjective* **1** not deep ♦ *shallow water.* **2** not showing or needing deep thought or feeling.
shallow *noun* a shallow place.
shallow *verb* to become shallow.
shallowly *adverb* **shallowness** *noun* [origin unknown]

shalt *verb* a form of **shall** used with *thou* ♦ *Thou shall not steal.*

sham *noun* a person or thing that is not what they claim to be, a pretence. SYNONYMS: pretence, deception.
sham *adjective* pretended, not genuine. SYNONYMS: pretended, bogus, fake; (*informal*) phoney.
sham *verb* (**shammed, shamming**) to pretend to be something ♦ *to sham illness.*
shammer *noun* [probably a different form of *shame*]

shaman (sham-ən) *noun* a person regarded as being able to contact and influence the world of good and evil spirits and to guide souls and cure illnesses, especially in parts of northern Asia and North America. **shamanism** *noun* [from a Siberian language]

shamble *verb* to walk or run in a slow or awkward way.
shamble *noun* a shambling movement. [perhaps from a phrase *shamble legs*, the legs of trestle tables in meat markets (see **shambles**)]

shambles *noun* (*informal*) a scene or state of great confusion or disorder. SYNONYMS: muddle, mess, chaos. [from an old word *shamble* meaning 'meat market' or 'slaughterhouse']

shambolic (sham-bol-ik) *adjective* (*informal*) chaotic or disorganized.

shame *noun* **1** a feeling of sorrow and guilt caused by having done something wrong or foolish. SYNONYMS: guilt, disgrace, humiliation, remorse. **2** the ability to feel this

♦ *They have no shame.* **3** a person or thing that causes shame. **4** something regrettable, a pity ♦ *It's a shame the weather's not better.*
shame *verb* to cause someone shame ♦ *They were shamed into contributing more.* [from an Old English word *sceamu*]

shamefaced *adjective* looking ashamed.

shameful *adjective* causing shame, disgraceful. SYNONYMS: disgraceful, deplorable, shocking. **shamefully** *adverb*

shameless *adjective* having or showing no feeling of shame. **shamelessly** *adverb*

shammy *noun* (**shammies**) (*informal*) a chamois leather.

shampoo *noun* (**shampoos**) **1** a liquid or cream used to lather and wash the hair. **2** a liquid or chemical for cleaning a carpet or upholstery, or for washing a car. **3** the act of washing with a shampoo.
shampoo *verb* (**shampoos, shampooed, shampooing**) to wash or clean something with a shampoo. [from a Hindi word *champo* meaning 'press!']

shamrock *noun* a clover-like plant with three leaves on each stem, the national emblem of Ireland.

shandy *noun* (**shandies**) a drink of beer mixed with lemonade or another soft drink. [origin unknown]

shanghai (shang-hiy) *verb* (**shanghais, shanghaied, shanghaiing**) to take someone by force or trickery and force them to do something. [from an earlier meaning 'to force someone to join a ship's crew', named after Shanghai, a seaport in China]

shank *noun* **1** a person's leg, especially the part below the knee. **2** the lower part of an animal's leg, especially as a cut of meat. **3** a long narrow part of something, a shaft. [from an Old English word *sceanca*]

Shanks's mare or **Shanks's pony** *noun* the legs as a means of conveyance.

shan't *verb* shall not.

shantung *noun* a kind of soft Chinese silk, or a fabric resembling this. [named after Shantung in China, where it was originally made]

shanty¹ *noun* (**shanties**) a roughly built shack.

shanty [2] noun (**shanties**) a traditional song sung by sailors. [from a French word *chantez* meaning 'sing!']

shanty town noun a settlement of shanty dwellings.

shape noun 1 an area or form with a definite outline, or the appearance produced by this. SYNONYMS: figure, form, profile, outline. 2 the form or condition in which something appears ♦ *a monster in human shape*. SYNONYMS: form, guise, appearance. 3 the general form or condition of something ♦ *the shape of British industry*. SYNONYMS: condition, state, health. 4 a proper form or condition ♦ *Try to get it into shape*.
shape verb 1 to give something a certain shape. SYNONYMS: form, fashion, mould. 2 to develop into a certain shape or condition ♦ *The plan is shaping well*. 3 to adapt or modify plans or ideas etc. SYNONYMS: affect, influence, govern, determine. **shaper** noun [from an Old English word *gesceap* meaning 'external form']

shapeless adjective not having a distinct or an attractive shape. **shapelessly** adverb

shapely adjective (**shapelier, shapeliest**) having an attractive shape, well formed or proportioned. **shapeliness** noun

shard noun a potsherd. [an Old English word]

share [1] noun 1 a part given to one person or thing out of a larger amount which is being divided or allocated, or a part that an individual is entitled to. SYNONYMS: part, portion, allowance, quota. 2 each of the equal parts that a business company's capital is divided into and that gives the person who holds it the right to receive a proportion (called a *dividend*) of the profits.
share verb 1 (also **share out**) to give portions of something to two or more people. SYNONYMS: divide, apportion, distribute. 2 to have a share of something, to possess or use something jointly with others ♦ *The sisters shared a room*. **sharer** noun [from an Old English word *scearu*]

share [2] noun a ploughshare.

shareholder noun a person who owns shares in a business company.

sharia (sha-**ree**-ə) noun the sacred law of Islam based on the teachings of the Koran. [from an Arabic word]

shark [1] noun a large sea fish with sharp teeth and a prominent fin on its back. [origin unknown]

shark [2] noun (*informal*) a person who extorts money from others. [same origin as for *shirk*]

sharkskin noun 1 the skin of a shark. 2 a synthetic fabric with a smooth slightly shiny finish.

sharp adjective 1 having a fine edge or point that is able to cut or pierce things. 2 narrowing to a point or edge ♦ *a sharp ridge*. 3 steep or angular, not gradual ♦ *a sharp slope* ♦ *a sharp bend*. SYNONYMS: abrupt, sudden, (of a height) steep, sheer. 4 distinct or well-defined ♦ *in sharp focus*. 5 forceful or severe ♦ *a sharp frost*. 6 (said about words) critical or angry. 7 (said about a sound) sudden and loud ♦ *We heard a sharp cry*. 8 (said about a feeling) intense or painful. 9 (said about a taste or smell) strong and slightly sour. 10 (said about a person) quick to perceive things, intelligent. SYNONYMS: bright, clever, astute, shrewd, acute. 11 (said about a person) quick to seize an advantage. 12 unscrupulous. 13 vigorous or brisk ♦ *a sharp walk*. 14 (*Music*) above the correct pitch ♦ *Our singing was sharp*.
sharp adverb 1 exactly, punctually ♦ *at six o'clock sharp*. 2 suddenly ♦ *The man stopped sharp*. 3 at a sharp angle ♦ *Turn sharp right at the lights*. 4 (*Music*) above the correct pitch ♦ *He was singing sharp*.
sharp noun (*Music*) a note that is a semitone higher than the natural note; the sign # indicating this. **sharply** adverb **sharpness** noun [from an Old English word *scarp*]

sharpen verb to make something sharp, or become sharp. **sharpener** noun

sharper noun (*informal*) a swindler, especially at cards.

sharp-eyed adjective quick at noticing things.

sharpish adjective (*informal*) fairly sharp. **sharpish** adverb (*informal*) quickly or briskly.

sharp practice noun dishonest or barely honest business dealings.

sharpshooter noun a person skilled in shooting.

shatter verb 1 to break something into small pieces, or to be broken in this way. SYNONYMS: smash, splinter, break. 2 to destroy something completely ♦ *The* *decision shattered all our hopes.* SYNONYMS: destroy, wreck, ruin, spoil. **3** to disturb or upset someone greatly ♦ *They were shattered by the news.* [origin unknown]

shave *verb* **1** to cut growing hair off the skin with a razor. **2** to cut or scrape thin slices from the surface of wood, metal, etc. **3** to graze something gently in passing. **4** to reduce something by a small amount ♦ *The Chancellor has shaved income tax by a half per cent.*
shave *noun* the process of shaving hair from the face ♦ *He needs a shave.* **a close shave** (*informal*) a narrow escape from injury or danger.

shaven *adjective* shaved.

shaver *noun* **1** a person or thing that shaves. **2** an electric razor.

Shavian (**shay-vi-an**) *adjective* to do with the Irish writer George Bernard Shaw (1856–1950). [from *Shavius*, the Latinized form of *Shaw*]

shavings *plural noun* thin strips shaved off the surface of a wood or metal.

shawl *noun* a large piece of material worn round the shoulders or head or wrapped round a baby. [from Urdu and Persian words]

she *pronoun* **1** the female person or animal mentioned. **2** a vehicle, ship, or aircraft regarded as female.
she *noun* a female animal ♦ *a she-bear.* [from an Old English word]

sheaf *noun* (**sheaves**) **1** a bundle of corn stalks tied together after reaping. **2** a bundle of arrows, papers, or other things laid lengthways together. [from an Old English word *sceaf*]

shear *verb* (past participle, **shorn** or **sheared**) **1** to cut or trim something with shears or another sharp device. **2** to cut the wool off a sheep or other animal. **3** to deprive someone of something ♦ *He was shorn of his glory.* **4** to break off, or cause something to break off, because of structural stress ♦ *The wing bolts have sheared off.*
shear *noun* a type of fracture or distortion produced by pressure, in which each successive layer (e.g. of a mass of rock) slides over the next. **shearer** *noun* [from an Old English word *sceran*]
◊ Do not confuse the verb with **sheer**, which has a different meaning.

shears *plural noun* a clipping or cutting instrument shaped like a large pair of scissors and worked with both hands.

shearwater *noun* a seabird with long wings, skimming close to the water as it flies.

sheath *noun* **1** a close-fitting covering. **2** a cover for a blade or tool. **3** a condom. [from an Old English word *sceath*]

sheathe (**shee**th) *verb* **1** to put a knife or sword into a sheath. **2** to enclose something, e.g. machinery, in a casing.

sheaves plural of **sheaf**.

shed[1] *noun* a simply-made building, usually made of wood, used for storing things or sheltering animals or as a workshop.

shed[2] *verb* (past tense and past participle **shed; shedding**) **1** to allow something to fall off ♦ *Trees shed their leaves in autumn.* **2** to take something off ♦ *to shed your clothes.* **3** to allow a liquid to pour ♦ *to shed tears.* **4** to give out light or heat. **to shed blood** to be wounded or killed, especially in battle. **to shed light on** to help to explain something. **to shed tears** to cry. [from an Old English word *sceadan*]

she'd *verb* (*informal*) she had or she would.

sheen *noun* a shine or gloss. **sheeny** *adjective* [from an Old English word *sciene* meaning 'beautiful']

sheep *noun* (**sheep**) a grass-eating animal with a thick fleecy coat, kept in flocks for its wool and its meat. **like sheep** (said about people) easily led or influenced. [from an Old English word *scep*]

sheep dip *noun* a liquid for cleansing sheep of vermin or preserving their wool.

sheepdog *noun* a dog trained to guard and herd sheep.

sheepfold *noun* an enclosure for sheep.

sheepish *adjective* shy or embarrassed, especially from shame. **sheepishly** *adverb* **sheepishness** *noun*

sheepshank *noun* a knot used to shorten a rope without cutting it.

sheepskin *noun* **1** a garment or rug made of sheep's skin with the fleece on. **2** leather made from a sheep's skin.

sheer[1] *adjective* **1** complete or pure, not mixed or qualified ♦ *sheer joy.* SYNONYMS: complete, pure, utter, absolute, total. **2** vertical or nearly vertical, with almost

no slope ♦ *a sheer drop*. SYNONYMS: abrupt, precipitous, sharp, vertical. **3** (said about fabric) very thin or transparent.
sheer *adverb* directly, straight up or down ♦ *The cliff rises sheer from the sea*. [from a dialect word *shire* meaning 'pure' or 'clean']

sheer² *verb* to swerve from a course, to move sharply away. [from a German word *scheren* meaning 'to shear']
◊ Do not confuse this word with **shear**, which has a different meaning.

sheet¹ *noun* **1** a large rectangular piece of cotton or similar fabric, used in pairs on a bed for a person to sleep between. **2** a large thin piece of paper, glass, metal, or other material. **3** a piece of paper for writing or printing on. **4** a wide expanse of water, snow, or flame etc.
sheet *verb* **1** to cover something with sheets. **2** (said about rain) to fall heavily. [from an Old English word *scete*]

sheet² *noun* a rope or chain attached to the lower corner of a sail, to secure or adjust it. [from an Old English word *sceata* meaning 'lower corner of a sail']

sheet anchor *noun* **1** an extra anchor for use in emergencies. **2** a person or thing to depend on in the last resort.

sheet lightning *noun* lightning that has its brightness spread across the sky because it is reflected within clouds.

sheet music *noun* printed music published on loose sheets of paper.

sheikh (shayk) *noun* an Arab leader, especially the head of an Arab tribe or village. **sheikhdom** *noun* [from an Arabic word meaning 'old man']

shekel (shek-əl) *noun* the unit of money in Israel.
shekels *plural noun* (*informal*) money or riches. [from a Hebrew word *shaqal* meaning 'to weigh']

shelduck *noun* (**shelducks** or **shelduck**) a wild duck with bright plumage, living on coasts. [probably from a dialect word *sheld* meaning 'pied']
◊ The male is sometimes called a *sheldrake*.

shelf *noun* (**shelves**) **1** a flat length of wood or other rigid material fixed horizontally to a wall or in a cupboard or bookcase for books or other objects to be placed on. **2** something resembling this, a ledge or step-like projection of land. **on the shelf 1** no longer useful or wanted. **2** (said about a person) past an age when they are

likely to get married. [from a German word *schelf*]

shelf life *noun* the length time for which something remains usable.

shell *noun* **1** the hard outer covering of an egg, nut, etc., or of an animal such as a snail, crab, or tortoise. **2** the walls or framework of an unfinished or derelict building or ship. **3** any structure that forms a firm framework or covering. **4** the metal framework of the body of a vehicle. **5** a light boat for rowing races. **6** a metal case filled with explosive, for firing from a large gun. **7** (*Physics*) a group of electrons in an atom, with almost equal energy.
shell *verb* **1** to take something out of its shell ♦ *to shell peas*. **2** to fire explosive shells at a target. **to come out of your shell** to become more sociable and less shy. **to shell out** (*informal*) to pay out money. [from an Old English word *sciell*]

she'll (*informal*) she will.

shellac (shəl-**ak**) *noun* thin flakes of a resinous substance used in making varnish.
shellac *verb* (**shellacs, shellacked, shellacking**) to varnish a surface with shellac.

shellfish *noun* (**shellfish**) a sea animal that has a shell, especially an edible kind such as an oyster, crab, or shrimp.

shell shock *noun* a nervous disorder caused by prolonged exposure to battle conditions.

shell suit *noun* a casual suit consisting of a loose jacket and trousers with a soft lining.

shelter *noun* **1** something that offers protection against bad weather or danger. **2** a place providing food and accommodation for homeless people. **3** protection ♦ *Seek shelter from the storm*. SYNONYMS: protection, refuge, safety.
shelter *verb* **1** to provide someone with shelter. **2** to protect someone from blame or difficulty. SYNONYMS: protect, shield. **3** to find a shelter ♦ *They sheltered under the trees*. [origin unknown]

sheltered housing *noun* housing provided for people who are elderly or handicapped, with special facilities or services.

shelve *verb* **1** to arrange something on a shelf or shelves. **2** to fit a wall or cupboard etc. with shelves. **3** to put an idea or plan aside until a later time. **4** to slope ♦ *The river bed shelves steeply here.* [from *shelf*]

shelves plural of **shelf**.

shelving *noun* shelves, or material for making them.

shemozzle *noun* (*informal*) a rumpus or loud brawl. [from a Yiddish word]

shenanigans (shin-an-i-gənz) *plural noun* (*North Amer.*) (*informal*) mischief or trickery. [origin unknown]

shepherd *noun* a person who looks after a flock of sheep.
shepherd *verb* to guide or direct people. [from *sheep* and *herd*]

shepherdess *noun* (*historical*) a woman who looks after a flock of sheep.

shepherd's pie *noun* a pie of minced meat under a layer of mashed potato.

sherbet *noun* **1** a cooling drink of weak sweetened fruit juice. **2** a fizzy sweet drink or the powder from which this is made. **3** a flavoured water ice. [from an Arabic word *sharba* meaning 'a drink']

sherd *noun* another spelling of **shard**.

sheriff *noun* **1** (in England and Wales) the chief executive officer of the Crown in a county, with certain legal and ceremonial duties. **2** (in Scotland) the chief judge of a district. **3** (in the USA) the chief law-enforcing officer of a county. [from *shire* and *reeve* meaning 'officer']

Sherpa *noun* (**Sherpa** or **Sherpas**) a member of a Himalayan people living on the borders of Nepal and Tibet. [from a Tibetan word *sharpa* meaning 'inhabitant of an eastern country']

sherry *noun* (**sherries**) a strong white sweet or dry wine originally from southern Spain. [from Jerez, a city in Spain]

she's (*informal*) she is or she has.

Shetland pony *noun* a small strong shaggy pony, originally from the Shetland Isles.

shibboleth (shib-ə-leth) *noun* a custom or principle that distinguishes a particular class or group of people. [from a Hebrew word *shibboleth* meaning 'ear of corn', used by the ancient Hebrews as a test of a person's nationality because it was hard for foreigners to pronounce (Judges 12:6)]

shield *noun* **1** a broad piece of armour carried on the arm to protect the body against missiles or blows in combat. **2** a representation of a shield used for displaying a coat of arms, or as a trophy. **3** an object, structure, or layer of material that protects something. SYNONYMS: protection, defence. **4** (*Geology*) a mass of ancient rock under a land area.
shield *verb* to protect someone or something from harm or discovery. SYNONYMS: protect, shelter. [from an Old English word *scild*]

shift *verb* **1** to change or move from one position to another, or to cause something to do this. SYNONYMS: move, budge, change position. **2** (said about a situation, opinion, etc.) to change slightly. **3** to transfer blame or responsibility to someone else. **4** (*informal*) to move quickly. **5** (*informal*) to sell goods in large quantities.
shift *noun* **1** a change of place, form, or condition. **2** a group of workers who start work as another group finishes, or the time when they work ♦ *the night shift.* **3** a woman's straight dress with no waist. **4** (*Computing*) a key that switches between two sets of characters or functions on a keyboard. **shifter** *noun* [from an Old English word *sciftan* meaning 'to divide or apportion']

shiftless *adjective* lazy, lacking resourcefulness and ambition. **shiftlessly** *adverb* **shiftlessness** *noun*

shifty *adjective* (**shiftier, shiftiest**) (*informal*) deceitful or evasive, untrustworthy. **shiftily** *adverb* **shiftiness** *noun*

Shiite (shee-iyt) *noun* a member of the Shiah, one of the two major groups in Islam, centred chiefly in Iran and based on the teachings of Muhammad and his son-in-law, Ali. (Compare **Sunnite**.) [from an Arabic word *shia* meaning 'the party of Ali']

shilling *noun* a former British coin, equal to 5p.

shilly-shally *verb* (**shilly-shallies, shilly-shallied, shilly-shallying**) to keep hesitating or changing your mind. [from *shall I? shall I?*]

shimmer *verb* to shine with a soft light that appears to quiver.
shimmer *noun* a shimmering effect. [from an Old English word *scymrian*]

shin *noun* **1** the front of the leg below the knee. **2** a cut of meat from the lower part of a cow's leg.
shin *verb* (**shinned, shinning**) to climb a steep surface by gripping with the arms and legs. [from an Old English word *scinu*]

shindig noun (*informal*) **1** a noisy or lively party. **2** a noisy disturbance. [origin unknown]

shindy noun (**shindies**) (*informal*) a noisy disturbance or quarrel. [origin unknown]

shine verb (past tense and past participle **shone** or (in meaning 5) **shined**) **1** to give out or reflect light, to glow or be bright. SYNONYMS: glow, glimmer, gleam. **2** (said about the sun etc.) to be visible and not obscured by clouds. **3** to excel in some way ♦ *He does not shine in maths.* **4** to direct a light ♦ *Shine the torch in the corner.* **5** (*informal*) to polish something to produce a shine.
shine noun **1** brightness. **2** a high polish. SYNONYMS: gleam, gloss, lustre, polish. **to take a shine to** (*informal*) to begin to like someone. [from an Old English word *scinan*]

shiner noun (*informal*) a black eye.

shingle [1] noun small rounded pebbles on a beach. [origin unknown]

shingle [2] noun **1** a rectangular piece of wood used as a roof tile. [from a Latin word *scindula* meaning 'a split piece of wood']

shingles noun a painful disease caused by the chicken pox virus, with blisters forming along the path of a nerve or nerves.

shin pad noun a pad worn to protect the shins in football and other sports.

Shinto noun a Japanese religion which includes the worship of ancestors and nature. [via Japanese from a Chinese phrase *shen dao* meaning 'way of the gods']

shinty noun a Scottish game resembling hockey. [origin unknown]

shiny adjective (**shinier, shiniest**) having a shining surface, rubbed until glossy. **shininess** noun

ship noun a large seagoing boat.
ship verb (**shipped, shipping**) to transport goods, especially by sea. **to ship oars** to take the oars from the rowlocks and lay them in the boat. **to take ship** to go on board a ship for a journey. [from an Old English word *scip*]

-ship suffix forming nouns (as in *friendship, hardship, citizenship, membership*). [from an Old English word *-scipe*]

shipboard noun **on shipboard** on board a ship.

shipbuilding noun the business of building ships. **shipbuilder** noun

ship canal noun a canal deep and wide enough for large ships to pass through.

shipload noun as much as a ship will hold.

shipmate noun a person travelling or working on the same ship as another.

shipment noun **1** the process of shipping goods. **2** a consignment of goods shipped.

shipowner noun a person who owns a ship or has shares in a shipping company.

shipper noun a person or firm that transports goods by ship.

shipping noun **1** a country's ships. **2** the process of transporting goods by ship.

shipshape adverb & adjective tidy and in good order.

shipwreck noun **1** the wrecking of a ship by a storm or accident at sea. **2** a wrecked ship. **shipwrecked** adjective

shipwright noun a shipbuilder.

shipyard noun a place where ships are built or repaired.

shire noun a county. **the Shires** the English counties, especially of central England, regarded as strongholds of rural culture. [from an Old English word *scir* meaning 'care' or 'official charge']

shire horse noun a heavy powerful breed of horse used, originally in the Midlands of England, for pulling loads.

shirk verb to avoid or neglect work or a duty. **shirker** noun [from an obsolete word *shirk* meaning 'sponger']

shirr verb to gather cloth into folds by means of parallel elastic threads that run through it. **shirring** noun [origin unknown]

shirt noun **1** a piece of men's clothing for the upper part of the body, made of a light material with a collar and sleeves and buttons down the front. **2** a piece of clothing worn on the upper part of the body in certain sports. **in your shirtsleeves** wearing a shirt without a jacket over it. **to keep your shirt on** (*informal*) to stay calm and not lose your temper. **to put your shirt on something** (*informal*) to bet all you have on something. [from an Old English word *scyrte*]

shirting noun material for making shirts.

shirtwaister noun a woman's dress with the top part shaped like a shirt.

shirty adjective (**shirtier, shirtiest**) (informal) bad-tempered or annoyed. **shirtily** adverb **shirtiness** noun

shish kebab (sheesh ki-**bab**) noun pieces of meat and vegetable grilled on skewers. [from Turkish words shish meaning 'skewer' and kebap meaning 'roast meat']

shiver[1] verb to tremble with cold or fear. SYNONYMS: tremble, shake, quake, quaver, shudder, quiver.
shiver noun a shivering movement. **to give you the shivers** to make you feel fearful or alarmed. **shivery** adjective [from an Old English word ceafl meaning 'jaw']

shiver[2] noun a splinter.
shiver verb to break into splinters. [from a Germanic word meaning 'to split']

shoal[1] noun a large number of fish swimming together.
shoal verb to form shoals. [same origin as for school[2]]

shoal[2] noun 1 an area of shallow water. 2 an underwater sandbank visible at low tide.
shoal verb to become shallow. [from an Old English word sceald, related to shallow]

shock[1] noun 1 a sudden unpleasant surprise, or the feeling that follows. SYNONYMS: surprise, blow; (informal) bombshell. 2 an acute state of weakness caused by physical injury or pain or by mental shock. 3 short for **electric shock**. 4 the effect of a violent shaking or impact. 5 a violent shake of the earth's crust in an earthquake.
shock verb 1 to make someone surprised and upset, to give someone a shock. SYNONYMS: shake, stun, appal, alarm, horrify, dismay. 2 to give someone an electric shock. 3 to cause someone to suffer from a state of shock. [from a French word choc (noun), choquer (verb)]

shock[2] noun a bushy mass of hair. [origin unknown]

shock absorber noun a device for absorbing jolts and vibrations in a vehicle.

shocker noun (informal) a person or thing that shocks.

shocking adjective 1 causing great shock or disgust. SYNONYMS: appalling, dreadful, deplorable, outrageous, scandalous. 2 (informal) very bad ♦ shocking weather.
shockingly adverb

shock tactics plural noun the use of sudden violent action to achieve a purpose.

shock troops plural noun troops specially trained for violent assaults.

shock wave noun a sharp change of atmospheric pressure, caused by an explosion or by a body moving faster than sound.

shod past tense and past participle of **shoe**.

shoddy adjective (**shoddier, shoddiest**) of poor quality, badly or cheaply made. SYNONYMS: inferior, poor-quality, substandard, tawdry, cheap.
shoddy noun a poor-quality fabric made from shredded woollen waste. **shoddily** adverb **shoddiness** noun [origin unknown]

shoe noun 1 an outer covering for the foot, with a fairly stiff sole. 2 a horseshoe. 3 something shaped or used like a shoe. 4 the part of a brake that presses against the wheel or its drum in a vehicle.
shoe verb (**shoes, shod, shoeing**) to fit a horse with a shoe or shoes. **to be in someone's shoes** to be in someone's situation or predicament. [from an Old English word scoh]

shoehorn noun a curved piece of stiff material for easing your heel into the back of a shoe.

shoelace noun a cord for fastening a shoe.

shoemaker noun a person who makes or mends boots and shoes.

shoestring noun on a shoestring with only a small amount of money or other resources.

shoe tree noun a shaped block put into a shoe to keep it in shape when it is not being worn.

shogun (shoh-gŏn) noun a hereditary commander in feudal Japan. [via Japanese from a Chinese word jiang jun meaning 'general']

shone past tense and past participle of **shine**.

shoo interjection a word used to frighten animals away.
shoo verb (**shooes, shooed, shooing**) to drive away an animal by saying this.

shook past tense of **shake**.

shoot verb (past tense and past participle **shot**) 1 to fire a gun or other weapon, or a missile. SYNONYMS: fire (a gun), launch (a missile). 2 to kill or wound a person or animal with a bullet or arrow. SYNONYMS:

hit, kill, wound. **3** to hunt animals with a gun for sport. **4** to move or send something out swiftly or violently ♦ *He shot the rubbish into the bin.* **5** to move very fast ♦ *A police car shot past us.* SYNONYMS: streak, flash, speed, fly, zoom, tear. **6** (said about a plant) to put forth buds or shoots. **7** to slide the bolt of a door to fasten or unfasten it. **8** (said about a boat) to move swiftly under a bridge or over rapids. **9** to take a shot at goal. **10** to film or photograph something ♦ *The film was shot in Africa.*
shoot noun **1** a young branch of new growth of a plant. **2** an expedition for shooting animals. **to have shot your bolt** to have made your last possible effort. **to shoot a line** (*informal*) to try to impress or convince someone by boastful talk. **to shoot it out** (*informal*) to engage in a battle or fight with guns. **to shoot your mouth off** (*informal*) to talk too freely. **to shoot up 1** to rise or increase suddenly. **2** (said about a person) to grow rapidly.   **shooter** noun [from an Old English word *sceotan*]

shooting gallery noun a place for shooting at targets with rifles, especially at a fairground.

shooting star noun a small rapidly moving meteor appearing like a star and then disappearing.

shooting stick noun a walking stick with a small folding seat at the handle end and a spike at the other.

shoot-out noun (*informal*) a battle or fight with guns.

shop noun **1** a building or room where goods or services are sold to the public. **2** a workshop. **3** (*informal*) a period of shopping.
shop verb (**shopped, shopping**) **1** to go to a shop or shops to buy goods. **2** (*informal*) to inform on someone, especially to the police. **all over the shop** (*informal*) in a mess, untidily scattered about. **to shop around** to look for the best bargain. **to talk shop** to talk at length or tediously about your own work. [from an Old French word *eschoppe* meaning 'lean-to booth']

shop floor noun the part of a factory or workshop where production of goods is carried on, as distinct from administration.

shopkeeper noun a person who owns or manages a shop.

shoplifter noun a person who steals goods in a shop, after pretending to be a customer. **shoplifting** noun

shopper noun **1** a person who shops. **2** a shopping bag attached to wheels.

shopping noun **1** the process of buying goods in shops. **2** the goods bought in shops.

shopping centre noun a part of a town or other area where shops are concentrated.

shop-soiled adjective dirty, faded, or slightly damaged from being displayed or handled in a shop.

shop steward noun a trade-union official elected by workers in a factory to represent them in dealings with the management.

shore [1] noun the land beside the sea or beside a lake.

shore [2] verb to support a building or other structure with a beam or prop set at a slant.
shore noun a support of this kind. [from a German or Dutch word *schoren*]

shoreline noun the line where the land meets the edge of the sea or a lake.

shoreward adjective & adverb towards the shore. **shorewards** adverb

shorn past participle of **shear**.

short adjective **1** small in length, measuring little from one end to the other. **2** taking a small amount of time ♦ *a short rest.* **3** (said about a person) small in height, not tall. **4** not lasting, not going far into the past or future ♦ *a short memory.* **5** not enough, or not having enough ♦ *Water is short* ♦ *We are short of water.* **6** (*informal*) having little of a certain quality ♦ *He seems rather short on tact.* **7** concise or brief ♦ *a short story.* **8** (said about a person or their manner) impolite or curt. **9** (said about vowel sounds) having a pronunciation that is considered to last less than that of a corresponding 'long' vowel (e.g. *oo* is short in *book* but long in *moon*). **10** (said about an alcoholic drink) small and concentrated, made with spirits. **11** (said about a person's temper) easily lost. **12** (said about pastry) rich and crumbly because it contains a lot of fat. **13** (said about odds in betting) nearly even, reflecting a high level of probability.
short adverb suddenly or abruptly ♦ *She heard a cry and stopped short.*

short noun (informal) **1** a short drink. **2** a short circuit.

short verb (informal) to short-circuit, or to cause something to short-circuit. **for short** as an abbreviation ♦ *Samantha is called Sam for short.* **in short supply** scarce. **in the short run** or **term** as regards the immediate future only. **to make short work of** to deal with a task rapidly and efficiently. **short for** an abbreviation of ♦ *'Sam' is short for 'Samantha'.* **short of** without going to the length of ♦ *We will do anything for her short of having her to stay.*
shortish adjective [from an Old English word *sceort*]

shortage noun a lack or scarcity of something that is needed. SYNONYMS: lack, scarcity, deficiency, insufficiency, want, dearth, paucity.

shortbread or **shortcake** noun a rich sweet biscuit made with butter.

short change noun not enough money given as change.
short-change verb **1** to give someone too little money as change, especially deliberately. **2** to cheat someone.

short circuit noun a fault in an electrical circuit in which current flows by a shorter route than the normal one.
short-circuit verb **1** to have a short circuit, or to cause something to do this. **2** to shorten or get round a process or procedure.

shortcoming noun a fault or failure to reach the right standard. SYNONYMS: fault, failing, defect, flaw, imperfection, weakness.

short cut noun a route or method that is quicker than the usual one.

short division noun the process of dividing one number by another without writing down the calculations.

shorten verb to make something shorter, or to become shorter. SYNONYMS: curtail, cut, reduce, abbreviate.

shortening noun fat used to make pastry rich and crumbly.

shortfall noun a shortage, or an amount by which something is less than it should be.

shorthand noun a method of quick writing using special abbreviations and symbols, especially to write words down while someone is saying them.

short-handed adjective having an insufficient number of workers or helpers.

shorthorn noun an animal of a breed of cattle with short horns.

shortlist noun a list of selected candidates from whom the final choice is made.
shortlist verb to put a candidate on a shortlist.

short-lived adjective lasting a short time.

shortly adverb **1** in a short time, soon ♦ *They will be here shortly* ♦ *It happened shortly afterwards.* **2** in a few words. **3** in an impolite or curt manner.

short rations plural noun small or strictly limited rations.

shorts plural noun **1** short trousers that do not reach to the knee. **2** (*North Amer.*) men's underpants.

short shrift noun impolite or curt treatment. [originally a short time allowed for a condemned person to confess to a priest before being executed, from an Old English word *scrift*]

short-sighted adjective **1** able to see things clearly only when they are close. **2** lacking foresight or imagination.
short-sightedly adverb **short-sightedness** noun

short-tempered adjective easily made angry.

short-term adjective affecting only the immediate future, temporary.

short time noun a reduced working day or week.

short ton see ton.

short wave noun a radio wave of a wavelength between 10 and 100 metres and a frequency of about 3 to 30 megahertz.

shot [1] past tense and past participle of shoot.
shot adjective (said about cloth) woven or dyed so that different colours show at different angles.

shot [2] noun **1** the firing of a gun or cannon, or the sound of this. **2** a person judged by their skill in shooting ♦ *He's a good shot.* **3** (**shot**) a single missile for a cannon or gun, a non-explosive projectile. **4** (**shot**) lead pellets for firing from small guns. **5** (**shot**) a heavy ball thrown as a sport. **6** the launching of a rocket or spacecraft. **7** a stroke in tennis, cricket, or billiards etc. **8** an attempt to hit something or reach a target. **9** (informal) an attempt to do something ♦ *Let's have a shot at the quiz.*

SYNONYMS: attempt, try, go; (*informal*) stab. **10** (*informal*) an injection. **11** (*informal*) a small drink of spirits. **12** a photograph, or a scene photographed or filmed. **like a shot** (*informal*) without hesitation, willingly. **a shot in the arm** (*informal*) a stimulus or encouragement. **a shot in the dark** a wild guess. [from an Old English word *sceot*]

shotgun *noun* a gun for firing small shot at close range.

should *auxiliary verb* used to express **1** an obligation or duty (= ought to) ♦ *You should have told me.* **2** something expected to happen ♦ *They should be here by ten o'clock.* **3** a possible event ♦ *If you should happen to see them.* **4** with *I* and *we* to make a polite statement ♦ *I should like to come*, or in a conditional clause ♦ *If they had supported us we should have won.* [the past tense of *shall*, from an Old English word *sceolde*]

◊ The use in meaning 4 is rather formal, and many people now use *would* after *I* and *we* as well as after other words such as *he*, *she*, *it*, and *they*: ♦ *If they had supported us we would have won.* There is also the problem that *should* seems to suggest an obligation (because meaning 1 is so common) rather than something that might have happened, whereas there is no such problem with *would*.

shoulder *noun* **1** the part of the body at which an arm, or in animals a foreleg or wing, is attached. **2** the part of the human body between this and the neck. **3** the upper foreleg and adjacent parts of an animal as a cut of meat. **4** a part that levels out below a slope or vertical surface ♦ *the shoulder of a bottle.* **5** short for **hard shoulder**.
shoulder *verb* **1** to push someone or something with your shoulder. **2** to carry something on your shoulder or shoulders. **3** to take the blame or responsibility for something. **put your shoulder to the wheel** to make an effort. **to shoulder arms** to hold a rifle with the barrel against your shoulder. [from an Old English word *sculdor*]

shoulder bag *noun* a bag hung on a long strap over the shoulder.

shoulder blade *noun* each of the two large flat bones at the top of the back.

shoulder strap *noun* a strap that passes over the shoulder, either as part of a dress etc. or to support something.

shouldn't *verb* (*informal*) should not.

shout *noun* a loud cry or call. SYNONYMS: yell, cry, call.
shout *verb* to give a shout, to call out loudly. SYNONYMS: yell, call out, cry out. **to shout someone down** to prevent someone from speaking by speaking loudly yourself. [origin unknown]

shove (shuv) *noun* a rough push.
shove *verb* **1** to push someone or something roughly. **2** (*informal*) to put something somewhere ♦ *Just shove it in the drawer.* [from an Old English word *scufan*]

shovel *noun* a tool like a spade with the sides turned up, used for lifting earth, coal, snow, etc.
shovel *verb* (**shovelled, shovelling**) **1** to move or clear something with a shovel. **2** to scoop or push something roughly ♦ *He sat shovelling food into his mouth.* [from an Old English word *scofl*]

shoveller *noun* a duck with a long broad beak.

show *verb* (past participle, **shown** or **showed**) **1** to allow or cause something to be seen ♦ *Show me your new car.* **2** to explain something or make someone understand it ♦ *Show us how to do it.* SYNONYMS: explain, tell, demonstrate. **3** to demonstrate or prove something ♦ *The evidence shows that he was speaking the truth.* SYNONYMS: demonstrate, prove, indicate, establish, confirm, verify. **4** to guide or escort someone ♦ *I will show you out.* SYNONYMS: escort, guide, conduct. **5** to give an image of something ♦ *The picture shows the hotel.* **6** to exhibit something in a show. SYNONYMS: exhibit, display, present. **7** to present a film or television programme for viewing. SYNONYMS: present, put on, screen (a film), broadcast (a television programme). **8** to display a certain feeling or quality ♦ *They showed genuine concern.* SYNONYMS: display, reveal, evince. **9** to be able to be seen ♦ *The lining is showing.* **10** (*informal*) to prove your ability or worth to someone ♦ *We'll show them!* **11** (*informal*) to appear, to come when expected ♦ *I wonder if they'll show.*
show *noun* **1** a display or exhibition. **2** a public entertainment or performance. **3** (*informal*) a business or undertaking ♦ *She runs the whole show now.* **4** an outward appearance or display ♦ *a show of friendship.* **to give the show away** to reveal things that were intended to be secret. **to show off** to try to impress people boastfully. **to show something off** to

display something well or conspicuously **a show of hands** the raising of hands to vote for or against something. **to show yourself** to be seen in public. **to show your face** to let yourself be seen. **to show up 1** to be clearly visible. **2** (*informal*) to appear, to come when expected. [from an Old English word *sceawian* meaning 'to look at']

show business *noun* the entertainment industry; the theatre, cinema, and broadcasting as a profession.

showcase *noun* **1** a glass case for displaying articles in a shop, museum, etc. **2** an opportunity for presenting something publicly ♦ *The programme is a showcase for new talent.*

showdown *noun* a final test or confrontation.

shower *noun* **1** a brief fall of rain or snow. **2** a lot of small things falling or arriving like rain ♦ *a shower of stones* ♦ *a shower of letters.* **3** a device or cubicle in which a person stands under a spray of water to wash, or a wash in this. **4** (*informal*) an incompetent person or group.
shower *verb* **1** to fall or arrive in a shower. **2** to send or give a large number of letters or gifts to someone. SYNONYMS: inundate, overwhelm. **3** to wash yourself in a shower. [from an Old English word *scur* meaning 'light fall of rain']

showerproof *adjective* (said about fabric) able to keep out slight rain.

showery *adjective* (said about the weather) with many showers.

show house *noun* a house on a newly built estate, furnished so that prospective buyers can view it.

showing *noun* **1** the presentation of a cinema film or television programme. **2** the evidence or quality that someone shows ♦ *On today's showing, he will succeed.*

showjumping *noun* the sport of riding horses over fences and other obstacles, with penalty points for errors.

showman *noun* (**showmen**) **1** a person who manages or organizes a circus, fair, or similar entertainment. **2** a person who is good at entertaining. **showmanship** *noun*

shown past participle of **show**.

show-off *noun* (*informal*) a person who tries to impress people boastfully.

showpiece *noun* a fine example of something displayed for people to admire.

showroom *noun* a large room where goods are displayed for people to look at.

showy *adjective* (**showier, showiest**) likely to attract attention, bright and colourful. SYNONYMS: bright, colourful, gaudy, striking. **showily** *adverb* **showiness** *noun*

shrank past tense of **shrink**.

shrapnel *noun* **1** pieces of metal scattered from an exploding bomb. **2** a bomb designed to scatter pieces in this way. [named after the British soldier General Henry Shrapnel (1761–1842), who invented it in about 1806]

shred *noun* **1** a small piece torn or cut off something. SYNONYMS: bit, piece, scrap. **2** a small amount ♦ *There is not a shred of evidence.* SYNONYMS: jot, iota, speck, trace.
shred *verb* (**shredded, shredding**) to tear or cut something into shreds. **shredder** *noun* [from an Old English word *scread* meaning 'piece cut off']

shrew *noun* **1** a small mouse-like animal. **2** (*old use*) a bad-tempered or nagging woman. **shrewish** *adjective* [from an Old English word *screawa*]

shrewd *adjective* having good sense or judgement, clever or astute. SYNONYMS: clever, astute, perceptive, sharp. **shrewdly** *adverb* **shrewdness** *noun* [from *shrew* in an old meaning 'spiteful or cunning person']

shriek *noun* a shrill cry or scream. SYNONYMS: scream, screech, yell, cry.
shriek *verb* to give a shriek. SYNONYMS: scream, screech, yell, cry out. [an imitation of the sound]

shrift *noun* see **short shrift**.

shrike *noun* a bird with a strong hooked beak that impales its prey on thorns. [origin unknown]

shrill *adjective* (said about a voice or sound) piercing and high-pitched. SYNONYMS: high, high-pitched, piercing, harsh.
shrill *verb* to make a shrill sound. **shrilly** *adverb* **shrillness** *noun* [probably from Old English]

shrimp *noun* **1** a small shellfish that turns pink when boiled. **2** (*informal*) a very small person. [origin unknown]

shrimping *noun* fishing for shrimps.

shrine *noun* an altar or chapel or other place that is considered to be holy because of its special associations. [from an Old English word *scrin* meaning 'cabinet']

shrink *verb* (**shrank, shrunk**) 1 to make something smaller, or to become smaller; to contract. SYNONYMS: contract, shrivel, diminish, reduce. 2 (said about clothes or material) to become smaller after being immersed in water. 3 to move back or away from something out of fear or disgust. [from an Old English word *scrincan*]

shrinkage *noun* 1 the process of shrinking, or the amount by which something has shrunk. 2 an allowance made for loss of income in business due to theft or wastage.

shrink wrap *noun* transparent plastic film that clings to an article it is wrapped round.
shrink-wrap *verb* (**shrink-wrapped, shrink-wrapping**) to wrap something in this material.

shrivel *verb* (**shrivelled, shrivelling**) to become wrinkled and contract, or to make something do this, through lack of moisture. [probably from Old Norse]

shroud *noun* 1 a sheet in which a dead body is wrapped for burial. 2 a thing that conceals or obscures something ♦ *The event was wrapped in a shroud of secrecy.* 3 each of a set of ropes supporting the mast of a ship.
shroud *verb* 1 to wrap a body in a shroud. 2 to protect or conceal something in wrappings. 3 to conceal or obscure something ♦ *His past life is shrouded in mystery.* [from an Old English word *scrud* meaning 'clothing']

Shrove Tuesday *noun* the day before Ash Wednesday.

shrub *noun* a woody plant smaller than a tree and usually having separate stems starting at or near the ground. **shrubby** *adjective* [from an Old English word *scrubb*]

shrubbery *noun* (**shrubberies**) an area planted with shrubs.

shrug *verb* (**shrugged, shrugging**) to raise the shoulders slightly to show indifference, doubt, or helplessness.
shrug *noun* an act of shrugging the shoulders. **to shrug something off** to dismiss something as unimportant. [origin unknown]

shrunk past participle of **shrink**.

shrunken *adjective* having shrunk.

shudder *verb* 1 to shiver violently with horror, fear, or cold. SYNONYMS: tremble, shake, quake, quaver, shiver, quiver. 2 to make a strong shaking movement.
shudder *noun* a shuddering movement. [from German and Dutch words, meaning 'to shake']

shuffle *verb* 1 to walk without lifting the feet clear of the ground. 2 to slide playing cards over each other to get them in a random order. 3 to rearrange or jumble things. 4 to keep changing one's position.
shuffle *noun* 1 a shuffling movement or walk. 2 an act of shuffling playing cards. 3 a rearrangement of people or things.
shuffler *noun* [probably from an early German word *schuffeln* meaning 'to walk clumsily']

shun *verb* (**shunned, shunning**) to avoid or keep away from someone or something. [from an Old English word *scunian*]

shunt *verb* 1 to move a train or wagons to another track. 2 to divert someone or something to a less important place or position. 3 (*Electricity*) to provide an electrical circuit with a shunt.
shunt *noun* 1 the process of shunting. 2 (*Electricity*) a conductor joining two points of a circuit. **shunter** *noun* [from an earlier meaning 'to move suddenly aside', perhaps related to *shun*]

shut *verb* (past tense and past participle **shut; shutting**) 1 to move something so as to cover or block an opening, to close something. 2 to move or be moved into this position ♦ *The door shut with a bang.* 3 to bring two parts of something together ♦ *She shut the book.* 4 to keep something (e.g. noise) in or out by shutting a door or window. 5 to trap a finger or piece of clothing by shutting something on it. **to shut down** to stop working or doing business, either for the day or permanently. **to shut your eyes to something** to pretend not to notice something. **to shut someone in** or **out** to confine or exclude someone by shutting a door. **to shut something off** to stop the flow of water or gas etc. by shutting a valve. **to shut up** (*informal*) to stop talking. **to shut someone up** (*informal*) to make someone stop talking. **to shut something up** to shut a place securely. [from an Old English word *scyttan* meaning 'to put a bolt in position']

shutdown *noun* **1** the closing of a factory or business. **2** the turning off of a computer or other device.

shut-eye *noun* (*informal*) sleep.

shutter *noun* **1** a panel or screen that can be closed over a window. **2** a device in a camera that opens and closes to allow light to fall on the film. **shuttered** *adjective* [from *shut*]

shuttle *noun* **1** a form of public transport that travels regularly between two places. **2** a holder carrying the weft thread to and fro across the loom in weaving, or the lower thread in a sewing machine. **3** a shuttlecock.
shuttle *verb* to move or travel or send something backwards and forwards. [from an Old English word *scytel* meaning 'a dart']

shuttlecock *noun* a small rounded piece of cork with a crown of feathers or similar materials, struck to and fro by players in badminton.

shuttle diplomacy *noun* diplomacy that involves travelling between the countries involved in a dispute.

shy¹ *adjective* (**shyer, shyest**) **1** (said about a person) timid and reserved in the presence of other people. SYNONYMS: timid, reserved, coy, nervous, bashful, reticent, withdrawn. **2** showing shyness ♦ *a shy smile*. **3** (said about a wild animal) avoiding contact with humans.
shy *verb* (**shies, shied, shying**) to jump or move suddenly in alarm. **shyly** *adverb* **shyness** *noun* [from an Old English word *sceoh*, referring to a horse]

shy² *verb* (**shies, shied, shying**) to fling or throw something at a target.
shy *noun* (**shies**) a throw. [origin unknown]

shyster *noun* (*informal*) a cheat or rogue. [perhaps from Scheuster, the name of a lawyer]

SI *abbreviation* an internationally recognized system of metric units and measurements, including the metre, kilogram, ampere, and kelvin. [short for French *Système International d'Unités* meaning 'International System of Units']

Si *abbreviation* (*Chemistry*) the symbol for silicon.

Siamese *adjective* to do with or coming from Siam (now called Thailand) or its people or language.

Siamese cat *noun* a cat with short pale fur and a darker face, ears, tail, and feet.

Siamese twins *plural noun* twins born with their bodies partially joined.

sibilant *adjective* having a hissing sound ♦ *She spoke in a sibilant whisper*.
sibilant *noun* a speech sound that sounds like hissing, e.g. *s* and *sh*. **sibilance** *noun* [from a Latin word *sibilans* meaning 'hissing']

sibling *noun* a brother or sister. [from an Old English word *sib* meaning 'related by birth' and *-ling*]

sibyl (**sib**-il) *noun* an ancient Greek or Roman prophetess. [from a Greek name *Sibulla*]

sic *adverb* used or spelt in the way given. [a Latin word meaning 'so, thus']
◊ This word is placed in brackets after a word that seems odd or is wrongly spelt, to show that it is being quoted exactly as in the original.

sick *adjective* **1** ill; physically or mentally unwell. SYNONYMS: ill, unwell, poorly. **2** likely to vomit ♦ *He said he felt sick*. SYNONYMS: nauseous, queasy. **3** distressed or disgusted ♦ *Their attitude makes me sick*. **4** (said about humour) making fun of something unpleasant or upsetting ♦ *sick jokes*.
sick *verb* (*informal*) to bring something up by vomiting ♦ *The cat sicked up its food on the carpet*.
sick *noun* (*informal*) vomit. **to be sick** to vomit. **sick of** tired of something or someone because you have had too much of them. [from an Old English word *seoc*]

sickbay *noun* a room or building for people who are sick, especially in a ship or school.

sickbed *noun* a sick person's bed.

sicken *verb* to make someone disgusted or appalled, or to become disgusted or appalled. **to be sickening for** to show the first symptoms of a disease.

sickening *adjective* **1** disgusting or appalling ♦ *His head hit the wall with a sickening thud*. **2** (*informal*) annoying or irritating.

sickle *noun* a tool with a curved blade and a short handle, used for cutting corn etc. [from an Old English word *sicol*, from a Latin word *secare* meaning 'to cut']

sick leave *noun* leave of absence allowed to someone who is sick.

sickly *adjective* (**sicklier, sickliest**) **1** often ill or in poor health ♦ *a sickly child*. SYNONYMS: frail, infirm, weak, delicate, unhealthy. **2** causing poor health ♦ *a sickly climate*. **3** causing sickness or nausea ♦ *a sickly smell*. **4** feeble or sentimental ♦ *a sickly smile*.

sickness *noun* **1** illness. **2** a disease. **3** nausea or vomiting.

sickroom *noun* a room for a person who is sick.

side *noun* **1** a surface of something, especially one joining the top and bottom, front and back, or ends. SYNONYMS: surface, face. **2** each of the surfaces of a flat object, e.g. a piece of paper. **3** (*Geometry*) each of the bounding lines of a plane figure such as a triangle or square. **4** each of the two halves into which something can be divided by a line down its centre. **5** the part near the edge and away from the centre of something. SYNONYMS: edge, boundary, verge. **6** a slope of a hill or ridge. **7** the place or region next to a person or thing ♦ *Her husband stood at her side*. **8** one aspect or view of something ♦ *We have to study all sides of the problem*. SYNONYMS: aspect, facet, element, factor, view. **9** each of two groups or teams who oppose each other. **10** a person's line of descent traced through their father or mother ♦ *He was of German origin on his mother's side of the family*.
side *adjective* at or on the side ♦ *Leave by the side door*.
side *verb* to support someone in a dispute or disagreement ♦ *She sided with her son*. **on the side** as a separate activity or sideline, especially a secret or illicit one. **to take someone's side** to support someone in a dispute or disagreement. **side by side** standing close together. [from an Old English word *side*]

sideboard *noun* a long piece of furniture with a flat top and drawers and cupboards for cutlery and other things for a dining table.

sideburns *plural noun* a strip of hair growing on the side of a man's face in front of his ears.

sidecar *noun* a small low vehicle attached to the side of a motorcycle, for carrying a passenger.

side drum *noun* a small drum with a surface on each side.

side effect *noun* a secondary and usually unwanted effect that a drug or medicine has as well as the main effect.

side issue *noun* a secondary point or issue in addition to the main one.

sidekick *noun* (*informal*) a close associate or subordinate.

sidelight *noun* **1** a small light on each side of a vehicle, beside the headlight. **2** a light at either side of a moving ship. **3** a narrow piece of glass beside a door or window.

sideline *noun* **1** something done in addition to your main work or activity. **2** each of the lines on the two long sides of a sports pitch. **on the sidelines** in a position of watching events rather than taking part in them.

sidelong *adverb & adjective* to one side, sideways ♦ *a sidelong glance*. [from *side* and an Old English word *-ling* meaning 'extending in a certain direction']

sidereal (siy-**deer**-iəl) *adjective* to do with the stars, or measured by the stars. [from a Latin word *sideris* meaning 'of a star']

side road *noun* a minor road, especially one leading off a main road.

side saddle *noun* a saddle for a rider to sit with both legs on the same side of the horse, used by women wearing skirts. **side-saddle** *adverb* sitting in this position on a horse.

sideshow *noun* **1** a small show or display at a fair or exhibition. **2** a minor but interesting or diverting incident or activity.

sidesman *noun* (**sidesmen**) a person who acts as an usher or attendant at a church service.

sidestep *verb* (**sidestepped, sidestepping**) **1** to avoid something by stepping sideways. **2** to evade a question or responsibility.

side street *noun* a minor street off a main one.

sidestroke *noun* a swimming stroke in which the swimmer lies on their side.

sidetrack *verb* to divert someone's attention from the main subject or issue.

sidewalk *noun* (*North Amer.*) a pavement.

sideways *adverb & adjective* **1** to or from one side ♦ *Move it sideways*. **2** with one side facing forward ♦ *She sat sideways*.

siding *noun* a short track at the side of a railway line and linked to it with points.

sidle *verb* to walk in a shy or nervous manner. [from *sidelong*]

siege *noun* 1 a military operation in which a force surrounds and blockades an enemy town or fortified position to force its surrender. 2 an operation by a police team to force an armed person occupying a building to surrender. **to lay siege to** to begin a siege of a place. [from an Old French word *sege*]

siemens (see-mǝnz) *noun* (*Physics*) the SI unit of electrical conductance, the reciprocal of the ohm. [named after the German electrical engineer E. W. von Siemens (1816–92)]

sienna (si-en-ǝ) *noun* a kind of clay used in making brownish paints, either reddish-brown (**burnt sienna**) or yellowish-brown (**raw sienna**). [from an Italian phrase *terra di Siena*, meaning 'earth of Siena' (in Italy)]

sierra (si-e-rǝ) *noun* a long mountain chain with sharp slopes and a jagged outline, in Spain or parts of America. [via Spanish from a Latin word *serra* meaning 'a saw']

siesta (si-est-ǝ) *noun* (**siestas**) a short afternoon rest, especially in hot countries. [via Spanish from a Latin word *sexta* meaning 'sixth (hour)']

sieve (siv) *noun* a utensil consisting of wire or plastic mesh in a frame, used for sorting solid or coarse matter from liquid or fine matter, or for reducing a soft mixture squeezed through it to a pulp. **sieve** *verb* to put something through a sieve. [from an Old English word *sife*]

sift *verb* 1 to put something dry through a sieve in order to remove lumps and large particles. 2 to sprinkle something lightly from a perforated container. 3 to examine and analyse facts or evidence etc. carefully. 4 (said about snow or light) to fall as if from a sieve. **sifter** *noun* [from an Old English word *siftan*]

sigh *noun* 1 a long sound made by breathing out heavily when you are sad, tired, relieved, etc. 2 a sound like this, e.g. made by the wind. **sigh** *verb* 1 to give a sigh, or to express something with a sigh. 2 (said about the wind etc.) to make a sound like someone sighing. **to sigh for** (*literary*) to yearn for someone or something. [from an Old English word *sican* (verb)]

sight *noun* 1 the faculty or power of seeing with the eyes. SYNONYMS: eyesight, vision. 2 the action or fact of seeing or being seen ♦ *We lost sight of it.* 3 the range over which a person can see or an object can be seen ♦ *The group were now within sight of the castle.* 4 a thing that is seen or worth seeing, an attractive display ♦ *The garden is a wonderful sight in the spring.* SYNONYMS: scene, spectacle. 5 (*informal*) a person or thing that looks unsightly or ridiculous ♦ *He looks a sight in that old coat.* 6 a device you look through to observe with a telescope or take aim with a weapon, or an aim or observation you make using this device. **sight** *verb* 1 to see or observe something ♦ *On the fourth day we sighted land.* SYNONYMS: observe, spot, glimpse, see, discern, recognize. 2 to aim or observe something with the sight of a gun or telescope. **at** or **on sight** as soon as a person or thing has been seen ♦ *The guards were instructed to shoot on sight.* **to catch sight of** to glimpse something or someone briefly. **in sight** visible, or near at hand ♦ *Victory was in sight.* **to lose sight of** 1 to be no longer able to see something. 2 to forget about something or no longer consider it. **to lower your sights** to be less ambitious. **to set your sights on** to aim to get or achieve something. **sight unseen** without having an opportunity to see something beforehand. [from an Old English word *sihth* meaning 'something seen'] ◊ Do not confuse this word with **site**, which has a different meaning.

sighted *adjective* able to see, not blind.

sightless *adjective* unable to see, blind.

sightly *adjective* pleasing to look at. **sightliness** *noun*

sight-reading *noun* playing or singing music at sight, without preparation.

sightseeing *noun* visiting interesting places in a town etc. **sightseer** *noun*

sign *noun* 1 an object, event, or thing said that shows the existence of something ♦ *There are signs of corrosion in the bodywork.* SYNONYMS: indication, suggestion, clue, hint; (of something about to happen) portent, omen, presage. 2 a mark, device, or symbol that has a special meaning. SYNONYMS: mark, device, symbol, emblem. 3 a board or notice that gives information or an instruction ♦ *a road sign.* 4 an action or movement that gives information or a command etc.

SYNONYMS: signal, gesture, cue. **5** each of the twelve divisions of the zodiac, or the symbol representing it.

sign *verb* **1** to write your name on a document as an identification or authorization. **2** to agree to a contract by signing your name. **3** to engage someone, or to be engaged, as an employee by signing a contract of employment. **4** to make a sign ♦ *She signed to me to come.* **5** to use sign language. **to sign off** (in broadcasting) to announce the end of a programme or transmission. **to sign on** to register as unemployed and claim state benefit. **to sign up** to sign a contract of employment, enrol for a course, etc. [from a Latin word *signum* meaning 'a mark']

signal *noun* **1** an action, sound, or gesture giving information or an instruction. SYNONYMS: sign, gesture, cue. **2** a message made up of such things. **3** an act or event that provides a stimulus for something to happen ♦ *The athletes' arrival was the signal for an outburst of cheering.* **4** a semaphore or set of lights on a road or railway, giving instructions to drivers as to whether they can continue. **5** a sequence of electrical impulses or radio waves.
signal *verb* (**signalled, signalling**) **1** to make a signal or signals. SYNONYMS: gesture, indicate, motion. **2** to give someone information or an instruction in this way.
signal *adjective* very good or bad ♦ *a signal success.* **signaller** *noun* **signally** *adverb* [same origin as for *sign*]

signal box *noun* a building from which railway signals, points, etc., are controlled.

signalman *noun* (**signalmen**) a person who controls railway signals.

signatory (sig-nə-ter-i) *noun* (**signatories**) a person, organization, or country that signs a treaty or agreement.

signature *noun* **1** a person's name or initials written in signing something. **2** (*Music*) a set of sharps and flats after the clef in a score, showing the key in which the music is written (the **key signature**), or the sign, often a fraction such as $\frac{3}{4}$ (the **time signature**), showing the number of beats in the bar and their rhythm. [same origin as for *sign*]

signature tune *noun* a special tune used to announce a particular programme or performer.

signboard *noun* a board showing the name or logo of a shop or business.

signet (sig-nit) *noun* a small seal used with or instead of a signature. [same origin as for *sign*]

signet ring *noun* a ring with an engraved design, formerly used as a seal.

significance *noun* **1** what something means ♦ *What is the significance of this symbol?* SYNONYMS: meaning, signification. **2** importance ♦ *The event is of no significance.* SYNONYMS: importance, consequence, moment, relevance.

significant *adjective* **1** having a meaning, indicating something. **2** full of meaning ♦ *She gave him a significant glance.* **3** important or noteworthy ♦ *There have been some significant developments.* **significantly** *adverb*

signification *noun* meaning.

signify *verb* (**signifies, signified, signifying**) **1** to be a sign or symbol of something. SYNONYMS: represent, indicate, stand for, betoken. **2** to have something as a meaning. SYNONYMS: mean, denote. **3** to indicate something or make it known ♦ *She signified her approval.* **4** to be important, to matter ♦ *It doesn't signify.* [from a Latin word *signum* meaning 'sign']

sign language or **signing** *noun* a system of communication by gestures with the face and hands, used by and to deaf people.

signor (seen-yor) *noun* the title of an Italian-speaking man, equivalent to 'Mr' or 'sir'.

signora (seen-yor-ə) *noun* the title of an Italian-speaking married woman, equivalent to 'Mrs' or 'madam'.

signorina (seen-yor-een-ə) *noun* the title of an Italian-speaking unmarried woman or girl, equivalent to 'Miss'.

signpost *noun* a sign on a post at a road junction etc. showing the names of places along each road.
signpost *verb* to provide a road with a signpost.

Sikh (seek) *noun* a member of an Indian religion founded in northern India, believing in one God and including some beliefs of Hinduism and Islam. **Sikhism** *noun* [from a Hindi word meaning 'disciple']

silage (siy-lij) *noun* fodder made from green crops stored and fermented in a silo.

silence *noun* 1 absence of sound. SYNONYMS: quiet, stillness, hush. 2 avoidance or absence of speaking or of making a sound. 3 not mentioning something or revealing information.
silence *verb* to make a person or thing silent. **in silence** without speaking or making a sound.

silencer *noun* a device for reducing the sound made by something, especially a gun or a vehicle's exhaust system.

silent *adjective* 1 not making or accompanied by a sound. SYNONYMS: quiet, noiseless. 2 not speaking. 3 (said about a person) tending to say little. **silently** *adverb* [from a Latin word *silere* meaning 'to be silent']

silhouette (sil-oo-et) *noun* 1 a dark shadow or outline seen against a light background. 2 a portrait of a person in profile, showing the shape and outline only in solid black.
silhouette *verb* to show a person or thing as a silhouette ♦ *He was silhouetted against the screen.* [named after the French author and politician Étienne de Silhouette (1709–67), who made paper cut-outs of people's profiles from their shadows]

silica (sil-i-kə) *noun* a hard white compound of silicon which occurs as quartz or flint and in sandstone and other rocks. **siliceous** (sil-ish-əs) *adjective* [from a Latin word *silicis* meaning 'of flint']

silicate (sil-i-kayt) *noun* a mineral consisting of silica combined with metal oxides, which occurs in rocks.

silicon (sil-i-kən) *noun* a chemical element (symbol Si), found widely in the earth's crust and used to make transistors and electrical circuits.

silicon chip *noun* a microchip made of silicon.

silicone (sil-i-kohn) *noun* a compound of silicon used in paints, varnish, and lubricants.

silicosis (sil-i-koh-sis) *noun* an abnormal condition of the lungs caused by breathing in dust that contains silica.

silk *noun* 1 a fine strong soft fibre produced by silkworms in making cocoons. 2 thread or cloth made from this fibre. 3 clothing made from silk. 4 (*informal*) a Queen's Counsel, entitled to wear a silk gown. 5 fine soft strands like threads of silk. **to take silk** to become a Queen's Counsel. [from an Old English word *sioloc*, from a Latin word *sericum*]

silken *adjective* like silk.

silkworm *noun* the caterpillar of a kind of moth, which feeds on mulberry leaves and spins a cocoon of silk.

silky *adjective* (**silkier, silkiest**) soft, fine, or smooth like silk. **silkily** *adverb* **silkiness** *noun*

sill *noun* 1 a strip of stone, wood, or metal at the foot of a window or door. 2 (*Geology*) a sheet of igneous rock that intrudes between existing strata. [from an Old English word *syll*]

silly *adjective* (**sillier, silliest**) 1 lacking good sense, foolish or unwise. SYNONYMS: foolish, unwise, senseless, ridiculous, absurd; (*informal*) crazy, mad. 2 feeble-minded. 3 (in cricket, said about a fielder's position) close to the batsman ♦ *silly mid-on*.
silly *noun* (**sillies**) (*informal*) a foolish person. **silliness** *noun* [from an earlier meaning 'feeble', from an older word *seely* meaning 'happy or fortunate']

silo (siy-loh) *noun* (**silos**) 1 an airtight pit or other container in which green crops are pressed and fermented for use as fodder. 2 a pit or tower for storing grain, cement, or radioactive waste. 3 an underground place where a missile is kept ready for firing. [via Spanish from a Greek word *siros* meaning 'corn pit']

silt *noun* sediment deposited by running water in a channel or harbour etc.
silt *verb* to fill or block a place with silt, or to become blocked with silt. [origin unknown]

silver *noun* 1 a shiny white precious metal, a chemical element (symbol Ag). 2 coins made of this or of a silver-coloured metal. 3 silver dishes or ornaments, or household cutlery of any metal. 4 a silver medal, usually given as second prize. 5 the colour of silver.
silver *adjective* made of silver; coloured like silver.
silver *verb* 1 to coat or plate something with silver. 2 to give a silvery appearance to something. 3 to become silvery or grey. **born with a silver spoon in your mouth** to be born into a wealthy family of high social standing. [from an Old English word *seolfor*]

silver birch noun a birch tree with a silver-coloured bark.

silverfish noun (**silverfish** or **silverfishes**) a small insect with a fish-like body found in books and damp places.

silver jubilee noun the 25th anniversary of an event.

silver plate noun a thin layer of silver applied as a coating to another metal.

silver sand noun very fine sand used in gardening.

silverside noun a joint of beef cut from the upper part of the leg.

silversmith noun a person who makes articles in silver.

silverware noun articles made of silver.

silver wedding noun the 25th anniversary of a wedding.

silvery adjective 1 like silver in colour or appearance. 2 having a clear gentle ringing sound.

simian (sim-iən) adjective like a monkey. [from a Latin word simia meaning 'monkey']

similar adjective 1 like or resembling another person or thing but not identical. 2 of the same kind, nature, or amount. 3 (Geometry) (said about figures) having the same shape but not the same size. **similarly** adverb **similarity** (sim-i-la-riti) noun [from a Latin word similis meaning 'like']

simile (sim-i-li) noun a figure of speech in which one thing is compared to another, as in He's as fit as a fiddle and They went through it like a hot knife through butter. [same origin as for similar]

similitude (sim-il-i-tewd) noun being similar, similarity.

simmer verb 1 to boil something gently. 2 to be in a state of excitement or anger which is only just kept under control. **to simmer down** to become less excited or agitated. [from a dialect word simper]

simnel cake noun a rich fruit cake covered with marzipan, eaten at Easter or during Lent. [via French from a Latin word simila meaning 'fine flour']

simony (siy-mən-i) noun the buying or selling of church positions or privileges. [named after Simon Magus, who offered the apostles money in exchange for the gift of healing (Acts 8:18)]

simoom (sim-oom) noun a hot dry dust-laden wind in the desert. [from an Arabic word samma meaning 'to poison']

simper verb to smile in a coy or affected way.
simper noun an affected smile. [origin unknown]

simple adjective 1 not complicated or difficult, easy to understand or do ♦ a simple question. SYNONYMS: easy, straightforward, elementary. 2 not elaborate or luxurious, plain ♦ a simple house. SYNONYMS: plain, undecorated, modest, austere. 3 consisting of one element or kind, not compound or complex. 4 foolish or inexperienced. 5 feeble-minded. 6 of humble rank ♦ simple ordinary people. [from a Latin word simplus]

simple harmonic motion noun (Physics) a regular oscillating motion such as that of a weight bouncing from a spring or a string vibrating on a musical instrument.

simple interest noun interest paid only on the original capital, not on the interest added to it.

simple-minded adjective unintelligent or foolish.

simple time noun (Music) time with two, three, or four crotchets or quavers in each bar.

simpleton noun a foolish or gullible person.

simplicity noun being simple.

simplify verb (**simplifies, simplified, simplifying**) to make something simple or more simple. **simplification** noun

simplistic adjective treating complicated things as being more simple than they are.
◊ This word does not mean the same as simple.

simply adverb 1 in a simple manner. 2 absolutely, without doubt ♦ The food was simply delicious. 3 merely ♦ It is simply the truth.

simulate verb 1 to reproduce the appearance or conditions of something. SYNONYMS: reproduce, replicate. 2 to pretend to have or feel something ♦ They simulated indignation. SYNONYMS: pretend, affect, feign, fake. **simulation** noun **simulator** noun [same origin as for similar]

simultaneous (sim-əl-tayn-iəs) adjective occurring or done at the same time.

simultaneously adverb **simultaneity** (sim-əl-tən-ee-iti) noun [from a Latin word simul meaning 'at the same time']

simultaneous equations plural noun (Mathematics) equations involving two or more variables that have the same value in each equation.

sin[1] noun 1 the breaking of a religious or moral law, or an act which does this. SYNONYMS: wrong, wrongdoing. 2 a serious fault or offence.
sin verb (**sinned, sinning**) to commit a sin. [from an Old English word synn]

sin[2] abbreviation (Mathematics) sine.

sin bin noun (informal) 1 (in hockey and some other games) a place by the side of the pitch where players who have committed an offence are sent for a time as a penalty. 2 a detention centre.

since conjunction 1 from the time when ♦ Where have you been since we last met? 2 because ♦ Since we've missed the bus we'll have to walk home.
since preposition from a certain time ♦ She has been here since Sunday.
since adverb 1 between then and now ♦ He ran away and hasn't been seen since. 2 ago ♦ It all happened long since. [from an Old English word sithon meaning 'then']

sincere adjective having or arising from genuine feelings, free from pretence ♦ my sincere thanks. SYNONYMS: genuine, frank, honest, earnest, heartfelt. **sincerity** (sin-se-ri-ti) noun **sincerely** adverb [from a Latin word sincerus meaning 'pure']

sine noun (Mathematics) (in a right-angled triangle) the ratio of the length of a side opposite one of the acute angles to the length of the hypotenuse. [from a Latin word sinus meaning 'curve']

sinecure (siy-ni-kewr) noun a position that gives payment or honour without the need for any work. [from a Latin phrase sine cura meaning 'without care']

sinew (sin-yoo) noun 1 tough fibrous tissue that connects muscle to bone. 2 a tendon. **sinews** plural noun the part of a structure that gives it its strength. **sinewy** adjective [from an Old English word sinewe meaning 'tendon']

sinful adjective 1 guilty of sin. 2 wicked. **sinfully** adverb **sinfulness** noun

sing verb (**sang, sung**) 1 to make musical sounds with the voice, especially in a set tune. 2 to perform a song. 3 to make an attractive whistling or humming sound. 4 (informal) to act as an informer. **to sing someone's praises** to praise someone greatly. **to sing out** to call out loudly. [from an Old English word singan]

singe (sinj) verb (**singed, singeing**) to burn something slightly, or to become burnt, especially at the edges.
singe noun a slight burn. [from an Old English word sencgan]

singer noun a person who sings, especially as a professional.

Singhalese another spelling of Sinhalese.

single adjective 1 one only, not double or multiple. SYNONYMS: sole, solitary. 2 designed for one person or thing ♦ a single bed. 3 taken separately ♦ every single thing. 4 (said about a person) unmarried. 5 (said about a ticket) valid for a journey to a place but not to return. 6 (said about a flower) having only one circle of petals.
single noun 1 a single person or thing. 2 a short record with one piece of music on each side. 3 a room etc. for one person. 4 a single ticket. 5 (in cricket) a hit for one run.
single verb to choose or distinguish one from others ♦ They singled him out for comment. SYNONYMS: choose, pick, decide on, opt for, select.
singles plural noun a game of tennis or badminton with one player on each side.
singly adverb [via Old French from a Latin word singulus]

single-breasted adjective (said about a jacket or coat) fastening at the front with a single row of buttons down the centre and not overlapping across the breast.

single combat noun fighting between two people.

single-decker noun a bus with one deck.

single figures noun any of the numbers from 1 to 9, as a total.

single file noun a line of people one behind the other.

single-handed adjective without help from anyone else. SYNONYMS: unaided, unassisted. **single-handedly** adverb

single-minded adjective with your mind set on a single purpose. SYNONYMS: resolute, determined, dogged.

single parent noun a person bringing up a child or children without a partner.

singlet noun a vest or similar sleeveless piece of clothing worn by a man.

singleton (sing-gəl-tən) *noun* something occurring singly, not as one of a group.

sing-song *adjective* having a monotonous tone of voice or rhythm.
sing-song *noun* (*informal*) an informal gathering for singing.

singular *adjective* 1 (*Grammar*) (said about a form of a noun or verb) used when it refers to one person or thing ♦ *The singular form is 'child' and the plural form is 'children'.* 2 unusual or exceptional ♦ *A person of singular courage.* SYNONYMS: unusual, exceptional, remarkable, peculiar.
singular *noun* (*Grammar*) a singular form or word. **singularity** (sing-gyoo-la-riti) *noun* **singularly** *adverb* [from a Latin word *singulus* meaning 'single']

Sinhalese (sin-hə-leez) *adjective* to do with an Indian people who form the majority of the population of Sri Lanka, or to do with their language.
Sinhalese *noun* (**Sinhalese**) 1 a Sinhalese person. 2 the Sinhalese language. [from a Sanskrit word *Sinhala* meaning 'Sri Lanka']

sinister *adjective* 1 suggestive of harm or evil. SYNONYMS: menacing, threatening, ominous. 2 involving wickedness, criminal ♦ *sinister motives.* SYNONYMS: criminal, wicked, evil, nefarious. [from a Latin word *sinister* meaning 'on the left' (which was thought to be unlucky)]

sink *verb* (**sank, sunk**) 1 to go down below the surface of a liquid or (said about a ship) to the bottom of the sea; to cause something to do this. 2 to fall slowly downwards, to come gradually to a lower level or pitch. SYNONYMS: drop, fall, descend, go down. 3 to pass into a less active state or condition ♦ *She gradually sank into sleep.* 4 to decline in amount or strength gradually. SYNONYMS: decline, deteriorate, decrease, fade, languish. 5 to suppress or ignore a feeling ♦ *They agreed to sink their differences.* 6 to cause something sharp to penetrate a surface. 7 to dig a well or bore a shaft. 8 to engrave a die. 9 to send a ball into a pocket or hole in billiards, golf, etc. 10 to invest money.
sink *noun* a fixed basin with a water supply and drainage pipe. **to sink in** 1 to penetrate a surface. 2 to become understood. **a sinking feeling** a feeling caused by worry or fear. [from an Old English word *sincan*]

sinker *noun* a weight used to sink a fishing line or a line used in taking soundings.

sinkhole *noun* a pool or marsh into which the water from a stream flows and disappears by evaporating or by percolating into the underlying soil.

sinking fund *noun* a fund formed by putting aside money over a period of time in order to repay a debt or replace an asset.

sinless *adjective* free from sin.

sinner *noun* a person who sins.

Sino- (siy-noh-) *prefix* Chinese (and) ♦ *Sino-Japanese* ♦ *Sino-Tibetan.* [from a Greek word *Sinai* meaning 'the Chinese']

sinter *noun* (*Geology*) a solid mass or hard deposit.
sinter *verb* to cause a powdery substance to form into a solid mass by heating, or (said about the substance) to become solid in this way. [from a German word *Sinter* (noun)]

sinuous (sin-yoo-əs) *adjective* having many curves or bends. **sinuously** *adverb* [same origin as for *sinus*]

sinus (siy-nəs) *noun* a cavity in bone or tissue, especially that in the skull connecting with the nostrils. [a Latin word meaning 'curve']

sinusitis (siy-nəs-iy-tiss) *noun* inflammation of a sinus.

sip *verb* (**sipped, sipping**) to take a small mouthful of liquid; to drink liquid in small mouthfuls.
sip *noun* 1 the act of sipping. 2 a small mouthful of liquid. [probably from *sup*]

siphon (siy-fən) *noun* 1 a pipe or tube in the form of an upside-down U, used for forcing liquid to flow from one container to another at a lower level by means of atmospheric pressure. 2 a bottle from which aerated water is forced out through a tube by pressure of gas. 3 the sucking tube of some insects or small animals.
siphon *verb* 1 to flow through a siphon, or to draw liquid through a siphon. 2 to take small amounts of something, especially illicitly ♦ *We have been siphoning off funds for this purpose.* [from a Greek word meaning 'pipe']

sir *noun* a polite form of address to a man.
Sir *noun* a title used before the name of a knight or baronet ♦ *Sir John Moore.* [from *sire*]

sire *noun* 1 the male parent of an animal. 2 (*literary*) a father or male ancestor. 3 (*old* *use*) a title used to address a king.

sire *verb* (said about an animal) to be the sire of young. [same origin as for *senior*]

siren *noun* **1** a device that makes a long loud sound as a signal. **2** a dangerously attractive woman. [named after the Sirens in Greek legend, women who lived on an island and by their singing lured seafarers to destruction on the rocks]

sirloin *noun* the best part of a loin of beef. [from *sur-* meaning 'over' and *loin*]

sirocco (si-rok-oh) *noun* (**siroccos**) a hot dry wind that reaches southern Europe from Africa. [from an Arabic word meaning 'east wind']

sisal (siy-səl) *noun* fibre made from the leaves of a tropical plant, used for making ropes. [named after Sisal, a port in Morocco from which it was exported]

sissy *noun* (**sissies**) (*informal*) a timid or cowardly person. [from *sis* meaning 'sister']

sister *noun* **1** a daughter of the same parents as another person. **2** a woman who is a fellow member of a group or organization. **3** a member of a religious order of women. **4** a female hospital nurse in charge of other nurses. **5** (used before a noun) denoting an organization that is of the same kind as another or under the same ownership ♦ *a sister company*. **sisterly** *adjective* [from an Old English word]

sisterhood *noun* **1** the relationship of sisters. **2** friendliness and companionship between women. **3** a society or association of women, or its members.

sister-in-law *noun* (**sisters-in-law**) the sister of a married person's husband or wife, or the wife of a person's brother.

sit *verb* (past tense and past participle **sat**; **sitting**) **1** to take a position or be in a position in which the body rests more or less upright on the buttocks. **2** to put someone in a sitting position ♦ *She sat him down on a stool.* **3** to pose for a portrait. **4** (said about an animal) to rest with its legs bent and its body close to the ground. **5** (said about a bird) to stay on its nest to hatch eggs. **6** to be situated, to lie. **7** to be a candidate for an examination ♦ *She wants to sit for a scholarship.* **8** to occupy a seat as a member of a committee etc. **9** (said about Parliament or a law court or committee) to be assembled for business. **10** (said about clothes) to fit in a certain

way ♦ *The coat sits badly on the shoulders.* **to sit back** to relax your efforts. **to sit down** to take a seat after standing. **to sit on the fence** to avoid taking sides in a dispute. **to sit something out 1** to take no part in a dance etc. **2** to stay till the end of something unpleasant or not enjoyable. **to sit tight** (*informal*) **1** to remain firmly where you are. **2** to take no action and not give way. **to sit up 1** to rise to a sitting posture from lying down or slouching. **2** to refrain from going to bed until later than usual ♦ *They sat up late watching television.* [from an Old English word *sittan*]

sitar (sit-ar or si-tar) *noun* an Indian stringed musical instrument with a long neck, played by plucking. [a Hindi word meaning 'three-stringed']

sitcom *noun* (*informal*) a situation comedy.

sit-down *adjective* **1** (said about a meal) eaten sitting down at a table. **2** (said about a protest or strike) in which the people demonstrating occupy a place or sit on the ground, refusing to leave until their demands are met.

site *noun* **1** an area of ground on which a town or building stood or stands or is going to be built. SYNONYMS: location, position. **2** the place where a certain activity or event takes place or took place ♦ *a camping site* ♦ *the site of the battle.* **site** *verb* to locate or build something in a certain place. SYNONYMS: locate, position, situate, place. [from a Latin word *situs* meaning 'position']
◊ Do not confuse this word with **sight**, which has a different meaning.

sit-in *noun* the occupation of a building by protesters or demonstrators.

sitter *noun* **1** a person who is sitting, especially for a portrait. **2** a hen that is sitting on a nest. **3** a person who looks after children, pets, or a house while the owners are away. **4** (*informal*) something very easy, especially in sport.

sitting *noun* **1** the time when people are served a meal. **2** the time when a parliament or committee is conducting business.

sitting duck *noun* (*informal*) a person or thing that is a helpless victim of attack.

sitting room *noun* a room used for sitting in comfortably.

sitting tenant *noun* a tenant who is already living in premises when there is a change of owner.

situate *verb* to place or put something in a certain position. SYNONYMS: locate, position, site, place. **to be situated** to be in a certain position or circumstances. [from a Latin word *situs* meaning 'site']

situation *noun* 1 a place, together with its surroundings, that is occupied by something. SYNONYMS: location, position, site. 2 a set of circumstances. 3 a job. [same origin as for *site*]

situation comedy *noun* a radio or television comedy in which the humour comes from the characters' misunderstandings and embarrassments.

six *adjective & noun* the number 6, one more than five. **at sixes and sevens** in disorder. **to hit** or **knock someone for six** (*informal*) to surprise or defeat someone utterly.

sixer *noun* the leader of a group of six Brownies or Cub Scouts.

sixfold *adjective & adverb* 1 six times as much or as many. 2 consisting of six parts.

sixpence *noun* (*old use*) the sum of 6d. (2½ p), or a coin worth this, before decimalization (1971).

sixpenny *adjective* costing sixpence, especially before decimalization (1971).

sixteen *adjective & noun* the number 16, one more than fifteen. **sixteenth** *adjective & noun*

sixth *adjective & noun* 1 next after fifth. 2 one of six equal parts of a thing. 3 (*Music*) an interval or chord spanning six alphabetical notes, e.g. C to A. **sixthly** *adverb*

sixth form *noun* a form for pupils aged 16–18 in a secondary school.

sixth sense *noun* a supposed extra power of perception other than the five physical ones, intuition.

sixty *adjective & noun* (**sixties**) the number 60, six times ten. **sixties** *plural noun* the numbers from 60 to 69, especially representing years of age or degrees of temperature. **sixtieth** *adjective & noun*

size [1] *noun* 1 the measurements or extent of something. SYNONYMS: extent, dimensions, magnitude, proportions. 2 any of a series of standard measurements in which some things are made ♦ *a size eight shoe.*

size *verb* to group or sort things according to their size. **to size something** or **someone up** 1 to estimate the size of a person or thing. 2 (*informal*) to form a judgement of a person or situation etc. **that's the size of it** (*informal*) that's the way it is, those are the facts about it. [from an earlier meaning 'a law fixing the amount of a tax', from an Old French word *assise* meaning 'law' or 'court session']

size [2] *noun* a gluey substance used to glaze paper or stiffen cloth etc.
size *verb* to treat something with size. [origin unknown]

sizeable *adjective* large or fairly large in size.

sizzle *verb* 1 (said about food) to make a hissing sound when frying or roasting. 2 (*informal*) to be very hot. 3 (*informal*) to be angry or resentful. [an imitation of the sound]

sjambok (**sham**-bok) *noun* (in South Africa) a whip made of rhinoceros hide.
sjambok *verb* (**sjambokked, sjambokking**) to hit or beat someone with a sjambok. [an Afrikaans word]

skate [1] *noun* 1 a shoe or boot with a steel blade attached to the sole, used for sliding smoothly on ice. 2 a rollerskate.
skate *verb* 1 to move on skates. 2 to perform a figure in this way. **to get your skates on** (*informal*) to make haste. **to skate over** to ignore a subject or refer to it only briefly. **skater** *noun* [from a Dutch word *schaats*]

skate [2] *noun* (**skate**) a large flat sea fish used for food. [from an Old Norse word *skata*]

skateboard *noun* a short narrow board with wheels like rollerskates, for riding on while standing or crouching. **skateboarder** *noun* **skateboarding** *noun*

skating rink *noun* 1 a stretch of natural or artificial ice used for skating. 2 a smooth area used for rollerskating.

skedaddle *verb* (*informal*) to go away quickly. [origin unknown]

skein (skayn) *noun* 1 a loosely coiled bundle of yarn or thread. 2 a number of wild geese or swans in flight. [origin unknown]

skeletal (**skel**-i-təl) *adjective* 1 of or like a skeleton. 2 existing only as an outline or framework.

skeleton noun 1 the framework of bones that support a human or animal body. 2 the shell or other hard structure covering or supporting an invertebrate animal. 3 a very thin or emaciated person or animal. 4 a framework, e.g. of a building. 5 an outline of a literary work etc. 6 (used before a noun) reduced to the minimum needed ♦ a skeleton crew. **a skeleton in the cupboard** a discreditable secret. [from a Greek word skeletos meaning 'dried up']

skeleton key noun a key designed to fit several locks.

sketch noun 1 a rough drawing or painting. 2 a brief account or description of something. SYNONYMS: outline, summary, draft. 3 a short humorous play. **sketch** verb to make a sketch of something. **sketcher** noun [from a Greek word skhedios meaning 'done without preparation']

sketchbook noun a pad of drawing paper for sketching on.

sketch map noun a roughly drawn map.

sketchy adjective (**sketchier, sketchiest**) rough and lacking detail. **sketchily** adverb **sketchiness** noun

skew adjective slanting or askew. **skew** verb to make something skew, to turn or twist something round. **on the skew** askew. [from an Old French word eskiuwer]

skewbald adjective (said about a horse) having irregular patches of white and another colour (strictly, not including black). (Compare **piebald**.) [from an obsolete word skewed, with the same meaning]

skewed distribution noun (Statistics) a statistical distribution that is not symmetrical.

skewer noun a long pin for holding pieces of food together during cooking. **skewer** verb to pierce or hold something in place with a skewer or other pointed object. [origin unknown]

ski noun (**skis**) 1 each of a pair of long narrow strips of wood, metal, or plastic fitted under the feet for travelling over snow. 2 a similar device fitted to a vehicle or aircraft.

ski verb (**skis, skied, skiing**) to travel over snow on skis. **skier** noun [a Norwegian word, from an Old Norse word skith meaning 'snow shoe']

skid verb (**skidded, skidding**) (said about a vehicle) to slide on slippery ground, usually after severe braking or sharp turning. **skid** noun 1 an act of skidding, a skidding movement. 2 (North Amer.) a log or beam over which heavy objects are dragged or rolled. 3 a runner on a helicopter, for use in landing. 4 a wooden or metal shoe that acts as a braking device on the wheel of a cart. **on the skids** (informal) in a bad state; failing. **to put the skids under someone** (informal) to hasten the downfall of someone or something. [probably related to ski]

skidpan noun a slippery surface where drivers can practise controlling skidding vehicles.

skid row noun (informal) a slum area where vagrants live.

skiff noun a small light boat for one person, used for rowing or sculling. [from a French word esquif, related to ship]

ski jump noun a steep slope with a sharp drop where it levels out at the bottom, for skiers to leap through the air and land further down, as a sport.

skilful adjective having or showing skill. SYNONYMS: capable, able, expert, accomplished, proficient, competent, adept, talented. **skilfully** adverb

ski lift noun a device for carrying skiers up a slope, usually on seats hanging from an overhead cable.

skill noun ability to do something well, expertise. SYNONYMS: ability, expertise, proficiency, competence, talent. [from an Old Norse word skil meaning 'knowledge']

skilled adjective 1 having or showing skill, skilful. 2 (said about work) needing a special skill or training.

skillet noun 1 a metal cooking pot with a long handle and usually legs. 2 (North Amer.) a frying pan. [via Old French from a Latin word scutella]

skim verb (**skimmed, skimming**) 1 to remove something from the surface of a liquid, or to clear a liquid in this way. 2 to move lightly and quickly over a surface or through the air. 3 to read something quickly to get the main points. [from an Old French word *escume* meaning 'scum']

skimmed milk *noun* milk from which the cream has been removed.

skimp *verb* to supply or use less than is needed, to scrimp ♦ *Don't skimp on food.* [origin unknown]

skimpy *adjective* (**skimpier, skimpiest**) scanty or too small. **skimpily** *adverb* **skimpiness** *noun*

skin *noun* 1 the thin layer of tissue covering the body of a human or animal. 2 the skin removed from a dead animal, used as a material for clothing or other covering. SYNONYMS: hide, fleece, pelt. 3 a vessel for water or wine, made from an animal's whole skin. 4 a person's complexion. 5 an outer layer or covering, e.g. of a fruit. SYNONYMS: covering, film; (of fruit) peel, rind. 6 a thin film that forms on the surface of a liquid. **skin** *verb* (**skinned, skinning**) 1 to strip or scrape the skin from something. 2 to cover something with new skin, or to become covered with new skin ♦ *The wound had skinned over.* **by the skin of your teeth** only just, barely. **to get under someone's skin** (*informal*) to annoy or obsess someone. **to save your skin** to escape injury or loss. [via Old English from an Old Norse word *skinn*]

skin-deep *adjective* not substantial or lasting, superficial.

skin diving *noun* the sport of swimming underwater without a diving suit, using flippers and a breathing apparatus. **skin diver** *noun*

skinflint *noun* (*informal*) a miserly person.

skinhead *noun* a young person with closely cropped hair.

skinny *adjective* (**skinnier, skinniest**) 1 (said about a person or animal) very thin. SYNONYMS: bony, gaunt, emaciated. 2 (said about clothing) tight-fitting.

skinny-dip *verb* (**skinny-dipped, skinny-dipping**) (*informal*) to swim naked.

skint *adjective* (*informal*) having no money left.

skintight *adjective* (said about clothing) very close-fitting.

skip [1] *verb* (**skipped, skipping**) 1 to move along lightly, especially by hopping on each foot in turn. 2 to jump with a skipping rope. 3 to pass quickly from one subject or point to another. 4 to omit something ♦ *You can skip chapter six.* SYNONYMS: omit, disregard, leave out, ignore, pass over. 5 (*informal*) to go away hastily or secretly. **skip** *noun* a skipping movement. [probably from a Scandinavian language]

skip [2] *noun* 1 a large open-topped metal container for carrying away builders' rubbish or other bulky refuse. 2 a cage or bucket in which people or materials are raised and lowered in mines and quarries. [from an Old Norse word *skeppa* meaning 'basket']

skipper [1] *noun* (*informal*) a captain. **skipper** *verb* to captain a crew or team. [from a German or Dutch word *schip* meaning 'ship']

skipper [2] *noun* 1 someone who skips. 2 a small dark butterfly with a thick body.

skipping rope *noun* a length of rope with a handle at each end, that you turn over your head and under your feet as you jump, for exercise or play.

skirl *noun* a shrill sound like that made by bagpipes. **skirl** *verb* to make this sound. [probably from a Scandinavian language]

skirmish *noun* a small fight or conflict. **skirmish** *verb* to take part in a skirmish. [from an Old French word *eskirmir*]

skirt *noun* 1 a woman's piece of clothing hanging from the waist. 2 the part of a dress or coat below the waist. 3 a covering that protects the wheels or underside of a vehicle or aircraft. 4 the hanging part round the base of a hovercraft, containing the air cushion. 5 a cut of beef from the lower flank. 6 a flap on a horse's saddle covering the bar from which the stirrup hangs. **skirt** *verb* 1 to go or be situated along the edge of something. 2 to avoid dealing directly with a difficult question, controversial topic, etc. [from an Old Norse word *skyrta* meaning 'shirt']

skirting or **skirting board** *noun* a wooden board running round the wall of a room, close to the floor.

ski run *noun* a slope suitable for skiing down as a sport.

skit *noun* a short comedy sketch or parody ♦ *He wrote a skit on Hamlet.* [origin unknown]

skittish *adjective* playful or frisky.

skittishly adverb **skittishness** noun [origin unknown]

skittle noun each of the wooden bottle-shaped objects that players try to knock down in a game of **skittles**.
skittle verb to knock something over as if in a game of skittles. [origin unknown]

skive verb (informal) to avoid work or a duty. **skiver** noun [probably from a French word esquiver meaning 'to dodge']

skivvy noun (**skivvies**) (informal) 1 a lowly female servant. 2 a person doing menial work. [origin unknown]

skua (**skew-ǝ**) noun a seabird like a large gull. [from an Old Norse word skufr]

skulduggery noun dishonest behaviour or trickery. [from a Scots word sculduddery]

skulk verb to loiter or move about stealthily. [probably from a Scandinavian language]

skull noun 1 a framework of bones in the head, or the part of this protecting the brain. 2 a representation of a skull. **skull and crossbones** a picture of a skull with two thigh bones crossed below it as an emblem of death or piracy, or as a warning symbol. [probably from a Scandinavian language]

skullcap noun a small close-fitting cap with no peak, worn on top of the head.

skunk noun a North American animal with black and white fur that can spray a bad-smelling liquid from glands near its tail. [from an Abnaki (Native American) word]

sky noun (**skies**) 1 the region of the atmosphere seen from the earth, appearing blue in fine weather. 2 a climate or type of weather seen in the sky ♦ the sunny skies of Italy.
sky verb (**skies, skied, skying**) to hit a ball high in the air. [from an Old Norse word sky meaning 'cloud']

sky blue adjective & noun bright clear blue.

skydiving noun the sport of jumping from an aircraft and floating down or performing acrobatics in the air under free fall, opening a parachute at the last safe moment.

sky-high adjective & adverb very high.

skyjack verb to hijack an aircraft.

skylark noun a lark that sings while it hovers high in the air.

skylark verb to play about light-heartedly.

skylight noun a window in a roof or ceiling.

skyline noun the outline of land or buildings seen against the sky.

skyrocket noun a rocket that rises high into the air before exploding, used as a signal or firework.
skyrocket verb (**skyrocketed, skyrocketing**) (informal) to increase sharply.

skyscape noun a picture or view of the sky.

skyscraper noun a very tall building of many storeys.

skyward adjective & adverb towards the sky. **skywards** adverb

slab noun a thick flat piece of something solid. SYNONYMS: block, chunk. [origin unknown]

slack [1] adjective 1 loose, not held tight. SYNONYMS: loose, limp. 2 careless or negligent. SYNONYMS: careless, negligent, lax. 3 (said about trade or business) with little happening, not busy.
slack noun the slack part of a rope etc. ♦ to pull in the slack.
slack verb 1 to slacken. 2 to avoid work or be lazy. **slacker** noun **slackly** adverb **slackness** noun [from an Old English word slæc meaning 'inclined to be lazy']

slack [2] noun coal dust or small pieces of coal. [origin unknown]

slacken verb to make something slack, or to become slack.

slacks plural noun trousers for casual or sports wear.

slag noun waste matter separated from metal in smelting.

slag heap noun a mound of waste matter from a mine or industrial site.

slain past participle of **slay**.

slake verb 1 to quench your thirst. 2 to combine quicklime chemically with water to produce calcium hydroxide. [from an Old English word slacian meaning 'to become less eager']

slalom (**slah-lǝm**) noun 1 a ski race down a winding course marked by poles. 2 an obstacle race in canoes. [from Norwegian words sla meaning 'sloping' and lom meaning 'track']

slam verb (**slammed, slamming**) 1 to shut something forcefully with a loud noise. 2 to put or hit something forcefully. 3 (informal) to criticize someone severely.

slam noun 1 a slamming noise. 2 (in bridge) the winning of 12 tricks (**small slam**) or 13 tricks (**grand slam**). [probably from a Scandinavian language]

slander noun the act or crime of making a false spoken statement that damages a person's reputation.
slander verb to utter a slander about someone. **slanderous** adjective **slanderously** adverb [from an Old French word esclandre, related to scandal]

slang noun informal language used mostly in speech and often restricted to a particular social group ♦ youth slang. **slangy** adjective [origin unknown]

slanging match noun a long noisy argument in which people exchange insults.

slant verb 1 to slope. SYNONYMS: slope, incline, lean. 2 to present news or information from a particular point of view. SYNONYMS: misrepresent, colour, twist. **slant** noun 1 a slope. SYNONYMS: slope, incline, gradient. 2 the way something is presented, an attitude or bias. SYNONYMS: attitude, angle, bias, viewpoint, perspective. [probably from a Scandinavian language]

slantwise adjective & adverb in a slanting position.

slap verb (**slapped, slapping**) 1 to strike someone with the open hand or with something flat. SYNONYMS: smack, hit. 2 to put something down forcefully ♦ She slapped the money on the table. 3 to apply something hastily or carelessly ♦ We'll have to slap some paint on the walls. **slap** noun a blow with the open hand or with something flat. **slap** adverb suddenly or directly ♦ Then I ran slap into him. [an imitation of the sound]

slapdash adjective hasty and careless. SYNONYMS: careless, slovenly. **slapdash** adverb in a slapdash way.

slap-happy adjective (informal) cheerfully casual or irresponsible.

slapstick noun comedy with contrived mishaps and playful fighting.

slap-up adjective (informal) large and lavish ♦ a slap-up meal.

slash verb 1 to cut or strike something with a long sweeping stroke or strokes. 2 to make large cuts in something ♦ The painting had been slashed by vandals. SYNONYMS: rip, gash, hack. 3 (informal) to reduce a price or total by a large amount. **slash** noun 1 a cut made with a long sweeping stroke. 2 an oblique stroke (/) used in writing and printing. [perhaps from an Old French word eslachier meaning 'to break in pieces']

slat noun each of a series of thin narrow strips of wood, metal, or plastic arranged so as to overlap, e.g. in a Venetian blind or wooden fence. [from an Old French word esclat meaning 'splinter']

slate noun 1 a kind of grey rock that is easily split into flat smooth plates. 2 a piece of this used for covering a roof or (formerly) for writing on. **slate** verb 1 to cover a roof or surface with slates. 2 (informal) to criticize someone severely. **to have a clean slate** to have a record of good conduct with nothing discreditable. **slaty** adjective [same origin as for slat]

slattern noun (old use) a dirty untidy woman. **slatternly** adjective [from a dialect word slatter meaning 'to spill or slop']

slaughter noun 1 the killing of animals for food. 2 the ruthless killing of a great number of people or animals, a massacre. SYNONYMS: massacre, carnage, butchery, extermination.
slaughter verb 1 to kill animals for food. 2 to kill people or animals ruthlessly or in great numbers. SYNONYMS: massacre, butcher, exterminate. 3 (informal) to defeat an opponent decisively. **slaughterer** noun [from an Old Norse word slátr meaning 'butcher's meat', related to slay]

slaughterhouse noun a place where animals are killed for food.

Slav noun a member of a group of peoples of central and eastern Europe who speak a Slavonic language. [from a Latin word Sclavus]

slave noun 1 a person who is the legal property of another person and obliged to work for that person. 2 someone who is dominated or greatly influenced by another person or thing ♦ a slave to fashion. 3 a mechanism that is controlled by another mechanism and repeats its actions.
slave verb to work very hard. [from a Latin word sclavus meaning 'captive']

slave-driver noun (informal) a person who makes others work very hard.

slave labour noun labour that is forced on people and not adequately paid.

slaver (**slav**-er or **slay**-ver) *verb* to have saliva running from the mouth. **slaver** *noun* saliva running from the mouth. [origin unknown]

slavery *noun* 1 the condition of a slave. SYNONYMS: servitude, bondage, captivity. 2 the practice of owning or using slaves. 3 hard work or drudgery.

slave trade *noun* (*historical*) the trade in procuring, transporting, and selling slaves, especially from Africa.

Slavic (**slah**-vik) *adjective* to do with the group of languages that includes Russian, Czech, Polish, and Serbo-Croat.

slavish *adjective* 1 like a slave, excessively submissive. SYNONYMS: servile, submissive, obsequious, deferential. 2 showing no independence or originality. SYNONYMS: unimaginative, unoriginal. **slavishly** *adverb* **slavishness** *noun*

Slavonic (slǝ-**von**-ik) *adjective* another word for **Slavic**.

slay *verb* (**slew, slain**) (*literary*) to kill a person or animal violently.

sleaze *noun* (*informal*) immoral or corrupt behaviour, especially in public life. [a back-formation from *sleazy*]

sleazy *adjective* (**sleazier, sleaziest**) (*informal*) 1 corrupt or immoral. 2 (said about a place) dirty and squalid. [origin unknown]

sled *noun* (*North Amer.*) a sledge.

sledge *noun* a vehicle with runners instead of wheels, used for travelling over snow. **sledging** *noun* [from a Dutch word, related to *sled*]

sledgehammer *noun* a large heavy hammer swung with both hands. [from an Old English word *slecg*]

sleek *adjective* 1 (often said about hair or fur) smooth and glossy. 2 looking prosperous. **sleek** *verb* to make hair sleek by smoothing. **sleekly** *adverb* **sleekness** *noun* [a different spelling of *slick*]

sleep *noun* 1 the natural condition of rest in animals, in which the eyes are closed, the muscles are relaxed, and the mind is unconscious. 2 a period of this condition ♦ *a long sleep.* 3 the inert condition of hibernating animals. **sleep** *verb* (past tense and past participle **slept**) 1 to rest in a state of sleep. SYNONYMS: snooze, doze, slumber. 2 to provide people with sleeping

accommodation ♦ *The cottage sleeps four.* **to sleep in** to remain asleep later in the morning than usual. **to sleep something off** to recover from something by sleeping. **to sleep on it** to delay deciding about something until the next day. [from an Old English word *slep*]

sleeper *noun* 1 someone who is sleeping. 2 each of the wooden or concrete beams on which the rails of a railway rest. 3 a sleeping car, or a train including sleeping cars. 4 a ring worn in a pierced ear to keep the hole from closing.

sleeping bag *noun* a padded bag for sleeping in, especially while camping.

sleeping car or **sleeping carriage** *noun* a railway coach fitted with berths or beds for passengers.

sleeping partner *noun* a partner in a business firm who does not take part in its actual work.

sleeping sickness *noun* a tropical disease with symptoms that include extreme sleepiness, spread by the bite of the tsetse fly.

sleepless *adjective* 1 without sleep ♦ *a sleepless night.* 2 unable to sleep ♦ *feeling sleepless.* **sleeplessly** *adverb* **sleeplessness** *noun*

sleepover *noun* a night spent away from home, especially after a party.

sleepwalk *verb* to walk around while asleep. **sleepwalker** *noun*

sleepy *adjective* (**sleepier, sleepiest**) 1 feeling a need or wish to sleep. SYNONYMS: drowsy, tired, weary; (*formal*) somnolent. 2 quiet and lacking activity ♦ *a sleepy little town.* **sleepily** *adverb* **sleepiness** *noun*

sleepyhead *noun* (*informal*) a sleepy person.

sleet *noun* a mixture of rain and snow or hail falling at the same time. **sleet** *verb* to fall as sleet ♦ *It's been sleeting.* **sleety** *adjective* [probably from Old English]

sleeve *noun* 1 the part of a piece of clothing that covers the arm or part of it. 2 a paper or cardboard cover for a record. 3 a protective tube fitting over a rod or another tube. 4 a windsock. **up your sleeve** kept hidden or put aside for use when needed. **sleeved** *adjective* **sleeveless** *adjective* [from an Old English word *slefe*]

sleigh (slay) *noun* a large sledge drawn by horses. [from a Dutch word *slee*, related to *sled*]

sleight (slyt) *noun* **sleight of hand** skill in using the hands to do conjuring tricks etc. [from an Old Norse word *slægth* meaning 'slyness']

slender *adjective* **1** slim and graceful. **2** barely enough ♦ *people of slender means.* SYNONYMS: slim, meagre, scanty, slight. **slenderness** *noun* [origin unknown]

slept past tense and past participle of **sleep**.

sleuth (slooth) *noun* a detective. [from an Old Norse word *slóth*]

sleuthing (slooth-ing) *noun* searching for information as a detective does.

slew [1] *verb* to turn or swing round.

slew [2] past tense of **slay**.

slice *noun* **1** a thin broad piece cut from something, especially a piece of food. **2** a portion or share ♦ *a slice of the profits.* **3** a utensil with a thin broad blade for lifting or serving fish or cake. **4** (in sports) a stroke or shot that veers off to the right or left.
slice *verb* **1** to cut something into slices. **2** to cut something from a larger piece ♦ *Slice the top off the egg.* **3** to cut cleanly or easily ♦ *The knife sliced through the apple.* **4** (in golf) to strike the ball so that it veers away from the direction intended, going to the right of a right-handed player. **5** (in other sports) to hit the ball so that it goes forward spinning. **slicer** *noun* [from an Old French word *esclice* meaning 'splinter']

slick *adjective* **1** done or doing things in a noticeably smooth and efficient way. **2** glibly smooth in manner or speech. **3** smooth and slippery ♦ *The roads were slick with mud.*
slick *noun* **1** a thick patch of oil floating on the sea. **2** a slippery place.
slick *verb* to make something sleek. [probably from an Old English word]

slide *verb* (past tense and past participle **slid**) **1** to move along a smooth surface keeping continuous contact with it, or to cause something to do this. SYNONYMS: glide, skim. **2** to move quietly or discreetly, or to cause something to do this ♦ *She slid a note into his hand.* **3** to change gradually into a worse condition or habit ♦ *The country slid into anarchy.*
slide *noun* **1** the act of sliding. **2** a smooth surface for sliding on. **3** a structure with a smooth sloping surface for children to slide down, or a similar device for sending goods from one part of a building to another. **4** a sliding part of a machine or instrument. **5** a small glass plate on which an object is mounted to be looked at under a microscope. **6** a mounted picture or transparency for showing on a screen with a projector. **7** a hairslide. **to let things slide** to fail to give matters proper attention. [from an Old English word *slidan*]

slide rule *noun* a ruler with a sliding central strip, marked with logarithmic scales and used for making calculations rapidly.

sliding scale *noun* a scale of fees, taxes, or payment that varies in accordance with the variation of some standard.

slight *adjective* **1** not much or great; not serious or important. SYNONYMS: small, little, modest, faint, minor. **2** slender, not heavily built.
slight *verb* to offend someone by not treating them with proper respect or courtesy. SYNONYMS: offend, affront, insult, snub.
slight *noun* an act of slighting someone, a minor insult. SYNONYMS: affront, insult, snub. **slightly** *adverb* **slightness** *noun* [from an Old Norse word *sléttr* meaning 'smooth']

slim *adjective* (**slimmer, slimmest**) **1** attractively or gracefully thin or small in thickness. **2** slight or inadequate ♦ *There is only a slim chance of rescuing any survivors.*
slim *verb* (**slimmed, slimming**) **1** to make yourself slimmer, especially by dieting or exercise. **2** to reduce the size or scale of an organization to make it more efficient. **slimly** *adverb* **slimness** *noun* **slimmer** *noun* [from a German or Dutch word]

slime *noun* an unpleasantly wet and thick substance. [from an Old English word]

slimline *adjective* slender in build or design.

slimy *adjective* (**slimier, slimiest**) **1** unpleasantly wet and thick like slime. **2** covered or smeared with slime. **3** (*informal*) revoltingly servile or obsequious. **slimily** *adverb* **sliminess** *noun*

sling *noun* **1** a belt or strap looped round an object to support or lift it. **2** a bandage looped round the neck to form a support for an injured arm. **3** a looped strap used to throw a stone or other small missile.
sling *verb* (past tense and past participle

slung) **1** to suspend or lift something with a sling. **2** to hurl a stone with a sling. **3** (*informal*) to throw something forcefully or carelessly. SYNONYMS: hurl, fling, toss, throw; (*informal*) chuck. **to sling your hook** (*informal*) to abscond or leave abruptly. [from a Dutch or Old Norse word]

slink *verb* (past tense and past participle **slunk**) to move quietly in a stealthy or shamefaced way. SYNONYMS: sneak, creep, steal, slip, skulk. [from an Old English word *slincan* meaning 'to crawl']

slinky *adjective* (**slinkier, slinkiest**) (*informal*) smooth and sinuous in movement or form. **slinkily** *adverb*

slip¹ *verb* (**slipped, slipping**) **1** to slide accidentally, or to lose your balance in this way. SYNONYMS: slide, skid, slither; stumble. **2** to go quickly and discreetly, or to cause something to do this ♦ *She slipped slowly through the crowd* ♦ *John slipped a note under the door.* SYNONYMS: (without an object) sneak, creep, steal, slink, skulk. **3** to escape hold or capture by being slippery or not grasped firmly. **4** (in knitting) to transfer a stitch to the other needle without looping the yarn through it. **5** to escape or become detached from a restraint ♦ *The dog slipped its leash* ♦ *I'm afraid it slipped my memory.*
slip *noun* **1** an act of slipping. **2** an accidental or casual mistake. **3** a loose covering or piece of clothing. **4** a petticoat. **5** a pillowslip. **6** (in cricket) a fielding position on the off side just behind the wicket. **to give someone the slip** to escape from someone or succeed in avoiding them. **to let something slip** to reveal something by mistake in conversation. **a slip of the pen** or **tongue** a small mistake in writing or speaking. **to slip up** (*informal*) to make an accidental or casual mistake. [from an early German word *slippen* (verb)]

slip² *noun* **1** a small piece of paper for writing on. **2** a cutting taken from a plant for grafting or planting. **a slip of a girl** a small slim girl. [from an early German word *slippe* meaning 'strip']

slip³ *noun* a thin liquid containing fine clay, used for coating pottery. [origin unknown]

slip knot *noun* a knot that can slide along the rope etc. on which it is tied, or one that can be undone by pulling.

slipped disc *noun* a displaced layer of cartilage between vertebrae in the spine, pressing on nerves and causing pain.

slipper *noun* a soft light comfortable shoe for wearing indoors.

slippery *adjective* **1** smooth and difficult to hold. **2** causing slipping by being wet or smooth. **3** (said about a person) untrustworthy. **slipperiness** *noun*

slippy *adjective* (*informal*) slippery.

slip road *noun* a road entering or leaving a motorway or other main road.

slipshod *adjective* **1** not doing things carefully. SYNONYMS: careless, slapdash, sloppy. **2** not done or arranged carefully.

slip stitch *noun* **1** a loose stitch joining several layers in sewing. **2** a slipped stitch in knitting.

slipstream *noun* a current of air driven backward as something is propelled forward.

slip-up *noun* (*informal*) an accidental or casual mistake.

slipway *noun* a slope into water, used as a landing stage or for building or repairing ships.

slit *noun* a long narrow cut or opening. SYNONYMS: opening, crack, chink.
slit *verb* (past tense and past participle **slit; slitting**) **1** to cut a slit in something. **2** to cut something into strips. [from an Old English word *slite*]

slither *verb* (*informal*) to slip or slide unsteadily or with an irregular movement. [from a dialect word *slidder*, related to *slide*]

slithery *adjective* causing things to slither, or liable to slither.

sliver (sliv-er) *noun* a thin strip cut or split off a larger piece of wood or glass etc. [from a dialect word *slive* meaning 'to split' or 'to cut a piece off']

slob *noun* (*informal*) an untidy or lazy person. [from an old word *slab* meaning 'mud or slime', and *slobber*]

slobber *verb* to dribble a lot from the mouth. [probably from an early Dutch word *slobbern* meaning 'to wade through mud']

sloe *noun* the small dark plum-like fruit of the blackthorn. [from an Old English word *slah*]

slog verb (**slogged, slogging**) 1 to hit something hard. 2 to work hard for a long period. 3 to walk with great effort over a long distance.
slog noun 1 a hard hit. 2 a spell of hard tiring work or walking. **to slog it out** to fight or compete fiercely. **slogger** noun [origin unknown]

slogan noun a word or phrase used to advertise something or to represent the aims of a campaign, political party, etc. [from a Scottish Gaelic word *sluagh-ghairm* meaning 'battle cry']

sloop noun a kind of sailing ship with one mast. [from a Dutch word *sloep*]

slop verb (**slopped, slopping**) 1 (said about a liquid) to spill over the edge of its container. 2 to make liquid spill over, to splash liquid on a surface. 3 to wade clumsily through mud or puddles.
slop noun 1 weak unappetizing drink or liquid food. 2 an amount of slopped liquid. 3 swill fed to pigs.
slops plural noun 1 liquid refuse in a kitchen. 2 the contents of chamber pots. 3 dregs from teacups. **to slop out** (in prison) to carry slops out from cells. [probably from an Old English word]

slope verb 1 to lie or turn at an angle from the horizontal or vertical. SYNONYMS: slant, incline, lean. 2 to place something in this position.
slope noun 1 a sloping surface. SYNONYMS: incline, gradient, slant. 2 a stretch of rising or falling ground. 3 the amount by which something slopes. **to slope off** (informal) to go away. [a shortening of an earlier word *aslope*, of unknown origin]

sloppy adjective (**sloppier, sloppiest**) 1 having a liquid consistency and splashing easily. 2 careless or slipshod. SYNONYMS: careless, slapdash, slipshod. 3 weakly sentimental. **sloppily** adverb **sloppiness** noun

slosh verb 1 (informal) to hit someone ♦ *She felt like sloshing him on the chin.* 2 to pour liquid clumsily. 3 to splash or slop about.
slosh noun 1 (informal) a blow. 2 a splashing sound. [a different spelling of *slush*]

slot noun 1 a narrow opening to put something through. 2 a groove, channel, or slit into which something fits. 3 a regular position in a scheme or schedule ♦ *The programme has been moved to the 6.00 p.m. slot.* SYNONYMS: niche, space, spot.
slot verb (**slotted, slotting**) 1 to make a slot or slots in something. 2 to put something into a slot. [from an Old French word *esclot*]

slot machine noun a machine worked by putting a coin in a slot.

sloth (slohth) noun 1 reluctance to make an effort, laziness. 2 a South American animal that lives in trees and can only move very slowly.

slothful adjective reluctant to make an effort, lazy. SYNONYMS: lazy, idle, indolent. **slothfully** adverb

slouch verb to stand or sit or move in a lazy awkward way, not with an upright posture.
slouch noun a slouching movement or posture. **sloucher** noun [origin unknown]

slough [1] (slow) noun a swamp or marshy place. [from an Old English word *sloh*]

slough [2] (sluf) verb (said about an animal) to shed its skin.
slough noun dead tissue that has dropped away. [origin unknown]

sloven (sluv-ən) noun a slovenly person.

slovenly (sluv-ən-li) adjective 1 dirty and untidy. 2 unmethodical in work. SYNONYMS: slipshod, slapdash, careless. **slovenliness** noun [perhaps from a Dutch word *slof* meaning 'careless']

slow adjective 1 not quick or fast, taking more time than is usual. 2 (said about a clock or watch) showing a time earlier than the correct time. 3 not able to understand things quickly or easily. 4 sluggish, not lively ♦ *Business is slow today.* 5 (in photography, said about a film or lens) needing a long exposure. 6 tending to cause slowness.
slow adverb slowly ♦ *to go slow.*
◊ The normal adverb from *slow* is *slowly*: ♦ *The traffic was moving very slowly.* The adverb *slow* is now only used in the expression *to go slow.*
slow verb (usually **slow down** or **slow up**) to go more slowly, or to make something go more slowly. SYNONYMS: brake, decelerate; retard, impede. **slowish** adjective **slowly** adverb **slowness** noun [from an Old English word *slaw* meaning 'slow-witted']

slowcoach noun (informal) a person who is slow in actions or work.

slow motion noun the process of showing cinema or video film at a lower speed than the recording speed, so that movements appear to be slower than in real life.

slow-worm noun a small European legless lizard that looks like a snake and gives birth to live young.

slub noun a thick lump in yarn or thread. [origin unknown]

sludge noun thick greasy mud, or something like this. [origin unknown]

slug[1] noun 1 a small slimy animal like a snail without a shell. 2 a roundish lump of metal, especially a pellet for firing from a gun. 3 an amount of alcoholic drink. [probably from a Scandinavian language]

slug[2] verb (**slugged, slugging**) (informal) to strike someone or something with a hard heavy blow.
slug noun a blow of this kind. [origin unknown]

sluggard noun a slow or lazy person. [from an old word slug meaning 'to be lazy or slow']

sluggish adjective 1 slow-moving or inactive. SYNONYMS: slow-moving, inactive, lethargic, listless. 2 not alert or lively. **sluggishly** adverb **sluggishness** noun [from slug[1]]

sluice (slooss) noun 1 (also **sluice gate**) a sliding gate for controlling the volume or flow of water. 2 the water controlled by this. 3 a channel carrying off water. 4 a place where objects are rinsed. 5 the act of rinsing.
sluice verb 1 to let out water by means of a sluice. 2 to flood or wash something with a flow of water. [from an Old French word escluse, related to exclude]

slum noun an area of poor run-down and overcrowded houses. [origin unknown]

slumber verb (literary) to sleep.
slumber noun a period of sleep. **slumberer** noun [from a Scots word sloom, with the same meaning]

slump verb 1 to sit or fall down heavily and limply. 2 to suffer a sudden great decline ♦ Sales have slumped recently.
slump noun a sudden or great fall in prices, business activity, the demand for goods, etc. ♦ a slump in the property market. [origin unknown]

slung past tense and past participle of sling.

slunk past tense and past participle of slink.

slur verb (**slurred, slurring**) 1 to pronounce words indistinctly with each sound running into the next. 2 (Music) to mark notes with a slur; to perform a group of notes in the way indicated by this. 3 to speak ill of someone. 4 to pass lightly over something ♦ The minister slurred over some important facts in the interview.
slur noun 1 an insinuation or allegation ♦ a slur on his reputation. 2 a slurred sound. 3 (Music) a curved line placed over notes to show that they are to be sung to one syllable or played smoothly without a break. **slurred** adjective [origin unknown]

slurp verb to eat or drink with a loud sucking sound.
slurp noun this sound. [from a Dutch word slurpen]

slurry noun (**slurries**) a semi-liquid mixture, especially of cement or manure. [origin unknown]

slush noun 1 partly melted snow or ice on the ground. 2 (informal) excessively sentimental talk or writing. **slushy** adjective [an imitation of the sound when you walk in it]

slush fund noun a fund of money used for illegal purposes such as bribery.

slut noun a slovenly or promiscuous woman. **sluttish** adjective [origin unknown]

sly adjective (**slyer, slyest**) 1 done or doing things in an unpleasantly cunning and secretive way. SYNONYMS: crafty, wily, devious, surreptitious, underhand; (informal) sneaky, shifty. 2 mischievous and knowing ♦ a sly smile. **on the sly** in a secretive way. **slyly** or **slily** adverb **slyness** noun [from an Old Norse word]

smack[1] noun 1 a sharp blow or slap, especially one given with the palm of the hand. 2 a loud sharp sound ♦ It hit the wall with a smack. 3 a loud kiss.
smack verb 1 to slap someone. 2 to hit something hard.
smack adverb (informal) directly and forcefully ♦ The ball went smack through the window. **to smack your lips** to part your lips noisily in enjoyment. [from an Old Dutch word smacken]

smack[2] noun a slight flavour or trace of something.
smack verb 1 to have a slight flavour of something. 2 to suggest the presence or effects of something ♦ His manner smacks of conceit. [from an Old English word]

smack [3] noun a sailing boat with a single mast used for coasting or fishing. [from a Dutch word *smak*]

small adjective 1 less than normal in size, not large or big. 2 not great in number, strength, etc. 3 not fully grown, young. 4 not important or significant ♦ a small complaint. SYNONYMS: minor, trivial, trifling, petty, slight, inconsequential. 5 doing things on a small scale ♦ a small business. 6 humble ♦ small beginnings.
small adverb into small pieces; in a small size or way ♦ Chop it up small.
smalls plural noun (informal) underwear. **to look** or **feel small** to be humiliated. **the small of the back** the part of a person's back at the waist. **smallness** noun [from an Old English word]

small change noun coins as opposed to notes.

small fry plural noun 1 people or things of little importance. 2 children.

smallholding noun a small area of land sold or let for farming. **smallholder** noun

small hours noun the early hours of the morning, after midnight.

small intestine noun (Anatomy) the part of the intestine between the stomach and the large intestine.

small-minded adjective having a narrow or selfish outlook.

smallpox noun a highly contagious disease caused by a virus, with fever and pustules that leave permanent scars.

small print noun the details of a contract, especially if printed in small type or difficult to understand.

small-scale adjective 1 drawn to a small scale so that few details are shown. 2 not extensive, involving only small quantities etc.

small screen noun television ♦ stars of the small screen.

small talk noun social conversation about unimportant subjects.

small-time adjective of an unimportant level ♦ small-time crooks.

smarmy adjective (**smarmier, smarmiest**) (informal) trying to win favour by flattery or excessive politeness. **smarmily** adverb **smarminess** noun [origin unknown]

smart adjective 1 neat, elegant, and well-dressed. 2 fashionable and upmarket ♦ a smart restaurant. 3 clever, shrewd, or witty. 4 (said about a device) controlled or guided by a computer and capable of some independent and seemingly intelligent action ♦ a smart bomb. 5 forceful, brisk ♦ a smart pace.
smart verb 1 to feel a stinging pain. 2 to feel upset and annoyed.
smart noun a stinging pain. **smartly** adverb **smartness** noun [from an Old English word *smeortan*]

smart alec noun (informal) a know-all.

smart card noun a plastic card with a microprocessor built in, which stores information or enables you to draw or spend money from your bank account.

smarten verb to make a person or thing smarter or to become smarter.

smash verb 1 to break something or become broken suddenly and noisily into pieces. 2 to hit or move something with great force. 3 (in tennis etc.) to strike a ball forcefully downwards. 4 to crash a vehicle. 5 to destroy something or defeat someone completely ♦ Police smashed the drug ring.
smash noun 1 the act or sound of smashing. 2 a collision. 3 (also **smash hit**) (informal) a very successful song, show, etc.
smash adverb with a sudden smash. [an imitation of the sound]

smash-and-grab adjective (said about a robbery) done by smashing a shop window and grabbing goods.

smasher noun (informal) an excellent or very attractive person or thing.

smashing adjective (informal) excellent. [from *smash*]

smattering noun a slight knowledge of a language or subject. [origin unknown]

smear verb 1 to spread something with a greasy or sticky substance. 2 to try to damage someone's reputation by making false allegations.
smear noun 1 a greasy or sticky mark. 2 a false accusation intended to damage a person's reputation. 3 a specimen of material smeared on a slide to be examined under a microscope. 4 a smear test. **smeary** adjective [from an Old English word *smeoru* meaning 'ointment, grease']

smear test noun the taking and examination of a sample of the cervix lining, to check for faulty cells which may cause cancer.

smell noun 1 the faculty of perceiving odours by their action on the sense organs of the nose. 2 the quality that is perceived in this way. 3 an unpleasant quality of this kind. SYNONYMS: stench, stink, reek, whiff; (informal) pong. 4 an act of smelling something.
smell verb (past tense and past participle **smelt** or **smelled**) 1 to perceive the smell of something; to detect or test something by your sense of smell. 2 to give off a smell. 3 to give off an unpleasant smell. 4 to detect or suspect something by intuition or instinct ♦ I was sure I could smell a cover-up. **to smell a rat** (informal) to suspect trickery. [origin unknown]

smelling salts plural noun a solid preparation of ammonia used for smelling as a stimulant to relieve faintness.

smelly adjective (**smellier**, **smelliest**) having a strong or unpleasant smell.

smelt [1] past tense and past participle of **smell**.

smelt [2] verb to heat and melt ore to obtain the metal it contains; to obtain metal in this way. [from an Old German or Old Dutch word smelten]

smelt [3] noun a small silvery fish related to the salmon. [from an Old English word]

smidgen noun (informal) a tiny amount. [perhaps from a Scots word]

smile noun a facial expression showing pleasure, friendliness, or amusement, with the corners of the mouth turned up.
smile verb 1 to give a smile. 2 to look favourably on something ♦ Fortune smiled on us. **smiler** noun [probably from a Scandinavian word]

smirch verb 1 to make something dirty. 2 to disgrace or dishonour a reputation. **smirch** noun 1 a dirty mark or stain. 2 a flaw. [origin unknown]

smirk noun a self-satisfied or silly smile. **smirk** verb to give a smirk. [from an Old English word]

smite verb (**smote**, **smitten**) 1 (old use) to hit something hard. 2 (old use) to defeat or conquer someone. 3 to afflict someone. [from an Old English word]

smith noun 1 a person who makes things in metal. 2 a blacksmith. [from an Old English word]

smithereens plural noun (informal) small fragments. [from an Irish word]

smithy noun (**smithies**) a blacksmith's workshop. [from an Old Norse word]

smitten past participle of **smite**. **to be smitten (with)** 1 to be affected by love for someone, especially suddenly and powerfully ♦ He only met her last week but he's completely smitten. 2 to be deeply affected by an emotion ♦ She is smitten with remorse.

smock noun 1 an overall shaped like a long loose shirt ♦ an artist's smock. 2 a woman's long loose top.
smock verb to decorate a piece of clothing with smocking. [from an Old English word smoc meaning 'woman's loose-fitting piece of underclothing']

smocking noun a decoration made by gathering a section of material into tight pleats and stitching them together into a honeycomb pattern.

smog noun fog polluted by smoke. [from smoke and fog]

smoke noun 1 the mixture of gas and solid particles that forms a visible vapour given off by a burning substance. 2 an act of smoking tobacco ♦ He went outside for a smoke. 3 (informal) a cigarette or cigar.
smoke verb 1 to give off smoke. 2 (said about a fireplace) to send smoke into a room instead of up the chimney. 3 to have a lighted cigarette, cigar, or pipe between your lips and draw its smoke into your mouth; to do this as a habit. 4 to preserve meat or fish by treating it with smoke ♦ smoked salmon. 5 to darken something with smoke ♦ smoked glass. **to go up in smoke** (informal) 1 to be destroyed by fire. 2 to come to nothing. **the Smoke** or **the Big Smoke** a big city, especially London. **to smoke someone** or **something out** to drive a person or animal out of a place by using smoke. [from an Old English word smoca]

smoke alarm noun a device that detects and warns of the presence of smoke.

smoke bomb noun a bomb that gives out dense smoke when it explodes.

smokeless adjective 1 free from smoke. 2 producing little or no smoke ♦ smokeless fuel.

smoker noun a person who smokes tobacco as a habit.

smokescreen noun 1 a cloud of smoke used to conceal the movement of troops or ships. 2 something intended to conceal or disguise what someone is really doing.

smokestack noun a chimney or funnel on a locomotive, ship, factory building, etc.

smoky adjective (**smokier, smokiest**) 1 giving off much smoke. 2 covered or filled with smoke ♦ *a smoky pub.* 3 having the taste or smell of smoked food.

smolt noun a young salmon at the stage between parr and grilse, when it is covered with silvery scales and migrates to the sea for the first time. [origin unknown]

smooth adjective 1 having an even surface without any lumps, wrinkles, roughness, etc. 2 moving evenly without bumps or jolts ♦ *a smooth ride.* 3 without problems or difficulties. 4 not harsh in sound or taste. 5 pleasantly polite but perhaps insincere. SYNONYMS: slick, urbane, suave, glib.
smooth adverb (*old use*) in a way that is without difficulties ♦ *The course of true love never did run smooth.*
smooth verb 1 to make something smooth. 2 to remove problems or dangers from something ♦ *A number of factors helped to smooth her path to the top.*
smooth noun a smoothing touch or stroke. **smoothly** adverb **smoothness** noun [from an Old English word]

smooth-talking or **smooth-tongued** adjective pleasantly polite or convincing but insincere.

smorgasbord (**smor-gəs-bord**) noun a variety of open sandwiches and savoury dishes served as hors d'oeuvres or a buffet. [a Swedish word]

smote past tense of **smite**.

smother verb 1 to suffocate someone by covering the nose and mouth. 2 to put out a fire by covering it. 3 to cover something thickly ♦ *chips smothered in ketchup.* 4 to restrain or suppress something ♦ *She managed to smother a smile.*
smother noun a dense cloud of dust, smoke, etc. [from an Old English word *smorian* meaning 'to suffocate']

smoulder verb 1 to burn slowly with smoke but no flame. 2 to feel strong but concealed hostile feelings, especially anger or hatred ♦ *He was smouldering with jealousy.* **smouldering** adjective [origin unknown]

smudge verb 1 to make something blurred or smeared. 2 to become blurred or smeared.

smudge noun a smudged mark. **smudgy** adjective [origin unknown]

smug adjective (**smugger, smuggest**) self-satisfied; too pleased with your own good fortune or abilities. **smugly** adverb **smugness** noun [from an Old German word *smuk* meaning 'pretty']

smuggle verb 1 to bring goods into or out of a country illegally, especially without paying customs duties. 2 to bring something into or out of a place secretly. **smuggler** noun [from an Old German or Old Dutch word]

smut noun 1 a small flake of soot or dirt. 2 indecent or obscene talk, pictures, or writing. [from an old word *smotten* meaning 'to stain']

smutty adjective (**smuttier, smuttiest**) 1 (said about talk, pictures, or writing) indecent or obscene. 2 marked with smuts. **smuttily** adverb **smuttiness** noun

snack noun 1 a small meal. 2 food eaten between meals.
snack verb to eat a snack. [from an Old Dutch word *snacken* meaning 'to bite']

snack bar noun a small café where snacks are sold.

snaffle noun a simple bit on a bridle, used with a single set of reins.
snaffle verb (*informal*) to take something for yourself hastily, before anyone else has a chance to. [probably from an Old German or Old Dutch word]

snag noun 1 an unexpected difficulty. 2 a sharp or jagged part sticking out from something. 3 a tear in fabric that has caught on something sharp.
snag verb (**snagged, snagging**) to catch or tear or be caught on a snag. **snaggy** adjective [probably from a Scandinavian word]

snail noun a soft-bodied animal with a spiral shell that can enclose its whole body. [from an Old English word]

snail mail noun (*informal*) the ordinary post as opposed to email.

snail's pace noun a very slow pace.

snake noun 1 a reptile with a long narrow body and no legs. 2 (also **snake in the grass**) a treacherous person.
snake verb to move or stretch out with the twisting motion of a snake. **snaky** adjective [from an Old English word *snaca*]

snake charmer noun an entertainer who seems to make snakes move by playing music.

snakes and ladders noun a children's board game in which the players' pieces go up ladders and down snakes pictured on the board.

snap verb (**snapped, snapping**) 1 to break or make something break with a sharp cracking sound ♦ *The rope snapped.* 2 to bite or try to bite something with a snatching movement. 3 to open or close with a sharp sound, or to make something do this ♦ *The lid snapped shut.* 4 to speak with sudden irritation; to suddenly lose your self-control. 5 to take or accept something eagerly, especially something in short supply ♦ *shoppers snapping up bargains.* 6 to move suddenly or abruptly ♦ *Both the guards snapped to attention.* 7 to take a snapshot of something.
snap noun 1 the act or sound of snapping. 2 a snapshot. 3 a sudden brief spell of cold weather. 4 a card game in which players call 'Snap!' when two similar cards are exposed. 5 a crisp brittle biscuit ♦ *ginger snaps.*
snap adjective done or arranged on the spur of the moment ♦ *a snap decision.*
snap adverb with a snapping sound. **to snap your fingers** to make a cracking noise by flipping the thumb against a finger, usually in order to draw attention. **to snap out of it** (*informal*) to make yourself recover quickly from a bad mood. [probably from an Old German or Old Dutch word *snappen* meaning 'to seize']

snapdragon noun a garden plant with flowers that have a mouth-like opening.

snapper noun 1 any of several sea fish used as food. 2 a person or thing that snaps.

snappish adjective bad-tempered and inclined to snap at people. **snappishly** adverb

snappy adjective (**snappier, snappiest**) (*informal*) 1 neat and stylish ♦ *a snappy dresser.* 2 clever and concise ♦ *a snappy catchphrase.* **make it snappy** (*informal*) hurry up. **snappily** adverb

snapshot noun a photograph taken informally or casually.

snare noun 1 a trap for catching birds or animals, consisting of a loop of wire or cord that pulls tight. 2 something that is likely to trap someone or to expose them to danger or failure. 3 each of the strings of gut or coiled metal stretched across a side drum to produce a rattling effect. 4 a snare drum.
snare verb to catch or trap someone or something in a snare, or as if in a snare ♦ *How did she manage to snare that job?* [from an Old English word *sneare*]

snare drum noun a drum with snares.

snarl ¹ verb 1 to growl angrily with the teeth bared. 2 to say something aggressively.
snarl noun the act or sound of snarling. [an imitation of the sound]

snarl ² noun a tangle or knot. **to snarl something up** to make something jammed, blocked, or tangled ♦ *We got snarled up in traffic.* [from *snare*]

snarl-up noun (*informal*) 1 a muddle. 2 a traffic jam.

snatch verb 1 to seize something quickly or eagerly. 2 to take something quickly or when a chance occurs ♦ *We snatched a few hours' sleep on the plane.*
snatch noun 1 the act of snatching. 2 a short and incomplete part of a song, piece of music, or conversation. [from an old word *snacchen* meaning 'to snap at, to seize']

snazzy adjective (**snazzier, snazziest**) (*informal*) smart, stylish. **snazzily** adverb **snazziness** noun [origin unknown]

sneak verb 1 to move quietly and secretly ♦ *Her brother had sneaked up behind her.* 2 (*informal*) to take something secretly ♦ *He sneaked a look at the answers.* 3 (*informal*) to tell tales.
sneak noun (*informal*) a telltale.
sneak adjective acting or done without warning ♦ *a sneak preview.* **sneaky** adjective [probably from an Old English word]

sneakers plural noun (*North Amer.*) soft-soled shoes.

sneaking adjective persistent but not openly acknowledged ♦ *I had a sneaking affection for him.*

sneer noun a scornful expression or remark.
sneer verb to show contempt by a sneer. [probably from an Old English word]

sneeze noun a sudden audible involuntary expulsion of air through the nose and mouth, to get rid of something irritating the nostrils.

sneeze *verb* to give a sneeze. **not to be sneezed at** (*informal*) not to be disregarded; worth having or thinking about. [from an Old English word *fneosan*, an imitation of the sound]

snick *verb* 1 to make a small cut or notch in something. 2 (in cricket) to hit the ball with a light glancing stroke from the edge of the bat.
snick *noun* 1 a small cut or notch. 2 (in cricket) a batsman's light glancing stroke. [probably from an old phrase *snick or snee* meaning 'to fight with knives']

snicker *verb* to snigger.
snicker *noun* a snigger. [an imitation of the sound]

snide *adjective* 1 sneering in a sly or indirect way ♦ *a snide remark.* 2 counterfeit. [origin unknown]

sniff *verb* 1 to make a sound by drawing in air through the nose. 2 to smell something.
sniff *noun* 1 the act or sound of sniffing. 2 (*informal*) a hint or sign. **to sniff around** or **round** (*informal*) to secretly investigate something. **to sniff at** (*informal*) to show contempt for something. **sniffer** *noun* [an imitation of the sound]

sniffer dog *noun* (*informal*) a dog trained to find drugs or explosives by smell.

sniffle *verb* to sniff slightly or repeatedly.
sniffle *noun* 1 the act or sound of sniffling. 2 a slight cold. **sniffly** *adjective* [an imitation of the sound]

sniffy *adjective* (**sniffier, sniffiest**) (*informal*) contemptuous. **sniffily** *adverb*

snigger *noun* a sly or mocking giggle.
snigger *verb* to give a snigger. [a variation of *snicker*]

snip *verb* (**snipped, snipping**) to cut something with scissors or shears, with small quick strokes.
snip *noun* 1 the act or sound of snipping. 2 a piece snipped off. 3 (*informal*) a bargain. 4 (*informal*) something that is very easy to do.
snips *plural noun* a small pair of shears for cutting metal. [from an Old German or Old Dutch word]

snipe *noun* (**snipe**) a wading bird with a long straight bill, living in marshes.
snipe *verb* 1 to shoot at people from a hiding place. 2 to make sly critical remarks attacking a person or thing.

sniper *noun* [probably from a Scandinavian word; the verb because the birds are shot from a hiding place]

snippet *noun* 1 a small piece of information or news; a brief extract. 2 a small piece cut off. [from *snip*]

snitch *verb* (*informal*) 1 to inform on someone. 2 to steal something.
snitch *noun* an informer. [origin unknown]

snivel *verb* (**snivelled, snivelling**) 1 to cry or complain in a whining way. 2 to have a runny nose. [from an Old English word]

snob *noun* a person who has an exaggerated respect for social position or wealth or for certain tastes, and who looks down on people whom he or she considers inferior ♦ *a wine snob.* **snobbery** *noun* [origin unknown]

snobbish *adjective* to do with or like a snob. **snobbishly** *adverb* **snobbishness** *noun*

snog *verb* (**snogged, snogging**) (*informal*) to kiss and caress someone.
snog *noun* an act of snogging. [origin unknown]

snood *noun* 1 a loose bag-like ornamental net in which a woman's hair is held at the back. 2 a wide ring of material worn as a hood or scarf. [from an Old English word]

snook *noun* (*informal*) **to cock a snook** 1 to make a contemptuous gesture with your thumb touching your nose and the fingers spread out. 2 to show cheeky contempt or lack of respect for someone or something.   [origin unknown]

snooker *noun* 1 a game played on a billiard table with cues and 15 red and 6 other coloured balls. 2 a position in snooker in which a player cannot make a direct shot at a ball they are allowed to hit.
snooker *verb* 1 to subject an opponent to a snooker. 2 (*informal*) to thwart someone or put them in an impossible position. [origin unknown]

snoop *verb* (*informal*) to investigate or look around secretly in order to find something out.
snoop *noun* 1 the act of snooping. 2 a person who snoops. **snooper** *noun* **snoopy** *adjective* [from a Dutch word]

snooty *adjective* (**snootier, snootiest**) (*informal*) haughty and contemptuous. **snootily** *adverb* [from *snout*]

snooze *noun* (*informal*) a nap.
snooze *verb* (*informal*) to take a snooze. [origin unknown]

snore *verb* to make snorting or grunting sounds while sleeping.
snore *noun* one of these sounds. **snorer** *noun* [an imitation of the sound]

snorkel *noun* 1 a breathing tube to enable a person to swim under water. 2 a device by which a submerged submarine can take in and expel air.
snorkel *verb* (**snorkelled, snorkelling**) to swim using a snorkel. **snorkelling** *noun* [from a German word *Schnorchel*]

snort *noun* a rough sound made by forcing breath suddenly through the nose, usually expressing annoyance or disgust.
snort *verb* to make a snort. [an imitation of the sound]

snot *noun* (*informal*) mucus from the nose.
snotty *adjective* [probably from an Old German or Old Dutch word; related to *snout*]

snout *noun* 1 an animal's long projecting nose and jaws. 2 the projecting front part of something. [from an Old German or Old Dutch word]

snow *noun* 1 crystals of ice that form from atmospheric vapour and fall to earth in light white flakes. 2 a fall or layer of snow. 3 something resembling snow.
snow *verb* 1 to come down as snow ♦ *It is snowing.* 2 to scatter or fall like snow. **to be snowed in** or **up** to be blocked or unable to go out because of snow. **to be snowed under** to be overwhelmed with a large amount of work. [from an Old English word]

snowball *noun* snow pressed into a small compact ball for throwing in play.
snowball *verb* 1 to throw snowballs at someone. 2 to grow quickly in size, intensity, or importance, as a snowball does when rolled in more snow.

snow-blindness *noun* temporary blindness caused by the glare of light reflected by snow.

snowboard *noun* a board like a wide ski, used for sliding downhill on snow.
snowboard *verb* to slide downhill on a snowboard. **snowboarding** *noun*

snow boot *noun* a warm padded boot worn in the snow.

snowbound *adjective* 1 prevented by snow from going out or travelling. 2 (said about a place) cut off or blocked by snow.

snow-capped *adjective* (said about a mountain) with a covering of snow on top.

snowdrift *noun* a bank of deep snow piled up by the wind.

snowdrop *noun* a small flower growing from a bulb, with hanging white flowers blooming in early spring.

snowfall *noun* a fall of snow; the amount of snow that falls.

snowfield *noun* a permanent wide expanse of snow.

snowflake *noun* a flake of snow.

snow goose *noun* a white goose of Arctic areas.

snowline *noun* the level above which an area is covered permanently with snow.

snowman *noun* (**snowmen**) a shape of a human figure made of snow.

snowmobile (snoh-mə-beel) *noun* a motor vehicle, especially one with runners or tracks, for travelling over snow.

snowplough *noun* a vehicle or device for clearing a road or railway track by pushing snow aside.

snowshoe *noun* a frame rather like a tennis racket, attached to the sole of a boot and used for walking on snow.

snowstorm *noun* a storm in which snow falls.

snow white *adjective* pure white.

snowy *adjective* (**snowier, snowiest**) 1 with snow falling ♦ *snowy weather*. 2 covered with snow ♦ *snowy roofs*. 3 as white as snow.

SNP *abbreviation* Scottish National Party.

snub *verb* (**snubbed, snubbing**) to insult someone by deliberately ignoring them or treating them scornfully.
snub *noun* an act of snubbing someone.
snub *adjective* (said about a nose) short and turned up at the end. [from an Old Norse word *snubba* meaning 'to chide, check the growth of']

snub-nosed *adjective* having a short turned-up nose.

snuff¹ *verb* to put out a candle by covering or pinching the flame. **to snuff it** (*informal*) to die. [origin unknown]

snuff² *noun* powdered tobacco for sniffing into the nostrils. [from an Old Dutch word *snuffen* meaning 'to snuffle']

snuff box noun a small box for holding snuff.

snuffer noun a metal cone attached to a handle, used for putting out a candle.

snuffle verb to sniff in a noisy way, to breathe noisily through a partly blocked nose.
snuffle noun a snuffling sound.
the snuffles plural noun (informal) a cold.
snuffly adverb [same origin as for snuff²]

snug adjective (snugger, snuggest) 1 warm and cosy. 2 very tight or close-fitting.
snug noun a small cosy room in a pub or hotel. **snugly** adverb [probably from a Dutch word]

snuggery noun (snuggeries) a snug and private place.

snuggle verb to settle into a warm and comfortable position. [from snug]

so adverb 1 to such an extent ♦ It was so dark that we could not see. 2 very ♦ We are so pleased to see you. 3 also ♦ I was wrong, but then so were you.
so conjunction for that reason; therefore ♦ No one was in, so I left the keys next door.
so pronoun that, the same thing ♦ Do you think so? ♦ And so say all of us. **and so on** and other things of the same kind. **or so** approximately ♦ two hundred or so. **so as to** in order to. **so far** up to now. **so long!** (informal) goodbye. **so many** or **so much** nothing but ♦ They went down like so many skittles ♦ His promises were just so much nonsense. **so much for** no more need be said about something ♦ Well, so much for that idea. **so that** in order that; with the result that. **so what?** that is not important. [from an Old English word]

soak verb 1 to place something or lie in a liquid so as to become thoroughly wet. 2 to make something or someone extremely wet; to drench someone or something. 3 (said about liquid) to penetrate gradually ♦ The rain has soaked right through my jacket. 4 (informal) to extract money from someone by charging or taxing them very heavily.
soak noun the act or process of soaking.
to soak something up 1 to take in a liquid in the way that a sponge does. 2 to absorb something ♦ We walked around the stadium, soaking up the atmosphere. [from an Old English word socian]

so-and-so noun (so-and-sos) 1 a person or thing that need not be named. 2 (informal) an unpleasant or objectionable person ♦ a nosy so-and-so.

soap noun 1 a substance used with water for washing and cleaning things, made of fat or oil combined with an alkali. 2 (informal) a soap opera.
soap verb to put soap on something.
soapiness noun **soapy** adjective [from an Old English word]

soapbox noun a box or crate used as a platform for someone making a speech in a public place.

soap opera noun a television serial about the everyday lives of a group of people. [so called because the serials were originally sponsored in the USA by soap manufacturers]

soap powder noun powder of soap with additives, used for washing clothes.

soapstone noun a soft stone composed of talc, used for making ornaments.

soapsuds plural noun froth of soapy water.

soar verb 1 to fly or rise high in the air. 2 to rise very high ♦ Prices were soaring. [from an Old French word essorer; related to aura]

sob verb (sobbed, sobbing) to make a loud gasping sound when crying.
sob noun an act or sound of sobbing. [probably from an Old Dutch word]

sober adjective 1 not drunk. 2 serious and self-controlled, not frivolous. 3 (said about colour) not bright or conspicuous.
sober verb to make someone sober, or to become sober ♦ He soon sobered up.
soberly adverb [from a Latin word sobrius]

sobriety (sə-bry-əti) noun being sober. [same origin as for sober]

sobriquet (soh-brik-ay) noun a person's nickname. [a French word]

sob story noun (informal) an account of someone's experiences, told in order to get sympathy or help.

so-called adjective called by that name or description but perhaps not deserving it.

soccer noun Association Football. [short for Association]

sociable (soh-shə-bəl) adjective 1 liking to be with other people. SYNONYMS: friendly, outgoing, gregarious. 2 characterized by friendliness ♦ a sociable occasion. SYNONYM: convivial. **sociability** noun **sociably** adverb [same origin as for sociable]

social adjective 1 to do with human society or its organization; to do with the relationships between people or classes

living in a society ♦ *social problems* ♦ *her social background.* **2** helping people to meet each other ♦ *a social club.* **3** living in an organized community, not solitary ♦ *Bees are social insects.* **4** sociable.
social *noun* a social gathering. **socially** *adverb* [from a Latin word *socius* meaning 'companion']

social climber *noun* a person who is keen to gain a higher status in society.

social democrat *noun* a person who believes in achieving a socialist system of government by democratic rather than revolutionary means. **social democracy** *noun*

socialism *noun* **1** a political and economic theory advocating that land, transport, natural resources, and the chief industries should be owned and managed by the government. **2** a policy or practice based on this. **socialist** *noun & adjective* **socialistic** *adjective* [from a French word; related to *social*]

socialite (**soh-shǝ-liyt**) *noun* a person who is well known in fashionable society and often takes part in social activities.

socialize *verb* **1** to mix socially with other people, to take part in social activities. **2** to make someone behave in a way acceptable to society. **socialization** *noun*

social science *noun* the scientific study of human society and social relationships.

social security *noun* money and other assistance provided by the government for those in need through being unemployed, ill, or disabled.

social services *plural noun* welfare services provided by local or national government, including education, medical care, and housing.

social work *noun* work done by people trained to help people with social problems. **social worker** *noun*

society *noun* (**societies**) **1** an organized community of people in a particular country or region ♦ *We live in a multiracial society.* SYNONYMS: community, culture. **2** people in general ♦ *The judge said he was a danger to society.* **3** a group of people organized for some common purpose ♦ *the school debating society.* SYNONYMS: club, association, guild, league, union. **4** being in the company of other people ♦ *She shunned the society of others.* **5** people of the higher social classes ♦ *a society wedding.* [same origin as for *social*]

sociology (**soh-si-ol-ǝji**) *noun* the scientific study of human society and its development and institutions, or of social problems. **sociological** *adjective* **sociologist** *noun* [from a Latin word *socius* meaning 'companion, ally' and *-logy*]

sock *noun* **1** a knitted piece of clothing for the foot and lower part of the leg. **2** a loose insole. **3** (*informal*) a forceful blow. **sock** *verb* (*informal*) to hit someone hard. **to pull your socks up** (*informal*) to make an effort to do better. **to put a sock in it** (*informal*) to stop talking. [from an Old English word *socc* meaning 'light shoe']

socket *noun* **1** a hollow into which something fits ♦ *a tooth socket.* **2** a device into which an electric plug or bulb is put in order to make a connection. [from an Old French word *soc* meaning 'ploughshare']

socketed *adjective* fitted with a socket.

sockeye *noun* a kind of salmon. [from an American Indian word *sukai* meaning 'fish of fishes']

sod *noun* a piece of turf. [from an Old German or Old Dutch word *sode*]

soda *noun* **1** a compound of sodium in common use, especially sodium carbonate (*washing soda*), sodium bicarbonate (*baking soda*), or sodium hydroxide (*caustic soda*). **2** soda water ♦ *whisky and soda.* [probably from a Persian word]

soda bread *noun* bread made with baking soda, not yeast.

soda fountain *noun* (*North Amer.*) **1** an apparatus in which soda water is stored under pressure, ready to be drawn out. **2** a counter serving drinks, ice cream, and snacks.

soda siphon *noun* a bottle in which carbonated water is stored under pressure, ready to be drawn out.

soda water *noun* water made fizzy by being charged with carbon dioxide under pressure.

sodden *adjective* soaked through. [the old past participle of *seethe*]

sodium (**soh-di-ǝm**) *noun* a chemical element (symbol Na), a soft silver-white metal. [from *soda*, to which it is related]

sodium bicarbonate *noun* a soluble white powder used in fire extinguishers and fizzy drinks, and to make cakes rise; baking soda.

sodium carbonate noun white powder or crystals used to clean plates and in making soap and glass; washing soda.

sodium lamp noun a lamp using an electrical discharge in sodium vapour and giving a yellow light, often used in street lighting.

sofa noun a long upholstered seat with a back and arms. [from an Arabic word *suffa* meaning 'long stone bench']

sofa bed noun a sofa that can be converted into a bed.

soft adjective 1 not hard or firm. 2 smooth in texture, not rough or stiff. SYNONYMS: sleek, velvety, silky, fluffy, downy, furry, feathery. 3 not loud. SYNONYMS: low, faint, muted. 4 gentle or delicate ♦ *a soft breeze.* 5 lenient or tender-hearted. 6 not physically robust, feeble. 7 not extreme or radical ♦ *the soft left of the Labour party.* 8 not done with much force ♦ *a soft kick.* 9 (*informal*) easy, not needing much effort ♦ *a soft option* ♦ *soft living.* 10 (said about currency) likely to drop suddenly in value. 11 (said about drinks) not alcoholic. 12 (said about drugs) not likely to cause addiction. 13 (said about water) free from mineral salts that prevent soap from lathering. 14 (said about colour or light) not bright or dazzling. 15 (said about consonants) not hard. The letter 'g' is hard in 'gun' and soft in 'gin'.
soft adverb softly. **to have a soft spot for** to be fond of someone. **softly** adverb **softness** noun [from an Old English word]

soft-boiled adjective (said about eggs) lightly boiled so that the yolk does not become set.

soften verb 1 to make something soft, or to become soft. 2 to make something or become less severe ♦ *We did all we could to soften the blow* ♦ *His attitude has softened over the years.* **to soften someone up** to make someone weaker or less able to resist ♦ *Heavy bombing softened them up before the ground forces attacked.* **softener** noun

soft fruit noun a small stoneless fruit such as a strawberry or currant.

soft furnishings plural noun cushions, curtains, rugs, etc.

soft-hearted adjective kind and compassionate.

softie noun (*informal*) a person who is physically weak or not hardy, or who is soft-hearted.

softly-softly adjective cautious and patient.

soft option noun the easier alternative.

soft-pedal verb (**soft-pedalled, soft-pedalling**) (*informal*) to play down the unpleasant aspects of something.

soft soap noun 1 semi-liquid soap. 2 (*informal*) persuasive flattery.

software noun (*Computing*) programs for databases, word processing, and other tasks a computer performs, as distinct from the machinery in which these are loaded (called *hardware*).

softwood noun wood from coniferous trees.

soggy adjective (**soggier, soggiest**) very wet and soft. **soggily** adverb **sogginess** noun [from a dialect word *sog* meaning 'swamp']

soil¹ noun 1 the loose upper layer of earth in which plants grow. 2 the territory of a particular nation ♦ *on British soil.* [from an Old French word]

soil² verb to make something dirty. [from an Old French word *soillier*]

soirée (**swah-ray**) noun a social gathering in the evening for music or conversation. [a French word meaning 'evening']

sojourn (**soj-ern**) noun (*formal*) a temporary stay.
sojourn verb (*formal*) to stay at a place temporarily. [from an Old French word *sojourner*]

solace (**sol-əs**) noun comfort given to someone in distress.
solace verb to give solace to someone. [from a Latin word *solari* meaning 'to console']

solar (**soh-ler**) adjective 1 to do with or derived from the sun ♦ *solar energy.* 2 reckoned by the sun ♦ *solar time.* [from a Latin word *sol* meaning 'sun']

solar battery or **solar cell** noun a device converting solar radiation into electricity.

solarium (**sə-lair-iəm**) noun (**solariums** or **solaria**) 1 a room equipped with sunlamps or sunbeds. 2 a room enclosed with glass to let in a lot of sunlight. [from a Latin word *solarium* meaning 'sundial, place for sunning yourself']

solar panel noun a panel designed to catch the sun's rays and use their energy for heating or to make electricity.

solar plexus noun the network of nerves at the pit of the stomach; this area.

solar power noun electricity or other forms of power derived from the sun's rays.

solar system noun the sun together with the planets, asteroids, etc. that revolve around it.

sold past tense and past participle of **sell**.
to be sold on (*informal*) to be enthusiastic about something.

solder (**sohl**-der) noun a soft alloy that is melted to join metal parts together.
solder verb to join metal parts with solder. [from a Latin word *solidare* meaning 'to fasten together']

soldering iron noun an electrical tool for melting and applying solder.

soldier noun 1 a member of an army, especially one who is not an officer. 2 one of the strong-jawed ants or termites whose job is to defend the colony.
soldier verb to serve as a soldier. **to soldier on** (*informal*) to persevere with something despite difficulties. [from an Old French word *soldier*]

soldierly adjective like a soldier.

soldier of fortune noun a mercenary.

soldiery noun soldiers collectively or as a class.

sole [1] noun 1 the underside of a person's foot. 2 the part of a shoe or stocking etc. that covers this.
sole verb to put a sole on a shoe. [from a Latin word *solum*]

sole [2] noun a flat sea fish used as food. [from a Latin word *solea* meaning 'sandal' (because of the fish's shape)]

sole [3] adjective 1 one and only ♦ *She was the sole survivor.* SYNONYMS: single, lone, solitary. 2 belonging or restricted to one person or group ♦ *We have the sole right to sell these cars.* SYNONYM: exclusive. **solely** adverb [from a Latin word *solus* meaning 'alone']

solecism (**sol**-i-sizm) noun 1 a mistake in the use of language. 2 a piece of bad manners or incorrect behaviour. [from a Greek word *soloikos* meaning 'speaking incorrectly']

solemn adjective 1 formal and dignified ♦ *a solemn procession.* 2 (said about a person) not smiling or cheerful. SYNONYMS: serious, grave, sombre, unsmiling. **solemnity**

(sol-**em**-niti) noun **solemnly** adverb [from a Latin word *sollemnis* meaning 'customary, celebrated at a fixed date']

solemnize (**sol**-əm-niyz) verb 1 to mark something with a formal ceremony. 2 to perform a marriage ceremony with formal rites. **solemnization** noun

solenoid (**soh**-lin-oid) noun a coil of wire that becomes magnetic when an electrical current is passed through it. [from a Greek word *sōlēn* meaning 'channel']

sol-fa (**sol**-fah) noun the system of syllables (*doh, ray, me, fah, soh, la, te*) used to represent the notes of the musical scale. [*sol* was an earlier spelling of *soh*; the names of the notes came from syllables of a Latin hymn]

solicit (sə-**liss**-it) verb 1 to ask for or try to obtain something ♦ *She's been soliciting opinions from rail users* ♦ *All the candidates were soliciting for votes.* 2 to approach someone as a prostitute. **solicitation** noun [same origin as for *solicitous*]

solicitor noun a lawyer who advises on legal matters, prepares legal documents, and represents clients in lower courts.

solicitous (sə-**liss**-it-əs) adjective anxious and concerned about a person's welfare or comfort. **solicitously** adverb [from a Latin word *sollicitus* meaning 'worrying']

solicitude (sə-**liss**-i-tewd) noun care or concern. [same origin as for *solicitous*]

solid adjective 1 keeping its shape, firm; not liquid or gas. 2 not hollow. 3 of the same substance throughout ♦ *solid silver.* SYNONYMS: pure, unadulterated, unalloyed. 4 continuous, without a break ♦ *for two solid hours.* 5 strongly built or made, not flimsy ♦ *a solid foundation.* SYNONYMS: robust, sturdy, stout, sound. 6 having three dimensions; concerned with three-dimensional objects ♦ *solid geometry.* 7 sound and reliable ♦ *There are solid arguments against it.* 8 unanimous, showing solidarity ♦ *The miners are solid on this issue.*
solid noun 1 a solid substance or object. 2 (*Geometry*) a body or shape with three dimensions.
solids plural noun food that is not liquid ♦ *Is your baby eating solids yet?* **solidity** (sə-**id**-iti) noun **solidly** adverb [from a Latin word *solidus*]

solidarity noun unity resulting from common interests, feelings, or sympathies. [from a French word]

solidify (sol-id-i-fiy) verb (**solidifies, solidified, solidifying**) to make something hard or solid, or to become hard or solid.

solid state noun a state of matter in which the constituent atoms or molecules occupy fixed positions with respect to each other and cannot move freely.

solid-state adjective making use of the electronic properties of solid semiconductors, instead of valves.

soliloquize (sol-il-o-kwiyz) verb to make a soliloquy.

soliloquy (sol-il-o-kwi) noun (**soliloquies**) a speech in which a person expresses thoughts aloud when alone or without addressing anyone. [from Latin words solus meaning 'alone' and loqui meaning 'to speak']

solitaire (sol-i-tair) noun 1 a game for one person, in which marbles or pegs are removed from their places on a special board after jumping others over them. 2 the card game patience. 3 a diamond or other gem set by itself. [from a French word; related to solitary]

solitary adjective 1 alone, without companions. 2 single, only ♦ a solitary example. 3 secluded or isolated ♦ a solitary valley.
solitary noun (**solitaries**) 1 a recluse. 2 (informal) solitary confinement.
solitarily adverb [from a Latin word solus meaning 'alone']

solitary confinement noun isolation of a prisoner in a separate cell as a punishment.

solitude noun being alone. SYNONYMS: seclusion, isolation, loneliness. [same origin as for solitary]

solo noun (**solos**) 1 a piece of music, song, or dance for one performer. 2 a pilot's flight in an aircraft without an instructor or companion. 3 (also **solo whist**) a card game like whist in which one player may oppose the others.
solo adjective & adverb for or done by one person ♦ for solo flute ♦ flying solo. [an Italian word meaning 'alone']

soloist noun a person who performs a solo.

solstice (sol-stis) noun each of the two times in the year when the sun is furthest from the equator. The **summer solstice** is the longest day of the year, around 21 June. The **winter solstice** is the shortest day of the year, around 22 December. [from Latin words sol meaning 'sun' and sistere meaning 'to stand still']

soluble (sol-yoo-bəl) adjective 1 able to be dissolved in liquid. 2 able to be solved. **solubility** (sol-yoo-bil-iti) noun **solubly** adverb [same origin as for solve]

solute (sol-yoot) noun a substance that is dissolved in another substance.

solution noun 1 the answer to a problem or puzzle. 2 a liquid in which something is dissolved. 3 dissolving or being dissolved into liquid form. [same origin as for solve]

solvable adjective able to be solved.

solve verb to find the answer to a problem or puzzle or the way out of a difficulty. SYNONYMS: answer, resolve, unravel, decipher, work out, clear up; (informal) crack. **solver** noun [from a Latin word solvere meaning 'to unfasten']

solvent adjective 1 having enough money to pay your debts and liabilities. 2 able to dissolve another substance.
solvent noun a substance, especially a liquid, used for dissolving something. **solvency** noun [from a Latin word solvere meaning 'to unfasten']

solvent abuse noun the inhaling of the fumes from certain solvents for their intoxicating effect, e.g. glue-sniffing.

somatic (sə-mat-ik) adjective to do with the body. [from a Greek word sōma meaning 'body']

sombre (som-ber) adjective 1 dark or dull. 2 solemn or gloomy ♦ a sombre mood. **sombrely** adverb [from Latin words sub meaning 'under' and umbra meaning 'shade']

sombrero (som-brair-oh) noun (**sombreros**) a felt or straw hat with a very wide brim, worn especially in Mexico. [from a Spanish word sombra meaning 'shade'; related to sombre]

some adjective 1 an unspecified amount or number ♦ some apples ♦ some sugar. 2 an unspecified person or thing ♦ Some fool locked the door. 3 approximately ♦ We waited some 30 minutes. 4 a considerable amount or number ♦ That was some years ago. 5 (informal) used to express admiration ♦ That was some storm!
some pronoun an amount that is less than the whole ♦ Some of them were late. **some**

time 1 quite a long time ♦ *I may be some time* ♦ *I've been wondering about the job for some time.* **2** at some unspecified time; sometime ♦ *You must come round for a meal some time.* [from an Old English word *sum*]

◊ Note that *some time* must be written as two words when the meaning is 'quite a long time'. See also the notes on **sometime** and **sometimes**.

-some *suffix* **1** forms adjectives denoting a quality or manner (as in *handsome*, *quarrelsome*). **2** forms nouns from numbers, denoting a group of this many (as in *foursome*). [from an Old English word]

somebody *noun & pronoun* someone.

somehow *adverb* **1** in some unspecified or unexplained manner ♦ *I never liked her, somehow.* **2** by one means or another ♦ *We must get it finished somehow.*

someone *noun & pronoun* **1** an unspecified person. **2** a person of importance.

someplace *adverb* (*North Amer.*) somewhere.

somersault (**sum-er-solt**) *noun* an acrobatic movement in which a person rolls head over heels on the ground or in the air. **somersault** *verb* to do a somersault. [from Latin words *supra* meaning 'above' and *saltus* meaning 'a leap']

something *noun & pronoun* **1** an unspecified thing. **2** an impressive or praiseworthy thing ♦ *Winning a gold medal would be quite something.* **something like 1** approximately ♦ *It cost something like £10.* **2** rather like ♦ *It's something like a rabbit.* **something of** to some extent ♦ *He is something of an expert.*

sometime *adverb* (also **some time**) at some unspecified time.
sometime *adjective* former ♦ *her sometime friend.*
◊ When *sometime* is an adverb, it can also be spelt as two words, *some time*: *You must come round for a meal sometime* or *some time.* See the note on *some time* at the entry for **some**.

sometimes *adverb* at some times but not all the time ♦ *We sometimes go there by bus.*
◊ See the note on *some time* at the entry for **some**.

somewhat *adverb* to some extent ♦ *It is somewhat difficult.*

somewhere *adverb* **1** at, in, or to an unspecified place or position. **2** at an approximate point ♦ *It was somewhere between 5 and 6 o'clock.* **to get somewhere** (*informal*) to achieve some success ♦ *Now we are getting somewhere.*

somnambulist (som-**nam**-bew-list) *noun* a sleepwalker. **somnambulism** *noun* [from Latin words *somnus* meaning 'sleep' and *ambulare* meaning 'to walk']

somnolent (som-nŏl-ŏnt) *adjective* sleepy or drowsy. **somnolence** *noun* [from a Latin word *somnus* meaning 'sleep']

son *noun* **1** a male child in relation to his parents. **2** a male descendant. **3** a form of address to a boy or young man. [from an Old English word *sunu*]

sonar (soh-ner) *noun* a system or device for detecting objects under water by the reflection of sound waves. [from *sound navigation and ranging*]

sonata (sŏn-ah-tǎ) *noun* a musical composition for one instrument, often with a piano accompaniment, usually with three or four movements. [from an Italian word *sonare* meaning 'to sound']

sonatina (sonn-ǎ-teen-ǎ) *noun* a simple or short sonata.

son et lumière (sonn ay loom-yair) *noun* an entertainment given at night, giving a dramatic account of the history of a building or monument using lighting effects and recorded sound. [a French phrase meaning 'sound and light']

song *noun* **1** a musical composition for singing. **2** singing ♦ *He burst into song.* **3** the musical call of some birds, whales, and insects. **for a song** (*informal*) very cheaply. **to make a song and dance** (*informal*) to make a great fuss. [from an Old English word *sang*]

songbird *noun* a bird that sings sweetly.

sonic *adjective* to do with or involving sound waves. [from a Latin word *sonus* meaning 'sound']

sonic boom *noun* a loud noise heard when the shock wave caused by an aircraft travelling faster than the speed of sound reaches the hearer.

son-in-law *noun* (**sons-in-law**) a daughter's husband.

sonnet *noun* a poem of 14 lines with rhymes following any of several patterns. [from an Italian word *sonetto* meaning 'a little sound']

sonny noun (informal) a form of address to a boy or young man.

sonorous (sonn-er-os) adjective resonant, giving a deep powerful sound. [from a Latin word sonor meaning 'sound']

soon adverb 1 in a short time from now. 2 not long after something. 3 early, quickly ♦ You spoke too soon. **as soon as** readily, as willingly ♦ I'd just as soon stay here. **as soon as** at the moment that, as early as; as readily or willingly as. **no sooner ... than** as soon as; at the very moment that ♦ No sooner had I found my seat than the play ended. **sooner or later** at some time, eventually. [from an Old English word]

soot noun the black powdery substance that rises in the smoke of coal or wood etc. [from an Old English word]

soothe verb 1 to calm or comfort someone. 2 to ease pain or distress. SYNONYMS: ease, relieve, allay, assuage. **soothing** adjective [from an Old English word]

soothsayer noun a person who foretells the future. [from sooth and say]

sooty adjective (sootier, sootiest) 1 covered with soot. 2 like soot, black.

sop noun 1 a concession that is made in order to pacify or bribe someone. 2 a piece of bread dipped in gravy, soup, or sauce.
sop verb (sopped, sopping) to soak up liquid with something absorbent. [from an Old English word soppian meaning 'to dip bread in liquid']

sophism (sof-izm) noun a piece of sophistry.

sophist (sof-ist) noun a person who uses sophistry. [named after the Sophists, Greek philosophers of the 5th century BC, who taught rhetoric and skilled reasoning]

sophisticate (sof-ist-i-kayt) verb 1 to make someone become more discerning or worldy-wise through education or experience. 2 to develop something into a more complex form. **sophistication** noun [from a Latin word sophisticare meaning 'to tamper with, mix with something']

sophisticated (sof-ist-i-kaytid) adjective 1 having refined or cultured tastes or experienced about the world. 2 complex or elaborate ♦ sophisticated electronic devices. 3 able to understand complex issues ♦ a sophisticated electorate.

sophistry (sof-ist-ri) noun (sophistries) reasoning that is clever and subtle but unsound or misleading. [from a Greek word sophos meaning 'wise']

soporific (sop-er-if-ik) adjective causing sleep or drowsiness.
soporific noun a drug or other substance that causes sleep. [from a Latin word sopor meaning 'sleep' and facere meaning 'to make']

sopping adjective wet through. [from sop]

soppy adjective (soppier, soppiest) (informal) sentimental in a silly way. **soppily** adverb **soppiness** noun [from sop]

soprano (so-prah-noh) noun (sopranos) 1 the highest female or boy's singing voice, or a singer with such a voice. 2 a musical instrument of the highest pitch in its family. [from an Italian word sopra meaning 'above']

sorbet (sor-bay) noun a flavoured water ice. [same origin as for sherbet]

sorcerer noun a person believed to have magic powers. [from an Old French word sorcier]

sorceress noun a female sorcerer.

sorcery noun the art or use of magic, especially involving evil spirits.

sordid adjective 1 dirty or squalid. SYNONYMS: dingy; (informal) sleazy, seedy. 2 dishonourable and shameful ♦ sordid dealings. **sordidly** adverb **sordidness** noun [from a Latin word sordere meaning 'to be dirty']

sore adjective 1 (said about part of your body) hurting when you touch or use it. SYNONYMS: painful, tender, raw. 2 suffering pain ♦ I felt sore all over. 3 annoyed or upset. 4 serious or urgent ♦ in sore need of attention.
sore noun 1 a sore place, especially where the skin is raw. 2 a source of distress or annoyance. **a sore point** an issue about which someone feels distressed or annoyed. **soreness** noun [from an Old English word]

sorely adverb seriously, very ♦ I was sorely tempted.

sorghum (sor-gəm) noun a kind of tropical cereal grass. [from an Italian word sorgo]

sorrel [1] noun a herb with sharp-tasting leaves used in salads. [from an Old French word sur meaning 'sour']

sorrel[2] *noun* 1 a horse with a light reddish-brown coat. 2 a light reddish-brown colour. [from an Old French word *sor* meaning 'yellowish']

sorrow *noun* 1 mental suffering caused by loss or disappointment. 2 something that causes this.
sorrow *verb* to feel sorrow. [from an Old English word]

sorrowful *adjective* feeling or showing sorrow. **sorrowfully** *adverb*

sorry *adjective* (**sorrier, sorriest**) 1 feeling regret or shame for something you have done. SYNONYMS: apologetic, regretful, remorseful, repentant, penitent, contrite. 2 feeling sadness, pity, or sympathy about something. 3 pitiful or regrettable ♦ *His clothes were in a sorry state* ♦ *a sorry episode.*
sorry *interjection* used to express apology. [from an Old English word]

sort *noun* 1 a particular kind or variety. SYNONYMS: kind, type, category, form, variety, class, make (of product). 2 (*informal*) a person of a particular nature ♦ *She's quite a good sort.*
sort *verb* to arrange things in groups according to their kind, size, destination, etc. **of a sort** or **of sorts** not fully deserving the name given. **out of sorts** slightly unwell or unhappy. **sort of** (*informal*) to some extent ♦ *I sort of expected it.* **to sort someone out** (*informal*) to deal with or punish someone. **to sort something out** to resolve a problem or difficulty. **sorter** *noun* [from a Latin word *sors* meaning 'lot, condition']
◊ Correct usage is *this sort of thing* or *these sorts of things*, not *these sort of things.*

sortie (*sor-tee*) *noun* 1 an attack by troops coming out from a besieged place. 2 a flight of an aircraft on a military operation. 3 a short trip. [from a French word *sortir* meaning 'to go out']

SOS *noun* an urgent appeal for help or response. [the international Morse code signal of extreme distress]

so-so *adjective* neither very good nor very bad.

sot *noun* a drunkard. **sottish** *adjective* [from an Old English word *sott* meaning 'foolish person']

sotto voce (*sot-oh voh-chi*) *adverb* & *adjective* in a quiet voice. [an Italian phrase meaning 'under the voice']

sou (*soo*) *noun* 1 a former French coin of low value. 2 (*informal*) a very small amount of money. [from a French word]

soubriquet (*soo-bri-kay*) *noun* another spelling of **sobriquet**.

soufflé (*soo-flay*) *noun* a light spongy dish made with beaten egg white. [from a French word *souffler* meaning 'to blow']

sough (*sow* or *suf*) *verb* to make a moaning or whispering sound as the wind does in trees.
sough *noun* this sound. [from an Old English word]

sought past tense and past participle of **seek**.

sought after *adjective* much in demand.

souk (*sook*) *noun* an open-air market place in countries of the Middle East and North Africa. [from an Arabic word *suk*]

soul *noun* 1 the spiritual or immortal element in a person. 2 a person's mental, moral, or emotional nature. 3 a personification or embodiment of some quality ♦ *She is the soul of discretion.* 4 a person ♦ *There wasn't a soul about.* 5 soul music. [from an Old English word]

soul-destroying *adjective* unbearably monotonous or depressing.

soulful *adjective* having or showing deep and often sorrowful feeling. **soulfully** *adverb*

soulless *adjective* 1 lacking human feelings. 2 dull, uninteresting.

soulmate *noun* a person ideally suited to another.

soul music *noun* a kind of music combining elements of rhythm and blues and gospel music.

soul-searching *noun* close examination of your emotions and motives.

sound[1] *noun* 1 vibrations that travel through the air and can be detected by the ear. 2 something that can be heard ♦ *the sound of drums.* 3 sound reproduced in a film etc. 4 the volume on a television set ♦ *Can you put the sound up?* 5 the mental impression produced by a statement or description etc. ♦ *I don't like the sound of the new scheme.*
sound *verb* 1 to produce or cause something to produce a sound ♦ *Sound the trumpet!* 2 to utter or pronounce something ♦ *The 'h' in 'hour' is not sounded.* 3 to give an impression when heard ♦ *It sounds like an owl* ♦ *The news sounds good.* 4 to give an audible signal for something ♦ *Sound the retreat!* 5 to test something by noting the sound produced ♦ *The doctor*

sounds a patient's lungs with a stethoscope. **to sound off** (*informal*) to express your opinions loudly and freely. **sounder** *noun* [from a Latin word *sonus* meaning 'a sound']

sound [2] *adjective* **1** in good condition, not damaged. **2** healthy, not diseased. **3** logical and well-founded ♦ *sound reasoning.* **4** showing good judgement, sensible ♦ *sound advice.* **5** financially secure ♦ *a sound investment.* **6** thorough or severe ♦ *a sound thrashing.* **7** (said about sleep) deep and unbroken.
sound *adverb* soundly ♦ *The baby is sound asleep.* **soundly** *adverb* **soundness** *noun* [from an Old English word *gesund* meaning 'healthy']

sound [3] *verb* **1** to test the depth or quality of the bottom of the sea or a river etc., using a weighted line (called a *sounding line*) or sound echoes. **2** to examine part of the body with a surgical probe.
sound *noun* a surgical probe. **to sound someone out** to question someone cautiously to find out what they think or feel about something. **sounder** *noun* [from Latin words *sub* meaning 'under' and *unda* meaning 'wave']

sound [4] *noun* a strait of water ♦ *Plymouth Sound.* [from an Old Norse word *sund* meaning 'swimming or sea']

sound barrier *noun* the high resistance of air to aircraft moving at speeds close to that of sound.

sound bite *noun* a very short part of a speech, interview, or statement broadcast on radio or television because it seems to sum up the person's opinion in a few words.

sound effect *noun* a sound other than speech or music made artificially for use in a play, film, etc.

sounding *noun* measurement of the depth of water.
soundings *plural noun* the checking of opinions or intentions before taking action.

sounding board *noun* a person whose reactions to ideas are used to test how good the ideas are.

soundproof *adjective* not able to be penetrated by sound.
soundproof *verb* to make a room etc. soundproof.

soundtrack *noun* **1** the sound that goes with a cinema film. **2** a strip on the edge of cinema film for recording sound.

soup *noun* liquid food made of stock from stewed meat, fish, or vegetables etc.
soup *verb* **to soup something up** (*informal*) **1** to increase the power of an engine. **2** to make something more lively or elaborate. **in the soup** (*informal*) in difficulties or trouble. **soupy** *adjective* [from an Old French word *soupe* meaning 'sop or broth']

soupçon (**soop**-sawn) *noun* a very small quantity ♦ *Add a soupçon of garlic.* [a French word meaning 'suspicion']

soup kitchen *noun* a place where free food is supplied to the homeless or needy.

sour *adjective* **1** tasting sharp like lemon or vinegar. SYNONYMS: sharp, tart, tangy, acid, acidic. **2** not fresh, tasting or smelling sharp or unpleasant from fermentation or staleness ♦ *sour milk.* **3** showing resentment or anger ♦ *He gave me a sour look.* **4** (said about soil) excessively acid, deficient in lime.
sour *verb* to make something sour, or to become sour ♦ *He had been soured by misfortune.* **to go** or **turn sour** to turn out badly. **sourly** *adverb* **sourness** *noun* [from an Old English word]

source *noun* **1** the place from which something comes or is obtained. **2** the starting point of a river. **3** a person, book, etc. providing information. **at source** at the point of origin. [from an Old French word; related to *surge*]

sour cream *noun* cream deliberately fermented by the action of bacteria.

sour grapes *noun* pretending to despise something you want because you know you cannot have it yourself. [from the fable of the fox who wanted some grapes but found that they were out of reach and so pretended that they were sour and undesirable anyway]

sourpuss *noun* (*informal*) a bad-tempered or sullen person.

souse (sows) *verb* **1** to soak something in liquid; to drench something with liquid. **2** to soak fish etc. in pickle or a marinade ♦ *soused herrings.* [from an Old French word *sous* meaning 'pickle']

south *noun* **1** the point or direction opposite north. **2** the part of a place or building that is towards the south.
south *adjective* & *adverb* **1** towards or in the south. **2** (said about a wind) blowing

from the south. [from an Old English word]

south-east *noun* the point or direction midway between south and east.
south-east *adjective* **1** situated in the south-east. **2** (said about a wind) blowing from the south-east.
south-east *adverb* in or towards the south-east. **south-easterly** *adjective & noun* **south-eastern** *adjective*

southeaster *noun* a south-east wind.

southerly *adjective* **1** in or towards the south. **2** (said about a wind) blowing from the south.
southerly *noun* (**southerlies**) a southerly wind.

southern *adjective* of or in the south.

southerner *noun* someone who lives in the south of a country or region.

Southern Lights *plural noun* the aurora australis, which appears in the southern hemisphere.

southernmost *adjective* furthest south.

southpaw *noun* a left-handed person, especially in boxing.

South Pole *noun* the southernmost point of the earth.

southward *adjective & adverb* towards the south. **southwards** *adverb*

south-west *noun* the point or direction midway between south and west.
south-west *adjective* **1** situated in the south-west. **2** (said about a wind) blowing from the south-west.
south-west *adverb* in or towards the south-west. **south-westerly** *adjective & noun* **south-western** *adjective*

southwester *noun* a south-west wind.

souvenir (soo-vən-eer) *noun* something bought or kept as a reminder of an incident or a place visited. [from a French word *se souvenir* meaning 'to remember']

sou'wester *noun* a waterproof hat, usually of oilskin, with a broad flap at the back. [from *southwester*, a wind often bringing rain]

sovereign (sov-rin) *noun* **1** a king or queen who is the supreme ruler of a country. **2** an old British gold coin, originally worth £1.
sovereign *adjective* **1** possessing supreme power or authority. **2** (said about a nation) independent ♦ *sovereign states.* [from a Latin word *super* meaning 'over']

sovereignty *noun* (**sovereignties**)
1 supreme power or authority. **2** the authority of a state to govern itself or another state. **3** an independent state.

soviet (soh-vi-ət or sov-i-ət) *noun* an elected council in the former USSR.
Soviet *adjective* to do with the former Soviet Union. [from a Russian word *sovet* meaning 'council']

sow[1] (soh) *verb* (past participle, **sown** or **sowed**) **1** to plant seed by scattering it on or in the ground. **2** to spread or introduce feelings or ideas ♦ *Her words sowed doubt in my mind.* **sower** *noun* [from an Old English word *sawan*]
◊ Do not confuse this word with **sew**, which has a different meaning.

sow[2] (sow) *noun* an adult female pig. [from an Old English word *sugu*]

soya bean *noun* a kind of bean, originally from SE Asia, from which an edible oil and flour are obtained. [via Dutch from a Japanese word]

soy sauce or **soya sauce** *noun* a salty brown sauce made by fermenting soya beans in brine, used in Chinese and Japanese cooking.

sozzled *adjective* (*informal*) very drunk. [from an old word *sozzle* meaning 'to mix sloppily']

spa (spah) *noun* a health resort where there is a spring of water containing mineral salts. [from Spa, a town in Belgium with a mineral spring]

space *noun* **1** the limitless expanse in which all objects exist and move. **2** an area or volume that is available to be used ♦ *The table takes up too much space* ♦ *storage space.* **3** an interval between points or objects, an empty area ♦ *There's a space here for your signature* ♦ *The posts are separated by a space of 10 ft.* **4** a large area ♦ *a country of wide open spaces.* **5** the universe beyond the earth's atmosphere. **6** an interval of time ♦ *within the space of an hour.*
space *verb* to arrange things with spaces between ♦ *Space the chairs out.* [from a Latin word *spatium* meaning 'a space']

space bar *noun* the horizontal bar on a keyboard which you press to make a space.

spacecraft *noun* (**spacecraft**) a vehicle for travelling in outer space.

spaceman *noun* (**spacemen**) an astronaut.

space probe *noun* an unmanned rocket with instruments to detect conditions in outer space.

spaceship *noun* a spacecraft.

space shuttle *noun* a spacecraft designed for repeated use, e.g. between earth and a space station.

space station *noun* an artificial satellite which orbits the earth and is used as a base for operations and experiments in space.

spacesuit *noun* a sealed pressurized suit allowing an astronaut to survive in space.

space-time continuum *noun* (*Physics*) the fusion of the concepts of space and time, with time as a fourth dimension, that allows any physical object to be precisely located.

spacious (spay-shəs) *adjective* providing a lot of space. SYNONYMS: roomy, sizeable, commodious, capacious. **spaciousness** *noun* [same origin as for *space*]

spade [1] *noun* **1** a tool for digging ground, with a broad metal blade and a wooden handle. **2** a tool of similar shape for other purposes.
spade *verb* to dig or move something with a spade. **to call a spade a spade** to call a thing by its proper name; to speak plainly or bluntly. **spadeful** *noun* (**spadefuls**) [from an Old English word *spadu*]

spade [2] *noun* a playing card of the suit (called **spades**) marked with black figures shaped like an inverted heart with a short stem. **in spades** (*informal*) in large amounts or to a high degree. [from an Italian word *spada* meaning 'sword']

spadework *noun* hard or dull work done in preparation for something.

spaghetti (spə-get-i) *noun* pasta made in long thin solid sticks. [from an Italian word meaning 'little strings']

spam *noun* (*trademark*) tinned pork luncheon meat. [from *spiced ham*]

span [1] *noun* **1** the extent from end to end or across something. **2** the distance or part between the uprights supporting an arch or bridge. **3** the length of time that something lasts ♦ *the span of life*. **4** the distance (reckoned as 9 inches or 23 cm) between the tips of a person's thumb and little finger when these are stretched apart.
span *verb* (**spanned, spanning**) **1** to reach or extend across something ♦ *A bridge spans the river*. **2** to stretch your hand across something in one span ♦ *Can you span an octave on the piano?* [from an Old English word meaning 'distance between thumb and little finger']

span [2] *noun* a team of two or more pairs of oxen or horses. [from an Old Dutch word]

span [3] see **spick**.

spandrel *noun* (*Architecture*) the space between the curve of an arch and the surrounding rectangular moulding or framework, or between the curves of adjoining arches and the moulding above. [from an Old French word]

spangle *noun* a small piece of glittering material, especially one of many decorating a dress etc.
spangle *verb* to cover something with spangles or sparkling objects. **spangly** *adjective* [from an Old Dutch word *spange* meaning 'buckle']

Spaniard *noun* a person born in Spain or descended from people born there.

spaniel *noun* a dog with long drooping ears and a silky coat. [from an Old French word *espaigneul* meaning 'Spanish dog']

Spanish *adjective* to do with or coming from Spain.
Spanish *noun* the language of Spain, also spoken in much of Central and South America.

spank *verb* to smack a person on the bottom as a punishment. [an imitation of the sound]

spanking *adjective* (*informal*) brisk and lively ♦ *a spanking pace*. [from *spank*]

spanner *noun* a tool for gripping and turning a nut or bolt. **to throw a spanner into the works** to sabotage a scheme. [from a German word *spannen* meaning 'to tighten']

spar [1] *noun* a strong pole used for a mast, yard, or boom on a ship. [from an Old Norse word *sperra*]

spar [2] *verb* (**sparred, sparring**) **1** to practise boxing. **2** to argue with someone, especially in a friendly way. [from an Old English word *sperran* meaning 'to strike out']

spar [3] *noun* any of several kinds of non-metallic mineral that split easily. [from an Old German word]

spare *verb* **1** to part with or afford to give something ♦ *We can't spare him until next*

week ♦ *I can only spare a couple of hours.*
2 to be merciful towards someone, to
refrain from hurting or harming a person
or thing. **3** to choose not to inflict
something on someone ♦ *Spare me the gory
details.*
spare *adjective* **1** additional to what is
usually needed or used; kept for use when
needed ♦ *a spare wheel* ♦ *the spare room.*
2 thin or lean. **3** elegantly simple ♦ *a spare
style of writing.*
spare *noun* a spare part or thing kept in
reserve for use when needed. **to go spare**
(*informal*) to become very annoyed. **to
spare no expense** to be prepared to pay as
much as is necessary. **to spare** left over.
sparely *adverb* **spareness** *noun* [from an
Old English word]

spare rib *noun* a cut of pork from the lower
ribs.

spare tyre *noun* **1** an extra tyre carried in a
vehicle in case of a puncture. **2** (*informal*)
a roll of fat round a person's waist.

sparing (spair-ing) *adjective* economical,
not generous or wasteful. **sparingly**
adverb [from *spare*]

spark *noun* **1** a small fiery particle, e.g. one
thrown off by something burning or
caused by friction. **2** a flash of light
produced by an electrical discharge. **3** a
small amount of a quality ♦ *He hasn't a
spark of generosity in him.* **4** liveliness and
excitement.
spark *verb* to give off a spark or sparks. **a
bright spark** a lively person. **to spark
something off** to trigger something off.
sparky *adjective* [from an Old English
word]

sparkle *verb* **1** to shine brightly with tiny
flashes of light. SYNONYMS: glitter, glisten,
twinkle, flash, gleam, glint. **2** to be witty and
lively.
sparkle *noun* **1** a glittering flash of light.
2 liveliness and wit. **sparkly** *adjective*
[from *spark*]

sparkler *noun* a hand-held firework that
gives off sparks.

sparkling wine *noun* wine that is
effervescent.

spark plug or **sparking plug** *noun* a
device producing an electrical spark to
ignite the fuel in an internal-combustion
engine.

sparrow *noun* a small brownish-grey bird.
[from an Old English word *spearwa*]

sparrowhawk *noun* a small hawk that
preys on small birds.

sparse *adjective* thinly scattered, not dense
♦ *a sparse population.* **sparsely** *adverb*
sparseness *noun* **sparsity** *noun* [from a
Latin word *sparsum* meaning 'scattered']

spartan *adjective* (said about conditions)
simple and sometimes harsh, without
comfort or luxuries. [from Sparta, a city
in the southern Peloponnese in Greece,
whose citizens in ancient times were
renowned for hardiness]

spasm *noun* **1** a sudden involuntary
contraction of a muscle. **2** a sudden brief
spell of activity or emotion ♦ *a spasm of
coughing.* [from a Greek word *spasmos*
meaning 'contraction']

spasmodic (spaz-mod-ik) *adjective*
1 happening or done at irregular
intervals. **2** to do with or caused by a
spasm or spasms. **spasmodically** *adverb*
[from *spasm*]

spastic *adjective* (*old use*) **1** to do with
muscle spasm. **2** affected by cerebral
palsy.
spastic *noun* a person suffering from
cerebral palsy. **spasticity** (spas-tiss-iti)
noun [from a Greek word *spastikos*
meaning 'pulling']
◊ This word can be offensive to some
people. It is better to use *person with
cerebral palsy* instead.

spat¹ past tense and past participle of
spit¹.

spat² *noun* a short gaiter covering the
instep and ankle. [from *spatter*]

spat³ *noun* a petty quarrel. [probably an
imitation of the sound]

spate (spayt) *noun* a sudden flood or rush
♦ *a spate of orders.* **in spate** (said about a
river) flowing strongly at an abnormally
high level. [origin unknown]

spathe (spayth) *noun* a large petal-like part
of a flower, surrounding a central spike.
[from a Greek word meaning 'broad
blade']

spatial (spay-shǝl) *adjective* to do with or
relating to space; existing in space.
spatially *adverb* [same origin as for *space*]

spatter *verb* to scatter drops of liquid over
something; to be splashed in this way
♦ *The side of the car was spattered with mud*
♦ *Blood spattered everywhere.*

spatter *noun* a splash or splashes; the sound of spattering. [an imitation of the sound]

spatula (spat-yoo-lə) *noun* **1** a tool like a knife with a broad blunt flexible blade, used for spreading or mixing things. **2** a strip of stiff material used by a doctor for pressing down the tongue etc. [from a Latin word *spathula* meaning 'small spear']

spatulate (spat-yoo-lət) *adjective* shaped like a spatula, with a broad rounded end.

spawn *noun* **1** the eggs of fish, frogs, or shellfish. **2** (*derogatory*) offspring. **3** the thread-like matter from which fungi grow ♦ *mushroom spawn.*
spawn *verb* **1** to release or deposit spawn. **2** (*derogatory*) to produce offspring. **3** to produce something ♦ *The film has spawned a series of feeble imitations.* [from an Old French word *espaundre* meaning 'to shed roe']

spay *verb* to sterilize a female animal by removing the ovaries. [from an Old French word *espeer* meaning 'to cut with a sword']

speak *verb* (**spoke**, **spoken**) **1** to say something, to talk. **2** to have a conversation with someone ♦ *I need to speak to you for a minute.* **3** to make a speech ♦ *He spoke for an hour.* **4** to use or be able to use a foreign language ♦ *Do you speak French?* **5** to express something or make it known ♦ *She spoke the truth.* **6** to be evidence of something ♦ *The facts speak for themselves.* **to be on speaking terms** to be on friendly terms with each other. **to speak for** to express someone's views on their behalf ♦ *I believe I speak for the rest of the team.* **to speak for yourself** to give your own opinion. **to speak your mind** to give your opinion frankly. **to speak out** to give your opinion frankly. **to speak up** **1** to speak more loudly. **2** to give your opinion frankly. **to speak volumes** to convey a lot without using words ♦ *Her expression spoke volumes.* [from an Old English word *sprecan*]

speaker *noun* **1** a person who speaks or makes a speech. **2** a loudspeaker.
the Speaker the person who controls the debates in the House of Commons or a similar assembly.

spear *noun* **1** a weapon for throwing or stabbing, with a long shaft and a pointed tip. **2** a pointed stem, e.g. of asparagus or broccoli.

spear *verb* to pierce something with a spear or with something pointed. [from an Old English word *spere*]

spearhead *noun* **1** the point of a spear. **2** the person or group that leads an attacking or advancing force.
spearhead *verb* to be the spearhead of something.

spearmint *noun* a common garden mint used in cookery and to flavour chewing gum. [from *spear* and *mint*[1] (probably because the leaves are shaped like spearheads)]

spec *noun* **on spec** (*informal*) in the hope of being successful but without any preparation or plan ♦ *We thought we'd call round on spec to see if you were in.* [short for *speculation*]

special *adjective* **1** of a particular kind, different from the usual or normal kind ♦ *special training* ♦ *This is a special occasion.* **2** designed for a particular purpose ♦ *You need a special key to open it.* **3** exceptional in amount, quality, or intensity ♦ *Take special care of it.*
special *noun* **1** a special thing; a special train or edition etc. **2** a dish not on the regular menu but served on a particular day. [same origin as for *species*]

Special Branch *noun* the police department that deals with problems of national security.

special constable *noun* a person trained to act as a police officer on particular occasions, especially in an emergency.

special effects *plural noun* illusions created for films or television by using props, trick photography, or computer images.

specialist *noun* a person who is an expert in a particular branch of a subject, especially of medicine ♦ *a skin specialist.*
specialism *noun*

speciality (spesh-i-al-iti) *noun* (**specialities**) **1** a product for which a person or region is famous. **2** something in which a person specializes.

specialize *verb* **1** to study a subject with special intensity; to become a specialist ♦ *She specialized in the biology of moths.* **2** to have a product etc. to which you devote special attention ♦ *The shop specializes in sports goods.* **specialization** *noun*

specialized *adjective* **1** designed or adapted for a particular purpose ♦ *specialized* organs such as the ear. **2** to do with a specialist ♦ *specialized knowledge.*

specially *adverb* **1** in a special way. **2** for a special purpose.

special needs *plural noun* educational requirements resulting from learning difficulties, physical disability, or emotional and behavioural difficulties.

species (spee-shiz) *noun* (**species**) **1** a group of animals or plants within a genus, differing only in minor details from the others. **2** a kind or sort ♦ *a species of sledge.* [a Latin word meaning 'appearance']

specific (spi-sif-ik) *adjective* **1** particular, clearly distinguished from others ♦ *The money was given for a specific purpose.* **2** expressing yourself in precise and clear terms, not vague ♦ *Please be specific about your requirements.*
specific *noun* **1** a precise detail ♦ *Let me give you some specifics.* **2** (*old use*) a remedy for a specific disease or condition.
specifically *adverb* [same origin as for *species*]

specification *noun* **1** specifying, or being specified. **2** a detailed description of how to make or do something.

specific gravity *noun* another term for relative density.

specific heat capacity *noun* (*Physics*) the amount of heat needed to raise the temperature of one gram (or one pound etc.) of a substance by one degree.

specify *verb* (**specifies, specified, specifying**) **1** to mention details, ingredients, etc. clearly and definitely ♦ *The recipe specified cream, not milk.* **2** to include something in a list of specifications. [same origin as for *species*]

specimen *noun* **1** a part or individual taken as an example of a whole or of a class, especially for investigation or scientific examination ♦ *a specimen signature.* **2** a quantity of a person's urine etc. taken for testing. **3** (*informal*) a person of a special sort ♦ *He seems a peculiar specimen.* [from a Latin word *specere* meaning 'to look']

specious (spee-shəs) *adjective* seeming to be true or plausible at first sight but actually wrong or false ♦ *specious reasoning.* **speciously** *adverb* [from a Latin word *speciosus* meaning 'attractive']

speck *noun* a tiny spot or particle. [from an Old English word *specca*]

speckle *noun* a small spot or patch, especially as a natural marking. [from an Old Dutch word *spekkel*]

speckled *adjective* marked with speckles.

specs *plural noun* (*informal*) spectacles.

spectacle *noun* **1** a striking or impressive sight ♦ *a magnificent spectacle.* **2** a lavish public show or performance.
spectacles *plural noun* (*formal*) a pair of glasses. **to make a spectacle of yourself** to draw attention to yourself by behaving in a ridiculous way in public. **spectacled** *adjective* [from a Latin word *spectare* meaning 'to look at']

spectacular *adjective* striking or impressive. SYNONYMS: stunning, sensational, magnificent, breathtaking, dazzling, eye-catching.
spectacular *noun* a performance or event produced on a large scale and with striking effects. **spectacularly** *adverb* [same origin as for *spectacle*]

spectate *verb* to be a spectator.

spectator *noun* a person who watches a show, game, or other event. [same origin as for *spectacle*]

spectator sports *noun* sports that attract many spectators.

spectra plural of **spectrum.**

spectral *adjective* **1** to do with or like a spectre. **2** to do with the spectrum. **spectrally** *adverb*

spectre (spek-ter) *noun* **1** a ghost. **2** a haunting fear of future trouble ♦ *The spectre of defeat loomed over them.* [same origin as for *spectrum*]

spectrometer (spek-trom-it-er) *noun* an instrument used for recording and measuring spectra. [from *spectrum* and *meter*]

spectroscope (spek-trə-skohp) *noun* an instrument for producing and examining spectra. [from *spectrum* and a Greek word *skopein* meaning 'to look at']

spectroscopy (spek-tros-kəpi) *noun* the examination and investigation of spectra.

spectrum *noun* (**spectra**) **1** the bands of colour as seen in a rainbow, forming a series according to their wavelengths. **2** a similar series of bands of sound. **3** an entire range of related qualities or ideas ♦ *the political spectrum.* [a Latin word meaning 'image']

speculate verb 1 to form a theory or opinion about something without having definite knowledge or evidence. 2 to invest in stocks, property, etc. in the hope of making a profit but with the risk of loss. **speculation** noun **speculator** noun [from a Latin word speculari meaning 'to spy out']

speculative (spek-yoo-lə-tiv) adjective 1 to do with or based on speculation ♦ speculative reasoning. 2 (said about an investment) involving financial speculation and the risk of loss. **speculatively** adverb

sped past tense and past participle of **speed**.

speech noun 1 the act, power, or manner of speaking. 2 a formal talk given to an audience. SYNONYMS: address, oration, talk, sermon, homily. 3 a sequence of lines spoken by a character in a play. [from an Old English word]

speech day noun an annual day of celebration at some schools, when speeches are made and prizes are presented.

speechless adjective unable to speak because of great emotion or shock. **speechlessly** adverb

speech therapy noun treatment to improve a stammer or other defect of speech. **speech therapist** noun

speed noun 1 the rate in time at which something moves or happens. SYNONYMS: rate, pace, tempo, velocity. 2 rapidity of movement or action. SYNONYMS: rapidity, speediness, swiftness, alacrity, haste. 3 the sensitivity of photographic film to light, the power of a lens to let in light. **speed** verb (past tense and past participle **sped** or (in meanings 2 and 3) **speeded**) 1 to move or pass quickly ♦ The years sped by. 2 to make something move or happen quickly ♦ These drugs will help speed her recovery. 3 to travel at a speed greater than the legal limit. **at speed** quickly. **to speed up** to move or work at greater speed. **to speed something up** to make something move or work at greater speed. [from an Old English word]

speedboat noun a fast motor boat.

speed bump or **speed hump** noun a ridge built across a road to make vehicles slow down.

speed camera noun a camera by the side of a road which automatically photographs

any vehicle which is exceeding a speed limit.

speed limit noun the maximum speed at which vehicles may legally travel on a particular stretch of road.

speedo noun (**speedos**) (informal) a speedometer.

speedometer (spee-dom-it-er) noun a device in a motor vehicle, showing its speed. [from speed and meter]

speedway noun 1 a form of motorcycle racing in which the riders travel round an oval dirt track. 2 a stadium or track used for this sport. 3 (North Amer.) a road or track reserved for fast traffic.

speedwell noun a wild plant with small blue flowers.

speedy adjective (**speedier, speediest**) 1 moving quickly. 2 done or coming without delay. **speedily** adverb **speediness** noun

speleology (spel-i-ol-əji) noun the exploration and scientific study of caves. **speleological** adjective **speleologist** noun [from a Greek word spēlaion meaning 'cave' and -logy]

spell ¹ verb (past tense and past participle **spelt** or **spelled**) 1 to write or name the letters that form a word in their correct sequence. 2 (said about letters) to form a word ♦ C-A-T spells 'cat'. 3 to have something as a necessary result ♦ These proposals would spell disaster for the farmer. **to spell something out** to explain something simply and in detail. **speller** noun **spelling** noun [via Old French from a Germanic word]

spell ² noun 1 words supposed to have magic power. 2 the state of being influenced by this ♦ The wizard put them all under a spell. 3 a fascination or attraction that something has ♦ the spell of eastern countries. [from an Old English word spel meaning 'speech, story']

spell ³ noun 1 a period of time during which something lasts ♦ during the cold spell. 2 a period of a certain activity ♦ We each did a spell of driving. SYNONYMS: stint, turn, session. [from an Old English word spelian meaning 'to take someone's place, to take over a task']

spellbinding adjective holding your attention as if by a spell.

spellbound adjective with the attention held as if by a spell, entranced.

spellchecker or **spelling checker** *noun* a computer program which checks the spelling of words in files of text.

spelt[1] *past tense and past participle of* **spell**[1].

spelt[2] *noun* a kind of wheat. [from an Old English word]

spend *verb* (*past tense and past participle* **spent**) **1** to pay out money in buying something. SYNONYMS: (*informal*) fork out, shell out, splash out, cough up. **2** to use something for a certain purpose, to use something up ♦ *Don't spend too much time on it.* **3** to pass time ♦ *We spent a holiday in Greece.* **spender** *noun* [from an Old English word *spendan*]

spendthrift *noun* a person who spends money extravagantly and wastefully. [from *spend* and an old sense of *thrift* meaning 'prosperity, earnings']

spent *past tense and past participle of* **spend**.
spent *adjective* used up, having lost its force or strength.

sperm *noun* (**sperms** or **sperm**) **1** semen. **2** a spermatozoon. [from a Greek word *sperma* meaning 'seed']

spermatic *adjective* to do with sperm.

spermatic cord *noun* (in mammals) a cord connecting the testicles to the abdominal cavity.

spermatozoon (sper-mə-tə-**zoh**-ən) *noun* (**spermatozoa**) (*Biology*) a male reproductive cell in semen, capable of fertilizing an ovum. [from *sperm* and a Greek word *zōion* meaning 'animal']

spermicide (**sperm**-i-siyd) *noun* a substance that kills sperm, used as a contraceptive. **spermicidal** *adjective* [from *sperm* and a Latin word *caedere* meaning 'to kill']

sperm whale *noun* a large whale from which a waxy oil can be obtained.

spew *verb* **1** to vomit. **2** to cast something out in a stream ♦ *The volcano spewed out lava.* [from an Old English word]

sphagnum (**sfag**-nəm) *noun* a kind of moss that grows on bogs. [from a Greek word *sphagnos*, denoting a kind of moss]

sphere (sfeer) *noun* **1** a perfectly round solid geometric figure. **2** something shaped like this. **3** a field of activity, influence, or interest. [from a Greek word *sphaira* meaning 'ball']

spherical (**sfe**-ri-kəl) *adjective* shaped like a sphere. **spherically** *adverb* **sphericity** *noun*

spheroid (**sfeer**-oid) *noun* a sphere-like but not perfectly spherical solid. **spheroidal** *adjective*

sphincter (**sfink**-ter) *noun* (*Anatomy*) a ring of muscle surrounding an opening in the body and able to close it by contracting. [from a Greek word *sphingein* meaning 'to bind tight']

sphinx *noun* **1** any of the ancient stone statues in Egypt with a lion's body and a human or animal's head, especially the large one near the pyramids at Giza. **2** a person who does not reveal their thoughts and feelings. [from the Sphinx in Greek mythology, a winged creature at Thebes that killed anyone who could not answer a riddle]

spice *noun* **1** a substance, often obtained from dried parts of plants, with a strong taste or smell, used for flavouring food. **2** such substances collectively. **3** something that adds interest or excitement ♦ *Variety is the spice of life.* **spice** *verb* to flavour something with spice. **to spice something up** to make something more interesting or exciting. [from an Old French word *espice*]

spick and span *adjective* neat and clean. [*span* is from an Old Norse word and *spick* is probably from an Old Dutch word]

spicy *adjective* (**spicier**, **spiciest**) **1** flavoured with spice. **2** (said about stories) slightly scandalous or indecent. **spicily** *adverb* **spiciness** *noun*

spider *noun* an insect-like animal with eight legs, spinning webs to trap insects on which it feeds. [from an Old English word *spithra* meaning 'spinner']

spider plant *noun* a house plant of the lily family with long narrow leaves and a central yellow stripe.

spidery *adjective* having thin angular lines like a spider's legs ♦ *spidery handwriting.*

spied *past tense and past participle of* **spy**.

spiel (shpeel or speel) *noun* (*informal*) a glib or lengthy speech, usually when trying to persuade someone or sell them something. [from a German word *Spiel* meaning 'a game']

spigot (spig-ət) *noun* a peg or plug used to stop up the vent hole of a cask or to control the flow of a tap. [via Old French from a Latin word *spica* meaning 'an ear of corn']

spike [1] *noun* a sharp point sticking out; a pointed piece of metal.
spike *verb* 1 to put spikes on something ♦ *spiked running shoes.* 2 to pierce or fasten something with a spike. 3 (*informal*) to secretly add alcohol or a drug to a drink or food. **to spike someone's guns** to spoil someone's plans. [origin unknown]

spike [2] *noun* (*Botany*) a long cluster of flowers with short stalks, or no stalks, on a central stem. [from a Latin word *spica* meaning 'an ear of corn']

spiky *adjective* (**spikier, spikiest**) 1 like a spike or having many spikes. 2 (*informal*) easily offended or annoyed. **spikily** *adverb* **spikiness** *noun*

spill [1] *verb* (past tense and past participle **spilt** or **spilled**) 1 to allow or cause a liquid etc. to run over the edge of its container ♦ *Try not to spill the coffee.* 2 to become spilt ♦ *Some of the ink must have spilt.* 3 to go somewhere in large numbers and quickly ♦ *The coins came spilling out* ♦ *The fans started to spill onto the pitch.*
spill *noun* 1 a quantity of liquid that has spilt; an instance of spilling ♦ *an acid spill.* 2 a fall from a horse, bicycle, etc. **to spill blood** to shed blood in killing or wounding. **to spill over** to overflow from something that is full ♦ *The crowd spilt over from the town hall into the street outside.* **to spill the beans** (*informal*) to let out information, especially without meaning to. [from an Old English word *spillan* meaning 'to kill, waste, shed (blood)']

spill [2] *noun* a thin strip of wood or of twisted paper used for lighting a fire or pipe. [from an old word *spille* meaning 'splinter']

spillage *noun* 1 spilling. 2 the amount spilt.

spin *verb* (past tense and past participle **spun; spinning**) 1 to turn or make something turn round quickly on its axis. SYNONYMS: revolve, rotate, whirl, (of dancers) pirouette. 2 (said about a ball) to revolve in the air and change direction when it bounces; to bowl or hit a ball so that it does this. 3 to make raw cotton or wool etc. into threads by pulling and twisting its fibres; to make thread in this way. 4 (said about a spider or silkworm) to make a web or cocoon from a fine

thread-like material it produces from its body. 5 (said about a person's head) to give a feeling of dizziness. SYNONYMS: swim, reel. 6 to dry washing in a washing machine or spin dryer. 7 (*informal*) to present news, information, etc. in a way favourable to a particular person or group, usually a politician or political party.
spin *noun* 1 a spinning movement. 2 (*informal*) a short drive in a vehicle. 3 (*informal*) a bias or slant given to a piece of news or information intended to be favourable to a particular person or group, usually a politician or political party. **in a flat spin** (*informal*) in a state of agitation. **to spin a yarn** to tell an invented story, especially in order to deceive someone. **to spin something out** to make something last as long as possible. [from an Old English word *spinnan* meaning 'to draw out and twist fibre']

spina bifida (spiy-nə bif-id-ə) *noun* a congenital condition in which certain bones of the spine are not properly developed and allow part of the spinal cord to stick out, sometimes causing paralysis and mental handicap. [Latin words meaning 'cleft spine']

spinach *noun* a vegetable with dark green leaves. [via Spanish and Arabic from a Persian word]

spinal *adjective* to do with the spine.

spinal column *noun* the spine.

spinal cord *noun* the rope-like bundle of nerve fibres enclosed within the spinal column, that carries impulses to and from the brain.

spin bowler *noun* (in cricket) a bowler who gives the ball a spinning movement so that it changes direction after bouncing.

spindle *noun* a thin rod on which thread is twisted or wound in spinning. 2 a pin or axis that revolves or on which something revolves. [from an Old English word *spinel*]

spindly *adjective* long or tall and thin. [from *spindle*]

spin doctor *noun* (*informal*) a person whose job is to present information or events in a way that is favourable to their employer, usually a politician or political party.

spindrift *noun* spray blown along the surface of the sea. [from an old word *spoon* meaning 'to be blown by the wind' and *drift*]

spin-dry *verb* (**spin-dries, spin-dried, spin-drying**) to dry something in a spin dryer.

spin dryer *noun* a machine in which moisture is removed from wet clothes by spinning them in a rapidly rotating drum.

spine *noun* 1 the backbone. 2 any of the sharp needle-like parts on certain plants (e.g. cacti) and animals (e.g. hedgehogs). 3 the part of a book where the pages are joined together; this section of the jacket or cover. [from a Latin word *spina* meaning 'thorn, backbone']

spine-chiller *noun* a spine-chilling story or film.

spine-chilling *adjective* causing a thrill of terror ♦ *a spine-chilling horror film.*

spineless *adjective* 1 without a backbone. 2 lacking determination or strength of character. **spinelessness** *noun*

spinet (spin-et) *noun* a kind of small harpsichord with one string to each note. [from an Old French word *espinette*]

spine-tingling *adjective* (*informal*) thrilling or pleasantly frightening.

spinnaker (spin-ǝ-ker) *noun* a large triangular extra sail on a racing yacht. [perhaps from Sphinx, the name of the yacht first using it]

spinner *noun* 1 a person or thing that spins. 2 a spin bowler. 3 (in fishing) a lure that spins round when pulled through the water.

spinney *noun* (**spinneys**) a small area of trees and bushes; a thicket. [from an Old French word *espinei*]

spinning jenny *noun* (*historical*) an early spinning machine operating several spindles at a time.

spinning wheel *noun* a household device for spinning fibre into yarn, with a spindle driven by a wheel.

spin-off *noun* 1 a benefit or product produced incidentally from a larger process or while developing this; a by-product. 2 a book, film, television series, etc. that is derived from an earlier successful one ♦ *a TV spin-off from the film of the same name.*

spinster *noun* an unmarried woman. [the original meaning was 'someone who spins' (because many unmarried women used to earn their living by spinning, which could be done at home)]

spiny *adjective* (**spinier, spiniest**) covered with spines, prickly.

spiny anteater *noun* another term for **echidna**.

spiracle (spiy-rǝ-kǝl) *noun* (*Zoology*) 1 any of the external openings through which an insect breathes. 2 the blowhole of a whale etc. [from a Latin word *spirare* meaning 'to breathe']

spiral *adjective* 1 going round and round a central point or axis and becoming gradually closer to it or further from it. 2 winding in a continuous curve round a central line or cylinder.
spiral *noun* 1 a spiral curve or shape; a thing of spiral form. 2 a continuous increase or decrease in two or more quantities alternately because of their dependence on each other ♦ *the spiral of rising wages and prices.*
spiral *verb* (**spiralled, spiralling**) 1 to move in a spiral. 2 to increase or decrease continuously and quickly ♦ *Prices were spiralling.* **spirally** *adverb* [from a Greek word *speira* meaning 'winding']

spire *noun* a pointed structure in the form of a tall cone or pyramid, especially on a church tower. [from an Old English word]

spirit *noun* 1 a person's mind, feelings, or character as distinct from the body. 2 the soul, believed by some people to remain after death ♦ *He may be dead but his spirit lives on.* 3 a ghost or supernatural being. 4 a person's nature. 5 a person with specified mental or moral qualities ♦ *A few brave spirits went swimming.* 6 the characteristic quality or mood of something ♦ *the spirit of the times.* 7 the real meaning or intention of something as distinct from a strict interpretation of the words used to express it ♦ *the spirit of the law.* 8 liveliness or courage, readiness to assert yourself ♦ *She answered with spirit* ♦ *team spirit.* 9 a distilled extract; purified alcohol.
spirits *plural noun* 1 a person's mood ♦ *He was in good spirits.* 2 strong distilled alcoholic drink, e.g. whisky or gin.
spirit *verb* (**spirited, spiriting**) to carry a person or thing off swiftly and secretly ♦ *The airport staff spirited him away before anyone noticed.* **in spirit** in thought or

intention though not physically ♦ *We shall be with you in spirit.* **the Spirit** the Holy Spirit. [from a Latin word *spiritus* meaning 'breath']

spirited *adjective* **1** full of liveliness and courage ♦ *a spirited response.* **2** having a character or mood of a specified kind ♦ *a generous-spirited person.* **spiritedly** *adverb*

spirit lamp *noun* a lamp that burns methylated spirit or a similar fluid.

spiritless *adjective* not spirited.

spirit level *noun* a glass tube nearly filled with alcohol or other liquid and containing an air bubble, used to test whether a surface is perfectly level by means of the position of this bubble.

spiritual *adjective* **1** to do with the human spirit or soul, not physical or worldly. **2** to do with religion or religious belief. **spiritual** *noun* a religious folk song associated with black Christians of the southern USA. **spirituality** *noun* **spiritually** *adverb*

spiritualism *noun* the belief that spirits of the dead can and do communicate with the living; practices based on this. **spiritualist** *noun* **spiritualistic** *adjective*

spirituous *adjective* (*formal* or *old use*) containing a lot of alcohol; distilled ♦ *spirituous liquors.* [same origin as for *spirit*]

spirogyra (spiyr-ə-jiyr-ə) *noun* (*Botany*) a simple freshwater plant that has spiral bands of chlorophyll. [from Greek words *speira* meaning 'coil' and *gura* meaning 'round']

spit[1] *verb* (past tense and past participle **spat** or **spit**; **spitting**) **1** to send out saliva, food, or liquid forcibly from the mouth. **2** (said about fire, hot fat, etc.) to throw out sparks, fat, etc. with a series of explosive noises. **3** to utter something violently ♦ *He spat curses at me.* **4** (said about a cat) to make a hissing noise to show it is angry or hostile. **5** to fall lightly ♦ *It's spitting with rain.* **spit** *noun* **1** saliva or spittle. **2** the act of spitting. **to be the spit** or **dead spit of** (*informal*) to look exactly like someone ♦ *He's the dead spit of his father.* **to spit it out** (*informal*) to say something without delay. [from an Old English word *spittan*]

spit[2] *noun* **1** a long thin metal spike put through meat to hold and turn it while it is being roasted. **2** a long narrow strip of land sticking out into the sea.

spit *verb* (**spitted, spitting**) to put a spit through meat. [from an Old English word *spitu*]

spit and polish *noun* thorough cleaning and polishing, especially by soldiers.

spite *noun* a malicious desire to hurt, annoy, or humiliate another person. **spite** *verb* to hurt, annoy, or humiliate someone from spite. **in spite of** not being prevented by ♦ *We enjoyed ourselves in spite of the weather.* **in spite of yourself** although you did not want or expect to do so. [same origin as for *despite*]

spiteful *adjective* full of spite; showing or caused by spite. SYNONYMS: malicious, vindictive, vicious; (*informal*) bitchy, catty. **spitefully** *adverb* **spitefulness** *noun*

spitfire *noun* a person with a fierce temper.

spitting image *noun* an exact likeness. [an alteration of *spit and image*]

spittle *noun* saliva, especially when it is spat out. [from an Old English word]

spittoon *noun* a container for spitting into.

spiv *noun* (*informal*) a smartly-dressed man who makes money by shady dealings or by selling goods on the black market. **spivvy** *adjective* [perhaps from a dialect word *spiff* meaning 'well dressed']

splash *verb* **1** to make liquid fly about or fall on something in drops ♦ *The bus splashed us.* **2** (said about liquid) to fall or be scattered in drops. **3** to move or fall with splashing ♦ *We splashed through the puddles.* **4** to display a story or photograph in a prominent place in a newspaper or magazine ♦ *The news was splashed across the Sunday papers.* **5** to decorate something with irregular patches of colour etc. **splash** *noun* **1** splashing, or the sound made by this. **2** a quantity of liquid splashed on to a surface. **3** a small quantity of liquid added to a drink ♦ *a whisky with a splash of soda.* **4** a bright patch of colour or light. **to make a splash** (*informal*) to attract a lot of attention. **to splash down** (said about a spacecraft) to land on the sea. **to splash out** (*informal*) to spend money freely. **splashy** *adjective* [an imitation of the sound]

splashback *noun* a panel behind a sink or cooker to protect a wall from splashes.

splashdown *noun* the landing of a spacecraft on the sea.

splat noun (informal) the sound of something soft and wet or heavy striking a surface. [short for splatter]

splatter verb to splash or make something splash with large drops ♦ A passing bus splattered him with mud.
splatter noun a noisy splashing sound. [an imitation of the sound]

splay verb 1 to spread something apart or be spread apart ♦ He splayed his fingers wide. 2 to slant the sides of an opening so that the inside is wider than the outside or vice versa.
splay adjective turned outward or widened. [from display]

spleen noun 1 (Anatomy) an organ of the body situated at the left of the stomach and involved in keeping the blood in good condition. 2 bad temper, spite ♦ He vented his spleen on us. [from a Greek word splēn. The second meaning comes from the former belief that the spleen was what made people bad-tempered]

splendid adjective 1 magnificent, very impressive. 2 excellent ♦ a splendid achievement. **splendidly** adverb [from a Latin word splendidus meaning 'shining']

splendiferous adjective (informal) splendid.

splendour noun magnificent display or appearance. SYNONYMS: magnificence, grandeur, glory, majesty. [from a Latin word splendere meaning 'to shine brightly']

splenetic (splin-et-ik) adjective bad-tempered or spiteful. [from spleen]

splice verb 1 to join two ends of rope by untwisting and interweaving the strands of each. 2 to join pieces of film, tape, or timber by overlapping them.
splice noun a join made by splicing. **to get spliced** (informal) to get married. [probably from an Old Dutch word splissen]

splint noun 1 a strip of wood or metal tied to an injured part of the body to prevent movement, e.g. while a broken bone heals. 2 a thin strip of wood used to light a fire.
splint verb to hold something firm with a splint. [from an Old German or Old Dutch word splinte meaning 'metal plate or pin']

splinter noun a small thin sharp piece of wood, stone, glass, etc. broken off from a larger piece.
splinter verb to break something or become broken into splinters. **splintery** adjective [from an Old German or Old Dutch word]

splinter group noun a small group of people that has broken away from a larger one, e.g. in a political party.

split verb (past tense and past participle **split**; **splitting**) 1 to break something or become broken into parts, especially lengthways or along the grain of wood etc. SYNONYMS: cleave, slice. 2 to divide something or become divided into parts. 3 to divide and share something ♦ We split the prize money between us. 4 to come apart, to tear ♦ This coat has split at the seams. 5 to divide or become divided into disagreeing or hostile groups ♦ This issue has split the party. 6 (informal) to leave somewhere suddenly.
split noun 1 a division or separation, especially one resulting from a disagreement. SYNONYMS: rift, schism. 2 a crack or tear made by splitting. 3 the splitting or dividing of something.
splits noun an acrobatic position in which the legs are stretched in opposite directions and at right angles to the trunk. **to split on** (informal) to inform on someone or betray their secrets. **to split your sides** to laugh very heartily. **to split the difference** to decide on an amount half-way between two proposed amounts. **to split up** to end a marriage or other relationship. [from a Dutch word splitten]

split end noun a tip of a person's hair which has split, often because of dryness.

split infinitive noun an infinitive with a word or words placed between to and the verb, e.g. to thoroughly understand. ◊ Although a split infinitive is not strictly speaking a grammatical error, many people dislike this construction. For this reason it is probably best to avoid it in formal writing, e.g. by putting to understand thoroughly.

split-level adjective 1 (said about a building) having adjoining rooms at a level midway between successive storeys in other parts. 2 (said about a cooker) having the oven and the hob as separate units.

split pin noun a metal pin with split ends that hold it in position when they are splayed.

split screen noun the showing of two or more images simultaneously on separate parts of a film or television screen.

split second noun a very brief moment of time.

split-second *adjective* extremely rapid or precise ♦ *split-second timing.*

splitting *adjective* (*informal*) (said about a headache) very severe.

splodge *noun & verb* another word for **splotch**.

splosh *verb* (*informal*) to move with a soft splashing sound.
splosh *noun* (*informal*) a splash or splashing sound. [an imitation of the sound]

splotch *noun* a splash or blotch on something.
splotch *verb* to mark something with splotches. **splotchy** *adjective* [perhaps from *spot* and *blotch*]

splurge *verb* (*informal*) to spend a lot of money on something, especially as a luxury ♦ *She splurged her first week's wages on a new coat.*
splurge *noun* (*informal*) a sudden burst of extravagance. [originally American; origin unknown]

splutter *verb* 1 to make a rapid series of spitting or choking sounds. 2 to speak rapidly but not clearly, e.g. in rage.
splutter *noun* a spluttering sound. [an imitation of the sound]

Spode *noun* (*trademark*) a kind of fine pottery or porcelain named after the English potter Josiah Spode (1755–1827), its original maker.

spoil *verb* (past tense and past participle **spoilt** or **spoiled**) 1 to damage something and make it useless or unsatisfactory. SYNONYMS: wreck, ruin, mar; (*informal*) mess up, scupper. 2 to become unfit for eating or use. 3 to mark a ballot paper incorrectly so that the vote does not count. 4 to make a child selfish by always letting them have what they want. 5 to treat someone with great or too much kindness or generosity.
spoil *noun* earth etc. brought up during excavation or dredging.
spoils *plural noun* 1 plunder or other benefits taken by force ♦ *the spoils of war.* 2 benefits or rewards of an official position. **to be spoiling for** to desire something eagerly ♦ *He is spoiling for a fight.* **to be spoilt for choice** to have so many options that it is difficult to make a choice. **spoilage** *noun* [from a Latin word *spolium* meaning 'plunder']

spoiler *noun* 1 a device on an aircraft to slow it down by interrupting the airflow. 2 a similar device on a vehicle to prevent it from being lifted off the road when travelling very fast. 3 a news story published to spoil the impact of a similar story published by a rival newspaper.

spoilsport *noun* a person who spoils the enjoyment of other people.

spoke [1] *noun* each of the bars or wire rods that connect the centre or hub of a wheel to its rim. **to put a spoke in someone's wheel** to thwart someone's intentions. [from an Old English word]

spoke [2] past tense of **speak**.

spoken past participle of **speak**. **to be spoken for** 1 to be already claimed or reserved. 2 to already have a boyfriend or girlfriend.

spokeshave *noun* a tool for planing something curved.

spokesman *noun* (**spokesmen**) a spokesperson, especially a man.

spokesperson *noun* (**spokespersons** or **spokespeople**) a person who speaks on behalf of a group.

spokeswoman *noun* (**spokeswomen**) a female spokesperson.

spoliation (spoh-li-ay-shən) *noun* 1 pillaging. 2 spoiling. [same origin as for *spoil*]

spondee *noun* (in poetry) a metrical foot with two long or stressed syllables, as in the phrase *no hope.* [from an Old French word]

sponge *noun* 1 a sea creature with a soft porous body. 2 the skeleton of this, or a substance of similar texture, used for washing, cleaning, or padding. 3 (also **sponge cake**) a soft light cake made with little or no fat. 4 a wipe or wash with a sponge.
sponge *verb* 1 to wipe or wash something with a sponge. 2 (*informal*) to get money or food off other people without giving anything in return ♦ *He's always sponging off his friends.* **spongeable** *adjective* [via Old English from a Greek word *spongia*]

sponge bag *noun* a bag for holding soap and other items for washing.

sponge pudding *noun* a steamed or baked pudding of fat, flour, and eggs.

sponger *noun* (*informal*) a person who lives at other people's expense.

spongy *adjective* (**spongier, spongiest**) like a sponge in texture, soft and springy.

sponsor *noun* **1** a person or organization that provides funds for a musical, artistic, or sporting event or for a broadcast in return for advertising. **2** a person who promises to give money to a charity in return for something achieved by another person. **3** a person who puts forward a proposal, e.g. for a new law. **4** a person who supports someone undergoing training etc. **5** a godparent.
sponsor *verb* to act as sponsor for someone or something. **sponsorship** *noun* [from a Latin word *sponsum* meaning 'promised']

spontaneous (spon-**tay**-niəs) *adjective* **1** occurring or developing naturally, without an external cause. **2** done on impulse without planning ♦ *a spontaneous gesture*. **spontaneity** (spon-tən-**ee**-iti) *noun* **spontaneously** *adverb* [from a Latin word *sponte* meaning 'of your own accord']

spontaneous combustion *noun* the bursting into flame of a substance because of heat produced by its own rapid oxidation and not by heat from an external source.

spoof *noun* (*informal*) **1** a parody, especially of a type of film. **2** a hoax. [originally denoting a card game invented and named by an English comedian, Arthur Roberts (1852-1933)]

spook *noun* (*informal*) **1** a ghost. **2** a spy.
spook *verb* to frighten someone, or to become frightened. [from a Dutch word]

spooky *adjective* (**spookier, spookiest**) (*informal*) ghostly or eerie. **spookiness** *noun*

spool *noun* a rod or cylinder on which something is wound, e.g. thread, film, or magnetic tape.
spool *verb* to wind something or become wound on a spool. [via Old French from a Germanic word]

spoon *noun* a utensil consisting of an oval or round bowl and a handle, used for lifting food to the mouth or for stirring or measuring things.
spoon *verb* **1** to take or lift something with a spoon. **2** to hit a ball upwards with a soft or weak stroke. [from an Old English word]

spoonbill *noun* a wading bird with a very broad flat tip to its bill.

spoonerism *noun* an accidental exchange of the initial sounds of two words, usually as a slip of the tongue, e.g. saying *a boiled sprat* instead of *a spoiled brat*. [named after the English scholar Rev. W. A. Spooner (1844–1930), said to have made such errors in speaking]

spoon-feed *verb* (past tense and past participle **spoon-fed**) **1** to feed a baby or invalid with liquid food from a spoon. **2** to give so much help or information to someone that they do not need to think for themselves.

spoonful *noun* (**spoonfuls**) as much as a spoon will hold.

spoor *noun* the track or scent left by an animal. [from an Afrikaans word]

sporadic (sper-**ad**-ik) *adjective* occurring here and there, scattered. **sporadically** *adverb* [from a Greek word *sporas* meaning 'sown, scattered']

sporangium (sper-**an**-ji-əm) *noun* (**sporangia**) (*Botany*) the receptacle in which spores are formed in some plants, e.g. ferns. [from a Greek word *spora* meaning 'spore' and *angeion* meaning 'vessel']

spore *noun* (*Biology*) one of the tiny reproductive cells of plants such as fungi and ferns. [from a Greek word *spora* meaning 'seed']

sporran (**spo**-rən) *noun* a pouch worn hanging in front of the kilt as part of Scottish Highland dress. [from a Scottish Gaelic word *sporan*]

sport *noun* **1** a competitive activity involving physical activity and skill, especially one outdoors. **2** such activities collectively ♦ *Do you like sport?* **3** amusement or fun ♦ *We said it in sport.* **4** (*informal*) a person who behaves well in response to teasing or defeat ♦ *Thanks for being such a good sport.* **5** (*Biology*) an animal or plant that is strikingly different from its parents.
sport *verb* **1** to wear or display something ♦ *He sported a gold tiepin.* **2** to play or amuse yourself. [from an Old French word; related to *disport*]

sporting *adjective* **1** interested in or connected with sport ♦ *a sporting man.* **2** behaving fairly and generously. **sportingly** *adverb*

sporting chance *noun* a reasonable chance of success.

sportive adjective playful. **sportively** adverb

sports car noun an open low-built fast car.

sports jacket noun a man's jacket for informal wear, not part of a suit.

sportsman or **sportswoman** noun (**sportsmen** or **sportswomen**) **1** a person who takes part in a sport, especially professionally. **2** a person who shows sportsmanship.

sportsmanlike adjective behaving fairly and generously.

sportsmanship noun sporting behaviour; behaving fairly and generously to rivals.

sportswear noun clothes worn for sport or for casual outdoor use.

sporty adjective (**sportier, sportiest**) (informal) **1** fond of or good at sport. **2** (said about a car) compact and fast. **sportily** adverb **sportiness** noun

spot noun **1** a round area different in colour from the rest of a surface. **2** a roundish mark or stain. SYNONYMS: blotch, blot, speck. **3** a pimple or other red mark on the skin. **4** a particular place or locality. **5** (informal) a small amount of something ◆ We had a spot of trouble. **6** a drop ◆ a few spots of rain. **7** a spotlight.
spot verb (**spotted, spotting**) **1** to mark something with spots. **2** to notice or recognize someone or something ◆ We spotted him in the crowd ◆ I can spot a tourist a mile off. **3** to watch for and take note of something, especially as a hobby ◆ train-spotting. **4** (in snooker or billiards) to place a ball on its proper spot on the table. **to hit the spot** (informal) to be exactly what is needed. **in a spot** (informal) in difficulties. **on the spot** **1** without delay or change of place. **2** at the scene of an incident. **to put someone on the spot** to force someone into a situation in which they must respond or take action. **spot on** (informal) exactly right or accurate. **spotted** adjective **spotter** noun [probably from an Old German or Old Dutch word]

spot check noun a check made without warning on something chosen at random.

spot-check verb to do a spot check.

spotless adjective **1** free from stains or marks, perfectly clean. SYNONYMS: immaculate, pristine. **2** free from moral faults ◆ a spotless reputation. SYNONYMS: unblemished, untarnished. **spotlessly** adverb

spotlight noun **1** a beam of light directed on to a small area, or a lamp giving this. **2** public attention ◆ She is not used to being in the spotlight.
spotlight verb (past tense and past participle **spotlighted** or **spotlit**) **1** to direct a spotlight on something. **2** to draw attention to something.

spotted dick noun a suet pudding containing currants.

spotty adjective (**spottier, spottiest**) marked with spots. **spottiness** noun

spot-weld verb to weld small areas that are in contact. **spot-welder** noun **spot-welding** noun

spouse noun a person's husband or wife. **spousal** adjective [from a Latin word sponsus meaning 'betrothed']

spout noun **1** a projecting tube through which liquid can be poured. **2** a jet of liquid.
spout verb **1** to come or send something out forcefully as a jet of liquid. **2** to speak for a long time, expressing your views. **up the spout** (informal) broken, ruined, or useless. [from an Old Dutch word spouten]

sprain verb to injure a joint or its muscles or ligaments by twisting it violently. **sprain** noun an injury caused in this way. [origin unknown]

sprang past tense of **spring**.

sprat noun a small herring-like fish used for food. [from an Old English word sprot]

sprawl verb **1** to sit, lie, or fall with the arms and legs spread out loosely. SYNONYMS: lounge, slouch, recline. **2** to spread out over a large area in an irregular way.
sprawl noun **1** a sprawling attitude, movement, or arrangement. **2** an irregular or disorganized expansion of something ◆ an urban sprawl. **sprawling** adjective [from an Old English word spreawlian meaning 'to move the limbs convulsively']

spray¹ noun **1** liquid sent through the air in very small drops. **2** a liquid preparation for spraying. **3** a device for spraying liquid.
spray verb **1** to put liquid on something in a spray. **2** (said about a liquid) to be sent through the air in very small drops. **3** to scatter something over an area with force. **sprayer** noun [origin unknown]

spray² noun **1** a single shoot or branch with

its leaves, twigs, and flowers. **2** a small bunch of cut flowers arranged decoratively. **3** a brooch in this form. [from an Old English word]

spray gun noun a gun-like device for spraying a liquid such as paint.

spread verb (past tense and past participle **spread**) **1** to open or stretch something out, to unroll or unfold something ♦ The peacock spread its tail ♦ Spread the map out. **2** to become longer or wider ♦ The stain began to spread. **3** to make something cover a surface, to apply something as a layer ♦ He spread the bread with jam ♦ Spread the paint evenly. **4** to be able to be spread ♦ It spreads like butter. **5** to make something or become more widely known, felt, or suffered ♦ You'd better spread the news ♦ Rats spread disease ♦ Panic spread. SYNONYMS: pass on, circulate, transmit, disperse, disseminate. **6** to distribute something or become distributed over a large area ♦ Settlers soon spread inland. **7** to distribute something over a period ♦ You can spread the payments over 12 months.
spread noun **1** spreading, or being spread. **2** the extent, expanse, or breadth of something. **3** the range of something. **4** (informal) a lavish meal. **5** a sweet or savoury paste for spreading on bread. **6** an article or feature covering several columns or pages of a newspaper or magazine. **to spread out** (said about a group of people) to move apart so that they cover a wider area. [from an Old English word]

spreadeagled adjective with arms and legs stretched out ♦ He lay spreadeagled on the bed. [originally referring to a picture of an eagle with legs and wings stretched out, used as an emblem on a knight's shield, inn sign, etc.]

spreadsheet noun a computer program that allows numerical, especially financial, data to be displayed in a table and manipulated.

spree noun a period in which you do something freely ♦ a shopping spree ♦ a spending spree. [origin unknown]

sprig noun **1** a small stem with leaves or flowers on it. **2** an ornament or decoration in this form. [from an Old German word sprick]

sprightly adjective (**sprightlier, sprightliest**) lively and full of energy. **sprightliness** noun [from sprite]

spring verb (**sprang, sprung**) **1** to move rapidly or suddenly upwards or forwards ♦ He sprang to his feet. SYNONYMS: leap, jump. **2** to grow, originate, or arise ♦ Weeds had started to spring up ♦ Their discontent springs from distrust of their leaders. **3** (informal) to help a prisoner escape. **4** to cause something to operate suddenly ♦ Just then they sprang their trap. **5** (said about wood) to become warped or split.
spring noun **1** the season in which most plants begin to grow, from March to May in the northern hemisphere. **2** a device, usually of bent or coiled metal, that returns to its original position after being compressed or tightened or stretched, used to drive clockwork or in groups to make a seat etc. more comfortable. **3** elasticity. **4** a sudden jump upwards or forwards. **5** a place where water comes up naturally from the ground. **to spring a leak** to develop a leak. **to spring something on** to present something suddenly or unexpectedly to someone ♦ They sprang a surprise on us. [from an Old English word]

spring balance noun a device that measures weight by the tension of a spring.

springboard noun **1** a flexible board that a gymnast or diver jumps on to gain height or impetus. **2** something that is used to get an activity started.

springbok noun a South African gazelle that can spring high into the air. **Springbok** noun a member of a sports team representing South Africa, especially in rugby union. [an Afrikaans word, from Dutch words springen meaning 'to spring' and bok meaning 'antelope']

spring clean noun a thorough cleaning of your home, especially in spring. **spring-clean** verb

spring onion noun a young onion with a long green stem, eaten raw in salads.

spring roll noun a Chinese pancake filled with vegetables and sometimes meat, and fried until crisp.

spring tide noun the tide when there is the largest rise and fall of water, occurring shortly after the new and full moon.

springtime noun the season of spring.

springy adjective (**springier, springiest**) able to spring back easily after being squeezed or stretched. **springiness** noun

sprinkle verb 1 to scatter or fall in small drops or pieces. 2 to scatter small drops or pieces on a surface. 3 to distribute something randomly throughout a thing. **sprinkle** noun a small amount of something that is sprinkled. [probably from an Old Dutch word *sprenkelen*]

sprinkler noun a device for sprinkling water.

sprinkling noun 1 a few here and there. 2 something sprinkled.

sprint verb to run very fast over a short distance. **sprint** noun 1 a run or race of this kind. 2 a short fast race in swimming, cycling, etc. **sprinter** noun [from a Scandinavian word]

sprite noun an elf or fairy. [from *spirit*]

sprocket noun each of the row of teeth round a wheel, fitting into links on a chain or holes in film, tape, or paper. [origin unknown]

sprout verb 1 to put out new leaves or shoots. 2 to begin to grow or develop ♦ *Small businesses have been sprouting up in the area.* SYNONYMS: shoot up, spring up, emerge. 3 to start to grow or develop something ♦ *Eventually the deer sprouts antlers.* **sprout** noun 1 a new shoot or bud. 2 a Brussels sprout. [probably from an Old English word]

spruce [1] adjective neat and smart. **spruce** verb to make a person or place smarter ♦ *Spruce yourself up a bit.* **sprucely** adverb **spruceness** noun [probably from *spruce jerkin*, made of leather from Prussia (see *spruce*[2])]

spruce [2] noun a kind of fir tree with dense foliage, or its wood. [from *Pruce*, the old name of Prussia, an area in central Europe, where it was grown]

sprung past participle of **spring**. **sprung** adjective fitted with springs ♦ *a sprung seat.*

spry adjective (**spryer, spryest**) active, nimble, and lively. **spryly** adverb **spryness** noun [origin unknown]

spud noun (*informal*) a potato. [origin unknown]

spume noun (*literary*) froth or foam, especially on waves. **spumy** adjective [from a Latin word *spuma*]

spun past tense and past participle of **spin**.

spunk noun (*informal*) courage and determination. **spunky** adjective [origin unknown]

spun silk noun a cheap material made from waste silk.

spun sugar noun a fluffy mass made from boiled sugar drawn into long threads, used to make candyfloss.

spur noun 1 a pricking device with a small spike or toothed wheel, worn on the heel of a rider's boot to urge a horse to go faster. 2 a stimulus or incentive. 3 something shaped like a spur, such as a hard spike on the back of a cock's leg or a slender hollow projection on a flower. 4 a ridge sticking out from a mountain. 5 a short branch road or railway line. **spur** verb (**spurred, spurring**) 1 to urge a horse on by pricking it with spurs. 2 to encourage someone or urge them on ♦ *He spurred the men to greater effort.* 3 to stimulate something ♦ *The programme had spurred my interest.* **on the spur of the moment** on an impulse, without previous planning. **spurred** adjective [from an Old English word *spora*]

spurge noun a kind of plant or bush with a bitter milky juice. [from an Old French word]

spurious (spewr-iəs) adjective not genuine or authentic. **spuriously** adverb **spuriousness** noun [from a Latin word *spurius* meaning 'false']

spurn verb to reject something with disdain or contempt. [from an Old English word *spurnan*]

spurt verb 1 to gush out, to send out a liquid suddenly. 2 to increase your speed suddenly. **spurt** noun 1 a sudden gush. 2 a short burst of speed or activity. [origin unknown]

sputnik (sput-nik or spoot-nik) noun a Soviet artificial satellite orbiting the earth. [a Russian word meaning 'fellow-traveller']

sputter verb to splutter; to make a series of quick explosive sounds ♦ *Sausages sputtered in the pan.* **sputter** noun a sputtering sound. [from a Dutch word *sputteren*, an imitation of the sound]

sputum (spew-təm) noun saliva or phlegm. [from a Latin word *spuere* meaning 'to spit']

spy noun (**spies**) 1 a person employed by a government or organization to gather and report secret information about the activities of an enemy or competitor. 2 someone who watches other people secretly.
spy verb (**spies, spied, spying**) 1 to be a spy. 2 to keep watch secretly ♦ *Have you been spying on me?* 3 to see or notice something. [from an Old French word *espier* meaning 'to espy']

spyglass noun a small telescope.

spyhole noun a peephole.

sq abbreviation square.

squab (skwob) noun 1 a young pigeon. 2 a stuffed seat or cushion, especially as part of a car seat. [origin unknown]

squabble verb to quarrel in a petty or noisy way, as children do.
squabble noun a quarrel of this kind. [origin unknown]

squad noun 1 a small group of soldiers or police officers working together. 2 a group of sports players from which a team is chosen. [from an Old French word *escouade*; related to *squadron*]

squadron noun 1 a unit of an air force, consisting of between 10 and 18 aircraft. 2 a division of an armoured or cavalry regiment, consisting of two troops. 3 a detachment of warships. [from an Italian word *squadrone*, denoting a group of soldiers in square formation; related to *squad*]

squadron leader noun an officer commanding a squadron in the RAF.

squalid adjective 1 dirty and unpleasant, especially because of neglect or poverty. SYNONYMS: dingy, sordid, insalubrious; (informal) sleazy. 2 showing a lack of moral standards. **squalidly** adverb [from a Latin word *squalidus* meaning 'rough, dirty']

squall noun 1 a sudden storm of wind, especially with rain, snow, or sleet. 2 a baby's loud cry.
squall verb (said about a baby) to cry loudly. **squally** adjective [probably from *squeal* and *bawl*]

squalor noun the state of being squalid. [from a Latin word *squalere* meaning 'to be dirty']

squander verb to spend money or time etc. wastefully. SYNONYMS: waste; (informal) fritter, blow. [origin unknown]

square noun 1 a geometric figure with four equal sides and four right angles. 2 an area or object shaped like this. 3 a four-sided area surrounded by buildings ♦ *Leicester Square.* 4 the product obtained when a number is multiplied by itself ♦ *9 is the square of 3 (9 = 3 × 3).* 5 an L-shaped or T-shaped instrument used for obtaining or testing right angles. 6 (informal) a person considered to be old-fashioned or boringly conventional.
square adjective 1 having the shape of a square. 2 right-angled ♦ *The desk has square corners.* 3 measuring the specified amount on each of four sides ♦ *a carpet six metres square.* 4 of or using units that express the measurement of an area ♦ *one square metre.* 5 level or parallel. 6 properly arranged or organized ♦ *We need to get things square before we leave.* 7 (also **all square**) equal or even, with no balance of advantage or debt etc. on either side ♦ *Are we square now?* ♦ *The teams are all square with six points each.* 8 (informal) old-fashioned or boringly conventional.
square adverb straight, directly ♦ *I hit him square on the jaw.*
square verb 1 to make something right-angled or square ♦ *Next square the corners.* 2 to mark something out in squares ♦ *squared paper.* 3 to multiply a number by itself ♦ *3 squared is 9 i.e. 3² = 9 (3 × 3 = 9).* 4 to settle or pay something ♦ *That squares the account.* 5 to make the score of a match even. 6 to be or make something consistent ♦ *His story doesn't square with yours* ♦ *It's impossible to square the two stories.* 7 to place your shoulders into a position in which they appear square and broad. 8 (informal) to get someone to cooperate by paying or bribing them ♦ *I'll try and square the porter.* **back to square one** back to where you started, with no progress made. **to square up to 1** to assume a boxer's fighting attitude. 2 to face and tackle a difficulty resolutely. **squareness** noun **squarish** adjective [from a Latin word *quadra* meaning 'a square']

square dance noun a country dance in which four couples face inwards from four sides.

square deal noun a deal that is honest and fair.

square leg noun (in cricket) a fielding position on the batsman's leg side and nearly in line with the wicket.

squarely adverb 1 directly centred, not to one side. 2 directly or unequivocally ♦ *Responsibility for this mess rests squarely with the local authority.*

square meal *noun* a large satisfying meal.

square-rigged *adjective* (said about a sailing ship) with the principal sails at right angles to the length of the ship.

square root *noun* a number that produces a given number when it is multiplied by itself ◆ *3 is the square root of 9 (3 × 3 = 9).*

square wave *noun* (*Electronics*) a wave form in which the variable takes each of two constant values in turn, jumping abruptly from one to the other, so that all lines are straight.

squash¹ *verb* **1** to crush or squeeze something so that it becomes flat, soft, or out of shape. **2** to become squeezed in this way ◆ *Tomatoes squash very easily.* **3** to squeeze or force something into a small space ◆ *She seems to have squashed half her wardrobe into her suitcase.* **4** to suppress or overcome a rebellion etc. **5** to firmly reject an idea or suggestion. **6** to silence someone with a crushing reply.
squash *noun* **1** a crowd of people squashed together; a state of being squashed. **2** a fruit-flavoured soft drink. **3** (also **squash rackets**) a game played with rackets and a small rubber ball in a closed court.
squashy *adjective* [from *quash*]

squash² *noun* a kind of gourd used as a vegetable, or the plant that bears it. [from a Native American word]

squat *verb* (**squatted, squatting**) **1** to sit on your heels or crouch with your knees drawn up closely. **2** (said about an animal) to crouch close to the ground. **3** to live in an unoccupied building without authority.
squat *noun* **1** a squatting posture. **2** a building occupied by squatters; occupying a building as a squatter.
squat *adjective* short and fat. [from an Old French word *esquatir* meaning 'to flatten']

squatter *noun* **1** a person who is living in an unoccupied building without authority. **2** a person who settles on unoccupied land in order to acquire a legal right to it.

squaw *noun* an American Indian woman or wife. [from a Native American word meaning 'woman']
◊ This word is now considered to be offensive.

squawk *noun* a loud harsh cry.
squawk *verb* **1** to make a loud harsh cry. **2** (*informal*) to complain. [an imitation of the sound]

squeak *noun* **1** a short high-pitched cry or sound. **2** a single word or slight sound ◆ *I've not heard a squeak from them all evening.*
squeak *verb* **1** to make a squeak. **2** to say something in a high-pitched voice. **3** (*informal*) to inform on someone. **a narrow squeak** (*informal*) a narrow escape from danger or failure. **to squeak through** (*informal*) to achieve or pass something by a narrow margin ◆ *The bill just squeaked through.* **squeaker** *noun* [an imitation of the sound]

squeaky *adjective* (**squeakier, squeakiest**) making a squeaking sound. **squeakily** *adverb* **squeakiness** *noun*

squeaky clean *adjective* (*informal*) **1** completely clean. **2** morally beyond reproach.

squeal *noun* a long shrill cry or sound.
squeal *verb* **1** to make this cry or sound. **2** (*informal*) to protest sharply. **3** (*informal*) to inform on someone. **squealer** *noun* [an imitation of the sound]

squeamish *adjective* **1** easily sickened or disgusted. **2** excessively scrupulous about moral principles. **squeamishly** *adverb* **squeamishness** *noun* [from an Old French word *escoymos*]

squeegee (skwee-jee) *noun* a tool with a rubber blade or roller on a handle, used for scraping away water, especially when cleaning windows. [from an old word *squeege* meaning 'to press']

squeeze *verb* **1** to press something firmly from opposite or all sides. **2** to get moisture or juice out of something by squeezing. **3** to force something into or through a place; to manage to get into or through a small or narrow place ◆ *We squeezed six people into the car* ◆ *She squeezed through the gap in the hedge.* **4** to press a person's hand etc. gently as a sign of affection or reassurance. **5** to obtain something from someone with difficulty ◆ *We managed to squeeze a promise out of him.* **6** (*informal*) to put pressure on someone to give money or information. **7** to put someone under financial pressure ◆ *Heavy taxation is squeezing small firms.*
squeeze *noun* **1** squeezing, or being squeezed. **2** an affectionate clasp or hug. **3** a small amount of liquid squeezed out ◆ *Add a squeeze of lemon.* **4** a crowd or crush, the experience of this ◆ *We all got in, but it was a tight squeeze.* **5** restrictions on borrowing or spending imposed during a financial crisis ◆ *a credit squeeze.* **to**

squeeze something in to manage to find time for something. [origin unknown]

squeezer noun a device for squeezing juice from fruit by pressure.

squelch verb to make a sound like someone treading in thick mud. **squelch** noun this sound. [an imitation of the sound]

squib noun a small firework that hisses and then explodes. **a damp squib** something intended to impress people but failing to do so. [origin unknown]

squid noun a sea creature related to the cuttlefish, with eight arms and two long tentacles. [origin unknown]

squidgy adjective (**squidgier, squidgiest**) (informal) soft and moist. [perhaps an imitation of the sound]

squiffy adjective (**squiffier, squiffiest**) (informal) slightly drunk. [origin unknown]

squiggle noun a short curly line, especially in handwriting. **squiggly** adverb [probably from squirm and wriggle]

squint verb 1 to look at something with partly closed eyes. 2 to have a squint affecting one eye.
squint noun 1 a condition in which one eye is permanently turned from the line of gaze of the other. 2 (informal) a quick or casual look ♦ Have a squint at this.
squint adjective (informal) not straight or level. [origin unknown]

squire noun 1 a country gentleman, especially the chief landowner in a district. 2 a young nobleman in the Middle Ages who served a knight before becoming a knight himself. 3 (informal) used as a friendly form of address by one man to another. [from esquire]

squirearchy noun landowners collectively, especially when thought of as having political or social influence. [from squire and hierarchy]

squirm verb 1 to wriggle or twist your body from side to side. 2 to feel embarrassed or ashamed.
squirm noun a wriggling movement. [origin unknown]

squirrel noun 1 a tree-climbing rodent with a bushy tail and red or grey fur. 2 the fur of this animal.
squirrel verb (**squirrelled, squirrelling**) to move about busily. **to squirrel something away** to hide money etc. in a safe place. [from a Greek word skiouros]

squirt verb 1 to send out liquid or be sent out in a thin jet. 2 to wet something with a jet of liquid.
squirt noun 1 a thin jet of liquid. 2 a syringe. 3 (informal) a small or insignificant person. [an imitation of the sound]

squish verb to make a soft squelching sound.
squish noun a soft squelching sound. **squishy** adjective [an imitation of the sound]

SRN abbreviation State Registered Nurse.

SS abbreviation 1 saints. 2 steamship. 3 the Nazi special police force (German Schutzstaffel).

St abbreviation 1 Saint. 2 Street.

stab verb (**stabbed, stabbing**) 1 to wound or pierce someone or something with a pointed tool or weapon. 2 to aim a blow with or as if with a pointed weapon. 3 to cause a sensation of being stabbed ♦ a stabbing pain.
stab noun an act of stabbing; a wound made by stabbing. 2 a sudden sharp pain ♦ She felt a stab of fear. 3 (informal) an attempt ♦ I'll have a stab at it. **to stab someone in the back** to betray someone. [origin unknown]

stability (stə-bil-iti) noun being stable.

stabilize (stay-bə-liyz) verb to make something stable, or to become stable. **stabilization** noun

stabilizer noun 1 a device to prevent a ship from rolling. 2 the horizontal tailplane of an aircraft. 3 a substance to prevent the breakdown of emulsions in food or paint. **stabilizers** plural noun a pair of small wheels fitted to a child's bicycle to help keep it upright.

stable¹ adjective (**stabler, stablest**) 1 steady and firmly fixed or balanced. 2 strong and lasting; not likely to change or collapse ♦ a stable government. 3 sensible and dependable. **stably** adverb [from a Latin word stabilis meaning 'standing firm']

stable² noun 1 a building in which horses are kept. 2 an establishment for training racehorses; the horses from a particular establishment; 3 an establishment managing, training, or producing a group of people or things ♦ two snooker players *from the same stable.*

stable *verb* to put or keep a horse in a stable. [from an Old French word *estable* meaning 'stable, pigsty'; related to *stable*[1]]

stable boy or **stable lad** or **stable girl** *noun* a person who works in a stable.

stabling *noun* accommodation for horses.

staccato (stə-**kah**-toh) *adjective* & *adverb* 1 (*Music*) with each note sounded in a sharp disconnected manner, not running on smoothly. 2 with short sharp sounds ♦ *a staccato voice.* [an Italian word meaning 'detached']

stack *noun* 1 an orderly pile or heap. 2 a haystack. 3 (*informal*) a large quantity ♦ *There's a whole stack of work to get through* ♦ *I still have stacks to do.* 4 a tall factory chimney; a chimney or funnel for smoke on a steamer etc. 5 a number of chimneys standing together. 6 an isolated pillar of rock just off a coast where there are cliffs. 7 a number of aircraft stacked for landing. **stack** *verb* 1 to pile things up; to arrange things in a stack. 2 to fill something with stacks of things ♦ *a job stacking supermarket shelves.* 3 to instruct aircraft to fly round the same point at different altitudes while waiting to land. 4 to arrange cards secretly for cheating ♦ *a stacked deck.* **to be stacked against** to be extremely likely to lead to a bad result for someone. **to stack up** (*informal*) to compare with something ♦ *Let's see how well we stack up against some of our competitors.* [from an Old Norse word *stakkr* meaning 'haystack']

stadium *noun* (**stadiums** or **stadia**) a sports ground surrounded by tiers of seats for spectators. [from a Latin word]

staff *noun* 1 the people who work in a particular organization, shop, etc. 2 the teachers in a school or college. 3 a group of officers assisting a commanding officer and concerned with an army, regiment, or fleet etc. as a whole. 4 a stick or pole used as a weapon, support, or measuring stick, or as a symbol of authority. 5 (**staves**) another word for **stave**. **staff** *verb* to provide an organization with a staff of employees or assistants ♦ *The centre is staffed by volunteers.* [from an Old English word]

staff nurse *noun* a qualified nurse less senior than a sister.

staff officer *noun* a member of a military staff.

staffroom *noun* a common room for teachers in a school or college.

stag *noun* a fully-grown male deer. [probably from an Old English word]

stag beetle *noun* a large beetle with branched jaws that resemble a stag's antlers.

stage *noun* 1 a point, period, or step in the course or development of something ♦ *The talks have reached a critical stage.* SYNONYMS: point, phase, juncture. 2 a section of a journey or race. 3 a platform on which plays etc. are performed before an audience. 4 theatrical work, the profession of actors and actresses. 5 a raised floor or platform, e.g. on scaffolding. 6 a section of a rocket or spacecraft with a separate engine, jettisoned when its fuel is exhausted. **stage** *verb* 1 to present a play or other performance on a stage. 2 to arrange something and carry it out ♦ *The students decided to stage a sit-in.* **to go on the stage** to become an actor or actress. **to set the stage for** to prepare the conditions for something. **stage left** on the left side of the stage when facing the audience. **stage right** on the right side of the stage when facing the audience. [from an Old French word *estage* meaning 'dwelling']

stagecoach *noun* a horse-drawn coach that formerly ran regularly along the same route, carrying passengers and often mail. [so called because it ran in stages, picking up passengers at points along the route]

stagecraft *noun* skill in writing or staging plays.

stage fright *noun* nervousness before or while performing to an audience.

stage-manage *verb* 1 to be the stage manager of a play. 2 to organize and control an event in order to create a particular effect.

stage manager *noun* the person responsible for the scenery, props, and other practical arrangements in the production of a play.

stage-struck *adjective* having an overwhelming desire to become a stage actor or actress.

stage whisper *noun* a loud whisper that is meant to be overheard.

stagey *adjective* another spelling of **stagy**.

stagflation noun (*Economics*) a state of inflation without a corresponding increase in demand and employment. [from *stagnation* and *inflation*]

stagger verb 1 to walk unsteadily, as if you are about to fall. SYNONYMS: totter, lurch, reel, stumble. 2 to astonish or shock someone ♦ *We were staggered by the news.* SYNONYMS: astound, startle, stun, dumbfound. 3 to place things in an alternating or overlapping arrangement, not in a line ♦ *a staggered junction.* 4 to arrange people's holidays or hours of work etc. so that their times do not coincide exactly. **stagger** noun 1 an unsteady staggering movement. 2 the staggered arrangement of the runners on a track at the start of a race. [from an Old Norse word *staka* meaning 'to push, stagger']

staggering adjective astonishing ♦ *The total cost is staggering.* **staggeringly** adverb

staging noun 1 an instance or method of putting on a play or other performance. 2 scaffolding; a temporary platform or support. 3 a platform of boards for plants to stand on in a greenhouse.

staging post noun a regular stopping place on a long route.

stagnant adjective 1 (said about water) not flowing, still and stale. 2 showing no activity ♦ *Business was stagnant.* **stagnancy** noun [from a Latin word *stagnum* meaning 'a pool']

stagnate (stag-nayt) verb 1 to become stagnant. 2 (said about a person) to become dull through lack of activity, variety, or opportunity. **stagnation** noun [same origin as for *stagnant*]

stag night or **stag party** noun a celebration for a man who is about to get married, attended only by men.

stagy (stay-ji) adjective (**stagier, stagiest**) theatrical in style or manner. **staginess** noun

staid (stayd) adjective steady and serious in manner, tastes, etc. [old past tense of *stay*]

stain verb 1 to make a dirty or coloured mark on something; to become discoloured by a substance. 2 to damage someone's reputation. SYNONYMS: blacken, besmirch, sully, taint, tarnish. 3 to colour something with a dye or pigment that penetrates. **stain** noun 1 a mark caused by staining. 2 something that damages someone's

reputation or past record ♦ *without a stain on his character.* 3 a liquid used for staining things. [from an old word *distain* meaning 'dye']

stained glass noun glass coloured with transparent colouring, often used for church windows.

stainless adjective free from stains or blemishes.

stainless steel noun steel containing chromium and not liable to rust or tarnish under ordinary conditions.

stair noun each of a set of fixed indoor steps. **stairs** plural noun a set of these. [from an Old English word]

staircase noun a set of stairs, often with banisters, and its supporting structure.

stairway noun a staircase.

stairwell noun the space going up through a building, which contains the staircase.

stake noun 1 a stick or post with a point at one end, driven into the ground as a support or marker. 2 a post to which people used to be tied for execution by being burnt alive. 3 an amount of money bet on the result of a race or other event. 4 a share or interest in a business or situation. **stake** verb 1 to fasten or support something with stakes. 2 to mark an area with stakes. 3 to bet or risk money etc. on an event. 4 (*North Amer.*) (*informal*) to give financial or other support to a person or business. **stakes** plural noun (in horse races) prize money; the race itself ♦ *the Queen Anne Stakes.* **at stake** being risked, depending on the outcome of an event. **to stake a claim** to claim or obtain a right to something. **to stake something out** (*informal*) to keep a place under surveillance. [from an Old English word *staca*]

stakeholder noun 1 an independent person or party that holds a stake in a bet. 2 someone with an interest in a business or concern.

stake-out noun (*informal*) a period of secret surveillance.

stalactite (stal-ək-tiyt) noun a deposit of calcium carbonate hanging like an icicle from the roof of a cave etc. [from a Greek word *stalaktos* meaning 'dripping'] ◊ Do not confuse this word with

stalagmite, which has a different meaning.

stalagmite (stal-əg-miyt) *noun* a deposit like a stalactite but standing like a pillar on the floor of a cave etc. [from a Greek word *stalagma* meaning 'a drop']
◊ Do not confuse this word with **stalactite**, which has a different meaning.

stale *adjective* (**staler, stalest**) 1 (said about food) no longer fresh or pleasant to eat. 2 (said about air) not fresh; musty. 3 no longer new and interesting ♦ *stale news* ♦ *stale jokes*. 4 no longer able to perform well or have new ideas because you have been doing something for too long.
stale *verb* to make something stale, or to become stale. **stalely** *adverb* **staleness** *noun* [from an Old French word *stale* meaning 'at a standstill']

stalemate *noun* 1 a drawn position in chess, in which a player cannot make a move without putting their own king in check. 2 a situation on which neither side in an argument will give way and progress seems impossible.
stalemate *verb* to bring something to a position of stalemate or deadlock. [from an Old French word *stale* meaning 'at a standstill' and *mate*[2]]

stalk[1] *noun* 1 the main stem of a plant. 2 a stem attaching a leaf, flower, or fruit to another stem or to a twig. 3 a similar support of a part or organ in animals or of a device. [probably from an Old English word *stalu* meaning 'upright piece of wood']

stalk[2] *verb* 1 to track or hunt an animal or person stealthily. 2 to harass someone, especially a celebrity, with unwanted and obsessive attention. 3 to walk in a stiff, dignified, or angry manner. **stalker** *noun* [from an Old English word *stealcian*]

stalking horse *noun* a candidate for the leadership of a political party who stands only in order to bring about the election and so allow a stronger candidate to come forward.

stall[1] *noun* 1 a stand, table, or counter from which things are sold, especially in a market. 2 an individual compartment for an animal in a stable or cowshed. 3 a compartment for one person. 4 a seat with its back and sides more or less enclosed, in a church etc. 5 the stalling of an engine or aircraft.
stalls *plural noun* the set of seats on the ground floor of a theatre.

stall *verb* 1 (said about an engine or vehicle) to stop suddenly because of an overload or insufficient fuel. 2 (said about an aircraft) to begin to drop because the speed is too low for it to respond to its controls. 3 to cause an engine or aircraft to stall. 4 to stop making progress, or to prevent something from making progress ♦ *The peace talks seem to have stalled.* 5 to delay someone deliberately in order to gain time ♦ *See if you can stall them for a minute.* 6 to avoid acting or giving a definite answer in order to gain time ♦ *Stop stalling and give me an answer.* [from an Old English word *steall* meaning 'stable or cattle shed']

stallion (stal-yən) *noun* an uncastrated male horse, especially one kept for breeding. [from an Old French word *estalon*]

stalwart (stawl-wert) *adjective* 1 strong and faithful ♦ *stalwart supporters.* 2 (*old use*) sturdy.
stalwart *noun* a stalwart supporter or member of an organization. [from an Old English word]

stamen (stay-men) *noun* (*Botany*) the male fertilizing organ of a flower, bearing pollen. [from a Latin word meaning 'thread']

stamina (stam-in-ə) *noun* staying power, the ability to withstand prolonged physical or mental effort. [from a Latin word meaning 'threads', referring to the threads of life spun by the Fates]

stammer *verb* to speak with involuntary pauses or rapid repetitions of the same syllable.
stammer *noun* a tendency to stammer.
stammerer *noun* [from an Old English word *stamerian*]

stamp *verb* 1 to bring your foot down heavily on the ground ♦ *The crowd stamped their feet in approval.* 2 to walk with loud heavy steps. 3 to stick a postage stamp on something. 4 to strike or press something with a device that leaves a mark or pattern etc.; to cut or shape something in this way. 5 to mark something with an official design, seal, etc. ♦ *They didn't stamp my passport.* 6 to give a certain character to something ♦ *This achievement stamps him as a genius.*
stamp *noun* 1 a postage stamp. 2 a piece of paper bearing a special design, for sticking on to a document to show that a fee etc. has been paid. 3 a device for

stamping a pattern or mark; the mark itself. **4** a distinguishing mark, a clear indication ♦ *His story bears the stamp of truth*. **5** the act or sound of stamping. **to stamp on** to quell something. **to stamp something out** **1** to put out a fire by stamping on it. **2** to put an end to something.   [from an Old English word]

stamp-collecting *noun* the collecting of postage stamps as objects of interest or value.

stamp duty *noun* a tax imposed on certain kinds of legal documents.

stampede *noun* **1** a sudden rush of a herd of frightened animals. **2** a rush of people under a sudden common impulse. **stampede** *verb* to take part in or cause animals or people to take part in a stampede. [from a Spanish word *estampida* meaning 'crash, uproar']

stamping ground *noun* a person's or animal's usual haunt or place of action.

stance *noun* **1** the position in which a person stands. **2** a person's attitude to something. [via French from an Italian word *stanza*]

stanch *verb* another spelling of **staunch**[2].

stanchion (stan-shǝn) *noun* an upright bar or post forming a support. [from an Old French word *estance* meaning 'a support']

stand *verb* (past tense and past participle **stood**) **1** to be in or rise to an upright position on your feet ♦ *We were standing at the back of the hall*. **2** to move in this position ♦ *Could you stand to the right, please?* **3** to place something or be situated in a particular position ♦ *Stand the vase on the table* ♦ *A statue stands in the square*. **4** (said about food, liquid, etc.) to be left undisturbed ♦ *Leave the mixture to stand for 15 minutes*. **5** to remain stationary or upright ♦ *After the earthquake few buildings were left standing*. **6** to stay the same, to remain valid ♦ *My offer still stands*. **7** to be in a particular condition or at a particular value ♦ *The thermometer stood at 90°*. **8** to be a candidate in an election ♦ *She stood for Parliament*. **9** to be likely to do something ♦ *Investors stood to lose thousands of pounds*. **10** to put up with or endure something ♦ *I can't stand that noise*. SYNONYMS: bear, abide, endure, tolerate. **11** to withstand being damaged. **12** to provide and pay for something ♦ *I'll stand you a drink*.

stand *noun* **1** a rack or pedestal etc. on which something may be held or displayed ♦ *an umbrella stand* ♦ *a music stand*. **2** a stall, booth, or other structure where things are sold or displayed. **3** a raised structure with seats at a sports ground etc. **4** a place where vehicles wait for passengers ♦ *a taxi stand*. **5** the place where someone usually stands ♦ *He took his stand near the door*. **6** an attitude towards a particular issue. **7** a determined effort to resist an attack, or the period of this ♦ *The time has come to make a stand*. **8** (in cricket) a partnership. **9** a witness box. **as it stands 1** in the present state of affairs. **2** in its present condition, unaltered. **it stands to reason** it is obvious or logical. **to stand a chance** to have a chance of success. **to stand alone** to be unequalled. **to stand by 1** to look on without interfering. **2** to support or side with a person in a difficulty or dispute. **3** to keep to a promise or agreement. **4** to be ready to take action if needed. **to stand down** or **stand aside** to resign from a position or office. **to stand for 1** to represent or be an abbreviation for something ♦ *'US' stands for 'United States'*. **2** (*informal*) to tolerate something ♦ *I won't stand for it!* **to stand in** to deputize. **to stand off** to remain at a distance. **to stand on ceremony** to insist on behaving formally ♦ *There's no need to stand on ceremony*. **to stand on end** (said about hair) to become erect from fear or horror. **to stand on your own (two) feet** to be independent. **to stand your ground** to refuse to yield. **to stand out 1** to stick out or be conspicuous. **2** to be clearly better than others. **3** to persist in opposition or in your demands ♦ *They stood out for a ten per cent rise*. **to stand over** to be postponed. **to stand to** to stand ready for action. **to stand trial** to be tried in a court of law. **to stand up** to be valid ♦ *That argument won't stand up in court*. **to stand someone up** (*informal*) to fail to keep a date or appointment with someone. **to stand up and be counted** to state publicly your support for someone or something. **to stand up for** to defend or support a person or opinion. **to stand up to 1** to resist someone bravely. **2** to stay in good condition despite the harmful effects of something. **to take the stand** to enter a witness box and give evidence. [from an Old English word]

stand-alone *adjective* (said of computing equipment) able to be used independently.

standard noun 1 how good something is ♦ *The standard of her work is high.* 2 a specified level of quality, attainment, or proficiency ♦ *Your work does not reach the required standard.* 3 a thing, quality, or specification by which something may be tested or measured. 4 a special flag ♦ *the royal standard.* 5 an upright support. 6 a shrub that has been grafted on an upright stem ♦ *standard roses.*
standards plural noun principles of decent honourable behaviour.
standard adjective 1 used as or conforming to a standard ♦ *standard measures of length.* 2 of average or usual quality or type ♦ *the standard model of this car.* 3 accepted as being authoritative and so widely used ♦ *the standard book on spiders.* 4 widely accepted as the usual form ♦ *standard English.* [from an Old French word *estendre* meaning 'to extend']

standard assessment task noun a standard test given to schoolchildren to assess their progress in one of the subjects of the national curriculum.

standard deviation noun (*Statistics*) a quantity used for measuring the extent to which a group of values deviate from the mean value.

standardize verb to make things conform to a standard size, quality, etc. **standardization** noun

standard lamp noun a household lamp set on a tall pillar on a base.

standard of living noun the level of material comfort that a person, community, or country has.

standby noun (**standbys**) 1 a person or thing available to be used as a substitute or in an emergency. 2 a system by which seats for a play, on an aircraft, etc. that have not yet been reserved can be bought at the last minute. **on standby** ready to be used as a substitute or in an emergency ♦ *Troops were on standby during the crisis.*

stand-in noun a substitute or deputy.

standing noun 1 a person's status or reputation ♦ *people of high standing.* 2 the period for which something has existed ♦ *a friendship of long standing.*
standing adjective 1 (said about a jump) performed without a run. 2 permanent or regularly repeated ♦ *a standing invitation.* 3 (said about water) stagnant or still. 4 (said about corn) not yet harvested.

standing order noun an instruction to a bank to make regular payments to someone, or to a trader to supply something regularly.

stand-off noun a deadlock between two equally matched opponents.

stand-offish adjective (*informal*) aloof, distant, and unfriendly in manner.

standpipe noun a vertical pipe connected directly to a water supply, especially one set up in the street to provide water in an emergency.

standpoint noun a point of view. SYNONYMS: stance, view, perspective, viewpoint, angle.

standstill noun a complete stop ♦ *Traffic has come to a virtual standstill.*

stand-up adjective 1 (said about a comedian or comedy) performing or performed solo in front of a live audience. 2 (said about a fight or argument) vigorous, involving direct confrontation ♦ *a stand-up row.*

stank past tense of **stink**.

stanza noun a verse of poetry. [from an Italian word *stanza* meaning 'standing place']

staphylococcus noun (**staphylococci** (staf-il-ə-**kok**-iy)) a kind of micro-organism that causes pus to form. [from Greek words *staphulē* meaning 'bunch of grapes' and *kokkos* meaning 'berry']

staple [1] noun 1 a U-shaped piece of metal or wire pushed through papers and clenched to fasten them together. 2 a U-shaped metal nail for holding wires etc. in place.
staple verb to fix something with a staple or staples. **stapler** noun [from an Old English word *stapol*]

staple [2] adjective main or important ♦ *Rice is their staple food.*
staple noun a staple food or product etc. [from an Old French word *estaple* meaning 'market']

star noun 1 a large mass of burning gas that is seen as a point of light in the night sky. 2 a figure, object, or ornament with rays or radiating points; an asterisk. 3 a star-shaped symbol indicating a category of excellence ♦ *a five-star hotel.* 4 a famous or brilliant actor, singer, sports player, etc. 5 one of the chief performers in a film, play, or show. 6 a planet or constellation regarded as influencing a person's fortunes or personality ♦ *Thank your lucky stars.*
stars plural noun a horoscope.

star *verb* (**starred, starring**) 1 to perform or have someone as one of the main actors ♦ *She is to star in a new production of Cabaret* ♦ *The film stars Russell Crowe as Maximus.* 2 to put an asterisk or star symbol beside a name or item in a list etc. **starless** *adjective* [from an Old English word *steorra*]

starboard *noun* the right-hand side of a ship or aircraft when facing forward, the opposite to **port**.
starboard *verb* to turn a ship or its helm to the starboard side. [from an Old English word *stear* meaning 'paddle for steering' (usually mounted on the right-hand side) and *board*]

starch *noun* 1 a white carbohydrate that is an important element in human food. It is found in bread, potatoes, etc. 2 a preparation of this or a similar substance used for stiffening fabric. 3 stiffness of manner.
starch *verb* to stiffen something with starch. [from an Old English word]

starchy *adjective* (**starchier, starchiest**) 1 like or containing starch. 2 stiff and formal in manner. **starchily** *adverb* **starchiness** *noun*

star-crossed *adjective* (*literary*) ill-fated.

stardom *noun* being a star actor or performer.

stare *verb* 1 to look fixedly at someone or something with the eyes wide open, especially in astonishment. SYNONYMS: gape, gaze, goggle; (*informal*) gawp. 2 (said about the eyes) to be wide open with fixed gaze.
stare *noun* a staring gaze. **to be staring you in the face** to be glaringly obvious. [from an Old English word *starian*]

starfish *noun* (**starfishes** or **starfish**) a sea creature shaped like a star with five or more points.

stargazing *noun* (*informal*) astronomy or astrology. **stargazer** *noun*

stark *adjective* 1 severe or bare in appearance; desolate ♦ *a stark moorland.* 2 sharply evident ♦ *in stark contrast.* 3 downright, complete ♦ *stark madness.* **starkly** *adverb* **starkness** *noun* **stark naked** completely naked. **stark raving** or **staring mad** (*informal*) completely mad. [from an Old English word *stearc* meaning 'unyielding, severe']

starlight *noun* light from the stars.

starling *noun* a noisy bird with glossy blackish speckled feathers, that forms large flocks. [from an Old English word]

starlit *adjective* lit by starlight.

Star of David *noun* the six pointed star used as a Jewish and Israeli symbol.

starry *adjective* (**starrier, starriest**) 1 full of stars. 2 shining like stars. 3 (*informal*) to do with film stars, pop stars, etc. ♦ *a starry cast.*

starry-eyed *adjective* naively optimistic or idealistic.

Stars and Stripes *noun* the national flag of the USA.

star sign *noun* a sign of the zodiac.

start *verb* 1 to begin or cause something to begin a process or course of action. 2 to make an engine or machine begin running; to begin running ♦ *I'll start the car.* 3 to establish or found something; to be established or founded ♦ *We started our own business in 2000.* 4 to begin a journey. SYNONYMS: leave, depart, set off, set out; (*informal*) get going, hit the road. 5 to make a sudden movement because of pain or surprise. 6 to spring suddenly ♦ *The man started from his seat.* 7 (said about timber) to spring from its proper position. 8 to rouse game from its lair. 9 (*informal*) to begin quarrelling or complaining ♦ *Now please don't start!*
start *noun* 1 the beginning of a journey, activity, or race. 2 the place where a race starts. 3 an opportunity for or assistance in starting a career etc. ♦ *Your family background should give you a good start in broadcasting.* 4 an advantage given in starting a race ♦ *We gave the young ones 10 seconds start.* 5 a sudden movement of surprise or pain. **for a start** in the first place. **to start at** to cost at least the amount mentioned. **to start off** or **out** 1 to be at the outset ♦ *The play starts off in the present day.* 2 to begin a journey or undertaking. **to start something off** 1 to make something begin working or operating. 2 to be the cause of something ♦ *What started off the unrest?* **to start something up** to make something begin working or operating ♦ *How do you start up the computer?* **to start with** in the first place. [from an Old English word *styrtan* meaning 'to leap']

starter *noun* 1 a person or thing that starts something. 2 a person who gives the signal for a race to start. 3 a horse or competitor at the start of a race ♦ *the list of* *probable starters.* **4** the first course of a meal. **for starters** (*informal*) to start with.

starting gate *noun* a removable barrier behind which horses are lined up at the start of a race.

startle *verb* to surprise or alarm someone. [from an Old English word *steartlian* meaning 'to kick or struggle']

startling *adjective* surprising or alarming.

star turn *noun* the principal item in an entertainment.

starve *verb* **1** to die or suffer acutely from lack of food; to cause someone to do this. **2** to deprive someone of something they need ♦ *starved of affection.* **to be starving** or **starved** (*informal*) to feel very hungry. **starvation** *noun* [from an Old English word *steorfan* meaning 'to die']

stash *verb* (*informal*) to store something safely in a secret place. **stash** *noun* (*informal*) a secret store. [origin unknown]

state *noun* **1** the condition of someone or something ♦ *a poor state of health* ♦ *She was in a state of shock.* **2** the physical structure or form of a substance ♦ *a liquid state.* **3** (often **State**) an organized community under one government (e.g. *the State of Israel*) or forming part of a federal republic (e.g. *the state of Texas*). **4** (often **State**) a country's civil government ♦ *These benefits are provided by the State* ♦ *matters of state.* **5** pomp and ceremony associated with monarchy or government. **6** an excited or agitated condition of mind ♦ *Don't get into a state about it.* **7** a dirty or disorderly condition ♦ *I'm afraid the house is in a bit of a state.* **state** *adjective* **1** to do with or for the State. **2** involving ceremony, used or done on ceremonial occasions ♦ *the state apartments.* **state** *verb* **1** to express something in spoken or written words. SYNONYMS: assert, declare, remark, aver. **2** to specify something ♦ *The office is only open at the stated times.* **to lie in state** see **lie**². **state of affairs** a situation. **the state of play** the current situation. **the States** the USA. [from a Latin word *status* meaning 'a standing']

stateless *adjective* (said about a person) not a citizen or subject of any country.

stately *adjective* (**statelier, stateliest**) dignified, imposing, or grand. **stateliness** *noun* [from *state*]

stately home *noun* a large and magnificent house belonging to an aristocratic family.

statement *noun* **1** something expressed in spoken or written words. **2** a formal account of facts or events ♦ *The witness made a statement to the police.* **3** a written report of a financial account ♦ *a bank statement.*

state of emergency *noun* a situation of national disaster or danger in which a government suspends normal law and order procedures.

state-of-the-art *adjective* using the newest ideas and most up-to-date features.

stateroom *noun* **1** a large room in a palace or public building used on formal occasions. **2** a passenger's private compartment on a ship.

state school *noun* a school which is funded by the government and which does not charge fees to pupils.

statesman or **stateswoman** *noun* (**statesmen** or **stateswomen**) an experienced or respected politician, especially a leader. **statesmanlike** *adjective* **statesmanship** *noun*

static *adjective* **1** not moving, stationary. **2** not changing. **3** (*Physics*) (said about force) not producing motion (as opposed to *dynamic*). **static** *noun* **1** static electricity. **2** atmospherics. **statics** *noun* a branch of physics that deals with bodies at rest and forces in equilibrium. [from a Greek word *statikos* meaning 'standing']

static electricity *noun* electricity that is present in something and not flowing as current.

station *noun* **1** a regular stopping place for trains, buses, etc. with platforms and buildings for passengers and goods. **2** an establishment or building where a public service is based or which is equipped for certain activities ♦ *the fire station* ♦ *an agricultural research station.* **3** a broadcasting company with its own frequency. **4** a place where a person or thing stands or is stationed. **5** a person's social rank or position ♦ *She's getting ideas above her station.* **6** (*Austral.*) a large sheep or cattle farm. **station** *verb* to put someone at or in a certain place for a purpose ♦ *The regiment was stationed in Germany.* [from a Latin word *statio* meaning 'a stand, standing']

stationary *adjective* 1 not moving ♦ *The car was stationary when the van hit it.* SYNONYMS: at a standstill, at rest, immobile, motionless, static. 2 not changing in condition or quantity.
◊ Do not confuse this word with **stationery**, which has a different meaning.

stationer *noun* someone who sells stationery. [from a Latin word *stationarius* denoting a tradesman (usually a bookseller) who had a shop or stand, as opposed to someone who sold goods wherever they could]

stationery *noun* writing paper, envelopes, and other materials used for writing.
◊ Do not confuse this word with **stationary**, which has a different meaning.

stationmaster *noun* the official in charge of a railway station.

statistic (stə-**tist**-ik) *noun* a piece of information expressed as a number. [from a German word *Statistik*]

statistical *adjective* to do with statistics. **statistically** *adverb*

statistician (stat-iss-**tish**-ən) *noun* an expert in statistics.

statistics (stə-**tist**-iks) *noun* the science of collecting and interpreting information based on numerical data.

stats *noun* (*informal*) statistics.

statuary (**stat**-yoo-er-i) *noun* statues.

statue *noun* a carved, cast, or moulded figure of a person or animal, usually of life size or larger. [from a Latin word *stare* meaning 'to stand']

statuesque (stat-yoo-**esk**) *adjective* looking like a statue in size, dignity, or stillness.

statuette (stat-yoo-**et**) *noun* a small statue.

stature (**stat**-yer) *noun* 1 a person's natural height. 2 greatness gained by ability or achievement. [same origin as for *statue*]

status (**stay**-təs) *noun* 1 a person's position or rank in relation to others. 2 a person's or thing's legal position or official classification. 3 the state of affairs at a particular time. 4 high rank or prestige. [from a Latin word *status* meaning 'a standing']

status quo (stay-təs **kwoh**) the existing state of affairs ♦ *A majority voted to maintain the status quo.* [a Latin phrase meaning 'the state in which']

status symbol *noun* something you own or have that shows off your wealth or position in society.

statute (**stat**-yoot) *noun* 1 a law passed by a parliament. 2 a rule of an organization or institution. [from a Latin word *statutum* meaning 'set up']

statutory (**stat**-yoo-ter-i) *adjective* 1 fixed, done, or required by statute ♦ *statutory rights.* 2 required or expected because of being done regularly. **statutorily** *adverb*

staunch[1] *adjective* firm in attitude or loyalty ♦ *our staunch supporters.* **staunchly** *adverb* [from an Old French word *estanche* meaning 'watertight']

staunch[2] *verb* to stop the flow of blood from a wound. [from an Old French word *estanchier*]

stave *noun* 1 one of the curved strips of wood forming the side of a cask or tub. 2 (also **staff**) (*Music*) a set of five horizontal lines on which music is written.
stave *verb* to stave something in to dent or break a hole in something. to stave something off to ward something off permanently or temporarily ♦ *We staved off disaster.* [from *staves* (see *staff*)]
◊ The past tense and past participle for *stave something in* can be either *staved* or *stove.* For *stave something off* the past tense and past participle is *staved*, and *stove* cannot be used in this meaning.

stay[1] *verb* 1 to remain in the same place or state ♦ *Stay here* ♦ *I can hardly stay awake* ♦ *He decided to stay away from the meeting.* 2 to spend time in a place as a guest or visitor. 3 to postpone carrying something out ♦ *The disciplinary committee has agreed to stay judgement.* 4 to satisfy something temporarily ♦ *We stayed our hunger with a sandwich.* 5 (*old use*) to pause in movement, action, or speech.
stay *noun* 1 a time spent somewhere ♦ *We made a short stay in Athens.* 2 a postponement, e.g. of carrying out a judgement ♦ *He was granted a stay of execution.*
stays *plural noun* (*old use*) a corset. to stay put to remain somewhere without moving. to stay the course or distance 1 to keep going to the end of a race or contest. 2 to continue with a difficult task or activity to the end. to stay up to not go to bed. [same origin as for *stable*[1]]

stay[2] *noun* 1 a rope or wire supporting or bracing a mast, spar, pole, etc. 2 any prop or support. [via Old French from a Germanic word]

stayer noun a person with great staying power.

staying power noun endurance or stamina.

stay stitching noun stitching close to a curved or bias-cut edge to prevent it from stretching when worked on.

STD abbreviation 1 subscriber trunk dialling. 2 sexually transmitted disease.

stead (sted) noun in a person's or thing's stead instead of this person or thing. to stand someone in good stead to be of advantage to someone over time. [from an Old English word stede meaning 'place']

steadfast (sted-fahst) adjective firm and not changing or yielding ◆ a steadfast refusal. **steadfastly** adverb **steadfastness** noun [from an Old English word meaning 'standing firm']

steady adjective (**steadier, steadiest**) 1 firmly supported or balanced, not shaking or tottering ◆ Hold the camera steady. 2 constant and regular, not changing ◆ a steady pace. 3 continuing in an even and regular way without being interrupted ◆ She's making steady progress at school. 4 behaving in a serious and dependable manner, not frivolous or excitable.
steady noun (**steadies**) (informal) a regular boyfriend or girlfriend.
steady verb (**steadies, steadied, steadying**) to make something steady, or to become steady.
steady adverb steadily. to go steady (informal) to have a regular romantic or sexual relationship with someone. **steady on!** calm down; be more reasonable. **steadily** adverb **steadiness** noun [from stead]

steak noun 1 a thick slice of beef or other meat, cut for grilling or frying. 2 beef from the front of an animal, cut for stewing or braising. 3 a thick slice of fish ◆ salmon steaks. [from an Old Norse word steik]

steal verb (**stole, stolen**) 1 to take another person's property without right or permission. SYNONYMS: thieve, rob, pilfer, purloin;(informal) nick, pinch, swipe, lift, filch, knock off. 2 to take someone else's ideas and dishonestly pretend they are yours. SYNONYM: plagiarize; (informal) rip off. 3 to obtain something by surprise or a trick or surreptitiously ◆ I stole a quick kiss ◆ She stole a look at him. 4 to move somewhere secretly or without being noticed ◆ She stole out of the room.
steal noun (informal) a bargain. to steal a march on to gain an advantage over someone by doing something ahead of them. to steal the show to attract the most attention. [from an Old English word stelan]

stealth (stelth) noun stealthiness.
stealth adjective (said about aircraft, missiles, etc.) designed using advanced technology that makes detection by radar or sonar difficult ◆ a stealth bomber. [probably from an Old English word and related to steal]

stealthy (stel-thi) adjective (**stealthier, stealthiest**) acting or done in a quiet or secret way so as to avoid being noticed. **stealthily** adverb **stealthiness** noun

steam noun 1 invisible gas into which water is changed by boiling, used to drive machinery. 2 the mist that forms when steam condenses in the air. 3 energy or momentum ◆ The dispute gathered steam. **steam** verb 1 to give off steam or vapour. 2 to cook or treat something by steam ◆ a steamed pudding. 3 to move by the power of steam ◆ The ship steamed down the river. to be or get steamed up (informal) to be or become angry or upset. to get up or pick up steam 1 to generate enough pressure to drive a steam engine. 2 (informal) to gradually gain speed or momentum. to let off steam (informal) to release pent-up energy or strong emotion. to run out of steam (informal) to become exhausted or lose enthusiasm before something is finished. to steam up or steam something up to become covered or cover something with condensed steam ◆ Her glasses started to steam up. under your own steam without help from other people. **steamy** adjective [from an Old English word]

steamboat noun a steam-driven boat, especially a paddle-wheel craft used widely on rivers in the 19th century.

steam engine noun an engine or locomotive driven by steam.

steamer noun 1 a ship or boat driven by steam. 2 a container in which things are cooked or treated by steam.

steaming noun (informal) robbery by a gang who rush through a crowd of people, especially in a railway carriage.

steam iron noun an electric iron that can send out jets of steam from its flat surface.

steamroller noun a heavy slow-moving engine with a large roller, used to flatten surfaces when making roads.
steamroller or **steamroll** verb 1 to force something to be accepted by being too powerful for any opposition. 2 to force someone into doing something. [so called because the first ones were powered by steam]

steamship noun a ship driven by steam.

stearate (steer-ayt) noun a salt or ester of stearic acid.

stearic acid (sti-a-rik) noun a white fatty acid obtained from animal or vegetable fats. [from a Greek word *stear* meaning 'tallow']

steed noun (literary) a horse. [from an Old English word]

steel noun 1 a very strong alloy of iron and carbon much used for making vehicles, tools, weapons etc. 2 a tapered usually roughened steel rod for sharpening knives. 3 strength and determination ♦ nerves of steel.
steel verb to mentally prepare yourself to face something difficult ♦ You'd better steel yourself for some bad news. [from an Old English word]

steel band noun a band playing music on steel drums.

steel drum or **steel pan** noun a percussion instrument, originally from Trinidad, which is made out of an oil drum, with the top beaten into sections that produce different notes.

steel wool noun fine shavings of steel massed together, used as an abrasive.

steelworks noun a factory where steel is manufactured.

steely adjective (**steelier, steeliest**) 1 like steel in colour or strength. 2 cold, determined, and severe ♦ a steely glare.

steelyard noun a weighing apparatus with a graduated arm along which a weight slides. [from *steel* and an old sense of *yard* meaning 'measuring stick']

steep [1] adjective 1 sloping sharply not gradually. SYNONYMS: sheer, precipitous. 2 (said about a rise or fall) very large or rapid. 3 (informal) (said about a price) unreasonably high. **steeply** adverb

steepness noun [from an Old English word meaning 'extending to a great height']

steep [2] verb to soak something or be soaked in liquid. **to be steeped in** to be filled with or heavily involved in something ♦ The story is steeped in mystery. [probably from a Scandinavian word]

steepen verb to make something steeper, or to become steeper.

steeple noun 1 a tall tower with a spire on top, rising above the roof of a church. 2 a spire. [from an Old English word]

steeplechase noun 1 a horse race on a course with hedges and ditches to jump. 2 a long running race in which runners must jump over hurdles and water jumps. [so called because the race originally had a distant steeple in view as its goal]

steeplechaser noun a person or horse that takes part in a steeplechase; a horse trained for this.

steeplechasing noun the sport of riding in steeplechases.

steeplejack noun a person who climbs tall chimneys or steeples to do repairs.

steer [1] verb 1 to make a vehicle or ship etc. go in the direction you want. 2 to direct the course of something ♦ I steered the conversation round to the subject of holidays. SYNONYMS: direct, guide. 3 to be able to be steered ♦ The car steers well. **to steer clear of** to take care to avoid something. **steerer** noun [from an Old English word *stieran*]

steer [2] noun a young castrated bull raised for its beef. [from an Old English word *steor*]

steerage noun (historical) the cheapest section of accommodation for passengers in a ship, situated below decks.

steering noun the mechanism by which a vehicle or boat etc. is steered.

steering wheel noun a wheel for controlling the steering mechanism.

steersman noun (**steersmen**) a person who steers a ship.

stegosaurus (ste-gə-sor-əs) noun a large dinosaur with bony plates along its back, which fed on plants. [from a Greek word *stegē* meaning 'roof' and *sauros* meaning 'lizard']

stellar adjective to do with a star or stars. [from a Latin word *stella* meaning 'star']

stem [1] *noun* **1** the main central part of a plant or shrub. **2** a slender part supporting a fruit, flower, or leaf. **3** any slender part of something, e.g. the thin part of a wine glass between the bowl and the foot. **4** (*Grammar*) the main part of a noun or verb, from which other parts or words are made, e.g. by altering the endings. **5** the curved timber or metal piece at the bow of a ship.
stem *verb* (**stemmed, stemming**) to remove the stems from something. **to stem from** to arise from something. [from an Old English word *stemn*]

stem [2] *verb* (**stemmed, stemming**) to stop or restrict the flow of something. [from an Old Norse word *stemma*]

stench *noun* a strong and unpleasant smell. [from an Old English word *stenc* meaning 'smell']

stencil *noun* **1** a sheet of metal or card etc. with a design cut out, which can be painted or inked over to produce a corresponding design on the surface below. **2** the decoration or lettering etc. produced by a stencil.
stencil *verb* (**stencilled, stencilling**) to produce or decorate something by means of a stencil. [from an old word *stanselen* meaning 'to decorate with various colours']

stenography (sten-og-rəfi) *noun* (*North Amer.*) the process or technique of writing in shorthand. **stenographer** *noun* [from a Greek word *stenos* meaning 'narrow' and -*graphy*]

stentorian (sten-tor-iən) *adjective* (said about a voice) loud and powerful. [from the name of Stentor, a herald in ancient Greek legend]

step *noun* **1** a movement made by lifting the foot and setting it down. **2** the distance covered by this. **3** the sound of a step ♦ *I heard steps behind me.* SYNONYMS: footstep, footfall. **4** a short distance ♦ *It's only a step to the bus stop.* **5** a series of steps forming a particular pattern in dancing. **6** a level surface for placing the foot on in climbing up or down. **7** a rhythm of stepping, as in marching. **8** each of a series of things done in some process or course of action ♦ *The first step is to find somewhere to rehearse.* SYNONYMS: stage, phase, procedure. **9** a stage in a scale or hierarchy.
steps *plural noun* a stepladder.
step *verb* (**stepped, stepping**) **1** to lift and set down the foot or alternate feet as you do when you walk. **2** to move a short distance in this way ♦ *Please step aside.* **in step 1** stepping in time with other people in marching or dancing. **2** conforming to what others are doing. **out of step** not in step. **step by step 1** one step at a time. **2** proceeding steadily from one stage to the next. **to step down** to resign from a position or office. **to step forward** to offer your help or services. **to step in 1** to intervene. **2** to act as a substitute for someone. **to step on it** (*informal*) to hurry. **to step something up** to increase the level of something ♦ *It's time we stepped up the campaign.* **watch your step** be careful. [from an Old English word *steppan*]

step- *prefix* related by remarriage of one parent. [from an Old English word *steop-*]

stepbrother *noun* the son of one of your parents from an earlier or later marriage.

stepchild *noun* (**stepchildren**) a child that a person's wife or husband has from an earlier marriage. **stepdaughter** *noun* **stepson** *noun*

stepfather *noun* a man who is married to your mother but is not your natural father.

step-in *adjective* (said about a piece of clothing) put on by being stepped into, without fastenings.

stepladder *noun* a short folding ladder with flat steps and a small platform.

stepmother *noun* a woman who is married to your father but is not your natural mother.

steppe (step) *noun* a level grassy plain with few trees, especially in SE Europe and Siberia. [from a Russian word]

stepping stone *noun* **1** a raised stone providing a place to step on in crossing a stream or muddy area. **2** a means or stage of progress towards achieving a goal.

stepsister *noun* the daughter of one of your parents from an earlier or later marriage.

stereo (ste-ri-oh) *noun* (**stereos**) **1** stereophonic sound or recording. **2** a stereophonic CD player, record player, etc.
stereo *adjective* stereophonic. [from *stereophonic*]

stereophonic (ste-ri-ə-**fon**-ik) *adjective* (said about sound reproduction) using two or more transmission channels so that the reproduced sound seems to surround the listener and to come from more than one source. (Compare **monophonic**.) **stereophonically** adverb [from Greek words *stereos* meaning 'solid' and *phone* meaning 'sound']

stereoscope (ste-ri-ǝ-skohp) noun a device for giving a stereoscopic effect.

stereoscopic (ste-ri-ǝ-skop-ik) adjective giving a three-dimensional effect, e.g. in photographs. **stereoscopically** adverb [from Greek words *stereos* meaning 'solid' and *skopein* meaning 'to look at']

stereotype (ste-ri-ǝ-tiyp or steer-ri-ǝ-tiyp) noun 1 an over-simplified image or idea of a type of person or thing that has become fixed through being widely held. 2 a relief printing plate cast from a mould. **stereotype** verb to represent or view something as a stereotype. [from a Greek word *stereos* meaning 'solid' and *type*, referring to fixed type formerly used in printing]

sterile (ste-riyl) adjective 1 not able to produce children, young, fruit, or seeds. 2 free from bacteria or other living micro-organisms. 3 unproductive, lacking new ideas ♦ *a sterile discussion*. SYNONYMS: fruitless, unprofitable. **sterility** (ster-il-iti) noun [from a Latin word *sterilis*]

sterilize (ste-ri-liyz) verb 1 to make something sterile or free from micro-organisms, e.g. by heating it. 2 to make a person or animal unable to produce offspring by removing or blocking the reproductive organs. **sterilization** noun

sterling noun British money. **sterling** adjective excellent, of great value ♦ *her sterling qualities*. [probably from an Old English word *steorra* meaning 'star' and *-ling* (because some early coins had a star on them)]

sterling silver noun silver of a level of purity of at least 92.25%.

stern[1] adjective 1 strict and severe, not lenient, cheerful, or kindly. 2 demanding or rigorous ♦ *a stern test*. **sternly** adverb **sternness** noun [from an Old English word *styrne*]

stern[2] noun the rear end of a ship or boat. [from an Old Norse word]

sternum noun the breastbone. **sternal** adjective [from a Greek word *sternon* meaning 'chest']

steroid (steer-oid) noun (Biochemistry) 1 any of a group of organic compounds that includes certain hormones and other bodily secretions. 2 short for **anabolic steroid**. [from *sterol*]

sterol (steer-ol or sterr-ol) noun any of a group of steroid alcohols that includes cholesterol. [from the ending of *cholesterol*]

stertorous (ster-ter-ǝs) adjective (said about breathing) noisy and laboured. **stertorously** adverb [from a Latin word *stertere* meaning 'to snore']

stet verb (**stetted, stetting**) (placed beside a word that has been crossed out by mistake) let it stand as written or printed. [a Latin word meaning 'let it stand']

stethoscope (steth-ǝ-skohp) noun a medical instrument for listening to sounds within the body, e.g. breathing and heartbeats. [from a Greek word *stēthos* meaning 'breast' and *skopein* meaning 'to look at']

stetson noun a hat with a very wide brim and a high crown, of the type traditionally worn by cowboys. [named after the American hat manufacturer J. B. Stetson (1830–1906)]

stevedore (stee-vǝ-dor) noun a person employed at a dock to load and unload ships. [from a Spanish word *estivador*]

stew noun a dish of food, especially meat and vegetables, cooked slowly in liquid in a closed dish or pan. **stew** verb 1 to cook something or be cooked slowly in liquid in a closed dish or pan. 2 (said about tea) to become too strong and bitter because it has been brewing too long. 3 (informal) to be very worried or agitated. **in a stew** (informal) very worried or agitated. **to stew in your own juice** (informal) to be left to suffer the consequence of your own actions. [from an Old French word *estuve*]

steward noun 1 a person who looks after the passengers on a ship or aircraft. 2 an official who keeps order or supervises the arrangements at a large public event. 3 a person whose job is to arrange for the supply of food to a college, club, etc. 4 a person employed to manage someone else's property, especially a large house or estate. **stewardship** noun [from an Old English word *stig* meaning 'house or hall' and *ward*]

stewardess noun a woman who looks after the passengers on a ship or aircraft.

stick [1] *noun* **1** a small thin branch from a tree. **2** a thin piece of wood for use as a support or weapon etc. **3** a walking stick. **4** a long implement used to hit the ball in hockey, polo, etc. **5** a long thin object or piece of a substance ◆ *a stick of celery* ◆ *a stick of dynamite.* **6** the threat of punishment used to persuade someone to do something, as distinct from the 'carrot' used to entice them to do it. **7** (*informal, old use*) a person of a particular kind ◆ *She's not such a bad old stick.* **the sticks** *plural noun* (*informal*) rural areas. **to get hold of the wrong end of the stick** (*informal*) to misunderstand a remark or situation. **to give someone stick** (*informal*) to criticize someone. [from an Old English word *sticca* meaning 'peg, stick, spoon']

stick [2] *verb* (past tense and past participle **stuck**) **1** to push a thing or its point into something ◆ *Stick a pin in it.* **2** to fix something by means of a pointed object ◆ *A sign was stuck to the door with pins.* **3** to extend upwards or outwards ◆ *His hair was sticking up at the back* ◆ *I stuck my head round the door.* **4** (*informal*) to put something somewhere ◆ *Just stick the parcel on the table.* **5** to fix something or be fixed by glue or suction etc. or as if by these. **6** to become fixed in one place and unable to move ◆ *This drawer keeps sticking.* **7** to remain in the same place or for a long time ◆ *His name sticks in my mind.* **8** (*informal*) (said about an accusation) to be recognized as valid ◆ *We couldn't make the charges stick.* **9** (*informal*) to endure or tolerate something ◆ *I can't stick all this noise.* **to stick around** (*informal*) to remain in an area. **to stick at** (*informal*) to persevere with something. **to stick by** to continue to support someone. **to stick in your throat** to be against your principles or difficult to accept. **to stick it out** to persevere with something to the end in spite of difficulty or unpleasantness. **to stick your neck out** to expose yourself deliberately to danger or argument. **to stick out 1** to stand out from the surrounding surface. **2** to be very noticeable. **to stick out for** to refuse to accept less than you have been demanding. **to stick to 1** to keep to and not alter something ◆ *He stuck to his story.* **2** to remain faithful to a friend or promise etc. **to stick to your guns** to hold your position against attack or argument. **to stick together 1** to stay together. **2** to support each other. **to stick someone up** to rob someone by threatening them with

a gun. **to stick up for** to support or defend a person or opinion. **to stick with** to persevere or continue with something. [from an Old English word *stician*]

sticker *noun* **1** an adhesive label or sign for sticking to something. **2** (*informal*) someone who persists in their efforts.

sticking plaster *noun* a strip of fabric with an adhesive on one side, used for covering small cuts.

sticking point *noun* an issue that prevents an agreement being reached.

stick insect *noun* an insect with a twig-like body.

stick-in-the-mud *noun* (*informal*) a person who does not like doing anything new.

stickleback *noun* a small fish with sharp spines along its back. [from an Old English word *sticel* meaning 'thorn']

stickler *noun* a person who insists on something ◆ *a stickler for punctuality.* [from an Old English word *stihtan* meaning 'to put in order']

stick-up *noun* (*informal*) an armed robbery in which a gun is used to threaten people.

sticky *adjective* (**stickier**, **stickiest**) **1** able or tending to stick to things. SYNONYMS: adhesive, tacky. **2** (said about weather) hot and humid, causing perspiration. **3** (*informal*) difficult or awkward. **to come to a sticky end** (*informal*) to die or end in a painful or unpleasant way. **sticky fingers** (*informal*) a tendency to steal things. **stickily** *adverb* **stickiness** *noun*

stiff *adjective* **1** not bending or moving or changing its shape easily. **2** not fluid, thick and hard to stir ◆ *a stiff dough.* **3** difficult to do or beat ◆ *a stiff examination* ◆ *stiff opposition.* **4** formal in manner, not relaxed or friendly. **5** (said about a price or penalty) high, severe ◆ *a stiff fine.* **6** (said about a breeze) blowing strongly. **7** (said about a drink or dose) strong. **8** (*informal*) to an extreme degree ◆ *I was bored stiff.* **stiff** *noun* (*informal*) **1** a corpse. **2** (*North Amer.*) a boringly conventional person. **a stiff upper lip** emotional self-control when facing grief or loss. **stiffly** *adverb* **stiffness** *noun* [from an Old English word]

stiffen *verb* to make something stiff, or to become stiff. **stiffener** *noun*

stiff-necked *adjective* obstinate or haughty.

stifle *verb* 1 to prevent someone from breathing freely; to suffocate someone. 2 to restrain or suppress something ♦ *She stifled a yawn.* **stifling** *adjective* [from an Old French word *estouffer* meaning 'to smother, stifle']

stigma *noun* (**stigmas**) 1 a mark of disgrace associated with something. 2 (*Botany*) the part of a pistil that receives the pollen in pollination. [a Greek word meaning 'a mark made by a pointed instrument']

stigmata (**stig-mə-tə**) *plural noun* marks on the body corresponding to those left on Christ's body by the nails and spear at his crucifixion. [same origin as for *stigma*]

stigmatize (**stig-mə-tyz**) *verb* to brand a person or thing as something disgraceful ♦ *He was stigmatized as a coward.*

stile *noun* an arrangement of steps or bars for people to climb in order to get over a fence or wall. [from an Old English word *stigel*]

stiletto *noun* (**stilettos**) 1 a high pointed heel on a woman's shoe. 2 a dagger with a narrow blade. 3 a pointed tool for making eyelet holes. [an Italian word meaning 'little dagger']

still ¹ *adjective* 1 not moving. 2 not disturbed by motion, wind, or sound ♦ *a still evening.* 3 (said about drinks) not sparkling or fizzy.
still *adverb* 1 without or almost without moving ♦ *Stand still.* 2 continuing then, now, or in the future as before ♦ *It's still raining.* ♦ *She was still living with her parents.* 3 nevertheless ♦ *They've lost. Still, they tried, and that was good.* 4 in a greater amount or degree ♦ *I'm sure you could do better still.*
still *verb* to make something still, or to become still ♦ *a god with the power to still the waves.*
still *noun* 1 silence and calm ♦ *in the still of the night.* 2 a photograph of a scene from a cinema film. **stillness** *noun* [from an Old English word *stille*]

still ² *noun* an apparatus for distilling alcoholic drinks such as whisky. [from *distil*]

stillbirth *noun* a birth in which the child is born dead.

stillborn *adjective* 1 (said about an infant) born dead.

still life *noun* (**still lifes**) a painting or drawing of an arrangement of objects such as flowers, fruit, or ornaments.

still room *noun* (*historical*) a housekeeper's storeroom in a large house.

stilt *noun* 1 either of a pair of poles with a rest for the foot some way up it, enabling the user to walk with their feet at a distance above the ground. 2 each of a set of posts supporting a building, often above marshy ground. 3 a long-legged marsh bird. [from an old word *stilte* meaning 'plough handle']

stilted *adjective* stiffly or artificially formal ♦ *written in stilted language.* [originally meaning 'raised on stilts']

Stilton *noun* (*trademark*) a rich blue-veined cheese. [named after Stilton in Cambridgeshire]

stimulant *noun* 1 a drug or drink that increases physiological or nervous activity in the body ♦ *Caffeine is a stimulant.* 2 something that makes people more enthusiastic, interested, or active.
stimulant *adjective* acting as a stimulant.

stimulate *verb* 1 to make something more lively or active ♦ *The programme has stimulated a lot of interest in her work.*
SYNONYMS: prompt, provoke, arouse, inspire, kindle, stir up, whet. 2 to make someone interested or excited. 3 to apply a stimulus to something. **stimulating** *adjective* **stimulation** *noun* **stimulator** *noun* [from a Latin word *stimulare* meaning 'to urge, goad']

stimulative (**stim-yoo-lə-tiv**) *adjective* stimulating.

stimulus *noun* (**stimuli** (**stim-yool-iy**)) 1 something that produces a reaction in an organ or tissue of the body. 2 something that rouses a person or thing to activity or energy. [a Latin word meaning 'goad']

sting *noun* 1 a sharp-pointed part or organ of an insect, plant, etc. that can cause a wound or inflammation by injecting poison. 2 a wound from a sting. 3 a sharp tingling sensation or hurtful effect ♦ *the sting of remorse.*
sting *verb* (past tense and past participle **stung**) 1 to wound or affect a person or animal with a sting; to be able to do this. 2 to make someone feel a sharp bodily or mental pain. 3 to goad someone into doing something ♦ *I was stung into answering rudely.* 4 (*informal*) to swindle or overcharge someone. [from an Old English word *sting*]

stinging nettle *noun* a nettle covered in stinging hairs.

stingray *noun* a tropical fish with a flat body, fins like wings, and a long tail with sharp spines that can cause severe wounds.

stingy (stin-ji) *adjective* (**stingier, stingiest**) (*informal*) mean, not generous. **stingily** *adverb* **stinginess** *noun* [from *sting*]

stink *noun* 1 a strong unpleasant smell. SYNONYMS: stench, reek, whiff; (*informal*) pong. 2 (*informal*) an unpleasant fuss or protest ♦ They kicked up a stink about it.
stink *verb* (past tense **stank** or **stunk**; past participle **stunk**) 1 to give off a strong unpleasant smell. 2 (*informal*) to seem very unpleasant or unsavoury ♦ This idea of yours stinks. 3 (*informal*) to suggest or indicate something dishonest ♦ The whole business stinks of corruption. [from an Old English word *stincan* meaning 'to stink']

stinker *noun* (*informal*) 1 a person or thing that stinks. 2 (*informal*) something offensive or severe or difficult to do.

stinking *adjective* 1 foul-smelling. 2 (*informal*) very unpleasant.
stinking *adverb* (*informal*) extremely ♦ stinking rich.

stint *noun* 1 a fixed or allotted amount of work to be done ♦ Could you do a stint of delivering leaflets?. 2 a limitation of supply or effort ♦ She gave help without stint.
stint *verb* 1 to be sparing with something ♦ You didn't stint on the cream, did you?. 2 to restrict someone to a small amount ♦ Fill your plate up. Don't stint yourself. [from an Old English word *styntan* meaning 'to make blunt']

stipend (stiy-pend) *noun* a salary or allowance, especially the official income of a member of the clergy. [from Latin words *stips* meaning 'wages' and *pendere* meaning 'to pay']

stipendiary (stip-end-i-er-i) *adjective* receiving a stipend.

stipple *verb* 1 to paint, draw, or engrave something with small dots instead of lines or strokes. 2 to roughen the surface of cement, plaster, etc. [from a Dutch word *stippen* meaning 'to prick']

stipulate *verb* to demand or insist on something as part of an agreement. [from a Latin word *stipulari* meaning 'to demand as a formal promise']

stipulation *noun* 1 stipulating. 2 something stipulated.

stir [1] *verb* (**stirred, stirring**) 1 to mix or move a liquid or soft mixture by moving a spoon etc. round and round in it. 2 to move slightly or cause something to move slightly ♦ Not a leaf stirred ♦ Wind stirred the sand. 3 to wake up or begin to be active. 4 to arouse, stimulate, or excite someone or something ♦ The story stirred their interest ♦ They are always stirring up trouble.
stir *noun* 1 the act or process of stirring ♦ Give the soup a stir. 2 a commotion or disturbance ♦ The news caused a stir. [from an Old English word *styrian*]

stir [2] *noun* (*informal*) prison. [perhaps from a Romany word *sturbin* meaning 'jail']

stir-fry *verb* (**stir-fries, stir-fried, stir-frying**) to cook something by frying it quickly over a high heat while stirring and tossing.
stir-fry *noun* (**stir-fries**) a stir-fried dish.

stirring *adjective* exciting or stimulating.

stirrup *noun* a metal or leather support for a rider's foot, hanging from the saddle. [from an Old English word]

stitch *noun* 1 a single movement of a threaded needle in and out of fabric in sewing or tissue in surgery. 2 a single complete movement of a needle or hook in knitting or crochet. 3 the loop of thread, wool, etc. made in this way. 4 a particular method of arranging the thread ♦ a cross stitch ♦ an embroidery stitch. 5 the least bit of clothing ♦ without a stitch on. 6 a sudden sharp pain in the muscles at the side of the body, caused by running.
stitch *verb* to sew, join, or close something with stitches. **in stitches** (*informal*) laughing uncontrollably. **to stitch someone up** (*informal*) to betray or incriminate someone. [from an Old English word *stice*]

stoat *noun* an animal of the weasel family, with brown fur that turns white in winter (when the animal is known as an *ermine*). [origin unknown]

stock *noun* 1 all the goods or raw materials kept on the premises of a shop, business, etc. ♦ The shop has an excellent stock of art materials. 2 an amount of something kept ready for use ♦ a stock of jokes. 3 livestock. 4 a line of ancestry ♦ a woman of Irish stock. 5 the capital raised by a company by selling shares. 6 a portion of this held in the form of shares by an individual shareholder. 7 securities issued by the

government in fixed units with a fixed rate of interest. **8** a person's standing in the opinion of others ♦ *His stock is high.* **9** liquid made by stewing bones, meat, fish, or vegetables, used as a basis for making soup, sauce, etc. **10** a garden plant with fragrant single or double flowers. **11** the lower and thicker part of a tree trunk. **12** a growing plant into which a graft is inserted. **13** a part serving as the base, holder, or handle for the working parts of an implement or machine. **14** the wooden or metal part of a rifle to which the barrel is attached. **15** a cravat worn as part of a riding outfit. **16** a piece of black or purple fabric worn under a clerical collar.
stock *adjective* **1** kept in stock and regularly available ♦ *one of our stock items.* **2** commonly used, constantly recurring ♦ *a stock phrase.*
stock *verb* **1** to keep goods in stock. **2** to provide a place with goods, livestock, or a supply of something ♦ *He stocked his farm with Jersey cows* ♦ *a well-stocked library.* **in stock** available in a shop etc. without needing to be obtained specially. **out of stock** sold out. **to stock up** to assemble a stock of goods etc. **to take stock** to make an overall assessment of a situation. [from an Old English word *stoc* meaning 'trunk, block of wood']

stockade *noun* a protective fence made of upright stakes. [from a Spanish word *estacada*]

stockbreeder *noun* a farmer who raises livestock. **stockbreeding** *noun*

stockbroker *noun* a broker who deals in stocks and shares. **stockbroking** *noun*

stock car *noun* an ordinary car strengthened for use in racing where deliberate bumping is allowed.

stock cube *noun* a cube of concentrated dehydrated meat, vegetable, or fish stock used in cooking.

stock exchange *noun* a place where stocks and shares are publicly bought and sold ♦ *He lost a lot of money on the stock exchange.*

stockholder *noun* a person who holds financial stock or shares.

stockinet *noun* fine stretchable machine-knitted fabric formerly used for making stockings and underwear. [probably an alteration of *stocking-net*]

stocking *noun* **1** a close-fitting covering for the foot and part or all of the leg. **2** (*old use*) a long sock. **in your stockinged feet** wearing stockings but not shoes. [from *stock*]

stocking mask *noun* a nylon stocking pulled over the head to cover the face, used as a disguise by criminals.

stocking stitch *noun* alternate rows of plain and purl in knitting, giving a plain smooth surface on one side.

stock-in-trade *noun* **1** the typical subject or commodity someone uses or deals in. **2** the type of stock kept regularly by a shop.

stockist *noun* a shop or business that stocks goods of a certain type for sale.

stockman *noun* (**stockmen**) a person who looks after livestock.

stock market *noun* **1** a stock exchange. **2** the buying and selling of stocks and shares.

stockpile *noun* a large stock of goods or materials etc. built up and kept in reserve. **stockpile** *verb* to build up a stockpile of something.

stockpot *noun* a cooking pot in which stock is made and kept.

stockroom *noun* a room where goods kept in stock are stored.

stocks *plural noun* **1** (*historical*) a wooden framework with holes for the legs of a seated person, used like the pillory. **2** a framework on which a ship rests during construction. [from *stock*]

stock-still *adverb* completely still, motionless.

stocktaking *noun* the counting, listing, and checking of the amount of stock held by a shop or business. **stocktake** *noun*

stocky *adjective* (**stockier, stockiest**) short and solidly built. **stockily** *adverb* **stockiness** *noun* [from *stock*]

stockyard *noun* (*North Amer.*) an enclosure with pens and sheds for keeping and sorting livestock.

stodge *noun* (*informal*) stodgy food. [probably from *stuff* and *podgy*]

stodgy *adjective* (**stodgier, stodgiest**) **1** (said about food) heavy and filling, indigestible. **2** (said about a book etc.) written in a heavy uninteresting way. **3** (said about a person) dull, not lively. **stodgily** *adverb* **stodginess** *noun*

stoep (stoop) *noun* (in South Africa) a veranda at the front of a house. [an Afrikaans word]

stoic (stoh-ik) *noun* a stoical person. **stoic** *adjective* stoical. [named after the Stoics, Greek and Roman philosophers of the 3rd century BC onwards, who taught that goodness is based on knowledge and that the truly wise man is indifferent to changes of fortune]

stoical (stoh-ikəl) *adjective* bearing difficulties, pain, or discomfort calmly or without complaining. **stoically** *adverb*

stoicism (stoh-i-sizm) *noun* being stoical.

stoke *verb* 1 to tend and add fuel to a furnace or fire etc. 2 to encourage a strong emotion. **to stoke up** (*informal*) to eat a large quantity of food to give yourself energy. [from a Dutch word *stoken* meaning 'to stoke a furnace']

stoker *noun* 1 a person who stokes a furnace etc. on a steamship or steam train. 2 a mechanical device for doing this.

STOL *abbreviation* short take-off and landing, a system in which an aircraft needs only a short distance to take off and land.

stole ¹ *noun* 1 a scarf or shawl worn loosely round the shoulders by women. 2 a clerical vestment consisting of a long strip of silk or other material worn round the neck with the ends hanging down in front. [from an Old English word]

stole ² past tense of **steal**.

stolen past participle of **steal**.

stolid *adjective* not showing much emotion or interest. **stolidity** (stə-lid-iti) *noun* **stolidly** *adverb* [from a Latin word *stolidus* meaning 'dull']

stoma (stoh-mə) *noun* (**stomata**) 1 (*Zoology*) a small mouth-like opening in some lower animals. 2 (*Botany*) one of the tiny openings in the outer surface of a leaf or stem. [from a Greek word meaning 'mouth']

stomach *noun* 1 the internal organ in which the first part of digestion takes place. 2 the abdomen. 3 an appetite or desire for something ♦ *Frankly I had no stomach for the fight.* **stomach** *verb* to endure or tolerate something ♦ *I can't stomach all that violence.* **a strong stomach** an ability to see or do something unpleasant without feeling sick or squeamish. [from a Greek word *stomakhos* meaning 'gullet']

stomach ache *noun* a pain in the stomach or bowels.

stomach pump *noun* a suction pump used in medicine for emptying a patient's stomach.

stomp *verb* to tread heavily and noisily. [a variation of *stamp*]

stone *noun* 1 a piece of rock, usually detached from the earth's crust and of fairly small size. 2 stones or rock as a substance or material, e.g. for building. 3 a piece of stone shaped for a particular purpose, e.g. a tombstone or millstone. 4 a jewel or gem. 5 a gallstone or kidney stone. 6 the hard seed in a plum, peach, cherry, etc. 7 (**stone**) a unit of weight equal to 14 lb (6.35 kg) ♦ *She weighs ten stone.*
stone *adjective* made of stone ♦ *stone floors.* **stone** *verb* 1 to pelt someone with stones. 2 to remove the stone from a fruit.
stone *adverb* extremely or totally ♦ *stone cold* ♦ *stone deaf.* **to leave no stone unturned** to try every possible means to achieve something. **a stone's throw** a short distance. **stoneless** *adjective* [from an Old English word]

Stone Age *noun* the very early period of human history, when tools and weapons were made of stone not metal.

stonechat *noun* a small black-and-white songbird with a rattling cry.

stone circle *noun* a circle of large stones or boulders, put up in prehistoric times.

stone cold *adjective* completely cold.

stoned *adjective* (*informal*) under the influence of drugs or alcohol.

stone deaf *adjective* completely deaf.

stoneground *adjective* (said about flour) ground with millstones.

stonemason *noun* a person who cuts and prepares stone or builds in stone. **stonemasonry** *noun*

stonewall *verb* 1 to delay or obstruct something by refusing to answer questions or by giving non-committal replies. 2 (in cricket) to bat without attempting to score runs. **stonewaller** *noun*

stoneware *noun* a kind of pottery with a hard shiny surface.

stonewashed *adjective* (said about denim etc.) washed with abrasives to make it look worn or faded.

stonework *noun* the parts of a building or other structure that are made of stone.

stony *adjective* (**stonier, stoniest**) 1 full of stones. 2 like stone, especially in being hard. 3 unfeeling or unresponsive ♦ *a stony gaze*. **stonily** *adverb*

stony broke *adjective* (*informal*) without any money at all.

stood past tense and past participle of **stand**.

stooge *noun* 1 a comedian's assistant, used as a target for jokes. 2 (*informal*) a person who is given dull or routine work to do by someone more powerful.
stooge *verb* (*informal*) 1 to act as a stooge. 2 to wander about aimlessly. [originally American; origin unknown]

stool *noun* 1 a seat without arms or a back. 2 a footstool. 3 a lump of faeces. 4 the base of a plant from which new stems or foliage shoot up. [from an Old English word]

stool pigeon *noun* 1 a police informer. 2 a person acting as a decoy. [so called because a pigeon fixed to a stool was used as a decoy]

stoop¹ *verb* 1 to bend your head or body forwards and down. 2 to do something that is below your dignity or moral standards ♦ *He would never stoop to cheating.* **stoop** *noun* a posture of the body with shoulders bent forwards ♦ *He walks with a stoop.* [from an Old English word, related to **steep**¹]

stoop² *noun* (*North Amer.*) a porch with steps in front of a house or other building. [from a Dutch word *stoep*]

stop *verb* (**stopped, stopping**) 1 to put an end to something; to cause something to halt or pause. SYNONYMS: end, finish, halt, suspend, terminate. 2 to no longer continue doing something ♦ *I'm trying to stop smoking.* SYNONYMS: finish, cease, desist from, discontinue, quit; (*informal*) pack in. 3 to come to an end; to not continue moving or working. 4 to prevent or obstruct something. 5 (*informal*) to stay somewhere for a short time ♦ *Are you stopping for tea?* 6 to keep something back, to refuse to give or allow something ♦ *The cost of the damage will be stopped out of your wages.* 7 to instruct a bank not to honour a cheque. 8 (said about a bus or train) to call at a place to pick up or put down passengers. 9 to block or close up a hole or leak. 10 to press down a string or block a hole in a musical instrument in order to obtain the desired pitch.

stop *noun* 1 an act of stopping. 2 a place where a bus or train regularly stops. 3 a full stop. 4 an obstruction or device that stops or regulates movement or operation. 5 a row of organ pipes providing a particular tone and range of pitch; the knob or lever controlling these. 6 any of the standard sizes of aperture in an adjustable lens. **to pull out all the stops** to make all possible efforts to achieve something. **to put a stop to** to cause something to end. **to stop at nothing** to be completely ruthless or unscrupulous. **to stop by** to visit somewhere briefly. **to stop dead** to suddenly stop moving or speaking. **to stop something down** (in photography) to reduce the aperture of a lens. **to stop off** or **over** to break your journey somewhere. [from an Old English word *stoppian* meaning 'to block up']

stopcock *noun* a valve controlling the flow of liquid or gas through a pipe, usually operated by a handle on the outside of the pipe.

stopgap *noun* a temporary substitute.

stop-go *noun* (*Economics*) the alternate restriction and stimulation of economic demand by a government.

stop light *noun* a red traffic signal.

stopover *noun* a break in your journey, especially for a night.

stoppage *noun* 1 stopping, or being stopped. 2 an interruption in the work of a factory etc. 3 an obstruction.
stoppages *plural noun* an amount taken off someone's wages by an employer for paying tax, National Insurance, etc.

stopper *noun* a plug for closing a bottle etc.
stopper *verb* to close something with a stopper. **to put a stopper on** (*informal*) to prevent something.

stop press *noun* late news put into a newspaper just before printing or after printing has begun. [so called because the printing presses are stopped to allow the late news to be added]

stopwatch *noun* a watch with a mechanism for starting and stopping it when you wish, used to time races etc.

storage noun 1 the storing of goods etc. or of information. 2 space available for storing. 3 a charge for storing things.

storage battery or **storage cell** noun an apparatus for storing electrical energy, consisting of a group of rechargeable electric cells.

storage heater noun an electric heater that accumulates heat in off-peak periods.

store noun 1 a quantity or supply of something available for use when needed. SYNONYMS: reserve, stock, supply, cache, hoard, stockpile. 2 a place where things are stored. 3 a large shop selling goods of many kinds. 4 (*North Amer.*) a shop. 5 a computer memory.
store verb 1 to collect and keep things until they are needed. 2 to put something into a store. 3 to put furniture etc. into a warehouse for a while. 4 to have a useful supply of something ♦ *a mind well stored with information.* **in store 1** kept available for use. **2** about to happen ♦ *There's a surprise in store for you.* **to set store by** to value something greatly. [from an Old French word *estore*]

store card noun a credit card that can be used only in one store or chain of stores.

storehouse noun 1 a building where things are stored. 2 a rich source or supply of something ♦ *The book is a storehouse of information.*

storekeeper noun 1 a person in charge of a store or stores. 2 (*North Amer.*) a shopkeeper.

storeroom noun a room where things are stored.

storey noun (**storeys**) one horizontal section of a building, all the rooms at the same level. **storeyed** adjective [from a Latin word]
◊ Do not confuse this word with **story**, which has a different meaning.

stork noun a large long-legged wading bird with a long straight bill, sometimes nesting on buildings. [from an Old English word *storc*]

storm noun 1 a violent disturbance of the atmosphere with strong winds and usually rain, thunder, lightning, or snow. 2 a great outbreak of strong feeling ♦ *a storm of protest.* 3 a violent military attack on a place.
storm verb 1 to move violently or angrily ♦ *He stormed out of the room.* 2 to shout angrily ♦ *She stormed at us for being late.* 3 to suddenly attack and capture a place ♦ *They stormed the citadel.* 4 (said about wind or rain) to rage, to be stormy. **to go down a storm** to be enthusiastically received. **a storm in a teacup** a great fuss over a trivial matter. **to take something by storm 1** to capture a place by a sudden violent attack. 2 to have great and rapid success. [from an Old English word]

storm cloud noun 1 a heavy black rain cloud. 2 a sign of something dangerous or threatening.

storm lantern noun a hurricane lamp.

storm petrel noun a kind of petrel said to be active before storms.

storm trooper noun a soldier specially trained for violent attacks.

stormy adjective (**stormier, stormiest**) 1 full of storms, affected by storms ♦ *a stormy night* ♦ *stormy coasts.* 2 full of violent anger or outbursts ♦ *a stormy interview.* **stormily** adverb **storminess** noun

stormy petrel noun 1 (*old use*) a storm petrel. 2 a person who seems to attract trouble or controversy.

story noun (**stories**) 1 an account of an incident or of a series of incidents, either true or invented. SYNONYMS: tale, yarn, narrative. 2 the plot of a novel, play, film, etc. 3 a report of an item of news. 4 (*informal*) a lie ♦ *Don't tell stories!* [same origin as for *history*]
◊ Do not confuse this word with **storey**, which has a different meaning.

storyboard noun a sequence of drawings outlining the plan of a film, television advertisement, etc.

storybook noun a book of stories for children.

storyline noun the plot of a novel, play, film, etc.

storyteller noun a person who tells stories.

stoup (stoop) noun a stone basin for holy water, especially in the wall of a church. [from an Old Norse word *staup* meaning 'small cask']

stout adjective 1 (said about a person) solidly built and rather fat. SYNONYMS: stocky, solid, heavy, thick-set. 2 sturdy and thick ♦ *a stout stick.* 3 brave and determined ♦ *a stout defender of human rights.* SYNONYMS: fearless, spirited, resolute, plucky.
stout noun a strong dark beer brewed with roasted malt or barley. **stoutly** adverb **stoutness** noun [from an Old French word]

stout-hearted *adjective* brave and determined.

stove¹ *noun* 1 a device containing one or more ovens. 2 a closed device used for heating rooms etc. [from an Old German or Old Dutch word]

stove² past tense and past participle of **stave**.

stow *verb* to pack or store something tidily away. **to stow away** to conceal yourself on a ship or aircraft etc. so as to travel without paying or unseen. [from *bestow*]

stowage *noun* 1 stowing, or being stowed. 2 space available for this. 3 the charge for stowing something.

stowaway *noun* a person who stows away.

straddle *verb* 1 to sit or stand across something with one leg on either side. 2 to extend across both sides of something ♦ *A long bridge straddles the river.* **straddle** *noun* an act of straddling. [from an Old English word; related to *stride*]

strafe (strahf or strayf) *verb* to attack people or a place with gunfire or bombs from a low-flying aircraft. [from a German word *strafen* meaning 'to punish']

straggle *verb* 1 to move along slowly and drop behind the people in front. 2 to grow or spread out in an irregular or untidy manner. **straggler** *noun* **straggly** *adjective* [origin unknown]

straight *adjective* 1 extending or moving continuously in one direction, not curved or bent. 2 level, horizontal, or upright ♦ *Is the picture straight?* 3 correctly arranged, in proper order. 4 in unbroken succession ♦ *ten straight wins.* 5 not evasive; honest and frank ♦ *Just give me a straight answer.* 6 simple, not modified or elaborate ♦ *a straight choice.* 7 (said about an alcoholic drink) not diluted. 8 to do with serious drama, not comedy ♦ *a straight role.* 9 (*informal*) conventional or respectable. 10 (*informal*) heterosexual. **straight** *adverb* 1 in a straight line ♦ *It's a good thing you can't shoot straight.* 2 directly, without delay ♦ *Go straight home.* 3 straightforwardly ♦ *I told him straight.* **straight** *noun* 1 the straight part of something, especially the last section of a racecourse. 2 (in poker) a continuous sequence of five cards. 3 (*informal*) a heterosexual person. **to go straight** to live an honest life after being a criminal. **a straight face** a blank or serious expression on your face, especially when

you are trying not to laugh. **straightness** *noun* [an old past participle of *stretch*] ◊ Do not confuse this word with **strait**, which has a different meaning.

straight angle *noun* (*Mathematics*) an angle of 180°.

straightaway or **straight away** *adverb* without delay, immediately.

straight edge *noun* a bar with one edge accurately straight, used for testing straightness.

straighten *verb* to make something straight, or to become straight. ◊ Do not confuse this word with **straitened**, which has a different meaning.

straightforward *adjective* 1 honest and frank. SYNONYMS: plain, straight, direct, candid, blunt. 2 easy to do or understand. **straightforwardly** *adverb* **straightforwardness** *noun*

straight man *noun* a comedian's stooge.

strain¹ *verb* 1 to injure or weaken part of your body by excessive stretching or by too much effort ♦ *Don't strain your eyes.* 2 to make an intense effort ♦ *People were straining to hear what she was saying.* 3 to pull or push forcefully at something. 4 to stretch something tightly. 5 to apply a meaning or rule etc. beyond its true application. 6 to put something through a sieve or filter in order to separate solids from the liquid containing them. **strain** *noun* 1 straining, or being strained; the force of straining. 2 an injury caused by straining a muscle or limb. 3 a severe demand on your mental or physical strength or on your resources; exhaustion caused by this. 4 a passage from a tune. 5 the tone or style of something written or spoken ♦ *She then continued in a more cheerful strain.* **to be straining at the leash** to be eager to begin doing something. [from an Old French word *estreindre*]

strain² *noun* 1 a line of descent of animals, plants, or micro-organisms; a variety or breed of these ♦ *a new strain of flu virus.* 2 a slight or inherited characteristic ♦ *There's a strain of insanity in the family.* [from an Old English word]

strained *adjective* 1 (said about behaviour or manner) produced by effort, not natural or genuine. 2 unpleasantly tense, showing signs of strain ♦ *strained relations.*

strainer *noun* a device for straining liquids ♦ *a tea strainer.*

strait noun (also **straits**) a narrow stretch of water connecting two seas ♦ *the Strait of Gibraltar* ♦ *the Menai Straits*.
straits plural noun a difficult state of affairs ♦ *in dire straits*.
strait adjective (old use) narrow or restricted. [from a Latin word *strictus* meaning 'tightened']
◊ Do not confuse this word with **straight**, which has a different meaning.

straitened adjective made narrow, restricted. **in straitened circumstances** with barely enough money to live on. [from *strait*]
◊ Do not confuse this word with **straighten**, which has a different meaning.

straitjacket noun 1 a strong jacket-like piece of clothing with long sleeves that can be tied together to restrain the arms of a violent person. 2 a severe restriction.

strait-laced adjective very prim and proper.

strake noun a continuous line of planking or metal plates from the stem to the stern of a ship. [related to an Old English word *streccan* meaning 'to stretch']

strand[1] noun 1 a single length of thread, wire, etc., twisted together to form a rope, yarn, or cable. 2 an element that forms part of a whole ♦ *a novel with several interwoven strands*. [origin unknown]

strand[2] noun (literary) a shore.
strand verb 1 to run or cause a ship to run onto sand or rocks in shallow water. 2 to leave someone in a difficult or helpless position. SYNONYMS: abandon, desert, maroon. [from an Old English word]

stranded adjective left somewhere in difficulties, e.g. without any money or means of transport.

strange adjective 1 unusual or surprising ♦ *It's strange that you haven't heard*. SYNONYMS: unusual, extraordinary, odd, peculiar, curious, weird, bizarre, eccentric (behaviour). 2 not known, seen, or encountered before ♦ *the problems of adapting to a strange culture*. SYNONYMS: new, unfamiliar, alien, foreign. **strangely** adverb **strangeness** noun [from a Latin word *extraneus* meaning 'external' or 'strange']

stranger noun 1 a person you do not know. 2 a person who does not know or is not known in a particular place. 3 someone who is not used to a certain feeling, experience, or situation ♦ *He was no stranger to poverty*. [same origin as for *strange*]

strangle verb 1 to squeeze a person's throat, especially in order to kill them. 2 to restrict or suppress something so that it does not develop. **strangler** noun [from a Greek word *strangalē* meaning 'a halter']

stranglehold noun 1 a strangling grip. 2 complete control over something.

strangulate verb (Medicine) to compress a vein or intestine etc. so that nothing can pass through it. [from a Latin word *strangulare* meaning 'to strangle']

strangulated adjective sounding as though your throat is constricted ♦ *a strangulated cry*.

strangulation noun 1 strangling, or being strangled. 2 strangulating, or being strangulated.

strap noun 1 a strip of leather, cloth, or other flexible material, often with a buckle, for holding things together or in place. 2 a shoulder strap. 3 a loop for holding on to in a moving vehicle.
strap verb (**strapped**, **strapping**) 1 to fasten something with a strap or straps. 2 to bind an injury ♦ *We'd better strap it up*. 3 to beat someone with a strap. [via Old German or Old Dutch from a Latin word]

strapless adjective without shoulder straps.

strapping adjective big and strong ♦ *a strapping lad*.
strapping noun 1 straps, or material for making straps. 2 sticking plaster etc. used for binding wounds or injuries.

strata plural of **stratum**.

stratagem (strat-ə-jəm) noun a cunning method of achieving something; a plan or trick. [same origin as for *strategy*]

strategic (strə-tee-jik) adjective 1 to do with strategy. (Compare **tactical**.) 2 giving an advantage ♦ *a strategic position*. 3 (said about weapons) used against an enemy's home territory (as distinct from *tactical weapons* which are for use in a battle or at close quarters). **strategical** adjective **strategically** adverb

strategist (strat-i-jist) noun an expert in strategy.

strategy (strat-i-ji) noun (**strategies**) 1 a broad plan or policy for achieving something ♦ *our economic strategy*. 2 the planning and directing of the whole operation of a campaign or war. [from a Greek word *stratēgos* meaning 'a general']
◊ See the note at **tactics**.

stratified *adjective* formed or arranged into strata. **stratification** *noun*

stratosphere (strat-ə-sfeer) *noun* **1** a layer of the earth's atmosphere between about 10 and 60 km above the earth's surface. **2** (*informal*) the very highest levels of something. [from *stratum* and *sphere*]

stratum (strah-təm or stray-təm) *noun* (**strata**) **1** one of a series of layers, especially of rock in the earth's crust. **2** a social level or class ♦ *the various strata of society*. [a Latin word meaning 'thing spread']
◊ The word *strata* is the plural of *stratum*. It is incorrect to speak of *a strata* or *this strata*, or of *stratas*.

stratus (strah-təs or stray-təs) *noun* (**strati**) a continuous horizontal sheet of cloud. [a Latin word meaning 'strewn']

straw *noun* **1** dry cut stalks of grain used as material for thatching, fodder, packing, etc. **2** a single stalk or piece of this. **3** a thin tube of paper or plastic for sucking up a drink. **to clutch** or **grasp at straws** to be so desperate that you will try something even though it seems unlikely to succeed. **to draw the short straw** to be chosen to do an unpleasant task. **the last** or **final straw** a further difficulty coming after a series of other difficulties and making a situation unbearable. [from an Old English word]

strawberry *noun* (**strawberries**) **1** a soft juicy edible red fruit with yellow seeds on the surface. **2** the plant that bears this fruit. [from an Old English word]

straw poll *noun* an unofficial poll taken as a rough test of general opinion.

stray *verb* **1** to wander away from the proper path or place. **2** to go aside from a direct course; to depart from a subject.
stray *adjective* **1** having strayed ♦ *a stray cat*. **2** separated from a group, isolated ♦ *a stray taxi*.
stray *noun* a person or domestic animal that has strayed; a stray thing. [from an Old French word *estrayer*]

streak *noun* **1** a thin line or band of a different colour or substance from its surroundings. **2** an element in a person's character ♦ *He has a ruthless streak*. **3** a spell of success, luck, etc. ♦ *We are on a winning streak at the moment*.
streak *verb* **1** to mark something with streaks. **2** to move very rapidly. **3** (*informal*) to run naked in a public place for fun or to get attention. **like a streak**

(*informal*) very fast. **streak of lightning** a flash of lightning. **streaker** *noun* [from an Old English word *strica*]

streaky *adjective* (**streakier, streakiest**) **1** full of streaks. **2** (said about bacon) with alternate strips of fat and lean. **streakily** *adverb* **streakiness** *noun*

stream *noun* **1** a small narrow river. **2** a flow of liquid or of a mass of things or people. **3** (in certain schools) a section into which children with the same level of ability are placed.
stream *verb* **1** to run or move in a continuous flow. **2** to produce a stream of liquid, to run with liquid ♦ *The wound streamed blood* ♦ *My eyes were streaming*. **3** to float or wave at full length ♦ *Flags were streaming in the wind*. **4** to arrange schoolchildren in streams according to their ability. [from an Old English word]

streamer *noun* a long narrow strip of paper or material used as a decoration or flag.

streamline *verb* **1** to give something a streamlined shape. **2** to make an organization or system more efficient by using simpler or faster methods.

streamlined *adjective* having a smooth even shape that offers very little resistance to movement through air or water.

street *noun* a public road in a town or village with buildings on one or both sides. **to be streets ahead of** (*informal*) to be much superior to someone or something. **on the streets** (*informal*) homeless. **up your street** (*informal*) well suited to your field of knowledge or interests. [via Old English from a Latin phrase *strata via* meaning 'paved way']

streetcar *noun* (*North Amer.*) a tram.

streetwise *adjective* (*informal*) having the skills and knowledge needed to deal with modern city life.

strength *noun* **1** the quality of being strong; the intensity of this. **2** an ability or good quality ♦ *Patience is your great strength*. **3** the number of people present or available, the full complement ♦ *The department is below strength*. **to go from strength to strength** to progress with increasing success. **in strength** in large numbers ♦ *Supporters were present in strength*. **on the strength of** on the basis of, using a fact etc. as your support. [from an Old English word *strengthu*]

strengthen *verb* to make something stronger, or to become stronger. SYNONYMS: fortify, reinforce, bolster, build up, toughen.

strenuous *adjective* 1 energetic and wholehearted. 2 needing great effort ♦ *a strenuous task.* SYNONYMS: arduous, laborious, gruelling, demanding, taxing, hard, stiff. **strenuously** *adverb* **strenuousness** *noun* [from a Latin word *strenuus* meaning 'brisk']

streptococcus *noun* (**streptococci** (strep-tə-**kok**-iy)) any of a group of bacteria that cause serious infections. **streptococcal** *adjective* [from Greek words *streptos* meaning 'twisted' and *kokkos* meaning 'berry']

streptomycin (strep-tə-**miy**-sin) *noun* a kind of antibiotic drug used against tuberculosis. [from Greek words *streptos* meaning 'twisted' and *mykēs* meaning 'fungus']

stress *noun* 1 a force that acts on or within a thing and tends to distort it, e.g. by pressing, pulling, or twisting it. 2 mental distress caused by having too many problems or too much to do. SYNONYMS: strain, pressure, tension. 3 emphasis, especially the extra force with which you pronounce part of a word or phrase. **stress** *verb* 1 to give emphasis to something ♦ *I must stress the importance of arriving on time.* SYNONYMS: emphasize, underline, accentuate, highlight, draw attention to. 2 to put stress on part of a word or phrase. 3 to cause stress to someone. [from *distress*]

stressful *adjective* causing stress to someone.

stretch *verb* 1 to pull something or be pulled so that it becomes longer or wider. 2 to be able to be stretched without tearing or breaking; to tend to become stretched ♦ *Knitted fabrics stretch.* 3 to straighten out your body or part of it to its full length and tighten the muscles after being relaxed. 4 to extend in area, length, or time ♦ *The wall stretches right round the estate.* 5 to make great demands on a person's abilities. 6 to last or be enough ♦ *Will our money stretch to a meal out?* 7 to exaggerate something ♦ *That's stretching the truth a bit.* **stretch** *noun* 1 stretching, or being stretched. 2 the ability to be stretched ♦ *This elastic has lost its stretch.* 3 a continuous expanse or period of time. 4 (*informal*) a period of time in prison. **stretch** *adjective* able to be stretched ♦ *stretch fabrics.* **at a stretch** 1 in one continuous period. 2 just possible but with difficulty. **at full stretch** or **fully stretched** working to the utmost of your powers. **to stretch your legs** to go for a short walk after sitting for some time. **to stretch a point** 1 to agree to something that is not normally allowed. 2 to exaggerate. [from an Old English word *streccan*]

stretcher *noun* 1 a framework of poles, canvas, etc. for carrying a sick or injured person in a lying position. 2 a wooden frame over which a canvas is stretched ready for painting. 3 a board in a boat against which a rower braces his or her feet. **stretcher** *verb* to carry someone on a stretcher.

strew *verb* (past participle, **strewn** or **strewed**) to scatter things over a surface; to cover something with scattered things ♦ *Confetti was strewn over the pavement* ♦ *The floor was strewn with paper cups.* [from an Old English word *strewian*]

strewth *interjection* (*informal*) an exclamation of surprise. [short for *God's truth*]

striated (striy-**ay**-tid) *adjective* marked with striations.

striation (striy-**ay**-shən) *noun* any of a series of ridges, furrows, or lines. [from a Latin word *stria* meaning 'a furrow']

stricken *adjective* affected or overcome by an illness, shock, or grief ♦ *The whole family has been stricken with flu* ♦ *grief-stricken.* [an old past participle of *strike*]

strict *adjective* 1 demanding that rules concerning behaviour are obeyed ♦ *a strict teacher.* SYNONYMS: stern, severe, harsh, firm. 2 following rules or beliefs exactly. 3 precisely limited or defined, exact or complete ♦ *the strict truth.* **strictly** *adverb* **strictness** *noun* [from a Latin word *stringere* meaning 'to tighten']

stricture *noun* 1 severe criticism or condemnation. 2 a rule restricting behaviour or action. 3 (*Medicine*) abnormal narrowing of a tube-like part of the body. [same origin as for *strict*]

stride *verb* (**strode**, **stridden**) 1 to walk with long steps. 2 to cross something with one long step.

stride noun 1 a single long step, or the length of this. 2 a person's manner of striding. 3 a step in progress ◆ *The country has made great strides towards independence.* **to get into your stride** to settle into a fast and steady rate or progress. **to take something in your stride** to manage or deal with something without difficulty or fuss. [from an Old English word *stride* meaning 'single long step']

strident (striy-dənt) adjective loud and harsh. **stridency** noun **stridently** adverb [from a Latin word *stridens* meaning 'creaking']

strife noun conflict; fighting or quarrelling. [from an Old French word *estrif*]

strike verb (past tense and past participle **struck**) 1 to hit something, deliberately or accidentally. 2 (said about a disease, disaster, etc.) to afflict someone. 3 to attack suddenly. 4 to bring someone into a specified state suddenly ◆ *He was struck blind.* 5 to fill someone with a sudden strong emotion ◆ *It was a sound that struck fear into me.* 6 to occur to someone, to make an impression on someone's mind ◆ *An idea struck me* ◆ *She strikes me as being efficient.* 7 to refuse to work as a form of protest. 8 to reach an agreement, balance, or compromise ◆ *We finally struck a bargain.* 9 to light a match by rubbing it against a rough surface. 10 to indicate the time by making a sound ◆ *The clock struck ten* ◆ *Two o'clock struck.* 11 (said about lightning) to descend upon and blast something. 12 to produce sparks or a sound etc. by striking something; to produce a musical note by pressing a key. 13 to make a coin or medal by stamping metal. 14 to reach gold or oil etc. by digging or drilling. 15 to take down a tent, camp, or theatrical set; to take down a flag or sail. 16 (said about plant cuttings) to put down roots. 17 to cancel something as if crossing it out with a pen ◆ *Okay, strike that idea.* 18 to go in a certain direction ◆ *We struck north through the forest.* **strike** noun 1 a workers' refusal to work, as a form of protest. 2 a sudden attack ◆ *an air strike.* 3 an act or instance of striking, a hit. 4 a sudden discovery of gold or oil etc. 5 (in tenpin bowling) knocking down all the pins with your first ball. **on strike** (said about workers) striking. **to strike an attitude** or **pose** to hold your body in a certain position to create an impression. **to strike back** to retaliate. **to strike someone off** to officially remove a person from membership of a professional group, usually because of misconduct. **to strike something off** or **out** to cross something off or out. **to strike on** or **upon** to discover something, especially unexpectedly. **to strike out** to start out on a new or independent course. **to strike up** to begin to play a piece of music. **to strike something up** to start a friendship or conversation with someone. [from an Old English word]

strike force noun a military force equipped for sudden attack.

striker noun 1 a worker who is on strike. 2 a football player whose main function is to try to score goals. 3 the player striking the ball in a game.

striking adjective 1 noticeable or conspicuous ◆ *a striking omission.* 2 very good-looking or impressive. **strikingly** adverb

string noun 1 thin cord made of twisted threads. 2 a length of this or some other material used to fasten or lace or pull something. 3 a piece of catgut or wire stretched and vibrated to produce tones in a musical instrument. 4 a piece of catgut, nylon, etc. interwoven with others in a frame to form the head of a racket. 5 a strip of tough fibre on a bean etc. 6 a set of objects threaded or tied together on a cord ◆ *a string of pearls.* 7 a series of things coming after one another ◆ *a string of buses* ◆ *a string of coincidences.* 8 the racehorses trained at one stable. 9 something ranked as your first or second etc. resource. 10 a condition that is insisted upon ◆ *The offer has no strings attached.*
string verb (past tense and past participle **strung**) 1 to fit a string or strings to something ◆ *an archer stringing his bow.* 2 to thread beads etc. on a string. 3 to remove the tough fibre from beans. **strings** plural noun the stringed instruments in an orchestra. **to have several strings to your bow** (informal) to have more than one skill or other resource that you can call on. **to pull strings** see pull. **to string along** (informal) to stay with someone while it is convenient. **to string someone along** (informal) to mislead someone over a length of time. **to string something out** 1 to cause something to last a long time. 2 to spread something out in a line. **to string someone up** to kill someone by

hanging. [from an Old English word *streng*]

string bag *noun* a shopping bag made of net.

string bean *noun* a bean eaten in its pod, such as a runner bean or French bean.

stringed *adjective* (said about musical instruments) having strings that are played by being touched, or with a bow or a plectrum.

stringent (strin-jənt) *adjective* (said about rules or conditions) strictly enforced. **stringency** *noun* **stringently** *adverb* [from a Latin word *stringere* meaning 'to bind']

string quartet *noun* a quartet for stringed instruments, made up of two violins, a cello, and a viola.

string vest *noun* a vest made of large mesh.

stringy *adjective* (**stringier, stringiest**) 1 like string. 2 (said about meat, beans, etc.) having tough fibres. 3 (said about liquid) viscous, forming strings.

strip[1] *verb* (**stripped, stripping**) 1 to take a covering or layer off something ♦ *a solvent for stripping paint.* 2 to take off your clothes or another person's clothes. 3 to deprive someone of something, especially a title or position. 4 to take a machine to pieces in order to inspect it ♦ *We stripped the engine.* 5 to tear the thread from a screw or the tooth from a gearwheel.
strip *noun* 1 an act of undressing, especially in a striptease. 2 the distinctive clothes worn by a sports team while playing. **to strip something down** to take a machine apart to inspect or adjust it. [probably from an Old English word]

strip[2] *noun* a long narrow piece or area ♦ *Tear the paper into strips* ♦ *a strip of land.* **to tear someone off a strip** (*informal*) to rebuke someone angrily. [from an Old German word *strippe* meaning 'strap']

strip cartoon *noun* a humorous or adventure story in the form of a series of drawings.

stripe *noun* 1 a long narrow band on a surface, having a different colour or texture from its surroundings. 2 a band or chevron of cloth worn on the sleeve of a uniform to show the wearer's rank. **stripy** *adjective* [probably from an Old German word and related to *strip*[2]]

striped *adjective* marked with stripes.

strip light *noun* a tubular fluorescent lamp.

stripling *noun* a young man. [from *strip*[2] and *-ling*]

stripper *noun* 1 a device or solvent for removing paint etc. 2 a person who performs striptease.

striptease *noun* an entertainment in which a person slowly undresses to music.

strive *verb* (**strove, striven**) 1 to make great efforts to do something. SYNONYMS: endeavour, struggle, strain. 2 to fight against someone or something. [from an Old French word *estriver*]

strobe *noun* (*informal*) a stroboscope.

stroboscope (stroh-bə-skohp) *noun* an apparatus for producing a rapidly flashing light. **stroboscopic** (-skop-ik) *adjective* [from Greek words *strobos* meaning 'whirling' and *skopein* meaning 'to look at']

strode past tense of **stride**.

stroke *noun* 1 the act or process of striking something. 2 a single successful or effective action or effort ♦ *a stroke of luck* ♦ *a stroke of genius* ♦ *He hasn't done a stroke of work all day.* 3 each of a series of repeated movements. 4 a style of swimming. 5 (in golf) a hit at the ball with a club as a unit of scoring. 6 one hit at the ball in various games ♦ *a forehand stroke.* 7 an act or spell of stroking. 8 the oarsman nearest the stern of a racing boat, setting the time of the stroke. 9 a mark made by a movement of a pen, pencil, or paintbrush. 10 the sound made by a striking clock ♦ *on the stroke of ten.* 11 an attack of apoplexy or paralysis, caused by an interruption in the flow of blood to the brain.
stroke *verb* 1 to move your hand gently along the surface of something. 2 to act as stroke to a boat or crew. [from an Old English word meaning 'to caress lightly'; related to *strike*]

stroll *verb* to walk in a leisurely way. SYNONYMS: amble, saunter.
stroll *noun* a leisurely walk. **stroller** *noun* [probably from a German dialect word *strollen*]

strong *adjective* 1 physically powerful or healthy; done with great power ♦ *strong muscles* ♦ *a strong kick.* SYNONYMS: mighty, powerful; (*informal*) hefty. 2 able to withstand rough treatment or great force. SYNONYMS: robust, durable. 3 great in degree or intensity ♦ *a strong smell* ♦ *strong* *colours.* **4** felt, held, or expressed with intensity ♦ *strong beliefs* ♦ *I have strong feelings about this matter.* SYNONYMS: fervent, keen, passionate, fierce. **5** (said about an argument, evidence, etc.) forceful and convincing. **6** having a lot of power or influence ♦ *a strong country.* **7** good and likely to succeed ♦ *a strong candidate.* **8** having a specified number of members ♦ *an army 5,000 strong.* **9** (said about a drink) concentrated, not weak or diluted. **10** (said about language) forceful and extreme. **11** (said about a verb) changing the vowel in the past tense (as in *ring, rang; strike, struck*), not adding a suffix (as in *float, floated*). (Compare **weak**.) **going strong** (*informal*) continuing to be effective or successful. **strongly** *adverb* [from an Old English word]

strong-arm *adjective* using force or violence ♦ *strong-arm tactics.*

strongbox *noun* a lockable box or safe for storing valuables.

stronghold *noun* **1** a fortified place. **2** a place of strong support for a cause or political party ♦ *a Labour stronghold.*

strong-minded *adjective* having a determined mind.

strongpoint *noun* a specially fortified position in a system of defences.

strongroom *noun* a room designed to protect valuables from fire or theft.

strontium (stron-ti-əm) *noun* a chemical element (symbol Sr), a soft silver-white metal, having a radioactive isotope that concentrates in bones when taken into an animal's body. [named after Strontian in the Scottish highlands, where it was discovered]

strop *noun* a strip of leather or other device for sharpening razors.
strop *verb* (**stropped, stropping**) to sharpen something on or with a strop. [probably from a Latin word *stroppus* meaning 'thong']

stroppy *adjective* (*informal*) (**stroppier, stroppiest**) bad-tempered, awkward to deal with. [perhaps an abbreviation of *obstreperous*]

strove past tense of **strive**.

struck past tense and past participle of **strike**. **to be struck by** or **with** to find something particularly interesting or impressive. **to be struck on** (*informal*) to be very fond of a person or thing.

structural *adjective* **1** to do with or forming part of a structure. **2** used in the construction of buildings ♦ *structural steel.* **structurally** *adverb*

structure *noun* **1** a building or other thing that has been constructed or built. SYNONYMS: construction, edifice. **2** the way in which something is constructed or organized. SYNONYMS: composition, organization, constitution, (*informal*) make-up. [from a Latin word *structura* meaning 'thing built']

strudel (stroo-dəl) *noun* thin pastry filled with fruit, especially apple. [from a German word *Strudel* meaning 'whirlpool']

struggle *verb* **1** to move your limbs or body in a strong effort to get free. **2** to make a strong effort under difficult circumstances. **3** to make your way or a living etc. with difficulty. **4** to try to overcome an opponent or problem etc.
struggle *noun* **1** a spell of struggling. **2** a hard fight or difficult task. [origin unknown]

strum *verb* (**strummed, strumming**) **1** to sound a guitar by running your fingers up and down its strings. **2** to play a stringed instrument badly or casually.
strum *noun* the sound made by strumming. [an imitation of the sound]

strumpet *noun* (*old use*) a prostitute. [origin unknown]

strung past tense and past participle of **string**. **strung up** tense or nervous.

strut *noun* **1** a bar of wood or metal put into a framework to strengthen and brace it. **2** a strutting walk.
strut *verb* (**strutted, strutting**) to walk in a pompous self-satisfied way. [from an Old English word]

struth *interjection* (*informal*) another spelling of **strewth**.

strychnine (strik-neen) *noun* a bitter and highly poisonous substance, used in very small doses as a stimulant. [from a Greek word *strukhnos*, denoting a kind of nightshade]

stub *noun* **1** a short stump left when the rest has been used or worn down ♦ *a cigarette stub.* **2** the counterfoil of a cheque, receipt, ticket, etc.
stub *verb* (**stubbed, stubbing**) to accidentally hit your toe against something. **to stub something out** to put out a cigarette by pressing it against

something hard. [an Old English word meaning 'stump of a tree']

stubble noun **1** the lower ends of the stalks of cereal plants left in the ground after the harvest is cut. **2** short stiff hairs growing on a man's face when he has not shaved for a while. **stubbly** adjective [from an Old French word stuble]

stubborn adjective **1** determined not to give in or change your opinion. SYNONYMS: obstinate, obdurate, intransigent, inflexible, wilful, headstrong; (informal) pig-headed, bloody-minded. **2** difficult to remove or deal with ♦ stubborn stains. **stubbornly** adverb **stubbornness** noun [origin unknown]

stubby adjective (**stubbier, stubbiest**) short and thick.

stucco noun plaster or cement used for coating surfaces of walls or moulding to form architectural decorations. **stuccoed** adjective [from an Italian word]

stuck past tense and past participle of **stuck²**.
stuck adjective unable to move or make progress ♦ I'm stuck! **to get stuck into** (informal) to begin working seriously at a job etc. **to be stuck for** (informal) to be at a loss for something ♦ I'm stuck for words. **to be stuck with** (informal) to be unable to get rid of someone or something.

stuck-up adjective (informal) conceited or snobbish.

stud¹ noun **1** a short large-headed nail or other short piece of metal sticking out from a surface. **2** one of a number of small knobs on the base of a shoe or boot to give better grip. **3** a device like a button on a stalk, used e.g. to fasten a detachable shirt collar.
stud verb (**studded, studding**) **1** to decorate something with studs or precious stones set into a surface ♦ The necklace was studded with jewels. **2** to strew or scatter something ♦ The sky was studded with stars. [from an Old English word studu meaning 'post']

stud² noun **1** the place where a number of horses are kept for breeding. **2** a stallion. **at stud** (said about a male horse) available for breeding on payment of a fee. [from an Old English word stod]

student noun a person who studies a subject, especially at a college or university ♦ medical students. [from a Latin word studens meaning 'studying']

studied adjective done with deliberate and careful effort ♦ She answered with studied indifference.

studio noun (**studios**) **1** the room where a painter, sculptor, photographer, etc. works. **2** a room from which radio or television programmes are regularly broadcast or in which recordings are made. **3** a place where cinema films are made. [same origin as for study]

studious adjective **1** spending a lot of time studying or reading. SYNONYMS: bookish, academic, scholarly. **2** deliberate or painstaking ♦ studious politeness. **studiously** adverb **studiousness** noun

study verb (**studies, studied, studying**) **1** to spend time learning about a subject. **2** to look at or consider something carefully ♦ We studied the map.
study noun (**studies**) **1** the process of studying; the pursuit of some branch of knowledge ♦ a course in business studies. **2** a detailed investigation into a particular subject ♦ The programme is a study of race relations in Britain. **3** a room used by a person for writing or academic work. **4** a musical composition designed to develop a player's skill. **5** a drawing done for practice or in preparation for another work ♦ a study of a woman's head. [from a Latin word studium meaning 'zeal']

stuff noun **1** a substance or material. **2** (informal) unnamed things, belongings, subject matter, activities, etc. ♦ Leave your stuff in the hall ♦ A comedian came on and did his stuff. **3** (informal) (old use) nonsense or rubbish ♦ That's just stuff and nonsense!
stuff verb **1** to fill something tightly; to cram something in. **2** to push a thing hastily into something ♦ He stuffed his hands into his pockets. **3** to fill poultry or other food with savoury stuffing. **4** to fill the empty skin etc. of a bird or animal with material to restore its original shape, e.g. for exhibition in a museum. **5** to fill something with padding. **6** (informal) to eat greedily ♦ The kids stuffed themselves with chips. **to be stuffed up** (informal) to have your nose blocked with catarrh. **to know your stuff** (informal) to be an expert in your subject or trade. [from an Old French word estoffe meaning 'material' or 'furniture']

stuffing noun **1** padding used to stuff cushions, furniture, or soft toys. **2** a savoury mixture put as a filling into poultry, meat, vegetables, etc. before cooking. **to knock the stuffing out of**

(*informal*) to make someone feel weak or lacking in confidence.

stuffy *adjective* (**stuffier, stuffiest**) **1** lacking fresh air or enough ventilation. **2** formal and boring ♦ *a stuffy occasion.* **3** old-fashioned and narrow-minded ♦ *Don't be so stuffy.* **4** (said about a person's nose) with blocked breathing passages. **stuffily** *adverb* **stuffiness** *noun*

stultify *verb* (**stultifies, stultified, stultifying**) **1** to prevent something from being effective ♦ *Their uncooperative approach has stultified the discussions.* **2** to make someone bored or feel bored. **stultification** *noun* [from a Latin word *stultus* meaning 'foolish']

stumble *verb* **1** to strike your foot on something and lose your balance. **2** to walk unsteadily. **3** to make a mistake or frequent mistakes in speaking or playing music etc. ♦ *She stumbled through her speech.* **stumble** *noun* an act of stumbling. **to stumble across** or **on** to find something by chance. [from an Old Norse word]

stumbling block *noun* an obstacle, something that causes difficulty or hesitation.

stump *noun* **1** the base of a tree trunk left in the ground when the rest has fallen or been cut down. **2** something left when the main part has worn down or been cut off. **3** (in cricket) each of the three upright sticks of a wicket. **stump** *verb* **1** to baffle or be too difficult for someone ♦ *The last question stumped me completely.* **2** (said about a wicketkeeper) to get a batsman out by knocking the bails off the stumps while he or she is out of the crease. **3** to walk stiffly or noisily. **to stump something up** (*informal*) to produce the money to pay for something. [from an Old German or Old Dutch word]

stumpy *adjective* (**stumpier, stumpiest**) short and thick. **stumpiness** *noun*

stun *verb* (**stunned, stunning**) **1** to knock a person unconscious or into a dazed state. **2** to astonish or shock someone so much that they cannot think clearly ♦ *She was stunned by the news.* [from an Old French word *estoner* meaning 'to astonish']

stung past tense and past participle of **sting**.

stunk past tense and past participle of **stink**.

stunner *noun* (*informal*) an extremely attractive person or thing.

stunning *adjective* extremely attractive. **stunningly** *adverb*

stunt¹ *verb* to prevent something from growing or developing normally. [probably from an Old English word meaning 'foolish']

stunt² *noun* **1** something difficult and daring done as a performance or as part of the action of a film. **2** something unusual done to attract attention ♦ *a publicity stunt.* [originally American; origin unknown]

stuntman or **stuntwoman** *noun* (**stuntmen** or **stuntwomen**) a person employed to take an actor's place in performing dangerous stunts.

stupa (**stew**-pə) *noun* a round usually domed Buddhist monument, usually containing a sacred relic. [a Sanskrit word]

stupefy *verb* (**stupefies, stupefied, stupefying**) **1** to make someone unable to think or feel properly. **2** to astonish and shock someone. **stupefaction** *noun* [from a Latin word *stupere* meaning 'to be struck senseless']

stupendous (stew-**pend**-əs) *adjective* extremely impressive. **stupendously** *adverb* [same origin as for *stupefy*]

stupid *adjective* **1** not intelligent or clever, slow at learning or understanding things. SYNONYMS: dim, dense, slow; (*informal*) thick. **2** without reason or common sense. SYNONYMS: foolish, idiotic, crazy. **3** dazed and unable to think clearly ♦ *He was knocked stupid.* **stupidity** *noun* **stupidly** *adverb* [from a Latin word *stupidus* meaning 'dazed']

stupor (**stew**-per) *noun* a dazed or almost unconscious condition brought on by shock, drugs, drink, etc. [same origin as for *stupefy*]

sturdy *adjective* (**sturdier, sturdiest**) strongly built or made. **sturdily** *adverb* **sturdiness** *noun* [originally meaning 'reckless', from an Old French word *esturdi* meaning 'dazed']

sturgeon *noun* (**sturgeon**) a large shark-like fish with flesh that is valued as food and roe that is made into caviare. [via Old French from a Germanic word]

stutter *verb* **1** to speak with rapid repetitions of the same sound, especially the first consonants of words. **2** to make a series of short sharp sounds ♦ *a stuttering engine.*

stutter *noun* a tendency to stutter when speaking. [an imitation of the sound]

sty[1] *noun* (**sties**) a pigsty. [from an Old English word *stig*]

sty[2] or **stye** *noun* (**sties** or **styes**) an inflamed swelling on the edge of the eyelid. [from an Old English word *stigend* meaning 'rising' or 'swelling']

Stygian (stij-iən) *adjective* (*literary*) very dark or gloomy. [from Styx, the name of one of the rivers of the Underworld in Greek mythology]

style *noun* 1 the way in which something is written, said, or done. 2 a distinctive design or arrangement ♦ *a new style of coat.* 3 elegance and confidence in doing things. SYNONYMS: dash, flair, panache. 4 (*Botany*) a narrow extension of the ovary in a plant, supporting the stigma. **style** *verb* to design, shape, or arrange something, especially in a fashionable style. **in style** elegantly or luxuriously. [same origin as for *stylus*]

stylish *adjective* in a fashionable style. SYNONYMS: chic, smart; (*informal*) trendy, snazzy, natty. **stylishly** *adverb* **stylishness** *noun*

stylist *noun* 1 a person who does something with style. 2 a person who cuts hair or designs fashionable clothes.

stylistic *adjective* to do with literary or artistic style. **stylistically** *adverb*

stylized *adjective* represented in a way that is deliberately not realistic.

stylus *noun* (**styli** or **styluses**) 1 a needle-like device, usually a polished jewel, used to follow a groove in a gramophone record and transmit the recorded sound for reproduction. 2 an ancient writing instrument for scratching letters on wax-covered tablets. 3 (*Computing*) a pen-like device used to write or draw directly into a computer. [from a Latin word *stilus* meaning 'pointed writing instrument']

stymie *verb* (*informal*) to prevent a person or thing from progressing. [origin unknown]

styptic (stip-tik) *adjective* stopping bleeding by causing blood vessels to contract. [from a Greek word *stuphein* meaning 'to contract']

styrene *noun* (*Chemistry*) a liquid hydrocarbon used in plastics. [from a Greek word *sturax*, denoting a type of tree]

suave (swahv) *adjective* (said about a man) confident and smooth-mannered. **suavity** *noun* **suavely** *adverb* [from a Latin word *suavis* meaning 'agreeable']

sub *noun* (*informal*) 1 a submarine. 2 a subscription. 3 a substitute. 4 a small loan or advance payment.

sub- *prefix* (changing to suc-, suf-, sum-, sup-, sur-, sus- before certain consonants) 1 under (as in *submarine*). 2 subordinate, secondary (as in *subsection*). [from a Latin word *sub* meaning 'under']

subaltern (sub-əl-tern) *noun* an army officer ranking below a captain, especially a second lieutenant. [from a Latin word *subalternus* meaning 'inferior, lower in rank']

sub-aqua *adjective* to do with underwater sports, such as diving. [from *sub-* and a Latin word *aqua* meaning 'water']

subarctic *adjective* to do with regions bordering on the Arctic Circle.

subatomic *adjective* smaller than or forming part of an atom.

subcommittee *noun* a committee formed for a special purpose from some members of the main committee.

subconscious *adjective* to do with mental processes of which we are not fully aware but which influence our actions. **subconscious** *noun* the part of the mind in which these processes take place. **subconsciously** *adverb*

subcontinent *noun* a large land mass that forms part of a continent ♦ *the Indian subcontinent.*

subcontract (sub-kən-trakt) *verb* to hire a company or person outside your company to do a particular part of your work.

subcontractor *noun* a company or person hired by another company to do a particular part of their work.

subculture *noun* a social culture within a larger culture.

subcutaneous (sub-kew-tay-niəs) *adjective* (*Medicine*) under the skin. [from *sub-* and a Latin word *cutis* meaning 'skin']

subdivide *verb* to divide something into smaller parts after a first division. **subdivision** *noun*

subdominant *noun* (*Music*) the fourth note of a major or minor scale.

subduction noun (Geology) the process by which the edge of one plate of the earth's crust passes under the edge of another where they collide. [from sub- and a Latin word ductum meaning 'conveyed']

subdue verb 1 to overcome someone or bring them under control. SYNONYMS: quell, suppress. 2 to make something quieter or less intense. [from an Old French word suduire]

subdued adjective 1 (said about a person) quiet, shy, or slightly depressed. 2 not loud, harsh, or bright ♦ subdued lighting.

subeditor noun a person who checks and corrects material before it is printed in a newspaper, magazine, or book.

sub-heading noun a subordinate heading.

subhuman adjective less than human; not fully human.

subject[1] (sub-jikt) noun 1 the thing that is being discussed or dealt with. SYNONYMS: topic, matter, issue, question, business, affair. 2 a branch of knowledge that is studied or taught. SYNONYMS: field, area, discipline. 3 (Grammar) the word or words in a sentence that name who or what does the action or undergoes what is stated by the verb, e.g. 'the book' in the book fell off the table. 4 someone who is ruled by a monarch or government ♦ British subjects. 5 (Music) each of the principal themes in a sonata etc.
subject adjective not politically independent ♦ subject peoples. **subject to** 1 likely to be affected by something ♦ Trains are subject to delay because of flooding. 2 having to obey something ♦ We are all subject to the laws of the land. 3 depending upon something as a condition ♦ Our decision is subject to your approval. [from sub- and a Latin word -jectum meaning 'thrown']

subject[2] (səb-jekt) verb 1 to make a person or thing undergo something ♦ He was subjected to torture ♦ Scientists have subjected the metal to severe tests. 2 to bring a country under your control. **subjection** noun

subjective (səb-jek-tiv) adjective 1 influenced by personal feelings or opinions. 2 existing in a person's mind and not produced by things outside it, not objective. **subjectively** adverb

subject matter noun the matter treated in a book, speech, work of art, etc.

sub judice (sub joo-dis-i) adjective (Law) being decided by a judge or law court and therefore not able to be discussed publicly. [a Latin phrase meaning 'under a judge']

subjugate (sub-jə-gayt) verb to bring a country or group of people under your control, especially by conquest. **subjugation** noun [from Latin words sub meaning 'under' and jugum meaning 'a yoke']

subjunctive adjective (said about the form of a verb) used to express what is imagined, wished, or possible. There are only a few cases where the subjunctive form is commonly used in English, e.g. 'were' in if I were you and 'save' in God save the Queen.
subjunctive noun the subjunctive form of a verb. [from sub- and a Latin word junctum meaning 'joined']

sublet verb (past tense and past participle **sublet; subletting**) to let to another person accommodation that is let to you by a landlord.

sublimate (sub-lim-ayt) verb 1 (in psychoanalytic theory) to direct your instincts, urges, or energies into other activities, especially more socially acceptable ones. 2 (Chemistry) to sublime a substance. 3 to purify or refine something. **sublimation** noun

sublime adjective 1 of the most noble or impressive kind. 2 extreme; not caring about the consequences ♦ with sublime indifference.
sublime verb (Chemistry) to convert a solid substance into a vapour by heat and usually allow it to solidify again; to undergo this process. **sublimely** adverb **sublimity** (səb-lim-iti) noun [from a Latin word sublimis meaning 'in a high position']

subliminal (sub-lim-inəl) adjective (Psychology) perceived by someone's mind without their being aware of it. [from sub- and a Latin word limen meaning 'threshold']

sub-machine gun noun a lightweight machine gun held in the hands for firing.

submarine noun a ship that can operate under the sea for long periods.
submarine adjective under the surface of the sea ♦ submarine cables.

submediant (sub-mee-di-ənt) *noun* (Music) the sixth note of a major or minor scale.

submerge *verb* 1 to cause something to be under water. 2 (said about a submarine) to go below the surface. 3 to hide or cover something completely. **submergence** *noun* **submersion** *noun* [from *sub-* and a Latin word *mergere* meaning 'to dip']

submersible *noun* a small boat or other craft that can operate under water.

submicroscopic *adjective* too small to be seen by an ordinary microscope.

submission *noun* 1 submitting, or being submitted. 2 something submitted for consideration. 3 a theory or argument submitted by counsel to a judge or jury.

submissive *adjective* meekly obedient, willing to submit to others. **submissively** *adverb* **submissiveness** *noun*

submit *verb* (**submitted, submitting**) 1 to surrender or yield to someone stronger than you. 2 to subject a person or thing to a process. 3 to present something for consideration or decision ♦ *Submit your plans to the committee.* [from *sub-* and a Latin word *mittere* meaning 'to send']

subnormal *adjective* 1 less than normal. 2 below the normal level of intelligence or development.

subordinate [1] (sə-or-din-ət) *adjective* 1 of lesser importance or rank. 2 working under the control or authority of another person.
subordinate *noun* a person in a subordinate position. [from *sub-* and a Latin word *ordinare* meaning 'to arrange']

subordinate [2] (sə-or-din-ayt) *verb* to treat something as of lesser importance than something else. **subordination** *noun*

subordinate clause *noun* a clause which adds details to the main clause of the sentence, but cannot be used as a sentence itself.

suborn (sə-orn) *verb* to induce a person by bribery or other means to commit perjury or some other unlawful act. **subornation** *noun* [from *sub-* and a Latin word *ornare* meaning 'to equip']

sub-plot *noun* a secondary plot in a play, novel, etc.

subpoena (sub-pee-nə) *noun* (Law) a writ commanding a person to appear in court. **subpoena** *verb* (**subpoenas, subpoenaed,** subpoenaing) to summon a person with a subpoena. [from a Latin phrase *sub poena* meaning 'under a penalty' (because there is a punishment for not obeying)]

sub-post office *noun* a small local post office, often in a shop, which offers fewer services than a main post office.

subroutine *noun* (Computing) a set of instructions designed to perform a commonly used operation within a program.

subscribe *verb* 1 to pay in advance or at regular intervals in order to receive a periodical, be a member of a society, have the use of a telephone, etc. 2 to apply to take part in something ♦ *The course is already fully subscribed.* 3 to contribute money to a project or cause. 4 to express your agreement ♦ *I do not myself subscribe to this theory.* 5 (formal) to sign your name at the end of a document ♦ *He neglected to subscribe the contract.* [from *sub-* and a Latin word *scribere* meaning 'to write']

subscriber *noun* 1 a person who subscribes. 2 someone who rents a telephone.

subscriber trunk dialling *noun* a telephone system by which long-distance calls can be made directly by dialling instead of needing an operator to connect them.

subscript *adjective* written or printed below the level of a letter etc. (e.g. 2 in H_2O).

subscription *noun* 1 subscribing. 2 a payment to subscribe to something. 3 a fee for membership of a society etc.

subsection *noun* a division of a section.

subsequent *adjective* coming after something in time. **subsequently** *adverb* [from *sub-* and a Latin word *sequens* meaning 'following']

subservient *adjective* 1 prepared to obey others without question, obsequious. 2 subordinate. **subservience** *noun* [from *sub-* and a Latin word *serviens* meaning 'serving']

subset *noun* 1 a part of a larger group of related things. 2 (Mathematics) a set contained within a larger set.

subside *verb* 1 to become less active or intense ♦ *The excitement subsided.* SYNONYMS: abate, dwindle, ebb, die down. 2 to go down to a lower or to the normal level. 3 (said about land) to sink, e.g. because of

mining operations underneath.
4 (*informal*) (said about a person) to sink into a chair etc. [from *sub-* and a Latin word *sidere* meaning 'to settle']

subsidence (sǝb-**siy**-dǝns or **sub**-sid-ǝns) *noun* the gradual sinking or caving in of an area of land.

subsidiary *adjective* **1** of secondary importance. **2** (said about a company) controlled by another company. **subsidiary** *noun* (**subsidiaries**) a subsidiary company. [same origin as for *subsidy*]

subsidize *verb* **1** to pay part of the cost of producing something to reduce its price ♦ *All our meals at college are subsidized.* **2** to support something financially.

subsidy *noun* (**subsidies**) a grant of money paid to an industry or other cause needing help, or to keep down the price of a commodity or service. [from a Latin word *subsidium* meaning 'assistance']

subsist *verb* to exist or continue to exist; to keep yourself alive ♦ *They managed to subsist on a diet of vegetables.* [from a Latin word *subsistere* meaning 'to stand firm']

subsistence *noun* subsisting; a means of doing this.

subsistence farming *noun* farming in which almost all the crops etc. are consumed by the farmer's household.

subsistence level *noun* a standard of living that supplies only the bare necessities of life.

subsoil *noun* soil lying just beneath the surface layer.

subsonic *adjective* **1** (said about speed) less than the speed of sound. **2** (said about aircraft) flying at subsonic speeds, not supersonic. **subsonically** *adverb*

substance *noun* **1** matter of a particular kind. SYNONYMS: material, stuff, matter. **2** the essence of something spoken or written ♦ *We agree with the substance of your report but not with its details.* **3** solid basis in reality or fact ♦ *The claim has no substance.* [from a Latin word *substantia* meaning 'essence']

sub-standard *adjective* below the usual or required standard.

substantial *adjective* **1** of considerable importance, amount, or worth ♦ *a substantial fee* ♦ *substantial reasons.* **2** solidly built or made. **3** in essentials, virtual ♦ *We are in substantial agreement.* **substantially** *adverb* [same origin as for *substance*]

substantiate (sǝb-**stan**-shi-ayt) *verb* to produce evidence to support or prove a statement or claim. **substantiation** *noun* [same origin as for *substance*]

substantive [1] (sǝb-**stan**-tiv) *adjective* **1** having a firm basis in reality; substantial, important, or meaningful. **2** (said about a rank) permanent, not temporary.

substantive [2] (**sub**-stǝn-tiv) *noun* (*Grammar*) (*old use*) a noun.

substation *noun* a subsidiary station, e.g. for the distribution of electric current.

substitute *noun* **1** a person or thing that acts or is used in place of another. SYNONYMS: replacement, stand-in. **2** a sports player who replaces another during a match. **substitute** *verb* **1** to put or use something as a substitute. SYNONYMS: replace, exchange, swap. **2** to serve as a substitute. **substitution** *noun* [from *sub-* and a Latin word *statuere* meaning 'to set up']

substratum (sub-**strah**-tǝm or sub-**stray**-tǝm) *noun* (**substrata**) an underlying layer or substance.

substructure *noun* an underlying or supporting structure.

subsume *verb* to include or absorb something in something else ♦ *The three committees have now been subsumed under a single body.* [from *sub-* and a Latin word *sumere* meaning 'to take up']

subtenant *noun* a person who leases accommodation etc. from a tenant. **subtenancy** *noun*

subtend *verb* (said about a line or arc) to form an angle at a point where lines drawn from each end of it meet. [from *sub-* and a Latin word *tendere* meaning 'to stretch']

subterfuge (**sub**-ter-fewj) *noun* a trick or deception used in order to achieve something. [from a Latin word *subterfugere* meaning 'to escape secretly']

subterranean (sub-ter-**ayn**-iǝn) *adjective* underground. [from *sub-* and a Latin word *terra* meaning 'ground']

subtitle *noun* a secondary or additional title.

subtitles *plural noun* words shown at the bottom of the screen during a film, e.g. to translate the dialogue from a foreign language.

subtitle *verb* to provide something with a subtitle or subtitles.

subtle (**sut**əl) *adjective* **1** not immediately obvious or understandable ♦ *a subtle argument.* SYNONYMS: ingenious, sophisticated, arcane. **2** slight and difficult to detect or describe ♦ *a subtle distinction.* **3** (said about a smell, flavour, shade, etc.) delicate or faint ♦ *a subtle perfume.* **4** able to perceive and make fine distinctions ♦ *a subtle mind.* **subtlety** (**sut**-əl-ti) *noun* **subtly** *adverb* [from a Latin word *subtilis*]

subtotal *noun* the total of part of a group of figures.

subtract *verb* **1** to take away a quantity or number from another to calculate the difference. **2** to remove a part of something. **subtraction** *noun* [from *sub-* and a Latin word *tractum* meaning 'pulled']

subtropical *adjective* to do with regions bordering on the tropics.

suburb *noun* a residential district lying outside the central part of a town. **suburban** *adjective* [from *sub-* and a Latin word *urbs* meaning 'city']

suburbia *noun* **1** the suburbs. **2** the way people in the suburbs live and think.

subvention (səb-**ven**-shən) *noun* a grant of money, especially from a government. [from a Latin word *subvenire* meaning 'to assist']

subversion *noun* subverting.

subversive *adjective* tending to subvert an established idea, system, or institution.

subvert (səb-**vert**) *verb* to undermine the authority of an established idea, system, or institution. [from *sub-* and a Latin word *vertere* meaning 'to turn']

subway *noun* **1** an underground passage, e.g. for pedestrians to cross below a road. **2** (*North Amer.*) an underground railway.

sub-zero *adjective* (said about temperatures) below zero.

succeed *verb* **1** to achieve an aim or purpose; to be successful ♦ *Our plan succeeded brilliantly* ♦ *She is determined to succeed in life.* **2** to come after and take the place of another person or thing. **3** to become the next holder of an office, especially the monarchy ♦ *Edward the Seventh succeeded Queen Victoria* ♦ *Who succeeded to the throne?* [from *sub-* and a Latin word *cedere* meaning 'to go']

success *noun* **1** doing or getting what you

wanted or intended. **2** the attainment of wealth, fame, or position. **3** a person or thing that is successful ♦ *The show was a great success.* [same origin as for *succeed*]

successful *adjective* having success. **successfully** *adverb*

succession *noun* **1** a series of people or things following one after the other. **2** succeeding to the throne or to another position or title; the right of doing this; the sequence of people with this right. **3** the sequence of plant and animal communities which replace one another in an area. **in succession** one after another. [same origin as for *succeed*]

successive *adjective* following one after another, in an unbroken series ♦ *on five successive days.* **successively** *adverb*

successor *noun* a person or thing that succeeds another.

succinct (sək-**sinkt**) *adjective* expressed briefly and clearly. **succinctly** *adverb* **succinctness** *noun* [from a Latin word *succinctum* meaning 'tucked up']

Succoth (**suuk**-oht) *noun* the Jewish autumn festival of thanksgiving (the Feast of Tabernacles), commemorating the time when the Israelites sheltered in the wilderness. [from a Hebrew word]

succour (**suk**-er) *noun* help and support given in time of need. **succour** *verb* to give such help to someone. [from a Latin word *succurrere* meaning 'to run to someone's help']

succulent (**suk**-yoo-lənt) *adjective* **1** juicy and tasty. **2** (said about plants) having thick fleshy leaves or stems. **succulent** *noun* a succulent plant. **succulence** *noun* [from a Latin word *succus* meaning 'juice']

succumb (sə-**kum**) *verb* to give way to something overpowering ♦ *In the end he succumbed to temptation.* [from *sub-* and a Latin word *cumbere* meaning 'to lie']

such *adjective* **1** of the same kind ♦ *I love weddings, christenings, and all such occasions.* **2** of the kind or degree described ♦ *There's no such person.* **3** so great or intense ♦ *It gave her such a fright.* **such** *pronoun* the action or thing just mentioned ♦ *Such being the case, we can do nothing.* **as such** in the exact sense of the word ♦ *He's not an artist as such, but he does paint now and again.* **such as 1** for example. **2** of a similar kind as ♦ *people such as our* *neighbours.* [from an Old English word *swilc*]

such-and-such *adjective* particular but not now specified ♦ *He says he will arrive at such-and-such a time but is always late.*

suchlike *noun* things of the type mentioned.

suck *verb* 1 to draw liquid or air etc. into the mouth by using the lip muscles. 2 to squeeze something in the mouth by using the tongue ♦ *She was sucking a toffee.* 3 to draw something in ♦ *Plants suck moisture from the soil* ♦ *The canoe was sucked into the whirlpool.*
suck *noun* the act or process of sucking.
to suck up to (*informal*) to flatter someone in the hope of winning their favour. [from an Old English word]

sucker *noun* 1 an organ of certain animals, or a device of rubber etc., that can stick to a surface by suction. 2 a shoot coming up from the roots or underground stem of a tree or shrub. 3 (*informal*) a person who is easily deceived. **to be a sucker for** to be very fond of a particular thing.

sucking *adjective* not yet weaned ♦ *a sucking pig.*

suckle *verb* 1 to feed a baby or young animal at the breast or udder. 2 (said about young) to take milk in this way. [from *suckling*]

suckling *noun* a child or animal that is not yet weaned. [from *suck* and *-ling*]

sucrose (sewk-rohz) *noun* (*Chemistry*) sugar obtained from plants such as sugar cane or sugar beet. [from a French word *sucre* meaning 'sugar']

suction *noun* 1 sucking. 2 producing a partial or complete vacuum so that external atmospheric pressure forces fluid etc. into the empty space or causes adhesion of surfaces ♦ *Vacuum cleaners work by suction.* [from a Latin word *sugere* meaning 'to suck']

sudden *adjective* happening or done quickly and unexpectedly. SYNONYMS: abrupt, sharp, swift. **all of a sudden** suddenly. **suddenness** *noun* [from an Old French word *sudein*, from a Latin word *subitus*]

sudden death *noun* (*informal*) a way of deciding a drawn or tied contest by playing one more game or point, whoever wins it being the winner of the whole contest.

suddenly *adverb* quickly and unexpectedly.

suds *plural noun* froth on soapy water. [probably from an Old German or Old Dutch word meaning 'marsh']

sue *verb* (**sues, sued, suing**) 1 to begin legal proceedings against someone to claim money from them. 2 (*formal*) to appeal formally to someone for something ♦ *The ambassador was dispatched to sue for peace.* [from an Old French word *suer*]

suede (swayd) *noun* leather with the flesh side rubbed to make it velvety. [from Suède, the French name for Sweden, where it was first made]

suet *noun* the hard fat from round the kidneys of cattle and sheep, used in cooking. [from an Old French word; related to *sebum*]

suet pudding *noun* a boiled or steamed pudding made with flour and suet.

suffer *verb* 1 to undergo or be subjected to pain, loss, grief, damage, etc. 2 to be affected by an illness ♦ *She suffers from arthritis.* 3 to become worse or be badly affected ♦ *I'm not sleeping and my work is suffering.* 4 (old use) to allow or tolerate something. **sufferer** *noun* **suffering** *noun* [from *sub-* and a Latin word *ferre* meaning 'to bear']

sufferance *noun* **on sufferance** tolerated but only grudgingly or because there is no positive objection. [from a Latin word *sufferentia* meaning 'suffering']

suffice (sə-fyss) *verb* to be enough for someone's needs. [from *sub-* and a Latin word *facere* meaning 'to make or do']

sufficient *adjective* enough. **sufficiency** *noun* **sufficiently** *adverb* [same origin as for *suffice*]

suffix *noun* a letter or set of letters added at the end of a word to make another word (e.g. *y* added to *rust* to make *rusty*) or as an inflexion (e.g. *ing* added to *suck* to make *sucking*). [from *sub-* and a Latin word *figere* meaning 'to fasten']

suffocate *verb* 1 to kill someone by stopping them breathing; to be killed in this way. 2 to have difficulty in breathing because of heat and lack of air. **suffocation** *noun* [from *sub-* and a Latin word *fauces* meaning 'throat']

suffragan (suf-rə-gən) or **suffragan bishop** noun a bishop appointed to help the bishop of a diocese. [from a Latin word suffraganeus meaning 'assistant']

suffrage (suf-rij) noun the right to vote in political elections. [from a Latin word meaning 'vote']

suffragette (suf-rə-jet) noun a woman who, in the early 20th century, campaigned for women to have the right to vote.

suffragist noun a person who favours giving the right to vote to more people or groups, e.g. women or young people.

suffuse (sə-fewz) verb to spread throughout or over something gradually ♦ A blush suffused her cheeks. **suffusion** noun [from sub- and a Latin word fusum meaning 'poured']

Sufi (soo-fi) noun (**Sufis**) a Muslim ascetic and mystic. **Sufic** adjective **Sufism** noun [from an Arabic word]

sugar noun 1 a sweet crystalline substance obtained from the juices of various plants. 2 (Biochemistry) any of a class of sweet-tasting carbohydrates such as glucose and sucrose.
sugar verb to sweeten or coat something with sugar. [from an Arabic word sukkar]

sugar beet noun the kind of beet from which sugar is extracted.

sugar cane noun a tropical grass with tall jointed stems from which sugar is obtained.

sugar soap noun an abrasive compound for cleaning or removing paint.

sugary adjective 1 containing or resembling sugar. 2 too sentimental. **sugariness** noun

suggest verb 1 to put forward an idea or plan for someone to consider. SYNONYMS: propose, moot, raise, recommend, advocate. 2 to cause an idea or possibility to come into the mind. SYNONYMS: indicate, imply. [from a Latin word suggerere meaning 'to suggest']

suggestible adjective easily influenced by people's suggestions. **suggestibility** noun

suggestion noun 1 suggesting, or being suggested. 2 something suggested. 3 a slight trace ♦ a suggestion of a French accent.

suggestive adjective 1 conveying a suggestion. 2 tending to convey an indecent or improper meaning.

suggestively adverb **suggestiveness** noun

suicidal adjective 1 to do with suicide. 2 (said about a person) liable to commit suicide. 3 destructive to your own interests. **suicidally** adverb

suicide noun 1 the intentional killing of yourself; an instance of this. 2 a person who commits suicide. 3 a course of action that is destructive to your own interests ♦ The announcement of tax increases was political suicide.
suicide verb to commit suicide. **to commit suicide** to kill yourself intentionally. [from a Latin word sui meaning 'of yourself' and caedere meaning 'to kill']

suit noun 1 a set of clothing to be worn together, especially a jacket and trousers or a jacket and skirt. 2 clothing for use in a particular activity ♦ a diving suit ♦ a suit of armour. 3 any of the four sets (spades, hearts, diamonds, and clubs) into which a pack of cards is divided. 4 a lawsuit. 5 (formal) a request or appeal.
suit verb 1 to look attractive on someone; to go well with something ♦ Red doesn't suit her. 2 to be acceptable to or convenient for a person or thing ♦ 7 o'clock suits me fine. 3 to meet the demands or needs of someone. 4 to adapt something, to make something suitable ♦ Suit your style to your audience. [from a Latin word sequi meaning 'to follow']
◊ Do not confuse this word with **suite**, which has a different meaning.

suitable adjective satisfactory or right for a particular person, purpose, or occasion. SYNONYMS: appropriate, acceptable, fitting, fit, apt, convenient. **suitability** noun **suitably** adverb

suitcase noun a rectangular case for carrying clothes, usually with a hinged lid and a handle.

suite noun 1 a set of connected rooms. 2 a set of matching furniture. 3 a set of musical pieces or extracts. [from an Old French word; related to suit]
◊ Do not confuse this word with **suit**, which has a different meaning.

suiting noun material for making suits.

suitor noun a man who is courting a woman. [from a Latin word secutor meaning 'follower']

sulk verb to be sulky.
sulks plural noun a fit of sulkiness. [from sulky]

sulky *adjective* (**sulkier, sulkiest**) bad-tempered and silent because of resentment. **sulkily** *adverb* **sulkiness** *noun* [origin unknown]

sullen *adjective* **1** silent, bad-tempered, and gloomy. **2** dark and dismal ♦ *a sullen sky.* **sullenly** *adverb* **sullenness** *noun* [from an Old French word *sulein*; related to *sole*³]

sully *verb* (**sullies, sullied, sullying**) to stain, blemish, or spoil the purity of something ♦ *The scandal sullied his reputation.* [same origin as for *soil*²]

sulpha *adjective* sulphonamide ♦ *sulpha drugs.*

sulphate *noun* (*Chemistry*) a salt of sulphuric acid.

sulphonamide (sul-**fon**-ə-miyd) *noun* (*Medicine*) any of a group of chemical compounds with anti-bacterial properties.

sulphur *noun* a chemical element (symbol S), a pale-yellow substance that burns with a blue flame and a stifling smell, used in industry and medicine. [from a Latin word *sulfur*]

sulphuric (sul-**fewr**-ik) *adjective* containing a proportion of sulphur.

sulphuric acid *noun* a strong corrosive acid.

sulphurous (sul-**fewr**-əs) *adjective* **1** to do with or like sulphur. **2** containing a proportion of sulphur.

sultan *noun* the ruler of certain Muslim countries. [from an Arabic word meaning 'ruler']

sultana *noun* **1** a light brown seedless raisin. **2** the wife, mother, sister, or daughter of a sultan. [from an Italian word meaning 'sultan's wife']

sultanate *noun* the territory of a sultan.

sultry *adjective* (**sultrier, sultriest**) **1** hot and humid ♦ *sultry weather.* **2** passionate and sensual ♦ *her sultry smile.* **sultriness** *noun* [from an old word *sulter* meaning 'to swelter']

sum *noun* **1** a total. **2** a particular amount of money ♦ *for the sum of £5.* **3** a problem in arithmetic ♦ *She's good at sums.*
sum *verb* (**summed, summing**) to find the sum of two or more amounts. **in sum** briefly, in summary. **to sum up 1** to summarize, especially at the end of a talk etc. **2** (said about a judge) to summarize the evidence or argument. **to sum**

someone or something **up** to concisely describe or form a quick opinion of someone or something ♦ *How would you sum him up?* [from a Latin word *summa* meaning 'main part']

Sumerian (soo-**meer**-iən) *noun* **1** a member of an ancient people of Sumer in southern Mesopotamia in the 4th millennium BC. **2** the language of ancient Sumer. **Sumerian** *adjective* to do with ancient Sumer.

summarize *verb* to make or be a summary of something. **summarizer** *noun*

summary *noun* (**summaries**) a statement giving the main points of something briefly. SYNONYMS: outline, synopsis, précis, résumé, digest, gist.
summary *adjective* **1** giving the main points only, not the details ♦ *a summary account.* **2** done or given without delay or attention to the formal procedures ♦ *summary punishment.* **summarily** *adverb* [same origin as for *sum*]

summation (sum-**ay**-shən) *noun* **1** finding of a total or sum. **2** summing up.

summer *noun* the season between spring and autumn, when the weather is warmest. [from an Old English word *sumor*]

summer house *noun* a small building providing shade in a garden or park.

summer school *noun* a course of study held during school and university summer vacations.

summertime *noun* the season of summer.

summer time *noun* time shown by clocks that are put one hour ahead of standard time in summer to give longer light evenings during the summer months. In Britain, British Summer Time is one hour ahead of Greenwich Mean Time.

summery *adjective* like summer; suitable for summer.

summing-up *noun* **1** a summary. **2** (*Law*) a judge's review of the evidence at the end of a case, in which points of law are explained to the jury.

summit *noun* **1** the top of a mountain or hill. **2** the highest level of achievement. **3** (also **summit conference**) a meeting between heads of two or more governments. [from a Latin word *summus* meaning 'highest']

summon *verb* **1** to order someone to come or appear. **2** to call people together ♦ *A* meeting of the governors was quickly summoned. SYNONYMS: assemble, convene. **to summon something up** to gather together your strength or courage in order to do something ♦ I couldn't even summon up the energy to get out of bed. [from sub- and a Latin word monere meaning 'to warn']

summons noun (**summonses**) **1** an order to appear in a law court, or a document containing this. **2** a command to do something or appear somewhere. **summons** verb to serve someone with a summons. [same origin as for summon]

sumo (**soo-moh**) noun a form of Japanese heavyweight wrestling. [from a Japanese word]

sump noun **1** an inner casing holding lubricating oil in a petrol engine. **2** a hole or pit into which waste material drains. [an Old German or Old Dutch word meaning 'marsh']

sumptuous adjective splendid and expensive-looking. SYNONYMS: lavish, magnificent, rich, grand. **sumptuously** adverb **sumptuousness** noun [from a Latin word sumptus meaning 'cost']

sum total noun a total.

sun noun **1** the star round which the earth travels and from which it receives light and warmth. **2** the light and warmth from the sun ♦ Go and sit in the sun. **3** any star in the universe, with or without planets. **sun** verb (**sunned, sunning**) to expose yourself to the sun ♦ People were sunning themselves on the beach. **under the sun** in existence ♦ There's nothing new under the sun. **sunless** adjective [from an Old English word sunne]

sunbathe verb to sit or lie in the sun, especially to get a suntan.

sunbeam noun a ray of sunlight.

sunbed noun **1** a bench that you lie on under sunlamps. **2** a lounger used for sunbathing.

sunblock noun a cream or lotion that you put on your skin to protect it from sunburn.

sunburn noun redness and inflammation of the skin caused by exposure to the sun. **sunburnt** or **sunburned** adjective

suncream noun a cream for protecting the skin from sunburn.

sundae (**sun-day**) noun a dish of ice cream and crushed fruit, nuts, syrup, etc. [perhaps from Sunday (because sundaes were originally sold then, possibly to use up ice cream not sold during the week)]

Sunday noun the first day of the week, observed by Christians as a day of rest and worship. [from an Old English word sunnandæg meaning 'day of the sun']

Sunday school noun a class held on Sundays to teach children about Christianity.

sunder verb (literary) to break or tear something apart. [from an Old English word sundrian]

sundew noun a small bog plant with sticky hairs that trap insects.

sundial noun an instrument that shows the time by means of the shadow of a rod or plate on a scaled dial.

sundown noun sunset.

sundry adjective of various kinds. **sundries** plural noun various small items not named individually. **all and sundry** everyone. [from an Old English word syndrig meaning 'distinct or separate']

sunfish noun (**sunfish** or **sunfishes**) a large sea fish with an almost spherical body.

sunflower noun a tall garden plant bearing large flowers with golden petals round a dark centre, producing seeds that yield an edible oil.

sung past participle of sing.

sunglasses plural noun glasses with tinted lenses to protect the eyes from sunlight or glare.

sunk past participle of sink.

sunken adjective **1** lying below the level of the surrounding area ♦ a sunken bath. **2** submerged in water ♦ sunken treasure. **3** (said about a person's eyes or cheeks) hollow or recessed.

sunk fence noun another term for ha-ha.

sunlamp noun a lamp producing ultraviolet rays, used to give people an artificial suntan.

sunlight noun light from the sun.

sunlit adjective lit by sunlight.

Sunna noun the traditional portion of Muslim law, based on Muhammad's words or acts but not written by him. [an Arabic word meaning 'form' or 'way' or 'rule']

Sunnite *noun* a member of the Sunni, one of the two major groups in Islam, comprising the main community in most Muslim countries other than Iran. (Compare **Shiite**.) [from an Arabic word meaning 'law or custom']

sunny *adjective* (**sunnier, sunniest**) **1** bright with sunlight, full of sunshine. **2** (said about a person or mood) cheerful. **sunnily** *adverb*

sunrise *noun* **1** the rising of the sun, or the time of this. **2** the sky full of colour at sunrise.

sunrise industry *noun* a new and expanding industry.

sunroof *noun* a panel in the roof of a car that can be opened to let in fresh air and sunlight.

sunscreen *noun* a cream or lotion that you put on your skin to protect it from the sun.

sunset *noun* **1** the setting of the sun, or the time of this. **2** the sky full of colour at sunset.

sunshade *noun* a parasol, awning, or other device giving protection from the sun.

sunshine *noun* **1** direct sunlight with no cloud between the sun and the earth. **2** cheerfulness or happiness.

sunspot *noun* one of the dark patches sometimes observed on the sun's surface, associated with the sun's magnetic field.

sunstroke *noun* illness caused by being in the sun too long.

suntan *noun* a brown colour in skin that has been exposed to the sun. **suntanned** *adjective*

suntrap *noun* a sunny place, especially a sheltered one.

sunup *noun* (*North Amer.*) sunrise.

sun visor *noun* a flap at the top of a vehicle's windscreen that shields your eyes from the sun.

sup *verb* (**supped, supping**) **1** (*old use or N. England*) to drink liquid by sips or spoonfuls. **2** (*old use*) to eat supper. **sup** *noun* a mouthful of liquid. [from an Old English word]

super *adjective* (*informal*) excellent or superb. **super** *noun* (*informal*) a superintendent, especially in the police force. [from *super-*]

super- *prefix* **1** over or beyond (as in *superimpose*, *superhuman*). **2** of greater size or quality etc. (as in *supermarket*). **3** extremely (as in *superabundant*). **4** beyond (as in *supernatural*). [from a Latin word *super* meaning 'over']

superabundant *adjective* (*formal*) very abundant, more than enough. **superabundance** *noun*

superannuate *verb* to make an employee retire with a pension. [from *super-* and a Latin word *annus* meaning 'a year']

superannuated *adjective* **1** belonging to a superannuation scheme. **2** too old or outdated to be used.

superannuation *noun* **1** regular payments made by an employee towards a pension. **2** a pension of this type.

superb *adjective* **1** excellent. **2** splendid or magnificent. **superbly** *adverb* [from a Latin word *superbus* meaning 'proud']

supercharge *verb* to increase the efficiency and power of an engine by using a device that supplies air or fuel at above the normal pressure. **supercharger** *noun*

supercilious (soo-per-**sil**-iəs) *adjective* with an air of superiority; haughty and scornful. **superciliously** *adverb* **superciliousness** *noun* [from a Latin word *supercilium* meaning 'eyebrow']

supercomputer *noun* a very powerful mainframe computer.

superconductivity *noun* (*Physics*) the property of certain metals of having no electrical resistance at temperatures near absolute zero. **superconductive** *adjective* **superconductor** *noun*

supercool *verb* (*Chemistry*) to cool a liquid below its freezing point without its becoming solid or crystalline.

superego (soo-per-**eg**-oh) *noun* (**superegos**) (*Psychology*) an individual's personal ideals, acting like a conscience in directing behaviour.

superficial *adjective* **1** existing or happening on the surface ♦ *a superficial wound.* **2** not deep or thorough ♦ *superficial knowledge.* **3** apparent but not real or significant ♦ *The changes are only superficial.* **4** (said about a person) having no depth of character or feeling. **superficiality** (soo-per-**fish**-i-al-iti) *noun* **superficially** *adverb* [from *super-* and a Latin word *facies* meaning 'face']

superfluity (soo-per-**floo**-iti) *noun* (**superfluities**) a superfluous amount.

superfluous (soo-per-floo-əs) *adjective* unnecessary, more than is needed. **superfluously** *adverb* [from super- and a Latin word *fluere* meaning 'to flow']

superglue *noun* a kind of strong glue that sticks very quickly.

supergrass *noun* (*informal*) a police informer who gives information about a large number of criminals.

superheat *verb* (*Physics*) to heat a liquid above its boiling point without allowing it to vaporize; to heat steam or other vapour above boiling point.

superhuman *adjective* beyond ordinary human ability or power ♦ *superhuman strength*.

superimpose *verb* to place or lay one thing on top of something else. **superimposition** *noun*

superintend *verb* to supervise or be in charge of something or someone. **superintendence** *noun* [from super- and a Latin word *intendere* meaning 'to direct or intend']

superintendent *noun* 1 a person who superintends something or someone. 2 a police officer ranking above chief inspector.

superior *adjective* 1 higher in position or rank. 2 better or more important than another; higher in quality or ability. 3 showing that you feel yourself to be above or better than others. SYNONYMS: supercilious, self-important, conceited. **superior** *noun* 1 a person who is higher than another in rank or ability. 2 the head of a monastery or other religious community. **superiority** *noun* [a Latin word meaning 'higher']

superlative (soo-per-lə-tiv) *adjective* 1 of the highest degree or quality ♦ *with superlative skill*. 2 describing a form of an adjective or adverb that means 'most', such as *dearest, shyest, best*. **superlative** *noun* a superlative form of an adjective or adverb. **superlatively** *adverb* [from a Latin word *superlatum* meaning 'carried above']

superman *noun* (**supermen**) a man who appears to have superhuman powers.

supermarket *noun* a large self-service shop selling groceries and household goods.

supermodel *noun* a highly successful fashion model.

supernatural *adjective* to do with events that are apparently caused by forces beyond the laws of nature or science. **the supernatural** *noun* the world of supernatural events and forces. **supernaturally** *adverb*

supernova *noun* (**supernovae**) (*Astronomy*) a star that suddenly increases very greatly in brightness because of an explosion disrupting its structure.

supernumerary (soo-per-new-mer-er-i) *adjective* in excess of the normal number, extra. **supernumerary** *noun* (**supernumeraries**) a supernumerary person or thing. [from a Latin word *supernumerarius* meaning 'soldier added to a legion after it is complete']

superpose *verb* to put one thing on top of another so that their outlines coincide. **superposition** *noun* [from super- and a Latin word *positum* meaning 'placed']

superpower *noun* one of the most powerful nations of the world.

superscribe *verb* to write a word or words at the top of or on the outside of a document. **superscription** *noun* [from super- and a Latin word *scribere* meaning 'to write']

superscript *adjective* written or printed just above and to the right of a word, figure, or symbol (e.g. 2 in 3^2 meaning 9). [from a Latin word *superscribere* meaning 'to write above']

supersede (soo-per-**seed**) *verb* to take the place of another person or thing ♦ *Cars have superseded horse-drawn carriages*. [from super- and a Latin word *sedere* meaning 'to sit'] ◊ Note that this word ends -*sede* and not -*cede*.

supersonic *adjective* 1 (said about speed) greater than the speed of sound. 2 (said about aircraft) flying at supersonic speeds. **supersonically** *adverb*

superstar *noun* an extremely successful performer in entertainment or sport.

superstition *noun* 1 belief that events can be influenced by certain acts, objects, or circumstances, although the connection has no rational basis. 2 an idea or practice based on such belief. [from a Latin word *superstare* meaning 'to stand over']

superstitious *adjective* based on or influenced by superstition.

superstitiously adverb **superstitiousness** noun

superstore noun a very large out-of-town supermarket.

superstructure noun a structure built on top of something else; a building as distinct from its foundations.

supertanker noun a very large oil tanker.

supervene (soo-per-**veen**) verb to happen and interrupt or change something ♦ *The country was prosperous until an earthquake supervened.* **supervention** (soo-per-ven-shən) noun [from *super-* and a Latin word *venire* meaning 'to come']

supervise verb to be in charge of a person or task and inspect the work that is done. SYNONYMS: oversee, superintend, preside over, watch over, invigilate (an exam). **supervision** noun **supervisor** noun [from *super-* and a Latin word *visum* meaning 'seen']

supervisory (soo-per-**viy**-zer-i) adjective supervising ♦ *supervisory duties.*

superwoman noun (**superwomen**) a woman who appears to have superhuman powers.

supine (soo-**piyn**) adjective **1** lying face upwards (contrasted with *prone*). **2** not taking action, indolent. **supinely** adverb [from a Latin word *supinus* meaning 'bent backwards']

supper noun a light or informal evening meal. [from an Old French word *super* meaning 'to sup']

supplant verb to oust and take the place of a person or thing. [from a Latin word *supplantare* meaning 'to trip someone up']

supple adjective (**suppler**, **supplest**) bending easily; flexible, not stiff. **supplely** adverb **suppleness** noun [from *sub-* and a Latin word *plicare* meaning 'to fold or bend']

supplement[1] (**sup**-li-mənt) noun **1** a thing added to something as an extra or to make up for a deficiency. **2** a separate section, especially a colour magazine, added to a newspaper. **3** an additional charge paid for an extra service. **supplemental** adjective [same origin as for *supply*]

supplement[2] (**sup**-li-ment) verb to provide or be a supplement to something ♦ *She supplements her pocket money by working on Saturdays.* SYNONYMS: augment, boost; (*informal*) top up. **supplementation** noun

supplementary adjective serving as a supplement.

supplementary angle noun (*Mathematics*) either of two angles which add up to 180°.

supplementary benefit noun a payment made by the state to people with very low incomes, now replaced by income support.

suppliant (**sup**-li-ənt) noun a person asking humbly for something. [from an Old French word; related to *supplicate*]

supplicate verb to ask or beg humbly for something. **supplicant** noun **supplication** noun [from a Latin word *supplicare* meaning 'to kneel']

supplier noun someone who supplies something.

supply verb (**supplies**, **supplied**, **supplying**) **1** to give someone or provide them with what is needed; to make something available for use. SYNONYMS: provide, furnish, equip, purvey. **2** to satisfy or make up for something ♦ *supply a need.*
supply noun (**supplies**)
1 providing of what is needed. **2** a stock or amount of something provided or available ♦ *the water supply* ♦ *an inexhaustible supply of fish.*
supply adjective (said about a schoolteacher etc.) acting as a temporary substitute for another. **on supply** (said about a schoolteacher) acting as a temporary substitute for another. [from a Latin word *supplere* meaning 'to fill up']

support verb **1** to keep something from falling or sinking; to bear the weight of something. **2** to give strength, help, or encouragement to someone or something. **3** to supply someone with the necessities of life ♦ *She has a family to support.* **4** to enable something to last or continue ♦ *The planet may once have supported life.* **5** to be a fan of a particular sports team. **6** to take a secondary part ♦ *The play has a strong supporting cast.* **7** to bring facts to confirm a statement, claim, theory, etc. ♦ *All the available evidence supports this view.* SYNONYMS: corroborate, substantiate, endorse, verify. **8** to endure or tolerate something ♦ *We cannot support such insolence.*
support noun **1** assistance, encouragement, or approval ♦ *Thank you for your support.* SYNONYMS: backing, help, aid. **2** supporting, or being supported. **3** a person or thing that supports someone or

something. **supporter** noun [from sub- and a Latin word *portare* meaning 'to carry']

supportive adjective providing help or support.

suppose verb 1 to think that something is likely to happen or be true, though without proof ♦ *I don't suppose they will come.* SYNONYMS: believe, expect, think, guess, imagine, assume, presume. 2 to assume something as true for the purpose of argument ♦ *Suppose the world were flat.* 3 to consider something as a proposal or suggestion ♦ *Suppose we try another firm.* **to be supposed to** to be expected or required to do something ♦ *You were supposed to be here an hour ago.* [from an Old French word *supposer*]

supposed adjective believed to exist or to have a certain character or identity ♦ *his supposed brother.*

supposedly (sə-**poh**-zidli) adverb according to what is generally believed or supposed.

supposition noun an assumption or hypothesis ♦ *The article is based on supposition not on fact.*

supposititious (sup-ə-**zish**-əs) adjective hypothetical, based on supposition.

suppress verb 1 to put an end to something, especially by force or authority ♦ *Troops suppressed the rebellion.* SYNONYMS: subdue, quell, quash, crush, put down, stamp out; (informal) crack down on. 2 to prevent something from being known, published, or seen ♦ *The police were accused of suppressing evidence.* 3 to prevent your feelings from being expressed ♦ *She managed to suppress her anger.* **suppressible** adjective **suppression** noun [from sub- and a Latin word *pressus* meaning 'pressed']

suppressor noun a person or thing that suppresses something, especially a device for suppressing electrical interference.

suppurate (**sup**-yoor-ayt) verb to form or produce pus. **suppuration** noun [from sub- and a Latin word *pus* meaning 'pus']

supra- prefix above, over. [from a Latin word *supra* meaning 'above']

supranational adjective transcending national boundaries or governments.

supremacy (soo-**prem**-əsi) noun being supreme; the position of supreme authority or power.

supreme adjective 1 highest in authority or rank ♦ *the supreme commander.* 2 highest in importance, intensity, or quality ♦ *supreme courage.* 3 involving death ♦ *the supreme sacrifice.* 4 (said about food) served in a rich cream sauce ♦ *chicken supreme.* **supremely** adverb [from a Latin word *supremus* meaning 'highest']

supreme court noun the highest court in a country or state.

supremo noun (**supremos**) (informal) a person in overall charge. [a Spanish word meaning 'supreme']

sur- prefix equivalent to super- (as in surcharge, surface). [from a French word]

sura (soor-ə) noun a chapter or section of the Koran. [an Arabic word]

surcharge noun 1 payment demanded in addition to the usual charge. 2 a mark printed over a postage stamp, changing its value. **surcharge** verb 1 to make a surcharge on something; to charge someone extra. 2 to print a surcharge on a stamp.

surd noun (Mathematics) a number or quantity (especially a root) that cannot be expressed in finite terms of whole numbers or quantities; an irrational number. [from a Latin word *surdus* meaning 'deaf' or 'mute']

sure adjective 1 completely confident that you are right, free from doubt. SYNONYMS: certain, definite, positive, convinced. 2 certain to do something or to happen ♦ *The book is sure to be a success.* SYNONYMS: certain, bound. 3 undoubtedly true ♦ *One thing is sure.* 4 completely reliable ♦ *There's only one sure way to do it.* **sure** adverb (informal) certainly ♦ *It sure was cold.* **to make sure** 1 to confirm something ♦ *Just make sure you've locked the door.* 2 to make something happen or be true ♦ *Make sure no one comes in.* **sureness** noun [from an Old French word *sur*; related to *secure*]

sure-fire adjective (informal) certain to succeed.

sure-footed adjective 1 never slipping or stumbling. 2 confident and competent.

surely adverb 1 without doubt, certainly. 2 used for emphasis ♦ *Surely you don't mean that?* 3 (as an answer) certainly, of course ♦ *'Will you help?' 'Surely.'*

surety (**shoor**-ti or **shoor**-ri-ti) noun (**sureties**) 1 a person who promises to pay a debt or fulfil a contract etc. if another person fails to do so. 2 money given as a guarantee that someone will do something. [from an Old French word *surte*; related to *security*]

surf noun the white foam of waves breaking on a rock or shore.
surf verb 1 to stand or lie on a surfboard while being carried on waves to the shore. 2 to spend time moving from site to site on the Internet. **surfer** noun **surfing** noun [origin unknown]

surface noun 1 the outside of something. 2 the uppermost area, the top of a table or desk etc. ♦ *a working surface.* 3 the top of a body of water or other liquid. 4 the outward appearance of something; the qualities perceived by casual observation (as distinct from deeper or hidden ones) ♦ *On the surface he was a charming man.*
surface adjective 1 to do with or on the surface only. 2 to do with or carried by the surface of the earth or sea (as distinct from in the air or underground, or under water).
surface verb 1 to rise or come up to the surface, especially from under water. 2 to become apparent. 3 to put a surface on a road or path. 4 (*informal*) to appear after being asleep. [from a French word]

surface tension noun tension of the surface film of a liquid, tending to make its surface area as small as possible.

surface-to-air adjective (said about a missile) designed to be fired from the ground or a vessel at an aircraft.

surface-to-surface adjective (said about a missile) designed to be fired from the ground or a vessel at another point on the ground or another vessel.

surfboard noun a long narrow board used in surfing.

surfeit (ser-fit) noun too much of something. SYNONYMS: excess, surplus, superfluity, plethora, glut.
surfeit verb to give someone too much of something, especially food. [from *sur-* and a Latin word *facere* meaning 'to do']

surge noun 1 a sudden powerful movement forwards or upwards ♦ *tidal surges.* 2 a sudden increase in something or rush of feeling. SYNONYMS: burst, onrush, upsurge.
surge verb 1 to move forwards or upwards like waves. 2 to increase suddenly and powerfully. [from a Latin word *surgere* meaning 'to rise']

surgeon noun a medical practitioner who performs surgical operations. [same origin as for *surgery*]

surgery noun (**surgeries**) 1 the treatment of injuries, disorders, and disease by cutting or manipulating the affected parts. 2 the place where a doctor or dentist etc. treats or advises patients. 3 the hours during which a doctor or dentist etc. is available to patients at a surgery. 4 the place where an MP, lawyer, etc. is regularly available for consultation. [from a Greek word *kheirourgia* meaning 'handiwork']

surgical adjective 1 to do with or used in surgery. 2 worn to correct an injury, illness, or deformity ♦ *a surgical stocking.* **surgically** adverb

surgical spirit noun methylated spirits used for cleansing the skin before injections or surgery.

surly adjective (**surlier, surliest**) bad-tempered and unfriendly. **surlily** adverb **surliness** noun [originally meaning 'majestic' or 'haughty': from *sir* and *-ly*]

surmise (ser-myz) verb to conclude something without much evidence, to guess something.
surmise noun a guess or conjecture. [from an Old French word *surmettre* meaning 'to accuse']

surmount verb to overcome a difficulty or obstacle. **be surmounted by** to have something on or over the top ♦ *The spire is surmounted by a weather vane.*
surmountable adjective [from an Old French word *surmonter*]

surname noun the name held by all members of a family. [from a French word]

surpass verb to do or be better than all others. SYNONYMS: beat, better, exceed, excel, outdo, outclass, top, eclipse, transcend. [from a French word *surpasser*]

surpassing adjective (*literary*) greatly excelling others, outstanding. **surpassingly** adverb

surplice (ser-plis) noun a loose white vestment, worn over the cassock by clergy and choir at a Christian church service. [from an Old French word *sourpelis*]

surplus (ser-plǝs) noun 1 an amount left over after spending or using all that was needed. 2 the amount by which income is greater than expenditure over a given period.

surplus adjective excess or extra. [from sur- and a Latin word plus meaning 'more']

surprise noun 1 the feeling caused by something unexpected happening. 2 something unexpected. 3 the process of catching a person etc. unprepared ♦ a surprise attack ♦ a surprise visit.
surprise verb 1 to cause someone to feel surprise, to be a surprise to someone. 2 to come upon or attack someone suddenly and without warning. **to take someone by surprise** to happen unexpectedly to someone. **surprised** adjective [from an Old French word surprendre meaning 'to overtake']

surprising adjective causing surprise. **surprisingly** adverb

surreal adjective typical of surrealism; bizarre.

surrealism (sə-ree-əl-izm) noun a 20th-century movement in art and literature that seeks to express what is in the unconscious mind, for example by depicting objects and events as seen in dreams. **surrealist** noun **surrealistic** adjective [from sur- and real]

surrender verb 1 to stop fighting and give yourself up to an enemy or agree that they have won. SYNONYMS: concede, yield, capitulate. 2 to hand something over or give something up, especially on demand or under compulsion ♦ We were ordered to surrender our passports. SYNONYM: relinquish. 3 to let a powerful emotion take control of you ♦ She surrendered herself to grief. SYNONYMS: succumb, submit, yield, give in. 4 to give up your rights under a life insurance policy in return for a smaller sum payable immediately.
surrender noun surrendering, or being surrendered. [from sur- and render]

surreptitious (su-rəp-tish-əs) adjective acting or done stealthily. **surreptitiously** adverb [from a Latin word surrepticius meaning 'seized secretly']

surrogate (su-rə-gət) noun a deputy or substitute. **surrogacy** noun [from a Latin word surrogare meaning 'to elect as a substitute']

surrogate mother noun a woman who carries and gives birth to a baby for a woman who cannot do so herself, using a fertilized egg from the other woman or sperm from the other woman's partner.

surround verb 1 to be all round something. SYNONYMS: encircle, circle, ring, enclose. 2 to move into position all round something ♦ Police quickly surrounded the building. 3 to place something all round something ♦ The new president surrounded himself with trusted advisors. 4 to be associated with something ♦ Controversy surrounds this appointment.
surround noun a border or edging. **to be surrounded by** or **with** to have something on all sides. [from sur- and a Latin word undare meaning 'to rise in waves']

surroundings plural noun the conditions or area around a person or thing.

surtax noun an additional tax, especially on income above a certain level.

surveillance (ser-vayl-əns) noun a close watch kept on a person or thing, especially on a suspected person. [from sur- and a French word veiller meaning 'to watch']

survey[1] (ser-vay) noun 1 a general look at something. 2 a general examination of a situation or subject; an account of this. 3 an investigation of the opinions or experience of a group of people, in which they are asked a series of questions. 4 the surveying of land or property; a map, plan, or report produced by this. [from sur- and a Latin word videre meaning 'to see']

survey[2] (ser-vay) verb 1 to look carefully and thoroughly at something. SYNONYMS: view, examine, assess, inspect, scrutinize. 2 to make or present a survey of something ♦ The report surveys progress made in the past year. 3 to examine and report on the condition of a building etc. 4 to conduct a survey among a group of people. 5 to measure and map out the size, shape, position, and elevation etc. of an area of land.

surveyor noun a person whose job is to survey land or buildings.

survival noun 1 surviving. 2 something that has survived from an earlier time.

survive verb 1 to continue to live or exist. 2 to remain alive or in existence after something ♦ Few flowers survived the frost. 3 to remain alive after someone's death ♦ He is survived by his wife and two children. [from sur- and a Latin word vivere meaning 'to live']

survivor noun someone who has survived.

susceptibility noun being susceptible.

susceptibilities *plural noun* a person's feelings that may be hurt or offended.

susceptible (sə-**sep**-ti-bəl) *adjective* 1 likely to be affected or harmed by something ♦ *She is susceptible to colds.* 2 easily affected by feelings or emotions. 3 open to or capable of something ♦ *Is the charge susceptible of proof?* **susceptibly** *adverb* [from a Latin word *susceptum* meaning 'caught up']

suspect[1] (sə-**spekt**) *verb* 1 to have a feeling that something is likely or possible ♦ *We suspected a trap.* 2 to feel that a person is guilty of something but have little or no proof. 3 to doubt that something is genuine or true ♦ *I can't help but suspect their motives.* [from *sub-* and a Latin word *specere* meaning 'to look']

suspect[2] (**sus**-pekt) *noun* a person who is suspected of a crime or other offence. **suspect** *adjective* possibly dangerous or false; open to suspicion.

suspend *verb* 1 to hang something from somewhere. 2 to put a temporary stop to something. 3 to postpone or delay something ♦ *The committee has decided to suspend judgement.* 4 to remove a person temporarily from a job ♦ *Two officers have been suspended from duty while the investigation takes place.* 5 to keep something from falling or sinking in air or liquid etc. ♦ *Particles are suspended in the fluid.* **to suspend payment** (said about a company) to stop paying any of its debts when it recognizes that it is insolvent and unable to pay them all. [from *sub-* and a Latin word *pendere* meaning 'to hang']

suspended animation *noun* a state in which the vital body functions stop for a time, without actually resulting in death.

suspended sentence *noun* a sentence of imprisonment that is not to be enforced as long as no further offence is committed within a specified period.

suspender *noun* an elastic strap fastened to the top of a stocking to hold it up.

suspender belt *noun* a woman's piece of underwear with suspenders for holding up stockings.

suspense *noun* a state or feeling of anxious uncertainty while waiting for something to happen or become known. [same origin as for *suspend*]

suspension *noun* 1 suspending, or being suspended. 2 the system of springs and shock absorbers by which a vehicle is supported on its axles. 3 a mixture consisting of a fluid containing small pieces of solid material which do not dissolve.

suspension bridge *noun* a bridge suspended from cables that pass over supporting towers near each end.

suspicion *noun* 1 the feeling that someone is guilty of something or that something is wrong ♦ *He was arrested on suspicion of fraud.* 2 a feeling that something is likely or possible ♦ *I have a suspicion that she hasn't told me everything.* 3 a slight trace ♦ *a suspicion of a smile.* **above suspicion** too good or honest to be thought to have done something wrong. **under suspicion** suspected of doing wrong. [same origin as for *suspect*]

suspicious *adjective* 1 feeling suspicion. SYNONYMS: wary, uneasy, sceptical, distrustful. 2 causing suspicion ♦ *a suspicious character.* SYNONYMS: doubtful, dubious, questionable, suspect; (*informal*) fishy, shady. **suspiciously** *adverb*

suss *verb* (*informal*) to understand or realize something. [short for *suspect*]

sustain *verb* 1 to support or strengthen someone, physically or mentally. 2 to keep something going continuously. 3 to undergo or suffer something ♦ *We sustained a heavy defeat.* 4 to confirm or uphold the validity of something ♦ *The objection was sustained.* **sustainable** *adjective* [from *sub-* and a Latin word *tenere* meaning 'to hold']

sustenance (**sus**-tin-əns) *noun* 1 food and drink that sustains life. 2 the process of sustaining life by food. [same origin as for *sustain*]

sutra (**soo**-trə) *noun* 1 a short saying or a collection of these in Hindu literature. 2 a Buddhist or Jainist scripture. [a Sanskrit word meaning 'thread']

suttee (sut-**ee**) *noun* the former Hindu practice of a widow sacrificing herself on her husband's funeral pyre. [from a Sanskrit word *sati* meaning 'faithful wife']

suture (**soo**-cher) *noun* 1 a stitch or thread etc. used to hold together the edges of a wound. 2 surgical stitching of a wound. **suture** *verb* to stitch up a wound. [from a Latin word *sutura* meaning 'sewing']

suzerain (**soo**-zer-ayn) *noun* 1 a country or ruler that has some control over another country which is self-governing in its internal affairs. 2 an overlord in feudal times. **suzerainty** *noun* [from a French word]

svelte (svelt) *adjective* (said about a person) slim and elegant. [via French from an Italian word *svelto*]

SW *abbreviation* south-west or south-western.

swab (swob) *noun* **1** a mop or absorbent pad for cleaning, drying, or mopping things up. **2** a specimen of a fluid from the body taken on a swab for testing.
swab *verb* (**swabbed, swabbing**) to clean or wipe something with a swab. [from a Dutch word]

swaddle (swod-ǝl) *verb* to wrap someone or something in cloth or warm clothes. [from *swathe*²]

swaddling clothes *plural noun* strips of cloth formerly wrapped round a newborn baby to restrain its movements.

swag *noun* **1** (*informal*) money or goods taken by a thief or burglar. **2** a carved ornamental garland of flowers and fruit, hung by its ends. **3** (*Austral.*) a traveller's bundle of personal belongings. [probably from a Scandinavian language]

swagger *verb* to walk or behave in a self-important or arrogant way, to strut.
swagger *noun* a swaggering walk or manner. [probably from a Scandinavian language]

swagman *noun* (**swagmen**) (*Austral.*) a worker who travels from place to place. [from *swag*]

Swahili (swah-hee-li) *noun* **1** a Bantu language widely used in East Africa. **2** a Bantu people of Zanzibar and the adjacent coasts. [from an Arabic word]

swain *noun* (*literary*) a young lover or suitor. [from an Old Norse word *sveinn* meaning 'lad']

swallow¹ *verb* **1** to make food, drink, etc. go down your throat. **2** to work the muscles of the throat in the same way, because of fear or nervousness. **3** to accept or believe something meekly or unquestioningly ♦ *How could anyone swallow that story?* **4** to repress or resist expressing something ♦ *He swallowed a sob* ♦ *She will have to swallow her pride.*
swallow *noun* an act of swallowing something, or the amount swallowed. **to swallow something up** to take something in so as to engulf or absorb it ♦ *She was* swallowed up in the crowd. [from an Old English word *swelgan*]

swallow² *noun* a small migratory insect-eating bird with a forked tail and pointed wings whose arrival in Britain is associated with the beginning of summer. [from an Old English word *swealwe*]

swallow dive *noun* a dive with arms outspread at the start.

swallow-tailed *adjective* having a deeply forked tail.

swam past tense of **swim**.

swami (swah-mi) *noun* (**swamis**) a Hindu religious teacher or holy man. [a Hindi word]

swamp *noun* a bog or marsh.
swamp *verb* **1** to flood a place; to submerge something in water. **2** to overwhelm someone or something with too much of something. **swampy** *adjective* [origin unknown]

swan *noun* a large usually white water bird with a long slender neck.
swan *verb* (**swanned, swanning**) (*informal*) to go around in a casual or showy way ♦ *They've been swanning around the shops all day.* [from an Old English word]

swank *verb* (*informal*) to show off your possessions or achievements in order to impress others.
swank *noun* (*informal*) boastful behaviour, talk, or display. **swanky** *adjective* [origin unknown]

swannery *noun* (**swanneries**) a place where swans are kept or bred.

swansdown *noun* a swan's fine soft down, used for trimmings and powder puffs.

swansong *noun* a person's last performance, achievement, or composition. [from the old belief that a swan sang sweetly when about to die]

swap *verb* (**swapped, swapping**) (*informal*) to exchange one thing for another.
swap *noun* (*informal*) **1** an act of exchanging one thing for another. **2** a thing suitable for swapping. [formerly meaning 'to seal a bargain by slapping each other's hands'; an imitation of the sound]

sward (swawd) *noun* an expanse of short grass. [from an Old English word *sweard* meaning 'skin']

swarf (sworf) *noun* fine chips or filings of wood, metal, etc. [from an Old Norse word *svarf* meaning 'file dust']

swarm[1] *noun* 1 a large number of insects, birds, small animals, or people flying or moving about together. 2 a cluster of honeybees leaving the hive with a queen bee to establish a new home.
swarm *verb* 1 to move in a swarm, to come together in large numbers. 2 (said about bees) to cluster in a swarm. 3 (said about a place) to be crowded or overrun with insects, people, etc. ♦ *The town centre was swarming with tourists*. SYNONYMS: teem, seethe, crawl. [from an Old English word *swearm*]

swarm[2] *verb* **to swarm up** to climb by gripping with your hands and legs. [origin unknown]

swarthy (swor-thi) *adjective* (**swarthier, swarthiest**) having a dark complexion. **swarthiness** *noun* [from an Old English word *swart*]

swashbuckling *adjective* 1 daring; loving adventure and fighting. 2 (said about a film etc.) showing daring adventures set in the past. **swashbuckler** *noun* [from an old word *swash* meaning 'to hit' and *buckler*]

swastika (swos-tik-ə) *noun* an ancient symbol formed by a cross with the ends bent at right angles, adopted (in clockwise form) by the German Nazi party as its emblem. [from a Sanskrit word *svasti* meaning 'well-being']

swat *verb* (**swatted, swatting**) to hit or crush a fly etc. with something flat. **swat** *noun* a sharp blow with a flat object. **swatter** *noun* [originally American, a different spelling of *squat*]

swathe[1] (swawth) *noun* 1 a line of grass, corn, etc. as it falls after being cut. 2 a broad strip or area ♦ *vast swathes of countryside*. **to cut a swathe through** to pass through an area causing destruction or upheaval. [from an Old English word *swathu* meaning 'track' or 'trace']

swathe[2] (swayth) *verb* to wrap a person or thing in layers of bandage, wrappings, or warm clothes. [from an Old English word *swathian*]

sway *verb* 1 to move or swing gently from side to side. 2 to influence the opinions, sympathy, or actions of someone ♦ *His speech swayed many voters*. **sway** *noun* a swaying movement. **to hold**

sway to have great power or influence. [origin unknown]

swear *verb* (**swore, sworn**) 1 to use offensive language, especially because you are angry. 2 to promise something solemnly or on oath ♦ *She swore to tell the truth*. SYNONYMS: vow, pledge, give your word. 3 (*informal*) to state something emphatically ♦ *He swore he hadn't touched it*. 4 to make someone promise to do something ♦ *We swore him to secrecy*. **to swear by** (*informal*) to have or express great confidence in a person or thing. **to swear someone in** to admit someone to an office or position by getting them to take a formal oath. **to swear off** (*informal*) to promise to abstain from something. **to swear to** to guarantee that something is the case ♦ *I wouldn't swear to it*. **swearer** *noun* [from an Old English word *swerian*]

swear word *noun* a word considered offensive or obscene.

sweat *noun* 1 moisture given off by the body through the pores of the skin. 2 a state of sweating or being covered by sweat ♦ *Just thinking about the accident makes me break out in a sweat*. 3 (*informal*) a state of great anxiety. 4 (*informal*) a laborious task.
sweat *verb* 1 to give off sweat; to cause a person or animal to do this. 2 to be in a state of great anxiety. 3 to work long and hard ♦ *I really sweated over that essay*. 4 (said about a substance) to form moisture in drops on the surface, e.g. by condensation. **to sweat blood** (*informal*) to work very hard at something. **to sweat it out** (*informal*) to wait anxiously for something to happen or end. [from an Old English word]

sweatband *noun* a band of absorbent material worn to soak up sweat.

sweated labour *noun* the use of manual workers who have to work for long hours and under poor conditions.

sweater *noun* a jumper or pullover.

sweatshirt *noun* a loose cotton sweater worn for sports or casual wear.

sweatshop *noun* a place where sweated labour is used.

sweaty *adjective* (**sweatier, sweatiest**) damp with sweat.

Swede *noun* a person born in Sweden or descended from people born there.

swede noun a large variety of turnip with purple skin and yellow flesh. [short for Swedish turnip (because it originally came from Sweden)]

Swedish adjective to do with or coming from Sweden.
Swedish noun the language of Sweden.

sweep verb (past tense and past participle **swept**) 1 to clear something away with a broom or brush. 2 to clean or clear a surface or area by doing this. 3 to move or remove something quickly by pushing ♦ The floods swept away the bridge ♦ We were almost swept off our feet by the waves. 4 to remove something swiftly and suddenly ♦ All objections were swept aside. 5 to go smoothly and swiftly ♦ She swept out of the room. 6 to move or travel quickly over or along an area ♦ Winds sweep the hillside ♦ A new fashion is sweeping America. 7 to pass over something, especially when searching for something ♦ Searchlights swept the sky. 8 to extend in a continuous line or slope ♦ The mountains sweep down to the sea. 9 to move over something, touching it lightly ♦ Her gown swept the ground as she walked.
sweep noun 1 a sweeping movement. 2 a sweeping line or slope. 3 the act of sweeping with a broom etc. ♦ Give the drive a good sweep. 4 a chimney sweep. 5 a sweepstake. **to make a clean sweep** 1 to get rid of everything or of all staff etc. in order to start afresh. 2 (also **to sweep the board**) to win all the events or prizes in a contest. [from an Old English word]

sweeper noun 1 a person or device that sweeps ♦ a carpet sweeper. 2 (in football) a player positioned just in front of the goalkeeper and free to defend at any point across the field.

sweeping adjective 1 wide-ranging ♦ The new manager made sweeping changes. 2 (said about a statement) making no exceptions or limitations; too general ♦ sweeping generalizations.
sweepings plural noun dust or scraps etc. collected by sweeping. **sweepingly** adverb

sweepstake noun 1 a form of gambling on sporting events in which all the money staked is divided among the winners. 2 a horse race with betting of this kind.

sweet adjective 1 tasting as if it contains sugar, not sour or bitter. 2 smelling pleasant; fragrant. 3 pleasant to listen to ♦ a sweet song. 4 (said about air, water, etc.) fresh and pure. 5 making you feel pleased and satisfied ♦ Revenge is sweet. 6 attractive and charming ♦ a sweet face. 7 having a pleasant and kind nature.
sweet noun 1 a small shaped piece of sweet food, usually made with sugar or chocolate. 2 a sweet dish forming a course of a meal. **sweetish** adjective **sweetly** adverb **sweetness** noun [from an Old English word]

sweet-and-sour adjective cooked in a sauce containing sugar and a sour substance such as vinegar or lemon.

sweetbread noun an animal's thymus gland or pancreas used as food.

sweetbriar noun a small fragrant wild rose.

sweetcorn noun a type of maize with juicy yellow kernels.

sweeten verb 1 to make something sweet, or to become sweet. 2 to make something more pleasant or acceptable.

sweetener noun 1 a substance used to sweeten food or drink. 2 (informal) something given to induce someone to do something; a bribe.

sweetheart noun 1 a person you are in love with, one of a pair of people in love with each other. 2 used as a term of endearment.

sweetmeal adjective (said about biscuits) sweetened wholemeal.

sweetmeat noun (old use) a sweet or a very small fancy cake. [from an old sense of meat meaning 'food']

sweet pea noun a climbing garden plant with fragrant flowers in many colours.

sweet potato noun a root vegetable with reddish skin and sweet yellow flesh.

sweet-talk verb (informal) to persuade someone to do something by flattering them.

sweet tooth noun a liking for sweet things.

sweet william noun a garden plant with clusters of fragrant flowers.

swell verb (past participle, **swollen** or **swelled**) 1 to make something larger, or to become larger, because of pressure from within; to curve outwards ♦ My ankle was starting to swell. SYNONYMS: bulge, distend, puff up, inflate, billow. 2 to make something or become larger in amount, volume, numbers, or intensity.
swell noun 1 the act or state of swelling. 2 the rise and fall of the sea's surface in waves that do not break. 3 a gradual

increase in sound, amount, or intensity.
4 (*informal*) (*old use*) a stylish person of
high social position.
swell *adjective* (*North Amer.*) (*informal, old
use*) very good. **to swell with pride** to feel
very proud. [from an Old English word
swellan]

swelling *noun* a swollen place on the body.

swelter *verb* to feel uncomfortably hot.
sweltering *adjective* [from an Old English
word]

swept past tense and past participle of
sweep.

swept-wing *noun* (said about an aircraft)
with wings slanting backwards from the
direction of flight.

swerve *verb* to turn or make something
turn to one side suddenly.
swerve *noun* a swerving movement or
direction. [from an Old English word
sweorfan meaning 'to depart' or 'to turn
aside']

swift *adjective* **1** happening quickly or
promptly ♦ *a swift response*. **2** able to move
fast ♦ *a swift runner*.
swift *noun* a swiftly-flying insect-eating
bird with long narrow wings. **swiftly**
adverb **swiftness** *noun* [from an Old English
word]

swig *verb* (**swigged, swigging**) (*informal*) to
drink something quickly, taking large
mouthfuls.
swig *noun* (*informal*) a large mouthful of a
drink. [origin unknown]

swill *verb* **1** to wash or rinse something by
pouring water over or through it. **2** to
drink something in large quantities.
swill *noun* **1** a sloppy mixture of waste
food fed to pigs. **2** (*informal*) disgusting
food or drink. **3** a rinse ♦ *Give it a swill
under the tap*. [from an Old English word
swillan]

swim *verb* (**swam, swum, swimming**) **1** to
move the body through water by
movements of the limbs, fins, or tail etc.
2 to cross a stretch of water by swimming
♦ *the youngest person to swim the Channel*.
3 to float. **4** to be covered with or full of
liquid ♦ *The floor was swimming in water*.
5 to seem to be whirling or waving, to feel
dizzy ♦ *Everything swam before her eyes* ♦ *My
head is swimming*.
swim *noun* **1** a period of swimming ♦ *Let's
go for a swim*. **2** a deep pool in a river
which is a good spot for fishing. **in the
swim** active in or aware of what is going

on. **swimmer** *noun* [from an Old English
word *swimman*]

swimming costume *noun* a bikini or
swimsuit.

swimmingly *adverb* with smooth progress.

swimming pool *noun* an artificial pool for
swimming in.

swimming trunks *plural noun* shorts worn
by men for swimming.

swimsuit *noun* a woman's one-piece
swimming costume.

swimwear *noun* clothing worn for
swimming.

swindle *verb* **1** to cheat someone in a
business transaction. SYNONYMS: defraud;
(*informal*) con, diddle, fleece. **2** to obtain
something by fraud.
swindle *noun* a piece of swindling.
swindler *noun* [from a German word
Schwindler meaning 'a fool or cheat']

swine *plural noun* pigs.
swine *noun* (**swine** or **swines**) (*informal*) **1** a
very unpleasant person. **2** a difficult
thing. [from an Old English word]

swineherd *noun* (*old use*) a person taking
care of a number of pigs.

swing *verb* (past tense and past participle
swung) **1** to move to and fro while
hanging or supported; to make
something do this. **2** to move or make
something move in a curve ♦ *The car
swung into the drive*. **3** to try to hit or punch
someone with a wide curving movement
♦ *He swung at me but I managed to duck*. **4** to
lift or move something with a swinging
movement. **5** to change from one opinion
or mood etc. to another. **6** to have a
decisive influence on an election, a deal,
etc. ♦ *That speech last night may have swung
it for us*. **7** (*informal*) to be executed by
hanging. **8** to play music with a flowing
but vigorous rhythm. **9** to be lively or
exciting.
swing *noun* **1** a seat hung on ropes or
chains so that it can be moved backwards
and forwards. **2** a swinging movement,
action, or rhythm. **3** the amount by which
votes, opinions, or points scored etc.
change from one side to the other. **4** a
kind of jazz music with a flowing but
vigorous rhythm. **to get (back) into the
swing of things** to get used to or return to
an activity or routine. **in full swing** at the
height of activity.

to swing the lead see **lead**². **swinger** *noun* [from an Old English word *swingan* meaning 'to beat or whip']

swingbin *noun* a rubbish bin with a lid that swings shut.

swing bridge *noun* a bridge that can be swung aside to allow ships to pass.

swing door *noun* a door that opens in either direction and closes itself when released.

swingeing (swinj-ing) *adjective* severe or drastic ♦ *a swingeing increase in taxation.* [from an Old English word *swengan* meaning 'to shake']

swinging *adjective* (*informal*) lively and fashionable.

swing-wing *noun* an aircraft wing that can be moved to slant backwards.

swinish *adjective* like a swine.

swipe *verb* (*informal*) 1 to hit or try to hit something with a swinging blow. 2 to steal something, especially by snatching. 3 to slide a swipe card through an electronic device.
swipe *noun* (*informal*) 1 a swinging blow. 2 an attack or criticism. [a different spelling of *sweep*]

swipe card *noun* a plastic card with magnetically encoded information on it which can be read by sliding the card through an electronic device.

swirl *verb* to move round quickly in circles; to make something do this.
swirl *noun* a swirling movement or pattern. [probably from an Old Dutch word]

swish *verb* to move something with a hissing sound.
swish *noun* a swishing sound.
swish *adjective* (*informal*) smart and fashionable. [an imitation of the sound]

Swiss *adjective* to do with or coming from Switzerland.
Swiss *noun* (**Swiss**) a person born in Switzerland or descended from people born there.

Swiss roll *noun* a thin flat sponge cake spread with jam etc. and rolled up.

switch *noun* 1 a device that is pressed or turned to start or stop something working, usually by opening or closing an electric circuit. 2 a shift or change in something. 3 the replacing of one thing with something else, especially in order

to deceive people. 4 a flexible shoot cut from a tree. 5 a tress of real or false hair tied at one end. 6 (*North Amer.*) a railway point.
switch *verb* 1 to turn an electrical or other device on or off by means of a switch. 2 to change over to a different side, method, system, etc. ♦ *Can we switch over to Channel 4?* 3 to replace something with something else; to exchange places ♦ *The blackmailer must have switched the bags somehow.* [probably from an Old German word]

switchback *noun* 1 a road with alternate sharp ascents and descents. 2 a roller coaster.

switchboard *noun* a panel with a set of switches for making telephone connections or operating electric circuits.

swivel *noun* a link or pivot between two parts enabling one of them to revolve without turning the other.
swivel *verb* (**swivelled, swivelling**) to turn round or make something turn round, as if on a swivel ♦ *She swivelled round in her chair to face us.* [from an Old English word]

swivel chair *noun* a chair with a seat that can turn to face in any direction.

swizz or **swizzle** *noun* (*informal*) an instance of being cheated or disappointed. [from *swizzle*, an alteration of *swindle*]

swollen past participle of **swell**.

swoon *verb* to faint.
swoon *noun* a faint. [from an Old English word]

swoop *verb* 1 to come down with a rushing movement like a bird upon its prey. 2 to make a sudden attack.
swoop *noun* a swooping movement or attack. **at one fell swoop** see **fell**⁴. [probably from *sweep*]

swop *verb* (**swopped, swopping**) & *noun* another spelling of **swap**.

sword (sord) *noun* a weapon with a long metal blade and a hilt. [from an Old English word *sweord*]

swordfish *noun* (**swordfish** or **swordfishes**) a large sea fish with a long sword-like upper jaw.

swordsman *noun* (**swordsmen**) a person who fights or is skilful with a sword.
swordsmanship *noun*

swordstick *noun* a hollow walking stick containing a blade that can be used as a sword.

swore past tense of **swear**.

sworn past participle of **swear**.
　sworn *adjective* **1** given under oath ♦ *sworn testimony*. **2** determined to remain so ♦ *They are sworn enemies*.

swot *verb* (**swotted, swotting**) (*informal*) to study hard.
　swot *noun* (*informal*) a person who spends a lot of time studying. [a dialect word for *sweat*]

swum past participle of **swim**.

swung past tense and past participle of **swing**.

sybarite (**sib-er-riyt**) *noun* a person who is excessively fond of comfort and luxury. **sybaritic** (**sib-er-it-ik**) *adjective* [from Sybaris, an ancient Greek city in southern Italy, noted for its luxury]

sycamore (**sik-ə-mor**) *noun* a tall tree with winged seeds, often grown for its timber. [from a Greek word *sukomoros*]

sycophant (**sik-ə-fant**) *noun* a person who tries to win people's favour by flattering them. **sycophancy** *noun* **sycophantic** (**sik-ə-fan-tik**) *adjective* **sycophantically** *adverb* [from a Greek word *sukophantēs* meaning 'informer']

syllabic (**sil-ab-ik**) *adjective* to do with or in syllables. **syllabically** *adverb*

syllable (**sil-ə-bəl**) *noun* a word or part of a word that has one vowel sound when you say it, with or without surrounding consonants. There are two syllables in 'without', three in 'consonant', and one in 'say'. [from Greek words *sun-* meaning 'together' and *lambanein* meaning 'to take']

syllabub (**sil-ə-bub**) *noun* a dessert made of sweetened whipped cream, usually flavoured with wine or sherry. [origin unknown]

syllabus (**sil-ə-bəs**) *noun* (**syllabuses**) a summary of the subjects that are included in a course of study. [from a Greek word *sittuba* meaning 'title slip' or 'label']

syllogism (**sil-ə-jizm**) *noun* a form of reasoning in which a conclusion is reached from two statements, as in ♦ *'All men must die; I am a man; therefore I must die'*. [from *syn-* and a Greek word *logos* meaning 'reason']

sylph (silf) *noun* a slender girl or woman. **sylphlike** *adjective* [probably from a Latin phrase *sylvestris nympha* meaning 'nymph of the woods']

symbiosis (**sim-bi-oh-sis**) *noun* **1** (*Biology*) an association of two different organisms living attached to each other or one within the other, usually to the advantage of both. **2** a similar relationship between people or groups. **symbiotic** (**sim-bi-ot-ik**) *adjective* [from a Greek word *sumbiōsis* meaning 'living together']

symbol *noun* **1** a thing thought of as representing or standing for something else ♦ *The cross is a symbol of Christianity* ♦ *The lion is the symbol of courage*. SYNONYMS: emblem, sign, mark. **2** a mark or sign with a special meaning, such as mathematical signs (e.g. + and – for addition and subtraction), letters representing chemical elements, or written forms of notes in music. [from a Greek word *sumbolon* meaning 'token'] ◊ Do not confuse this word with **cymbal**, which has a different meaning.

symbolic *adjective* to do with, using, or used as a symbol. **symbolical** *adjective* **symbolically** *adverb*

symbolism *noun* the use of symbols to represent things. **symbolist** *noun* & *adjective*

symbolize *verb* **1** to be a symbol of something. **2** to represent something by means of a symbol. **symbolization** *noun*

symmetrical (**sim-et-rik-əl**) *adjective* able to be divided into parts that are the same in size and shape and similar in position on either side of a dividing line (**line symmetry**) or a central point (**radial symmetry** or **rotational symmetry**). **symmetrically** *adverb* [from *syn-* and a Greek word *metron* meaning 'a measure']

symmetry (**sim-it-ri**) *noun* **1** being symmetrical. **2** pleasing proportion between parts of a whole. **3** similarity or exact correspondence.

sympathetic *adjective* **1** feeling, expressing, or resulting from sympathy. **2** likeable ♦ *He's not a sympathetic character*. **3** showing approval or support ♦ *He is sympathetic to our plan*. **sympathetically** *adverb*

sympathize *verb* **1** to feel or show sympathy. **2** to agree with an opinion or sentiment. **sympathizer** *noun*

sympathy noun (**sympathies**) 1 a feeling of pity or tenderness towards someone suffering pain, grief, or trouble. 2 the sharing or understanding of another person's feelings or sensations. 3 liking for each other produced in people who have similar opinions or tastes. **to be in sympathy with** to feel approval of an opinion or desire. [from *syn-* and a Greek word *pathos* meaning 'feeling']

symphonic (sim-fon-ik) *adjective* to do with or like a symphony. **symphonically** *adverb*

symphonic poem noun another term for **tone poem**.

symphony (sim-fǝn-i) noun (**symphonies**) a long elaborate musical composition (usually in several movements) for a full orchestra. [from *syn-* and a Greek word *phōnē* meaning 'sound']

symphony orchestra noun a large classical orchestra.

symposium (sim-poh-ziǝm) noun (**symposia** or **symposiums**) a meeting or conference to discuss a particular subject. [originally denoting a drinking party held in ancient Greece, from a Greek word *sumpotēs* meaning 'fellow drinker']

symptom noun 1 (*Medicine*) a perceptible change from what is normal in the body or its functioning, indicating the existence of a condition or disease ♦ *Red spots are a symptom of measles.* 2 an indication of something undesirable. [from a Greek word *sumptōma* meaning 'chance or accident']

symptomatic (simp-tǝm-at-ik) *adjective* serving as a symptom.

syn- prefix (changing to **syl-** or **sym-** before certain consonants) 1 with, together (as in *synchronize*). 2 alike (as in *synonym*). [from a Greek word *sun* meaning 'with']

synagogue (sin-ǝ-gog) noun a building for public Jewish worship. [from a Greek word *sunagōgē* meaning 'assembly']

synapse (sy-naps) noun (*Biology*) a gap between two nerve cells, across which impulses are transmitted. **synaptic** *adjective* [from Greek words *sun-* meaning 'together' and *hapsis* meaning 'joining']

sync or **synch** (sink) noun (*informal*) synchronization.

synchromesh (sink-roh-mesh) noun a device that makes parts of a gear revolve at the same speed while they are being brought into contact. [shortened from *synchronized mesh*]

synchronic (sink-ron-ik) *adjective* concerned with a subject as it exists at a particular time, not with the way it has developed through time. **synchronically** *adverb*

synchronicity (sink-rǝ-nis-it-ee) noun when two things happen simultaneously and there is no obvious causal link between them.

synchronism (sink-rǝn-izm) noun another term for **synchrony**.

synchronize (sink-rǝ-niyz) verb 1 to make things happen or operate at the same time or rate. 2 to make watches or clocks show the same time. **synchronization** noun **synchronizer** noun [from *syn-* and a Greek word *khronos* meaning 'time']

synchronized swimming noun a sport in which teams of swimmers perform the same coordinated movements in time to music.

synchronous (sink-rǝn-ǝs) *adjective* 1 existing or happening at the same time. 2 operating at the same rate and simultaneously.

synchrony (sink-rǝn-ee) noun 1 acting or happening simultaneously. 2 synchronic treatment.

syncopate (sink-ǝ-payt) verb to change the beats or accents in a passage of music by making the strong beats weak ones, and vice versa. **syncopated** *adjective* **syncopation** noun [from a Latin word]

syncope (sink-ǝ-pi) noun (*Medicine*) fainting caused by low blood pressure. [from *syn-* and a Greek word *koptein* meaning 'to cut off']

syncretism (sink-rǝt-izm) noun the combining of different beliefs or principles. [from a Greek word]

syndicate[1] (sin-dik-ǝt) noun 1 a group of people or firms who work together in business. 2 a group of people who gamble together, sharing the cost and any gains. [from *syn-* and a Greek word *dikē* meaning 'judgement']

syndicate[2] (sin-dik-ayt) verb 1 to sell a story, photograph, cartoon strip, etc. to several newspapers and periodicals for simultaneous publication. 2 to manage something by a syndicate. **syndication** noun

syndrome (sin-drohm) noun 1 a group of symptoms that together indicate the presence of a disease or abnormal condition. **2** a combination of opinions, behaviour, etc. that are characteristic of a particular condition. [from *syn-* and a Greek word *dramein* meaning 'to run']

synergy (sin-ə-jee) *noun* the cooperation of two or more organizations etc. to produce a combined effect that is greater than the sum of their separate effects. [from a Greek word *sunergos* meaning 'working together']

synod (sin-əd) *noun* a council of senior members of the clergy or church officials (and sometimes also lay people) to discuss questions of policy, teaching, etc. [from a Greek word *sunodos* meaning 'meeting']

synonym (sin-ə-nim) *noun* a word or phrase that means the same or almost the same as another word or phrase in the same language. 'Large' and 'great' are synonyms of 'big'. [from *syn-* and a Greek word *onoma* meaning 'name']

synonymous (sin-on-im-əs) *adjective* (said about a word or phrase) having the same or almost the same meaning as another word or phrase in the same language.

synopsis (sin-op-sis) *noun* (**synopses**) a brief summary of something. [from *syn-* and a Greek word *opsis* meaning 'seeing']

synoptic (sin-op-tik) *adjective* **1** to do with or forming a synopsis. **2** to do with the **Synoptic Gospels**, those of Matthew, Mark, and Luke which have many similarities.

synovial (siy-noh-vi-əl) *adjective* denoting a type of joint surrounded by a thick membrane containing a thick sticky fluid that lubricates the joint. [from a modern Latin word *synovia*]

syntax (sin-taks) *noun* **1** the way in which words are arranged to form phrases and sentences. **2** (*Computing*) the structure of statements in a computer language. **syntactic** (sin-**tak**-tik) *adjective* **syntactically** *adverb* [from *syn-* and a Greek word *taxis* meaning 'arrangement']

synthesis (sin-thi-sis) *noun* (**syntheses**) **1** the combining of separate parts or elements to form a complex whole. **2** the combining of substances to form a compound; artificial production of a substance that occurs naturally in plants or animals. [from *syn-* and a Greek word *thesis* meaning 'placing']

synthesize (sin-thi-siyz) *verb* **1** to make something by synthesis. **2** to produce sound electronically.

synthesizer *noun* an electronic musical instrument operated by a keyboard and able to reproduce the musical tones of conventional instruments or produce a variety of artificial ones.

synthetic *adjective* **1** made by chemical synthesis; artificially made, not natural ♦ *synthetic rubber.* SYNONYMS: artificial, man-made. **2** (*informal*) not genuine or natural ♦ *decorated in synthetic Tudor style.* **synthetic** *noun* a synthetic substance or fabric, e.g. nylon. **synthetically** *adverb* [same origin as for *synthesis*]

syphilis (sif-i-lis) *noun* a serious venereal disease that if untreated can affect the bones, muscles, and brain. [from Syphilus, the name of a character in a poem of 1530 who is portrayed as the first sufferer of the disease]

syphon *noun & verb* another spelling of **siphon**.

syringe (sə-rinj) *noun* **1** a device for drawing in liquid and forcing it out again in a fine stream. **2** a hypodermic syringe. **syringe** *verb* to spray liquid into or over something with a syringe. [from a Greek word *surinx* meaning 'pipe or tube']

syrinx (si-rinks) *noun* the part of a bird's throat where its song is produced. [same origin as for *syringe*]

syrup *noun* a thick sweet liquid; water in which sugar is dissolved. **syrupy** *adjective* [from an Arabic word meaning 'a drink']

system *noun* **1** a set of connected things or parts that form a whole or work together ♦ *a railway system* ♦ *the nervous system.* **2** an organized scheme or method. SYNONYMS: approach, process, procedure, technique, method, methodology, routine. **3** a method of classification or notation or measurement etc. ♦ *the metric system.* **4** orderliness, being systematic ♦ *She works without system.* **5** a set of rules, principles, or practices forming a particular philosophy or form of government etc. **to get something out of your system** to be rid of its effects. [from a Greek word *sustēma* meaning 'setting up']

systematic *adjective* methodical, according to a plan or system and not casually or at random. **systematically** *adverb* [same origin as for *system*]

systematize (sis-təm-ə-tiyz) *verb* to arrange something according to a system. **systematization** *noun*

systemic (sis-**tem**-ik) *adjective* 1 to do with or affecting the body or a system as a whole. 2 (said about a fungicide etc.) entering a plant by way of the roots or shoots and passing into the tissues. **systemically** *adverb*

systemize *verb* another word for **systematize**. **systemization** *noun*

systems analysis *noun* analysis of a complex process or operation in order to decide how computers may be used to perform it more efficiently.

systems analyst *noun* an expert in systems analysis.

systole (sis-**tǝl**-i) *noun* the rhythmical contraction of chambers of the heart, alternating with diastole to form the pulse (compare **diastole**). **systolic** (sis-**tol**-ik) *adjective* [from a Greek word *sustellein* meaning 'to contract']

Tt

T the twentieth letter of the English alphabet.

T *abbreviation* 1 tera- (10^{12}). 2 tesla.

TA *abbreviation* Territorial Army.

Ta *abbreviation* (*Chemistry*) the symbol for tantalum.

ta *interjection* (*informal*) thank you.

tab *noun* a small flap or strip that sticks out, especially for getting hold of something or for putting information about it or identifying it.
tab *verb* (**tabbed, tabbing**) to provide something with tabs. **keep a tab** or **tabs on** (*informal*) to keep account of something or keep it under observation. [origin unknown]

tabard (**tab**-ard) *noun* 1 a short kind of tunic open at the sides, worn by a herald and decorated with the sovereign's coat of arms. 2 a jerkin shaped like this. [from an Old French word *tabart*]

tabby *noun* (**tabbies**) a cat with grey or dark brown fur and dark stripes. [from an earlier meaning 'a kind of striped material', named after al-Attabiyya, a district of Baghdad, where it was made]

tabernacle *noun* 1 (in the Bible) the portable shrine used by the Israelites during their wanderings in the wilderness. 2 (in the Roman Catholic Church) an ornamental receptacle or cabinet containing the consecrated elements of the Eucharist. 3 a meeting place for worship used by Nonconformists (e.g. Baptists) or Mormons. [from a Latin word *tabernaculum* meaning 'tent or shed']

tabla *noun* a pair of small Indian drums played with the hands. [from an Arabic word *tabl* meaning 'drum']

table *noun* 1 a piece of furniture with a flat top supported on one or more legs. 2 food provided in a household or restaurant. 3 a list of facts or figures systematically arranged, especially in columns. 4 (*Architecture*) a flat vertical surface.
table *verb* to put forward a proposal for discussion at a meeting. **on the table** put forward for consideration or discussion. **to turn the tables** to reverse a situation and put yourself at an advantage in relation to someone else. [from a Latin word *tabula* meaning 'plank']

tableau (**tab**-loh) *noun* (**tableaux** (**tab**-lohz)) a dramatic or picturesque scene, especially a group of still figures representing a scene on a stage. [a French word meaning 'little table']

tablecloth *noun* a cloth for covering a table, especially at meals.

table d'hôte (tahbl **doht**) *noun* a restaurant meal served at a fixed price. [a French phrase, meaning 'host's table']

tableland *noun* a high level region of land, a plateau.

table manners *plural noun* behaviour that is socially acceptable while eating a meal.

tablespoon *noun* a large spoon for serving food. **tablespoonful** *noun* (**tablespoonfuls**)

tablet *noun* 1 a slab or panel bearing an inscription or picture, especially one fixed to a wall as a memorial. 2 a small measured amount of a medicine or drug compressed into a solid form, a pill. 3 a small flattish piece of a solid substance such as soap. SYNONYMS: bar, block, cake. [from an Old French word *tablete* meaning 'small table or slab', related to *table*]

table tennis *noun* a game played with bats and a light hollow ball on a table with a net across it.

tabloid *noun* a newspaper having pages that are half the size of broadsheet newspapers, usually popular in style with many photographs and large headlines. [originally the trade name for a type of pill, later 'something in a more compact form than usual']

taboo *noun* a ban or prohibition on something that is regarded by religion or custom as not to be done, used, spoken, etc.
taboo *adjective* prohibited by a taboo ♦ *taboo words.* [from a Tongan word *tabu* meaning 'sacred']

tabor (tay-ber) *noun* (*historical*) a small drum formerly used to accompany a pipe. [from an Old French word *tabour* meaning 'drum']

tabular (tab-yoo-ler) *adjective* arranged or displayed in a table or in columns.

tabulate (tab-yoo-layt) *verb* to arrange figures or other information in a table or in columns. **tabulation** *noun*

tabulator *noun* a device on a typewriter or word processor for moving to a set position across the page in tabular work.

tachograph (tak-ə-grahf) *noun* a device that automatically records the speed and travelling time of a motor vehicle in which it is fitted. [from a Greek word *takhos* meaning 'speed' and *-graph*]

tachometer (tə-kom-it-er) *noun* an instrument for measuring the speed of a vehicle's engine. [from a Greek word *takhos* meaning 'speed' and *meter*]

tacit (tas-it) *adjective* implied or understood without being put into words ♦ *We understood their silence to mean tacit approval.* **tacitly** *adverb* [from a Latin word *tacitus* meaning 'silent']

taciturn (tas-i-tern) *adjective* saying very little, reserved and uncommunicative. **taciturnity** (tas-i-tern-iti) *noun* [same origin as for *tacit*]

tack [1] *noun* 1 a small nail with a broad flat head. 2 a long stitch used to hold fabric in position lightly or temporarily. 3 (in sailing) the direction of a ship's course as determined by the position of its sails; a temporary oblique course followed to take advantage of a wind. 4 a course of action or policy ♦ *We seem to be on the wrong tack.*
tack *verb* 1 to nail something with a tack or tacks. 2 to stitch fabric temporarily with long stitches. 3 to add something as

an extra ♦ *A service charge had been tacked on to the bill.* 4 (in sailing) to follow a zigzag course to take advantage of a wind; to make a tack or tacks. [from an Old French word *tache* meaning 'a clasp' or 'a large nail']

tack [2] *noun* riding equipment including harness, saddles, etc. [from *tackle* meaning 'equipment']

tackle *noun* 1 a set of ropes and pulleys for lifting weights or working a ship's sails. 2 equipment for a task or sport, especially fishing. 3 the act of tackling in football or hockey.
tackle *verb* 1 to intercept another player and try to get the ball in football or hockey. 2 to open a discussion with someone on a difficult or awkward matter. 3 to try to deal with or overcome something difficult or awkward.
SYNONYMS: deal with, attend to, sort out, face up to, have a go at. **tackler** *noun* [probably from an early German word *taken* meaning 'to lay hold of']

tacky [1] *adjective* (tackier, tackiest) (said about paint, glue, etc.) slightly sticky, not quite dry. **tackiness** *noun* [from *tack*[1]]

tacky [2] *adjective* (tackier, tackiest) (*informal*) cheaply made, in poor taste. [from an earlier (American) meaning denoting a worthless horse]

tact *noun* skill and care in dealing with people sensitively and not offending them. SYNONYMS: understanding, diplomacy, discretion, sensitivity. [from a Latin word *tactus* meaning 'sense of touch']

tactful *adjective* having or showing tact. SYNONYMS: diplomatic, discreet, sensitive, considerate, polite. **tactfully** *adverb*

tactic *noun* a piece of tactics.

tactical *adjective* 1 to do with tactics, especially as distinct from strategy. (Compare **strategic**.) 2 (said about weapons) intended to support the immediate needs of a military operation. 3 (said about voting in elections) intended to prevent a strong candidate from winning rather than to support a candidate for reasons based on principle. **tactically** *adverb*

tactician (tak-tish-ən) *noun* an expert in tactics.

tactics *plural noun* 1 the organization and deployment of military forces in battle. 2 the methods used to achieve something. [from a Greek word *taktika* meaning 'things arranged']

◊ Note that *tactics* refers to arrangements made for a particular objective, whereas *strategy* refers to a broader plan or policy. Both words originally relate to military activities and have been extended in use to refer to general situations.

tactile (tak-tyil) *adjective* to do with or involving the sense of touch ♦ *tactile organs.* [from a Latin word *tactum* meaning 'touched']

tactless *adjective* having or showing a lack of tact. SYNONYMS: undiplomatic, indiscreet, insensitive, inconsiderate, thoughtless, impolite. **tactlessly** *adverb* **tactlessness** *noun*

tadpole *noun* the larva of a frog or toad at the stage when it lives in water and has gills and a tail. [from old words *tad* meaning 'toad' and *poll* meaning 'head']

taffeta *noun* a shiny silk-like dress fabric. [from a Persian word *taftan* meaning 'to shine']

tag[1] *noun* 1 a label attached or stuck to something to identify it or give information about it. 2 a metal or plastic point fixed to the end of a shoelace. 3 a stock phrase or often repeated quotation. 4 a loose or ragged end or projection. **tag** *verb* (**tagged, tagging**) 1 to label something with a tag. 2 to attach something or add it as an extra thing ♦ *A postscript was tagged on to her letter.* 3 (*informal*) to follow or trail behind. **to tag along** (*informal*) to go along with another person or group, especially without being asked. [origin unknown]

tag[2] *noun* a children's game in which one chases the rest, and anyone who is caught becomes the next chaser. [origin unknown]

tagliatelle (tahl-yah-**tel**-i) *plural noun* pasta in ribbon-shaped strips. [an Italian word, from *tagliare* meaning 'to cut']

t'ai chi ch'uan or **t'ai chi** (tiy-chee-**chwahn**-ə) *noun* a Chinese martial art and system of exercises. [from Chinese words meaning 'great ultimate boxing']

taiga (**tiy**-gə) *noun* swampy coniferous forest lying between tundra and steppe, especially in Siberia. [from a Russian word *taiga*, from Mongolian]

tail *noun* 1 the hindmost part of an animal, especially when this extends beyond the rest of the body. 2 something resembling an animal's tail in shape or position; the rear part of something, or a part that

hangs down or behind. 3 (*informal*) a person who is following or shadowing another.
tail *verb* 1 to remove the stalks of fruit or vegetables. 2 (*informal*) to follow someone closely. **on someone's tail** following someone closely. **to tail away** or **off** to become fewer, smaller, or slighter; to fall behind in a straggling line; (said about remarks etc.) to end inconclusively. **to turn tail** see **turn**. **with your tail between your legs** (*informal*) feeling dejected or humiliated. [from an Old English word *tægel*]

tailback *noun* a long line of traffic stretching back from an obstruction.

tailboard *noun* a door or flap at the back of a cart or lorry, which opens downwards.

tailcoat *noun* a man's coat with a long skirt cut away at the front and tapering and divided at the back, worn as part of formal evening or morning dress.

tailgate *noun* 1 a door at the back of an estate car or hatchback, hinged at the top. 2 a tailboard.

tailless *adjective* having no tail.

tail light or **tail lamp** *noun* a red light at the back of a vehicle or bicycle.

tailor *noun* a person who makes men's clothes.
tailor *verb* 1 to make or fit clothes as a tailor. 2 to make or adapt something for a special purpose ♦ *The new offices are tailored to our needs.* [from an early French word *taillour*, from a Latin word *taliare* meaning 'to cut']

tailor-made *adjective* 1 made by a tailor for a particular person. 2 specially made or suited for a purpose.

tailpipe *noun* the exhaust pipe of a motor vehicle.

tailplane *noun* the horizontal surface of the tail of an aircraft.

tails *plural noun* 1 a tailcoat, or a set of evening dress including a tailcoat. 2 the side of a coin without the head on it, turned upwards after being tossed.

tailspin *noun* a spiral dive made by an aircraft with the tail making wider circles than the front.

tailwind *noun* a wind blowing from behind a vehicle or aircraft, in the direction of its travel.

taint *noun* a trace of a bad quality or condition. SYNONYMS: blemish, blot, flaw.

taint *verb* to affect something with a taint. SYNONYMS: blemish, tarnish, blot. [from an early French word *teint* meaning 'tinged']

take *verb* (**took, taken**) **1** to get something into your hands by effort ♦ *Take a leaflet if you need more information.* SYNONYMS: grasp, get hold of, seize, grab. **2** to remove something from its place, to steal something ♦ *Who has taken my pen?* SYNONYMS: steal, pick up, remove; (*informal*) swipe, pinch, nick. **3** to get possession of something, to capture or win something or someone ♦ *The soldiers took many prisoners.* SYNONYMS: capture, seize; arrest, detain, abduct, kidnap. **4** to win or achieve something ♦ *She took first prize.* SYNONYMS: win, achieve, gain. **5** to obtain something after fulfilling the conditions needed ♦ *to take a degree.* **6** to be successful or effective ♦ *The inoculation did not take.* SYNONYMS: work, take effect. **7** to subtract one number from another. SYNONYMS: subtract, deduct. **8** to make use of something ♦ *to take a seat* ♦ *to take an opportunity* ♦ *to take a holiday.* **9** to occupy a position, especially as your right. **10** to use something as a means of transport ♦ *Let's take the train.* SYNONYMS: catch, use. **11** to use something habitually ♦ *Which newspaper do you take?* ♦ *I don't take sugar in tea.* **12** to eat a meal ♦ *We'll take tea now.* SYNONYMS: eat, have. **13** to have something as a requirement ♦ *It takes a strong man to lift that.* SYNONYMS: need, require, call for. **14** to carry or remove something to a place ♦ *Please take these letters to the post.* SYNONYMS: convey, carry. **15** to accompany someone, or make them go with you ♦ *I'll take you to the station.* SYNONYMS: accompany, escort. **16** to experience or exert a feeling or effort ♦ *She took pity on him* ♦ *Do take care.* **17** to find out and record information ♦ *The police officer took his name* ♦ *I'll take your measurements.* **18** to interpret something in a certain way ♦ *I take it that you are satisfied.* **19** to accept or deal with something ♦ *The corner shop doesn't take credit cards.* **20** to accept something in a certain way ♦ *They took the news well.* **21** to accept or endure something ♦ *We will just have to take the consequences.* SYNONYMS: accept, put up with, endure, suffer. **22** to perform or deal with something ♦ *to take a decision* ♦ *to take an exam* ♦ *He took the corner too fast.* **23** to make a photograph with a camera.

take *noun* **1** a scene or sequence of actions photographed at one time, in making a cinema or television film. **2** the amount of game or fish taken or caught in one session. **to be taken by** or **with someone** or **something** to find someone or something attractive. **to be taken ill** to become ill. **to take after** to resemble a parent etc. **to take against** to begin to dislike someone or something. **to take something away 1** to remove something or carry it away. **2** to subtract an amount from a total. SYNONYMS: subtract, deduct. **to take someone back** to make a person think back to a past time. **to take something back** to withdraw something you have said. **to take something down 1** to write down words that are spoken. **2** to remove a building or structure by demolishing it. **to take someone in 1** to provide someone with accommodation in your house. **2** to deceive or cheat someone. SYNONYMS: deceive, fool, cheat. **to take something in 1** to understand something. **2** to visit a place briefly during a longer journey ♦ *We could take in Naples on the way south.* **3** to make a piece of clothing tighter. **to take it into your head** to decide to do something impulsively or unexpectedly. **to take it out of** to exhaust the strength of someone. **to take it out on** to relieve a feeling of frustration by attacking or maltreating someone. **to take it upon yourself** to undertake or assume a responsibility. **to take someone's life** to kill someone. **to take off 1** (said about an aircraft) to leave the ground and become airborne. **2** (*informal*) to leave abruptly. **3** (*informal*) to become successful. **to take someone off** to mimic someone. SYNONYMS: mimic, caricature, mock, parody. **to take something off** to remove a piece of clothing from the body. **to take on** (*informal*) to show feeling or emotion. **to take someone on 1** to give someone a job. **2** to agree to compete with someone in a game etc. **to take something on** to agree to do work or accept a responsibility. **to take your time** to do something at a comfortable pace without hurrying. **to take someone out** to escort someone on a date or outing. **to take something out** to pay for a business service, especially an insurance policy. **to take something over** to take control of a business or activity. **to take part** to share in an activity. **to take place** to happen or occur. SYNONYMS: happen, occur, come about, be held. **to take sides** to support one side in a dispute or disagreement. **to take stock 1** to make an inventory of the stock in a shop etc. **2** to examine your position and resources. **to**

take to doing something to begin to do something as a habit. **to take to someone or something** to form a liking for someone or something. **to take to something 1** to develop an ability for something. **2** to go to a place to hide or take refuge ♦ *The bandits took to the hills.* **to take to pieces** to separate something into the pieces from which it was made. SYNONYMS: dismantle, take apart. **to take someone up** to adopt someone as a protégé. **to take someone up on something** to accept someone's offer or challenge. **to take something up 1** to begin to pursue an interest or activity. **2** to accept an offer. **3** to begin to hold a post or position. **4** to occupy time or space. **5** to investigate or pursue a matter further ♦ *We will take up your complaints and let you know the outcome.* **6** to shorten a piece of clothing. **to take up with someone** to begin to associate with someone. [via Old English from an Old Norse word *taka* meaning 'to lay hold of']

takeaway *noun* **1** a place that sells cooked meals for customers to take away. **2** a meal from a takeaway.

take-home pay *noun* the amount an employee receives in wages after tax and insurance have been deducted.

take-off *noun* **1** the process by which an aircraft becomes airborne. **2** an act of mimicking.

takeover *noun* the act of taking control of something, especially of one business company by another.

taker *noun* a person who takes or accepts something, especially a bet ♦ *There are no takers.*

taking *adjective* (*old use*) attractive or charming.

takings *plural noun* money taken for goods or services, receipts.

talc *noun* **1** a soft smooth mineral that is powdered for use as a lubricant. **2** talcum powder. [via Latin from an Arabic word *talk*]

talcum powder *noun* powdered and scented talc for use on the skin to make it feel smooth and dry.

tale *noun* a narrative or story, especially one imaginatively told. SYNONYMS: story, narrative, account. [from an Old English word *talu*]

talent *noun* **1** a great or special natural

ability. SYNONYMS: ability, aptitude, gift, flair. **2** a unit of money used in certain ancient countries. [via Latin from a Greek word *talanton* meaning 'sum of money']

talented *adjective* having a natural talent or skill.

talisman (tal-iz-mən) *noun* (**talismans**) an object supposed to bring good luck. **talismanic** *adjective* [from a Greek word *telesma* meaning 'consecrated object']

talk *verb* **1** to use spoken words to convey ideas, to hold a conversation. SYNONYMS: speak, converse, chat; (*informal*) natter. **2** to express or utter something in words ♦ *You are talking nonsense.* **3** to speak in a particular language ♦ *I think they are talking Urdu.* **4** to influence or persuade someone by talking ♦ *She talked him into marrying her.* **5** to give away information ♦ *Do you think he'll talk?* **6** (*informal*) to be specifically concerned with something ♦ *We are talking big money here.*
talk *noun* **1** talking or conversation. **2** an informal lecture. **3** rumour or gossip ♦ *There is talk of an autumn election.* **4** talking or promises without action or results. **to talk someone down** to silence someone by talking loudly or persistently. **to talk down to** to speak to someone in condescendingly simple language. **to talk something over** to discuss something. SYNONYMS: discuss, debate, confer about. **to talk through one's hat** to talk nonsense. **talker** *noun* [from a Germanic language, related to *tale* and *tell*]

talkative *adjective* (*informal*) talking very much. SYNONYMS: garrulous, loquacious; (*informal*) chatty.

talking-to *noun* (*informal*) a scolding or reprimand.

tall *adjective* **1** of more than average height. SYNONYMS: (building) high, lofty; (person) big, lanky. **2** having a certain height ♦ *He is six feet tall.* **tall order** (*informal*) a difficult thing to do. **a tall story** (*informal*) a story that is difficult to believe and probably untrue. **tallness** *noun* [from earlier meanings 'swift' and 'bold', probably from an Old English word]

tallboy *noun* a tall chest of drawers.

tallish *adjective* rather tall.

tallow *noun* animal fat used to make candles, soap, lubricants, etc. [from a Germanic language]

tally *noun* (**tallies**) the total amount of a debt or score.

tally *verb* (**tallies, tallied, tallying**) to agree or correspond ♦ *The two witnesses' stories do not tally.* SYNONYMS: agree, correspond, match, square. [via French from a Latin word *talea* meaning 'twig' or 'cutting']

tally-ho *interjection* a huntsman's cry to the hounds on sighting a fox.

Talmud (tal-məd) *noun* a collection of ancient writings on Jewish civil and religious law and tradition. [from a Hebrew word meaning 'instruction']

talon (tal-ən) *noun* a claw, especially of a bird of prey. [from a Latin word *talus* meaning 'ankle bone' or 'heel']

tamarind (tam-er-ind) *noun* **1** the fruit of a tropical tree, with a sour pulp. **2** this tree. [from an Arabic word *tamr-hindi* meaning 'Indian date']

tamarisk (tam-er-isk) *noun* a shrub or small tree with feathery branches and spikes of pink or white flowers. [from a Latin word *tamarix*]

tambour (tam-boor) *noun* **1** a small drum. **2** a circular frame for holding fabric taut while it is being embroidered. [a French word meaning 'drum']

tambourine (tam-ber-**een**) *noun* a percussion instrument like a shallow drum, with metal discs in slots round the edge, played by being shaken or hit with the hand. [a diminutive form of *tambour*]

tame *adjective* **1** (said about an animal) gentle and not afraid of human beings, not wild or dangerous. SYNONYMS: friendly, domesticated. **2** docile. SYNONYMS: docile, gentle. **3** not exciting or interesting. SYNONYMS: dull, uninteresting, feeble, boring. **tame** *verb* to make an animal or person tame or manageable. SYNONYMS: domesticate, train. **tameable** *adjective* **tamely** *adverb* **tameness** *noun* **tamer** *noun* [from an Old English word *tam*]

Tamil (tam-il) *noun* **1** a member of a people of southern India and Sri Lanka. **2** the language of the Tamils.

tam-o'-shanter *noun* a round Scottish cap with a bobble in the middle. [named after Tam o'Shanter, hero of a poem by Robert Burns]

tamp *verb* to pack something or ram it down tightly. [from a French word, related to *tampon*]

tamper *verb* to meddle or interfere with something. SYNONYMS: meddle, interfere, tinker. [another form of *temper*]

tampon *noun* a plug of absorbent material that a woman inserts into her vagina to absorb blood during her menstrual period. [from a French word *tampon* or *tapon* meaning 'plug']

tan¹ *verb* (**tanned, tanning**) **1** to make the skin brown, or to become brown, by exposure to the sun. **2** to convert an animal hide into leather by treating it with tannic acid. **3** (*informal*) to beat someone as a punishment.
tan *noun* **1** yellowish brown. **2** a brown colour in skin that has been exposed to the sun. **3** tree bark used in tanning hides.
tan *adjective* yellowish-brown. [probably from a Latin word *tannare*]

tan² *abbreviation* (*Mathematics*) tangent.

tandem *noun* **1** a bicycle for two riders, sitting one behind another. **2** an arrangement of people or things one behind another. **in tandem** one behind another. [a Latin word meaning 'at length']

tandoori *noun* a style of Indian cooking in which food is cooked in a clay oven (called a *tandoor*). [via Urdu from an Arabic word *tannur* meaning 'oven']

tang *noun* **1** a strong flavour or smell. SYNONYMS: taste, flavour, savour. **2** a projection on the blade of a knife or tool by which it is fixed in the handle. [from an Old Norse word *tangi* meaning 'point']

tangent (tan-jənt) *noun* **1** a straight line that touches the outside of a curve but does not cross it. **2** (*Mathematics*) the ratio of the length of the side opposite the right angle (in a right-angled triangle) to the side opposite the other acute angle. **to go off at a tangent** to diverge suddenly from a subject or line of thought being considered. [from a Latin word *tangens* meaning 'touching']

tangential (tan-jen-shəl) *adjective* **1** of or along a tangent. **2** not relevant or only slightly relevant to a subject being considered. **3** diverging from a line of thought.

tangerine (tan-jer-**een**) *noun* **1** a kind of small flattened orange with a loose skin. **2** a deep orange-red colour. [named after Tangier in North Africa, from where the fruit was exported]

tangible (tan-ji-bəl) *adjective* **1** able to be perceived by touch. **2** clear and definite, real ♦ *The scheme has tangible advantages.* **tangibility** *noun* **tangibly** *adverb* [from a Latin word *tangere* meaning 'to touch']

tangle *verb* **1** to twist strands, or to become twisted, into a confused mass. **2** (*informal*) to come into conflict with someone ♦ *They are people you should not tangle with.* **tangle** *noun* a tangled mass or condition. [probably from a Scandinavian language]

tango *noun* (**tangos**) a ballroom dance with gliding steps, or the music for this. **tango** *verb* (**tangoes, tangoed, tangoing**) to dance the tango. [an American Spanish word, perhaps from an African language]

tangram *noun* a Chinese puzzle consisting of a square cut into seven pieces which can be combined to form other figures. [origin unknown]

tangy (tang-i) *adjective* (**tangier, tangiest**) having a strong flavour or smell.

tank *noun* **1** a large container for holding liquid or gas. **2** a heavy armoured fighting vehicle carrying guns and moving on a continuous metal track round its wheels.

tankard *noun* a tall drinking mug with one handle, usually of silver or pewter and often with a lid. [origin unknown]

tanker *noun* a ship, aircraft, or road vehicle for carrying oil or other liquid in bulk.

tanner *noun* a person who tans hides into leather.

tannery *noun* (**tanneries**) a place where hides are tanned into leather.

tannin *noun* a compound obtained from oak galls and various tree barks and also found in tea, used chiefly in tanning and dyeing. [from a French word *tanin*, related to *tan*]

Tannoy *noun* (*trademark*) a type of public address system.

tantalize *verb* to tease or torment someone by showing them something they want but cannot reach. SYNONYMS: torment, taunt, tease. [from the name of Tantalus in Greek mythology, who was punished by being condemned to stand near water and fruit that moved away when he tried to reach them]

tantalum (tan-tə-ləm) *noun* a hard white metallic element (symbol Ta). [same origin as for *tantalize* (because it is frustratingly insoluble in acids)]

tantamount (tant-ə-mownt) *adjective* equivalent, virtually the same ♦ *The Queen's request was tantamount to a command.* [from an Italian phrase *tanto montare* meaning 'to amount to so much']

tantra *noun* each of a class of Hindu, Buddhist, or Jain sacred texts that deal with mystical and magical practices. **tantric** *adjective* [from a Sanskrit word meaning 'doctrine']

tantrum *noun* (**tantrums**) a wild outburst of bad temper or frustration, especially in a young child. [origin unknown]

Taoiseach (tee-shək) *noun* the title of the prime minister of the Republic of Ireland.

Taoism (tah-oh-izm) *noun* a moral and religious system based on the Tao, the code of behaviour in harmony with the natural order. **Taoist** *noun & adjective*

tap [1] *noun* **1** a device for letting out liquid or gas in a controllable flow. **2** a device for cutting a screw thread inside a cavity. **3** a device for listening secretly to a telephone conversation. **tap** *verb* (**tapped, tapping**) **1** to fit a tap into a cask in order to draw out its contents. **2** to draw off liquid by means of a tap or through an incision. **3** to extract or obtain supplies or information from a source. **4** to cut a screw thread inside a cavity. **5** to connect a device to a telephone in order to listen secretly to conversations. **on tap 1** (said about a liquid or gas) ready to be drawn off by a tap. **2** (*informal*) readily available. [from an Old English word *tæppa* meaning 'stopper for a cask']

tap [2] *verb* (**tapped, tapping**) **1** to hit something or someone with a quick light blow. **2** to strike an object lightly against something. **tap** *noun* **1** a quick light blow, or the sound of this. **2** tap-dancing. [from an Old French word *taper*]

tapas (tap-əs) *noun* Spanish savoury snacks served with drinks at a bar. [from a Spanish word meaning 'cover' or 'lid' (because they were served on a small dish placed over a drink)]

tap dance *noun* a dance performed wearing shoes with metal caps, in which an elaborate rhythm is tapped with the toes and heels. **tap-dance** *verb* to perform a tap dance. **tap dancer** *noun*

tape *noun* **1** a narrow strip of cloth, paper, plastic, etc., used especially for tying or

fastening. **2** a strip of adhesive paper or plastic for sticking things together. **3** a plastic strip coated with a magnetic substance used for recording sound or pictures or storing computer data. **4** a cassette or reel of magnetic tape. **5** a tape measure.
tape *verb* **1** to tie or fasten something with tape. **2** to record something on magnetic tape. **to have someone or something taped** (*informal*) to understand someone or something fully, or to have an effective way of dealing with them.

tape measure *noun* a length of tape or flexible metal marked in inches or centimetres for measuring length.

taper *noun* a thin candle, burnt to give a light or to light other candles.
taper *verb* to become gradually narrower, or to make something narrower. **to taper off** to become less in amount or cease gradually, or to make something do this. [via Old English from a Latin word *papyrus* (see *papyrus*). The pith of the papyrus plant was used to make candle wicks]

tape recorder *noun* an apparatus for recording and reproducing sounds on magnetic tape. **tape-record** *verb* **tape recording** *noun*

tapestry (tap-i-stri) *noun* (**tapestries**) a piece of strong cloth with a picture or design woven into it or embroidered on it, used for hanging on walls or as an upholstery fabric. [from a French word *tapis* meaning 'carpet']

tapeworm *noun* a long flat worm that can live as a parasite in the intestines of humans and animals.

tapioca (tap-i-**oh**-kə) *noun* a starchy substance in hard white grains obtained from cassava, used for making puddings. [from a Tupi (South American) word]

tapir (**tay**-per) *noun* an animal like a pig, with a long flexible snout. [via Spanish and Portuguese from a Tupi (South American) word *tapyra*]

tappet *noun* a projecting part in a piece of machinery, which makes intermittent contact with another part and causes a movement, e.g. opening and closing a valve. [probably from *tap*²]

taproot *noun* the chief root of a plant, growing straight downwards.

tar *noun* **1** a thick dark inflammable liquid obtained by distilling wood or coal, used in making roads and for preserving timber. **2** a similar substance formed by burning tobacco.
tar *verb* (**tarred, tarring**) to coat something with tar. **to be tarred with the same brush** to be thought of as having the same faults as someone else. [from an Old English word *teru*]

taramasalata (ta-rə-mə-sə-**lah**-tə) *noun* a soft paste made from the roe of certain fish, mixed with olive oil and seasoning. [from modern Greek words *taramas* meaning 'roe' and *salata* meaning 'salad']

tarantella (ta-rən-**tel**-ə) *noun* a rapid whirling South Italian dance. [an Italian word, named after Taranto in southern Italy (because the dance was thought to be a cure for a psychological illness called tarantism, which was also associated with Taranto)]

tarantula (tə-**ran**-tew-lə) *noun* **1** a large black spider of southern Europe. **2** a large hairy tropical spider, whose bite was once thought to cause a psychological illness called tarantism (see **tarantella**).

tarboosh (tar-**boosh**) *noun* a cap like a fez, often made of red felt with a tassle at the top. [from an Arabic word *tarbush*]

tardy *adjective* (**tardier, tardiest**) **1** slow to act or move. SYNONYMS: slow, sluggish, dilatory. **2** not happening quickly or on time. SYNONYMS: belated, overdue. **tardily** *adverb* **tardiness** *noun* [from a Latin word *tardus* meaning 'slow']

tare ¹ *noun* a kind of vetch. [origin unknown]

tare ² *noun* an allowance made for the weight of the container in which goods are packed or for the vehicle transporting them, when the goods are weighed together with them. [via French from an Arabic word *taraha* meaning 'to deduct']

target *noun* **1** the object or mark that someone tries to hit in shooting, especially a disc painted with concentric circles used in archery. **2** a person, place, or object that is aimed at in an attack. **3** a person or thing that is being criticized. **4** an aim or objective ♦ *sales targets*. SYNONYMS: aim, objective, goal, ambition. **target** *verb* (**targeted, targeting**) **1** to select something or someone as an object of attack or attention. **2** to aim a weapon etc. at a target. [from an Old English word *targa*]

tariff *noun* **1** a list of fixed charges made by a business, hotel, etc. **2** a tax or duty to be paid on imports or exports. **3** (*Law*) a scale of judicial sentences for certain crimes. [via French and Italian from an Arabic word *arrafa* meaning 'to notify']

tarmac *noun* an area surfaced with tarmacadam, especially on an airfield. **tarmac** *verb* (**tarmacked, tarmacking**) to surface an area with tarmacadam.

tarmacadam *noun* a mixture of tar and broken stone, used as a material for surfacing roads. [from *tar* and *macadam*]

tarn *noun* a small mountain lake. [from an Old Norse word *tjorn*]

tarnish *verb* 1 to lose lustre, or to cause metal to lose its lustre, by exposure to the air or to damp. SYNONYMS: discolour, dull. 2 to stain or blemish a reputation etc. **tarnish** *noun* loss of lustre, a stain or blemish. [from a French word *terne* meaning 'dark' or 'dull']

tarot cards (ta-roh) *plural noun* a pack of 78 special cards used for fortune telling. [via French from an Italian word *tarocchi*]

tarpaulin (tar-paw-lin) *noun* a large sheet of waterproof canvas. [from *tar*¹ and *pall*¹]

tarragon (ta-rə-gən) *noun* a plant with leaves that are used for flavouring salads and in cooking. [from a late Latin word *tragonia*, perhaps ultimately from a Greek word *drakōn* meaning 'dragon']

tarry¹ (tar-i) *adjective* (**tarrier, tarriest**) like or covered in tar.

tarry² (ta-ri) *verb* (**tarries, tarried, tarrying**) (*old use*) to delay leaving, to stay longer. [origin unknown]

tarsal *adjective* to do with the tarsus or ankle. **tarsal** *noun* any of the bones forming the ankles.

tarsus *noun* (*Anatomy*) the seven small bones that make up the ankle. [via Latin from a Greek word *tarsos*]

tart¹ *noun* an open pastry case with a sweet or savoury filling. **tart** *verb* **to tart oneself up** (*informal*) to dress smartly or attractively. **to tart something up** (*informal*) to decorate or smarten something. [from a Latin word *tarta*]

tart² *adjective* 1 sharp or acid in taste. SYNONYMS: sharp, sour, acid. 2 sharp in manner, sarcastic ♦ *a tart reply*. SYNONYMS: sharp, sarcastic, caustic, cutting, biting. **tartly** *adverb* **tartness** *noun* [from an Old English word *teart* meaning 'harsh, severe']

tart³ *noun* (*informal*) a prostitute. [probably a shortening of *sweetheart*]

tartan *noun* a woollen cloth woven in a pattern of coloured stripes crossing at right angles, especially one associated with a particular Scottish Highland clan. [from an Old French word *tertaine* for a kind of material]

Tartar *noun* a member of a group of Central Asian peoples including Mongols and Turks. **tartar** *noun* a person who is fierce or difficult to deal with.

tartar *noun* 1 a hard chalky deposit that forms on the teeth and causes decay. 2 a reddish deposit that forms on the side of a cask in which wine is fermented. [origin unknown]

tartaric acid (tar-ta-rik) *noun* an organic acid used as a food additive and in baking powders.

tartar sauce (tar-ter) *noun* a sauce made from mayonnaise with pieces of chopped gherkin etc.

tartlet *noun* a small pastry tart.

task *noun* a piece of work that has to be done. SYNONYMS: job, assignment, undertaking, chore **task** *verb* 1 to make great demands on someone's powers, patience, etc. 2 to assign a task to someone. **to take someone to task** to scold or rebuke someone. SYNONYMS: scold, rebuke, reprimand, chide. [from an Old French word, related to *tax*]

task force *noun* a group and resources specially organized for a particular task.

taskmaster *noun* a person who imposes difficult tasks on people ♦ *a hard taskmaster.*

tassel *noun* 1 a bunch of threads tied together at the top and hanging loosely as an ornament. 2 the tufted head of certain plants. **tasselled** *adjective* [an Old French word meaning 'clasp']

taste *noun* 1 the sensation caused in the tongue by things placed on it, or the particular sensation something has. SYNONYMS: flavour, savour. 2 the ability to perceive this sensation. 3 a small quantity of food or drink taken as a sample. SYNONYMS: sample, morsel, bit. 4 a slight experience of something ♦ *a taste of success.* SYNONYMS: touch, hint. 5 a liking for something ♦ *I have developed a taste for*

jazz. SYNONYMS: liking, fondness, partiality.
6 the ability to enjoy beautiful things or to
know what is suitable for an occasion
♦ *She shows good taste in her choice of
clothes.*
taste *verb* **1** to discover or test the flavour
of a thing by putting it in the mouth. **2** to
be able to perceive flavours. **3** to have a
certain flavour ♦ *That tastes sour.* **4** to
experience something ♦ *to taste the joys of
freedom.* **taster** *noun* [from an Old French
word *tast* (noun)]

taste bud *noun* any of the small
projections on the tongue which provide
the sense of flavour.

tasteful *adjective* showing good taste.
SYNONYMS: attractive, elegant, seemly,
pleasing. **tastefully** *adverb* **tastefulness** *noun*

tasteless *adjective* **1** having no flavour.
SYNONYMS: bland, flavourless, insipid.
2 showing poor taste ♦ *The decor was
tasteless.* SYNONYMS: crude, vulgar, garish.
tastelessly *adverb* **tastelessness** *noun*

tasty *adjective* (**tastier, tastiest**) having a
pleasant strong flavour. SYNONYMS:
delicious, appetizing; (*informal*) yummy.
tastily *adverb* **tastiness** *noun*

tat [1] *verb* (**tatted, tatting**) to do tatting, or to
make something by tatting.

tat [2] *noun* tawdry or tasteless things.
[probably a back-formation from *tatty*]

tat [3] see **tit** [2].

tattered *adjective* old and ragged, torn into
tatters. SYNONYMS: ragged, torn, frayed,
threadbare.

tatters *plural noun* torn pieces of cloth,
paper, etc.

tatting *noun* **1** a kind of lace made by hand
with a small shuttle. **2** the process of
making this. [origin unknown]

tattle *noun* idle chatter or gossip.
tattle *verb* to chatter or gossip idly. [from
an early Flemish word *tatelen*]

tattoo [1] *noun* (**tattoos**) **1** an evening drum
or bugle signal calling soldiers back to
their quarters. **2** a military display with
music and marching, as an
entertainment. **3** a drumming or tapping
sound. [from a Dutch word *taptoe!*
meaning 'close the tap (of the cask)']

tattoo [2] *verb* (**tattoos, tattooed, tattooing**) to
mark the skin with indelible patterns by
puncturing and inserting a dye.
tattoo *noun* (**tattoos**) a pattern made by
tattooing. [from a Polynesian language]

tatty *adjective* (**tattier, tattiest**) (*informal*)
shabby and worn. SYNONYMS: shabby, worn,
scruffy. **tattily** *adverb* **tattiness** *noun* [from
an Old English word *tættec* meaning 'rag']

taught past tense and past participle of
teach.

taunt *verb* to provoke someone with
scornful remarks or criticism. SYNONYMS:
torment, tease, mock.
taunt *noun* a taunting remark. SYNONYMS:
jibe, dig. [from a French phrase *tant pour
tant* meaning 'tit for tat']

Taurus (tor-əs) *noun* **1** a group of stars (the
Bull), seen as representing a figure of a
bull. **2** a sign of the zodiac which the sun
enters about 21 April. [a Latin word
meaning 'bull']

taut *adjective* stretched tightly, not slack.
SYNONYMS: tight, stretched, tense. **tautly**
adverb [probably from *tough*]

tauten *verb* to make something taut, or to
become taut.

tautology (taw-tol-əji) *noun* (**tautologies**)
saying the same thing over again in
different words, as in 'free, gratis, and for
nothing'. **tautological** (taw-tə-loj-ikəl)
adjective **tautologous** (taw-tol-ə-gəs)
adjective [from Greek words *tauto* meaning
'the same' and *logos* meaning 'word']

tavern *noun* (*old use*) an inn or public
house. [from a Latin word *taberna*
meaning 'hut']

tawdry (taw-dri) *adjective* (**tawdrier,
tawdriest**) showy or gaudy but cheap.
SYNONYMS: gaudy, showy, tasteless. **tawdrily**
adverb **tawdriness** *noun* [from *St Audrey's
lace*, cheap finery formerly sold at St
Audrey's fair at Ely]

tawny *adjective* brownish-yellow or
brownish-orange. [from an Old French
word *tane*, related to *tan* [1]]

tawse (tawz) *noun* (*Scottish*) a leather strap
with a slit at one end, formerly used for
punishing children in schools. [from *taw*
meaning 'to make hide into leather']

tax *noun* **1** money that people or business
firms are required to pay to a
government, to be used for public
purposes. **2** something that makes a
heavy demand ♦ *a tax on one's strength.*
tax *verb* **1** to impose a tax on someone.
2 to pay the tax on something ♦ *The car is
taxed until June.* **3** to make heavy demands
on someone. SYNONYMS: strain, burden,
stretch. **4** to accuse someone in a

challenging or reproving way ♦ *She taxed him with having left the door unlocked.* [from a Latin word *taxare* meaning 'to calculate']

taxable *adjective* able or liable to be taxed.

taxation *noun* the imposition or payment of tax.

tax-free *adjective* exempt from tax.

tax haven *noun* a country where taxes are low.

taxi *noun* (**taxis**) a car that carries passengers for payment, usually with a meter to record the fare payable.
taxi *verb* (**taxies, taxied, taxiing**) 1 to go in a taxi. 2 (said about an aircraft) to move slowly along the ground under its own power, especially before take-off or after landing. [short for *taximeter cab*]

taxicab *noun* a taxi.

taxidermy (tak-si-derm-i) *noun* the art of preparing, stuffing, and mounting the skins of animals so as to look lifelike.
taxidermist *noun* [from Greek words *taxis* meaning 'arrangement' and *derma* meaning 'skin']

taxman *noun* (**taxmen**) an inspector or collector of taxes.

taxonomy (taks-on-əmi) *noun* the scientific process of classifying living things. [from Greek words *taxis* meaning 'arrangement' and *-nomia* meaning 'distribution']

taxpayer *noun* a person who pays tax, especially income tax.

TB *abbreviation* (*informal*) tuberculosis.

tea *noun* 1 a hot drink made by pouring boiling water over the dried leaves of an evergreen shrub grown in parts of south and east Asia (called *tea plant*). 2 these dried leaves. 3 a similar drink made with the leaves of other plants ♦ *camomile tea.* 4 a meal at which tea is served, especially a light meal in the afternoon or early evening. [from a Chinese word *t'e*]

tea bag *noun* a small porous sachet containing tea leaves for making tea.

tea break *noun* a short break from work for drinking tea.

teacake *noun* a kind of sweet bun usually served toasted and buttered.

teach *verb* (past tense and past participle **taught**) 1 to give someone knowledge or skill about a subject, especially in a school or college as part of a programme of study. SYNONYMS: instruct, educate, coach,

train. 2 to put something forward as a fact or principle ♦ *Christ taught forgiveness.* 3 to cause someone to learn a principle or way of behaving by example or experience. 4 (*informal*) to discourage someone from doing something ♦ *That will teach you not to meddle.* **teachable** *adjective* [from an Old English word *tæcan* meaning 'to show' or 'to point out']

teacher *noun* a person who teaches in a school.

tea chest *noun* a light wooden box lined with thin sheets of lead or tin, in which tea is transported.

teaching *noun* things that are taught ♦ *the teachings of Plato.*

tea cloth *noun* a cloth for a tea table, a tea towel.

tea cosy *noun* a cover placed over a teapot to keep the tea hot.

teacup *noun* a cup from which tea or other hot liquids are drunk.

teak *noun* 1 the hard strong wood of a tall evergreen Asian tree, used for making furniture and in shipbuilding. 2 this tree. [via Portuguese from a south Indian language]

teal *noun* (**teal**) a small freshwater duck. [origin unknown]

team *noun* 1 a group of players forming one side in certain games and sports. SYNONYMS: side, squad. 2 a group of people working together. 3 two or more animals harnessed together to pull a vehicle or farm implement.
team *verb* to combine into a team or set or for a common purpose. [from an Old English word *team* meaning 'a team of draught animals']

team spirit *noun* willingness to act for the good of the group you belong to.

teamwork *noun* organized cooperation between members of a team.

teapot *noun* a pot with a handle, lid, and spout, for making and pouring out tea.

tear [1] (tair) *verb* (**tore, torn**) 1 to pull something forcibly apart or to pieces. SYNONYMS: rip, split, slit. 2 to make a hole or a split in this way. 3 to become torn, or be able to be easily torn ♦ *This kind of paper tends to tear.* 4 to subject someone to conflicting desires or demands ♦ *I was torn between love and duty.* 5 to run or travel hurriedly. SYNONYMS: dash, rush, hurry, race, speed.

tear noun a hole or split caused by tearing. SYNONYMS: split, slit, hole, gash. **to tear into** (informal) to criticize someone harshly. **to tear your hair out** (informal) to feel extreme frustration or despair. **that's torn it** (informal) an expression of dismay when something has gone wrong. [from an Old English word teran]

tear [2] (teer) noun a drop of clear salty water that comes to the surface of the eyes when they are sore or when someone is crying. **in tears** crying. [from an Old English word tæher]

tearaway noun someone who behaves wildly or recklessly.

teardrop noun a single tear.

tearful adjective upset and starting to cry. **tearfully** adverb

tear gas noun a gas that causes severe irritation of the eyes, used especially for riot control.

tearing (tair-ing) adjective extreme or overwhelming ♦ in a tearing hurry.

tea rose noun a kind of delicately-scented rose.

tease verb 1 to provoke someone in a playful or unkind way. SYNONYMS: taunt, make fun of, goad. 2 to pick tangled wool or hair etc. into separate strands. 3 to brush up the nap on cloth. **tease** noun a person who likes teasing others. [from an Old English word tæsan]

teasel (tee-zəl) noun a plant with bristly heads formerly used to brush up the nap on cloth. [from tease]

teaser noun (informal) a tricky problem.

tea set noun a set of cups and plates for serving tea.

teashop noun a shop where tea is served to the public.

teaspoon noun a small spoon for stirring tea. **teaspoonful** noun (**teaspoonfuls**)

teat noun 1 a nipple on the milk-secreting organ of an animal. 2 a rubber or plastic bulb on a feeding bottle, pierced with a hole for sucking the contents. [from an Old French word tete]

tea towel noun a towel for drying washed dishes, cutlery, etc.

tech (tek) noun (informal) a technical college.

technical adjective 1 to do with the mechanical arts and applied sciences. 2 to do with a particular subject or its techniques ♦ the technical terms of chemistry. 3 (said about a book etc.) needing special knowledge to be understood. 4 in a strict legal sense ♦ technical assault. **technically** adverb [from a Greek word tekhnikos meaning 'skilful']

technical college noun a college of further education providing courses in technical and practical subjects.

technicality (tek-ni-kal-iti) noun (**technicalities**) 1 being technical. 2 a technical word, phrase, or point ♦ He was acquitted on a technicality.

technician (tek-nish-ən) noun 1 an expert in the techniques of a particular subject. 2 a skilled mechanic.

Technicolor noun (trademark) a process of producing cinema films in colour. **technicolor** noun (informal) bright or vivid colour.

technique (tek-neek) noun 1 a method of doing or performing something, especially in an art or science. 2 skill in doing something. [a French word, related to technical]

technologist noun an expert in technology.

technology noun (**technologies**) 1 the practical application of scientific knowledge, e.g. in industry. 2 the scientific study of mechanical arts and applied sciences, such as engineering. **technological** adjective **technologically** adverb [from a Greek word tekhnē meaning 'skill' and -logy]

tectonics (tek-tonn-iks) noun the scientific study of the earth's crust and structural features. [from a Greek word tektōn meaning 'carpenter']

teddy bear noun a soft furry toy bear. [named after the American President Theodore ('Teddy') Roosevelt (1858–1919), who liked hunting bears]

tedious (tee-di-əs) adjective tiresome because of its length or dullness, boring. SYNONYMS: dull, tiresome, boring, uninteresting, dreary, monotonous. **tediously** adverb **tediousness** noun [from a Latin word taedium meaning 'tiresomeness']

tedium (tee-di-əm) noun tediousness.

tee noun 1 a cleared space on a golf course, from which each player strikes the ball at the beginning of play for each hole. 2 a small peg with a shallow dip on its head, on which a golf ball is placed for being struck. **3** the mark aimed at in quoits, bowls, and curling.

tee *verb* (**tees, teed, teeing**) to place a ball on a tee in golf. **to tee off** to begin a hole of golf by playing the ball from a tee. [originally a Scots word; origin unknown]

teem [1] *verb* to be full of something ♦ *The river was teeming with fish.* [from an Old English word *teman* meaning 'to give birth to']

teem [2] *verb* (said about water or rain etc.) to flow in large quantities, to pour. [from an Old Norse word *tæma* meaning 'to empty']

teenage *adjective* to do with teenagers.

teenaged *adjective* in your teens.

teenager *noun* a person aged between 13 and 19 years.

teens *plural noun* the years of a person's age from 13 to 19.

teeny *adjective* (**teenier, teeniest**) (*informal*) tiny.

tee-shirt *noun* another spelling of **T-shirt**.

teeter *verb* to stand or move unsteadily. SYNONYMS: stumble, stagger, totter.

teeth plural of **tooth**.

teethe *verb* (said about a baby) to have its first teeth beginning to grow through the gums.

teething troubles *plural noun* short-term problems that arise in the early stages of an enterprise.

teetotal *adjective* abstaining completely from alcoholic drink. **teetotaller** *noun*

TEFL *abbreviation* teaching of English as a foreign language.

tele- *prefix* far, at a distance (as in ♦ *telescope*). [from a Greek word *tēle* meaning 'far off']

telecommunications *plural noun* communications over long distances, such as telephone, radio, or television.

teleconference *noun* a conference or discussion in which the participants are in different locations linked by telecommunication devices.

telegram *noun* a message sent by telegraph. [from *tele-* and *-gram*]

telegraph *noun* a system or apparatus for sending messages over a distance,

especially by transmitting electrical impulses along wires.
telegraph *verb* to send a message by telegraph. [from *tele-* and *-graph*]

telegraphist (til-**eg**-rə-fist) *noun* a person who sends and receives messages by telegraph.

telegraph pole *noun* a pole for carrying overhead telegraph and telephone wires.

telegraphy (til-**eg**-rə-fi) *noun* communication by telegraph. **telegraphic** (tel-i-**graf**-ik) *adjective*

teleology (tel-i-**ol**-əji) *noun* (*Philosophy*) the doctrine that there is evidence of design or purpose in nature. **teleological** (tel-i-ə-**loj**-ikəl) *adjective* [from a Greek word *telos* meaning 'purpose' and *-logy*]

telepathic (tel-i-**path**-ik) *adjective* to do with telepathy, able to communicate by telepathy.

telepathy (til-**ep**-ə-thi) *noun* supposed communication of thoughts and ideas other than by the normal senses. [from *tele-* and a Greek word *pathos* meaning 'feeling']

telephone *noun* **1** a system of transmitting voices over a distance by wire or radio, converting sound to electrical signals and back again. **2** a device used in this, with a receiver and mouthpiece and a set of numbered buttons for making a connection.
telephone *verb* to speak to someone by telephone. **telephonic** (teli-**fon**-ik) *adjective* **telephonically** *adverb* [from *tele-* and a Greek word *phōnē* meaning 'voice']

telephone directory or **telephone book** *noun* a book listing the names and numbers of people who have a telephone.

telephone number *noun* a number assigned to a particular telephone line and used in making connections to it.

telephonist (til-**ef**-ən-ist) *noun* an operator of a telephone switchboard.

telephony (til-**ef**-əni) *noun* the system or use of telephones.

telephoto lens *noun* a lens used to produce a large image of a distant object.

teleprinter (tel-i-**print**-er) *noun* a device for transmitting messages by telegraph as they are keyed, and for printing messages received.

telescope *noun* an optical instrument using lenses and mirrors to make distant objects appear larger when viewed through it.

telescope verb **1** to make something shorter, or to become shorter, by sliding overlapping sections one inside another. **2** to compress something, or to become compressed. **3** to condense something so as to occupy less space or time. [from *tele-* and a Greek word *skopein* meaning 'to look at']

telescopic adjective **1** magnifying like a telescope. **2** visible only through a telescope ♦ *telescopic stars.* **telescopically** adverb

teleshopping noun shopping by means of a telephone or Internet link.

teletext noun a system for displaying news and information on a television screen.

televangelist (te-li-van-jə-list) noun (especially in the USA) an evangelical preacher who appears regularly on television.

televise verb to broadcast a programme by television.

television noun **1** a system for transmitting visual images and sound by means of radio waves so that they can be reproduced on a screen. **2** (also **television set**) an apparatus with a screen for receiving television pictures. **3** television as a medium of communication, or material seen by means of television. [from *tele-* and *vision*]

teleworking noun working from home by means of telecommunications, email, and the Internet.

telex noun a system of international telegraphy in which printed messages are transmitted and received by teleprinters using public transmission lines. **telex** verb to send a message by telex. [a blend of *teleprinter* and *exchange*]

tell verb (past tense and past participle **told**) **1** to make something known to someone, especially in spoken or written words ♦ *I told them we would be late.* SYNONYMS: inform, advise, let know. **2** to give information to someone ♦ *Can you tell me what happened?* SYNONYMS: explain, reveal, disclose, divulge. **3** to give someone a command or order ♦ *Tell them to wait.* SYNONYMS: instruct, order, command, direct. **4** to utter or express something ♦ *Always tell the truth.* **5** to relate a story or narrative. SYNONYMS: relate, narrate, recount. **6** to reveal a secret ♦ *Promise me you won't tell.* **7** to decide or

determine something ♦ *How do you tell which button to press?* **8** to distinguish one person or thing from another ♦ *I can't tell him from his brother.* **9** to produce a noticeable effect ♦ *The strain was beginning to tell on them.* **to tell someone's fortune** see **fortune. to tell someone off** (informal) to scold or reprimand someone. SYNONYMS: scold, rebuke, reprimand, chide, upbraid; (informal) tick off. **to tell on someone** (informal) to reveal the activities of a person by telling others. **to tell tales** to report someone's bad behaviour or wrongdoing. **to tell the time** to read the time from a clock. [from an Old English word *tellan* meaning 'to relate' or 'to count']

teller noun **1** a person who deals with customers' routine transactions in a bank. **2** a person appointed to count votes. **3** a person who tells or gives an account of something.

telling adjective having a noticeable effect, significant or noteworthy ♦ *a telling argument.*

telltale noun **1** a person who tells tales. **2** a device that gives a visual indication of the state of something. **telltale** adjective revealing or indicating something ♦ *a telltale blush.*

telly noun (**tellies**) (informal) television, or a television set.

temerity (tim-e-riti) noun boldness or rashness. SYNONYMS: boldness, audacity, rashness. [from a Latin word *temeritas*, from *temere* meaning 'rashly']

temp noun (informal) a secretary or other worker who works for short periods in different companies. **temp** verb (informal) to work as a temp. [a shortening of *temporary*]

temper noun **1** the state of a person's mind in terms of being calm or angry ♦ *in a good temper.* SYNONYMS: mood, humour. **2** a fit of anger ♦ *in a temper.* SYNONYMS: rage, fury. **3** a tendency to have fits of anger ♦ *He has a temper.* **4** the degree of hardness and elasticity in metal. **temper** verb **1** to harden or strengthen metal by heating and then cooling it. **2** to bring clay etc. to the right consistency by moistening and mixing it. **3** to moderate or soften the effects of something ♦ *to temper justice with mercy.* SYNONYMS: moderate, soften, modify, mitigate. **to keep your temper** to remain calm and restrained when feeling angry. **to lose**

your temper to lose your calmness and become openly angry. [via Old English from a Latin word *temperare* meaning 'to mix']

tempera *noun* a method of painting with powdered colours mixed with egg or size, used in Europe chiefly in the 12th–15th centuries. [from an Italian phrase *pingere a tempera* meaning 'to paint in distemper']

temperament *noun* a person's nature as it affects their behaviour and attitudes ♦ *a nervous temperament.* SYNONYMS: disposition, nature, character. [same origin as for *temper*]

temperamental *adjective* **1** having unpredictable changes of mood or behaviour. SYNONYMS: changeable, moody, volatile. **2** (said of a machine etc.) liable to work erratically, unreliable. **3** to do with a person's temperament. **temperamentally** *adverb*

temperance *noun* **1** self-restraint in behaviour. **2** drinking little or no alcohol. [from a Latin word *temperantia* meaning 'moderation']

temperate *adjective* **1** (said about climate) having a mild temperature without extremes of heat and cold. **2** self-restrained or moderate in behaviour. SYNONYMS: moderate, self-restrained, self-controlled, disciplined. **temperately** *adverb* [from an earlier meaning 'not affected by strong emotions'; same origin as for *temper*]

temperature *noun* **1** the degree or intensity of heat or cold in a substance or place. **2** an abnormally high body temperature ♦ *She has a temperature.* [from a Latin word *temperatus* meaning 'tempered']

tempest *noun* a violent storm. [from a Latin word *tempestas* meaning 'weather']

tempestuous (tem-**pest**-yoo-əs) *adjective* **1** very stormy. SYNONYMS: stormy, turbulent, wild. **2** full of commotion or strong emotion.

template *noun* **1** a piece of specially prepared rigid material used as a guide for cutting or shaping things. **2** a timber or metal plate used to distribute the weight in a wall or under a beam. [from an earlier spelling *templet*, from *temple*, a device in a loom for keeping the cloth stretched]

temple [1] *noun* a building for the worship of a god or gods. [from a Latin word *templum* meaning 'consecrated place']

temple [2] *noun* the flat part at each side of the head between the forehead and the ear. [from a Latin word *tempora* meaning 'sides of the head']

tempo *noun* (**tempos** or **tempi**) **1** the speed at which a piece of music is played. **2** the pace of any movement or activity. [an Italian word, from a Latin word *tempus* meaning 'time']

temporal (temp-er-əl) *adjective* **1** to do with worldly affairs, secular. SYNONYMS: earthly, worldly, secular. **2** to do with time. **3** to do with the temples of the head. [via French from a Latin word *temporis* meaning 'of time']

temporary *adjective* lasting or meant to last for a limited time only, not permanent. **temporary** *noun* (**temporaries**) a person employed temporarily. **temporarily** (temp-er-er-ili) *adverb* [same origin as for *temporal*]

temporize *verb* to avoid giving a definite answer or decision, in order to gain time. **temporization** *noun* **temporizer** *noun*

tempt *verb* **1** to try to persuade or entice someone, especially into doing something wrong or unwise. SYNONYMS: coax, entice, persuade. **2** to arouse a desire in someone ♦ *I'm tempted to tell them.* **to tempt fate** or **providence** to do something rash or reckless. **tempter** *noun* **temptress** *noun* [from a Latin word *temptare* meaning 'to test']

temptation *noun* **1** the process of tempting or being tempted. **2** something that tempts or attracts someone.

tempting *adjective* attractive or appealing ♦ *a tempting offer.* SYNONYMS: attractive, appealing, alluring, enticing, seductive.

ten *adjective* & *noun* the number 10, one more than nine.

tenable (**ten**-əbəl) *adjective* **1** able to be maintained or defended against attack or objection ♦ *a tenable argument.* SYNONYMS: plausible, reasonable, defensible. **2** (said about a job or office) able to be held for a certain time or by a certain type of person etc. **tenability** *noun* [from a Latin word *tenere* meaning 'to hold']

tenacious (tin-**ay**-shəs) *adjective* **1** holding or clinging firmly to something, especially to rights or principles. SYNONYMS: determined, dogged, resolute, persistent. **tenaciously** *adverb* **tenacity** (tin-**ass**-iti) *noun* [same origin as for *tenable*]

tenancy *noun* (**tenancies**) **1** the use of land or buildings as a tenant. **2** the period for which this lasts.

tenant *noun* **1** a person who rents land or buildings from a landlord. **2** (*Law*) an occupant or owner of land or a building. [from a Latin word *tenens* meaning 'holding']

tend[1] *verb* to take care of or look after a person or thing. [from *attend*]

tend[2] *verb* **1** to behave frequently in a certain way or to have a certain characteristic ♦ *He tends to be rude* ♦ *The figures tend to show an increase in profits.* **2** to take a certain direction ♦ *The track tends upwards.* [from a Latin word *tendere* meaning 'to stretch']

tendency *noun* (**tendencies**) **1** the way a person or thing tends to be or behave ♦ *He has a tendency to be rude* ♦ *He has a tendency to rudeness.* **2** the direction in which something moves or changes, a trend ♦ *an upward tendency.*

tendentious (ten-den-shəs) *adjective* meant to promote a particular cause or point of view, not impartial.

tender[1] *adjective* **1** gentle and loving ♦ *a tender smile.* SYNONYMS: gentle, loving, fond. **2** (said about food, especially meat) not tough or hard, easy to chew. **3** delicate or easily damaged ♦ *tender plants.* SYNONYMS: delicate, fragile. **4** (said about a part of the body) sensitive, painful when touched. SYNONYMS: sensitive, sore. **tenderly** *adverb* **tenderness** *noun* [from a Latin word *tener* meaning 'soft' or 'delicate']

tender[2] *verb* **1** to offer something formally ♦ *to tender one's resignation.* SYNONYMS: offer, submit. **2** to make a tender for goods or work.
tender *noun* a formal offer to supply goods or carry out work at a stated price. **legal tender** kinds of money that are legal for making payment ♦ *Are pound notes still legal tender?* [from a Latin word *tendere* meaning 'to stretch' or 'to hold out']

tender[3] *noun* **1** a truck attached to a steam locomotive, carrying its fuel and water. **2** a small boat carrying stores or passengers to and from a ship. **3** a person who tends or looks after something. [from *tend*[1]]

tenderize *verb* to make meat more tender by beating it or by slow cooking.
tenderizer *noun*

tenderloin *noun* the tender middle part of a pork loin.

tendon *noun* a strong band or cord of tissue that connects a muscle to a bone. [same origin as for *tender*[2]]

tendril *noun* **1** a thread-like part by which a climbing plant clings to a support. **2** a thin curl of hair etc. [from an Old French word, related to *tender*[1]]

tenement (ten-i-mənt) *noun* **1** (in Scotland and the USA) a separate residence in a house or block of flats. **2** a large house or building divided into apartments or rooms that are let to a number of tenants. **3** (*Law*) land or other permanent property held by a tenant ♦ *lands and tenements.* [from a Latin word *tenementum*]

tenet (ten-it) *noun* a firm belief or principle held by a person or group. SYNONYMS: belief, principle, doctrine, precept, conviction. [a Latin word meaning 'he or she holds']

tenfold *adjective & adverb* ten times as much or as many.

tenner *noun* (*informal*) a ten-pound note, or the sum of ten pounds.

tennis *noun* either of two ball games for two or four players, played with rackets over a net with a soft ball on an open court (**lawn tennis**) or with a hard ball in a walled court (**real tennis**). [from a French word *tenez!* meaning 'receive!' (called by the person serving)]

tenon (ten-ən) *noun* a piece of wood or other material shaped to fit into a mortise. [a French word, from *tenir* meaning 'to hold']

tenor (ten-er) *noun* **1** the general meaning or drift ♦ *What was the tenor of her speech?* **2** the general routine or course of something ♦ *They were disrupting the even tenor of his life.* **3** the highest ordinary adult male singing voice, or a singer with such a voice. **4** a musical instrument with approximately the range of a tenor voice ♦ *a tenor saxophone.* [from a Latin word *tenere* meaning 'to hold']

tenpin bowling *noun* a game in which players try to knock over ten pins set up at the end of a track by rolling hard balls down it.

tense[1] *noun* a form of a verb that indicates the time of action or state as being past, present, or future, e.g *they came* (**past**

tense), they come or they are coming (**present tense**), they will come (**future tense**). [from a Latin word *tempus* meaning 'time']

tense [2] *adjective* **1** stretched tightly. SYNONYMS: tight, stretched, taut. **2** with muscles tight, ready for what might happen. **3** anxious and unable to relax. SYNONYMS: anxious, nervous, edgy. **4** causing tenseness ♦ *a tense moment.*
tense *verb* to make something tense, or to become tense. **tensely** *adverb* **tenseness** *noun* [from a Latin word *tensum* meaning 'stretched']

tensile (ten-siyl) *adjective* **1** to do with tension. **2** able to be stretched.

tension *noun* **1** the process of stretching or being stretched. **2** tenseness, the condition when feelings are tense. SYNONYMS: anxiety, nervousness, strain. **3** the effect produced by forces pulling against each other. **4** electromotive force or voltage ♦ *high-tension cables.* **5** (in knitting) the number of stitches and rows to a unit of measurement (e.g. 10 cm or 1 inch). [from a Latin word *tensio* meaning 'stretching']

tent *noun* a portable shelter made of canvas or cloth, supported by poles and fixed to the ground with pegs, used in camping. [same origin as for *tense*[2]]

tentacle *noun* a thin flexible part extending from the body of certain animals (e.g. snails and octopuses), used for feeling or grasping things or for moving. **tentacled** *adjective* [from a Latin word *tentaculum*, from *tentare* meaning 'to feel' or 'to try']

tentative (tent-ə-tiv) *adjective* hesitant or provisional ♦ *a tentative suggestion.* **tentatively** *adverb* [same origin as for *tempt*]

tenterhook *noun* on tenterhooks in a state of anxious suspense or strain. [from *tenter* meaning 'a hook used to stretch cloth for drying']

tenth *adjective & noun* **1** next after ninth. **2** one of ten equal parts of a thing. **tenthly** *adverb*

tenuous (ten-yoo-əs) *adjective* **1** very thin ♦ *tenuous threads.* **2** having little substance or validity, very slight ♦ *a tenuous connection.* SYNONYMS: insubstantial, flimsy, weak. **tenuously** *adverb* **tenuousness** *noun* [from a Latin word *tenuis* meaning 'thin']

tenure (ten-yer) *noun* the holding of a position of employment, or of land, property, etc. [from an Old French word, from *tenir* meaning 'to hold']

tepee (tee-pee) *noun* a kind of tent formerly used by Native Americans, made by fastening skins over mats or poles. [a Native American word]

tepid *adjective* only slightly warm, lukewarm. **tepidity** (ti-pid-iti) *noun* **tepidly** *adverb* [from a Latin word *tepidus*, from *tepere* meaning 'to be warm']

tercentenary (ter-sen-teen-er-i) *noun* (**tercentenaries**) a 300th anniversary. [from a Latin word *ter* meaning 'three times' and *centenary*]

terebinth (te-ri-binth) *noun* a small tree of southern Europe, used to produce turpentine. [from a Greek word *terebinthos*]

term *noun* **1** a word or expression that names or identifies something ♦ *'Larceny' is a legal term for 'theft'.* **2** each of the periods of several weeks in which teaching is done in a school, college, or university. **3** the time for which something lasts, a fixed or limited time ♦ *The President is seeking re-election for a second term* ♦ *She narrowly escaped a term of imprisonment.* SYNONYMS: period, spell. **4** (also **full term**) completion of a normal period of pregnancy. **5** each of the periods in which a law court holds sessions. **6** (*Mathematics*) each of the quantities in a series, ratio, or expression.
term *verb* to call something by a certain term or expression ♦ *This music is termed plainsong.*
terms *plural noun* **1** agreed stipulations or conditions ♦ *peace terms.* SYNONYMS: stipulations, conditions, requirements. **2** conditions or methods of payment ♦ *We offer a wide range of terms.* **3** a relation between people ♦ *They ended up on friendly terms.* **4** language or the way it is used ♦ *She protested in the strongest terms.* **to come to terms with 1** to reach an agreement with someone. **2** to become reconciled to a difficulty or unwelcome situation. SYNONYMS: accept, face up to, be reconciled to. **terms of reference** the defined scope of an inquiry or other activity. [from a Latin word *terminus* meaning 'boundary']

termagant (ter-mə-gənt) *noun* a bad-tempered bullying woman. [named after Tervagant, a fierce god in medieval plays]

terminable *adjective* able to be terminated.

terminal *adjective* **1** to do with or situated at the end or boundary of something. **2** in the last stage of a fatal disease ♦ *terminal cancer.* **3** done each term ♦ *terminal examinations.*
terminal *noun* **1** the end of a railway line or long-distance bus route. **2** a building at an airport or in a town where air passengers arrive and depart. **3** a point of connection in an electric circuit or device. **4** a device by which a user enters data into a computer and which displays the output on a screen. **terminally** *adverb* [same origin as for *terminus*]

terminal velocity *noun* (*Physics*) the maximum speed reached by a falling body when the frictional resistance of the medium through which it is falling matches the gravitational pull.

terminate *verb* to end something, or to come to an end. SYNONYMS: stop, conclude, end, close. **termination** *noun* **terminator** *noun* [same origin as for *terminus*]

terminology *noun* (**terminologies**) a set of technical terms relating to a subject. **terminological** *adjective* [from *term* and *-logy*]

terminus *noun* (**termini** (ter-min-iy) or **terminuses**) **1** the end of something. **2** the last station at the end of a railway line or bus route. [a Latin word meaning 'the end']

termite *noun* a small insect that is very destructive to timber, especially in tropical regions. [from a Latin word *termes* meaning 'woodworm']

tern *noun* a seabird with long pointed wings and a forked tail. [probably from a Scandinavian language]

ternary *adjective* **1** involving sets of three; consisting of three parts. **2** (*Mathematics*) using three as a base. [from a Latin word *terni* meaning 'three each']

terrace *noun* **1** a raised level place, especially each of a series of these into which a slope or hillside is formed for cultivation. **2** a flight of wide shallow steps for spectators to stand on at a sports ground. **3** a paved area beside a house. **4** a row of houses forming a continuous block.

terrace *verb* to form sloping land into a terrace or terraces. [from a Latin word *terra* meaning 'earth']

terracotta *noun* **1** a kind of brownish-red unglazed pottery. **2** this colour. [from an Italian phrase *terra cotta* meaning 'baked earth']

terra firma *noun* dry land, the ground. [a Latin phrase, meaning 'firm land']

terrain (te-rayn) *noun* a stretch of land with regard to its natural features ♦ *walking over rugged terrain.* [same origin as for *terrace*]

terrapin (te-rə-pin) *noun* an edible freshwater tortoise of North America. [from a Native American word]

terrarium (te-rair-iəm) *noun* (**terrariums**) **1** a place for keeping small land animals. **2** a sealed transparent globe or other container for growing plants. [from a Latin word *terra* meaning 'earth' and *aquarium*]

terrestrial (tə-rest-riəl) *adjective* **1** to do with the earth. **2** of or living on land. [same origin as for *terrace*]

terrible *adjective* **1** very bad or distressing. SYNONYMS: dreadful, awful, distressing, appalling, horrible, ghastly. **2** extreme, hard to bear ♦ *The heat was terrible.* **3** (*informal*) very bad ♦ *I'm terrible at tennis.* SYNONYMS: inept, hopeless, incompetent. **terribly** *adverb* [from a Latin word *terrere* meaning 'to frighten']

terrier *noun* a kind of small lively dog. [from a French phrase *chien terrier* meaning 'earth dog' (because terriers were used to dig foxes out of their earths)]

terrific *adjective* (*informal*) **1** very great or powerful ♦ *a terrific storm.* SYNONYMS: powerful, tremendous. **2** excellent ♦ *You did a terrific job.* SYNONYMS: excellent, marvellous, splendid, wonderful. **terrifically** *adverb* [from a Latin word *terrificus* meaning 'frightening']

terrify *verb* (**terrifies, terrified, terrifying**) to make someone feel terror. SYNONYMS: frighten, scare, petrify.

terrine (tə-reen) *noun* **1** pâté or a similar food cooked or prepared in its dish. **2** an earthenware or other dish holding this. [a French word meaning 'large earthenware pot', related to *tureen*]

territorial *adjective* to do with or belonging to a country's territory. **Territorial** *noun* a member of the Territorial Army. **territorially** *adverb*

Territorial Army noun a trained force of volunteers for use in an emergency.

territorial waters plural noun the sea within a certain distance (usually three miles) of a country's coast and subject to its control.

territory noun (**territories**) 1 an area of land under the control of a ruler or state. 2 an area for which a person has responsibility or in which a person conducts an activity. 3 a special sphere of thought or experience ◆ Criminal law was not her territory. 4 (Zoology) an area which an animal defends against others of the same species.
Territory noun (**Territories**) a country or area forming part of the USA, Canada, or Australia but not ranking as a state or province. [from a Latin word territorium, from terra meaning 'earth']

terror noun 1 extreme fear. SYNONYMS: horror, fright, fear, alarm, dread, trepidation, panic. 2 a terrifying person or thing. 3 (informal) a formidable or troublesome person or thing. [from a Latin word terrere meaning 'to frighten']

terrorism noun use of violence and intimidation, especially for political purposes. **terrorist** noun & adjective

terrorize verb to use terror to coerce people. **terrorization** noun

terror-stricken adjective extremely frightened.

terry noun a cotton fabric with raised loops left uncut, used especially for towels. [origin unknown]

terse adjective concise or curt. **tersely** adverb **terseness** noun [from a Latin word tersum meaning 'polished']

tertiary (ter-sher-i) adjective coming after something that is secondary, third in rank or order.
Tertiary adjective (Geology) to do with the first period of the Cenozoic era, extending from about 65 to 1.64 million years ago. [from a Latin word tertius meaning 'third']

tertiary education noun education coming after that provided by schools, e.g. at a university or college.

Terylene noun (trademark) a kind of synthetic textile fibre used to make clothes, bed linen, and sails. [from the full name polyethylene terephthalate]

TESL abbreviation teaching of English as a second language.

tessellate (tess-il-ayt) verb 1 to cover a floor with mosaics. 2 (Mathematics) to fit shapes into a pattern without overlapping or leaving gaps. [from a Latin word tessella meaning 'a small piece of wood or stone used in a mosaic']

test noun 1 a short examination, especially in a school, on a particular topic. 2 a procedure for finding out how good a person or thing is ◆ a test of good character ◆ an eye test. SYNONYMS: examination, check-up. 3 a means or procedure for testing something. 4 a test match.
test verb to carry out a test on a person or thing. SYNONYMS: check, examine, try out.
tester noun [from an earlier meaning 'a container used to treat gold or silver alloys or ore', from a Latin word testum meaning 'earthen pot']

testament noun 1 a person's will, or other formal statement. 2 evidence or proof of a fact or event.
Testament noun each of the two main divisions of the Bible (see **Old Testament**, **New Testament**). [from a Latin word testis meaning 'witness']

testamentary adjective to do with a person's will, or given in a will.

testate (tes-tayt) adjective (said about a person) having left a valid will at death.

testator (tes-tay-ter) noun a person who has made a will.

test case noun a lawsuit that provides a precedent for similar cases in the future.

testes plural noun of **testis**.

testicle noun either of the two glands that produce sperm in male mammals, contained in the scrotum behind the penis. [from a Latin word testiculus, from testis meaning 'witness (to virility)']

testify verb (**testifies, testified, testifying**) 1 to give evidence in a law court. 2 to be evidence or proof of something. [from a Latin word testis meaning 'witness']

testimonial noun 1 a formal statement testifying to a person's character or qualifications. 2 a gift or public recognition of a person's services or achievements.

testimony noun (**testimonies**) 1 a declaration or statement, especially one made under oath. 2 evidence in support of something.

testis noun (**testes** (tes-teez)) (*Anatomy and Zoology*) an organ that produces sperm. [same origin as for *testicle*]

test match noun an international cricket or rugby match between teams of two countries, usually one of a series in a tour.

testosterone (test-ost-er-ohn) noun a male sex hormone. [from *testis* and *sterol*]

test pilot noun (*informal*) a pilot who flies new aircraft in order to test their performance.

test tube noun a tube of thin glass with one end closed, used to hold materials for study or experiment in laboratories.

test-tube baby noun a baby that develops from an egg that has been fertilized outside the mother's body and then placed in the womb.

testy adjective (**testier, testiest**) easily annoyed, irritable. SYNONYMS: irritable, tetchy, crotchety, cross;(*informal*) grumpy. **testily** adverb **testiness** noun [from a French word *testif* meaning 'headstrong']

tetanus (tet-ən-əs) noun a disease caused by bacteria, which makes the muscles contract and stiffen. [from a Greek word *tetanos* meaning 'spasm']

tetchy adjective (**tetchier, tetchiest**) peevish or irritable. SYNONYMS: irritable, testy, crotchety, cross;(*informal*) grumpy. **tetchily** adverb [probably from a Scots word *tache* meaning 'blotch' or 'fault']

tête-à-tête (tayt-ah-tayt) noun (**tête-à-têtes**) a private conversation, especially between two people.
tête-à-tête adverb & adjective together in private. [a French word meaning 'head to head']

tether noun a rope or chain for tying an animal while it is grazing.
tether verb to tie an animal with a tether.
at the end of your tether unable to endure something any longer. [from an Old Norse word *tjothr*]

tetra- prefix four. [from a Greek word meaning 'four']

tetrahedron (tet-rə-hee-drən) noun (**tetrahedra** or **tetrahedrons**) a solid with four triangular faces forming a pyramid. [from *tetra-* and a Greek word *hedra* meaning 'base']

Teutonic (tew-tonn-ik) adjective to do with the Teutons, an ancient Germanic people, or their languages.

text noun 1 the words of something written or printed. 2 the main body of a book or page as distinct from illustrations, notes, appendices, etc. 3 a passage from the Bible used as the subject of a sermon or discussion. 4 a literary work that has been prescribed for study. [from a Latin word *textus* meaning 'literary style']

textbook noun a book of information for use in studying a subject.

textile noun a cloth or woven fabric.
textile adjective to do with textiles. [from a Latin word *textum* meaning 'woven']

text message noun a message sent from one mobile phone to another and able to be read on the screen.

textual adjective to do with a text, or in a text. **textually** adverb

texture noun 1 the way the surface of something feels to the touch. 2 the character of a fabric in feeling and appearance, as determined by its threads. [from a Latin word *textura* meaning 'weaving', from *texere* meaning 'to weave']

textured adjective 1 having a certain texture ♦ *coarse-textured*. 2 (said about yarn or fabric) curled or looped.

textured vegetable protein noun a protein obtained from soya beans, made to look like minced meat.

Th abbreviation (*Chemistry*) the symbol for thorium.

Thai (tiy) adjective to do with or coming from Thailand in SE Asia.
Thai noun (**Thais**) 1 a person born in Thailand or descended from people born there. 2 the language of Thailand.

thalidomide (thə-lid-ə-miyd) noun a sedative drug that was found (in 1961) to cause babies to be born with malformed limbs when the mothers took it during pregnancy. [from its chemical name]

thallium noun a chemical element (symbol Tl), a soft white poisonous metallic substance. [from a Greek word *thallos* meaning 'green shoot' (because it has a green line in its spectrum)]

than conjunction used to introduce the second part of a comparison ♦ *She is older than me* or ♦ *She is older than I am.*
◊ You can say ♦ *She is older than me* or ♦ *She is older than I am*, and these are preferred to ♦ *She is older than I*. Note that a sentence such as ♦ *She likes him better than me* means

'She likes him better than she likes me' and not 'She likes him better than I do' (if you intend this second meaning, you have to express it in full like this).

thane *noun* 1 (in Anglo-Saxon England) a man who held land from the king or other superior in return for performing military service. 2 (in Scotland until the 15th century) a man who held land from the Scottish king, a Scottish nobleman, or chief of a clan. [from an Old English word *thegen* meaning 'servant' or ' soldier']

thank *verb* to express gratitude to someone for something they have done or said. [from an Old English word *thancian*]

thankful *adjective* feeling or expressing gratitude. SYNONYMS: grateful, appreciative, indebted.

thankfully *adverb* 1 in a thankful way. 2 fortunately ♦ *Thankfully it has stopped raining.*

thankless *adjective* (said about a task) unpleasant or unappealing, and unlikely to win thanks.

thank-offering *noun* an offering made as an act of thanks.

thanks *plural noun* an expression of gratitude to someone. **thanks to** because of or as a result of ♦ *Thanks to their help we can finish the work in time.*

thanksgiving *noun* an expression of gratitude, especially to God. **Thanksgiving** or **Thanksgiving Day** *noun* (in North America) a holiday for giving thanks to God, in the USA on the fourth Thursday in November, in Canada on the second Monday in October.

thank you *noun & interjection* an expression of thanks ♦ *He left without so much as a thank you.*

that *adjective & pronoun* (**those**) the one there, the person or thing referred to or pointed to or understood ♦ *That book is mine* ♦ *Whose is that?*
that *adverb* so or to such an extent ♦ *I'll go that far.*
that *relative pronoun* which, who, or whom, used to introduce a clause that defines or identifies something or someone ♦ *The book that I sent you* ♦ *The woman that he married.*
that *conjunction* introducing a dependent clause ♦ *We hope that you enjoy your holiday.* **that's that** that is settled or finished. [from an Old English word *thæt*]
◊ Note that *that*, when it is a relative

pronoun or conjunction, is often omitted, especially in speaking: ♦ *The book I sent you* ♦ *We hope you enjoy your holiday.*

thatch *noun* a roof or roof-covering made of straw, reeds, or similar material. **thatch** *verb* to make a roof with thatch. **thatcher** *noun* [from an Old English word *theccan* meaning 'to cover']

Thatcherism *noun* the political and economic policies associated with Margaret Thatcher (now Baroness Thatcher), Prime Minister of the UK 1979–90, including the privatization of public services and a market economy governed by principles of monetarism.

thaw *verb* 1 to become liquid or unfrozen after being frozen, or to cause a substance to do this. SYNONYMS: melt, unfreeze, soften. 2 (said about the weather) to become warm enough for snow or ice to melt. 3 (said about a person) to become less aloof or formal in manner. **thaw** *noun* 1 the process of thawing. 2 weather that is warm enough for snow or ice to melt. [from an Old English word *thawian* (verb)]

the *adjective* (called the *definite article*) used before a noun to indicate: 1 a specific person or a thing ♦ *the President* ♦ *the woman in blue.* 2 something that denotes a class or group ♦ *diseases of the eye* ♦ *the unemployed.* 3 an occupation or activity ♦ *a bit too fond of the bottle.* 4 (*informal*) something that you own or that is connected with you ♦ *I'll go and wash the car* ♦ *Have you met the wife?* 5 (*thee*) the most famous or important bearer of a name ♦ *Do you mean the Sharon Stone?* 6 an amount, especially for a certain price ♦ *Speakers cost £500 for the pair.*
the *adverb* by such an amount ♦ *They felt all the better for their walk.* [from Old English words]

theatre *noun* 1 a building where plays or other forms of entertainment are performed before an audience. 2 a room or hall for lectures, with seats in tiers. 3 an operating theatre. 4 a scene of important events ♦ *a theatre of war.* 5 the writing, acting, and producing of plays. [from a Greek word *theatron* meaning 'place for seeing things']

theatrical *adjective* 1 to do with plays or the theatre. 2 (said about a person or behaviour) exaggerated and designed to make a showy effect.

theatricals *plural noun* the performance of plays in a theatre. **theatrically** *adverb* **theatricality** *noun*

theca (theek-ə) *noun* 1 (*Zoology*) a case or sheath enclosing an organ or part of an animal's body. 2 (*Botany*) a part of a plant serving as a receptacle. [via Latin from a Greek word *thēkē*]

thee *pronoun* a form of **thou** used as the object of a verb or after a preposition.

theft *noun* the act of stealing. SYNONYMS: robbery, (from a building) burglary, (from a shop) shoplifting. [from Old English words]

their *adjective* of or belonging to them. ◊ Do not confuse this word with **there** or **they're**, which have different meanings. [from an Old Norse word]

theirs *possessive pronoun* belonging to them ♦ *This luggage is theirs.* ◊ It is incorrect to write *their's*.

theism (thee-izm) *noun* belief in the existence of gods or a god, especially a creator who maintains a personal relation to the universe. **theist** *noun* **theistic** *adjective* [from Greek *theos* meaning 'a god']

them *pronoun* the form of **they** used as the object of a verb or after a preposition ♦ *We saw them.* [from an Old Norse word]

thematic (thee-mat-ik) *adjective* to do with or forming a theme or themes. **thematically** *adverb*

theme (theem) *noun* 1 the subject about which a person speaks, writes, or thinks. SYNONYMS: topic, subject, issue, matter. 2 (*Music*) a melody which occurs often in a piece or forms the basis for a set of variations. [via Latin from a Greek word *thema* meaning 'proposition']

theme park *noun* an amusement park with activities related to a particular theme or subject.

themselves *pronoun* the form of **them** used in reflexive constructions (e.g. *They hurt themselves*) and for emphasis (e.g. *They themselves wanted it* and *They did it themselves*).

then *adverb* 1 at that time. 2 next, after that; and also. 3 in that case, therefore ♦ *If she said so, then it must be true.*
then *adjective* belonging to that time ♦ *the then duke.*
then *noun* that time ♦ *from then on.* [from Old English]

thence *adverb* (*formal*) 1 from that place. 2 as a result, therefore. [from Old English]

thenceforth or **thenceforward** *adverb* (*formal*) from then on.

theocracy (thi-ok-rə-si) *noun* (**theocracies**) 1 government of a country by priests who rule in the name of God or a god. 2 a country governed in this way. [from a Greek word *theos* meaning 'god' and -*cracy*]

theodolite (thi-od-ə-liyt) *noun* an instrument used in surveying, with a rotating telescope used for measuring horizontal and vertical angles. [origin unknown]

theologian (thi-ə-loh-jiən) *noun* a person who studies theology.

theology (thi-ol-əji) *noun* (**theologies**) 1 the study of religion. 2 a system of religion. **theological** *adjective* **theologically** *adverb* [from a Greek word *theos* meaning 'god' and -*logy*]

theorem *noun* (*Physics and Mathematics*) 1 a statement that has to be proved by reasoning. 2 a rule in algebra and other branches of mathematics, especially one expressed as a formula. [from a Greek word *theōrēma* meaning 'theory']

theoretical *adjective* based on theory and not on practice or experience. SYNONYMS: hypothetical, conjectural. **theoretically** *adverb*

theorize *verb* to form a theory or theories.

theory *noun* (**theories**) 1 a set of ideas proposed by reasoning from known facts to explain something ♦ *Darwin's theory of evolution.* SYNONYMS: hypothesis, conjecture, thesis. 2 an opinion or supposition. 3 ideas or suppositions in general, as contrasted with *practice*. 4 a statement of the principles on which a subject is based ♦ *music theory.* [from a Greek word *theōria* meaning 'thinking, contemplation']

theosophy (thi-oss-əfi) *noun* any of several systems of philosophy that aim at a direct knowledge of God by means of spiritual ecstasy and contemplation. **theosophical** *adjective* **theosophist** *noun* [from Greek words *theos* meaning 'god' and *sophia* meaning 'wisdom']

therapeutic (the-rə-pew-tik) *adjective* helping to relieve or cure a disease or disability.
therapeutics *plural noun* medical treatment of disease.

therapist *noun* a medical specialist who treats diseases and disorders by means of therapy.

therapy *noun* (**therapies**) **1** a form of medical treatment designed to relieve or cure a disease or disability. **2** physiotherapy; psychotherapy. [from Greek *therapeia* meaning 'healing']

Theravada (the-rə-vah-də) *noun* a more conservative form of Buddhism practised in Sri Lanka and parts of SE Asia. [from a Pali (Asian) word *theravada* meaning 'doctrine of the elders']

there *adverb* **1** in or at or to that place. **2** at that point in a process or a series of events. **3** in that matter ♦ *I can't agree with you there.* **4** used to call attention ♦ *Hey, you there!* **5** used to introduce a sentence when the verb comes before its subject ♦ *There was plenty to eat.*
there *noun* that place ♦ *We live near there.*
there *interjection* **1** used to express satisfaction or dismay ♦ *There! what did I tell you!* **2** used to give comfort ♦ *There, there!* [from Old English]
◊ Do not confuse this word with **their** or **they're**, which have different meanings.

thereabouts *adverb* **1** near that place. **2** somewhere near that number or quantity or time etc.

thereafter *adverb* (*formal*) after that.

thereby *adverb* by that means, because of that.

therefore *adverb* for that reason. SYNONYMS: consequently, accordingly, so, thus.

therein *adverb* (*formal*) **1** in that place. **2** in that respect.

thereof *adverb* (*formal*) of that, of it.

thereto *adverb* (*formal*) to that, to it.

thereupon *adverb* (*formal*) **1** as a result of that. **2** immediately after that.

therm *noun* a unit of heat equal to 100,000 thermal units, used especially in measuring a gas supply. [from a Greek word *thermē* meaning 'heat']

thermal *adjective* **1** to do with heat, or using or operated by heat. **2** warm or hot ♦ *thermal springs.*
therm *noun* a rising current of hot air.

thermal unit *noun* a unit for measuring heat.

thermionic valve *noun* (thermi-on-ik) (*Electronics*) a vacuum tube used in radio communication, in which a flow of

electrons is emitted by heated electrodes. [from *thermo-* and *ion*]

thermistor (ther-mist-er) *noun* an electrical resistor whose resistance decreases as its temperature increases, used for measuring and controlling the passage of an electric current. [from *thermal resistor*]

thermo- *prefix* heat. [same origin as for *therm*]

thermocouple *noun* a device for measuring differences in temperature, by means of the thermoelectric voltage developing between two pieces of wire of different metals joined to each other at each end.

thermodynamics *noun* a branch of science dealing with the relations between heat and other forms of energy.
thermodynamic *adjective*

thermoelectric *adjective* producing electricity by a difference of temperatures.

thermometer *noun* an instrument for measuring temperature, especially a graduated glass tube containing mercury or alcohol which expands when heated. [from *thermo-* and *meter*]

thermonuclear *adjective* to do with nuclear reactions that occur at very high temperatures.

thermopile *noun* a set of connected thermocouples used for measuring small quantities of radiant heat.

thermoplastic *adjective* (said especially about synthetic resins) becoming soft and plastic when heated and hardening when cooled.

Thermos *noun* (*trademark*) a vacuum flask.

thermosetting *adjective* (said especially about synthetic resins) setting permanently when heated.

thermosphere *noun* the upper region of the earth's atmosphere above the mesosphere.

thermostat *noun* a device that automatically regulates temperature or activates a device when a certain temperature is reached. **thermostatic** *adjective* **thermostatically** *adverb* [from *thermo-* and a Greek word *statos* meaning 'standing']

thesaurus (thi-sor-əs) *noun* (**thesauruses** or **thesauri** (thi-sor-iy)) **1** a dictionary of synonyms, a book containing words listed in sets according to their meanings. **2** (*old* *use*) a dictionary or encyclopedia. [from a Greek word *thēsauros* meaning 'treasury']

these plural of **this**.

thesis (thee-sis) *noun* (**theses** (-seez)) **1** a statement or theory put forward and supported by arguments. SYNONYMS: theory, argument, premiss, proposition. **2** a long written essay based on personally done research and submitted by a candidate for a university degree. [from a Greek word meaning 'placing' or 'a proposition']

thespian (thess-pi-ən) *adjective* to do with the theatre and acting.
thespian *noun* an actor or actress. [named after the Greek tragic dramatist Thespis (6th century BC)]

thews *plural noun* (*literary*) muscles, or muscular strength. [from an Old English word *thēaw* meaning 'usage' or 'custom']

they *pronoun* **1** the people or things mentioned. **2** people in general ♦ *They say that wildlife is coming back to the cities.* **3** those in authority ♦ *They are planning to increase fees for students.* **4** used to refer to a person of either sex, instead of 'he or she' ♦ *If anyone has lost an umbrella would they please come to the cloakroom.*

they'd *verb* (*informal*) they had or they would.

they'll *verb* (*informal*) they will.

they're *verb* (*informal*) they are.
◊ Do not confuse this word with **their** or **there**, which have different meanings.

they've *verb* (*informal*) they have.

thiamine (thiy-ə-meen) *noun* vitamin B1.

thick *adjective* **1** having its opposite surfaces far apart ♦ *The castle's outer walls were thick and massive.* SYNONYMS: broad, wide, solid, substantial. **2** having its opposite surfaces a certain distance apart ♦ *The tree trunk was six feet thick.* **3** (said about a line) broad and not fine. **4** made of thick material ♦ *a thick coat.* **5** dense or crowded ♦ *a thick forest* ♦ *thick fog.* SYNONYMS: dense, solid. **6** densely covered or filled ♦ *The square was thick with holidaymakers.* SYNONYMS: crowded, packed. **7** (said about a liquid or paste) relatively stiff in consistency, not flowing easily. SYNONYMS: stiff, heavy, glutinous. **8** (said about a person's voice) not sounding clear. **9** (said about an accent) marked or noticeable ♦ *a thick brogue.* **10** (said about a person) stupid. **11** (*informal*) having a close

relationship ♦ *Her parents are very thick with mine.*
thick *adverb* thickly ♦ *Blows came thick and fast.*
thick *noun* the busiest part of a crowd or activity ♦ *They wanted to be in the thick of the local musical scene.* SYNONYMS: centre, heart, core. **a bit thick** (*informal*) unreasonable or excessive. **a thick ear** (*informal*) an ear that is swollen as the result of a blow. **through thick and thin** no matter what the difficulties ♦ *They promised to stand by each other through thick and thin.* **thickly** *adverb* [from an Old English word *thicce*]

thicken *verb* to become thicker or of a stiffer consistency, or to make something do this. **the plot thickens** the situation becomes more interesting or complicated. **thickener** *noun*

thicket *noun* a number of shrubs and small trees growing close together. [from an Old English word *thiccet*, related to **thick**]

thick-headed *adjective* stupid.

thickish *adjective* rather thick.

thickness *noun* **1** the quality of being thick. **2** the distance between the surfaces of something. **3** a layer ♦ *The bed had three thicknesses of blankets.* **4** the part between opposite surfaces ♦ *Steps had been cut in the thickness of the wall.*

thickset *adjective* **1** having a stocky or burly body. **2** with parts placed or growing close together.

thick-skinned *adjective* insensitive to criticism or insults.

thief *noun* (**thieves**) a person who steals someone else's property. SYNONYMS: robber, (from a building) burglar, (from a shop) shoplifter. **thievish** *adjective* **thievery** *noun* [from an Old English word *thiof*]

thieve *verb* to be a thief, to steal things.

thigh *noun* the part of the leg between the hip and the knee. [from an Old English word *theh*]

thimble *noun* a small metal or plastic cap worn on the end of the finger to push the needle in sewing. [from an Old English word *thymel* meaning 'finger stall']

thimbleful *noun* (**thimblefuls**) a small quantity of liquid to drink.

thin *adjective* (**thinner, thinnest**) **1** having its opposite surfaces close together, not thick. **2** (said about a line etc.) narrow and not broad. SYNONYMS: narrow, fine. **3** made of thin material ♦ *a thin dress.* **4** (said

about a person) lean and not plump. SYNONYMS: slim, slender, lean, slight. **5** not dense or plentiful ♦ *The audience on the first night was fairly thin.* SYNONYMS: sparse, scanty, meagre, small. **6** having units that are not crowded or numerous. **7** (said about a liquid or paste) flowing easily, not thick. SYNONYMS: runny, watery, weak. **8** feeble or unconvincing ♦ *a thin excuse.* SYNONYMS: feeble, unconvincing, lame, weak.
thin *adverb* thinly ♦ *Cut the bread thin.*
thin *verb* (**thinned, thinning**) to become thinner, or to make something thinner. **the thin end of the wedge** a change that will lead to more extensive or significant changes. **to thin out** to become less dense or crowded. **to thin something out** to make something less dense or crowded. **thinly** *adverb* **thinness** *noun* thinnish *adjective* [from an Old English word *thynne*]

thine *possessive pronoun* (*old use*) yours (referring to one person).
thine *adjective* a form of **thy** used before a vowel. [from an Old English word *thin*]

thing *noun* **1** something that can be seen or known about. **2** an object or item that cannot or need not be named more precisely ♦ *There were six things on the shelf.* SYNONYMS: item, article, object. **3** an inanimate object as distinct from something living. **4** a person or animal you express a feeling about ♦ *You silly thing!* **5** an act or circumstance, or a task to be done ♦ *That was a funny thing to happen* ♦ *She takes things too seriously.* SYNONYMS: circumstance, occurrence, happening, event. **6** (**the thing**) (*informal*) something suitable or fashionable ♦ *A huge umbrella was just the thing for a wet day.*
things *plural noun* **1** personal belongings or clothing ♦ *I'll go and pack my things.* SYNONYMS: belongings, property, possessions, effects. **2** implements or utensils ♦ *Did you bring your painting things?* **3** circumstances or conditions ♦ *Things began to improve.* **to do your own thing** (*informal*) to follow your own wishes or interests. **to have a thing about** (*informal*) to be preoccupied with something or someone or be obsessed by them. [from an Old English word]

thingamabob or **thingamajig** *noun* (*informal*) another word for **thingummy**.

thingummy *noun* (**thingummies**) (*informal*) a person or thing you do not want or need to name more precisely.

thingy *noun* (**thingies**) (*informal*) another word for **thingummy**.

think *verb* (past tense and past participle **thought**) **1** to use your mind to form ideas. SYNONYMS: contemplate, ponder, cogitate, deliberate, reflect. **2** to have an idea or opinion ♦ *Do you think we will be in time?* ♦ *It is thought to be a fake.* SYNONYMS: consider, believe, suppose, imagine. **3** to form a plan or intention ♦ *We are thinking of moving to London* ♦ *I wouldn't think of disturbing them.* SYNONYMS: consider, contemplate, intend, plan. **4** to consider something ♦ *Think how nice it would be.* **5** to remember something ♦ *I can't think where I put it.* SYNONYMS: remember, recall.
think *noun* (*informal*) an act of thinking ♦ *I had better have a think about that.* **to think better of** to change your mind about something you were going to do. **to think something out** to consider something thoroughly before acting. **to think something over** to consider something carefully. **to think twice** to be cautious about doing something. **to think something up** (*informal*) to invent or produce something by thought. **thinker** *noun* [from an Old English word *thencan*]

think tank *noun* an organization providing advice and ideas, especially on national and commercial problems.

thinner *noun* a substance for thinning paint.

thin-skinned *adjective* sensitive to criticism or insults.

third *adjective* next after second.
third *noun* **1** a person or thing that is third. **2** the third day of a month. **3** third-class honours in a university degree. **4** third gear in a motor vehicle. **5** one of three equal parts of a thing. **thirdly** *adverb* [from an Old English word *thridda*]

third degree *noun* long and severe questioning to get information or a confession.

third party *noun* another person besides the two principal ones involved.

third person *noun* see **person**.

third-rate *adjective* of very inferior or poor quality.

Third World *noun* the poorest and underdeveloped countries of Asia, Africa, and South America. [originally called 'third' because they were not considered to be politically connected with the USA and its allies (*the First World*) or with the Communist countries led by Russia (*the Second World*)]

thirst *noun* 1 the feeling of needing or wanting to drink. 2 a strong desire ♦ *a thirst for adventure.* SYNONYMS: appetite, craving, yearning, hankering, desire.
thirst *verb* to feel a thirst. [from an Old English word *thurst*]

thirsty *adjective* (**thirstier, thirstiest**) 1 needing or wanting to drink. 2 (said about land) in need of water. 3 (*informal*) causing thirst ♦ *thirsty work.* **thirstily** *adverb*

thirteen *adjective & noun* the number 13, one more than twelve. **thirteenth** *adjective & noun*

thirty *adjective & noun* (**thirties**) the number 30, equal to three times ten.
thirties *plural noun* the numbers from 30 to 39, especially representing years of age or degrees of temperature. **thirtieth** *adjective & noun*

this *adjective & pronoun* (**these**) the one here, the person or thing close at hand or just mentioned.
this *adverb* (*informal*) to such an extent ♦ *I'm surprised he got this far.* **this and that** various things. [from an Old English word]

thistle *noun* a prickly wild plant with purple, white, or yellow flowers. [from an Old English word *thistel*]

thistledown *noun* a light fluff on thistle seeds, causing them to be blown about by the wind.

thither *adverb* (old use) to or towards that place.

thong *noun* 1 a narrow strip of hide or leather used as a fastening or as the lash of a whip. 2 a skimpy piece of clothing worn as the lower half of a bikini or as underwear. [from an Old English word *thwong*]

thorax (**thor**-aks) *noun* the part of the body between the head or neck and the abdomen. **thoracic** (thor-**ass**-ik) *adjective* [from a Greek word meaning 'breastplate']

thorium (**thor**-iəm) *noun* a radioactive metallic element (symbol Th). [named after Thor, the Scandinavian god of thunder]

thorn *noun* 1 a sharp pointed growth on the stem of a plant. SYNONYMS: prickle, spine. 2 a thorny tree or shrub. **a thorn in your flesh** something or someone that gives constant trouble. [from an Old English word]

thorny *adjective* (**thornier, thorniest**) 1 having many thorns. 2 causing trouble or difficulty ♦ *a thorny problem.*

thorough *adjective* 1 complete in every detail. SYNONYMS: complete, exhaustive, comprehensive. 2 done or doing things with great care or completeness. SYNONYMS: careful, meticulous, methodical, conscientious. **thoroughly** *adverb* **thoroughness** *noun* [a different spelling of *through*]

thoroughbred *adjective* (said about a horse) bred of pure or pedigree stock.
thoroughbred *noun* a thoroughbred animal.

thoroughfare *noun* a public road or path that is open at both ends. [from *thorough* in an old meaning 'through' and *fare* meaning 'to progress']

thoroughgoing *adjective* thorough.

those plural of *that*.

thou *pronoun* (old use) you (referring to one person). [from an Old English word *thu*]

though *conjunction* in spite of the fact that, even if ♦ *We can run for the train, though it may be too late.*
though *adverb* however ♦ *They were right, though.* [from an Old English word *theah*]

thought[1] *noun* 1 the power of thinking. SYNONYMS: intelligence, reason. 2 the process of thinking. SYNONYMS: meditation, deliberation, contemplation, reflection. 3 a way of thinking that is associated with a particular time or group of people ♦ *in modern thought.* 4 an idea or piece of reasoning produced by thinking. SYNONYMS: idea, brainwave. 5 an intention ♦ *We had no thought of giving offence.* 6 consideration ♦ *They will give the proposal serious thought.* SYNONYMS: consideration, attention. [from an Old English word *thoht*]

thought[2] past tense and past participle of **think**.

thoughtful *adjective* 1 thinking carefully about what other people need and want, considerate. SYNONYMS: considerate, caring, kind, helpful, obliging, attentive. 2 thinking hard and carefully, often absorbed in thought. SYNONYMS: pensive, reflective, absorbed. 3 (said about a book, writer, or remark) showing signs of careful thought. SYNONYMS: reasoned, intelligent. **thoughtfully** *adverb* **thoughtfulness** *noun*

thoughtless *adjective* 1 not thinking about other people, inconsiderate. SYNONYMS: inconsiderate, uncaring, inattentive. 2 not thinking about the possible effects or consequences of something. **thoughtlessly** *adverb* **thoughtlessness** *noun*

thousand *adjective & noun* the number 1,000, equal to ten times a hundred ♦ *a few thousand.* **thousandth** *adjective & noun* [from an Old English word *thusend*] ◊ Notice that you say ♦ *three thousand* and ♦ *a few thousand*, not *thousands*.

thousandfold *adjective & adverb* one thousand times as much or as many.

thrall (thrawl) *noun* (old use) **in thrall** in bondage. [from an Old English word *thræl* meaning 'slave']

thrash *verb* 1 to beat someone with a stick or whip. SYNONYMS: beat, whip, flog. 2 to defeat an opponent or opposing side heavily. SYNONYMS: trounce, crush, overwhelm. 3 to move around in a violent or uncontrolled way ♦ *He was on the floor, thrashing around in pain.* SYNONYMS: wave, toss, flail. 4 to move something violently or threateningly ♦ *The crocodile was thrashing its tail.* **to thrash something out** to discuss a matter thoroughly. [from an Old English word, a different spelling of *thresh*]

thread *noun* 1 a length of spun cotton, wool, or other fibre used in making cloth or in sewing or knitting. SYNONYMS: fibre, strand. 2 a thin length of any substance. 3 the spiral ridge round the edge of a screw. 4 a theme or argument running through a piece of writing or speaking ♦ *I'm afraid I've lost the thread.* **thread** *verb* 1 to put a thread through the eye of a needle. 2 to put beads on a thread. 3 to pass a strip of film or other material through or round something into the right position for use. 4 to cut a thread on a screw. **to thread your way** to make your way carefully through a crowded street or area. **threader** *noun* [from an Old English word *thræd*]

threadbare *adjective* (said about cloth) having a surface worn with age and the threads showing. SYNONYMS: worn, shabby, tattered.

threadworm *noun* a small worm like a thread, especially one sometimes found in the intestines of children.

threat *noun* 1 an expression of a person's intention to punish, hurt, or harm someone or something. 2 a sign of something unwelcome ♦ *There's a slight threat of rain.* **danger**, risk. 3 a person or thing that might cause danger or catastrophe ♦ *Technology was seen as a*

threat to people's jobs. [from an Old English word *threat* meaning 'oppression']

threaten *verb* 1 to make a threat or threats against someone, to try to influence someone by using threats. SYNONYMS: intimidate, menace, bully, browbeat. 2 to be a warning of something unwelcome ♦ *The clouds threatened rain.* 3 to seem likely to be or do something unwelcome ♦ *The costs are threatening to increase rapidly.* 4 to be a threat or danger to someone ♦ *Money problems are threatening us.*

three *adjective & noun* the number 3, one more than two. **the three Rs** reading, writing, and arithmetic, as the basis of elementary education. [from an Old English word *thrie*]

three-dimensional *adjective* having the three dimensions of length, breadth, and depth, or appearing to.

threefold *adjective & adverb* 1 three times as much or as many. 2 consisting of three parts.

three-legged race *noun* a race between pairs of runners with the right leg of one tied to the left leg of the other.

three-line whip *noun* a written notice, underlined three times to indicate urgency, to members of a party in parliament to attend a vote.

three-piece suite *noun* a matching sofa and two chairs.

three-ply *adjective* made of three strands or layers.

three-quarter *adjective* consisting of three-quarters of something in size, length, etc. **three-quarter** *noun* (in rugby) a position just behind the half-backs.

three quarters *plural noun* three out of four parts of something. **three-quarters** *adverb* to the extent of three quarters ♦ *After two hours we were three-quarters finished.*

threesome *noun* a group of three people.

three-wheeler *noun* a vehicle with three wheels.

thresh *verb* to beat corn with a flail or a machine in order to separate the grain from the husks. [from an Old English word *therscan*]

threshold *noun* 1 a piece of wood or stone forming the bottom of a doorway, or (more generally) the entrance as a whole. **2** the point at which something begins to happen ♦ *Scientists are on the threshold of a new discovery.* **3** the point at which something has an effect ♦ *a low pain threshold.* [from an Old English word *threscold*]

threw past tense of **throw**.

thrice *adverb* (old use) three times.

thrift *noun* **1** careful management and use of money or other resources. SYNONYMS: frugality, economy, prudence. **2** a plant with pink flowers, often growing on sea cliffs and hills. [same origin as for *thrive*]

thriftless *adjective* not thrifty, using money or resources extravagantly.

thrifty *adjective* (**thriftier, thriftiest**) practising thrift, using money or other resources carefully. SYNONYMS: frugal, economic, prudent. **thriftily** *adverb*

thrill *noun* **1** a sudden feeling of pleasure and excitement. SYNONYM: excitement; (*informal*) buzz. **2** a wave of feeling or emotion.
thrill *verb* to feel a thrill, or to give someone a thrill. SYNONYMS: (with object) delight, excite. [from a dialect word *thirl* meaning 'to pierce']

thriller *noun* an exciting story, play, or film, usually involving crime or espionage.

thrive *verb* (past tense **thrived** or **throve**; past participle **thrived** or **thriven**) **1** to grow or develop strongly. **2** to prosper or be successful ♦ *The business is thriving.* SYNONYMS: prosper, flourish, succeed, do well. [from an Old Norse word *thrifask* meaning 'to prosper']

throat *noun* **1** the passage in the neck through which food and air pass into the body. **2** the front part of the neck. **to be at each other's throats** to fight or quarrel. [from an Old English word *throte*]

throaty *adjective* (**throatier, throatiest**) **1** produced deep in the throat ♦ *a throaty laugh.* **2** hoarse. **throatily** *adverb* **throatiness** *noun*

throb *verb* (**throbbed, throbbing**) **1** to beat or sound with a strong steady rhythm ♦ *My heart was throbbing with excitement.* SYNONYMS: pound, beat, pulsate. **2** to give pain in a steady rhythm ♦ *a throbbing wound.*
throb *noun* a strong regular beat or rhythm. [an imitation of the sound]

throes *plural noun* severe pangs of pain. in

the throes of struggling with ♦ *We are in the throes of moving house.* [origin unknown]

thrombosis (throm-boh-sis) *noun* (**thromboses**) formation of a clot of blood in a blood vessel or organ of the body. [from a Greek word *thrombos* meaning 'lump']

throne *noun* **1** a ceremonial chair used by a king, queen, or bishop on formal occasions. **2** (**the throne**) the power or position of a sovereign ♦ *the heir to the throne.* [from a Greek word *thronos* meaning 'high seat']

throng *noun* a crowded mass of people. SYNONYMS: crowd, mass, mob, horde.
throng *verb* **1** to come or go or press in a throng. SYNONYMS: crowd, swarm, flock. **2** to fill a place with a crowd of people ♦ *Tourists thronged the main square.* SYNONYMS: crowd, pack. [from an Old English word]

throttle *noun* a device that controls the flow of fuel to an engine, or the lever or pedal that operates this.
throttle *verb* to strangle someone. SYNONYMS: strangle, choke, suffocate, stifle. [perhaps related to *throat*]

through *preposition* **1** from one end or side of to the other end or side of ♦ *The dog climbed through a window* ♦ *Cars raced through the tunnel.* **2** between or among ♦ *scuffling through fallen leaves.* **3** from beginning to end of, so as to have finished or completed ♦ *They are all through their exams.* **4** (North Amer.) up to and including ♦ *Monday through Friday.* **5** because of ♦ *We lost it through carelessness.*
through *adverb* **1** from one end or side to the other ♦ *The cat jumped up to the window and squeezed through.* **2** connected by telephone ♦ *I think I'm through at last.* **3** finished ♦ *Wait till we're through with our meeting.*
through *adjective* **1** going through something. **2** (said about traffic or passengers etc.) going all the way to a destination. **3** having finished a relationship or activity ♦ *She said they were through.* **through and through** thoroughly, completely. [from an Old English word *thurh*]

throughout *preposition & adverb* all the way through, from beginning to end.

throughput *noun* the amount of material dealt with by a process or system.

throve past tense of **thrive**.

throw verb (**threw, thrown**) 1 to send something or someone through the air or in a certain direction. SYNONYMS: fling, toss, hurl, cast, pitch, heave; (informal) chuck, sling. 2 (said about a horse) to send its rider to the ground. 3 to force an opponent to the ground in wrestling, judo, etc. 4 (informal) to confuse or disconcert someone ♦ Your question threw me. SYNONYMS: confuse, disconcert, unnerve; (informal) flummox, stump, rattle. 5 (informal) to lose a race or match deliberately, especially by being bribed. 6 to put clothes on or off hurriedly or casually. 7 to move or turn a part of the body quickly ♦ He threw his head back and laughed. 8 to project your voice so that it seems to come from another source. 9 to put someone in a certain state ♦ They will be thrown out of work ♦ We were thrown into confusion. 10 to apply or make use of something ♦ They threw all their energy into the task. 11 to build a structure that projects or extends ♦ The army threw a bridge across the river. 12 to score a number by throwing a dice in a game ♦ I've thrown another six. 13 to shape rounded pottery on a wheel. 14 to move a switch or lever so as to operate it. 15 to have a fit or tantrum. 16 (informal) to hold a party.
throw noun 1 the act of throwing. 2 the distance something is or may be thrown. **to throw something away** 1 to get rid of something because it is useless or unwanted. SYNONYMS: discard, get rid of, dispose of, jettison, scrap; (informal) dump, ditch. 2 to waste or fail to use an opportunity or advantage. **to throw something in** 1 to include something extra without further charge. 2 to add a remark to a conversation or discussion. **to throw in the towel** or **sponge** to give up or admit failure. **to throw light on** to make something clearer or easier to understand. **to throw someone off** to manage to escape from people. **to throw something off** 1 to manage to get rid of something ♦ to throw off a cold. 2 to write something hurriedly or casually ♦ He threw off a few lines of verse. **to throw yourself into** to start doing something with energy or enthusiasm. **to throw someone out** to expel someone forcibly. **to throw something out** 1 to get rid of something no longer wanted. 2 to cause calculations to become wrong or inaccurate. **to throw someone over** to desert or abandon someone. **to throw the book at** (informal) to charge or punish someone severely. **to throw people together** to bring people into contact by

chance. **to throw something together** to make something hurriedly or in an improvised way. **to throw up** (informal) to vomit. **to throw something up** 1 to bring something to people's notice ♦ Their researches threw up some interesting facts. 2 to abandon or discontinue something ♦ She decided to throw up her job. **thrower** noun [from an Old English word thrawan meaning 'to twist' or 'to turn']

throwaway adjective 1 designed to be thrown away after use. 2 (said about a remark) said casually or in an offhand way.

throwback noun an animal or custom having characteristics of an older ancestor or practice.

throw-in noun (in football) the throwing in of a ball after it has gone out of play over the touchline.

thrum verb (**thrummed, thrumming**) to strum the strings of a musical instrument, to sound monotonously. **thrum** noun a thrumming sound. [an imitation of the sound]

thrush [1] noun a songbird with a brownish back and speckled breast. [from an Old English word thrysce]

thrush [2] noun 1 a fungus infection causing white patches in the mouth and throat, especially in children. 2 an infection of the female genitals caused by the same fungus. [origin unknown]

thrust verb (past tense and past participle **thrust**) 1 to push something suddenly and forcibly. SYNONYMS: push, shove, force, ram. 2 to make a forward stroke with a sword or other weapon. 3 to force something unwelcome on someone ♦ They were angry at having these ideas thrust on them. **thrust** noun 1 a thrusting movement or force. 2 a hostile remark aimed at a person. **thruster** noun [from an Old Norse word thrysta]

thud noun a low dull sound like that of something heavy hitting the ground. **thud** verb (**thudded, thudding**) to make a thud, or to fall with a thud. [probably from an Old English word thyddan meaning 'to thrust']

thug noun a violent and brutal man, especially a criminal. SYNONYMS: ruffian, hooligan, hoodlum. **thuggery** noun [from a Hindi word thag meaning 'swindler' or 'thief'. The Thugs were robbers and murderers in India in the 17th to 19th centuries]

thulium *noun* a chemical element (symbol Tm), a soft silvery-white metallic substance. [from Latin *Thule*, a name for the most northern part of the world]

thumb *noun* the short thick finger of the hand, set apart from the other four. **thumb** *verb* to turn the pages of a book with your thumb. **to be all thumbs** to handle things clumsily. **to thumb a lift** to get a lift by signalling with your thumb, to hitch-hike. **to thumb your nose** (*informal*) to show contempt or disapproval. **thumbs down** a gesture of disapproval or rejection. **thumbs up** a gesture of approval or satisfaction. **under someone's thumb** completely under someone's influence. [from an Old English word *thuma*]

thumbnail *noun* the nail on a thumb. **thumbnail** *adjective* brief and succinct ♦ *a thumbnail sketch.*

thumbscrew *noun* 1 a former instrument of torture for crushing the thumb. 2 a screw with a flattened head for turning with the thumb and forefinger.

thump *verb* 1 to strike or knock something heavily. SYNONYMS: hit, strike, punch, knock, slap, clout. 2 to beat or punch someone. 3 to throb or beat with a strong pulse ♦ *My heart was thumping.* **thump** *noun* a heavy blow, or the sound made by this. [an imitation of the sound]

thumping *adjective* (*informal*) very large ♦ *Labour won the election with a thumping majority.*

thunder *noun* 1 the loud noise heard after a flash of lightning during an electrical storm. 2 a loud or enthusiastic noise ♦ *The concert ended with thunders of applause.* **thunder** *verb* 1 to make the sound of thunder ♦ *It was thundering in the distance.* 2 to make a loud rumbling noise ♦ *The train thundered past.* 3 to speak loudly or angrily. SYNONYMS: bellow, roar. **to steal someone's thunder** to use someone's ideas or words before they can do so themselves. **thunderer** *noun* **thundery** *adjective* [from an Old English word *thunor*. The idiom *to steal someone's thunder* comes from the remark of an 18th-century dramatist when the stage thunder intended for his play was taken and used for another]

thunderbolt *noun* 1 a lightning flash and a

clap of thunder occurring together. 2 something startling or immensely powerful in effect.

thunderclap *noun* a clap of thunder.

thunderous *adjective* like thunder.

thunderstorm *noun* a storm with thunder.

thunderstruck *adjective* very surprised or shocked.

Thursday *noun* the day of the week following Wednesday. [from an Old English word *thuresdæg* meaning 'day of thunder', named after the god Thor]

thus *adverb* (*formal*) 1 in this way, like this ♦ *Hold the book thus.* 2 as a result of this ♦ *He was the eldest son and thus heir to the title.* 3 to this extent ♦ *thus far.*

thwack *verb* to strike someone or something with a heavy blow. **thwack** *noun* a heavy blow, or the sound of this. [an imitation of the sound]

thwart *verb* to prevent someone from doing what they want or intend; to prevent a plan from being achieved. SYNONYMS: frustrate, hinder, foil, baulk. **thwart** *noun* a piece of wood across a boat, for a rower to sit on. [from an Old Norse word *thvert* meaning 'going across']

thy *adjective* (*old use*) your (referring to one person).

thyme (tiym) *noun* a herb with fragrant leaves, used in cooking. [from a Greek word *thumon*]

thymus *noun* a gland near the base of the neck, which in humans becomes smaller at the beginning of puberty.

thyristor (thiy-**rist**-er) *noun* (*Electronics*) a switch in the form of a semiconductor device in which a small electric current is used to start the flow of a large current. [from a Greek word *thura* meaning 'gate' and *transistor*]

thyroid or **thyroid gland** *noun* a large gland at the front of the neck, which secretes hormones regulating the body's growth and development. [from a Greek word *thureos* meaning 'shield' (because of the shape of the gland)]

thyself *pronoun* (*old use*) yourself.

Ti *abbreviation* (*Chemistry*) the symbol for titanium.

tiara (ti-**ar**-ə) *noun* 1 a jewelled band worn by a woman at the front of her hair on formal occasions. 2 a diadem worn by the pope, pointed at the top and surrounded by three crowns. [from a Greek word]

tibia *noun* (**tibiae**) (*Anatomy*) the bone on the inner side of the leg between the knee and the ankle, parallel to the fibula. [a Latin word meaning 'shin bone']

tic *noun* an involuntary twitching of the muscles, especially of the face. [via French from an Italian word *ticchio*]

tick [1] *noun* **1** a mark (✓) placed against something written or printed to show that it is correct or that it has been dealt with. **2** a regularly repeated clicking sound, especially that made by a watch or clock. **3** (*informal*) a moment.
tick *verb* **1** (said about a clock or watch) to make a series of ticks. **2** to put a tick beside something written or printed. **to tick someone off** (*informal*) to scold or reprimand someone. SYNONYMS: scold, rebuke, reprimand, chide, upbraid, tell off. **to tick something off** to mark something with a tick to show that it has been dealt with. **to tick over 1** (said about an engine) to run slowly without being connected. **2** (said about an activity) to continue in a routine way. **what makes someone tick** what makes someone behave in a certain way. [probably from German and Dutch words]

tick [2] *noun* **1** a mite or parasitic insect that attaches itself to the skin and sucks blood. [from an Old English word *ticia*]

tick [3] *noun* (*informal*) credit ♦ *I bought it on tick.* [thought to be a shortening of *ticket* (because the credit arrangement was recorded on a ticket)]

ticker *noun* (*informal*) **1** a watch. **2** a person's heart.

ticker tape *noun* a paper strip on which messages are issued from a teleprinter.

ticket *noun* **1** a written or printed piece of card or paper that entitles a person to go into a place or travel on public transport etc. **2** a label attached to something to show its price or give other information about it. **3** an official notification of a traffic offence ♦ *a parking ticket.* **4** (*North Amer.*) a party's list of candidates in an election.
ticket *verb* (**ticketed, ticketing**) to put a ticket or label on something. **just the ticket** (*informal*) exactly what is right or wanted. [from an Old French word *estiquier* meaning 'to fix']

tickle *verb* **1** to touch or stroke a person's skin lightly so as to cause a slight tingling sensation, usually making them wriggle or laugh. **2** to feel this sensation ♦ *My foot tickles.* **3** to amuse or please someone. SYNONYMS: amuse, cheer, delight, please. **tickle** *noun* the act of tickling or the feeling of being tickled. [origin unknown]

ticklish *adjective* **1** sensitive to tickling, likely to wriggle or laugh when tickled. **2** (said about a problem) needing careful handling. **ticklishness** *noun*

tidal *adjective* to do with or affected by a tide or tides. **tidally** *adverb*

tidal wave *noun* **1** a huge and powerful wave in the sea, especially one caused by an earthquake. **2** a great wave of enthusiasm or indignation etc.

tiddler *noun* (*informal*) **1** a small fish. **2** an unusually small person or thing. [origin unknown]

tiddly [1] *adjective* (**tiddlier, tiddliest**) (*informal*) very small. [origin unknown]

tiddly [2] *adjective* (**tiddlier, tiddliest**) (*informal*) slightly drunk. [origin unknown]

tiddlywink *noun* a small counter flicked into a cup by pressing the edge of it with another counter in the game called *tiddlywinks.* [origin unknown]

tide *noun* **1** the regular rise and fall in the level of the sea, which usually happens twice a day and is caused by the attraction of the moon and the sun. **2** a powerful trend of opinion or feeling ♦ *a tide of excitement.* **3** (old use) a season ♦ *Christmas-tide.*
tide *verb* to float with the tide. **to tide someone over** to help someone through a difficult period by providing what they need. **tideless** *adjective* [from an Old English word *tid* meaning 'time' or 'period']

tidemark *noun* **1** a line left on the shore by the tide. **2** a dirty mark left on the inside of a bath or washbasin when the water has been emptied.

tideway *noun* a channel in which a tide runs, especially the tidal part of a river.

tidings *plural noun* (*literary*) news or information. [from an Old English word *tidung* meaning 'piece of news', probably from Old Norse words]

tidy *adjective* (**tidier, tidiest**) **1** arranged in a neat and orderly way. SYNONYMS: neat, orderly, shipshape, smart. **2** (said about a person) neat and orderly in appearance or behaviour. **3** (*informal*) (usually said about a sum of money) fairly large ♦ *She left a tidy fortune when she died.*

tidy *noun* (**tidies**)
1 a spell of tidying. **2** a receptacle for odds and ends.

tidy *verb* (**tidies, tidied, tidying**) to make something tidy. **tidily** *adverb* **tidiness** *noun* [from an earlier meaning 'at the right time or season', from *tide*]

tie *verb* (**ties, tied, tying**) **1** to attach or fasten something with string, cord, etc. SYNONYMS: attach, fasten, bind, secure, tether. **2** to arrange string, ribbon, a tie, etc. to form a knot or bow. SYNONYM: knot. **3** (*Music*) to link notes with a tie. **4** in a game or competition, to reach the same score as another competitor or team ♦ *They tied for second place.* SYNONYM: draw. **5** to restrict or limit what a person can do or where they can live.

tie *noun* **1** (also **necktie**) a strip of material worn round the neck, passing under the collar and knotted in front. **2** a string or cord used for tying something. **3** something that unites things or people, a bond. **4** something that restricts a person's freedom of action. **5** (*Music*) a curved line over two notes of the same pitch in a score, indicating that the second is not sounded separately. **6** a result of a game or competition in which two or more competitors have achieved the same score. SYNONYM: draw. **7** a sports match between two competing teams or players, the winner passing on to the next round. **to tie in** (said about information or facts) to agree or be connected with something else. **to tie someone up 1** to restrain someone by binding them. **2** to occupy someone so that they have no time for other activities. **to tie something up 1** to fasten something with cord etc. **2** to invest money or impose restrictions on it so that it cannot be freely used. [from an Old English word *tigan*]

tie beam *noun* a horizontal beam connecting rafters.

tie-break or **tie-breaker** *noun* a means of deciding a winner in a game or competition in which two or more competitors have tied.

tie clip *noun* an ornamental clip for keeping a tie in place.

tied *adjective* **1** (said about a house) for use by a person who works for its owner. **2** (said about a public house) owned and

controlled by one brewery. **3** (said about a loan) given for a particular purpose and not to be used for another.

tie-dye *noun* a method of producing dyed patterns by tying parts of a fabric to mask them from the dye.

tiepin *noun* an ornamental pin for holding a tie in place.

tie-up *noun* a connection or link.

tier (teer) *noun* each of a series of rows or levels placed one above the other. **tiered** *adjective* [from a French word *tire* meaning 'order' or 'sequence']

tiff *noun* a brief or minor quarrel. [probably from a dialect word]

tiger *noun* a large animal of the cat family native to Asia, with yellow-brown and black stripes. [via Latin from a Greek word *tigris*]

tiger lily *noun* a tall garden lily with dark-spotted orange flowers.

tiger moth *noun* a moth with wings that are streaked like a tiger's face.

tight *adjective* **1** fixed or fastened firmly, hard to move or undo or open. SYNONYMS: secure, form, fast, fixed. **2** fitting very closely ♦ *She was wearing a tight dress.* **3** well sealed against liquid or air. **4** severe or strictly imposed ♦ *Security was tight at the airport* ♦ *We are all working to a tight schedule.* SYNONYMS: severe, strict. **5** (said about a group or organization) well organized and controlled. **6** (said about a rope, cord, etc., or a surface) stretched so as to leave no slack. SYNONYMS: stretched, tight, tense. **7** not easy to obtain, in short supply ♦ *Money is tight at the moment.* **8** (*informal*) drunk. **9** stingy ♦ *He is rather tight with his money.*
tight *adverb* tightly or firmly ♦ *Please hold tight* ♦ *The top is screwed down tight.* **in a tight corner** or **spot** in a difficult or dangerous situation. **tightly** *adverb* **tightness** *noun* [from an earlier meaning 'healthy' or 'vigorous', from an early word *thight* meaning 'firm' or 'solid']

tighten *verb* to make something tighter, or to become tighter. **to tighten your belt** to spend less, to live more frugally or economically.

tight-fisted *adjective* stingy with money.

tight-lipped *adjective* with the lips firmly closed, not saying anything or showing any feelings.

tightrope *noun* a rope stretched tightly high above the ground, on which acrobats perform.

tights *plural noun* a close-fitting piece of clothing covering the feet, legs, and lower part of the body.

tigress *noun* a female tiger.

tilde (til-də) *noun* a mark (˜) put over a letter in some languages, especially over Spanish *n* when this is pronounced as in ♦ *señor* or over Portuguese *a* or *o* when these are nasalized. [via Spanish from a Latin word *titulus*, related to *title*]

tile *noun* 1 a thin square piece of baked clay or other hard material, used in rows for covering roofs, walls, or floors. 2 any of the small flat pieces used in mah-jong and some other games.
tile *verb* to cover a surface with tiles. [via Old English from a Latin word *tegula*]

till¹ *preposition & conjunction* until. [from an Old English word *til* meaning 'to']
◊ See the note at **until.**

till² a drawer or box for money in a shop, a cash register. [origin unknown]

till³ *verb* to prepare and use land for growing crops. [from an Old English word *tilian* meaning 'to try for']

tiller *noun* a horizontal bar attached to the rudder of a boat, used for steering. [from an Old English word *telga* meaning 'bough']

tilt *verb* 1 to move into a sloping position, or to make something do this. SYNONYMS: lean, slant, tip, slope, list. 2 to run or thrust with a lance in jousting.
tilt *noun* a sloping position or movement.
at full tilt at full speed or with full force. **to tilt at windmills** to fight with imaginary enemies. [origin unknown. The phrase *to tilt at windmills* comes from the story of Don Quixote, who attacked windmills thinking they were giants.]

timber *noun* 1 wood prepared for use in building or carpentry. 2 trees grown for producing this type of wood. 3 a wooden beam used in building a house or ship. [from an Old English word meaning 'building' or 'building material']

timbered *adjective* 1 (said about a building) built of timber or with a timber framework. 2 (said about land) wooded.

timberline *noun* the level of land above which no trees grow.

timbre (tambr) *noun* the characteristic quality of a voice or musical sound. [via French from a Greek word *tumpanon* meaning 'drum']

time *noun* 1 all the years of the past, present, and future regarded as a whole. 2 the passing of time ♦ *Time will show who is right.* 3 a particular point or portion of time associated with certain events or conditions ♦ *in Tudor times* ♦ *in times of hardship.* SYNONYMS: age, period, day. 4 an experience or period of activity ♦ *We all had a good time* ♦ *She spent a long time in the library.* 5 a point or portion of time taken or allowed for something ♦ *How much time did it take?* ♦ *Now is the time to speak out* ♦ *It's nearly lunch time.* 6 the point of time when something must occur or end. 7 an occasion or instance ♦ *That was the last time we saw him* ♦ *A bus goes to the village three times a day.* SYNONYMS: occasion, instance, opportunity. 8 a point of time stated in hours and minutes ♦ *The time is exactly two o'clock.* 9 any of the standard systems by which time is reckoned ♦ *Greenwich Mean Time.* 10 measured time spent in work or other activity, especially as a basis for payment ♦ *They are being paid double time.* 11 (*Music*) tempo or rhythm depending on the number and accentuation of beats in a bar.
time *verb* 1 to choose or arrange the time or moment for something ♦ *The meeting has been timed for Monday afternoon.* 2 to measure the time taken by a person or activity.
times *plural noun* 1 present-day conditions and customs ♦ *Times are bad.* 2 used to express multiplication ♦ *Three times four is twelve.* **to do time** (*informal*) to serve a prison sentence. **for the time being** until some other arrangement is made. **from time to time** at intervals. **to have no time for** 1 to be unable or unwilling to spend time on something. 2 to dislike or disapprove of someone or something. **in no time** very soon or very quickly. **in time** 1 punctually, not late. 2 eventually, sooner or later. **on time** punctually, not late. [from an Old English word *tima*]

time-and-motion study *noun* a procedure for measuring the efficiency of business or industrial activities.

time bomb *noun* a bomb that can be set to explode at a certain time.

time-consuming *adjective* needing a lot of time to do.

time-honoured adjective (said about a practice or custom) established and valued because it has existed for a long time.

timekeeper noun 1 a person who records the amount of time taken by a process or of work done by people. 2 a person considered in terms of how punctual they are, or a watch or clock in terms of how accurate it is ♦ a good timekeeper.

time lag noun an interval of time between two connected events.

timeless adjective not affected by the passage of time or by changes of taste or fashion.

time limit noun a limit of time within which something must be done.

timely adjective occurring at a suitable or useful time ♦ a timely warning. **timeliness** noun

timepiece noun (formal) a clock or watch.

timer noun 1 a device for timing things. 2 a device for activating something at a preset time.

timeshare noun 1 an arrangement by which several people own a holiday home and have the right to use it at agreed times each year. 2 a property owned and used in this way. **timesharing** noun

time signature noun see **signature**.

time switch noun a switch that can be set to act automatically at a certain time.

timetable noun a list showing the time at which certain events will happen, e.g. when buses or trains leave and arrive, or when lessons take place in a school. **timetable** verb to organize events in a timetable.

time zone noun a region between two lines of longitude, in which a common standard time is used.

timid adjective shy or easily frightened. SYNONYMS: shy, coy, diffident, bashful, sheepish. **timidly** adverb **timidity** (tim-id-iti) noun [from a Latin word timidus meaning 'nervous']

timing noun 1 the choice and control of when something is going to happen. 2 a particular time when something happens.

timorous (tim-er-əs) adjective nervous or timid. **timorously** adverb **timorousness** noun [from a Latin word timor meaning 'fear']

timpani (timp-ən-ee) plural noun kettledrums. [an Italian word]

timpanist noun a person who plays the timpani in an orchestra.

tin noun 1 a silvery-white metal, a chemical element (symbol Sn). 2 iron or steel sheets coated with tin. 3 an airtight container for preserved food, made of tinplate. **tin** verb (**tinned, tinning**) 1 to seal food in a tin in order to preserve it. 2 to cover a surface with a thin layer of tin. [from an Old English word]

tin can noun a tin for preserving food.

tincture noun 1 a solution consisting of a medicinal substance dissolved in alcohol, ♦ tincture of quinine. 2 a slight tinge or trace of some element or quality. **tincture** verb to tinge. [same origin as tint]

tinder noun a dry material such as wood or paper that catches fire easily. [from an Old English word]

tinderbox noun (historical) a metal box containing dry material, flint and steel, and other things used for lighting a fire.

tine noun a point or prong of a fork, harrow, or antler. [from an Old English word tind]

tinfoil noun a thin sheet of tin, aluminium, or tin alloy, used for wrapping and packing things.

ting verb to make a sharp ringing sound. **ting** noun a tinging sound. [an imitation of the sound]

tinge (tinj) verb (**tinging** or **tingeing**) 1 to colour something slightly ♦ white tinged with pink. 2 to influence or affect something, especially a feeling, slightly ♦ Their admiration was tinged with envy. **tinge** noun a slight colouring or trace. [same origin as for tint]

tingle verb to have a slight pricking or stinging sensation. **tingle** noun this sensation. [probably from tinkle]

tin god noun a self-important person, especially a minor official.

tinker noun 1 a person who travels about mending people's pots and pans. 2 (informal) a mischievous person or animal. 3 a spell of tinkering ♦ have a tinker at it. **tinker** verb to work at something casually, trying to improve it or mend it. [origin unknown]

tinkle *verb* to make a series of short light ringing sounds.
tinkle *noun* **1** a tinkling sound. **2** (*informal*) a telephone call. [from an obsolete word *tink* meaning 'to chink or clink', an imitation of the sound]

tinny *adjective* (**tinnier, tinniest**) **1** like tin, especially in not looking strong or solid. **2** having a metallic taste or a thin metallic sound.

tin-opener *noun* a tool for opening tins of food.

tinplate *noun* sheet iron or steel coated thinly with tin. **tin-plated** *adjective*

tinpot *adjective* (*informal*) having no real value or power ♦ *a tinpot dictator.*

tinsel *noun* strips of glittering material used for decoration. **tinselled** *adjective* [from an Old French word *estincele* meaning 'spark', related to *scintillate*]

tint *noun* **1** a shade or variety of a particular colour. SYNONYMS: shade, hue, tinge, tone. **2** a slight trace of a different colour ♦ *blue with a green tint.*
tint *verb* to give a tint to something, to colour something slightly. [from a Latin word *tinctum* meaning 'stained']

tintinnabulation *noun* (*formal*) a ringing or tinkling sound, especially of bells. [from a Latin word *tintinnabulum* meaning 'tinkling bell']

tiny *adjective* (**tinier, tiniest**) very small. SYNONYMS: minute, minuscule, miniature, diminutive. [from an obsolete word *tine* meaning 'very small']

tip[1] *noun* **1** the part at the very end or top of something, especially something small or tapering. **2** a small part or piece fitted to the end of something.
tip *verb* (**tipped, tipping**) to provide something with a tip. **on the tip of your tongue** almost remembered or spoken but not quite. **tip of the iceberg** see **iceberg**. [from an Old Norse word *typpi*]

tip[2] *verb* (**tipped, tipping**) **1** to tilt or topple, or to make something do this. SYNONYMS: lean, tilt, topple, slant. **2** to empty the contents of a container by tilting it ♦ *She tipped the dirty water down the drain.* **3** to strike or touch something lightly. **4** to name someone or something as likely to win or succeed. **5** to make a small present of money to a person, especially to someone who has done you a service.
tip *noun* **1** a small present of money given to someone who has done you a service. **2** a small but useful piece of advice on how to do something. **3** a recommendation or piece of information about someone or something that is likely to win or succeed. **4** a slight tilt or push. **5** a place where rubbish or refuse is tipped. **6** (*informal*) a messy or untidy place. **to tip someone off** to give someone special information about something that is likely to happen. SYNONYMS: warn, alert, forewarn. **to tip the balance** or **scale** to be the deciding factor in an activity or decision. **tipper** *noun* [probably from a Scandinavian language]

tip-off *noun* (*informal*) special information given to someone about something that is likely to happen.

tipple *verb* to drink alcoholic drinks.
tipple *noun* (*informal*) a spell of drinking alcoholic drinks. **tippler** *noun* [origin unknown]

tipster *noun* a person who gives tips, especially about horse races.

tipsy *adjective* (**tipsier, tipsiest**) slightly drunk. **tipsily** *adverb* **tipsiness** *noun* [from *tip*[2]]

tiptoe *verb* (**tiptoes, tiptoed, tiptoeing**) to walk very quietly or carefully, with your heels not touching the ground. **on tiptoe** walking or standing on your toes.

tiptop *adjective* (*informal*) excellent, very best ♦ *in tiptop condition.* [from *tip*[1] and *top*[1]]

TIR *abbreviation* Transport International Routier. [a French abbreviation, meaning 'international road transport']

tiramisu (ti-rə-mi-**soo**) *noun* an Italian dessert made from sponge cake soaked in coffee and brandy or liqueur, with powdered chocolate on top. [an Italian word, from *tira mi sù* meaning 'pick me up']

tirade (tiy-**rayd**) *noun* a long angry or hostile speech or piece of criticism. [from a French word *tirade* meaning 'long speech']

tire[1] *verb* to become tired, or to make someone tired. [from an Old English word *teorian*]

tire[2] *noun* an American spelling of **tyre**.

tired *adjective* feeling that you need to sleep or rest. **to be tired of** to have had enough of something ♦ *They were tired of waiting.*

tireless *adjective* not tiring easily, having a lot of energy. SYNONYMS: energetic, indefatigable, unflagging. **tirelessly** *adverb*

tiresome *adjective* making you feel impatient, annoying. SYNONYMS: trying, irksome, tedious, exasperating.

tiro *noun* another spelling of **tyro**.

'tis (*literary*) it is.

tissue (tiss-yoo or tish-oo) *noun* 1 the substance forming any part of the body of an animal or plant ♦ *bone tissue*. 2 (also **tissue paper**) very thin soft paper used for wrapping and packing things. 3 a piece of soft absorbent paper used as a disposable handkerchief. 4 a fabric with a fine gauzy texture. 5 a series of connected things ♦ *They told us a tissue of lies*. [from an Old French word *tissu* meaning 'woven', related to *textile*]

tit [1] *noun* a small bird, often with a dark patch on top of the head. [probably from a Scandinavian language]

tit [2] *noun* **tit for tat** something equal given in return, especially in revenge. [from an earlier phrase *tip for tap*, from *tip* [1] and *tap* [2]]

Titan (tiy-tən) *noun* (*Greek Mythology*) each of a family of giant gods who came before Zeus and the other Olympian gods. **titan** *noun* a person of great size, strength, or importance.

titanic (tiy-tan-ik) *adjective* gigantic or immense.

titanium (ti-tay-nium or tiy-tay-nium) *noun* a grey metallic element (symbol Ti), used to make light alloys that are free from corrosion. [from *Titan*, on the pattern of *uranium*]

titbit *noun* an attractive or delicious piece of something, especially food or information. [from a dialect word *tid* meaning 'tender' and *bit* [1]]

tithe (tiyth) *noun* one-tenth of the annual produce from a farm etc., formerly paid as tax to support the clergy and church. [from an Old English word *teotha* meaning 'tenth']

titillate (tit-i-layt) *verb* to excite or stimulate someone in a pleasant way. **titillation** *noun* [from a Latin word *titillare* meaning 'to tickle']
◊ Do not confuse this word with **titivate**, which has a different meaning.

titivate (tit-i-vayt) *verb* (*informal*) to smarten something up, or put the finishing touches to it. **titivation** *noun* [origin unknown]
◊ Do not confuse this word with **titillate**, which has a different meaning.

title *noun* 1 the name of a book, poem, piece of music, or other artistic work. 2 a word used to show a person's rank or office (e.g. *queen, mayor, captain*) or used to address or refer to a person (e.g. *Lord, Mrs, Doctor*). 3 the legal right to ownership of property, or a document conferring this. 4 a championship in sport ♦ *the world heavyweight title*. **title** *verb* to give a title to a book or other artistic work. [from a Latin word *titulus* meaning 'title']

titled *adjective* having a title as a member of the nobility ♦ *titled landowners*.

title deed *noun* a legal document providing evidence of a person's right, especially to owning a property.

title page *noun* a page at the beginning of a book giving the title, the name of the author, and other details.

title role *noun* the part in a play, film, or opera that gives its name to the title, e.g. the part of Macbeth in Shakespeare's play called *Macbeth*.

titmouse *noun* (**titmice**) another name for **tit** [1].

titrate (tiy-trayt) *verb* (*Chemistry*) to calculate the amount of a substance in a solution by using a standard reagent. **titration** *noun* [from a French word *titrer*, from *titre* meaning 'fineness of alloyed gold or silver']

titre (tiy-ter) *noun* (*Chemistry*) the strength of a solution as calculated by titrating.

titter *verb* to laugh quietly or furtively. **titter** *noun* a quiet or furtive laugh. [an imitation of the sound]

tittle-tattle *noun* idle chatter or gossip. **tittle-tattle** *verb* to chatter or gossip idly. [a variation on *tattle*]

titular (tit-yoo-ler) *adjective* 1 belonging to a title. 2 holding a title without any real power or authority ♦ *The king had titular command of the army*.

tizzy *noun* (*informal*) a state of nervous agitation or confusion ♦ *in a tizzy*. [origin unknown]

T-junction *noun* a road junction forming the shape of a T, at which one road meets another at right angles but does not cross it.

TI *abbreviation* (*Chemistry*) the symbol for thallium.

TM *abbreviation* Transcendental Meditation.

Tm *abbreviation* (*Chemistry*) the symbol for thulium.

TNT *abbreviation* trinitrotoluene, a powerful explosive.

to *preposition* used to show **1** direction in relation to a place or state ♦ *Shall we walk to the station?* ♦ *He was sent to prison* ♦ *They stood back to back.* **2** extent or degree ♦ *Surgery is from 10 to 4 o'clock* ♦ *goods to the value of £10* ♦ *The dinner was cooked to perfection.* **3** comparison ♦ *We won by 3 goals to 2.* **4** a person or thing affected by an action or feeling ♦ *I gave it to Tom* ♦ *Have you spoken to her?* ♦ *They are kind to the animals.*

to *preposition* **1** used before a verb to form an infinitive or to express a purpose or result ♦ *They only do it to annoy.* **2** used alone when a verb is understood ♦ *I meant to call but I forgot to.*

to *adverb* **1** in or into the closed position ♦ *Push the door to.* **2** into a state of consciousness ♦ *After a while she came to.* **3** into a state of activity ♦ *Let's set to.* **to and fro** backwards and forwards. **toing and froing** going to and fro. [from an Old English word *to*]

toad *noun* a frog-like animal that lives mainly on land. [from an Old English word *tadde*]

toadflax *noun* a wild plant with spurred yellow or purple flowers and slender leaves.

toad-in-the-hole *noun* a dish of sausages baked in batter.

toadstool *noun* a fungus, usually poisonous, with a round top and a slender stalk.

toady *noun* (**toadies**) a person who flatters other people and behaves obsequiously towards them in the hope of getting favours.
toady *verb* (**toadies, toadied, toadying**) to behave as a toady. [short for *toad-eater* (because quack healers used to have assistants who ate toads (which people thought were poisonous) so that the quack healer could demonstrate a 'cure')]

toast *noun* **1** a slice of bread that has been warmed to make it crisp and brown. **2** a call to a group of people to drink in honour of someone, or the person or thing in whose honour this is done.
toast *verb* **1** to brown the surface of bread by placing it against a source of direct heat. **2** to warm yourself in this way. **3** to drink a toast to someone or something. [from a Latin word *tostum* meaning 'dried up']

toaster *noun* an electrical device for toasting bread.

toasting fork *noun* a long-handled fork for holding a slice of bread in front of a fire to toast it.

toastmaster *noun* a person who announces the toasts at a public function.

toast rack *noun* a rack for holding slices of toast.

tobacco *noun* (**tobaccos**) **1** the dried leaves of certain plants, used for smoking or for making snuff. **2** the plant that produces these leaves. [from a Spanish word *tabaco*, perhaps from a Carib word]

tobacconist *noun* a shopkeeper who sells cigarettes, cigars, and tobacco.

-to-be soon to become ♦ *the bride-to-be.*

toboggan *noun* a light narrow sledge curved upwards at the front, used for sliding downhill on snow or ice.
tobogganing *noun* [via Canadian French from a Native American word *topagan* meaning 'sled']

toby jug *noun* a mug or jug in the form of a plump old man wearing a three-cornered hat. [from the name *Toby*, used in a poem about a soldier who liked drinking]

toccata (tə-kah-tə) *noun* (*Music*) a composition for a keyboard instrument, written in a free style with rapid running passages. [an Italian word meaning 'touched']

tocsin *noun* (*old use*) an alarm bell or signal. [from an Old French word *toquassen*]

today *noun* **1** this present day ♦ *Today is Monday.* **2** the present age, nowadays ♦ *The youth of today.*
today *adverb* **1** on this present day. **2** at the present time. [from *to* (preposition) and *day*]

toddle *verb* **1** (said about a young child) to walk with short unsteady steps. **2** (*informal*) to walk or go casually somewhere. [origin unknown]

toddler *noun* a child who is just beginning to walk.

toddy *noun* (**toddies**) a sweetened drink made with spirits and hot water. [from a Sanskrit word *tadi*, a tree with a sugary sap that was made into an alcoholic drink]

to-do *noun* (*informal*) a fuss or commotion.

toe *noun* 1 each of the five divisions of the front part of the human foot, or each of the divisions of the foot of an animal. 2 the part of a shoe or sock that covers the toes. 3 the lower end or tip of a tool etc. **toe** *verb* (**toes, toed, toeing**) to touch or reach something with the toes. **to be on your toes** to be alert or eager. **to toe the line** to follow instructions or authority, especially under pressure. [from an Old English word *ta*]

toecap *noun* the outer covering of the toe of a boot or shoe.

toehold *noun* 1 a slight foothold. 2 a small beginning from which progress can be made.

toenail *noun* the nail on a toe.

toffee *noun* a sticky or hard sweet made from heated butter and sugar. [origin unknown]

toffee apple *noun* an apple coated thinly with toffee and fixed on a stick.

toffee-nosed *adjective* (*informal*) snobbish or pretentious.

tofu (toh-foo) *noun* a curd originally made in Japan and China from mashed soya beans. [from Japanese and Chinese words]

tog *verb* (**togged, togging**) (*informal*) **to be togged up** or **out** to put on clothes, to dress.
tog *noun* a unit used in measuring the insulating and warming power of clothing or bedding.
togs *plural noun* (*informal*) clothes. [from an obsolete slang word *togeman* meaning 'light cloak', ultimately from a Latin word *toga* (see *toga*)]

toga (toh-gə) *noun* a loose flowing outer garment worn by men in ancient Rome. [a Latin word, from *tegere* meaning 'to cover']

together *adverb* 1 with another person or thing, with each other ♦ *They went to the disco together.* 2 at the same time ♦ *They both cried out together.* 3 without a break or interruption ♦ *She is away for weeks together.* 4 married or having a personal relationship ♦ *They have been together for three years now.* **together with** as well as, and also. [from *to* and *gather*]

togetherness *noun* a feeling of belonging together.

toggle *noun* 1 a fastening for a piece of clothing, made of a short piece of wood or plastic that is passed through a loop. 2 (*Computing*) a key that switches a function on and off successively with the same action. [origin unknown]

toil *verb* 1 to work hard and continuously. SYNONYMS: labour, slave, slog. 2 to move with great effort or difficulty ♦ *The walkers toiled up the hill.*
toil *noun* hard or difficult work. **toiler** *noun* [from an Old French word *toiler* meaning 'to strive']

toilet *noun* 1 a large bowl for urinating and defecating into, usually plumbed into a sewage system. 2 a room or compartment containing a toilet. 3 the process of washing and dressing yourself. [from a French word *toilette* meaning 'cloth']

toilet paper *noun* paper for wiping the body clean after using a toilet.

toilet roll *noun* a roll of toilet paper.

toiletries *plural noun* things used in washing and caring for the body, such as soap and shampoo.

token *noun* 1 a sign or indication of something ♦ *a token of our friendship.* SYNONYMS: sign, symbol, mark, emblem, indication. 2 a voucher or coupon that can be exchanged for goods ♦ *a book token.* 3 a piece of metal or plastic shaped like a coin and used to operate a machine or in exchange for goods or services.
token *adjective* serving as a token or gesture rather than for real effect ♦ *The enemy put up token resistance.* SYNONYMS: nominal, symbolic. **by the same token** similarly; moreover. [from an Old English word *tacen*]

told past tense and past participle of **tell**. **all told** counting everything or everyone ♦ *There are 16 people all told.*

tolerable *adjective* 1 able to be tolerated, endurable. 2 fairly good, passable. SYNONYMS: passable, satisfactory, acceptable. **tolerably** *adverb*

tolerance *noun* 1 being tolerant, willing to accept what other people say and do. 2 the permitted variation in the measurement or weight of an object.

tolerant *adjective* willing to accept or tolerate what other people say and do when you don't necessarily agree with them. SYNONYMS: broad-minded, easygoing, understanding, indulgent. **tolerantly** *adverb*

tolerate *verb* 1 to allow something to happen or to be said although you don't necessarily agree with it. SYNONYMS: permit, accept, allow. 2 to bear pain or suffering. SYNONYMS: bear, put up with, stand. 3 to be able to take a drug or medical treatment without bad effects. **toleration** *noun* [from a Latin word *tolerare* meaning 'to endure']

toll[1] (tohl) *noun* 1 a charge you have to pay to use a public road or bridge. 2 (*North Amer.*) a charge for making a long-distance telephone call. 3 the number of deaths or amount of damage caused by an accident or disaster. **to take its toll** to cause loss or injury. [via Old English and Latin from a Greek word *telos* meaning 'tax']

toll[2] (tohl) *verb* 1 to ring a bell with a slow sequence of strokes, especially for a death or funeral. 2 (said about a bell) to sound in this way, or to indicate a death or funeral by tolling. **toll** *noun* the stroke of a tolling bell. [probably from a dialect word *toll* meaning 'to drag' or 'to pull']

tollbooth *noun* 1 a roadside booth at which tolls are paid. 2 (*Scottish*) (*old use*) a town hall or town prison.

toll gate *noun* a gate across a road where a toll has to be paid for vehicles to continue.

tom *noun* a male animal, especially a cat. [short for Thomas, a man's name]

tomahawk *noun* 1 a light axe formerly used as a tool or weapon by Native Americans. 2 (*Austral.*) a hatchet. [from an Algonquian (North American) word meaning 'he cuts']

tomato *noun* (**tomatoes**) 1 a soft round red or yellow fruit with a shiny skin, eaten as a vegetable. 2 the plant on which this grows. [via Spanish and Portuguese from a Nahuatl (Central American) word]

tomb (toom) *noun* 1 a burial place, especially a large underground one. 2 a monument built over a grave or burial place. [via Old French and Latin from a Greek word *tumbos*]

tombola (tom-boh-lə) *noun* a game played at a fair or fête, in which tickets are drawn from a revolving drum for prizes. [from an Italian word *tombolare* meaning 'to tumble round']

tomboy *noun* a girl who enjoys rough noisy games and activities. [from *tom* (short for *Thomas*) and *boy*]

tombstone *noun* a memorial stone set up over a grave.

tomcat *noun* a male cat.

Tom, Dick, and Harry *noun* ordinary people, people in general.

tome *noun* a book or volume, especially a large heavy one. [from a Greek word *tomos* meaning 'roll of papyrus']

tomfoolery *adjective* silly or foolish behaviour. [from the name *Tom* (short for *Thomas*) and *fool*]

Tommy *noun* (**Tommies**) (*informal*) a British private soldier. [from the name *Tommy Atkins*, used in specimens of completed official forms in the British army]

tommy gun *noun* (*informal*) a type of sub-machine gun. [from the name of its American inventor, J. T. Thompson (1860–1940)]

tomorrow *noun* 1 the day after today. 2 the near future.
tomorrow *adverb* 1 on the day after today. 2 in the near future. [from *to* and *morrow*]

tomtit *noun* a blue tit or titmouse.

tom-tom *noun* a drum beaten with the hands, especially in music of African or Asian origin. [from a Hindi word *tam-tam*, imitating the sound it makes]

ton (tun) *noun* 1 a measure of weight, either 2,240 lb. (**long ton**) or 2,000 lb. (**short ton**). 2 a measure of capacity for various materials; 40 cubic feet of timber. 3 a unit of volume in shipping. 4 (*informal*) a large amount ♦ *There's tons of time.* 5 (*informal*) a speed of 100 m.p.h. [a different spelling of *tun*]

tonal (toh-nəl) *adjective* 1 to do with tone or tones. 2 said about music written in the conventional system of keys and harmony. **tonally** *adverb*

tonality (tə-nal-iti) *noun* 1 the character of a piece of music, depending on the scale or key in which it is written. 2 the colour scheme of a picture.

tone *noun* 1 a musical or vocal sound, especially with reference to its pitch,

quality, and strength. **2** a manner of expression in speaking or writing ♦ *an apologetic tone*. **3** a tint or shade of a colour, or the general effect of colour or of light and shade in a picture. SYNONYMS: tint, shade, hue. **4** the general character or quality of something ♦ *He set the tone with a witty speech*. SYNONYMS: mood, atmosphere, spirit. **5** (*Music*) a basic interval, equal to two semitones, separating two notes in an ordinary scale. **6** (also **muscle tone**) the normal firmness of a resting muscle.
tone *verb* **1** to give a particular tone of sound or colour to something. **2** to be harmonious in colour ♦ *The carpet tones in with the wallpaper*. **3** to give proper firmness to the body or to a muscle. **to tone something down 1** to make something softer in sound or colour. **2** to make a statement less strong or harsh. SYNONYMS: moderate, soften, modify. **toneless** *adjective* [from a Greek word *tonos* meaning 'tension']

tone-deaf *adjective* unable to perceive differences of musical pitch accurately.

tone poem *noun* a piece of music, usually in a single movement, on a descriptive or poetic theme.

toner *noun* **1** a liquid put on the skin to improve its condition. **2** a chemical used to change the tone of a photographic print during development. **3** a powder used to produce tones in photocopying.

tongs *plural noun* an instrument with two arms joined at one end, used to pick up or hold things. [from an Old English word *tange* (singular)]

tongue *noun* **1** the fleshy muscular organ in the mouth, used for tasting, licking, swallowing, and (in humans) speaking. **2** the tongue of an ox or other animal as food. **3** a particular language ♦ *Their native tongue is German*. **4** the ability to speak or a manner of speaking ♦ *She has a persuasive tongue*. **5** a strip of leather or other material under the laces of a shoe or boot. **6** a projecting strip on a piece of wood, which fits into a groove on another piece. **7** a pointed flame.
tongue *verb* (**tongues, tongued, tonguing**) (*Music*) to use the tongue to interrupt the flow of air when playing a wind instrument, so as to produce staccato or other effects. [from an Old English word *tunge*]

tongue-in-cheek *adjective* said or written with irony or sarcasm.

tongue-lashing *noun* a severe reprimand or scolding.

tongue-tied *adjective* too shy or embarrassed to speak.

tongue-twister *noun* a sequence of words that is difficult to pronounce quickly and correctly, e.g. *She sells sea shells*.

tonic *noun* **1** a medicine that gives strength and vigour, especially after an illness. **2** anything that restores people's energy or good spirits. **3** (*Music*) the first note in a scale, providing the keynote in a piece of music. **4** short for **tonic water**.
tonic *adjective* **1** having the effect of a tonic. **2** relating to the tonic in music. [same origin as for *tone*]

tonic sol-fa *noun* (*Music*) the system of syllables (*doh, ray, me, fah, soh, la, te*) used to represent the notes of the musical scale, especially in teaching singing.

tonic water *noun* a fizzy mineral water with a bitter taste, often mixed with a spirit such as gin.

tonight *noun* this present or coming evening or night.
tonight *adverb* on the present or coming evening or night. [from *to* (preposition) and *night*]

tonnage (**tun-ij**) *noun* **1** the amount that a ship or ships can carry, expressed in tons. **2** the charge per ton for carrying cargo or freight.

tonne (**tun**) *noun* another word for **metric ton**.

tonsil *noun* each of two small organs at the sides of the throat near the root of the tongue. [from a Latin word *tonsillae* (plural)]

tonsillitis *noun* inflammation of the tonsils.

tonsure (**ton-sher**) *noun* **1** the top part of a monk's or priest's head made bare by shaving the hair. **2** the act of having the hair shaved in this way on entering certain holy orders. **tonsured** *adjective* [from a Latin word *tonsor* meaning 'barber']

too *adverb* **1** more than is wanted or desirable. **2** (*informal*) very ♦ *She's not too well today*. **3** also, as well ♦ *Please take the others too*. **too bad** (*informal*) regrettable, a pity. [from an Old English form of *to*]

took past tense of **take**.

tool *noun* **1** a device, held in the hand or in

a machine, for performing a particular function. SYNONYMS: instrument, implement, device, utensil, gadget. **2** a simple machine, e.g. a lathe. **3** a thing used for a particular purpose ♦ *An encyclopedia is a useful study tool.* **4** a person who is manipulated by another person.

tool verb **1** to shape or decorate something by using a tool. **2** (often **tool up**) to equip a factory or other place with the tools needed, or to be equipped with tools. [from an Old English word *tol*]

toot verb to make or cause something to make the short sharp sound of a horn or whistle.

toot noun a tooting sound.

tooth noun (**teeth**) **1** each of the hard white bony structures that are rooted in the gums, used for biting and chewing. **2** a tooth-like part or projection on a gear, saw, comb, or rake. **3** a liking for a particular type of food ♦ *a sweet tooth.* **to fight tooth and nail** to fight very fiercely. **in the teeth of** in spite of or in opposition to ♦ *They continued the campaign in the teeth of strong criticism.* **toothed** adjective [from an Old English word *toth*]

toothache noun pain in a tooth or teeth.

toothbrush noun a brush for cleaning the teeth.

toothcomb noun **with a fine toothcomb** very thoroughly, in great detail. [from a misreading of *fine-tooth comb*, i.e. a comb with fine teeth]

toothless adjective having no teeth.

toothpaste noun a paste for cleaning the teeth.

toothpick noun a small pointed piece of wood etc. for removing bits of food from between the teeth.

toothy adjective (**toothier, toothiest**) having or showing large or prominent teeth.

tootle verb **1** to toot gently or repeatedly. **2** (informal) to go in a casual or leisurely way ♦ *to tootle around.* [from *tool*]

top [1] noun **1** the highest part of something. SYNONYMS: peak, tip, summit, crown. **2** the upper surface of something. **3** the covering or stopper of a container. SYNONYMS: lid, cap, cover, stopper. **4** the highest position or rank ♦ *She is at the top of her profession.* SYNONYMS: peak, summit. **5** the utmost degree of intensity ♦ *He shouted at the top of his voice.* **6** a thing forming the upper part of something,

such as the creamy part of milk. **7** a piece of clothing covering the upper part of the body. **8** the highest gear in a motor vehicle.

top adjective highest in position, rank, or degree ♦ *at top speed* ♦ *top prices.*

top verb (**topped, topping**) **1** to provide or be a top for something. **2** to exceed or be more than something. SYNONYMS: exceed, surpass, beat. **3** to reach the top of a piece of high ground. **4** to be the highest in rank or position ♦ *Who topped the list?* **5** to add something as a final thing or finishing touch. **6** to remove the top of a plant or fruit. **7** (informal) to kill or execute someone. **on top 1** above, at the highest point. **2** in a superior or advantageous position. **3** in addition, as well. **on top of 1** in addition to. **2** in control of. **to top something up** to fill up a container that is partly empty. [from an Old English word *topp*]

top [2] noun a toy that can be made to spin on its point. **to sleep like a top** to sleep soundly. [from an Old English word]

topaz (toh-paz) noun a precious stone, usually yellow or pale blue. [via French and Latin from a Greek word *topazos*]

top brass noun (informal) high-ranking officers or officials.

topcoat noun **1** an overcoat. **2** an outer or final coat of paint.

toper (toh-per) noun (literary) someone who is habitually drunk. [from an old verb *tope* meaning 'to drink excessively']

top gear noun the highest gear in a motor vehicle.

top hat noun a man's tall stiff black or grey hat worn with formal dress.

top-heavy adjective too heavy at the top and likely to fall over.

topiary (toh-pi-er-i) noun the art of clipping shrubs or trees into ornamental shapes. [from a Latin word *topiarius* meaning 'ornamental gardener']

topic noun the subject of a discussion or piece of writing. SYNONYMS: subject, theme, issue. [from a Greek word *topos* meaning 'place']

topical adjective to do with current events. **topicality** (top-i-kal-iti) noun **topically** adverb

topknot noun a knot of hair, or a knotted ribbon, on top of the head.

topless adjective (said about a woman or her clothing) having or leaving the breasts uncovered.

topmost adjective highest.

top-notch adjective (informal) excellent, first-rate.

topography (tə-**pog**-rəfi) noun the arrangement of the features of a place or district, including the position of its rivers, mountains, roads, and buildings. **topographical** (top-ə-**graf**-ikəl) adjective [from a Greek word topos meaning 'place' and -graphy]

topology (təp-**ol**-ə-ji) noun (Mathematics) the study of geometrical properties which remain unaffected by certain changes in the shape or size of the figures and surfaces concerned. **topological** adjective [from a Greek word topos meaning 'place' and -logy]

topper noun (informal) a top hat.

topple verb 1 to overbalance and fall, or to make something do this. SYNONYMS: tip, tumble, overbalance. 2 to overthrow people in authority, or cause them to fall ♦ Several guerrilla organizations want to topple the government. SYNONYMS: overthrow, crush. [from top[1]]

top secret adjective extremely secret.

topside noun 1 a joint of beef cut from the upper part of the haunch. 2 the side of a ship above the waterline.

topsoil noun the top layer of soil, as distinct from the subsoil.

topsy-turvy adjective & adverb 1 in a muddle. SYNONYMS: confused, chaotic, disorderly, disorganized, jumbled, untidy, mixed up. 2 upside down. [probably from top[1] and an old word terve meaning 'to turn upside down']

toque (tohk) noun a woman's close-fitting hat with a small turned-up brim and a high crown. [a French word]

tor noun a hill or rocky peak, especially in Devon and Cornwall. [from an Old English word torr, perhaps from a Celtic language]

Torah (**tor**-ə) noun the revealed will of God, especially the laws given to Moses and recorded in the Pentateuch. [from a Hebrew word torah meaning 'instruction']

torch noun 1 a small battery-powered electric lamp held in the hand. 2 a stick with burning material at the end, used as a light. [via French from a Latin word torqua, from torquere meaning 'to twist']

torchlight noun the light of a torch or torches ♦ a torchlight procession.

tore past tense of tear[1].

toreador (torri-ə-dor) noun a bullfighter, especially one on horseback. [a Spanish word, from toro meaning 'bull']

torment[1] (**tor**-ment) noun 1 intense physical or mental suffering. SYNONYMS: agony, torture, suffering. 2 something causing this. SYNONYMS: affliction, bane, nuisance. [from a Latin word tortum meaning 'twisted']

torment[2] (**tor**-ment) verb 1 to cause someone intense physical or mental suffering. SYNONYMS: afflict, torture, persecute. 2 to tease or try to provoke someone by annoying or teasing them. SYNONYMS: annoy, tease, bait, provoke, taunt. **tormentor** noun

torn past participle of tear[1].

tornado (tor-**nay**-doh) noun (tornadoes) a destructive whirlwind advancing in a narrow path with the appearance of a funnel-shaped cloud. [a Spanish word meaning 'thunderstorm']

torpedo noun (torpedoes) a cigar-shaped explosive underwater missile, launched against a ship from a submarine or surface ship or from an aircraft. **torpedo** verb (torpedoes, torpedoed, torpedoing) 1 to destroy or attack something with a torpedo. 2 to ruin or wreck a plan or policy. [from a Latin word meaning 'stiffness' or 'numbness', used to refer to a large sea fish that can give an electric shock which causes numbness]

torpid adjective slow or inactive. **torpidity** (tor-**pid**-iti) noun **torpidly** adverb [from a Latin word torpidus meaning 'numb']

torpor (**tor**-per) noun a state of slowness or inactivity.

torque (tork) noun (Physics) a force causing rotation in a mechanism. [from a Latin word torquere meaning 'to twist']

torrent noun 1 a rushing stream of water or lava. SYNONYMS: flood, deluge, stream. 2 a downpour of rain. 3 an overwhelming flow ♦ a torrent of abuse. [from a Latin word torrere meaning 'to scorch']

torrential (ter-en-shəl) adjective like a torrent, flowing in torrents.

torrid *adjective* 1 (said about a climate or land) very hot and dry. 2 intense or passionate. [from a Latin word *torridus* meaning 'parched']

torrid zone *noun* the hot central belt of the earth, between the tropics of Cancer and Capricorn.

torsion (tor-shən) *noun* the action of twisting, especially of one end of a thing while the other is held fixed. [same origin as for *torture*]

torso (tor-soh) *noun* (**torsos**) 1 the trunk of the human body. 2 the trunk of a statue, without the head and limbs. 3 an incomplete thing, especially a work of art. [an Italian word meaning 'stump']

tort *noun* (*Law*) a private or civil wrong (other than breach of contract) for which the wronged person may claim damages. [same origin as for *torture*]

torte (tor-tə) *noun* a kind of rich round layer cake. [a German word, from a Latin word *torta* meaning 'cake']

tortilla (tor-tee-yə) *noun* in Mexican cookery, a flat maize cake eaten hot. [a Spanish word meaning 'little cake']

tortoise (tor-təs) *noun* a slow-moving reptile having four legs and a body enclosed in a hard shell. [via Old French and Spanish from a Latin word *tortuca*]

tortoiseshell *noun* 1 the semi-transparent mottled yellow and brown shell of certain turtles, used for making combs and jewellery. 2 a cat or butterfly with mottled colouring resembling this.

tortuous (tor-tew-əs) *adjective* 1 full of twists and turns. SYNONYMS: twisting, winding, meandering, zigzag, serpentine. 2 (said about a policy, argument, etc.) devious, not straightforward. **tortuously** *adverb* [from a Latin word *tortum* meaning 'twisted']

torture *noun* 1 the action of inflicting severe pain as a punishment or means of coercing someone. 2 severe physical or mental pain. SYNONYMS: torment, agony. **torture** *verb* 1 to inflict torture on someone. 2 to subject someone to great pain or anxiety ♦ *tortured by doubts and fears.* **torturer** *noun* [same origin as for *tortuous*]

Tory *noun* (**Tories**) 1 (*informal*) a member of the Conservative Party. 2 a member of the political party in the 17th–19th centuries that was opposed to the Whigs and from which the Conservative Party was formed in the 1830s. **Tory** *adjective* (*informal*) Conservative. **Toryism** *noun* [originally used of Irish outlaws, from an Irish word *toraidhe* meaning 'outlaw']

tosh *noun* (*informal*) nonsense. [origin unknown]

toss *verb* 1 to throw something lightly or casually. SYNONYMS: fling, hurl, cast, pitch, throw, heave; (*informal*) chuck, sling. 2 to throw your head back, especially in impatience or disapproval. 3 to send a coin spinning in the air to decide something according to which way up it lands. 4 to move restlessly or unevenly from side to side, or to make something do this. 5 to shake food in a dressing or liquid to coat it lightly. **toss** *noun* 1 a tossing action or movement. 2 the result obtained by tossing a coin. **to toss something off** to produce or complete something rapidly or casually. [origin unknown]

toss-up *noun* (*informal*) 1 the tossing of a coin. 2 an even chance.

tot[1] *noun* 1 a small child. 2 (*informal*) a small amount of spirits ♦ *a tot of rum.* [origin unknown]

tot[2] *verb* (**totted, totting**) **tot up** (*informal*) to add up numbers or amounts. [short for *total*]

total *adjective* 1 including the whole number or amount. SYNONYMS: entire, complete, overall. 2 utter or complete ♦ *in total darkness* ♦ *a total eclipse.* **total** *noun* the total number or amount. SYNONYMS: sum, amount. **total** *verb* (**totalled, totalling**) 1 to reckon the total of something. 2 to amount to a certain total ♦ *The damage totalled a million dollars.* **totally** *adverb* [from a Latin word *totum* meaning 'the whole']

totalitarian (toh-tal-i-**tair**-iən) *adjective* to do with a form of government which demands total submission to the state and does not allow rival politics.

totality (toh-**tal**-iti) *noun* 1 a total number or amount. 2 the period when the sun or moon is totally obscured during an eclipse.

totalizator *noun* a device that automatically records the number and amount of bets staked, in order to divide the total amount among those betting on the winner.

totalize *verb* to find the total of something.

tote *noun* (*informal*) a totalizator.

totem (toh-təm) *noun* an animal or other natural object adopted in certain societies as an emblem having spiritual significance. [from an Ojibwa (North American) word *nindoodem* meaning 'my totem']

totem pole *noun* a tall pole carved or painted with images of totems.

totter *verb* 1 to walk unsteadily. SYNONYMS: stagger, stumble, teeter. 2 to rock or shake as if about to collapse.
totter *noun* an unsteady walk or movement. **tottery** *adjective* [from a Dutch word *touteren* meaning 'to swing']

totting-up *noun* the adding together of penalty points from successive convictions for driving offences, leading to disqualification if the total reaches a certain level in a fixed period.

toucan (too-kən) *noun* a tropical American bird with a very large beak. [via French and Portuguese from a Tupi (South American) word]

touch *verb* 1 to be or come together so that there is no space between. 2 to come into contact with something. SYNONYMS: brush, graze. 3 to put your fingers lightly on something. SYNONYMS: feel, stroke, pat, finger. 4 to press or strike something lightly. 5 to move or meddle with something. 6 to attempt or deal with something ♦ *The firm doesn't touch business of that kind.* 7 (*informal*) to eat or drink any of something ♦ *She has hardly touched her breakfast.* 8 (*informal*) to match or equal something or someone in quality ♦ *No other cloth can touch it for quality.* 9 to reach a certain level ♦ *The thermometer touched 100°.* SYNONYMS: reach, rise to. 10 to affect someone slightly. 11 to rouse a person's sympathy or feelings ♦ *He was touched by the generosity people showed him.* SYNONYMS: move, affect. 12 (*informal*) to persuade someone to give money as a loan or gift ♦ *He touched her for a fiver.*
touch *noun* 1 the act of touching. 2 the ability to perceive things or their qualities by touching them. 3 small things done in producing a piece of work ♦ *the finishing touches.* 4 a musician's manner of using the keys or strings of an instrument. 5 a special skill or style of workmanship ♦ *She hasn't lost her touch.* SYNONYMS: style, technique, skill. 6 a slight trace ♦ *a touch of frost.* 7 the part of a football field outside

the touchlines. **in touch with 1** in communication with someone. **2** having an interest in or knowledge about something. **to lose touch** to be no longer in communication with someone. **out of touch** no longer in touch with a person or subject etc. **a soft touch** (*informal*) someone who readily agrees to give money or help. **touch and go** having an uncertain outcome. **to touch bottom** to reach the worst point in your misfortune. **to touch down 1** (said about an aircraft) to land. **2** (in rugby) to touch the ball on the ground behind the goal line. **to touch something off 1** to make something explode. **2** to cause something to start ♦ *Their arrest touched off a riot.* **to touch on** to deal with or mention a subject briefly. **to touch something up** to improve something by making small alterations or additions. **to touch wood** to touch something made of wood as a superstition averting bad luck.
touchable *adjective* [from an Old French word *tochier*]

touchdown *noun* the act of touching down in an aircraft.

touché (too-shay) *interjection* used to acknowledge a true or clever point made against you in an argument. [a French word meaning 'touched', originally referring to a hit in fencing]

touched *adjective* 1 caused to feel warm sympathy or gratitude. 2 slightly mad.

touching *adjective* rousing kindly feelings or sympathy or pity.
touching *preposition* concerning.
touchingly *adverb*

touch judge *noun* a linesman in rugby.

touchline *noun* the boundary on each side of a football or rugby pitch.

touchpaper *noun* paper impregnated with a substance that will make it burn slowly, used for lighting fireworks.

touchstone *noun* a standard or criterion by which something is judged. [from an earlier meaning, a kind of stone against which gold and silver were rubbed to test their purity]

touch-type *verb* to type using all the fingers and without looking at the keys.

touchy *adjective* (**touchier, touchiest**) quick to take offence, oversensitive. SYNONYMS: testy, sensitive, peevish, grumpy. **touchily** *adverb* **touchiness** *noun* [origin unknown]

tough adjective **1** strong enough to endure hard wear ♦ *shoes made of tough leather.* SYNONYMS: durable, hard-wearing, sturdy, strong, stout. **2** difficult to break or cut. **3** (said about food) difficult to chew. SYNONYMS: chewy, gristly, leathery. **4** (said about a person) able to endure hardship, not easily hurt or injured. SYNONYMS: hardy, robust, strong. **5** firm or resolute ♦ *a tough policy on fighting crime.* SYNONYMS: firm, resolute, strict. **6** difficult to do ♦ *a tough job.* SYNONYMS: hard, difficult, gruelling, arduous, onerous, exacting. **7** (*informal*) hard or unpleasant.
tough noun (*informal*) a rough and violent person. **toughly** adverb **toughness** noun [from an Old English word *toh*]

toughen verb to make something tough, or to become tough.

tough-minded adjective firm and realistic, and not sentimental.

toupee (too-pay) noun a small wig or piece of artificial hair worn to cover a bald spot. [from a French word *toupet* meaning 'tuft of hair']

tour noun **1** a journey made for pleasure, visiting several places. **2** a series of performances in different places by a theatrical or musical company, or a series of sports fixtures by a travelling team.
tour verb to make a tour of an area. **on tour** touring. [same origin as for *turn*]

tour de force (toor də **forss**) noun an outstandingly skilful performance or achievement. [a French phrase, meaning 'feat of strength']

tourism noun the business of organizing and providing services for tourists.

tourist noun a person who travels for pleasure.

tourist class noun the cheapest class of accommodation on a ship or aircraft.

tourmaline (toor-mə-leen) noun a mineral of various colours, having unusual electric properties and used as a gem. [from a Sinhalese word *toramalli* meaning 'carnelian']

tournament (toor-nə-mənt) noun a series of contests between a number of competitors. [from an Old French word *torneiement*, related to *turn*]

tournedos (toor-nə-doh) noun (**tournedos**) a round piece cut from a fillet of beef and cooked with a strip of fat wrapped round it. [a French word, from *tourner* meaning 'to turn' and *dos* meaning 'back']

tourney noun (**tourneys**) a medieval jousting tournament. [same origin as for *tournament*]

tourniquet (toor-ni-kay) noun a strip of material wrapped tightly round a leg or arm to stop the flow of blood from an artery. [a French word, related to *turn*]

tousle (tow-zəl) verb to make someone's hair untidy by ruffling it. [from a dialect word *touse* meaning 'to handle roughly']

tout (towt) verb **1** to try to sell something or get business. **2** to urge people to buy or use something.
tout noun **1** a person who sells tickets for a sports match or concert at inflated prices. **2** a person who touts things. [from an Old English word]

tow¹ (toh) verb to pull something along behind. SYNONYMS: pull, haul, drag, draw.
tow noun the action of towing something. **in tow** being towed. **2** accompanying someone, or in their charge ♦ *He arrived with his family in tow.* **on tow** being towed. [from an Old English word *togian*]

tow² (toh) noun short coarse fibres of flax or hemp, used for making yarn. [from an Old English word *tow*]

toward preposition in the direction of, towards.
◊ *Toward* is mainly used in American English. *Towards* is the usual word in British English.

towards preposition **1** in the direction of ♦ *She guided them towards the door.* **2** regarding or in relation to ♦ *attitudes towards terrorism.* **3** as a contribution to the cost of ♦ *I'll put the money towards a new computer.* **4** near or approaching ♦ *towards evening.* [from an Old English word *toweardes*]

tow bar noun a bar fitted to the back of a vehicle for towing a caravan or trailer.

towel noun a piece of absorbent cloth or paper for drying yourself or wiping things dry.
towel verb (**towelled, towelling**) to wipe or dry something with a towel. [from an Old French word *toaille*, from a Germanic language]

towelling noun thick absorbent cloth used for making towels.

tower noun a tall narrow building standing alone or forming part of a larger building such as a church or castle.
tower verb to have a great height, to be taller or more eminent than others ♦ *He towered above everyone.* **a tower of strength** a person who gives strong and reliable support. [from an Old English word *torr*]

tower block noun a tall modern building containing many floors of offices or flats.

towering adjective **1** very tall or high. **2** (said about an emotion) very strong or intense ♦ *a towering rage.*

town noun **1** a place with many houses and other buildings that is larger than a village and usually smaller than a city. **2** the inhabitants of a town. **3** the central business and shopping part of a neighbourhood ♦ *Are you going into town?* **4** urban areas as distinct from the country. **to go to town** (*informal*) to do something thoroughly or enthusiastically. **on the town** (*informal*) enjoying a town's social life. [from an Old English word *tun* meaning 'enclosure']

town clerk noun **1** (*North Amer.*) an official in charge of records of a town. **2** (in Britain until 1974) the secretary and legal adviser of a town corporation.

town council noun the body of elected people who govern a municipality.

town crier noun (*historical*) an official who formerly made public announcements in the streets.

town hall noun a building containing local government offices and usually a hall for public events.

town house noun **1** a house in town as distinct from the country. **2** a house forming part of a row or group of similar houses in a town.

townie noun (*informal*) an inhabitant of a town, especially when regarded as being ignorant of country affairs.

town planning noun the planning and control of building and development in a town.

townscape noun **1** a picture of a town. **2** the general appearance of a town.

townsfolk plural noun the people of a town.

township noun **1** a small town. **2** (in South Africa) a residential area occupied by black people, and formerly (under apartheid legislation) set aside for them.

townsman or **townswoman** noun (**townsmen** or **townswomen**) a man or woman who lives in a town.

townspeople plural noun the people of a town.

towpath noun a path beside a canal or river, originally used by horses towing barges.

toxaemia (tok- see- mia) noun (*Medicine*) blood poisoning caused by a local bacterial infection. [from *toxic* and a Greek word *haima* meaning 'blood']

toxic adjective **1** of or caused by poison. **2** poisonous. **toxicity** (toks-**iss**-iti) noun [via Latin from a Greek phrase *toxikon pharmakon* meaning 'poison for arrows', from *toxon* meaning 'bow']

toxicology noun the study of poisons. **toxicological** adjective **toxicologist** noun [from *toxic* and *-logy*]

toxin noun a poisonous substance of animal or vegetable origin, especially one formed by micro-organisms in the body. [from *toxic*]

toy noun **1** an object for a child to play with, especially a model or small-scale replica. **2** a gadget or device intended for amusement rather than for serious use. **toy** adjective **1** serving as a toy. **2** (said about a dog) of a miniature breed or variety, kept as a pet. **toy** verb **to toy with 1** to handle or finger something casually. **2** to consider an idea casually or intermittently ♦ *We are toying with the idea of going to China.* [origin unknown]

toyshop noun a shop that sells toys.

trace [1] noun **1** a mark or indication showing that a person or thing exists or has been present at a place ♦ *There was no trace of the thief.* SYNONYMS: sign, vestige, clue, hint. **2** a very small amount ♦ *There were traces of poison in the food.* SYNONYMS: speck, dash, suggestion.
trace verb **1** to follow or discover someone or something by looking for marks, tracks, or other evidence. SYNONYMS: discover, track, unearth. **2** to copy a picture or outline by drawing over it on transparent paper. **3** to mark out or form the outline of something ♦ *She traced her signature shakily.* **traceable** adjective [via Old French from a Latin word *tractus*, related to *tract* [1]]

trace [2] noun each of the two straps or ropes by which a horse pulls a cart or other vehicle. **to kick over the traces** (said about a person) to become disobedient or reckless. [from an Old French word, related to *traction*]

trace element *noun* a substance present or required only in minute amounts, especially in soil.

tracer *noun* 1 a bullet or shell that leaves a trail of coloured light or smoke, so that its course can be followed for aiming. 2 a substance introduced into the human body and able to be traced through the system by its colour or the radiation it produces. 3 a device that transmits a signal, left in a moving vehicle so that its movements can be traced.

tracery *noun* (**traceries**) (*Architecture*) a decorative open-work pattern in stone, especially in a church window. [from *trace*[1]]

trachea (trə-**kee**-ə or **tray**-kiə) *noun* (*Anatomy*) the windpipe.

tracing *noun* a copy of a map or drawing made by tracing it.

tracing paper *noun* transparent paper for making tracings.

track *noun* 1 a rough path or road, especially one made by people or animals or vehicles passing along it. 2 a road or area of ground prepared for something, especially racing. 3 a mark or series of marks left by a person, animal, or thing moving along. SYNONYMS: mark, trace, trail. 4 a course taken by someone or something. SYNONYMS: route, path, course. 5 a course of action or procedure ♦ *Are we on the right track?* 6 each of the items on a CD or other recording. 7 a set of rails on which a train or tram runs. 8 a continuous band round the wheels of a tank or other heavy vehicle. 9 (*Electronics*) a continuous line of material connecting parts of a circuit on a printed circuit.
track *verb* 1 to follow the tracks left by a person or animal. SYNONYMS: follow, pursue, trace, trail, stalk. 2 to follow or observe something as it moves. 3 (said about a film or television camera) to follow the subject being filmed. 4 (said about a stylus of a record player) to follow the groove in a record. **to stop someone in their tracks** (*informal*) to bring them to a halt. **to keep** or **lose track of** to keep or fail to keep yourself aware of something or informed about it. **to make tracks** (*informal*) to go away. **make tracks for** (*informal*) to go to or towards a place. **to**

track someone or **something down** to find someone or something after a long or difficult search. **tracker** *noun* [from an Old French word *trac*]

track events *plural noun* (in sports) races as distinct from field events.

track record *noun* a person's past achievements, as a guide to their competence.

tracksuit *noun* a warm loose suit worn when exercising or as casual wear.

tract[1] *noun* 1 a large area of land. 2 (*Anatomy*) a passage or series of connected parts in an animal body along which something passes ♦ *the digestive tract.* [from a Latin word *tractus* meaning 'drawing' or 'draught']

tract[2] *noun* a pamphlet containing a short essay, especially on a religious subject. [via Old English from a Latin word *tractare* meaning 'to handle']

tractable *adjective* (said about a person) easy to control or deal with, docile. **tractability** *noun* [same origin as for *tract*[2]]

traction *noun* 1 the action of pulling something along a surface. 2 a medical treatment in which an arm, leg, or muscle is pulled gently for a long period by means of weights and pulleys, especially to set a fractured bone or to correct a deformity. [from a Latin word *tractum* meaning 'pulled']

traction engine *noun* a steam or diesel engine formerly used for drawing a heavy load along a road or across a field etc.

tractor *noun* a powerful motor vehicle with large rear wheels, used for pulling farm machinery or other heavy equipment. [same origin as for *traction*]

trad *adjective* (*informal*) (said about music) traditional.

trade *noun* 1 the buying and selling of goods and services. SYNONYMS: commerce, business. 2 business of a particular kind ♦ *the tourist trade.* 3 a skilled job or occupation ♦ *He's a butcher by trade* ♦ *to learn a trade.* 4 (**the trade**) the people involved in a particular trade. 5 a trade wind.
trade *verb* 1 to take part in trade, to buy and sell goods or services. SYNONYMS: deal, do business. 2 to exchange goods in trading. SYNONYM: barter. **to trade something in** to give something you have used as part payment for something you are buying ♦ *He traded in his motorbike for a*

new car. **to trade on** to make use of something for your own advantage ♦ *He tends to trade on his good luck*. **trader** *noun* [from a Germanic language, related to *tread*]

trademark *noun* a company's legally registered name or emblem, used to identify its products or services.

trade name *noun* 1 a name used as a trademark for a company's products or services. 2 the name by which a thing is known in a particular trade.

tradesman *noun* (**tradesmen**) a person employed in a trade, especially one who sells or delivers goods.

trade union *noun* an organized association of workers employed in a particular trade or profession, formed to protect and promote their rights and interests. **trade unionist** *noun*

trade wind *noun* a wind blowing steadily towards the equator over most of the tropics, from the north-east in the northern hemisphere and south-east in the southern hemisphere.

tradition *noun* 1 the passing down of beliefs or customs from one generation to another. 2 a belief or custom that has been handed down in this way, especially an established custom or way of doing things. [from a Latin word *traditum* meaning 'handed on']

traditional *noun* (said about a belief or custom) following tradition, or passed down by tradition. **traditionally** *adverb*

traditionalist *noun* a person who follows or supports traditional beliefs and ways of doing things. **traditionalism** *noun*

traduce (trə-**dewss**) *verb* to speak badly or untruthfully about someone or something. [from a Latin word *traducere* meaning 'to lead in front' and 'to ridicule']

traffic *noun* 1 vehicles, ships, or aircraft moving along a route. 2 trading, especially when it is illegal or wrong ♦ *the traffic in drugs*.
traffic *verb* (**traffics, trafficked, trafficking**) to buy and sell something illegal, especially drugs. **trafficker** *noun* [from a French word *traffique*]

traffic calming *noun* measures taken to slow down traffic in residential areas by making roads narrow or building speed bumps or other obstacles.

traffic lights *plural noun* coloured lights used as a signal controlling traffic at road junctions, road works, and pedestrian crossings.

traffic warden *noun* an official who monitors the parking of road vehicles and reports on infringements.

tragedian (trə-**jeed**-iən) *noun* 1 a person who writes tragedies. 2 an actor in tragedies.

tragedy *noun* (**tragedies**) 1 an event that causes great destruction or suffering. SYNONYMS: disaster, calamity, catastrophe. 2 a serious play with an unhappy ending, especially the death or downfall of the main character. 3 the branch of drama that consists of such plays. [from Greek words *tragos* meaning 'goat' and *ōidē* meaning 'song', but it is not clear why Greek tragedies were called 'goat songs']

tragic *adjective* 1 causing great distress or disaster. SYNONYMS: disastrous, catastrophic. 2 suffering great sadness. 3 to do with tragedy ♦ *a tragic actor*. **tragical** *adjective* **tragically** *adverb*

trail *noun* 1 a series of marks or signs left where someone or something has passed, a trace. SYNONYMS: traces, tracks, marks. 2 an improvised path or track, especially through a wild region. 3 a route followed for a particular purpose ♦ *Turn left for the tourist trail through the lakes.* 4 a long thin part hanging down or behind something. 5 a line of people or things following behind something. 6 a track or scent used in following someone or something.
trail *verb* 1 to follow the trail of someone or something, to track or hunt them. SYNONYMS: follow, pursue, track, trace, stalk. 2 to drag something behind along the ground, or to be dragged behind. SYNONYMS: drag, tow, pull. 3 to hang down or float loosely. SYNONYMS: dangle, hang. 4 to walk or move slowly or wearily, to lag or straggle. SYNONYMS: lag, straggle, dawdle, linger. 5 to be losing in a game or contest. 6 to become less or fainter ♦ *The voice trailed away.* [from a Latin word *tragula* meaning 'net for dragging a river']

trailer *noun* 1 a truck or other container pulled along by a vehicle. 2 (*North Amer.*) a caravan. 3 a short extract from a film or television programme, shown in advance to advertise it.

trailing edge *noun* the rear edge of a moving body.

train *noun* 1 a series of linked railway carriages or trucks pulled by a locomotive or having built-in motors. 2 a number of people or animals moving in a line ♦ *a camel train.* 3 a body of followers, a retinue. SYNONYMS: retinue, entourage, escort. 4 part of a long dress or robe that trails on the ground at the back. 5 a series of things ♦ *a train of events* ♦ *a train of thought.* 6 a set of connected parts in machinery. 7 a line of gunpowder for firing an explosive charge.
train *verb* 1 to give someone instruction or practice in a particular skill. SYNONYMS: instruct, coach, teach. 2 to be given instruction ♦ *She is training as an accountant.* 3 to bring a person, team, etc. to the right level of physical fitness, especially for sport. SYNONYMS: coach, drill. 4 to practise in order to come to the right level of physical fitness. SYNONYMS: practise, exercise, work out. 5 to teach a person or animal to do something or behave in a particular way. 6 to aim a gun or camera at a particular object. 7 to make a plant grow in a particular direction. **to put something in train** to make preparations for something. **in training** undergoing training for a sport. **trainable** *adjective* [same origin as for *traction*]

trainee *noun* a person who is being trained for a particular job or profession.

trainer *noun* 1 a person who trains people or animals. 2 a soft shoe with a rubber sole, used for sports or casual wear. 3 an aircraft used to train pilots, or a machine simulating an aircraft.

trainspotter *noun* a person who goes to see and record details of railway locomotives as a hobby.

traipse *verb* (*informal*) to walk or wearily, to trudge. [origin unknown]

trait (tray) *noun* a distinguishing characteristic. SYNONYMS: characteristic, peculiarity, idiosyncrasy. [from a French word, related to *tract*[1]]

traitor *noun* a person who betrays their country. **traitorous** *adjective* [from an Old French word *traitour*, related to *tradition*]

trajectory (trǝ-jek-ter-i) *noun* (**trajectories**) the path taken by an object moving under force, especially a bullet or rocket. [from *trans-* and a Latin word *jactum* meaning 'thrown']

tram or **tramcar** *noun* a public passenger vehicle powered by electricity and running on rails laid in the road. [from a German or Dutch word *trame* meaning 'beam' or 'shaft of a cart']

tramlines *plural noun* 1 rails for a tram. 2 (*informal*) a pair of parallel lines, especially the ones at each side of a tennis or badminton court.

trammel *noun* a kind of net with three layers forming pockets for catching fish. **trammel** *verb* (**trammelled, trammelling**) to hamper or impede someone. [via Old French *tramail* from Latin words *tri-* meaning 'three' and *macula* meaning 'mesh']

tramp *noun* 1 a homeless person who goes from place to place begging or doing casual work. 2 a cargo boat that travels on different routes. 3 the sound of heavy footsteps. 4 a long walk. SYNONYMS: trudge, traipse, plod.
tramp *verb* 1 to walk with heavy steps. 2 to travel on foot across rough country. [probably from a German or Dutch word]

trample *verb* to tread on something repeatedly and crush it. SYNONYMS: crush, squash, flatten. [from *tramp*]

trampoline (tramp-ǝ-leen) *noun* a piece of gymnastic equipment consisting of a sheet of strong canvas attached by springs to a horizontal frame, used as a springboard for acrobatic jumping. [from an Italian word *trampolino*, from *trampoli* meaning 'stilts']

tramway *noun* a set of rails for a tram.

trance *noun* 1 a semi-conscious state of the kind induced by hypnosis. 2 a dreamy self-absorbed state. [from an Old French word *transir* meaning 'to fall into a trance', related to *transient*]

tranquil *adjective* calm and quiet, without disturbance. SYNONYMS: calm, quiet, peaceful, serene, placid. **tranquillity** *noun* **tranquilly** *adverb* [via French from a Latin word *tranquillus*]

tranquillize *verb* (said about a drug) to make someone feel calm.

tranquillizer *noun* a drug used to relieve anxiety and make a person feel calm.

trans- *prefix* across or beyond (as in *transatlantic*). [from a Latin word *trans* meaning 'across']

transact *verb* to carry out business.
transactor *noun*

transaction *noun* **1** the process of carrying out business. **2** a piece of business carried out.
transactions *plural noun* a published report of the proceedings of a learned society.
transactional *adjective* [from *trans-* and a Latin word *agere* meaning 'to do']

transatlantic *adjective* **1** crossing the Atlantic ♦ *a transatlantic flight.* **2** on or from the other side of the Atlantic.

transceiver (tran-**seev**-er) *noun* a combined radio transmitter and receiver.

transcend (tran-**send**) *verb* **1** to go or be beyond the range or limits of something ♦ *The experience transcended her wildest expectations.* SYNONYMS: surpass, exceed. **2** to surpass something. [from *trans-* and a Latin word *scandere* meaning 'to climb']

transcendent (tran-**sen**-dənt) *adjective* going beyond the limits of ordinary experience, surpassing. **transcendence** *noun* **transcendently** *adverb*

transcendental (tran-sen-**den**-təl) *adjective* belonging to a spiritual or visionary world. **transcendentally** *adverb*

transcendental meditation *noun* a technique of relaxation based on meditation and repetition of a mantra.

transcontinental *adjective* extending or travelling across a continent.

transcribe *verb* **1** to copy something in writing, or to write something out in another system of writing. **2** to record sound for later reproduction or broadcasting. **3** (*Music*) to arrange a composition for a different instrument. **transcriber** *noun* **transcription** *noun* [from *trans-* and a Latin word *scribere* meaning 'to write']

transcript *noun* a written or printed version of something originally in a different medium.

transducer *noun* an electrical device that converts one type of energy into another, such as a radio or microphone. [from *trans-* and a Latin word *ducere* meaning 'to lead']

transect *noun* (*Ecology*) a line or belt of vegetation marked out for observation or measurement. [from *trans-* and a Latin word *sectum* meaning 'cut']

transept (**tran**-sept) *noun* each of the two parts at right angles to the nave in a cross-shaped church ♦ *the north and south transepts.* [from *trans-* and a Latin word *septum* meaning 'partition']

transfer[1] (**trans**-fer) *verb* (**transferred, transferring**) **1** to move or convey something from one place or person to another. SYNONYMS: convey, move, carry, pass on. **2** to connect a telephone caller to another line or extension. **3** to change from one station, route, or means of transport to another during a journey. **4** to move or make someone move to another group or activity ♦ *She has transferred to the new branch.* **5** to copy a drawing or pattern from one surface to another. **transference** *noun* **transferral** *noun* [from *trans-* and a Latin word *ferre* meaning 'to carry']

transfer[2] (**trans**-fer) *noun* **1** the process of transferring or being transferred. **2** (*Law*) a document that transfers property or a right from one person to another. **3** a design that can be transferred from one surface to another, or a piece of paper bearing this design.

transferable (trans-**fer**-əbəl) *adjective* able to be transferred; (said about a ticket or permit) able to be used by another person. **transferability** *noun*

transfigure *verb* to transform something, especially to make it nobler or more beautiful ♦ *Her face was transfigured by happiness.* **transfiguration** *noun* [from *trans-* and a Latin word *figura* meaning 'figure']

transfix *verb* **1** to pierce something with a pointed object. **2** to make a person or animal unable to move through fear or wonder. [from a Latin word *transfigere* meaning 'to pierce through']

transform *verb* **1** to make a great change in the appearance or character of something. **2** to become greatly changed in appearance or character. **3** to change the voltage of an electric current. **transformation** *noun* **transformational** *adjective* [from *trans-* and a Latin word *formare* meaning 'to form']

transformer *noun* a device for changing the voltage of alternating current.

transfuse *verb* to transfer blood from one person or animal to another. [from *trans-* and a Latin word *fusum* meaning 'poured']

transfusion *noun* an injection of blood into the bloodstream of a person or animal.

transgress *verb* 1 to break a rule or law. 2 to go beyond a restriction or limit. 3 (*old use*) to commit a sin. **transgression** *noun* **transgressor** *noun* [from *trans-* and a Latin word *gressus* meaning 'gone']

transient (**tran-zi-ənt**) *adjective* 1 lasting only a short time, not permanent. 2 staying in a place for a short period only. **transient** *noun* a temporary visitor or worker. **transience** *noun* [from *trans-* and a Latin word *iens* meaning 'going']

transistor *noun* 1 a semiconductor device with three electrodes, used in electronic amplification and control circuits. 2 (in full **transistor radio**) a portable radio using circuits with transistors. **transistorize** *verb* [from *transfer* and *resistor*]

transit *noun* 1 the process of going or taking things from one place to another. 2 the movement of a planet across the face of the sun, or of a moon across the face of a planet.
transit *verb* (**transited, transiting**) to pass across or through a place. [from *trans-* and a Latin word *itum* meaning 'gone']

transition (**tran-si-zhən**) *noun* the process of changing from one condition or form to another. **transitional** *adjective* **transitionally** *adverb*

transitive *adjective* (said about a verb or a meaning of a verb) used with a direct object, e.g. *play* in *The teams will play each other on Saturday* (but not in *The teams will play on Saturday*). **transitively** *adverb*

transitory *adjective* existing for a time but not lasting. **transitorily** *adverb* **transitoriness** *noun*

translate *verb* 1 to express something in another language. 2 to be capable of being expressed in another language ♦ *The novel does not translate well*. 3 to move something from one place or state to another. 4 (*formal*) to move a bishop to another see, or to move a saint's relics to another place. **translatable** *adjective* **translation** *noun* **translator** *noun* [from *trans-* and a Latin word *latum* meaning 'carried']

transliterate *verb* to represent letters or words in the most closely corresponding letters of a different alphabet. **transliteration** *noun* [from *trans-* and a Latin word *littera* meaning 'letter']

translucent (**tranz-loo-sənt**) *adjective* allowing light to pass through without being completely transparent. **translucence** *noun* **translucency** *noun* [from *trans-* and a Latin word *lucens* meaning 'shining']

transmigration *noun* the passing of a person's soul into another body after death.

transmission *noun* 1 the process of transmitting a message or broadcast. 2 a broadcast transmitted. 3 the set of gears by which power is transmitted from the engine to the wheels of a motor vehicle.

transmit *verb* (**transmitted, transmitting**) 1 to send or pass something from one person, place, or thing to another. SYNONYMS: convey, deliver, transfer, pass on. 2 to be a medium for a form of energy ♦ *Iron transmits heat*. 3 to send out a signal or broadcast by telegraph wire or radio waves. **transmissible** *adjective* **transmittable** *adjective* [from *trans-* and a Latin word *mittere* meaning 'to send']

transmitter *noun* a device or set of equipment for transmitting radio or television signals.

transmogrify *verb* (**transmogrifies, transmogrified, transmogrifying**) to transform something, especially in a magical or surprising way. **transmogrification** *noun* [origin unknown]

transmute *verb* to cause something to change in form or substance. **transmutation** *noun* [from *trans-* and a Latin word *mutare* meaning 'to change']

transoceanic *adjective* 1 crossing an ocean. 2 on or from the other side of an ocean.

transom *noun* (*Architecture*) 1 a horizontal bar of wood or stone across the top of a door or window. 2 a small window above a door. [from an Old French word *traversin*, related to *traverse*]

transparency (**trans-pa-rən-si**) *noun* (**transparencies**) 1 a state of being transparent. 2 a positive photograph printed on film or glass, a slide.

transparent (**trans-pa-rənt**) *adjective* 1 allowing light to pass through so that objects behind can be seen clearly. 2 easily understood, clear or obvious. SYNONYMS: clear, obvious, apparent. **transparently** *adverb* [from *trans-* and a Latin word *parens* meaning 'appearing']

transpire verb 1 (said about information) to become known ♦ It transpired that during the war he had been a member of the resistance. 2 to happen ♦ It's hard to know exactly what transpired. 3 (said about plants) to give off watery vapour from the surface of leaves etc. **transpiration** noun [from trans- and a Latin word spirare meaning 'to breathe'] ◊ Some people dislike meaning 2,'to happen', but it is very common.

transplant [1] (trans-plaht) verb 1 to remove a plant and put it to grow somewhere else. 2 to transfer an organ or living tissue from one part of the body or one person or animal to another. **transplantation** noun

transplant [2] (trans-plaht) noun 1 the process of transplanting an organ or tissue. 2 something transplanted.

transport [1] (trans-port) verb 1 to take or convey someone or something from one place to another. SYNONYMS: convey, transfer. 2 to overcome someone with strong emotion ♦ She was transported with joy. 3 (historical) to deport a criminal to a penal settlement. **transportable** adjective **transportation** noun [from trans- and a Latin word portare meaning 'to carry']

transport [2] (trans-port) noun 1 the act or process of transporting people or things. 2 a means of transporting people or things ♦ We'll have to use public transport. 3 a ship or aircraft for carrying troops or supplies. 4 the condition of being carried away by strong emotion ♦ in transports of rage.

transporter noun a vehicle used to transport heavy loads.

transpose verb 1 to cause two or more things to change places, or to change one thing to a different position in a series. SYNONYMS: exchange, switch, interchange, reverse. 2 to put a piece of music into a different key. **transposition** noun [from trans- and a Latin word positum meaning 'placed']

transsexual noun a person who feels emotionally and psychologically that they belong to the sex opposite to their own.

trans-ship verb (**trans-shipped**, **trans-shipping**) to transfer cargo from one ship or form of transport to another. **trans-shipment** noun

transubstantiation noun the process of changing one substance into another. [from trans- and substance]

transuranic (trans-yoor-an-ik) adjective (Chemistry) belonging to a group of radioactive elements with atoms heavier than those of uranium.

transverse adjective lying or extending across something. **transversely** adverb [from trans- and a Latin word versum meaning 'turned']

transvestite noun a person who enjoys dressing in the clothing of the opposite sex. **transvestism** noun [from trans- and a Latin word vestire meaning 'to clothe']

trap noun 1 a device for catching and holding animals. SYNONYM: snare. 2 a plan or trick for capturing or detecting a person unawares or for making a person betray themselves. 3 an unpleasant situation from which you cannot easily escape. 4 a device for preventing the passage of water or steam or silt etc. 5 a U-shaped or S-shaped section of a pipe that holds liquid to prevent gases from rising up from a drain. 6 a device for hurling an object into the air to be shot at. 7 a compartment from which a greyhound is released at the start of a race. 8 a two-wheeled carriage drawn by a horse. 9 a trapdoor.
trap verb (**trapped**, **trapping**) 1 to catch or hold an animal in a trap. SYNONYMS: snare, catch. 2 to trick or deceive someone into doing something. SYNONYMS: trick, deceive, dupe. 3 to prevent someone from escaping, or from avoiding an unpleasant situation. [from an Old English word træppe]

trapdoor noun a small hinged or removable flap in a floor, ceiling, or roof.

trapeze noun a horizontal bar hanging by long ropes as a swing for acrobatics.

trapezium (trə-pee-ziəm) noun (**trapezia** or **trapeziums**) a quadrilateral in which two opposite sides are parallel and the other two are not. [from a Greek word trapeza meaning 'table']

trapezoid (trap-i-zoid) noun a quadrilateral in which no sides are parallel. **trapezoidal** (trap-i-**zoi**-dəl) adjective

trapper noun a person who traps wild animals, especially for their fur.

trappings plural noun 1 the clothes and other things that indicate a person's status or position ♦ all the trappings of respectability. 2 the ornamental harness of a horse. [from an Old French word drap meaning 'cloth']

Trappist noun a monk of a Cistercian order founded at La Trappe in France, following an austere rule including a vow of silence.

trash noun 1 worthless stuff, rubbish. 2 worthless people.
trash verb (informal) to wreck a place.
trashy adjective [origin unknown]

trauma (traw-mə) noun 1 an emotional shock that leaves a lasting effect on a person's mind. 2 a distressing experience. 3 (Medicine) a wound or injury. [a Greek word meaning 'a wound']

traumatic (traw-mat-ik) adjective 1 causing trauma. 2 (said about an experience) very distressing or unpleasant. SYNONYMS: distressing, unpleasant, upsetting.

travail (trav-ayl) noun 1 (literary) painful or laborious effort. 2 (old use) the pains of childbirth.
travail verb (literary) to make a painful or laborious effort. [via Old French from a late Latin word trepalium meaning 'instrument of torture']

travel verb (travelled, travelling) 1 to go from one place to another, to make a journey. 2 to journey along or through a region or distance.
travel noun 1 the action of travelling, especially abroad. 2 the range, rate, or method of movement of a machine part. [another form of travail, which was the original meaning]

travel agent or **travel agency** noun a business that makes travel and holiday arrangements for travellers.

traveller noun 1 a person who is travelling or who travels a lot. 2 a person who travels from place to place, especially as a member of a New Age community.

traveller's cheque noun a cheque for a fixed amount of money that is sold by banks and can be cashed for foreign currency abroad.

travelogue (trav-əl-og) noun a book, film, or illustrated lecture about travel. [from travel and a Greek word logos meaning 'word']

traverse [1] (trə-vers) verb 1 to travel across an area. 2 to lie or extend across something. **traversal** noun [same origin as for transverse]

traverse [2] (trav-ers) noun 1 a part of a building or structure that lies across another part. 2 a zigzag course that a ship follows because conditions prevent it

sailing in a direct line. 3 a lateral movement across something. 4 a steep mountain slope that has to be crossed from side to side.

travesty (trav-iss-ti) noun (travesties) a ridiculous or poor version of something worthwhile ♦ The trial was a travesty of justice.
travesty verb (travesties, travestied, travestying) to represent something as a travesty. [from a French word travesti meaning 'having changed clothes']

trawl verb 1 to fish from a boat by dragging a large net along the seabed. 2 to search a place thoroughly.
trawl noun a large net used in trawling for fish. [from a Dutch word traghelen meaning 'to drag']

trawler noun a fishing boat used for trawling.

tray noun 1 a flat piece of wood, metal, or plastic, usually with a raised edge, for carrying a number of small articles such as cups, plates, and food. 2 an open container for holding letters and papers in an office. [from an Old English word trig]

treacherous adjective 1 behaving with or showing deception or betrayal. SYNONYMS: disloyal, faithless. 2 dangerous or unsafe ♦ The roads are icy and treacherous. SYNONYMS: dangerous, hazardous, unsafe.
treacherously adverb **treacherousness** noun [from an Old French word trechier meaning 'to cheat']

treachery noun betrayal of a person or cause, an act of disloyalty.

treacle noun a thick sticky dark liquid produced when sugar is refined. **treacly** adjective [from an earlier meaning 'ointment for an animal bite', from a Greek word thērion meaning 'wild animal']

tread verb (trod, trodden) 1 to set your foot down, to walk or step on the ground. 2 to press or crush something with the feet. SYNONYMS: press, crush, squash, trample. 3 to make a path or trail by walking.
tread noun 1 a manner or the sound of walking ♦ walking with a heavy tread. 2 the top surface of a step or stair. 3 the part of a wheel or tyre that makes contact with the ground. **to tread on air** to walk buoyantly because of happiness. **to tread on someone's toes** to anger or offend someone. **to tread water** to keep yourself upright in water by making treading

movements with the legs. [from an Old English word *tredan*]

treadle (tred-ǝl) *noun* a lever worked with the foot to drive a wheel, especially in a sewing machine.
treadle *verb* to work a machine with a treadle. [from an Old English word *tredel*, related to *tread*]

treadmill *noun* 1 a wide mill wheel turned by the weight of people or animals treading on steps fixed round its edge. 2 an exercise machine with a moving belt for walking or running on. 3 a job or task that is tedious or routine.

treason *noun* the act of betraying your country, especially by overthrowing the monarch or government. **treasonous** *adjective* [from a Latin word *traditum* meaning 'handed over' or 'betrayed', related to *tradition*]

treasonable *adjective* involving or amounting to treason ♦ *a treasonable offence.* **treasonably** *adverb*

treasure *noun* 1 precious metals, gems, or other valuable objects, or a store of these. 2 an object of great worth or value ♦ *art treasures.* 3 a much loved or highly valued person.
treasure *verb* 1 to value something or someone highly. SYNONYMS: cherish, value, prize, hold dear. 2 to keep something valuable carefully. [from a Greek word *thēsauros* meaning 'treasury']

treasure hunt *noun* a game in which players try to find hidden objects by following a series of clues.

treasurer *noun* a person appointed to manage the funds of an organization, society, etc.

treasure trove *noun* gold or silver coins or objects found hidden and with no known owner.

treasury *noun* (**treasuries**) 1 a place where money and valuables are stored. 2 a collection of valuable or useful things ♦ *The book is a treasury of information.* 3 (**Treasury**) a government department that manages the public finances of a country.

treat *verb* 1 to behave in a certain way towards a person or thing. SYNONYMS: deal with, handle, manage, consider. 2 to present or discuss a subject ♦ *The author treats recent events in detail.* 3 to give medical care to a person or illness. SYNONYM: tend. 4 to put something through a chemical or other process ♦ *The fabric has been treated to make it waterproof.* 5 to provide someone with food or entertainment at your own expense in order to give pleasure ♦ *I'll treat you to a drink.* 6 to discuss terms ♦ *The government are treating with the guerrillas to agree a ceasefire.*
treat *noun* 1 something special that gives a lot of pleasure. 2 the act of providing someone with food or entertainment at your own expense ♦ *It's my treat.* [from a Latin word *tractare* meaning 'to handle']

treatise (tree-tiss) *noun* a book or pamphlet on a particular subject. [same origin as for *treat*]

treatment *noun* 1 the process or manner of dealing with a person, animal, or thing. 2 medical care for a person or illness.

treaty *noun* (**treaties**) a formal agreement between two or more countries. [same origin as for *treat*]

treble *adjective* three times as much or three times as many.
treble *noun* 1 a treble quantity or thing. 2 a high-pitched singing voice, or a singer (usually a boy) with such a voice. 3 a high-pitched member of a group of musical instruments.
treble *verb* to make something, or become, three times as much or as many. **trebly** *adverb* [same origin as for *triple*]

tree *noun* 1 a tall perennial plant with a single thick hard stem or trunk that is usually without branches for some distance above the ground. 2 a wooden framework of wood for various purposes ♦ *a shoe tree.* **treeless** *adjective* [from an Old English word *treow*]

tree diagram *noun* a diagram with information organized in branches like a tree.

tree house *noun* a small hut or cabin built in a tree for children to play in.

treeline *noun* a line or altitude above which no trees grow.

tree surgeon *noun* a person who treats old or decayed trees in order to preserve them.

treetop *noun* the highest part of a tree.

trefoil (tref-oil) *noun* 1 a plant with three small leaves, e.g. clover. 2 an ornament or design having three lobes like a trefoil. [from a Latin word *trifolium*, from *tres* meaning 'three' and *folium* meaning 'leaf']

trek *noun* a long difficult journey on foot. **trek** *verb* (**trekked, trekking**) to go on a trek. [from a Dutch word *trekken* meaning 'to pull']

trellis *noun* a light framework of crossing wooden or metal bars, used to support climbing plants. [via Old French from a Latin word *trilix* meaning 'three-ply']

trematode (trem-ə-tohd) *noun* a parasitic flatworm. [from a Greek word *trēmatōdēs* meaning 'perforated']

tremble *verb* 1 to shake involuntarily, especially from fear or excitement. SYNONYMS: quiver, shake, shudder, shiver. 2 to be in a state of great anxiety or agitation ♦ *I tremble to think what all this might cost.* **tremble** *noun* a trembling movement or feeling. SYNONYMS: tremor, quiver, shudder. [via French from a Latin word *tremulare*, related to *tremulous*]

tremendous *adjective* 1 very large or immense. SYNONYMS: immense, huge, colossal, enormous. 2 (*informal*) excellent or impressive ♦ *They gave a tremendous performance.* **tremendously** *adverb* **tremendousness** *noun* [from a Latin word *tremendus* meaning 'causing people to tremble']

tremolo (trem-ə-loh) *noun* (**tremolos**) (*Music*) a trembling or vibrating effect made by a voice or instrument. [an Italian word]

tremor (trem-er) *noun* 1 a shaking or trembling movement, a vibration. 2 (also **earth tremor**) a slight earthquake. 3 a sudden feeling of fear or excitement. [a Latin word, from *tremere* meaning 'to tremble']

tremulous (trem-yoo-ləs) *adjective* 1 trembling from nervousness or weakness ♦ *She drew in a tremulous breath.* 2 quivering gently. **tremulously** *adverb* [from a Latin word *tremulus* meaning 'trembling']

trench *noun* a long narrow ditch cut in the ground, often used for drainage or to give troops shelter from enemy fire. **trench** *verb* to dig trenches in the ground. [from an Old French word *trenche*, related to *truncate*]

trenchant (tren-chənt) *adjective* (said about comments or actions) strong and effective ♦ *They have made some trenchant criticisms.* **trenchancy** *noun* **trenchantly** *adverb* [from an Old French word meaning 'cutting']

trench coat *noun* a belted double-breasted coat with pockets and flaps like those worn by soldiers.

trencherman *noun* (**trenchermen**) a person who eats heartily ♦ *a good trencherman.* [from an old word *trencher* meaning 'wooden plate']

trend *noun* 1 a general direction in which something is developing, a continuing tendency. 2 a fashion. [from an Old English word *trendan* meaning 'to rotate']

trendsetter *noun* a person who leads the way in fashion or ideas.

trendy *adjective* (**trendier, trendiest**) (*informal*) fashionable, following the latest trends. **trendily** *adverb* **trendiness** *noun*

trepidation (trep-i-day-shən) *noun* a state of nervous fear or anxiety. [from a Latin word *trepidare* meaning 'to be afraid']

trespass *verb* 1 to enter a person's land or property without their authority. 2 to intrude on someone or take unfair advantage of them ♦ *I don't want to trespass on your hospitality.* 3 (*old use*) to sin or do wrong.
trespass *noun* 1 the act of trespassing. 2 (*old use*) a sin or wrongdoing ♦ *Forgive us our trespasses.* **trespasser** *noun* [from an Old French word *trespasser* meaning 'to pass over', from *trans-* and *pass*[1]]

tress *noun* a lock of a woman's hair. [from an Old French word *tresse*]

trestle *noun* 1 a board resting on two sets of sloping legs to form a table or working surface. 2 each of a pair of sloping legs supporting a board. 3 an open braced framework used to support a bridge. [via Old French from a Latin word *transtrum* meaning 'beam']

trews *plural noun* close-fitting tartan trousers. [from Irish and Scottish Gaelic words]

tri- *prefix* three or triple (as in *tricycle*, *triathlon*). [from a Latin word *tres* or a Greek word *treis* meaning 'three']

triacetate (triy-ass-i-tayt) *noun* (also **cellulose triacetate**) a form of cellulose acetate having a very large molecule built up of units each containing three acetate groups, used for making synthetic fibres.

triad (triy-ad) *noun* 1 a group or set of three. 2 a Chinese secret organization involved in organized crime. [via French from a Greek word *trias* meaning 'group of three']

trial *noun* **1** the process of examining the evidence in a law court to determine whether an accused person has committed a crime. **2** the process of testing the qualities or performance of something by trying it out. SYNONYMS: test, experiment. **3** a sports match to test the ability of players who may be selected for a team. **4** a test of individual ability on a motorcycle over rough ground or on a road. **5** a person or thing that tests your patience or endurance. SYNONYMS: nuisance, worry, bane. **on trial 1** being tried in a law court. **2** on approval. **trial and error** the process of trying out different methods until you find the one most suitable. [from *try*]

triangle *noun* **1** a flat figure with three sides and three angles. **2** something shaped like a triangle. **3** a percussion instrument consisting of a steel rod bent into the shape of a triangle and struck with a small steel bar. [from *tri-* and *angle*[1]]

triangular *adjective* **1** shaped like a triangle. **2** involving three people ♦ *a triangular contest*.

triangulate *verb* **1** to divide something into triangles. **2** to measure or map out an area by triangulation.

triangulation *noun* (in surveying) the process of measuring or mapping out an area by means of calculations based on a network of triangles measured from a baseline.

tribal *adjective* to do with a tribe or tribes.

tribe *noun* **1** a traditional social division in some societies, consisting of a group of families living in one area as a community and sharing a common culture. **2** a set or class of people ♦ *He despises the whole tribe of journalists.* **3** a division of the people (originally one of three) in ancient Rome. [via Old French from a Latin word *tribus*]

tribesman or **tribeswoman** *noun* (**tribesmen** or **tribeswomen**) a member of a tribe.

tribulation (trib-yoo-lay-shən) *noun* great trouble or suffering, or something that causes this. [from a Latin word *tribulare* meaning 'to press' or 'to oppress']

tribunal (triy-bew-nəl) *noun* a body of officials appointed to make certain judgements or settle certain disputes. [from a Latin word *tribunale* meaning 'tribune's seat']

tribune (trib-yoon) *noun* **1** an official in ancient Rome chosen by the people to protect their interests. **2** an officer in command of a Roman legion. **3** a leader of the people. [from a Latin word *tribunus*, literally 'leader of a tribe' (in the Roman sense)]

tributary *noun* (**tributaries**) a river or stream that flows into a larger river or a lake. [same origin as for *tribute*]

tribute *noun* **1** something said, done, or given as a mark of respect or admiration. SYNONYMS: eulogy, appreciation. **2** something that shows how effective or worthwhile a thing was ♦ *Her success was a tribute to her determination.* **3** (*historical*) payment that one country or ruler paid to another, especially as a mark of dependence. **to pay tribute to** to express respect or admiration for someone or something. [from a Latin word *tributum* meaning 'assigned']

trice *noun* **in a trice** in an instant. [from a Dutch word *trisen* meaning 'to pull quickly']

triceps (triy-seps) *noun* (**triceps**) (*Anatomy*) the large muscle at the back of the upper arm, which straightens the elbow. [a Latin word meaning 'three-headed' (because the end of the muscle is attached at three points)]

triceratops (triy-se-rə-tops) *noun* a large dinosaur with a huge head and two large horns, which fed on plants. [from Greek words *trikeratos* meaning 'with three horns' and *ōps* meaning 'face']

trick *noun* **1** a clever or cunning action intended to deceive or outwit someone. SYNONYMS: ploy, ruse, subterfuge. **2** a mischievous or foolish practical joke. SYNONYMS: prank, stunt, hoax. **3** a deception or illusion ♦ *a trick of the light.* **4** a particular technique, the exact or best way of doing something. **5** a skilful action done for entertainment ♦ *a conjuring trick.* **6** a mannerism ♦ *He has a trick of tapping his fingers.* **7** the cards played in one round of a card game such as bridge or whist. **trick** *verb* **1** to deceive or mislead someone by means of a trick. SYNONYMS: deceive, mislead, dupe, fool, hoodwink. **do the trick** (*informal*) to achieve the result that is wanted. **trick or treat** a children's custom of calling at houses at Hallowe'en and threatening to do mischief if they do not get a small reward. **to trick something**

out or **up** to decorate something. [from an Old French word *trichier* meaning 'to deceive']

trickery noun the use of tricks, deception.

trickle verb 1 to flow or cause a liquid to flow in a thin stream. 2 to move slowly or gradually ♦ *People trickled into the hall.* **trickle** noun 1 a slow gentle flow. 2 a small number of people or things moving slowly ♦ *a trickle of information.* [an imitation of the sound]

trickster noun a person who tricks or cheats people.

tricky adjective (**trickier, trickiest**) 1 difficult or needing skill ♦ *a tricky job.* SYNONYMS: difficult, awkward. 2 cunning or deceitful. SYNONYMS: cunning, deceitful, devious, scheming. **trickily** adverb **trickiness** noun

tricolour (trik-əl-er) noun a flag with three coloured stripes, especially the national flags of France and Ireland. [from *tri-* and *colour*]

tricuspid (triy-kus-pid) adjective having three points ♦ *a tricuspid valve.* [from *tri-* and a Latin word *cuspis* meaning 'cusp']

tricycle noun a vehicle like a bicycle with two wheels at the back and one at the front.

trident (triy-dənt) noun a three-pronged spear, carried by Poseidon (Neptune) and Britannia as a symbol of their power over the sea. [*tri-* and a Latin word *dens* meaning 'tooth']

tried past tense and past participle of **try**.

triennial (triy-en-iəl) adjective 1 lasting for three years. 2 happening every third year. **triennially** adverb [from *tri-* and a Latin word *annus* meaning 'year']

trier noun 1 a person who tries hard. 2 a tester.

trifle noun 1 something of little value or importance. 2 a slight amount ♦ *They seem a trifle upset.* 3 a sweet food made of sponge cake and fruit with layers of jelly, custard, and cream.
trifle verb to behave or talk frivolously. **to trifle with** to treat someone casually or without proper seriousness. **trifler** noun [from an Old French word *trufle*, from *trufe* meaning 'deceit']

trifling adjective trivial or unimportant. SYNONYMS: trivial, unimportant, insignificant, petty.

trigger noun a lever or catch that releases a spring to activate a mechanism, especially to fire a gun.
trigger verb 1 to activate a mechanism. 2 to cause something to start. **to trigger something off** to be the immediate cause of something. [from a Dutch word *trekker* meaning 'puller']

trigger-happy adjective apt to fire a gun or take other action impulsively.

trigonometry (trig-ən-om-itri) noun the branch of mathematics dealing with the relationship of sides and angles of triangles. **trigonometric** adjective **trigonometrical** adjective [from Greek *trigōnon* meaning 'triangle' and *-metria* meaning 'measurement']

trike noun (*informal*) a tricycle.

trilateral (triy-lat-er-əl) adjective 1 having or to do with three sides. 2 between three people or groups ♦ *a trilateral agreement.* [from *tri-* and *lateral*]

trilby noun (**trilbies**) a man's soft felt hat with a narrow brim and a dent in the crown. [named after the heroine of George du Maurier's novel *Trilby* (1894), who wore such a hat in a play based on the book]

trilingual (triy-ling-gwəl) adjective 1 able to speak three languages. 2 written in three languages. [from *tri-* and a Latin word *lingua* meaning 'language']

trill noun 1 a vibrating sound made by the voice or in birdsong. 2 a quick alternation of two notes in music that are a tone or semitone apart.
trill verb to sound or sing with a trill. [from an Italian word *trillo*]

trillion noun 1 a million million. 2 (*old use*) a million million million. **trillionth** adjective noun [from *tri-* and *million*]
◊ Now that *billion* means 'a thousand million', most people use *trillion* to mean 'a million million'. In the past, though, the word was used to mean 'a million million million'.

trilogy (tril-əji) noun (**trilogies**) a group of three novels, plays, or poems about the same people or on the same subject. [from *tri-* and a Greek word *-logia* meaning 'writings']

trim verb (**trimmed, trimming**) 1 to make something neat or smooth by cutting away unwanted or untidy parts. 2 to remove or reduce something by cutting. 3 to decorate a piece of clothing by adding decorations such as lace, ribbons, etc. 4 to arrange the sails of a boat to suit the wind. 5 to make a boat or aircraft evenly balanced by arranging the position of its cargo or passengers or ballast.
trim noun 1 how fit or in what condition a person or thing is ♦ *in good trim*. 2 extra decoration on a piece of clothing or furniture. 3 the colour or type of upholstery and other fittings in a car. 4 the cutting or trimming of hair ♦ *Your beard needs a trim*. 5 the balance or level position of a ship in the water or an aircraft in the air.
trim adjective (**trimmer, trimmest**) neat and smart, having a smooth outline or compact structure. SYNONYMS: neat, smart, spruce. **trimly** adverb **trimmer** noun **trimness** noun [from an Old English word *trymman* meaning 'to arrange']

trimaran (triy-mǝ-ran) noun a yacht with three hulls side by side. [from *tri-* and *catamaran*]

trimming noun something added as an ornament or decoration on a piece of clothing or furniture.
trimmings plural noun 1 pieces cut off when something is trimmed. 2 the usual accompaniments or extras ♦ *roast turkey and all the trimmings*.

trinity noun (**trinities**) 1 a group of three people or things.
Trinity noun (in Christian belief) the three persons of the Godhead: Father, Son, and Holy Spirit. [from a Latin word *trinitas* meaning 'group of three']

trinket noun a small ornament or piece of jewellery that does not have much value. [origin unknown]

trinomial (triy-noh-mi-ǝl) noun an algebraic expression consisting of three terms joined by + or −. [from *tri-* and *binomial*]

trio (tree-oh) noun (**trios**) 1 a group or set of three. 2 a group of three musicians or singers. 3 a piece of music for three musicians. [via Italian from a Latin word *tres* meaning 'three']

triode (triy-ohd) noun (*Electronics*) 1 a thermionic valve with three electrodes. 2 a semiconductor rectifier with three terminals. [from *tri-* and *electrode*]

trip verb (**tripped, tripping**) 1 to catch your foot on something and stumble or fall, or to make someone do this. SYNONYMS: stumble, slip, fall. 2 to make a mistake. 3 to move or dance with quick light steps. SYNONYMS: cavort, caper, dance. 4 (said about a rhythm) to run lightly. 5 to go on a short journey. 6 (*informal*) to have hallucinations caused by a drug. 7 to release a switch or catch in order to activate a mechanism.
trip noun 1 a journey or excursion, especially for pleasure. SYNONYMS: excursion, outing, journey. 2 (*informal*) an experience of hallucinations caused by a drug. 3 an act of tripping or falling over. 4 a device for activating a mechanism. **to trip up** 1 to stumble or fall. 2 to make a mistake. **to trip someone up** 1 to make someone stumble. 2 to show that someone has made a mistake. [from a Dutch word *trippen* meaning 'to hop']

tripartite (triy-par-tiyt) adjective 1 consisting of three parts. 2 involving three people or groups ♦ *tripartite talks*. [from *tri-* and a Latin word *partitus* meaning 'divided']

tripe noun 1 the part of the stomach of an ox used for food. 2 (*informal*) nonsense or rubbish. [from an Old French word meaning 'entrails of an animal']

Tripitaka (trip-i-tah-kǝ) noun the sacred canon of Theravada Buddhism. [from a Sanskrit word meaning 'the three baskets (or collections)']

triple adjective 1 three times as much or three times as many. 2 consisting of three things or parts. 3 involving three people or groups.
triple verb to make something, or become, three times as much or as many. **triply** adverb [from a Latin word *triplus* meaning 'three times as much']

triple jump noun an athletic event in which competitors make a hop, a step, and a long jump from a running start.

triplet noun 1 each of three children or animals born at one birth. 2 a set of three rhyming lines of verse. [from *triple*]

triple time noun (*Music*) time with three beats to the bar.

triplicate (trip-li-kǝt) noun each of three things that are exactly the same. **triplicate** adjective threefold; being a triplicate. **in triplicate** as three identical copies. [from a Latin word *triplex* meaning 'triple']

tripod (triy-pod) *noun* a three-legged stand for a camera, surveying instrument, or other device. [from *tri-* and a Greek word *podos* meaning 'of a foot']

tripper *noun* (*informal*) a person who goes on a pleasure trip.

triptych (trip-tik) *noun* a picture or carving on three wooden panels, usually fixed or hinged side by side and used as an altarpiece. [from *tri-* and *diptych*]

trireme (triy-reem) *noun* an ancient Greek or Roman warship with three banks of oars. [from *tri-* and a Latin word *remus* meaning 'oar']

trisect (triy-sekt) *verb* to divide something into three equal parts. **trisection** *noun* [from *tri-* and a Latin word *sectum* meaning 'cut']

trite *adjective* (said about a phrase or opinion) overused and having little meaning. SYNONYMS: hackneyed, banal; (*informal*) corny. [from a Latin word *tritum* meaning 'worn by use']

triton (triy-tən) *noun* (*Greek Mythology*) a minor sea god, represented as a man with a fish's tail carrying a trident and a shell trumpet. [named after Triton, the son of Poseidon]

triumph *noun* 1 a great success or victory. 2 a celebration of a success. SYNONYMS: jubilation, exultation, rejoicing.
triumph *verb* 1 to be successful or victorious. SYNONYMS: prevail, succeed. 2 to celebrate a success. [from a Latin word *triumphus*]

triumphal *adjective* celebrating a triumph
♦ *a triumphal arch.*

triumphant *adjective* 1 successful or victorious. 2 celebrating a success. **triumphantly** *adverb*

triumvirate (triy-um-ver-ət) *noun* a group of three people having power or authority. [from a Latin phrase *trium virorum* meaning 'of three men']

trivet (triv-it) *noun* an iron stand for a kettle or pot placed over a fire. [from a Latin word *tripes* meaning 'three-footed']

trivia *plural noun* unimportant details or pieces of information. [same origin as for *trivial*]

trivial *adjective* having little value or importance. SYNONYMS: trifling, unimportant, insignificant, petty. **triviality** (triv-i-al-iti)

noun **trivially** *adjective* [from a Latin word *trivialis*, literally meaning 'at a crossroads', and then 'commonplace']

trochee (troh-kee) *noun* (in poetry) a metrical foot with one long or stressed syllable followed by one short or unstressed syllable. [from a Greek phrase *trokhaios pous* meaning 'running foot']

trod past tense of **tread.**

trodden past participle of **tread.**

troglodyte (trog-lə-diyt) *noun* a person living in a cave in ancient times. [from a Greek word *trōglē* meaning 'hole']

Trojan *adjective* to do with or coming from ancient Troy in Asia minor (modern Turkey).
Trojan *noun* a person born or living in ancient Troy.

troll [1] *noun* (in folklore) an ugly dwarf or giant living in a cave or under a bridge. [from an Old Norse word]

troll [2] *verb* 1 to sing in a happy carefree way. 2 to fish by pulling a baited line along behind a boat. [from an earlier meaning 'stroll' or 'roll', from an Old French word *troller*]

trolley *noun* (**trolleys**) 1 a metal basket or platform on wheels for carrying or moving things. 2 a small table on wheels or castors for carrying food or drink indoors. [probably the same origin as for *troll*[2]]

trolleybus *noun* an electrically powered bus with a roof pole that is connected to an overhead wire by means of a contact wheel.

trollop *noun* (*old use*) a promiscuous woman or prostitute. [origin unknown]

trombone *noun* a large brass wind instrument with a sliding tube. [from an Italian word *tromba* meaning 'trumpet']

trompe l'œil (trawmp-lu-ee) *noun* a painting or design that makes the objects represented appear three-dimensional. [a French phrase meaning 'deceives the eye']

troop *noun* 1 a moving group of people or animals. SYNONYMS: band, company, group, squad. 2 a cavalry unit commanded by a captain, or a unit of artillery. 3 a group of three or more Scout patrols.
troop *verb* to assemble or move in large numbers.
troops *plural noun* soldiers or armed forces.
to troop the colour in Britain, to perform

the ceremony of parading the regimental flag along ranks of soldiers. [via French from a Latin word *troppus* meaning 'herd']
◊ Do not confuse this word with **troupe**, which has a different meaning.

trooper *noun* **1** a soldier in the cavalry or in an armoured unit. **2** (*North Amer.*) a member of a State police force.

trophic *adjective* (in ecology) to do with feeding or nutrition. [from a Greek word *trophē* meaning 'nourishment']

trophic level *noun* (*Ecology*) the position occupied by a group of plants or animals in a food chain.

trophy *noun* (**trophies**) **1** a cup or other object given as a prize for victory or success. **2** something taken in war or hunting as a souvenir of success.

tropic *noun* a line of latitude 23° 26' north of the equator (**tropic of Cancer**) or the same latitude south of it (**tropic of Capricorn**).
tropics *plural noun* the hot regions between these two latitudes. [from a Greek word *tropē* meaning 'turning' (because the sun seems to turn back when it reaches these points)]

tropical *adjective* **1** to do with or located in the tropics. **2** (said about the climate) hot and humid.

tropism (**troh**-pizm) *noun* (*Biology*) the turning or movement of an organism in response to an external stimulus such as light. [same origin as for *tropic*]

troposphere (**trop**-ə-sfeer) *noun* the lowest region of the atmosphere, extending to a height of 6–10 km from the earth's surface. [from a Greek word *tropos* meaning 'turning' and *sphere*]

trot *verb* (**trotted, trotting**) **1** (said about a horse) to go at a pace faster than a walk. **2** (*informal*) to walk or go ♦ *I'll just trot round to the chemist.*
trot *noun* **1** the action of a horse when trotting. **2** a slow gentle run. **on the trot** (*informal*) one after the other without a break ♦ *She worked for ten days on the trot.* **to trot something out** (*informal*) to say something that has been said many times before ♦ *They trotted out the same old excuses.* [via Old French from a Germanic language]

Trotskyist *noun* a supporter of the Russian leader and revolutionary Leon Trotsky (1879–1940), who urged worldwide socialist revolution. **Trotskyism** *noun* **Trotskyite** *noun*

trotter *noun* **1** a pig's foot used for food. **2** a horse of a special breed trained for trotting.

troubadour (**troo**-bəd-oor) *noun* a poet and singer in southern France in the 11th–13th centuries, singing mainly of chivalry and courtly love. [from an early French word *trover* meaning 'to write in verse']

trouble *noun* **1** difficulty or misfortune. SYNONYMS: difficulty, misfortune, bother, distress. **2** something that causes worry or difficulty. SYNONYMS: nuisance, worry, pest. **3** (often **troubles**) conflict or public unrest. SYNONYMS: disturbance, conflict, disorder, strife, turmoil. **4** (often **in trouble**) unpleasantness involving punishment or rebuke. **5** bad functioning of a mechanism or of the body or mind ♦ *engine trouble* ♦ *stomach trouble.*
trouble *verb* **1** to cause someone trouble or difficulty. SYNONYMS: worry, bother, upset, disturb, afflict. **2** to disturb or interrupt someone ♦ *I'm sorry to trouble you.* SYNONYMS: bother, annoy, disturb. **3** to be worried or inconvenienced ♦ *Please don't trouble about it.* **to make trouble** to cause difficulty or unpleasantness. **to take trouble** to use much care and effort in doing something. [from an Old French word *truble*, related to *turbid*]

troublemaker *noun* someone who constantly causes trouble.

troubleshooter *noun* someone employed to deal with faults in machinery or to act as a mediator in disputes.

troublesome *adjective* causing trouble or difficulty. SYNONYMS: bothersome, annoying, tiresome, trying.

trouble spot *noun* a place where trouble often occurs.

trough (trof) *noun* **1** a long narrow open container, especially one holding water or food for animals. **2** a channel for liquid. **3** a low part between two waves or ridges. **4** an extended region of low atmospheric pressure. **5** a point of low value, achievement, or activity. [from an Old English word *trog*]

trounce *verb* **1** to defeat an opponent heavily. **2** to thrash someone.

troupe (troop) *noun* a company of actors or other performers. [a French word meaning 'troop']
◊ Do not confuse this word with **troop**, which has a different meaning.

trouper (troop-er) *noun* 1 a member of a theatrical troupe. 2 someone who is reliable and supportive.

trousers *plural noun* a piece of clothing worn over the lower part of the body, with a separate part for each leg. [from Irish and Scottish Gaelic words]

trousseau (troo-soh) *noun* clothes and household belongings collected by a bride for her married life. [a French word meaning 'bundle']

trout *noun* (**trout**) a freshwater fish that is caught as a sport and for food.

trowel *noun* 1 a small garden tool with a curved blade for lifting plants or scooping things. 2 a small tool with a flat blade for spreading mortar etc. [from a Latin word *trulla* meaning 'scoop']

troy weight *noun* a system of weights used for precious metals and gems, in which 1 pound equals 12 ounces or 5,760 grains. [said to be from a weight used at Troyes in France]

truant *noun* a child who stays away from school without permission. **to play truant** to stay away as a truant. **truancy** *noun* [from an earlier meaning 'idle rogue', from a Celtic word related to Welsh *truan* meaning 'miserable']

truce *noun* an agreement to stop fighting for a time. SYNONYMS: ceasefire, armistice. [from an Old English word *treowa*]

truck[1] *noun* 1 a lorry. 2 an open container on wheels for transporting loads. 3 an open railway wagon. [from *truckle*]

truck[2] *noun* **to have no truck with** to refuse to have anything to do with someone or something. [origin unknown]

truculent (truk-yoo-lənt) *adjective* defiant and aggressive. SYNONYMS: aggressive, bad-tempered, surly. **truculence** *noun* **truculently** *adverb* [from a Latin word *truculentus*, from *trux* meaning 'fierce']

trudge *verb* to walk slowly and heavily. **trudge** *noun* a slow heavy walk. [origin unknown]

true *adjective* 1 in accordance with what has happened or is real. SYNONYMS: real, factual, actual. 2 genuine and proper ♦ *He was the true heir.* SYNONYMS: genuine, authentic, proper. 3 exact or accurate ♦ *a true voice.* 4 accurately placed or balanced or shaped. 5 loyal or faithful ♦ *She is a true friend.* SYNONYMS: loyal, faithful, staunch, constant. [from an Old English word *treowe*]

truffle *noun* 1 a soft sweet made of a chocolate mixture. 2 a fungus that grows underground and is eaten as a delicacy because of its rich flavour. [via Dutch and French from a Latin word *tuber* meaning 'swelling']

trug *noun* a long shallow basket used in gardening.

truism (troo-izm) *noun* 1 a statement that is obviously true but says very little, e.g. *Nothing lasts for ever.* 2 (in logic) a statement that merely repeats an idea already implied in one of its words, e.g. ♦ *There's no need to be unnecessarily careful.*

truly *adverb* 1 in a truthful way. 2 sincerely or genuinely ♦ *We are truly grateful.* 3 faithfully or loyally. **Yours truly** see **yours**.

trump *noun* 1 a playing card of a suit temporarily ranking above others. 2 (*informal*) a person who behaves in a helpful or useful way. **trump** *verb* to take a card or trick with a trump; to play a trump. **to trump something up** to invent a false excuse or accusation. **to turn up trumps** (*informal*) to turn out much better than expected. [from *triumph*]

trumpet *noun* 1 a metal wind instrument with a bright ringing tone, consisting of a narrow straight or curved tube flared at the end. 2 something shaped like this. **trumpet** *verb* (**trumpeted, trumpeting**) 1 to blow a trumpet. 2 to proclaim something loudly. 3 (said about an elephant) to make a loud resounding sound with its trunk. [from an Old French word *trompette*, related to *trombone*]

trumpeter *noun* a person who plays or sounds a trumpet.

truncate (trunk-ayt) *verb* to shorten something by cutting off its top or end. **truncation** *noun* [from a Latin word *truncare* meaning 'to maim']

truncheon (trun-chən) *noun* a short thick stick carried as a weapon by a police officer. [from a Latin word *truncus* meaning 'tree trunk']

trundle *verb* to move along or roll something heavily along on a wheel or wheels. [from an obsolete word *trendle* meaning 'to revolve']

trunk *noun* 1 the main stem of a tree. 2 the long flexible nose of an elephant. 3 a person's body apart from the head, arms, and legs. 4 a large box with a hinged lid, used for transporting or storing clothes etc.

trunks plural noun men's shorts, used especially for swimming or boxing. [from a Latin word *truncus*]

trunk call noun (old use) a long-distance telephone call within the same country.

trunk road noun an important main road between large towns and cities.

truss noun 1 a framework of beams or bars supporting a roof or bridge etc. 2 a bundle of hay or straw. 3 a small cluster of flowers or fruit. 4 a padded belt or other device worn to support a hernia. **truss** verb 1 to tie or bind a person or thing securely. 2 to support a roof, bridge, or other structure with trusses. [from an Old French word *trusse*]

trust noun 1 a firm belief that a person or thing is reliable, truthful, or honest. 2 confident expectation. 3 responsibility associated with a trust placed on someone ♦ *a position of trust*. 4 a legal arrangement by which a person (called a *trustee*) is given charge of money or property with instructions to use it for another person's benefit or for a specified purpose. 5 an organization managed by trustees to promote or preserve something ♦ *a wildlife trust*. 6 a large company or association of business firms formed to establish a monopoly or reduce competition. **trust** verb 1 to believe that a person or thing is reliable, truthful, or honest. SYNONYMS: rely on, have faith in, believe in, bank on, be sure of. 2 to give something to someone for safe keeping. 3 to hope ♦ *I trust you are well.* **on trust** accepted without investigation ♦ *Don't take the statement on trust.* **to trust to something** to rely on something ♦ *to trust to luck.* [from an Old Norse word *traustr* meaning 'strong']

trustee noun 1 a person who has charge of money or property in trust for another. 2 a member of a group of people managing the business affairs of an institution.

trustful adjective willing to trust people. **trustfully** adverb **trustfulness** noun

trusting adjective having trust, trustful.

trustworthy adjective worthy of trust, reliable. SYNONYMS: reliable, dependable, responsible, trusty. **trustworthiness** noun

trusty adjective (trustier, trustiest) (old use) reliable and trustworthy ♦ *his trusty steed.*

truth noun 1 the quality or state of being true. 2 something that is true. [from an Old English word *treowth*]

truthful adjective 1 (said about a person) always telling the truth. SYNONYMS: honest, sincere, frank. 2 true or accurate ♦ *a truthful account of what happened.* SYNONYMS: true, accurate, factual, correct. **truthfully** adverb **truthfulness** noun

try verb (tries, tried, trying) 1 to make an effort to do something, to attempt something. SYNONYMS: attempt, seek, endeavour, strive, venture. 2 to use or test something to see how effective or satisfactory it is ♦ *Try the shop on the corner* ♦ *Try sleeping on your back.* 3 to try to open a door or window in order to discover whether it is locked. 4 to be a strain on a part of the body ♦ *Small print tries the eyes.* 5 to examine the accusations against someone in a law court.

try noun (tries) 1 an attempt. SYNONYMS: attempt, go, effort; (informal) shot, stab. 2 (in rugby) an act of touching the ball down behind the opposing goal line, scoring points and entitling the scoring side to a kick at goal. **to try something on** to put on a piece of clothing to see if it fits and looks suitable. **to try your hand** or **luck** to attempt something for the first time. **to try something out** to test something by using it. [from an Old French word *trier* meaning 'to sift']

trying adjective putting a strain on your temper or patience, annoying.

tsar (zah) noun the title of an emperor of Russia before the Revolution of 1917. [a Russian word, from the Latin name Caesar]

tsetse fly (tset-si or tet-si) noun a tropical African fly that transmits sleeping sickness or other diseases by its bite. [from a word in Setswana (a southern African language)]

T-shirt noun a short-sleeved casual top having the shape of a T when spread out flat.

T-square noun a T-shaped instrument for measuring or drawing right angles.

tsunami (tsoo-nah-mi) noun (tsunami or tsunamis) a long high sea wave caused by an underwater earthquake. [from Japanese words *tsu* meaning 'harbour' and *nami* meaning 'wave']

Tuareg (twah-reg) noun (Tuareg or Tuaregs) 1 a member of a Berber people of North Africa. 2 the language of this people.

tub *noun* a round open container with a flat bottom, used for washing or for holding liquids, soil for plants, etc. [probably from German and Dutch words]

tuba (tew-bə) *noun* a large brass wind instrument with a low pitch and deep tone. [a Latin word meaning 'trumpet']

tubby *adjective* (**tubbier, tubbiest**) short and rather fat. SYNONYMS: plump, podgy, dumpy, chubby. **tubbiness** *noun* [from *tub*]

tube *noun* 1 a long hollow piece of metal, plastic, rubber, glass, etc., especially for air or liquids to pass along. 2 a container made of a flexible material with a screw cap ♦ *a tube of toothpaste*. 3 (**the tube**) (*informal*) the underground railway system in London. [from a Latin word *tubus*]

tuber *noun* a short thick rounded root (e.g. of a dahlia) or underground stem (e.g. of a potato) that produces buds from which new plants will grow. **tuberous** *adjective* [a Latin word meaning 'a swelling']

tubercle (tew-ber-kəl) *noun* a small rounded projection or swelling, e.g. on a bone or plant.

tubercular (tew-ber-kew-ler) *adjective* to do with or affected with tuberculosis.

tuberculin-tested (tew-ber-kew-lin) *adjective* (said about milk) taken from cows that have been tested with a sterile protein (called *tuberculin*) and found to be free from tuberculosis.

tuberculosis (tew-ber-kew-loh-sis) *noun* an infectious disease of people and animals, affecting various parts of the body, especially the lungs, and causing swellings (called *tubercles*) to appear on body tissue. [from a Latin word *tuberculum* meaning 'little swelling']

tubing *noun* tubes, or a length of tube.

tubular *adjective* shaped like a tube or like tubes.

tubule (tew-bewl) *noun* (*Anatomy*) a small tube or tube-shaped part in the body.

TUC *abbreviation* Trades Union Congress.

tuck *verb* 1 to put a flat fold in a piece of clothing or other material. 2 to put or fold a loose end or edge into something to hide it or hold it in place. 3 to put something away neatly or in a small space ♦ *Tuck this in your pocket.* **tuck** *noun* 1 a flat fold stitched in a piece of clothing or other material. 2 (*informal*) food, especially sweets and cakes that children enjoy. **to tuck in** (*informal*) to eat food heartily. **to tuck someone in** or **up** to settle someone comfortably in bed by folding the edges of the bedclothes securely. [from an Old English word *tucian* meaning 'to ill-treat' and later 'to tug or pull at']

Tudor *noun* a member of the royal family of England from Henry VII to Elizabeth I. **Tudor** *adjective* 1 to do with the Tudors. 2 imitating the style of houses etc. of that period.

Tuesday *noun* the day of the week following Monday. [from an Old English word *Tiwesdæg* meaning 'day of Tiw', named after the god Tyr]

tufa (tew-fə) *noun* 1 porous rock formed round mineral springs. 2 another word for **tuff**.

tuff *noun* rock formed from volcanic ashes. [via Italian from a Latin word *tophus*]

tuft *noun* a bunch of threads, grass, feathers, or hair etc. held or growing close together. SYNONYMS: clump, knot, bunch. **tuft** *verb* to make depressions in a mattress or cushion by stitching tightly through it at a number of points to hold the stuffing in place. **tufted** *adjective* [from an Old French word *tofe*]

tug *verb* (**tugged, tugging**) 1 to pull something vigorously or with great effort. SYNONYMS: drag, pull, jerk; (*informal*) yank. 2 to tow a ship by means of a tug. **tug** *noun* 1 a hard or sudden pull. 2 (also **tugboat**) a small powerful boat for towing large ships. [related to *tow*[1]]

tug of war *noun* a contest between two teams tugging a rope from opposite ends until one team manages to pull the other across a line.

tuition (tew-ish-ən) *noun* the process of teaching, instruction. [from a Latin word *tuitio* meaning 'looking after something', from *tueri* meaning 'to watch over']

tulip *noun* a garden plant growing from a bulb, with a large cup-shaped flower on a tall stem. [from a Turkish word *tuliband* meaning 'turban' (because the flowers are this shape)]

tulle (tewl) *noun* a fine silky net material used for veils, wedding dresses, etc. [named after Tulle, a town in France where it was first made]

tumble *verb* 1 to fall or roll over suddenly or clumsily, or to make someone or something do this. SYNONYMS: topple, fall,

stumble. **2** to fall suddenly in value or amount. **3** to move or rush in a hasty careless way ♦ *After supper we all tumbled into bed.* **4** to move or push something quickly or carelessly. **5** to rumple or disarrange something.
tumble *noun* **1** a tumbling fall. **2** an untidy or confused state ♦ *Things were all in a tumble.* **to tumble to** (*informal*) to realize suddenly or eventually what something means. [from a German word *tummelen* and a French word *tomber* meaning 'to fall']

tumbledown *adjective* falling into ruins, dilapidated.

tumble-dryer *noun* a machine that dries washing by rotating it in a drum through which heated air passes.

tumbler *noun* **1** a drinking glass with straight sides and no handle or stem. **2** a part of a lock that holds the bolt until it is lifted by the action of a key. **3** an electrical switch operated by pushing a small spring-loaded lever. **4** an acrobat.

tumbril or **tumbrel** *noun* (*historical*) an open cart of the kind used to carry condemned people to the guillotine during the French Revolution. [from an Old French word *tomberel*, from *tomber* meaning 'to fall']

tumescent (tew-**mess**-ənt) *adjective* swollen or swelling. **tumescence** *noun* [same origin as for *tumour*]

tumid (tew-mid) *adjective* (said about a part of the body) swollen or bulging. [same origin as for *tumour*]

tummy *noun* (**tummies**) (*informal*) the stomach.

tumour (tew-mer) *noun* a swelling in the body, caused by an abnormal growth of tissue. [from a Latin word *tumere* meaning 'to swell']

tumult (tew-mult) *noun* **1** a loud confused noise made by a crowd of people. SYNONYMS: commotion, uproar, disturbance, rumpus. **2** a state of confusion ♦ *Her mind was in a tumult.* [from a Latin word *tumultus*]

tumultuous (tew-mul-tew-əs) *adjective* **1** making a loud confused noise. **2** excited or confused. **tumultuously** *adverb*

tun *noun* a large cask for wine or beer. [from a Latin word *tunna*]

tuna (tew-nə) *noun* (**tuna**) a large seafish with pink flesh, used for food. [from an American Spanish word *atún*, related to *tunny*]

tundra *noun* a vast level Arctic region of Europe, Asia, and North America, where there are no trees and the subsoil is always frozen. [from a Lappish word (the language of Lapland)]

tune *noun* a pleasant sequence of musical notes, a melody. SYNONYMS: melody, air, theme.
tune *verb* **1** to put a musical instrument in tune. **2** to adjust a radio or television set to receive a certain channel. **3** to adjust an engine to run smoothly. **in tune** playing or singing at the correct musical pitch. **out of tune** not playing or singing in tune. **to the tune of** amounting to ♦ *They received compensation to the tune of £5,000.* **to tune up** (said about an orchestra) to bring the instruments to the correct pitch. **tunable** *adjective* [a different spelling of *tone*]

tuneful *adjective* having a pleasing tune. SYNONYMS: melodious, musical. **tunefully** *adverb* **tunefulness** *noun*

tuneless *adjective* not having a pleasant or recognizable tune. **tunelessly** *adverb*

tuner *noun* **1** a person who tunes a piano or other musical instrument. **2** a unit for receiving radio broadcasts.

tungsten (tung-stən) *noun* a heavy grey metal and chemical element (symbol W), used for making the filaments of electric lamps and for making a kind of steel. [from a Swedish word *tung* meaning 'heavy' and *sten* meaning 'stone']

tunic *noun* **1** a loose sleeveless piece of clothing reaching the hips or knees. **2** a close-fitting short coat worn as part of a uniform. [from a Latin word *tunica*]

tunicate (tew-ni-kayt) *noun* a small sea creature with a hard outer skin. [from *tunic* (because of its skin)]

tuning fork *noun* a steel device with two prongs, which when struck vibrates to produce a note of fixed pitch (usually middle C).

tunnel *noun* an underground passage built through a hill or under a building, or made by a burrowing animal.
tunnel *verb* (**tunnelled, tunnelling**) to make a tunnel through something. [from an Old French word *tonel* meaning 'barrel']

tunny noun (tunny or tunnies) another word for tuna.

tuppence noun another spelling of twopence.

tuppenny adjective another spelling of twopenny.

turban noun a man's headdress made by wrapping a strip of cloth round a cap, worn especially by Muslims and Sikhs. [from a Persian word *dulband*, related to *tulip*]

turbid adjective 1 (said about a liquid) muddy, not clear. 2 confused or obscure ♦ *a turbid imagination.* **turbidity** (ter-**bid**-iti) noun **turbidly** adverb [from a Latin word *turba* meaning 'crowd' or 'disturbance']

turbine (ter-byn) noun a machine or motor driven by a wheel or rotor that is turned by a flow of water or gas. [from a Latin word *turbinis* meaning 'of a whirlwind']

turbo noun (turbos) short for **turbocharger**.

turbocharger noun a supercharger driven by a turbine that is powered by the engine's exhausts.

turbofan noun a jet engine equipped with a turbine-driven fan for additional thrust.

turbojet noun a jet engine in which the jet gases also operate a compressor for compressing the air taken into the engine.

turboprop noun a jet engine in which a turbine is used to drive a propeller.

turbot noun (turbot or turbots) a large flat seafish used for food. [from a Scandinavian language]

turbulent (ter-bew-lənt) adjective 1 (said about air or water) moving violently and unevenly. 2 confused or unruly. **turbulence** noun **turbulently** adverb [same origin as for *turbid*]

tureen (tewr-een) noun a deep dish with a lid, for serving soup at a table. [from a French word *terrine* meaning 'earthenware pot']

turf noun (turfs or turves) 1 short grass and earth round its roots. 2 a piece of this cut from the ground. 3 (the turf) horse racing. **turf** verb to cover a surface with turf. **to turf someone** or **something out** (informal) to get rid of someone or something.

turgid (ter-jid) adjective 1 swollen and thick. 2 (said about language or style) tedious and pompous. **turgidity** (ter-jid-iti) noun

turgidly adverb [from a Latin word *turgere* meaning 'to swell']

Turk noun a person born in Turkey in Asia Minor and SE Europe, or descended from people born there.

turkey noun (turkeys) a large game bird kept for its meat. [originally the name of a different bird that was imported from Turkey]

Turkish adjective to do with or coming from Turkey. **Turkish** noun the language of Turkey.

Turkish bath noun a kind of bath in which the whole body is exposed to hot air or steam to induce sweating, followed by washing.

Turkish delight noun a sweet made from flavoured gelatine coated in powdered sugar.

turmeric (ter-mer-ik) noun a bright yellow powder obtained from a plant of the ginger family, used in cookery for flavouring and colouring. [perhaps from a French phrase *terre mérite* meaning 'deserving earth']

turmoil (ter-moil) noun a state of great disturbance or confusion. SYNONYMS: confusion, disturbance, havoc. [origin unknown]

turn verb 1 to move or make something move round a point or axis. SYNONYMS: rotate, revolve, roll, spin. 2 to change or make something change its position so that a different side is on top or in front. 3 to take a new direction or make something do this ♦ *Turn left at the lights* ♦ *The tide has turned.* SYNONYMS: swing, veer. 4 to go or move round something ♦ *Turn the corner.* 5 to pass a certain time or age ♦ *She turned eighteen last week.* 6 to make an animal go somewhere ♦ *The farmer turned the horse into the field.* 7 to change something or become changed in nature, form, or appearance ♦ *The witch turned him into a frog* ♦ *The caterpillar will turn into a chrysalis* ♦ *She turned pale at the news.* SYNONYMS: change, transform. 8 (said about leaves) to change colour in the autumn. 9 (said about milk) to become sour. 10 to shape something in a lathe. 11 to give an elegant form to something.
turn noun 1 an act of turning or of being turned, a turning movement. SYNONYMS: rotation, revolution. 2 a bend or curve in a road, river, etc. SYNONYMS: bend, curve, corner. 3 a place where you leave one road

to join another. SYNONYMS: junction, turning. **4** a change of direction or condition. SYNONYMS: change, alteration, shift. **5** an opportunity or obligation to do something that comes to each of a number of people or things in succession ♦ *It's my turn to pay.* **6** a short performance in an entertainment. **7** (*informal*) a short feeling of shock or illness ♦ *He had a funny turn.* **at every turn** in every place, all the time. **in turn** in succession, when your turn comes. **out of turn** in an indiscreet or presumptuous way ♦ *to speak out of turn.* **to turn something down 1** to adjust a device to reduce the volume, heat, etc. **2** to reject an offer or application. SYNONYMS: reject, decline, refuse. **to turn someone in** to hand someone over to the authorities. SYNONYM: surrender. **to turn off** to drive a vehicle from a main road into a side road. **to turn someone off** (*informal*) to make someone less interested. **to turn something off** to use a control to stop a device from operating. **turn of mind** a particular way of thinking ♦ *a practical turn of mind.* **turn of speed** the ability to go fast when necessary. **to turn someone on** (*informal*) to make someone interested or excited. **to turn something on** to use a control to start a device operating. **to turn your back on** to abandon or ignore someone or something. **to turn out** to happen in the end ♦ *We'll see how things turn out.* **to turn someone out** to expel someone from a place. SYNONYMS: expel, evict, throw out. **to turn something out 1** to turn off an electric light. **2** to clear and clean a place thoroughly ♦ *We'll have to turn out the attic.* **to turn something over** to think carefully about something. SYNONYMS: consider, ponder on. **to turn something round** to make something successful when it was failing before. **to turn tail** to run away. **to turn to** to start a task or piece of work. **to turn up** to appear or be discovered in the end. SYNONYMS: appear, come to light. **to turn something up** to adjust a device to increase the volume, heat, etc. [from a Greek word *tornos* meaning 'lathe']

turncoat *noun* a person who abandons one party or group in order to support an opposing one.

turner *noun* a person who makes things on a lathe.

turning *noun* a place where one road meets another, forming a corner.

turning circle *noun* the smallest circle in which a vehicle or ship can turn in one direction.

turnip *noun* a plant with a round white root used as a vegetable. [from a Latin word *napus*, but the first part of the word is unknown]

turnkey *noun* (**turnkeys**) (*old use*) a jailer.

turn-off *noun* (*informal*) **1** a junction at which a road leaves another. **2** something that puts you off; a disincentive.

turnover *noun* **1** the amount of money a business takes in a particular period. **2** the rate at which goods are sold. **3** the rate at which workers leave and are replaced. **4** a small pie in which a piece of pastry is folded over a filling.

turnpike *noun* (*historical*) a road on which a toll was charged.

turnstile *noun* a mechanical gate with barriers that revolve to allow people through one at a time.

turntable *noun* a circular revolving platform or support, e.g. for the record in a record player.

turpentine (ter-pǝn-tiyn) *noun* an oil made from the resin of certain trees, used for thinning paint, cleaning brushes, etc. [from a Latin phrase *terebinthia resina* meaning 'resin of the terebinth']

turpitude (ter-pi-tewd) *noun* (*formal*) wickedness. [from a Latin word *turpis* meaning 'shameful']

turps *noun* (*informal*) short for **turpentine.**

turquoise (ter-kwoiz) *noun* **1** a bright blue precious stone. **2** a bright or greenish blue colour. [a French word meaning 'Turkish stone']

turret *noun* **1** a small tower on a castle or other building or wall. **2** a rotating structure protecting a gun and gunners in a ship, aircraft, fort, or tank. **3** a rotating holder for tools in a lathe or drill. **turreted** *adjective* [from a French word *tour* meaning 'tower']

turtle *noun* a sea creature like a tortoise, with flippers used in swimming. **to turn turtle** (said about a boat) to turn upside down in the water. [probably from a French word *tortue* meaning 'turtle']

turtle dove *noun* a wild dove with a soft cooing call. [via Old English from a Latin word *turtur*]

turtleneck *noun* a high round close-fitting neck on a knitted top.

Tuscan *adjective* to do with or coming from Tuscany in central Italy.

tusk *noun* a long pointed tooth, one of a pair that project from the mouth of an elephant, walrus, etc. [from an Old English word *tux*]

tussle *noun* a struggle or conflict.
SYNONYMS: struggle, conflict, scuffle, fight.
tussle *verb* to take part in a tussle. [probably from a dialect word *touse* meaning 'to handle roughly']

tussock *noun* a tuft or clump of grass. [origin unknown]

tutelage (tew-til-ij) *noun* 1 guardianship or protection of someone or something. 2 instruction or tuition. [from a Latin word *tutela* meaning 'keeping']

tutor *noun* 1 a private teacher, especially of one pupil or a small group. 2 a university teacher responsible for a number of students. 3 an instruction book ♦ *a guitar tutor.*
tutor *verb* to teach or be a tutor to someone. [a Latin word meaning 'guardian']

tutorial (tew-tor-iəl) *noun* a period of tuition given by a university or college tutor.
tutorial *adjective* to do with a tutor or tuition.

tutu (too-too) (**tutus**) a ballet dancer's short skirt made of layers of stiffened frills. [a French word]

TV *abbreviation* television.

twaddle *noun* (*informal*) nonsense. [origin unknown]

twain *adjective* & *noun* (*old use*) two. [from an Old English word *twegen* meaning 'two']

twang *noun* 1 a sharp ringing sound like that made by a tense wire when plucked. 2 a nasal intonation in speech.
twang *verb* to make or cause something to make a twang; to play a guitar etc. by plucking the strings.

tweak *verb* 1 to pinch and twist something with a quick sharp jerk. 2 to improve something by making fine adjustments.
tweak *noun* a sharp twist or pull. [probably from a dialect word *twick* meaning 'to pull sharply']

twee *adjective* affectedly quaint or pretty. [supposedly a child's pronunciation of *sweet*]

tweed *noun* a thick woollen cloth, often woven of mixed colours.
tweeds *plural noun* clothes made of tweed. [originally a mistake: the Scottish word *tweel* (= twill) was wrongly read as *tweed* by being confused with the River Tweed]

tweet *verb* to make the chirp of a small bird.
tweet *noun* a tweeting sound. [an imitation of the sound]

tweeter *noun* a loudspeaker designed to reproduce high-frequency signals.

tweezers *plural noun* small pincers for picking up or pulling very small things. [from an old word *tweeze* meaning 'case of surgical instruments' (including tweezers)]

twelfth *adjective* & *noun* 1 next after eleventh. 2 one of twelve equal parts of a thing. **twelfthly** *adverb*

twelve *adjective* & *noun* the number 12, one more than eleven. [from an Old English word *twelfe*]

twenty *adjective* & *noun* (**twenties**) the number 20, equal to two times ten.
twenties *plural noun* the numbers from 20 to 29, especially representing years of age or degrees of temperature. **twentieth** *adjective* & *noun* [from an Old English word *twentig*]

twice *adverb* 1 two times, on two occasions. 2 double the amount or degree ♦ *twice as strong.* [from an Old English word *twiges*, related to *two*]

twiddle *verb* to turn or fiddle with something aimlessly.
twiddle *noun* 1 a slight twirl. 2 a rapid series of musical notes. **to twiddle your thumbs** to have nothing to do. **twiddly** *adjective* [from *twirl* and *fiddle*]

twig [1] *noun* a small shoot on a branch or stem of a tree or shrub. [from an Old English word]

twig [2] (**twigged, twigging**) (*informal*) to come to realize what something means.

twilight *noun* dim light from the sky after sunset. [from an Old English word *twi*-meaning 'two' (but here probably 'half') and *light*]

twill *noun* cloth that is woven to produce a surface pattern of diagonal lines. **twilled** *adjective* [from an old word *twilly*, from an Old English word *twi* meaning 'two']

twin noun 1 either of two children or animals born at one birth. 2 either of two people or things that are exactly alike. **twin** adjective being a twin or twins ♦ twin sisters.
twin verb (**twinned, twinning**) 1 to put things together as a pair. 2 to link a town or city in one country with a similar one in another country for cultural exchanges. [from an Old English word twinn meaning 'double']

twine noun strong thread or string made of two or more strands twisted together. **twine** verb to twist or wind one thing round another. [from an Old English word]

twinge noun a sudden short pain. [from an Old English word twengan meaning 'to pinch']

twinkle verb 1 (said about a star or light) to shine with a light that flickers rapidly, to sparkle. 2 (said about the eyes) to be bright or sparkling with amusement. 3 to move with short rapid movements. **twinkle** noun a twinkling light. [from an Old English word twinclian]

twirl verb to spin round lightly or rapidly, or to make something do this. SYNONYMS: spin, whirl, twist.
twirl noun 1 a twirling movement. 2 a twirling mark or sign. **twirly** adjective [origin unknown]

twist verb 1 to turn the ends of something in opposite directions. 2 to wrench something out of its normal shape ♦ a heap of twisted metal ♦ a twisted ankle. 3 to wind threads or strands round something, or round each other to form a single cord. SYNONYMS: coil, wind, curl. 4 to take a spiral or winding form or course ♦ The road twisted through the hills. SYNONYMS: curve, meander, zigzag. 5 to rotate or revolve round something that is not moving, or to make something do this. SYNONYMS: rotate, revolve, spin, twirl. 6 to distort the meaning of something ♦ Don't try to twist my words. SYNONYMS: distort, misrepresent. 7 (informal) to swindle someone.
twist noun 1 the action or movement of twisting or being twisted. 2 something formed by twisting, a turn in a twisting course. 3 a strange or unexpected development in a series of events. 4 (**the twist**) a dance with twisting of the body, popular in the 1960s. **to twist a person's arm** (informal) to persuade someone to do something they are reluctant to do.

twister noun **twisty** adjective [from an Old English word]

twit [1] verb (**twitted, twitting**) (informal) to taunt someone. [from an Old English word ætwitan meaning 'to blame or reproach']

twit [2] noun (informal) a silly or foolish person.

twitch verb 1 to pull something with a light jerk. 2 to move with a jerk or series of jerks.
twitch noun a twitching movement. [probably from a German word]

twitchy adjective (**twitchier, twitchiest**) (informal) 1 twitching a lot. 2 nervous or agitated. **twitchiness** noun

twitter verb 1 to make a series of quick chirping sounds. 2 to talk quickly in an anxious or nervous way.
twitter noun a twittering sound. [an imitation of the sound]

two adjective & noun the number 2, one more than one. **to be in two minds** to be undecided about something. [from an Old English word twa]

two-dimensional adjective having the two dimensions of length and breadth.

two-faced adjective insincere or deceitful.

twofold adjective & adverb 1 twice as much or as many. 2 consisting of two parts.

twopence (tup-əns) noun the sum of two pence (before decimalization).

twopenny (tup-əni) adjective costing or worth twopence (before decimalization).

twopenny-halfpenny adjective insignificant or worthless.

twosome noun two people together, a couple or pair.

two-time verb (informal) to be unfaithful to someone.

two-way adjective 1 involving two directions ♦ two-way traffic. 2 (said about a switch) allowing electric current to be turned on or off from either of two points.

tycoon noun a wealthy and influential business person or industrialist. [from a Japanese word taikun meaning 'great prince']

tying present participle of **tie**.

tyke noun an annoying or mischievous person, especially a child. [from an Old Norse word tik meaning 'bitch']

Tynwald (**tin**-wolld) *noun* the parliament of the Isle of Man. [from Old Norse words meaning 'place of assembly']

type *noun* 1 a class or sort of people or things with the same characteristics. SYNONYMS: class, sort, category. 2 a typical example or instance. 3 (*informal*) a person of specified character or nature ◆ *brainy types*. 4 printed characters or letters ◆ *It is printed in large type.*
type *verb* 1 to classify people or things according to their type. 2 to write something with a typewriter. [from a Greek word *tupos* meaning 'impression']

typecast *verb* (past tense and past participle **typecast**) to choose an actor to play a role that is like them in character.

typeface *noun* a set of printing types of one design.

typescript *noun* a typed copy of a text or document.

typesetting *noun* arranging type for printing. **typesetter** *noun*

typewriter *noun* a manual or electronic machine with keys for producing characters like print.

typewritten *adjective* written with a typewriter.

typhoid fever *noun* a serious infectious disease with fever, caused by harmful bacteria taken into the body in food or drink. [from *typhus*]

typhoon (tiy-**foon**) *noun* a violent hurricane in the western Pacific or East Asian seas. [from a Chinese phrase *tai fung* meaning 'great wind']

typhus *noun* an infectious disease with fever, weakness, and a rash on the body. [from a Greek word *tuphos* meaning 'vapour']

typical *adjective* 1 having the usual qualities of a particular type of person or thing ◆ *a typical suburban house.* 2 characteristic of a person ◆ *He answered with typical curtness.* **typically** *adverb* [same origin as for *type*]

typify (**tip**-i-fiy) *verb* (**typifies, typified, typifying**) to be a representative specimen of someone or something. SYNONYMS: represent, characterize, epitomize.

typist *noun* a person who types letters and documents, especially in an office.

typography (tiy-**pog**-rafi) *noun* 1 the art or process of printing. 2 the style or

appearance of printed matter.
typographical (tiy-pə-**graf**-ikəl) *adjective* [from *type* and *-graphy*]

tyrannical (ti-**ran**-ikəl) *adjective* like a tyrant, enforcing obedience by force or threats. SYNONYMS: domineering, authoritarian, autocratic. **tyrannically** *adverb*

tyrannize (ti-rə-niyz) *verb* to behave like a tyrant to people.

tyrannosaurus (ti-ran-ə-sor-us) *noun* a large dinosaur (also called *Tyrannosaurus rex*) that walked on its hind legs and fed on flesh. [from Greek words *turannos* meaning 'tyrant' and *sauros* meaning 'lizard']

tyranny (**ti**-rə-ni) *noun* (**tyrannies**) 1 government by a tyrannical ruler. 2 oppressive use of power, like that of a tyrant.

tyrant (**tiy**-rənt) *noun* a person who rules or uses authority harshly or cruelly. SYNONYMS: despot, autocrat, dictator, martinet. [from a Greek word *turannos* meaning 'ruler with full power']

tyre *noun* a rubber covering, usually filled with air, fitted round the rim of a wheel to make it grip the road and run smoothly. [from *attire* (because a tyre was a kind of clothing for a wheel)]

tyro (**tiy**-roh) *noun* (**tyros**) a beginner or novice. [a Latin word meaning 'recruit']

U the twenty-first letter of the English alphabet.

Uu

U *abbreviation* 1 (in film classification) universal. 2 (*Chemistry*) the symbol for uranium.

UB 40 *noun* a card issued to a person who is registered as unemployed.

ubiquitous (yoo-**bik**-wit-əs) *adjective* found everywhere ◆ *Mobile phones are ubiquitous these days.* **ubiquity** *noun* [from a Latin word *ubique* meaning 'everywhere']

U-boat *noun* a German submarine, especially of the kind used in the Second World War. [short for a German word *Unterseeboot* meaning 'undersea boat']

UCAS *abbreviation* Universities and Colleges Admissions Service.

udder *noun* a bag-like milk-producing organ of a cow, ewe, female goat, etc., with two or more teats. [from an Old English word]

UDI *abbreviation* unilateral declaration of independence.

UEFA *abbreviation* Union of European Football Associations.

UFO *noun* (**UFOs**) a mysterious object seen in the sky, especially one believed to be a vehicle piloted by beings from outer space. [short for *unidentified flying object*]

ugh (uh) *interjection* an exclamation of disgust or horror.

Ugli fruit (ug-li) *noun* (**Ugli fruit**) (*trademark*) a citrus fruit that is a hybrid of a grapefruit and tangerine. [from *ugly*]

ugly *adjective* (**uglier, ugliest**) **1** unpleasant to look at or to hear. SYNONYMS: unattractive, hideous, unsightly, repulsive, grotesque. **2** hostile and threatening; likely to be unpleasant ♦ *The crowd was in an ugly mood.* **ugliness** *noun* [from an Old Norse word *uggligr* meaning 'frightening']

ugly duckling *noun* a person who at first seems unattractive or unpromising but later turns out to be beautiful or much admired. [like the cygnet in the brood of ducks in Hans Christian Andersen's story]

UHF *abbreviation* ultra-high frequency.

UHT *abbreviation* ultra heat treated; used to describe milk that has been treated at a very high temperature so that it will keep for a long time.

UK *abbreviation* United Kingdom.

ukulele (yoo-kə-lay-li) *noun* a small four-stringed guitar. [from a Hawaiian word meaning 'jumping flea']

ulcer *noun* an open sore on the surface of the body or one of its organs. **ulcerous** *adjective* [from a Latin word *ulcus*]

ulcerate *verb* to make an ulcer form in or on something; to become affected with an ulcer. **ulceration** *noun*

ulna (ul-nə) *noun* (*Anatomy and Zoology*) the thinner of the two long bones in the forearm; the corresponding bone in an animal. **ulnar** *adjective* [from a Latin word]

ulterior *adjective* beyond what is obvious or admitted ♦ *She had some ulterior motive in coming to see me.* [from a Latin word meaning 'further' (compare *ultra-*)]

ultimate *adjective* **1** furthest in a series of things; last or final ♦ *Our ultimate destination is London.* **2** being the best or most extreme example of something ♦ *the ultimate accolade.* **3** basic or fundamental ♦ *the ultimate cause.* **ultimately** *adverb* [from a Latin word *ultimus* meaning 'last']

ultimatum (ulti-**may**-təm) *noun* (**ultimatums**) a final demand or statement of terms, rejection of which will lead to the ending of friendly relations or to hostile action. [same origin as for *ultimate*]

ultra- *prefix* **1** beyond (as in *ultraviolet*). **2** extremely, excessively (as in *ultra-conservative, ultra-modern*). [from a Latin word *ultra* meaning 'beyond']

ultra-high frequency *adjective* a radio frequency in the range of 300 to 3,000 MHz.

ultramarine (ultrə-mə-**reen**) *noun & adjective* bright deep blue. [*ultra-* and a Latin word *mare* meaning 'sea' (because the pigment was originally imported 'across the sea' from the East)]

ultrasonic (ultrə-**sonn**-ik) *adjective* to do with sound waves with a frequency that is above the upper limit of normal human hearing.
ultrasonics *noun* the science and application of ultrasonic waves.

ultrasound *noun* **1** sound with an ultrasonic frequency, used in medical examinations. **2** an examination of an internal part of the body, especially a fetus, using ultrasound; an image produced by this.

ultraviolet *adjective* **1** (said about radiation) having a wavelength that is slightly shorter than that of visible light rays at the violet end of the spectrum. **2** to do with or using this radiation.

umbel (**um**-bəl) *noun* (*Botany*) a flower cluster in which the flowers are on stalks of nearly equal length springing from the same point on the main stem. [from a Latin word *umbella* meaning 'sunshade']

umber *noun* a natural pigment like ochre but darker and browner. [from an Italian phrase *terra di ombra* meaning 'earth of shadow']

umbilical (um-**bil**-ikəl) *adjective* to do with the navel. [from a Latin word *umbilicus* meaning 'navel']

umbilical cord *noun* the flexible tube of tissue connecting the placenta to the navel of the fetus and carrying nourishment to the fetus while it is in the womb.

umbra *noun* (**umbrae** (um-bree) or **umbras**) the dark central part of the shadow cast by the earth or the moon in an eclipse, or of a sunspot. [a Latin word meaning 'shade']

umbrage (um-**brij**) *noun* a feeling of being offended. **to take umbrage** to take offence. [from a Latin word *umbra* meaning 'shadow']

umbrella *noun* 1 a circular piece of fabric stretched over a folding frame of spokes attached to a central stick used as a handle, or a central pole, which you open to protect yourself from rain. 2 any kind of protecting force or influence. 3 a thing that includes or contains many different parts ♦ *an umbrella organization*. [from an Italian word *ombrella* meaning 'a little shade']

umlaut (**uum**-lowt) *noun* 1 a mark (¨) placed over a vowel in German to show a change in its pronunciation. 2 a vowel change in related words in Germanic languages (e.g. *man/men*, or in German *Mann/Männer*). [from German words *um* meaning 'about' and *Laut* meaning 'sound']

umpire *noun* 1 a person appointed to see that the rules of a game or contest are followed and to settle any disputes that arise. 2 a person chosen to give a decision on any disputed question.
umpire *verb* to act as an umpire in a game or match. [from French words *non* meaning 'not' and *per* meaning 'an equal']

umpteen *adjective* (*informal*) very many.
umpteenth *adjective* [a made-up word intended to be humorous]

UN *abbreviation* United Nations.

'un *pronoun* (*informal*) one ♦ *a good 'un.*

un- *prefix* 1 not (as in *uncertain*). 2 reversing the action indicated by a verb (as in *unlock*). [from an Old English word]
◊ The number of words with this prefix is almost unlimited, and many of those whose meaning is obvious are not listed below.

unable *adjective* not able to do something.

unaccompanied *adjective* 1 not accompanied. 2 without musical accompaniment.

unaccountable *adjective* 1 unable to be explained or accounted for ♦ *for some unaccountable reason.* 2 not required to account for your actions. **unaccountably** *adverb*

unaccustomed *adjective* not accustomed or used to something ♦ *unaccustomed to hard work.*

unadopted *adjective* (said about a road) not taken over for maintenance by a local authority.

unadulterated *adjective* pure; not mixed with things that are less good. [from *un-* and *adulterate*]

unaided *adjective* without help.

unalloyed (un-ə-**loid**) *adjective* 1 (said about metal) not alloyed. 2 pure or complete ♦ *unalloyed joy.*

unanimous (yoo-**nan**-im-əs) *adjective* with everyone agreeing ♦ *a unanimous decision.* **unanimity** (yoo-nən-**im**-iti) *noun* **unanimously** *adverb* [from Latin words *unus* meaning 'one' and *animus* meaning 'mind']

unanswerable *adjective* unable to be answered or refuted by a good argument to the contrary. **unanswerably** *adverb*

unappealing *adjective* not very attractive or interesting.

unapproachable *adjective* (said about a person) not very friendly or welcoming.

unarmed *adjective* not armed, without weapons.

unashamed *adjective* feeling no guilt or embarrassment. **unashamedly** (un-ə-**shaym**-idli) *adverb*

unasked *adjective* not asked, without being requested.

unassailable *adjective* unable to be attacked or questioned. **unassailably** *adverb*

unassuming *adjective* not arrogant or pretentious. [from *un-* and *assume*]

unattached *adjective* 1 not attached to another thing, person, or organization. 2 not married or in a relationship.

unattended *adjective* (said about a vehicle, piece of baggage, etc.) having no person in charge of it.

unavailing adjective achieving little or nothing.

unavoidable adjective not able to be avoided or prevented.

unaware adjective having no knowledge of something.

unawares adverb unexpectedly; without warning ♦ His question caught me unawares.

unbalanced adjective 1 not balanced. 2 mentally disordered or irrational.

unbearable adjective not able to be endured or tolerated. SYNONYMS: intolerable, insufferable, unendurable. **unbearably** adverb

unbeatable adjective impossible to defeat or surpass.

unbeaten adjective not defeated or surpassed.

unbecoming adjective 1 not making a person look attractive ♦ an unbecoming hat. 2 not suitable or fitting ♦ behaviour unbecoming to a gentleman. [from un- and become]

unbeknown or **unbeknownst** adjective (informal) without someone knowing about or being aware of it ♦ Unbeknown to us, they had planned a surprise party. [from un- and an old word beknown meaning 'known']

unbelief noun lack of religious belief.

unbelievable adjective 1 unlikely to be true. 2 extraordinary. **unbelievably** adverb

unbeliever noun a person who has no religious belief. **unbelieving** adjective

unbend verb (past tense and past participle unbent) 1 to change something or become changed from a bent position. 2 to relax and become friendly.

unbending adjective inflexible, refusing to alter your demands.

unbiased adjective showing no prejudice; impartial.

unbidden adjective not commanded or invited. [from un- and bid²]

unblock verb to remove an obstruction from something.

unbolt verb to open a door etc. by drawing back a bolt.

unborn adjective not yet born.

unbosom verb **to unbosom yourself** to reveal your thoughts or feelings.

unbounded adjective having no limits.

unbridled adjective not controlled or restrained ♦ unbridled rage.

unbroken adjective not broken or interrupted.

unburden verb to remove a burden from the person carrying it. **to unburden yourself** to tell someone your secrets or problems so that you feel better.

uncalled-for adjective not necessary or deserved ♦ uncalled-for rudeness.

uncanny adjective (**uncannier, uncanniest**) 1 strange and difficult to explain ♦ an uncanny coincidence. 2 beyond what is thought normal for a human being ♦ They predicted the results with uncanny accuracy. **uncannily** adverb **uncanniness** noun [from un- and an old sense of canny meaning 'knowing, able to be known']

uncared-for adjective not looked after, neglected.

unceasing adjective not ceasing, continuous. **unceasingly** adverb

unceremonious adjective 1 without proper formality or ceremony. 2 offhand, abrupt, or rude. **unceremoniously** adverb

uncertain adjective 1 not known certainly. 2 not completely confident or sure about something. SYNONYMS: unsure, doubtful, undecided. 3 not to be depended on, not reliable ♦ His aim is rather uncertain. SYNONYMS: unreliable, erratic, unpredictable. **in no uncertain terms** clearly and forcefully. **uncertainly** adverb **uncertainty** noun

unchangeable adjective unable to be changed.

uncharacteristic adjective not characteristic or typical ♦ She spoke with uncharacteristic sharpness.

uncharitable adjective making unkind or severe judgements about people or acts.

unchristian adjective contrary to the teachings of Christianity, uncharitable.

unclassified adjective 1 not classified. 2 (said about a grade in an examination) denoting a fail.

uncle noun 1 the brother of your father or mother or the husband of your aunt. 2 (informal) a term of address used by a child to an adult male friend. [from a Latin word avunculus meaning 'uncle']

Uncle Sam *noun* (*informal*) a personification of the government or people of the USA.

unclothed *adjective* naked.

uncoil *verb* to straighten something out that was coiled up; to staighten out in this way ♦ *Slowly the snake uncoiled.*

uncomfortable *adjective* **1** not comfortable. **2** feeling or causing unease ♦ *an uncomfortable silence.* **uncomfortably** *adverb*

uncommon *adjective* out of the ordinary, unusual.

uncommunicative *adjective* not inclined to talk or give information.

uncompromising (un-kom-prə-miy-zing) *adjective* not willing to make a compromise, inflexible.

unconcerned *adjective* not feeling or showing concern about something, not worried. **unconcernedly** *adverb*

unconditional *adjective* not subject to any conditions or limitations ♦ *unconditional surrender.* **unconditionally** *adverb*

unconscionable (un-kon-shən-əbl) *adjective* (*formal*) **1** unscrupulous. **2** unreasonable or excessive. **unconscionably** *adverb*

unconscious *adjective* **1** not conscious, not aware. **2** done or said etc. without you realizing it ♦ *unconscious humour.* **unconscious** *noun* the unconscious mind, the part of the mind which is not normally accessible to the conscious mind but which affects behaviour. **unconsciously** *adverb* **unconsciousness** *noun*

unconstitutional *adjective* not in accordance with the constitution of a country etc. **unconstitutionally** *adverb*

uncontrollable *adjective* not able to be controlled or stopped. **uncontrollably** *adverb*

uncooperative *adjective* not willing to work helpfully with another person.

uncoordinated *adjective* not coordinated, clumsy.

uncouple (un-kup-əl) *verb* to disconnect railway carriages etc. from being connected by a coupling.

uncouth (un-kooth) *adjective* rude and rough in manner, boorish. [from *un-* and an Old English word *cuth* meaning 'known']

uncover *verb* **1** to remove the covering from something. **2** to discover, reveal, or expose something ♦ *They uncovered a plot to kill the president.*

uncritical *adjective* not expressing criticism; accepting faults too readily.

uncrowned *adjective* not yet crowned as a monarch. **uncrowned king** or **queen** a person who is acknowledged as a champion or expert in a specified group or subject etc.

unction (unk-shən) *noun* **1** (*formal*) anointing with oil, especially in a religious ceremony for consecration or healing. **2** pretended earnestness; excessive politeness. [from a Latin word *unctum* meaning 'oiled']

unctuous (unk-tew-əs) *adjective* polite and charming in an exaggerated and insincere way. **unctuously** *adverb* **unctuousness** *noun* [same origin as for *unction* and *unguent*]

uncurl *verb* to straighten something out or be straightened out from a curled state.

uncut *adjective* **1** not cut. **2** with no parts cut out, not abridged ♦ *the uncut version of the film.* **3** (said about a gem) not shaped by cutting.

undaunted *adjective* not discouraged by difficulty or danger.

undecided *adjective* **1** not yet settled or certain ♦ *The point is still undecided.* **2** not yet having made up your mind.

undemonstrative *adjective* not expressing your feelings openly.

undeniable *adjective* impossible to deny, undoubtedly true. **undeniably** *adverb*

under *preposition* **1** below or beneath ♦ *Hide it under the table.* **2** less than ♦ *children under 5 years old.* **3** lower in rank than ♦ *No one under a bishop can attend.* **4** governed or controlled by ♦ *The country prospered under his rule.* **5** undergoing a process ♦ *The road is under repair.* **6** in accordance with ♦ *It is permissible under our agreement.* **7** subject to ♦ *He is under contract to our firm.* **8** in view of ♦ *Under the circumstances, I think you had better leave.* **9** known by ♦ *Charles Dodgson wrote under the name 'Lewis Carroll'.* **10** in the category of ♦ *File it under 'miscellaneous'.*
under *adverb* **1** in or to a lower position or subordinate condition ♦ *Slowly the diver went under.* **2** in or into a state of unconsciousness. **3** below a certain quantity, rank, or age etc. ♦ *children of five*

and under. **under way** in motion or in progress. [from an Old English word]

under- *prefix* **1** below or beneath (as in *underwear*). **2** lower or subordinate (as in *undermanager*). **3** insufficient, incompletely (as in *undercooked*).

underachieve *verb* to do less well than was expected, especially in school work. **underachiever** *noun*

under age *adjective* not old enough, especially for some legal right; not yet of adult status.

underarm *adjective & adverb* **1** (in cricket etc.) bowling or bowled with the hand brought forward and upwards and not raised above shoulder level. **2** (in tennis) with the racket moved similarly. **3** in or for the armpit.

underbelly *noun* (**underbellies**) the soft underside of an animal.

underbid *verb* (past tense and past participle **underbid; underbidding**) **1** to make a lower bid than another person. **2** to bid less than is justified in the game of bridge.

undercarriage *noun* an aircraft's landing wheels and their supports.

undercharge *verb* to charge someone too low a price.

underclass *noun* the lowest social group in a community, consisting of the poor and the unemployed.

underclothes *plural noun* or **underclothing** *noun* underwear.

undercoat *noun* **1** a layer of paint under a finishing coat; the paint used for this. **2** (in animals) a coat of hair under another.

undercover *adjective & adverb* done or working in secret, especially when this involves spying or police work ♦ *an undercover agent.*

undercroft *noun* a church crypt.

undercurrent *noun* **1** a current that is below a surface or below another current. **2** an underlying feeling or influence ♦ *an undercurrent of fear.*

undercut *verb* (past tense and past participle **undercut; undercutting**) **1** to sell something or work for a lower price than another person does. **2** to cut away the part below.

underdeveloped *adjective* **1** not fully

developed or grown. **2** (said about a country) not having reached its potential level in economic development.

underdog *noun* a person or team that is expected to lose a contest or struggle.

underdone *adjective* (said about food) not completely cooked throughout.

underdressed *adjective* dressed too plainly or informally for an occasion.

underestimate *verb* to estimate something to be smaller or less important than it really is. **underestimate** *noun* an estimate that is too low. **underestimation** *noun*

underexpose *verb* to expose photographic film for too short a time. **underexposure** *noun*

underfed *adjective* not sufficiently fed.

underfloor *adjective* situated beneath the floor ♦ *underfloor heating.*

underfoot *adverb* on the ground, under your feet.

undergarment *noun* a piece of underwear.

undergo *verb* (**undergoes, underwent, undergone, undergoing**) to experience or be subjected to something ♦ *The new aircraft underwent intensive trials.* SYNONYMS: experience, endure, bear, suffer, stand, withstand, go through, put up with.

undergraduate *noun* a student at a university who has not yet taken a degree.

underground *adverb* **1** under the surface of the ground. **2** done or working in secret; into secrecy or hiding. **underground** *adjective* **1** under the surface of the ground. **2** secret or hidden; to do with a secret political organization or one for resisting enemy forces controlling a country. **underground** *noun* **1** an underground railway. **2** an underground organization.

undergrowth *noun* shrubs and bushes etc. growing closely, especially under trees.

underhand *adjective* done or doing things in a secret or dishonest way.

underlay[1] (un-der-lay) *verb* (past tense and past participle **underlaid**) to lay something under a thing as a support or in order to raise it. **underlay** *noun* a layer of material, e.g. felt or rubber, laid under a carpet as a protection or support.

underlay [2] (un-der-lay) past tense of **underlie**.

underlie verb (**underlay, underlain, underlying**) 1 to lie or be situated under something. 2 to be the cause or basis of something ♦ *It is a theme that underlies much of her work.*

underline verb 1 to draw a line under a word etc. 2 to emphasize something.

underling noun a person working under someone's authority or control; a subordinate.

underlying adjective basic or hidden ♦ *the underlying reasons for her behaviour.*

undermanned adjective having too few people to operate it properly, understaffed.

undermine verb 1 to damage or weaken something gradually ♦ *His confidence was undermined.* SYNONYMS: erode, subvert. 2 to make a mine or tunnel beneath something, especially one causing weakness at the base.

underneath preposition below or beneath; on the inside of something. **underneath** adverb at, in, or to a position underneath something. [from under- and an Old English word *neothan* meaning 'beneath']

underpaid adjective paid too little.

underpants plural noun a piece of men's underwear covering the lower part of the body and part of the legs.

underpart noun the part underneath.

underpass noun a road or tunnel that passes under another road or a railway.

underpay verb (past tense and past participle **underpaid**) to pay someone too little.

underpin verb (**underpinned, underpinning**) 1 to support or form the basis for something. 2 to strengthen something from below.

underprivileged adjective less privileged than others, having less than the normal standard of living or rights in a community.

underrate verb to have too low an opinion of a person or thing.

underscore verb to underline something.

undersea adjective below the surface of the sea.

underseal verb to coat the lower surface of a motor vehicle etc. with a protective sealing layer. **underseal** noun a substance used for this.

undersecretary noun (**undersecretaries**) a junior minister or senior civil servant.

undersell verb (past tense and past participle **undersold**) to sell something at a lower price than another person.

undershoot verb (past tense and past participle **undershot**) (said about an aircraft) to land short of something ♦ *The plane undershot the runway.*

undershot adjective (said about a waterwheel) turned by water flowing under it.

underside adjective the side or surface underneath.

undersigned adjective (formal) who has or have signed at the bottom of this document ♦ *We, the undersigned, wish to protest.*

undersized adjective of less than the normal size.

underskirt noun a skirt worn beneath another, a petticoat.

underspend verb (past tense and past participle **underspent**) to spend too little or less than you planned to.

understaffed adjective having less than the necessary number of staff.

understand verb (past tense and past participle **understood**) 1 to know the meaning of words or what someone says. SYNONYMS: comprehend, see, know, grasp, follow, fathom. 2 to realize how or why something happens or why it is important ♦ *Do you understand how computers work?* ♦ *I don't understand what all the fuss is about.* 3 to know what someone is like and why they behave as they do; to sympathize with how someone feels ♦ *She doesn't understand children* ♦ *Believe me, I understand the difficulty of your position.* 4 to know the explanation and not be offended ♦ *We shall understand if you can't come.* 5 to know a lot about something and how to deal with it ♦ *I don't understand finance at all.* 6 to have been told something or to draw a conclusion from the information you have ♦ *I understand that you want to speak to me.* 7 to supply a word or words mentally ♦ *Before 'coming?' the words 'are you' are understood.* 8 to take something for granted ♦ *Your expenses will* be paid, that's understood. [from an Old English word understandan]

understandable adjective able to be understood. **understandably** adverb

understanding noun 1 the ability to understand something. SYNONYMS: grasp, appreciation, awareness, comprehension, insight, perception. 2 the power of thought, intelligence. 3 sympathetic awareness of the point of view of others ♦ a better understanding between nations. 4 an informal agreement or arrangement ♦ I thought we had reached an understanding. **understanding** adjective having or showing sympathy towards other people's feelings and points of view.

understate verb 1 to state a thing in very restrained terms. 2 to represent something as being less than it really is. **understatement** noun

understudy noun (**understudies**) an actor who learns a part in order to be able to play it if the usual actor is ill or absent. **understudy** verb (**understudies, understudied, understudying**) to act as an understudy to someone; to learn a part as an understudy.

undertake verb (**undertook, undertaken**) 1 to make yourself responsible for doing something and start to do it ♦ She volunteered to undertake the mission. SYNONYMS: take on, tackle, handle, deal with, attend to. 2 to agree or promise that you will do something ♦ He undertook to pay all the money back by the end of the year.

undertaker verb a person whose job is to prepare the dead for burial or cremation and make arrangements for funerals.

undertaking noun 1 a job or task that is being undertaken. SYNONYMS: business, enterprise, venture. 2 a promise or guarantee. 3 the business of an undertaker.

under-the-counter adjective (said about goods) bought or sold dishonestly or illegally.

undertone noun 1 a low or quiet tone ♦ They spoke in undertones. 2 a colour that modifies another ♦ pink with mauve undertones. 3 an underlying quality or feeling ♦ His letter has a threatening undertone.

undertow (un-der-toh) noun a current below the surface of the sea, moving in an opposite direction to the surface current.

undervalue verb to put too low a value on something.

underwater adjective situated, used, or done beneath the surface of water. **underwater** adverb beneath the surface of water.

underwear noun clothes worn under other clothes next to the skin.

underweight adjective weighing less than is normal, desirable, or allowed.

underwent past tense of **undergo**.

underworld noun 1 (in mythology) the place for the spirits of the dead, under the earth. 2 the part of society regularly involved in crime.

underwrite verb (**underwrote, underwritten**) 1 to sign and accept liability under an insurance policy, especially for ships, thus guaranteeing payment in the event of loss or damage. 2 to undertake to finance an enterprise. 3 to undertake to buy all the shares in a company etc. that are not bought by the public. **underwriter** noun [so called because the underwriter used to sign his or her name underneath the names of the other people in the agreement]

undeserved adjective not deserved as reward or punishment. **undeservedly** (un-di-**zerv**-idli) adverb

undesirable adjective not desirable, objectionable. **undesirable** noun a person thought of as objectionable in some way. **undesirability** noun **undesirably** adverb

undetermined adjective not yet decided or settled.

undeveloped adjective not developed.

undies plural noun (informal) underwear.

undignified adjective lacking in dignity.

undiscriminating adjective lacking good judgement or taste.

undistinguished adjective not particularly good or remarkable.

undivided adjective complete ♦ I'll give this my undivided attention.

undo verb (**undid, undone, undoing**) 1 to unfasten, untie, or loosen something. 2 to cancel or reverse the effect of something ♦ She has undone all our careful work.

undoing noun a person's ruin or downfall, or the cause of this ♦ Drink was his undoing.

undone *adjective* 1 not tied or fastened. 2 not done or finished ♦ *Most of the work was left undone.* 3 (*old use*) brought to ruin or destruction ♦ *We are undone!*

undoubted *adjective* not regarded as doubtful, not questioned or disputed ♦ *She has undoubted talent.* **undoubtedly** *adverb*

undreamed-of or **undreamt-of** *adjective* not previously thought to be possible.

undress *verb* to take off your clothes or the clothes of another person.
undress *noun* the state of being naked or not fully clothed.

undue *adjective* excessive, more than is appropriate.

undulate (un-dew-layt) *verb* to move like a wave or waves; to have a wavy appearance. **undulation** *noun* **undulatory** *adjective* [from a Latin word *unda* meaning 'a wave']

unduly *adverb* excessively, more than is appropriate.

undying *adjective* lasting forever ♦ *You have my undying gratitude.*

unearned *adjective* not earned or deserved.

unearned income *noun* income from interest on investments and similar sources, not from work.

unearth *verb* 1 to uncover or obtain something from the ground by digging. 2 to find something by searching or investigation.

unearthly *adjective* 1 unnatural or mysterious, especially in a frightening way. 2 (*informal*) unreasonably early or inconvenient ♦ *We had to get up at an unearthly hour.* **unearthliness** *noun*

uneasy *adjective* (**uneasier, uneasiest**) 1 worried or anxious. 2 worrying ♦ *They had an uneasy suspicion that all was not well.* 3 not comfortable ♦ *She passed an uneasy night.* **uneasily** *adverb* **uneasiness** *noun*

uneatable *adjective* not fit to be eaten.

uneconomic *adjective* not profitable; not likely to be profitable.

uneducated *adjective* poorly educated.

unemployable *adjective* not likely to get paid employment, e.g. because of lack of skills or qualifications.

unemployed *adjective* 1 without a paid job. 2 not in use. **unemployment** *noun*

unencumbered *adjective* 1 not having a burden. 2 free of debt or other financial liability.

unending *adjective* not coming to an end; endless.

unenterprising *adjective* not showing initiative.

unenviable *adjective* difficult or unpleasant.

unequal *adjective* 1 not equal. 2 not with equal advantage to both sides, not evenly balanced ♦ *an unequal contest.* **to be unequal to** (said about a person) to be not strong enough or not clever enough etc. for something ♦ *He was unequal to the task.* **unequally** *adverb*

unequalled *adjective* without an equal.

unequivocal (un-i-kwiv-ə-kəl) *adjective* clear and unmistakable, not at all ambiguous ♦ *an unequivocal reply.* **unequivocally** *adverb*

unerring *adjective* making no mistake ♦ *with unerring accuracy.* **unerringly** *adverb* [from *un-* and *err*]

UNESCO (yoo-ness-koh) *abbreviation* United Nations Educational, Scientific, and Cultural Organization.

unethical *adjective* not ethical, unscrupulous in business or professional conduct. **unethically** *adverb*

uneven *adjective* 1 not level or smooth. SYNONYMS: bumpy, rough, irregular. 2 not regular or uniform ♦ *an uneven rhythm.* 3 not equally balanced ♦ *an uneven contest.* **unevenly** *adverb* **unevenness** *noun*

uneventful *adjective* (said of an occasion or period of time) without much happening, uninteresting.

unexceptionable *adjective* with which no fault can be found. **unexceptionably** *adverb* [from *un-* and *exception*, as in 'take exception']
◊ Do not confuse this word with **unexceptional**, which has a different meaning.

unexceptional *adjective* not exceptional, quite ordinary.
◊ Do not confuse this word with **unexceptionable**, which has a different meaning.

unexpected *adjective* not expected. **unexpectedly** *adverb* **unexpectedness** *noun*

unfailing *adjective* constant or reliable ♦ *his unfailing good humour.*

unfair *adjective* 1 not based on or showing fairness; unjust. 2 against the rules of a game. **unfairly** *adverb* **unfairness** *noun*

unfaithful *adjective* 1 not loyal or trustworthy. 2 not sexually loyal to your partner. **unfaithfully** *adverb* **unfaithfulness** *noun*

unfamiliar *adjective* 1 not known or recognized. 2 not knowing something well. **unfamiliarity** *noun*

unfasten *verb* to open the fastenings of something.

unfazed *adjective* not bothered or disconcerted by something.

unfeeling *adjective* 1 unsympathetic, not caring about other people's feelings. 2 lacking the power of sensation or sensitivity. **unfeelingly** *adverb*

unfit *adjective* 1 unsuitable for something. 2 not in good physical condition because you do not take enough exercise. **unfit** *verb* (**unfitted, unfitting**) (*old use*) to make a person or thing unsuitable.

unflappable *adjective* (*informal*) remaining calm in a crisis, not getting into a flap. **unflappability** *noun*

unfold *verb* 1 to open or spread a thing out or become opened or spread out. 2 to reveal something or become known slowly ♦ *as the story unfolds.*

unforeseen *adjective* not predicted or anticipated.

unforgettable *adjective* highly memorable.

unforgivable *adjective* not able to be forgiven.

unforgiving *adjective* not willing to forgive or excuse faults.

unformed *adjective* not formed; shapeless.

unfortunate *adjective* 1 having bad luck, unlucky. 2 unsuitable or regrettable ♦ *a most unfortunate choice of words.* **unfortunate** *noun* a person who suffers bad luck. **unfortunately** *adverb*

unfounded *adjective* not based on facts. [from *un-* and *found*[2]]

unfreeze *verb* (**unfroze, unfrozen**) to thaw, to cause something to thaw.

unfriendly *adjective* (**unfriendlier, unfriendliest**) not friendly. SYNONYMS: cool, distant, aloof, stand-offish, stern, unwelcoming, hostile. **unfriendliness** *noun*

unfrock *verb* to dismiss a priest from the priesthood. [from *un-* and an old sense of *frock* meaning 'a priest's robe']

unfurl *verb* to unroll something or spread it out ♦ *They unfurled a large flag.*

unfurnished *adverb* without furniture ♦ *an unfurnished flat.*

ungainly *adjective* awkward-looking or clumsy. **ungainliness** *noun* [from *un-* and an old word *gainly* meaning 'graceful']

unget-at-able *adjective* (*informal*) difficult or impossible to reach, inaccessible.

ungodly *adjective* 1 not religious. 2 (*informal*) unreasonably early or inconvenient ♦ *Why are you phoning me at this ungodly hour?* **ungodliness** *noun*

ungovernable *adjective* impossible to control or govern ♦ *an ungovernable temper.*

ungracious *adjective* not kindly or courteous. **ungraciously** *adverb*

ungrateful *adjective* feeling no gratitude. **ungratefully** *adjective*

unguarded *adjective* 1 not guarded. 2 without thought or caution, careless ♦ *in an unguarded moment.*

unguent (*ung-gwənt*) *noun* an ointment or lubricant. [from a Latin word *unguere* meaning 'to oil or anoint']

unhand *verb* (*old use*) to take your hands off a person.

unhappy *adjective* (**unhappier, unhappiest**) 1 not happy; sad or depressed. SYNONYMS: sad, miserable, depressed, despondent, down-hearted, dejected, downcast, glum. 2 unfortunate or unsuitable ♦ *an unhappy coincidence.* **unhappily** *adverb* **unhappiness** *noun*

unhealthy *adjective* (**unhealthier, unhealthiest**) 1 in poor health. 2 harmful to health. 3 unwise or dangerous. **unhealthily** *adverb* **unhealthiness** *noun*

unheard *adjective* not heard.

unheard-of *adjective* not previously known of or done.

unhinge *verb* to cause a person's mind to become unbalanced ♦ *The shock unhinged him.*

unhitch *verb* to release something from being hitched or fastened.

unholy *adjective* (**unholier, unholiest**) 1 wicked or unnatural. 2 (*informal*) very great, dreadful ♦ *Stop making that unholy row.* **unholiness** *noun*

unhook *verb* 1 to detach something from a hook or hooks. 2 to unfasten something by releasing the hooks.

unhoped-for *adjective* not hoped for or expected.

unhorse *verb* to throw or drag a rider from a horse.

uni- *prefix* one; single (as in *unicorn*). [from a Latin word *unus* meaning 'one']

unicameral (yoo-ni-**kam**-er-əl) *adjective* having only one legislative chamber. [from *uni-* and a Latin word *camera* meaning 'chamber']

UNICEF (**yoo**-ni-sef) *abbreviation* United Nations Children's Fund. [formerly the United Nations International Children's Emergency Fund]

unicellular (yoo-ni-**sel**-yoo-ler) *adjective* (*Biology*) (said about an organism) consisting of one cell.

unicorn *noun* a mythical animal resembling a horse with a single straight horn growing from its forehead. [from *uni-* and a Latin word *cornu* meaning 'horn']

unicycle *noun* a cycle with a single wheel.

unidentified *adjective* not identified.

unification *noun* the process of being united.

Unification Church *noun* a religious and political organization founded by Sun Myung Moon in Korea in 1954.

uniform *noun* the distinctive clothing worn to identify the wearer as a member of a certain organization, group, school, etc. **uniform** *adjective* always the same, not varying ♦ *planks of uniform thickness.* SYNONYMS: consistent, regular, standard, homogeneous. **uniformity** (yoo-ni-**form**-iti) *noun* **uniformly** *adverb* [from *uni-* and a Latin word *forma* meaning 'form']

uniformed *adjective* wearing a uniform.

unify *verb* (**unifies, unified, unifying**) to make a number of things into a single unit; to form into a single unit. **unifier** *noun* [same origin as for *unit*]

unilateral (yoo-ni-**lat**-erəl) *adjective* done by or affecting only one person, group, country, etc. ♦ *a unilateral decision.* **unilateralism** *noun* **unilaterally** *adverb* [from *uni-* and *lateral*]

unimaginable *adjective* too unpleasant or unusual to imagine.

unimaginative *adjective* not having or showing much imagination.

unimpaired *adjective* not weakened or damaged.

unimpeachable *adjective* not open to doubt or question, beyond reproach ♦ *unimpeachable honesty.* **unimpeachably** *adverb* [from *un-* and *impeach*]

unimportant *adjective* not important. SYNONYMS: insignificant, trivial, negligible, inconsequential, minor, petty.

uninformed *adjective* not aware of the facts.

uninhabitable *adjective* unfit to live in.

uninhabited *adjective* with nobody living there.

uninhibited *adjective* not inhibited, having no inhibitions.

uninspired *adjective* **1** dull, not imaginative. **2** not filled with excitement.

unintelligent *adjective* not having or showing much intelligence.

unintelligible *adjective* impossible to understand. **unintelligibly** *adverb*

uninterested *adjective* not interested; showing or feeling no concern. ◊ See the note at **disinterested.**

uninteresting *adjective* not interesting.

uninviting *adjective* not attractive, unpleasant.

union *noun* **1** the joining of things together; uniting or being united. **2** a whole formed by uniting parts. **3** an association of people with a common purpose. **4** a trade union. **5** (*Mathematics*) the combination of two or more sets, with repeated elements counted once only. **6** a joint or coupling for pipes. **7** a fabric with mixed materials, e.g. cotton with linen or silk. [from a Latin word *unio* meaning 'unity']

unionist *noun* **1** a member of a trade union. **2** (in specific uses **Unionist**) a person who wishes to unite one country with another, especially a supporter of the political union between Great Britain and Northern Ireland. **unionism** *noun*

unionize *verb* to organize into a trade union or cause people to join a trade union. **unionization** *noun*

Union Jack *noun* the national flag of the United Kingdom.

unique (yoo-**neek**) *adjective* **1** being the only one of its kind ♦ *This vase is unique.* **2** (*informal*) remarkable or unusual ♦ *This makes it even more unique.* **uniquely** *adverb* [from a Latin word *unus* meaning 'one'] ◊ Many people regard the use in meaning 2 as illogical and incorrect, and it should be avoided in formal contexts.

unisex (**yoo**-ni-seks) *adjective* designed to be suitable for both sexes ♦ *a unisex hairdresser's.*

unison *noun* **in unison 1** speaking, singing, or doing something together at the same time. **2** in agreement or concord ♦ *All the firms acted in unison.* [from *uni-* and a Latin word *sonus* meaning 'sound']

unit *noun* **1** a quantity chosen as a standard in terms of which other quantities may be expressed or measured ♦ *Centimetres are units of length.* **2** an individual thing, person, or group regarded as single and complete, or as part of a complex whole ♦ *the family as the unit of society.* **3** a device or machine part with a specified function ♦ *a waste disposal unit.* **4** a group with a specified function within an organization or army. **5** a piece of furniture for fitting with others like it or made of complementary parts. **6** any whole number less than 10. [from a Latin word *unus* meaning 'one']

Unitarian (yoo-ni-**tair**-iən) *noun* a member of a Christian religious sect maintaining that God is one person, not a Trinity. [from a Latin word *unitas* meaning 'unity']

unitary *adjective* to do with a unit or units.

unite *verb* **1** to join things or be joined together, to make things into or become a single unit or whole. SYNONYMS: combine, unify, amalgamate, coalesce, fuse. **2** to agree or cooperate ♦ *They all united in condemning the action.* [same origin as for *unit*]

United Kingdom *noun* Great Britain and Northern Ireland.

unit trust *noun* an investment company investing contributions from a number of people in various securities and paying them a dividend (calculated on the average return from these) in proportion to their holdings.

unity *noun* (**unities**) **1** the state of being one or a unit. **2** a complex whole made up of parts. **3** (*Mathematics*) the number one. **4** harmony, agreement in feelings, ideas, or aims etc. ♦ *Can we ever live together in unity?* [same origin as for *unit*]

univalent (yoo-ni-**vay**-lənt) *adjective* (*Chemistry*) another word for **monovalent**. [from *uni-* and *valency*]

univalve (**yoo**-ni-valv) *noun* a shellfish with a shell consisting of only one part (called a *valve*).

universal *adjective* to do with or including or done by everyone or everything. **universally** *adverb* [same origin as for *universe*]

universal joint *noun* a joint that connects two shafts in such a way that they can be at any angle to each other.

universe *noun* everything that exists, including the whole of space and all the stars, planets, etc. in it. [from a Latin word *universus* meaning 'combined into one']

university *noun* (**universities**) an educational institution that provides instruction and facilities for research in many branches of advanced learning and awards degrees. [same origin as for *universe*]

unjust *adjective* not just or fair. **unjustly** *adverb*

unkempt *adjective* looking untidy or neglected. [from *un-* and an old word *kempt* meaning 'combed']

unkind *adjective* not kind, harsh. SYNONYMS: nasty, mean, uncharitable, uncaring, heartless, callous. **unkindly** *adverb* **unkindness** *noun*

unknown *adjective* not known, not identified.
unknown *noun* **1** an unknown person or thing. **2** (*Mathematics*) an unknown quantity or variable.
unknown *adverb* **unknown to** without the knowledge of.

unknown quantity *noun* a person or thing whose nature, value, or significance is unknown.

unladen *adjective* not carrying a load.

unleaded *adjective* (said about petrol) without added lead.

unlearn *verb* (past tense and past participle **unlearned** or **unlearnt**) to cause a thing to be no longer in your knowledge or memory.

unleash *verb* **1** to set a dog free from a leash. **2** to release something so it is no longer under restraint.

unleavened (un-lev-ənd) *adjective* (said about bread) made without yeast or other raising agent.

unless *conjunction* if not, except when ♦ *Don't move unless I say so.* [from an old word *onlesse*, from *on* and *less*]

unlettered *adjective* illiterate or poorly educated.

unlike *preposition* **1** not like, different from ♦ *This is unlike anything I've ever read before* ♦ *Unlike her mother, she enjoys shopping.* **2** not typical of ♦ *It's unlike you to be so gloomy.*

unlike *adjective* not alike, different ♦ *The two children are very unlike.*

unlikely *adjective* (**unlikelier, unlikeliest**) **1** not likely to be true ♦ *an unlikely tale.* SYNONYMS: far-fetched, implausible, improbable, incredible. **2** not likely to happen.

unlimited *adjective* not limited; very great in number or quantity.

unlined *adjective* **1** without a lining. **2** not marked with lines.

unlisted *adjective* not included on a list, especially a published list of telephone numbers or stock exchange prices.

unload *verb* **1** to remove a load from someone or something; to remove goods from a vehicle, ship, etc. **2** to get rid of something. **3** to remove ammunition from a gun or film from a camera.

unlock *verb* **1** to open something by releasing a lock. **2** to release something by or as if by unlocking.

unlooked-for *adjective* unexpected.

unloose or **unloosen** *verb* to undo something or let it free.

unlucky *adjective* (**unluckier, unluckiest**) **1** bringing or resulting from bad luck. **2** having bad luck. SYNONYMS: luckless, hapless, accident-prone. **unluckily** *adverb*

unmade *adjective* **1** not made. **2** (said about a bed) not yet arranged ready for sleeping in.

unmanageable *adjective* not easy to manage or control. **unmanageably** *adverb*

unmanned *adjective* operated without a crew ♦ *an unmanned spacecraft.*

unmannerly *adjective* not well mannered.

unmarked *adjective* **1** not marked; with no mark of identification. **2** not noticed.

unmarried *adjective* not married, single.

unmask *verb* **1** to remove a person's mask or disguise. **2** to expose the true character of something.

unmentionable *adjective* too bad, embarrassing, or shocking to be spoken about.

unmistakable *adjective* clear and obvious, not able to be mistaken for anything else.

unmistakably *adverb*

unmitigated (un-mit-i-gayt-id) *adjective* absolute, not modified at all ♦ *an unmitigated disaster.*

unmoved *adjective* not changed in your purpose or affected by emotion.

unnatural *adjective* **1** not natural or normal. **2** artificial, not spontaneous. **unnaturally** *adverb*

unnecessary *adjective* **1** not necessary. **2** more than is necessary ♦ *with unnecessary care.* **unnecessarily** *adverb*

unnerve *verb* to make someone lose courage or determination. **unnerving** *adjective*

unnumbered *adjective* **1** not marked with a number. **2** countless.

unobtrusive (un-ǝb-troo-siv) *adjective* not obtrusive, not attracting attention. **unobtrusively** *adverb*

unoccupied *adjective* not occupied.

unofficial *adjective* not officially confirmed or authorized. **unofficially** *adverb*

unorthodox *adjective* not generally accepted ♦ *an unorthodox method.*

unpack *verb* to open and remove the contents of a suitcase etc.; to take something out from its packaging or from a suitcase etc.

unpaid *adjective* **1** (said about a debt) not yet paid. **2** not receiving payment for work done.

unpalatable *adjective* **1** not pleasant to eat or drink. **2** difficult to accept or tolerate.

unparalleled *adjective* not paralleled, never yet equalled ♦ *unparalleled enthusiasm.*

unparliamentary *adjective* (said especially about language) contrary to the rules or customs of parliament.

unperson *noun* (**unpersons**) a person whose name or existence is officially ignored or denied.

unperturbed *adjective* not bothered or concerned.

unpick *verb* to undo the stitching of something.

unplaced *adjective* not placed as one of the first three to finish in a race.

unplayable *adjective* (said about a ball in games) impossible to play or return etc.

unpleasant *adjective* not pleasant. **unpleasantly** *adverb* **unpleasantness** *noun*

unplug *verb* (**unplugged, unplugging**) 1 to disconnect an electrical device by removing its plug from the socket. 2 to remove an obstacle or blockage from something.

unplumbed *adjective* 1 without plumbing. 2 not fully explored or understood.

unpopular *adjective* not liked or popular. **unpopularity** *noun* **unpopularly** *adverb*

unpowered *adjective* not driven by an engine.

unprecedented (un-**press**-i-dent-id) *adjective* never done or known before. [from *un-* and *precedent*]

unpredictable *adjective* not able to be predicted; apt to change.

unprejudiced *adjective* without prejudice, impartial.

unpremeditated (un-pri-**med**-i-tayt-id) *adjective* not planned beforehand.

unprepared *adjective* 1 not prepared beforehand. 2 not ready or able to deal with something.

unprepossessing (un-pree-pə-**zess**-ing) *adjective* unattractive, not likely to make a good impression.

unpretentious (un-pri-**ten**-shəs) *adjective* not pretentious, not showy or pompous.

unprincipled *adjective* acting without good moral principles.

unprintable *adjective* too rude or offensive to be printed.

unprofessional *adjective* not worthy of a member of a profession; contrary to professional standards of behaviour. **unprofessionally** *adverb*

unprofitable *adjective* 1 not producing a profit. 2 serving no useful purpose.

unprompted *adjective* without being prompted, spontaneous.

unprotected *adjective* 1 not protected or kept safe. 2 (said about sexual intercourse) done without using a condom.

unproven *adjective* 1 not established by evidence. 2 not tested or known to be reliable.

unqualified *adjective* 1 (said about a person) not legally or officially qualified to do something. 2 not limited or modified ♦ *We gave it our unqualified approval.*

unquestionable *adjective* not questionable, too clear to be doubted. **unquestionably** *adverb*

unquestioned *adverb* not disputed or doubted.

unravel *verb* (**unravelled, unravelling**) 1 to disentangle something. 2 to undo something that is knitted. 3 to investigate and solve a mystery or puzzle. 4 to become unravelled.

unreadable *adjective* 1 too difficult or dull to read. 2 illegible.

unready *adjective* 1 not ready or prepared. 2 not prompt in action, hesitant. **unreadily** *adverb* **unreadiness** *noun*

unreal *adjective* not real, existing in the imagination only. **unreality** (un-ri-**al**-iti) *noun*

unreasonable *adjective* 1 not reasonable in your attitude etc. 2 excessive, going beyond the limits of what is reasonable or just. **unreasonably** *adverb*

unreel *verb* to unwind something from a reel.

unrelated *adjective* not related or connected.

unrelenting *adjective* not becoming less in intensity or severity.

unrelieved *adjective* without anything to vary it ♦ *unrelieved gloom* ♦ *a plain black dress unrelieved by any touches of colour.*

unremarkable *adjective* not particularly remarkable or interesting.

unremitting (un-ri-**mit**-ing) *adjective* not relaxing or stopping, persistent. [from *un-* and *remit*]

unrepeatable *adjective* 1 that cannot be done or offered etc. again ♦ *an unrepeatable bargain.* 2 too rude or offensive to be said again.

unrepentant *adjective* showing no regret for one's wrongs.

unrequited (un-ri-**kwiy**-tid) *adjective* (said about love) not returned or rewarded. [from *un-* and *requited* meaning 'paid back']

unreserved *adjective* 1 without reservation or restriction, complete ♦ *unreserved support.* 2 not reserved in advance ♦ *unreserved seats.* **unreservedly** (un-ri-**zerv**-idli) *adverb*

unresolved *adjective* (said about a problem or dispute) not resolved or settled.

unrest noun trouble or rioting caused because people are dissatisfied.

unrestrained adjective not restrained.

unripe adjective not yet ripe.

unrivalled (un-riy-vəld) adjective having no equal, better than all others.

unroll verb to open something that has been rolled up; to become opened after being rolled.

unruffled adjective not disturbed, calm.

unruly (un-roo-li) adjective (**unrulier, unruliest**) not easy to control or discipline, disorderly. **unruliness** noun [from un- and rule]

unsaddle verb 1 to remove the saddle from a horse. 2 to unseat a rider.

unsaid (un-sed) past tense and past participle of **unsay**.
unsaid adjective not spoken or expressed ◆ Many things were left unsaid.

unsalted adjective not seasoned with salt.

unsatisfactory adjective not good enough to be acceptable.

unsaturated adjective (Chemistry) (said about a substance) able to combine chemically with hydrogen to form a third substance by the joining of molecules.

unsavoury adjective 1 unpleasant to the taste or smell. 2 morally unpleasant or disgusting ◆ an unsavoury reputation.

unsay verb (past tense and past participle **unsaid**) to take back or retract something you have said ◆ What's said can't be unsaid.

unscathed (un-skaythd) adjective without suffering any injury. [from un- and an old word scathed meaning 'harmed']

unscientific adjective not in accordance with scientific principles or methods. **unscientifically** adverb

unscramble verb 1 to sort something out from a scrambled state. 2 to make a scrambled transmission intelligible.

unscrew verb 1 to unfasten something by turning or removing screws, or by twisting it. 2 to loosen a screw or lid by turning it. 3 (said about a screw, lid, etc.) to become unscrewed.

unscripted adjective without a prepared script.

unscrupulous (un-skroo-pew-ləs) adjective without moral scruples. **unscrupulously** adverb **unscrupulousness** noun

unseal verb to open a sealed letter or container etc.

unseasonable adjective 1 unusual for a particular season. 2 untimely. **unseasonably** adverb

unseat verb 1 to throw a rider from horseback or from a bicycle etc. 2 to remove an MP from a parliamentary seat ◆ She was unseated at the last election.

unsecured adjective (said about a loan) made without anything offered as security.

unseeded adjective (said about a tennis player etc.) not seeded.

unseeing adjective not seeing anything.

unseemly adjective not proper or suitable. **unseemliness** noun

unseen adjective 1 not seen or noticed. 2 (said about translation) done without previous preparation.

unselfconscious adjective not self-conscious.

unselfish adjective not selfish, considering the needs of others before your own. **unselfishly** adverb **unselfishness** noun

unsettle verb to make someone feel uneasy or anxious. **unsettling** adjective

unsettled adjective 1 not settled or calm. 2 (said about weather) likely to change.

unshackle verb to release someone from shackles, to set someone free.

unshakeable adjective not able to be shaken, firm ◆ an unshakeable belief.

unshaven adjective (said about a man) not recently shaved.

unsheathe verb to remove a knife etc. from a sheath.

unshockable adjective impossible to shock.

unsightly adjective not pleasant to look at, ugly. **unsightliness** noun

unsigned adjective not signed; not having a signature.

unskilled adjective not having or needing skill or special training.

unsociable adjective not sociable, not enjoying the company of other people. **unsociably** adverb

unsocial adjective 1 (said about hours of work) falling outside the normal working

day, when most people are not working.
2 unsociable. **unsocially** adverb

unsolicited (un-sə-**liss**-it-id) adjective not
asked for; given or done voluntarily
♦ unsolicited advice. [from un- and solicit]

unsophisticated adjective not
sophisticated, simple and natural or
naive.

unsound adjective **1** not reliable, not based
on sound evidence or reasoning ♦ unsound
advice. **2** not firm or strong. **3** not healthy
♦ of unsound mind. [from un- and sound[2]]

unsparing (un-**spair**-ing) adjective giving
freely and lavishly ♦ unsparing in your
efforts.

unspeakable adjective too bad or too
horrific to be described in words.

unspecified adjective not stated clearly or
exactly.

unstable adjective (**unstabler, unstablest**)
1 not stable, tending to change suddenly.
2 mentally or emotionally unbalanced.
unstably adverb

unsteady adjective (**unsteadier, unsteadiest**)
1 not firm or steady. SYNONYMS: unstable,
rickety, wobbly. **2** not regular. SYNONYMS:
irregular, erratic, fluctuating. **unsteadily**
adverb **unsteadiness** noun

unstick verb (past tense and past participle
unstuck) to separate a thing stuck to
another.

unstinting adjective given or giving freely
and lavishly. [from un- and stint]

unstop verb (**unstopped, unstopping**) verb
1 to free something from an obstruction.
2 to remove the stopper from a container.

unstoppable adjective impossible to stop
or prevent.

unstressed adjective not pronounced with
a stress.

unstructured adjective without a formal
structure.

unstuck adjective detached after being
stuck on or together. **to come unstuck**
(informal) to fail.

unstudied adjective natural in manner, not
affected ♦ with unstudied elegance.

unsubstantial adjective not substantial,
flimsy; having little or no factual basis.

unsuccessful adjective not successful.

unsuitable adjective not suitable.
unsuitability noun **unsuitably** adverb

unsuited adjective not right or appropriate.

unsullied (un-**sul**-id) adjective not sullied,
pure.

unsure adjective not confident or certain.

unsuspecting adjective feeling no
suspicion.

unswerving adjective not turning aside,
unchanging ♦ unswerving loyalty.

untangle verb **1** to disentangle something.
2 to free something from complications or
confusion.

untapped adjective not yet made use of
♦ the country's untapped resources.

untaught adjective **1** not instructed by
teaching. **2** not acquired by teaching.

untenable (un-**ten**-əbəl) adjective (said
about a theory) not able to be held or
defended against attack.

unthinkable adjective too unlikely or
undesirable to be considered.

unthinking adjective thoughtless, done or
said etc. without consideration.
unthinkingly adverb

untidy adjective (**untidier, untidiest**) not
neat or properly arranged. **untidily** adverb
untidiness noun

untie verb (**unties, untied, untying**) to undo
something that has been tied; to release
someone from being tied up.

until preposition & conjunction up to a
particular time or event ♦ Until last year we
had never been abroad ♦ This matter can wait
until I return. [from an Old Norse word]
◊ Until is used in preference to till when it
is the first word in the sentence and also
in more formal contexts.

untimely adjective **1** happening at an
unsuitable time. **2** happening too soon or
sooner than is normal ♦ his untimely death.
untimeliness noun

unto preposition (old use) to. [from until and
the preposition to]

untold adjective **1** too much or too many to
be counted ♦ untold wealth. **2** not told.
[from an Old English word unteald
meaning 'not counted']

untouchable adjective **1** not able to be
touched. **2** not able to be matched or
rivalled.
untouchable noun a member of the lowest
Hindu group in India, or a person outside
the caste system.
◊ Use of the term, and the social

restrictions associated with it, were declared illegal in India in 1949 and in Pakistan in 1953.

untoward (un-tə-**word**) *adjective* unexpected and inconvenient or unfortunate ♦ *if nothing untoward happens.* [from *un-* and an old sense of *toward* meaning 'fortunate, promising']

untraceable *adjective* unable to be found or traced.

untrammelled *adjective* not hampered.

untried *adjective* not yet tried or tested.

untroubled *adjective* not troubled, calm.

untrue *adjective* 1 not true, contrary to facts. 2 not faithful or loyal.

untruth *noun* 1 a lie. 2 lack of truth. **untruthful** *adjective* **untruthfully** *adverb*

untwist *verb* to open something from a twisted position.

unused *adjective* 1 (un-**yoozd**) not yet used ♦ *an unused stamp.* 2 (un-**yoost**) not accustomed ♦ *He is unused to such attention.*

unusual *adjective* not usual; strange or exceptional. SYNONYMS: strange, abnormal, uncommon, rare, odd, peculiar, curious. **unusually** *adverb*

unutterable *adjective* too great or too intense to be expressed in words ♦ *unutterable joy.* **unutterably** *adverb* [*un-* and *utter* and *-able*]

unvarnished *adjective* 1 not varnished. 2 plain and straightforward ♦ *the unvarnished truth.*

unveil *verb* 1 to remove a veil or covering from something ♦ *The Queen unveiled the portrait.* 2 to reveal or disclose something, to make something publicly known.

unversed *adjective* not experienced in something ♦ *He was unversed in court etiquette.*

unvoiced *adjective* not spoken or voiced.

unwaged *adjective* not in paid employment.

unwanted *adjective* not wanted.

unwarrantable *adjective* not justifiable. **unwarrantably** *adverb* [*un-* and *warrant*]

unwarranted *adjective* not justified, uncalled-for.

unwary (un-**wair**-i) *adjective* not cautious or careful about danger. **unwarily** *adverb* **unwariness** *noun*

unwearying *adjective* never tiring; persistent.

unwell *adjective* not in good health.

unwholesome *adjective* 1 harmful to health or to moral well-being. 2 unhealthy-looking. **unwholesomeness** *noun*

unwieldy (un-**weel**-di) *adjective* (**unwieldier, unwieldiest**) awkward to move or control because of its size, shape, or weight. **unwieldiness** *noun* [*un-* and *wield*]

unwilling *adjective* not willing, reluctant to do something. SYNONYMS: reluctant, averse, disinclined, loath. **unwillingly** *adverb*

unwind *verb* (past tense and past participle **unwound**) 1 to draw something out or become drawn out from being wound. 2 (*informal*) to relax after a period of work or tension.

unwinking *adjective* not winking; gazing or shining steadily.

unwise *adjective* not wise, foolish. **unwisely** *adverb*

unwitting *adjective* 1 unintentional. 2 unaware ♦ *She was an unwitting accomplice.* **unwittingly** *adverb* [from an Old English word *unwitende* meaning 'not knowing or realizing']

unwonted (un-**wohn**-tid) *adjective* not customary or usual ♦ *She spoke with unwonted rudeness.* **unwontedly** *adverb* [from *un-* and *wont*]

unworkable *adjective* (said about an idea or scheme) not able to be done, not practical.

unworldly *adjective* 1 having little awareness of the realities of life; naive. 2 not concerned with material things. **unworldliness** *noun*

unworn *adjective* not yet worn.

unworthy *adjective* (**unworthier, unworthiest**) 1 not worthy, lacking worth or excellence. 2 not deserving ♦ *He is unworthy of this honour.* 3 unsuitable to the character of a person or thing ♦ *Such conduct is unworthy of a king.* **unworthily** *adverb* **unworthiness** *noun*

unwrap *verb* (**unwrapped, unwrapping**) to remove the wrapping from something.

unwritten *adjective* 1 not written. 2 (said about a law) resting on custom or tradition rather than on statute.

unyielding *adjective* firm, not yielding to pressure or influence.

unzip *verb* (**unzipped, unzipping**) to unfasten the zip on something.

up *adverb* 1 to, in, or at a higher place, level, value, or condition ♦ *Prices have gone up.* 2 to an upright position ♦ *Stand up.* 3 so as to be inflated ♦ *Pump up the tyres.* 4 winning by a specified margin ♦ *United are two goals up.* 5 at or towards a central place or a university. 6 to the place, time, or amount etc. in question ♦ *I walked up to one of the boys.* 7 out of bed ♦ *It's time to get up.* 8 into a condition of activity ♦ *She's been stirring up trouble.* 9 apart, into pieces ♦ *I tore up the letter.* 10 into a compact state, securely ♦ *Tie it up.* 11 completely ♦ *Eat up your carrots.* 12 finished ♦ *Your time is up.* 13 (*informal*) happening (especially of something unusual or undesirable) ♦ *Something is up.*
up *preposition* 1 upwards along or through or into; from a lower to a higher point of ♦ *Water came up the pipes.* 2 at a higher part of ♦ *Fix it further up the wall.*
up *adjective* 1 directed towards a higher place ♦ *an up stroke.* 2 travelling towards a central place ♦ *an up train.* 3 (said about a computer system) working properly. 4 (said about a road) being repaired.
up *verb* (**upped, upping**) (*informal*) 1 to begin to do something suddenly or unexpectedly ♦ *He upped and demanded an inquiry.* 2 to increase something ♦ *They promptly upped the price.* **up against** 1 close to or touching. 2 (*informal*) faced with a difficulty or an opponent. **up and down** in various places throughout. **up for** 1 available for ♦ *The house is up for sale.* 2 being considered for. 3 (*informal*) ready to take part in. **up on** (*informal*) well informed about. **ups and downs** alternate good and bad luck. **up to** 1 as far as. 2 (also **up until**) until. 3 indicating a maximum amount ♦ *The taxi can take up to four passengers.* 4 busy with or doing something ♦ *What are you up to?* 5 capable of ♦ *I don't feel up to a long walk.* 6 required as a duty or obligation from ♦ *It's up to us to help her.* **what's up?** 1 what is going on? 2 what is the matter? [from an Old English word]

up-and-coming *adjective* (*informal*) likely to become successful.

Upanishad (uup-an-i-shad) *noun* each of a series of Sanskrit philosophical writings in prose and verse, based on the Vedas and forming the main part of Hindu scriptures. [from a Sanskrit word]

upbeat *noun* an unaccented beat in music, when the conductor's baton moves upwards.
upbeat *adjective* cheerful or optimistic.

upbraid *verb* to scold or reproach someone. [from an Old English word]

upbringing *noun* training and education during childhood.

upcountry *adverb* towards the interior of a country.

update *verb* 1 to make something more modern or up-to-date. 2 to give someone the latest information.

upend *verb* to set something or be set up on end.

upfront *adjective* & *adverb* (said about payments) made in advance, e.g. as a deposit.
upfront *adjective* open and frank.

upgrade *verb* to raise something to a higher standard or rank.
upgrade *noun* an upgraded version of something.

upheaval *noun* a sudden violent change or disturbance. [from *up-* and *heave*]

uphill *adverb* towards the top of a slope.
uphill *adjective* 1 sloping upwards. 2 difficult ♦ *It was an uphill struggle.*

uphold *verb* (past tense and past participle **upheld**) to support or maintain a decision, statement, or belief.

upholster *verb* to put a soft padded covering on furniture. **upholsterer** *noun* [from *uphold* meaning 'to maintain and repair']

upholstery *noun* 1 the work of upholstering furniture. 2 the material used for this.

upkeep *noun* keeping something in good condition and repair; the cost of this.

uplands *plural noun* the higher parts of a country or region.
upland *adjective* to do with uplands.

uplift *verb* to raise something.
uplift *noun* 1 being raised. 2 a morally or spiritually elevating influence.

uplifting *adjective* making you feel more cheerful or morally or spiritually elevated.

upmarket *adjective & adverb* to do with or towards the more expensive end of the market.

upon *preposition* on ♦ Stratford-upon-Avon ♦ Christmas is almost upon us. [from the adverb *up* and the preposition *on*]

upper *adjective* 1 higher in place or position. 2 situated on higher ground or to the north ♦ Upper Egypt. 3 ranking above others. 4 (said about a geological or archaeological period) later in its occurrence.
upper *noun* the part of a boot or shoe above the sole. **on your uppers** (*informal*) very short of money. **the upper crust** *noun* (*informal*) the upper classes. **the upper hand** *noun* control or dominance ♦ In the second half City gained the upper hand.

upper case *noun* capital letters.

Upper Chamber or **Upper House** *noun* the House of Lords as an assembly.

upper class *noun* the highest class in society, especially the aristocracy.
upper-class *adjective*

upper crust *noun* (*informal*) the upper class.

uppercut *noun* a punch in boxing, delivered upwards with the arm bent.

uppermost *adjective* highest in place or rank.
uppermost *adjective* on or to the top or the most prominent position ♦ Keep the painted side uppermost. [from *upper* and *most*]

uppish *adjective* arrogant.

uppity *adjective* (*informal*) self-important. [from *up*]

upright *adjective* 1 in a vertical position. 2 (said about a piano) with the strings mounted vertically. 3 strictly honest or honourable.
upright *adverb* in or into an upright position.
upright *noun* 1 a post or rod placed upright, especially as a support. 2 an upright piano. **uprightness** *noun* [from an Old English word *upriht*]

uprising *noun* a rebellion or revolt.

uproar *noun* an outburst of noise and excitement or anger. SYNONYMS: bedlam, commotion, pandemonium, furore, rumpus, hubbub; (*informal*) hullabaloo. [from an Old Dutch word *uproer*]

uproarious *adjective* 1 very noisy; with loud laughter. 2 extremely funny.
uproariously *adverb*

uproot *verb* 1 to remove a plant and its roots from the ground. 2 to force someone to leave the place where they have lived for a long time ♦ We don't want to uproot ourselves and go to live abroad.

uprush *noun* a sudden upward surge or flow.

upset [1] (up-set) *verb* (past tense and past participle **upset; upsetting**) 1 to make someone unhappy or distressed. SYNONYMS: agitate, disconcert, distress, disturb, perturb, bother. 2 to knock something over. 3 to disturb the normal working of something; to disrupt something ♦ Fog upset the timetable. 4 to disturb the digestion of someone.
upset *adjective* 1 unhappy or distressed. 2 slightly ill ♦ an upset stomach. **to upset the applecart** to spoil a situation or someone's plans.

upset [2] (up-set) *noun* 1 a slight illness ♦ a stomach upset. 2 an unexpected result or setback ♦ There has been a major upset in the quarter-finals.

upshot *noun* the eventual outcome. [originally denoting the final shot in an archery contest]

upside down *adverb & adjective* 1 with the upper part underneath instead of on top. 2 in great disorder ♦ His flat had been turned upside down.

upstage *adjective & adverb* towards the back of a theatre stage.
upstage *verb* 1 to move upstage from another actor and make them face away from the audience. 2 to divert attention from someone towards yourself.

upstairs *adverb* up the stairs, to or on an upper floor.
upstairs *adjective* situated upstairs.

upstanding *adjective* 1 respectable. 2 strong and healthy.

upstart *noun* a person who has risen suddenly to a high position, especially one who behaves arrogantly. [from an old verb *upstart* meaning 'to spring up suddenly']

upstate *adjective* (in the USA) in a part of a state that is away from the principal city ♦ upstate New York.

upstream *adjective & adverb* in the direction from which a stream flows.

upsurge *noun* an upward surge, an increase.

upswept *adjective* (said about the hair) brushed upwards and off the face.

upswing *noun* an upward movement or trend.

uptake *noun* the action of taking up or making use of something. **quick on the uptake** quick to understand. **slow on the uptake** slow to understand.

uptight *adjective* (*informal*) nervously tense or angry.

up-to-date *adjective* **1** in current fashion ♦ *up-to-date clothes*. SYNONYMS: fashionable, contemporary; (*informal*) trendy, in. **2** containing the latest information or making use of the latest developments ♦ *the most up-to-date edition*. SYNONYMS: advanced, current, latest, modern, new.

upturn *noun* an upward trend in business or fortune etc., an improvement. **upturn** *verb* to turn something upwards or upside down.

upward *adjective* moving, leading, or pointing towards a higher point or level. **upwards** or **upward** *adverb* towards a higher point or level.

upwind *adjective & adverb* in the direction from which the wind is blowing.

uranium (yoor-**ay**-niəm) *noun* a chemical element (symbol U), a heavy grey metal used as a fuel in nuclear reactors. [from the name of the planet Uranus]

urban *adjective* to do with or situated in a city or town. [from a Latin word *urbs* meaning 'city']

urbane (er-**bayn**) *adjective* smooth and courteous in manner, suave. **urbanity** (er-**ban**-iti) *noun* **urbanely** *adverb* [same origin as for *urban*]

urbanize *verb* to change a place into a town-like area. **urbanization** *noun*

urchin *noun* **1** a mischievous child, especially one who is dirty and poorly dressed. **2** a sea urchin. [from a Latin word *hericius* meaning 'hedgehog']

Urdu (oor-**doo**) *noun* a language related to Hindi, spoken in northern India and Pakistan. [from a Persian word]

urea (yoor-iə or yoor-**ee**-ə) *noun* (*Biochemistry*) a soluble colourless compound contained especially in urine. [from a Greek word *ouron* meaning 'urine']

ureter (yoor-**ee**-ter) *noun* either of the two ducts by which urine passes from the kidneys to the bladder. [from a Greek word *ourētēr*]

urethra (yoor-**ee**-thrə) *noun* the duct by which urine is passed out of the body. [from a Greek word *ourēthra*]

urge *verb* **1** to try hard or persistently to persuade someone to do something ♦ *I urged him to accept the job*. **2** to encourage someone to continue ♦ *The runners were urged on by the huge crowd*. **3** to recommend something strongly ♦ *I urge caution in this matter*. **4** to force an animal to go more quickly ♦ *She urged her horse forward*. **urge** *noun* a strong desire or feeling that drives you to do something. SYNONYMS: compulsion, impulse, inclination; (*informal*) itch. [from a Latin word *urgere* meaning 'to press' or 'to drive']

urgent *adjective* **1** needing to be done or dealt with immediately. SYNONYMS: pressing, high-priority, immediate. **2** showing that something is urgent ♦ *She spoke in an urgent whisper*. SYNONYMS: insistent, importunate. **urgency** *noun* **urgently** *adverb* [from a Latin word *urgens* meaning 'urging']

uric (yoor-**ik**) *adjective* to do with urine ♦ *uric acid*. [same origin as for *urine*]

urinal (yoor-in-əl or yoor-**iy**-nəl) *noun* a bowl or trough fixed to the wall in a men's public toilet, for men to urinate into. [from a Latin word *urinalis* meaning 'urinary']

urinary (yoor-in-er-i) *adjective* to do with urine or its excretion ♦ *urinary organs*.

urinate (yoor-in-ayt) *verb* to pass urine out of your body. **urination** *noun* [from a Latin word *urinare* meaning 'to urinate']

urine (yoor-in) *noun* waste liquid that collects in the bladder and is passed out of the body. [from a Latin word *urina*]

URL *abbreviation* (*Computing*) uniform (or universal) resource locator, the address of a website or web page.

urn *noun* **1** a tall vase with a stem and base, especially one used for holding the ashes of a cremated person. **2** a large metal container with a tap, in which tea or coffee is made and kept hot. [from a Latin word *urna*]

US *abbreviation* United States.

us *pronoun* the form of *we* used as the object of a verb or after a preposition. [from an Old English word]

USA *abbreviation* United States of America.

usable *adjective* able to be used; fit for use.

usage (yoo-sij) *noun* 1 use; the way something is used or treated ♦ *It has been damaged by rough usage.* 2 a habitual or customary practice, especially in the way words are used ♦ *English usage often differs from American usage.*

use [1] (yooz) *verb* 1 to perform an action or job with something, to put something to a purpose. SYNONYMS: employ, utilize, apply, exercise. 2 to consume or be fuelled by something. 3 to treat someone in a particular way ♦ *They used her shamefully.* 4 to exploit someone selfishly. **could use** (*informal*) would like to have or benefit from ♦ *I could use a drink.* **to use something up** 1 to use all of something. 2 to finish off what is left over. **user** *noun* [from a Latin word *uti* meaning 'to use']

use [2] (yooss) *noun* 1 using something or being used ♦ *the use of computers in schools.* SYNONYMS: usage, appliance, application, employment. 2 the ability or right to use something ♦ *He lost the use of his legs.* 3 the quality of being useful ♦ *These scissors are no use at all.* SYNONYMS: usefulness, utility. 4 the purpose for which something is used; work that a person or thing is able to do ♦ *Can you find a use for this crate?* **to have no use for** 1 to have no purpose for which a thing can be used. 2 to refuse to tolerate someone or something. **to make use of** to benefit from something.

use-by date *noun* the recommended date by which food or other perishable goods should be used.

used [1] (yoozd) *adjective* 1 having already been used. 2 (said about clothes or vehicles) second-hand.

used [2] (yoost) *verb* was or were accustomed in the past ♦ *We used to go by train.* **used** *adjective* having become familiar with a thing by experience or habit ♦ *I am used to getting up early.*

useful *adjective* 1 able to be used a lot or to do something that needs doing. SYNONYMS: helpful, beneficial, valuable, advantageous, worthwhile, profitable, productive. 2 (*informal*) good or skilful at something. **to make yourself useful** to do something that is of some benefit or value. **usefully** *adverb* **usefulness** *noun*

useless *adjective* 1 serving no useful purpose, not able to produce good results ♦ *Their efforts were useless.* 2 (*informal*) poor at doing something. **uselessly** *adverb* **uselessness** *noun*

user-friendly *adjective* easy to use or understand.

usher *noun* 1 a person who shows people to their seats in a cinema or theatre or at a wedding. 2 a person who walks before a person of high rank on special occasions. 3 an official who swears in jurors and witnesses in a law court. **usher** *verb* to lead or guide someone to a place. [from a Latin word *ostiarius* meaning 'doorkeeper']

usherette *noun* a woman who shows people to their seats in a cinema or theatre.

USSR *abbreviation* (*historical*) Union of Soviet Socialist Republics.

usual *adjective* happening or done most often. SYNONYMS: customary, habitual, normal, regular, ordinary, common, standard, orthodox. **usual** *noun* (*informal*) a person's usual drink. **usually** *adverb* [from a Latin word *usum* meaning 'used']

usurer (yoo-zher-er) *noun* a person who lends money at excessively high rates of interest. [same origin as for *usury*]

usurious (yooz-yoor-iəs) *adjective* to do with or involving usury.

usurp (yoo-zerp) *verb* to take a position of power from someone illegally or by force. **usurpation** *noun* **usurper** *noun* [from a Latin word *usurpare* meaning 'to seize in order to use']

usury (yoo-zher-i) *noun* the lending of money at excessively high rates of interest. [from a Latin word *usura* meaning 'usage']

utensil (yoo-ten-səl) *noun* a tool, device, or container, especially one for use in the house ♦ *cooking utensils.* [from a Latin word *utensilis* meaning 'fit for use']

uterine (yoo-teriyn) *adjective* to do with the uterus.

uterus (yoo-ter-əs) *noun* (**uteri**) (yoo-ter-iy) the womb. [a Latin word meaning 'womb']

utilitarian (yoo-tili-**tair**-iən) *adjective* designed to be useful or practical rather than decorative or luxurious. [from *utility*]

utility *noun* (**utilities**) **1** usefulness. **2** a useful thing, especially a public service such as the supply of water, gas, or electricity etc.
utility *adjective* **1** useful, especially through having several functions. **2** functional rather than attractive. [from a Latin word *utilis* meaning 'useful']

utility room *noun* a room containing one or more large domestic appliances, e.g. a washing machine.

utilize *verb* to make use of something. **utilization** *noun* [from a French word *utiliser*]

utmost *adjective* greatest or most extreme ♦ *Look after it with the utmost care.*
the utmost *noun* the greatest or most extreme amount or extent. **to do your utmost** to do the most that you are able to. [from an Old English word *utemest* meaning 'furthest out']

Utopia (yoo-**toh**-piə) *noun* an imaginary place or state of things where everything is perfect. **Utopian** *adjective* [the title of a book (1516) by Sir Thomas More, meaning 'Nowhere', based on Greek words *ou* meaning 'not' and *topos* meaning 'place']

utter¹ *adjective* complete or absolute ♦ *utter bliss.* **utterly** *adverb* [from an Old English word *uttra* meaning 'outer']

utter² *verb* to make a sound or say something ♦ *I heard him utter a sigh.* **utterance** *noun* [from an Old Dutch word]

uttermost *adjective & noun* utmost.

U-turn *noun* **1** the turning of a vehicle in a U-shaped course so that it then faces the opposite way. **2** a complete change or reversal of policy.

UV *abbreviation* ultraviolet.

uvula (yoov-yoo-lə) *noun* (**uvulae**) (*Anatomy*) the small fleshy extension at the back of the roof of the mouth which hangs above the throat. [from a Latin word *uva* meaning 'grape']

uxorious (uks-**or**-iəs) *adjective* showing great or excessive fondness for your wife. [from a Latin word *uxor* meaning 'wife']

Vv

V 1 the twenty-second letter of the English alphabet. **2** the Roman numeral for 5.

V *abbreviation* **1** volt(s). **2** (*Physics*) the symbol for volume. **3** (*Chemistry*) the symbol for vanadium.

v *abbreviation* **1** verse. **2** versus. **3** (*Physics*) the symbol for velocity.

vac *noun* (*informal*) a vacation.

vacancy *noun* (**vacancies**) **1** the condition of being vacant, emptiness. **2** an unoccupied position or job ♦ *We have a vacancy for a typist.* **3** an available room in a hotel, guest house, etc. ♦ *We have no vacancies.*

vacant *adjective* **1** empty, not filled or occupied ♦ *a vacant seat* ♦ *a vacant post.* **2** showing no sign of thought or intelligence, having a blank expression. **vacantly** *adverb* [from a Latin word *vacans* meaning 'being empty']

vacate (və-**kayt**) *verb* to leave or give up a place or position. [from a Latin word *vacare* meaning 'to leave empty']

vacation (və-**kay**-shən) *noun* **1** a holiday period between terms in universities and law courts. **2** (*North Amer.*) a holiday. **3** vacating a place ♦ *Immediate vacation of the house is essential.* [same origin as for *vacate*]

vaccinate (vak-sin-ayt) *verb* to inoculate someone with a vaccine in order to give them immunity against a disease. **vaccination** *noun*

vaccine (vak-seen) *noun* a substance used to give someone immunity against a disease. [from a Latin word *vacca* meaning 'cow' (because serum from cows was used to protect people from smallpox)]

vacillate (**vass**-il-ayt) *verb* to keep changing your mind, to waver. **vacillation** *noun* **vacillator** *noun* [from a Latin word *vacillare* meaning 'to sway']

vacuity (və-**kew**-iti) *noun* **1** emptiness. **2** vacuousness.

vacuole (vak-yoo-ohl) *noun* (*Biology*) a tiny cavity in an organ or cell of the body, containing air or fluid etc. [same origin as for *vacuum*]

vacuous (vak-yoo-əs) *adjective* showing a lack of thought or intelligence.

vacuously adverb **vacuousness** noun [same origin as for vacuum]

vacuum noun (**vacuums** or **vacua**) 1 space completely empty of matter; space in a container from which the air has been removed. 2 a gap or feeling of emptiness left by the loss of something important ♦ His resignation has created a power vacuum. 3 (informal) a vacuum cleaner. **vacuum** verb (informal) to clean something with a vacuum cleaner. [from a Latin word vacuus meaning 'empty']
◊ The plural form vacua can be used in scientific contexts. It cannot be used as the plural of meaning 3.

vacuum cleaner noun an electrical appliance that takes up dust, dirt, etc. by suction.

vacuum flask noun a flask with a double wall that encloses a vacuum, used for keeping liquids hot or cold.

vacuum-packed adjective sealed in a pack or wrapping from which the air has been removed.

vacuum tube noun a sealed glass tube with an almost perfect vacuum, allowing the free passage of electric current.

vagabond noun a person without a settled home or regular work, a vagrant. [from a Latin word vagari meaning 'to wander']

vagary (vayg-er-i) noun (**vagaries**) an erratic and unexpected change or whim ♦ the vagaries of fashion. [from a Latin word vagari meaning 'to wander']

vagina (və-jiy-nə) noun the passage leading from the vulva to the womb in women and most female mammals. **vaginal** adjective [a Latin word meaning 'sheath']

vagrant (vay-grənt) noun a person without a settled home or regular work. **vagrancy** noun [probably from an Old French word waucrant meaning 'wandering about']

vague adjective 1 not clearly expressed or explained ♦ a vague promise. SYNONYMS: indefinite, uncertain, unclear, imprecise, undefined; (informal) woolly. 2 not clearly seen or remembered ♦ I have a vague memory of what happened. SYNONYMS: indistinct, hazy, dim. 3 not thinking or expressing your thoughts clearly or precisely. **vaguely** adverb **vagueness** noun [from a Latin word vagus meaning 'wandering']

vain adjective 1 conceited, especially about your appearance. SYNONYM: narcissistic. 2 useless or futile ♦ They made vain attempts to rescue her. SYNONYMS: futile, fruitless, ineffective, unsuccessful, abortive. 3 having no value or significance ♦ a vain boast. **in vain** without success ♦ We tried, but in vain. **to take someone's name in vain** to use someone's name in a way that shows a lack of respect. **vainly** adverb [from a Latin word vanus meaning 'empty']
◊ Do not confuse this word with **vane** or **vein**, which have different meanings.

vainglory noun (literary) extreme vanity or boastfulness. **vainglorious** adjective [via Old French from a Latin phrase vana gloria meaning 'empty glory']

valance (val-əns) noun a short curtain round the frame or canopy of a bed, or above a window or under a shelf. [from an Old French word avaler meaning 'to hang down']

vale noun a valley ♦ the Vale of Evesham. [from a Latin word vallis meaning 'valley']

valediction (vali-dik-shən) noun saying farewell; the words used in this. [from a Latin word vale meaning 'farewell' and dicere meaning 'to say' (compare benediction)]

valedictory (vali-dik-ter-i) adjective saying farewell ♦ a valedictory speech.

valence [1] (vay-ləns) noun (Chemistry) another term for **valency**.

valence [2] noun another spelling of **valance**.

valency (vay-lən-si) noun (**valencies**) (Chemistry) the combining power of an element, measured by the number of hydrogen atoms it is capable of combining with ♦ Carbon has a valency of four. [from a Latin word valentia meaning 'power']

valentine noun 1 a card sent, often anonymously, on St Valentine's day (14 February) to a person you love or are attracted to. 2 the person to whom you send this card. [named after St Valentine, an early Italian saint (possibly a Roman priest martyred c.269), who is regarded as the patron of lovers. His feast day is 14 February]

valerian (və-leer-iən) noun a strong-smelling herb with pink or white flowers. [from an Old French word valeriane]

valet (val-it or val-ay) noun 1 a man's personal attendant who takes care of his clothes and appearance. **2** a hotel employee who performs similar duties for guests.

valet *verb* (**valeted, valeting**) **1** to clean a car, especially on the inside. **2** to act as a valet to someone. [from a French word; related to *vassal*]

valetudinarian (vali-tew-din-**air**-iən) *noun* a person who pays excessive attention to keeping healthy. **valetudinarianism** *noun* [from a Latin word *valetudo* meaning 'health']

valiant *adjective* brave or courageous. **valiantly** *adverb* [from an Old French word; related to *value*]

valid (**val**-id) *adjective* **1** legally or officially able to be used or accepted ♦ *a valid passport*. **2** supporting a point or argument well, based on sound reasoning ♦ *a valid criticism*. **validity** (və-**lid**-iti) *noun* **validly** *adverb* [from a Latin word *validus* meaning 'strong']

validate (**val**-id-ayt) *verb* to confirm or prove that something is valid; to make something valid ♦ *Is there enough evidence to validate this theory?* **validation** *noun*

Valium (**val**- iəm) *noun* (*trademark*) a name for **diazepam**.

valley *noun* (**valleys**) **1** a long low area between hills or mountains, usually with a river flowing through it. **2** an area that a river flows through ♦ *the Thames valley*. [same origin as for *vale*]

valour (**val**-er) *noun* bravery, especially in battle. **valorous** *adjective* [from a Latin word *valor* meaning 'strength']

valuable *adjective* **1** worth a lot of money. SYNONYMS: costly, expensive, precious. **2** extremely useful or important. SYNONYMS: beneficial, invaluable, worthwhile. **valuables** *plural noun* valuable things, especially small personal possessions. **valuably** *adverb*

valuation *noun* an estimation of a thing's value, especially by a professional valuer; the value decided upon.

value *noun* **1** the amount of money etc. thought to be equivalent to something else or for which a thing can be exchanged. SYNONYMS: cost, worth, price. **2** how useful or important something is ♦ *He learnt the value of regular exercise.* SYNONYMS: worth, merit, benefit, use. **3** the amount or quantity denoted by a figure etc. **4** (*Music*) the duration of a sound indicated by a note.

values *plural noun* standards or principles considered valuable or important in life ♦ *moral values.*

value *verb* **1** to estimate the value of something. **2** to consider something to be of great worth or importance. SYNONYMS: appreciate, cherish, prize, esteem. **valueless** *adjective* [from a Latin word *valere* meaning 'to be strong']

value added tax *noun* a tax on the amount by which the value of an article has been increased at each stage of its production.

valuer *noun* a person who estimates values professionally.

valve *noun* **1** a device for controlling the flow of gas or liquid through a pipe or tube, especially one that allows movement in one direction only. **2** (*Anatomy and Zoology*) a structure in the heart or in a blood vessel allowing blood to flow in one direction only. **3** a device for varying the length of the tube in a brass wind instrument. **4** each piece of the shell of molluscs such as oysters. **5** a thermionic valve. [from a Latin word *valva* meaning 'section of a folding door']

vamoose *verb* (*informal*) to go away hurriedly. [from a Spanish word *vamos* meaning 'let us go']

vamp [1] *noun* the upper front part of a boot or shoe.
vamp *verb* **1** to make or repair something from odds and ends ♦ *I'm sure we can vamp something up.* **2** to improvise a musical accompaniment to a tune. [from Old French words *avant* meaning 'before' and *pie* meaning 'foot']

vamp [2] *noun* (*informal*) a woman who uses her sexual attractions to exploit men. [from *vampire*]

vampire *noun* **1** a corpse that is supposed to leave its grave at night and drink the blood of living people. **2** a person who preys on others. [from a Hungarian word *vampir*]

vampire bat *noun* a tropical bat that bites animals and people with its sharp teeth and sucks their blood.

van [1] *noun* **1** a covered vehicle for transporting goods or people. **2** a railway carriage for luggage, mail, etc., or for the use of the guard. [short for *caravan*]

van [2] *noun* the vanguard or forefront. [short for *vanguard*]

vanadium (və-**nay**-diəm) *noun* a hard grey metallic element (symbol V) used in certain steels as a hardener. [named after Vanadis, a name of the Scandinavian goddess Freyja]

Van Allen belt *noun* each of two regions of intense radiation partly surrounding the earth at heights of several thousand kilometres. [named after the American physicist J. A. Van Allen (b. 1914)]

vandal *noun* a person who deliberately destroys or damages things, especially public property. **vandalism** *noun* [named after the *Vandals*, a Germanic people who invaded Gaul, Spain, North Africa, and Rome in the 4th–5th centuries, destroying many books and works of art]

vandalize *verb* to deliberately destroy or damage property etc.

vane *noun* 1 the blade of a propeller, sail of a windmill, or other device acting on or moved by wind or water. 2 a weathervane. [from an old word *fane* meaning 'banner']
◊ Do not confuse this word with **vain** or **vein**, which have different meanings.

vanguard *noun* 1 the leading part of an army or fleet advancing or ready to do so. 2 the group of people leading the way in a new fashion, movement, or idea. [from French words *avant* meaning 'before' and *garde* meaning 'guard']

vanilla *noun* a flavouring obtained from the pods of a tropical climbing orchid. [from a Spanish word *vainilla* meaning 'little pod']

vanish *verb* to disappear suddenly and completely. SYNONYMS: disappear, evaporate, dissolve, fade, pass. [from a Latin word *evanescere* meaning 'to die away']

vanishing point *noun* the point at which parallel lines receding into the distance appear to meet.

vanity *noun* (**vanities**) 1 conceit, especially about your appearance. 2 futility, worthlessness, something vain ♦ *the pomp and vanity of this world*. [same origin as for *vain*]

vanity case *noun* a small case used by a woman for carrying a mirror and make-up.

vanquish *verb* to defeat someone thoroughly. [from a Latin word *vincere* meaning 'to conquer']

vantage point *noun* a place from which you have a good view of something. [from an old word *vantage* meaning 'advantage']

vapid (**vap**-id) *adjective* not lively or interesting, insipid. **vapidity** *noun* [from a Latin word *vapidus* meaning 'without flavour']

vaporize *verb* to change something into vapour, or to be changed into vapour. **vaporization** *noun* **vaporizer** *noun*

vapour *noun* 1 moisture or other substance diffused or suspended in the air in the form of clouds, mist, smoke, etc. 2 (*Physics*) a substance in the form of a gas that can be turned into a liquid by pressure alone. **vaporous** *adjective* [from a Latin word *vapor* meaning 'steam']

variable *adjective* 1 likely to vary; not steady or regular. SYNONYMS: changeable, inconsistent, unsteady, volatile, unpredictable. 2 able to be changed or adapted. **variable** *noun* 1 something that varies or can vary, a variable quantity. 2 (*Astronomy*) a star that periodically varies in brightness. **variability** *noun* **variably** *adverb*

variance *noun* 1 the amount by which things differ. 2 (*Mathematics*) a quantity equal to the square of the standard deviation. **at variance with** in disagreement or conflict with something. [from a Latin word *variare* meaning 'to vary']

variant *adjective* differing from something or from a standard ♦ *'Gipsy' is a variant spelling of 'gypsy'.* **variant** *noun* a variant form or spelling etc. [same origin as for *variance*]

variation *noun* 1 a change or slight difference in something. 2 a different form of something, a variant. 3 a repetition of a melody in a different (usually more elaborate) form.

varicoloured (**vair**-i-kul-erd) *adjective* consisting of several different colours.

varicose (**va**-ri-kohs) *adjective* (said about a vein) permanently swollen or enlarged. [from a Latin word *varix* meaning 'varicose vein']

varied past tense and past participle of **vary**. **varied** *adjective* of different sorts, full of variety.

variegated (vair-i-gayt-id) *adjective* marked with irregular patches or streaks of different colours. **variegation** *noun* [same origin as for *various*]

variety *noun* (**varieties**) **1** a quantity or range of different things ♦ *for a variety of reasons.* SYNONYMS: mixture, combination, assortment, array, miscellany. **2** the quality of not being the same or of not being the same at all times. SYNONYMS: variation, diversity. **3** a thing that differs from others in the same general class ♦ *There are several varieties of spaniel.* **4** a form of entertainment consisting of a series of different types of act, such as singing, dancing, and comedy. [same origin as for *various*]

various *adjective* **1** of several kinds, different from one another ♦ *for various reasons.* SYNONYMS: varied, miscellaneous, assorted, diverse, sundry. **2** more than one, individual and separate ♦ *We met various people.* **variously** *adverb* [from a Latin word *varius* meaning 'changing']

varlet *noun* (*old use*) **1** an attendant or servant. **2** a rascal or rogue. [from an Old French word]

varmint *noun* (*North Amer.*) (*dialect*) a troublesome or mischievous person or animal. [an alteration of *vermin*]

varnish *noun* a liquid that dries to form a hard shiny transparent coating, used on wood or metal etc.
varnish *verb* to coat something with varnish. [from an Old French word *vernis*]

vary *verb* (**varies, varied, varying**) **1** to make something change or make sure it is not always the same ♦ *You can vary the pressure* ♦ *Try to vary your diet.* **2** to become different ♦ *His mood varies from day to day.* SYNONYMS: change, fluctuate. **3** to be different or of different kinds ♦ *Opinions vary on this point.* [same origin as for *various*]

vascular (vas-kew-ler) *adjective* consisting of vessels or tubes for circulating blood or sap within an organism ♦ *the vascular system.* [from a Latin word *vasculum* meaning 'little vessel']

vascular bundle *noun* (*Botany*) a strand of conducting vessels in the stem or leaves of a plant, typically with phloem on the outside and xylem on the inside.

vase (vahz) *noun* an open usually tall container of glass, pottery, etc. used for holding cut flowers or as an ornament. [from a Latin word *vas* meaning 'vessel']

vasectomy (və-sekt-əmi) *noun* (**vasectomies**) surgical removal of part of each of the ducts through which semen passes from the testicles, especially as a means of sterilization. [from a Latin word *vas* meaning 'vessel' and a Greek word *ektomē* meaning 'cutting out']

Vaseline (vas-i-leen) *noun* (*trademark*) petroleum jelly used as an ointment or lubricant. [from a German word *Wasser* meaning 'water' and a Greek word *elaion* meaning 'oil']

vaso- (vay-soh) *prefix* to do with or affecting a blood vessel ♦ *vasoconstriction.* [same origin as for *vase*]

vasoconstriction *noun* the constriction of the blood vessels, which increases blood pressure.

vasodilation *noun* the widening of the blood vessels, which reduces blood pressure.

vassal *noun* a person in the Middle Ages who gave service to a lord in return for land or protection. **vassalage** *noun* [from a Latin word *vassallus* meaning 'manservant']

vast *adjective* **1** very great in area or size ♦ *a vast expanse of water.* SYNONYMS: immense, huge, enormous, massive, great. **2** (*informal*) very great ♦ *It makes a vast difference.* **vastly** *adverb* **vastness** *noun* [from a Latin word *vastus* meaning 'unoccupied, desert']

VAT *abbreviation* value added tax.

vat *noun* a tank or other very large container for holding liquids. [from an Old English word]

Vatican *noun* **1** the palace and official residence of the Pope in Rome. **2** the papal government.

vaudeville (vaw-də-vil) *noun* a kind of entertainment popular in the early 20th century, consisting of a mixture of musical and comedy acts. [from a French word]

vault[1] *noun* **1** an arched roof. **2** a cellar or underground room used to store things. **3** a secure room in a bank for storing money or valuables. **4** a burial chamber ♦ *the family vault.* **vaulted** *adjective* [from a Latin word *volvere* meaning 'to roll']

vault[2] *verb* to jump or leap over something, especially while supporting yourself on your hands or with the help of

a pole ♦ *She easily vaulted the gate* ♦ *He vaulted over the fence.*
vault *noun* a leap performed in this way. [from an Old French word *volter* meaning 'to turn a horse']

vaulting horse *noun* a padded wooden block for vaulting over in gymnastics.

vaunt *verb* to boast about something. [from a Latin word *vanus* meaning 'vain']

VC *abbreviation* Victoria Cross.

VCR *abbreviation* video cassette recorder.

VD *abbreviation* venereal disease.

VDU *abbreviation* visual display unit.

veal *noun* calf's flesh used as food. [from a Latin word *vitulus* meaning 'calf']

vector *noun* 1 (*Mathematics and Physics*) a quantity (such as velocity or force) that has both magnitude and direction. 2 the carrier of a disease or infection. **vectorial** *adjective* [a Latin word meaning 'carrier']

Veda (vay-də or vee-də) *noun* any or all of the most ancient and sacred writings of the Hindus. [a Sanskrit word meaning 'sacred knowledge']

Vedanta (ved-ahn-tə) *noun* 1 the Upanishads. 2 a Hindu philosophy founded on these.

Vedic (vay-dik or vee-dik) *adjective* to do with the Vedas.
Vedic *noun* the language of the Vedas, an early form of Sanskrit.

veena (vee-nə) *noun* an Indian musical instrument with four strings and a half-gourd at each end. [from a Sanskrit word]

veer *verb* 1 to change direction or course suddenly. 2 (said about the wind) to change gradually in a clockwise direction. (Compare **back**[2].) [from a French word *virer*]

veg (vej) *noun* (*informal*) a vegetable or vegetables.

vegan (vee-gən) *noun* a person who does not eat or use animal products at all. [from *vegetarian*]

vegetable *noun* 1 a plant or part of a plant used as food. 2 (*informal*) a person who is not capable of normal physical or mental activity, especially because of brain damage. 3 (*informal*) a person leading a dull monotonous life. [from a Latin word *vegetare* meaning 'to enliven']

vegetarian *noun* a person who does not eat meat.
vegetarian *adjective* suitable for vegetarians. **vegetarianism** *noun*

vegetate (vej-i-tayt) *verb* to live an uneventful or monotonous life. [originally meaning 'to grow like a vegetable': same origin as for *vegetable*]

vegetation *noun* plants collectively.

vegetative (vej-i-tə-tiv) *adjective* 1 to do with vegetation. 2 (*Biology*) to do with reproduction or propagation by other than sexual means, as in the propagation of plants from cuttings or runners etc., not from seeds (which involve fusion of male and female cells).

vehement (vee-i-mənt) *adjective* showing strong feeling ♦ *a vehement denial.*
vehemence *noun* **vehemently** *adverb* [from a Latin word *vehemens* meaning 'impetuous' or 'ardent']

vehicle (vee-i-kəl) *noun* 1 a means of transporting people or goods, especially on land. 2 a means by which something is communicated or displayed ♦ *The play was the perfect vehicle for this actor's talents.* [from a Latin word *vehere* meaning 'to carry']

vehicular (vi-hik-yoo-ler) *adjective* to do with vehicles ♦ *vehicular traffic.*

veil *noun* a piece of fine net or other material worn as part of a headdress or to protect or conceal the face.
veil *verb* 1 to cover something with a veil. 2 to partially conceal something ♦ *a thinly veiled threat.* **to draw a veil over** to avoid discussing or calling attention to something. **to take the veil** to become a nun. [from a Latin word *velum* meaning 'veil']

vein *noun* 1 any of the tubes carrying blood from all parts of the body to the heart. 2 any of the thread-like structures forming the framework of a leaf or of an insect's wing. 3 a narrow strip or streak of a different colour in marble, cheese, etc. 4 a long continuous or branching deposit of mineral or ore, especially in a fissure. 5 a source of something ♦ *a rich vein of satire.* 6 a mood, quality, or manner ♦ *She continued in the same humorous vein.* [from a Latin word *vena* meaning 'vein']
◊ Do not confuse this word with **vain** or **vane**, which have different meanings.

veined *adjective* filled or marked with veins.

Velcro noun (trademark) a fastener for clothes etc. consisting of two strips of fabric, one covered with tiny hooks and the other with tiny loops, which cling together when pressed. [from a French phrase velours croché meaning 'hooked velvet']

veld (velt) noun an area of open grassland in southern Africa. [an Afrikaans word, from a Dutch word veld meaning 'field']

vellum noun 1 a kind of fine parchment. 2 smooth writing paper. [same origin as for veal (because parchment was originally made from the skin of a calf)]

velocity noun (velocities) 1 the speed of something in a given direction. 2 speed. [from a Latin word velox meaning 'swift']

velodrome noun a cycle-racing track with steeply banked curves. [from a French word]

velour (vil-oor) noun a thick velvety material. [from a French word velours meaning 'velvet']

velvet noun 1 a woven fabric of silk, cotton, or nylon with a thick short pile on one side. 2 a soft furry skin covering a growing antler. **velvety** adjective [from a Latin word villus meaning 'soft fur']

velveteen noun cotton velvet.

vena cava (vee-nə kay-və) (venae cavae (vee-nee kay-vee)) noun each of the two veins carrying deoxygenated blood into the heart. [a Latin phrase meaning 'hollow vein']

venal (veen-əl) adjective 1 able to be bribed. 2 (said about conduct) influenced by bribery. **venality** (veen-al-iti) noun **venally** adverb [from a Latin word venalis meaning 'for sale']
◊ Do not confuse this word with **venial**, which has a different meaning.

vend verb to sell something or offer it for sale, especially from a slot machine. [from a Latin word vendere meaning 'to sell']

vendetta (ven-det-ə) noun a long-lasting bitter quarrel; a feud. [an Italian word, from a Latin word vindicta meaning 'vengeance']

vending machine noun a slot machine from which you can obtain drinks, chocolate, cigarettes, etc.

vendor noun (Law) a person selling something, especially a house or other property. [from vend]

veneer noun 1 a thin layer of finer wood covering the surface of a cheaper wood in furniture etc. 2 an outward show of some good quality, concealing your true nature or feelings ♦ a veneer of politeness.
veneer verb to cover something with a veneer. [via German from an Old French word fournir meaning 'to furnish']

venerable (ven-er-əbəl) adjective 1 worthy of or given great respect, especially because of age ♦ these venerable ruins. 2 the title of an archdeacon in the Church of England. **venerability** noun **venerably** adverb [same origin as for venerate]

venerate verb to regard someone or something with great respect. **veneration** noun **venerator** noun [from a Latin word venerari meaning 'to revere']

venereal (vin-eer-iəl) adjective 1 to do with venereal disease. 2 to do with sexual desire or sexual intercourse. **venereally** adverb [from the name of Venus, the Roman goddess of love]

venereal disease noun a disease contracted by sexual intercourse with a person who is already infected.

Venetian (vin-ee-shən) adjective to do with or coming from Venice.
Venetian noun a person born or living in Venice. [from a Latin word Venetia meaning 'Venice']

venetian blind noun a window blind consisting of horizontal strips that can be adjusted to let light in or shut it out.

vengeance noun punishment or retaliation for hurt or harm done to you or to someone close to you ♦ He swore to take vengeance on his wife's killers. **with a vengeance** with great intensity. [from an Old French word; related to vindictive]

vengeful adjective seeking vengeance. **vengefully** adverb **vengefulness** noun

venial (veen-iəl) adjective (said about a sin or fault) pardonable, not serious. **venially** adverb **veniality** noun [from a Latin word venia meaning 'forgiveness']
◊ Do not confuse this word with **venal**, which has a different meaning.

venison (ven-i-sən) noun meat from a deer. [from a Latin word venatio meaning 'hunting']

Venn diagram noun (Mathematics) a diagram using overlapping and intersecting circles to show the relationships between different sets of things. [named after an English mathematician J. Venn (1834–1923)]

venom (ven-əm) *noun* **1** the poisonous fluid produced by certain snakes, scorpions, etc. and injected into a victim by a bite or sting. **2** strong bitterness or aggression. [from a Latin word *venenum* meaning 'poison']

venomous (ven-əm-əs) *adjective* **1** secreting venom ♦ *venomous snakes.* **2** full of bitterness or aggression. **venomously** *adverb*

vent[1] *noun* an opening allowing air, gas, or liquid to pass out of or into a confined space ♦ *a smoke vent.*
vent *verb* **1** to express your feelings freely and openly ♦ *She vented her anger on the receptionist.* **2** to send air, gas, or liquid out through an opening. **3** to make a vent in something. **to give vent to** to express your feelings freely and openly ♦ *He finally gave vent to his anger.* [from a Latin word *ventus* meaning 'wind']

vent[2] *noun* a slit in a piece of clothing, especially a coat or jacket, at the bottom of a back or side seam. [from an Old French word *fente* meaning 'slit']

ventilate *verb* **1** to let air enter and circulate freely in a room or building. **2** to discuss an opinion or issue in public. **ventilation** *noun* [same origin as for vent[1]]

ventilator *noun* **1** a device for ventilating a room etc. **2** an apparatus for giving artificial respiration.

ventral *adjective* to do with or on the underside of an animal or plant ♦ *This fish has a ventral fin.* **ventrally** *adverb* [from a Latin word *venter* meaning 'abdomen']

ventricle (ven-trik-əl) *noun* (*Anatomy*) a cavity or chamber in an organ of the body, especially one of the two in the heart that pump blood into the arteries by contracting. [from a Latin word *ventriculus* meaning 'little belly']

ventriloquist (ven-tril-ə-kwist) *noun* an entertainer who makes their voice sound as if it comes from another source, such as a dummy. **ventriloquism** *noun* [from Latin words *venter* meaning 'abdomen' and *loqui* meaning 'to speak']

ventriloquize *verb* to use ventriloquism.

venture *noun* something you decide to do that involves risk, especially a business enterprise. SYNONYMS: enterprise, undertaking.
venture *verb* **1** to dare or be bold enough to do something ♦ *No one ventured to tell him he was mistaken.* **2** to express something although others may disagree ♦ *I wonder if I might venture an opinion.* **to venture out** or **forth** to dare to go out ♦ *We ventured out into the snow.* [from *adventure*]

venture capital *noun* capital invested in a project that involves risk. **venture capitalist** *noun*

Venture Scout *noun* a member of the senior section of the Scout Association.

venturesome *adjective* ready to take risks or do something daring.

venturi tube *noun* a device consisting of a tube with a narrow section, used to produce suction or in measuring a rate of flow. [named after the Italian physicist G. B. Venturi (1746–1822)]

venue (ven-yoo) *noun* the place where a meeting, concert, sports match, etc. is held. [from a French word *venir* meaning 'to come']

venule *noun* (*Anatomy*) a small blood vessel that joins up with others to form a vein. [from a Latin word *venula* meaning 'little vein']

veracious (ver-ay-shəs) *adjective* (*formal*) **1** truthful. **2** true. **veraciously** *adverb* [same origin as for veracity]

veracity (ver-ass-iti) *noun* truth, accuracy, or truthfulness. [from a Latin word *verus* meaning 'true']

veranda or **verandah** *noun* a roofed terrace along the side of a house. [via Hindi from a Portuguese word *varanda* meaning 'railing' or 'balcony']

verb *noun* a word used to describe an action, occurrence, or state, e.g. *bring, came, exists.* [from a Latin word *verbum* meaning 'word']

verbal *adjective* **1** to do with or in words ♦ *verbal accuracy.* **2** spoken, not written ♦ *a verbal statement.* **3** to do with verbs ♦ *verbal inflections.* **verbally** *adverb* [same origin as for verb]

verbalize *verb* to put something into words. **verbalization** *noun*

verbal noun *noun* a noun derived from a verb, such as *smoking* in *smoking is forbidden.*

verbatim (ver-**bay**-tim) *adverb & adjective* in exactly the same words, word for word ♦ *He copied down the whole paragraph verbatim.* [from a Latin word *verb* meaning 'word']

verbena (ver-**been**-ə) *noun* a kind of plant with brightly coloured and fragrant flowers. [from a Latin word meaning 'sacred bough']

verbiage (**verb**-i-ij) *noun* an excessive number of words used to express an idea. [from an Old French word *verbeier* meaning 'to chatter']

verbose (ver-**bohs**) *adjective* using more words than are needed. **verbosely** *adverb* **verbosity** (ver-**boss**-iti) *noun* [same origin as for *verb*]

verdant *adjective* green with grass or other vegetation. [from an Old French word *verd* meaning 'green']

verdict *noun* **1** the decision reached by a jury. **2** a decision or opinion given after examining, testing, or experiencing something. SYNONYMS: conclusion, finding, assessment, judgement. [from Latin words *verus* meaning 'true' and *dictum* meaning 'said']

verdigris (**verd**-i-grees) *noun* green rust on copper or brass. [from a French phrase *vert-de-gris* meaning 'green of Greece']

verdure *noun* lush green vegetation. [same origin as for *verdant*]

verge *noun* **1** an edge or border. **2** a strip of grass along the edge of a road or path. **3** the point beyond which something will begin or happen ♦ *I was on the verge of tears.*
verge *verb* **to verge on** to be very close or similar to something ♦ *Sometimes her determination verges on ruthlessness.* [via Old French from a Latin word *virga* meaning 'rod'; related to *verger*]

verger (**ver**-jer) *noun* **1** an official in a church who acts as a caretaker and attendant. **2** an official who carries the mace etc. before a bishop or other dignitary. [from a Latin word *virga* meaning 'rod']

verify *verb* (**verifies, verified, verifying**) to make sure or show that something is true or correct ♦ *Please verify these figures.* **verifiable** *adjective* **verification** *noun* **verifier** *noun* [from a Latin word *verus* meaning 'true']

verily *adverb* (old use) in truth. [from *very*]

verisimilitude (ve-ri-sim-il-i-tewd) *noun* the appearance of being true or lifelike. [from Latin words *verus* meaning 'true' and *similis* meaning 'like']

veritable *adjective* real, rightly named ♦ *a veritable villain.* **veritably** *adverb* [same origin as for *verity*]

verity *noun* (**verities**) the truth of something; a true principle or belief. [from a Latin word *veritas* meaning 'truth']

vermicelli (verm-i-**chel**-i or verm-i-**sel**-i) *noun* **1** pasta made in long thin threads. **2** very small rod-shaped pieces of chocolate used for decorating cakes etc. [an Italian word meaning 'little worms']

vermiform (**verm**-i-form) *adjective* (Zoology and Anatomy) worm-like in shape ♦ *the vermiform appendix.* [from a Latin word *vermis* meaning 'worm' and *form*]

vermilion *noun & adjective* bright red. [from a Latin word *vermiculus* meaning 'little worm']

vermin *plural noun* **1** wild animals and birds (such as foxes, rats, mice, and owls) that are harmful to crops, food, or domestic animals. **2** parasitic insects, e.g. lice. **3** people who are unpleasant or harmful to society. [from a Latin word *vermis* meaning 'worm']

verminous *adjective* infested with vermin.

vermouth (**ver**-məth) *noun* white wine flavoured with fragrant herbs, usually drunk mixed with gin. [from a French word *vermout*]

vernacular (ver-**nak**-yoo-ler) *noun* **1** the language or dialect spoken by the ordinary people of a country or region, as distinct from an official or formal language. **2** slang or indecent language. [from a Latin word *vernaculus* meaning 'domestic']

vernal *adjective* to do with or happening in the season of spring. **vernally** *adverb* [from a Latin word *ver* meaning 'spring']

vernier (**ver**-ni-er) *noun* a small movable graduated scale for indicating fractions of the main scale on a measuring instrument such as a barometer. [named after the French mathematician P. Vernier (1580–1637)]

veronica *noun* any of a number of plants with small blue, white, or pink flowers, including the speedwell. [from the name Veronica]

verruca (ver-oo-kə) *noun* a wart, especially one on the sole of the foot. [from a Latin word meaning 'wart']

versatile (ver-sə-tiyl) *adjective* able to do, or be used for, many different things. **versatility** (ver-sə-**til**-iti) *noun* [from a Latin word *versare* meaning 'to turn']

verse *noun* 1 writing arranged in short lines, usually with a particular rhythm and often with rhymes; poetry. 2 a group of lines forming a unit in a poem or song. 3 each of the short numbered sections of a chapter of the Bible. [via Old English from a Latin word *versus* meaning 'a line of writing']

versed *adjective* **versed in** experienced or skilled in something; having a knowledge of something. [from a Latin word *versatus* meaning 'engaged in something']

versify *verb* (**versifies, versified, versifying**) to express something in verse; to write verse. **versification** *noun*

version *noun* 1 a form of something that is different from the original or usual form ♦ *the de luxe version of this car* ♦ *the film version of the play.* 2 a particular person's account of something that happened. 3 a translation into another language ♦ *the Revised Version of the Bible.* [from a Latin word *versum* meaning 'turned']

verso *noun* (**versos**) the left-hand page of an open book, or the back of a sheet of paper. (Compare **recto**.) [from a Latin phrase *verso folio* meaning 'on the turned leaf']

versus *preposition* against ♦ *France versus Brazil.* [a Latin word]

vertebra (ver-tib-rə) *noun* (**vertebrae** (ver-tib-ree)) any of the series of small bones that form the backbone. **vertebral** *adjective* [from a Latin word *vertere* meaning 'to turn']

vertebrate (vert-i-brət) *noun* (*Zoology*) an animal that has a backbone. [from *vertebra*]

vertex *noun* (**vertices** (ver-ti-seez)) 1 the highest point of something. 2 (*Geometry*) the meeting point of lines that form an angle, e.g. any point of a triangle or polygon. [from a Latin word *vertex* meaning 'top of the head']

vertical *adjective* 1 at right angles to the horizontal; upright. 2 going from top to bottom, not side to side.

vertical *noun* a vertical line, part, or position. **vertically** *adverb* [from *vertex*]

vertigo (vert-i-goh) *noun* a feeling of dizziness and of losing your balance, usually caused by looking down from a great height. [a Latin word meaning 'whirling around', from *vertere* meaning 'to turn']

verve (verv) *noun* enthusiasm and liveliness. [from a French word meaning 'vigour']

very *adverb* 1 in a high degree ♦ *very good.* SYNONYMS: extremely, highly, greatly, enormously, exceedingly, really, most, truly. 2 in the fullest sense ♦ *Drink it to the very last drop.* 3 exactly ♦ *I sat in the very same seat.* **very** *adjective* 1 exact or actual ♦ *Those were her very words.* 2 extreme, utter ♦ *at the very end.* **very good** or **very well** an expression of consent. [from an Old French word *verai* meaning 'true']

Very light (vair-i or veer-i) *noun* a flare fired from a pistol for signalling or to give temporary light. [named after the American inventor E. W. Very (1847–1910)]

vesicle (vess-i-kəl) *noun* 1 (*Anatomy and Botany*) a small hollow structure in a plant or animal body. 2 (*Medicine*) a blister. **vesicular** (vis-ik-yoo-ler) *adjective* [from a Latin word *vesicula* meaning 'little bladder']

vespers *noun* a service of evening prayer in some Christian churches. [from a Latin word *vesper* meaning 'evening']

vessel *noun* 1 a hollow structure designed to travel on water and carry people or goods; a ship or boat. 2 a hollow container, especially for liquid. 3 (*Anatomy and Botany*) a tube in the body of an animal or plant, carrying or holding blood or other fluid. [same origin as for *vase*]

vest *noun* 1 a piece of underwear covering the trunk of the body. 2 (*North Amer.*) a waistcoat. **vest** *verb* to give something as an official or legal right ♦ *The power of making laws is vested in Parliament* ♦ *Parliament is vested with this power.* [from a Latin word *vestis* meaning 'piece of clothing']

vestal *adjective* to do with Vesta, the Roman goddess of the hearth and household.

vestal or **vestal virgin** *noun* (in ancient Rome) a virgin consecrated to the goddess Vesta and vowed to chastity.

vested interest *noun* a strong personal reason for wanting something to happen, usually because you will benefit from it.

vestibule (vest-i-bewl) *noun* an entrance hall or lobby of a building. [from a Latin word *vestibulum* meaning 'entrance court']

vestige *noun* **1** a trace, a small remaining bit of what once existed ♦ *Not a vestige of the abbey remains.* **2** a very small amount ♦ *There is not a vestige of truth in it.* [from a Latin word *vestigium* meaning 'footprint']

vestigial (ves-tij-iəl) *adjective* remaining as the last part of what once existed.

vestment *noun* a ceremonial robe or other piece of clothing, especially one worn by the clergy or choir at a religious service. [same origin as for *vest*]

vestry *noun* (**vestries**) a room in a church where the clergy and choir put their vestments on. [from a Latin word *vestiarium* meaning 'wardrobe']

vet *noun* a veterinary surgeon.
vet *verb* (**vetted, vetting**) to make a careful and critical examination of a person or thing, especially of someone's background and qualifications before employing them. [short for *veterinary surgeon*]

vetch *noun* a plant of the pea family, used as fodder for cattle. [from a Latin word *vicia*]

veteran *noun* a person with long experience, especially in the armed forces. [from a Latin word *vetus* meaning 'old']

veteran car *noun* a car made before 1919, or before 1905. (Compare **vintage car**.)

veterinary (vet-rin-ri) *adjective* to do with or for the medical and surgical treatment of animals. [from a Latin word *veterinae* meaning 'cattle']

veterinary surgeon *noun* a person trained to give medical and surgical treatment to animals.

veto (veet-oh) *noun* (**vetoes**) **1** the right to reject or forbid something that is proposed ♦ *the presidential veto.* **2** any refusal or prohibition.
veto *verb* (**vetoes, vetoed, vetoing**) **1** to use a veto against something. **2** to refuse to allow or accept something. [a Latin word meaning 'I forbid']

vex *verb* to make someone feel annoyed or worried. [from a Latin word *vexare* meaning 'to shake']

vexation *noun* **1** a state of annoyance or worry. **2** something that causes this.

vexatious (veks-ay-shəs) *adjective* causing annoyance or worry. **vexatiously** *adverb* **vexatiousness** *noun*

vexed question *noun* a problem that is difficult and much discussed.

VHF *abbreviation* very high frequency.

VHS *abbreviation* (*trademark*) video home system.

via (viy-ə) *preposition* **1** by way of, through ♦ *from Exeter to York via London.* **2** by means of. [a Latin word meaning 'by way of']

viable (viy-əbəl) *adjective* **1** able to work or exist successfully ♦ *a viable plan* ♦ *There is no viable alternative.* **2** (said about plants) able to live or grow. **3** (said about a fetus) sufficiently developed to be able to survive after birth. **viability** *noun* **viably** *adverb* [from a French word *vie* meaning 'life']

viaduct (viy-ə-dukt) *noun* a long bridge-like structure, usually with a series of arches, for carrying a road or railway over a valley or low ground. [from Latin words *via* meaning 'way' and *ducere* meaning 'to lead' (compare *aqueduct*)]

vial (viy-əl) *noun* a small glass bottle, especially for liquid medicine. [an alteration of *phial*]

viands (viy-əndz) *plural noun* (*old use*) items of food. [from an Old French word *viande* meaning 'food']

vibes *plural noun* (*informal*) **1** (also **vibe**) the atmosphere or mood produced by a person, place, or situation and felt by people ♦ *I get bad vibes from this place.* **2** a vibraphone. [the first meaning is short for *vibrations*]

vibrant (viy-brənt) *adjective* **1** full of energy or activity. **2** bold and strong ♦ *vibrant colours.* **vibrancy** *noun* [same origin as for *vibrate*]

vibraphone (vy-brə-fohn) *noun* a percussion instrument like a xylophone but with resonators underneath the bars that open and close electronically to give a vibrating effect. [from *vibrate* and a Greek word *phōnē* meaning 'voice']

vibrate *verb* **1** to move rapidly and continuously with small movements to

and fro; to make something do this.
2 (said about a sound) to resonate. [from a Latin word *vibrare* meaning 'to shake']

vibration *noun* a vibrating movement, sensation, or sound.
vibrations *plural noun* (*informal*) the atmosphere of a place. (Compare **vibes**.)

vibrato (vi-**brah**-toh) *noun* (**vibratos**) (*Music*) a vibrating effect in music, with rapid slight variation of pitch. [an Italian word, from *vibrare* meaning 'to vibrate']

vibrator (viy-**bray**-ter) *noun* a device that vibrates or causes vibration.

vibratory (viy-brǝ-ter-i) *adjective* causing vibration.

viburnum (viy-**ber**-nǝm) *noun* a kind of shrub, usually with white flowers. [from a Latin word meaning 'wayfaring tree']

vicar *noun* (in the Church of England) a member of the clergy in charge of a parish. [same origin as for *vicarious* (because originally a vicar looked after a parish for another clergyman, or for a monastery)]

vicarage *noun* the house of a vicar.

vicarious (vik-**air**-iǝs) *adjective* (said about feelings or emotions) not experienced yourself but felt by imagining you share someone else's experience ♦ *vicarious pleasure*. **vicariously** *adverb* **vicariousness** *noun* [from a Latin word *vicarius* meaning 'substitute']

vice [1] *noun* **1** immoral or wicked behaviour. **2** a particular form of this, a fault or bad habit ♦ *Smoking isn't one of my vices.* **3** criminal activities involving prostitution, pornography, or drugs. [from a Latin word *vitium* meaning 'fault']

vice [2] *noun* a device with two jaws that grip something and hold it firmly while you work on it, used especially in carpentry and metal-working. **vice-like** *adjective* [from a Latin word *vitis* meaning 'vine']

vice- *prefix* **1** acting as substitute or deputy for (as in *vice-captain*, *vice-president*). **2** next in rank to (as in *vice-admiral*). [from a Latin word *vice* meaning 'in place of']

viceregal (viys-**ree**-gǝl) *adjective* to do with a viceroy.

viceroy *noun* a person governing a colony or province as the sovereign's representative. [from *vice-* and an Old French word *roy* meaning 'king']

vice versa (viy-si **ver**-sǝ) *adverb* the other way round ♦ *Which do you prefer: blue spots on a yellow background or vice versa?* [a Latin phrase meaning 'the position being reversed']

vicinity (vis-**in**-iti) *noun* (**vicinities**) the area near or surrounding a particular place ♦ *Is there a library in the vicinity?* [from a Latin word *vicinus* meaning 'neighbour']

vicious (**vish**-ǝs) *adjective* **1** cruel or violent ♦ *a vicious attack.* SYNONYMS: savage, ferocious, brutal, barbaric. **2** (said about an animal) wild and dangerous. **3** spiteful or malicious ♦ *vicious lies.* **viciously** *adverb* **viciousness** *noun* [same origin as for *vice* [1]]

vicious circle *noun* a situation in which a problem produces an effect which in turn produces or intensifies the original problem.

vicissitude (viss-**iss**-i-tewd) *noun* a change of circumstances or fortune affecting your life, usually for the worse. [from a Latin word *vicissim* meaning 'in turn']

victim *noun* **1** a person who is injured, killed, robbed, etc. as the result of a crime, accident, or disaster ♦ *victims of the earthquake.* **2** a person who is tricked or swindled. **3** a living creature killed and offered as a religious sacrifice. [from a Latin word *victima*]

victimize *verb* to single someone out for cruel or unfair treatment. **victimization** *noun*

victor *noun* the winner in a battle or contest. [same origin as for *victory*]

Victorian *adjective* during or to do with the reign of Queen Victoria (1837–1901). **Victorian** *noun* a person living at this time.

Victoriana (vik-tor-i-**ah**-nǝ) *plural noun* objects from Victorian times.

Victoria plum *noun* a large red juicy variety of plum.

Victoria sandwich *noun* a kind of sponge cake with a jam filling.

victorious *adjective* having gained a victory.

victory *noun* (**victories**) success in a battle, contest, or game etc. achieved by defeating your opponent or achieving the highest score. [from a Latin word *victum* meaning 'conquered']

victualler (vit-ler) *noun* **1** a person who is licensed to sell alcoholic drinks. **2** (*old use*) a person who supplies victuals.

victuals (vit-lz) *plural noun* (*old use*) food and drink. [from a Latin word *victus* meaning 'food']

vicuña (vik-yoo-nə) *noun* **1** a South American animal related to the llama, with fine silky wool. **2** cloth made from this wool. [a Spanish word]

video (vid-i-oh) *noun* (**videos**) **1** the system of recording or broadcasting pictures on videotape. **2** a film or other recording on videotape. **3** a video cassette or video recorder.
video *verb* (**videoes, videoed, videoing**) to record something on videotape. [a Latin word meaning 'I see']

video cassette *noun* a cassette containing videotape.

videodisc *noun* a CD-ROM or other disc used to store visual images.

video game *noun* a game in which you use electronic controls to move images produced by a computer program on a monitor or television screen.

video recorder or **video cassette recorder** *noun* a device for recording television programmes on videotape and for playing video cassettes.

videotape *noun* **1** magnetic tape suitable for recording television pictures and sound. **2** a video cassette.

vie *verb* (**vies, vied, vying**) to compete eagerly with someone to achieve something ♦ *All the reporters were vying for her attention* ♦ *The children were vying with each other to see who knew the most jokes.* [probably from *envy*]

view *noun* **1** what can be seen from one place, e.g. beautiful natural scenery ♦ *the view from the summit.* SYNONYMS: scene, prospect, outlook, vista, panorama. **2** sight, range of vision ♦ *The ship sailed into view.* **3** an attitude or opinion ♦ *They have strong views about education.* **4** an inspection of something for sale ♦ *We had a private view of the exhibition before it was opened.*
view *verb* **1** to look at something. **2** to inspect something; to look over a house etc. with the idea of buying it. **3** to watch television. **4** to regard something in a particular way ♦ *We view the matter seriously.* **in full view** clearly visible. **in view of** because or as a result of ♦ *In view of the excellence of the work, we are not too concerned about the cost.* **on view** being shown or exhibited to the public. **with a**

view to with the hope or intention of. [from a Latin word *videre* meaning 'to see']

viewer *noun* **1** a person who views something. **2** a person watching a television programme. **3** a device used to look at photographic slides etc.

viewfinder *noun* a device on a camera by which the user can see the area that will be photographed through the lens.

viewpoint *noun* **1** an opinion or point of view. SYNONYMS: perspective, angle, slant, standpoint, stance, position. **2** a place giving a good view.

vigil (vij-il) *noun* **1** a period of staying awake to keep watch or to pray ♦ *We kept vigil all night* ♦ *a long vigil.* **2** an occasion when a large number of people stand outside a building at night as a peaceful demonstration. **3** the eve of a religious festival. [a Latin word meaning 'awake']

vigilant (vij-i-lənt) *adjective* watching out for possible danger or difficulties.
vigilance *noun* **vigilantly** *adverb* [from a Latin word *vigilans* meaning 'keeping watch']

vigilante (vij-il-**an**-ti) *noun* a member of a self-appointed group of people who try to prevent crime and disorder in their community, usually because they believe the official system of law enforcement is not working properly. [a Spanish word meaning 'vigilant']

vignette (veen-yet) *noun* **1** a short description or character sketch. **2** a photograph or portrait which fades into its background without a definite edge. [from a French word meaning 'little vine']

vigorous *adjective* full of strength and energy. **vigorously** *adverb* **vigorousness** *noun* [same origin as for *vigour*]

vigour *noun* **1** physical strength and good health. **2** forcefulness and energy ♦ *She continued her campaign with renewed vigour.* [from a Latin word *vigor* meaning 'strength']

Viking (viy-king) *noun* a Scandinavian trader and pirate of the 8th–11th centuries. [from an Old Norse word]

vile *adjective* **1** disgusting or foul ♦ *a vile smell.* **2** morally bad or wicked. **3** (*informal*) bad or unpleasant ♦ *this vile weather.* **vilely** *adverb* **vileness** *noun* [from a Latin word *vilis* meaning 'cheap' or 'unworthy']

vilify (vil-i-fiy) *verb* (**vilifies, vilified, vilifying**) to say unpleasant things about a person or thing. **vilification** *noun* [same origin as for *vile*]

villa *noun* 1 a large country house, especially in Italy or southern France. 2 a detached or semi-detached house in a residential district. 3 a rented holiday home abroad. [from a Latin word meaning 'country house']

village *noun* 1 a group of houses and other buildings in a country district, smaller than a town and usually having a church. 2 an area or community within a town or city. **villager** *noun* [from an Old French word; related to *villa*]

villain (vil-ən) *noun* 1 a wicked person; a person who is guilty of a crime. 2 a character in a story or play whose evil actions or motives are important in the plot. **villainy** *noun* [from a Latin word *villanus* meaning 'villager']

villainous (vil-ən-əs) *adjective* wicked, worthy of a villain. **villainously** *adverb*

villein (vil-ən or vil-ayn) *noun* a feudal tenant in the Middle Ages. [a different spelling of *villain*]

villus *noun* (**villi**) (*Anatomy*) each of the many short thin finger-like growths of tissue on some membranes of the body, especially the small intestine. [a Latin word meaning 'shaggy hair']

vim *noun* (*informal*) vigour or energy. [originally American; probably from a Latin word *vis* meaning 'energy']

vinaigrette (vin-i-gret) *noun* salad dressing made of oil and vinegar. [a French word, from *vinaigre* meaning 'vinegar']

vindicate (vin-dik-ayt) *verb* 1 to clear someone of blame or suspicion. 2 to show something to be right or justified. **vindication** *noun* **vindicator** *noun* [from a Latin word *vindicare* meaning 'to set free']

vindictive (vin-dik-tiv) *adjective* having or showing a desire for revenge; spiteful. **vindictively** *adverb* **vindictiveness** *noun* [from a Latin word *vindicta* meaning 'vengeance']

vine *noun* 1 a climbing or trailing woody-stemmed plant whose fruit is the grape. 2 a slender climbing or trailing stem. [from a Latin word *vinum* meaning 'wine']

vinegar *noun* a sour liquid made from wine, cider, malt, etc. by fermentation, used in flavouring food and for pickling. [from a Latin word *vinum* meaning 'wine' and *acer* meaning 'sour']

vinegary *adjective* 1 like vinegar. 2 sour-tempered.

vineyard (vin-yard) *noun* a plantation of vines producing grapes for making wine.

vintage (vint-ij) *noun* 1 the harvest of a season's grapes for wine-making. 2 wine made from a particular season's grapes, especially in a good year; the date of this as an indication of the wine's quality. 3 the date or period when something was produced or existed.
vintage *adjective* 1 (said about wine) of high quality and from a specified year. 2 being typical of the best of something from a past period ♦ *vintage TV drama*. [from a French word; related to *vine*]

vintage car *noun* a car made between 1919 and 1930. (Compare **veteran car**.)

vintner (vint-ner) *noun* a wine merchant. [from a Latin word *vinetum* meaning 'vineyard']

vinyl (viy-nil) *noun* a kind of plastic, especially polyvinyl chloride. [from a Latin word *vinum* meaning 'wine']

viol (viy-əl) *noun* a stringed musical instrument popular especially in the 16th–17th centuries, similar to a violin but held vertically. [from an Old French word *viele*]

viola [1] (vee-oh-lə) *noun* a stringed musical instrument slightly larger than a violin and of lower pitch. [from a Spanish or Italian word]

viola [2] (viy-ə-lə) *noun* a plant of the genus to which pansies and violets belong, especially a hybrid cultivated variety. [a Latin word meaning 'violet']

violate *verb* 1 to break or fail to follow an oath, rule, treaty, etc. 2 to treat a person or place with disrespect. 3 to rape someone. **violation** *noun* **violator** *noun* [from a Latin word *violare* meaning 'to treat violently']

violence *noun* 1 physical force intended to hurt or damage. 2 strength of feeling. 3 the strength of a natural force ♦ *the violence of the storm*. **to do violence to** 1 to use violence on someone. 2 to distort the meaning of something. [from a Latin word *violentus* meaning 'violent']

violent *adjective* **1** using or involving violence ♦ *violent crime* ♦ *a violent death.* **2** involving great force, strength, or intensity ♦ *I took a violent dislike to him.* **violently** *adverb*

violet *noun* **1** a small wild or garden plant, often with purple flowers. **2** a bluish-purple colour seen at the opposite end of the spectrum from red. **violet** *adjective* bluish-purple. [from an Old French word; related to *viola*²]

violin *noun* a musical instrument with four strings of treble pitch, played with a bow. [from an Italian word *violino* meaning 'small viola']

violinist *noun* a person who plays the violin.

violoncello (viy-ə-lən-**chel**-oh) *noun* (**violoncellos**) a formal word for a **cello**.

VIP *abbreviation* very important person.

viper *noun* a small poisonous snake. [from a Latin word *vipera* meaning 'snake']

virago (vi-**rah**-goh) *noun* (**viragos**) a fierce or bullying woman. [a Latin word meaning 'female warrior']

viral (**viy**-rəl) *adjective* to do with or caused by a virus.

virgin *noun* **1** a person, especially a woman, who has never had sexual intercourse. **2** a person who is inexperienced in a particular context ♦ *a political virgin.* **the Virgin** *noun* the Virgin Mary, mother of Christ. **virgin** *adjective* **1** to do with, being, or suitable for a virgin. **2** in its original state, not yet touched or used ♦ *virgin snow.* **virginity** *noun* [from a Latin word *virgo*]

virginal *adjective* relating to or suitable for a virgin. **virginal** *noun* a keyboard instrument of the 16th–17th centuries, the earliest form of harpsichord. [from a Latin word *virginalis* meaning 'to do with virgins' (because it was often played by young women)]

Virgo (**ver**-goh) **1** a group of stars (the Virgin), seen as representing a young woman. **2** the sign of the zodiac which the sun enters about 23 August. **Virgoan** (ver-**goh**-ən) *adjective & noun* [from a Latin word]

virile (**vi**-riyl) *adjective* having masculine strength or vigour, especially sexually. **virility** (vi-**ril**-iti) *noun* [from a Latin word *vir* meaning 'man']

virology (viyr-**ol**-əji) *noun* the scientific study of viruses. **virological** *adjective* **virologist** *noun* [from *virus* and *-logy*]

virtual *adjective* **1** almost or nearly, but not according to strict definition ♦ *She is the virtual head of the firm* ♦ *His silence was a virtual admission of guilt.* **2** (*Computing*) not physically existing as such but made by software to appear to exist. [same origin as for *virtue*]

virtual image *noun* an image (e.g. in a mirror) that appears to exist as a result of reflection or refraction.

virtually *adverb* nearly or almost.

virtual reality *noun* (*Computing*) a three-dimensional image or environment produced by a computer, that a user can interact with by means of special equipment.

virtue *noun* **1** moral goodness; a quality thought to be morally good ♦ *Patience is a virtue.* **2** an advantage or useful quality ♦ *My plan has the virtue of being simple.* **3** (*old use*) chastity or virginity. **by** or **in virtue of** because or as a result of. **to make a virtue of** to get some benefit from something unpleasant that you have to do. [from a Latin word *virtus* meaning 'worth']

virtuoso (ver-tew-**oh**-soh) *noun* (**virtuosos** or **virtuosi**) a person who excels in the technique of doing something, especially singing or playing music. **virtuosity** (ver-tew-**oss**-iti) *noun* [an Italian word meaning 'skilful']

virtuous *adjective* having or showing moral virtue. SYNONYMS: good, moral, noble, righteous, upright. **virtuously** *adverb* **virtuousness** *noun*

virulent (**vi**-rew-lənt) *adjective* **1** (said about a poison or disease) extremely strong or severe. **2** strongly and bitterly hostile ♦ *virulent abuse.* **virulence** *noun* [same origin as for *virus*]

virus (**viy**-rəs) *noun* (**viruses**) **1** a very simple organism (smaller than bacteria) capable of causing disease. **2** a disease caused by a virus. **3** (also **computer virus**) a set of instructions hidden within a computer program that is designed to destroy data. [a Latin word meaning 'poison']

visa (**vee**-zə) *noun* an official stamp or mark put on a passport by officials of a foreign country to show that the holder has permission to enter or stay in that country. [Latin word meaning 'things seen']

visage (viz-ij) *noun* a person's face or expression. [from a Latin word *visus* meaning 'sight']

vis-à-vis (veez-ah-vee) *preposition* in relation to, as compared with. [a French phrase meaning 'face to face']

viscera (vis-er-ə) *plural noun* the internal organs of the body, especially the intestines. [a Latin word meaning 'soft parts']

visceral (vis-er-əl) *adjective* 1 to do with the viscera. 2 to do with deep inward feelings, not the intellect.

viscid (vis-id) *adjective* (said about liquid) thick and gluey. **viscidity** (vis-id-iti) *noun* [same origin as for *viscous*]

viscose (vis-kohz) *noun* 1 cellulose in a viscous state, used in the manufacture of rayon etc. 2 fabric made of this.

viscount (viy-kownt) *noun* 1 a British nobleman ranking between an earl and a baron ♦ *Viscount Samuel.* 2 the courtesy title of an earl's eldest son ♦ *Viscount Linley.* **viscountess** *noun* **viscounty** *noun* [from an Old French word *visconte* meaning 'vice-count']

viscous (vis-kəs) *adjective* thick and gluey, not pouring easily. **viscosity** (vis-kos-iti) *noun* [from a Latin word *viscus* denoting a sticky substance spread on branches to catch birds]

visibility *noun* 1 being visible. 2 the distance you can see as determined by conditions of light and atmosphere ♦ *The aircraft turned back because of poor visibility.*

visible *adjective* able to be seen or noticed ♦ *The ship was still visible on the horizon.* **visibly** *adverb* [same origin as for *vision*] ◊ Do not confuse this word with **visual**, which has a different meaning.

vision *noun* 1 the ability to see, sight. 2 the ability to think about the future with imagination, insight, and wisdom ♦ *a statesman with vision.* 3 a mental image of what the future could be like. 4 something seen in a person's imagination, in a dream, or as a supernatural apparition. 5 a person or sight of unusual beauty. [from a Latin word *visum* meaning 'seen']

visionary *adjective* 1 thinking about the future with imagination, insight, and wisdom. ♦ *visionary schemes.* 3 to do with supernatural visions etc.

visionary *noun* (**visionaries**) a person with extremely imaginative ideas about the future.

visit *verb* 1 to go to see a person or place either socially or on business or for some other purpose. 2 to stay somewhere for a while. 3 (in the Bible) to inflict punishment for something on someone ♦ *The sins of the fathers will be visited upon the children.*
visit *noun* 1 going to see a person or place. 2 a short stay somewhere. [from a Latin word *visitare* meaning 'to go to see']

visitant *noun* 1 a visitor, especially a supernatural one. 2 a bird that is a visitor to an area while migrating.

visitation *noun* 1 an official visit, especially to inspect something. 2 trouble or disaster looked upon as punishment from God.

visitor *noun* 1 someone who visits a person or place. 2 a migratory bird that lives in an area for only part of the year.

visor (viy-zer) *noun* 1 the movable front part of a helmet, covering the face. 2 a fixed or movable shield at the top of a vehicle windscreen, protecting the eyes from bright sunshine. [from an Old French word; related to *visage*]

vista *noun* 1 a pleasant view, especially one seen through a long narrow opening such as an avenue of trees. 2 a mental view of a stretch of time or long series of events, especially in the future. [an Italian word meaning 'view']

visual *adjective* to do with seeing or sight ♦ *a good visual memory.* **visually** *adverb* [from a Latin word *visus* meaning 'sight'] ◊ Do not confuse this word with **visible**, which has a different meaning.

visual aid *noun* a picture, slide, film, etc. used as an aid to teaching.

visual display unit *noun* a screen that displays data being received from a computer.

visualize *verb* to form a mental picture of something. **visualization** *noun*

vital *adjective* 1 essential to the existence, success, or operation of something; extremely important. SYNONYMS: essential, crucial, indispensable, imperative. 2 connected with life, essential to life ♦ *vital functions.* 3 full of vitality ♦ *She's a very vital sort of person.*

vitals *plural noun* the important internal organs of the body. [from a Latin word *vita* meaning 'life']

vitality (viy-**tal**-iti) *noun* liveliness or energy.

vitalize *verb* to fill someone with energy and strength. **vitalization** *noun*

vitally *adverb* in a vital way, essentially.

vital statistics *noun* 1 statistics relating to population figures or births and deaths. 2 (*informal*) the measurements of a woman's bust, waist, and hips.

vitamin (**vit**-ə-min or **viy**-tə-min) *noun* any of a number of organic substances present in many foods and essential to the nutrition of people and animals. [same origin as for *vital*]

vitiate (**vish**-i-ayt) *verb* (*formal*) 1 to spoil something or make it less efficient. 2 to weaken the force of something, to make something no longer valid ♦ *This admission vitiates your claim*. **vitiation** *noun* [from a Latin word *vitium* meaning 'fault']

viticulture (**vit**-i-kul-cher) *noun* the cultivation of grapes for making wine. [from a Latin word *vitis* meaning 'vine']

vitreous (**vit**-ri-əs) *adjective* having a glass-like texture or appearance ♦ *vitreous enamel*. [from a Latin word *vitrum* meaning 'glass']

vitreous humour *noun* the transparent substance filling the eyeball.

vitrify (**vit**-ri-fiy) *verb* (**vitrifies**, **vitrified**, **vitrifying**) to convert something or be converted into glass or a glass-like substance, especially by heat. **vitrifaction** *noun* **vitrification** *noun* [from a Latin word *vitrum* meaning 'glass']

vitriol (**vit**-ri-ol) *noun* 1 sulphuric acid or one of its salts. 2 savagely hostile comments or criticism. **vitriolic** (vit-ri-**ol**-ik) *adjective* [from a Latin word *vitrum* meaning 'glass']

vituperate (vi-**tew**-per-ayt) *verb* 1 to scold someone angrily or abusively. 2 to use abusive language. **vituperation** *noun* [from a Latin word *vituperare* meaning 'to blame or find fault']

vituperative *adjective* bitter and abusive.

viva (**viy**-va) *noun* an oral examination, usually for an academic qualification. [short for *viva voce*]

vivacious (viv-**ay**-shəs) *adjective* attractively lively and high-spirited. SYNONYMS: exuberant, ebullient, lively, animated, bubbly, sparkling. **vivaciously** *adverb* **vivacity** (viv-**ass**-iti) *noun* [from a Latin word *vivere* meaning 'to live']

vivarium (viy-**vair**-iəm) *noun* (**vivaria**) a place prepared for keeping animals in conditions as similar as possible to their natural environment, for purposes of study etc. [from a Latin word *vivus* meaning 'alive']

viva voce (viy-və **voh**-chi) *adjective & adverb* (said about an examination in universities) oral rather than written; conducted orally.
viva voce *noun* an oral examination. [a Latin phrase meaning 'with the living voice']

vivid *adjective* 1 (said about light or colour) bright and strong, intense. SYNONYMS: vibrant, brilliant, dazzling. 2 producing strong and clear mental pictures ♦ *a vivid description*. SYNONYMS: graphic, powerful. 3 (said about the imagination) creating ideas or feelings in an active and lively way. **vividly** *adverb* **vividness** *noun* [from a Latin word *vividus* meaning 'full of life']

viviparous (vi-**vip**-er-əs) *adjective* producing young in a developed state from the mother's body, not hatching by means of an egg (in contrast to *oviparous*). [from Latin words *vivus* meaning 'alive' and *parere* meaning 'to bring forth']

vivisection *noun* doing surgical experiments on live animals. [from a Latin word *vivus* meaning 'alive' and *dissection*]

vixen *noun* a female fox. [from an Old English word]

viz. *adverb* namely ♦ *The case is made in three sizes, viz. large, medium, and small*. [short for a Latin word *videlicet*]
◊ In reading aloud, the word 'namely' is usually spoken where *viz.* is written.

vizier (viz-**eer**) *noun* in former times, an official of high rank in certain Muslim countries. [from an Arabic word *wazir* meaning 'chief counsellor']

V-neck *noun* a V-shaped neckline on a pullover etc.

vocabulary *noun* (**vocabularies**) 1 the body of words used in a particular subject or language. 2 the body of words known to an individual person ♦ *She has a good vocabulary*. 3 a list of difficult or foreign words with their meanings. [from a Latin word *vocabulum* meaning 'name']

vocal (voh-kəl) *adjective* **1** to do with, for, or using the voice. **2** expressing your feelings freely in speech ♦ *He was very vocal about his rights.*
vocal *noun* a piece of sung music. **vocally** *adverb* [from a Latin word *vocis* meaning 'of the voice']

vocal cords *plural noun* two strap-like membranes in the throat that can be made to vibrate and produce sounds.

vocalist (voh-kəl-ist) *noun* a singer, especially in jazz or pop music.

vocalize (voh-kə-liyz) *verb* to use your voice.

vocation (və-kay-shən) *noun* **1** a strong desire to do or a natural liking for a particular kind of work. **2** a person's job or occupation. **3** a feeling of being called by God to do something. [from a Latin word *vocare* meaning 'to call']

vocational *adjective* teaching you the skills you need for a particular job or profession ♦ *vocational training.*

vocational guidance *noun* advice about suitable careers.

vociferate (və-sif-er-ayt) *verb* to say something loudly or noisily. **vociferation** *noun* [from Latin words *vocis* meaning 'of the voice' and *ferre* meaning 'to carry']

vociferous (və-sif-er-əs) *adjective* expressing your views loudly and forcibly. **vociferously** *adverb* **vociferousness** *noun* [same origin as for *vociferate*]

vodka *noun* an alcoholic spirit of Russian origin, distilled chiefly from rye. [from a Russian word *voda* meaning 'water']

vogue *noun* **1** the current fashion or style ♦ *Large hats are the vogue.* **2** a period of being popular or fashionable. **in vogue** in fashion ♦ *Stripy dresses seem to be in vogue.* [via French from an Italian word *voga* meaning 'rowing' or 'fashion']

voice *noun* **1** sounds formed in the larynx and uttered by the mouth, especially in speaking or singing. **2** the ability to produce such sounds ♦ *She has a cold and has lost her voice.* ♦ *The tenor is in good voice.* **3** someone expressing a particular opinion about something ♦ *Ruth's the only dissenting voice.* **4** expression of your opinion, the right to express it, or the opinion itself ♦ *He lost no time in giving voice to his indignation.* ♦ *I have no voice in the*

matter. **5** (*Grammar*) either of the sets of forms of a verb that show the relation of the subject to the action, either the *active voice* or the *passive voice* (see the entries for **active** and **passive**).
voice *verb* **1** to put something into words ♦ *We all voiced our opinions.* **2** to utter something with resonance of the vocal cords, not only with the breath. [from a Latin word *vox* meaning 'voice']

voicemail *noun* an electronic system that can store messages from telephone callers.

voice-over *noun* narration in a film or broadcast by a voice not accompanied by a picture of the speaker.

void *adjective* **1** not legally valid or binding. **2** empty or vacant. **3** lacking something ♦ *an act void of all humour.*
void *noun* an empty space or hole.
void *verb* **1** to make something legally void ♦ *The contract was voided by his death.* **2** to empty the bowels or bladder. [from an Old French word *vuide* meaning 'unoccupied'; related to *vacant*]

voile (voil) *noun* a very thin almost transparent dress material. [a French word meaning 'veil']

volatile (vol-ə-tiyl) *adjective* **1** (said about a liquid) evaporating quickly. **2** (said about a person) changing quickly from one mood or emotion to another. **3** changing quickly and unpredictably. **volatility** (vol-ə-til-iti) *noun* [from a Latin word *volatilis* meaning 'flying']

vol-au-vent (vol-oh-vahn) *noun* a pie of puff pastry filled with a sauce containing meat or fish. [a French word meaning 'flight in the wind']

volcanic *adjective* to do with or from a volcano. **volcanically** *adverb*

volcano *noun* (**volcanoes** or **volcanos**) a mountain or hill with openings through which lava, cinders, hot gases, etc., from below the earth's crust are or have been thrown out. [an Italian word, from the name of Vulcan, the Roman god of fire]

vole (vohl) *noun* a small mouse-like rodent with a rounded snout and small ears. [from an Old Norse word]

volition (və-lish-ən) *noun* using your own will in choosing to do something ♦ *She left of her own volition.* [from a Latin word *volo* meaning 'I wish']

volley *noun* (**volleys**) **1** a number of bullets,

shells, arrows, etc. fired at the same time.
2 a number of questions or remarks
directed in quick succession at someone
♦ *a volley of abuse.* **3** hitting the ball in
tennis, football, etc. before it touches the
ground.
volley *verb* (**volleys, volleyed, volleying**)
1 to hit a ball before it touches the
ground. **2** to fire or say things in a volley.
[from a Latin word *volare* meaning 'to fly']

volleyball *noun* a game for two teams of
players who hit a large ball to and fro over
a high net with their hands.

volt *noun* a unit of electromotive force, the
force sufficient to carry one ampere of
current against one ohm resistance.
[named after the Italian physicist A. Volta
(1745–1824), who discovered how to
produce electricity by a chemical
reaction]

voltage (**vohl**-tij) *noun* electromotive force
expressed in volts.

voltaic (vol-**tay**-ik) *adjective* an old word for
galvanic.

volte-face (volt-**fahs**) *noun* a sudden and
complete reversal in your attitude
towards something. [a French phrase
meaning 'turning face']

voltmeter *noun* an instrument for
measuring electric potential in volts.

voluble (**vol**-yoo-bəl) *adjective* talking very
much; speaking or spoken with great
fluency. **volubility** (vol-yoo-**bil**-iti) *noun*
volubly *adverb* [from a Latin word *volubilis*
meaning 'rolling']

volume *noun* **1** the amount of space (often
expressed in cubic units) that a
three-dimensional thing occupies or
contains. **2** an amount or quantity of
something ♦ *The volume of business has
increased.* **3** the strength or power of
sound ♦ *Turn the volume up.* **4** a book,
especially one of a set. [from a Latin word
volumen meaning 'a roll' (because ancient
books were made in a rolled form)]

volumetric (vol-yoo-**met**-rik) *adjective* to do
with the measurement of volume.
volumetrically *adverb* [from *volume* and
metric]

voluminous (vəl-yoo-min-əs) *adjective*
1 (said about a piece of clothing) large and
full, billowing out ♦ *a voluminous skirt.*
2 having great volume, able to hold a lot
♦ *a voluminous bag.* **3** (said about writings)
great in quantity. **voluminously** *adverb*

voluminousness *noun* [from a Latin word
voluminosus meaning 'having many coils']

voluntary *adjective* **1** done or doing
something willingly and not because you
are forced to do it. **2** working or done
without payment ♦ *voluntary work.* **3** (said
about an organization) maintained by
voluntary contributions or voluntary
workers. **4** (said about bodily movements)
consciously controlled by the brain.
voluntary *noun* (**voluntaries**) an organ solo
played before, during, or after a church
service. **voluntarily** *adverb* **voluntariness**
noun [from a Latin word *voluntas* meaning
'the will']

volunteer *noun* **1** a person who offers to do
something. **2** a person who enrols for
military service voluntarily, not as a
conscript. **3** a person who works for an
organization without being paid.
volunteer *verb* **1** to give or offer to do
something of your own accord, without
being asked or forced to ♦ *Michael
volunteered to do the cooking* ♦ *Several people
volunteered advice.* **2** to be a volunteer.
[from a French word *volontaire* meaning
'voluntary']

voluptuous (vəl-up-**tew**-əs) *adjective*
1 giving a sensation of luxury and sensual
pleasure. **2** fond of luxury or sumptuous
living. **3** (said about a woman) having an
attractively curved figure. **voluptuously**
adverb **voluptuousness** *noun* [from a Latin
word *voluptas* meaning 'pleasure']

volute (vəl-**yoot**) *noun* (Architecture) a spiral
scroll in stonework. [from a Latin word
volutum meaning 'rolled']

vomit *verb* (**vomited, vomiting**) **1** to bring
up matter from the stomach and out
through the mouth, to be sick. **2** to throw
something out violently.
vomit *noun* matter vomited from the
stomach. [from a Latin word *vomere*
meaning 'to vomit']

voodoo *noun* a form of religion based on
belief in witchcraft and magical rites,
practised in the Caribbean and the
southern US. **voodooism** *noun* **voodooist**
noun [via American French from a West
African language]

voracious (ver-**ay**-shəs) *adjective* **1** wanting
or eating great quantities of food.
2 eagerly consuming something ♦ *a
voracious reader.* **voraciously** *adverb* **voracity**
(ver-**ass**-iti) *noun* [from a Latin word *vorare*
meaning 'to devour']

-vore *suffix* forming nouns meaning 'eating or feeding on something' (as in *carnivore*). [same origin as for *voracious*]

-vorous *suffix* forming adjectives corresponding to nouns ending in *-vore* (as in *carnivorous*).

vortex *noun* (**vortices** (vor-ti-seez) or **vortexes**) a whirling mass of water or air, a whirlpool or whirlwind. [a Latin word]

vote *noun* 1 a formal expression of your opinion or choice on a matter under discussion, e.g. by ballot or show of hands. SYNONYMS: ballot, election, poll, referendum. 2 an opinion or choice expressed in this way ♦ *The vote went against accepting the plan.* 3 the total number of votes given by a certain group ♦ *Such a policy will lose us the middle-class vote.* 4 the right to vote ♦ *Today people get the vote at 18.*
vote *verb* 1 to express an opinion or choice by a vote. 2 to decide something by a majority of votes ♦ *The union voted to accept the deal.* 3 (*informal*) to declare something by general consent ♦ *The party was voted a great success.* 4 (*informal*) to suggest something ♦ *I vote that we scrap the whole idea.* **voter** *noun* [from a Latin word *votum* meaning 'a wish or vow']

votive (voh-tiv) *adjective* given in fulfilment of a vow ♦ *votive offerings at the shrine.* [same origin as for *vote*]

vouch *verb* **to vouch for** to guarantee that someone or something is reliable, genuine, or true ♦ *I will vouch for his honesty.* [from an Old French word *voucher* meaning 'to summon'; related to *vocation*]

voucher *noun* 1 a piece of paper that can be exchanged for certain goods or services. 2 a document establishing that money has been paid or goods delivered. [from *vouch*]

vouchsafe *verb* to give or grant something in a gracious or condescending manner ♦ *She did not vouchsafe a reply.* [from *vouch* and *safe*]

vow *noun* a solemn promise or undertaking, especially in the form of an oath to God or a god or saint.
vow *verb* to promise solemnly to do something, to make a vow ♦ *They vowed vengeance against their oppressor.* SYNONYMS: pledge, swear. [from an Old French word *vou*; related to *vote*]

vowel *noun* 1 any of the letters of the alphabet a, e, i, o, and u. 2 a speech sound made without audible stopping of the breath. [from a Latin phrase *vocalis littera* meaning 'vocal letter']

voyage *noun* a journey by water or in space, especially a long one.
voyage *verb* to go on a voyage. **voyager** *noun* [from an Old French word *voiage*]

vs *abbreviation* versus.

VSO *abbreviation* Voluntary Service Overseas.

VTO *abbreviation* vertical take-off.

VTOL *abbreviation* vertical take-off and landing.

vulcanite *noun* hard black vulcanized rubber.

vulcanize *verb* to treat rubber or similar material with sulphur at a high temperature in order to increase its elasticity and strength. **vulcanization** *noun* [same origin as for *volcano*]

vulgar *adjective* 1 lacking refinement or good taste. 2 rude or coarse. 3 (*old use*) to do with or used by ordinary people. **vulgarity** *noun* **vulgarly** *adverb* [from a Latin word *vulgus* meaning 'the ordinary people']

vulgar fraction *noun* a fraction represented by numbers above and below a line (e.g. $\frac{2}{3}$, $\frac{5}{8}$), not a decimal fraction.

vulgarian (vul-gair-iǝn) *noun* a vulgar person, especially someone who is rich.

vulgarism *noun* 1 a coarse word or phrase. 2 a word or phrase used mainly by people who are ignorant of standard usage.

vulgarize *verb* 1 to make a person or manners etc. less refined. 2 to reduce something to the level of being usual or ordinary, to spoil something by making it ordinary or too well known. **vulgarization** *noun*

Vulgate (vul-gayt) *noun* the 4th-century Latin version of the Bible. [from a Latin phrase *vulgata editio* meaning 'edition prepared for the public']

vulnerable (vul-ner-ǝbǝl) *adjective* 1 able to be hurt or harmed. 2 unprotected, exposed to danger or attack. **vulnerability** *noun* **vulnerably** *adverb* [from a Latin word *vulnus* meaning 'wound']

vulpine (vul-piyn) *adjective* to do with or like a fox. [from a Latin word *vulpes* meaning 'fox']

vulture *noun* 1 a large bird of prey that lives on the flesh of dead animals. 2 a greedy person seeking to profit from the misfortunes of others. [from a Latin word *vulturius*]

vulva *noun* the external parts of the female genitals. [a Latin word meaning 'womb']

vying present participle of **vie**.

Ww

W the twenty-third letter of the English alphabet.

W *abbreviation* 1 watt(s). 2 west or western. 3 (*Chemistry*) the symbol for tungsten.

wacky *adjective* (**wackier, wackiest**) crazy or silly. **wackiness** *noun* [from *whack* and -*y*]

wad (wod) *noun* 1 a lump or bundle of soft material used to keep things apart or in place, stop up a hole, etc. 2 a bundle of banknotes or documents.
wad *verb* (**wadded, wadding**) to pad, line, or stuff something with soft material. [from a Dutch word]

wadding *noun* soft material used for padding, packing, or lining things.

waddle *verb* to walk with short steps, swaying from side to side.
waddle *noun* a waddling walk. [probably from *wade*]

wade *verb* 1 to walk through water or mud etc. 2 to read through something with effort because it is dull, difficult, or long ♦ *I've been wading through his latest novel.* [from an Old English word *wadan* meaning 'to move onward']

wader or **wading bird** *noun* any long-legged waterbird that wades in shallow water.
waders *plural noun* high waterproof boots worn by anglers.

wadi (wod-i) *noun* (**wadis**) a rocky river bed in North Africa and neighbouring countries that is dry except in the rainy season. [an Arabic word]

wafer *noun* 1 a kind of thin light biscuit. 2 a thin disc of unleavened bread used in the Eucharist. [from an Old French word *waufre*; related to *waffle*²]

wafer-thin *adjective* very thin.

waffle¹ (wof-əl) *noun* (*informal*) vague wordy talk or writing.
waffle *verb* to talk or write waffle. [from a dialect word *waff* meaning 'to yelp']

waffle² (wof-əl) *noun* a small cake made of batter and eaten hot, cooked in a waffle iron. [from a Dutch word *wafel*]

waffle iron *noun* a utensil for baking waffles, which has two shallow metal pans hinged together.

waft (woft) *verb* to float gently and easily through the air or over water; to make something do this.
waft *noun* 1 a gentle movement of air. 2 a scent carried in the air. [from an Old German or Dutch word *wachten* meaning 'to guard']

wag¹ *verb* (**wagged, wagging**) 1 to move or make something move briskly to and fro ♦ *a dog wagging its tail.* 2 (said about the tongue) to move rapidly in talk or gossip ♦ *Tongues are wagging, you know.*
wag *noun* a single wagging movement. [from an Old English word *wagian* meaning 'to sway']

wag² *noun* a person who is fond of making jokes or playing practical jokes. [from an old word *waghalter* meaning 'someone likely to be hanged']

wage *noun* or **wages** *plural noun* a regular payment to an employee in return for work or services ♦ *He earns a good wage* ♦ *He earns good wages.*
wage *verb* to carry on a war or campaign. SYNONYMS: conduct, fight, pursue, (*formal*) prosecute. [via Old French from a Germanic word]

wage-earner *noun* the person who earns money by working in order to support a household.

wager (way-jer) *noun* a bet.
wager *verb* to bet. [from an Old French word *wageure*; related to *wage*]

waggish *adjective* to do with or like a wag, humorous. **waggishly** *adverb* **waggishness** *noun*

waggle *verb* to move or make something move quickly to and fro ♦ *Can you waggle your ears?*
waggle *noun* a waggling or wobbling movement. [from *wag*¹]

wagon or **waggon** *noun* 1 a four-wheeled vehicle for carrying goods, pulled by horses or oxen. 2 an open railway truck, e.g. for coal. [from a Dutch word *wagen*]

wagon-lit (vag-awn-**lee**) noun (**wagons-lits** (vag-awn-**lee**)) a sleeping car on a continental railway. [a French word]

wagon train noun a convoy of covered horse-drawn wagons, used by settlers in North America.

wagtail noun any of several small birds with a long tail that moves up and down constantly when the bird is standing.

waif noun a homeless and helpless person, especially a child. [from an Old French word]

wail verb 1 to make a long sad cry. 2 (said about the wind) to make a sound like a person wailing.
wail noun a wailing cry, sound, or utterance. [from an Old Norse word]

wain noun (old use) a farm wagon. [from an Old English word]

wainscot noun wooden panelling on the wall of a room. [from an Old German word]

wainscoting noun a wainscot, or material used for this.

waist noun 1 the part of the human body below the ribs and above the bones of the pelvis, normally narrower than the rest of the body. 2 the part of a piece of clothing covering this. 3 a narrow part in the middle of something ♦ the waist of an hourglass. **waisted** adjective [probably from an Old English word]

waistband noun a strip of cloth that fits round the waist, e.g. at the top of a skirt.

waistcoat noun a close-fitting waist-length piece of clothing with no sleeves or collar, buttoned down the front and usually worn over a shirt and under a jacket.

waistline noun 1 the amount you measure around your waist. 2 the narrowest part of a piece of clothing, fitting at or just above or below the waist.

wait verb 1 to stay somewhere or delay doing something for a specified time or until something happens ♦ We waited until evening ♦ You'll have to wait your turn. 2 to be left to be dealt with at a later time ♦ This question will have to wait until our next meeting. 3 to be ready for someone ♦ A lovely stew is waiting for you when you get here. 4 to wait on people at a meal.
wait noun an act or period of waiting ♦ We had a long wait for the train. **to lie in wait** to be hiding ready to surprise or attack

someone. **to wait on 1** to hand food and drink to people at a meal. **2** to fetch and carry for someone as an attendant. **to wait up** to delay going to bed until someone has come home. [from an Old French word waitier; related to **wake**[1]]

waiter noun a man who serves people with food and drink in a restaurant.

waiting list noun a list of people waiting for a chance to obtain something when it becomes available.

waiting room noun a room for people to wait in, e.g. at a railway station or a doctor's or dentist's premises.

waitress noun a woman who serves people with food and drink in a restaurant.

waive verb to refrain from using or insisting upon a right or claim ♦ She waived her right to first class travel. [from an Old French word meaning 'to abandon' (compare waif)]
◊ Do not confuse this word with **wave**, which has a different meaning.

waiver noun the waiving of a right or claim; a document recording this.
◊ Do not confuse this word with **waver**, which has a different meaning.

wake[1] verb (**woke**, **woken**) (also **wake up**) to stop sleeping, or to make someone stop sleeping. SYNONYMS: (with object) waken, awaken, rouse, arouse, stir, call.
wake noun (Irish) a watch by a corpse before burial, or a party held after a funeral.
wakes plural noun an annual holiday in some parts of northern England ♦ wakes week. **to wake up** to become alert. **to wake someone up** to make someone feel more lively or pay attention. **to wake up to** to become aware of something ♦ He has finally woken up to the seriousness of the situation. [from an Old English word]

wake[2] noun 1 the track left on the water's surface by a moving ship etc. 2 air-currents left behind an aircraft etc. moving through air. **in the wake of** behind; following after. [probably from an Old Norse word]

wakeful adjective 1 (said about a person) unable to sleep. 2 (said about a night etc.) with little sleep.

waken verb to wake or make someone wake from sleep.

waking adjective being awake ♦ in his waking hours.

walk *verb* **1** to move along by lifting and setting down each foot in turn so that one foot is on the ground while the other is being lifted. **2** (said about quadrupeds) to go with the slowest gait, always having at least two feet on the ground. **3** to travel or go on foot; to take exercise in this way. **4** to go over somewhere on foot ♦ *We used to walk the fields in search of wild flowers.* **5** to cause someone to walk with you; to go with someone on foot ♦ *I'll walk you to your car.* **6** to take a dog out for exercise. **7** (said about a ghost) to appear.
walk *noun* **1** a journey on foot, especially for pleasure or exercise ♦ *Let's go for a walk.* **2** the manner or style of walking; a walking pace. **3** a path or route for walking. **to walk all over** (*informal*) **1** to treat someone badly or with disrespect ♦ *She lets her husband walk all over her.* **2** to defeat someone easily. **to walk away** to leave a difficult situation instead of staying to deal with it. **to walk off with** (*informal*) **3** to win something easily ♦ *She walked off with the first prize.* **4** to steal something. **to walk out 1** to depart suddenly and angrily. **2** to go on strike. **3** (*old use*) to go for walks with a person in courtship. **to walk out on** to abandon or desert someone. **to walk tall** to feel justifiable pride. [from an Old English word *wealcan* meaning 'to roll' or 'to toss']

walkabout *noun* **1** an informal stroll among a crowd by an important visitor. **2** a journey on foot in the bush made by an Australian Aboriginal.

walker *noun* **1** a person who walks. **2** a framework that supports a baby learning to walk. **3** a walking frame.

walkie-talkie *noun* a portable radio transmitter and receiver.

walking frame *noun* a frame used by an infirm or disabled person for support while walking.

walking stick *noun* a stick carried or used as a support while walking.

Walkman *noun* (**Walkmans** or **Walkmen**) (*trademark*) a personal stereo.

walk of life *noun* a person's occupation or social position.

walkout *noun* a sudden angry departure, especially as a protest or strike.

walkover *noun* an easy victory.

walkway *noun* a passage or path for walking along, especially one connecting different sections of a building.

wall *noun* **1** a continuous upright structure forming one of the sides of a building or room, or serving to enclose, protect, or divide an area. **2** something thought of as resembling this in form or function ♦ *a wall of fire* ♦ *a wall of silence.* **3** the outside part of a hollow structure; tissue surrounding an organ of the body etc. ♦ *the stomach wall.*
wall *verb* to surround, enclose, or block something with a wall ♦ *a walled garden* ♦ *We are going to wall up the fireplace.* **to drive someone up the wall** (*informal*) to make someone very irritated or furious. **to go to the wall** (*informal*) (said about a business) to fail. [from an Old English word]

wallaby (wol-ǝ-bi) *noun* (**wallabies**) a kind of small kangaroo. [from an Australian Aboriginal word]

wallet *noun* a small flat folding case for holding banknotes, credit cards, etc. [via Old French from a Germanic word]

wall-eyed *adjective* **1** having eyes that show an abnormal amount of white, especially because of a squint. **2** having eyes with a white iris.

wallflower *noun* **1** a garden plant blooming in spring, with clusters of fragrant flowers. **2** (*informal*) a shy person who no one talks to or dances with at a party. [so called because it is often found growing on old walls]

Walloon (wol-oon) *noun* **1** a member of a people living in southern Belgium and neighbouring parts of France. **2** their language, a French dialect. [from a French word *Wallon*]

wallop *verb* (**walloped, walloping**) (*informal*) **1** to strike or hit someone or something very hard. **2** to heavily defeat someone. **wallop** *noun* (*informal*) a heavy blow or punch. [from an Old French word; related to *gallop*]

walloping *adjective* (*informal*) big ♦ *a walloping lie.*
walloping *noun* (*informal*) a beating or defeat.

wallow *verb* **1** to roll about in water or mud. **2** to get great pleasure by being surrounded by something ♦ *a weekend wallowing in luxury.*
wallow *noun* **1** the act of wallowing. **2** an area of mud or shallow water where mammals go to wallow. [from an Old English word *walwian* meaning 'to roll about']

wall painting *noun* a painting applied directly to the surface of a wall.

wallpaper *noun* paper used for covering the inside walls of rooms.
wallpaper *verb* to put wallpaper on the walls of a room.

wall-to-wall *adjective* 1 (said about a carpet) covering the whole floor of a room. 2 (*informal*) numerous or plentiful.

wally *noun* (**wallies**) (*informal*) a stupid person. [perhaps from the name Walter]

walnut *noun* 1 a nut containing an edible kernel with a wrinkled surface. 2 the tree that bears this nut. 3 the wood of this tree, used in making furniture, especially as a veneer. [from an Old English word *walh-hnutu*]

walrus *noun* a large amphibious animal of Arctic regions, related to the seal and having a pair of long tusks. [probably from a Dutch word]

waltz *noun* 1 a ballroom dance for couples, with a graceful flowing melody in triple time. 2 a piece of music for this.
waltz *verb* 1 to dance a waltz; to lead someone in a waltz. 2 (*informal*) to move somewhere in a very casual or confident way ♦ *You can't just waltz in and expect a warm welcome.* **waltzer** *noun* [from a German word *walzen* meaning 'to revolve']

wan (wonn) *adjective* 1 pale from being ill or tired. 2 (said about a smile) faint and strained. **wanly** *adverb* **wanness** *noun* [from an Old English word *wann* meaning 'dark']

wand *noun* 1 a slender stick carried in the hand, used by someone performing magic or magic tricks. 2 a pen-like photoelectric device for passing over a bar code. [from an Old Norse word]

wander *verb* 1 to go from place to place without a settled route or destination or a special purpose. SYNONYMS: ramble, roam, rove, range, stray. 2 to go off course; to stray from your group or from a place ♦ *Don't wander from the path or you'll get lost.* 3 to be distracted or digress from a subject ♦ *He let his attention wander* ♦ *You're wandering off the point again.* 4 (said about eyes) to move slowly from looking at one thing to looking at something else. 5 (said about a road or river) to wind or meander.
wander *noun* an act of wandering.
wanderer *noun* [from an Old English word *wandrian*]

wanderlust *noun* a strong desire to travel. [from a German word]

wane *verb* 1 (said about the moon) to show a gradually decreasing area of brightness after being full. 2 to become less, smaller, or weaker ♦ *His popularity was waning.*
wane *noun* **on the wane** becoming less or weaker. [from an Old English word *wanian* meaning 'to reduce']

wangle *verb* (*informal*) to get or arrange something by using trickery, clever planning, or persuasion ♦ *He's managed to wangle himself a trip to Paris.* [origin unknown]

want *verb* 1 to have a desire or wish for something. SYNONYMS: desire, fancy, covet, crave, wish for, hanker after, long for, yearn for. 2 to wish to speak to someone or need their presence ♦ *You are wanted upstairs.* 3 (*informal*) to require or need something ♦ *Your hair wants cutting* ♦ *You want to be more careful.* 4 (*formal*) to be lacking in something ♦ *She doesn't want confidence.*
want *noun* 1 a desire or wish to have something ♦ *a man of few wants.* 2 lack or need of something, deficiency ♦ *The plants died from want of water.* 3 being poor and lacking the necessities of life ♦ *Many families here are living in great want.* **to want for** to lack something that you need ♦ *Her children want for nothing.* [from an Old Norse word]

wanted *adjective* (said about a suspected criminal) being sought by the police for questioning or arrest.

wanting *adjective* lacking in what is needed or usual; deficient.

wanton (wonn-tən) *adjective* 1 done deliberately without any provocation or motive ♦ *wanton vandalism.* 2 sexually immoral or promiscuous. **wantonly** *adverb* **wantonness** *noun* [from an Old English word]

WAP *abbreviation* Wireless Application Protocol, a means of connecting a mobile phone to the Internet.

wapiti (wop-it-i) *noun* a North American elk. [a Native American word]

war *noun* 1 fighting between nations or groups, especially using armed forces. SYNONYMS: conflict, hostilities, warfare. 2 a state of competition or hostility between people ♦ *a price war.* 3 a strong campaign against something ♦ *a war on drugs.* **at war** taking part in a war. **to have been in the wars** (*humorous*) to show signs of injury or rough usage. [via Old French from a Germanic word]

warble *verb* to sing, especially with a gentle trilling note as some birds do. **warble** *noun* a warbling sound. [via Old French from a Germanic word]

warble fly *noun* a kind of fly whose larvae burrow under the skin of cattle, producing painful swellings called *warbles*. [origin unknown]

warbler *noun* any of several small songbirds.

war crime *noun* a crime committed during a war that breaks international rules of war, such as genocide. **war criminal** *noun*

war cry *noun* **1** a word or cry shouted in attacking or in rallying your side. **2** the slogan of a political or other party.

ward *noun* **1** a room with beds for a particular group of patients in a hospital. **2** an area of a city or borough electing a councillor to represent it. **3** a child or young person under the care of a guardian or the protection of a law court. **4** each of the notches and ridges in a key (or the corresponding parts in a lock) designed to prevent the lock from being opened by a key other than the right one. **ward** *verb* **to ward someone** or **something off** to keep at a distance a person or thing that threatens danger. [from an Old English word *weard* meaning 'guard']

-ward *suffix* forming adjectives and adverbs showing direction (e.g. *backward, forward, homeward*). [from an Old English word]

war dance *noun* a ceremonial dance performed before a battle or after a victory.

warden *noun* **1** an official who supervises a place or procedure. **2** the head of certain schools, colleges, or other institutions. **3** (*North Amer.*) a prison governor. [from an Old French word; related to *guardian*]

warder *noun* a prison guard. **wardress** *noun* [from an Old French word; related to *guard*]

wardrobe *noun* **1** a large cupboard where clothes are hung or stored. **2** a person's stock of clothes. **3** the stock of costumes of a theatre or film company, or the department in charge of this. [from an Old French word *warder* meaning 'to guard' and *robe*]

wardroom *noun* the mess room for commissioned officers on a warship.

-wards *suffix* forming adverbs showing direction (e.g. *backwards, forwards*). [from an Old English word *-weardes* meaning '-ward']

ware *noun* **1** (used in compound words) manufactured articles of a particular type ♦ *hardware* ♦ *silverware*. **2** (used in compound words) pottery of a particular type ♦ *delftware*. **wares** *plural noun* goods offered for sale ♦ *traders displaying their wares*. [from an Old English word *waru* meaning 'commodities']

warehouse *noun* a large building for storing goods or for storing furniture on behalf of its owners. [from *ware*¹ and *house*]

warfare *noun* fighting a war; a particular form of this ♦ *guerrilla warfare*.

war game *noun* **1** a training exercise in which sets of armed forces take part in mock opposition to each other. **2** a game in which models representing troops etc. are moved about on maps.

warhead *noun* the explosive head of a missile, torpedo, or similar weapon.

warlike *adjective* **1** fond of making war, aggressive ♦ *a warlike people*. **2** to do with or for war ♦ *warlike preparations*.

warlock *noun* a man who practises witchcraft. [from an Old English word *wær-loga* meaning 'traitor']

warlord *noun* a powerful military commander in charge of a region.

warm *adjective* **1** fairly hot, not cold or cool. **2** (said about clothes etc.) keeping the body warm. **3** friendly or enthusiastic ♦ *a warm supporter* ♦ *a warm welcome*. **4** kindly and affectionate ♦ *She has a warm heart*. **5** (said about colours) suggesting warmth. **6** (said about the scent in hunting) still fairly fresh and strong. **7** (in children's games) close to finding or guessing what is sought. **warm** *verb* to make something warm, or to become warm. **warm** *noun* **1** a warm place or area. **2** an act of warming. **to warm to 1** to start to like someone more. **2** to become more enthusiastic about a task. **to warm up 1** to become warm. **2** (said about an engine etc.) to reach a temperature high enough for it to work properly. **3** to prepare for athletic exercise by practice beforehand. **4** to become more lively or receptive. **to warm someone up** to put an audience into a receptive mood before a performance. **to warm something up 1** to make something warm. **2** to reheat food or drink. **3** to make something more lively. **warmish** adjective **warmly** adverb **warmness** noun [from an Old English word]

warm-blooded adjective having a body temperature that remains warm (ranging from 36° to 42°C) permanently.

war memorial noun a memorial erected to those who died in a war.

warm-hearted noun sympathetic and kind.

warming pan noun a covered metal pan with a long handle, formerly filled with hot coals and used for warming beds.

warmonger (wor-mung-ger) noun a person who seeks to bring about war. **warmongering** noun & adjective

warmth noun **1** the state or quality of being warm. **2** friendliness or affection.

warm-up noun preparing for athletic exercise by practice beforehand.

warn verb to tell someone about a danger or problem; to advise someone about what they should do in such circumstances ♦ We warned them to take waterproof clothing. SYNONYMS: caution, alert, forewarn, advise; (informal) tip off. **to warn someone off** to tell someone to keep away or to avoid a thing. [from an Old English word]

warning noun **1** something that serves to warn ♦ We had no warning of the blizzard. SYNONYMS: notice, forewarning; (informal) tip-off. **2** advice to someone that they will be punished if they continue doing something.

war of nerves noun an effort to wear down your opponent by gradually destroying their morale.

warp (worp) verb **1** to become bent or twisted out of shape, usually because of heat or damp; to bend or twist something in this way. **2** to distort a person's judgement or principles. **warp** noun **1** a warped condition. **2** the lengthwise threads in weaving, crossed by the weft. [from an Old English word]

warpaint noun paint traditionally put on the face and body before battle by certain peoples.

warpath noun **on the warpath** angry and getting ready for a fight or argument.

warrant (wo-rənt) noun **1** written authorization to do something ♦ The police have a warrant for his arrest ♦ a search warrant. **2** a document entitling the holder to receive certain goods or services ♦ a travel warrant. **3** a justification or authorization for something ♦ He had no warrant for saying this. **warrant** verb **1** to justify something ♦ Nothing can warrant such rudeness. **2** to guarantee or confidently assert something ♦ He'll be back, I'll warrant you. [from an Old French word; related to guarantee]

warrant officer noun a member of the armed services ranking between commissioned officers and NCOs.

warrantor (wo-rən-ter) noun a person who makes a warranty.

warranty (wo-rən-ti) noun (**warranties**) a written guarantee, especially one given to the buyer of an article by its manufacturer, promising to repair or replace it if necessary within a specified period. [from an Old French word; related to guarantee]

warren noun **1** a piece of ground in which there are many burrows in which rabbits live and breed. **2** a building or place with many narrow winding passages. [from an Old French word garenne meaning 'game park']

warring adjective involved in war.

warrior noun a person who fights in battle; a soldier. [from an Old French word guerreier meaning 'to make war']

warship noun a ship equipped with weapons and used in war.

wart noun **1** a small hard lump on the skin, caused by a virus. **2** a similar growth on an animal or plant. **warts and all** including all faults or unattractive features. **warty** adjective [from an Old English word wearte]

warthog noun an African wild pig with two large tusks and wart-like growths on its face.

wartime noun a time of war.

war-torn adjective (said about a place) devastated by war.

wary (wair-i) adjective (**warier, wariest**) cautious about possible danger or difficulty. **warily** adverb **wariness** noun [from an Old English word]

was past tense of **be**, used with a singular noun and with *I, he, she,* and *it.*

wash *verb* 1 to clean something with water or other liquid. 2 to be washable ♦ *Cotton washes easily.* 3 to do your laundry. 4 to flow against or over something, to go splashing or flowing ♦ *The sea washes the base of the cliffs* ♦ *Waves washed over the deck.* 5 (said about moving liquid) to carry something in a specified direction ♦ *A wave washed him overboard.* 6 to sift ore by running water through it. 7 to brush something with a thin coat of paint or ink. 8 (*informal*) (said about an excuse, piece of reasoning, etc.) to seem convincing or genuine ♦ *That argument just won't wash.*
wash *noun* 1 washing, or being washed ♦ *Give it a good wash.* 2 a quantity of clothes that need to be washed or have just been washed. 3 the process of doing your laundry. 4 the disturbed water or air behind a moving ship or aircraft. 5 a thin coating of colour painted over a surface. 6 liquid food or swill fed to pigs. **to come out in the wash** (*informal*) (said about mistakes etc.) to be eliminated during the progress of work etc. **to wash your dirty linen in public** to discuss your family scandals or quarrels publicly. **to wash something down with** to accompany food with a drink ♦ *We washed the curry down with beer.* **to wash your hands of** to refuse to take responsibility for something. **to wash something out** to cause an event to be cancelled or postponed because of rain. **to wash over** to happen all around without affecting you much. **to wash something up** 1 (also **wash up**) to clean dishes and cutlery etc. after use. 2 to cast something up on shore. [from an Old English word]

washable *adjective* able to be washed without becoming damaged.

washbasin *noun* a basin, usually fixed to a wall, for washing your hands and face.

washed out *adjective* 1 faded by washing; faded-looking. 2 pale and tired.

washed-up *adjective* no longer effective or successful.

washer *noun* 1 a ring of rubber or metal etc. placed between two surfaces (e.g. under a bolt or screw) to give tightness or prevent leakage. 2 a washing machine.

washerwoman *noun* (**washerwomen**) a woman whose occupation is washing clothes.

washhouse *noun* an outbuilding where washing is done.

washing *noun* a quantity of clothes etc. that is to be washed or has just been washed.

washing machine *noun* a machine for washing clothes etc.

washing powder *noun* powder of soap or detergent for washing clothes etc.

washing soda *noun* sodium carbonate, used for washing and cleaning.

washing-up *noun* the process of washing dishes etc. after use; the dishes etc. that are to be washed.

washout *noun* (*informal*) a complete failure.

washroom *noun* (*North Amer.*) a room containing toilet facilities.

washstand *noun* a piece of furniture to hold a basin and jug of water etc. for washing.

washy *adjective* (**washier, washiest**) 1 (said about colours) having a faded look. 2 (said about food or drink) too watery.

wasn't *verb* (*informal*) was not.

wasp *noun* a stinging insect with black and yellow stripes round its body. [from an Old English word]

waspish *adjective* making sharp or irritable comments. **waspishly** *adverb* **waspishness** *noun*

wassail (**woss**-ayl) *verb* (*old use*) to make merry and drink a lot of alcohol. [from an Old Norse phrase *ves heill* meaning 'be in good health']

wast (*old use*) the past tense of **be**, used with *thou.*

wastage *noun* 1 loss of something by waste. 2 (also **natural wastage**) the loss of employees through retirement or resignation, not through making them redundant.

waste *verb* 1 to use something extravagantly or needlessly or without getting an adequate result. SYNONYMS: squander, fritter, dissipate, misuse. 2 to fail to use an opportunity. 3 to become gradually weaker or thinner ♦ *She was wasting away for lack of food.*
waste *adjective* 1 left over or thrown away because it is no longer wanted ♦ *waste products.* 2 (said about land) not used, cultivated, or built on ♦ *waste ground.*
waste *noun* 1 wasting a thing or not using

it effectively ♦ *a waste of time*. SYNONYMS: profligacy, prodigality, extravagance. **2** waste material or food; waste products. **3** a stretch of barren uninhabited land ♦ *the wastes of the Sahara desert*. **to go to waste** to be wasted. **to lay waste** to or **lay something to waste** to destroy the crops and buildings etc. of an area. **to waste your breath** to talk uselessly. [from a Latin word *vastus* meaning 'empty']

wasteful *adjective* using more than is needed, showing waste. SYNONYMS: profligate, improvident, prodigal, extravagant, uneconomical. **wastefully** *adverb* **wastefulness** *noun*

wasteland *noun* a barren or empty area of land.

waste pipe *noun* a pipe that carries off water etc. that has been used or is not required.

waster (**wayst-er**) *noun* **1** a wasteful person. **2** (*informal*) a person who does nothing useful.

wastrel (**wayst-rəl**) *noun* (*literary*) someone who wastes their life and does nothing useful. [from *waste*]

watch *verb* **1** to look at or observe something for some time, to keep your eyes fixed on something. **2** to be on the alert or ready for something to happen ♦ *Watch for the traffic lights to turn green* ♦ *I'm watching for an opportunity*. **3** to pay careful attention to something ♦ *Watch where you put your feet* ♦ *I'll watch his progress with interest*. **4** to safeguard or take care of something ♦ *She employed a solicitor to watch her interests*.
watch *noun* **1** a small portable device indicating the time, usually worn on the wrist or carried in the pocket. **2** the act of watching, especially to see that all is well. **3** a fixed period of being on duty on a ship, usually lasting four hours; the officers and crew on duty during a watch. **4** a shift worked by firefighters or police officers. **to be on the watch** to be on the alert for trouble or danger. **to keep watch** to stay on the lookout for trouble or danger. **to watch out** to be careful or on your guard. **to watch over** to guard or look after someone or something. **to watch your step** to be careful not to stumble or fall or do something wrong. **watcher** *noun* [from an Old English word]

watchdog *noun* **1** a dog kept to guard property. **2** a person or committee whose job is to make sure that companies

providing a service or utility do not do anything harmful or illegal.

watchful *adjective* watching or observing closely. **watchfully** *adverb* **watchfulness** *noun*

watchmaker *noun* a person who makes and repairs watches.

watchman *noun* (**watchmen**) a person employed to look after an empty building at night.

watchtower *noun* a tower from which a sentry keeps watch.

watchword *noun* a word or phrase expressing briefly the principles or policy of a party or group ♦ *Our watchword is 'safety first'*.

water *noun* **1** a colourless odourless tasteless liquid that is a compound of oxygen and hydrogen. **2** a stretch or body of water, such as a lake, sea, or river. **3** a solution of a substance in water ♦ *lavender water* ♦ *soda water*. **4** urine. **5** the level of the tide ♦ *at high water*. **6** the transparency and brilliance of a diamond or other gem. **waters** *plural noun* the amniotic fluid surrounding a fetus in the womb.
water *verb* **1** to sprinkle something with water. **2** to supply something with water; to give drinking water to an animal. **3** to produce tears or saliva ♦ *It makes my mouth water*. **4** (said about a ship etc.) to take on board a supply of water. **by water** (said about travel) in a boat, ship, or barge etc. **to pass water** to urinate. **to water something down 1** to dilute something. **2** to make something less forceful or controversial. **waterless** *adjective* [from an Old English word]

waterbed *noun* a mattress filled with water.

waterbird *noun* a bird that swims on or wades in water.

water biscuit *noun* a thin unsweetened biscuit made from flour and water.

water boatman *noun* a bug that lives in still water and swims upside-down on the surface.

water buffalo *noun* the common domestic buffalo of India and SE Asia.

water bus *noun* a boat carrying passengers on a regular route on a lake or river.

water butt *noun* a barrel used to catch and store rainwater.

water cannon noun a device for shooting a powerful jet of water to disperse a crowd.

water closet noun (old use) a toilet with a pan that is flushed by water.

watercolour noun 1 artists' paint in which the pigment is diluted with water rather than oil. 2 a picture painted with this kind of paint.

watercourse noun a stream, brook, or artificial waterway; the channel along which it flows.

watercress noun a kind of cress that grows in streams or ponds, with strong-tasting leaves that are used in salads.

watered silk noun silk that has been treated to give it an irregular wavy marking.

waterfall noun a cascade of water where a river or stream flows over the edge of a cliff or large rock.

waterfowl plural noun waterbirds, especially ducks, geese, and swans.

waterfront noun the part of a town that borders on a river, lake, or sea.

waterhole noun a hollow in which water collects, especially one where animals drink.

water ice noun a dessert of frozen fruit juice.

watering can noun a container with a long tubular spout, for watering plants.

watering place noun 1 (also **watering hole**) a pool etc. where animals go to drink water. 2 a spa or a seaside resort.

water jump noun a place where a horse in a steeplechase or showjumping competition must jump over water.

water level noun 1 the height reached by a body of water. 2 another term for **water table**.

water lily noun a plant that grows in water, with broad floating leaves and white, yellow, blue, or red flowers.

waterline noun 1 the line along which the surface of the water touches a ship's side. 2 a line on a shore or riverbank that marks the level reached by the sea or a river.

waterlogged adjective 1 (said about ground) so saturated with water that it is useless or unable to be worked. 2 (said about a ship) so filled with water that it will barely float. [from water and log[1] (because water was said to 'lie like a log' in the hold of a waterlogged ship)]

Waterloo noun **to meet your Waterloo** to lose a decisive contest. [from Waterloo, a village in Belgium where in 1815 Napoleon's army was finally defeated by the British and Prussians]

water main noun the main pipe in a water supply system.

waterman noun (**watermen**) a boatman.

watermark noun 1 a manufacturer's design in some kinds of paper, visible when the paper is held against light. 2 a mark showing how high a river or tide rises or how low it falls. **watermarked** adjective

water meadow noun a meadow that is kept fertile by being flooded periodically by a stream.

watermelon noun a melon with a smooth green skin, red pulp, and watery juice.

watermill noun a mill worked by a waterwheel.

water pistol noun a toy pistol that shoots a jet of water.

water polo noun a game played by teams of swimmers with a ball like a football.

water power noun power obtained from flowing or falling water, used to drive machinery or generate electric current.

waterproof adjective that keeps out water. **waterproof** noun a waterproof piece of clothing. **waterproof** verb to make something waterproof.

water rat noun a rat-like rodent that lives beside a lake or stream.

water rate noun the charge made for use of a public water supply.

watershed noun 1 a turning point in the course of events. 2 a line of high land where streams on one side flow into one river or sea and streams on the other side flow into another. 3 the time after which programmes that are thought to be unsuitable for children are broadcast on television ♦ the 9 o'clock watershed. [from water and an Old English word scead meaning 'separation']

waterside noun the edge of a river, lake, or sea.

waterski noun (**waterskis**) each of a pair of flat boards on which someone stands so that they can skim over the surface of water while being towed by a motor boat. **waterski** verb (**waterskis, waterskied, waterskiing**) to travel on waterskis. **waterskier** noun

water softener noun a device or substance for softening hard water.

water sports plural noun sports that are carried out on water, such as waterskiing and windsurfing.

waterspout noun a funnel-shaped column of water between sea and cloud, formed when a whirlwind draws up a whirling mass of water.

water table noun the level below which the ground is saturated with water.

watertight adjective 1 made, fastened, or sealed so that water cannot get in or out. 2 (said about an argument, alibi, agreement, etc.) so carefully put together that it is impossible to dispute; containing no weaknesses or loopholes ♦ a watertight excuse.

water tower noun a tower that holds a water tank at a height that provides the pressure needed for distributing water.

waterway noun 1 a river or canal that ships or boats can travel on. 2 any navigable channel.

waterweed noun a weed growing in water.

waterwheel noun a large wheel turned by a flow of water, used to work machinery.

water wings plural noun inflated floats worn on the shoulders by a person learning to swim.

waterworks noun a place with pumping machinery etc. for supplying water to a district.

watery adjective 1 to do with or like water. 2 made weak or thin by too much water. 3 full of water or moisture ♦ watery eyes. 4 pale or weak ♦ a watery moon. **a watery grave** death by drowning.

watt (wot) noun a unit of electric power, equivalent to one joule per second. [named after the Scottish engineer J. Watt (1736–1819)]

wattage (wot-ij) noun an amount of electric power, expressed in watts.

wattle [1] (wot-əl) noun a structure of interwoven sticks and twigs used as material for fences, walls, etc. [from an Old English word watul]

wattle [2] (wot-əl) noun a red fleshy fold of skin hanging from the head or throat of turkeys and some other birds. [origin unknown]

wattle and daub noun wattle covered with mud or clay, used as a building material.

wave noun 1 a ridge of water moving along the surface of the sea etc. or arching and breaking on the shore. 2 (Physics) the wave-like motion by which heat, light, sound, or electricity etc. is spread or carried; a single curve in the course of this motion. 3 an act of waving your hand. 4 an advancing group of people, especially attackers. 5 a sudden increase in or occurrence of something ♦ a wave of anger ♦ a crime wave. 6 a wave-like curve or arrangement of curves, e.g. in a line or in hair.

wave verb 1 to move your arm or hand or something held to and fro as a signal or greeting. 2 to signal or express something in this way ♦ I waved him away ♦ We stood on the platform, waving goodbye. 3 to move loosely to and fro or up and down. SYNONYMS: flap, flutter, sway, wag, billow, ripple. 4 to make something wavy. 5 to be wavy. **to make waves** to make a great impression or cause trouble. **to wave something aside** to dismiss an objection etc. as unimportant or irrelevant. **to wave someone or something down** to signal a vehicle or its driver to stop, by waving your hand. [from an Old English word] ◊ Do not confuse this word with **waive**, which has a different meaning.

waveband noun a range of wavelengths between certain limits, used in radio transmissions.

waveform noun (Physics) a curve showing the shape of a wave at a given time.

wavefront noun (Physics) a surface containing all the points affected in the same way by a wave at a given time.

wavelength noun (Physics) the distance between corresponding points (e.g. peaks) in a sound wave or an electromagnetic wave. **on the same wavelength** having the same point of view as someone else ♦ We don't seem to be on the same wavelength at all.

wavelet noun a small wave.

waver verb 1 to be or become unsteady, to begin to give way or weaken ♦ The line of troops wavered and then broke ♦ His courage was beginning to waver. SYNONYMS: falter, wobble. 2 to hesitate or be uncertain ♦ She wavered between two opinions. 3 to move to

and fro. **4** (said about light) to flicker.
waverer noun [from an Old Norse word
vafra meaning 'to flicker']
◊ Do not confuse this word with **waiver**,
which has a different meaning.

wavy adjective (**wavier, waviest**) full of
waves or wave-like curves. **waviness** noun

wax [1] noun **1** beeswax. **2** any of various soft
sticky substances that melt easily (e.g.
obtained from petroleum), used for
various purposes such as making candles,
crayons, and polish. **3** a yellow wax-like
substance secreted in the ears.
wax verb to coat, polish, or treat
something with wax. [from an Old
English word *weax*]

wax [2] verb **1** (said about the moon) to show
a bright area that becomes gradually
larger until the moon becomes full.
2 (literary) to become stronger or more
important ♦ *Kingdoms waxed and waned.*
3 to speak or write in a particular way
♦ *He waxed lyrical about his childhood.* [from
an Old English word *weaxan*]

waxen adjective **1** like wax in its paleness or
smoothness. **2** made of wax.

waxwing noun any of several small birds
with small red tips (like sealing wax) on
some wing feathers.

waxwork noun a lifelike model of a person
made in wax.
waxworks noun an exhibition of
waxworks.

waxy adjective (**waxier, waxiest**) like wax.
waxiness noun

way noun **1** how something is done; a
method or style of doing something ♦ *This
is the best way to make scrambled eggs.*
SYNONYMS: method, approach, procedure,
technique, means, style, manner. **2** a manner
♦ *She spoke in a kindly way.* SYNONYMS:
manner, fashion, style, mode. **3** a habitual
manner or course of action or events
♦ *You'll soon get into our ways.* SYNONYMS:
custom, habit, practice, routine. **4** a road,
path, or track. **5** a route or direction ♦ *Can
you tell me the way to the station?* ♦ *Which way
is she looking?* **6** the route over which a
person or thing is moving or would
naturally move ♦ *Don't get in the way of the
trucks.* **7** space free of obstacles so that
people can pass ♦ *Make way!* **8** a distance
to be travelled ♦ *It's a long way to the summit
from here.* **9** the amount of difference
between two states or conditions ♦ *His
work is a long way from being perfect.* **10** a

talent or skill ♦ *She has a way with flowers.*
11 advance in some direction, progress
♦ *We made our way to the front.* **12** a
particular aspect of something ♦ *It's a
good idea in some ways.* **13** a condition or
state ♦ *Things are in a bad way.*
ways plural noun parts into which
something is divided ♦ *We'll split the money
three ways.*
way adverb (informal) far, to a great extent
♦ *The shot was way off the target* ♦ *That is way
beyond what we can afford.* **by the way**
incidentally. **by way of 1** via ♦ *London by
way of Reading.* **2** as a substitute for or a
form of ♦ *He smiled by way of greeting.* **to
get** or **have your own way** to manage to
get or do what you want. **to give way 1** to
be replaced by something else. **2** to yield
to someone else's wishes or demands.
3 to allow other traffic to go first. **4** to
collapse. **to go out of your way** to make a
special effort to do something. **to go your
way** (said about events etc.) to happen in
a way that is favourable to you. **in a way**
to a certain extent; in some respects. **in
no way** not at all. **in the way** forming an
obstacle or hindrance. **to look the other
way** to deliberately ignore a person or
thing. **no way** (informal) that is impossible.
on the way 1 about to arrive or happen.
2 (said about a baby) conceived but not
yet born. **on your way** in the process of
travelling or approaching. **out of the way
1** remote. **2** dealt with or finished. **under
way** see **under**. [from an Old English
word *weg*]

waybill noun a list of the passengers or
goods carried by a vehicle.

wayfarer noun a person travelling on foot.

waylay verb (past tense and past participle
waylaid) to lie in wait for someone,
especially in order to talk to them or rob
them.

way-out adjective unconventional in style.

-ways suffix forming adjectives and adverbs
showing direction or manner (e.g.
sideways). [from *way*]

wayside noun the edge of a road or path.
to fall by the wayside to fail to continue
doing something.

wayward adjective self-willed and
unpredictable, not obedient or easily
controlled. **waywardness** noun [from *away*
and *-ward*]

Wb abbreviation weber.

WC abbreviation water closet (a toilet).

we *pronoun* **1** used by a person referring to himself or herself and one or more other people, or speaking on behalf of a nation, group, or firm etc. **2** used instead of 'I' by a royal person in formal contexts and by an editor or writer in a newspaper etc. [from an Old English word]

weak *adjective* **1** lacking physical strength and energy. SYNONYMS: feeble, frail, infirm, delicate, sickly, puny, weedy. **2** easily broken or bent; not able to withstand rough treatment or great force. **3** (said about an argument, evidence, etc.) not forceful or convincing. SYNONYMS: lame, unconvincing, pathetic. **4** having little power or influence. SYNONYMS: impotent, ineffectual. **5** lacking firmness of character; easily led by others. **6** lacking intensity ♦ *a weak signal.* **7** not functioning well ♦ *weak eyesight.* **8** poor and unlikely to succeed ♦ *a weak candidate.* **9** heavily diluted, having little of a certain substance in proportion to the amount of water ♦ *weak tea* ♦ *a weak solution of salt and water.* **10** (said about a verb) forming the past tense by adding a suffix (as in *float,' floated*; *waste, wasted*), not by changing the vowel (as in *ring, rang*). (Compare **strong**.) [from an Old English word]

weaken *verb* **1** to make something weaker. SYNONYMS: debilitate, enfeeble, sap, erode, undermine. **2** to become weaker. SYNONYMS: fade, abate, ebb, decline, dwindle, wane.

weak-kneed *adjective* giving way weakly, especially when intimidated.

weakling *noun* a weak person or animal.

weakly *adverb* in a weak manner.
weakly *adjective* (**weaklier, weakliest**) weak or sickly.

weakness *noun* **1** the state of being weak. **2** a weak point; a disadvantage or fault. **3** inability to resist something, a particular fondness for something.

weal [1] *noun* a ridge raised on the flesh by a stroke of a cane or whip etc. [from an Old English word *walu* meaning 'ridge']

weal [2] *noun* (*formal*) welfare or prosperity ♦ *for the public weal.* [from an Old English word *wela* meaning 'wealth' or 'well-being']

wealth *noun* **1** a lot of money or property. **2** the state of being rich. **3** a great quantity ♦ *a book with a wealth of illustrations.* SYNONYMS: profusion, abundance, cornucopia. [from *well* [2]]

wealthy *adjective* (**wealthier, wealthiest**) having wealth, rich. SYNONYMS: rich, affluent, prosperous, well-off, well-to-do; (*informal*) loaded, well-heeled. **wealthily** *adverb*

wean *verb* to get a baby used to taking food other than milk. **to be weaned on** to be strongly influenced by something from an early age. **to wean someone off** to make someone give up a habit, addiction, or interest gradually. [from an Old English word *wenian*]

weapon *noun* **1** a thing designed or used as a means of inflicting bodily harm or physical damage. **2** a means of getting the better of someone in a conflict ♦ *the weapon of a general strike.* [from an Old English word]

weaponry *noun* weapons collectively.

wear [1] *verb* (**wore, worn**) **1** to have clothes, jewellery, etc. on your body ♦ *He wears his hair long.* **2** to have a certain look on your face ♦ *She wore a frown.* **3** to damage something by rubbing or using it often; to become damaged in this way ♦ *The carpet has worn thin.* **4** to withstand continued use ♦ *This fabric wears well wash after wash.* **5** (*informal*) to accept or tolerate something ♦ *We suggested working shorter hours but the boss wouldn't wear it.*
wear *noun* **1** wearing or being worn as clothing ♦ *Choose cotton for summer wear.* **2** clothing ♦ *Men's wear is on the ground floor* ♦ *evening wear.* **3** (also **wear and tear**) damage resulting from continuous use. **4** capacity to withstand being used ♦ *There's a lot of wear left in that coat.* **to wear someone or something down** to exhaust or overcome someone or something by persistence ♦ *She gradually wore down the opposition.* **to wear your heart on your sleeve** to show your affections quite openly. **to wear off** **1** to be removed by wear or use. **2** to become gradually less intense or effective. **to wear on** (said about time) to pass gradually ♦ *The night wore on.* **to wear out** to be used until it is no longer usable. **to wear someone out** to exhaust someone. **to wear something out** to use something until it is no longer usable. **to wear thin** to gradually become less effective or be used up. **wearer** *noun* [from an Old English word *werian*]

wear [2] *verb* (past tense and past participle **wore**) to bring a ship about by turning its head away from the wind. [origin unknown]

wearable *adjective* able to be worn. **wearability** *noun*

wearing *adjective* mentally or physically tiring.

wearisome *adjective* causing weariness.

weary *adjective* (**wearier, weariest**) **1** very tired, especially from exertion or endurance. **2** tired of something ♦ *People are weary of war.* **3** causing tiredness ♦ *It's weary work.*
weary *verb* (**wearies, wearied, wearying**) **1** to make someone weary. **2** to grow tired of something. **wearily** *adverb* **weariness** *noun* [from an Old English word]

weasel *noun* a small fierce mammal with a slender body and reddish-brown fur, living on small animals, birds' eggs, etc. [from an Old English word]

weather *noun* the condition of the atmosphere at a certain place and time, with reference to the presence or absence of sunshine, rain, wind, etc.
weather *adjective* windward ♦ *on the weather side.*
weather *verb* **1** to wear something away or change its appearance by exposing it to the effects of the weather. **2** to become worn or altered in this way. **3** to come through something safely or successfully ♦ *The ship weathered the storm.* **4** to sail to the windward of a place ♦ *The ship weathered the Cape.* **to keep a weather eye on** to be watchful for developments. **to make heavy weather of** to have more difficulty in dealing with something than you need to. **under the weather** feeling ill or depressed. [from an Old English word *weder*]

weather-beaten *adjective* damaged, worn, or tanned by exposure to the weather.

weatherboard *noun* a sloping board for keeping out the rain, especially one attached to the bottom of a door.

weatherboarding *noun* a series of weatherboards with each overlapping the one below, fixed to the outside wall of light buildings.

weathercock *noun* a weathervane in the shape of a cockerel.

weatherproof *adjective* unable to be penetrated by rain or wind.

weathervane *noun* a revolving pointer mounted in a high place and turning easily in the wind to show from which direction the wind is blowing.

weave [1] *verb* (**wove, woven**) **1** to make fabric or baskets etc. by crossing threads or strips under and over each other. **2** to form thread into fabric in this way, especially with a loom. **3** to put a story together ♦ *She wove a thrilling tale.*
weave *noun* a style or pattern of weaving ♦ *a loose weave.* **weaver** *noun* [from an Old English word *wefan*]

weave [2] *verb* (past tense and past participle **weaved**) to move from side to side to get round things in the way ♦ *He weaved through the traffic.* **to get weaving** (*informal*) to set to work energetically. [probably from an Old Norse word *veifa* meaning 'to brandish']

weaver bird or **weaver** *noun* a tropical bird that builds a nest of elaborately interwoven twigs.

web *noun* **1** the network of fine strands made by a spider. **2** a network ♦ *a web of deceit.* **3** skin filling the spaces between the toes of birds such as ducks and animals such as frogs.
the Web *noun* the World Wide Web.
webbed *adjective* [from an Old English word *webb* meaning 'a piece of woven cloth']

webbing *noun* strong bands of woven fabric used in upholstery, belts, etc.

weber (vay-ber) *noun* a unit of magnetic flux. [named after the German physicist W. E. Weber (1804–91)]

web-footed *adjective* having the toes joined by webs.

web page *noun* a page on a website.

website *noun* a location on the World Wide Web, giving information about a company, subject, etc.

wed *verb* (past tense and past participle **wedded** or **wed; wedding**) **1** to marry. **2** to combine or unite two different things ♦ *We need to wed efficiency to economy.* **to be wedded to** to be devoted to and unable to abandon an activity or opinion. [from an Old English word *weddian*]

we'd *verb* (*informal*) we had, we should, or we would.

wedded *adjective* to do with marriage ♦ *wedded bliss.*

wedding *noun* the ceremony and celebration when a couple get married.

wedding cake *noun* a rich iced cake cut and eaten at a wedding.

wedding ring *noun* a ring worn by a married person, given to them by their spouse at their wedding.

wedge *noun* 1 a piece of wood or metal etc. thick at one end and tapered to a thin edge at the other, pushed between things to force them apart or to prevent something from moving. 2 a wedge-shaped thing.
wedge *verb* 1 to keep something in place with a wedge. 2 to force something into a narrow space ♦ *Ten of us were wedged in the lift.* [from an Old English word]

Wedgwood *noun* (*trademark*) a kind of fine pottery named after Josiah Wedgwood (1730–95), its original 18th-century manufacturer.

wedlock *noun* being married. **born out of wedlock** born of unmarried parents. [from an Old English word *wedlac* meaning 'marriage vow']

Wednesday *noun* the day of the week following Tuesday. [from an Old English word *Wodnesdæg* meaning 'day of Woden', named after the god Odin]

wee *adjective* (**weer, weest**) (*Scottish*) little ♦ *wee Georgie.* [from an Old English word]

weed *noun* 1 a wild plant that grows where it is not wanted. 2 a thin weak-looking person.
weed *verb* to remove weeds from the ground. **to weed something out** to remove people or things that are inferior or undesirable. [from an Old English word *weod*]

weedkiller *noun* a substance used to destroy weeds.

weedy *adjective* (**weedier, weediest**) 1 full of weeds. 2 thin and puny.

week *noun* 1 a period of seven days, especially from Sunday to the following Saturday. 2 the five days other than Saturday and Sunday ♦ *I never go there during the week.* 3 the period for which you regularly work during a week ♦ *a 40-hour week.* [from an Old English word *wice*]

weekday *noun* a day other than Saturday or Sunday.

weekend *noun* Saturday and Sunday.

weekly *adjective* happening, done, or produced once a week.
weekly *adverb* once a week.
weekly *noun* (**weeklies**) a newspaper or magazine published once a week.

weeny *adjective* (**weenier, weeniest**) (*informal*) tiny. [from *wee* and *tiny*]

weep *verb* (past tense and past participle **wept**) 1 to shed tears, to cry. 2 to ooze moisture in drops.
weep *noun* a spell of weeping. [from an Old English word *wepan*]

weeping *adjective* (said about a tree) having drooping branches ♦ *a weeping willow.*

weepy *adjective* (**weepier, weepiest**) (*informal*) inclined to weep, tearful.

weevil *noun* a kind of small beetle that feeds on grain, nuts, tree bark, etc. [from an Old English word *wifel* meaning 'beetle']

weft *noun* the threads on a loom that are woven under and over the warp to make fabric. [from an Old English word]

weigh *verb* 1 to measure the weight of something, especially by means of scales or a similar instrument. 2 to have a certain weight ♦ *What do you weigh?* 3 to consider carefully the relative importance or value of something ♦ *Let's weigh the pros and cons.* 4 to be important or have influence ♦ *Her evidence weighed with the jury.* 5 to be a burden ♦ *The responsibility weighed heavily on him.* **to weigh anchor** to raise the anchor and start a voyage. **to weigh someone down** to depress or trouble someone ♦ *He seemed weighed down with cares.* **to weigh something down** to bring or keep something down by its weight. **to weigh in** to be weighed (in the case of a boxer) before a contest or (in the case of a jockey) after a race. **to weigh in with** (*informal*) to contribute a comment to a discussion. **to weigh something out** to take a specified weight of a substance from a larger quantity. **to weigh something up** to assess the nature or importance of something. **to weigh your words** to choose carefully the words that express exactly what you mean. [from an Old English word *wegan*]

weighbridge *noun* a weighing machine with a plate set in a road etc. on to which vehicles can be driven to be weighed.

weigh-in *noun* an official weighing, especially of boxers before a fight.

weight *noun* 1 how heavy something is; the amount that something weighs. 2 the quality of being heavy. 3 a unit or system of units used to express how much something weighs ♦ *tables of weights and measures* ♦ *troy weight.* 4 a piece of metal of

known weight used on scales for weighing things. **5** a heavy object, especially one used to bring or keep something down ♦ *The clock is worked by weights.* **6** a load to be supported or lifted ♦ *The pillars carry a great weight.* **7** a heavy burden of responsibility or worry. **8** importance or influence ♦ *The weight of the evidence is against you.* **9** (*Statistics*) a value given to one of a set of items to indicate its relative importance.
weight *verb* **1** to attach a weight to something; to hold something down with a heavy object. **2** to arrange something in a way that gives someone an advantage or creates a bias ♦ *The test was weighted in favour of candidates with scientific knowledge.* **to carry weight** to be influential. **to throw your weight about** (*informal*) to use your influence aggressively. [from an Old English word *wiht*]

weighting *noun* extra pay given to compensate for the higher cost of living in a place ♦ *a London weighting.*

weightless *adjective* having no weight, or with no weight relative to its surroundings (e.g. in a spacecraft moving under the action of gravity). **weightlessness** *noun*

weightlifting *noun* the athletic sport of lifting heavy weights. **weightlifter** *noun*

weight training *noun* physical training that involves lifting weights.

weighty *adjective* (**weightier, weightiest**) **1** having great weight, heavy. **2** important or influential. **3** serious or worrying. **weightily** *adverb* **weightiness** *noun*

weir (weer) *noun* a low dam built across a river so that water flows over it, serving to regulate the flow or to raise the level of water upstream. [from an Old English word *wer*]

weird *adjective* strange and uncanny or bizarre. **weirdly** *adverb* **weirdness** *noun* [from an Old English word *wyrd* meaning 'destiny']

weirdo *noun* (**weirdos**) (*informal*) a strange or eccentric person.

welcome *noun* a greeting or reception, especially a kindly one.
welcome *adjective* **1** received with pleasure ♦ *a welcome guest.* **2** pleasing because it is much needed or wanted ♦ *a welcome change.* **3** allowed or invited to do something ♦ *Anyone is welcome to try it.*
welcome *verb* **1** to show that you are

pleased when a person or thing arrives. **2** to be glad to receive or hear of something ♦ *The decision has been widely welcomed.*
welcome *interjection* a greeting expressing pleasure at a person's arrival. **to make someone welcome** to make someone feel welcome. **you're welcome** a polite phrase replying to thanks for something. [from an Old English word *wilcuma* meaning 'a person whose coming is pleasing']

weld *verb* **1** to join pieces of metal or plastic by heating and hammering or pressing them together. **2** to combine people or things into a whole.
weld *noun* a joint made by welding. **welder** *noun* [from an old word *well* meaning 'to melt']

welfare *noun* **1** people's health, happiness, and comfort; well-being. **2** organized efforts to ensure the physical and material well-being of a group of people in need. **3** financial support given to people in need. [from *well*[1] and *fare*]

welfare state *noun* a system in which a country's government seeks to ensure the welfare of all its citizens by providing money to pay for health care, old-age pensions, benefits, etc.

well[1] *adverb* (**better, best**) **1** in a good or suitable way, satisfactorily, rightly. **2** thoroughly or carefully ♦ *Polish it well.* **3** by a considerable margin; very much ♦ *She is well over forty.* **4** with good reason, probably ♦ *You may well ask* ♦ *It may well be our last chance.* **5** favourably or kindly ♦ *They think well of him.*
well *adjective* **1** in good health. **2** in a satisfactory state or position ♦ *All's well.* **3** sensible or advisable.
well *interjection* used to express surprise, relief, resignation, etc., or used to introduce a remark when you are hesitating. **as well, as well as** see **as. to leave** or **let well alone** to leave things as they are and not meddle unnecessarily. [from an Old English word *wel* meaning 'prosperously']
◊ The adverb *well* is often used in combination with past participles of verbs, e.g. *well advised* and *well known*. It is usual to use a hyphen when the combination comes before a noun (e.g. *a well-known singer*), but not when it comes after a verb (e.g. *a singer who is well known*).

well[2] *noun* **1** a deep shaft dug in the ground to obtain water or oil etc. from underground. **2** (*old use*) a spring serving

as a source of water. **3** an enclosed space in the middle of a building, especially one containing a staircase or lift. **4** a plentiful supply or source of something ♦ *a deep well of sympathy*.
well *verb* to rise or flow up ♦ *Tears welled up in her eyes*. [from an Old English word *wella* meaning 'spring of water']

we'll *verb* (*informal*) we shall or we will.

well advised *adjective* showing good sense.

well-being *noun* good health, happiness, and comfort.

well born *adjective* born of good family.

well bred *adjective* **1** showing good breeding, having good manners. **2** (said about a horse etc.) of good stock.

well connected *adjective* related to good families.

well disposed *adjective* having kindly or favourable feelings towards a person or plan etc.

well done *adjective* (said about food, especially meat) cooked thoroughly.

well earned *adjective* fully deserved ♦ *a well-earned rest*.

well favoured *adjective* good-looking.

well groomed *adjective* neat and clean in your personal appearance.

well head *noun* **1** the place where a spring comes out of the ground. **2** the structure over a well.

well-heeled *adjective* (*informal*) wealthy.

wellies *plural noun* (*informal*) wellingtons.

wellingtons *plural noun* rubber or plastic waterproof boots, usually reaching almost to the knee. [named after the first Duke of Wellington (1769–1852), who wore long leather boots]

well intentioned *adjective* having or showing good intentions.

well judged *adjective* (said about an action) showing judgement, tact, or aim.

well known *adjective* **1** known to many people. **2** known thoroughly.

well mannered *adjective* having or showing good manners.

well meaning or **well meant** *adjective* having good intentions but not having a good effect.

well-nigh *adverb* almost.

well off *adjective* **1** fairly rich. **2** in a satisfactory or good situation.

well read *adjective* having read a lot of good books.

well spoken *adjective* speaking in an educated and refined way.

well-to-do *adjective* fairly rich.

well tried *adjective* used often and so known to be reliable.

well-wisher *noun* a person who wishes another well.

well worn *adjective* **1** much worn by use. **2** (said about a phrase or idea) used so much that it is no longer interesting or significant; hackneyed.

Welsh *adjective* to do with or coming from Wales.
Welsh *noun* the Celtic language of Wales. [from an Old English word]

welsh *verb* **to welsh on** to fail to honour a debt or obligation ♦ *You're not going to welsh on our agreement, are you?* **welsher** *noun* [origin unknown]

Welshman or **Welshwoman** *noun* (**Welshmen** or **Welshwomen**) a man or woman born in Wales or descended from people born there.

Welsh rarebit or **Welsh rabbit** *noun* another term for **rarebit**.
◊ *Welsh rabbit* is the original name for this dish. *Rabbit* was later altered to *rarebit* to make it sound more understandable, but the word *rarebit* does not otherwise exist.

welt *noun* **1** a strip of leather sewn round the edge of the upper of a boot or shoe for attaching it to the sole. **2** a ribbed or strengthened border of a knitted piece of clothing, e.g. at the waist. **3** a weal, the mark of a heavy blow. [origin unknown]

welter *noun* a disorderly or confused mass ♦ *a welter of information*.
welter *verb* (*literary*) (said about a ship) to be tossed to and fro by waves. [from an Old German or Old Dutch word]

welterweight *noun* in boxing, a weight (67 kg) between middleweight and lightweight. [from an old word *welter* meaning 'a heavy person']

wen *noun* a large but harmless swelling or growth on the skin, especially on the head. [from an Old English word]

wench *noun* (*old use*) a girl or young woman. [from an Old English word *wencel* meaning 'child']

wend *verb* **to wend your way** to go slowly or by an indirect route. [from an Old English word *wendan* meaning 'to turn or depart']

Wendy house *noun* a toy house large enough for children to play in. [named after a character in J. M. Barrie's *Peter Pan*]

went past tense of **go**.

wept past tense and past participle of **weep**.

were past tense of **be**, used with a plural noun and with *we*, *you*, and *they*.

we're *verb* (*informal*) we are.

weren't *verb* (*informal*) were not.

werewolf (weer-wuulf) *noun* (**werewolves**) (in legends) a person who at times turns into a wolf. [from an Old English word *wer* meaning 'man' and *wolf*]

wert (*old use*) the past subjunctive of **be**, used with *thou*.

west *noun* **1** the point of the horizon where the sun sets, opposite east, or the direction in which this point lies. **2** the part of a place or building that is towards the west.
west *adjective* & *adverb* **1** towards or in the west. **2** (said about a wind) blowing from the west. **to go west** (*informal*) to be destroyed, lost, or killed. **the West 1** Europe and North America seen in contrast to other civilizations. **2** (*historical*) the non-Communist countries of Europe and America. [from an Old English word]

westerly *adjective* **1** in or towards the west. **2** (said about a wind) blowing from the west.
westerly *noun* (**westerlies**) a westerly wind.

western *adjective* **1** of or in the west. **2** to do with westerns.
western *noun* a film or story dealing with cowboys in western North America.

westerner *noun* someone who lives in the west of a country or region.

westernize *verb* to bring a person, country, etc. under the influence of ideas, customs, and institutions from Europe and North America. **westernization** *noun*

westernmost *adjective* furthest west.

westing *noun* **1** a distance travelled or measured westward, especially at sea. **2** a westerly direction.

Westminster *noun* the British Parliament. [named after the district of London where the Houses of Parliament (or Palace of Westminster) are situated]

westward *adjective* & *adverb* in or towards the west.
westwards *adverb* towards the west.

wet *adjective* (**wetter, wettest**) **1** soaked, covered, or moistened with water or other liquid. **2** not yet dry ♦ *wet paint*. **3** rainy ♦ *wet weather*. **4** (*informal*) (said about a person) lacking strength of character or firmness of purpose. **5** (said about a part of a country) allowing the sale of alcohol.
wet *verb* (past tense and past participle **wetted** or **wet**; **wetting**) **1** to make something wet. **2** to urinate in something.
wet *noun* **1** liquid that makes something damp. **2** rainy weather. **3** (*informal*) a drink. **4** (*informal*) a feeble or ineffectual person. **5** a moderate Conservative politician. **wet behind the ears** immature or inexperienced. **wetly** *adverb* **wetness** *noun* [from an Old English word *wæt* meaning 'wet']
◊ Do not confuse this word with **whet**, which has a different meaning.

wet blanket *noun* a gloomy person who prevents other people from enjoying themselves.

wet dock *noun* a dock in which a ship can float.

wet dream *noun* a sexually exciting dream that causes ejaculation of semen during sleep.

wether *noun* a castrated ram. [from an Old English word]

wetlands *plural noun* swampy or marshy land.

wet nurse *noun* a woman employed to suckle another woman's child.
wet-nurse *verb* **1** to act as a wet nurse to a child. **2** to look after or coddle someone as if they were helpless.

wetsuit *noun* a close-fitting rubber suit worn in skin diving etc. to keep the wearer warm.

wettish *adjective* rather wet.

we've *verb* (*informal*) we have.

whack *noun* (*informal*) **1** a heavy resounding blow. **2** an attempt ♦ *I'll have a whack at it.* **3** a share or contribution ♦ *Everyone did their whack.*

whack *verb* to hit someone or something hard. [an imitation of the sound]

whacked *adjective* (*informal*) tired out.

whacking *adjective* (*informal*) very large. **whacking** *adverb* (*informal*) very ♦ *a whacking great car.*

whale *noun* any of several very large sea mammals with a horizontal tail fin and a blowhole on top of the head for breathing. **to have a whale of a time** (*informal*) to enjoy yourself very much. [from an Old English word]

whalebone *noun* a horny springy substance from the upper jaw of some kinds of whale, formerly used as stays in corsets and dresses.

whaler *noun* a person or ship that hunts whales.

whaling *noun* hunting whales.

wham *interjection & noun* (*informal*) the sound of a forcible impact.

wharf (worf) *noun* (**wharves** or **wharfs**) a landing stage where ships may moor for loading and unloading. [from an Old English word *hwearf*]

what *adjective* 1 asking for a statement of amount, number, or kind ♦ *What vegetables have we got?* 2 which ♦ *What languages does he speak?* 3 how great or strange or remarkable ♦ *What a fool you are!* 4 the or any that, whatever ♦ *Lend me what money you can spare.*
what *pronoun* 1 what thing or things; the thing that ♦ *What did you say?* ♦ *This is what you must do.* 2 a request for something to be repeated because you have not heard or understood.
what *adverb* to what extent or degree ♦ *What does it matter?*
what *interjection* an exclamation of surprise. **and what not** and other similar things. **to give someone what for** (*informal*) to punish or scold someone. **what about** 1 what is the news about a subject. 2 what do you think of, how would you deal with. 3 used to make a suggestion ♦ *What about some tea?* **what-d'you-call-it** or **what's-its-name** used as a substitute for a name that you cannot remember. **what for?** for what reason? **what have you** other similar things. **what is more** as an additional point, moreover. **what's what** what things are useful or important ♦ *She knows what's what.* **what with** on account of ♦ *What with working too hard and not eating he fell ill.* [from an Old English word]

whatever *pronoun* 1 anything or everything ♦ *Do whatever you like.* 2 no matter what ♦ *Keep calm, whatever happens.*
whatever *adjective* 1 of any kind or number ♦ *Take whatever books you need.* 2 at all ♦ *There is no doubt whatever.* **or whatever** or anything similar.

whatnot *noun* other things of the same kind ♦ *a drawer full of pens, paper, and whatnot.*

whatsoever *adjective & pronoun* whatever.

wheat *noun* 1 grain from which flour is made. 2 the cereal plant that produces this. [from an Old English word]

wheatear *noun* a small songbird with a white rump.

wheaten *adjective* made from wheat flour.

wheatmeal *noun* flour made from wheat from which some of the bran and germ has been removed.

wheedle *verb* to persuade someone to do something by coaxing or flattering them. [probably from a German word *wedeln* meaning 'to fawn']

wheel *noun* 1 a circular object that revolves on a shaft or axle that passes through its centre. 2 something resembling this or having a wheel as an essential part. 3 a steering wheel ♦ *Who was at the wheel?* 4 a horizontal revolving disc on which clay is made into a pot. 5 motion like that of a wheel, or of a line of people that pivots on one end.
wheel *verb* 1 to push or pull a bicycle or cart etc. along on its wheels. 2 to turn round quickly to face another way ♦ *He wheeled round in astonishment.* 3 to move or fly in a wide circle or curve.
wheels *plural noun* (*informal*) a car. **to wheel and deal** to be involved in business or political activities in an unscrupulous or dishonest way. **wheels within wheels** secret or indirect motives and influences interacting with one another. [from an Old English word]

wheelbarrow *noun* an open container for moving small loads, with a wheel beneath one end, and two straight handles (by which it is pushed) and legs at the other.

wheelbase *noun* the distance between the front and rear axles of a vehicle.

wheelchair *noun* a chair on wheels, used by a person who cannot walk.

wheel clamp *noun* a device that can be locked around a vehicle's wheel to stop it from moving, used on cars that have been parked illegally.

wheeler dealer noun a person who is clever and unscrupulous in business dealings.

wheelhouse noun a shelter for the person at the wheel of a boat or ship.

wheelie noun (informal) the stunt of riding a bicycle or motorcycle for a short distance with the front wheel off the ground.

wheelie bin noun (informal) a tall refuse bin on wheels.

wheeze verb to breathe with a hoarse whistling or rattling sound in the chest. **wheeze** noun 1 the sound of wheezing. 2 (informal) a clever or amusing scheme or plan. **wheezy** adjective [probably from an Old Norse word meaning 'to hiss']

whelk noun a shellfish that looks like a snail. [from an Old English word wioloc]

whelp noun a young dog or wolf, a pup or cub.
whelp verb to give birth to a whelp or whelps. [from an Old English word hwelp]

when adverb 1 at what time?; on what occasion? 2 at which time ♦ There are times when joking is out of place.
when conjunction 1 at the time that, on the occasion that. 2 although; considering that, since ♦ Why risk it when you know it's dangerous?
when pronoun what or which time ♦ From when does the agreement date? [from an Old English word]

whence adverb & conjunction (formal) 1 from where, from what place or source; from which. 2 to the place from which ♦ They returned whence they came. [from an Old English word]

whenever conjunction & adverb 1 at whatever time; on whatever occasion. 2 every time that.

whensoever conjunction & adverb (formal) whenever.

where adverb & conjunction 1 at or in what or which place, position, or circumstances. 2 in what respect; from what place, source, or origin. 3 to what place. 4 in or at or to the place in which ♦ Leave it where it is.
where pronoun what place ♦ Where does she come from? [from an Old English word]

whereabouts adverb in or near what place.
whereabouts noun & plural noun the place where someone or something is ♦ Can you tell me his whereabouts?

whereas conjunction 1 but in contrast ♦ He is English, whereas his wife is French. 2 since it is the fact that.

whereby adverb by which.

wherefore adverb (old use) why. [from where and for (preposition)]

wherein adverb in what; in which.

whereof adverb & conjunction of what or which.

wheresoever adjective (formal) wherever.

whereupon conjunction immediately after which.

wherever adverb at or to whatever place.
wherever conjunction in every place that; in every case when.

wherewithal noun (informal) the money or other resources needed for a particular purpose.

whet verb (whetted, whetting) 1 to sharpen something by rubbing it against a stone etc. 2 to stimulate something ♦ You've really whetted my appetite. [from an Old English word hwettan meaning 'to sharpen']
◊ Do not confuse this word with wet, which has a different meaning.

whether conjunction used to express a doubt or choice between two possibilities ♦ I don't know whether to believe her or not. [from an Old English word]

whetstone noun a shaped stone used for sharpening tools. [from whet and stone]

whew interjection used to express astonishment, relief, tiredness, etc.

whey (way) noun the watery liquid left when milk forms curds. [from an Old English word]

which adjective & pronoun 1 what particular one or ones of a set of things or people ♦ Which way did he go? ♦ Which is your desk? 2 and that ♦ We invited him to come, which he did very willingly.
which relative pronoun the thing referred to. [from an Old English word hwilc]
◊ You use which when it begins a clause giving incidental information that you could leave out, e.g. The house, which is for sale, is round the corner. You use that or which when it begins a clause that defines or identifies something and cannot be left out, e.g. The house that is for sale is round the corner.

whichever *adjective & pronoun* any which, that or those which ♦ *Get the 45 or 47 bus, whichever comes first* ♦ *Take whichever one you like.*

whiff *noun* 1 a puff or slight smell of smoke, gas, etc. 2 a trace of something ♦ *a whiff of danger.* [an imitation of the sound of a puff]

Whig *noun* a member of a political party in the 17th–19th centuries opposed to the Tories, succeeded in the 19th century by the Liberal Party. [from *whiggamore*, a name for Scottish Presbyterian rebels in 1648]

while *conjunction* 1 at the same time as ♦ *Whistle while you work.* 2 although ♦ *While I admit that he is sincere, I think he is mistaken.* 3 on the other hand, whereas ♦ *She is dark, while her sister is fair.*
while *noun* a period of time, the time spent in doing something ♦ *a long while ago* ♦ *We've waited all this while.*
while *verb* **to while something away** to pass time in a leisurely manner. **worth while** or **worth your while** worth the time or effort spent. [from an Old English word]

whilst *conjunction* while.

whim *noun* a sudden desire or change of mind. SYNONYMS: caprice, impulse, fancy, urge. [origin unknown]

whimper *verb* to cry or whine softly, to make feeble frightened or complaining sounds.
whimper *noun* a whimpering sound. [an imitation of the sound]

whimsical (**wim-zik-əl**) *adjective* 1 quaint or fanciful. 2 impulsive and playful. **whimsicality** (**wim-zi-kal-iti**) *noun* **whimsically** *adverb* [from *whim*]

whimsy *noun* (**whimsies**) 1 a whim. 2 playful or fanciful humour.

whine *verb* 1 to make a long high complaining cry like that of a child or dog. 2 to make a long high shrill sound resembling this. 3 to complain in a petty or feeble way.
whine *noun* a whining cry or sound or complaint. **whiner** *noun* **whiny** *adjective* [from an Old English word meaning 'to whistle through the air']

whinge *verb* (present participle **whingeing**) to grumble persistently.
whinge *noun* (*informal*) an act of grumbling. [from an Old English word *hwinsian*]

whinny *verb* (**whinnies, whinnied, whinnying**) (said about a horse) to neigh gently.
whinny *noun* (**whinnies**) a gentle neigh. [an imitation of the sound]

whip *noun* 1 a cord or strip of leather fastened to a handle, used for urging an animal on or for striking a person as a punishment. 2 an official of a political party in parliament with authority to maintain discipline among members of the party. 3 a written notice issued by party whips, requesting members to attend on a particular occasion. These are underlined with a number of lines indicating the degree of urgency, e.g. *three-line whip.* 4 party membership of a Member of Parliament. 5 a dessert made by whipping a mixture of cream etc. with fruit or flavouring.
whip *verb* (**whipped, whipping**) 1 to beat a person or animal with a whip. SYNONYMS: flog, scourge, lash, flagellate. 2 to beat cream or eggs etc. into a froth. 3 to move or take something suddenly ♦ *He whipped out a knife.* 4 (*informal*) to steal something. **to have the whip hand** to be in a controlling position. **to whip someone up** to deliberately excite or provoke someone. **to whip something up** 1 to stir up people's feelings ♦ *We've been trying to whip up support for the proposal.* 2 to make or prepare something quickly. [from an Old German and Old Dutch word *wippen* meaning 'to swing' or 'to leap']

whipcord *noun* 1 cord made of tightly twisted strands. 2 a kind of cotton or worsted fabric with diagonal ridges.

whiplash *noun* 1 the lash of a whip. 2 injury caused by a severe jerk to the head, especially in a motor accident.

whippersnapper *noun* (*old use*) a young and inexperienced person who behaves in a presumptuous way. [origin unknown]

whippet *noun* a small dog resembling a greyhound, used for racing. [from *whip*]

whipping boy *noun* a person who is blamed or punished when someone else is at fault. [originally denoting a boy who was educated with a young prince and whipped in his place for the prince's faults]

whippy *adjective* flexible or springy.

whip-round *noun* an appeal for contributions of money from a group of people.

whirl *verb* **1** to swing or spin round and round; to make something do this. SYNONYMS: spin, revolve, rotate, twirl, swivel, gyrate. **2** to travel swiftly in a curved course. **3** (said about the head or mind) to seem to spin round.
whirl *noun* **1** a whirling movement. **2** frantic or bustling activity ♦ *a mad social whirl.* **3** a sweet or biscuit with a spiral shape. **to give something a whirl** (*informal*) to give something a try. **in a whirl** in a state of confusion. [from an Old Norse word]

whirlpool *noun* a current of water whirling in a circle, often drawing floating objects towards its centre.

whirlwind *noun* a mass of air whirling rapidly about a central point.
whirlwind *adjective* very rapid and unexpected ♦ *a whirlwind romance.*

whirr *verb* to make a continuous buzzing or vibrating sound like that of a wheel etc. turning rapidly.
whirr *noun* a whirring sound. [probably from a Scandinavian word]

whisk *verb* **1** to take someone or something rapidly, especially in a vehicle ♦ *A taxi whisked us off to the theatre.* **2** to brush or sweep something lightly from a surface ♦ *I'll just whisk away the crumbs.* **3** to move something with a quick light sweeping movement ♦ *a horse whisking its tail.* **4** to beat eggs etc. until they are frothy.
whisk *noun* **1** a whisking movement. **2** a kitchen tool used for whisking eggs or cream. **3** a bunch of strips of straw etc. tied to a handle, used for flicking flies away. [from an Old Norse word]

whisker *noun* **1** each of the long hair-like bristles growing near the mouth of a cat and certain other animals. **2** (*informal*) a very small amount or distance ♦ *within a whisker of it.*
whiskers *plural noun* the hair growing on a man's face, especially on his cheeks. [from *whisk*]

whiskery or **whiskered** *adjectives* having whiskers.

whiskey *noun* Irish whisky.

whisky *noun* (**whiskies**) **1** spirit distilled from malted grain, especially barley. **2** a drink of this. [from a Scottish phrase *uisge beatha* meaning 'water of life']

whisper *verb* **1** to speak softly, using the breath but not the vocal cords. **2** to talk privately or secretly; to spread a rumour ♦ *It is whispered that she had an affair a few years ago.* **3** (said about leaves or fabrics etc.) to rustle softly.
whisper *noun* **1** a whispering tone of voice ♦ *She spoke in a whisper.* **2** a rumour. **3** a soft rustling sound. **4** a slight trace.
whisperer *noun* [from an Old English word *hwisprian*]

whispering gallery *noun* a gallery or dome in which the slightest sound made at a particular point can be heard at another far off.

whist *noun* a card game usually for two pairs of players. [origin unknown]

whistle *noun* **1** a shrill sound made by forcing breath through a narrow opening in your lips or through your teeth. **2** a similar sound made by a bird or the wind or produced by a flute, kettle, train, etc. **3** an instrument that makes a shrill sound when air or steam is forced through it, especially for giving a signal.
whistle *verb* **1** to make a whistle; to produce a tune in this way. **2** to move with a whistling sound ♦ *Bullets whistled through the air.* **to whistle for** (*informal*) to wish for or expect something in vain.
whistler *noun* [from an Old English word]

whistle-stop *adjective* very fast and with only brief pauses ♦ *a whistle-stop tour.*

Whit *adjective* to do with Whitsuntide.

whit *noun* the least possible amount ♦ *not a whit better.* [from an old word *wight* meaning 'an amount']

white *adjective* **1** of the very lightest colour, like snow or salt. SYNONYMS: snowy, snow-white, ivory, chalky, milky. **2** having a light-coloured skin. **3** (said about coffee or tea) with milk. **4** (said about wine) made from pale grapes or skinned black grapes, and yellowish in colour. **5** pale in the face from illness or fear or other emotion.
white *noun* **1** a white colour. **2** white clothes ♦ *The bride was all in white.* **3** a person with a light-coloured skin. **4** the transparent substance (called *albumen*) round the yolk of an egg, turning white when cooked. **5** the white part of the eyeball, round the iris. **6** the player using the white pieces in chess. **whitely** *adverb* **whiteness** *noun* **whitish** *adjective* [from an Old English word]

white admiral *noun* a butterfly with dark brown wings that have a broad white band on them.

white ant *noun* a termite.

whitebait *noun* (**whitebait**) a small silvery-white fish, used for food. [from *white* and *bait* (because it was used as bait to catch larger fish)]

white blood cell *noun* another term for leucocyte.

white Christmas *noun* a Christmas during which there is snow on the ground.

white-collar *adjective* (said about a worker) involved in clerical or professional work done in an office, especially as opposed to manual work.

white dwarf *noun* (in astronomy) a small dense star about the size of a planet.

white elephant *noun* a useless or unwanted possession, especially one that is expensive to maintain.

white flag *noun* a white flag or cloth used as a symbol of surrender or truce.

white heat *noun* the temperature at which heated metal looks white.

white hope *noun* a person who is expected to bring success or glory to a team or group.

white horses *plural noun* white-crested waves at sea.

white-hot *adjective* so hot that it glows white.

white lie *noun* a harmless or trivial lie that you tell in order to avoid hurting someone's feelings.

white magic *noun* magic used only for good purposes.

white meat *noun* pale meat such as poultry, veal, rabbit, and pork.

whiten *verb* to make something white, or to become white.

White Paper *noun* a report issued by the government to give information on a subject.

white spirit *noun* a colourless liquid made from petroleum, used as a paint thinner and solvent.

white tie *noun* a man's white bow tie worn with full evening dress.

whitewash *noun* 1 a liquid containing quicklime or powdered chalk, used for painting walls white. 2 deliberately concealing someone's mistakes or faults so that they will not be punished. 3 a victory by the same side in every game of a series.
whitewash *verb* 1 to paint a wall with whitewash. 2 to clear someone's reputation by glossing over their mistakes or faults.

whither *adverb* (*old use*) to what place or state ♦ *Whither did they go?*
whither *conjunction* (*old use*) to the particular place that; to whatever place. [from an Old English word *hwider*]
◊ Do not confuse this word with *wither*, which has a different meaning.

whiting [1] *noun* (**whiting**) a small sea fish with white flesh, used for food. [from a Dutch word *wijt* meaning 'white']

whiting [2] *noun* ground chalk used in whitewashing, plate-cleaning, etc.

whitlow (wit-loh) *noun* a small abscess under or near a nail. [from an old word *whitflaw* meaning 'white flaw']

Whitsun *noun* Whitsuntide. [from *Whit Sunday*]

Whit Sunday *noun* the seventh Sunday after Easter, commemorating the descent of the Holy Spirit on the apostles at Pentecost. [from an Old English word *hwit* meaning 'white' (because people used to be baptized on that day and wore white clothes)]

Whitsuntide *noun* the weekend or week including Whit Sunday.

whittle *verb* 1 to trim or shape wood by cutting thin slices from the surface. 2 to reduce something by removing various amounts from it ♦ *We whittled down the cost by cutting out all but the essential items.* [from an Old English word meaning 'to cut']

whizz or **whiz** *verb* (**whizzed, whizzing**) 1 to move or make something move at great speed through the air with a whistling or buzzing sound. 2 to move very quickly.
whizz *noun* a whizzing sound. **to whizz through** to do or deal with something quickly. [an imitation of the sound]

whizz-kid or **whiz-kid** *noun* (*informal*) an exceptionally brilliant or successful young person.

WHO *abbreviation* World Health Organization.

who *pronoun* 1 what or which person or persons. 2 the particular person or

persons ♦ *This is the man who wanted to see you.* [from an Old English word]
◊ See the note at **whom**.

whoa *interjection* a command to a horse to stop or slow down. [origin unknown]

who'd *verb* (*informal*) **1** who had. **2** who would.

whodunnit *noun* (*informal*) a story or play about a murder and the attempt to identify the murderer. [from *who done it?*, a nonstandard form of *who did it?*]

whoever *pronoun* **1** any or every person who. **2** no matter who.

whole *adjective* **1** with no part removed or left out ♦ *I told them the whole story.* SYNONYMS: full, entire, complete, total. **2** not injured or broken ♦ *There's not a plate left whole.*
whole *adverb* **1** in one piece ♦ *The snake swallowed the bird whole.* **2** completely ♦ *a whole new approach.*
whole *noun* **1** the full or complete amount, all of something. **2** something that is complete in itself. **as a whole** in general. **on the whole** taking everything into account; in general. **a whole lot** (*informal*) a great amount. [from an Old English word]

wholefood *noun* food that has been processed as little as possible and is free of additives.

wholehearted *adjective* without doubts or reservations ♦ *You have my wholehearted support.*

wholemeal *adjective* made from the whole grain of wheat ♦ *wholemeal bread.* [from *whole* and *meal²*]

whole number *noun* a number without fractions.

wholesale *noun* the selling of goods in large quantities to be retailed by others.
wholesale *adjective* & *adverb* **1** being sold in this way. **2** on a large scale ♦ *wholesale destruction.*
wholesale *verb* to sell goods wholesale.
wholesaler *noun* [originally in the phrase *by whole sale* meaning 'in large quantities']

wholesome *adjective* **1** good for physical health; showing a healthy condition. **2** good for moral well-being.
wholesomeness *noun* [from an old sense of *whole* meaning 'healthy' and *-some*]

wholewheat *noun* whole grains of wheat including the husk.

who'll *verb* (*informal*) who will.

wholly *adverb* completely or entirely, with nothing excepted or removed.

whom *pronoun* the form of *who* used when it is the object of a verb or comes after a preposition, as in *the boy whom I saw* or *To whom did you speak?*
◊ *Whom* can sound rather formal. In modern English, especially in speech and less formal writing, it often sounds more natural to use *who*, as in *the boy who I saw* (or simply *the boy I saw*) and *Who did you speak to?*

whomever *pronoun* (*formal*) the form of *whoever* used when it is the object of a verb or comes after a preposition.

whomsoever *pronoun* (*formal*) the form of *whosoever* used when it is the object of a verb or comes after a preposition.

whoop (woop) *noun* a loud cry of excitement.
whoop *verb* to give a whoop. [an imitation of the sound]

whoopee *interjection* a cry of wild excitement or joy.

whooping cough (hoop-ing) *noun* an infectious disease that mainly affects children, causing a cough that is followed by a long rasping indrawn breath. [so called because of the sound the person makes gasping for breath]

whoops (woops) *interjection* (*informal*) an exclamation of apology or dismay.

whopper *noun* (*informal*) **1** something very large. **2** a blatant lie. [from an old word *wap* meaning 'to strike or beat']

whopping *adjective* (*informal*) extremely large. [from *whopper*]

whore (hor) *noun* a prostitute; a sexually immoral woman. [from an Old English word]

whorl *noun* **1** a coiled form; a single turn of a spiral. **2** a complete circle formed by ridges in a fingerprint. **3** (*Botany*) a ring of leaves or petals round a stem or central point. [a different spelling of *whirl*]

who's *verb* (*informal*) **1** who is. **2** who has.
◊ Do not confuse this word with **whose**, which has a different meaning.

whose *pronoun* of whom, of which ♦ *Whose house is that?* ♦ *the boy whose bike we found.* [from an Old English word]
◊ Do not confuse this word with **who's**, which has a different meaning.

whosoever *pronoun* (*formal*) whoever.

who's who *noun* a book listing notable people and facts about them.

why *adverb* **1** for what reason or purpose. **2** on account of which ♦ *The reasons why it happened are not clear*.
why *interjection* an exclamation of surprise or indignation.
why *noun* (**whys**) a reason. **whys and wherefores** reasons. [from an Old English word]

WI *abbreviation* **1** West Indies. **2** Women's Institute.

wick *noun* a length of thread in the centre of a candle, oil lamp, or cigarette lighter etc. by which the flame is kept supplied with melted grease or fuel. [from an Old English word]

wicked *adjective* **1** morally bad or cruel. SYNONYMS: evil, heinous, villainous, foul. **2** playfully mischievous ♦ *a wicked grin*. **3** (*informal*) excellent. **wickedly** *adverb* **wickedness** *noun* [from an Old English word *wicca* meaning 'witch']

wicker *noun* thin canes or twigs woven together to make furniture or baskets etc. **wickerwork** *noun* [from a Scandinavian word]

wicket *noun* **1** a set of three stumps and two bails used in cricket, defended by the batsman. **2** the strip of ground between the two wickets. **3** getting a batsman out ♦ *We took three wickets in the last over*. **4** a small door or gate, especially one next to or within a larger one used for when this is not open. [from an Old French word]

wicketkeeper *noun* a fielder in cricket who stands behind the batsman's wicket.

widdershins *adverb* (*Scottish*) in a direction contrary to the apparent course of the sun, considered unlucky; anticlockwise. [from Old German words *wider* meaning 'against' and *sin* meaning 'direction']

wide *adjective* **1** measuring a lot from side to side, not narrow ♦ *a wide river*. **2** in width, measuring from side to side ♦ *one metre wide*. **3** extending far, covering a great range ♦ *a wide knowledge of art*. SYNONYMS: extensive, broad, wide-ranging, comprehensive, catholic. **4** open to the full extent ♦ *She stared at me with wide eyes*. **5** missing a point or target ♦ *His header was a metre wide*.
wide *adverb* **1** widely. **2** to the full extent ♦ *Open wide*. **3** missing the target ♦ *The shot went wide*.

wide *noun* a bowled ball in cricket that passes the wicket beyond the batsman's reach and counts one run to the batsman's team. **wide awake** fully awake. **wide of the mark 1** a long way from the target. **2** not correct or accurate ♦ *His guess was wide of the mark*. **wide open 1** (said about a place) exposed to attack. **2** (said about a contest) in which it is not predictable who will win. **widely** *adverb* **wideness** *noun* [from an Old English word]

wide-angle *adjective* (said about a lens) able to include a wider field of vision than a standard lens does.

wide-eyed *noun* **1** with your eyes wide open in amazement. **2** inexperienced or innocent.

widen *verb* to make something wider, or to become wider.

widespread *adjective* found or distributed over a wide area or among a large number of people ♦ *a widespread belief*. SYNONYMS: common, pervasive, prevalent, rife.

widgeon *noun* another spelling of **wigeon**.

widow *noun* a woman whose husband has died and who has not married again. **widowhood** *noun* [from an Old English word *widewe*]

widowed *adjective* made a widow or widower.

widower *noun* a man whose wife has died and who has not married again.

width *noun* **1** how wide something is; the distance or measurement of something from side to side. **2** a piece of material at its full extent from side to side ♦ *Use two widths to make this curtain*. **3** a wide range or extent. [from *wide*]

wield (weeld) *verb* **1** to hold and use a weapon or tool. **2** to have and use power or influence. [from an Old English word *wieldan* meaning 'to govern' or 'to subdue']

wife *noun* (**wives**) the woman to whom a man is married. **wifely** *adjective* [from an Old English word *wif* meaning 'woman']

wig *noun* a covering for the head made of real or artificial hair. [short for *periwig*]

wigeon (wij-ən) *noun* any of several kinds of wild duck, the male of which has a whistling call. [perhaps an imitation of its call, and suggested by *pigeon*]

wiggle *verb* to move or make something move repeatedly from side to side.

wiggle *noun* a wiggling movement. [from an Old German or Old Dutch word *wiggelen*]

wigwam (wig-wam) *noun* a hut or tent made by fastening skins or mats over a framework of poles, as formerly used by some American Indians. [from a Native American word meaning 'their house']

wilco *interjection* used in radio communication to indicate that directions received will be carried out. [short for *will comply*]

wild *adjective* 1 living or growing in its original natural state; not domesticated, tame, or cultivated. 2 (said about people) not civilized, barbarous ♦ *wild tribes.* 3 (said about scenery) looking very desolate; not cultivated ♦ *a wild moor.* 4 lacking restraint or control ♦ *wild behaviour.* SYNONYMS: disorderly, unruly, boisterous, riotous. 5 stormy or windy ♦ *a wild night.* 6 full of strong unrestrained feeling; very excited, enthusiastic, or angry. 7 extremely foolish or unreasonable ♦ *these wild ideas.* 8 haphazard ♦ *a wild guess.* **the wild** *noun* a natural environment ♦ *a chance to see lions in the wild.* **the wilds** *plural noun* a remote area, far from civilization. **to run wild** to grow or live without being disciplined or restrained. **to sow your wild oats** see oats. **wildly** *adverb* **wildness** *noun* [from an Old English word *wilde*]

wild card *noun* 1 a playing card that can have any value chosen by the player holding it in a game. 2 (*Computing*) a special character, such as an asterisk, that can be used in a search to match any character or sequence of characters.

wildcat *adjective* 1 (said about strikes) sudden and unofficial. 2 risky, especially financially ♦ *a wildcat scheme.*

wildebeest (wil-di-beest) *noun* (**wildebeest** or **wildebeests**) a gnu. [an Afrikaans word meaning 'wild beast']

wilderness *noun* a wild uncultivated area. [from an Old English phrase *wild deor* meaning 'wild deer' and *-ness*]

wildfire *noun* **to spread like wildfire** (said about rumours etc.) to spread very fast.

wildfowl *noun* birds that are hunted as game, such as ducks and geese, quail, and pheasants.

wild goose chase *noun* a hopeless or pointless search for something.

wildlife *noun* wild animals collectively.

Wild West *noun* the western states of the USA during the period when they were lawless frontier districts.

wile *noun* a piece of trickery intended to deceive or attract someone. [origin unknown]

wilful *adjective* 1 stubbornly determined to do what you want ♦ *a wilful child.* SYNONYMS: headstrong, self-willed, refractory, stubborn, wayward. 2 done deliberately and not as an accident ♦ *wilful murder.* SYNONYMS: deliberate, intentional, premeditated, calculated. **wilfully** *adverb* **wilfulness** *noun* [from *will²* and *full*]

will ¹ *auxiliary verb* 1 used to express the future tense ♦ *They will arrive soon.* 2 used in questions, especially requests ♦ *Will you shut the door?* 3 used to express a promise, intention, or obligation ♦ *I will never let you down.* [from an Old English word *wyllan*] ◊ See the note at **shall.**

will ² *noun* 1 the mental power to decide on and control your own actions or those of others. 2 will power. 3 a desire; a chosen decision ♦ *I wrote the letter against my will.* 4 a document containing instructions from a person on how their money and property are to be disposed of after their death. **will** *verb* 1 to use your will power; to bring something about by doing this ♦ *I was willing you to win.* 2 (*formal*) to intend something to happen ♦ *God has willed it.* 3 to bequeath something in a will ♦ *She willed her money to the local hospital.* **at will** whenever you like ♦ *He comes and goes at will.* **to have a will of your own** to be stubbornly determined in character. **with the best will in the world** however good your intentions are. **with a will** with determination ♦ *They set to work with a will.* [from an Old English word *willa*]

willies *plural noun* **the willies** (*informal*) nervous discomfort ♦ *This house gives me the willies.* [origin unknown]

willing *adjective* 1 ready and happy to do what was wanted. 2 given or done readily ♦ *We received willing help.* **willingly** *adverb* **willingness** *noun* [from *will²*]

will-o'-the-wisp *noun* 1 a flickering spot of light seen on marshy ground. 2 an elusive person, hope, or goal. [from *William* and *of* and *the* and an old sense of *wisp* meaning 'small bundle of straw burned as a torch']

willow *noun* 1 any of several trees or shrubs

with flexible branches, usually growing near water. **2** the wood of this tree. [from an Old English word *welig*]

willowherb *noun* any of several wild flowers usually with pink petals.

willow pattern *noun* a Chinese design on pottery, usually in blue on a white background and including a willow tree, a river, and a bridge.

willowy *adjective* **1** full of willow trees. **2** (said about a person) tall, slim, and supple.

will power *noun* strength of mind to control what you do or resist temptation.

willy-nilly *adverb* **1** whether you want to or not. **2** haphazardly. [a later spelling of *will I, nill I* meaning 'I am willing, I am unwilling']

wilt¹ *verb* **1** (said about plants or flowers) to lose freshness and droop. **2** (said about a person) to lose your energy because of exhaustion.
wilt *noun* a plant disease that causes wilting. [originally a dialect word; probably from an Old Dutch word]

wilt² an old form of **will**¹, used with *thou*.

wily (wiy-li) *adjective* (**wilier, wiliest**) crafty or cunning. **wiliness** *noun* [from *wile*]

wimp *noun* (*informal*) a weak or timid person. [perhaps from *whimper*]

wimple *noun* a cloth headdress folded round the head, neck, and cheeks, worn by women in the Middle Ages and still worn by some nuns. [from an Old English word *wimpel*]

win *verb* (past tense and past participle **won**; **winning**) **1** to defeat your opponents in a battle, game, or contest; to gain a victory. **2** to get or achieve something as the result of a battle, contest, bet, etc. **3** to gain something as a result of effort or perseverance ♦ *Gradually he won their confidence.* **4** to gain the favour or support of someone ♦ *By the end the audience was completely won over.*
win *noun* a victory in a game or contest. [from an Old English word *winnan* meaning 'to strive']

wince *verb* to make a slight involuntary movement because of pain, distress, or embarrassment.
wince *noun* a wincing movement. [from an Old French word *guenchir* meaning 'to turn aside']

winceyette *noun* a soft fabric woven of cotton and wool, used especially for nightclothes.

winch *noun* a device for lifting or pulling things by means of a cable which winds round a revolving drum or wheel.
winch *verb* to lift or pull something with a winch. [from an Old English word *wince* meaning 'reel' or 'pulley']

wind¹ (wind) *noun* **1** a movement or current of air, especially one occurring naturally in the atmosphere and blowing horizontally. **2** the breath you need in exertion or speech or for playing a musical instrument. **3** gas forming in the stomach or intestines and causing discomfort. **4** the wind instruments of an orchestra. **5** a trend or influence ♦ *the winds of change.* **6** meaningless or boastful talk. **7** a scent carried by the wind ♦ *The deer we were stalking had got our wind.*
wind *verb* **1** to make someone short of breath ♦ *We were quite winded by the climb.* **2** to make a baby bring up wind by patting its back. **3** to detect something by the presence of its scent ♦ *The hounds had winded the fox.* **to get wind of** to hear a rumour of something. **in the wind** happening or about to happen. **like the wind** very swiftly. **to put or have the wind up** (*informal*) to alarm someone or to become alarmed. **to take the wind out of someone's sails** to frustrate someone by anticipating what they will say or do.
windless *adjective* [from an Old English word]

wind² (wiynd) *verb* (past tense and past participle **wound**) **1** to go or turn something in a twisting or spiral course ♦ *The road winds through the hills.* **2** to wrap or encircle something ♦ *She wound a bandage round her finger.* **3** to twist or wrap something closely round and round upon itself so that it forms a ball. **4** to haul, hoist, or move something by turning a handle or windlass ♦ *I can't wind the car window down.* **5** (also **wind up**) to set or keep a watch, clock, etc. going by turning a key or handle.
wind *noun* **1** a bend or turn in a course. **2** a single turn in winding a clock or string etc. **to wind down** **1** to gradually lose power. **2** to relax. **to wind something down** to bring something to an end. **to wind up** **1** to come to an end. **2** (*informal*) to end up in a place or condition ♦ *He'll wind up in jail.* **to wind someone up** (*informal*) to tease someone. **to wind something up** **1** to bring something to an end. **2** to close down a

business. **winder** noun [from an Old English word windan meaning 'to go rapidly']

windbag noun (informal) a person who talks too much.

windbreak noun a screen or row of trees shielding something from the full force of the wind.

windcheater noun a jacket of thin but wind-proof material fitting closely at the waist and cuffs.

wind chill noun the cooling effect of wind blowing on a surface.

windfall noun 1 an apple or other fruit blown off a tree by the wind. 2 a piece of unexpected good fortune, especially in the form of a sum of money.

wind farm noun a group of windmills or wind turbines for generating electricity.

winding sheet noun a sheet in which a dead body is wrapped for burial; a shroud.

wind instrument noun a musical instrument played by blowing, such as a trumpet or flute.

windjammer noun a merchant sailing ship.

windlass (wind-ləs) noun a device for lifting or pulling things (e.g. a bucket of water from a well) by means of a rope or chain that is wound round a drum-shaped axle by turning a handle. [via Old French from an Old Norse word vindass meaning 'winding pole']

windmill noun 1 a mill worked by the wind turning the arms (called sails or vanes) that radiate from a central shaft. 2 a similar structure used to generate electricity or pump water. 3 a toy consisting of a stick with curved vanes that turn in the wind.

window noun 1 an opening in a wall or roof to let in light and often air, usually fitted with glass in a frame. 2 an opening through which customers are served in a post office, ticket office, etc. 3 a space behind the window of a shop where goods are displayed. 4 a framed area on a computer screen used for a particular purpose. 5 an interval or opportunity to do something. [from Old Norse words vind meaning 'wind' and auga meaning 'eye']

window box noun a long narrow box fixed outside a window, for growing plants and flowers.

window dressing noun 1 the displaying of goods attractively in a shop window. 2 presentation of facts in a way that creates a more favourable impression.

windowpane noun a pane of glass in a window.

window seat noun a seat below a window an alcove or bay of a room.

window-shopping noun looking at the goods displayed in shop windows without necessarily intending to buy anything.

windpipe noun the tube by which air reaches the lungs, leading from the throat to the bronchial tubes.

windscreen noun the glass in the window at the front of a motor vehicle.

windscreen wiper noun a device for clearing the windscreen of a motor vehicle from rain, consisting of a rubber blade that moves in an arc across the screen.

windshield noun (North Amer.) a windscreen.

windsock noun a tube-shaped piece of canvas open at both ends, flown on a mast at an airfield to show the direction and strength of the wind.

windsurfing noun the sport of surfing on a board that has a sail fixed to it (called a sailboard). **windsurfer** noun

windswept adjective exposed to strong winds.

wind tunnel noun a tunnel-like apparatus in which an air stream can be produced past models of aircraft etc. for studying the effects of wind.

wind-up noun (informal) an attempt to tease or play a trick on someone.

windward adjective situated on the side facing the wind.
windward noun the windward side.

windy adjective (windier, windiest) 1 with strong winds ♦ a windy night. 2 exposed to strong winds. 3 wordy, full of useless talk ♦ a windy speaker. **windiness** noun

wine noun 1 an alcoholic drink made from fermented grape juice. 2 a fermented drink made from other fruits or plants ♦ ginger wine. 3 dark purplish red.
wine verb to wine and dine someone to entertain someone with drinks and a meal. [same origin as for vine]

wine bar noun a bar or small restaurant where wine is the main drink sold.

wine glass *noun* a glass with a stem and foot, for drinking wine from.

wineskin *noun* the whole skin of a goat etc. sewn up and used to hold wine.

wing *noun* **1** each of the pair of parts of a bird, bat, or insect etc. that it uses for flying. **2** one of the pair of long flat parts that stick out from the sides of an aircraft and support it in the air. **3** something resembling a wing in appearance or position, such as the thin projection on maple and sycamore seeds. **4** a part of a large building, especially one that extends from the main part. **5** the part of a motor vehicle's bodywork immediately above a wheel. **6** a section of a political party or other group, usually one with more extreme views than those of the majority. **7** the part of a football, rugby, or hockey field close to either of the sides. **8** an attacking player whose place is at one of the far ends of the forward line. **9** either end of an army lined up for battle. SYNONYM: flank. **10** an air force unit of several squadrons.
wings *plural noun* **1** the sides of a theatre stage out of sight of the audience. **2** a pilot's badge representing a pair of wings. **wing** *verb* **1** to fly, to travel by means of wings ♦ *a bird winging its way home.* **2** to shoot a bird in the wing; to wound a person slightly in the arm or shoulder. **in the wings** ready to do something or to be used at the appropriate time. **on the wing** flying. **to spread your wings** to become more independent and try something new. **to take wing** to fly away. **under your wing** under your protection. **to wing its way** to be sent somewhere quickly ♦ *Your prize will be winging its way to you soon.* [from an Old Norse word]

wing chair *noun* an armchair with side pieces sticking out at the top of a high back.

wing commander *noun* an officer of the RAF.

winged *adjective* having wings.

winger *noun* an attacking player on the wing in football, hockey, etc.

wingless *adjective* without wings.

wing nut *noun* a nut with two parts that stick out so that the fingers can turn it on a bolt.

wingspan *noun* the length from the tip of one wing of an aircraft, bird, etc. to the tip of the other.

wink *verb* **1** to close and open one eye quickly, often as a private signal to someone. **2** (said about a light or star etc.) to shine with a light that flashes quickly on and off or twinkles.
wink *noun* **1** an act of winking. **2** a brief period of sleep ♦ *I didn't sleep a wink.* **to wink at** to pretend not to notice something that should be stopped or condemned. [from an Old English word *wincian* meaning 'to close the eyes']

winkle *noun* a kind of edible shellfish with a spiral shell.
winkle *verb* **to winkle something out** to extract or obtain something with difficulty ♦ *I managed to winkle out some information.* [short for *periwinkle*²]

winner *noun* **1** a person, animal, or thing that wins. SYNONYMS: victor, champion; (*informal*) champ. **2** something successful ♦ *Her latest novel is a winner.*

winning present participle of **win**.
winning *adjective* charming and attractive ♦ *a winning smile.*
winnings *plural noun* money won, especially in gambling.

winning post *noun* a post marking the end of a race.

winnow *verb* **1** to toss or fan grain etc. so that the loose dry outer part is blown away; to separate chaff in this way. **2** to sift or separate something from the parts that are not wanted ♦ *The purpose of this inquiry is to winnow out the truth from the falsehoods.* [from an Old English word *windwian*]

winsome *adjective* charming and attractive. [from an Old English word *wyn* meaning 'joy' and *-some*]

winter *noun* the coldest season of the year, between autumn and spring.
winter *verb* to spend the winter somewhere ♦ *We decided to winter in Egypt.* [from an Old English word]

winter sports *plural noun* sports performed on snow or ice, such as skiing and skating.

wintry *adjective* (**wintrier, wintriest**) **1** to do with or like winter, cold ♦ *wintry weather.* **2** lacking warmth or friendliness ♦ *a wintry smile.*

wipe *verb* **1** to clean or dry the surface of something by rubbing something over it. **2** to remove something by wiping ♦ *Now wipe your tears away.* **3** to spread a substance thinly over a surface. **4** to erase data from a tape etc. ♦ *I accidentally wiped our holiday video.*

wipe noun the act of wiping ♦ *Give this plate a wipe.* **to wipe something out 1** to cancel or eliminate something ♦ *He has agreed to wipe out the debt.* **2** to destroy something completely ♦ *The whole army was wiped out.* [from an Old English word]

wiper noun **1** a rubber strip mechanically moved in an arc across a windscreen to remove rain etc. **2** something that wipes or is used for wiping.

wire noun **1** metal drawn out into a thin flexible thread or rod. **2** a piece of wire used to carry electric current, for fencing, etc. **3** a fence made from wire. **4** (*informal*) a telegram.
wire verb **1** to fit or connect something with wires to carry electric current; to install wiring in a house. **2** to fasten or strengthen something with wire. **3** (*informal*) to send a telegram to someone. **to get your wires crossed** (said about two people) to have a misunderstanding. [from an Old English word]

wire-haired adjective (said about a dog) having stiff wiry hair.

wireless noun (*old use*) a radio. [so called because it does not need wires to conduct sound]

wiretapping noun the tapping of telephone lines in order to listen secretly to conversations.

wire wool noun another term for **steel wool**.

wireworm noun the destructive worm-like larva of a kind of beetle.

wiring noun a system of wires for conducting electricity in a building or device.

wiry adjective (**wirier, wiriest**) **1** like wire. **2** (said about a person) lean but strong.

wisdom noun **1** being wise, soundness of judgement and good sense. SYNONYMS: sagacity, shrewdness, astuteness. **2** the knowledge and experience that develops within a period or society. [same origin as for *wise*]

wisdom tooth noun a molar tooth that may grow at the back of the jaw of a person after the age of 20.

wise[1] adjective **1** having or showing soundness of judgement and good sense. SYNONYMS: sage, sagacious, shrewd, astute. **2** knowledgeable or well-informed. **3** (*informal*) aware of or informed about something ♦ *I'm wise to his scheming* ♦ *She put me wise to it.*

wise verb **to wise up** (*informal*) to become aware of the truth of a situation. **to be none the wiser 1** to know no more than you did before. **2** to be unaware of what has happened. **wisely** adverb [from an Old English word *wis*]

wise[2] noun (*old use*) way or manner ♦ *in no wise.* [from an Old English word]

-wise suffix forming adjectives and adverbs meaning **1** 'in this manner or direction' (as in *otherwise, clockwise*). **2** 'with respect to' (as in *price-wise*).

wiseacre (wiy-zay-ker) noun a person who pretends to have great wisdom or knowledge. [from an Old Dutch word]

wisecrack noun (*informal*) a witty or clever remark.
wisecrack verb (*informal*) to make a wisecrack.

wise guy noun (*informal*) a person who makes sarcastic or cocky remarks to show how clever they are.

wish verb **1** to feel or say that you would like to have or do something or would like something to happen, even though this might be impossible ♦ *I wish I was taller.* **2** (*formal*) to want something ♦ *I wish to speak to the manager.* **3** to make a wish ♦ *What did you just wish for?* **4** to say that you hope someone will have success, happiness, etc. ♦ *Wish me luck* ♦ *We wish her well.* **5** to greet someone ♦ *They wished us good afternoon.*
wish noun **1** a desire or hope; something wished for. **2** an attempt to make something happen by thinking about it, as in fairy tales ♦ *She threw a coin in the fountain and made a wish.* **3** an expression of hope about another person's success or welfare ♦ *with best wishes.* **to wish something on** to hope that something unpleasant will happen to someone. [from an Old English word]

wishbone noun a forked bone between the neck and breast of a cooked bird. When it is pulled in two between two people, the one who gets the longer part has the right to make a wish.

wishful adjective desiring something.

wishful thinking noun believing something because you wish it were true rather than on the facts.

wishy-washy adjective weak or feeble in colour, character, etc.

wisp noun 1 a small thin bunch or strand of something ♦ *wisps of hair.* 2 a small streak of smoke or cloud etc. 3 a small thin person. **wispy** adjective [origin unknown]

wisteria (wis-teer-iǝ) noun a climbing plant with hanging clusters of blue, purple, or white flowers. [named after an American anatomist C. Wistar (1761–1818)]

wistful adjective sadly longing for something. **wistfully** adverb **wistfulness** noun [from an old word *wistly* meaning 'intently']

wit[1] noun 1 the ability to use words or ideas cleverly for humorous effect. 2 a witty person. 3 intelligence or understanding ♦ *Use your wits* ♦ *No one had the wit to see what was needed.* **at your wits' end** feeling desperate because you do not know what to do. **to have** or **keep your wits about you** to be or remain mentally alert. **scared out of your wits** extremely frightened. [from an Old English word *wit*]

wit[2] (old use) **to wit** that is to say. [from an Old English word *witan*]

witch noun 1 a woman thought to have evil magic powers. 2 a person who practises modern witchcraft. 3 (informal) an ugly or unpleasant old woman. [from an Old English word *wicca*]

witchcraft noun the use of magic, especially for evil purposes. SYNONYMS: sorcery, black magic, wizardry, voodoo.

witch doctor noun (among some peoples) a person who is believed to use magic powers to treat illness and to harm people.

witch elm noun another spelling of **wych elm**.

witch hazel noun 1 a North American shrub with yellow flowers. 2 an astringent lotion made from the leaves and bark of this plant.

witch-hunt noun a campaign to find and punish people suspected of holding views that are considered to be unacceptable or dangerous.

with preposition 1 in the company of, among ♦ *Come with me.* 2 having, characterized by ♦ *a man with a beard.* 3 using ♦ *Hit it with the hammer.* 4 in the care or charge of ♦ *Can I leave a message with you?* 5 employed by ♦ *How long have you been with IBM?* 6 on the side of, of the same opinion as ♦ *We're all with you on this matter.* 7 at the same time as, in the same way or direction or

degree as ♦ *She rises with the sun* ♦ *I was swimming with the tide.* 8 because of ♦ *He was shaking with laughter.* 9 feeling or showing ♦ *I heard the news with calmness.* 10 under the conditions of; in the manner specified ♦ *She sleeps with the window open* ♦ *They won with ease.* 11 by addition or possession of ♦ *Fill it with water* ♦ *a woman laden with baggage.* 12 concerning or towards ♦ *I lost my temper with him.* 13 in opposition to ♦ *She argues with me all the time.* 14 in spite of ♦ *With all his roughness, he's very good-natured.* 15 being separated from ♦ *We didn't want to part with our luggage.* **to be with child** (old use) to be pregnant. **I'm not with you** (informal) I cannot follow your meaning. **with it** (informal) 1 up to date or fashionable. 2 alert and able to understand something. [from an Old English word]

withal adverb (old use) in addition; moreover. [originally with *all*]

withdraw verb (**withdrew, withdrawn**) 1 to pull or take something back or away ♦ *She withdrew her hand from his.* 2 to take money out of an account. 3 to cancel a promise or offer or retract a statement. 4 to leave a place, to retreat ♦ *The troops were forced to withdraw.* 5 to stop taking part in something ♦ *He angrily said he was withdrawing from the discussions.* 6 to become unresponsive or unsociable ♦ *She began to withdraw into herself.* [from an Old English word *with-* meaning 'away' and *draw*]

withdrawal noun 1 withdrawing. 2 the process of stopping taking drugs to which you are addicted, often with unpleasant reactions ♦ *withdrawal symptoms.*

withdrawn adjective (said about a person) very shy or reserved.

wither verb 1 (said about a plant) to become dried up and shrivelled. 2 to become shrunken or wrinkled from age or disease. 3 to fade away or fall into decline ♦ *Our hopes withered away.* 4 to subdue someone with a scornful look or remark ♦ *She withered him with a glance.* [from *weather*]

◊ Do not confuse this word with **whither**, which has a different meaning.

withering adjective scornful or sarcastic ♦ *a withering remark.*

withers (with-erz) plural noun the ridge between a horse's shoulder blades. [origin unknown]

withhold verb (past tense and past

participle withheld) **1** to refuse to give or allow something ♦ *She may withhold her permission.* **2** to hold something back, to restrain something ♦ *We could not withhold our laughter.* [from an Old English word *with-* meaning 'away, back' and *hold*[1]]

within *preposition* **1** inside, enclosed by. **2** not beyond the limit or scope of ♦ *Success is within our grasp* ♦ *He acted within his rights.* **3** in a time no longer than ♦ *We shall finish within an hour.*
within *adverb* inside ♦ *Apply within.* [from an Old English word *withinnan* meaning 'on the inside']

without *preposition* **1** not having, feeling, or showing ♦ *two days without food* ♦ *They are without fear.* **2** in the absence of ♦ *There's no smoke without fire.* **3** with no action of ♦ *We can't leave without thanking them.* **4** (*old use*) outside ♦ *without the city wall.*
without *adverb* (*old use*) outside ♦ *the house as seen from without.* [from an Old English word]

withstand *verb* (*past tense and past participle* **withstood**) to endure or resist something successfully. SYNONYMS: endure, bear, tolerate, stand, take, put up with, weather. [from an Old English word *with-* meaning 'against' and *stand*]

witless *adjective* foolish or stupid.

witness *noun* **1** a person who sees or hears something happen ♦ *There were no witnesses to the accident.* **2** a person who gives evidence in a law court. **3** a person who is present at the signing of a document and confirms this by adding their own signature. **4** something that serves as evidence ♦ *His tattered clothes were a witness to his poverty.*
witness *verb* **1** to be a witness to something ♦ *Did anyone witness the incident?* **2** to be the place or period in which something takes place ♦ *The 20th century witnessed a revolution in communications.* **3** to sign a document as a witness. **to bear witness** see **bear**[2]. [from *wit*[1]]

witness box *noun* the place in a law court where a witness stands to give evidence.

witness stand *noun* (*North Amer.*) a witness box.

witted *adjective* having wits of a certain kind ♦ *quick-witted.*

witter *verb* (*informal*) to speak at annoying length about trivial matters. [probably an imitation of the sound]

witticism (wit-i-sizm) *noun* a witty remark. [coined by the poet Dryden from *witty* and *criticism*]

wittingly *adverb* intentionally. [from *wit*[2]]

witty *adjective* (**wittier, wittiest**) full of wit. **wittily** *adverb* **wittiness** *noun*

wives plural of **wife**.

wizard *noun* **1** a man with magical powers, especially in legends and stories. **2** a person with amazing abilities ♦ *a financial wizard.* **wizardry** *noun* [from an old sense of *wise* meaning 'a wise person']

wizened (wiz-ənd) *adjective* full of wrinkles, shrivelled with age ♦ *a wizened face.* [from an old word *wizen* meaning 'to shrivel']

woad *noun* **1** a kind of blue dye formerly obtained from a plant of the mustard family. **2** this plant. [from an Old English word]

wobble *verb* **1** to rock unsteadily from side to side. SYNONYMS: shake, rock, tremble, quiver, quake, vibrate. **2** to make something rock or shake ♦ *Don't wobble the table.* **3** (said about the voice) to be unsteady. **wobble** *noun* a wobbling movement or sound. **wobbly** *adjective* [origin unknown]

wodge *noun* (*informal*) a large piece or amount. [from *wedge*]

woe *noun* **1** great sorrow or distress. **2** trouble or misfortune. [from an Old English word]

woebegone (woh-big-on) *adjective* looking unhappy. [from *woe* and an old word *bego* meaning 'to attack or surround']

woeful *adjective* **1** full of woe, sad. **2** deplorable ♦ *woeful ignorance.* **woefully** *adverb*

wok *noun* a Chinese cooking pan shaped like a large bowl. [a Chinese word]

woke past tense of **wake**[1].

woken past participle of **wake**[1].

wold *noun* an area of open upland country. [from an Old English word *wald* meaning 'wooded upland']

wolf *noun* (**wolves**) a fierce wild animal of the dog family, feeding on the flesh of other animals and often hunting in packs. **wolf** *verb* to eat food quickly and greedily. **to cry wolf** to raise false alarms so often that a real cry for help is ignored. **to keep the wolf from the door** to have enough

money to ward off hunger or starvation.
a wolf in sheep's clothing a person who
appears friendly or harmless but is really
an enemy. [from an Old English word
wulf]

wolfhound *noun* any of several large dogs
of a kind originally used for hunting
wolves.

wolfram (wuul-frəm) *noun* tungsten or its
ore. [from a German word]

wolf whistle *noun* a whistle whose pitch
rises then falls, used to express sexual
attraction or admiration.

wolverine (wuul-ver-een) *noun* an animal
that is the largest of the weasel family,
common in the north of North America.
[from *wolf*]

woman *noun* (**women**) 1 an adult female
human being. SYNONYMS: lady, female;
(*informal*) girl, lass. 2 (*informal*) a female
worker or employee. **woman to woman**
openly and frankly. [from an Old English
word]

womanhood *noun* 1 the state or time of
being an adult woman. 2 the qualities
traditionally associated with women.

womanish *adjective* 1 suitable for a woman
but not for a man. 2 (said about a man)
effeminate.

womanize *verb* (said about a man) to have
sexual affairs with many women.
womanizer *noun*

womankind *noun* women collectively.

womanly *adjective* 1 having the qualities
traditionally associated with women.
2 suitable for a woman. **womanliness** *noun*

womb (woom) *noun* the hollow organ in
the body of a woman or female animal in
which a child or the young may be
conceived and nourished while
developing before birth; the uterus.
[from an Old English word]

wombat *noun* an Australian marsupial
animal resembling a small bear. [from an
Aboriginal word]

women plural of **woman**.

womenfolk *noun* women in general; the
women of your family.

women's lib *noun* (*informal*) women's
liberation.

women's liberation *noun* the freedom of
women to have a status and rights equal
to those of men; feminism.

women's rights *plural noun* the right of
women to have a position of legal and
social equality with men.

won past tense and past participle of **win**.

wonder *noun* 1 a feeling of surprise and
admiration. SYNONYMS: awe, amazement,
astonishment, wonderment. 2 something that
causes this feeling, a remarkable thing or
event. SYNONYMS: marvel, miracle,
phenomenon.
wonder *verb* 1 to feel that you want to
know something; to try to form an
opinion or decision about something
♦ *We're still wondering what to do next.* 2 to
feel wonder or doubt ♦ *I wonder that he
wasn't killed.* **no wonder** it is not surprising.
to work or **do wonders** to have a very good
effect. [from an Old English word *wundor*]

wonderful *adjective* marvellous or
excellent. SYNONYMS: marvellous, excellent,
outstanding, remarkable, admirable,
exceptional. **wonderfully** *adverb*

wonderland *noun* a place full of wonderful
things.

wonderment *noun* a feeling of awe and
admiration.

wondrous *adjective* (*old use*) wonderful.
wondrously *adverb*

wonky *adjective* (**wonkier, wonkiest**) (*informal*)
faulty, unsteady, or crooked. [from a
dialect word]

wont (wohnt) *adjective* (*old use*) accustomed
♦ *He was wont to go to bed early.*
wont *noun* a habit or custom ♦ *He went to
bed early, as was his wont.* [from an Old
English word]

won't *verb* (*informal*) will not.

wonted (wohn-tid) *adjective* (*old use*)
customary ♦ *He listened with his wonted
courtesy.* [from *wont*]

woo *verb* (**woos, wooed, wooing**) 1 (said
about a man) to try to win the love of a
woman, especially in order to marry her.
2 to try to win someone's favour, support,
or custom ♦ *a special offer designed to woo
customers into the shop.* [from an Old
English word]

wood *noun* 1 the tough fibrous substance
that the trunk and branches of trees are
made of. 2 this substance cut for use as
timber or fuel. 3 (also **woods**) a small
forest. 4 a ball of wood or other material
used in the game of bowls. 5 a golf club
with a wooden head. **can't see the wood
for the trees** cannot get a clear view of the

main issue because of giving too much attention to details. **out of the wood** or **woods** clear of danger or difficulty. [from an Old English word *wudu*]

woodbine *noun* wild honeysuckle.

woodcock *noun* a kind of game bird with a long bill, related to the snipe.

woodcut *noun* 1 an engraving made on wood. 2 a print made from this, especially as an illustration in a book.

wooded *adjective* covered with growing trees.

wooden *adjective* 1 made of wood. 2 stiff and awkward in manner, showing no expression or liveliness. **woodenly** *adverb*

wooden spoon *noun* a real or imaginary prize given to a competitor who comes last; a booby prize.

woodland *noun* or **woodlands** *plural noun* land covered with trees.

woodlouse *noun* (**woodlice**) a small wingless creature with seven pairs of legs, living in decaying wood, damp soil, etc.

woodman *noun* (**woodmen**) (*old use*) a forester.

woodpecker *noun* a bird that clings to tree trunks and taps them with its beak to find insects.

wood pigeon *noun* a kind of large pigeon.

woodwind *noun* the wind instruments of an orchestra that are not made of brass, such as the flutes, clarinets, and oboes.

woodwork *noun* 1 making things out of wood. 2 things made out of wood, especially the wooden fittings of a house.

woodworm *noun* 1 the larva of a kind of beetle that bores into wooden furniture and fittings. 2 the damage done to wood by this larva.

woody *adjective* (**woodier, woodiest**) 1 like or consisting of wood ♦ *the woody parts of a plant*. 2 covered with trees ♦ *a woody area*. **woodiness** *noun*

woof *verb* to make the bark of a dog. **woof** *noun* a barking sound. [an imitation of the sound]

woofer *noun* a loudspeaker for reproducing low frequencies.

wool *noun* 1 the fine soft hair that forms the fleece of sheep and goats etc. 2 thread or cloth made from this. 3 a mass of fine fibres ♦ *steel wool*. **to pull the wool over someone's eyes** to deceive someone. [from an Old English word *wull*]

wool-gathering *noun* being in a dreamy or absent-minded state.

woollen *adjective* made of wool. **woollens** *plural noun* woollen clothing.

woolly *adjective* (**woollier, woolliest**) 1 made of or like wool ♦ *a woolly hat*. 2 covered with wool or wool-like hair. 3 not thinking clearly, not clearly expressed or thought out ♦ *woolly ideas*. **woolly** *noun* (**woollies**) (*informal*) a woollen piece of clothing, especially a pullover. **woolliness** *noun*

woolly bear *noun* a large hairy caterpillar.

Woolsack *noun* the large wool-stuffed cushion on which the Lord Chancellor sits in the House of Lords. [said to have been adopted in Edward III's reign as a symbol of the importance of the wool trade]

woozy *adjective* (**woozier, wooziest**) (*informal*) dizzy or dazed. [origin unknown]

Worcester sauce (**wuus**-ter) *noun* a pungent sauce containing soy sauce and vinegar, first made in the city of Worcester.

word *noun* 1 a single unit of speech or writing expressing an independent meaning. 2 a brief conversation with someone ♦ *Can I have a word with you?*. 3 a remark or statement ♦ *He didn't utter a word*. 4 even the smallest amount of something spoken or written ♦ *I don't believe a word of it*. 5 news or information ♦ *We sent word of our safe arrival*. 6 a promise or assurance ♦ *He kept his word* ♦ *Take my word for it*. 7 a command or spoken signal ♦ *Don't fire till I give you the word*. **word** *verb* to put something into words ♦ *I don't like the way the question is worded*. SYNONYMS: express, phrase. **by word of mouth** in spoken not written words. **to have words** to quarrel. **in a word** briefly. **a man of his word** or **a woman of her word** someone who keeps their promises. **to take someone at their word** to act on the assumption that someone means what they say. **the Word (of God)** the Bible, or part of it. **word for word** in exactly the same or equivalent words . **wordless** *adjective* **wordlessly** *adverb* [from an Old English word]

word class *noun* one of the categories into which words are divided in grammar, e.g. noun, verb, adjective, adverb, pronoun, preposition, conjunction, and interjection; a part of speech.

wording *noun* the way something is worded. SYNONYMS: phraseology, choice of words.

word of honour *noun* a solemn promise.

word-perfect *adjective* having memorized every word perfectly.

wordplay *noun* the witty use of words, especially in puns.

word processor *noun* a type of computer or program used for editing and printing text. **word-processing** *noun*

wordy *adjective* (**wordier, wordiest**) using too many words; not concise. **wordily** *adverb* **wordiness** *noun*

wore past tense of **wear**[1,2].

work *noun* 1 physical or mental effort made in order to do or make something ◆ *His good results are down to hard work.* SYNONYMS: toil, labour. 2 a task or duty that needs doing, or the materials used for this ◆ *Get on with your work.* SYNONYMS: task, job, assignment. 3 something done or produced by work; the result of action ◆ *The teacher marked our work.* 4 what a person does to earn a living, employment. 5 the place where someone is employed ◆ *She leaves work around 5 o'clock.* 6 a piece of writing, painting, music, etc. ◆ *one of Mozart's later works.* 7 activities or experiences of a certain kind ◆ *Nice work!.* 8 (*Physics*) the transfer of energy calculated by multiplying a force by the distance moved by an object in the direction of that force, measured in joules. 9 ornamentation of a specified kind; things or parts made of certain materials or with certain tools ◆ *fine filigree work.*

works *plural noun* 1 a place where industrial or manufacturing processes are carried out. 2 operations of building or repair. 3 the mechanism of a machine.

work *verb* 1 to do work ◆ *If you work hard, you'll pass.* 2 to be employed or have a job ◆ *She works in a bank.* 3 to make efforts ◆ *a lifetime working for peace.* 4 to function or operate properly or effectively ◆ *Is the lift working?* ◆ *It works by electricity.* SYNONYMS: go, run, operate, function. 5 to make something function or operate; to make someone work ◆ *Can you work the lift?* ◆ *He works his staff very hard.* 6 to have the desired result ◆ *I hope this is going to work.* 7 to cultivate land or extract something from a mine or quarry. 8 to bring something about ◆ *I can't work miracles.* 9 to shape, knead, or hammer etc. something into a desired form or consistency ◆ *Work the mixture into a paste.* 10 to produce paintings, sculptures, etc. ◆ *She usually works in oils.* 11 to do or make something by needlework or fretwork etc. ◆ *Now work your initials on it.* 12 to move

gradually or with effort into a particular position; to make something do this ◆ *The grub works its way into timber* ◆ *The screw had worked loose.* 13 to bring someone into a state of excitement, anger, etc. ◆ *She had worked herself into a frenzy.* 14 to be in motion ◆ *His face worked violently.* **at work** 1 working. 2 at your place of employment. 3 operating, having an effect ◆ *There are secret influences at work.* **to have your work cut out** to be faced with a hard task. **out of work** having no job or work. **the works** everything. **to work something in** to try to include something. **to work on** to use your influence on a person. **to work out** 1 to be calculated ◆ *It works out at £5 each.* 2 to have a particular result ◆ *It worked out very well.* 3 to spend time doing strenuous physical exercise. **to work something out** 1 to solve something by calculation or thinking. 2 to plan something in detail ◆ *We're trying to work out a plan.* **to work someone over** (*informal*) to beat someone up. **to work your passage** to pay for your journey on a ship by working on board. **to work to rule** to follow the official rules of your job with excessive strictness in order to cause delay, as a form of industrial protest. **to work up to** to gradually progress to something more difficult or advanced. **to work someone up** to excite or arouse someone. **to work something up** to bring something gradually to a more developed state. [from an Old English word *weorc*]

workable *adjective* 1 able to be worked. 2 that is likely to work ◆ *a workable plan.*

workaday *adjective* ordinary, everyday.

workaholic *noun* (*informal*) a person who works extremely hard and finds it difficult to stop. **workaholism** *noun* [from *work* and *alcoholic*]

worker *noun* 1 a person who works ◆ *a slow worker.* 2 a neuter or undeveloped female bee or ant etc. that does the work of the hive or colony. 3 a member of the working class.

work experience *noun* a short period of experience of employment arranged for school students.

workforce *noun* the total number of workers in a particular firm, industry, country, etc.

workhouse *noun* a former public institution where people unable to support themselves were housed in return for work.

working adjective 1 having paid employment ♦ working mothers. 2 (said about an animal) used in farming, hunting, etc. ♦ a working dog. 3 adequate for the time being or for normal purposes ♦ the play's working title ♦ a working knowledge of Spanish.
working noun a record of steps taken in solving a mathematical problem.
workings plural noun 1 a mechanism or way of operating ♦ I don't understand the workings of the stock exchange. 2 excavations at a mine or quarry.

working capital noun capital used in the day-to-day running of a business, not invested in its buildings and equipment.

working class noun the class of people who are employed for wages, especially in manual or industrial work. **working-class** adjective

working order noun a condition in which a machine etc. works satisfactorily.

working party noun a group of people appointed to investigate and report or advise on something.

workload noun the amount of work to be done.

workman noun (**workmen**) 1 a man employed to do manual labour. 2 a person who works in a certain way ♦ a conscientious workman.

workmanlike adjective efficient or competent but not outstanding.

workmanship noun the degree of skill shown in making or producing something.

workmate noun a person with whom you work.

work of art noun a fine painting, sculpture, or composition etc.

workout noun a session of strenuous physical exercise.

work permit noun a document giving a foreigner permission to work in a country.

workpiece noun a thing for working on with a tool or machine.

worksheet noun 1 a paper with a set of questions about a subject for students to work through, often used with a textbook. 2 a paper on which work done is recorded.

workshop noun 1 a room or building where things are made or repaired. 2 a meeting at which a group comes together to discuss a subject and take part in activities relating to it.

work-shy adjective avoiding work.

workstation noun a computer terminal and keyboard, especially one linked to a network.

worktop noun a flat surface for working on, especially in the kitchen.

work-to-rule noun the practice of following the official rules of your job with excessive strictness in order to cause delay, as a form of industrial protest.

world noun 1 the earth with all its countries and peoples. 2 a planet ♦ creatures from another world. 3 a region or section of the earth ♦ the western world ♦ the English-speaking world. 4 all the people on the earth; everyone ♦ He felt that the world was against him. 5 a person's life and activities ♦ Your world is a lot more exciting than mine. 6 the people or things belonging to a certain class, historical period, or sphere of activity ♦ the world of sport ♦ the insect world. 7 material things and occupations, as opposed to spiritual ones ♦ She renounced the world and became a nun. 8 a very great amount ♦ It will do him a world of good ♦ She is worlds better today. **for all the world like** precisely like. **man of woman of the world** a person who is experienced in the ways of human society. **not for the world** not for anything no matter how great. **out of this world** (informal) extremely enjoyable or impressive. **to think the world of** to have the highest possible opinion of someone. [from an Old English word]

world-famous adjective famous throughout the world.

worldly adjective (**worldlier, worldliest**) 1 to do with material things, not spiritual ones. 2 experienced about people and life. **worldliness** noun

worldly goods plural noun or **worldly wealth** noun everything that you own.

worldly-wise adjective having enough experience about people and life not to be easily deceived or impressed.

world music noun various kinds of music using styles from different nations or ethnic groups, especially in developing countries.

world power noun a country with influence in international politics.

world war *noun* a war involving many large nations in different parts of the world ♦ *the Second World War.*

world-weary *adjective* bored with or cynical about life. **world-weariness** *noun*

worldwide *adjective & adverb* extending throughout the whole world.

World Wide Web *noun* (*Computing*) an extensive information system that connects related sites and documents which can be accessed using the Internet.

worm *noun* 1 any of several types of animal with a long soft rounded or flattened body and no backbone or limbs. 2 the worm-like larva of certain insects. 3 an insignificant or contemptible person. 4 the spiral part of a screw.
worm *verb* 1 to move along by wriggling or crawling. 2 to rid an animal of parasitic worms. **to worm something out** to gradually get someone to tell you something by constantly and cleverly questioning them ♦ *We eventually managed to worm the truth out of them.* **to worm your way into** to insinuate your way into a person's affections etc. [from an Old English word *wyrm*]

worm cast *noun* a tubular pile of earth sent up by an earthworm on to the surface of the ground.

worm-eaten *adjective* (said about wood) full of holes made by woodworm.

worm's-eye view *noun* a view as seen from below or from a humble position.

wormwood *noun* 1 a woody plant with a bitter flavour. 2 bitterness or grief. [from an Old English word]

wormy *adjective* (**wormier, wormiest**) full of worms; worm-eaten.

worn past participle of **wear**[1].
worn *adjective* 1 damaged by use or wear. SYNONYMS: shabby, threadbare, frayed; (*informal*) tatty. 2 very tired.

worn out *adjective* 1 exhausted. 2 damaged by too much use.

worried *adjective* feeling or showing worry. SYNONYMS: anxious, concerned, apprehensive, uneasy, perturbed, agitated, fretful.

worrisome *adjective* causing worry.

worry *verb* (**worries, worried, worrying**) 1 to make someone anxious or disturb their peace of mind. SYNONYMS: concern, perturb, alarm, trouble, bother, disturb. 2 to feel anxious. SYNONYMS: fret, agonize. 3 to hold

something in the teeth and shake it ♦ *The dog was worrying a rat.* 4 (said about a dog) to chase and attack sheep etc.
worry *noun* (**worries**) 1 a state of worrying, mental uneasiness. SYNONYMS: anxiety, apprehension, concern, agitation, disquiet. 2 something that makes a person worry. SYNONYMS: care, concern, problem, trouble. **to worry something out** to obtain a solution to a problem etc. by persistent effort. **worrier** *noun* [from an Old English word *wyrgan* meaning 'to strangle']

worry beads *plural noun* a string of beads for fiddling with to calm yourself.

worse *adjective & adverb* 1 more bad or more badly. 2 less good or less well. **worse** *noun* something worse ♦ *There's worse to come.* **the worse for wear** 1 damaged by use. 2 feeling unwell, especially because of drinking too much alcohol. **worse off** less fortunate or well off. [from an Old English word; related to *war*]

worsen *verb* 1 to make something worse. SYNONYMS: aggravate, exacerbate, compound. 2 to become worse. SYNONYMS: deteriorate, decline, degenerate.

worship *noun* 1 reverence and respect paid to God or a god. 2 acts or ceremonies displaying this. 3 great admiration or devotion. SYNONYMS: adoration, veneration, glorification, adulation, homage. 4 a title of respect used to or of a mayor or magistrate ♦ *his worship the mayor* ♦ *their worships.*
worship *verb* (**worshipped, worshipping**) 1 to give praise or respect to God or a god. 2 to take part in an act of worship. 3 to feel great admiration or devotion for someone or something. SYNONYMS: adore, revere, venerate, idolize, lionize, exalt. **worshipper** *noun* [from an Old English word *weorth* meaning 'worth' and *-ship*]

worshipful *adjective* (in certain titles of respect) honourable ♦ *the Worshipful Company of Goldsmiths.*

worst *adjective & adverb* 1 most bad or most badly. 2 least good or least well. **worst** *noun* the worst part, event, situation, etc. ♦ *We are prepared for the worst.*
worst *verb* to get the better of someone. **at worst** in the worst possible case. **to get or have the worst of it** to suffer the most. [from an Old English word *wierresta*]

worsted (wuu-stid) *noun* fine smooth yarn spun from long strands of wool; fabric made from this. [named after Worstead, a place in Norfolk, where it was made]

wort (wert) *noun* (used in names) a plant or herb ♦ *St John's wort.* [from an Old English word *wyrt*; related to *root*[1]]

worth *adjective* 1 having a certain value ♦ *a book worth £10.* 2 deserving something; good or important enough for something ♦ *That book is worth reading.* 3 having wealth or property to a certain value ♦ *He was worth a million pounds when he died.* **worth** *noun* 1 value or usefulness ♦ *people of great worth to the community.* 2 the amount of something that a specified sum will buy ♦ *Give me a pound's worth of stamps.* **for all you are worth** (*informal*) with all your energy, making every effort. [from an Old English word]

worthless *adjective* having no value or usefulness. **worthlessness** *noun*

worthwhile *adjective* important or good enough to deserve the time, money, or effort needed or spent ♦ *a worthwhile job.* [from *worth the while* meaning 'worth the time']

worthy *adjective* (**worthier, worthiest**) having great merit, deserving respect or support ♦ *a worthy cause.* **worthy** *noun* (**worthies**) a worthy or important person ♦ *local worthies.* **worthy of** deserving ♦ *This charity is worthy of your support.* **worthily** *adverb* **worthiness** *noun* [from *worth*]

would *auxiliary verb* 1 used as the past tense of *will*[1] ♦ *We said we would do it.* 2 used in questions and polite requests ♦ *Would they like it?* ♦ *Would you come in please?* 3 used to make a polite statement ♦ *I would like to come,* or in a conditional clause ♦ *If they had supported us we would have won.* 4 used to give advice ♦ *I would phone the doctor straight away.* 5 used to express something to be expected or something that happens from time to time ♦ *That's just what he would do!* ♦ *Occasionally the machine would go wrong.* [from an Old English word *wolde*] ◊ See the note at **should**.

would-be *adjective* desiring or pretending to be something ♦ *a would-be humorist.*

wouldn't *verb* (*informal*) would not.

wound[1] (woond) *noun* 1 an injury done by a cut, stab, or blow. 2 a hurt done to a person's reputation or feelings. **wound** *verb* 1 to cause a wound to a person

or animal. 2 to hurt a person's feelings ♦ *She was wounded by these remarks.* **wounding** *adjective* [from an Old English word *wund*]

wound[2] (wownd) past tense and past participle of **wind**[2].

wove past tense of **weave**[1]. **wove** *adjective* (said about paper) made on a frame of closely woven wire.

woven past participle of **weave**[1].

wow[1] *interjection* an exclamation of astonishment or admiration. **wow** *noun* (*informal*) a sensational success. **wow** *verb* (*informal*) to impress or excite someone greatly.

wow[2] *noun* (*Electronics*) a slow fluctuation of pitch in reproduced sound, most perceptible in long notes or piano music. [an imitation of the sound]

WPC *abbreviation* woman police constable.

wpm *abbreviation* words per minute.

WRAC *abbreviation* Women's Royal Army Corps.

wrack *noun* a coarse brown seaweed thrown up on the shore or growing there. [from an old word *wrack* meaning 'shipwreck']

WRAF *abbreviation* Women's Royal Air Force.

wraith (rayth) *noun* a ghost. [originally Scots: origin unknown]

wrangle *verb* to have a noisy angry argument or quarrel. **wrangle** *noun* an argument or quarrel of this kind. [probably from an Old German word *wrangeln*]

wrap *verb* (**wrapped, wrapping**) 1 to put paper or cloth etc. round something as a covering. 2 to arrange a flexible covering or a piece of clothing round a person or thing ♦ *Wrap a scarf round your neck.* 3 (*Computing*) to make text carry over to a new line automatically; to be carried over in this way. **wrap** *noun* a shawl, coat, or cloak etc. worn for warmth. **to be wrapped up in** with your attention deeply occupied by something; deeply involved in something ♦ *She is completely wrapped up in her children* ♦ *The country's prosperity is wrapped up in its mineral trade.* **under wraps** kept secret. **to wrap round** or **over** (said about a piece of clothing) to overlap at the edges when worn. **to wrap up** 1 to put on warm clothes. 2 (*informal*) to stop talking. **to wrap something up 1** to enclose something in wrapping paper. **2** to finish or settle something. **3** to win something. [origin unknown]

wrapper *noun* a cover of paper or other material wrapped round something.

wrapping *noun* material used to wrap something.

wrasse (rass) *noun* a brightly-coloured sea fish with thick lips and strong teeth. [from a Cornish word *wrah*]

wrath (roth) *noun* extreme anger. [from an Old English word]

wrathful *adjective* full of extreme anger. **wrathfully** *adverb*

wreak (reek) *verb* to inflict or cause something ♦ *Flooding wreaked havoc with the running of trains.* [from an Old English word *wrecan* meaning 'to avenge']
◊ Note that the past form of *wreak* is *wreaked* and not *wrought*. The adjective *wrought* is used to describe metal that has been shaped by hammering or rolling.

wreath (reeth) *noun* (**wreaths** (reethz))
1 flowers or leaves etc. fastened into a ring and used as a decoration or placed on a grave as a mark of respect ♦ *wreaths of holly.* **2** a curving line of smoke or cloud. [from an Old English word *writhan* meaning 'to writhe']

wreathe (reeth) *verb* **1** to surround or decorate something with or as if with a wreath. **2** to wind round something ♦ *The snake wreathed itself round the branch.* **3** to form flowers etc. into a wreath. **4** to move in a curving line ♦ *Smoke wreathed upwards.* [from *wreath* and *writhe*]

wreck *noun* **1** the destruction of a ship by storms or accidental damage. **2** a ship that has suffered wreck. **3** the remains of a vehicle, building, etc. that has been badly damaged. **4** a person whose physical or mental health has been damaged or destroyed ♦ *a nervous wreck.* **wreck** *verb* **1** to cause the wreck of a ship. **2** to damage or ruin something so badly that it cannot be used again. SYNONYMS: spoil, demolish, shatter, devastate. [via Old French from an Old Norse word *reka* meaning 'to drive'; related to *wreak*]

wreckage *noun* the remains of something that has been badly damaged or destroyed.

wrecker *noun* **1** a person who wrecks

something. **2** a person employed in demolition work.

Wren *noun* a member of the former Women's Royal Naval Service. [from the abbreviation WRNS]

wren *noun* a small usually brown songbird. [from an Old English word *wrenna*]

wrench *verb* **1** to twist or pull something violently. **2** to injure part of your body by making a sudden twisting movement. **wrench** *noun* **1** a violent twist or twisting pull. **2** pain caused by parting ♦ *Leaving home was a great wrench.* **3** an adjustable tool like a spanner, used for gripping and turning nuts or bolts. [from an Old English word *wrencan* meaning 'to twist']

wrest (rest) *verb* **1** to take or pull something away from someone using force ♦ *A policeman managed to wrest the gun from him.* **2** to obtain something with effort or difficulty ♦ *We finally wrested a confession from him.* [from an Old English word]

wrestle *verb* **1** to fight by grappling with a person and trying to throw them to the ground. **2** to force someone into a position by fighting them like this ♦ *Police wrestled him to the ground.* **3** to struggle to deal with or overcome something ♦ *I've been wrestling with this problem all week.* SYNONYMS: grapple, struggle. **wrestle** *noun* **1** a wrestling match. **2** a hard struggle. **wrestler** *noun* [from an Old English word]

wretch *noun* **1** a very unfortunate or miserable person. **2** a despicable person. [from an Old English word *wrecca*]
◊ Do not confuse this word with **retch**, which has a different meaning.

wretched (rech-id) *adjective* **1** miserable or unhappy. **2** of poor quality, unsatisfactory. **3** used to express anger or annoyance ♦ *This wretched car won't start.* **wretchedly** *adverb* **wretchedness** *noun* [from *wretch*]

wriggle *verb* to move with short twisting movements. **wriggle** *noun* a wriggling movement. **to wriggle out of** to avoid a task etc. on some pretext or by some devious means. **wriggly** *adverb* [from an Old German word *wriggen* meaning 'to twist or turn']

wring *verb* (past tense and past participle **wrung**) **1** to twist and squeeze a wet thing to remove liquid from it. **2** to remove liquid in this way. **3** to break an animal's neck by twisting it. **4** to squeeze

someone's hand tightly. **5** to obtain something with effort or difficulty ♦ *We wrung a promise out of him.*
wring noun a wringing movement, a squeeze or twist. **to wring your hands** to twist them together in despair or distress. **wringing wet** so wet that water can be squeezed out of it. [from an Old English word *wringan*]

wringer noun a device with a pair of rollers between which washed clothes etc. are passed so that water is squeezed out.

wrinkle noun **1** a small furrow or ridge in the skin, especially the kind produced by age. **2** a small crease in something. **wrinkle** verb to make wrinkles in something; to form wrinkles. **wrinkly** adverb [origin unknown]

wrist noun the joint connecting the hand and forearm. [from an Old English word]

wristband noun a band worn round the wrist, especially as a form of identification or as a sweatband.

wristwatch noun a watch worn on a strap round the wrist.

writ[1] (rit) noun a formal written command issued by a law court or other legal authority directing a person to act or refrain from acting in a certain way. **Holy Writ** the Bible. [from an Old English word]

writ[2] an old past participle of **write**. **writ large** in an obvious or exaggerated form.

write verb (**wrote**, **written**) **1** to put letters, words, or other symbols on a surface, especially with a pen or pencil on paper. **2** to have the ability to do this ♦ *She couldn't read or write.* **3** to be the author or composer of something ♦ *How many books have you written?* ♦ *He makes a living by writing.* **4** to write and send a letter ♦ *Promise you'll write to me often.* **5** (North Amer.) to write to someone ♦ *I will write you soon.* **6** to indicate something clearly ♦ *Guilt was written all over her face.* **7** to enter data into a computer memory or storage device; to transfer data from one memory or storage device to another. **to write a cheque** to write the appropriate figures, words, and signature on a cheque to make it valid. **to write something down 1** to put something into writing. **2** to reduce the accounting value of an asset. **to write something off 1** to damage a vehicle so badly that it is not worth repairing. **2** to cancel a debt. **3** to acknowledge that something is bound to

fail or be lost ♦ *The supporters seem to have written off this season.* **4** to dismiss something as not being significant. **to write something out** to write a thing in full or in a finished form. **to write something up 1** to write an account of something. **2** to write entries in a diary etc. so it is up to date. **3** to praise something in writing. [from an Old English word]

write-off noun **1** a vehicle too badly damaged to be worth repairing. **2** something written off as completely lost, such as a debt that will never be paid.

writer noun **1** a person who writes or has written something. **2** a person who writes books, an author.

writer's cramp noun cramp in the muscles of the hand.

write-up noun a published written account of something; a review.

writhe (riyth) verb **1** to twist your body about, especially because of pain. **2** to wriggle ♦ *writhing snakes.* **3** to suffer because of great shame or embarrassment. [from an Old English word]

writing noun **1** handwriting ♦ *I can't read your writing.* **2** literary work, a piece of this ♦ *Do you like Orwell's writing?* ♦ *the writings of Charles Dickens.* **in writing** in written form. **the writing is on the wall** there are clear signs that something is doomed. [The phrase *the writing is on the wall* comes from the biblical story of the writing that appeared on the wall of Belshazzar's palace, foretelling his doom]

writing paper noun paper for writing on, especially for writing letters.

written past participle of **write**.

WRNS abbreviation Women's Royal Naval Service.

wrong adjective **1** not correct or true ♦ *the wrong answer.* SYNONYMS: incorrect, inaccurate, untrue, false, mistaken, erroneous. **2** (said about conduct or actions etc.) morally bad, unfair or unjust ♦ *It is wrong to cheat.* SYNONYMS: immoral, unethical, dishonest, sinful. **3** not working properly ♦ *There's something wrong with the engine.* SYNONYMS: amiss, faulty. **4** not based on good judgement ♦ *I think you've made the wrong decision.* SYNONYMS: misguided, ill-considered, misjudged. **5** not what is required, suitable, or most desirable ♦ *That's the wrong colour* ♦ *We must have gone the wrong way.*

wrong adverb not correctly or appropriately; mistakenly ♦ *You guessed wrong.*

wrong noun what is morally wrong or unjust ♦ *They have done me a great wrong.*

wrong verb 1 to do wrong to someone, to treat someone unfairly ♦ *a wronged wife.* 2 to attribute bad motives to a person mistakenly. **to get someone wrong** to misunderstand someone. **to get the wrong end of the stick** to misunderstand a remark or situation. **in the wrong** not having justice or truth on your side. **on the wrong side of 1** out of favour with someone. 2 more than the age mentioned ♦ *He's on the wrong side of 40.* **wrongly** adverb **wrongness** noun [probably from an Old Norse word *rangr* meaning 'awry' or 'unjust']

wrongdoing noun illegal or dishonest behaviour. **wrongdoer** noun

wrong-foot verb to catch someone unprepared.

wrongful adjective unfair or unjust; illegal ♦ *wrongful arrest.* **wrongfully** adverb

wrong-headed adjective showing bad judgement; misguided.

wrong'un noun (*informal*) a person of bad character. [from *wrong one*]

wrote past tense of **write**.

wrought (rawt) adjective (said about metals) beaten out or shaped by hammering. [the old past participle of *work*] ◊ See the note at **wreak**.

wrought iron noun iron made by forging or rolling rather than casting.

wrung past tense and past participle of **wring**.

WRVS abbreviation Women's Royal Voluntary Service.

wry (riy) adjective (**wryer** or **wrier**, **wryest** or **wriest**) 1 (said about humour) dry and mocking. SYNONYMS: droll, sardonic. 2 (said about a person's face or features) twisted into an expression of disgust, disappointment, or mockery. 3 twisted or bent to one side. **wryly** adverb **wryness** noun [from an Old English word]

wryneck noun a small bird related to the woodpecker, able to twist its head over its shoulder.

wt abbreviation weight.

WW abbreviation World War.

WWF abbreviation World Wide Fund for Nature.

WWW abbreviation World Wide Web.

wych elm noun a kind of elm with broader leaves and more spreading branches than the common elm. [from an Old English word]

wych hazel noun another spelling of **witch hazel**.

WYSIWYG (wiz-i-wig) adjective (*Computing*) representing text on-screen in a form that is exactly the same as its appearance on a printout. [from the initial letters of *what you see is what you get*]

wyvern noun (*Heraldry*) a dragon with wings, two legs, and a barbed tail. [via Old French from a Latin word *vipera* meaning 'viper']

Xx

X 1 the twenty-fourth letter of the English alphabet. 2 the Roman numeral for 10. 3 an unknown or unnamed thing or person.

x abbreviation (*Mathematics*) a symbol for an unknown quantity or variable.

x-axis noun (*Mathematics*) the horizontal axis in a system of coordinates.

x-coordinate noun (*Mathematics*) a coordinate measured parallel to the x-axis of a graph.

xenon (zen-on) noun a chemical element (symbol Xe), a colourless odourless gas. [from a Greek word *xenos* meaning 'strange']

xenophobia (zen-ə-foh-biə) noun strong dislike or distrust of foreigners. **xenophobe** noun **xenophobic** adjective [from a Greek word *xenos* meaning 'foreigner' and *phobia*]

Xerox (zeer-oks) noun (*trademark*) 1 a process for producing photocopies without the use of wet chemicals. 2 a photocopy made in this way.
xerox verb to photocopy a document by a process of this kind. [from a Greek word *xēros* meaning 'dry' (because the process

does not use liquid chemicals, as earlier photocopiers did)]

Xhosa (koh-sə or kaw-sə) *noun* 1 a member of a South African people of the Cape Province. 2 the Bantu language of this people.

Xmas *noun* an informal word for **Christmas**. ◊ The *X* represents the Greek letter chi, the first letter of *Khristos*, the Greek word for *Christ*.

X-ray *noun* 1 a kind of electromagnetic radiation that can penetrate solid things and make it possible to see into or through them. 2 a photograph or examination made by passing X-rays through something.
X-ray *verb* to photograph or examine something with X-rays. [so called because the nature of the rays was unknown when they were discovered in 1895]

xylem (ziy-lom) *noun* (*Botany*) the woody tissue in the stem of a plant, that carries water and dissolved minerals upwards from the ground. [from a Greek word *xulon* meaning 'wood']

xylene (ziy-leen) *noun* (*Chemistry*) any of three substances derived from benzene by substitution of two methyl groups, used in solvents and fuels. [same origin as for *xylem*]

xylophone (ziy-lə-fohn) *noun* a musical instrument consisting of flat wooden bars of graduated length which produce different notes when you hit them with small hammers. [from Greek words *xulon* meaning 'wood' and *phōnē* meaning 'sound']

Yy

Y the twenty-fifth letter of the English alphabet.

y *abbreviation* (*Mathematics*) a symbol for the second of two or three unknown quantities or variables.

-y[1] *suffix* forming adjectives meaning 'to do with' or 'like' (as in *angry*, *horsy*, *messy*, *sticky*). [from an Old English word]

-y[2] *suffix* forming diminutives or pet names (as in *aunty*, *pussy*). [origin unknown]

Y2K *abbreviation* year 2000 (with reference to the millennium bug).

yacht (yot) *noun* 1 a sailing boat used for racing or cruising. 2 a powered boat used for cruising. **yachtsman** *noun* (**yachtsmen**) **yachtswoman** *noun* (**yachtswomen**) [from a Dutch word *jaghtschip* meaning 'fast pirate ship']

yachting *noun* racing or cruising in a yacht.

yahoo (yə-hoo) *noun* a rude or brutish person. [the name of an imaginary race in *Gulliver's Travels* by Swift]

Yahweh (yah-way) *noun* see **Jehovah**.

yak *noun* a large long-haired Tibetan ox. [from a Tibetan word]

Yale lock *noun* (*trademark*) a type of lock for doors, using a flat key with a toothed edge. [named after the American locksmith L. Yale (1821–68)]

yam *noun* 1 the edible starchy tuber of a tropical climbing plant; the plant itself. 2 (*North Amer.*) a sweet potato. [from a Portuguese or Spanish word]

yang *noun* (in Chinese philosophy) the active principle of the universe (complemented by *yin*). [from a Chinese word]

Yank *noun* (*informal*) an American.

yank *verb* (*informal*) to pull something with a sudden sharp tug.
yank *noun* (*informal*) a sudden sharp tug. [origin unknown]

Yankee *noun* (*informal*) 1 an American. 2 (*North Amer.*) an inhabitant of the northern states of the USA. [probably from a Dutch word *Janke* meaning 'Johnny']

yap *noun* a shrill bark.
yap *verb* (**yapped**, **yapping**) 1 to give a shrill bark. 2 (*informal*) to talk at length in an annoying way. [an imitation of the sound]

yard[1] *noun* 1 a measure of length, equal to 3 feet (0.9144 metre). 2 a long pole stretched horizontally or crosswise from a mast to support a sail. [from an Old English word *gerd*]

yard[2] *noun* a piece of enclosed ground, especially one attached to a building, surrounded by buildings, or used for a particular purpose or business ♦ *a timber yard*. [from an Old English word *geard* meaning 'building' or 'home']

yardarm *noun* either end of a yard supporting a sail.

yardstick *noun* a standard of comparison. [from *yard*¹]

yarmulke or **yarmulka** (yar-mul-kə) *noun* a skullcap worn by Jewish men. [a Yiddish word]

yarn *noun* 1 thread spun by twisting fibres together, used for knitting, weaving, or sewing. 2 (*informal*) a tale or story, especially a far-fetched one.
yarn *verb* (*informal*) to tell yarns. **to spin a yarn** (*informal*) to tell a yarn. [from an Old English word *gearn*]

yarrow (ya-roh) *noun* a plant with feathery leaves and strong-smelling white or pinkish flowers. [from an Old English word *gearwe*]

yashmak *noun* a veil concealing all of the face except for the eyes, worn by some Muslim women in public. [an Arabic word]

yaw *verb* (said about a ship or aircraft) to fail to hold a straight course, to turn from side to side.
yaw *noun* a yawing movement or course. [origin unknown]

yawl *noun* 1 a kind of sailing boat with two masts. 2 a kind of fishing boat. [from an Old German or Dutch word]

yawn *verb* 1 to open your mouth wide and draw in breath (often involuntarily), because of tiredness or boredom. 2 to form a wide opening ♦ *a yawning chasm*.
yawn *noun* 1 an act of yawning. 2 (*informal*) something boring. [from an Old English word *geonian*]

y-axis *noun* (*Mathematics*) the vertical axis in a system of coordinates.

y-coordinate *noun* (*Mathematics*) a coordinate measured parallel to the y-axis of a graph.

ye ¹ *pronoun* (*old use*) you (referring to more than one person). [from an Old English word]

ye ² *adjective* (*supposed old use*) the ♦ *ye olde tea shoppe*. [from an Old English letter that represented the sound *th* but resembled the letter *y*]

yea (yay) *adverb* & *noun* (*old use*) yes. [from an Old English word]

yeah (yair) *adverb* (*informal*) yes.

year *noun* 1 the time taken by the earth to make one revolution around the sun, about 365¼ days. 2 the period from 1 January to 31 December inclusive. 3 any period of twelve months. 4 a group of students of roughly the same age ♦ *Is she in your year?*
years *plural noun* 1 a person's age or time of life ♦ *He looks younger than his years.* 2 (*informal*) a very long time ♦ *We've been waiting for years.* [from an Old English word]

yearbook *noun* an annual publication containing current information about a particular subject.

yearling (yer-ling) *noun* an animal between one and two years old.

yearly *adjective* happening or produced once a year or every year. SYNONYM: annual.
yearly *adverb* annually.

yearn *verb* to long for something. SYNONYMS: long, ache, hunger, pine, hanker. [from an Old English word *giernan*]

yeast *noun* a kind of fungus that causes alcohol and carbon dioxide to be produced while it is developing, used to cause fermentation in making beer and wines and as a raising agent in baking. [from an Old English word]

yeasty *adjective* (**yeastier, yeastiest**) frothy like yeast when it is developing.
yeastiness *noun*

yell *noun* a loud sharp cry.
yell *verb* to shout loudly. [from an Old English word]

yellow *adjective* 1 of the colour of egg yolks and ripe lemons. 2 (*informal*) cowardly.
yellow *noun* 1 yellow colour. 2 a yellow substance or material, yellow clothes.
yellow *verb* to become yellow, especially with age ♦ *a book with yellowing pages.*
yellowish *adjective* **yellowness** *noun* [from an Old English word *geolu*]

yellow card *noun* a yellow card shown by the referee in a football match to a player being cautioned.

yellow fever *noun* a tropical disease with fever and jaundice.

yellowhammer *noun* a kind of bunting, the male of which has a yellow head, neck, and breast.

Yellow Pages *plural noun* (*trademark*) a telephone directory printed on yellow paper and giving addresses and telephone numbers of businesses, arranged according to what services they provide.

yellow streak noun (*informal*) cowardice in a person's character.

yelp verb to make a short sharp cry or bark. **yelp** noun a yelping sound. [from an Old English word *gielpan* meaning 'to boast']

yen ¹ noun (**yen**) the unit of money in Japan. [from a Japanese word *en* meaning 'round']

yen ² noun a longing for something. [a Chinese dialect word]

yeoman (yoh-mən) noun (**yeomen**) (in the past) a man who owned and farmed a small estate. **yeoman service** long and useful service. [probably from *young* and *man*]

Yeoman of the Guard noun a member of the ceremonial bodyguard of the British monarch, who wear Tudor dress as uniform.

yeomanry (yoh-mən-ri) noun 1 yeomen collectively. 2 a volunteer cavalry force from 1794 to 1908, composed chiefly of yeomen.

yes adverb 1 used to agree to or give a positive reply to something. 2 used as an answer, meaning 'I am here'. **yes** noun (**yeses** or **yesses**) a positive reply or decision. [from an Old English word]

yes-man noun (**yes-men**) a person who always agrees with their superiors, especially in a sycophantic way.

yesterday noun 1 the day before today. 2 the recent past. **yesterday** adverb 1 on the day before today. 2 in the recent past. [from an old word *yester-* and *day*]

yesteryear noun (*literary*) 1 last year. 2 the recent past.

yet adverb 1 up to this time and continuing, still ♦ *There's life in the old dog yet.* 2 by this time, so far ♦ *It hasn't happened yet.* 3 before the matter is done with, eventually ♦ *I'll get even with you yet.* 4 in addition, even ♦ *She became yet more excited.* 5 nevertheless ♦ *strange yet true.* **yet** conjunction nevertheless, but in spite of that ♦ *He worked hard, yet he failed.* [from an Old English word]

yeti (yet-i) noun (**yetis**) a large animal like a bear, said to exist in the Himalayas, also known as the *Abominable Snowman*. [from a Tibetan word]

yew noun 1 an evergreen tree with dark-green needle-like leaves and red berries. 2 the wood of this tree. [from an Old English word]

Yiddish noun a language used by Jews of central and eastern Europe, based on a German dialect and with words from Hebrew and various modern languages. [from a German word *jüdisch* meaning 'Jewish']

yield verb 1 to produce something as a crop or other natural product ♦ *The land yields good crops* ♦ *How much milk does your herd yield?* 2 to produce a sum as profit, interest, etc. ♦ *The investment yields 15%.* 3 to give way to pressure or demands, to agree to do what is requested or ordered ♦ *The town yielded* ♦ *He yielded to persuasion.* SYNONYMS: surrender, succumb, give in, give way, capitulate, acquiesce, cave in. 4 to acknowledge inferiority ♦ *I yield to no one in my admiration for his achievements.* 5 (said about traffic) to allow other traffic to have right of way. 6 to be able to be forced out of shape, e.g. under pressure. **yield** noun the amount yielded or produced; the quantity obtained ♦ *What is the yield of wheat per acre?* [from an Old English word meaning 'to pay']

yin noun (in Chinese philosophy) the passive principle of the universe (complemented by *yang*). [from a Chinese word]

yippee interjection an exclamation of excitement.

YMCA abbreviation Young Men's Christian Association.

yob noun (*informal*) a bad-mannered or aggressive young man, a lout. [from *boy*, written backwards]

yobbo noun (**yobbos** or **yobboes**) (*informal*) a yob.

yodel (yoh-dəl) verb (**yodelled, yodelling**) to sing or call with the voice alternating rapidly between a very high pitch and its normal pitch. **yodel** noun a yodelling cry. **yodeller** noun [from a German word *jodeln*]

yoga (yoh-gə) noun 1 a Hindu system of meditation and self-control designed to produce mystical experience and spiritual insight. 2 a system of physical exercises based on this, practised for health and relaxation. [a Sanskrit word meaning 'union']

yogi (yoh-gi) noun (**yogis**) a person who is a master of yoga. [a Sanskrit word]

yogurt or **yoghurt** (yog-ert) *noun* a food prepared from milk that has been thickened by the action of certain bacteria, giving it a sharp taste. [from a Turkish word]

yoke *noun* 1 a wooden crosspiece fastened over the necks of two oxen or other animals pulling a cart or plough. 2 a piece of timber shaped to fit a person's shoulders and to hold a pail or basket hung at each end. 3 a part of a piece of clothing that fits over the shoulders and from which the rest hangs. 4 something thought of as oppressive or burdensome ♦ *Now is the time to throw off the yoke of servitude.*
yoke *verb* 1 to harness or join things together by means of a yoke ♦ *He yoked his oxen to the plough.* 2 to join two or more things together ♦ *a couple yoked together in marriage.* [from an Old English word *geoc*]
◊ Do not confuse this word with **yolk**, which has a different meaning.

yokel (yoh-kəl) *noun* a simple and unsophisticated country person. [origin unknown]

yolk (yohk) *noun* the round yellow part inside an egg. [from an Old English word *geolu* meaning 'yellow']
◊ Do not confuse this word with **yoke**, which has a different meaning.

Yom Kippur (yom kip-oor) *noun* the Day of Atonement, a solemn Jewish religious festival, a day of fasting and repentance. [a Hebrew phrase]

yomp *verb* (*informal*) to march across rough country while carrying heavy equipment on your back.
yomp *noun* (*informal*) a march of this kind. [origin unknown]

yon *adjective & adverb* (*dialect*) yonder. [from an Old English word]

yonder *adverb* (*old use or dialect*) over there.
yonder *adjective* situated or able to be seen over there. [from an Old English word; related to *yon*]

yonks *noun* (*informal*) a long time, ages ♦ *I haven't seen him for yonks.* [origin unknown]

yore *noun* **of yore** (*literary*) formerly; of long ago ♦ *in days of yore.* [from an Old English word]

yorker *noun* a ball bowled in cricket so that it pitches immediately under the bat. [probably from the name of Yorkshire County Cricket Club]

Yorkist *noun* a follower of the House of York in the Wars of the Roses.
Yorkist *adjective* to do with the House of York.

Yorkshire pudding *noun* a baked batter pudding eaten with roast beef. [from Yorkshire, a former county in northern England, where it was first made]

Yorkshire terrier *noun* a small long-haired terrier.

Yoruba (yo-ruu-bə) *noun* (**Yoruba** or **Yorubas**) 1 a member of an African people of SW Nigeria and Benin. 2 the language of this people.

you *pronoun* 1 the person or people being spoken to. 2 one, anyone, or everyone ♦ *You never know when it might come in useful.* [from an Old English word]

you'd *verb* (*informal*) 1 you had. 2 you would.

you'll *verb* (*informal*) you will.

young *adjective* 1 having lived or existed for only a short time; not old. 2 not far advanced in time ♦ *The night is young.* 3 to do with or for young people. SYNONYM: juvenile.
young *noun* young children or animals ♦ *a robin feeding its young.* SYNONYMS: offspring, brood, progeny. **youngish** *adjective* [from an Old English word]

youngster *noun* a young person, a child.

your *adjective* of or belonging to you. [from an Old English word]
◊ Do not confuse this word with **you're**, which has a different meaning.

you're *verb* (*informal*) you are.
◊ Do not confuse this word with **your**, which has a different meaning.

yours *possessive pronoun* belonging to you; the thing(s) belonging to you. **Yours faithfully** a more formal ending to a business letter.
Yours sincerely a less formal ending to a business letter, also used in personal correspondence.
Yours truly 1 a fairly formal ending to a business letter. 2 (*informal*) the person speaking ♦ *The awkward jobs are always left for yours truly.*
◊ It is incorrect to write *your's.*

yourself *pronoun* (**yourselves**) 1 the form of *you* used in reflexive constructions (e.g. *You've cut yourself* and for emphasis (e.g. *You told me yourself*).

youth *noun* (**youths** (yoothz)) 1 the period

between childhood and adult age; being young. **2** the vigour or lack of experience etc. characteristic of being young. **3** a young man ♦ *a youth of 16.* **4** young people collectively ♦ *the youth of the country.* [from an Old English word *geoguth*]

youth club or **youth centre** *noun* a place providing leisure activities for young people.

youthful *adjective* **1** young; looking or seeming young. **2** characteristic of young people ♦ *youthful impatience.* **youthfully** *adverb* **youthfulness** *noun*

youth hostel *noun* a place providing cheap accommodation, especially for young people who are hiking or on holiday.

youth hostelling *noun* staying in youth hostels.

you've *verb* (*informal*) you have.

yowl *verb* to make a loud wailing cry or howl.
yowl *noun* this cry. [an imitation of the sound]

yo-yo *noun* (**yo-yos**) (*trademark*) a toy consisting of two circular parts with a deep groove between them, which can be made to rise and fall on a string attached to it when this is jerked by a finger.
yo-yo *verb* (**yo-yoes, yo-yoed, yo-yoing**) to move up and down repeatedly. [probably from a language spoken in the Philippines]

yrs *abbreviation* **1** years. **2** (in letters) yours.

YTS *abbreviation* Youth Training Scheme.

yuan (yu-ahn) *noun* (**yuan**) the unit of money in China. [a Chinese word meaning 'round']

yucca (yuk-ə) *noun* a tall plant with white bell-like flowers and stiff spiky leaves. [a Carib word]

Yule or **Yuletide** *noun* (*old use*) the Christmas festival. [from an Old English word]

yule log *noun* a large log traditionally burnt in the hearth on Christmas Eve.

yummy *adjective* (**yummier, yummiest**) (*informal*) delicious.

yum-yum *interjection* an exclamation of pleasure at eating delicious food. [an imitation of the sound]

yuppie *noun* (*informal*) a young middle-class person with a well-paid professional job. [from the initial letters of *young urban professional*]

YWCA *abbreviation* Young Women's Christian Association.

Zz

Z the twenty-sixth letter of the English alphabet.

z *abbreviation* (*Mathematics*) a symbol for the third of three unknown quantities or variables.

zany *adjective* (**zanier, zaniest**) crazily funny.
zany *noun* (**zanies**) a comical or eccentric person. [from an Italian word *zanni*, denoting a type of clown]

zap *verb* (**zapped, zapping**) (*informal*) **1** to attack or destroy something forcefully. **2** to use a remote control to change television channels quickly. **zapper** *noun* [an imitation of the sound of a blow or shot]

zeal (zeel) *noun* enthusiasm or energy. [from a Greek word *zēlos*]

zealot (zel-ət) *noun* a zealous person, a fanatic. **zealotry** *noun*

zealous (zel-əs) *adjective* full of zeal.
SYNONYMS: keen, enthusiastic, fanatical, fervent, passionate. **zealously** *adverb*

zebra *noun* an African animal of the horse family, with black and white stripes all over its body. [from an Italian, Spanish, or Portuguese word]

zebra crossing *noun* a pedestrian crossing where the road is marked with broad white stripes.

zebu (zee-bew) *noun* an ox with a humped back, used in India and East Asia for pulling loads. [from a French word *zébu*]

Zen *noun* a form of Buddhism emphasizing the value of meditation and intuition. [a Japanese word meaning 'meditation']

Zend-Avesta noun the Zoroastrian sacred writings consisting of the Avesta (the text) and the Zend (the commentary). [from a Persian word *zand* meaning 'interpretation' and *Avesta*]

zenith (zen-ith) 1 (in astronomy) the part of the sky that is directly above the observer. 2 the highest or most successful point ♦ *His power was at its zenith.* [from an Arabic phrase *samt ar-ras* meaning 'path over the head']

zephyr (zef-er) noun a soft gentle breeze. [from a Greek word *Zephuros*, denoting a god of the west wind]

Zeppelin noun a large German airship of the early 20th century. [named after the German airship pioneer Count F. von Zeppelin (1838–1917)]

zero noun (zeros) 1 nought, the figure 0. 2 nothing, nil. 3 a temperature of 0°C, marking the freezing point of water. **zero** verb (zeroes, zeroed, zeroing) to adjust an instrument to zero. **to zero in on** 1 to focus your aim or attention on something. 2 to go purposefully towards a place. [from an Arabic word *sifr* meaning 'cipher']

zero hour noun the time at which something is timed to begin.

zero tolerance noun strict enforcement of the law in social matters such as street crime.

zest noun 1 keen enjoyment or enthusiasm ♦ *a zest for life.* 2 a pleasantly stimulating quality ♦ *The risk added zest to the whole adventure.* 3 the coloured part of the peel of an orange or lemon etc., used as flavouring. 4 a pleasantly sharp flavour. **zestful** adjective **zestfully** adverb [from a French word *zeste* meaning 'orange or lemon peel']

zigzag noun a line or course that turns sharply from side to side. **zigzag** adjective & adverb forming or in a zigzag. **zigzag** verb (zigzagged, zigzagging) to move in a zigzag course. [via French from a German word]

zillion noun (informal) an extremely large number. [based on *million*]

Zimmer or **Zimmer frame** noun (trademark) a frame that a lame or frail person uses as a support in walking. [from the name of the manufacturer]

zinc noun a white metallic element (symbol Zn), used in alloys and to coat iron and steel as a protection against corrosion. [from a German word *Zink*]

zinnia (zin-ia) noun a daisy-like garden plant with brightly-coloured flowers. [named after the German botanist J. Zinn (1727–59)]

Zionism (ziy-ən-izm) noun a movement for the development and protection of a Jewish nation in Israel. **Zionist** noun [from Zion, the name of the holy hill of ancient Jerusalem]

zip noun 1 a fastening device consisting of two flexible strips of metal or plastic, each with rows of small teeth that interlock when a sliding tab brings them together. 2 (informal) liveliness or vigour. **zip** verb (zipped, zipping) 1 to fasten or close something with a zip. 2 to move quickly with a sharp sound. [an imitation of the sound]

zip code noun (North Amer.) a type of postcode. [from the initial letters of *zone improvement plan*]

zipper noun (North Amer.) a zip fastener.

zippy adjective (zippier, zippiest) lively and vigorous. **zippiness** noun

zip-up adjective fastened with a zip.

zircon (zer-kon) noun a bluish-white gem cut from a translucent mineral. [from a German word *Zirkon*]

zither (zith-er) noun a musical instrument with many strings stretched over a shallow box-like body, played by plucking with the fingers of both hands. [from a Greek word *kithara*, denoting a type of harp]

Zn abbreviation (Chemistry) the symbol for zinc.

zodiac (zoh-di-ak) noun 1 (in astrology) a band of the sky containing the paths of the sun, moon, and main planets, divided into twelve equal parts (called the *signs of the zodiac*) each named after a constellation that was formerly situated in it. 2 a chart or diagram of these signs. **zodiacal** (zə-diy-əkəl) adjective [from a Greek word *zōidion* meaning 'image of an animal']

zombie noun 1 (in voodoo) a corpse said to have been brought back to life by witchcraft. 2 (informal) a person who seems to be doing things without thinking, usually because they are very tired. [from a West African word *zumbi* meaning 'fetish']

zone *noun* an area that has a particular characteristic, purpose, or use ♦ *a war zone* ♦ *a no-parking zone.*
zone *verb* **1** to divide a place into zones. **2** to assign something to a particular zone. **zonal** *adjective* [from a Greek word *zōnē* meaning 'girdle']

zoo *verb* a place where wild animals are kept for exhibition, conservation, and study. [short for *zoological garden*]

zoological garden *noun* (*old use*) a zoo.

zoology (zoh-ol-əji or zoo-ol-əji) *noun* the scientific study of animals. **zoological** *adjective* **zoologist** *noun* [from a Greek word *zōion* meaning 'animal' and *-logy*]

zoom *verb* **1** to move or travel very quickly. SYNONYMS: shoot, hurtle, career. **2** to rise or increase rapidly ♦ *The population is likely to zoom.* **3** (in photography) to change smoothly from a long shot to a close-up or vice versa.
zoom *noun* the action of a camera zooming. [an imitation of the sound]

zoom lens *noun* a camera lens that can be adjusted continuously to focus on things that are close up or far away.

zooplankton (zoh-ə-**plank**-tən) *noun* (*Biology*) plankton consisting of tiny animals. [from a Greek word *zōion* meaning 'animal' and *plankton*]

Zoroastrianism (zo-roh-**ast**-ri-ən-izm) *noun* an ancient Persian religion based on the teachings of the prophet Zoroaster (or Zarathustra) and his followers. **Zoroastrian** *noun* & *adjective* .

zucchini (zuuk-**ee**-ni) *noun* (**zucchini** or **zucchinis**) (*North Amer.*) a courgette. [an Italian word]

Zulu *noun* (**Zulus**) **1** a member of a South African people. **2** the Bantu language of this people.

zygospore (**ziy**-gə-spor) *noun* (*Biology*) a spore formed by the union of two similar gametes. [from a Greek word *zugon* meaning 'yoke' and *spore*]

zygote (**ziy**-goht) *noun* (*Biology*) a cell formed by the union of two gametes. [from a Greek word *zugon* meaning 'yoke']

zymase (**ziy**-mayz) *noun* (*Biochemistry*) an enzyme of a group originally found in yeast, that causes the breakdown of glucose and some other sugars. [from a Greek word *zumē* meaning 'leaven']

Countries and Peoples of the World

Country	People	Country	People
Afghanistan	Afghans	Denmark	Danes
Albania	Albanians	Djibouti	Djiboutians
Algeria	Algerians	Dominica	Dominicans
Andorra	Andorrans	Dominican	Dominicans
Angola	Angolans	Republic	
Antigua and Barbuda	Antiguans, Barbudans	East Timor	East Timorese
Argentina	Argentinians	Ecuador	Ecuadoreans
Armenia	Armenians	Egypt	Egyptians
Australia	Australians	El Salvador	Salvadoreans
Austria	Austrians	Equatorial Guinea	Equatorial Guineans
Azerbaijan	Azerbaijanis or Azeris	Eritrea	Eritreans
		Estonia	Estonians
Bahamas	Bahamians	Ethiopia	Ethiopians
Bahrain	Bahrainis		
Bangladesh	Bangladeshis	Fiji	Fijians
Barbados	Barbadians	Finland	Finns
Belarus	Belorussians	France	French
Belgium	Belgians		
Belize	Belizians	Gabon	Gabonese
Benin	Beninese	Gambia, The	Gambians
Bhutan	Bhutanese	Georgia	Georgians
Bolivia	Bolivians	Germany	Germans
Bosnia- Herzegovina	Bosnians	Ghana	Ghanaians
Botswana	Batswana or Citizens of Botswana	Greece	Greeks
		Grenada	Grenadians
Brazil	Brazilians	Guatemala	Guatemalans
Brunei Darussalam	People of Brunei	Guinea	Guineans
Bulgaria	Bulgarians	Guinea- Bissau	People of Guinea-Bissau
Burkina Faso	Burkinans		
Burundi	People of Burundi	Guyana	Guyanese
Cambodia	Cambodians	Haiti	Haitians
Cameroon	Cameroonians	Honduras	Hondurans
Canada	Canadians	Hungary	Hungarians
Cape Verde	Cape Verdeans		
Central African Republic	People of the Central African Republic	Iceland	Icelanders
		India	Indians
Chad	Chadians	Indonesia	Indonesians
Chile	Chileans	Iran	Iranians
China, People's Republic of	Chinese	Iraq	Iraqis
		Ireland, Republic of	Irish
Colombia	Colombians	Israel	Israelis
Comoros	Comorans	Italy	Italians
Congo, Democratic Republic of the	Congolese		
		Jamaica	Jamaicans
Congo, Republic of the	Congolese	Japan	Japanese
		Jordan	Jordanians
Costa Rica	Costa Ricans		
Côte d'Ivoire	People of the Côte d'Ivoire	Kazakhstan	Kazakhs
		Kenya	Kenyans
Croatia	Croats	Kiribati	Kiribatians
Cuba	Cubans	Kuwait	Kuwaitis
Cyprus	Cypriots	Kyrgyzstan	Kyrgyz
Czech Republic	Czechs		

Country	People	Country	People
Laos	Laotians	Romania	Romanians
Latvia	Latvians	Russia (Russian Federation)	Russians
Lebanon	Lebanese	Rwanda	Rwandans
Lesotho	Basotho		
Liberia	Liberians		
Libya	Libyans	St Kitts and Nevis	People of St Kitts and Nevis
Liechtenstein	Liechtensteiners		
Lithuania	Lithuanians	St Lucia	St Lucians
Luxembourg	Luxembourgers	St Vincent and the Grenadines	St Vincentians
Macedonia (Former Yugoslav Republic of Macedonia)	Macedonians	Samoa	Samoans
		San Marino	People of San Marino
		São Tomé and Príncipe	People of São Tomé and Príncipe
Madagascar	Malagasies	Saudi Arabia	Saudi Arabians
Malawi	Malawians	Senegal	Senegalese
Malaysia	Malaysians	Seychelles	Seychellois
Maldives	Maldivians	Sierra Leone	Sierra Leoneans
Mali	Malians	Singapore	Singaporeans
Malta	Maltese	Slovakia	Slovaks
Marshall Islands	Marshall Islanders	Slovenia	Slovenes
Mauritania	Mauritanians	Solomon Islands	Solomon Islanders
Mauritius	Mauritians	Somalia	Somalis
Mexico	Mexicans	South Africa	South Africans
Micronesia	Micronesians	South Korea (Republic of Korea)	South Koreans
Moldova	Moldovans		
Monaco	Monégasques	Spain	Spaniards
Mongolia	Mongolians	Sri Lanka	Sri Lankans
Morocco	Moroccans	Sudan	Sudanese
Mozambique	Mozambicans	Suriname	Surinamers
Myanmar (Burma)	Burmese	Swaziland	Swazis
		Sweden	Swedes
Namibia	Namibians	Switzerland	Swiss
Nauru	Nauruans	Syria	Syrians
Nepal	Nepalese		
Netherlands	Dutch	Taiwan	Taiwanese
New Zealand	New Zealanders	Tajikistan	Tajiks
Nicaragua	Nicaraguans	Tanzania	Tanzanians
Niger	Nigeriens	Thailand	Thais
Nigeria	Nigerians	Togo	Togolese
North Korea (People's Democratic Republic of Korea)	North Koreans	Tonga	Tongans
		Trinidad and Tobago	Trinidadians and Tobagans or Tobagonians
Norway	Norwegians		
		Tunisia	Tunisians
Oman	Omanis	Turkey	Turks
		Turkmenistan	Turkmens
Pakistan	Pakistanis	Tuvalu	Tuvaluans
Palau	Palauans		
Panama	Panamanians	Uganda	Ugandans
Papua New Guinea	Papua New Guineans	Ukraine	Ukrainians
Paraguay	Paraguayans	United Arab Emirates	People of the United Arab Emirates
Peru	Peruvians	United Kingdom	British
Philippines	Filipinos	United States of America	Americans
Poland	Poles	Uruguay	Uruguayans
Portugal	Portuguese	Uzbekistan	Uzbeks
Qatar	Qataris		

Country	People	Country	People
Vanuatu	People of Vanuatu	Yugoslavia (Montenegro and Serbia)	Yugoslavians (Montenegrins and Serbians)
Vatican City	Vatican citizens		
Venezuela	Venezuelans		
Vietnam	Vietnamese		
		Zambia	Zambians
Yemen	Yemenis	Zimbabwe	Zimbabweans

...mical Elements

element	symbol	atomic number	element	symbol	atomic number
actinium	Ac	89	mendelevium	Md	101
aluminium	Al	13	mercury	Hg	80
americium	Am	95	molybdenum	Mo	42
antimony	Sb	51	neodymium	Nd	60
argon	Ar	18	neon	Ne	10
arsenic	As	33	neptunium	Np	93
astatine	At	85	nickel	Ni	28
barium	Ba	56	niobium	Nb	41
berkelium	Bk	97	nitrogen	N	7
beryllium	Be	4	nobelium	No	102
bismuth	Bi	83	osmium	Os	76
boron	B	5	oxygen	O	8
bromine	Br	35	palladium	Pd	46
cadmium	Cd	48	phosphorus	P	15
caesium	Cs	55	platinum	Pt	78
calcium	Ca	20	plutonium	Pu	94
californium	Cf	98	polonium	Po	84
carbon	C	6	potassium	K	19
cerium	Ce	58	praseodymium	Pr	59
chlorine	Cl	17	promethium	Pm	61
chromium	Cr	24	protactinium	Pa	91
cobalt	Co	27	radium	Ra	88
copper	Cu	29	radon	Rn	86
curium	Cm	96	rhenium	Re	75
dysprosium	Dy	66	rhodium	Rh	45
einsteinium	Es	99	rubidium	Rb	37
erbium	Er	68	ruthenium	Ru	44
europium	Eu	63	rutherfordium	Rf	104
fermium	Fm	100	samarium	Sm	62
fluorine	F	9	scandium	Sc	21
francium	Fr	87	selenium	Se	34
gadolinium	Gd	64	silicon	Si	14
gallium	Ga	31	silver	Ag	47
germanium	Ge	32	sodium	Na	11
gold	Au	79	strontium	Sr	38
hafnium	Hf	72	sulphur	S	16
hahnium	Ha	105	tantalum	Ta	73
helium	He	2	technetium	Tc	43
holmium	Ho	67	tellurium	Te	52
hydrogen	H	1	terbium	Tb	65
indium	In	49	thallium	Tl	81
iodine	I	53	thorium	Th	90
iridium	Ir	77	thulium	Tm	69
iron	Fe	26	tin	Sn	50
krypton	Kr	36	titanium	Ti	22
kurchatovium	Ku	104	tungsten	W	74
lanthanum	La	57	uranium	U	92
lawrencium	Lr	103	vanadium	V	23
lead	Pb	82	xenon	Xe	54
lithium	Li	3	ytterbium	Yb	70
lutetium	Lu	71	yttrium	Y	39
magnesium	Mg	12	zinc	Zn	30
manganese	Mn	25	zirconium	Zr	40